The Sporting News®

OFFICIAL BASEBALL REGISTER

1 9 9 2   E D I T I O N

Editor / Baseball Register
MARK SHIMABUKURO

Contributing Editor / Baseball Register
JOHN DUXBURY

The Sporting News

—PUBLISHING CO.—

Thomas G. Osenton, President and Chief Operating Officer; **Kathy Kinkeade**, Vice President / Production; **William N. Topaz**, Director / Information Development; **Gary Levy**, Editor; **Mike Nahrstedt**, Managing Editor; **Joe Hoppel**, Senior Editor; **Jef Fletcher, Tom Grady, Kevin Hormuth, Craig Mulcahy, Paul Santistevan, Terry Shea and Marc Witengier**, Editorial Assistants; **Bill Perry**, Director of Graphic Presentation; **Mike Bruner**, Art Director / Yearbooks and Books; **Gary Brinker**, Director of Information Systems; **Mike Bibler**, Database Analyst.

▼▲ A Times Mirror
◤◣ Company

Major league statistics compiled by MLB-IBM Baseball Information System.

Minor league statistics compiled by Howe Sportsdata International Inc., Boston.

Published in the United States by THE SPORTING NEWS Publishing Co., 1212 North Lindbergh Boulevard, St. Louis, Missouri 63132.

ISBN: 0-89204-419-5

10 9 8 7 6 5 4 3 2 1

CONTENTS

EXPLANATION OF FOOTNOTES AND ABBREVIATIONS

Note for statistical comparisons: Player strikes forced the cancellation of games in the 1972 season (10 days missed) and the 1981 season (50 days missed).

Positions are listed in descending order of games played.

* ★ Led league. For fielding statistics, the player led the league at the position shown.
* • Tied for league lead. For fielding statistics, the player tied for the league lead at the position shown.
* † Led league, but number indicated is total figure for two or more positions. Actual league-leading figure for first position is mentioned in "Statistical Notes" section.
* ‡ Tied for league lead, but number indicated is total figure for two or more positions. Actual figure with which player shared league lead for first position is mentioned in "Statistical Notes" section.
* ■ Indicates a player's movement from one major league organization to another major league organization or to an independent minor league organization.
* ... Statistic unavailable, unofficial or mathematically impossible to calculate.

LEAGUES: Alabama-Florida: Ala.-Fla. **American:** A.L. **American Association:** Am. Association, Am. Assoc., A.A. **Appalachian:** Appal. **Arizona:** Ariz. **California:** Calif. **Canadian-American:** Can.-Am. **Carolina:** Caro. **Cocoa Rookie:** Coc. Rk. **Eastern:** East. **Florida East Coast:** Fla. E.C. **Florida Rookie:** Fla. Rk. **Florida State:** Florida St., Fla. St., FSL. **Georgia-Florida:** Georgia-Fla. **Gulf Coast:** GCL. **Gulf States:** Gulf St. **Inter-American:** Int.-Amer. **International:** Int'l. **Japanese Central:** Japanese Cen., Jap. Cen., Jp. Cn. **Japanese Pacific:** Japanese Pac., Jap. Pacific, Jap. Pac. **Mexican:** Mex. **Mexican Center:** Mex. Cen. **Midwest:** Midw. **National:** N.L. **New York-Pennsylvania:** New York-Penn, N.Y.-Penn, NYP. **North Carolina State:** N.Carolina St. **Northwest:** N'west. **Pacific Coast:** Pac. Coast, PCL. **Piedmont:** Pied. **South Atlantic:** S. Atlantic, S. Atl., SAL, Sally. **Southern:** South. **Texas:** Tex. **Western Carolinas:** West. Carolinas, W. Carolinas, W. Caro.

TEAMS: Albuquerque: Albuq. **Alexandria:** Alexand., Alex. **Appleton:** Apple. **Atlanta:** Atl. **Baltimore:** Balt. **Bradenton:** Brad., Braden. **Calgary:** Calg. **California:** Calif. **Charleston, S.C.:** Charles., S.C. **Charlotte:** Charlot. **Chicago:** Chi. **Chunichi Dragons:** Chunichi **Cincinnati:** Cin. **Cleveland:** Clev. **Colorado Springs:** Colo. Springs, Colo. Spgs. **Columbus:** Colum. **Coos Bay/North Bend:** C. Bay/N. Bend, Coos Bay/N. Bend. **Daytona Beach:** Day. Beach, Day B. **Detroit:** Det. **Edmonton:** Edmon., Edm. **Everett:** Ever. **Fukuoka Daiei Hawks:** Fukuoka. **Hagerstown:** Hagers. **Harrisburg:** Harris. **Hiroshima Toyo Carp:** Hiroshima. **Houston:** Hou. **Indianapolis:** Ind. **Jacksonville:** Jackson. **Kansas City:** K.C. **Kissimmee:** Kissim. **Las Vegas:** L.V. **Los Angeles:** L.A. **Lynchburg:** Lynch. **Memphis:** Mem. **Mexico City Tigers:** Mex. City Tigers. **Milwaukee:** Mil. **Minnesota:** Minn. **Montreal:** Mont. **Nankai Hawks:** Nankai. **Nashville:** Nash. **New York:** N.Y. **Oakland:** Oak. **Oklahoma City:** Okla. City. **Philadelphia:** Phil. **Pittsburgh:** Pitts. **Quad City:** Q. City. **Reading:** Read. **Redwood:** Red. **Richmond:** Rich. **Rochester:** Roch. **San Bernardino:** San Bern. **San Diego:** S.D. **San Francisco:** San Fran., S.F. **Santo Domingo:** San. Domin. **Sarasota:** Sara. **Sarasota Astros-Orange:** Sara. Astros-Or. **Sarasota Cardinals:** Sara. Cards. **Scranton/Wilkes-Barre:** Scranton/W.B., Scran./W.B., Scr./W.B. **Seattle:** Sea. **Southern Oregon:** South. Oregon. **Spokane:** Spok. **Stockton:** Stock. **Tacoma:** Tac. **Tidewater:** Tide. **Toronto:** Tor. **Tri-Cities:** Tri-Cit. **Vancouver:** Vanc. **Waterbury:** Water. **Wichita:** Wich. **Williamsport:** Williams. **Winter Haven:** Win. Hav. **Wisconsin Rapids:** Wis. Rapids. **Yakult Swallows:** Yakult. **Yomiuri Giants:** Yomiuri.

STATISTICS: A: assists. **AB:** at-bats. **Avg.:** average. **BB:** bases on balls. **E:** errors. **ER:** earned runs. **ERA:** earned-run average. **G:** games. **H:** hits. **HR:** home runs. **IP:** innings pitched. **L:** losses. **Pct.:** winning percentage. **PO:** putouts. **Pos.:** position. **R:** runs. **RBI:** runs batted in. **SB:** stolen bases. **SO:** strikeouts. **Sv.:** saves. **W:** wins. **2B:** doubles. **3B:** triples.

ON THE COVER: One of baseball's rising stars is Chicago White Sox first baseman Frank Thomas, who batted .318, smacked 32 home runs and drove in 109 runs in 1991, his first full major league season. (Photo by Tom DiPace)

PLAYERS

ABBOTT, JIM
P, ANGELS

PERSONAL: Born September 19, 1967, at Flint, Mich. . . . 6-3/210. . . . Throws left, bats left. . . . Full name: James Anthony Abbott.
HIGH SCHOOL: Flint Central (Mich.).
COLLEGE: Michigan.
TRANSACTIONS/CAREER NOTES: Selected by Toronto Blue Jays organization in 36th round of free-agent draft (June 3, 1985). . . . Selected by California Angels organization in first round (eighth pick overall) of free-agent draft (June 1, 1988).
RECORDS/HONORS: Named lefthanded pitcher on THE SPORTING NEWS college All-America team (1988). . . . Named lefthanded pitcher on THE SPORTING NEWS A.L. All-Star team (1991).
STATISTICAL NOTES: Tied for A.L. lead with four balks in 1991.
MISCELLANEOUS: Member of 1988 U.S. Olympic baseball team.

Year Team (League)	G	W	L	Pct.	ERA	Sv.	IP	H	R	ER	BB	SO
1989 — California (A.L.)	29	12	12	.500	3.92	0	181⅓	190	95	79	74	115
1990 — California (A.L.)	33	10	14	.417	4.51	0	211⅔	*246	116	106	72	105
1991 — California (A.L.)	34	18	11	.621	2.89	0	243	222	85	78	73	158
Major league totals (3 years)	96	40	37	.519	3.72	0	636	658	296	263	219	378

ABBOTT, KYLE
P, PHILLIES

PERSONAL: Born February 18, 1968, at Newbury Port, Mass. . . . 6-4/200. . . . Throws left, bats left. . . . Full name: Lawrence Kyle Abbott. . . . Son of Larry Abbott, former minor league pitcher (1964-70).
HIGH SCHOOL: Mission Viejo (Calif.).
COLLEGE: UC San Diego and Long Beach State.
TRANSACTIONS/CAREER NOTES: Selected by California Angels organization in first round (ninth pick overall) of free-agent draft (June 2, 1989). . . . Traded by Angels with OF Ruben Amaro to Philadelphia Phillies for OF Von Hayes (December 8, 1991).
STATISTICAL NOTES: Led Pacific Coast League with 22 home runs allowed in 1991.

Year Team (League)	G	W	L	Pct.	ERA	Sv.	IP	H	R	ER	BB	SO
1989 — Quad City (Midwest)	13	5	4	.556	2.57	0	73⅔	55	26	21	30	95
1990 — Midland (Texas)	24	6	9	.400	4.14	0	128⅓	124	75	59	73	91
— Edmonton (Pacific Coast)	3	1	0	1.000	14.81	0	10⅓	26	18	17	4	14
1991 — Edmonton (Pacific Coast)	27	•14	10	.583	3.99	0	*180⅓	173	84	80	46	120
— California (A.L.)	5	1	2	.333	4.58	0	19⅔	22	11	10	13	12
Major league totals (1 year)	5	1	2	.333	4.58	0	19⅔	22	11	10	13	12

ABBOTT, PAUL
P, TWINS

PERSONAL: Born September 15, 1967, at Van Nuys, Calif. . . . 6-3/193. . . . Throws right, bats right. . . . Full name: Paul David Abbott.
HIGH SCHOOL: Sunny Hills (Fullerton, Calif.).
TRANSACTIONS/CAREER NOTES: Selected by Minnesota Twins organization in third round of free-agent draft (June 3, 1985).
STATISTICAL NOTES: Pitched 3-0 no-hit victory against Palm Springs (June 26, 1988, seven innings). . . . Tied for California League lead in games started by pitcher with 28 in 1988.

Year Team (League)	G	W	L	Pct.	ERA	Sv.	IP	H	R	ER	BB	SO
1985 — Elizabethton (Appalachian)	10	1	5	.167	6.94	0	35	33	32	27	32	34
1986 — Kenosha (Midwest)	25	6	10	.375	4.50	0	98	102	62	49	73	73
1987 — Kenosha (Midwest)	26	13	6	.684	3.65	0	145⅓	102	76	59	103	138
1988 — Visalia (California)	28	11	9	.550	4.18	0	172⅓	141	95	80	*143	*205
1989 — Orlando (Southern)	17	9	3	.750	4.37	0	90⅔	71	44	44	48	102
1990 — Portland (Pacific Coast)	23	5	14	.263	4.56	0	128⅓	110	75	65	82	129
— Minnesota (A.L.)	7	0	5	.000	5.97	0	34⅔	37	24	23	28	25
1991 — Portland (Pacific Coast)	8	2	3	.400	3.89	0	44	36	19	19	28	40
— Minnesota (A.L.)	15	3	1	.750	4.75	0	47⅓	38	27	25	36	43
Major league totals (2 years)	22	3	6	.333	5.27	0	82	75	51	48	64	68

ABNER, SHAWN
OF, ANGELS

PERSONAL: Born June 17, 1966, at Hamilton, O. . . . 6-1/194. . . . Throws right, bats right. . . . Full name: Shawn Wesley Abner. . . . Brother of Ben Abner, minor league outfielder (1984-87).
HIGH SCHOOL: Mechanicsburg (Pa.).
TRANSACTIONS/CAREER NOTES: Selected by New York Mets organization in first round (first pick overall) of free-agent draft (June 4, 1984). . . . Traded by Mets with OF Stanley Jefferson, OF Kevin Mitchell, P Kevin Armstrong and P Kevin Brown to San Diego Padres for OF Kevin McReynolds, P Gene Walter and IF Adam Ging (December 11, 1986). . . . Traded by Padres to California Angels for 3B Jack Howell (July 30, 1991).
RECORDS/HONORS: Named Carolina League Player of the Year (1985).
STATISTICAL NOTES: Led Carolina League outfielders with 352 total chances in 1985. . . . Led Texas League outfielders with 352 total chances in 1986. . . . Tied for Texas League lead in being hit by pitch with seven in 1986.

Year Team (League)	Pos.	G	AB	R	H	2B	3B	HR	RBI	Avg.	SB	PO	A	E	Avg.
1984—Kingsport (Appalachian)..	OF	46	183	32	50	8	0	10	35	.273	9	87	1	1	.989
—Little Falls (N.Y.-Penn)....	OF	18	68	7	18	2	0	1	5	.265	3	40	2	1	.977
1985—Lynchburg (Carolina).......	OF	139	*542	71	*163	*30	*11	16	*89	.301	8	*332	8	12	.966
1986—Jackson (Texas).............	OF	*134	511	80	136	29	•8	14	76	.266	8	*338	10	4	.989
1987—Las Vegas (Pac. Coast)■..	OF	105	406	60	122	14	11	11	85	.300	11	238	9	4	.984
—San Diego (N.L.).............	OF	16	47	5	13	3	1	2	7	.277	1	23	2	2	.926
1988—San Diego (N.L.).............	OF	37	83	6	15	3	0	2	5	.181	0	55	1	1	.982
—Las Vegas (Pac. Coast)....	OF	63	252	35	64	16	2	4	34	.254	0	147	1	6	.961
1989—Las Vegas (Pac. Coast)....	OF	56	223	31	60	11	2	8	31	.269	3	129	6	1	.993
—San Diego (N.L.).............	OF	57	102	13	18	4	0	2	14	.176	1	67	0	0	1.000
1990—San Diego (N.L.).............	OF	91	184	17	45	9	0	1	15	.245	2	108	1	1	.991
1991—San Diego (N.L.)■............	OF	53	115	15	19	4	1	1	5	.165	0	86	1	0	1.000
—California (A.L.)■...........	OF	41	101	12	23	6	1	2	9	.228	1	72	3	0	1.000
American League totals (1 year)		41	101	12	23	6	1	2	9	.228	1	72	3	0	1.000
National League totals (5 years)		254	531	56	110	23	2	8	46	.207	4	339	5	4	.989
Major league totals (5 years)		295	632	68	133	29	3	10	55	.210	5	411	8	4	.991

ACKER, JIM
P, MARINERS

PERSONAL: Born September 24, 1958, at Freer, Tex.... 6-2/212.... Throws right, bats right.... Full name: James Justin Acker.... Brother of Bill Acker, National Football League player (1980-84).
HIGH SCHOOL: Freer (Tex.).
COLLEGE: Texas.
TRANSACTIONS/CAREER NOTES: Selected by Atlanta Braves organization in first round (21st pick overall) of free-agent draft (June 3, 1980).... On disabled list (April 9-20, 1982).... Drafted by Toronto Blue Jays (December 6, 1982).... On disabled list (August 16-September 1, 1984).... Traded by Toronto Blue Jays to Atlanta Braves for P Joe Johnson (July 6, 1986).... On Atlanta disabled list (May 9-August 19, 1988; included rehabilitation disability assignment to Greenville (July 30-August 18, 1988).... Granted free agency (November 4, 1988).... Re-signed by Richmond, Braves organization (January 6, 1989). ... Traded by Braves organization to Blue Jays for P Tony Castillo and a player to be named later (August 24, 1989); Braves organization acquired C Francisco Cabrera to complete deal (August 24, 1989).... Granted free agency (October 31, 1991). ...Signed by Seattle Mariners organization (February 2, 1992).

Year Team (League)	G	W	L	Pct.	ERA	Sv.	IP	H	R	ER	BB	SO
1980—Bradenton Braves (GCL)...........	1	1	0	1.000	0.00	0	5	1	0	0	0	5
—Savannah (Southern).............	13	5	5	.500	2.65	0	95	84	33	28	29	47
1981—Savannah (Southern).............	10	5	5	.500	2.69	0	77	57	34	23	34	37
—Richmond (International).........	21	8	7	.533	4.19	0	118	112	63	55	74	72
1982—Savannah (Southern).............	26	9	14	.391	4.44	1	142	120	96	70	86	96
1983—Toronto (A.L.)■...............	38	5	1	.833	4.33	1	$97\frac{2}{3}$	103	52	47	38	44
1984—Toronto (A.L.)..............	32	3	5	.375	4.38	1	72	79	39	35	25	33
1985—Toronto (A.L.)..............	61	7	2	.778	3.23	10	$86\frac{1}{3}$	86	35	31	43	42
1986—Toronto (A.L.)..............	23	2	4	.333	4.35	0	60	63	34	29	22	32
—Atlanta (N.L.)■..............	21	3	8	.273	3.79	0	95	100	47	40	26	37
1987—Atlanta (N.L.)..............	68	4	9	.308	4.16	14	$114\frac{2}{3}$	109	57	53	51	68
1988—Atlanta (N.L.)..............	21	0	4	.000	4.71	0	42	45	26	22	14	25
—Greenville (Southern)........	8	0	0	...	1.72	0	$15\frac{2}{3}$	7	3	3	3	5
1989—Atlanta (N.L.)..............	59	0	6	.000	2.67	2	$97\frac{2}{3}$	84	29	29	20	68
—Toronto (A.L.)■..............	14	2	1	.667	1.59	0	$28\frac{1}{3}$	24	7	5	12	24
1990—Toronto (A.L.)..............	59	4	4	.500	3.83	0	$91\frac{2}{3}$	103	49	39	30	54
1991—Toronto (A.L.)..............	54	3	5	.375	5.20	0	$88\frac{1}{3}$	77	51	51	36	44
American League totals (7 years)	281	26	22	.542	4.07	14	$524\frac{1}{3}$	535	269	237	206	273
National League totals (4 years)	169	7	27	.206	3.71	16	$349\frac{1}{3}$	338	159	144	111	198
Major league totals (9 years)	450	33	49	.402	3.92	30	$873\frac{2}{3}$	873	428	381	317	471

CHAMPIONSHIP SERIES RECORD
CHAMPIONSHIP SERIES NOTES: Shares single-series record for most games pitched—5 (1989).

Year Team (League)	G	W	L	Pct.	ERA	Sv.	IP	H	R	ER	BB	SO
1985—Toronto (A.L.)...........................	2	0	0	...	0.00	0	6	2	0	0	0	5
1989—Toronto (A.L.)...........................	5	0	0	...	1.42	0	$6\frac{1}{3}$	4	2	1	1	4
1991—Toronto (A.L.)...........................	1	0	0	...	0.00	0	$\frac{2}{3}$	1	0	0	0	1
Championship Series totals (3 years)	8	0	0	...	0.69	0	13	7	2	1	1	10

AFENIR, TROY
C, REDS

PERSONAL: Born September 21, 1963, at Escondido, Calif. ... 6-4/200. ... Throws right, bats right.... Full name: Michael Troy Afenir.... Name pronounced AFF-nur.
HIGH SCHOOL: Escondido (Calif.).
COLLEGE: Palomar College (Calif.).
TRANSACTIONS/CAREER NOTES: Selected by Chicago Cubs organization in first round (second pick overall) of free-agent draft (January 12, 1982).... Selected by Baltimore Orioles organization in secondary phase of free-agent draft (June 7, 1982).... Selected by Houston Astros organization in secondary phase of free-agent draft (January 11, 1983).... On disabled list (June 21-July 7, 1986).... Traded by Columbus (Astros organization) to Huntsville (Oakland Athletics organization) for C Matt Sinatro (April 6, 1989).... On disabled list (April 22-May 1 and May 9-June 14, 1989).... On Tacoma disabled list (May 12-May 28, 1991).... Granted free agency (October 16, 1991).... Signed by Cincinnati Reds organization (November 15, 1991).
STATISTICAL NOTES: Led South Atlantic League with 32 passed balls in 1984.... Led Florida State League catchers with 16 errors in 1985.

Year	Team (League)	Pos.	G	AB	R	H	2B	3B	HR	RBI	Avg.	SB	PO	A	E	Avg.
1983	—Sarasota Astros (GCL).....	C	27	89	16	26	5	1	5	24	.292	2	101	19	3	.976
	—Auburn (N.Y.-Penn).........	C	7	26	2	3	0	0	0	0	.115	0	48	2	0	1.000
1984	—Asheville (S. Atlantic).......	C-1B	115	358	44	69	16	0	16	69	.193	1	656	61	12	.984
1985	—Osceola (Florida State).....	C-SS	99	323	38	80	19	1	6	41	.248	3	557	72	†16	.975
1986	—Columbus (Southern)........	C-1B	91	313	50	68	15	3	14	45	.217	0	492	38	14	.974
1987	—Osceola (Florida State).....	C-1B	79	294	60	81	20	1	14	68	.276	1	353	30	5	.987
	—Columbus (Southern)........	C-1B	31	99	15	20	8	0	2	11	.202	0	142	16	3	.981
	—Houston (N.L.).............	C	10	20	1	6	1	0	0	1	.300	0	35	2	1	.974
1988	—Columbus (Southern)........	OF-C-1B	137	494	61	122	21	5	16	66	.247	11	313	29	9	.974
1989	—Huntsville (Southern)■....	OF-C-1B	65	225	31	57	15	1	13	45	.253	1	142	11	3	.981
1990	—Tacoma (Pacific Coast)....	C	88	289	44	72	14	2	15	47	.249	1	457	60	7	.987
	—Oakland (A.L.).............	C	14	14	0	2	0	0	0	2	.143	0	13	0	0	1.000
1991	—Tacoma (Pacific Coast)....	C-1B	80	262	35	64	12	3	10	38	.244	0	405	37	6	.987
	—Oakland (A.L.).............	C	5	11	0	1	0	0	0	0	.091	0	18	1	0	1.000
American League totals (2 years)....................			19	25	0	3	0	0	0	2	.120	0	31	1	0	1.000
National League totals (1 year)....................			10	20	1	6	1	0	0	1	.300	0	35	2	1	.974
Major league totals (3 years)........................			29	45	1	9	1	0	0	3	.200	0	66	3	1	.986

AGOSTO, JUAN
P, CARDINALS

PERSONAL: Born February 23, 1958, at Rio Piedras, Puerto Rico.... 6-2/190.... Throws left, bats left.... Full name: Juan Roberto Agosto.
TRANSACTIONS/CAREER NOTES: Signed as free agent by Boston Red Sox organization (August 29, 1974).... Released by Red Sox organization (September 21, 1978).... Signed by Puerto Rico of Inter-American League (March 10, 1979).... Declared free agent when Inter-American League folded (June 30, 1979).... Signed by Chicago White Sox organization (January 18, 1980).... Sold by White Sox organization to Minnesota Twins in exchange for Twins loaning P Pete Filson to Buffalo, White Sox organization (April 30, 1986); Filson was returned to Minnesota and traded to White Sox for P Kurt Walker (September 3, 1986).... Released by Twins organization (December 20, 1986).... Signed by Tucson, Houston Astros organization (February 13, 1987).... Granted free agency (November 5, 1990). ...Signed by St. Louis Cardinals (December 14, 1990).
STATISTICAL NOTES: Led Carolina League with four balks in 1977 and five in 1978.

Year	Team (League)	G	W	L	Pct.	ERA	Sv.	IP	H	R	ER	BB	SO
1975	—Winter Haven (Florida State) ...	6	0	4	.000	5.79	0	28	35	23	18	24	19
	—Elmira (New York-Penn)	9	1	4	.200	8.61	0	23	27	37	22	34	22
1976	—Winter Haven (Florida State) ...	28	5	11	.313	4.63	0	107	97	70	55	69	80
1977	—Winston-Salem (Carolina)	30	4	9	.308	5.97	0	119	128	106	79	*111	98
1978	—Winter Haven (Florida State) ...	1	0	0	...	18.00	0	1	5	2	2	0	0
	—Winston-Salem (Carolina)	23	5	11	.313	3.83	0	120	114	76	51	89	74
1979	—Puerto Rico (Inter-American)■.	10	3	2	.600	2.61	...	31	31	13	9	17	9
1980	—Glens Falls (Eastern)■.............	8	1	0	1.000	6.95	1	22	26	18	17	18	8
	—Appleton (Midwest).............	23	11	6	.647	2.69	1	144	118	60	43	52	93
1981	—Edmonton (Pacific Coast)........	48	7	10	.412	3.90	7	120	128	61	52	49	57
	—Chicago (A.L.).................	2	0	0	...	4.50	0	6	5	3	3	0	3
1982	—Edmonton (Pacific Coast)........	50	3	4	.429	5.00	11	95⅓	101	63	53	49	39
	—Chicago (A.L.).................	1	0	0	...	18.00	0	2	7	4	4	0	1
1983	—Denver (American Assoc.)	19	4	1	.800	2.08	7	26	19	8	6	10	19
	—Chicago (A.L.).................	39	2	2	.500	4.10	7	41⅔	41	20	19	11	29
1984	—Chicago (A.L.).................	49	2	1	.667	3.09	7	55⅓	54	20	19	34	26
1985	—Chicago (A.L.).................	54	4	3	.571	3.58	1	60⅓	45	27	24	23	39
	—Buffalo (American Assoc.)	6	0	0	...	2.13	2	12⅔	13	3	3	2	11
1986	—Chicago-Minnesota (A.L.)■....	26	1	4	.200	8.64	1	25	49	30	24	18	12
	—Toledo (International).............	21	4	3	.571	2.31	6	35	33	11	9	14	29
1987	—Tucson (Pacific Coast)■..........	44	4	2	.667	1.98	7	50	48	16	11	19	31
	—Houston (N.L.).................	27	1	1	.500	2.63	2	27⅓	26	12	8	10	6
1988	—Houston (N.L.).................	75	10	2	.833	2.26	4	91⅔	74	27	23	30	33
1989	—Houston (N.L.).................	71	4	5	.444	2.93	1	83	81	32	27	32	46
1990	—Houston (N.L.).................	*82	9	8	.529	4.29	4	92⅓	91	46	44	39	50
1991	—St. Louis (N.L.)■.	72	5	3	.625	4.81	2	86	92	52	46	39	34
American League totals (6 years)		171	9	10	.474	4.40	16	190⅓	201	104	93	86	110
National League totals (5 years)		327	29	19	.604	3.50	13	380⅓	364	169	148	150	169
Major league totals (11 years)		498	38	29	.567	3.80	29	570⅔	565	273	241	236	279

CHAMPIONSHIP SERIES RECORD

Year	Team (League)	G	W	L	Pct.	ERA	Sv.	IP	H	R	ER	BB	SO
1983	—Chicago (A.L.)	1	0	0	...	0.00	0	⅓	0	0	0	0	0

AGUILERA, RICK
P, TWINS

PERSONAL: Born December 31, 1961, at San Gabriel, Calif.... 6-5/205.... Throws right, bats right.... Full name: Richard Warren Aguilera.... Name pronounced AG-ah-LAIR-uh.
HIGH SCHOOL: Edgewood (West Covina, Calif.).
COLLEGE: Brigham Young.

TRANSACTIONS/CAREER NOTES: Selected by St. Louis Cardinals organization in 37th round of free-agent draft (June 3, 1980). . . . Selected by New York Mets organization in third round of free-agent draft (June 6, 1983). . . . On New York disabled list (September 3- 15, 1985). . . . On New York disabled list (May 23-August 24, 1987); included rehabilitation disability assignment to Tidewater (August 10-24, 1987). . . . On New York disabled list (April 19-June 19 and July 12-September 7, 1988); included rehabilitation disability assignment to St. Lucie (June 7- 14, 1988) and Tidewater (June 15- 19, 1988). . . . Traded by Mets with P David West and three players to be named later to Minnesota Twins for P Frank Viola (July 31, 1989); Portland (Twins organization) acquired P Kevin Tapani and P Tim Drummond (August 1, 1989), and Twins acquired P Jack Savage to complete deal (October 16, 1989).

STATISTICAL NOTES: Tied for New York-Pennsylvania League lead with two shutouts in 1983. . . . Tied for Carolina League lead with three shutouts in 1984.

Year	Team (League)	G	W	L	Pct.	ERA	Sv.	IP	H	R	ER	BB	SO
1983	Little Falls (New York-Penn)....	16	5	6	.455	3.72	0	104	★109	55	43	26	84
1984	Lynchburg (Carolina)	13	8	3	.727	2.34	0	88⅓	72	29	23	28	101
	—Jackson (Texas)	11	4	4	.500	4.57	0	67	68	37	34	19	71
1985	—Tidewater (International)	11	6	4	.600	2.51	0	79	64	24	22	17	55
	—New York (N.L.)	21	10	7	.588	3.24	0	122⅓	118	49	44	37	74
1986	—New York (N.L.)	28	10	7	.588	3.88	0	141⅔	145	70	61	36	104
1987	—New York (N.L.)	18	11	3	.786	3.60	0	115	124	53	46	33	77
	—Tidewater (International)	3	1	1	.500	0.69	0	13	8	2	1	1	10
1988	—New York (N.L.)	11	0	4	.000	6.93	0	24⅔	29	20	19	10	16
	—St. Lucie (Florida State)	2	0	0	. . .	1.29	0	7	8	1	1	1	5
	—Tidewater (International)	1	0	0	. . .	1.50	0	6	6	1	1	1	4
1989	—New York (N.L.)	36	6	6	.500	2.34	7	69⅓	59	19	18	21	80
	—Minnesota (A.L.)■	11	3	5	.375	3.21	0	75⅔	71	32	27	17	57
1990	—Minnesota (A.L.)	56	5	3	.625	2.76	32	65⅓	55	27	20	19	61
1991	—Minnesota (A.L.)	63	4	5	.444	2.35	42	69	44	20	18	30	61
American League totals (3 years)		130	12	13	.480	2.79	74	210	170	79	65	66	179
National League totals (5 years)		114	37	27	.578	3.58	7	473	475	211	188	137	351
Major league totals (7 years)		244	49	40	.551	3.33	81	683	645	290	253	203	530

CHAMPIONSHIP SERIES RECORD

Year	Team (League)	G	W	L	Pct.	ERA	Sv.	IP	H	R	ER	BB	SO
1986	—New York (N.L.)	2	0	0	. . .	0.00	0	5	2	1	0	2	2
1988	—New York (N.L.)	3	0	0	. . .	1.29	0	7	3	1	1	2	4
1991	—Minnesota (A.L.)	3	0	0	. . .	0.00	3	3⅓	1	0	0	0	3
Championship Series totals (3 years)		8	0	0	. . .	0.59	3	15⅓	6	2	1	4	9

WORLD SERIES RECORD

WORLD SERIES NOTES: Flied out in only appearance as pinch-hitter (1991).

Year	Team (League)	G	W	L	Pct.	ERA	Sv.	IP	H	R	ER	BB	SO
1986	—New York (N.L.)	2	1	0	1.000	12.00	0	3	8	4	4	1	4
1991	—Minnesota (A.L.)	4	1	1	.500	1.80	2	5	6	1	1	1	3
World Series totals (2 years)		6	2	1	.667	5.63	2	8	14	5	5	2	7

ALL-STAR GAME RECORD

Year	League	W	L	Pct.	ERA	Sv.	IP	H	R	ER	BB	SO
1991	—American	0	0	. . .	0.00	0	1⅓	2	0	0	0	3

AKERFELDS, DARREL
P, ORIOLES

PERSONAL: Born June 12, 1962, at Denver. . . . 6-2/210. . . . Throws right, bats right. . . . Full name: Darrel Wayne Akerfelds.
HIGH SCHOOL: Columbine (Littleton, Colo.).
COLLEGE: Mesa College (Colo.) and Arkansas.

TRANSACTIONS/CAREER NOTES: Selected by Atlanta Braves organization in ninth round of free-agent draft (June 3, 1980). . . . Selected by Seattle Mariners organization in first round (seventh pick overall) of free-agent draft (June 6, 1983). . . . Traded by Mariners to Oakland Athletics (December 7, 1983), completing deal in which Mariners traded P Bill Caudill and a player to be named later to A's for P Dave Beard and C Bob Kearney (November 21, 1983). . . . On disabled list (May 22-June 13 and July 5- August 20, 1985). . . . Traded by A's with C Brian Dorsett to Cleveland Indians for 2B Tony Bernazard (July 15, 1987). . . . Drafted by Texas Rangers (December 5, 1988); deal settled with future considerations. . . . Sold by Rangers to Philadelphia Phillies (March 31, 1990). . . . Granted free agency (October 7, 1991). . . . Signed by Baltimore Orioles organization (January 23, 1992).

STATISTICAL NOTES: Tied for Midwest League lead with 19 wild pitches in 1984.

Year	Team (League)	G	W	L	Pct.	ERA	Sv.	IP	H	R	ER	BB	SO
1983	—Bellingham (Northwest)............	12	5	3	.625	4.48	1	68⅓	62	36	34	36	85
1984	—Madison (Midwest)■	24	11	6	.647	4.41	0	151	156	86	74	74	137
1985	—Huntsville (Southern)	17	9	6	.600	3.46	0	96⅓	75	42	37	64	56
1986	—Tacoma (Pacific Coast)	25	8	12	.400	4.74	0	150	158	91	79	62	91
	—Oakland (A.L.)	2	0	0	. . .	6.75	0	5⅓	7	5	4	3	5
1987	—Tacoma (Pacific Coast)	19	10	3	.769	3.54	0	129⅔	117	52	51	57	84
	—Cleveland (A.L.)■	16	2	6	.250	6.75	0	74⅔	84	60	56	38	42
1988	—Colorado Springs (Pac. Coast) ..	49	3	7	.300	4.34	6	58	70	43	28	26	50
1989	—Oklahoma City (Am. Assoc.)■ ..	33	5	5	.500	3.33	4	108	89	45	40	59	75
	—Texas (A.L.)	6	1	0	.000	3.27	0	11	11	6	4	5	9

Year Team (League)	G	W	L	Pct.	ERA	Sv.	IP	H	R	ER	BB	SO
1990 —Philadelphia (N.L.)■...............	71	5	2	.714	3.77	3	93	65	45	39	54	42
1991 —Philadelphia (N.L.)..................	30	2	1	.667	5.26	0	49⅔	49	30	29	27	31
—Scranton/Wilkes-Barre (Int'l) ..	11	3	3	.500	6.32	0	52⅔	52	37	37	39	36
American League totals (3 years)..........	24	2	7	.222	6.33	0	91	102	71	64	46	56
National League totals (2 years)..........	101	7	3	.700	4.29	3	142⅔	114	75	68	81	73
Major league totals (5 years)...............	125	9	10	.474	5.08	3	233⅔	216	146	132	127	129

ALDRED, SCOTT
P, TIGERS

PERSONAL: Born June 12, 1968, at Flint, Mich. . . . 6-4/195. . . . Throws left, bats left. . . . Full name: Scott Phillip Aldred.
HIGH SCHOOL: Hill McCloy (Montrose, Mich.).
TRANSACTIONS/CAREER NOTES: Selected by Detroit Tigers organization in 16th round of free-agent draft (June 2, 1986).
STATISTICAL NOTES: Led International League pitchers with 29 games started in 1990.

Year Team (League)	G	W	L	Pct.	ERA	Sv.	IP	H	R	ER	BB	SO
1987 —Fayetteville (South Atlantic)	21	4	9	.308	3.60	0	110	101	56	44	69	91
1988 —Lakeland (Florida State)...........	25	8	7	.533	3.56	0	131⅓	122	61	52	72	102
1989 —London (Eastern)	20	10	6	.625	3.84	0	122	98	55	52	59	97
1990 —Toledo (International)...............	29	6	15	.286	4.90	0	158	145	93	86	81	133
—Detroit (A.L.)	4	1	2	.333	3.77	0	14⅓	13	6	6	10	7
1991 —Toledo (International)	22	8	8	.500	3.92	1	135⅓	127	65	59	72	95
—Detroit (A.L.)	11	2	4	.333	5.18	0	57⅓	58	37	33	30	35
Major league totals (2 years)	15	3	6	.333	4.90	0	71⅔	71	43	39	40	42

ALDRETE, MIKE
OF/1B, INDIANS

PERSONAL: Born January 29, 1961, at Carmel, Calif. . . . 5-11/185. . . . Throws left, bats left. . . . Full name: Michael Peter Aldrete. . . . Brother of Rich Aldrete, first baseman, San Francisco Giants organization. . . . Name pronounced owl-DRET-ee.
HIGH SCHOOL: Monterey (Calif.).
COLLEGE: Stanford (bachelor of arts degree in communication).
TRANSACTIONS/CAREER NOTES: Selected by San Francisco Giants organization in seventh round of free-agent draft (June 6, 1983). . . . Traded by Giants to Montreal Expos for OF Tracy Jones (December 8, 1988). . . . On Montreal disabled list (August 16-September 1, 1989); included rehabilitation disability assignment to Indianapolis (August 21-September 1, 1989). . . . Released by Expos (March 30, 1991). . . . Signed by San Diego Padres (April 5, 1991). . . . Released by Padres (May 10, 1991). . . . Signed by Colorado Springs, Cleveland Indians organization (May 17, 1991).
STATISTICAL NOTES: Led California League with 225 total bases in 1984.

Year Team (League)	Pos.	G	AB	R	H	2B	3B	HR	RBI	Avg.	SB	PO	A	E	Avg.
1983 —Great Falls (Pioneer)	1B-OF	38	132	30	55	11	2	4	31	.417	7	257	17	4	.986
—Fresno (California)	1B	20	68	5	14	4	0	1	12	.206	2	189	9	2	.990
1984 —Fresno (California)	1B	136	457	89	155	28	3	12	72	.339	14	1180	74	8	*.994
1985 —Shreveport (Texas)	1B-OF	127	441	80	147	32	1	15	77	.333	16	854	41	9	.990
—Phoenix (Pacific Coast)	OF	3	8	0	1	1	0	0	1	.125	0	3	0	0	1.000
1986 —Phoenix (Pacific Coast)	OF-1B	47	159	36	59	14	0	6	35	.371	0	131	8	1	.993
—San Francisco (N.L.)	1B-OF	84	216	27	54	18	3	2	25	.250	1	317	36	1	.997
1987 —San Francisco (N.L.)	OF-1B	126	357	50	116	18	2	9	51	.325	6	328	18	3	.991
1988 —San Francisco (N.L.)	OF-1B	139	389	44	104	15	0	3	50	.267	6	272	8	4	.986
1989 —Montreal (N.L.)■..............	OF-1B	76	136	12	30	8	1	1	12	.221	1	109	9	1	.992
—Indianapolis (A.A.)	1B-OF	10	31	4	4	1	0	0	2	.129	0	41	3	0	1.000
1990 —Montreal (N.L.)■..............	OF-1B	96	161	22	39	7	1	1	18	.242	1	160	12	1	.994
1991 —San Diego (N.L.)■..	OF	12	15	2	0	0	0	0	1	.000	0	7	1	0	1.000
—Colorado Springs (PCL)■..	OF-1B	23	76	4	22	5	0	0	8	.289	0	77	8	1	.988
—Cleveland (A.L.)	1B-OF	85	183	22	48	6	1	1	19	.262	1	334	23	2	.994
American League totals (1 year)		85	183	22	48	6	1	1	19	.262	1	334	23	2	.994
National League totals (6 years)		533	1274	157	343	66	7	16	157	.269	15	1193	84	10	.992
Major league totals (6 years)		618	1457	179	391	72	8	17	176	.268	16	1527	107	12	.993

CHAMPIONSHIP SERIES RECORD

Year Team (League)	Pos.	G	AB	R	H	2B	3B	HR	RBI	Avg.	SB	PO	A	E	Avg.
1987 —San Francisco (N.L.)	PH-OF	5	10	0	1	0	0	0	1	.100	0	5	0	0	1.000

ALEXANDER, GERALD
P, RANGERS

PERSONAL: Born March 26, 1968, at Baton Rouge, La. . . . 5-11/200. . . . Throws right, bats right. . . . Full name: Gerald Paul Alexander.
HIGH SCHOOL: Donaldsville (La.).
COLLEGE: Tulane.
TRANSACTIONS/CAREER NOTES: Selected by Texas Rangers organization in 21st round of free-agent draft (June 5, 1989). . . . On Texas disabled list (August 15-September 12, 1991).

Year Team (League)	G	W	L	Pct.	ERA	Sv.	IP	H	R	ER	BB	SO
1989 —Sarasota Rangers (GCL)...........	6	0	0	. . .	0.00	4	6⅓	3	0	0	0	9
—Port Charlotte (Florida State) ...	14	2	3	.400	1.70	2	53	36	12	10	16	41

Year	Team (League)	G	W	L	Pct.	ERA	Sv.	IP	H	R	ER	BB	SO
1990	—Charlotte (Florida State)	7	6	1	.857	0.63	0	42⅔	24	7	3	14	39
	—Oklahoma City (Am. Assoc.)	20	13	2	.867	4.10	0	118⅔	126	58	54	45	94
	—Texas (A.L.)	3	0	0	...	7.71	0	7	14	6	6	5	8
1991	—Oklahoma City (Am. Assoc.)	2	1	1	.500	4.22	0	10⅔	10	5	5	4	10
	—Texas (A.L.)	30	5	3	.625	5.24	0	89⅓	93	56	52	48	50
Major league totals (2 years)		33	5	3	.625	5.42	0	96⅓	107	62	58	53	58

ALEXANDER, MANNY

SS, ORIOLES

PERSONAL: Born March 20, 1971, at San Pedro De Macoris, Dominican Republic. . . . 5- 10/ 150. . . . Throws right, bats right. . . . Full name: Manuel DeJesus Alexander.
TRANSACTIONS/CAREER NOTES: Signed as free agent by Baltimore Orioles organization (February 4, 1988). . . . On disabled list (April 26-July 23, 1990).
STATISTICAL NOTES: Led Appalachian League shortstops with 349 total chances in 1989. . . . Led Carolina League shortstops with 651 total chances and 93 double plays in 1991.

							BATTING						FIELDING			
Year	Team (League)	Pos.	G	AB	R	H	2B	3B	HR	RBI	Avg.	SB	PO	A	E	Avg.
1989	—Bluefield (Appalachian)	SS	65	*274	49	*85	13	2	2	34	.310	19	*140	177	*32	.908
1990	—Wausau (Midwest)	SS	44	152	16	27	3	1	0	11	.178	8	66	99	11	.938
1991	—Hagerstown (Eastern)	SS	3	9	3	3	1	0	0	2	.333	0	5	4	0	1.000
	—Frederick (Carolina)..........	SS	134	548	*81	*143	17	3	3	42	.261	47	*226	*393	32	.951

ALICEA, LUIS

2B, CARDINALS

PERSONAL: Born July 29, 1965, at Santurce, Puerto Rico. . . . 5-9/ 177. . . . Throws right, bats both. . . . Full name: Luis Rene Alicea.
HIGH SCHOOL: Liceo Castro (Rio Piedras, Puerto Rico).
COLLEGE: Florida State.
TRANSACTIONS/CAREER NOTES: Selected by St. Louis Cardinals organization in first round (23rd pick overall) of free-agent draft (June 2, 1986). . . . On disabled list (April 6-June 4, 1990).
RECORDS/HONORS: Named second baseman on THE SPORTING NEWS college All-America team (1986).

							BATTING						FIELDING			
Year	Team (League)	Pos.	G	AB	R	H	2B	3B	HR	RBI	Avg.	SB	PO	A	E	Avg.
1986	—Erie (New York-Penn)	2B	47	163	40	46	6	1	3	18	.282	27	94	163	12	.955
	—Arkansas (Texas)	2B-SS	25	68	8	16	3	0	0	3	.235	0	39	63	4	.962
1987	—Arkansas (Texas)	2B	101	337	57	91	14	3	4	47	.270	13	184	251	11	*.975
	—Louisville (Am. Assoc.)	2B	29	105	18	32	10	2	2	20	.305	4	69	81	4	.974
1988	—Louisville (Am. Assoc.)	2B-SS-OF	49	191	21	53	11	6	1	21	.277	8	116	165	0	1.000
	—St. Louis (N.L.)	2B	93	297	20	63	10	4	1	24	.212	1	206	240	14	.970
1989	—Louisville (Am. Assoc.)	2B	124	412	53	102	20	3	8	48	.248	13	240	310	16	.972
1990	—Arkansas (Texas)	2B	14	49	11	14	3	1	0	4	.286	2	24	34	4	.935
	—St. Petersburg (Fla. St.)	2B	29	95	14	22	1	4	0	12	.232	9	20	23	0	1.000
	—Louisville (Am. Assoc.)	3B	25	92	10	32	6	3	0	10	.348	0	14	39	6	.898
1991	—Louisville (Am. Assoc.)	2B	31	112	26	44	6	3	4	16	.393	5	68	95	5	.970
	—St. Louis (N.L.)	2B-3B-SS	56	68	5	13	3	0	0	0	.191	0	19	23	0	1.000
Major league totals (2 years)			149	365	25	76	13	4	1	24	.208	1	225	263	14	.972

ALLANSON, ANDY

C

PERSONAL: Born December 22, 1961, at Richmond, Va. . . . 6-5/225. . . . Throws right, bats right. . . . Full name: Andrew Neal Allanson.
HIGH SCHOOL: Varina (Richmond, Va.).
COLLEGE: Richmond.
TRANSACTIONS/CAREER NOTES: Selected by Cleveland Indians organization in second round of free-agent draft (June 6, 1983). . . . On Cleveland disabled list (June 19-29, 1984 and July 16-August 5, 1988). . . . Released by Indians (March 27, 1990). . . . Signed by Oklahoma City, Texas Rangers organization (April 2, 1990). . . . Released by Oklahoma City (May 8, 1990). . . . Signed by Salinas, independent (July 23, 1990). . . . Released by Salinas (August 29, 1990). . . . Signed by Omaha, Kansas City Royals organization (January 18, 1991). . . . Traded by Royals to Detroit Tigers organization for C Jim Baxter (March 30, 1991). . . . Granted free agency (December 20, 1991).
STATISTICAL NOTES: Led A.L. catchers with 762 total chances and 11 double plays in 1988.

							BATTING						FIELDING			
Year	Team (League)	Pos.	G	AB	R	H	2B	3B	HR	RBI	Avg.	SB	PO	A	E	Avg.
1983	—Waterloo (Midwest)	C	17	50	4	10	0	0	0	0	.200	1	99	8	3	.973
	—Batavia (N.Y.-Penn)	C	51	145	27	38	3	0	0	6	.262	3	372	27	5	.988
1984	—Buffalo (Eastern)	C	39	111	12	28	4	0	0	11	.252	0	154	15	3	.983
	—Waterloo (Midwest)	C	46	144	14	39	5	0	0	10	.271	6	68	9	1	.987
1985	—Waterbury (Eastern)........	C	120	420	69	131	17	1	0	47	*.312	22	578	64	10	.985
1986	—Cleveland (A.L.)	C	101	293	30	66	7	3	1	29	.225	10	446	33	*20	.960
1987	—Buffalo (Am. Assoc.)	C	76	276	21	75	8	0	4	39	.272	2	428	30	*12	.974
	—Cleveland (A.L.)	C	50	154	17	41	6	0	3	16	.266	1	252	22	4	.986
1988	—Cleveland (A.L.)	C	133	434	44	114	11	0	5	50	.263	5	*691	60	•11	.986
1989	—Cleveland (A.L.)	C	111	323	30	75	9	1	3	17	.232	4	570	53	9	.986
1990	—Oklahoma City (A.A.)■.......	C	13	40	3	4	0	0	0	4	.100	0	79	12	2	.978
	—Salinas (California)■.........	C	36	127	21	37	6	1	3	19	.291	6	223	28	2	.992
1991	—Detroit (A.L.)■	C-1B	60	151	10	35	10	0	1	16	.232	0	219	22	5	.980
Major league totals (5 years)			455	1355	131	331	43	4	13	128	.244	20	2178	190	49	.980

ALLISON, DANA
P, ATHLETICS

PERSONAL: Born August 14, 1966, at Front Royal, Va. . . . 6-3/215. . . . Throws left, bats right. . . . Full name: Dana Eric Allison.
HIGH SCHOOL: Warren County (Front Royal, Va.).
COLLEGE: James Madison (degree in political science).
TRANSACTIONS/CAREER NOTES: Selected by Los Angeles Dodgers organization in 14th round of free-agent draft (June 1, 1988). . . . Selected by Oakland Athletics organization in 21st round of free-agent draft (June 5, 1989). . . . On Tacoma disabled list (July 10-23 and July 28-August 18, 1991).

Year	Team (League)	G	W	L	Pct.	ERA	Sv.	IP	H	R	ER	BB	SO
1989	— Madison (Midwest)	13	2	3	.400	1.13	1	24	24	6	3	3	16
	— Southern Oregon (Northwest)	11	0	2	.000	1.84	4	29⅓	17	8	6	4	27
1990	— Modesto (California)	10	0	0	. . .	2.33	4	19⅓	13	9	5	3	19
	— Huntsville (Southern)	35	7	1	.875	2.39	2	52⅔	52	14	14	6	38
	— Tacoma (Pacific Coast)	2	0	0	. . .	0.00	0	1⅓	1	0	0	1	2
1991	— Oakland (A.L.)	11	1	1	.500	7.36	0	11	16	9	9	5	4
	— Tacoma (Pacific Coast)	18	3	1	.750	4.37	0	22⅔	25	12	11	11	13
Major league totals (1 year)		11	1	1	.500	7.36	0	11	16	9	9	5	4

ALLRED, BEAU
OF, INDIANS

PERSONAL: Born June 4, 1965, at Mesa, Ariz. . . . 6-0/195. . . . Throws left, bats left. . . . Full name: Dale LeBeau Allred.
HIGH SCHOOL: Safford (Ariz.).
COLLEGE: Cochise County Community College (Ariz.) and Lamar.
TRANSACTIONS/CAREER NOTES: Selected by Cleveland Indians organization in 25th round of free-agent draft (June 2, 1987).

Year	Team (League)	Pos.	G	AB	R	H	2B	3B	HR	RBI	Avg.	SB	PO	A	E	Avg.
1987	— Burlington (W. Caro.)	OF	54	167	39	57	14	1	10	38 ★.341		4	61	2	4	.940
1988	— Kinston (Carolina)	OF	126	397	66	100	23	3	15	74	.252	6	187	10	10	.952
1989	— Canton/Akron (Eastern)	OF	118	412	67	125	23	5	14	75	.303	16	204	7	8	.963
	— Colorado Springs (PCL)	OF	11	47	8	13	3	0	1	4	.277	0	27	1	0	1.000
	— Cleveland (A.L.)	OF	13	24	0	6	3	0	0	1	.250	0	11	1	0	1.000
1990	— Colorado Springs (PCL)	OF	115	378	79	105	23	6	13	74	.278	6	203	12	•11	.951
	— Cleveland (A.L.)	OF	4	16	2	3	1	0	1	2	.188	0	5	0	1	.833
1991	— Colorado Springs (PCL)	OF	53	148	39	37	12	3	6	21	.250	1	92	4	2	.980
	— Cleveland (A.L.)	OF	48	125	17	29	3	0	3	21	.232	2	105	1	3	.972
Major league totals (3 years)			65	165	19	38	7	0	4	24	.230	2	121	2	4	.969

ALOMAR, ROBERTO
2B, BLUE JAYS

PERSONAL: Born February 5, 1968, at Salinas, Puerto Rico. . . . 6-0/185. . . . Throws right, bats both. . . . Full name: Roberto Velazquez Alomar. . . . Son of Sandy Alomar Sr., major league infielder for six teams (1964-78) and coach, San Diego Padres (1986-90); and brother of Sandy Alomar Jr., catcher, Cleveland Indians.
TRANSACTIONS/CAREER NOTES: Signed as free agent by San Diego Padres organization (February 16, 1985). . . . Traded by Padres with OF Joe Carter to Toronto Blue Jays for 1B Fred McGriff and SS Tony Fernandez (December 5, 1990).
RECORDS/HONORS: Won A.L. Gold Glove at second base (1991).
STATISTICAL NOTES: Led South Atlantic League second basemen with 35 errors in 1985. . . . Led Texas League shortstops with 167 putouts and 34 errors in 1987. . . . Led N.L. with 17 sacrifice hits in 1989. . . . Led N.L. second basemen with 17 errors in 1990. . . . Switch hit home runs in a game (May 10, 1991).

Year	Team (League)	Pos.	G	AB	R	H	2B	3B	HR	RBI	Avg.	SB	PO	A	E	Avg.
1985	— Charleston, S.C. (S. Atl.)	2B-SS	★137	★546	89	160	14	3	0	54	.293	36	298	339	†36	.947
1986	— Reno (California)	2B	90	356	53	123	16	4	4	49 ★.346		14	198	265	18	.963
1987	— Wichita (Texas)	SS-2B	130	536	88	171	41	4	12	68	.319	43	†188	309	†36	.932
1988	— Las Vegas (Pac. Coast)	2B	9	37	5	10	1	0	2	14	.270	3	22	29	1	.981
	— San Diego (N.L.)	2B	143	545	84	145	24	6	9	41	.266	24	319	459	16	.980
1989	— San Diego (N.L.)	2B	158	623	82	184	27	1	7	56	.295	42	341	472	★28	.967
1990	— San Diego (N.L.)	2B-SS	147	586	80	168	27	5	6	60	.287	24	316	404	†19	.974
1991	— Toronto (A.L.)■	2B	161	637	88	188	41	11	9	69	.295	53	333	447	15	.981
American League totals (1 year)			161	637	88	188	41	11	9	69	.295	53	333	447	15	.981
National League totals (3 years)			448	1754	246	497	78	12	22	157	.283	90	976	1335	63	.973
Major league totals (4 years)			609	2391	334	685	119	23	31	226	.286	143	1309	1782	78	.975

CHAMPIONSHIP SERIES RECORD
CHAMPIONSHIP SERIES NOTES: Shares single-series record for most singles—9 (1991).

Year	Team (League)	Pos.	G	AB	R	H	2B	3B	HR	RBI	Avg.	SB	PO	A	E	Avg.
1991	— Toronto (A.L.)	2B	5	19	3	9	0	0	0	4	.474	2	14	9	0	1.000

ALL-STAR GAME RECORD

Year	League	Pos.	AB	R	H	2B	3B	HR	RBI	Avg.	SB	PO	A	E	Avg.
1990	— National	2B	1	0	0	0	0	0	0	.000	0	1	0	0	1.000
1991	— American	2B	4	0	0	0	0	0	0	.000	0	2	5	0	1.000
All-Star Game totals (2 years)			5	0	0	0	0	0	0	.000	0	3	7	0	1.000

ALOMAR, SANDY
C, INDIANS

PERSONAL: Born June 18, 1966, at Salinas, Puerto Rico.... 6-5/200.... Throws right, bats right.... Full name: Santos Velazquez Alomar Jr.... Son of Sandy Alomar Sr., major league infielder for six teams (1964-78) and coach, San Diego Padres (1986-90); and brother of Roberto Alomar, second baseman, Toronto Blue Jays.

TRANSACTIONS/CAREER NOTES: Signed as free agent by San Diego Padres organization (October 21, 1983).... Traded by Padres with OF Chris James and 3B Carlos Baerga to Cleveland Indians for OF Joe Carter (December 6, 1989).... On Cleveland disabled list (May 15-June 17 and July 29, 1991-remainder of season); included rehabilitation disability assignment to Colorado Springs (June 8-17 and August 9-12, 1991).

RECORDS/HONORS: Named Minor League Co-Player of the Year by THE SPORTING NEWS (1988).... Named Pacific Coast League Player of the Year (1988-89).... Named Minor League Player of the Year by THE SPORTING NEWS (1989).... Named A.L. Rookie Player of the Year by THE SPORTING NEWS (1990).... Won A.L. Gold Glove at catcher (1990).... Named A.L. Rookie of the Year by Baseball Writers' Association of America (1990).

STATISTICAL NOTES: Led Northwest League catchers with .985 fielding percentage and 421 putouts in 1984.... Led Pacific Coast League catchers with 14 errors in 1988.... Led Pacific Coast League catchers with 573 putouts in 1988 and 702 in 1989. .... Led Pacific Coast League catchers with 633 total chances in 1988 and 761 in 1989.

MISCELLANEOUS: Batted as switch-hitter (1984-1986).

Year	Team (League)	Pos.	G	AB	R	H	2B	3B	HR	RBI	Avg.	SB	PO	A	E	Avg.
1984	Spokane (Northwest)	C-1B	59	219	13	47	5	0	0	21	.215	3	†465	51	8	†.985
1985	Charleston, S.C. (S. Atl.)	C-OF	100	352	38	73	7	0	3	43	.207	3	779	75	18	.979
1986	Beaumont (Texas)	C	100	346	36	83	15	1	4	27	.240	2	505	60	★18	.969
1987	Wichita (Texas)	C	103	375	50	115	19	1	8	65	.307	1	★606	50	★15	.978
1988	Las Vegas (Pac. Coast)	C-OF	93	337	59	100	9	5	16	71	.297	1	†574	46	†14	.978
	San Diego (N.L.)	PH	1	1	0	0	0	0	0	0	.000	0	0	0	0	...
1989	Las Vegas (Pac. Coast)	C-OF	131	★523	88	160	33	8	13	101	.306	3	†706	47	12	.984
	San Diego (N.L.)	C	7	19	1	4	1	0	1	6	.211	0	33	1	0	1.000
1990	Cleveland (A.L.)■	C	132	445	60	129	26	2	9	66	.290	4	686	46	★14	.981
1991	Cleveland (A.L.)	C	51	184	10	40	9	0	0	7	.217	0	280	19	4	.987
	Colorado Springs (PCL)	C	12	35	5	14	2	0	1	10	.400	0	5	0	1	.833
American League totals (2 years)			183	629	70	169	35	2	9	73	.269	4	966	65	18	.983
National League totals (2 years)			8	20	1	4	1	0	1	6	.200	0	33	1	0	1.000
Major league totals (4 years)			191	649	71	173	36	2	10	79	.267	4	999	66	18	.983

ALL-STAR GAME RECORD

Year	League	Pos.	AB	R	H	2B	3B	HR	RBI	Avg.	SB	PO	A	E	Avg.
1990	American	C	3	1	2	0	0	0	0	.667	0	3	0	0	1.000
1991	American	C	2	0	0	0	0	0	0	.000	0	2	0	0	1.000
All-Star Game totals (2 years)			5	1	2	0	0	0	0	.400	0	5	0	0	1.000

ALOU, MOISES
OF, EXPOS

PERSONAL: Born July 3, 1966, at Atlanta.... 6-3/190.... Throws right, bats right.... Full name: Moises Rojas Alou.... Son of Felipe Alou, major league outfielder-first baseman for six teams (1958-74) and coach, Montreal Expos (1979-80 and 1984); nephew of Jesus Alou, major league outfielder for four teams (1963-75 and 1978-79); and nephew of Matty Alou, major league outfielder for six teams (1960-74).... Name pronounced MOY-ses.

HIGH SCHOOL: C.E.E. (Santo Domingo, Dominican Republic).

COLLEGE: Canada College (Calif.).

TRANSACTIONS/CAREER NOTES: Selected by Pittsburgh Pirates organization in first round (second pick overall) of free-agent draft (January 14, 1986).... Traded by Pirates organization to Montreal Expos (August 16, 1990), completing deal in which Expos traded P Zane Smith to Pirates for P Scott Ruskin, SS Willie Greene and a player to be named later (August 8, 1990).... On disabled list (March 19, 1991-entire season).

STATISTICAL NOTES: Led American Association outfielders with seven double plays in 1990.

Year	Team (League)	Pos.	G	AB	R	H	2B	3B	HR	RBI	Avg.	SB	PO	A	E	Avg.
1986	Watertown (N.Y.-Penn)	OF	69	254	30	60	9	★8	6	35	.236	14	134	6	7	.952
1987	Macon (South Atlantic)	OF	4	8	1	1	0	0	0	0	.125	24	6	0	0	1.000
	Watertown (N.Y.-Penn)	OF	39	117	20	25	6	2	4	8	.214	6	43	1	2	.957
1988	Augusta (S. Atlantic)	OF	105	358	58	112	23	5	7	62	.313	12	220	10	9	.962
1989	Salem (Carolina)	OF	86	321	50	97	29	2	14	53	.302	8	166	12	10	.947
	Harrisburg (Eastern)	OF	54	205	36	60	5	2	3	19	.293	7	89	1	2	.978
1990	Harrisburg (Eastern)	OF	36	132	19	39	12	2	3	22	.295	7	93	2	1	.990
	Buffalo-Ind. (A.A.)■	OF	90	326	44	86	5	6	5	37	.264	13	196	12	8	.963
	Pitts.-Montreal (N.L.)	OF	16	20	4	4	0	1	0	0	.200	0	9	1	0	1.000
1991							Did not play									
Major league totals (1 year)			16	20	4	4	0	1	0	0	.200	0	9	1	0	1.000

ALVAREZ, WILSON
P, WHITE SOX

PERSONAL: Born March 24, 1970, at Maracaibo, Venezuela.... 6-1/175.... Throws left, bats left.... Full name: Wilson Eduardo Alvarez.

TRANSACTIONS/CAREER NOTES: Signed as free agent by Texas Rangers organization (September 23, 1986).... Traded by Rangers with IF Scott Fletcher and OF Sammy Sosa to Chicago White Sox for OF Harold Baines and IF Fred Manrique (July 29, 1989).

STATISTICAL NOTES: Tied for Gulf Coast League lead with six home runs allowed in 1987. . . . Pitched 7-0 no-hit victory against Baltimore Orioles (August 11, 1991).

Year	Team (League)	G	W	L	Pct.	ERA	Sv.	IP	H	R	ER	BB	SO
1987	—Gastonia (South Atlantic).........	8	1	5	.167	6.47	0	32	39	24	23	23	19
	—Sarasota Rangers (GCL)...........	10	2	5	.286	5.24	0	44⅔	41	29	26	21	46
1988	—Gastonia (South Atlantic).........	23	4	11	.267	2.98	0	127	113	63	42	49	134
	—Oklahoma City (Am. Assoc.).....	5	1	1	.500	3.78	0	16⅔	17	8	7	6	9
1989	—Tulsa (Texas)	7	2	2	.500	2.06	0	48	40	14	11	16	29
	—Texas (A.L.)	1	0	1	.000	. . .	0	0	3	3	3	2	0
	—Birmingham (Southern)■.........	6	2	1	.667	3.03	0	35⅔	32	12	12	16	18
1990	—Birmingham (Southern)	7	5	1	.833	4.27	0	46⅓	44	24	22	25	36
	—Vancouver (Pacific Coast)	17	7	7	.500	6.00	0	75	91	54	50	51	35
1991	—Birmingham (Southern)	23	10	6	.625	1.83	0	152⅓	109	46	31	74	165
	—Chicago (A.L.)	10	3	2	.600	3.51	0	56⅓	47	26	22	29	32
Major league totals (2 years)		11	3	3	.500	3.99	0	56⅓	50	29	25	31	32

AMARAL, RICH
SS/2B, MARINERS

PERSONAL: Born April 1, 1962, at Visalia, Calif. . . . 6-0/175. . . . Throws right, bats right. . . . Full name: Richard Louis Amaral.
HIGH SCHOOL: Estancia (Costa Mesa, Calif.).
COLLEGE: Orange Coast College (Calif.) and UCLA.
TRANSACTIONS/CAREER NOTES: Selected by Chicago Cubs organization in second round of free-agent draft (June 6, 1983). . . . Drafted by Chicago White Sox organization (December 6, 1988). . . . Granted free agency (October 15, 1990). . . . Signed by Seattle Mariners organization (November 25, 1990). . . . On Seattle disabled list (May 29-July 17, 1991); included rehabilitation disability assignment to Calgary (July 11-17, 1991).
RECORDS/HONORS: Named second baseman on THE SPORTING NEWS college All-America team (1983).
STATISTICAL NOTES: Tied for New York-Pennsylvania League lead with 39 double plays by second basemen in 1984. . . . Tied for Carolina League lead with 25 errors by second basemen in 1985. . . . Led Pacific Coast League with .433 on base percentage in 1991.

Year	Team (League)	Pos.	G	AB	R	H	2B	3B	HR	RBI	Avg.	SB	PO	A	E	Avg.
1983	—Geneva (N.Y.-Penn)	2B-3B-SS	67	269	63	68	17	3	1	24	.253	22	135	205	14	.960
1984	—Quad Cities (Midwest).......	2B-SS	34	119	21	25	1	0	0	7	.210	12	62	73	6	.957
1985	—Winston-Salem (Caro.)	2B-3B	124	428	62	116	15	5	3	36	.271	26	228	318	‡27	.953
1986	—Pittsfield (Eastern)..........	2B	114	355	43	89	12	0	0	24	.251	25	228	266	14	.972
1987	—Pittsfield (Eastern)..........	2B-1B	104	315	45	80	8	5	0	28	.254	28	242	274	18	.966
1988	—Pittsfield (Eastern)..........	2-3-1-S-0	122	422	66	117	15	4	4	47	.277	54	288	262	19	.967
1989	—Birmingham (Southern)■..	2B-SS-3B	122	432	*90	123	15	6	4	48	.285	57	198	256	23	.952
1990	—Vancouver (Pac. Coast)...	S-3-2-0-1	130	462	87	139	*39	4	4	56	.301	20	154	260	15	.965
1991	—Calgary (Pacific Coast)■..	SS-2B	86	347	79	120	26	2	3	36	*.346	30	148	284	15	.966
	—Seattle (A.L.)	2-3-S-1	14	16	2	1	0	0	0	0	.063	0	13	16	2	.935
Major league totals (1 year)			14	16	2	1	0	0	0	0	.063	0	13	16	2	.935

AMARO, RUBEN
OF, PHILLIES

PERSONAL: Born February 12, 1965, at Philadelphia. . . . 5-10/170. . . . Throws right, bats both. . . . Full name: Ruben Amaro Jr. . . . Son of Ruben Amaro Sr., major league infielder for four teams (1958 and 1960-69) and current scout with Detroit Tigers.
HIGH SCHOOL: William Penn Charter (Philadelphia).
COLLEGE: Stanford (bachelor of science degree in human biology, 1987).
TRANSACTIONS/CAREER NOTES: Selected by California Angels organization in 11th round of free-agent draft (June 2, 1987). . . . Traded by Angels with P Kyle Abbott to Philadelphia Phillies for OF Von Hayes (December 8, 1991).
STATISTICAL NOTES: Led Northwest League in caught stealing with 11 in 1987. . . . Tied for Texas League lead in being hit by pitch with nine in 1990.

Year	Team (League)	Pos.	G	AB	R	H	2B	3B	HR	RBI	Avg.	SB	PO	A	E	Avg.
1987	—Salem (Northwest)	0-3-1-S-2	71	241	51	68	7	3	3	41	.282	27	243	53	17	.946
1988	—Palm Springs (Calif.)........	2-0-C-S	115	417	96	111	13	3	4	50	.266	42	258	188	18	.961
	—Midland (Texas)	2B	13	31	5	4	1	0	0	2	.129	4	14	30	1	.978
1989	—Quad City (Midwest)	OF-2B	59	200	50	72	9	4	3	27	.360	20	94	34	4	.970
	—Midland (Texas)	OF	29	110	28	42	9	2	3	9	.382	7	34	2	2	.947
1990	—Midland (Texas)	OF	57	224	50	80	15	6	4	38	.357	8	97	8	0	1.000
	—Edmonton (Pac. Coast).....	OF-1B	82	318	53	92	15	4	3	32	.289	32	161	5	2	.988
1991	—Edmonton (Pac. Coast).....	0F-2B-1B	121	472	*95	154	*42	6	3	42	.326	36	167	23	5	.974
	—California (A.L.)	OF-2B	10	23	0	5	1	0	0	2	.217	0	9	6	1	.938
Major league totals (1 year)			10	23	0	5	1	0	0	2	.217	0	9	6	1	.938

ANDERSEN, LARRY
P, PADRES

PERSONAL: Born May 6, 1953, at Portland, Ore. . . . 6-3/205. . . . Throws right, bats right. . . . Full name: Larry Eugene Andersen.
HIGH SCHOOL: Interlake (Seattle).
COLLEGE: Bellevue Community College (Wash.).
TRANSACTIONS/CAREER NOTES: Selected by Cleveland Indians organization in seventh round of free-agent draft (June 8, 1971).

... Traded by Indians to Pittsburgh Pirates for OF Larry Littleton and P John Burden (December 21, 1979).... Traded by Pirates organization to Seattle Mariners (October 29, 1980), completing deal in which Mariners traded P Odell Jones to Pirates for a player to be named later (April 1, 1980).... On Seattle disabled list (August 11-September 1, 1982); included rehabilitation disability assignment to Salt Lake City (August 11-31, 1982).... Loaned by Mariners organization to Portland, Philadelphia Phillies organization (April 1, 1983).... Sold by Mariners to Philadelphia Phillies (July 29, 1983).... Released by Phillies (May 13, 1986).... Signed by Houston Astros (May 16, 1986).... Granted free agency (November 12, 1986).... Re-signed by Astros (December 21, 1986).... Granted free agency (November 9, 1987).... Re-signed by Astros (January 8, 1988).... On disabled list (April 26-May 11, 1988; April 25-May 10 and August 20-September 4, 1989).... Traded by Astros to Boston Red Sox for 3B Jeff Bagwell (August 30, 1990).... Granted free agency (December 7, 1990).... Signed by San Diego Padres (December 21, 1990).... On disabled list (May 8-30 and August 20-September 9, 1991).

STATISTICAL NOTES: Pitched 6-0 no-hit victory against Victoria (June 1, 1974).... Led American Association with four balks in 1975.

MISCELLANEOUS: Appeared as first baseman with no chances with Toledo (1977).

Year	Team (League)	G	W	L	Pct.	ERA	Sv.	IP	H	R	ER	BB	SO
1971	—Reno (California)	7	1	0	1.000	6.75	0	24	37	20	18	9	10
	—Sarasota Indians (Gulf Coast)	4	0	3	.000	3.00	0	15	15	7	5	7	10
1972	—Reno (California)	27	4	14	.222	6.53	0	124	166	102	90	57	79
1973	—Reno (California)	29	10	8	.556	3.95	0	164	173	91	72	67	115
1974	—San Antonio (Texas)	25	10	6	.625	3.83	0	169	176	84	72	51	64
1975	—Oklahoma City (Am. Assoc.)	25	10	11	.476	4.21	0	156	179	87	73	52	64
	—Cleveland (A.L.)	3	0	0	...	4.50	0	6	4	3	3	2	4
1976	—Toledo (International)	6	0	2	.000	12.91	0	23	47	33	33	6	8
	—Williamsport (Eastern)	21	9	6	.600	2.71	0	133	117	47	40	34	74
1977	—Toledo (International)	45	5	6	.455	1.94	9	65	52	20	14	37	40
	—Cleveland (A.L.)	11	0	1	.000	3.21	0	14	10	7	5	9	8
1978	—Portland (Pacific Coast)	57	10	7	.588	3.45	*25	99	92	42	38	45	65
1979	—Tacoma (Pacific Coast)	27	10	6	.625	4.02	4	112	124	59	50	32	52
	—Cleveland (A.L.)	8	0	0	.000	7.41	0	17	25	14	14	4	7
1980	—Portland (Pacific Coast)■	52	5	7	.417	1.74	15	93	78	24	18	16	65
1981	—Seattle (A.L.)■	41	3	3	.500	2.65	5	68	57	27	20	18	40
1982	—Seattle (A.L.)	40	0	0	...	5.99	1	79 2/3	100	56	53	23	32
	—Salt Lake City (Pacific Coast)	5	1	0	1.000	0.00	4	6 2/3	2	0	0	3	8
1983	—Portland (Pacific Coast)■	52	7	8	.467	2.05	*22	70 1/3	63	35	16	30	64
	—Philadelphia (N.L.)	17	1	0	1.000	2.39	0	26 1/3	19	7	7	9	14
1984	—Philadelphia (N.L.)	64	3	7	.300	2.38	4	90 2/3	85	32	24	25	54
1985	—Philadelphia (N.L.)	57	3	3	.500	4.32	3	73	78	41	35	26	50
1986	—Philadelphia-Houston (N.L.)■■	48	2	1	.667	3.03	1	77 1/3	83	30	26	26	42
1987	—Houston (N.L.)	67	9	5	.643	3.45	5	101 2/3	95	46	39	41	94
1988	—Houston (N.L.)	53	2	4	.333	2.94	5	82 2/3	82	29	27	20	66
1989	—Houston (N.L.)	60	4	4	.500	1.54	3	87 2/3	63	19	15	24	85
1990	—Houston (N.L.)	50	5	2	.714	1.95	6	73 2/3	61	19	16	24	68
	—Boston (A.L.)■	15	0	0	...	1.23	1	22	18	3	3	3	25
1991	—San Diego (N.L.)■	38	3	4	.429	2.30	13	47	39	13	12	13	40
American League totals (6 years)		118	3	4	.429	4.27	7	206 2/3	214	110	98	59	116
National League totals (9 years)		454	32	30	.516	2.74	40	660	605	236	201	208	513
Major league totals (14 years)		572	35	34	.507	3.11	47	866 2/3	819	346	299	267	629

CHAMPIONSHIP SERIES RECORD

Year	Team (League)	G	W	L	Pct.	ERA	Sv.	IP	H	R	ER	BB	SO
1986	—Houston (N.L.)	2	0	0	...	0.00	0	5	1	0	0	2	3
1990	—Boston (A.L.)	3	0	1	.000	6.00	0	3	3	2	2	3	3
Championship Series totals (2 years)		5	0	1	.000	2.25	0	8	4	2	2	5	6

WORLD SERIES RECORD

Year	Team (League)	G	W	L	Pct.	ERA	Sv.	IP	H	R	ER	BB	SO
1983	—Philadelphia (N.L.)	2	0	0	...	2.25	0	4	4	1	1	0	1

ANDERSON, ALLAN

P, YANKEES

PERSONAL: Born January 7, 1964, at Lancaster, O.... 6-0/201.... Throws left, bats left.... Full name: Allan Lee Anderson.

HIGH SCHOOL: Lancaster (O.).

TRANSACTIONS/CAREER NOTES: Selected by Minnesota Twins organization in second round of free-agent draft (June 7, 1982).... Granted free agency (December 20, 1991).... Signed by New York Yankees organization (January 29, 1992).

STATISTICAL NOTES: Led California League with five shutouts in 1984.

MISCELLANEOUS: Appeared in one game as a pinch-runner with Minnesota (1986).... Struck out in only appearance as a pinch-hitter (1989).

Year	Team (League)	G	W	L	Pct.	ERA	Sv.	IP	H	R	ER	BB	SO
1983	—Wisconsin Rapids (Midwest)	7	0	4	.000	6.82	0	30 1/3	36	28	23	17	46
	—Elizabethton (Appalachian)	6	1	3	.250	8.53	0	12 2/3	17	12	12	7	12
1984	—Visalia (California)	26	12	7	.632	2.86	0	188 2/3	152	80	60	105	151
1985	—Toledo (International)	27	7	11	.389	3.43	0	176	176	81	67	79	94
1986	—Minnesota (A.L.)	21	3	6	.333	5.55	0	84 1/3	106	54	52	30	51
	—Toledo (International)	11	2	5	.286	4.57	0	67	78	39	34	31	37
1987	—Portland (Pacific Coast)	19	4	8	.333	5.60	0	98	127	77	61	49	45
	—Minnesota (A.L.)	4	1	0	1.000	10.95	0	12 1/3	20	15	15	10	3

Year Team (League)	G	W	L	Pct.	ERA	Sv.	IP	H	R	ER	BB	SO
1988 —Portland (Pacific Coast)	3	1	1	.500	1.26	0	14⅓	11	4	2	5	9
—Minnesota (A.L.)	30	16	9	.640	*2.45	0	202⅓	199	70	55	37	83
1989 —Minnesota (A.L.)	33	17	10	.630	3.80	0	196⅔	214	97	83	53	69
1990 —Minnesota (A.L.)	31	7	18	.280	4.53	0	188⅔	214	106	95	39	82
1991 —Minnesota (A.L.)	29	5	11	.313	4.96	0	134⅓	148	82	74	42	51
—Portland (Pacific Coast)	5	4	1	.800	3.06	0	32⅓	33	15	11	7	16
Major league totals (6 years)	148	49	54	.476	4.11	0	818⅔	901	424	374	211	339

ANDERSON, BRADY
OF, ORIOLES

PERSONAL: Born January 18, 1964, at Silver Spring, Md. . . . 6-1/185. . . . Throws left, bats left. . . . Full name: Brady Kevin Anderson.
HIGH SCHOOL: Carlsbad (Calif.).
COLLEGE: UC Irvine.
TRANSACTIONS/CAREER NOTES: Selected by Boston Red Sox organization in 10th round of free-agent draft (June 3, 1985). . . . Traded by Red Sox with P Curt Schilling to Baltimore Orioles for P Mike Boddicker (July 29, 1988). . . . On Baltimore disabled list (June 8-July 20, 1990); included rehabilitation disability assignment to Hagerstown (July 5-12, 1990) and Frederick (July 13-17, 1990). . . . On Baltimore disabled list (May 28-June 14, 1991).
STATISTICAL NOTES: Led New York-Pennsylvania League with 67 bases on balls received in 1985. . . . Led Florida State League with 107 bases on balls received in 1986.

Year Team (League)	Pos.	G	AB	R	H	2B	3B	HR	RBI	Avg.	SB	PO	A	E	Avg.
1985 —Elmira (New York-Penn) ..	OF	71	215	36	55	7	•6	5	21	.256	13	119	5	3	.976
1986 —Winter Haven (Fla. St.) ...	OF	126	417	86	133	19	11	12	87	.319	44	280	5	1	*.997
1987 —New Britain (Eastern)	OF	52	170	30	50	4	3	6	35	.294	7	127	2	2	.985
—Pawtucket (Int'l)	OF	23	79	18	30	4	0	2	8	.380	2	48	1	0	1.000
1988 —Pawtucket (Int'l)	OF	49	167	27	48	6	1	4	19	.287	8	115	4	2	.983
—Boston-Baltimore (A.L.)■.	OF	94	325	31	69	13	4	1	21	.212	10	243	4	4	.984
1989 —Baltimore (A.L.)...............	OF	94	266	44	55	12	2	4	16	.207	16	191	3	3	.985
—Rochester (Int'l)	OF	21	70	14	14	1	2	1	8	.200	2	1	0	0	1.000
1990 —Baltimore (A.L.)...............	OF	89	234	24	54	5	2	3	24	.231	15	149	3	2	.987
—Hagerstown (Eastern)	OF	9	34	8	13	0	2	1	5	.382	2	8	1	0	1.000
—Frederick (Carolina)..........	OF	2	7	2	3	1	0	0	3	.429	0	1	0	0	1.000
1991 —Baltimore (A.L.)...............	OF	113	256	40	59	12	3	2	27	.230	12	150	3	3	.981
—Rochester (Int'l)	OF	7	26	5	10	3	0	0	2	.385	4	19	1	0	1.000
Major league totals (4 years)		390	1081	139	237	42	11	10	88	.219	53	733	13	12	.984

ANDERSON, DAVE
IF, DODGERS

PERSONAL: Born August 1, 1960, at Louisville, Ky. . . . 6-2/184. . . . Throws right, bats right. . . . Full name: David Carter Anderson.
HIGH SCHOOL: Gibbs (St. Petersburg, Fla.).
COLLEGE: Memphis State.
TRANSACTIONS/CAREER NOTES: Selected by Los Angeles Dodgers organization in first round (22nd pick overall) of free-agent draft (June 8, 1981). . . . On Los Angeles disabled list (April 29-June 2 and July 31-September 1, 1985); included rehabilitation disability assignment to Albuquerque (May 17-June 1 and August 17-31, 1985). . . . On disabled list (June 22-August 19, 1986 and August 11-September 2, 1987). . . . Granted free agency (November 13, 1989). . . . Signed by San Francisco Giants (November 29, 1989). . . . Granted free agency (October 31, 1991). . . . Signed by Dodgers organization (January 28, 1992).
STATISTICAL NOTES: Led Pacific Coast League shortstops with 81 double plays in 1982.

Year Team (League)	Pos.	G	AB	R	H	2B	3B	HR	RBI	Avg.	SB	PO	A	E	Avg.
1981 —Vero Beach (Florida St.) ...	SS	65	200	44	54	8	1	0	18	.270	15	109	218	23	.934
1982 —Albuquerque (PCL)	SS	132	507	100	174	19	7	5	76	.343	43	223	397	*34	.948
1983 —Albuquerque (PCL)	SS	9	27	10	11	1	1	0	3	.407	4	17	26	1	.977
—Los Angeles (N.L.)	SS-3B	61	115	12	19	4	2	1	2	.165	6	56	100	5	.969
1984 —Los Angeles (N.L.)	SS-3B	121	374	51	94	16	2	3	34	.251	15	176	359	19	.966
1985 —Los Angeles (N.L.)	3B-SS-2B	77	221	24	44	6	0	4	18	.199	5	61	187	9	.965
—Albuquerque (PCL)	SS-3B-2B	28	97	23	28	7	0	3	16	.289	10	29	62	11	.892
1986 —Los Angeles (N.L.)	3B-SS-2B	92	216	31	53	9	0	1	15	.245	5	77	159	11	.955
1987 —Los Angeles (N.L.)	SS-3B-2B	108	265	32	62	12	3	1	13	.234	9	103	207	7	.978
1988 —Los Angeles (N.L.)	SS-3B-2B	116	285	31	71	10	2	2	20	.249	4	139	244	5	.987
1989 —Los Angeles (N.L.)	SS-3B-2B	87	140	15	32	2	0	1	14	.229	2	61	73	1	.993
1990 —San Francisco (N.L.)■...	S-2-1-3	60	100	14	35	5	1	1	6	.350	1	33	59	1	.989
1991 —San Francisco (N.L.)	S-1-3-2	100	226	24	56	5	2	2	13	.248	2	167	127	11	.964
Major league totals (9 years)		822	1942	234	466	69	12	16	135	.240	49	873	1515	69	.972

CHAMPIONSHIP SERIES RECORD

Year Team (League)	Pos.	G	AB	R	H	2B	3B	HR	RBI	Avg.	SB	PO	A	E	Avg.
1983 —Los Angeles (N.L.)............						Did not play									
1985 —Los Angeles (N.L.)............	PR-SS-3B	4	5	1	0	0	0	0	0	.000	0	3	4	0	1.000
1988 —Los Angeles (N.L.)............						Did not play									

WORLD SERIES RECORD

Year Team (League)	Pos.	G	AB	R	H	2B	3B	HR	RBI	Avg.	SB	PO	A	E	Avg.
1988 —Los Angeles (N.L.)............	PH-DH	1	1	0	0	0	0	0	0	.000	0	0	0	0	...

— 14 —

ANTHONY, ERIC
OF, ASTROS

PERSONAL: Born November 8, 1967, at San Diego. . . . 6-2/195. . . . Throws left, bats left. . . . Full name: Eric Todd Anthony.

TRANSACTIONS/CAREER NOTES: Selected by Houston Astros organization in 34th round of free-agent draft (June 2, 1986). . . . On Houston disabled list (April 10-30, 1990); included rehabilitation disability assignment to Columbus (April 25-30, 1990).

RECORDS/HONORS: Named Southern League Most Valuable Player (1989).

STATISTICAL NOTES: Led Gulf Coast League with 110 total bases in 1987. . . . Led South Atlantic League with .558 slugging percentage in 1988. . . . Led Southern League with .558 slugging percentage in 1989.

Year Team (League)	Pos.	G	AB	R	H	2B	3B	HR	RBI	Avg.	SB	PO	A	E	Avg.
1986—Sarasota Astros (GCL)	OF	13	12	2	3	0	0	0	0	.250	1	2	1	0	1.000
1987—Sarasota Astros (GCL)	OF	60	216	38	57	11	6	∗10	∗46	.264	2	100	∗11	5	.957
1988—Asheville (S. Atlantic)	OF	115	439	73	120	∗36	1	∗29	89	.273	10	152	8	14	.920
1989—Columbus (Southern)	OF	107	403	67	121	16	2	∗28	79	.300	14	178	17	8	.961
—Houston (N.L.)	OF	25	61	7	11	2	0	4	7	.180	0	34	1	0	1.000
—Tucson (Pacific Coast)	OF	12	46	10	10	3	0	3	11	.217	0	21	0	0	1.000
1990—Houston (N.L.)	OF	84	239	26	46	8	0	10	29	.192	5	124	5	4	.970
—Columbus (Southern)	OF	4	12	2	2	0	0	1	3	.167	0	3	0	0	1.000
—Tucson (Pacific Coast)	OF	40	161	28	46	10	2	6	26	.286	8	84	7	4	.958
1991—Houston (N.L.)	OF	39	118	11	18	6	0	1	7	.153	1	64	5	1	.986
Major league totals (3 years)		148	418	44	75	16	0	15	43	.179	6	222	11	5	.979

APPIER, KEVIN
P, ROYALS

PERSONAL: Born December 6, 1967, at Lancaster, Calif. . . . 6-2/200. . . . Throws right, bats right. . . . Full name: Robert Kevin Appier.

HIGH SCHOOL: Antelope Valley (Calif.).

COLLEGE: Fresno State and Antelope Valley College (Calif.).

TRANSACTIONS/CAREER NOTES: Selected by Kansas City Royals organization in first round (ninth pick overall) of free-agent draft (June 2, 1987).

RECORDS/HONORS: Named A.L. Rookie Pitcher of the Year by THE SPORTING NEWS (1990).

STATISTICAL NOTES: Tied for Northwest League lead in games started by pitcher with 15 in 1987.

Year Team (League)	G	W	L	Pct.	ERA	Sv.	IP	H	R	ER	BB	SO
1987—Eugene (Northwest)	15	5	2	.714	3.04	0	77	81	43	26	29	72
1988—Baseball City (Florida State)	24	10	9	.526	2.75	0	147⅓	134	58	45	39	112
—Memphis (Southern)	3	2	0	1.000	1.83	0	19⅔	11	5	4	7	18
1989—Omaha (American Assoc.)	22	8	8	.500	3.95	0	139	141	70	61	42	109
—Kansas City (A.L.)	6	1	4	.200	9.14	0	21⅔	34	22	22	12	10
1990—Omaha (American Assoc.)	3	2	0	1.000	1.50	0	18	15	3	3	3	17
—Kansas City (A.L.)	32	12	8	.600	2.76	0	185⅔	179	67	57	54	127
1991—Kansas City (A.L.)	34	13	10	.565	3.42	0	207⅔	205	97	79	61	158
Major league totals (3 years)	72	26	22	.542	3.43	0	415	418	186	158	127	295

AQUINO, LUIS
P, ROYALS

PERSONAL: Born May 19, 1965, at Rio Piedras, Puerto Rico. . . . 6-1/195. . . . Throws right, bats right. . . . Full name: Luis Antonio Colon Aquino. . . . Name pronounced uh-KEE-no.

HIGH SCHOOL: Gabriela Mistra (Rio Piedras, Puerto Rico).

TRANSACTIONS/CAREER NOTES: Signed as free agent by Toronto Blue Jays organization (June 15, 1981). . . . Traded by Blue Jays organization to Kansas City Royals organization for OF Juan Beniquez (July 14, 1987). . . . On disabled list (May 31-June 15, 1989 and July 21-September 24, 1990).

STATISTICAL NOTES: Pitched 2-0 no-hit victory against Columbus (June 20, 1988).

Year Team (League)	G	W	L	Pct.	ERA	Sv.	IP	H	R	ER	BB	SO
1982—Bradenton Blue Jays (GCL)	13	4	7	.364	3.31	0	73⅓	60	33	27	17	52
1983—Florence (South Atlantic)	29	7	9	.438	5.25	0	133⅔	128	91	78	61	104
1984—Kinston (Carolina)	∗53	5	6	.455	2.70	20	70	50	21	21	37	78
—Knoxville (Southern)	3	0	0	. . .	9.00	0	4	3	4	4	3	7
1985—Knoxville (Southern)	50	5	7	.417	2.60	∗20	83	58	29	24	32	82
1986—Syracuse (International)	43	3	7	.300	2.88	10	84⅓	70	30	27	34	60
—Toronto (A.L.)	7	1	1	.500	6.35	0	11⅓	14	8	8	3	5
1987—Syracuse (International)	26	6	7	.462	4.78	0	84⅔	75	46	45	51	68
—Omaha (American Assoc.)■	14	3	2	.600	2.31	1	50⅔	42	15	13	16	29
1988—Omaha (American Assoc.)	25	8	3	.727	2.85	0	129½	106	43	41	50	93
—Kansas City (A.L.)	7	1	0	1.000	2.79	0	29	33	15	9	17	11
1989—Kansas City (A.L.)	34	6	8	.429	3.50	0	141⅓	148	62	55	35	68
1990—Kansas City (A.L.)	20	4	1	.800	3.16	0	68⅓	59	25	24	27	28
1991—Kansas City (A.L.)	38	8	4	.667	3.44	3	157	152	67	60	47	80
Major league totals (5 years)	106	20	14	.588	3.45	3	407	406	177	156	129	192

ARD, JOHNNY
P, GIANTS

PERSONAL: Born June 1, 1967, at Las Vegas. . . . 6-5/220. . . . Throws right, bats right. . . . Full name: Broni John Ard.

HIGH SCHOOL: Hemingway (S.C.).

COLLEGE: Francis Marion (S.C.) and Manatee Junior College (Fla.).

TRANSACTIONS/CAREER NOTES: Selected by Minnesota Twins organization in first round (20th pick overall) of free-agent draft (June 1, 1988).... Traded by Twins organization with a player to be named later to San Francisco Giants for P Steve Bedrosian (December 5, 1990); Giants acquired P Jimmy Williams to complete deal (December 18, 1990).... On Phoenix disabled list (April 11-May 4, 1991).
STATISTICAL NOTES: Tied for California League lead in games started by pitcher with 28 in 1989.... Pitched 2-0 no-hit victory against Chattanooga (August 30, 1990, first game).... Tied for Texas League lead with three shutouts in 1991.

Year	Team (League)	G	W	L	Pct.	ERA	Sv.	IP	H	R	ER	BB	SO
1988	—Elizabethton (Appalachian)	9	4	1	.800	1.97	0	59⅓	40	17	13	26	71
	—Kenosha (Midwest)	4	3	0	1.000	1.05	0	25⅔	14	3	3	4	16
1989	—Visalia (California)	28	•13	7	.650	3.29	0	186	155	87	68	84	153
1990	—Orlando (Southern)	29	12	9	.571	3.79	0	180⅓	167	90	76	85	101
1991	—Phoenix (Pacific Coast)■	10	3	5	.375	5.78	0	62⅓	76	42	40	33	30
	—Shreveport (Texas)	13	9	3	.750	2.74	0	88⅔	77	31	27	36	58

ARIAS, ALEX
SS, CUBS

PERSONAL: Born November 20, 1967, at New York.... 6-3/185.... Throws right, bats right.... Full name: Alejandro Arias.
HIGH SCHOOL: George Washington (New York).
TRANSACTIONS/CAREER NOTES: Selected by Chicago Cubs organization in third round of free-agent draft (June 2, 1987).
STATISTICAL NOTES: Led Midwest League shortstops with 655 total chances and 83 double plays in 1989.... Led Southern League shortstops with 583 total chances and 81 double plays in 1991.

				BATTING									FIELDING			
Year	Team (League)	Pos.	G	AB	R	H	2B	3B	HR	RBI	Avg.	SB	PO	A	E	Avg.
1987	—Wytheville (Appal.)	SS-3B	61	233	41	69	7	0	0	24	.296	16	77	141	16	.932
1988	—Charleston, W.Va. (SAL)	SS-3B-2B	127	472	57	122	12	1	0	33	.258	41	184	396	32	.948
1989	—Peoria (Midwest)	SS	*136	506	74	140	10	*11	2	64	.277	31	*210	*408	37	.944
1990	—Charlotte (Southern)	SS	119	419	55	103	16	3	4	38	.246	12	171	284	*42	.915
1991	—Charlotte (Southern)	SS	134	488	69	134	26	0	4	47	.275	23	*203	*351	29	*.950

ARMSTRONG, JACK
P, INDIANS

PERSONAL: Born March 7, 1965, at Englewood, N.J.... 6-5/215.... Throws right, bats right.... Full name: Jack William Armstrong.
HIGH SCHOOL: Neptune (N.J.).
COLLEGE: Rider (N.J.) and Oklahoma (degree in economics, 1987).
TRANSACTIONS/CAREER NOTES: Selected by San Francisco Giants organization in third round of free-agent draft (June 2, 1986).... Selected by Cincinnati Reds organization in first round (18th pick overall) of free-agent draft (June 2, 1987).... On Cincinnati disabled list (August 25-September 9, 1990).... Traded by Reds with P Scott Scudder and P Joe Turek to Cleveland Indians for P Greg Swindell (November 15, 1991).
STATISTICAL NOTES: Pitched 4-0 no-hit victory against Indianapolis (August 7, 1988).... Led American Association with six shutouts and 12 complete games in 1989.... Tied for N.L. lead with five balks in 1990.

Year	Team (League)	G	W	L	Pct.	ERA	Sv.	IP	H	R	ER	BB	SO
1987	—Billings (Pioneer)	5	2	1	.667	2.66	0	20⅓	16	7	6	12	29
	—Vermont (Eastern)	5	1	2	.333	3.03	0	35⅔	24	12	12	23	39
1988	—Nashville (American Assoc.)	17	5	5	.500	3.00	0	120	84	44	40	38	116
	—Cincinnati (N.L.)	14	4	7	.364	5.79	0	65⅓	63	44	42	38	45
1989	—Nashville (American Assoc.)	25	•13	9	.591	2.91	0	182⅔	144	63	59	58	152
	—Cincinnati (N.L.)	9	2	3	.400	4.64	0	42⅔	40	24	22	21	23
1990	—Cincinnati (N.L.)	29	12	9	.571	3.42	0	166	151	72	63	59	110
1991	—Cincinnati (N.L.)	27	7	13	.350	5.48	0	139⅔	158	90	85	54	93
	—Nashville (American Assoc.)	6	2	0	1.000	2.65	0	37⅓	31	14	11	5	28
Major league totals (4 years)		79	25	32	.439	4.61	0	413⅔	412	230	212	172	271

WORLD SERIES RECORD

Year	Team (League)	G	W	L	Pct.	ERA	Sv.	IP	H	R	ER	BB	SO
1990	—Cincinnati (N.L.)	1	0	0	...	0.00	0	3	1	0	0	0	3

ALL-STAR GAME RECORD

Year	League	W	L	Pct.	ERA	Sv.	IP	H	R	ER	BB	SO
1990	—National	0	0	...	0.00	0	2	1	0	0	0	2

ARNSBERG, BRAD
P

PERSONAL: Born August 20, 1963, at Seattle.... 6-4/210.... Throws right, bats right.... Full name: Bradley James Arnsberg.... Brother of Tim Arnsberg, minor league pitcher (1985-87).
HIGH SCHOOL: Medford (Ore.).
COLLEGE: Merced (Calif.) College.
TRANSACTIONS/CAREER NOTES: Selected by Cleveland Indians organization in 19th round of free-agent draft (June 8, 1981).... Selected by St. Louis Cardinals organization in secondary phase of free-agent draft (January 12, 1982).... Selected by Baltimore Orioles organization in secondary phase of free-agent draft (June 7, 1982).... Selected by California Angels organization in secondary phase of free-agent draft (January 11, 1983).... Selected by New York Yankees organization in secondary phase of free-agent draft (June 6, 1983).... On disabled list (May 12-24 and June 23-July 22, 1985).... On New York disabled list (August 23-September 14, 1987).... Traded by Yankees organization to Texas Rangers (November 10, 1987), com-

pleting deal in which Rangers traded C Don Slaught to Yankees for a player to be named later (November 2, 1987).... On disabled list (March 29-September 1, 1988).... On Texas disabled list (May 6-July 28 and August 2, 1991-remainder of season); included rehabilitation disability assignment to Oklahoma City (July 11-28, 1991).... Granted free agency (October 17, 1991).
RECORDS/HONORS: Named Eastern League Pitcher of the Year (1985). ... Named International League Pitcher of the Year (1987).
STATISTICAL NOTES: Pitched 5-0 no-hit victory against Savannah (May 24, 1984).... Tied for South Atlantic League lead with 10 complete games and four shutouts in 1984. ... Led International League pitchers with 28 games started and five balks in 1986.... Led International League with nine complete games and tied for lead with two shutouts in 1987.

Year	Team (League)	G	W	L	Pct.	ERA	Sv.	IP	H	R	ER	BB	SO
1984	Greensboro (South Atlantic)	23	12	5	.706	2.95	0	158⅔	121	61	52	59	112
1985	Albany (Eastern)	20	•14	2	.875	★1.59	0	141⅓	105	34	25	35	82
1986	Columbus (International)	28	8	•12	.400	4.21	0	★177⅓	168	★106	•83	53	96
—	New York (A.L.)	2	0	0	...	3.38	0	8	13	3	3	1	3
1987	Columbus (International)	19	12	5	.706	2.88	0	144	140	55	46	37	83
—	New York (A.L.)	6	1	3	.250	5.59	0	19⅓	22	12	12	13	14
1988	■					Did not play							
1989	Texas (A.L.)	16	2	1	.667	4.13	1	48	45	27	22	22	26
—	Oklahoma City (Am. Assoc.).....	18	6	8	.429	4.06	0	115⅓	117	58	52	34	61
1990	Oklahoma City (Am. Assoc.).....	14	0	4	.000	5.16	2	29⅔	35	19	17	10	17
—	Texas (A.L.)	53	6	1	.857	2.15	5	62⅔	56	20	15	33	44
1991	Texas (A.L.)	9	0	1	.000	8.38	0	9⅔	10	9	9	5	8
—	Oklahoma City (Am. Assoc.).....	9	1	0	1.000	1.69	1	10⅔	3	2	2	3	10
Major league totals (5 years)		86	9	6	.600	3.72	6	147⅔	146	71	61	74	95

ASHBY, ANDY
P, PHILLIES

PERSONAL: Born July 11, 1967, at Kansas City, Mo.... 6-5/180.... Throws right, bats right.... Full name: Andrew Jason Ashby.
HIGH SCHOOL: Park Hill (Kansas City, Mo.).
COLLEGE: Crowder College (Mo.).
TRANSACTIONS/CAREER NOTES: Signed as free agent by Philadelphia Phillies organization (May 4, 1986).... On Spartanburg disabled list (April 7-July 10, 1988).... On disabled list (April 6-26, 1989).
RECORDS/HONORS: Shares major league record by striking out side on nine pitches (June 15, 1991, fourth inning).
STATISTICAL NOTES: Tied for International League lead with six complete games and three shutouts in 1991.

Year	Team (League)	G	W	L	Pct.	ERA	Sv.	IP	H	R	ER	BB	SO
1986	Bend (Northwest)	16	1	2	.333	4.95	2	60	56	40	33	34	45
1987	Spartanburg (South Atlantic) ..	13	4	6	.400	5.60	0	64⅓	73	45	40	38	52
—	Utica (New York-Penn)	13	3	7	.300	4.05	0	60	56	38	27	36	51
1988	Spartanburg (South Atlantic) ..	3	1	1	.500	2.70	0	16⅔	13	7	5	7	16
—	Batavia (New York-Penn)	6	3	1	.750	1.61	0	44⅔	25	11	8	16	32
1989	Spartanburg (South Atlantic) ..	17	5	9	.357	2.87	0	106⅔	95	48	34	49	100
—	Clearwater (Florida State)	6	1	4	.200	1.24	0	43⅔	28	9	6	21	44
1990	Reading (Eastern)	23	10	7	.588	3.42	0	139⅔	134	65	53	48	94
1991	Scranton/Wilkes-Barre (Int'l) ..	26	11	11	.500	3.46	0	161⅓	144	78	62	60	113
—	Philadelphia (N.L.)	8	1	5	.167	6.00	0	42	41	28	28	19	26
Major league totals (1 year)		8	1	5	.167	6.00	0	42	41	28	28	19	26

ASHLEY, BILLY
OF, DODGERS

PERSONAL: Born July 11, 1970, at Taylor, Mich.... 6-7/220.... Throws right, bats right.... Full name: Billy Manual Ashley.
HIGH SCHOOL: Belleville (Mich.).
TRANSACTIONS/CAREER NOTES: Selected by Los Angeles Dodgers organization in third round of free-agent draft (June 1, 1988).... On disabled list (April 10-May 31 and June 8-July 8, 1991).

						BATTING						FIELDING			
Year	Team (League)	Pos.	G	AB	R	H	2B	3B	HR	RBI	Avg.	SB	PO	A	E	Avg.
1988	Sarasota Dodgers (GCL) ...	OF	9	26	3	4	0	0	0	0	.154	1	8	2	0	1.000
1989	Kissimm. Dodgers (GCL) ...	OF	48	160	23	38	6	2	1	19	.238	9	50	3	5	.914
1990	Bakersfield (California)	OF	99	331	48	72	13	1	9	40	.218	17	122	3	10	.926
1991	Vero Beach (Florida St.) ...	OF	61	206	18	52	11	2	7	42	.252	9	39	1	0	1.000

ASSENMACHER, PAUL
P, CUBS

PERSONAL: Born December 10, 1960, at Detroit.... 6-3/200.... Throws left, bats left. ... Full name: Paul Andre Assenmacher. ... Name pronounced OSS-en-MOCK-er.
HIGH SCHOOL: Aquinas (Southgate, Mich.).
COLLEGE: Aquinas, Mich. (degree in business administration).
TRANSACTIONS/CAREER NOTES: Signed as free agent by Atlanta Braves organization (July 10, 1983).... On Atlanta disabled list (April 29-May 9, 1987 and August 10-25, 1988).... Traded by Braves organization to Chicago Cubs for two players to be named later (August 24, 1989); Braves acquired C Kelly Mann and P Pat Gomez to complete deal (September 1, 1989).
RECORDS/HONORS: Shares major league record for most strikeouts, inning—4 (August 22, 1989, fifth inning).

Year	Team (League)	G	W	L	Pct.	ERA	Sv.	IP	H	R	ER	BB	SO
1983	Bradenton Braves (GCL)	10	1	0	1.000	2.21	2	36⅔	35	14	9	4	44

Year Team (League)	G	W	L	Pct.	ERA	Sv.	IP	H	R	ER	BB	SO
1984—Durham (Carolina)	26	6	11	.353	4.28	0	147⅓	153	78	70	52	147
1985—Durham (Carolina)	14	3	2	.600	3.29	1	38⅓	38	16	14	13	36
—Greenville (Southern)	29	6	0	1.000	2.56	4	52⅔	47	16	15	11	59
1986—Atlanta (N.L.)	61	7	3	.700	2.50	7	68⅓	61	23	19	26	56
1987—Atlanta (N.L.)	52	1	1	.500	5.10	2	54⅔	58	41	31	24	39
—Richmond (International)	4	1	2	.333	3.65	0	24⅔	30	11	10	8	21
1988—Atlanta (N.L.)	64	8	7	.533	3.06	5	79⅓	72	28	27	32	71
1989—Atlanta-Chicago (N.L.)■	63	3	4	.429	3.99	0	76⅔	74	37	34	28	79
1990—Chicago (N.L.)	74	7	2	.778	2.80	10	103	90	33	32	36	95
1991—Chicago (N.L.)	75	7	8	.467	3.24	15	102⅔	85	41	37	31	117
Major league totals (6 years)	389	33	25	.569	3.34	39	484⅔	440	203	180	177	457

CHAMPIONSHIP SERIES RECORD

Year Team (League)	G	W	L	Pct.	ERA	Sv.	IP	H	R	ER	BB	SO
1989—Chicago (N.L.)	2	0	0	...	13.50	0	⅔	3	1	1	0	0

ASTACIO, PEDRO
P, DODGERS

PERSONAL: Born November 28, 1969, at Hato Mayor, Dominican Republic.... 6-2/174.... Throws right, bats right.... Full name: Pedro Julio Astacio.
HIGH SCHOOL: Pilar Rondon (Dominican Republic).
TRANSACTIONS/CAREER NOTES: Signed as free agent by Los Angeles Dodgers organization (November 21, 1987).
STATISTICAL NOTES: Tied for Florida State League lead with one shutout in 1990.

Year Team (League)	G	W	L	Pct.	ERA	Sv.	IP	H	R	ER	BB	SO
1989—Kissimmee Dodgers (GCL)	12	7	3	.700	3.17	0	76⅔	77	30	27	12	52
1990—Vero Beach (Florida State)	8	1	5	.167	6.32	0	47	54	39	33	23	41
—Yakima (Northwest)	3	2	0	1.000	1.74	0	20⅔	9	8	4	4	22
—Bakersfield (California)	10	5	2	.714	2.77	0	52	46	22	16	15	34
1991—Vero Beach (Florida State)	9	5	3	.625	1.67	0	59⅓	44	19	11	8	45
—San Antonio (Texas)	19	4	11	.267	4.78	0	113	142	67	60	39	62

AUGUST, DON
P, GIANTS

PERSONAL: Born July 3, 1963, at Inglewood, Calif.... 6-3/190.... Throws right, bats right.... Full name: Donald Glenn August.
HIGH SCHOOL: Capistrano Valley (Mission Viejo, Calif.).
COLLEGE: Chapman (Calif.).
TRANSACTIONS/CAREER NOTES: Selected by Houston Astros organization in first round (17th pick overall) of free-agent draft (June 4, 1984).... Traded by Astros organization with a player to be named later to Milwaukee Brewers for P Danny Darwin (August 15, 1986); Brewers organization acquired P Mark Knudson to complete deal (August 21, 1986).... Granted free agency (October 15, 1991).... Signed by San Francisco Giants organization (December 8, 1991).
STATISTICAL NOTES: Tied for Pacific Coast League lead in games started by pitcher with 27 in 1986.
MISCELLANEOUS: Member of 1984 U.S. Olympic baseball team.

Year Team (League)	G	W	L	Pct.	ERA	Sv.	IP	H	R	ER	BB	SO
1985—Columbus (International)	27	14	8	.636	2.96	0	176⅓	183	77	58	49	78
1986—Tucson-Vancouver (PCL)■	27	10	10	.500	3.37	0	179	192	88	67	51	70
1987—Denver (American Assoc.)	28	10	9	.526	5.57	0	179⅓	*220	*124	*111	55	91
1988—Denver (American Assoc.)	10	4	1	.800	3.52	0	71⅔	79	37	28	14	58
—Milwaukee (A.L.)	24	13	7	.650	3.09	0	148⅓	137	55	51	48	66
1989—Milwaukee (A.L.)	31	12	12	.500	5.31	0	142⅓	175	93	84	58	51
—Denver (American Assoc.)	4	1	1	.500	4.94	0	23⅔	35	18	13	5	12
1990—Milwaukee (A.L.)	5	0	3	.000	6.55	0	11	13	10	8	5	2
—Denver (American Assoc.)	22	7	7	.500	6.75	0	124	164	98	*93	27	67
1991—Denver (American Assoc.)	1	1	0	1.000	0.00	0	5	3	0	0	0	1
—Milwaukee (A.L.)	28	9	8	.529	5.47	0	138⅓	166	87	84	47	62
Major league totals (4 years)	88	34	30	.531	4.64	0	440	491	245	227	158	181

AUSANIO, JOE
P, PIRATES

PERSONAL: Born December 9, 1965, at Kingston, N.Y.... 6-1/205.... Throws right, bats right. ... Full name: Joseph John Ausanio Jr.
HIGH SCHOOL: Kingston (N.Y.).
COLLEGE: Jacksonville.
TRANSACTIONS/CAREER NOTES: Selected by Atlanta Braves organization in 30th round of free-agent draft (June 4, 1984).... Selected by Pittsburgh Pirates organization in 11th round of free-agent draft (June 1, 1988).... On Buffalo disabled list (June 24, 1991-remainder of season).

Year Team (League)	G	W	L	Pct.	ERA	Sv.	IP	H	R	ER	BB	SO
1988—Watertown (New York-Penn)	28	2	4	.333	1.32	*13	47⅔	29	10	7	27	56
1989—Salem (Carolina)	54	5	4	.556	2.12	*20	89	51	29	21	44	97
1990—Harrisburg (Eastern)	43	3	2	.600	1.83	15	54	36	15	11	16	50
1991—Carolina (Southern)	3	0	0	...	0.00	2	3	0	0	0	0	2
—Buffalo (American Assoc.)	22	2	2	.500	3.86	3	30⅓	33	17	13	19	26

AUSMUS, BRAD
C, YANKEES

PERSONAL: Born April 14, 1969, at New Haven, Conn. . . . 5-11/185. . . . Throws right, bats right.
HIGH SCHOOL: Cheshire (Conn.).
COLLEGE: Dartmouth.
TRANSACTIONS/CAREER NOTES: Selected by New York Yankees organization in 47th round of free-agent draft (June 2, 1987).
STATISTICAL NOTES: Led Gulf Coast League catchers with 434 total chances in 1988.

Year Team (League)	Pos.	G	AB	R	H	2B	3B	HR	RBI	Avg.	SB	PO	A	E	Avg.
1988—Oneonta (N.Y.-Penn)	C	2	4	0	1	0	0	0	0	.250	0	0	0	0	...
—Sarasota (Florida State) ...	C	43	133	22	34	2	0	0	15	.256	5	*378	*47	9	.979
1989—Oneonta (N.Y.-Penn)	C-3B	52	165	29	43	6	0	1	18	.261	6	401	43	7	.984
1990—Prince William (Caro.).......	C	107	364	46	86	12	2	0	27	.236	2	662	84	5	*.993
1991—Prince William (Caro.).......	C	63	230	28	70	14	3	2	30	.304	17	419	54	5	.990
—Albany (Eastern)	C	67	229	36	61	9	2	1	29	.266	14	470	56	4	.992

AUSTIN, JAMES
P, BREWERS

PERSONAL: Born December 7, 1963, at Farmville, Va. . . . 6-2/200. . . . Throws right, bats right. . . . Full name: James Parker Austin.
HIGH SCHOOL: Dinwiddie Senior (Va.).
COLLEGE: Virginia Commonwealth.
TRANSACTIONS/CAREER NOTES: Selected by San Diego Padres organization in sixth round of free-agent draft (June 2, 1986). . . . Traded by Padres organization with P Todd Simmons to Milwaukee Brewers organization for P Dan Murphy (February 15, 1989). . . . On Denver disabled list (May 7-June 23, 1991). . . . On Milwaukee disabled list (July 30-August 31, 1991).

Year Team (League)	G	W	L	Pct.	ERA	Sv.	IP	H	R	ER	BB	SO
1986—Spokane (Northwest)	28	5	4	.556	2.26	5	59⅔	53	24	15	22	74
1987—Charleston, S.C. (S. Atlantic)	31	7	10	.412	4.20	0	152	138	89	71	56	123
1988—Riverside (California)	12	6	2	.750	2.70	0	80	65	31	24	35	73
—Wichita (Texas)	12	5	6	.455	4.81	0	73	76	46	39	23	52
1989—Stockton (California)■	7	3	3	.500	2.61	0	48⅓	51	19	14	14	44
—El Paso (Texas)	22	3	10	.231	5.82	1	85	121	60	55	34	69
1990—El Paso (Texas)	38	11	3	.786	2.44	6	92⅓	91	36	25	26	77
1991—Denver (American Assoc.)	20	6	3	.667	2.45	3	44	35	12	12	24	37
—Milwaukee (A.L.)	5	0	0	...	8.31	0	8⅔	8	8	8	11	3
Major league totals (1 year)	**5**	**0**	**0**	**...**	**8.31**	**0**	**8⅔**	**8**	**8**	**8**	**11**	**3**

AVERY, STEVE
P, BRAVES

PERSONAL: Born April 14, 1970, at Trenton, Mich. . . . 6-4/190. . . . Throws left, bats left. . . . Full name: Steven Thomas Avery. . . . Son of Ken Avery, minor league pitcher (1962-63).
HIGH SCHOOL: John F. Kennedy (Taylor, Mich.).
TRANSACTIONS/CAREER NOTES: Selected by Atlanta Braves organization in first round (third pick overall) of free-agent draft (June 1, 1988).
STATISTICAL NOTES: Tied for Appalachian League lead with two shutouts in 1988.
MISCELLANEOUS: Received base on balls in only appearance as pinch-hitter and appeared in one game as pinch-runner (1991).

Year Team (League)	G	W	L	Pct.	ERA	Sv.	IP	H	R	ER	BB	SO
1988—Pulaski (Appalachian)	10	7	1	.875	1.50	0	66	38	16	11	19	80
1989—Durham (Carolina)	13	6	4	.600	1.45	0	86⅔	59	22	14	20	90
—Greenville (Southern)	13	6	3	.667	2.77	0	84⅓	68	32	26	34	75
1990—Richmond (International)	13	5	5	.500	3.39	0	82⅓	85	35	31	21	69
—Atlanta (N.L.)	21	3	11	.214	5.64	0	99	121	79	62	45	75
1991—Atlanta (N.L.)	35	18	8	.692	3.38	0	210⅓	189	89	79	65	137
Major league totals (2 years)	**56**	**21**	**19**	**.525**	**4.10**	**0**	**309⅓**	**310**	**168**	**141**	**110**	**212**

CHAMPIONSHIP SERIES RECORD

CHAMPIONSHIP SERIES NOTES: Holds single-series record for most consecutive scoreless innings—16⅓ (1991). . . . Holds N.L. career record for most consecutive scoreless innings—16⅓ (1991).

Year Team (League)	G	W	L	Pct.	ERA	Sv.	IP	H	R	ER	BB	SO
1991—Atlanta (N.L.)	2	2	0	1.000	0.00	0	16⅓	9	0	0	4	17

WORLD SERIES RECORD

Year Team (League)	G	W	L	Pct.	ERA	Sv.	IP	H	R	ER	BB	SO
1991—Atlanta (N.L.)	2	0	0	...	3.46	0	13	10	6	5	1	8

AYALA, BOBBY
P, REDS

PERSONAL: Born July 8, 1969, at Ventura, Calif. . . . 6-2/190. . . . Throws right, bats right. . . . Full name: Robert Joesph Ayala.
HIGH SCHOOL: Rio Mesa (Oxnard, Calif.).
TRANSACTIONS/CAREER NOTES: Signed as free agent by Cincinnati Reds organization (June 27, 1988).

Year Team (League)	G	W	L	Pct.	ERA	Sv.	IP	H	R	ER	BB	SO
1988—Sarasota Reds (Gulf Coast)	20	0	4	.000	3.82	3	33	34	23	14	12	24
1989—Greensboro (South Atlantic)	22	5	8	.385	4.10	0	105⅓	97	73	48	50	70
1990—Cedar Rapids (Midwest)	18	3	2	.600	3.38	1	53⅓	40	24	20	18	59
—Charleston, W.Va. (S. Atl.)	21	6	1	.857	2.43	2	74	48	23	20	21	73
1991—Chattanooga (Southern)	39	3	1	.750	4.67	4	90⅔	79	52	47	58	92

AYRAULT, BOB
P, PHILLIES

PERSONAL: Born April 27, 1966, at Lake Tahoe, Calif. . . . 6-4/230. . . . Throws right, bats right. . . . Full name: Robert Cunningham Ayrault. **HIGH SCHOOL:** Carson City (Nev.). **COLLEGE:** Moorpark Junior College (Calif.) and UNLV.

TRANSACTIONS/CAREER NOTES: Selected by San Diego Padres organization in ninth round of free-agent draft (January 14, 1986). . . . Selected by Pittsburgh Pirates organization in 26th round of free-agent draft (June 2, 1987). . . . Signed as free agent by Reno, independent (June 2, 1989). . . . Sold by Reno to Philadelphia Phillies organization (July 29, 1989).

Year	Team (League)	G	W	L	Pct.	ERA	Sv.	IP	H	R	ER	BB	SO
1989	—Reno (California)	24	7	4	.636	3.78	0	109⅔	104	56	46	57	91
	—Batavia (New York-Penn)■	4	2	1	.667	1.38	0	26	13	5	4	7	20
	—Reading (Eastern)	2	0	0	. . .	1.04	0	8⅔	3	1	1	4	8
1990	—Reading (Eastern)	44	4	6	.400	2.30	10	109⅓	77	33	28	34	84
1991	—Scranton/Wilkes-Barre (Int'l)	68	8	5	.615	4.83	3	98⅔	91	58	53	47	103

AZOCAR, OSCAR
OF/1B, PADRES

PERSONAL: Born February 21, 1965, at Caracas, Venezuela. . . . 6-1/195. . . . Throws left, bats left. . . . Full name: Oscar Azocar Azocar. . . . Name pronounced ah-ZO-car. **TRANSACTIONS/CAREER NOTES:** Signed as free agent by New York Yankees organization (November 22, 1983). . . . Traded by Yankees organization to San Diego Padres for a player to be named later (December 3, 1990); Yankees acquired OF Mike Humphreys to complete deal (February 7, 1991). **STATISTICAL NOTES:** Led Eastern League outfielders with 15 errors in 1988.

Year	Team (League)	Pos.	G	AB	R	H	2B	3B	HR	RBI	Avg.	SB	PO	A	E	Avg.
1987	—Fort Lauderdale (FSL)	OF-1B	53	192	25	69	11	3	6	39	.359	5	112	4	3	.975
1988	—Albany (Eastern)	OF-P	★138	★543	60	148	22	★9	6	66	.273	21	264	13	†15	.949
1989	—Albany (Eastern)	OF	92	362	50	101	15	2	4	47	.279	11	158	2	4	.976
	—Columbus (Int'l)	OF	37	130	14	38	9	3	1	12	.292	3	41	2	1	.977
1990	—Columbus (Int'l)	OF-1B	94	374	49	109	20	5	5	52	.291	8	228	10	4	.983
	—New York (A.L.)	OF	65	214	18	53	8	0	5	19	.248	7	105	4	1	.991
1991	—Las Vegas (Pac. Coast)■	OF-1B	107	361	51	107	23	3	7	50	.296	4	260	9	4	.985
	—San Diego (N.L.)	OF-1B	38	57	5	14	2	0	0	9	.246	2	19	0	2	.905
American League totals (1 year)			65	214	18	53	8	0	5	19	.248	7	105	4	1	.991
National League totals (1 year)			38	57	5	14	2	0	0	9	.246	2	19	0	2	.905
Major league totals (2 years)			103	271	23	67	10	0	5	28	.247	9	124	4	3	.977

RECORD AS PITCHER

Year	Team (League)	G	W	L	Pct.	ERA	Sv.	IP	H	R	ER	BB	SO
1984	—Sarasota Yankees (GCL)	11	4	1	.800	1.28	0	56⅓	37	12	8	17	60
1985	—Oneonta (New York-Penn)	14	0	2	.000	4.86	0	16⅔	21	16	9	9	13
	—Sarasota Yankees (GCL)	5	4	0	1.000	1.45	0	37⅓	30	8	6	14	36
1986	—Sarasota Yankees (GCL)	6	4	2	.667	3.25	0	36	29	17	13	12	22
	—Oneonta (New York-Penn)	10	2	0	1.000	2.86	2	22	27	9	7	9	19
1988	—Albany (Eastern)	3	0	0	. . .	3.00	0	3	4	1	1	1	1

BAAR, BRYAN
C, DODGERS

PERSONAL: Born April 10, 1968, at Zeeland, Mich. . . . 6-3/205. . . . Throws right, bats right. . . . Full name: Bryan David Baar. **HIGH SCHOOL:** Jennison (Mich.). **COLLEGE:** Western Michigan.

TRANSACTIONS/CAREER NOTES: Selected by Los Angeles Dodgers organization in seventh round of free-agent draft (June 5, 1989).
STATISTICAL NOTES: Led California League catchers with 857 total chances and 29 passed balls in 1990. . . . Led Texas League catchers with 10 double plays and 14 passed balls in 1991.

Year	Team (League)	Pos.	G	AB	R	H	2B	3B	HR	RBI	Avg.	SB	PO	A	E	Avg.
1989	—Great Falls (Pioneer)	C	48	139	31	40	9	1	10	38	.288	1	252	27	2	★.993
1990	—Bakersfield (California)	C	111	389	53	111	23	1	20	71	.285	1	★741	★98	★18	.979
1991	—San Antonio (Texas)	C	101	348	33	78	19	0	10	51	.224	3	513	57	11	.981

BACKMAN, WALLY
IF, PHILLIES

PERSONAL: Born September 22, 1959, at Hillsboro, Ore. . . . 5-9/168. . . . Throws right, bats both. . . . Full name: Walter Wayne Backman. **HIGH SCHOOL:** Aloha (Beaverton, Ore.).
TRANSACTIONS/CAREER NOTES: Selected by New York Mets organization in first round (16th pick overall) of free-agent draft (June 7, 1977). . . . On suspended list (June 18-20, 1981). . . . On Tidewater disabled list (July 9-September 1, 1981). . . . On New York disabled list (August 15-September 8, 1982; June 9-29, 1987; and August 27-September 11, 1988). . . . Traded by Mets with P Mike Santiago to Minnesota Twins for P Jeff Bumgarner, P Steve Gasser and P Toby Nivens (December 7, 1988). . . . On disabled list (May 8-25 and July 9-August 4, 1989). . . . Granted free agency (November 13, 1989). . . . Signed by Pittsburgh Pirates (January 31, 1990). . . . Granted free agency (November 5, 1990). . . . Signed by Philadelphia Phillies (January 10, 1991).
STATISTICAL NOTES: Led Carolina League in caught stealing with 17 in 1978. . . . Led International League with 87 bases on balls received in 1980. . . . Tied for N.L. lead with 14 sacrifice hits in 1985. . . . Led N.L second basemen with .989 fielding percentage in 1985. . . . Collected six hits in one game (April 27, 1990).

Year	Team (League)	Pos.	G	AB	R	H	2B	3B	HR	RBI	Avg.	SB	PO	A	E	Avg.
1977	Little Falls (N.Y.-Penn)	SS-3B	69	255	44	83	10	2	6	30	.325	20	96	185	19	.937
1978	Lynchburg (Carolina)	SS	132	494	86	149	19	•9	3	38	.302	42	★202	★329	30	★.947
1979	Jackson (Texas)	SS-2B	110	404	63	114	11	5	2	19	.282	23	184	259	31	.935
1980	Tidewater (Int'l)	2B-SS	125	400	53	117	15	5	1	51	.293	11	237	320	22	.962
	New York (N.L.)	2B-SS	27	93	12	30	1	1	0	9	.323	2	62	55	1	.992
1981	New York (N.L.)	2B-3B	26	36	5	10	2	0	0	4	.278	1	14	21	2	.946
	Tidewater (Int'l)	SS-3B-2B	21	59	6	9	3	1	0	6	.153	2	12	38	1	.980
1982	New York (N.L.)	2B-3B-SS	96	261	37	71	13	2	3	22	.272	8	173	209	16	.960
1983	New York (N.L.)	2B-3B	26	42	6	7	0	1	0	3	.167	0	16	15	2	.939
	Tidewater (Int'l)	2B-SS-3B	101	361	69	114	11	3	1	28	.316	37	175	278	13	.972
1984	New York (N.L.)	2B-SS	128	436	68	122	19	2	1	26	.280	32	223	306	10	.981
1985	New York (N.L.)	2B-SS	145	520	77	142	24	5	1	38	.273	30	273	370	7	†.989
1986	New York (N.L.)	2B	124	387	67	124	18	2	1	27	.320	13	186	290	17	.966
1987	New York (N.L.)	2B	94	300	43	75	6	1	1	23	.250	11	131	210	6	.983
1988	New York (N.L.)	2B	99	294	44	89	12	0	0	17	.303	9	128	219	4	.989
1989	Minnesota (A.L.)■	2B	87	299	33	69	9	2	1	26	.231	1	146	187	6	.982
1990	Pittsburgh (N.L.)■	3B-2B	104	315	62	92	21	3	2	28	.292	6	56	136	12	.941
1991	Philadelphia (N.L.)■	2B-3B	94	185	20	45	12	0	0	15	.243	3	54	79	4	.971
	American League totals (1 year)		87	299	33	69	9	2	1	26	.231	1	146	187	6	.982
	National League totals (11 years)		963	2869	441	807	128	17	9	208	.281	115	1316	1910	81	.976
	Major league totals (12 years)		1050	3168	474	876	137	19	10	234	.277	116	1462	2097	87	.976

CHAMPIONSHIP SERIES RECORD

Year	Team (League)	Pos.	G	AB	R	H	2B	3B	HR	RBI	Avg.	SB	PO	A	E	Avg.
1986	New York (N.L.)	2B-PH	6	21	5	5	0	0	0	2	.238	1	9	17	0	1.000
1988	New York (N.L.)	2B	7	22	2	6	1	0	0	2	.273	1	7	19	2	.929
1990	Pittsburgh (N.L.)	3B-PH	3	7	1	1	1	0	0	0	.143	1	1	3	0	1.000
	Championship Series totals (3 years)		16	50	8	12	2	0	0	4	.240	3	17	39	2	.966

WORLD SERIES RECORD

Year	Team (League)	Pos.	G	AB	R	H	2B	3B	HR	RBI	Avg.	SB	PO	A	E	Avg.
1986	New York (N.L.)	PR-2B	6	18	4	6	0	0	0	1	.333	1	9	13	0	1.000

BAERGA, CARLOS
2B/3B, INDIANS

PERSONAL: Born November 4, 1968, at San Juan, Puerto Rico. . . . 5-11/165. . . . Throws right, bats both. . . . Full name: Carlos Obed Ortiz Baerga. . . . Name pronounced by-AIR-guh.
TRANSACTIONS/CAREER NOTES: Signed as free agent by San Diego Padres organization (November 4, 1985). . . . Traded by Padres organization with C Sandy Alomar and OF Chris James to Cleveland Indians for OF Joe Carter (December 6, 1989).
STATISTICAL NOTES: Led South Atlantic League second basemen with 29 errors in 1987. . . . Led Texas League shortstops with 61 double plays in 1988. . . . Led Pacific Coast League third basemen with 380 total chances in 1989.

Year	Team (League)	Pos.	G	AB	R	H	2B	3B	HR	RBI	Avg.	SB	PO	A	E	Avg.
1986	Charleston, S.C. (S. Atl.) ...	2B-SS	111	378	57	102	14	4	7	41	.270	6	202	245	27	.943
1987	Charleston, S.C. (S. Atl.) ...	2B-SS	134	515	83	157	23	•9	7	50	.305	26	253	341	†36	.943
1988	Wichita (Texas)	SS-2B	122	444	67	121	28	1	12	65	.273	4	221	325	33	.943
1989	Las Vegas (Pac. Coast)	3B	132	520	63	143	28	2	10	74	.275	6	★92	256	★32	.916
1990	Cleveland (A.L.)	3B-SS-2B	108	312	46	81	17	2	7	47	.260	0	79	164	17	.935
	Colorado Springs (PCL)	3B	12	50	11	19	2	1	1	11	.380	1	18	31	4	.925
1991	Cleveland (A.L.)	3B-2B-SS	158	593	80	171	28	2	11	69	.288	3	217	421	27	.959
	Major league totals (2 years)		266	905	126	252	45	4	18	116	.278	3	296	585	44	.952

BAEZ, KEVIN
SS, METS

PERSONAL: Born January 10, 1967, at Brooklyn, N.Y. . . . 6-0/170. . . . Throws right, bats right. . . . Full name: Kevin Richard Baez. . . . Name pronounced BY-EZ.
COLLEGE: Dominican College (N.Y.).
TRANSACTIONS/CAREER NOTES: Selected by New York Mets organization in seventh round of free-agent draft (June 1, 1988). . . . On Jackson disabled list (July 26-August 12, 1990). . . . On disabled list (June 24, 1991-remainder of season).
STATISTICAL NOTES: Led New York-Pennsylvania League shortstops with 317 total chances in 1988. . . . Led Texas League shortstops with 509 total chances in 1990.

Year	Team (League)	Pos.	G	AB	R	H	2B	3B	HR	RBI	Avg.	SB	PO	A	E	Avg.
1988	Little Falls (N.Y.-Penn)	SS	70	218	23	58	7	1	1	19	.266	7	93	198	26	.918
1989	Columbia (S. Atlantic)	SS	123	426	59	108	20	1	5	44	.254	11	181	327	36	★.934
1990	Jackson (Texas)	SS	106	326	29	76	11	0	2	29	.233	3	★184	301	24	.953
	New York (N.L.)	SS	5	12	0	2	1	0	0	0	.167	0	5	7	0	1.000
1991	Tidewater (Int'l)	SS	65	210	18	36	8	0	0	13	.171	0	128	227	15	.959
	Major league totals (1 year)		5	12	0	2	1	0	0	0	.167	0	5	7	0	1.000

BAGWELL, JEFF

1B, ASTROS

PERSONAL: Born May 27, 1968, at Boston.... 6-0/195.... Throws right, bats right.... Full name: Jeffrey Robert Bagwell.
HIGH SCHOOL: Xavier (Middletown, Conn.).
COLLEGE: Hartford.
TRANSACTIONS/CAREER NOTES: Selected by Boston Red Sox organization in fourth round of free-agent draft (June 5, 1989)....
Traded by Red Sox to Houston Astros for P Larry Andersen (August 31, 1990).
RECORDS/HONORS: Named Eastern League Most Valuable Player (1990).... Named N.L. Rookie Player of the Year by THE SPORTING NEWS (1991).... Named N.L. Rookie of the Year by the Baseball Writers' Association of America (1991).
STATISTICAL NOTES: Led Eastern League with 220 total bases and 12 intentional bases on balls received in 1990.... Led N.L. in being hit by pitch with 13 in 1991.

Year Team (League)	Pos.	G	AB	R	H	2B	3B	HR	RBI	Avg.	SB	PO	A	E	Avg.
1989—Sarasota Red Sox (GCL) ...	3B-2B	5	19	3	6	1	0	0	3	.316	0	2	12	2	.875
—Winter Haven (Fla. St.) ...	3B-2B-1B	64	210	27	65	13	2	2	19	.310	1	53	109	12	.931
1990—New Britain (Eastern)	3B	136	481	63	•160	•34	7	4	61	.333	5	93	267	34	.914
1991—Houston (N.L.)■...............	1B	156	554	79	163	26	4	15	82	.294	7	1270	106	12	.991
Major league totals (1 year)........................		156	554	79	163	26	4	15	82	.294	7	1270	106	12	.991

BAILES, SCOTT

P, ANGELS

PERSONAL: Born December 18, 1962, at Chillicothe, O.... 6-2/171.... Throws left, bats left. ... Full name: Scott Alan Bailes.
HIGH SCHOOL: Parkview (Springfield, Mo.).
COLLEGE: St. Louis Community College at Meramec (Mo.).
TRANSACTIONS/CAREER NOTES: Selected by Texas Rangers organization in seventh round of free-agent draft (January 12, 1982).... Selected by Pittsburgh Pirates organization in secondary phase of free-agent draft (June 7, 1982).... On disabled list (August 12, 1982-remainder of season).... Traded by Pirates organization to Cleveland Indians organization (July 3, 1985), completing deal in which Indians traded SS Johnnie LeMaster to Pirates for a player to be named later (May 30, 1985). ... On disabled list (August 13-September 6, 1989).... Traded by Indians to California Angels for IF Jeff Manto and P Colin Charland (January 9, 1990).... On disabled list (June 30-July 15, 1991).

Year Team (League)	G	W	L	Pct.	ERA	Sv.	IP	H	R	ER	BB	SO
1982—Greenwood (South Atlantic)	3	0	1	.000	7.24	0	13⅔	17	12	11	6	8
1983—Alexandria (Carolina)	52	5	2	.714	3.36	7	75	67	38	28	45	101
1984—Nashua (Eastern)...................	54	6	8	.429	3.41	3	87	80	43	33	46	61
1985—Nashua-Waterbury (Eastern)■	42	9	6	.600	2.71	9	126⅓	123	58	38	43	93
1986—Cleveland (A.L.)	62	10	10	.500	4.95	7	112⅔	123	70	62	43	60
1987—Cleveland (A.L.)	39	7	8	.467	4.64	6	120⅓	145	75	62	47	65
1988—Cleveland (A.L.)	37	9	14	.391	4.90	0	145	149	89	79	46	53
1989—Cleveland (A.L.)	34	5	9	.357	4.28	0	113⅔	116	57	54	29	47
1990—California (A.L.)■	27	2	0	1.000	6.37	0	35⅓	46	30	25	20	16
—Edmonton (Pacific Coast)........	9	0	1	.000	6.00	0	18	21	13	12	8	12
1991—California (A.L.)	42	1	2	.333	4.18	0	51⅔	41	26	24	22	41
Major league totals (6 years)	241	34	43	.442	4.76	13	578⅔	620	347	306	207	282

BAINES, HAROLD

DH/OF, ATHLETICS

PERSONAL: Born March 15, 1959, at Easton, Md.... 6-2/195.... Throws left, bats left. ... Full name: Harold Douglas Baines.
HIGH SCHOOL: St. Michaels (Easton, Md.).
TRANSACTIONS/CAREER NOTES: Selected by Chicago White Sox organization in first round (first pick overall) of free-agent draft (June 7, 1977).... On disabled list (April 7-May 8, 1987).... Traded by White Sox with IF Fred Manrique to Texas Rangers for SS Scott Fletcher, OF Sammy Sosa and P Wilson Alvarez (July 29, 1989).... Traded by Rangers to Oakland Athletics for two players to be named later (August 29, 1990); Rangers acquired P Joe Bitker and P Scott Chiamparino to complete deal (September 4, 1990).
RECORDS/HONORS: Shares major league single-game record for most plate appearances—12 (May 8, finished May 9, 1984, 25 innings).... Shares A.L. record for longest errorless game by outfielder—25 innings (May 8, finished May 9, 1984).... Shares A.L. single-game record for most innings by outfielder—25 (May 8, finished May 9, 1984).... Named outfielder on THE SPORTING NEWS A.L. All-Star team (1985).... Named designated hitter on THE SPORTING NEWS A.L. All-Star team (1988-89).... Named designated hitter on THE SPORTING NEWS A.L. Silver Slugger team (1989).
STATISTICAL NOTES: Tied for American Association lead with four double plays by outfielder in 1979.... Hit three home runs in a game (July 7, 1982; September 17, 1984 and May 7, 1991).... Led A.L. with 22 game-winning RBIs in 1983.... Led A.L. with .541 slugging percentage in 1984.

Year Team (League)	Pos.	G	AB	R	H	2B	3B	HR	RBI	Avg.	SB	PO	A	E	Avg.
1977—Appleton (Midwest)...........	OF	69	222	37	58	11	2	5	29	.261	2	94	10	7	.937
1978—Knoxville (Southern)........	OF-1B	137	502	70	138	16	6	13	72	.275	3	291	22	13	.960
1979—Iowa (American Assoc.) ...	OF	125	466	87	139	25	8	22	87	.298	5	222	•16	11	.956
1980—Chicago (A.L.)	OF	141	491	55	125	23	6	13	49	.255	2	229	6	9	.963
1981—Chicago (A.L.)	OF	82	280	42	80	11	7	10	41	.286	6	120	10	2	.985
1982—Chicago (A.L.)	OF	161	608	89	165	29	8	25	105	.271	10	326	10	7	.980
1983—Chicago (A.L.)	OF	156	596	76	167	33	2	20	99	.280	7	312	10	9	.973
1984—Chicago (A.L.)	OF	147	569	72	173	28	10	29	94	.304	1	307	8	6	.981
1985—Chicago (A.L.)	OF	160	640	86	198	29	3	22	113	.309	1	318	8	2	.994
1986—Chicago (A.L.)	OF	145	570	72	169	29	2	21	88	.296	2	295	15	5	.984
1987—Chicago (A.L.)	OF	132	505	59	148	26	4	20	93	.293	0	13	0	0	1.000

Year	Team (League)	Pos.	G	AB	R	H	2B	3B	HR	RBI	Avg.	SB	PO	A	E	Avg.
1988 —Chicago (A.L.)	OF	158	599	55	166	39	1	13	81	.277	0	14	1	2	.882
1989 —Chicago-Texas (A.L.)■.....	OF	146	505	73	156	29	1	16	72	.309	0	54	0	2	.964
1990 —Texas-Oakland (A.L.)■...	OF	135	415	52	118	15	1	16	65	.284	0	5	0	1	.833
1991 —Oakland (A.L.)	OF	141	488	76	144	25	1	20	90	.295	0	11	1	1	.923
Major league totals (12 years)		1704	6266	807	1809	316	46	225	990	.289	29	2004	69	46	.978

CHAMPIONSHIP SERIES RECORD

Year	Team (League)	Pos.	G	AB	R	H	2B	3B	HR	RBI	Avg.	SB	PO	A	E	Avg.
1983 —Chicago (A.L.)	OF	4	16	0	2	0	0	0	0	.125	0	5	1	0	1.000
1990 —Oakland (A.L.)	DH	4	14	2	5	1	0	0	3	.357	1	0	0	0	...
Championship Series totals (2 years)		8	30	2	7	1	0	0	3	.233	1	5	1	0	1.000

WORLD SERIES RECORD

Year	Team (League)	Pos.	G	AB	R	H	2B	3B	HR	RBI	Avg.	SB	PO	A	E	Avg.
1990 —Oakland (A.L.)	PH-DH	3	7	1	1	0	0	1	2	.143	0	0	0	0	...

ALL-STAR GAME RECORD

Year	League	Pos.	AB	R	H	2B	3B	HR	RBI	Avg.	SB	PO	A	E	Avg.
1985 —American	PH	1	0	1	0	0	0	0	1.000	0	0	0	0	...
1986 —American	PH	1	0	0	0	0	0	0	.000	0	0	0	0	...
1987 —American	PH	1	0	0	0	0	0	0	.000	0	0	0	0	...
1989 —American	DH	3	1	1	0	0	0	1	.333	0	0	0	0	...
1991 —American	DH	1	0	0	0	0	0	1	.000	0	0	0	0	...
All-Star Game totals (5 years)		7	1	2	0	0	0	2	.286	0	0	0	0	...

BALLARD, JEFF
P

PERSONAL: Born August 13, 1963, at Billings, Mont. . . . 6-2/203. . . . Throws left, bats left. . . . Full name: Jeffrey Scott Ballard.
HIGH SCHOOL: Billings West (Mont.).
COLLEGE: Stanford (degree in geophysics).
TRANSACTIONS/CAREER NOTES: Selected by Milwaukee Brewers organization in 16th round of free-agent draft (June 8, 1981). . . . Selected by Baltimore Orioles organization in 27th round of free-agent draft (June 4, 1984). . . . Selected by Orioles organization in seventh round of free-agent draft (June 3, 1985). . . . Granted free agency (October 18, 1991).
STATISTICAL NOTES: Tied for New York-Pennsylvania League lead with three shutouts in 1985.

Year	Team (League)	G	W	L	Pct.	ERA	Sv.	IP	H	R	ER	BB	SO
1985 —Newark (New York-Penn)	13	•10	2	.833	1.41	0	96	78	20	15	20	91
1986 —Hagerstown (Carolina)	17	9	5	.643	★1.85	0	112	106	39	23	32	115
—Charlotte (Southern)	10	5	2	.714	3.32	0	59⅔	70	29	22	20	35
—Rochester (International)	2	0	2	.000	7.11	0	6⅓	11	6	5	3	7
1987 —Rochester (International)	23	13	4	.765	3.09	0	160⅓	151	60	55	35	114
—Baltimore (A.L.)	14	2	8	.200	6.59	0	69⅔	100	60	51	35	27
1988 —Rochester (International)	9	4	3	.571	2.97	0	60⅔	56	26	20	11	32
—Baltimore (A.L.)	25	8	12	.400	4.40	0	153⅓	167	83	75	42	41
1989 —Baltimore (A.L.)	35	18	8	.692	3.43	0	215⅓	240	95	82	57	62
1990 —Baltimore (A.L.)	44	2	11	.154	4.93	0	133⅓	152	79	73	42	50
1991 —Baltimore (A.L.)	26	6	12	.333	5.60	0	123⅔	153	91	77	28	37
—Rochester (International)	7	3	3	.500	4.41	0	51	63	27	25	10	19
Major league totals (5 years)	144	36	51	.414	4.63	0	695⅓	812	408	358	204	217

BANISTER, JEFFERY
C/1B, PIRATES

PERSONAL: Born January 15, 1965, at Weatherford, Okla. . . . 6-2/200. . . . Throws right, bats right. . . . Full name: Jeffery Todd Banister.
HIGH SCHOOL: La Marque (Tex.).
COLLEGE: Houston.
TRANSACTIONS/CAREER NOTES: Selected by Pittsburgh Pirates organization in 25th round of free-agent draft (June 2, 1986).
STATISTICAL NOTES: Led South Atlantic League catchers with seven double plays in 1987. . . . Led Eastern League catchers with .988 fielding percentage in 1989.

Year	Team (League)	Pos.	G	AB	R	H	2B	3B	HR	RBI	Avg.	SB	PO	A	E	Avg.
1986 —Watertown (N.Y.-Penn)....	C-1B-OF	41	124	9	18	4	0	0	8	.145	4	189	41	2	.991
1987 —Macon (South Atlantic)	C-1B	101	307	35	78	20	0	6	37	.254	1	540	53	15	.975
1988 —Harrisburg (Eastern)	C	71	205	9	53	6	0	6	26	.259	0	348	26	•17	.957
1989 —Harrisburg (Eastern)	C-1B	102	336	48	80	13	0	12	48	.238	2	558	31	7	†.988
1990 —Harrisburg (Eastern)	C-1B	101	368	43	99	13	0	10	57	.269	2	514	47	8	.986
—Buffalo (Am. Assoc.)	C-1B	12	25	3	8	2	0	1	3	.320	0	40	4	3	.936
1991 —Buffalo (Am. Assoc.)	C-1B	79	234	23	57	7	1	2	21	.244	1	303	23	10	.970
—Pittsburgh (N.L.)	PH	1	1	0	1	0	0	0	0	1.000	0	0	0	0	...
Major league totals (1 year)		1	1	0	1	0	0	0	0	1.000	0	0	0	0	...

BANKHEAD, SCOTT
P, REDS

PERSONAL: Born July 31, 1963, at Raleigh, N.C. . . . 5-10/185. . . . Throws right, bats right. . . . Full name: Michael Scott Bankhead.
COLLEGE: North Carolina.
TRANSACTIONS/CAREER NOTES: Selected by Pittsburgh Pirates organization in 17th round of free-agent draft (June 8, 1981). . . . Selected by Kansas City Royals organization in first round (16th pick overall) of free-agent draft (June 4, 1984). . . . Traded by Royals with P Steve Shields and OF Mike Kingery to Seattle Mariners for OF Danny Tartabull and P Rick Luecken (December 10, 1986). . . . On disabled list (June 24-July 13, 1987). . . . On Seattle disabled list (March 20-May 14, 1988); included rehabilitation disability assignment to San Bernardino (April 23-May 2, 1988) and Calgary (May 3-10, 1988). . . . On Seattle disabled list (April 16-May 18 and June 3, 1990-remainder of season); included rehabilitation disability assignment to Calgary (May 1-7, 1990). . . . On disabled list (May 11-31 and June 12-September 1, 1991); included rehabilitation disability assignment to San Bernardino (August 5-14, 1991), Bellingham (August 14-18, 1991) and Calgary (August 18-September 1, 1991). . . . Granted free agency (December 20, 1991). . . . Signed by Cincinnati Reds (January 22, 1992).
MISCELLANEOUS: Member of 1984 U.S. Olympic baseball team.

Year	Team (League)	G	W	L	Pct.	ERA	Sv.	IP	H	R	ER	BB	SO
1985	—Memphis (Southern)	24	8	6	.571	3.59	0	140⅓	117	63	56	56	•128
1986	—Omaha (American Assoc.)	7	2	2	.500	1.49	0	48⅓	31	11	8	14	34
	—Kansas City (A.L.)	24	8	9	.471	4.61	0	121	121	66	62	37	94
1987	—Seattle (A.L.)■	27	9	8	.529	5.42	0	149⅓	168	96	90	37	95
1988	—San Bernardino (California)	2	0	0	. . .	1.64	0	11	6	3	2	4	6
	—Calgary (Pacific Coast)	2	1	1	.500	7.36	0	11	15	9	9	5	5
	—Seattle (A.L.)	21	7	9	.438	3.07	0	135	115	53	46	38	102
1989	—Seattle (A.L.)	33	14	6	.700	3.34	0	210⅓	187	84	78	63	140
1990	—Seattle (A.L.)	4	0	2	.000	11.08	0	13	18	16	16	7	10
	—Calgary (Pacific Coast)	2	0	1	.000	6.43	0	7	9	6	5	3	7
1991	—Seattle (A.L.)	17	3	6	.333	4.90	0	60⅔	73	35	33	21	28
	—San Bernardino (California)	2	0	1	.000	5.06	0	5⅓	4	4	3	2	4
	—Bellingham (Northwest)	1	1	0	1.000	0.00	0	4	1	0	0	1	8
	—Calgary (Pacific Coast)	5	0	0	. . .	1.04	1	8⅔	7	1	1	1	10
Major league totals (6 years)		126	41	40	.506	4.24	0	689⅓	682	350	325	203	469

BANKS, WILLIE
P, TWINS

PERSONAL: Born February 27, 1969, at Jersey City, N.J. . . . 6-1/190. . . . Throws right, bats right. . . . Full name: Willie Anthony Banks.
HIGH SCHOOL: St. Anthony's (Jersey City, N.J.).
TRANSACTIONS/CAREER NOTES: Selected by Minnesota Twins organization in first round (third pick overall) of free-agent draft (June 2, 1987).
STATISTICAL NOTES: Led Appalachian League with 28 wild pitches and tied for lead with three balks in 1987. . . . Pitched 1-0 no-hit victory against Palm Springs (May 24, 1989). . . . Led California League with 22 wild pitches and tied for lead with four shutouts in 1989. . . . Tied for Pacific Coast League lead with 14 wild pitches in 1991.

Year	Team (League)	G	W	L	Pct.	ERA	Sv.	IP	H	R	ER	BB	SO
1987	—Elizabethton (Appalachian)	13	1	8	.111	6.99	0	65⅔	73	★71	★51	★62	71
1988	—Kenosha (Midwest)	24	10	10	.500	3.72	0	125⅔	109	73	52	★107	113
1989	—Visalia (California)	27	12	9	.571	2.59	0	174	122	70	50	85	★173
	—Orlando (Southern)	1	1	0	1.000	5.14	0	7	10	4	4	0	9
1990	—Orlando (Southern)	28	7	9	.438	3.93	0	162⅔	161	93	71	98	114
1991	—Portland (Pacific Coast)	25	9	8	.529	4.55	0	146⅓	156	81	74	76	63
	—Minnesota (A.L.)	5	1	1	.500	5.71	0	17⅓	21	15	11	12	16
Major league totals (1 year)		5	1	1	.500	5.71	0	17⅓	21	15	11	12	16

BANNISTER, FLOYD
P

PERSONAL: Born June 10, 1955, at Pierre, S.D. . . . 6-1/190. . . . Throws left, bats left. . . . Full name: Floyd Franklin Bannister.
HIGH SCHOOL: John F. Kennedy (Seattle).
COLLEGE: Arizona State.
TRANSACTIONS/CAREER NOTES: Selected by Oakland Athletics organization in third round of free-agent draft (June 5, 1973). . . . Selected by Houston Astros organization in first round (first pick overall) of free-agent draft (June 8, 1976). . . . On disabled list (July 26-August 22, 1977). . . . Traded by Astros to Seattle Mariners for SS Craig Reynolds (December 8, 1978). . . . On disabled list (August 8-29, 1981). . . . Granted free agency (November 10, 1982). . . . Signed by Chicago White Sox (December 13, 1982). . . . On disabled list (May 19-June 17, 1986). . . . Traded by White Sox with IF Dave Cochrane to Kansas City Royals for P John Davis, P Melido Perez, P Chuck Mount and P Greg Hibbard (December 10, 1987). . . . On disabled list (June 12, 1989-remainder of season). . . . Granted free agency (November 13, 1989). . . . Signed by Yakult Swallows of Japan Central League (December 4, 1989). . . . Signed as free agent by California Angels (December 12, 1990). . . . On California disabled list (May 18-June 18, 1991); included rehabilitation disability assignment to Palm Springs (June 13-18, 1991). . . . Released by Angels (August 29, 1991).
RECORDS/HONORS: Named lefthanded pitcher on THE SPORTING NEWS college All-America team (1975-76). . . . Named College Player of the Year by THE SPORTING NEWS (1976).
MISCELLANEOUS: Had one at-bat with no hits (1984).

Year	Team (League)	G	W	L	Pct.	ERA	Sv.	IP	H	R	ER	BB	SO
1976	—Covington (App'l'ch'n)	3	0	0	. . .	0.00	1	13	3	0	0	2	27
	—Columbus (Southern)	3	1	0	1.000	1.50	0	24	16	4	4	14	20
	—Memphis (International)	1	1	0	1.000	1.50	0	6	7	1	1	3	6
1977	—Houston (N.L.)	24	8	9	.471	4.03	0	143	138	70	64	68	112

Year	Team (League)	G	W	L	Pct.	ERA	Sv.	IP	H	R	ER	BB	SO
1978	—Houston (N.L.)	28	3	9	.250	4.83	0	110	120	59	59	63	94
1979	—Seattle (A.L.)■	30	10	15	.400	4.05	0	182	185	92	82	68	115
1980	—Seattle (A.L.)	32	9	13	.409	3.47	0	218	200	96	84	66	155
1981	—Seattle (A.L.)	21	9	9	.500	4.46	0	121	128	62	60	39	85
1982	—Seattle (A.L.)	35	12	13	.480	3.43	0	247	225	112	94	77	★209
1983	—Chicago (A.L.)■	34	16	10	.615	3.35	0	217⅓	191	88	81	71	193
1984	—Chicago (A.L.)	34	14	11	.560	4.83	0	218	211	127	117	80	152
1985	—Chicago (A.L.)	34	10	14	.417	4.87	0	210⅔	211	121	114	100	198
1986	—Chicago (A.L.)	28	10	14	.417	3.54	0	165⅓	162	81	65	48	92
1987	—Chicago (A.L.)	34	16	11	.593	3.58	0	228⅔	216	100	91	49	124
1988	—Kansas City (A.L.)■	31	12	13	.480	4.33	0	189½	182	102	91	68	113
1989	—Kansas City (A.L.)	14	4	1	.800	4.66	0	75⅓	87	40	39	18	35
1990	—Yakult Swallows (Jap. Cen.)■...	9	3	2	.600	4.04	0	49	52	25	22	22	31
1991	—California (A.L.)■	16	0	0	...	3.96	0	25	25	12	11	10	16
	—Palm Springs (California)	7	0	3	.000	6.59	1	28⅔	32	24	21	9	27
	American League totals (12 years)	343	122	124	.496	3.99	0	2097⅔	2023	1033	929	694	1487
	National League totals (2 years)	52	11	18	.379	4.38	0	253	258	129	123	131	206
	Major league totals (14 years)	395	133	142	.484	4.03	0	2350⅔	2281	1162	1052	825	1693

CHAMPIONSHIP SERIES RECORD

Year	Team (League)	G	W	L	Pct.	ERA	Sv.	IP	H	R	ER	BB	SO
1983	—Chicago (A.L.)	1	0	1	.000	4.50	0	6	5	4	3	1	5

ALL-STAR GAME RECORD

Year	League	W	L	Pct.	ERA	Sv.	IP	H	R	ER	BB	SO
1982	—American	0	0	...	0.00	0	1	1	0	0	0	0

BARBERIE, BRET
IF, EXPOS

PERSONAL: Born August 16, 1967, at Long Beach, Calif. ... 5-11/180. ... Throws right, bats both. ... Full name: Bret Edward Barberie. ... Son of Edward Barberie, minor league catcher-shortstop (1961-66).
HIGH SCHOOL: Gahr (Cerritos, Calif.).
COLLEGE: Cerritos Junior College (Calif.) and Southern California (received degree, 1988).
TRANSACTIONS/CAREER NOTES: Selected by St. Louis Cardinals organization in second round of free-agent draft (January 14, 1986). ... Selected by Oakland Athletics organization in secondary phase of free-agent draft (June 2, 1986). ... Selected by Kansas City Royals organization in 65th round of free-agent draft (June 2, 1987). ... Selected by Montreal Expos organization in seventh round of free-agent draft (June 1, 1988).
STATISTICAL NOTES: Switch-hit home runs in one game (August 2, 1991).
MISCELLANEOUS: Member of 1988 U.S. Olympic baseball team.

Year	Team (League)	Pos.	G	AB	R	H	2B	3B	HR	RBI	Avg.	SB	PO	A	E	Avg.
1989	—West Palm Beach (FSL)	2B	124	457	63	122	16	4	4	34	.267	10	247	343	16	.974
1990	—Jacksonville (Southern)	2B	133	431	71	112	18	3	7	56	.260	20	263	322	14	★.977
1991	—Indianapolis (A.A.)	3-2-S-1	71	218	45	68	10	4	10	48	.312	10	83	162	13	.950
	—Montreal (N.L.)	S-2-3-1	57	136	16	48	12	2	2	18	.353	0	53	90	5	.966
	Major league totals (1 year)		57	136	16	48	12	2	2	18	.353	0	53	90	5	.966

BARFIELD, JESSE
OF, YANKEES

PERSONAL: Born October 29, 1959, at Joliet, Ill. ... 6-1/201. ... Throws right, bats right. ... Full name: Jesse Lee Barfield.
HIGH SCHOOL: Joliet Central (Ill.).
TRANSACTIONS/CAREER NOTES: Selected by Toronto Blue Jays organization in ninth round of free-agent draft (June 7, 1977). ... On disabled list (August 15-29, 1980 and May 16-31, 1988). ... Traded by Blue Jays to New York Yankees for P Al Leiter (April 30, 1989). ... On disabled list (July 29, 1991-remainder of season).
RECORDS/HONORS: Won A.L. Gold Glove as outfielder (1986-87). ... Named outfielder on THE SPORTING NEWS A.L. Silver-Slugger team (1986).
STATISTICAL NOTES: Led Florida State League batters with 125 strikeouts in 1978. ... Led A.L. outfielders with eight double plays in 1985 and 1986.

Year	Team (League)	Pos.	G	AB	R	H	2B	3B	HR	RBI	Avg.	SB	PO	A	E	Avg.
1977	—Utica (New York-Penn)	OF	70	234	37	53	9	3	5	35	.226	4	122	6	•13	.908
1978	—Dunedin (Florida State)	OF	133	441	40	91	12	3	2	34	.206	1	229	★22	★15	.944
1979	—Kinston (Carolina)	OF	136	477	66	126	24	5	8	71	.264	6	284	19	17	.947
1980	—Knoxville (Southern)	OF	124	433	63	104	12	8	14	65	.240	11	309	14	12	.964
1981	—Knoxville (Southern)	OF	141	524	83	137	24	13	16	70	.261	25	270	★23	6	.980
	—Toronto (A.L.)	OF	25	95	7	22	3	2	2	9	.232	4	71	2	0	1.000
1982	—Toronto (A.L.)	OF	139	394	54	97	13	2	18	58	.246	1	217	15	9	.963
1983	—Toronto (A.L.)	OF	128	388	58	98	13	3	27	68	.253	2	213	16	8	.966
1984	—Toronto (A.L.)	OF	110	320	51	91	14	1	14	49	.284	8	190	9	10	.952
1985	—Toronto (A.L.)	OF	155	539	94	156	34	9	27	84	.289	22	349	★22	4	.989
1986	—Toronto (A.L.)	OF	158	589	107	170	35	2	★40	108	.289	8	368	★20	3	.992

Year	Team (League)	Pos.	G	AB	R	H	2B	3B	HR	RBI	Avg.	SB	PO	A	E	Avg.
1987	—Toronto (A.L.)	OF	159	590	89	155	25	3	28	84	.263	3	341	•17	3	.992
1988	—Toronto (A.L.)	OF	137	468	62	114	21	5	18	56	.244	7	325	12	4	.988
1989	—Toronto-New York (A.L.)■	OF	150	521	79	122	23	1	23	67	.234	5	340	★20	•10	.973
1990	—New York (A.L.)	OF	153	476	69	117	21	2	25	78	.246	4	305	★16	9	.973
1991	—New York (A.L.)	OF	84	284	37	64	12	0	17	48	.225	1	178	10	0	1.000
	Major league totals (11 years)		1398	4664	707	1206	214	30	239	709	.259	65	2897	159	60	.981

CHAMPIONSHIP SERIES RECORD

Year	Team (League)	Pos.	G	AB	R	H	2B	3B	HR	RBI	Avg.	SB	PO	A	E	Avg.
1985	—Toronto (A.L.)	OF	7	25	3	7	1	0	1	4	.280	1	21	0	1	.955

ALL-STAR GAME RECORD

Year	League	Pos.	AB	R	H	2B	3B	HR	RBI	Avg.	SB	PO	A	E	Avg.
1986	—American	PH-OF	3	0	0	0	0	0	0		.000	0	2	0	0	1.000

BARFIELD, JOHN
P, RANGERS

PERSONAL: Born October 15, 1964, at Little Rock, Ark. . . . 6-1/195. . . . Throws left, bats left. . . . Full name: John David Barfield.
HIGH SCHOOL: Pine Bluff (Ark.).
COLLEGE: Crowder College (Mo.) and Oklahoma City University.
TRANSACTIONS/CAREER NOTES: Selected by Philadelphia Phillies organization in 17th round of free-agent draft (January 9, 1985). . . . Selected by Texas Rangers organization in 11th round of free-agent draft (June 2, 1986). . . . On disabled list (August 2, 1991-remainder of season).

Year	Team (League)	G	W	L	Pct.	ERA	Sv.	IP	H	R	ER	BB	SO
1986	—Daytona Beach (Florida State)	3	1	1	.500	4.15	0	17⅓	14	9	8	1	13
	—Salem (Carolina)	13	2	5	.286	4.98	0	56	71	43	31	22	39
1987	—Charlotte (Florida State)	25	10	7	.588	3.69	0	153⅔	145	75	63	55	79
1988	—Tulsa (Texas)	24	9	9	.500	2.88	0	169	159	69	54	66	125
1989	—Oklahoma City (Am. Assoc.)	28	10	8	.556	4.06	0	175⅓	178	93	79	68	58
	—Texas (A.L.)	4	0	1	.000	6.17	0	11⅔	15	10	8	4	9
1990	—Oklahoma City (Am. Assoc.)	19	1	6	.143	3.53	1	43⅓	44	21	17	21	25
	—Texas (A.L.)	33	4	3	.571	4.67	1	44⅓	42	25	23	13	17
1991	—Texas (A.L.)	28	4	4	.500	4.54	1	83⅓	96	51	42	22	27
	Major league totals (3 years)	65	8	8	.500	4.72	2	139⅓	153	86	73	39	53

BARNES, BRIAN
P, EXPOS

PERSONAL: Born March 25, 1967, at Roanoke Rapids, N.C. . . . 5-9/170. . . . Throws left, bats left. . . . Full name: Brian Keith Barnes.
HIGH SCHOOL: Roanoke Rapids (N.C.).
COLLEGE: Clemson.
TRANSACTIONS/CAREER NOTES: Selected by Baltimore Orioles organization in 25th round of free-agent draft (June 1, 1988). . . . Selected by Montreal Expos organization in fourth round of free-agent draft (June 5, 1989). . . . On Expos disabled list (March 28-May 5, 1991); included rehabilitation disability assignment to West Palm Beach (April 15-21, 1991) and Indianapolis (April 21-May 5, 1991).
RECORDS/HONORS: Named Southern League Pitcher of the Year (1990).

Year	Team (League)	G	W	L	Pct.	ERA	Sv.	IP	H	R	ER	BB	SO
1989	—Jamestown (New York-Penn)	2	1	0	1.000	1.00	0	9	4	1	1	3	15
	—West Palm Beach (Florida St.)	7	4	3	.571	0.72	0	50	25	9	4	16	67
	—Indianapolis (Am. Assoc.)	1	1	0	1.000	1.50	0	6	5	1	1	2	5
1990	—Jacksonville (Southern)	29	13	7	.650	2.77	0	★201⅓	144	78	62	87	★213
	—Montreal (N.L.)	4	1	1	.500	2.89	0	28	25	10	9	7	23
1991	—Montreal (N.L.)	28	5	8	.385	4.22	0	160	135	82	75	84	117
	—West Palm Beach (Florida St.)	2	0	0	. . .	0.00	0	7	3	0	0	4	6
	—Indianapolis (Am. Assoc.)	2	2	0	1.000	1.64	0	11	6	2	2	8	10
	Major league totals (2 years)	32	6	9	.400	4.02	0	188	160	92	84	91	140

BARNES, SKEETER
OF/IF, TIGERS

PERSONAL: Born March 7, 1957, at Cincinnati. . . . 5-10/180. . . . Throws right, bats right. . . . Full name: William Henry Barnes III.
HIGH SCHOOL: Woodward (Cincinnati).
COLLEGE: Cincinnati.
TRANSACTIONS/CAREER NOTES: Selected by Cincinnati Reds organization in 16th round of free-agent draft (June 6, 1978). . . . Traded by Reds organization to Montreal Expos organization for OF Max Venable (April 26, 1985). . . . Traded by Expos organization with P Dan Schatzeder to Philadelphia Phillies for IF Tom Foley and P Larry Sorensen (July 24, 1986). . . . Granted free agency (October 15, 1986). . . . Signed by Louisville, St. Louis Cardinals organization (January 26, 1987). . . . Sold by Cardinals to Denver, Milwaukee Brewers organization (July 16, 1987). . . . Granted free agency (October 15, 1987). . . . Signed by Buffalo, Pittsburgh Pirates organization (November 20, 1987). . . . Released by Pirates organization (May 7, 1988). . . . Signed by Nashville, Reds organization (May 14, 1988). . . . Granted free agency (October 15, 1988). . . . Re-signed by Reds (November 5, 1988). . . . Granted free agency (October 22, 1989). . . . Re-signed by Reds (January 29, 1990). . . . Granted free agency (October 15, 1990). . . . Signed by Toledo, Detroit Tigers organization (January 21, 1991).

STATISTICAL NOTES: Tied for Pioneer League lead with six sacrifice flies in 1978. . . . Led Eastern League third basemen with 104 putouts in 1981 and .947 fielding percentage in 1982. . . . Tied for American Association lead with eight sacrifice flies in 1989.

Year	Team (League)	Pos.	G	AB	R	H	2B	3B	HR	RBI	Avg.	SB	PO	A	E	Avg.
1978	—Billings (Pioneer)	0-3-S-2-1	68	277	66	102	★22	5	3	★76	.368	21	56	50	16	.869
1979	—Nashville (Southern)	3B	★145	500	54	133	19	4	12	77	.266	5	123	★291	★35	.922
1980	—Waterbury (Eastern)	OF	★138	533	62	156	27	6	4	64	.293	18	264	15	13	.955
1981	—Indianapolis (A.A.)	1B-OF-3B	36	118	10	31	6	1	1	11	.263	1	254	23	3	.989
	—Waterbury (Eastern)	3-0-1-2	96	363	45	93	17	0	6	49	.256	15	†115	185	15	.952
1982	—Waterbury (Eastern)	3B-1B-SS	112	418	67	128	24	6	12	72	.306	31	252	192	19	†.959
	—Indianapolis (A.A.)	3B-1B	18	59	8	18	5	1	1	3	.305	1	25	25	2	.962
1983	—Indianapolis (A.A.)	3-1-0-2	109	377	67	127	19	6	7	56	.337	10	203	140	16	.955
	—Cincinnati (N.L.)	1B-3B	15	34	5	7	0	0	1	4	.206	2	45	11	1	.982
1984	—Wichita (Am. Assoc.)	3-1-0-2	92	360	59	118	23	4	14	67	.328	24	143	122	13	.953
	—Cincinnati (N.L.)	3B-OF	32	42	5	5	0	0	1	3	.119	0	7	15	0	1.000
1985	—Denver-Ind. (A.A.)■	3-1-0-2	95	340	51	95	16	0	8	63	.279	20	308	154	10	.979
	—Montreal (N.L.)	3B-OF-1B	19	26	0	4	1	0	0	0	.154	0	13	6	0	1.000
1986	—Indianapolis (A.A.)	3B-OF-1B	85	300	40	80	18	5	5	40	.267	16	95	137	18	.928
	—Portland (Pacific Coast)■	3-0-S-1	38	141	21	52	8	4	1	29	.369	3	44	60	6	.945
1987	—Louisville-Denver (A.A.)■	3B-1B-OF	110	431	79	131	33	5	16	76	.304	17	315	127	7	.963
	—St. Louis (N.L.)	3B	4	4	1	1	0	0	1	3	.250	0	0	0	0	...
1988	—Buffalo-Nashville (A.A.)■	1-0-3-P	122	379	47	96	16	0	6	39	.253	15	461	38	3	.994
1989	—Nashville (Am. Assoc.)	3-1-0-2	124	472	57	143	★39	3	6	55	.303	15	305	24	7	.979
	—Cincinnati (N.L.)	PR-PH	5	3	1	0	0	0	0	0	.000	0	0	0	0	...
1990	—Nashville (Am. Assoc.)■	OF-1B-3B	★144	★548	83	★156	21	2	7	66	.285	34	281	30	5	.984
1991	—Toledo (International)■	OF-3B-1B	62	233	48	77	14	0	9	40	.330	27	209	69	7	.975
	—Detroit (A.L.)	0-3-1-2	75	159	28	46	13	2	5	17	.289	10	92	38	2	.985
American League totals (1 year)			75	159	28	46	13	2	5	17	.289	10	92	38	2	.985
National League totals (5 years)			75	109	12	17	1	0	3	10	.156	2	65	32	1	.990
Major league totals (6 years)			150	268	40	63	14	2	8	27	.235	12	157	70	3	.987

RECORD AS PITCHER

Year	Team (League)	G	W	L	Pct.	ERA	Sv.	IP	H	R	ER	BB	SO
1988	—Nashville (American Assoc.)	1	0	0	...	...	0	0	4	6	6	3	0

BARRETT, MARTY

2B

PERSONAL: Born June 23, 1958, at Arcadia, Calif. . . . 5-10/175. . . . Throws right, bats right. . . . Full name: Martin Glenn Barrett. . . . Brother of Tom Barrett, second baseman, Philadelphia Phillies (1988-89); and brother of Charlie Barrett, minor league pitcher (1973-78).

HIGH SCHOOL: Rancho (Las Vegas).
COLLEGE: Mesa Community College (Ariz.) and Arizona State.
TRANSACTIONS/CAREER NOTES: Selected by California Angels organization in 11th round of free-agent draft (January 11, 1977). . . . Selected by New York Mets organization in third round of free-agent draft (January 10, 1978). . . . Selected by Boston Red Sox organization in secondary phase of free-agent draft (June 5, 1979). . . . On Pawtucket disabled list (June 25-July 15 and July 17-August 4, 1981; and April 11-27, 1987). . . . On Boston disabled list (June 5-August 5, 1989); included rehabilitation disability assignment to Pawtucket (July 24-August 5, 1989). . . . Released by Red Sox (December 14, 1990). . . . Signed by San Diego Padres (January 8, 1991). . . . On San Diego disabled list (May 8-June 10, 1991); included rehabilitation disability assignment to Las Vegas (May 24-June 10, 1991). . . . Released by Padres (June 14, 1991).
STATISTICAL NOTES: Led Florida State League with nine sacrifice flies nine in 1979. . . . Led Eastern League with 15 sacrifice hits in 1980. . . . Led Eastern League second basemen with .985 fielding percentage in 1980. . . . Led International League second basemen with 99 double plays in 1982. . . . Led A.L. second basemen with 110 double plays in 1985. . . . Led A.L. with 18 sacrifice hits in 1986, 22 in 1987 and 20 in 1988.

Year	Team (League)	Pos.	G	AB	R	H	2B	3B	HR	RBI	Avg.	SB	PO	A	E	Avg.
1979	—Winter Haven (Fla. St.)	2B	57	178	25	53	7	0	1	28	.298	4	124	144	6	.978
1980	—Bristol (Eastern)	2B-SS	128	475	72	130	17	2	1	41	.274	22	279	372	10	†.985
1981	—Pawtucket (Int'l)	2B	88	343	36	91	12	2	1	28	.265	9	186	254	10	.978
1982	—Pawtucket (Int'l)	2B	131	477	72	143	27	1	5	57	.300	28	303	★415	11	★.985
	—Boston (A.L.)	2B	8	18	0	1	0	0	0	0	.056	0	11	21	0	1.000
1983	—Boston (A.L.)	2B	33	44	7	10	1	1	0	2	.227	1	32	28	1	.984
	—Pawtucket (Int'l)	2B	36	119	24	41	4	2	1	18	.345	5	70	115	1	.995
1984	—Boston (A.L.)	2B	139	475	56	144	23	3	3	45	.303	5	245	417	9	★.987
1985	—Boston (A.L.)	2B	156	534	59	142	26	0	5	56	.266	7	★355	479	11	.987
1986	—Boston (A.L.)	2B	158	625	94	179	39	4	4	60	.286	15	303	★450	14	.982
1987	—Boston (A.L.)	2B	137	559	72	164	23	0	3	43	.293	15	320	438	9	★.988
1988	—Boston (A.L.)	2B	150	612	83	173	28	1	1	65	.283	7	312	402	7	.990
1989	—Boston (A.L.)	2B	86	336	31	86	18	0	1	27	.256	4	152	245	10	.975
	—Pawtucket (Int'l)	2B	11	35	4	10	1	1	0	4	.286	0	22	25	2	.959
1990	—Boston (A.L.)	2B-3B	62	159	15	36	4	0	0	13	.226	4	90	148	2	.992
1991	—San Diego (N.L.)■	2B-3B	12	16	1	3	1	0	1	3	.188	0	7	6	0	1.000
	—Las Vegas (Pac. Coast)	2B	16	47	5	15	4	1	0	4	.319	0	28	39	0	1.000
American League totals (9 years)			929	3362	417	935	162	9	17	311	.278	57	1820	2628	63	.986
National League totals (1 year)			12	16	1	3	1	0	1	3	.188	0	7	6	0	1.000
Major league totals (10 years)			941	3378	418	938	163	9	18	314	.278	57	1827	2634	63	.986

CHAMPIONSHIP SERIES RECORD

CHAMPIONSHIP SERIES NOTES: Shares A.L. single-series record for most singles—9 (1986).

Year Team (League)	Pos.	G	AB	R	H	2B	3B	HR	RBI	Avg.	SB	PO	A	E	Avg.
1986—Boston (A.L.)	2B	7	30	4	11	2	0	0	5	.367	0	19	21	0	1.000
1988—Boston (A.L.)	2B	4	15	2	1	0	0	0	0	.067	0	6	8	0	1.000
1990—Boston (A.L.)	2B	3	0	0	0	0	0	0	0	. . .	0	2	0	0	1.000
Championship Series totals (3 years)		14	45	6	12	2	0	0	5	.267	0	27	29	0	1.000

WORLD SERIES RECORD

WORLD SERIES NOTES: Shares single-series record for most hits—13 (1986).

Year Team (League)	Pos.	G	AB	R	H	2B	3B	HR	RBI	Avg.	SB	PO	A	E	Avg.
1986—Boston (A.L.)	2B	7	30	1	13	2	0	0	4	.433	0	13	25	0	1.000

BASS, KEVIN
OF, GIANTS

PERSONAL: Born May 12, 1959, at Redwood City, Calif. . . . 6-0/190. . . . Throws right, bats both. . . . Full name: Kevin Charles Bass. . . . Brother of Richard Bass, minor league outfielder (1976-77); and cousin of James Lofton, Buffalo Bills, National Football League.
HIGH SCHOOL: Menlo Park (Calif.).
TRANSACTIONS/CAREER NOTES: Selected by Milwaukee Brewers organization in second round of free-agent draft (June 7, 1977). . . . On disabled list (July 29-September 1, 1981). . . . Traded by Brewers organization with P Mike Madden and P Frank DiPino to Houston Astros (September 3, 1982), completing deal in which Houston traded P Don Sutton to Brewers for three players to be named later (August 30, 1982). . . . On disabled list (March 29-April 13, 1984). . . . On Houston disabled list (May 28-August 11, 1989); included rehabilitation disability assignment to Tucson (August 4-22, 1989). . . . Granted free agency (November 13, 1989). . . . Signed by San Francisco Giants (November 16, 1989). . . . On San Francisco disabled list (May 27-September 3, 1990); included rehabilitation disability assignment to San Jose (August 20-26, 1990) and Phoenix (August 27-September 3, 1990). . . . On San Francisco disabled list (June 19-July 23, 1991); included rehabilitation disability assignment to San Jose (July 4-10, 1991) and Phoenix (July 10-23, 1991).
RECORDS/HONORS: Shares major league single-season record for most games with switch-hit home runs—2 (1987). . . . Shares N.L. career record for most games with switch-hit home runs—3.
STATISTICAL NOTES: Led Midwest League in being hit by pitch with 10 in 1978. . . . Led Eastern League outfielders with seven double plays in 1980. . . . Switch-hit home runs in one game (August 3, 1987, September 2, 1987 and August 20, 1989).

Year Team (League)	Pos.	G	AB	R	H	2B	3B	HR	RBI	Avg.	SB	PO	A	E	Avg.
1977—Newark (N.Y.-Penn)	OF	48	189	30	56	11	•7	1	33	.296	11	56	2	3	.951
1978—Burlington (Midwest)........	OF	129	499	81	132	27	5	18	69	.265	36	★281	14	11	.964
1979—Holyoke (Eastern)	OF	135	490	69	129	15	4	8	54	.263	17	280	•16	★17	.946
1980—Holyoke (Eastern)	OF	136	490	79	147	★31	7	4	51	.300	35	305	14	★18	.947
1981—Vancouver (Pac. Coast)....	OF	97	339	40	87	10	5	2	30	.257	29	175	14	7	.964
1982—Milwaukee (A.L.)	OF	18	9	4	0	0	0	0	0	.000	0	7	0	0	1.000
—Vancouver (Pac. Coast)....	OF	102	413	70	130	23	7	17	65	.315	23	199	15	10	.955
—Houston (N.L.)■...............	OF	12	24	2	1	0	0	0	1	.042	0	11	0	1	.917
1983—Houston (N.L.)	OF	88	195	25	46	7	3	2	18	.236	2	68	1	4	.945
1984—Houston (N.L.)	OF	121	331	33	86	17	5	2	29	.260	5	149	4	4	.975
1985—Houston (N.L.)	OF	150	539	72	145	27	5	16	68	.269	19	328	10	1	★.997
1986—Houston (N.L.)	OF	157	591	83	184	33	5	20	79	.311	22	303	12	5	.984
1987—Houston (N.L.)	OF	157	592	83	168	31	5	19	85	.284	21	287	11	4	.987
1988—Houston (N.L.)	OF	157	541	57	138	27	2	14	72	.255	31	267	7	6	.979
1989—Houston (N.L.)	OF	87	313	42	94	19	4	5	44	.300	11	186	6	3	.985
—Tucson (Pacific Coast)	OF	6	17	1	5	1	0	0	2	.294	0	8	0	0	1.000
1990—San Francisco (N.L.)■......	OF	61	214	25	54	9	1	7	32	.252	2	88	2	3	.968
—San Jose (California)	OF	6	22	2	8	1	0	0	4	.364	1	3	0	0	1.000
—Phoenix (Pacific Coast)	OF	8	33	2	8	2	0	0	4	.242	1	5	2	0	1.000
1991—San Francisco (N.L.)	OF	124	361	43	84	10	4	10	40	.233	7	159	9	4	.977
—San Jose (California)	OF	5	19	1	2	2	0	0	1	.105	2	7	1	1	.889
—Phoenix (Pacific Coast)	OF	10	41	8	13	3	1	2	7	.317	1	20	0	0	1.000
American League totals (1 year)		18	9	4	0	0	0	0	0	.000	0	7	0	0	1.000
National League totals (10 years)		1114	3701	465	1000	180	34	95	468	.270	120	1846	62	35	.982
Major league totals (10 years)		1132	3710	469	1000	180	34	95	468	.270	120	1853	62	35	.982

CHAMPIONSHIP SERIES RECORD

CHAMPIONSHIP SERIES NOTES: Shares single-series record for most times caught stealing—3 (1986). . . . Shares single-game record for most times caught stealing—2 (October 15, 1986, 16 innings).

Year Team (League)	Pos.	G	AB	R	H	2B	3B	HR	RBI	Avg.	SB	PO	A	E	Avg.
1986—Houston (N.L.)	OF	6	24	0	7	2	0	0	0	.292	2	16	0	1	.941

ALL-STAR GAME RECORD

Year League	Pos.	AB	R	H	2B	3B	HR	RBI	Avg.	SB	PO	A	E	Avg.
1986—National	PH	1	0	0	0	0	0	0	.000	0	0	0	0	. . .

BATISTA, MIGUEL
P, PIRATES

PERSONAL: Born February 19, 1971, at Santo Domingo, Dominican Republic. . . . 6-0/ 160. . . . Throws right, bats right. . . . Full name: Miguel Jerez Batista.
TRANSACTIONS/CAREER NOTES: Signed as free agent by Montreal Expos organization (February 29, 1988). . . . Played in Dominican Summer League (1988-89). . . . Drafted by Pittsburgh Pirates organization (December 9, 1991).

Year	Team (League)	G	W	L	Pct.	ERA	Sv.	IP	H	R	ER	BB	SO
1988	—						Dominican Summer League						
1989	—						Dominican Summer League						
1990	—Bradenton Expos (Gulf Coast)..	9	4	3	.571	2.06	0	39⅓	33	16	9	17	21
	—Rockford (Midwest)	3	0	1	.000	8.76	0	12⅓	16	13	12	5	7
1991	—Rockford (Midwest)	23	11	5	.688	4.04	0	133⅔	126	74	60	57	90

BATISTE, KIM
SS, PHILLIES

PERSONAL: Born March 15, 1968, at New Orleans. . . . 6-0/175. . . . Throws right, bats right. . . . Full name: Kimothy Emil Batiste. . . . Name pronounced buh-TEEST.
HIGH SCHOOL: St. Amant High (La.).
TRANSACTIONS/CAREER NOTES: Selected by Philadelphia Phillies organization in third round of free-agent draft (June 2, 1987).
STATISTICAL NOTES: Led Eastern League shortstops with 550 total chances in 1990.

Year	Team (League)	Pos.	G	AB	R	H	2B	3B	HR	RBI	Avg.	SB	PO	A	E	Avg.
							BATTING							FIELDING		
1987	—Utica (New York-Penn)	S-3	46	150	15	26	8	1	2	10	.173	4	64	90	16	.906
1988	—Spartanburg (S. Atl.)	SS	122	430	51	107	19	6	6	52	.249	16	202	363	60	.904
1989	—Clearwater (Florida St.)	SS-3B	114	385	36	90	12	4	3	33	.234	13	168	309	35	.932
1990	—Reading (Eastern)	SS	125	486	57	134	14	4	6	33	.276	28	*182	*333	*35	.936
1991	—Scranton/W.B. (Int'l)	SS	122	462	54	135	25	6	1	41	.292	18	181	344	*37	.934
	—Philadelphia (N.L.)	SS	10	27	2	6	0	0	0	1	.222	0	10	22	1	.970
Major league totals (1 year)			10	27	2	6	0	0	0	1	.222	0	10	22	1	.970

BAUTISTA, JOSE
P, ROYALS

PERSONAL: Born July 25, 1964, at Bani, Dominican Republic. . . . 6-2/207. . . . Throws right, bats right. . . . Full name: Jose Joaquin Bautista. . . . Name pronounced bough-TEES-tuh.
HIGH SCHOOL: Bani School (Bani, Dominican Republic).
TRANSACTIONS/CAREER NOTES: Signed as free agent by New York Mets organization (April 25, 1981). . . . Drafted by Baltimore Orioles (December 7, 1987). . . . On Baltimore disabled list (May 20-June 11, 1989); included rehabilitation disability assignment to Rochester (May 29-June 11, 1989). . . . Sent by Orioles outright to Miami, independent (April 24, 1991); returned to Orioles organization (June 1, 1991). . . . Loaned by Orioles organization to Oklahoma City (June 1, 1991); returned (July 11, 1991). . . . Granted free agency (September 23, 1991). . . . Signed by Omaha, Kansas City Royals organization (December 20, 1991).
STATISTICAL NOTES: Pitched 6-0 no-hit victory against Prince William (May 26, 1985, first game). . . . Tied for Florida State League lead with three shutouts in 1991.

Year	Team (League)	G	W	L	Pct.	ERA	Sv.	IP	H	R	ER	BB	SO
1981	—Kingsport (Appalachian)	13	3	6	.333	4.64	0	66	84	54	34	17	34
1982	—Kingsport (Appalachian)	14	0	4	.000	8.92	5	38⅓	61	44	38	19	13
1983	—Sarasota Mets (Gulf Coast)	13	4	3	.571	2.31	0	81⅔	66	31	21	32	44
1984	—Columbia (South Atlantic)	19	13	4	.765	3.13	0	135	121	52	47	35	96
1985	—Lynchburg (Carolina)	27	15	8	.652	2.34	1	169	145	49	44	33	109
1986	—Jackson (Texas)	7	0	1	.000	8.31	0	21⅔	36	22	20	8	13
	—Lynchburg (Carolina)	18	8	8	.500	3.94	0	118⅔	120	58	52	24	62
1987	—Jackson (Texas)	28	10	5	.667	3.24	0	169⅓	174	76	61	43	95
1988	—Baltimore (A.L.)■	33	6	15	.286	4.30	0	171⅔	171	86	82	45	76
1989	—Baltimore (A.L.)	15	3	4	.429	5.31	0	78	84	46	46	15	30
	—Rochester (International)	15	4	4	.500	2.83	0	98⅔	84	41	31	26	47
1990	—Baltimore (A.L.)	22	1	0	1.000	4.05	0	26⅔	28	15	12	7	15
	—Rochester (International)	27	7	8	.467	4.06	2	108⅔	115	51	49	15	50
1991	—Baltimore (A.L.)	5	0	1	.000	16.88	0	5⅓	13	10	10	5	3
	—Miami (Florida State)■.............	11	8	2	*.800	2.71	0	76⅓	63	23	23	11	69
	—Oklahoma City (Am. Assoc.)■ ..	11	0	3	.000	5.29	0	32⅓	38	19	19	6	22
	—Rochester (International)■.......	6	1	0	1.000	0.59	1	15⅓	8	1	1	3	7
Major league totals (4 years)		75	10	20	.333	4.79	0	281⅔	296	157	150	72	124

BEASLEY, CHRIS
P

PERSONAL: Born June 23, 1962, at Jackson, Tenn. . . . 6-2/190. . . . Throws right, bats right. . . . Full name: Christopher Charles Beasley.
HIGH SCHOOL: Costa Mesa (Calif.).
COLLEGE: Orange Coast (Calif.) and Arizona State.
TRANSACTIONS/CAREER NOTES: Selected by Chicago White Sox organization in sixth round of free-agent draft (January 12, 1982). . . . Selected by California Angels organization in 27th round of free-agent draft (June 6, 1983). . . . Selected by Cleveland Indians organization in ninth round of free-agent draft (June 4, 1984). . . . Released by Indians (June 15, 1987). . . . Signed by Seattle Mariners organization (June 30, 1987). . . . Released by Mariners (March 23, 1988). . . . Signed by California Angels organization (February 10, 1989). . . . Granted free agency (October 15, 1990). . . . Re-signed by Angels (January 15, 1991). . . . Granted free agency (December 20, 1991).

STATISTICAL NOTES: Tied for New York-Pennsylvania League lead with 11 home runs allowed in 1984.... Led Pacific Coast League with 16 hit batsmen in 1990.

Year	Team (League)	G	W	L	Pct.	ERA	Sv.	IP	H	R	ER	BB	SO
1984—Batavia (New York-Penn)		14	6	5	.545	4.01	0	89⅔	97	54	40	33	70
1985—Waterloo (Midwest)		17	6	7	.462	3.30	0	120	110	55	44	47	87
—Waterbury (Eastern)		9	2	6	.250	4.18	0	56	44	28	26	35	27
1986—Waterbury (Eastern)		27	8	9	.471	3.82	0	155⅔	152	83	66	67	105
1987—Williamsport (N.Y.-Penn)		11	2	6	.250	6.65	0	66⅓	93	63	49	30	37
—Chattanooga (Southern)■		14	2	4	.333	3.67	0	56⅓	73	33	23	22	26
1988—						Out of Organized Baseball							
1989—Palm Springs (California)■		10	4	3	.571	2.66	0	71	60	31	21	18	44
—Midland (Texas)		16	8	4	.667	3.88	1	104⅓	101	53	45	33	48
1990—Edmonton (Pacific Coast)		28	12	9	.571	4.49	0	176⅓	★201	107	88	70	108
1991—Edmonton (Pacific Coast)		23	3	5	.375	5.26	1	89	99	55	52	26	51
—California (A.L.)		22	0	1	.000	3.38	0	26⅔	26	14	10	10	14
Major league totals (1 year)		22	0	1	.000	3.38	0	26⅔	26	14	10	10	14

BEATTY, BLAINE
P, EXPOS

PERSONAL: Born April 25, 1964, at Victoria, Tex.... 6-2/190.... Throws left, bats left.... Full name: Gordon Blaine Beatty.
HIGH SCHOOL: Victoria (Tex.).
COLLEGE: San Jacinto (Tex.) and Baylor.
TRANSACTIONS/CAREER NOTES: Selected by Baltimore Orioles organization in fifth round of free-agent draft (January 17, 1984).... Selected by Orioles organization in secondary phase of free-agent draft (June 4, 1984).... Selected by St. Louis Cardinals organization in secondary phase of free-agent draft (June 3, 1985).... Selected by Orioles organization in ninth round of free-agent draft (June 2, 1986).... Traded by Orioles organization with a player to be named later to New York Mets for P Doug Sisk (December 8, 1987); Mets acquired P Greg Talamantez to complete deal (December 11, 1987).... On disabled list (April 6, 1990-entire season).... Traded by Mets to Montreal Expos for OF Jeff Barry (December 9, 1991).
RECORDS/HONORS: Named Carolina League Pitcher of the Year (1987).... Named Texas League Pitcher of the Year (1988).
STATISTICAL NOTES: Led New York-Pennsylvania League with eight complete games in 1986.... Led Texas League with five shutouts, 12 complete games and tied for lead in games started by pitcher with 28 in 1988.... Tied for International League lead with three shutouts and 27 games started by pitcher in 1989.... Tied for International League lead in games started by pitcher with 28 in 1991.

Year	Team (League)	G	W	L	Pct.	ERA	Sv.	IP	H	R	ER	BB	SO
1986—Newark (New York-Penn)		15	★11	3	.786	2.11	0	★119⅓	98	37	28	30	93
1987—Hagerstown (Carolina)		13	11	1	★.917	2.52	0	100	81	32	28	11	65
—Charlotte (Southern)		15	6	5	.545	3.07	0	105⅔	110	38	36	20	57
1988—Jackson (Texas)■		30	★16	8	.667	2.46	0	★208⅔	191	64	57	34	103
1989—Tidewater (International)		27	12	10	.545	3.31	0	185	173	86	68	43	90
—New York (N.L.)		2	0	0	...	1.50	0	6	5	1	1	2	3
1990—						Did not play							
1991—Tidewater (International)		28	•12	9	.571	4.11	0	175⅓	192	86	80	43	74
—New York (N.L.)		5	0	0	...	2.79	0	9⅔	9	3	3	4	7
Major league totals (2 years)		7	0	0	...	2.30	0	15⅔	14	4	4	6	10

BECK, ROD
P, GIANTS

PERSONAL: Born August 3, 1968, at Burbank, Calif.... 6-1/215.... Throws right, bats right.... Full name: Rodney Roy Beck.
HIGH SCHOOL: Grant (Sherman Oaks, Calif.).
TRANSACTIONS/CAREER NOTES: Selected by Oakland Athletics organization in 13th round of free-agent draft (June 2, 1986).... Traded by A's organization to San Francisco Giants organization for P Charlie Corbell (March 23, 1988).

Year	Team (League)	G	W	L	Pct.	ERA	Sv.	IP	H	R	ER	BB	SO
1986—Medford (Northwest)		13	1	3	.250	5.23	1	32⅔	47	25	19	11	21
1987—Medford (Northwest)		17	5	8	.385	5.18	0	92	106	74	53	26	69
1988—Clinton (Midwest)■		28	12	7	.632	3.00	0	177	177	68	59	27	123
1989—San Jose (California)		13	11	2	★.846	2.40	0	97⅓	91	29	26	26	88
—Shreveport (Texas)		16	7	3	.700	3.55	0	99	108	45	39	16	74
1990—Shreveport (Texas)		14	10	3	.769	2.23	0	93	85	26	23	17	71
—Phoenix (Pacific Coast)		12	4	7	.364	4.93	0	76⅔	100	51	42	18	43
1991—Phoenix (Pacific Coast)		23	4	3	.571	2.02	6	71⅓	56	18	16	13	35
—San Francisco (N.L.)		31	1	1	.500	3.78	1	52⅓	53	22	22	13	38
Major league totals (1 year)		31	1	1	.500	3.78	1	52⅓	53	22	22	13	38

BEDROSIAN, STEVE
P

PERSONAL: Born December 6, 1957, at Methuen, Mass. ... 6-3/210. ... Throws right, bats right. ... Full name: Stephen Wayne Bedrosian. ... Name pronounced bed-ROHZ-ee-un.
HIGH SCHOOL: Methuen (Mass.).
COLLEGE: North Essex Community College (Mass.) and New Haven (Conn.).
TRANSACTIONS/CAREER NOTES: Selected by Atlanta Braves organization in third round of free-agent draft (June 6, 1978).... On disabled list (June 24-September 18, 1979 and August 20-September 4, 1984).... Traded by Braves with OF Milt Thompson to

Philadelphia Phillies for C Ozzie Virgil and P Pete Smith (December 10, 1985).... On Philadelphia disabled list (March 21-May 20, 1988); included rehabilitation disability assignment to Maine (May 9-19, 1988).... Traded by Phillies with a player to be named later to San Francisco Giants for P Dennis Cook, P Terry Mulholland and 3B Charlie Hayes (June 18, 1989); Giants organization acquired IF Rick Parker to complete deal (August 7, 1989).... Traded by Giants to Minnesota Twins for P Johnny Ard and a player to be named later (December 5, 1990); Giants acquired P Jimmy Williams to complete deal (December 18, 1990).... Granted free agency (November 7, 1991).

RECORDS/HONORS: Named N.L. Rookie Pitcher of the Year by THE SPORTING NEWS (1982).... Named N.L. Fireman of the Year by THE SPORTING NEWS (1987). ... Named N.L. Cy Young Award winner by Baseball Writers' Association of America (1987).

STATISTICAL NOTES: Tied for Southern League lead in games started by pitcher with 29 in 1980.

Year	Team (League)	G	W	L	Pct.	ERA	Sv.	IP	H	R	ER	BB	SO
1978	—Kingsport (Appalachian)	6	2	2	.500	3.08	0	38	38	18	13	25	29
	—Greenwood (W. Carolinas)	8	5	1	.833	2.13	0	55	45	17	13	34	58
1979	—Savannah (Southern)	13	5	5	.500	3.03	0	89	71	36	30	58	73
1980	—Savannah (Southern)	29	14	10	.583	3.19	0	*203	167	91	72	96	*161
1981	—Richmond (International)	26	10	10	.500	2.69	0	184	143	76	55	99	144
	—Atlanta (N.L.)	15	1	2	.333	4.50	0	24	15	14	12	15	9
1982	—Atlanta (N.L.)	64	8	6	.571	2.42	11	137⅔	102	39	37	57	123
1983	—Atlanta (N.L.)	70	9	10	.474	3.60	19	120	100	50	48	51	114
1984	—Atlanta (N.L.)	40	9	6	.600	2.37	11	83⅔	65	23	22	33	81
1985	—Atlanta (N.L.)	37	7	15	.318	3.83	0	206⅔	198	101	88	111	134
1986	—Philadelphia (N.L.)■	68	8	6	.571	3.39	29	90⅓	79	39	34	34	82
1987	—Philadelphia (N.L.)	65	5	3	.625	2.83	40	89	79	31	28	28	74
1988	—Maine (International)	5	0	0	...	0.00	0	6⅔	6	0	0	2	5
	—Philadelphia (N.L.)	57	6	6	.500	3.75	28	74⅓	75	34	31	27	61
1989	—Phil.-San Francisco (N.L.)■	68	3	7	.300	2.87	23	84⅔	56	31	27	39	58
1990	—San Francisco (N.L.)	68	9	9	.500	4.20	17	79⅓	72	40	37	44	43
1991	—Minnesota (A.L.)■	56	5	3	.625	4.42	6	77⅓	70	42	38	35	44
	American League totals (1 year)	56	5	3	.625	4.42	6	77⅓	70	42	38	35	44
	National League totals (10 years)	552	65	70	.481	3.31	178	989⅔	841	402	364	439	779
	Major league totals (11 years)	608	70	73	.490	3.39	184	1067	911	444	402	474	823

CHAMPIONSHIP SERIES RECORD

CHAMPIONSHIP SERIES NOTES: Shares N.L. single-series record for most saves—3 (1989).

Year	Team (League)	G	W	L	Pct.	ERA	Sv.	IP	H	R	ER	BB	SO
1982	—Atlanta (N.L.)	2	0	0	...	18.00	0	1	3	2	2	1	2
1989	—San Francisco (N.L.)	4	0	0	...	2.70	3	3⅓	4	1	1	2	2
1991	—Minnesota (A.L.)	2	0	0	...	0.00	0	1⅓	3	2	0	2	2
	Championship Series totals (3 years)	8	0	0	...	4.76	0	5⅔	10	5	3	5	6

WORLD SERIES RECORD

Year	Team (League)	G	W	L	Pct.	ERA	Sv.	IP	H	R	ER	BB	SO
1989	—San Francisco (N.L.)	2	0	0	...	0.00	0	2⅔	0	0	0	2	2
1991	—Minnesota (A.L.)	3	0	0	...	5.40	0	3⅓	3	2	2	0	2
	World Series totals (2 years)	5	0	0	...	3.00	0	6	3	2	2	2	4

ALL-STAR GAME RECORD

Year	League	W	L	Pct.	ERA	Sv.	IP	H	R	ER	BB	SO
1987	—National	0	0	...	0.00	0	1	0	0	0	2	0

BELCHER, TIM

P, REDS

PERSONAL: Born October 19, 1961, at Mount Gilead, O.... 6-3/223.... Throws right, bats right. ... Full name: Timothy Wayne Belcher.
HIGH SCHOOL: Highland (Sparta, O.).
COLLEGE: Mt. Vernon Nazarene (O.).
TRANSACTIONS/CAREER NOTES: Selected by Minnesota Twins organization in first round (first pick overall) of free-agent draft (June 6, 1983).... Selected by New York Yankees organization in secondary phase of free-agent draft (January 17, 1984).... Selected by Oakland Athletics organization in player compensation pool draft (February 8, 1984); A's received compensation for Baltimore Orioles' signing of free-agent P Tom Underwood, a Type A player (February 7, 1984).... On disabled list (April 10-May 4 and May 5-July 23, 1986).... Traded by A's organization to Los Angeles Dodgers (September 3, 1987), completing deal in which Dodgers traded P Rick Honeycutt to A's for a player to be named later (August 29, 1987).... On disabled list (August 17, 1990-remainder of season).... Traded by Dodgers with P John Wetteland to Cincinnati Reds for OF Eric Davis and P Kip Gross (November 27, 1991).
RECORDS/HONORS: Named righthanded pitcher on THE SPORTING NEWS college All-America team (1983).... Named N.L. Rookie Pitcher of the Year by THE SPORTING NEWS (1988).
STATISTICAL NOTES: Led N.L. with eight shutouts and tied for lead with 10 complete games in 1989.

Year	Team (League)	G	W	L	Pct.	ERA	Sv.	IP	H	R	ER	BB	SO
1984	—Madison (Midwest)	16	9	4	.692	3.57	0	98⅓	80	45	39	48	111
	—Albany (Eastern)	10	3	4	.429	3.33	0	54	37	30	20	41	40
1985	—Huntsville (Southern)	29	11	10	.524	4.69	0	149⅔	145	99	78	99	90
1986	—Huntsville (Southern)	9	2	5	.286	6.57	0	37	50	28	27	22	25
1987	—Tacoma (Pacific Coast)	29	9	11	.450	4.42	0	163	143	89	80	*133	136
	—Los Angeles (N.L.)■	6	4	2	.667	2.38	0	34	30	11	9	7	23
1988	—Los Angeles (N.L.)	36	12	6	.667	2.91	4	179⅔	143	65	58	51	152

Year	Team (League)	G	W	L	Pct.	ERA	Sv.	IP	H	R	ER	BB	SO
1989 — Los Angeles (N.L.)		39	15	12	.556	2.82	1	230	182	81	72	80	200
1990 — Los Angeles (N.L.)		24	9	9	.500	4.00	0	153	136	76	68	48	102
1991 — Los Angeles (N.L.)		33	10	9	.526	2.62	0	209⅓	189	76	61	75	156
Major league totals (5 years)		138	50	38	.568	2.99	5	806	680	309	268	261	633

CHAMPIONSHIP SERIES RECORD

Year	Team (League)	G	W	L	Pct.	ERA	Sv.	IP	H	R	ER	BB	SO
1988 — Los Angeles (N.L.)		2	2	0	1.000	4.11	0	15⅓	12	7	7	4	16

WORLD SERIES RECORD

Year	Team (League)	G	W	L	Pct.	ERA	Sv.	IP	H	R	ER	BB	SO
1988 — Los Angeles (N.L.)		2	1	0	1.000	6.23	0	8⅔	10	7	6	6	10

BELINDA, STAN
P, PIRATES

PERSONAL: Born August 6, 1966, at State College, Pa.... 6-3/200.... Throws right, bats right.... Full name: Stanley Peter Belinda.
HIGH SCHOOL: State College Area (State College, Pa.).
COLLEGE: Allegany Community (Md.).
TRANSACTIONS/CAREER NOTES: Selected by Pittsburgh Pirates organization in 10th round of free-agent draft (June 2, 1986).... On Bradenton disabled list (June 21-30, 1986).

Year	Team (League)	G	W	L	Pct.	ERA	Sv.	IP	H	R	ER	BB	SO
1986 — Watertown (New York-Penn)		5	0	0	...	3.38	2	8	5	3	3	2	5
— Bradenton Pirates (GCL)		17	3	2	.600	2.66	7	20⅓	23	12	6	2	17
1987 — Macon (South Atlantic)		50	6	4	.600	2.09	16	82	59	26	19	27	75
1988 — Salem (Carolina)		53	6	4	.600	2.76	14	71⅔	54	33	22	32	63
1989 — Harrisburg (Eastern)		32	1	4	.200	2.33	13	38⅔	32	13	10	25	33
— Buffalo (American Assoc.)		19	2	2	.500	0.95	9	28⅓	13	5	3	13	28
— Pittsburgh (N.L.)		8	0	1	.000	6.10	0	10⅓	13	8	7	2	10
1990 — Buffalo (American Assoc.)		15	3	1	.750	1.90	5	23⅔	20	8	5	8	25
— Pittsburgh (N.L.)		55	3	4	.429	3.55	8	58⅓	48	23	23	29	55
1991 — Pittsburgh (N.L.)		60	7	5	.583	3.45	16	78⅓	50	30	30	35	71
Major league totals (3 years)		123	10	10	.500	3.67	24	147	111	61	60	66	136

CHAMPIONSHIP SERIES RECORD

Year	Team (League)	G	W	L	Pct.	ERA	Sv.	IP	H	R	ER	BB	SO
1990 — Pittsburgh (N.L.)		3	0	0	...	2.45	0	3⅔	3	1	1	0	4
1991 — Pittsburgh (N.L.)		3	1	0	1.000	0.00	0	5	0	0	0	3	4
Championship Series totals (2 years)		6	1	0	1.000	1.04	0	8⅔	3	1	1	3	8

BELL, DEREK
OF, BLUE JAYS

PERSONAL: Born December 11, 1968, at Tampa, Fla.... 6-2/200.... Throws right, bats right.... Full name: Derek Nathaniel Bell.
HIGH SCHOOL: King (Tampa, Fla.).
TRANSACTIONS/CAREER NOTES: Selected by Toronto Blue Jays organization in second round of free-agent draft (June 2, 1987).... On Knoxville disabled list (July 30, 1988-remainder of season; June 13-21 and July 2-12, 1990).
RECORDS/HONORS: Named International League Most Valuable Player (1991).
STATISTICAL NOTES: Led International League with 243 total bases in 1991.... Led International League outfielders with seven double plays in 1991.

Year	Team (League)	Pos.	G	AB	R	H	2B	3B	HR	RBI	Avg.	SB	PO	A	E	Avg.
						BATTING								FIELDING		
1987 — St. Catharines (NYP)		OF	74	273	46	72	11	3	10	42	.264	12	126	6	2	.985
1988 — Knoxville (Southern)		OF	14	52	5	13	3	1	0	4	.250	2	18	2	2	.909
1989 — Knoxville (Southern)		OF	136	513	72	124	22	6	16	75	.242	15	216	12	9	.962
1990 — Syracuse (International)		OF	109	402	57	105	13	5	7	56	.261	21	220	9	5	.979
1991 — Syracuse (International)		OF	119	457	*89	*158	22	*12	13	*93	*.346	27	278	*15	*16	.948
— Toronto (A.L.)		OF	18	28	5	4	0	0	0	1	.143	3	16	0	2	.889
Major league totals (1 year)			18	28	5	4	0	0	0	1	.143	3	16	0	2	.889

BELL, ERIC
P, INDIANS

PERSONAL: Born October 27, 1963, at Modesto, Calif.... 6-0/165.... Throws left, bats left.... Full name: Eric Alvin Bell.
HIGH SCHOOL: Beyer (Modesto, Calif.).
TRANSACTIONS/CAREER NOTES: Selected by Baltimore Orioles organization in ninth round of free-agent draft (June 7, 1982).... On Orioles disabled list (May 3-June 18, 1984; May 9, 1988-remainder of season; and April 5-June 10, 1989).... Granted free agency (October 4, 1990).... Signed by Cleveland Indians (October 14, 1990).
STATISTICAL NOTES: Tied for Carolina League lead in games started by pitcher with 26 in 1985.

Year	Team (League)	G	W	L	Pct.	ERA	Sv.	IP	H	R	ER	BB	SO
1982 — Bluefield (Appalachian)		11	4	1	.800	2.10	0	51⅓	42	19	12	36	30
1983 — Newark (New York-Penn)		18	3	2	.600	4.95	6	60	71	44	33	30	56
1984 — Hagerstown (Carolina)		3	0	0	...	9.82	0	3⅔	6	4	4	5	6
— Newark (New York-Penn)		15	8	3	.727	2.46	0	102⅓	82	40	28	26	114

Year Team (League)	G	W	L	Pct.	ERA	Sv.	IP	H	R	ER	BB	SO
1985—Hagerstown (Carolina)	26	11	6	.647	3.13	0	158⅓	141	73	55	63	★162
—Baltimore (A.L.)	4	0	0	...	4.76	0	5⅔	4	3	3	4	4
1986—Charlotte (Southern)	18	9	6	.600	★3.05	0	129⅔	109	49	44	66	104
—Rochester (International)	11	7	3	★.700	3.05	0	76⅓	68	26	26	35	59
—Baltimore (A.L.)	4	1	2	.333	5.01	0	23⅓	23	14	13	14	18
1987—Baltimore (A.L.)	33	10	13	.435	5.45	0	165	174	113	100	78	111
1988—Rochester (International)	7	3	1	.750	1.98	0	36⅓	28	10	8	13	33
1989—Rochester (International)	7	1	2	.333	4.99	0	39⅔	40	24	22	15	27
—Hagerstown (Carolina)	9	4	2	.667	1.88	1	43	32	11	9	11	35
1990—Rochester (International)	27	9	6	.600	4.86	0	148	168	90	80	65	90
1991—Canton/Akron (Eastern)	18	9	5	.643	2.89	0	93⅓	82	47	30	37	84
—Colorado Springs (Pac. Coast)	4	2	1	.667	2.13	0	25⅓	23	6	6	11	16
—Cleveland (A.L.)	10	4	0	1.000	0.50	0	18	5	2	1	5	7
Major league totals (4 years)	51	15	15	.500	4.97	0	212	206	132	117	101	140

BELL, GEORGE
OF, CUBS

PERSONAL: Born October 21, 1959, at San Pedro de Macoris, Dominican Republic. . . . 6-1/202. . . . Throws right, bats right. . . . Full name: George Antonio Mathey Bell. . . . Brother of Juan Bell, infielder, Baltimore Orioles; and brother of Rolando Bell, minor league infielder (1985-87).
TRANSACTIONS/CAREER NOTES: Signed as free agent by Philadelphia Phillies organization (June 23, 1978). . . . On disabled list (June 22, 1980-remainder of season). . . . Drafted by Toronto Blue Jays (December 8, 1980). . . . On disabled list (April 20-May 1, June 14-30 and July 8, 1982-remainder of season). . . . On suspended list (July 31-August 2, 1989). . . . Granted free agency (November 5, 1990). . . . Signed by Chicago Cubs (December 6, 1990).
RECORDS/HONORS: Shares major league single-game record for most sacrifice flies—3 (August 14, 1990). . . . Named outfielder on THE SPORTING NEWS A.L. Silver Slugger team (1985-87). . . . Named outfielder on THE SPORTING NEWS A.L. All-Star team (1986-87). . . . Named Major League Player of the Year by THE SPORTING NEWS (1987). . . . Named A.L. Player of the Year by THE SPORTING NEWS (1987). . . . Named A.L. Most Valuable Player by Baseball Writers' Association of America (1987).
STATISTICAL NOTES: Led Western Carolinas League with 270 total bases in 1979. . . . Tied for International League lead in double plays by outfielders with four in 1983. . . . Tied for A.L. lead in errors by outfielder with 11 in 1985. . . . Tied for A.L. lead with 15 game-winning RBIs in 1986. . . . Led A.L. with 369 total bases in 1987. . . . Hit three home runs in a game (April 4, 1988). . . . Led A.L. with 14 sacrifice flies in 1989.

Year Team (League)	Pos.	G	AB	R	H	2B	3B	HR	RBI	Avg.	SB	PO	A	E	Avg.
1978—Helena (Pioneer)	OF	33	106	20	33	6	1	0	14	.311	3	39	4	4	.915
1979—Spartanburg (W. Caro.)	OF	130	491	78	150	24	★15	22	★102	.305	10	206	14	8	.965
1980—Reading (Eastern)	OF	22	55	11	17	5	2	0	11	.309	3	24	0	1	.960
1981—Toronto (A.L.)	OF	60	163	19	38	2	1	5	12	.233	3	92	3	3	.969
1982—Syracuse (International)	OF	37	125	11	25	5	4	3	19	.200	2	72	3	1	.987
1983—Syracuse (International)	OF	85	317	37	86	11	4	15	59	.271	5	135	12	6	.961
—Toronto (A.L.)	OF	39	112	5	30	5	4	2	17	.268	1	61	1	3	.954
1984—Toronto (A.L.)	OF-3B	159	606	85	177	39	4	26	87	.292	11	289	13	9	.971
1985—Toronto (A.L.)	OF-1B	157	607	87	167	28	6	28	95	.275	21	320	14	‡11	.968
1986—Toronto (A.L.)	OF-3B	159	641	101	198	38	6	31	108	.309	7	270	17	10	.966
1987—Toronto (A.L.)	OF-2B-3B	156	610	111	188	32	4	47	★134	.308	5	249	14	11	.960
1988—Toronto (A.L.)	OF	156	614	78	165	27	5	24	97	.269	4	253	8	15	.946
1989—Toronto (A.L.)	OF	153	613	88	182	41	2	18	104	.297	4	258	4	•10	.963
1990—Toronto (A.L.)	OF	142	562	67	149	25	0	21	86	.265	3	226	4	5	.979
1991—Chicago (N.L.)■	OF	149	558	63	159	27	0	25	86	.285	2	249	6	★10	.962
American League totals (9 years)		1181	4528	641	1294	237	32	202	740	.286	59	2018	78	77	.965
National League totals (1 year)		149	558	63	159	27	0	25	86	.285	2	249	6	10	.962
Major league totals (10 years)		1330	5086	704	1453	264	32	227	826	.286	61	2267	84	87	.964

CHAMPIONSHIP SERIES RECORD

Year Team (League)	Pos.	G	AB	R	H	2B	3B	HR	RBI	Avg.	SB	PO	A	E	Avg.
1985—Toronto (A.L.)	OF	7	28	4	9	3	0	0	1	.321	21	13	0	0	1.000
1989—Toronto (A.L.)	OF-DH	5	20	2	4	0	0	1	2	.200	4	3	1	0	1.000
Championship Series totals (2 years)		12	48	6	13	3	0	1	3	.271	25	16	1	0	1.000

ALL-STAR GAME RECORD

Year League	Pos.	AB	R	H	2B	3B	HR	RBI	Avg.	SB	PO	A	E	Avg.
1987—American	OF	3	0	0	0	0	0	0	.000	5	1	0	0	1.000
1990—American	PH-OF	2	0	0	0	0	0	0	.000	3	2	0	0	1.000
1991—National	PH	1	0	0	0	0	0	0	.000	0	0	0	0	...
All-Star Game totals (3 years)		6	0	0	0	0	0	0	.000	8	3	0	0	1.000

BELL, JAY
SS, PIRATES

PERSONAL: Born December 11, 1965, at Pensacola, Fla. . . . 6-1/185. . . . Throws right, bats right. . . . Full name: Jay Stuart Bell.
HIGH SCHOOL: Tate (Gonzalez, Fla.).
TRANSACTIONS/CAREER NOTES: Selected by Minnesota Twins organization in first round (eighth pick

overall) of free-agent draft (June 4, 1984). . . . Traded by Twins with P Curt Wardle, OF Jim Weaver and a player to be named later to Cleveland Indians for P Bert Blyleven (August 1, 1985); Indians organization acquired P Rich Yett to complete deal (September 17, 1985). . . . Traded by Indians to Pittsburgh Pirates for SS Felix Fermin (March 25, 1989).

STATISTICAL NOTES: Led Appalachian League shortstops with 352 total chances and 43 double plays in 1984. . . . Led California League shortstops with 84 double plays in 1985. . . . Hit home run in first major league at-bat on first pitch (September 29, 1986). . . . Led Eastern League shortstops with 613 total chances in 1986. . . . Led American Association shortstops with 198 putouts, 322 assists, 550 total chances and 30 errors in 1987. . . . Led N.L. with 39 sacrifice hits in 1990. . . . Led N.L. shortstops with 741 total chances in 1990 and 754 in 1991. . . . Led N.L. with 30 sacrifice hits in 1991.

						BATTING							FIELDING			
Year	Team (League)	Pos.	G	AB	R	H	2B	3B	HR	RBI	Avg.	SB	PO	A	E	Avg.
1984 —Elizabethton (Appal.)		SS	66	245	43	54	12	1	6	30	.220	4	★109	★218	25	.929
1985 —Visalia (California)		SS	106	376	56	106	16	6	9	59	.282	10	176	330	53	.905
—Waterbury (Eastern)■		SS	29	114	13	34	11	2	1	14	.298	3	41	79	6	.952
1986 —Waterbury (Eastern)		SS	138	494	86	137	28	4	7	74	.277	10	197	★371	★45	.927
—Cleveland (A.L.)		2B	5	14	3	5	2	0	1	4	.357	0	1	6	2	.778
1987 —Buffalo (Am. Assoc.)		SS-2B	110	362	71	94	15	4	17	60	.260	6	†201	†325	†30	.946
—Cleveland (A.L.)		SS	38	125	14	27	9	1	2	13	.216	2	67	93	9	.947
1988 —Cleveland (A.L.)		SS	73	211	23	46	5	1	2	21	.218	4	103	170	10	.965
—Colorado Springs (PCL)		SS	49	181	35	50	12	2	7	24	.276	3	87	171	18	.935
1989 —Pittsburgh (N.L.)■...........		SS	78	271	33	70	13	3	2	27	.258	5	109	197	10	.968
—Buffalo (Am. Assoc.)		SS-3B	86	298	49	85	15	3	10	54	.285	12	110	223	16	.954
1990 —Pittsburgh (N.L.)		SS	159	583	93	148	28	7	7	52	.254	10	★260	459	22	.970
1991 —Pittsburgh (N.L.)		SS	157	608	96	164	32	8	16	67	.270	10	239	★491	★24	.968
American League totals (3 years)			116	350	40	78	16	2	5	38	.223	6	171	269	21	.954
National League totals (3 years)			394	1462	222	382	73	18	25	146	.261	25	608	1147	56	.969
Major league totals (6 years)			510	1812	262	460	89	20	30	184	.254	31	779	1416	77	.966

CHAMPIONSHIP SERIES RECORD

CHAMPIONSHIP SERIES NOTES: Shares single-series record for most singles—9 (1991).

						BATTING							FIELDING			
Year	Team (League)	Pos.	G	AB	R	H	2B	3B	HR	RBI	Avg.	SB	PO	A	E	Avg.
1990 —Pittsburgh (N.L.)		SS	6	20	3	5	1	0	1	1	.250	0	4	22	1	.963
1991 —Pittsburgh (N.L.)		SS	7	29	2	12	2	0	1	1	.414	0	13	19	1	.970

BELL, JUAN

2B/SS, ORIOLES

PERSONAL: Born March 29, 1968, at San Pedro de Macoris, Dominican Republic. . . . 5-11/175. . . . Throws right, bats both. . . . Full name: Juan Mathey Bell. . . . Brother of George Bell, outfielder, Chicago Cubs; and brother of Rolando Bell, minor league infielder (1985-87).
HIGH SCHOOL: Gastone F. Deligne (San Pedro de Macoris, Dominican Republic).

TRANSACTIONS/CAREER NOTES: Signed as free agent by Los Angeles Dodgers organization (September 1, 1984). . . . Traded by Dodgers organization with P Brian Holton and P Ken Howell to Baltimore Orioles for 1B Eddie Murray (December 4, 1988). . . . On Rochester disabled list (July 6-August 27, 1990).
STATISTICAL NOTES: Led Gulf Coast League shortstops with 293 total chances in 1986. . . . Led California League shortstops with 719 total chances in 1987.
MISCELLANEOUS: Batted righthanded only with Sarasota (1986) and San Antonio (1988).

						BATTING							FIELDING			
Year	Team (League)	Pos.	G	AB	R	H	2B	3B	HR	RBI	Avg.	SB	PO	A	E	Avg.
1985 —Braden. Dod. (GCL)		SS-2B	42	106	11	17	0	0	0	8	.160	2	56	73	20	.866
1986 —Sarasota Dodgers (GCL) ...		SS	59	217	38	52	6	2	0	26	.240	12	78	★193	22	.925
1987 —Bakersfield (California)		SS	134	473	54	116	15	3	4	58	.245	21	235	★431	★53	.926
1988 —San Antonio (Texas)		SS	61	215	37	60	4	2	5	21	.279	11	106	182	20	.935
—Albuquerque (PCL)		SS	73	257	42	77	9	3	8	45	.300	7	114	249	23	.940
1989 —Rochester (Int'l)■.............		SS	116	408	50	107	15	6	2	32	.262	17	190	297	36	.931
—Baltimore (A.L.)		2B-SS	8	4	2	0	0	0	0	0	.000	1	2	6	0	1.000
1990 —Rochester (Int'l)		SS	82	326	59	93	12	5	6	35	.285	16	131	240	22	.944
—Baltimore (A.L.)		SS	5	2	1	0	0	0	0	0	.000	0	1	1	0	1.000
1991 —Baltimore (A.L.)		2B-SS-OF	100	209	26	36	9	2	1	15	.172	0	107	199	9	.971
Major league totals (3 years)			113	215	29	36	9	2	1	15	.167	1	110	206	9	.972

BELL, MIKE

1B/OF, BRAVES

PERSONAL: Born April 22, 1968, at Lewiston, N.J. . . . 6-1/175. . . . Throws left, bats left. . . . Full name: Michael Allen Bell.
HIGH SCHOOL: Newton (N.J.).
TRANSACTIONS/CAREER NOTES: Selected by Atlanta Braves organization in fourth round of free-agent draft (June 2, 1986).
STATISTICAL NOTES: Led Carolina League first basemen with 1,014 total chances in 1988. . . . Led Southern League first basemen with 1,316 total chances in 1989.

						BATTING							FIELDING			
Year	Team (League)	Pos.	G	AB	R	H	2B	3B	HR	RBI	Avg.	SB	PO	A	E	Avg.
1987 —Sumter (So. Atl.)		1B	133	443	54	108	17	3	5	51	.244	11	1007	70	16	.985
1988 —Durham (Carolina)		1B	126	440	72	113	18	3	17	84	.257	11	★924	76	14	★.986
—Greenville (Southern)		1B	4	12	1	3	1	0	0	4	.250	0	44	1	0	1.000

— 34 —

Year	Team (League)	Pos.	G	AB	R	H	2B	3B	HR	RBI	Avg.	SB	PO	A	E	Avg.
1989	—Greenville (Southern)........	1B	132	472	63	115	26	3	6	57	.244	10	*1209	*94	13	.990
1990	—Greenville (Southern)........	1B	106	405	50	118	24	2	6	42	.291	10	981	85	8	*.993
	—Atlanta (N.L.)..................	1B	36	45	8	11	5	1	1	5	.244	0	97	9	2	.981
1991	—Richmond (Int'l)	1B-OF	91	341	37	85	12	2	5	29	.249	2	645	44	4	.994
	—Atlanta (N.L.)..................	1B	17	30	4	4	0	0	1	1	.133	1	72	5	2	.975
	Major league totals (2 years)		53	75	12	15	5	1	2	6	.200	1	169	14	4	.979

BELLE, ALBERT

OF/DH, INDIANS

PERSONAL: Born August 25, 1966, at Shreveport, La. . . . 6-2/200. . . . Throws right, bats right. . . . Full name: Albert Jojuan Belle. . . . Formerly known as Joey Belle.
COLLEGE: Louisiana State.
TRANSACTIONS/CAREER NOTES: Selected by Cleveland Indians organization in second round of free-agent draft (June 2, 1987). . . . On suspended list (July 12-18, 1991).
RECORDS/HONORS: Shares major league single-season record for fewest errors by outfielder who led league in errors—9 (1991).

Year	Team (League)	Pos.	G	AB	R	H	2B	3B	HR	RBI	Avg.	SB	PO	A	E	Avg.
1987	—Kinston (Carolina)...........	OF	10	37	5	12	2	0	3	9	.324	0	5	0	0	1.000
1988	—Kinston (Carolina)...........	OF	41	153	21	46	16	0	8	39	.301	2	43	5	5	.906
	—Waterloo (Midwest).........	OF	9	28	2	7	1	0	1	2	.250	0	11	1	0	1.000
1989	—Canton/Akron (Eastern) ..	OF	89	312	48	88	20	0	20	69	.282	8	136	4	3	.979
	—Cleveland (A.L.)	OF	62	218	22	49	8	4	7	37	.225	2	92	3	2	.979
1990	—Cleveland (A.L.)	OF	9	23	1	4	0	0	1	3	.174	0	0	0	0	...
	—Colorado Springs (PCL)	OF	24	96	16	33	3	1	5	19	.344	4	31	0	2	.939
	—Canton/Akron (Eastern) ..	DH	9	32	4	8	1	0	0	3	.250	0	0	0	0	...
1991	—Cleveland (A.L.)	OF	123	461	60	130	31	2	28	95	.282	3	170	8	•9	.952
	—Colorado Springs (PCL)	OF	16	61	9	20	3	2	2	16	.328	1	19	1	1	.952
	Major league totals (3 years)		194	702	83	183	39	6	36	135	.261	5	262	11	11	.961

BELLIARD, RAFAEL

SS, BRAVES

PERSONAL: Born October 24, 1961, at Pueblo Nuevo, Mao, Dominican Republic. . . . 5-6/160. . . . Throws right, bats right. . . . Full name: Rafael Leonidas Matias Belliard. . . . Name pronounced BELL-ee-ard.
TRANSACTIONS/CAREER NOTES: Signed as free agent by Pittsburgh Pirates organization (July 10, 1980). . . . On Buffalo disabled list (April 19-July 24, 1982). . . . On Pittsburgh disabled list (June 28-August 28, 1984; July 28-August 12, 1986; August 27, 1987-remainder of season; and May 19-June 3, 1988). . . . Granted free agency (November 5, 1990). . . . Signed by Atlanta Braves (December 18, 1990).
STATISTICAL NOTES: Led Carolina League with 12 sacrifice hits and tied for lead in caught stealing with 15 in 1981. . . . Tied for Eastern League lead in double plays by shortstops with 69 in 1983. . . . Led N.L. shortstops with .977 fielding percentage in 1988.

Year	Team (League)	Pos.	G	AB	R	H	2B	3B	HR	RBI	Avg.	SB	PO	A	E	Avg.
1980	—Brad. Pir. GCL	SS-2B-3B	12	42	6	9	1	0	0	2	.214	1	24	39	1	.984
	—Shelby (South Atlantic)	SS	8	24	1	3	0	0	0	2	.125	0	10	27	5	.881
1981	—Alexandria (Carolina)	SS	127	472	58	102	6	5	0	33	.216	42	•205	330	29	.949
1982	—Buffalo (Eastern)	SS	40	124	14	34	1	1	0	19	.274	6	56	87	5	.966
	—Pittsburgh (N.L.)	SS	9	2	3	1	0	0	0	0	.500	1	2	2	0	1.000
1983	—Lynn (Eastern)	SS-2B	127	431	63	113	13	2	2	37	.262	12	203	307	26	.951
	—Pittsburgh (N.L.)	SS	4	1	1	0	0	0	0	0	.000	0	1	3	0	1.000
1984	—Pittsburgh (N.L.)	SS-2B	20	22	3	5	0	0	0	0	.227	0	12	13	3	.893
1985	—Pittsburgh (N.L.)	SS	17	20	1	4	0	0	0	1	.200	0	13	23	2	.947
	—Hawaii (Pacific Coast)	SS-2B	100	341	35	84	12	4	1	18	.246	9	172	289	5	.989
1986	—Pittsburgh (N.L.)	SS-2B	117	309	33	72	5	2	0	31	.233	12	147	317	12	.975
1987	—Pittsburgh (N.L.)	SS-2B	81	203	26	42	4	3	1	15	.207	5	113	191	6	.981
	—Harrisburg (Eastern)	SS	37	145	24	49	5	2	0	9	.338	7	59	115	7	.961
1988	—Pittsburgh (N.L.)	SS-2B	122	286	28	61	0	4	0	11	.213	7	134	261	9	†.978
1989	—Pittsburgh (N.L.)	SS-2B-3B	67	154	10	33	4	0	0	8	.214	5	71	138	3	.986
1990	—Pittsburgh (N.L.)	2B-SS-3B	47	54	10	11	3	0	0	6	.204	1	37	36	2	.973
1991	—Atlanta (N.L.)■	SS	149	353	36	88	9	2	0	27	.249	3	168	361	18	.967
	Major league totals (10 years)		633	1404	151	317	25	11	1	99	.226	34	698	1345	55	.974

CHAMPIONSHIP SERIES RECORD

Year	Team (League)	Pos.	G	AB	R	H	2B	3B	HR	RBI	Avg.	SB	PO	A	E	Avg.
1991	—Atlanta (N.L.)	SS	7	19	0	4	0	0	0	1	.211	0	9	15	1	.960

WORLD SERIES RECORD

Year	Team (League)	Pos.	G	AB	R	H	2B	3B	HR	RBI	Avg.	SB	PO	A	E	Avg.
1991	—Atlanta (N.L.)	SS	7	16	0	6	1	0	0	4	.375	0	8	21	0	1.000

BELTRE, ESTEBAN
SS, WHITE SOX

PERSONAL: Born December 26, 1967, at Ingenio Quisfella, Dominican Republic. . . . 5-10/ 155. . . . Throws right, bats right. . . . Full name: Esteban Velera Beltre. . . . Name pronounced BELL-tray.
HIGH SCHOOL: Eugenio Mariade Hostos (Dominican Republic).
TRANSACTIONS/CAREER NOTES: Signed as a free agent by the Montreal Expos (May 9, 1989). . . . Loaned to Utica, independent (June 16, 1985); returned to Expos (September 16, 1985). . . . Granted free agency (January 1, 1991). . . . Signed by Vancouver, Milwaukee Brewers organization (March 16, 1991). . . . Traded by Brewers organization to Chicago White Sox organization for OF John Cangelosi (May 23, 1991).
STATISTICAL NOTES: Led American Association shortstops with 580 total chances in 1990.

Year	Team (League)	Pos.	G	AB	R	H	2B	3B	HR	RBI	Avg.	SB	PO	A	E	Avg.
1984	Calgary (Pioneer)	SS	18	20	1	4	0	0	0	2	.200	1	13	13	10	.722
1985	Utica (New York-Penn)■..	SS	72	241	19	48	6	2	0	22	.199	8	106	206	26	.923
1986	West Palm Beach (FSL)■..	SS	97	285	24	69	11	1	1	20	.242	4	116	273	23	.944
1987	Jacksonville (Southern) ...	SS	142	491	55	104	15	4	4	34	.212	9	★198	★358	★35	.941
1988	Jacksonville (Southern) ...	SS	35	113	5	17	2	0	0	6	.150	1	39	87	11	.920
	West Palm Beach (FSL) ...	SS	69	226	23	63	5	6	0	15	.279	4	99	204	19	.941
1989	Rockford (Midwest)	SS	104	375	42	80	15	3	2	33	.213	9	183	336	30	★.945
1990	Indianapolis (A.A.)	SS	133	407	33	92	11	2	1	37	.226	8	215	★335	★30	.948
1991	Denver (Am. Assoc.)■	SS	27	78	11	14	1	3	0	9	.179	3	52	64	13	.899
	Vancouver (Pac. Coast)■..	SS-2B	88	347	48	94	11	3	0	30	.271	8	129	243	26	.935
	Chicago (A.L.)	SS	8	6	0	1	0	0	0	0	.167	1	1	5	0	1.000
Major league totals (1 year)			8	6	0	1	0	0	0	0	.167	1	1	5	0	1.000

BENAVIDES, FREDDIE
SS/2B, REDS

PERSONAL: Born April 7, 1966, at Laredo, Tex. . . . 6-2/185. . . . Throws right, bats right. . . . Full name: Alfredo Benavides III. . . . Name pronounced ben-uh-VEE-dees.
HIGH SCHOOL: Nixon (Laredo, Tex.).
COLLEGE: Texas Christian.
TRANSACTIONS/CAREER NOTES: Selected by Cincinnati Reds organization in second round of free-agent draft (June 2, 1987).

Year	Team (League)	Pos.	G	AB	R	H	2B	3B	HR	RBI	Avg.	SB	PO	A	E	Avg.
1987	Cedar Rapids (Midwest) ...	SS	5	15	2	2	1	0	0	0	.133	0	7	7	4	.778
1988	Cedar Rapids (Midwest) ...	SS	88	314	38	70	9	2	1	32	.223	18	118	210	24	.932
1989	Chattanooga (Southern)...	SS	88	284	25	71	14	3	0	27	.250	1	129	230	20	.947
	Nashville (Am. Assoc.)	SS	31	94	9	16	4	0	1	12	.170	0	40	73	7	.942
1990	Chattanooga (Southern)	SS	55	197	20	51	10	1	1	28	.259	4	76	157	7	.971
	Nashville (Am. Assoc.)	SS	77	266	30	56	7	3	2	20	.211	3	134	200	16	.954
1991	Nashville (Am. Assoc.)	SS-2B	94	331	24	80	8	0	0	21	.242	7	148	269	11	.974
	Cincinnati (N.L.)	SS-2B	24	63	11	18	1	0	0	3	.286	1	33	53	2	.977
Major league totals (1 year)			24	63	11	18	1	0	0	3	.286	1	33	53	2	.977

BENES, ANDY
P, PADRES

PERSONAL: Born August 20, 1967, at Evansville, Ind. . . . 6-6/240. . . . Throws right, bats right. . . . Full name: Andrew Charles Benes. . . . Name pronounced BEN-ess.
HIGH SCHOOL: Central (Evansville, Ind.).
COLLEGE: Evansville.
TRANSACTIONS/CAREER NOTES: Selected by San Diego Padres organization in first round (first pick overall) of free-agent draft (June 1, 1988).
RECORDS/HONORS: Named N.L. Rookie Pitcher of the Year by THE SPORTING NEWS (1989). . . . Named Texas League Pitcher of the Year (1989).
STATISTICAL NOTES: Led Texas League with three shutouts in 1989. . . . Tied for N.L. lead with five balks in 1990.
MISCELLANEOUS: Member of 1988 U.S. Olympic baseball team.

Year	Team (League)	G	W	L	Pct.	ERA	Sv.	IP	H	R	ER	BB	SO
1989	Wichita (Texas)	16	8	4	.667	2.16	0	108⅓	79	32	26	39	115
	Las Vegas (Pacific Coast)	5	2	1	.667	8.10	0	26⅔	41	29	24	12	29
	San Diego (N.L.)	10	6	3	.667	3.51	0	66⅔	51	28	26	31	66
1990	San Diego (N.L.)	32	10	11	.476	3.60	0	192⅓	177	87	77	69	140
1991	San Diego (N.L.)	33	15	11	.577	3.03	0	223	194	76	75	59	167
Major league totals (3 years)		75	31	25	.554	3.32	0	482	422	191	178	159	373

BENJAMIN, MIKE
SS, GIANTS

PERSONAL: Born November 22, 1965, at Euclid, O. . . . 6-2/175. . . . Throws right, bats right. . . . Full name: Michael Paul Benjamin.
HIGH SCHOOL: Bellflower (Calif.).
COLLEGE: Cerritos College (Calif.) and Arizona State.
TRANSACTIONS/CAREER NOTES: Selected by Minnesota Twins organization in seventh round of free-agent draft (January 9, 1985). . . . Selected by San Francisco Giants organization in third round of free-agent draft (June 2, 1987).
STATISTICAL NOTES: Led Pacific Coast League shortstops with 676 total chances in 1990.

Year	Team (League)	Pos.	G	AB	R	H	2B	3B	HR	RBI	Avg.	SB	PO	A	E	Avg.
1987 —Fresno (California)	SS	64	212	25	51	6	4	6	24	.241	6	89	188	21	.930
1988 —Shreveport (Texas)	SS	89	309	48	73	19	5	6	37	.236	14	134	248	11	.972
—Phoenix (Pacific Coast)	SS	37	106	13	18	4	1	0	6	.170	2	41	74	4	.966
1989 —Phoenix (Pacific Coast)	SS-2B	113	363	44	94	17	6	3	36	.259	10	149	332	15	.970
—San Francisco (N.L.)	SS	14	6	6	1	0	0	0	0	.167	0	4	4	0	1.000
1990 —Phoenix (Pacific Coast)	SS	118	419	61	105	21	7	5	39	.251	13	*216	*386	24	.962
—San Francisco (N.L.)	SS	22	56	7	12	3	1	2	3	.214	1	29	53	1	.988
1991 —San Francisco (N.L.)	SS-3B	54	106	12	13	3	0	2	8	.123	2	64	123	3	.984
—Phoenix (Pacific Coast)	SS	64	226	34	46	13	2	6	31	.204	3	109	252	9	.976
Major league totals (3 years)		90	168	25	26	6	1	4	11	.155	4	97	180	4	.986

BENZINGER, TODD

1B/OF, DODGERS

PERSONAL: Born February 11, 1963, at Dayton, Ky.... 6-1/190.... Throws right, bats both.... Full name: Todd Eric Benzinger.... Nephew of Don Gross, pitcher, Cincinnati Reds and Pittsburgh Pirates (1955-60).

HIGH SCHOOL: New Richmond (Richmond, O.).

TRANSACTIONS/CAREER NOTES: Selected by Boston Red Sox organization in fourth round of free-agent draft (June 8, 1981).... On disabled list (August 10, 1984-remainder of season; April 10-June 11, 1985; April 11-21 and June 26-July 17, 1986; and June 3-22, 1988).... Traded by Red Sox with P Jeff Sellers and a player to be named later to Cincinnati Reds for 1B Nick Esasky and P Rob Murphy (December 13, 1988); Reds acquired P Luis Vasquez to complete deal (January 12, 1989).... Traded by Reds to Kansas City Royals for 1B-OF Carmelo Martinez (July 11, 1991).... Traded by Royals to Los Angeles Dodgers for OF Chris Gwynn and 2B Domingo Mota (December 11, 1991).

Year	Team (League)	Pos.	G	AB	R	H	2B	3B	HR	RBI	Avg.	SB	PO	A	E	Avg.
1981 —Elmira (New York-Penn) ..	OF-1B	41	141	21	34	10	1	2	8	.241	4	131	9	2	.986
1982 —Winston-Salem (Caro.)	OF-1B	121	443	54	97	19	1	5	46	.219	4	438	28	8	.983
1983 —Winter Haven (Fla. St.)	OF-1B-3B	125	480	56	134	34	5	7	68	.279	4	206	10	8	.964
1984 —New Britain (Eastern)	OF-1B	110	391	49	101	25	5	10	60	.258	0	465	29	14	.972
1985 —Pawtucket (Int'l)	OF	70	256	31	64	13	1	11	47	.250	0	106	3	3	.973
1986 —Pawtucket (Int'l)	OF-1B	90	314	41	79	13	2	11	32	.252	7	156	4	2	.988
1987 —Pawtucket (Int'l)	OF-1B	65	257	47	83	17	3	13	49	.323	7	256	16	2	.993
—Boston (A.L.)	OF-1B	73	223	36	62	11	1	8	43	.278	5	155	7	2	.988
1988 —Boston (A.L.)	1B-OF	120	405	47	103	28	1	13	70	.254	2	602	38	6	.991
1989 —Cincinnati (N.L.)■.............	1B	161	*628	79	154	28	3	17	76	.245	3	1417	73	7	.995
1990 —Cincinnati (N.L.)	1B-OF	118	376	35	95	14	2	5	46	.253	3	733	52	6	.992
1991 —Cincinnati (N.L.)	1B-OF	51	123	7	23	3	2	1	11	.187	2	146	13	2	.988
—Kansas City (A.L.)■........	1B	78	293	29	86	15	3	2	40	.294	2	651	38	3	.996
American League totals (3 years)		271	921	112	251	54	5	23	153	.273	9	1408	83	11	.993
National League totals (3 years)		330	1127	121	272	45	7	23	133	.241	8	2296	138	15	.994
Major league totals (5 years)		601	2048	233	523	99	12	46	286	.255	17	3704	221	26	.993

CHAMPIONSHIP SERIES RECORD

Year	Team (League)	Pos.	G	AB	R	H	2B	3B	HR	RBI	Avg.	SB	PO	A	E	Avg.
1988 —Boston (A.L.)	1B-PH	4	11	0	1	0	0	0	0	.091	0	21	1	0	1.000
1990 —Cincinnati (N.L.)	PH-1B	5	9	0	3	0	0	0	0	.333	0	17	0	0	1.000
Championship Series totals (2 years)		9	20	0	4	0	0	0	0	.200	0	38	1	0	1.000

WORLD SERIES RECORD

Year	Team (League)	Pos.	G	AB	R	H	2B	3B	HR	RBI	Avg.	SB	PO	A	E	Avg.
1990 —Cincinnati (N.L.)	PH-1B	4	11	1	2	0	0	0	0	.182	0	24	0	0	1.000

BERENGUER, JUAN

P, BRAVES

PERSONAL: Born November 30, 1954, at Aguadulce, Panama. ... 5-11/220. ... Throws right, bats right.... Full name: Juan Bautista Berenguer Jr.... Name pronounced BARE-en-GARE.

HIGH SCHOOL: Artesy Mecanica (Aguadulce, Panama).

TRANSACTIONS/CAREER NOTES: Signed as free agent by New York Mets organization (February 22, 1975).... Loaned by Mets to Tacoma, Cleveland Indians organization (March 24, 1979); returned to Mets organization (August 29, 1979).... Traded by Mets to Kansas City Royals for OF Marvell Wynne and P John Skinner (March 31, 1981).... Sold by Royals on waivers to Toronto Blue Jays (August 8, 1981).... Released by Blue Jays (March 28, 1982).... Signed by Evansville, Detroit Tigers organization (April 4, 1982).... Traded by Tigers with C Bob Melvin and a player to be named later to San Francisco Giants for P Dave LaPoint, P Eric King and C Matt Nokes (October 7, 1985); Giants acquired P Scott Medvin to complete deal (December 11, 1985).... On disabled list (April 7-28, 1986).... Released by Giants (December 9, 1986).... Signed by Minnesota Twins (January 9, 1987).... On disabled list (August 3-22, 1987).... Granted free agency (November 9, 1987).... Re-signed by Twins (December 22, 1987).... Granted free agency (December 7, 1990).... Signed by Atlanta Braves (January 29, 1991). ... On disabled list (August 13-September 1, 1991).

RECORDS/HONORS: Named International League Pitcher of the Year (1978).

STATISTICAL NOTES: Tied for Midwest League lead with eight hit batsmen in 1975.... Led Carolina League with 28 games started by pitcher and 13 hit batsmen in 1976.... Tied for Texas League lead in games started by pitcher with 26 in 1977.... Tied for American Association lead with nine complete games in 1982.

Year	Team (League)	G	W	L	Pct.	ERA	Sv.	IP	H	R	ER	BB	SO
1975	—Wausau (Midwest)	18	5	4	.556	2.94	1	95	83	41	31	50	58
1976	—Lynchburg (Carolina)	28	10	13	.435	3.61	0	187	★175	89	★75	★118	114
1977	—Jackson (Texas)	26	9	8	.529	3.43	0	181	143	89	69	★126	★160
1978	—Tidewater (International)	24	10	7	.588	3.67	0	147	117	60	60	91	130
	—New York (N.L.)	5	0	2	.000	8.31	0	13	17	12	12	11	8
1979	—Tacoma (Pacific Coast)■	26	8	8	.500	4.88	0	166	128	101	90	129	★220
	—New York (N.L.)■	5	1	1	.500	2.90	0	31	28	13	10	12	25
1980	—Tidewater (International)	27	9	★15	.375	3.84	2	157	122	78	67	76	★178
	—New York (N.L.)	6	0	1	.000	6.00	0	9	9	9	6	10	7
1981	—Kansas City-Toronto (A.L.)■	20	2	★13	.133	5.24	0	91	84	62	53	51	49
1982	—Evansville (Am. Assoc.)■	25	11	10	.524	4.61	0	156⅓	152	85	80	80	127
	—Detroit (A.L.)	2	0	0	. . .	6.75	0	6⅔	5	5	5	9	8
1983	—Detroit (A.L.)	37	9	5	.643	3.14	1	157⅔	110	58	55	71	129
1984	—Detroit (A.L.)	31	11	10	.524	3.48	0	168⅓	146	75	65	79	118
1985	—Detroit (A.L.)	31	5	6	.455	5.59	0	95	96	67	59	48	82
1986	—San Francisco (N.L.)■	46	2	3	.400	2.70	4	73⅓	64	23	22	44	72
1987	—Minnesota (A.L.)■	47	8	1	.889	3.94	4	112	100	51	49	47	110
1988	—Minnesota (A.L.)	57	8	4	.667	3.96	2	100	74	44	44	61	99
1989	—Minnesota (A.L.)	56	9	3	.750	3.48	3	106	96	44	41	47	93
1990	—Minnesota (A.L.)	51	8	5	.615	3.41	0	100⅓	85	43	38	58	77
1991	—Atlanta (N.L.)■	49	0	3	.000	2.24	17	64⅓	43	18	16	20	53
	American League totals (9 years)	332	60	47	.561	3.93	10	937	796	449	409	471	765
	National League totals (5 years)	111	3	10	.231	3.12	21	190⅔	161	75	66	97	165
	Major league totals (14 years)	443	63	57	.525	3.79	31	1127⅔	957	524	475	568	930

CHAMPIONSHIP SERIES RECORD

CHAMPIONSHIP SERIES NOTES: Shares A.L. single-series record for most games pitched—4 (1987).

Year	Team (League)	G	W	L	Pct.	ERA	Sv.	IP	H	R	ER	BB	SO
1987	—Minnesota (A.L.)	4	0	0	. . .	1.50	1	6	1	1	1	3	6

WORLD SERIES RECORD

Year	Team (League)	G	W	L	Pct.	ERA	Sv.	IP	H	R	ER	BB	SO
1984	—Detroit (A.L.)						Did not play						
1987	—Minnesota (A.L.)	3	0	1	.000	10.38	0	4⅓	10	5	5	0	1

BERGMAN, DAVE
1B/DH, TIGERS

PERSONAL: Born June 6, 1953, at Evanston, Ill. . . . 6-2/190. . . . Throws left, bats left. . . . Full name: David Bruce Bergman.
HIGH SCHOOL: Maine (Park Ridge, Ill.).
COLLEGE: Illinois State (bachelor of arts degree in business administration, 1974).
TRANSACTIONS/CAREER NOTES: Selected by Chicago Cubs organization in 12th round of free-agent draft (June 8, 1971). . . . Selected by New York Yankees organization in second round of free-agent draft (June 5, 1974). . . . Traded by Yankees to Houston Astros (November 23, 1977), completing deal in which Astros traded 1B-C Cliff Johnson to Yankees for IF Mike Fischlin, P Randy Niemann and a player to be named later (June 15, 1977). . . . Traded by Astros with OF Jeff Leonard to San Francisco Giants for 1B Mike Ivie (April 20, 1981). . . . Traded by Giants to Philadelphia Phillies for OF Alejandro Sanchez (March 24, 1984); traded by Phillies with P Willie Hernandez to Detroit Tigers for OF Glenn Wilson and C-1B John Wockenfuss (March 24, 1984). . . . On Detroit disabled list (April 22-May 29, 1985); included rehabilitation disability assignment to Nashville (May 15-29, 1985). . . . On disabled list (June 7-22, 1987). . . . Granted free agency (November 4, 1988). . . . Re-signed by Tigers (December 7, 1988). . . . Granted free agency (November 8, 1991). . . . Re-signed by Tigers (December 10, 1991).
RECORDS/HONORS: Named outfielder on THE SPORTING NEWS college All-America team (1974). . . . Named Eastern League Most Valuable Player (1975).
STATISTICAL NOTES: Led Eastern League first basemen with 58 assists in 1975. . . . Led International League first basemen with .992 fielding percentage and 1,199 putouts in 1976. . . . Led International League with 95 bases on balls received in 1979.

								—BATTING—						—FIELDING—			
Year	Team (League)	Pos.	G	AB	R	H	2B	3B	HR	RBI	Avg.	SB	PO	A	E	Avg.
1974	—Oneonta (N.Y.-Penn)	1B	56	201	60	70	6	•7	10	48 ★.348		20	494	★29	8	★.985
1975	—West Haven (Eastern)	1B-OF	124	399	76	124	15	6	11	60 ★.311		15	610	†61	5	.993
	—New York (A.L.)	OF	7	17	0	0	0	0	0	0	.000	0	10	1	1	.917
1976	—Syracuse (International)	1B-OF	134	455	68	134	23	2	7	65	.295	17 †1201		82	10	†.992
1977	—Syracuse (International)	OF-1B	132	468	88	146	29	4	16	59	.312	29	534	39	8	.986
	—New York (A.L.)	OF-1B	5	4	1	1	0	0	0	1	.250	0	8	0	0	1.000
1978	—Houston (N.L.)■	1B-OF	104	186	15	43	5	1	0	12	.231	2	328	16	4	.989
1979	—Charleston, W.Va. (Int'l)	1B-OF	138	461	78	129	23	3	6	58	.280	9	910	61	11	.989
	—Houston (N.L.)	1B	13	15	4	6	0	0	1	2	.400	0	8	0	0	1.000
1980	—Houston (N.L.)	1B-OF	90	78	12	20	6	1	0	3	.256	1	187	16	1	.995
1981	—Hou.-S.F. (N.L.)■	1B-OF	69	151	17	38	9	0	4	14	.252	2	255	25	3	.989
1982	—San Francisco (N.L.)	1B-OF	100	121	22	33	3	1	4	14	.273	3	321	20	4	.988
1983	—San Francisco (N.L.)	1B-OF	90	140	16	40	4	1	6	24	.286	2	299	27	2	.994
1984	—Detroit (A.L.)■	1B-OF	120	271	42	74	8	5	7	44	.273	3	658	75	8	.989
1985	—Detroit (A.L.)	1B-OF	69	140	8	25	2	0	3	7	.179	0	306	25	3	.991
	—Nashville (Am. Assoc.)	1B	11	39	6	9	1	0	1	6	.231	0	87	8	1	.990
1986	—Detroit (A.L.)	1B-OF	65	130	14	30	6	1	1	9	.231	0	255	29	4	.986
1987	—Detroit (A.L.)	1B-OF	91	172	25	47	7	3	6	22	.273	0	357	29	3	.992
1988	—Detroit (A.L.)	1B-OF	116	289	37	85	14	0	5	35	.294	0	386	37	4	.991

Year Team (League)	Pos.	G	AB	R	H	2B	3B	HR	RBI	Avg.	SB	PO	A	E	Avg.
1989—Detroit (A.L.)	1B-OF	137	385	38	103	13	1	7	37	.268	1	912	85	7	.993
1990—Detroit (A.L.)	1B-OF	100	205	21	57	10	1	2	26	.278	3	203	13	1	.995
1991—Detroit (A.L.)	1B-OF	86	194	23	46	10	1	7	29	.237	1	365	29	1	.997
American League totals (10 years)		796	1807	209	468	70	12	38	210	.259	8	3460	323	32	.992
National League totals (6 years)		466	691	86	180	27	4	15	69	.260	10	1398	104	14	.991
Major league totals (16 years)		1262	2498	295	648	97	16	53	279	.259	18	4858	427	46	.991

CHAMPIONSHIP SERIES RECORD

Year Team (League)	Pos.	G	AB	R	H	2B	3B	HR	RBI	Avg.	SB	PO	A	E	Avg.
1980—Houston (N.L.)	PR-1B	4	3	0	1	0	1	0	2	.333	0	8	2	1	.909
1984—Detroit (A.L.)	PR-1B	2	1	1	1	0	0	0	0	1.000	0	5	0	0	1.000
1987—Detroit (A.L.)	PH-DH-1B	4	4	0	1	0	0	0	2	.250	1	6	0	0	1.000
Championship Series totals (3 years)		10	8	1	3	0	1	0	4	.375	1	19	2	1	.955

WORLD SERIES RECORD

Year Team (League)	Pos.	G	AB	R	H	2B	3B	HR	RBI	Avg.	SB	PO	A	E	Avg.
1984—Detroit (A.L.)	PR-1B	5	5	0	0	0	0	0	0	.000	1	22	4	0	1.000

BERNAZARD, TONY
2B

PERSONAL: Born August 24, 1956, at Caguas, Puerto Rico. . . . 5-9/160. . . . Throws right, bats both. . . . Full name: Antonio Garcia Bernazard. . . . Brother of Oscar Bernazard, minor league outfielder (1975-78).
COLLEGE: Florida and Humacao College (P.R.).
TRANSACTIONS/CAREER NOTES: Signed as free agent by Montreal Expos organization (November 13, 1973). . . . On Kinston disabled list (June 10-17, 1974). . . . On Sarasota temporary inactive list (August 15-September 25, 1974). . . . Traded by Expos to Chicago White Sox for P Richard Wortham (December 12, 1980). . . . On disabled list (September 13, 1982-remainder of season). . . . Traded by White Sox to Seattle Mariners for 2B Julio Cruz (June 15, 1983). . . . Traded by Mariners to Cleveland Indians for OF Gorman Thomas and 2B Jack Perconte (December 7, 1983). . . . Granted free agency (November 12, 1985). . . . Re-signed by Indians (January 8, 1986). . . . Traded by Indians to Oakland Athletics for P Darrel Akerfelds and C Brian Dorsett (July 15, 1987). . . . Released by A's (December 21, 1987). . . . Signed by Nankai Hawks of Japanese Baseball League (February, 1988). . . . Nankai Hawks moved from Osoka to Fukuoka for 1989 . . . Signed by Detroit Tigers (December 5, 1990). . . . Released by Tigers (May 7, 1991).
RECORDS/HONORS: Named second baseman on THE SPORTING NEWS A.L. All-Star team (1986).
STATISTICAL NOTES: Led Florida State League second basemen with 386 assists in 1975. . . . Led Eastern League second basemen with 70 double plays in 1976. . . . Led Eastern League in caught stealing with 20 in 1977. . . . Led American Association second basemen with 297 putouts, 386 assists, 32 errors and 101 double plays in 1978. . . . Led A.L. second basemen with 810 total chances in 1986. . . . Switch-hit home runs in one game (July 1, 1986).

Year Team (League)	Pos.	G	AB	R	H	2B	3B	HR	RBI	Avg.	SB	PO	A	E	Avg.
1974—Kinston (Carolina)	2B	56	225	22	45	3	1	0	16	.200	11	129	142	19	.934
—Sarasota Expos (GCL)	2B	34	109	11	18	2	1	1	6	.165	5	95	71	7	.960
1975—West Palm Beach (FSL)	2B-SS	★134	★509	65	121	16	2	6	50	.238	27	282	†389	28	.960
1976—Quebec City (Eastern)	2B	106	334	35	72	8	3	1	26	.216	6	227	257	18	.964
1977—Quebec City (Eastern)	2B	125	425	68	119	11	6	1	34	.280	31	273	379	25	.963
1978—Denver (Am. Assoc.)	2B-3B-OF	128	479	★107	137	30	9	9	65	.286	33	†302	†390	†32	.956
1979—Denver (Am. Assoc.)	2B	82	273	58	82	15	2	3	29	.300	19	178	275	•19	.960
—Montreal (N.L.)	2B	22	40	11	12	2	0	1	8	.300	1	22	34	1	.982
1980—Montreal (N.L.)	2B-SS	82	183	26	41	7	1	5	18	.224	9	82	151	9	.963
1981—Chicago (A.L.)■	2B-SS	106	384	53	106	14	4	6	34	.276	4	228	320	7	.987
1982—Chicago (A.L.)	2B	137	540	90	138	25	9	11	56	.256	11	353	443	12	.985
1983—Chicago-Seattle (A.L.)■	2B	139	533	65	141	34	3	8	56	.265	23	262	422	19	.973
1984—Cleveland (A.L.)■	2B	140	439	44	97	15	4	2	38	.221	20	264	397	★20	.971
1985—Cleveland (A.L.)	2B-SS	153	500	73	137	26	3	11	59	.274	9	313	399	16	.978
1986—Cleveland (A.L.)	2B	146	562	88	169	28	4	17	73	.301	17	★351	442	17	.979
1987—Clev.-Oakland (A.L.)■•	2B	140	507	73	127	26	2	14	49	.250	11	243	335	17	.971
1988—Nankai (Japanese Pac.)■•		111	438	71	138	23	1	20	60	.315	6	. . .	. . .	. . .	. . .
1989—Fukuoka (Jap. Pacific)		122	446	71	121	19	0	34	93	.271	2	. . .	. . .	. . .	. . .
1990—Fukuoka (Jap. Pacific)		75	276	36	76	18	0	13	40	.275	3	. . .	. . .	. . .	. . .
1991—Detroit (A.L.)■	2B	6	12	0	2	0	0	0	0	.167	0	3	6	1	.900
American League totals (8 years)		967	3477	486	917	168	29	69	365	.264	95	2017	2764	109	.978
National League totals (2 years)		104	223	37	53	9	1	6	26	.238	10	104	185	10	.967
Major league totals (10 years)		1071	3700	523	970	177	30	75	391	.262	105	2121	2949	119	.977

BERRY, SEAN
3B, ROYALS

PERSONAL: Born March 22, 1966, at Santa Monica, Calif. . . . 5-11/210. . . . Throws right, bats right. . . . Full name: Sean Robert Berry.
HIGH SCHOOL: West Torrance (Calif.).
COLLEGE: UCLA.
TRANSACTIONS/CAREER NOTES: Selected by Boston Red Sox organization in fourth round of free-agent draft (June 4, 1984). . . .

Selected by Kansas City Royals organization in secondary phase of free-agent draft (January 14, 1986).... On disabled list (April 16-May 3, 1987).
STATISTICAL NOTES: Led Northwest League third basemen with 11 double plays in 1986.

Year	Team (League)	Pos.	G	AB	R	H	2B	3B	HR	RBI	Avg.	SB	PO	A	E	Avg.
1986	Eugene (Northwest)	3B	65	238	53	76	20	2	5	44	.319	10	★63	96	21	.883
1987	Fort Myers (Florida St.)	3B	66	205	26	52	7	2	2	30	.254	5	39	101	23	.859
1988	Baseball City (Fla. St.)	3B-SS-OF	94	304	34	71	6	4	4	30	.234	24	84	161	28	.897
1989	Baseball City (Fla. St.)	3-0-2-S	116	399	67	106	19	7	4	44	.266	37	100	199	24	.926
1990	Memphis (Southern)	3B	135	487	73	142	25	4	14	77	.292	18	79	238	27	.922
	Kansas City (A.L.)	3B	8	23	2	5	1	1	0	4	.217	0	7	10	1	.944
1991	Omaha (Am. Assoc.)	3B-SS-2B	103	368	62	97	21	9	11	54	.264	8	75	206	20	.934
	Kansas City (A.L.)	3B	31	60	5	8	3	0	0	1	.133	0	13	52	2	.970
Major league totals (2 years)			39	83	7	13	4	1	0	5	.157	0	20	62	3	.965

BERRYHILL, DAMON
C, BRAVES

PERSONAL: Born December 3, 1963, at South Laguna, Calif. ... 6-0/205. ... Throws right, bats both.... Full name: Damon Scott Berryhill. **HIGH SCHOOL:** Laguna Beach (Calif.). **COLLEGE:** Orange Coast (Calif.).
TRANSACTIONS/CAREER NOTES: Selected by Chicago White Sox organization in 13th round of free-agent draft (January 11, 1983).... Selected by Chicago Cubs organization in first round (fourth pick overall) of free-agent draft (January 17, 1984). ... On Chicago disabled list (June 30-July 15, 1988).... On Chicago disabled list (March 9-May 1 and August 19-September 29, 1989); included rehabilitation disability assignment to Iowa (April 24-May 1, 1989).... On Chicago disabled list (April 8-August 15, 1990); included rehabilitation disability assignment to Peoria (July 16-23, 1990) and Iowa (July 24-August 4, 1990).... Traded by Cubs with P Mike Bielecki to Atlanta Braves for P Turk Wendell and P Yorkis Perez (September 29, 1991).
STATISTICAL NOTES: Led Carolina League with 18 passed balls in 1985.... Led American Association catchers with .990 fielding percentage, 603 putouts, 66 assists, 676 total chances, 15 passed balls and 11 double plays in 1987.
MISCELLANEOUS: Batted righthanded only with Quad Cities (1984).

Year	Team (League)	Pos.	G	AB	R	H	2B	3B	HR	RBI	Avg.	SB	PO	A	E	Avg.
1984	Quad Cities (Midwest)	C-1B	62	217	30	60	14	0	0	31	.276	4	314	31	8	.977
1985	Winston-Salem (Caro.)	C-1B	117	386	31	90	25	1	9	50	.233	4	625	71	11	.984
1986	Pittsfield (Eastern)	C-OF	112	345	33	71	13	1	6	35	.206	2	449	61	12	.977
1987	Iowa (American Assoc.)	C-1B	121	429	54	123	22	1	18	67	.287	5	†607	†67	7	†.990
	Chicago (N.L.)	C	12	28	2	5	1	0	0	1	.179	0	37	3	4	.909
1988	Iowa (American Assoc.)	C	21	73	11	16	5	1	2	11	.219	0	117	15	0	1.000
	Chicago (N.L.)	C	95	309	19	80	19	1	7	38	.259	1	448	54	9	.982
1989	Iowa (American Assoc.)	C	7	30	4	6	1	0	2	4	.200	0	40	5	2	.957
	Chicago (N.L.)	C	91	334	37	86	13	0	5	41	.257	1	473	41	4	.992
1990	Peoria (Midwest)	C	7	26	10	10	2	0	3	8	.385	0	75	4	1	.988
	Iowa (American Assoc.)	C	22	79	8	17	1	0	3	6	.215	0	115	13	2	.985
	Chicago (N.L.)	C	17	53	6	10	4	0	1	9	.189	0	87	3	2	.978
1991	Chicago-Atlanta (N.L.)■	C	63	160	13	30	7	0	5	14	.188	1	214	24	8	.967
	Iowa (American Assoc.)	C	26	97	20	32	4	1	8	24	.330	0	90	14	2	.981
Major league totals (5 years)			278	884	77	211	44	1	18	103	.239	3	1259	125	27	.981

BICHETTE, DANTE
OF, BREWERS

PERSONAL: Born November 18, 1963, at West Palm Beach, Fla. ... 6-3/225. ... Throws right, bats right. ... Full name: Alphonse Dante Bichette. ... Name pronounced bi-SHETT. **HIGH SCHOOL:** Jupiter (Fla.).
COLLEGE: Palm Beach Junior College (Fla.).
TRANSACTIONS/CAREER NOTES: Selected by California Angels organization in 16th round of free-agent draft (June 4, 1984).... Traded by Angels to Milwaukee Brewers for DH Dave Parker (March 14, 1991).
STATISTICAL NOTES: Led A.L. outfielders with seven double plays in 1991.

Year	Team (League)	Pos.	G	AB	R	H	2B	3B	HR	RBI	Avg.	SB	PO	A	E	Avg.
1984	Salem (Carolina)	OF-1B-3B	64	250	27	58	9	2	4	30	.232	6	224	24	11	.958
1985	Quad Cities (Midwest)	1B-OF-C	137	547	58	145	28	4	11	78	.265	25	300	21	15	.955
1986	Palm Springs (Calif.)	OF-3B	68	290	39	79	15	0	10	73	.272	2	78	68	11	.930
	Midland (Texas)	OF-3B	62	243	43	69	16	2	12	36	.284	3	131	30	11	.936
1987	Edmonton (Pac. Coast)	OF-3B	92	360	54	108	20	3	13	50	.300	3	169	21	9	.955
1988	Edmonton (Pac. Coast)	OF	132	509	64	136	29	•10	14	81	.267	7	218	★22	★15	.941
	California (A.L.)	OF	21	46	1	12	2	0	0	8	.261	0	44	2	1	.979
1989	California (A.L.)	OF	48	138	13	29	7	0	3	15	.210	3	95	6	1	.990
	Edmonton (Pac. Coast)	OF	61	226	39	55	11	2	11	40	.243	4	92	9	1	.990
1990	California (A.L.)	OF	109	349	40	89	15	1	15	53	.255	5	183	12	7	.965
1991	Milwaukee (A.L.)■	OF-3B	134	445	53	106	18	3	15	59	.238	14	270	14	7	.976
Major league totals (4 years)			312	978	107	236	42	4	33	135	.241	22	592	34	16	.975

BIELECKI, MIKE
P, BRAVES

PERSONAL: Born July 31, 1959, at Baltimore. . . . 6-3/195. . . . Throws right, bats right. . . . Full name: Michael Joseph Bielecki. . . . Name pronounced bill-LECK-ee.
HIGH SCHOOL: Dundalk (Baltimore).
COLLEGE: Loyola College (Md.) and Valencia Community College (Fla.).
TRANSACTIONS/CAREER NOTES: Selected by Kansas City Royals organization in sixth round of free-agent draft (January 9, 1979). . . . Selected by Pittsburgh Pirates organization in secondary phase of free-agent draft (June 5, 1979). . . . Traded by Pirates to Chicago Cubs for P Mike Curtis (March 31, 1988). . . . Traded by Cubs with C Damon Berryhill to Atlanta Braves for P Turk Wendell and P Yorkis Perez (September 29, 1991).
STATISTICAL NOTES: Tied for South Atlantic League lead in games started by pitcher with 28 in 1981. . . . Tied for Eastern League lead with 24 home runs allowed in 1982.

Year Team (League)	G	W	L	Pct.	ERA	Sv.	IP	H	R	ER	BB	SO
1979—Bradenton Pirates (GCL)	9	1	4	.200	2.29	0	51	48	21	13	21	35
1980—Shelby (South Atlantic)	29	3	5	.375	4.55	3	99	106	60	50	58	78
1981—Greenwood (South Atlantic)	28	12	11	.522	3.42	0	192	172	95	73	82	163
1982—Buffalo (Eastern)	25	7	12	.368	4.86	0	157⅓	165	96	•85	75	135
1983—Lynn (Eastern)	25	•15	7	.682	3.19	0	163⅔	126	73	58	69	★143
1984—Hawaii (Pacific Coast)	28	★19	3	.864	2.97	0	187⅓	162	70	62	88	★162
—Pittsburgh (N.L.)	4	0	0	...	0.00	0	4⅓	4	0	0	0	1
1985—Pittsburgh (N.L.)	12	2	3	.400	4.53	0	45⅔	45	26	23	31	22
—Hawaii (Pacific Coast)	20	8	6	.571	3.83	0	129⅓	117	58	55	56	111
1986—Pittsburgh (N.L.)	31	6	11	.353	4.66	0	148⅔	149	87	77	83	83
1987—Vancouver (Pacific Coast)	26	12	10	.545	3.78	0	181	194	89	76	78	140
—Pittsburgh (N.L.)	8	2	3	.400	4.73	0	45⅔	43	25	24	12	25
1988—Chicago (N.L.)■	19	2	2	.500	3.35	0	48⅓	55	22	18	16	33
—Iowa (American Association) ...	23	3	2	.600	2.63	5	54⅔	34	19	16	20	50
1989—Chicago (N.L.)	33	18	7	.720	3.14	0	212⅓	187	82	74	81	147
1990—Chicago (N.L.)	36	8	11	.421	4.93	1	168	188	101	92	70	103
1991—Chicago-Atlanta (N.L.)■..........	41	13	11	.542	4.46	0	173⅔	171	91	86	56	75
Major league totals (8 years)	184	51	48	.515	4.19	1	846⅔	842	434	394	349	489

CHAMPIONSHIP SERIES RECORD

Year Team (League)	G	W	L	Pct.	ERA	Sv.	IP	H	R	ER	BB	SO
1989—Chicago (N.L.)	2	0	1	.000	3.65	0	12⅓	7	5	5	6	11

BIGGIO, CRAIG
2B/C, ASTROS

PERSONAL: Born December 14, 1965, at Smithtown, N.Y. . . . 5-11/180. . . . Throws right, bats right. . . . Full name: Craig Alan Biggio. . . . Name pronounced BEE-jee-oh.
HIGH SCHOOL: Kings Park (N.Y.).
COLLEGE: Seton Hall.
TRANSACTIONS/CAREER NOTES: Selected by Houston Astros organization in first round (22nd pick overall) of free-agent draft (June 2, 1987).
RECORDS/HONORS: Named catcher on THE SPORTING NEWS college All-America team (1987). . . . Named catcher on THE SPORTING NEWS N.L. Silver Slugger team (1989).
STATISTICAL NOTES: Led N.L. catchers with 889 putouts, 963 total chances and 13 passed balls in 1991.

Year Team (League)	Pos.	G	AB	R	H	2B	3B	HR	RBI	Avg.	SB	PO	A	E	Avg.
1987—Asheville (S. Atlantic)	C-OF	64	216	59	81	17	2	9	49	.375	31	378	46	2	.995
1988—Tucson (Pacific Coast)	C-OF	77	281	60	90	21	4	3	41	.320	19	318	33	6	.983
—Houston (N.L.)	C	50	123	14	26	6	1	3	5	.211	6	292	28	3	.991
1989—Houston (N.L.)	C-OF	134	443	64	114	21	2	13	60	.257	21	742	56	9	.989
1990—Houston (N.L.)	C-OF	150	555	53	153	24	2	4	42	.276	25	657	60	13	.982
1991—Houston (N.L.)	C-2B-OF	149	546	79	161	23	4	4	46	.295	19	†894	73	11	.989
Major league totals (4 years)		483	1667	210	454	74	9	24	153	.272	71	2585	217	36	.987

ALL-STAR GAME RECORD

Year League	Pos.	AB	R	H	2B	3B	HR	RBI	Avg.	SB	PO	A	E	Avg.
1991—National	C	1	0	0	0	0	0	0	.000	0	2	0	1	.667

BILARDELLO, DANN
C, PADRES

PERSONAL: Born May 26, 1959, at Santa Cruz, Calif. . . . 6-0/190. . . . Throws right, bats right. . . . Full name: Dann James Bilardello. . . . Name pronounced BILL-ar-DELL-oh.
HIGH SCHOOL: Marello Prep (Marello, Calif.).
COLLEGE: Cabrillo College (Calif.).
TRANSACTIONS/CAREER NOTES: Selected by Seattle Mariners organization in third round of free-agent draft (January 10, 1978). . . . Selected by Los Angeles Dodgers organization in secondary phase of free-agent draft (June 6, 1978). . . . On disabled list (May 9-June 14, 1979 and June 12-August 13, 1980). . . . Drafted by Cincinnati Reds (December 6, 1982). . . . Traded by Reds with P Jay Tibbs, P Andy McGaffigan and P John Stuper to Montreal Expos for P Bill Gullickson and C Sal Butera (December 19, 1985). . . . Released by Expos organization (December 20, 1986). . . . Re-signed by Expos organization (March 22, 1987). . . . Sold by Expos organization to Pittsburgh Pirates (March 22, 1987). . . . Sold by Pirates to Omaha, Kansas City Royals organization (July 23, 1987). . . . Granted free agency (October 15, 1988). . . . Signed by Buffalo, Pittsburgh Pirates organization (January 25, 1989). . . . Released by Pirates (November 21, 1989). . . . Re-signed by Pirates organization (January 30, 1990). . . . Granted free agency (December 20, 1990). . . . Signed by San Diego Padres (January 15, 1991).

STATISTICAL NOTES: Led Pioneer League catchers with five double plays in 1978. . . . Led Texas League catchers with 15 double plays in 1982.

Year	Team (League)	Pos.	G	AB	R	H	2B	3B	HR	RBI	Avg.	SB	PO	A	E	Avg.
							BATTING							FIELDING		
1978	—Lethbridge (Pioneer)	C	42	133	21	33	8	1	2	20	.248	0	210	36	7	.972
1979	—Clinton (Midwest)	C	52	142	18	34	4	0	2	15	.239	2	283	31	3	.991
1980	—Lodi (California)	C	41	117	22	36	4	0	6	15	.308	4	169	30	8	.961
1981	—Lodi (California)	C	105	352	72	108	19	2	21	80	.307	1	203	39	9	.964
	—San Antonio (Texas)	C	6	19	0	1	0	0	0	1	.053	0	34	2	1	.973
1982	—San Antonio (Texas)	C	103	347	49	99	14	2	17	48	.285	2	546	*80	15	.977
1983	—Cincinnati (N.L.)■	C	109	298	27	71	18	0	9	38	.238	2	494	72	5	.991
1984	—Cincinnati (N.L.)	C	68	182	16	38	7	0	2	10	.209	0	323	34	3	.992
	—Wichita (Am. Assoc.)	C	49	167	21	40	9	0	5	17	.240	2	290	31	3	.991
1985	—Cincinnati (N.L.)	C	42	102	6	17	0	0	1	9	.167	0	198	20	3	.986
	—Denver (Am. Assoc.)	C-1B-3B	67	236	41	57	5	3	10	37	.242	4	365	50	6	.986
1986	—Montreal (N.L.)■	C	79	191	12	37	5	0	4	17	.194	1	391	38	8	.982
	—Indianapolis (A.A.)	C	2	5	1	3	0	1	0	0	.600	0	6	0	0	1.000
1987	—Vancouver (Pac. Coast)■.	C	37	97	7	21	3	0	1	11	.216	0	186	30	4	.982
	—Omaha (Am. Assoc.)■	C-3B	22	71	6	13	5	1	2	7	.183	0	96	13	1	.991
1988	—Omaha (Am. Assoc.)	C	71	235	27	57	14	0	8	45	.243	0	395	31	5	.988
1989	—Buffalo (Am. Assoc.)■	C-1B	66	180	11	37	8	0	3	17	.206	3	364	33	7	.983
	—Pittsburgh (N.L.)	C	33	80	11	18	6	0	2	8	.225	1	150	14	5	.970
1990	—Buffalo (Am. Assoc.)	C-1B	52	154	19	44	8	1	5	26	.286	0	295	26	5	.985
	—Pittsburgh (N.L.)	C	19	37	1	2	0	0	0	3	.054	0	69	9	0	1.000
1991	—Las Vegas (Pac. Coast)■..	C-1B-3B	44	140	17	44	13	1	4	29	.314	2	200	33	9	.963
	—San Diego (N.L.)	C	15	26	4	7	2	1	0	5	.269	0	59	6	0	1.000
Major league totals (7 years)			365	916	77	190	38	1	18	90	.207	4	1684	193	24	.987

BITKER, JOE

P

PERSONAL: Born February 12, 1964, at Glendale, Calif. . . . 6-1/175. . . . Throws right, bats right. . . . Full name: Joseph Anthony Bitker.
HIGH SCHOOL: Porduoso (Shingle Springs, Calif.).
COLLEGE: Sacramento City College (Calif.).
TRANSACTIONS/CAREER NOTES: Selected by Detroit Tigers organization in third round of free-agent draft (January 11, 1983). . . . Selected by Minnesota Twins organization in sixth round of free-agent draft (January 17, 1984). . . . Selected by San Diego Padres organization in secondary phase of free-agent draft (June 4, 1984). . . . Released by Padres organization (June 1, 1989). . . . Signed by Tacoma, Oakland Athletics organization (June 22, 1989). . . . Traded by A's organization with P Scott Chiamparino to Texas Rangers (September 4, 1990), completing deal in which Texas traded OF-DH Harold Baines to A's for two players to be named later (August 29, 1990). . . . On Oklahoma City disabled list (July 16-September 6, 1991). . . . Granted free agency (October 15, 1991).
STATISTICAL NOTES: Tied for South Atlantic League lead with four shutouts in 1985.

Year	Team (League)	G	W	L	Pct.	ERA	Sv.	IP	H	R	ER	BB	SO
1984	—Spokane (Northwest)	14	4	4	.500	3.41	0	87	85	48	33	33	60
1985	—Charleston, S.C. (S. Atlantic)	13	9	3	.750	2.59	0	90⅓	74	35	26	31	85
	—Beaumont (Texas)	15	8	1	.889	3.12	0	98	91	43	34	41	64
1986	—Beaumont (Texas)	18	7	7	.500	3.53	0	114⅔	114	55	45	52	91
	—Las Vegas (Pacific Coast)	5	2	0	1.000	3.29	0	27⅓	24	10	10	9	19
1987	—Las Vegas (Pacific Coast)	36	11	9	.550	4.83	1	160⅓	184	97	86	79	80
1988	—Las Vegas (Pacific Coast)	28	8	10	.444	3.58	0	178⅓	195	98	71	41	106
1989	—Las Vegas-Tacoma (PCL)■	42	3	4	.429	3.67	3	73⅔	67	38	30	20	48
1990	—Tacoma (Pacific Coast)	48	2	3	.400	3.20	*26	56⅓	51	22	20	20	52
	—Oakland-Texas (A.L.)■	6	0	0	...	2.25	0	12	8	3	3	4	8
1991	—Oklahoma City (Am. Assoc.)	23	0	5	.000	4.00	7	27	30	16	12	9	33
	—Texas (A.L.)	9	1	0	1.000	6.75	0	14⅔	17	11	11	8	16
Major league totals (2 years)		15	1	0	1.000	4.73	0	26⅔	25	14	14	12	24

BLACK, BUD

P, GIANTS

PERSONAL: Born June 30, 1957, at San Mateo, Calif. . . . 6-2/185. . . . Throws left, bats left. . . . Full name: Harry Ralston Black.
HIGH SCHOOL: Mark Morris (Longview, Wash.).
COLLEGE: Lower Columbia College (Wash.) and San Diego State (bachelor of arts degree in finance, 1979).
TRANSACTIONS/CAREER NOTES: Selected by San Francisco Giants organization in third round of free-agent draft (January 11, 1977). . . . Selected by New York Mets organization in secondary phase of free-agent draft (June 7, 1977). . . . Selected by Seattle Mariners organization in 17th round of free-agent draft (June 5, 1979). . . . Traded by Mariners to Kansas City Royals (March 2, 1982), completing deal in which Royals traded IF Manny Castillo to Mariners for a player to be named later (October 23, 1981). . . . On disabled list (June 8-July 4, 1987). . . . Traded by Royals to Cleveland Indians for 1B Pat Tabler (June 3, 1988). . . . On Cleveland disabled list (July 19-August 21, 1988); included rehabilitation disability assignment to Williamsport (August 16-21, 1988). . . . Granted free agency (November 4, 1988). . . . Re-signed by Indians (December 5, 1988). . . . Traded by Indians to Toronto Blue Jays for P Mauro Gozzo and two players to be named later (September 16, 1990); Indians acquired P Steve Cummings (September 21, 1990) and P Alex Sanchez (September 24, 1990) to complete deal. . . . Granted free agency (November 5, 1990). . . . Signed by San Francisco Giants (November 9, 1990).
STATISTICAL NOTES: Led A.L. with seven balks in 1982. . . . Led N.L. with six balks in 1991.
MISCELLANEOUS: Appeared in one game as pinch-hitter (1991).

Year Team (League)	G	W	L	Pct.	ERA	Sv.	IP	H	R	ER	BB	SO
1979 —Bellingham (Northwest)............	2	0	0	...	0.00	0	5	3	0	0	5	8
—San Jose (California)	17	0	1	.000	3.00	1	27	17	11	9	16	24
1980 —San Jose (California)	32	5	3	.625	3.45	2	86	67	34	33	49	73
1981 —Lynn (Eastern)	22	2	6	.250	3.00	2	87	78	38	29	23	86
—Spokane (Pacific Coast)	4	1	0	1.000	4.50	0	8	12	4	4	2	4
—Seattle (A.L.)	2	0	0	...	0.00	0	1	2	0	0	3	0
1982 —Kansas City (A.L.)■...........	22	4	6	.400	4.58	0	88⅓	92	48	45	34	40
—Omaha (American Assoc.)........	4	3	1	.750	2.48	0	29	23	9	8	10	20
1983 —Omaha (American Assoc.)........	5	3	1	.750	3.34	0	35	31	13	13	13	32
—Kansas City (A.L.)	24	10	7	.588	3.79	0	161⅓	159	75	68	43	58
1984 —Kansas City (A.L.)	35	17	12	.586	3.12	0	257	226	99	89	64	140
1985 —Kansas City (A.L.)	33	10	15	.400	4.33	0	205⅔	216	111	99	59	122
1986 —Kansas City (A.L.)	56	5	10	.333	3.20	9	121	100	49	43	43	68
1987 —Kansas City (A.L.)	29	8	6	.571	3.60	1	122⅓	126	63	49	35	61
1988 —Kansas City-Cleveland (A.L.)■.	33	4	4	.500	5.00	1	81	82	47	45	34	63
—Williamsport (Eastern)	1	1	0	1.000	0.00	0	5	0	0	0	0	5
1989 —Cleveland (A.L.)	33	12	11	.522	3.36	0	222⅓	213	95	83	52	88
1990 —Cleveland-Toronto (A.L.)■.......	32	13	11	.542	3.57	0	206⅔	181	86	82	61	106
1991 —San Francisco (N.L.)■	34	12	*16	.429	3.99	0	214⅓	201	104	95	71	104
American League totals (10 years)........	299	83	82	.503	3.70	11	1466⅔	1397	673	603	428	746
National League totals (1 year)	34	12	16	.429	3.99	0	214⅓	201	104	95	71	104
Major league totals (11 years)	333	95	98	.492	3.74	11	1681	1598	777	698	499	850

CHAMPIONSHIP SERIES RECORD

Year Team (League)	G	W	L	Pct.	ERA	Sv.	IP	H	R	ER	BB	SO
1984 —Kansas City (A.L.)	1	0	1	.000	7.20	0	5	7	4	4	1	3
1985 —Kansas City (A.L.)	3	0	0	...	1.69	0	10⅔	11	3	2	4	8
Championship Series totals (2 years)	4	0	1	.000	3.45	0	15⅔	18	7	6	5	11

WORLD SERIES RECORD

Year Team (League)	G	W	L	Pct.	ERA	Sv.	IP	H	R	ER	BB	SO
1985 —Kansas City (A.L.)	2	0	1	.000	5.06	0	5⅓	4	3	3	5	4

BLAIR, WILLIE
P, ASTROS

PERSONAL: Born December 18, 1965, at Paintsville, Ky. ... 6-1/185. ... Throws right, bats right.... Full name: William Allen Blair.
HIGH SCHOOL: Johnson Central (Paintsville, Ky.).
COLLEGE: Morehead State.
TRANSACTIONS/CAREER NOTES: Selected by Toronto Blue Jays organization in 11th round of free-agent draft (June 2, 1986).... Traded by Blue Jays to Cleveland Indians for P Alex Sanchez (November 6, 1990).... Traded by Indians with C Eddie Taubensee to Houston Astros for OF Kenny Lofton and IF Dave Rohde (December 10, 1991).

Year Team (League)	G	W	L	Pct.	ERA	Sv.	IP	H	R	ER	BB	SO
1986 —St. Catharines (N.Y.-Penn)	21	5	0	1.000	1.68	*12	53⅔	32	10	10	20	55
1987 —Dunedin (Florida State)	50	2	9	.182	4.43	13	85⅓	99	51	42	29	72
1988 —Dunedin (Florida State)	4	2	0	1.000	2.70	0	6⅔	5	2	2	4	5
—Knoxville (Southern)	34	5	5	.500	3.62	3	102	94	49	41	35	76
1989 —Syracuse (International)	19	5	6	.455	3.97	0	106⅔	94	55	47	38	76
1990 —Toronto (A.L.)	27	3	5	.375	4.06	0	68⅔	66	33	31	28	43
—Syracuse (International)	3	0	2	.000	4.74	0	19	20	13	10	8	6
1991 —Colorado Springs (Pac. Coast)■	26	9	6	.600	4.99	4	113⅔	130	74	63	30	57
—Cleveland (A.L.)	11	2	3	.400	6.75	0	36	58	27	27	10	13
Major league totals (2 years)	38	5	8	.385	4.99	0	104⅔	124	60	58	38	56

BLANKENSHIP, LANCE
2B/OF/3B, ATHLETICS

PERSONAL: Born December 6, 1963, at Portland, Ore.... 6-0/185.... Throws right, bats right.... Full name: Lance Robert Blankenship.
HIGH SCHOOL: Ygnacio Valley (Concord, Calif.).
COLLEGE: California.
TRANSACTIONS/CAREER NOTES: Selected by Oakland Athletics organization in 10th round of free-agent draft (June 2, 1986).
RECORDS/HONORS: Named third baseman on THE SPORTING NEWS college All-America team (1985).
STATISTICAL NOTES: Led Pacific Coast League with 96 bases on balls received in 1988. ... Led Pacific Coast League second basemen with 390 assists and 682 total chances in 1988.

Year Team (League)	Pos.	G	AB	R	H	2B	3B	HR	RBI	Avg.	SB	PO	A	E	Avg.
1986 —Medford (Northwest)	OF	14	52	22	21	3	0	2	17	.404	10	22	1	1	.958
—Modesto (California)	OF-3B	55	171	47	50	5	3	6	25	.292	15	88	27	7	.943
1987 —Modesto (California)	3-O-S-2	22	84	14	23	9	2	0	17	.274	12	26	30	8	.875
—Huntsville (Southern)	OF-2B-3B	107	390	64	99	21	3	4	39	.254	34	185	99	8	.973
1988 —Tacoma (Pacific Coast)	2B-OF	131	437	84	116	21	8	9	52	.265	40	272	†390	21	.969
—Oakland (A.L.)	2B	10	3	1	0	0	0	0	0	.000	0	1	1	0	1.000
1989 —Tacoma (Pacific Coast)	2B	25	98	25	29	8	2	2	9	.296	5	39	81	2	.984
—Oakland (A.L.)	OF-2B	58	125	22	29	5	1	1	4	.232	5	69	49	1	.992

Year Team (League)	Pos.	G	AB	R	H	2B	3B	HR	RBI	Avg.	SB	PO	A	E	Avg.
					BATTING								FIELDING		
1990—Oakland (A.L.)	3-0-2-1	86	136	18	26	3	0	0	10	.191	3	66	69	5	.964
—Tacoma (Pacific Coast)	2B-OF-3B	24	93	18	24	7	1	1	9	.258	7	39	57	2	.980
1991—Oakland (A.L.)	2B-OF-3B	90	185	33	46	8	0	3	21	.249	12	123	122	3	.988
—Tacoma (Pacific Coast)	S-2-3-0	30	109	19	32	7	0	1	11	.294	9	51	90	8	.946
Major league totals (4 years)		244	449	74	101	16	1	4	35	.225	20	259	241	9	.982

CHAMPIONSHIP SERIES RECORD

Year Team (League)	Pos.	G	AB	R	H	2B	3B	HR	RBI	Avg.	SB	PO	A	E	Avg.
					BATTING								FIELDING		
1989—Oakland (A.L.)	2B	1	0	0	0	0	0	0	0	...	0	0	1	0	1.000
1990—Oakland (A.L.)	PR	3	0	1	0	0	0	0	0	...	1	0	0	0	...
Championship Series totals (2 years)		4	0	1	0	0	0	0	0	...	1	0	1	0	1.000

WORLD SERIES RECORD

Year Team (League)	Pos.	G	AB	R	H	2B	3B	HR	RBI	Avg.	SB	PO	A	E	Avg.
					BATTING								FIELDING		
1989—Oakland (A.L.)	PH-2B	1	2	1	1	0	0	0	0	.500	0	1	0	0	1.000
1990—Oakland (A.L.)	PH	1	1	0	0	0	0	0	0	.000	0	0	0	0	...
World Series totals (2 years)		2	3	1	1	0	0	0	0	.333	0	1	0	0	1.000

BLAUSER, JEFF

IF, BRAVES

PERSONAL: Born November 8, 1965, at Los Gatos, Calif. . . . 6-0/170. . . . Throws right, bats right. . . . Full name: Jeffrey Michael Blauser.
HIGH SCHOOL: Placer (Sacramento, Calif.).
COLLEGE: Sacramento City College (Calif.).
TRANSACTIONS/CAREER NOTES: Selected by St. Louis Cardinals organization in first round (eighth pick overall) of free-agent draft (January 17, 1984). . . . Selected by Atlanta Braves organization in secondary phase of free-agent draft (June 4, 1984). . . . On disabled list (May 14-30, 1990).
STATISTICAL NOTES: Led Carolina League shortstops with 506 total chances in 1986.

Year Team (League)	Pos.	G	AB	R	H	2B	3B	HR	RBI	Avg.	SB	PO	A	E	Avg.
					BATTING								FIELDING		
1984—Pulaski (Appalachian)	SS	62	217	41	54	6	1	3	24	.249	14	61	162	24	.903
1985—Sumter (South Atlantic)	SS	125	422	74	99	19	0	5	49	.235	36	150	306	35	.929
1986—Durham (Carolina)	SS	123	447	94	128	27	3	13	52	.286	36	167	*314	25	*.951
1987—Richmond (Int'l)	SS-2B	33	113	11	20	1	0	1	12	.177	3	56	106	9	.947
—Atlanta (N.L.)	SS	51	165	11	40	6	3	2	15	.242	7	65	166	9	.963
—Greenville (Southern)	SS	72	265	35	66	13	3	4	32	.249	5	101	225	8	.976
1988—Richmond (Int'l)	SS	69	271	40	77	19	1	5	23	.284	6	93	156	15	.943
—Atlanta (N.L.)	2B-SS	18	67	7	16	3	1	2	7	.239	0	35	59	4	.959
1989—Atlanta (N.L.)	3-2-S-0	142	456	63	123	24	2	12	46	.270	5	137	254	21	.949
1990—Atlanta (N.L.)	S-2-3-0	115	386	46	104	24	3	8	39	.269	3	169	288	16	.966
1991—Atlanta (N.L.)	SS-2B-3B	129	352	49	91	14	3	11	54	.259	5	136	219	17	.954
Major league totals (5 years)		455	1426	176	374	71	12	35	161	.262	20	542	986	67	.958

CHAMPIONSHIP SERIES RECORD

Year Team (League)	Pos.	G	AB	R	H	2B	3B	HR	RBI	Avg.	SB	PO	A	E	Avg.
					BATTING								FIELDING		
1991—Atlanta (N.L.)	PH	2	2	0	0	0	0	0	0	.000	0	0	1	1	.500

WORLD SERIES RECORD

Year Team (League)	Pos.	G	AB	R	H	2B	3B	HR	RBI	Avg.	SB	PO	A	E	Avg.
					BATTING								FIELDING		
1991—Atlanta (N.L.)	PH-SS	5	6	0	1	0	0	0	0	.167	0	3	3	0	1.000

BLOWERS, MIKE

IF, MARINERS

PERSONAL: Born April 24, 1965, at Wurzburg, West Germany. . . . 6-2/210. . . . Throws right, bats right. . . . Full name: Michael Roy Blowers.
HIGH SCHOOL: Bethel (Wash.).
COLLEGE: Tacoma Community College (Wash.) and Washington.
TRANSACTIONS/CAREER NOTES: Selected by Seattle Mariners organization in eighth round of free-agent draft (January 17, 1984). . . . Selected by San Francisco Giants organization in secondary phase of free-agent draft (June 4, 1984). . . . Selected by Baltimore Orioles organization in secondary phase of free-agent draft (January 9, 1985). . . . Selected by Montreal Expos organization in 10th round of free-agent draft (June 2, 1986). . . . Traded by Expos to New York Yankees (August 31, 1989), completing deal in which Yankees traded P John Candelaria to Expos for a player to be named later (August 29, 1989). . . . Traded by Yankees to Mariners for a player to be named later and cash (May 17, 1991); Yankees acquired P Jim Blueberg to complete deal (June 22, 1991).
RECORDS/HONORS: Shares A.L. single-game record for most errors—4 (May 3, 1990).
STATISTICAL NOTES: Led Florida State League third basemen with .944 fielding percentage and 27 double plays in 1987. . . . Led Southern League third basemen with 125 putouts and 27 double plays in 1988. . . . Led American Association third basemen with .930 fielding percentage in 1989.

Year	Team (League)	Pos.	G	AB	R	H	2B	3B	HR	RBI	Avg.	SB	PO	A	E	Avg.
1986	—Jamestown (N.Y.-Penn) ...	SS-3B	32	95	13	24	9	2	1	6	.253	3	48	73	16	.883
	—Bradenton Expos (GCL)	SS	31	115	14	25	3	1	2	17	.217	2	50	84	15	.899
1987	—West Palm Beach (FSL) ...	3B-SS-1B	136	491	68	124	30	3	16	71	.253	4	75	239	18	†.946
1988	—Jacksonville (South.)	3B-SS-2B	137	460	58	115	20	6	15	60	.250	6	†125	241	34	.915
1989	—Indianapolis (A.A.)	3B-SS	131	461	49	123	29	6	14	56	.267	3	91	214	23	†.930
	—New York (A.L.)■	3B	13	38	2	10	0	0	0	3	.263	0	9	14	4	.852
1990	—New York (A.L.)	3B	48	144	16	27	4	0	5	21	.188	1	26	63	10	.899
	—Columbus (Int'l)	3B-1B-2B	62	230	30	78	20	6	6	50	.339	3	64	89	8	.950
1991	—New York (A.L.)	3B	15	35	3	7	0	0	1	1	.200	0	4	16	3	.870
	—Calgary (Pacific Coast)■ ..	3B-SS-1B	90	329	56	95	20	2	9	59	.289	3	56	163	19	.920
Major league totals (3 years)			76	217	21	44	4	0	6	25	.203	1	39	93	17	.886

BLYLEVEN, BERT

P, ANGELS

PERSONAL: Born April 6, 1951, at Zeist, The Netherlands. ... 6-3/220. ... Throws right, bats right. ... Full name: Rik Aalbert Blyleven.
HIGH SCHOOL: Santiago (Garden Grove, Calif.).
TRANSACTIONS/CAREER NOTES: Selected by Minnesota Twins organization in third round of free-agent draft (June 5, 1969). ... Traded by Twins with SS Danny Thompson to Texas Rangers for P Bill Singer, IF Roy Smalley, IF Mike Cubbage, P Jim Gideon and cash (June 1, 1976). ... Traded by Rangers with 1B-OF John Milner to Pittsburgh Pirates for OF-1B Al Oliver and IF Nelson Norman (December 8, 1977). ... Traded by Pirates with C Manny Sanguillen to Cleveland Indians for P Bob Owchinko, P Rafael Vasquez, P Victor Cruz and C Gary Alexander (December 9, 1980). ... On disabled list (May 2, 1982-remainder of season and May 23-June 10, 1984). ... Traded by Indians to Minnesota Twins for P Curt Wardle, OF Jim Weaver, IF Jay Bell and a player to be named later (August 1, 1985); Indians organization acquired P Rich Yett to complete deal (September 17, 1985). ... On disabled list (July 30-August 15, 1988). ... Traded by Twins with P Kevin Trudeau to California Angels for P Mike Cook, P Rob Wassenaar and 1B Paul Sorrento (November 3, 1988). ... On disabled list (August 11, 1990-remainder of season and March 26, 1991-entire season). ... Granted free agency (November 1, 1991). ... Re-signed by Angels organization (January 22, 1992).
RECORDS/HONORS: Holds major league single-season record for most home runs allowed—50 (1986). ... Shares major league single-game record (nine innings) for most putouts by pitcher—6 (June 24, 1984). ... Shares A.L. single-game record for longest one-hit complete game—10 innings (June 21, 1976). ... Named A.L. Rookie Pitcher of the Year by THE SPORTING NEWS (1970). ... Named A.L. Comeback Player of the Year by THE SPORTING NEWS (1989).
STATISTICAL NOTES: Tied for A.L. lead with three balks in 1970. ... Pitched 6-0 no-hit victory against California Angels (September 22, 1977). ... Led A.L. with nine shutouts in 1973 and 5 in both 1985 and 1989. ... Led A.L. with 24 complete games and tied for lead in games started by pitcher with 37 in 1985. ... Led A.L. with 50 home runs allowed in 1986 and 46 in 1987. ... Led A.L. with 12 hit batsmen in 1976 and 16 in 1988.

Year	Team (League)	G	W	L	Pct.	ERA	Sv.	IP	H	R	ER	BB	SO
1969	—Sarasota Twins (Gulf Coast)	7	2	2	.500	2.81	1	32	31	13	10	11	39
	—Orlando (Florida State)	6	5	0	1.000	1.46	0	37	36	6	6	14	41
1970	—Evansville (Am. Assoc.)	8	4	2	.667	2.50	0	54	48	18	15	12	63
	—Minnesota (A.L.)	27	10	9	.526	3.18	0	164	143	66	58	47	135
1971	—Minnesota (A.L.)	38	16	15	.516	2.82	0	278	267	95	87	59	224
1972	—Minnesota (A.L.)	39	17	17	.500	2.73	0	287	247	93	87	69	228
1973	—Minnesota (A.L.)	40	20	17	.541	2.52	0	325	296	109	91	67	258
1974	—Minnesota (A.L.)	37	17	17	.500	2.66	0	281	244	99	83	77	249
1975	—Minnesota (A.L.)	35	15	10	.600	3.00	0	276	219	104	92	84	233
1976	—Minnesota-Texas (A.L.)■	36	13	16	.448	2.87	0	298	283	106	95	81	219
1977	—Texas (A.L.)	30	14	12	.538	2.72	0	235	181	81	71	69	182
1978	—Pittsburgh (N.L.)■	34	14	10	.583	3.02	0	244	217	94	82	66	182
1979	—Pittsburgh (N.L.)	37	12	5	.706	3.61	0	237	238	102	95	92	172
1980	—Pittsburgh (N.L.)	34	8	13	.381	3.82	0	217	219	102	92	59	168
1981	—Cleveland (A.L.)■	20	11	7	.611	2.89	0	159	145	52	51	40	107
1982	—Cleveland (A.L.)	4	2	2	.500	4.87	0	$20\frac{1}{3}$	16	14	11	11	19
1983	—Cleveland (A.L.)	24	7	10	.412	3.91	0	$156\frac{1}{3}$	160	74	68	44	123
1984	—Cleveland (A.L.)	33	19	7	.731	2.87	0	245	204	86	78	74	170
1985	—Cleveland-Minnesota (A.L.)■...	37	17	16	.515	3.16	0	★$293\frac{2}{3}$	264	121	103	75	★206
1986	—Minnesota (A.L.)	36	17	14	.548	4.01	0	★$271\frac{2}{3}$	262	134	121	58	215
1987	—Minnesota (A.L.)	37	15	12	.556	4.01	0	267	249	132	119	101	196
1988	—Minnesota (A.L.)	33	10	★17	.370	5.43	0	$207\frac{1}{3}$	240	128	★125	51	145
1989	—California (A.L.)■	33	17	5	.773	2.73	0	241	225	76	73	44	131
1990	—California (A.L.)	23	8	7	.533	5.24	0	134	163	85	78	25	69
1991	—California (A.L.)					Did not play							
American League totals (18 years)		562	245	210	.538	3.24	0	$4139\frac{1}{3}$	3808	1655	1491	1076	3109
National League totals (3 years)		105	34	28	.548	3.47	0	698	674	298	269	217	522
Major league totals (21 years)		667	279	238	.540	3.27	0	$4837\frac{1}{3}$	4482	1953	1760	1293	3631

CHAMPIONSHIP SERIES RECORD

Year	Team (League)	G	W	L	Pct.	ERA	Sv.	IP	H	R	ER	BB	SO
1970	—Minnesota (A.L.)	1	0	0	...	0.00	0	2	2	1	0	0	2
1979	—Pittsburgh (N.L.)	1	1	0	1.000	1.00	0	9	8	1	1	0	9
1987	—Minnesota (A.L.)	2	2	0	1.000	4.05	0	$13\frac{1}{3}$	12	6	6	3	9
Championship Series totals (3 years)		4	3	1	1.000	2.59	0	$24\frac{1}{3}$	22	8	7	3	20

Year	Team (League)	G	W	L	Pct.	ERA	Sv.	IP	H	R	ER	BB	SO
1979 —Pittsburgh (N.L.)		2	1	0	1.000	1.80	0	10	8	2	2	3	4
1987 —Minnesota (A.L.)		2	1	1	.500	2.77	0	13	13	5	4	2	12
World Series totals (2 years)		4	2	1	.667	2.35	0	23	21	7	6	5	16

ALL-STAR GAME RECORD

Year	League	W	L	Pct.	ERA	Sv.	IP	H	R	ER	BB	SO
1973 —American	0	1	.000	18.00	0	1	2	2	2	2	0
1985 —American	0	0	. . .	9.00	0	2	3	2	2	1	1
All-Star totals (2 years)	0	1	.000	12.00	0	3	5	4	4	3	1

BODDICKER, MIKE
P, ROYALS

PERSONAL: Born August 23, 1957, at Cedar Rapids, Ia. . . . 5-11/185. . . . Throws right, bats right. . . . Full name: Michael James Boddicker. . . . Name pronounced BOD-dicker.
HIGH SCHOOL: Norway Community (Ia.).
COLLEGE: Iowa.
TRANSACTIONS/CAREER NOTES: Selected by Montreal Expos organization in eighth round of free-agent draft (June 4, 1975). . . . Selected by Baltimore Orioles organization in sixth round of free-agent draft (June 6, 1978). . . . On disabled list (April 20-May 10, 1986). . . . Traded by Orioles to Boston Red Sox for OF Brady Anderson and P Curt Schilling (July 29, 1988). . . . Granted free agency (November 5, 1990). . . . Signed by Kansas City Royals (November 21, 1990). . . . On disabled list (May 13-29, 1991).
RECORDS/HONORS: Shares modern major league single-season record for most putouts by pitcher—49 (1984). . . . Named A.L. Rookie Pitcher of the Year by THE SPORTING NEWS (1983). . . . Named righthanded pitcher on THE SPORTING NEWS A.L. All-Star team (1984). . . . Won A.L. Gold Glove at pitcher (1990).
STATISTICAL NOTES: Led A.L. with five shutouts in 1983. . . . Tied for A.L. lead with 13 hit batsmen in 1991.
MISCELLANEOUS: Appeared in one game as a pinch-runner (1984) and in two games as a pinch-runner (1985).

Year	Team (League)	G	W	L	Pct.	ERA	Sv.	IP	H	R	ER	BB	SO
1978 —Bluefield (Appalachian)		8	2	1	.667	0.47	2	19	9	2	1	10	28
—Charlotte (Southern)		10	4	3	.571	1.94	0	65	42	15	14	17	48
—Rochester (International)		1	1	0	1.000	1.80	0	5	4	1	1	2	3
1979 —Charlotte (Southern)		14	9	3	.750	3.00	0	102	82	40	34	36	89
—Rochester (International)		15	4	6	.400	6.00	0	72	88	48	48	27	48
1980 —Rochester (International)		25	12	9	.571	2.18	0	190	149	57	46	35	109
—Baltimore (A.L.)		1	0	1	.000	6.43	0	7	6	6	5	5	4
1981 —Rochester (International)		30	10	10	.500	4.20	0	182	182	91	85	66	109
—Baltimore (A.L.)		2	0	0	. . .	4.50	0	6	6	4	3	2	2
1982 —Rochester (International)		20	10	5	.667	3.58	0	133⅓	121	59	53	36	82
—Baltimore (A.L.)		7	1	0	1.000	3.51	0	25⅔	25	10	10	12	20
1983 —Rochester (International)		4	3	1	.750	1.90	0	23⅔	17	6	5	13	18
—Baltimore (A.L.)		27	16	8	.667	2.77	0	179	141	65	55	52	120
1984 —Baltimore (A.L.)		34	*20	11	.645	*2.79	0	261⅓	218	95	81	81	128
1985 —Baltimore (A.L.)		32	12	17	.414	4.07	0	203⅓	227	104	92	89	135
1986 —Baltimore (A.L.)		33	14	12	.538	4.70	0	218⅓	214	125	114	74	175
1987 —Baltimore (A.L.)		33	10	12	.455	4.18	0	226	212	114	105	78	152
1988 —Baltimore-Boston (A.L.)■		36	13	15	.464	3.39	0	236	234	102	89	77	156
1989 —Boston (A.L.)		34	15	11	.577	4.00	0	211⅔	217	101	94	71	145
1990 —Boston (A.L.)		34	17	8	.680	3.36	0	228	225	92	85	69	143
1991 —Kansas City (A.L.)■		30	12	12	.500	4.08	0	180⅔	188	89	82	59	79
Major league totals (12 years)		303	130	107	.549	3.70	0	1983	1913	907	815	669	1259

CHAMPIONSHIP SERIES RECORD

CHAMPIONSHIP SERIES NOTES: Shares single-game record for most strikeouts—14 (October 6, 1983).

Year	Team (League)	G	W	L	Pct.	ERA	Sv.	IP	H	R	ER	BB	SO
1983 —Baltimore (A.L.)		1	1	0	1.000	0.00	0	9	5	0	0	3	14
1988 —Boston (A.L.)		1	0	1	.000	20.25	0	2⅔	8	6	6	1	2
1990 —Boston (A.L.)		1	0	1	.000	2.25	0	8	6	4	2	3	7
Championship Series totals (3 years)		3	1	2	.333	3.66	0	19⅔	19	10	8	7	23

WORLD SERIES RECORD

Year	Team (League)	G	W	L	Pct.	ERA	Sv.	IP	H	R	ER	BB	SO
1983 —Baltimore (A.L.)		1	1	0	1.000	0.00	0	9	3	1	0	0	6

ALL-STAR GAME RECORD

Year	League	W	L	Pct.	ERA	Sv.	IP	H	R	ER	BB	SO
1984 —American						Did not play						

BOEVER, JOE
P, ASTROS

PERSONAL: Born October 4, 1960, at St. Louis. . . . 6-1/212. . . . Throws right, bats right. . . . Full name: Joseph Martin Boever. . . . Name pronounced BAY-vur.
HIGH SCHOOL: Lindbergh (St. Louis).
COLLEGE: Crowder College (Mo.), St. Louis Community College at Meramec (Mo.) and UNLV.

TRANSACTIONS/CAREER NOTES: Signed as free agent by St. Louis Cardinals organization (June 25, 1982). . . . Traded by Cardinals to Atlanta Braves for P Randy O'Neal (July 25, 1987). . . . Traded by Braves to Philadelphia Phillies for P Marvin Freeman (July 23, 1990). . . . Granted free agency (December 20, 1991). . . . Signed by Houston Astros organization (January 27, 1992).

Year Team (League)	G	W	L	Pct.	ERA	Sv.	IP	H	R	ER	BB	SO
1982—Erie (New York-Penn)	19	2	3	.400	1.93	9	32⅔	20	8	7	12	63
—Springfield (Midwest)	3	0	0	...	2.25	0	4	3	1	1	2	7
1983—St. Petersburg (Florida State)	53	5	6	.455	3.02	*26	80⅓	61	29	27	37	57
1984—Arkansas (Texas)	8	0	1	.000	8.18	3	11	10	11	10	12	12
—St. Petersburg (Florida State)	48	6	4	.600	3.01	*14	77⅔	52	31	26	45	81
1985—Arkansas (Texas)	27	3	1	.750	1.19	9	37⅔	21	5	5	23	45
—Louisville (American Assoc.)	21	3	2	.600	2.04	1	35⅓	28	11	8	22	37
—St. Louis (N.L.)	13	0	0	...	4.41	0	16⅓	17	8	8	4	20
1986—St. Louis (N.L.)	11	0	1	.000	1.66	0	21⅔	19	5	4	11	8
—Louisville (American Assoc.)	51	4	5	.444	2.25	5	88	71	25	22	48	75
1987—Louisville (American Assoc.)	43	3	2	.600	3.36	*21	59	52	22	22	27	79
—Atlanta (N.L.)■	14	1	0	1.000	7.36	0	18⅓	29	15	15	12	18
—Richmond (International)	6	1	0	1.000	1.00	1	9	8	1	1	4	8
1988—Richmond (International)	48	6	3	.667	2.14	*22	71⅓	47	17	17	22	71
—Atlanta (N.L.)	16	0	2	.000	1.77	1	20⅓	12	4	4	1	7
1989—Atlanta (N.L.)	66	4	11	.267	3.94	21	82⅓	78	37	36	34	68
1990—Atlanta-Philadelphia (N.L.)■	67	3	6	.333	3.36	14	88⅓	77	35	33	51	75
1991—Philadelphia (N.L.)	68	3	5	.375	3.84	0	98⅓	90	45	42	54	89
Major league totals (7 years)	255	11	25	.306	3.70	36	345⅔	322	149	142	167	285

BOGGS, WADE
3B, RED SOX

PERSONAL: Born June 15, 1958, at Omaha, Neb. . . . 6-2/197. . . . Throws right, bats left. . . . Full name: Wade Anthony Boggs.
HIGH SCHOOL: H.B. Plant (Tampa, Fla.).
COLLEGE: Hillsborough Community College (Fla.).
TRANSACTIONS/CAREER NOTES: Selected by Boston Red Sox organization in seventh round of free-agent draft (June 8, 1976). . . . On disabled list (April 20-May 2, 1979).
RECORDS/HONORS: Holds major league records for most seasons and most consecutive seasons leading league in intentional bases on balls—5. . . . Holds A.L. record for most consecutive years with 200 or more hits—7. . . . Holds A.L. rookie single-season record for highest batting average (100 or more games)—.349 (1982). . . . Shares major league single-season record for most games, one or more hits—135 (1985). . . . Holds A.L. single-season record for most singles—187 (1985). . . . Shares A.L. single-season record for fewest double plays by third baseman (150 or more games)—17 (1988). . . . Shares major league single-season record for fewest chances accepted by third baseman (150 or more games)—349 (1990). . . . Named third baseman on THE SPORTING NEWS A.L. All-Star team (1983, 1985-88 and 1991). . . . Named third baseman on THE SPORTING NEWS A.L. Silver Slugger team (1983, 1986-89 and 1991).
STATISTICAL NOTES: Led Eastern League third basemen with .953 fielding percentage in 1979. . . . Led A.L with .449 on base percentage in 1983, .450 in 1985, .453 in 1986, .461 in 1987, .476 in 1988 and .430 in 1989. . . . Led A.L. third basemen with 30 double plays in 1984, 37 in 1987 and 29 in 1989. . . . Led A.L. third basemen with 486 total chances in 1985. . . . Led A.L. with 105 bases on balls received in 1986 and 125 in 1988. . . . Led A.L. with 19 intentional bases on balls received in 1987, 1989 and 1990 and with 25 in 1991 and tied for lead with 18 in 1988. . . . Led A.L. in grounding into double plays with 23 in 1988.

Year Team (League)	Pos.	G	AB	R	H	2B	3B	HR	RBI	Avg.	SB	PO	A	E	Avg.
1976—Elmira (New York-Penn)	3B	57	179	29	47	6	0	0	15	.263	2	36	75	16	.874
1977—Win.-Salem (Caro.)	3B-2B-SS	117	422	67	140	13	1	2	55	.332	8	145	223	27	.932
1978—Bristol (Eastern)	3-S-2-0	109	354	63	110	14	2	1	32	.311	1	62	107	7	.960
1979—Bristol (Eastern)	3B-SS-2B	113	406	56	132	17	2	0	41	.325	11	94	213	15	†.953
1980—Pawtucket (Int'l)	3B-1B	129	418	51	128	21	0	1	45	.306	3	108	156	12	.957
1981—Pawtucket (Int'l)	3B-1B	137	498	67	*167	*41	3	5	60	*.335	4	359	238	26	.958
1982—Boston (A.L.)	1B-3B-OF	104	338	51	118	14	1	5	44	.349	1	489	168	8	.988
1983—Boston (A.L.)	3B	153	582	100	210	44	7	5	74	*.361	3	118	368	*27	.947
1984—Boston (A.L.)	3B	158	625	109	203	31	4	6	55	.325	3	141	330	•20	.959
1985—Boston (A.L.)	3B	161	653	107	*240	42	3	8	78	*.368	2	134	335	17	.965
1986—Boston (A.L.)	3B	149	580	107	207	47	2	8	71	*.357	0	*121	267	19	.953
1987—Boston (A.L.)	3B-1B	147	551	108	200	40	6	24	89	*.363	1	112	277	14	.965
1988—Boston (A.L.)	3B	155	584	*128	214	*45	6	5	58	*.366	2	*122	250	11	.971
1989—Boston (A.L.)	3B	156	621	•113	205	*51	7	3	54	.330	2	*123	264	17	.958
1990—Boston (A.L.)	3B	155	619	89	187	44	5	6	63	.302	0	108	241	20	.946
1991—Boston (A.L.)	3B	144	546	93	181	42	2	8	51	.332	1	89	276	12	.968
Major league totals (10 years)		1482	5699	1005	1965	400	43	78	637	.345	15	1557	2776	165	.963

CHAMPIONSHIP SERIES RECORD

CHAMPIONSHIP SERIES NOTES: Shares single-series record for most sacrifice flies—2 (1988).

Year Team (League)	Pos.	G	AB	R	H	2B	3B	HR	RBI	Avg.	SB	PO	A	E	Avg.
1986—Boston (A.L.)	3B	7	30	3	7	1	1	0	2	.233	0	7	13	2	.909
1988—Boston (A.L.)	3B	4	13	2	5	0	0	0	3	.385	0	6	6	0	1.000
1990—Boston (A.L.)	3B	4	16	1	7	1	0	1	1	.438	0	6	10	0	1.000
Championship Series totals (3 years)		15	59	6	19	2	1	1	6	.322	0	19	29	2	.960

WORLD SERIES RECORD

Year	Team (League)	Pos.	G	AB	R	H	2B	3B	HR	RBI	Avg.	SB	PO	A	E	Avg.
1986 —Boston (A.L.)		3B	7	31	3	9	3	0	0	3	.290	0	4	15	0	1.000

ALL-STAR GAME RECORD

Year	League	Pos.	AB	R	H	2B	3B	HR	RBI	Avg.	SB	PO	A	E	Avg.
1985 —American		3B	0	0	0	0	0	0	0	...	0	0	0	0	...
1986 —American		3B	3	0	1	0	0	0	0	.333	0	0	1	0	1.000
1987 —American		3B	3	0	0	0	0	0	0	.000	0	0	3	0	1.000
1988 —American		3B	3	0	1	0	0	0	0	.333	0	0	1	0	1.000
1989 —American		3B	3	1	1	0	0	1	1	.333	0	1	1	0	1.000
1990 —American		3B	2	0	2	0	0	0	0	1.000	0	0	4	0	1.000
1991 —American		3B	2	1	1	0	0	0	0	.500	0	1	2	0	1.000
All-Star Game totals (7 years)			16	2	6	0	0	1	1	.375	0	2	12	0	1.000

BOHANON, BRIAN
P, RANGERS

PERSONAL: Born August 1, 1968, at Denton, Tex.... 6-2/220.... Throws left, bats left. ... Full name: Brian Edward Bohanon.
HIGH SCHOOL: North Shore (Houston).
TRANSACTIONS/CAREER NOTES: Selected by Texas Rangers organization in first round (19th pick overall) of free-agent draft (June 2, 1987).... On disabled list (April 17, 1988-remainder of season).... On Charlotte disabled list (April 7-May 2, 1989).... On Texas disabled list (April 7-July 1, 1991); included rehabilitation disability assignment to Port Charlotte (June 1- 10, 1991), Tulsa (June 10-23, 1991) and Oklahoma City (June 23-30, 1991).

Year	Team (League)	G	W	L	Pct.	ERA	Sv.	IP	H	R	ER	BB	SO
1987 —Sarasota Rangers (GCL)	5	0	2	.000	4.71	0	21	15	13	11	5	21
1988 —Port Charlotte (Florida State) ...	2	0	1	.000	5.40	0	6⅔	6	4	4	5	9
1989 —Charlotte (Florida State)	11	0	3	.000	1.81	1	54⅔	40	16	11	20	33
—Tulsa (Texas)	11	5	0	1.000	2.20	0	73⅔	59	20	18	27	44
1990 —Texas (A.L.)	11	0	3	.000	6.62	0	34	40	30	25	18	15
—Oklahoma City (Am. Assoc.)	14	1	2	.333	3.66	1	32	35	16	13	8	22
1991 —Charlotte (Florida State)	2	1	0	1.000	3.86	0	11⅔	6	5	5	4	7
—Tulsa (Texas)	2	0	1	.000	2.31	0	11⅔	9	8	3	11	6
—Oklahoma City (Am. Assoc.)	7	0	4	.000	2.91	0	46⅓	49	19	15	15	37
—Texas (A.L.)	11	4	3	.571	4.84	0	61⅓	66	35	33	23	34
Major league totals (2 years)	22	4	6	.400	5.48	0	95⅓	106	65	58	41	49

BOLICK, FRANK
3B, MARINERS

PERSONAL: Born June 28, 1966, at Ashland, Pa.... 5-10/175.... Throws right, bats both. ... Full name: Frank Charles Bolick.... Son of Frank Bolick, minor league pitcher (1966-77).
HIGH SCHOOL: Mt. Carmel (Pa.).
COLLEGE: Georgia Tech.
TRANSACTIONS/CAREER NOTES: Selected by Montreal Expos organization in 23rd round of free-agent draft (June 3, 1985).... Selected by Milwaukee Brewers organization in ninth round of free-agent draft (June 2, 1987).... Traded by Brewers organization to Seattle Mariners organization for OF Mickey Brantley (June 6, 1990).
STATISTICAL NOTES: Tied for California League lead with 13 sacrifice flies in 1990.... Led Southern League batters with 84 bases on balls received in 1991.

Year	Team (League)	Pos.	G	AB	R	H	2B	3B	HR	RBI	Avg.	SB	PO	A	E	Avg.
1987 —Helena (Pioneer)		3B	52	156	41	39	8	1	10	28	.250	4	5	13	1	.947
1988 —Beloit (Midwest)		3B	55	180	28	41	14	1	2	16	.228	3	38	81	14	.895
—Peoria Brewers (Ariz.).......		3B	23	80	20	30	9	3	1	20	.375	1	23	55	4	.951
—Helena (Pioneer)		3B	40	131	35	39	10	1	10	38	.298	5	28	65	10	.903
1989 —Beloit (Midwest)	3B-1B-OF	88	299	44	90	23	0	9	41	.301	9	47	108	15	.912
1990 —Stock.-San Bern. (Calif.)■	3B-1B	128	441	100	143	33	5	18	*102	.324	8	114	209	20	.942
1991 —Jacksonville (Southern) ...	3B-SS	136	468	69	119	19	0	16	73	.254	5	88	256	17	.953

BOLTON, TOM
P, RED SOX

PERSONAL: Born May 6, 1962, at Nashville, Tenn.... 6-3/185.... Throws left, bats left.... Full name: Thomas Edward Bolton.
HIGH SCHOOL: Antioch (Tenn.).
TRANSACTIONS/CAREER NOTES: Selected by Boston Red Sox organization in 20th round of free-agent draft (June 3, 1980).... On New Britain disabled list (June 27-July 9, 1983).... On disabled list (April 11-May 26, 1986 and July 22-August 13, 1991).

Year	Team (League)	G	W	L	Pct.	ERA	Sv.	IP	H	R	ER	BB	SO
1980 —Elmira (New York-Penn)	23	6	2	.750	2.41	5	56	43	26	15	22	43
1981 —Winter Haven (Florida State) ...	24	2	9	.182	4.50	0	92	125	62	46	41	47
1982 —Winter Haven (Florida State) ...	28	9	8	.529	2.99	0	162⅔	161	67	54	63	77
1983 —New Britain (Eastern)	16	7	3	.700	2.89	0	99⅔	93	36	32	41	62
—Pawtucket (International)	6	0	5	.000	6.52	0	29	33	26	21	25	20

Year	Team (League)	G	W	L	Pct.	ERA	Sv.	IP	H	R	ER	BB	SO
1984 — New Britain (Eastern)		33	4	5	.444	4.14	1	87	87	54	40	34	66
1985 — New Britain (Eastern)		34	5	6	.455	4.28	1	101	106	53	48	40	74
1986 — Pawtucket (International)		29	3	4	.429	2.72	2	86	80	30	26	25	58
1987 — Pawtucket (International)		5	2	1	.667	5.40	0	21⅔	25	14	13	12	8
— Boston (A.L.)		29	1	0	1.000	4.38	0	61⅔	83	33	30	27	49
1988 — Pawtucket (International)		18	3	0	1.000	2.79	0	19⅓	17	7	6	10	15
— Boston (A.L.)		28	1	3	.250	4.75	0	30⅓	35	17	16	14	21
1989 — Pawtucket (International)		25	12	5	.706	2.89	1	143⅓	140	57	46	47	99
— Boston (A.L.)		4	0	4	.000	8.31	0	17⅓	21	18	16	10	9
1990 — Pawtucket (International)		4	1	0	1.000	3.86	0	11⅔	9	6	5	7	8
— Boston (A.L.)		21	10	5	.667	3.38	0	119⅔	111	46	45	47	65
1991 — Boston (A.L.)		25	8	9	.471	5.24	0	110	136	72	64	51	64
Major league totals (5 years)		107	20	21	.488	4.54	1	339	386	186	171	149	208

CHAMPIONSHIP SERIES RECORD

Year	Team (League)	G	W	L	Pct.	ERA	Sv.	IP	H	R	ER	BB	SO
1990 — Boston (A.L.)		2	0	0	. . .	0.00	0	3	2	0	0	2	3

BONDS, BARRY
OF, PIRATES

PERSONAL: Born July 24, 1964, at Riverside, Calif. . . . 6-1/190. . . . Throws left, bats left. . . . Full name: Barry Lamar Bonds. . . . Son of Bobby Bonds, major league outfielder for eight teams (1968-81) and coach, Cleveland Indians (1984-87).
HIGH SCHOOL: Serra (San Mateo, Calif.).
COLLEGE: Arizona State.
TRANSACTIONS/CAREER NOTES: Selected by San Francisco Giants organization in second round of free-agent draft (June 7, 1982). . . . Selected by Pittsburgh Pirates organization in first round (sixth pick overall) of free-agent draft (June 3, 1985).
RECORDS/HONORS: Shares major league single-season record for fewest assists by outfielder who led league in assists—14 (1990). . . . Named outfielder on THE SPORTING NEWS college All-America team (1985). . . . Named Major League Player of the Year by THE SPORTING NEWS (1990). . . . Named N.L. Player of the Year by THE SPORTING NEWS (1990-91). . . . Named outfielder on THE SPORTING NEWS N.L. All-Star team (1990-91). . . . Won N.L. Gold Glove as outfielder (1990-91). . . . Named outfielder on THE SPORTING NEWS N.L. Silver Slugger team (1990-91). . . . Named N.L. Most Valuable Player by Baseball Writers' Association of America (1990).
STATISTICAL NOTES: Led N.L. with .565 slugging percentage in 1990.

								BATTING						FIELDING		
Year	Team (League)	Pos.	G	AB	R	H	2B	3B	HR	RBI	Avg.	SB	PO	A	E	Avg.
1985 — Prince William (Caro.).......		OF	71	254	49	76	16	4	13	37	.299	15	202	4	5	.976
1986 — Hawaii (Pacific Coast)		OF	44	148	30	46	7	2	7	37	.311	16	109	4	2	.983
— Pittsburgh (N.L.)		OF	113	413	72	92	26	3	16	48	.223	36	280	9	5	.983
1987 — Pittsburgh (N.L.)		OF	150	551	99	144	34	9	25	59	.261	32	330	15	5	.986
1988 — Pittsburgh (N.L.)		OF	144	538	97	152	30	5	24	58	.283	17	292	5	6	.980
1989 — Pittsburgh (N.L.)		OF	159	580	96	144	34	6	19	58	.248	32	365	14	6	.984
1990 — Pittsburgh (N.L.)		OF	151	519	104	156	32	3	33	114	.301	52	338	•14	6	.983
1991 — Pittsburgh (N.L.)		OF	153	510	95	149	28	5	25	116	.292	43	321	13	3	.991
Major league totals (6 years)			870	3111	563	837	184	31	142	453	.269	212	1926	70	31	.985

CHAMPIONSHIP SERIES RECORD

								BATTING						FIELDING		
Year	Team (League)	Pos.	G	AB	R	H	2B	3B	HR	RBI	Avg.	SB	PO	A	E	Avg.
1990 — Pittsburgh (N.L.)		OF	6	18	4	3	0	0	0	1	.167	2	13	0	0	1.000
1991 — Pittsburgh (N.L.)		OF	7	27	1	4	1	0	0	0	.148	3	14	1	1	.938
Championship Series totals (2 years)			13	45	5	7	1	0	0	1	.156	5	27	1	1	.966

ALL-STAR GAME RECORD

						BATTING							FIELDING		
Year	League	Pos.	AB	R	H	2B	3B	HR	RBI	Avg.	SB	PO	A	E	Avg.
1990 — National		OF	1	0	0	0	0	0	0	.000	0	2	0	0	1.000

BONES, RICKY
P, PADRES

PERSONAL: Born April 7, 1969, at Salinas, Puerto Rico. . . . 6-0/190. . . . Throws right, bats right. . . . Full name: Ricardo Bones. . . . Name pronounced bo-NAY.
TRANSACTIONS/CAREER NOTES: Signed as free agent by San Diego Padres organization (May 13, 1986).
STATISTICAL NOTES: Led Texas League with 22 home runs allowed in 1989.

Year	Team (League)	G	W	L	Pct.	ERA	Sv.	IP	H	R	ER	BB	SO
1986 — Spokane (Northwest)		18	1	3	.250	5.59	0	58	63	44	36	29	46
1987 — Charleston, S.C. (S. Atlantic)		26	12	5	.706	3.65	0	170⅓	★183	81	69	45	130
1988 — Riverside (California)		25	15	6	.714	3.64	0	175⅓	162	80	71	64	129
1989 — Wichita (Texas)		24	10	9	.526	5.74	0	136⅓	162	103	87	47	88
1990 — Wichita (Texas)		21	6	4	.600	3.48	0	137	138	66	53	45	96
— Las Vegas (Pacific Coast)		5	2	1	.667	3.47	0	36⅓	45	17	14	10	25
1991 — Las Vegas (Pacific Coast)		23	8	6	.571	4.22	0	136⅓	155	90	64	43	95
— San Diego (N.L.)		11	4	6	.400	4.83	0	54	57	33	29	18	31
Major league totals (1 year)		11	4	6	.400	4.83	0	54	57	33	29	18	31

BONILLA, BOBBY
OF, METS

PERSONAL: Born February 23, 1963, at New York. . . . 6-3/240. . . . Throws right, bats both. . . . Full name: Roberto Martin Antonio Bonilla. . . . Name pronounced bo-NEE-yah.
HIGH SCHOOL: Lehman (Bronx, N.Y.).
COLLEGE: New York Technical College.
TRANSACTIONS/CAREER NOTES: Signed as free agent by Pittsburgh Pirates organization (July 11, 1981). . . . On Pittsburgh disabled list (March 25-July 19, 1985). . . . Drafted by Chicago White Sox (December 10, 1985). . . . Traded by White Sox to Pittsburgh Pirates for P Jose DeLeon (July 23, 1986). . . . Granted free agency (October 28, 1991). . . . Signed by New York Mets (December 2, 1991).
RECORDS/HONORS: Named third baseman on THE SPORTING NEWS N.L. All-Star team (1988). . . . Named third baseman on THE SPORTING NEWS N.L. Silver Slugger team (1988). . . . Named outfielder on THE SPORTING NEWS N.L. All-Star team (1990-91). . . . Named outfielder on THE SPORTING NEWS N.L. Silver Slugger team (1990-91).
STATISTICAL NOTES: Led Eastern League outfielders with 15 errors in 1984. . . . Switch-hit home runs in one game (July 3, 1987 and April 6, 1988). . . . Led N.L. third basemen with 489 total chances in 1988. . . . Led N.L. third basemen with 35 errors in 1989. . . . Led N.L. third basemen with 31 double plays in 1989. . . . Led N.L. with 15 sacrifice flies in 1990.

							BATTING								FIELDING		
Year	Team (League)	Pos.	G	AB	R	H	2B	3B	HR	RBI	Avg.	SB	PO	A	E	Avg.
1981—Bradenton Pirates (GCL) ..	1B-C-3B	22	69	6	15	5	0	0	7	.217	2	124	23	5	.967
1982—Bradenton Pirates (GCL) ..	1B	47	167	20	38	3	0	5	26	.228	2	318	36	★14	.962
1983—Alexandria (Carolina)	OF-1B	•136	504	88	129	19	7	11	59	.256	28	259	12	15	.948
1984—Nashua (Eastern)........	OF-1B	136	484	74	128	19	5	11	71	.264	15	312	8	†15	.955
1985—Prince William (Caro.).......	1B-3B	39	130	15	34	4	1	3	11	.262	1	180	9	2	.990
1986—Chicago (A.L.)■..............	OF-1B	75	234	27	63	10	2	2	26	.269	4	361	22	2	.995
—Pittsburgh (N.L.)■..........	OF-1B-3B	63	192	28	46	6	2	1	17	.240	4	90	16	3	.972
1987—Pittsburgh (N.L.)	3B-OF-1B	141	466	58	140	33	3	15	77	.300	3	142	139	16	.946
1988—Pittsburgh (N.L.)	3B	159	584	87	160	32	7	24	100	.274	3	121	★336	★32	.935
1989—Pittsburgh (N.L.)	3B-1B-OF	•163	616	96	173	37	10	24	86	.281	8	190	334	†35	.937
1990—Pittsburgh (N.L.)	OF-3B-1B	160	625	112	175	39	7	32	120	.280	4	315	35	15	.959
1991—Pittsburgh (N.L.)	OF-3B-1B	157	577	102	174	★44	6	18	100	.302	2	247	144	15	.963
American League totals (1 year)		75	234	27	63	10	2	2	26	.269	4	361	22	2	.995
National League totals (6 years)		843	3060	483	868	191	35	114	500	.284	24	1105	1004	116	.948
Major league totals (6 years)		918	3294	510	931	201	37	116	526	.283	28	1466	1026	118	.955

CHAMPIONSHIP SERIES RECORD

							BATTING								FIELDING		
Year	Team (League)	Pos.	G	AB	R	H	2B	3B	HR	RBI	Avg.	SB	PO	A	E	Avg.
1990—Pittsburgh (N.L.)	OF-3B	6	21	0	4	1	0	0	1	.190	0	4	5	1	.900
1991—Pittsburgh (N.L.)	OF	7	23	2	7	2	0	0	1	.304	0	12	1	0	1.000
Championship Series totals (2 years)		13	44	2	11	3	0	0	2	.250	0	16	6	1	.957

ALL-STAR GAME RECORD

					BATTING						FIELDING		
Year	League	Pos.	AB	R	H	2B	3B	HR	RBI	Avg.	SB	PO	A	E	Avg.
1988—National	3B	4	0	0	0	0	0	0	.000	0	0	2	0	1.000
1989—National	DH	2	0	2	0	0	0	0	1.000	0	0	0	0	. . .
1990—National	1B	1	0	0	0	0	0	0	.000	0	1	0	0	1.000
1991—National	DH	4	0	2	0	0	0	1	.500	0	0	0	0	. . .
All-Star Game totals (4 years)		11	0	4	0	0	0	1	.364	0	1	2	0	1.000

BOOKER, ROD
IF, ASTROS

PERSONAL: Born September 4, 1958, at Los Angeles. . . . 6-0/175. . . . Throws right, bats left. . . . Full name: Roderick Stewart Booker.
HIGH SCHOOL: Pasadena (Pasadena, Calif.).
COLLEGE: Pasadena City College (Calif.) and California.
TRANSACTIONS/CAREER NOTES: Selected by Detroit Tigers organization in 14th round of free-agent draft (June 8, 1976). . . . Selected by Baltimore Orioles organization in 10th round of free-agent draft (June 5, 1979). . . . Selected by Minnesota Twins organization in fourth round of free-agent draft (June 3, 1980). . . . Sold by Twins organization to St. Louis Cardinals organization (April 5, 1983). . . . Released by Cardinals organization (October 5, 1989). . . . Signed by Scranton/Wilkes-Barre, Philadelphia Phillies organization (December 14, 1989). . . . Released by Phillies organization (July 30, 1991). . . . Signed by Houston Astros organization (January 10, 1992).

							BATTING								FIELDING		
Year	Team (League)	Pos.	G	AB	R	H	2B	3B	HR	RBI	Avg.	SB	PO	A	E	Avg.
1980—Visalia (California)...........	SS	69	242	45	68	5	4	0	26	.281	9	91	198	18	.941
1981—Orlando (Southern).........	SS-3B	111	331	56	85	8	3	0	33	.257	10	145	304	30	.937
1982—Toledo (International).......	SS-2B-3B	104	292	38	73	8	1	0	19	.250	5	177	272	36	.926
1983—Arkansas (Texas)■..........	SS-3B-2B	127	469	75	128	15	3	3	60	.273	20	153	343	19	.963
1984—Louisville (Am. Assoc.).....	2B-SS-3B	63	185	19	47	3	1	0	14	.254	3	100	167	8	.971
—Arkansas (Texas)...........	SS	52	209	10	43	4	3	0	22	.206	8	87	160	15	.943
1985—Arkansas (Texas)...........	SS	129	466	59	123	18	3	1	47	.264	13	198	362	26	★.956
1986—Arkansas (Texas)...........	SS	36	151	20	48	7	2	0	20	.318	4	66	121	10	.949
—Louisville (Am. Assoc.)....	2B-SS-3B	78	289	51	81	11	5	1	30	.280	18	151	205	10	.973
1987—Arkansas (Texas)...........	SS	34	135	25	47	3	1	1	21	.348	5	50	95	5	.967
—St. Louis (N.L.)	2B-3B-SS	44	47	9	13	1	1	0	8	.277	2	25	28	2	.964
1988—St. Louis (N.L.)	3B-2B	18	35	6	12	3	0	0	3	.343	2	3	15	2	.900
—Louisville (Am. Assoc.)....	2B-SS-OF	111	370	50	96	12	1	4	31	.259	15	197	330	20	.963

Year	Team (League)	Pos.	G	AB	R	H	2B	3B	HR	RBI	Avg.	SB	PO	A	E	Avg.
1989	—St. Louis (N.L.)	2B-3B	10	8	1	2	0	0	0	0	.250	0	4	9	2	.867
	—Louisville (Am. Assoc.)	SS-3B-2B	94	276	37	64	9	2	2	30	.232	9	123	232	14	.962
1990	—Philadelphia (N.L.)■	SS-2B-3B	73	131	19	29	5	2	0	10	.221	3	57	74	4	.970
1991	—Philadelphia (N.L.)	SS-3B	28	53	3	12	1	0	0	7	.226	0	17	33	0	1.000
	Major league totals (5 years)		173	274	38	68	10	3	0	28	.248	7	106	159	10	.964

BORDERS, PAT

C, BLUE JAYS

PERSONAL: Born May 14, 1963, at Columbus, O. . . . 6-2/200. . . . Throws right, bats right. . . . Full name: Patrick Lance Borders. . . . Brother of Todd Borders, minor league catcher (1988).
HIGH SCHOOL: Lake Wales (Fla.).
TRANSACTIONS/CAREER NOTES: Selected by Toronto Blue Jays organization in sixth round of free-agent draft (June 7, 1982). . . . On Toronto disabled list (July 5-August 19, 1988); included rehabilitation disability assignment to Syracuse (July 30-August 19, 1988).
STATISTICAL NOTES: Tied for Southern League lead with 16 passed balls in 1987.

Year	Team (League)	Pos.	G	AB	R	H	2B	3B	HR	RBI	Avg.	SB	PO	A	E	Avg.
1982	—Medicine Hat (Pioneer)	3B	61	217	30	66	12	2	5	33	.304	1	23	96	★25	.826
1983	—Florence (S. Atlantic)	3B	131	457	62	125	31	4	5	54	.274	4	70	233	★41	.881
1984	—Florence (S. Atlantic)	1B-3B-OF	131	467	69	129	32	5	12	85	.276	3	650	77	25	.967
1985	—Kinston (Carolina)	1B	127	460	43	120	16	1	10	60	.261	6	854	42	★20	.978
1986	—Florence (S. Atlantic)	C-OF	16	40	8	15	7	0	3	9	.375	0	22	1	0	1.000
	—Knoxville (Southern)	C-1B	12	34	3	12	1	0	2	5	.353	4	45	5	3	.943
	—Kinston (Carolina)	C-1B-OF	49	174	24	57	10	0	6	26	.328	0	211	26	7	.971
1987	—Dunedin (Florida State)	C	3	11	0	4	0	0	0	1	.364	0	21	1	0	1.000
	—Knoxville (Southern)	C-3B	94	349	44	102	14	1	11	51	.292	2	432	49	12	.976
1988	—Toronto (A.L.)	C-2B-3B	56	154	15	42	6	3	5	21	.273	0	205	19	7	.970
	—Syracuse (International)	C	35	120	11	29	8	0	3	14	.242	0	202	17	2	.991
1989	—Toronto (A.L.)	C	94	241	22	62	11	1	3	29	.257	2	261	27	6	.980
1990	—Toronto (A.L.)	C	125	346	36	99	24	2	15	49	.286	0	515	46	4	.993
1991	—Toronto (A.L.)	C	105	291	22	71	17	0	5	36	.244	0	505	48	4	.993
	Major league totals (4 years)		380	1032	95	274	58	6	28	135	.266	2	1486	140	21	.987

CHAMPIONSHIP SERIES RECORD

Year	Team (League)	Pos.	G	AB	R	H	2B	3B	HR	RBI	Avg.	SB	PO	A	E	Avg.
1989	—Toronto (A.L.)	PH-C	1	1	0	1	0	0	0	1	1.000	0	1	0	0	1.000
1991	—Toronto (A.L.)	C	5	19	0	5	1	0	0	2	.263	0	38	4	2	.955
	Championship Series totals (2 years)		6	20	0	6	1	0	0	3	.300	0	39	4	2	.956

BORDICK, MIKE

SS, ATHLETICS

PERSONAL: Born July 21, 1965, at Marquette, Mich. . . . 5-11/175. . . . Throws right, bats right. . . . Full name: Michael Todd Bordick.
HIGH SCHOOL: Hampden Academy (Me.).
COLLEGE: Maine.
TRANSACTIONS/CAREER NOTES: Signed as free agent by Oakland Athletics organization (July 10, 1986). . . . On Tacoma disabled list (April 14-May 13, 1991).
STATISTICAL NOTES: Led Pacific Coast League shortstops with .972 fielding percentage and 82 double plays in 1990.

Year	Team (League)	Pos.	G	AB	R	H	2B	3B	HR	RBI	Avg.	SB	PO	A	E	Avg.
1986	—Medford (Northwest)	SS	46	187	30	48	3	1	0	19	.257	6	68	143	18	.921
1987	—Modesto (California)	SS	133	497	73	133	17	0	3	75	.268	8	216	305	17	★.968
1988	—Huntsville (Southern)	2B-SS-3B	132	481	48	130	13	2	0	28	.270	7	260	406	24	.965
1989	—Tacoma (Pacific Coast)	2B-SS-3B	136	487	55	117	17	1	1	43	.240	4	261	431	33	.954
1990	—Oakland (A.L.)	3B-SS-2B	25	14	0	1	0	0	0	0	.071	0	9	8	0	1.000
	—Tacoma (Pacific Coast)	SS-2B	111	348	49	79	16	1	2	30	.227	3	210	366	16	†.973
1991	—Tacoma (Pacific Coast)	SS	26	81	15	22	4	1	2	14	.272	0	35	79	3	.974
	—Oakland (A.L.)	SS-2B-3B	90	235	21	56	5	1	0	21	.238	3	146	213	11	.970
	Major league totals (2 years)		115	249	21	57	5	1	0	21	.229	3	155	221	11	.972

WORLD SERIES RECORD

Year	Team (League)	Pos.	G	AB	R	H	2B	3B	HR	RBI	Avg.	SB	PO	A	E	Avg.
1990	—Oakland (A.L.)	PR-SS	3	0	0	0	0	0	0	0	. . .	0	0	2	0	1.000

BORLAND, TOBY

P, PHILLIES

PERSONAL: Born May 19, 1969, at Quitman, La. . . . 6-6/180. . . . Throws right, bats right. . . . Full name: Toby Shawn Borland.
HIGH SCHOOL: Quitman (La.).
TRANSACTIONS/CAREER NOTES: Selected by Philadelphia Phillies organization in 27th round of free-agent draft (June 2, 1987).
STATISTICAL NOTES: Tied for Eastern League lead with three balks in 1991.

Year	Team (League)	G	W	L	Pct.	ERA	Sv.	IP	H	R	ER	BB	SO
1988	—Martinsville (Appalachian).......	34	2	3	.400	4.04	*12	49	42	26	22	29	43
1989	—Spartanburg (South Atlantic) ..	47	4	5	.444	2.97	9	66⅔	62	29	22	35	48
1990	—Clearwater (Florida State)........	44	1	2	.333	2.26	5	59⅔	44	21	15	35	44
	—Reading (Eastern)..................	14	4	1	.800	1.44	0	25	16	6	4	11	26
1991	—Reading (Eastern)..................	*59	8	3	.727	2.70	•24	76⅔	68	31	23	56	72

BOSIO, CHRIS
P, BREWERS

PERSONAL: Born April 3, 1963, at Carmichael, Calif.... 6-3/225.... Throws right, bats right.... Full name: Christopher Louis Bosio.... Name pronounced BOZ-ee-o.
HIGH SCHOOL: Cordova (Calif.).
COLLEGE: Sacramento City College (Calif.).
TRANSACTIONS/CAREER NOTES: Selected by Pittsburgh Pirates organization in 29th round of free-agent draft (June 8, 1981).... Selected by Milwaukee Brewers organization in secondary phase of free-agent draft (January 12, 1982).... On Milwaukee disabled list (June 29-July 15 and August 2, 1990-remainder of season); included rehabilitation disability assignment to Beloit (July 9-15, 1990).... On disabled list (July 1-16, 1991).

Year	Team (League)	G	W	L	Pct.	ERA	Sv.	IP	H	R	ER	BB	SO
1982	—Pikeville (Appalachian)	13	3	2	.600	4.91	1	51⅓	60	31	28	17	53
1983	—Beloit (Midwest)	17	3	10	.231	5.60	0	107⅔	125	82	67	41	71
	—Paintsville (Appalachian)	7	2	2	.500	2.84	0	44⅓	30	18	14	18	43
1984	—Beloit (Midwest)	26	*17	6	.739	2.73	0	181	159	83	55	56	156
1985	—El Paso (Texas)	28	11	6	.647	3.82	2	181⅓	186	108	77	49	*155
1986	—Milwaukee (A.L.)	10	0	4	.000	7.01	0	34⅔	41	27	27	13	29
	—Vancouver (Pacific Coast)	44	7	3	.700	2.28	•16	67	47	18	17	13	60
1987	—Milwaukee (A.L.)	46	11	8	.579	5.24	2	170	187	102	99	50	150
1988	—Milwaukee (A.L.)	38	7	15	.318	3.36	6	182	190	80	68	38	84
	—Denver (American Assoc.)	2	1	0	1.000	3.86	0	14	13	6	6	4	12
1989	—Milwaukee (A.L.)	33	15	10	.600	2.95	0	234⅔	225	90	77	48	173
1990	—Milwaukee (A.L.)	20	4	9	.308	4.00	0	132⅔	131	67	59	38	76
	—Beloit (Midwest)	1	0	0	...	3.00	0	3	4	2	1	1	2
1991	—Milwaukee (A.L.)	32	14	10	.583	3.25	0	204⅔	187	80	74	58	117
	Major league totals (6 years)	179	51	56	.477	3.79	8	958⅔	961	446	404	245	629

BOSKIE, SHAWN
P, CUBS

PERSONAL: Born March 28, 1967, at Hawthorne, Nev.... 6-3/205.... Throws right, bats right.... Full name: Shawn Kealoha Boskie.
HIGH SCHOOL: Reno (Nev.).
COLLEGE: Modesto Junior College (Calif.).
TRANSACTIONS/CAREER NOTES: Selected by Chicago Cubs organization in first round (10th pick overall) of free-agent draft (January 14, 1986).... On Chicago disabled list (August 5-September 26, 1990).
STATISTICAL NOTES: Led Appalachian League with 15 wild pitches in 1986.... Led Carolina League with 17 hit batsmen in 1988.... Led Southern League with 19 hit batsmen in 1989.
MISCELLANEOUS: Appeared in one game as pinch-runner and one game as pinch-hitter (1991).

Year	Team (League)	G	W	L	Pct.	ERA	Sv.	IP	H	R	ER	BB	SO
1986	—Wytheville (Appalachian)	14	4	4	.500	5.33	0	54	42	41	32	57	40
1987	—Peoria (Midwest)	26	9	11	.450	4.35	0	149	149	91	72	56	100
1988	—Winston-Salem (Carolina)	27	12	7	.632	3.39	0	186	176	83	70	89	164
1989	—Charlotte (Southern)	28	11	8	.579	4.38	0	181	*196	105	88	84	*164
1990	—Iowa (American Association) ...	8	4	2	.667	3.18	0	51	46	22	18	21	51
	—Chicago (N.L.)	15	5	6	.455	3.69	0	97⅔	99	42	40	31	49
1991	—Chicago (N.L.)	28	4	9	.308	5.23	0	129	150	78	75	52	62
	—Iowa (American Association) ...	7	2	2	.500	3.57	0	45⅓	43	19	18	11	29
	Major league totals (2 years)	43	9	15	.375	4.57	0	226⅔	249	120	115	83	111

BOSTON, DARYL
OF, METS

PERSONAL: Born January 4, 1963, at Cincinnati.... 6-3/195.... Throws left, bats left.... Full name: Daryl Lamont Boston.
HIGH SCHOOL: Woodward (Cincinnati).
TRANSACTIONS/CAREER NOTES: Selected by Chicago White Sox organization in first round (seventh pick overall) of free-agent draft (June 8, 1981).... Claimed on waivers by New York Mets (April 30, 1990).... Granted free agency (October 31, 1991).
STATISTICAL NOTES: Led Midwest League outfielders with 312 total chances in 1982.... Led Eastern League batters with 133 strikeouts in 1983.... Tied for American Association lead with 11 sacrifice flies in 1984.... Tied for American Association lead in double plays by outfielder with four in 1984.

Year	Team (League)	Pos.	G	AB	R	H	2B	3B	HR	RBI	Avg.	SB	PO	A	E	Avg.
1981	—Sara. White Sox (GCL)	OF	56	189	30	55	6	3	1	30	.291	12	84	9	3	.969
1982	—Appleton (Midwest).........	OF	*139	512	86	143	19	9	15	77	.279	28	*293	9	10	.968
1983	—Glens Falls (Eastern)	OF	113	435	65	104	15	1	18	50	.239	21	271	8	13	.955
	—Denver (Am. Assoc.)	OF	14	51	11	13	4	1	2	7	.255	0	26	1	5	.844
1984	—Denver (Am. Assoc.)	OF	127	471	94	147	21	*19	15	82	.312	40	311	11	•10	.970
	—Chicago (A.L.)	OF	35	83	8	14	3	1	0	3	.169	6	59	2	6	.910

Year	Team (League)	Pos.	G	AB	R	H	2B	3B	HR	RBI	Avg.	SB	PO	A	E	Avg.
1985	—Chicago (A.L.)	OF	95	232	20	53	13	1	3	15	.228	8	179	7	2	.989
	—Buffalo (Am. Assoc.)	OF	63	241	45	66	12	1	10	36	.274	16	151	3	3	.981
1986	—Buffalo (Am. Assoc.)	OF	96	360	57	109	16	3	5	41	.303	37	210	1	5	.977
	—Chicago (A.L.)	OF	56	199	29	53	11	3	5	22	.266	9	152	3	5	.969
1987	—Chicago (A.L.)	OF	103	337	51	87	21	2	10	29	.258	12	207	3	2	.991
	—Hawaii (Pacific Coast)	OF	21	77	14	23	3	0	5	13	.299	10	43	3	0	1.000
1988	—Chicago (A.L.)	OF	105	281	37	61	12	2	15	31	.217	9	190	4	10	.951
1989	—Chicago (A.L.)	OF	101	218	34	55	3	4	5	23	.252	7	134	2	4	.971
1990	—Chicago (A.L.)	OF	5	1	0	0	0	0	0	0	.000	1	0	0	0	. . .
	—New York (N.L.)■............	OF	115	366	65	100	21	2	12	45	.273	18	203	3	3	.986
1991	—New York (N.L.)	OF	137	255	40	70	16	4	4	21	.275	15	156	2	3	.981
	American League totals (7 years)		500	1351	179	323	63	13	38	123	.239	52	921	21	29	.970
	National League totals (2 years)		252	621	105	170	37	6	16	66	.274	33	359	5	6	.984
	Major league totals (8 years)		752	1972	284	493	100	19	54	189	.250	85	1280	26	35	.974

BOTTENFIELD, KENT
P, EXPOS

PERSONAL: Born November 14, 1968, at Portland, Ore. . . . 6-3/225. . . . Throws right, bats both. . . . Full name: Kent Dennis Bottenfield. . . . Twin brother of Keven Bottenfield, minor league catcher-infielder (1986-87).
HIGH SCHOOL: James Madison (Portland, Ore.).
TRANSACTIONS/CAREER NOTES: Selected by Montreal Expos organization in fourth round of free-agent draft (June 2, 1986).
STATISTICAL NOTES: Tied for American Association lead with five complete games in 1991.

Year	Team (League)	G	W	L	Pct.	ERA	Sv.	IP	H	R	ER	BB	SO
1986	—Bradenton Expos (Gulf Coast) ..	13	5	6	.455	3.27	0	74⅓	73	•42	27	30	41
1987	—Burlington (Midwest)	27	9	13	.409	4.53	0	161	175	98	81	42	103
1988	—West Palm Beach (Florida St.) ..	27	10	8	.556	3.33	0	181	165	80	67	47	120
1989	—Jacksonville (Southern)	25	3	★17	.150	5.26	0	138⅔	137	101	81	73	91
1990	—Jacksonville (Southern)	29	12	10	.545	3.41	0	169	158	72	64	67	121
1991	—Indianapolis (Am. Assoc.)	29	8	15	.348	4.06	0	166⅓	155	97	75	61	108

BOUCHER, DENIS
P, INDIANS

PERSONAL: Born March 7, 1968, at Montreal, Que. . . . 6-1/195. . . . Throws left, bats right. . . . Full name: Denis Boucher. . . . Name pronounced DEN-ee BOO-shay.
TRANSACTIONS/CAREER NOTES: Signed as a free agent by the Toronto Blue Jays organization (August 18, 1987). . . . Traded by Blue Jays with OF Glenallen Hill, OF Mark Whiten and a player to be named later to Cleveland Indians for P Tom Candiotti and OF Turner Ward (June 27, 1991); Indians acquired cash instead of player to complete deal (October 15, 1991).
STATISTICAL NOTES: Tied for South Atlantic League lead in games started by pitcher with 32 in 1988. . . . Led South Atlantic League with 21 balks in 1988. . . . Tied for A.L. lead with four balks in 1991.

Year	Team (League)	G	W	L	Pct.	ERA	Sv.	IP	H	R	ER	BB	SO
1988	—Myrtle Beach (South Atlantic) ..	33	13	12	.520	2.84	0	196⅔	161	81	62	63	169
1989	—Dunedin (Florida State)	33	10	10	.500	3.06	0	164⅔	142	80	56	58	117
1990	—Dunedin (Florida State)	9	7	0	1.000	0.75	0	60	45	8	5	8	62
	—Syracuse (International)	17	8	5	.615	3.85	0	107⅔	100	52	46	37	80
1991	—Toronto-Cleveland (A.L.)■.......	12	1	7	.125	6.05	0	58	74	41	39	24	29
	—Syracuse (International)	8	2	1	.667	3.18	0	56⅔	57	24	20	19	28
	—Colorado Springs (Pac. Coast) ..	3	1	0	1.000	5.02	0	14⅓	14	8	8	2	9
	Major league totals (1 year)	12	1	7	.125	6.05	0	58	74	41	39	24	29

BOWEN, RYAN
P, ASTROS

PERSONAL: Born February 10, 1968, at Hanford, Calif. . . . 6-0/185. . . . Throws right, bats right. . . . Full name: Ryan Eugene Bowen.
HIGH SCHOOL: Hanford (Calif.).
TRANSACTIONS/CAREER NOTES: Selected by Houston Astros organization in first round (13th pick overall) of free-agent draft (June 2, 1986).
MISCELLANEOUS: Appeared in three games as pinch-runner (1991).

Year	Team (League)	G	W	L	Pct.	ERA	Sv.	IP	H	R	ER	BB	SO
1987	—Asheville (South Atlantic)	26	12	5	.706	4.04	0	160⅓	143	86	72	78	126
1988	—Osceola (Florida State)	4	1	0	1.000	3.95	0	13⅔	12	8	6	10	12
1989	—Columbus (Southern)	27	8	6	.571	4.25	0	139⅔	123	83	66	116	136
1990	—Columbus (Southern)	18	8	4	.667	3.74	0	113	103	59	47	49	109
	—Tucson (Pacific Coast)	10	1	3	.250	9.35	0	34⅔	41	36	36	38	29
1991	—Tucson (Pacific Coast)	18	5	5	.500	4.38	0	98⅔	114	56	48	56	78
	—Houston (N.L.)	14	6	4	.600	5.15	0	71⅔	73	43	41	36	49
	Major league totals (1 year)	14	6	4	.600	5.15	0	71⅔	73	43	41	36	49

BOYD, OIL CAN
P

PERSONAL: Born October 6, 1959, at Meridian, Miss. . . . 6-1/160. . . . Throws right, bats right. . . . Full name: Dennis Ray Boyd. . . . Brother of Don Boyd, minor league outfielder (1973).
HIGH SCHOOL: Meridian (Miss.).
COLLEGE: Jackson State.
TRANSACTIONS/CAREER NOTES: Selected by Boston Red Sox organization in 16th round of free-agent draft (June 3, 1980). . . .

On Boston disabled list (March 29-June 22 and July 31, 1987-remainder of season); included rehabilitation disability assignment to Pawtucket (June 8-22, 1987).... On disabled list (July 27-August 20 and August 31, 1988-remainder of season).... On Boston disabled list (May 2-September 1, 1989); included rehabilitation disability assignment to Pawtucket (August 18-27, 1989) and New Britain (August 28-September 1, 1989).... Granted free agency (November 13, 1989).... Signed by Montreal Expos (December 7, 1989).... Traded by Expos to Texas Rangers for P Jonathan Hurst, P Joey Eischen and a player to be named later (July 21, 1991); Expos acquired P Travis Buckley to complete deal (September 1, 1991).... Granted free agency (October 31, 1991).

STATISTICAL NOTES: Led Florida State League pitchers with 28 games started and 11 home runs allowed in 1981.... Tied for Eastern League lead in games started by pitcher with 27 and complete games with 13 in 1982.

MISCELLANEOUS: Given nickname from beer drinking friends in Meridian, Miss. where beer is referred to as oil.

Year	Team (League)	G	W	L	Pct.	ERA	Sv.	IP	H	R	ER	BB	SO
1980	Elmira (New York-Penn)	12	7	1	.875	2.48	0	69	54	20	19	30	79
1981	Winter Haven (Florida State)	28	14	8	.636	3.63	0	186	★195	90	75	54	154
1982	Bristol (Eastern)	27	14	8	.636	2.81	0	★205	190	71	64	49	★191
	Boston (A.L.)	3	0	1	.000	5.40	0	8⅓	11	5	5	2	2
1983	Pawtucket (International)	20	5	8	.385	4.04	1	122⅔	119	69	55	41	129
	Boston (A.L.)	15	4	8	.333	3.28	0	98⅔	103	46	36	23	43
1984	Boston (A.L.)	29	12	12	.500	4.37	0	197⅔	207	109	96	53	134
	Pawtucket (International)	5	3	1	.750	2.89	0	37⅓	30	12	12	12	45
1985	Boston (A.L.)	35	15	13	.536	3.70	0	272⅓	★273	117	112	67	154
1986	Boston (A.L.)	30	16	10	.615	3.78	0	214⅓	222	99	90	45	129
1987	Pawtucket (International)	3	1	1	.500	4.50	0	12	12	6	6	4	8
	Boston (A.L.)	7	1	3	.250	5.89	0	36⅔	47	31	24	9	12
1988	Boston (A.L.)	23	9	7	.563	5.34	0	129⅓	147	82	77	41	71
1989	Boston (A.L.)	10	3	2	.600	4.42	0	59	57	31	29	19	26
	Pawtucket (International)	2	0	0	...	0.00	0	7	4	0	0	0	11
	New Britain (Eastern)	1	0	1	.000	1.80	0	5	3	1	1	1	8
1990	Montreal (N.L.)■	31	10	6	.625	2.93	0	190⅔	164	64	62	52	113
1991	Montreal (N.L.)	19	6	8	.429	3.52	0	120⅓	115	49	47	40	82
	Texas (A.L.)■	12	2	7	.222	6.68	0	62	81	47	46	17	33
American League totals (9 years)		164	62	63	.496	4.30	0	1078⅔	1148	567	515	276	604
National League totals (2 years)		50	16	14	.533	3.15	0	311	279	113	109	92	195
Major league totals (10 years)		214	78	77	.503	4.04	0	1389⅔	1427	680	624	368	799

CHAMPIONSHIP SERIES RECORD

Year	Team (League)	G	W	L	Pct.	ERA	Sv.	IP	H	R	ER	BB	SO
1986	Boston (A.L.)	2	1	1	.500	4.61	0	13⅔	17	7	7	3	8

WORLD SERIES RECORD

Year	Team (League)	G	W	L	Pct.	ERA	Sv.	IP	H	R	ER	BB	SO
1986	Boston (A.L.)	1	0	1	.000	7.71	0	7	9	6	6	1	3

BRADLEY, SCOTT
C, MARINERS

PERSONAL: Born March 22, 1960, at Montclair, N.J.... 5-11/185.... Throws right, bats left.... Full name: Scott William Bradley.

COLLEGE: North Carolina (bachelor of science degree in business administration).

TRANSACTIONS/CAREER NOTES: Selected by Minnesota Twins organization in 12th round of free-agent draft (June 6, 1978).... Selected by New York Yankees organization in third round of free-agent draft (June 8, 1981).... On New York disabled list (April 24-June 17, 1985); included rehabilitation disability assignment to Sarasota (June 5-6, 1985) and Albany (June 7-17, 1985).... Traded by Yankees with P Neil Allen, OF Glen Braxton and cash to Chicago White Sox for C Ron Hassey, C Chris Alvarez, P Eric Schmidt and OF Matt Winters (February 13, 1986).... Traded by White Sox to Seattle Mariners for a player to be named later (June 26, 1986); White Sox organization acquired OF Ivan Calderon to complete deal (July 1, 1986).

RECORDS/HONORS: Named International League Player of the Year (1984).

Year	Team (League)	Pos.	G	AB	R	H	2B	3B	HR	RBI	Avg.	SB	PO	A	E	Avg.
1981	Oneonta (N.Y.-Penn)	C-OF	71	276	48	85	17	4	4	54	.308	7	323	40	9	.976
1982	Nashville (Am. Assoc.)	C	5	19	2	2	1	0	0	0	.105	0	44	2	2	.958
	Fort Lauderdale (FSL)	C-1B-3B	121	439	52	130	28	4	3	66	.296	5	407	57	10	.979
1983	Nashville (Am. Assoc.)	C-3B	137	525	83	142	33	4	8	76	.270	3	475	88	13	.977
1984	Columbus (Int'l)	C-OF-3B	★138	★538	84	★180	31	2	6	•84	.335	1	432	50	9	.982
	New York (A.L.)	OF-C	9	21	3	6	1	0	0	2	.286	0	10	0	0	1.000
1985	New York (A.L.)	C	19	49	4	8	2	1	0	1	.163	0	12	0	1	.923
	Albany (Eastern)	3B	6	24	2	3	1	0	0	2	.125	0	8	14	4	.846
	Columbus (Int'l)	C-3B	43	163	17	49	10	0	4	27	.301	2	118	53	4	.977
1986	Buffalo (Am. Assoc.)■	C-OF	33	126	14	42	3	3	5	20	.333	2	165	9	0	1.000
	Chicago-Seattle (A.L.)■	C-OF	77	220	20	66	8	3	5	28	.300	1	281	21	3	.990
1987	Seattle (A.L.)	C-3B-OF	102	342	34	95	15	1	5	43	.278	0	438	39	8	.984
1988	Seattle (A.L.)	C-0-3-1	103	335	45	86	17	1	4	33	.257	1	543	42	6	.990
1989	Seattle (A.L.)	C-1B-OF	103	270	21	74	16	0	3	37	.274	1	400	26	4	.991
1990	Seattle (A.L.)	C-3B-1B	101	233	11	52	9	0	1	28	.223	0	354	30	2	.995
1991	Seattle (A.L.)	C-3B-1B	83	172	10	35	7	0	0	11	.203	0	288	18	4	.987
Major league totals (8 years)			597	1642	148	422	75	6	18	183	.257	3	2326	176	28	.989

BRAGGS, GLENN
OF, REDS

PERSONAL: Born October 17, 1962, at San Bernardino, Calif. . . . 6-4/220. . . . Throws right, bats right. . . . Full name: Glenn Erick Braggs. **HIGH SCHOOL:** San Bernardino (Calif.). **COLLEGE:** Hawaii.

TRANSACTIONS/CAREER NOTES: Selected by New York Yankees organization in sixth round of free-agent draft (June 3, 1980). . . . Selected by Milwaukee Brewers organization in second round of free-agent draft (June 6, 1983). . . . On disabled list (July 2, 1988-remainder of season). . . . Traded by Brewers with IF Billy Bates to Cincinnati Reds for P Ron Robinson and P Bob Sebra (June 9, 1990). . . . On disabled list (August 26, 1991-remainder of season).

RECORDS/HONORS: Named Appalachian League Player of the Year (1983). . . . Named California League Most Valuable Player (1984).

STATISTICAL NOTES: Led Appalachian League with 164 total bases, 54 bases on balls received and six intentional bases on balls received in 1983. . . . Led Texas League in being hit by pitch with 10 in 1985.

Year	Team (League)	Pos.	G	AB	R	H	2B	3B	HR	RBI	Avg.	SB	PO	A	E	Avg.
1983	—Paintsville (Appal.)	OF	•73	241	*65	*94	*20	*1	•16	*74	*.390	22	115	8	6	.953
1984	—Stockton (California)	OF	108	399	76	118	29	2	15	86	.296	9	158	4	6	.964
1985	—El Paso (Texas)	OF	117	448	105	139	26	4	20	103	.310	20	239	10	11	.958
1986	—Vancouver (Pac. Coast)....	OF	90	325	80	117	26	6	15	75	.360	22	218	8	2	.991
	—Milwaukee (A.L.)	OF	58	215	19	51	8	2	4	18	.237	1	116	5	12	.910
1987	—Milwaukee (A.L.)	OF	132	505	67	136	28	7	13	77	.269	12	301	6	9	.972
1988	—Milwaukee (A.L.)	OF	72	272	30	71	14	0	10	42	.261	6	134	1	3	.978
1989	—Milwaukee (A.L.)	OF	144	514	77	127	12	3	15	66	.247	17	267	6	8	.972
1990	—Milwaukee (A.L.)	OF	37	113	17	28	5	0	3	13	.248	5	81	1	3	.965
	—Cincinnati (N.L.)■.........	OF	72	201	22	60	9	1	6	28	.299	3	110	10	4	.968
1991	—Cincinnati (N.L.)	OF	85	250	36	65	10	0	11	39	.260	11	139	2	5	.966
	American League totals (5 years)		443	1619	210	413	67	12	45	216	.255	41	899	19	35	.963
	National League totals (2 years)		157	451	58	125	19	1	17	67	.277	14	249	12	9	.967
	Major league totals (6 years)		600	2070	268	538	86	13	62	283	.260	55	1148	31	44	.964

CHAMPIONSHIP SERIES RECORD

Year	Team (League)	Pos.	G	AB	R	H	2B	3B	HR	RBI	Avg.	SB	PO	A	E	Avg.
1990	—Cincinnati (N.L.)	OF	2	5	0	1	0	0	0	0	.200	0	2	0	0	1.000

WORLD SERIES RECORD

Year	Team (League)	Pos.	G	AB	R	H	2B	3B	HR	RBI	Avg.	SB	PO	A	E	Avg.
1990	—Cincinnati (N.L.)	PH-OF	2	4	0	0	0	0	0	2	.000	0	0	0	0	...

BRANSON, JEFF
IF, REDS

PERSONAL: Born January 26, 1967, at Waynesboro, Miss. . . . 6-0/180. . . . Throws left, bats right. . . . Full name: Jeffery Glenn Branson. **HIGH SCHOOL:** Southern Choctaw (Silas, Ala.). **COLLEGE:** Livingston University (Ala.).

TRANSACTIONS/CAREER NOTES: Selected by Cincinnati Reds organization in second round of free-agent draft (June 1, 1988).

Year	Team (League)	Pos.	G	AB	R	H	2B	3B	HR	RBI	Avg.	SB	PO	A	E	Avg.
1989	—Cedar Rapids (Midwest) ...	SS	127	469	70	132	28	1	10	68	.281	5	172	394	33	.945
1990	—Cedar Rapids (Midwest) ...	SS	62	239	37	60	13	4	6	24	.251	11	96	152	7	.973
	—Chattanooga (Southern)...	2B-SS	63	233	19	49	9	1	2	29	.210	3	122	151	13	.955
1991	—Chattanooga (Southern)...	SS-2B	88	304	35	80	13	3	2	28	.263	3	126	212	12	.966
	—Nashville (Am. Assoc.)	SS-2B-OF	43	145	10	35	4	1	0	11	.241	5	61	93	8	.951

BRANTLEY, CLIFF
P, PHILLIES

PERSONAL: Born April 12, 1968, at Staten Island, N.Y. . . . 6-1/190. . . . Throws right, bats right. . . . Full name: Clifford Brantley. **HIGH SCHOOL:** Port Richmond (Staten Island, N.Y.).

TRANSACTIONS/CAREER NOTES: Selected by Philadelphia Phillies organization in second round of free-agent draft (June 2, 1986). . . . On Scranton/Wilkes-Barre disabled list (July 16-August 20, 1991).

STATISTICAL NOTES: Led Florida State League with 20 wild pitches in 1988.

Year	Team (League)	G	W	L	Pct.	ERA	Sv.	IP	H	R	ER	BB	SO
1986	—Utica (New York-Penn)	11	3	5	.375	4.30	0	60⅔	68	37	29	25	42
1987	—Spartanburg (South Atlantic) ..	20	3	10	.231	4.81	0	110⅓	114	69	59	58	86
1988	—Clearwater (Florida State)	24	8	11	.421	2.59	0	166⅔	126	55	48	74	124
	—Reading (Eastern)	1	1	0	1.000	6.00	0	6	5	4	4	2	5
1989	—Reading (Eastern)	11	3	4	.429	3.31	0	49	49	29	18	28	35
	—Clearwater (Florida State)	8	0	5	.000	4.35	0	49⅔	60	31	24	19	33
1990	—Clearwater (Florida State)	8	1	4	.200	2.94	0	49	44	20	16	17	37
	—Reading (Eastern)	17	4	9	.308	4.55	0	87	93	51	44	39	69
1991	—Reading (Eastern)	11	4	3	.571	1.94	0	69⅔	50	17	15	25	51
	—Scranton/Wilkes-Barre (Int'l) ..	8	2	4	.333	3.80	0	47⅓	44	26	20	25	28
	—Philadelphia (N.L.)	6	2	2	.500	3.41	0	31⅔	26	12	12	19	25
	Major league totals (1 year)	6	2	2	.500	3.41	0	31⅔	26	12	12	19	25

BRANTLEY, JEFF
P, GIANTS

PERSONAL: Born September 5, 1963, at Florence, Ala. . . . 5-11/190. . . . Throws right, bats right. . . . Full name: Jeffrey Hoke Brantley.
HIGH SCHOOL: W. A. Berry (Florence, Ala.).
COLLEGE: Mississippi State.
TRANSACTIONS/CAREER NOTES: Selected by Montreal Expos organization in 13th round of free-agent draft (June 4, 1984). . . . Selected by San Francisco Giants organization in sixth round of free-agent draft (June 3, 1985).
STATISTICAL NOTES: Tied for Texas League lead with eight complete games in 1986. . . . Tied for Pacific Coast League lead with 11 hit batsmen in 1987.

Year	Team (League)	G	W	L	Pct.	ERA	Sv.	IP	H	R	ER	BB	SO
1985	Fresno (California)	14	8	2	.800	3.33	0	94⅔	83	39	35	37	85
1986	Shreveport (Texas)	26	8	10	.444	3.48	0	165⅔	139	78	64	68	125
1987	Shreveport (Texas)	2	0	1	.000	3.09	0	11⅔	12	7	4	4	7
	Phoenix (Pacific Coast)	29	6	11	.353	4.65	0	170⅓	187	110	88	82	111
1988	Phoenix (Pacific Coast)	27	9	5	.643	4.33	0	122⅔	130	65	59	39	83
	San Francisco (N.L.)	9	0	1	.000	5.66	1	20⅔	22	13	13	6	11
1989	San Francisco (N.L.)	59	7	1	.875	4.07	0	97⅓	101	50	44	37	69
	Phoenix (Pacific Coast)	7	1	1	.500	1.26	3	14⅓	6	2	2	6	20
1990	San Francisco (N.L.)	55	5	3	.625	1.56	19	86⅔	77	18	15	33	61
1991	San Francisco (N.L.)	67	5	2	.714	2.45	15	95⅓	78	27	26	52	81
Major league totals (4 years)		190	17	7	.708	2.94	35	300	278	108	98	128	222

CHAMPIONSHIP SERIES RECORD

Year	Team (League)	G	W	L	Pct.	ERA	Sv.	IP	H	R	ER	BB	SO
1989	San Francisco (N.L.)	3	0	0	. . .	0.00	0	5	1	0	0	2	3

WORLD SERIES RECORD

Year	Team (League)	G	W	L	Pct.	ERA	Sv.	IP	H	R	ER	BB	SO
1989	San Francisco (N.L.)	3	0	0	. . .	4.15	0	4⅓	5	2	2	3	1

ALL-STAR GAME RECORD

Year	League	W	L	Pct.	ERA	Sv.	IP	H	R	ER	BB	SO
1990	National	0	1	.000	54.00	0	⅓	2	2	2	0	0

BREAM, SID
1B, BRAVES

PERSONAL: Born August 3, 1960, at Carlisle, Pa. . . . 6-4/220. . . . Throws left, bats left. . . . Full name: Sidney Eugene Bream.
HIGH SCHOOL: Carlisle (Pa.).
COLLEGE: Liberty Baptist College (Va.).
TRANSACTIONS/CAREER NOTES: Selected by Los Angeles Dodgers organization in second round of free-agent draft (June 8, 1981). . . . Traded by Dodgers with OF Cecil Espy to Pittsburgh Pirates (September 9, 1985), completing deal in which Dodgers traded 3B Bill Madlock to Dodgers for three players to be named later (August 31, 1985); Pirates acquired OF R.J. Reynolds as partial completion of deal (September 3, 1985). . . . On disabled list (April 16-May 9 and May 29, 1989-remainder of season). . . . Granted free agency (November 5, 1990). . . . Signed by Atlanta Braves (December 5, 1990). . . . On disabled list (June 26-August 2 and August 5-29, 1991).
RECORDS/HONORS: Holds N.L. single-season record for most assists by first baseman—166 (1986).
STATISTICAL NOTES: Led Pacific Coast League first basemen with 1,411 total chances in 1983 and 1,200 in 1984. . . . Led Pacific Coast League first basemen with 106 double plays in 1984. . . . Led N.L. first basemen with 166 assists in 1986. . . . Led N.L. first basemen with 1,503 total chances in 1986. . . . Led N.L. first basemen with 17 errors in 1986.

Year	Team (League)	Pos.	G	AB	R	H	2B	3B	HR	RBI	Avg.	SB	PO	A	E	Avg.
1981	Vero Beach (Florida St.)	1B	70	260	35	85	12	5	1	47	.327	0	613	45	10	.985
1982	Vero Beach (Florida St.)	1B	63	226	41	70	13	5	4	43	.310	1	523	40	5	.991
	San Antonio (Texas)	1B	70	259	43	83	18	0	8	50	.320	0	621	40	12	.982
	Albuquerque (PCL)	1B	3	8	3	3	1	0	1	2	.375	6	11	0	0	1.000
1983	Albuquerque (PCL)	1B	138	485	115	149	23	4	•32	★118	.307	0	1264	★123	24	.983
	Los Angeles (N.L.)	1B	15	11	0	2	0	0	0	2	.182	0	8	0	0	1.000
1984	Albuquerque (PCL)	1B	114	429	82	147	25	4	20	90	.343	1	1071	★143	17	.986
	Los Angeles (N.L.)	1B	27	49	2	9	3	0	0	6	.184	5	95	11	0	1.000
1985	Albuquerque (PCL)	1B-OF	85	297	51	110	25	3	17	57	.370	2	381	51	2	.995
	Los Angeles-Pitts. (N.L.)■	1B	50	148	18	34	7	0	6	21	.230	1	367	35	3	.993
1986	Pittsburgh (N.L.)	1B-OF	154	522	73	140	37	5	16	77	.268	13	1320	†166	†17	.989
1987	Pittsburgh (N.L.)	1B	149	516	64	142	25	3	13	65	.275	13	1236	127	★17	.988
1988	Pittsburgh (N.L.)	1B	148	462	50	122	37	0	10	65	.264	9	1118	★140	6	.995
1989	Pittsburgh (N.L.)	1B	19	36	3	8	3	0	0	4	.222	9	111	7	1	.992
1990	Pittsburgh (N.L.)	1B	147	389	39	105	23	2	15	67	.270	8	971	104	8	.993
1991	Atlanta (N.L.)■	1B	91	265	32	67	12	0	11	45	.253	0	668	50	3	.996
Major league totals (9 years)			800	2398	281	629	147	10	71	352	.262	37	5894	640	55	.992

CHAMPIONSHIP SERIES RECORD

Year	Team (League)	Pos.	G	AB	R	H	2B	3B	HR	RBI	Avg.	SB	PO	A	E	Avg.
1990	Pittsburgh (N.L.)	1B-PH	4	8	1	4	1	0	1	3	.500	0	26	3	0	1.000
1991	Atlanta (N.L.)	1B-PH	4	10	1	3	0	0	1	3	.300	0	19	4	0	1.000
Championship Series totals (2 years)			8	18	2	7	1	0	2	6	.389	0	45	7	0	1.000

WORLD SERIES RECORD

Year	Team (League)	Pos.	G	AB	R	H	2B	3B	HR	RBI	Avg.	SB	PO	A	E	Avg.
1991	Atlanta (N.L.)	1B	7	24	0	3	2	0	0	0	.125		69	7	0	1.000

BRETT, GEORGE
DH/1B, ROYALS

PERSONAL: Born May 15, 1953, at Glen Dale, W.Va. . . . 6-0/205. . . . Throws right, bats left. . . . Full name: George Howard Brett. . . . Brother of Ken Brett, major league pitcher for 10 teams (1967 and 1969-81); brother of John Brett, minor league infielder (1968); and brother of Bob Brett, minor league outfielder (1972).

HIGH SCHOOL: El Segundo (Calif.).

COLLEGE: Longview Community College (Mo.) and El Camino College (Calif.).

TRANSACTIONS/CAREER NOTES: Selected by Kansas City Royals organization in second round of free-agent draft (June 8, 1971). . . . On disabled list (April 29-May 11, 1972; May 4-19 and July 27-August 14, 1978; June 11-July 10, 1980; June 8-29, 1983; April 1-May 18, 1984; April 20-May 13 and May 16-June 12, 1987; April 30-June 10, 1989; and April 26-May 24, 1991).

RECORDS/HONORS: Holds major league single-season record for most consecutive games, three or more hits—6 (May 8-13, 1976). . . . Shares major league record for most home runs, month of October—4 (1985). . . . Holds A.L. career record for most intentional bases on balls received—214. . . . Holds A.L. record for most seasons with 10 or more intentional bases on balls received—11. . . . Holds A.L. single-season record for fewest putouts by third baseman who led league in putouts—140 (1976). . . . Named third baseman on THE SPORTING NEWS A.L. All-Star team (1976, 1979 and 1980). . . . Named Man of the Year by THE SPORTING NEWS (1980). . . . Named Major League Player of the Year by THE SPORTING NEWS (1980). . . . Named A.L. Player of the Year by THE SPORTING NEWS (1980). . . . Named third baseman on THE SPORTING NEWS Silver Slugger team (1980 and 1985). . . . Named A.L. Most Valuable Player by Baseball Writers' Association of America (1980). . . . Won A.L. Gold Glove at third base (1985). . . . Named first baseman on THE SPORTING NEWS A.L. All-Star team (1988). . . . Named first baseman on THE SPORTING NEWS A.L. Silver Slugger team (1988).

STATISTICAL NOTES: Led California League with eight sacrifice hits in 1972. . . . Led California League third basemen with 172 assists and 30 errors in 1972. . . . Tied for A.L. lead in errors by third basemen with 26 in 1975. . . . Led A.L. with 298 total bases in 1976. . . . Led A.L. third basemen with 140 putouts in 1976. . . . Led A.L. third basemen with 373 assists, 30 errors and 532 total chances in 1979. . . . Hit three home runs in a game (July 22, 1979 and April 20, 1983). . . . Led A.L. .461 on base percentage in 1980. . . . Led A.L. with .664 slugging percentage in 1980, .563 in 1983 and .585 in 1985. . . . Led A.L. third basemen with 33 double plays in 1985. . . . Led A.L. with 31 intentional bases on balls received in 1985 and 18 in 1986. . . . Hit for the cycle (May 28, 1979 and July 25, 1990).

Year	Team (League)	Pos.	G	AB	R	H	2B	3B	HR	RBI	Avg.	SB	PO	A	E	Avg.
1971	Billings (Pioneer)	SS-3B	68	258	44	75	8	5	5	44	.291	3	87	140	28	.890
1972	San Jose (California)	3B-SS-2B	117	431	66	118	13	5	10	68	.274	2	101	†213	†30	.913
1973	Omaha (Am. Assoc.)	3B-OF	117	405	66	115	16	4	8	64	.284	3	92	219	26	.923
	Kansas City (A.L.)	3B	13	40	2	5	2	0	0	0	.125	0	9	28	1	.974
1974	Omaha (Am. Assoc.)	3B	16	64	9	17	2	0	2	14	.266	1	8	31	4	.907
	Kansas City (A.L.)	3B-SS	133	457	49	129	21	5	2	47	.282	8	102	279	21	.948
1975	Kansas City (A.L.)	3B-SS	159	*634	84	*195	35	•13	11	89	.308	13	132	356	‡26	.949
1976	Kansas City (A.L.)	3B-SS	159	*645	94	*215	34	*14	7	67	*.333	21	†146	350	26	.950
1977	Kansas City (A.L.)	3B-SS	139	564	105	176	32	13	22	88	.312	14	115	325	21	.954
1978	Kansas City (A.L.)	3B-SS	128	510	79	150	*45	8	9	62	.294	23	104	289	16	.961
1979	Kansas City (A.L.)	3B-1B	154	645	119	*212	42	*20	23	107	.329	17	176	†378	†31	.947
1980	Kansas City (A.L.)	3B-1B	117	449	87	175	33	9	24	118	*.390	15	107	256	17	.955
1981	Kansas City (A.L.)	3B	89	347	42	109	27	7	6	43	.314	14	74	170	14	.946
1982	Kansas City (A.L.)	3B-OF	144	552	101	166	32	9	21	82	.301	6	130	295	17	.962
1983	Kansas City (A.L.)	3B-1B-OF	123	464	90	144	38	2	25	93	.310	0	210	192	25	.941
1984	Kansas City (A.L.)	3B	104	377	42	107	21	3	13	69	.284	0	59	201	14	.949
1985	Kansas City (A.L.)	3B	155	550	108	184	38	5	30	112	.335	9	107	*339	15	.967
1986	Kansas City (A.L.)	3B-SS	124	441	70	128	28	4	16	73	.290	1	97	218	16	.952
1987	Kansas City (A.L.)	1B-SS	115	427	71	124	18	2	22	78	.290	6	805	69	9	.990
1988	Kansas City (A.L.)	1B-SS	157	589	90	180	42	3	24	103	.306	14	1126	70	10	.992
1989	Kansas City (A.L.)	1B-OF	124	457	67	129	26	3	12	80	.282	14	898	80	2	.998
1990	Kansas City (A.L.)	1B-OF-3B	142	544	82	179	*45	7	14	87	*.329	9	880	67	7	.993
1991	Kansas City (A.L.)	1B	131	505	77	129	40	2	10	61	.255	2	87	5	1	.989
Major league totals (19 years)			2410	9197	1459	2836	599	129	291	1459	.308	186	5364	3967	289	.970

DIVISION SERIES RECORD

Year	Team (League)	Pos.	G	AB	R	H	2B	3B	HR	RBI	Avg.	SB	PO	A	E	Avg.
1981	Kansas City (A.L.)	3B	3	12	0	2	0	0	0	0	.167	0	1	6	1	.875

CHAMPIONSHIP SERIES RECORD

CHAMPIONSHIP SERIES NOTES: Holds career records for highest slugging average, 50 or more at-bats—.728; runs—22; triples—4; home runs—9; total bases—75; long hits—18. . . . Holds single-game record for most total bases—12 (October 6, 1978). . . . Shares career record for most game-winning RBIs—3. . . . Shares single-series record for most triples—2 (1977); game-winning RBIs—2 (1985); bases on balls received—7 (1985). . . . Shares single-game record for most runs—4 (October 11, 1985); home runs—3 (October 6, 1978). . . . Holds A.L. single-series record for highest slugging average—1.056 (1978). . . . Shares A.L. single-series record for most home runs—3 (1978 and 1985). . . . Shares A.L. single-game record for most long hits—3 (October 6, 1978 and October 11, 1985).

Year	Team (League)	Pos.	G	AB	R	H	2B	3B	HR	RBI	Avg.	SB	PO	A	E	Avg.
1976	Kansas City (A.L.)	3B	5	18	4	8	1	1	1	5	.444	0	3	7	3	.769
1977	Kansas City (A.L.)	3B	5	20	2	6	0	2	0	2	.300	0	5	12	2	.895

Year	Team (League)	Pos.	G	AB	R	H	2B	3B	HR	RBI	Avg.	SB	PO	A	E	Avg.
1978 — Kansas City (A.L.)		3B	4	18	7	7	1	1	3	3	.389	0	3	8	1	.917
1980 — Kansas City (A.L.)		3B	3	11	3	3	1	0	2	4	.273	0	2	7	0	1.000
1984 — Kansas City (A.L.)		3B	3	13	0	3	0	0	0	0	.231	0	2	7	0	1.000
1985 — Kansas City (A.L.)		3B	7	23	6	8	2	0	3	5	.348	0	7	8	2	.882
Championship Series totals (6 years)			27	103	22	35	5	4	9	19	.340	0	22	49	8	.899

WORLD SERIES RECORD

Year	Team (League)	Pos.	G	AB	R	H	2B	3B	HR	RBI	Avg.	SB	PO	A	E	Avg.
1980 — Kansas City (A.L.)		3B	6	24	3	9	2	1	1	3	.375	1	4	17	1	.955
1985 — Kansas City (A.L.)		3B	7	27	5	10	1	0	0	1	.370	0	10	19	1	.967
World Series totals (2 years)			13	51	8	19	3	1	1	4	.373	1	14	36	2	.962

ALL-STAR GAME RECORD

ALL-STAR GAME NOTES: Holds career record for most sacrifice flies—3. . . . Named to A.L. All-Star team in 1980 game; replaced due to injury. . . . Named to A.L. All-Star team for 1986 game; replaced due to injury by Brook Jacoby. . . . Named to A.L. All-Star team for 1987 game; replaced due to injury by Kevin Seitzer.

Year	League	Pos.	AB	R	H	2B	3B	HR	RBI	Avg.	SB	PO	A	E	Avg.
1976 — American		3B	2	0	0	0	0	0	0	.000	0	0	1	0	1.000
1977 — American		3B	2	0	0	0	0	0	0	.000	0	2	1	0	1.000
1978 — American		3B	3	1	2	1	0	0	2	.667	1	0	2	0	1.000
1979 — American		3B	3	1	0	0	0	0	0	.000	0	1	2	0	1.000
1981 — American		3B	3	0	0	0	0	0	0	.000	0	0	1	0	1.000
1982 — American		3B	2	0	2	0	0	0	0	1.000	0	0	0	0	. . .
1983 — American		3B	4	2	2	1	1	0	1	.500	0	1	5	0	1.000
1984 — American		3B	3	1	1	0	0	1	1	.333	0	3	0	0	1.000
1985 — American		3B	1	0	0	0	0	0	0	.000	0	2	1	0	1.000
1988 — American		PH	1	0	0	0	0	0	0	.000	0	0	0	0	. . .
All-Star Game totals (10 years)			24	5	7	2	1	1	5	.292	1	9	13	0	1.000

BREWER, ROD
1B/OF, CARDINALS

PERSONAL: Born February 24, 1966, at Zellwood, Fla. . . . 6-3/218. . . . Throws left, bats left. . . . Full name: Rodney Lee Brewer.
HIGH SCHOOL: Apopka (Fla.).
COLLEGE: Florida.
TRANSACTIONS/CAREER NOTES: Selected by Toronto Blue Jays organization in 25th round of free-agent draft (June 4, 1984). . . . Selected by St. Louis Cardinals organization in fifth round of free-agent draft (June 2, 1987).
RECORDS/HONORS: Named first baseman on THE SPORTING NEWS college All-America team (1987).
STATISTICAL NOTES: Led Appalachian League first basemen with .990 fielding percentage, 554 putouts, 45 assists and 605 total chances in 1987. . . . Led Appalachian League with five intentional bases on balls received in 1987. . . . Led Midwest League first basemen with 106 double plays in 1988. . . . Led American Association first basemen with 1,153 putouts, 126 assists, 1,292 total chances and 118 double plays in 1990.

Year	Team (League)	Pos.	G	AB	R	H	2B	3B	HR	RBI	Avg.	SB	PO	A	E	Avg.
1987 — Johnson City (Appal.)		1B-OF	67	238	33	60	11	2	10	42	.252	2	†557	†45	6	†.990
1988 — Springfield (Midwest)		1B	133	457	57	136	25	2	8	64	.298	6	★1249	78	10	★.993
1989 — Arkansas (Texas)		1B	128	470	71	130	25	2	10	93	.277	2	1084	97	•12	.990
1990 — Louisville (Am. Assoc.)		1B-P	•144	514	60	129	15	5	12	83	.251	0	†1153	†126	13	.990
— St. Louis (N.L.)		1B	14	25	4	6	1	0	0	2	.240	0	46	6	1	.981
1991 — Louisville (Am. Assoc.)		1B-OF	104	382	39	86	21	1	8	52	.225	4	588	42	3	.995
— St. Louis (N.L.)		1B-OF	19	13	0	1	0	0	0	1	.077	0	30	3	1	.971
Major league totals (2 years)			33	38	4	7	1	0	0	3	.184	0	76	9	2	.977

RECORD AS PITCHER

Year	Team (League)	G	W	L	Pct.	ERA	Sv.	IP	H	R	ER	BB	SO
1990 — Louisville (American Assoc.)	1	0	0	. . .	0.00	0	1	0	0	0	0	0

BRILEY, GREG
OF, MARINERS

PERSONAL: Born May 24, 1965, at Bethel, N.C. . . . 5-8/165. . . . Throws right, bats left. . . . Full name: Gregory Briley.
HIGH SCHOOL: North Pitt (N.C.).
COLLEGE: Louisburg College (N.C.) and North Carolina State.
TRANSACTIONS/CAREER NOTES: Selected by Los Angeles Dodgers organization in third round of free-agent draft (January 9, 1985). . . . Selected by Cleveland Indians organization in secondary phase of free-agent draft (June 3, 1985). . . . Selected by Seattle Mariners organization in secondary phase of free-agent draft (June 2, 1986).

Year	Team (League)	Pos.	G	AB	R	H	2B	3B	HR	RBI	Avg.	SB	PO	A	E	Avg.
1986 — Bellingham (Northwest)		2B	63	218	52	65	12	•4	7	46	.298	26	132	146	24	.921
1987 — Chattanooga (Southern)		2B	137	539	81	148	21	5	7	61	.275	34	221	346	★29	.951
1988 — Calgary (Pacific Coast)		OF-2B	112	445	74	139	29	9	11	66	.312	27	237	132	15	.961

Year	Team (League)	Pos.	G	AB	R	H	2B	3B	HR	RBI	Avg.	SB	PO	A	E	Avg.
	—Seattle (A.L.)	OF	13	36	6	9	2	0	1	4	.250	0	13	0	1	.929
1989	—Seattle (A.L.)	OF-2B	115	394	52	105	22	4	13	52	.266	11	197	38	9	.963
	—Calgary (Pacific Coast)	3B-2B-0F	25	94	27	32	8	1	4	20	.340	14	22	44	5	.930
1990	—Seattle (A.L.)	OF	125	337	40	83	18	2	5	29	.246	16	177	4	2	.989
1991	—Seattle (A.L.)	OF-2B-3B	139	381	39	99	17	3	2	26	.260	23	187	5	4	.980
	Major league totals (4 years)		392	1148	137	296	59	9	21	111	.258	50	574	47	16	.975

BRISCOE, JOHN
P, ATHLETICS

PERSONAL: Born September 22, 1967, at LaGrange, Ill. . . . 6-3/185. . . . Throws right, bats right. . . . Full name: John Eric Briscoe.
HIGH SCHOOL: Berkner (Tex.).
COLLEGE: Texarkana College and Texas Christian.
TRANSACTIONS/CAREER NOTES: Selected by Milwaukee Brewers organization in third round of free-agent draft (January 14, 1986). . . . Selected by Toronto Blue Jays organization in secondary phase of free-agent draft (June 2, 1986). . . . Selected by Oakland Athletics organization in third round of free-agent draft (June 1, 1989).

Year	Team (League)	G	W	L	Pct.	ERA	Sv.	IP	H	R	ER	BB	SO
1988	—Scottsdale (Arizona)	7	1	1	.500	3.51	0	25 2/3	26	14	10	6	23
1989	—Madison (Midwest)	21	7	5	.583	4.21	0	117 2/3	121	66	55	57	69
1990	—Modesto (California)	29	3	6	.333	4.59	4	86 1/3	72	50	44	52	66
	—Huntsville (Southern)	3	0	0	...	13.50	0	4 2/3	9	7	7	7	7
1991	—Huntsville (Southern)	2	2	0	1.000	0.00	0	4 1/3	1	2	0	2	6
	—Oakland (A.L.)	11	0	0	...	7.07	0	14	12	11	11	10	9
	—Tacoma (Pacific Coast)	22	3	5	.375	3.66	1	76 1/3	73	35	31	44	66
	Major league totals (1 year)	11	0	0	...	7.07	0	14	12	11	11	10	9

BROCAIL, DOUG
P, PADRES

PERSONAL: Born May 16, 1967, at Clearfield, Pa. . . . 6-5/220. . . . Throws right, bats left. . . . Full name: Douglas Keith Brocail.
HIGH SCHOOL: Lamar (Colo.).
COLLEGE: Lamar Community College (Colo.).
TRANSACTIONS/CAREER NOTES: Selected by San Diego Padres organization in first round (12th pick overall) of free-agent draft (January 14, 1986).
STATISTICAL NOTES: Tied for Northwest League lead in games started by pitcher with 15 in 1986. . . . Tied for Texas League lead with three shutouts in 1991.

Year	Team (League)	G	W	L	Pct.	ERA	Sv.	IP	H	R	ER	BB	SO
1986	—Spokane (Northwest)	16	5	4	.556	3.81	0	85	85	52	36	53	77
1987	—Charleston, S.C. (S. Atlantic)	19	2	6	.250	4.09	0	92 1/3	94	51	42	28	68
1988	—Charleston, S.C. (S. Atlantic)	22	8	6	.571	2.69	2	107	107	40	32	25	107
1989	—Wichita (Texas)	23	5	9	.357	5.21	0	134 2/3	158	88	78	50	95
1990	—Wichita (Texas)	12	2	2	.500	4.33	0	52	53	30	25	24	27
1991	—Wichita (Texas)	34	10	7	.588	3.87	6	146 1/3	147	77	63	43	108

BROCK, GREG
1B, WHITE SOX

PERSONAL: Born June 14, 1957, at McMinnville, Ore. . . . 6-3/205. . . . Throws right, bats left. . . . Full name: Gregory Allen Brock. . . . Brother of Eric Brock, minor league shortstop (1983-84).
HIGH SCHOOL: Slayton Union (Ore.).
COLLEGE: Wyoming.
TRANSACTIONS/CAREER NOTES: Selected by Los Angeles Dodgers organization in 13th round of free-agent draft (June 5, 1979). . . . On Los Angeles disabled list (May 12-June 7, 1984 and June 19-July 10, 1986). . . . Traded by Dodgers to Milwaukee Brewers for P Tim Leary and P Tim Crews (December 10, 1986). . . . On disabled list (June 12-27, 1987 and June 7-July 23, 1988). . . . On Milwaukee disabled list (April 2-May 31, 1989); included rehabilitation disability assignment to Beloit (May 10-28, 1989). . . . Released by Brewers (July 3, 1991). . . . Signed by Chicago White Sox organization (August 12, 1991).
STATISTICAL NOTES: Led Pioneer League with 54 bases on balls received in 1979. . . . Led Pacific Coast League with 105 bases on balls received and 15 intentional bases on balls received in 1982. . . . Led Pacific Coast League first basemen with 106 double plays in 1982.

Year	Team (League)	Pos.	G	AB	R	H	2B	3B	HR	RBI	Avg.	SB	PO	A	E	Avg.
1979	—Lethbridge (Pioneer)	1B	66	247	61	88	18	2	16	77	.356	7	543	*36	8	*.986
1980	—Lodi (California)	1B	121	418	72	125	19	3	*29	95	.299	3	906	*79	5	*.995
1981	—San Antonio (Texas)	1B	128	499	86	147	25	3	*32	106	.295	3	1071	*90	9	.992
1982	—Albuquerque (PCL)	1B	135	480	118	149	21	8	44	138	.310	4	*1076	*106	*20	.983
	—Los Angeles (N.L.)	1B	18	17	1	2	1	0	0	1	.118	0	9	0	0	1.000
1983	—Los Angeles (N.L.)	1B	146	455	64	102	14	2	20	66	.224	5	1162	106	12	.991
1984	—Los Angeles (N.L.)	1B	88	271	33	61	6	0	14	34	.225	8	703	65	4	.995
	—Albuquerque (PCL)	1B-3B	24	93	19	29	7	0	6	15	.312	2	134	38	11	.940
1985	—Los Angeles (N.L.)	1B	129	438	64	110	19	0	21	66	.251	4	1113	84	7	.994
1986	—Los Angeles (N.L.)	1B	115	325	33	76	13	0	16	52	.234	2	726	87	3	.996
1987	—Milwaukee (A.L.)■	1B	141	532	81	159	29	3	13	85	.299	5	1065	109	8	.993
1988	—Milwaukee (A.L.)	1B	115	364	53	77	16	1	6	50	.212	6	915	102	7	.993
1989	—Beloit (Midwest)	1B	16	52	10	18	2	0	2	10	.346	2	80	8	2	.978
	—Milwaukee (A.L.)	1B	107	373	40	99	16	0	12	52	.265	6	850	58	5	.995

Year	Team (League)	Pos.	G	AB	R	H	2B	3B	HR	RBI	Avg.	SB	PO	A	E	Avg.
1990 — Milwaukee (A.L.)		1B	123	367	42	91	23	0	7	50	.248	4	885	63	5	.995
1991 — Milwaukee (A.L.)		1B	31	60	9	17	4	0	1	6	.283	1	150	10	0	1.000
— Vancouver (Pac. Coast)■..		1B	2	7	0	1	0	0	0	0	.143	0	5	1	0	1.000
American League totals (5 years)			517	1696	225	443	88	4	39	243	.261	22	3865	342	25	.994
National League totals (5 years)			496	1506	195	351	53	2	71	219	.233	19	3713	342	26	.994
Major league totals (10 years)			1013	3202	420	794	141	6	110	462	.248	41	7578	684	51	.994

CHAMPIONSHIP SERIES RECORD

Year	Team (League)	Pos.	G	AB	R	H	2B	3B	HR	RBI	Avg.	SB	PO	A	E	Avg.
1983 — Los Angeles (N.L.)		1B	3	9	1	0	0	0	0	0	.000	0	13	0	0	1.000
1985 — Los Angeles (N.L.)		1B-PH	5	12	2	1	0	0	1	2	.083	0	35	4	0	1.000
Championship Series totals (2 years)			8	21	3	1	0	0	1	2	.048	0	48	4	0	1.000

BROGNA, RICO

1B, TIGERS

PERSONAL: Born April 18, 1970, at Turner Falls, Mass. . . . 6-2/190. . . . Throws left, bats left. . . . Full name: Rico Joseph Brogna.
HIGH SCHOOL: Watertown (Conn.).
TRANSACTIONS/CAREER NOTES: Selected by Detroit Tigers organization in first round (26th pick overall) of free-agent draft (June 1, 1988).
STATISTICAL NOTES: Led Eastern League first basemen with 1,261 total chances and 117 double plays in 1990.

Year	Team (League)	Pos.	G	AB	R	H	2B	3B	HR	RBI	Avg.	SB	PO	A	E	Avg.
1988 — Bristol (Appalachian)		1B-OF	60	209	37	53	11	2	7	33	.254	3	319	26	6	.983
1989 — Lakeland (Florida State)		1B	128	459	47	108	20	7	5	51	.235	2	1098	83	13	.989
1990 — London (Eastern)		1B	137	488	70	128	21	3	*21	•77	.262	1	*1155	*93	13	.990
1991 — Toledo (International)		1B	41	132	13	29	6	1	2	13	.220	2	311	37	5	.986
— London (Eastern)		1B-OF	77	293	40	80	13	1	13	51	.273	0	368	46	6	.986

BROOKS, HUBIE

OF, ANGELS

PERSONAL: Born September 24, 1956, at Los Angeles. . . . 6-0/205. . . . Throws right, bats right. . . . Full name: Hubert Brooks. . . . Cousin of Donnie Moore, major league pitcher for five teams (1975 and 1977-88).
HIGH SCHOOL: Dominguez (Los Angeles).
COLLEGE: Mesa Community College (Ariz.) and Arizona State (bachelor of science degree in health science).
TRANSACTIONS/CAREER NOTES: Selected by Montreal Expos organization in 19th round of free-agent draft (June 5, 1974). . . . Selected by Kansas City Royals organization in secondary phase of free-agent draft (January 7, 1976). . . . Selected by Chicago White Sox organization in secondary phase of free-agent draft (June 8, 1976). . . . Selected by Oakland Athletics organization in secondary phase of free-agent draft (January 11, 1977). . . . Selected by White Sox organization in secondary phase of free-agent draft (June 7, 1977). . . . Selected by New York Mets organization in first round (third pick overall) of free-agent draft (June 6, 1978). . . . On disabled list (June 28-July 22, 1982). . . . Traded by Mets with C Mike Fitzgerald, OF Herm Winningham and P Floyd Youmans to Montreal Expos for C Gary Carter (December 10, 1984). . . . On disabled list (August 2, 1986-remainder of season and April 11-May 25, 1987). . . . Granted free agency (November 13, 1989). . . . Signed by Los Angeles Dodgers (December 21, 1989). . . . Traded by Dodgers to Mets for P Bob Ojeda and P Greg Hansell (December 15, 1990). . . . On disabled list (August 19, 1991-remainder of season). . . . Traded by Mets to California Angels for OF Dave Gallagher (December 10, 1991).
RECORDS/HONORS: Named outfielder on THE SPORTING NEWS college All-America team (1977). . . . Named shortstop on THE SPORTING NEWS college All-America team (1978). . . . Named shortstop on THE SPORTING NEWS N.L. Silver Slugger team (1985-86).
STATISTICAL NOTES: Led N.L. third basemen with 21 errors in 1981.

Year	Team (League)	Pos.	G	AB	R	H	2B	3B	HR	RBI	Avg.	SB	PO	A	E	Avg.
1978 — Jackson (Texas)	SS-OF-3B		45	153	19	33	8	1	3	16	.216	3	49	84	14	.905
1979 — Jackson (Texas)	3B-SS		112	406	68	124	21	2	3	28	.305	14	92	218	29	.914
— Tidewater (Int'l)	SS-3B-OF		5	15	1	6	1	0	1	3	.400	0	4	8	1	.923
1980 — Tidewater (Int'l)	OF-3B-SS		113	417	50	124	18	5	3	50	.297	14	152	90	18	.931
— New York (N.L.)	3B		24	81	8	25	2	1	1	10	.309	1	16	40	2	.966
1981 — New York (N.L.)	3B-OF-SS		98	358	34	110	21	2	4	38	.307	9	67	193	†21	.925
1982 — New York (N.L.)	3B		126	457	40	114	21	2	2	40	.249	6	89	237	24	.931
1983 — New York (N.L.)	3B-2B		150	586	53	147	18	4	5	58	.251	6	116	303	21	.952
1984 — New York (N.L.)	3B-SS		153	561	61	159	23	2	16	73	.283	6	112	284	29	.932
1985 — Montreal (N.L.)■	SS		156	605	67	163	34	7	13	100	.269	6	203	441	28	.958
1986 — Montreal (N.L.)	SS		80	306	50	104	18	5	14	58	.340	4	116	222	15	.958
1987 — Montreal (N.L.)	SS		112	430	57	113	22	3	14	72	.263	4	131	271	20	.953
1988 — Montreal (N.L.)	OF		151	588	61	164	35	2	20	90	.279	7	261	8	9	.968
1989 — Montreal (N.L.)	OF		148	542	56	145	30	1	14	70	.268	6	234	6	9	.964
1990 — Los Angeles (N.L.)■	OF		153	568	74	151	28	1	20	91	.266	2	255	9	10	.964
1991 — New York (N.L.)	OF		103	357	48	85	11	1	16	50	.238	3	166	6	5	.972
Major league totals (12 years)			1454	5439	609	1480	263	31	139	750	.272	60	1766	2020	193	.951

ALL-STAR GAME RECORD

Year	League	Pos.	AB	R	H	2B	3B	HR	RBI	Avg.	SB	PO	A	E	Avg.
1986 — National		PH-SS	2	1	0	0	0	0	0	.000	0	1	0	0	1.000
1987 — National		SS	3	1	1	0	0	0	0	.333	0	1	2	0	1.000
All-Star Game totals (2 years)			5	2	1	0	0	0	0	.200	0	2	2	0	1.000

BROSIUS, SCOTT
2B/OF/3B, ATHLETICS

PERSONAL: Born August 15, 1966, at Hillsboro, Ore. . . . 6-1/185. . . . Throws right, bats right. . . . Full name: Scott David Brosius.
HIGH SCHOOL: Rex Putnam (Milwaukie, Ore.).
COLLEGE: Linfield College (Ore.).
TRANSACTIONS/CAREER NOTES: Selected by Oakland Athletics organization in 20th round of free-agent draft (June 2, 1987). . . . On Tacoma disabled list (April 17-May 29, 1991).
STATISTICAL NOTES: Led Northwest League with seven sacrifice flies in 1987. . . . Led Southern League with 274 total bases in 1990.

Year	Team (League)	Pos.	G	AB	R	H	2B	3B	HR	RBI	Avg.	SB	PO	A	E	Avg.
1987 — Medford (Northwest)		IF-P	65	255	34	73	18	1	3	49	.286	5	123	148	38	.877
1988 — Madison (Midwest)		S-3-0-1	132	504	82	153	28	2	9	58	.304	13	151	305	61	.882
1989 — Huntsville (Southern)		2-3-S-1	128	461	68	125	22	2	7	60	.271	4	225	316	34	.941
1990 — Huntsville (Southern)		SS-2B-3B	•142	547	94	*162	*39	2	23	88	.296	12	253	419	41	.942
— Tacoma (Pacific Coast)		2B	3	7	2	1	0	1	0	0	.143	0	3	5	0	1.000
1991 — Tacoma (Pacific Coast)		3B-SS-2B	65	245	28	70	16	3	8	31	.286	4	49	168	14	.939
— Oakland (A.L.)		2B-OF-3B	36	68	9	16	5	0	2	4	.235	3	31	16	0	1.000
Major league totals (1 year)			36	68	9	16	5	0	2	4	.235	3	31	16	0	1.000

RECORD AS PITCHER

Year	Team (League)	G	W	L	Pct.	ERA	Sv.	IP	H	R	ER	BB	SO
1987 — Medford (Northwest)		1	0	0	. . .	0.00	0	2	0	0	0	0	1

BROSS, TERRY
P, METS

PERSONAL: Born March 30, 1966, at El Paso, Tex. . . . 6-9/230. . . . Throws right, bats right. . . . Full name: Terrence Paul Bross.
HIGH SCHOOL: Immaculata (Somerville, N.J.).
COLLEGE: St. John's.
TRANSACTIONS/CAREER NOTES: Selected by New York Mets organization in 13th round of free-agent draft (June 2, 1987). . . . On disabled list (May 31-June 29, 1989). . . . On Tidewater disabled list (April 10-April 17, 1991).

Year	Team (League)	G	W	L	Pct.	ERA	Sv.	IP	H	R	ER	BB	SO
1987 — Little Falls (New York-Penn)		10	2	0	1.000	3.86	0	28	22	23	12	20	21
1988 — Little Falls (New York-Penn)		20	2	1	.667	3.09	1	55 1/3	43	25	19	38	59
1989 — St. Lucie (Florida State)		35	8	2	•.800	2.79	11	58	39	21	18	26	47
1990 — Jackson (Texas)		58	3	4	.429	2.64	*28	71 2/3	46	21	21	40	51
1991 — Tidewater (International)		27	2	0	1.000	4.36	2	33	31	21	16	32	23
— Williamsport (Eastern)		20	2	0	1.000	2.49	5	25 1/3	13	12	7	11	27
— New York (N.L.)		8	0	0	. . .	1.80	0	10	7	2	2	3	5
Major league totals (1 year)		8	0	0	. . .	1.80	0	10	7	2	2	3	5

BROWN, JARVIS
OF, TWINS

PERSONAL: Born March 26, 1967, at Waukegan, Ill. . . . 5-7/177. . . . Throws right, bats right. . . . Full name: Jarvis Ardel Brown.
HIGH SCHOOL: St. Joseph (Kenosha, Wis.).
COLLEGE: Triton (Ill.).
TRANSACTIONS/CAREER NOTES: Selected by Minnesota Twins organization in first round (ninth pick overall) of free-agent draft (January 14, 1986).
STATISTICAL NOTES: Led Midwest League outfielders with 334 total chances in 1988. . . . Led California League outfielders with seven double plays in 1989. . . . Tied for Southern League lead in double plays by outfielder with four in 1990.

Year	Team (League)	Pos.	G	AB	R	H	2B	3B	HR	RBI	Avg.	SB	PO	A	E	Avg.
1986 — Elizabethton (Appal.)		2B-OF-SS	49	180	28	41	4	0	3	23	.228	15	90	107	17	.921
1987 — Kenosha (Midwest)		2B-OF	43	117	22	37	4	1	3	16	.316	6	74	82	15	.912
— Elizabethton (Appal.)		OF	67	258	52	63	9	1	1	15	.244	30	106	6	*16	.875
1988 — Kenosha (Midwest)		OF	138	531	*108	*156	25	7	7	45	.294	72	311	15	8	.976
1989 — Visalia (California)		OF	141	545	*95	131	21	6	4	46	.240	49	291	16	6	.981
1990 — Orlando (Southern)		OF	135	527	*104	137	22	7	14	57	.260	33	316	12	10	.970
1991 — Portland (Pacific Coast)		OF	108	436	62	126	5	8	3	37	.289	27	243	11	4	.984
— Minnesota (A.L.)		OF	38	37	10	8	0	0	0	0	.216	7	21	0	1	.955
Major league totals (1 year)			38	37	10	8	0	0	0	0	.216	7	21	0	1	.955

CHAMPIONSHIP SERIES RECORD

Year	Team (League)	Pos.	G	AB	R	H	2B	3B	HR	RBI	Avg.	SB	PO	A	E	Avg.
1991 — Minnesota (A.L.)		PR-DH	1	0	1	0	0	0	0	0	. . .	0	0	0	0	. . .

Year	Team (League)	Pos.	G	AB	R	H	2B	3B	HR	RBI	Avg.	SB	PO	A	E	Avg.
1991—Minnesota (A.L.)	....	O-PH-PR	3	2	0	0	0	0	0	0	.000	0	0	0	0	...

BROWN, KEITH
P, REDS

PERSONAL: Born February 14, 1964, at Flagstaff, Ariz. . . . 6-4/210. . . . Throws right, bats both. . . . Full name: Keith Edward Brown.
HIGH SCHOOL: Central Valley (Calif.).
COLLEGE: College of the Siskiyous (Calif.) and Cal State Sacramento.
TRANSACTIONS/CAREER NOTES: Selected by Cincinnati Reds organization in 21st round of free-agent draft (June 2, 1986).

Year	Team (League)	G	W	L	Pct.	ERA	Sv.	IP	H	R	ER	BB	SO
1986—Sarasota Reds (Gulf Coast)		7	4	1	.800	.95	0	47⅓	29	15	5	5	26
—Billings (Pioneer)		4	2	0	1.000	2.11	0	21⅓	18	6	5	7	14
—Vermont (Eastern)		4	1	1	.500	5.14	0	14	12	10	8	8	11
1987—Cedar Rapids (Midwest)		17	13	4	.765	*1.59	0	124⅓	91	28	22	27	86
1988—Chattanooga (Southern)		10	9	1	.900	1.42	0	69⅔	47	11	11	20	34
—Nashville (American Assoc.)		12	6	3	.667	1.90	0	85⅓	72	33	18	28	43
—Cincinnati (N.L.)		4	2	1	.667	2.76	0	16⅓	14	5	5	4	6
1989—Nashville (American Assoc.)		29	8	13	.381	4.80	0	161⅓	171	99	86	51	85
1990—Nashville (American Assoc.)		39	7	8	.467	2.39	9	94⅓	83	37	25	24	50
—Cincinnati (N.L.)		8	0	0	...	4.76	0	11⅓	12	6	6	3	8
1991—Nashville (American Assoc.)		47	2	5	.286	3.48	16	62	64	26	24	32	53
—Cincinnati (N.L.)		11	0	0	...	2.25	0	12	15	4	3	6	4
Major league totals (3 years)		23	2	1	.667	3.18	0	39⅔	41	15	14	13	18

BROWN, KEVIN
P, RANGERS

PERSONAL: Born March 14, 1965, at McIntyre, Ga. . . . 6-4/195. . . . Throws right, bats right. . . . Full name: James Kevin Brown.
HIGH SCHOOL: Wilkinson County (Irwinton, Ga.).
COLLEGE: Georgia Tech.
TRANSACTIONS/CAREER NOTES: Selected by Texas Rangers organization in first round (fourth pick overall) of free-agent draft (June 2, 1986). . . . On disabled list (August 14-29, 1990).
RECORDS/HONORS: Named as righthanded pitcher on THE SPORTING NEWS college All-America team (1986).
STATISTICAL NOTES: Tied for A.L. lead with 13 hit batsmen in 1991.
MISCELLANEOUS: Made an out in only appearance as pinch-hitter (1990).

Year	Team (League)	G	W	L	Pct.	ERA	Sv.	IP	H	R	ER	BB	SO
1986—Sarasota Rangers (GCL)		3	0	0	...	6.00	0	6	7	4	4	2	1
—Tulsa (Texas)		3	0	0	...	4.50	0	10	9	7	5	5	10
—Texas (A.L.)		1	1	0	1.000	3.60	0	5	6	2	2	0	4
1987—Tulsa (Texas)		8	1	4	.200	7.29	0	42	53	36	34	18	26
—Oklahoma City (Am. Assoc.)......		5	0	5	.000	10.73	0	24⅓	32	32	29	17	9
—Port Charlotte (Florida State) ...		6	0	2	.000	2.72	0	36⅓	33	14	11	17	21
1988—Tulsa (Texas)		26	12	10	.545	3.51	0	174⅓	174	94	68	61	118
—Texas (A.L.)		4	1	1	.500	4.24	0	23⅓	33	15	11	8	12
1989—Texas (A.L.)		28	12	9	.571	3.35	0	191	167	81	71	70	104
1990—Texas (A.L.)		26	12	10	.545	3.60	0	180	175	84	72	60	88
1991—Texas (A.L.)		33	9	12	.429	4.40	0	210⅔	233	116	103	90	96
Major league totals (5 years)		92	35	32	.522	3.82	0	610	614	298	259	228	304

BROWN, KEVIN
P, BREWERS

PERSONAL: Born March 5, 1966, at Oroville, Calif. . . . 6-1/185. . . . Throws left, bats left. . . . Full name: Kevin Dewayne Brown.
HIGH SCHOOL: Oroville (Calif.).
COLLEGE: Sacramento City College (Calif.).
TRANSACTIONS/CAREER NOTES: Selected by Kansas City Royals organization in fourth round of free-agent draft (January 9, 1985). . . . Selected by Philadelphia Phillies organization in secondary phase of free-agent draft (June 3, 1985). . . . Selected by Atlanta Braves organization in secondary phase of free-agent draft (January 14, 1986). . . . Traded by Braves organization to New York Mets (December 8, 1987), completing deal in which Atlanta Braves acquired OF Terry Blocker for a player to be named later (November 11, 1987). . . . Traded by Mets with P Julio Machado to Milwaukee Brewers (September 7, 1990) as partial completion of deal in which Brewers traded C Charlie O'Brien and a player to be named later to Mets for two players to be named later (August 30, 1990); Mets acquired P Kevin Carmody to complete deal (September 11, 1990). . . . On Denver disabled list (August 2-16, 1991).

Year	Team (League)	G	W	L	Pct.	ERA	Sv.	IP	H	R	ER	BB	SO
1986—Idaho Falls (Pioneer)		12	3	6	.333	5.03	0	68	65	48	38	41	44
1987—Sumter (South Atlantic)		9	7	1	.875	1.93	0	56	53	14	12	19	45
—Durham (Carolina)		13	4	4	.500	5.20	0	72⅔	78	46	42	42	48
1988—St. Lucie (Florida State)■.........		20	5	7	.417	*1.81	0	134	96	42	27	37	113
—Jackson (Texas)		5	1	2	.333	2.20	0	32⅔	24	9	8	11	24
1989—Jackson (Texas)		8	5	2	.714	2.26	0	51⅔	51	15	13	11	40
—Tidewater (International)		13	6	6	.500	4.44	0	75	81	41	37	31	46

Year	Team (League)	G	W	L	Pct.	ERA	Sv.	IP	H	R	ER	BB	SO
1990	—Tidewater (International)	26	10	6	.625	3.55	0	134⅓	138	71	53	60	109
	—New York (N.L.)	2	0	0	...	0.00	0	2	2	0	0	1	0
	—Milwaukee (A.L.)■..................	5	1	1	.500	2.57	0	21	14	7	6	7	12
1991	—Milwaukee (A.L.)	15	2	4	.333	5.51	0	63⅔	66	39	39	34	30
	—Denver (American Assoc.)	12	4	3	.571	4.67	0	61⅔	71	36	32	34	31
American League totals (2 years)		20	3	5	.375	4.78	0	84⅔	80	46	45	41	42
National League totals (1 year)		2	0	0	...	0.00	0	2	2	0	0	1	0
Major league totals (2 years)		22	3	5	.375	4.67	0	86⅔	82	46	45	42	42

BROWNE, JERRY

2B, INDIANS

PERSONAL: Born February 13, 1966, at St. Croix, Virgin Islands. . . . 5-10/170. . . . Throws right, bats both.
HIGH SCHOOL: Central (Killshill, Va.).
TRANSACTIONS/CAREER NOTES: Signed as free agent by Texas Rangers organization (March 3, 1983). . . . On disabled list (August 24-September 8, 1987). . . . Traded by Rangers with 1B Pete O'Brien and OF Oddibe McDowell to Cleveland Indians for 2B Julio Franco (December 6, 1988).
RECORDS/HONORS: Holds A.L. single-season record for fewest double plays by second baseman (150 or more games)—67 (1989).
STATISTICAL NOTES: Led Carolina League second basemen with 675 total chances in 1985. . . . Led Texas League second basemen with .984 fielding percentage in 1986.

							—BATTING—							—FIELDING—			
Year	Team (League)	Pos.	G	AB	R	H	2B	3B	HR	RBI	Avg.	SB	PO	A	E	Avg.
1983	—Sarasota Rangers (GCL)...	2B	48	181	34	51	2	2	0	20	.282	8	92	123	14	.939
1984	—Burlington (Midwest)	SS-2B	127	420	70	99	10	1	0	18	.236	31	231	311	43	.926
1985	—Salem (Carolina)	2B	122	460	69	123	18	4	3	58	.267	24	★265	★390	20	.970
1986	—Tulsa (Texas)	2B-SS	128	491	82	149	15	7	2	57	.303	39	282	307	19	†.969
	—Texas (A.L.)	2B	12	24	6	10	2	0	0	3	.417	0	9	15	2	.923
1987	—Texas (A.L.)	2B	132	454	63	123	16	6	1	38	.271	27	258	338	12	.980
1988	—Oklahoma City (A.A.)	2B	76	286	45	72	15	2	5	34	.252	14	190	231	10	.977
	—Texas (A.L.)	2B	73	214	26	49	9	2	1	17	.229	7	112	139	11	.958
1989	—Cleveland (A.L.)■	2B	153	598	83	179	31	4	5	45	.299	14	305	380	15	.979
1990	—Cleveland (A.L.)	2B	140	513	92	137	26	5	6	50	.267	12	286	382	10	.985
1991	—Cleveland (A.L.)	2-0-3	107	290	28	66	5	2	1	29	.228	2	113	141	14	.948
Major league totals (6 years)			617	2093	298	564	89	19	14	182	.269	62	1083	1395	64	.975

BROWNING, TOM

P, REDS

PERSONAL: Born April 28, 1960, at Casper, Wyo. . . . 6-1/195. . . . Throws left, bats left. . . . Full name: Thomas Leo Browning.
HIGH SCHOOL: Franklin Academy (Malone, N.Y.).
COLLEGE: Tennessee Wesleyan College and Le Moyne College (N.Y.).
TRANSACTIONS/CAREER NOTES: Selected by Cincinnati Reds organization in ninth round of free-agent draft (June 7, 1982). . . . Granted free agency (November 5, 1990). . . . Re-signed by Reds (November 21, 1990).
RECORDS/HONORS: Named N.L. Rookie Pitcher of the Year by THE SPORTING NEWS (1985).
STATISTICAL NOTES: Pitched seven-inning, 2-0 no-hit victory against Iowa (July 31, 1984). . . . Tied for American Association lead with 24 home runs allowed in 1984. . . . Pitched 1-0 perfect game against Los Angeles Dodgers (September 16, 1988). . . . Led N.L. with 36 home runs allowed in 1988, 31 in 1989 and 32 in 1991. . . . Led N.L. pitchers with 37 games started in 1989 and tied for lead with 39 in 1986, 36 in 1988 and 35 in 1990.

Year	Team (League)	G	W	L	Pct.	ERA	Sv.	IP	H	R	ER	BB	SO
1982	—Billings (Pioneer).......................	14	4	●8	.333	3.89	0	88	96	53	38	41	★87
1983	—Tampa (Florida State)...............	11	8	1	.889	1.49	0	78⅔	53	19	13	36	101
	—Waterbury (Eastern)...............	18	4	10	.286	3.53	0	117⅓	100	62	46	63	101
1984	—Wichita (American Assoc.)	30	12	10	.545	3.95	0	189⅓	169	88	83	73	★160
	—Cincinnati (N.L.)	3	1	0	1.000	1.54	0	23⅓	27	4	4	5	14
1985	—Cincinnati (N.L.)	38	20	9	.690	3.55	0	261⅓	242	111	103	73	155
1986	—Cincinnati (N.L.)	39	14	13	.519	3.81	0	243⅓	225	123	103	70	147
1987	—Cincinnati (N.L.)	32	10	13	.435	5.02	0	183	201	107	102	61	117
	—Nashville (American Assoc.)....	5	2	3	.400	6.07	0	29⅔	37	22	20	12	28
1988	—Cincinnati (N.L.)	36	18	5	.783	3.41	0	250⅔	205	98	95	64	124
1989	—Cincinnati (N.L.)	37	15	12	.556	3.39	0	249⅔	241	109	94	64	118
1990	—Cincinnati (N.L.)	35	15	9	.625	3.80	0	227⅔	235	98	96	52	99
1991	—Cincinnati (N.L.)	36	14	14	.500	4.18	0	230⅓	241	★124	★107	56	115
Major league totals (8 years)		256	107	75	.588	3.80	0	1669⅓	1617	774	704	445	889

CHAMPIONSHIP SERIES RECORD

Year	Team (League)	G	W	L	Pct.	ERA	Sv.	IP	H	R	ER	BB	SO
1990	—Cincinnati (N.L.)	2	1	1	.500	3.27	0	11	9	4	4	6	5

WORLD SERIES RECORD

Year	Team (League)	G	W	L	Pct.	ERA	Sv.	IP	H	R	ER	BB	SO
1990	—Cincinnati (N.L.)	1	1	0	1.000	4.50	0	6	6	3	3	2	2

Year	League	W	L	Pct.	ERA	Sv.	IP	H	R	ER	BB	SO
1991—National						Did not play						

BRUETT, J.T.
OF, TWINS

PERSONAL: Born October 8, 1967, at Milwaukee. . . . 5-11/175. . . . Throws left, bats left. . . . Full name: Joseph Timothy Bruett.
HIGH SCHOOL: Oconomowoc (Wis.).
COLLEGE: Minnesota.
TRANSACTIONS/CAREER NOTES: Selected by Minnesota Twins organization in 11th round of free-agent draft (June 1, 1988).
STATISTICAL NOTES: Led Midwest League in caught stealing with 27 in 1989. . . . Tied for Midwest League lead in double plays by outfielder with five in 1989.

							BATTING							FIELDING			
Year	Team (League)	Pos.	G	AB	R	H	2B	3B	HR	RBI	Avg.	SB	PO	A	E	Avg.
1988—Elizabethton (Appal.)		OF	28	91	23	27	3	0	0	3	.297	17	53	2	2	.965
—Kenosha (Midwest)		OF	3	10	2	2	0	0	0	0	.200	1	6	1	0	1.000
1989—Kenosha (Midwest)		OF	120	445	82	119	9	1	3	29	.267	★61	234	10	3	★.988
1990—Visalia (California)		OF	123	437	86	134	15	3	1	33	.307	50	268	13	4	.986
—Portland (Pacific Coast) ...		OF	10	34	8	8	2	0	0	3	.235	2	20	0	0	1.000
1991—Portland (Pacific Coast) ...		OF	99	345	51	98	6	3	0	35	.284	21	211	10	2	.991

BRUMFIELD, JACOB
OF, REDS

PERSONAL: Born May 27, 1965, at Bogalusa, La. . . . 6-0/170. . . . Throws right, bats right. . . . Full name: Jacob Donnell Brumfield.
HIGH SCHOOL: Hammond (La.).
TRANSACTIONS/CAREER NOTES: Selected by Chicago Cubs organization in seventh round of free-agent draft (June 6, 1983). . . . On disabled list (June 21, 1984-remainder of season). . . . Released by Cubs organization (April 9, 1985). . . . Signed by Kansas City Royals organization (August 16, 1986). . . . Granted free agency (October 15, 1991). . . . Signed by Cincinnati Reds organization (November 12, 1991).
STATISTICAL NOTES: Led American Association in caught stealing with 16 in 1991.

							BATTING							FIELDING			
Year	Team (League)	Pos.	G	AB	R	H	2B	3B	HR	RBI	Avg.	SB	PO	A	E	Avg.
1983—Pikeville (Appalachian)		OF	42	113	17	29	0	1	3	15	.257	8	34	3	5	.881
1984—							Did not play									
1985—							Did not play									
1986—Fort Myers (Florida St.)■..		SS	12	41	3	13	3	1	1	5	.317	0	18	16	8	.810
1987—Fort Myers (Florida St.) ...		OF-3B	114	379	56	93	14	★10	6	34	.245	43	235	53	19	.938
—Memphis (Southern)		OF	9	39	7	13	3	2	1	6	.333	2	35	0	2	.946
1988—Memphis (Southern)		OF	128	433	70	98	15	5	6	28	.226	47	239	2	6	.976
1989—Memphis (Southern)		OF	104	346	43	79	14	2	1	25	.228	28	217	2	8	.965
1990—Baseball City (Fla. St.)		OF	109	372	66	125	24	3	0	40	★.336	47	186	★17	8	.962
—Omaha (Am. Assoc.)		OF	24	77	10	25	6	1	2	11	.325	10	45	3	0	1.000
1991—Omaha (Am. Assoc.)		OF	111	397	62	106	14	7	3	43	.267	★36	227	10	2	.992

BRUMLEY, MIKE
SS/3B, RED SOX

PERSONAL: Born April 9, 1963, at Oklahoma City. . . . 5-10/175. . . . Throws right, bats both. . . . Full name: Anthony Michael Brumley. . . . Son of Mike Brumley, catcher, Washington Senators (1964-66).
HIGH SCHOOL: Union (Broken Arrow, Okla.).
COLLEGE: Texas.
TRANSACTIONS/CAREER NOTES: Selected by Philadelphia Phillies organization in 16th round of free-agent draft (June 3, 1980). . . . Selected by Boston Red Sox organization in second round of free-agent draft (June 6, 1983). . . . Traded by Red Sox organization with P Dennis Eckersley to Chicago Cubs for 1B-OF Bill Buckner (May 25, 1984). . . . Traded by Cubs with IF Keith Moreland to San Diego Padres for P Rich Gossage and P Ray Hayward (February 12, 1988). . . . Traded by Padres organization to Detroit Tigers for IF Luis Salazar (March 23, 1989). . . . Traded by Tigers organization to Baltimore Orioles for DH Larry Sheets (January 10, 1990). . . . Released by Orioles (April 3, 1990). . . . Signed by Seattle Mariners (April 6, 1990). . . . On Seattle disabled list (June 6-July 11, 1990); included rehabilitation disability assignment to Calgary (July 4-11, 1990). . . . Released by Mariners (September 27, 1990). . . . Signed by Pawtucket, Red Sox organization (January 23, 1991).
STATISTICAL NOTES: Led American Association shortstops with 597 total chances in 1986.

							BATTING							FIELDING			
Year	Team (League)	Pos.	G	AB	R	H	2B	3B	HR	RBI	Avg.	SB	PO	A	E	Avg.
1983—Winter Haven (Fla. St.)		SS-OF	44	153	25	48	6	4	1	18	.314	4	51	92	20	.877
1984—New Britain (Eastern)		OF-SS	34	121	14	28	6	2	0	9	.231	3	71	6	6	.928
—Midland (Texas)■............		OF	73	255	37	55	11	3	6	21	.216	5	128	4	5	.964
1985—Pittsfield (Eastern)		SS-OF	131	460	66	127	23	★14	3	58	.276	29	182	333	33	.940
1986—Iowa (American Assoc.)		SS	139	458	74	103	21	5	10	44	.225	35	177	★400	20	.966
1987—Iowa (American Assoc.) ...	SS-2B-OF	92	319	44	81	20	5	6	42	.254	27	147	240	24	.942
—Chicago (N.L.)		SS-2B	39	104	8	21	2	2	1	9	.202	9	43	93	5	.965
1988—Las Vegas (Pac. Coast)■..		S-O-3-2	113	425	77	134	16	7	3	41	.315	41	139	322	28	.943
1989—Detroit (A.L.)■		S-2-3-0	92	212	33	42	5	2	1	11	.198	8	80	160	12	.952
—Toledo (International)		SS	8	26	4	6	2	2	0	1	.231	1	9	14	2	.920
1990—Seattle (A.L.)■		S-2-3-0	62	147	19	33	5	4	0	7	.224	2	63	123	5	.974
—Calgary (Pacific Coast)		SS	8	28	4	9	1	0	0	1	.321	3	13	23	2	.947

Year Team (League)	Pos.	G	AB	R	H	2B	3B	HR	RBI	Avg.	SB	PO	A	E	Avg.
1991—Pawtucket (Int'l)■............	SS-2B-OF	32	108	25	29	2	2	4	16	.269	8	49	77	7	.947
—Boston (A.L.)	S-3-2-0	63	118	16	25	5	0	0	5	.212	2	46	116	7	.959
American League totals (3 years)		217	477	68	100	15	6	1	23	.210	12	189	399	24	.961
National League totals (1 year)		39	104	8	21	2	2	1	9	.202	7	43	93	5	.965
Major league totals (4 years)		256	581	76	121	17	8	2	32	.208	19	232	492	29	.961

BRUNANSKY, TOM
OF, RED SOX

PERSONAL: Born August 20, 1960, at Covina, Calif.... 6-4/220.... Throws right, bats right.... Full name: Thomas Andrew Brunansky.
HIGH SCHOOL: West Covina (Calif.).
COLLEGE: Cal Poly Pomona.
TRANSACTIONS/CAREER NOTES: Selected by California Angels organization in first round (14th pick overall) of free-agent draft (June 6, 1978).... On Salt Lake disabled list (August 8-31, 1981).... Traded by Angels organization with P Mike Walters and cash to Minnesota Twins for P Doug Corbett and 2B Rob Wilfong (May 12, 1982).... Traded by Twins to St. Louis Cardinals for 2B Tom Herr (April 22, 1988).... Traded by Cardinals to Boston Red Sox for P Lee Smith (May 4, 1990).... Granted free agency (November 5, 1990).... Re-signed by Red Sox (December 19, 1990).
STATISTICAL NOTES: Tied for Texas League lead in double plays by outfielders with four in 1980.... Led A.L. outfielders with eight double plays in 1983 and six in 1984.... Hit three home runs in a game (September 29, 1990).

Year Team (League)	Pos.	G	AB	R	H	2B	3B	HR	RBI	Avg.	SB	PO	A	E	Avg.
1978—Idaho Falls (Pioneer)........	OF	48	190	55	63	14	4	6	45	.332	17	85	1	8	.915
1979—Salinas (California)..........	OF	★140	485	85	131	23	1	23	76	.270	20	279	11	6	.980
1980—El Paso (Texas).............	OF	128	495	103	160	24	8	24	97	.323	23	306	17	★14	.958
—Salt Lake City (PCL).........	OF	9	32	7	11	2	2	1	8	.344	0	28	1	0	1.000
1981—Salt Lake City (PCL)........	OF	96	343	61	114	17	10	22	81	.332	6	250	14	5	.981
—California (A.L.)	OF	11	33	7	5	0	0	3	6	.152	1	27	3	2	.938
1982—Spokane (Pacific Coast) ...	OF	25	88	12	18	6	1	1	6	.205	4	44	7	1	.981
—Minnesota (A.L.)■...........	OF	127	463	77	126	30	1	20	46	.272	1	343	8	5	.986
1983—Minnesota (A.L.)	OF	151	542	70	123	24	5	28	82	.227	2	375	16	6	.985
1984—Minnesota (A.L.)	OF	155	567	75	144	21	0	32	85	.254	4	304	13	5	.984
1985—Minnesota (A.L.)	OF	157	567	71	137	28	4	27	90	.242	5	300	14	5	.984
1986—Minnesota (A.L.)	OF	157	593	69	152	28	1	23	75	.256	12	315	10	6	.982
1987—Minnesota (A.L.)	OF	155	532	83	138	22	2	32	85	.259	11	273	10	3	.990
1988—Minnesota (A.L.)	OF	14	49	5	9	1	0	1	6	.184	1	19	0	3	.864
—St. Louis (N.L.)■.............	OF	143	523	69	128	22	4	22	79	.245	16	267	10	1	★.996
1989—St. Louis (N.L.)	OF-1B	158	556	67	133	29	3	20	85	.239	5	291	9	7	.977
1990—St. Louis (N.L.)	OF	19	57	5	9	3	0	1	2	.158	0	37	1	2	.950
—Boston (A.L.)■.................	OF	129	461	61	123	24	5	15	71	.267	5	267	7	5	.982
1991—Boston (A.L.)	OF	142	459	54	105	24	1	16	70	.229	1	265	5	3	.989
American League totals (10 years)		1198	4266	572	1062	202	19	197	616	.249	43	2488	86	43	.984
National League totals (3 years)		320	1136	141	270	54	7	43	166	.238	21	595	20	10	.984
Major league totals (11 years)		1518	5402	713	1332	256	26	240	782	.247	64	3083	106	53	.984

CHAMPIONSHIP SERIES RECORD

Year Team (League)	Pos.	G	AB	R	H	2B	3B	HR	RBI	Avg.	SB	PO	A	E	Avg.
1987—Minnesota (A.L.)	OF	5	17	5	7	4	0	2	9	.412	0	10	0	0	1.000
1990—Boston (A.L.)	OF	4	12	0	1	0	0	0	1	.083	0	13	0	0	1.000
Championship Series totals (2 years)		9	29	5	8	4	0	2	10	.276	0	23	0	0	1.000

WORLD SERIES RECORD

Year Team (League)	Pos.	G	AB	R	H	2B	3B	HR	RBI	Avg.	SB	PO	A	E	Avg.
1987—Minnesota (A.L.)	OF	7	25	5	5	0	0	0	2	.200	1	14	0	0	1.000

ALL-STAR GAME RECORD

Year League	Pos.	AB	R	H	2B	3B	HR	RBI	Avg.	SB	PO	A	E	Avg.
1985—American	OF	1	0	0	0	0	0	0	.000	0	0	0	0	...

BUECHELE, STEVE
3B, PIRATES

PERSONAL: Born September 26, 1961, at Lancaster, Calif.... 6-2/200.... Throws right, bats right.... Full name: Steven Bernard Buechele.... Name pronounced BOO-shell.
HIGH SCHOOL: Servite (Anaheim, Calif.).
COLLEGE: Stanford.
TRANSACTIONS/CAREER NOTES: Selected by Chicago White Sox organization in first round (ninth pick overall) of free-agent draft (June 5, 1979).... Selected by Texas Rangers organization in fifth round of free-agent draft (June 7, 1982).... On Texas disabled list (April 22-May 25 and June 18-July 20, 1990); included rehabilitation disability assignment to Oklahoma City (July 16-20, 1990).... On suspended list (August 24-27, 1990).... Traded by Rangers to Pittsburgh Pirates for P Kurt Miller and a player to be named later (August 30, 1991); Rangers acquired P Hector Fajardo to complete deal (September 6, 1991).... Granted free agency (October 28, 1991).... Re-signed by Pirates (December 12, 1991).

RECORDS/HONORS: Named American Association Most Valuable Player (1985).
STATISTICAL NOTES: Lead A.L. third basemen with .991 fielding percentage in 1991.

Year	Team (League)	Pos.	G	AB	R	H	2B	3B	HR	RBI	Avg.	SB	PO	A	E	Avg.
1982	—Tulsa (Texas)	2B-3B	62	213	21	63	12	2	5	33	.296	2	111	174	8	.973
1983	—Tulsa (Texas)	2B-3B	117	437	62	121	12	4	14	62	.277	5	182	259	18	.961
	—Oklahoma City (A.A.)	2B-3B	9	34	6	9	5	0	1	4	.265	0	17	22	1	.975
1984	—Oklahoma City (A.A.)	2B-3B	131	447	48	118	25	3	7	59	.264	7	236	329	17	.971
1985	—Oklahoma City (A.A.)	3B-2B	89	350	56	104	20	7	9	64	.297	6	84	170	7	.973
	—Texas (A.L.)	3B-2B	69	219	22	48	6	3	6	21	.219	3	52	138	6	.969
1986	—Texas (A.L.)	3B-2B-OF	153	461	54	112	19	2	18	54	.243	5	174	292	12	.975
1987	—Texas (A.L.)	3B-2B-OF	136	363	45	86	20	0	13	50	.237	2	89	211	9	.971
1988	—Texas (A.L.)	3B-2B	155	503	68	126	21	4	16	58	.250	2	114	300	16	.963
1989	—Texas (A.L.)	3B-2B-SS	155	486	60	114	22	2	16	59	.235	1	128	288	12	.972
1990	—Texas (A.L.)	3B-2B	91	251	30	54	10	0	7	30	.215	1	72	160	8	.967
	—Oklahoma City (A.A.)	3B	6	21	1	3	0	0	1	1	.143	0	4	15	0	1.000
1991	—Texas (A.L.)	3B-2B-SS	121	416	58	111	17	2	18	66	.267	0	99	275	3	†.992
	—Pittsburgh (N.L.)■	3B	31	114	16	28	5	1	4	19	.246	0	22	64	4	.956
	American League totals (7 years)		880	2699	337	651	115	13	94	338	.241	14	728	1664	66	.973
	National League totals (1 year)		31	114	16	28	5	1	4	19	.246	0	22	64	4	.956
	Major league totals (7 years)		911	2813	353	679	120	14	98	357	.241	14	750	1728	70	.973

CHAMPIONSHIP SERIES RECORD

Year	Team (League)	Pos.	G	AB	R	H	2B	3B	HR	RBI	Avg.	SB	PO	A	E	Avg.
1991	—Pittsburgh (N.L.)	3B	7	23	2	7	2	0	0	0	.304	0	8	14	0	1.000

BUHNER, JAY
OF, MARINERS

PERSONAL: Born August 13, 1964, at Louisville, Ky.... 6-3/205.... Throws right, bats right.... Full name: Jay Campbell Buhner.... Name Pronounced BYOO-ner.
HIGH SCHOOL: Clear Creek (League City, Tex.).
COLLEGE: McLennan Community College (Tex.).
TRANSACTIONS/CAREER NOTES: Selected by Atlanta Braves organization in ninth round of free-agent draft (June 6, 1983).... Selected by Pittsburgh Pirates organization in secondary phase of free-agent draft (January 17, 1984).... Traded by Pirates organization with IF Dale Berra and P Alfonso Pulido to New York Yankees for OF Steve Kemp, IF Tim Foli and cash (December 20, 1984).... On disabled list (April 11-July 28, 1986).... Traded by Yankees with P Rich Balabon and a player to be named later to Seattle Mariners for DH Ken Phelps (July 21, 1988); Mariners acquired P Troy Evers to complete deal (October 12, 1988).... On Seattle disabled list (June 29-August 19, 1989); included rehabilitation disability assignment to Calgary (August 16-19, 1989).... On Seattle disabled list (March 31-June 1 and June 17-August 23, 1990); included rehabilitation disability assignment to Calgary (May 18-June 1, 1990).
RECORDS/HONORS: Shares major league records for most strikeouts in two consecutive nine-inning games—8 (August 23-24, 1990); most strikeouts in three consecutive games—10 (August 23-25, 1990).
STATISTICAL NOTES: Tied for International League lead in double plays by outfielders with six in 1987.

Year	Team (League)	Pos.	G	AB	R	H	2B	3B	HR	RBI	Avg.	SB	PO	A	E	Avg.
1984	—Watertown (N.Y.-Penn)	OF	65	229	43	74	16	3	9	•58	.323	3	106	8	1	.991
1985	—Fort Lauderdale (FSL)■	OF	117	409	65	121	18	10	11	76	.296	6	235	12	7	.972
1986	—Fort Lauderdale (FSL)	OF	36	139	24	42	9	1	7	31	.302	1	84	7	3	.968
1987	—Columbus (Int'l)	OF	134	502	83	140	23	1	★31	85	.279	4	275	★20	6	.980
	—New York (A.L.)	OF	7	22	0	5	2	0	0	1	.227	0	11	1	0	1.000
1988	—Columbus (Int'l)	OF	38	129	26	33	5	0	8	18	.256	1	83	3	1	.989
	—New York-Seattle (A.L.)■	OF	85	261	36	56	13	1	13	38	.215	1	186	9	3	.985
1989	—Calgary (Pacific Coast)	OF	56	196	43	61	12	1	11	45	.311	4	97	8	2	.981
	—Seattle (A.L.)	OF	58	204	27	56	15	1	9	33	.275	1	106	6	4	.966
1990	—Calgary (Pacific Coast)	OF	13	34	6	7	1	0	2	5	.206	0	14	1	0	1.000
	—Seattle (A.L.)	OF	51	163	16	45	12	0	7	33	.276	2	55	1	2	.966
1991	—Seattle (A.L.)	OF	137	406	64	99	14	4	27	77	.244	0	244	15	5	.981
	Major league totals (5 years)		338	1056	143	261	56	6	56	182	.247	4	602	32	14	.978

BULLETT, SCOTT
OF, PIRATES

PERSONAL: Born December 25, 1968, at Martinsburg, W.Va.... 6-2/200.... Throws left, bats left.... Full name: Scott Douglas Bullett.
HIGH SCHOOL: Martinsburg (W.Va.).
TRANSACTIONS/CAREER NOTES: Signed as free agent by Pittsburgh Pirates organization (June 20, 1988).

Year	Team (League)	Pos.	G	AB	R	H	2B	3B	HR	RBI	Avg.	SB	PO	A	E	Avg.
1988	—Bradenton (Gulf Coast)	OF	21	61	6	11	1	0	0	8	.180	2	28	2	1	.968
1989	—Bradenton (Gulf Coast)	OF-1B	46	165	24	42	7	3	1	16	.255	15	141	4	7	.954
1990	—Welland (N.Y.-Penn)	OF	74	255	46	77	11	4	3	33	.302	30	110	5	5	.958
1991	—Augusta (S. Atlantic)	OF	95	384	61	109	22	6	1	36	.284	48	195	8	5	.976
	—Salem (Carolina)	OF	39	156	22	52	7	5	2	15	.333	15	87	3	4	.957
	—Pittsburgh (N.L.)	OF	11	4	2	0	0	0	0	0	.000	1	2	0	0	1.000
	Major league totals (1 year)		11	4	2	0	0	0	0	0	.000	1	2	0	0	1.000

BULLINGER, JIM
P, CUBS

PERSONAL: Born August 21, 1965, at New Orleans. . . . 6-2/185. . . . Throws right, bats right. . . . Full name: James Eric Bullinger.
HIGH SCHOOL: Archbishop Rummel (Metairie, La.).
COLLEGE: New Orleans.
TRANSACTIONS/CAREER NOTES: Selected by Chicago Cubs organization in ninth round of free-agent draft (June 2, 1986).
STATISTICAL NOTES: Led New York-Pennsylvania League with 48 bases on balls received in 1986. . . . Led Carolina League shortstops with 92 double plays in 1987. . . . Tied for Southern League lead with eight complete games in 1991.

Year	Team (League)	G	W	L	Pct.	ERA	Sv.	IP	H	R	ER	BB	SO
1989	—Charlotte (Southern)	124	0	0	...	0.00	0	3	3	0	0	3	5
1990	—Winston-Salem (Carolina)	14	7	6	.538	3.70	0	90	81	43	37	46	85
	—Charlotte (Southern)	9	3	4	.429	5.11	0	44	42	30	25	18	33
1991	—Iowa (American Association)	8	3	4	.429	5.40	0	46⅔	47	32	28	23	30
	—Charlotte (Southern)	20	9	9	.500	3.53	0	142⅔	132	62	56	61	128

RECORD AS POSITION PLAYER

Year	Team (League)	Pos.	G	AB	R	H	2B	3B	HR	RBI	Avg.	SB	PO	A	E	Avg.
1986	—Geneva (N.Y.-Penn)	SS	★78	248	35	61	•16	1	3	33	.246	7	104	207	26	.923
1987	—Winston-Salem (Caro.)	SS	129	437	58	112	12	3	9	48	.256	3	210	383	28	.955
1988	—Pittsfield (Eastern)	SS	88	242	21	41	6	1	3	33	.169	1	129	256	21	.948
	—Winston-Salem (Caro.)	SS	32	104	13	20	4	2	1	11	.192	4	49	80	11	.921
1989	—Charlotte (Southern)	SS-3B-P	124	320	34	69	13	1	3	28	.216	3	188	281	26	.947

BULLOCK, ERIC
OF/1B, EXPOS

PERSONAL: Born February 16, 1960, at Los Angeles. . . . 5-11/185. . . . Throws left, bats left. . . . Full name: Eric Jerald Bullock. . . . Son of Eddie Bullock, minor league outfielder (1955).
HIGH SCHOOL: South Gate (Calif.).
COLLEGE: Los Angeles Harbor Junior College and Cal State Fullerton.
TRANSACTIONS/CAREER NOTES: Selected by Los Angeles Dodgers organization in 18th round of free-agent draft (June 6, 1978). . . . Selected by San Diego Padres organization in first round (fifth pick overall) of free-agent draft (January 13, 1981). . . . Selected by Houston Astros organization in secondary phase of free-agent draft (June 8, 1981). . . . On Tuscon disabled list (May 6-July 7, 1986). . . . Traded by Astros organization to Minnesota Twins organization for P Clay Christiansen (June 2, 1987). . . . Granted free agency (October 15, 1987). . . . Re-signed by Twins organization (November 7, 1987). . . . Traded by Twins with 2B Tom Herr and C Tom Nieto to Philadelphia Phillies for P Shane Rawley and cash (October 24, 1988). . . . On Scranton/Wilkes-Barre disabled list (April 6-May 27, 1989). . . . Granted free agency (October 15, 1989). . . . Signed by Indianapolis, Montreal Expos organization (March 17, 1990).
STATISTICAL NOTES: Tied for Pacific Coast League lead in being hit by pitch with seven in 1985. . . . Led Pacific Coast League in caught stealing with 18 in 1988.

Year	Team (League)	Pos.	G	AB	R	H	2B	3B	HR	RBI	Avg.	SB	PO	A	E	Avg.
1981	—Sara. Astros-Or. (GCL)	OF	56	184	38	54	8	3	1	15	.293	24	67	6	3	.961
	—Daytona Beach (Fla. St.)	DH	1	2	1	1	0	0	0	1	.500	0	0	0	0	...
1982	—Daytona Beach (Fla. St.)	OF	117	442	90	150	24	11	5	•85	.339	45	180	11	5	.974
	—Columbus (Southern)	OF	18	66	6	20	1	0	2	13	.303	5	21	1	0	1.000
1983	—Columbus (Southern)	OF	130	475	65	131	15	6	9	59	.276	35	196	9	3	.986
1984	—Columbus (Southern)	OF	71	265	47	77	15	2	3	41	.291	41	133	3	4	.971
	—Tucson (Pacific Coast)	OF	60	185	22	51	6	2	1	16	.276	7	96	2	5	.951
1985	—Tucson (Pacific Coast)	OF	124	467	81	149	26	8	4	57	.319	48	199	5	7	.967
	—Houston (N.L.)	OF	18	25	3	7	2	0	0	2	.280	0	6	0	2	.750
1986	—Houston (N.L.)	OF	6	21	0	1	0	0	0	1	.048	2	7	0	1	.875
	—Tucson (Pacific Coast)	OF	42	151	28	58	8	2	3	21	.384	14	73	2	1	.987
1987	—Tucson-Portland (PCL)■	OF	106	330	42	88	13	6	2	34	.267	14	145	5	2	.987
1988	—Portland (Pacific Coast)	OF	117	434	69	134	20	8	2	46	.309	★51	211	11	3	★.987
	—Minnesota (A.L.)	OF	16	17	3	5	0	0	0	3	.294	1	7	0	1	.875
1989	—Scranton/W.B. (Int'l)■	OF	80	281	37	77	10	8	3	40	.274	16	119	4	1	.992
	—Philadelphia (N.L.)	OF	6	4	1	0	0	0	0	0	.000	0	2	0	0	1.000
1990	—Indianapolis (A.A.)■	OF	107	434	62	122	19	7	3	32	.281	40	185	5	5	.974
	—Montreal (N.L.)	PH-PR	4	2	0	1	0	0	0	0	.500	0	0	0	0	...
1991	—Montreal (N.L.)	OF-1B	73	72	6	16	4	0	1	6	.222	6	22	3	1	.962
	American League totals (1 year)		16	17	3	5	0	0	0	3	.294	1	7	0	1	.875
	National League totals (5 years)		107	124	10	25	6	0	1	9	.202	8	37	3	4	.909
	Major league totals (6 years)		123	141	13	30	6	0	1	12	.213	9	44	3	5	.904

BURBA, DAVE
P, GIANTS

PERSONAL: Born July 7, 1966, at Dayton, O. . . . 6-4/220. . . . Throws right, bats right. . . . Full name: David Allen Burba. . . . Nephew of Ray Hathaway, pitcher, Brooklyn Dodgers (1945).
HIGH SCHOOL: Kenton Ridge (Springfield, O.).
COLLEGE: Ohio State.
TRANSACTIONS/CAREER NOTES: Selected by Seattle Mariners organization in second round of free-agent draft (June 2, 1987). . . . Traded by Mariners with P Bill Swift and P Mike Jackson to San Francisco Giants for OF Kevin Mitchell and P Mike Remlinger (December 11, 1991).

Year	Team (League)	G	W	L	Pct.	ERA	Sv.	IP	H	R	ER	BB	SO
1987	—Bellingham (Northwest)	5	3	1	.750	1.93	0	23⅓	20	10	5	3	24
	—Salinas (California)	9	1	6	.143	4.61	0	54⅔	53	31	28	29	46

Year	Team (League)	G	W	L	Pct.	ERA	Sv.	IP	H	R	ER	BB	SO
1988	—San Bernardino (California)	20	5	7	.417	2.68	0	114	106	41	34	54	102
1989	—Williamsport (Eastern)	25	11	7	.611	3.16	0	156⅔	138	69	55	55	89
1990	—Calgary (Pacific Coast)	31	10	6	.625	4.67	2	113⅔	124	64	59	45	47
	—Seattle (A.L.)	6	0	0	...	4.50	0	8	8	6	4	2	4
1991	—Calgary (Pacific Coast)	23	6	4	.600	3.53	4	71⅓	82	35	28	27	42
	—Seattle (A.L.)	22	2	2	.500	3.68	1	36⅔	34	16	15	14	16
Major league totals (2 years)		28	2	2	.500	3.83	1	44⅔	42	22	19	16	20

BURKE, TIM
P, METS

PERSONAL: Born February 19, 1959, at Omaha, Neb. ... 6-3/205. ... Throws right, bats right. ... Full name: Timothy Philip Burke.
HIGH SCHOOL: Roncalli (Omaha, Neb.).
COLLEGE: Nebraska.

TRANSACTIONS/CAREER NOTES: Selected by Pittsburgh Pirates organization in second round of free-agent draft (June 3, 1980). ... On disabled list (July 12, 1980-remainder of season). ... Traded by Pirates organization with C John Holland, IF Jose Rivera and OF Don Aubin to New York Yankees organization for OF Lee Mazzilli (December 22, 1982). ... On Nashville disabled list (May 4-23, 1983). ... Traded by Yankees organization to Montreal Expos organization for OF Pat Rooney (December 19, 1983). ... On disabled list (March 28-April 22, 1987 and May 31-July 12, 1990). ... Traded by Expos to New York Mets for P Ron Darling and P Mike Thomas (July 15, 1991).
RECORDS/HONORS: Holds N.L. rookie-season record for most games pitched—78 (1985).

Year	Team (League)	G	W	L	Pct.	ERA	Sv.	IP	H	R	ER	BB	SO
1980	—...						Did not play						
1981	—Alexandria (Carolina)	23	8	10	.444	3.44	0	149	139	67	57	48	111
1982	—Buffalo (Eastern)	25	7	10	.412	5.19	0	144	162	93	83	57	93
1983	—Columbus (International)■	4	1	0	1.000	6.75	0	12	15	9	9	8	6
	—Nashville (Southern)	20	12	4	.750	3.21	0	129	124	63	46	37	64
1984	—Indianapolis (Am. Assoc.)■	35	11	8	.579	3.49	2	180⅔	192	81	70	61	108
1985	—Montreal (N.L.)	★78	9	4	.692	2.39	8	120⅓	86	32	32	44	87
1986	—Montreal (N.L.)	68	9	7	.563	2.93	4	101⅓	103	37	33	46	82
1987	—Montreal (N.L.)	55	7	0	1.000	1.19	18	91	64	18	12	17	58
1988	—Montreal (N.L.)	61	3	5	.375	3.40	18	82	84	36	31	25	42
1989	—Montreal (N.L.)	68	9	3	.750	2.55	28	84⅔	68	24	24	22	54
1990	—Montreal (N.L.)	58	3	3	.500	2.52	20	75	71	29	21	21	47
1991	—Montreal-New York (N.L.)■	72	6	7	.462	3.36	6	101⅔	96	46	38	26	59
Major league totals (7 years)		460	46	29	.613	2.62	102	656	572	222	191	201	429

ALL-STAR GAME RECORD

Year	League	W	L	Pct.	ERA	Sv.	IP	H	R	ER	BB	SO
1989	—National	0	0	...	0.00	0	2	2	0	0	0	1

BURKETT, JOHN
P, GIANTS

PERSONAL: Born November 28, 1964, at New Brighton, Pa. ... 6-2/210. ... Throws right, bats right. ... Full name: John David Burkett.
HIGH SCHOOL: Beaver (Penn.).
TRANSACTIONS/CAREER NOTES: Selected by San Francisco Giants organization in sixth round of free-agent draft (June 6, 1983).
STATISTICAL NOTES: Tied for Pacific Coast League lead in games started by pitcher with 28 in 1989. ... Led N.L. with 10 hit batsmen in 1991.

Year	Team (League)	G	W	L	Pct.	ERA	Sv.	IP	H	R	ER	BB	SO
1983	—Great Falls (Pioneer)	13	2	6	.250	6.26	0	50⅓	73	44	35	30	38
1984	—Clinton (Midwest)	20	7	6	.538	4.33	0	126⅔	128	81	61	38	83
1985	—Fresno (California)	20	7	4	.636	2.87	0	109⅔	98	43	35	46	72
1986	—Fresno (California)	4	0	3	.000	5.47	0	24⅔	34	19	15	8	14
	—Shreveport (Texas)	22	10	6	.625	2.66	0	128⅔	99	46	38	42	73
1987	—Shreveport (Texas)	27	•14	8	.636	3.34	0	★177⅔	181	75	66	53	126
	—San Francisco (N.L.)	3	0	0	...	4.50	0	6	7	4	3	3	5
1988	—Phoenix (Pacific Coast)	21	5	11	.313	5.21	0	114	141	79	66	49	74
	—Shreveport (Texas)	7	5	1	.833	2.13	0	50⅔	33	15	12	18	34
1989	—Phoenix (Pacific Coast)	28	10	11	.476	5.05	0	167⅔	197	111	94	59	105
1990	—Phoenix (Pacific Coast)	3	2	1	.667	2.74	0	23	18	8	7	3	9
	—San Francisco (N.L.)	33	14	7	.667	3.79	1	204	201	92	86	61	118
1991	—San Francisco (N.L.)	36	12	11	.522	4.18	0	206⅔	223	103	96	60	131
Major league totals (3 years)		72	26	18	.591	4.00	1	416⅔	431	199	185	124	254

BURKS, ELLIS
OF, RED SOX

PERSONAL: Born September 11, 1964, at Vicksburg, Miss. ... 6-2/205. ... Throws right, bats right. ... Full name: Ellis Rena Burks.
HIGH SCHOOL: Everman (Tex.).
COLLEGE: Ranger Junior College (Tex.).

TRANSACTIONS/CAREER NOTES: Selected by Boston Red Sox organization in first round (20th pick overall) of free-agent draft (January 11, 1983). ... On disabled list (March 26-April 12, 1988). ... On Boston disabled list (June 15-August 1, 1989); included rehabilitation disability assignment to Pawtucket (July 26-August 1, 1989).
RECORDS/HONORS: Shares major league record for most home runs in one inning—2 (August 27, 1990, fourth inning). ... Named outfielder on THE SPORTING NEWS A.L. All-Star team (1990). ... Won A.L. Gold Glove as outfielder (1990). ...

Named outfielder on THE SPORTING NEWS A.L. Silver Slugger team (1990).
STATISTICAL NOTES: Tied for Florida State League lead in double plays by outfielders with six in 1984.

Year	Team (League)	Pos.	G	AB	R	H	2B	3B	HR	RBI	Avg.	SB	PO	A	E	Avg.
							BATTING							FIELDING		
1983 —Elmira (New York-Penn) ..	OF	53	174	30	42	9	0	2	23	.241	9	89	5	2	.979
1984 —Winter Haven (Fla. St.)	OF	112	375	52	96	15	4	6	43	.256	29	196	12	5	.977
1985 —New Britain (Eastern)	OF	133	476	66	121	25	7	10	61	.254	17	306	9	8	.975
1986 —New Britain (Eastern)	OF	124	462	70	126	20	3	14	55	.273	31	318	5	5	.985
1987 —Pawtucket (Int'l)	OF	11	40	11	9	3	1	3	6	.225	1	25	0	0	1.000
—Boston (A.L.)	OF	133	558	94	152	30	2	20	59	.272	27	320	15	4	.988
1988 —Boston (A.L.)	OF	144	540	93	159	37	5	18	92	.294	25	370	9	9	.977
1989 —Boston (A.L.)	OF	97	399	73	121	19	6	12	61	.303	21	245	7	6	.977
—Pawtucket (Int'l)	OF	5	21	4	3	1	0	0	0	.143	0	16	0	0	1.000
1990 —Boston (A.L.)	OF	152	588	89	174	33	8	21	89	.296	9	324	7	2	.994
1991 —Boston (A.L.)	OF	130	474	56	119	33	3	14	56	.251	6	283	2	2	.993
Major league totals (5 years)		656	2559	405	725	152	24	85	357	.283	88	1542	40	23	.986

CHAMPIONSHIP SERIES RECORD

Year	Team (League)	Pos.	G	AB	R	H	2B	3B	HR	RBI	Avg.	SB	PO	A	E	Avg.
							BATTING							FIELDING		
1988 —Boston (A.L.)	OF	4	17	2	4	1	0	0	1	.235	0	10	0	0	1.000
1990 —Boston (A.L.)	OF	4	15	1	4	2	0	0	0	.267	1	9	1	0	1.000
Championship Series totals (2 years)		8	32	3	8	3	0	0	1	.250	1	19	1	0	1.000

ALL-STAR GAME RECORD

ALL-STAR GAME NOTES: Named to A.L. All-Star team for 1990 game; replaced due to injury by Brook Jacoby.

BURLINGAME, DENNIS
P, BRAVES

PERSONAL: Born June 17, 1969, at Woodbury, N.J. . . . 6-4/200. . . . Throws right, bats right. . . . Full name: Dennis Arthur Burlingame.
HIGH SCHOOL: Kingsway Regional (Swedesboro, N.J.).
TRANSACTIONS/CAREER NOTES: Selected by Atlanta Braves organization in fifth round of free-agent draft (June 2, 1987). . . . On disabled list (April 12-July 7, 1990).
STATISTICAL NOTES: Led South Atlantic League with four shutouts in 1988. . . . Pitched seven-inning, 4-0 perfect game against Frederick (April 9, 1989).

Year	Team (League)	G	W	L	Pct.	ERA	Sv.	IP	H	R	ER	BB	SO
1988 —Sumter (South Atlantic)............	24	9	11	.450	2.49	0	162⅔	132	59	45	43	89
1989 —Durham (Carolina)	11	4	0	1.000	0.50	0	54⅓	28	8	3	5	42
1990 —Sumter (South Atlantic)............	12	1	3	.250	2.27	0	35⅔	36	14	9	6	20
1991 —Durham (Carolina)	26	11	7	.611	3.01	0	161⅓	143	60	54	80	95

BURNS, TODD
P, RANGERS

PERSONAL: Born July 6, 1963, at Maywood, Calif. . . . 6-2/190. . . . Throws right, bats right. . . . Full name: Todd Edward Burns.
HIGH SCHOOL: Santa Fe (Calif.).
COLLEGE: Oral Roberts.
TRANSACTIONS/CAREER NOTES: Selected by Oakland Athletics organization in seventh round of free-agent draft (June 4, 1984). . . . On A's disabled list (April 13-June 13, 1991; included rehabilitation disability assignment to Modesto (June 6-13, 1991). . . . Granted free agency (October 18, 1991). . . . Signed by Texas Rangers organization (December 20, 1991).
STATISTICAL NOTES: Tied for Southern League lead with three shutouts in 1986.

Year	Team (League)	G	W	L	Pct.	ERA	Sv.	IP	H	R	ER	BB	SO
1984 —Medford (Northwest)	22	3	0	1.000	0.50	8	36⅓	21	4	2	12	63
—Madison (Midwest)	10	3	2	.600	2.57	1	14	11	4	4	3	20
1985 —Madison (Midwest)	20	8	8	.500	3.66	0	123	109	55	50	40	94
—Huntsville (Southern)	4	3	1	.750	1.19	0	22⅔	16	6	3	13	8
1986 —Huntsville (Southern)	20	7	7	.500	3.75	0	124⅔	122	59	52	39	77
—Tacoma (Pacific Coast)	11	0	0	.000	2.16	2	16⅔	11	4	4	12	14
1987 —Huntsville (Southern)	34	3	4	.429	2.97	7	63⅔	49	24	21	17	54
—Tacoma (Pacific Coast)	21	2	2	.500	4.88	0	27⅔	27	16	15	16	30
1988 —Tacoma (Pacific Coast)	21	4	3	.571	3.68	1	73⅓	74	39	30	26	59
—Oakland (A.L.)	17	8	2	.800	3.16	1	102⅔	93	38	36	34	57
1989 —Oakland (A.L.)	50	6	5	.545	2.24	8	96⅓	66	27	24	28	49
1990 —Oakland (A.L.)	43	3	3	.500	2.97	3	78⅔	78	28	26	32	43
1991 —Oakland (A.L.)	9	1	0	1.000	3.38	0	13⅓	10	5	5	8	3
—Modesto (California)	2	1	0	1.000	10.50	0	6	9	7	7	3	8
—Tacoma (Pacific Coast)	13	0	2	.000	5.33	2	25⅓	30	16	15	7	24
Major league totals (4 years)	119	18	10	.643	2.81	12	291	247	98	91	102	152

WORLD SERIES RECORD

Year	Team (League)	G	W	L	Pct.	ERA	Sv.	IP	H	R	ER	BB	SO
1988 —Oakland (A.L.)	1	0	0	...	0.00	0	⅓	0	0	0	0	0
1989 —Oakland (A.L.)	2	0	0	...	0.00	0	1⅔	1	0	0	1	0
1990 —Oakland (A.L.)	2	0	0	...	16.20	0	1⅔	5	3	3	2	0
World Series totals (3 years)	5	0	0	...	7.36	0	3⅔	6	3	3	3	0

BUSH, RANDY
OF/1B, TWINS

PERSONAL: Born October 5, 1958, at Dover, Del. . . . 6-1/190. . . . Throws left, bats left. . . . Full name: Robert Randall Bush.
HIGH SCHOOL: Carol City (Fla.).
COLLEGE: Miami-Dade Community College, North (Fla.) and New Orleans.
TRANSACTIONS/CAREER NOTES: Selected by Minnesota Twins organization in second round of free-agent draft (June 5, 1979). . . . On Toledo disabled list (May 25-June 27, 1980). . . . Granted free agency (November 4, 1988). . . . Re-signed by Twins (December 12, 1988). . . . On Minnesota disabled list (May 19-July 19 and August 23-September 7, 1990); included rehabilitation disability assignment to Portland (June 27-30, 1990). . . . Granted free agency (November 5, 1990). . . . Re-signed by Twins (December 18, 1990).
RECORDS/HONORS: Shares A.L. record for most home runs by pinch-hitter in consecutive at-bats—2 (June 20 and 23, 1986).
STATISTICAL NOTES: Led Southern League in being hit by pitch with eight in 1979 and 12 in 1981.

| | | | | | | |—BATTING—| | | | | | |—FIELDING—| | |
Year	Team (League)	Pos.	G	AB	R	H	2B	3B	HR	RBI	Avg.	SB	PO	A	E	Avg.
1979—Orlando (Southern)		1B	76	243	33	62	12	2	6	34	.255	1	653	38	13	.982
1980—Toledo (International)		OF-1B	40	108	11	21	1	0	1	7	.194	2	112	6	1	.992
—Orlando (Southern)		1B	51	175	32	41	2	1	7	26	.234	1	458	28	4	.992
1981—Orlando (Southern)		OF-1B	136	482	98	140	26	3	22	94	.290	14	174	7	5	.973
1982—Toledo (International)		OF	49	160	21	52	14	0	8	27	.325	2	68	0	1	.986
—Minnesota (A.L.)		OF	55	119	13	29	6	1	4	13	.244	0	7	0	0	1.000
1983—Minnesota (A.L.)		1B	124	373	43	93	24	3	11	56	.249	0	21	3	0	1.000
1984—Minnesota (A.L.)		1B	113	311	46	69	17	1	11	43	.222	1	5	0	0	1.000
1985—Minnesota (A.L.)		OF-1B	97	234	26	56	13	3	10	35	.239	3	79	0	2	.975
1986—Minnesota (A.L.)		OF-1B	130	357	50	96	19	7	7	45	.269	5	182	2	4	.979
1987—Minnesota (A.L.)		OF-1B	122	293	46	74	10	2	11	46	.253	10	164	5	4	.977
1988—Minnesota (A.L.)		OF-1B	136	394	51	103	20	3	14	51	.261	8	206	5	4	.981
1989—Minnesota (A.L.)		OF-1B	141	391	60	103	17	4	14	54	.263	5	339	14	3	.992
1990—Minnesota (A.L.)		OF-1B	73	181	17	44	8	0	6	18	.243	0	64	3	0	1.000
—Portland (Pacific Coast) ...		OF	3	9	2	2	2	0	0	1	.222	0	0	0	0	...
1991—Minnesota (A.L.)		OF-1B	93	165	21	50	10	1	6	23	.303	0	85	5	2	.978
Major league totals (10 years)			1084	2818	373	717	144	25	94	384	.254	32	1152	37	19	.984

CHAMPIONSHIP SERIES RECORD

CHAMPIONSHIP SERIES NOTES: Shares record for most stolen bases in one inning—2 (October 8, 1987, fourth inning).

| | | | | | | |—BATTING—| | | | | | |—FIELDING—| | |
Year	Team (League)	Pos.	G	AB	R	H	2B	3B	HR	RBI	Avg.	SB	PO	A	E	Avg.
1987—Minnesota (A.L.)		DH	4	12	4	3	0	1	0	2	.250	3	0	0	0	...
1991—Minnesota (A.L.)							Did not play									
Championship Series totals (2 years)			4	12	4	3	0	1	0	2	.250	3	0	0	0	...

WORLD SERIES RECORD

| | | | | | | |—BATTING—| | | | | | |—FIELDING—| | |
Year	Team (League)	Pos.	G	AB	R	H	2B	3B	HR	RBI	Avg.	SB	PO	A	E	Avg.
1987—Minnesota (A.L.)		DH-PH	4	6	1	1	1	0	0	2	.167	0	0	0	0	...
1991—Minnesota (A.L.)		PH-3B	3	4	0	1	0	0	0	0	.250	0	0	0	0	...
World Series totals (2 years)			7	10	1	2	1	0	0	2	.200	0	0	0	0	...

BUTCHER, MIKE
P, ANGELS

PERSONAL: Born May 10, 1965, at Davenport, Ia. . . . 6-1/200. . . . Throws right, bats right. . . . Full name: Michael Dana Butcher.
HIGH SCHOOL: United Township (East Moline, Ill.).
COLLEGE: Northeastern Oklahoma A&M.
TRANSACTIONS/CAREER NOTES: Selected by Cincinnati Reds organization in fourth round of free-agent draft (January 14, 1986). . . . Selected by Kansas City Royals organization in secondary phase of free-agent draft (June 2, 1986). . . . Released by Royals organization (July 3, 1988). . . . Signed by California Angels organization (July 8, 1988).

Year	Team (League)	G	W	L	Pct.	ERA	Sv.	IP	H	R	ER	BB	SO
1986—Eugene (Northwest)		14	5	4	.556	3.86	0	72⅓	51	39	31	49	68
1987—Appleton (Midwest)		20	10	4	.714	2.67	0	121⅓	101	50	36	56	89
—Fort Myers (Florida State)		5	2	2	.500	5.46	0	31⅓	33	20	19	8	17
1988—Baseball City (Florida State)		6	1	4	.200	3.86	0	32⅔	32	19	14	10	20
—Appleton-Quad City (Midw.)■..		7	0	1	.000	3.38	0	24	23	10	9	9	14
—Palm Springs (California)		7	3	2	.600	5.70	0	42⅔	57	33	27	19	37
1989—Midland (Texas)		15	2	6	.250	6.55	0	68⅔	92	54	50	41	49
1990—Midland (Texas)		35	3	7	.300	6.21	0	87	109	68	60	55	84
1991—Midland (Texas)		41	9	6	.600	5.22	3	88	93	54	51	46	70

BUTLER, BRETT
OF, DODGERS

PERSONAL: Born June 15, 1957, at Los Angeles. . . . 5-10/160. . . . Throws left, bats left. . . . Full name: Brett Morgan Butler.
HIGH SCHOOL: Libertyville (Ill.).
TRANSACTIONS/CAREER NOTES: Selected by Atlanta Braves organization in 23rd round of free-agent draft (June 5, 1979). . . . Traded by Braves with IF Brook Jacoby to Cleveland Indians (October 21, 1983), completing deal in which Indians traded P Len Barker to Braves for three players to be named later (August 28, 1983); Indians acquired P Rick Behenna as partial completion of deal (September 2, 1983). . . . On disabled list (April 11-30, 1987). . . . Granted free agency (November 9, 1987). . . . Signed by San Francisco Giants (December 1, 1987). . . . Granted free agency (December 7,

1990).... Signed by Los Angeles Dodgers (December 14, 1990).

RECORDS/HONORS: Shares major league single-season records for fewest double plays by outfielder who led league in double plays—3 (1991); fewest double plays by outfielder (150 or more games)—0 (1990); highest fielding percentage by outfielder (150 or more games)—1.000 (1991); and fewest errors by outfielder (150 games or more)—0 (1991).... Shares N.L. single-season record for fewest assists by outfielder (150 or more games)—3 (1988).... Shares modern N.L. single-game record for most bases on balls—5 (April 12, 1990).... Named International League Most Valuable Player (1981).

STATISTICAL NOTES: Led International League with 103 bases on balls received in 1981.... Tied for N.L. lead in double plays by outfielders with four in 1983 and three in 1991.... Led A.L. in caught stealing with 22 in 1984 and 20 in 1985.... Led N.L. with 108 bases on balls received and in caught stealing with 28 in 1991.... Tied for N.L. lead in total chances by outfielders with 380 in 1991.

Year Team (League)	Pos.	G	AB	R	H	2B	3B	HR	RBI	Avg.	SB	PO	A	E	Avg.
1979—Greenwood (W. Caro.)	OF	35	117	26	37	2	4	1	11	.316	20	45	2	0	1.000
—Bradenton (Gulf Coast)	OF	30	111	36	41	7	5	3	20	.369	5	66	5	0	1.000
1980—Anderson (S. Atlantic)	OF	70	255	73	76	12	6	1	26	.298	44	190	5	1	.995
—Durham (Carolina)	OF	66	224	47	82	15	6	2	39	.366	36	156	4	3	.982
1981—Richmond (Int'l)	OF	125	466	*93	156	19	4	3	36	.335	44	286	15	3	.990
—Atlanta (N.L.)	OF	40	126	17	32	2	3	0	4	.254	9	76	2	1	.987
1982—Atlanta (N.L.)	OF	89	240	35	52	2	0	0	7	.217	21	129	2	0	1.000
—Richmond (Int'l)	OF	41	157	22	57	8	3	1	22	.363	12	101	2	1	.990
1983—Atlanta (N.L.)	OF	151	549	84	154	21	*13	5	37	.281	39	284	13	4	.987
1984—Cleveland (A.L.)■	OF	159	602	108	162	25	9	3	49	.269	52	448	13	4	.991
1985—Cleveland (A.L.)	OF	152	591	106	184	28	14	5	50	.311	47	437	19	1	*.998
1986—Cleveland (A.L.)	OF	161	587	92	163	17	*14	4	51	.278	32	434	9	3	.993
1987—Cleveland (A.L.)	OF	137	522	91	154	25	8	9	41	.295	33	393	4	4	.990
1988—San Francisco (N.L.)■	OF	157	568	*109	163	27	9	6	43	.287	43	395	3	5	.988
1989—San Francisco (N.L.)	OF	154	594	100	168	22	4	4	36	.283	31	407	11	6	.986
1990—San Francisco (N.L.)	OF	160	622	108	•192	20	9	3	44	.309	51	420	4	6	.986
1991—Los Angeles (N.L.)■	OF	*161	615	*112	182	13	5	2	38	.296	38	*372	8	0	*1.000
American League totals (4 years)		609	2302	397	663	95	45	21	191	.288	164	1712	45	12	.993
National League totals (7 years)		912	3314	565	943	107	43	20	209	.285	232	2083	43	22	.990
Major league totals (11 years)		1521	5616	962	1606	202	88	41	400	.286	396	3795	88	34	.991

CHAMPIONSHIP SERIES RECORD

Year Team (League)	Pos.	G	AB	R	H	2B	3B	HR	RBI	Avg.	SB	PO	A	E	Avg.
1982—Atlanta (N.L.)	OF-PH	2	1	0	0	0	0	0	0	.000	0	0	0	0	...
1989—San Francisco (N.L.)	OF	5	19	6	4	0	0	0	0	.211	0	9	0	0	1.000
Championship Series totals (2 years)		7	20	6	4	0	0	0	0	.200	0	9	0	0	1.000

WORLD SERIES RECORD

Year Team (League)	Pos.	G	AB	R	H	2B	3B	HR	RBI	Avg.	SB	PO	A	E	Avg.
1989—San Francisco (N.L.)	OF	4	14	1	4	1	0	0	1	.286	2	9	0	0	1.000

ALL-STAR GAME RECORD

Year League	Pos.	AB	R	H	2B	3B	HR	RBI	Avg.	SB	PO	A	E	Avg.
1991—National	PR-OF	1	0	0	0	0	0	0	.000	0	0	0	0	...

CABRERA, FRANCISCO
C/1B, BRAVES

PERSONAL: Born October 10, 1966, at Santo Domingo, Dominican Republic.... 6-4/193.... Throws right, bats right.... Full name: Francisco Paulino Cabrera.

HIGH SCHOOL: Santa Cruz (Santo Domingo, Dominican Republic).

TRANSACTIONS/CAREER NOTES: Signed as free agent by Toronto Blue Jays organization (February 28, 1986).... Traded by Blue Jays to Atlanta Braves organization (August 24, 1989), completing deal in which Braves traded P Jim Acker to Blue Jays for P Tony Castillo and a player to be named later (August 24, 1989).

STATISTICAL NOTES: Led South Atlantic League catchers with 959 total chances in 1987.... Led Southern League catchers with 874 total chances and tied for lead with six double plays in 1988.... Led International League with eight sacrifice flies in 1989.... Led International League catchers with 12 errors and 13 passed balls in 1989.

Year Team (League)	Pos.	G	AB	R	H	2B	3B	HR	RBI	Avg.	SB	PO	A	E	Avg.
1986—Ventura County (Calif.)	C	6	12	2	2	1	0	0	3	.167	1	26	3	1	.967
—St. Catharines (NYP)	C	68	246	31	73	13	2	6	35	.297	7	449	50	6	.988
1987—Myrtle Beach (S. Atl.)	C	129	449	61	124	27	1	14	72	.276	4	*849	89	•21	.978
1988—Dunedin (Florida State)	C	9	35	2	14	4	0	1	9	.400	0	74	9	3	.965
—Knoxville (Southern)	C	119	429	59	122	19	1	20	54	.284	4	*783	*68	*23	.974
1989—Syracuse-Rich. (Int'l)	C-1B	116	434	59	130	31	5	9	72	.300	4	554	35	†12	.980
—Toronto (A.L.)	DH	3	12	1	2	1	0	0	0	.167	0	0	0	0	...
—Atlanta (N.L.)■	C-1B	4	14	0	3	2	0	0	0	.214	0	27	1	1	.966
1990—Richmond (Int'l)	1B-C-OF	35	132	12	30	3	1	7	20	.227	2	269	25	4	.987
—Atlanta (N.L.)	1B-C	63	137	14	38	5	1	7	25	.277	1	269	19	3	.990

Year	Team (League)	Pos.	G	AB	R	H	2B	3B	HR	RBI	Avg.	SB	PO	A	E	Avg.
1991—Atlanta (N.L.)		C-1B	44	95	7	23	6	0	4	23	.242	1	137	13	3	.980
—Richmond (Int'l)		1B-C-OF	32	119	22	31	7	1	7	24	.261	0	145	13	2	.988
American League totals (1 year)			3	12	1	2	1	0	0	0	.167	0	0	0	0	...
National League totals (3 years)			111	246	21	64	13	1	11	48	.260	2	433	33	7	.985
Major league totals (3 years)			114	258	22	66	14	1	11	48	.256	2	433	33	7	.985

CHAMPIONSHIP SERIES RECORD

Year	Team (League)	Pos.	G	AB	R	H	2B	3B	HR	RBI	Avg.	SB	PO	A	E	Avg.
1991—Atlanta (N.L.)							Did not play									

WORLD SERIES RECORD

Year	Team (League)	Pos.	G	AB	R	H	2B	3B	HR	RBI	Avg.	SB	PO	A	E	Avg.
1991—Atlanta (N.L.)		PH-C	3	1	0	0	0	0	0	0	.000	0	0	0	0	...

CADARET, GREG
P, YANKEES

PERSONAL: Born February 27, 1962, at Detroit.... 6-3/215.... Throws left, bats left.... Full name: Gregory James Cadaret.... Name pronounced CAD-uh-ray.
HIGH SCHOOL: Central Montacalm (Stanton, Mich.).
COLLEGE: Grand Valley State (Mich.).
TRANSACTIONS/CAREER NOTES: Selected by Oakland Athletics organization in 11th round of free-agent draft (June 6, 1983).... Traded by A's organization with P Eric Plunk and OF Luis Polonia to New York Yankees for OF Rickey Henderson (June 21, 1989).

Year	Team (League)	G	W	L	Pct.	ERA	Sv.	IP	H	R	ER	BB	SO
1983—Medford (Northwest)		12	7	3	.700	4.36	0	64	73	36	31	36	51
1984—Modesto (California)		26	13	8	.619	3.05	0	171⅓	162	79	58	82	138
1985—Huntsville (Southern)		17	3	7	.300	6.12	0	82⅓	96	61	56	57	60
—Modesto (California)		12	3	9	.250	5.87	0	61⅓	59	50	40	54	43
1986—Huntsville (Southern)		28	12	5	.706	5.41	0	141⅓	166	106	85	98	113
1987—Huntsville (Southern)		24	5	2	.714	2.90	9	40⅓	31	16	13	20	48
—Tacoma (Pacific Coast)		7	1	2	.333	3.46	1	13	5	6	5	13	12
—Oakland (A.L.)		29	6	2	.750	4.54	0	39⅔	37	22	20	24	30
1988—Oakland (A.L.)		58	5	2	.714	2.89	3	71⅔	60	26	23	36	64
1989—Oakland-New York (A.L.)■		46	5	5	.500	4.05	0	120	130	62	54	57	80
1990—New York (A.L.)		54	5	4	.556	4.15	3	121⅓	120	62	56	64	80
1991—New York (A.L.)		68	8	6	.571	3.62	3	121⅔	110	52	49	59	105
Major league totals (5 years)		255	29	19	.604	3.83	9	474⅓	457	224	202	240	359

CHAMPIONSHIP SERIES RECORD

Year	Team (League)	G	W	L	Pct.	ERA	Sv.	IP	H	R	ER	BB	SO
1988—Oakland (A.L.)		1	0	0	...	27.00	0	⅓	1	1	1	0	0

WORLD SERIES RECORD

Year	Team (League)	G	W	L	Pct.	ERA	Sv.	IP	H	R	ER	BB	SO
1988—Oakland (A.L.)		3	0	0	...	0.00	0	2	2	0	0	0	3

CALDERON, IVAN
OF/1B, EXPOS

PERSONAL: Born March 19, 1962, at Fajardo, Puerto Rico.... 6-1/221.... Throws right, bats right.... Full name: Ivan Perez Calderon.... Name pronounced CALL-dur-OWN.
HIGH SCHOOL: Madiania Alta Intermediate (Luiza, Puerto Rico).
TRANSACTIONS/CAREER NOTES: Signed as free agent by Seattle Mariners organization (July 30, 1979).... On Salt Lake City disabled list (May 25-July 2, 1984).... On Seattle disabled list (August 26-September 12, 1984).... Traded by Mariners to Chicago White Sox organization (July 1, 1986), completing deal in which White Sox traded C Scott Bradley to Mariners for a player to be named later (June 26, 1986).... On disabled list (May 16-31, 1987; June 27-July 12 and July 31, 1988-remainder of season).... Traded by White Sox with P Barry Jones to Montreal Expos for OF Tim Raines, P Jeff Carter and a player to be named later (December 23, 1990); White Sox acquired P Mario Brito to complete deal (February 15, 1991).
STATISTICAL NOTES: Tied for Southern League lead with 267 total bases in 1983.... Led A.L. in grounding into double plays with 26 in 1990.

Year	Team (League)	Pos.	G	AB	R	H	2B	3B	HR	RBI	Avg.	SB	PO	A	E	Avg.
1980—Bellingham (Northwest)		OF	57	195	44	62	7	*9	4	32	.318	7	56	4	7	.896
1981—Wausau (Midwest)		OF-SS	117	402	79	123	19	1	20	62	.306	26	130	17	6	.961
1982—Wausau (Midwest)		S-0-3-1	126	461	91	132	22	5	24	89	.286	26	215	202	45	.903
1983—Chattanooga (Southern)		OF	139	546	92	•170	34	*15	11	80*	.311	25	251	10	13	.953
1984—Salt Lake City (PCL)		OF	66	255	61	93	7	9	4	45	.365	18	132	9	8	.946
—Seattle (A.L.)		OF	11	24	2	5	1	0	1	1	.208	1	22	0	0	1.000
1985—Seattle (A.L.)		OF-1B	67	210	37	60	16	4	8	28	.286	4	108	5	5	.983
1986—Calgary (Pacific Coast)		OF	24	81	17	27	3	0	3	18	.333	5	34	2	1	.973
—Seattle-Chicago (A.L.)■		OF	50	164	16	41	7	1	2	15	.250	3	64	4	5	.932
—Buffalo (Am. Assoc.)		OF	27	105	11	23	9	0	5	22	.219	0	30	1	5	.861

Year Team (League)	Pos.	G	AB	R	H	2B	3B	HR	RBI	Avg.	SB	PO	A	E	Avg.
1987—Chicago (A.L.)	OF	144	542	93	159	38	2	28	83	.293	10	295	8	5	.984
1988—Chicago (A.L.)	OF	73	264	40	56	14	0	14	35	.212	4	141	5	7	.954
1989—Chicago (A.L.)	OF-1B	157	622	83	178	34	9	14	87	.286	7	384	17	9	.978
1990—Chicago (A.L.)	OF	158	607	85	166	44	2	14	74	.273	32	269	7	7	.975
1991—Montreal (N.L.)■..............	OF-1B	134	470	69	141	22	3	19	75	.300	31	284	5	7	.976
American League totals (7 years)		660	2433	356	665	154	18	81	323	.273	61	1283	46	35	.974
National League totals (1 year)		134	470	69	141	22	3	19	75	.300	31	284	5	7	.976
Major league totals (8 years)		794	2903	425	806	176	21	100	398	.278	92	1567	51	42	.975

ALL-STAR GAME RECORD

Year League	Pos.	AB	R	H	2B	3B	HR	RBI	Avg.	SB	PO	A	E	Avg.
1991—National	OF	2	0	1	0	0	0	0	.500	1	1	0	0	1.000

CAMINITI, KEN
3B, ASTROS

PERSONAL: Born April 21, 1963, at Hanford, Calif.... 6-0/200.... Throws right, bats both.... Full name: Kenneth Gene Caminiti.
HIGH SCHOOL: Leigh (San Jose, Calif.).
COLLEGE: San Jose State.
TRANSACTIONS/CAREER NOTES: Selected by Houston Astros organization in third round of free-agent draft (June 4, 1984).
RECORDS/HONORS: Named third baseman on THE SPORTING NEWS college All-America team (1984).
STATISTICAL NOTES: Led Southern League third basemen with 34 double plays in 1986.... Led Pacific Coast League third basemen with 382 total chances and 25 double plays in 1988.

Year Team (League)	Pos.	G	AB	R	H	2B	3B	HR	RBI	Avg.	SB	PO	A	E	Avg.
1985—Osceola (Florida State)	3B	126	468	83	133	26	9	4	73	.284	14	53	193	20	.925
1986—Columbus (Southern)	3B	137	513	82	154	29	3	12	81	.300	5	105	*299	33	.924
1987—Columbus (Southern)	3B	95	375	66	122	25	2	15	69	.325	11	55	205	21	.925
—Houston (N.L.)	3B	63	203	10	50	7	1	3	23	.246	0	50	98	8	.949
1988—Tucson (Pacific Coast)	3B	109	416	54	113	24	7	5	66	.272	13	*105	*250	27	.929
—Houston (N.L.)	3B	30	83	5	15	2	0	1	7	.181	0	12	43	3	.948
1989—Houston (N.L.)	3B	161	585	71	149	31	3	10	72	.255	4	126	335	22	.954
1990—Houston (N.L.)	3B	153	541	52	131	20	2	4	51	.242	9	118	243	21	.945
1991—Houston (N.L.)	3B	152	574	65	145	30	3	13	80	.253	4	129	293	23	.948
Major league totals (5 years)		559	1986	203	490	90	9	31	233	.247	17	435	1012	77	.949

CAMPANIS, JIM
C, MARINERS

PERSONAL: Born August 27, 1967, at Fullerton, Calif.... 6-1/200.... Throws right, bats right.... Full name: James Alexander Campanis Jr.... Son of Jim Campanis, catcher, Los Angeles Dodgers, Kansas City Royals, Pittsburgh Pirates (1966-70, 1973); grandson of Al Campanis, second baseman, Brooklyn Dodgers (1943) and executive, Los Angeles Dodgers (1968-87).
HIGH SCHOOL: Valencia (Calif.).
COLLEGE: Southern California.
TRANSACTIONS/CAREER NOTES: Selected by Seattle Mariners organization in third round of free-agent draft (June 1, 1988).
STATISTICAL NOTES: Led California League catchers with 16 errors and 34 passed balls in 1989.... Led Carolina League in being hit by pitch with 18 in 1990.... Led Southern League catchers with 714 putouts, 93 assists, 14 errors, 821 total chances and eight double plays in 1991.

Year Team (League)	Pos.	G	AB	R	H	2B	3B	HR	RBI	Avg.	SB	PO	A	E	Avg.
1989—San Bernardino (Calif.)	C-1B	133	455	49	116	26	0	11	58	.255	0	806	93	†17	.981
1990—Peninsula (Carolina)	C	112	364	47	91	22	0	14	60	.250	3	604	*87	•14	.980
1991—Jacksonville (Southern) ...	C-3B-1B	118	387	36	96	10	0	15	49	.248	0	†722	†94	†14	.983

CAMPBELL, KEVIN
P, ATHLETICS

PERSONAL: Born December 6, 1964, at Marianna, Ark.... 6-2/225.... Throws right, bats right.... Full name: Kevin Wade Campbell.
COLLEGE: Arkansas.
TRANSACTIONS/CAREER NOTES: Selected by Philadelphia Phillies organization in 13th round of free-agent draft (June 6, 1983).... Selected by Los Angeles Dodgers organization in fifth round of free-agent draft (June 2, 1986).... Traded by Dodgers organization to Oakland Athletics organization for P David Veres (January 15, 1991).

Year Team (League)	G	W	L	Pct.	ERA	Sv.	IP	H	R	ER	BB	SO
1986—Great Falls (Pioneer)	15	5	6	.455	4.66	0	85	99	62	44	32	66
1987—Vero Beach (Florida State)	28	7	14	.333	3.91	0	184	200	100	80	64	112
1988—Vero Beach (Florida State)	26	8	12	.400	2.75	0	163⅔	166	67	50	49	115
1989—San Antonio (Texas)	17	1	5	.167	6.67	2	27	29	22	20	16	28
—Bakersfield (California)	31	5	3	.625	2.54	6	60⅓	43	23	17	28	63
1990—San Antonio (Texas)	49	2	6	.250	2.33	8	81	67	29	21	25	84
1991—Tacoma (Pacific Coast)■........	35	9	2	*.818	1.80	2	75	53	18	15	35	56
—Oakland (A.L.)	14	1	0	1.000	2.74	0	23	13	7	7	14	16
Major league totals (1 year)	14	1	0	1.000	2.74	0	23	13	7	7	14	16

CAMPUSANO, SIL
OF

PERSONAL: Born December 31, 1966, at Mano Guayabo, Dominican Republic.... 6-0/190.... Throws right, bats right.... Full name: Silvestre Campusano.
TRANSACTIONS/CAREER NOTES: Signed as free agent by Toronto Blue Jays organization (November 14, 1983).... On Toronto disabled list (August 4-September 2, 1988); included rehabilitation disability assignment to Syracuse (August 19-September 2, 1988).... Drafted by Philadelphia Phillies (December 4, 1989).... On Philadelphia disabled list (April 1-26, 1991).... Granted free agency (October 7, 1991).
RECORDS/HONORS: Named South Atlantic League Most Valuable Player (1985).
STATISTICAL NOTES: Led South Atlantic League outfielders with five double plays in 1985.... Led Southern League outfielders with 437 total chances and tied for lead with six double plays in 1986.... Tied for International League lead in caught stealing with 15 in 1987.

Year	Team (League)	Pos.	G	AB	R	H	2B	3B	HR	RBI	Avg.	SB	PO	A	E	Avg.
1984 — Brad. Blue Jays (GCL)	OF	•63	236	42	63	17	2	0	22	.267	•21	128	7	•8	.944
1985 — Florence (S. Atlantic)	OF	88	348	80	109	31	1	15	56	.313	21	188	12	4	.980
— Knoxville (Southern)	OF	45	178	30	54	9	0	6	29	.303	10	135	3	4	.972
1986 — Knoxville (Southern)	OF	132	493	89	126	32	6	14	59	.256	18	*401	21	15	.966
1987 — Syracuse (International)	OF	129	481	70	127	28	•10	14	63	.264	26	324	8	*11	.968
1988 — Toronto (A.L.)	OF	73	142	14	31	10	2	2	12	.218	0	111	2	8	.934
— Syracuse (International)	OF	17	62	8	13	3	0	0	3	.210	1	44	0	1	.978
1989 — Syracuse (International)	OF	112	356	46	86	19	4	6	30	.242	17	256	9	5	.981
1990 — Philadelphia (N.L.)■	OF	66	85	10	18	1	1	2	9	.212	1	40	1	1	.976
1991 — Philadelphia (N.L.)	OF	15	35	2	4	0	0	1	2	.114	0	27	1	0	1.000
— Scranton/W.B. (Int'l)	OF	94	305	44	80	12	1	8	47	.262	9	161	8	7	.960
American League totals (1 year)		73	142	14	31	10	2	2	12	.218	0	111	2	8	.934
National League totals (2 years)		81	120	12	22	1	1	3	11	.183	1	67	2	1	.986
Major league totals (3 years)		154	262	26	53	11	3	5	23	.202	1	178	4	9	.953

CANALE, GEORGE
1B, EXPOS

PERSONAL: Born August 11, 1965, at Memphis, Tenn.... 6-1/190.... Throws right, bats left.... Full name: George Anthony Canale IV.... Name pronounced ca-NAL-lee.
HIGH SCHOOL: Cave Spring (Roanoke, Va.).
COLLEGE: Virginia Tech.
TRANSACTIONS/CAREER NOTES: Selected by Milwaukee Brewers organization in sixth round of free-agent draft (June 2, 1986).... On Denver disabled list (June 23-July 14, 1991).... Traded by Brewers to Montreal Expos for OF Alex Diaz (October 15, 1991).
RECORDS/HONORS: Named first baseman on THE SPORTING NEWS college All-America team (1986).
STATISTICAL NOTES: Led Pioneer League with 54 bases on balls received in 1986.... Led Pioneer League first basemen with 47 double plays in 1986.... Led Texas League batters with 152 strikeouts in 1988.... Led Texas League first basemen with 106 double plays in 1988.... Led American Association batters with 134 strikeouts and 245 total bases in 1989.... Led American Association first basemen with .993 fielding percentage, 1,287 putouts, 94 assists, 1,391 total chances and 122 double plays in 1989.

Year	Team (League)	Pos.	G	AB	R	H	2B	3B	HR	RBI	Avg.	SB	PO	A	E	Avg.
1986 — Helena (Pioneer)	1B	65	221	48	72	19	0	9	49	.326	6	*554	29	6	*.990
1987 — El Paso (Texas)	1B	65	253	38	65	10	2	7	36	.257	3	639	35	3	.996
— Stockton (California)	1B	66	246	42	69	18	1	7	48	.280	5	615	33	4	.994
1988 — El Paso (Texas)	1B-3B-OF	132	496	77	120	23	2	23	93	.242	9	1231	71	12	.991
1989 — Denver (Am. Assoc.)	1B-3B	•144	503	80	140	33	•9	18	71	.278	5	†1287	†94	10	†.993
— Milwaukee (A.L.)	1B	13	26	5	5	1	0	1	3	.192	0	86	4	1	.989
1990 — Denver (Am. Assoc.)	1B	134	468	76	119	17	6	12	60	.254	12	1073	63	10	*.991
— Milwaukee (A.L.)	1B	10	13	4	1	1	0	0	0	.077	0	32	4	0	1.000
1991 — Denver (Am. Assoc.)	1B-3B	88	274	36	64	10	2	10	47	.234	6	489	46	6	.989
— Milwaukee (A.L.)	1B	21	34	6	6	2	0	3	10	.176	0	101	16	15	.886
Major league totals (3 years)		44	73	15	12	4	0	4	13	.164	0	219	24	16	.938

CANDAELE, CASEY
2B/OF, ASTROS

PERSONAL: Born January 12, 1961, at Lompoc, Calif.... 5-9/165.... Throws right, bats both.... Full name: Casey Todd Candaele.... Son of Helen St. Aubin, former women's professional baseball player.... Name pronounced kan-DELL.
HIGH SCHOOL: Lompoc (Calif.).
COLLEGE: Arizona.
TRANSACTIONS/CAREER NOTES: Signed as free agent by Montreal Expos organization (August 15, 1982).... Traded by Expos to Houston Astros for C Mark Bailey (July 23, 1988).... On disabled list (June 9-July 22, 1989).
STATISTICAL NOTES: Led Florida State League second basemen with 391 assists, 30 errors and 87 double plays in 1983.... Led American Association with 11 sacrifice hits in 1986.... Tied for American Association lead in double plays by second basemen with 68 in 1986.

Year	Team (League)	Pos.	G	AB	R	H	2B	3B	HR	RBI	Avg.	SB	PO	A	E	Avg.
1983 — West Palm Beach (FSL)	2-0-3-S	127	*511	77	156	26	9	0	45	.305	22	271	†403	†32	.955
— Memphis (Southern)	3B	5	19	4	4	1	0	0	1	.211	1	2	11	0	1.000
1984 — Jacksonville (Southern)	S-0-2-3	132	532	68	145	23	2	2	53	.273	26	224	352	18	.970
1985 — Indianapolis (A.A.)	0-2-S-3	127	390	55	101	13	5	0	35	.259	13	266	160	6	.986
1986 — Indianapolis (A.A.)	2B-OF	119	480	77	145	32	6	2	42	.302	16	240	319	13	.977
— Montreal (N.L.)	2B-3B	30	104	9	24	4	1	0	6	.231	3	45	74	2	.983

— 74 —

Year	Team (League)	Pos.	G	AB	R	H	2B	3B	HR	RBI	Avg.	SB	PO	A	E	Avg.
1987	—Montreal (N.L.)	2-0-S-1	138	449	62	122	23	4	1	23	.272	7	237	176	8	.981
1988	—Indianapolis (A.A.)	SS-2B-OF	60	239	23	63	11	6	2	36	.264	5	105	161	3	.989
	—Montreal-Houston (N.L.)■	2B-OF-3B	57	147	11	25	8	1	0	5	.170	1	79	126	2	.990
	—Tucson (Pacific Coast)	0-2-S-3	17	66	8	17	3	0	0	5	.258	4	35	29	3	.955
1989	—Tucson (Pacific Coast)	0-3-2-S-1	68	206	22	45	6	1	0	17	.218	6	94	59	5	.968
1990	—Tucson (Pacific Coast)	2B	7	28	2	6	1	0	0	2	.214	1	14	24	1	.974
	—Houston (N.L.)	0-2-S-3	130	262	30	75	8	6	3	22	.286	7	147	120	3	.989
1991	—Houston (N.L.)	2B-OF-3B	151	461	44	121	20	7	4	50	.262	9	244	318	10	.983
	Major league totals (5 years)		506	1423	156	367	63	19	8	106	.258	27	752	814	25	.984

CANDELARIA, JOHN

P, DODGERS

PERSONAL: Born November 6, 1953, at Brooklyn, N.Y. . . . 6-6/225. . . . Throws left, bats right. . . . Full name: John Robert Candelaria.
HIGH SCHOOL: LaSalle Academy (New York).
TRANSACTIONS/CAREER NOTES: Selected by Pittsburgh Pirates organization in second round of free-agent draft (June 6, 1972). . . . On disabled list (May 11, 1981-remainder of season). . . . Traded by Pirates with P Al Holland and OF George Hendrick to California Angels for P Pat Clements, OF Mike Brown and a player to be named later (August 2, 1985); Pirates organization acquired P Bob Kipper to complete deal (August 16, 1985). . . . On California disabled list (April 15-July 8, 1986); included rehabilitation disability assignment to Palm Springs (June 26-July 2, 1986). . . . On disabled list (May 14-29 and June 19-August 5, 1987). . . . Traded by Angels to New York Mets for P Shane Young and P Jeff Richardson (September 15, 1987). . . . Granted free agency (November 9, 1987). . . . Signed by New York Yankees (January 15, 1988). . . . On New York disabled list (May 6-August 19, 1989); included rehabilitation disability assignment to Sarasota Yankees (August 11-19, 1989). . . . Traded by Yankees to Montreal Expos for a player to be named later (August 29, 1989); Yankees acquired 3B Mike Blowers to complete deal (August 31, 1989). . . . Released by Expos (January 24, 1990). . . . Signed by Minnesota Twins (February 28, 1990). . . . Traded by Twins to Toronto Blue Jays for 2B Nelson Liriano and OF Pedro Munoz (July 27, 1990). . . . Granted free agency (November 5, 1990). . . . Signed by Los Angeles Dodgers (March 25, 1991).
RECORDS/HONORS: Named A.L. Comeback Player of the Year by THE SPORTING NEWS (1986).
STATISTICAL NOTES: Led Carolina League with 17 home runs allowed in 1974. . . . Pitched 2-0 no-hit victory against Los Angeles Dodgers (August 9, 1976). . . . Tied for N.L. lead with 29 home runs allowed in 1977.

Year	Team (League)	G	W	L	Pct.	ERA	Sv.	IP	H	R	ER	BB	SO
1973	—Charleston, S.C. (W. Caro.)	18	10	2	*.833	3.79	0	95	84	45	40	38	60
1974	—Salem (Carolina)	25	11	8	.579	3.68	1	154	146	80	63	63	147
	—Charleston, W.Va. (Int'l)	1	0	0	...	1.64	0	11	7	2	2	1	10
1975	—Pittsburgh (N.L.)	18	8	6	.571	2.75	0	121	95	47	37	36	95
	—Charleston, W.Va. (Int'l)	10	7	1	.875	1.77	1	61	53	15	12	17	48
1976	—Pittsburgh (N.L.)	32	16	7	.696	3.15	1	220	173	87	77	60	138
1977	—Pittsburgh (N.L.)	33	20	5	*.800	*2.34	0	231	197	64	60	52	133
1978	—Pittsburgh (N.L.)	30	12	11	.522	3.24	1	189	191	73	68	49	94
1979	—Pittsburgh (N.L.)	33	14	9	.609	3.22	0	207	201	83	74	41	101
1980	—Pittsburgh (N.L.)	35	11	14	.440	4.02	1	233	246	114	104	50	97
1981	—Pittsburgh (N.L.)	6	2	2	.500	3.51	0	41	42	17	16	11	14
1982	—Pittsburgh (N.L.)	31	12	7	.632	2.94	1	174⅔	166	62	57	37	133
1983	—Pittsburgh (N.L.)	33	15	8	.652	3.23	0	197⅔	191	73	71	45	157
1984	—Pittsburgh (N.L.)	33	12	11	.522	2.72	2	185⅓	179	69	56	34	133
1985	—Pittsburgh (N.L.)	37	2	4	.333	3.64	9	54⅓	57	23	22	14	47
	—California (A.L.)■	13	7	3	.700	3.80	0	71	70	33	30	24	53
1986	—California (A.L.)	16	10	2	.833	2.55	0	91⅔	68	30	26	26	81
	—Palm Springs (California)	2	0	0	...	2.57	0	7	4	2	2	2	8
1987	—California (A.L.)	20	8	6	.571	4.71	0	116⅔	127	70	61	20	74
	—New York (N.L.)■	3	2	0	1.000	5.84	0	12⅓	17	8	8	3	10
1988	—New York (A.L.)	25	13	7	.650	3.38	1	157	150	69	59	23	121
1989	—New York (A.L.)	10	3	3	.500	5.14	0	49	49	28	28	12	37
	—Sarasota Yankees (GCL)	2	1	0	1.000	0.00	0	8	6	0	0	1	12
	—Montreal (N.L.)■	12	0	2	.000	3.31	0	16⅓	17	8	6	4	14
1990	—Minnesota-Toronto (A.L.)■	47	7	6	.538	3.95	5	79⅔	87	36	35	20	63
1991	—Los Angeles (N.L.)■	59	1	1	.500	3.74	2	33⅔	31	16	14	11	38
	American League totals (6 years)	131	48	27	.640	3.81	6	565	551	266	239	125	429
	National League totals (14 years)	395	127	87	.593	3.15	17	1916⅓	1803	744	670	447	1204
	Major league totals (17 years)	526	175	114	.606	3.30	23	2481⅓	2354	1010	909	572	1633

CHAMPIONSHIP SERIES RECORD

CHAMPIONSHIP SERIES NOTES: Shares single-game records for most strikeouts—14; most consecutive strikeouts—4 (October 7, 1975).

Year	Team (League)	G	W	L	Pct.	ERA	Sv.	IP	H	R	ER	BB	SO
1975	—Pittsburgh (N.L.)	1	0	0	...	3.52	0	7⅔	3	3	3	2	14
1979	—Pittsburgh (N.L.)	1	0	0	...	2.57	0	7	5	2	2	1	4
1986	—California (A.L.)	2	1	1	.500	0.84	0	10⅔	11	8	1	6	7
	Championship Series totals (3 years)	4	1	1	.500	2.13	0	25⅓	19	13	6	9	25

WORLD SERIES RECORD

Year	Team (League)	G	W	L	Pct.	ERA	Sv.	IP	H	R	ER	BB	SO
1979	—Pittsburgh (N.L.)	2	1	1	.500	5.00	0	9	14	6	5	2	4

Year	League	W	L	Pct.	ERA	Sv.	IP	H	R	ER	BB	SO
1977	—National					Did not play						

CANDIOTTI, TOM
P, DODGERS

PERSONAL: Born August 31, 1957, at Walnut Creek, Calif. . . . 6-2/200. . . . Throws right, bats right. . . . Full name: Thomas Caesar Candiotti.
HIGH SCHOOL: St. Mary's (Calif.).
COLLEGE: St. Mary's, Calif. (bachelor of science degree in business administration, 1979).
TRANSACTIONS/CAREER NOTES: Signed as free agent by Victoria, independent (July 17, 1979). . . . Released by Victoria (January 4, 1980). . . . Signed by Ft. Myers, Kansas City Royals organization (January 5, 1980). . . . On Jacksonville disabled list (June 7-26, 1980). . . . Drafted by Vancouver, Milwaukee Brewers organization (December 9, 1980). . . . On disabled list (April 10-May 12, 1981 and April 13, 1982-remainder of season). . . . On Vancouver disabled list (May 30-June 15, 1984). . . . On Milwaukee disabled list (August 2-September 1, 1984); included rehabilitation disability assignment to Beloit (August 24-31, 1984). . . . Granted free agency (October 15, 1985). . . . Signed by Cleveland Indians (December 12, 1985). . . . On disabled list (August 4-19, 1988; July 2-17, 1989; and May 7-22, 1990). . . . Traded by Indians with OF Turner Ward to Toronto Blue Jays for P Denis Boucher, OF Glenallen Hill, OF Mark Whiten and a player to be named later (June 27, 1991); Indians acquired cash instead of player to complete deal (October 15, 1991). . . . Granted free agency (November 7, 1991). . . . Signed by Los Angeles Dodgers (December 3, 1991).
STATISTICAL NOTES: Led A.L. with 17 complete games in 1986.

Year	Team (League)	G	W	L	Pct.	ERA	Sv.	IP	H	R	ER	BB	SO
1979	—Victoria (Northwest)	12	5	1	.833	2.44	1	70	63	23	19	16	66
1980	—Fort Myers (Florida State)■.....	7	3	2	.600	2.25	0	44	32	16	11	9	31
	—Jacksonville (Southern)	17	7	8	.467	2.77	0	117	98	45	36	40	93
1981	—El Paso (Texas)■....................	21	7	6	.538	2.80	0	119	137	51	37	27	68
1982	—						Did not play						
1983	—El Paso (Texas)	7	1	0	1.000	2.92	2	24⅔	23	10	8	7	18
	—Vancouver (Pacific Coast)	15	6	4	.600	2.81	0	99⅓	87	35	31	16	61
	—Milwaukee (A.L.)	10	4	4	.500	3.23	0	55⅔	62	21	20	16	21
1984	—Vancouver (Pacific Coast)	15	8	4	.667	2.89	0	96⅔	96	36	31	22	53
	—Milwaukee (A.L.)	8	2	2	.500	5.29	0	32⅓	38	21	19	10	23
	—Beloit (Midwest)	2	0	1	.000	2.70	0	10	12	5	3	5	12
1985	—El Paso (Texas)	4	1	0	1.000	2.76	0	29⅓	29	11	9	7	16
	—Vancouver (Pacific Coast)	24	9	13	.409	3.94	0	150⅔	178	83	66	36	97
1986	—Cleveland (A.L.)■	36	16	12	.571	3.57	0	252⅓	234	112	100	106	167
1987	—Cleveland (A.L.)	32	7	18	.280	4.78	0	201⅔	193	132	107	93	111
1988	—Cleveland (A.L.)	31	14	8	.636	3.28	0	216⅔	225	86	79	53	137
1989	—Cleveland (A.L.)	31	13	10	.565	3.10	0	206	188	80	71	55	124
1990	—Cleveland (A.L.)	31	15	11	.577	3.65	0	202	207	92	82	55	128
1991	—Cleveland-Toronto (A.L.)■......	34	13	13	.500	2.65	0	238	202	82	70	73	167
	Major league totals (8 years)	213	84	78	.519	3.51	0	1404⅔	1349	626	548	461	878

CHAMPIONSHIP SERIES RECORD

Year	Team (League)	G	W	L	Pct.	ERA	Sv.	IP	H	R	ER	BB	SO
1991	—Toronto (A.L.)..........................	2	0	1	.000	8.22	0	7⅔	17	9	7	2	5

CANSECO, JOSE
OF, ATHLETICS

PERSONAL: Born July 2, 1964, at Havana, Cuba. . . . 6-3/240. . . . Throws right, bats right. . . . Full name: Jose Canseco Jr. . . . Identical twin of Ozzie Canseco, minor league outfielder (1983-90) and Japanese professional player (1991). . . . Name pronounced can-SAY-co.
HIGH SCHOOL: Coral Park (Miami).
TRANSACTIONS/CAREER NOTES: Selected by Oakland Athletics organization in 15th round of free-agent draft (June 7, 1982). . . . On Huntsville disabled list (May 14-June 3, 1985). . . . On Oakland disabled list (March 23-July 13, 1989); included rehabilitation disability assignment to Huntsville (May 6, 1989 and June 28-July 13, 1989). . . . On disabled list (June 8-23, 1990).
RECORDS/HONORS: Shares major league single-season record for fewest errors by outfielder who led league in errors—9 (1991). . . . Named Minor League Player of the Year by THE SPORTING NEWS (1985). . . . Named Southern League Most Valuable Player (1985). . . . Named A.L. Rookie Player of the Year by THE SPORTING NEWS (1986). . . . Named A.L. Rookie of the Year by Baseball Writers' Association of America (1986). . . . Named A.L. Player of the Year by THE SPORTING NEWS (1988). . . . Named outfielder on THE SPORTING NEWS A.L. All-Star team (1988 and 1990-91). . . . Named outfielder on THE SPORTING NEWS A.L. Silver Slugger team (1988 and 1990-91). . . . Named A.L. Most Valuable Player by Baseball Writers' Association of America (1988).
STATISTICAL NOTES: Led Northwest League batters with 78 strikeouts in 1983. . . . Led California League outfielders with eight double plays in 1984. . . . Hit three home runs in a game (July 3, 1988). . . . Led A.L. with .569 slugging percentage in 1988.

Year	Team (League)	Pos.	G	AB	R	H	2B	3B	HR	RBI	Avg.	SB	PO	A	E	Avg.
						BATTING								FIELDING		
1982	—Miami (Florida State)	3B	6	9	0	1	0	0	0	0	.111	0	3	1	1	.800
	—Idaho Falls (Pioneer)........	3B-OF	28	57	13	15	3	0	2	7	.263	3	6	17	3	.885
1983	—Madison (Midwest)	OF	34	88	8	14	4	0	3	10	.159	2	23	2	1	.962
	—Medford (Northwest)	OF	59	197	34	53	15	2	11	40	.269	6	46	5	5	.911
1984	—Modesto (California)	OF	116	410	61	113	21	2	15	73	.276	10	216	17	9	.963
1985	—Huntsville (Southern)	OF	58	211	47	67	10	2	25	80	.318	6	117	9	7	.947
	—Tacoma (Pacific Coast)	OF	60	233	41	81	16	1	11	47	.348	5	81	7	2	.978
	—Oakland (A.L.)	OF	29	96	16	29	3	0	5	13	.302	1	56	4	3	.951

Year	Team (League)	Pos.	G	AB	R	H	2B	3B	HR	RBI	Avg.	SB	PO	A	E	Avg.
1986—Oakland (A.L.)	OF	157	600	85	144	29	1	33	117	.240	15	319	4	•14	.958
1987—Oakland (A.L.)	OF	159	630	81	162	35	3	31	113	.257	15	263	12	7	.975
1988—Oakland (A.L.)	OF	158	610	120	187	34	0	★42	★124	.307	40	304	11	7	.978
1989—Huntsville (Southern)	OF	9	29	2	6	0	0	0	3	.207	1	9	0	0	1.000
—Oakland (A.L.)	OF	65	227	40	61	9	1	17	57	.269	6	119	5	3	.976
1990—Oakland (A.L.)	OF	131	481	83	132	14	2	37	101	.274	19	182	7	1	.995
1991—Oakland (A.L.)	OF	154	572	115	152	32	1	•44	122	.266	26	245	5	•9	.965
Major league totals (7 years)		853	3216	540	867	156	8	209	647	.270	122	1488	46	44	.972

CHAMPIONSHIP SERIES RECORD

CHAMPIONSHIP SERIES NOTES: Shares A.L. single-series record for most home runs—3 (1988).

Year	Team (League)	Pos.	G	AB	R	H	2B	3B	HR	RBI	Avg.	SB	PO	A	E	Avg.
1988—Oakland (A.L.)	OF	4	16	4	5	1	0	3	4	.313	1	6	0	0	1.000
1989—Oakland (A.L.)	OF-PH	5	17	1	5	0	0	1	3	.294	0	6	1	1	.875
1990—Oakland (A.L.)	OF	4	11	3	2	0	0	0	1	.182	2	14	0	0	1.000
Championship Series totals (3 years)		13	44	8	12	1	0	4	8	.273	3	26	1	1	.964

WORLD SERIES RECORD

WORLD SERIES NOTES: Hit home run in first series at-bat (October 15, 1988).... Shares single-game record for most grand slams—1 (October 15, 1988).... Shares record for most runs batted in in one inning—4 (October 15, 1988, second inning).

Year	Team (League)	Pos.	G	AB	R	H	2B	3B	HR	RBI	Avg.	SB	PO	A	E	Avg.
1988—Oakland (A.L.)	OF	5	19	1	1	0	0	1	5	.053	1	8	0	0	1.000
1989—Oakland (A.L.)	OF	4	14	5	5	0	0	1	3	.357	1	6	0	0	1.000
1990—Oakland (A.L.)	O-PH-DH	4	12	1	1	0	0	1	2	.083	0	4	0	0	1.000
World Series totals (3 years)		13	45	7	7	0	0	3	10	.156	2	18	0	0	1.000

ALL-STAR GAME RECORD

ALL-STAR GAME NOTES: Named to A.L. All-Star team for 1989 game; replaced due to injury.

Year	League	Pos.	AB	R	H	2B	3B	HR	RBI	Avg.	SB	PO	A	E	Avg.
1986—American							Did not play								
1988—American	OF	4	0	0	0	0	0	0	.000	0	3	0	0	1.000
1990—American	OF	4	0	0	0	0	0	0	.000	1	1	0	0	1.000
All-Star Game totals (2 years)		8	0	0	0	0	0	0	.000	1	4	0	0	1.000

CAPEL, MIKE
P, ASTROS

PERSONAL: Born October 13, 1961, at Marshall, Tex.... 6-1/175.... Throws right, bats right.... Full name: Michael Lee Capel.
HIGH SCHOOL: Spring (Tex.).
COLLEGE: Texas.
TRANSACTIONS/CAREER NOTES: Selected by Philadelphia Phillies organization in 24th round of free-agent draft (June 3, 1980).... Selected by Chicago Cubs organization in 13th round of free-agent draft (June 6, 1983).... On disabled list (May 26-June 16, 1986).... Granted free agency (October 15, 1989).... Signed by Denver, Milwaukee Brewers organization (December 13, 1989).... Granted free agency (October 4, 1990).... Signed by Houston Astros (January 5, 1991).

Year	Team (League)	G	W	L	Pct.	ERA	Sv.	IP	H	R	ER	BB	SO
1983—Midland (Texas)	3	1	1	.500	6.91	0	14⅓	22	12	11	8	8
—Quad Cities (Midwest)	8	3	2	.600	2.42	1	44⅔	32	15	12	14	35
1984—Midland (Texas)	16	1	10	.091	6.31	0	61⅓	69	53	43	37	20
—Lodi (California)	20	0	7	.000	3.65	1	69	54	38	28	35	46
1985—Pittsfield (Eastern)	33	3	6	.333	4.91	0	73⅓	74	44	40	47	53
1986—Pittsfield (Eastern)	38	4	4	.500	1.87	13	62⅔	51	20	13	22	50
1987—Iowa (American Association)	53	7	10	.412	5.73	4	108⅓	117	72	69	43	75
1988—Iowa (American Association)	32	3	2	.600	3.43	3	57⅔	60	24	22	23	49
—Chicago (N.L.)	22	2	1	.667	4.91	0	29⅓	34	19	16	13	19
1989—Iowa (American Association)	64	4	7	.364	3.25	5	97	87	43	35	41	62
1990—Denver (American Assoc.)■	41	4	3	.571	4.26	2	101⅓	98	55	48	39	60
—Milwaukee (A.L.)	2	0	0	...	135.00	0	⅓	6	6	5	1	1
1991—Tucson (Pacific Coast)■	30	4	2	.667	2.40	3	56⅓	49	16	15	17	44
—Houston (N.L.)	25	1	3	.250	3.03	3	32⅔	33	14	11	15	23
American League totals (1 year)	2	0	0	...	135.00	0	⅓	6	6	5	1	1
National League totals (2 years)	47	3	4	.429	3.92	3	62	67	33	27	28	42
Major league totals (3 years)	49	3	4	.429	4.62	3	62⅓	73	39	32	29	43

CAPRA, NICK
OF/3B, REDS

PERSONAL: Born March 8, 1958, at Denver.... 5-8/165.... Throws right, bats right.... Full name: Nick Lee Capra.
HIGH SCHOOL: Lincoln (Denver).
COLLEGE: Blinn College (Tex.), Lamar Community College (Colo.) and Oklahoma.
TRANSACTIONS/CAREER NOTES: Selected by Montreal Expos organization in 12th round of free-agent draft (June 8, 1976)....

Selected by Texas Rangers organization in third round of free-agent draft (June 5, 1979).... On disabled list (July 4-19, 1979 and May 14-June 1, 1984).... Granted free agency (October 15, 1985).... Signed by Chicago White Sox organization (January 18, 1986).... Loaned by White Sox organization to Oklahoma City, Texas Rangers organization (June 17, 1986); returned (September 2, 1986).... Granted free agency (October 15, 1986).... Signed by Oklahoma City (January 10, 1987).... Granted free agency (October 15, 1987).... Signed by Omaha, Kansas City Royals organization (December 18, 1987).... Granted free agency (October 15, 1988).... Re-signed by Omaha (January 12, 1989).... Granted free agency (October 15, 1989).... Signed by Oklahoma City (January 9, 1990).... Granted free agency (October 15, 1991).... Signed by Cincinnati Reds organization (November 12, 1991).

RECORDS/HONORS: Named second baseman on THE SPORTING NEWS college All-America team (1979).

STATISTICAL NOTES: Led American Association outfielders with 330 total chances in 1983.

Year	Team (League)	Pos.	G	AB	R	H	2B	3B	HR	RBI	Avg.	SB	PO	A	E	Avg.
1979	Tulsa (Texas)	3B-2B-SS	66	212	29	59	7	0	3	26	.278	16	60	173	22	.914
1980	Tulsa (Texas)	2B-OF-SS	117	440	90	127	25	9	6	53	.289	★55	288	303	19	.969
1981	Wichita (Am. Assoc.)	OF	123	398	74	104	16	4	4	38	.261	41	226	6	7	.971
1982	Denver (Am. Assoc.)	OF	121	416	82	117	15	10	9	40	.281	29	275	11	3	.990
	Texas (A.L.)	OF	13	15	2	4	0	0	1	1	.267	2	14	2	0	1.000
1983	Oklahoma City (A.A.)	OF	124	441	84	113	17	4	13	41	.256	27	★307	12	11	.967
	Texas (A.L.)	OF	8	2	0	0	0	0	0	0	.000	0	0	0	0	...
1984	Oklahoma City (A.A.)	OF-2B	123	442	68	113	18	1	2	21	.256	47	329	13	4	.988
1985	Oklahoma City (A.A.)	OF-2B	97	353	53	96	17	1	0	27	.272	25	201	70	2	.993
	Texas (A.L.)	OF	8	8	1	1	0	0	0	0	.125	0	11	0	0	1.000
1986	Buffalo-Okla. City (A.A.)■	OF-2B	108	406	68	105	18	2	7	31	.259	32	231	58	6	.980
1987	Oklahoma City (A.A.)■	OF	97	353	69	107	18	3	1	39	.303	21	250	11	2	.992
1988	Omaha (Am. Assoc.)■	OF	93	346	53	100	11	6	1	43	.289	28	169	10	4	.978
	Kansas City (A.L.)	OF	14	29	3	4	1	0	0	0	.138	1	15	0	0	1.000
1989	Omaha (Am. Assoc.)	0-S-2-3	128	500	★84	145	27	3	7	44	.290	31	236	64	12	.962
1990	Oklahoma City (A.A.)■	OF-3B	122	451	80	125	26	3	5	45	.277	35	228	16	5	.980
1991	Oklahoma City (A.A.)	0-3-2-S-P	127	485	74	132	34	4	5	39	.272	27	219	33	11	.958
Major league totals (4 years)			43	54	8	9	1	0	1	1	.167	3	40	2	0	1.000

RECORD AS PITCHER

Year	Team (League)	G	W	L	Pct.	ERA	Sv.	IP	H	R	ER	BB	SO
1991	Oklahoma City (Am. Assoc.)	1	0	0	...	0.00	0	3	3	2	0	0	1

CARABALLO, RAMON
SS, BRAVES

PERSONAL: Born May 23, 1969, at Rio San Juan, Dominican Republic.... 5-7/150.... Throws right, bats both.... Full name: Ramon Caraballo.
HIGH SCHOOL: Liceo Antorcha del Futero (Dominican Republic).
TRANSACTIONS/CAREER NOTES: Signed as free agent by Atlanta Braves organization (April 10, 1988).

Year	Team (League)	Pos.	G	AB	R	H	2B	3B	HR	RBI	Avg.	SB	PO	A	E	Avg.
1989	Bradenton Braves (GCL)	SS-OF-2B	20	77	9	19	3	1	1	10	.247	5	39	47	6	.935
	Sumter (South Atlantic)	SS	45	171	22	45	10	5	1	32	.263	9	57	151	18	.920
1990	Burlington (Midwest)	SS	102	390	83	113	18	★14	7	55	.290	41	139	280	35	.923
1991	Durham (Carolina)	2B	120	444	73	111	13	8	6	52	.250	★53	217	341	28	.952

CARMAN, DON
P, RANGERS

PERSONAL: Born August 14, 1959, at Oklahoma City.... 6-3/201.... Throws left, bats left.... Full name: Donald Wayne Carman.
HIGH SCHOOL: Leedey (Okla.).
COLLEGE: Seminole Junior College (Okla.) and Oklahoma.
TRANSACTIONS/CAREER NOTES: Signed as free agent by Philadelphia Phillies organization (August 25, 1978).... Granted free agency (November 5, 1990).... Signed by Houston Astros (February 6, 1991).... Released by Astros (April 2, 1991).... Signed by Cincinnati Reds (April 7, 1991).... Released by Reds (July 18, 1991).... Signed by Omaha, Kansas City Royals organization (August 2, 1991).... Granted free agency (October 15, 1991).... Signed by Oklahoma City, Texas Rangers organization (February 4, 1992).
RECORDS/HONORS: Shares N.L. single-season record for fewest games lost for pitcher who led league in games lost—15 (1989).... Shares N.L. record for most consecutive home runs allowed in one inning—3 (April 17, 1989, third inning).

Year	Team (League)	G	W	L	Pct.	ERA	Sv.	IP	H	R	ER	BB	SO
1979	Spartanburg (W. Carolinas)	37	6	3	.667	3.92	0	78	72	36	34	28	70
1980	Peninsula (Carolina)	27	14	5	.737	3.42	0	150	149	73	57	53	★141
1981	Reading (Eastern)	28	12	13	.480	4.04	0	176	167	93	79	75	105
1982	Oklahoma City (Am. Assoc.)	10	0	1	.000	6.82	0	33	37	29	25	23	29
	Reading (Eastern)	20	6	7	.462	4.16	0	97⅓	99	58	45	62	81
1983	Reading (Eastern)	★56	8	5	.615	2.97	23	124⅓	85	51	41	71	93
	Philadelphia (N.L.)	1	0	0	...	0.00	1	1	0	0	0	0	0
1984	Portland (Pacific Coast)	39	3	3	.500	5.34	3	55⅔	66	36	33	22	53
	Philadelphia (N.L.)	11	0	1	.000	5.40	0	13⅓	14	9	8	6	16
1985	Philadelphia (N.L.)	71	9	4	.692	2.08	7	86⅓	52	25	20	38	87
1986	Philadelphia (N.L.)	50	10	5	.667	3.22	1	134⅓	113	50	48	52	98
1987	Philadelphia (N.L.)	35	13	11	.542	4.22	0	211	194	110	99	69	125
1988	Philadelphia (N.L.)	36	10	14	.417	4.29	0	201⅓	211	101	96	70	116

Year	Team (League)	G	W	L	Pct.	ERA	Sv.	IP	H	R	ER	BB	SO
1989—Philadelphia (N.L.)		49	5	•15	.250	5.24	0	149⅓	152	98	87	86	81
1990—Philadelphia (N.L.)		59	6	2	.750	4.15	1	86⅔	69	43	40	38	58
1991—Cincinnati (N.L.)■..................		28	0	2	.000	5.25	1	36	40	23	21	19	15
—Omaha (American Assoc.)■....		14	3	3	.500	3.96	0	25	29	12	11	13	14
Major league totals (9 years)		340	53	54	.495	4.10	11	919⅓	845	459	419	378	596

CARMONA, GREG
SS, CARDINALS

PERSONAL: Born May 9, 1968, at Bani, Dominican Republic.... 6-0/150.... Throws right, bats both.... Full name: Gregorio Carmona.
HIGH SCHOOL: Bani (Dominican Republic).
TRANSACTIONS/CAREER NOTES: Signed as free agent by St. Louis Cardinals organization (October 14, 1986).
STATISTICAL NOTES: Led Florida State League shortstops with 48 errors in 1989.

						BATTING						FIELDING			
Year	Team (League)	Pos.	G	AB	R	H	2B	3B	HR	RBI	Avg.	SB	PO	A	E	Avg.
1987—Johnson City (Appal.)		3B-2B-SS	47	120	35	21	4	1	0	9	.175	14	30	87	13	.900
1988—Johnson City (Appal.)		SS	21	64	15	21	1	1	0	8	.328	8	20	71	7	.929
—Savannah (S. Atlantic)		SS	33	100	11	16	1	0	0	4	.160	2	51	102	16	.905
1989—St. Petersburg (Fla. St.)		SS-3B	116	348	52	78	4	3	1	30	.224	31	152	373	†48	.916
1990—Arkansas (Texas)		SS	114	319	29	74	3	3	0	20	.232	20	110	★321	★55	.887
1991—Arkansas (Texas)		SS	13	33	1	6	0	0	0	1	.182	0	13	33	3	.939
—Louisville (Am. Assoc.)		SS	56	143	16	25	2	1	2	10	.175	7	67	134	17	.922

CARPENTER, CRIS
P, CARDINALS

PERSONAL: Born April 5, 1965, at St. Augustine, Fla.... 6-1/185.... Throws right, bats right.... Full name: Cris Howell Carpenter.
HIGH SCHOOL: Gainesville (Fla.).
COLLEGE: Georgia.
TRANSACTIONS/CAREER NOTES: Selected by Toronto Blue Jays organization in seventh round of free-agent draft (June 2, 1986). ... Selected by St. Louis Cardinals organization in first round (14th pick overall) of free-agent draft (June 2, 1987).

Year	Team (League)	G	W	L	Pct.	ERA	Sv.	IP	H	R	ER	BB	SO
1988—Louisville (American Assoc.) ...		13	6	2	.750	2.87	0	87⅔	81	28	28	26	45
—St. Louis (N.L.)		8	2	3	.400	4.72	0	47⅔	56	27	25	9	24
1989—St. Louis (N.L.)		36	4	4	.500	3.18	0	68	70	30	24	26	35
—Louisville (American Assoc.) ...		27	5	3	.625	3.19	11	36⅔	39	17	13	9	29
1990—St. Louis (N.L.)		4	0	0	. . .	4.50	0	8	5	4	4	2	6
—Louisville (American Assoc.) ...		22	10	8	.556	3.70	0	143⅓	146	61	59	21	100
1991—St. Louis (N.L.)		59	10	4	.714	4.23	0	66	53	31	31	20	47
Major league totals (4 years)		107	16	11	.593	3.99	0	189⅔	184	92	84	57	112

CARR, CHUCK
OF, CARDINALS

PERSONAL: Born August 10, 1968, at San Bernardino, Calif.... 5-10/155.... Throws right, bats both.... Full name: Charles Lee Glenn Carr Jr.
HIGH SCHOOL: Fontana (Fontana, Calif.).
TRANSACTIONS/CAREER NOTES: Selected by Cincinnati Reds organization in ninth round of free-agent draft (June 2, 1986).... Released by Reds organization (March, 1987).... Signed by Bellingham, Seattle Mariners organization (June 15, 1987).... Traded by Mariners organization to New York Mets organization for P Reggie Dobie (November 18, 1988).... On Tidewater disabled list (April 10-17 and July 15-August 9, 1991).... On New York disabled list (August 29-September 13, 1991).... Traded by Mets to St. Louis Cardinals for P Clyde Keller (December 13, 1991).

						BATTING						FIELDING			
Year	Team (League)	Pos.	G	AB	R	H	2B	3B	HR	RBI	Avg.	SB	PO	A	E	Avg.
1986—Sarasota Reds (GCL)		2B	44	123	13	21	5	0	0	10	.171	9	75	100	11	.941
1987—Bellingham (Northwest)■.		S-O-2-3	44	165	31	40	1	1	1	11	.242	20	50	58	14	.885
1988—Wausau (Midwest)		OF-SS	82	304	58	91	14	2	6	30	.299	41	170	17	12	.940
—Vermont (Eastern)		OF	41	159	26	39	4	2	1	13	.245	21	105	6	6	.949
1989—Jackson (Texas)■		OF	116	444	45	107	13	1	0	22	.241	47	280	11	8	.973
1990—Jackson (Texas)		OF	93	361	60	93	19	9	3	24	.258	48	226	12	8	.967
—Tidewater (Int'l)		OF	20	81	13	21	5	1	0	8	.259	6	40	3	0	1.000
—New York (N.L.)		OF	4	2	0	0	0	0	0	0	.000	1	0	0	0	. . .
1991—Tidewater (Int'l)		OF	64	246	34	48	6	1	1	11	.195	27	141	8	6	.961
—New York (N.L.)		OF	12	11	1	2	0	0	0	1	.182	1	9	0	0	1.000
Major league totals (2 years)			16	13	1	2	0	0	0	1	.154	2	9	0	0	1.000

CARRENO, AMALIO
P, ORIOLES

PERSONAL: Born April 11, 1964, at Chacachacare, Venezuela. ... 6-0/170. ... Throws right, bats right.... Full name: Amalio Rafael Adrian Carreno.
TRANSACTIONS/CAREER NOTES: Signed as free agent by New York Yankees organization (November 22, 1983).... On New York disabled list (June 4-25, 1988).... Traded by Yankees organization to Philadelphia Phillies organization for IF Luis Aguayo (July 15, 1988).... On Scranton/Wilkes-Barre disabled list (June 3-25, 1991).... Granted free agency (October 7, 1991).... Signed by Rochester, Baltimore Orioles organization (January 7, 1992).

Year Team (League)	G	W	L	Pct.	ERA	Sv.	IP	H	R	ER	BB	SO
1984 —Sarasota Yankees (GCL)	9	1	6	.143	4.91	0	33	37	28	18	26	31
1985 —Sarasota Yankees (GCL)	1	0	0	...	4.50	0	2	1	1	1	1	1
1986 —Sarasota Yankees (GCL)	7	5	0	1.000	1.70	0	47⅔	36	12	9	12	27
—Fort Lauderdale (Florida St.)	3	1	1	.500	4.02	0	15⅔	16	11	7	7	8
1987 —Prince William (Carolina)	26	5	2	.714	3.03	2	62⅓	53	30	21	30	49
—Albany (Eastern)	9	0	3	.000	7.88	0	24	32	23	21	15	18
—Columbus (International)	11	1	1	.500	7.79	1	17⅓	26	15	15	5	11
1988 —Columbus (International)	1	0	0	...	10.80	0	3⅓	8	4	4	0	2
—Albany-Reading (Eastern)■.....	14	3	4	.429	4.07	0	59⅔	60	32	27	32	31
1989 —Reading (Eastern)	31	5	7	.417	4.34	1	101⅔	99	57	49	41	56
1990 —Reading (Eastern)	25	4	13	.235	3.66	1	128	137	62	52	47	86
1991 —Scranton/Wilkes-Barre (Int'l) ..	33	4	8	.333	5.33	0	81	88	51	48	26	52
—Philadelphia (N.L.)	3	0	0	...	16.20	0	3⅓	5	6	6	3	2
Major league totals (1 year)	3	0	0	.000	16.20	0	3⅓	5	6	6	3	2

CARREON, MARK
OF, TIGERS

PERSONAL: Born July 9, 1963, at Chicago.... 6-0/195.... Throws left, bats right.... Full name: Mark Steven Carreon.... Son of Camilo Carreon, catcher, Chicago White Sox, Cleveland Indians and Baltimore Orioles (1959-66).... Name pronounced CARE-ee-on.
HIGH SCHOOL: Salpointe (Tucson, Ariz.).
TRANSACTIONS/CAREER NOTES: Selected by New York Mets organization in eighth round of free-agent draft (June 8, 1981)....
On New York disabled list (March 28-April 24, 1989); included rehabilitation disability assignment to Tidewater (April 5-24, 1989).... On disabled list (August 21, 1990-remainder of season).... Traded by Mets with P Tony Castillo to Detroit Tigers for P Paul Gibson and P Randy Marshall (January 22, 1992).
STATISTICAL NOTES: Led Carolina League with 11 sacrifice flies in 1983.

Year Team (League)	Pos.	G	AB	R	H	2B	3B	HR	RBI	Avg.	SB	PO	A	E	Avg.
1981—Kingsport (Appalachian) ..	OF-C	64	232	30	67	8	0	1	36	.289	12	101	7	4	.964
1982—Shelby (South Atlantic)	OF	133	486	★120	160	29	6	2	79	.329	33	183	8	5	.974
1983—Lynchburg (Carolina)	OF	128	491	94	164	13	8	1	67	.334	36	173	8	14	.928
1984—Jackson (Texas)	OF	119	435	64	122	14	3	1	43	.280	12	146	1	4	.974
1985—Tidewater (Int'l)	OF	7	15	1	2	1	0	1	2	.133	0	2	0	0	1.000
—Jackson (Texas)	OF	123	447	96	140	23	5	6	51	.313	23	201	8	1	.995
1986—Tidewater (Int'l)	OF	115	426	62	123	23	2	10	64	.289	11	192	6	6	.971
1987—Tidewater (Int'l)	OF	133	525	83	164	★41	5	10	89	.312	31	237	8	5	.980
—New York (N.L.)	OF	9	12	0	3	0	0	0	1	.250	0	4	0	1	.800
1988—Tidewater (Int'l)	OF	102	365	48	96	13	3	14	55	.263	11	111	6	2	.983
—New York (N.L.)	OF	7	9	5	5	2	0	1	1	.556	0	1	0	0	1.000
1989—Tidewater (Int'l)	OF-1B	32	122	22	34	4	0	1	21	.279	8	26	0	0	1.000
—New York (N.L.)	OF	68	133	20	41	6	0	6	16	.308	2	57	0	1	.983
1990—New York (N.L.)	OF	82	188	30	47	12	0	10	26	.250	1	87	1	0	1.000
1991—New York (N.L.)	OF	106	254	18	66	6	0	4	21	.260	4	96	4	3	.971
Major league totals (5 years)		272	596	73	162	26	0	21	65	.272	5	245	5	5	.980

CARRILLO, MATIAS
OF, BREWERS

PERSONAL: Born February 24, 1963, at Los Mochis Sinaloa, Mexico.... 5-11/190. ... Throws left, bats left.... Full name: Matias Garcia Carrillo.
HIGH SCHOOL: Los Mochis Sinaloa (Mexico).
TRANSACTIONS/CAREER NOTES: Signed by Poza Rica of Mexican League (1982)....
Sold to Hawaii, Pittsburgh Pirates organization (December 15, 1985).... Loaned by Pittsburgh organization to Mexico City Tigers of Mexican League (May 8, 1986); returned (September, 1986).... Drafted by Milwaukee Brewers organization (December 8, 1987).... On suspended list (May 15-29, 1988).... On Denver disabled list (May 9, 1990-remainder of season).
STATISTICAL NOTES: Tied for Mexican League lead with 16 intentional bases on balls received in 1984.... Tied for Mexican League lead in double plays by outfielders with four in 1985.

Year Team (League)	Pos.	G	AB	R	H	2B	3B	HR	RBI	Avg.	SB	PO	A	E	Avg.
1982—Poza Rica (Mexican)	OF-1B	99	301	59	93	9	5	0	29	.309	17	150	13	6	.964
1983—Poza Rica (Mexican)	OF	91	360	54	112	13	11	6	39	.311	25	128	12	1	.993
1984—Mex. City Tigers (Mex.)	OF	113	442	100	154	32	6	14	76	.348	30	281	13	12	.961
1985—Mex. City Tigers (Mex.)	OF	126	465	114	164	21	8	20	102	.353	46	320	13	10	.971
1986—Nashua (Eastern)■.........	OF	15	52	3	8	1	0	0	0	.154	2	28	0	0	1.000
—Mex. City Tigers (Mex.)■ ..	OF	60	216	39	70	15	5	11	64	.324	8	123	6	1	.992
1987—Salem (Carolina)■..........	OF	90	284	42	77	11	3	8	37	.271	15	55	3	3	.951
1988—El Paso (Texas)■............	OF	106	396	76	118	17	2	12	55	.298	11	232	★18	2	★.992
1989—Denver (Am. Assoc.)	OF-1B	125	400	46	104	14	4	10	43	.260	21	236	15	7	.973
1990—Denver (Am. Assoc.)	OF	21	75	15	20	6	2	2	10	.267	0	47	1	1	.980
1991—Denver (Am. Assoc.)	OF-1B	120	421	56	116	18	5	8	56	.276	10	279	7	5	.983

CARTER, GARY
C/1B, EXPOS

PERSONAL: Born April 8, 1954, at Culver City, Calif.... 6-2/214.... Throws right, bats right. ... Full name: Gary Edmund Carter.... Brother of Gordon Carter, minor league outfielder (1972-73).
HIGH SCHOOL: Sunny Hills (Fullerton, Calif.).

TRANSACTIONS/CAREER NOTES: Selected by Montreal Expos organization in third round of free-agent draft (June 6, 1972).... On disabled list (June 6-July 22, 1976).... Traded by Expos to New York Mets for IF Hubie Brooks, C Mike Fitzgerald, OF Herm Winningham and P Floyd Youmans (December 10, 1984).... On disabled list (August 17-September 1, 1986).... On New York disabled list (May 10-July 25, 1989); included rehabilitation disability assignment to Tidewater (July 19-25, 1989).... Released by Mets (November 14, 1989).... Signed by San Francisco Giants (January 19, 1990).... On disabled list (July 9-25, 1990).... Granted free agency (November 5, 1990).... Signed by Los Angeles Dodgers (March 26, 1991).... Claimed on waivers by Expos (November 15, 1991).

RECORDS/HONORS: Holds major league career record for putouts by catcher—11,304.... Holds major league single-season record for fewest passed balls (150 or more games)—1 (1978).... Shares major league records for most home runs in two consecutive games—5 (September 3 and 4, 1985); most years leading league in chances accepted by catcher—8.... Holds N.L. career records for most seasons leading league in games by catcher—6; most years leading league in putouts by catcher—8; most years leading league in chances accepted by catcher—7; most games by catcher—1,971; and most chances accepted by catcher—12,455.... Named N.L. Rookie Player of the Year by THE SPORTING NEWS (1975).... Named catcher on THE SPORTING NEWS N.L. All-Star team (1980-82 and 1984-86).... Won N.L. Gold Glove at catcher (1980-82).... Named catcher on THE SPORTING NEWS N.L. Silver Slugger team (1981-82 and 1984-86).

STATISTICAL NOTES: Led International League catchers with .990 fielding percentage, 794 putouts, 65 assists and 15 double plays in 1974.... Led N.L. catchers with 811 putouts in 1977, 781 in 1978, 509 in 1981, 956 in 1985 and 797 in 1988.... Led N.L. catchers with 101 assists in 1977.... Led N.L. catchers with 921 total chances in 1977, 874 in 1978, 848 in 1979, 937 in 1980, 571 in 1981, 1,068 in 1982 and 860 in 1988.... Led N.L. catchers with 14 double plays in 1977, 9 in 1978, 12 in 1979, 14 in 1983 and 13 in 1987.... Hit three home runs in a game (April 20, 1977 and September 3, 1985).... Led N.L. with 12 passed balls in 1979.... Led N.L. catchers with .995 fielding percentage in 1983.... Led N.L. catchers with 107 assists in 1983.... Led N.L. with 15 sacrifice flies and tied for lead with 16 game-winning RBIs and in grounding into double plays with 21 in 1986.

Year	Team (League)	Pos.	G	AB	R	H	2B	3B	HR	RBI	Avg.	SB	PO	A	E	Avg.
1972 —Cocoa Expos (Fla. E.C.)		C-1B-3B	18	71	6	17	3	0	2	9	.239	1	111	12	10	.925
—West Palm Beach (FSL) ...		C	20	50	9	16	2	2	0	5	.320	1	84	12	2	.980
1973 —Quebec City (Eastern).......		C-1B-OF	130	439	65	111	16	1	15	68	.253	5	823	75	20	.978
—Peninsula (Int'l)		C	8	25	2	7	2	0	0	1	.280	0	5	1	0	1.000
1974 —Memphis (International) ...		C-1B-3B	135	441	62	118	14	7	23	83	.268	6	†908	†76	12	†.988
—Montreal (N.L.)		C-OF	9	27	5	11	0	1	1	6	.407	0	28	4	0	1.000
1975 —Montreal (N.L.)		OF-C-3B	144	503	58	136	20	1	17	68	.270	5	430	38	9	.981
1976 —Montreal (N.L.)		C-OF	91	311	31	68	8	1	6	38	.219	0	364	42	2	.995
1977 —Montreal (N.L.)		C-OF	154	522	86	148	29	2	31	84	.284	5	†813	†101	9	.990
1978 —Montreal (N.L.)		C-1B	157	533	76	136	27	1	20	72	.255	10	†787	83	10	.989
1979 —Montreal (N.L.)		C	141	505	74	143	26	5	22	75	.283	3	★751	★88	9	.989
1980 —Montreal (N.L.)		C	154	549	76	145	25	5	29	101	.264	3	★822	★108	7	★.993
1981 —Montreal (N.L.)		C-1B	100	374	48	94	20	2	16	68	.251	1	†515	58	4	.993
1982 —Montreal (N.L.)		C	154	557	91	163	32	1	29	97	.293	2	★954	★104	10	.991
1983 —Montreal (N.L.)		C-1B	145	541	63	146	37	3	17	79	.270	1	855	†108	5	†.995
1984 —Montreal (N.L.)		C-1B	159	596	75	175	32	1	27	•106	.294	2	990	78	7	.993
1985 —New York (N.L.)■		C-1B-OF	149	555	83	156	17	1	32	100	.281	1	†987	70	8	.992
1986 —New York (N.L.)		C-1-0-3	132	490	81	125	14	2	24	105	.255	1	943	70	9	.991
1987 —New York (N.L.)		C-1B-OF	139	523	55	123	18	2	20	83	.235	0	886	70	9	.991
1988 —New York (N.L.)		C-1B-3B	130	455	39	110	16	2	11	46	.242	0	†842	58	10	.989
1989 —New York (N.L.)		C-1B	50	153	14	28	8	0	2	15	.183	0	266	31	6	.980
—Tidewater (Int'l)		C-1B	5	16	2	3	0	0	1	3	.188	0	26	1	1	.964
1990 —San Francisco (N.L.)■.......		C-1B	92	244	24	62	10	0	9	27	.254	1	348	31	3	.992
1991 —Los Angeles (N.L.)■.........		C-1B	101	248	22	61	14	0	6	26	.246	2	402	52	5	.989
Major league totals (18 years)			2201	7686	1001	2030	353	30	319	1196	.264	37	11983	1194	122	.991

DIVISION SERIES RECORD

Year	Team (League)	Pos.	G	AB	R	H	2B	3B	HR	RBI	Avg.	SB	PO	A	E	Avg.
1981 —Montreal (N.L.)		C	5	19	3	8	3	0	2	6	.421	0	21	5	0	1.000

CHAMPIONSHIP SERIES RECORD

CHAMPIONSHIP SERIES NOTES: Shares career record for most game-winning RBIs—3.... Shares single-series record for most game-winning RBIs—2 (1986).

Year	Team (League)	Pos.	G	AB	R	H	2B	3B	HR	RBI	Avg.	SB	PO	A	E	Avg.
1981 —Montreal (N.L.)		C	5	16	3	7	1	0	0	0	.438	0	27	3	0	1.000
1986 —New York (N.L.)		C	6	27	1	4	1	0	2	2	.148	0	42	5	0	1.000
1988 —New York (N.L.)		C	7	27	0	6	1	1	0	4	.222	0	58	1	0	1.000
Championship Series totals (3 years)			18	70	4	17	3	1	0	6	.243	0	127	9	0	1.000

WORLD SERIES RECORD

Year	Team (League)	Pos.	G	AB	R	H	2B	3B	HR	RBI	Avg.	SB	PO	A	E	Avg.
1986 —New York (N.L.)		C	7	29	4	8	2	0	2	9	.276	0	57	1	0	1.000

ALL-STAR GAME RECORD

ALL-STAR GAME NOTES: Shares single-game record for most home runs—2 (August 9, 1981).... Named to N.L. All-Star team for 1985 game; replaced due to injury by Terry Kennedy.

Year	League	Pos.	AB	R	H	2B	3B	HR	RBI	Avg.	SB	PO	A	E	Avg.
										BATTING			FIELDING		
1975 —National		OF	0	0	0	0	0	0	0	...	0	1	0	0	1.000
1979 —National		C	2	0	1	0	0	0	1	.500	0	6	1	0	1.000
1980 —National		C	1	0	0	0	0	0	0	.000	0	1	0	0	1.000
1981 —National		C	3	2	2	0	0	2	2	.667	0	5	1	0	1.000
1982 —National		C	3	0	1	0	0	0	1	.333	0	7	0	0	1.000
1983 —National		C	2	0	0	0	0	0	0	.000	0	3	0	0	1.000
1984 —National		C	2	1	1	0	0	1	1	.500	0	9	0	0	1.000
1986 —National		C	3	0	0	0	0	0	0	.000	0	9	0	0	1.000
1987 —National		C	1	0	0	0	0	0	0	.000	0	1	0	0	1.000
1988 —National		C	3	0	1	0	0	0	0	.333	0	3	0	0	1.000
All-Star Game totals (10 years)			20	3	6	0	0	3	5	.300	0	45	2	0	1.000

CARTER, JEFF

P, WHITE SOX

PERSONAL: Born December 3, 1964, at Tampa, Fla.... 6-3/195.... Throws right, bats right.... Full name: Jeffrey Allen Carter.
HIGH SCHOOL: Brandon (Fla.).
COLLEGE: South Florida Community College and Tampa (received degree).
TRANSACTIONS/CAREER NOTES: Selected by Montreal Expos organization in 19th round of free-agent draft (June 2, 1987).... Traded by Expos with OF Tim Raines and a player to be named later to Chicago White Sox for OF Ivan Calderon and P Barry Jones (December 24, 1990); White Sox acquired P Mario Brito to complete deal (February 15, 1991).

Year	Team (League)	G	W	L	Pct.	ERA	Sv.	IP	H	R	ER	BB	SO
1987 —Jamestown (New York-Penn) ..		31	2	3	.400	2.34	5	42⅓	39	15	11	17	42
1988 —Rockford (Midwest)		39	11	5	.688	2.77	3	107⅓	100	38	33	35	91
1989 —West Palm Beach (Florida St.) ..		7	4	1	.800	2.57	0	35	36	14	10	8	29
—Jacksonville (Southern)		6	1	4	.200	2.50	0	36	23	11	10	14	21
1990 —Jacksonville (Southern)		52	8	3	.727	★1.84	15	117⅓	90	36	24	33	76
1991 —Vancouver (Pacific Coast)■		41	3	7	.300	3.05	4	79⅔	78	33	27	35	40
—Chicago (A.L.)		5	0	1	.000	5.25	0	12	8	8	7	5	2
Major league totals (1 year)		5	0	1	.000	5.25	0	12	8	8	7	5	2

CARTER, JOE

OF, BLUE JAYS

PERSONAL: Born March 7, 1960, at Oklahoma City.... 6-3/225.... Throws right, bats right.... Full name: Joseph Carter.... Brother of Fred Carter, minor league outfielder (1985-1988).
HIGH SCHOOL: Millwood (Oklahoma City).
COLLEGE: Wichita State.
TRANSACTIONS/CAREER NOTES: Selected by Chicago Cubs organization in first round (second pick overall) of free-agent draft (June 8, 1981).... On disabled list (April 9-19, 1982).... Traded by Cubs organization with OF Mel Hall, P Don Schulze and P Darryl Banks to Cleveland Indians for C Ron Hassey, P Rick Sutcliffe and P George Frazier (June 13, 1984).... On Cleveland disabled list (July 2-17, 1984).... Traded by Indians to San Diego Padres for C Sandy Alomar, OF Chris James and 3B Carlos Baerga (December 6, 1989).... Traded by Padres with 2B Roberto Alomar to Toronto Blue Jays for 1B Fred McGriff and SS Tony Fernandez (December 5, 1990).
RECORDS/HONORS: Shares major league records for most home runs in two consecutive games—5 (July 18 [2], 19 [3], 1989). ... Shares major league single season record for most games with three or more home runs—2 (1989).... Shares A.L. career record for most games with three or more home runs—4.... Named outfielder on THE SPORTING NEWS college All-America team (1980-81).... Named College Player of the Year by THE SPORTING NEWS (1981).... Named outfielder on THE SPORTING NEWS A.L. All-Star team (1991).... Named outfielder on THE SPORTING NEWS A.L. Silver Slugger team (1991).
STATISTICAL NOTES: Led American Association with 265 total bases and tied for lead in strikeouts by batters with 103 in 1983. ... Hit three home runs in a game (August 29, 1986; May 28, 1987; June 24, 1989; and July 19, 1989).... Led A.L. first basemen with 12 errors in 1987.... Led A.L. in being hit by pitch with 10 in 1991.

Year	Team (League)	Pos.	G	AB	R	H	2B	3B	HR	RBI	Avg.	SB	PO	A	E	Avg.
							BATTING							FIELDING		
1981 —Midland (Texas)		OF	67	249	42	67	15	3	5	35	.269	12	100	10	4	.965
1982 —Midland (Texas)		OF	110	427	84	136	22	8	25	98	.319	15	182	6	5	.974
1983 —Iowa (American Assoc.) ...		OF	124	★522	82	160	27	6	22	83	.307	40	204	9	12	.947
—Chicago (N.L.)		OF	23	51	6	9	1	1	0	1	.176	1	26	0	0	1.000
1984 —Iowa (American Assoc.) ...		OF	61	248	45	77	12	7	14	67	.310	11	142	6	2	.987
—Cleveland (A.L.)■		OF-1B	66	244	32	67	6	1	13	41	.275	2	169	11	6	.968
1985 —Cleveland (A.L.)		0-1-2-3	143	489	64	128	27	0	15	59	.262	24	311	17	6	.982
1986 —Cleveland (A.L.)		OF-1B	162	663	108	200	36	9	29 •121	.302	29	800	55	10	.988
1987 —Cleveland (A.L.)		1B-OF	149	588	83	155	27	2	32	106	.264	31	782	46	†17	.980
1988 —Cleveland (A.L.)		OF	157	621	85	168	36	6	27	98	.271	27	444	8	7	.985
1989 —Cleveland (A.L.)		OF-1B	•162	•651	84	158	32	4	35	105	.243	13	443	20	9	.981
1990 —San Diego (N.L.)■		OF-1B	★162	★634	79	147	27	1	24	115	.232	22	492	16	11	.979
1991 —Toronto (A.L.)■		OF	•162	638	89	174	42	3	33	108	.273	20	283	13	8	.974
American League totals (7 years)			1001	3894	545	1050	206	25	184	638	.270	146	3232	170	63	.982
National League totals (2 years)			185	685	85	156	28	2	24	116	.228	23	518	16	11	.980
Major league totals (9 years)			1186	4579	630	1206	234	27	208	754	.263	169	3750	186	74	.982

CHAMPIONSHIP SERIES RECORD

Year	Team (League)	Pos.	G	AB	R	H	2B	3B	HR	RBI	Avg.	SB	PO	A	E	Avg.
							BATTING							FIELDING		
1991 —Toronto (A.L.)		OF-DH	5	19	3	5	2	0	1	4	.263	0	4	1	0	1.000

ALL-STAR GAME RECORD

					BATTING								FIELDING		
Year	League	Pos.	AB	R	H	2B	3B	HR	RBI	Avg.	SB	PO	A	E	Avg.
1991 — American		OF	1	1	1	0	0	0	0	1.000	0	1	0	0	1.000

CARY, CHUCK
P

PERSONAL: Born March 3, 1960, at Whittier, Calif.... 6-4/216.... Throws left, bats left.... Full name: Charles Douglas Cary.
HIGH SCHOOL: California (San Ramon, Calif.).
COLLEGE: California.
TRANSACTIONS/CAREER NOTES: Selected by Detroit Tigers organization in seventh round of free-agent draft (June 8, 1981)....
On Birmingham disabled list (April 18-May 12, 1983; June 24-July 11 and August 4-17, 1984).... Traded by Tigers organization with P Randy O'Neal to Atlanta Braves for OF Terry Harper and OF Freddy Tiburcio (January 27, 1987).... On Atlanta disabled list (April 10-August 17, 1988); included rehabilitation disability assignment to Bradenton (July 29-August 10, 1988) and Richmond (August 11-17, 1988).... Released by Braves organization (December 4, 1988).... Signed by Columbus, New York Yankees organization (January 26, 1989).... On New York disabled list (June 15-July 11, 1989); included rehabilitation disability assignment to Columbus (July 4-11, 1989).... On New York disabled list (April 9-May 15, 1990); included rehabilitation disability assignment to Tampa but did not play (May 1-14, 1990).... Released by Yankees (October 28, 1991).
STATISTICAL NOTES: Tied for Southern League lead with three balks in 1982.

Year	Team (League)	G	W	L	Pct.	ERA	Sv.	IP	H	R	ER	BB	SO
1981 — Macon (South Atlantic)		13	5	5	.500	2.59	0	87	77	32	25	19	55
1982 — Birmingham (Southern)		28	8	14	.364	4.17	0	166	162	93	77	64	125
1983 — Birmingham (Southern)		17	6	8	.429	3.61	0	104⅔	103	50	42	42	69
— Evansville (Am. Assoc.)		15	1	1	.500	4.41	1	16⅓	21	10	8	8	8
1984 — Birmingham (Southern)		22	6	4	.600	4.82	0	108⅓	118	61	58	46	62
1985 — Nashville (American Assoc.)		48	2	1	.667	3.00	8	66	55	27	22	27	54
— Detroit (A.L.)		16	0	1	.000	3.42	2	23⅔	16	9	9	8	22
1986 — Detroit (A.L.)		22	1	2	.333	3.41	0	31⅔	33	18	12	15	21
— Nashville (American Assoc.)		22	1	4	.200	5.47	0	26⅓	29	21	16	15	19
1987 — Richmond (International)■		40	4	6	.400	4.68	3	105⅔	104	64	55	43	128
— Atlanta (N.L.)		13	1	1	.500	3.78	1	16⅔	17	7	7	4	15
1988 — Atlanta (N.L.)		7	0	0	...	6.48	0	8⅓	8	6	6	4	7
— Bradenton Braves (GCL)		4	0	2	.000	3.75	0	12	11	10	5	2	18
— Richmond (International)		5	0	0	...	1.42	1	6⅓	4	1	1	2	3
1989 — Columbus (International)■		11	1	1	.500	3.09	0	23⅓	17	9	8	13	27
— New York (A.L.)		22	4	4	.500	3.26	0	99⅓	78	42	36	29	79
1990 — New York (A.L.)		28	6	12	.333	4.19	0	156⅔	155	77	73	55	134
1991 — New York (A.L.)		10	1	6	.143	5.91	0	53⅓	61	35	35	32	34
— Columbus (International)		8	5	3	.625	5.72	0	45⅔	44	31	29	26	27
American League totals (5 years)		98	12	25	.324	4.07	2	364⅔	343	181	165	139	290
National League totals (2 years)		20	1	1	.500	4.68	1	25	25	13	13	8	22
Major league totals (7 years)		118	13	26	.333	4.11	3	389⅔	368	194	178	147	312

CASIAN, LARRY
P, TWINS

PERSONAL: Born October 28, 1965, at Lynwood, Calif. ... 6-0/170. ... Throws left, bats right.... Full name: Lawrence Paul Casian.... Name pronounced CASS-ee-un.
HIGH SCHOOL: Lakewood (Calif.).
COLLEGE: Cal State Fullerton.
TRANSACTIONS/CAREER NOTES: Selected by Minnesota Twins organization in sixth round of free-agent draft (June 2, 1987).

Year	Team (League)	G	W	L	Pct.	ERA	Sv.	IP	H	R	ER	BB	SO
1987 — Visalia (California)		18	10	3	.769	2.51	2	97	89	35	27	49	96
1988 — Orlando (Southern)		27	9	9	.500	2.95	0	174	165	72	57	62	104
— Portland (Pacific Coast)		1	0	1	.000	0.00	0	2⅔	5	3	0	0	2
1989 — Portland (Pacific Coast)		28	7	12	.368	4.52	0	169⅓	201	97	85	63	65
1990 — Portland (Pacific Coast)		37	9	9	.500	4.48	0	156⅔	171	90	78	59	89
— Minnesota (A.L.)		5	2	1	.667	3.22	0	22⅓	26	9	8	4	11
1991 — Minnesota (A.L.)		15	0	0	...	7.36	0	18⅓	28	16	15	7	6
— Portland (Pacific Coast)		34	3	2	.600	3.46	1	52	51	25	20	16	24
Major league totals (2 years)		20	2	1	.667	5.09	0	40⅔	54	25	23	11	17

CASTELLANO, PEDRO
3B, CUBS

PERSONAL: Born March 11, 1970, at Lara, Venezuela.... 6-1/175.... Throws right, bats right.... Full name: Pedro Orlando Castellano.
HIGH SCHOOL: Jose Dominguez (Lara, Venezuela).
TRANSACTIONS/CAREER NOTES: Signed as free agent by Chicago Cubs organization (April 14, 1988).
RECORDS/HONORS: Named Carolina League Most Valuable Player (1991).

						BATTING						FIELDING			
Year	Team (League)	Pos.	G	AB	R	H	2B	3B	HR	RBI	Avg.	SB	PO	A	E	Avg.
1989 — Wytheville (Appal.)		S-3-1	66	244	•55	76	17	4	9	42	.311	5	91	138	19	.923
1990 — Peoria (Midwest)		3B-SS	117	417	61	115	27	4	2	44	.276	7	93	213	17	.947
— Winston-Salem (Caro.)		3B	19	66	6	13	0	0	1	8	.197	1	14	37	2	.962
1991 — Charlotte (Southern)		3B	7	19	2	8	0	0	0	2	.421	0	2	11	0	1.000
— Winston-Salem (Caro.)		3B-SS	129	459	59	139	25	3	10	*87	.303	11	132	318	26	.945

CASTILLA, VINNY
SS, BRAVES

PERSONAL: Born June 4, 1967, at Oaxaca, Mexico. . . . 6-1/175. . . . Throws right, bats right. . . . Full name: Vinicio Soria Castilla.
HIGH SCHOOL: Instituto Carlos Graciga (Oaxaca, Mexico).
TRANSACTIONS/CAREER NOTES: Signed as free agent by Saltillo of the Mexican League. . . . Sold by Saltillo to Atlanta Braves organization (March 19, 1990).

Year	Team (League)	Pos.	G	AB	R	H	2B	3B	HR	RBI	Avg.	SB	PO	A	E	Avg.
1987	—Saltillo (Mexican)............	3B	13	27	0	5	2	0	0	1	.185	0	10	31	1	.976
1988	—Saltillo-Monclova (Mex.)■	SS	50	124	22	30	2	2	5	18	.242	1	53	105	13	.924
1989	—Saltillo (Mexican)■..........	SS-3B	128	462	70	142	25	13	10	58	.307	11	224	427	34	.950
1990	—Sumter (South Atlantic)■ .	SS	93	339	47	91	15	2	9	53	.268	2	139	320	23	.952
	—Greenville (Southern)........	SS	46	170	20	40	5	1	4	16	.235	4	71	167	7	.971
1991	—Greenville (Southern)........	SS	66	259	34	70	17	3	7	44	.270	1	86	221	11	.965
	—Richmond (Int'l)	SS	67	240	25	54	7	4	7	36	.225	1	93	208	12	.962
	—Atlanta (N.L.)	SS	12	5	1	1	0	0	00	0	.200	0	6	6	0	1.000
Major league totals (1 year)			12	5	1	1	0	0	0	0	.200	0	6	6	0	1.000

CHAMPIONSHIP SERIES RECORD

Year	Team (League)	Pos.	G	AB	R	H	2B	3B	HR	RBI	Avg.	SB	PO	A	E	Avg.
1991	—Atlanta (N.L.)						Did not play									

WORLD SERIES RECORD

Year	Team (League)	Pos.	G	AB	R	H	2B	3B	HR	RBI	Avg.	SB	PO	A	E	Avg.
1991	—Atlanta (N.L.)						Did not play									

CASTILLO, BRAULIO
OF, PHILLIES

PERSONAL: Born May 13, 1968, at Elias Pina, Dominican Republic. . . . 6-0/160. . . . Throws right, bats right. . . . Full name: Braulio Robinson Medrano Castillo. . . . Name pronounced cas-TEE-yo.
HIGH SCHOOL: Licey Miguel Angel Garrido (Dominican Republic).
TRANSACTIONS/CAREER NOTES: Signed as free agent by Los Angeles Dodgers organization (October 10, 1985). . . . On disabled list (August 9, 1990-remainder of season). . . . Traded by Dodgers with P Mike Hartley to Philadelphia Phillies for P Roger McDowell (July 31, 1991).

Year	Team (League)	Pos.	G	AB	R	H	2B	3B	HR	RBI	Avg.	SB	PO	A	E	Avg.
1987	—Sarasota Dodgers (GCL)...	OF	49	140	21	28	4	2	1	19	.200	7	40	2	2	.955
1988	—Salem (Northwest)	OF	73	306	51	86	20	•5	8	40	.281	16	•180	40	6	.973
1989	—Bakersfield (California)	OF	126	494	83	147	28	•8	18	82	.298	31	232	9	*11	.956
1990	—San Antonio (Texas)	OF	75	241	34	55	11	3	3	24	.228	11	125	7	8	.943
1991	—San Antonio (Texas)	OF	87	297	49	89	19	3	8	48	.300	22	187	4	5	.974
	—Scranton/W.B. (Int'l)■......	OF	16	60	14	21	9	1	0	15	.350	2	29	1	0	1.000
	—Philadelphia (N.L.)	OF	28	52	3	9	3	0	0	2	.173	1	40	2	1	.977
Major league totals (1 year)			28	52	3	9	3	0	0	2	.173	1	40	2	1	.977

CASTILLO, CARMEN
OF

PERSONAL: Born June 8, 1958, at San Francisco de Macoris, Dominican Republic. . . . 6-1/201. . . . Throws right, bats right. . . . Full name: Monte Carmelo Castillo. . . . Name pronounced cas-TEE-yo.
HIGH SCHOOL: Liceo Hercilia Pepin (Santo Domingo, Dominican Republic).
COLLEGE: Univercidad Autonoma (Dominican Republic).
TRANSACTIONS/CAREER NOTES: Signed as free agent by Philadelphia Phillies organization (June 30, 1978). . . . Drafted by Chattanooga, Cleveland Indians organization (December 5, 1978). . . . On Cleveland disabled list (May 5-July 4, 1983). . . . Traded by Indians to Minnesota Twins for P Keith Atherton (March 26, 1989). . . . Granted free agency (November 13, 1989). . . . Re-signed by Twins (January 8, 1990). . . . Released by Twins (May 10, 1991). . . . Signed by Denver, Milwaukee Brewers organization (May 25, 1991). . . . Granted free agency (October 15, 1991).

Year	Team (League)	Pos.	G	AB	R	H	2B	3B	HR	RBI	Avg.	SB	PO	A	E	Avg.
1978	—Auburn (N.Y.-Penn)..........	OF	53	174	37	41	10	2	4	21	.236	13	109	6	11	.913
	—Helena (Pioneer)■............	OF	5	15	1	6	2	0	0	2	.400	0	2	0	1	.667
1979	—Waterloo (Midwest)■..........	OF	49	138	25	28	5	1	3	12	.203	15	54	1	7	.887
	—Batavia (N.Y.-Penn)	OF	36	128	29	43	8	1	8	28	.336	7	56	4	5	.923
1980	—Waterloo (Midwest)...........	OF	117	390	69	103	14	1	14	64	.264	46	173	10	14	.929
1981	—Chattanooga (Southern)...	OF	119	441	63	124	17	6	11	58	.281	25	236	13	15	.943
1982	—Charleston, W.Va. (Int'l) ...	OF	71	281	46	78	12	1	9	39	.278	12	159	10	11	.939
	—Cleveland (A.L.)	OF	47	120	11	25	4	0	2	11	.208	0	91	0	2	.978
1983	—Charleston, W.Va. (Int'l) ...	OF	36	148	29	40	5	2	4	22	.270	4	85	6	6	.938
	—Cleveland (A.L.)	OF	23	36	9	10	2	1	1	3	.278	1	23	3	2	.929
1984	—Cleveland (A.L.)	OF	87	211	36	55	9	2	10	36	.261	1	123	2	9	.933
1985	—Cleveland (A.L.)	OF	67	184	27	45	5	1	11	25	.245	3	101	0	5	.953
	—Maine (International)	OF	26	96	12	23	2	2	2	18	.240	2	9	0	0	1.000
1986	—Cleveland (A.L.)	OF	85	205	34	57	9	0	8	32	.278	2	58	4	4	.939
1987	—Cleveland (A.L.)	OF	89	220	27	55	17	0	11	31	.250	1	29	3	0	1.000
1988	—Cleveland (A.L.)	OF	66	176	12	48	8	0	4	14	.273	6	69	1	5	.933
1989	—Minnesota (A.L.)■............	OF	94	218	23	56	13	3	8	33	.257	1	119	3	3	.976

Year	Team (League)	Pos.	G	AB	R	H	2B	3B	HR	RBI	Avg.	SB	PO	A	E	Avg.
							BATTING							FIELDING		
1990—Minnesota (A.L.)		OF	64	137	11	30	4	0	0	12	.219	0	24	0	2	.923
1991—Minnesota (A.L.)		OF	9	12	0	2	0	1	0	0	.167	0	3	0	0	1.000
—Denver (Am. Assoc.)■		OF	92	334	41	103	19	5	14	72	.308	2	26	0	1	.963
Major league totals (10 years)			631	1519	190	383	71	8	55	197	.252	15	640	16	32	.953

CASTILLO, FRANK
P, CUBS

PERSONAL: Born April 1, 1969, at El Paso, Tex. . . . 6-1/180. . . . Throws right, bats right. . . . Full name: Frank Anthony Castillo. . . . Name pronounced cas-TEE-yo.
HIGH SCHOOL: Eastwood (El Paso, Tex.).
TRANSACTIONS/CAREER NOTES: Selected by Chicago Cubs organization in sixth round of free-agent draft (June 2, 1987). . . . On disabled list (April 1-July 23, 1988). . . . On Iowa disabled list (April 12-June 6, 1991). . . . On Chicago disabled list (August 11-27, 1991).
RECORDS/HONORS: Named Appalachian League Player of the Year (1987).
STATISTICAL NOTES: Tied for Appalachian League lead with five complete games in 1987. . . . Pitched 4-0 no-hit victory against Huntsville (July 13, 1990, first game).

Year	Team (League)	G	W	L	Pct.	ERA	Sv.	IP	H	R	ER	BB	SO
1987—Wytheville (Appalachian)		12	*10	1	*.909	2.29	0	90⅓	86	31	23	21	83
—Geneva (New York-Penn)		1	1	0	1.000	0.00	0	6	3	1	0	1	6
1988—Peoria (Midwest)		9	6	1	.857	0.71	0	51	25	5	4	10	58
1989—Winston-Salem (Carolina)		18	9	6	.600	2.51	0	129⅓	118	42	36	24	114
—Charlotte (Southern)		10	3	4	.429	3.84	0	68	73	35	29	12	43
1990—Charlotte (Southern)		18	6	6	.500	3.88	0	111⅓	113	54	48	27	112
1991—Iowa (American Association)		4	3	1	.750	2.52	0	25	20	7	7	7	20
—Chicago (N.L.)		18	6	7	.462	4.35	0	111⅔	107	56	54	33	73
Major league totals (1 year)		18	6	7	.462	4.35	0	111⅔	107	56	54	33	73

CASTILLO, TONY
P, TIGERS

PERSONAL: Born March 1, 1963, at Lara, Venezuela. . . . 5-10/188. . . . Throws left, bats left. . . . Full name: Antonio Castillo. . . . Name pronounced cas-TEE-yo.
TRANSACTIONS/CAREER NOTES: Signed as free agent by Toronto Blue Jays organization (February 16, 1983). . . . On disabled list (April 10, 1986-entire season). . . . Traded by Blue Jays organization with a player to be named later to Atlanta Braves for P Jim Acker (August 24, 1989); Braves organization acquired C Francisco Cabrera to complete deal (August 24, 1989). . . . Traded by Braves with a player to be named later to New York Mets for P Alejandro Pena (August 28, 1991); Mets acquired P Joe Roa to complete deal (August 29, 1991). . . . Traded by Mets with OF Mark Carreon to Detroit Tigers for P Paul Gibson and P Randy Marshall (January 22, 1992).

Year	Team (League)	G	W	L	Pct.	ERA	Sv.	IP	H	R	ER	BB	SO
1983—Bradenton Blue Jays (GCL)		1	0	0	...	3.00	1	3	3	1	1	0	4
1984—Florence (South Atlantic)		25	11	8	.579	3.41	0	137⅓	123	71	52	50	96
1985—Kinston (Carolina)		36	11	7	.611	1.90	3	127⅔	111	44	27	48	136
1986—						Did not play							
1987—Dunedin (Florida State)		39	6	2	.750	3.36	6	69⅓	62	30	26	19	62
1988—Dunedin (Florida State)		30	4	3	.571	1.48	12	42⅔	31	9	7	10	46
—Knoxville (Southern)		5	1	0	1.000	0.00	2	8	2	0	0	1	11
—Toronto (A.L.)		14	1	0	1.000	3.00	0	15	10	5	5	2	14
1989—Toronto (A.L.)		17	1	1	.500	6.11	1	17⅔	23	14	12	10	10
—Syracuse (International)		27	1	3	.250	2.81	5	41⅔	33	15	13	15	37
—Atlanta (N.L.)■		12	0	1	.000	4.82	0	9⅓	8	5	5	4	5
1990—Atlanta (N.L.)		52	5	1	.833	4.23	1	76⅔	93	41	36	20	64
—Richmond (International)		5	3	1	.750	2.52	0	25	14	7	7	6	27
1991—Richmond (International)		23	5	6	.455	2.90	0	118	89	47	38	32	78
—Atlanta-New York (N.L.)■		17	2	1	.667	3.34	0	32⅓	40	16	12	11	18
American League totals (2 years)		31	2	1	.667	4.68	1	32⅔	33	19	17	12	24
National League totals (3 years)		81	7	3	.700	4.03	1	118⅓	141	62	53	35	87
Major league totals (4 years)		112	9	4	.692	4.17	2	151	174	81	70	47	111

CEDENO, ANDUJAR
SS, ASTROS

PERSONAL: Born August 21, 1969, at La Romana, Dominican Republic. . . . 6-1/168. . . . Throws right, bats right. . . . Full name: Andujar Cedeno. . . . Name pronounced seh-DAIN-yo.
TRANSACTIONS/CAREER NOTES: Signed as free agent by Houston Astros organization (October 1, 1986).
STATISTICAL NOTES: Led Southern League shortstops with 572 total chances in 1990. . . . Led Southern League with 12 sacrifice hits in 1991.

Year	Team (League)	Pos.	G	AB	R	H	2B	3B	HR	RBI	Avg.	SB	PO	A	E	Avg.
							BATTING							FIELDING		
1988—Sarasota Rangers (GCL)		SS	46	165	25	47	5	2	1	20	.285	10	58	145	25	.890
1989—Asheville (S. Atlantic)		SS-3B	126	487	76	*146	23	6	14	93	.300	23	182	346	62	.895
1990—Columbus (Southern)		SS	132	495	57	119	21	*11	19	64	.240	6	167	354	*51	.911
—Houston (N.L.)		SS	7	8	0	0	0	0	0	0	.000	0	3	2	1	.833
1991—Tucson (Pacific Coast)		SS	93	347	49	105	19	6	7	55	.303	5	131	262	31	.927
—Houston (N.L.)		SS	67	251	27	61	13	2	9	36	.243	4	88	151	18	.930
Major league totals (2 years)			74	259	27	61	13	2	9	36	.236	4	91	153	19	.928

CERONE, RICK

C

PERSONAL: Born May 19, 1954, at Newark, N.J. ... 5-11/195. ... Throws right, bats right. ... Full name: Richard Aldo Cerone. ... Name pronounced seh-RONE.
HIGH SCHOOL: Essex Catholic (East Orange, N.J.).
COLLEGE: Seton Hall (bachelor of science degree in physical education, 1975).
TRANSACTIONS/CAREER NOTES: Selected by Cleveland Indians organization in first round (seventh pick overall) of free-agent draft (June 4, 1975). ... On Toledo disabled list (May 13-24, 1976). ... Traded by Indians with IF-OF John Lowenstein to Toronto Blue Jays for OF Rico Carty (December 6, 1976). ... Traded by Blue Jays with P Tom Underwood and OF Ted Wilborn to New York Yankees for 1B Chris Chambliss, IF Damaso Garcia and P Paul Mirabella (November 1, 1979). ... On disabled list (April 19-May 24, 1981 and May 12-July 15, 1982). ... On New York disabled list (May 7-July 5, 1984); included rehabilitation disability assignment to Columbus (June 25-July 5, 1984). ... Traded by Yankees to Atlanta Braves for P Brian Fisher (December 5, 1984). ... On disabled list (June 17-July 2, 1985). ... Traded by Braves with P David Clay and SS Flavio Alfaro to Milwaukee Brewers for C Ted Simmons (March 5, 1986). ... Granted free agency (November 12, 1986). ... Signed by New York Yankees (February 13, 1987). ... Released by Yankees (April 4, 1988). ... Signed by Boston Red Sox (April 15, 1988). ... Released by Red Sox (December 19, 1989). ... Signed by New York Yankees (December 20, 1989). ... On New York disabled list (June 8-August 11, 1990); included rehabilitation disability assignment to Sarasota Yankees (July 9-11, 1990) and Columbus (July 12-24, 1990). ... Released by Yankees (January 13, 1991). ... Signed by New York Mets (January 21, 1991). ... Granted free agency (October 7, 1991).
RECORDS/HONORS: Holds major league career record for most consecutive errorless games by catcher—159 (July 5, 1987-May 8, 1989). ... Named catcher on THE SPORTING NEWS A.L. All-Star team (1980).
STATISTICAL NOTES: Led A.L. catchers with .998 fielding percentage in 1987.

Year	Team (League)	Pos.	G	AB	R	H	2B	3B	HR	RBI	Avg.	SB	PO	A	E	Avg.
1975	—Oklahoma City (A.A.)	C-OF	46	140	22	35	6	1	2	13	.250	0	178	30	3	.986
	—Cleveland (A.L.)	C	7	12	1	3	1	0	0	0	.250	0	18	1	0	1.000
1976	—Toledo (International)	C	96	339	38	86	19	0	11	49	.254	2	351	50	*18	.957
	—Cleveland (A.L.)	C	7	16	1	2	0	0	0	1	.125	0	25	1	1	.963
1977	—Charleston, W.Va. (Int'l)■	C-OF	70	231	30	54	10	1	6	40	.234	1	254	32	5	.983
	—Toronto (A.L.)	C	31	100	7	20	4	0	1	10	.200	1	146	15	1	.994
1978	—Toronto (A.L.)	C	88	282	25	63	8	2	3	20	.223	1	426	44	4	.992
1979	—Toronto (A.L.)	C	136	469	47	112	27	4	7	61	.239	1	560	68	13	.980
1980	—New York (A.L.)■	C	147	519	70	144	30	4	14	85	.277	1	800	73	9	.990
1981	—New York (A.L.)	C	71	234	23	57	13	2	2	21	.244	0	353	26	3	.992
1982	—New York (A.L.)	C	89	300	29	68	10	0	5	28	.227	1	509	25	6	.989
1983	—New York (A.L.)	C-3B	80	246	18	54	7	0	2	22	.220	4	412	18	4	.991
1984	—New York (A.L.)	C	38	120	8	25	3	0	2	13	.208	1	230	9	1	.996
	—Columbus (Int'l)	C	8	25	2	5	2	0	0	1	.200	0	42	5	1	.979
1985	—Atlanta (N.L.)■	C	96	282	15	61	9	0	3	25	.216	0	384	48	6	.986
1986	—Milwaukee (A.L.)■	C	68	216	22	56	14	0	4	18	.259	1	391	44	4	.991
1987	—New York (A.L.)■	C-1B-P	113	284	28	69	12	1	4	23	.243	0	542	38	1	†.998
1988	—Boston (A.L.)■	C	84	264	31	71	13	1	3	27	.269	0	471	28	0	*1.000
1989	—Boston (A.L.)	C-OF	102	296	28	72	16	1	4	48	.243	0	579	41	10	.984
1990	—New York (A.L.)■	C-2B	49	139	12	42	6	0	2	11	.302	0	179	14	1	.995
	—Sarasota Yankees (GCL)	C	3	7	0	1	0	0	0	0	.143	0	11	1	0	1.000
	—Columbus (Int'l)	C	4	11	0	1	0	0	0	1	.091	0	13	0	1	.929
1991	—New York (N.L.)■	C	90	227	18	62	13	0	2	16	.273	1	424	36	6	.987
	American League totals (15 years)		1110	3497	350	858	164	15	53	388	.245	4	5641	445	58	.991
	National League totals (2 years)		186	509	33	123	22	0	5	41	.242	1	808	84	12	.987
	Major league totals (17 years)		1296	4006	383	981	186	15	58	429	.245	5	6449	529	70	.990

DIVISION SERIES RECORD

Year	Team (League)	Pos.	G	AB	R	H	2B	3B	HR	RBI	Avg.	SB	PO	A	E	Avg.
1981	—New York (A.L.)	C	5	18	1	6	2	0	1	5	.333	0	42	1	1	.977

CHAMPIONSHIP SERIES RECORD

CHAMPIONSHIP SERIES NOTES: Hit home run in first series at-bat (October 8, 1980).

Year	Team (League)	Pos.	G	AB	R	H	2B	3B	HR	RBI	Avg.	SB	PO	A	E	Avg.
1980	—New York (A.L.)■	C	3	12	1	4	0	0	1	2	.333	0	14	4	0	1.000
1981	—New York (A.L.)	C	3	10	1	1	0	0	0	0	.100	0	23	2	0	1.000
	Championship Series totals (2 years)		6	22	2	5	0	0	1	2	.227	0	37	6	0	1.000

WORLD SERIES RECORD

Year	Team (League)	Pos.	G	AB	R	H	2B	3B	HR	RBI	Avg.	SB	PO	A	E	Avg.
1981	—New York (A.L.)	C	6	21	2	4	1	0	1	3	.190	00	42	4	0	1.000

RECORD AS PITCHER

Year	Team (League)	G	W	L	Pct.	ERA	Sv.	IP	H	R	ER	BB	SO
1987	—New York (A.L.)■	2	0	0	...	0.00	0	2	0	0	0	1	1

CERUTTI, JOHN

P

PERSONAL: Born April 28, 1960, at Albany, N.Y. ... 6-2/195. ... Throws left, bats left. ... Full name: John Joseph Cerutti.
HIGH SCHOOL: Christian Brothers Academy (Albany, N.Y.).
COLLEGE: Amherst College, Mass. (bachelor of arts degree in economics).

TRANSACTIONS/CAREER NOTES: Selected by Toronto Blue Jays organization in first round (21st pick overall) of free-agent draft (June 8, 1981).... Granted free agency (December 20, 1990).... Signed by Detroit Tigers (January 14, 1991).... Granted free agency (October 31, 1991).
STATISTICAL NOTES: Tied for Pioneer League lead in home runs allowed with eight and games started by pitcher with 14 in 1981. ... Tied for Southern League lead with three shutouts in 1983.

Year Team (League)	G	W	L	Pct.	ERA	Sv.	IP	H	R	ER	BB	SO
1981—Medicine Hat (Pioneer)	14	8	4	.667	3.03	0	*107	87	45	36	43	120
1982—Kinston (Carolina)	16	10	5	.667	3.19	0	113	88	47	40	49	136
—Knoxville (Southern)	4	4	0	1.000	1.11	0	32⅓	18	4	4	10	17
—Syracuse (International)	6	0	3	.000	6.60	0	30	42	25	22	16	20
1983—Knoxville (Southern)	29	9	13	.409	3.43	1	188⅔	182	89	72	65	131
1984—Syracuse (International)	29	7	•13	.350	4.44	3	148	152	89	73	52	114
1985—Syracuse (International)	28	11	9	.550	2.97	0	182	165	84	60	60	110
—Toronto (A.L.)	4	0	2	.000	5.40	0	6⅔	10	7	4	4	5
1986—Syracuse (International)	7	1	3	.250	4.12	0	43⅔	44	27	20	16	22
—Toronto (A.L.)	34	9	4	.692	4.15	1	145⅓	150	73	67	47	89
1987—Toronto (A.L.)	44	11	4	*.733	4.40	0	151⅓	144	75	74	59	92
1988—Toronto (A.L.)	46	6	7	.462	3.13	1	123⅔	120	56	43	42	65
1989—Toronto (A.L.)	33	11	11	.500	3.07	0	205⅓	214	90	70	53	69
1990—Toronto (A.L.)	30	9	9	.500	4.76	0	140	162	77	74	49	49
1991—Detroit (A.L.)■	38	3	6	.333	4.57	2	88⅔	94	49	45	37	29
Major league totals (7 years)	229	49	43	.533	3.94	4	861	894	427	377	291	398

CHAMPIONSHIP SERIES RECORD

Year Team (League)	G	W	L	Pct.	ERA	Sv.	IP	H	R	ER	BB	SO
1989—Toronto (A.L.)	2	0	0	...	0.00	0	2⅔	0	0	0	3	1

CHAMBERLAIN, WES
OF, PHILLIES

PERSONAL: Born April 13, 1966, at Chicago.... 6-2/210.... Throws right, bats right.... Full name: Wesley Polk Chamberlain.
HIGH SCHOOL: Simeon (Chicago).
COLLEGE: Jackson State.
TRANSACTIONS/CAREER NOTES: Selected by Pittsburgh Pirates organization in fifth round of free-agent draft (June 4, 1984).... Selected by Pittsburgh Pirates organization in fourth round of free-agent draft (June 2, 1987).... Traded by Pirates organization with OF Julio Peguero and a player to be named later to Philadelphia Phillies for OF-1B Carmelo Martinez (August 30, 1990); Phillies acquired OF Tony Longmire to complete deal (September 28, 1990).
RECORDS/HONORS: Named Eastern League Most Valuable Player (1989).
STATISTICAL NOTES: Tied for New York-Pennsylvania League lead in double plays by outfielders with three in 1987.... Led Eastern League with 239 total bases in 1989.

Year Team (League)	Pos.	G	AB	R	H	2B	3B	HR	RBI	Avg.	SB	PO	A	E	Avg.
1987—Watertown (N.Y.-Penn)	OF	66	258	50	67	13	4	5	35	.260	22	121	9	7	.949
1988—Augusta (S. Atlantic)	OF	27	107	22	36	7	2	1	17	.336	1	49	4	1	.981
—Salem (Carolina)	OF	92	365	66	100	15	1	11	50	.274	14	161	11	9	.950
1989—Harrisburg (Eastern)	OF	129	471	65	*144	26	3	21	*87	.306	11	205	*14	*15	.936
1990—Buffalo (Am. Assoc.)	OF	123	416	43	104	24	2	6	52	.250	14	203	16	9	.961
—Philadelphia (N.L.)■	OF	18	46	9	13	3	0	2	4	.283	4	23	0	1	.958
1991—Philadelphia (N.L.)	OF	101	383	51	92	16	3	13	50	.240	9	199	4	3	.985
—Scranton/W.B. (Int'l)	OF	39	144	12	37	7	2	2	20	.257	7	63	2	3	.956
Major league totals (2 years)		119	429	60	105	19	3	15	54	.245	13	222	4	4	.983

CHAPIN, DARRIN
P, PHILLIES

PERSONAL: Born February 1, 1966, at Warren, O.... 6-0/170.... Throws right, bats right. ... Full name: Darrin John Chapin.
COLLEGE: Cuyahoga Community College (O.) and Cleveland State.
TRANSACTIONS/CAREER NOTES: Selected by New York Yankees organization in sixth round of free-agent draft (January 14, 1986).... Traded by Yankees to Philadelphia Phillies for a player to be named later (January 8, 1992).

Year Team (League)	G	W	L	Pct.	ERA	Sv.	IP	H	R	ER	BB	SO
1986—Sarasota Yankees (GCL)	13	4	3	.571	3.24	0	83⅓	71	•42	30	27	67
1987—Oneonta (New York-Penn)	25	1	1	.500	0.68	12	40	31	8	3	17	26
1988—Fort Lauderdale (Florida St.)	38	6	4	.600	0.86	15	63	39	8	6	19	57
—Albany (Eastern)	3	0	0	...	11.25	0	4	11	7	5	2	4
1989—Albany (Eastern)	7	1	0	1.000	0.00	3	8⅔	5	0	0	1	16
—Columbus (International)	27	2	4	.333	2.93	5	40	33	15	13	15	38
1990—Albany (Eastern)	43	3	2	.600	2.73	*21	52⅔	43	20	16	21	61
—Columbus (International)	6	1	0	1.000	7.27	2	8⅔	10	8	7	6	8
1991—Columbus (International)	55	10	3	.769	1.95	12	78⅓	54	23	17	40	69
—New York (A.L.)	3	0	1	.000	5.06	0	5⅓	3	3	3	6	5
Major league totals (1 year)	3	0	1	.000	5.06	0	5⅓	3	3	3	6	5

CHARLTON, NORM
P, REDS

PERSONAL: Born January 6, 1963, at Fort Polk, La. . . . 6-3/205. . . . Throws left, bats both. . . . Full name: Norman Wood Charlton III.
HIGH SCHOOL: James Madison (San Antonio).
COLLEGE: Rice (degree in political science, religion, and physical education, 1986).
TRANSACTIONS/CAREER NOTES: Selected by Montreal Expos organization in first round (27th pick overall) of free-agent draft (June 4, 1984). . . . Traded by Expos organization with a player to be named later to Cincinnati Reds for IF Wayne Krenchicki (March 31, 1986); Reds acquired 2B Tim Barker to complete deal (April 2, 1986). . . . On Cincinnati disabled list (April 6-June 26, 1987); included rehabilitation disability assignment to Nashville (June 9-26, 1987). . . . On disabled list (May 26-June 11, 1991 and June 17-July 19, 1991). . . . On suspended list (September 29 and October 4-6, 1991).
STATISTICAL NOTES: Led American Association with 13 wild pitches in 1988.
MISCELLANEOUS: Appeared in two games as pinch-runner (1991).

Year	Team (League)	G	W	L	Pct.	ERA	Sv.	IP	H	R	ER	BB	SO
1984	West Palm Beach (Florida St.) ..	8	1	4	.200	4.58	0	39⅓	51	27	20	22	27
1985	West Palm Beach (Florida St.) ..	24	7	10	.412	4.57	0	128	135	79	65	79	71
1986	Vermont (Eastern)■	22	10	6	.625	2.83	0	136⅔	109	55	43	74	96
1987	Nashville (American Assoc.)	18	2	8	.200	4.30	0	98⅓	97	57	47	44	74
1988	Nashville (American Assoc.)	27	11	10	.524	3.02	0	182	149	69	61	56	*161
	Cincinnati (N.L.)	10	4	5	.444	3.96	0	61⅓	60	27	27	20	39
1989	Cincinnati (N.L.)	69	8	3	.727	2.93	0	95⅓	67	38	31	40	98
1990	Cincinnati (N.L.)	56	12	9	.571	2.74	2	154⅓	131	53	47	70	117
1991	Cincinnati (N.L.)	39	3	5	.375	2.91	1	108⅓	92	37	35	34	77
Major league totals (4 years)		174	27	22	.551	3.00	3	419⅓	350	155	140	164	331

CHAMPIONSHIP SERIES RECORD

Year	Team (League)	G	W	L	Pct.	ERA	Sv.	IP	H	R	ER	BB	SO
1990	Cincinnati (N.L.)	4	1	1	.500	1.80	0	5	4	2	1	3	3

WORLD SERIES RECORD

Year	Team (League)	G	W	L	Pct.	ERA	Sv.	IP	H	R	ER	BB	SO
1990	Cincinnati (N.L.)	1	0	0	. . .	0.00	0	1	1	0	0	0	0

CHIAMPARINO, SCOTT
P, RANGERS

PERSONAL: Born August 22, 1966, at San Mateo, Calif. . . . 6-2/205. . . . Throws right, bats left. . . . Full name: Scott Michael Chiamparino. . . . Name pronounced CHAMP-uh-ree-no.
HIGH SCHOOL: Serra (San Mateo, Calif.).
COLLEGE: Santa Clara.
TRANSACTIONS/CAREER NOTES: Selected by Oakland Athletics organization in fourth round of free-agent draft (June 2, 1987). . . . Traded by A's with P Joe Bitker to Texas Rangers (September 4, 1990), completing deal in which Rangers traded OF-DH Harold Baines to A's for two players to be named later (August 29, 1990). . . . On disabled list (May 26, 1991-remainder of season).
STATISTICAL NOTES: Tied for Pacific Coast League lead with two shutouts in 1990.

Year	Team (League)	G	W	L	Pct.	ERA	Sv.	IP	H	R	ER	BB	SO
1987	Medford (Northwest)	13	5	4	.556	2.53	0	67⅔	64	29	19	20	65
1988	Modesto (California)	16	5	7	.417	2.70	0	106⅔	89	40	32	56	117
	Huntsville (Southern)	13	4	5	.444	3.21	0	84	88	36	30	26	49
1989	Huntsville (Southern)	17	8	6	.571	4.60	0	101⅔	109	60	52	29	87
1990	Tacoma (Pacific Coast)	26	13	9	.591	3.28	0	173	174	79	63	72	110
	Texas (A.L.)■	6	1	2	.333	2.63	0	37⅔	36	14	11	12	19
1991	Texas (A.L.)	5	1	0	1.000	4.03	0	22⅓	26	11	10	12	8
Major league totals (2 years)		11	2	2	.500	3.15	0	60	62	25	21	24	27

CHITREN, STEVE
P, ATHLETICS

PERSONAL: Born June 8, 1967, at Tokyo, Japan. . . . 6-0/180. . . . Throws right, bats right. . . . Full name: Stephen Vincent Chitren.
HIGH SCHOOL: Valley (Las Vegas).
COLLEGE: Stanford.
TRANSACTIONS/CAREER NOTES: Selected by Seattle Mariners organization in ninth round of free-agent draft (June 1, 1988). . . . Selected by Oakland Athletics organization in sixth round of free-agent draft (June 5, 1989).

Year	Team (League)	G	W	L	Pct.	ERA	Sv.	IP	H	R	ER	BB	SO
1989	Madison (Midwest)	20	2	1	.667	1.19	7	22⅔	13	3	3	4	17
	Southern Oregon (Northwest) ..	2	0	0	. . .	1.80	0	5	3	2	1	2	3
1990	Huntsville (Southern)	48	2	4	.333	1.68	*27	53⅔	32	18	10	22	61
	Tacoma (Pacific Coast)	1	0	0	. . .	0.00	0	⅔	1	0	0	0	2
	Oakland (A.L.)	8	1	0	1.000	1.02	0	17⅔	7	2	2	4	19
1991	Oakland (A.L.)	56	1	4	.200	4.33	4	60⅓	59	31	29	32	47
Major league totals (2 years)		64	2	4	.333	3.58	4	78	66	33	31	36	66

CHRISTOPHER, MIKE
P, INDIANS

PERSONAL: Born November 3, 1963, at Petersburg, Va. . . . 6-5/205. . . . Throws right, bats right. . . . Full name: Michael Wayne Christopher.
COLLEGE: East Carolina.
TRANSACTIONS/CAREER NOTES: Selected by New York Yankees organization in

seventh round of free-agent draft (June 3, 1985).... On Albany disabled list (May 2-20, 1989).... Drafted by Los Angeles Dodgers organization (December 5, 1989).... Traded by Dodgers with P Dennis Cook to Cleveland Indians for P Rudy Seanez (December 10, 1991).

Year	Team (League)	G	W	L	Pct.	ERA	Sv.	IP	H	R	ER	BB	SO
1985	—Oneonta (New York-Penn)	15	8	1	.889	1.46	0	80⅓	58	21	13	22	84
1986	—Fort Lauderdale (Florida St.)	15	7	3	.700	2.63	0	102⅔	92	37	30	36	56
	—Albany (Eastern)	11	3	5	.375	5.04	0	60⅔	75	48	34	12	34
1987	—Fort Lauderdale (Florida St.)	24	13	8	.619	2.44	0	169⅓	183	63	46	28	81
1988	—Albany (Eastern)	24	13	7	.650	3.83	0	152⅔	166	75	65	44	67
1989	—Albany (Eastern)	8	6	1	.857	2.52	0	53⅔	48	17	15	7	33
	—Columbus (International)	13	5	6	.455	4.81	0	73	95	45	39	21	42
1990	—Albuquerque (Pacific Coast)■	54	6	1	.857	1.97	8	68⅔	62	20	15	23	47
1991	—Albuquerque (Pacific Coast)	63	7	2	.778	2.44	16	77⅓	73	25	21	30	67
	—Los Angeles (N.L.)	3	0	0	...	0.00	0	4	2	0	0	3	2
Major league totals (1 year)		3	0	0	...	0.00	0	4	2	0	0	3	2

CLANCY, JIM
P, CUBS

PERSONAL: Born December 18, 1955, at Chicago.... 6-4/220.... Throws right, bats right.... Full name: James Clancy.
HIGH SCHOOL: St. Rita (Chicago).
TRANSACTIONS/CAREER NOTES: Selected by Texas Rangers organization in fourth round of free-agent draft (June 5, 1974).... On disabled list (June 15-26, 1976).... Selected by Toronto Blue Jays from Texas Rangers in A.L. expansion draft (November 5, 1976).... On disabled list (May 12-July 4 and August 5, 1979-remainder of season).... On Toronto disabled list (March 25-April 30 and July 27-September 2, 1985); included rehabilitation disability assignment to Knoxville (April 21-30, 1985).... Granted free agency (November 12, 1986).... Re-signed by Blue Jays (January 6, 1987). ... Granted free agency (October 24, 1988).... Signed by Houston Astros (December 16, 1988).... Traded by Astros to Atlanta Braves for P Matt Turner and a player to be named later (July 31, 1991); Astros acquired P Earl Sanders to complete deal (November 15, 1991).... Granted free agency (November 4, 1991).... Signed by Chicago Cubs organization (January 30, 1992).
STATISTICAL NOTES: Tied for Gulf Coast League lead with two shutouts in 1974.... Led A.L. pitchers with 40 games started in 1982 and tied for lead with 36 in 1984.

Year	Team (League)	G	W	L	Pct.	ERA	Sv.	IP	H	R	ER	BB	SO
1974	—Sarasota Rangers (GCL)	9	3	3	.500	2.72	0	53	40	21	16	28	58
1975	—Anderson (Western Carolinas)	23	6	13	.316	3.83	0	148	139	85	63	91	109
1976	—San Antonio (Texas)	23	6	8	.429	6.41	0	125	133	94	*89	98	77
1977	—Jersey City (Eastern)■	20	5	13	.278	4.88	0	118	116	87	64	75	99
	—Toronto (A.L.)	13	4	9	.308	5.03	0	77	80	47	43	47	44
1978	—Toronto (A.L.)	31	10	12	.455	4.08	0	194	199	96	88	91	106
1979	—Toronto (A.L.)	12	2	7	.222	5.48	0	64	65	44	39	31	33
1980	—Toronto (A.L.)	34	13	16	.448	3.30	0	251	217	108	92	*128	152
1981	—Toronto (A.L.)	22	6	12	.333	4.90	0	125	126	77	68	64	56
1982	—Toronto (A.L.)	40	16	14	.533	3.71	0	266⅔	251	122	110	77	139
1983	—Toronto (A.L.)	34	15	11	.577	3.91	0	223	238	115	97	61	99
1984	—Toronto (A.L.)	36	13	15	.464	5.12	0	219⅔	249	*132	*125	88	118
1985	—Toronto (A.L.)	23	9	6	.600	3.78	0	128⅔	117	54	54	37	66
	—Knoxville (Southern)	2	1	0	1.000	3.38	0	8	7	3	3	2	2
1986	—Toronto (A.L.)	34	14	14	.500	3.94	0	219⅓	202	100	96	63	126
1987	—Toronto (A.L.)	37	15	11	.577	3.54	0	241⅓	234	103	95	80	180
1988	—Toronto (A.L.)	36	11	13	.458	4.49	1	196⅓	207	106	98	47	118
1989	—Houston (N.L.)■	33	7	14	.333	5.08	0	147	155	100	83	66	91
1990	—Houston (N.L.)	33	2	8	.200	6.51	1	76	100	58	55	33	44
	—Tucson (Pacific Coast)	10	3	2	.600	2.98	0	42⅓	48	17	14	9	34
1991	—Houston-Atlanta (N.L.)■	54	3	5	.375	3.91	8	89⅔	73	42	39	34	50
American League totals (12 years)		352	128	140	.478	4.10	1	2206	2185	1104	1005	814	1237
National League totals (3 years)		120	12	27	.308	5.09	9	312⅔	328	200	177	133	185
Major league totals (15 years)		472	140	167	.456	4.22	10	2518⅔	2513	1304	1182	947	1422

CHAMPIONSHIP SERIES RECORD

Year	Team (League)	G	W	L	Pct.	ERA	Sv.	IP	H	R	ER	BB	SO
1985	—Toronto (A.L.)	1	0	1	.000	9.00	0	1	2	1	1	1	0
1991	—Atlanta (N.L.)	1	0	0	...	0.00	0	⅓	0	0	0	0	0
Championship Series totals (2 years)		2	0	1	.000	6.75	0	1⅓	2	1	1	1	0

WORLD SERIES RECORD

Year	Team (League)	G	W	L	Pct.	ERA	Sv.	IP	H	R	ER	BB	SO
1991	—Atlanta (N.L.)	3	1	0	1.000	4.15	0	4⅓	3	2	2	4	2

ALL-STAR GAME RECORD

Year	League	W	L	Pct.	ERA	Sv.	IP	H	R	ER	BB	SO
1982	—American	0	0	...	0.00	0	1	0	0	0	0	0

CLARK, DAVE
OF, PIRATES

PERSONAL: Born September 3, 1962, at Tupelo, Miss.... 6-2/210.... Throws right, bats left.... Full name: David Earl Clark.... Brother of Louis Clark, Seattle Seahawks, National Football League.
HIGH SCHOOL: Shannon (Miss.).

COLLEGE: Jackson State.
TRANSACTIONS/CAREER NOTES: Selected by Cleveland Indians organization in first round (11th pick overall) of free-agent draft (June 6, 1983).... Traded by Indians to Chicago Cubs for OF Mitch Webster (November 20, 1989).... Released by Cubs (April 1, 1991).... Signed by Omaha, Kansas City Royals organization (April 29, 1991).... Granted free agency (December 10, 1991).... Signed by Pittsburgh Pirates organization (January 29, 1992).
RECORDS/HONORS: Named outfielder on THE SPORTING NEWS college All-America team (1983).

Year	Team (League)	Pos.	G	AB	R	H	2B	3B	HR	RBI	Avg.	SB	PO	A	E	Avg.
1983 —Waterloo (Midwest)		OF	58	159	20	44	8	1	4	20	.277	2	37	4	1	.976
1984 —Waterloo (Midwest)		OF	110	363	74	112	16	3	15	63	.309	20	128	10	4	.972
—Buffalo (Eastern)		OF	17	56	12	10	1	0	3	10	.179	1	23	2	1	.962
1985 —Waterbury (Eastern).......		OF	132	463	75	140	24	7	12	64	.302	27	204	11	11	.951
1986 —Maine (International)		OF	106	355	56	99	17	2	19	58	.279	6	150	4	6	.963
—Cleveland (A.L.)		OF	18	58	10	16	1	0	3	9	.276	1	26	0	0	1.000
1987 —Buffalo (Am. Assoc.)........		OF	108	420	83	143	22	3	30	80	.340	14	181	★22	6	.971
—Cleveland (A.L.)		OF	29	87	11	18	5	0	3	12	.207	1	24	1	0	1.000
1988 —Cleveland (A.L.)		OF	63	156	11	41	4	1	3	18	.263	0	36	0	2	.947
—Colorado Springs (PCL)		OF	47	165	27	49	10	2	4	31	.297	4	85	6	3	.968
1989 —Cleveland (A.L.)		OF	102	253	21	60	12	0	8	29	.237	0	27	0	1	.964
1990 —Chicago (N.L.)■...........		OF	84	171	22	47	4	2	5	20	.275	7	60	2	0	1.000
1991 —Omaha (Am. Assoc.)■......	OF-1B	104	359	45	108	24	3	13	64	.301	6	264	11	4	.986
—Kansas City (A.L.)		OF	11	10	1	2	0	0	0	1	.200	0	0	0	0	...
American League totals (5 years)			223	564	54	137	22	1	17	69	.243	2	113	1	3	.974
National League totals (1 year)			84	171	22	47	4	2	5	20	.275	7	60	2	0	1.000
Major league totals (6 years)			307	735	76	184	26	3	22	89	.250	9	173	3	3	.983

CLARK, DERA
P, ROYALS

PERSONAL: Born January 8, 1966, at Monahans, Tex.... 6-1/205.... Throws right, bats right. ...Full name: Dera Jennings Clark.
HIGH SCHOOL: Artesia (N.M.).
COLLEGE: Arkansas, then Oklahoma.
TRANSACTIONS/CAREER NOTES: Selected by Atlanta Braves organization in fifth round of free-agent draft (June 6, 1983).... Signed as free agent by Kansas City Royals organization (June 10, 1987).
STATISTICAL NOTES: Led American Association with 17 wild pitches in 1991.

Year	Team (League)	G	W	L	Pct.	ERA	Sv.	IP	H	R	ER	BB	SO
1987 —Sarasota Royals (Gulf Coast) ...		21	3	4	.429	2.24	4	56⅓	42	20	14	17	51
1988 —Baseball City (Florida State)		34	5	2	.714	2.71	4	79⅔	73	28	24	31	46
1989 —Memphis (Southern)		30	5	5	.500	4.40	1	106⅓	103	63	52	29	93
1990 —Omaha (American Assoc.)........		17	8	3	.727	3.73	0	91⅔	82	40	38	44	66
1991 —Omaha (American Assoc.)........		25	6	9	.400	4.51	0	129⅔	126	76	65	73	108

CLARK, JACK
DH, RED SOX

PERSONAL: Born November 10, 1955, at New Brighton, Pa.... 6-3/210.... Throws right, bats right.... Full name: Jack Anthony Clark.
HIGH SCHOOL: Gladstone (Azusa, Calif.).
TRANSACTIONS/CAREER NOTES: Selected by San Francisco Giants organization in 13th round of free-agent draft (June 5, 1973).... On disabled list (August 23-September 8, 1980 and June 25-September 5, 1984).... Traded by Giants to St. Louis Cardinals for 1B David Green, 1B Gary Rajsich, SS Jose Gonzalez (Jose Uribe) and P Dave LaPoint (February 1, 1985).... On disabled list (August 24-September 8, 1985 and June 25, 1986-remainder of season).... Granted free agency (November 9, 1987).... Signed by New York Yankees (January 6, 1988).... On disabled list (March 21-April 15, 1988).... Traded by Yankees with P Pat Clements to San Diego Padres for P Jimmy Jones, P Lance McCullers and OF Stan Jefferson (October 24, 1988).... On disabled list (May 6-June 4, 1990).... On suspended list (October 2-3, 1990).... Granted free agency (December 7, 1990).... Signed by Boston Red Sox (December 15, 1990).... On suspended list for one game (May 24, 1991).
RECORDS/HONORS: Shares major league record for most strikeouts, two consecutive games—9 (June 11, 12 innings [5], and June 13 [4], 1989).... Shares major league record for most errors by first baseman in one inning—3 (May 25, 1987, second inning).... Holds N.L. record for most consecutive games, one or more bases on balls—16 (July 18-August 10, 1987).... Shares N.L. record for most bases on balls in doubleheader—6 (July 8, 1987, 19 innings).... Named outfielder on THE SPORTING NEWS N.L. All-Star team (1978).... Named first baseman on THE SPORTING NEWS N.L. Silver Slugger team (1985 and 1987).... Named first baseman on THE SPORTING NEWS N.L. All-Star team (1987).
STATISTICAL NOTES: Led California League with 254 total bases in 1974.... Led Texas League with 239 total bases in 1975.... Led Texas League third basemen with .872 fielding percentage, 102 putouts, 278 assists, 56 errors, 436 total chances and 29 double plays in 1975.... Tied for N.L. lead in double plays by outfielders with five in 1978, 7 in 1979 and 4 in 1981.... Led N.L. with 18 game-winning RBIs in 1980 and tied for lead with 21 in 1982.... Led N.L. first basemen with 14 errors in 1985.... Led N.L. with 136 bases on balls received in 1987, 132 in 1989 and 104 in 1990.... Led N.L. with .597 slugging percentage and .459 on base percentage in 1987.... Tied for N.L. lead in errors by first basemen with 15 in 1989.... Hit three home runs in a game (July 31, 1991).

Year	Team (League)	Pos.	G	AB	R	H	2B	3B	HR	RBI	Avg.	SB	PO	A	E	Avg.
1973 —Great Falls (Pioneer)	OF-P-3B	65	234	46	75	20	1	9	54	.321	5	73	9	1	.988
1974 —Fresno (California)	3B	131	495	88	156	23	9	19	★117	.315	3	100	204	★53	.852
1975 —Lafayette (Texas)	3B-OF	126	466	94	141	25	2	•23	77	.303	9	†107	†279	†56	†.873
—San Francisco (N.L.)	OF-3B	8	17	3	4	0	0	0	2	.235	1	8	1	0	1.000
1976 —Phoenix (Pacific Coast)	OF-3B	131	470	111	152	29	★16	17	86	.323	16	188	23	9	.959
—San Francisco (N.L.)	OF	26	102	14	23	6	2	2	10	.225	6	71	3	1	.987

Year — Team (League)	Pos.	G	AB	R	H	2B	3B	HR	RBI	Avg.	SB	PO	A	E	Avg.
1977 —San Francisco (N.L.)	OF	136	413	64	104	17	4	13	51	.252	12	226	11	6	.975
1978 —San Francisco (N.L.)	OF	156	592	90	181	46	8	25	98	.306	15	320	16	6	.982
1979 —San Francisco (N.L.)	OF-3B	143	527	84	144	25	2	26	86	.273	11	262	13	5	.982
1980 —San Francisco (N.L.)	OF	127	437	77	124	20	8	22	82	.284	2	229	7	8	.967
1981 —San Francisco (N.L.)	OF	99	385	60	103	19	2	17	53	.268	1	193	•14	4	.981
1982 —San Francisco (N.L.)	OF	157	563	90	154	30	3	27	103	.274	6	281	10	6	.980
1983 —San Francisco (N.L.)	OF-1B	135	492	82	132	25	0	20	66	.268	5	262	20	9	.969
1984 —San Francisco (N.L.)	OF-1B	57	203	33	65	9	1	11	44	.320	1	120	9	2	.985
1985 —St. Louis (N.L.)■	1B-OF	126	442	71	124	26	3	22	87	.281	1	1128	66	†14	.988
1986 —St. Louis (N.L.)	1B	65	232	34	55	12	2	9	23	.237	1	623	35	3	.995
1987 —St. Louis (N.L.)	1B-OF	131	419	93	120	23	1	35	106	.286	1	1152	77	14	.989
1988 —New York (A.L.)■	OF-1B	150	496	81	120	14	0	27	93	.242	3	129	8	5	.965
1989 —San Diego (N.L.)■	1B-OF	142	455	76	110	19	1	26	94	.242	6	1157	89	‡15	.988
1990 —San Diego (N.L.)	1B	115	334	59	89	12	1	25	62	.266	4	855	69	6	.994
1991 —Boston (A.L.)■	DH	140	481	75	120	18	1	28	87	.249	0	0	0	0	...
American League totals (2 years)		290	977	156	240	32	1	55	180	.246	3	129	8	5	.965
National League totals (15 years)		1623	5613	930	1532	289	38	280	967	.273	73	6887	440	99	.987
Major league totals (17 years)		1913	6590	1086	1772	321	39	335	1147	.269	76	7016	448	104	.986

CHAMPIONSHIP SERIES RECORD

CHAMPIONSHIP SERIES NOTES: Shares records for most at-bats in one inning—2; most hits in one inning—2; most singles in one inning—2 (October 13, 1985, second inning).

Year — Team (League)	Pos.	G	AB	R	H	2B	3B	HR	RBI	Avg.	SB	PO	A	E	Avg.
1985 —St. Louis (N.L.)	1B	6	21	4	8	0	0	1	4	.381	2	55	0	0	1.000
1987 —St. Louis (N.L.)	PH	1	1	0	0	0	0	0	0	.000	0	0	0	0	...
Championship Series totals (2 years)		7	22	4	8	0	0	1	4	.364	2	55	0	0	1.000

WORLD SERIES RECORD

Year — Team (League)	Pos.	G	AB	R	H	2B	3B	HR	RBI	Avg.	SB	PO	A	E	Avg.
1985 —St. Louis (N.L.)	1B	7	25	1	6	2	0	0	4	.240	0	49	4	0	1.000

ALL-STAR GAME RECORD

Year — League	Pos.	AB	R	H	2B	3B	HR	RBI	Avg.	SB	PO	A	E	Avg.
1978 —National	OF	1	0	0	0	0	0	0	.000	0	0	0	0	...
1979 —National	PH	1	0	0	0	0	0	0	.000	0	0	0	0	...
All-Star Game totals (2 years)		2	0	0	0	0	0	0	.000	0	0	0	0	...

CLARK, JERALD
OF/1B, PADRES

PERSONAL: Born August 10, 1963, at Crockett, Tex. . . . 6-4/205. . . . Throws right, bats right. . . . Full name: Jerald Dwayne Clark. . . . Brother of Phil Clark, outfielder-catcher, Detroit Tigers organization.
HIGH SCHOOL: Crockett (Tex.).
COLLEGE: Lamar.
TRANSACTIONS/CAREER NOTES: Selected by Los Angeles Dodgers organization in 23rd round of free-agent draft (June 4, 1984). . . . Selected by San Diego Padres organization in 12th round of free-agent draft (June 3, 1985). . . . On disabled list (May 1-20, 1991).
RECORDS/HONORS: Named Northwest League Most Valuable Player (1985).

Year — Team (League)	Pos.	G	AB	R	H	2B	3B	HR	RBI	Avg.	SB	PO	A	E	Avg.
1985 —Spokane (Northwest)	OF	73	283	45	92	•24	3	2	50	.325	9	145	7	6	.962
1986 —Reno (California)	OF	95	389	76	118	34	3	7	58	.303	5	135	6	5	.966
—Beaumont (Texas)	OF	16	56	9	18	4	1	0	6	.321	1	39	1	2	.952
1987 —Wichita (Texas)	OF	132	531	86	165	36	8	18	95	.311	6	262	10	3	.989
1988 —Las Vegas (Pac. Coast)	OF-3B-1B	107	408	65	123	27	7	9	67	.301	6	194	11	7	.967
—San Diego (N.L.)	OF	6	15	0	3	1	0	0	3	.200	0	10	1	0	1.000
1989 —Las Vegas (Pac. Coast)	OF-1B	107	419	84	131	27	4	22	83	.313	5	213	8	8	.965
—San Diego (N.L.)	OF	17	41	5	8	2	0	1	7	.195	0	16	2	1	.947
1990 —San Diego (N.L.)	1B-OF	53	101	12	27	4	1	5	11	.267	0	102	6	1	.991
—Las Vegas (Pac. Coast)	1B-OF	40	161	30	49	7	4	12	32	.304	2	236	10	2	.992
1991 —San Diego (N.L.)	OF-1B	118	369	26	84	16	0	10	47	.228	2	245	10	2	.992
Major league totals (4 years)		194	526	43	122	23	1	16	68	.232	2	373	19	4	.990

CLARK, MARK
P, CARDINALS

PERSONAL: Born May 12, 1968, at Bath, Ill. . . . 6-5/225. . . . Throws right, bats right. . . . Full name: Mark William Clark.
HIGH SCHOOL: Balyki (Bath, Ill.).
COLLEGE: Lincoln Land Community College (Ill.).

TRANSACTIONS/CAREER NOTES: Selected by St. Louis Cardinals organization in ninth round of free-agent draft (June 1, 1988). . . . On Arkansas disabled list (April 12-May 8, 1991).
STATISTICAL NOTES: Led Texas League with five complete games in 1990.

Year	Team (League)	G	W	L	Pct.	ERA	Sv.	IP	H	R	ER	BB	SO
1988 —Hamilton (New York-Penn)		15	6	7	.462	3.05	0	94⅓	88	39	32	32	60
1989 —Savannah (South Atlantic)		27	•14	9	.609	2.44	0	173⅔	143	61	47	52	132
1990 —St. Petersburg (Florida State) ..		10	3	2	.600	3.05	0	62	63	33	21	14	58
—Arkansas (Texas)		19	5	11	.313	3.82	0	115⅓	111	56	49	37	87
1991 —Arkansas (Texas)		15	5	5	.500	4.00	0	92⅓	99	50	41	30	76
—Louisville (American Assoc.) ...		7	3	2	.600	2.98	0	45⅓	43	17	15	15	29
—St. Louis (N.L.)		7	1	1	.500	4.03	0	22⅓	17	10	10	11	13
Major league totals (1 year)		7	1	1	.500	4.03	0	22⅓	17	10	10	11	13

CLARK, WILL
1B, GIANTS

PERSONAL: Born March 13, 1964, at New Orleans. . . . 6-1/190. . . . Throws left, bats left. . . . Full name: William Nuschler Clark Jr.
HIGH SCHOOL: Jesuit (New Orleans).
COLLEGE: Mississippi State.

TRANSACTIONS/CAREER NOTES: Selected by Kansas City Royals organization in fourth round of free-agent draft (June 7, 1982). . . . Selected by San Francisco Giants organization in first round (second pick overall) of free-agent draft (June 3, 1985). . . . On San Francisco disabled list (June 4-July 24, 1986); included rehabilitation disability assignment to Phoenix (July 7-24, 1986).

RECORDS/HONORS: Named designated hitter on THE SPORTING NEWS college All-America team (1984). . . . Named first baseman on THE SPORTING NEWS college All-America team (1985). . . . Named first baseman on THE SPORTING NEWS N.L. All-Star team (1988-89 and 1991). . . . Named first baseman on THE SPORTING NEWS N.L. Silver Slugger team (1989 and 1991). . . . Won N.L. Gold Glove at first base (1991).

STATISTICAL NOTES: Hit home run in first major league at-bat (April 8, 1986). . . . Led N.L. first baseman with 130 double plays in 1987, 126 in 1988, 118 in 1990 and 115 in 1991. . . . Led N.L. with 100 bases on balls received and 27 intentional bases on balls received in 1988. . . . Led N.L. first basemen with 1,608 total chances in 1988, 1,566 in 1989 and 1,587 in 1990. . . . Led N.L. with .536 slugging percentage and tied for lead with 303 total bases in 1991.
MISCELLANEOUS: Member of 1984 U.S. Olympic baseball team.

						BATTING						FIELDING			
Year	Team (League)	Pos.	G	AB	R	H	2B	3B	HR	RBI	Avg.	SB	PO	A	E	Avg.
1985 —Fresno (California)		1B-OF	65	217	41	67	14	0	10	48	.309	11	523	51	6	.990
1986 —San Francisco (N.L.)		1B	111	408	66	117	27	2	11	41	.287	4	942	72	11	.989
—Phoenix (Pacific Coast)		DH	6	20	3	5	0	0	0	1	.250	1	0	0	0	...
1987 —San Francisco (N.L.)		1B	150	529	89	163	29	5	35	91	.308	5	1253	103	13	.991
1988 —San Francisco (N.L.)		1B	★162	575	102	162	31	6	29	★109	.282	9	★1492	104	12	.993
1989 —San Francisco (N.L.)		1B	159	588	•104	196	38	9	23	111	.333	8	★1445	111	10	.994
1990 —San Francisco (N.L.)		1B	154	600	91	177	25	5	19	95	.295	8	★1456	119	12	.992
1991 —San Francisco (N.L.)		1B	148	565	84	170	32	7	29	116	.301	4	1273	110	4	★.997
Major league totals (6 years)			884	3265	536	985	182	34	146	563	.302	38	7861	619	62	.993

CHAMPIONSHIP SERIES RECORD

CHAMPIONSHIP SERIES NOTES: Holds single-series records for most hits—13; total bases—24 (1989). . . . Holds single-game record for most runs batted in—6 (October 4, 1989). . . . Shares single-series records for most runs—8; consecutive hits—5; long hits—6 (1989). . . . Shares single-game records for most runs—4; grand slams—1 (October 4, 1989). . . . Shares record for most runs batted in one inning—4 (October 4, 1989, fourth inning). . . . Shares N.L. single-game record for most hits—4 (October 4, 1989).

						BATTING						FIELDING			
Year	Team (League)	Pos.	G	AB	R	H	2B	3B	HR	RBI	Avg.	SB	PO	A	E	Avg.
1987 —San Francisco (N.L.)		1B	7	25	3	9	2	0	1	3	.360	1	63	7	1	.986
1989 —San Francisco (N.L.)		1B	5	20	8	13	3	1	2	8	.650	0	43	6	0	1.000
Championship Series totals (2 years)			12	45	11	22	5	1	3	11	.489	1	106	13	1	.992

WORLD SERIES RECORD

						BATTING						FIELDING			
Year	Team (League)	Pos.	G	AB	R	H	2B	3B	HR	RBI	Avg.	SB	PO	A	E	Avg.
1989 —San Francisco (N.L.)		1B	4	16	2	4	1	0	0	0	.250	0	40	2	0	1.000

ALL-STAR GAME RECORD

					BATTING						FIELDING			
Year	League	Pos.	AB	R	H	2B	3B	HR	RBI	Avg.	SB	PO	A	E	Avg.
1988 —National		1B	2	0	0	0	0	0	0	.000	0	4	1	0	1.000
1989 —National		1B	2	0	0	0	0	0	0	.000	0	5	0	0	1.000
1990 —National		1B	3	0	1	0	0	0	0	.333	0	6	0	0	1.000
1991 —National		1B	2	0	1	0	0	0	0	.500	0	2	0	0	1.000
All-Star Game totals (4 years)			9	0	2	0	0	0	0	.222	0	17	1	0	1.000

CLAYTON, ROYCE
SS, GIANTS

PERSONAL: Born January 2, 1970, at Burbank, Calif. . . . 6-0/175. . . . Throws right, bats right. . . . Full name: Royce Spencer Clayton.
HIGH SCHOOL: St. Bernard (Inglewood, Calif.).
TRANSACTIONS/CAREER NOTES: Selected by San Francisco Giants organization in first

round (15th pick overall) of free-agent draft (June 1, 1988).
STATISTICAL NOTES: Led Texas League shortstops with 80 double plays in 1991.

Year	Team (League)	Pos.	G	AB	R	H	2B	3B	HR	RBI	Avg.	SB	PO	A	E	Avg.
								BATTING						FIELDING		
1988	—Everett (Northwest)	SS	60	212	35	55	4	0	3	29	.259	10	75	166	35	.873
1989	—Clinton (Midwest)	SS	104	385	39	91	13	3	0	24	.236	28	182	332	31	.943
	—San Jose (California)	SS	28	92	5	11	2	0	0	4	.120	10	53	71	8	.939
1990	—San Jose (California)	SS	123	460	80	123	15	10	7	71	.267	33	★202	358	37	.938
1991	—Shreveport (Texas)	SS	126	485	84	136	22	8	5	68	.280	36	174	379	29	.950
	—San Francisco (N.L.)	SS	9	26	0	3	1	0	0	2	.115	0	16	6	3	.880
Major league totals (1 year)			9	26	0	3	1	0	0	2	.115	0	16	6	3	.880

CLEMENS, ROGER

P, RED SOX

PERSONAL: Born August 4, 1962, at Dayton, O. . . . 6-4/220. . . . Throws right, bats right. . . . Full name: William Roger Clemens.
HIGH SCHOOL: Spring Woods (Houston).
COLLEGE: San Jacinto College, North (Tex.) and Texas.

TRANSACTIONS/CAREER NOTES: Selected by New York Mets organization in 12th round of free-agent draft (June 8, 1981). . . . Selected by Boston Red Sox organization in first round (19th pick overall) of free-agent draft (June 6, 1983). . . . On disabled list (July 8-August 3 and August 21, 1985-remainder of season). . . . On suspended list (April 26-May 3, 1991).
RECORDS/HONORS: Holds major league single-game record for most strikeouts (nine-inning game)—20 (April 29, 1986). . . . Shares A.L. single-game record for most consecutive strikeouts—8 (April 29, 1986). . . . Named Major League Player of the Year by THE SPORTING NEWS (1986). . . . Named A.L. Pitcher of the Year by THE SPORTING NEWS (1986 and 1991). . . . Named righthanded pitcher on THE SPORTING NEWS A.L. All-Star team (1986-87 and 1991). . . . Named A.L. Most Valuable Player by Baseball Writers' Association of America (1986). . . . Named A.L. Cy Young Award winner by Baseball Writers' Association of America (1986-87 and 1991).
STATISTICAL NOTES: Led A.L. with seven shutouts in 1987, eight in 1988, four in 1991 and tied for lead with four in 1990. . . . Led A.L. with 18 complete games in 1987 and tied for lead with 14 in 1988. . . . Tied for A.L. lead in games started by pitcher with 35 in 1991.

Year	Team (League)	G	W	L	Pct.	ERA	Sv.	IP	H	R	ER	BB	SO
1983	—Winter Haven (Florida State)	4	3	1	.750	1.24	0	29	22	4	4	0	36
	—New Britain (Eastern)	7	4	1	.800	1.38	0	52	31	8	8	12	59
1984	—Pawtucket (International)	7	2	3	.400	1.93	0	46⅔	39	12	10	14	50
	—Boston (A.L.)	21	9	4	.692	4.32	0	133⅓	146	67	64	29	126
1985	—Boston (A.L.)	15	7	5	.583	3.29	0	98⅓	83	38	36	37	74
1986	—Boston (A.L.)	33	★24	4	★.857	★2.48	0	254	179	77	70	67	238
1987	—Boston (A.L.)	36	•20	9	.690	2.97	0	281⅔	248	100	93	83	256
1988	—Boston (A.L.)	35	18	12	.600	2.93	0	264	217	93	86	62	★291
1989	—Boston (A.L.)	35	17	11	.607	3.13	0	253⅓	215	101	88	93	230
1990	—Boston (A.L.)	31	21	6	.778	★1.93	0	228⅓	193	59	49	54	209
1991	—Boston (A.L.)	35	18	10	.643	★2.62	0	★271⅓	219	93	79	65	★241
Major league totals (8 years)		241	134	61	.687	2.85	0	1784⅓	1500	628	565	490	1665

CHAMPIONSHIP SERIES RECORD

CHAMPIONSHIP SERIES NOTES: Holds single-series record for most hits allowed—22 (1986). . . . Shares single-series record for most earned runs allowed—11 (1986). . . . Shares single-game record for most earned runs allowed—7 (October 7, 1986); most consecutive strikeouts—4 (October 6, 1988). . . . Holds A.L. single-series record for most innings pitched—22 ⅔ (1986). . . . Shares A.L. single-game record for most runs allowed—8 (October 7, 1986).

Year	Team (League)	G	W	L	Pct.	ERA	Sv.	IP	H	R	ER	BB	SO
1986	—Boston (A.L.)	3	1	1	.500	4.37	0	22⅔	22	12	11	7	17
1988	—Boston (A.L.)	1	0	0	...	3.86	0	7	6	3	3	0	8
1990	—Boston (A.L.)	2	0	1	.000	3.52	0	7⅔	7	3	3	5	4
Championship Series totals (3 years)		6	1	2	.333	4.10	0	37⅓	35	18	17	12	29

WORLD SERIES RECORD

Year	Team (League)	G	W	L	Pct.	ERA	Sv.	IP	H	R	ER	BB	SO
1986	—Boston (A.L.)	2	0	0	...	3.18	0	11⅓	9	5	4	6	11

ALL-STAR GAME RECORD

Year	League	W	L	Pct.	ERA	Sv.	IP	H	R	ER	BB	SO
1986	—American	1	0	1.000	0.00	0	3	0	0	0	0	2
1988	—American	0	0	...	0.00	0	1	0	0	0	0	1
1990	—American						Did not play					
1991	—American	0	0	...	9.00	0	1	1	1	1	0	0
All-Star totals (3 years)		1	0	1.000	1.80	0	5	1	1	1	0	3

CLEMENTS, PAT

P, PADRES

PERSONAL: Born February 2, 1962, at McCloud, Calif. . . . 6-0/187. . . . Throws left, bats right. . . . Full name: Patrick Brian Clements.
HIGH SCHOOL: Pleasant Valley (Chico, Calif.).
COLLEGE: UCLA.

TRANSACTIONS/CAREER NOTES: Selected by New York Yankees organization in 32nd round of free-agent draft (June 3, 1980). . . . Selected by California Angels organization in fourth round of free-agent draft (June 6, 1983). . . . Traded by Angels with OF

Mike Brown and a player to be named later to Pittsburgh Pirates for P John Candelaria, P Al Holland and OF George Hendrick (August 2, 1985); Pirates organization acquired P Bob Kipper to complete deal (August 16, 1985).... Traded by Pirates with P Rick Rhoden and P Cecilio Guante to New York Yankees for P Doug Drabek, P Brian Fisher and P Logan Easley (November 26, 1986).... Traded by Yankees with 1B-OF Jack Clark to San Diego Padres for P Jimmy Jones, P Lance McCullers and OF Stan Jefferson (October 24, 1988).... Granted free agency (December 20, 1990).... Signed by Las Vegas, San Diego Padres organization (February 9, 1991).... On San Diego disabled list (April 25-September 3, 1991); included rehabilitation disability assignment to Las Vegas (August 11-September 3, 1991).

Year	Team (League)	G	W	L	Pct.	ERA	Sv.	IP	H	R	ER	BB	SO
1983	—Peoria (Midwest)	15	4	7	.364	4.48	0	92 ⅓	113	56	46	24	67
1984	—Waterbury (Eastern)	43	4	2	.667	2.69	9	67	59	28	20	29	44
1985	—California (A.L.)	41	5	0	1.000	3.34	1	62	47	23	23	25	19
	—Pittsburgh (N.L.)■	27	0	2	.000	3.67	2	34 ⅓	39	14	14	15	17
1986	—Pittsburgh (N.L.)	65	0	4	.000	2.80	2	61	53	20	19	32	31
1987	—New York (A.L.)■	55	3	3	.500	4.95	7	80	91	45	44	30	36
	—Columbus (International)	4	1	0	1.000	3.79	0	19	19	8	8	2	7
1988	—Columbus (International)	32	6	7	.462	2.75	5	144	136	55	44	34	69
	—New York (A.L.)	6	0	0	...	6.48	0	8 ⅓	12	8	6	4	3
1989	—Las Vegas (Pacific Coast)■	18	3	1	.750	4.09	2	55	57	31	25	24	34
	—San Diego (N.L.)	23	4	1	.800	3.92	0	39	39	17	17	15	18
1990	—San Diego (N.L.)	9	0	0	...	4.15	0	13	20	9	6	7	6
	—Las Vegas (Pacific Coast)	26	4	3	.571	6.05	0	86 ⅓	106	68	58	34	57
1991	—Las Vegas (Pacific Coast)	11	0	0	...	6.75	0	12	15	9	9	5	4
	—San Diego (N.L.)	12	1	0	1.000	3.77	0	14 ⅓	13	8	6	9	8
American League totals (3 years)		102	8	3	.727	4.37	8	150 ⅓	150	76	73	59	58
National League totals (5 years)		136	5	7	.417	3.45	4	161 ⅔	164	68	62	78	80
Major league totals (7 years)		238	13	10	.565	3.89	12	312	314	144	135	137	138

COCHRANE, DAVE
C/3B/OF, MARINERS

PERSONAL: Born January 31, 1963, at Riverside, Calif.... 6-2/180.... Throws right, bats both.... Full name: David Carter Cochrane.
COLLEGE: Cal State Fullerton.
TRANSACTIONS/CAREER NOTES: Selected by New York Mets organization in fourth round of free-agent draft (June 8, 1981).... On disabled list (May 25-July 16, 1985).... Traded by Mets organization to Chicago White Sox organization for OF Tom Paciorek (July 16, 1985).... On Glens Falls disabled list (July 16, 1985-remainder of season).... Traded by White Sox organization with P Floyd Bannister to Kansas City Royals for P John Davis, P Melido Perez, P Chuck Mount and P Greg Hibbard (December 10, 1987).... Traded by Royals organization to Calgary (Seattle Mariners organization) for P Ken Spratke (February 3, 1988).... Granted free agency (April 4, 1991).... Re-signed by Calgary (April 8, 1991).
STATISTICAL NOTES: Led New York-Pennsylvania League batters with 117 strikeouts and seven intentional bases on balls received in 1982.... Led Texas League batters with 133 strikeouts in 1984.

Year	Team (League)	Pos.	G	AB	R	H	2B	3B	HR	RBI	Avg.	SB	PO	A	E	Avg.
1982	—Little Falls (N.Y.-Penn)	3B	70	269	51	81	16	2	22	62	.301	3	49	110	*29	.846
1983	—Lynchburg (Carolina)	3B	120	445	73	117	16	1	25	*102	.263	4	66	167	26	.900
1984	—Jackson (Texas)	3B-SS	129	454	66	121	29	3	22	77	.267	2	79	167	32	.885
1985	—Jackson (Texas)	SS	33	103	14	23	1	0	4	20	.223	0	39	87	14	.900
1986	—Birmingham (Southern)■	3B-SS	93	349	66	95	23	5	17	74	.272	4	82	201	36	.887
	—Buffalo (Am. Assoc.)	3B-SS-OF	38	124	15	28	7	0	6	16	.226	0	25	58	4	.954
	—Chicago (A.L.)	3B-SS	19	62	4	12	2	0	1	2	.194	0	10	31	6	.872
1987	—Hawaii (Pacific Coast)	3-O-P-1	129	451	60	122	23	3	15	66	.271	7	106	83	15	.926
1988	—Calgary (Pacific Coast)■	1-0-3-C-S	120	406	55	116	27	3	15	61	.286	4	387	106	29	.944
1989	—Calgary (Pacific Coast)	3-1-S-C-0	32	125	22	34	10	0	6	35	.272	2	86	43	6	.956
	—Seattle (A.L.)	IF-OF-C	54	102	13	24	4	1	3	7	.235	0	78	41	5	.960
1990	—Calgary (Pacific Coast)	3-0-S-2-C	69	262	43	72	14	4	8	36	.275	2	104	101	14	.936
	—Seattle (A.L.)	S-3-1-C	15	20	0	3	0	0	0	0	.150	0	8	10	0	1.000
1991	—Calgary (Pacific Coast)	C-I-0	47	190	25	61	11	0	3	37	.321	2	146	47	17	.919
	—Seattle (A.L.)	0-C-3-1	65	178	16	44	13	0	2	22	.247	0	105	25	7	.949
Major league totals (4 years)			153	362	33	83	19	1	6	31	.229	0	201	107	18	.945

RECORD AS PITCHER

Year	Team (League)	G	W	L	Pct.	ERA	Sv.	IP	H	R	ER	BB	SO
1987	—Hawaii (Pacific Coast)	8	1	1	.500	7.15	0	11 ⅓	15	9	9	11	6

COLBRUNN, GREG
C, EXPOS

PERSONAL: Born July 26, 1969, at Fontana, Calif.... 6-0/190.... Throws right, bats right.... Full name: Gregory Joseph Colbrunn.
HIGH SCHOOL: Fontana (Calif.).
TRANSACTIONS/CAREER NOTES: Selected by Montreal Expos organization in sixth round of free-agent draft (June 2, 1987).... On disabled list (entire 1991 season).

Year	Team (League)	Pos.	G	AB	R	H	2B	3B	HR	RBI	Avg.	SB	PO	A	E	Avg.
1988	—Rockford (Midwest)	C	115	417	55	111	18	2	7	46	.266	5	595	81	15	.978
1989	—West Palm Beach (FSL)	C	59	228	20	54	8	0	0	25	.237	3	376	49	5	.988
	—Jacksonville (Southern)	C	55	178	21	49	11	1	3	18	.275	0	304	34	4	.988

	Pos.	G	AB	R	H	2B	3B	HR	RBI	Avg.	SB	PO	A	E	Avg.
1990—Jacksonville (Southern) ...	C	125	458	57	138	29	1	13	76	.301	1	698	58	15	.981
1991—					Did not play										

COLE, ALEX
OF, INDIANS

PERSONAL: Born August 17, 1965, at Fayetteville, N.C. . . . 6-2/170. . . . Throws left, bats left. . . . Full name: Alexander Cole Jr.
HIGH SCHOOL: George Wythe (Richmond, Va.).
COLLEGE: Manatee Junior College (Fla.).
TRANSACTIONS/CAREER NOTES: Selected by Pittsburgh Pirates organization in 11th round of free-agent draft (January 17, 1984). . . . Selected by St. Louis Cardinals organization in second round of free-agent draft (January 9, 1985). . . . Traded by Cardinals organization with P Steve Peters to San Diego Padres for P Omar Olivares (February 27, 1990). . . . Traded by Padres organization to Cleveland Indians for C Tom Lampkin (July 11, 1990). . . . On Cleveland disabled list (May 4-26, 1991); included rehabilitation disability assignment to Colorado Springs (May 17-26, 1991).
STATISTICAL NOTES: Led Appalachian League outfielders with 142 total chances in 1985. . . . Led Appalachian League in caught stealing with eight in 1985. . . . Led Florida State League in caught stealing with 22 in 1986. . . . Led Texas League in caught stealing with 29 in 1987. . . . Tied for Texas League lead in double plays by outfielders with five in 1987. . . . Led American Association outfielders with 342 total chances in 1989. . . . Tied for Pacific Coast League lead in caught stealing with 18 in 1990.

						BATTING						FIELDING			
Year Team (League)	Pos.	G	AB	R	H	2B	3B	HR	RBI	Avg.	SB	PO	A	E	Avg.
1985—Johnson City (Appal.)	OF	66	232	*60	61	5	1	1	13	.263	*46	*127	*12	3	.979
1986—St. Petersburg (Fla. St.)	OF	74	286	76	98	9	1	0	26	.343	56	201	4	8	.962
—Louisville (Am. Assoc.)	OF	63	200	25	50	2	4	1	16	.250	24	135	6	9	.940
1987—Arkansas (Texas)	OF	125	477	68	122	12	4	2	27	.256	*68	289	14	10	.968
1988—Louisville (Am. Assoc.)	OF	120	392	44	91	7	8	0	24	.232	40	276	13	1	.997
1989—St. Petersburg (Fla. St.)	OF	8	32	2	6	0	0	0	1	.188	4	13	0	0	1.000
—Louisville (Am. Assoc.)	OF	127	455	75	128	5	5	2	29	.281	*47	*320	14	8	.977
1990—L.V.-Colo. Spgs. (PCL)■...	OF	104	390	71	120	9	4	0	31	.308	38	181	6	9	.954
—Cleveland (A.L.)	OF	63	227	43	68	5	4	0	13	.300	40	145	3	6	.961
1991—Cleveland (A.L.)	OF	122	387	58	114	17	3	0	21	.295	27	256	6	8	.970
—Colorado Springs (PCL)	OF	8	32	6	6	0	1	0	3	.188	1	18	2	2	.909
Major league totals (2 years)		185	614	101	182	22	7	0	34	.296	67	401	9	14	.967

COLE, STU
IF, ROYALS

PERSONAL: Born February 7, 1966, at Charlotte, N.C. . . . 6-1/175. . . . Throws right, bats right. . . . Full name: Stewart Bryan Cole.
HIGH SCHOOL: South Meek (Charlotte, N.C.).
COLLEGE: UNC Charlotte.
TRANSACTIONS/CAREER NOTES: Selected by Pittsburgh Pirates organization in 19th round of free-agent draft (June 4, 1984). . . . Selected by Kansas City Royals organization in third round of free-agent draft (June 2, 1987).

						BATTING						FIELDING			
Year Team (League)	Pos.	G	AB	R	H	2B	3B	HR	RBI	Avg.	SB	PO	A	E	Avg.
1987—Eugene (Northwest)	2B-SS-3B	63	243	42	74	17	1	3	51	.305	3	87	161	16	.939
1988—Virginia (Carolina)	SS-3B	70	257	41	70	10	0	1	22	.272	10	94	182	74	.789
—Baseball City (Fla. St.)	SS-3B	15	41	7	6	0	0	0	4	.146	2	10	30	3	.930
1989—Memphis (Southern)	3B-SS-2B	90	299	30	64	8	3	6	32	.214	11	93	193	25	.920
1990—Memphis (Southern)	S-2-3-0	113	357	61	110	18	2	1	49	.308	20	114	188	19	.941
1991—Omaha (Am. Assoc.)	S-2-3-0-1	120	441	64	115	13	7	3	39	.261	11	195	266	18	.962
—Kansas City (A.L.)	2B-SS	9	7	1	1	0	0	0	0	.143	0	2	4	0	1.000
Major league totals (1 year)		9	7	1	1	0	0	0	0	.143	0	2	4	0	1.000

COLE, VICTOR
P, PIRATES

PERSONAL: Born January 23, 1968, at Leningrad, Russia. . . . 5-10/160. . . . Throws right, bats both. . . . Full name: Victor Alexander Cole.
HIGH SCHOOL: Monterey (Calif.).
COLLEGE: Santa Clara.
TRANSACTIONS/CAREER NOTES: Selected by Kansas City Royals organization in 14th round of free-agent draft (June 1, 1988). . . . Traded by Royals to Pittsburgh Pirates for 1B-OF Carmelo Martinez (May 3, 1991).

Year Team (League)	G	W	L	Pct.	ERA	Sv.	IP	H	R	ER	BB	SO
1988—Eugene (Northwest)	15	1	0	1.000	1.52	9	23⅔	16	6	4	8	39
—Baseball City (Florida State)	10	5	0	1.000	2.06	1	35	27	9	8	21	29
1989—Baseball City (Florida State)	9	3	1	.750	3.86	0	42	43	23	18	22	30
—Memphis (Southern)	13	1	9	.100	6.36	0	63⅔	67	53	45	51	52
1990—Memphis (Southern)	46	3	8	.273	4.35	4	107⅔	91	61	52	70	102
1991—Omaha-Buffalo (Am. Assoc.)■..	25	2	3	.400	3.89	0	37	32	17	16	29	36
—Carolina (Southern)	13	0	2	.000	1.91	12	28⅓	13	8	6	19	32

COLEMAN, VINCE
OF, METS

PERSONAL: Born September 22, 1961, at Jacksonville, Fla. . . . 6-0/185. . . . Throws right, bats both. . . . Full name: Vincent Maurice Coleman. . . . Cousin of Greg Coleman, National Football League player (1977-1988).
HIGH SCHOOL: Raines (Jacksonville, Fla.).

COLLEGE: Florida A&M (degree in physical education).
TRANSACTIONS/CAREER NOTES: Selected by Philadelphia Phillies organization in 20th round of free-agent draft (June 8, 1981). . . . Selected by St. Louis Cardinals organization in 10th round of free-agent draft (June 7, 1982). . . . Granted free agency (November 5, 1990). . . . Signed by New York Mets (December 5, 1990). . . . On disabled list (June 15-July 25 and August 14-September 27, 1991).
RECORDS/HONORS: Holds major league rookie season records for most stolen bases—110; most caught stealing—25 (1985). . . . Holds major league career record for most consecutive stolen bases without caught stealing—50 (September 18, 1988-July 26, 1989). . . . Shares major league single-game record for most sacrifice flies—3 (May 1, 1986). . . . Shares major league single-season record for fewest errors by outfielder who led league in errors—9 (1986). . . . Shares N.L. record for most consecutive years leading league in stolen bases—6 (1985-1990). . . . Named South Atlantic League Most Valuable Player (1983). . . . Named N.L. Rookie Player of the Year by THE SPORTING NEWS (1985). . . . Named N.L. Rookie of the Year by Baseball Writers' Association of America (1985).
STATISTICAL NOTES: Led South Atlantic League in caught stealing with 31 in 1983. . . . Led American Association in caught stealing with 36 in 1984. . . . Led American Association outfielders with 381 total chances in 1984. . . . Led N.L. in caught stealing with 25 in 1985, 22 in 1987 and tied for lead with 27 in 1988.

Year	Team (League)	Pos.	G	AB	R	H	2B	3B	HR	RBI	Avg.	SB	PO	A	E	Avg.
1982—Johnson City (Appal.)		OF	58	212	40	53	2	1	0	16	.250	•43	123	7	8	.942
1983—Macon (South Atlantic)		OF	113	446	99	156	8	7	0	53	★.350	★145	225	18	8	.968
1984—Louisville (Am. Assoc.)		OF	152	★608	★97	156	21	7	4	48	.257	★101	357	14	•10	.974
1985—Louisville (Am. Assoc.)		OF	5	21	1	3	0	0	0	0	.143	0	8	0	0	1.000
—St. Louis (N.L.)		OF	151	636	107	170	20	10	1	40	.267	★110	305	16	7	.979
1986—St. Louis (N.L.)		OF	154	600	94	139	13	8	0	29	.232	★107	300	12	•9	.972
1987—St. Louis (N.L.)		OF	151	623	121	180	14	10	3	43	.289	★109	274	16	9	.970
1988—St. Louis (N.L.)		OF	153	616	77	160	20	10	3	38	.260	★81	290	14	9	.971
1989—St. Louis (N.L.)		OF	145	563	94	143	21	9	2	28	.254	★65	247	5	•10	.962
1990—St. Louis (N.L.)		OF	124	497	73	145	18	9	6	39	.292	★77	244	12	5	.981
1991—New York (N.L.) ■............		OF	72	278	45	71	7	5	1	17	.255	37	132	5	3	.979
Major league totals (7 years)			950	3813	611	1008	113	61	16	234	.264	586	1792	80	52	.973

CHAMPIONSHIP SERIES RECORD

CHAMPIONSHIP SERIES NOTES: Shares N.L. career record for most times caught stealing—4.

Year	Team (League)	Pos.	G	AB	R	H	2B	3B	HR	RBI	Avg.	SB	PO	A	E	Avg.
1985—St. Louis (N.L.)		OF	3	14	2	4	0	0	0	1	.286	1	8	0	0	1.000
1987—St. Louis (N.L.)		OF	7	26	3	7	1	0	0	4	.269	1	9	1	0	1.000
Championship Series totals (2 years)			10	40	5	11	1	0	0	5	.275	2	17	1	0	1.000

WORLD SERIES RECORD

Year	Team (League)	Pos.	G	AB	R	H	2B	3B	HR	RBI	Avg.	SB	PO	A	E	Avg.
1985—St. Louis (N.L.)						Did not play										
1987—St. Louis (N.L.)		OF	7	28	5	4	2	0	0	2	.143	6	10	2	0	1.000

ALL-STAR GAME RECORD

Year	League	Pos.	AB	R	H	2B	3B	HR	RBI	Avg.	SB	PO	A	E	Avg.
1988—National		OF	2	1	1	0	0	0	0	.500	1	3	0	0	1.000
1989—National		PR-OF	0	0	0	0	0	0	0	...	0	0	0	0	...
All-Star Game totals (2 years)			2	1	1	0	0	0	0	.500	1	3	0	0	1.000

COLES, DARNELL
OF/IF, REDS

PERSONAL: Born June 2, 1962, at San Bernardino, Calif. . . . 6-1/185. . . . Throws right, bats right. . . . Full name: Darnell Coles. . . . Name pronounced dar-NELL.
HIGH SCHOOL: Eisenhower (Rialto, Calif.).
COLLEGE: Orange Coast College (Calif.).
TRANSACTIONS/CAREER NOTES: Selected by Seattle Mariners organization in first round (sixth pick overall) of free-agent draft (June 3, 1980). . . . On Seattle disabled list (March 29-April 24, 1984); included rehabilitation disability assignment to Salt Lake City (April 12-24, 1984). . . . On Calgary disabled list (August 8-September 9, 1985). . . . Traded by Mariners to Detroit Tigers for P Rich Monteleone (December 12, 1985). . . . On disabled list (June 16-July 1, 1986). . . . On Detroit disabled list (May 25-June 27, 1987); included rehabilitation disability assignment to Toledo (June 16-27, 1987). . . . Traded by Tigers organization with a player to be named later to Pittsburgh Pirates for 3B Jim Morrison (August 7, 1987); Pirates organization acquired P Morris Madden to complete deal (August 12, 1987). . . . Traded by Pirates to Mariners for OF Glenn Wilson (July 22, 1988). . . . Traded by Mariners to Tigers for OF Tracy Jones (June 18, 1990). . . . Granted free agency (November 5, 1990). . . . Signed by Phoenix, San Francisco Giants organization (March 30, 1991). . . . Granted free agency (October 16, 1991). . . . Signed by Cincinnati Reds organization (November 12, 1991).
STATISTICAL NOTES: Led Midwest League shortstops with 66 double plays in 1981. . . . Hit three home runs in a game (September 30, 1987, second game).

Year	Team (League)	Pos.	G	AB	R	H	2B	3B	HR	RBI	Avg.	SB	PO	A	E	Avg.
1980—Bellingham (Northwest)....		SS	35	117	23	25	3	1	2	12	.214	1	37	80	★28	.807
1981—Wausau (Midwest)..........		SS	111	354	53	97	20	3	9	48	.274	9	154	335	52	.904
1982—Bakersfield (California)		SS	136	482	91	146	24	4	11	55	.303	27	200	419	★73	.895

Year	Team (League)	Pos.	G	AB	R	H	2B	3B	HR	RBI	Avg.	SB	PO	A	E	Avg.
1983	—Chattanooga (Southern)...	SS	72	261	49	75	10	4	5	24	.287	12	131	232	30	.924
	—Salt Lake City (PCL)........	SS	61	234	43	74	12	5	10	41	.316	11	100	178	25	.917
	—Seattle (A.L.)..................	3B	27	92	9	26	7	0	1	6	.283	0	17	47	4	.941
1984	—Salt Lake City (PCL)........	3B	69	242	57	77	22	3	14	68	.318	7	45	164	16	.929
	—Seattle (A.L.)..................	3B-OF	48	143	15	23	3	1	0	6	.161	2	31	63	8	.922
1985	—Calgary (Pacific Coast)	3B-SS-OF	31	97	16	31	8	0	4	24	.320	2	16	49	5	.929
	—Seattle (A.L.)..................	SS-3B-OF	27	59	8	14	4	0	1	5	.237	0	25	44	6	.920
1986	—Detroit (A.L.)■................	3B-OF-SS	142	521	67	142	30	2	20	86	.273	6	111	242	23	.939
1987	—Detroit (A.L.)	3-1-0-S	53	149	14	27	5	1	4	15	.181	6	84	67	17	.899
	—Toledo (International)	3B-OF-SS	10	37	7	12	5	0	1	8	.324	0	7	8	1	.938
	—Pittsburgh (N.L.)■...........	OF-3B-1B	40	119	20	27	8	0	6	24	.227	1	39	20	3	.952
1988	—Pittsburgh (N.L.)	OF-1B-3B	68	211	20	49	13	1	5	36	.232	1	100	0	2	.980
	—Seattle (A.L.)■................	OF-1B	55	195	32	57	10	1	10	34	.292	3	66	3	1	.986
1989	—Seattle (A.L.)	OF-3B-1B	146	535	54	135	21	3	10	59	.252	5	317	76	12	.970
1990	—Seattle-Detroit (A.L.)■.....	OF-1B	89	215	22	45	7	1	3	20	.209	0	69	42	9	.925
1991	—Phoenix (Pacific Coast) ■..	3B-OF-1B	83	328	43	95	23	2	6	65	.290	0	102	118	17	.928
	—San Francisco (N.L.)	OF-1B	11	14	1	3	0	0	0	0	.214	0	4	0	0	1.000
American League totals (8 years)			587	1909	221	469	87	9	49	231	.246	22	720	584	80	.942
National League totals (3 years)			119	344	41	79	21	1	11	60	.230	2	143	20	5	.970
Major league totals (9 years)			706	2253	262	548	108	10	60	291	.243	24	863	604	85	.945

COLON, CRIS
SS, RANGERS

PERSONAL: Born January 3, 1969, at LaGuaira, Venezuela. ... 6-2/180. ... Throws right, bats both. ... Full name: Cristobal Colon.
HIGH SCHOOL: Fey Alegria.
TRANSACTIONS/CAREER NOTES: Signed as free agent by Texas Rangers organization (October 6, 1986). ... On Port Charlotte disabled list (June 11-July 17, 1991).
STATISTICAL NOTES: Led Pioneer League shortstops with 38 double plays in 1988.

Year	Team (League)	Pos.	G	AB	R	H	2B	3B	HR	RBI	Avg.	SB	PO	A	E	Avg.
1987	—Sarasota Rangers (GCL)...	SS	46	136	12	35	3	0	0	9	.257	2	40	102	20	.877
1988	—Gastonia (S. Atlantic)	SS	75	232	23	46	12	0	1	11	.198	6	104	205	48	.866
	—Butte (Pioneer)	SS	49	190	21	37	3	4	1	19	.195	3	68	136	27	.883
1989	—Gastonia (S. Atlantic)	SS	125	473	58	107	9	8	3	49	.226	9	183	320	47	.915
1990	—Gastonia (S. Atlantic)	SS-3B	38	140	23	45	2	4	4	16	.321	7	50	79	14	.902
	—Tulsa (Texas)	SS	65	234	24	57	9	1	3	29	.244	6	108	192	27	.917
1991	—Charlotte (Florida State)...	SS	66	249	33	78	9	5	3	27	.313	4	118	157	20	.932
	—Tulsa (Texas)	SS	26	102	20	40	6	2	3	28	.392	0	50	82	12	.917

COMBS, PAT
P, PHILLIES

PERSONAL: Born September 29, 1966, at Newport, R.I. ... 6-4/207. ... Throws left, bats left. ... Full name: Patrick Dennis Combs.
HIGH SCHOOL: Alief-Hastings (Houston).
COLLEGE: Rice and Baylor.
TRANSACTIONS/CAREER NOTES: Selected by Philadelphia Phillies organization in first round (11th pick overall) of free-agent draft (June 1, 1988). ... On Philadelphia disabled list (June 27, 1991-remainder of season); included rehabilitation disability assignment to Scranton/Wilkes-Barre (July 14-August 12, 1991).
STATISTICAL NOTES: Led Eastern League with 16 home runs allowed in 1989.

Year	Team (League)	G	W	L	Pct.	ERA	Sv.	IP	H	R	ER	BB	SO
1989	—Clearwater (Florida State)	6	2	1	.667	1.30	0	41⅔	35	8	6	11	24
	—Reading (Eastern)	19	8	7	.533	3.38	0	125	104	57	47	40	77
	—Scranton/Wilkes-Barre (Int'l) ..	3	3	0	1.000	0.37	0	24⅓	15	4	1	7	20
	—Philadelphia (N.L.)	6	4	0	1.000	2.09	0	38⅔	36	10	9	6	30
1990	—Philadelphia (N.L.)	32	10	10	.500	4.07	0	183⅓	179	90	83	86	108
1991	—Philadelphia (N.L.)	14	2	6	.250	4.90	0	64⅓	64	41	35	43	41
	—Scranton/Wilkes-Barre (Int'l) ..	6	2	2	.500	6.67	0	27	39	23	20	16	14
Major league totals (3 years)		52	16	16	.500	3.99	0	286⅓	279	141	127	135	179

COMPRES, FIDEL
P, CARDINALS

PERSONAL: Born May 10, 1965, at Bacuibaso, Dominican Republic. ... 6-0/165. ... Throws right, bats right.
TRANSACTIONS/CAREER NOTES: Signed as a free agent by Cleveland Indians organization (November 21, 1983). ... Loaned to Utica, independent (August 2, 1984); returned (September 4, 1984). ... Drafted by Chicago White Sox (December 6, 1988). ... Released by White Sox (April 1, 1989). ... Signed by Texas Rangers organization (July 23, 1989). ... Granted free agency (October 15, 1990). ... Signed by St. Louis Cardinals organization (January 18, 1991). ... Granted free agency (October 15, 1991). ... Re-signed by Cardinals organization (November 4, 1991).

Year	Team (League)	G	W	L	Pct.	ERA	Sv.	IP	H	R	ER	BB	SO
1984	—Batavia-Utica (N.Y.-Penn)■....	8	2	2	.500	6.97	0	31	35	29	24	25	18
1985	—Batavia (New York-Penn)■......	4	0	1	.000	13.50	0	4	5	6	6	6	4

Year Team (League)	G	W	L	Pct.	ERA	Sv.	IP	H	R	ER	BB	SO
1986—Batavia (New York-Penn)	18	2	5	.286	4.08	0	39⅔	50	29	18	17	34
1987—Waterloo (Midwest)	21	3	2	.600	3.71	0	63	60	29	26	23	56
1988—Waterloo (Midwest)	29	5	5	.500	4.41	2	67⅓	69	41	33	31	65
1989—Gastonia (South Atlantic)■	8	0	1	.000	0.92	1	19⅔	12	4	2	5	13
1990—Charlotte (Florida State)	22	9	2	.818	2.24	1	116⅔	89	38	29	43	69
—Tulsa (Texas)	6	0	1	.000	6.10	0	10⅓	12	10	7	11	9
1991—Arkansas (Texas)■	27	4	2	.667	3.94	9	32	37	17	14	12	18
—Louisville (American Assoc.)	10	0	2	.000	3.07	0	14⅔	22	5	5	8	7

COMSTOCK, KEITH
P

PERSONAL: Born December 23, 1955, at San Francisco. . . . 6-0/174. . . . Throws left, bats left. . . . Full name: Keith Martin Comstock. . . . Brother of Brad Comstock, minor league pitcher (1987-88).
HIGH SCHOOL: San Carlos (Calif.).
COLLEGE: Canada College (Calif.).
TRANSACTIONS/CAREER NOTES: Selected by California Angels organization in fifth round of free-agent draft (January 7, 1976). . . . On disabled list (July 29, 1976-remainder of season). . . . Released by Angels organization (July 6, 1979). . . . Signed by West Haven, Oakland Athletics organization (February 29, 1980). . . . Sold by A's organization to Detroit Tigers organization (March 28, 1983). . . . Granted free agency (October 23, 1983). . . . Signed by Minnesota Twins organization (October 23, 1983). . . . Released by Twins organization (November 6, 1984). . . . Signed by Yomiuri Giants of Japan Central League for 1985. . . . Released by Yomiuri Giants. . . . Signed by San Francisco Giants (November 24, 1986). . . . Traded by Giants with 3B Chris Brown, P Mark Davis and P Mark Grant to San Diego Padres for P Dave Dravecky, P Craig Lefferts and IF Kevin Mitchell (July 4, 1987). . . . Released by Padres organization (June 18, 1989). . . . Signed by Seattle Mariners (June 20, 1989). . . . On Calgary disabled list (May 20-July 11, 1991). . . . On Seattle disabled list (August 6, 1991-remainder of season). . . . Granted free agency (October 10, 1991).
STATISTICAL NOTES: Tied for Southern League lead with three shutouts in 1983.
MISCELLANEOUS: Appeared in one game as an outfielder with San Francisco with no chances (1987).

Year Team (League)	G	W	L	Pct.	ERA	Sv.	IP	H	R	ER	BB	SO
1976—Idaho Falls (Pioneer)	15	1	4	.200	3.89	5	37	33	18	16	32	45
1977—Quad Cities (Midwest)	18	1	0	1.000	5.06	5	32	22	18	18	18	39
—Salinas (California)	23	1	1	.500	4.64	6	33	35	26	17	18	41
1978—Salinas (California)	27	6	4	.600	2.85	2	82	70	31	26	46	71
1979—El Paso (Texas)	16	2	5	.286	7.14	0	63	95	64	50	35	18
1980—West Haven (Eastern)■	29	2	4	.333	4.19	1	73	64	40	34	37	52
1981—West Haven (Eastern)	35	8	7	.533	4.10	0	145	123	76	66	80	133
1982—West Haven (Eastern)	24	9	5	.643	3.02	0	125	99	48	42	69	132
—Tacoma (Pacific Coast)	5	1	2	.333	7.16	0	27⅔	34	24	22	12	22
1983—Birmingham (Southern)■	37	12	3	•.800	3.21	1	145⅔	130	58	52	63	136
1984—Minnesota (A.L.)■	4	0	0	…	8.53	0	6⅓	6	6	6	4	2
—Toledo (International)	23	12	6	.667	2.79	0	164⅓	132	58	51	56	154
1985—Yomiuri Giants (Japan. Cen.)■	21	8	8	.500	4.21	…	124	…	…	58	76	87
1986—Yomiuri Giants (Japan. Cen.)	3	0	2	.000	8.10	…	10	…	…	9	7	7
1987—Phoenix (Pacific Coast)■	17	4	2	.667	2.77	2	39	24	12	12	23	35
—San Fran.-San Diego (N.L.)■	41	2	1	.667	4.61	1	56⅔	52	30	29	31	59
1988—Las Vegas (Pacific Coast)	50	5	4	.556	3.14	17	71⅔	67	32	25	31	78
—San Diego (N.L.)	7	0	0	…	6.75	0	8	8	6	6	3	9
1989—Las Vegas-Calgary (PCL)■	33	9	2	.818	2.93	10	55⅓	45	19	18	21	64
—Seattle (A.L.)	31	1	2	.333	2.81	0	25⅔	26	8	8	10	22
1990—Seattle (A.L.)	60	7	4	.636	2.89	2	56	40	22	18	26	50
1991—Calgary (Pacific Coast)	15	3	1	.750	3.28	2	35⅔	25	16	13	16	38
—Seattle (A.L.)	1	0	0	…	54.00	0	⅓	2	2	2	1	0
American League totals (4 years)	96	8	6	.571	3.46	2	88⅓	74	38	34	41	74
National League totals (2 years)	48	2	1	.667	4.87	1	64⅔	60	36	35	34	68
Major league totals (6 years)	144	10	7	.588	4.06	3	153	134	74	69	75	142

CONE, DAVID
P, METS

PERSONAL: Born January 2, 1963, at Kansas City, Mo. . . . 6-1/190. . . . Throws right, bats left. . . . Full name: David Brian Cone.
HIGH SCHOOL: Rockhurst (Kansas City, Mo.).
TRANSACTIONS/CAREER NOTES: Selected by Kansas City Royals organization in third round of free-agent draft (June 8, 1981). . . . On disabled list (April 8, 1983-entire season). . . . Traded by Royals with C Chris Jelic to New York Mets for C Ed Hearn, P Rick Anderson and P Mauro Gozzo (March 27, 1987). . . . On New York disabled list (May 28-August 14, 1987); included rehabilitation disability assignment to Tidewater (July 30-August 14, 1987).
RECORDS/HONORS: Shares N.L. single-game record for most strikeouts—19 (October 6, 1991).
STATISTICAL NOTES: Led Southern League with 27 wild pitches in 1984. . . . Tied for N.L. lead with 10 balks in 1988.

Year Team (League)	G	W	L	Pct.	ERA	Sv.	IP	H	R	ER	BB	SO
1981—Sarasota Royals-Blue (GCL)	14	6	4	.600	2.55	0	67	52	24	19	33	45
1982—Charleston, S.C. (S. Atlantic)	16	9	2	.818	2.06	0	104⅔	84	38	24	47	87
—Fort Myers (Florida State)	10	7	1	.875	2.12	0	72⅓	56	21	17	25	57
1983—						Did not play						
1984—Memphis (Southern)	29	8	12	.400	4.28	0	178⅔	162	103	85	114	110
1985—Omaha (American Assoc.)	28	9	15	.375	4.65	0	158⅔	157	90	82	★93	115

Year	Team (League)	G	W	L	Pct.	ERA	Sv.	IP	H	R	ER	BB	SO
1986	—Omaha (American Assoc.)	39	8	4	.667	2.79	14	71	60	23	22	25	63
	—Kansas City (A.L.)	11	0	0	...	5.56	0	22⅔	29	14	14	13	21
1987	—New York (N.L.)■	21	5	6	.455	3.71	1	99⅓	87	46	41	44	68
	—Tidewater (International)	3	0	1	.000	5.73	0	11	10	8	7	6	7
1988	—New York (N.L.)	35	20	3	*.870	2.22	0	231⅓	178	67	57	80	213
1989	—New York (N.L.)	34	14	8	.636	3.52	0	219⅔	183	92	86	74	190
1990	—New York (N.L.)	31	14	10	.583	3.23	0	211⅔	177	84	76	65	*233
1991	—New York (N.L.)	34	14	14	.500	3.29	0	232⅔	204	95	85	73	*241
	American League totals (1 year)	11	0	0	...	5.56	0	22⅔	29	14	14	13	21
	National League totals (5 years)	155	67	41	.620	3.12	1	994⅔	829	384	345	336	945
	Major league totals (6 years)	166	67	41	.620	3.18	1	1017⅓	858	398	359	349	966

CHAMPIONSHIP SERIES RECORD

Year	Team (League)	G	W	L	Pct.	ERA	Sv.	IP	H	R	ER	BB	SO
1988	—New York (N.L.)	3	1	1	.500	4.50	0	12	10	6	6	5	9

ALL-STAR GAME RECORD

Year	League	W	L	Pct.	ERA	Sv.	IP	H	R	ER	BB	SO
1988	—National	0	0	...	0.00	0	1	0	0	0	0	1

CONINE, JEFF
1B/OF, ROYALS

PERSONAL: Born June 27, 1966, at Tacoma, Wash.... 6-1/220.... Throws right, bats right.... Full name: Jeffrey Guy Conine.
HIGH SCHOOL: Eisenhower (Yakima, Wash.).
COLLEGE: UCLA.
TRANSACTIONS/CAREER NOTES: Selected by Kansas City Royals organization in 58th round of free-agent draft (June 2, 1987). ... On disabled list (June 28, 1991-remainder of season).
RECORDS/HONORS: Named Southern League Most Valuable Player (1990).
STATISTICAL NOTES: Led Southern League first basemen with 1,164 putouts, 95 assists, 22 errors, 1,281 total chances and 108 double plays in 1990.

Year	Team (League)	Pos.	G	AB	R	H	2B	3B	HR	RBI	Avg.	SB	PO	A	E	Avg.
1988	—Baseball City (Fla. St.)	1B-3B	118	415	63	113	23	9	10	59	.272	26	661	51	22	.970
1989	—Baseball City (Fla. St.)	1B	113	425	68	116	12	7	14	60	.273	32	830	65	18	.980
1990	—Memphis (Southern)	1B-3B	137	487	89	156	37	8	15	95	.320	21	†1164	†95	†22	.983
	—Kansas City (A.L.)	1B	9	20	3	5	2	0	0	2	.250	0	39	4	1	.977
1991	—Omaha (Am. Assoc.)	1B-OF	51	171	23	44	9	1	3	15	.257	0	392	41	7	.984
	Major league totals (1 year)		9	20	3	5	2	0	0	2	.250	0	39	4	1	.977

COOK, DENNIS
P, INDIANS

PERSONAL: Born October 4, 1962, at Lamarque, Tex.... 6-3/185.... Throws left, bats left.... Full name: Dennis Bryan Cook.
HIGH SCHOOL: Dickinson (Tex.).
COLLEGE: Angelina College (Tex.) and Texas.
TRANSACTIONS/CAREER NOTES: Selected by San Diego Padres organization in sixth round of free-agent draft (January 11, 1983).... Selected by San Francisco Giants organization in 18th round of free-agent draft (June 3, 1985).... Traded by Giants with P Terry Mulholland and 3B Charlie Hayes to Philadelphia Phillies for P Steve Bedrosian and a player to be named later (June, 18, 1989); Giants organization acquired IF Rick Parker to complete deal (August 7, 1989).... Traded by Phillies to Los Angeles Dodgers for C Darrin Fletcher (September 13, 1990).... Traded by Dodgers with P Mike Christopher to Cleveland Indians for P Rudy Seanez (December 10, 1991).
RECORDS/HONORS: Named Texas League Pitcher of the Year (1987).

Year	Team (League)	G	W	L	Pct.	ERA	Sv.	IP	H	R	ER	BB	SO
1985	—Clinton (Midwest)	13	5	4	.556	3.36	0	83	73	35	31	27	40
1986	—Fresno (California)	27	12	7	.632	3.97	1	170	141	92	75	100	*173
1987	—Shreveport (Texas)	16	9	2	.818	2.13	0	105⅔	94	32	25	20	98
	—Phoenix (Pacific Coast)	12	2	5	.286	5.23	0	62	72	45	36	26	24
1988	—Phoenix (Pacific Coast)	26	11	9	.550	3.88	0	141⅓	138	73	61	51	110
	—San Francisco (N.L.)	4	2	1	.667	2.86	0	22	9	8	7	11	13
1989	—Phoenix (Pacific Coast)	12	7	4	.636	3.12	0	78	73	29	27	19	85
	—San Francisco-Phil. (N.L.)■	23	7	8	.467	3.72	0	121	110	59	50	38	67
1990	—Phil.-Los Angeles (N.L.)■	47	9	4	.692	3.92	1	156	155	74	68	56	64
1991	—Albuquerque (Pacific Coast)	14	7	3	.700	3.63	0	91⅔	73	46	37	32	84
	—Los Angeles (N.L.)	20	1	0	1.000	0.51	0	17⅔	12	3	1	7	8
	—San Antonio (Texas)	7	1	3	.250	2.49	0	50⅔	43	20	14	10	45
	Major league totals (4 years)	94	19	13	.594	3.58	1	316⅔	286	144	126	112	152

COOLBAUGH, SCOTT
3B, PADRES

PERSONAL: Born June 13, 1966, at Binghamton, N.Y.... 5-11/195.... Throws right, bats right.... Full name: Scott Robert Coolbaugh.... Name pronounced COOL-bah.
HIGH SCHOOL: Roosevelt (San Antonio).
COLLEGE: Texas.

TRANSACTIONS/CAREER NOTES: Selected by Texas Rangers organization in third round of free-agent draft (June 2, 1987).... Traded by Rangers to San Diego Padres for C Mark Parent (December 12, 1990).
STATISTICAL NOTES: Tied for Texas League lead with eight sacrifice flies in 1988.... Led Texas League third basemen with 421 total chances and 28 double plays in 1988.... Led American Association third basemen with 105 putouts, 278 assists, 413 total chances and 32 double plays in 1989.

Year	Team (League)	Pos.	G	AB	R	H	2B	3B	HR	RBI	Avg.	SB	PO	A	E	Avg.
1987	—Charlotte (Florida State)...	3B-2B	66	233	27	64	21	0	2	20	.275	0	42	151	16	.923
1988	—Tulsa (Texas)	3B	136	470	52	127	15	4	13	75	.270	2	72	★324	25	.941
1989	—Oklahoma City (A.A.)	3B-2B	•144	★527	66	137	28	0	18	74	.260	1	†108	†279	30	.928
	—Texas (A.L.)......................	3B	25	51	7	14	1	0	2	7	.275	0	7	39	2	.958
1990	—Oklahoma City (A.A.)	3-1-2-0	76	293	39	66	17	2	6	30	.225	0	91	144	15	.940
	—Texas (A.L.)......................	3B	67	180	21	36	6	0	2	13	.200	1	42	118	10	.941
1991	—Las Vegas (Pac. Coast)■..	3B	60	209	29	60	9	2	7	29	.287	2	36	112	19	.886
	—San Diego (N.L.)...............	3B	60	180	12	39	8	1	2	15	.217	0	32	108	7	.952
	American League totals (2 years)		92	231	28	50	7	0	4	20	.216	1	49	157	12	.945
	National League totals (1 year)		60	180	12	39	8	1	2	15	.217	0	32	108	7	.952
	Major league totals (3 years)		152	411	40	89	15	1	6	35	.217	1	81	265	19	.948

COOPER, GARY

3B/OF/1B, ASTROS

PERSONAL: Born August 13, 1964, at Lynwood, Calif.... 6-1/200.... Throws right, bats right. ... Full name: Gary Clifton Cooper.
HIGH SCHOOL: Lafayette (Ellisville, Mo.).
COLLEGE: Brigham Young.
TRANSACTIONS/CAREER NOTES: Selected by Houston Astros organization in seventh round of free-agent draft (June 2, 1986).
STATISTICAL NOTES: Led New York-Pennsylvania League with 141 total bases in 1986.... Led New York-Pennsylvania League outfielders with 1.000 fielding percentage in 1986.

Year	Team (League)	Pos.	G	AB	R	H	2B	3B	HR	RBI	Avg.	SB	PO	A	E	Avg.
1986	—Auburn (N.Y.-Penn)..........	OF-1B	76	275	52	86	•16	3	11	54	.313	16	127	11	1	†.993
1987	—Osceola (Florida State)	OF-1B-3B	123	427	66	119	17	4	4	73	.279	14	421	51	9	.981
1988	—Columbus (Southern)	OF-3B-1B	140	474	65	128	25	7	7	69	.270	13	355	78	11	.975
1989	—Tucson (Pacific Coast)	OF-3B-1B	118	376	51	102	23	3	1	50	.271	5	210	2	3	.986
1990	—Osceola (Florida State)	OF	8	26	4	4	4	0	0	2	.154	0	5	0	0	1.000
	—Columbus (Southern)	OF-1B-3B	54	160	29	42	7	0	8	30	.263	1	75	15	3	.968
1991	—Tucson (Pacific Coast)	3B-OF-1B	120	406	86	124	25	6	14	75	.305	7	183	125	8	.975
	—Houston (N.L.)	3B	9	16	1	4	1	0	0	2	.250	0	3	2	1	.833
	Major league totals (1 year)		9	16	1	4	1	0	0	2	.250	0	3	2	1	.833

COOPER, SCOTT

3B, RED SOX

PERSONAL: Born October 13, 1967, at St. Louis.... 6-3/205.... Throws right, bats left.... Full name: Scott Kendrick Cooper.
HIGH SCHOOL: Pattonville (St. Louis).
TRANSACTIONS/CAREER NOTES: Selected by Boston Red Sox organization in third round of free-agent draft (June 2, 1986).
STATISTICAL NOTES: Led Carolina League with 234 total bases in 1988.... Led International League third basemen with 94 putouts and tied for lead with 240 assists in 1990.... Led International League with 11 intentional bases on balls received in 1991. ... Led International League third basemen with 364 total chances in 1991.

Year	Team (League)	Pos.	G	AB	R	H	2B	3B	HR	RBI	Avg.	SB	PO	A	E	Avg.
1986	—Elmira (New York-Penn) ..	3B	51	191	23	55	9	0	9	43	.288	1	22	62	9	.903
1987	—Greensboro (S. Atlantic) ...	3B-1B-P	119	370	52	93	21	2	15	63	.251	1	150	153	21	.935
1988	—Lynchburg (Carolina)	3B-1B-OF	130	497	90	•148	★45	7	9	73	.298	0	116	198	27	.921
1989	—New Britain (Eastern)	3B	124	421	50	104	24	2	7	39	.247	1	91	212	22	.932
1990	—Pawtucket (Int'l)	3B-SS	124	433	56	115	17	1	12	44	.266	2	†96	†244	22	.939
	—Boston (A.L.)	PH-PR	2	1	0	0	0	0	0	0	.000	0	0	0	0	...
1991	—Pawtucket (Int'l)	3B-SS	137	483	55	134	21	2	15	72	.277	3	†115	†241	†26	.932
	—Boston (A.L.)	3B	14	35	6	16	4	2	0	7	.457	0	6	22	2	.933
	Major league totals (2 years)		16	36	6	16	4	2	0	7	.444	0	6	22	2	.933

RECORD AS PITCHER

Year	Team (League)	G	W	L	Pct.	ERA	Sv.	IP	H	R	ER	BB	SO
1987	—Greensboro (South Atlantic)	2	0	0	...	0.00	0	2	2	1	0	2	3

CORA, JOEY

2B, WHITE SOX

PERSONAL: Born May 14, 1965, at Cuguas, Puerto Rico.... 5-8/152.... Throws right, bats both.... Full name: Jose Manuel Cora.
COLLEGE: Vanderbilt.
TRANSACTIONS/CAREER NOTES: Selected by San Diego Padres organization in first round (23rd pick overall) of free-agent draft (June 3, 1985).... On disabled list (June 22-August 15, 1986).... Traded by Padres with IF Kevin Garner and OF Warren Newson to Chicago White Sox for P Adam Peterson and P Steve Rosenberg (March 31, 1991).... On Chicago disabled list (June 22-July 11, 1991); included rehabilitation disability assignment to South Bend (July 9-11, 1991).
STATISTICAL NOTES: Led Pacific Coast League second basemen with 24 errors in both 1988 and 1989.

Year	Team (League)	Pos.	G	AB	R	H	2B	3B	HR	RBI	Avg.	SB	PO	A	E	Avg.
1985	Spokane (Northwest)	2B	43	170	48	55	11	2	3	26	.324	13	92	123	9	.960
1986	Beaumont (Texas)	2B-SS	81	315	54	96	5	5	3	41	.305	24	217	267	19	.962
1987	San Diego (N.L.)	2B-SS	77	241	23	57	7	2	0	13	.237	15	123	200	10	.970
	Las Vegas (Pac. Coast)	2B-SS	81	293	50	81	9	1	1	24	.276	12	186	249	9	.980
1988	Las Vegas (Pac. Coast)	2B-3B-OF	127	460	73	136	15	3	3	55	.296	31	285	346	†26	.960
1989	Las Vegas (Pac. Coast)	2B-SS	119	507	79	157	25	4	0	37	.310	★40	245	349	†27	.957
	San Diego (N.L.)	SS-3B-2B	12	19	5	6	1	0	0	1	.316	1	11	15	2	.929
1990	San Diego (N.L.)	SS-2B-C	51	100	12	27	3	0	0	2	.270	8	59	49	11	.908
	Las Vegas (Pac. Coast)	2B-SS	51	211	41	74	13	9	0	24	.351	15	125	148	14	.951
1991	Chicago (A.L.)■	2B-SS	100	228	37	55	2	3	0	18	.241	11	107	192	10	.968
	South Bend (Midwest)	2B	1	5	1	1	0	0	0	0	.200	1	2	4	0	1.000
American League totals (1 year)			100	228	37	55	2	3	0	18	.241	11	107	192	10	.968
National League totals (3 years)			140	360	40	90	11	2	0	16	.250	24	193	264	23	.952
Major league totals (4 years)			240	588	77	145	13	5	0	34	.247	35	300	456	33	.958

CORBIN, ARCHIE
P, ROYALS

PERSONAL: Born December 30, 1967, at Beaumont, Tex. . . . 6-4/190. . . . Throws right, bats right. . . . Full name: Archie Ray Corbin.
HIGH SCHOOL: Pellard (Beaumont, Tex.).
TRANSACTIONS/CAREER NOTES: Selected by New York Mets organization in 16th round of free-agent draft (June 2, 1986). . . . On disabled list (April 6-May 4, 1990). . . . Traded by Mets organization to Kansas City Royals organization for 1B-OF Pat Tabler (August 31, 1990).

Year	Team (League)	G	W	L	Pct.	ERA	Sv.	IP	H	R	ER	BB	SO
1986	Kingsport (Appalachian)	18	1	1	.500	4.75	0	30⅓	31	23	16	28	30
1987	Kingsport (Appalachian)	6	2	3	.400	6.31	0	25⅔	24	21	18	26	17
1988	Kingsport (Appalachian)	11	7	2	.778	1.56	0	69⅓	47	23	12	17	47
1989	Columbia (South Atlantic)	27	9	9	.500	4.51	1	153⅔	149	86	77	72	130
1990	St. Lucie (Florida State)	20	7	8	.467	2.97	0	118	97	47	39	59	105
1991	Memphis (Southern)■	28	8	8	.500	4.66	0	156⅓	139	90	★81	90	166
	Kansas City (A.L.)	2	0	0	. . .	3.86	0	2⅓	3	1	1	2	1
Major league totals (1 year)		2	0	0	. . .	3.86	0	2⅓	3	1	1	2	1

CORDERO, WILFREDO
SS, EXPOS

PERSONAL: Born October 3, 1971, at Mayaguez, Puerto Rico. . . . 6-2/185. . . . Throws right, bats right. . . . Full name: Wilfredo Cordero.
HIGH SCHOOL: Centro de Servicios Education de Mayaguez (Puerto Rico).
TRANSACTIONS/CAREER NOTES: Signed as free agent by Montreal Expos organization (May 24, 1988). . . . On disabled list (August 1, 1991-remainder of season).

Year	Team (League)	Pos.	G	AB	R	H	2B	3B	HR	RBI	Avg.	SB	PO	A	E	Avg.
1988	Jamestown (N.Y.-Penn) ...	SS	52	190	18	49	3	0	2	22	.258	3	82	159	31	.886
1989	West Palm Beach (FSL)	SS	78	289	37	80	12	2	6	29	.277	2	121	224	29	.922
	Jacksonville (Southern) ...	SS	39	121	9	26	6	1	3	17	.215	1	62	93	7	.957
1990	Jacksonville (Southern) ...	SS	131	444	63	104	18	4	7	40	.234	9	179	349	41	.928
1991	Indianapolis (A.A.)	SS	98	360	48	94	16	4	11	52	.261	9	157	287	27	.943

CORMIER, RHEAL
P, CARDINALS

PERSONAL: Born April 23, 1967, at Monteon, New Brunswick, Canada. . . . 5-10/185. . . . Throws left, bats left. . . . Full name: Rheal Paul Cormier. . . . Name pronounced re-AL COR-mee-AY.
COLLEGE: Community College of Rhode Island.
TRANSACTIONS/CAREER NOTES: Selected by St. Louis Cardinals organization in sixth round of free-agent draft (June 6, 1988).
STATISTICAL NOTES: Led American Association pitchers with three shutouts in 1991.
MISCELLANEOUS: Member of 1988 Canadian Olympic baseball team.

Year	Team (League)	G	W	L	Pct.	ERA	Sv.	IP	H	R	ER	BB	SO
1989	St. Petersburg (Florida State) ..	26	12	7	.632	2.23	0	169⅔	141	63	42	33	122
1990	Arkansas (Texas)	22	5	•12	.294	5.04	0	121⅓	133	81	68	30	102
	Louisville (American Assoc.) ...	4	1	1	.500	2.25	0	24	18	8	6	3	9
1991	Louisville (American Assoc.) ...	21	7	9	.438	4.23	0	127⅔	140	64	60	31	74
	St. Louis (N.L.)	11	4	5	.444	4.12	0	67⅔	74	35	31	8	38
Major league totals (1 year)		11	4	5	.444	4.12	0	67⅔	74	35	31	8	38

CORSI, JIM
P

PERSONAL: Born September 9, 1961, at Newton, Mass. . . . 6-1/210. . . . Throws right, bats right. . . . Full name: James Bernard Corsi.
HIGH SCHOOL: Newton North (Mass.).
COLLEGE: St. Leo (Fla.) College (bachelor of arts degree in management).
TRANSACTIONS/CAREER NOTES: Selected by New York Yankees organization in 25th round of free-agent draft (June 7, 1982). . . . On Fort Lauderdale disabled list (April 8-May 11, 1983). . . . Released by Yankees organization (April 3, 1984). . . . Signed by

Greensboro, Boston Red Sox organization (April 1, 1985).... Released by Red Sox organization (January 31, 1986).... Re-signed by Red Sox organization (April 5, 1986).... Released by Red Sox organization (April 2, 1987).... Signed by Modesto, Oakland Athletics organization (April 12, 1987).... On Oakland disabled list (March 29, 1990-entire season); included reha-bilitation disability assignment to Tacoma (June 29-July 25, 1990).... Granted free agency (December 20, 1990).... Signed by Tucson, Houston Astros organization (March 19, 1991).... Released by Astros (November 18, 1991).

Year	Team (League)	G	W	L	Pct.	ERA	Sv.	IP	H	R	ER	BB	SO
1982	—Oneonta (New York-Penn)	1	0	0	...	10.80	0	3⅓	5	4	4	2	6
	—Paintsville (Appalachian)	8	0	2	.000	2.90	0	31	32	11	10	13	20
1983	—Greensboro (South Atlantic)	12	2	2	.500	4.09	1	50⅔	59	37	23	33	37
	—Oneonta (New York-Penn)	11	3	6	.333	4.25	0	59⅓	76	38	28	21	47
1984	—					Out of Organized Baseball							
1985	—Greensboro (South Atlantic)■	41	5	8	.385	4.23	9	78⅔	94	49	37	23	84
1986	—New Britain (Eastern)	29	2	3	.400	2.28	3	51⅓	52	13	13	20	38
1987	—Modesto (California)■	19	3	1	.750	3.60	6	30	23	16	12	10	45
	—Huntsville (Southern)	28	8	1	.889	2.81	4	48	30	17	15	15	33
1988	—Tacoma (Pacific Coast)	50	2	5	.286	2.75	16	59	60	25	18	23	48
	—Oakland (A.L.)	11	0	1	.000	3.80	0	21⅓	20	10	9	6	10
1989	—Tacoma (Pacific Coast)	23	2	3	.400	4.13	8	28⅓	40	17	13	9	23
	—Oakland (A.L.)	22	1	2	.333	1.88	0	38⅓	26	8	8	10	21
1990	—Tacoma (Pacific Coast)	5	0	0	...	1.50	0	6	9	2	1	1	3
1991	—Tucson (Pacific Coast)■	2	0	0	...	0.00	0	3	2	0	0	0	4
	—Houston (N.L.)	47	0	5	.000	3.71	0	77⅔	76	37	32	23	53
	American League totals (2 years)	33	1	3	.250	2.56	0	59⅔	46	18	17	16	31
	National League totals (1 year)	47	0	5	.000	3.71	0	77⅔	76	37	32	23	53
	Major league totals (3 years)	80	1	8	.111	3.21	0	137⅓	122	55	49	39	84

COSTELLO, JOHN
P

PERSONAL: Born December 24, 1960, at New York.... 6-1/180.... Throws right, bats right.... Full name: John Reilly Costello.
HIGH SCHOOL: Oceanside (New York).
COLLEGE: Mercyhurst College, Pa. (degree in police science).
TRANSACTIONS/CAREER NOTES: Selected by St. Louis Cardinals organization in 24th round of free-agent draft (June 6, 1983).... On St. Louis disabled list (April 30-May 21, 1989); included rehabilitation disability assignment to Louisville (May 13-21, 1989).... On St. Louis disabled list (March 31-April 15, 1990).... Traded by Cardinals to Montreal Expos for IF Rex Hudler (April 23, 1990).... On Montreal disabled list (April 25-May 26 and May 27-June 10, 1990); included rehabilitation disability assignment to Indianapolis (May 17-24 and June 8-9, 1990).... Traded by Expos to San Diego Padres for P Brian Harrison (November 9, 1990).... Released by Padres (November 19, 1991).

Year	Team (League)	G	W	L	Pct.	ERA	Sv.	IP	H	R	ER	BB	SO
1983	—Erie (New York-Penn)	15	2	5	.286	6.64	2	63⅔	79	51	47	21	41
1984	—Savannah (South Atlantic)	26	13	9	.591	3.36	0	166	142	80	62	86	114
1985	—Springfield (Midwest)	28	8	13	.381	4.16	0	188	188	105	★87	60	127
1986	—St. Petersburg (Florida State)	15	8	2	.800	2.39	1	71⅔	65	21	19	24	32
	—Arkansas (Texas)	10	0	0	...	5.40	1	15	17	11	9	6	10
1987	—Arkansas (Texas)	44	5	2	.714	2.31	7	74	64	27	19	22	67
	—Louisville (American Assoc.)	6	2	0	1.000	4.35	0	10⅓	14	6	5	7	8
1988	—Louisville (American Assoc.)	20	1	1	.500	1.84	11	29⅓	17	7	6	7	34
	—St. Louis (N.L.)	36	5	2	.714	1.81	1	49⅔	44	15	10	25	38
1989	—St. Louis (N.L.)	48	5	4	.556	3.32	3	62⅓	48	24	23	20	40
	—Louisville (American Assoc.)	4	0	0	...	1.80	1	5	5	1	1	1	4
1990	—St. Louis-Montreal (N.L.)■	8	0	0	...	5.91	0	10⅔	12	8	7	2	2
	—Indianapolis (Am. Assoc.)	22	0	3	.000	7.04	0	30⅔	36	26	24	20	32
1991	—Las Vegas (Pacific Coast)■	17	1	2	.333	2.15	3	29⅓	31	16	7	7	24
	—San Diego (N.L.)	27	1	0	1.000	3.09	0	35	37	15	12	17	24
	Major league totals (4 years)	119	11	6	.647	2.97	4	157⅔	141	62	52	64	104

COTTO, HENRY
OF, MARINERS

PERSONAL: Born January 5, 1961, at New York.... 6-2/180.... Throws right, bats right.... Full name: Henry Suarez Cotto.... Name pronounced KOTT-oh.
TRANSACTIONS/CAREER NOTES: Signed as free agent by Chicago Cubs organization (June 7, 1980).... On disabled list (May 10-30, 1983).... Traded by Cubs organization with C Ron Hassey, P Rich Bordi and P Porfi Altamirano to New York Yankees for P Ray Fontenot and OF Brian Dayett (December 4, 1984).... On New York disabled list (May 25-July 5, 1985); included rehabilitation disability assignment to Columbus (June 19-July 5, 1985).... Traded by Yankees with P Steve Trout to Seattle Mariners for P Lee Guetterman, P Clay Parker and P Wade Taylor (December 22, 1987).... On disabled list (August 3, 1991-remainder of season).
STATISTICAL NOTES: Led Texas League outfielders with 333 total chances in 1982.... Tied for American Association lead in caught stealing with 17 in 1983.... Tied for International League lead in double plays by outfielders with three in 1986.

						BATTING						FIELDING			
Year	Team (League)	Pos.	G	AB	R	H	2B	3B	HR	RBI	Avg.	SB	PO	A	E	Avg.
1980	—Sarasota Cubs (GCL)	OF	43	166	24	47	7	5	0	30	.283	12	93	6	3	.971
	—Quad Cities (Midwest)	OF	19	78	9	22	1	1	0	5	.282	8	27	2	4	.879
1981	—Quad Cities (Midwest)	OF	128	493	80	144	15	6	1	46	.292	52	249	★23	13	.954
1982	—Midland (Texas)	OF	130	524	103	161	12	5	1	36	.307	52	★310	16	7	.979
1983	—Iowa (American Assoc.)	OF	104	426	52	111	7	10	0	35	.261	32	253	8	7	.974

Year Team (League)	Pos.	G	AB	R	H	2B	3B	HR	RBI	Avg.	SB	PO	A	E	Avg.
1984—Chicago (N.L.)	OF	105	146	24	40	5	0	0	8	.274	9	117	3	2	.984
—Iowa (American Assoc.) ...	OF	8	30	3	6	2	0	0	0	.200	1	12	3	0	1.000
1985—New York (A.L.)■.............	OF	34	56	4	17	1	0	1	6	.304	1	41	2	1	.977
—Columbus (Int'l)	OF	75	272	38	70	16	2	7	36	.257	16	158	5	2	.988
1986—New York (A.L.)	OF	35	80	11	17	3	0	1	6	.213	3	59	1	0	1.000
—Columbus (Int'l)	OF	97	359	45	89	17	6	7	48	.248	16	215	5	8	.965
1987—Columbus (Int'l)	OF	34	129	26	39	13	2	3	20	.302	14	73	3	2	.974
—New York (A.L.)	OF	68	149	21	35	10	0	5	20	.235	4	89	2	1	.989
1988—Seattle (A.L.)■	OF	133	386	50	100	18	1	8	33	.259	27	253	6	2	.992
1989—Seattle (A.L.)	OF	100	295	44	78	11	2	9	33	.264	10	153	9	2	.988
1990—Seattle (A.L.)	OF	127	355	40	92	14	3	4	33	.259	21	194	4	2	.990
1991—Seattle (A.L.)	OF	66	177	35	54	6	2	6	23	.305	16	104	2	2	.981
American League totals (7 years)		563	1498	205	393	63	8	34	154	.262	82	893	26	10	.989
National League totals (1 year)		105	146	24	40	5	0	0	8	.274	9	117	3	2	.984
Major league totals (8 years)		668	1644	229	433	68	8	34	162	.263	91	1010	29	12	.989

CHAMPIONSHIP SERIES RECORD

Year Team (League)	Pos.	G	AB	R	H	2B	3B	HR	RBI	Avg.	SB	PO	A	E	Avg.
1984—Chicago (N.L.)	OF-PR	3	1	1	1	0	0	0	0	1.000	0	2	0	0	1.000

COX, DANNY
P, PHILLIES

PERSONAL: Born September 21, 1959, at Northhampton, England. . . . 6-4/225. . . . Throws right, bats right. . . . Full name: Danny Bradford Cox.
HIGH SCHOOL: Warner Robins (Ga.).
COLLEGE: Chattahoochee Valley Community College (Ala.) and Troy State.
TRANSACTIONS/CAREER NOTES: Selected by St. Louis Cardinals organization in 13th round of free-agent draft (June 8, 1981). . . . On Arkansas disabled list (April 8-21, 1983). . . . On St. Louis disabled list (March 30-April 24, 1986); included rehabilitation disability assignment to Louisville (April 17-24, 1986). . . . On disabled list (July 10-August 8, 1987). . . . On St. Louis disabled list (April 30-June 27 and August 7, 1988-remainder of season); included rehabilitation disability assignment to Louisville (June 16-27, 1988). . . . On disabled list (March 27, 1989-entire season). . . . Granted free agency (November 13, 1989). . . . Re-signed by Cardinals (November 30, 1989). . . . On St. Louis disabled list (March 31, 1990-entire season); included rehabilitation disability assignment to Louisville (May 17-31 and June 13-18, 1990), Springfield (June 6-7, 1990) and Arkansas (June 8-12, 1990). . . . Granted free agency (October 19, 1990). . . . Signed by Scranton/Wilkes-Barre, Philadelphia Phillies organization (December 17, 1990). . . . On Philadelphia disabled list (May 19-June 17, 1991); included rehabilitation disability assignment to Scranton/Wilkes-Barre (June 14-15, 1991). . . . Granted free agency (October 31, 1991). . . . Re-signed by Phillies organization (December 9, 1991).
RECORDS/HONORS: Named Appalachian League Player of the Year (1981).
STATISTICAL NOTES: Pitched 11-0 no-hit victory against Bristol (August 9, 1981). . . . Led Appalachian League with 10 complete games and four shutouts in 1981. . . . Tied for N.L. lead with seven hit batsmen in 1984. . . . Pitched seven innings, combining with Bob Gaddy in nine inning no-hit victory against Baseball City Royals (April 21, 1991).

Year Team (League)	G	W	L	Pct.	ERA	Sv.	IP	H	R	ER	BB	SO
1981—Johnson City (Appalachian)	13	9	4	.692	*2.06	0	*109	80	27	25	36	*87
1982—Springfield (Midwest)	15	5	3	.625	2.56	0	84⅓	82	46	24	29	68
1983—St. Petersburg (Florida State) ..	5	2	2	.500	2.53	0	32	26	10	9	14	22
—Arkansas (Texas)	11	8	3	.727	2.29	0	86⅓	60	31	22	24	73
—Louisville (American Assoc.) ...	2	0	0	...	2.45	0	11	10	3	3	0	8
—St. Louis (N.L.)	12	3	6	.333	3.25	0	83	92	38	30	23	36
1984—St. Louis (N.L.)	29	9	11	.450	4.03	0	156⅓	171	81	70	54	70
—Louisville (American Assoc.) ...	6	4	1	.800	2.13	0	42⅓	34	16	10	7	34
1985—St. Louis (N.L.)	35	18	9	.667	2.88	0	241	226	91	77	64	131
1986—St. Louis (N.L.)	32	12	13	.480	2.90	0	220	189	85	71	60	108
1987—St. Louis (N.L.)	31	11	9	.550	3.88	0	199⅓	224	99	86	71	101
1988—St. Louis (N.L.)	13	3	8	.273	3.98	0	86	89	40	38	25	47
—Louisville (American Assoc.) ...	3	0	0	...	3.09	0	11⅔	11	7	4	6	7
1989—						Did not play						
1990—Louisville (American Assoc.) ...	4	0	3	.000	15.55	0	11	22	20	19	10	6
—Springfield (Midwest)	1	0	0	...	0.00	0	5	1	0	0	0	3
—Arkansas (Texas)	1	1	0	1.000	1.29	0	7	3	1	1	1	3
1991—Clearwater (Florida State)■■....	3	3	0	1.000	0.00	0	18	4	0	0	4	15
—Philadelphia (N.L.)	23	4	6	.400	4.57	0	102⅓	98	57	52	39	46
—Scranton/Wilkes-Barre (Int'l) ..	1	1	0	1.000	3.00	0	6	5	2	2	2	3
Major league totals (7 years)	175	60	62	.492	3.51	0	1088	1089	491	424	336	539

CHAMPIONSHIP SERIES RECORD

CHAMPIONSHIP SERIES NOTES: Shares single-series record for most complete games pitched—2 (1987). . . . Shares N.L. career record for most complete games pitched—2.

Year Team (League)	G	W	L	Pct.	ERA	Sv.	IP	H	R	ER	BB	SO
1985—St. Louis (N.L.)	1	1	0	1.000	1.50	0	6	4	1	1	5	4
1987—St. Louis (N.L.)	2	1	1	.500	2.12	0	17	17	4	4	3	11
Championship Series totals (2 years)	3	2	1	.667	1.96	0	23	21	5	5	8	15

WORLD SERIES NOTES: Shares single-game record for most earned runs allowed—7 (October 18, 1987). . . . Shares record for most earned runs allowed in one inning—6 (October 18, 1987, fourth inning).

Year	Team (League)	G	W	L	Pct.	ERA	Sv.	IP	H	R	ER	BB	SO
1985	St. Louis (N.L.)	2	0	0	...	1.29	0	14	14	2	2	4	13
1987	St. Louis (N.L.)	3	1	2	.333	7.71	0	11⅔	13	10	10	8	9
World Series totals (2 years)		5	1	2	.333	4.21	0	25⅔	27	12	12	12	22

CRAWFORD, STEVE
P

PERSONAL: Born April 29, 1958, at Pryor, Okla. . . . 6-5/225. . . . Throws right, bats right. . . . Full name: Steven Ray Crawford.
HIGH SCHOOL: Salina (Okla.).
COLLEGE: Claremore Junior College (Okla.) and Northeastern Oklahoma State.

TRANSACTIONS/CAREER NOTES: Signed as free agent by Boston Red Sox organization (May 6, 1978). . . . On Bristol disabled list (April 14-May 2, 1980). . . . On Boston disabled list (April 1-August 12, 1982); included rehabilitation disability assignment to Pawtucket (July 21-August 9, 1982). . . . On Pawtucket disabled list (July 26-August 5, 1983). . . . On disabled list (May 7-22 and June 23-July 8, 1985). . . . On Boston disabled list (July 18-September 1, 1986); included rehabilitation disability assignment to Pawtucket (August 15-September 1, 1986). . . . On disabled list (July 16-31, 1987). . . . Granted free agency (November 9, 1987). . . . Signed by San Antonio, Los Angeles Dodgers organization (May 12, 1988). . . . On San Antonio disabled list (May 12-25, 1988). . . . Granted free agency (October 15, 1988). . . . Signed by Omaha, Kansas City Royals organization (March 7, 1989). . . . Granted free agency (November 13, 1989). . . . Re-signed by Royals (December 5, 1989). . . . On Kansas City disabled list (April 25-May 24, 1990); included rehabilitation disability assignment to Omaha (May 12-23, 1990). . . . Granted free agency (November 5, 1990). . . . Re-signed by Royals (December 6, 1990). . . . On disabled list (June 24-July 11 and July 18-September 9, 1991). . . . Granted free agency (October 29, 1991).
STATISTICAL NOTES: Led Carolina League pitchers with 28 games started and 15 complete games in 1979. . . . Tied for Carolina League lead with three shutouts in 1979.

Year	Team (League)	G	W	L	Pct.	ERA	Sv.	IP	H	R	ER	BB	SO
1978	Winston-Salem (Carolina)	19	9	5	.643	3.44	0	110	109	53	42	48	60
1979	Winston-Salem (Carolina)	29	11	11	.500	2.94	0	*211	*208	88	•69	67	127
1980	Bristol (Eastern)	24	9	7	.563	2.64	0	177	170	68	52	64	97
	Boston (A.L.)	6	2	0	1.000	3.66	0	32	41	14	13	8	10
1981	Boston (A.L.)	14	0	5	.000	4.97	0	58	69	38	32	18	29
1982	Boston (A.L.)	5	1	0	1.000	2.00	0	9	14	3	2	0	2
	Pawtucket (International)	10	1	4	.200	4.11	0	46	55	25	21	15	20
1983	Pawtucket (International)	27	8	11	.421	5.18	0	154⅔	181	98	89	80	104
1984	Pawtucket (International)	7	2	1	.667	1.96	2	18⅓	11	10	4	9	8
	Boston (A.L.)	35	5	0	1.000	3.34	1	62	69	31	23	21	21
1985	Boston (A.L.)	44	6	5	.545	3.76	12	91	103	47	38	28	58
1986	Boston (A.L.)	40	0	2	.000	3.92	4	57⅓	69	29	25	19	32
	Pawtucket (International)	5	1	1	.500	6.00	2	6	10	4	4	1	2
1987	Boston (A.L.)	29	5	4	.556	5.33	0	72⅔	91	48	43	32	43
1988	San Antonio (Texas)■	3	1	0	1.000	0.00	1	6	2	0	0	0	4
	Albuquerque (Pacific Coast)	32	3	6	.333	3.81	3	54⅓	59	31	23	25	36
1989	Omaha (American Assoc.)■	22	3	1	.750	2.93	2	43	41	18	14	9	32
	Kansas City (A.L.)	25	3	1	.750	2.83	0	54	48	19	17	19	33
1990	Kansas City (A.L.)	46	5	4	.556	4.16	1	80	79	38	37	23	54
	Omaha (American Assoc.)	4	0	0	...	0.00	0	6	2	0	0	2	11
1991	Kansas City (A.L.)	33	3	2	.600	5.98	1	46⅔	60	31	31	18	38
Major league totals (10 years)		277	30	23	.566	4.17	19	562⅔	643	298	261	186	320

CHAMPIONSHIP SERIES RECORD

Year	Team (League)	G	W	L	Pct.	ERA	Sv.	IP	H	R	ER	BB	SO
1986	Boston (A.L.)	1	1	0	1.000	0.00	0	1⅔	1	0	0	2	1

WORLD SERIES RECORD

Year	Team (League)	G	W	L	Pct.	ERA	Sv.	IP	H	R	ER	BB	SO
1986	Boston (A.L.)	3	1	0	1.000	6.23	0	4⅓	5	3	3	0	4

CREWS, TIM
P, DODGERS

PERSONAL: Born April 3, 1961, at Tampa, Fla. . . . 6-0/195. . . . Throws right, bats right. . . . Full name: Stanley Timothy Crews.
HIGH SCHOOL: King (Tampa, Fla.).
COLLEGE: Valencia Community College (Fla.).

TRANSACTIONS/CAREER NOTES: Selected by Kansas City Royals organization in second round of free-agent draft (January 8, 1980). . . . Selected by Milwaukee Brewers organization in second round of free-agent draft (January 13, 1981). . . . On disabled list (June 9, 1984-remainder of season and May 17-July 12, 1985). . . . Traded by Brewers organization with P Tim Leary to Los Angeles Dodgers for 1B Greg Brock (December 10, 1986).
STATISTICAL NOTES: Tied for Midwest League lead with 16 home runs allowed in 1981. . . . Led Texas League with 25 home runs allowed and tied for lead with four balks in 1983.

Year	Team (League)	G	W	L	Pct.	ERA	Sv.	IP	H	R	ER	BB	SO
1981	Burlington (Midwest)	21	10	4	.714	4.19	0	144	148	82	67	27	98
1982	Stockton (California)	19	10	4	.714	3.37	0	139	151	66	52	28	83
1983	El Paso (Texas)	27	9	8	.529	6.56	0	163⅓	*207	*129	*119	53	99

Year Team (League)	G	W	L	Pct.	ERA	Sv.	IP	H	R	ER	BB	SO
1984—El Paso (Texas)	8	2	3	.400	6.75	0	36	56	32	27	10	22
1985—Stockton (California)	16	8	1	.889	3.30	0	90	101	46	33	17	56
1986—El Paso (Texas)	15	5	5	.500	4.76	0	90⅔	114	53	48	18	50
—Vancouver (Pacific Coast)	10	2	1	.667	4.05	1	33⅓	39	15	15	14	28
1987—Albuquerque (Pacific Coast)■..	42	7	2	.778	3.63	12	72	73	34	29	25	60
—Los Angeles (N.L.)	20	1	1	.500	2.48	3	29	30	9	8	8	20
1988—Albuquerque (Pacific Coast)	10	1	1	.500	2.70	3	13⅓	13	5	4	2	7
—Los Angeles (N.L.)	42	4	0	1.000	3.14	0	71⅔	77	29	25	16	45
1989—Los Angeles (N.L.)	44	0	1	.000	3.21	1	61⅔	69	27	22	23	56
—Albuquerque (Pacific Coast)	2	0	1	.000	7.71	0	2⅓	3	2	2	0	2
1990—Los Angeles (N.L.)	66	4	5	.444	2.77	5	107⅓	98	40	33	24	76
1991—Los Angeles (N.L.)	60	2	3	.400	3.43	6	76	75	30	29	19	53
Major league totals (5 years)	232	11	10	.524	3.05	15	345⅔	349	135	117	90	250

CRIM, CHUCK
P, ANGELS

PERSONAL: Born July 23, 1961, at Van Nuys, Calif. . . . 6-0/185. . . . Throws right, bats right. . . . Full name: Charles Robert Crim.
HIGH SCHOOL: Thousands Oaks (Calif.).
COLLEGE: Hawaii.
TRANSACTIONS/CAREER NOTES: Selected by Chicago Cubs organization in third round of free-agent draft (June 5, 1979). . . . Selected by Milwaukee Brewers organization in 17th round of free-agent draft (June 7, 1982). . . . On Milwaukee disabled list (July 22-August 10, 1990); included rehabilitation disability assignment to Beloit (August 7, 1990). . . . Traded by Brewers to California Angels for P Mike Fetters and P Glenn Carter (December 10, 1991).
STATISTICAL NOTES: Led Appalachian League with eight complete games in 1982. . . . Tied for Midwest League lead with 11 complete games in 1983.
MISCELLANEOUS: Appeared as first baseman in one game with no chances (1989).

Year Team (League)	G	W	L	Pct.	ERA	Sv.	IP	H	R	ER	BB	SO
1982—Pikeville (Appalachian)	11	4	6	.400	2.56	0	77⅓	62	32	22	18	76
1983—Beloit (Midwest)	25	11	10	.524	3.47	0	163⅓	150	83	63	50	154
1984—El Paso (Texas)	55	7	4	.636	1.50	17	90	77	20	15	25	69
1985—Vancouver (Pacific Coast)	48	3	6	.333	4.56	6	106⅔	110	58	54	38	68
1986—Vancouver (Pacific Coast)	26	0	3	.000	4.96	1	45⅓	64	32	25	15	26
—El Paso (Texas)	16	2	4	.333	2.77	6	39	35	16	12	2	32
1987—Milwaukee (A.L.)	53	6	8	.429	3.67	12	130	133	60	53	39	56
1988—Milwaukee (A.L.)	*70	7	6	.538	2.91	9	105	95	38	34	28	58
1989—Milwaukee (A.L.)	*76	9	7	.563	2.83	7	117⅔	114	42	37	36	59
1990—Milwaukee (A.L.)	67	3	5	.375	3.47	11	85⅔	88	39	33	23	39
—Beloit (Midwest)	1	0	0	...	4.50	0	2	3	2	1	0	0
1991—Milwaukee (A.L.)	66	8	5	.615	4.63	3	91⅓	115	52	47	25	39
Major league totals (5 years)	332	33	31	.516	3.47	42	529⅔	545	231	204	151	251

CROMARTIE, WARREN
1B/OF

PERSONAL: Born September 29, 1953, at Miami. . . . 6-0/200. . . . Throws left, bats left. . . . Full name: Warren Livingston Cromartie. . . . Name pronounced cro-MAR-tee.
HIGH SCHOOL: Miami Jackson (Miami).
COLLEGE: Miami-Dade (North) Community College.
TRANSACTIONS/CAREER NOTES: Selected by Chicago White Sox organization in seventh round of free-agent draft (June 8, 1971). . . . Selected by Minnesota Twins organization in secondary phase of free-agent draft (January 12, 1972). . . . Selected by San Diego Padres organization in secondary phase of free-agent (June 6, 1972). . . . Selected by Oakland Athletics organization in secondary phase of free-agent draft (January 10, 1973). . . . Selected by Montreal Expos organization in secondary phase of free-agent draft (June 5, 1973). . . . On suspended list (May 19-21, 1976). . . . Granted free agency (November 7, 1983). . . . Signed by Yomiuri Giants of Japan Central League. . . . Signed as free agent by Kansas City Royals (April 5, 1991). . . . On voluntarily retired list (September 15, 1991).
STATISTICAL NOTES: Led Eastern League with 235 total bases in 1974. . . . Tied for N.L. lead in double plays by outfielders with five in 1978. . . . Tied for N.L. lead in assists by outfielders with 24 in 1978. . . . Tied for N.L. lead in grounding into double plays with 24 in 1980. . . . Led N.L. with 24 intentional bases on balls received in 1980. . . . Led N.L. first baseman with 14 errors in 1980.

Year Team (League)	Pos.	G	AB	R	H	2B	3B	HR	RBI	Avg.	SB	PO	A	E	Avg.
1974—Quebec City (Eastern)	OF-1B	129	482	*94	162	20	7	13	61	.336	30	389	22	9	.979
—Montreal (N.L.)	OF	8	17	2	3	0	0	0	0	.176	1	8	0	0	1.000
1975—Memphis (International)	OF-1B	119	400	42	107	16	6	3	38	.268	5	478	35	15	.972
1976—Denver (Am. Assoc.)	OF-1B	107	415	69	140	12	5	8	60	.337	27	274	13	6	.980
—Montreal (N.L.)	OF	33	81	8	17	1	0	0	2	.210	1	61	1	2	.969
1977—Montreal (N.L.)	OF	155	620	64	175	41	7	5	50	.282	10	319	10	8	.976
1978—Montreal (N.L.)	OF-1B	159	607	77	180	32	6	10	56	.297	8	351	†24	8	.979
1979—Montreal (N.L.)	OF	158	659	84	181	46	5	8	46	.275	8	343	16	9	.976
1980—Montreal (N.L.)	1B-OF	162	597	74	172	33	5	14	70	.288	8	1459	93	†14	.991
1981—Montreal (N.L.)	1B-OF	99	358	41	109	19	2	6	42	.304	2	570	33	4	.993
1982—Montreal (N.L.)	OF-1B	144	497	59	126	24	3	14	62	.254	3	308	13	6	.982
1983—Montreal (N.L.)	OF-1B	120	360	37	100	26	2	3	43	.278	8	209	12	6	.974
1984—Yomiuri (Jap. Cen.)■	OF	122	457	...	128	...	...	35	93	.280	...	...	...	...	...

Year Team (League)	Pos.	G	AB	R	H	2B	3B	HR	RBI	Avg.	SB	PO	A	E	Avg.
1985—Yomiuri (Jap. Cen.)	OF	119	482	...	149	...	...	32	112	.309	...	...	...	...	...
1986—Yomiuri (Jap. Cen.)	OF	124	471	...	171	...	...	37	98	.363	...	...	...	...	...
1987—Yomiuri (Jap. Cen.)	OF	124	476	...	143	...	...	28	92	.300	...	...	...	...	...
1988—Yomiuri (Jap. Cen.)	OF	49	186	31	62	...	...	10	36	.333	...	...	...	...	...
1989—Yomiuri (Jap. Cen.)	OF	124	439	70	*166	...	...	15	72	*.378	...	...	...	...	...
1990—Yomiuri (Jap. Cen.)	OF	117	450	68	132	23	1	14	55	.293	...	...	...	...	...
1991—Kansas City (A.L.)■..........	1B-OF	69	131	13	41	7	2	1	20	.313	1	221	9	1	.996
American League totals (1 year)		69	131	13	41	7	2	1	20	.313	1	221	9	1	.996
National League totals (9 years)		1038	3796	446	1063	222	30	60	371	.280	49	3628	202	57	.985
Major league totals (10 years)		1107	3927	459	1104	229	32	61	391	.281	50	3849	211	58	.986

CRON, CHRIS
1B/3B, WHITE SOX

PERSONAL: Born March 31, 1964, at Albuquerque, N.M. ... 6-2/200. ... Throws right, bats right. ... Full name: Christopher John Cron.
HIGH SCHOOL: El Dorado (Calif.).
COLLEGE: Santa Ana Junior College (Calif.).
TRANSACTIONS/CAREER NOTES: Selected by Atlanta Braves organization in seventh round of free-agent draft (January 11, 1983). ... Selected by Detroit Tigers organization in secondary phase of free-agent draft (June 6, 1983). ... Selected by Braves organization in secondary phase of free-agent draft (January 17, 1984). ... Released by Braves organization (October 16, 1986). ... Signed by California Angels organization (January 19, 1987). ... Released by Angels (November 13, 1991). ... Signed by Chicago White Sox organization (December 6, 1991).
STATISTICAL NOTES: Tied for South Atlantic League lead in being hit by pitch with 18 in 1985. ... Led Midwest League in being hit by pitch with 17 in 1987. ... Led California League in being hit by pitch with 27 in 1988. ... Led California League third basemen with 31 errors in 1988. ... Led California League third basemen in double plays with 27 in 1988. ... Tied for Texas League lead in errors by first baseman with 12 in 1989. ... Led Pacific Coast League in sacrifice flies with 11 in 1991.

Year Team (League)	Pos.	G	AB	R	H	2B	3B	HR	RBI	Avg.	SB	PO	A	E	Avg.
1984—Pulaski (Appalachian)	1B	32	114	22	42	8	0	7	37	.368	2	241	18	5	.981
1985—Sumter (South Atlantic)....	1B	119	425	53	102	20	0	7	59	.240	5	930	68	*25	.976
1986—Durham (Carolina)	1B	90	265	26	55	10	0	7	34	.208	0	527	41	9	.984
1987—Palm Springs (Calif.)■.......	3B	26	92	6	25	3	0	2	9	.272	2	21	60	8	.910
—Quad City (Midwest)	3B-SS	111	398	53	110	20	1	11	62	.276	1	88	225	36	.897
1988—Palm Springs (Calif.)	3B-1B	127	467	71	117	28	3	14	84	.251	4	99	225	†31	.913
1989—Midland (Texas)	1B-3B	128	491	80	148	*33	3	22	*103	.301	0	932	116	‡17	.984
1990—Edmonton (Pac. Coast)	1B-3B	104	401	54	115	31	0	17	75	.287	7	847	84	7	.993
1991—Edmonton (Pac. Coast)	1B-3B-P	123	461	74	135	21	1	22	91	.293	6	757	125	22	.976
—California (A.L.)	1B	6	15	0	2	0	0	0	0	.133	0	32	6	0	1.000
Major league totals (1 year)		6	15	0	2	0	0	0	0	.133	0	32	6	0	1.000

RECORD AS PITCHER

Year Team (League)	G	W	L	Pct.	ERA	Sv.	IP	H	R	ER	BB	SO
1991—Edmonton (Pacific Coast)	1	0	0	...	0.00	0	⅔	2	0	0	0	0

CROSS, JESSE
P, TWINS

PERSONAL: Born January 15, 1968, at Chattanooga, Tenn. ... 5-10/195. ... Throws right, bats right. ... Full name: Jesse William Cross.
HIGH SCHOOL: Ringgold (Ga.).
COLLEGE: Middle Georgia.
TRANSACTIONS/CAREER NOTES: Selected by Boston Red Sox organization in 30th round of free-agent draft (June 2, 1987). ... Selected by Toronto Blue Jays organization in 62nd round of free-agent draft (June 1, 1988). ... Drafted by Minnesota Twins (December 9, 1991).
STATISTICAL NOTES: Led Southern League pitchers with six errors in 1991.

Year Team (League)	G	W	L	Pct.	ERA	Sv.	IP	H	R	ER	BB	SO
1989—Myrtle Beach (South Atlantic) ..	36	7	8	.467	3.51	4	100	61	46	39	81	139
1990—Dunedin (Florida State)	28	13	7	.650	3.29	0	139⅓	100	54	51	70	126
1991—Knoxville (Southern)	31	10	9	.526	2.83	1	172	141	72	54	71	128

CUMMINGS, STEVE
P, TIGERS

PERSONAL: Born July 15, 1964, at Houston. ... 6-2/205. ... Throws right, bats both. ... Full name: Steven Brent Cummings.
HIGH SCHOOL: J. Frank Dobie (Houston).
COLLEGE: Blinn College (Tex.) and Houston.
TRANSACTIONS/CAREER NOTES: Selected by Texas Rangers organization in fifth round of free-agent draft (January 17, 1984). ... Selected by Atlanta Braves organization in secondary phase of free-agent draft (June 4, 1984). ... Selected by Toronto Blue Jays organization in second round of free-agent draft (June 2, 1986). ... Traded by Blue Jays to Cleveland Indians (September 21, 1990) as partial completion of deal in which Indians traded P Bud Black to Blue Jays for P Mauro Gozzo and two players to be named later (September 16, 1990); Indians acquired P Alex Sanchez to complete deal (September 24, 1990). ... Traded by Indians to Detroit Tigers for a player to be named later (May 21, 1991); Indians acquired P Eric Stone to complete deal (July 8, 1991).
STATISTICAL NOTES: Tied for New York-Pennsylvania League lead in games started by pitcher with 18 in 1986. ... Led Florida State League pitchers with 29 games started in 1987. ... Led Southern League pitchers with 33 games started in 1988.

Year	Team (League)	G	W	L	Pct.	ERA	Sv.	IP	H	R	ER	BB	SO
1986	—St. Catharines (N.Y.-Penn)	18	9	5	.643	2.04	0	110⅓	80	36	25	34	86
1987	—Dunedin (Florida State)	32	★18	8	.692	2.94	0	186⅔	189	80	61	60	111
1988	—Knoxville (Southern)	35	14	11	.560	2.75	0	★212⅔	★206	88	65	64	131
1989	—Syracuse (International)	19	7	5	.583	3.14	0	106	97	46	37	41	60
	—Toronto (A.L.)	5	2	0	1.000	3.00	0	21	18	9	7	11	8
1990	—Syracuse (International)	16	5	3	.625	3.11	0	81	76	31	28	37	34
	—Toronto (A.L.)	6	0	0	...	5.11	0	12⅓	22	7	7	5	4
1991	—Colorado Springs (Pac. Coast)■	5	0	4	.000	6.08	0	26⅔	36	24	18	6	15
	—Toledo (International)■............	30	5	5	.500	4.68	5	75	72	42	39	29	41
	Major league totals (2 years)	11	2	0	1.000	3.78	0	33⅓	40	16	14	16	12

CURTIS, CHAD
OF/3B, ANGELS

PERSONAL: Born November 6, 1968, at Marion, Ind.... 5-10/175.... Throws right, bats right. ... Full name: Chad David Curtis.
HIGH SCHOOL: Benson Union (Benson, Ariz.).
COLLEGE: Grand Canyon University (Ariz.).
TRANSACTIONS/CAREER NOTES: Selected by California Angels organization in 45th round of free-agent draft (June 5, 1989).
STATISTICAL NOTES: Led Midwest League with 223 total bases in 1990.

						BATTING							FIELDING		
Year	Team (League)	Pos.	G	AB	R	H	2B	3B	HR	RBI	Avg.	SB	PO	A	E	Avg.
1989	—Mesa Angels (Arizona)	2B-OF	32	122	30	37	4	4	3	20	.303	17	62	58	6	.952
	—Quad City (Midwest)	OF	23	78	7	19	3	0	2	11	.244	7	34	1	1	.972
1990	—Quad City (Midwest)	2B-OF	135	★492	87	★151	28	1	14	65	.307	64	216	221	26	.944
1991	—Edmonton (Pac. Coast)	3B-2B-OF	115	431	81	136	28	7	9	61	.316	46	124	220	25	.932

CUYLER, MILT
OF, TIGERS

PERSONAL: Born October 7, 1968, at Macon, Ga.... 5-10/175.... Throws right, bats both.... Full name: Milton Cuyler Jr.
HIGH SCHOOL: Southwest Macon (Macon, Ga.).
TRANSACTIONS/CAREER NOTES: Selected by Detroit Tigers organization in second round of free-agent draft (June 2, 1986).
STATISTICAL NOTES: Led South Atlantic League with 17 sacrifice hits in 1987.... Led Florida State League in caught stealing with 25 in 1988.... Led Eastern League outfielders with 293 total chances in 1989.... Led International League in caught stealing with 14 in 1990.

						BATTING							FIELDING		
Year	Team (League)	Pos.	G	AB	R	H	2B	3B	HR	RBI	Avg.	SB	PO	A	E	Avg.
1986	—Bristol (Appalachian)	OF	45	174	24	40	3	5	1	11	.230	12	97	0	4	.960
1987	—Fayetteville (S. Atl.)	OF	94	366	65	107	8	4	2	34	.292	27	237	13	7	.973
1988	—Lakeland (Florida State) ...	OF	132	483	★100	143	11	3	2	32	.296	50	257	8	4	.985
1989	—Toledo (International)	OF	24	83	4	14	3	2	0	6	.169	4	48	3	2	.962
	—London (Eastern)	OF	98	366	69	96	8	7	7	34	.262	32	★272	13	8	.973
1990	—Toledo (International)	OF	124	461	77	119	11	8	2	42	.258	★52	290	4	7	.977
	—Detroit (A.L.)	OF	19	51	8	13	3	1	0	8	.255	1	38	2	1	.976
1991	—Detroit (A.L.)	OF	154	475	77	122	15	7	3	33	.257	41	411	7	6	.986
	Major league totals (2 years)		173	526	85	135	18	8	3	41	.257	42	449	9	7	.985

DALTON, MIKE
P, PIRATES

PERSONAL: Born March 27, 1963, at Palo Alto, Calif.... 6-0/215.... Throws left, bats right. ... Full name: Michael Edward Dalton.
HIGH SCHOOL: Mountain View (Calif.).
COLLEGE: DeAnza Junior College (Calif.) and San Diego State.
TRANSACTIONS/CAREER NOTES: Selected by Boston Red Sox organization in 15th round of free-agent draft (June 6, 1983).... Granted free agency (October 22, 1989).... Re-signed by Red Sox (February 6, 1990).... Granted free agency (October 15, 1990).... Signed by Detroit Tigers organization (December 19, 1990).... Granted free agency (October 15, 1991).... Signed by Pittsburgh Pirates organization (January 22, 1992).

Year	Team (League)	G	W	L	Pct.	ERA	Sv.	IP	H	R	ER	BB	SO
1983	—Elmira (New York-Penn)	21	3	1	.750	2.65	5	51	48	19	15	15	49
1984	—Winter Haven (Florida State) ...	38	5	8	.385	3.18	6	107⅔	115	56	38	52	43
1985	—Winter Haven (Florida State) ...	49	2	3	.400	1.13	18	72	45	14	9	27	41
1986	—Pawtucket (International)	37	6	2	.750	5.02	1	71⅔	84	43	40	34	49
1987	—New Britain (Eastern)	4	1	0	1.000	.00	1	5	1	0	0	2	7
	—Pawtucket (International)	39	1	2	.333	4.16	2	88⅔	83	49	41	40	45
1988	—New Britain (Eastern)	52	6	5	.545	2.24	8	84⅓	65	32	21	39	61
1989	—New Britain (Eastern)	18	3	1	.750	2.48	3	32⅔	25	13	9	15	15
	—Pawtucket (International)	26	1	3	.250	5.12	4	45⅔	55	26	26	16	20
1990	—Pawtucket (International)	49	7	4	.636	2.55	5	99	94	42	28	22	49
1991	—Toledo (International)■............	39	3	3	.500	4.13	4	65⅓	72	33	30	24	28
	—Detroit (A.L.)	4	0	0	...	3.38	0	8	12	3	3	2	4
	Major league totals (1 year)	4	0	0	...	3.38	0	8	12	3	3	2	4

DANIELS, KAL
OF, DODGERS

PERSONAL: Born August 20, 1963, at Vienna, Ga. . . . 5-11/205. . . . Throws right, bats left. . . . Full name: Kalvoski Daniels.
HIGH SCHOOL: Northside (Warner Robins, Ga.).
COLLEGE: Middle Georgia College.
TRANSACTIONS/CAREER NOTES: Selected by New York Mets organization in third round of free-agent draft (January 12, 1982). . . . Selected by Cincinnati Reds organization in secondary phase of free-agent draft (June 7, 1982). . . . On disabled list (July 7, 1985-remainder of season). . . . On Cincinnati disabled list (July 6-August 6, 1987 and May 15-June 21, 1989). . . . Traded by Reds with IF Lenny Harris to Los Angeles Dodgers for P Tim Leary and SS Mariano Duncan (July 18, 1989). . . . On Los Angeles disabled list (August 7, 1989-remainder of season).
STATISTICAL NOTES: Led Eastern League with .525 slugging percentage in 1984. . . . Led N.L. with .397 on base percentage in 1988.

Year Team (League)	Pos.	G	AB	R	H	2B	3B	HR	RBI	Avg.	SB	PO	A	E	Avg.
1982—Billings (Pioneer)	OF	67	240	43	88	19	4	3	38	.367	★27	104	4	5	.956
1983—Cedar Rapids (Midwest) ...	OF	101	342	51	86	14	5	5	28	.251	31	130	5	2	.985
1984—Vermont (Eastern)	OF	122	415	81	130	29	4	17	62	.313	43	143	2	5	.967
1985—Denver (Am. Assoc.)	OF	76	285	59	86	12	9	15	43	.302	10	83	5	4	.957
1986—Cincinnati (N.L.)	OF	74	181	34	58	10	4	6	23	.320	15	88	0	3	.967
—Denver (Am. Assoc.)	OF	42	132	33	49	12	2	8	32	.371	12	78	4	3	.965
1987—Cincinnati (N.L.)	OF	108	368	73	123	24	1	26	64	.334	26	178	5	6	.968
1988—Cincinnati (N.L.)	OF	140	495	95	144	29	1	18	64	.291	27	256	10	5	.982
1989—Cincinnati-L.A. (N.L.)■	OF	55	171	33	42	13	0	4	17	.246	9	88	4	0	1.000
1990—Los Angeles (N.L.)	OF	130	450	81	133	23	1	27	94	.296	4	207	13	3	.987
1991—Los Angeles (N.L.)	OF	137	461	54	115	15	1	17	73	.249	6	220	9	5	.979
Major league totals (6 years)		644	2126	370	615	114	8	98	335	.289	87	1037	41	22	.980

DARLING, RON
P, ATHLETICS

PERSONAL: Born August 19, 1960, at Honolulu. . . . 6-3/195. . . . Throws right, bats right. . . . Full name: Ronald Maurice Darling Jr. . . . Brother of Eddie Darling, minor league first baseman (1981-82).
HIGH SCHOOL: St. John's (Worcester, Mass.).
COLLEGE: Yale.
TRANSACTIONS/CAREER NOTES: Selected by Texas Rangers organization in first round (ninth pick overall) of free-agent draft (June 8, 1981). . . . Traded by Rangers organization with P Walt Terrell to New York Mets organization for OF Lee Mazzilli (April 1, 1982). . . . On disabled list (September 12, 1987-remainder of season). . . . Traded by Mets with P Mike Thomas to Montreal Expos for P Tim Burke (July 15, 1991). . . . Traded by Expos to Oakland Athletics for P Matt Grott and P Russell Cormier (July 31, 1991). . . . Granted free agency (October 31, 1991). . . . Re-signed by A's (January 17, 1992).
RECORDS/HONORS: Shares N.L. single-season record for fewest assists by pitcher who led league in assists—47 (1985-86). . . . Won N.L. Gold Glove at pitcher (1989).

Year Team (League)	G	W	L	Pct.	ERA	Sv.	IP	H	R	ER	BB	SO
1981—Tulsa (Texas)	13	4	3	.667	4.44	0	71	72	43	35	33	53
1982—Tidewater (International)	26	7	9	.438	3.73	0	152	143	76	63	95	114
1983—Tidewater (International)	27	10	9	.526	4.02	0	159	137	83	71	102	107
—New York (N.L.)	5	1	3	.250	2.80	0	35⅓	31	11	11	17	23
1984—New York (N.L.)	33	12	9	.571	3.81	0	205⅔	179	97	87	104	136
1985—New York (N.L.)	36	16	6	.727	2.90	0	248	214	93	80	★114	167
1986—New York (N.L.)	34	15	6	.714	2.81	0	237	203	84	74	81	184
1987—New York (N.L.)	32	12	8	.600	4.29	0	207⅔	183	111	99	96	167
1988—New York (N.L.)	34	17	9	.654	3.25	0	240⅔	218	97	87	60	161
1989—New York (N.L.)	33	14	14	.500	3.52	0	217⅓	214	100	85	70	153
1990—New York (N.L.)	33	7	9	.438	4.50	0	126	135	73	63	44	99
1991—New York-Montreal (N.L.)■	20	5	8	.385	4.37	0	119⅓	121	66	58	33	69
—Oakland (A.L.)■	12	3	7	.300	4.08	0	75	64	34	34	38	60
American League totals (1 year)	12	3	7	.300	4.08	0	75	64	34	34	38	60
National League totals (9 years)	260	99	72	.579	3.54	0	1637	1498	732	644	619	1159
Major league totals (9 years)	272	102	79	.564	3.56	0	1712	1562	766	678	657	1219

CHAMPIONSHIP SERIES RECORD
CHAMPIONSHIP SERIES NOTES: Appeared as pinch-runner for New York Mets in one game (1988).

Year Team (League)	G	W	L	Pct.	ERA	Sv.	IP	H	R	ER	BB	SO
1986—New York (N.L.)	1	0	0	...	7.20	0	5	6	4	4	2	5
1988—New York (N.L.)	2	0	1	.000	7.71	0	7	11	9	6	4	7
Championship Series totals (2 years)	3	0	1	.000	7.50	0	12	17	13	10	6	12

WORLD SERIES RECORD
WORLD SERIES NOTES: Shares single-game record for most wild pitches—2 (October 18, 1986).

Year Team (League)	G	W	L	Pct.	ERA	Sv.	IP	H	R	ER	BB	SO
1986—New York (N.L.)	3	1	1	.500	1.53	0	17⅔	13	4	3	10	12

ALL-STAR GAME RECORD

Year League	W	L	Pct.	ERA	Sv.	IP	H	R	ER	BB	SO
1985—National					Did not play						

DARWIN, DANNY
P, RED SOX

PERSONAL: Born October 25, 1955, at Bonham, Tex. . . . 6-3/195. . . . Throws right, bats right. . . . Full name: Daniel Wayne Darwin. . . . Brother of Jeff Darwin, pitcher, Seattle Mariners organization.
HIGH SCHOOL: Bonham (Tex.).
COLLEGE: Grayson County College (Tex.).
TRANSACTIONS/CAREER NOTES: Signed as free agent by Texas Rangers organization (May 10, 1976). . . . On disabled list (April 25-May 4 and May 22-June 11, 1977; June 5-26, 1980; March 25-April 10 and August 9-September 1, 1983). . . . Traded by Rangers with a player to be named later to Milwaukee Brewers as part of a six-player, four-team deal in which Kansas City Royals acquired C Jim Sundberg from Brewers, Rangers acquired C Don Slaught from Royals, New York Mets organization acquired P Frank Wills from Royals and Brewers organization acquired P Tim Leary from Mets (January 18, 1985); Brewers organization acquired C Bill Hance from Rangers to complete deal (January 30, 1985). . . . Granted free agency (November 12, 1985). . . . Re-signed by Brewers (December 22, 1985). . . . Traded by Brewers organization to Houston Astros for P Don August and a player to be named later (August 15, 1986); Milwaukee Brewers organization acquired P Mark Knudson to complete deal (August 21, 1986). . . . Granted free agency (November 9, 1987). . . . Re-signed by Astros (January 8, 1988). . . . Granted free agency (December 7, 1990). . . . Signed by Boston Red Sox (December 19, 1990). . . . On disabled list (April 23-May 22, 1991 and July 5, 1991-remainder of season).
STATISTICAL NOTES: Tied for Western Carolinas League lead with five balks in 1976. . . . Tied for Texas League lead with four shutouts and eight hit batsmen in 1977. . . . Tied for A.L. lead with 34 home runs allowed in 1985.

Year	Team (League)	G	W	L	Pct.	ERA	Sv.	IP	H	R	ER	BB	SO
1976	—Asheville (Western Carolinas) ..	16	6	3	.667	3.62	0	102	96	54	41	48	76
1977	—Tulsa (Texas)	23	13	4	.765	2.51	0	154	130	53	43	72	129
1978	—Tucson (Pacific Coast)	23	8	9	.471	6.26	0	125	147	100	87	83	126
	—Texas (A.L.)...................	3	1	0	1.000	4.00	0	9	11	4	4	1	8
1979	—Tucson (Pacific Coast)	13	6	6	.500	3.60	0	95	89	43	38	42	65
	—Texas (A.L.)...................	20	4	4	.500	4.04	0	78	50	36	35	30	58
1980	—Texas (A.L.)...................	53	13	4	.765	2.62	8	110	98	37	32	50	104
1981	—Texas (A.L.)...................	22	9	9	.500	3.64	0	146	115	67	59	57	98
1982	—Texas (A.L.)...................	56	10	8	.556	3.44	7	89	95	38	34	37	61
1983	—Texas (A.L.)...................	28	8	13	.381	3.49	0	183	175	86	71	62	92
1984	—Texas (A.L.)...................	35	8	12	.400	3.94	0	223⅔	249	110	98	54	123
1985	—Milwaukee (A.L.)■............	39	8	18	.308	3.80	2	217⅔	212	112	92	65	125
1986	—Milwaukee (A.L.)	27	6	8	.429	3.52	0	130⅓	120	62	51	35	80
	—Houston (N.L.)■............	12	5	2	.714	2.32	0	54⅓	50	19	14	9	40
1987	—Houston (N.L.)	33	9	10	.474	3.59	0	195⅔	184	87	78	69	134
1988	—Houston (N.L.)	44	8	13	.381	3.84	3	192	189	86	82	48	129
1989	—Houston (N.L.)	68	11	4	.733	2.36	7	122	92	34	32	33	104
1990	—Houston (N.L.)	48	11	4	.733	★2.21	2	162⅔	136	42	40	31	109
1991	—Boston (A.L.)■..............	12	3	6	.333	5.16	0	68	71	39	39	15	42
	American League totals (10 years)	295	70	82	.461	3.69	17	1254⅔	1196	591	515	406	791
	National League totals (5 years)	205	44	33	.571	3.05	12	726⅔	651	268	246	190	516
	Major league totals (14 years)	500	114	115	.498	3.46	29	1981⅓	1847	859	761	596	1307

DASCENZO, DOUG
OF, CUBS

PERSONAL: Born June 30, 1964, at Cleveland. . . . 5-8/160. . . . Throws left, bats both. . . . Full name: Douglas Craig Dascenzo. . . . Name pronounced duh-SEN-zo.
HIGH SCHOOL: Brownsville (Pa.).
COLLEGE: Florida College and Oklahoma State.
TRANSACTIONS/CAREER NOTES: Selected by Chicago Cubs organization in 12th round of free-agent draft (June 3, 1985).
RECORDS/HONORS: Holds N.L. career record for most consecutive errorless games by outfielder—242 (September 2, 1988 through August 21, 1991).
STATISTICAL NOTES: Led Carolina League with 12 sacrifice hits in 1986. . . . Led Eastern League outfielders with 308 total chances in 1987. . . . Led American Association in caught stealing with 21 in 1989.

Year	Team (League)	Pos.	G	AB	R	H	2B	3B	HR	RBI	Avg.	SB	PO	A	E	Avg.
1985	—Geneva (N.Y.-Penn)	OF-1B	70	252	★59	84	15	1	3	23	.333	33	133	7	4	.972
1986	—Winston-Salem (Caro.)	OF	138	545	107	★178	29	11	6	83	.327	57	299	15	8	.975
1987	—Pittsfield (Eastern)	OF	134	496	84	152	32	6	3	56	.306	36	★299	5	4	★.987
1988	—Iowa (American Assoc.)	OF	132	505	73	149	22	5	6	49	.295	30	261	6	4	.985
	—Chicago (N.L.)	OF	26	75	9	16	3	0	0	4	.213	6	55	1	0	1.000
1989	—Iowa (American Assoc.)	OF	111	431	59	121	18	4	4	33	.281	34	273	15	6	.980
	—Chicago (N.L.)	OF	47	139	20	23	1	0	1	12	.165	6	96	0	0	1.000
1990	—Chicago (N.L.)	OF-P	113	241	27	61	9	5	1	26	.253	15	174	2	0	1.000
1991	—Chicago (N.L.)	OF-P	118	239	40	61	11	0	1	18	.255	14	134	0	2	.985
	Major league totals (4 years)		304	694	96	161	24	5	3	60	.232	41	459	3	2	.996

RECORD AS PITCHER

Year	Team (League)	G	W	L	Pct.	ERA	Sv.	IP	H	R	ER	BB	SO
1990	—Chicago (N.L.)	1	0	0	...	0.00	0	1	1	0	0	0	0
1991	—Chicago (N.L.)	3	0	0	...	0.00	0	4	2	0	0	2	2
	Major league totals (2 years)	4	0	0	...	0.00	0	5	3	0	0	2	2

DAUGHERTY, JACK
OF/1B, RANGERS

PERSONAL: Born July 3, 1960, at Hialeah, Fla. . . . 6-0/190. . . . Throws left, bats both. . . . Full name: John Michael Daugherty. . . . Name pronounced DAW-er-tee.
HIGH SCHOOL: Kearny (San Diego).
COLLEGE: San Diego Mesa College (Calif.) and Arizona.

TRANSACTIONS/CAREER NOTES: Signed as free agent by Oakland Athletics organization (October 9, 1982). . . . Released by A's organization (January 16, 1984). . . . Signed by Helena, independent (June 13, 1984). . . . Sold by Helena to West Palm Beach, Montreal Expos organization (December 4, 1984). . . . Traded by Expos organization to Texas Rangers organization (September 13, 1988), completing deal in which Rangers traded IF Tom O'Malley to Expos for a player to be named later (September 1, 1988). . . . On Texas disabled list (June 6-22 and June 23-September 1, 1991); included rehabilitation disability assignment to Oklahoma City (June 19-22 and August 9-28, 1991).
RECORDS/HONORS: Named Florida State League Most Valuable Player (1985).
STATISTICAL NOTES: Led Pioneer League with 179 total bases and 10 intentional bases on balls received and tied for lead with 52 bases on balls received in 1984. . . . Led Pioneer League first basemen with 624 total chances in 1984. . . . Led Florida State League with 213 total bases in 1985.

Year	Team (League)	Pos.	G	AB	R	H	2B	3B	HR	RBI	Avg.	SB	PO	A	E	Avg.
1983	San Jose (California)	1B	116	364	46	95	17	2	2	45	.261	2	670	25	7	.990
1984	Helena (Pioneer)■	1B	66	259	*77	*104	*26	2	15	*82	*.402	16	*583	33	8	.987
1985	West Palm Beach (FSL)■	1B	133	481	76	152	25	3	10	*87	.316	33	1041	50	14	.987
1986	Jacksonville (Southern)	1B	138	502	87	159	37	4	4	63	.317	15	1007	64	*19	.983
1987	Indianapolis (A.A.)	1B-OF	117	420	65	131	35	3	7	50	.312	11	754	76	7	.992
	Montreal (N.L.)	1B	11	10	1	1	1	0	0	1	.100	0	1	1	0	1.000
1988	Indianapolis (A.A.)	1B-OF	137	481	82	137	33	2	6	67	.285	18	896	62	8	.992
1989	Oklahoma City (A.A.)■	1B-OF	82	311	28	78	15	3	3	32	.251	2	728	54	6	.992
	Texas (A.L.)	1B-OF	52	106	15	32	4	2	1	10	.302	2	132	14	0	1.000
1990	Texas (A.L.)	OF-1B	125	310	36	93	20	2	6	47	.300	0	225	22	3	.988
1991	Texas (A.L.)	OF-1B	58	144	8	28	3	2	1	11	.194	1	120	4	1	.992
	Oklahoma City (A.A.)	OF	22	77	4	11	2	0	0	4	.143	1	27	2	1	.967
American League totals (3 years)			235	560	59	153	27	6	8	68	.273	3	477	40	4	.992
National League totals (1 year)			11	10	1	1	1	0	0	1	.100	0	1	1	0	1.000
Major league totals (4 years)			246	570	60	154	28	6	8	69	.270	3	478	41	4	.992

DAULTON, DARREN
C, PHILLIES

PERSONAL: Born January 3, 1962, at Arkansas City, Kan. . . . 6-2/200. . . . Throws right, bats left. . . . Full name: Darren Arthur Daulton.
HIGH SCHOOL: Arkansas City (Kan.).
COLLEGE: Crowley County Community College (Kan.).

TRANSACTIONS/CAREER NOTES: Selected by Philadelphia Phillies organization in 25th round of free-agent draft (June 3, 1980). . . . On disabled list (July 20-August 28, 1984). . . . On Philadelphia disabled list (May 17-August 9, 1985); included rehabilitation disability assignment to Portland (July 20-August 7, 1985). . . . On Philadelphia disabled list (June 22, 1986-remainder of season; April 1-16, 1987; August 28, 1988-remainder of season; and May 6-21, 1991). . . . On Philadelphia disabled list (May 28-June 18, 1991); included rehabilitation disability assignment to Scranton/Wilkes-Barre (June 15-17, 1991) and Reading (June 17-18, 1991). . . . On disabled list (September 7, 1991-remainder of season).
STATISTICAL NOTES: Tied for Eastern League lead with 10 sacrifice flies in 1983. . . . Tied for N.L. lead in double plays by catchers with 10 in 1990.

Year	Team (League)	Pos.	G	AB	R	H	2B	3B	HR	RBI	Avg.	SB	PO	A	E	Avg.
1980	Helena (Pioneer)	C	37	100	13	20	2	1	1	10	.200	5	224	17	4	.984
1981	Spartanburg (S. Atl.)	C-OF-3B	98	270	44	62	11	1	3	29	.230	14	378	34	4	.990
1982	Peninsula (Carolina)	C-1B	110	324	65	78	21	2	11	44	.241	17	654	63	9	.988
1983	Reading (Eastern)	C-1B-OF	113	362	77	95	16	4	19	83	.262	28	557	57	14	.978
	Philadelphia (N.L.)	C	2	3	1	1	0	0	0	0	.333	0	8	0	0	1.000
1984	Portland (Pacific Coast)	C	80	252	45	75	19	4	7	38	.298	3	322	26	6	.983
1985	Portland (Pacific Coast)	C	23	64	13	19	5	3	2	10	.297	6	110	9	0	1.000
	Philadelphia (N.L.)	C	36	103	14	21	3	1	4	11	.204	3	160	15	1	.994
1986	Philadelphia (N.L.)	C	49	138	18	31	4	0	8	21	.225	2	244	21	4	.985
1987	Clearwater (Florida St.)	C-1B	9	22	1	5	3	0	1	5	.227	0	27	5	3	.914
	Maine (International)	C-1B	20	70	9	15	1	1	3	10	.214	5	138	12	0	1.000
	Philadelphia (N.L.)	C-1B	53	129	10	25	6	0	3	13	.194	0	210	13	2	.991
1988	Philadelphia (N.L.)	C-1B	58	144	13	30	6	0	1	12	.208	2	205	15	6	.973
1989	Philadelphia (N.L.)	C	131	368	29	74	12	2	8	44	.201	2	627	56	11	.984
1990	Philadelphia (N.L.)	C	143	459	62	123	30	1	12	57	.268	7	683	*70	8	.989
1991	Philadelphia (N.L.)	C	89	285	36	56	12	0	12	42	.196	5	493	33	8	.985
	Scranton/W.B. (Int'l)	C	2	9	1	2	0	0	1	1	.222	0	14	1	0	1.000
	Reading (Eastern)	C	1	4	0	1	0	0	0	0	.250	0	6	2	0	1.000
Major league totals (8 years)			561	1629	183	361	73	4	48	200	.222	21	2630	223	40	.986

DAVIDSON, MARK
OF

PERSONAL: Born February 15, 1961, at Knoxville, Tenn. . . . 6-2/190. . . . Throws right, bats right. . . . Full name: John Mark Davidson. . . . Son of Max Davidson, minor league outfielder (1947-54).
HIGH SCHOOL: Garinger (Charlotte, N.C.).
COLLEGE: UNC Charlotte and Clemson.

TRANSACTIONS/CAREER NOTES: Selected by Minnesota Twins organization in 11th round of free-agent draft (June 7, 1982)....
On disabled list (April 15-May 4, 1983; and July 16-26, 1984).... Traded by Twins organization to Tucson (Houston Astros organization) for a player to be named later (May 16, 1989); Twins acquired P Greg Johnson to complete deal (September 6, 1989).... On Houston disabled list (April 30-May 28, 1990); included rehabilitation disability assignment to Tucson (May 10-28, 1990).... Granted free agency (October 16, 1991).

						—BATTING—						—FIELDING—			
Year	Team (League)	Pos.	G	AB	R	H	2B	3B	HR	RBI	Avg.	SB	PO	A	E	Avg.
1982 —Wis. Rapids (Midwest)		OF	79	247	54	74	11	0	10	41	.300	12	166	13	5	.973
1983 —Wis. Rapids (Midwest)		OF	111	363	63	80	15	1	13	48	.220	26	181	6	6	.969
1984 —Orlando (Southern)		O-1-3	114	348	55	99	11	6	4	37	.284	15	243	13	3	.988
1985 —Orlando (Southern)		OF-3B	134	453	93	137	17	2	25	106	.302	13	305	14	6	.982
1986 —Toledo (International)		OF	108	383	55	95	16	1	10	38	.248	4	290	8	8	.974
—Minnesota (A.L.)		OF	36	68	5	8	3	0	0	2	.118	2	48	0	1	.980
1987 —Minnesota (A.L.)		OF	102	150	32	40	4	1	1	14	.267	9	102	3	0	1.000
1988 —Minnesota (A.L.)		OF-3B	100	106	22	23	7	0	1	10	.217	3	103	3	5	.955
—Portland (Pacific Coast)		OF-P	15	56	6	18	4	2	0	5	.321	1	35	2	0	1.000
1989 —Portland-Tucson (PCL)■		OF	69	237	26	58	9	2	5	24	.245	1	145	9	0	1.000
—Houston (N.L.)		OF	33	65	7	13	2	1	1	5	.200	1	36	0	0	1.000
1990 —Tucson (Pacific Coast)		OF	56	182	35	61	13	1	6	46	.335	5	98	4	1	.990
—Houston (N.L.)		OF	57	130	12	38	5	1	1	11	.292	0	103	1	2	.981
1991 —Houston (N.L.)		OF	85	142	10	27	6	0	2	15	.190	0	71	1	0	1.000
American League totals (3 years)			238	324	59	71	14	1	2	26	.219	14	253	6	6	.977
National League totals (3 years)			175	337	29	78	13	2	4	31	.231	1	210	2	2	.991
Major league totals (6 years)			413	661	88	149	27	3	6	57	.225	15	463	8	8	.983

CHAMPIONSHIP SERIES RECORD

						—BATTING—						—FIELDING—			
Year	Team (League)	Pos.	G	AB	R	H	2B	3B	HR	RBI	Avg.	SB	PO	A	E	Avg.
1987 —Minnesota (A.L.)		PR	1	0	0	0	0	0	0	0	...	0	0	0	0	...

WORLD SERIES RECORD

						—BATTING—						—FIELDING—			
Year	Team (League)	Pos.	G	AB	R	H	2B	3B	HR	RBI	Avg.	SB	PO	A	E	Avg.
1987 —Minnesota (A.L.)		OF-PH	2	1	0	0	0	0	0	0	.000	0	0	0	0	...

RECORD AS PITCHER

Year	Team (League)	G	W	L	Pct.	ERA	Sv.	IP	H	R	ER	BB	SO
1988 —Portland (Pacific Coast)		1	0	1	.000	6.75	0	1⅓	2	1	1	2	0

DAVIS, ALVIN
1B/DH

PERSONAL: Born September 9, 1960, at Riverside, Calif.... 6-1/190.... Throws right, bats left. ...Full name: Alvin Glenn Davis.
HIGH SCHOOL: John W. North (Riverside, Calif.).
COLLEGE: Arizona State (bachelor of science degree in finance).
TRANSACTIONS/CAREER NOTES: Selected by San Francisco Giants organization in eighth round of free-agent draft (June 6, 1978).... Selected by Oakland Athletics organization in sixth round of free-agent draft (June 8, 1981).... Selected by Seattle Mariners organization in sixth round of free-agent draft (June 7, 1982).... On Chattanooga disabled list (July 21-31, 1983). ... On Seattle disabled list (June 25-July 17, 1986; June 26-July 15, 1988; May 21-June 6, 1989; and June 26-July 11, 1990). ... Granted free agency (October 29, 1991).
RECORDS/HONORS: Shares major league single-game (nine innings) record for most putouts by first baseman—22 (May 28, 1988).... Shares A.L. record for most home runs in first two major league games—2 (April 11 and 13, 1984).... Named A.L. Rookie Player of the Year by THE SPORTING NEWS (1984).... Named A.L. Rookie of the Year by Baseball Writers' Association of America (1984).
STATISTICAL NOTES: Led Southern League with 120 bases on balls received and 12 sacrifice flies in 1983. ... Led Southern League first basemen with 1,233 putouts, 99 assists, 1,348 total chances and 118 double plays and tied for lead with 16 errors in 1983. ... Tied for A.L. lead with 10 sacrifice flies in 1991.

						—BATTING—						—FIELDING—			
Year	Team (League)	Pos.	G	AB	R	H	2B	3B	HR	RBI	Avg.	SB	PO	A	E	Avg.
1982 —Lynn (Eastern)		1B	74	225	37	64	10	1	12	56	.284	1	579	51	6	.991
1983 —Chattanooga (Southern)		1B-OF	131	422	87	125	24	3	18	83	.296	7	†1233	†99	‡16	.988
1984 —Salt Lake City (PCL)		1B	1	3	2	2	0	0	0	1	.667	0	2	0	0	1.000
—Seattle (A.L.)		1B	152	567	80	161	34	3	27	116	.284	5	1271	94	11	.992
1985 —Seattle (A.L.)		1B	155	578	78	166	33	1	18	78	.287	1	1438	103	13	.992
1986 —Seattle (A.L.)		1B	135	479	66	130	18	1	18	72	.271	0	880	82	14	.986
1987 —Seattle (A.L.)		1B	157	580	86	171	37	2	29	100	.295	0	1386	96	9	.994
1988 —Seattle (A.L.)		1B	140	478	67	141	24	1	18	69	.295	1	980	65	6	.994
1989 —Seattle (A.L.)		1B	142	498	84	152	30	1	21	95	.305	0	1106	81	10	.992
1990 —Seattle (A.L.)		1B	140	494	63	140	21	0	17	68	.283	0	435	31	3	.994
1991 —Seattle (A.L.)		1B	145	462	39	102	15	1	12	69	.221	0	116	7	0	1.000
Major league totals (8 years)			1166	4136	563	1163	212	10	160	667	.281	7	7612	559	66	.992

ALL-STAR GAME RECORD

					—BATTING—						—FIELDING—			
Year	League	Pos.	AB	R	H	2B	3B	HR	RBI	Avg.	SB	PO	A	E	Avg.
1984 —American		PH	1	0	0	0	0	0	0	.000	0	0	0	0	...

DAVIS, BUTCH
OF, BLUE JAYS

PERSONAL: Born June 19, 1958, at Williamston, N.C. . . . . 6-0/196. . . . Throws right, bats right. . . . Full name: Wallace McArthur Davis.
HIGH SCHOOL: Williamston (N.C.).
COLLEGE: St. Augustine's College (N.C.) and East Carolina (bachelor of science degree, 1980).
TRANSACTIONS/CAREER NOTES: Selected by Kansas City Royals organization in 12th round of free-agent draft (June 3, 1980). . . . On disabled list (April 11, 1986-entire season). . . . Granted free agency (October 15, 1986). . . . Signed by Pittsburgh Pirates (December 4, 1986). . . . Granted free agency (October 15, 1987). . . . Signed by Charlotte, Baltimore Orioles organization (May 3, 1988). . . . Granted free agency (October 15, 1988). . . . Re-signed by Orioles organization (November 21, 1988). . . . Released by Orioles (December 20, 1989). . . . Signed by Los Angeles Dodgers organization (January 9, 1990). . . . Granted free agency (October 16, 1991). . . . Signed by Toronto Blue Jays organization (December 11, 1991).
STATISTICAL NOTES: Led Gulf Coast League with 105 total bases. . . . Led International League outfielders with 272 total chances in 1989. . . . Led Pacific Coast League with 243 total bases and 11 sacrifice flies in 1990.

Year	Team (League)	Pos.	G	AB	R	H	2B	3B	HR	RBI	Avg.	SB	PO	A	E	Avg.
1980	—Sarasota Royals (GCL)	OF	61	235	46	*74	*17	4	2	35	.315	31	117	5	3	.976
1981	—Fort Myers (Florida St.) ..	OF	126	464	*89	139	17	10	13	70	.300	44	239	5	12	.953
1982	—Jacksonville (Southern) ...	OF	122	450	64	115	18	4	10	57	.256	17	231	7	2	.992
1983	—Jacksonville (Southern) ...	OF-1B	90	331	51	105	15	7	14	63	.317	29	117	4	4	.968
	—Omaha (Am. Assoc.)	OF	46	171	27	54	10	3	5	21	.316	13	10	0	1	.909
	—Kansas City (A.L.)	OF	33	122	13	42	2	6	2	18	.344	4	83	1	2	.977
1984	—Kansas City (A.L.)	OF	41	116	11	17	3	0	2	12	.147	4	69	2	3	.959
	—Omaha (Am. Assoc.)	OF-1B	83	314	45	102	15	5	7	43	.325	9	153	13	6	.965
1985	—Omaha (Am. Assoc.)	OF-1B	109	403	58	106	26	10	6	34	.263	15	209	3	9	.959
1987	—Vancouver (Pac. Coast)■..	OF	111	424	58	115	17	7	7	57	.271	22	232	8	4	.984
	—Pittsburgh (N.L.)	OF	7	7	3	1	1	0	0	0	.143	0	3	0	0	1.000
1988	—Charlotte (Florida State)■.	OF	101	412	62	124	23	7	13	82	*.301	17	116	3	3	.975
	—Rochester (Int'l)	OF	8	28	4	4	0	2	0	0	.143	0	10	0	0	1.000
	—Baltimore (A.L.)	OF	13	25	2	6	1	0	0	0	.240	1	16	1	0	1.000
1989	—Rochester (Int'l)	OF	127	479	81	145	29	9	10	64	.303	19	*258	8	6	.978
	—Baltimore (A.L.)	OF	5	6	1	1	0	0	0	0	.167	0	3	0	0	1.000
1990	—Albuquerque (PCL)■.........	OF	124	480	87	164	31	9	10	85	.342	25	131	4	2	.985
1991	—Albuquerque (PCL)	OF	91	284	55	89	19	10	7	44	.313	12	56	2	0	1.000
	—Los Angeles (N.L.)	PH	1	1	0	0	0	0	0	0	.000	0	0	0	0	...
	American League totals (4 years)		92	269	27	66	7	6	4	30	.245	9	171	4	5	.972
	National League totals (2 years)		8	8	3	1	1	0	0	0	.125	0	3	0	0	1.000
	Major league totals (6 years)		100	277	30	67	8	6	4	30	.242	9	174	4	5	.973

DAVIS, CHILI
DH/OF, TWINS

PERSONAL: Born January 17, 1960, at Kingston, Jamaica. . . . . 6-3/219. . . . Throws right, bats both. . . . Full name: Charles Theodore Davis.
HIGH SCHOOL: Dorsey (Los Angeles).
TRANSACTIONS/CAREER NOTES: Selected by San Francisco Giants organization in 11th round of free-agent draft (June 7, 1977). . . . On Phoenix disabled list (August 19-28, 1981). . . . Granted free agency (November 9, 1987). . . . Signed by California Angels (December 1, 1987). . . . On disabled list (July 17-August 9, 1990). . . . Granted free agency (December 7, 1990). . . . Signed by Minnesota Twins (January 29, 1991).
RECORDS/HONORS: Shares major league single-season record for fewest errors by outfielder who led league—9 (1986). . . . Holds N.L. career record for most games with switch-hit home runs—3. . . . Shares N.L. single-season record for most games with switch-hit home runs—2 (1987).
STATISTICAL NOTES: Switch-hit home runs in one game (June 5, 1983; June 27, 1987; September 15, 1987; July 30, 1988; and July 1, 1989). . . . Tied for A.L. lead with 10 sacrifice flies in 1988.
MISCELLANEOUS: Original nickname was Chili Bowl, which was prompted by a friend who saw Davis after he received a haircut back in the sixth grade. The nickname was later shortened to Chili.

Year	Team (League)	Pos.	G	AB	R	H	2B	3B	HR	RBI	Avg.	SB	PO	A	E	Avg.
1978	—Cedar Rapids (Midwest) ...	C-OF	124	424	63	119	18	5	16	73	.281	15	365	45	25	.943
1979	—Fresno (California)	OF-C	134	490	91	132	24	5	21	95	.269	30	339	43	20	.950
1980	—Shreveport (Texas)	OF-C	129	442	50	130	30	4	12	67	.294	19	184	20	12	.944
1981	—San Francisco (N.L.)	OF	8	15	1	2	0	0	0	0	.133	2	7	0	0	1.000
	—Phoenix (Pacific Coast)	OF	88	334	76	117	16	6	19	75	.350	40	175	7	6	.968
1982	—San Francisco (N.L.)	OF	154	641	86	167	27	6	19	76	.261	24	404	•16	12	.972
1983	—San Francisco (N.L.)	OF	137	486	54	113	21	2	11	59	.233	10	357	7	9	.976
	—Phoenix (Pacific Coast)	OF	10	44	12	13	2	0	2	9	.295	4	15	0	2	.882
1984	—San Francisco (N.L.)	OF	137	499	87	157	21	6	21	81	.315	12	292	9	9	.971
1985	—San Francisco (N.L.)	OF	136	481	53	130	25	2	13	56	.270	15	279	10	6	.980
1986	—San Francisco (N.L.)	OF	153	526	71	146	28	3	13	70	.278	16	303	9	•9	.972
1987	—San Francisco (N.L.)	OF	149	500	80	125	22	1	24	76	.250	16	265	4	7	.975
1988	—California (A.L.)■	OF	158	600	81	161	29	3	21	93	.268	9	299	10	*19	.942
1989	—California (A.L.)	OF	154	560	81	152	24	1	22	90	.271	3	270	5	6	.979
1990	—California (A.L.)	OF	113	412	58	109	17	1	12	58	.265	1	77	5	3	.965
1991	—Minnesota (A.L.)	OF	153	534	84	148	34	1	29	93	.277	5	2	0	0	1.000
	American League totals (4 years)		578	2106	304	570	104	6	84	334	.271	18	648	20	28	.960
	National League totals (7 years)		874	3148	432	840	144	26	101	418	.267	95	1907	57	52	.974
	Major league totals (11 years)		1452	5254	736	1410	248	26	185	752	.268	113	2555	77	80	.971

CHAMPIONSHIP SERIES RECORD

CHAMPIONSHIP SERIES NOTES: Shares A.L. single-series record for most strikeouts—8 (1991).

Year Team (League)	Pos.	G	AB	R	H	2B	3B	HR	RBI	Avg.	SB	PO	A	E	Avg.
1987—San Francisco (N.L.)	OF	6	20	2	3	1	0	0	0	.150	0	11	1	1	.923
1991—Minnesota (A.L.)	DH	5	17	3	5	2	0	0	2	.294	1	0	0	0	...
Championship Series totals (2 years)		11	37	5	8	3	0	0	2	.216	1	11	1	1	.923

WORLD SERIES RECORD

Year Team (League)	Pos.	G	AB	R	H	2B	3B	HR	RBI	Avg.	SB	PO	A	E	Avg.
1991—Minnesota (A.L.)	DH-PH-O	6	18	4	4	0	0	2	4	.222	0	1	0	0	1.000

ALL-STAR GAME RECORD

Year League	Pos.	AB	R	H	2B	3B	HR	RBI	Avg.	SB	PO	A	E	Avg.
1984—National	PH	1	0	0	0	0	0	0	.000	0	0	0	0	...
1986—National	OF	1	0	0	0	0	0	0	.000	0	0	0	0	...
All-Star Game totals (2 years)		2	0	0	0	0	0	0	.000	0	0	0	0	...

DAVIS, ERIC
OF, DODGERS

PERSONAL: Born May 29, 1962, at Los Angeles. . . . 6-3/200. . . . Throws right, bats right. . . . Full name: Eric Keith Davis.
HIGH SCHOOL: Fremont (Los Angeles).
TRANSACTIONS/CAREER NOTES: Selected by Cincinnati Reds organization in eighth round of free-agent draft (June 3, 1980). . . . On disabled list (August 16-September 1, 1984; May 3-18, 1989; April 25-May 19, 1990; June 12-27 and July 31-August 26, 1991). . . . Traded by Reds with P Kip Gross to Los Angeles Dodgers for P Tim Belcher and P John Wetteland (November 27, 1991).
RECORDS/HONORS: Holds major league record for most strikeouts in two consecutive games—9 (April 24 and 25, 1987, 21 innings). . . . Shares major league single-month record for most grand slams—3 (May, 1987). . . . Named outfielder on THE SPORTING NEWS N.L. All-Star team (1987 and 1989). . . . Won N.L. Gold Glove as outfielder (1987-89). . . . Named outfielder on THE SPORTING NEWS N.L. Silver Slugger team (1987 and 1989).
STATISTICAL NOTES: Hit three home runs in a game (September 10, 1986 and May 3, 1987). . . . Led N.L. outfielders with 394 total chances in 1987. . . . Led N.L. with 21 game-winning RBIs in 1988. . . . Hit for the cycle (June 2, 1989).

Year Team (League)	Pos.	G	AB	R	H	2B	3B	HR	RBI	Avg.	SB	PO	A	E	Avg.
1980—Eugene (Northwest)	SS-2B-OF	33	73	12	16	1	0	1	11	.219	10	29	36	11	.855
1981—Eugene (Northwest)	OF	62	214	*67	69	10	4	11	39	.322	*40	94	11	4	.963
1982—Cedar Rapids (Midwest) ...	OF	111	434	80	120	20	5	15	56	.276	53	239	9	9	.965
1983—Waterbury (Eastern)	OF	89	293	56	85	13	1	15	43	.290	39	214	8	2	.991
—Indianapolis (A.A.)	OF	19	77	18	23	4	0	7	19	.299	9	61	1	1	.984
1984—Wichita (Am. Assoc.)	OF	52	194	42	61	9	5	14	34	.314	27	110	5	5	.958
—Cincinnati (N.L.)	OF	57	174	33	39	10	1	10	30	.224	10	125	4	1	.992
1985—Cincinnati (N.L.)	OF	56	122	26	30	3	3	8	18	.246	16	75	3	1	.987
—Denver (Am. Assoc.)	OF	64	206	48	57	10	2	15	38	.277	35	94	5	3	.971
1986—Cincinnati (N.L.)	OF	132	415	97	115	15	3	27	71	.277	80	274	2	7	.975
1987—Cincinnati (N.L.)	OF	129	474	120	139	23	4	37	100	.293	50	*380	10	4	.990
1988—Cincinnati (N.L.)	OF	135	472	81	129	18	3	26	93	.273	35	300	2	6	.981
1989—Cincinnati (N.L.)	OF	131	462	74	130	14	2	34	101	.281	21	298	2	5	.984
1990—Cincinnati (N.L.)	OF	127	453	84	118	26	2	24	86	.260	21	257	11	2	.993
1991—Cincinnati (N.L.)	OF	89	285	39	67	10	0	11	33	.235	14	190	5	3	.985
Major league totals (8 years)		856	2857	554	767	119	18	177	532	.268	247	1899	39	29	.985

CHAMPIONSHIP SERIES RECORD

Year Team (League)	Pos.	G	AB	R	H	2B	3B	HR	RBI	Avg.	SB	PO	A	E	Avg.
1990—Cincinnati (N.L.)	OF	6	23	2	4	1	0	0	2	.174	0	12	1	0	1.000

WORLD SERIES RECORD

WORLD SERIES NOTES: Hit home run in first series at-bat (October 16, 1990).

Year Team (League)	Pos.	G	AB	R	H	2B	3B	HR	RBI	Avg.	SB	PO	A	E	Avg.
1990—Cincinnati (N.L.)	OF	4	14	3	4	0	0	1	5	.286	0	4	0	0	1.000

ALL-STAR GAME RECORD

Year League	Pos.	AB	R	H	2B	3B	HR	RBI	Avg.	SB	PO	A	E	Avg.
1987—National	OF	3	0	0	0	0	0	0	.000	0	1	0	0	1.000
1989—National	OF	2	0	0	0	0	0	0	.000	1	1	0	0	1.000
All-Star Game totals (2 years)		5	0	0	0	0	0	0	.000	1	2	0	0	1.000

DAVIS, GLENN
1B/DH, ORIOLES

PERSONAL: Born March 28, 1961, at Jacksonville, Fla. . . . 6-3/211. . . . Throws right, bats right. . . . Full name: Glenn Earl Davis.
HIGH SCHOOL: University Christian (Jacksonville, Fla.).
COLLEGE: Manatee Junior College (Fla.) and Georgia.

TRANSACTIONS/CAREER NOTES: Selected by Baltimore Orioles organization in 32nd round of free-agent draft (June 5, 1979).... Selected by Houston Astros organization in secondary phase of free-agent draft (January 13, 1981).... On Houston disabled list (June 25-August 29, 1990); included rehabilitation disability assignment to Columbus (July 28-August 3 and August 18-28, 1990).... Traded by Astros to Baltimore Orioles for P Pete Harnisch, P Curt Schilling and OF Steve Finley (January 10, 1991).... On Baltimore disabled list (April 25-August 19, 1991); included rehabilitation disability assignment to Hagerstown (August 10-19, 1991).... Granted free agency (November 1, 1991).... Re-signed by Orioles (November 12, 1991).

RECORDS/HONORS: Shares major league single-game record for most times hit by pitch—3 (April 9, 1990).... Shares A.L. single-game record for most errors by first baseman—4 (April 18, 1991).... Shares N.L. single-season record for fewest double plays by first baseman (150 or more games)—89 (1987).... Named first baseman on THE SPORTING NEWS N.L. Silver Slugger team (1986).

STATISTICAL NOTES: Led Gulf Coast League first basemen with 469 putouts, 37 assists, 14 errors and 520 total chances and tied for lead with 35 double plays in 1981.... Tied for N.L. lead with 16 game-winning RBIs in 1986.... Hit three home runs in a game (September 10, 1987 and June 1, 1990).... Led N.L. in being hit by pitch with eight in 1990.

							BATTING							FIELDING		
Year	Team (League)	Pos.	G	AB	R	H	2B	3B	HR	RBI	Avg.	SB	PO	A	E	Avg.
1981	Sara. Astros-Or. (GCL)	1B-OF	54	188	27	49	7	1	6	35	.261	0	†469	†37	†14	.973
1982	Daytona Beach (Fla. St.)	1B-3B	103	378	70	119	28	3	•19	79	.315	1	759	70	16	.981
	Columbus (Southern)	1B	26	97	14	24	6	1	4	8	.247	7	257	11	2	.993
1983	Columbus (Southern)	OF	118	445	68	133	19	3	•25	85	.299	1	186	17	9	.958
	Tucson (Pacific Coast)	OF-1B-3B	15	57	5	12	3	0	1	8	.211	0	52	4	2	.966
1984	Tucson (Pacific Coast)	1B-OF	131	471	66	140	28	7	16	94	.297	2	922	94	22	.979
	Houston (N.L.)	1B	18	61	6	13	5	0	2	8	.213	0	151	15	2	.988
1985	Tucson (Pacific Coast)	1B-OF	60	220	22	67	24	2	5	35	.305	0	420	29	5	.989
	Houston (N.L.)	1B-OF	100	350	51	95	11	0	20	64	.271	0	766	57	12	.986
1986	Houston (N.L.)	1B	158	574	91	152	32	3	31	101	.265	3	1253	111	11	.992
1987	Houston (N.L.)	1B	151	578	70	145	35	2	27	93	.251	4	1283	112	12	.991
1988	Houston (N.L.)	1B	152	561	78	152	26	0	30	99	.271	4	1355	103	6	•.996
1989	Houston (N.L.)	1B	158	581	87	156	26	1	34	89	.269	4	1347	113	12	.992
1990	Houston (N.L.)	1B	93	327	44	82	15	4	22	64	.251	8	796	55	4	.995
	Columbus (Southern)	1B	12	37	3	11	0	0	1	8	.297	1	79	7	3	.966
1991	Baltimore (A.L.)■	1B	49	176	29	40	9	1	10	28	.227	4	288	38	8	.976
	Hagerstown (Eastern)	1B	7	24	4	6	1	0	1	3	.250	1	38	1	0	1.000
American League totals (1 year)			49	176	29	40	9	1	10	28	.227	4	288	38	8	.976
National League totals (7 years)			830	3032	427	795	150	10	166	518	.262	23	6951	566	59	.992
Major league totals (8 years)			879	3208	456	835	159	11	176	546	.260	27	7239	604	67	.992

CHAMPIONSHIP SERIES RECORD

CHAMPIONSHIP SERIES NOTES: Hit home run in first series at-bat (October 8, 1986).... Shares single-game record for most at-bats—7 (October 15, 1986, 16 innings).

							BATTING							FIELDING		
Year	Team (League)	Pos.	G	AB	R	H	2B	3B	HR	RBI	Avg.	SB	PO	A	E	Avg.
1986	Houston (N.L.)	1B	6	26	3	7	1	0	1	3	.269	0	62	3	1	.985

ALL-STAR GAME RECORD

					BATTING							FIELDING		
Year	League	Pos.	AB	R	H	2B	3B	HR	RBI	Avg.	SB	PO	A	E	Avg.
1986	National	PH	1	0	0	0	0	0	0	.000	0	0	0	0	...
1989	National	1B	1	1	1	0	0	0	0	1.000	0	7	0	0	1.000
All-Star Game totals (2 years)			2	1	1	0	0	0	0	.500	0	7	0	0	1.000

DAVIS, MARK
OF, ANGELS

PERSONAL: Born November 25, 1964, at Lemon Grove, Calif.... 6-0/170.... Throws right, bats right.... Full name: Mark Anthony Davis.... Brother of Mike Davis, outfielder, Oakland A's and Los Angeles Dodgers (1980-89); and cousin of Dave Grayson Sr., American Football League and National Football League player (1961-70).

HIGH SCHOOL: Hoover (Calif.).

COLLEGE: Stanford.

TRANSACTIONS/CAREER NOTES: Selected by St. Louis Cardinals organization in fifth round of free-agent draft (June 7, 1982).... Selected by San Diego Padres organization in ninth round of free-agent draft (June 3, 1985).... Selected by Chicago White Sox organization in 12th round of free-agent draft (June 2, 1986).... Traded by White Sox organization to Midland (California Angels organization) for OF Mark Doran (August 4, 1989).

STATISTICAL NOTES: Led Pacific Coast League batters with 114 strikeouts in 1991.

							BATTING							FIELDING		
Year	Team (League)	Pos.	G	AB	R	H	2B	3B	HR	RBI	Avg.	SB	PO	A	E	Avg.
1986	Appleton (Midwest)	OF	77	272	37	62	10	4	3	22	.228	19	105	5	3	.973
1987	Peninsula (Carolina)	OF	134	507	91	149	24	6	16	72	.294	37	214	9	7	.970
1988	Birmingham (Southern)	OF	66	248	52	72	18	3	6	27	.290	32	142	5	6	.961
	Vancouver (Pac. Coast)	OF	68	241	24	51	9	2	4	29	.212	8	114	6	5	.960
1989	Vancouver (Pac. Coast)	OF	39	123	13	16	4	1	0	8	.130	6	64	2	0	1.000
	Birmingham (Southern)	OF	56	192	35	49	10	3	5	26	.255	16	102	1	3	.972
	Midland (Texas)■	OF	19	58	9	14	1	0	1	7	.241	6	37	1	0	1.000
1990	Midland (Texas)	OF	92	353	66	94	16	1	12	41	.266	16	194	8	2	.990
	Edmonton (Pac. Coast)	OF	35	133	30	49	10	5	9	34	.368	7	56	2	3	.951

Year Team (League)	Pos.	G	AB	R	H	BATTING 2B	3B	HR	RBI	Avg.	SB	FIELDING PO	A	E	Avg.
1991—Edmonton (Pac. Coast).....	OF	116	424	86	118	20	6	13	58	.278	32	207	9	4	.982
—California (A.L.)	OF	3	2	0	0	0	0	0	0	.000	0	1	0	1	.500
Major league totals (1 year)		3	2	0	0	0	0	0	0	.000	0	1	0	1	.500

DAVIS, MARK
P, ROYALS

PERSONAL: Born October 19, 1960, at Livermore, Calif.... 6-4/210.... Throws left, bats left.... Full name: Mark William Davis.
HIGH SCHOOL: Granada (Livermore, Calif.).
COLLEGE: Chabot College (Calif.).
TRANSACTIONS/CAREER NOTES: Selected by New York Mets organization in 21st round of free-agent draft (June 6, 1978).... Selected by Philadelphia Phillies organization in secondary phase of free-agent draft (January 9, 1979).... On Oklahoma City disabled list (April 14-June 11, 1981 and August 3-30, 1982).... Traded by Phillies organization with P Mike Krukow and OF Charles Penigar to San Francisco Giants for 2B Joe Morgan and P Al Holland (December 14, 1982).... Traded by Giants with 3B Chris Brown, P Keith Comstock and P Mark Grant to San Diego Padres for P Dave Dravecky, P Craig Lefferts and IF Kevin Mitchell (July 4, 1987).... Granted free agency (November 13, 1989).... Signed by Kansas City Royals (December 11, 1989). ... On disabled list (August 10-September 5, 1990 and April 20-May 5, 1991).... On Kansas City disabled list (June 18-August 5, 1991); included rehabilitation disability assignment to Omaha (July 6-August 4, 1991).
RECORDS/HONORS: Named Eastern League Most Valuable Player (1980).... Named N.L. Pitcher of the Year by THE SPORTING NEWS (1989).... Named N.L. Fireman of the Year by THE SPORTING NEWS (1989).... Named lefthanded pitcher on THE SPORTING NEWS N.L. All-Star team (1989).... Named N.L. Cy Young Award winner by Baseball Writers' Association of America (1989).
STATISTICAL NOTES: Led Western Carolinas League with five shutouts and 18 home runs allowed and tied for lead with five balks in 1979.... Tied for Eastern League lead in shutouts with four and games started by pitcher with 28 in 1980.

Year Team (League)	G	W	L	Pct.	ERA	Sv.	IP	H	R	ER	BB	SO
1979—Spartanburg (W. Caro)	26	11	9	.550	3.20	0	166	147	76	59	49	135
1980—Reading (Eastern)	28	*19	6	.760	*2.47	0	*193	140	63	53	75	*185
—Philadelphia (N.L.)	2	0	0	...	2.57	0	7	4	2	2	5	5
1981—Oklahoma City (Am. Assoc.).....	13	5	2	.714	3.88	0	65	66	34	28	47	56
—Philadelphia (N.L.)	9	1	4	.200	7.74	0	43	49	37	37	24	29
1982—Oklahoma City (Am. Assoc.).....	21	5	12	.294	6.24	0	96⅔	111	75	67	50	95
1983—Phoenix (Pacific Coast)■	13	6	3	.667	6.32	0	72⅔	89	57	51	33	64
—San Francisco (N.L.)	20	6	4	.600	3.49	0	111	93	51	43	50	83
1984—San Francisco (N.L.)	46	5	17	.227	5.36	0	174⅔	201	113	*104	54	124
1985—San Francisco (N.L.)	77	5	12	.294	3.54	7	114⅓	89	49	45	41	131
1986—San Francisco (N.L.)	67	5	7	.417	2.99	4	84⅓	63	33	28	34	90
1987—San Fran.-San Diego (N.L.)■...	63	9	8	.529	3.99	2	133	123	64	59	59	98
1988—San Diego (N.L.)	62	5	10	.333	2.01	28	98⅓	70	24	22	42	102
1989—San Diego (N.L.)	70	4	3	.571	1.85	*44	92⅔	66	21	19	31	92
1990—Kansas City (A.L.)■...............	53	2	7	.222	5.11	6	68⅔	71	43	39	52	73
1991—Kansas City (A.L.)	29	6	3	.667	4.45	1	62⅔	55	36	31	39	47
—Omaha (American Assoc.)........	6	4	1	.800	2.02	0	35⅔	27	11	8	9	36
American League totals (2 years)	82	8	10	.444	4.80	7	131⅓	126	79	70	91	120
National League totals (9 years)	416	40	65	.381	3.76	85	858⅓	758	394	359	340	754
Major league totals (11 years)	498	48	75	.390	3.90	92	989⅔	884	473	429	431	874

ALL-STAR GAME RECORD

Year League	W	L	Pct.	ERA	Sv.	IP	H	R	ER	BB	SO
1988—National	0	0	...	0.00	0	⅔	1	0	0	0	0
1989—National	0	0	...	0.00	0	1	0	0	0	0	2
All-Star totals (2 years)	0	0	...	0.00	0	1⅔	1	0	0	0	2

DAVIS, STORM
P, ORIOLES

PERSONAL: Born December 26, 1961, at Dallas.... 6-4/225.... Throws right, bats right.... Full name: George Earl Davis Jr.
HIGH SCHOOL: University Christian (Jacksonville, Fla.).
TRANSACTIONS/CAREER NOTES: Selected by Baltimore Orioles organization in seventh round of free-agent draft (June 5, 1979).... On Baltimore disabled list (July 4-22, 1986); included rehabilitation disability assignment to Hagerstown (July 18-22, 1986).... Traded by Orioles to San Diego Padres for C Terry Kennedy and P Mark Williamson (October 30, 1986).... On San Diego disabled list (June 30-August 17, 1987); included rehabilitation disability assignment to Wichita (August 7-11) and Reno (August 12-17, 1987).... Traded by Padres to Oakland Athletics for two players to be named later (August 30, 1987); Padres acquired P Dave Leiper (August 31, 1987) and 1B Rob Nelson (September 8, 1987) to complete deal.... On disabled list (May 18-June 10, 1989).... Granted free agency (November 13, 1989).... Signed by Kansas City Royals (December 7, 1989).... On disabled list (May 31-June 21 and July 1-17, 1990).... Traded by Royals to Orioles for C Bob Melvin (December 11, 1991).
RECORDS/HONORS: Named A.L. Comeback Player of the Year by THE SPORTING NEWS (1988).
STATISTICAL NOTES: Tied for A.L. lead with 16 wild pitches in 1988.
MISCELLANEOUS: Nicknamed by mother after Dr. Storm, a character in "Dates on Trial," a book she was reading while pregnant with Storm.

Year Team (League)	G	W	L	Pct.	ERA	Sv.	IP	H	R	ER	BB	SO
1979—Bluefield (Appalachian)	10	4	4	.500	3.88	0	58	44	34	25	30	54
1980—Miami (Florida State)	25	9	12	.429	3.52	0	151	157	85	59	55	90
1981—Charlotte (Southern)	28	14	10	.583	3.47	0	187	*215	86	72	65	119

Year	Team (League)	G	W	L	Pct.	ERA	Sv.	IP	H	R	ER	BB	SO
1982	—Rochester (International)	4	2	1	.667	3.71	0	26⅔	25	13	11	7	27
	—Baltimore (A.L.)	29	8	4	.667	3.49	0	100⅔	96	40	39	28	67
1983	—Baltimore (A.L.)	34	13	7	.650	3.59	0	200⅓	180	90	80	64	125
1984	—Baltimore (A.L.)	35	14	9	.609	3.12	1	225	205	86	78	71	105
1985	—Baltimore (A.L.)	31	10	8	.556	4.53	0	175	172	92	88	70	93
1986	—Baltimore (A.L.)	25	9	12	.429	3.62	0	154	166	70	62	49	96
	—Hagerstown (Carolina)	1	0	0	...	0.00	0	4	3	0	0	3	6
1987	—San Diego (N.L.)	21	2	7	.222	6.18	0	62⅔	70	48	43	36	37
	—Wichita (Texas)	1	0	1	.000	0.00	0	4	4	3	0	0	2
	—Reno (California)	1	0	0	...	3.60	0	5	2	2	2	6	5
	—Oakland (A.L.)■	5	1	1	.500	3.26	0	30⅓	28	13	11	11	28
1988	—Oakland (A.L.)	33	16	7	.696	3.70	0	201⅔	211	86	83	91	127
1989	—Oakland (A.L.)	31	19	7	.731	4.36	0	169⅓	187	91	82	68	91
1990	—Kansas City (A.L.)■	21	7	10	.412	4.74	0	112	129	66	59	35	62
1991	—Kansas City (A.L.)	51	3	9	.250	4.96	2	114⅓	140	69	63	46	53
	American League totals (10 years)	295	100	74	.575	3.92	3	1482⅔	1514	703	645	533	847
	National League totals (1 year)	21	2	7	.222	6.18	0	62⅔	70	48	43	36	37
	Major league totals (10 years)	316	102	81	.557	4.01	3	1545⅓	1584	751	688	569	884

CHAMPIONSHIP SERIES RECORD

Year	Team (League)	G	W	L	Pct.	ERA	Sv.	IP	H	R	ER	BB	SO
1983	—Baltimore (A.L.)	1	0	0	...	0.00	0	6	5	0	0	2	2
1988	—Oakland (A.L.)	1	0	0	...	0.00	0	6⅓	2	2	0	5	4
1989	—Oakland (A.L.)	1	0	1	.000	7.11	0	6⅓	5	6	5	2	3
	Championship Series totals (3 years)	3	0	1	.000	2.41	0	18⅔	12	8	5	9	9

WORLD SERIES RECORD

Year	Team (League)	G	W	L	Pct.	ERA	Sv.	IP	H	R	ER	BB	SO
1983	—Baltimore (A.L.)	1	1	0	1.000	5.40	0	5	6	3	3	1	3
1988	—Oakland (A.L.)	2	0	2	.000	11.25	0	8	14	10	10	1	7
1989	—Oakland (A.L.)							Did not play					
	World Series totals (2 years)	3	1	2	.333	9.00	0	13	20	13	13	2	10

DAWSON, ANDRE
OF, CUBS

PERSONAL: Born July 10, 1954, at Miami. . . . 6-3/197. . . . Throws right, bats right. . . . Full name: Andre Nolan Dawson.
HIGH SCHOOL: Southwest Miami (Fla.).
COLLEGE: Florida A&M.
TRANSACTIONS/CAREER NOTES: Selected by Montreal Expos organization in 11th round of free-agent draft (June 4, 1975). . . . On disabled list (June 5-30, 1986). . . . Granted free agency (November 12, 1986). . . . Signed by Chicago Cubs (March 9, 1987). . . . On disabled list (May 7-June 12, 1989). . . . On suspended list for one game (September 17, 1991).
RECORDS/HONORS: Holds major league single-game record for most intentional bases on balls received—5 (May 22, 1990, 16 innings). . . . Shares major league records for most total bases in one inning—8; most home runs in one inning—2 (July 30, 1978, third inning and September 24, 1985, fifth inning); most runs batted in in one inning—6 (September 24, 1985, fifth inning). . . . Shares major league single-season record for fewest double plays by outfielder (150 or more games)—0 (1987). . . . Named N.L. Rookie Player of the Year by THE SPORTING NEWS (1977). . . . Named N.L. Rookie of the Year by Baseball Writers' Association of America (1977). . . . Won N.L. Gold Glove as outfielder (1980-85 and 1987-88). . . . Named outfielder on THE SPORTING NEWS N.L. Silver Slugger team (1980-81, 1983 and 1987). . . . Named N.L. Player of the Year by THE SPORTING NEWS (1981 and 1987). . . . Named outfielder on THE SPORTING NEWS N.L. All-Star team (1981, 1983 and 1987). . . . Named N.L. Most Valuable Player by Baseball Writers' Association of America (1987).
STATISTICAL NOTES: Led Pioneer League with total bases with 166, in being hit by pitch with six and tied for lead in sacrifice flies with five in 1975. . . . Led N.L. in being hit by pitch with 12 in 1978, 7 in 1981 and tied for lead with six in 1980 and 9 in 1983. . . . Led N.L. outfielders with 344 total chances in 1981, 435 in 1982 and 450 in 1983. . . . Hit for the cycle (April 29, 1987). . . . Led N.L. with 341 total bases in 1983 and 353 in 1987. . . . Led N.L. with 18 sacrifice flies in 1983. . . . Hit three home runs in a game (September 24, 1985 and August 1, 1987). . . . Tied for N.L. lead with 16 game-winning RBIs in 1987. . . . Tied for N.L. lead with 21 intentional bases on balls received in 1990.

							BATTING						FIELDING			
Year	Team (League)	Pos.	G	AB	R	H	2B	3B	HR	RBI	Avg.	SB	PO	A	E	Avg.
1975	—Lethbridge (Pioneer)	OF	•72	*300	52	*99	14	7	*13	50	.330	11	*142	7	*10	.937
1976	—Denver (Am. Assoc.)	OF	74	240	51	84	19	4	20	46	.350	10	97	2	2	.980
	—Montreal (N.L.)	OF	24	85	9	20	4	1	0	7	.235	1	61	1	2	.969
1977	—Montreal (N.L.)	OF	139	525	64	148	26	9	19	65	.282	21	352	9	4	.989
1978	—Montreal (N.L.)	OF	157	609	84	154	24	8	25	72	.253	28	411	17	5	.988
1979	—Montreal (N.L.)	OF	155	639	90	176	24	12	25	92	.275	35	394	7	5	.988
1980	—Montreal (N.L.)	OF	151	577	96	178	41	7	17	87	.308	34	410	14	6	.986
1981	—Montreal (N.L.)	OF	103	394	71	119	21	3	24	64	.302	26	*327	10	7	.980
1982	—Montreal (N.L.)	OF	148	608	107	183	37	7	23	83	.301	39	*419	8	8	.982
1983	—Montreal (N.L.)	OF	159	633	104	•189	36	10	32	113	.299	25	*435	6	9	.980
1984	—Montreal (N.L.)	OF	138	533	73	132	23	6	17	86	.248	13	297	11	8	.975
1985	—Montreal (N.L.)	OF	139	529	65	135	27	2	23	91	.255	13	248	9	7	.973
1986	—Montreal (N.L.)	OF	130	496	65	141	32	2	20	78	.284	18	200	11	3	.986
1987	—Chicago (N.L.)■	OF	153	621	90	178	24	2	*49	*137	.287	11	271	12	4	.986
1988	—Chicago (N.L.)	OF	157	591	78	179	31	8	24	79	.303	12	267	7	3	.989

Year	Team (League)	Pos.	G	AB	R	H	2B	3B	HR	RBI	Avg.	SB	PO	A	E	Avg.
							BATTING						FIELDING			
1989	—Chicago (N.L.)	OF	118	416	62	105	18	6	21	77	.252	8	227	4	3	.987
1990	—Chicago (N.L.)	OF	147	529	72	164	28	5	27	100	.310	16	250	10	5	.981
1991	—Chicago (N.L.)	OF	149	563	69	153	21	4	31	104	.272	4	243	7	3	.988
	Major league totals (16 years)		2167	8348	1199	2354	417	92	377	1335	.282	304	4812	143	82	.984

DIVISION SERIES RECORD

Year	Team (League)	Pos.	G	AB	R	H	2B	3B	HR	RBI	Avg.	SB	PO	A	E	Avg.
							BATTING						FIELDING			
1981	—Montreal (N.L.)	OF	5	20	1	6	0	1	0	0	.300	2	12	1	1	.929

CHAMPIONSHIP SERIES RECORD

Year	Team (League)	Pos.	G	AB	R	H	2B	3B	HR	RBI	Avg.	SB	PO	A	E	Avg.
							BATTING						FIELDING			
1981	—Montreal (N.L.)	OF	5	20	2	3	0	0	0	0	.150	0	12	0	0	1.000
1989	—Chicago (N.L.)	OF	5	19	0	2	1	0	0	3	.105	0	4	0	0	1.000
	Championship Series totals (2 years)		10	39	2	5	1	0	0	3	.128	0	16	0	0	1.000

ALL-STAR GAME RECORD

Year	League	Pos.	AB	R	H	2B	3B	HR	RBI	Avg.	SB	PO	A	E	Avg.
						BATTING							FIELDING		
1981	—National	OF	4	0	1	0	0	0	0	.250	1	4	0	0	1.000
1982	—National	OF	4	0	1	0	0	0	0	.250	0	4	0	0	1.000
1983	—National	OF	3	0	0	0	0	0	0	.000	0	3	0	0	1.000
1987	—National	OF	3	0	1	1	0	0	0	.333	0	3	0	0	1.000
1988	—National	OF	2	0	1	0	0	0	0	.500	0	0	0	0	...
1989	—National	OF	1	0	0	0	0	0	0	.000	0	1	0	0	1.000
1990	—National	OF	2	0	0	0	0	0	0	.000	0	1	0	0	1.000
1991	—National	OF	2	1	1	0	0	1	1	.500	0	0	0	0	...
	All-Star Game totals (8 years)		21	1	5	1	0	1	1	.238	1	16	0	0	1.000

DAYLEY, KEN

P, BLUE JAYS

PERSONAL: Born February 25, 1959, at Jerome, Idaho.... 6-0/180.... Throws left, bats left.... Full name: Kenneth Grant Dayley II.
HIGH SCHOOL: Dalles (Ore.).
COLLEGE: Portland.
TRANSACTIONS/CAREER NOTES: Selected by Atlanta Braves organization in first round (third pick overall) of free-agent draft (June 3, 1980).... Traded by Braves with 1B Mike Jorgensen to St. Louis Cardinals for 3B Ken Oberkfell (June 15, 1984).... On disabled list (July 13, 1986-remainder of season).... Released by Cardinals (December 20, 1986).... Re-signed by Cardinals (January 19, 1987).... On St. Louis disabled list (April 5-May 21, 1987); included rehabilitation disability assignment to Louisville (May 12-21, 1987).... On disabled list (April 5-May 9, 1988).... Granted free agency (November 5, 1990).... Signed by Toronto Blue Jays (November 26, 1990).... On Toronto disabled list (April 3-May 24 and June 12, 1991-remainder of season); included rehabilitation disability assignment to Dunedin (May 18-24, 1991) and Syracuse (June 18-July 8 and September 1-5, 1991).
RECORDS/HONORS: Named lefthanded pitcher on THE SPORTING NEWS college All-America team (1980).
STATISTICAL NOTES: Led International League pitchers with 31 games started in 1981.

Year	Team (League)	G	W	L	Pct.	ERA	Sv.	IP	H	R	ER	BB	SO
1980	—Savannah (Southern)	16	8	3	.727	2.57	0	105	86	38	30	54	104
1981	—Richmond (International)	31	•13	8	.619	3.33	0	★200	180	82	74	★117	★162
1982	—Richmond (International)	13	8	3	.727	3.11	0	98⅓	89	43	34	47	79
	—Atlanta (N.L.)	20	5	6	.455	4.54	0	71⅓	79	39	36	25	34
1983	—Richmond (International)	14	9	3	.750	3.28	0	90⅔	79	39	33	49	74
	—Atlanta (N.L.)	24	5	8	.385	4.30	0	104⅔	100	59	50	39	70
1984	—Richmond (International)	9	5	1	.833	4.14	0	62⅓	66	31	28	24	45
	—Atlanta-St. Louis (N.L.)■......	7	0	5	.000	7.99	0	23⅔	44	28	21	11	10
	—Louisville (American Assoc.) ...	13	4	6	.400	3.27	0	96⅓	86	42	35	22	79
1985	—St. Louis (N.L.)	57	4	4	.500	2.76	11	65⅓	65	24	20	18	62
1986	—St. Louis (N.L.)	31	0	3	.000	3.26	5	38⅔	42	19	14	11	33
1987	—Louisville (American Assoc.) ...	1	0	0	...	4.50	0	2	1	1	1	1	1
	—Springfield (Midwest)	2	0	0	...	0.00	0	3⅔	1	0	0	1	3
	—St. Louis (N.L.)	53	9	5	.643	2.66	4	61	52	21	18	33	63
1988	—St. Louis (N.L.)	54	2	7	.222	2.77	5	55⅓	48	20	17	19	38
1989	—St. Louis (N.L.)	71	4	3	.571	2.87	12	75⅓	63	26	24	30	40
1990	—St. Louis (N.L.)	58	4	4	.500	3.56	4	73⅓	63	32	29	30	51
1991	—Dunedin (Florida State)■	3	0	0	...	0.00	0	6	1	000	0	2	2
	—Toronto (A.L.)	8	0	0	...	6.23	0	4⅓	7	3	3	5	3
	—Syracuse (International)	10	0	1	.000	9.64	1	14	26	16	15	11	13
	American League totals (1 year)	8	0	0	.000	6.23	0	4⅓	7	3	3	5	3
	National League totals (9 years)	375	33	45	.423	3.62	41	568⅔	556	268	229	216	401
	Major league totals (10 years)	383	33	45	.423	3.64	41	573	563	271	232	221	404

CHAMPIONSHIP SERIES NOTES: Shares single-series record for most games pitched—5 (1985).

Year Team (League)	G	W	L	Pct.	ERA	Sv.	IP	H	R	ER	BB	SO
1985 —St. Louis (N.L.)	5	0	0	...	0.00	2	6	2	0	0	1	3
1987 —St. Louis (N.L.)	3	0	0	...	0.00	2	4	1	0	0	2	4
Championship Series totals (2 years)	8	0	0	...	0.00	4	10	3	0	0	3	7

WORLD SERIES RECORD

Year Team (League)	G	W	L	Pct.	ERA	Sv.	IP	H	R	ER	BB	SO
1985 —St. Louis (N.L.)	4	1	0	1.000	0.00	0	6	1	0	0	3	5
1987 —St. Louis (N.L.)	4	0	0	...	1.93	1	4⅔	2	1	1	0	3
World Series totals (2 years)	8	1	0	1.000	0.84	1	10⅔	3	1	1	3	8

DECKER, STEVE
C, GIANTS

PERSONAL: Born October 25, 1965, at Rock Island, Ill. . . . 6-3/205. . . . Throws right, bats right. . . . Full name: Steven M. Decker.
HIGH SCHOOL: Rock Island (Ill.).
COLLEGE: Lewis-Clark State College (Ida.).
TRANSACTIONS/CAREER NOTES: Selected by San Francisco Giants organization in 21st round of free-agent draft (June 1, 1988).

Year Team (League)	Pos.	G	AB	R	H	2B	3B	HR	RBI	Avg.	SB	PO	A	E	Avg.
1988 —Everett (Northwest)	C	13	42	11	22	2	0	2	13	.524	0	37	3	2	.952
—San Jose (Pacific Coast) ...	C	47	175	31	56	9	0	4	34	.320	0	199	26	5	.978
1989 —San Jose (Pacific Coast) ...	C-1B	64	225	27	65	12	0	3	46	.289	8	417	51	7	.985
—Shreveport (Texas)	C-1B	44	142	19	46	8	0	1	18	.324	0	229	22	5	.980
1990 —Shreveport (Texas)	C	116	403	52	118	22	1	15	80	.293	3	650	71	10	.986
—San Francisco (N.L.)	C	15	54	5	16	2	0	3	8	.296	0	75	11	1	.989
1991 —San Francisco (N.L.)	C	79	233	11	48	7	1	5	24	.206	0	385	41	7	.984
—Phoenix (Pacific Coast)	C	31	111	20	28	5	1	6	14	.252	0	156	16	1	.994
Major league totals (2 years)		94	287	16	64	9	1	8	32	.223	0	460	52	8	.985

DEER, ROB
OF, TIGERS

PERSONAL: Born September 29, 1960, at Orange, Calif. . . . 6-3/225. . . . Throws right, bats right. . . . Full name: Robert George Deer.
HIGH SCHOOL: Canyon (Anaheim, Calif.).
COLLEGE: Fresno City College (Calif.).
TRANSACTIONS/CAREER NOTES: Selected by San Francisco Giants organization in fourth round of free-agent draft (June 6, 1978). . . . Traded by Giants to Milwaukee Brewers for P Dean Freeland and P Eric Pilkington (December 18, 1985). . . . On disabled list (July 4-27, 1988 and August 9-25, 1989). . . . Granted free agency (November 5, 1990). . . . Signed by Detroit Tigers (November 23, 1990).
RECORDS/HONORS: Shares major league records for most grand slams in two consecutive games—2 (August 19 and 20, 1987); most strikeouts in nine-inning game—5 (August 8, 1987, first game). . . . Holds A.L. single-season record for most strikeouts—186 (1987).
STATISTICAL NOTES: Led California League batters with 146 strikeouts in 1981. . . . Led Texas League batters with 177 strikeouts in 1982 and 185 in 1983. . . . Led Pacific Coast League batters with 175 strikeouts in 1984. . . . Led A.L. batters with 186 strikeouts in 1987 and 175 in 1991 and tied for lead with 153 in 1988. . . . Led A.L. outfielders with seven double plays in 1990.

Year Team (League)	Pos.	G	AB	R	H	2B	3B	HR	RBI	Avg.	SB	PO	A	E	Avg.
1978 —Great Falls (Pioneer)	OF	48	137	20	34	6	5	0	18	.248	2	83	3	4	.956
1979 —Cedar Rapids (Midwest) ...	OF	29	86	7	18	0	1	1	16	.209	3	35	1	4	.900
—Great Falls (Pioneer)	OF	63	218	49	69	18	7	7	44	.317	4	95	10	5	.955
1980 —Clinton (Midwest)	OF	127	434	60	114	31	5	13	58	.263	20	184	•17	11	.948
1981 —Fresno (California)	OF	135	479	86	137	24	4	*33	107	.286	18	211	14	6	.974
1982 —Shreveport (Texas)	OF-1B	128	410	58	85	26	0	27	73	.207	4	184	10	11	.946
1983 —Shreveport (Texas)	OF	132	448	89	97	15	1	*35	99	.217	18	252	13	7	.974
1984 —Phoenix (Pacific Coast)	OF	133	449	88	102	21	1	*31	69	.227	9	251	•19	9	.968
—San Francisco (N.L.)	OF	13	24	5	4	0	0	3	3	.167	1	19	0	2	.905
1985 —San Francisco (N.L.)	OF-1B	78	162	22	30	5	1	8	20	.185	0	127	2	2	.985
1986 —Milwaukee (A.L.)■	OF-1B	134	466	75	108	17	3	33	86	.232	5	312	8	8	.976
1987 —Milwaukee (A.L.)	OF-1B	134	474	71	113	15	2	28	80	.238	12	304	16	8	.976
1988 —Milwaukee (A.L.)	OF	135	492	71	124	24	0	23	85	.252	9	284	10	3	.990
1989 —Milwaukee (A.L.)	OF	130	466	72	98	18	2	26	65	.210	4	267	10	8	.972
1990 —Milwaukee (A.L.)	OF-1B	134	440	57	92	15	1	27	69	.209	2	373	25	10	.975
1991 —Detroit (A.L.)■	OF	134	448	64	80	14	2	25	64	.179	1	310	8	7	.978
American League totals (6 years)		801	2786	410	615	103	10	162	449	.221	33	1850	77	44	.978
National League totals (2 years)		91	186	27	34	5	1	11	23	.183	1	146	2	4	.974
Major league totals (8 years)		892	2972	437	649	108	11	173	472	.218	34	1996	79	48	.977

DeJESUS, JOSE
P, PHILLIES

PERSONAL: Born January 6, 1965, at Brooklyn, N.Y. . . . 6-5/213. . . . Throws right, bats right. . . . Full name: Jose Luis Velazquez DeJesus.
HIGH SCHOOL: Luis Munoz Iglesias.
TRANSACTIONS/CAREER NOTES: Signed as free agent by Kansas City Royals organization

(May 9, 1983).... Drafted by Toronto Blue Jays (December 10, 1985); returned to Royals (April 3, 1986).... Traded by Royals to Philadelphia Phillies for SS Steve Jeltz (March 31, 1990).

Year	Team (League)	G	W	L	Pct.	ERA	Sv.	IP	H	R	ER	BB	SO
1983—Sarasota Royals (Gulf Coast) ...		10	1	2	.333	4.13	0	24	17	18	11	17	10
1984—Charleston, S.C. (S. Atlantic)		27	11	12	.478	4.42	0	163	152	98	80	69	85
1985—Fort Myers (Florida State)		27	8	10	.444	4.30	0	129⅔	119	70	62	59	94
1986—Fort Myers (Florida State)		22	4	9	.308	3.44	0	110	87	64	42	82	97
1987—Memphis (Southern)		25	4	11	.267	4.49	0	130⅓	106	78	65	99	79
1988—Memphis (Southern)		20	9	9	.500	3.88	0	116	88	56	50	70	149
—Omaha (American Assoc.).......		7	2	3	.400	3.44	0	49⅔	44	22	19	14	57
—Kansas City (A.L.)		2	0	1	.000	27.00	0	2⅔	6	10	8	5	2
1989—Omaha (American Assoc.).......		31	8	11	.421	3.78	1	145⅓	112	78	61	*98	158
—Kansas City (A.L.)		3	0	0	...	4.50	0	8	7	4	4	8	2
1990—Scranton/Wilkes-Barre (Int'l)■		10	1	4	.200	3.38	0	56	41	30	21	39	45
—Philadelphia (N.L.)		22	7	8	.467	3.74	0	130	97	63	54	73	87
1991—Philadelphia (N.L.)		31	10	9	.526	3.42	1	181⅔	147	74	69	*128	118
American League totals (2 years)		5	0	1	.000	10.13	0	10⅔	13	14	12	13	4
National League totals (2 years)		53	17	17	.500	3.55	1	311⅔	244	137	123	201	205
Major league totals (4 years)		58	17	18	.486	3.77	1	322⅓	257	151	135	214	209

DeLaROSA, FRANCISCO
P, ORIOLES

PERSONAL: Born March 3, 1966, at La Romana, Dominican Republic.... 5-11/195.... Throws right, bats both.... Full name: Francisco DeLaRosa.
TRANSACTIONS/CAREER NOTES: Signed as free agent by Toronto Blue Jays organization (March 4, 1985).... Released by Blue Jays organization (September 28, 1985).... Signed by Baltimore Orioles organization (October 24, 1987).... On Rochester disabled list (June 10-18, 1991).

Year	Team (League)	G	W	L	Pct.	ERA	Sv.	IP	H	R	ER	BB	SO
1985—Bradenton Blue Jays (GCL)		16	0	1	.000	5.52	1	31	43	24	19	5	19
1986—						Out of Organized Baseball							
1987—						Out of Organized Baseball							
1988—Hagerstown (Carolina)■...........		29	3	4	.429	4.61	2	41	34	21	21	29	47
1989—Frederick (Carolina).................		23	3	4	.429	2.38	5	22⅔	17	9	6	11	31
—Hagerstown (Eastern)		18	1	1	.500	4.55	8	29⅔	27	15	15	20	34
1990—Hagerstown (Eastern).............		23	9	5	.643	2.06	0	131	97	42	30	51	105
—Rochester (International)		2	0	0	...	0.00	1	⅔	0	0	0	1	1
1991—Rochester (International)		38	4	1	.800	2.67	3	84⅓	71	28	25	33	61
—Baltimore (A.L.)		2	0	0	...	4.50	0	4	6	3	2	2	1
Major league totals (1 year)		2	0	0	...	4.50	0	4	6	3	2	2	1

DeLEON, JOSE
P, CARDINALS

PERSONAL: Born December 20, 1960, at Rancho Viejo, LaVega, Dominican Republic.... 6-3/226.... Throws right, bats right.... Full name: Jose Chestaro DeLeon.
HIGH SCHOOL: Perth Amboy (N.J.).
TRANSACTIONS/CAREER NOTES: Selected by Pittsburgh Pirates organization in third round of free-agent draft (June 5, 1979).... On disabled list (July 5-29, 1982).... Traded by Pirates organization to Chicago White Sox for OF Bobby Bonilla (July 23, 1986).... Traded by White Sox to St. Louis Cardinals for P Rick Horton, OF Lance Johnson and cash (February 9, 1988).
STATISTICAL NOTES: Led Gulf Coast League with seven home runs allowed and tied for lead with nine wild pitches in 1979.... Tied for South Atlantic League lead with 19 home runs allowed in 1980.
MISCELLANEOUS: Appeared in one game as outfielder with one putout (1988).

Year	Team (League)	G	W	L	Pct.	ERA	Sv.	IP	H	R	ER	BB	SO
1979—Bradenton Pirates (GCL)		11	2	4	.333	6.41	1	59	76	47	42	38	33
1980—Shelby (South Atlantic)		26	10	15	.400	4.82	0	168	160	108	*90	69	118
1981—Buffalo (Eastern)		25	12	6	.667	3.11	0	159	136	72	55	94	158
1982—Portland (Pacific Coast)		24	10	7	.588	5.97	0	119	138	81	79	65	94
1983—Hawaii (Pacific Coast)		20	11	6	.647	*3.04	0	127⅓	90	50	43	68	128
—Pittsburgh (N.L.)		15	7	3	.700	2.83	0	108	75	36	34	47	118
1984—Pittsburgh (N.L.)		30	7	13	.350	3.74	0	192⅓	147	86	80	92	153
1985—Pittsburgh (N.L.)		31	2	*19	.095	4.70	3	162⅓	138	93	85	89	149
—Hawaii (Pacific Coast)		5	4	0	1.000	0.88	0	41	15	4	4	10	45
1986—Hawaii (Pacific Coast)		15	5	8	.385	2.46	0	106	87	32	29	44	83
—Pittsburgh (N.L.)		9	1	3	.250	8.27	1	16⅓	17	16	15	17	11
—Chicago (A.L.)■..................		13	4	5	.444	2.96	0	79	49	30	26	42	68
1987—Chicago (A.L.)		33	11	12	.478	4.02	0	206	177	106	92	97	153
1988—St. Louis (N.L.)■..................		34	13	10	.565	3.67	0	225⅓	198	95	92	86	208
1989—St. Louis (N.L.)		36	16	12	.571	3.05	0	244⅔	173	96	83	80	*201
1990—St. Louis (N.L.)		32	7	*19	.269	4.43	0	182⅔	168	96	90	86	164
1991—St. Louis (N.L.)		28	5	9	.357	2.71	0	162⅔	144	57	49	61	118
American League totals (2 years)		46	15	17	.469	3.73	0	285	226	136	118	139	221
National League totals (8 years)		215	58	88	.397	3.67	4	1294⅔	1060	575	528	558	1122
Major league totals (9 years)		261	73	105	.410	3.68	4	1579⅔	1286	711	646	697	1343

de los SANTOS, LUIS

IF/OF

PERSONAL: Born December 29, 1966, at San Cristobal, Dominican Republic.... 6-5/200.... Throws right, bats right.... Full name: Luis Manuel de los Santos. **HIGH SCHOOL:** Newton (Elmhurst, N.Y.). **TRANSACTIONS/CAREER NOTES:** Selected by Kansas City Royals organization in second round of free-agent draft (June 4, 1984).... Claimed on waivers by Detroit Tigers (April 5, 1991).... Granted free agency (October 15, 1991).
RECORDS/HONORS: Named American Association Most Valuable Player (1988).
STATISTICAL NOTES: Led American Association in grounding into double plays with 20 in 1987, 17 in 1988 and 19 in 1989.... Led American Association first basemen with 1,050 total chances in 1988.... Led American Association with 12 sacrifice flies in 1990.

Year	Team (League)	Pos.	G	AB	R	H	2B	3B	HR	RBI	Avg.	SB	PO	A	E	Avg.
							BATTING						FIELDING			
1984—Eugene (Northwest)	3B	67	257	27	69	10	2	2	30	.268	5	67	93	22	.879	
1985—Fort Myers (Florida St.)	3B	123	454	44	120	18	2	0	48	.264	2	87	141	32	.877	
1986—Memphis (Southern)	3B	135	525	72	159	21	5	3	84	.303	5	*136	244	*50	.884	
1987—Omaha (Am. Assoc.)	3B-1B	135	518	53	152	29	6	2	67	.293	2	401	116	27	.950	
1988—Omaha (Am. Assoc.)	1B	136	*535	62	*164	25	4	6	•87	.307	2	*971	68	*11	.990	
—Kansas City (A.L.)	1B	11	22	1	2	1	1	0	1	.091	0	31	1	0	1.000	
1989—Omaha (Am. Assoc.)	1B-3B	99	387	45	115	31	3	3	62	.297	1	842	57	9	.990	
—Kansas City (A.L.)	1B	28	87	6	22	3	1	0	6	.253	0	203	16	3	.986	
1990—Omaha (Am. Assoc.)	1B	135	521	55	146	23	1	5	74	.280	2	242	171	16	.963	
1991—Detroit (A.L.)■	OF-3B-1B	16	30	1	5	2	0	0	0	.167	0	8	1	1	.900	
—Toledo (International)	1B-3B	41	141	12	40	8	0	2	22	.284	0	249	18	4	.985	
Major league totals (3 years)		55	139	8	29	6	2	0	7	.209	0	242	18	4	.985	

DeLUCIA, RICH

P, MARINERS

PERSONAL: Born October 7, 1964, at Wyomissing, Pa.... 6-0/180.... Throws right, bats right.... Full name: Richard Anthony DeLucia. **HIGH SCHOOL:** Wyomissing Area (Wyomissing, Pa.). **COLLEGE:** Tennessee.
TRANSACTIONS/CAREER NOTES: Selected by Toronto Blue Jays organization in 15th round of free-agent draft (June 3, 1985).... Selected by Seattle Mariners organization in sixth round of free-agent draft (June 2, 1986).... On disabled list (April 10, 1987-remainder of season).... On Williamsport disabled list (May 31-July 2 and July 7, 1989-remainder of season).
STATISTICAL NOTES: Pitched seven-inning, 1-0 no-hit victory against Everett (July 17, 1986).... Tied for Northwest League lead with one shutout in 1986.... Led A.L. with 31 home runs allowed in 1991.

Year	Team (League)	G	W	L	Pct.	ERA	Sv.	IP	H	R	ER	BB	SO
1986—Bellingham (Northwest)	13	8	2	.800	*1.70	0	74	44	20	14	24	69	
1987—Salinas (California)	1	0	0	...	9.00	0	1	2	1	1	0	1	
1988—San Bernardino (California)	22	7	8	.467	3.10	0	127⅔	110	57	44	59	118	
1989—Williamsport (Eastern)	10	3	4	.429	3.79	0	54⅔	59	28	23	13	41	
1990—San Bernardino (California)	5	4	1	.800	2.05	0	30⅔	19	9	7	3	35	
—Williamsport (Eastern)	18	6	6	.500	2.11	0	115	92	30	27	30	76	
—Calgary (Pacific Coast)	5	2	2	.500	3.62	0	32⅓	30	17	13	12	23	
—Seattle (A.L.)	5	1	2	.333	2.00	0	36	30	9	8	9	20	
1991—Seattle (A.L.)	32	12	13	.480	5.09	0	182	176	107	103	78	98	
Major league totals (2 years)	37	13	15	.464	4.58	0	218	206	116	111	87	118	

DEMPSEY, RICK

C

PERSONAL: Born September 13, 1949, at Fayetteville, Tenn.... 6-0/199.... Throws right, bats right.... Full name: John Rikard Dempsey.... Brother of Pat Dempsey, minor league catcher (1977-87). **HIGH SCHOOL:** Crespi (Encino, Calif.).
COLLEGE: Pierce Junior College (Calif.).
TRANSACTIONS/CAREER NOTES: Selected by Minnesota Twins organization in 12th round of free-agent draft (June 6, 1967).... Traded by Twins to New York Yankees organization for OF Danny Walton (October 27, 1972).... Traded by Yankees with P Rudy May, P Tippy Martinez, P Dave Pagan and P Scott McGregor to Baltimore Orioles for P Ken Holtzman, P Doyle Alexander, P Grant Jackson, C Ellie Hendricks and P Jimmy Freeman (June 15, 1976).... On disabled list (July 9-August 21, 1977).... Granted free agency (November 12, 1986).... Signed by Cleveland Indians (February 6, 1987).... On disabled list (July 22-September 11, 1987).... Released by Indians (October 29, 1987).... Signed by Los Angeles Dodgers (March 30, 1988).... On disabled list (April 16-May 3, 1990).... Granted free agency (November 5, 1990).... Signed by Milwaukee Brewers (April 2, 1991).... Released by Brewers (October 9, 1991).
RECORDS/HONORS: Shares major league single-game record for most double plays by catcher—3 (June 1, 1977).
STATISTICAL NOTES: Led New York-Pennsylvania League catchers with .990 fielding percentage, 468 putouts and 35 assists and tied for lead with four double plays in 1968.... Led International League with 14 passed balls in 1973.... Tied for A.L. lead in double plays by catchers with 14 in 1978.

Year	Team (League)	Pos.	G	AB	R	H	2B	3B	HR	RBI	Avg.	SB	PO	A	E	Avg.
							BATTING						FIELDING			
1967—Sarasota Twins (GCL)	C-OF-1B	40	102	9	21	4	3	0	9	.206	1	133	16	2	.987	
1968—Wis. Rapids (Midwest)	C	11	35	12	8	2	0	1	6	.229	0	68	2	1	.986	
—Auburn (N.Y.-Penn)	C-1B-OF	73	270	48	79	10	7	7	61	.293	3	†505	†38	7	.†987	
1969—Wis. Rapids (Midwest)	C	50	151	35	55	11	2	6	31	.364	7	341	30	•13	.966	
—Minnesota (A.L.)	C	5	6	1	3	1	0	0	0	.500	0	5	0	1	.833	
1970—Charlotte (Southern)	C-OF-2B	105	351	28	86	20	6	4	42	.245	4	506	76	18	.970	
—Minnesota (A.L.)	C	5	7	1	0	0	0	0	0	.000	0	12	0	1	.923	

Year	Team (League)	Pos.	G	AB	R	H	2B	3B	HR	RBI	Avg.	SB	PO	A	E	Avg.
1971	—Charlotte (Southern)	C-OF	105	338	39	82	16	2	8	47	.243	3	599	65	8	.988
	—Minnesota (A.L.)	C	6	13	2	4	1	0	0	0	.308	0	30	4	2	.944
1972	—Minnesota (A.L.)	C	25	40	0	8	1	0	0	0	.200	0	67	5	1	.986
	—Tacoma (Pacific Coast)	C-OF	48	161	13	38	6	2	3	18	.236	2	284	33	5	.984
1973	—Syracuse (International)■	C-OF-3B	122	387	53	96	14	4	6	47	.248	11	585	69	9	.986
	—New York (A.L.)	C	6	11	0	2	0	0	0	0	.182	0	9	0	2	.818
1974	—New York (A.L.)	C-OF	43	109	12	26	3	0	2	12	.239	1	152	22	4	.978
1975	—New York (A.L.)	C-OF-3B	71	145	18	38	8	0	1	11	.262	0	92	9	3	.971
1976	—New York-Balt. (A.L.)■.....	C-OF	80	216	12	42	2	0	0	12	.194	1	302	39	4	.988
1977	—Baltimore (A.L.)	C	91	270	27	61	7	4	3	34	.226	2	416	52	11	.977
1978	—Baltimore (A.L.)	C	136	441	41	114	25	0	6	32	.259	7	636	79	11	.985
1979	—Baltimore (A.L.)	C	124	368	48	88	23	0	6	41	.239	0	615	*81	7	.990
1980	—Baltimore (A.L.)	C-OF-1B	119	362	51	95	26	3	9	40	.262	3	544	55	8	.987
1981	—Baltimore (A.L.)	C	92	251	24	54	10	1	6	15	.215	0	384	35	1	*.998
1982	—Baltimore (A.L.)	C	125	344	35	88	15	1	5	36	.256	1	491	46	5	.991
1983	—Baltimore (A.L.)	C	128	347	33	80	16	2	4	32	.231	1	591	65	2	*.997
1984	—Baltimore (A.L.)	C	109	330	37	76	11	0	11	34	.230	1	453	43	4	.992
1985	—Baltimore (A.L.)	C	132	362	54	92	19	0	12	52	.254	0	575	49	8	.987
1986	—Baltimore (A.L.)	C	122	327	42	68	15	1	13	29	.208	1	659	53	7	.990
1987	—Cleveland (A.L.)■	C	60	141	16	25	10	0	1	9	.177	0	293	18	5	.984
1988	—Los Angeles (N.L.)■............	C	77	167	25	42	13	0	7	30	.251	1	333	29	4	.989
1989	—Los Angeles (N.L.)	C	79	151	16	27	7	0	4	16	.179	1	265	35	5	.984
1990	—Los Angeles (N.L.)	C	62	128	13	25	5	0	2	15	.195	1	213	27	2	.992
1991	—Milwaukee (A.L.)■.............	C-1B-P	61	147	15	34	5	0	4	21	.231	0	246	23	2	.993
American League totals (20 years)			1540	4237	469	998	198	12	83	410	.236	17	6572	678	89	.988
National League totals (3 years)			218	446	54	94	25	0	13	61	.211	3	811	91	11	.988
Major league totals (23 years)			1758	4683	523	1092	223	12	96	471	.233	20	7383	769	100	.988

CHAMPIONSHIP SERIES RECORD

Year	Team (League)	Pos.	G	AB	R	H	2B	3B	HR	RBI	Avg.	SB	PO	A	E	Avg.
1979	—Baltimore (A.L.)	C	3	10	3	4	2	0	0	2	.400	1	10	1	0	1.000
1983	—Baltimore (A.L.)	C	4	12	1	2	0	0	0	0	.167	0	29	5	1	.971
1988	—Los Angeles (N.L.)	PH-C	4	5	1	2	2	0	0	2	.400	0	7	0	0	1.000
Championship Series totals (3 years)			11	27	5	8	4	0	0	4	.296	1	46	6	1	.981

WORLD SERIES RECORD

Year	Team (League)	Pos.	G	AB	R	H	2B	3B	HR	RBI	Avg.	SB	PO	A	E	Avg.
1979	—Baltimore (A.L.)	C-PR	7	21	3	6	2	0	0	0	.286	0	38	2	0	1.000
1983	—Baltimore (A.L.)	C	5	13	3	5	4	0	1	2	.385	0	27	4	0	1.000
1988	—Los Angeles (N.L.)	C	2	5	0	1	1	0	0	1	.200	0	13	1	0	1.000
World Series totals (3 years)			14	39	6	12	7	0	1	3	.308	0	78	7	0	1.000

RECORD AS PITCHER

Year	Team (League)	G	W	L	Pct.	ERA	Sv.	IP	H	R	ER	BB	SO
1991	—Milwaukee (A.L.)	2	0	0	...	4.50	0	2	3	1	1	1	0

DESHAIES, JIM

P

PERSONAL: Born June 23, 1960, at Massena, N.Y. ... 6-4/222. ... Throws left, bats left. ... Full name: James Joseph Deshaies. ... Name pronounced duh-SHAYS.

HIGH SCHOOL: Massena Central (Massena, N.Y.).

COLLEGE: Le Moyne College, N.Y. (bachelor of arts degree, 1982).

TRANSACTIONS/CAREER NOTES: Selected by Montreal Expos organization in 13th round of free-agent draft (June 6, 1978). ... Selected by New York Yankees organization in 21st round of free-agent draft (June 7, 1982). ... On Columbus disabled list (April 10-25 and August 4-14, 1985). ... Traded by Yankees organization with a player to be named later to Houston Astros for P Joe Niekro (September 15, 1985); Astros organization acquired IF Neder Horta (September 24, 1985) and P Dody Rather (January 11, 1986) to complete deal. ... On disabled list (April 21-May 7, 1986 and July 26-August 16, 1987). ... Granted free agency (October 28, 1991).

RECORDS/HONORS: Holds modern major league record for most consecutive strikeouts at start of game—8 (September 23, 1986).

STATISTICAL NOTES: Pitched seven-inning, 5-1 no-hit victory for Nashville against Columbus (May 4, 1984). ... Tied for International League lead with four shutouts in 1984. ... Led International League with four balks in 1985. ... Led N.L. with seven balks in 1986.

Year	Team (League)	G	W	L	Pct.	ERA	Sv.	IP	H	R	ER	BB	SO
1982	—Oneonta (New York-Penn)	15	6	5	.545	3.32	0	108⅓	93	50	40	40	*137
1983	—Fort Lauderdale (Florida St.)	20	11	3	.786	2.52	0	117⅔	105	44	33	58	128
1984	—Nashville (Southern)	7	3	2	.600	2.80	0	45	33	20	14	29	42
	—Columbus (International)	18	10	5	.667	*2.39	0	135⅔	99	45	36	62	117
	—New York (A.L.)	2	0	1	.000	11.57	0	7	14	9	9	7	5
1985	—Columbus (International)	21	8	6	.571	4.31	0	131⅔	124	67	63	59	106
	—Houston (N.L.)■......................	2	0	0	...	0.00	0	3	1	0	0	0	2

Year	Team (League)	G	W	L	Pct.	ERA	Sv.	IP	H	R	ER	BB	SO
1986—Houston (N.L.)		26	12	5	.706	3.25	0	144	124	58	52	59	128
1987—Houston (N.L.)		26	11	6	.647	4.62	0	152	149	81	78	57	104
1988—Houston (N.L.)		31	11	14	.440	3.00	0	207	164	77	69	72	127
1989—Houston (N.L.)		34	15	10	.600	2.91	0	225⅔	180	80	73	79	153
1990—Houston (N.L.)		34	7	12	.368	3.78	0	209⅓	186	93	88	84	119
1991—Houston (N.L.)		28	5	12	.294	4.98	0	161	156	90	89	72	98
American League totals (1 year)		2	0	1	.000	11.57	0	7	14	9	9	7	5
National League totals (7 years)		181	61	59	.508	3.67	0	1102	960	479	449	423	731
Major league totals (8 years)		183	61	60	.504	3.72	0	1109	974	488	458	430	736

DeSHIELDS, DELINO
2B, EXPOS

PERSONAL: Born January 15, 1969, at Seaford, Del. . . . 6-1/170. . . . Throws right, bats left. . . . Full name: Delino Lamont DeShields. . . . Name pronounced duh-LINE-oh.
HIGH SCHOOL: Seaford (Del.).
COLLEGE: Villanova.
TRANSACTIONS/CAREER NOTES: Selected by Montreal Expos organization in first round (12th pick overall) of free-agent draft (June 2, 1987). . . . On disabled list (June 16-July 12, 1990).
RECORDS/HONORS: Shares modern N.L. record for most hits in first major league game—4 (April 9, 1990).
STATISTICAL NOTES: Led Gulf Coast League shortstops with 22 errors in 1987. . . . Led N.L. batters with 151 strikeouts in 1991.

Year	Team (League)	Pos.	G	AB	R	H	2B	3B	HR	RBI	Avg.	SB	PO	A	E	Avg.
1987—Bradenton Expos (GCL)		SS-3B	31	111	17	24	5	2	1	4	.216	16	47	90	†22	.862
—Jamestown (N.Y.-Penn)		SS	34	96	16	21	1	2	1	5	.219	14	25	57	21	.796
1988—Rockford (Midwest)		SS	129	460	97	116	26	6	12	46	.252	59	173	344	42	.925
1989—Jacksonville (Southern)		SS	93	307	55	83	10	6	3	35	.270	37	127	218	34	.910
—Indianapolis (A.A.)		SS	47	181	29	47	8	4	2	14	.260	16	73	101	13	.930
1990—Montreal (N.L.)		2B	129	499	69	144	28	6	4	45	.289	42	236	371	12	.981
1991—Montreal (N.L.)		2B	151	563	83	134	15	4	10	51	.238	56	285	405	*27	.962
Major league totals (2 years)			280	1062	152	278	43	10	14	96	.262	98	521	776	39	.971

DeSILVA, JOHN
P, TIGERS

PERSONAL: Born September 30, 1967, at Fort Bragg, Calif. . . . 6-0/193. . . . Throws right, bats right. . . . Full name: John Reed DeSilva.
COLLEGE: Brigham Young.
TRANSACTIONS/CAREER NOTES: Selected by Chicago White Sox organization in 30th round of free-agent draft (June 1, 1988). . . . Selected by Detroit Tigers organization in eighth round of free-agent draft (June 5, 1989).

Year	Team (League)	G	W	L	Pct.	ERA	Sv.	IP	H	R	ER	BB	SO
1989—Niagara Falls (N.Y.-Penn)		4	3	0	1.000	1.88	0	24	15	5	5	8	24
—Fayetteville (South Atlantic)		9	2	2	.500	2.68	0	53⅔	40	23	16	21	54
1990—Lakeland (Florida State)		14	8	1	.889	1.48	0	91	54	18	15	25	113
—London (Eastern)		14	5	6	.455	3.84	0	89	87	47	38	27	76
1991—London (Eastern)		11	5	4	.556	2.81	0	73⅔	51	24	23	24	80
—Toledo (International)		11	5	5	.556	4.60	0	58⅔	62	33	30	21	56

DEVARES, CESAR
C, ORIOLES

PERSONAL: Born September 22, 1969, at San Pedro de Macoris, Dominican Republic. . . . 5-10/175. . . . Throws right, bats right. . . . Full name: Cesar Salvatore Devares.
TRANSACTIONS/CAREER NOTES: Signed as free agent by Baltimore Orioles organization (February 6, 1988). . . . On disabled list (July 16-August 29, 1991).

Year	Team (League)	Pos.	G	AB	R	H	2B	3B	HR	RBI	Avg.	SB	PO	A	E	Avg.
1989—Bluefield (Appalachian)		C	12	42	3	9	4	0	0	7	.214	0	59	12	3	.959
1990—Wausau (Midwest)		C-3B	56	171	7	34	4	1	3	19	.199	2	320	31	8	.978
1991—Frederick (Carolina)		C-OF	74	235	25	59	13	2	3	29	.251	2	443	70	5	.990

DEVEREAUX, MIKE
OF, ORIOLES

PERSONAL: Born April 10, 1963, at Casper, Wyo. . . . 6-0/195. . . . Throws right, bats right. . . . Full name: Michael Devereaux. . . . Name pronounced DEH-ver-oh.
HIGH SCHOOL: Kelly Walsh (Casper, Wyo.).
COLLEGE: Mesa Community College (Ariz.) and Arizona State (bachelor of arts degree in finance).
TRANSACTIONS/CAREER NOTES: Selected by Cleveland Indians organization in 26th round of free-agent draft (June 4, 1984). . . . Selected by Los Angeles Dodgers organization in fifth round of free-agent draft (June 3, 1985). . . . Traded by Dodgers to Baltimore Orioles for P Mike Morgan (March 12, 1989). . . . On Baltimore disabled list (May 17-June 15, 1990); included rehabilitation disability assignment to Frederick (June 9-10, 1990) and Hagerstown (June 11-15, 1990).
STATISTICAL NOTES: Led Pioneer League with 152 total bases in 1985. . . . Led Texas League with 11 sacrifice flies in 1987. . . . Led Texas League outfielders with 349 total chances in 1987.

Year — Team (League)	Pos.	G	AB	R	H	2B	3B	HR	RBI	Avg.	SB	PO	A	E	Avg.
1985 — Great Falls (Pioneer)	OF	•70	★289	★73	★103	17	10	4	★67	.356	★40	100	4	5	.954
1986 — San Antonio (Texas)	OF	115	431	69	130	22	2	10	53	.302	31	292	13	4	.987
1987 — San Antonio (Texas)	OF	★135	★562	90	169	28	9	26	91	.301	33	★339	7	3	★.991
— Albuquerque (PCL)	OF	3	11	2	3	1	0	1	1	.273	1	4	1	0	1.000
— Los Angeles (N.L.)	OF	19	54	7	12	3	0	0	4	.222	3	21	1	0	1.000
1988 — Albuquerque (PCL)	OF	109	423	88	144	26	4	13	76	.340	33	211	5	7	.969
— Los Angeles (N.L.)	OF	30	43	4	5	1	0	0	2	.116	0	29	0	0	1.000
1989 — Baltimore (A.L.)■	OF	122	391	55	104	14	3	8	46	.266	22	288	1	5	.983
1990 — Baltimore (A.L.)	OF	108	367	48	88	18	1	12	49	.240	13	281	4	5	.983
— Frederick (Carolina)	OF	2	8	3	4	0	0	1	3	.500	1	4	2	0	1.000
— Hagerstown (Eastern)	OF	4	20	4	5	3	0	0	3	.250	1	13	0	1	.929
1991 — Baltimore (A.L.)	OF	149	608	82	158	27	10	19	59	.260	16	399	10	3	.993
American League totals (3 years)		379	1366	185	350	59	14	39	154	.256	51	968	15	13	.987
National League totals (2 years)		49	97	11	17	4	0	0	6	.175	3	50	1	0	1.000
Major league totals (5 years)		428	1463	196	367	63	14	39	160	.251	54	1018	16	13	.988

DIAZ, MARIO
IF, BREWERS

PERSONAL: Born January 10, 1962, at Humacao, Puerto Rico. . . . 5- 10/160. . . . Throws right, bats right. . . . Full name: Mario Rafael Torres Diaz. . . . Name pronounced DEE-az.
HIGH SCHOOL: Teodor Aguilar Mora (Humacao, Puerto Rico).
TRANSACTIONS/CAREER NOTES: Signed as free agent by Seattle Mariners organization (December 21, 1978). . . . On Seattle disabled list (May 6-23, 1988); included rehabilitation disability assignment to Calgary (May 16-23, 1988). . . . On Seattle disabled list (March 31-May 4, 1990). . . . Traded by Mariners organization to Tidewater (New York Mets organization) for P Brian Givens (June 19, 1990). . . . Granted free agency (October 15, 1990). . . . Signed by Texas Rangers (December 14, 1990). . . . On disabled list (June 24-July 11, 1991). . . . Granted free agency (October 15, 1991). . . . Signed by Denver, Milwaukee Brewers organization (December 16, 1991).
STATISTICAL NOTES: Led Southern League with 14 sacrifice hits in 1985.

Year — Team (League)	Pos.	G	AB	R	H	2B	3B	HR	RBI	Avg.	SB	PO	A	E	Avg.
1979 — Bellingham (Northwest)	SS-3B-2B	32	96	12	19	2	0	1	5	.198	0	28	69	8	.924
1980 — Wausau (Midwest)	SS-2B	110	349	28	63	5	0	3	21	.181	5	172	328	41	.924
1981 — Lynn (Eastern)	SS	106	314	16	63	8	1	1	22	.201	1	163	318	18	★.964
1982 — Lynn (Eastern)	SS-1B	53	162	19	35	7	1	1	13	.216	2	384	172	18	.969
— Salt Lake City (PCL)	SS	5	19	2	7	1	0	0	2	.368	0	4	15	1	.950
— Wausau (Midwest)	SS	56	187	15	49	8	1	1	23	.262	3	78	148	16	.934
1983 — Bakersfield (California)	SS-2B	51	171	23	41	5	1	0	10	.240	3	92	146	22	.915
— Chattanooga (Southern)	SS	33	111	18	30	6	5	2	13	.270	4	48	80	10	.928
1984 — Chattanooga (Southern)	SS-2B	108	322	23	67	7	1	1	19	.208	6	179	313	26	.950
1985 — Chattanooga (Southern)	SS	115	400	38	101	6	7	0	38	.253	3	186	314	31	.942
1986 — Calgary (Pacific Coast)	SS	109	379	40	107	17	6	1	41	.282	1	194	302	16	.969
1987 — Calgary (Pacific Coast)	SS	108	376	52	106	17	3	4	52	.282	1	195	280	21	.958
— Seattle (A.L.)	SS	11	23	4	7	0	1	0	3	.304	0	10	25	1	.972
1988 — Calgary (Pacific Coast)	SS	46	164	16	54	18	0	1	30	.329	1	65	138	12	.944
— Seattle (A.L.)	S-2-1-3	28	72	6	22	5	0	0	9	.306	0	31	47	1	.987
1989 — Seattle (A.L.)	SS-2B-3B	52	74	9	10	0	0	1	7	.135	0	35	54	5	.947
— Calgary (Pacific Coast)	2B-SS-1B	37	127	22	43	8	1	2	9	.339	1	64	73	9	.938
1990 — Calgary (Pacific Coast)	3B-SS-2B	32	105	10	35	5	1	1	19	.333	0	35	61	2	.980
— Tidewater (Int'l)■	SS-3B	29	104	15	33	8	0	1	9	.317	1	38	92	6	.956
— New York (N.L.)	SS-2B	16	22	0	3	1	0	0	1	.136	0	5	18	1	.958
1991 — Texas (A.L.)■	SS-2B-3B	96	182	24	48	7	0	1	22	.264	0	93	143	7	.971
American League totals (4 years)		187	351	43	87	12	1	2	41	.248	0	169	269	14	.969
National League totals (1 year)		16	22	0	3	1	0	0	1	.136	0	5	18	1	.958
Major league totals (5 years)		203	373	43	90	13	1	2	42	.241	0	174	287	15	.968

DIBBLE, ROB
P, REDS

PERSONAL: Born January 24, 1964, at Bridgeport, Conn. . . . 6-4/230. . . . Throws right, bats left. . . . Full name: Robert Keith Dibble.
HIGH SCHOOL: Southington (Conn.).
COLLEGE: Florida Southern.
TRANSACTIONS/CAREER NOTES: Selected by St. Louis Cardinals organization in 11th round of free-agent draft (June 7, 1982). . . . Selected by Cincinnati Reds organization in secondary phase of free-agent draft (June 6, 1983). . . . On suspended list (May 31-June 2 and July 25-28, 1989). . . . On disabled list (July 10-25, 1989). . . . On suspended list (July 19-23 and July 31-August 3, 1991).
RECORDS/HONORS: Shares major league record by striking out side on nine pitches (June 4, 1989, eighth inning). . . . Shares N.L. single-game record for most consecutive strikeouts by a relief pitcher—6 (April 23, 1991).

Year — Team (League)	G	W	L	Pct.	ERA	Sv.	IP	H	R	ER	BB	SO
1983 — Billings (Pioneer)	5	0	1	.000	7.82	0	12⅔	18	13	11	11	7
— Eugene (Northwest)	7	3	2	.600	5.73	0	37⅔	38	28	24	18	17
1984 — Tampa (Florida State)	15	5	2	.714	2.92	0	64⅔	59	31	21	29	39
1985 — Cedar Rapids (Midwest)	45	5	5	.500	3.84	12	65⅔	67	37	28	28	73
1986 — Vermont (Eastern)	31	3	2	.600	3.09	10	55⅓	53	29	19	28	37
— Denver (American Assoc.)	5	1	0	1.000	5.40	0	6⅔	9	4	4	2	3

Year Team (League)	G	W	L	Pct.	ERA	Sv.	IP	H	R	ER	BB	SO
1987—Nashville (American Assoc.)....	44	2	4	.333	4.72	4	61	72	34	32	27	51
1988—Nashville (American Assoc.)....	31	2	1	.667	2.31	13	35	21	9	9	14	41
—Cincinnati (N.L.)	37	1	1	.500	1.82	0	59⅓	43	12	12	21	59
1989—Cincinnati (N.L.)	74	10	5	.667	2.09	2	99	62	23	23	39	141
1990—Cincinnati (N.L.)	68	8	3	.727	1.74	11	98	62	22	19	34	136
1991—Cincinnati (N.L.)	67	3	5	.375	3.17	31	82⅓	67	32	29	25	124
Major league totals (4 years)	246	22	14	.611	2.21	44	338⅔	234	89	83	119	460

CHAMPIONSHIP SERIES RECORD

Year Team (League)	G	W	L	Pct.	ERA	Sv.	IP	H	R	ER	BB	SO
1990—Cincinnati (N.L.)	4	0	0	...	0.00	1	5	0	0	0	1	10

WORLD SERIES RECORD

Year Team (League)	G	W	L	Pct.	ERA	Sv.	IP	H	R	ER	BB	SO
1990—Cincinnati (N.L.)	3	1	0	1.000	0.00	0	4⅔	3	0	0	1	4

ALL-STAR GAME RECORD

Year League	W	L	Pct.	ERA	Sv.	IP	H	R	ER	BB	SO
1990—National	0	0	...	0.00	0	1	1	0	0	1	0
1991—National	0	0	...	0.00	0	1	0	0	0	1	1
All-Star totals (2 years)	0	0	...	0.00	0	2	1	0	0	2	1

DICKSON, LANCE
P, CUBS

PERSONAL: Born October 19, 1969, at Fullerton, Calif.... 6-1/185.... Throws left, bats right.... Full name: Lance Michael Dickson.
HIGH SCHOOL: Grossmont (La Mesa, Calif.).
COLLEGE: Arizona.
TRANSACTIONS/CAREER NOTES: Selected by Houston Astros organization in 37th round of free-agent draft (June 2, 1987).... Selected by Chicago Cubs organization in first round (23rd pick overall) of free-agent draft (June 4, 1990).... On Chicago disabled list (August 19-September 11, 1990).... On disabled list (June 13-August 25, 1991).

Year Team (League)	G	W	L	Pct.	ERA	Sv.	IP	H	R	ER	BB	SO
1990—Geneva (New York-Penn)	3	2	1	.667	0.53	0	17	5	1	1	4	29
—Peoria (Midwest)	5	3	1	.750	1.51	0	35⅔	22	9	6	11	54
—Charlotte (Southern)	3	2	1	.667	0.38	0	23⅔	13	1	1	3	28
—Chicago (N.L.)	3	0	3	.000	7.24	0	13⅔	20	12	11	4	4
1991—Iowa (American Association) ...	18	4	4	.500	3.11	0	101⅓	85	39	35	57	101
Major league totals (1 year)	3	0	3	.000	7.24	0	13⅔	20	12	11	4	4

DiPINO, FRANK
P, CARDINALS

PERSONAL: Born October 22, 1956, at Syracuse, N.Y.... 6-0/194.... Throws left, bats left. ... Full name: Frank Michael DiPino.
HIGH SCHOOL: West Genesee (Camillus, N.Y.).
COLLEGE: St. Leo College (Fla.).
TRANSACTIONS/CAREER NOTES: Signed as free agent by Milwaukee Brewers organization (July 11, 1977).... On disabled list (May 19-June 11, 1979).... On Vancouver disabled list (May 9-June 10, 1981).... Traded by Brewers organization with OF Kevin Bass and P Mike Madden to Houston Astros (September 3, 1982), completing deal in which Astros traded P Don Sutton to Brewers for three players to be named later (August 30, 1982).... Traded by Astros to Chicago Cubs for OF Davey Lopes (July 21, 1986).... Granted free agency (November 4, 1988).... Signed by St. Louis Cardinals (December 21, 1988).... Granted free agency (November 13, 1989).... Re-signed by Cardinals (December 13, 1989).... On St. Louis disabled list (March 25, 1991-entire season); included rehabilitation disability assignment to Louisville (May 3-6, 1991).
STATISTICAL NOTES: Pitched seven-inning, 6-0 no-hit victory against Reading (June 8, 1980, second game).

Year Team (League)	G	W	L	Pct.	ERA	Sv.	IP	H	R	ER	BB	SO
1977—Newark (New York-Penn)	14	1	3	.250	2.48	2	29	14	12	8	22	41
1978—Burlington (Midwest)	15	5	4	.556	4.70	0	88	98	58	46	36	68
1979—Stockton (California)	16	5	3	.625	3.45	0	99	92	45	38	46	67
1980—Holyoke (Eastern)	16	7	0	1.000	1.30	0	76	46	13	11	27	58
—Vancouver (Pacific Coast)	24	3	1	.750	2.25	2	28	24	10	7	14	32
1981—Vancouver (Pacific Coast)	27	3	5	.375	4.33	4	81	83	45	39	39	81
—Milwaukee (A.L.)	2	0	0	...	0.00	0	2	0	0	0	3	3
1982—Vancouver (Pacific Coast)	26	13	9	.591	4.03	0	189⅔	187	102	85	86	115
—Houston (N.L.)■	6	2	2	.500	6.04	0	28⅓	32	20	19	11	25
1983—Houston (N.L.)	53	3	4	.429	2.65	20	71⅓	52	21	21	20	67
1984—Houston (N.L.)	57	4	9	.308	3.35	14	75⅓	74	32	28	36	65
1985—Houston (N.L.)	54	3	7	.300	4.03	6	76	69	44	34	43	49
1986—Houston-Chicago (N.L.)■	61	3	7	.300	4.37	3	80⅓	74	45	39	30	75
1987—Chicago (N.L.)	69	3	3	.500	3.15	4	80	75	31	28	34	61
1988—Chicago (N.L.)	63	2	2	.500	4.98	6	90⅓	102	54	50	32	69
1989—St. Louis (N.L.)■	67	9	0	1.000	2.45	0	88⅓	73	26	24	20	44
1990—St. Louis (N.L.)	62	5	2	.714	4.56	3	81	92	45	41	31	49
1991—Louisville (American Assoc.) ...	2	0	0	...	36.00	0	1	2	4	4	3	0
American League totals (1 year)	2	0	0	...	0.00	0	2	0	0	0	3	3
National League totals (9 years)	492	34	37	.479	3.81	56	671	643	318	284	257	499
Major league totals (10 years)	494	34	37	.479	3.80	56	673	643	318	284	260	502

DiPOTO, GERRY
P, INDIANS

PERSONAL: Born May 24, 1968, at Jersey City, N.J. . . . 6-2/203. . . . Throws right, bats right. . . . Full name: Gerard Peter DiPoto III.
HIGH SCHOOL: Toms River (N.J.).
COLLEGE: Virginia Commonwealth.
TRANSACTIONS/CAREER NOTES: Selected by Cleveland Indians organization in third round of free-agent draft (June 5, 1989).
STATISTICAL NOTES: Tied for Eastern League lead in balks with three and led league in wild pitches with 15 in 1991.

Year	Team (League)	G	W	L	Pct.	ERA	Sv.	IP	H	R	ER	BB	SO
1989	—Watertown (New York-Penn)...	14	6	5	.545	3.61	0	87⅓	75	42	35	39	98
1990	—Kinston (Carolina)	24	11	4	.733	3.78	0	145⅓	129	75	61	77	143
	—Canton/Akron (Eastern)	3	1	0	1.000	2.57	0	14	11	5	4	4	12
1991	—Canton/Akron (Eastern)	28	6	11	.353	3.81	0	156	143	83	66	74	97

DiSARCINA, GARY
2B/SS, ANGELS

PERSONAL: Born November 19, 1967, at Malden, Mass. . . . 6-1/178. . . . Throws right, bats right. . . . Full name: Gary Thomas DiSarcina. . . . Name pronounced DEE-sar-SEE-na.
HIGH SCHOOL: Bellerica (Mass.).
COLLEGE: Massachusetts.
TRANSACTIONS/CAREER NOTES: Selected by California Angels organization in sixth round of free-agent draft (June 1, 1988).
STATISTICAL NOTES: Led Pacific Coast League shortstops with .968 fielding percentage and 419 assists in 1991.

Year	Team (League)	Pos.	G	AB	R	H	2B	3B	HR	RBI	Avg.	SB	PO	A	E	Avg.
1988	—Bend (Northwest)	SS	71	295	40	90	11	•5	2	39	.305	7	104	★237	27	.927
1989	—Midland (Texas)	SS	126	441	65	126	18	7	4	54	.286	11	206	★411	30	★.954
1990	—Edmonton (Pac. Coast)	SS	97	330	46	70	12	2	4	37	.212	5	165	289	24	.950
	—California (A.L.)	SS-2B	18	57	8	8	1	1	0	0	.140	1	17	57	4	.949
1991	—Edmonton (Pac. Coast)	SS-2B	119	390	61	121	21	4	4	58	.310	16	191	†425	20	†.969
	—California (A.L.)	SS-2B-3B	18	57	5	12	2	0	0	3	.211	0	29	45	4	.949
	Major league totals (2 years)		36	114	13	20	3	1	0	3	.175	1	46	102	8	.949

DOHERTY, JOHN
P, TIGERS

PERSONAL: Born June 11, 1967, at Bronx, N.Y. . . . 6-4/190. . . . Throws right, bats right. . . . Full name: John H. Doherty.
COLLEGE: Concordia, N.Y. (received degree).
TRANSACTIONS/CAREER NOTES: Selected by Detroit Tigers organization in 19th round of free-agent draft (June 5, 1989).
STATISTICAL NOTES: Tied for Eastern League lead with three balks in 1991.

Year	Team (League)	G	W	L	Pct.	ERA	Sv.	IP	H	R	ER	BB	SO
1989	—Niagara Falls (N.Y.-Penn)	26	1	1	.500	0.95	14	47⅓	30	7	5	6	45
1990	—Fayetteville (South Atlantic)	7	1	0	1.000	5.79	1	9⅓	17	12	6	1	6
	—Lakeland (Florida State)	30	5	1	.833	1.10	10	41	33	7	5	5	23
1991	—London (Eastern)	53	3	3	.500	2.22	15	65	62	29	16	21	42

DONNELS, CHRIS
3B/1B, METS

PERSONAL: Born April 21, 1966, at Los Angeles. . . . 6-0/185. . . . Throws right, bats left. . . . Full name: Chris Barton Donnels. . . . Name pronounced DONN-uls.
HIGH SCHOOL: South Torrance (Calif.).
COLLEGE: Loyola Marymount.
TRANSACTIONS/CAREER NOTES: Selected by New York Mets organization in first round (24th pick overall) of free-agent draft (June 2, 1987). . . . On Tidewater disabled list (June 20-28, 1991).
RECORDS/HONORS: Named Florida State League Most Valuable Player (1989).
STATISTICAL NOTES: Led Florida State League with .510 slugging percentage and 15 intentional bases on balls received in 1989. . . . Led Florida State League third basemen with 93 putouts, 202 assists and 320 total chances in 1989. . . . Led Texas League with 111 bases on balls received in 1990. . . . Led Texas League third basemen with 79 putouts, 242 assists, 31 errors, 352 total chances and 24 double plays in 1990.

Year	Team (League)	Pos.	G	AB	R	H	2B	3B	HR	RBI	Avg.	SB	PO	A	E	Avg.
1987	—Kingsport (Appalachian)	3B	26	86	18	26	4	0	3	16	.302	4	16	44	6	.909
	—Columbia (S. Atlantic)	3B	41	136	20	35	7	0	2	17	.257	3	32	86	10	.922
1988	—St. Lucie (Florida State)	3B	65	198	25	43	14	2	3	22	.217	4	40	116	15	.912
	—Columbia (S. Atlantic)	3B	42	133	19	32	6	0	2	13	.241	5	29	84	7	.942
1989	—St. Lucie (Florida State)	3B-1B	117	386	70	121	23	1	17	★78	.313	18	†242	†209	28	.942
1990	—Jackson (Texas)	3B-1B-2B	130	419	66	114	24	0	12	63	.272	11	†95	†244	†32	.914
1991	—Tidewater (Int'l)	3B-2B	84	287	45	87	19	2	8	56	.303	1	88	189	14	.952
	—New York (N.L.)	1B-3B	37	89	7	20	2	0	0	5	.225	1	131	34	2	.988
	Major league totals (1 year)		37	89	7	20	2	0	0	5	.225	1	131	34	2	.988

DOPSON, JOHN
P, RED SOX

PERSONAL: Born July 14, 1963, at Baltimore. . . . 6-4/235. . . . Throws right, bats left. . . . Full name: John Robert Dopson Jr.
HIGH SCHOOL: Delone Catholic (Hanover, Pa.).
TRANSACTIONS/CAREER NOTES: Selected by Montreal Expos organization in second round of

free-agent draft (June 7, 1982).... On suspended list (May 24-31, 1984).... On Indianapolis disabled list (June 24-July 15, 1985; April 10-May 12, May 29-June 23 and July 7, 1986-remainder of season).... Traded by Expos with SS Luis Rivera to Boston Red Sox for SS Spike Owen and P Dan Gakeler (December 8, 1988).... On Boston disabled list (August 2-28, 1989); included rehabilitation disability assignment to Pawtucket (August 18-28, 1989).... On Boston disabled list (April 28, 1990-remainder of season); included rehabilitation disability assignment to Pawtucket (May 15-June 4 and August 10-22, 1990). .... On Boston disabled list (April 5-September 3, 1991); included rehabilitation disability assignment to Winter Haven (August 2-31, 1991).

STATISTICAL NOTES: Led A.L. with 15 balks in 1989.

Year	Team (League)	G	W	L	Pct.	ERA	Sv.	IP	H	R	ER	BB	SO
1982	Jamestown (New York-Penn) ..	15	6	•8	.429	3.97	0	106⅔	117	58	47	34	62
1983	West Palm Beach (Florida St.) ..	23	13	6	.684	3.44	0	146⅔	141	82	56	38	69
1984	Jacksonville (Southern)	26	10	8	.556	3.69	0	170⅔	198	83	70	41	76
1985	Jacksonville (Southern)	5	3	0	1.000	1.11	0	32⅓	27	5	4	10	20
	Indianapolis (Am. Assoc.)	18	4	7	.364	3.78	0	95⅓	88	44	40	44	48
	Montreal (N.L.)	4	0	2	.000	11.08	0	13	25	17	16	4	4
1986	West Palm Beach (Florida St.) ..	2	2	0	1.000	0.00	0	10⅔	8	0	0	4	8
	Indianapolis (Am. Assoc.)	4	0	3	.000	4.50	0	16	18	12	8	11	6
1987	Jacksonville (Southern)	21	7	5	.583	3.80	0	118⅓	123	58	50	30	75
1988	Indianapolis (Am. Assoc.)	3	0	0	...	3.50	0	18	19	7	7	5	15
	Montreal (N.L.)	26	3	11	.214	3.04	0	168⅔	150	69	57	58	101
1989	Boston (A.L.)■	29	12	8	.600	3.99	0	169⅓	166	84	75	69	95
	Pawtucket (International)	2	0	2	.000	7.27	0	8⅔	13	9	7	1	9
1990	Boston (A.L.)	4	0	0	...	2.04	0	17⅔	13	7	4	9	9
	Pawtucket (International)	5	2	1	.667	4.91	0	22	28	12	12	8	13
1991	Boston (A.L.)	1	0	0	...	18.00	0	1	2	2	2	1	0
	Winter Haven (Florida State) ...	6	2	2	.500	3.38	0	26⅔	26	14	10	8	26
American League totals (3 years)		34	12	8	.600	3.88	0	188	181	93	81	79	104
National League totals (2 years)		30	3	13	.188	3.62	0	181⅔	175	86	73	62	105
Major league totals (5 years)		64	15	21	.417	3.75	0	369⅔	356	179	154	141	209

DORAN, BILL
2B, REDS

PERSONAL: Born May 28, 1958, at Cincinnati. ... 6-0/180. ... Throws right, bats both. ... Full name: William Donald Doran. ... Name pronounced DOOR-un.
HIGH SCHOOL: Mt. Healthy (Cincinnati).
COLLEGE: Miami of Ohio.
TRANSACTIONS/CAREER NOTES: Selected by Houston Astros organization in sixth round of free-agent draft (June 5, 1979).... On Houston disabled list (July 4-19, 1990).... Traded by Astros to Cincinnati Reds for three players to be named later (August 30, 1990); Astros acquired C Terry McGriff, P Keith Kaiser and P Butch Henry to complete deal (September 7, 1990).... Granted free agency (November 5, 1990).... Re-signed by Reds (December 5, 1990).... On disabled list (May 13-June 4, 1991).
STATISTICAL NOTES: Led Gulf Coast League second basemen with 33 double plays in 1979.... Led Pacific Coast League second basemen with 123 double plays in 1982.... Led N.L. in caught stealing with 19 in 1986.... Led N.L. second basemen with .992 fielding percentage in 1987.

						BATTING						FIELDING			
Year	Team (League)	Pos.	G	AB	R	H	2B	3B	HR	RBI	Avg.	SB	PO	A	E	Avg.
1979	Sarasota Astros (GCL)......	2B	44	164	21	42	6	0	1	16	.256	3	107	★144	11	.958
1980	Daytona Beach (Fla. St.) ..	2B-SS	102	369	62	90	11	3	2	45	.244	20	232	259	21	.959
1981	Columbus (Southern)........	2B-SS	124	427	83	120	17	7	5	56	.281	18	263	355	17	.973
1982	Tucson (Pacific Coast)	2B	★142	559	100	169	32	7	1	65	.302	48	★361	★424	★23	.972
	Houston (N.L.)	2B	26	97	11	27	3	0	0	6	.278	5	41	78	3	.975
1983	Houston (N.L.)	2B	154	535	70	145	12	7	8	39	.271	12	★347	461	17	.979
1984	Houston (N.L.)	2B-SS	147	548	92	143	18	11	4	41	.261	21	274	440	12	.983
1985	Houston (N.L.)	2B	148	578	84	166	31	6	14	59	.287	23	345	440	16	.980
1986	Houston (N.L.)	2B	145	550	92	152	29	3	6	37	.276	42	262	329	16	.974
1987	Houston (N.L.)	2B-SS	★162	625	82	177	23	3	16	79	.283	31	300	432	7	†.991
1988	Houston (N.L.)	2B	132	480	66	119	18	1	7	53	.248	17	260	371	8	★.987
1989	Houston (N.L.)	2B	142	507	65	111	25	2	8	58	.219	22	254	345	12	.980
1990	Houston-Cin. (N.L.)■	2B-3B	126	403	59	121	29	2	7	37	.300	23	198	306	8	.984
1991	Cincinnati (N.L.)	2B-OF-1B	111	361	51	101	12	2	6	35	.280	5	183	208	7	.982
Major league totals (10 years)			1293	4684	672	1262	200	37	76	444	.269	201	2464	3410	106	.982

CHAMPIONSHIP SERIES RECORD
CHAMPIONSHIP SERIES NOTES: Shares single-game record for most at-bats—7 (October 15, 1986, 16 innings).

						BATTING						FIELDING			
Year	Team (League)	Pos.	G	AB	R	H	2B	3B	HR	RBI	Avg.	SB	PO	A	E	Avg.
1986	Houston (N.L.)	2B	6	27	3	6	0	0	1	3	.222	2	9	17	0	1.000

DORSETT, BRIAN
1B/C, PIRATES

PERSONAL: Born April 9, 1961, at Terre Haute, Ind. ... 6-3/215. ... Throws right, bats right.... Full name: Brian Richard Dorsett.
HIGH SCHOOL: Terre Haute North (Ind.).
COLLEGE: Indiana State.
TRANSACTIONS/CAREER NOTES: Selected by Oakland Athletics organization in 10th round of free-agent draft (June 6, 1983)....

On disabled list (June 18-July 24, 1984).... Traded by A's organization with P Darrel Akerfelds to Cleveland Indians for 2B Tony Bernazard (July 15, 1987).... On Cleveland disabled list (March 26-June 7, 1988).... Traded by Indians organization to California Angels for a player to be named later (June 7, 1988); Indians acquired P Colby Ward to complete deal (July 15, 1989).... Traded by Angels to New York Yankees for P Eric Schmidt (November 17, 1988).... Released by Yankees (November 19, 1990).... Signed by San Diego Padres (January 15, 1991).... Traded by Padres organization to Pittsburgh Pirates organization for P Lynn Carlson (August 2, 1991).... Granted free agency (October 15, 1991).... Signed by Pittsburgh Pirates organization (January 22, 1992).

STATISTICAL NOTES: Led International League with 13 passed balls in 1990.

Year	Team (League)	Pos.	G	AB	R	H	2B	3B	HR	RBI	Avg.	SB	PO	A	E	Avg.
1983	—Medford (Northwest)	C	14	48	11	13	2	1	1	10	.271	0	85	8	2	.979
	—Madison (Midwest)	C	58	204	16	52	7	0	3	27	.255	2	337	51	6	.985
1984	—Modesto (California)	C-1B	99	375	39	99	19	0	8	52	.264	0	511	76	13	.978
1985	—Madison (Midwest)	C	40	161	15	43	11	0	2	30	.267	0	194	40	5	.979
	—Huntsville (Southern)	C	88	313	38	84	18	3	11	43	.268	2	437	51	10	.980
1986	—Tacoma (Pacific Coast)	C	117	426	49	111	33	1	10	51	.261	0	420	54	18	.963
1987	—Tacoma (Pacific Coast)	C	78	282	31	66	14	1	6	39	.234	0	341	51	4	.990
	—Buffalo (Am. Assoc.)■......	C	26	86	9	22	5	1	4	14	.256	0	119	9	1	.992
	—Cleveland (A.L.)	C	5	11	2	3	0	0	1	3	.273	0	12	0	0	1.000
1988	—Colo. Spgs.-Edm. (PCL)■..	C-1B	53	163	21	43	7	0	11	32	.264	0	283	37	5	.985
	—California (A.L.)	C	7	11	0	1	0	0	0	2	.091	0	19	3	0	1.000
1989	—Columbus (Int'l)■	C	110	388	45	97	21	1	17	62	.250	2	482	47	7	.987
	—New York (A.L.)	C	8	22	3	8	1	0	0	4	.364	0	29	3	0	1.000
1990	—Columbus (Int'l)	C	114	415	44	113	28	1	14	67	.272	1	548	37	11	.982
	—New York (A.L.)	C	14	35	2	5	2	0	0	0	.143	0	31	0	0	1.000
1991	—Las Vegas (Pac. Coast)■..	C-1B-3B	62	215	36	66	13	1	13	38	.307	0	312	29	6	.983
	—San Diego (N.L.)	1B	11	12	0	1	0	0	0	1	.083	0	4	1	0	1.000
	—Buffalo (Am. Assoc.)■......	1B-C	29	103	17	28	6	0	2	18	.272	0	186	20	7	.967
American League totals (4 years)			34	79	7	17	3	0	1	9	.215	0	91	6	0	1.000
National League totals (1 year)			11	12	0	1	0	0	0	1	.083	0	4	1	0	1.000
Major league totals (5 years)			45	91	7	18	3	0	1	10	.198	0	95	7	0	1.000

DOSTAL, BRUCE
OF, PHILLIES

PERSONAL: Born March 10, 1965, at Montville, N.J. ... 6-0/195. ... Throws right, bats left. ... Full name: Bruce Wayne Dostal.
HIGH SCHOOL: Montville (N.J.).
COLLEGE: William Patterson College (N.J.).
TRANSACTIONS/CAREER NOTES: Selected by Los Angeles Dodgers organization in 17th round of free-agent draft (June 2, 1987). ... Drafted by Philadelphia Phillies organization (December 4, 1990). ... On disabled list (June 14-27 and July 2-25, 1991).

Year	Team (League)	Pos.	G	AB	R	H	2B	3B	HR	RBI	Avg.	SB	PO	A	E	Avg.
1987	—Great Falls (Pioneer)	OF	62	201	27	56	6	1	1	27	.279	14	78	4	3	.965
1988	—Bakersfield (California) ...	OF	122	367	59	92	14	2	1	34	.251	32	163	8	8	.955
1989	—Vero Beach (Florida St.) ...	OF	118	348	58	86	10	5	2	24	.247	41	160	8	6	.966
1990	—Vero Beach (Florida St.) ...	OF	58	192	43	58	9	2	6	29	.302	31	112	3	0	1.000
	—San Antonio (Texas)	OF	53	127	16	33	3	4	0	16	.260	10	43	1	1	.978
1991	—Reading (Eastern)■..........	OF	96	364	68	114	11	5	5	34	.313	38	224	7	6	.975

DOWNING, BRIAN
DH, RANGERS

PERSONAL: Born October 9, 1950, at Los Angeles. ... 5-10/194. ... Throws right, bats right. ... Full name: Brian Jay Downing.
HIGH SCHOOL: Magnolia (Anaheim, Calif.).
COLLEGE: Cypress Junior College (Calif.).
TRANSACTIONS/CAREER NOTES: Signed as free agent by Chicago White Sox organization (August 19, 1969). ... On disabled list (June 1-July 9, 1973 and July 30-August 15, 1976). ... Traded by White Sox with P Chris Knapp and P Dave Frost to California Angels for OF Bobby Bonds, OF Thad Bosley and P Richard Dotson (December 5, 1977). ... On disabled list (April 20-September 1, 1980 and May 10-June 20, 1983). ... Granted free agency (November 12, 1986). ... Re-signed by Angels (January 8, 1987). ... On disabled list (April 20-May 6, 1988). ... Granted free agency (November 5, 1990). ... Signed by Texas Rangers (April 13, 1991). ... Granted free agency (October 30, 1991). ... Re-signed by Rangers (December 7, 1991).
RECORDS/HONORS: Holds A.L. record for most consecutive errorless games by an outfielder—244 (May 25, 1981-July 21, second game, 1983). ... Shares major league single-season records for highest fielding percentage by outfielder (150 or more games)—1,000 (1982); fewest errors by outfielder (150 or more games)—0 (1982); and fewest double plays by outfielder (150 or more games)—0 (1982).
STATISTICAL NOTES: Tied for A.L. lead with 106 bases on balls received in 1987.

Year	Team (League)	Pos.	G	AB	R	H	2B	3B	HR	RBI	Avg.	SB	PO	A	E	Avg.
1970	—Sara. White Sox (GCL)	C-OF	34	96	16	21	1	1	0	14	.219	2	167	11	1	.994
1971	—Appleton (Midwest)	3B-OF	99	333	51	82	6	3	3	22	.246	5	353	98	13	.972
1972	—Knoxville (Southern)	OF-3B-C	135	442	75	123	24	7	15	67	.278	3	250	123	21	.947
1973	—Iowa (American Assoc.) ...	3B-OF-C	68	228	34	56	6	1	7	27	.246	1	84	90	6	.956
	—Chicago (A.L.)	OF-C-3B	34	73	5	13	1	0	2	4	.178	0	72	17	5	.947
1974	—Chicago (A.L.)	C-OF	108	293	41	66	12	1	10	39	.225	0	337	30	2	.995
1975	—Chicago (A.L.)	C	138	420	58	101	12	1	7	41	.240	13	730	84	8	.990

Year	Team (League)	Pos.	G	AB	R	H	2B	3B	HR	RBI	Avg.	SB	PO	A	E	Avg.
1976 —Chicago (A.L.)		C	104	317	38	81	14	0	3	30	.256	7	450	38	6	.988
1977 —Chicago (A.L.)		C-OF	69	169	28	48	4	2	4	25	.284	1	325	28	6	.983
1978 —California (A.L.)■		C	133	412	42	105	15	0	7	46	.255	3	681	82	5	.993
1979 —California (A.L.)		C	148	509	87	166	27	3	12	75	.326	3	669	35	11	.985
1980 —California (A.L.)		C	30	93	5	27	6	0	2	25	.290	0	69	6	0	1.000
1981 —California (A.L.)		OF-C	93	317	47	79	14	0	9	41	.249	1	237	18	2	.992
1982 —California (A.L.)		OF	158	623	109	175	37	2	28	84	.281	2	321	9	0•1.000
1983 —California (A.L.)		OF	113	403	68	99	15	1	19	53	.246	1	160	9	1	.994
1984 —California (A.L.)		OF	156	539	65	148	28	2	23	91	.275	0	272	5	0 ∗1.000
1985 —California (A.L.)		OF	150	520	80	137	23	1	20	85	.263	5	244	5	2	.992
1986 —California (A.L.)		OF	152	513	90	137	27	4	20	95	.267	5	267	5	3	.989
1987 —California (A.L.)		OF	155	567	110	154	29	3	29	77	.272	5	47	2	0	1.000
1988 —California (A.L.)		DH	135	484	80	117	18	2	25	64	.242	3	0	0	0	...
1989 —California (A.L.)		DH	142	544	59	154	25	2	14	59	.283	0	0	0	0	...
1990 —California (A.L.)		DH	96	330	47	90	18	2	14	51	.273	0	0	0	0	...
1991 —Texas (A.L.)■		DH	123	407	76	113	17	2	17	49	.278	1	0	0	0	...
Major league totals (19 years)			2237	7533	1135	2010	342	28	265	1034	.267	49	4881	373	51	.990

CHAMPIONSHIP SERIES RECORD

Year	Team (League)	Pos.	G	AB	R	H	2B	3B	HR	RBI	Avg.	SB	PO	A	E	Avg.
1979 —California (A.L.)		C	4	15	1	3	0	0	0	1	.200	0	27	0	0	1.000
1982 —California (A.L.)		OF	5	19	3	3	1	0	0	0	.158	0	5	0	0	1.000
1986 —California (A.L.)		OF	7	27	2	6	0	0	1	7	.222	0	18	0	0	1.000
Championship Series totals (3 years)			16	61	6	12	1	0	1	8	.197	0	50	0	0	1.000

ALL-STAR GAME RECORD

Year	League	Pos.	AB	R	H	2B	3B	HR	RBI	Avg.	SB	PO	A	E	Avg.
1979 —American		C	1	0	1	0	0	0	0	1.000	0	3	0	0	1.000

DOWNS, KELLY
P, GIANTS

PERSONAL: Born October 25, 1960, at Ogden, Utah.... 6-4/205.... Throws right, bats right. ... Full name: Kelly Robert Downs.... Brother of Dave Downs, pitcher, Philadelphia Phillies (1972).

HIGH SCHOOL: Viewmont (Bountiful, Utah).

TRANSACTIONS/CAREER NOTES: Selected by Philadelphia Phillies organization in 26th round of free-agent draft (June 5, 1979). ... Traded by Phillies organization with P George Riley to San Francisco Giants for 1B Al Oliver and a player to be named later (August 20, 1984); Phillies acquired P Renie Martin to complete deal (August 30, 1984).... On disabled list (August 31, 1988- remainder of season).... On San Francisco disabled list (May 2-August 13, 1989); included rehabilitation disability assign- ment to Phoenix (May 17-23 and August 7, 1989) and San Jose (August 8-12, 1989).... On San Francisco disabled list (April 3-August 10, 1990); included rehabilitation disability assignment to San Jose (July 31-August 6, 1990) and Phoenix (August 7-9, 1990).... On disabled list (April 2-17, 1991).

STATISTICAL NOTES: Tied for Pacific Coast League lead in games started by pitcher with 29 in 1983.

Year	Team (League)	G	W	L	Pct.	ERA	Sv.	IP	H	R	ER	BB	SO
1980 —Spartanburg (South Atlantic) ..	14	5	7	.417	2.60	0	90	85	41	26	17	40
1981 —Peninsula (Carolina)	25	13	7	.650	2.98	0	175	176	79	58	35	124
1982 —Oklahoma City (Am. Assoc.).....	32	2	∗15	.118	5.34	1	156⅔	182	∗116	93	72	70
1983 —Portland (Pacific Coast)	29	9	∗13	.409	4.46	0	159⅓	186	98	79	61	71
1984 —Portland (Pacific Coast)	30	7	12	.368	5.30	0	163	166	106	96	65	104
1985 —Phoenix (Pacific Coast)■	37	9	10	.474	4.01	1	137	138	69	61	56	109
1986 —Phoenix (Pacific Coast)	18	8	5	.615	3.42	0	108	116	54	41	28	68
—San Francisco (N.L.)	14	4	4	.500	2.75	0	88⅓	78	29	27	30	64
1987 —San Francisco (N.L.)	41	12	9	.571	3.63	1	186	185	83	75	67	137
1988 —San Francisco (N.L.)	27	13	9	.591	3.32	0	168	140	67	62	47	118
1989 —San Francisco (N.L.)	18	4	8	.333	4.79	0	82⅔	82	47	44	26	49
—Phoenix (Pacific Coast)	3	1	1	.500	8.68	0	9⅓	11	9	9	5	9
—San Jose (California)	1	0	0	...	0.00	0	5	1	0	0	4	7
1990 —San Jose (California)	1	0	1	.000	1.80	0	5	5	2	1	0	3
—Phoenix (Pacific Coast)	1	0	0	...	1.80	0	5	5	3	1	0	4
—San Francisco (N.L.)	13	3	2	.600	3.43	0	63	56	26	24	20	31
1991 —San Francisco (N.L.)	45	10	4	.714	4.19	0	111⅔	99	59	52	53	62
Major league totals (6 years)	158	46	36	.561	3.65	1	699⅔	640	311	284	243	461

CHAMPIONSHIP SERIES RECORD

Year	Team (League)	G	W	L	Pct.	ERA	Sv.	IP	H	R	ER	BB	SO
1987 —San Francisco (N.L.)	1	0	0	...	0.00	0	1⅓	1	0	0	0	0
1989 —San Francisco (N.L.)	2	1	0	1.000	3.12	0	8⅔	8	3	3	6	6
Championship Series totals (2 years)	3	1	0	1.000	2.70	0	10	9	3	3	6	6

WORLD SERIES RECORD

Year	Team (League)	G	W	L	Pct.	ERA	Sv.	IP	H	R	ER	BB	SO
1989 —San Francisco (N.L.)	3	0	0	...	7.71	0	4⅔	3	4	4	2	4

DRABEK, DOUG
P, PIRATES

PERSONAL: Born July 25, 1962, at Victoria, Tex. . . . 6-1/185. . . . Throws right, bats right. . . . Full name: Douglas Dean Drabek.
HIGH SCHOOL: St. Joseph (Victoria, Tex.).
COLLEGE: Houston.
TRANSACTIONS/CAREER NOTES: Selected by Cleveland Indians organization in fourth round of free-agent draft (June 3, 1980). . . . Selected by Chicago White Sox organization in 11th round of free-agent draft (June 6, 1983). . . . Traded by White Sox with P Kevin Hickey to New York Yankees organization (August 13, 1984), completing deal in which Yankess traded IF Roy Smalley to White Sox for two players to be named later (July 18, 1984). . . . Traded by Yankees with P Brian Fisher and P Logan Easley to Pittsburgh Pirates for P Rick Rhoden, P Cecilio Guante and P Pat Clements (November 26, 1986). . . . On disabled list (April 26-May 18, 1987).
RECORDS/HONORS: Named N.L. Pitcher of the Year by THE SPORTING NEWS (1990). . . . Named righthanded pitcher on THE SPORTING NEWS N.L. All-Star team (1990). . . . Named N.L. Cy Young Award winner by Baseball Writers' Association of America (1990).
MISCELLANEOUS: Appeared in one game as pinch-runner (1991).

Year	Team (League)	G	W	L	Pct.	ERA	Sv.	IP	H	R	ER	BB	SO
1983	—Niagara Falls (N.Y.-Penn)	16	6	7	.462	3.65	0	103⅔	99	52	42	48	103
1984	—Appleton (Midwest)	1	1	0	1.000	1.80	0	5	3	1	1	3	6
	—Glens Falls (Eastern)	19	12	5	.706	2.24	0	124⅔	90	34	31	44	75
	—Nashville (Southern)■	4	1	2	.333	2.32	0	31	30	11	8	10	22
1985	—Albany (Eastern)	26	13	7	.650	2.99	0	★192⅔	153	71	64	55	★153
1986	—Columbus (International)	8	1	4	.200	7.29	0	42	50	36	34	25	23
	—New York (A.L.)	27	7	8	.467	4.10	0	131⅔	126	64	60	50	76
1987	—Pittsburgh (N.L.)■	29	11	12	.478	3.88	0	176⅓	165	86	76	46	120
1988	—Pittsburgh (N.L.)	33	15	7	.682	3.08	0	219⅓	194	83	75	50	127
1989	—Pittsburgh (N.L.)	35	14	12	.538	2.80	0	244⅓	215	83	76	69	123
1990	—Pittsburgh (N.L.)	33	★22	6	.786	2.76	0	231⅓	190	78	71	56	131
1991	—Pittsburgh (N.L.)	35	15	14	.517	3.07	0	234⅔	245	92	80	62	142
	American League totals (1 year)	27	7	8	.467	4.10	0	131⅔	126	64	60	50	76
	National League totals (5 years)	165	77	51	.602	3.08	0	1106	1009	422	378	283	643
	Major league totals (6 years)	192	84	59	.587	3.19	0	1237⅔	1135	486	438	333	719

CHAMPIONSHIP SERIES RECORD
CHAMPIONSHIP SERIES NOTES: Shares N.L. career record for most complete games pitched—2.

Year	Team (League)	G	W	L	Pct.	ERA	Sv.	IP	H	R	ER	BB	SO
1990	—Pittsburgh (N.L.)	2	1	1	.500	1.65	0	16⅓	12	4	3	3	13
1991	—Pittsburgh (N.L.)	2	1	1	.500	0.60	0	15	10	1	1	5	10
	Championship Series totals (2 years)	4	2	2	.500	1.15	0	31⅓	22	5	4	8	23

DRAHMAN, BRIAN
P, WHITE SOX

PERSONAL: Born November 7, 1966, at Kenton, Ky. . . . 6-3/205. . . . Throws right, bats right. . . . Full name: Brian Stacy Drahman. . . . Name pronounced DRAY-man.
HIGH SCHOOL: Northeast (Fort Lauderdale, Fla.).
COLLEGE: Miami-Dade (South) Community College (Fla.).
TRANSACTIONS/CAREER NOTES: Selected by Cleveland Indians organization in 13th round of free-agent draft (January 14, 1986). . . . Selected by Milwaukee Brewers organization in secondary phase of free-agent draft (June 2, 1986). . . . Traded by Brewers organization to Chicago White Sox organization for P Jerry Reuss (July 31, 1989).

Year	Team (League)	G	W	L	Pct.	ERA	Sv.	IP	H	R	ER	BB	SO
1986	—Helena (Pioneer)	18	4	6	.400	5.92	2	65⅓	79	49	43	33	40
1987	—Beloit (Midwest)	46	6	5	.545	2.16	18	79	63	28	19	22	60
1988	—Stockton (California)	44	4	5	.444	2.02	14	62⅓	57	17	14	27	50
1989	—El Paso (Texas)	19	3	4	.429	7.26	2	31	52	31	25	11	23
	—Stockton (California)	12	3	2	.600	3.25	4	27⅔	22	11	10	9	30
	—Sarasota (Florida State)■	7	0	1	.000	3.24	1	16⅔	18	9	6	5	9
1990	—Birmingham (Southern)	50	6	4	.600	4.08	17	90⅓	90	50	41	24	72
1991	—Chicago (A.L.)	28	3	2	.600	3.23	0	30⅔	21	12	11	13	18
	—Vancouver (Pacific Coast)	22	2	3	.400	4.44	12	24⅓	21	12	12	13	17
	Major league totals (1 year)	28	3	2	.600	3.23	0	30⅔	21	12	11	13	18

DREES, TOM
P, RANGERS

PERSONAL: Born June 17, 1963, at Des Moines, Ia. . . . 6-6/210. . . . Throws left, bats both. . . . Full name: Thomas Kent Drees.
HIGH SCHOOL: Edina East (Minn.).
COLLEGE: Creighton (received degree, 1985).
TRANSACTIONS/CAREER NOTES: Selected by Chicago White Sox organization in 17th round of free-agent draft (June 3, 1985). . . . Granted free agency (October 15, 1991). . . . Signed by Texas Rangers organization (December 5, 1991).
STATISTICAL NOTES: Pitched 1-0 no-hit victory against Calgary (May 23, 1989). . . . Pitched 1-0 no-hit victory against Edmonton (May 28, 1989, first game). . . . Pitched 5-0 no-hit victory against Las Vegas (August 16, 1989, first game). . . . Led Pacific Coast League with 10 balks in 1989. . . . Led Pacific Coast League with three shutouts in 1991.

Year	Team (League)	G	W	L	Pct.	ERA	Sv.	IP	H	R	ER	BB	SO
1985	—Sarasota White Sox (GCL)	12	6	3	.667	2.78	0	74⅓	75	29	23	17	75
1986	—Peninsula (Carolina)	37	5	7	.417	4.75	2	94⅔	108	64	50	61	54
1987	—Daytona Beach (Florida State)	27	10	★14	.417	3.74	0	168⅔	195	87	70	58	76

Year	Team (League)	G	W	L	Pct.	ERA	Sv.	IP	H	R	ER	BB	SO
1988 —Birmingham (Southern)	22	9	7	.563	2.79	0	158	149	63	49	52	94
1989 —Vancouver (Pacific Coast)	26	12	11	.522	3.37	0	168⅓	142	76	63	72	66
1990 —Vancouver (Pacific Coast)	17	8	5	.615	3.98	0	97⅓	94	49	43	51	63
1991 —Vancouver (Pacific Coast)	22	8	8	.500	3.52	0	143	130	70	56	62	89
—Chicago (A.L.)	4	0	0	...	12.27	0	7⅓	10	10	10	6	2
Major league totals (1 year)	**4**	**0**	**0**	**...**	**12.27**	**0**	**7⅓**	**10**	**10**	**10**	**6**	**2**

DRESSENDORFER, KIRK

P, ATHLETICS

PERSONAL: Born April 8, 1969, at Houston. . . . 5-11/190. . . . Throws right, bats right. . . . Full name: Kirk Richard Dressendorfer.
HIGH SCHOOL: Pearland (Tex.).
COLLEGE: Texas.

TRANSACTIONS/CAREER NOTES: Selected by Baltimore Orioles organization in 34th round of free-agent draft (June 2, 1987). . . . Selected by Oakland Athletics organization in first round (36th pick overall) of free-agent draft (June 4, 1990). . . . On Oakland disabled list (May 22-July 2, 1991); included rehabilitation disability assignment to Tacoma (June 24-July 2, 1991).

Year	Team (League)	G	W	L	Pct.	ERA	Sv.	IP	H	R	ER	BB	SO
1990 —Southern Oregon (Northwest) ..	7	0	1	.000	2.33	0	19⅓	18	7	5	2	22
1991 —Oakland (A.L.)	7	3	3	.500	5.45	0	34⅔	33	28	21	21	17
—Tacoma (Pacific Coast)	8	1	3	.250	10.88	0	24	31	29	29	20	19
Major league totals (1 year)	**7**	**3**	**3**	**.500**	**5.45**	**0**	**34⅔**	**33**	**28**	**21**	**21**	**17**

DUCEY, ROB

OF, BLUE JAYS

PERSONAL: Born May 24, 1965, at Toronto. . . . 6-2/180. . . . Throws right, bats left. . . . Full name: Robert Thomas Ducey.
HIGH SCHOOL: Glenview Park (Toronto).
COLLEGE: Seminole Community College (Fla.).

TRANSACTIONS/CAREER NOTES: Signed as free agent by Toronto Blue Jays organization (May 16, 1984). . . . On Toronto disabled list (June 9-September 2, 1989); included rehabilitation disability assignment to Syracuse (July 5-14 and August 24-September 2, 1989).

STATISTICAL NOTES: Tied for Southern League lead in double plays by outfielders with six in 1986. . . . Tied for International League lead in double plays by outfielders with four in 1990.

							BATTING						FIELDING			
Year	Team (League)	Pos.	G	AB	R	H	2B	3B	HR	RBI	Avg.	SB	PO	A	E	Avg.
1984 —Medicine Hat (Pioneer)	OF-1B	63	235	49	71	10	3	12	49	.302	13	185	11	6	.970
1985 —Florence (S. Atlantic)	OF-1B	134	529	78	133	22	2	13	86	.251	12	228	8	9	.963
1986 —Ventura (California)	OF-1B	47	178	36	60	11	3	12	38	.337	17	97	3	2	.980
—Knoxville (Southern)	OF	88	344	49	106	22	3	11	58	.308	7	186	10	6	.970
1987 —Syracuse (International) ..	OF	100	359	62	102	14	•10	10	60	.284	8	171	13	6	.968
—Toronto (A.L.)	OF	34	48	12	9	1	0	1	6	.188	2	31	0	0	1.000
1988 —Syracuse (International) ..	OF	90	317	40	81	14	4	7	42	.256	7	233	6	4	.984
—Toronto (A.L.)	OF	27	54	15	17	4	1	0	6	.315	1	35	1	0	1.000
1989 —Toronto (A.L.)	OF	41	76	5	16	4	0	0	7	.211	2	56	3	0	1.000
—Syracuse (International) ..	OF	10	29	0	3	0	1	0	3	.103	0	14	0	1	.933
1990 —Syracuse (International) ..	OF	127	438	53	117	32	7	7	47	.267	13	262	13	13	.955
—Toronto (A.L.)	OF	19	53	7	16	5	0	0	7	.302	1	37	0	0	1.000
1991 —Syracuse (International) ..	OF	72	266	53	78	10	3	8	40	.293	5	120	1	0	1.000
—Toronto (A.L.)	OF	39	68	8	16	2	2	1	4	.235	2	32	1	4	.892
Major league totals (5 years)		160	299	47	74	16	3	2	30	.247	8	191	5	4	.980

CHAMPIONSHIP SERIES RECORD

							BATTING						FIELDING			
Year	Team (League)	Pos.	G	AB	R	H	2B	3B	HR	RBI	Avg.	SB	PO	A	E	Avg.
1991 —Toronto (A.L.)	PR-OF	1	1	0	0	0	0	0	0	.000	0	0	0	0	...

DUNCAN, MARIANO

IF/OF, PHILLIES

PERSONAL: Born March 13, 1963, at San Pedro de Macoris, Dominican Republic. . . . 6-0/185. . . . Throws right, bats right. . . . Full name: Mariano Duncan.
TRANSACTIONS/CAREER NOTES: Signed as free agent by Los Angeles Dodgers organization (January 17, 1982). . . . On Los Angeles disabled list (August 19-September 17, 1986; June 19-July 4 and August 16, 1987-remainder of season; May 28-June 12 and July 1-16, 1989). . . . Traded by Dodgers with P Tim Leary to Cincinnati Reds for OF Kal Daniels and IF Lenny Harris (July 18, 1989). . . . On disabled list (May 14-30, 1990 and August 8-23, 1991). . . . Granted free agency (October 30, 1991). . . . Signed by Philadelphia Phillies (December 10, 1991).

STATISTICAL NOTES: Led Texas League second basemen with 84 double plays in 1984. . . . Led N.L. shortstops with 21 errors in 1987.

MISCELLANEOUS: Batted as switch-hitter (1982-1988).

							BATTING						FIELDING			
Year	Team (League)	Pos.	G	AB	R	H	2B	3B	HR	RBI	Avg.	SB	PO	A	E	Avg.
1982 —Lethbridge (Pioneer)	SS-2B	30	55	9	13	3	1	1	8	.236	1	23	35	15	.795
1983 —Vero Beach (Florida St.) ...	OF-SS-2B	109	384	73	102	10	*15	0	42	.266	*56	169	157	37	.898
1984 —San Antonio (Texas)	2B-OF-SS	125	502	80	127	14	•11	2	44	.253	41	283	335	22	.966

Year	Team (League)	Pos.	G	AB	R	H	2B	3B	HR	RBI	Avg.	SB	PO	A	E	Avg.
1985—Los Angeles (N.L.)		SS-2B	142	562	74	137	24	6	6	39	.244	38	224	430	30	.956
1986—Los Angeles (N.L.)		SS	109	407	47	93	7	0	8	30	.229	48	172	317	25	.951
1987—Los Angeles (N.L.)		SS-2B-OF	76	261	31	56	8	1	6	18	.215	11	101	213	†21	.937
—Albuquerque (PCL)		SS	6	22	6	6	0	0	0	0	.273	3	8	15	2	.920
1988—Albuquerque (PCL)		SS-2B	56	227	48	65	4	8	0	25	.286	33	104	153	18	.935
1989—Los Angeles-Cin. (N.L.)■		SS-2B-OF	94	258	32	64	15	2	3	21	.248	9	101	155	14	.948
1990—Cincinnati (N.L.)		2B-SS-OF	125	435	67	133	22	★11	10	55	.306	13	265	303	18	.969
1991—Cincinnati (N.L.)		2B-SS-OF	100	333	46	86	7	4	12	40	.258	5	169	212	9	.977
Major league totals (6 years)			646	2256	297	569	83	24	45	203	.252	124	1032	1630	117	.958

CHAMPIONSHIP SERIES RECORD

Year	Team (League)	Pos.	G	AB	R	H	2B	3B	HR	RBI	Avg.	SB	PO	A	E	Avg.
1985—Los Angeles (N.L.)		SS	5	18	2	4	2	1	0	1	.222	1	7	16	1	.958
1990—Cincinnati (N.L.)		2B	6	20	1	6	0	0	1	4	.300	0	6	11	1	.944
Championship Series totals (2 years)			11	38	3	10	2	1	1	5	.263	1	13	27	2	.952

WORLD SERIES RECORD

Year	Team (League)	Pos.	G	AB	R	H	2B	3B	HR	RBI	Avg.	SB	PO	A	E	Avg.
1990—Cincinnati (N.L.)		2B	4	14	1	2	0	0	0	1	.143	1	9	9	0	1.000

DUNSTON, SHAWON
SS, CUBS

PERSONAL: Born March 21, 1963, at Brooklyn, N.Y.... 6-1/175.... Throws right, bats right.... Full name: Shawon Donnell Dunston.
HIGH SCHOOL: Thomas Jefferson (Brooklyn, N.Y.).
TRANSACTIONS/CAREER NOTES: Selected by Chicago Cubs organization in first round (first pick overall) of free-agent draft (June 7, 1982).... On disabled list (May 31-June 10, 1983).... On Chicago disabled list (June 16-August 21, 1987); included rehabilitation disability assignment to Iowa (August 14-21, 1987).
RECORDS/HONORS: Shares modern major league single-game record for most triples—3 (July 28, 1990).... Named shortstop on THE SPORTING NEWS N.L. All-Star team (1989).
STATISTICAL NOTES: Led N.L. shortstops with 817 total chances and tied for lead in double plays with 96 in 1986.

Year	Team (League)	Pos.	G	AB	R	H	2B	3B	HR	RBI	Avg.	SB	PO	A	E	Avg.
1982—Sarasota Cubs (GCL)		SS-3B	53	190	27	61	11	0	2	28	.321	32	61	129	24	.888
1983—Quad Cities (Midwest)		SS	117	455	65	141	17	8	4	62	.310	58	172	326	47	.914
1984—Midland (Texas)		SS	73	298	44	98	13	3	3	34	.329	11	164	203	32	.920
—Iowa (American Assoc.)		SS	61	210	25	49	11	1	7	27	.233	9	90	165	26	.907
1985—Chicago (N.L.)		SS	74	250	40	65	12	4	4	18	.260	11	144	248	17	.958
—Iowa (American Assoc.)		SS	73	272	24	73	9	6	2	28	.268	17	138	176	12	.963
1986—Chicago (N.L.)		SS	150	581	66	145	36	3	17	68	.250	13	★320	★465	★32	.961
1987—Chicago (N.L.)		SS	95	346	40	85	18	3	5	22	.246	12	160	271	14	.969
—Iowa (American Assoc.)		SS	5	19	1	8	1	0	0	2	.421	1	6	12	1	.947
1988—Chicago (N.L.)		SS	155	575	69	143	23	6	9	56	.249	30	★257	455	20	.973
1989—Chicago (N.L.)		SS	138	471	52	131	20	6	9	60	.278	19	213	379	17	.972
1990—Chicago (N.L.)		SS	146	545	73	143	22	8	17	66	.262	25	255	392	20	.970
1991—Chicago (N.L.)		SS	142	492	59	128	22	7	12	50	.260	21	★261	383	21	.968
Major league totals (7 years)			900	3260	399	840	153	37	73	340	.258	131	1610	2593	141	.968

CHAMPIONSHIP SERIES RECORD

Year	Team (League)	Pos.	G	AB	R	H	2B	3B	HR	RBI	Avg.	SB	PO	A	E	Avg.
1989—Chicago (N.L.)		SS	5	19	2	6	0	0	0	0	.316	1	10	14	1	.960

ALL-STAR GAME RECORD

Year	League	Pos.	AB	R	H	2B	3B	HR	RBI	Avg.	SB	PO	A	E	Avg.
1988—National							Did not play								
1990—National		SS	2	0	0	0	0	0	0	.000	0	0	0	0	...

DYKSTRA, LENNY
OF, PHILLIES

PERSONAL: Born February 10, 1963, at Santa Ana, Calif.... 5-10/185.... Throws left, bats left.... Full name: Leonard Kyle Dykstra.... Grandson of Pete Leswick, National Hockey League player (1936-37 and 1944-45); nephew of Tony Leswick, NHL player (1945-46 through 1955-56 and 1957-58).... Name pronounced DIKE-struh.
HIGH SCHOOL: Garden Grove (Calif.).
TRANSACTIONS/CAREER NOTES: Selected by New York Mets organization in 12th round of free-agent draft (June 8, 1981).... Traded by Mets with P Roger McDowell and a player to be named later to Philadelphia Phillies for OF Juan Samuel (June 18, 1989); Phillies organization acquired P Tom Edens to complete deal (July 27, 1989).... On disabled list (May 6-July 15 and August 27, 1991-remainder of season).
RECORDS/HONORS: Named Carolina League Player of the Year (1983).
STATISTICAL NOTES: Led Carolina League in bases on balls received with 107 and in caught stealing with 23 in 1983.... Led N.L. outfielders with 452 total chances in 1990.... Led N.L. with .418 on base percentage in 1990.

Year	Team (League)	Pos.	G	AB	R	H	2B	3B	HR	RBI	Avg.	SB	PO	A	E	Avg.
1981—Shelby (South Atlantic)	OF-SS	48	157	34	41	7	2	0	18	.261	15	86	3	4	.957
1982—Shelby (South Atlantic)	OF	120	413	95	120	13	7	3	38	.291	77	239	11	14	.947
1983—Lynchburg (Carolina)	OF	•136	*525	*132	*188	24	*14	8	81	*.358	*105	268	9	7	.975
1984—Jackson (Texas)	OF	131	501	*100	138	25	7	6	52	.275	53	256	5	2	*.992
1985—Tidewater (Int'l)	OF	58	229	44	71	8	6	1	25	.310	26	184	4	5	.974
—New York (N.L.)	OF	83	236	40	60	9	3	1	19	.254	15	165	6	1	.994
1986—New York (N.L.)	OF	147	431	77	127	27	7	8	45	.295	31	283	8	3	.990
1987—New York (N.L.)	OF	132	431	86	123	37	3	10	43	.285	27	239	4	3	.988
1988—New York (N.L.)	OF	126	429	57	116	19	3	8	33	.270	30	270	3	1	.996
1989—New York-Phil. (N.L.)■	OF	146	511	66	121	32	4	7	32	.237	30	332	10	4	.988
1990—Philadelphia (N.L.)	OF	149	590	106	•192	35	3	9	60	.325	33	*439	7	6	.987
1991—Philadelphia (N.L.)	OF	63	246	48	73	13	5	3	12	.297	24	167	3	4	.977
Major league totals (7 years)		846	2874	480	812	172	28	46	244	.283	190	1895	41	22	.989

CHAMPIONSHIP SERIES RECORD

CHAMPIONSHIP SERIES NOTES: Shares single-series record for most times hit by pitch—2 (1988).

Year	Team (League)	Pos.	G	AB	R	H	2B	3B	HR	RBI	Avg.	SB	PO	A	E	Avg.
1986—New York (N.L.)	OF-PH	6	23	3	7	1	1	1	3	.304	1	10	0	0	1.000
1988—New York (N.L.)	PH-OF	7	14	6	6	3	0	1	3	.429	0	9	0	0	1.000
Championship Series totals (2 years)		13	37	9	13	4	1	2	6	.351	1	19	0	0	1.000

WORLD SERIES RECORD

Year	Team (League)	Pos.	G	AB	R	H	2B	3B	HR	RBI	Avg.	SB	PO	A	E	Avg.
1986—New York (N.L.)	OF-PH	7	27	4	8	0	0	2	3	.296	0	14	0	0	1.000

ALL-STAR GAME RECORD

Year	League	Pos.	AB	R	H	2B	3B	HR	RBI	Avg.	SB	PO	A	E	Avg.
1990—National	OF	4	0	1	0	0	0	0	.250	0	3	0	0	1.000

ECKERSLEY, DENNIS
P, ATHLETICS

PERSONAL: Born October 3, 1954, at Oakland, Calif.... 6-2/195.... Throws right, bats right.... Full name: Dennis Lee Eckersley.
HIGH SCHOOL: Washington (Fremont, Calif.).
TRANSACTIONS/CAREER NOTES: Selected by Cleveland Indians organization in third round of free-agent draft (June 6, 1972).... Traded by Indians with C Fred Kendall to Boston Red Sox for P Rick Wise, P Mike Paxton, 3B Ted Cox and C Bo Diaz (March 30, 1978).... Traded by Red Sox with OF Mike Brumley to Chicago Cubs for 1B-OF Bill Buckner (May 25, 1984).... Granted free agency (November 8, 1984).... Re-signed by Cubs (November 28, 1984).... On disabled list (August 11-September 7, 1985).... Traded by Cubs with IF Dan Rohn to Oakland Athletics for OF Dave Wilder, IF Brian Guinn and P Mark Leonette (April 3, 1987).... On disabled list (May 29-July 13, 1989).
RECORDS/HONORS: Named A.L. Rookie Pitcher of the Year by THE SPORTING NEWS (1975).... Named A.L. Fireman of the Year by THE SPORTING NEWS (1988).... Named A.L. co-Fireman of the Year by THE SPORTING NEWS (1991).
STATISTICAL NOTES: Led California League pitchers with 31 games started and tied for lead with five shutouts in 1973.... Led Texas League with 10 hit batsmen in 1974.... Pitched 1-0 no-hit victory against California Angels (May 30, 1977).... Led A.L. with 30 home runs allowed in 1978.

Year	Team (League)	G	W	L	Pct.	ERA	Sv.	IP	H	R	ER	BB	SO
1972—Reno (California)	12	5	5	.500	4.80	0	75	87	46	40	33	56
1973—Reno (California)	31	12	8	.600	3.65	0	202	182	97	82	91	218
1974—San Antonio (Texas)	23	•14	3	.824	3.40	0	167	141	66	63	60	*163
1975—Cleveland (A.L.)	34	13	7	.650	2.60	2	187	147	61	54	90	152
1976—Cleveland (A.L.)	36	13	12	.520	3.44	1	199	155	82	76	78	200
1977—Cleveland (A.L.)	33	14	13	.519	3.53	0	247	214	100	97	54	191
1978—Boston (A.L.)■	35	20	8	.714	2.99	0	268	258	99	89	71	162
1979—Boston (A.L.)	33	17	10	.630	2.99	0	247	234	89	82	59	150
1980—Boston (A.L.)	30	12	14	.462	4.27	0	198	188	101	94	44	121
1981—Boston (A.L.)	23	9	8	.529	4.27	0	154	160	82	73	35	79
1982—Boston (A.L.)	33	13	13	.500	3.73	0	224⅓	228	101	93	43	127
1983—Boston (A.L.)	28	9	13	.409	5.61	0	176⅓	223	119	110	39	77
1984—Boston (A.L.)	9	4	4	.500	5.01	0	64⅔	71	38	36	13	33
—Chicago (N.L.)■	24	10	8	.556	3.03	0	160⅓	152	59	54	36	81
1985—Chicago (N.L.)	25	11	7	.611	3.08	0	169⅓	145	61	58	19	117
1986—Chicago (N.L.)	33	6	11	.353	4.57	0	201	226	109	102	43	137
1987—Oakland (A.L.)■	54	6	8	.429	3.03	16	115⅔	99	41	39	17	113
1988—Oakland (A.L.)	60	4	2	.667	2.35	45	72⅔	52	20	19	11	70
1989—Oakland (A.L.)	51	4	0	1.000	1.56	33	57⅔	32	10	10	3	55
1990—Oakland (A.L.)	63	4	2	.667	0.61	48	73⅓	41	9	5	9	73
1991—Oakland (A.L.)	67	5	4	.556	2.96	43	76	60	26	25	9	87
American League totals (15 years)	589	147	118	.555	3.44	188	2360⅔	2162	978	902	570	1690
National League totals (3 years)	82	27	26	.509	3.63	0	530⅓	523	229	214	98	335
Major league totals (17 years)	671	174	144	.547	3.47	188	2891⅓	2685	1207	1116	668	2025

CHAMPIONSHIP SERIES RECORD

CHAMPIONSHIP SERIES NOTES: Holds career record for most saves—9. . . . Holds single-series record for most saves—4 (1988). . . . Shares A.L. career record for most games pitched—11. . . . Shares A.L. single-series record for most games pitched—4 (1988).

Year	Team (League)	G	W	L	Pct.	ERA	Sv.	IP	H	R	ER	BB	SO
1984	Chicago (N.L.)	1	0	1	.000	8.44	0	5⅓	9	5	5	0	0
1988	Oakland (A.L.)	4	0	0	...	0.00	4	6	1	0	0	2	5
1989	Oakland (A.L.)	4	0	0	...	1.59	3	5⅔	4	1	1	0	2
1990	Oakland (A.L.)	3	0	0	...	0.00	2	3⅓	2	0	0	0	3
Championship Series totals (4 years)		12	0	1	.000	2.66	9	20⅓	16	6	6	2	10

WORLD SERIES RECORD

Year	Team (League)	G	W	L	Pct.	ERA	Sv.	IP	H	R	ER	BB	SO
1988	Oakland (A.L.)	2	0	1	.000	10.80	0	1⅔	2	2	2	1	2
1989	Oakland (A.L.)	2	0	0	...	0.00	1	1⅔	0	0	0	0	0
1990	Oakland (A.L.)	2	0	1	.000	6.75	0	1⅓	3	1	1	0	1
World Series totals (3 years)		6	0	2	.000	5.79	1	4⅔	5	3	3	1	3

ALL-STAR GAME RECORD

Year	League	W	L	Pct.	ERA	Sv.	IP	H	R	ER	BB	SO
1977	American	0	0	...	0.00	0	2	0	0	0	0	1
1982	American	0	1	.000	9.00	0	3	2	3	3	2	1
1988	American	0	0	...	0.00	1	1	0	0	0	0	1
1990	American	0	0	...	0.00	1	1	1	0	0	0	1
1991	American	0	0	...	0.00	1	1	0	0	0	0	1
All-Star totals (5 years)		0	1	...	3.38	3	8	3	3	3	2	5

EDENS, TOM
P, TWINS

PERSONAL: Born June 9, 1961, at Ontario, Ore. . . . 6-2/185. . . . Throws right, bats right. . . . Full name: Thomas Patrick Edens.
HIGH SCHOOL: Fruitland (Idaho).
COLLEGE: Lewis-Clark State College, Idaho (degree in business).
TRANSACTIONS/CAREER NOTES: Selected by Cincinnati Reds organization in 12th round of free-agent draft (June 5, 1979). . . . Selected by Kansas City Royals organization in 14th round of free-agent draft (June 6, 1983). . . . Traded by Royals organization to New York Mets organization for IF Tucker Ashford (April 1, 1984). . . . On Columbia disabled list (April 9-19 and May 21-June 18, 1984). . . . On disabled list (June 25-August 12, 1985). . . . Traded by Mets organization to Philadelphia Phillies organization (July 27, 1989), completing deal in which Phillies traded 2B Juan Samuel to Mets for OF Lenny Dykstra, P Roger McDowell and a player to be named later (June 18, 1989). . . . Granted free agency (October 15, 1989). . . . Signed by Denver, Milwaukee Brewers organization (December 6, 1989). . . . Granted free agency (December 20, 1990). . . . Signed by Minnesota Twins (January 14, 1991).
STATISTICAL NOTES: Pitched seven-inning, 6-1 no-hit victory against Helena (August 22, 1983, second game).

Year	Team (League)	G	W	L	Pct.	ERA	Sv.	IP	H	R	ER	BB	SO
1983	Butte (Pioneer)	13	2	3	.400	4.32	0	58⅓	65	47	28	33	44
1984	Columbia (South Atlantic)■	16	7	4	.636	3.12	0	95⅓	65	44	33	58	60
	Lynchburg (Carolina)	3	1	1	.500	2.51	0	14⅓	11	6	4	8	15
1985	Lynchburg (Carolina)	16	6	4	.600	3.84	0	82	86	40	35	34	48
1986	Jackson (Texas)	16	9	4	.692	2.55	0	106	76	36	30	41	72
	Tidewater (International)	11	5	3	.625	4.55	0	61⅓	71	33	31	28	31
1987	Tidewater (International)	25	9	7	.563	3.59	1	138	140	69	55	55	61
	New York (N.L.)	2	0	0	...	6.75	0	8	15	6	6	4	4
1988	Tidewater (International)	24	7	6	.538	3.46	0	135⅓	128	67	52	53	89
1989	Tide.-Scran./W.B. (Int'l)■	25	2	6	.250	4.44	1	107⅓	121	59	53	39	47
1990	Denver (American Assoc.)■	19	1	1	.500	5.40	4	36⅔	32	23	22	22	26
	Milwaukee (A.L.)	35	4	5	.444	4.45	2	89	89	52	44	33	40
1991	Portland (Pacific Coast)■	25	10	7	.588	3.01	0	161⅓	145	67	54	62	100
	Minnesota (A.L.)	8	2	2	.500	4.09	0	33	34	15	15	10	19
American League totals (2 years)		43	6	7	.462	4.35	2	122	123	67	59	43	59
National League totals (1 year)		2	0	0	...	6.75	0	8	15	6	6	4	4
Major league totals (3 years)		45	6	7	.462	4.50	2	130	138	73	65	47	63

EDMONDS, JIM
OF, ANGELS

PERSONAL: Born June 27, 1970, at Fullerton, Calif. . . . 6-1/190. . . . Throws left, bats left. . . . Full name: James Patrick Edmonds.
HIGH SCHOOL: Diamond Bar (Calif.).
TRANSACTIONS/CAREER NOTES: Selected by California Angels organization in 7th round of free-agent draft (June 1, 1988). . . . On disabled list (June 19-September 2, 1989; April 10-May 7 and May 23, 1991-remainder of season).

Year	Team (League)	Pos.	G	AB	R	H	2B	3B	HR	RBI	Avg.	SB	PO	A	E	Avg.
1988	Bend (Northwest)	OF	35	122	23	27	4	0	0	13	.221	4	59	1	1	.984
1989	Quad City (Midwest)	OF	31	92	11	24	4	0	1	4	.261	1	47	2	3	.942
1990	Palm Springs (Calif.)	OF	91	314	36	92	18	6	3	56	.293	5	199	9	10	.954
1991	Palm Springs (Calif.)	OF-1B-P	60	187	28	55	15	1	2	27	.294	2	97	6	0	1.000

Year	Team (League)	G	W	L	Pct.	ERA	Sv.	IP	H	R	ER	BB	SO
1991 —Palm Springs (California)		1	0	0	...	0.00	0	2	1	0	0	3	2

EDWARDS, WAYNE
P, WHITE SOX

PERSONAL: Born March 7, 1964, at Burbank, Calif.... 6-5/185.... Throws left, bats left.... Full name: Wayne Maurice Edwards. **HIGH SCHOOL:** Village Christian (Sun Valley, Calif.). **COLLEGE:** Azusa Pacific University (Calif.).
TRANSACTIONS/CAREER NOTES: Selected by Chicago White Sox organization in 10th round of free-agent draft (June 3, 1985).
STATISTICAL NOTES: Led Florida State League with 15 complete games and tied for lead with 17 wild pitches in 1987.... Led Southern League with 16 wild pitches in 1988.

Year	Team (League)	G	W	L	Pct.	ERA	Sv.	IP	H	R	ER	BB	SO
1985 —Sarasota White Sox (GCL)		11	•7	3	.700	2.49	0	68⅔	52	26	19	18	61
1986 —Peninsula (Carolina)		24	8	8	.500	4.21	0	128⅓	149	80	60	68	86
1987 —Daytona Beach (Florida State)..		29	16	8	.667	3.61	0	★199⅔	★211	91	80	68	121
1988 —Birmingham (Southern)		27	9	12	.429	4.90	0	167	176	108	91	92	136
—Vancouver (Pacific Coast)		2	0	0	...	0.00	0	3	0	0	0	0	2
1989 —Birmingham (Southern)		24	10	4	.714	3.19	1	158	131	69	56	65	122
—Chicago (A.L.)		7	0	0	...	3.68	0	7⅓	7	3	3	3	9
1990 —Chicago (A.L.)		42	5	3	.625	3.22	2	95	81	39	34	41	63
1991 —Chicago (A.L.)		13	0	2	.000	3.86	0	23⅓	22	14	10	17	12
—Vancouver (Pacific Coast)		14	3	9	.250	6.26	0	64⅔	73	50	45	37	35
Major league totals (3 years)		62	5	5	.500	3.37	2	125⅔	110	56	47	61	84

EGLOFF, BRUCE
P, INDIANS

PERSONAL: Born April 10, 1965, at Denver.... 6-2/215.... Throws right, bats right.... Full name: Bruce Edward Egloff. **HIGH SCHOOL:** East Denver (Denver). **COLLEGE:** Merced College (Calif.) and UC Santa Barbara.
TRANSACTIONS/CAREER NOTES: Selected by Cleveland Indians organization in fifth round of free-agent draft (June 2, 1986).... On disabled list (June 11-August 8, 1987 and June 19, 1988-remainder of season).... On Canton-Akron disabled list (April 7-June 16, 1989; July 12-August 2 and August 10, 1990-remainder of season).

Year	Team (League)	G	W	L	Pct.	ERA	Sv.	IP	H	R	ER	BB	SO
1986 —Batavia (New York-Penn)		12	1	2	.333	3.99	0	70	79	42	31	17	62
1987 —Waterloo (Midwest)		7	1	2	.333	5.16	0	22⅔	30	14	13	10	14
1988 —							Did not play						
1989 —Watertown (New York-Penn)...		22	1	1	.500	2.59	8	48⅔	33	19	14	24	63
1990 —Canton/Akron (Eastern)		34	3	2	.600	1.98	15	54⅔	44	16	12	15	53
1991 —Cleveland (A.L.)		6	0	0	...	4.76	0	5⅔	8	3	3	4	8
—Colorado Springs (Pac. Coast) ..		15	1	2	.333	3.38	2	29⅓	31	14	11	13	17
Major league totals (1 year)		6	0	0	...	4.76	0	5⅔	8	3	3	4	8

EICHHORN, MARK
P, ANGELS

PERSONAL: Born November 21, 1960, at San Jose, Calif.... 6-3/210.... Throws right, bats right.... Full name: Mark Anthony Eichhorn.... Name pronounced IKE-horn. **HIGH SCHOOL:** Watsonville (Calif.). **COLLEGE:** Cabrillo Junior College (Calif.).
TRANSACTIONS/CAREER NOTES: Selected by Toronto Blue Jays organization in second round of free-agent draft (January 9, 1979).... On disabled list (June 16-July 1, 1986).... Sold by Blue Jays to Atlanta Braves (March 29, 1989).... Released by Braves (November 20, 1989).... Signed by Edmonton, California Angels organization (December 19, 1989).
RECORDS/HONORS: Shares A.L. single-season record for most games by relief pitcher—89 (1987).... Named A.L. Rookie Pitcher of the Year by THE SPORTING NEWS (1986).
STATISTICAL NOTES: Tied for Southern League lead in games started by pitcher with 29 in 1981.

Year	Team (League)	G	W	L	Pct.	ERA	Sv.	IP	H	R	ER	BB	SO
1979 —Medicine Hat (Pioneer)		16	7	6	.538	3.39	0	93	101	62	35	26	66
1980 —Kinston (Carolina)		26	14	10	.583	2.90	0	183	158	72	59	56	119
1981 —Knoxville (Southern)		30	10	14	.417	3.98	0	192	202	112	85	57	99
1982 —Syracuse (International)		27	10	11	.476	4.54	0	156⅔	158	92	79	83	71
—Toronto (A.L.)		7	0	3	.000	5.45	0	38	40	28	23	14	16
1983 —Syracuse (International)		7	0	5	.000	7.92	0	30⅔	36	32	27	21	12
—Knoxville (Southern)		21	6	12	.333	4.33	0	120⅔	124	65	58	47	54
1984 —Syracuse (International)		36	5	9	.357	5.97	0	117⅔	147	92	78	51	54
1985 —Knoxville (Southern)		26	5	1	.833	3.02	0	116⅓	101	49	39	34	76
—Syracuse (International)		8	2	5	.286	4.82	0	37⅓	38	24	20	7	27
1986 —Toronto (A.L.)		69	14	6	.700	1.72	10	157	105	32	30	45	166
1987 —Toronto (A.L.)		★89	10	6	.625	3.17	4	127⅔	110	47	45	52	96
1988 —Toronto (A.L.)		37	0	0	.000	4.19	1	66⅔	79	32	31	27	28
—Syracuse (International)		18	4	4	.500	1.17	1	38⅓	35	9	5	15	34
1989 —Atlanta (N.L.)■		45	5	5	.500	4.35	0	68⅓	70	36	33	19	49
—Richmond (International)		25	1	0	1.000	1.32	★19	41	29	6	6	6	33

Year Team (League)	G	W	L	Pct.	ERA	Sv.	IP	H	R	ER	BB	SO
1990 —California (A.L.)■	60	2	5	.286	3.08	13	84⅔	98	36	29	23	69
1991 —California (A.L.)	70	3	3	.500	1.98	1	81⅔	63	21	18	13	49
American League totals (6 years)	332	29	26	.527	2.85	29	555⅔	495	196	176	174	424
National League totals (1 year)	45	5	5	.500	4.35	0	68⅓	70	36	33	19	49
Major league totals (7 years)	377	34	31	.523	3.01	29	624	565	232	209	193	473

EILAND, DAVE
P, PADRES

PERSONAL: Born July 5, 1966, at Dade City, Fla. . . . 6-3/212. . . . Throws right, bats right. . . . Full name: David William Eiland. . . . Name pronounced EYE-land.
COLLEGE: Florida and South Florida.
TRANSACTIONS/CAREER NOTES: Selected by New York Yankees organization in seventh round of free-agent draft (June 2, 1987). . . . On disabled list (May 28-July 12, 1991); included rehabilitation disability assignment to Columbus (June 16-July 12, 1991). . . . Released by Yankees (January 7, 1992). . . . Signed by San Diego Padres organization (January 27, 1992).
RECORDS/HONORS: Named International League Pitcher of the Year (1990).
STATISTICAL NOTES: Tied for Eastern League lead with seven complete games in 1988. . . . Led International League with 11 complete games and tied for lead with three shutouts in 1990.

Year Team (League)	G	W	L	Pct.	ERA	Sv.	IP	H	R	ER	BB	SO
1987 —Oneonta (New York-Penn)	5	4	0	1.000	1.84	0	29⅓	20	6	6	3	16
—Fort Lauderdale (Florida St.)	8	5	3	.625	1.88	0	62⅓	57	17	13	8	28
1988 —Albany (Eastern)	18	9	5	.643	2.56	0	119⅓	95	39	34	22	66
—Columbus (International)	4	1	1	.500	2.59	0	24⅓	25	8	7	6	13
—New York (A.L.)	3	0	0	. . .	6.39	0	12⅔	15	9	9	4	7
1989 —Columbus (International)	18	9	4	.692	3.76	0	103	107	47	43	21	45
—New York (A.L.)	6	1	3	.250	5.77	0	34⅓	44	25	22	13	11
1990 —Columbus (International)	27	★16	5	.762	2.87	0	175⅓	155	63	56	32	96
—New York (A.L.)	5	2	1	.667	3.56	0	30⅓	31	14	12	5	16
1991 —New York (A.L.)	18	2	5	.286	5.33	0	72⅔	87	51	43	23	18
—Columbus (International)	9	6	1	.857	2.40	0	60	54	22	16	7	18
Major league totals (4 years)	32	5	9	.357	5.16	0	150	177	99	86	45	52

EISENREICH, JIM
OF, ROYALS

PERSONAL: Born April 18, 1959, at St. Cloud, Minn. . . . 5-11/195. . . . Throws left, bats left. . . . Full name: James Michael Eisenreich. . . . Name pronounced EYES-en-rike.
HIGH SCHOOL: St. Cloud Technical (Minn.).
COLLEGE: St. Cloud State (Minn.).
TRANSACTIONS/CAREER NOTES: Selected by Minnesota Twins organization in 16th round of free-agent draft (June 3, 1980). . . . On disabled list (May 6-28 and June 18-September 1, 1982). . . . On disabled list (April 7, 1983); then transferred to voluntarily retired list (May 27, 1983-remainder of season). . . . On disabled list (April 26-May 18, 1984). . . . On voluntarily retired list (June 4, 1984-September 29, 1986). . . . Claimed on waivers by Kansas City Royals (October 2, 1986). . . . On Kansas City disabled list (August 25-September 9, 1987 and July 22-August 6, 1989). . . . Granted free agency (October 30, 1991). . . . Re-signed by Royals (January 31, 1992).
RECORDS/HONORS: Named Appalachian League Co-Player of the Year (1980).

Year Team (League)	Pos.	G	AB	R	H	2B	3B	HR	RBI	Avg.	SB	PO	A	E	Avg.
1980 —Elizabethton (Appal.)	OF	67	258	47	77	12	•4	3	41	.298	12	151	7	3	.981
—Wis. Rapids (Midwest)	DH	5	16	4	7	0	0	0	5	.438	1	0	0	0	.000
1981 —Wis. Rapids (Midwest)	OF	★134	489	101	•152	★27	0	23	99	.311	9	★295	17	9	.972
1982 —Minnesota (A.L.)	OF	34	99	10	30	6	0	2	9	.303	0	72	0	2	.973
1983 —Minnesota (A.L.)	OF	2	7	1	2	1	0	0	0	.286	0	6	1	0	1.000
1984 —Minnesota (A.L.)	OF	12	32	1	7	1	0	0	3	.219	2	5	0	0	1.000
1985 —					Out of Organized Baseball										
1986 —					Out of Organized Baseball										
1987 —Memphis (Southern)■	DH	70	275	60	105	36	•10	11	57	.382	13	0	0	0	. . .
—Kansas City (A.L.)	DH	44	105	10	25	8	2	4	21	.238	1	0	0	0	. . .
1988 —Kansas City (A.L.)	OF	82	202	26	44	8	1	1	19	.218	9	109	0	4	.965
—Omaha (Am. Assoc.)	OF	36	142	28	41	8	3	4	14	.289	9	73	1	1	.987
1989 —Kansas City (A.L.)	OF	134	475	64	139	33	7	9	59	.293	27	273	4	3	.989
1990 —Kansas City (A.L.)	OF	142	496	61	139	29	7	5	51	.280	12	261	6	1	★.996
1991 —Kansas City (A.L.)	OF-1B	135	375	47	113	22	3	2	47	.301	5	243	12	5	.981
Major league totals (8 years)		585	1791	220	499	108	20	23	209	.279	56	969	23	15	.985

ELDRED, CAL
P, BREWERS

PERSONAL: Born November 24, 1967, at Cedar Rapids, Ia. . . . 6-4/215. . . . Throws right, bats right. . . . Full name: Calvin John Eldred.
HIGH SCHOOL: Urbana Community (Ia.).
COLLEGE: Iowa.
TRANSACTIONS/CAREER NOTES: Selected by Milwaukee Brewers organization in first round (17th pick overall) of free-agent draft (June 5, 1989).
STATISTICAL NOTES: Led American Association pitchers with 29 games started and 12 hit batsmen in 1991.

Year Team (League)	G	W	L	Pct.	ERA	Sv.	IP	H	R	ER	BB	SO
1989 —Beloit (Midwest)	5	2	1	.667	2.30	0	31⅓	23	10	8	11	32
1990 —Stockton (California)	7	4	2	.667	1.62	0	50	31	12	9	19	75
—El Paso (Texas)	19	5	4	.556	4.49	0	110⅓	126	61	55	47	93

Year Team (League)	G	W	L	Pct.	ERA	Sv.	IP	H	R	ER	BB	SO
1991—Denver (American Assoc.)	29	13	9	.591	3.75	0	*185	161	82	77	84	*168
—Milwaukee (A.L.)	3	2	0	1.000	4.50	0	16	20	9	8	6	10
Major league totals (1 year)	3	2	0	1.000	4.50	0	16	20	9	8	6	10

ELLIOTT, DONNIE
P, MARINERS

PERSONAL: Born September 20, 1968, at Pasadena, Tex. . . . 6-4/190. . . . Throws right, bats right. . . . Full name: Donald Glenn Elliott.
HIGH SCHOOL: Deer Park (Tex.).
COLLEGE: San Jacinto College (Tex.).
TRANSACTIONS/CAREER NOTES: Selected by Philadelphia Phillies organization in seventh round of free-agent draft (June 2, 1987). . . . Drafted by Seattle Mariners (December 9, 1991).
STATISTICAL NOTES: Tied for Appalachian League lead with nine balks in 1988.

Year Team (League)	G	W	L	Pct.	ERA	Sv.	IP	H	R	ER	BB	SO
1988—Martinsville (Appalachian)	15	4	2	.667	3.66	1	59	47	37	24	31	77
1989—Batavia (New York-Penn)	8	4	1	.800	1.42	0	57	45	21	9	14	48
—Spartanburg (South Atlantic)	7	2	3	.400	2.47	0	43⅔	46	19	12	14	36
1990—Spartanburg (South Atlantic)	20	4	8	.333	3.50	0	105⅓	101	52	41	46	109
1991—Spartanburg (South Atlantic)	10	3	4	.429	4.24	0	51	42	37	24	36	81
—Clearwater (Florida State)	18	8	5	.615	2.78	0	107	78	34	33	51	103

ELSTER, KEVIN
SS, METS

PERSONAL: Born August 3, 1964, at San Pedro, Calif. . . . 6-2/200. . . . Throws right, bats right. . . . Full name: Kevin Daniel Elster.
HIGH SCHOOL: Marina (Huntington Beach, Calif.).
COLLEGE: Golden West College (Calif.).
TRANSACTIONS/CAREER NOTES: Selected by New York Mets organization in second round of free-agent draft (January 17, 1984). . . . On Jackson disabled list (August 11, 1985-remainder of season). . . . On disabled list (August 4, 1990-remainder of season and May 6-21, 1991).
RECORDS/HONORS: Holds major league single-season record for fewest putouts by shortstop who led league—235 (1989). . . . Holds N.L. career record for most consecutive errorless games by shortstop—88 (July 20, 1988-May 8, 1989).
STATISTICAL NOTES: Led New York-Pennsylvania League shortstops with 358 total chances and 45 double plays in 1984. . . . Led Texas League shortstops with 589 total chances and 83 double plays in 1986.

Year Team (League)	Pos.	G	AB	R	H	2B	3B	HR	RBI	Avg.	SB	PO	A	E	Avg.
1984—Little Falls (N.Y.-Penn)	SS	71	257	35	66	7	3	3	35	.257	13	*128	214	16	*.955
1985—Lynchburg (Carolina)	SS	59	224	41	66	9	0	7	26	.295	8	82	195	16	.945
—Jackson (Texas)	SS	59	214	30	55	13	0	2	22	.257	2	107	220	10	.970
1986—Jackson (Texas)	SS	127	435	69	117	19	3	2	52	.269	6	*196	*365	28	*.952
—New York (N.L.)	SS	19	30	3	5	1	0	0	0	.167	0	16	35	2	.962
1987—Tidewater (Int'l)	SS	134	*549	83	*170	33	7	8	74	.310	7	219	419	21	.968
—New York (N.L.)	SS	5	10	1	4	2	0	0	1	.400	0	4	6	1	.909
1988—New York (N.L.)	SS	149	406	41	87	11	1	9	37	.214	2	196	345	13	.977
1989—New York (N.L.)	SS	151	458	52	106	25	2	10	55	.231	4	*235	374	15	.976
1990—New York (N.L.)	SS	92	314	36	65	20	1	9	45	.207	2	159	251	17	.960
1991—New York (N.L.)	SS	115	348	33	84	16	2	6	36	.241	2	149	299	14	.970
Major league totals (6 years)		531	1566	166	351	75	6	34	174	.224	10	759	1310	62	.971

CHAMPIONSHIP SERIES RECORD

Year Team (League)	Pos.	G	AB	R	H	2B	3B	HR	RBI	Avg.	SB	PO	A	E	Avg.
1986—New York (N.L.)	PR-SS	4	3	0	0	0	0	0	0	.000	0	2	3	0	1.000
1988—New York (N.L.)	SS-PR	5	8	1	2	1	0	0	1	.250	0	7	7	2	.875
Championship Series totals (2 years)		9	11	1	2	1	0	0	1	.182	0	9	10	2	.905

WORLD SERIES RECORD

Year Team (League)	Pos.	G	AB	R	H	2B	3B	HR	RBI	Avg.	SB	PO	A	E	Avg.
1986—New York (N.L.)	SS	1	1	0	0	0	0	0	0	.000	0	3	3	1	.857

ELVIRA, NARCISO
P, BREWERS

PERSONAL: Born October 29, 1967, at Vera Cruz, Mexico. . . . 5-10/160. . . . Throws left, bats left. . . . Full name: Narciso Elvira.
HIGH SCHOOL: Pasteje Academy (Pasteje, Mexico).
TRANSACTIONS/CAREER NOTES: Signed by Leon of Mexican League for 1986. . . . Sold to Milwaukee Brewers organization (December, 1986). . . . Loaned to Leon of Mexican League (1987). . . . On El Paso disabled list (May 17-July 20, 1990). . . . On Denver disabled list (June 28-July 7, 1991). . . . On El Paso disabled list (July 18-September 17, 1991).

Year Team (League)	G	W	L	Pct.	ERA	Sv.	IP	H	R	ER	BB	SO
1986—Leon (Mexican)	31	8	5	.615	4.81	1	127⅓	128	81	68	84	86
1987—Beloit (Midwest)	4	3	0	1.000	1.33	0	27	15	5	4	12	29
—Leon (Mexican)■	33	6	8	.429	5.27	1	109⅓	104	75	64	62	80

Year	Team (League)	G	W	L	Pct.	ERA	Sv.	IP	H	R	ER	BB	SO
1988	—Stockton (California)■	25	7	6	.538	2.93	0	135⅓	87	49	44	79	161
1989	—El Paso (Texas)	7	2	2	.500	7.64	0	33	48	34	28	23	18
	—Stockton (California)	17	8	5	.615	3.04	0	115⅓	92	45	39	43	135
1990	—El Paso (Texas)	4	0	2	.000	4.50	0	18	17	11	9	6	12
	—Beloit (Midwest)	8	3	2	.600	2.35	1	38⅓	37	16	10	9	45
	—Milwaukee (A.L.)	4	0	0	...	5.40	0	5	6	3	3	5	6
1991	—Denver (American Assoc.)	18	0	4	.000	5.96	0	80	100	62	53	40	52
	Major league totals (1 year)	4	0	0	...	5.40	0	5	6	3	3	5	6

ERB, MIKE
P, ANGELS

PERSONAL: Born March 19, 1966, at San Diego. . . . 6-4/210. . . . Throws right, bats right. . . . Full name: Michael William Erb.
HIGH SCHOOL: Madison (San Diego).
COLLEGE: San Diego State.
TRANSACTIONS/CAREER NOTES: Selected by Milwaukee Brewers organization in 17th round of free-agent draft (June 4, 1984). . . . Selected by California Angels organization in second round of free-agent draft (June 2, 1987).

Year	Team (League)	G	W	L	Pct.	ERA	Sv.	IP	H	R	ER	BB	SO
1987	—Salem (Northwest)	12	6	3	.667	2.44	0	85	65	33	23	20	98
1988	—Palm Springs (California)	19	10	7	.588	4.40	0	108⅓	102	66	53	62	86
1989	—Quad City (Midwest)	25	11	4	.733	2.69	0	147⅓	113	57	44	43	161
1990	—Edmonton (Pacific Coast)	16	4	4	.500	4.26	0	82⅓	90	46	39	60	45
	—Midland (Texas)	6	1	1	.500	5.17	0	31⅓	39	20	18	24	25
1991	—Edmonton (Pacific Coast)	31	1	0	1.000	3.76	5	40⅔	40	18	17	23	26

ERICKS, JOHN
P, CARDINALS

PERSONAL: Born September 16, 1967, at Oak Lawn, Ill. . . . 6-7/220. . . . Throws right, bats right. . . . Full name: John Edward Ericks.
HIGH SCHOOL: Chicago Christian (Palos Heights, Ill.).
COLLEGE: Illinois.
TRANSACTIONS/CAREER NOTES: Selected by St. Louis Cardinals organization in first round (22nd pick overall) of free-agent draft (June 1, 1988). . . . On Arkansas disabled list (May 19, 1990-remainder of season).

Year	Team (League)	G	W	L	Pct.	ERA	Sv.	IP	H	R	ER	BB	SO
1988	—Johnson City (Appalachian)	9	3	2	.600	3.73	0	41	27	20	17	27	41
1989	—Savannah (Southern)	28	11	10	.524	2.04	0	167⅓	90	59	38	101	★211
1990	—St. Petersburg (Florida State)	4	2	1	.667	1.57	0	23	16	5	4	6	25
	—Arkansas (Texas)	4	1	2	.333	9.39	0	15⅓	17	19	16	19	19
1991	—Arkansas (Texas)	25	5	14	.263	4.77	0	139⅔	138	94	74	84	103

ERICKSON, SCOTT
P, TWINS

PERSONAL: Born February 2, 1968, at Long Beach, Calif. . . . 6-4/225. . . . Throws right, bats right. . . . Full name: Scott Gavin Erickson III.
HIGH SCHOOL: Homestead (Cupertino, Calif.).
COLLEGE: San Jose City College (Calif.) and Arizona.
TRANSACTIONS/CAREER NOTES: Selected by New York Mets organization in 36th round of free-agent draft (June 2, 1986). . . . Selected by Houston Astros organization in 34th round of free-agent draft (June 2, 1987). . . . Selected by Toronto Blue Jays organization in 44th round of free-agent draft (June 1, 1988). . . . Selected by Minnesota Twins organization in fourth round of free-agent draft (June 5, 1989). . . . On disabled list (June 30-July 15, 1991).

Year	Team (League)	G	W	L	Pct.	ERA	Sv.	IP	H	R	ER	BB	SO
1989	—Visalia (California)	12	3	4	.429	2.97	0	78⅔	79	29	26	22	59
1990	—Orlando (Southern)	15	8	3	.727	3.03	0	101	75	38	34	24	69
	—Minnesota (A.L.)	19	8	4	.667	2.87	0	113	108	49	36	51	53
1991	—Minnesota (A.L.)	32	•20	8	.714	3.18	0	204	189	80	72	71	108
	Major league totals (2 years)	51	28	12	.700	3.07	0	317	297	129	108	122	161

CHAMPIONSHIP SERIES RECORD

Year	Team (League)	G	W	L	Pct.	ERA	Sv.	IP	H	R	ER	BB	SO
1991	—Minnesota (A.L.)	1	0	0	.000	4.50	0	4	3	2	2	5	2

WORLD SERIES RECORD

Year	Team (League)	G	W	L	Pct.	ERA	Sv.	IP	H	R	ER	BB	SO
1991	—Minnesota (A.L.)	2	0	0	.000	5.06	0	10⅔	10	7	6	4	5

ERWIN, SCOTT
P, ATHLETICS

PERSONAL: Born August 21, 1967, at Tampa, Fla. . . . 6-2/210. . . . Throws right, bats right. . . . Full name: Scott Douglas Erwin.
HIGH SCHOOL: H.B. Plant (Tampa, Fla.).
COLLEGE: Georgia Tech.
TRANSACTIONS/CAREER NOTES: Selected by Los Angeles Dodgers organization in eighth round of free-agent draft (June 1, 1988). . . . Selected by Oakland Athletics organization in fifth round of free-agent draft (June 5, 1989). . . . On Modesto disabled list (April 10-June 12, 1991).

Year	Team (League)	G	W	L	Pct.	ERA	Sv.	IP	H	R	ER	BB	SO
1989—Southern Oregon (Northwest) ..		15	6	3	.667	3.36	0	83	68	36	31	43	83
1990—Modesto (California)		25	6	11	.353	4.32	0	131⅓	122	89	63	78	128
1991—Modesto (California)		11	1	0	1.000	2.70	2	13⅓	7	4	4	6	22
—Huntsville (Southern)		19	1	4	.200	3.63	2	22⅓	15	10	9	17	30

ESASKY, NICK

1B, BRAVES

PERSONAL: Born February 24, 1960, at Hialeah, Fla.... 6-3/215.... Throws right, bats right. ... Full name: Nicholas Andrew Esasky.... Name pronounced ih-SASS-kee.
HIGH SCHOOL: Carol City (Miami).
TRANSACTIONS/CAREER NOTES: Selected by Cincinnati Reds organization in first round (17th pick overall) of free-agent draft (June 6, 1978).... On disabled list (June 15-July 17, 1986).... On Cincinnati disabled list (March 23-May 19, 1987); included rehabilitation disability assignment to Nashville (May 5-19, 1987).... On disabled list (May 11-June 3, 1988).... Traded by Reds with P Rob Murphy to Boston Red Sox for 1B Todd Benzinger, P Jeff Sellers and a player to be named later (December 13, 1988); Reds acquired P Luis Vasquez to complete deal (January 12, 1989).... Granted free agency (November 13, 1989).... Signed by Atlanta Braves (November 17, 1989).... On disabled list (April 22, 1990-remainder of season and March 30, 1991-entire season).
STATISTICAL NOTES: Led Eastern League batters with 131 strikeouts in 1980.

Year	Team (League)	Pos.	G	AB	R	H	2B	3B	HR	RBI	Avg.	SB	PO	A	E	Avg.
1978—Billings (Pioneer)		3B	64	213	38	65	10	5	4	48	.305	8	*62	88	22	.872
1979—Tampa (Florida State).......		3B	124	439	52	118	16	3	10	66	.269	3	91	234	27	.923
1980—Waterbury (Eastern)........		3B	135	425	79	115	18	4	*30	79	.271	2	98	241	23	.936
1981—Indianapolis (A.A.)		3B	121	423	55	112	22	4	17	62	.265	1	99	220	*37	.896
1982—Indianapolis (A.A.)		3B	105	341	59	90	15	3	27	62	.264	1	77	150	21	*.915
1983—Indianapolis (A.A.)		3B	49	158	33	44	5	0	14	37	.278	6	27	71	14	.875
—Cincinnati (N.L.)		3B	85	302	41	80	10	5	12	46	.265	6	53	133	13	.935
1984—Cincinnati (N.L.)		3B-1B	113	322	30	62	10	5	10	45	.193	1	220	137	18	.952
1985—Cincinnati (N.L.)		3B-OF-1B	125	413	61	108	21	0	21	66	.262	3	169	106	8	.972
1986—Cincinnati (N.L.)		1B-OF-3B	102	330	35	76	17	2	12	41	.230	5	585	33	5	.992
1987—Nashville (Am. Assoc.)		1B	13	52	13	23	6	0	5	18	.442	0	102	7	0	1.000
—Cincinnati (N.L.)		1B-3B-OF	100	346	48	94	19	2	22	59	.272	0	773	41	6	.993
1988—Cincinnati (N.L.)		1B	122	391	40	95	17	2	15	62	.243	7	982	52	6	.994
1989—Boston (A.L.)■		1B-OF	154	564	79	156	26	5	30	108	.277	1	1319	107	6	.996
1990—Atlanta (N.L.)■		1B	9	35	2	6	0	0	0	0	.171	0	79	5	5	.944
1991—									Did not play							
American League totals (1 year)			154	564	79	156	26	5	30	108	.277	1	1319	107	6	.996
National League totals (7 years)			656	2139	257	521	94	16	92	319	.244	17	2861	507	61	.982
Major league totals (8 years)			810	2703	336	677	120	21	122	427	.250	18	4180	614	67	.986

ESCOBAR, JOSE

SS/2B

PERSONAL: Born October 30, 1960, at Las Flores, Venezuela.... 5-10/140.... Throws right, bats right.... Full name: Jose Elias Sanchez Escobar.
TRANSACTIONS/CAREER NOTES: Signed as free agent by Toronto Blue Jays organization (November 27, 1978).... Traded by Blue Jays organization with OF Ken Kinnard and P Dave Shipanoff to Philadelphia Phillies organization for IF Len Matuszek (April 1, 1985).... Released by Phillies organization (December 12, 1985).... Signed by Blue Jays organization (January 6, 1986).... Loaned by Blue Jays organization to Omaha, Kansas City Royals organization (June 28, 1989); returned (August, 1989).... Granted free agency (October 15, 1990).... Signed by Cleveland Indians organization (November 25, 1990).... Released by Canton-Akron, Indians organization (July 29, 1991).

Year	Team (League)	Pos.	G	AB	R	H	2B	3B	HR	RBI	Avg.	SB	PO	A	E	Avg.
1979—Utica (New York-Penn)		SS-2B	62	204	44	54	5	3	2	21	.265	4	123	131	22	.920
1980—Utica (New York-Penn)		SS-2B	67	231	23	54	5	3	2	27	.234	13	90	182	24	.919
1981—Kinston (Carolina)..........		SS-2B	56	192	22	48	5	0	1	16	.250	5	75	154	16	.935
—Florence (S. Atlantic)........		SS-3B	35	105	12	25	3	0	0	4	.238	0	31	72	12	.896
1982—Kinston (Carolina)..........		SS-2B	84	225	30	54	9	0	0	16	.240	2	89	175	17	.940
1983—Kinston (Carolina)..........		SS-2B-3B	125	458	47	122	18	4	2	49	.266	7	211	382	27	.956
1984—Knoxville (Southern)		S-3-2-0	96	340	40	80	13	4	1	45	.235	6	119	275	15	.963
1985—Reading (Eastern)■.........		SS-3B-2B	40	122	17	31	4	0	1	8	.254	3	39	85	10	.925
—Portland (Pacific Coast) ..		SS-3B-2B	46	109	21	35	4	2	1	8	.321	4	50	114	7	.959
1986—Knoxville (Southern)■.......		3B-SS	19	66	9	16	1	0	0	5	.242	1	17	32	4	.925
—Syracuse (International) ..		SS-3B-2B	62	143	12	35	5	0	2	14	.245	2	56	131	7	.964
1987—Syracuse (International) ..		SS-3B-2B	37	68	12	24	2	0	2	14	.353	0	24	46	4	.946
—Knoxville (Southern)		SS	26	92	4	13	3	0	0	4	.141	2	38	77	5	.958
1988—Knoxville (Southern)		SS-2B	11	24	1	7	1	0	0	2	.292	0	10	19	5	.853
—Syracuse (International) ..		3B-SS-2B	46	124	8	26	1	1	0	12	.210	2	39	103	12	.922
1989—Syracuse (International) ..		SS-2B-3B	46	142	12	33	3	1	0	14	.232	2	81	135	14	.939
—Omaha (Am. Assoc.)■.......		SS	23	76	3	6	0	0	0	1	.079	2	22	66	4	.957
1990—Syracuse (International)■ ..		SS-2B	79	252	16	68	6	2	0	17	.270	3	130	191	8	.976
1991—Cleveland (A.L.)■		SS-2B	10	15	0	3	0	0	0	0	.200	0	15	13	0	1.000
—Colorado Springs (PCL)		SS-2B	33	93	12	19	5	1	0	11	.204	0	40	84	7	.947
—Canton/Akron (Eastern) ..		SS-2B	12	34	0	2	1	0	0	1	.059	0	11	29	3	.930
Major league totals (1 year)			10	15	0	3	0	0	0	0	.200	0	15	13	0	1.000

ESPINOZA, ALVARO
SS, YANKEES

PERSONAL: Born February 19, 1962, at Valencia, Carabobo, Venezuela. . . . 6-0/190. . . . Throws right, bats right. . . . Full name: Alvaro Alberto Ramirez Espinoza. . . . Name pronounced ESS-pin-OH-zuh.
HIGH SCHOOL: Valencia (Carabobo, Venezuela).

TRANSACTIONS/CAREER NOTES: Signed as free agent by Houston Astros organization (October 30, 1978). . . . Released by Astros organization (September 30, 1980). . . . Signed by Wisconsin Rapids, Minnesota Twins organization (March 18, 1982). . . . On Toledo disabled list (June 7-25, 1984 and June 6-July 2, 1985). . . . Granted free agency (October 15, 1987). . . . Signed by Columbus, New York Yankees organization (November 17, 1987).
RECORDS/HONORS: Shares major league single-season record for fewest runs batted in (150 or more games) —20 (1990).
STATISTICAL NOTES: Led Gulf Coast League shortstops with 114 putouts, 217 assists, 25 errors, 356 total chances and 33 double plays in 1980. . . . Led California League shortstops with 660 total chances in 1983. . . . Tied for International League lead with 16 sacrifice hits in 1984. . . . Led International League shortstops with 159 putouts in 1986.

Year	Team (League)	Pos.	G	AB	R	H	2B	3B	HR	RBI	Avg.	SB	PO	A	E	Avg.
1979	—Sarasota Astros (GCL)	SS-2B-3B	11	32	3	7	0	0	0	5	.219	0	18	27	1	.978
1980	—Sara. Astros-Or. (GCL)	SS-3B	59	200	24	43	5	0	0	14	.215	6	†114	†219	†25	.930
1981	—						Out of Organized Baseball									
1982	—Wis. Rapids (Midwest)■	SS-3B-1B	112	379	41	101	9	0	5	29	.266	9	237	241	33	.935
1983	—Visalia (California)	SS	130	486	57	155	20	1	4	57	.319	3	★256	364	40	.939
1984	—Toledo (International)	SS	104	344	22	80	12	5	0	30	.233	3	157	293	19	.959
1985	—Toledo (International)	SS	82	266	24	61	11	0	1	33	.229	1	132	245	16	.959
	—Minnesota (A.L.)	SS	32	57	5	15	2	0	0	9	.263	0	25	69	5	.949
1986	—Toledo (International)	SS-2B	73	253	18	71	8	1	2	27	.281	1	†170	205	12	.969
	—Minnesota (A.L.)	2B-SS	37	42	4	9	1	0	0	1	.214	0	23	52	4	.949
1987	—Portland (Pacific Coast)	SS-3B-1B	91	291	28	80	3	2	4	28	.275	37	158	236	20	.952
1988	—Columbus (Int'l)■	SS-2B-3B	119	435	42	107	10	5	2	30	.246	4	221	404	19	.970
	—New York (A.L.)	2B-SS	3	3	0	0	0	0	0	0	.000	0	5	2	0	1.000
1989	—New York (A.L.)	SS	146	503	51	142	23	1	0	41	.282	3	237	471	22	.970
1990	—New York (A.L.)	SS	150	438	31	98	12	2	2	20	.224	1	268	447	17	.977
1991	—New York (A.L.)	SS-3B-P	148	480	51	123	23	2	5	33	.256	4	225	441	21	.969
	Major league totals (6 years)		516	1523	142	387	61	5	7	104	.254	8	783	1482	69	.970

RECORD AS PITCHER

Year	Team (League)	G	W	L	Pct.	ERA	Sv.	IP	H	R	ER	BB	SO
1991	—New York (A.L.)	1	0	0	. . .	0.00	0	2/3	0	0	0	0	0

ESPY, CECIL
OF, PIRATES

PERSONAL: Born January 20, 1963, at San Diego. . . . 6-3/195. . . . Throws right, bats both. . . . Full name: Cecil Edward Espy.
HIGH SCHOOL: Point Loma (Calif.).
TRANSACTIONS/CAREER NOTES: Selected by Chicago White Sox organization in first round (eighth pick overall) of free-agent draft (June 3, 1980). . . . Traded by White Sox organization with P Burt Geiger to Los Angeles Dodgers organization for OF Rudy Law (March 30, 1982). . . . Traded by Dodgers organization with 1B Sid Bream to Pittsburgh Pirates (September 9, 1985), completing deal in which Dodgers acquired 3B Bill Madlock for three players to be named later; Pirates acquired OF R.J. Reynolds as partial completion of deal (September 3, 1985). . . . Drafted by Texas Rangers (December 8, 1986). . . . On disabled list (May 3-18, 1988). . . . Granted free agency (October 15, 1990). . . . Signed by Pirates organization (February 11, 1991).
STATISTICAL NOTES: Led Texas League outfielders with 348 putouts and 365 total chances in 1984. . . . Led Texas League shortstops with 50 errors in 1985. . . . Tied for Texas League lead in caught stealing with 17 in 1985. . . . Led A.L. in caught stealing with 20 in 1989.

Year	Team (League)	Pos.	G	AB	R	H	2B	3B	HR	RBI	Avg.	SB	PO	A	E	Avg.
1980	—Sara. White Sox (GCL)	OF	58	212	33	58	7	3	0	26	.274	23	138	4	7	.953
1981	—Appleton (Midwest)	OF	72	273	37	55	2	2	1	19	.201	11	143	5	5	.967
	—Sara. White Sox (GCL)	OF	43	142	24	40	3	1	0	16	.282	9	54	1	4	.932
1982	—Vero Beach (Florida St.)■	OF	131	★523	★100	★166	14	7	1	34	.317	★74	275	9	10	.966
1983	—San Antonio (Texas)	OF	133	★564	88	151	16	11	4	38	.268	51	258	12	10	.964
	—Los Angeles (N.L.)	OF	20	11	4	3	1	0	0	1	.273	0	11	0	0	1.000
1984	—San Antonio (Texas)	OF-2B-SS	★133	★535	99	146	19	8	8	60	.273	48	†348	16	5	.986
1985	—San Antonio (Texas)	SS-OF	124	461	64	129	24	3	5	49	.280	20	183	346	†51	.912
1986	—Hawaii (Pacific Coast)■	OF-2B-SS	106	384	49	101	19	3	4	38	.263	41	172	8	5	.973
1987	—Oklahoma City (A.A.)■	OF-SS	118	443	76	134	18	6	1	37	.302	46	195	161	16	.957
	—Texas (A.L.)	OF	14	8	1	0	0	0	0	0	.000	2	8	1	0	1.000
1988	—Texas (A.L.)	O-S-C-1-2	123	347	46	86	17	6	2	39	.248	33	200	11	7	.968
1989	—Texas (A.L.)	OF	142	475	65	122	12	7	3	31	.257	45	281	5	3	.990
1990	—Texas (A.L.)	OF-2B	52	71	10	9	0	0	1	1	.127	11	56	1	0	1.000
	—Oklahoma City (A.A.)	OF-SS	34	126	15	34	4	1	2	20	.270	7	69	8	5	.939
1991	—Buffalo (Am. Assoc.)■	OF	102	398	69	124	27	10	2	43	.312	22	215	10	7	.970
	—Pittsburgh (N.L.)	OF	43	82	7	20	4	0	1	11	.244	4	54	3	2	.966
	American League totals (4 years)		331	901	122	217	29	13	5	71	.241	91	545	18	10	.983
	National League totals (2 years)		63	93	11	23	5	0	1	12	.247	4	65	3	2	.971
	Major league totals (6 years)		394	994	133	240	34	13	6	83	.241	95	610	21	12	.981

Year	Team (League)	Pos.	G	AB	R	H	2B	3B	HR	RBI	Avg.	SB	PO	A	E	Avg.
							BATTING							FIELDING		
1991—Pittsburgh (N.L.)		PH	2	2	0	0	0	0	0	0	.000	0	0	0	0	...

EUSEBIO, TONY
C, ASTROS

PERSONAL: Born April 27, 1967, at Boca Chica, Dominican Republic.... 6-2/180.... Throws right, bats right.... Full name: Raul Antonio Eusebio.
HIGH SCHOOL: San Rafael (Dominican Republic).
TRANSACTIONS/CAREER NOTES: Signed as free agent by Houston Astros organization (May 30, 1985).... On disabled list (August 5, 1990-remainder of season).
STATISTICAL NOTES: Tied for Southern League lead in double plays by catchers with eight in 1989.

Year	Team (League)	Pos.	G	AB	R	H	2B	3B	HR	RBI	Avg.	SB	PO	A	E	Avg.
							BATTING							FIELDING		
1985—Sarasota Astros (GCL)......		C	1	1	0	0	0	0	0	0	.000	0	4	0	0	1.000
1986—							Dominican Republic Summer League									
1987—Sarasota Astros (GCL)......		C-1B	42	125	26	26	1	2	1	15	.208	8	204	24	4	.983
1988—Osceola (Florida State)....		C-OF	118	392	45	96	6	3	0	40	.245	19	611	66	8	.988
1989—Columbus (Southern).......		C	65	203	20	38	6	1	0	18	.187	7	355	46	7	.983
—Osceola (Florida State)		C	52	175	22	50	6	3	0	30	.286	5	290	40	5	.985
1990—Columbus (Southern)........		C	92	318	36	90	18	0	4	37	.283	6	558	69	4	*.994
1991—Jackson (Texas)		C	66	222	27	58	8	3	2	31	.261	3	424	48	7	.985
—Tucson (Pacific Coast)		C	5	20	5	8	1	0	0	2	.400	1	40	1	0	1.000
—Houston (N.L.)		C	10	19	4	2	1	0	0	0	.105	0	49	4	1	.981
Major league totals (1 year)...........................			10	19	4	2	1	0	0	0	.105	0	49	4	1	.981

EVANS, DWIGHT
OF/DH, ORIOLES

PERSONAL: Born November 3, 1951, at Santa Monica, Calif.... 6-3/208.... Throws right, bats right.... Full name: Dwight Michael Evans.
HIGH SCHOOL: Chatsworth (Los Angeles).
TRANSACTIONS/CAREER NOTES: Selected by Boston Red Sox organization in fifth round of free-agent draft (June 5, 1969).... On disabled list (June 21-July 8 and August 25-September 21, 1977; August 13-September 1, 1983; and July 14-30, 1990).... Released by Red Sox (October 26, 1990).... Signed by Baltimore Orioles (December 6, 1990).... On disabled list (June 14-July 11, 1991).... Granted free agency (November 4, 1991).... Re-signed by Orioles (December 10, 1991).
RECORDS/HONORS: Named International League Most Valuable Player (1972).... Won A.L. Gold Glove as outfielder (1976, 1978-79 and 1981-85).... Named outfielder on THE SPORTING NEWS A.L. Silver Slugger team (1981 and 1987).... Named outfielder on THE SPORTING NEWS A.L. All-Star team (1982, 1984 and 1987).
STATISTICAL NOTES: Led Western Carolinas League with eight sacrifice flies in 1970.... Tied for Carolina League lead in double plays by outfielders with three in 1971.... Led A.L. outfielders with eight double plays in 1975 and seven in 1980.... Led A.L. with 215 total bases in 1981.... Led A.L. with 85 bases on balls received in 1981, 114 in 1985 and tied for lead with 106 in 1987. ... Led A.L. with .403 on base percentage in 1982.... Hit for the cycle (June 28, 1984).... Tied for A.L. lead in errors by first basemen with 12 in 1987.

Year	Team (League)	Pos.	G	AB	R	H	2B	3B	HR	RBI	Avg.	SB	PO	A	E	Avg.
							BATTING							FIELDING		
1969—Jamestown (N.Y.-Penn) ...		OF-3B	34	100	13	28	3	2	1	12	.280	0	44	10	3	.947
1970—Greenville (W. Carolinas)..		OF-3B	108	355	69	98	14	*11	7	68	.276	1	130	11	7	.953
1971—Winston-Salem (Caro.) ...		OF-1B	118	402	63	115	20	4	12	63	.286	7	219	17	10	.959
1972—Louisville (International) ..		OF	•144	496	90	149	23	8	17	*95	.300	1	270	12	6	.979
—Boston (A.L.)		OF	18	57	2	15	3	1	1	6	.263	0	25	3	0	1.000
1973—Boston (A.L.)		OF	119	282	46	63	13	1	10	32	.223	5	178	4	1	.995
1974—Boston (A.L.)		OF	133	463	60	130	19	8	10	70	.281	4	294	8	3	.990
1975—Boston (A.L.)		OF	128	412	61	113	24	6	13	56	.274	3	281	15	4	.987
1976—Boston (A.L.)		OF	146	501	61	121	34	5	17	62	.242	6	324	15	2	*.994
1977—Boston (A.L.)		OF	73	230	39	66	9	2	14	36	.287	4	126	2	1	.992
1978—Boston (A.L.)		OF	147	497	75	123	24	2	24	63	.247	8	305	14	6	.982
1979—Boston (A.L.)		OF	152	489	69	134	24	1	21	58	.274	6	307	15	4	.988
1980—Boston (A.L.)		OF	148	463	72	123	37	5	18	60	.266	3	268	11	5	.982
1981—Boston (A.L.)		OF	108	412	84	122	19	4	•22	71	.296	3	259	9	2	.993
1982—Boston (A.L.)		OF	•162	609	122	178	37	7	32	98	.292	3	346	9	10	.973
1983—Boston (A.L.)		OF	126	470	74	112	19	4	22	58	.238	3	222	6	3	.987
1984—Boston (A.L.)		OF	•162	630	*121	186	37	8	32	104	.295	3	311	7	2	.994
1985—Boston (A.L.)		OF	159	617	110	162	29	1	29	78	.263	7	291	9	3	.990
1986—Boston (A.L.)		OF	152	529	86	137	33	2	26	97	.259	3	280	10	5	.983
1987—Boston (A.L.)		1B-OF	154	541	109	165	37	2	34	123	.305	4	753	46	‡13	.984
1988—Boston (A.L.)		OF-1B	149	559	96	164	31	7	21	111	.293	5	611	34	9	.986
1989—Boston (A.L.)		OF	146	520	82	148	27	3	20	100	.285	3	153	5	3	.981
1990—Boston (A.L.)		DH	123	445	66	111	18	3	13	63	.249	3	0	0	0	...
1991—Baltimore (A.L.).■.............		OF	101	270	35	73	9	1	6	38	.270	2	116	6	2	.984
Major league totals (20 years)			2606	8996	1470	2446	483	73	385	1384	.272	78	5450	228	78	.986

CHAMPIONSHIP SERIES RECORD

Year	Team (League)	Pos.	G	AB	R	H	2B	3B	HR	RBI	Avg.	SB	PO	A	E	Avg.
1975 —Boston (A.L.)	OF	3	10	1	1	1	0	0	0	.100	0	7	0	0	1.000
1986 —Boston (A.L.)	OF	7	28	2	6	1	0	1	4	.214	0	11	0	0	1.000
1988 —Boston (A.L.)	OF	4	12	1	2	1	0	0	1	.167	0	11	0	0	1.000
1990 —Boston (A.L.)	DH	4	13	0	3	1	0	0	0	.231	0	0	0	0	...
Championship Series totals (4 years)		18	63	4	12	4	0	1	5	.190	0	29	0	0	1.000

WORLD SERIES RECORD

Year	Team (League)	Pos.	G	AB	R	H	2B	3B	HR	RBI	Avg.	SB	PO	A	E	Avg.
1975 —Boston (A.L.)	OF	7	24	3	7	1	1	1	5	.292	0	23	1	0	1.000
1986 —Boston (A.L.)	OF	7	26	4	8	2	0	2	9	.308	0	16	1	1	.944
World Series totals (2 years)		14	50	7	15	3	1	3	14	.300	0	39	2	1	.976

ALL-STAR GAME RECORD

Year	League	Pos.	AB	R	H	2B	3B	HR	RBI	Avg.	SB	PO	A	E	Avg.
1978 —American	OF	1	0	0	0	0	0	0	.000	0	3	0	0	1.000
1981 —American	PH-OF	2	1	1	0	0	0	0	.500	0	2	0	0	1.000
1987 —American	OF	2	0	2	0	0	0	0	1.000	0	2	0	0	1.000
All-Star Game totals (3 years)		5	1	3	0	0	0	0	.600	0	7	0	0	1.000

FAJARDO, HECTOR
P, RANGERS

PERSONAL: Born November 6, 1970, at Michoacan, Mexico. ... 6-4/200. ... Throws right, bats right. ... Full name: Hector Fajardo.
TRANSACTIONS/CAREER NOTES: Purchased by Pittsburgh Pirates organization from Mexico City Reds (April 2, 1989). ... Traded by Pirates to Texas Rangers (September 6, 1991), completing deal in which Rangers traded 3B Steve Buechele to Pirates for P Kurt Miller and a player to be named later (August 30, 1991).

Year	Team (League)	G	W	L	Pct.	ERA	Sv.	IP	H	R	ER	BB	SO
1989 —Bradenton Pirates (GCL)	10	0	5	.000	5.97	0	34⅔	38	24	23	20	19
1990 —Bradenton Pirates (GCL)	5	1	1	.500	3.86	0	21	23	10	9	8	17
—Augusta (South Atlantic)	7	2	2	.500	3.86	0	39⅔	41	18	17	15	28
1991 —Augusta (South Atlantic)	11	4	3	.571	2.69	0	60⅓	44	26	18	24	79
—Salem (Carolina)	1	0	1	.000	2.35	0	7⅔	4	3	2	1	7
—Carolina (Southern)	10	3	4	.429	4.13	0	61	55	32	28	24	53
—Pittsburgh (N.L.)	2	0	0	...	9.95	0	6⅓	10	7	7	7	8
—Buffalo (American Assoc.)	8	1	0	1.000	0.96	1	9⅓	6	1	1	3	12
—Texas (A.L.)■..........................	4	0	2	.000	5.68	0	19	25	13	12	4	15
American League totals (1 year)	4	0	2	.000	5.68	0	19	25	13	12	4	15
National League totals (1 year)	2	0	0	...	9.95	0	6⅓	10	7	7	7	8
Major league totals (1 year)	6	0	2	.000	6.75	0	25⅓	35	20	19	11	23

FARIES, PAUL
3B, PADRES

PERSONAL: Born February 20, 1965, at Berkeley, Calif. ... 5-10/170. ... Throws right, bats right. ... Full name: Paul Tyrrell Faries. ... Name pronounced FAIR-ees.
HIGH SCHOOL: Campolindo (Moraga, Calif.).
COLLEGE: Pepperdine.
TRANSACTIONS/CAREER NOTES: Selected by San Diego Padres organization in 22nd round of free-agent draft (June 2, 1987). ... On San Diego disabled list (May 23-June 17, 1991); included rehabilitation disability assignment to High Desert (June 8-17, 1991).
RECORDS/HONORS: Named California League Most Valuable Player (1988).
STATISTICAL NOTES: Led Northwest League second basemen with 377 total chances in 1987. ... Led California League second basemen with .975 fielding percentage, 469 assists, 764 total chances and 81 double plays in 1988. ... Led Texas League second basemen with .979 fielding percentage and 258 putouts in 1989. ... Led Pacific Coast League second basemen with 363 assists in 1990.

Year	Team (League)	Pos.	G	AB	R	H	2B	3B	HR	RBI	Avg.	SB	PO	A	E	Avg.
1987 —Spokane (Northwest)	2B	74	280	★67	86	9	3	0	27	.307	★30	★169	★197	11	★.971
1988 —Riverside (California)	2B-SS	141	★579	108	183	39	4	2	77	.316	65	288	†486	20	†.975
1989 —Wichita (Texas)	2B-SS	130	★513	79	136	25	8	6	52	.265	41	†284	391	18	†.974
1990 —Las Vegas (Pac. Coast)	2B-SS-3B	137	★552	★109	★172	29	3	5	64	.312	47	277	†418	25	.965
—San Diego (N.L.)	2B-SS-3B	14	37	4	7	1	0	0	2	.189	0	21	34	2	.965
1991 —San Diego (N.L.)	2B-3B-SS	57	130	13	23	3	1	0	7	.177	3	80	117	2	.990
—High Desert (California) SS-2B-3B	10	42	6	13	2	2	0	5	.310	1	14	22	6	.857
—Las Vegas (Pac. Coast)	SS	20	75	16	23	2	1	1	12	.307	7	33	65	2	.980
Major league totals (2 years)		71	167	17	30	4	1	0	9	.180	3	101	151	4	.984

FARISS, MONTY
2B/OF, RANGERS

PERSONAL: Born October 13, 1967, at Cordell, Okla. ... 6-4/205. ... Throws right, bats right. ... Full name: Monty Ted Fariss.
HIGH SCHOOL: Leedey (Okla.).
COLLEGE: Oklahoma State.

Year	Team (League)	Pos.	G	AB	R	H	2B	3B	HR	RBI	Avg.	SB	PO	A	E	Avg.
1988	—Butte (Pioneer)	SS	17	53	16	21	1	0	4	22	.396	2	36	52	4	.957
	—Tulsa (Texas)	SS	49	165	21	37	6	6	3	31	.224	2	77	147	18	.926
1989	—Tulsa (Texas)	SS	132	497	72	135	27	2	5	52	.272	12	*260	401	*51	.928
1990	—Tulsa (Texas)	SS	71	244	45	73	15	6	7	34	.299	8	141	190	24	.932
	—Oklahoma City (A.A.)	S-2-1-3	62	225	30	68	12	3	4	31	.302	1	138	151	22	.929
1991	—Oklahoma City (A.A.)	2B-OF	137	494	84	134	31	9	13	73	.271	5	†288	368	†28	.959
	—Texas (A.L.)	OF-2B	19	31	6	8	1	0	1	6	.258	0	25	9	0	1.000
Major league totals (1 year)			19	31	6	8	1	0	1	6	.258	0	25	9	0	1.000

FARMER, HOWARD

P, EXPOS

PERSONAL: Born January 18, 1966, at Gary, Ind.... 6-3/192.... Throws right, bats right.... Full name: Howard Earl Farmer.
HIGH SCHOOL: Horace Mann (Gary, Ind.).
COLLEGE: Utica Junior College (Miss.) and Jackson State.

Year	Team (League)	G	W	L	Pct.	ERA	Sv.	IP	H	R	ER	BB	SO
1987	—Jamestown (New York-Penn)	15	9	6	.600	3.27	0	96⅓	93	42	35	30	63
1988	—Rockford (Midwest)	27	15	7	.682	2.51	0	193⅔	153	70	54	58	145
1989	—Jacksonville (Southern)	26	12	9	.571	2.20	0	184	122	59	45	50	151
	—Indianapolis (Am. Assoc.)	1	1	0	1.000	0.00	0	7	3	1	0	3	3
1990	—Indianapolis (Am. Assoc.)	26	7	9	.438	3.89	0	148	150	84	64	48	99
	—Montreal (N.L.)	6	0	3	.000	7.04	0	23	26	18	18	10	14
1991	—Indianapolis (Am. Assoc.)	20	6	4	.600	3.86	0	105	93	55	45	37	67
Major league totals (1 year)		6	0	3	.000	7.04	0	23	26	18	18	10	14

FARR, STEVE

P, YANKEES

PERSONAL: Born December 12, 1956, at Cheverly, Md.... 5-11/206.... Throws right, bats right.... Full name: Steven Michael Farr.
HIGH SCHOOL: DeMatha Catholic (Hyattsville, Md.).
COLLEGE: American and Charles County Community College (Md.).

Year	Team (League)	G	W	L	Pct.	ERA	Sv.	IP	H	R	ER	BB	SO
1977	—Niagara Falls (N.Y.-Penn)	10	1	5	.167	3.98	0	52	53	30	23	30	43
1978	—Charleston, S.C. (W. Caro.)	21	5	3	.625	4.21	2	77	72	45	36	63	54
	—Salem (Carolina)	2	2	0	1.000	0.56	0	16	13	2	1	1	12
1979	—Salem (Carolina)	26	3	10	.231	4.99	1	119	138	81	66	47	105
1980	—Buffalo (Eastern)	23	11	6	.647	3.97	0	161	158	84	71	64	71
	—Portland (Pacific Coast)	2	0	1	.000	10.29	0	7	11	9	8	2	0
1981	—Buffalo (Eastern)	29	8	3	.727	3.74	3	106	102	50	44	48	82
	—Portland (Pacific Coast)	4	0	3	.000	7.83	0	23	39	28	20	12	19
1982	—Buffalo (Eastern)	25	5	8	.385	4.01	5	76⅓	72	40	34	38	84
1983	—Buffalo (Eastern)	18	13	1	.929	*1.61	1	112	88	28	20	50	108
1984	—Maine (International)■	6	4	0	1.000	2.60	0	45	37	14	13	8	40
	—Cleveland (A.L.)	31	3	11	.214	4.58	1	116	106	61	59	46	83
1985	—Omaha (American Assoc.)■	17	10	4	.714	*2.02	0	133⅔	105	36	30	41	98
	—Kansas City (A.L.)	16	2	1	.667	3.11	1	37⅔	34	15	13	20	36
1986	—Kansas City (A.L.)	56	8	4	.667	3.13	8	109⅓	90	39	38	39	83
1987	—Kansas City (A.L.)	47	4	3	.571	4.15	1	91	97	47	42	44	88
	—Omaha (American Assoc.)	8	0	0	...	1.42	4	12⅔	6	3	2	6	15
1988	—Kansas City (A.L.)	62	5	4	.556	2.50	20	82⅔	74	25	23	30	72
1989	—Kansas City (A.L.)	51	2	5	.286	4.12	18	63⅓	75	35	29	22	56
1990	—Kansas City (A.L.)	57	13	7	.650	1.98	1	127	99	32	28	48	94
1991	—New York (A.L.)■	60	5	5	.500	2.19	23	70	57	19	17	20	60
Major league totals (8 years)		380	42	40	.512	3.22	73	697	632	273	249	269	572

Year	Team (League)	G	W	L	Pct.	ERA	Sv.	IP	H	R	ER	BB	SO
1985 — Kansas City (A.L.)		2	1	0	1.000	1.42	0	6⅓	4	1	1	1	3

WORLD SERIES RECORD

Year	Team (League)	G	W	L	Pct.	ERA	Sv.	IP	H	R	ER	BB	SO
1985 — Kansas City (A.L.)							Did not play						

FASSERO, JEFF
P, EXPOS

PERSONAL: Born January 5, 1963, at Springfield, Ill. . . . 6-1/195. . . . Throws left, bats left. . . . Full name: Jeffrey Joseph Fassero.
HIGH SCHOOL: Griffin (Springfield, Ill.).
COLLEGE: Lincoln Land Community College (Ill.) and Mississippi.
TRANSACTIONS/CAREER NOTES: Selected by St. Louis Cardinals organization in 22nd round of free-agent draft (June 4, 1984). . . . Drafted by Chicago White Sox organization (December 5, 1989). . . . Released by White Sox organization (April 3, 1990). . . . Signed by Cleveland Indians organization (April 9, 1990). . . . Granted free agency (October 15, 1990). . . . Signed by India-napolis, Montreal Expos organization (January 3, 1991).
STATISTICAL NOTES: Tied for Florida State League lead in games started by pitcher with 26 in 1986. . . . Pitched 5-0 no-hit victory against Jackson (June 12, 1989).

Year	Team (League)	G	W	L	Pct.	ERA	Sv.	IP	H	R	ER	BB	SO
1984 — Johnson City (Appalachian)		13	4	7	.364	4.59	1	66⅔	65	42	34	39	59
1985 — Springfield (Midwest)		29	4	8	.333	4.01	1	119	125	78	53	45	65
1986 — St. Petersburg (Florida State)		26	13	7	.650	2.45	0	★176	156	63	48	56	112
1987 — Arkansas (Texas)		28	10	7	.588	4.10	0	151⅓	168	90	69	67	118
1988 — Arkansas (Texas)		70	5	5	.500	3.58	17	78	97	48	31	41	72
1989 — Louisville (American Assoc.)		22	3	10	.231	5.22	0	112	136	79	65	47	73
— Arkansas (Texas)		6	4	1	.800	1.64	0	44	32	11	8	12	38
1990 — Canton/Akron (Eastern)■		★61	5	4	.556	2.80	6	64⅓	66	24	20	24	61
1991 — Indianapolis (Am. Assoc.)■		18	3	0	1.000	1.47	4	18⅓	11	3	3	7	12
— Montreal (N.L.)		51	2	5	.286	2.44	8	55⅓	39	17	15	17	42
Major league totals (1 year)		51	2	5	.286	2.44	8	55⅓	39	17	15	17	42

FELDER, MIKE
OF, GIANTS

PERSONAL: Born November 18, 1962, at Richmond, Calif. . . . 5-8/160. . . . Throws right, bats both. . . . Full name: Michael Otis Felder.
HIGH SCHOOL: John F. Kennedy (Richmond, Calif.).
COLLEGE: Contra Costa College (Calif.).
TRANSACTIONS/CAREER NOTES: Selected by Milwaukee Brewers organization in third round of free-agent draft (January 13, 1981). . . . On disabled list (April 15-26, 1984). . . . On Milwaukee disabled list (May 3-June 5, 1986); included rehabilitation disability assignment to El Paso (May 23-June 5, 1986). . . . On Milwaukee disabled list (May 31-August 2, 1988); included rehabilitation disability assignment to Denver (June 24-July 1 and July 15-28, 1988). . . . On suspended list (August 27-30, 1990). . . . Released by Brewers (April 2, 1991). . . . Signed by San Francisco Giants (April 5, 1991). . . . On disabled list (August 19-September 3, 1991).
STATISTICAL NOTES: Led Texas League outfielders with 332 putouts and 363 total chances and tied for lead with 18 assists and 13 errors in 1983. . . . Led Texas League with nine sacrifice flies in 1984.

Year	Team (League)	Pos.	G	AB	R	H	2B	3B	HR	RBI	Avg.	SB	PO	A	E	Avg.
1981 — Stockton (California)	2B-OF	91	338	66	91	8	1	3	30	.269	41	172	162	13	.963
1982 — Stockton (California)	OF	137	524	102	138	18	11	7	47	.263	★92	314	9	10	.970
1983 — El Paso (Texas)	OF-2B	133	554	108	156	23	10	9	78	.282	★71	†334	‡24	‡13	.965
1984 — El Paso (Texas)	OF	122	496	98	144	19	2	9	72	.290	★58	321	13	6	.982
1985 — Vancouver (Pac. Coast)	OF-2B	137	563	91	177	16	11	2	43	.314	★61	294	15	4	.987
— Milwaukee (A.L.)	OF	15	56	8	11	1	0	0	0	.196	4	32	1	0	1.000
1986 — Milwaukee (A.L.)	OF	44	155	24	37	2	4	1	13	.239	16	98	0	0	1.000
— El Paso (Texas)	OF	8	31	10	14	3	0	0	2	.452	7	14	0	0	1.000
— Vancouver (Pac. Coast)	OF	39	153	21	40	3	4	1	15	.261	4	83	4	4	.956
1987 — Milwaukee (A.L.)	OF-2B	108	289	48	77	5	7	2	31	.266	34	190	10	5	.976
— Denver (Am. Assoc.)	OF-2B	27	113	26	41	6	2	2	20	.363	17	75	3	1	.987
1988 — Milwaukee (A.L.)	OF-2B	50	81	14	14	1	0	0	5	.173	8	40	1	1	.976
— Denver (Am. Assoc.)	OF	20	78	10	21	4	1	0	5	.269	8	55	1	1	.982
1989 — Milwaukee (A.L.)	OF-2B	117	315	50	76	11	3	3	23	.241	26	203	24	4	.983
1990 — Milwaukee (A.L.)	OF-2B-3B	121	237	38	65	7	2	3	27	.274	20	167	9	5	.972
1991 — San Francisco (N.L.)■	OF-3B	132	348	51	92	10	6	0	18	.264	21	193	8	4	.980
American League totals (6 years)		455	1133	182	280	27	16	9	99	.247	108	730	45	15	.981
National League totals (1 year)		132	348	51	92	10	6	0	18	.264	21	193	8	4	.980
Major league totals (7 years)		587	1481	233	372	37	22	9	117	.251	129	923	53	19	.981

FELIX, JUNIOR
OF, ANGELS

PERSONAL: Born October 3, 1967, at Laguna Sabada, Dominican Republic. . . . 5-11/165. . . . Throws right, bats both. . . . Full name: Junior Francisco Sanchez Felix.
TRANSACTIONS/CAREER NOTES: Signed as free agent by Toronto Blue Jays organization (September 15, 1985). . . . On suspended list (July 15, 1988-remainder of season). . . . On disabled

list (July 13-August 9, 1990).... Traded by Blue Jays with IF Luis Sojo and a player to be named later to California Angels for OF Devon White, P Willie Fraser and a player to be named later (December 2, 1990); Blue Jays acquired P Marcus Moore and Angels acquired C Ken Rivers to complete deal (December 4, 1990).... On California disabled list (June 2-17, 1991).... On California disabled list (June 20-August 25, 1991); included rehabilitation disability assignment to Palm Springs (August 5-24, 1991)..

STATISTICAL NOTES: Led Pioneer League outfielders with 165 total chances in 1986.... Led Pioneer League batters in strikeouts with 84 and caught stealing with nine and tied for lead in being hit by pitch with six in 1986.... Led South Atlantic League in caught stealing with 28 in 1987.... Hit home run in first major league at-bat on first pitch (May 4, 1989).

Year	Team (League)	Pos.	G	AB	R	H	2B	3B	HR	RBI	Avg.	SB	PO	A	E	Avg.
1986	Medicine Hat (Pioneer)	OF	67	263	57	75	9	3	4	28	.285	*37	*152	8	5	.970
1987	Myrtle Beach (S. Atl.)........	OF	124	466	70	135	15	•9	12	51	.290	64	188	8	9	.956
1988	Knoxville (Southern)	OF	93	360	52	91	16	5	3	25	.253	40	190	13	11	.949
1989	Syracuse (International) ..	OF	21	87	17	24	4	2	1	10	.276	13	42	0	1	.977
	Toronto (A.L.)....................	OF	110	415	62	107	14	8	9	46	.258	18	243	9	9	.966
1990	Toronto (A.L.)....................	OF	127	463	73	122	23	7	15	65	.263	13	244	11	9	.966
1991	California (A.L.)■	OF	66	230	32	65	10	2	2	26	.283	7	126	1	3	.977
	Palm Springs (Calif.)	OF	18	64	12	23	3	0	2	10	.359	8	30	0	1	.968
Major league totals (3 years)			303	1108	167	294	47	17	26	137	.265	38	613	21	21	.968

CHAMPIONSHIP SERIES RECORD

Year	Team (League)	Pos.	G	AB	R	H	2B	3B	HR	RBI	Avg.	SB	PO	A	E	Avg.
1989	Toronto (A.L.)....................	OF	3	11	0	3	1	0	0	3	.273	0	8	0	0	1.000

FERMIN, FELIX
SS, INDIANS

PERSONAL: Born October 9, 1963, at Mao, Valverde, Dominican Republic.... 5-11/170... Throws right, bats right.... Full name: Felix Jose Fermin.
COLLEGE: U.C.E. College (San Pedro de Macoris, Dominican Republic).
TRANSACTIONS/CAREER NOTES: Signed as free agent by Pittsburgh Pirates organization (June 11, 1983).... On Pittsburgh disabled list (July 19-August 24, 1987); included rehabilitation disability assignment to Harrisburg (August 12-24, 1987).... Traded by Pirates to Cleveland Indians for SS Jay Bell (March 25, 1989).... On Cleveland disabled list (April 23-May 12, 1991); included rehabilitation disability assignment to Colorado Springs (May 5-12, 1991).
RECORDS/HONORS: Shares major league single-game record for most sacrifice hits—4 (August 22, 1989, 10 innings).... Holds A.L. single-season record for fewest long hits (150 or more games)—10 (1989).
STATISTICAL NOTES: Tied for New York-Pennsylvania League lead in double plays by shortstops with 38 in 1983.... Led Eastern League shortstops with .964 fielding percentage, 251 putouts and 661 total chances in 1985.... Led Eastern League shortstops in fielding percentage with .968 in 1987.... Led A.L. with 32 sacrifice hits in 1989.... Led A.L. shortstops with 26 errors in 1989.

Year	Team (League)	Pos.	G	AB	R	H	2B	3B	HR	RBI	Avg.	SB	PO	A	E	Avg.
1983	Watertown (N.Y.-Penn)....	SS	67	234	27	46	6	1	0	14	.197	5	94	223	30	.914
	Bradenton Pirates (GCL) ..	SS	1	4	1	1	0	0	0	1	.250	0	1	4	0	1.000
1984	Prince William (Caro.).......	SS	119	382	34	94	13	1	0	41	.246	32	181	376	23	*.960
1985	Nashua (Eastern)	SS-2B	137	443	32	100	10	2	0	27	.226	29	†251	387	24	†.964
1986	Hawaii (Pacific Coast)	SS-2B	39	125	13	32	5	0	0	9	.256	1	60	99	7	.958
	Prince William (Caro.)	SS	84	322	58	90	10	1	0	26	.280	40	158	205	19	.950
1987	Harrisburg (Eastern)	SS-2B	100	399	62	107	9	5	0	35	.268	22	177	288	15	†.969
	Pittsburgh (N.L.)	SS	23	68	6	17	0	0	0	4	.250	0	36	62	2	.980
1988	Buffalo (Am. Assoc.)	SS	87	352	38	92	11	1	0	31	.261	8	131	268	10	.976
	Pittsburgh (N.L.)	SS	43	87	9	24	0	1	0	2	.276	3	51	76	6	.955
1989	Cleveland (A.L.)■...........	SS-2B	156	484	50	115	9	1	0	21	.238	6	253	517	†26	.967
1990	Cleveland (A.L.)	SS-2B	148	414	47	106	13	2	1	40	.256	3	214	423	16	.975
1991	Cleveland (A.L.)	SS	129	424	30	111	13	2	0	31	.262	5	214	372	12	.980
	Colorado Springs (PCL)	SS	2	8	1	2	0	0	0	1	.250	0	2	5	0	1.000
American League totals (3 years)			433	1322	127	332	35	5	1	92	.251	14	681	1312	54	.974
National League totals (2 years)			66	155	15	41	0	2	0	6	.265	3	87	138	8	.966
Major league totals (5 years)			499	1477	142	373	35	7	1	98	.253	17	768	1450	62	.973

FERNANDEZ, ALEX
P, WHITE SOX

PERSONAL: Born August 13, 1969, at Miami Beach, Fla.... 6-1/205.... Throws right, bats right.... Full name: Alexander Fernandez.
HIGH SCHOOL: Pace (Miami).
COLLEGE: Miami (Fla.) and Miami-Dade (South) Community College.
TRANSACTIONS/CAREER NOTES: Selected by Milwaukee Brewers organization in first round (24th pick overall) of free-agent draft (June 1, 1988).... Selected by Chicago White Sox organization in first round (fourth pick overall) of free-agent draft (June 4, 1990).

Year	Team (League)	G	W	L	Pct.	ERA	Sv.	IP	H	R	ER	BB	SO
1990	Sarasota White Sox (GCL)	2	1	0	1.000	3.60	0	10	11	4	4	1	16
	Sarasota (Florida State)	2	1	1	.500	1.84	0	14⅔	8	4	3	3	23
	Birmingham (Southern)	4	3	0	1.000	1.08	0	25	20	7	3	6	27
	Chicago (A.L.)	13	5	5	.500	3.80	0	87⅔	89	40	37	34	61
1991	Chicago (A.L.)	34	9	13	.409	4.51	0	191⅔	186	100	96	88	145
Major league totals (2 years)	47	14	18	.438	4.29	0	279⅓	275	140	133	122	206

FERNANDEZ, JOSE
C, CARDINALS

PERSONAL: Born August 24, 1967, at New York. . . . 6-3/210. . . . Throws right, bats left. . . . Full name: Jose Ignacio Fernandez.
HIGH SCHOOL: Cardinal Newman (West Palm Beach, Fla.).
COLLEGE: Palm Beach Junior College (Fla.) and Florida.
TRANSACTIONS/CAREER NOTES: Selected by Houston Astros organization in 36th round of free-agent draft (June 2, 1986). . . . Selected by St. Louis Cardinals organization in 14th round of free-agent draft (June 5, 1989).

						BATTING						FIELDING		
Year Team (League)	Pos.	G	AB	R	H	2B	3B	HR	RBI	Avg.	SB	PO	A	E	Avg.
1989—Hamilton (N.Y.-Penn)	C	52	165	24	33	7	1	5	23	.200	3	369	35	6	.985
1990—St. Petersburg (Fla. St.)	C	42	138	12	35	10	0	1	19	.254	0	300	32	5	.985
—Arkansas (Texas)	C	55	177	13	30	5	1	4	25	.169	0	349	40	3	.992
1991—Arkansas (Texas)	C	94	285	46	65	14	1	12	28	.228	0	538	58	13	.979

FERNANDEZ, SID
P, METS

PERSONAL: Born October 12, 1962, at Honolulu. . . . 6-1/230. . . . Throws left, bats left. . . . Full name: Charles Sidney Fernandez.
HIGH SCHOOL: Kaiser (Honolulu).
TRANSACTIONS/CAREER NOTES: Selected by Los Angeles Dodgers organization in third round of free-agent draft (June 8, 1981). . . . Traded by Dodgers with IF Ross Jones to New York Mets for P Carlos Diaz and a player to be named later (December 8, 1983); Dodgers acquired IF Bob Bailor to complete deal (December 12, 1983). . . . On disabled list (August 4-22, 1987). . . . On New York disabled list (March 12-July 18, 1991); included rehabilitation disability assignment to St. Lucie (June 22-27, 1991), Tidewater (June 27-July 7 and July 14-16, 1991) and Williamsport (July 7-14, 1991).
RECORDS/HONORS: Named Texas League Pitcher of the Year (1983).
STATISTICAL NOTES: Pitched 5-0 no-hit victory against Winter Haven (April 24, 1982). . . . Pitched 1-0 no-hit victory against Fort Lauderdale (June 8, 1982).

Year Team (League)	G	W	L	Pct.	ERA	Sv.	IP	H	R	ER	BB	SO
1981—Lethbridge (Pioneer)	11	5	1	.833	★1.54	0	76	43	21	13	31	★128
1982—Vero Beach (Florida State)	12	8	1	.889	1.91	0	84⅔	38	19	18	38	★137
—Albuquerque (Pacific Coast)	13	6	5	.545	5.42	0	88	76	54	53	52	86
1983—San Antonio (Texas)	24	•13	4	.765	★2.82	0	153	111	61	48	96	★209
—Los Angeles (N.L.)	2	0	1	.000	6.00	0	6	7	4	4	7	9
1984—Tidewater (International)■.......	17	6	5	.545	2.56	0	105⅔	69	39	30	63	123
—New York (N.L.)	15	6	6	.500	3.50	0	90	74	40	35	34	62
1985—Tidewater (International)	5	4	1	.800	2.04	0	35⅓	17	8	8	21	42
—New York (N.L.)	26	9	9	.500	2.80	0	170⅓	108	56	53	80	180
1986—New York (N.L.)	32	16	6	.727	3.52	1	204⅓	161	82	80	91	200
1987—New York (N.L.)	28	12	8	.600	3.81	0	156	130	75	66	67	134
1988—New York (N.L.)	31	12	10	.545	3.03	0	187	127	69	63	70	189
1989—New York (N.L.)	35	14	5	.737	2.83	0	219⅓	157	73	69	75	198
1990—New York (N.L.)	30	9	14	.391	3.46	0	179⅓	130	79	69	67	181
1991—St. Lucie (Florida State)	1	0	0	...	0.00	0	3	1	0	0	1	4
—Tidewater (International)	3	1	0	1.000	1.15	0	15⅔	9	2	2	6	22
—Williamsport (Eastern)	1	0	0	...	0.00	0	6	3	0	0	1	5
—New York (N.L.)	8	1	3	.250	2.86	0	44	36	18	14	9	31
Major league totals (9 years)	207	79	62	.560	3.25	1	1256⅓	930	496	453	500	1184

CHAMPIONSHIP SERIES RECORD

Year Team (League)	G	W	L	Pct.	ERA	Sv.	IP	H	R	ER	BB	SO
1986—New York (N.L.)	1	0	1	.000	4.50	0	6	3	3	3	1	5
1988—New York (N.L.)	1	0	1	.000	13.50	0	4	7	6	6	1	5
Championship Series totals (2 years)	2	0	2	.000	8.10	0	10	10	9	9	2	10

WORLD SERIES RECORD

Year Team (League)	G	W	L	Pct.	ERA	Sv.	IP	H	R	ER	BB	SO
1986—New York (N.L.)	3	0	0	...	1.35	0	6⅔	6	1	1	1	10

ALL-STAR GAME RECORD

Year League	W	L	Pct.	ERA	Sv.	IP	H	R	ER	BB	SO
1986—National	0	0	...	0.00	0	1	0	0	0	2	3
1987—National	0	0	...	0.00	1	1	0	0	0	1	1
All-Star totals (2 years)	0	0	...	0.00	1	2	0	0	0	3	4

FERNANDEZ, TONY
SS, PADRES

PERSONAL: Born June 30, 1962, at San Pedro de Macoris, Dominican Republic. . . . 6-2/175. . . . Throws right, bats both. . . . Full name: Octavio Antonio Castro Fernandez.
HIGH SCHOOL: Gasto Fernando (San Pedro de Macoris, Dominican Republic).
TRANSACTIONS/CAREER NOTES: Signed as free agent by Toronto Blue Jays organization (April 24, 1979). . . . On Syracuse disabled list (August 10-27, 1981). . . . On disabled list (April 8-May 2, 1989). . . . Traded by Blue Jays with 1B Fred McGriff to San Diego Padres for OF Joe Carter and 2B Roberto Alomar (December 5, 1990).
RECORDS/HONORS: Holds A.L. career record for highest fielding percentage by shortstop (1000 or more games)—.980. . . . Holds A.L. single-season record for most games by shortstop—163 (1986). . . . Shares A.L. single-season record for most games by switch-hitter—163 (1986). . . . Named shortstop on THE SPORTING NEWS A.L. All-Star team (1986). . . . Won A.L. Gold Glove at shortstop (1986-89).

STATISTICAL NOTES: Led International League shortstops with 87 double plays in 1983. . . . Led A.L. shortstops with 791 total chances in 1985 and 786 in 1990.

Year	Team (League)	Pos.	G	AB	R	H	2B	3B	HR	RBI	Avg.	SB	PO	A	E	Avg.
1980	—Kinston (Carolina)............	SS	62	187	28	52	6	2	0	12	.278	7	93	205	28	.914
1981	—Kinston (Carolina)............	SS	75	280	57	89	10	6	1	13	.318	15	121	227	19	.948
	—Syracuse (International) ..	SS	31	115	13	32	6	2	1	9	.278	9	69	80	3	.980
1982	—Syracuse (International) ..	SS	134	523	78	158	21	6	4	56	.302	22	★246	364	23	★.964
1983	—Syracuse (International) ..	SS	117	437	65	131	18	6	5	38	.300	35	★211	361	26	.957
	—Toronto (A.L.).................	SS	15	34	5	9	1	1	0	2	.265	0	16	17	0	1.000
1984	—Syracuse (International) ..	SS	26	94	12	24	1	0	0	6	.255	1	46	72	5	.959
	—Toronto (A.L.).................	SS-3B	88	233	29	63	5	3	3	19	.270	5	119	195	9	.972
1985	—Toronto (A.L.).................	SS	161	564	71	163	31	10	2	51	.289	13	283	★478	30	.962
1986	—Toronto (A.L.).................	SS	★163	★687	91	213	33	9	10	65	.310	25	★294	445	13	★.983
1987	—Toronto (A.L.).................	SS	146	578	90	186	29	8	5	67	.322	32	★270	396	14	.979
1988	—Toronto (A.L.).................	SS	154	648	76	186	41	4	5	70	.287	15	247	470	14	.981
1989	—Toronto (A.L.).................	SS	140	573	64	147	25	9	11	64	.257	22	260	475	6	★.992
1990	—Toronto (A.L.).................	SS	161	635	84	175	27	★17	4	66	.276	26	★297	★480	9	.989
1991	—San Diego (N.L.)■.........	SS	145	558	81	152	27	5	4	38	.272	23	247	440	20	.972
American League totals (8 years)..............			1028	3952	510	1142	192	61	40	404	.289	138	1786	2956	95	.980
National League totals (1 year)..............			145	558	81	152	27	5	4	38	.272	23	247	440	20	.972
Major league totals (9 years)..............			1173	4510	591	1294	219	66	44	442	.287	161	2033	3396	115	.979

CHAMPIONSHIP SERIES RECORD

Year	Team (League)	Pos.	G	AB	R	H	2B	3B	HR	RBI	Avg.	SB	PO	A	E	Avg.
1985	—Toronto (A.L.).................	SS	7	24	2	8	2	0	0	2	.333	1	11	15	2	.929
1989	—Toronto (A.L.).................	SS	5	20	6	7	3	0	0	1	.350	5	9	15	0	1.000
Championship Series totals (2 years)..............			12	44	8	15	5	0	0	3	.341	5	20	30	2	.962

ALL-STAR GAME RECORD

Year	League	Pos.	AB	R	H	2B	3B	HR	RBI	Avg.	SB	PO	A	E	Avg.
1986	—American	SS	0	0	0	0	0	0	0	. . .	0	0	0	0	. . .
1987	—American	SS	2	0	0	0	0	0	0	.000	0	1	3	0	1.000
1989	—American	PR-SS	1	0	0	0	0	0	0	.000	0	2	2	0	1.000
All-Star Game totals (3 years)..............			3	0	0	0	0	0	0	.000	0	3	5	0	1.000

FETTERS, MIKE
P, BREWERS

PERSONAL: Born December 19, 1964, at Van Nuys, Calif. . . . 6-4/212. . . . Throws right, bats right. . . . Full name: Michael Lee Fetters.
HIGH SCHOOL: Iolani (Hawaii).
COLLEGE: Pepperdine.
TRANSACTIONS/CAREER NOTES: Selected by Los Angeles Dodgers organization in 22nd round of free-agent draft (June 6, 1983). . . . Selected by California Angels organization in first round (compensation selection) of free-agent draft (June 2, 1986). . . . Traded by Angels with P Glenn Carter to Milwaukee Brewers for P Chuck Crim (December 10, 1991). . . .
STATISTICAL NOTES: Tied for Pacific Coast League lead with six complete games in 1989.

Year	Team (League)	G	W	L	Pct.	ERA	Sv.	IP	H	R	ER	BB	SO
1986	—Salem (Northwest)	12	4	2	.667	3.38	0	72	60	39	27	51	72
1987	—Palm Springs (California)	19	9	7	.563	3.57	0	116	106	62	46	73	105
1988	—Midland (Texas)	20	8	8	.500	5.92	0	114	116	78	75	67	101
	—Edmonton (Pacific Coast).........	2	2	0	1.000	1.93	0	14	8	3	3	10	11
1989	—Edmonton (Pacific Coast).........	26	12	8	.600	3.80	0	168	160	80	71	72	★144
	—California (A.L.)	1	0	0	. . .	8.10	0	3⅓	5	4	3	1	4
1990	—Edmonton (Pacific Coast).........	5	1	1	.500	0.99	0	27⅓	22	9	3	13	26
	—California (A.L.)	26	1	1	.500	4.12	1	67⅔	77	33	31	20	35
1991	—Edmonton (Pacific Coast).........	11	2	7	.222	4.87	0	61	65	39	33	26	43
	—California (A.L.)	19	2	5	.286	4.84	0	44⅔	53	29	24	28	24
Major league totals (3 years)		46	3	6	.333	4.51	1	115⅔	135	66	58	49	63

FIELDER, CECIL
1B, TIGERS

PERSONAL: Born September 21, 1963, at Los Angeles. . . . 6-3/245. . . . Throws right, bats right. . . . Full name: Cecil Grant Fielder.
HIGH SCHOOL: Nogales (Los Angeles).
COLLEGE: UNLV.
TRANSACTIONS/CAREER NOTES: Selected by Baltimore Orioles organization in 31st round of free-agent draft (June 8, 1981). . . . Selected by Kansas City Royals organization in secondary phase of free-agent draft (June 7, 1982). . . . Traded by Royals organization to Toronto Blue Jays organization for OF Leon Roberts (February 4, 1983). . . . Sold by Blue Jays to Hanshin Tigers of Japanese League (December 22, 1988). . . . Signed by Detroit Tigers (January 15, 1990).
RECORDS/HONORS: Shares major league single-season record for most games with three home runs—2 (1990). . . . Named A.L. Player of the Year by THE SPORTING NEWS (1990). . . . Named first baseman on THE SPORTING NEWS A.L. All-Star team (1990-91). . . . Named first baseman on THE SPORTING NEWS A.L. Silver Slugger team (1990-91).

STATISTICAL NOTES: Led Pioneer League in total bases with 176 and being hit by pitch with eight in 1982. . . . Led A.L. batters with 339 total bases, .592 slugging percentage and 182 strikeouts in 1990. . . . Led A.L. first basemen with 137 double plays in 1990. . . . Hit three home runs in a game (May 6 and June 6, 1990).

Year	Team (League)	Pos.	G	AB	R	H	2B	3B	HR	RBI	Avg.	SB	PO	A	E	Avg.
1982	—Butte (Pioneer)	1B	69	273	73	88	★28	0	★20	68	.322	3	247	18	4	.985
1983	—Florence (S. Atlantic)■	1B	140	500	81	156	28	2	16	94	.312	2	957	64	16	.985
1984	—Kinston (Carolina)	1B	61	222	42	63	12	1	19	49	.284	2	533	24	9	.984
	—Knoxville (Southern)	1B	64	236	33	60	12	2	9	44	.254	0	173	10	4	.979
1985	—Knoxville (Southern)	1B	96	361	52	106	26	2	18	81	.294	0	444	26	6	.987
	—Toronto (A.L.)	1B	30	74	6	23	4	0	4	16	.311	0	171	17	4	.979
1986	—Toronto (A.L.)	1B-3B-OF	34	83	7	13	2	0	4	13	.157	0	37	4	1	.976
	—Syracuse (International)	OF-1B	88	325	47	91	13	3	18	68	.280	0	117	5	1	.992
1987	—Toronto (A.L.)	1B-3B	82	175	30	47	7	1	14	32	.269	0	98	6	0	1.000
1988	—Toronto (A.L.)	1B-3B-2B	74	174	24	40	6	1	9	23	.230	0	101	12	1	.991
1989	—Hanshin Tgrs (Jap. Cen.)■	...	106	384	60	116	11	0	38	81	.302	0	...	...	...	...
1990	—Detroit (A.L.)■	1B	159	573	104	159	25	1	★51	★132	.277	0	1190	111	14	.989
1991	—Detroit (A.L.)	1B	★162	624	102	163	25	0	●44	★133	.261	0	1055	83	8	.993
	Major league totals (6 years)		541	1703	273	445	69	3	126	349	.261	0	2652	233	28	.990

CHAMPIONSHIP SERIES RECORD

Year	Team (League)	Pos.	G	AB	R	H	2B	3B	HR	RBI	Avg.	SB	PO	A	E	Avg.
1985	—Toronto (A.L.)	PH	3	3	0	1	1	0	0	0	.333	0	0	0	0	...

ALL-STAR GAME RECORD

Year	League	Pos.	AB	R	H	2B	3B	HR	RBI	Avg.	SB	PO	A	E	Avg.
1990	—American	PH-1B	1	0	0	0	0	0	0	.000	0	3	1	0	1.000
1991	—American	1B	3	0	0	0	0	0	0	.000	0	6	2	0	1.000
	All-Star Game totals (2 years)		4	0	0	0	0	0	0	.000	0	9	3	0	1.000

FINLEY, CHUCK
P, ANGELS

PERSONAL: Born November 26, 1962, at Monroe, La. . . . 6-6/214. . . . Throws left, bats left. . . . Full name: Charles Edward Finley.
HIGH SCHOOL: West Monroe (La.).
COLLEGE: Northeast Louisiana State.
TRANSACTIONS/CAREER NOTES: Selected by California Angels organization in 15th round of free-agent draft (June 4, 1984). . . . Selected by California Angels organization in secondary phase of free-agent draft (January 9, 1985). . . . On disabled list (August 22-September 15, 1989).
RECORDS/HONORS: Named lefthanded pitcher on THE SPORTING NEWS A.L. All-Star team (1989-90).

Year	Team (League)	G	W	L	Pct.	ERA	Sv.	IP	H	R	ER	BB	SO
1985	—Salem (Northwest)	18	3	1	.750	4.66	5	29	34	21	15	10	32
1986	—Quad Cities (Midwest)	10	1	0	1.000	.00	6	12	4	0	0	3	16
	—California (A.L.)	25	3	1	.750	3.30	0	46⅓	40	17	17	23	37
1987	—California (A.L.)	35	2	7	.222	4.67	0	90⅔	102	54	47	43	63
1988	—California (A.L.)	31	9	15	.375	4.17	0	194⅓	191	95	90	82	111
1989	—California (A.L.)	29	16	9	.640	2.57	0	199⅔	171	64	57	82	156
1990	—California (A.L.)	32	18	9	.667	2.40	0	236	210	77	63	81	177
1991	—California (A.L.)	34	18	9	.667	3.80	0	227⅓	205	102	96	101	171
	Major league totals (6 years)	186	66	50	.569	3.35	0	994⅓	919	409	370	412	715

ALL-STAR GAME RECORD

Year	League	W	L	Pct.	ERA	Sv.	IP	H	R	ER	BB	SO
1989	—American					Did not play						
1990	—American	0	0	...	0.00	0	1	1	0	0	1	1

FINLEY, STEVE
OF, ASTROS

PERSONAL: Born March 12, 1965, at Union City, Tenn. . . . 6-2/180. . . . Throws left, bats left. . . . Full name: Steven Allen Finley.
HIGH SCHOOL: Paducah Tilghman (Paducah, Ky.).
COLLEGE: Southern Illinois (degree in physiology).
TRANSACTIONS/CAREER NOTES: Selected by Atlanta Braves organization in 11th round of free-agent draft (June 2, 1986). . . . Selected by Baltimore Orioles organization in 13th round of free-agent draft (June 2, 1987). . . . On Baltimore disabled list (April 4-22 and July 29-September 1, 1989; included rehabilitation disability assignment to Hagerstown (August 21-23, 1989). . . . Traded by Orioles with P Pete Harnisch and P Curt Schilling to Houston Astros for 1B Glenn Davis (January 10, 1991).
STATISTICAL NOTES: Led International League outfielders with 315 total chances in 1988.

Year	Team (League)	Pos.	G	AB	R	H	2B	3B	HR	RBI	Avg.	SB	PO	A	E	Avg.
1987	—Newark (N.Y.-Penn)	OF	54	222	40	65	13	2	3	33	.293	26	122	7	4	.970
	—Hagerstown (Carolina)	OF	15	65	9	22	3	2	1	5	.338	7	32	3	0	1.000

Year	Team (League)	Pos.	G	AB	R	H	2B	3B	HR	RBI	Avg.	SB	PO	A	E	Avg.
1988	—Hagerstown (Carolina)	OF	8	28	2	6	2	0	0	3	.214	4	17	0	0	1.000
	—Charlotte (Southern)	OF	10	40	7	12	4	2	1	6	.300	2	14	0	0	1.000
	—Rochester (Int'l)	OF	120	456	61	★143	19	7	5	54	★.314	20	★289	14	★12	.962
1989	—Baltimore (A.L.)	OF	81	217	35	54	5	2	2	25	.249	17	144	1	2	.986
	—Rochester (Int'l)	OF	7	25	2	4	0	0	0	2	.160	3	17	2	0	1.000
	—Hagerstown (Eastern)	OF	11	48	11	20	3	1	0	7	.417	4	35	2	3	.925
1990	—Baltimore (A.L.)	OF	142	464	46	119	16	4	3	37	.256	22	298	4	7	.977
1991	—Houston (N.L.)■.............	OF	159	596	84	170	28	10	8	54	.285	34	323	13	5	.985
American League totals (2 years)			223	681	81	173	21	6	5	62	.254	39	442	5	9	.980
National League totals (1 year)			159	596	84	170	28	10	8	54	.285	34	323	13	5	.985
Major league totals (3 years)			382	1277	165	343	49	16	13	116	.269	73	765	18	14	.982

FISK, CARLTON
C, WHITE SOX

PERSONAL: Born December 26, 1947, at Bellows Falls, Vt. . . . 6-2/225. . . . Throws right, bats right. . . . Full name: Carlton Ernest Fisk.
HIGH SCHOOL: Charlestown (N.H.).
COLLEGE: New Hampshire.

TRANSACTIONS/CAREER NOTES: Selected by Baltimore Orioles organization in 36th round of free-agent draft (June, 1965). . . . Selected by Boston Red Sox organization in first round (fourth pick overall) of free-agent draft (January, 1967). . . . On temporary inactive list (April 17, 1967; transferred to military list (May 18, 1967-April 19, 1968). . . . On temporary inactive list (August 5-20, 1968). . . . On disabled list (March 21-April 26 and June 28, 1974-remainder of season; March 24-June 23, 1975; and April 14-May 21, 1979). . . . Granted free agency by arbitrator's ruling (February 12, 1981). . . . Signed by Chicago White Sox (March 18, 1981). . . . On disabled list (June 13-July 5, 1984). . . . Granted free agency (November 12, 1985). . . . Re-signed by White Sox (January 8, 1986). . . . Granted free agency (January 22, 1988). . . . Re-signed by White Sox (February 9, 1988). . . . On disabled list (May 11-July 28, 1988 and April 11-June 1, 1989). . . . Granted free agency (November 4, 1991). . . . Re-signed by White Sox (December 11, 1991).

RECORDS/HONORS: Holds major league career record for most home runs by catcher—347. . . . Holds major league records for longest game with no passed balls—25 innings; most innings played by catcher in game—25 (May 8, finished May 9, 1984). . . . Shares major league single-game records for most at-bats—11; plate appearances—12 (May 8, finished May 9, 1984, 25 innings). . . . Shares modern major league record for most long hits in one inning—2 (May 15, 1975, eighth inning, and June 30, 1977, eighth inning). . . . Holds A.L. career catching records for most years—22; games—2,147; putouts—11,040; chances accepted—12,059. . . . Holds A.L. single-season record for most home runs by catcher—33 (1985). . . . Holds A.L. single-season record for fewest assists by catcher (150 or more games)—69 (1977). . . . Shares A.L. single-season record for fewest passed balls (150 or more games)—4 (1977). . . . Named THE SPORTING NEWS A.L. Rookie Player of the Year (1972). . . . Named catcher on THE SPORTING NEWS A.L. All-Star team (1972, 1977, 1983, 1985 and 1990). . . . Won A.L. Gold Glove at catcher (1972). . . . Named A.L. Rookie of the Year by Baseball Writers' Association of America (1972). . . . Named catcher on THE SPORTING NEWS A.L. Silver Slugger team (1981, 1985 and 1988).

STATISTICAL NOTES: Led International League catchers with 12 double plays in 1971. . . . Led A.L. catchers with 933 total chances in 1972; 803 in 1973; 519 in 1981; and 871 in 1985. . . . Led A.L. catchers with 17 errors in 1978 and 10 in 1980. . . . Led A.L. in being hit by pitch with 13 in 1980. . . . Led A.L. catchers with 470 putouts in 1981. . . . Led A.L. catchers with 10 double plays in 1981 and 15 in 1987. . . . Led A.L. with 11 passed balls in 1983. . . . Hit for the cycle (May 16, 1984).

Year	Team (League)	Pos.	G	AB	R	H	2B	3B	HR	RBI	Avg.	SB	PO	A	E	Avg.
1967	—				In military service											
1968	—Waterloo (Midwest)	C	62	195	31	66	11	2	12	34	.338	2	385	42	8	.982
1969	—Pittsfield (Eastern)..........	C	97	309	38	75	18	3	10	41	.243	2	551	65	★22	.966
	—Boston (A.L.)	C	2	5	0	0	0	0	0	0	.000	0	2	0	0	1.000
1970	—Pawtucket (Eastern)........	C-OF-1B	93	284	43	65	18	1	12	44	.229	6	482	50	7	.987
1971	—Louisville (International) ..	C-OF-3B	94	308	45	81	10	4	10	43	.263	4	588	51	13	.980
	—Boston (A.L.)	C	14	48	7	15	2	1	2	6	.313	0	72	6	2	.975
1972	—Boston (A.L.)	C	131	457	74	134	28	•9	22	61	.293	5	★846	★72	•15	.984
1973	—Boston (A.L.)	C	135	508	65	125	21	0	26	71	.246	7	★739	50	★14	.983
1974	—Boston (A.L.)	C	52	187	36	56	12	1	11	26	.299	5	267	26	6	.980
1975	—Boston (A.L.)	C	79	263	47	87	14	4	10	52	.331	4	347	30	8	.979
1976	—Boston (A.L.)	C	134	487	76	124	17	5	17	58	.255	12	649	73	12	.984
1977	—Boston (A.L.)	C	152	536	106	169	26	3	26	102	.315	7	779	69	11	.987
1978	—Boston (A.L.)	C-OF	157	571	94	162	39	5	20	88	.284	7	734	90	†17	.980
1979	—Boston (A.L.)	C-OF	91	320	49	87	23	2	10	42	.272	3	155	8	3	.982
1980	—Boston (A.L.) ■...............	C-1-0-3	131	478	73	138	25	3	18	62	.289	11	543	56	†11	.982
1981	—Chicago (A.L.)■..............	C-1-3-0	96	338	44	89	12	0	7	45	.263	3	†479	46	6	.989
1982	—Chicago (A.L.)	C-1B	135	476	66	127	17	3	14	65	.267	17	648	63	5	.993
1983	—Chicago (A.L.)	C	138	488	85	141	26	4	26	86	.289	9	★709	46	7	.991
1984	—Chicago (A.L.)	C	102	359	54	83	20	1	21	43	.231	6	421	38	6	.987
1985	—Chicago (A.L.)	C	153	543	85	129	23	1	37	107	.238	17	★801	60	10	.989
1986	—Chicago (A.L.)	C-OF	125	457	42	101	11	0	14	63	.221	2	455	44	8	.984
1987	—Chicago (A.L.)	C-1B-OF	135	454	68	116	22	1	23	71	.256	1	597	66	7	.990
1988	—Chicago (A.L.)	C	76	253	37	70	8	1	19	50	.277	0	338	36	2	.995
1989	—Chicago (A.L.)	C	103	375	47	110	25	2	13	68	.293	1	419	37	3	★.993
1990	—Chicago (A.L.)	C	137	452	65	129	21	0	18	65	.285	7	660	63	4	.994
1991	—Chicago (A.L.)	C-1B	134	460	42	111	25	0	18	74	.241	1	625	65	6	.991
Major league totals (22 years)			2412	8515	1262	2303	417	46	372	1305	.270	125	11285	1044	163	.987

CHAMPIONSHIP SERIES RECORD

Year	Team (League)	Pos.	G	AB	R	H	2B	3B	HR	RBI	Avg.	SB	PO	A	E	Avg.
1975 —Boston (A.L.)	C	3	12	4	5	1	0	0	2	.417	0	15	0	0	1.000
1983 —Chicago (A.L.)	C	4	17	0	3	1	0	0	0	.176	0	27	3	0	1.000
Championship Series totals (2 years)		7	29	4	8	2	0	0	2	.276	0	42	3	0	1.000

WORLD SERIES RECORD

WORLD SERIES NOTES: Shares record for most at-bats in one inning—2 (October 15, 1975, fourth inning).

Year	Team (League)	Pos.	G	AB	R	H	2B	3B	HR	RBI	Avg.	SB	PO	A	E	Avg.
1975 —Boston (A.L.)	C	7	25	5	6	0	0	0	2	4	.240	0	37	3	2	.952

ALL-STAR GAME RECORD

ALL-STAR GAME NOTES: Named to A.L. All-Star team for 1974 game; replaced due to injury.

Year	League	Pos.	AB	R	H	2B	3B	HR	RBI	Avg.	SB	PO	A	E	Avg.
1972 —American	C	2	1	1	0	0	0	0	.500	0	2	0	0	1.000
1973 —American	C	2	0	0	0	0	0	0	.000	0	3	0	0	1.000
1976 —American	C	1	0	0	0	0	0	0	.000	0	1	0	0	1.000
1977 —American	C	2	0	0	0	0	0	0	.000	0	6	1	0	1.000
1978 —American	C	2	0	0	0	0	0	1	.000	0	4	0	0	1.000
1980 —American	C	2	0	0	0	0	0	0	.000	0	5	0	0	1.000
1981 —American	C	3	1	1	0	0	0	0	.333	0	4	0	0	1.000
1982 —American	C	2	0	0	0	0	0	0	.000	0	2	0	0	1.000
1985 —American	C	2	0	0	0	0	0	0	.000	0	2	0	0	1.000
1991 —American	C	2	0	1	0	0	0	0	.500	0	5	0	0	1.000
All-Star Game totals (10 years)		20	2	3	0	0	0	1	.150	0	34	1	0	1.000

FITZGERALD, MIKE
C

PERSONAL: Born July 13, 1960, at Long Beach, Calif. . . . 5-11/190. . . . Throws right, bats right. . . . Full name: Michael Roy Fitzgerald.
HIGH SCHOOL: Lakewood (Calif.).
TRANSACTIONS/CAREER NOTES: Selected by New York Mets organization in sixth round of free-agent draft (June 6, 1978). . . . Loaned by Mets organization to Alexandria, co-op (April 8, 1980); returned to Mets (May 31, 1980). . . . Traded by Mets organization with IF Hubie Brooks, OF Herm Winningham and P Floyd Youmans to Montreal Expos for C Gary Carter (December 10, 1984). . . . On disabled list (August 2, 1986-remainder of season and March 28-April 20, 1987). . . . On Montreal disabled list (March 29-May 27, 1991); included rehabilitation disability assignment to Indianapolis (April 18-24 and May 19-27, 1991). . . . Granted free agency (October 29, 1991).
STATISTICAL NOTES: Led Carolina League with 11 sacrifice flies in 1979. . . . Hit home run in first major league at-bat (September 13, 1983). . . . Tied for N.L. lead in double plays by catchers with 10 in 1990.

Year	Team (League)	Pos.	G	AB	R	H	2B	3B	HR	RBI	Avg.	SB	PO	A	E	Avg.
1978 —Little Falls (N.Y.-Penn)	C	48	140	25	36	10	0	5	21	.257	4	230	37	1	.996
1979 —Lynchburg (Carolina)	C	117	368	55	93	16	4	13	★75	.253	0	424	60	10	.980
1980 —Alex.-Lynch. (Caro.)■.......	C-1B-OF	105	338	36	71	10	2	10	44	.210	5	438	45	7	.986
1981 —Jackson (Texas)	C-1-0-3	66	218	28	68	14	2	4	29	.312	1	344	52	3	.992
—Tidewater (Int'l)	C-OF	24	58	9	9	2	0	1	3	.155	2	124	9	2	.985
1982 —Tidewater (Int'l)	C-1-0-3	94	302	33	74	9	2	4	36	.245	9	451	34	7	.986
1983 —Tidewater (Int'l)	C-1-3-0	111	370	64	105	17	1	14	65	.284	2	588	62	8	.988
—New York (N.L.)	C	8	20	1	2	0	0	1	2	.100	0	37	8	2	.957
1984 —New York (N.L.)	C	112	360	20	87	15	1	2	33	.242	1	715	47	4	★.995
1985 —Montreal (N.L.)■............	C	108	295	25	61	7	1	5	34	.207	5	542	46	8	.987
1986 —Indianapolis (A.A.)	C	10	32	4	11	3	0	0	4	.344	0	58	5	1	.984
—Montreal (N.L.)	C	73	209	20	59	13	1	6	37	.282	3	415	35	3	.993
1987 —Montreal (N.L.)	C-1B-2B	107	287	32	69	11	0	3	36	.240	3	603	27	12	.981
1988 —Montreal (N.L.)	C-OF	63	155	17	42	6	1	5	23	.271	2	262	21	6	.979
—Indianapolis (A.A.)	C	32	96	12	24	6	1	1	13	.250	1	234	11	2	.992
1989 —Montreal (N.L.)	C-3B-OF	100	290	33	69	18	2	7	42	.238	3	465	44	8	.985
1990 —Montreal (N.L.)	C-OF	111	313	36	76	18	1	9	41	.243	6	565	42	6	.990
1991 —Indianapolis (A.A.)	C-OF	10	27	5	6	1	0	1	4	.222	0	31	2	0	1.000
—Montreal (N.L.)	C-1B-OF	71	198	17	40	5	2	4	28	.202	4	331	27	2	.994
Major league totals (9 years)		753	2127	201	505	93	9	42	276	.237	29	3935	297	51	.988

FLANAGAN, MIKE
P, ORIOLES

PERSONAL: Born December 16, 1951, at Manchester, N.H. . . . 6-0/199. . . . Throws left, bats left. . . . Full name: Michael Kendall Flanagan. . . . Son of Ed Flanagan Jr., minor league pitcher (1947-52).
HIGH SCHOOL: Memorial (Manchester, N.H.).
COLLEGE: Massachusetts.
TRANSACTIONS/CAREER NOTES: Selected by Houston Astros organization in 15th round of free-agent draft (June 8, 1971). . . . Selected by Baltimore Orioles organization in seventh round of free-agent draft (June 5, 1973). . . . On disabled list (May 18-August 7, 1983). . . . On Baltimore disabled list (March 26-July 20, 1985); included rehabilitation disability assignment to

Hagerstown (July 10-20, 1985).... On disabled list (May 31-June 19, 1986).... On Baltimore disabled list (May 18-July 17, 1987); included rehabilitation disability assignment to Rochester (July 3-17, 1987).... Traded by Orioles to Toronto Blue Jays for P Oswald Peraza and a player to be named later (August 31, 1987); Orioles acquired P Jose Mesa to complete deal (September 4, 1987).... Granted free agency (November 4, 1988).... Re-signed by Blue Jays (December 24, 1988).... Released by Blue Jays (May 8, 1990).... Signed by Orioles (April 2, 1991).

RECORDS/HONORS: Named A.L. Pitcher of the Year by THE SPORTING NEWS (1979).... Named lefthanded pitcher on THE SPORTING NEWS A.L. All-Star team (1979).... Named A.L. Cy Young Award winner by Baseball Writers' Association of America (1979).

STATISTICAL NOTES: Tied for Southern League lead with three shutouts in 1974.... Tied for International League lead with four shutouts in 1975.... Tied for A.L. lead in games started by pitcher with 40 in 1978.... Tied for A.L. lead with five shutouts in 1979.... Pitched one inning, combining with Bob Milacki, Mark Williamson and Gregg Olson in 2-0 nine-inning no-hit victory against Oakland Athletics (July 13, 1991).

Year — Team (League)	G	W	L	Pct.	ERA	Sv.	IP	H	R	ER	BB	SO
1973 — Miami (Florida State)	11	4	1	.800	2.21	0	61	39	21	15	25	61
1974 — Miami (Florida State)	14	6	6	.500	2.10	0	103	67	32	24	48	119
— Asheville (South Atlantic)	11	6	4	.600	1.82	0	84	61	19	17	18	62
1975 — Rochester (International)	27	13	4	.765	2.50	0	173	155	58	48	56	135
— Baltimore (A.L.)	2	0	1	.000	2.70	0	10	9	4	3	6	7
1976 — Baltimore (A.L.)	20	3	5	.375	4.13	0	85	83	41	39	33	56
— Rochester (International)	7	6	1	.857	2.12	0	51	40	16	12	14	24
1977 — Baltimore (A.L.)	36	15	10	.600	3.64	1	235	235	100	95	70	149
1978 — Baltimore (A.L.)	40	19	15	.559	4.04	0	281	271	128	★126	87	167
1979 — Baltimore (A.L.)	39	★23	9	.719	3.08	0	266	245	107	91	70	190
1980 — Baltimore (A.L.)	37	16	13	.552	4.12	0	251	★278	121	115	71	128
1981 — Baltimore (A.L.)	20	9	6	.600	4.19	0	116	108	55	54	37	72
1982 — Baltimore (A.L.)	36	15	11	.577	3.97	0	236	233	110	104	76	103
1983 — Baltimore (A.L.)	20	12	4	.750	3.30	0	125⅓	135	53	46	31	50
1984 — Baltimore (A.L.)	34	13	13	.500	3.53	0	226⅔	213	103	89	81	115
1985 — Hagerstown (Eastern)	1	0	0	...	0.00	0	6	1	0	0	4	5
— Baltimore (A.L.)	15	4	5	.444	5.13	0	86	101	49	49	28	42
1986 — Baltimore (A.L.)	29	7	11	.389	4.24	0	172	179	95	81	66	96
1987 — Baltimore-Toronto (A.L.)■	23	6	8	.429	4.06	0	144	148	72	65	51	93
— Rochester (International)	3	0	0	...	3.00	0	12	12	5	4	3	10
1988 — Toronto (A.L.)	34	13	13	.500	4.18	0	211	220	106	98	80	99
1989 — Toronto (A.L.)	30	8	10	.444	3.93	0	171⅔	186	82	75	47	47
1990 — Toronto (A.L.)	5	2	2	.500	5.31	0	20⅓	28	14	12	8	5
1991 — Baltimore (A.L.)■	64	2	7	.222	2.38	3	98⅓	84	27	26	25	55
Major league totals (17 years)	484	167	143	.539	3.84	4	2735⅓	2756	1267	1168	867	1474

CHAMPIONSHIP SERIES RECORD

Year — Team (League)	G	W	L	Pct.	ERA	Sv.	IP	H	R	ER	BB	SO
1979 — Baltimore (A.L.)	1	1	0	1.000	5.14	0	7	6	6	4	1	2
1983 — Baltimore (A.L.)	1	1	0	1.000	1.80	0	5	5	1	1	0	1
1989 — Toronto (A.L.)	1	0	1	.000	10.38	0	4⅓	7	5	5	1	3
Championship Series totals (3 years)	3	2	1	.667	5.51	0	16⅓	18	12	10	2	6

WORLD SERIES RECORD

Year — Team (League)	G	W	L	Pct.	ERA	Sv.	IP	H	R	ER	BB	SO
1979 — Baltimore (A.L.)	3	1	1	.500	3.00	0	15	18	7	5	2	13
1983 — Baltimore (A.L.)	1	0	0	...	4.50	0	4	6	2	2	1	1
World Series totals (2 years)	4	1	1	.500	3.32	0	19	24	9	7	3	14

ALL-STAR GAME RECORD

Year — League	W	L	Pct.	ERA	Sv.	IP	H	R	ER	BB	SO
1978 — American						Did not play					

FLEMING, DAVE
P, MARINERS

PERSONAL: Born November 7, 1969, at Queens, N.Y.... 6-3/200.... Throws left, bats left. ... Full name: David Anthony Fleming.
HIGH SCHOOL: Mahopac (N.Y.).
COLLEGE: Georgia.
TRANSACTIONS/CAREER NOTES: Selected by Seattle Mariners organization in third round of free-agent draft (June 4, 1990).

Year — Team (League)	G	W	L	Pct.	ERA	Sv.	IP	H	R	ER	BB	SO
1990 — San Bernardino (California)	12	7	3	.700	2.60	0	79⅔	64	29	23	30	77
1991 — Jacksonville (Southern)	21	10	6	.625	2.64	0	140	129	50	41	25	109
— Seattle (A.L.)	9	1	0	1.000	6.62	0	17⅔	19	13	13	3	11
— Calgary (Pacific Coast)	3	2	0	1.000	1.13	0	16	11	2	2	3	16
Major league totals (1 year)	9	1	0	1.000	6.62	0	17⅔	19	13	13	3	11

FLETCHER, DARRIN
C, EXPOS

PERSONAL: Born October 3, 1966, at Elmhurst, Ill.... 6-1/199.... Throws right, bats left.... Full name: Darrin Glen Fletcher.... Son of Tom Fletcher, pitcher, Detroit Tigers (1962).
HIGH SCHOOL: Oakwood (Ill.).

COLLEGE: Illinois.
TRANSACTIONS/CAREER NOTES: Selected by Los Angeles Dodgers organization in sixth round of free-agent draft (June 2, 1987). . . . Traded by Dodgers to Philadelphia Phillies for P Dennis Cook (September 13, 1990). . . . Traded by Phillies with cash to Montreal Expos for P Barry Jones (December 9, 1991).
STATISTICAL NOTES: Tied for Texas League lead in double plays by catchers with nine in 1988. . . . Led Pacific Coast League catchers with 787 total chances in 1990.

Year	Team (League)	Pos.	G	AB	R	H	2B	3B	HR	RBI	Avg.	SB	PO	A	E	Avg.
1987	Vero Beach (Florida St.) ...	C	43	124	13	33	7	0	0	15	.266	0	212	35	3	.988
1988	San Antonio (Texas)	C	89	279	19	58	8	0	1	20	.208	2	529	64	5	★.992
1989	Albuquerque (PCL)	C	100	315	34	86	16	1	5	44	.273	1	632	63	9	.987
	Los Angeles (N.L.)	C	5	8	1	4	0	0	1	2	.500	0	16	1	0	1.000
1990	Albuquerque (PCL)	C	105	350	58	102	23	1	13	65	.291	1	★715	64	8	.990
	Los Angeles-Phil. (N.L.)■.	C	11	23	3	3	1	0	0	1	.130	0	30	3	0	1.000
1991	Scranton/W.B. (Int'l)	C-1B	90	306	39	87	13	1	8	50	.284	1	491	44	5	.991
	Philadelphia (N.L.)	C	46	136	5	31	8	0	1	12	.228	0	242	22	2	.992
	Major league totals (3 years)		62	167	9	38	9	0	2	15	.228	0	288	26	2	.994

FLETCHER, SCOTT
2B

PERSONAL: Born July 30, 1958, at Fort Walton Beach, Fla. . . . 5-11/173. . . . Throws right, bats right. . . . Full name: Scott Brian Fletcher. . . . Son of Richard Fletcher, minor league pitcher (1952-59).
HIGH SCHOOL: Wadsworth (O.).
COLLEGE: Toledo, Valencia Community College (Fla.) and Georgia Southern.
TRANSACTIONS/CAREER NOTES: Selected by Los Angeles Dodgers organization in 33rd round of free-agent draft (June 8, 1976). . . . Selected by Oakland Athletics organization in secondary phase of free-agent draft (January 10, 1978). . . . Selected by Houston Astros organization in secondary phase of free-agent draft (June 6, 1978). . . . Selected by Chicago Cubs organization in secondary phase of free-agent draft (June 5, 1979). . . . Traded by Cubs with P Dick Tidrow, P Randy Martz and IF Pat Tabler to Chicago White Sox for P Steve Trout and P Warren Brusstar (January 25, 1983). . . . Traded by White Sox with P Ed Correa and a player to be named later to Texas Rangers for IF Wayne Tolleson and P Dave Schmidt (November 25, 1985); Rangers acquired IF Jose Mota to complete deal (December 12, 1985). . . . Granted free agency (November 4, 1988). . . . Re-signed by Rangers (November 30, 1988). . . . On Texas disabled list (July 5-20, 1989). . . . Traded by Rangers with OF Sammy Sosa and P Wilson Alvarez to Chicago White Sox for OF Harold Baines and IF Fred Manrique (July 29, 1989). . . . Granted free agency (November 4, 1991).
STATISTICAL NOTES: Led Texas League second basemen with 354 putouts, 390 assists, 29 errors and 112 double plays in 1980. . . . Led American Association in being hit by pitch with nine and grounding into double plays with 20 in 1981. . . . Led American Association shortstops with 607 total chances in 1982. . . . Led A.L. second basemen with 115 double plays in 1990.

Year	Team (League)	Pos.	G	AB	R	H	2B	3B	HR	RBI	Avg.	SB	PO	A	E	Avg.
1979	Geneva (N.Y.-Penn)	SS	67	261	59	81	12	3	4	43	.310	10	99	195	18	★.942
1980	Midland (Texas)	2B-SS	130	501	★111	164	16	★11	6	65	.327	20	†354	†390	†29	.962
1981	Iowa (American Assoc.) ...	SS	119	458	66	117	26	4	4	33	.255	24	★222	337	28	.952
	Chicago (N.L.)	2B-SS-3B	19	46	6	10	4	0	0	1	.217	0	34	44	3	.963
1982	Iowa (American Assoc.) ...	SS	129	502	90	157	26	3	4	60	.313	20	224	•357	26	.957
	Chicago (N.L.)	SS	11	24	4	4	0	0	0	1	.167	1	11	23	0	1.000
1983	Chicago (A.L.)■	SS-2B-3B	114	262	42	62	16	5	3	31	.237	5	126	308	16	.964
1984	Chicago (A.L.)	SS-2B-3B	149	456	46	114	13	3	3	35	.250	10	234	439	19	.973
1985	Chicago (A.L.)	3B-SS-2B	119	301	38	77	8	1	2	31	.256	5	123	208	8	.976
1986	Texas (A.L.)■	SS-3B-2B	147	530	82	159	34	5	3	50	.300	12	216	388	16	.974
1987	Texas (A.L.)	SS	156	588	82	169	28	4	5	63	.287	13	249	413	23	.966
1988	Texas (A.L.)	SS	140	515	59	142	19	4	0	47	.276	8	215	414	11	.983
1989	Texas-Chicago (A.L.)■...	SS-2B	142	546	77	138	25	2	1	43	.253	2	241	362	15	.976
1990	Chicago (A.L.)	2B	151	509	54	123	18	3	4	56	.242	1	305	436	9	.988
1991	Chicago (A.L.)	2B-3B	90	248	14	51	10	1	1	28	.206	0	178	192	3	.992
	American League totals (9 years)		1208	3955	494	1035	171	28	22	384	.262	56	1887	3160	120	.977
	National League totals (2 years)		30	70	10	14	4	0	0	2	.200	1	45	67	3	.974
	Major league totals (11 years)		1238	4025	504	1049	175	28	22	386	.261	57	1932	3227	123	.977

CHAMPIONSHIP SERIES RECORD

Year	Team (League)	Pos.	G	AB	R	H	2B	3B	HR	RBI	Avg.	SB	PO	A	E	Avg.
1983	Chicago (A.L.)	SS	3	7	0	0	0	0	0	0	.000	0	3	8	0	1.000

FLORA, KEVIN
2B, ANGELS

PERSONAL: Born June 10, 1969, at Fontana, Calif. . . . 6-0/180. . . . Throws right, bats right. . . . Full name: Kevin Scot Flora.
HIGH SCHOOL: Bonita (Calif.).
TRANSACTIONS/CAREER NOTES: Selected by California Angels organization in second round of free-agent draft (June 2, 1987). . . . On disabled list (June 21, 1988-remainder of season).
STATISTICAL NOTES: Led Midwest League shortstops with 46 errors (1989).

Year	Team (League)	Pos.	G	AB	R	H	2B	3B	HR	RBI	Avg.	SB	PO	A	E	Avg.
1987	Salem (Northwest)	SS	35	88	17	24	5	1	0	12	.273	8	35	81	22	.841
1988	Quad City (Midwest)	SS	48	152	19	33	3	4	0	15	.217	5	64	121	23	.889

Year Team (League)	Pos.	G	AB	R	H	2B	3B	HR	RBI	Avg.	SB	PO	A	E	Avg.
1989—Quad City (Midwest)	SS-2B	120	372	46	81	8	4	1	21	.218	30	156	281	†46	.905
1990—Midland (Texas)	SS-2B	71	232	35	53	17	5	5	32	.228	11	98	213	26	.923
1991—Midland (Texas)	2B	124	484	97	138	14	★15	12	67	.285	40	272	★348	24	.963
—California (A.L.)	2B	3	8	1	1	0	0	0	0	.125	1	8	3	2	.846
Major league totals (1 year)		3	8	1	1	0	0	0	0	.125	1	8	3	2	.846

FOLEY, TOM
SS/1B, EXPOS

PERSONAL: Born September 9, 1959, at Columbus, Ga. . . . 6-1/175. . . . Throws right, bats left. . . . Full name: Thomas Michael Foley.
HIGH SCHOOL: Palmetto (Miami).
COLLEGE: Miami-Dade (South) Community College.
TRANSACTIONS/CAREER NOTES: Selected by Cincinnati Reds organization in seventh round of free-agent draft (June 7, 1977). . . . Traded by Reds with C Alan Knicely, a player to be named later and cash to Philadelphia Phillies for C Bo Diaz and P Greg Simpson (August 8, 1985); Phillies acquired P Freddie Toliver to complete deal (August 27, 1985). . . . On Philadelphia disabled list (March 23-April 29, 1986); included rehabilitation disability assignment to Reading (April 25-29, 1986). . . . Traded by Phillies with P Larry Sorensen to Montreal Expos for P Dan Schatzeder and IF Skeeter Barnes (July 24, 1986). . . . On disabled list (May 17-June 2, 1987 and July 26-August 12, 1989).
STATISTICAL NOTES: Led Pioneer League in caught stealing with 10 in 1977. . . . Led Western Carolinas League shortstops with 98 double plays in 1978. . . . Led Florida State League shortstops with 71 double plays in 1979.

Year Team (League)	Pos.	G	AB	R	H	2B	3B	HR	RBI	Avg.	SB	PO	A	E	Avg.
1977—Billings (Pioneer)	3B-SS	59	209	37	53	7	1	2	21	.254	7	53	109	24	.871
1978—Shelby (W. Carolinas)	SS	124	424	55	98	19	1	2	41	.231	8	★217	★352	30	★.950
1979—Tampa (Florida State)	SS	125	414	38	95	12	6	0	37	.229	5	223	345	35	.946
1980—Waterbury (Eastern)	2B	131	477	49	119	16	4	4	41	.249	3	★222	329	31	.947
1981—Indianapolis (A.A.)	SS	103	347	47	81	12	2	6	27	.233	6	175	267	27	.942
1982—Indianapolis (A.A.)	SS	129	427	65	115	20	9	8	63	.269	1	★227	343	27	.955
1983—Cincinnati (N.L.)	SS-2B	68	98	7	20	4	1	0	9	.204	1	54	76	2	.985
1984—Cincinnati (N.L.)	SS-2B-3B	106	277	26	70	8	3	5	27	.253	3	119	228	11	.969
1985—Cin.-Phil. (N.L.)■	SS-2B-3B	89	250	24	60	13	1	3	23	.240	2	127	202	7	.979
1986—Reading (Eastern)	SS-2B	3	11	2	2	2	0	0	0	.182	0	2	11	0	1.000
—Phil.-Montreal (N.L.)■	SS-2B-3B	103	263	26	70	15	3	1	23	.266	10	117	190	6	.981
1987—Montreal (N.L.)	SS-2B-3B	106	280	35	82	18	3	5	28	.293	6	134	190	9	.973
1988—Montreal (N.L.)	2B-SS-3B	127	377	33	100	21	3	5	43	.265	2	204	324	15	.972
1989—Montreal (N.L.)	2-3-S-P	122	375	34	86	19	2	7	39	.229	2	203	317	8	.985
1990—Montreal (N.L.)	S-2-3-1	73	164	11	35	2	1	0	12	.213	0	80	123	5	.976
1991—Montreal (N.L.)	SS-3B-2B	86	168	12	35	11	1	0	15	.208	2	52	84	5	.965
Major league totals (9 years)		880	2252	208	558	111	18	26	219	.248	28	1090	1734	68	.976

RECORD AS PITCHER

Year Team (League)	G	W	L	Pct.	ERA	Sv.	IP	H	R	ER	BB	SO
1989—Montreal (N.L.)	1	0	0	...	27.00	0	⅓	1	1	1	0	0

FORDYCE, BROOK
C, METS

PERSONAL: Born May 7, 1970, at New London, Conn. . . . 6-1/185. . . . Throws right, bats right. . . . Full name: Brook Alexander Fordyce.
HIGH SCHOOL: St. Bernard's (Uncasville, Conn.).
TRANSACTIONS/CAREER NOTES: Selected by New York Mets organization in third round of free-agent draft (June 5, 1989).
STATISTICAL NOTES: Led Appalachian League catchers with .991 fielding percentage in 1989. . . . Led South Atlantic League with 30 passed balls in 1990.

Year Team (League)	Pos.	G	AB	R	H	2B	3B	HR	RBI	Avg.	SB	PO	A	E	Avg.
1989—Kingsport (Appalachian)	C-OF-3B	69	226	45	74	15	0	9	38	.327	10	311	28	4	†.988
1990—Columbia (S. Atlantic)	C	104	372	45	117	29	1	10	54	.315	4	574	63	15	.977
1991—St. Lucie (Florida State)	C	115	406	42	97	19	3	7	55	.239	4	630	87	13	.982

FORTUGNO, TIMOTHY
P, ANGELS

PERSONAL: Born April 11, 1962, at Clinton, Mass. . . . 6-1/195. . . . Throws left, bats left. . . . Full name: Timothy Shawn Fortugno.
HIGH SCHOOL: Uxbridge (Mass.).
COLLEGE: Golden West College (Calif.).
TRANSACTIONS/CAREER NOTES: Selected by Oakland Athletics organization in first round (ninth pick overall) of free-agent draft (January 17, 1984). . . . Selected by Cleveland Indians organization in secondary phase of free-agent draft (June 4, 1984). . . . Signed as free agent by Seattle Mariners organization (June 6, 1986). . . . Traded by Mariners with OF Phil Bradley to Philadelphia Phillies organization for OF Glenn Wilson, OF Dave Brundage and P Mike Jackson (December 9, 1987). . . . Released by Phillies (March 30, 1989). . . . Signed as free agent by Reno, independent (April 3, 1989). . . . Sold by Reno to Milwaukee Brewers organization (May 5, 1989). . . . Drafted by California Angels (December 9, 1991).
STATISTICAL NOTES: Pitched seven-inning 6-0 no-hit victory against Modesto (August 12, 1987).

Year	Team (League)	G	W	L	Pct.	ERA	Sv.	IP	H	R	ER	BB	SO
1986	—Bellingham (Northwest)	6	0	0	...	1.13	1	8	2	2	1	12	11
	—Wausau (Midwest)	19	1	1	.500	2.61	3	31	18	17	9	26	38
1987	—Salinas (California)	46	8	2	.800	2.80	6	93⅓	43	36	29	84	141
1988	—Reading (Eastern)■	29	1	4	.200	4.44	0	50⅔	42	29	25	36	48
	—Clearwater (Florida State)	9	1	3	.250	2.42	0	26	17	10	7	15	28
1989	—Reno-Stockton (California)■	18	4	4	.500	1.97	1	68⅔	37	26	15	40	90
	—El Paso (Texas)■	10	0	3	.000	7.96	0	26	29	24	23	21	22
1990	—Beloit (Midwest)	31	8	4	.667	1.56	7	63⅓	38	16	11	38	106
	—El Paso (Texas)	12	2	3	.400	3.14	2	28⅔	23	12	10	22	24
1991	—El Paso (Texas)	20	5	1	.833	1.99	1	54⅓	40	15	12	25	73
	—Denver (American Assoc.)	26	0	1	.000	3.57	2	35⅓	30	15	14	20	39

FOSSAS, TONY

P, RED SOX

PERSONAL: Born September 23, 1957, at Havana, Cuba. . . . 6-0/ 187. . . . Throws left, bats left. . . . Full name: Emilo Anthony Fossas.

HIGH SCHOOL: St. Mary's (Brookline, Mass.).

COLLEGE: South Florida.

TRANSACTIONS/CAREER NOTES: Selected by Minnesota Twins organization in ninth round of free-agent draft (June 6, 1978). . . . Selected by Texas Rangers organization in 12th round of free-agent draft (June 5, 1979). . . . Released by Rangers organization (February 18, 1982). . . . Signed by Midland, Chicago Cubs organization (March 11, 1982). . . . Loaned by Cubs organization to Tabasco of Mexican League (March 15, 1982); returned to Cubs (April 7, 1982). . . . Released by Cubs organization (April 7, 1982). . . . Signed by Burlington, Rangers organization (May 3, 1982). . . . Granted free agency (October 15, 1985). . . . Signed by Edmonton, California Angels organization (December 13, 1985). . . . On disabled list (June 2, 1986-remainder of season). . . . Granted free agency (October 15, 1987). . . . Signed by Oklahoma City, Rangers organization (December 1, 1987). . . . Granted free agency (October 15, 1988). . . . Signed by Denver, Milwaukee Brewers organization (January 21, 1989). . . . Released by Brewers organization (December 6, 1990). . . . Signed by Boston Red Sox organization (January 23, 1991).

STATISTICAL NOTES: Tied for South Atlantic League in games started by pitcher with 27 in 1980.

Year	Team (League)	G	W	L	Pct.	ERA	Sv.	IP	H	R	ER	BB	SO
1979	—Sarasota Rangers (GCL)	10	6	3	.667	3.00	0	60	54	28	20	26	49
	—Tulsa (Texas)	2	1	1	.500	6.55	0	11	14	10	8	4	3
1980	—Asheville (South Atlantic)	30	8	2	.800	3.15	2	★197	★187	84	69	69	140
1981	—Tulsa (Texas)	38	5	6	.455	4.16	2	106	113	65	49	44	57
1982	—Burlington (Midwest)	25	8	9	.471	3.08	0	146⅓	121	63	50	33	115
1983	—Tulsa (Texas)	24	8	7	.533	4.20	0	133	123	77	62	46	103
	—Oklahoma City (Am. Assoc.)	10	1	2	.333	7.90	0	35⅓	55	33	31	12	23
1984	—Tulsa (Texas)	4	0	1	.000	4.50	2	10	12	5	5	3	7
	—Oklahoma City (Am. Assoc.)	29	5	9	.357	4.31	0	121	143	65	58	34	74
1985	—Oklahoma City (Am. Assoc.)	30	7	6	.538	4.75	2	110	121	65	58	36	49
1986	—Edmonton (Pacific Coast)■	7	3	3	.500	4.57	0	43⅓	53	23	22	12	15
1987	—Edmonton (Pacific Coast)	40	6	8	.429	4.99	0	117⅓	152	76	65	29	54
1988	—Oklahoma City (Am. Assoc.)■	52	3	0	1.000	2.84	4	66⅔	64	21	21	16	42
	—Texas (A.L.)	5	0	0	...	4.76	0	5⅔	11	3	3	2	0
1989	—Denver (American Assoc.)■	24	5	1	.833	2.04	0	35⅓	27	9	8	11	35
	—Milwaukee (A.L.)	51	2	2	.500	3.54	1	61	57	27	24	22	42
1990	—Milwaukee (A.L.)	32	2	3	.400	6.44	0	29⅓	44	23	21	10	24
	—Denver (American Assoc.)	25	5	2	.714	1.51	4	35⅔	29	8	6	10	45
1991	—Boston (A.L.)■	64	3	2	.600	3.47	1	57	49	27	22	28	29
	Major league totals (4 years)	152	7	7	.500	4.12	2	153	161	80	70	62	95

FOSTER, STEVE

P, REDS

PERSONAL: Born August 16, 1966, at Dallas. . . . 6-0/ 180. . . . Throws right, bats right. . . . Full name: Stephen Eugene Foster Jr.

HIGH SCHOOL: DeSoto (Tex.).

COLLEGE: Blinn College (Tex.) and Texas-Arlington.

TRANSACTIONS/CAREER NOTES: Selected by Cincinnati Reds organization in 12th round of free-agent draft (June 1, 1988).

Year	Team (League)	G	W	L	Pct.	ERA	Sv.	IP	H	R	ER	BB	SO
1988	—Billings (Pioneer)	18	2	3	.400	1.19	7	30⅓	15	5	4	7	27
1989	—Cedar Rapids (Midwest)	51	0	3	.000	2.14	23	59	46	16	14	19	55
1990	—Chattanooga (Southern)	50	5	10	.333	5.34	20	59	69	38	35	33	52
1991	—Chattanooga (Southern)	17	0	2	.000	1.15	10	15⅔	10	4	2	4	18
	—Nashville (American Assoc.)	41	2	3	.400	2.14	12	54⅔	46	17	13	29	52
	—Cincinnati (N.L.)	11	0	0	...	1.93	0	14	7	5	3	4	11
	Major league totals (1 year)	11	0	0	...	1.93	0	14	7	5	3	4	11

FRANCO, JOHN

P, METS

PERSONAL: Born September 17, 1960, at Brooklyn, N.Y. . . . 5-10/ 185. . . . Throws left, bats left. . . . Full name: John Anthony Franco.

HIGH SCHOOL: Lafayette (Brooklyn, N.Y.).

COLLEGE: St. John's.

TRANSACTIONS/CAREER NOTES: Selected by Los Angeles Dodgers organization in fifth round of free-agent draft (June 8, 1981). . . . Traded by Dodgers organization with P Brett Wise to Cincinnati Reds organization for IF Rafael Landestoy (May 9, 1983). . . . Traded by Reds with OF Don Brown to New York Mets for P Randy Myers and P Kip Gross (December 6, 1989).

RECORDS/HONORS: Named N.L. Fireman of the Year by THE SPORTING NEWS (1988 and 1990).

Year — Team (League)	G	W	L	Pct.	ERA	Sv.	IP	H	R	ER	BB	SO
1981 — Vero Beach (Florida State)	13	7	4	.636	3.53	0	79	78	41	31	41	60
1982 — Albuquerque (Pacific Coast)	5	1	2	.333	7.24	0	27⅓	41	22	22	15	24
— San Antonio (Texas)	17	10	5	.667	4.96	0	105⅓	137	70	58	46	76
1983 — Albuquerque (Pacific Coast)	11	0	0	...	5.40	0	15	10	11	9	11	8
— Indianapolis (Am. Assoc.)■	23	6	10	.375	4.85	2	115	148	69	62	42	54
1984 — Wichita (American Assoc.)	6	1	0	1.000	5.79	0	9⅓	8	6	6	4	11
— Cincinnati (N.L.)	54	6	2	.750	2.61	4	79⅓	74	28	23	36	55
1985 — Cincinnati (N.L.)	67	12	3	.800	2.18	12	99	83	27	24	40	61
1986 — Cincinnati (N.L.)	74	6	6	.500	2.94	29	101	90	40	33	44	84
1987 — Cincinnati (N.L.)	68	8	5	.615	2.52	32	82	76	26	23	27	61
1988 — Cincinnati (N.L.)	70	6	6	.500	1.57	★39	86	60	18	15	27	46
1989 — Cincinnati (N.L.)	60	4	8	.333	3.12	32	80⅔	77	35	28	36	60
1990 — New York (N.L.)■	55	5	3	.625	2.53	★33	67⅔	66	22	19	21	56
1991 — New York (N.L.)	52	5	9	.357	2.93	30	55⅓	61	27	18	18	45
Major league totals (8 years)	500	52	42	.553	2.53	211	651	587	223	183	249	468

ALL-STAR GAME RECORD

Year — League	W	L	Pct.	ERA	Sv.	IP	H	R	ER	BB	SO
1986 — National					Did not play						
1987 — National	0	0	...	0.00	0	⅔	0	0	0	0	0
1989 — National					Did not play						
1990 — National	0	0	...	0.00	0	1	0	0	0	0	0
1991 — National					Did not play						
All-Star totals (2 years)	0	0	...	0.00	0	1⅔	0	0	0	0	0

FRANCO, JULIO
2B, RANGERS

PERSONAL: Born August 23, 1961, at San Pedro de Macoris, Dominican Republic. . . . 6-1/ 190. . . . Throws right, bats right. . . . Full name: Julio Cesar Franco.
HIGH SCHOOL: Divine Providence (San Pedro de Macoris, Dominican Republic).
TRANSACTIONS/CAREER NOTES: Signed as free agent by Philadelphia Phillies organization (June 23, 1978). . . . Traded by Phillies with 2B Manny Trillo, OF George Vukovich, P Jay Baller and C Jerry Willard to Cleveland Indians for OF Von Hayes (December 9, 1982). . . . On disabled list (July 13-August 8, 1987). . . . Traded by Indians to Texas Rangers for 1B Pete O'Brien, OF Oddibe McDowell and 2B Jerry Browne (December 6, 1988).
RECORDS/HONORS: Named Carolina League Most Valuable Player (1980). . . . Named second baseman on THE SPORTING NEWS A.L. Silver Slugger team (1988-1991). . . . Named second baseman on THE SPORTING NEWS A.L. All-Star team (1989-1991).
STATISTICAL NOTES: Led Northwest League with 153 total bases in 1979. . . . Led Northwest League shortstops with 45 double plays in 1979. . . . Led Carolina League shortstops with 73 double plays in 1980. . . . Led American Association shortstops with 42 errors in 1982. . . . Led A.L. shortstops with 35 errors in 1985. . . . Led A.L. in grounding into double plays with 28 in 1986 and 27 in 1989.

Year — Team (League)	Pos.	G	AB	R	H	2B	3B	HR	RBI	Avg.	SB	PO	A	E	Avg.
1978 — Butte (Pioneer)	SS	47	141	34	43	5	2	3	28	.305	4	37	52	25	.781
1979 — Central Oregon (N'West) ..	SS	★71	299	57	★98	15	5	●10	45	.328	22	103	★256	31	.921
1980 — Peninsula (Carolina)	SS	●140	★555	105	178	25	6	11	★99	.321	44	179	★412	42	.934
1981 — Reading (Eastern)	SS	★139	★532	70	160	17	3	8	74	.301	27	246	437	30	.958
1982 — Oklahoma City (A.A.)	SS-3B	120	463	80	139	19	5	21	66	.300	33	211	350	†42	.930
— Philadelphia (N.L.)	SS-3B	16	29	3	8	1	0	0	3	.276	0	8	25	0	1.000
1983 — Cleveland (A.L.)■	SS	149	560	68	153	24	8	8	80	.273	32	247	438	28	.961
1984 — Cleveland (A.L.)	SS	160	★658	82	188	22	5	3	79	.286	19	280	481	●36	.955
1985 — Cleveland (A.L.)	SS-2B	160	636	97	183	33	4	6	90	.288	13	252	437	†36	.950
1986 — Cleveland (A.L.)	SS-2B	149	599	80	183	30	5	10	74	.306	10	248	413	19	.972
1987 — Cleveland (A.L.)	SS-2B	128	495	86	158	24	3	8	52	.319	32	175	313	18	.964
1988 — Cleveland (A.L.)	2B	152	613	88	186	23	6	10	54	.303	25	310	434	14	.982
1989 — Texas (A.L.)■	2B	150	548	80	173	31	5	13	92	.316	21	256	386	13	.980
1990 — Texas (A.L.)	2B	157	582	96	172	27	1	11	69	.296	31	310	444	●19	.975
1991 — Texas (A.L.)	2B	146	589	108	201	27	3	15	78	★.341	36	294	372	14	.979
American League totals (9 years)		1351	5280	785	1597	241	40	84	668	.302	219	2372	3718	197	.969
National League totals (1 year)		16	29	3	8	1	0	0	3	.276	0	8	25	0	1.000
Major league totals (10 years)		1367	5309	788	1605	242	40	84	671	.302	219	2380	3743	197	.969

ALL-STAR GAME RECORD

Year — League	Pos.	AB	R	H	2B	3B	HR	RBI	Avg.	SB	PO	A	E	Avg.
1989 — American	2B	3	0	1	0	0	0	0	.333	0	1	1	0	1.000
1990 — American	PH-2B	3	0	1	1	0	0	2	.333	0	1	0	0	1.000
1991 — American							Did not play							
All-Star Game totals (2 years)		6	0	2	1	0	0	2	.333	0	2	1	0	1.000

FRASER, WILLIE
P, ANGELS

PERSONAL: Born May 26, 1964, at New York. . . . 6-1/206. . . . Throws right, bats right. . . . Full name: William Patrick Fraser.
HIGH SCHOOL: Newburgh (N.Y.).
COLLEGE: Concordia College (N.Y.).

TRANSACTIONS/CAREER NOTES: Selected by California Angels organization in first round (15th pick overall) of free-agent draft (June 3, 1985).... Traded by Angels organization with OF Devon White and a player to be named later to Toronto Blue Jays for OF Junior Felix, IF Luis Sojo and a player to be named later (December 2, 1990); Blue Jays acquired P Marcus Moore and Angels acquired C Ken Rivers to complete deal (December 4, 1990).... Claimed on waivers by St. Louis Cardinals (June 26, 1991).... Granted free agency (December 20, 1991)....Signed by Angels organization (January 14, 1992).
STATISTICAL NOTES: Led A.L. with 33 home runs allowed in 1988.

Year	Team (League)	G	W	L	Pct.	ERA	Sv.	IP	H	R	ER	BB	SO
1985	—Quad Cities (Midwest)	13	2	6	.250	5.40	0	81 2/3	95	53	49	32	72
1986	—Palm Springs (California)	19	9	2	.818	3.55	0	124 1/3	115	60	49	29	99
	—Edmonton (Pacific Coast)	6	4	1	.800	3.15	0	40	25	15	14	8	24
	—California (A.L.)	1	0	0	...	8.31	0	4 1/3	6	4	4	1	2
1987	—California (A.L.)	36	10	10	.500	3.92	1	176 2/3	160	85	77	63	106
1988	—California (A.L.)	34	12	13	.480	5.41	0	194 2/3	203	129	117	80	86
1989	—California (A.L.)	44	4	7	.364	3.24	2	91 2/3	80	33	33	23	46
1990	—California (A.L.)	45	5	4	.556	3.08	2	76	69	29	26	24	32
	—Edmonton (Pacific Coast)	3	1	0	1.000	3.14	0	14 1/3	11	8	5	6	12
1991	—Syracuse (International)■	7	0	1	.000	3.68	1	14 2/3	12	7	6	6	12
	—Toronto (A.L.)	13	0	2	.000	6.15	0	26 1/3	33	20	18	11	12
	—St. Louis (N.L.)■	35	3	3	.500	4.93	0	49 1/3	44	28	27	21	25
	American League totals (6 years)	173	31	36	.463	4.34	5	569 2/3	551	300	275	202	284
	National League totals (1 year)	35	3	3	.500	4.93	0	49 1/3	44	28	27	21	25
	Major league totals (6 years)	208	34	39	.466	4.39	5	619	595	328	302	223	309

FREEMAN, MARVIN
P, BRAVES

PERSONAL: Born April 10, 1963, at Chicago.... 6-7/222.... Throws right, bats right. ... Full name: Marvin Freeman.
HIGH SCHOOL: Chicago Vocational (Chicago, Ill.).
COLLEGE: Jackson State.
TRANSACTIONS/CAREER NOTES: Selected by Montreal Expos organization in ninth round of free-agent draft (June 8, 1981).... Selected by Philadelphia Phillies organization in second round of free-agent (June 4, 1984).... On Philadelphia disabled list (April 25, 1989-remainder of season); included rehabilitation disability assignment to Scranton/Wilkes-Barre (August 24-September 1, 1989).... Traded by Phillies organization to Richmond (Atlanta Braves organization) for P Joe Boever (July 23, 1990).... On disabled list (August 18, 1991-remainder of season).
STATISTICAL NOTES: Tied for Northwest League lead in games started by pitcher with 15 in 1984.... Tied for Eastern League lead in games started by pitcher with 27 in 1986.... Pitched 6-0 no-hit victory against Richmond (July 28, 1988, second game).

Year	Team (League)	G	W	L	Pct.	ERA	Sv.	IP	H	R	ER	BB	SO
1984	—Bend (Northwest)	15	8	5	.615	2.61	0	89 2/3	64	41	26	52	79
1985	—Clearwater (Florida State)	14	6	5	.545	3.06	0	88 1/3	72	32	30	36	55
	—Reading (Eastern)	11	1	7	.125	5.37	0	65 1/3	51	41	39	52	35
1986	—Reading (Eastern)	27	13	6	.684	4.03	0	163	130	89	73	★111	113
	—Philadelphia (N.L.)	3	2	0	1.000	2.25	0	16	6	4	4	10	8
1987	—Maine (International)	10	0	7	.000	6.26	0	46	56	38	32	30	29
	—Reading (Eastern)	9	3	3	.500	5.07	0	49 2/3	45	30	28	32	40
1988	—Maine (International)	18	5	5	.500	4.62	0	74	62	43	38	46	37
	—Philadelphia (N.L.)	11	2	3	.400	6.10	0	51 2/3	55	36	35	43	37
1989	—Philadelphia (N.L.)	1	0	0	...	6.00	0	3	2	2	2	5	0
	—Scranton/Wilkes-Barre (Int'l)	5	1	1	.500	4.50	0	14	11	8	7	5	8
1990	—Scran./W.B.-Rich. (Int'l)■	14	4	7	.364	4.84	0	74 1/3	72	43	40	41	56
	—Philadelphia-Atlanta (N.L.)	25	1	2	.333	4.31	1	48	41	24	23	17	38
1991	—Atlanta (N.L.)	34	1	0	1.000	3.00	1	48	37	19	16	13	34
	Major league totals (5 years)	74	6	5	.545	4.32	2	166 2/3	141	85	80	88	117

FREY, STEVE
P, EXPOS

PERSONAL: Born July 29, 1963, at Meadowbrook, Pa.... 5-9/170.... Throws left, bats right. ... Full name: Steven Francis Frey.
HIGH SCHOOL: William Tennent (Warminster, Pa.).
COLLEGE: Bucks County Community College (Pa.).
TRANSACTIONS/CAREER NOTES: Selected by New York Yankees organization in 15th round of free-agent draft (June 6, 1983).... Traded by Yankees organization with OF Darren Reed and C Phil Lombardi to New York Mets for SS Rafael Santana and P Victor Garica (December 11, 1987).... Traded by Mets organization to Indianapolis (Montreal Expos organization) for C Mark Bailey and 3B Tom O'Malley (March 28, 1989).... On Montreal disabled list (May 25-June 15, 1990); included rehabilitation disability assignment to Indianapolis (June 11-15, 1990).

Year	Team (League)	G	W	L	Pct.	ERA	Sv.	IP	H	R	ER	BB	SO
1983	—Oneonta (New York-Penn)	28	4	6	.400	2.74	9	72 1/3	47	27	22	35	86
1984	—Fort Lauderdale (Florida St.)	47	4	2	.667	2.09	4	64 2/3	46	26	15	34	66
1985	—Fort Lauderdale (Florida St.)	19	1	1	.500	1.21	7	22 1/3	11	4	3	12	15
	—Albany (Eastern)	40	4	7	.364	3.82	3	61 1/3	53	30	26	25	54
1986	—Albany (Eastern)	40	3	4	.429	2.10	4	73	50	25	17	18	62
	—Columbus (International)	11	0	2	.000	8.05	0	19	29	17	17	10	11
1987	—Albany (Eastern)	14	0	2	.000	1.93	1	28	20	6	6	7	19
	—Columbus (International)	23	2	1	.667	3.04	6	47 1/3	45	19	16	10	35

Year	Team (League)	G	W	L	Pct.	ERA	Sv.	IP	H	R	ER	BB	SO
1988	—Tidewater (International)■......	58	6	3	.667	3.13	6	54⅔	38	23	19	25	58
1989	—Indianapolis (Am. Assoc.)■......	21	2	1	.667	1.78	3	25⅓	18	7	5	6	23
	—Montreal (N.L.).....................	20	3	2	.600	5.48	0	21⅓	29	15	13	11	15
1990	—Montreal (N.L.).....................	51	8	2	.800	2.10	9	55⅔	44	15	13	29	29
	—Indianapolis (Am. Assoc.).......	2	0	0	...	0.00	1	3	0	0	0	1	3
1991	—Montreal (N.L.).....................	31	0	1	.000	4.99	1	39⅔	43	31	22	23	21
	—Indianapolis (Am. Assoc.).......	30	3	1	.750	1.51	3	35⅔	25	6	6	15	45
	Major league totals (3 years)................	102	11	5	.688	3.70	10	116⅔	116	61	48	63	65

FROHWIRTH, TODD
P, ORIOLES

PERSONAL: Born September 28, 1962, at Milwaukee. . . . 6-4/205. . . . Throws right, bats right. . . . Full name: Todd Gerald Frohwirth.
HIGH SCHOOL: Messmer (Milwaukee).
COLLEGE: Northwest Missouri State.

TRANSACTIONS/CAREER NOTES: Selected by Philadelphia Phillies organization in 13th round of free-agent draft (June 4, 1984). . . . Granted free agency (October 15, 1990). . . . Signed by Baltimore Orioles (December 12, 1990).

Year	Team (League)	G	W	L	Pct.	ERA	Sv.	IP	H	R	ER	BB	SO
1984	—Bend (Northwest).....................	29	4	4	.500	1.63	•11	49⅔	26	17	9	31	60
1985	—Peninsula (Carolina)................	★54	7	5	.583	2.20	★18	82	70	33	20	48	74
1986	—Clearwater (Florida State)........	32	3	3	.500	3.98	10	52	54	29	23	18	39
	—Reading (Eastern)...................	29	0	4	.000	3.21	12	42	39	20	15	10	23
1987	—Reading (Eastern)...................	36	2	4	.333	1.86	★19	58	36	14	12	13	44
	—Maine (International)................	27	1	4	.200	2.51	10	32⅓	30	12	9	15	21
	—Philadelphia (N.L.).................	10	1	0	1.000	0.00	0	11	12	0	0	2	9
1988	—Philadelphia (N.L.).................	12	1	2	.333	8.25	0	12	16	11	11	11	11
	—Maine (International)................	49	7	3	.700	2.44	13	62⅔	52	21	17	19	39
1989	—Scranton/Wilkes-Barre (Int'l) ..	21	3	2	.600	2.23	7	32⅓	29	11	8	11	29
	—Philadelphia (N.L.).................	45	1	0	1.000	3.59	0	62⅔	56	26	25	18	39
1990	—Philadelphia (N.L.).................	5	0	1	.000	18.00	0	1	3	2	2	6	1
	—Scranton/Wilkes-Barre (Int'l) ..	★67	9	7	.563	3.04	★21	83	76	34	28	32	56
1991	—Rochester (International)■........	20	1	3	.250	3.65	8	24⅔	17	12	10	5	15
	—Baltimore (A.L.)....................	51	7	3	.700	1.87	3	96⅓	64	24	20	29	77
	American League totals (1 year)...........	51	7	3	.700	1.87	3	96⅓	64	24	20	29	77
	National League totals (4 years)...........	72	3	3	.500	3.95	0	86⅔	87	39	38	37	60
	Major league totals (5 years)................	123	10	6	.625	2.85	3	183	151	63	58	66	137

FRYE, JEFF
2B, RANGERS

PERSONAL: Born August 31, 1966, at Oakland, Calif. . . . 5-9/180. . . . Throws right, bats right. . . . Full name: Jeffrey Dustin Frye.
HIGH SCHOOL: Panama (Okla.).
COLLEGE: Southeastern Oklahoma.
TRANSACTIONS/CAREER NOTES: Selected by Texas Rangers organization in 30th round of free-agent draft (June 1, 1988).
STATISTICAL NOTES: Led Pioneer League second basemen with 44 double plays in 1988.

Year	Team (League)	Pos.	G	AB	R	H	2B	3B	HR	RBI	Avg.	SB	PO	A	E	Avg.
1988	—Butte (Pioneer)................	2B	54	185	47	53	7	1	0	14	.286	16	96	149	7	.972
1989	—Gastonia (S. Atlantic).......	2B	125	464	85	145	26	3	1	40	★.313	33	242	340	14	★.977
1990	—Charlotte (Florida State)...	2B	131	503	77	137	16	7	0	50	.272	29	252	350	13	★.979
1991	—Tulsa (Texas)..................	2B	131	503	92	152	32	11	4	41	.302	15	262	322	★26	.957

FRYMAN, TRAVIS
3B/SS, TIGERS

PERSONAL: Born April 25, 1969, at Lexington, Ky. . . . 6-1/180. . . . Throws right, bats right. . . . Full name: David Travis Fryman.
HIGH SCHOOL: Tate (Ky.).
TRANSACTIONS/CAREER NOTES: Selected by Detroit Tigers organization in first round (30th pick overall) of free-agent draft (June 2, 1987).
STATISTICAL NOTES: Led Appalachian League shortstops with 313 total chances in 1987.

Year	Team (League)	Pos.	G	AB	R	H	2B	3B	HR	RBI	Avg.	SB	PO	A	E	Avg.
1987	—Bristol (Appalachian).......	SS	67	248	25	58	9	0	2	20	.234	6	★103	187	•23	.927
1988	—Fayetteville (S. Atl.)..........	SS-2B	123	411	44	96	17	4	0	47	.234	16	174	390	32	.946
1989	—London (Eastern)...........	SS	118	426	52	113	★30	1	9	56	.265	5	192	346	★27	.952
1990	—Toledo (International).......	SS	87	327	38	84	22	2	10	53	.257	4	128	277	26	.940
	—Detroit (A.L.)....................	3B-SS	66	232	32	69	11	1	9	27	.297	3	47	145	14	.932
1991	—Detroit (A.L.)....................	3B-SS	149	557	65	144	36	3	21	91	.259	12	153	354	23	.957
	Major league totals (2 years)........................		215	789	97	213	47	4	30	118	.270	15	200	499	37	.950

GAETTI, GARY
3B, ANGELS

PERSONAL: Born August 19, 1958, at Centralia, Ill. . . . 6-0/200. . . . Throws right, bats right. . . . Full name: Gary Joseph Gaetti. . . . Name pronounced guy-ETT-ee.
HIGH SCHOOL: Centralia (Ill.).
COLLEGE: Lake Land College (Ill.) and Northwest Missouri State.

TRANSACTIONS/CAREER NOTES: Selected by St. Louis Cardinals organization in fourth round of free-agent draft (January 10, 1978).... Selected by Chicago White Sox organization in secondary phase of free-agent draft (June 6, 1978).... Selected by Minnesota Twins organization in secondary phase of free-agent draft (June 5, 1979).... Granted free agency (November 9, 1987).... Re-signed by Twins (January 7, 1988).... On disabled list (August 21-September 5, 1988 and August 26-September 13, 1989).... Granted free agency (December 7, 1990).... Signed by California Angels (January 23, 1991).
RECORDS/HONORS: Shares major league record for most sacrifice flies, rookie season—13 (1982).... Won A.L. Gold Glove at third base (1986-89).
STATISTICAL NOTES: Tied for Appalachian League lead in errors by third basemen with 18 in 1979.... Led Midwest League third basemen with 492 total chances and 35 double plays in 1980.... Hit home run in first major league at-bat (September 20, 1981).... Led Southern League third basemen with 122 putouts, 281 assists, 32 errors and 435 total chances in 1981.... Led A.L. with 13 sacrifice flies in 1982.... Led A.L. third basemen with 131 putouts in 1983, 142 in 1984 and 146 in 1985.... Led A.L. third basemen with 46 double plays in 1983, 36 in both 1986 and 1990 and 39 in 1991.... Led A.L. third basemen with 496 total chances in 1984, 473 in 1986, 438 in 1990 and 481 in 1991.... Led A.L. third basemen with 334 assists in both 1984 and 1986 and 318 in 1990.... Tied for A.L. lead in errors by third basemen with 20 in 1984.... Led A.L. in grounding into double plays with 25 in 1987.

Year	Team (League)	Pos.	G	AB	R	H	2B	3B	HR	RBI	Avg.	SB	PO	A	E	Avg.
1979 —Elizabethton (Appal.)		3B-SS	66	230	50	59	15	2	14	42	.257	6	70	134	‡21	.907
1980 —Wis. Rapids (Midwest)		3B	138	503	77	134	27	3	★22	82	.266	24	★94	★363	•35	.929
1981 —Orlando (Southern)		3B-1B	137	495	92	137	19	2	30	93	.277	15	†143	†283	†32	.930
—Minnesota (A.L.)		3B	9	26	4	5	0	0	2	3	.192	0	5	17	0	1.000
1982 —Minnesota (A.L.)		3B-SS	145	508	59	117	25	4	25	84	.230	0	106	291	17	.959
1983 —Minnesota (A.L.)		3B	157	584	81	143	30	3	21	78	.245	7	†131	361	17	.967
1984 —Minnesota (A.L.)		3B-OF-SS	★162	588	55	154	29	4	5	65	.262	11	†163	†335	‡21	.960
1985 —Minnesota (A.L.)		3B-OF-1B	160	560	71	138	31	0	20	63	.246	13	†162	316	18	.964
1986 —Minnesota (A.L.)		3-S-0-2	157	596	91	171	34	1	34	108	.287	14	120	†335	21	.956
1987 —Minnesota (A.L.)		3B	154	584	95	150	36	2	31	109	.257	10	•134	261	11	.973
1988 —Minnesota (A.L.)		3B-SS	133	468	66	141	29	2	28	88	.301	7	105	191	7	.977
1989 —Minnesota (A.L.)		3B-1B	130	498	63	125	11	4	19	75	.251	6	115	253	10	.974
1990 —Minnesota (A.L.)		3B-SS	154	577	61	132	27	5	16	85	.229	6	125	†319	18	.961
1991 —California (A.L.)■		3B	152	586	58	144	22	1	18	66	.246	5	111	★353	17	.965
Major league totals (11 years)			1513	5575	704	1420	274	26	219	824	.255	79	1277	3032	157	.965

CHAMPIONSHIP SERIES RECORD

CHAMPIONSHIP SERIES NOTES: Hit home run in first at-bat (October 7, 1987).

Year	Team (League)	Pos.	G	AB	R	H	2B	3B	HR	RBI	Avg.	SB	PO	A	E	Avg.
1987 —Minnesota (A.L.)		3B	5	20	5	6	1	0	2	5	.300	0	8	7	0	1.000

WORLD SERIES RECORD

WORLD SERIES NOTES: Shares records for most at-bats in one inning—2; most hits in one inning—2 (October 17, 1987, fourth inning).

Year	Team (League)	Pos.	G	AB	R	H	2B	3B	HR	RBI	Avg.	SB	PO	A	E	Avg.
1987 —Minnesota (A.L.)		3B	7	27	4	7	2	1	1	4	.259	2	6	15	0	1.000

ALL-STAR GAME RECORD

Year	League	Pos.	AB	R	H	2B	3B	HR	RBI	Avg.	SB	PO	A	E	Avg.
1988 —American		PH	1	0	0	0	0	0	0	.000	0	0	0	0	. . .
1989 —American		3B	1	0	0	0	0	0	0	.000	0	0	1	0	1.000
All-Star Game totals (2 years)			2	0	0	0	0	0	0	.000	0	0	1	0	1.000

GAGNE, GREG
SS, TWINS

PERSONAL: Born November 12, 1961, at Fall River, Mass. ... 5-11/172. ... Throws right, bats right.... Full name: Gregory Carpenter Gagne.... Name pronounced GAG-nee.
HIGH SCHOOL: Somerset (Mass.).
TRANSACTIONS/CAREER NOTES: Selected by New York Yankees organization in fifth round of free-agent draft (June 5, 1979).... On disabled list (September 4-22, 1980).... Traded by Yankees organization with P Ron Davis, P Paul Boris and cash to Minnesota Twins for SS Roy Smalley (April 10, 1982).... On Toledo disabled list (June 13-July 18, 1984).... On disabled list (August 10-September 1, 1985).
RECORDS/HONORS: Shares major league single-game record for most inside-the-park home runs—2 (October 4, 1986).
STATISTICAL NOTES: Led International League shortstops with 599 total chances in 1983.... Led A.L. shortstops with 26 errors in 1986.

Year	Team (League)	Pos.	G	AB	R	H	2B	3B	HR	RBI	Avg.	SB	PO	A	E	Avg.
1979 —Paintsville (Appal.)		SS	41	106	10	19	2	3	0	7	.179	2	28	62	14	.865
1980 —Greensboro (S. Atlantic)		SS-3B-2B	98	337	39	91	20	5	3	32	.270	8	133	233	35	.913
1981 —Greensboro (S. Atlantic)		2B-SS-3B	104	364	71	108	21	3	9	48	.297	14	172	280	25	.948
1982 —Fort Lauderdale (FSL)		SS	1	3	0	1	0	0	0	0	.333	0	3	5	0	1.000
—Orlando (Southern)■		SS-2B	136	504	73	117	23	5	11	57	.232	8	185	403	39	.938
1983 —Toledo (International)		SS	119	392	61	100	22	4	17	66	.255	6	201	★364	★34	.943
—Minnesota (A.L.)		SS	10	27	2	3	1	0	0	3	.111	0	10	14	2	.923
1984 —Toledo (International)		3B-SS-2B	70	236	31	66	7	2	9	27	.280	2	58	168	20	.919
—Minnesota (A.L.)		PR-PH	2	1	0	0	0	0	0	0	.000	0	0	0	0	. . .

— 157 —

Year	Team (League)	Pos.	G	AB	R	H	2B	3B	HR	RBI	Avg.	SB	PO	A	E	Avg.
1985—Minnesota (A.L.)		SS	114	293	37	66	15	3	2	23	.225	10	149	269	14	.968
1986—Minnesota (A.L.)		SS-2B	156	472	63	118	22	6	12	54	.250	12	228	381	†26	.959
1987—Minnesota (A.L.)		SS-OF-2B	137	437	68	116	28	7	10	40	.265	6	196	391	18	.970
1988—Minnesota (A.L.)		S-0-2-3	149	461	70	109	20	6	14	48	.236	15	202	373	18	.970
1989—Minnesota (A.L.)		SS-OF	149	460	69	125	29	7	9	48	.272	11	218	389	18	.971
1990—Minnesota (A.L.)		SS-OF	138	388	38	91	22	3	7	38	.235	8	184	377	14	.976
1991—Minnesota (A.L.)		SS-3B	139	408	52	108	23	3	8	42	.265	11	181	377	9	.984
Major league totals (9 years)			994	2947	399	736	160	35	62	296	.250	73	1368	2571	119	.971

CHAMPIONSHIP SERIES RECORD

				BATTING									FIELDING			
Year	Team (League)	Pos.	G	AB	R	H	2B	3B	HR	RBI	Avg.	SB	PO	A	E	Avg.
1987—Minnesota (A.L.)		SS	5	18	5	5	3	0	2	3	.278	0	9	13	2	.917
1991—Minnesota (A.L.)		SS	5	17	1	4	0	0	0	1	.235	0	9	9	2	.900
Championship Series totals (2 years)			10	35	6	9	3	0	2	4	.257	0	18	22	4	.909

WORLD SERIES RECORD

WORLD SERIES NOTES: Shares record for most at-bats in one inning—2 (October 18, 1987, fourth inning).

				BATTING									FIELDING			
Year	Team (League)	Pos.	G	AB	R	H	2B	3B	HR	RBI	Avg.	SB	PO	A	E	Avg.
1987—Minnesota (A.L.)		SS	7	30	5	6	1	0	1	3	.200	0	6	20	2	.929
1991—Minnesota (A.L.)		SS	7	24	1	4	1	0	1	3	.167	0	13	24	0	1.000
World Series totals (2 years)			14	54	6	10	2	0	2	6	.185	0	19	44	2	.969

GAKELER, DAN
P, TIGERS

PERSONAL: Born May 1, 1964, at Mt. Holly, N.J. . . . 6-6/210. . . . Throws right, bats right. . . . Full name: Daniel Michael Gakeler.
COLLEGE: Mercer County Community College (N.J.).
TRANSACTIONS/CAREER NOTES: Selected by Milwaukee Brewers organization in 31st round of free-agent draft (June 6, 1983). . . . Selected by Boston Red Sox organization in secondary phase of free-agent draft (January 17, 1984). . . . Traded by Red Sox with SS Spike Owen to Montreal Expos for P John Dopson and SS Luis Rivera (December 8, 1988). . . . Granted free agency (October 15, 1990). . . . Signed by Detroit Tigers organization (November 19, 1990).

Year	Team (League)	G	W	L	Pct.	ERA	Sv.	IP	H	R	ER	BB	SO
1984—Elmira (New York-Penn)		14	4	6	.400	4.11	0	76⅔	67	47	35	41	54
1985—Greensboro (South Atlantic)		23	7	5	.583	5.50	0	108	135	86	66	54	51
1986—Greensboro (South Atlantic)		24	7	6	.538	3.32	1	154⅓	158	73	57	69	154
1987—New Britain (Eastern)		30	8	13	.381	4.63	0	173	188	112	89	63	90
1988—New Britain (Eastern)		26	6	13	.316	3.69	0	153⅔	157	74	63	54	110
1989—Jacksonville (Southern)■		14	5	4	.556	2.39	0	86⅔	70	31	23	39	76
—Indianapolis (Am. Assoc.)		11	3	6	.333	3.12	0	66⅓	53	29	23	28	41
1990—Indianapolis (Am. Assoc.)		22	5	5	.500	3.23	0	120	101	55	43	55	89
1991—Toledo (International)■		23	2	3	.400	3.50	4	43⅔	44	22	17	13	32
—Detroit (A.L.)		31	1	4	.200	5.74	2	73⅔	73	52	47	39	43
Major league totals (1 year)		31	1	4	.200	5.74	2	73⅔	73	52	47	39	43

GALARRAGA, ANDRES
1B, CARDINALS

PERSONAL: Born June 18, 1961, at Caracas, Venezuela. . . . 6-3/235. . . . Throws right, bats right. . . . Full name: Andres Jose Galarraga. . . . Name pronounced gahl-ah-RAH-guh.
HIGH SCHOOL: Enrique Felmi (Caracas, Venezuela).
TRANSACTIONS/CAREER NOTES: Signed as free agent by Montreal Expos organization (January 19, 1979). . . . On disabled list (July 10-August 19 and August 20-September 4, 1986; and May 26-July 4, 1991). . . . Traded by Expos to St. Louis Cardinals for P Ken Hill (November 25, 1991).
RECORDS/HONORS: Named Southern League Most Valuable Player (1984). . . . Named first baseman on THE SPORTING NEWS N.L. Silver Slugger team (1988). . . . Won N.L. Gold Glove at first base (1989-90).
STATISTICAL NOTES: Led Southern League with 271 total bases, .508 slugging percentage and 10 intentional bases on balls received and tied for lead in being hit by pitch with nine in 1984. . . . Led Southern League first basemen with 1,428 total chances and 130 double plays in 1984. . . . Led N.L. in being hit by pitch with 10 in 1987 and tied for lead with 13 in 1989. . . . Led N.L. with 329 total bases in 1988. . . . Led N.L. batters with 153 strikeouts in 1988, 158 in 1989 and 169 in 1990.

				BATTING									FIELDING			
Year	Team (League)	Pos.	G	AB	R	H	2B	3B	HR	RBI	Avg.	SB	PO	A	E	Avg.
1979—West Palm Beach (FSL)		1B	7	23	3	3	0	0	0	1	.130	0	2	1	0	1.000
—Calgary (Pioneer)		1B-3B-C	42	112	14	24	3	1	4	16	.214	1	187	21	5	.977
1980—Calgary (Pioneer)		1-3-C-O	59	190	27	50	11	4	4	22	.263	4	287	52	21	.942
1981—Jamestown (N.Y.-Penn)		C-1-O-3	47	154	24	40	4	6	4	26	.260	0	154	15	0	1.000
1982—West Palm Beach (FSL)		1B-OF	105	338	39	95	20	2	14	51	.281	2	462	36	9	.982
1983—West Palm Beach (FSL)		1B-OF-3B	104	401	55	116	18	3	10	66	.289	7	861	77	13	.986
1984—Jacksonville (Southern)		1B	143	533	81	154	28	4	27	87	.289	2	★1302	★110	16	.989
1985—Indianapolis (A.A.)		1B-OF	121	439	★75	118	15	8	25	87	.269	3	930	63	14	.986
—Montreal (N.L.)		1B	24	75	9	14	1	0	2	4	.187	1	173	22	1	.995
1986—Montreal (N.L.)		1B	105	321	39	87	13	0	10	42	.271	6	805	40	4	.995

— 158 —

Year	Team (League)	Pos.	G	AB	R	H	2B	3B	HR	RBI	Avg.	SB	PO	A	E	Avg.
1987	—Montreal (N.L.)	1B	147	551	72	168	40	3	13	90	.305	7	*1300	103	10	.993
1988	—Montreal (N.L.)	1B	157	609	99	*184	*42	8	29	92	.302	13	1464	103	15	.991
1989	—Montreal (N.L.)	1B	152	572	76	147	30	1	23	85	.257	12	1335	91	11	.992
1990	—Montreal (N.L.)	1B	155	579	65	148	29	0	20	87	.256	10	1300	94	10	.993
1991	—Montreal (N.L.)	1B	107	375	34	82	13	2	9	33	.219	5	887	80	9	.991
Major league totals (7 years)			847	3082	394	830	168	14	106	433	.269	54	7264	533	60	.992

ALL-STAR GAME RECORD

Year	League	Pos.	AB	R	H	2B	3B	HR	RBI	Avg.	SB	PO	A	E	Avg.
1988	—National	1B	2	0	0	0	0	0	0	.000	0	6	0	0	1.000

GALLAGHER, DAVE
OF, METS

PERSONAL: Born September 20, 1960, at Trenton, N.J. . . . 6-0/184. . . . Throws right, bats right. . . . Full name: David Thomas Gallagher.
HIGH SCHOOL: Steinert (Trenton, N.J.).
COLLEGE: Mercer County Community College (N.J.).
TRANSACTIONS/CAREER NOTES: Selected by Oakland Athletics organization in first round (third pick overall) of free-agent draft (January 8, 1980). . . . Selected by Cleveland Indians organization in secondary phase of free-agent draft (June 3, 1980). . . . On disabled list (May 2-June 6, 1983). . . . Traded by Indians organization to Seattle Mariners organization for P Mark Huismann (May 12, 1987). . . . Released by Mariners organization (September 30, 1987). . . . Signed by Vancouver, Chicago White Sox organization (December 7, 1987). . . . On Chicago disabled list (April 29-May 28, 1990). . . . Claimed on waivers by Baltimore Orioles (August 1, 1990). . . . Traded by Orioles to California Angels for P David Martinez and P Mike Hook (December 4, 1990). . . . Traded by Angels to New York Mets for OF Hubie Brooks (December 10, 1991).
STATISTICAL NOTES: Led Midwest League with 21 sacrifice hits in 1982. . . . Tied for Eastern League lead in double plays by outfielders with four in 1983. . . . Led International League outfielders with 369 total chances in 1985. . . . Led International League with 12 sacrifice hits in 1986.

Year	Team (League)	Pos.	G	AB	R	H	2B	3B	HR	RBI	Avg.	SB	PO	A	E	Avg.
1980	—Batavia (N.Y.-Penn)	OF	69	241	33	66	6	3	5	36	.274	11	114	4	2	.983
1981	—Waterloo (Midwest)	OF-3B	127	435	55	102	22	1	3	34	.234	12	224	22	7	.972
1982	—Chattanooga (Southern) ...	OF	15	54	10	12	2	1	0	4	.222	2	32	1	0	1.000
	—Waterloo (Midwest)	OF	110	409	61	118	25	7	6	47	.289	19	232	15	4	*.984
1983	—Buffalo (Eastern)	OF-3B	107	376	64	127	21	3	2	47	*.338	12	223	13	5	.979
1984	—Maine (International)	OF	116	380	49	94	19	5	6	49	.247	4	208	7	3	.986
1985	—Maine (International)	OF	132	488	71	118	22	3	9	55	.242	16	*357	9	3	*.992
1986	—Maine (International)	OF	132	497	59	145	23	5	8	44	.292	19	341	*14	1	*.997
1987	—Cleveland (A.L.)	OF	15	36	2	4	1	1	0	1	.111	2	34	1	1	.972
	—Buffalo (Am. Assoc.)	OF	12	46	10	12	4	0	0	6	.261	1	34	1	0	1.000
	—Calgary (Pacific Coast)■..	OF	75	268	45	82	27	2	3	46	.306	12	143	5	4	.974
1988	—Vancouver (Pac. Coast)■..	OF	34	131	23	44	8	1	4	27	.336	5	79	2	0	1.000
	—Chicago (A.L.)	OF	101	347	59	105	15	3	5	31	.303	5	228	5	0	1.000
1989	—Chicago (A.L.)	OF	161	601	74	160	22	2	1	46	.266	5	390	8	3	.993
1990	—Chicago-Balt. (A.L.)■■......	OF	68	126	12	32	4	1	0	7	.254	1	96	3	2	.980
1991	—California (A.L.)■	OF	90	270	32	79	17	0	1	30	.293	2	180	8	0	1.000
Major league totals (5 years)			435	1380	179	380	59	7	7	115	.275	15	928	25	6	.994

GALLEGO, MIKE
IF, YANKEES

PERSONAL: Born October 31, 1960, at Whittier, Calif. . . . 5-8/160. . . . Throws right, bats right. . . . Full name: Michael Anthony Gallego. . . . Name pronounced guy-YAY-go.
HIGH SCHOOL: St. Paul (Sante Fe Springs, Calif.).
COLLEGE: UCLA.
TRANSACTIONS/CAREER NOTES: Selected by Oakland Athletics organization in second round of free-agent draft (June 8, 1981). . . . On Tacoma temporary inactive list (April 10-May 20, 1983). . . . On Oakland disabled list (June 13-July 29, 1987). . . . Granted free agency (October 28, 1991). . . . Signed by New York Yankees (January 7, 1992).
STATISTICAL NOTES: Led Pacific Coast League in being hit by pitch with eight in 1986. . . . Tied for A.L. lead with 17 sacrifice hits in 1990.

Year	Team (League)	Pos.	G	AB	R	H	2B	3B	HR	RBI	Avg.	SB	PO	A	E	Avg.
1981	—Modesto (California)	2B	60	202	38	55	9	3	0	23	.272	9	127	161	13	.957
1982	—West Haven (Eastern)	2B-SS	54	139	17	25	1	0	0	5	.180	3	85	111	4	.980
	—Tacoma (Pacific Coast)	2B-3B-SS	44	136	12	30	3	1	0	11	.221	4	73	111	8	.958
1983	—Tacoma (Pacific Coast)	2B	2	2	0	0	0	0	0	0	.000	0	0	1	0	1.000
	—Albany (Eastern)	2B-SS-3B	90	274	31	61	6	0	0	18	.223	3	184	260	4	.991
1984	—Tacoma (Pacific Coast)	2B-SS-3B	101	288	29	70	8	1	0	18	.243	7	167	231	13	.968
1985	—Oakland (A.L.)	2B-SS-3B	76	77	13	16	5	1	1	9	.208	1	57	94	1	.993
	—Modesto (California)	2B-SS-3B	6	25	1	5	1	0	0	2	.200	1	12	11	1	.958
1986	—Tacoma (Pacific Coast)	SS-3B-2B	132	443	58	122	16	5	4	46	.275	3	197	417	23	.964
	—Oakland (A.L.)	2B-3B-SS	20	37	2	10	2	0	0	4	.270	0	24	51	1	.987
1987	—Tacoma (Pacific Coast)	2B	10	41	6	11	0	2	0	6	.268	1	15	25	1	.976
	—Oakland (A.L.)	2B-3B-SS	72	124	18	31	6	0	2	14	.250	0	75	122	8	.961
1988	—Oakland (A.L.)	2B-SS-3B	129	277	38	58	8	0	2	20	.209	2	155	254	8	.981

Year	Team (League)	Pos.	G	AB	R	H	2B	3B	HR	RBI	Avg.	SB	PO	A	E	Avg.
1989—Oakland (A.L.)		SS-2B-3B	133	357	45	90	14	2	3	30	.252	7	211	363	19	.968
1990—Oakland (A.L.)		2-S-3-0	140	389	36	80	13	2	3	34	.206	5	207	379	13	.978
1991—Oakland (A.L.)		2B-SS	159	482	67	119	15	4	12	49	.247	6	283	446	12	.984
Major league totals (7 years)			729	1743	219	404	63	9	23	160	.232	21	1012	1709	62	.978

CHAMPIONSHIP SERIES RECORD

CHAMPIONSHIP SERIES NOTES: Shares A.L. single-series record for most sacrifice hits—2 (1989).

Year	Team (League)	Pos.	G	AB	R	H	2B	3B	HR	RBI	Avg.	SB	PO	A	E	Avg.
1988—Oakland (A.L.)		2B	4	12	1	1	0	0	0	0	.083	0	7	6	0	1.000
1989—Oakland (A.L.)		SS-2B	4	11	3	3	1	0	0	1	.273	0	6	14	0	1.000
1990—Oakland (A.L.)		2B-SS	4	10	1	4	1	0	0	2	.400	0	8	9	0	1.000
Championship Series totals (3 years)			12	33	5	8	2	0	0	3	.242	0	21	29	0	1.000

WORLD SERIES RECORD

Year	Team (League)	Pos.	G	AB	R	H	2B	3B	HR	RBI	Avg.	SB	PO	A	E	Avg.
1988—Oakland (A.L.)		PR-2B	1	0	0	0	0	0	0	0	...	0	0	0	0	...
1989—Oakland (A.L.)		2B-3B	2	1	0	0	0	0	0	0	.000	0	0	0	0	...
1990—Oakland (A.L.)		SS	4	11	0	1	0	0	0	1	.091	1	7	10	1	.944
World Series totals (3 years)			7	12	0	1	0	0	0	1	.083	1	7	10	1	.944

GANT, RON
OF, BRAVES

PERSONAL: Born March 2, 1965, at Victoria, Tex. . . . 6-0/172. *. . . Throws right, bats right. . . . Full name: Ronald Edwin Gant.
HIGH SCHOOL: Victoria (Tex.).
TRANSACTIONS/CAREER NOTES: Selected by Atlanta Braves organization in fourth round of free-agent draft (June 6, 1983). . . . On suspended list for one game (July 31, 1991).
RECORDS/HONORS: Named outfielder on THE SPORTING NEWS N.L. All-Star team (1991). . . . Named outfielder on THE SPORTING NEWS N.L. Silver Slugger team (1991).
STATISTICAL NOTES: Led South Atlantic League second basemen with 75 double plays in 1984. . . . Led Carolina League with 271 total bases in 1986. . . . Led Southern League second basemen with 783 total chances and 108 double plays in 1987. . . . Led N.L. second basemen with 26 errors in 1988.

Year	Team (League)	Pos.	G	AB	R	H	2B	3B	HR	RBI	Avg.	SB	PO	A	E	Avg.
1983—Bradenton Braves (GCL)		SS	56	193	32	45	2	2	1	14	.233	4	68	134	22	.902
1984—Anderson (S. Atlantic)		2B	105	359	44	85	14	6	3	38	.237	13	248	263	31	.943
1985—Sumter (South Atlantic)		2B-SS-OF	102	305	46	78	14	4	7	37	.256	19	160	200	10	.973
1986—Durham (Carolina)		2B	137	512	108	142	31	10	*26	102	.277	35	240	384	26	.960
1987—Greenville (Southern)		2B	140	527	78	130	27	3	14	82	.247	24	*328	*434	21	*.973
—Atlanta (N.L.)		2B	21	83	9	22	4	0	2	9	.265	4	45	59	3	.972
1988—Richmond (Int'l)		2B	12	45	3	14	2	2	0	4	.311	1	22	23	5	.900
—Atlanta (N.L.)		2B-3B	146	563	85	146	28	8	19	60	.259	19	316	417	†31	.959
1989—Atlanta (N.L.)		3B-OF	75	260	26	46	8	3	9	25	.177	9	70	103	17	.911
—Sumter (South Atlantic)		OF	12	39	13	15	4	1	1	5	.385	4	19	1	2	.909
—Richmond (Int'l)		OF-3B	63	225	42	59	13	2	11	27	.262	6	111	14	5	.962
1990—Atlanta (N.L.)		OF	152	575	107	174	34	3	32	84	.303	33	357	7	8	.978
1991—Atlanta (N.L.)		OF	154	561	101	141	35	3	32	105	.251	34	338	7	6	.983
Major league totals (5 years)			548	2042	328	529	109	17	94	283	.259	99	1126	593	65	.964

CHAMPIONSHIP SERIES RECORD

CHAMPIONSHIP SERIES NOTES: Shares major league record for most stolen bases in one inning—2 (October 10, 1991, third inning). . . . Holds N.L. single-series record for most stolen bases—7 (1991). . . . Shares N.L. single-game record for most stolen bases—3 (October 10, 1991).

Year	Team (League)	Pos.	G	AB	R	H	2B	3B	HR	RBI	Avg.	SB	PO	A	E	Avg.
1991—Atlanta (N.L.)		OF	7	27	4	7	1	0	1	3	.259	7	15	2	0	1.000

WORLD SERIES RECORD

Year	Team (League)	Pos.	G	AB	R	H	2B	3B	HR	RBI	Avg.	SB	PO	A	E	Avg.
1991—Atlanta (N.L.)		OF	7	30	3	8	0	1	0	4	.267	1	19	0	0	1.000

GANTNER, JIM
2B, BREWERS

PERSONAL: Born January 5, 1954, at Eden, Wis. . . . 5-11/175. . . . Throws right, bats left. . . . Full name: James Elmer Gantner.
HIGH SCHOOL: Campbellsport (Wisc.).
COLLEGE: Wisconsin-Oshkosh.
TRANSACTIONS/CAREER NOTES: Selected by Milwaukee Brewers organization in 12th round of free-agent draft (June 5, 1974). . . . On disabled list (July 31-September 3, 1987). . . . Granted free agency (November 4, 1988). . . . Re-signed by Brewers (December 20, 1988). . . . On disabled list (August 16, 1989-remainder of season). . . . On Milwaukee disabled list (March 31-June

14, 1990); included rehabilitation disability assignment to Beloit (May 24-June 5, 1990) and Denver (June 6-12, 1990)....
Granted free agency (November 4, 1991).... Re-signed by Brewers (December 20, 1991).

RECORDS/HONORS: Shares major league record for longest errorless game by second baseman—25 innings (May 8, finished May 9, 1984); fielded 24.1 innings.... Holds A.L. career record for highest fielding percentage by second baseman—.984....
Shares A.L. single-game record for most innings played by second baseman—25 (May 8, finished May 9, 1984); fielded 24.1 innings.

STATISTICAL NOTES: Led Eastern League third basemen with 118 putouts and 310 assists in 1975.... Led Eastern League third basemen with .953 fielding percentage in 1976.... Led Pacific Coast League third basemen with .936 fielding percentage, 136 putouts and 321 assists in 1977.... Led A.L. second basemen with 613 total chances in 1981, 900 in 1983 and 844 in 1984....
Led A.L. second basemen with 95 double plays in 1981 and 128 in 1983.... Led A.L. second basemen with 325 putouts in 1988.
... Led A.L. in being hit by pitch with 10 in 1989.

Year	Team (League)	Pos.	G	AB	R	H	2B	3B	HR	RBI	Avg.	SB	PO	A	E	Avg.
1974 —Newark (N.Y.-Penn)	SS-3B	62	177	35	54	6	2	5	21	.305	7	64	134	14	.934
1975 —Thetford Mines (East.)......	3B-SS	•138	456	61	117	17	0	12	48	.257	20	†129	†317	33	.931
1976 —Berkshire (Eastern)	3B-SS	126	403	56	118	21	1	6	53	.293	25	120	294	20	†.954
—Milwaukee (A.L.)	3B	26	69	6	17	1	0	0	7	.246	1	17	37	1	.982
1977 —Spokane (Pacific Coast) ...	3B-OF	•143	541	98	152	35	5	15	80	.281	19	†137	†321	31	†.937
—Milwaukee (A.L.)	3B	14	47	4	14	1	0	1	2	.298	2	8	29	4	.902
1978 —Milwaukee (A.L.)	2-3-S-1	43	97	14	21	1	0	1	8	.216	2	46	82	5	.962
1979 —Milwaukee (A.L.)	3-2-S-P	70	208	29	59	10	3	2	22	.284	3	80	161	7	.972
1980 —Milwaukee (A.L.)	3B-2B-SS	132	415	47	117	21	3	4	40	.282	11	159	335	15	.971
1981 —Milwaukee (A.L.)	2B	107	352	35	94	14	1	2	33	.267	3	251	352	10	.984
1982 —Milwaukee (A.L.)	2B	132	447	48	132	17	2	4	43	.295	6	307	398	13	.982
1983 —Milwaukee (A.L.)	2B	161	603	85	170	23	8	11	74	.282	5	374	★512	14	.984
1984 —Milwaukee (A.L.)	2B	153	613	61	173	27	1	3	56	.282	6	★362	469	13	.985
1985 —Milwaukee (A.L.)	2B-3B-SS	143	523	63	133	15	4	5	44	.254	11	278	436	11	.985
1986 —Milwaukee (A.L.)	2B-3B-SS	139	497	58	136	25	1	7	38	.274	13	309	353	10	.985
1987 —Milwaukee (A.L.)	2B-3B	81	265	37	72	14	0	4	30	.272	6	119	193	6	.981
1988 —Milwaukee (A.L.)	2B-3B	155	539	67	149	28	2	0	47	.276	20	†325	430	11	.986
1989 —Milwaukee (A.L.)	2B	116	409	51	112	18	3	0	34	.274	20	241	362	8	.987
1990 —Milwaukee (A.L.)	2B-3B	88	323	36	85	8	5	0	25	.263	18	167	240	9	.978
—Beloit (Midwest)	2B	9	29	10	11	1	0	2	6	.379	2	2	1	1	.750
—Denver (Am. Assoc.)	2B-3B	6	22	1	8	1	0	0	1	.364	1	7	14	0	1.000
1991 —Milwaukee (A.L.)	3B-2B	140	526	63	149	27	4	2	47	.283	4	160	345	12	.977
Major league totals (16 years)		1700	5933	704	1633	250	37	46	550	.275	131	3203	4734	149	.982

DIVISION SERIES RECORD

Year	Team (League)	Pos.	G	AB	R	H	2B	3B	HR	RBI	Avg.	SB	PO	A	E	Avg.
1981 —Milwaukee (A.L.)	2B	4	14	1	2	1	0	0	0	.143	0	3	15	2	.900
Division Series totals (1 year)		4	14	1	2	1	0	0	0	.143	0	3	15	2	.900

CHAMPIONSHIP SERIES RECORD

Year	Team (League)	Pos.	G	AB	R	H	2B	3B	HR	RBI	Avg.	SB	PO	A	E	Avg.
1982 —Milwaukee (A.L.)	2B	5	16	1	3	0	0	0	2	.188	0	12	8	0	1.000

WORLD SERIES RECORD

Year	Team (League)	Pos.	G	AB	R	H	2B	3B	HR	RBI	Avg.	SB	PO	A	E	Avg.
1982 —Milwaukee (A.L.)	2B	7	24	5	8	4	1	0	4	.333	0	9	33	5	.894

PITCHING RECORD

Year	Team (League)	G	W	L	Pct.	ERA	Sv.	IP	H	R	ER	BB	SO
1979 —Milwaukee (A.L.)	1	0	0	. . .	0.00	0	1	2	0	0	0	0

GARCES, RICH
P, TWINS

PERSONAL: Born May 18, 1971, at Maracay, Venezuela. ... 6-0/212. ... Throws right, bats right.... Full name: Richard Aron Garces.
HIGH SCHOOL: Jose Felix Rivas (Maracay, Venezuela).
TRANSACTIONS/CAREER NOTES: Signed as free agent by Minnesota Twins organization (December 29, 1987). ... On Portland suspended list (May 17-September 16, 1991). ... On Portland disabled list (July 28-September 16, 1991).

Year	Team (League)	G	W	L	Pct.	ERA	Sv.	IP	H	R	ER	BB	SO
1988 —Elizabethton (Appalachian)	17	5	4	.556	2.29	5	59	51	22	15	27	69
1989 —Kenosha (Midwest)	24	9	10	.474	3.41	0	142⅔	117	70	54	62	84
1990 —Visalia (California)	47	2	2	.500	1.81	★28	54⅔	33	14	11	16	75
—Orlando (Southern)	15	2	1	.667	2.08	8	17⅓	17	4	4	14	22
—Minnesota (A.L.)	5	0	0	. . .	1.59	2	5⅔	4	2	1	4	1
1991 —Portland (Pacific Coast)	10	0	1	.000	4.85	3	13	10	7	7	8	13
—Orlando (Southern)	10	2	1	.667	3.31	0	16⅓	12	6	6	14	17
Major league totals (1 year)	5	0	0	. . .	1.59	2	5⅔	4	2	1	4	1

GARCIA, CARLOS
SS/3B, PIRATES

PERSONAL: Born October 15, 1967, at Tachira, Venezuela. . . . 6-1/185. . . . Throws right, bats right. . . . Full name: Carlos Jesus Garcia.
HIGH SCHOOL: Bolivar (Venezuela).
TRANSACTIONS/CAREER NOTES: Signed as free agent by Pittsburgh Pirates organization (January 9, 1987).

						—BATTING—							—FIELDING—			
Year	Team (League)	Pos.	G	AB	R	H	2B	3B	HR	RBI	Avg.	SB	PO	A	E	Avg.
1987 —Macon (South Atlantic)		SS	110	373	44	95	14	3	3	38	.255	20	161	262	42	.910
1988 — Augusta (S. Atlantic)		SS	73	269	32	78	13	2	1	45	.290	14	138	207	29	.922
—Salem (Carolina)		SS	62	236	21	65	9	3	1	28	.275	8	131	151	24	.922
1989 —Salem (Carolina)		SS	81	304	45	86	12	4	7	49	.283	19	137	262	32	.926
—Harrisburg (Eastern)		SS	54	188	28	53	5	5	3	25	.282	6	84	131	7	.968
1990 —Harrisburg (Eastern)		SS	65	242	36	67	11	2	5	25	.277	12	101	209	14	.957
—Buffalo (Am. Assoc.)		SS	63	197	23	52	10	0	5	18	.264	7	106	170	19	.936
—Pittsburgh (N.L.)		SS	4	4	1	2	0	0	0	0	.500	0	0	4	0	1.000
1991 —Buffalo (Am. Assoc.)		SS	127	463	62	123	21	6	7	60	.266	30	*212	332	*31	.946
—Pittsburgh (N.L.)	SS-3B-2B	12	24	2	6	0	2	0	1	.250	00	11	18	1	.967
Major league totals (2 years)			16	28	3	8	0	2	0	1	.286	0	11	22	1	.971

GARCIA, CHEO
3B, TWINS

PERSONAL: Born April 27, 1968, at Maracaibo, Venezuela. . . . 5-11/165. . . . Throws right, bats both. . . . Full name: Jose Antonio Garcia.
HIGH SCHOOL: Arquidiosesand San Francisco (Maracaibo, Venezuela).
TRANSACTIONS/CAREER NOTES: Signed as a free agent by Minnesota Twins organization (September 4, 1987).
STATISTICAL NOTES: Led California League third basemen with 236 assists, 337 total chances and 24 double plays in 1990.

						—BATTING—							—FIELDING—			
Year	Team (League)	Pos.	G	AB	R	H	2B	3B	HR	RBI	Avg.	SB	PO	A	E	Avg.
1988 —Elizabethton (Appal.)		OF-2B	59	228	31	59	9	3	2	27	.259	9	106	55	9	.947
1989 —Kenosha (Midwest)		2B-3B	123	468	58	110	24	4	6	49	.235	16	241	314	18	.969
1990 —Visalia (California)	3B-2B-OF	137	486	68	133	29	4	10	71	.274	10	113	†280	34	.920
1991 —Orlando (Southern)		3B	137	496	57	140	24	4	9	75	.282	13	93	*281	18	.954

GARCIA, RAMON
P, WHITE SOX

PERSONAL: Born December 9, 1969, at Guanare, Venezuela. . . . 6-2/200. . . . Throws right, bats right. . . . Full name: Ramon Antonio Garcia.
HIGH SCHOOL: Cesar Lizardo (Guanare, Venezuela).
TRANSACTIONS/CAREER NOTES: Signed as free agent by Chicago White Sox organization (June 30, 1987).
STATISTICAL NOTES: Pitched 2-0 no-hit victory against Sarasota Mets (August 3, 1989). . . . Tied for Gulf Coast League lead with one shutout in 1989. . . . Led Florida State League with 10 home runs allowed in 1990.

Year	Team (League)	G	W	L	Pct.	ERA	Sv.	IP	H	R	ER	BB	SO
1987 —Sarasota White Sox (GCL)		6	1	0	1.000	1.50	0	12	8	3	2	5	6
1988 —Sarasota White Sox (GCL)		13	2	1	.667	2.45	0	22	15	9	6	4	17
1989 —Sarasota White Sox (GCL)		14	6	4	.600	3.06	0	53	34	21	18	17	52
1990 —Sarasota (Florida State)		26	9	*14	.391	3.95	0	157⅓	155	84	69	45	130
—Vancouver (Pacific Coast)		1	0	0	...	0.00	0	1	2	0	0	0	1
1991 —Birmingham (Southern)		6	4	0	1.000	0.93	0	38⅔	27	5	4	11	38
—Vancouver (Pacific Coast)		4	2	2	.500	4.05	0	26⅔	24	13	12	7	17
—Chicago (A.L.)		16	4	4	.500	5.40	0	78⅓	79	50	47	31	40
Major league totals (1 year)		16	4	4	.500	5.40	0	78⅓	79	50	47	31	40

GARCIA, VICTOR
P, REDS

PERSONAL: Born September 15, 1969, at Bonao, Dominican Republic. . . . 6-2/195. . . . Throws right, bats right. . . . Full name: Victoriano Garcia.
TRANSACTIONS/CAREER NOTES: Signed as free agent by Cincinnati Reds organization (February 9, 1988).

Year	Team (League)	G	W	L	Pct.	ERA	Sv.	IP	H	R	ER	BB	SO
1988 —Sarasota Reds (Gulf Coast)		13	4	4	.500	2.27	0	71⅓	60	27	18	30	47
1989 —Greensboro (South Atlantic)		43	10	1	*.909	2.75	5	85	54	36	26	39	108
1990 —Cedar Rapids (Midwest)		49	8	3	.727	1.52	15	71	36	15	12	18	106
1991 —Chattanooga (Southern)		40	5	3	.625	1.98	5	50	41	12	11	20	51
—Nashville (American Assoc.)		15	2	0	1.000	2.63	0	24	15	7	7	14	12

GARDELLA, MIKE
P, YANKEES

PERSONAL: Born January 18, 1967, at Bronx, N.Y. . . . 5-10/195. . . . Throws left, bats left. . . . Full name: Michael Jeremy Gardella.
HIGH SCHOOL: St. Raymond's (New York).
COLLEGE: Oklahoma State.
TRANSACTIONS/CAREER NOTES: Selected by New York Yankees organization in 13th round of free-agent draft (June 5, 1989).

Year	Team (League)	G	W	L	Pct.	ERA	Sv.	IP	H	R	ER	BB	SO
1989 —Oneonta (New York-Penn)		28	2	0	1.000	1.67	★19	37⅔	23	8	7	15	66
1990 —Prince William (Carolina)		★62	4	3	.571	2.01	★30	71⅔	61	18	16	31	86
1991 —Albany (Eastern)		53	4	5	.444	3.82	11	77⅔	70	37	33	55	76

GARDINER, MIKE
P, RED SOX

PERSONAL: Born October 19, 1965, at Sarnia, Ont. . . . 6-0/200. . . . Throws right, bats both. . . . Full name: Michael James Gardiner.
HIGH SCHOOL: Sarnia Collegiate (Sarnia, Ont.).
COLLEGE: Indiana State (bachelor's degree in business, 1987).
TRANSACTIONS/CAREER NOTES: Selected by Seattle Mariners organization in 18th round of free-agent draft (June 2, 1987). . . . On disabled list (May 9-June 10, 1988). . . . Traded by Mariners to Boston Red Sox for P Rob Murphy (April 1, 1991). . . . On Boston disabled list (June 27-July 15, 1991).
RECORDS/HONORS: Named Eastern League Pitcher of the Year (1990).
MISCELLANEOUS: Member of Canadian Olympic Baseball team (1984).

Year	Team (League)	G	W	L	Pct.	ERA	Sv.	IP	H	R	ER	BB	SO
1987 —Bellingham (Northwest)...........		2	2	0	1.000	0.00	0	10	6	0	0	1	11
—Wausau (Midwest)		13	3	5	.375	5.22	0	81	91	54	47	33	80
1988 —Wausau (Midwest)		11	2	1	.667	3.16	1	31⅓	31	16	11	13	24
1989 —Wausau (Midwest)		15	4	0	1.000	0.59	7	30⅓	21	5	2	11	48
—Williamsport (Eastern)		30	4	6	.400	2.84	2	63⅓	54	25	20	32	60
1990 —Williamsport (Eastern)		26	12	8	.600	★1.90	0	★179⅔	136	47	38	29	★149
—Seattle (A.L.)		5	0	2	.000	10.66	0	12⅔	22	17	15	5	6
1991 —Pawtucket (International)■......		8	7	1	.875	2.34	0	57⅔	39	16	15	11	42
—Boston (A.L.)		22	9	10	.474	4.85	0	130	140	79	70	47	91
Major league totals (2 years)		27	9	12	.429	5.36	0	142⅔	162	96	85	52	97

GARDNER, CHRIS
P, ASTROS

PERSONAL: Born March 30, 1969, at Long Beach, Calif. . . . 6-0/175. . . . Throws right, bats right. . . . Full name: Christopher John Gardner.
COLLEGE: Cuesta College (Calif.).
TRANSACTIONS/CAREER NOTES: Selected by Houston Astros organization in sixth round of free-agent draft (June 1, 1988). . . . On Jackson disabled list (April 11-May 6, 1991).

Year	Team (League)	G	W	L	Pct.	ERA	Sv.	IP	H	R	ER	BB	SO
1988 —Sarasota Astros (Gulf Coast) ...		12	4	3	.571	1.46	0	55⅓	37	18	9	23	41
1989 —Asheville (South Atlantic)		15	3	8	.273	3.84	0	77⅓	76	53	33	58	49
1990 —Asheville (South Atlantic)		23	5	10	.333	2.62	0	134	102	57	39	69	81
1991 —Jackson (Texas)		22	13	5	.722	3.15	0	131⅓	116	57	46	75	72
—Houston (N.L.)		5	1	2	.333	4.01	0	24⅔	19	12	11	14	12
Major league totals (1 year)		5	1	2	.333	4.01	0	24⅔	19	12	11	14	12

GARDNER, JEFF
SS/2B, PADRES

PERSONAL: Born February 4, 1964, at Newport Beach, Calif. . . . 5-11/165. . . . Throws right, bats left. . . . Full name: Jeffrey Scott Gardner.
HIGH SCHOOL: Estancia (Costa Mesa, Calif.).
COLLEGE: Orange Coast College (Calif.).
TRANSACTIONS/CAREER NOTES: Selected by Houston Astros organization in 14th round of free-agent draft (January 17, 1984). . . . Signed as free agent by New York Mets organization (August 28, 1984). . . . Traded by Mets to San Diego Padres for P Steve Rosenberg (December 11, 1991).
STATISTICAL NOTES: Led South Atlantic League with 142 base on balls received in 1985. . . . Led South Atlantic League second basemen with 86 double plays in 1985. . . . Led Texas League with 14 sacrifice hits in 1988. . . . Led Texas League second basemen with .983 fielding percentage, 297 putouts, 398 assists, 707 total chances and 97 double plays in 1988. . . . Led International League second basemen with .995 fielding percentage in 1991.

Year	Team (League)	Pos.	G	AB	R	H	2B	3B	HR	RBI	Avg.	SB	PO	A	E	Avg.
1985 —Columbia (S. Atlantic).......		2B	123	401	80	118	9	1	0	50	.294	31	284	★349	19	★.971
1986 —Lynchburg (Carolina)		2B	111	334	59	91	11	2	1	39	.272	6	212	321	9	★.983
1987 —Jackson (Texas)		2B-SS	119	399	55	109	10	3	0	30	.273	1	244	343	20	.967
1988 —Jackson (Texas)		2B-SS	134	432	46	109	15	2	0	33	.252	13	†300	†404	12	†.983
—Tidewater (Int'l)		2B	2	8	3	3	1	1	0	2	.375	0	3	4	0	1.000
1989 —Tidewater (Int'l)		2B	101	269	28	75	11	0	0	24	.279	0	145	234	8	.979
1990 —Tidewater (Int'l)		2B-SS-3B	138	463	55	125	11	1	0	33	.270	3	271	385	13	.981
1991 —Tidewater (Int'l)		2B-SS-3B	136	504	73	147	23	4	1	56	.292	6	286	446	9	†.988
—New York (N.L.)		SS-2B	13	37	3	6	0	0	0	1	.162	0	11	29	6	.870
Major league totals (1 year)			13	37	3	6	0	0	0	1	.162	0	11	29	6	.870

GARDNER, MARK
P, EXPOS

PERSONAL: Born March 1, 1962, at Clovis, Calif. . . . 6-1/200. . . . Throws right, bats right. . . . Full name: Mark Allan Gardner.
HIGH SCHOOL: Clovis (Calif.).
COLLEGE: Fresno City College (Calif.) and Fresno State.

TRANSACTIONS/CAREER NOTES: Selected by California Angels organization in sixth round of free-agent draft (January 11, 1983).... Selected by Cleveland Indians organization in 17th round of free-agent draft (June 4, 1984).... Selected by Montreal Expos organization in eighth round of free-agent draft (June 3, 1985).... On disabled list (September 20, 1990-remainder of season).... On Montreal disabled list (April 2-May 14, 1991); included rehabilitation disability assignment to Indianapolis (April 11-May 8, 1991).

RECORDS/HONORS: Named American Association Pitcher of the Year (1989).

STATISTICAL NOTES: Led N.L. with nine hit batsmen in 1990.... Pitched nine hitless innings against Los Angeles Dodgers, but gave up two hits in 10th inning and lost, 1-0, when reliever Jeff Fassero gave up game-winning hit in 10th (July 26, 1991).

Year	Team (League)	G	W	L	Pct.	ERA	Sv.	IP	H	R	ER	BB	SO
1985	—Jamestown (New York-Penn)	3	0	0	...	2.77	0	13	9	4	4	4	16
	—West Palm Beach (Florida St.)	10	5	4	.556	2.37	0	60⅔	54	24	16	18	44
1986	—Jacksonville (Southern)	29	10	11	.476	3.84	0	168⅔	144	88	72	90	140
1987	—Indianapolis (Am. Assoc.)	9	3	3	.500	5.67	0	46	48	32	29	28	41
	—Jacksonville (Southern)	17	4	6	.400	4.19	0	101	101	50	47	42	78
1988	—Jacksonville (Southern)	15	6	3	.667	1.60	0	112⅓	72	24	20	36	130
	—Indianapolis (Am. Assoc.)	13	4	2	.667	2.77	0	84⅓	65	30	26	32	71
1989	—Indianapolis (Am. Assoc.)	24	12	4	★.750	2.37	0	163⅓	122	51	43	59	★175
	—Montreal (N.L.)	7	0	3	.000	5.13	0	26⅓	26	16	15	11	21
1990	—Montreal (N.L.)	27	7	9	.438	3.42	0	152⅔	129	62	58	61	135
1991	—Indianapolis (Am. Assoc.)	6	2	0	1.000	3.48	0	31	26	13	12	16	38
	—Montreal (N.L.)	27	9	11	.450	3.85	0	168⅓	139	78	72	75	107
Major league totals (3 years)		61	16	23	.410	3.76	0	347⅓	294	156	145	147	263

GARDNER, WES

P

PERSONAL: Born April 29, 1961, at Benton, Ark.... 6-4/203.... Throws right, bats right.... Full name: Wesley Brian Gardner.
HIGH SCHOOL: Benton (Ark.).
COLLEGE: Central Arkansas.

TRANSACTIONS/CAREER NOTES: Selected by New York Mets organization in 22nd round of free-agent draft (June 7, 1982).... Traded by Mets with P Calvin Schiraldi, OF John Christensen and OF LaSchelle Tarver to Boston Red Sox for P Bob Ojeda, P Tom McCarthy, P John Mitchell and P Chris Bayer (November 13, 1985).... On Boston disabled list (April 14, 1986-remainder of season); included rehabilitation disability assignment to Pawtucket (June 24-July 1, 1986).... On disabled list (May 29-June 13, 1988; May 21-June 12 and August 28, 1989-remainder of season; April 13-28 and July 28-August 12, 1990).... Traded by Red Sox to San Diego Padres for 1B-OF Steve Hendricks and P Brad Hoyer (December 15, 1990).... Released by Padres (May 31, 1991).... Signed by Omaha, Kansas City Royals organization (June 26, 1991).... Released by Royals (August 8, 1991).

Year	Team (League)	G	W	L	Pct.	ERA	Sv.	IP	H	R	ER	BB	SO
1982	—Little Falls (New York-Penn)	23	3	6	.333	3.71	6	77⅔	73	48	32	29	77
1983	—Lynchburg (Carolina)	49	6	3	.667	1.87	15	62⅔	55	16	13	32	67
1984	—Tidewater (International)	40	1	2	.333	1.61	★20	56	40	11	10	19	36
	—New York (N.L.)	21	1	1	.500	6.39	1	25⅓	34	19	18	8	19
1985	—Tidewater (International)	53	7	6	.538	2.82	•18	76⅔	57	31	24	34	75
	—New York (N.L.)	9	0	2	.000	5.25	0	12	18	14	7	8	11
1986	—Boston (A.L.)■	1	0	0	...	9.00	0	1	1	1	1	0	1
1987	—Boston (A.L.)	49	3	6	.333	5.42	10	89⅔	98	55	54	42	70
	—Pawtucket (International)	5	1	0	1.000	3.12	2	8⅔	8	3	3	3	9
1988	—Boston (A.L.)	36	8	6	.571	3.50	2	149	119	61	58	64	106
1989	—Boston (A.L.)	22	3	7	.300	5.97	0	86	97	64	57	47	81
1990	—Boston (A.L.)	34	3	7	.300	4.89	0	77⅓	77	43	42	35	58
1991	—San Diego (N.L.)■	14	0	1	.000	7.08	1	20⅓	27	16	16	12	9
	—Omaha (American Assoc.)■	9	3	1	.750	4.91	1	18⅓	27	11	10	5	12
	—Kansas City (A.L.)	3	0	0	...	1.59	0	5⅔	5	4	1	2	3
American League totals (6 years)		145	17	26	.395	4.69	12	408⅔	397	228	213	190	319
National League totals (3 years)		44	1	4	.200	6.40	2	57⅔	79	49	41	28	39
Major league totals (8 years)		189	18	30	.375	4.90	14	466⅓	476	277	254	218	358

CHAMPIONSHIP SERIES RECORD

Year	Team (League)	G	W	L	Pct.	ERA	Sv.	IP	H	R	ER	BB	SO
1988	—Boston (A.L.)	1	0	0	...	5.79	0	4⅔	6	3	3	2	8

GARRELTS, SCOTT

P, GIANTS

PERSONAL: Born October 30, 1961, at Urbana, Ill.... 6-4/210.... Throws right, bats right.... Full name: Scott William Garrelts.... Name pronounced guh-RELTZ.
HIGH SCHOOL: Buckley-Loda (Buckley, Ill.).
TRANSACTIONS/CAREER NOTES: Selected by San Francisco Giants organization in first round (15th pick overall) of free-agent draft (June 5, 1979).... On disabled list (July 15-August 16, 1981).... On Phoenix disabled list (May 12-June 6 and July 24, 1983).... On disabled list (June 30-July 16, 1989; April 24-May 16 and June 11-October 6, 1991).
STATISTICAL NOTES: Tied for Midwest League lead in games started by pitcher with 27 in 1980.... Pitched seven-inning, 1-0 no-hit victory against Tacoma (August 20, 1983).
MISCELLANEOUS: Appeared in three games as pinch-runner (1991).

Year	Team (League)	G	W	L	Pct.	ERA	Sv.	IP	H	R	ER	BB	SO
1979	—Great Falls (Pioneer)	8	1	4	.200	5.86	0	43	45	37	28	40	26
1980	—Clinton (Midwest)	27	11	11	.500	3.89	0	176	155	98	76	★149	★159

Year Team (League)	G	W	L	Pct.	ERA	Sv.	IP	H	R	ER	BB	SO
1981—Shreveport (Texas)	14	3	8	.273	4.44	0	71	56	43	35	43	73
1982—Shreveport (Texas)	27	9	10	.474	3.81	0	151⅓	131	76	64	90	159
—San Francisco (N.L.)	1	0	0	...	13.50	0	2	3	3	3	2	4
1983—Phoenix (Pacific Coast)	21	5	5	.500	4.61	0	97⅔	86	64	50	81	89
—San Francisco (N.L.)	5	2	2	.500	2.52	0	35⅔	33	11	10	19	16
1984—Phoenix (Pacific Coast)	21	5	7	.417	5.90	0	97⅔	97	75	64	82	69
—San Francisco (N.L.)	21	2	3	.400	5.65	0	43	45	33	27	34	32
1985—San Francisco (N.L.)	74	9	6	.600	2.30	13	105⅔	76	37	27	58	106
1986—San Francisco (N.L.)	53	13	9	.591	3.11	10	173⅔	144	65	60	74	125
1987—San Francisco (N.L.)	64	11	7	.611	3.22	12	106⅓	70	41	38	55	127
1988—San Francisco (N.L.)	65	5	9	.357	3.58	13	98	80	42	39	46	86
1989—San Francisco (N.L.)	30	14	5	.737	★2.28	0	193⅓	149	58	49	46	119
1990—San Francisco (N.L.)	31	12	11	.522	4.15	0	182	190	91	84	70	80
1991—San Francisco (N.L.)	8	1	1	.500	6.41	0	19⅔	25	14	14	9	8
Major league totals (10 years)	352	69	53	.566	3.29	48	959⅓	815	395	351	413	703

CHAMPIONSHIP SERIES RECORD

Year Team (League)	G	W	L	Pct.	ERA	Sv.	IP	H	R	ER	BB	SO
1987—San Francisco (N.L.)	2	0	0	...	6.75	0	2⅔	2	2	2	4	4
1989—San Francisco (N.L.)	2	1	0	1.000	5.40	0	11⅔	16	7	7	2	8
Championship Series totals (2 years)	4	1	0	1.000	5.65	0	14⅓	18	9	9	6	12

WORLD SERIES RECORD

Year Team (League)	G	W	L	Pct.	ERA	Sv.	IP	H	R	ER	BB	SO
1989—San Francisco (N.L.)	2	0	2	.000	9.82	0	7⅓	13	9	8	1	8

ALL-STAR GAME RECORD

Year League	W	L	Pct.	ERA	Sv.	IP	H	R	ER	BB	SO
1985—National						Did not play					

GEDMAN, RICH
C, CARDINALS

PERSONAL: Born September 26, 1959, at Worcester, Mass.... 6-0/211.... Throws right, bats left.... Full name: Richard Leo Gedman Jr.

HIGH SCHOOL: St Peter's (Worcester, Mass.).

TRANSACTIONS/CAREER NOTES: Signed as free agent by Boston Red Sox organization (August 5, 1977).... Granted free agency (November 12, 1986).... Re-signed by Red Sox (May 2, 1987).... On disabled list (July 7-22 and July 30, 1987-remainder of season).... On Boston disabled list (April 26-May 20, 1988); included rehabilitation disability assignment to Pawtucket (May 14-20, 1988).... Traded by Red Sox to Houston Astros for a player to be named later (June 8, 1990); deal settled with cash.... Granted free agency (November 5, 1990).... Signed by Louisville, St. Louis Cardinals organization (February 15, 1991).

RECORDS/HONORS: Holds major league records for most putouts—36; chances accepted—37, by catcher in two consecutive nine-inning games (April 29-30, 1986).... Shares major league single-game record for most putouts by catcher (nine-inning game)—20 (April 29, 1986). ... Shares A.L. single-game record for most chances accepted by catcher (nine-inning game)—20 (April 29, 1986).... Named A.L. Rookie Player of the Year by THE SPORTING NEWS (1981).... Named catcher on THE SPORTING NEWS A.L. All-Star team (1986).

STATISTICAL NOTES: Led International League catchers with 13 double plays in 1980.... Hit for the cycle (September 18, 1985). ... Led A.L. catchers with 937 total chances and 14 passed balls in 1986.

Year Team (League)	Pos.	G	AB	R	H	2B	3B	HR	RBI	Avg.	SB	PO	A	E	Avg.
1978—Winter Haven (Fla. St.)	C	98	297	35	89	17	3	3	32	.300	0	377	39	2	★.995
1979—Bristol (Eastern)	C	130	470	48	129	25	1	12	63	.274	0	497	58	11	★.981
1980—Pawtucket (Int'l)	C	111	347	43	82	18	2	11	29	.236	0	367	★65	7	.984
—Boston (A.L.)	C	9	24	2	5	0	0	1	1	.208	0	13	0	2	.867
1981—Pawtucket (Int'l)	C	25	81	8	24	3	0	2	11	.296	0	176	20	6	.970
—Boston (A.L.)	C	62	205	22	59	15	0	5	26	.288	0	275	30	3	.990
1982—Boston (A.L.)	C	92	289	30	72	17	2	4	26	.249	0	397	29	10	.977
1983—Boston (A.L.)	C	81	204	21	60	16	1	2	18	.294	0	274	26	6	.980
1984—Boston (A.L.)	C	133	449	54	121	26	4	24	72	.269	0	693	58	★18	.977
1985—Boston (A.L.)	C	144	498	66	147	30	5	18	80	.295	2	768	★78	★15	.983
1986—Boston (A.L.)	C	135	462	49	119	29	0	16	65	.258	1	★866	65	6	.994
1987—Boston (A.L.)	C	52	151	11	31	8	0	1	13	.205	0	306	14	8	.976
1988—Boston (A.L.)	C	95	299	33	69	14	0	9	39	.231	0	570	40	5	.992
—Pawtucket (Int'l)	C	4	15	2	7	1	0	1	1	.467	0	13	1	1	.933
1989—Boston (A.L.)	C	93	260	24	55	9	0	4	16	.212	0	486	36	10	.981
1990—Boston (A.L.)	C	10	15	3	3	0	0	0	0	.200	0	27	5	1	.970
—Houston (N.L.)■	C	40	104	4	21	7	0	1	10	.202	0	180	25	0	1.000
1991—St. Louis (N.L.)■	C	46	94	7	10	1	0	3	8	.106	0	192	13	5	.976
American League totals (11 years)		906	2856	315	741	164	12	83	356	.259	3	4675	381	84	.984
National League totals (2 years)		86	198	11	31	8	0	4	18	.157	0	372	38	5	.988
Major league totals (12 years)		992	3054	326	772	172	12	87	374	.253	3	5047	419	89	.984

CHAMPIONSHIP SERIES RECORD

Year Team (League)	Pos.	G	AB	R	H	2B	3B	HR	RBI	Avg.	SB	PO	A	E	Avg.
1986—Boston (A.L.)	C	7	28	4	10	1	0	1	6	.357	0	45	4	0	1.000
1988—Boston (A.L.)	C	4	14	1	5	0	0	1	1	.357	0	34	5	0	1.000
Championship Series totals (2 years)		11	42	5	15	1	0	2	7	.357	0	79	9	0	1.000

WORLD SERIES RECORD

Year Team (League)	Pos.	G	AB	R	H	2B	3B	HR	RBI	Avg.	SB	PO	A	E	Avg.
1986—Boston (A.L.)	C	7	30	1	6	1	0	1	1	.200	0	46	3	2	.961

ALL-STAR GAME RECORD

Year League	Pos.	AB	R	H	2B	3B	HR	RBI	Avg.	SB	PO	A	E	Avg.
1985—American	C	1	0	0	0	0	0	0	.000	0	4	0	0	1.000
1986—American	C	0	0	0	0	0	0	0	. . .	0	1	1	0	1.000
All-Star Game totals (2 years)		1	0	0	0	0	0	0	.000	0	5	1	0	1.000

GEORGE, CHRIS
P, BREWERS

PERSONAL: Born September 24, 1966, at Pittsburgh.... 6-2/200.... Throws right, bats right. ... Full name: Christopher Sean George.
HIGH SCHOOL: Plum (Pittsburgh).
COLLEGE: Kent State.
TRANSACTIONS/CAREER NOTES: Selected by Milwaukee Brewers organization in seventh round of free-agent draft (June 1, 1988).

Year Team (League)	G	W	L	Pct.	ERA	Sv.	IP	H	R	ER	BB	SO
1988—Beloit (Midwest)	22	7	4	.636	2.95	6	58	52	27	19	14	58
1989—Stockton (California)	55	7	7	.500	2.15	22	79⅔	61	30	19	37	85
1990—El Paso (Texas)	39	8	3	.727	1.78	13	55⅔	41	16	11	20	38
—Denver (American Assoc.)	7	1	1	.500	18.56	0	5⅓	17	11	11	4	4
1991—Denver (American Assoc.)	43	4	5	.444	2.33	4	85	74	31	22	26	65
—Milwaukee (A.L.)	2	0	0	. . .	3.00	0	6	8	2	2	0	2
Major league totals (1 year)	2	0	0	. . .	3.00	0	6	8	2	2	0	2

GEREN, BOB
C, REDS

PERSONAL: Born September 22, 1961, at San Diego.... 6-3/228.... Throws right, bats right.... Full name: Robert Peter Geren III.
TRANSACTIONS/CAREER NOTES: Selected by San Diego Padres organization in first round (24th pick overall) of free-agent draft (June 5, 1979).... Traded by Padres organization to St. Louis Cardinals organization (December 10, 1980), completing deal in which Padres traded P Rollie Fingers, P Bob Shirley, C-1B Gene Tenace and a player to be named later to Cardinals for C Terry Kennedy, C Steve Swisher, P John Littlefield, P Al Olmsted, P Kim Seaman, P John Urrea and IF Mike Phillips (December 8, 1980).... Granted free agency (October 15, 1985).... Signed by Columbus, New York Yankees organization (November 7, 1985).... Claimed on waivers by Cincinnati Reds (December 2, 1991).
STATISTICAL NOTES: Led Florida State League catchers with 72 assists in 1982.... Led Midwest League catchers with 826 putouts, 102 assists and 939 total chances in 1983.... Led Texas League catchers with .996 fielding percentage in 1985.... Led Eastern League catchers with .994 fielding percentage in 1987.

Year Team (League)	Pos.	G	AB	R	H	2B	3B	HR	RBI	Avg.	SB	PO	A	E	Avg.
1979—Walla Walla (Northwest) ..	C	54	151	19	26	5	0	0	16	.172	0	183	23	9	.958
1980—Reno (California)	C	48	157	24	45	7	1	4	23	.287	1	89	17	4	.964
—Walla Walla (Northwest) ..	C	51	177	19	45	8	1	2	28	.254	1	306	40	10	.972
1981—St. Petersburg (Fla. St.)■..	C	64	167	15	37	9	1	0	13	.222	0	204	24	3	.987
1982—St. Petersburg (Fla. St.)	C-OF-1B	110	352	38	86	24	1	1	45	.244	3	500	†72	10	.983
1983—Springfield (Midwest)	C-1B	124	434	67	115	21	3	24	73	.265	0	†829	†104	11	.988
1984—Arkansas (Texas)	C-1B-3B	86	292	39	72	12	0	15	40	.247	1	545	56	8	.987
—Louisville (Am. Assoc.)	C	15	40	3	7	1	0	0	3	.175	0	80	6	1	.989
1985—Arkansas (Texas)	C-1B-OF	103	315	38	71	18	1	5	40	.225	3	562	60	4	†.994
—Louisville (Am. Assoc.)	C	5	14	2	5	2	0	1	3	.357	0	27	1	0	1.000
1986—Albany (Eastern)■...........	C-1B	27	27	3	4	1	0	0	0	.148	1	51	7	0	1.000
—Columbus (Int'l)	C-1B	68	205	24	52	15	3	7	25	.254	1	270	36	5	.984
1987—Albany (Eastern)	C-1B-3B	78	213	33	47	7	2	11	31	.221	1	319	45	3	†.992
—Columbus (Int'l)	C	5	20	1	3	0	0	1	3	.150	0	20	3	1	.958
1988—Columbus (Int'l)	C	95	321	37	87	13	2	8	35	.271	0	478	72	8	.986
—New York (A.L.)	C	10	10	0	1	0	0	0	0	.100	0	18	3	0	1.000
1989—Columbus (Int'l)	C	27	95	11	24	4	1	2	13	.253	1	137	18	2	.987
—New York (A.L.)	C	65	205	26	59	5	1	9	27	.288	0	308	24	3	.991
1990—New York (A.L.)	C	110	277	21	59	7	0	8	31	.213	0	487	55	4	.993
1991—New York (A.L.)	C	64	128	7	28	3	0	2	12	.219	0	255	18	3	.989
Major league totals (4 years)		249	620	54	147	15	1	19	70	.237	0	1068	100	10	.992

GIANELLI, RAY
3B/1B, BLUE JAYS

PERSONAL: Born February 5, 1966, at Brooklyn, N.Y.... 6-0/195.... Throws right, bats left. ... Full name: Raymond John Gianelli.
HIGH SCHOOL: Copiague (N.Y.).
COLLEGE: New York Institute of Technology.

TRANSACTIONS/CAREER NOTES: Selected by Baltimore Orioles organization in 22nd round of free-agent draft (June 2, 1987)....
Selected by Toronto Blue Jays organization in 38th round of free-agent draft (June 1, 1988).

Year	Team (League)	Pos.	G	AB	R	H	2B	3B	HR	RBI	Avg.	SB	PO	A	E	Avg.
1988	Medicine Hat (Pioneer)	3B-C	47	123	17	30	8	3	4	28	.244	0	29	30	6	.908
1989	Myrtle Beach (S. Atl.)........	3B	127	458	76	138	17	1	18	84	.301	2	65	161	22	.911
1990	Dunedin (Florida State)	1B-3B	118	416	64	120	18	1	*18	57	.288	5	711	120	13	.985
1991	Knoxville (Southern)	3B	112	362	53	100	14	3	7	37	.276	8	70	161	21	.917
	Toronto (A.L.).................	3B	9	24	2	4	1	0	0	0	.167	1	0	12	1	.923
Major league totals (1 year)..........................			9	24	2	4	1	0	0	0	.167	1	0	12	1	.923

GIBSON, KIRK
OF/DH, ROYALS

PERSONAL: Born May 28, 1957, at Pontiac, Mich.... 6-3/225.... Throws left, bats left.... Full name: Kirk Harold Gibson.
HIGH SCHOOL: Kettering (Detroit).
COLLEGE: Michigan State.
TRANSACTIONS/CAREER NOTES: Selected by Detroit Tigers organization in first round (12th pick overall) of free-agent draft (June 6, 1978).... On restricted list (August 15, 1978-March 1, 1979).... On disabled list (April 13-May 21, 1979; June 18-October 6, 1980; and July 11, 1982-remainder of season).... Granted free agency (November 12, 1985).... Re-signed by Tigers (January 8, 1986).... On disabled list (April 23-June 2, 1986).... On Detroit disabled list (March 30-May 5, 1987); included rehabilitation disability assignment to Toledo (April 28-May 5, 1987).... Granted free agency (January 22, 1988)....
Signed by Los Angeles Dodgers (January 29, 1988).... On disabled list (April 26-May 23 and July 23, 1989-remainder of season).... On Los Angeles disabled list (March 31-June 2, 1990); included rehabilitation disability assignment to Albuquerque (May 24-June 2, 1990).... Granted free agency (November 5, 1990).... Signed by Kansas City Royals (December 1, 1990).
RECORDS/HONORS: Named outfielder on THE SPORTING NEWS college All-America team (1978).... Named outfielder on THE SPORTING NEWS N.L. Silver Slugger team (1988).... Named N.L. Most Valuable Player by Baseball Writers' Association of America (1988).
MISCELLANEOUS: Named as wide receiver on THE SPORTING NEWS college football All-America team (1978).... Selected by St. Louis Cardinals in seventh round (173rd pick overall) of 1979 NFL draft.

Year	Team (League)	Pos.	G	AB	R	H	2B	3B	HR	RBI	Avg.	SB	PO	A	E	Avg.
1978	Lakeland (Florida State) ...	OF	54	175	27	42	5	4	8	40	.240	13	115	2	6	.951
1979	Evansville (A.A.)	OF	89	327	50	80	13	5	9	42	.245	20	100	5	9	.921
	Detroit (A.L.)	OF	12	38	3	9	3	0	1	4	.237	3	15	0	0	1.000
1980	Detroit (A.L.)	OF	51	175	23	46	2	1	9	16	.263	4	122	1	1	.992
1981	Detroit (A.L.)	OF	83	290	41	95	11	3	9	40	.328	17	142	1	4	.973
1982	Detroit (A.L.)	OF	69	266	34	74	16	2	8	35	.278	9	167	4	1	.994
1983	Detroit (A.L.)	OF	128	401	60	91	12	9	15	51	.227	14	116	2	3	.975
1984	Detroit (A.L.)	OF	149	531	92	150	23	10	27	91	.282	29	245	4	•12	.954
1985	Detroit (A.L.)	OF	154	581	96	167	37	5	29	97	.287	30	286	1	•11	.963
1986	Detroit (A.L.)	OF	119	441	84	118	11	2	28	86	.268	34	190	2	2	.990
1987	Toledo (International)	DH	6	17	2	4	0	0	0	3	.235	2	0	0	0	.000
	Detroit (A.L.)	OF	128	487	95	135	25	3	24	79	.277	26	253	6	7	.974
1988	Los Angeles (N.L.)■........	OF	150	542	106	157	28	1	25	76	.290	31	311	6	*12	.964
1989	Los Angeles (N.L.)	OF	71	253	35	54	8	2	9	28	.213	12	146	3	3	.980
1990	Albuquerque (PCL)	OF	5	14	6	6	2	0	1	4	.429	1	2	0	1	.667
	Los Angeles (N.L.)	OF	89	315	59	82	20	0	8	38	.260	26	191	4	1	.995
1991	Kansas City (A.L.)■........	OF	132	462	81	109	17	6	16	55	.236	18	162	3	4	.976
American League totals (10 years)................			1025	3672	609	994	157	41	166	554	.271	184	1698	24	45	.975
National League totals (3 years)....................			310	1110	200	293	56	3	42	142	.264	69	648	13	16	.976
Major league totals (13 years)........................			1335	4782	809	1287	213	44	208	696	.269	253	2346	37	61	.975

CHAMPIONSHIP SERIES RECORD

CHAMPIONSHIP SERIES NOTES: Shares single-series record for most game-winning RBIs—2 (1988).... Shares A.L. single-series record for most strikeouts—8 (1987).

Year	Team (League)	Pos.	G	AB	R	H	2B	3B	HR	RBI	Avg.	SB	PO	A	E	Avg.
1984	Detroit (A.L.)	OF	3	12	2	5	1	0	1	2	.417	1	7	0	0	1.000
1987	Detroit (A.L.)	OF	5	21	4	6	1	0	1	4	.286	3	10	1	0	1.000
1988	Los Angeles (N.L.)............	OF	7	26	2	4	0	0	2	6	.154	2	17	1	1	.947
Championship Series totals (3 years)..............			15	59	8	15	2	0	4	12	.254	6	34	2	1	.973

WORLD SERIES RECORD

Year	Team (League)	Pos.	G	AB	R	H	2B	3B	HR	RBI	Avg.	SB	PO	A	E	Avg.
1984	Detroit (A.L.)	OF	5	18	4	6	0	0	2	7	.333	3	5	1	2	.750
1988	Los Angeles (N.L.).............	PH	1	1	1	1	0	0	1	2	1.000	0	0	0	0	...
World Series totals (2 years)........................			6	19	5	7	0	0	3	9	.368	3	5	1	2	.750

GIBSON, PAUL
P, METS

PERSONAL: Born January 4, 1960, at Southampton, N.Y.... 6-0/185.... Throws left, bats right.... Full name: Paul Marshall Gibson.
HIGH SCHOOL: Center Moriches (N.Y.).
COLLEGE: Suffolk County Community College (N.Y.).

TRANSACTIONS/CAREER NOTES: Selected by Cincinnati Reds organization in third round of free-agent draft (January 10, 1978). ... Released by Reds organization (April 8, 1981). ... Signed by Lakeland, Detroit Tigers organization (May 23, 1981). ... Drafted by Minnesota Twins (December 6, 1982). ... On disabled list (August 4-14, 1983). ... Granted free agency (October 15, 1984). ... Signed by Birmingham, Tigers organization (November 9, 1984). ... Traded by Tigers with P Randy Marshall to New York Mets for OF Mark Carreon and P Tony Castillo (January 22, 1992).
STATISTICAL NOTES: Tied for International League lead with two shutouts in 1987.

Year Team (League)	G	W	L	Pct.	ERA	Sv.	IP	H	R	ER	BB	SO
1978—Shelby (Western Carolinas)	24	9	6	.600	3.02	0	140	106	57	47	71	71
1979—Tampa (Florida State)	24	3	8	.273	3.07	0	129	121	56	44	46	58
1980—Cedar Rapids (Midwest)	28	6	*15	.286	4.93	0	146	171	97	80	53	74
1981—Lakeland (Florida State)■	20	4	3	.571	2.95	0	64	64	25	21	21	38
1982—Birmingham (Southern)	44	3	3	.500	2.68	12	77⅓	60	25	23	39	71
1983—Orlando (Southern)■	40	1	7	.125	6.10	3	76⅔	91	59	52	56	45
1984—Orlando (Southern)	27	7	7	.500	3.87	1	121	125	71	52	54	64
1985—Birmingham (Southern)■	36	8	8	.500	4.12	1	144⅓	135	73	66	63	79
1986—Glens Falls (Eastern)	9	3	1	.750	1.37	1	19⅔	16	3	3	7	21
—Nashville (American Assoc.)	30	5	6	.455	3.97	2	113⅓	121	58	50	40	91
1987—Toledo (International)	27	*14	7	.667	3.47	0	179	173	83	69	57	118
1988—Detroit (A.L.)	40	4	2	.667	2.93	0	92	83	33	30	34	50
1989—Detroit (A.L.)	45	4	8	.333	4.64	0	132	129	71	68	57	77
1990—Detroit (A.L.)	61	5	4	.556	3.05	3	97⅓	99	36	33	44	56
1991—Detroit (A.L.)	68	5	7	.417	4.59	8	96	112	51	49	48	52
Major league totals (4 years)	214	18	21	.462	3.88	11	417⅓	423	191	180	183	235

GILBERT, SHAWN
SS, TWINS

PERSONAL: Born March 12, 1965, at Camden, N.J. ... 5-9/170. ... Throws right, bats right. ... Full name: Albert Shawn Gilbert Jr.
HIGH SCHOOL: Agua Fria Union (Avondale, Ariz.).
COLLEGE: Golden West (Calif.) and Fresno State.
TRANSACTIONS/CAREER NOTES: Selected by Los Angeles Dodgers organization in 21st round of free-agent draft (June 6, 1983). ... Selected by Cincinnati Reds organization in secondary phase of free-agent draft (January 9, 1985). ... Selected by Minnesota Twins organization in secondary phase of free-agent draft (June 5, 1985). ... Selected by Minnesota Twins organization in 12th round of free-agent draft (June 2, 1987).
STATISTICAL NOTES: Led Midwest League shortstops with 80 double plays in 1988. ... Led Southern League in caught stealing with 19 in 1991.

Year Team (League)	Pos.	G	AB	R	H	2B	3B	HR	RBI	Avg.	SB	PO	A	E	Avg.
1987—Visalia (California)	SS	82	272	39	61	5	0	5	27	.224	6	122	214	30	.918
1988—Visalia (California)	SS-2B	14	43	10	16	3	2	0	8	.372	1	18	34	10	.839
—Kenosha (Midwest)	SS	108	402	80	112	21	2	3	44	.279	49	151	325	41	.921
1989—Visalia (California)	SS	125	453	52	113	17	1	2	43	.249	42	204	382	39	.938
1990—Orlando (Southern)	SS	123	433	68	110	18	2	4	44	.254	31	157	*361	41	.927
1991—Orlando (Southern)	O-S-2-3	138	529	69	136	12	5	3	38	.257	*43	247	250	20	.961

GILKEY, BERNARD
OF, CARDINALS

PERSONAL: Born September 24, 1966, at St. Louis. ... 6-0/190. ... Throws right, bats right. ... Full name: Otis Bernard Gilkey.
HIGH SCHOOL: University City (Mo.).
TRANSACTIONS/CAREER NOTES: Signed as free agent by St. Louis Cardinals organization (August 22, 1984). ... On disabled list (April 10-25, 1986 and May 29, 1987-remainder of season). ... On St. Louis disabled list (June 14-July 11, 1991).
STATISTICAL NOTES: Led New York-Pennsylvania League outfielders with 185 total chances in 1985. ... Led Texas League in caught stealing with 22 in 1989. ... Led American Association batters in bases on balls received with 75 and caught stealing with 33 in 1990.

Year Team (League)	Pos.	G	AB	R	H	2B	3B	HR	RBI	Avg.	SB	PO	A	E	Avg.
1985—Erie (New York-Penn)	OF	•77	*294	57	60	9	1	7	27	.204	34	*164	*13	*8	.957
1986—Savannah (Southern)	OF	105	374	64	88	15	4	6	36	.235	32	220	7	5	.978
1987—Springfield (Midwest)	OF	46	162	30	37	5	0	0	9	.228	18	79	5	4	.955
1988—Springfield (Midwest)	OF	125	491	84	120	18	7	6	36	.244	54	165	10	6	.967
1989—Arkansas (Texas)	OF	131	500	*104	139	25	3	6	57	.278	*53	236	*22	9	.966
1990—Louisville (Am. Assoc.)	OF	132	499	83	147	26	8	3	46	.295	45	236	18	•11	.958
—St. Louis (N.L.)	OF	18	64	11	19	5	2	1	3	.297	6	47	2	2	.961
1991—St. Louis (N.L.)	OF	81	268	28	58	7	2	5	20	.216	14	164	6	1	.994
—Louisville (Am. Assoc.)	OF	11	41	5	6	2	0	0	2	.146	1	33	1	0	1.000
Major league totals (2 years)		99	332	39	77	12	4	6	23	.232	20	211	8	3	.986

GIRARDI, JOE
C, CUBS

PERSONAL: Born October 14, 1964, at Peoria, Ill. ... 5-11/195. ... Throws right, bats right. ... Full name: Joseph Elliott Girardi.
HIGH SCHOOL: Spalding Institute (Peoria, Ill.).
COLLEGE: Northwestern (degree in industrial engineering, 1986).

TRANSACTIONS/CAREER NOTES: Selected by Chicago Cubs organization in fifth round of free-agent draft (June 2, 1986).... On disabled list (August 27, 1986-remainder of season and August 7, 1988-remainder of season).... On Chicago disabled list (April 17-August 6, 1991); included rehabilitation disability assignment to Iowa (July 23-August 6, 1991).
STATISTICAL NOTES: Led Carolina League catchers with 661 total chances and tied for lead with 17 passed balls in 1987.... Led Eastern League catchers with .992 fielding percentage, 448 putouts, 76 assists and 528 total chances and tied for lead with five double plays in 1988.... Tied for N.L. lead with 16 passed balls in 1990.

Year	Team (League)	Pos.	G	AB	R	H	2B	3B	HR	RBI	Avg.	SB	PO	A	E	Avg.
1986	—Peoria (Midwest)	C	68	230	36	71	13	1	3	28	.309	6	405	34	5	.989
1987	—Winston-Salem (Caro.)	C	99	364	51	102	9	8	8	46	.280	9	★569	★74	18	.973
1988	—Pittsfield (Eastern)	C-OF	104	357	44	97	14	1	7	41	.272	7	†460	†76	6	†.989
1989	—Chicago (N.L.)	C	59	157	15	39	10	0	1	14	.248	2	332	28	7	.981
	—Iowa (American Assoc.)	C	32	110	12	27	4	2	2	11	.245	3	172	21	1	.995
1990	—Chicago (N.L.)	C	133	419	36	113	24	2	1	38	.270	0	653	61	11	.985
1991	—Chicago (N.L.)	C	21	47	3	9	2	0	0	6	.191	0	95	11	3	.972
	—Iowa (American Assoc.)	C	12	36	3	8	1	0	0	4	.222	2	62	5	3	.957
Major league totals (3 years)			213	623	54	161	36	2	2	58	.258	10	1080	100	21	.983

CHAMPIONSHIP SERIES RECORD

Year	Team (League)	Pos.	G	AB	R	H	2B	3B	HR	RBI	Avg.	SB	PO	A	E	Avg.
1989	—Chicago (N.L.)	C	4	10	1	1	0	0	0	0	.100	0	20	0	0	1.000

GLADDEN, DAN
OF, TIGERS

PERSONAL: Born July 7, 1957, at San Jose, Calif.... 5-11/181.... Throws right, bats right. ... Full name: Clinton Daniel Gladden III.... Brother of Jeff Gladden, minor league pitcher (1980-84).
HIGH SCHOOL: Monte Vista (Cupertino, Calif.).
COLLEGE: DeAnza College (Calif.) and Fresno State.
TRANSACTIONS/CAREER NOTES: Signed as free agent by San Francisco Giants organization (June 17, 1979).... On Phoenix disabled list (April 19-May 1, 1984).... On San Francisco disabled list (June 4-July 23, 1986); included rehabilitation disability assignment to Phoenix (July 14-23, 1986).... Traded by Giants with P David Blakley to Minnesota Twins for P Jose Dominguez, P Ray Velasquez and a player to be named later (March 31, 1987); Giants organization acquired P Bryan Hickerson to complete deal (June 15, 1987).... On disabled list (June 25-July 10 and July 17-August 7, 1989; and June 29-July 24, 1991).... Granted free agency (November 5, 1991).... Signed by Detroit Tigers (December 20, 1991).
STATISTICAL NOTES: Led Texas League in caught stealing with 26 in 1981.... Tied for A.L. lead in double plays by outfielders with five in 1988.
MISCELLANEOUS: Batted as switch-hitter with Phoenix (1986).

Year	Team (League)	Pos.	G	AB	R	H	2B	3B	HR	RBI	Avg.	SB	PO	A	E	Avg.
1979	—Fresno (California)	OF-2B-SS	60	228	41	70	9	1	3	31	.307	17	56	16	3	.960
1980	—Fresno (California)	OF	62	237	46	72	10	2	9	41	.304	15	68	3	1	.986
	—Shreveport (Texas)	OF-SS	74	292	51	86	11	2	9	35	.295	22	169	14	5	.973
1981	—Shreveport (Texas)	OF-SS-2B	124	472	81	148	23	9	8	44	.314	★52	211	12	3	.987
1982	—Phoenix (Pacific Coast)	OF	130	503	93	155	40	5	10	74	.308	41	264	16	7	.976
1983	—Phoenix (Pacific Coast)	OF	127	505	113	153	30	9	12	80	.303	50	319	6	7	.979
	—San Francisco (N.L.)	OF	18	63	6	14	2	0	1	9	.222	4	53	0	0	1.000
1984	—Phoenix (Pacific Coast)	OF	59	234	70	93	11	7	3	27	.397	32	130	4	2	.985
	—San Francisco (N.L.)	OF	86	342	71	120	17	2	4	31	.351	31	232	8	3	.988
1985	—San Francisco (N.L.)	OF	142	502	64	122	15	8	7	41	.243	32	273	3	7	.975
1986	—San Francisco (N.L.)	OF	102	351	55	97	16	1	4	29	.276	27	226	7	3	.987
	—Phoenix (Pacific Coast)	OF	7	27	5	9	4	0	0	0	.333	1	11	0	0	1.000
1987	—Minnesota (A.L.)■	OF	121	438	69	109	21	2	8	38	.249	25	223	9	3	.987
1988	—Minnesota (A.L.)	0-2-3-P	141	576	91	155	32	6	11	62	.269	28	319	12	3	.991
1989	—Minnesota (A.L.)	OF-P	121	461	69	136	23	3	8	46	.295	23	245	8	9	.966
1990	—Minnesota (A.L.)	OF	136	534	64	147	27	6	5	40	.275	25	286	12	6	.980
1991	—Minnesota (A.L.)	OF	126	461	65	114	14	9	6	52	.247	15	240	4	3	.988
American League totals (5 years)			645	2470	358	661	117	26	38	238	.268	116	1313	45	24	.983
National League totals (4 years)			348	1258	196	353	50	11	16	110	.281	94	784	18	13	.984
Major league totals (9 years)			993	3728	554	1014	167	37	54	348	.272	210	2097	63	37	.983

CHAMPIONSHIP SERIES RECORD

Year	Team (League)	Pos.	G	AB	R	H	2B	3B	HR	RBI	Avg.	SB	PO	A	E	Avg.
1987	—Minnesota (A.L.)	OF	5	20	5	7	2	0	0	5	.350	0	12	0	0	1.000
1991	—Minnesota (A.L.)	OF	5	23	4	6	0	0	0	3	.261	3	20	0	0	1.000
Championship Series totals (2 years)			10	43	9	13	2	0	0	8	.302	3	32	0	0	1.000

WORLD SERIES RECORD

WORLD SERIES NOTES: Shares single-game record for most grand slams—1 (October 17, 1987).... Shares record for most runs batted in in one inning—4 (October 17, 1987, fourth inning).

Year	Team (League)	Pos.	G	AB	R	H	2B	3B	HR	RBI	Avg.	SB	PO	A	E	Avg.
							BATTING							FIELDING		
1987 —Minnesota (A.L.)		OF	7	31	3	9	2	1	1	7	.290	2	12	0	0	1.000
1991 —Minnesota (A.L.)		OF	7	30	5	7	2	2	0	0	.233	2	25	1	1	.963
World Series totals (2 years)			14	61	8	16	4	3	1	7	.262	4	37	1	1	.974

RECORD AS PITCHER

Year	Team (League)	G	W	L	Pct.	ERA	Sv.	IP	H	R	ER	BB	SO
1988 —Minnesota (A.L.)	141	0	0	...	0.00	0	1	0	0	0	0	0
1989 —Minnesota (A.L.)	121	0	0	...	9.00	0	1	2	1	1	1	0
Major league totals (2 years)	262	0	0	...	4.50	0	2	2	1	1	1	0

GLAVINE, TOM
P, BRAVES

PERSONAL: Born March 25, 1966, at Concord, Mass. . . . 6-1/190. . . . Throws left, bats left. . . . Full name: Thomas Michael Glavine. . . . Name pronounced GLAV-in.
HIGH SCHOOL: Billerica (Mass.).
TRANSACTIONS/CAREER NOTES: Selected by Atlanta Braves organization in second round of free-agent draft (June 4, 1984).
RECORDS/HONORS: Shares major league single-season record for fewest complete games by pitcher who led league—9 (1991). . . . Named N.L. Pitcher of the Year by THE SPORTING NEWS (1991). . . . Named lefthanded pitcher on THE SPORTING NEWS N.L. All-Star team (1991). . . . Named pitcher on THE SPORTING NEWS Silver Slugger team (1991). . . . Named N.L. Cy Young Award winner by Baseball Writers' Association of America (1991).
STATISTICAL NOTES: Led Gulf Coast League with 12 wild pitches in 1984. . . . Tied for N.L. lead with nine complete games in 1991.
MISCELLANEOUS: Drafted by Los Angeles Kings in fourth round of 1984 NHL entry draft (fourth Kings pick, 69th pick overall). . . . Appeared in one game as pinch-runner and one game as pinch-hitter, base on balls and scored (1991).

Year	Team (League)	G	W	L	Pct.	ERA	Sv.	IP	H	R	ER	BB	SO
1984 —Bradenton Braves (GCL)..........	8	2	3	.400	3.34	0	32⅓	29	17	12	13	34
1985 —Sumter (South Atlantic)............	26	9	6	.600	*2.35	0	168⅔	114	58	44	73	174
1986 —Greenville (Southern)	22	11	6	.647	3.41	0	145⅓	129	62	55	70	114
—Richmond (International)	7	1	5	.167	5.63	0	40	40	29	25	27	12
1987 —Richmond (International)	22	6	12	.333	3.35	0	150⅓	142	70	56	56	91
—Atlanta (N.L.)	9	2	4	.333	5.54	0	50⅓	55	34	31	33	20
1988 —Atlanta (N.L.)	34	7	*17	.292	4.56	0	195⅓	201	111	99	63	84
1989 —Atlanta (N.L.)	29	14	8	.636	3.68	0	186	172	88	76	40	90
1990 —Atlanta (N.L.)	33	10	12	.455	4.28	0	214⅓	232	111	102	78	129
1991 —Atlanta (N.L.)	34	•20	11	.645	2.55	0	246⅔	201	83	70	69	192
Major league totals (5 years)	139	53	52	.505	3.81	0	892⅔	861	427	378	283	515

CHAMPIONSHIP SERIES RECORD

CHAMPIONSHIP SERIES NOTES: Shares single-series record for most games lost—2 (1991).

Year	Team (League)	G	W	L	Pct.	ERA	Sv.	IP	H	R	ER	BB	SO
1991 —Atlanta (N.L.)	2	0	2	.000	3.21	0	14	12	5	5	6	11

WORLD SERIES RECORD

WORLD SERIES NOTES: Shares records for most bases on balls in one inning—4 (October 24, 1991, sixth inning); most consecutive bases on balls in one inning—3 (October 24, 1991, sixth inning).

Year	Team (League)	G	W	L	Pct.	ERA	Sv.	IP	H	R	ER	BB	SO
1991 —Atlanta (N.L.)	2	1	1	.500	2.70	0	13⅓	8	6	4	7	8

ALL-STAR GAME RECORD

Year	League	W	L	Pct.	ERA	Sv.	IP	H	R	ER	BB	SO
1991 —National	0	0	...	0.00	0	2	1	0	0	1	3

GLEATON, JERRY DON
P, ROYALS

PERSONAL: Born September 14, 1957, at Brownwood, Tex. . . . 6-3/210. . . . Throws left, bats left. . . . Full name: Jerry Don Gleaton.
HIGH SCHOOL: Brownwood (Tex.).
COLLEGE: Texas.
TRANSACTIONS/CAREER NOTES: Selected by Baltimore Orioles organization in second round of free-agent draft (June 8, 1976). . . . Selected by Texas Rangers organization in first round (17th pick overall) of free-agent draft (June 5, 1979). . . . Traded by Rangers with P Brian Allard, P Ken Clay, P Steve Finch, SS Rick Auerbach and OF Richie Zisk to Seattle Mariners for C Larry Cox, P Rick Honeycutt, OF Willie Horton, OF Leon Roberts and SS Mario Mendoza (December 12, 1980). . . . Traded by Mariners organization with P Gene Nelson to Chicago White Sox for P Salome Barojas (June 27, 1984). . . . Granted free agency (October 15, 1986). . . . Signed by Kansas City Royals (November 15, 1986). . . . Traded by Royals organization to Detroit Tigers for P Greg Everson (April 2, 1990). . . . On disabled list (June 18-July 18, 1991). . . . Granted free agency (November 1, 1991). . . . Signed by Royals organization (January 31, 1992).
STATISTICAL NOTES: Tied for Texas League lead with 17 home runs allowed in 1980. . . . Tied for Eastern League lead with 13 complete games in 1982.

Year	Team (League)	G	W	L	Pct.	ERA	Sv.	IP	H	R	ER	BB	SO
1979 —Tulsa (Texas)	5	3	2	.600	4.89	0	35	37	19	19	15	21
—Texas (A.L.).............................	5	0	1	.000	6.30	0	10	15	7	7	2	2
1980 —Tulsa (Texas)	25	13	7	.650	3.64	0	178	179	83	72	68	138
—Texas (A.L.).............................	5	0	0	...	2.57	0	7	5	2	2	4	2

Year Team (League)	G	W	L	Pct.	ERA	Sv.	IP	H	R	ER	BB	SO
1981—Seattle (A.L.)■	20	4	7	.364	4.76	0	85	88	50	45	38	31
—Spokane (Pacific Coast)	13	5	7	.417	4.15	0	91	104	53	42	39	57
1982—Lynn (Eastern)	24	15	7	.682	2.72	0	182	175	71	55	54	132
—Seattle (A.L.)	3	0	0	...	13.50	0	4⅔	7	7	7	2	1
1983—Salt Lake City (Pacific Coast) ..	24	9	9	.500	6.68	0	137⅓	189	112	102	81	73
1984—Salt Lake City (Pacific Coast) ..	29	4	1	.800	5.80	2	49⅔	62	39	32	17	39
—Denver (American Assoc.)■	12	1	1	.500	1.80	3	20	20	5	4	4	10
—Chicago (A.L.)	11	1	2	.333	3.44	2	18⅓	20	12	7	6	4
1985—Buffalo (American Assoc.)	38	8	2	*.800	2.44	7	55⅓	62	17	15	21	37
—Chicago (A.L.)	31	1	0	1.000	5.76	1	29⅔	37	19	19	13	22
1986—Buffalo (American Assoc.)	46	4	3	.571	3.22	7	78⅓	79	34	28	35	77
1987—Omaha (American Assoc.)■	6	2	0	1.000	3.00	0	15	14	6	5	6	9
—Kansas City (A.L.)	48	4	4	.500	4.26	5	50⅔	38	28	24	28	44
1988—Omaha (American Assoc.)	15	4	2	.667	1.45	0	37⅓	30	7	6	14	40
—Kansas City (A.L.)	42	0	4	.000	3.55	3	38	33	17	15	17	29
1989—Kansas City (A.L.)	15	0	0	...	5.65	0	14⅓	20	10	9	6	9
—Omaha (American Assoc.)	24	3	3	.500	1.11	4	56⅔	40	12	7	22	57
1990—Detroit (A.L.)■	57	1	3	.250	2.94	13	82⅔	62	27	27	25	56
1991—Detroit (A.L.)	47	3	2	.600	4.06	2	75⅓	74	37	34	39	47
Major league totals (11 years)	284	14	23	.378	4.24	26	415⅔	399	216	196	180	247

GOHR, GREG
P, TIGERS

PERSONAL: Born October 29, 1967, at Santa Clara, Calif. . . . 6-3/210. . . . Throws right, bats right. . . . Full name: Gregory James Gohr.
COLLEGE: Santa Clara.
TRANSACTIONS/CAREER NOTES: Selected by Detroit Tigers organization in first round (21st pick overall) of free-agent draft (June 5, 1989).
STATISTICAL NOTES: Led International League with 14 wild pitches in 1991.

Year Team (League)	G	W	L	Pct.	ERA	Sv.	IP	H	R	ER	BB	SO
1989—Fayetteville (South Atlantic)	4	0	2	.000	7.15	0	11⅓	11	9	9	6	10
1990—Lakeland (Florida State)	25	13	5	.722	2.62	0	137⅔	125	52	40	50	90
1991—London (Eastern)	2	0	0	...	0.00	0	11	9	0	0	2	10
—Toledo (International)	26	10	8	.556	4.61	0	148⅓	125	86	76	66	96

GOMEZ, LEO
3B, ORIOLES

PERSONAL: Born March 2, 1967, at Carnovanas, Puerto Rico. . . . 6-0/202. . . . Throws right, bats right. . . . Full name: Leonardo Gomez.
HIGH SCHOOL: Luis Hernaes Nevones (Carnovanas, Puerto Rico).
TRANSACTIONS/CAREER NOTES: Signed as free agent by Baltimore Orioles organization (December 13, 1985). . . . On disabled list (July 3-31, 1986 and May 3, 1988-remainder of season).
STATISTICAL NOTES: Led Eastern League with 89 bases on balls received in 1989. . . . Led Eastern League third basemen with 256 assists in 1989. . . . Led International League third basemen with 26 double plays in 1990.

Year Team (League)	Pos.	G	AB	R	H	2B	3B	HR	RBI	Avg.	SB	PO	A	E	Avg.
1986—Bluefield (Appalachian)	3B-2B-SS	27	88	23	31	7	1	7	28	.352	1	15	38	7	.883
1987—Hagerstown (Carolina)	3B-SS	131	466	94	152	*38	2	19	110*	.326	6	75	233	33	.903
1988—Charlotte (Southern)	3B-1B	24	89	6	26	5	0	1	10	.292	1	19	50	8	.896
1989—Hagerstown (Eastern)	3B-SS	134	448	71	126	23	3	18	78	.281	2	79	†257	25	.931
1990—Rochester (Int'l)	3B-1B	131	430	*97	119	26	4	26	*97	.277	2	92	204	20	.937
—Baltimore (A.L.)	3B	12	39	3	9	0	0	0	1	.231	0	11	20	4	.886
1991—Baltimore (A.L.)	3B-1B	118	391	40	91	17	2	16	45	.233	1	78	184	7	.974
—Rochester (Int'l)	3B-1B	28	101	13	26	6	0	6	19	.257	0	24	46	4	.946
Major league totals (2 years)		130	430	43	100	17	2	16	46	.233	1	89	204	11	.964

GOMEZ, PAT
P, BRAVES

PERSONAL: Born March 17, 1968, at Roseville, Calif. . . . 5-11/185. . . . Throws left, bats left. . . . Full name: Patrick Alexander Gomez.
HIGH SCHOOL: San Juan (Citrus Heights, Calif.).
TRANSACTIONS/CAREER NOTES: Selected by Chicago Cubs organization in fourth round of free-agent draft (June 2, 1986). . . . Traded by Cubs organization with C Kelly Mann to Atlanta Braves (September 1, 1989), completing deal in which Braves traded P Paul Assenmacher to Cubs for two players to be named later (August 24, 1989).

Year Team (League)	G	W	L	Pct.	ERA	Sv.	IP	H	R	ER	BB	SO
1986—Wytheville (Appalachian)	11	3	6	.333	5.17	0	54	57	51	31	46	55
1987—Peoria (Midwest)	20	3	6	.333	4.31	0	94	88	55	45	71	95
1988—Charleston, W.Va. (S. Atl.)	36	2	7	.222	5.38	5	78⅔	75	53	47	52	97
1989—Winston-Salem (Carolina) ...	23	11	6	.647	2.75	0	137⅔	115	59	42	60	127
—Charlotte (Southern)■............	2	1	0	1.000	2.51	0	14⅓	14	5	4	3	11
1990—Richmond (International)	4	1	1	.500	8.80	0	15⅓	19	16	15	10	8
—Greenville (Southern)	23	6	8	.429	4.49	0	124⅓	126	75	62	71	94
1991—Greenville (Southern)	13	5	2	.714	1.81	0	79⅔	58	20	16	31	71
—Richmond (International)	16	2	9	.182	4.39	0	82	99	55	40	41	41

GONZALES, RENE
IF, ANGELS

PERSONAL: Born September 3, 1961, at Austin, Tex. . . . 6-3/201. . . . Throws right, bats right. . . . Full name: Rene Adrian Gonzales.
HIGH SCHOOL: Rosemead (Calif.).
COLLEGE: Glendale College (Calif.) and Cal State Los Angeles.
TRANSACTIONS/CAREER NOTES: Selected by Montreal Expos organization in fifth round of free-agent draft (June 7, 1982). . . . Traded by Expos to Baltimore Orioles (December 16, 1986), completing deals in which Orioles traded P Dennis Martinez (June 16, 1986) and C John Stefero (December 8, 1986) to Expos for a player to be named later. . . . Traded by Orioles to Toronto Blue Jays for P Rob Blumberg (January 15, 1991). . . . Granted free agency (November 18, 1991). . . . Signed by California Angels organization (January 10, 1992).
STATISTICAL NOTES: Led Southern League shortstops with 102 double plays in 1983. . . . Led American Association shortstops with 79 double plays in 1985.

Year Team (League)	Pos.	G	AB	R	H	2B	3B	HR	RBI	Avg.	SB	PO	A	E	Avg.
1982—Memphis (Southern)	SS	56	183	10	39	3	1	1	11	.213	2	77	183	14	.949
1983—Memphis (Southern)	SS	144	476	67	128	12	2	2	44	.269	5	★258	449	20	★.972
1984—Indianapolis (A.A.)	SS-3B-2B	114	359	41	84	12	2	2	32	.234	10	161	349	13	.975
—Montreal (N.L.)	SS	29	30	5	7	1	0	0	2	.233	0	17	28	2	.957
1985—Indianapolis (A.A.)	SS	130	340	21	77	11	1	0	25	.226	3	203	★345	23	.960
1986—Indianapolis (A.A.)	3B-SS-2B	116	395	57	108	14	2	3	43	.273	8	208	297	23	.956
—Montreal (N.L.)	SS-3B	11	26	1	3	0	0	0	0	.115	0	7	19	0	1.000
1987—Baltimore (A.L.)■.............	3B-2B-SS	37	60	14	16	2	1	1	7	.267	1	22	43	2	.970
—Rochester (Int'l)	3-S-2-1-0	42	170	20	51	9	3	0	24	.300	4	72	108	3	.984
1988—Baltimore (A.L.)	3-2-S-1-0	92	237	13	51	6	0	2	15	.215	2	66	185	8	.969
1989—Baltimore (A.L.)	2B-3B-SS	71	166	16	36	4	0	1	11	.217	5	103	146	7	.973
1990—Baltimore (A.L.)	2-3-S-0	67	103	13	22	3	1	1	12	.214	1	68	114	2	.989
1991—Toronto (A.L.)■.............	S-3-2-1	71	118	16	23	3	0	1	6	.195	0	61	118	7	.962
American League totals (5 years)		338	684	72	148	18	2	6	51	.216	9	320	606	26	.973
National League totals (2 years)		40	56	6	10	1	0	0	2	.179	0	24	47	2	.973
Major league totals (7 years)		378	740	78	158	19	2	6	53	.214	9	344	653	28	.973

CHAMPIONSHIP SERIES RECORD

Year Team (League)	Pos.	G	AB	R	H	2B	3B	HR	RBI	Avg.	SB	PO	A	E	Avg.
1991—Toronto (A.L.)	PR-1B-SS	2	0	0	0	0	0	0	0	...	0	2	0	0	1.000

GONZALEZ, JOSE
OF, ANGELS

PERSONAL: Born November 23, 1964, at Puerto Plata, Dominican Republic. . . . 6-2/201. . . . Throws right, bats right. . . . Full name: Jose Rafael Gonzalez.
HIGH SCHOOL: Virginia Elena Ortea (Puerto Plata, Dominican Republic).
TRANSACTIONS/CAREER NOTES: Signed as free agent by Los Angeles Dodgers organization (August 12, 1980). . . . On disabled list (July 7, 1983-remainder of season). . . . Traded by Dodgers to Pittsburgh Pirates for OF Mitch Webster (July 3, 1991). . . . Claimed on waivers by Cleveland Indians (August 15, 1991). . . . Released by Indians (November 20, 1991). . . . Signed by California Angels organization (January 22, 1992).
STATISTICAL NOTES: Tied for Texas League lead in caught stealing with 17 in 1985. . . . Led Texas League outfielders with 320 total chances in 1985.

Year Team (League)	Pos.	G	AB	R	H	2B	3B	HR	RBI	Avg.	SB	PO	A	E	Avg.
1981—Lethbridge (Pioneer)	OF	34	103	11	14	1	1	0	7	.136	3	65	6	5	.934
1982—Lethbridge (Pioneer)	OF	55	209	35	63	14	1	4	47	.301	11	112	7	1	.992
1983—Lodi (California)	OF	76	310	48	91	17	4	6	36	.294	21	182	7	4	.979
1984—Bakersfield (California)	OF	129	484	86	107	26	1	11	59	.221	49	264	13	9	.969
1985—San Antonio (Texas)	OF	128	448	82	137	22	6	13	62	.306	34	★294	15	11	.966
—Los Angeles (N.L.)	OF	23	11	6	3	2	0	0	0	.273	1	10	0	0	1.000
1986—Albuquerque (PCL)	OF	89	303	39	84	20	3	6	37	.277	11	171	10	6	.968
—Los Angeles (N.L.)	OF	57	93	15	20	5	1	2	6	.215	4	73	0	6	.924
1987—Albuquerque (PCL)	OF	116	339	67	95	22	3	13	61	.280	19	225	10	9	.963
—Los Angeles (N.L.)	OF	19	16	2	3	2	0	0	1	.188	5	19	1	0	1.000
1988—Albuquerque (PCL)	OF	84	288	57	88	15	2	5	22	.306	44	177	7	6	.968
—Los Angeles (N.L.)	OF	37	24	7	2	1	0	0	0	.083	2	15	0	1	.938
1989—Albuquerque (PCL)	OF	50	180	32	48	12	4	4	31	.267	10	98	3	2	.981
—Los Angeles (N.L.)	OF	95	261	31	70	11	2	3	18	.268	9	171	8	6	.968
1990—Los Angeles (N.L.)	OF	106	99	15	23	5	3	2	8	.232	3	62	1	0	1.000
1991—Los Angeles-Pitts. (N.L.)■	OF	58	48	5	2	0	0	1	3	.042	0	38	1	0	1.000
—Cleveland (A.L.)■	OF	33	69	10	11	2	1	1	4	.159	8	52	1	1	.981
American League totals (1 year)		33	69	10	11	2	1	1	4	.159	8	52	1	1	.981
National League totals (7 years)		395	552	81	123	26	6	8	36	.223	25	388	11	13	.968
Major league totals (7 years)		428	621	91	134	28	7	9	40	.216	33	440	12	14	.970

CHAMPIONSHIP SERIES RECORD

Year Team (League)	Pos.	G	AB	R	H	2B	3B	HR	RBI	Avg.	SB	PO	A	E	Avg.
1988—Los Angeles (N.L.)	OF-PR	5	0	2	0	0	0	0	0	...	0	3	0	0	1.000

Year	Team (League)	Pos.	G	AB	R	H	2B	3B	HR	RBI	Avg.	SB	PO	A	E	Avg.
1988—Los Angeles (N.L.)............		PH-OF	4	2	0	0	0	0	0	0	.000	0	2	0	0	1.000

GONZALEZ, JUAN
OF, RANGERS

PERSONAL: Born October 16, 1969, at Vega Baja, Puerto Rico.... 6-3/210.... Throws right, bats right.
HIGH SCHOOL: Vega Baja (Puerto Rico).
TRANSACTIONS/CAREER NOTES: Signed as free agent by Texas Rangers organization (May 30, 1986).... On disabled list (April 27-June 17, 1988 and March 30-April 26, 1991).
RECORDS/HONORS: Named American Association Most Valuable Player (1990).
STATISTICAL NOTES: Led Texas League with 254 total bases in 1989.... Led American Association with 252 total bases in 1990.

Year	Team (League)	Pos.	G	AB	R	H	2B	3B	HR	RBI	Avg.	SB	PO	A	E	Avg.
1986—Sarasota Rangers (GCL)...		OF	60	*233	24	56	4	1	0	36	.240	7	89	6	•6	.941
1987—Gastonia (S. Atlantic)		OF	127	509	69	135	21	2	14	74	.265	9	234	10	12	.953
1988—Port Charlotte (Fla. St.)		OF	77	277	25	71	14	3	8	43	.256	5	139	5	4	.973
1989—Tulsa (Texas)		OF	133	502	73	147	30	7	21	85	.293	1	292	15	9	.972
—Texas (A.L.)......................		OF	24	60	6	9	3	0	1	7	.150	0	53	0	2	.964
1990—Oklahoma City (A.A.)		OF	128	496	78	128	29	4	*29	*101	.258	2	220	7	8	.966
—Texas (A.L.)......................		OF	25	90	11	26	7	1	4	12	.289	0	33	0	0	1.000
1991—Texas (A.L.)......................		OF	142	545	78	144	34	1	27	102	.264	4	310	6	6	.981
Major league totals (3 years)			191	695	95	179	44	2	32	121	.258	4	396	6	8	.980

GONZALEZ, LUIS
OF, ASTROS

PERSONAL: Born September 3, 1967, at Tampa, Fla.... 6-2/180.... Throws right, bats left.... Full name: Luis Emilio Gonzalez.
HIGH SCHOOL: Jefferson (Tampa, Fla.).
COLLEGE: South Alabama.
TRANSACTIONS/CAREER NOTES: Selected by Houston Astros organization in fourth round of free-agent draft (June 1, 1988)....
On disabled list (August 29-September 13, 1991).
STATISTICAL NOTES: Tied for Southern League lead with 12 sacrifice flies and nine intentional bases on balls received in 1990.

Year	Team (League)	Pos.	G	AB	R	H	2B	3B	HR	RBI	Avg.	SB	PO	A	E	Avg.
1988—Asheville (S. Atlantic)		3B	31	115	13	29	7	1	2	14	.252	2	19	62	6	.931
—Auburn (N.Y.-Penn)..........		3B-SS-1B	39	157	32	49	10	3	5	27	.312	2	37	83	13	.902
1989—Osceola (Florida State)		DH	86	287	46	82	16	7	6	38	.286	2	0	0	0	...
1990—Columbus (Southern)		1B-3B	138	495	86	131	30	6	•24	89	.265	27	1039	88	23	.980
—Houston (N.L.)		3B-1B	12	21	1	4	2	0	0	0	.190	0	22	10	0	1.000
1991—Houston (N.L.)		OF	137	473	51	120	28	9	13	69	.254	10	294	6	5	.984
Major league totals (2 years)			149	494	52	124	30	9	13	69	.251	10	316	16	5	.985

GOODEN, DWIGHT
P, METS

PERSONAL: Born November 16, 1964, at Tampa, Fla.... 6-3/210.... Throws right, bats right.... Full name: Dwight Eugene Gooden.... Uncle of Gary Sheffield, third baseman, Milwaukee Brewers.
HIGH SCHOOL: Hillsborough (Tampa, Fla.).
TRANSACTIONS/CAREER NOTES: Selected by New York Mets organization in first round (fifth pick overall) of free-agent draft (June 7, 1982).... On New York disabled list (April 1-June 5, 1987); included rehabilitation disability assignment to Tidewater (May 12-17 and May 21-June 1, 1987).... On disabled list (July 2-September 2, 1989 and August 24, 1991-remainder of season).
RECORDS/HONORS: Holds major league rookie-season record for most strikeouts—276 (1984).... Shares modern major league record for most strikeouts in two consecutive games—32 (September 12 and 17, 1984).... Holds N.L. record for most strikeouts in three consecutive games—43 (September 7, 12 and 17, 1984).... Named Carolina League Pitcher of the Year (1983).
... Named N.L. Rookie Pitcher of the Year by THE SPORTING NEWS (1984).... Named N.L. Rookie of the Year by Baseball Writers' Association of America (1984).... Named N.L. Pitcher of the Year by THE SPORTING NEWS (1985).... Named righthanded pitcher on THE SPORTING NEWS N.L. All-Star team (1985).... Named N.L. Cy Young Award winner by Baseball Writers' Association of America (1985).
STATISTICAL NOTES: Led Carolina League with six shutouts in 1983.... Tied for N.L. lead with seven balks in 1984.... Led N.L. with 16 complete games in 1985.

Year	Team (League)	G	W	L	Pct.	ERA	Sv.	IP	H	R	ER	BB	SO
1982—Kingsport (Appalachian)		9	5	4	.556	2.47	0	65⅔	53	34	18	25	66
—Little Falls (New York-Penn)....		2	0	1	.000	4.15	0	13	11	6	6	3	18
1983—Lynchburg (Carolina)		27	*19	4	.826	*2.50	0	191	121	58	53	*112	*300
1984—New York (N.L.)		31	17	9	.654	2.60	0	218	161	72	63	73	*276
1985—New York (N.L.)		35	*24	4	.857	*1.53	0	*276⅔	198	51	47	69	*268
1986—New York (N.L.)		33	17	6	.739	2.84	0	250	197	92	79	80	200
1987—Tidewater (International)		4	3	0	1.000	2.05	0	22	20	7	5	9	24
—Lynchburg (Carolina)		1	0	0	...	0.00	0	4	2	0	0	2	3
—New York (N.L.)		25	15	7	.682	3.21	0	179⅔	162	68	64	53	148
1988—New York (N.L.)		34	18	9	.667	3.19	0	248⅓	242	98	88	57	175

Year	Team (League)	G	W	L	Pct.	ERA	Sv.	IP	H	R	ER	BB	SO
1989 —New York (N.L.)		19	9	4	.692	2.89	1	118⅓	93	42	38	47	101
1990 —New York (N.L.)		34	19	7	.731	3.83	0	232⅔	229	106	99	70	223
1991 —New York (N.L.)		27	13	7	.650	3.60	0	190	185	80	76	56	150
Major league totals (8 years)		238	132	53	.714	2.91	1	1713⅔	1467	609	554	505	1541

CHAMPIONSHIP SERIES RECORD

CHAMPIONSHIP SERIES NOTES: Holds single-series record for most strikeouts—20 (1988).... Shares N.L. single-game record for most innings pitched—10 (October 14, 1986).

Year	Team (League)	G	W	L	Pct.	ERA	Sv.	IP	H	R	ER	BB	SO
1986 —New York (N.L.)		2	0	1	.000	1.06	0	17	16	2	2	5	9
1988 —New York (N.L.)		3	0	0	...	2.95	0	18⅓	10	6	6	8	20
Championship Series totals (2 years)		5	0	1	.000	2.04	0	35⅓	26	8	8	13	29

WORLD SERIES RECORD

Year	Team (League)	G	W	L	Pct.	ERA	Sv.	IP	H	R	ER	BB	SO
1986 —New York (N.L.)		2	0	2	.000	8.00	0	9	17	10	8	4	9

ALL-STAR GAME RECORD

ALL-STAR GAME NOTES: Holds career record for most balks—2.... Shares career record for most games lost—2.

Year	League	W	L	Pct.	ERA	Sv.	IP	H	R	ER	BB	SO
1984 —National		0	0	...	0.00	0	2	1	0	0	0	3
1985 —National					Did not play							
1986 —National		0	1	...	6.00	0	3	3	2	2	0	2
1988 —National		0	1	...	3.00	0	3	3	1	1	1	1
All-Star totals (3 years)		0	2	...	3.38	0	8	7	3	3	1	6

GOODWIN, TOM
OF, DODGERS

PERSONAL: Born July 27, 1968, at Fresno, Calif.... 6-1/165.... Throws right, bats left.... Full name: Thomas Jones Goodwin.
COLLEGE: Fresno State.
TRANSACTIONS/CAREER NOTES: Selected by Pittsburgh Pirates organization in sixth round of free-agent draft (June 2, 1986).... Selected by Los Angeles Dodgers organization in first round (22nd pick overall) of free-agent draft (June 5, 1989).
STATISTICAL NOTES: Tied for Pacific Coast League lead in caught stealing with 23 in 1991.

Year	Team (League)	Pos.	G	AB	R	H	2B	3B	HR	RBI	Avg.	SB	PO	A	E	Avg.
1989 —Great Falls (Pioneer)	OF	63	240	★55	74	12	3	2	33	.308	★60	67	3	1	.986
1990 —San Antonio (Texas)	OF	102	428	76	119	15	4	0	28	.278	★60	264	7	3	★.989
—Bakersfield (California)	OF	32	134	24	39	6	2	0	13	.291	22	55	2	0	1.000
1991 —Albuquerque (PCL)	OF	132	509	84	139	19	4	1	45	.273	48	284	6	3	.990
—Los Angeles (N.L.)	OF	16	7	3	1	0	0	0	0	.143	1	8	0	1	1.000
Major league totals (1 year)		16	7	3	1	0	0	0	0	.143	1	8	0	1	1.000

GORDON, TOM
P, ROYALS

PERSONAL: Born November 18, 1967, at Sebring, Fla.... 5-9/180.... Throws right, bats right.... Full name: Thomas Gordon.
HIGH SCHOOL: Avon Park (Fla.).
TRANSACTIONS/CAREER NOTES: Selected by Kansas City Royals organization in sixth round of free-agent draft (June 2, 1986).
RECORDS/HONORS: Named A.L. Rookie Pitcher of the Year by THE SPORTING NEWS (1989).
STATISTICAL NOTES: Tied for Northwest League lead with four balks in 1987.
MISCELLANEOUS: Appeared in one game as pinch-runner (1991).

Year	Team (League)	G	W	L	Pct.	ERA	Sv.	IP	H	R	ER	BB	SO
1986 —Sarasota Royals (Gulf Coast)	9	3	1	.750	1.02	0	44	31	12	5	23	47
—Omaha (American Assoc.)	1	0	0	...	47.25	0	1⅓	6	7	7	2	3
1987 —Eugene (Northwest)	15	•9	0	•1.000	2.86	1	72⅓	48	33	23	47	91
—Fort Myers (Florida State)	3	1	0	1.000	2.63	0	13⅔	5	4	4	17	11
1988 —Appleton (Midwest)	17	7	5	.583	2.06	0	118	69	30	27	43	★172
—Memphis (Southern)	6	6	0	1.000	0.38	0	47⅓	16	3	2	17	62
—Omaha (American Assoc.)	3	3	0	1.000	1.33	0	20⅓	11	3	3	15	29
—Kansas City (A.L.)	5	0	2	.000	5.17	0	15⅔	16	9	9	7	18
1989 —Kansas City (A.L.)	49	17	9	.654	3.64	1	163	122	67	66	86	153
1990 —Kansas City (A.L.)	32	12	11	.522	3.73	0	195⅓	192	99	81	99	175
1991 —Kansas City (A.L.)	45	9	14	.391	3.87	0	158	129	76	68	87	167
Major league totals (4 years)	131	38	36	.514	3.79	2	532	459	251	224	279	513

GOSSAGE, GOOSE
P

PERSONAL: Born July 5, 1951, at Colorado Springs, Colo.... 6-0/226.... Throws right, bats right.... Full name: Richard Michael Gossage.
HIGH SCHOOL: Wasson (Colorado Springs, Colo.).
COLLEGE: Southern Colorado.

TRANSACTIONS/CAREER NOTES: Selected by Chicago White Sox organization in ninth round of free-agent draft (June 4, 1970). ... Traded by White Sox with P Terry Forster to Pittsburgh Pirates for OF Richie Zisk and P Silvio Martinez (December 10, 1976).... Granted free agency (October 28, 1977).... Signed by New York Yankees (November 23, 1977).... On disabled list (April 21-July 9, 1979).... Granted free agency (November 7, 1983).... Signed by San Diego Padres (January 6, 1984).... On disabled list (August 8-September 1, 1985).... On suspended list (August 29-September 1, 1986).... On disabled list (April 14-May 4, 1987).... Traded by Padres with P Ray Hayward to Chicago Cubs for IF Keith Moreland and IF Mike Brumley (February 12, 1988).... On disabled list (June 16-July 1, 1988).... Released by Cubs (March 28, 1989).... Signed by San Francisco Giants (April 14, 1989).... Claimed on waivers by New York Yankees (August 10, 1989).... Granted free agency (November 13, 1989).... Signed by Fukuoka, Japan Pacific League (July 4, 1990).... Signed as free agent by Texas Rangers organization (January 25, 1991). ... On disabled list (June 17-July 11, 1991). ... On Texas disabled list (August 5-September 1, 1991); included rehabilitation disability assignment to Oklahoma City (August 28-September 1, 1991). ... Granted free agency (October 30, 1991).

RECORDS/HONORS: Holds N.L. single-season record for most strikeouts by relief pitcher— 151 (1977).... Named Midwest League Player of the Year (1971).... Named A.L. Fireman of the Year by THE SPORTING NEWS (1975 and 1978).

STATISTICAL NOTES: Led Midwest League with 15 complete games and seven shutouts in 1971.

Year	Team (League)	G	W	L	Pct.	ERA	Sv.	IP	H	R	ER	BB	SO
1970	—Sarasota White Sox (GCL)	3	0	0	...	2.81	0	16	11	6	5	4	21
	—Appleton (Midwest)	10	0	3	.000	5.91	0	35	41	27	23	19	21
1971	—Appleton (Midwest)	25	★18	2	★.900	★1.83	0	187	141	48	38	50	149
1972	—Chicago (A.L.)	36	7	1	.875	4.28	2	80	72	44	38	44	57
1973	—Iowa (American Association) ...	12	5	4	.556	3.68	1	71	59	32	29	28	66
	—Chicago (A.L.)	20	0	4	.000	7.38	0	50	57	44	41	37	33
1974	—Appleton (Midwest)	2	0	2	.000	3.38	0	8	8	6	3	4	5
	—Chicago (A.L.)	39	4	6	.400	4.15	1	89	92	45	41	47	64
1975	—Chicago (A.L.)	61	9	8	.529	1.84	★26	142	99	32	29	70	130
1976	—Chicago (A.L.)	31	9	17	.346	3.94	1	224	214	104	98	90	135
1977	—Pittsburgh (N.L.)■	72	11	9	.550	1.62	26	133	78	27	24	49	151
1978	—New York (A.L.)■■	63	10	11	.476	2.01	★27	134	87	41	30	59	122
1979	—New York (A.L.)	36	5	3	.625	2.64	18	58	48	18	17	19	41
1980	—New York (A.L.)	64	6	2	.750	2.27	★33	99	74	29	25	37	103
1981	—New York (A.L.)	32	3	2	.600	0.77	20	47	22	6	4	14	48
1982	—New York (A.L.)	56	4	5	.444	2.23	30	93	63	23	23	28	102
1983	—New York (A.L.)	57	13	5	.722	2.27	22	87⅓	82	27	22	25	90
1984	—San Diego (N.L.)■	62	10	6	.625	2.90	25	102⅓	75	34	33	36	84
1985	—San Diego (N.L.)	50	5	3	.625	1.82	26	79	64	21	16	17	52
1986	—San Diego (N.L.)	45	5	7	.417	4.45	21	64⅔	69	36	32	20	63
1987	—San Diego (N.L.)	40	5	4	.556	3.12	11	52	47	18	18	19	44
1988	—Chicago (N.L.)■	46	4	4	.500	4.33	13	43⅔	50	23	21	15	30
1989	—San Francisco (N.L.)■	31	2	1	.667	2.68	4	43⅔	32	16	13	27	24
	—New York (A.L.)■	11	1	0	1.000	3.77	1	14⅓	14	6	6	3	6
1990	—Fukuoka (Japanese Pacific)■...	23	2	3	.400	4.40	8	47	...	...	23	15	40
1991	—Texas (A.L.)■	44	4	2	.667	3.57	1	40⅓	33	16	16	16	28
	—Oklahoma City (Am. Assoc.) ...	2	0	0	...	18.00	0	2	2	4	4	1	3
American League totals (13 years)		550	75	66	.532	3.03	182	1158	957	435	390	489	959
National League totals (7 years)		346	42	34	.553	2.73	126	518⅓	415	175	157	183	448
Major league totals (19 years)		896	117	100	.539	2.94	308	1676⅓	1372	610	547	672	1407

DIVISION SERIES RECORD

Year	Team (League)	G	W	L	Pct.	ERA	Sv.	IP	H	R	ER	BB	SO
1981	—New York (A.L.)	3	0	0	...	0.00	2	6⅔	3	0	0	2	8

CHAMPIONSHIP SERIES RECORD

Year	Team (League)	G	W	L	Pct.	ERA	Sv.	IP	H	R	ER	BB	SO
1978	—New York (A.L.)	2	1	0	1.000	4.50	1	4	3	2	2	0	3
1980	—New York (A.L.)	1	0	1	.000	54.00	0	0⅓	3	2	2	0	0
1981	—New York (A.L.)	2	0	0	...	0.00	2	2⅔	1	0	0	0	2
1984	—San Diego (N.L.)	3	0	0	...	4.50	1	4	5	2	2	1	5
Championship Series totals (4 years)		8	1	1	.500	4.91	4	11	12	6	6	1	10

WORLD SERIES RECORD

Year	Team (League)	G	W	L	Pct.	ERA	Sv.	IP	H	R	ER	BB	SO
1978	—New York (A.L.)	3	1	0	1.000	0.00	0	6	1	0	0	1	4
1981	—New York (A.L.)	3	0	0	...	0.00	2	5	2	0	0	2	5
1984	—San Diego (N.L.)	2	0	0	...	13.50	0	2⅔	3	4	4	1	2
World Series totals (3 years)		8	1	0	1.000	2.63	2	13⅔	6	4	4	4	11

ALL-STAR GAME RECORD

ALL-STAR GAME NOTES: Named to A.L. All-Star team in 1981; replaced due to injury.

Year	League	W	L	Pct.	ERA	Sv.	IP	H	R	ER	BB	SO
1975	—American	0	0	...	9.00	0	1	1	1	1	0	0
1976	—American					Did not play						
1977	—National	0	0	...	18.00	0	1	1	2	2	1	2
1978	—American	0	1	.000	36.00	0	1	4	4	4	1	1
1980	—American	0	0	...	0.00	0	1	1	0	0	0	0

Year	League	W	L	Pct.	ERA	Sv.	IP	H	R	ER	BB	SO
1982	—American					Did not play						
1984	—National	0	0	...	0.00	1	1	1	0	0	0	2
1985	—National	0	0	...	0.00	0	1	0	0	0	1	2
	All-Star totals (6 years)	0	1	.000	10.50	1	6	8	7	7	3	7

GOTT, JIM
P, DODGERS

PERSONAL: Born August 3, 1959, at Hollywood, Calif. . . . 6-4/220. . . . Throws right, bats right. . . . Full name: James William Gott.
HIGH SCHOOL: San Marino (Calif.).
COLLEGE: Brigham Young.
TRANSACTIONS/CAREER NOTES: Selected by St. Louis Cardinals organization in fourth round of free-agent draft (June 7, 1977). . . . On Arkansas disabled list (August 16-September 1, 1979). . . . Drafted by Toronto Blue Jays (December 7, 1981). . . . Traded by Blue Jays with P Jack McKnight and IF Augie Schmidt to San Francisco Giants for P Gary Lavelle (January 26, 1985). . . . On San Francisco disabled list (May 9, 1986-remainder of season); included rehabilitation disability assignment to Phoenix (June 9-24, 1986). . . . Released by Giants organization (December 19, 1986). . . . Re-signed by Giants (April 7, 1987). . . . Claimed on waivers by Pittsburgh Pirates (August 3, 1987). . . . On disabled list (April 7, 1989-remainder of season). . . . Granted free agency (November 13, 1989). . . . Signed by Los Angeles Dodgers (December 7, 1989). . . . On Los Angeles disabled list (April 7-May 25, 1990); included rehabilitation disability assignment to Bakersfield (May 4-25, 1990).
STATISTICAL NOTES: Tied for Pioneer League lead in games started by pitcher with 14 in 1977. . . . Led Western Carolinas League with 21 wild pitches in 1979.

Year	Team (League)	G	W	L	Pct.	ERA	Sv.	IP	H	R	ER	BB	SO
1977	—Calgary (Pioneer)	14	3	4	.429	9.55	0	65	71	★82	★69	★83	60
1978	—Gastonia (Western Carolinas) ..	22	9	6	.600	3.97	0	145	100	67	64	•113	130
	—St. Petersburg (Florida State) ..	5	1	3	.250	1.29	0	28	23	9	4	12	15
1979	—St. Petersburg (Florida State) ..	4	0	3	.000	6.50	0	18	18	13	13	13	9
	—Gastonia (Western Carolinas) ..	19	5	5	.500	5.61	0	77	63	57	48	88	102
	—Arkansas (Texas)	2	0	1	.000	5.40	0	5	3	6	3	13	7
1980	—St. Petersburg (Florida State) ..	25	5	11	.313	4.60	0	137	138	96	70	113	103
1981	—Arkansas (Texas)	28	5	9	.357	3.44	0	131	133	68	50	65	93
1982	—Toronto (A.L.)■	30	5	10	.333	4.43	0	136	134	76	67	66	82
1983	—Toronto (A.L.)	34	9	14	.391	4.74	0	176⅔	195	103	93	68	121
1984	—Toronto (A.L.)	35	7	6	.538	4.02	2	109⅔	93	54	49	49	73
1985	—San Francisco (N.L.)■	26	7	10	.412	3.88	0	148⅓	144	73	64	51	78
1986	—San Francisco (N.L.)	9	0	0	...	7.62	1	13	16	12	11	13	9
	—Phoenix (Pacific Coast)	2	0	0	...	6.75	0	2⅔	2	2	2	3	2
1987	—San Francisco-Pitts. (N.L.)■	55	1	2	.333	3.41	13	87	81	43	33	40	90
1988	—Pittsburgh (N.L.)	67	6	6	.500	3.49	34	77⅓	68	30	30	22	76
1989	—Pittsburgh (N.L.)	1	0	0	...	0.00	0	⅔	1	0	0	1	1
1990	—Bakersfield (California)■	7	0	0	...	2.77	0	13	13	5	4	4	16
	—Los Angeles (N.L.)	50	3	5	.375	2.90	3	62	59	27	20	34	44
1991	—Los Angeles (N.L.)	55	4	3	.571	2.96	2	76	63	28	25	32	73
	American League totals (3 years)	99	21	30	.412	4.45	2	422⅓	422	233	209	183	276
	National League totals (7 years)	263	21	26	.447	3.55	53	464⅓	432	213	183	193	371
	Major league totals (10 years)	362	42	56	.429	3.98	55	886⅔	854	446	392	376	647

GOZZO, MAURO
P, TWINS

PERSONAL: Born March 7, 1966, at New Britain, Conn. . . . 6-3/210. . . . Throws right, bats right. . . . Full name: Mauro Paul Gozzo.
HIGH SCHOOL: Berlin (Conn.).
TRANSACTIONS/CAREER NOTES: Selected by New York Mets organization in 13th round of free-agent draft (June 4, 1984). . . . Traded by Mets organization with C Ed Hearn and P Rich Anderson to Kansas City Royals for C Chris Jelic and P David Cone (March 27, 1987). . . . Drafted by Toronto Blue Jays organization (December 6, 1988). . . . Traded by Blue Jays with two players to be named later to Cleveland Indians for P Bud Black (September 16, 1990); Indians acquired P Steve Cummings (September 21, 1990) and P Alex Sanchez (September 24, 1990) to complete deal. . . . Granted free agency (October 15, 1991). . . . Signed by Portland, Minnesota Twins organization (January 7, 1992).

Year	Team (League)	G	W	L	Pct.	ERA	Sv.	IP	H	R	ER	BB	SO
1984	—Little Falls (New York-Penn)....	24	4	3	.571	5.63	2	38⅓	40	27	24	28	30
1985	—Columbia (South Atlantic)	49	11	4	.733	2.54	14	78	62	22	22	39	66
1986	—Lynchburg (Carolina)	60	9	4	.692	3.10	9	78½	80	30	27	35	50
1987	—Memphis (Southern)■	19	6	5	.545	4.53	0	91⅓	95	58	46	36	56
1988	—Memphis (Southern)	33	4	9	.308	5.73	3	92⅔	127	64	59	36	48
1989	—Knoxville (Southern)■	18	7	0	1.000	2.98	0	60⅓	59	27	20	12	37
	—Syracuse (International)	12	5	1	.833	2.76	2	62	56	22	19	19	34
	—Toronto (A.L.)	9	4	1	.800	4.83	0	31⅔	35	19	17	9	10
1990	—Syracuse (International)	34	3	8	.273	3.58	7	98	87	46	39	44	62
	—Cleveland (A.L.)■	2	0	0	...	0.00	0	3	2	0	0	2	2
1991	—Colorado Springs (Pac. Coast) ..	25	10	6	.625	5.25	1	130⅓	143	86	76	68	81
	—Cleveland (A.L.)	2	0	0	...	19.29	0	4⅔	9	10	10	7	3
	Major league totals (3 years)	13	4	1	.800	6.18	0	39⅓	46	29	27	18	15

GRACE, MARK
1B, CUBS

PERSONAL: Born June 28, 1964, at Winston-Salem, N.C. . . . 6-2/190. . . . Full name: Mark Eugene Grace.
HIGH SCHOOL: Tustin (Calif.).
COLLEGE: Saddleback College (Calif.) and San Diego State.

TRANSACTIONS/CAREER NOTES: Selected by Minnesota Twins organization in 15th round of free-agent draft (January 17, 1984). ... Selected by Chicago Cubs organization in 24th round of free-agent draft (June 3, 1985).... On disabled list (June 5-23, 1989).
RECORDS/HONORS: Shares major league record for most assists by first baseman in one inning—3 (May 23, 1990, fourth inning).... Holds major league single-season record for most assists by first baseman— 180 (1990).... Named Eastern League Most Valuable Player (1987).... Named N.L. Rookie Player of the Year by THE SPORTING NEWS (1988).
STATISTICAL NOTES: Led Midwest League first basemen with 103 double plays in 1986.... Led Eastern League with .545 slugging percentage in 1987.... Led N.L. first basemen with 1,695 total chances in 1991.

Year Team (League)	Pos.	G	AB	R	H	2B	3B	HR	RBI	Avg.	SB	PO	A	E	Avg.
1986 —Peoria (Midwest)	1B-OF	126	465	81	159	30	4	15	95	★.342	6	1050	69	13	.989
1987 —Pittsfield (Eastern)	1B	123	453	81	151	29	8	17	★101	.333	5	1054	★96	6	★.995
1988 —Iowa (American Assoc.) ...	1B	21	67	11	17	4	0	0	14	.254	1	189	20	1	.995
—Chicago (N.L.)	1B	134	486	65	144	23	4	7	57	.296	3	1182	87	•17	.987
1989 —Chicago (N.L.)	1B	142	510	74	160	28	3	13	79	.314	14	1230	126	6	.996
1990 —Chicago (N.L.)	1B	157	589	72	182	32	1	9	82	.309	15	1324	★180	12	.992
1991 —Chicago (N.L.)	1B	160	★619	87	169	28	5	8	58	.273	3	★1520	★167	8	.995
Major league totals (4 years)		593	2204	298	655	111	13	37	276	.297	35	5256	560	43	.993

CHAMPIONSHIP SERIES RECORD

CHAMPIONSHIP SERIES NOTES: Hit home run in first series at-bat (October 4, 1989).

Year Team (League)	Pos.	G	AB	R	H	2B	3B	HR	RBI	Avg.	SB	PO	A	E	Avg.
1989 —Chicago (N.L.)	1B	5	17	3	11	3	1	1	8	.647	1	44	3	0	1.000

GRAHE, JOE
P, ANGELS

PERSONAL: Born June 14, 1967, at West Palm Beach, Fla.... 6-0/200.... Throws right, bats right. ... Full name: Joseph Milton Grahe.
HIGH SCHOOL: Palm Beach Gardens (West Palm Beach, Fla.).
COLLEGE: Palm Beach Junior College (Fla.) and Miami (Fla.).
TRANSACTIONS/CAREER NOTES: Selected by Milwaukee Brewers organization in 28th round of free-agent draft (June 2, 1986). ... Selected by Oakland Athletics organization in fifth round of free-agent draft (June 1, 1988).... Selected by California Angels organization in second round of free-agent draft (June 5, 1989).

Year Team (League)	G	W	L	Pct.	ERA	Sv.	IP	H	R	ER	BB	SO
1990 —Midland (Texas)	18	7	5	.583	5.29	0	119	145	75	70	34	58
—Edmonton (Pacific Coast)	5	3	0	1.000	1.35	0	40	35	10	6	11	21
—California (A.L.)	8	3	4	.429	4.98	0	43⅓	51	30	24	23	25
1991 —Edmonton (Pacific Coast)	14	9	3	.750	4.01	0	94⅓	121	55	42	30	55
—California (A.L.)	18	3	7	.300	4.81	0	73	84	43	39	33	40
Major league totals (2 years)	26	6	11	.353	4.87	0	116⅓	135	73	63	56	65

GRATER, MARK
P, CARDINALS

PERSONAL: Born January 19, 1964, at Rochester, Pa.... 5-10/205.... Throws right, bats right.... Full name: Mark Grater.
HIGH SCHOOL: Monaca (Pa.).
COLLEGE: Community College of Beaver County (Pa.) and Florida International.
TRANSACTIONS/CAREER NOTES: Selected by St. Louis Cardinals organization in 23rd round of free-agent draft (June 2, 1986).

Year Team (League)	G	W	L	Pct.	ERA	Sv.	IP	H	R	ER	BB	SO
1986 —Johnson City (Appalachian)	24	5	2	.714	2.40	8	41⅓	25	14	11	14	46
1987 —Savannah (South Atlantic)	50	6	10	.375	3.04	6	74	54	35	25	48	59
1988 —Springfield (Midwest)	53	7	2	.778	1.78	11	81	60	23	16	27	66
1989 —St. Petersburg (Florida State) ..	56	3	8	.273	1.87	★32	67⅓	44	23	14	24	59
1990 —Arkansas (Texas)	29	2	0	1.000	2.86	17	44	31	18	14	18	43
—Louisville (American Assoc.) ...	24	0	2	.000	3.18	3	28⅓	24	13	10	15	18
1991 —Louisville (American Assoc.) ...	58	3	5	.375	2.02	12	80⅓	68	20	18	33	54
—St. Louis (N.L.)	3	0	0	...	0.00	0	3	5	0	0	2	0
Major league totals (1 year)	3	0	0	...	0.00	0	3	5	0	0	2	0

GRAY, JEFF
P, RED SOX

PERSONAL: Born April 10, 1963, at Richmond, Va.... 6-1/190.... Throws right, bats right.... Full name: Jeffrey Edward Gray.
HIGH SCHOOL: Miami Southride (Fla.).
COLLEGE: Florida State.
TRANSACTIONS/CAREER NOTES: Signed as free agent by Philadelphia Phillies organization (June 14, 1984).... Traded by Phillies organization with P John Denny to Cincinnati Reds for OF Gary Redus and P Tom Hume (December 11, 1985).... Traded by Reds organization to Phillies organization (September 6, 1989), completing deal in which Phillies traded P Bob Sebra to Reds for a player to be named later (July 13, 1989).... Released by Phillies organization (March 30, 1990).... Signed by Pawtucket, Boston Red Sox organization (April 7, 1990).... On disabled list (July 29, 1991-remainder of season).

Year Team (League)	G	W	L	Pct.	ERA	Sv.	IP	H	R	ER	BB	SO
1984 —Sarasota Phillies (Gulf Coast) ..	26	6	4	.600	1.31	7	41⅓	35	9	6	10	26
1985 —Clearwater (Florida State)	55	5	9	.357	3.18	23	87⅔	80	38	31	33	80

Year Team (League)	G	W	L	Pct.	ERA	Sv.	IP	H	R	ER	BB	SO
1986—Vermont (Eastern)■	*55	*14	2	*.875	2.35	15	84⅓	71	24	22	26	65
1987—Nashville (American Assoc.)	53	4	10	.286	4.86	14	83⅓	97	52	45	26	70
1988—Nashville (American Assoc.)	42	8	5	.615	1.97	5	73	59	17	16	18	73
—Cincinnati (N.L.)	5	0	0	...	3.86	0	9⅓	12	4	4	4	5
1989—Nashville (American Assoc.)	44	4	4	.500	3.66	7	66⅓	76	33	27	12	58
1990—Pawtucket (International)■	21	0	0	...	3.41	0	31⅔	20	14	12	7	35
—Boston (A.L.)	41	2	4	.333	4.44	9	50⅔	53	27	25	15	50
1991—Boston (A.L.)	50	2	3	.400	2.34	1	61⅔	39	17	16	10	41
American League totals (2 years)	91	4	7	.364	3.28	10	112⅓	92	44	41	25	91
National League totals (1 year)	5	0	0	...	3.86	0	9⅓	12	4	4	4	5
Major league totals (3 years)	96	4	7	.364	3.33	10	121⅔	104	48	45	29	96

CHAMPIONSHIP SERIES RECORD

Year Team (League)	G	W	L	Pct.	ERA	Sv.	IP	H	R	ER	BB	SO
1990—Boston (A.L.)	2	0	0	...	2.70	0	3⅓	4	2	1	1	2

GREBECK, CRAIG
IF, WHITE SOX

PERSONAL: Born December 29, 1964, at Cerritos, Calif. . . . 5-7/160. . . . Throws right, bats right. . . . Full name: Craig Allen Grebeck. . . . Name pronounced GRAY-bek.
HIGH SCHOOL: Lakewood (Calif.).
COLLEGE: Cal State Dominguez Hills.
TRANSACTIONS/CAREER NOTES: Signed as free agent by Chicago White Sox organization (August 13, 1986).
STATISTICAL NOTES: Led Southern League in grounding into double plays with 15 in 1989.

Year Team (League)	Pos.	G	AB	R	H	2B	3B	HR	RBI	Avg.	SB	PO	A	E	Avg.
1987—Peninsula (Carolina)	SS-3B	104	378	63	106	22	3	15	67	.280	3	137	278	16	.963
1988—Birmingham (Southern)	2B	133	450	57	126	21	1	9	53	.280	5	238	368	19	.970
1989—Birmingham (Southern)	SS-3B-2B	*143	*533	85	*153	25	4	5	80	.287	14	234	364	28	.955
1990—Chicago (A.L.)	3B-SS-2B	59	119	7	20	3	1	1	9	.168	0	36	98	3	.978
—Vancouver (Pac. Coast)	SS-3B-2B	12	41	8	8	0	0	1	3	.195	1	28	26	1	.982
1991—Chicago (A.L.)	3B-2B-SS	107	224	37	63	16	3	6	31	.281	1	104	183	10	.966
Major league totals (2 years)		166	343	44	83	19	4	7	40	.242	1	140	281	13	.970

GREEN, GARY
SS, REDS

PERSONAL: Born January 14, 1962, at Pittsburgh. . . . 6-3/175. . . . Throws right, bats right. . . . Full name: Gary Allan Green. . . . Son of Fred Green, pitcher, Pittsburgh Pirates and Washington Senators (1959-62 and 1964).
HIGH SCHOOL: Taylor-Allderdice (Pittsburgh).
COLLEGE: Oklahoma State.
TRANSACTIONS/CAREER NOTES: Selected by San Francisco Giants organization in 29th round of free-agent draft (June 3, 1980). . . . Selected by St. Louis Cardinals organization in second round of free-agent draft (June 6, 1983). . . . Selected by San Diego Padres organization in first round (26th pick overall) of free-agent draft (June 4, 1984). . . . On disabled list (July 19-28, 1985). . . . Drafted by Texas Rangers organization (December 5, 1989). . . . On Texas disabled list (March 31-May 17, 1991); included rehabilitation disability assignment to Oklahoma City (April 29-May 17, 1991). . . . Granted free agency (October 14, 1991). . . . Signed by Cincinnati Reds organization (November 12, 1991).
STATISTICAL NOTES: Led Texas League with 15 sacrifice hits in 1985. . . . Led Pacific Coast League with 14 sacrifice hits in 1987. . . . Led Pacific Coast League shortstops with 75 double plays in 1987.
MISCELLANEOUS: Member of 1984 U.S. Olympic baseball team.

Year Team (League)	Pos.	G	AB	R	H	2B	3B	HR	RBI	Avg.	SB	PO	A	E	Avg.
1985—Beaumont (Texas)	SS	119	409	44	105	17	1	1	51	.257	8	157	405	30	.949
1986—Las Vegas (Pac. Coast)	SS	129	416	42	104	11	3	0	41	.250	3	158	390	24	.958
—San Diego (N.L.)	SS	13	33	2	7	1	0	0	2	.212	0	16	35	0	1.000
1987—Las Vegas (Pac. Coast)	SS	111	337	32	80	8	2	1	32	.237	2	164	306	13	*.973
1988—Las Vegas (Pac. Coast)	SS-3B	88	302	39	82	16	2	0	37	.272	4	79	194	18	.938
1989—San Diego (N.L.)	SS-3B	15	27	4	7	3	0	0	0	.259	0	6	29	3	.921
—Las Vegas (Pac. Coast)	SS-1B	62	191	18	40	6	0	0	18	.209	2	71	177	19	.929
1990—Oklahoma City (A.A.)■	SS	55	167	19	39	11	0	4	25	.234	1	101	145	10	.961
—Texas (A.L.)	SS	62	88	10	19	3	0	0	8	.216	1	61	112	5	.972
1991—Oklahoma City (A.A.)	SS	100	308	36	67	4	2	2	30	.218	1	171	245	19	.956
—Texas (A.L.)	SS	8	20	0	3	1	0	0	1	.150	0	10	20	1	.968
American League totals (2 years)		70	108	10	22	4	0	0	9	.204	1	71	132	6	.971
National League totals (2 years)		28	60	6	14	4	0	0	2	.233	0	22	64	3	.966
Major league totals (4 years)		98	168	16	36	8	0	0	11	.214	1	93	196	9	.970

GREEN, OTIS
P, BREWERS

PERSONAL: Born March 11, 1964, at Miami. . . . 6-2/192. . . . Throws left, bats left. . . . Full name: Otis Andre Green.
HIGH SCHOOL: Miami Carol City Sr. (Miami).
COLLEGE: Miami-Dade Community College (North).
TRANSACTIONS/CAREER NOTES: Selected by Chicago White Sox organization in fifth round of free-agent draft (June 7, 1982). . . .

Selected by White Sox organization in secondary phase of free-agent draft (January 11, 1983).... Selected by Toronto Blue Jays organization in secondary phase of free-agent draft (June 6, 1983).... On disabled list (July 18-August 14, 1985).... Granted free agency (October 22, 1989).... Signed by Montreal Expos organization (April 23, 1990).... Traded by Expos organization to San Francisco Giants organization for OF James Steels (August 19, 1990).... Granted free agency (October 15, 1990).... Signed by Milwaukee Brewers organization (November 13, 1990).

STATISTICAL NOTES: Tied for International League lead in double plays by outfielders with three in 1986.... Led International League first basemen with 111 double plays and tied for lead with 14 errors in 1987.

Year	Team (League)	G	W	L	Pct.	ERA	Sv.	IP	H	R	ER	BB	SO
1991	—Stockton (California)■	12	9	1	*.900	1.92	0	75	41	18	16	33	106
	—El Paso (Texas)	9	3	3	.500	3.18	0	51	35	21	18	25	49

RECORD AS POSITION PLAYER

Year	Team (League)	Pos.	G	AB	R	H	2B	3B	HR	RBI	Avg.	SB	PO	A	E	Avg.
1983	—Medicine Hat (Pioneer)	OF	59	241	44	76	8	2	10	37	.315	10	102	1	7	.936
1984	—Florence (S. Atlantic)........	OF	43	158	31	42	6	4	5	26	.266	9	70	4	2	.974
	—Kinston (Carolina)............	OF	84	305	40	79	18	3	6	34	.259	9	120	7	5	.962
1985	—Knoxville (Southern)	OF	115	442	68	128	19	5	11	68	.290	9	221	4	3	.987
1986	—Syracuse (International) ..	OF	122	480	66	135	24	8	5	53	.281	12	226	13	8	.968
1987	—Syracuse (International) ..	1B-OF	131	473	62	121	21	6	5	60	.256	15	939	79	‡16	.985
1988	—Syracuse (International) ..	1B-OF	109	410	59	109	23	7	10	41	.266	13	705	47	8	.989
1989	—Syracuse (International) ..	1B-OF	87	306	45	81	11	1	5	28	.265	14	600	36	6	.991
1990	—Indianapolis (A.A.)■........	OF-1B	76	197	34	54	12	3	1	16	.274	5	184	7	5	.974
	—Phoenix (Pacific Coast)■..	OF	8	22	4	6	2	0	0	0	.273	0	16	1	0	1.000

GREENE, TOMMY
P, PHILLIES

PERSONAL: Born April 6, 1967, at Lumberton, N.C. ... 6-5/227. ... Throws right, bats right.... Full name: Ira Thomas Greene.
HIGH SCHOOL: Whiteville (N.C.).
TRANSACTIONS/CAREER NOTES: Selected by Atlanta Braves organization in first round (14th pick overall) of free-agent draft (June 3, 1985).... Traded by Braves to Scranton/Wilkes-Barre, Philadelphia Phillies organization (August 9, 1990), as partial completion of deal in which Braves traded OF Dale Murphy and a player to be named later to Phillies for P Jeff Parrett and two players to be named later (August 3, 1990); Braves acquired OF Jim Vatcher (August 9, 1990) and SS Victor Rosario (September 4, 1990) to complete deal.
STATISTICAL NOTES: Led South Atlantic League pitchers with 28 games started and tied for lead with three shutouts in 1986.... Tied for International League lead with three shutouts in 1988.... Pitched 2-0 no-hit victory against Montreal Expos (May 23, 1991).
MISCELLANEOUS: Appeared in two games as pinch-hitter (1991).

Year	Team (League)	G	W	L	Pct.	ERA	Sv.	IP	H	R	ER	BB	SO
1985	—Pulaski (Appalachian)	12	2	5	.286	7.64	0	50⅔	49	45	43	27	32
1986	—Sumter (South Atlantic)............	28	11	7	.611	4.69	0	174⅔	162	95	91	82	169
1987	—Greenville (Southern)	23	11	8	.579	3.29	0	142½	103	60	52	66	101
1988	—Richmond (International)	29	7	17	.292	4.77	0	177⅓	169	98	94	70	130
1989	—Richmond (International)	26	9	12	.429	3.61	0	152	136	74	61	50	125
	—Atlanta (N.L.)	4	1	2	.333	4.10	0	26⅓	22	12	12	6	17
1990	—Atlanta-Philadelphia (N.L.)■ ...	15	3	3	.500	5.08	0	51⅓	50	31	29	26	21
	—Rich.-Scran./W.B. (Int'l)	20	5	8	.385	3.49	0	116	93	49	45	67	69
1991	—Philadelphia (N.L.)	36	13	7	.650	3.38	0	207⅔	177	85	78	66	154
	Major league totals (3 years)	55	17	12	.586	3.75	0	285⅓	249	128	119	98	192

GREENWELL, MIKE
OF, RED SOX

PERSONAL: Born July 18, 1963, at Louisville, Ky. ... 6-0/205. ... Throws right, bats left.... Full name: Michael Lewis Greenwell.
HIGH SCHOOL: North Ft. Myers (Fla.).
TRANSACTIONS/CAREER NOTES: Selected by Boston Red Sox organization in third round of free-agent draft (June 7, 1982).... On disabled list (April 21-May 2 and May 13-July 25, 1983; and July 30-August 14, 1989).
RECORDS/HONORS: Holds A.L. single-season record for most game-winning runs batted in—23 (1988).... Named outfielder on THE SPORTING NEWS A.L. All-Star team (1988).... Named outfielder on THE SPORTING NEWS A.L. Silver Slugger team (1988).
STATISTICAL NOTES: Led Carolina League in being hit by pitch with 15 in 1984.... Hit for the cycle (September 14, 1988).... Led A.L. with 23 game-winning RBIs and tied for lead with 18 intentional bases on balls received in 1988.

Year	Team (League)	Pos.	G	AB	R	H	2B	3B	HR	RBI	Avg.	SB	PO	A	E	Avg.
1982	—Elmira (New York-Penn) ..	3B-2B	72	268	57	72	10	1	6	36	.269	5	96	151	31	.888
1983	—Winston-Salem (Caro.)	OF	48	158	23	44	8	0	3	21	.278	4	28	1	1	.967
1984	—Winston-Salem (Caro.)	3B-OF	130	454	70	139	23	6	16	84	.306	9	126	132	30	.896
1985	—Pawtucket (Int'l)	OF	117	418	47	107	21	1	13	52	.256	3	178	8	7	.964
	—Boston (A.L.)	OF	17	31	7	10	1	0	4	8	.323	1	14	0	0	1.000
1986	—Pawtucket (Int'l)	OF-3B	89	320	62	96	21	1	18	59	.300	6	130	20	8	.949
	—Boston (A.L.)	OF	31	35	4	11	2	0	4	4	.314	0	18	1	0	1.000
1987	—Boston (A.L.)	OF-C	125	412	71	135	31	6	19	89	.328	5	165	6	6	.966
1988	—Boston (A.L.)	OF	158	590	86	192	39	8	22	119	.325	16	302	6	6	.981

Year Team (League)	Pos.	G	AB	R	H	2B	3B	HR	RBI	Avg.	SB	PO	A	E	Avg.
					—BATTING—								—FIELDING—		
1989—Boston (A.L.)	OF	145	578	87	178	36	0	14	95	.308	13	220	11	8	.967
1990—Boston (A.L.)	OF	159	610	71	181	30	6	14	73	.297	8	287	13	7	.977
1991—Boston (A.L.)	OF	147	544	76	163	26	6	9	83	.300	15	263	9	3	.989
Major league totals (7 years)		782	2800	402	870	165	26	82	471	.311	58	1269	48	30	.978

CHAMPIONSHIP SERIES RECORD

Year Team (League)	Pos.	G	AB	R	H	2B	3B	HR	RBI	Avg.	SB	PO	A	E	Avg.
1986—Boston (A.L.)	PH	2	2	0	1	0	0	0	0	.500	0	0	0	0	...
1988—Boston (A.L.)	OF	4	14	2	3	1	0	1	3	.214	0	4	0	0	1.000
1990—Boston (A.L.)	OF	4	14	1	0	0	0	0	0	.000	0	3	0	1	.750
Championship Series totals (3 years)		10	30	3	4	1	0	1	3	.133	0	7	0	1	.875

WORLD SERIES RECORD

Year Team (League)	Pos.	G	AB	R	H	2B	3B	HR	RBI	Avg.	SB	PO	A	E	Avg.
1986—Boston (A.L.)	PH	4	3	0	0	0	0	0	0	.000	0	0	0	0	...

ALL-STAR GAME RECORD

Year League	Pos.	AB	R	H	2B	3B	HR	RBI	Avg.	SB	PO	A	E	Avg.
1988—American	OF	1	0	0	0	0	0	0	.000	0	1	0	0	1.000
1989—American	OF	0	0	0	0	0	0	0	...	0	1	0	0	1.000
All-Star Game totals (2 years)		1	0	0	0	0	0	0	.000	0	2	0	0	1.000

GREGG, TOMMY
OF/1B, BRAVES

PERSONAL: Born July 29, 1963, at Boone, N.C. . . . 6-1/190. . . . Throws left, bats left. . . . Full name: William Thomas Gregg.
HIGH SCHOOL: R.J. Reynolds (Winston-Salem, N.C.).
COLLEGE: Wake Forest.
TRANSACTIONS/CAREER NOTES: Selected by Cleveland Indians organization in ninth round of free-agent draft (June 8, 1981). . . . Selected by Indians organization in 32nd round of free-agent draft (June 4, 1984). . . . Selected by Pittsburgh Pirates organization in seventh round of free-agent draft (June 3, 1985). . . . Traded by Pirates to Atlanta Braves (September 1, 1988), completing deal in which Braves traded IF Ken Oberkfell and cash to Pirates for a player to be named later (August 28, 1988). . . . On disabled list (April 20-June 2, 1989). . . . On Atlanta disabled list (April 28-June 9, 1991); included rehabilitation disability assignment to Richmond (June 5-9, 1991).
STATISTICAL NOTES: Led Eastern League with 14 intentional bases on balls received in 1987.

Year Team (League)	Pos.	G	AB	R	H	2B	3B	HR	RBI	Avg.	SB	PO	A	E	Avg.
1985—Macon (South Atlantic)	OF	72	259	43	81	14	2	1	18	.313	16	117	4	1	.992
1986—Nashua (Eastern)	OF-1B	126	421	55	113	13	4	1	29	.268	11	216	7	4	.982
1987—Harrisburg (Eastern)	OF	133	461	99	171	22	9	10	82	*.371	35	242	12	7	.973
—Pittsburgh (N.L.)	OF	10	8	3	2	1	0	0	0	.250	0	1	0	0	1.000
1988—Buffalo (Am. Assoc.)	OF	72	252	34	74	12	0	6	27	.294	7	134	3	2	.986
—Pitts.-Atlanta (N.L.)■	OF	25	44	5	13	4	0	1	7	.295	0	26	1	0	1.000
1989—Atlanta (N.L.)	OF-1B	102	276	24	67	8	0	6	23	.243	3	321	17	2	.994
1990—Atlanta (N.L.)	1B-OF	124	239	18	63	13	1	5	32	.264	4	356	34	6	.985
1991—Atlanta (N.L.)	OF-1B	72	107	13	20	8	1	1	4	.187	2	121	9	0	1.000
—Richmond (Int'l)	OF	3	13	3	6	0	0	1	4	.462	1	5	0	0	1.000
Major league totals (5 years)		333	674	63	165	34	2	13	66	.245	9	825	61	8	.991

CHAMPIONSHIP SERIES RECORD

Year Team (League)	Pos.	G	AB	R	H	2B	3B	HR	RBI	Avg.	SB	PO	A	E	Avg.
1991—Atlanta (N.L.)	PH	4	4	0	1	0	0	0	0	.250	0	0	0	0	...

WORLD SERIES RECORD

Year Team (League)	Pos.	G	AB	R	H	2B	3B	HR	RBI	Avg.	SB	PO	A	E	Avg.
1991—Atlanta (N.L.)	PH	4	3	0	0	0	0	0	0	.000	0	0	0	0	...

GRIFFEY JR., KEN
OF, MARINERS

PERSONAL: Born November 21, 1969, at Donora, Pa. . . . 6-3/200. . . . Throws left, bats left. . . . Full name: George Kenneth Griffey Jr. . . . Son of Ken Griffey Sr., major league outfielder for four teams (1973-91).
HIGH SCHOOL: Moeller (Cincinnati).
TRANSACTIONS/CAREER NOTES: Selected by Seattle Mariners organization in first round (first pick overall) of free-agent draft (June 2, 1987). . . . On San Bernardino disabled list (June 9-August 15, 1988). . . . On disabled list (July 24-August 20, 1989).
RECORDS/HONORS: Won A.L. Gold Glove as outfielder (1990-91). . . . Named outfielder on THE SPORTING NEWS A.L. All-Star team (1991). . . . Named outfielder on THE SPORTING NEWS A.L. Silver Slugger team (1991).
STATISTICAL NOTES: Led A.L. outfielders with six double plays in 1989.

Year	Team (League)	Pos.	G	AB	R	H	2B	3B	HR	RBI	Avg.	SB	PO	A	E	Avg.
1987	—Bellingham (Northwest)....	OF	54	182	43	57	9	1	14	40	.313	13	117	4	1	*.992
1988	—San Bernardino (Calif.).....	OF	58	219	50	74	13	3	11	42	.338	32	145	3	2	.987
	—Vermont (Eastern)	OF	17	61	10	17	5	1	2	10	.279	4	40	2	1	.977
1989	—Seattle (A.L.)	OF	127	455	61	120	23	0	16	61	.264	16	302	12	•10	.969
1990	—Seattle (A.L.)	OF	155	597	91	179	28	7	22	80	.300	16	330	8	7	.980
1991	—Seattle (A.L.)	OF	154	548	76	179	42	1	22	100	.327	18	360	15	4	.989
Major league totals (3 years)			436	1600	228	478	93	8	60	241	.299	50	992	35	21	.980

ALL-STAR GAME RECORD

Year	League	Pos.	AB	R	H	2B	3B	HR	RBI	Avg.	SB	PO	A	E	Avg.
1990	—American	OF	2	0	0	0	0	0	0	.000	0	2	0	0	1.000
1991	—American	OF	3	0	2	0	0	0	0	.667	0	2	0	0	1.000
All-Star Game totals (2 years)			5	0	2	0	0	0	0	.400	0	4	0	0	1.000

GRIFFEY SR., KEN
OF

PERSONAL: Born April 10, 1950, at Donora, Pa. . . . 6-0/210. . . . Throws left, bats left. . . . Full name: George Kenneth Griffey. . . . Father of Ken Griffey Jr., outfielder, Seattle Mariners.
HIGH SCHOOL: Donora (Pa.).

TRANSACTIONS/CAREER NOTES: Selected by Cincinnati Reds organization in 29th round of free-agent draft (June 5, 1969). . . . On disabled list (August 14-September 7, 1979). . . . Traded by Reds to New York Yankees for P Brian Ryder and a player to be named later (November 4, 1981); Reds organization acquired P Freddie Toliver to complete deal (December 10, 1981). . . . On disabled list (July 2-August 2, 1983 and May 28-June 12, 1985). . . . Traded by Yankees to Atlanta Braves for OF Claudell Washington and SS Paul Zuvella (June 30, 1986). . . . On disabled list (May 5-20, 1987). . . . Granted free agency (November 9, 1987). . . . Re-signed by Braves (November 13, 1987). . . . Released by Braves (July 28, 1988). . . . Signed by Cincinnati Reds (August 2, 1988). . . . Released by Reds (December 21, 1988). . . . Re-signed by Reds (March 30, 1989). . . . On voluntarily retired list (August 18, 1990). . . . Released by Reds (August 24, 1990). . . . Signed by Seattle Mariners (August 29, 1990). . . . Granted free agency (November 5, 1990). . . . Re-signed by Mariners (December 17, 1990). . . . On disabled list (April 1-16, 1991 and June 1, 1991-remainder of season). . . . On voluntarily retired list (November 1, 1991).
RECORDS/HONORS: Shares modern major league single-game (nine innings) record for most at-bats—7 (June 13, 1975). . . . Named as outfielder on THE SPORTING NEWS N.L. All-Star team (1976).
STATISTICAL NOTES: Led Gulf Coast League outfielders with 10 errors in 1969. . . . Tied for Eastern League lead in errors by outfielder with 15 in 1972. . . . Tied for Eastern League lead in double plays by outfielders with six in 1972. . . . Hit three home runs in a game (July 22, 1986).

Year	Team (League)	Pos.	G	AB	R	H	2B	3B	HR	RBI	Avg.	SB	PO	A	E	Avg.
1969	—Bradenton Reds (GCL)	OF-1B	49	153	22	43	*11	1	1	12	.281	11	57	4	†10	.859
1970	—Sioux Falls (Northern)	OF	51	164	20	40	2	1	2	24	.244	10	76	2	7	.918
1971	—Tampa (Florida State).......	OF	88	281	60	96	7	11	3	33	.342	25	137	13	8	.949
	—Three Rivers (Eastern)	OF	9	32	1	13	1	2	0	4	.406	4	17	0	1	.944
1972	—Three Rivers (Eastern)	OF-SS	128	472	*96	150	21	3	14	52	.318	31	212	10	‡15	.937
1973	—Indianapolis (A.A.)	OF	107	397	88	130	18	5	10	58	.327	*43	171	11	6	.968
	—Cincinnati (N.L.)	OF	25	86	19	33	5	1	3	14	.384	4	25	1	0	1.000
1974	—Indianapolis (A.A.)	OF	43	162	34	54	6	4	5	18	.333	12	70	4	1	.987
	—Cincinnati (N.L.)	OF	88	227	24	57	9	5	2	19	.251	9	115	5	0	1.000
1975	—Cincinnati (N.L.)	OF	132	463	95	141	15	9	4	46	.305	16	202	6	7	.967
1976	—Cincinnati (N.L.)	OF	148	562	111	189	28	9	6	74	.336	34	270	10	6	.979
1977	—Cincinnati (N.L.)	OF	154	585	117	186	35	8	12	57	.318	17	298	10	3	.990
1978	—Cincinnati (N.L.)	OF	158	614	90	177	33	8	10	63	.288	23	296	13	10	.969
1979	—Cincinnati (N.L.)	OF	95	380	62	120	27	4	8	32	.316	12	175	8	3	.984
1980	—Cincinnati (N.L.)	OF	146	544	89	160	28	10	13	85	.294	23	266	5	6	.978
1981	—Cincinnati (N.L.)	OF	101	396	65	123	21	6	2	34	.311	12	268	8	3	.989
1982	—New York (A.L.)■	OF	127	484	70	134	23	2	12	54	.277	10	282	8	5	.983
1983	—New York (A.L.)	1B-OF	118	458	60	140	21	3	11	46	.306	6	870	57	8	.991
1984	—New York (A.L.)	OF-1B	120	399	44	109	20	1	7	56	.273	2	422	22	16	.965
1985	—New York (A.L.)	OF-1B	127	438	68	120	28	4	10	69	.274	7	227	8	7	.971
1986	—New York (A.L.)	OF	59	198	33	60	7	0	9	26	.303	2	96	5	3	.971
	—Atlanta (N.L.)■	OF-1B	80	292	36	90	15	3	12	32	.308	12	136	2	2	.986
1987	—Atlanta (N.L.)	OF-1B	122	399	65	114	24	1	14	64	.286	4	205	8	2	.991
1988	—Atlanta-Cin. (N.L.)■........	OF-1B	94	243	26	62	6	0	4	23	.255	1	193	16	4	.981
1989	—Cincinnati (N.L.)	OF-1B	106	236	26	62	8	3	8	30	.263	4	122	2	2	.984
1990	—Cincinnati (N.L.)	1B-OF	46	63	6	13	2	0	1	8	.206	2	54	1	1	.983
	—Seattle (A.L.)■	OF	21	77	13	29	2	0	3	18	.377	0	25	1	1	.963
1991	—Seattle (A.L.)	OF	30	85	10	24	7	0	1	9	.282	0	31	0	0	1.000
American League totals (7 years)			602	2139	298	616	108	10	53	278	.288	27	1953	101	40	.981
National League totals (14 years)			1495	5090	831	1527	256	67	99	581	.300	173	2625	98	49	.982
Major league totals (19 years)			2097	7229	1129	2143	364	77	152	859	.296	200	4578	199	89	.982

CHAMPIONSHIP SERIES RECORD

CHAMPIONSHIP SERIES NOTES: Shares record for most stolen bases in one inning—2 (October 5, 1975, sixth inning). . . . Shares N.L. single-game record for most stolen bases—3 (October 5, 1975).

Year	Team (League)	Pos.	G	AB	R	H	2B	3B	HR	RBI	Avg.	SB	PO	A	E	Avg.
1973 —Cincinnati (N.L.)		OF-PH	3	7	0	1	1	0	0	0	.143	0	2	0	0	1.000
1975 —Cincinnati (N.L.)		OF	3	12	3	4	1	0	0	4	.333	3	4	1	0	1.000
1976 —Cincinnati (N.L.)		OF	3	13	2	5	0	1	0	2	.385	2	11	0	0	1.000
Championship Series totals (3 years)			9	32	5	10	2	1	0	6	.313	5	17	1	0	1.000

WORLD SERIES RECORD

Year	Team (League)	Pos.	G	AB	R	H	2B	3B	HR	RBI	Avg.	SB	PO	A	E	Avg.
1975 —Cincinnati (N.L.)		OF	7	26	4	7	3	1	0	4	.269	2	10	1	0	1.000
1976 —Cincinnati (N.L.)		OF	4	17	2	1	0	0	0	1	.059	1	5	0	0	1.000
World Series totals (2 years)			11	43	6	8	3	1	0	5	.186	3	15	1	0	1.000

ALL-STAR GAME RECORD

Year	League	Pos.	AB	R	H	2B	3B	HR	RBI	Avg.	SB	PO	A	E	Avg.
1976 —National		OF	1	1	1	0	0	0	1	1.000	0	1	0	0	1.000
1977 —National							Did not play								
1980 —National		OF	3	1	2	0	0	1	1	.667	0	0	0	0	...
All-Star Game totals (2 years)			4	2	3	0	0	1	2	.750	0	1	0	0	1.000

GRIFFIN, ALFREDO
SS

PERSONAL: Born March 6, 1957, at Santo Domingo, Dominican Republic.... 5-11/165. ... Throws right, bats both.... Full name: Alfredo Claudino Griffin.
HIGH SCHOOL: San Esteban (Santo Domingo, Dominican Republic).
TRANSACTIONS/CAREER NOTES: Signed as free agent by Cleveland Indians organization (August 22, 1973).... Traded by Indians with 3B Phil Lansford to Toronto Blue Jays for P Victor Cruz (December 6, 1978).... Traded by Blue Jays with OF Dave Collins and cash to Oakland Athletics for P Bill Caudill (December 8, 1984).... Traded as part of an eight-player, three-team deal in which New York Mets traded P Jesse Orosco to A's (December 11, 1987). A's then traded Orosco with Griffin and P Jay Howell to Los Angeles Dodgers for P Bob Welch, P Matt Young and P Jack Savage. A's then traded Savage with P Wally Whitehurst and P Kevin Tapani to Mets.... On disabled list (May 22-July 25, 1988).... Granted free agency (November 4, 1988).... Re-signed by Dodgers (November 7, 1988).... On disabled list (May 8-28, 1989; May 10-15 and August 6-31, 1991).... Granted free agency (October 31, 1991).
RECORDS/HONORS: Named A.L. Co-Rookie of the Year by the Baseball Writers' Association of America (1979).... Won A.L. Gold Glove at shortstop (1985).
STATISTICAL NOTES: Led Pacific Coast League shortstops with 40 errors in 1978.... Led A.L. shortstops with 31 errors in 1981. ... Led A.L. shortstops with 824 total chances in 1982.... Led A.L. shortstops with 280 putouts in 1983.

Year	Team (League)	Pos.	G	AB	R	H	2B	3B	HR	RBI	Avg.	SB	PO	A	E	Avg.
1974 —Reno (California)		SS	11	35	4	9	0	0	0	1	.257	3	10	22	9	.780
—Sarasota Indians (GCL)		SS	49	158	17	41	1	0	0	11	.259	7	67	133	*25	.889
1975 —San Jose (California)		SS	124	358	42	82	4	3	0	25	.229	11	189	281	47	.909
1976 —San Jose (California)		SS	64	224	40	58	3	1	0	17	.259	9	91	145	24	.908
—Williamsport (Eastern)		SS	58	200	22	55	3	0	0	17	.275	13	86	172	17	.938
—Toledo (International)		SS	22	88	5	19	7	1	0	6	.216	0	44	71	7	.943
—Cleveland (A.L.)		SS	12	4	0	1	0	0	0	0	.250	0	1	2	1	.750
1977 —Toledo (International)		SS	125	457	60	114	14	5	1	32	.249	26	*223	398	*49	.927
—Cleveland (A.L.)		SS	14	41	5	6	1	0	0	3	.146	2	17	30	3	.940
1978 —Portland (Pacific Coast)		SS-OF	133	474	82	138	22	10	5	48	.291	35	201	395	†40	.937
—Cleveland (A.L.)		SS	5	4	1	2	1	0	0	0	.500	0	4	7	1	.917
1979 —Toronto (A.L.)■		SS	153	624	81	179	22	10	2	31	.287	21	272	501	*36	.956
1980 —Toronto (A.L.)		SS	155	653	63	166	26	•15	2	41	.254	18	295	489	*37	.955
1981 —Toronto (A.L.)		SS-3B-2B	101	388	30	81	19	6	0	21	.209	8	191	279	†31	.938
1982 —Toronto (A.L.)		SS	•162	539	57	130	20	8	1	48	.241	10	*319	470	*26	.968
1983 —Toronto (A.L.)		SS-2B	•162	528	62	132	22	9	4	47	.250	8	†287	422	25	.966
1984 —Toronto (A.L.)		SS-2B	140	419	53	101	8	2	4	30	.241	11	230	320	21	.963
1985 —Oakland (A.L.)■		SS	162	614	75	166	18	7	2	64	.270	24	278	440	30	.960
1986 —Oakland (A.L.)		SS	162	594	74	169	23	6	4	51	.285	33	282	421	25	.966
1987 —Oakland (A.L.)		SS-2B	144	494	69	130	23	3	3	60	.263	26	250	389	24	.964
1988 —Los Angeles (N.L.)■		SS	95	316	39	63	8	3	1	27	.199	7	145	264	15	.965
1989 —Los Angeles (N.L.)		SS	136	506	49	125	27	2	0	29	.247	10	208	333	14	.975
1990 —Los Angeles (N.L.)		SS	141	461	38	97	11	3	1	35	.210	6	221	382	•26	.959
1991 —Los Angeles (N.L.)		SS	109	350	27	85	6	2	0	27	.243	5	186	349	22	.961
American League totals (12 years)			1372	4902	570	1263	183	68	22	396	.258	161	2426	3779	260	.960
National League totals (4 years)			481	1633	153	370	52	10	2	118	.227	28	760	1328	77	.964
Major league totals (16 years)			1853	6535	723	1633	235	78	24	514	.250	189	3186	5107	337	.961

CHAMPIONSHIP SERIES RECORD

Year	Team (League)	Pos.	G	AB	R	H	2B	3B	HR	RBI	Avg.	SB	PO	A	E	Avg.
1988 —Los Angeles (N.L.)		SS	7	25	1	4	1	0	0	3	.160	0	17	13	0	1.000

Year	Team (League)	Pos.	G	AB	R	H	2B	3B	HR	RBI	Avg.	SB	PO	A	E	Avg.
1988 — Los Angeles (N.L.)...........		SS	5	16	2	3	0	0	0	0	.188	0	7	13	1	.952

ALL-STAR GAME RECORD

Year	League	Pos.	AB	R	H	2B	3B	HR	RBI	Avg.	SB	PO	A	E	Avg.
1984 — American		SS	0	0	0	0	0	0	0	...	0	0	1	0	1.000

GRIFFITHS, BRIAN
P, ASTROS

PERSONAL: Born May 29, 1968, at Portland, Ore. . . . 6-2/190. . . . Throws right, bats right. . . . Full name: Brian David Griffiths.
HIGH SCHOOL: Milwaukie (Ore.).
COLLEGE: Mount Hood Community College (Ore.).
TRANSACTIONS/CAREER NOTES: Selected by Houston Astros organization in ninth round of free-agent draft (June 1, 1988). . . . On disabled list (April 11-May 27, 1991).

Year	Team (League)	G	W	L	Pct.	ERA	Sv.	IP	H	R	ER	BB	SO
1988 — Sarasota Astros (Gulf Coast) ...		14	2	6	.250	2.95	0	55	46	26	18	16	43
1989 — Asheville (South Atlantic)		22	6	9	.400	6.14	0	110	125	85	75	76	95
1990 — Osceola (Florida State)		28	5	10	.333	4.81	0	129	129	88	69	75	79
1991 — Osceola (Florida State)		18	4	3	.571	1.92	0	61	43	18	13	17	44

GRIMSLEY, JASON
P, PHILLIES

PERSONAL: Born August 7, 1967, at Cleveland, Tex. . . . 6-3/182. . . . Throws right, bats right. . . . Full name: Jason Alan Grimsley.
HIGH SCHOOL: Tarkington (Cleveland, Tex.).
TRANSACTIONS/CAREER NOTES: Selected by Philadelphia Phillies organization in 10th round of free-agent draft (June 3, 1985). . . . On Philadelphia disabled list (June 6-August 22, 1991); included rehabilitation disability assignment to Scranton/Wilkes-Barre (June 15-30 and August 7-21, 1991).
STATISTICAL NOTES: Led New York-Pennsylvania League with 11 hit batsmen and 18 wild pitches in 1986. . . . Pitched 3-0 no-hit victory against Harrisburg (May 3, 1989, first game). . . . Tied for Eastern League lead in games started by pitcher with 26 in 1989. . . . Led International League with 18 wild pitches in 1990.

Year	Team (League)	G	W	L	Pct.	ERA	Sv.	IP	H	R	ER	BB	SO
1985 — Bend (Northwest)		6	0	1	.000	13.50	0	11⅓	12	21	17	25	10
1986 — Utica (New York-Penn)		14	1	•10	.091	6.40	0	64⅔	63	61	46	*77	46
1987 — Spartanburg (South Atlantic) ..		23	7	4	.636	3.16	0	88⅓	59	48	31	54	98
1988 — Clearwater (Florida State)........		16	4	7	.364	3.73	0	101⅓	80	48	42	37	90
— Reading (Eastern)		5	1	3	.250	7.17	0	21⅓	20	19	17	13	14
1989 — Reading (Eastern)		26	11	8	.579	2.98	0	172	121	65	57	*109	134
— Philadelphia (N.L.)		4	1	3	.250	5.89	0	18⅓	19	13	12	19	7
1990 — Scranton/Wilkes-Barre (Int'l) ..		22	8	5	.615	3.93	0	128⅓	111	68	56	78	99
— Philadelphia (N.L.)		11	3	2	.600	3.30	0	57⅓	47	21	21	43	41
1991 — Philadelphia (N.L.)		12	1	7	.125	4.87	0	61	54	34	33	41	42
— Scranton/Wilkes-Barre (Int'l) ..		9	2	3	.400	4.35	0	51⅔	48	28	25	37	43
Major league totals (3 years)		27	5	12	.294	4.35	0	136⅔	120	68	66	103	90

GRISSOM, MARQUIS
OF, EXPOS

PERSONAL: Born April 17, 1967, at Atlanta. . . . 5-11/190. . . . Throws right, bats right. . . . Full name: Marquis Dean Grissom. . . . Name pronounced mar-KEESE.
HIGH SCHOOL: Lakeshore (College Park, Ga.).
COLLEGE: Florida A&M.
TRANSACTIONS/CAREER NOTES: Selected by Montreal Expos organization in third round of free-agent draft (June 1, 1988). . . . On Montreal disabled list (May 29-June 30, 1990); included rehabilitation disability assignment to Indianapolis (June 25-30, 1990).
STATISTICAL NOTES: Led New York-Pennsylvania League with 146 total bases in 1988.

Year	Team (League)	Pos.	G	AB	R	H	2B	3B	HR	RBI	Avg.	SB	PO	A	E	Avg.
1988 — Jamestown (N.Y.-Penn) ...		OF	74	*291	*69	94	14	7	8	39	.323	23	123	•11	3	.978
1989 — Jacksonville (Southern) ...		OF	78	278	43	83	15	4	3	31	.299	24	141	7	3	.980
— Indianapolis (A.A.)		OF	49	187	28	52	10	4	2	21	.278	16	106	5	0	1.000
— Montreal (N.L.)		OF	26	74	16	19	2	0	1	2	.257	1	32	1	2	.943
1990 — Montreal (N.L.)		OF	98	288	42	74	14	2	3	29	.257	22	165	5	2	.988
— Indianapolis (A.A.)		OF	5	22	3	4	0	0	2	3	.182	1	16	0	0	1.000
1991 — Montreal (N.L.)		OF	148	558	73	149	23	9	6	39	.267	*76	350	•15	6	.984
Major league totals (3 years)			272	920	131	242	39	11	10	70	.263	99	547	21	10	.983

GROOM, BUDDY
P, TIGERS

PERSONAL: Born June 10, 1965, at Dallas. . . . 6-2/200. . . . Throws left, bats left. . . . Full name: Wedsel Gary Groom.
COLLEGE: Mary Hardin-Baylor (Tex.).
TRANSACTIONS/CAREER NOTES: Selected by Chicago White Sox organization in 12th round of free-agent draft (June 2, 1987). . . . Drafted by Detroit Tigers organization (December 3, 1990).

Year	Team (League)	G	W	L	Pct.	ERA	Sv.	IP	H	R	ER	BB	SO
1987	—Sarasota White Sox (GCL)	4	1	0	1.000	0.75	1	12	12	1	1	2	8
	—Daytona Beach (Florida State)..	11	7	2	.778	3.59	0	67⅔	60	30	27	33	29
1988	—Tampa (Florida State)...............	27	13	10	.565	2.54	0	★195	181	69	55	51	118
1989	—Birmingham (Southern)	26	13	8	.619	4.52	0	167⅓	172	101	84	78	94
1990	—Birmingham (Southern)	20	6	8	.429	5.07	0	115⅓	135	81	65	48	66
1991	—Toledo (International)■.............	24	2	5	.286	4.32	1	75	75	39	36	25	49
	—London (Eastern)	11	7	1	.875	3.48	0	51⅔	51	20	20	12	39

GROSS, KEVIN
P, DODGERS

PERSONAL: Born June 8, 1961, at Downey, Calif. . . . 6-5/215. . . . Throws right, bats right. . . . Full name: Kevin Frank Gross.
HIGH SCHOOL: Fillmore (Calif.).
COLLEGE: Oxnard College (Calif.) and California Lutheran College.
TRANSACTIONS/CAREER NOTES: Selected by Baltimore Orioles organization in 32nd round of free-agent draft (June 5, 1979). . . . Selected by Philadelphia Phillies organization in secondary phase of free-agent draft (January 13, 1981). . . . Traded by Phillies to Montreal Expos for P Floyd Youmans and P Jeff Parrett (December 6, 1988). . . . On disabled list (June 28-July 20, 1990). . . . Granted free agency (November 5, 1990). . . . Signed by Los Angeles Dodgers (December 3, 1990).
STATISTICAL NOTES: Tied for South Atlantic League lead in games started by pitcher with 28 in 1981. . . . Led N.L. with 28 home runs allowed in 1986. . . . Led N.L. with 11 hit batsmen in 1988 and tied for lead with eight in 1986 and 10 in 1987.
MISCELLANEOUS: Singled and scored and struck out in two appearances as pinch-hitter (1991).

Year	Team (League)	G	W	L	Pct.	ERA	Sv.	IP	H	R	ER	BB	SO
1981	—Spartanburg (South Atlantic) ..	28	13	12	.520	3.56	0	192	173	94	76	62	123
1982	—Reading (Eastern)	26	10	15	.400	4.23	0	151	138	81	71	89	136
1983	—Portland (Pacific Coast)	15	3	5	.375	6.75	0	80	82	60	60	45	61
	—Philadelphia (N.L.)	17	4	6	.400	3.56	0	96	100	46	38	35	66
1984	—Philadelphia (N.L.)	44	8	5	.615	4.12	1	129	140	66	59	44	84
1985	—Philadelphia (N.L.)	38	15	13	.536	3.41	0	205⅔	194	86	78	81	151
1986	—Philadelphia (N.L.)	37	12	12	.500	4.02	0	241⅔	240	115	108	94	154
1987	—Philadelphia (N.L.)	34	9	16	.360	4.35	0	200⅔	205	107	97	87	110
1988	—Philadelphia (N.L.)	33	12	14	.462	3.69	0	231⅔	209	101	★89	101	162
1989	—Montreal (N.L.)■........................	31	11	12	.478	4.38	0	201⅓	188	105	★98	88	158
1990	—Montreal (N.L.)	31	9	12	.429	4.57	0	163⅓	171	86	83	65	111
1991	—Los Angeles (N.L.)■..................	46	10	11	.476	3.58	3	115⅔	123	55	46	50	95
	Major league totals (9 years)	311	90	101	.471	3.99	4	1585	1570	767	702	633	1091

WORLD SERIES RECORD

Year	Team (League)	G	W	L	Pct.	ERA	Sv.	IP	H	R	ER	BB	SO
1983	—Philadelphia (N.L.)						Did not play						

ALL-STAR GAME RECORD

Year	League	W	L	Pct.	ERA	Sv.	IP	H	R	ER	BB	SO
1988	—National	0	0	. . .	0.00	0	1	0	0	0	0	1

GROSS, KIP
P, DODGERS

PERSONAL: Born August 24, 1964, at Scottsbluff, Neb. . . . 6-2/190. . . . Throws right, bats right. . . . Full name: Kip Lee Gross.
HIGH SCHOOL: Gering (Neb.).
COLLEGE: Murray State and Nebraska.
TRANSACTIONS/CAREER NOTES: Selected by St. Louis Cardinals organization in third round of free-agent draft (January 9, 1985). . . . Selected by New York Mets organization in fourth round of free-agent draft (June 2, 1986). . . . Traded by Mets organization with P Randy Myers to Cincinnati Reds for P John Franco and OF Don Brown (December 6, 1989). . . . Traded by Reds with OF Eric Davis to Los Angeles Dodgers for P Tim Belcher and P John Wetteland (November 27, 1991).

Year	Team (League)	G	W	L	Pct.	ERA	Sv.	IP	H	R	ER	BB	SO
1987	—Lynchburg (Carolina)	16	7	4	.636	2.72	0	89⅓	92	37	27	22	39
1988	—St. Lucie (Florida State)...........	28	13	9	.591	2.62	0	178⅓	153	72	52	53	124
1989	—Jackson (Texas)	16	6	5	.545	2.49	0	112	96	47	31	13	60
	—Tidewater (International)	12	4	4	.500	3.97	0	70⅓	72	33	31	17	39
1990	—Nashville (American Assoc.)■..	40	12	7	.632	3.33	3	127	113	54	47	47	62
	—Cincinnati (N.L.)	5	0	0	. . .	4.26	0	6⅓	6	3	3	2	3
1991	—Nashville (American Assoc.)	14	5	3	.625	2.08	0	47⅔	39	13	11	16	28
	—Cincinnati (N.L.)	29	6	4	.600	3.47	0	85⅔	93	43	33	40	40
	Major league totals (2 years)	34	6	4	.600	3.52	0	92	99	46	36	42	43

GRUBER, KELLY
3B, BLUE JAYS

PERSONAL: Born February 26, 1962, at Bellaire, Tex. . . . 6-0/185. . . . Throws right, bats right. . . . Full name: Kelly Wayne Gruber.
HIGH SCHOOL: Westlake (Tex.).
COLLEGE: Texas.
TRANSACTIONS/CAREER NOTES: Selected by Cleveland Indians organization in first round (10th pick overall) of free-agent draft (June 3, 1980). . . . Drafted by Toronto Blue Jays (December 5, 1983). . . . On disabled list (August 10-25, 1989 and May 2-June 12, 1991).

RECORDS/HONORS: Named third baseman on THE SPORTING NEWS A.L. All-Star team (1990).... Won A.L. Gold Glove at third base (1990).... Named third baseman on THE SPORTING NEWS A.L. Silver Slugger team (1990).
STATISTICAL NOTES: Led Southern League shortstops with 43 errors in 1982. ... Led International League with .500 slugging percentage in 1984.... Led International League third basemen with 309 total chances in 1985.... Led A.L. third basemen with 349 assists and 477 total chances in 1988.... Led A.L. third basemen with 22 errors in 1989.... Hit for the cycle (April 16, 1989).... Led A.L. third basemen with 123 putouts in 1990.

Year	Team (League)	Pos.	G	AB	R	H	2B	3B	HR	RBI	Avg.	SB	PO	A	E	Avg.
1980 — Batavia (N.Y.-Penn)		SS	61	212	27	46	3	2	2	19	.217	6	87	155	21	.920
1981 — Waterloo (Midwest)		SS	127	458	64	133	25	4	14	59	.290	15	*180	*389	*56	.910
1982 — Chattanooga (Southern)		SS-3B	128	441	53	107	18	4	13	54	.243	11	161	333	†44	.918
1983 — Buffalo (Am. Assoc.)		3B-SS-OF	111	403	60	106	20	4	15	54	.263	15	98	170	27	.908
1984 — Toronto (A.L.)■		3B-OF-SS	15	16	1	1	0	0	1	2	.063	0	6	12	2	.900
— Syracuse (International)		3B-OF	97	342	53	92	12	2	21	55	.269	12	76	156	18	.928
1985 — Syracuse (International)		3B	121	473	71	118	16	5	21	69	.249	20	78	*217	14	.955
— Toronto (A.L.)		3B-2B	5	13	0	3	0	0	0	1	.231	0	2	6	0	1.000
1986 — Toronto (A.L.)		3-2-0-S	87	143	20	28	4	1	5	15	.196	2	43	77	7	.945
1987 — Toronto (A.L.)		3-S-2-0	138	341	50	80	14	3	12	36	.235	12	76	200	13	.955
1988 — Toronto (A.L.)		3-2-0-S	158	569	75	158	33	5	16	81	.278	23	121	†365	16	.968
1989 — Toronto (A.L.)		3B-OF-SS	135	545	83	158	24	4	18	73	.290	10	121	295	†22	.950
1990 — Toronto (A.L.)		3B-OF	150	592	92	162	36	6	31	118	.274	14	†129	280	19	.956
1991 — Toronto (A.L.)		3B	113	429	58	108	18	2	20	65	.252	12	97	231	13	.962
Major league totals (8 years)			801	2648	379	698	129	21	103	391	.264	73	595	1466	92	.957

CHAMPIONSHIP SERIES RECORD
CHAMPIONSHIP SERIES NOTES: Shares single-game record for most singles—4 (October 7, 1989).

Year	Team (League)	Pos.	G	AB	R	H	2B	3B	HR	RBI	Avg.	SB	PO	A	E	Avg.
1989 — Toronto (A.L.)		3B	5	17	2	5	1	0	0	1	.294	1	4	8	0	1.000
1991 — Toronto (A.L.)		3B	5	21	1	6	1	0	0	4	.286	1	3	6	3	.750
Championship Series totals (2 years)			10	38	3	11	2	0	0	5	.289	2	7	14	3	.875

ALL-STAR GAME RECORD
ALL-STAR GAME NOTES: Shares single-game record for most stolen bases—2 (July 10, 1990).

Year	League	Pos.	AB	R	H	2B	3B	HR	RBI	Avg.	SB	PO	A	E	Avg.
1989 — American							Did not play								
1990 — American		PR-3B	1	0	0	0	0	0	0	.000	0	0	1	0	1.000

GUBICZA, MARK
P, ROYALS

PERSONAL: Born August 14, 1962, at Philadelphia.... 6-5/225.... Throws right, bats right.... Full name: Mark Steven Gubicza.... Son of Anthony Gubicza, minor league pitcher (1950-51).... Name pronounced GOO-ba-zah.
HIGH SCHOOL: William Penn Charter (Philadelphia).
TRANSACTIONS/CAREER NOTES: Selected by Kansas City Royals organization in second round of free-agent draft (June 8, 1981). ...On disabled list (June 29, 1982-remainder of season; June 6-21, 1986; and July 1, 1990-remainder of season).... On Kansas City disabled list (March 30-May 14, 1991); included rehabilitation disability assignment to Omaha (April 20-May 13, 1991).
STATISTICAL NOTES: Tied for A.L. lead in games started by pitcher with 36 in 1989.

Year	Team (League)	G	W	L	Pct.	ERA	Sv.	IP	H	R	ER	BB	SO
1981 — Sarasota Royals-Gold (GCL)	11	•8	1	.889	2.25	0	56	39	18	14	23	40
1982 — Fort Myers (Florida State)	11	2	5	.286	4.13	0	48	49	33	22	25	36
1983 — Jacksonville (Southern)	28	14	12	.538	3.08	0	196	146	81	67	93	*146
1984 — Kansas City (A.L.)	29	10	14	.417	4.05	0	189	172	90	85	75	111
1985 — Kansas City (A.L.)	29	14	10	.583	4.06	0	177⅓	160	88	80	77	99
1986 — Kansas City (A.L.)	35	12	6	.667	3.64	0	180⅔	155	77	73	84	118
1987 — Kansas City (A.L.)	35	13	18	.419	3.98	0	241⅔	231	114	107	120	166
1988 — Kansas City (A.L.)	35	20	8	.714	2.70	0	269⅔	237	94	81	83	183
1989 — Kansas City (A.L.)	36	15	11	.577	3.04	0	255	252	100	86	63	173
1990 — Kansas City (A.L.)	16	4	7	.364	4.50	0	94	101	48	47	38	71
1991 — Omaha (American Assoc.)	3	2	1	.667	3.31	0	16⅓	20	7	6	4	12
— Kansas City (A.L.)	26	9	12	.429	5.68	0	133	168	90	84	42	89
Major league totals (8 years)	241	97	86	.530	3.76	0	1540⅓	1476	701	643	582	1010

WORLD SERIES RECORD

Year	Team (League)	G	W	L	Pct.	ERA	Sv.	IP	H	R	ER	BB	SO
1985 — Kansas City (A.L.)							Did not play						

CHAMPIONSHIP SERIES RECORD

Year	Team (League)	G	W	L	Pct.	ERA	Sv.	IP	H	R	ER	BB	SO
1985 — Kansas City (A.L.)	2	1	0	1.000	3.24	0	8⅓	4	3	3	4	4

Year	League	W	L	Pct.	ERA	Sv.	IP	H	R	ER	BB	SO
1988 —American		0	0	...	4.50	0	2	3	1	1	0	2
1989 —American		0	0	...	0.00	0	1	0	0	0	0	1
All-Star totals (2 years)		0	0	...	3.00	0	3	3	1	1	0	3

GUERRERO, JUAN

3B/OF, ASTROS

PERSONAL: Born February 1, 1967, at Los Llanos, Domican Republic. ... 5-11/160. ... Throws right, bats right. ... Full name: Juan Antonio Guerrero.
HIGH SCHOOL: Haina (Bajos de Haina, Dominican Republic).
TRANSACTIONS/CAREER NOTES: Signed as free agent by San Francisco Giants organization (September 13, 1986). ... Drafted by Houston Astros (December 9, 1991).

							BATTING							FIELDING		
Year	Team (League)	Pos.	G	AB	R	H	2B	3B	HR	RBI	Avg.	SB	PO	A	E	Avg.
1987 —Pocatello (Pioneer)		2B	34	81	13	17	5	1	1	7	.210	1	59	62	4	.968
1988 —Clinton (Midwest)		2B-OF-3B	111	385	57	106	17	3	13	54	.275	7	111	150	14	.949
1989 —San Jose (California)		3B-2B	108	409	61	115	24	2	13	78	.281	7	81	174	24	.914
1990 —Shreveport (Texas)		2B-SS	118	390	55	94	21	1	16	47	.241	4	214	278	19	.963
1991 —Shreveport (Texas)		3B-OF-2B	128	479	78	160	★40	2	19	94	.334	14	131	121	25	.910

GUERRERO, PEDRO

OF/1B, CARDINALS

PERSONAL: Born June 29, 1956, at San Pedro de Macoris, Dominican Republic. ... 6-0/195. ... Throws right, bats right. ... Full name: Pedro Guerrero. ... Name pronounced guh-RARE-oh.
TRANSACTIONS/CAREER NOTES: Signed as free agent by Cleveland Indians organization (January 15, 1973). ... Traded by Indians organization to Los Angeles Dodgers for P Bruce Ellingson (April 4, 1974). ... On disabled list (May 19-August 30, 1977; August 23-September 15, 1980; July 22-August 6, 1984; and April 4-July 30 and August 11-September 3, 1986). ... On suspended list (May 24-28, 1988). ... On Los Angeles disabled list (June 5-July 29, 1988); included rehabilitation disability assignment to Albuquerque (July 23-29, 1988). ... Traded by Dodgers to St. Louis Cardinals for P John Tudor (August 16, 1988). ... On disabled list (August 19-September 3, 1990). ... On St. Louis disabled list (July 8-August 19, 1991); included rehabilitation disability assignment to Louisville (August 15-19, 1991). ... Granted free agency (October 30, 1991). ... Re-signed by Cardinals (January 7, 1992).
RECORDS/HONORS: Holds N.L. record for most home runs in month of June— 15 (1985). ... Holds N.L. single-season record for most consecutive times reached base safely— 14 (July 23-26, 1985). ... Shares N.L. single-season record for fewest errors by first baseman who led league— 13 (1990). ... Named outfielder on THE SPORTING NEWS N.L. All-Star team (1981-82). ... Named outfielder on THE SPORTING NEWS N.L. Silver Slugger team (1982).
STATISTICAL NOTES: Tied for Northwest League lead in double plays by third basemen with 13 in 1974. ... Led Pacific Coast League with 15 sacrifice flies in 1978. ... Led N.L. third basemen with 30 errors and tied for lead with 458 total chances in 1983. ... Led N.L. with .577 slugging percentage and .422 on-base percentage in 1985. ... Led N.L. with 12 sacrifice flies in 1989.

							BATTING							FIELDING		
Year	Team (League)	Pos.	G	AB	R	H	2B	3B	HR	RBI	Avg.	SB	PO	A	E	Avg.
1973 —Sarasota Indians (GCL)		3B-SS	44	153	13	39	2	3	2	22	.255	1	32	82	11	.912
1974 —Orangeburg (W. Caro.)■		3B	19	55	3	8	1	0	0	1	.145	0	11	22	5	.868
—Bellingham (Northwest)		3B	82	297	49	94	★23	2	3	55	.316	4	★69	124	23	.894
1975 —Danville (Midwest)		3B-OF	104	351	81	121	25	5	10	76	★.345	10	111	168	31	.900
1976 —Waterbury (Eastern)		1B	132	495	73	115	★30	10	5	66	.305	23	1129	★96	★19	.985
1977 —Albuquerque (PCL)		1B	32	129	30	52	11	4	4	39	.403	0	329	17	10	.972
1978 —Albuquerque (PCL)		1B-3B	134	492	92	166	28	4	14	★116	.337	17	982	80	10	.991
—Los Angeles (N.L.)		1B	5	8	3	5	0	1	0	1	.625	0	25	1	0	1.000
1979 —Albuquerque (PCL)		OF-3B-1B	113	453	94	151	33	9	22	★103	.333	26	188	9	5	.975
—Los Angeles (N.L.)		OF-1B-3B	25	62	7	15	2	0	2	9	.242	2	53	4	1	.983
1980 —Los Angeles (N.L.)		0-2-3-1	75	183	27	59	9	1	7	31	.322	2	103	110	3	.986
1981 —Los Angeles (N.L.)		OF-3B-1B	98	347	46	104	17	2	12	48	.300	5	165	55	11	.952
1982 —Los Angeles (N.L.)		OF-3B	150	575	87	175	27	5	32	100	.304	22	282	53	12	.965
1983 —Los Angeles (N.L.)		3B-1B	160	584	87	174	28	6	32	103	.298	23	130	308	†31	.934
1984 —Los Angeles (N.L.)		3B-OF-1B	144	535	85	162	29	4	16	72	.303	9	271	151	22	.950
1985 —Los Angeles (N.L.)		OF-3B-1B	137	487	99	156	22	2	33	87	.320	12	251	123	13	.966
1986 —Los Angeles (N.L.)		OF-1B	31	61	7	15	3	0	5	10	.246	0	39	1	0	1.000
1987 —Los Angeles (N.L.)		OF-1B	152	545	89	184	25	2	27	89	.338	9	482	44	12	.978
1988 —Albuquerque (PCL)		1B	5	12	3	5	0	0	1	4	.417	0	30	2	0	1.000
—L.A.-St. Louis (N.L.)■		1B-3B-OF	103	364	40	104	14	2	10	65	.286	4	466	99	12	.979
1989 —St. Louis (N.L.)		1B	162	570	60	177	★42	1	17	117	.311	2	★1445	72	★15	.990
1990 —St. Louis (N.L.)		1B	136	498	42	140	31	1	13	80	.281	1	1083	73	★13	.989
1991 —St. Louis (N.L.)		1B	115	427	41	116	12	1	8	70	.272	4	953	66	★16	.985
—Louisville (Am. Assoc.)		1B	3	11	2	5	0	0	1	2	.455	0	14	0	1	.933
Major league totals (14 years)			1493	5246	720	1586	261	28	214	882	.302	95	5748	1160	161	.977

DIVISION SERIES RECORD

							BATTING							FIELDING		
Year	Team (League)	Pos.	G	AB	R	H	2B	3B	HR	RBI	Avg.	SB	PO	A	E	Avg.
1981 —Los Angeles (N.L.)		3B	5	17	1	3	1	0	1	1	.176	1	3	15	0	1.000

CHAMPIONSHIP SERIES RECORD

CHAMPIONSHIP SERIES NOTES: Holds career record for most times grounded into double play—5. ... Holds single-series record for most times grounded into double play—4 (1981). ... Shares N.L. single-game record for most times grounded into double play—2 (October 16, 1981).

Year	Team (League)	Pos.	G	AB	R	H	2B	3B	HR	RBI	Avg.	SB	PO	A	E	Avg.
1981—Los Angeles (N.L.)...........		OF	5	19	1	2	0	0	1	2	.105	0	9	2	0	1.000
1983—Los Angeles (N.L.)...........		3B	4	12	1	3	1	1	0	2	.250	0	0	9	0	1.000
1985—Los Angeles (N.L.)...........		OF	6	20	2	5	1	0	0	4	.250	2	11	0	0	1.000
Championship Series totals (3 years).............			15	51	4	10	2	1	1	8	.196	2	20	11	0	1.000

WORLD SERIES RECORD

Year	Team (League)	Pos.	G	AB	R	H	2B	3B	HR	RBI	Avg.	SB	PO	A	E	Avg.
1981—Los Angeles (N.L.)...........		OF	6	21	2	7	1	1	2	7	.333	0	17	1	0	1.000

ALL-STAR GAME RECORD

ALL-STAR GAME NOTES: Named to N.L. All-Star team for 1985 game; replaced due to injury by Glenn Wilson.

Year	League	Pos.	AB	R	H	2B	3B	HR	RBI	Avg.	SB	PO	A	E	Avg.
1981—National................	PH	1	0	0	0	0	0	0	.000	0	0	0	0	...
1983—National................	3B-OF	1	0	0	0	0	0	0	.000	0	0	0	1	.000
1987—National................	PH	1	0	0	0	0	0	0	.000	0	0	0	0	...
1989—National................	DH	2	0	0	0	0	0	0	.000	0	0	0	0	....
All-Star Game totals (4 years)................		5	0	0	0	0	0	0	.000	0	0	0	1	.000

GUETTERMAN, LEE
P, YANKEES

PERSONAL: Born November 22, 1958, at Chattanooga, Tenn.... 6-8/230.... Throws left, bats left.... Full name: Arthur Lee Guetterman.
HIGH SCHOOL: Oceanside (Calif.).
COLLEGE: Liberty Baptist, Va. (bachelor of science degree in physical education, 1981).
TRANSACTIONS/CAREER NOTES: Selected by Seattle Mariners organization in fourth round of free-agent draft (June 8, 1981).... On Chattanooga disabled list (August 1-15, 1984).... On disabled list (April 11-May 31, 1985).... Traded by Mariners with P Clay Parker and P Wade Taylor to New York Yankees for P Steve Trout and OF Henry Cotto (December 22, 1987).... On disabled list (July 19-August 3, 1990).

Year	Team (League)	G	W	L	Pct.	ERA	Sv.	IP	H	R	ER	BB	SO
1981—Bellingham (Northwest)...........	13	6	4	.600	2.68	0	84	85	36	25	42	55
1982—Bakersfield (California)...........	26	7	11	.389	4.44	0	154	172	100	76	69	82
1983—Bakersfield (California)...........	25	12	6	.667	3.22	0	156⅓	164	72	56	45	93
1984—Chattanooga (Southern)...........	24	11	7	.611	3.38	0	157	174	68	59	38	47
—Seattle (A.L.)...........	3	0	0	...	4.15	0	4⅓	9	2	2	2	2
1985—Calgary (Pacific Coast)...........	20	5	8	.385	5.79	0	110⅓	138	86	71	44	48
1986—Seattle (A.L.)...........	41	0	4	.000	7.34	0	76	108	67	62	30	38
—Calgary (Pacific Coast)...........	4	1	0	1.000	5.59	0	19⅓	24	12	12	7	8
1987—Calgary (Pacific Coast)...........	16	5	1	.833	2.86	1	44	41	14	14	17	29
—Seattle (A.L.)...........	25	11	4	★.733	3.81	0	113⅓	117	60	48	35	42
1988—New York (A.L.)■.......	20	1	2	.333	4.65	0	40⅔	49	21	21	14	15
—Columbus (International)...........	18	9	6	.600	2.76	0	120⅔	109	46	37	26	49
1989—New York (A.L.)................	70	5	5	.500	2.45	13	103	98	31	28	26	51
1990—New York (A.L.)................	64	11	7	.611	3.39	2	93	80	37	35	26	48
1991—New York (A.L.)................	64	3	4	.429	3.68	6	88	91	42	36	25	35
Major league totals (7 years)................	287	31	26	.544	4.03	21	518⅓	552	260	232	158	231

GUILLEN, OZZIE
SS, WHITE SOX

PERSONAL: Born January 20, 1964, at Ocumare del Tuy, Miranda, Venezuela.... 5-11/150.... Throws right, bats left.... Full name: Oswaldo Jose Barrios Guillen.... Name pronounced GHEE-un.
TRANSACTIONS/CAREER NOTES: Signed as free agent by San Diego Padres organization (December 17, 1980).... Traded by Padres organization with P Tim Lollar, P Bill Long and 3B Luis Salazar to Chicago White Sox for P LaMarr Hoyt, P Kevin Kristan and P Todd Simmons (December 6, 1984).
RECORDS/HONORS: Shares major league single-season record for fewest bases on balls received (150 or more games)—12 (1985-86).... Holds A.L. single-season record for fewest putouts by shortstop (150 or more games)—220 (1985).... Named A.L. Rookie Player of the Year by THE SPORTING NEWS (1985).... Named A.L. Rookie of the Year by Baseball Writers' Association of America (1985).... Won A.L. Gold Glove at shortstop (1990).
STATISTICAL NOTES: Tied for California League lead with 14 sacrifice hits in 1982.... Led Pacific Coast League shortstops with 362 assists and 549 total chances in 1984.... Led A.L. shortstops with 760 total chances in 1987 and 863 in 1988.... Led A.L. shortstops with 105 double plays in 1987.
MISCELLANEOUS: Batted as switch-hitter (1981-1984).

Year	Team (League)	Pos.	G	AB	R	H	2B	3B	HR	RBI	Avg.	SB	PO	A	E	Avg.
1981—Bradenton Padres (GCL)...	SS-2B	55	189	26	49	4	1	0	16	.259	8	105	135	15	.941
1982—Reno (California)...........	SS	130	528	★103	★183	33	1	2	54	.347	25	★240	399	41	.940
1983—Beaumont (Texas)...........	SS	114	427	62	126	20	4	2	48	.295	7	185	327	★38	.931
1984—Las Vegas (Pac. Coast)....	SS-2B	122	463	81	137	26	6	5	53	.296	9	172	†364	17	.969
1985—Chicago (A.L.)■................	SS	150	491	71	134	21	9	1	33	.273	7	220	382	12	★.980
1986—Chicago (A.L.)................	SS	159	547	58	137	19	4	2	47	.250	8	261	459	22	.970

— 187 —

Year	Team (League)	Pos.	G	AB	R	H	2B	3B	HR	RBI	Avg.	SB	PO	A	E	Avg.
								BATTING							**FIELDING**	
1987	—Chicago (A.L.)	SS	149	560	64	156	22	7	2	51	.279	25	266	475	19	.975
1988	—Chicago (A.L.)	SS	156	566	58	148	16	7	0	39	.261	25	273	★570	20	.977
1989	—Chicago (A.L.)	SS	155	597	63	151	20	8	1	54	.253	36	272	512	22	.973
1990	—Chicago (A.L.)	SS	160	516	61	144	21	4	1	58	.279	13	252	474	17	.977
1991	—Chicago (A.L.)	SS	154	524	52	143	20	3	3	49	.273	21	249	439	21	.970
Major league totals (7 years)			1083	3801	427	1013	139	42	10	331	.267	135	1793	3311	133	.975

ALL-STAR GAME RECORD

ALL-STAR GAME NOTES: Named to A.L. All-Star team for 1988 game; replaced due to injury by Kurt Stillwell.

Year	League	Pos.	AB	R	H	2B	3B	HR	RBI	Avg.	SB	PO	A	E	Avg.
						BATTING							**FIELDING**		
1990	—American	SS	2	0	0	0	0	0	0	.000	0	0	2	0	1.000
1991	—American	SS	0	0	0	0	0	0	0	. . .	0	1	0	0	1.000
All-Star Game totals (2 years)			2	0	0	0	0	0	0	.000	0	1	2	0	1.000

GULLICKSON, BILL

P, TIGERS

PERSONAL: Born February 20, 1959, at Marshall, Minn. . . . 6-3/220. . . . Throws right, bats right. . . . Full name: William Lee Gullickson.
HIGH SCHOOL: Joliet (Ill.).
TRANSACTIONS/CAREER NOTES: Selected by Montreal Expos organization in first round (second pick overall) of free-agent draft (June 7, 1977). . . . On disabled list (April 20-May 8, 1984 and June 17-July 8, 1985). . . . Traded by Expos with C Sal Butera to Cincinnati Reds for P Jay Tibbs, P Andy McGaffigan, P John Stuper and C Dann Bilardello (December 19, 1985). . . . Traded by Reds to New York Yankees for P Dennis Rasmussen (August 26, 1987). . . . Granted free agency (November 9, 1987). . . . Signed by Yomiuri Giants of Japan Central League (January 13, 1988). . . . Signed as free agent by Houston Astros (December 6, 1989). . . . Released by Astros (October 4, 1990). . . . Signed by Detroit Tigers (December 3, 1990).
RECORDS/HONORS: Shares modern major league single-game record for most wild pitches—6 (April 10, 1982). . . . Named N.L. Rookie Pitcher of the Year by THE SPORTING NEWS (1980).
STATISTICAL NOTES: Led N.L. with 27 home runs allowed in 1984. . . . Tied for A.L. lead in games started by pitcher with 35 in 1991.
MISCELLANEOUS: Had sacrifice hit in one appearance as pinch-hitter (1991).

Year	Team (League)	G	W	L	Pct.	ERA	Sv.	IP	H	R	ER	BB	SO
1977	—West Palm Beach (Florida St.) ..	10	3	3	.500	4.02	0	56	67	30	25	17	35
1978	—West Palm Beach (Florida St.) ..	20	9	9	.500	1.82	0	148	121	45	30	52	127
	—Memphis (Southern)	8	1	4	.200	3.06	1	50	44	19	17	19	43
1979	—Denver (American Assoc.)	11	3	3	.500	6.67	0	54	65	44	40	26	31
	—Memphis (Southern)	16	10	3	.769	3.65	0	116	110	52	47	42	115
	—Montreal (N.L.)	1	0	0	. . .	0.00	0	1	2	0	0	0	0
1980	—Denver (American Assoc.)	9	6	2	.750	1.91	0	66	47	14	14	29	64
	—Montreal (N.L.)	24	10	5	.667	3.00	0	141	127	53	47	50	120
1981	—Montreal (N.L.)	22	7	9	.438	2.81	0	157	142	54	49	34	115
1982	—Montreal (N.L.)	34	12	14	.462	3.57	0	236⅔	231	101	94	61	155
1983	—Montreal (N.L.)	34	17	12	.586	3.75	0	242⅓	230	108	101	59	120
1984	—Montreal (N.L.)	32	12	9	.571	3.61	0	226⅔	230	100	91	37	100
1985	—Montreal (N.L.)	29	14	12	.538	3.52	0	181⅓	187	78	71	47	68
1986	—Cincinnati (N.L.)■	37	15	12	.556	3.38	0	244⅔	245	103	92	60	121
1987	—Cincinnati (N.L.)	27	10	11	.476	4.85	0	165	172	99	89	39	89
	—New York (A.L.) ■	8	4	2	.667	4.88	0	48	46	29	26	11	28
1988	—Yomiuri Giants (Japan. Cen.)■ ..	26	14	9	.609	3.10	0	203⅓	173	77	70	51	134
1989	—Yomiuri Giants (Japan. Cen.) ...	15	7	5	.583	3.65	0	111	97	47	45	34	97
1990	—Houston (N.L.)■	32	10	14	.417	3.82	0	193⅓	221	100	82	61	73
1991	—Detroit (A.L.)■	35	•20	9	.690	3.90	0	226⅓	256	109	98	44	91
American League totals (2 years)		43	24	11	.686	4.07	0	274⅓	302	138	124	55	119
National League totals (10 years)		272	107	98	.522	3.60	0	1789	1787	796	716	448	961
Major league totals (11 years)		315	131	109	.546	3.66	0	2063⅓	2089	934	840	503	1080

DIVISION SERIES RECORD

Year	Team (League)	G	W	L	Pct.	ERA	Sv.	IP	H	R	ER	BB	SO
1981	—Montreal (N.L.)	1	1	0	1.000	1.17	0	7⅔	6	1	1	1	3

CHAMPIONSHIP SERIES RECORD

CHAMPIONSHIP SERIES NOTES: Shares single-series record for most games lost—2 (1981).

Year	Team (League)	G	W	L	Pct.	ERA	Sv.	IP	H	R	ER	BB	SO
1981	—Montreal (N.L.)	2	0	2	.000	2.51	0	14⅓	12	5	4	6	12

GUNDERSON, ERIC

P, GIANTS

PERSONAL: Born March 29, 1966, at Portland, Ore. . . . 6-0/175. . . . Throws left, bats right. . . . Full name: Eric Andrew Gunderson.
HIGH SCHOOL: Aloha (Portland, Ore.).
COLLEGE: Portland State (Ore.).

TRANSACTIONS/CAREER NOTES: Selected by San Francisco Giants organization in second round of free-agent draft (June 2, 1987).
STATISTICAL NOTES: Led Northwest League pitchers with five complete games and tied for lead with 15 games started and three shutouts in 1987.... Led California League with 17 hit batsmen in 1988.

Year Team (League)	G	W	L	Pct.	ERA	Sv.	IP	H	R	ER	BB	SO
1987—Everett (Northwest)	15	8	4	.667	2.46	0	98⅔	80	34	27	34	*99
1988—San Jose (California)	20	12	5	.706	2.65	0	149⅓	131	56	44	52	151
—Shreveport (Texas)	7	1	2	.333	5.15	0	36⅔	45	25	21	13	28
1989—Shreveport (Texas)	11	8	2	*.800	2.72	0	72⅔	68	24	22	23	61
—Phoenix (Pacific Coast)	14	2	4	.333	5.04	0	85⅔	93	51	48	36	56
1990—San Francisco (N.L.)	7	1	2	.333	5.49	0	19⅔	24	14	12	11	14
—Phoenix (Pacific Coast)	16	5	7	.417	8.23	0	82	137	87	75	46	41
—Shreveport (Texas)	8	2	2	.500	3.25	0	52⅔	51	24	19	17	44
1991—San Francisco (N.L.)	2	0	0	...	5.40	1	3⅓	6	4	2	1	2
—Phoenix (Pacific Coast)	40	7	6	.538	6.14	3	107	153	85	73	44	53
Major league totals (2 years)	9	1	2	.333	5.48	1	23	30	18	14	12	16

GUTHRIE, MARK
P, TWINS

PERSONAL: Born September 22, 1965, at Buffalo, N.Y. . . . 6-4/196. . . . Throws left, bats both. . . . Full name: Mark Andrew Guthrie.
HIGH SCHOOL: Venice (Fla.).
COLLEGE: Louisiana State.
TRANSACTIONS/CAREER NOTES: Selected by St. Louis Cardinals organization in fourth round of free-agent draft (June 2, 1986). . . . Selected by Minnesota Twins organization in seventh round of free-agent draft (June 2, 1987).
MISCELLANEOUS: Appeared in one game as pinch-runner (1991).

Year Team (League)	G	W	L	Pct.	ERA	Sv.	IP	H	R	ER	BB	SO
1987—Visalia (California)	4	2	1	.667	4.50	0	12	10	7	6	5	9
1988—Visalia (California)	25	12	9	.571	3.31	0	171⅓	169	81	63	86	182
1989—Orlando (Southern)	14	8	3	.727	1.97	0	96	75	32	21	38	103
—Portland (Pacific Coast)	7	3	4	.429	3.65	0	44⅓	45	21	18	16	35
—Minnesota (A.L.)	13	2	4	.333	4.55	0	57⅓	66	32	29	21	38
1990—Minnesota (A.L.)	24	7	9	.438	3.79	0	144⅔	154	65	61	39	101
—Portland (Pacific Coast)	9	1	3	.250	2.98	0	42⅓	47	19	14	12	39
1991—Minnesota (A.L.)	41	7	5	.583	4.32	2	98	116	52	47	41	72
Major league totals (3 years)	78	16	18	.471	4.11	2	300	336	149	137	101	211

CHAMPIONSHIP SERIES RECORD

Year Team (League)	G	W	L	Pct.	ERA	Sv.	IP	H	R	ER	BB	SO
1991—Minnesota (A.L.)	2	1	0	1.000	0.00	0	2⅔	0	0	0	0	0

WORLD SERIES RECORD

Year Team (League)	G	W	L	Pct.	ERA	Sv.	IP	H	R	ER	BB	SO
1991—Minnesota (A.L.)	4	0	1	.000	2.25	0	4	3	1	1	4	3

GUTIERREZ, RICKY
SS, ORIOLES

PERSONAL: Born May 23, 1970, at Miami. . . . 6-1/175. . . . Throws right, bats right. . . . Full name: Ricardo Gutierrez.
HIGH SCHOOL: American (Hialeah, Fla.).
TRANSACTIONS/CAREER NOTES: Selected by Baltimore Orioles organization in first round (28th pick overall) of free-agent draft (June 1, 1988).
STATISTICAL NOTES: Led Appalachian League shortstops with 309 total chances in 1988.

Year Team (League)	Pos.	G	AB	R	H	2B	3B	HR	RBI	Avg.	SB	PO	A	E	Avg.
1988—Bluefield (Appalachian)	SS	62	208	35	51	8	2	2	19	.245	5	*100	175	34	.890
1989—Frederick (Carolina)	SS	127	456	48	106	16	2	3	41	.232	15	190	372	34	*.943
1990—Frederick (Carolina)	SS	112	425	54	117	16	4	1	46	.275	12	192	286	26	.948
—Hagerstown (Eastern)	SS	20	64	4	15	0	1	0	6	.234	2	31	36	4	.944
1991—Hagerstown (Eastern)	SS	84	292	47	69	6	4	0	30	.236	11	158	196	22	.941
—Rochester (Int'l)	SS-3B	49	157	23	48	5	3	0	15	.306	4	61	129	8	.960

GUZMAN, JOHNNY
P, ATHLETICS

PERSONAL: Born January 21, 1971, at Hatillo Palma, Dominican Republic. . . . 5-10/155. . . . Throws left, bats right. . . . Full name: Ramon Dionny Estrella Guzman.
TRANSACTIONS/CAREER NOTES: Signed as free agent by the Oakland Athletics organization (February 18, 1988).
STATISTICAL NOTES: Led Pacific Coast League with six balks in 1991. . . . Tied for Southern League lead with five balks in 1991.

Year Team (League)	G	W	L	Pct.	ERA	Sv.	IP	H	R	ER	BB	SO
1988—Scottsdale (Arizona)	16	0	2	.000	10.57	1	23	37	27	27	8	18
1989—Modesto (California)	5	0	2	.000	4.86	0	16⅔	23	11	9	13	12
—Madison (Midwest)	9	3	3	.500	3.74	0	45⅔	41	26	19	21	36
—Southern Oregon (Northwest)	5	3	1	.750	2.63	0	27⅓	23	16	8	12	26

Year	Team (League)	G	W	L	Pct.	ERA	Sv.	IP	H	R	ER	BB	SO
1990	—Modesto (California)	13	7	4	.636	1.91	0	84⅔	67	25	18	23	58
	—Huntsville (Southern)	16	5	6	.455	3.58	0	105⅔	89	52	42	54	63
1991	—Tacoma (Pacific Coast)	17	2	5	.286	6.78	0	79⅔	113	74	60	51	40
	—Oakland (A.L.)	5	1	0	1.000	9.00	0	5	11	5	5	2	3
	—Huntsville (Southern)	7	2	1	.667	3.48	0	44	46	17	17	25	23
Major league totals (1 year)		5	1	0	1.000	9.00	0	5	11	5	5	2	3

GUZMAN, JOSE
P, RANGERS

PERSONAL: Born April 9, 1963, at Santa Isabel, Puerto Rico. . . . 6-3/195. . . . Throws right, bats right. . . . Full name: Jose Alberto Mirabel Guzman.
HIGH SCHOOL: John F. Kennedy (Santa Isabel, Puerto Rico).
TRANSACTIONS/CAREER NOTES: Signed as free agent by Texas Rangers organization (February 10, 1981). . . . On disabled list (March 26-September 1, 1989). . . . On Texas disabled list (March 31-August 9, 1990); included rehabilitation disability assignments to Charlotte (June 6-19, 1990), Oklahoma City (July 17-19 and July 29-30, 1990) and Tulsa (July 20-25, 1990). . . . Released by Rangers (April 2, 1991). . . . Re-signed by Rangers organization (April 8, 1991).
RECORDS/HONORS: Named A.L. Comeback Player of the Year by THE SPORTING NEWS (1991).

Year	Team (League)	G	W	L	Pct.	ERA	Sv.	IP	H	R	ER	BB	SO
1981	—Sarasota Rangers (GCL)	14	3	3	.500	5.31	0	39	44	30	23	14	13
1982	—Sarasota Rangers (GCL)	12	5	4	.556	2.18	0	66	51	21	16	13	42
1983	—Burlington (Midwest)	25	12	8	.600	2.97	0	154⅔	135	68	51	52	146
1984	—Tulsa (Texas)	25	7	9	.438	4.17	0	140½	137	75	65	55	82
1985	—Oklahoma City (Am. Assoc.)	25	10	5	.667	3.13	1	149⅔	131	60	52	40	76
	—Texas (A.L.)	5	3	2	.600	2.76	0	32⅔	27	13	10	14	24
1986	—Texas (A.L.)	29	9	15	.375	4.54	0	172½	199	101	87	60	87
1987	—Texas (A.L.)	37	14	14	.500	4.67	0	208⅓	196	115	108	82	143
1988	—Texas (A.L.)	30	11	13	.458	3.70	0	206⅔	180	99	85	82	157
1989	—					Did not play							
1990	—Charlotte (Florida State)	2	0	1	.000	2.16	0	8⅓	10	3	2	4	7
	—Oklahoma City (Am. Assoc.)	7	0	3	.000	5.65	0	28⅔	35	20	18	9	26
	—Tulsa (Texas)	1	0	0	. . .	6.00	0	3	3	2	2	0	2
1991	—Oklahoma City (Am. Assoc.)	3	1	1	.500	3.92	0	20⅔	18	9	9	4	18
	—Texas (A.L.)	25	13	7	.650	3.08	0	169⅔	152	67	58	84	125
Major league totals (5 years)		126	50	51	.495	3.97	0	789⅔	754	395	348	322	536

GUZMAN, JUAN
P, BLUE JAYS

PERSONAL: Born October 28, 1966, at Santo Domingo, Dominican Republic. . . . 5-11/195. . . . Throws right, bats right. . . . Full name: Juan Andres Correa Guzman.
HIGH SCHOOL: Liceo Las Americas (Dominican Republic).
TRANSACTIONS/CAREER NOTES: Signed as free agent by the Los Angeles Dodgers organization (March 16, 1985). . . . Traded by Dodgers to Toronto Blue Jays organization for IF Mike Sharperson (September 22, 1987).
RECORDS/HONORS: Named A.L. Rookie Pitcher of the Year by THE SPORTING NEWS (1991).
STATISTICAL NOTES: Led Gulf Coast League with 15 wild pitches in 1985. . . . Led Florida State League with 16 wild pitches in 1986. . . . Led Southern League with 21 wild pitches in 1990.

Year	Team (League)	G	W	L	Pct.	ERA	Sv.	IP	H	R	ER	BB	SO
1985	—Bradenton (Gulf Coast)	21	5	1	.833	3.86	4	42	39	26	18	25	43
1986	—Vero Beach (Florida State)	20	10	9	.526	3.49	0	131⅓	114	69	51	90	96
1987	—Bakersfield (California)	22	5	6	.455	4.75	0	110	106	71	58	84	113
1988	—Knoxville (Southern)■	46	4	5	.444	2.36	6	84	52	29	22	61	90
1989	—Syracuse (International)	14	1	1	.500	3.98	0	20⅓	13	9	9	30	28
	—Knoxville (Southern)	22	1	4	.200	6.23	0	47⅔	34	36	33	60	50
1990	—Knoxville (Southern)	37	11	9	.550	4.24	1	157	145	84	74	80	138
1991	—Syracuse (International)	12	4	5	.444	4.03	0	67	46	39	30	42	67
	—Toronto (A.L.)	23	10	3	.769	2.99	0	138⅔	98	53	46	66	123
Major league totals (1 year)		23	10	3	.769	2.99	0	138⅔	98	53	46	66	123

CHAMPIONSHIP SERIES RECORD

Year	Team (League)	G	W	L	Pct.	ERA	Sv.	IP	H	R	ER	BB	SO
1991	—Toronto (A.L.)	1	1	0	1.000	3.18	0	5⅔	4	2	2	4	2

GWYNN, CHRIS
OF, ROYALS

PERSONAL: Born October 13, 1964, at Los Angeles. . . . 6-0/210. . . . Throws left, bats left. . . . Full name: Christopher Karlton Gwynn. . . . Brother of Tony Gwynn, outfielder, San Diego Padres.
HIGH SCHOOL: Long Beach Polytechnic (Calif.).
COLLEGE: San Diego State.
TRANSACTIONS/CAREER NOTES: Selected by California Angels organization in fifth round of free-agent draft (June 7, 1982). . . . Selected by Los Angeles Dodgers organization in first round (10th pick overall) of free-agent draft (June 3, 1985). . . . On Los Angeles disabled list (June 12-July 6 and July 16, 1989-remainder of season); included rehabilitation disability assignment to Albuquerque (August 3-11, 1989). . . . Traded by Dodgers with 2B Domingo Mota to Kansas City Royals for 1B-OF Todd Benzinger (December 11, 1991).

RECORDS/HONORS: Named outfielder on THE SPORTING NEWS college All-America team (1985).
MISCELLANEOUS: Member of 1984 U.S. Olympic baseball team.

Year Team (League)	Pos.	G	AB	R	H	2B	3B	HR	RBI	Avg.	SB	PO	A	E	Avg.
1985—Vero Beach (Florida St.) ...	OF	52	179	19	46	8	6	0	17	.257	2	43	2	0	1.000
1986—San Antonio (Texas)	OF	111	401	46	115	22	1	6	67	.287	2	186	11	2	.990
1987—Albuquerque (PCL)	OF	110	362	54	101	12	3	5	41	.279	5	141	5	1	.993
—Los Angeles (N.L.)............	OF	17	32	2	7	1	0	0	2	.219	0	12	0	0	1.000
1988—Albuquerque (PCL)	OF	112	411	57	123	22	•10	5	61	.299	1	134	3	4	.972
—Los Angeles (N.L.)........	OF	12	11	1	2	0	0	0	0	.182	0	0	0	0	...
1989—Albuquerque (PCL)	OF	26	89	14	29	9	1	0	12	.326	3	27	0	0	1.000
—Los Angeles (N.L.)........	OF	32	68	8	16	4	1	0	7	.235	1	26	1	0	1.000
1990—Los Angeles (N.L.)........	OF	101	141	19	40	2	1	5	22	.284	0	39	1	0	1.000
1991—Los Angeles (N.L.)............	OF	94	139	18	35	5	1	5	22	.252	1	37	2	0	1.000
Major league totals (5 years)		256	391	48	100	12	3	10	53	.256	2	114	4	0	1.000

GWYNN, TONY
OF, PADRES

PERSONAL: Born May 9, 1960, at Los Angeles. . . . 5-11/215. . . . Throws left, bats left. . . . Full name: Anthony Keith Gwynn. . . . Brother of Chris Gwynn, outfielder, Kansas City Royals.
HIGH SCHOOL: Long Beach Polytechnic (Calif.).
COLLEGE: San Diego State.

TRANSACTIONS/CAREER NOTES: Selected by San Diego Padres organization in third round of free-agent draft (June 8, 1981). . . . On disabled list (August 26-September 10, 1982). . . . On San Diego disabled list (March 26-June 21, 1983); included rehabilitation assignment to Las Vegas (May 31-June 20, 1983). . . . On disabled list (May 8-29, 1988).
RECORDS/HONORS: Holds N.L. single-season record for lowest batting average by leader—.313 (1988). . . . Shares N.L. record for most years leading league in singles—4. . . . Named Northwest League Most Valuable Player (1981). . . . Named outfielder on THE SPORTING NEWS N.L. All-Star team (1984, 1986-87 and 1989). . . . Named outfielder on THE SPORTING NEWS N.L. Silver Slugger team (1984, 1986-87 and 1989). . . . Won N.L. Gold Glove as outfielder (1986-87 and 1989-91).
STATISTICAL NOTES: Led N.L. with .410 on base percentage in 1984. . . . Led N.L. outfielders with 360 total chances in 1986.
MISCELLANEOUS: Selected by San Diego Clippers in 10th round (210th pick overall) of 1981 NBA draft (June 9, 1981).

Year Team (League)	Pos.	G	AB	R	H	2B	3B	HR	RBI	Avg.	SB	PO	A	E	Avg.
1981—Walla Walla (Northwest) ..	OF	42	178	46	59	12	1	12	37	★.331	17	76	2	3	.963
—Amarillo (Texas)	OF	23	91	22	42	8	2	4	19	.462	5	41	1	0	1.000
1982—Hawaii (Pacific Coast)	OF	93	366	65	120	23	2	5	46	.328	14	208	11	4	.982
—San Diego (N.L.)	OF	54	190	33	55	12	2	1	17	.289	8	110	1	1	.991
1983—Las Vegas (Pac. Coast)	OF	17	73	15	25	6	0	0	7	.342	3	23	2	3	.893
—San Diego (N.L.)	OF	86	304	34	94	12	2	1	37	.309	7	163	9	1	.994
1984—San Diego (N.L.)	OF	158	606	88	★213	21	10	5	71	★.351	33	345	11	4	.989
1985—San Diego (N.L.)	OF	154	622	90	197	29	5	6	46	.317	14	337	14	4	.989
1986—San Diego (N.L.)	OF	160	★642	•107	★211	33	7	14	59	.329	37	★337	19	4	.989
1987—San Diego (N.L.)	OF	157	589	119	★218	36	13	7	54	★.370	56	298	13	6	.981
1988—San Diego (N.L.)	OF	133	521	64	163	22	5	7	70	★.313	26	264	8	5	.982
1989—San Diego (N.L.)	OF	158	604	82	★203	27	7	4	62	★.336	40	353	13	6	.984
1990—San Diego (N.L.)	OF	141	573	79	177	29	10	4	72	.309	17	327	11	5	.985
1991—San Diego (N.L.)	OF	134	530	69	168	27	11	4	62	.317	8	291	8	3	.990
Major league totals (10 years)		1335	5181	765	1699	248	72	53	550	.328	246	2825	107	39	.987

CHAMPIONSHIP SERIES RECORD

Year Team (League)	Pos.	G	AB	R	H	2B	3B	HR	RBI	Avg.	SB	PO	A	E	Avg.
1984—San Diego (N.L.)	OF	5	19	6	7	3	0	0	3	.368	0	9	0	0	1.000

WORLD SERIES RECORD

Year Team (League)	Pos.	G	AB	R	H	2B	3B	HR	RBI	Avg.	SB	PO	A	E	Avg.
1984—San Diego (N.L.)	OF	5	19	1	5	0	0	0	0	.263	1	12	1	1	.929

ALL-STAR GAME RECORD

Year League	Pos.	AB	R	H	2B	3B	HR	RBI	Avg.	SB	PO	A	E	Avg.
1984—National	OF	3	0	1	0	0	0	0	.333	0	0	0	0	...
1985—National	OF	1	0	0	0	0	0	0	.000	0	1	0	0	1.000
1986—National	OF	3	0	0	0	0	0	0	.000	0	1	0	0	1.000
1987—National	PH	1	0	0	0	0	0	0	.000	0	0	0	0	...
1989—National	OF	2	1	1	0	0	0	0	.500	1	2	0	0	1.000
1990—National	PH	0	0	0	0	0	0	0	...	0	0	0	0	...
1991—National	OF	4	1	2	0	0	0	0	.500	0	6	0	0	1.000
All-Star Game totals (7 years)		14	2	4	0	0	0	0	.286	1	10	0	0	1.000

HAAS, DAVE
P, TIGERS

PERSONAL: Born October 19, 1965, at Independence, Mo. . . . 6-1/200. . . . Throws right, bats right. . . . Full name: Robert David Haas.
COLLEGE: Wichita State.
TRANSACTIONS/CAREER NOTES: Selected by Baltimore Orioles organization in 28th round of free-

agent draft (June 4, 1984).... Selected by Toronto Blue Jays organization in 18th round of free-agent draft (June 2, 1987). ... Selected by Detroit Tigers organization in 15th round of free-agent draft (June 1, 1988).
STATISTICAL NOTES: Pitched 5-0 no-hit victory against Clearwater (April 14, 1989).... Led Eastern League pitchers with 27 games started in 1990.... Tied for International League lead in games started by pitcher with 28 in 1991.

Year	Team (League)	G	W	L	Pct.	ERA	Sv.	IP	H	R	ER	BB	SO
1988	Fayetteville (South Atlantic)	11	4	3	.571	1.81	0	54⅔	59	20	11	19	46
1989	Lakeland (Florida State)	10	4	1	.800	2.03	0	62	50	16	14	16	46
	London (Eastern)	18	3	11	.214	5.64	0	103⅓	107	69	65	51	75
1990	London (Eastern)	27	13	8	.619	2.99	0	177⅔	151	64	59	74	116
1991	Toledo (International)	28	8	10	.444	5.26	0	157⅓	187	103	92	77	133
	Detroit (A.L.)	11	1	0	1.000	6.75	0	10⅔	8	8	8	12	6
Major league totals (1 year)		11	1	0	1.000	6.75	0	10⅔	8	8	8	12	6

HABYAN, JOHN
P, YANKEES

PERSONAL: Born January 29, 1964, at Bayshore, N.Y.... 6-2/191.... Throws right, bats right.... Full name: John Gabriel Habyan.... Name pronounced HAY-bee-un.
HIGH SCHOOL: St. John the Baptist (Brentwood, N.Y.).
TRANSACTIONS/CAREER NOTES: Selected by Baltimore Orioles organization in third round of free-agent draft (June 7, 1982).... On Baltimore disabled list (March 30-June 9, 1989).... Traded by Orioles to New York Yankees organization for OF Stanley Jefferson (July 20, 1989).
STATISTICAL NOTES: Pitched 6-0 no-hit victory against Columbus (May 13, 1985).

Year	Team (League)	G	W	L	Pct.	ERA	Sv.	IP	H	R	ER	BB	SO
1982	Bluefield (Appalachian)	12	•9	2	.818	3.54	0	81⅓	68	35	32	24	55
	Hagerstown (Carolina)	1	0	0	...	67.50	0	⅔	5	5	5	2	1
1983	Hagerstown (Carolina)	11	2	3	.400	5.81	0	48	54	41	31	29	42
	Newark (New York-Penn)	11	5	3	.625	3.39	0	71⅔	68	34	27	29	64
1984	Hagerstown (Carolina)	13	9	4	.692	3.54	0	81⅓	64	41	32	33	81
	Charlotte (Southern)	13	4	7	.364	4.44	0	77	84	46	38	34	55
1985	Charlotte (Southern)	28	13	5	.722	3.27	0	189⅔	157	73	69	90	123
	Baltimore (A.L.)	2	1	0	1.000	0.00	0	2⅔	3	1	0	0	2
1986	Rochester (International)	26	12	7	.632	4.29	0	157⅓	168	82	75	69	93
	Baltimore (A.L.)	6	1	3	.250	4.44	0	26⅓	24	17	13	18	14
1987	Rochester (International)	7	3	2	.600	3.86	0	49	47	23	21	20	39
	Baltimore (A.L.)	27	6	7	.462	4.80	1	116⅓	110	67	62	40	64
1988	Rochester (International)	23	9	9	.500	4.46	0	147⅓	161	78	73	46	91
	Baltimore (A.L.)	7	1	0	1.000	4.30	0	14⅔	22	10	7	4	4
1989	Rochester-Columbus (Int'l)■ ..	15	3	5	.375	3.98	0	83⅔	103	44	37	14	52
1990	Columbus (International)	36	7	7	.500	3.21	6	112	99	52	40	30	77
	New York (A.L.)	6	0	0	...	2.08	0	8⅔	10	2	2	2	4
1991	New York (A.L.)	66	4	2	.667	2.30	2	90	73	28	23	20	70
Major league totals (6 years)		114	13	12	.520	3.72	3	258⅔	242	125	107	84	158

HALL, MEL
OF, YANKEES

PERSONAL: Born September 16, 1960, at Lyons, N.Y.... 6-1/214.... Throws left, bats left.... Full name: Melvin Hall Jr.
HIGH SCHOOL: Port Byron (N.Y.).
TRANSACTIONS/CAREER NOTES: Selected by Chicago Cubs organization in second round of free-agent draft (June 6, 1978).... On Chicago disabled list (April 15-May 31, 1983); included rehabilitation disability assignment to Midland (May 25-31, 1983).... Traded by Cubs with OF Joe Carter, P Don Schulze and P Darryl Banks to Cleveland Indians for C Ron Hassey, P Rick Sutcliffe and P George Frazier (June 13, 1984).... On disabled list (May 10, 1985-remainder of season). ... Traded by Indians to New York Yankees for C Joel Skinner and OF Turner Ward (March 19, 1989).... On disabled list (April 26-May 26, 1989).... Granted free agency (November 13, 1989).... Re-signed by Yankees (November 30, 1989).... On disabled list (July 16-August 1, 1990).
STATISTICAL NOTES: Led Texas League with 286 total bases in 1981.... Led Texas League outfielders with 324 total chances and five double plays in 1981.... Led American Association outfielders with 339 total chances in 1982.

Year	Team (League)	Pos.	G	AB	R	H	2B	3B	HR	RBI	Avg.	SB	PO	A	E	Avg.
1978	Bradenton Cubs (GCL)	OF	43	145	30	42	7	3	2	17	.290	4	★97	5	4	.962
1979	Geneva (N.Y.-Penn)	OF	66	251	49	79	18	5	3	53	.315	4	113	5	7	.944
1980	Midland (Texas)	OF	37	128	17	34	7	3	1	14	.266	2	58	3	3	.953
	Quad Cities (Midwest).......	OF	97	347	54	102	14	4	6	42	.294	21	171	9	5	.973
1981	Midland (Texas)	OF	131	533	★98	★170	34	5	24	95	.319	18	★302	14	8	.975
	Chicago (N.L.)	OF	10	11	1	1	0	0	1	2	.091	0	0	0	0	...
1982	Iowa (American Assoc.) ...	OF	133	502	★116	165	★34	6	32	125	.329	19	★317	13	•9	.973
	Chicago (N.L.)	OF	24	80	6	21	3	2	0	4	.263	0	42	4	3	.939
1983	Chicago (N.L.)	OF	112	410	60	116	23	5	17	56	.283	6	239	8	3	.988
	Midland (Texas)	OF	6	19	9	9	2	1	3	7	.474	2	8	0	0	1.000
1984	Chicago (N.L.)	OF	48	150	25	42	11	3	4	22	.280	2	69	5	3	.961
	Cleveland (A.L.)■	OF	83	257	43	66	13	1	7	30	.257	1	143	3	1	.993
1985	Cleveland (A.L.)	OF	23	66	7	21	6	0	0	12	.318	0	18	0	0	1.000
1986	Cleveland (A.L.)	OF	140	442	68	131	29	2	18	77	.296	6	233	7	7	.972
1987	Cleveland (A.L.)	OF	142	485	57	136	21	1	18	76	.280	5	264	3	3	.989
1988	Cleveland (A.L.)	OF	150	515	69	144	32	4	6	71	.280	7	288	3	10	.967

Year Team (League)	Pos.	G	AB	R	H	2B	3B	HR	RBI	Avg.	SB	PO	A	E	Avg.
1989—New York (A.L.)■	OF	113	361	54	94	9	0	17	58	.260	0	141	3	1	.993
1990—New York (A.L.)	OF	113	360	41	93	23	2	12	46	.258	0	70	2	2	.973
1991—New York (A.L.)	OF	141	492	67	140	23	2	19	80	.285	0	221	8	3	.987
American League totals (8 years)		905	2978	406	825	156	12	97	450	.277	19	1378	29	27	.981
National League totals (4 years)		194	651	92	180	37	10	22	84	.276	8	350	17	9	.976
Major league totals (11 years)		1099	3629	498	1005	193	22	119	534	.277	27	1728	46	36	.980

HAMILTON, DARRYL
OF, BREWERS

PERSONAL: Born December 3, 1964, at Baton Rouge, La. . . . 6-1/180. . . . Throws right, bats left. . . . Full name: Darryl Quinn Hamilton.
HIGH SCHOOL: University (Baton Rouge, La.).
COLLEGE: Nicholls State (La.).
TRANSACTIONS/CAREER NOTES: Selected by Milwaukee Brewers organization in 11th round of free-agent draft (June 2, 1986). . . . On disabled list (May 22-June 15, 1991).
STATISTICAL NOTES: Led California League with nine intentional bases on balls received in 1987.

Year Team (League)	Pos.	G	AB	R	H	2B	3B	HR	RBI	Avg.	SB	PO	A	E	Avg.
1986—Helena (Pioneer)	OF	65	248	★72	★97	12	★6	0	35	★.391	34	132	9	0	★1.000
1987—Stockton (California)	OF	125	494	102	162	17	6	8	61	.328	42	221	8	1	★.996
1988—Denver (Am. Assoc.)	OF	72	277	55	90	11	4	0	32	.325	28	160	2	2	.988
—Milwaukee (A.L.)	OF	44	103	14	19	4	0	1	11	.184	7	75	1	0	1.000
1989—Denver (Am. Assoc.)	OF	129	497	72	142	24	4	2	40	.286	20	263	11	0	★1.000
1990—Milwaukee (A.L.)	OF	89	156	27	46	5	0	1	18	.295	10	120	1	1	.992
1991—Milwaukee (A.L.)	OF	122	405	64	126	15	6	1	57	.311	16	234	3	1	.996
Major league totals (3 years)		255	664	105	191	24	6	3	86	.288	33	429	5	2	.995

HAMILTON, JEFF
3B, DODGERS

PERSONAL: Born March 19, 1964, at Flint, Mich. . . . 6-3/207. . . . Throws right, bats right. . . . Full name: Jeffrey Robert Hamilton.
HIGH SCHOOL: Flint Carman (Flint, Mich.).
TRANSACTIONS/CAREER NOTES: Selected by Los Angeles Dodgers organization in 29th round of free-agent draft (June 7, 1982). . . . On Los Angeles disabled list (August 14, 1987-remainder of season; July 27-September 1, 1988; and April 21, 1990-remainder of season). . . . On Los Angeles disabled list (June 19-September 6, 1991); included rehabilitation disability assignment to Albuquerque (August 9-13, 1991).
STATISTICAL NOTES: Led Pioneer League third basemen with 16 double plays in 1983. . . . Led Florida State League third basemen with 395 total chances and 25 double plays in 1984. . . . Led N.L. third basemen with 139 putouts in 1989.

Year Team (League)	Pos.	G	AB	R	H	2B	3B	HR	RBI	Avg.	SB	PO	A	E	Avg.
1983—Lodi (California)	3B-OF	44	141	15	28	4	0	0	10	.199	2	26	62	17	.838
—Lethbridge (Pioneer)	3B	68	★281	48	★94	★23	2	3	61	.335	3	38	118	17	.902
1984—Vero Beach (Florida St.)	3B	127	466	51	121	31	4	4	59	.260	7	★109	★259	★27	★.932
1985—San Antonio (Texas)	3B-OF	101	377	48	125	14	3	13	59	.332	1	69	186	16	.941
1986—Albuquerque (PCL)	3B	71	288	40	90	21	3	10	42	.313	1	39	151	19	.909
—Los Angeles (N.L.)	3B-SS	71	147	22	33	5	0	5	19	.224	0	40	87	4	.969
1987—Albuquerque (PCL)	3B	65	236	52	85	17	1	12	48	.360	0	43	102	11	.929
—Los Angeles (N.L.)	3B-SS	35	83	5	18	3	0	1	1	.217	0	27	60	6	.935
1988—Los Angeles (N.L.)	3B-SS-1B	111	309	34	73	14	2	6	33	.236	0	67	160	14	.942
1989—Los Angeles (N.L.)	3-P-2-S	151	548	45	134	35	1	12	56	.245	0	†139	234	19	.952
1990—Los Angeles (N.L.)	3B	7	24	1	3	0	0	0	1	.125	0	3	12	0	1.000
1991—Los Angeles (N.L.)	3B-SS	41	94	4	21	4	0	1	14	.223	0	21	43	5	.928
—Albuquerque (PCL)	DH	2	7	0	0	0	0	0	0	.000	0	0	0	0	. . .
Major league totals (6 years)		416	1205	111	282	61	3	24	124	.234	0	297	596	48	.949

CHAMPIONSHIP SERIES RECORD

CHAMPIONSHIP SERIES NOTES: Shares record for most at-bats in one inning—2 (October 12, 1988, second inning).

Year Team (League)	Pos.	G	AB	R	H	2B	3B	HR	RBI	Avg.	SB	PO	A	E	Avg.
1988—Los Angeles (N.L.)	3B	7	23	2	5	0	0	0	1	.217	0	9	10	2	.905

WORLD SERIES RECORD

Year Team (League)	Pos.	G	AB	R	H	2B	3B	HR	RBI	Avg.	SB	PO	A	E	Avg.
1988—Los Angeles (N.L.)	3B	5	19	1	2	0	0	0	0	.105	0	2	5	1	.875

RECORD AS PITCHER

Year Team (League)	G	W	L	Pct.	ERA	Sv.	IP	H	R	ER	BB	SO
1989—Los Angeles (N.L.)	1	0	1	.000	5.40	0	1⅔	2	1	1	1	2

HAMMAKER, ATLEE
P

PERSONAL: Born January 24, 1958, at Carmel, Calif. . . . 6-2/200. . . . Throws left, bats both. . . . Full name: Charlton Atlee Hammaker. . . . Name pronounced HAM-ek-er.
HIGH SCHOOL: Mt. Vernon (Alexandria, Va.).

COLLEGE: East Tennessee State.
TRANSACTIONS/CAREER NOTES: Selected by Kansas City Royals organization in first round (21st pick overall) of free-agent draft (June 5, 1979). . . . On disabled list (July 6-October 26, 1979 and August 3-22, 1980). . . . Traded by Royals with P Craig Chamberlain, P Renie Martin and a player to be named later to San Francisco Giants for P Vida Blue and P Bob Tufts (March 30, 1982); Giants organization acquired 2B Brad Wellman to complete deal (April 19, 1982). . . . On disabled list (July 26-August 21, 1983). . . . On San Francisco disabled list (April 2-June 26 and August 4-September 1, 1984); included rehabilitation disability assignment to Phoenix (June 16-25, 1984). . . . On disabled list (April 7, 1986-entire season). . . . Released by Giants (December 9, 1986). . . . Re-signed by Giants (February 4, 1987). . . . On San Francisco disabled list (April 2-30, 1987); included rehabilitation disability assignment to Phoenix (April 10-30, 1987). . . . Granted free agency (November 9, 1987). . . . Re-signed by Giants (January 8, 1988). . . . On San Francisco disabled list (June 19-July 17 and August 3-September 21, 1989; and June 18-July 11, 1990). . . . Released by Giants (August 12, 1990). . . . Signed by San Diego Padres (August 24, 1990). . . . On San Diego disabled list (March 31-June 9, 1991); included rehabilitation disability assignment to High Desert (May 12-23, 1991) and Las Vegas (May 23-June 9, 1991). . . . On San Diego disabled list (June 14-September 3, 1991); included rehabiliation disability assignment to Wichita (August 13-September 3, 1991). . . . Granted free agency (October 31, 1991).

Year	Team (League)	G	W	L	Pct.	ERA	Sv.	IP	H	R	ER	BB	SO
1979	—Sarasota Royals (Gulf Coast) ...	1	1	0	1.000	1.80	0	5	3	1	1	1	6
	—Fort Myers (Florida State)	1	0	1	.000	1.80	0	5	9	5	1	0	5
1980	—Jacksonville (Southern)	20	8	9	.471	3.35	0	137	131	64	51	37	88
1981	—Omaha (American Assoc.)........	21	11	5	.688	3.64	0	146	147	70	59	40	63
	—Kansas City (A.L.)	10	1	3	.250	5.54	0	39	44	24	24	12	11
1982	—Phoenix (Pacific Coast)■.........	1	0	1	.000	6.35	0	5⅔	13	5	4	2	6
	—San Francisco (N.L.)	29	12	8	.600	4.11	0	175	189	86	80	28	102
1983	—San Francisco (N.L.)	23	10	9	.526	★2.25	0	172⅓	147	57	43	32	127
1984	—Phoenix (Pacific Coast)	2	0	1	.000	4.50	0	8	14	7	4	2	5
	—San Francisco (N.L.)	6	2	0	1.000	2.18	0	33	32	10	8	9	24
1985	—San Francisco (N.L.)	29	5	12	.294	3.74	0	170⅔	161	81	71	47	100
1986	—					Did not play							
1987	—Phoenix (Pacific Coast)	3	1	2	.333	4.15	0	17⅓	19	9	8	6	8
	—Shreveport (Texas)	1	0	1	.000	1.29	0	7	6	2	1	0	3
	—San Francisco (N.L.)	31	10	10	.500	3.58	0	168⅓	159	73	67	57	107
1988	—San Francisco (N.L.)	43	9	9	.500	3.73	5	144⅔	136	68	60	41	65
1989	—San Francisco (N.L.)	28	6	6	.500	3.76	0	76⅔	78	34	32	23	30
1990	—San Fran.-San Diego (N.L.)■....	34	4	9	.308	4.36	0	86⅔	85	44	42	27	44
1991	—High Desert (California)	2	0	0	. . .	2.25	0	8	9	3	2	3	3
	—Las Vegas (Pacific Coast)	3	0	0	. . .	6.46	0	15⅓	21	11	11	3	9
	—San Diego (N.L.)	1	0	1	.000	5.79	0	4⅔	8	7	3	3	1
	—Wichita (Texas)	5	0	1	.000	3.52	0	7⅔	10	3	3	0	9
American League totals (1 year)		10	1	3	.250	5.54	0	39	44	24	24	12	11
National League totals (9 years)		224	58	64	.475	3.54	5	1032	995	460	406	267	600
Major league totals (10 years)		234	59	67	.468	3.61	5	1071	1039	484	430	279	611

CHAMPIONSHIP SERIES RECORD

Year	Team (League)	G	W	L	Pct.	ERA	Sv.	IP	H	R	ER	BB	SO
1987	—San Francisco (N.L.)	2	0	1	.000	7.88	0	8	12	7	7	0	7
1989	—San Francisco (N.L.)	1	0	0	. . .	0.00	0	1	1	0	0	0	0
Championship Series totals (2 years)	....	3	0	1	.000	7.00	0	9	13	7	7	0	7

WORLD SERIES RECORD

Year	Team (League)	G	W	L	Pct.	ERA	Sv.	IP	H	R	ER	BB	SO
1989	—San Francisco (N.L.)	2	0	0	. . .	15.43	0	2⅓	8	4	4	0	2

ALL-STAR GAME RECORD

ALL-STAR GAME NOTES: Holds single-game records for most runs—7; most earned runs allowed—7 (July 6, 1983). . . . Holds records for most runs in one inning—7; most earned runs in one inning—7; most hits allowed in one inning—6 (July 6, 1983, third inning). . . . Shares record for most home runs allowed in one inning—2 (July 6, 1983, third inning).

Year	League	W	L	Pct.	ERA	Sv.	IP	H	R	ER	BB	SO
1983	—National	0	0	. . .	94.50	0	⅔	6	7	7	1	0

HAMMOND, CHRIS
P, REDS

PERSONAL: Born January 21, 1966, at Atlanta. . . . 6-1/190. . . . Throws left, bats left. . . . Full name: Christopher Andrew Hammond. . . . Brother of Steve Hammond, outfielder, Kansas City Royals (1982).
HIGH SCHOOL: Vestavia Hills (Birmingham, Ala.).
COLLEGE: Gulf Coast Community College (Fla.) and Alabama-Birmingham.
TRANSACTIONS/CAREER NOTES: Selected by Cincinnati Reds organization in sixth round of free-agent draft (January 14, 1986). . . . On disabled list (July 27-September 1, 1991).
RECORDS/HONORS: Named American Association Pitcher of the Year (1990).
STATISTICAL NOTES: Led American Association with three shutouts in 1990.

Year	Team (League)	G	W	L	Pct.	ERA	Sv.	IP	H	R	ER	BB	SO
1986	—Sarasota Reds (Gulf Coast)	7	3	2	.600	2.81	0	41⅔	27	21	13	17	53
	—Tampa (Florida State)	5	0	2	.000	3.32	0	21⅔	25	8	8	13	5
1987	—Tampa (Florida State)	25	11	11	.500	3.55	0	170	174	81	67	60	126

Year Team (League)	G	W	L	Pct.	ERA	Sv.	IP	H	R	ER	BB	SO
1988—Chattanooga (Southern)	26	*16	5	.762	*1.72	0	182⅔	127	48	35	77	127
1989—Nashville (American Assoc.)	24	11	7	.611	3.38	0	157⅓	144	69	59	96	142
1990—Nashville (American Assoc.)	24	*15	1	*.938	*2.17	0	149	118	43	36	63	*149
—Cincinnati (N.L.)	3	0	2	.000	6.35	0	11⅓	13	9	8	12	4
1991—Cincinnati (N.L.)	20	7	7	.500	4.06	0	99⅔	92	51	45	48	50
Major league totals (2 years)	23	7	9	.438	4.30	0	111	105	60	53	60	54

HANCOCK, CHRISTOPHER
P, GIANTS

PERSONAL: Born September 12, 1969, at Lynwood, Calif. . . . 6-3/175. . . . Throws left, bats left. . . . Full name: Christopher Martin Hancock.
HIGH SCHOOL: Fontana (Calif.).
TRANSACTIONS/CAREER NOTES: Selected by San Francisco Giants organization in second round of free-agent draft (June 1, 1988). . . . On disabled list (April 10-July 4, 1991).

Year Team (League)	G	W	L	Pct.	ERA	Sv.	IP	H	R	ER	BB	SO
1988—Pocatello (Pioneer)	12	2	5	.286	8.86	0	42⅔	60	54	42	43	31
1989—Everett (Northwest)	11	2	5	.286	5.64	0	52⅔	47	52	33	53	50
—Clinton (Midwest)	18	4	7	.364	5.88	0	72	63	53	47	77	62
1990—Clinton (Midwest)	18	11	3	.786	2.28	0	110⅔	78	33	28	43	123
—San Jose (California)	1	0	0	. . .	1.17	0	7⅔	7	1	1	4	7
1991—San Jose (California)	9	4	3	.571	2.03	0	53⅓	42	16	12	33	59

HANEY, CHRIS
P, EXPOS

PERSONAL: Born November 16, 1968, at Baltimore. . . . 6-3/185. . . . Throws left, bats left. . . . Full name: Christopher Deane Haney. . . . Son of Larry Haney, major league catcher for five teams (1966-70 and 1972-78) and coach, Milwaukee Brewers (1978-91).
HIGH SCHOOL: Orange County (Va.).
COLLEGE: UNC Charlotte.
TRANSACTIONS/CAREER NOTES: Selected by Milwaukee Brewers organization in 25th round of free-agent draft (June 2, 1987). . . . Selected by Montreal Expos organization in second round of free-agent draft (June 4, 1990).

Year Team (League)	G	W	L	Pct.	ERA	Sv.	IP	H	R	ER	BB	SO
1990—Jamestown (New York-Penn)	6	3	0	1.000	0.96	1	28	17	3	3	10	26
—Rockford (Midwest)	8	2	4	.333	2.21	0	53	40	15	13	6	45
—Jacksonville (Southern)	1	1	0	1.000	0.00	0	6	6	0	0	3	6
1991—Harrisburg (Eastern)	12	5	3	.625	2.16	0	83⅓	65	21	20	31	68
—Montreal (N.L.)	16	3	7	.300	4.04	0	84⅔	94	49	38	43	51
—Indianapolis (Am. Assoc.)	2	1	1	.500	4.35	0	10⅓	14	10	5	6	8
Major league totals (1 year)	16	3	7	.300	4.04	0	84⅔	94	49	38	43	51

HANSEN, DAVE
3B, DODGERS

PERSONAL: Born November 24, 1968, at Long Beach, Calif. . . . 6-0/180. . . . Throws right, bats left. . . . Full name: David Andrew Hansen.
HIGH SCHOOL: Rowland (Long Beach, Calif.).
TRANSACTIONS/CAREER NOTES: Selected by Los Angeles Dodgers organization in second round of free-agent draft (June 2, 1986).
STATISTICAL NOTES: Led California League third basemen with 45 errors in 1987. . . . Led Florida State League with 210 total bases and tied for lead with nine sacrifice flies in 1988. . . . Led Florida State League third basemen with 383 total chances and 24 double plays in 1988. . . . Led Pacific Coast League with 90 bases on balls received in 1990. . . . Led Pacific Coast League third basemen with .926 fielding percentage, 254 assists, 349 total chances and 25 double plays in 1990.

Year Team (League)	Pos.	G	AB	R	H	2B	3B	HR	RBI	Avg.	SB	PO	A	E	Avg.
1986—Great Falls (Pioneer)	O-3-C-2	61	204	39	61	7	3	1	36	.299	9	54	10	7	.901
1987—Bakersfield (California)	3B-OF	132	432	68	113	22	1	3	38	.262	4	79	198	†45	.860
1988—Vero Beach (Florida St.)	3B	135	512	68	*149	*28	6	7	*81	.291	2	*102	*263	18	*.953
1989—San Antonio (Texas)	3B	121	464	72	138	21	4	6	52	.297	3	*92	208	16	*.949
—Albuquerque (PCL)	3B	6	30	6	8	1	0	2	10	.267	0	3	8	3	.786
1990—Albuquerque (PCL)	3-0-S	135	487	90	154	20	3	11	92	.316	9	71	†255	26	†.926
—Los Angeles (N.L.)	3B	5	7	0	1	0	0	0	1	.143	0	0	1	1	.500
1991—Albuquerque (PCL)	3B-SS	68	254	42	77	11	1	5	40	.303	4	43	125	6	.966
—Los Angeles (N.L.)	3B-SS	53	56	3	15	4	0	1	5	.268	1	5	19	0	1.000
Major league totals (2 years)		58	63	3	16	4	0	1	6	.254		5	20	1	.962

HANSEN, TERREL
1B/OF, METS

PERSONAL: Born September 25, 1966, at Bremerton, Wash. . . . 6-3/210. . . . Throws right, bats right. . . . Full name: Terrel Ernest Hansen.
HIGH SCHOOL: Bremerton (Wash.).
COLLEGE: Washington State.
TRANSACTIONS/CAREER NOTES: Selected by New York Mets organization in 14th round of free-agent draft (June 4, 1984). . . . Selected by Montreal Expos organization in 14th round of free-agent draft (June 2, 1987). . . . Traded by Expos with P David Sommer to Mets for OF Darren Reed and OF Alex Diaz (April 2, 1991).
STATISTICAL NOTES: Led Midwest League in being hit by pitch with 23 in 1989. . . . Led International league in being hit by pitch with 20 and grounding into double plays with 20 in 1991.

Year	Team (League)	Pos.	G	AB	R	H	2B	3B	HR	RBI	Avg.	SB	PO	A	E	Avg.
1987 —Jamestown (N.Y.-Penn) ...		OF-1B	29	67	8	16	3	0	1	14	.239	1	21	2	3	.885
1988 —West Palm Beach (FSL)		OF-1B	58	190	17	49	9	0	4	28	.258	2	80	4	2	.977
1989 —Rockford (Midwest)		OF-1B	125	468	60	126	24	3	16	•81	.269	5	205	14	4	.982
1990 —Jacksonville (Southern) ...		OF-1B	123	420	72	109	26	2	•24	83	.260	3	289	12	9	.971
1991 —Tidewater (Int'l)■		OF-1B	107	368	54	100	20	2	12	62	.272	0	217	11	5	.979

HANSON, ERIK
P, MARINERS

PERSONAL: Born May 18, 1965, at Kinnelon, N.J. . . . 6-6/210. . . . Throws right, bats right.
HIGH SCHOOL: Peddie Prep (Highstown, N.J.).
COLLEGE: Wake Forest.
TRANSACTIONS/CAREER NOTES: Selected by Montreal Expos organization in seventh round of free-agent draft (June 6, 1983). . . . Selected by Seattle Mariners organization in second round of free-agent draft (June 2, 1986). . . . On inactive list (June 12-August 18, 1986). . . . On Seattle disabled list (May 25-August 4, 1989); included rehabilitation disability assignment to Calgary (June 14-22 and July 24-August 4, 1989). . . . On Seattle disabled list (May 12-28 and May 29-June 22, 1991); included rehabilitation disability assignment to Calgary (June 16-20, 1991).
STATISTICAL NOTES: Pitched 5-0 no-hit victory against Las Vegas (August 21, 1988, second game).

Year	Team (League)	G	W	L	Pct.	ERA	Sv.	IP	H	R	ER	BB	SO
1986 —Chattanooga (Southern)		3	0	0	. . .	3.86	0	9⅓	10	4	4	4	11
1987 —Chattanooga (Southern)		21	8	10	.444	2.60	0	131⅓	102	56	38	43	131
—Calgary (Pacific Coast)		8	1	3	.250	3.61	0	47⅓	38	23	19	21	43
1988 —Calgary (Pacific Coast)		27	12	7	.632	4.23	0	161⅔	167	92	76	57	*154
—Seattle (A.L.)		6	2	3	.400	3.24	0	41⅔	35	17	15	12	36
1989 —Seattle (A.L.)		17	9	5	.643	3.18	0	113⅓	103	44	40	32	75
—Calgary (Pacific Coast)		8	4	2	.667	6.87	0	38	51	30	29	11	37
1990 —Seattle (A.L.)		33	18	9	.667	3.24	0	236	205	88	85	68	211
1991 —Seattle (A.L.)		27	8	8	.500	3.81	0	174⅔	182	82	74	56	143
—Calgary (Pacific Coast)		1	0	0	. . .	1.50	0	6	1	1	1	2	5
Major league totals (4 years)		83	37	25	.597	3.40	0	565⅔	525	231	214	168	465

HARE, SHAWN
OF, TIGERS

PERSONAL: Born March 26, 1967, at St. Louis. . . . 6-2/190. . . . Throws left, bats left. . . . Full name: Shawn Robert Hare.
HIGH SCHOOL: Rochester Adams (Mich.).
COLLEGE: Central Michigan.
TRANSACTIONS/CAREER NOTES: Signed as a free agent by Detroit Tigers organization (August 28, 1988). . . . On Toledo disabled list (April 26-May 11, 1991).

Year	Team (League)	Pos.	G	AB	R	H	2B	3B	HR	RBI	Avg.	SB	PO	A	E	Avg.
1989 —Lakeland (Florida State) ...		OF-1B	93	290	32	94	16	4	2	36	.324	11	142	4	2	.986
1990 —Toledo (International)		OF-1B	127	429	53	109	25	4	9	55	.254	9	198	6	7	.967
1991 —Toledo (International)		OF-1B	80	252	44	78	18	2	9	42	.310	1	231	19	5	.980
—London (Eastern)		OF	31	125	20	34	12	0	4	28	.272	2	55	5	3	.952
—Detroit (A.L.)		OF	9	19	0	1	1	0	0	0	.053	0	9	1	0	1.000
Major league totals (1 year)			9	19	0	1	1	0	0	0	.053	0	9	1	0	1.000

HARKEY, MIKE
P, CUBS

PERSONAL: Born October 25, 1966, at San Diego. . . . 6-5/220. . . . Throws right, bats right. . . . Full name: Michael Anthony Harkey.
HIGH SCHOOL: Ganesha (Pomona, Calif.).
COLLEGE: Cal State Fullerton.
TRANSACTIONS/CAREER NOTES: Selected by San Diego Padres organization in 18th round of free-agent draft (June 4, 1984). . . . Selected by Chicago Cubs organization in first round (fourth pick overall) of free-agent draft (June 2, 1987). . . . On disabled list (April 5-28 and July 4, 1989-remainder of season; May 29-June 13, 1990; and April 27, 1991-remainder of season).
RECORDS/HONORS: Shares major league record for most putouts by pitcher in one inning—3 (May 23, 1990, fourth inning). . . . Named N.L. Rookie Pitcher of the Year by THE SPORTING NEWS (1990).

Year	Team (League)	G	W	L	Pct.	ERA	Sv.	IP	H	R	ER	BB	SO
1987 —Peoria (Midwest)		12	2	3	.400	3.55	0	76	81	45	30	28	48
—Pittsfield (Eastern)		1	0	0	. . .	0.00	0	2	1	0	0	0	2
1988 —Pittsfield (Eastern)		13	9	2	*.818	1.37	0	85⅔	66	29	13	35	73
—Iowa (American Association) ...		12	7	2	.778	3.55	0	78⅔	55	36	31	33	62
—Chicago (N.L.)		5	0	3	.000	2.60	0	34⅔	33	14	10	15	18
1989 —Iowa (American Association) ...		12	2	7	.222	4.43	0	63	67	37	31	35	37
1990 —Chicago (N.L.)		27	12	6	.667	3.26	0	173⅔	153	71	63	59	94
1991 —Chicago (N.L.)		4	0	2	.000	5.30	0	18⅔	21	11	11	6	15
Major league totals (3 years)		36	12	11	.522	3.33	0	227	207	96	84	80	127

HARNISCH, PETE
P, ASTROS

PERSONAL: Born September 23, 1966, at Commack, N.Y. . . . 6-0/207. . . . Throws right, bats right. . . . Full name: Peter Thomas Harnisch.
HIGH SCHOOL: Commack (N.Y.).
COLLEGE: Fordham.

TRANSACTIONS/CAREER NOTES: Selected by Baltimore Orioles organization in first round (27th pick overall) of free-agent draft (June 2, 1987).... Traded by Orioles with P Curt Schilling and OF Steve Finley to Houston Astros for 1B Glenn Davis (January 10, 1991).
RECORDS/HONORS: Shares major league record for striking out side on nine pitches (September 6, 1991, seventh inning).

Year Team (League)	G	W	L	Pct.	ERA	Sv.	IP	H	R	ER	BB	SO
1987—Bluefield (Appalachian)	9	3	1	.750	2.56	0	52⅔	38	19	15	26	64
—Hagerstown (Carolina)	4	1	2	.333	2.25	0	20	17	7	5	14	18
1988—Charlotte (Southern)	20	7	6	.538	2.58	0	132⅓	113	55	38	52	141
—Rochester (International)	7	4	1	.800	2.16	0	58⅓	44	16	14	14	43
—Baltimore (A.L.)	2	0	2	.000	5.54	0	13	13	8	8	9	10
1989—Baltimore (A.L.)	18	5	9	.357	4.62	0	103⅓	97	55	53	64	70
—Rochester (International)	12	5	5	.500	2.58	0	87⅓	60	27	25	35	59
1990—Baltimore (A.L.)	31	11	11	.500	4.34	0	188⅔	189	96	91	86	122
1991—Houston (N.L.)■	33	12	9	.571	2.70	0	216⅔	169	71	65	83	172
American League totals (3 years)	51	16	22	.421	4.49	0	305	299	159	152	159	202
National League totals (1 year)	33	12	9	.571	2.70	0	216⅔	169	71	65	83	172
Major league totals (4 years)	84	28	31	.475	3.74	0	521⅔	468	230	217	242	374

ALL-STAR GAME RECORD

Year League	W	L	Pct.	ERA	Sv.	IP	H	R	ER	BB	SO
1991—National	0	0	...	0.00	0	1	2	0	0	0	1

HARPER, BRIAN
C, TWINS

PERSONAL: Born October 16, 1959, at Los Angeles.... 6-2/208.... Throws right, bats right. ... Full name: Brian David Harper.
HIGH SCHOOL: San Pedro (Calif.).
TRANSACTIONS/CAREER NOTES: Selected by California Angels organization in fourth round of free-agent draft (June 7, 1977).... On disabled list (July 1-17, 1980).... Traded by Angels to Pittsburgh Pirates for SS Tim Foli (December 11, 1981).... On disabled list (April 12-May 10 and May 16-June 4, 1984).... Traded by Pirates with P John Tudor to St. Louis Cardinals for OF-1B George Hendrick and C Steve Barnard (December 12, 1984).... Released by Cardinals (April 1, 1986).... Signed by Detroit Tigers (April 25, 1986).... Released by Tigers (March 23, 1987).... Signed by San Jose, independent (May 3, 1987).... Sold by San Jose to Oakland Athletics organization (May 12, 1987).... Released by A's organization (October 12, 1987).... Signed by Portland, Minnesota Twins organization (January 4, 1988).... Granted free agency (November 4, 1991).... Re-signed by Twins (December 19, 1991).
STATISTICAL NOTES: Led Texas League with 19 passed balls in 1979.... Led Pacific Coast League with 339 total bases in 1981. ... Led Pacific Coast League catchers with 19 errors in 1981.... Tied for American Association lead in errors by catchers with 13 in 1986.... Led Pacific Coast League with 12 sacrifice flies in 1987.... Led A.L. catchers with 11 errors in 1989.

Year Team (League)	Pos.	G	AB	R	H	2B	3B	HR	RBI	Avg.	SB	PO	A	E	Avg.
1977—Idaho Falls (Pioneer)	C	52	186	28	60	9	3	1	33	.323	4	352	36	13	.968
1978—Quad Cities (Midwest)	C	129	508	80	149	31	2	24	★101	.293	1	430	46	16	.967
1979—El Paso (Texas)	C	132	531	85	167	★37	3	14	90	.315	10	443	66	★29	.946
—California (A.L.)	DH	1	2	0	0	0	0	0	0	.000	0	0	0	0	...
1980—El Paso (Texas)	C	105	400	61	114	23	3	12	66	.285	3	214	30	7	.972
1981—Salt Lake City (PCL)	C-OF-1B	134	549	99	★192	45	9	28	122	.350	0	421	30	†24	.949
—California (A.L.)	OF	4	11	1	3	0	0	0	1	.273	1	5	0	1	.833
1982—Pittsburgh (N.L.)■	OF	20	29	4	8	1	0	2	4	.276	0	10	0	0	1.000
—Portland (Pacific Coast)	OF-3B-C	101	395	71	112	29	8	17	73	.284	3	164	36	8	.962
1983—Pittsburgh (N.L.)	OF-1B	61	131	16	29	4	1	7	20	.221	0	40	0	0	1.000
1984—Pittsburgh (N.L.)	OF-C	46	112	4	29	4	0	2	11	.259	0	57	3	1	.984
1985—St. Louis (N.L.)■	0-3-C-1	43	52	5	13	4	0	0	8	.250	0	15	5	0	1.000
1986—Nashville (Am. Assoc.)■	C-OF-1B	95	317	41	83	11	1	11	45	.262	3	377	55	‡15	.966
—Detroit (A.L.)	OF-1B-C	19	36	2	5	1	0	0	3	.139	0	25	2	1	.964
1987—San Jose (California)■	3B-OF-C	8	29	5	9	0	0	3	8	.310	0	21	12	5	.868
—Tacoma (Pacific Coast)■..	OF-C-P	94	323	41	100	17	0	9	62	.310	1	163	10	5	.972
—Oakland (A.L.)	OF	11	17	1	4	1	0	0	3	.235	0	0	0	0	...
1988—Portland (Pacific Coast)■.	C-3-0-P	46	170	34	60	10	1	13	42	.353	2	181	25	5	.976
—Minnesota (A.L.)	C-3B	60	166	15	49	11	1	3	20	.295	0	208	15	2	.991
1989—Minnesota (A.L.)	C-0-1-3	126	385	43	125	24	0	8	57	.325	2	462	36	†11	.978
1990—Minnesota (A.L.)	C-3B-1B	134	479	61	141	42	3	6	54	.294	3	686	58	11	.985
1991—Minnesota (A.L.)	C-1B	123	441	54	137	28	1	10	69	.311	1	643	33	8	.988
American League totals (8 years)		478	1537	177	464	107	5	27	207	.302	7	2029	144	34	.985
National League totals (4 years)		170	324	29	79	13	1	11	43	.244	0	122	8	1	.992
Major league totals (12 years)		648	1861	206	543	120	6	38	250	.292	7	2151	152	35	.985

CHAMPIONSHIP SERIES RECORD

Year Team (League)	Pos.	G	AB	R	H	2B	3B	HR	RBI	Avg.	SB	PO	A	E	Avg.
1985—St. Louis (N.L.)	PH	1	1	0	0	0	0	0	0	.000	0	0	0	0	...
1991—Minnesota (A.L.)	C	5	18	1	5	2	0	0	1	.278	0	23	1	1	.960
Championship Series totals (2 years)		6	19	1	5	2	0	0	1	.263	0	23	1	1	.960

WORLD SERIES RECORD

Year	Team (League)	Pos.	G	AB	R	H	2B	3B	HR	RBI	Avg.	SB	PO	A	E	Avg.
1985—St. Louis (N.L.)		PH	4	4	0	1	0	0	0	1	.250	0	0	0	0	...
1991—Minnesota (A.L.)		C-PH	7	21	2	8	2	0	0	1	.381	0	33	5	2	.950
World Series totals (2 years)			11	25	2	9	2	0	0	2	.360	0	33	5	2	.950

RECORD AS PITCHER

Year	Team (League)	G	W	L	Pct.	ERA	Sv.	IP	H	R	ER	BB	SO
1987—Tacoma (Pacific Coast)	1	0	0	...	3.00	0	3	3	1	1	0	1
1988—Portland (Pacific Coast)	1	0	0	...	9.00	0	1	2	1	1	2	0

HARRIS, DONALD
OF, RANGERS

PERSONAL: Born November 12, 1967, at Waco, Tex. . . . 6-1/185. . . . Throws right, bats right. . . . Full name: Donald Harris.
HIGH SCHOOL: Jefferson-Moore (Waco, Tex.).
COLLEGE: McLennan Community College (Tex.).
TRANSACTIONS/CAREER NOTES: Selected by Texas Rangers organization in first round (fifth pick overall) of free-agent draft (June 5, 1989).
STATISTICAL NOTES: Led Pioneer League outfielders with 124 total chances and three double plays in 1989.

Year	Team (League)	Pos.	G	AB	R	H	2B	3B	HR	RBI	Avg.	SB	PO	A	E	Avg.
1989—Butte (Pioneer)	OF	65	*264	50	75	7	*8	6	37	.284	14	*115	7	2	.984
1990—Tulsa (Texas)	OF	64	213	16	34	5	1	1	15	.160	7	123	6	8	.942
—Gastonia (S. Atlantic)	OF	58	221	27	46	10	0	3	13	.208	15	104	6	5	.957
1991—Tulsa (Texas)	OF	130	450	47	102	17	8	11	53	.227	9	283	11	9	.970
—Texas (A.L.)	OF	18	8	4	3	0	0	1	2	.375	1	7	0	0	1.000
Major league totals (1 year)		18	8	4	3	0	0	1	2	.375	1	7	0	0	1.000

HARRIS, GENE
P, MARINERS

PERSONAL: Born December 5, 1964, at Sebring, Fla. . . . 5-11/190. . . . Throws right, bats right. . . . Full name: Tyrone Eugene Harris.
HIGH SCHOOL: Okeechobee (Fla.).
COLLEGE: Tulane.
TRANSACTIONS/CAREER NOTES: Selected by Montreal Expos organization in fifth round of free-agent draft (June 2, 1986). . . . Traded by Expos organization with P Randy Johnson and P Brian Holman to Seattle Mariners for P Mark Langston and a player to be named later (May 25, 1989); Indianapolis (Expos organization) acquired P Mike Campbell to complete deal (July 31, 1989). . . . On Seattle disabled list (July 29, 1989-remainder of season). . . . On disqualified list (April 25-June 26, 1991).
STATISTICAL NOTES: Led Southern League with seven complete games in 1988.
MISCELLANEOUS: Appeared in one game as pinch-runner (1989).

Year	Team (League)	G	W	L	Pct.	ERA	Sv.	IP	H	R	ER	BB	SO
1986—Jamestown (New York-Penn) ..	4	0	2	.000	2.21	0	20⅓	15	8	5	11	16
—Burlington (Midwest)	7	4	2	.667	1.35	0	53⅓	37	12	8	15	32
—West Palm Beach (Florida St.) ..	2	0	0	...	4.09	0	11	14	7	5	7	5
1987—West Palm Beach (Florida St.) ..	26	9	7	.563	4.37	0	179	178	101	87	77	121
1988—Jacksonville (Southern)	18	9	5	.643	2.63	0	126⅔	95	43	37	45	103
1989—Montreal (N.L.)	11	1	1	.500	4.95	0	20	16	11	11	10	11
—Indianapolis (Am. Assoc.)	6	2	0	1.000	0.00	2	11	4	0	0	10	9
—Calgary (Pacific Coast)■	5	0	0	...	0.00	2	6	4	0	0	1	4
—Seattle (A.L.)	10	1	4	.200	6.48	1	33⅓	47	27	24	15	14
1990—Calgary (Pacific Coast)	6	3	0	1.000	2.35	2	7⅔	7	2	2	4	9
—Seattle (A.L.)	25	1	2	.333	4.74	0	38	31	25	20	30	43
1991—Seattle (A.L.)	8	0	0	...	4.05	1	13⅓	15	8	6	10	6
—Calgary (Pacific Coast)	25	4	0	1.000	3.34	4	35	37	16	13	11	23
American League totals (3 years)	43	2	6	.250	5.31	2	84⅔	93	60	50	55	63
National League totals (1 year)	11	1	1	.500	4.95	0	20	16	11	11	10	11
Major league totals (3 years)	54	3	7	.300	5.25	2	104⅔	109	71	61	65	74

HARRIS, GREG
P, RED SOX

PERSONAL: Born November 2, 1955, at Lynwood, Calif. . . . 6-0/175. . . . Throws right, bats right. . . . Full name: Greg Allen Harris.
HIGH SCHOOL: Los Alomitos (Calif.).
COLLEGE: Long Beach City College (Calif.).
TRANSACTIONS/CAREER NOTES: Selected by California Angels organization in 10th round of free-agent draft (June 5, 1974). . . . Selected by New York Mets organization in secondary phase of free-agent draft (January 9, 1975). . . . Selected by New York Mets organization in seventh round of free-agent draft (January 7, 1976). . . . Signed as free agent by New York Mets organization (September 17, 1976). . . . Traded by Mets with C Alex Trevino and P Jim Kern to Cincinnati Reds for OF George Foster (February 10, 1982). . . . Claimed on waivers by Montreal Expos (September 27, 1983). . . . Traded by Expos to San Diego Padres for IF Al Newman (July 20, 1984). . . . Sold by Padres to Texas Rangers (February 13, 1985). . . . Released by Rangers (December 21, 1987). . . . Signed by Cleveland Indians (January 19, 1988). . . . Released by Indians (March 24, 1988). . . . Signed by Maine, Philadelphia Phillies organization (April 1, 1988). . . . Granted free agency (November 4, 1988). . . . Re-

signed by Phillies (December 7, 1988).... Claimed on waivers by Boston Red Sox (August 7, 1989).... Granted free agency (November 13, 1989).... Re-signed by Red Sox (February 15, 1990).

Year	Team (League)	G	W	L	Pct.	ERA	Sv.	IP	H	R	ER	BB	SO
1977 —	Jackson (Texas)	30	3	6	.333	5.42	0	83	96	63	50	36	56
1978 —	Lynchburg (Carolina)	21	8	9	.471	2.16	0	154	114	52	37	74	102
—	Jackson (Texas)	6	2	3	.400	3.00	0	33	24	13	11	10	18
1979 —	Jackson (Texas)	25	9	11	.450	*2.26	0	163	125	58	41	81	89
1980 —	Tidewater (International)	39	2	9	.182	2.70	2	110	99	45	33	40	92
1981 —	Tidewater (International)	7	4	0	1.000	2.06	0	48	37	14	11	16	26
—	New York (N.L.)	16	3	5	.375	4.43	1	69	65	36	34	28	54
1982 —	Indianapolis (Am. Assoc.)■	8	4	1	.800	3.00	0	48	27	18	16	24	44
—	Cincinnati (N.L.)	34	2	6	.250	4.83	1	91⅓	96	56	49	37	67
1983 —	Indianapolis (Am. Assoc.)	28	9	12	.429	4.14	0	152⅓	155	83	70	66	*146
—	Cincinnati (N.L.)	1	0	0	...	27.00	0	1	2	3	3	3	1
1984 —	Montreal-San Diego (N.L.)■	34	2	2	.500	2.48	3	54⅓	38	18	15	25	45
—	Indianapolis (Am. Assoc.)	14	4	4	.500	4.43	1	44⅔	44	27	22	29	45
1985 —	Texas (A.L.)	58	5	4	.556	2.47	11	113	74	35	31	43	111
1986 —	Texas (A.L.)	73	10	8	.556	2.83	20	111⅓	103	40	35	42	95
1987 —	Texas (A.L.)	42	5	10	.333	4.86	0	140⅔	157	92	76	56	106
1988 —	Maine (International)■	3	0	1	1.000	1.93	1	4⅔	5	3	1	1	5
—	Philadelphia (N.L.)	66	4	6	.400	2.36	1	107	80	34	28	52	71
1989 —	Philadelphia (N.L.)	44	2	2	.500	3.58	1	75⅓	64	34	30	43	51
—	Boston (A.L.)■	15	2	2	.500	2.57	0	28	21	12	8	15	25
1990 —	Boston (A.L.)	34	13	9	.591	4.00	0	184⅓	186	90	82	77	117
1991 —	Boston (A.L.)	53	11	12	.478	3.85	2	173	157	79	74	69	127
American League totals (6 years)		275	46	45	.505	3.67	33	750⅓	698	348	306	302	581
National League totals (6 years)		195	13	21	.382	3.60	7	398	345	181	159	188	289
Major league totals (11 years)		470	59	66	.472	3.64	40	1148⅓	1043	529	465	490	870

CHAMPIONSHIP SERIES RECORD

CHAMPIONSHIP SERIES NOTES: Shares single-game record for most earned runs allowed—7 (October 2, 1984).... Shares record for most earned runs in one inning—6; most hits in one inning—6 (October 2, 1984, fifth inning).

Year	Team (League)	G	W	L	Pct.	ERA	Sv.	IP	H	R	ER	BB	SO
1984 —	San Diego (N.L.)	1	0	0	...	31.50	0	2	9	8	7	3	2
1990 —	Boston (A.L.)	1	0	1	.000	27.00	0	⅓	3	1	1	0	0
Championship Series totals (2 years)		2	0	1	.000	30.86	0	2⅓	12	9	8	3	2

HARRIS, GREG
P, PADRES

PERSONAL: Born December 1, 1963, at Greensboro, N.C.... 6-2/195.... Throws right, bats right.... Full name: Gregory Wade Harris.
HIGH SCHOOL: Jordan Matthews (Siler City, N.C.).
COLLEGE: Elon College (N.C.).
TRANSACTIONS/CAREER NOTES: Selected by San Diego Padres organization in 10th round of free-agent draft (June 3, 1985).... On San Diego disabled list (April 23-July 4, 1991); included rehabilitation disability assignment to Las Vegas (June 12-30, 1991).
STATISTICAL NOTES: Pitched 7-0 no-hit victory against Midland (August 26, 1987).... Led Texas League with seven complete games, 32 home runs allowed and six balks and tied for lead with two shutouts in 1987.

Year	Team (League)	G	W	L	Pct.	ERA	Sv.	IP	H	R	ER	BB	SO
1985 —	Spokane (Northwest)	13	5	4	.556	3.40	0	87⅓	80	36	33	36	90
1986 —	Charleston, S.C. (S. Atlantic)	27	13	7	.650	2.63	0	*191⅓	176	69	56	54	176
1987 —	Wichita (Texas)	27	12	11	.522	4.28	0	174⅓	205	103	83	49	170
1988 —	Las Vegas (Pacific Coast)	26	9	5	.643	4.11	0	159⅔	160	84	73	65	147
—	San Diego (N.L.)	3	2	0	1.000	1.50	0	18	13	3	3	3	15
1989 —	San Diego (N.L.)	56	8	9	.471	2.60	6	135	106	43	39	52	106
1990 —	San Diego (N.L.)	73	8	8	.500	2.30	9	117⅓	92	35	30	49	97
1991 —	San Diego (N.L.)	20	9	5	.643	2.23	0	133	116	42	33	27	95
—	Las Vegas (Pacific Coast)	4	1	2	.333	7.40	0	20⅔	24	20	17	8	16
Major league totals (4 years)		152	27	22	.551	2.34	15	403⅓	327	123	105	131	313

HARRIS, LENNY
3B, DODGERS

PERSONAL: Born October 28, 1964, at Miami.... 5-10/205.... Throws right, bats left.... Full name: Leonard Anthony Harris.
HIGH SCHOOL: Jackson (Miami).
COLLEGE: Miami-Dade (North) Community College.
TRANSACTIONS/CAREER NOTES: Selected by Cincinnati Reds organization in fifth round of free-agent draft (June 6, 1983).... Loaned by Reds organization to Glens Falls, Detroit Tigers organization (May 6, 1988); returned to Reds organization (June 26, 1988).... Traded by Reds with OF Kal Daniels to Los Angeles Dodgers for P Tim Leary and SS Mariano Duncan (July 18, 1989).
STATISTICAL NOTES: Led Florida State League third basemen with 34 double plays in 1985.... Led Eastern League third basemen with 116 putouts, 28 errors and 360 total chances in 1986.... Led American Association in caught stealing with 22 in 1988.... Led American Association second basemen with 23 errors in 1988.

Year	Team (League)	Pos.	G	AB	R	H	2B	3B	HR	RBI	Avg.	SB	PO	A	E	Avg.
1983 —Billings (Pioneer)		3B	56	224	37	63	8	1	1	26	.281	7	34	95	22	.854
1984 —Cedar Rapids (Midwest) ...		3B	132	468	52	115	15	3	6	53	.246	31	111	204	★34	.903
1985 —Tampa (Florida State)		3B	132	499	66	129	11	8	3	51	.259	15	89 ★277	★35		.913
1986 —Vermont (Eastern)	3B-SS		119	450	68	114	17	2	10	52	.253	36	†119	220	†28	.924
1987 —Nashville (Am. Assoc.)	SS-3B		120	403	45	100	12	3	2	31	.248	30	124	210	34	.908
1988 —Nashville (Am. Assoc.)	2B-SS-3B		107	422	46	117	20	2	0	35	.277	★45	203	247	†25	.947
—Glens Falls (Eastern)■		2B	17	65	9	22	5	1	1	7	.338	6	40	49	5	.947
—Cincinnati (N.L.)■		3B-2B	16	43	7	16	1	0	0	8	.372	4	14	33	1	.979
1989 —Nashville (Am. Assoc.)		2B	8	34	6	9	2	0	3	6	.265	0	23	20	0	1.000
—Cincinnati-L.A. (N.L.)■	2-3-0-S		115	335	36	79	10	1	3	26	.236	14	147	168	15	.955
1990 —Los Angeles (N.L.)	3-2-0-S		137	431	61	131	16	4	2	29	.304	15	140	205	11	.969
1991 —Los Angeles (N.L.)	3-2-S-0		145	429	59	123	16	1	3	38	.287	12	125	250	20	.949
Major league totals (4 years)			413	1238	163	349	43	6	8	101	.282	45	426	656	47	.958

HARRIS, REGGIE
P, ATHLETICS

PERSONAL: Born August 12, 1968, at Waynesboro, Va. . . . 6-1/190. . . . Throws right, bats right. . . . Full name: Reginald Allen Harris.
HIGH SCHOOL: Waynesboro (Va.).
TRANSACTIONS/CAREER NOTES: Selected by Boston Red Sox organization in first round (26th pick overall) of free-agent draft (June 2, 1987). . . . Drafted by Oakland Athletics (December 4, 1989). . . . On Oakland disabled list (March 29-July 3, 1990); included rehabilitation disability assignment to Huntsville (May 26-June 24, 1990). . . . On Tacoma disabled list (June 17-August 4, 1991).

Year	Team (League)	G	W	L	Pct.	ERA	Sv.	IP	H	R	ER	BB	SO
1987 —Elmira (New York-Penn)		9	2	3	.400	5.01	0	46⅔	50	29	26	22	25
1988 —Lynchburg (Carolina)		17	1	8	.111	7.45	0	64	86	60	53	34	48
—Elmira (New York-Penn)		10	3	6	.333	5.30	0	54⅓	56	37	32	28	46
1989 —Winter Haven (Florida State) ...		29	10	13	.435	3.99	0	153⅓	144	81	68	77	85
1990 —Huntsville (Southern)■		5	0	2	.000	3.03	0	29⅔	26	12	10	16	34
—Oakland (A.L.)		16	1	0	1.000	3.48	0	41⅓	25	16	16	21	31
1991 —Tacoma (Pacific Coast)		16	5	4	.556	4.99	0	83	83	55	46	58	72
—Oakland (A.L.)		2	0	0	. . .	12.00	0	3	5	4	4	3	2
Major league totals (2 years)		18	1	0	1.000	4.06	0	44⅓	30	20	20	24	33

HARRISON, BRIAN
P, WHITE SOX

PERSONAL: Born November 26, 1966, at Bluefield, W.Va. . . . 6-1/180. . . . Throws left, bats left. . . . Full name: Brian Lee Harrison.
COLLEGE: Ventura Junior College (Calif.).
TRANSACTIONS/CAREER NOTES: Selected by San Francisco Giants organization in 26th round of free-agent draft (June 3, 1985). . . . Selected by San Diego Padres organization in secondary phase of free-agent draft (January 14, 1986). . . . Loaned by Padres organization to Tri-Cities, co-op (July 16, 1986); returned to Padres organization (September 1, 1986). . . . Traded by Padres organization to Montreal Expos organization for P John Costello (November 9, 1990). . . . Drafted by Chicago White Sox (December 3, 1990). . . . On disabled list (March 24, 1991-entire of season).
STATISTICAL NOTES: Tied for Northwest League lead with three balks in 1986.

Year	Team (League)	G	W	L	Pct.	ERA	Sv.	IP	H	R	ER	BB	SO
1986 —Spokane-Tri-Cities (N'West)■..		22	3	5	.375	6.20	0	61	66	56	42	60	64
1987 —Charleston, S.C. (S. Atlantic)■ ..		37	4	0	1.000	2.72	4	72⅔	64	31	22	30	87
—Reno (California)		1	0	0	. . .	7.36	0	3⅔	6	5	3	5	2
1988 —Riverside (California)		21	5	8	.385	4.16	0	101⅔	92	61	47	60	95
1989 —Riverside (California)		42	2	7	.222	4.18	10	71	69	42	33	43	81
1990 —Riverside (California)		37	5	2	.714	1.19	18	45⅓	31	9	6	20	55
1991 —■						Did not play							

HARTLEY, MIKE
P, PHILLIES

PERSONAL: Born August 31, 1961, at Hawthorne, Calif. . . . 6-1/197. . . . Throws right, bats right. . . . Full name: Michael Edward Hartley.
HIGH SCHOOL: El Cajon Valley (Calif.).
COLLEGE: Grossmont College (Calif.).
TRANSACTIONS/CAREER NOTES: Signed as free agent by St. Louis Cardinals organization (November 27, 1981). . . . Drafted by Los Angeles Dodgers organization (December 9, 1986). . . . Traded by Dodgers with OF Braulio Castillo to Philadelphia Phillies for P Roger McDowell (July 31, 1991).

Year	Team (League)	G	W	L	Pct.	ERA	Sv.	IP	H	R	ER	BB	SO
1982 —Johnson City (Appalachian)		8	3	1	.750	2.79	0	29	32	12	9	8	13
1983 —St. Petersburg (Florida State) ..		9	1	3	.250	3.34	0	29⅔	25	14	11	24	18
—Macon (South Atlantic)		7	2	3	.400	10.24	0	29	36	36	33	30	12
—Erie (New York-Penn)		7	1	3	.250	6.75	0	32	36	27	24	31	25
1984 —St. Petersburg (Florida State) ..		31	8	14	.364	4.20	0	139⅓	142	81	65	84	88
1985 —Springfield (Midwest)		33	2	7	.222	5.12	0	114⅓	119	77	65	62	100
1986 —Springfield (Midwest)		8	0	0	. . .	9.60	1	15	22	17	16	14	10
—Savannah (South Atlantic)		39	5	7	.417	2.89	8	56	38	31	18	37	55

Year	Team (League)	G	W	L	Pct.	ERA	Sv.	IP	H	R	ER	BB	SO
1987	—Bakersfield (California)■	33	5	4	.556	2.57	15	56	44	19	16	24	72
	—San Antonio (Texas)	25	3	4	.429	1.32	3	41	21	8	6	18	37
	—Albuquerque (Pacific Coast)	2	0	1	.000	6.75	0	2⅔	5	3	2	3	3
1988	—San Antonio (Texas)	30	5	1	.833	0.80	9	45	25	5	4	18	57
	—Albuquerque (Pacific Coast)	18	2	2	.500	4.35	3	20⅔	22	11	10	12	16
1989	—Albuquerque (Pacific Coast)	58	7	4	.636	2.79	18	77⅓	53	31	24	34	76
	—Los Angeles (N.L.)	5	0	1	.000	1.50	0	6	2	1	1	0	4
1990	—Los Angeles (N.L.)	32	6	3	.667	2.95	1	79⅓	58	32	26	30	76
	—Albuquerque (Pacific Coast)	3	0	0	...	0.00	2	3	3	0	0	2	3
1991	—Los Angeles-Phil. (N.L.)■	58	4	1	.800	4.21	2	83⅓	74	40	39	47	63
	Major league totals (3 years)	95	10	5	.667	3.52	3	168⅔	134	73	66	77	143

HARTSOCK, JEFF
P, CUBS

PERSONAL: Born November 19, 1966, at Hamilton, O. . . . 6-0/190. . . . Throws right, bats right. . . . Full name: Jeffrey Roger Hartsock.
COLLEGE: North Carolina State.
TRANSACTIONS/CAREER NOTES: Selected by Los Angeles Dodgers in seventh round of free-agent draft (June 1, 1988). . . . Traded by Dodgers to Chicago Cubs organization for P Steve Wilson (September 6, 1991).

Year	Team (League)	G	W	L	Pct.	ERA	Sv.	IP	H	R	ER	BB	SO
1988	—Great Falls (Pioneer)	14	7	2	.778	2.67	0	81	62	30	24	26	★108
1989	—Bakersfield (California)	26	12	5	.706	2.63	0	164	123	64	48	62	146
1990	—San Antonio (Texas)	16	6	4	.600	3.93	0	94	88	42	41	42	68
	—Albuquerque (Pacific Coast)	11	3	3	.500	6.22	0	46⅓	62	38	32	30	33
1991	—Albuquerque (Pacific Coast)	29	12	6	.667	3.80	0	154	153	80	65	78	★123

HARVEY, BRYAN
P, ANGELS

PERSONAL: Born June 2, 1963, at Chattanooga, Tenn. . . . 6-2/212. . . . Throws right, bats right. . . . Full name: Bryan Stanley Harvey.
HIGH SCHOOL: Bandys (Catawba, N.C.).
COLLEGE: UNC Charlotte.
TRANSACTIONS/CAREER NOTES: Signed as free agent by California Angels organization (August 20, 1984). . . . On disabled list (April 12-22, 1985).
RECORDS/HONORS: Named A.L. Rookie Pitcher of the Year by THE SPORTING NEWS (1988). . . . Named A.L. co-Fireman of the Year by THE SPORTING NEWS (1991).

Year	Team (League)	G	W	L	Pct.	ERA	Sv.	IP	H	R	ER	BB	SO
1985	—Quad City (Midwest)	30	5	6	.455	3.53	4	81⅔	66	37	32	37	111
1986	—Palm Springs (California)	43	3	4	.429	2.68	15	57	38	24	17	38	68
1987	—Midland (Texas)	43	2	2	.500	2.04	20	53	40	14	12	28	78
	—California (A.L.)	3	0	0	...	0.00	0	5	6	0	0	2	3
1988	—Edmonton (Pacific Coast)	5	0	0	...	3.18	2	5⅔	7	2	2	4	10
	—California (A.L.)	50	7	5	.583	2.13	17	76	59	22	18	20	67
1989	—California (A.L.)	51	3	3	.500	3.44	25	55	36	21	21	41	78
1990	—California (A.L.)	54	4	4	.500	3.22	25	64⅓	45	24	23	35	82
1991	—California (A.L.)	67	2	4	.333	1.60	★46	78⅔	51	20	14	17	101
	Major league totals (5 years)	225	16	16	.500	2.45	113	279	197	87	76	115	331

ALL-STAR GAME RECORD

Year	League	W	L	Pct.	ERA	Sv.	IP	H	R	ER	BB	SO
1991	—American						Did not play					

HASELMAN, BILL
C, RANGERS

PERSONAL: Born May 25, 1966, at Long Branch, N.J. . . . 6-3/205. . . . Throws right, bats right. . . . Full name: William Joseph Haselman.
HIGH SCHOOL: Saratoga (Calif.).
COLLEGE: UCLA.
TRANSACTIONS/CAREER NOTES: Selected by Texas Rangers organization in first round (23rd pick overall) of free-agent draft (June 2, 1987).
STATISTICAL NOTES: Led Texas League with 12 passed balls in 1989. . . . Led Texas League catchers with 676 putouts, 90 assists, 20 errors, 786 total chances and 20 passed balls in 1990. . . . Led American Association catchers with 673 putouts and 751 total chances in 1991.

Year	Team (League)	Pos.	G	AB	R	H	2B	3B	HR	RBI	Avg.	SB	PO	A	E	Avg.
1987	—Gastonia (S. Atlantic)	C	61	235	35	72	13	1	8	33	.306	1	26	2	2	.933
1988	—Port Charlotte (Fla. St.)	C	122	453	56	111	17	2	10	54	.245	8	249	30	6	.979
1989	—Tulsa (Texas)	C	107	352	38	95	17	2	7	36	.270	5	508	63	9	.984
1990	—Tulsa (Texas)	C-1-0-3	120	430	68	137	36	2	18	80	.319	3	†722	†93	†20	.976
	—Texas (A.L.)	C	7	13	0	2	0	0	0	3	.154	0	8	0	0	1.000
1991	—Oklahoma City (A.A.)	C-0-1-3	126	442	57	113	22	2	9	60	.256	10	†706	71	11	.986
	Major league totals (1 year)		7	13	0	2	0	0	0	3	.154	0	8	0	0	1.000

HASSEY, RON
C

PERSONAL: Born February 27, 1953, at Tucson, Ariz. . . . 6-2/195. . . . Throws right, bats left. . . . Full name: Ronald William Hassey. . . . Son of Bill Hassey, minor league outfielder (1949-52).
COLLEGE: Arizona (degree in public administration).
TRANSACTIONS/CAREER NOTES: Selected by Cincinnati Reds organization in 23rd round of free-agent draft (June 6, 1972). . . . Selected by Kansas City Royals organization in 22nd round of free-agent draft (June 4, 1975). . . . Selected by Cleveland Indians organization in 18th round of free-agent draft (June 8, 1976). . . . Traded by Indians with P Rick Sutcliffe and P George Frazier to Chicago Cubs for OF Mel Hall, OF Joe Carter, P Don Schulze and P Darryl Banks (June 13, 1984). . . . On Chicago disabled list (July 5-September 1, 1984). . . . Traded by Cubs with OF Henry Cotto, P Rich Bordi and P Porfi Altamirano to New York Yankees for P Ray Fontenot and OF Brian Dayett (December 4, 1984). . . . Traded by Yankees with P Joe Cowley to Chicago White Sox for P Britt Burns, SS Mike Soper and OF Glen Braxton (December 12, 1985). . . . Traded by White Sox with C Chris Alvarez, P Eric Schmidt and OF Matt Winters to Yankees for P Neil Allen, C Scott Bradley, OF Glen Braxton and cash (February 13, 1986). . . . Traded by Yankees with SS Carlos Martinez and a player to be named later to White Sox for OF-DH Ron Kittle, IF Wayne Tolleson and C Joel Skinner (July 30, 1986); Yankees traded C Bill Lindsey to White Sox organization to complete deal (December 24, 1986). . . . On Chicago disabled list (June 1-August 7, 1987); included rehabilitation disability assignment to Hawaii (June 28-August 2, 1987). . . . Granted free agency (November 30, 1987). . . . Signed by Oakland Athletics (December 9, 1987). . . . Granted free agency (November 5, 1990). . . . Signed by Montreal Expos organization (February 15, 1991). . . . Granted free agency (October 28, 1991).
STATISTICAL NOTES: Led A.L. with 15 passed balls in 1985.

Year	Team (League)	Pos.	G	AB	R	H	2B	3B	HR	RBI	Avg.	SB	PO	A	E	Avg.
1976	—San Jose (California)	C-3B	22	62	7	19	4	0	1	7	.306	0	55	2	2	.966
	—Williamsport (Eastern)	C	21	68	6	19	3	0	0	8	.279	0	63	10	4	.948
1977	—Toledo (International)	C-3-1-0	129	446	50	132	21	1	10	57	.296	7	484	82	21	.964
1978	—Portland (Pacific Coast)	C-3B	72	235	42	76	12	1	12	52	.323	2	312	32	7	.980
	—Cleveland (A.L.)	C	25	74	5	15	0	0	2	9	.203	2	130	15	1	.993
1979	—Tacoma (Pacific Coast)	C-3B	44	157	25	53	10	0	3	27	.338	2	282	44	2	.994
	—Cleveland (A.L.)	C-1B	75	223	20	64	14	0	4	32	.287	1	368	29	3	.993
1980	—Cleveland (A.L.)	C-1B	130	390	43	124	18	4	8	65	.318	0	564	52	4	.994
1981	—Cleveland (A.L.)	C-1B	61	190	8	44	4	0	1	25	.232	0	327	44	3	.992
1982	—Cleveland (A.L.)	C-1B	113	323	33	81	18	0	5	34	.251	3	566	38	4	.993
1983	—Cleveland (A.L.)	C	117	341	48	92	21	0	6	42	.270	2	514	43	3	.995
1984	—Cleveland (A.L.)	C-1B	48	149	11	38	5	1	0	19	.255	1	210	16	1	.996
	—Chicago (N.L.)■	C-1B	19	33	5	11	0	0	2	5	.333	1	53	2	1	.982
1985	—New York (A.L.)	C-1B	92	267	31	79	16	1	13	42	.296	0	420	20	7	.984
1986	—New York-Chi. (A.L.)■	C	113	341	45	110	25	1	9	49	.323	1	318	14	4	.988
1987	—Chicago (A.L.)	C	49	145	15	31	9	0	3	12	.214	0	114	12	0	1.000
	—Hawaii (Pacific Coast)	DH	6	21	3	3	2	0	0	4	.143	0	0	0	0	. . .
1988	—Oakland (A.L.)■	C	107	323	32	83	15	0	7	45	.257	2	465	31	3	.994
1989	—Oakland (A.L.)	C-1B	97	268	29	61	12	0	5	23	.228	1	425	25	4	.991
1990	—Oakland (A.L.)	C-1B	94	254	18	54	7	0	5	22	.213	0	312	18	1	.997
1991	—Montreal (N.L.)■	C	52	119	5	27	8	0	1	14	.227	1	172	13	2	.989
American League totals (13 years)			1121	3288	338	876	164	7	68	419	.266	13	4733	357	38	.993
National League totals (2 years)			71	152	10	38	8	0	3	19	.250	1	225	15	3	.988
Major league totals (14 years)			1192	3440	348	914	172	7	71	438	.266	14	4958	372	41	.992

CHAMPIONSHIP SERIES RECORD

Year	Team (League)	Pos.	G	AB	R	H	2B	3B	HR	RBI	Avg.	SB	PO	A	E	Avg.
1988	—Oakland (A.L.)	C	4	8	2	4	1	0	1	3	.500	0	13	0	0	1.000
1989	—Oakland (A.L.)	C	2	6	0	1	0	0	0	1	.167	0	10	0	0	1.000
1990	—Oakland (A.L.)	C-PH	2	3	0	1	0	0	0	0	.333	0	6	0	0	1.000
Championship Series totals (3 years)			8	17	2	6	1	0	1	4	.353	0	29	0	0	1.000

WORLD SERIES RECORD

Year	Team (League)	Pos.	G	AB	R	H	2B	3B	HR	RBI	Avg.	SB	PO	A	E	Avg.
1988	—Oakland (A.L.)	C-PH	5	8	0	2	0	0	0	1	.250	0	28	1	0	1.000
1989	—Oakland (A.L.)						Did not play									
1990	—Oakland (A.L.)	PH-C	3	6	0	2	0	0	0	1	.333	0	2	0	1	.667
World Series totals (2 years)			8	14	0	4	0	0	0	2	.286	0	30	1	1	.969

HATCHER, BILLY
OF, REDS

PERSONAL: Born October 4, 1960, at Williams, Ariz. . . . 5-10/190. . . . Throws right, bats right. . . . Full name: William Augustus Hatcher.
HIGH SCHOOL: Williams (Ariz.).
COLLEGE: Yavapai Community College (Ariz.).
TRANSACTIONS/CAREER NOTES: Selected by Chicago Cubs organization in sixth round of free-agent draft (January 13, 1981). . . . On Chicago disabled list (August 19-September 3, 1985). . . . Traded by Cubs with a player to be named later to Houston Astros for OF Jerry Mumphrey (December 16, 1985); Astros organization acquired P Steve Engel to complete deal (July 24, 1986). . . . On disabled list (June 28-July 13, 1986 and July 7-22, 1987). . . . Traded by Astros to Pittsburgh Pirates for OF Glenn Wilson (August 18, 1989). . . . Traded by Pirates to Cincinnati Reds for P Mike Roesler and IF Jeff Richardson (April 3, 1990).
RECORDS/HONORS: Shares major league single-game record for most doubles—4 (August 21, 1990).
STATISTICAL NOTES: Led New York-Pennsylvania League in being hit by pitch with eight in 1981. . . . Led American Association in being hit by pitch with nine in 1984. . . . Tied for N.L. lead in double plays by outfielders with six in 1987.

Year	Team (League)	Pos.	G	AB	R	H	2B	3B	HR	RBI	Avg.	SB	PO	A	E	Avg.
								BATTING						FIELDING		
1981—Geneva (N.Y.-Penn)	OF	•75	289	57	81	15	3	4	40	.280	13	138	7	11	.929
1982—Salinas (California)	OF	138	549	92	171	18	8	8	59	.311	84	235	10	12	.953
1983—Midland (Texas)	OF	135	545	★132	163	33	11	10	80	.299	56	286	17	•13	.959
1984—Iowa (American Assoc.)	OF	150	595	96	164	27	18	9	59	.276	56	303	15	7	.978
—Chicago (N.L.)	OF	8	9	1	1	0	0	0	0	.111	2	2	1	0	1.000
1985—Iowa (American Assoc.)	OF	67	279	39	78	14	5	5	19	.280	17	157	4	4	.976
—Chicago (N.L.)	OF	53	163	24	40	12	1	2	10	.245	2	77	2	1	.988
1986—Houston (N.L.)■	OF	127	419	55	108	15	4	6	36	.258	38	226	7	4	.983
1987—Houston (N.L.)	OF	141	564	96	167	28	3	11	63	.296	53	276	16	4	.986
1988—Houston (N.L.)	OF	145	530	79	142	25	4	7	52	.268	32	280	7	5	.983
1989—Houston-Pitts. (N.L.)■	OF	135	481	59	111	19	3	4	51	.231	24	250	1	2	.992
1990—Cincinnati (N.L.)■	OF	139	504	68	139	28	5	5	25	.276	30	308	10	1	★.997
1991—Cincinnati (N.L.)	OF	138	442	45	116	25	3	4	41	.262	11	248	4	5	.981
Major league totals (8 years)		886	3112	427	824	152	23	39	278	.265	192	1667	48	22	.987

CHAMPIONSHIP SERIES RECORD

CHAMPIONSHIP SERIES NOTES: Shares single-game record for most at-bats—7 (October 15, 1986, 16 innings).

Year	Team (League)	Pos.	G	AB	R	H	2B	3B	HR	RBI	Avg.	SB	PO	A	E	Avg.
								BATTING						FIELDING		
1986—Houston (N.L.)	OF	6	25	4	7	0	0	1	2	.280	3	11	0	1	.917
1990—Cincinnati (N.L.)	OF	4	15	2	5	1	0	1	2	.333	0	5	1	0	1.000
Championship Series totals (2 years)		10	40	6	12	1	0	2	4	.300	3	16	1	1	.944

WORLD SERIES RECORD

WORLD SERIES NOTES: Holds single-series record for highest batting average—.750 (1990); most consecutive hits—7 (October 16 [3], 17 [4], 1990).... Shares record for most at-bats in one inning—2 (October 19, 1990, third inning).

Year	Team (League)	Pos.	G	AB	R	H	2B	3B	HR	RBI	Avg.	SB	PO	A	E	Avg.
								BATTING						FIELDING		
1990—Cincinnati (N.L.)	OF	4	12	6	9	4	1	0	2	.750	0	11	0	0	1.000

HAWKINS, ANDY
P

PERSONAL: Born January 21, 1960, at Waco, Tex. ... 6-3/223. ... Throws right, bats right. ... Full name: Melton Andrew Hawkins.
TRANSACTIONS/CAREER NOTES: Selected by San Diego Padres organization in first round (fifth pick overall) of free-agent draft (June 6, 1978). ... On disabled list (July 29-September 1, 1987). ... Granted free agency (November 4, 1988). ... Signed by New York Yankees (December 8, 1988). ... Released by Yankees (May 9, 1991). ... Signed by Oakland Athletics (May 18, 1991). ... Released by A's (August 20, 1991).
STATISTICAL NOTES: Led Northwest League with four balks in 1978. ... Led Texas League pitchers with 14 complete games and tied for lead with 27 games started in 1981. ... Led Pacific Coast League with six shutouts in 1982. ... Pitched no-hit game against Chicago White Sox in which he completed eight innings but lost, 4-0 (July 1, 1990).

Year	Team (League)	G	W	L	Pct.	ERA	Sv.	IP	H	R	ER	BB	SO
1978—Walla Walla (Northwest)	14	8	3	.727	2.12	0	102	95	52	24	45	73
1979—Reno (California)	27	8	13	.381	5.60	0	188	★232	143	★117	97	130
1980—Reno (California)	26	13	10	.565	4.26	0	171	183	108	81	79	124
1981—Amarillo (Texas)	27	11	10	.524	4.19	0	200	★209	100	★93	48	144
1982—Hawaii (Pacific Coast)	18	9	7	.563	2.17	0	132⅔	108	49	32	47	91
—San Diego (N.L.)	15	2	5	.286	4.10	0	63⅔	66	33	29	27	25
1983—Las Vegas (Pacific Coast)	14	6	4	.600	6.43	0	85⅓	110	67	61	27	50
—San Diego (N.L.)	21	5	7	.417	2.93	0	119⅔	106	50	39	48	59
1984—San Diego (N.L.)	36	8	9	.471	4.68	0	146	143	90	76	72	77
1985—San Diego (N.L.)	33	18	8	.692	3.15	0	228⅔	229	88	80	65	69
1986—San Diego (N.L.)	37	10	8	.556	4.30	0	209⅓	218	111	100	75	117
1987—San Diego (N.L.)	24	3	10	.231	5.05	0	117⅔	131	71	66	49	51
1988—San Diego (N.L.)	33	14	11	.560	3.35	0	217⅔	196	88	81	76	91
1989—New York (A.L.)■	34	15	15	.500	4.80	0	208⅓	238	★127	•111	76	98
1990—New York (A.L.)	28	5	12	.294	5.37	0	157⅔	156	101	94	82	74
1991—New York-Oakland (A.L.)■	19	4	6	.400	5.52	0	89⅔	91	56	55	42	45
American League totals (3 years)	81	24	33	.421	5.14	0	455⅔	485	284	260	200	217
National League totals (7 years)	199	60	58	.508	3.84	0	1102⅔	1089	531	471	412	489
Major league totals (10 years)	280	84	91	.480	4.22	0	1558⅓	1574	815	731	612	706

CHAMPIONSHIP SERIES RECORD

Year	Team (League)	G	W	L	Pct.	ERA	Sv.	IP	H	R	ER	BB	SO
1984—San Diego (N.L.)	3	0	0	...	0.00	0	3⅔	0	0	0	2	1

WORLD SERIES RECORD

Year	Team (League)	G	W	L	Pct.	ERA	Sv.	IP	H	R	ER	BB	SO
1984—San Diego (N.L.)	3	1	1	.500	0.75	0	12	4	1	1	6	4

HAYES, CHARLIE
3B, PHILLIES

PERSONAL: Born May 29, 1965, at Hattiesburg, Miss. ... 6-0/210. ... Throws right, bats right. ... Full name: Charles Dewayne Hayes.
HIGH SCHOOL: Forrest County Agricultural (Brooklyn, Miss.).
TRANSACTIONS/CAREER NOTES: Selected by San Francisco Giants organization in fourth

round of free-agent draft (June 6, 1983).... On disabled list (July 20, 1983-remainder of season).... Traded by Giants with P Dennis Cook and P Terry Mulholland to Philadelphia Phillies for P Steve Bedrosian and a player to be named later (June 18, 1989); Giants organization acquired IF Rick Parker to complete deal (August 7, 1989).

STATISTICAL NOTES: Led Texas League third basemen with 27 double plays in 1986.... Led Texas League third basemen with 334 total chances in 1987.... Led Pacific Coast League in grounding into double plays with 19 in 1988.... Led N.L. third basemen with 324 assists and tied for lead with 465 total chances in 1990.

Year	Team (League)	Pos.	G	AB	R	H	2B	3B	HR	RBI	Avg.	SB	PO	A	E	Avg.
1983—Great Falls (Pioneer)	3B-OF	34	111	9	29	4	2	0	9	.261	1	13	32	9	.833
1984—Clinton (Midwest)	3B	116	392	41	96	17	2	2	51	.245	4	68	216	28	.910
1985—Fresno (California)	3B	131	467	73	132	17	2	4	68	.283	7	*100	233	18	*.949
1986—Shreveport (Texas)	3B	121	434	52	107	23	2	5	45	.247	1	89	*259	25	.933
1987—Shreveport (Texas)	3B	128	487	66	148	33	3	14	75	.304	5	*100	*212	22	*.934
1988—Phoenix (Pacific Coast)	OF-3B	131	492	71	151	26	4	7	71	.307	4	206	100	23	.930
—San Francisco (N.L.)	OF-3B	7	11	0	1	0	0	0	0	.091	0	5	0	0	1.000
1989—Phoenix (Pacific Coast)	IF-OF	61	229	25	65	15	1	7	27	.284	5	76	76	8	.950
—San Fran.-Phil. (N.L.)■	3B	87	304	26	78	15	1	8	43	.257	3	51	174	22	.911
—Scranton/W.B. (Int'l)	3B	7	27	4	11	3	1	1	3	.407	0	8	8	0	1.000
1990—Philadelphia (N.L.)	3B-1B-2B	152	561	56	145	20	0	10	57	.258	4	151	†329	20	.960
1991—Philadelphia (N.L.)	3B-SS	142	460	34	106	23	1	12	53	.230	3	88	240	15	.956
Major league totals (4 years)		388	1336	116	330	58	2	30	153	.247	10	295	743	57	.948

HAYES, VON

OF, ANGELS

PERSONAL: Born August 31, 1958, at Stockton, Calif.... 6-5/188.... Throws right, bats left.... Full name: Von Francis Hayes.
HIGH SCHOOL: St. Mary's (Stockton, Calif.).
COLLEGE: St. Mary's (Calif.).

TRANSACTIONS/CAREER NOTES: Selected by Cleveland Indians organization in seventh round of free-agent draft (June 5, 1979). ... Traded by Indians to Philadelphia Phillies for 2B Baseman Manny Trillo, OF George Vukovich, IF Julio Franco, P Jay Baller and C Jerry Willard (December 9, 1982).... On disabled list (March 27-April 12, 1983 and July 15-September 2, 1988).... On Philadelphia disabled list (June 28-July 13, 1990); included rehabilitation disability assignment to Clearwater (July 9-13, 1990).... On Philadelphia disabled list (June 15-September 5, 1991); included rehabilitation disability assignment to Scranton/Wilkes-Barre (September 2-5, 1991).... Traded by Phillies to California Angels for P Kyle Abbott and OF Ruben Amaro (December 8, 1991).

RECORDS/HONORS: Shares major league record for most home runs—2 and most total bases—8, in one inning (June 11, 1985, first inning).... Named Midwest League Most Valuable Player (1980).

STATISTICAL NOTES: Led Midwest League third basemen with .930 fielding percentage in 1980.... Hit three home runs in a game (August 29, 1989).

Year	Team (League)	Pos.	G	AB	R	H	2B	3B	HR	RBI	Avg.	SB	PO	A	E	Avg.
1980—Waterloo (Midwest)	3B-SS	134	492	105	*162	*33	3	15	90	*.329	51	94	291	30	†.928
1981—Cleveland (A.L.)	OF-3B	43	109	21	28	8	2	1	17	.257	8	30	4	3	.919
—Charleston, W.Va. (Int'l)	3B-1B	105	382	58	120	19	6	10	73	.314	34	96	222	19	.944
1982—Cleveland (A.L.)	OF-3B-1B	150	527	65	132	25	3	14	82	.250	32	323	17	6	.983
1983—Philadelphia (N.L.)	OF	124	351	45	93	9	5	6	32	.265	20	165	7	5	.972
1984—Philadelphia (N.L.)	OF	152	561	85	164	27	6	16	67	.292	48	341	2	4	.988
1985—Philadelphia (N.L.)	OF	152	570	76	150	30	4	13	70	.263	21	368	9	6	.984
1986—Philadelphia (N.L.)	1B-OF	158	610	•107	186	*46	2	19	98	.305	24	1247	100	13	.990
1987—Philadelphia (N.L.)	1B-OF	158	556	84	154	36	5	21	84	.277	16	1216	80	13	.990
1988—Philadelphia (N.L.)	1B-OF-3B	104	367	43	100	28	2	6	45	.272	20	756	58	9	.989
1989—Philadelphia (N.L.)	OF-1B-3B	154	540	93	140	27	2	26	78	.259	28	426	47	9	.981
1990—Philadelphia (N.L.)	OF	129	467	70	122	14	3	17	73	.261	16	272	8	6	.979
—Clearwater (Florida St.)	OF	2	6	0	1	1	0	0	0	.167	0	3	0	0	1.000
1991—Philadelphia (N.L.)	OF	77	284	43	64	15	1	0	21	.225	9	202	3	2	.990
—Scranton/W.B. (Int'l)	OF	2	8	2	2	1	0	0	0	.250	0	3	0	0	1.000
American League totals (2 years)		193	636	86	160	33	5	15	99	.252	40	353	21	9	.977
National League totals (9 years)		1208	4306	646	1173	232	30	124	568	.272	202	4993	314	67	.988
Major league totals (11 years)		1401	4942	732	1333	265	35	139	667	.270	242	5346	335	76	.987

CHAMPIONSHIP SERIES RECORD

Year	Team (League)	Pos.	G	AB	R	H	2B	3B	HR	RBI	Avg.	SB	PO	A	E	Avg.
1983—Philadelphia (N.L.)	PH-OF	2	2	0	0	0	0	0	0	.000	0	0	0	0	...

WORLD SERIES RECORD

Year	Team (League)	Pos.	G	AB	R	H	2B	3B	HR	RBI	Avg.	SB	PO	A	E	Avg.
1983—Philadelphia (N.L.)	PH-OF	4	3	0	0	0	0	0	0	.000	0	1	0	0	1.000

ALL-STAR GAME RECORD

Year	League	Pos.	AB	R	H	2B	3B	HR	RBI	Avg.	SB	PO	A	E	Avg.
1989—National	OF	1	0	1	0	0	0	1	1.000	0	0	0	0	...

HEATH, MIKE
C, BRAVES

PERSONAL: Born February 5, 1955, at Tampa, Fla.... 5-11/180.... Throws right, bats right.... Full name: Michael Thomas Heath.
HIGH SCHOOL: Hillsborough (Tampa, Fla.).
TRANSACTIONS/CAREER NOTES: Selected by New York Yankees organization in second round of free-agent draft (June 5, 1973).... On disabled list (August 2-September 16, 1975 and June 29-July 13, 1976).... Traded by Yankees with P Sparky Lyle, P Larry McCall, P Dave Rajsich, SS Domingo Ramos and cash to Texas Rangers for OF Juan Beniquez, OF Greg Jemison, P Mike Griffin, P Paul Mirabella and P Dave Righetti (November 10, 1978).... Traded by Rangers organization with 3B Dave Chalk and cash to Oakland A's for P John Henry Johnson (June 15, 1979).... On disabled list (March 28-April 20, 1982 and April 25-May 25, 1983).... Traded by A's with P Tim Conroy to St. Louis Cardinals for P Joaquin Andujar (December 10, 1985).... Traded by Cardinals to Detroit Tigers for P Ken Hill and a player to be named later (August 10, 1986); Cardinals acquired 1B Mike Laga to complete deal (September 2, 1986).... Granted free agency (November 9, 1987).... Re-signed by Tigers, (December 1, 1987).... On disabled list (August 2-3, 1990).... Granted free agency (December 7, 1990).... Signed by Atlanta Braves (January 22, 1991).... On disabled list (July 13, 1991-remainder of season).
STATISTICAL NOTES: Tied for Appalachian League lead with seven sacrifice hits in 1973.... Led New York-Pennsylvania League shortstops with 42 double plays in 1974.... Led A.L. catchers with 10 errors in 1981.... Led A.L. catchers with 66 assists and 10 double plays in 1989.

Year	Team (League)	Pos.	G	AB	R	H	2B	3B	HR	RBI	Avg.	SB	PO	A	E	Avg.
1973—Johnson City (Appal.)		SS-2B-3B	48	166	17	29	5	2	0	10	.175	7	83	137	24	.902
1974—Oneonta (N.Y.-Penn)		SS	65	234	51	66	6	3	3	34	.282	6	114	170	★27	.913
1975—Fort Lauderdale (FSL)		SS	98	376	43	87	7	3	1	23	.231	13	184	256	31	.934
1976—Fort Lauderdale (FSL)		S-3-C-P	80	267	28	71	16	3	2	30	.266	0	143	121	16	.943
1977—West Haven (Eastern)		C-3B	98	352	58	94	13	5	8	42	.267	5	492	72	16	.972
1978—West Haven (Eastern)		C-SS	66	217	43	64	16	1	8	27	.295	9	335	53	10	.975
—New York (N.L.)		C	33	92	6	21	3	1	0	8	.228	0	151	11	5	.970
1979—Tucson (Pacific Coast)■		C	54	196	21	53	8	2	1	28	.270	2	183	24	7	.967
—Oakland (A.L.)■		OF-C-3B	74	258	19	66	8	0	3	27	.256	1	167	32	5	.975
1980—Oakland (A.L.)		C-OF	92	305	27	74	10	2	1	33	.243	3	292	20	4	.987
1981—Oakland (A.L.)		C-OF	84	301	26	71	7	1	8	30	.236	3	399	45	†10	.978
1982—Oakland (A.L.)		C-OF-3B	101	318	43	77	18	4	3	39	.242	8	368	54	12	.972
1983—Oakland (A.L.)		C-OF-3B	96	345	45	97	17	0	6	33	.281	3	362	47	11	.974
1984—Oakland (A.L.)		C-O-3-S	140	475	49	118	21	5	13	64	.248	7	495	56	8	.986
1985—Oakland (A.L.)		C-OF-3B	138	436	71	109	18	6	13	55	.250	7	539	67	12	.981
1986—St. Louis (N.L.)■		C-OF	65	190	19	39	8	1	4	25	.205	2	260	30	10	.967
—Detroit (A.L.)■		C-3B	30	98	11	26	3	0	4	11	.265	4	145	9	3	.981
1987—Detroit (A.L.)		C-OF-IF	93	270	34	76	16	0	8	33	.281	1	384	43	5	.988
1988—Detroit (A.L.)		C-OF	86	219	24	54	7	2	5	18	.247	1	361	24	6	.985
1989—Detroit (A.L.)		C-3B-OF	122	396	38	104	16	2	10	43	.263	7	584	†68	10	.985
1990—Detroit (A.L.)		C-OF-SS	122	370	46	100	18	2	7	38	.270	7	588	54	13	.980
1991—Atlanta (N.L.)■		C	49	139	4	29	3	1	1	12	.209	0	192	33	2	.991
American League totals (13 years)			1211	3883	439	993	162	25	81	432	.256	52	4835	530	104	.981
National League totals (2 years)			114	329	23	68	11	2	5	37	.207	2	452	63	12	.977
Major league totals (14 years)			1325	4212	462	1061	173	27	86	469	.252	54	5287	593	116	.981

DIVISION SERIES RECORD

Year	Team (League)	Pos.	G	AB	R	H	2B	3B	HR	RBI	Avg.	SB	PO	A	E	Avg.
1981—Oakland (A.L.)		C	2	8	0	0	0	0	0	0	.000	0	9	1	0	1.000

CHAMPIONSHIP SERIES RECORD

Year	Team (League)	Pos.	G	AB	R	H	2B	3B	HR	RBI	Avg.	SB	PO	A	E	Avg.
1981—Oakland (A.L.)		C-OF	3	6	1	2	0	0	0	0	.333	1	3	1	0	1.000
1987—Detroit (A.L.)		C	3	7	1	2	0	0	1	2	.286	0	14	0	0	1.000
Championship Series totals (2 years)			6	13	2	4	0	0	1	2	.308	1	17	1	0	1.000

WORLD SERIES RECORD

Year	Team (League)	Pos.	G	AB	R	H	2B	3B	HR	RBI	Avg.	SB	PO	A	E	Avg.
1978—New York (A.L.)		C	1	0	0	0	0	0	0	0	...	0	0	0	0	...

RECORD AS PITCHER

Year	Team (League)	G	W	L	Pct.	ERA	Sv.	IP	H	R	ER	BB	SO
1976—Fort Lauderdale (Florida St.)	1	0	0	...	0.00	0	1	1	0	0	0	1

HEATON, NEAL
P, PIRATES

PERSONAL: Born March 3, 1960, at Jamaica, N.Y.... 6-1/205.... Throws left, bats left.... Full name: Neal Heaton.
HIGH SCHOOL: Sachem (Lake Ronkonkoma, N.Y.).
COLLEGE: Miami (Fla.).
TRANSACTIONS/CAREER NOTES: Selected by New York Mets organization in first round (first pick overall) of free-agent draft (January 9, 1979).... Selected by Cleveland Indians organization in second round of free-agent draft (June 8, 1981).... Traded by Indians to Minnesota Twins for P John Butcher (June 20, 1986).... Traded by Twins with P Al Cardwood, P Yorkis Perez and C Jeff Reed to Montreal Expos for P Jeff Reardon and C Tom Nieto (February 3, 1987).... On disabled list (April 8-29, 1988).... Traded by Expos to Pittsburgh Pirates for a player to be named later (March 28, 1989); Expos acquired P Brett

Gideon to complete deal (March 30, 1989).... Granted free agency (November 13, 1989).... Re-signed by Pirates (December 6, 1989).

RECORDS/HONORS: Named lefthanded pitcher on THE SPORTING NEWS college All-America team (1981).
MISCELLANEOUS: Appeared in one game as pinch-runner and received base on balls in only appearance as pinch-hitter (1991).

Year	Team (League)	G	W	L	Pct.	ERA	Sv.	IP	H	R	ER	BB	SO
1981 — Chattanooga (Southern)		11	4	4	.500	3.97	0	77	61	42	34	27	50
1982 — Charleston, W.Va. (Int'l)		29	10	5	.667	4.01	0	172⅔	194	97	77	66	105
— Cleveland (A.L.)		8	0	2	.000	5.23	0	31	32	21	18	16	14
1983 — Cleveland (A.L.)		39	11	7	.611	4.16	7	149⅓	157	79	69	44	75
1984 — Cleveland (A.L.)		38	12	15	.444	5.21	0	198⅔	231	128	115	75	75
1985 — Cleveland (A.L.)		36	9	17	.346	4.90	0	207⅔	244	119	113	80	82
1986 — Cleveland-Minnesota (A.L.)■...		33	7	15	.318	4.08	1	198⅔	201	102	90	81	90
1987 — Montreal (N.L.)■		32	13	10	.565	4.52	0	193⅓	207	103	97	37	105
1988 — Montreal (N.L.)		32	3	10	.231	4.99	2	97⅓	98	54	54	43	43
1989 — Pittsburgh (N.L.)■		42	6	7	.462	3.05	0	147⅓	127	55	50	55	67
1990 — Pittsburgh (N.L.)		30	12	9	.571	3.45	0	146	143	66	56	38	68
1991 — Pittsburgh (N.L.)		42	3	3	.500	4.33	0	68⅔	72	37	33	21	34
American League totals (5 years)		154	39	56	.411	4.64	8	785⅓	865	449	405	296	336
National League totals (5 years)		178	37	39	.487	4.00	2	652⅔	647	315	290	194	317
Major league totals (10 years)		332	76	95	.444	4.35	10	1438	1512	764	695	490	653

ALL-STAR GAME RECORD

Year	League	W	L	Pct.	ERA	Sv.	IP	H	R	ER	BB	SO
1990 — National							Did not play					

HEEP, DANNY
1B/OF

PERSONAL: Born July 3, 1957, at San Antonio.... 5-11/177.... Throws left, bats left.... Full name: Daniel William Heep.
HIGH SCHOOL: Robert E. Lee (San Antonio).
COLLEGE: St. Mary's University, Tex. (degree in teaching and political science).
TRANSACTIONS/CAREER NOTES: Selected by Houston Astros organization in second round of free-agent draft (June 6, 1978)....
On Houston disabled list (April 19-May 4, 1981).... Traded by Astros to New York Mets for P Mike Scott (December 10, 1982).
... Granted free agency (November 12, 1986).... Signed by Los Angeles Dodgers organization (June 12, 1987).... Released by Dodgers (December 21, 1988).... Signed by Boston Red Sox (February 6, 1989).... On disabled list (June 28-September 2, 1990).... Granted free agency (November 5, 1990).... Signed by Vancouver, Chicago White Sox organization (April 12, 1991).... Traded by White Sox to Atlanta Braves for IF Kevin Castleberry (May 6, 1991).... Released by Braves (June 17, 1991).
RECORDS/HONORS: Named Southern League co-Most Valuable Player (1979).
STATISTICAL NOTES: Led Southern League with 274 total bases in 1979.

Year	Team (League)	Pos.	G	AB	R	H	2B	3B	HR	RBI	Avg.	SB	PO	A	E	Avg.
1978 — Daytona Beach (Fla. St.)		OF	66	212	29	72	18	2	2	24	.340	0	89	9	2	.980
1979 — Columbus (Southern)		OF	138	523	103	★171	30	5	21	84	.327	7	211	12	6	.974
— Houston (N.L.)		OF	14	14	0	2	0	0	0	2	.143	0	7	0	0	1.000
1980 — Tucson (Pacific Coast)		1B-OF	96	376	63	129	28	5	17	69	★.343	0	810	53	8	.991
— Houston (N.L.)		1B	33	87	6	24	8	0	6	.276		0	188	8	2	.990
1981 — Houston (N.L.)		1B-OF	33	96	6	24	3	0	0	11	.250	0	198	9	2	.990
— Tucson (Pacific Coast)		1B-OF	78	285	55	96	23	5	11	60	.337	3	635	44	12	.983
1982 — Houston (N.L.)		OF-1B	85	198	16	47	14	1	4	22	.237	0	192	6	1	.995
1983 — New York (N.L.)■		OF-1B	115	253	30	64	12	0	8	21	.253	3	159	11	0	1.000
1984 — New York (N.L.)		OF-1B	99	199	36	46	9	2	1	12	.231	3	137	7	4	.973
1985 — New York (N.L.)		OF-1B	95	271	26	76	17	0	7	42	.280	2	154	5	4	.975
1986 — New York (N.L.)		OF	86	195	24	55	8	2	5	33	.282	1	83	2	1	.988
1987 — San Antonio (Texas)■...		OF	11	47	6	16	1	0	2	9	.340	0	9	1	0	1.000
— Los Angeles (N.L.)		OF	60	98	7	16	4	0	0	9	.163	1	52	6	1	.983
1988 — Los Angeles (N.L.)		OF-1B-P	95	149	14	36	2	0	1	12	.242	2	129	10	3	.979
1989 — Boston (A.L.)■		OF-1B	113	320	36	96	17	0	5	49	.300	0	216	14	3	.987
1990 — Boston (A.L.)		OF-1B-P	41	69	3	12	1	1	0	8	.174	0	42	4	1	.979
1991 — Vancouver (Pac. Coast)■...		OF-1B	20	70	2	17	6	0	0	10	.243	1	39	5	0	1.000
— Atlanta (N.L.)■		1B-OF	14	12	4	5	1	0	0	3	.417	0	1	0	0	1.000
American League totals (2 years)			154	389	39	108	18	1	5	57	.278	0	258	18	4	.986
National League totals (11 years)			729	1572	169	395	78	5	25	172	.251	12	1300	64	18	.987
Major league totals (13 years)			883	1961	208	503	96	6	30	229	.257	12	1558	82	22	.987

CHAMPIONSHIP SERIES RECORD

Year	Team (League)	Pos.	G	AB	R	H	2B	3B	HR	RBI	Avg.	SB	PO	A	E	Avg.
1980 — Houston (N.L.)		PH	1	1	0	0	0	0	0	0	.000	0	0	0	0	...
1986 — New York (N.L.)		PH-OF	5	4	0	1	0	0	0	1	.250	0	0	0	0	...
1988 — Los Angeles (N.L.)		PH	3	1	0	0	0	0	0	0	.000	0	0	0	0	...
1990 — Boston (A.L.)		PH	2	2	0	0	0	0	0	0	.000	0	0	0	0	...
Championship Series totals (4 years)			11	8	0	1	0	0	0	1	.125	0	0	0	0	...

WORLD SERIES RECORD

Year	Team (League)	Pos.	G	AB	R	H	2B	3B	HR	RBI	Avg.	SB	PO	A	E	Avg.
1986—New York (N.L.)	PH-O-DH	5	11	0	1	0	0	0	2	.091	0	1	0	0	1.000
1988—Los Angeles (N.L.)	PH-O-DH	3	8	0	2	1	0	0	0	.250	0	0	0	0	...
World Series totals (2 years)		8	19	0	3	1	0	0	2	.158	0	1	0	0	1.000

RECORD AS PITCHER

Year	Team (League)	G	W	L	Pct.	ERA	Sv.	IP	H	R	ER	BB	SO
1988—Los Angeles (N.L.)		1	0	0	...	9.00	0	2	2	2	2	0	0
1990—Boston (A.L.)		1	0	0	...	9.00	0	1	4	1	1	0	0
American League totals (1 year)	1	0	0	...	9.00	0	1	4	1	1	0	0
National League totals (1 year)	1	0	0	...	9.00	0	2	2	2	2	0	0
Major league totals (2 years)	2	0	0	...	9.00	0	3	6	3	3	0	0

HEMOND, SCOTT
IF/C, ATHLETICS

PERSONAL: Born November 18, 1965, at Taunton, Mass. . . . 6-0/205. . . . Throws right, bats right. . . . Full name: Scott Matthew Hemond.
HIGH SCHOOL: Dunedin (Fla.).
COLLEGE: South Florida.
TRANSACTIONS/CAREER NOTES: Selected by Kansas City Royals organization in fifth round of free-agent draft (June 6, 1983). . . . Selected by Oakland Athletics organization in first round (12th pick overall) of free-agent draft, (June 2, 1986). . . . On Tacoma disabled list (May 18-July 6, 1990).
RECORDS/HONORS: Named catcher on THE SPORTING NEWS college All-America team (1986).
STATISTICAL NOTES: Led Southern League third basemen with 299 assists and 427 total chances in 1988.

Year	Team (League)	Pos.	G	AB	R	H	2B	3B	HR	RBI	Avg.	SB	PO	A	E	Avg.
1986—Madison (Midwest)	C	22	85	9	26	2	0	2	13	.306	2	121	11	2	.985
1987—Madison (Midwest)	C-OF	90	343	60	99	21	4	8	52	.289	27	408	53	16	.966
—Huntsville (Southern)	C-3B	33	110	10	20	3	1	1	8	.182	5	161	32	6	.970
1988—Huntsville (Southern)	3B-C	133	482	51	106	22	4	9	53	.220	29	93	†302	38	.912
1989—Huntsville (Southern)	3B-C	132	490	89	130	26	6	5	62	.265	45	272	198	31	.938
1990—Tacoma (Pacific Coast)	2-C-3-S	72	218	32	53	11	0	8	35	.243	11	138	177	12	.963
—Oakland (A.L.)	3B-2B	7	13	0	2	0	0	0	1	.154	0	2	5	0	1.000
1991—Tacoma (Pacific Coast)	2-C-3-S	92	327	50	89	19	5	3	31	.272	11	280	177	12	.974
—Oakland (A.L.)	C-2-3-S	23	23	4	5	0	0	0	0	.217	1	27	14	1	.976
Major league totals (2 years)		30	36	4	7	0	0	0	1	.194	1	29	19	1	.980

HENDERSON, DAVE
OF, ATHLETICS

PERSONAL: Born July 21, 1958, at Dos Palos, Calif. . . . 6-2/220. . . . Throws right, bats right. . . . Full name: David Lee Henderson. . . . Nephew of Joe Henderson, pitcher, Chicago White Sox, Cincinnati Reds (1974, 1976-77).
HIGH SCHOOL: Dos Palos (Calif.).
TRANSACTIONS/CAREER NOTES: Selected by Seattle Mariners organization in first round (26th pick overall) of free-agent draft (June 7, 1977). . . . On disabled list (June 26-July 22, 1980; May 3-18, 1982; and August 10-29, 1984). . . . Traded by Mariners with IF Spike Owen to Boston Red Sox for IF Rey Quinones, a player to be named later and cash (August 19, 1986); as part of deal, Mariners claimed P Mike Brown and P Mike Trujillo on waivers from Red Sox (August 22, 1986). Mariners acquired OF John Christensen to complete deal (September 25, 1986). . . . Traded by Red Sox to San Francisco Giants for a player to be named later (September 1, 1987); Red Sox acquired OF Randy Kutcher to complete deal (December 9, 1987). . . . Granted free agency (November 9, 1987). . . . Signed by Oakland Athletics (December 21, 1987). . . . Granted free agency (November 4, 1988). . . . Re-signed by A's (December 1, 1988). . . . On disabled list (August 21-September 21, 1990). . . . Granted free agency (December 7, 1990). . . . Re-signed by A's (December 11, 1990).
STATISTICAL NOTES: Hit three home runs in a game (August 3, 1991).

Year	Team (League)	Pos.	G	AB	R	H	2B	3B	HR	RBI	Avg.	SB	PO	A	E	Avg.
1977—Bellingham (Northwest)	OF	65	251	47	79	14	2	•16	63	.315	5	136	5	★11	.928
1978—Stockton (California)	OF	117	409	48	95	16	4	7	63	.232	11	204	12	14	.939
1979—San Jose (California)	OF	136	507	103	152	23	3	27	99	.300	19	264	18	4	.986
1980—Spokane (Pacific Coast)	OF	109	341	48	95	26	1	7	50	.279	16	258	9	7	.974
1981—Seattle (A.L.)	OF	59	126	17	21	3	0	6	13	.167	2	105	4	0	1.000
—Spokane (Pacific Coast)	OF	80	272	47	76	23	1	12	50	.279	3	146	7	3	.981
1982—Seattle (A.L.)	OF	104	324	47	82	17	1	14	48	.253	2	249	11	4	.985
1983—Seattle (A.L.)	OF	137	484	50	130	24	5	17	55	.269	9	304	17	6	.982
1984—Seattle (A.L.)	OF	112	350	42	98	23	0	14	43	.280	5	242	11	3	.988
1985—Seattle (A.L.)	OF	139	502	70	121	28	2	14	68	.241	6	335	8	5	.986
1986—Seattle-Boston (A.L.)■	OF	139	388	59	103	22	4	15	47	.265	2	231	11	5	.980
1987—Boston (A.L.)	OF	75	184	30	43	10	0	8	25	.234	1	114	0	5	.958
—San Francisco (N.L.)■	OF	15	21	2	5	2	0	0	1	.238	2	10	1	0	1.000
1988—Oakland (A.L.)■	OF	146	507	100	154	38	1	24	94	.304	2	382	5	7	.982
1989—Oakland (A.L.)	OF	152	579	77	145	24	3	15	80	.250	8	385	5	9	.977
1990—Oakland (A.L.)	OF	127	450	65	122	28	0	20	63	.271	3	319	5	4	.988
1991—Oakland (A.L.)	OF-2B	150	572	86	158	33	0	25	85	.276	6	362	10	1	.997
American League totals (11 years)		1340	4466	643	1177	250	16	172	621	.264	46	3028	87	49	.985
National League totals (1 year)		15	21	2	5	2	0	0	1	.238	2	10	1	0	1.000
Major league totals (11 years)		1355	4487	645	1182	252	16	172	622	.263	48	3038	88	49	.985

CHAMPIONSHIP SERIES RECORD

CHAMPIONSHIP SERIES NOTES: Holds single-series record (four games) for most strikeouts—7 (1988).

Year — Team (League)	Pos.	G	AB	R	H	2B	3B	HR	RBI	Avg.	SB	PO	A	E	Avg.
1986 — Boston (A.L.)	OF	5	9	3	1	0	0	1	4	.111	0	11	0	0	1.000
1988 — Oakland (A.L.)	OF	4	16	2	6	1	0	1	4	.375	0	11	0	2	.846
1989 — Oakland (A.L.)	OF	5	19	4	5	3	0	1	1	.263	0	22	0	0	1.000
1990 — Oakland (A.L.)	OF	2	6	0	1	0	0	0	1	.167	1	7	0	0	1.000
Championship Series totals (4 years)		16	50	9	13	4	0	3	10	.260	1	51	0	2	.962

WORLD SERIES RECORD

WORLD SERIES NOTES: Shares record for most home runs in two consecutive innings—2 (October 27, 1989; fourth and fifth innings).

Year — Team (League)	Pos.	G	AB	R	H	2B	3B	HR	RBI	Avg.	SB	PO	A	E	Avg.
1986 — Boston (A.L.)	OF	7	25	6	10	1	1	2	5	.400	0	22	0	0	1.000
1988 — Oakland (A.L.)	OF	5	20	1	6	2	0	1	1	.300	0	12	0	0	1.000
1989 — Oakland (A.L.)	OF	4	13	6	4	2	0	1	4	.308	0	13	0	0	1.000
1990 — Oakland (A.L.)	PH-OF	4	13	2	3	1	0	0	0	.231	0	7	0	0	1.000
World Series totals (4 years)		20	71	15	23	6	1	4	10	.324	0	54	0	0	1.000

ALL-STAR GAME RECORD

Year — League	Pos.	AB	R	H	2B	3B	HR	RBI	Avg.	SB	PO	A	E	Avg.
1991 — American	OF	2	0	0	0	0	0	0	.000	0	2	0	0	1.000

HENDERSON, RICKEY
OF, ATHLETICS

PERSONAL: Born December 25, 1958, at Chicago. . . . 5-10/190. . . . Throws left, bats right. . . . Full name: Rickey Henley Henderson.

HIGH SCHOOL: Technical (Oakland, Calif.).

TRANSACTIONS/CAREER NOTES: Selected by Oakland Athletics organization in fourth round of free-agent draft (June 8, 1976). . . . Traded by A's with P Bert Bradley and cash to New York Yankees for OF Stan Javier, P Jay Howell, P Jose Rijo, P Eric Plunk and P Tim Birtsas (December 5, 1984). . . . On New York disabled list (March 30-April 22, 1985); included rehabilitation disability assignment to Fort Lauderdale (April 19-22, 1985). . . . On disabled list (June 5-29 and July 26-September 1, 1987). . . . Traded by Yankees to A's for P Greg Cadaret, P Eric Plunk and OF Luis Polonia (June 21, 1989). . . . Granted free agency (November 13, 1989). . . . Re-signed by A's (November 28, 1989). . . . On disabled list (April 12-27, 1991).

RECORDS/HONORS: Holds major league career records for most home runs as leadoff batter—50; stolen bases—994. . . . Holds major league single-season records for most stolen bases—130 (1982); most times caught stealing—42 (1982). . . . Holds major league record for most years leading league in stolen bases—11. . . . Holds A.L. career record for most times caught stealing—211. . . . Holds A.L. single-season record for most home runs as leadoff batter—9 (1986). . . . Holds A.L. record for most consecutive years with 50 or more stolen bases—7. . . . Shares A.L. records for most stolen bases in two consecutive games—7 (July 3-4, 1983). . . . Named outfielder on THE SPORTING NEWS A.L. All-Star team (1981, 1985 and 1990). . . . Won A.L. Gold Glove as outfielder (1981). . . . Named outfielder on THE SPORTING NEWS A.L. Silver Slugger team (1981, 1985 and 1990). . . . Won THE SPORTING NEWS Silver Shoe Award (1982). . . . Won THE SPORTING NEWS Golden Shoe Award (1983). . . . Named A.L. Most Valuable Player by Baseball Writers' Association of America (1990).

STATISTICAL NOTES: Led California League in caught stealing with 22 in 1977. . . . Led Eastern League in caught stealing with 28 in 1978. . . . Led Eastern League outfielders with four double plays in 1978. . . . Led A.L. in caught stealing with 26 in 1980, 22 in 1981, 42 in 1982, 19 in 1983 and tied for lead with 18 in 1986. . . . Led A.L. outfielders with 341 total chances in 1981. . . . Led A.L. with 116 bases on balls received in 1982, 103 in 1983 and 126 in 1989. . . . Tied for A.L. lead in double plays by outfielders with five in 1988. . . . Led A.L. with .439 on base percentage in 1990.

Year — Team (League)	Pos.	G	AB	R	H	2B	3B	HR	RBI	Avg.	SB	PO	A	E	Avg.
1976 — Boise (Northwest)	OF	46	140	34	47	13	2	3	23	.336	29	99	3	*12	.895
1977 — Modesto (California)	OF	134	481	120	166	18	4	11	69	.345	*95	278	15	*20	.936
1978 — Jersey City (Eastern)	OF	133	455	81	141	14	4	0	34	.310	*81	305	•15	7	.979
1979 — Ogden (Pacific Coast)	OF	71	259	66	80	11	8	3	26	.309	44	149	6	6	.963
— Oakland (A.L.)	OF	89	351	49	96	13	3	1	26	.274	33	215	5	6	.973
1980 — Oakland (A.L.)	OF	158	591	111	179	22	4	9	53	.303	*100	407	15	7	.984
1981 — Oakland (A.L.)	OF	108	423	*89	*135	18	7	6	35	.319	*56	*327	7	7	.979
1982 — Oakland (A.L.)	OF	149	536	119	143	24	4	10	51	.267	*130	379	2	9	.977
1983 — Oakland (A.L.)	OF	145	513	105	150	25	7	9	48	.292	*108	349	9	3	.992
1984 — Oakland (A.L.)	OF	142	502	113	147	27	4	16	58	.293	*66	341	7	11	.969
1985 — Fort Lauderdale (FSL)■	OF	3	6	5	1	0	1	0	3	.167	1	6	0	0	1.000
— New York (A.L.)	OF	143	547	*146	172	28	5	24	72	.314	*80	439	7	9	.980
1986 — New York (A.L.)	OF	153	608	*130	160	31	5	28	74	.263	*87	426	4	6	.986
1987 — New York (A.L.)	OF	95	358	78	104	17	3	17	37	.291	41	189	3	4	.980
1988 — New York (A.L.)	OF	140	554	118	169	30	2	6	50	.305	*93	320	7	12	.965
1989 — New York-Oak. (A.L.)■	OF	150	541	•113	148	26	3	12	57	.274	*77	335	6	4	.988
1990 — Oakland (A.L.)	OF	136	489	*119	159	33	3	28	61	.325	*65	289	5	5	.983
1991 — Oakland (A.L.)	OF	134	470	105	126	17	1	18	57	.268	*58	249	10	8	.970
Major league totals (13 years)		1742	6483	1395	1888	311	51	184	679	.291	994	4265	87	91	.980

Year	Team (League)	Pos.	G	AB	R	H	2B	3B	HR	RBI	Avg.	SB	PO	A	E	Avg.
						BATTING								FIELDING		
1981—Oakland (A.L.)		OF	3	11	3	2	0	0	0	0	.182	2	8	0	0	1.000

CHAMPIONSHIP SERIES RECORD

CHAMPIONSHIP SERIES NOTES: Holds career record for most stolen bases—12. . . . Holds single-series record for most stolen bases—8 (1989); most runs—8 (1989). . . . Holds single-game record for most stolen bases—4 (October 4, 1989). . . . Shares records for most at-bats in one inning—2; most hits in one inning—2; and most singles in one inning—2 (October 6, 1990, ninth inning); most stolen bases in one inning—2 (October 4, 1989, fourth and seventh innings). . . . Shares A.L. single-series record for most bases on balls received—7 (1989).

Year	Team (League)	Pos.	G	AB	R	H	2B	3B	HR	RBI	Avg.	SB	PO	A	E	Avg.
						BATTING								FIELDING		
1981—Oakland (A.L.)		OF	3	11	0	4	2	1	0	1	.364	2	6	0	1	.857
1989—Oakland (A.L.)		OF	5	15	8	6	1	1	2	5	.400	8	13	0	1	.929
1990—Oakland (A.L.)		OF	4	17	1	5	0	0	0	3	.294	2	10	0	0	1.000
Championship Series totals (3 years)			12	43	9	15	3	2	2	9	.349	12	29	0	2	.935

WORLD SERIES RECORD

WORLD SERIES NOTES: Shares single-game record for most at-bats—6 (October 28, 1989).

Year	Team (League)	Pos.	G	AB	R	H	2B	3B	HR	RBI	Avg.	SB	PO	A	E	Avg.
						BATTING								FIELDING		
1989—Oakland (A.L.)		OF	4	19	4	9	1	2	1	3	.474	3	9	0	0	1.000
1990—Oakland (A.L.)		OF	4	15	2	5	2	0	1	1	.333	3	12	1	0	1.000
World Series totals (2 years)			8	34	6	14	3	2	2	4	.412	6	21	1	0	1.000

ALL-STAR GAME RECORD

ALL-STAR GAME NOTES: Shares single-game record for most singles—3 (July 13, 1982).

Year	League	Pos.	AB	R	H	2B	3B	HR	RBI	Avg.	SB	PO	A	E	Avg.
					BATTING								FIELDING		
1980—American		OF	1	0	0	0	0	0	0	.000	0	0	0	0	. . .
1982—American		OF	4	1	3	0	0	0	0	.750	1	3	0	1	.750
1983—American		OF	1	0	0	0	0	0	1	.000	0	0	0	0	. . .
1984—American		OF	2	0	0	0	0	0	0	.000	0	0	0	0	. . .
1985—American		OF	3	1	1	0	0	0	0	.333	1	1	0	0	1.000
1986—American		OF	3	0	0	0	0	0	0	.000	0	2	0	0	1.000
1987—American		OF	3	0	1	0	0	0	0	.333	0	0	0	0	. . .
1988—American		OF	2	0	1	0	0	0	0	.500	0	1	0	0	1.000
1990—American		OF	3	0	0	0	0	0	0	.000	0	2	0	0	1.000
1991—American		OF	2	1	1	0	0	0	0	.500	0	0	0	0	. . .
All-Star Game totals (10 years)			24	3	7	0	0	0	1	.292	2	9	0	1	.900

HENKE, TOM
P, BLUE JAYS

PERSONAL: Born December 21, 1957, at Kansas City, Mo. . . . 6-5/225. . . . Throws right, bats right. . . . Full name: Thomas Anthony Henke. . . . Name pronounced HEN-kee.
HIGH SCHOOL: Blair Oaks (Wardsville, Mo.).
COLLEGE: East Central College (Mo.).
TRANSACTIONS/CAREER NOTES: Selected by Seattle Mariners organization in 20th round of free-agent draft (June 5, 1979). . . . Selected by Chicago Cubs organization in secondary phase of free-agent draft (January 8, 1980). . . . Selected by Texas Rangers organization in secondary phase of free-agent draft (June 3, 1980). . . . Selected by Toronto Blue Jays organization in player compensation pool draft (January 24, 1985). Blue Jays received compensation for Rangers signing of free agent DH Cliff Johnson, a type A player (December 5, 1984). . . . On Toronto disabled list (April 12-May 17, 1991); included rehabilitation disability assignment to Dunedin, but did not pitch (May 13-17, 1991).
RECORDS/HONORS: Named International League Pitcher of the Year (1985).

Year	Team (League)	G	W	L	Pct.	ERA	Sv.	IP	H	R	ER	BB	SO
1980—Sarasota Rangers (GCL)		8	3	3	.500	0.95	0	38	33	11	4	12	34
—Asheville (South Atlantic)		5	0	2	.000	7.83	0	23	25	21	20	20	19
1981—Asheville (South Atlantic)		28	8	6	.571	2.93	3	92	77	36	30	35	67
—Tulsa (Texas)		15	4	3	.571	3.94	1	32	31	16	14	14	37
1982—Tulsa (Texas)		*52	3	6	.333	2.67	14	87⅔	69	35	26	40	100
—Texas (A.L.)		8	1	0	1.000	1.15	0	15⅔	14	2	2	8	9
1983—Oklahoma City (Am. Assoc.)		47	9	6	.600	3.01	2	77⅔	71	33	26	33	90
—Texas (A.L.)		8	1	0	1.000	3.38	1	16	16	6	6	4	17
1984—Texas (A.L.)		25	1	1	.500	6.35	2	28⅓	36	21	20	20	25
—Oklahoma City (Am. Assoc.)		39	6	2	.750	2.64	7	64⅔	59	21	19	25	65
1985—Syracuse (International)■		39	2	1	.667	0.88	•18	51⅓	13	5	5	18	60
—Toronto (A.L.)		28	3	3	.500	2.03	13	40	29	12	9	8	42
1986—Toronto (A.L.)		63	9	5	.643	3.35	27	91⅓	63	39	34	32	118
1987—Toronto (A.L.)		72	0	6	.000	2.49	*34	94	62	27	26	25	128
1988—Toronto (A.L.)		52	4	4	.500	2.91	25	68	60	23	22	24	66
1989—Toronto (A.L.)		64	8	3	.727	1.92	20	89	66	20	19	25	116
1990—Toronto (A.L.)		61	2	4	.333	2.17	32	74⅔	58	18	18	19	75
1991—Toronto (A.L.)		49	0	2	.000	2.32	32	50⅓	33	13	13	11	53
Major league totals (10 years)		430	29	28	.509	2.68	186	567⅓	437	181	169	176	649

CHAMPIONSHIP SERIES NOTES: Shares A.L. single-series record for most games won—2 (1985).

Year	Team (League)	G	W	L	Pct.	ERA	Sv.	IP	H	R	ER	BB	SO
1985 —Toronto (A.L.)		3	2	0	1.000	4.26	0	6⅓	5	3	3	4	4
1989 —Toronto (A.L.)		3	0	0	...	0.00	0	2⅔	0	0	0	0	3
1991 —Toronto (A.L.)		2	0	0	...	0.00	0	2⅔	0	0	0	1	5
Championship Series totals (3 years)		8	2	0	1.000	2.31	0	11⅔	5	3	3	5	12

ALL-STAR GAME RECORD

Year	League	W	L	Pct.	ERA	Sv.	IP	H	R	ER	BB	SO
1987 —American	0	0	...	0.00	0	2⅔	2	0	0	0	1

HENNEMAN, MIKE
P, TIGERS

PERSONAL: Born December 11, 1961, at St. Charles, Mo. . . . 6-4/195. . . . Throws right, bats right. . . . Full name: Michael Alan Henneman.
HIGH SCHOOL: St. Pius X (Festus, Mo.).
COLLEGE: Oklahoma State.
TRANSACTIONS/CAREER NOTES: Selected by Toronto Blue Jays organization in 27th round of free-agent draft (June 7, 1982). . . . Selected by Philadelphia Phillies organization in secondary phase of free-agent draft (June 6, 1983). . . . Selected by Detroit Tigers organization in fourth round of free-agent draft (June 4, 1984). . . . On disabled list (May 22-June 6, 1988 and April 24-May 15, 1989).
RECORDS/HONORS: Named A.L. Rookie Pitcher of the Year by THE SPORTING NEWS (1987).
MISCELLANEOUS: Struck out in only at-bat with Detroit (1987).

Year	Team (League)	G	W	L	Pct.	ERA	Sv.	IP	H	R	ER	BB	SO
1984 —Birmingham (Southern)		29	4	2	.667	2.43	6	59⅓	48	22	16	33	39
1985 —Birmingham (Southern)		46	3	5	.375	5.76	9	70⅓	88	50	45	28	40
1986 —Nashville (American Assoc.)		31	2	5	.286	2.95	1	58	57	27	19	23	39
1987 —Toledo (International)		11	1	1	.500	1.47	0	18⅓	5	3	3	3	19
—Detroit (A.L.)		55	11	3	.786	2.98	7	96⅔	86	36	32	30	75
1988 —Detroit (A.L.)		65	9	6	.600	1.87	22	91⅓	72	23	19	24	58
1989 —Detroit (A.L.)		60	11	4	.733	3.70	8	90	84	46	37	51	69
1990 —Detroit (A.L.)		69	8	6	.571	3.05	22	94⅓	90	36	32	33	50
1991 —Detroit (A.L.)		60	10	2	.833	2.88	21	84⅓	81	29	27	34	61
Major league totals (5 years)		309	49	21	.700	2.90	80	456⅔	413	170	147	172	313

CHAMPIONSHIP SERIES RECORD

Year	Team (League)	G	W	L	Pct.	ERA	Sv.	IP	H	R	ER	BB	SO
1987 —Detroit (A.L.)		3	1	0	1.000	10.80	0	5	6	6	6	6	3

ALL-STAR GAME RECORD

Year	League	W	L	Pct.	ERA	Sv.	IP	H	R	ER	BB	SO
1989 —American						Did not play						

HENRY, BUTCH
P, ASTROS

PERSONAL: Born October 7, 1968, at El Paso, Tex. . . . 6-1/195. . . . Throws left, bats left. . . . Full name: Floyd Bluford Henry III.
HIGH SCHOOL: Eastwood (El Paso, Tex.).
TRANSACTIONS/CAREER NOTES: Selected by Cincinnati Reds organization in 15th round of free-agent draft (June 2, 1987). . . . On disabled list (April 28, 1989-remainder of season). . . . Traded by Reds with C Terry McGriff and P Keith Kaiser to Houston Astros (September 7, 1990), completing deal in which Astros traded 2B Bill Doran to Reds for three players to be named later (August 30, 1990).

Year	Team (League)	G	W	L	Pct.	ERA	Sv.	IP	H	R	ER	BB	SO
1987 —Billings (Pioneer)		9	4	0	1.000	4.63	1	35	37	21	18	12	38
1988 —Cedar Rapids (Midwest)		27	16	2	*.889	2.26	0	187	144	59	47	56	163
1989 —Chattanooga (Southern)		7	1	3	.250	3.42	0	26⅓	22	12	10	12	19
1990 —Chattanooga (Southern)		24	8	8	.500	4.21	0	143⅓	151	74	67	58	95
1991 —Tucson (Pacific Coast)■		27	10	11	.476	4.80	0	153⅔	192	92	82	42	97

HENRY, DOUG
P, BREWERS

PERSONAL: Born December 10, 1963, at Sacramento, Calif. . . . 6-4/185. . . . Throws right, bats right. . . . Full name: Richard Douglas Henry.
HIGH SCHOOL: Tennyson (Hayward, Calif.).
COLLEGE: Arizona State.
TRANSACTIONS/CAREER NOTES: Selected by New York Mets organization in 16th round of free-agent draft (June 7, 1982). . . . Selected by Milwaukee Brewers organization in the eighth round of free-agent draft (June 3, 1985). . . . On El Paso disabled list (April 5-June 5 and June 18-August 9, 1989).
STATISTICAL NOTES: Combined with Michael Ignasiak in 6-3 no-hit victory against San Jose (April 15, 1990, first game).

Year	Team (League)	G	W	L	Pct.	ERA	Sv.	IP	H	R	ER	BB	SO
1986 —Beloit (Midwest)		27	7	8	.467	4.65	1	143⅓	153	95	74	56	115
1987 —Beloit (Midwest)		31	8	9	.471	4.88	2	132⅔	145	83	72	51	106
1988 —Stockton (California)		23	7	1	.875	1.78	7	70⅔	46	19	14	31	71
—El Paso (Texas)		14	4	0	1.000	3.15	0	45⅔	33	16	16	19	50

Year	Team (League)	G	W	L	Pct.	ERA	Sv.	IP	H	R	ER	BB	SO
1989	—Stockton (California)	4	0	1	.000	0.00	0	11	9	4	0	3	9
	—El Paso (Texas)	1	0	0	...	13.50	0	2	3	3	3	3	2
1990	—Stockton (California)	4	1	0	1.000	1.13	1	8	4	1	1	3	13
	—El Paso (Texas)	15	1	0	1.000	2.93	9	30⅔	31	13	10	11	25
	—Denver (American Assoc.)	27	2	3	.400	4.44	8	50⅔	46	26	25	27	54
1991	—Denver (American Assoc.)	32	3	2	.600	2.18	14	57⅔	47	16	14	20	47
	—Milwaukee (A.L.)	32	2	1	.667	1.00	15	36	16	4	4	14	28
Major league totals (1 year)		32	2	1	.667	1.00	15	36	16	4	4	14	28

HENRY, DWAYNE
P, REDS

PERSONAL: Born February 16, 1962, at Elkton, Md. . . . 6-3/205. . . . Throws right, bats right. . . . Full name: Dwayne Allen Henry.
HIGH SCHOOL: Middletown (Del.).
TRANSACTIONS/CAREER NOTES: Selected by Texas Rangers organization in second round of free-agent draft (June 3, 1980). . . . On disabled list (May 4, 1982-remainder of season). . . . On Tulsa disabled list (April 8-July 9, 1983). . . . On Texas disabled list (May 31-July 8, 1986); included rehabilitation disability assignment to Oklahoma City (June 18-July 8, 1986). . . . Traded by Rangers to Atlanta Braves for P David Miller and cash (March 30, 1989). . . . Released by Braves organization (November 13, 1990). . . . Signed by Tucson, Houston Astros organization (March 29, 1991). . . . Claimed on waivers by Cincinnati Reds (November 26, 1991).

Year	Team (League)	G	W	L	Pct.	ERA	Sv.	IP	H	R	ER	BB	SO
1980	—Sarasota Rangers (GCL)	11	5	1	.833	2.67	0	54	36	23	16	28	47
1981	—Asheville (South Atlantic)	25	8	7	.533	4.43	0	134	120	81	66	58	86
1982	—Burlington (W. Caro.)	4	2	0	1.000	0.00	0	18⅔	6	0	0	6	25
1983	—Tulsa (Texas)	9	0	0	...	5.79	1	14	16	14	9	19	14
	—Sarasota Rangers (GCL)	3	0	0	...	4.00	0	9	10	6	4	1	11
1984	—Tulsa (Texas)	33	5	8	.385	3.39	8	85	65	42	32	60	79
	—Texas (A.L.)	3	0	1	.000	8.31	0	4⅓	5	4	4	7	2
1985	—Tulsa (Texas)	34	7	6	.538	2.66	9	81⅓	51	32	24	44	97
	—Texas (A.L.)	16	2	2	.500	2.57	3	21	16	7	6	7	20
1986	—Tulsa (Texas)	19	1	0	1.000	4.66	0	19⅓	14	11	10	2	17
	—Oklahoma City (Am. Assoc.)	28	2	1	.667	5.89	3	44⅓	51	30	29	27	41
1987	—Oklahoma City (Am. Assoc.)	30	4	4	.500	4.96	3	69	66	39	38	50	55
	—Texas (A.L.)	5	0	0	...	9.00	0	10	12	10	10	9	7
1988	—Oklahoma City (Am. Assoc.)	46	5	5	.500	5.59	7	75⅔	57	51	47	54	98
	—Texas (A.L.)	11	0	1	.000	8.71	1	10⅓	15	10	10	9	10
1989	—Richmond (International)■	41	11	5	.688	2.44	1	84⅔	43	28	23	61	101
	—Atlanta (N.L.)	12	0	2	.000	4.26	1	12⅔	12	6	6	5	16
1990	—Atlanta (N.L.)	34	2	2	.500	5.63	0	38⅓	41	26	24	25	34
	—Richmond (International)	13	1	1	.500	2.33	2	27	12	7	7	16	36
1991	—Houston (N.L.)■	52	3	2	.600	3.19	2	67⅔	51	25	24	39	51
American League totals (5 years)		54	3	4	.429	5.54	4	65	62	42	40	34	56
National League totals (3 years)		98	5	6	.455	4.10	3	118⅔	104	57	54	69	101
Major league totals (8 years)		152	8	10	.444	4.61	7	183⅔	166	99	94	103	157

HENTGEN, PAT
P, BLUE JAYS

PERSONAL: Born November 13, 1968, at Detroit. . . . 6-2/200. . . . Throws right, bats right. . . . Full name: Patrick George Hentgen.
HIGH SCHOOL: Fraser (Mich.).
TRANSACTIONS/CAREER NOTES: Selected by Toronto Blue Jays organization in fifth round of free-agent draft (June 2, 1986).
STATISTICAL NOTES: Led South Atlantic League pitchers with 31 games started in 1987. . . . Led Florida State League pitchers with 30 games started in 1988. . . . Tied for International League lead in games started by pitcher with 28 in 1991.

Year	Team (League)	G	W	L	Pct.	ERA	Sv.	IP	H	R	ER	BB	SO
1986	—St. Catharines (N.Y.-Penn)	13	0	4	.000	4.50	1	40	38	27	20	30	30
1987	—Myrtle Beach (South Atlantic)	32	11	5	.688	2.35	0	★188	145	62	49	60	131
1988	—Dunedin (Florida State)	31	3	12	.200	3.45	0	151⅓	139	80	58	65	125
1989	—Dunedin (Florida State)	29	9	8	.529	2.68	0	151⅓	123	53	45	71	148
1990	—Knoxville (Southern)	28	9	5	.643	3.05	0	153⅓	121	57	52	68	142
1991	—Syracuse (International)	31	8	9	.471	4.47	0	171	146	91	85	★90	★155
	—Toronto (A.L.)	3	0	0	...	2.45	0	7⅓	5	2	2	3	3
Major league totals (1 year)		3	0	0	...	2.45	0	7⅓	5	2	2	3	3

HEREDIA, GIL
P, GIANTS

PERSONAL: Born October 26, 1965, at Nogales, Ariz. . . . 6-1/190. . . . Throws right, bats right. . . . Full name: Gilbert Heredia.
HIGH SCHOOL: Nogales (Ariz.).
COLLEGE: Pima Community College (Ariz.) and Arizona.
TRANSACTIONS/CAREER NOTES: Selected by Pittsburgh Pirates organization in first round (16th pick overall) of free-agent draft (January 17, 1984). . . . Selected by Baltimore Orioles organization in sixth round of free-agent draft (January 9, 1985). . . . Selected by San Francisco Giants organization in ninth round of free-agent draft (June 2, 1987). . . . Loaned by Giants organi-

zation to San Luis Potosi of Mexican League and returned (1989).
STATISTICAL NOTES: Tied for Pacific Coast League lead with five complete games in 1991.

Year	Team (League)	G	W	L	Pct.	ERA	Sv.	IP	H	R	ER	BB	SO
1987	—Everett (Northwest)	3	2	0	1.000	3.60	0	20	24	8	8	1	14
	—Fresno (California)	11	5	3	.625	2.90	0	80⅔	62	28	26	23	60
1988	—San Jose (California)	27	13	12	.520	3.49	0	*206⅓	*216	107	80	46	121
1989	—Shreveport (Texas)	7	1	0	1.000	2.55	0	24⅔	28	10	7	4	8
	—San Luis (Mexican)■	24	14	9	.609	2.99	0	180⅔	183	73	60	35	125
1990	—Phoenix (Pacific Coast)■	29	9	7	.563	4.10	1	147	159	81	67	37	75
1991	—Phoenix (Pacific Coast)	33	9	11	.450	*2.82	1	140⅓	155	60	44	28	75
	—San Francisco (N.L.)	7	0	2	.000	3.82	0	33	27	14	14	7	13
Major league totals (1 year)		7	0	2	.000	3.82	0	33	27	14	14	7	13

HERNANDEZ, CARLOS
C, DODGERS

PERSONAL: Born May 24, 1967, at Bolivar, Venezuela. . . . 5-11/185. . . . Throws right, bats right. . . . Full name: Carlos Alberto Hernandez.
HIGH SCHOOL: Escuela Tecnica Industrial (San Felix, Bolivar, Venezuela).
TRANSACTIONS/CAREER NOTES: Signed as free agent by Los Angeles Dodgers organization (October 10, 1984). . . . On Albuquerque disabled list (May 27-June 20, 1990).
STATISTICAL NOTES: Tied for Gulf Coast League lead in double plays by catcher with three in 1986. . . . Led Texas League catchers with 737 total chances in 1989. . . . Led Pacific Coast League catchers with 684 total chances in 1991.

Year	Team (League)	Pos.	G	AB	R	H	2B	3B	HR	RBI	Avg.	SB	PO	A	E	Avg.
1985	—Braden. Dodgers (GCL)	3B-1B	22	49	3	12	1	0	0	0	.245	0	48	16	2	.970
1986	—Sarasota Dodgers (GCL)	C-3B	57	205	19	64	7	0	1	31	.312	1	217	36	10	.962
1987	—Bakersfield (California)	C	48	162	22	37	6	1	3	22	.228	8	181	26	8	.963
1988	—Bakersfield (California)	C	92	333	37	103	15	2	5	52	.309	3	480	88	14	.976
	—Albuquerque (PCL)	C	3	8	0	1	0	0	0	1	.125	0	11	0	1	.917
1989	—San Antonio (Texas)	C	99	370	37	111	16	3	8	41	.300	2	*629	*90	*18	.976
	—Albuquerque (PCL)	C	4	14	1	3	0	0	0	1	.214	0	23	3	3	.897
1990	—Albuquerque (PCL)	C	52	143	11	45	8	1	0	16	.315	2	207	31	8	.967
	—Los Angeles (N.L.)	C	10	20	2	4	1	0	0	1	.200	0	37	2	0	1.000
1991	—Albuquerque (PCL)	C	95	345	60	119	24	2	8	44	.345	5	*592	*77	*15	.978
	—Los Angeles (N.L.)	C-3B	15	14	1	3	1	0	0	1	.214	1	24	4	1	.966
Major league totals (2 years)			25	34	3	7	2	0	0	2	.206	1	61	6	1	.985

HERNANDEZ, CESAR
OF, REDS

PERSONAL: Born September 28, 1966, at Yamasa, Dominican Republic. . . . 6-0/160. . . . Throws right, bats right. . . . Full name: Cesar Dario Perez Hernandez.
HIGH SCHOOL: Juan Pablo Duarte (Santo Domingo, Dominican Republic).
COLLEGE: University of Autonona (Santo Domingo, Dominican Republic).
TRANSACTIONS/CAREER NOTES: Selected by Montreal Expos (first overall) in Dominican Draft (March 2, 1985). . . . On disabled list (June 3, 1986-remainder of season). . . . Claimed on waivers by Cincinnati Reds (December 2, 1991).

Year	Team (League)	Pos.	G	AB	R	H	2B	3B	HR	RBI	Avg.	SB	PO	A	E	Avg.
1986	—Burlington (Midwest)	OF	38	104	12	26	11	0	1	12	.250	7	62	1	3	.955
1987	—West Palm Beach (FSL)	OF	32	106	14	25	3	1	2	6	.236	6	60	4	3	.955
1988	—Rockford (Midwest)	OF	117	411	71	101	20	4	19	60	.246	28	188	9	16	.925
1989	—West Palm Beach (FSL)	OF	42	158	16	45	8	3	1	15	.285	16	53	6	0	1.000
	—Jacksonville (Southern)	OF	81	222	25	47	9	1	3	13	.212	22	109	7	11	.913
1990	—Jacksonville (Southern)	OF	118	393	58	94	21	7	10	50	.239	17	203	14	3	.986
1991	—Harrisburg (Eastern)	OF	128	418	58	106	15	2	13	52	.254	34	222	*21	5	.980

HERNANDEZ, JEREMY
P, PADRES

PERSONAL: Born July 6, 1966, at Burbank, Calif. . . . 6-6/205. . . . Throws right, bats right. . . . Full name: Jeremy Stuart Hernandez.
HIGH SCHOOL: Francis Poly (Sun Valley, Calif.).
COLLEGE: Cal State Northridge.
TRANSACTIONS/CAREER NOTES: Selected by St. Louis Cardinals organization in second round of free-agent draft (June 2, 1987). . . . Traded by Cardinals organization to Charleston, S.C. (San Diego Padres organization) for OF Randell Byers (April 24, 1989).
STATISTICAL NOTES: Led Texas League with 18 home runs allowed in 1990.

Year	Team (League)	G	W	L	Pct.	ERA	Sv.	IP	H	R	ER	BB	SO
1987	—Erie (New York-Penn)	16	5	4	.556	2.81	0	99⅓	87	36	31	41	62
1988	—Springfield (Midwest)	24	12	6	.667	3.54	0	147⅓	133	73	58	34	97
1989	—St. Petersburg (Florida State)	3	0	2	.000	7.71	0	14	17	14	12	5	5
	—Charleston, S.C. (S. Atlantic)■	10	3	5	.375	3.53	0	58⅔	65	37	23	16	39
	—Riverside (California)	9	5	2	.714	1.75	0	67	55	17	13	11	65
	—Wichita (Texas)	4	2	1	.667	8.53	0	19	30	18	18	8	9
1990	—Wichita (Texas)	26	7	6	.538	4.53	0	155	163	92	78	50	101
1991	—Las Vegas (Pacific Coast)	56	4	8	.333	4.74	13	68⅓	76	36	36	25	67
	—San Diego (N.L.)	9	0	0	. . .	0.00	2	14⅓	8	1	0	5	9
Major league totals (1 year)		9	0	0	. . .	0.00	2	14⅓	8	1	0	5	9

HERNANDEZ, JOSE
SS, RANGERS

PERSONAL: Born July 14, 1969, at Vega Alta, Puerto Rico. . . . 6-1/180. . . . Throws right, bats right. . . . Full name: Jose Hernandez.
HIGH SCHOOL: Maestro Ladi (Vega Alta, Puerto Rico).
COLLEGE: American University (Puerto Rico).
TRANSACTIONS/CAREER NOTES: Signed as free agent by Texas Rangers organization (January 13, 1987).
STATISTICAL NOTES: Led Gulf Coast League third basemen with .950 fielding percentage, 47 putouts and 11 double plays in 1988. . . . Led Florida State League shortstops with .959 fielding percentage in 1990.

						BATTING								FIELDING			
Year	Team (League)	Pos.	G	AB	R	H	2B	3B	HR	RBI	Avg.	SB	PO	A	E	Avg.
1987	Sarasota Rangers (GCL)...	SS	24	52	5	9	1	1	0	2	.173	2	30	38	5	.932
1988	Sarasota Rangers (GCL)...	IF-OF	55	162	19	26	7	1	1	13	.160	4	†68	115	8	†.958
1989	Gastonia (S. Atlantic)	3-S-2-O	91	215	35	47	7	6	1	16	.219	9	101	169	17	.941
1990	Charlotte (Florida State)...	SS-OF	121	388	43	99	14	7	1	44	.255	11	192	372	25	†.958
1991	Tulsa (Texas)	SS	91	301	36	72	17	4	1	20	.239	4	151	300	15	★.968
	Oklahoma City (A.A.)	SS	14	46	6	14	1	1	1	3	.304	0	32	43	3	.962
	Texas (A.L.).....................	SS-3B	45	98	8	18	2	1	0	4	.184	0	49	111	4	.976
Major league totals (1 year)			45	98	8	18	2	1	0	4	.184	0	49	111	4	.976

HERNANDEZ, ROBERTO
P, WHITE SOX

PERSONAL: Born November 11, 1964, at Santurce, Puerto Rico. . . . 6-4/220. . . . Throws right, bats right. . . . Full name: Roberto Manuel Hernandez.
HIGH SCHOOL: New Hampton Prep.
COLLEGE: South Carolina.
TRANSACTIONS/CAREER NOTES: Selected by California Angels organization in first round (16th pick overall) of free-agent draft (June 2, 1986). . . . On disabled list (May 6-21 and June 4-August 14, 1987). . . . Traded by Angels with OF Mark Doran to Chicago White Sox organization for OF Mark Davis (August 2, 1989). . . . On Vancouver disabled list (May 17-August 10, 1991).

Year	Team (League)	G	W	L	Pct.	ERA	Sv.	IP	H	R	ER	BB	SO
1986	Salem (Northwest)	10	2	2	.500	4.58	0	55	57	37	28	42	38
1987	Quad City (Midwest)	7	2	3	.400	6.86	1	21	24	21	16	12	21
1988	Quad City (Midwest)	24	9	10	.474	3.17	0	164⅔	157	70	58	48	114
	Midland (Texas)	3	0	2	.000	6.57	0	12⅓	16	13	9	8	7
1989	Midland (Texas)	12	2	7	.222	6.89	0	64	94	57	49	30	42
	Palm Springs (California)	7	1	4	.200	4.64	0	42⅔	49	27	22	16	33
	South Bend (Midwest)■	4	1	1	.500	3.33	0	24⅓	19	9	9	7	17
1990	Birmingham (Southern)	17	8	5	.615	3.67	0	108	103	57	44	43	62
	Vancouver (Pacific Coast)	11	3	5	.375	2.84	0	79⅓	73	33	25	26	49
1991	Birmingham (Southern)	4	2	1	.667	1.99	0	22⅔	11	5	5	6	25
	Vancouver (Pacific Coast)	7	4	1	.800	3.22	0	44⅔	41	17	16	23	40
	Sarasota White Sox (GCL)	1	0	0	...	0.00	0	6	2	0	0	0	7
	Chicago (A.L.)	9	1	0	1.000	7.80	0	15	18	15	13	7	6
Major league totals (1 year)		9	1	0	1.000	7.80	0	15	18	15	13	7	6

HERNANDEZ, XAVIER
P, ASTROS

PERSONAL: Born August 16, 1965, at Port Arthur, Tex. . . . 6-2/185. . . . Throws right, bats left. . . . Full name: Francis Xavier Hernandez.
HIGH SCHOOL: Thomas Jefferson (Port Arthur, Tex.).
COLLEGE: Southwestern Louisiana.
TRANSACTIONS/CAREER NOTES: Selected by Toronto Blue Jays organization in fourth round of free-agent draft (June 2, 1986). . . . Drafted by Houston Astros (December 4, 1989). . . . On Houston disabled list (June 3-26, 1991); included rehabilitation disability assignment to Tucson (June 14-26, 1991).

Year	Team (League)	G	W	L	Pct.	ERA	Sv.	IP	H	R	ER	BB	SO
1986	St. Catharines (N.Y.-Penn)	13	5	5	.500	2.67	0	70⅔	55	27	21	16	69
1987	St. Catharines (N.Y.-Penn)	13	3	3	.500	5.07	0	55	57	39	31	16	49
1988	Myrtle Beach (South Atlantic) ..	23	13	6	.684	2.55	0	148	116	52	42	28	111
	Knoxville (Southern)	11	2	4	.333	2.90	0	68⅓	73	32	22	15	33
1989	Knoxville (Southern)	4	1	1	.500	4.13	0	24	25	11	11	11	17
	Syracuse (International)	15	5	6	.455	3.53	0	99⅓	95	42	39	22	47
	Toronto (A.L.)	7	1	0	1.000	4.76	0	22⅔	25	15	12	8	7
1990	Houston (N.L.)■...................	34	2	1	.667	4.62	0	62⅓	60	34	32	24	24
1991	Houston (N.L.)	32	2	7	.222	4.71	3	63	66	34	33	32	55
	Tucson (Pacific Coast)	16	2	1	.667	2.75	4	36	35	16	11	9	34
American League totals (1 year)		7	1	0	1.000	4.76	0	22⅔	25	15	12	8	7
National League totals (2 years)		66	4	8	.333	4.67	3	125⅓	126	68	65	56	79
Major league totals (3 years)		73	5	8	.385	4.68	3	148	151	83	77	64	86

HERR, TOM
2B

PERSONAL: Born April 4, 1956, at Lancaster, Pa. . . . 6-0/196. . . . Throws right, bats both. . . . Full name: Thomas Mitchell Herr.
HIGH SCHOOL: Hempfield (Ladisville, Pa.).
COLLEGE: Delaware.
TRANSACTIONS/CAREER NOTES: Signed as free agent by St. Louis Cardinals organization (August 22, 1974). . . . On St. Louis disabled list (March 25-April 29 and August 9, 1983-remainder of season); included rehabilitation disability assignment to Ar-

kansas (April 18-29, 1983).... On disabled list (April 24-May 12 1987).... Traded by Cardinals to Minnesota Twins for OF Tom Brunansky (April 22, 1988).... On Minnesota disabled list (June 21-July 22 and July 25-August 18, 1988).... Traded by Twins with C Tom Nieto and OF Eric Bullock to Philadelphia Phillies for P Shane Rawley and cash (October 24, 1988).... Granted free agency (November 4, 1988).... Re-signed by Phillies (November 17, 1988).... Traded by Phillies to New York Mets for P Rocky Elli and 1B Nikco Riesgo (August 30, 1990).... Released by Mets (August 5, 1991).... Signed by San Francisco Giants (August 15, 1991).... Released by Giants (October 6, 1991).

RECORDS/HONORS: Named second baseman on THE SPORTING NEWS N.L. All-Star team (1985).

STATISTICAL NOTES: Led Florida State League second basemen with 91 double plays in 1977.... Led N.L. second basemen with 590 total chances in 1981.... Led N.L. second basemen with 74 double plays in 1981, 106 in 1984, 121 in 1986 and tied for lead with 94 in 1990.... Led N.L. with 13 sacrifice flies in 1985 and 12 in 1987.

Year	Team (League)	Pos.	G	AB	R	H	2B	3B	HR	RBI	Avg.	SB	PO	A	E	Avg.
1975 —Johnson City (Appal.)		2B-SS	42	133	29	41	8	1	0	15	.308	10	74	125	5	.975
1976 —St. Petersburg (Fla. St.)		SS-2B	82	275	47	74	6	1	0	21	.269	12	133	211	18	.950
1977 —St. Petersburg (Fla. St.)		2B	136	*515	*80	*156	13	7	1	53	.303	*50	*348	*430	21	*.974
1978 —Arkansas (Texas)		2B	89	335	70	98	23	4	3	45	.293	30	207	280	13	.974
—Springfield (Am. Assoc.) ...		2B	33	86	16	24	6	1	0	8	.279	3	45	63	7	.939
1979 —Springfield (Am. Assoc.) ...		2B	109	423	74	124	20	6	6	48	.293	29	225	324	10	*.982
—St. Louis (N.L.)		2B	14	10	4	2	0	0	0	1	.200	1	12	11	0	1.000
1980 —Springfield (Am. Assoc.) ...		2B-3B	37	141	29	44	6	2	1	16	.312	19	29	52	1	.988
—St. Louis (N.L.)		2B-SS	76	222	29	55	12	5	0	15	.248	9	124	184	7	.978
1981 —St. Louis (N.L.)		2B	103	411	50	110	14	9	0	46	.268	23	211	*374	5	*.992
1982 —St. Louis (N.L.)		2B	135	493	83	131	19	4	0	36	.266	25	263	427	9	.987
1983 —St. Louis (N.L.)		2B	89	313	43	101	14	4	2	31	.323	6	178	245	6	.986
—Arkansas (Texas)		2B	3	9	0	4	3	0	0	1	.444	0	4	9	0	1.000
1984 —St. Louis (N.L.)		2B	145	558	67	154	23	2	4	49	.276	13	328	452	6	.992
1985 —St. Louis (N.L.)		2B	159	596	97	180	38	3	8	110	.302	31	337	448	12	.985
1986 —St. Louis (N.L.)		2B	152	559	48	141	30	4	2	61	.252	22	352	414	9	.988
1987 —St. Louis (N.L.)		2B	141	510	73	134	29	0	2	83	.263	19	306	350	7	.989
1988 —St. Louis (N.L.)		2B	15	50	4	13	0	0	1	3	.260	3	28	35	1	.984
—Minnesota (A.L.) ■		2B-SS	86	304	42	80	16	0	1	21	.263	10	140	195	4	.988
1989 —Philadelphia (N.L.) ■.....		2B	151	561	65	161	25	6	2	37	.287	10	281	415	7	.990
1990 —Phil.-New York (N.L.) ■.....		2B	146	547	48	143	26	3	5	60	.261	7	275	349	7	.989
1991 —New York-S.F. (N.L.) ■.....2B-3B-OF			102	215	23	45	8	1	1	21	.209	9	116	151	0	1.000
American League totals (1 year)			86	304	42	80	16	0	1	21	.263	10	140	195	4	.988
National League totals (13 years)			1428	5045	634	1370	238	41	27	553	.272	178	2811	3855	76	.989
Major league totals (13 years)			1514	5349	676	1450	254	41	28	574	.271	188	2951	4050	80	.989

CHAMPIONSHIP SERIES RECORD

CHAMPIONSHIP SERIES NOTES: Shares single-series record for most doubles—4 (1985).

Year	Team (League)	Pos.	G	AB	R	H	2B	3B	HR	RBI	Avg.	SB	PO	A	E	Avg.
1982 —St. Louis (N.L.)		2B	3	13	1	3	1	0	0	0	.231	0	6	10	0	1.000
1985 —St. Louis (N.L.)		2B	6	21	2	7	4	0	1	6	.333	1	13	12	0	1.000
1987 —St. Louis (N.L.)		2B	7	27	0	6	0	0	0	3	.222	0	12	11	1	.958
Championship Series totals (3 years)			16	61	3	16	5	0	1	9	.262	1	31	33	1	.985

WORLD SERIES RECORD

WORLD SERIES NOTES: Holds seven-game series record for most double plays started by second baseman—5 (1985).... Holds record for most runs batted in on sacrifice fly—2 (October 16, 1982, second inning).

Year	Team (League)	Pos.	G	AB	R	H	2B	3B	HR	RBI	Avg.	SB	PO	A	E	Avg.
1982 —St. Louis (N.L.)		2B	7	25	2	4	2	0	0	5	.160	0	11	19	1	.968
1985 —St. Louis (N.L.)		2B	7	26	2	4	2	0	0	0	.154	0	11	13	0	1.000
1987 —St. Louis (N.L.)		2B	7	28	2	7	0	0	1	1	.250	0	23	17	0	1.000
World Series totals (3 years)			21	79	6	15	4	0	1	6	.190	0	45	49	1	.989

ALL-STAR GAME RECORD

Year	League	Pos.	AB	R	H	2B	3B	HR	RBI	Avg.	SB	PO	A	E	Avg.
1985 —National		2B	3	1	1	1	0	0	0	.333	0	0	1	0	1.000

HERSHISER, OREL

P, DODGERS

PERSONAL: Born September 16, 1958, at Buffalo, N.Y. ... 6-3/190. ... Throws right, bats right. ... Full name: Orel Leonard Hershiser IV. ... Brother of Gordie Hershiser, minor league pitcher (1987-88).... Name pronounced her-SHY-zer.
HIGH SCHOOL: Cherry Hills East (N.J.).

COLLEGE: Bowling Green State.

TRANSACTIONS/CAREER NOTES: Selected by Los Angeles Dodgers organization in 17th round of free-agent draft (June 5, 1979). ... On disabled list (April 27, 1990-through remainder of season).... On Los Angeles disabled list (March 31-May 29, 1991); included rehabilitation disability assignment to Bakersfield (May 8-13, 1991 and May 18-24, 1991), Albuquerque (May 13-18, 1991) and San Antonio (May 24-29, 1991).... Granted free agency (November 1, 1991).... Re-signed by Dodgers (December 3, 1991).

RECORDS/HONORS: Holds major league single-season record for most consecutive scoreless innings—59 (August 30, sixth inning, through September 28, 10th inning, 1988).... Shares N.L. single-season record for fewest games lost by pitcher who led league—15 (1989).... Shares N.L. single-month record for most shutouts—5 (September, 1988).... Named Major League Player of the Year by THE SPORTING NEWS (1988).... Named N.L. Pitcher of the Year by THE SPORTING NEWS (1988).... Named righthanded pitcher on THE SPORTING NEWS N.L. All-Star team (1988).... Won N.L. Gold Glove at pitcher (1988). ... Named N.L. Cy Young Award winner by Baseball Writers' Association of America (1988).

STATISTICAL NOTES: Led N.L. with eight shutouts in 1988 and tied for lead with four in 1984.... Tied for N.L. lead with 15 complete games in 1988.... Tied for N.L. lead in sacrifice hits by batter with 19 in 1988.

Year	Team (League)	G	W	L	Pct.	ERA	Sv.	IP	H	R	ER	BB	SO
1979 —Clinton (Midwest)		15	4	0	1.000	2.09	2	43	33	15	10	17	33
1980 —San Antonio (Texas)		49	5	9	.357	3.55	14	109	120	59	43	59	75
1981 —San Antonio (Texas)		42	7	6	.538	4.68	★15	102	94	54	53	50	95
1982 —Albuquerque (Pacific Coast)		47	9	6	.600	3.71	4	123⅔	121	73	51	63	93
1983 —Albuquerque (Pacific Coast)		49	10	8	.556	4.09	16	134⅓	132	73	61	57	95
—Los Angeles (N.L.)		8	0	0	...	3.38	1	8	7	6	3	6	5
1984 —Los Angeles (N.L.)		45	11	8	.579	2.66	2	189⅔	160	65	56	50	150
1985 —Los Angeles (N.L.)		36	19	3	★.864	2.03	0	239⅔	179	72	54	68	157
1986 —Los Angeles (N.L.)		35	14	14	.500	3.85	0	231⅓	213	112	99	86	153
1987 —Los Angeles (N.L.)		37	16	16	.500	3.06	1	★264⅔	247	105	90	74	190
1988 —Los Angeles (N.L.)		35	•23	8	.742	2.26	1	★267	208	73	67	73	178
1989 —Los Angeles (N.L.)		35	15	•15	.500	2.31	0	★256⅔	226	75	66	77	178
1990 —Los Angeles (N.L.)		4	1	1	.500	4.26	0	25⅓	26	12	12	4	16
1991 —Bakersfield (California)		2	2	0	1.000	0.82	0	11	5	2	1	1	6
—Albuquerque (Pacific Coast)		1	0	0	...	0.00	0	5	5	0	0	0	5
—San Antonio (Texas)		1	0	1	.000	2.57	0	7	11	3	2	1	5
—Los Angeles (N.L.)		21	7	2	.778	3.46	0	112	112	43	43	32	73
Major league totals (9 years)		256	106	67	.613	2.77	5	1594⅓	1378	563	490	470	1100

CHAMPIONSHIP SERIES RECORD

CHAMPIONSHIP SERIES NOTES: Holds single-series record for most innings pitched—24⅔ (1988).... Holds N.L. single-game record for most hit batsmen—2 (October 12, 1988).... Shares N.L. career records for most complete games—2; most hit batsmen—2.... Shares N.L. single-series record for most hit batsmen—2 (1988).

Year	Team (League)	G	W	L	Pct.	ERA	Sv.	IP	H	R	ER	BB	SO
1985 —Los Angeles (N.L.)		2	1	0	1.000	3.52	0	15⅓	17	6	6	6	5
1988 —Los Angeles (N.L.)		4	1	0	1.000	1.09	1	24⅔	18	5	3	7	15
Championship Series totals (2 years)		6	2	0	1.000	2.03	1	40	35	11	9	13	20

WORLD SERIES RECORD

Year	Team (League)	G	W	L	Pct.	ERA	Sv.	IP	H	R	ER	BB	SO
1988 —Los Angeles (N.L.)		2	2	0	1.000	1.00	0	18	7	2	2	6	17

ALL-STAR GAME RECORD

Year	League	W	L	Pct.	ERA	Sv.	IP	H	R	ER	BB	SO
1987 —National		0	0	...	0.00	0	2	1	0	0	1	0
1988 —National		0	0	...	0.00	0	1	0	0	0	0	0
1989 —National						Did not play						
All-Star totals (2 years)		0	0	...	0.00	0	3	1	0	0	1	0

HESKETH, JOE

P, RED SOX

PERSONAL: Born February 15, 1959, at Lackawanna, N.Y.... 6-2/170.... Throws left, bats left.... Full name: Joseph Thomas Hesketh.

HIGH SCHOOL: Central (Hamburg, N.Y.).

COLLEGE: State University of New York.

TRANSACTIONS/CAREER NOTES: Selected by Montreal Expos organization in second round of free-agent draft (June 3, 1980).... On Memphis disabled list (April 9, 1981-remainder of season and April 8-July 8, 1982).... On Montreal disabled list (August 24, 1985-remainder of season; July 4, 1986-remainder of season; and August 18-September 8, 1989).... Claimed on waivers by Atlanta Braves (April 30, 1990).... Released by Braves (July 24, 1990).... Signed by Boston Red Sox (July 31, 1990).... Granted free agency (October 28, 1991).... Re-signed by Red Sox (December 19, 1991).

RECORDS/HONORS: Named American Association Pitcher of the Year (1984).

STATISTICAL NOTES: Tied for American Association lead with two shutouts in 1983.

Year	Team (League)	G	W	L	Pct.	ERA	Sv.	IP	H	R	ER	BB	SO
1980 —West Palm Beach (Florida St.)		11	8	2	.800	1.92	0	75	71	30	16	32	43
—Memphis (Southern)		3	1	0	1.000	4.05	0	20	20	13	9	7	20
1981 —							Did not play						
1982 —							Did not play						
—West Palm Beach (Florida St.)		8	3	2	.600	2.76	0	45⅔	41	16	14	16	24
1983 —Memphis (Southern)		11	6	4	.600	3.04	0	74	82	38	25	25	22
—Wichita (American Assoc.)		15	5	5	.500	5.09	0	88⅓	98	53	50	46	41
1984 —Indianapolis (Am. Assoc.)		22	12	3	.800	3.05	0	147⅔	120	60	50	54	135
—Montreal (N.L.)		11	2	2	.500	1.80	1	45	38	12	9	15	32
1985 —Montreal (N.L.)		25	10	5	.667	2.49	0	155⅓	125	52	43	45	113
1986 —Montreal (N.L.)		15	6	5	.545	5.01	0	82⅔	92	46	46	31	67
1987 —Bradenton Expos (Gulf Coast)		2	0	0	...	8.31	0	4⅓	7	4	4	0	8
—Jacksonville (Southern)		6	1	0	1.000	2.29	1	19⅔	18	6	5	4	22
—Montreal (N.L.)		18	0	0	...	3.14	1	28⅔	23	12	10	15	31

Year	Team (League)	G	W	L	Pct.	ERA	Sv.	IP	H	R	ER	BB	SO
1988	—Indianapolis (Am. Assoc.)	8	0	0	...	3.27	2	11	10	5	4	5	16
	—Montreal (N.L.)	60	4	3	.571	2.85	9	72⅔	63	30	23	35	64
1989	—Montreal (N.L.)	43	6	4	.600	5.77	3	48⅓	54	34	31	26	44
	—Indianapolis (Am. Assoc.)	5	0	0	...	3.86	1	9⅓	11	4	4	5	9
1990	—Montreal-Atlanta (N.L.)■........	33	1	2	.333	5.29	5	34	32	23	20	14	24
	—Boston (A.L.)■	12	0	4	.000	3.51	0	25⅔	37	12	10	11	26
1991	—Boston (A.L.)	39	12	4	*.750	3.29	0	153⅓	142	59	56	53	104
	American League totals (2 years)	51	12	8	.600	3.32	0	179	179	71	66	64	130
	National League totals (7 years)	205	29	21	.580	3.51	19	466⅔	427	209	182	181	375
	Major league totals (8 years)	256	41	29	.586	3.46	19	645⅔	606	280	248	245	505

HETZEL, ERIC

P, ORIOLES

PERSONAL: Born September 25, 1963, at Crowley, La.... 6-3/180.... Throws right, bats right. ... Full name: Eric Paul Hetzel.
HIGH SCHOOL: Notre Dame (Crowley, La.).
COLLEGE: Eastern Oklahoma State College and Louisiana State.
TRANSACTIONS/CAREER NOTES: Selected by Boston Red Sox organization in fifth round of free-agent draft (January 11, 1983). ... Selected by Kansas City Royals organization in second round of free-agent draft (January 17, 1984).... Selected by Pittsburgh Pirates organization in secondary phase of free-agent draft (June 4, 1984).... Selected by Boston Red Sox organization in secondary phase of free-agent draft (June 3, 1985).... On disabled list (April 9, 1986-entire season).... On Boston disabled list (August 3-24, 1989); included rehabilitation disability assignment to Pawtucket (August 18-24, 1989).... On Pawtucket disabled list (August 13, 1991-remainder of season).... Granted free agency (October 15, 1991).... Signed by Baltimore Orioles (November 13, 1991).

Year	Team (League)	G	W	L	Pct.	ERA	Sv.	IP	H	R	ER	BB	SO
1985	—Greensboro (South Atlantic)	15	7	5	.583	5.57	0	76	87	54	47	48	82
1986	—					Did not play							
1987	—Winter Haven (Florida State) ...	26	10	12	.455	3.55	0	192⅔	186	94	76	87	136
1988	—Pawtucket (International)	22	6	10	.375	3.96	0	127⅓	129	67	56	51	122
1989	—Pawtucket (International)	12	4	4	.500	2.48	0	80	65	27	22	32	79
	—Boston (A.L.)	12	2	3	.400	6.26	0	50⅓	61	39	35	28	33
1990	—Pawtucket (International)	19	6	5	.545	3.64	0	108⅔	85	51	44	74	90
	—Boston (A.L.)	9	1	4	.200	5.91	0	35	39	28	23	21	20
1991	—Pawtucket (International)	19	9	5	.643	3.57	0	116	110	60	46	58	83
	Major league totals (2 years)	21	3	7	.300	6.12	0	85⅓	100	67	58	49	53

HIBBARD, GREG

P, WHITE SOX

PERSONAL: Born September 13, 1964, at New Orleans.... 6-0/190.... Throws left, bats left. ... Full name: James Gregory Hibbard.
COLLEGE: Mississippi Gulf Coast Junior College and Alabama.
TRANSACTIONS/CAREER NOTES: Selected by Houston Astros organization in eighth round of free-agent draft (January 17, 1984).... Selected by Kansas City Royals organization in 16th round of free-agent draft (June 2, 1986).... Traded by Royals with P Melido Perez, P John Davis and P Chuck Mount to Chicago White Sox for P Floyd Bannister and 3B Dave Cochrane (December 10, 1987).

Year	Team (League)	G	W	L	Pct.	ERA	Sv.	IP	H	R	ER	BB	SO
1986	—Eugene (Northwest)	26	5	2	.714	3.46	5	39	30	23	15	19	44
1987	—Appleton (Midwest)	9	7	2	.778	1.11	0	64⅔	53	17	8	18	61
	—Fort Myers (Florida State)	3	2	1	.667	1.88	0	24	20	5	5	3	20
	—Memphis (Southern)	16	7	6	.538	3.23	0	106	102	48	38	21	56
1988	—Vancouver (Pacific Coast)■.....	25	11	11	.500	4.12	0	144⅓	155	74	66	44	65
1989	—Vancouver (Pacific Coast)	9	2	3	.400	2.64	0	58	47	24	17	11	45
	—Chicago (A.L.)	23	6	7	.462	3.21	0	137⅓	142	58	49	41	55
1990	—Chicago (A.L.)	33	14	9	.609	3.16	0	211	202	80	74	55	92
1991	—Chicago (A.L.)	32	11	11	.500	4.31	0	194	196	107	93	57	71
	—Vancouver (Pacific Coast)	1	0	0	...	3.38	0	5⅓	4	3	2	3	3
	Major league totals (3 years)	88	31	27	.534	3.58	0	542⅓	540	245	216	153	218

HICKERSON, BRYAN

P, GIANTS

PERSONAL: Born October 13, 1963, at Bemidji, Minn.... 6-2/195.... Throws left, bats left.... Full name: Bryan David Hickerson.
HIGH SCHOOL: Bemidji (Minn.).
COLLEGE: Minnesota (degree in sports and exercise science, 1987).
TRANSACTIONS/CAREER NOTES: Selected by St. Louis Cardinals organization in ninth round of free-agent draft (June 3, 1985). ... Selected by Minnesota Twins organization in seventh round of free-agent draft (June 2, 1986).... Loaned by Twins to San Francisco Giants organization (April 1, 1987); returned to Twins organization (June 14, 1987).... Traded by Twins organization to Giants organization (June 15, 1987), completing trade in which Twins traded P Jose Dominguez and P Ray Velasquez to Giants for P David Blakely and OF Dan Gladden (March 31, 1987).... On disabled list (entire 1988 season).

Year	Team (League)	G	W	L	Pct.	ERA	Sv.	IP	H	R	ER	BB	SO
1986	—Visalia (California)	11	4	3	.571	4.23	0	72⅓	72	37	34	25	69
1987	—Clinton (Midwest)■................	17	11	0	*1.000	1.24	1	94	60	17	13	37	103
	—Shreveport (Texas)■................	4	1	2	.333	3.94	0	16	20	7	7	4	23
1988	—					Did not play							

Year	Team (League)	G	W	L	Pct.	ERA	Sv.	IP	H	R	ER	BB	SO
1989 —San Jose (California)		21	11	6	.647	2.55	0	134	111	52	38	57	110
1990 —Shreveport (Texas)		27	3	6	.333	4.23	1	66	71	37	31	26	63
—Phoenix (Pacific Coast)		12	0	4	.000	5.50	0	34⅓	48	25	21	16	26
1991 —Shreveport (Texas)		23	3	4	.429	3.00	2	39	36	15	13	14	41
—Phoenix (Pacific Coast)		12	1	1	.500	3.80	2	21⅓	29	10	9	5	21
—San Francisco (N.L.)		17	2	2	.500	3.60	0	50	53	20	20	17	43
Major league totals (1 year)		17	2	2	.500	3.60	0	50	53	20	20	17	43

HICKEY, KEVIN
P

PERSONAL: Born February 25, 1956, at Chicago. . . . 6-1/200. . . . Throws left, bats left. . . . Full name: Kevin John Hickey.
HIGH SCHOOL: Kelly (Chicago).
TRANSACTIONS/CAREER NOTES: Signed as free agent by Chicago White Sox organization (August 18, 1977). . . . On disabled list (August 1-September 5, 1983). . . . Released by White Sox (March 26, 1984). . . . Re-signed by White Sox organization (April 2, 1984). . . . Traded by White Sox with P Doug Drabek to New York Yankees organization (August 13, 1984), completing deal in which Yankees traded IF Roy Smalley to White Sox for two players to be named later (July 18, 1984). . . . Released by Yankees organization (May 25, 1985). . . . Signed by Reading, Philadelphia Phillies organization (June 1, 1985). . . . Released by Phillies organization (September 30, 1986). . . . Signed by Hawaii, White Sox organization (March 11, 1987). . . . Released by White Sox organization (August 21, 1987). . . . Signed by Phoenix, San Francisco Giants organization (August 22, 1987). . . . Granted free agency (October 15, 1987). . . . Signed by Charlotte, Baltimore Orioles organization (December 18, 1987). . . . Released by Orioles (April 2, 1991). . . . Re-signed by Orioles organization (April 8, 1991). . . . Released by Orioles (July 11, 1991). . . . Signed by Phoenix, Giants organization (August 30, 1991). . . . Granted free agency (October 15, 1991).
STATISTICAL NOTES: Led Midwest League with five balks in 1979. . . . Led Eastern League with 20 home runs allowed and six balks in 1980.

Year	Team (League)	G	W	L	Pct.	ERA	Sv.	IP	H	R	ER	BB	SO
1978 —Paintsville (Appalachian)		9	2	4	.333	4.00	0	36	37	19	16	23	24
1979 —Appleton (Midwest)		29	5	10	.333	3.57	3	121	122	64	48	71	100
1980 —Glens Falls (Eastern)		26	9	7	.563	4.31	0	169	184	92	81	73	80
1981 —Chicago (A.L.)		41	0	2	.000	3.68	3	44	38	22	18	18	17
1982 —Chicago (A.L.)		60	4	4	.500	3.00	6	78	73	32	26	30	38
1983 —Chicago (A.L.)		23	1	2	.333	5.23	5	20⅔	23	14	12	11	8
1984 —Appleton (Midwest)		10	4	3	.571	2.36	1	49⅔	45	18	13	11	40
—Denver (American Assoc.)		16	2	2	.500	6.27	1	47⅓	61	39	33	23	20
—Columbus (International)		5	1	1	.500	8.68	0	9⅓	14	10	9	8	3
1985 —Albany-Reading (Eastern)■		44	5	5	.500	2.69	11	60⅓	53	22	18	22	44
1986 —Portland (Pacific Coast)		33	1	3	.250	6.51	2	65	76	54	47	29	44
1987 —Hawaii-Phoenix (Pac. Coast)■		46	4	5	.444	5.01	8	82⅔	88	52	46	36	48
1988 —Charlotte (Florida State)■		6	1	1	.500	3.72	0	9⅔	10	4	4	8	7
—Rochester (International)		27	2	0	1.000	1.46	2	37	31	7	6	9	24
1989 —Baltimore (A.L.)		51	2	3	.400	2.92	2	49⅓	38	16	16	23	28
1990 —Baltimore (A.L.)		37	1	3	.250	5.13	1	26⅓	26	16	15	13	17
—Rochester (International)		16	2	1	.667	5.79	3	23⅓	31	15	15	7	28
1991 —Hagerstown (Eastern)		15	0	1	.000	1.83	3	19⅔	15	6	4	6	20
—Baltimore (A.L.)		19	1	0	1.000	9.00	0	14	15	14	14	6	10
—Phoenix (Pacific Coast)■		5	0	0	...	20.65	0	5⅔	18	13	13	1	5
Major league totals (6 years)		231	9	14	.391	3.91	17	232⅓	213	114	101	101	118

HIGUERA, TEDDY
P, BREWERS

PERSONAL: Born November 9, 1958, at Los Mochis, Mexico. . . . 5-10/178. . . . Throws left, bats both. . . . Full name: Teodoro Valenzuela Higuera. . . . Name pronounced he-GARE-uh.
HIGH SCHOOL: Los Mochis (Los Mochis Sinaloa, Mexico).
TRANSACTIONS/CAREER NOTES: Sold to Vancouver, Milwaukee Brewers organization (September 13, 1983). . . . On Milwaukee disabled list (March 25-May 1, 1989); included rehabilitation disability assignment to El Paso (April 9-28, 1989). . . . On disabled list (June 14-29, 1990). . . . Granted free agency (November 5, 1990). . . . Re-signed by Brewers (December 5, 1990). . . . On Milwaukee disabled list (March 29-May 28, 1991); included rehabilitation disability assignment to Denver (May 19-28, 1991). . . . On disabled list (July 5, 1991-remainder of season).
RECORDS/HONORS: Named A.L. Rookie Pitcher of the Year by THE SPORTING NEWS (1985). . . . Named lefthanded pitcher on THE SPORTING NEWS A.L. All-Star team (1986).
STATISTICAL NOTES: Played a 20-team season and a 6-team short season with Ciudad Juarez of Mexican League (1980). . . . Tied for Mexican League lead in games started by pitcher with 27 and complete games with 18 in 1983.

Year	Team (League)	G	W	L	Pct.	ERA	Sv.	IP	H	R	ER	BB	SO
1979 —Ciudad Juarez (Mexican)		2	0	1	.000	45.00	0	1	4	5	5	4	1
1980 —Ciudad Juarez (Mexican)		19	8	3	.727	1.85	0	117	111	30	24	59	76
—Ciudad Juarez (Mexican)		8	2	5	.286	3.67	0	49	44	22	20	17	29
1981 —Ciudad Juarez (Mexican)		28	16	9	.640	3.10	0	203	207	81	70	69	157
1982 —Ciudad Juarez (Mexican)		24	9	12	.429	4.05	0	142⅓	163	77	64	53	74
1983 —Ciudad Juarez (Mexican)		27	•17	8	.680	2.03	0	*222	177	61	50	68	*165
1984 —El Paso (Texas)■		19	8	7	.533	*2.60	0	121	116	57	35	43	99
--Vancouver (Pacific Coast)		8	1	4	.200	4.73	0	40	49	26	21	14	29
1985 —Milwaukee (A.L.)		32	15	8	.652	3.90	0	212⅓	186	105	92	63	127

— 217 —

Year	Team (League)	G	W	L	Pct.	ERA	Sv.	IP	H	R	ER	BB	SO
1986 —Milwaukee (A.L.)		34	20	11	.645	2.79	0	248⅓	226	84	77	74	207
1987 —Milwaukee (A.L.)		35	18	10	.643	3.85	0	261⅔	236	120	112	87	240
1988 —Milwaukee (A.L.)		31	16	9	.640	2.45	0	227⅓	168	66	62	59	192
1989 —El Paso (Texas)		1	0	1	.000	1.80	0	5	5	2	1	1	4
—Milwaukee (A.L.)		22	9	6	.600	3.46	0	135⅓	125	56	52	48	91
1990 —Milwaukee (A.L.)		27	11	10	.524	3.76	0	170	167	80	71	50	129
1991 —Denver (American Assoc.)		2	1	0	1.000	2.08	0	8⅔	6	3	2	6	6
—Milwaukee (A.L.)		7	3	2	.600	4.46	0	36⅓	37	18	18	10	33
Major league totals (7 years)		**188**	**92**	**56**	**.622**	**3.37**	**0**	**1291⅓**	**1145**	**529**	**484**	**391**	**1019**

ALL-STAR GAME RECORD

Year	League	W	L	Pct.	ERA	Sv.	IP	H	R	ER	BB	SO
1986 —American	0	0	...	0.00	0	3	1	0	0	1	2

HILL, DONNIE
2B/SS, TWINS

PERSONAL: Born November 12, 1960, at Pomona, Calif. . . . 5-10/160. . . . Throws right, bats both. . . . Full name: Donald Earl Hill.
HIGH SCHOOL: Edison (Huntington Beach, Calif.).
COLLEGE: Orange Coast College (Calif.) and Arizona State.
TRANSACTIONS/CAREER NOTES: Selected by Houston Astros organization in fifth round of free-agent draft (January 8, 1980). . . . Selected by San Francisco Giants organization in secondary phase of free-agent draft (June 3, 1980). . . . Selected by Oakland A's organization in secondary phase of free-agent draft (June 8, 1981). . . . On temporary inactive list (April 13-23, 1982). . . . On Tacoma disabled list (April 30-May 10, 1983). . . . On Oakland disabled list (May 3-18, 1984). . . . Traded by A's to Chicago White Sox for P Gene Nelson and a player to be named later (December 18, 1986); A's acquired P Bruce Tanner to complete deal (December 18, 1986). . . . On Chicago disabled list (May 30-June 14 and July 29-August 13, 1987); included rehabilitation disability assignment to Hawaii (June 6-14, 1987). . . . Released by White Sox organization (March 9, 1989). . . . Signed by Tacoma, A's organization (March 22, 1989). . . . Released by A's organization (August 9, 1989). . . . Signed by Edmonton, California Angels organization (January 5, 1990). . . . On disabled list (August 25-September 11, 1990). . . . Granted free agency (November 5, 1990). . . . Re-signed by Angels (December 19, 1990). . . . Granted free agency (November 1, 1991). . . . Signed by Minnesota Twins organization (January 17, 1992).
STATISTICAL NOTES: Tied for Eastern League lead with eight sacrifice flies in 1982.

Year	Team (League)	Pos.	G	AB	R	H	2B	3B	HR	RBI	Avg.	SB	PO	A	E	Avg.
1981 —Modesto (California)	SS-2B	46	149	21	29	3	0	6	22	.195	9	44	84	22	.853
1982 —West Haven (Eastern)	SS-3B	132	405	66	103	21	3	10	59	.254	15	141	301	29	.938
1983 —Tacoma (Pacific Coast)	SS	93	322	45	101	19	2	14	63	.314	9	148	256	18	.957
—Oakland (A.L.)	SS	53	158	20	42	7	0	2	15	.266	1	87	136	9	.961
1984 —Oakland (A.L.)	SS-2B-3B	73	174	21	40	6	0	2	16	.230	1	102	128	12	.950
—Tacoma (Pacific Coast)	SS-2B	42	141	28	46	12	3	2	24	.326	7	71	92	4	.976
1985 —Oakland (A.L.)	2B	123	393	45	112	13	2	3	48	.285	4	228	320	15	.973
1986 —Oakland (A.L.)	2B-3B-SS	108	339	37	96	18	2	4	29	.283	5	104	213	9	.972
1987 —Chicago (A.L.)■	2B-3B	111	410	57	98	14	6	9	46	.239	1	167	278	14	.969
—Hawaii (Pacific Coast)	2B	7	23	10	9	2	0	2	6	.391	2	11	11	0	1.000
1988 —Chicago (A.L.)	2B-3B	83	221	17	48	6	1	2	20	.217	3	118	152	8	.971
—Vancouver (Pac. Coast)	2B	7	26	5	9	4	0	0	7	.346	1	4	10	1	.933
1989 —Tacoma (Pacific Coast)■	2-3-S-P	58	180	26	47	7	2	4	23	.261	4	69	102	7	.961
1990 —California (A.L.)■	IF-P	103	352	36	93	18	2	3	32	.264	1	194	255	11	.976
1991 —California (A.L.)	2B-SS-1B	77	209	36	50	8	1	1	20	.239	1	127	176	8	.974
Major league totals (8 years)		**731**	**2256**	**269**	**579**	**88**	**14**	**26**	**226**	**.257**	**21**	**1127**	**1658**	**86**	**.970**

RECORD AS PITCHER

Year	Team (League)	G	W	L	Pct.	ERA	Sv.	IP	H	R	ER	BB	SO
1989 —Tacoma (Pacific Coast)■	1	0	0	...	0.00	0	1	1	0	0	0	0
1990 —California (A.L.)■	1	0	0	...	0.00	0	1	0	0	0	1	1
Major league totals (1 year)	**1**	**0**	**0**	**...**	**0.00**	**0**	**1**	**0**	**0**	**0**	**1**	**1**

HILL, GLENALLEN
OF, INDIANS

PERSONAL: Born March 22, 1965, at Santa Cruz, Calif. . . . 6-2/210. . . . Throws right, bats right. . . . Full name: Glenallen Hill.
HIGH SCHOOL: Santa Cruz (Calif.).
TRANSACTIONS/CAREER NOTES: Selected by Toronto Blue Jays organization in ninth round of free-agent draft (June 6, 1983). . . . On disabled list (July 6-21, 1990). . . . Traded by Blue Jays with P Denis Boucher, OF Mark Whiten and a player to be named later to Cleveland Indians for P Tom Candiotti and OF Turner Ward (June 27, 1991); Indians acquired cash instead of player to complete deal (October 15, 1991). . . . On Cleveland disabled list (September 8, 1991-remainder of season).
STATISTICAL NOTES: Led South Atlantic League batters with 150 strikeouts in 1984. . . . Led Carolina League batters with 211 strikeouts in 1985. . . . Led Southern League batters with 287 total bases, 153 strikeouts and tied for lead with 13 sacrifice flies in 1986. . . . Led International League batters with 152 strikeouts in 1987. . . . Led International League with 279 total bases and .578 slugging percentage in 1989.

Year	Team (League)	Pos.	G	AB	R	H	2B	3B	HR	RBI	Avg.	SB	PO	A	E	Avg.
1983 —Medicine Hat (Pioneer)	OF	46	133	34	63	3	4	6	27	.474	4	63	3	6	.917
1984 —Florence (S. Atlantic)	OF	129	440	75	105	19	5	16	64	.239	30	281	9	16	.948
1985 —Kinston (Carolina)	OF	131	466	57	98	13	0	20	56	.210	42	234	12	13	.950

Year	Team (League)	Pos.	G	AB	R	H	2B	3B	HR	RBI	Avg.	SB	PO	A	E	Avg.
1986 —Knoxville (Southern)		OF	141	*570	87	159	23	6	*31	96	.279	18	230	9	*21	.919
1987 —Syracuse (International) ..		OF	*137	536	65	126	25	6	16	77	.235	22	176	10	10	.949
1988 —Syracuse (International) ..		OF	51	172	21	40	7	0	4	19	.233	7	101	2	1	.990
—Knoxville (Southern)		OF	79	269	37	71	13	2	12	38	.264	10	130	6	5	.965
1989 —Syracuse (International) ..		OF	125	483	*86	*155	31	*15	*21	72	.321	21	242	3	*7	.972
—Toronto (A.L.)		OF	19	52	4	15	0	0	1	7	.288	2	27	0	1	.964
1990 —Toronto (A.L.)		OF	84	260	47	60	11	3	12	32	.231	8	115	4	2	.983
1991 —Toronto-Clev. (A.L.)■		OF	72	221	29	57	8	2	8	25	.258	6	118	0	3	.975
Major league totals (3 years)			175	533	80	132	19	5	21	64	.248	16	260	4	6	.978

HILL, KEN
P, EXPOS

PERSONAL: Born December 14, 1965, at Lynn, Mass. . . . 6-2/175. . . . Throws right, bats right. . . . Full name: Kenneth Wade Hill.
HIGH SCHOOL: Classical (Lynn, Mass.).
TRANSACTIONS/CAREER NOTES: Signed as free agent by Detroit Tigers organization (February 14, 1985). . . . Traded by Tigers with a player to be named later to St. Louis Cardinals for C Mike Heath (August 10, 1986); Cardinals acquired 1B Mike Laga to complete deal (September 2, 1986). . . . On St. Louis disabled list (March 26-May 9, 1988). . . . On St. Louis disabled list (August 11-September 1, 1991); included rehabilitation disability assignment to Louisville (August 29-30, 1991). . . . Traded by Cardinals to Montreal Expos for 1B Andres Galarraga (November 25, 1991).
RECORDS/HONORS: Shares N.L. single-season record for fewest games lost by pitcher who led league—15 (1989).

Year	Team (League)	G	W	L	Pct.	ERA	Sv.	IP	H	R	ER	BB	SO
1985 —Gastonia (South Atlantic)		15	3	6	.333	4.96	0	69	60	51	38	57	48
1986 —Gastonia (South Atlantic)		22	9	5	.643	2.79	0	122⅔	95	51	38	80	86
—Glens Falls (Eastern)		1	0	1	.000	5.14	0	7	4	4	4	6	4
—Arkansas (Texas)■		3	1	2	.333	4.50	0	18	18	10	9	7	9
1987 —Arkansas (Texas)		18	3	5	.375	5.20	2	53⅔	60	33	31	30	48
—St. Petersburg (Florida State) ..		18	1	3	.250	4.17	2	41	38	19	19	17	32
1988 —St. Louis (N.L.)		4	0	1	.000	5.14	0	14	16	9	8	6	6
—Arkansas (Texas)		22	9	9	.500	4.92	0	115⅓	129	76	63	50	107
1989 —Louisville (American Assoc.) ...		3	0	2	.000	3.50	0	18	13	8	7	10	18
—St. Louis (N.L.)		33	7	•15	.318	3.80	0	196⅔	186	92	83	*99	112
1990 —St. Louis (N.L.)		17	5	6	.455	5.49	0	78⅔	79	49	48	33	58
—Louisville (American Assoc.) ...		12	6	1	.857	1.79	0	85⅓	47	20	17	27	104
1991 —St. Louis (N.L.)		30	11	10	.524	3.57	0	181⅓	147	76	72	67	121
—Louisville (American Assoc.) ...		1	0	0	. . .	0.00	0	1	0	0	0	0	2
Major league totals (4 years)		84	23	32	.418	4.03	0	470⅔	428	226	211	205	297

HILL, MILT
P, REDS

PERSONAL: Born August 22, 1965, at Atlanta. . . . 6-0/180. . . . Throws right, bats right. . . . Full name: Milton Giles Hill.
HIGH SCHOOL: Redan (Stone Mountain, Ga.).
COLLEGE: DeKalb Community College (Ga.) and Georgia College.
TRANSACTIONS/CAREER NOTES: Selected by Atlanta Braves organization in 23rd round of free-agent draft (June 3, 1985). . . . Selected by Cincinnati Reds organization in 28th round of free-agent draft (June 2, 1987). . . . On Nashville disabled list (June 11-20, 1991).

Year	Team (League)	G	W	L	Pct.	ERA	Sv.	IP	H	R	ER	BB	SO
1987 —Billings (Pioneer)		21	3	1	.750	1.65	7	32⅔	25	10	6	4	40
1988 —Cedar Rapids (Midwest)		44	9	4	.692	2.07	13	78⅓	52	21	18	17	69
1989 —Chattanooga (Southern)		51	6	5	.545	2.06	13	70	49	19	16	28	63
1990 —Nashville (American Assoc.)		48	4	4	.500	2.27	3	71⅓	51	20	18	18	58
1991 —Nashville (American Assoc.)		37	3	3	.500	2.94	3	67⅓	59	26	22	15	62
—Cincinnati (N.L.)		22	1	1	.500	3.78	0	33⅓	36	14	14	8	20
Major league totals (1 year)		22	1	1	.500	3.78	0	33⅓	36	14	14	8	20

HILLEGAS, SHAWN
P, INDIANS

PERSONAL: Born August 21, 1964, at Dos Palos, Calif. . . . 6-2/223. . . . Throws right, bats right. . . . Full name: Shawn Patrick Hillegas. . . . Name pronounced HILL-uh-gus.
HIGH SCHOOL: Forest Hills (Sidman, Pa.).
COLLEGE: Middle Georgia College.
TRANSACTIONS/CAREER NOTES: Selected by California Angels organization in 26th round of free-agent draft (June 6, 1983). . . . Selected by Los Angeles Dodgers organization in secondary phase of free-agent draft (January 17, 1984). . . . Traded by Dodgers to Chicago White Sox (September 2, 1988), completing deal in which White Sox traded P Rick Horton to Dodgers for a player to be named later (August 30, 1988). . . . Traded by White Sox with P Eric King to Cleveland Indians for OF Cory Snyder and IF Lindsay Foster (December 4, 1990).

Year	Team (League)	G	W	L	Pct.	ERA	Sv.	IP	H	R	ER	BB	SO
1984 —Vero Beach (Florida State)		13	5	3	.625	1.83	0	93⅓	71	25	19	33	64
1985 —San Antonio (Texas)		23	4	10	.286	3.17	0	139⅓	134	72	49	67	56
1986 —San Antonio (Texas)		17	9	5	.643	3.06	0	132⅓	107	60	45	58	97
—Albuquerque (Pacific Coast)		9	1	5	.167	6.17	0	46⅔	48	35	32	31	43

Year	Team (League)	G	W	L	Pct.	ERA	Sv.	IP	H	R	ER	BB	SO
1987 —Albuquerque (Pacific Coast)		24	13	5	.722	3.37	0	165⅔	172	79	62	64	105
—Los Angeles (N.L.)		12	4	3	.571	3.57	0	58	52	27	23	31	51
1988 —Albuquerque (Pacific Coast)		16	6	4	.600	3.49	0	100⅔	93	44	39	22	66
—Los Angeles (N.L.)		11	3	4	.429	4.13	0	56⅔	54	26	26	17	30
—Chicago (A.L.)■		6	3	2	.600	3.15	0	40	30	16	14	18	26
1989 —Chicago (A.L.)		50	7	11	.389	4.74	3	119⅔	132	67	63	51	76
1990 —Vancouver (Pacific Coast)		36	5	3	.625	1.74	9	67⅓	49	22	13	15	52
—Chicago (A.L.)		7	0	0	. . .	0.79	0	11⅓	4	1	1	5	5
1991 —Cleveland (A.L.)■		51	3	4	.429	4.34	7	83	67	42	40	46	66
American League totals (4 years)		114	13	17	.433	4.18	10	254	233	126	118	120	173
National League totals (2 years)		23	7	7	.500	3.85	0	114⅔	106	53	49	48	81
Major league totals (5 years)		137	20	24	.455	4.08	10	368⅔	339	179	167	168	254

HILLMAN, ERIC
P, METS

PERSONAL: Born April 27, 1966, at Gary, Ind. . . . 6-10/235. . . . Throws left, bats left. . . . Full name: John Eric Hillman.
HIGH SCHOOL: Homewood Flossmoor (Flossmoor, Ill.).
COLLEGE: Eastern Illinois.
TRANSACTIONS/CAREER NOTES: Selected by New York Mets organization in 16th round of free-agent draft (June 2, 1987).
STATISTICAL NOTES: Tied for International League lead with 10 hit batsmen in 1991.

Year	Team (League)	G	W	L	Pct.	ERA	Sv.	IP	H	R	ER	BB	SO
1987 —Little Falls (New York-Penn)....		13	6	4	.600	4.22	0	79	84	44	37	30	80
1988 —Columbia (South Atlantic)		17	1	6	.143	5.55	1	73	73	54	45	43	60
1989 —Columbia (South Atlantic)		9	2	1	.667	1.87	1	33⅔	28	17	7	21	33
—St. Lucie (Florida State)............		19	6	6	.500	5.50	0	88⅓	96	59	54	53	67
1990 —St. Lucie (Florida State)............		4	2	0	1.000	0.67	0	27	15	2	2	8	23
—Jackson (Texas)		15	6	5	.545	3.93	0	89⅓	92	42	39	30	61
1991 —Tidewater (International)		27	5	12	.294	4.01	0	161⅔	184	89	72	58	91

HOFFMAN, TREVOR
P, REDS

PERSONAL: Born October 13, 1967, at Bellflower, Calif. . . . 6-0/200. . . . Throws right, bats right. . . . Full name: Trevor William Hoffman.
HIGH SCHOOL: Savanna (Anaheim, Calif.).
COLLEGE: Cypress (Calif.) and Arizona.
TRANSACTIONS/CAREER NOTES: Selected by Cincinnati Reds organization in 11th round of free-agent draft (June 5, 1989).

Year	Team (League)	G	W	L	Pct.	ERA	Sv.	IP	H	R	ER	BB	SO
1991 —Cedar Rapids (Midwest)		27	1	1	.500	1.87	12	33⅔	22	8	7	13	52
—Chattanooga (Southern)		14	1	0	1.000	1.93	8	14	10	4	3	7	23

RECORD AS POSITION PLAYER

Year	Team (League)	Pos.	G	AB	R	H	2B	3B	HR	RBI	Avg.	SB	PO	A	E	Avg.
1989 —Billings (Pioneer)...............	SS	61	201	22	50	5	0	1	20	.249	1	*116	140	•25	.911
1990 —Charleston, W.Va. (SAL) ..	SS-3B	103	278	41	59	10	1	2	23	.212	3	114	209	30	.915

HOILES, CHRIS
C, ORIOLES

PERSONAL: Born March 20, 1965, at Bowling Green, O. . . . 6-0/206. . . . Throws right, bats right. . . . Full name: Christopher Allen Hoiles.
HIGH SCHOOL: Elmwood (Wayne, O.).
COLLEGE: Eastern Michigan.
TRANSACTIONS/CAREER NOTES: Selected by Detroit Tigers organization in 19th round of free-agent draft (June 2, 1986). . . . Traded by Tigers organization with P Cesar Mejia and P Robinson Garces to Baltimore Orioles (September 9, 1988), completing deal in which Orioles traded OF Fred Lynn to Tigers for three players to be named later (August 31, 1988). . . . On Rochester disabled list (June 18-July 7, 1989).
STATISTICAL NOTES: Led Appalachian League first basemen with .996 fielding percentage, 515 putouts and 551 total chances in 1986. . . . Led Appalachian League with 143 total bases in 1986. . . . Led Eastern League with .500 slugging percentage in 1988. . . . Tied for Eastern League lead in double plays by catchers with five in 1988. . . . Led A.L. catchers with .998 fielding percentage in 1991.

Year	Team (League)	Pos.	G	AB	R	H	2B	3B	HR	RBI	Avg.	SB	PO	A	E	Avg.
1986 —Bristol (Appalachian)	1B-C	•68	253	42	81	*19	2	13	*57	.320	10	†563	38	4	†.993
1987 —Glens Falls (Eastern)	C-1B-3B	108	380	47	105	12	0	13	53	.276	1	406	88	11	.978
1988 —Glens Falls (Eastern)	C-1B	103	360	67	102	21	3	•17	73	.283	4	438	57	7	.986
—Toledo (International)■.....	C	22	69	4	11	1	0	2	6	.159	1	71	2	1	.986
1989 —Rochester (Int'l)	C-1B	96	322	41	79	19	1	10	51	.245	1	431	33	7	.985
—Baltimore (A.L.)	C	6	9	0	1	1	0	0	1	.111	0	11	0	0	1.000
1990 —Rochester (Int'l)	C-1B	74	247	52	86	20	1	18	56	.348	4	268	13	5	.983
—Baltimore (A.L.)	C-1B	23	63	7	12	3	0	1	6	.190	0	62	6	0	1.000
1991 —Baltimore (A.L.)	C-1B	107	341	36	83	15	0	11	31	.243	0	443	44	1	†.998
Major league totals (3 years)		136	413	43	96	19	0	12	38	.232	0	516	50	1	.998

HOLBERT, RAY
SS, PADRES

PERSONAL: Born September 25, 1970, at Torrance, Calif. . . . 6-0/170. . . . Throws right, bats right. . . . Full name: Ray Arthur Holbert. . . . Brother of Aaron Holbert, shortstop, St. Louis Cardinals organization.
HIGH SCHOOL: David Starr Jordan (Long Beach, Calif.).
TRANSACTIONS/CAREER NOTES: Selected by San Diego Padres organization in third round of free-agent draft (June 1, 1988).
STATISTICAL NOTES: Led Arizona League shortstops with .927 fielding percentage and 132 assists in 1988. . . . Led Midwest League shortstops with 75 double plays and 642 total chances in 1990.

Year	Team (League)	Pos.	G	AB	R	H	2B	3B	HR	RBI	Avg.	SB	PO	A	E	Avg.
1988 — Scottsdale Padres (Ariz.)..		SS-3B	49	170	38	44	1	0	3	19	.259	20	59 †137	15 †.929
1989 — Waterloo (Midwest)		SS-3B	117	354	37	55	7	1	0	20	.155	13	205	303	32	.941
1990 — Waterloo (Midwest)		SS	133	411	51	84	10	1	3	39	.204	16	*233	*378	31	.952
1991 — High Desert (California)		SS	122	386	76	102	14	2	4	51	.264	19	196	331	*37	.934

HOLDRIDGE, DAVID
P, ANGELS

PERSONAL: Born February 5, 1968, at Wayne, Mich. . . . 6-3/185. . . . Throws right, bats right. . . . Full name: David Allen Holdridge.
HIGH SCHOOL: Ocean View (Huntington Beach, Calif.).
TRANSACTIONS/CAREER NOTES: Selected by California Angels organization in first round (31st pick overall) of free-agent draft (June 2, 1987). . . . Traded by Angels organization to Philadelphia Phillies organization for C Lance Parrish (October 3, 1988). . . . On Reading disabled list (May 27-June 25, 1991). . . . Drafted by Angels (December 9, 1991).
STATISTICAL NOTES: Tied for Florida State League lead with 11 home runs allowed in 1989. . . . Tied for Eastern League lead with 13 home runs allowed in 1990.

Year	Team (League)	G	W	L	Pct.	ERA	Sv.	IP	H	R	ER	BB	SO
1988 — Quad City (Midwest)	28	6	12	.333	3.87	0	153⅔	151	92	66	66	110
1989 — Clearwater (Florida State)■......	24	7	10	.412	5.71	0	132⅓	147	*100	*84	77	77
1990 — Reading (Eastern)	24	8	12	.400	4.58	0	127⅔	114	74	65	*79	78
1991 — Reading (Eastern)	7	0	2	.000	5.47	0	26⅓	26	24	16	34	19
— Clearwater (Florida State)	15	0	0	. . .	7.56	1	25	34	23	21	21	23

HOLLINS, DAVE
3B/1B, PHILLIES

PERSONAL: Born May 25, 1966, at Buffalo, N.Y. . . . 6-1/207. . . . Throws right, bats both. . . . Full name: David Michael Hollins.
HIGH SCHOOL: Orchard Park (N.Y.).
COLLEGE: South Carolina.
TRANSACTIONS/CAREER NOTES: Selected by San Diego Padres organization in sixth round of free-agent draft (June 2, 1987). . . . Drafted by Philadelphia Phillies (December 4, 1989). . . . On Philadelphia disabled list (August 16-September 6, 1991); included rehabilitation disability assignment to Scranton/Wilkes-Barre (September 2-5, 1991).
STATISTICAL NOTES: Led Northwest League third basemen with 241 total chances in 1987. . . . Led Northwest League with seven intentional bases on balls received in 1987. . . . Led Texas League with 10 sacrifice flies in 1989.

Year	Team (League)	Pos.	G	AB	R	H	2B	3B	HR	RBI	Avg.	SB	PO	A	E	Avg.
1987 — Spokane (Northwest)		3B	75	278	52	86	14	4	2	44	.309	20	*59	*167	15	*.938
1988 — Riverside (California)	3B-1B-SS	139	516	90	157	32	1	9	92	.304	13	102	248	29	.923
1989 — Wichita (Texas)		3B	131	459	69	126	29	4	9	79	.275	8	77	209	25	.920
1990 — Philadelphia (N.L.)■........	3B-1B	72	114	14	21	0	0	5	15	.184	0	27	37	4	.941
1991 — Philadelphia (N.L.)	3B-1B	56	151	18	45	10	2	6	21	.298	1	67	62	8	.942
— Scranton/W.B. (Int'l)	3B-1B	72	229	37	61	11	6	8	35	.266	4	67	105	10	.945
Major league totals (2 years)		128	265	32	66	10	2	11	36	.249	1	94	99	12	.941

HOLMAN, BRIAN
P, MARINERS

PERSONAL: Born January 25, 1965, at Denver. . . . 6-4/185. . . . Throws right, bats right. . . . Full name: Brian Scott Holman.
HIGH SCHOOL: Wichita North (Kan.).
TRANSACTIONS/CAREER NOTES: Selected by Montreal Expos organization in first round (16th pick overall) of free-agent draft (June 6, 1983). . . . On disabled list (August 3, 1983-remainder of season). . . . Traded by Expos with P Randy Johnson and P Gene Harris to Seattle Mariners for P Mark Langston and a player to be named later (May 25, 1989); Indianapolis (Expos organization) acquired P Mike Campbell to complete deal (July 31, 1989).
RECORDS/HONORS: Named Southern League Pitcher of the Year (1987).
STATISTICAL NOTES: Led Southern League with six complete games in 1987.
MISCELLANEOUS: Batted once in order (reached on error) after designated hitter moved to first base (1990).

Year	Team (League)	G	W	L	Pct.	ERA	Sv.	IP	H	R	ER	BB	SO
1983 — Jamestown (New York-Penn) ..	2	0	0	. . .	11.81	0	5⅓	7	7	7	4	5
1984 — West Palm Beach (Florida St.) ..	4	0	3	.000	18.00	0	8	14	19	16	21	14
— Gastonia (South Atlantic)	20	5	8	.385	4.76	0	90⅔	76	58	48	98	94
1985 — West Palm Beach (Florida St.) ..	25	9	9	.500	3.96	0	143⅓	124	79	63	90	103
1986 — Jacksonville (Southern)	27	11	9	.550	5.14	0	157⅔	146	111	90	*122	118
1987 — Jacksonville (Southern)	22	14	5	.737	*2.50	0	151⅓	114	52	42	56	115
— Indianapolis (Am. Assoc.)	6	0	4	.000	6.23	0	34⅔	41	28	24	33	27
1988 — Indianapolis (Am. Assoc.)	14	8	1	.889	2.36	0	91⅓	78	26	24	30	70
— Montreal (N.L.)	18	4	8	.333	3.23	0	100⅓	101	39	36	34	58

Year	Team (League)	G	W	L	Pct.	ERA	Sv.	IP	H	R	ER	BB	SO
1989	—Montreal (N.L.)	10	1	2	.333	4.83	0	31⅔	34	18	17	15	23
	—Seattle (A.L.)■	23	8	10	.444	3.44	0	159⅔	160	68	61	62	82
1990	—Seattle (A.L.)	28	11	11	.500	4.03	0	189⅔	188	92	85	66	121
1991	—Seattle (A.L.)	30	13	14	.481	3.69	0	195⅓	199	86	80	77	108
American League totals (3 years)		81	32	35	.478	3.73	0	544⅔	547	246	226	205	311
National League totals (2 years)		28	5	10	.333	3.61	0	132	135	57	53	49	81
Major league totals (4 years)		109	37	45	.451	3.71	0	676⅔	682	303	279	254	392

HOLMES, DARREN
P, BREWERS

PERSONAL: Born April 25, 1966, at Asheville, N.C. . . . 6-0/199. . . . Throws right, bats right. . . . Full name: Darren Lee Holmes.
HIGH SCHOOL: T.C. Roberson (Asheville, N.C.).
TRANSACTIONS/CAREER NOTES: Selected by Los Angeles Dodgers organization in 16th round of free-agent draft (June 4, 1984). . . . On disabled list (June 5, 1986-remainder of season). . . . Loaned by Dodgers organization to San Luis Potosi and returned (1988). . . . Traded by Dodgers to Milwaukee Brewers for C Bert Heffernan (December 20, 1990). . . . On Milwaukee disabled list (July 3-18, 1991); included rehabilitation disability assignment to Beloit (July 13-18, 1991).

Year	Team (League)	G	W	L	Pct.	ERA	Sv.	IP	H	R	ER	BB	SO
1984	—Great Falls (Pioneer)	18	2	5	.286	6.65	0	44⅔	53	41	33	30	29
1985	—Vero Beach (Florida State)	33	4	3	.571	3.11	2	63⅔	57	31	22	35	46
1986	—Vero Beach (Florida State)	11	3	6	.333	2.92	0	64⅔	55	30	21	39	59
1987	—Vero Beach (Florida State)	19	6	4	.600	4.52	0	99⅔	111	60	50	53	46
1988	—San Luis (Mexican)■	23	9	9	.500	4.64	0	139⅔	151	88	72	92	110
	—Albuquerque (Pacific Coast)■	2	0	1	.000	5.06	0	5⅓	6	3	3	1	1
1989	—San Antonio (Texas)	17	5	8	.385	3.83	1	110½	102	59	47	44	81
	—Albuquerque (Pacific Coast)	9	1	4	.200	7.45	0	38⅔	50	32	32	18	31
1990	—Albuquerque (Pacific Coast)	56	12	2	★.857	3.11	13	92⅔	78	34	32	39	99
	—Los Angeles (N.L.)	14	0	1	.000	5.19	0	17⅓	15	10	10	11	19
1991	—Denver (American Assoc.)■	1	0	0	. . .	9.00	0	1	1	1	1	2	2
	—Milwaukee (A.L.)	40	1	4	.200	4.72	3	76⅓	90	43	40	27	59
	—Beloit (Midwest)	2	0	0	. . .	0.00	2	2	0	0	0	0	3
American League totals (1 year)		40	1	4	.200	4.72	3	76⅓	90	43	40	27	59
National League totals (1 year)		14	0	1	.000	5.19	0	17⅓	15	10	10	11	19
Major league totals (2 years)		54	1	5	.167	4.80	3	93⅔	105	53	50	38	78

HONEYCUTT, RICK
P, ATHLETICS

PERSONAL: Born June 29, 1954, at Chattanooga, Tenn. . . . 6-1/191. . . . Throws left, bats left. . . . Full name: Frederick Wayne Honeycutt.
HIGH SCHOOL: Lakeview (Fort Oglethorpe, Ga.).
COLLEGE: Tennessee (bachelor of science degree in health education).
TRANSACTIONS/CAREER NOTES: Selected by Baltimore Orioles organization in 14th round of free-agent draft (June 6, 1972). . . . Selected by Pittsburgh Pirates organization in 17th round of free-agent draft (June 8, 1976). . . . Traded by Pirates organization to Seattle Mariners (August 22, 1977), completing deal in which Mariners traded P Dave Pagan to Pirates for a player to be named later (July 27, 1977). . . . On disabled list (May 20-June 26, 1978). . . . Traded by Mariners with C Larry Cox, OF Willie Horton, OF Leon Roberts and SS Mario Mendoza to Texas Rangers for P Brian Allard, P Ken Clay, P Steve Finch, P Jerry Don Gleaton, SS Rick Auerbach and OF Richie Zisk (December 12, 1980). . . . Traded by Rangers to Los Angeles Dodgers for P Dave Stewart and a player to be named later (August 19, 1983); Rangers acquired P Ricky Wright to complete deal (September 16, 1983). . . . Traded by Dodgers to Oakland Athletics for a player to be named later (August 29, 1987); Dodgers acquired P Tim Belcher to complete deal (September 3, 1987). . . . Granted free agency (November 4, 1988). . . . Re-signed by A's (December 21, 1988). . . . On Oakland disabled list (April 1-June 16, 1991); included rehabilitation disability assignment to Modesto (June 6-14, 1991) and Madison (June 14-16, 1991).
STATISTICAL NOTES: Tied for New York-Pennsylvania League lead with seven complete games in 1976.
MISCELLANEOUS: Played two games as first baseman and one game as shortstop (1976). . . . Appeared as shortstop with no chances with Shreveport (1977). . . . Made an out in both appearances as a pinch-hitter and appeared in one game as a pinch-runner (1990).

Year	Team (League)	G	W	L	Pct.	ERA	Sv.	IP	H	R	ER	BB	SO
1976	—Niagara Falls (N.Y.-Penn)	13	5	3	.625	2.60	0	★97	91	36	28	20	★98
1977	—Shreveport (Texas)	21	10	6	.625	★2.47	0	135	144	53	37	42	82
	—Seattle (A.L.)■	10	0	1	.000	4.34	0	29	26	16	14	11	17
1978	—Seattle (A.L.)	26	5	11	.313	4.90	0	134	150	81	73	49	50
1979	—Seattle (A.L.)	33	11	12	.478	4.04	0	194	201	103	87	67	83
1980	—Seattle (A.L.)	30	10	17	.370	3.95	0	203	221	99	89	60	79
1981	—Texas (A.L.)■	20	11	6	.647	3.30	0	128	120	49	47	17	40
1982	—Texas (A.L.)	30	5	17	.227	5.27	0	164	201	103	96	54	64
1983	—Texas (A.L.)	25	14	8	.636	★2.42	0	174⅔	168	59	47	37	56
	—Los Angeles (N.L.)■	9	2	3	.400	5.77	0	39	46	26	25	13	18
1984	—Los Angeles (N.L.)	29	10	9	.526	2.84	0	183⅔	180	72	58	51	75
1985	—Los Angeles (N.L.)	31	8	12	.400	3.42	1	142	141	71	54	49	67
1986	—Los Angeles (N.L.)	32	11	9	.550	3.32	0	171	164	71	63	45	100
1987	—Los Angeles (N.L.)	27	2	12	.143	4.59	0	115⅔	133	74	59	45	92
	—Oakland (A.L.)■	7	1	4	.200	5.32	0	23⅔	25	17	14	9	10

— 222 —

Year Team (League)	G	W	L	Pct.	ERA	Sv.	IP	H	R	ER	BB	SO
1988 —Oakland (A.L.)	55	3	2	.600	3.50	7	79 2/3	74	36	31	25	47
1989 —Oakland (A.L.)	64	2	2	.500	2.35	12	76 2/3	56	26	20	26	52
1990 —Oakland (A.L.)	63	2	2	.500	2.70	7	63 1/3	46	23	19	22	38
1991 —Oakland (A.L.)	43	2	4	.333	3.58	0	37 2/3	37	16	15	20	26
—Modesto (California)	3	0	0	...	0.00	0	5	4	1	0	1	5
—Madison (Midwest)	1	0	1	.000	18.00	0	1	4	2	2	0	2
American League totals (12 years)	406	66	86	.434	3.80	26	1307 2/3	1325	628	552	397	562
National League totals (5 years)	128	33	45	.423	3.58	1	651 1/3	664	314	259	203	352
Major league totals (15 years)	534	99	131	.430	3.73	27	1959	1989	942	811	600	914

CHAMPIONSHIP SERIES RECORD

Year Team (League)	G	W	L	Pct.	ERA	Sv.	IP	H	R	ER	BB	SO
1983 —Los Angeles (N.L.)	2	0	0	...	21.60	0	1 2/3	4	4	4	0	2
1985 —Los Angeles (N.L.)	2	0	0	...	13.50	0	1 1/3	4	2	2	2	1
1988 —Oakland (A.L.)	3	1	0	1.000	0.00	0	2	0	0	0	2	0
1989 —Oakland (A.L.)	3	0	0	...	32.40	0	1 2/3	6	6	6	5	1
1990 —Oakland (A.L.)	3	0	0	...	0.00	1	1 2/3	0	0	0	0	0
Championship Series totals (5 years)	13	1	0	1.000	12.96	1	8 1/3	14	12	12	9	4

WORLD SERIES RECORD

Year Team (League)	G	W	L	Pct.	ERA	Sv.	IP	H	R	ER	BB	SO
1988 —Oakland (A.L.)	3	1	0	1.000	0.00	0	3 1/3	0	0	0	0	5
1989 —Oakland (A.L.)	3	0	0	...	6.75	0	2 2/3	4	2	2	0	2
1990 —Oakland (A.L.)	1	0	0	...	0.00	0	1 2/3	2	0	0	1	0
World Series totals (3 years)	7	1	0	1.000	2.35	0	7 2/3	6	2	2	1	7

ALL-STAR GAME RECORD

Year League	W	L	Pct.	ERA	Sv.	IP	H	R	ER	BB	SO
1980 —American					Did not play						
1983 —American	0	0	...	9.00	0	2	5	2	2	0	0

HORN, SAM
DH/1B, ORIOLES

PERSONAL: Born November 2, 1963, at Dallas. . . . 6-5/247. . . . Throws left, bats left. . . . Full name: Samuel Lee Horn.
HIGH SCHOOL: Morse (San Diego).
TRANSACTIONS/CAREER NOTES: Selected by Boston Red Sox organization in first round (16th pick overall) of free-agent draft (June 7, 1982). . . . On disabled list (April 28-June 23, 1983). . . . On Boston disabled list (June 8-July 28, 1989); included rehabilitation disability assignment to Pawtucket (July 13-28, 1989). . . . Released by Red Sox organization (December 20, 1989). . . . Signed by Rochester, Baltimore Orioles organization (February 20, 1990). . . . On Baltimore disabled list (May 8-29, 1990); included rehabilitation disability assignment to Rochester (May 21-29, 1990).
RECORDS/HONORS: Shares major league single-game record for most strikeouts—6 (July 17, 1991, 15 innings). . . . Shares A.L. record for most home runs in first two major league games—2 (July 25-26 1987).
STATISTICAL NOTES: Led Carolina League with .538 slugging percentage in 1984. . . . Led International League with .649 slugging percentage in 1987. . . . Tied for International League lead with 10 intentional bases on balls received in 1988.

Year Team (League)	Pos.	G	AB	R	H	2B	3B	HR	RBI	Avg.	SB	PO	A	E	Avg.
1982 —Elmira (New York-Penn)	1B	61	213	47	64	13	1	11	48	.300	2	368	29	11	.973
1983 —Winston-Salem (Caro.)	1B	68	217	33	52	9	0	9	29	.240	0	363	24	10	.975
1984 —Winston-Salem (Caro.)	1B	127	403	67	126	22	3	21	89	.313	5	978	*70	*29	.973
1985 —New Britain (Eastern)	1B	134	457	64	129	*32	0	11	82	.282	4	751	63	*23	.973
1986 —New Britain (Eastern)	1B	100	345	41	85	13	0	8	46	.246	0	356	28	9	.977
—Pawtucket (Int'l)	1B	20	77	8	15	2	0	3	14	.195	1	61	4	0	1.000
1987 —Pawtucket (Int'l)	1B	94	333	57	107	19	0	30	84	.321	0	28	2	2	.938
—Boston (A.L.)	DH	46	158	31	44	7	0	14	34	.278	0	0	0	0	...
1988 —Boston (A.L.)	DH	24	61	4	9	0	0	2	8	.148	0	0	0	0	...
—Pawtucket (Int'l)	1B	83	279	33	65	10	0	10	31	.233	0	6	1	1	.875
1989 —Boston (A.L.)	1B	33	54	1	8	2	0	4	4	.148	0	5	0	0	1.000
—Pawtucket (Int'l)	DH	51	164	15	38	9	1	8	27	.232	0	0	0	0	...
1990 —Baltimore (A.L.)■	1B	79	246	30	61	13	0	14	45	.248	0	58	6	2	.970
—Rochester (Int'l)	1B	17	58	16	24	3	0	9	26	.414	0	27	1	2	.933
—Hagerstown (Eastern)	DH	7	23	2	6	2	0	1	3	.261	0	0	0	0	...
1991 —Baltimore (A.L.)	DH	121	317	45	74	16	0	23	61	.233	0	0	0	0	...
Major league totals (5 years)		303	836	111	196	38	0	53	152	.234	0	63	6	2	.972

HORSMAN, VINCE
P, BLUE JAYS

PERSONAL: Born March 9, 1967, at Halifax, Nova Scotia. . . . 6-2/180. . . . Throws left, bats right. . . . Full name: Vincent Stanley Joseph Horsman.
HIGH SCHOOL: Prince Andrew (Dartmouth, Nova Scotia).
TRANSACTIONS/CAREER NOTES: Signed as free agent by Toronto Blue Jays organization (September 26, 1984). . . . On Knoxville disabled list (April 11-24, 1991).
STATISTICAL NOTES: Led South Atlantic League with 20 home runs allowed in 1987.

Year	Team (League)	G	W	L	Pct.	ERA	Sv.	IP	H	R	ER	BB	SO
1985	—Medicine Hat (Pioneer)	18	0	3	.000	6.25	1	40⅓	56	31	28	23	30
1986	—Florence (South Atlantic)	29	4	3	.571	4.07	1	90⅔	93	56	41	49	64
1987	—Myrtle Beach (South Atlantic) ..	30	7	7	.500	3.32	0	149	144	74	55	37	109
1988	—Dunedin (Florida State)	14	3	1	.750	1.36	1	39⅔	28	7	6	12	34
	—Knoxville (Southern)	20	3	2	.600	4.63	0	58⅓	57	34	30	28	40
1989	—Dunedin (Florida State)	35	5	6	.455	2.51	8	79	72	24	22	27	60
	—Knoxville (Southern)	4	0	0	...	1.80	1	5	3	1	1	2	3
1990	—Dunedin (Florida State)	28	4	7	.364	3.24	1	50	53	21	18	15	41
	—Knoxville (Southern)	8	2	1	.667	4.63	0	11⅔	11	7	6	5	10
1991	—Knoxville (Southern)	42	4	1	.800	2.34	3	80⅔	79	23	21	19	80
	—Toronto (A.L.)	4	0	0	...	0.00	0	4	2	0	0	3	2
	Major league totals (1 year)	**4**	**0**	**0**	**...**	**0.00**	**0**	**4**	**2**	**0**	**0**	**3**	**2**

HOSEY, STEVE
OF, GIANTS

PERSONAL: Born April 2, 1969, at Oakland, Calif. ... 6-3/215. ... Throws right, bats right. ... Full name: Steven Bernard Hosey.
HIGH SCHOOL: Freemont (Oakland, Calif.).
COLLEGE: Fresno State.
TRANSACTIONS/CAREER NOTES: Selected by Cleveland Indians organization in 19th round of free-agent draft (June 2, 1986). ... Selected by San Francisco Giants organization in first round (14th pick overall) of free-agent draft (June 5, 1989).
STATISTICAL NOTES: Led Northwest League batters with 84 strikeouts in 1989. ... Led California League batters with 139 strikeouts in 1990.

Year	Team (League)	Pos.	G	AB	R	H	2B	3B	HR	RBI	Avg.	SB	PO	A	E	Avg.
1989	—Everett (Northwest)	OF	73	288	44	83	14	3	13	59	.288	15	143	8	4	.974
1990	—San Jose (California)	OF	•139	479	85	111	13	6	16	78	.232	16	239	11	8	.969
1991	—Shreveport (Texas)	OF	126	409	79	120	21	5	17	74	.293	26	243	5	7	.973

HOUGH, CHARLIE
P, WHITE SOX

PERSONAL: Born January 5, 1948, at Honolulu. ... 6-2/190. ... Throws right, bats right. ... Full name: Charles Oliver Hough. ... Son of Dick Hough, minor league third baseman (1933). ... Name pronounced HUFF.
HIGH SCHOOL: Hialeah (Fla.).
TRANSACTIONS/CAREER NOTES: Selected by Los Angeles Dodgers organization in eighth round of free-agent draft (June 9, 1966). ... On temporary inactive list (June 19-July 1, 1968). ... On Spokane temporary inactive list (July 10-24, 1971). ... On Albuquerque temporary inactive list (June 12-15, July 22-24 and August 7-12, 1972). ... Sold by Dodgers to Texas Rangers (July 11, 1980). ... On Texas disabled list (March 25-May 6, 1986); included rehabilitation disability assignment to Oklahoma City (May 2-6, 1986). ... On disabled list (July 20-August 4, 1989). ... Granted free agency (November 5, 1990). ... Signed by Chicago White Sox (December 20, 1990). ... On disabled list (March 29-April 13, 1991).
RECORDS/HONORS: Shares major league record for most strikeouts in one inning—4 (July 4, 1988, first inning). ... Holds A.L. single-season record for most balks—9 (1987). ... Named Pacific Coast League Pitcher of the Year (1972).
STATISTICAL NOTES: Led Texas League with 17 home runs allowed in 1969. ... Led A.L. pitchers with 40 games started in 1987 and tied for lead with 36 in 1984. ... Led A.L. with 17 complete games in 1984. ... Led A.L. with nine balks in 1987. ... Led A.L. with 19 hit batsmen in 1987 and 11 in 1990. ... Tied for A.L. lead with 28 home runs allowed in 1989.

Year	Team (League)	G	W	L	Pct.	ERA	Sv.	IP	H	R	ER	BB	SO
1966	—Ogden (Pioneer)	21	5	•7	.417	4.76	0	68	82	56	36	29	68
1967	—Santa Barbara (California)	20	14	4	*.778	2.24	0	165	129	50	41	43	138
	—Albuquerque (Texas)	7	2	1	.667	7.00	0	36	57	31	28	10	25
1968	—Albuquerque (Texas)	27	6	10	.375	3.94	0	121	145	72	53	26	74
1969	—Albuquerque (Texas)	27	10	9	.526	4.09	0	163	190	87	74	42	113
1970	—Spokane (Pacific Coast)	49	12	8	.600	1.95	*18	134	98	43	29	44	90
	—Los Angeles (N.L.)	8	0	0	...	5.29	2	17	18	11	10	11	8
1971	—Spokane (Pacific Coast)	47	10	8	.556	3.92	12	117	95	56	51	52	104
	—Los Angeles (N.L.)	4	0	0	...	4.50	0	4	3	3	2	3	4
1972	—Albuquerque (Pacific Coast)	58	14	5	.737	2.38	14	125	109	47	33	60	95
	—Los Angeles (N.L.)	2	0	0	...	3.00	0	3	2	1	1	2	4
1973	—Los Angeles (N.L.)	37	4	2	.667	2.75	5	72	52	24	22	45	70
1974	—Los Angeles (N.L.)	49	9	4	.692	3.75	1	96	65	45	40	40	63
1975	—Los Angeles (N.L.)	38	3	7	.300	2.95	4	61	43	25	20	34	34
1976	—Los Angeles (N.L.)	77	12	8	.600	2.20	18	143	102	43	35	77	81
1977	—Los Angeles (N.L.)	70	6	12	.333	3.33	22	127	98	53	47	70	105
1978	—Los Angeles (N.L.)	55	5	5	.500	3.29	7	93	69	38	34	48	66
1979	—Los Angeles (N.L.)	42	7	5	.583	4.77	0	151	152	88	80	66	76
1980	—Los Angeles (N.L.)	19	1	3	.250	5.63	1	32	37	21	20	21	25
	—Texas (A.L.)■	16	2	2	.500	3.98	0	61	54	30	27	37	47
1981	—Texas (A.L.)	21	4	1	.800	2.96	1	82	61	30	27	31	69
1982	—Texas (A.L.)	34	16	13	.552	3.95	0	228	217	111	100	72	128
1983	—Texas (A.L.)	34	15	13	.536	3.18	0	252	219	96	89	95	152
1984	—Texas (A.L.)	36	16	14	.533	3.76	0	266	*260	127	111	94	164
1985	—Texas (A.L.)	34	14	16	.467	3.31	0	250⅓	198	102	92	83	141
1986	—Oklahoma City (Am. Assoc.).....	1	0	1	.000	9.00	0	5	7	5	5	1	3
	—Texas (A.L.)	33	17	10	.630	3.79	0	230⅓	188	115	97	89	146
1987	—Texas (A.L.)	40	18	13	.581	3.79	0	*285⅓	238	*159	120	124	223

Year	Team (League)	G	W	L	Pct.	ERA	Sv.	IP	H	R	ER	BB	SO
1988 —Texas (A.L.)		34	15	16	.484	3.32	0	252	202	111	93	*126	174
1989 —Texas (A.L.)		30	10	13	.435	4.35	0	182	168	97	88	95	94
1990 —Texas (A.L.)		32	12	12	.500	4.07	0	218⅔	190	108	99	119	114
1991 —Chicago (A.L.)■		31	9	10	.474	4.02	0	199⅓	167	98	89	94	107
American League totals (12 years)		375	148	133	.527	3.70	1	2507	2162	1184	1032	1059	1559
National League totals (11 years)		401	47	46	.505	3.50	60	799	641	352	311	417	536
Major league totals (22 years)		776	195	179	.521	3.66	61	3306	2803	1536	1343	1476	2095

CHAMPIONSHIP SERIES RECORD

Year	Team (League)	G	W	L	Pct.	ERA	Sv.	IP	H	R	ER	BB	SO
1974 —Los Angeles (N.L.)		1	0	0	...	7.71	0	2⅓	4	2	2	0	2
1977 —Los Angeles (N.L.)		1	0	0	...	4.50	0	2	2	1	1	0	3
1978 —Los Angeles (N.L.)		1	0	0	...	4.50	0	2	1	1	1	0	1
Championship Series totals (3 years)		3	0	0	...	5.68	0	6⅓	7	4	4	0	6

WORLD SERIES RECORD

Year	Team (League)	G	W	L	Pct.	ERA	Sv.	IP	H	R	ER	BB	SO
1974 —Los Angeles (N.L.)		1	0	0	...	0.00	0	2	0	0	0	1	4
1977 —Los Angeles (N.L.)		2	0	0	...	1.80	0	5	3	1	1	0	5
1978 —Los Angeles (N.L.)		2	0	0	...	8.44	0	5⅓	10	5	5	2	5
World Series totals (3 years)		5	0	0	...	4.38	0	12⅓	13	6	6	3	14

ALL-STAR GAME RECORD

Year	League	W	L	Pct.	ERA	Sv.	IP	H	R	ER	BB	SO
1986 —American		0	0	...	5.40	0	1⅔	2	2	1	0	3

RECORD AS POSITION PLAYER

Year	Team (League)	Pos.	G	AB	R	H	2B	3B	HR	RBI	Avg.	SB	PO	A	E	Avg.
1967 —Santa Barbara (Calif.)		P-1B	28	72	8	14	2	0	0	4	.194	0	15	25	2	.952
1968 —Albuquerque (Texas)		P-1B-3B	56	83	10	21	4	0	6	6	.253	0	43	25	4	.944
1969 —Albuquerque (Texas)		P-3B	31	57	10	12	0	0	1	9	.211	1	10	19	2	.935
1970 —Spokane (Pacific Coast)		P-OF-1B	49	33	1	6	0	0	1	3	.182	0	7	28	3	.921
1971 —Spokane (Pacific Coast)		P-OF	48	36	2	10	0	0	0	3	.278	0	6	20	1	.963
1972 —Albuquerque (PCL)		P-OF	58	34	4	9	1	0	0	5	.265	0	3	27	0	1.000

HOUSIE, WAYNE
OF, RED SOX

PERSONAL: Born May 20, 1965, at Hampton, Va. . . . 5-9/165. . . . Throws right, bats both. . . . Full name: Wayne Tyrone Housie.
HIGH SCHOOL: Norte Vista (Riverside, Calif.).
COLLEGE: Riverside City College (Calif.).
TRANSACTIONS/CAREER NOTES: Selected by Detroit Tigers organization in eighth round of free-agent draft (January 14, 1986). . . . Released by Tigers organization (April 2, 1990). . . . Signed by Boston Red Sox organization (August 2, 1990).

Year	Team (League)	Pos.	G	AB	R	H	2B	3B	HR	RBI	Avg.	SB	PO	A	E	Avg.
1986 —Gastonia (S. Atlantic)		OF	90	336	55	87	10	6	2	29	.259	38	214	13	8	.966
1987 —Lakeland (Florida State)		OF	125	458	58	118	12	7	1	45	.258	26	248	13	6	.978
1988 —Glens Falls (Eastern)		OF	63	202	26	38	4	2	1	16	.188	9	128	5	1	.993
—Lakeland (Florida State)		OF	55	212	31	57	11	3	0	23	.269	24	113	6	4	.967
1989 —London (Eastern)		OF	127	434	56	103	17	2	5	28	.237	23	238	13	5	.980
1990 —New Britain (Eastern)■		OF	30	113	13	31	8	3	1	12	.274	7	83	4	1	.989
1991 —New Britain (Eastern)		OF	113	444	58	123	24	2	6	26	.277	43	261	10	4	.985
—Pawtucket (Int'l)		OF	21	79	14	26	9	0	2	8	.329	2	49	1	0	1.000
—Boston (A.L.)		OF	11	8	2	2	1	0	0	0	.250	1	3	0	0	1.000
Major league totals (1 year)			11	8	2	2	1	0	0	0	.250	1	3	0	0	1.000

HOWARD, CHRIS
C, MARINERS

PERSONAL: Born February 27, 1966, at San Diego. . . . 6-2/200. . . . Throws right, bats right. . . . Full name: Christopher Hugh Howard.
HIGH SCHOOL: Bishop (Kansas City, Mo.).
COLLEGE: Oklahoma and Southwestern Louisiana.
TRANSACTIONS/CAREER NOTES: Selected by Seattle Mariners organization in 41st round of free-agent draft (June 1, 1988). . . . On Calgary disabled list (July 11-27, 1991).
STATISTICAL NOTES: Led Eastern League with 21 passed balls in 1989. . . . Led Eastern League catchers with 783 total chances in 1990. . . . Led Pacific Coast League catchers with 18 passed balls and tied for lead in double plays with eight in 1991.

Year	Team (League)	Pos.	G	AB	R	H	2B	3B	HR	RBI	Avg.	SB	PO	A	E	Avg.
1988 —Bellingham (Northwest)		C	2	9	3	3	0	0	1	3	.333	0	10	0	1	.909
—Wausau (Midwest)		C-OF-1B	61	187	20	45	10	1	7	20	.241	1	248	33	9	.969
1989 —Williamsport (NYP)		C-3B	86	296	30	75	13	0	9	36	.253	0	443	57	8	.984

Year Team (League)	Pos.	G	AB	R	H	2B	3B	HR	RBI	Avg.	SB	PO	A	E	Avg.
1990—Williamsport (NYP)	C	118	401	48	95	19	1	5	49	.237	3	*680	*84	*19	.976
1991—Calgary (Pacific Coast)	C	82	293	32	72	12	1	8	36	.246	1	381	57	10	.978
—Seattle (A.L.)	C	9	6	1	1	1	0	0	0	.167	0	13	2	0	1.000
Major league totals (1 year)		9	6	1	1	1	0	0	0	.167	0	13	2	0	1.000

HOWARD, CHRIS
P, WHITE SOX

PERSONAL: Born November 18, 1965, at Lynn, Mass. . . . 6-0/185. . . . Throws left, bats right. . . . Full name: Christian Howard.
HIGH SCHOOL: St. Mary's (Lynn, Mass.).
COLLEGE: Miami-Dade South Community College (Fla.).
TRANSACTIONS/CAREER NOTES: Selected by Milwaukee Brewers organization in eighth round of free-agent draft (January 9, 1985). . . . Signed as a free agent by New York Yankees organization (June 16, 1986). . . . Released by Yankees organization (May 1, 1990). . . . Signed by Cleveland Indians organization (May 10, 1990). . . . Released by Indians organization (June 6, 1990). . . . Signed by Chicago White Sox organization (January 27, 1991).

Year Team (League)	G	W	L	Pct.	ERA	Sv.	IP	H	R	ER	BB	SO
1987—Prince William (Carolina)	4	0	0	...	10.29	0	7	9	8	8	8	1
1988—Prince William (Carolina)	31	2	2	.500	2.34	3	50	44	18	13	23	48
—Albany (Eastern)	2	0	0	...	13.50	0	1⅓	3	2	2	1	1
1989—Fort Lauderdale (Florida St.)	13	2	0	1.000	1.78	0	25⅓	19	6	5	13	25
—Albany (Eastern)	24	0	1	.000	3.44	2	34	29	14	13	17	33
1990—Albany (Eastern)	2	0	0	...	14.40	0	5	9	8	8	7	2
—Kinston (Carolina)■	8	1	1	.500	2.45	0	14⅔	21	5	4	6	16
1991—Birmingham (Southern)■	38	6	1	.857	2.04	9	53	43	14	12	16	52

RECORD AS POSITION PLAYER

Year Team (League)	Pos.	G	AB	R	H	2B	3B	HR	RBI	Avg.	SB	PO	A	E	Avg.
1986—Oneonta (N.Y.-Penn)	OF	9	23	2	2	0	0	0	4	.087	1	4	1	1	.833
—Sarasota Yankees (GCL)	OF-1B	43	131	15	39	5	1	0	16	.298	2	101	4	3	.972
1987—Prince William (Caro.)	OF-P	86	258	35	62	11	1	5	27	.240	2	135	15	7	.955
1988—Prince William (Caro.)	P-1B-OF	40	11	2	1	0	0	0	0	.091	0	10	9	0	1.000

HOWARD, DAVID
SS/2B, ROYALS

PERSONAL: Born February 26, 1967, at Sarasota, Fla. . . . 6-0/165. . . . Throws right, bats both. . . . Full name: David Wayne Howard. . . . Son of Bruce Howard, pitcher, Chicago White Sox, Baltimore Orioles and Washington Senators (1963-68).
HIGH SCHOOL: Riverview (Sarasota, Fla.).
COLLEGE: Manatee Junior College (Fla.).
TRANSACTIONS/CAREER NOTES: Selected by Kansas City Royals organization in 32nd round of free-agent draft (June 2, 1986). . . . On disabled list (May 12-31 and July 23-August 9, 1989).

Year Team (League)	Pos.	G	AB	R	H	2B	3B	HR	RBI	Avg.	SB	PO	A	E	Avg.
1987—Fort Myers (Florida St.)	SS	89	289	26	56	9	4	1	19	.194	11	123	273	28	.934
1988—Appleton (Midwest)	SS	110	368	48	82	9	4	1	22	.223	10	151	275	43	.908
1989—Baseball City (Fla. St.)	S-O-3-2	83	267	36	63	7	3	3	30	.236	12	141	225	18	.953
1990—Memphis (Southern)	SS-2B	116	384	41	96	10	4	5	44	.250	15	194	321	32	.941
1991—Omaha (Am. Assoc.)	SS-2B	14	41	2	5	0	0	0	2	.122	1	30	43	3	.961
—Kansas City (A.L.)	S-2-3-0	94	236	20	51	7	0	1	17	.216	3	129	248	12	.969
Major league totals (1 year)		94	236	20	51	7	0	1	17	.216	3	129	248	12	.969

HOWARD, THOMAS
OF, PADRES

PERSONAL: Born December 11, 1964, at Middletown, O. . . . 6-2/205. . . . Throws right, bats both. . . . Full name: Thomas Sylvester Howard.
HIGH SCHOOL: Valley View (Germantown, O.).
COLLEGE: Ball State.
TRANSACTIONS/CAREER NOTES: Selected by San Diego Padres organization in first round (11th pick overall) of free-agent draft (June 2, 1986). . . . On disabled list (June 5-July 17, 1989).
RECORDS/HONORS: Named outfielder on THE SPORTING NEWS college All-America team (1986).

Year Team (League)	Pos.	G	AB	R	H	2B	3B	HR	RBI	Avg.	SB	PO	A	E	Avg.
1986—Spokane (Northwest)	OF	13	55	16	23	3	3	2	17	.418	2	24	3	0	1.000
—Reno (California)	OF	61	223	35	57	7	3	10	39	.256	10	104	5	6	.948
1987—Wichita (Texas)	OF	113	401	72	133	27	4	14	60	.332	26	226	6	6	.975
1988—Wichita (Texas)	OF	29	103	15	31	9	2	0	16	.301	6	51	2	2	.964
—Las Vegas (Pac. Coast)	OF	44	167	29	42	9	1	0	15	.251	3	74	2	2	.975
1989—Las Vegas (Pac. Coast)	OF	80	303	45	91	18	3	3	31	.300	22	178	7	2	.989
1990—Las Vegas (Pac. Coast)	OF	89	341	58	112	26	8	5	51	.328	27	159	6	2	.988
—San Diego (N.L.)	OF	20	44	4	12	2	0	0	0	.273	0	19	0	1	.950
1991—San Diego (N.L.)	OF	106	281	30	70	14	3	4	22	.249	10	182	4	1	.995
Major league totals (2 years)		126	325	34	82	14	3	4	22	.252	10	201	4	2	.990

HOWE, STEVE

P, YANKEES

PERSONAL: Born March 10, 1958, at Pontiac, Mich. . . . 5-11/196. . . . Throws left, bats left. . . . Full name: Steven Roy Howe.
HIGH SCHOOL: Clarkston (Mich.).
COLLEGE: Michigan.

TRANSACTIONS/CAREER NOTES: Selected by Los Angeles Dodgers organization in first round (16th pick overall) of free-agent draft (June 5, 1979). . . . On disabled list (May 28-June 29, 1983). . . . On suspended list (July 16-17 and September 23, 1983-remainder of season; and December 15, 1983-entire 1984 season). . . . On restricted list (July 1-3, 1985). . . . Released by Dodgers (July 3, 1985). . . . Signed by Minnesota Twins (August 12, 1985). . . . Released by Twins (September 17, 1985). . . . Signed by San Jose, independent (March 20, 1986). . . . On suspended list (May 15-June 24 and July 15, 1986-remainder of season). . . . Released by San Jose (December 31, 1986). . . . Signed by Tabasco of Mexican League (1987). . . . Signed as free agent by Texas Rangers organization (July 12, 1987). . . . Released by Rangers (January 19, 1988). . . . Signed by Salinas, independent (April 7, 1990). . . . Released by Salinas (October 24, 1990). . . . Signed by New York Yankees organization (February 21, 1991). . . . On New York disabled list (August 11-September 2, 1991).
RECORDS/HONORS: Named lefthanded pitcher on THE SPORTING NEWS college All-America team (1979). . . . Named N.L. Rookie of the Year by Baseball Writers' Association of America (1980).

Year	Team (League)	G	W	L	Pct.	ERA	Sv.	IP	H	R	ER	BB	SO
1979	San Antonio (Texas)	13	6	2	.750	3.13	0	95	78	36	33	22	57
1980	Los Angeles (N.L.)	59	7	9	.438	2.65	17	85	83	33	25	22	39
1981	Los Angeles (N.L.)	41	5	3	.625	2.50	8	54	51	17	15	18	32
1982	Los Angeles (N.L.)	66	7	5	.583	2.08	13	99 1/3	87	27	23	17	49
1983	Los Angeles (N.L.)	46	4	7	.364	1.44	18	68 2/3	55	15	11	12	52
1984	—					Did not play							
1985	Los Angeles (N.L.)	19	1	1	.500	4.91	3	22	30	17	12	5	11
	Minnesota (A.L.)■	13	2	3	.400	6.16	0	19	28	16	13	7	10
1986	San Jose (California)■	14	3	2	.600	1.47	2	49	40	14	8	5	37
1987	Tabasco (Mexican)■	10	1	0	1.000	0.00	4	12 1/3	7	0	0	7	5
	Oklahoma City (Am. Assoc.)■	7	2	2	.500	3.48	0	20 2/3	26	8	8	5	14
	Texas (A.L.)	24	3	3	.500	4.31	1	31 1/3	33	15	15	8	19
1988	—					Out of Organized Baseball							
1989	—					Out of Organized Baseball							
1990	Salinas (California)■	10	0	1	.000	2.12	0	17	19	8	4	5	14
1991	Columbus (International)■	12	2	1	.667	0.00	5	18	11	1	0	8	13
	New York (A.L.)	37	3	1	.750	1.68	3	48 1/3	39	12	9	7	34
American League totals (3 years)		74	8	7	.533	3.38	4	98 2/3	100	43	37	22	63
National League totals (5 years)		231	24	25	.490	2.35	59	329	306	109	86	74	183
Major league totals (7 years)		305	32	32	.500	2.59	63	427 2/3	406	152	123	96	246

DIVISION SERIES RECORD

Year	Team (League)	G	W	L	Pct.	ERA	Sv.	IP	H	R	ER	BB	SO
1981	Los Angeles (N.L.)	2	0	0	. . .	0.00	0	2	1	0	0	0	2

CHAMPIONSHIP SERIES RECORD

Year	Team (League)	G	W	L	Pct.	ERA	Sv.	IP	H	R	ER	BB	SO
1981	Los Angeles (N.L.)	2	0	0	. . .	0.00	0	2	1	0	0	0	2

WORLD SERIES RECORD

Year	Team (League)	G	W	L	Pct.	ERA	Sv.	IP	H	R	ER	BB	SO
1981	Los Angeles (N.L.)	3	1	0	1.000	3.86	1	7	7	3	3	1	4

ALL-STAR GAME RECORD

Year	League	W	L	Pct.	ERA	Sv.	IP	H	R	ER	BB	SO
1982	National	0	0	. . .	0.00	0	1/3	0	0	0	0	0

HOWELL, JACK

3B

PERSONAL: Born August 18, 1961, at Tucson, Ariz. . . . 6-0/190. . . . Throws right, bats left. . . . Full name: Jack Robert Howell.
HIGH SCHOOL: Palo Verde (Tucson, Ariz.).
COLLEGE: Pima Community College (Ariz.) and Arizona.

TRANSACTIONS/CAREER NOTES: Signed as free agent by California Angels organization (August 6, 1983). . . . On Edmonton disabled list (June 21-July 7, 1985). . . . On California disabled list (May 23-June 9, 1990 and May 5-28, 1991). . . . Traded by Angels to San Diego Padres for OF Shawn Abner (July 30, 1991). . . . Granted free agency (October 28, 1991). . . . Signed by Yakult Swallows of Japan Central League (December 8, 1991).
STATISTICAL NOTES: Led California League third basemen with .943 fielding percentage, 259 assists, 368 total chances and 23 double plays in 1984. . . . Led A.L. third basemen with .974 fielding percentage, 322 assists and 428 total chances in 1989.

Year	Team (League)	Pos.	G	AB	R	H	2B	3B	HR	RBI	Avg.	SB	PO	A	E	Avg.
1983	Salem (Northwest)	3B-2B	21	76	23	30	2	5	3	12	.395	26	19	32	11	.823
1984	Redwood (California)	3B-1B	135	451	62	111	21	5	5	64	.246	12	96	†260	21	†.944
1985	Edmonton (Pac. Coast)	3B-SS	79	284	55	106	22	3	13	48	.373	3	67	130	12	.943
	California (A.L.)	3B	43	137	19	27	4	0	5	18	.197	1	33	75	8	.931
1986	Edmonton (Pac. Coast)	3B	44	156	39	56	17	3	3	28	.359	1	28	84	8	.933
	California (A.L.)	3B-OF	63	151	26	41	14	2	4	21	.272	2	38	57	2	.979
1987	California (A.L.)	OF-3B-2B	138	449	64	110	18	5	23	64	.245	4	185	95	7	.976
1988	California (A.L.)	3B-OF	154	500	59	127	32	2	16	63	.254	2	97	249	17	.953

Year	Team (League)	Pos.	G	AB	R	H	2B	3B	HR	RBI	Avg.	SB	PO	A	E	Avg.
								BATTING							FIELDING		
1989	California (A.L.)	3B-OF	144	474	56	108	19	4	20	52	.228	0	97	†322	11	†.974
1990	California (A.L.)	3B-SS-1B	105	316	35	72	19	1	8	33	.228	3	76	196	18	.938
	Edmonton (Pac. Coast)	3B-1B	20	75	14	25	7	1	2	15	.333	2	22	33	1	.982
1991	California (A.L.)	2-0-1-3	32	81	11	17	2	0	2	7	.210	1	53	55	2	.982
	San Diego (N.L.)■	3B	58	160	24	33	3	1	6	16	.206	0	33	98	2	.985
	American League totals (7 years)		679	2108	270	502	108	14	78	258	.238	13	579	1049	65	.962
	National League totals (1 year)		58	160	24	33	3	1	6	16	.206	0	33	98	2	.985
	Major league totals (7 years)		737	2268	294	535	111	15	84	274	.236	13	612	1147	67	.963

CHAMPIONSHIP SERIES RECORD

Year	Team (League)	Pos.	G	AB	R	H	2B	3B	HR	RBI	Avg.	SB	PO	A	E	Avg.
								BATTING							FIELDING		
1986	California (A.L.)	PH	2	1	0	0	0	0	0	0	.000	0	0	0	0	...

HOWELL, JAY
P, DODGERS

PERSONAL: Born November 26, 1955, at Miami. . . . 6-3/203. . . . Throws right, bats right. . . . Full name: Jay Canfield Howell.
HIGH SCHOOL: Fairview (Boulder, Colo.).
COLLEGE: Colorado.

TRANSACTIONS/CAREER NOTES: Selected by Cincinnati Reds organization in 12th round of free-agent draft (June 5, 1973). . . . Selected by Cincinnati Reds organization in 31st round of free-agent draft (June 8, 1976). . . . Traded by Reds to Chicago Cubs for C Mike O'Berry (October 17, 1980). . . . Traded by Cubs organization to New York Yankees organization (August 2, 1982), completing deal in which Cubs acquired 2B Pat Tabler from Yankees on waivers for two players to be designated (August 19, 1981); Yankees acquired P Bill Caudill as partial completion of deal (April 1, 1982). . . . On disabled list (August 3, 1983-remainder of season). . . . Traded by Yankees with OF Stan Javier, P Jose Rijo, P Eric Plunk and P Tim Birtsas to Oakland Athletics for OF Rickey Henderson, P Bert Bradley and cash (December 5, 1984). . . . On Oakland disabled list (April 30-May 18 and May 27-July 20, 1986); included rehabilitation disability assignment to Modesto (July 11-16, 1986). . . . On disabled list (August 25, 1987-remainder of season). . . . Traded as part of an eight-player, three-team deal in which New York Mets traded P Jesse Orosco to A's (December 11, 1987). A's then traded Orosco with Howell and SS Alfredo Griffin to Los Angeles Dodgers for P Bob Welch, P Matt Young and P Jack Savage; A's then traded Savage with P Wally Whitehurst and P Kevin Tapani to Mets. . . . On disabled list (June 21-July 7, 1988; April 23-May 17, 1990; and June 20-July 23, 1991). . . . Granted free agency (November 1, 1991).
RECORDS/HONORS: Named American Association Pitcher of the Year (1982).
STATISTICAL NOTES: Tied for American Association lead with six balks in 1981. . . . Tied for American Association lead with two shutouts in 1982.

Year	Team (League)	G	W	L	Pct.	ERA	Sv.	IP	H	R	ER	BB	SO
1976	Eugene (Northwest)	13	5	4	.556	2.96	1	73	65	30	24	34	79
1977	Tampa (Florida State)	23	7	13	.350	2.96	0	158	141	60	52	52	99
1978	Nashville (Southern)	28	9	14	.391	3.09	0	166	134	70	57	55	*173
1979	Indianapolis (Am. Assoc.)	24	10	10	.500	5.13	0	128	121	82	73	84	79
1980	Indianapolis (Am. Assoc.)	25	5	11	.313	5.05	0	98	95	70	55	71	73
	Cincinnati (N.L.)	5	0	0	...	15.00	0	3	8	5	5	0	1
1981	Iowa (American Association)■	23	5	10	.333	3.75	0	144	141	74	60	62	90
	Chicago (N.L.)	10	2	0	1.000	4.91	0	22	23	13	12	10	10
1982	Iowa (American Association)	20	13	4	*.765	*2.36	0	141⅓	102	45	37	48	139
	Columbus (International)■	5	2	1	.667	2.41	0	37⅓	18	13	10	19	33
	New York (A.L.)	6	2	3	.400	7.71	0	28	42	25	24	13	21
1983	New York (A.L.)	19	1	5	.167	5.38	0	82	89	53	49	35	61
1984	New York (A.L.)	61	9	4	.692	2.69	7	103⅔	86	33	31	34	109
1985	Oakland (A.L.)■	63	9	8	.529	2.85	29	98	98	32	31	31	68
1986	Oakland (A.L.)	38	3	6	.333	3.38	16	53⅓	53	23	20	23	42
	Modesto (California)	2	0	0	...	13.50	0	2	5	3	3	1	1
1987	Oakland (A.L.)	36	3	4	.429	5.89	16	44⅓	48	30	29	21	35
1988	Los Angeles (N.L.)■	50	5	3	.625	2.08	21	65	44	16	15	21	70
1989	Los Angeles (N.L.)	56	5	3	.625	1.58	28	79⅔	60	15	14	22	55
1990	Los Angeles (N.L.)	45	5	5	.500	2.18	16	66	59	17	16	20	59
1991	Los Angeles (N.L.)	44	6	5	.545	3.18	16	51	39	19	18	11	40
	American League totals (6 years)	223	27	30	.474	4.05	68	409⅓	416	196	184	157	336
	National League totals (6 years)	210	23	16	.590	2.51	81	286⅔	233	85	80	84	235
	Major league totals (12 years)	433	50	46	.521	3.41	149	696	649	281	264	241	571

CHAMPIONSHIP SERIES RECORD

Year	Team (League)	G	W	L	Pct.	ERA	Sv.	IP	H	R	ER	BB	SO
1988	Los Angeles (N.L.)	2	0	1	.000	27.00	0	⅔	1	2	2	2	1

WORLD SERIES RECORD

Year	Team (League)	G	W	L	Pct.	ERA	Sv.	IP	H	R	ER	BB	SO
1988	Los Angeles (N.L.)	2	0	1	.000	3.38	1	2⅔	3	1	1	1	2

Year	League	W	L	Pct.	ERA	Sv.	IP	H	R	ER	BB	SO
1985	— American					Did not play						
1987	— American	0	1	.000	9.00	0	2	3	2	2	0	3
1989	— National	0	0	...	0.00	0	1	1	0	0	0	1
All-Star totals (2 years)		0	1	.000	6.00	0	3	4	2	2	0	4

HOWELL, KEN
P, PHILLIES

PERSONAL: Born November 28, 1960, at Detroit. . . . 6-3/237. . . . Throws right, bats right. . . . Full name: Kenneth Howell Jr.
HIGH SCHOOL: Redford (Detroit).
COLLEGE: Tuskegee Institute (Ala.).
TRANSACTIONS/CAREER NOTES: Selected by Los Angeles Dodgers organization in third round of free-agent draft (June 7, 1982). . . . On Albuquerque disabled list (April 7-17, 1984). . . . On Los Angeles disabled list (March 20-May 25 and June 17-July 8, 1988); included rehabilitation disability assignment to Bakersfield (May 7-11 and May 17-25, 1988) and Albuquerque (May 12-16 and June 24-July 8, 1988). . . . Traded by Dodgers with P Brian Holton and SS Juan Bell to Baltimore Orioles for 1B Eddie Murray (December 4, 1988). . . . Traded by Orioles with P Gordon Dillard to Philadelphia Phillies for OF Phil Bradley (December 8, 1988). . . . On disabled list (July 6-31 and August 1, 1990-remainder of season). . . . On Philadelphia disabled list (March 19, 1991-entire season); included rehabilitation disability assignment to Scranton/Wilkes-Barre (July 16-August 12, 1991).
STATISTICAL NOTES: Tied for Texas League lead in games started by pitcher with 27 in 1983. . . . Led N.L. with 21 wild pitches in 1989.

Year	Team (League)	G	W	L	Pct.	ERA	Sv.	IP	H	R	ER	BB	SO
1982	— Vero Beach (Florida State)	11	5	4	.556	4.22	0	59⅔	58	40	28	36	37
1983	— San Antonio (Texas)	27	8	11	.421	4.41	0	169⅓	171	98	83	101	116
	— Albuquerque (Pacific Coast)	1	0	0	...	9.00	0	3	4	3	3	1	1
1984	— Albuquerque (Pacific Coast)	18	8	2	.800	4.60	2	72⅓	79	48	37	37	58
	— Los Angeles (N.L.)	32	5	5	.500	3.33	6	51⅓	51	21	19	9	54
1985	— Los Angeles (N.L.)	56	4	7	.364	3.77	12	86	66	41	36	35	85
1986	— Los Angeles (N.L.)	62	6	12	.333	3.87	12	97⅔	86	48	42	63	104
1987	— Los Angeles (N.L.)	40	3	4	.429	4.91	1	55	54	32	30	29	60
	— Albuquerque (Pacific Coast)	2	1	0	1.000	0.00	0	13	6	1	0	7	13
1988	— Bakersfield (California)	3	0	1	.000	1.32	0	13⅔	8	5	2	9	13
	— Albuquerque (Pacific Coast)	18	10	1	*.909	3.27	0	107⅓	92	43	39	42	95
	— Los Angeles (N.L.)	4	0	1	.000	6.39	0	12⅔	16	10	9	4	12
1989	— Philadelphia (N.L.)■..	33	12	12	.500	3.44	0	204	155	84	78	86	164
1990	— Philadelphia (N.L.)	18	8	7	.533	4.64	0	106⅔	106	60	55	49	70
1991	— Scranton/Wilkes-Barre (Int'l) ..	6	2	0	1.000	5.11	0	24⅔	30	15	14	16	20
Major league totals (7 years)		245	38	48	.442	3.95	31	613⅓	534	296	269	275	549

CHAMPIONSHIP SERIES RECORD

Year	Team (League)	G	W	L	Pct.	ERA	Sv.	IP	H	R	ER	BB	SO
1985	— Los Angeles (N.L.)	1	0	0	...	0.00	0	2	0	0	0	0	2

HOWELL, PAT
OF, METS

PERSONAL: Born August 31, 1968, at Mobile, Ala. . . . 5-11/155. . . . Throws right, bats both. . . . Full name: Patrick O'Neal Howell.
HIGH SCHOOL: Vigor (Prichard, Ala.).
TRANSACTIONS/CAREER NOTES: Selected by New York Mets organization in ninth round of free-agent draft (June 2, 1987). . . . Drafted by Minnesota Twins (December 3, 1990). . . . Returned to Mets (April 5, 1991).
STATISTICAL NOTES: Led South Atlantic League outfielders with 334 total chances in 1990.
MISCELLANEOUS: Batted righthanded only (1987-1989).

Year	Team (League)	Pos.	G	AB	R	H	2B	3B	HR	RBI	Avg.	SB	PO	A	E	Avg.
1987	— Kingsport (Appalachian) ..	OF	34	92	14	20	2	0	1	5	.217	8	35	4	1	.975
1988	— Kingsport (Appalachian) ..	OF	66	251	43	67	6	3	0	16	.267	27	122	5	1	*.992
1989	— Pittsfield (Eastern)	OF	56	231	41	67	4	3	1	26	.290	*45	113	5	3	.975
1990	— Columbia (S. Atlantic)	OF	135	*573	98	151	15	5	1	37	.264	*79	*303	16	15	.955
1991	— Williamsport (Eastern)	OF	70	274	43	77	5	1	1	26	.281	27	186	5	3	.985
	— St. Lucie (Florida State)....	OF	62	246	36	54	8	2	0	10	.220	37	139	8	0	1.000

HOWITT, DANN
1B/OF, ATHLETICS

PERSONAL: Born February 13, 1964, at Battle Creek, Mich. . . . 6-5/205. . . . Throws right, bats left. . . . Full name: Dann Paul John Howitt. . . . Brother of Shaun Howitt, minor league outfielder (1972).
HIGH SCHOOL: Hastings (Mich.).
COLLEGE: Michigan State and Cal State Fullerton.
TRANSACTIONS/CAREER NOTES: Selected by Oakland Athletics organization in 18th round of free-agent draft (June 2, 1986).
STATISTICAL NOTES: Tied for Northwest League lead in double plays by outfielders with two in 1986. . . . Led California League outfielders with six double plays in 1987. . . . Led Southern League with 253 total bases in 1989. . . . Led Southern League first basemen with .992 fielding percentage in 1989.

Year	Team (League)	Pos.	G	AB	R	H	2B	3B	HR	RBI	Avg.	SB	PO	A	E	Avg.
1986	— Medford (Northwest)	OF	66	208	36	66	9	2	6	37	.317	5	83	5	4	.957
1987	— Modesto (California)	OF-1B-P	109	336	44	70	11	2	8	42	.208	7	263	23	6	.979
1988	— Modesto (California)	OF-1B-P	132	480	75	121	20	2	18	86	.252	11	475	42	12	.977
	— Tacoma (Pacific Coast)	OF-1B	4	15	1	2	1	0	0	0	.133	0	14	0	0	1.000

Year	Team (League)	Pos.	G	AB	R	H	2B	3B	HR	RBI	Avg.	SB	PO	A	E	Avg.
1989	Huntsville (Southern)	1B-OF-P	138	509	78	143	28	2	26	111	.281	2	965	74	9	†.991
	Oakland (A.L.)	1B-OF	3	3	0	0	0	0	0	0	.000	0	2	0	0	1.000
1990	Tacoma (Pacific Coast)	1B-OF-3B	118	437	58	116	30	1	11	69	.265	4	608	74	11	.984
	Oakland (A.L.)	OF-1B-3B	14	22	3	3	0	1	0	1	.136	0	34	1	0	1.000
1991	Tacoma (Pacific Coast)	OF-1B	122	449	58	120	28	6	14	73	.267	6	429	33	4	.991
	Oakland (A.L.)	OF-1B	21	42	5	7	1	0	1	3	.167	0	36	0	0	1.000
Major league totals (3 years)			38	67	8	10	1	1	1	4	.149	0	72	1	0	1.000

RECORD AS PITCHER

Year	Team (League)	G	W	L	Pct.	ERA	Sv.	IP	H	R	ER	BB	SO
1987	Modesto (California)	2	0	0	...	1.80	0	5	7	1	1	3	3
1988	Modesto (California)	4	0	0	...	6.43	0	7	13	8	5	3	3
1989	Huntsville (Southern)	2	0	0	...	0.00	0	2	2	1	0	0	2

HOY, PETE

P, RED SOX

PERSONAL: Born June 29, 1966, at Brockville, Ont. . . . 6-7/220. . . . Throws right, bats left. . . . Full name: Peter Alexander Hoy. . . . Son of Jack Hoy, minor league pitcher (1955-56).
HIGH SCHOOL: South Greenville District (Prescott, Ont.).
COLLEGE: LeMoyne College (N.Y.).
TRANSACTIONS/CAREER NOTES: Selected by Boston Red Sox organization in 33rd round of free-agent draft (June 1, 1988).
MISCELLANEOUS: Member of 1988 Canadian Olympic baseball team.

Year	Team (League)	G	W	L	Pct.	ERA	Sv.	IP	H	R	ER	BB	SO
1989	Elmira (New York-Penn)	26	6	10	.375	2.82	1	118	109	52	37	37	73
1990	Winter Haven (Florida State)	52	2	10	.167	3.56	7	108⅔	110	54	43	30	48
1991	New Britain (Eastern)	47	4	4	.500	1.46	15	68	47	20	11	22	39
	Pawtucket (International)	15	1	2	.333	2.38	5	22⅔	18	8	6	10	12

HRBEK, KENT

1B, TWINS

PERSONAL: Born May 21, 1960, at Minneapolis. . . . 6-4/262. . . . Throws right, bats left. . . . Full name: Kent Alan Hrbek. . . . Name pronounced HER-beck.
HIGH SCHOOL: Kennedy (Bloomington, Minn.).
TRANSACTIONS/CAREER NOTES: Selected by Minnesota Twins organization in 17th round of free-agent draft (June 6, 1978). . . . On Wisconsin Rapids disabled list (April 13-June 21, 1979). . . . On Elizabethton disabled list (July 22-September 6, 1979). . . . On disabled list (May 27-June 6, 1980 and May 16-June 26, 1989). . . . Granted free agency (November 13, 1989). . . . Re-signed by Twins (December 6, 1989).
RECORDS/HONORS: Named California League Most Valuable Player (1981).
STATISTICAL NOTES: Led California League with .630 slugging percentage and tied for lead with nine sacrifice flies in 1981. . . . Led A.L. first basemen with .997 fielding percentage in 1990.

Year	Team (League)	Pos.	G	AB	R	H	2B	3B	HR	RBI	Avg.	SB	PO	A	E	Avg.
1979	Elizabethton (Appal.)	1B	17	59	5	12	2	0	1	11	.203	2	126	11	2	.986
1980	Wis. Rapids (Midwest)	1B	115	419	74	112	16	0	19	76	.267	1	1005	81	∗20	.982
1981	Visalia (California)	1B	121	462	119	175	25	5	27	111∗	.379	12	1034	53	11	∗.990
	Minnesota (A.L.)	1B	24	67	5	16	5	0	1	7	.239	0	124	4	0	1.000
1982	Minnesota (A.L.)	1B	140	532	82	160	21	4	23	92	.301	3	1174	88	9	.993
1983	Minnesota (A.L.)	1B	141	515	75	153	41	5	16	84	.297	4	1151	89	13	.990
1984	Minnesota (A.L.)	1B	149	559	80	174	31	3	27	107	.311	1	1320	99	14	.990
1985	Minnesota (A.L.)	1B	158	593	78	165	31	2	21	93	.278	1	1339	114	8	.995
1986	Minnesota (A.L.)	1B	149	550	85	147	27	1	29	91	.267	2	1218	104	10	.992
1987	Minnesota (A.L.)	1B	143	477	85	136	20	1	34	90	.285	5	1179	68	5	.996
1988	Minnesota (A.L.)	1B	143	510	75	159	31	0	25	76	.312	0	842	57	3	.997
1989	Minnesota (A.L.)	1B	109	375	59	102	17	0	25	84	.272	3	723	60	4	.995
1990	Minnesota (A.L.)	1B-3B	143	492	61	141	26	0	22	79	.287	5	1057	83	3	†.997
1991	Minnesota (A.L.)	1B	132	462	72	131	20	1	20	89	.284	4	1138	95	8	.994
Major league totals (11 years)			1431	5132	757	1484	270	17	243	892	.289	28	11265	861	77	.994

CHAMPIONSHIP SERIES RECORD

Year	Team (League)	Pos.	G	AB	R	H	2B	3B	HR	RBI	Avg.	SB	PO	A	E	Avg.
1987	Minnesota (A.L.)	1B	5	20	4	3	0	0	1	1	.150	0	40	3	0	1.000
1991	Minnesota (A.L.)	1B	5	21	0	3	0	0	0	3	.143	0	40	8	0	1.000
Championship Series totals (2 years)			10	41	4	6	0	0	1	4	.146	0	80	11	0	1.000

WORLD SERIES RECORD

WORLD SERIES NOTES: Shares single-game record for most grand slams—1 (October 24, 1987). . . . Shares record for most runs batted in in one inning—4 (October 24, 1987, sixth inning).

Year	Team (League)	Pos.	G	AB	R	H	2B	3B	HR	RBI	Avg.	SB	PO	A	E	Avg.
1987	Minnesota (A.L.)	1B	7	24	4	5	0	0	1	6	.208	0	68	2	0	1.000
1991	Minnesota (A.L.)	1B	7	26	2	3	1	0	1	2	.115	0	66	8	0	1.000
World Series totals (2 years)			14	50	6	8	1	0	2	8	.160	0	134	10	0	1.000

ALL-STAR GAME RECORD

Year	League	Pos.	AB	R	H	2B	3B	HR	RBI	Avg.	SB	PO	A	E	Avg.
1982—American		PH	1	0	0	0	0	0	0	.000	0	0	0	0	...

HUDLER, REX

`OF/1B, CARDINALS`

PERSONAL: Born September 2, 1960, at Tempe, Ariz. . . .6-0/195. . . . Throws right, bats right. . . . Full name: Rex Allen Hudler.
HIGH SCHOOL: Bullard (Fresno, Calif.).
TRANSACTIONS/CAREER NOTES: Selected by New York Yankees organization in first round (18th pick overall) of free-agent draft (June 6, 1978). . . . On Fort Lauderdale disabled list (May 18-31, 1979; May 10-June 15, 1980; and May 11-June 11, 1981). . . . Traded by Yankees with P Rich Bordi to Baltimore Orioles for OF Gary Roenicke and a player to be named later (December 12, 1985); Yankees acquired OF Leo Hernandez to complete deal (December 16, 1985). . . . On Baltimore disabled list (March 23-June 16, 1987); included rehabilitation disability assignment to Rochester (May 28-June 16, 1987). . . . Granted free agency (October 15, 1987). . . . Signed by Indianapolis, Montreal Expos organization (December 18, 1987). . . . Traded by Expos to St. Louis Cardinals for P John Costello (April 23, 1990).
STATISTICAL NOTES: Led International League second basemen with 95 double plays in 1984.

Year	Team (League)	Pos.	G	AB	R	H	2B	3B	HR	RBI	Avg.	SB	PO	A	E	Avg.
1978—Oneonta (N.Y.-Penn)		SS	58	221	33	62	5	5	0	24	.281	16	123	21	22	.867
1979—Fort Lauderdale (FSL)		S-3-2-0	116	414	37	104	14	1	1	25	.251	23	164	314	45	.914
1980—Fort Lauderdale (FSL)		3-2-0-1	37	125	14	26	4	0	0	6	.208	2	55	71	5	.962
—Greensboro (S. Atlantic) ...		2B	20	75	7	17	3	1	2	9	.227	1	51	52	5	.954
1981—Fort Lauderdale (FSL)		2-S-3-0	79	259	35	77	11	1	2	26	.297	6	104	238	19	.947
1982—Nashville (Southern)		2B-SS-OF	89	299	27	71	14	1	0	24	.237	9	136	219	20	.947
—Fort Lauderdale (FSL)		2B	9	32	2	8	1	0	1	6	.250	2	23	25	2	.960
1983—Fort Lauderdale (FSL)		2B-SS	91	345	55	93	15	2	2	50	.270	30	195	245	15	.967
—Columbus (Int'l)		2B-3B-SS	40	118	17	36	5	0	1	11	.305	1	55	95	4	.974
1984—Columbus (Int'l)		2B	114	394	49	115	26	1	1	35	.292	11	266	348	16	.975
—New York (A.L.)		2B	9	7	2	1	1	0	0	0	.143	0	4	7	0	1.000
1985—Columbus (Int'l)		IF-OF	106	380	62	95	13	4	3	18	.250	29	192	234	17	.962
—New York (A.L.)		2B-1B-SS	20	51	4	8	0	1	0	1	.157	0	42	51	2	.979
1986—Rochester (Int'l)■		2-3-0-S	77	219	29	57	12	3	2	13	.260	12	135	191	15	.956
—Baltimore (A.L.)		2B-3B	14	1	1	0	0	0	0	0	.000	1	2	3	1	.833
1987—Rochester (Int'l)		OF-2B-SS	31	106	22	27	5	1	5	10	.255	9	51	15	2	.971
1988—Indianapolis (A.A.)■		O-2-S-3	67	234	36	71	11	3	7	25	.303	14	102	96	4	.980
—Montreal (N.L.)		2B-SS-OF	77	216	38	59	14	2	4	14	.273	29	116	168	10	.966
1989—Montreal (N.L.)		2B-OF-SS	92	155	21	38	7	0	6	13	.245	15	59	59	7	.944
1990—Mont.-St. Louis (N.L.)■		OF-IF	93	220	31	62	11	2	7	22	.282	18	158	42	5	.976
1991—St. Louis (N.L.)		OF-1B-2B	101	207	21	47	10	2	1	15	.227	12	130	6	2	.986
American League totals (3 years)			43	59	7	9	1	1	0	1	.153	1	48	61	3	.973
National League totals (4 years)			363	798	111	206	42	6	18	64	.258	74	463	275	24	.969
Major league totals (7 years)			406	857	118	215	43	7	18	65	.251	75	511	336	27	.969

HUFF, MIKE

`OF, WHITE SOX`

PERSONAL: Born August 11, 1963, at Honolulu. . . . 6-1/180. . . . Throws right, bats right. . . . Full name: Míchael Kale Huff.
HIGH SCHOOL: New Trier (Winnetka, Ill.).
COLLEGE: Northwestern (bachelor of science degree in industrial engineering, 1985).
TRANSACTIONS/CAREER NOTES: Selected by Los Angeles Dodgers organization in 16th round of free-agent draft (June 3, 1985). . . . On disabled list (May 11, 1987-remainder of season). . . . Drafted by Cleveland Indians (December 3, 1990). . . . Claimed on waivers by Chicago White Sox (July 12, 1991). . . . On disabled list (August 25-September 9, 1991).
STATISTICAL NOTES: Tied for Texas League lead in double plays by outfielders with four in 1988.

Year	Team (League)	Pos.	G	AB	R	H	2B	3B	HR	RBI	Avg.	SB	PO	A	E	Avg.
1985—Great Falls (Pioneer)		OF	•70	247	70	78	6	6	0	35	.316	28	120	5	5	.962
1986—Vero Beach (Florida St.) ...		OF	113	362	73	106	6	8	2	32	.293	28	257	10	1	.996
1987—San Antonio (Texas)		OF	31	135	23	42	5	1	3	18	.311	2	52	2	2	.964
1988—San Antonio (Texas)		OF	102	395	68	120	18	10	2	40	.304	33	222	12	2	.992
—Albuquerque (PCL)		OF	2	4	0	1	1	0	0	0	.250	0	2	0	0	1.000
1989—Albuquerque (PCL)		OF-2B	115	471	75	150	29	7	10	78	.318	32	209	13	2	.991
—Los Angeles (N.L.)		OF	12	25	4	5	1	0	1	2	.200	0	18	0	0	1.000
1990—Albuquerque (PCL)		OF-2B	★138	474	99	154	28	11	7	84	.325	27	285	29	5	.984
1991—Clev.-Chicago (A.L.)■		OF-2B	102	243	42	61	10	2	3	25	.251	14	168	7	2	.989
American League totals (1 year)			102	243	42	61	10	2	3	25	.251	14	168	7	2	.989
National League totals (1 year)			12	25	4	5	1	0	1	2	.200	0	18	0	0	1.000
Major league totals (2 years)			114	268	46	66	11	2	4	27	.246	14	186	7	2	.990

HUISMANN, MARK

`P, ROYALS`

PERSONAL: Born May 11, 1958, at Lincoln, Neb. . . . 6-3/195. . . . Throws right, bats right. . . . Full name: Mark Lawrence Huismann. . . . Name pronounced HYOOS-mun.
HIGH SCHOOL: Doherty (Colo.).
COLLEGE: Colorado State (bachelor of science degree in business and finance, 1980).

— 231 —

TRANSACTIONS/CAREER NOTES: Selected by Chicago Cubs organization in 23rd round of free-agent draft (June 5, 1979)....
Signed as free agent by Kansas City Royals organization (June 16, 1980).... Traded by Royals to Seattle Mariners for C Terry
Bell (May 21, 1986).... Traded by Mariners to Cleveland Indians for OF Dave Gallagher (May 12, 1987).... Released by Indi-
ans organization (March 17, 1988).... Signed by Toledo, Detroit Tigers organization (March 23, 1988).... Released by Tigers
(February 22, 1989).... Signed by Rochester, Baltimore Orioles organization (March 1, 1989).... On Baltimore disabled list
(June 11, 1989-remainder of season).... Released by Orioles (October 3, 1989).... Signed by Buffalo, Pittsburgh Pirates or-
ganization (March 7, 1990).... Granted free agency (October 15, 1990).... Re-signed by Pirates organization (February 4,
1991).... Released by Buffalo (June 11, 1991).... Signed by Omaha, Kansas City Royals organization (June 20, 1991)....
Granted free agency (October 16, 1991).... Re-signed by Royals organization (December 30, 1991).
RECORDS/HONORS: Named American Association Pitcher of the Year (1985).

Year	Team (League)	G	W	L	Pct.	ERA	Sv.	IP	H	R	ER	BB	SO
1980	—Sarasota Royals-Blue (GCL)....	28	1	2	.333	2.44	0	59	50	20	16	14	46
1981	—Charleston, S.C. (S. Atlantic)....	28	3	2	.600	1.64	10	44	36	16	8	17	42
	—Fort Myers (Florida State)........	14	3	1	.750	3.43	2	21	15	9	8	16	19
1982	—Fort Myers (Florida State)........	14	3	1	.750	0.39	3	23	16	1	1	4	21
	—Jacksonville (Southern)...........	36	4	4	.500	2.14	9	54⅔	52	18	13	15	60
1983	—Jacksonville (Southern)...........	37	6	3	.667	3.23	10	61⅓	60	25	22	25	46
	—Omaha (American Assoc.)........	17	0	2	.000	1.85	8	24⅓	16	7	5	9	25
	—Kansas City (A.L.)............	13	2	1	.667	5.58	0	30⅔	29	20	19	17	20
1984	—Kansas City (A.L.)............	38	3	3	.500	4.20	3	75	84	38	35	21	54
	—Omaha (American Assoc.)........	15	2	0	1.000	0.00	3	19	11	0	0	5	18
1985	—Omaha (American Assoc.)........	*59	5	5	.500	2.01	*33	89⅓	70	20	20	14	70
	—Kansas City (A.L.)............	9	1	0	1.000	1.93	0	18⅔	14	4	4	3	9
1986	—Kansas City-Seattle (A.L.)■....	46	3	4	.429	3.79	5	97⅓	98	47	41	25	72
1987	—Seattle-Cleveland (A.L.)■........	26	2	3	.400	5.04	2	50	48	32	28	12	38
	—Buffalo (American Assoc.)........	13	1	1	.500	7.56	0	33⅓	43	32	28	8	31
1988	—Toledo (International)■...........	48	4	6	.400	1.87	21	57⅔	50	20	12	15	61
	—Detroit (A.L.)............	5	1	0	1.000	5.06	0	5⅓	6	3	3	2	6
1989	—Rochester (International)■.......	16	2	1	.667	1.71	8	21	9	4	4	3	20
	—Baltimore (A.L.)............	8	0	0	...	6.35	1	11⅓	13	8	8	0	13
1990	—Buffalo (American Assoc.)■....	49	6	2	.750	2.61	4	76	69	23	22	15	32
	—Pittsburgh (N.L.)............	2	1	0	1.000	9.00	0	3	6	5	3	1	2
1991	—Buffalo-Omaha (Am. Assoc.)■..	45	6	5	.545	3.16	17	68⅓	70	28	24	18	51
	—Pittsburgh (N.L.)............	5	0	0	...	7.20	0	5	7	6	4	2	5
American League totals (7 years)...........		145	12	11	.522	4.31	11	288⅓	292	152	138	80	212
National League totals (2 years)...........		7	1	0	1.000	7.88	0	8	13	11	7	3	7
Major league totals (9 years).................		152	13	11	.542	4.40	11	296⅓	305	163	145	83	219

CHAMPIONSHIP SERIES RECORD

Year	Team (League)	G	W	L	Pct.	ERA	Sv.	IP	H	R	ER	BB	SO
1984	—Kansas City (A.L.)...................	1	0	0	...	6.75	0	2⅔	6	3	2	1	2

HULETT, TIM

3B/2B, ORIOLES

PERSONAL: Born January 12, 1960, at Springfield, Ill.... 6-0/199.... Throws right, bats right....
Full name: Timothy Craig Hulett.... Name pronounced HYOO-lit.
HIGH SCHOOL: Lanphier (Springfield, Ill.).
COLLEGE: Miami-Dade (North) Community College and South Florida.

TRANSACTIONS/CAREER NOTES: Selected by Texas Rangers organization in 39th round of free-agent draft (June 6, 1978)....
Selected by Chicago White Sox organization in secondary phase of free-agent draft (January 8, 1980).... Traded by White
Sox organization to Montreal Expos for a player to be named later (April 13, 1988); White Sox acquired 2B Edgar Caceres to
complete deal (June 15, 1988).... Granted free agency (October 15, 1988).... Signed by Rochester, Baltimore Orioles organization (November 21, 1988).... On Baltimore disabled list (April 4-June 12, 1990); included rehabilitation disability assignment to Rochester (May 29-June 21, 1990).
STATISTICAL NOTES: Led Eastern League second basemen with 332 putouts, 415 assists, 763 total chances and 112 double
plays in 1981.... Led Eastern League second basemen with .975 fielding percentage, 343 putouts, 386 assists, 748 total
chances and 95 double plays in 1982.... Led American Association second basemen with 730 total chances in 1983.... Led
American Association with nine sacrifice flies in both 1983 and 1988.... Tied for A.L. lead in errors by third basemen with 23 in
1985.... Led International League third basemen with 23 double plays in 1989.

						—BATTING—						—FIELDING—			
Year	Team (League)	Pos.	G	AB	R	H	2B	3B	HR	RBI	Avg.	SB	PO	A	E	Avg.
1980	—Glens Falls (Eastern)........	SS	6	23	2	4	0	0	0	0	.174	0	14	13	2	.931
	—Iowa (American Assoc.)...	3B	3	8	1	2	0	0	0	0	.250	1	0	6	3	.667
	—Appleton (Midwest)..........	2B-3B-SS	79	278	49	72	11	1	13	47	.259	5	162	258	17	.961
1981	—Glens Falls (Eastern)........	2B-3B	134	437	59	99	27	1	10	55	.227	0	†333	†422	16	.979
1982	—Glens Falls (Eastern)........	2B-SS	•140	*536	*113	145	28	5	22	87	.271	1	†352	†398	21	†.973
1983	—Denver (Am. Assoc.)........	2B	133	477	77	130	19	4	21	88	.273	5	*286	*424	*20	.973
	—Chicago (A.L.)................	2B	6	5	0	1	0	0	0	0	.200	1	8	6	2	.875
1984	—Chicago (A.L.)................	2B	8	7	1	0	0	0	0	0	.000	1	4	15	0	1.000
	—Denver (Am. Assoc.)........	2B-3B-SS	139	475	72	125	32	6	16	80	.263	3	269	371	28	.958
1985	—Chicago (A.L.)................	3B-2B-0F	141	395	52	106	19	4	5	37	.268	6	117	256	‡24	.940
1986	—Chicago (A.L.)................	3B-2B	150	520	53	120	16	5	17	44	.231	4	179	331	15	.971
1987	—Chicago (A.L.)................	3B-2B	68	240	20	52	10	0	7	28	.217	0	55	142	9	.956
	—Hawaii (Pacific Coast)......	3B-2B	42	157	13	37	5	2	1	24	.236	4	47	81	11	.921
1988	—Indianapolis (A.A.)■........	3B-2B	126	427	36	100	29	2	7	59	.234	2	118	211	25	.929

Year	Team (League)	Pos.	G	AB	R	H	2B	3B	HR	RBI	Avg.	SB	PO	A	E	Avg.
1989	—Rochester (Int'l)■............	3-S-2-P	1	461	61	129	32	12	3	50	.280	2	149	289	20	.956
	—Baltimore (A.L.)...............	2B-3B	33	97	12	27	5	0	3	18	.278	0	70	71	4	.972
1990	—Rochester (Int'l)	2B-SS-3B	14	43	10	16	2	1	2	4	.372	0	22	35	1	.983
	—Baltimore (A.L.)	3B-2B	53	153	16	39	7	1	3	16	.255	1	44	101	4	.973
1991	—Baltimore (A.L.)	3B-2B-SS	79	206	29	42	9	0	7	18	.204	0	47	96	4	.973
	Major league totals (8 years)		538	1623	183	387	66	10	42	161	.238	13	524	1018	62	.961

RECORD AS PITCHER

Year	Team (League)	G	W	L	Pct.	ERA	Sv.	IP	H	R	ER	BB	SO
1989	—Rochester (International)	1	0	0	...	0.00	0	$\frac{2}{3}$	0	0	0	0	0

HUMPHREYS, MIKE
OF/3B, YANKEES

PERSONAL: Born April 10, 1967, at Dallas.... 6-0/185.... Throws right, bats right. ... Full name: Michael Butler Humphreys.
COLLEGE: Texas Tech.
TRANSACTIONS/CAREER NOTES: Selected by San Diego Padres organization in 15th round of free-agent draft (June 1, 1988).... Traded by Padres to New York Yankees (February 7, 1991), completing deal in which Yankees traded OF Oscar Azocar to Padres for a player to be named later (December 3, 1990).
STATISTICAL NOTES: Led Northwest League outfielders with .974 fielding percentage and tied for lead with 180 putouts in 1988.

Year	Team (League)	Pos.	G	AB	R	H	2B	3B	HR	RBI	Avg.	SB	PO	A	E	Avg.
1988	—Spokane (Northwest)	OF-1B	76	303	★67	93	16	•5	6	59	.307	21	‡181	6	5	†.974
1989	—Riverside (California)	OF-3B-1B	117	420	77	121	26	1	13	66	.288	23	251	10	7	.974
1990	—Wichita (Texas)	OF	116	421	★92	116	21	4	17	79	.276	38	277	8	5	.983
	—Las Vegas (Pac. Coast)	OF	12	42	7	10	1	0	2	6	.238	1	19	5	0	1.000
1991	—Columbus (Int'l)	OF-3B	117	413	71	117	23	5	9	53	.283	34	188	51	8	.968
	—New York (A.L.)	OF-3B	25	40	9	8	0	0	0	3	.200	2	10	8	1	.947
	Major league totals (1 year)		25	40	9	8	0	0	0	3	.200	2	10	8	1	.947

HUNDLEY, TODD
C, METS

PERSONAL: Born May 27, 1969, at Martinsville, Va.... 5-11/185.... Throws right, bats both.... Full name: Todd Randolph Hundley.... Son of Randy Hundley, major league catcher for four teams (1964-77).
HIGH SCHOOL: William Fremd (Palatine, Ill.).
COLLEGE: William Rainey Harper College (Ill.).
TRANSACTIONS/CAREER NOTES: Selected by New York Mets organization in second round of free-agent draft (June 2, 1987).... On Tidewater disabled list (June 29-July 6, 1991).
STATISTICAL NOTES: Led South Atlantic League in intentional bases on balls received with 10 and grounded into double plays with 20 in 1989.... Led South Atlantic League catchers with 826 putouts and 930 total chances in 1989.... Tied for International League lead in errors by catcher with nine and double plays with 12 in 1991.

Year	Team (League)	Pos.	G	AB	R	H	2B	3B	HR	RBI	Avg.	SB	PO	A	E	Avg.
1987	—Little Falls (N.Y.-Penn)	C	34	103	12	15	4	0	1	10	.146	0	181	25	7	.967
1988	—Little Falls (N.Y.-Penn)	C	52	176	23	33	8	0	2	18	.188	1	345	54	8	.980
	—St. Lucie (Florida State)	C	1	1	0	0	0	0	0	0	.000	0	4	0	1	.800
1989	—Columbia (S. Atlantic)	C-OF	125	439	67	118	23	4	11	66	.269	6	†829	91	13	.986
1990	—Jackson (Texas)	C-3B	81	279	27	74	12	2	1	35	.265	5	474	63	9	.984
	—New York (N.L.)	C	36	67	8	14	6	0	0	2	.209	0	162	8	2	.988
1991	—Tidewater (Int'l)	C-1B	125	454	62	124	24	4	14	66	.273	1	585	63	‡9	.986
	—New York (N.L.)	C	21	60	5	8	0	1	1	7	.133	0	85	11	0	1.000
	Major league totals (2 years)		57	127	13	22	6	1	1	9	.173	0	247	19	2	.993

HUNTER, BRIAN
1B/OF, BRAVES

PERSONAL: Born March 4, 1968, at El Toro, Calif.... 6-0/195.... Throws left, bats right.... Full name: Brian Ronald Hunter.
HIGH SCHOOL: Paramount (Calif.).
COLLEGE: Cerritos College (Calif.).
TRANSACTIONS/CAREER NOTES: Selected by Atlanta Braves organization in eighth round of free-agent draft (June 2, 1987).
STATISTICAL NOTES: Led Appalachian League first basemen with 43 double plays in 1987.... Led Midwest League first basemen with 21 errors in 1988.... Tied for Southern League lead with nine sacrifice flies in 1989.

Year	Team (League)	Pos.	G	AB	R	H	2B	3B	HR	RBI	Avg.	SB	PO	A	E	Avg.
1987	—Pulaski (Appalachian)	1B-OF	65	251	38	58	10	2	8	30	.231	3	498	29	11	.980
1988	—Burlington (Midwest)	1B-OF	117	417	58	108	17	0	•22	71	.259	7	987	69	†22	.980
	—Durham (Carolina)	OF-1B	13	49	13	17	3	0	3	9	.347	2	52	6	0	1.000
1989	—Greenville (Southern)	OF-1B	124	451	57	114	19	2	19	82	.253	5	248	15	4	.985
1990	—Richmond (Int'l)	OF-1B	43	137	13	27	4	0	5	16	.197	2	126	5	3	.978
	—Greenville (Southern)	OF-1B	88	320	45	77	13	1	14	55	.241	6	189	19	8	.963
1991	—Richmond (Int'l)	OF	48	181	28	47	7	0	10	30	.260	3	121	4	4	.969
	—Atlanta (N.L.)	1B-OF	97	271	32	68	16	1	12	50	.251	0	624	46	8	.988
	Major league totals (1 year)		97	271	32	68	16	1	12	50	.251	0	624	46	8	.988

Year	Team (League)	Pos.	G	AB	R	H	2B	3B	HR	RBI	Avg.	SB	PO	A	E	Avg.
							BATTING							FIELDING		
1991—Atlanta (N.L.)		1B	5	18	2	6	2	0	1	4	.333	0	30	4	0	1.000

WORLD SERIES RECORD

Year	Team (League)	Pos.	G	AB	R	H	2B	3B	HR	RBI	Avg.	SB	PO	A	E	Avg.
							BATTING							FIELDING		
1991—Atlanta (N.L.)		O-PH-1	7	21	2	4	1	0	1	3	.190	0	6	1	0	1.000

HUNTER, JIM
P

PERSONAL: Born June 22, 1964, at Jersey City, N.J. . . . . 6-3/205. . . . Throws right, bats right. . . . Full name: James MacGregor Hunter.
COLLEGE: Brookdale Community College (N.J.) and Georgia.
TRANSACTIONS/CAREER NOTES: Selected by Atlanta Braves organization in 23rd round of free-agent draft (June 6, 1986). . . . Selected by Baltimore Orioles organization in secondary phase of free-agent draft (January 17, 1984). . . . Selected by Baltimore Orioles organization in secondary phase of free-agent draft (June 4, 1984). . . . Selected by Montreal Expos organization in secondary phase of free-agent draft (June 3, 1985). . . . Sold by Expos organization to Milwaukee Brewers organization (June 9, 1986). . . . Granted free agency (October 15, 1991).

Year	Team (League)	G	W	L	Pct.	ERA	Sv.	IP	H	R	ER	BB	SO
1985—Jamestown (New York-Penn) ..		14	3	3	.500	2.80	0	70⅔	65	30	22	34	41
1986—Burlington-Beloit (Midwest)■..		24	6	8	.429	4.02	0	134⅓	143	75	60	47	80
1987—Stockton (California)		8	6	1	.857	2.45	0	51⅓	39	16	14	20	44
—El Paso (Texas)		16	5	5	.500	4.61	0	95⅔	117	60	49	33	62
1988—El Paso (Texas)		26	8	11	.421	5.67	0	147⅔	163	107	93	•77	103
1989—El Paso (Texas)		19	7	10	.412	4.19	0	124⅔	149	70	58	45	68
1990—El Paso (Texas)		9	6	3	.667	3.92	0	62	64	31	27	15	37
—Denver (American Assoc.)		20	6	8	.429	4.69	0	117	138	76	61	45	57
1991—Denver (American Assoc.)		14	7	4	.636	3.30	0	87⅓	94	38	32	27	43
—Milwaukee (A.L.)		8	0	5	.000	7.26	0	31	45	26	25	17	14
Major league totals (1 year)		8	0	5	.000	7.26	0	31	45	26	25	17	14

HURST, BRUCE
P, PADRES

PERSONAL: Born March 24, 1958, at St. George, Utah . . . 6-3/220. . . . Throws left, bats left. . . . Full name: Bruce Vee Hurst.
HIGH SCHOOL: Dixie (St. George, Utah).
COLLEGE: Dixie College (Utah).
TRANSACTIONS/CAREER NOTES: Selected by Boston Red Sox organization in first round (22nd pick overall) of free-agent draft (June 8, 1976). . . . On disabled list (August 8-September 14, 1977; May 23-September 21, 1978; June 3-July 18, 1986; and July 8-24, 1988). . . . Granted free agency (November 4, 1988). . . . Signed by San Diego Padres (December 8, 1988).
STATISTICAL NOTES: Led A.L. with four balks in 1985. . . . Tied for N.L. lead with 10 complete games in 1989. . . . Tied for N.L. lead with four shutouts in 1990.

Year	Team (League)	G	W	L	Pct.	ERA	Sv.	IP	H	R	ER	BB	SO
1976—Elmira (New York-Penn)		9	3	2	.600	3.00	0	42	25	18	14	38	40
1977—Winter Haven (Florida State) ...		13	5	4	.556	2.08	0	91	77	28	21	25	69
1978—Bristol (Eastern)		6	1	3	.250	2.73	0	33	32	15	10	17	35
1979—Winter Haven (Florida State) ...		12	8	2	.800	1.93	0	84	57	22	18	20	64
—Bristol (Eastern)		16	9	4	.692	3.58	0	113	108	56	45	49	91
1980—Pawtucket (International)		17	8	6	.571	3.94	0	105	101	52	46	50	54
—Boston (A.L.)		12	2	2	.500	9.00	0	31	39	33	31	16	16
1981—Pawtucket (International)		32	12	7	.632	2.87	0	157	143	68	50	71	99
—Boston (A.L.)		5	2	0	1.000	4.30	0	23	23	11	11	12	11
1982—Boston (A.L.)		28	3	7	.300	5.77	0	117	161	87	75	40	53
1983—Boston (A.L.)		33	12	12	.500	4.09	0	211⅓	241	102	96	62	115
1984—Boston (A.L.)		33	12	12	.500	3.92	0	218	232	106	95	88	136
1985—Boston (A.L.)		35	11	13	.458	4.51	0	229⅓	243	123	115	70	189
1986—Boston (A.L.)		25	13	8	.619	2.99	0	174⅓	169	63	58	50	167
1987—Boston (A.L.)		33	15	13	.536	4.41	0	238⅔	239	124	117	76	190
1988—Boston (A.L.)		33	18	6	.750	3.66	0	216⅔	222	98	88	65	166
1989—San Diego (N.L.)■		33	15	11	.577	2.69	0	244⅔	214	84	73	66	179
1990—San Diego (N.L.)		33	11	9	.550	3.14	0	223⅔	188	85	78	63	162
1991—San Diego (N.L.)		31	15	8	.652	3.29	0	221⅔	201	89	81	59	141
American League totals (9 years)		237	88	73	.547	4.23	0	1459⅓	1569	747	686	479	1043
National League totals (3 years)		97	41	28	.594	3.03	0	690	603	258	232	188	482
Major league totals (12 years)		334	129	101	.561	3.84	0	2149⅓	2172	1005	918	667	1525

CHAMPIONSHIP SERIES RECORD
CHAMPIONSHIP SERIES NOTES: Shares single-series record for most games lost—2 (1988).

Year	Team (League)	G	W	L	Pct.	ERA	Sv.	IP	H	R	ER	BB	SO
1986—Boston (A.L.)		2	1	0	1.000	2.40	0	15	18	5	4	1	8
1988—Boston (A.L.)		2	0	2	.000	2.77	0	13	10	4	4	5	12
Championship Series totals (2 years)		4	1	2	.333	2.57	0	28	28	9	8	6	20

WORLD SERIES RECORD

Year	Team (League)	G	W	L	Pct.	ERA	Sv.	IP	H	R	ER	BB	SO
1986 — Boston (A.L.)		3	2	0	1.000	1.96	0	23	18	5	5	6	17

ALL-STAR GAME RECORD

Year	League	W	L	Pct.	ERA	Sv.	IP	H	R	ER	BB	SO
1987 — American						Did not play						

HURST, JODY
OF, TIGERS

PERSONAL: Born March 11, 1967, at Meridian, Miss. . . . 6-4/190. . . . Throws right, bats left. . . . Full name: Joseph Foster Hurst.
HIGH SCHOOL: West Lauderdale (Collinsville, Miss.).
COLLEGE: Mississippi State.
TRANSACTIONS/CAREER NOTES: Selected by Minnesota Twins organization in 24th round of free-agent draft (June 1, 1988). . . . Selected by Detroit Tigers organization in 10th round of free-agent draft (June 5, 1989).

							BATTING							FIELDING			
Year	Team (League)	Pos.	G	AB	R	H	2B	3B	HR	RBI	Avg.	SB	PO	A	E	Avg.
1989 — Niagara Falls (NYP)		OF	55	198	41	56	9	0	10	38	.283	9	91	2	4	.959
1990 — Lakeland (Florida State) ...		OF	75	286	38	86	12	5	10	47	.301	16	143	5	4	.974
— London (Eastern)		OF	44	152	26	63	10	1	4	13	.414	6	97	1	1	.990
1991 — London (Eastern)		OF	54	187	33	52	8	0	8	25	.278	9	117	3	3	.976

HURST, JONATHAN
P, EXPOS

PERSONAL: Born October 20, 1966, at New York. . . . 6-3/175. . . . Throws right, bats right. . . . Full name: Jonathan Hurst.
HIGH SCHOOL: Spartanburg (S.C.).
COLLEGE: Spartanburg Methodist College (S.C.).
TRANSACTIONS/CAREER NOTES: Selected by Texas Rangers organization in fourth round of free-agent draft (June 2, 1987). . . . Loaned by Rangers organization to Miami, independent (April 5, 1991); returned to Rangers organization (June 28, 1991). . . . Traded by Rangers organization with P Joey Eischen and a player to be named later to Montreal Expos for P Oil Can Boyd (July 21, 1991); Expos acquired P Travis Buckley to complete deal (September 1, 1991).

Year	Team (League)	G	W	L	Pct.	ERA	Sv.	IP	H	R	ER	BB	SO
1987 — Sarasota Rangers (GCL)	12	4	3	.571	1.88	0	57⅓	34	19	12	32	59
1988 — Sarasota Rangers (GCL)	5	1	0	1.000	0.59	0	15⅓	5	1	1	4	13
— Port Charlotte (Florida State) ...	7	1	0	1.000	1.69	0	16	8	4	3	6	20
— Oklahoma City (Am. Assoc.)	1	0	0	. . .	10.80	0	1⅔	1	2	2	5	2
1989 — Port Charlotte (Florida State) ...	19	4	6	.400	4.45	1	58⅔	67	44	29	32	37
1990 — Gastonia (South Atlantic)	15	8	1	.889	2.64	1	61⅓	48	21	18	19	49
— Tulsa (Texas)	8	0	2	.000	9.47	0	25⅔	29	30	27	17	23
— Charlotte (Florida State)	6	0	1	.000	2.19	0	12⅓	8	3	3	5	8
1991 — Miami (Florida State)■..............	15	8	2	*.800	2.90	0	99⅓	89	41	32	31	91
— Tulsa (Texas)■.........................	5	2	1	.667	2.16	1	25	18	6	6	6	17
— Harrisburg (Eastern)■	6	5	0	1.000	0.86	0	42	26	4	4	12	34

HUSON, JEFF
SS, RANGERS

PERSONAL: Born August 15, 1964, at Scottsdale, Ariz. . . . 6-3/180. . . . Throws right, bats left. . . . Full name: Jeffrey Kent Huson.
HIGH SCHOOL: Mingus Union (Cottonwood, Ariz.).
COLLEGE: Glendale Community College (Ariz.) and Wyoming.
TRANSACTIONS/CAREER NOTES: Signed as free agent by Montreal Expos organization (August 18, 1985). . . . Traded by Expos to Oklahoma City (Texas Rangers organization) for P Drew Hall (April 2, 1990). . . . On Texas disabled list (August 8-31, 1991); included rehabiliation disability assignment to Oklahoma City (August 29-31, 1991).

							BATTING							FIELDING			
Year	Team (League)	Pos.	G	AB	R	H	2B	3B	HR	RBI	Avg.	SB	PO	A	E	Avg.
1986 — Burlington (Midwest)	SS-3B-2B	133	457	85	132	19	1	16	72	.289	32	183	324	37	.932
— Jacksonville (Southern) ...	3B	1	4	0	0	0	0	0	0	.000	0	0	1	0	1.000
1987 — West Palm Beach (FSL) ...	SS-OF-2B	131	455	54	130	15	4	1	53	.286	33	234	347	34	.945
1988 — Jacksonville (Southern) ...	S-2-0-3	128	471	72	117	18	1	0	34	.248	*56	217	285	26	.951
— Montreal (N.L.)	S-2-3-0	20	42	7	13	2	0	0	3	.310	2	18	41	4	.937
1989 — Indianapolis (A.A.)	SS-OF-2B	102	378	70	115	17	4	3	35	.304	30	172	214	17	.958
— Montreal (N.L.)	SS-2B-3B	32	74	1	12	5	0	0	2	.162	3	40	65	8	.929
1990 — Texas (A.L.)■.................	SS-3B-2B	145	396	57	95	12	2	0	28	.240	12	183	304	19	.962
1991 — Texas (A.L.)	SS-2B-3B	119	268	36	57	8	3	2	26	.213	8	143	269	15	.965
— Oklahoma City (A.A.)	SS	2	6	0	3	1	0	0	2	.500	0	5	3	0	1.000
American League totals (2 years)		264	664	93	152	20	5	2	54	.229	20	326	573	34	.964
National League totals (2 years)		52	116	8	25	7	0	0	5	.216	5	58	106	12	.932
Major league totals (4 years)		316	780	101	177	27	5	2	59	.227	25	384	679	46	.959

IGNASIAK, MIKE
P, BREWERS

PERSONAL: Born March 12, 1966, at Mt. Clemens, Mich. . . . 5-11/175. . . . Throws right, bats both. . . . Full name: Michael James Ignasiak. . . . Name pronounced ig-NASH-ik.
HIGH SCHOOL: St. Mary's (Orchard Lake, Mich.).
COLLEGE: Michigan.

TRANSACTIONS/CAREER NOTES: Selected by St. Louis Cardinals organization in fourth round of free-agent draft (June 2, 1987). . . . Selected by Milwaukee Brewers organization in eighth round of free-agent draft (June 1, 1988). . . . On Milwaukee disabled list (August 31-September 28, 1991).
STATISTICAL NOTES: Tied for Carolina League lead in games started by pitcher with 28 and in shutouts with three in 1989. . . . Pitched a 6-3 no-hit victory (combined with Doug Henry) against San Jose (April 15, 1990, first game).

Year	Team (League)	G	W	L	Pct.	ERA	Sv.	IP	H	R	ER	BB	SO
1988	—Beloit (Midwest)	9	2	4	.333	2.72	0	56⅓	52	21	17	12	66
	—Helena (Pioneer)	7	2	0	1.000	3.09	1	11⅔	10	5	4	7	18
1989	—Stockton (California)	28	11	6	.647	2.72	0	179	140	67	54	97	142
1990	—Stockton (California)	6	3	1	.750	3.94	0	32	18	14	14	17	23
	—El Paso (Texas)	15	6	3	.667	4.35	0	82⅔	96	45	40	34	39
1991	—Denver (American Assoc.)	24	9	5	.643	4.25	1	137⅔	119	68	65	57	103
	—Milwaukee (A.L.)	4	2	1	.667	5.68	0	12⅔	7	8	8	8	10
Major league totals (1 year)		4	2	1	.667	5.68	0	12⅔	7	8	8	8	10

INCAVIGLIA, PETE
OF, ASTROS

PERSONAL: Born April 2, 1964, at Pebble Beach, Calif. . . . 6-1/230. . . . Throws right, bats right. . . . Full name: Peter Joseph Incaviglia. . . . Son of Tom Incaviglia, minor league infielder (1948-55); and brother of Tony Invaciglia, minor league third baseman (1979-83).
HIGH SCHOOL: Monterrey (Pebble Beach, Calif.).
COLLEGE: Oklahoma State.
TRANSACTIONS/CAREER NOTES: Selected by San Francisco Giants organization in 10th round of free-agent draft (June 7, 1982). . . . Selected by Montreal Expos organization in first round (eighth pick overall) of free-agent draft (June 3, 1985). . . . Traded by Expos to Texas Rangers organization for P Bob Sebra and IF Jim Anderson (November 2, 1985). . . . On disabled list (June 15-30, 1989). . . . Released by Rangers (March 29, 1991). . . . Signed by Detroit Tigers (April 7, 1991). . . . On disabled list (June 13-July 5 and July 25-August 11, 1991). . . . Granted free agency (October 31, 1991). . . . Signed by Houston Astros organization (January 24, 1992).
RECORDS/HONORS: Shares major league record for most doubles in one inning—2 (May 11, 1986, second game, fourth inning). . . . Named designated hitter on THE SPORTING NEWS college All-America team (1985).
STATISTICAL NOTES: Led A.L. batters with 185 strikeouts in 1986 and tied for lead with 153 in 1988.

Year	Team (League)	Pos.	G	AB	R	H	2B	3B	HR	RBI	Avg.	SB	PO	A	E	Avg.
1986	—Texas (A.L.)	OF	153	540	82	135	21	2	30	88	.250	3	157	6	•14	.921
1987	—Texas (A.L.)	OF	139	509	85	138	26	4	27	80	.271	9	216	8	•13	.945
1988	—Texas (A.L.)	OF	116	418	59	104	19	3	22	54	.249	6	172	12	2	.989
1989	—Texas (A.L.)	OF	133	453	48	107	27	4	21	81	.236	5	213	7	6	.973
1990	—Texas (A.L.)	OF	153	529	59	123	27	0	24	85	.233	3	290	12	8	.974
1991	—Detroit (A.L.)■	OF	97	337	38	72	12	1	11	38	.214	1	106	4	3	.973
Major league totals (6 years)			791	2786	371	679	132	14	135	426	.244	27	1154	49	46	.963

INGRAM, RICCARDO
OF, TIGERS

PERSONAL: Born September 10, 1966, at Douglas, Ga. . . . 6-0/198. . . . Throws right, bats right. . . . Full name: Riccardo Benay Ingram.
HIGH SCHOOL: Coffee (Douglas, Ga.).
COLLEGE: Georgia Tech.
TRANSACTIONS/CAREER NOTES: Selected by Detroit Tigers organization in fourth round of free-agent draft (June 2, 1987).

Year	Team (League)	Pos.	G	AB	R	H	2B	3B	HR	RBI	Avg.	SB	PO	A	E	Avg.
1988	—Lakeland (Florida State)	OF	37	117	10	24	3	1	0	10	.205	2	33	2	0	1.000
	—Fayetteville (S. Atl.)	OF	17	50	7	9	2	1	0	3	.180	0	14	5	0	1.000
1989	—Lakeland (Florida State)	OF	109	365	40	88	13	3	6	30	.241	5	119	5	4	.969
1990	—London (Eastern)	OF	92	271	27	69	10	2	0	26	.255	3	108	8	4	.967
1991	—London (Eastern)	OF	118	421	58	114	14	1	18	64	.271	6	181	6	5	.974

INNIS, JEFF
P, METS

PERSONAL: Born July 5, 1962, at Decatur, Ill. . . . 6-1/180. . . . Throws right, bats right. . . . Full name: Jeffrey David Innis.
HIGH SCHOOL: Eisenhower (Decatur, Ill.).
COLLEGE: Illinois.
TRANSACTIONS/CAREER NOTES: Selected by New York Mets organization in 13th round of free-agent draft (June 6, 1983).

Year	Team (League)	G	W	L	Pct.	ERA	Sv.	IP	H	R	ER	BB	SO
1983	—Little Falls (New York-Penn)	28	8	0	1.000	1.37	8	46	29	8	7	28	68
1984	—Jackson (Texas)	42	6	5	.545	4.25	8	59⅓	65	34	28	40	63
1985	—Lynchburg (Carolina)	53	6	3	.667	2.34	14	77	46	26	20	40	91
1986	—Jackson (Texas)	56	4	5	.444	2.45	★25	92	69	30	25	24	75
1987	—Tidewater (International)	29	6	1	.857	2.03	5	44⅓	26	10	10	16	28
	—New York (N.L.)	17	0	1	.000	3.16	0	25⅔	29	9	9	4	28
1988	—Tidewater (International)	34	0	5	.000	3.54	4	48⅓	43	22	19	25	43
	—New York (N.L.)	12	1	1	.500	1.89	0	19	19	6	4	2	14
1989	—Tidewater (International)	25	3	1	.750	2.12	10	29⅔	28	9	7	8	14
	—New York (N.L.)	29	0	1	.000	3.18	0	39⅔	38	16	14	8	16

Year Team (League)	G	W	L	Pct.	ERA	Sv.	IP	H	R	ER	BB	SO
1990—New York (N.L.)	18	1	3	.250	2.39	1	26⅓	19	9	7	10	12
—Tidewater (International)	40	5	2	.714	1.71	19	52⅔	34	11	10	17	42
1991—New York (N.L.)	69	0	2	.000	2.66	0	84⅔	66	30	25	23	47
Major league totals (5 years)	145	2	8	.200	2.72	1	195⅓	171	70	59	47	117

IRVINE, DARYL
P, RED SOX

PERSONAL: Born November 15, 1964, at Harrisonburg, Va.... 6-3/195.... Throws right, bats right.... Full name: Daryl Keith Irvine.
HIGH SCHOOL: Spotswood (Penn Laird, Va.).
COLLEGE: Ferrum (Va.).
TRANSACTIONS/CAREER NOTES: Selected by Boston Red Sox organization in third round of free-agent draft (January 17, 1984). ... Selected by Toronto Blue Jays organization in secondary phase of free-agent draft (June 4, 1984).... Selected by Boston Red Sox organization in secondary phase of free-agent draft (January 9, 1985).... On disabled list (June 2-July 15, 1985 and August 1, 1991-remainder of season).
STATISTICAL NOTES: Led Eastern League with 16 wild pitches in 1987.

Year Team (League)	G	W	L	Pct.	ERA	Sv.	IP	H	R	ER	BB	SO
1985—Greensboro (South Atlantic)	8	4	2	.667	4.38	0	37	46	26	18	17	19
1986—Winter Haven (Florida State)	26	9	8	.529	3.19	0	161	162	73	57	67	73
1987—New Britain (Eastern)	37	4	13	.235	5.31	0	127	156	101	75	59	70
1988—New Britain (Eastern)	39	5	11	.313	3.09	0	125⅓	113	62	43	57	82
1989—New Britain (Eastern)	★54	4	6	.400	1.28	16	91⅓	74	24	13	23	50
1990—Pawtucket (International)	42	2	5	.286	3.24	12	50	47	24	18	19	35
—Boston (A.L.)	11	1	1	.500	4.67	0	17⅓	15	10	9	10	9
1991—Pawtucket (International)	27	1	1	.500	3.00	17	33	27	11	11	13	19
—Boston (A.L.)	9	0	0	...	6.00	0	18	25	13	12	9	8
Major league totals (2 years)	20	1	1	.500	5.35	0	35⅓	40	23	21	19	17

JACKSON, BO
DH/OF, WHITE SOX

PERSONAL: Born November 30, 1962, at Bessemer, Ala.... 6-1/235.... Throws right, bats right. ... Full name: Vincent Edward Jackson.
HIGH SCHOOL: McAdory (McCalla, Ala.)
COLLEGE: Auburn.
TRANSACTIONS/CAREER NOTES: Selected by New York Yankees organization in second round of free-agent draft (June 7, 1982). ... Selected by California Angels organization in 20th round of free-agent draft (June 3, 1985).... Selected by Kansas City Royals organization in fourth round of free-agent draft (June 2, 1986).... On Memphis temporary inactive list (June 20-30, 1986).... On disabled list (June 1-July 2, 1988; July 25-August 9, 1989; and July 18-August 26, 1990).... Released by Royals (March 18, 1991).... Signed by Chicago White Sox (April 3, 1991).... On Chicago disabled list (April 3-September 2, 1991); included rehabilitation disability assignments to Sarasota (August 25, 1991) and Birmingham (August 26-September 2, 1991).
RECORDS/HONORS: Shares major league record for most consecutive home runs—4 (July 17 [3], August 26 [1], 1990).... Shares major league single-game (nine innings) record for most strikeouts—5 (April 18, 1987).... Shares major league record for most strikeouts in one inning—2 (April 8, 1987, fourth inning).
STATISTICAL NOTES: Led A.L. batters with 172 strikeouts in 1989.... Hit three home runs in a game (July 17, 1990).

Year Team (League)	Pos.	G	AB	R	H	2B	3B	HR	RBI	Avg.	SB	PO	A	E	Avg.
						BATTING							FIELDING		
1986—Memphis (Southern)	OF	53	184	30	51	9	3	7	25	.277	3	116	8	7	.947
—Kansas City (A.L.)	OF	25	82	9	17	2	1	2	9	.207	3	29	2	4	.886
1987—Kansas City (A.L.)	OF	116	396	46	93	17	2	22	53	.235	10	180	9	9	.955
1988—Kansas City (A.L.)	OF	124	439	63	108	16	4	25	68	.246	27	246	11	7	.973
1989—Kansas City (A.L.)	OF	135	515	86	132	15	6	32	105	.256	26	224	11	8	.967
1990—Kansas City (A.L.)	OF	111	405	74	110	16	1	28	78	.272	15	230	8	12	.952
1991—Sarasota (Florida State)■	DH	2	6	1	2	0	0	2	2	.333	0	0	0	0	...
—Birmingham (Southern)	DH	4	13	2	4	0	0	0	0	.308	1	0	0	0	...
—Chicago (A.L.)	DH	23	71	8	16	4	0	3	14	.225	0	0	0	0	...
Major league totals (6 years)		534	1908	286	476	70	14	112	327	.249	81	909	41	40	.960

ALL-STAR GAME RECORD
ALL-STAR GAME NOTES: Hit home run in first at-bat (July 11, 1989).

Year League	Pos.	AB	R	H	2B	3B	HR	RBI	Avg.	SB	PO	A	E	Avg.
				BATTING							FIELDING			
1989—American	OF	4	1	2	0	0	1	2	.500	1	2	0	0	1.000

RECORD AS FOOTBALL PLAYER
TRANSACTIONS/CAREER NOTES: Selected by Tampa Bay Buccaneers in first round (first pick overall) of 1986 NFL draft.... Selected by Birmingham Stallions in 1986 USFL territorial draft. ... On reserve/did not sign list (entire 1986 season-April 27, 1987).... Selected by Los Angeles Raiders in seventh round (183rd pick overall) of 1987 NFL draft.... Signed by Raiders (July 17, 1987).... On reserve/did not report list (August 27-October 24, 1987).... On reserve/did not report list (August 22-October 12, 1988).... Activated from reserve/did not report list (October 15, 1988).... On reserve/did not report list (July 21-October 11, 1989).... On reserve/did not report list (July-October 21, 1990).... On reserve/did not report list (July-October, 1991).... On reserve/retired list (October, 1991-remainder of season).
CHAMPIONSHIP GAME EXPERIENCE: Member of Los Angeles Raiders for AFC championship game after 1990 season; inactive.
RECORDS/HONORS: Heisman Trophy winner (1985).... Named College Football Player of the Year by THE SPORTING NEWS (1985).... Named as running back on THE SPORTING NEWS college All-America team (1985).... Named to play in Pro Bowl

after 1990 season; replaced due to injury by John L. Williams.
PRO STATISTICS: 1987—Recovered one fumble. 1988—Recovered two fumbles.

Year	Team	G	Att.	Yds.	Avg.	TD	No.	Yds.	Avg.	TD	TD	Pts.	F.
			— RUSHING —				— RECEIVING —				— TOTAL —		
1987—	L.A. Raiders NFL	7	81	554	6.8	4	16	136	8.5	2	6	36	2
1988—	L.A. Raiders NFL	10	136	580	4.3	3	9	79	8.8	0	3	18	5
1989—	L.A. Raiders NFL	11	173	950	5.5	4	9	69	7.7	0	4	24	1
1990—	L.A. Raiders NFL	10	125	698	5.6	5	6	68	11.3	0	5	30	3
1991—	L.A. Raiders NFL						Did not play						
Pro totals (4 years)		38	515	2782	5.4	16	40	352	8.8	2	18	108	11

JACKSON, DANNY
P, CUBS

PERSONAL: Born January 5, 1962, at San Antonio. . . . 6-0/205. . . . Throws left, bats right. . . . Full name: Danny Lynn Jackson.
HIGH SCHOOL: Central (Aurora, Colo.).
COLLEGE: Oklahoma and Trinidad State Junior College (Colo.).
TRANSACTIONS/CAREER NOTES: Selected by Oakland A's organization in 24th round of free-agent draft (June 3, 1980). . . . Selected by Kansas City Royals organization in secondary phase of free-agent draft (January 17, 1982). . . . On Jacksonville disabled list (September 8, 1982-remainder of season). . . . On disabled list (April 4-21, 1986). . . . Traded by Royals with SS Angel Salazar to Cincinnati Reds for P Ted Power and SS Kurt Stillwell (November 6, 1987). . . . On disabled list (June 18-July 6 and July 25-September 1, 1989). . . . On Cincinnati disabled list (April 30-May 17, July 18-August 8 and August 14-30, 1990); included rehabilitation disability assignment to Nashville (May 13-17 and August 30, 1990) and Charleston, W.Va. (August 5-8, 1990). . . . Granted free agency (November 5, 1990). . . . Signed by Chicago Cubs (November 21, 1990). . . . On Chicago disabled list (April 20-June 9, 1991). . . . On Chicago disabled list (June 20-August 3, 1991); included rehabilitation disability assignment to Iowa (July 29-30, 1991).
RECORDS/HONORS: Named lefthanded pitcher on THE SPORTING NEWS N.L. All-Star team (1988).
STATISTICAL NOTES: Tied for American Association lead with two shutouts in 1983 and three in 1984. . . . Tied for American Association lead with 10 complete games in 1984. . . . Tied for N.L. lead with 15 complete games in 1988.

Year	Team (League)	G	W	L	Pct.	ERA	Sv.	IP	H	R	ER	BB	SO
1982 —Charleston, S.C. (S. Atlantic)		13	10	1	.909	2.62	0	96⅓	80	37	28	39	62
—Jacksonville (Southern)		14	7	2	.778	2.39	0	98	78	30	26	42	74
1983 —Omaha (American Assoc.)........		23	7	8	.467	3.97	0	136	126	74	60	73	93
—Kansas City (A.L.)		4	1	1	.500	5.21	0	19	26	12	11	6	9
1984 —Kansas City (A.L.)		15	2	6	.250	4.26	0	76	84	41	36	35	40
—Omaha (American Assoc.)........		16	5	8	.385	3.67	0	110⅓	91	50	45	45	82
1985 —Kansas City (A.L.)		32	14	12	.538	3.42	0	208	209	94	79	76	114
1986 —Kansas City (A.L.)		32	11	12	.478	3.20	1	185⅔	177	83	66	79	115
1987 —Kansas City (A.L.)		36	9	18	.333	4.02	0	224	219	115	100	109	152
1988 —Cincinnati (N.L.)■		35	•23	8	.742	2.73	0	260⅔	206	86	79	71	161
1989 —Cincinnati (N.L.)		20	6	11	.353	5.60	0	115⅔	122	78	72	57	70
1990 —Cincinnati (N.L.)		22	6	6	.500	3.61	0	117⅓	119	54	47	40	76
—Nashville (American Assoc.)....		2	1	0	1.000	0.00	0	11	9	0	0	4	3
—Charleston, W.Va. (Int'l)		1	0	0	. . .	6.00	0	3	2	2	2	1	2
1991 —Chicago (N.L.)■		17	1	5	.167	6.75	0	70⅔	89	59	53	48	31
—Iowa (American Association) ...		1	0	0	. . .	1.80	0	5	2	1	1	2	4
American League totals (5 years)		119	37	49	.430	3.69	1	712⅔	715	345	292	305	430
National League totals (4 years)		94	36	30	.545	4.00	0	564⅓	536	277	251	216	338
Major league totals (9 years)		213	73	79	.480	3.83	1	1277	1251	622	543	521	768

CHAMPIONSHIP SERIES RECORD

Year	Team (League)	G	W	L	Pct.	ERA	Sv.	IP	H	R	ER	BB	SO
1985 —Kansas City (A.L.)		2	1	0	1.000	0.00	0	10	10	0	0	1	7
1990 —Cincinnati (N.L.)		2	1	0	1.000	2.38	0	11⅓	8	3	3	7	8
Championship Series totals (2 years)		4	2	0	1.000	1.27	0	21⅓	18	3	3	8	15

WORLD SERIES RECORD

Year	Team (League)	G	W	L	Pct.	ERA	Sv.	IP	H	R	ER	BB	SO
1985 —Kansas City (A.L.)		2	1	1	.500	1.69	0	16	9	3	3	5	12
1990 —Cincinnati (N.L.)		1	0	0	. . .	10.13	0	2⅔	6	4	3	2	0
World Series totals (2 years)		3	1	1	.500	2.89	0	18⅔	15	7	6	7	12

ALL-STAR GAME RECORD

Year	League	W	L	Pct.	ERA	Sv.	IP	H	R	ER	BB	SO
1988 —National						Did not play						

JACKSON, DARRIN
OF, PADRES

PERSONAL: Born August 22, 1963, at Los Angeles. . . . 6-0/185. . . . Throws right, bats right. . . . Full name: Darrin Jay Jackson.
HIGH SCHOOL: Culver City (Calif.).
TRANSACTIONS/CAREER NOTES: Selected by Chicago Cubs organization in second round of free-agent draft (June 8, 1981). . . . Traded by Cubs with P Calvin Schiraldi and a player to be named later to San Diego Padres for OF Marvell Wynne and IF Luis Salazar (August 30, 1989); Padres acquired 1B Phil Stephenson to complete deal (September 5, 1989).

STATISTICAL NOTES: Led Gulf Coast League outfielders with 127 total chances in 1981.... Tied for Texas League lead in double plays by outfielders with six in 1984.... Tied for American Association lead in double plays by outfielders with six in 1987.

Year	Team (League)	Pos.	G	AB	R	H	2B	3B	HR	RBI	Avg.	SB	PO	A	E	Avg.
1981—Sarasota Cubs (GCL)		OF	62	210	29	39	5	0	1	15	.186	18	★121	5	1	.992
1982—Quad Cities (Midwest).......		OF	132	529	86	146	23	5	5	48	.276	58	266	9	8	.972
1983—Salinas (California)		OF	129	509	70	126	18	5	6	54	.248	36	237	15	13	.951
1984—Midland (Texas)		OF	132	496	63	134	18	2	15	54	.270	13	286	★19	8	.974
1985—Iowa (American Assoc.) ...		OF	10	40	0	7	2	1	0	1	.175	1	19	0	0	1.000
—Pittsfield (Eastern)..........		OF	91	325	38	82	10	1	3	30	.252	8	221	5	0	1.000
—Chicago (N.L.)		OF	5	11	0	1	0	0	0	0	.091	0	7	0	0	1.000
1986—Pittsfield (Eastern)..........		OF	137	•520	82	139	28	2	15	64	.267	42	320	★16	7	.980
1987—Iowa (American Assoc.) ...		OF	132	474	81	130	32	5	23	81	.274	13	290	15	6	.981
—Chicago (N.L.)		OF	7	5	2	4	1	0	0	0	.800	1	1	0	0	1.000
1988—Chicago (N.L.)		OF	100	188	29	50	11	3	6	20	.266	4	116	1	2	.983
1989—Chicago-S.D. (N.L.)■		OF	70	170	17	37	7	0	4	20	.218	1	121	5	5	.962
—Iowa (American Assoc.) ...		OF	30	120	18	31	4	1	7	17	.258	4	66	12	0	1.000
1990—San Diego (N.L.)		OF	58	113	10	29	3	0	3	9	.257	3	63	1	1	.985
—Las Vegas (Pac. Coast)		OF	29	98	14	27	4	0	5	15	.276	3	61	4	0	1.000
1991—San Diego (N.L.)		OF-P	122	359	51	94	12	1	21	49	.262	5	243	2	2	.992
Major league totals (6 years)			362	846	109	215	34	4	34	98	.254	13	551	9	10	.982

RECORD AS PITCHER

Year	Team (League)	G	W	L	Pct.	ERA	Sv.	IP	H	R	ER	BB	SO
1991—San Diego (N.L.)		1	0	0	...	9.00	0	2	3	2	2	2	0

JACKSON, MIKE
P, GIANTS

PERSONAL: Born December 22, 1964, at Houston.... 6-0/200.... Throws right, bats right. ... Full name: Michael Ray Jackson.
HIGH SCHOOL: Forest Brook (Houston).
COLLEGE: Hill Junior College (Tex.).
TRANSACTIONS/CAREER NOTES: Selected by Philadelphia Phillies organization in 29th round of free-agent draft (June 6, 1983). ... Selected by Philadelphia Phillies organization in secondary phase of free-agent draft (January 17, 1984).... On Philadelphia disabled list (August 6-21, 1987).... Traded by Phillies organization with OF Glenn Wilson and OF Dave Brundage to Seattle Mariners for OF Phil Bradley and P Tim Fortugno (December 9, 1987).... Traded by Mariners with P Bill Swift and P Dave Burba to San Francisco Giants for OF Kevin Mitchell and P Mike Remlinger (December 11, 1991).
STATISTICAL NOTES: Led Carolina League with seven balks in 1985.... Tied for N.L. lead with eight balks in 1987.

Year	Team (League)	G	W	L	Pct.	ERA	Sv.	IP	H	R	ER	BB	SO
1984—Spartanburg (South Atlantic) ..		14	7	2	.778	2.68	0	80⅔	53	35	24	50	77
1985—Peninsula (Carolina)		31	7	9	.438	4.60	1	125⅓	127	71	64	53	96
1986—Reading (Eastern)		30	2	3	.400	1.66	6	43⅓	25	9	8	22	42
—Portland (Pacific Coast)		17	3	1	.750	3.18	3	22⅔	18	8	8	13	23
—Philadelphia (N.L.)		9	0	0	...	3.38	0	13⅓	12	5	5	4	3
1987—Philadelphia (N.L.)		55	3	10	.231	4.20	1	109⅓	88	55	51	56	93
—Maine (International)		2	1	0	1.000	0.82	0	11	9	2	1	5	13
1988—Seattle (A.L.)■		62	6	5	.545	2.63	4	99⅓	74	37	29	43	76
1989—Seattle (A.L.)		65	4	6	.400	3.17	7	99⅓	81	43	35	54	94
1990—Seattle (A.L.)		63	5	7	.417	4.54	3	77⅓	64	42	39	44	69
1991—Seattle (A.L.)		72	7	7	.500	3.25	14	88⅔	64	35	32	34	74
American League totals (4 years)		262	22	25	.468	3.33	28	364⅔	283	157	135	175	313
National League totals (2 years)		64	3	10	.231	4.11	1	122⅔	100	60	56	60	96
Major league totals (6 years)		326	25	35	.417	3.53	29	487⅓	383	217	191	235	409

JACOBY, BROOK
3B/1B, INDIANS

PERSONAL: Born November 23, 1959, at Philadelphia.... 5-11/195.... Throws right, bats right.... Full name: Brook Wallace Jacoby Jr.... Son of Brook Jacoby Sr., minor league pitcher (1956-58).
HIGH SCHOOL: Ventura (Calif.).
COLLEGE: Ventura College (Calif.).
TRANSACTIONS/CAREER NOTES: Selected by Atlanta Braves organization in seventh round of free-agent draft (January 9, 1979). ... Traded by Braves with OF Brett Butler to Cleveland Indians (October 21, 1983), completing deal in which Indians traded P Len Barker to Braves for three players to be named later (August 28, 1983); Indians acquired P Rick Behenna as partial completion of deal (September 2, 1983).... On disabled list (August 20, 1984-remainder of season and April 28-May 16, 1991). ... Traded by Indians to Oakland Athletics for OF Lee Tinsley and P Apolinar Garcia (July 26, 1991).... Granted free agency (November 6, 1991).... Signed by Indians organization (January 27, 1992).
STATISTICAL NOTES: Led International League third basemen with 331 total chances and 22 double plays in 1982.... Hit three home runs in a game (July 3, 1987).... Tied for A.L. lead in putouts by third basemen with 134 and errors with 22 in 1987.

Year	Team (League)	Pos.	G	AB	R	H	2B	3B	HR	RBI	Avg.	SB	PO	A	E	Avg.
1979—Kingsport (Appalachian) ..		OF	8	28	3	7	2	0	0	1	.250	0	9	0	0	1.000
—Bradenton (Gulf Coast)		OF	42	160	24	43	11	1	3	35	.269	4	65	7	4	.947
1980—Anderson (S. Atlantic)		OF-3B	132	496	82	147	★40	4	19	★108	.296	4	219	30	10	.961
—Savannah (Southern)		3B	3	8	0	1	0	0	0	0	.125	0	0	2	0	1.000

Year—Team (League)	Pos.	G	AB	R	H	2B	3B	HR	RBI	Avg.	SB	PO	A	E	Avg.
1981—Savannah (Southern)	3B-OF	140	507	59	148	28	3	24	82	.292	0	103	232	31	.915
—Atlanta (N.L.)	3B	11	10	0	2	0	0	0	1	.200	0	3	4	0	1.000
1982—Richmond (Int'l)	3B	134	501	74	150	21	3	18	58	.299	1	83	★229	★19	★.943
1983—Richmond (Int'l)	3B	133	489	88	154	32	2	25	100	.315	1	62	247	18	.945
—Atlanta (N.L.)	3B	4	8	0	0	0	0	0	0	.000	0	0	2	0	1.000
1984—Cleveland (A.L.)■	3B-SS	126	439	64	116	19	3	7	40	.264	3	86	188	14	.951
1985—Cleveland (A.L.)	3B-2B	161	606	72	166	26	3	20	87	.274	2	114	319	19	.958
1986—Cleveland (A.L.)	3B	158	583	83	168	30	4	17	80	.288	2	109	292	25	.941
1987—Cleveland (A.L.)	3B-1B	155	540	73	162	26	4	32	69	.300	2	‡192	261	‡22	.954
1988—Cleveland (A.L.)	3B	152	552	59	133	25	0	9	49	.241	2	99	298	10	.975
1989—Cleveland (A.L.)	3B	147	519	49	141	26	5	13	64	.272	2	92	268	17	.955
1990—Cleveland (A.L.)	3B-1B	155	553	77	162	24	4	14	75	.293	1	628	186	6	.993
1991—Clev.-Oakland (A.L.)■..	3B-1B	122	419	28	94	21	1	4	44	.224	2	453	136	7	.988
American League totals (8 years)		1176	4211	505	1142	197	24	116	508	.271	16	1773	1948	120	.969
National League totals (2 years)		15	18	0	2	0	0	0	1	.111	0	3	6	0	1.000
Major league totals (10 years)		1191	4229	505	1144	197	24	116	509	.271	16	1776	1954	120	.969

ALL-STAR GAME RECORD

Year League	Pos.	AB	R	H	2B	3B	HR	RBI	Avg.	SB	PO	A	E	Avg.
1986—American	PH-3B	1	0	0	0	0	0	0	.000	0	1	1	0	1.000
1990—American	PH	1	0	0	0	0	0	0	.000	0	0	0	0	...
All-Star Game totals (2 years)		2	0	0	0	0	0	0	.000	0	1	1	0	1.000

JAHA, JOHN
1B, BREWERS

PERSONAL: Born May 27, 1966, at Portland, Ore. ... 6-1/195. ... Throws right, bats right. ... Full name: John Emile Jaha. ... Name pronounced JAH-ha.
HIGH SCHOOL: David Douglas (Portland, Ore.).
TRANSACTIONS/CAREER NOTES: Selected by Milwaukee Brewers organization in 14th round of free-agent draft (June 4, 1984). ... On disabled list (April 6-August 1, 1990).
RECORDS/HONORS: Named Texas League Most Valuable Player (1991).
STATISTICAL NOTES: Led Northwest League with 144 total bases and 70 bases on balls received and tied for lead with four intentional bases on balls received in 1986. ... Led California League with 112 bases on balls received in 1989. ... Led Texas League with 301 total bases and .619 slugging percentage in 1991. ... Led Texas League first basemen with 81 assists in 1991.

Year—Team (League)	Pos.	G	AB	R	H	2B	3B	HR	RBI	Avg.	SB	PO	A	E	Avg.
1985—Helena (Pioneer)	3B	24	68	13	18	3	0	2	14	.265	4	9	32	1	.976
1986—Tri-Cities (Northwest)	3B	●73	258	65	82	13	2	★15	67	.318	9	352	101	18	.962
1987—Beloit (Midwest)	3B-1B-SS	122	376	68	101	22	0	7	47	.269	10	493	113	18	.971
1988—Stockton (California)	1B	99	302	58	77	14	6	8	54	.255	10	793	60	5	★.994
1989—Stockton (California)	1B-3B	140	479	83	140	26	5	25	91	.292	8	1081	62	8	.993
1990—Stockton (California)	DH-PH	26	84	12	22	5	0	4	19	.262	0	0	0	0	...
1991—El Paso (Texas)	1B-3B	130	486	★121	167	38	3	★30	★134	.344	12	883	†87	10	.990

JAMES, CHRIS
OF, GIANTS

PERSONAL: Born October 4, 1962, at Rusk, Tex. ... 6-1/190. ... Throws right, bats right. ... Full name: Donald Christopher James. ... Brother of Craig James, United States Football League and National Football League player (1983-88).
HIGH SCHOOL: Stratford (Houston).
COLLEGE: Blinn College (Tex.).
TRANSACTIONS/CAREER NOTES: Signed as free agent by Philadelphia Phillies organization (October 30, 1981). ... On Philadelphia disabled list (May 6-July 21, 1986); included rehabilitation disability assignment to Portland (July 3-21, 1986). ... Traded by Phillies to San Diego Padres for IF Randy Ready and OF John Kruk (June 2, 1989). ... Traded by Padres with C Sandy Alomar and 3B Carlos Baerga to Cleveland Indians for OF Joe Carter (December 6, 1989). ... On disabled list (September 11, 1991-remainder of season). ... Granted free agency (December 20, 1991). ... Signed by San Francisco Giants (January 15, 1992).
STATISTICAL NOTES: Led South Atlantic League with 257 total bases and tied for lead in being hit by pitch with 12 in 1983. ... Led Eastern League third basemen with 39 errors in 1984. ... Led Pacific Coast League outfielders with 351 total chances in 1985. ... Tied for Pacific Coast League lead in being hit by pitch with seven in 1985.

Year—Team (League)	Pos.	G	AB	R	H	2B	3B	HR	RBI	Avg.	SB	PO	A	E	Avg.
1982—Bend (Northwest)	3B-OF	63	227	47	72	★19	3	12	50	.317	10	93	54	10	.936
1983—Spartanburg (S. Atl.)	OF-3B	129	499	94	148	23	4	26	★121	.297	11	150	88	16	.937
1984—Reading (Eastern)	3B-OF	128	457	66	117	19	★12	8	57	.256	19	104	209	†39	.889
1985—Portland (Pacific Coast) ...	OF	135	507	78	160	35	8	11	73	.316	23	★328	16	7	.980
1986—Portland (Pacific Coast) ...	OF-3B	69	266	30	64	6	2	12	41	.241	3	83	44	8	.941
—Philadelphia (N.L.)	OF	16	46	5	13	3	0	1	5	.283	0	19	0	0	1.000
1987—Philadelphia (N.L.)	OF	115	358	48	105	20	6	17	54	.293	3	198	5	2	.990
—Maine (International)	OF-3B	13	40	5	9	2	1	0	3	.225	0	22	4	0	1.000
1988—Philadelphia (N.L.)	OF-3B	150	566	57	137	24	1	19	66	.242	7	282	51	9	.974
1989—Phil.-San Diego (N.L.)■.....	OF-3B	132	482	55	117	17	2	13	65	.243	5	215	27	7	.972

Year	Team (League)	Pos.	G	AB	R	H	2B	3B	HR	RBI	Avg.	SB	PO	A	E	Avg.
1990—Cleveland (A.L.)■		OF	140	528	62	158	32	4	12	70	.299	4	25	1	0	1.000
1991—Cleveland (A.L.)		OF-1B	115	437	31	104	16	2	5	41	.238	3	173	10	0	1.000
American League totals (2 years)			255	965	93	262	48	6	17	111	.272	7	198	11	0	1.000
National League totals (4 years)			413	1452	165	372	64	9	50	190	.256	15	714	83	18	.978
Major league totals (6 years)			668	2417	258	634	112	15	67	301	.262	22	912	94	18	.982

JAMES, MIKE
P, DODGERS

PERSONAL: Born August 15, 1967, at Fort Walton Beach, Fla. . . . 6-3/180. . . . Throws right, bats right. . . . Full name: Michael Elmo James.
HIGH SCHOOL: Fort Walton Beach (Fla.).
COLLEGE: Lurleen B. Wallace State Junior College (Ala.).
TRANSACTIONS/CAREER NOTES: Selected by Los Angeles Dodgers organization in 43rd round of free-agent draft (June 2, 1987).

Year	Team (League)	G	W	L	Pct.	ERA	Sv.	IP	H	R	ER	BB	SO
1988—Great Falls (Pioneer)		14	7	1	*.875	3.76	0	67	61	36	28	41	59
1989—Bakersfield (California)		27	11	8	.579	3.78	0	159⅔	144	82	67	78	127
1990—San Antonio (Texas)		26	11	4	.733	3.32	0	157	144	73	58	78	97
1991—Albuquerque (Pacific Coast)		13	1	3	.250	6.60	0	45	51	36	33	30	39
—San Antonio (Texas)		15	9	5	.643	4.53	0	89⅓	88	54	45	51	74

JAVIER, STAN
OF, DODGERS

PERSONAL: Born September 1, 1965, at San Francisco de Macoris, Dominican Republic. . . . 6-0/185. . . . Throws right, bats both. . . . Full name: Stanley Julian Javier. . . . Son of Julian Javier, infielder, St. Louis Cardinals and Cincinnati Reds (1960-72). . . . Name pronounced HA-vee-AIR.
HIGH SCHOOL: La Altagracia (San Francisco de Macoris, Dominican Republic).
TRANSACTIONS/CAREER NOTES: Signed as free agent by St. Louis Cardinals organization (March 26, 1981). . . . Traded by Cardinals organization with SS Bob Meacham to New York Yankees organization for OF Bob Helsom, P Marty Mason and P Steve Fincher (December 14, 1982). . . . Traded by Yankees organization with P Jay Howell, P Jose Rijo, P Eric Plunk and P Tim Birtas to Oakland A's for OF Rickey Henderson, P Bert Bradley and cash (December 5, 1984). . . . On Oakland disabled list (August 3-September 1, 1987); included rehabilitation disability assignment to Tacoma (August 20-September 1, 1987). . . . On disabled list (August 18-September 2, 1988 and July 7-24, 1989). . . . Traded by A's to Los Angeles Dodgers for 2B Willie Randolph (May 13, 1990).
STATISTICAL NOTES: Led Southern League with 112 bases on balls received in 1985.

Year	Team (League)	Pos.	G	AB	R	H	2B	3B	HR	RBI	Avg.	SB	PO	A	E	Avg.
1981—Johnson City (Appal.)		OF	53	144	30	36	5	4	3	19	.250	2	53	2	3	.948
1982—Johnson City (Appal.)		OF	57	185	45	51	3	•4	8	36	.276	11	94	8	4	.962
1983—Greensboro (S. Atlantic)■		OF	129	489	109	152	*34	6	12	77	.311	33	250	10	15	.945
1984—New York (A.L.)		OF	7	7	1	1	0	0	0	0	.143	0	3	0	0	1.000
—Nashville (Southern)		OF	76	262	40	76	17	4	7	38	.290	17	202	4	7	.967
—Columbus (Int'l)		OF	32	99	12	22	3	1	0	7	.222	1	77	4	2	.976
1985—Huntsville (Southern)■		OF	140	486	105	138	21	8	9	64	.284	61	363	8	7	.981
1986—Tacoma (Pacific Coast)		OF-1B	69	248	50	81	16	2	4	51	.327	18	172	9	6	.968
—Oakland (A.L.)		OF	59	114	13	23	8	0	0	8	.202	8	118	1	0	1.000
1987—Oakland (A.L.)		OF-1B	81	151	22	28	3	1	2	9	.185	3	149	5	3	.981
—Tacoma (Pacific Coast)		OF-1B	15	51	6	11	2	0	2	2	.216	3	26	0	2	.929
1988—Oakland (A.L.)		OF-1B	125	397	49	102	13	3	2	35	.257	20	274	7	5	.983
1989—Oakland (A.L.)		OF-2B-1B	112	310	42	77	12	3	1	28	.248	12	221	8	2	.991
1990—Oakland (A.L.)		OF	19	33	4	8	0	2	0	3	.242	0	19	0	0	1.000
—Los Angeles (N.L.)■		OF	104	276	56	84	9	4	3	24	.304	15	204	2	0	1.000
1991—Los Angeles (N.L.)		OF-1B	121	176	21	36	5	3	1	11	.205	7	90	4	3	.969
American League totals (6 years)			403	1012	131	239	36	9	5	83	.236	43	784	21	10	.988
National League totals (2 years)			225	452	77	120	14	7	4	35	.265	22	294	6	3	.990
Major league totals (7 years)			628	1464	208	359	50	16	9	118	.245	65	1078	27	13	.988

CHAMPIONSHIP SERIES RECORD

Year	Team (League)	Pos.	G	AB	R	H	2B	3B	HR	RBI	Avg.	SB	PO	A	E	Avg.
1988—Oakland (A.L.)		OF-PR	2	4	0	2	0	0	0	1	.500	0	5	0	0	1.000
1989—Oakland (A.L.)		OF	1	2	0	0	0	0	0	0	.000	0	1	0	0	1.000
Championship Series totals (2 years)			3	6	0	2	0	0	0	1	.333	0	6	0	0	1.000

WORLD SERIES RECORD

Year	Team (League)	Pos.	G	AB	R	H	2B	3B	HR	RBI	Avg.	SB	PO	A	E	Avg.
1988—Oakland (A.L.)		PR-OF	3	4	0	2	0	0	0	2	.500	0	1	0	0	1.000
1989—Oakland (A.L.)		OF	1	0	0	0	0	0	0	0	...	0	0	0	0	...
World Series totals (2 years)			4	4	0	2	0	0	0	2	.500	0	1	0	0	1.000

JEFFCOAT, MIKE
P, RANGERS

PERSONAL: Born August 3, 1959, at Pine Bluff, Ark. . . . 6-2/189. . . . Throws left, bats left. . . . Full name: James Michael Jeffcoat.
HIGH SCHOOL: Pine Bluff (Ark.).
COLLEGE: Louisiana Tech.

TRANSACTIONS/CAREER NOTES: Selected by St. Louis Cardinals organization in 30th round of free-agent draft (June 7, 1977). . . . Selected by Cleveland Indians organization in 13th round of free-agent draft (June 3, 1980). . . . Traded by Indians with IF Luis Quinones to San Francisco Giants organization for SS Johnnie LeMaster (May 7, 1985). . . . Released by Giants organization (October 21, 1986). . . . Signed by Texas Rangers organization (December 18, 1986). . . . On disabled list (July 22-August 18 and August 21-September 5, 1990). . . . Granted free agency (October 8, 1991). . . . Re-signed by Rangers organization (January 28, 1992).

MISCELLANEOUS: Had RBI double and scored in only appearance as pinch-hitter (1991).

Year	Team (League)	G	W	L	Pct.	ERA	Sv.	IP	H	R	ER	BB	SO
1980	—Waterloo (Midwest)	4	0	0	...	6.00	0	6	12	12	4	3	7
	—Batavia (New York-Penn)	12	4	3	.571	3.97	0	68	65	40	30	45	71
1981	—Waterloo (Midwest)	25	10	8	.556	3.86	0	147	151	71	63	78	109
1982	—Waterloo (Midwest)	9	5	4	.556	4.06	0	62	58	29	28	15	68
	—Chattanooga (Southern)	18	8	8	.500	2.88	0	128⅓	122	49	41	51	107
1983	—Charleston, W.Va. (Int'l)	26	12	8	.600	4.53	0	167	187	95	84	46	96
	—Cleveland (A.L.)	11	1	3	.250	3.31	0	32⅔	32	13	12	13	9
1984	—Cleveland (A.L.)	63	5	2	.714	2.99	1	75⅓	82	28	25	24	41
1985	—Cleveland (A.L.)	9	0	0	...	2.79	0	9⅔	8	5	3	6	4
	—Phoenix (Pacific Coast)■	10	4	5	.444	3.62	0	59⅔	64	26	24	9	28
	—San Francisco (N.L.)	19	0	2	.000	5.32	0	22	27	13	13	6	10
1986	—Phoenix (Pacific Coast)	54	7	2	.778	4.20	7	75	81	40	35	31	57
1987	—Oklahoma City (Am. Assoc.)■	26	11	8	.579	4.79	0	159⅔	193	99	85	41	101
	—Texas (A.L.)	2	0	1	.000	12.86	0	7	11	10	10	4	1
1988	—Texas (A.L.)	5	0	2	.000	11.70	0	10	19	13	13	5	5
	—Oklahoma City (Am. Assoc.)	22	9	5	.643	2.80	0	157⅓	137	53	49	41	95
1989	—Oklahoma City (Am. Assoc.)	11	4	4	.500	3.22	0	72⅔	81	31	26	21	50
	—Texas (A.L.)	22	9	6	.600	3.58	0	130⅔	139	65	52	33	64
1990	—Texas (A.L.)	44	5	6	.455	4.47	5	110⅔	122	57	55	28	58
1991	—Texas (A.L.)	70	5	3	.625	4.63	1	79⅔	104	46	41	25	43
American League totals (8 years)		226	25	23	.521	4.17	7	455⅔	517	237	211	138	225
National League totals (1 year)		19	0	2	.000	5.32	0	22	27	13	13	6	10
Major league totals (8 years)		245	25	25	.500	4.22	7	477⅔	544	250	224	144	235

JEFFERIES, GREGG
IF, ROYALS

PERSONAL: Born August 1, 1967, at Burlingame, Calif. . . . 5-10/185. . . . Throws right, bats both. . . . Full name: Gregory Scott Jefferies.
HIGH SCHOOL: Serra (San Mateo, Calif.).
TRANSACTIONS/CAREER NOTES: Selected by New York Mets organization in first round (20th pick overall) of free-agent draft (June 3, 1985). . . . On disabled list (April 27-May 13, 1991). . . . Traded by Mets with OF Kevin McReynolds and 2B Keith Miller to Kansas City Royals for P Bret Saberhagen and IF Bill Pecota (December 11, 1991).
RECORDS/HONORS: Named Appalachian League Player of the Year (1985). . . . Named Carolina League Most Valuable Player (1986). . . . Named Texas League Most Valuable Player (1987).
STATISTICAL NOTES: Led Carolina League with .549 slugging percentage in 1986. . . . Led Texas League with 18 intentional bases on balls received in 1987. . . . Tied for International League lead with 10 intentional bases on balls received in 1988. . . . Led International League third basemen with 240 assists in 1988.

							BATTING						FIELDING			
Year	Team (League)	Pos.	G	AB	R	H	2B	3B	HR	RBI	Avg.	SB	PO	A	E	Avg.
1985	—Kingsport (Appalachian)	SS-2B	47	166	27	57	18	2	3	29	.343	21	78	130	21	.908
	—Columbia (S. Atlantic)	2B-SS	20	64	7	18	2	2	1	12	.281	7	28	26	2	.964
1986	—Columbia (S. Atlantic)	SS	25	112	29	38	6	1	5	24	.339	13	36	83	7	.944
	—Lynchburg (Carolina)	SS	95	390	66	138	25	9	11	80	*.354	43	138	273	20	.954
	—Jackson (Texas)	SS-3B	5	19	1	8	1	1	0	7	.421	1	7	9	1	.941
1987	—Jackson (Texas)	SS-3B	134	510	81	187	*48	5	20	101	.367	26	167	388	35	.941
	—New York (N.L.)	PH	6	6	0	3	1	0	0	2	.500	0	0	0	0	...
1988	—Tidewater (Int'l)	3-S-2-0	132	504	62	142	28	4	7	61	.282	32	110	†330	27	.942
	—New York (N.L.)	3B-2B	29	109	19	35	8	2	6	17	.321	5	33	46	2	.975
1989	—New York (N.L.)	2B-3B	141	508	72	131	28	2	12	56	.258	21	242	280	14	.974
1990	—New York (N.L.)	2B-3B	153	604	96	171	*40	3	15	68	.283	11	242	341	16	.973
1991	—New York (N.L.)	2B-3B	136	486	59	132	19	2	9	62	.272	26	170	271	17	.963
Major league totals (5 years)			465	1713	246	472	96	9	42	205	.276	63	687	938	49	.971

CHAMPIONSHIP SERIES RECORD

							BATTING						FIELDING			
Year	Team (League)	Pos.	G	AB	R	H	2B	3B	HR	RBI	Avg.	SB	PO	A	E	Avg.
1988	—New York (N.L.)	3B	7	27	2	9	2	0	0	1	.333	0	5	8	1	.929

JEFFERSON, REGGIE
1B, INDIANS

PERSONAL: Born September 25, 1968, at Tallahassee, Fla. . . . 6-4/210. . . . Throws left, bats both. . . . Full name: Reginald Jirod Jefferson.
HIGH SCHOOL: Lincoln (Tallahassee, Fla.).
TRANSACTIONS/CAREER NOTES: Selected by Cincinnati Reds organization in third round of free-agent draft (June 2, 1986). . . . On disabled list (May 25, 1990-remainder of season). . . . Traded by Reds to Cleveland Indians for 1B Tim Costo (June 14, 1991). . . . On Cleveland disabled list (June 24-July 1, 1991); included rehabilitation disability assignment to Canton-Akron (June 25-July 1, 1991).
STATISTICAL NOTES: Led Gulf Coast League first basemen with 624 total chances in 1986.
MISCELLANEOUS: Batted lefthanded only with Cedar Rapids (1987-88).

Year	Team (League)	Pos.	G	AB	R	H	2B	3B	HR	RBI	Avg.	SB	PO	A	E	Avg.
1986	—Sarasota Reds (GCL)	1B	59	208	28	54	4	•5	3	33	.260	10	★581	★36	7	.989
1987	—Billings (Pioneer).............	1B	8	22	10	8	1	0	1	9	.364	1	21	1	0	1.000
	—Cedar Rapids (Midwest) ...	1B	15	54	9	12	5	0	3	11	.222	1	120	11	1	.992
1988	—Cedar Rapids (Midwest) ...	1B	135	517	76	149	26	2	18	★90	.288	2	1084	91	13	.989
1989	—Chattanooga (Southern)...	1B	135	487	66	140	19	3	17	80	.287	2	1004	79	16	.985
1990	—Nashville (Am. Assoc.)	1B	37	126	24	34	11	2	5	23	.270	1	314	20	4	.988
1991	—Nashville (Am. Assoc.)	1B	28	103	15	33	3	1	3	20	.320	3	196	13	2	.991
	—Cincinnati (N.L.)..............	1B	5	7	1	1	0	0	1	1	.143	0	14	1	0	1.000
	—Cleveland (A.L.)■	1B	26	101	10	20	3	0	2	12	.198	0	252	24	2	.993
	—Canton/Akron (Eastern) ..	1B	6	25	2	7	1	0	0	4	.280	0	46	3	0	1.000
	—Colorado Springs (PCL)	1B	39	136	29	42	11	0	3	21	.309	0	289	25	3	.991
American League totals (1 year)			26	101	10	20	3	0	2	12	.198	0	252	24	2	.993
National League totals (1 year)			5	7	1	1	0	0	1	1	.143	0	14	1	0	1.000
Major league totals (1 year)			31	108	11	21	3	0	3	13	.194	0	266	25	2	.993

JEFFERSON, STAN
OF

PERSONAL: Born December 4, 1962, at New York. . . . 5-11/180. . . . Throws right, bats both. . . . Full name: Stanley Jefferson.
HIGH SCHOOL: Harry S. Truman (Bronx, N.Y.).
COLLEGE: Bethune-Cookman.
TRANSACTIONS/CAREER NOTES: Selected by New York Mets organization in first round (20th pick overall) of free-agent draft (June 6, 1983). . . . On Tidewater disabled list (July 25-August 14, 1986). . . . Traded by Mets with OF Shawn Abner, OF Kevin Mitchell, P Kevin Armstrong and P Kevin Brown to San Diego Padres for OF Kevin McReynolds, P Gene Walter and IF Adam Ging (December 11, 1986). . . . On disabled list (April 13-May 7 and May 30-June 14, 1987). . . . Traded by Padres organization with P Jimmy Jones and P Lance McCullers to New York Yankees for 1B-OF Jack Clark and P Pat Clements (October 24, 1988). . . . Traded by Yankees organization to Rochester (Baltimore Orioles organization) for P John Hayden (July 20, 1989). . . . Claimed on waivers by Cleveland Indians (May 7, 1990). . . . Released by Indians (July 5, 1991). . . . Signed by Nashville, Cincinnati Reds organization (July 18, 1991). . . . On Nashville disabled list (July 26-August 4, 1991). . . . Granted free agency (October 15, 1991).
RECORDS/HONORS: Named outfielder on THE SPORTING NEWS college All-America team (1983).
MISCELLANEOUS: Batted righthanded only (1983-84).

Year	Team (League)	Pos.	G	AB	R	H	2B	3B	HR	RBI	Avg.	SB	PO	A	E	Avg.
1983	—Little Falls (N.Y.-Penn)	OF	71	281	57	90	5	1	9	36	.320	★35	★153	7	4	.976
1984	—Lynchburg (Carolina)	OF	128	493	★113	142	20	•9	5	47	.288	45	265	11	8	.972
1985	—Jackson (Texas)	OF	133	524	97	145	21	6	8	30	.277	★39	276	9	7	.976
1986	—Tidewater (Int'l)	OF	95	369	60	107	19	4	2	37	.290	25	219	5	2	.991
	—New York (N.L.)	OF	14	24	6	5	1	0	1	3	.208	0	13	0	0	1.000
1987	—San Diego (N.L.)■	OF	116	422	59	97	8	7	8	29	.230	34	232	3	3	.987
1988	—San Diego (N.L.)	OF	49	111	16	16	1	2	1	4	.144	5	62	0	0	1.000
	—Las Vegas (Pac. Coast) ...	OF	74	278	60	88	14	6	4	33	.317	19	163	4	7	.960
1989	—New York-Balt. (A.L.)■	OF	45	139	20	34	7	0	4	21	.245	10	82	3	1	.988
	—Columbus-Roch. (Int'l)	OF	84	321	43	83	14	9	3	36	.259	18	150	3	4	.975
1990	—Baltimore-Clev. (A.L.)■ ..	OF	59	117	22	27	8	0	2	10	.231	10	70	4	1	.987
	—Colorado Springs (PCL)	OF	33	119	27	41	9	3	3	17	.345	8	69	6	0	1.000
1991	—Colorado Springs (PCL)	OF	28	74	11	21	2	1	2	9	.284	3	27	3	1	.968
	—Nashville (Am. Assoc.)■ ...	OF	27	78	10	19	4	3	2	5	.244	2	45	4	0	1.000
	—Cincinnati (N.L.)	OF	13	19	2	1	0	0	0	0	.053	2	4	0	0	1.000
American League totals (2 years)			104	256	42	61	15	0	6	31	.238	20	152	7	2	.988
National League totals (4 years)			192	576	83	119	10	9	10	36	.207	41	311	3	3	.991
Major league totals (6 years)			296	832	125	180	25	9	16	67	.216	61	463	10	5	.990

JENNINGS, DOUG
OF, ATHLETICS

PERSONAL: Born September 30, 1964, at Atlanta. . . . 5-10/175. . . . Throws left, bats left. . . . Full name: James Douglas Jennings.
HIGH SCHOOL: Leon (Tallahassee, Fla.).
COLLEGE: Brevard Community College (Fla.).
TRANSACTIONS/CAREER NOTES: Selected by California Angels organization in second round of free-agent draft (January 17, 1984). . . . Drafted by Oakland Athletics (December 7, 1987). . . . On Oakland disabled list (June 27-July 31, 1988); included rehabilitation disability assignment to Tacoma (July 15-31, 1988).
STATISTICAL NOTES: Led California League with 117 bases on balls received in 1986. . . . Led Texas League in bases on balls received with 94 and being hit by pitch with 13 in 1987. . . . Led Pacific Coast League in bases on balls received with 93 and being hit by pitch with 16 in 1989. . . . Led Pacific Coast League first basemen with 12 errors in 1989. . . . Led Pacific Coast League in being hit by pitch with 11 in 1991.

Year	Team (League)	Pos.	G	AB	R	H	2B	3B	HR	RBI	Avg.	SB	PO	A	E	Avg.
1984	—Salem (Northwest)	OF	52	173	29	45	7	1	1	17	.260	12	82	5	9	.906
1985	—Quad Cities (Midwest).......	OF	95	319	50	81	17	7	5	54	.254	10	187	12	11	.948
1986	—Palm Springs (Calif.)........	OF	129	429	95	136	31	6	17	89	.317	7	205	10	6	.973
1987	—Midland (Texas)	OF	126	464	106	157	33	1	•30	104	.338	7	145	6	6	.962

Year	Team (League)	Pos.	G	AB	R	H	2B	3B	HR	RBI	Avg.	SB	PO	A	E	Avg.
							BATTING								FIELDING	
1988	—Oakland (A.L.)	OF-1B	71	101	9	21	6	0	1	15	.208	0	85	5	1	.989
	—Tacoma (Pacific Coast)	OF-1B	16	49	12	16	1	0	0	9	.327	5	26	1	1	.964
1989	—Tacoma (Pacific Coast)	1B-OF-P	137	497	*99	136	35	5	11	64	.274	10	842	34	†14	.984
	—Oakland (A.L.)	OF	4	4	0	0	0	0	0	0	.000	0	2	0	0	1.000
1990	—Tacoma (Pacific Coast)	OF-1B	60	208	32	72	19	1	6	30	.346	4	123	7	5	.963
	—Oakland (A.L.)	OF-1B	64	156	19	30	7	2	2	14	.192	0	90	1	1	.989
1991	—Tacoma (Pacific Coast)	OF	95	332	43	89	17	2	3	44	.268	5	145	11	10	.940
	—Oakland (A.L.)	OF	8	9	0	1	0	0	0	0	.111	0	8	0	0	1.000
Major league totals (4 years)			147	270	28	52	13	2	3	29	.193	0	185	6	2	.990

CHAMPIONSHIP SERIES RECORD

Year	Team (League)	Pos.	G	AB	R	H	2B	3B	HR	RBI	Avg.	SB	PO	A	E	Avg.
							BATTING								FIELDING	
1990	—Oakland (A.L.)	OF	1	1	0	0	0	0	0	0	.000	0	0	0	0	...

WORLD SERIES RECORD

Year	Team (League)	Pos.	G	AB	R	H	2B	3B	HR	RBI	Avg.	SB	PO	A	E	Avg.
							BATTING								FIELDING	
1990	—Oakland (A.L.)	PH	1	1	0	1	0	0	0	0	1.000	0	0	0	0	...

RECORD AS PITCHER

Year	Team (League)	G	W	L	Pct.	ERA	Sv.	IP	H	R	ER	BB	SO
1989	—Tacoma (Pacific Coast)	2	0	0	...	3.00	0	3	4	1	1	0	0

JOHNSON, DAVE
P, ANGELS

PERSONAL: Born October 24, 1959, at Baltimore. ... 5-11/179. ... Throws right, bats right. ... Full name: David Wayne Johnson.
HIGH SCHOOL: Overlea (Baltimore).
COLLEGE: Community College of Baltimore.
TRANSACTIONS/CAREER NOTES: Selected by Kansas City Royals organization in fifth round of free-agent draft (January 13, 1981). ... Signed as free agent by Pittsburgh Pirates organization (June 10, 1982). ... Granted free agency (October 15, 1988). ... Signed by Houston Astros (December 22, 1988). ... Traded by Astros organization with OF Victor Hithe to Baltimore Orioles for C Carl Nichols (March 31, 1989). ... On disabled list (August 15-September 4, 1990). ... On Baltimore disabled list (May 19-July 26, 1991); included rehabilitation disability assignment to Hagerstown (July 2-17, 1991) and Rochester (July 17-26, 1991). ... Released by Orioles (November 20, 1991). ... Signed by California Angels (January 8, 1992).
STATISTICAL NOTES: Pitched 3-0 no-hit victory against Portland (July 23, 1987). ... Tied for Pacific Coast League lead with nine complete games in 1987. ... Led American Association pitchers with nine complete games and tied for lead with 29 games started in 1988. ... Led A.L. with 30 home runs allowed in 1990.

Year	Team (League)	G	W	L	Pct.	ERA	Sv.	IP	H	R	ER	BB	SO
1982	—Greenwood (South Atlantic)	16	4	4	.500	3.86	0	58 1/3	50	32	25	41	41
1983	—Alexandria (Carolina)	46	7	5	.583	3.01	8	113 2/3	100	52	38	42	95
1984	—Prince William (Carolina)	13	7	5	.583	1.32	0	88 1/3	60	22	13	35	48
	—Nashua (Eastern)	12	1	8	.111	4.84	0	83 2/3	95	52	45	31	47
1985	—Nashua (Eastern)	34	6	9	.400	3.12	2	153	129	66	53	45	84
1986	—Hawaii (Pacific Coast)	22	8	7	.533	*3.17	0	150 1/3	150	68	53	35	71
1987	—Vancouver (Pacific Coast)	23	8	10	.444	3.51	0	153 2/3	133	74	60	68	76
	—Pittsburgh (N.L.)	5	0	0	...	9.95	0	6 1/3	13	7	7	2	4
1988	—Buffalo (American Assoc.)	29	*15	12	.556	3.51	0	192 1/3	*213	93	75	55	90
1989	—Rochester (International)■	18	7	6	.538	3.26	1	105	104	45	38	31	60
	—Baltimore (A.L.)	14	4	7	.364	4.23	0	89 1/3	90	44	42	28	26
1990	—Baltimore (A.L.)	30	13	9	.591	4.10	0	180	196	83	82	43	68
1991	—Baltimore (A.L.)	22	4	8	.333	7.07	0	84	127	68	66	24	38
	—Hagerstown (Eastern)	3	3	0	1.000	1.00	0	18	13	3	2	3	9
	—Rochester (International)	2	0	1	.000	4.15	0	13	18	7	6	5	8
American League totals (3 years)		66	21	24	.467	4.84	0	353 1/3	413	195	190	95	132
National League totals (1 year)		5	0	0	...	9.95	0	6 1/3	13	7	7	2	4
Major league totals (4 years)		71	21	24	.467	4.93	0	359 2/3	426	202	197	97	136

JOHNSON, HOWARD
OF/3B, METS

PERSONAL: Born November 29, 1960, at Clearwater, Fla. ... 5-10/195. ... Throws right, bats both. ... Full name: Howard Michael Johnson.
HIGH SCHOOL: Clearwater (Fla.).
COLLEGE: St. Petersburg Junior College (Fla.).
TRANSACTIONS/CAREER NOTES: Selected by New York Yankees organization in 23rd round of free-agent draft (June 6, 1978). ... Selected by Detroit Tigers organization in secondary phase of free-agent draft (January 9, 1979). ... On Evansville disabled list (June 2-August 8, 1983). ... Traded by Tigers to New York Mets for P Walt Terrell (December 7, 1984). ... On disabled list (June 2-23, 1986).
RECORDS/HONORS: Holds N.L. single-season record for most home runs by switch-hitter—38 (1991). ... Shares N.L. record for most home runs by switch-hitter in two consecutive seasons—61 (1990-1991). ... Named third baseman on THE SPORTING NEWS N.L. All-Star team (1989). ... Named third baseman on THE SPORTING NEWS N.L. Silver Slugger team (1989 and 1991).
STATISTICAL NOTES: Led Florida State League with 16 sacrifice hits in 1980. ... Led Florida State League third basemen with 21

double plays in 1980. . . . Led American Association third basemen with 19 double plays in 1982. . . . Tied for N.L. lead with 16 game-winning RBIs in 1987. . . . Switch-hit home runs in a game (August 31, 1991). . . . Led N.L. with 15 sacrifice flies in 1991.

							BATTING							FIELDING			
Year	Team (League)	Pos.	G	AB	R	H	2B	3B	HR	RBI	Avg.	SB	PO	A	E	Avg.
1979—Lakeland (Florida State) ...		3B-SS-OF	132	456	49	107	9	6	3	49	.235	18	130	240	36	.911
1980—Lakeland (Florida State) ...		3B	130	474	83	135	*28	1	10	69	.285	31	*110	*264	13	*.966
1981—Birmingham (Southern)		3B	138	488	84	130	28	7	22	83	.266	19	103	218	26	.925
1982—Evansville (A.A.)		3B-OF	98	366	70	116	16	4	23	67	.317	35	69	139	23	.900
—Detroit (A.L.)		3B-OF	54	155	23	49	5	0	4	14	.316	7	36	40	7	.916
1983—Detroit (A.L.)		3B	27	66	11	14	0	0	3	5	.212	0	10	30	7	.851
—Evansville (A.A.)		3B	3	9	1	2	1	0	0	0	.222	0	1	11	2	.857
1984—Detroit (A.L.)		3-S-1-0	116	355	43	88	14	1	12	50	.248	10	63	150	14	.938
1985—New York (N.L.)■		3B-SS-OF	126	389	38	94	18	4	11	46	.242	6	78	190	18	.937
1986—New York (N.L.)		3B-SS-OF	88	220	30	54	14	0	10	39	.245	8	52	136	20	.904
1987—New York (N.L.)		3B-SS-OF	157	554	93	147	22	1	36	99	.265	32	118	305	26	.942
1988—New York (N.L.)		3B-SS	148	495	85	114	21	1	24	68	.230	23	110	274	18	.955
1989—New York (N.L.)		3B-SS	153	571	•104	164	41	3	36	101	.287	41	97	217	24	.929
1990—New York (N.L.)		3B-SS	154	590	89	144	37	3	23	90	.244	34	150	335	28	.945
1991—New York (N.L.)		3B-OF-SS	156	564	108	146	34	4	*38	*117	.259	30	161	264	31	.932
American League totals (3 years)			197	576	77	151	19	1	19	69	.262	17	109	220	28	.922
National League totals (7 years)			982	3383	547	863	187	16	178	560	.255	174	766	1721	165	.938
Major league totals (10 years)			1179	3959	624	1014	206	17	197	629	.256	191	875	1941	193	.936

CHAMPIONSHIP SERIES RECORD

							BATTING							FIELDING			
Year	Team (League)	Pos.	G	AB	R	H	2B	3B	HR	RBI	Avg.	SB	PO	A	E	Avg.
1986—New York (N.L.)		PH	2	2	0	0	0	0	0	0	.000	0	0	0	0	...
1988—New York (N.L.)		SS-3B-PH	6	18	3	1	0	0	0	0	.056	1	6	9	1	.938
Championship Series totals (2 years)			8	20	3	1	0	0	0	0	.050	1	6	9	1	.938

WORLD SERIES RECORD

							BATTING							FIELDING			
Year	Team (League)	Pos.	G	AB	R	H	2B	3B	HR	RBI	Avg.	SB	PO	A	E	Avg.
1984—Detroit (A.L.)		PH	1	1	0	0	0	0	0	0	.000	0	0	0	0	...
1986—New York (N.L.)		3B-PH-SS	2	5	0	0	0	0	0	0	.000	0	1	0	0	1.000
World Series totals (2 years)			3	6	0	0	0	0	0	0	.000	0	1	0	0	1.000

ALL-STAR GAME RECORD

						BATTING							FIELDING		
Year	League	Pos.	AB	R	H	2B	3B	HR	RBI	Avg.	SB	PO	A	E	Avg.
1989—National		3B	3	0	1	0	0	0	1	.333	1	0	0	0	...
1991—National		3B	2	0	0	0	0	0	0	.000	0	0	0	0	...
All-Star Game totals (2 years)			5	0	1	0	0	0	1	.200	1	0	0	0	...

JOHNSON, JEFF
P, YANKEES

PERSONAL: Born August 4, 1966, at Durham, N.C. . . . 6-3/206. . . . Throws left, bats right. . . . Full name: William Jeffrey Johnson.
COLLEGE: UNC Durham.
TRANSACTIONS/CAREER NOTES: Selected by New York Yankees organization in sixth round of free-agent draft (June 1, 1988).

Year	Team (League)	G	W	L	Pct.	ERA	Sv.	IP	H	R	ER	BB	SO
1988—Oneonta (New York-Penn)		14	6	1	.857	2.98	0	87⅔	67	35	29	39	91
1989—Prince William (Carolina)		25	4	10	.286	2.92	0	138⅔	125	59	45	55	99
1990—Fort Lauderdale (Florida St.)		17	6	8	.429	3.65	0	103⅔	101	55	42	25	84
—Albany (Eastern)		9	4	3	.571	1.63	0	60⅔	44	14	11	15	41
1991—Columbus (International)		10	4	0	1.000	2.61	0	62	58	27	18	25	40
—New York (A.L.)		23	6	11	.353	5.95	0	127	156	89	84	33	62
Major league totals (1 year)		23	6	11	.353	5.95	0	127	156	89	84	33	62

JOHNSON, LANCE
OF, WHITE SOX

PERSONAL: Born July 7, 1963, at Lincoln Heights, O. . . . 5-11/160. . . . Throws left, bats left. . . . Full name: Kenneth Lance Johnson.
HIGH SCHOOL: Princeton (Cincinnati).
COLLEGE: Triton College (Ill.) and South Alabama.
TRANSACTIONS/CAREER NOTES: Selected by Pittsburgh Pirates organization in 30th round of free-agent draft (June 8, 1981). . . . Selected by Seattle Mariners organization in 31st round of free-agent draft (June 7, 1982). . . . Selected by St. Louis Cardinals organization in sixth round of free-agent draft (June 4, 1984). . . . Traded by Cardinals with P Rick Horton and cash to Chicago White Sox for P Jose DeLeon (February 9, 1988).
RECORDS/HONORS: Named American Association Most Valuable Player (1987).
STATISTICAL NOTES: Led New York-Pennsylvania League outfielders with 201 total chances in 1984. . . . Led Texas League in caught stealing with 15 in 1986. . . . Led American Association outfielders with 333 total chances in 1987. . . . Led Pacific Coast League outfielders with five double plays in 1988. . . . Led Pacific Coast League outfielders with 273 total chances in 1989. . . . Led Pacific Coast League in caught stealing with 18 in 1989. . . . Led A.L. in caught stealing with 22 in 1990.

Year	Team (League)	Pos.	G	AB	R	H	2B	3B	HR	RBI	Avg.	SB	PO	A	E	Avg.
1984	Erie (New York-Penn)	OF	71	283	*63	*96	7	5	1	28	.339	29	*188	5	8	.960
1985	St. Petersburg (Fla. St.)	OF	129	497	68	134	17	10	2	55	.270	33	338	16	5	.986
1986	Arkansas (Texas)	OF	127	445	82	128	24	6	2	33	.288	*49	262	11	7	.975
1987	Louisville (Am. Assoc.)	OF	116	477	89	159	21	11	5	50	.333	42	*319	6	•8	.976
	St. Louis (N.L.)	OF	33	59	4	13	2	1	0	7	.220	6	27	0	2	.931
1988	Chicago (A.L.)■	OF	33	124	11	23	4	1	0	6	.185	6	63	1	2	.970
	Vancouver (Pac. Coast)	OF	100	411	71	126	12	6	2	36	.307	49	262	9	5	.982
1989	Vancouver (Pac. Coast)	OF	106	408	69	124	11	7	0	28	.304	33	*261	7	5	.982
	Chicago (A.L.)	OF	50	180	28	54	8	2	0	16	.300	16	113	0	2	.983
1990	Chicago (A.L.)	OF	151	541	76	154	18	9	1	51	.285	36	353	5	10	.973
1991	Chicago (A.L.)	OF	159	588	72	161	14	•13	0	49	.274	26	425	11	2	.995
American League totals (4 years)			393	1433	187	392	44	25	1	122	.274	84	954	17	16	.984
National League totals (1 year)			33	59	4	13	2	1	0	7	.220	6	27	0	2	.931
Major league totals (5 years)			426	1492	191	405	46	26	1	129	.271	90	981	17	18	.982

CHAMPIONSHIP SERIES RECORD

Year	Team (League)	Pos.	G	AB	R	H	2B	3B	HR	RBI	Avg.	SB	PO	A	E	Avg.
1987	St. Louis (N.L.)	PR	1	00	1	0	0	0	0	0	...	0	0	0	0	...

WORLD SERIES RECORD

Year	Team (League)	Pos.	G	AB	R	H	2B	3B	HR	RBI	Avg.	SB	PO	A	E	Avg.
1987	St. Louis (N.L.)	PR	1	0	0	0	0	0	0	0	...	0	0	0	0	...

JOHNSON, RANDY
P, MARINERS

PERSONAL: Born September 10, 1963, at Walnut Creek, Calif.... 6-10/225.... Throws left, bats right.... Full name: Randall David Johnson.
HIGH SCHOOL: Livermore (Calif.).
COLLEGE: Southern California.
TRANSACTIONS/CAREER NOTES: Selected by Atlanta Braves organization in third round of free-agent draft (June 7, 1982).... Selected by Montreal Expos organization in second round of free-agent draft (June 3, 1985).... Traded by Expos organization with P Brian Holman and P Gene Harris to Seattle Mariners for P Mark Langston and a player to be named later (May 25, 1989); Indianapolis (Expos organization) acquired P Mike Campbell to complete deal (July 31, 1989).
STATISTICAL NOTES: Tied for Florida State League lead in games started by pitcher with 26 in 1986.... Led American Association with 20 balks in 1988.... Pitched 2-0 no-hit victory against Detroit Tigers (June 2, 1990).

Year	Team (League)	G	W	L	Pct.	ERA	Sv.	IP	H	R	ER	BB	SO
1985	Jamestown (New York-Penn)	8	0	3	.000	5.93	0	27⅓	29	22	18	24	21
1986	West Palm Beach (Florida St.)	26	8	7	.533	3.16	0	119⅔	89	49	42	*94	133
1987	Jacksonville (Southern)	25	11	8	.579	3.73	0	140	100	63	58	128	*163
1988	Indianapolis (Am. Assoc.)	20	8	7	.533	3.26	0	113⅓	85	52	41	72	111
	Montreal (N.L.)	4	3	0	1.000	2.42	0	26	23	8	7	7	25
1989	Montreal (N.L.)	7	0	4	.000	6.67	0	29⅔	29	25	22	26	26
	Indianapolis (Am. Assoc.)	3	1	1	.500	2.00	0	18	13	5	4	9	17
	Seattle (A.L.)■	22	7	9	.438	4.40	0	131	118	75	64	70	104
1990	Seattle (A.L.)	33	14	11	.560	3.65	0	219⅔	174	103	89	*120	194
1991	Seattle (A.L.)	33	13	10	.565	3.98	0	201⅓	151	96	89	*152	228
American League totals (3 years)		88	34	30	.531	3.95	0	552	443	274	242	342	526
National League totals (2 years)		11	3	4	.429	4.69	0	55⅔	52	33	29	33	51
Major league totals (4 years)		99	37	34	.521	4.01	0	607⅔	495	307	271	375	577

ALL-STAR GAME RECORD

Year	League	W	L	Pct.	ERA	Sv.	IP	H	R	ER	BB	SO
1990	American						Did not play					

JOHNSTON, JOEL
P, ROYALS

PERSONAL: Born March 8, 1967, at West Chester, Pa.... 6-4/220.... Throws right, bats right.... Full name: Joel Raymond Johnston.
HIGH SCHOOL: Newtown (West Chester, Pa.).
COLLEGE: Penn State.
TRANSACTIONS/CAREER NOTES: Selected by Kansas City Royals organization in third round of free-agent draft (June 1, 1988).

Year	Team (League)	G	W	L	Pct.	ERA	Sv.	IP	H	R	ER	BB	SO
1988	Eugene (Northwest)	14	4	7	.364	5.20	0	64	64	49	37	34	64
1989	Baseball City (Florida State)	26	9	4	.692	4.92	0	131⅔	135	84	72	63	76
1990	Memphis (Southern)	4	0	0	...	6.75	0	6⅔	5	9	5	16	6
	Baseball City (Florida State)	31	2	4	.333	4.88	7	55⅓	36	37	30	49	60
	Omaha (American Assoc.)	2	0	0	...	0.00	0	3	1	0	0	1	3
1991	Omaha (American Assoc.)	47	4	7	.364	5.21	8	74⅓	60	43	43	42	63
	Kansas City (A.L.)	13	1	0	1.000	0.40	0	22⅓	9	1	1	9	21
Major league totals (1 year)		13	1	0	1.000	0.40	0	22⅓	9	1	1	9	21

JOHNSTONE, JOHN
P, METS

PERSONAL: Born November 25, 1968, at Liverpool, N.Y. .... 6-3/195. ... Throws right, bats right. ... Full name: John William Johnstone. **HIGH SCHOOL:** Bishop Ludden (Syracuse, N.Y.). **COLLEGE:** Onondaga Community College (N.Y.).

TRANSACTIONS/CAREER NOTES: Selected by New York Mets organization in 20th round of free-agent draft (June 2, 1987). **STATISTICAL NOTES:** Led Florida State League with nine complete games in 1990. ... Tied for Eastern League lead in games started by pitcher with 27 in 1991.

Year	Team (League)	G	W	L	Pct.	ERA	Sv.	IP	H	R	ER	BB	SO
1987	Kingsport (Appalachian)	17	1	1	.500	7.45	0	29	42	28	24	20	21
1988	Sarasota Mets (Gulf Coast)	12	3	4	.429	2.68	0	74	65	29	22	25	57
1989	Pittsfield (New York-Penn)	15	*11	2	.846	2.77	0	104	101	47	32	28	60
1990	St. Lucie (Florida State)	25	*15	6	.714	2.24	0	172²/₃	145	53	43	60	120
1991	Williamsport (Eastern)	27	7	9	.438	3.97	0	165¹/₃	159	94	73	79	100

JONES, BARRY
P, PHILLIES

PERSONAL: Born February 15, 1963, at Centerville, Ind. ... 6-4/225. ... Throws right, bats right. ... Full name: Barry Louis Jones. **HIGH SCHOOL:** Centerville (Ind.). **COLLEGE:** Indiana.

TRANSACTIONS/CAREER NOTES: Selected by Texas Rangers organization in sixth round of free-agent draft (June 8, 1981). .... Selected by Pittsburgh Pirates organization in third round of free-agent draft (June 4, 1984). .... Traded by Pirates to Chicago White Sox for P Dave LaPoint (August 13, 1988). .... On Chicago disabled list (May 4-August 24, 1989); included rehabilitation disability assignment to Sarasota (June 29-July 18, 1989). .... Traded by White Sox with OF Ivan Calderon to Montreal Expos for OF Tim Raines, P Jeff Carter and a player to be named later (December 23, 1990); White Sox acquired P Mario Brito to complete deal (February 15, 1991). .... Traded by Expos to Philadelphia Phillies for C Darrin Fletcher and cash (December 9, 1991).

Year	Team (League)	G	W	L	Pct.	ERA	Sv.	IP	H	R	ER	BB	SO
1984	Watertown (New York-Penn)	14	6	3	.667	3.43	0	86²/₃	75	41	33	49	61
1985	Prince William (Carolina)	28	3	2	.600	1.21	10	37¹/₃	26	7	5	19	42
	Nashua (Eastern)	23	3	2	.600	1.55	12	29	19	6	5	10	24
	Hawaii (Pacific Coast)	1	0	0	...	9.00	0	3	5	5	3	1	2
1986	Hawaii (Pacific Coast)	35	3	6	.333	3.56	7	48	41	20	19	20	28
	Pittsburgh (N.L.)	26	3	4	.429	2.89	3	37¹/₃	29	16	12	21	29
1987	Pittsburgh (N.L.)	32	2	4	.333	5.61	1	43¹/₃	55	34	27	23	28
	Vancouver (Pacific Coast)	20	1	2	.333	3.20	11	25¹/₃	21	9	9	14	27
1988	Pittsburgh (N.L.)■	42	1	1	.500	3.04	2	56¹/₃	57	21	19	21	31
	Chicago (A.L.)	17	2	2	.500	2.42	1	26	15	7	7	17	17
1989	South Bend (Midwest)	3	0	0	...	4.91	0	3²/₃	6	3	2	0	2
	Sarasota White Sox (GCL)	7	0	1	.000	1.47	1	18¹/₃	12	7	3	5	14
	Chicago (A.L.)	22	3	2	.600	2.37	1	30¹/₃	22	12	8	8	17
1990	Chicago (A.L.)	65	11	4	.733	2.31	1	74	62	20	19	33	45
1991	Montreal (N.L.)■	*77	4	9	.308	3.35	13	88²/₃	76	35	33	33	46
	American League totals (3 years)	104	16	8	.667	2.35	3	130¹/₃	99	39	34	58	79
	National League totals (4 years)	177	10	18	.357	3.63	19	225²/₃	217	106	91	98	134
	Major league totals (6 years)	281	26	26	.500	3.16	22	356	316	145	125	156	213

JONES, CALVIN
P, MARINERS

PERSONAL: Born September 26, 1963, at Compton, Calif. ... 6-3/185. ... Throws right, bats right. ... Full name: Calvin Douglas Jones. **HIGH SCHOOL:** Verbum Dei (Los Angeles). **COLLEGE:** California Riverside and Chaffey College (Calif.).

TRANSACTIONS/CAREER NOTES: Selected by Seattle Mariners organization in first round (first pick overall) in free-agent draft (January 17, 1984). .... On disabled list (August 7-17, 1985).

Year	Team (League)	G	W	L	Pct.	ERA	Sv.	IP	H	R	ER	BB	SO
1984	Bellingham (Northwest)	10	5	0	1.000	2.41	0	59²/₃	29	23	16	36	59
1985	Wausau (Midwest)	20	4	11	.267	3.91	0	106	96	59	46	65	71
1986	Salinas (California)	26	11	8	.579	3.60	0	157¹/₃	141	76	63	90	137
1987	Chattanooga (Southern)	26	2	9	.182	4.98	2	81¹/₃	90	58	45	38	77
1988	Vermont (Eastern)	24	7	5	.583	2.65	0	74²/₃	52	26	22	47	58
1989	San Bernardino (California)	5	2	0	1.000	0.73	1	12¹/₃	8	1	1	7	15
	Williamsport (N.Y.-Penn)	5	0	0	...	12.15	0	6²/₃	13	9	9	4	5
1990	San Bernardino (California)	53	5	3	.625	2.96	8	67	43	32	22	54	94
1991	Calgary (Pacific Coast)	20	1	1	.500	3.91	7	23	19	12	10	19	25
	Seattle (A.L.)	27	2	2	.500	2.53	2	46¹/₃	33	14	13	29	42
	Major league totals (1 year)	27	2	2	.500	2.53	2	46¹/₃	33	14	13	29	42

JONES, CHRIS
OF, ASTROS

PERSONAL: Born December 16, 1965, at Utica, N.Y. .... 6-2/205. .... Throws right, bats right. .... Full name: Christopher Carlos Jones. **HIGH SCHOOL:** Liverpool (N.Y.).

TRANSACTIONS/CAREER NOTES: Selected by the Cincinnati Reds organization in third round of free-agent draft (June 4, 1984). .... Released by Reds (December 13, 1991). .... Signed by Houston Astros organization (December 19, 1991).

Year Team (League)	Pos.	G	AB	R	H	2B	3B	HR	RBI	Avg.	SB	PO	A	E	Avg.
1984 — Billings (Pioneer)	3B	21	73	8	11	2	0	2	13	.151	4	6	27	5	.868
1985 — Billings (Pioneer)	OF	63	240	43	62	12	5	4	33	.258	13	112	4	*13	.899
1986 — Cedar Rapids (Midwest) ...	OF	128	473	65	117	13	9	20	78	.247	23	218	15	11	.955
1987 — Vermont (Eastern)	OF	113	383	50	88	11	4	10	39	.230	13	207	12	8	.965
1988 — Chattanooga (Southern) ...	OF	116	410	50	111	20	7	4	61	.271	11	185	15	8	.962
1989 — Chattanooga (Southern) ...	OF	103	378	47	95	18	2	10	54	.251	10	197	8	7	.967
— Nashville (Am. Assoc.)	OF	21	49	8	8	1	0	2	5	.163	2	25	0	1	.962
1990 — Nashville (Am. Assoc.)	OF	134	436	53	114	23	3	10	52	.261	12	209	17	8	.966
1991 — Nashville (Am. Assoc.)	OF	73	267	29	65	5	4	9	33	.243	10	110	5	6	.950
— Cincinnati (N.L.)	OF	52	89	14	26	1	2	2	6	.292	2	27	1	0	1.000
Major league totals (1 year)		52	89	14	26	1	2	2	6	.292	2	27	1	0	1.000

JONES, DOUG
P, ASTROS

PERSONAL: Born June 24, 1957, at Covina, Calif. ... 6-2/195. ... Throws right, bats right. ... Full name: Douglas Reid Jones.
HIGH SCHOOL: Lebanon (Ind.).
COLLEGE: Central Arizona College and Butler.
TRANSACTIONS/CAREER NOTES: Selected by Milwaukee Brewers organization in third round of free-agent draft (January 10, 1978). ... On disabled list (June 20-July 12, 1978). ... On Vancouver disabled list (April 11-September 1, 1983 and April 25-May 30, 1984). ... Granted free agency (October 15, 1984). ... Signed by Waterbury, Cleveland Indians organization (April 3, 1985). ... Granted free agency (December 20, 1991). ... Signed by Houston Astros organization (January 24, 1992).
STATISTICAL NOTES: Led Midwest League with 16 complete games and tied for lead with three shutouts in 1979.

Year Team (League)	G	W	L	Pct.	ERA	Sv.	IP	H	R	ER	BB	SO
1978 — Newark (New York-Penn)	15	2	4	.333	5.21	2	38	49	30	22	15	27
1979 — Burlington (Midwest)	28	10	10	.500	*1.75	0	*190	144	63	37	73	115
1980 — Stockton (California)	11	6	2	.750	2.84	0	76	63	32	24	31	54
— Vancouver (Pacific Coast)	8	3	2	.600	3.23	0	53	52	19	19	15	28
— Holyoke (Eastern)	8	5	3	.625	2.90	0	62	57	23	20	26	39
1981 — El Paso (Texas)	15	5	7	.417	5.80	0	90	121	67	58	28	62
— Vancouver (Pacific Coast)	11	5	3	.625	3.04	0	80	79	29	27	22	38
1982 — Milwaukee (A.L.)	4	0	0	...	10.13	0	2⅔	5	3	3	1	1
— Vancouver (Pacific Coast)	23	5	8	.385	2.97	2	106	109	48	35	31	60
1983 — Vancouver (Pacific Coast)	3	0	1	.000	10.29	0	7	10	8	8	5	4
1984 — Vancouver (Pacific Coast)	3	1	0	1.000	10.13	0	8	9	9	9	3	2
— El Paso (Texas)	16	6	8	.429	4.28	0	109⅓	120	61	52	35	62
1985 — Waterbury (Eastern)■	39	9	4	.692	3.65	7	116	123	59	47	36	113
1986 — Maine (International)	43	5	6	.455	*2.09	9	116⅓	105	35	27	27	98
— Cleveland (A.L.)	11	1	0	1.000	2.50	1	18	18	5	5	6	12
1987 — Cleveland (A.L.)	49	6	5	.545	3.15	8	91⅓	101	45	32	24	87
— Buffalo (American Assoc.)	23	5	2	.714	2.04	7	61⅔	49	18	14	12	61
1988 — Cleveland (A.L.)	51	3	4	.429	2.27	37	83⅓	69	26	21	16	72
1989 — Cleveland (A.L.)	59	7	10	.412	2.34	32	80⅔	76	25	21	13	65
1990 — Cleveland (A.L.)	66	5	5	.500	2.56	43	84⅓	66	26	24	22	55
1991 — Cleveland (A.L.)	36	4	8	.333	5.54	7	63⅓	87	42	39	17	48
— Colorado Springs (Pac. Coast) ..	17	2	2	.500	3.28	7	35⅔	30	14	13	5	29
Major league totals (7 years)	276	26	32	.448	3.08	128	423⅔	422	172	145	99	340

ALL-STAR GAME RECORD

Year League	W	L	Pct.	ERA	Sv.	IP	H	R	ER	BB	SO
1988 — American	0	0	...	0.00	0	⅔	0	0	0	0	1
1989 — American	0	0	...	0.00	1	1⅓	1	0	0	0	0
1990 — American					Did not play						
All-Star totals (2 years)	0	0	...	0.00	1	2	1	0	0	0	1

JONES, JIMMY
P, ASTROS

PERSONAL: Born April 20, 1964, at Dallas. ... 6-2/190. ... Throws right, bats right. ... Full name: James Condia Jones.
HIGH SCHOOL: Thomas Jefferson (Dallas).
TRANSACTIONS/CAREER NOTES: Selected by San Diego Padres organization in first round (third pick overall) of free-agent draft (June 7, 1982). ... On disabled list (July 13, 1984-remainder of season; and June 29-July 11 and July 28, 1985-remainder of season). ... Traded by Padres with P Lance McCullers and OF Stan Jefferson to New York Yankees for 1B-OF Jack Clark and P Pat Clements (October 24, 1988). ... Granted free agency (October 4, 1990). ... Signed by Tucson, Houston Astros organization (March 19, 1991). ... On disabled list (August 21, 1991-remainder of season).
RECORDS/HONORS: Shares modern major league record for fewest hits allowed in first major league game (nine innings) — 1 (September 21, 1986).
STATISTICAL NOTES: Tied for Pacific Coast League lead in games started by pitcher with 27 in 1986.

Year Team (League)	G	W	L	Pct.	ERA	Sv.	IP	H	R	ER	BB	SO
1982 — Walla Walla (Northwest)	14	4	6	.400	3.22	0	78⅓	64	49	28	71	78
1983 — Reno (California)	17	7	5	.583	2.70	0	116⅔	96	50	35	49	79
1984 — Beaumont (Texas)	13	7	2	.778	2.10	0	85⅔	63	28	20	39	49

Year	Team (League)	G	W	L	Pct.	ERA	Sv.	IP	H	R	ER	BB	SO
1985	—Beaumont (Texas)	16	7	5	.583	4.66	0	85	84	51	44	66	57
1986	—Las Vegas (Pacific Coast)	28	9	10	.474	4.40	0	157⅔	168	84	77	72	114
	—San Diego (N.L.)	3	2	0	1.000	2.50	0	18	10	6	5	3	15
1987	—Las Vegas (Pacific Coast)	4	2	0	1.000	5.92	0	24⅓	24	16	16	8	11
	—San Diego (N.L.)	30	9	7	.563	4.14	0	145⅔	154	85	67	54	51
1988	—San Diego (N.L.)	29	9	14	.391	4.12	0	179	192	98	82	44	82
1989	—Columbus (International)■	20	8	6	.571	3.77	0	124	110	54	52	31	94
	—New York (A.L.)	11	2	1	.667	5.25	0	48	56	29	28	16	25
1990	—Columbus (International)	11	5	2	.714	2.34	0	73	46	20	19	35	78
	—New York (A.L.)	17	1	2	.333	6.30	0	50	72	42	35	23	25
1991	—Houston (N.L.)■	26	6	8	.429	4.39	0	135⅓	143	73	66	51	88
American League totals (2 years)		28	3	3	.500	5.79	0	98	128	71	63	39	50
National League totals (4 years)		88	26	29	.473	4.14	0	478	499	262	220	152	236
Major league totals (6 years)		116	29	32	.475	4.42	0	576	627	333	283	191	286

JONES, RON
OF, INDIANS

PERSONAL: Born June 11, 1964, at Seguin, Tex. . . . 5-10/214. . . . Throws right, bats left. . . . Full name: Ronald Glen Jones.
HIGH SCHOOL: Seguin (Tex.).
COLLEGE: Wharton County Junior College (Tex.).
TRANSACTIONS/CAREER NOTES: Selected by Toronto Blue Jays organization in 14th round of free-agent draft (June 7, 1982). . . . Selected by Montreal Expos organization in secondary phase of free-agent draft (January 11, 1983). . . . Signed as free agent by Philadelphia Phillies organization (October 20, 1984). . . . On Portland disabled list (August 8, 1986-remainder of season). . . . On Philadelphia disabled list (April 19, 1989-remainder of season and July 1, 1990-remainder of season). . . . On Philadelphia disabled list (April 3-June 3, 1991; included rehabilitation disability assignment to Clearwater (May 14-30, 1991) and Scranton/Wilkes-Barre (May 30-June 3, 1991). . . . Granted free agency (October 18, 1991). . . . Signed by Cleveland Indians organization (December 13, 1991).
RECORDS/HONORS: Named Florida State League Most Valuable Player (1986).
STATISTICAL NOTES: Led Florida State League with 216 total bases and .524 slugging percentage in 1986. . . . Tied for International League lead with eight sacrifice flies in 1988. . . . Tied for International League lead in double plays by outfielders with four in 1988.

						BATTING						FIELDING			
Year	Team (League)	Pos.	G	AB	R	H	2B	3B	HR	RBI	Avg.	SB	PO	A	E	Avg.
1985	—Bend (Northwest)	OF	73	286	54	90	13	1	10	60	.315	9	88	4	*11	.893
1986	—Clearwater (Florida St.)	OF	108	412	76	•153	18	*12	7	73*	.371	33	196	9	2	.990
	—Portland (Pacific Coast)	OF	11	34	4	4	1	0	0	2	.118	0	11	2	0	1.000
1987	—Maine (International)	OF	90	316	33	78	13	4	7	32	.247	13	178	4	3	.984
1988	—Maine (International)	OF	125	445	64	119	15	3	16	*75	.267	16	191	14	7	.967
	—Philadelphia (N.L.)	OF	33	124	15	36	6	1	8	26	.290	0	70	1	0	1.000
1989	—Philadelphia (N.L.)	OF	12	31	7	9	0	0	2	4	.290	1	27	1	0	1.000
1990	—Scranton/W.B. (Int'l)	OF	44	148	13	39	4	1	3	26	.264	5	46	1	1	.979
	—Philadelphia (N.L.)	OF	24	58	5	16	2	0	3	7	.276	0	25	1	0	1.000
1991	—Clearwater (Florida St.)	OF	12	38	8	6	4	0	1	6	.158	2	3	0	0	1.000
	—Scranton/W.B. (Int'l)	OF	48	150	17	38	7	0	4	26	.253	3	44	0	3	.936
	—Philadelphia (N.L.)	PH	28	26	0	4	2	0	0	3	.154	0	0	0	0	. . .
Major league totals (4 years)			97	239	27	65	10	1	13	40	.272	1	122	3	0	1.000

JONES, STACY
P, ORIOLES

PERSONAL: Born May 26, 1967, at Gadsden, Ala. . . . 6-6/230. . . . Throws right, bats right. . . . Full name: Joseph Stacy Jones.
HIGH SCHOOL: Etowah (Ala.).
COLLEGE: Auburn.
TRANSACTIONS/CAREER NOTES: Selected by Baltimore Orioles organization in third round of free-agent draft (June 1, 1988).

Year	Team (League)	G	W	L	Pct.	ERA	Sv.	IP	H	R	ER	BB	SO
1988	—Erie (New York-Penn)	7	3	3	.500	1.33	0	54⅓	51	12	8	15	40
	—Hagerstown (Eastern)	6	3	1	.750	2.87	0	37⅔	35	14	12	12	23
1989	—Frederick (Carolina)	15	5	6	.455	4.90	0	82⅔	93	57	45	35	58
1990	—Frederick (Carolina)	15	1	2	.333	3.38	2	26⅔	31	13	10	7	24
	—Hagerstown (Eastern)	19	1	6	.143	5.13	0	40⅓	46	27	23	11	41
1991	—Hagerstown (Eastern)	12	0	1	.000	1.78	1	30⅓	24	6	6	15	26
	—Rochester (International)	33	4	4	.500	3.38	8	50⅔	53	22	19	20	47
	—Baltimore (A.L.)	4	0	0	. . .	4.09	0	11	11	6	5	5	10
Major league totals (1 year)		4	0	0	. . .	4.09	0	11	11	6	5	5	10

JONES, TIM
SS/2B, CARDINALS

PERSONAL: Born December 1, 1962, at Sumter, S.C. . . . 5-10/175. . . . Throws right, bats left. . . . Full name: William Timothy Jones.
HIGH SCHOOL: Sumter (S.C.).
COLLEGE: The Citadel (degree in health service, 1985).
TRANSACTIONS/CAREER NOTES: Selected by St. Louis Cardinals organization in second round of free-agent draft (June 3, 1985).
STATISTICAL NOTES: Tied for Appalachian League lead with five sacrifice flies in 1985. . . . Led Appalachian League shortstops with 105 putouts and 30 double plays in 1985.

Year	Team (League)	Pos.	G	AB	R	H	2B	3B	HR	RBI	Avg.	SB	PO	A	E	Avg.
1985 —Johnson City (Appal.)	SS-3B	68	*235	33	75	10	1	3	48	.319	28	†109	148	23	.918
1986 —St. Petersburg (Fla. St.)	SS	39	142	19	43	3	2	0	27	.303	8	67	125	8	.960
—Arkansas (Texas)	SS	96	284	36	76	15	1	2	27	.268	7	142	277	24	.946
1987 —Arkansas (Texas)	SS-2B	61	176	23	58	12	0	3	26	.330	15	80	151	9	.963
—Louisville (Am. Assoc.)	SS	73	276	48	78	14	3	4	43	.283	11	112	221	13	.962
1988 —Louisville (Am. Assoc.)	SS	103	370	63	95	21	2	6	38	.257	39	145	302	15	*.968
—St. Louis (N.L.)	SS-2B-3B	31	52	2	14	0	0	0	3	.269	4	26	40	1	.985
1989 —St. Louis (N.L.)	2-S-3-0-C	42	75	11	22	6	0	0	7	.293	1	33	48	2	.976
1990 —St. Louis (N.L.)	S-2-3-P	1	128	9	28	7	1	1	12	.219	3	43	105	7	.955
1991 —Louisville (Am. Assoc.)	S-2-0-3	86	306	34	78	9	1	5	29	.255	19	120	207	12	.965
—St. Louis (N.L.)	SS-2B	16	24	1	4	2	0	0	2	.167	0	5	16	0	1.000
Major league totals (4 years)		90	279	23	68	15	1	1	24	.244	8	107	209	10	.969

RECORD AS PITCHER

Year	Team (League)	G	W	L	Pct.	ERA	Sv.	IP	H	R	ER	BB	SO
1990 —St. Louis (N.L.)	1	0	0	...	6.75	0	1⅓	1	2	1	2	0

JONES, TODD
P, ASTROS

PERSONAL: Born April 24, 1968, at Marietta, Ga. . . . 6-3/200. . . . Throws right, bats right. . . . Full name: Todd Barton Jones.
HIGH SCHOOL: Osborne (Ga.).
COLLEGE: Jacksonville State (Ala.).
TRANSACTIONS/CAREER NOTES: Selected by New York Mets organization in 41st round of free-agent draft (June 2, 1986). . . . Selected by Houston Astros organization in first round (27th pick overall) of free-agent draft (June 5, 1989).
STATISTICAL NOTES: Tied for Florida State League lead in games started by pitcher with 27 in 1990.

Year	Team (League)	G	W	L	Pct.	ERA	Sv.	IP	H	R	ER	BB	SO
1989 —Auburn (New York-Penn)	11	2	3	.400	5.44	0	49⅔	47	39	30	42	71
1990 —Osceola (Florida State)	27	12	10	.545	3.51	0	151⅓	124	81	59	109	106
1991 —Osceola (Florida State)	14	4	4	.500	4.35	0	72⅓	69	38	35	35	51
—Jackson (Texas)	10	4	3	.571	4.88	0	55⅓	51	37	30	39	37

JONES, TRACY
OF

PERSONAL: Born March 31, 1961, at Inglewood, Calif. . . . 6-3/220. . . . Throws right, bats right. . . . Full name: Tracy Donald Jones. . . . Brother of Terry Jones, minor league infielder (1984-88).
HIGH SCHOOL: Lawndale (Hawthorne, Calif.).
COLLEGE: Loyola Marymount.
TRANSACTIONS/CAREER NOTES: Selected by New York Mets organization in fourth round of free-agent draft (June 7, 1982). . . . Selected by Cincinnati Reds organization in secondary phase of free-agent draft (January 11, 1983). . . . On disabled list (July 18-September 18, 1984; and May 23-June 15 and July 10-September 1, 1986). . . . On Cincinnati disabled list (May 5-22 and May 26-June 20, 1988); included rehabilitation disability assignment to Nashville (June 18 and June 19, 1988). . . . Traded by Reds with P Pat Pacillo to Montreal Expos for C Jeff Reed, OF Herm Winningham and P Randy St. Claire (July 13, 1988). . . . Traded by Expos to San Francisco Giants for OF Mike Aldrete (December 8, 1988). . . . Traded by Giants to Detroit Tigers for OF Pat Sheridan (June 18, 1989). . . . On Detroit disabled list (August 17, 1989-remainder of season). . . . Traded by Tigers to Seattle Mariners for OF Darnell Coles (June 18, 1990). . . . On disabled list (August 9, 1990-remainder of season and June 18-July 13, 1991). . . . Granted free agency (November 7, 1991).

Year	Team (League)	Pos.	G	AB	R	H	2B	3B	HR	RBI	Avg.	SB	PO	A	E	Avg.
1983 —Tampa (Florida State)	0-3-1-S	53	118	27	32	5	3	1	15	.271	3	54	12	11	.857
—Eugene (Northwest)	2-3-0-S	55	203	42	54	12	0	1	26	.266	14	83	70	12	.927
1984 —Tampa (Florida State)	OF	86	307	50	95	14	3	4	41	.309	24	150	6	0	1.000
1985 —Vermont (Eastern)	OF	75	284	40	90	12	3	4	31	.317	26	117	4	1	.992
—Denver (Am. Assoc.)	OF	51	205	43	69	12	0	10	31	.337	20	93	2	0	1.000
1986 —Cincinnati (N.L.)	OF-1B	46	86	16	30	3	0	2	10	.349	7	46	1	0	1.000
1987 —Cincinnati (N.L.)	OF	117	359	53	104	17	3	10	44	.290	31	189	2	2	.990
1988 —Cin.-Montreal (N.L.)■	OF	90	224	29	66	6	1	3	24	.295	18	96	2	2	.980
—Nashville (Am. Assoc.)	OF	2	6	2	3	1	0	0	1	.500	0	2	1	0	1.000
1989 —San Francisco (N.L.)■	OF	40	97	5	18	4	0	0	12	.186	2	35	0	0	1.000
—Detroit (A.L.)■	OF	46	158	17	41	10	0	3	26	.259	1	72	0	1	.986
1990 —Detroit-Seattle (A.L.)■	OF	75	204	23	53	8	1	6	24	.260	1	68	3	2	.973
1991 —Seattle (A.L.)	OF	79	175	30	44	8	1	3	24	.251	2	49	0	0	1.000
American League totals (3 years)		200	537	70	138	26	2	12	74	.257	4	189	3	3	.985
National League totals (4 years)		293	766	103	218	30	4	15	90	.285	58	366	5	4	.989
Major league totals (6 years)		493	1303	173	356	56	6	27	164	.273	62	555	8	7	.988

JORDAN, BRIAN
OF, CARDINALS

PERSONAL: Born March 26, 1967, at Baltimore. . . . 6-1/205. . . . Throws right, bats right. . . . Full name: Brian O'Neil Jordan.
HIGH SCHOOL: Milford (Baltimore).
COLLEGE: Richmond.

TRANSACTIONS/CAREER NOTES: Selected by Cleveland Indians organization in 20th round of free-agent draft (June 3, 1985).... Selected by St. Louis Cardinals organization in first round (30th pick overall) of free-agent draft (June 1, 1988).... On temporary inactive list (July 3, 1991-remainder of season).

Year	Team (League)	Pos.	G	AB	R	H	2B	3B	HR	RBI	Avg.	SB	PO	A	E	Avg.
1988 —Hamilton (N.Y.-Penn)		OF	19	71	12	22	3	1	4	12	.310	3	32	1	1	.971
1989 —St. Petersburg (Fla. St.)		OF	11	43	7	15	4	1	2	11	.349	0	22	2	0	1.000
1990 —Arkansas (Texas)		OF	16	50	4	8	1	0	0	0	.160	0	28	0	2	.933
—St. Petersburg (Fla. St.)		OF	9	30	3	5	0	1	0	1	.167	0	23	0	0	1.000
1991 —Louisville (Am. Assoc.)		OF	61	212	35	56	11	4	4	24	.264	10	144	3	2	.987

RECORD AS FOOTBALL PLAYER

TRANSACTIONS/CAREER NOTES: Selected by Buffalo Bills in seventh round (173rd pick overall) of 1989 NFL draft.... Signed by Bills (July 17, 1989).... Released by Bills (September 4, 1989).... Awarded on waivers to Atlanta Falcons (September 5, 1989).... On injured reserve with ankle injury (September 9-October 22, 1989).... Transferred to developmental squad (October 23-December 2, 1989).

PRO STATISTICS: 1989—Recovered two fumbles. 1990—Recovered one fumble. 1991—Credited with a safety and recovered one fumble.

Year	Team	G	No.	Yds.	Avg.	TD	No.	Yds.	Avg.	TD	No.	Yds.	Avg.	TD	TD	Pts.	F.
			— INTERCEPTIONS—				— PUNT RETURNS —				– KICKOFF RETURNS–				— TOTAL—		
1989— Atlanta NFL		4	0	0	. . .	0	4	34	8.5	0	3	27	9.0	0	0	0	1
1990— Atlanta NFL		16	3	14	4.7	0	2	19	9.5	0	0	0	. . .	0	0	0	0
1991— Atlanta NFL		16	2	3	1.5	0	14	116	8.3	0	5	100	20.0	0	0	2	0
Pro totals (3 years)		36	5	17	3.4	0	20	169	8.5	0	8	127	15.6	0	0	2	1

JORDAN, RICKY
1B, PHILLIES

PERSONAL: Born May 26, 1965, at Richmond, Calif.... 6-3/209.... Throws right, bats right. ... Full name: Paul Scott Jordan.
HIGH SCHOOL: Grant (Sacramento, Calif.).
TRANSACTIONS/CAREER NOTES: Selected by Philadelphia Phillies organization in first round (22nd pick overall) of free-agent draft (June 6, 1983).... On Philadelphia disabled list (June 13-July 4, 1990); included rehabilitation disability assignment to Scranton/Wilkes-Barre (June 29-July 4, 1990).
STATISTICAL NOTES: Led Eastern League first basemen with 17 errors and 100 double plays in 1986.... Tied for Eastern League lead with nine sacrifice flies in 1987.... Led Eastern League first basemen with 1,255 total chances and 110 double plays in 1987.... Hit home run in first major league at-bat (July 17, 1988).

Year	Team (League)	Pos.	G	AB	R	H	2B	3B	HR	RBI	Avg.	SB	PO	A	E	Avg.
1983 —Helena (Pioneer)		1B	60	247	32	73	7	1	5	33	.296	3	486	35	7	.987
1984 —Spartanburg (S. Atl.)		1B	128	490	72	143	23	4	10	76	.292	8	1129	69	14	.988
1985 —Clearwater (Florida St.)		1B	★139	528	60	146	22	8	7	62	.277	26	1252	86	★20	.985
1986 —Reading (Eastern)		1B-OF	133	478	44	131	19	3	2	60	.274	17	1052	87	†17	.985
1987 —Reading (Eastern)		1B	132	475	78	151	28	3	16	95	.318	15	★1193	54	8	.994
1988 —Maine (International)		1B	87	338	42	104	23	1	7	36	.308	10	809	41	4	.995
—Philadelphia (N.L.)		1B	69	273	41	84	15	1	11	43	.308	1	579	35	5	.992
1989 —Philadelphia (N.L.)		1B	144	523	63	149	22	3	12	75	.285	4	1271	61	9	.993
1990 —Philadelphia (N.L.)		1B	92	324	32	78	21	0	5	44	.241	2	743	37	4	.995
—Scranton/W.B. (Int'l)		1B	27	104	8	29	1	0	2	11	.279	0	225	8	1	.996
1991 —Philadelphia (N.L.)		1B	101	301	38	82	21	3	9	49	.272	0	626	37	9	.987
Major league totals (4 years)			406	1421	174	393	79	7	37	211	.277	7	3219	170	27	.992

JORGENSEN, TERRY
3B, TWINS

PERSONAL: Born September 2, 1966, at Kewaunee, Wis.... 6-4/213.... Throws right, bats right.... Full name: Terry Allen Jorgensen.
HIGH SCHOOL: Luxemburg-Casco (Luxemburg, Wis.).
COLLEGE: Wisconsin-Oshkosh.
TRANSACTIONS/CAREER NOTES: Selected by Minnesota Twins organization in second round of free-agent draft (June 2, 1987).
STATISTICAL NOTES: Led Southern League third basemen with 406 total chances and tied for lead with 21 double plays in 1989. ... Tied for Southern League lead with nine sacrifice flies in 1989.... Led Pacific Coast League third basemen with 102 putouts and 34 errors in 1990.... Led Pacific Coast League third basemen with 398 total chances and 32 double plays in 1991.

Year	Team (League)	Pos.	G	AB	R	H	2B	3B	HR	RBI	Avg.	SB	PO	A	E	Avg.
1987 —Kenosha (Midwest)		OF	67	254	37	80	17	0	7	33	.315	1	54	4	5	.921
1988 —Orlando (Southern)		3B	135	472	53	116	27	4	3	43	.246	4	101	216	★39	.890
1989 —Orlando (Southern)		3B	135	514	84	135	27	5	13	101	.263	1	★99	★274	33	.919
—Minnesota (A.L.)		3B	10	23	1	4	1	0	0	2	.174	0	4	19	1	.958
1990 —Portland (Pacific Coast) ...	3B-SS-2B	123	440	43	114	28	3	10	50	.259	0	†104	206	†35	.899
1991 —Portland (Pacific Coast) ...		3B	126	456	74	136	29	0	11	59	.298	1	★91	★277	★30	.925
Major league totals (1 year)			10	23	1	4	1	0	0	2	.174	0	4	19	1	.958

JOSE, FELIX
OF, CARDINALS

PERSONAL: Born May 8, 1965, at Santo Domingo, Dominican Republic.... 6-1/221.... Throws right, bats both.... Full name: Domingo Felix Jose.
HIGH SCHOOL: Eldo Foreda Reyez de Munoz (Santo Domingo, Dominican Republic).
TRANSACTIONS/CAREER NOTES: Signed as free agent by Oakland Athletics organization (January 3, 1984).... Traded by A's with 3B Stan Royer and P Daryl Green to St. Louis Cardinals for OF Willie McGee (August 29, 1990).

Year	Team (League)	Pos.	G	AB	R	H	2B	3B	HR	RBI	Avg.	SB	PO	A	E	Avg.
1984	Idaho Falls (Pioneer)	OF	45	152	16	33	6	0	1	18	.217	5	48	6	1	.982
1985	Madison (Midwest)	OF	117	409	46	89	13	3	3	33	.218	6	187	9	12	.942
1986	Modesto (California)	OF	127	516	77	147	22	8	14	77	.285	14	215	12	14	.942
1987	Huntsville (Southern)	OF	91	296	29	67	11	1	5	42	.226	9	131	7	8	.945
1988	Tacoma (Pacific Coast)	OF	134	508	72	161	29	5	12	83	.317	16	253	11	8	.971
	Oakland (A.L.)	OF	8	6	2	2	1	0	0	1	.333	1	8	0	0	1.000
1989	Tacoma (Pacific Coast)	OF	104	387	59	111	26	0	14	63	.287	11	186	7	*10	.951
	Oakland (A.L.)	OF	20	57	3	11	2	0	0	5	.193	0	35	2	1	.974
1990	Oakland (A.L.)	OF	101	341	42	90	12	0	8	39	.264	8	212	5	5	.977
	St. Louis (N.L.)■	OF	25	85	12	23	4	1	3	13	.271	4	42	0	0	1.000
1991	St. Louis (N.L.)	OF	154	568	69	173	40	6	8	77	.305	20	268	•15	3	.990
American League totals (3 years)			129	404	47	103	15	0	8	45	.255	9	255	7	6	.978
National League totals (2 years)			179	653	81	196	44	7	11	90	.300	24	310	15	3	.991
Major league totals (4 years)			308	1057	128	299	59	7	19	135	.283	33	565	22	9	.985

ALL-STAR GAME RECORD

Year	League	Pos.	AB	R	H	2B	3B	HR	RBI	Avg.	SB	PO	A	E	Avg.
1991	National	OF	2	0	1	0	0	0	0	.500	0	1	0	0	1.000

JOYNER, WALLY
1B, ROYALS

PERSONAL: Born June 16, 1962, at Atlanta.... 6-2/203.... Throws left, bats left.... Full name: Wallace Keith Joyner.
HIGH SCHOOL: Redan (Stone Mountain, Ga.).
COLLEGE: Brigham Young.
TRANSACTIONS/CAREER NOTES: Selected by California Angels organization in third round of free-agent draft (June 6, 1983).... On disabled list (July 12, 1990-remainder of season).... Granted free agency (October 28, 1991).... Signed by Kansas City Royals (December 9, 1991).
RECORDS/HONORS: Shares major league record for most home runs in month of October—4 (1987).
STATISTICAL NOTES: Tied for Eastern League lead with eight intentional bases on balls received in 1984.... Led Pacific Coast League first basemen with 1,229 total chances and 121 double plays in 1985.... Led A.L. with 12 sacrifice flies in 1986.... Hit three home runs in a game (October 3, 1987).... Led A.L. first basemen with 1,520 total chances and 148 double plays in 1988. ... Led A.L. first basemen with 1,441 total chances in 1991.

Year	Team (League)	Pos.	G	AB	R	H	2B	3B	HR	RBI	Avg.	SB	PO	A	E	Avg.
1983	Peoria (Midwest)	1B	54	192	25	63	16	2	3	33	.328	1	480	45	6	.989
1984	Waterbury (Eastern)	1B-OF	134	467	81	148	24	7	12	72	.317	0	906	86	9	.991
1985	Edmonton (Pac. Coast)	1B	126	477	68	135	29	5	12	73	.283	2	*1107	*107	•15	.988
1986	California (A.L.)	1B	154	593	82	172	27	3	22	100	.290	5	1222	139	15	.989
1987	California (A.L.)	1B	149	564	100	161	33	1	34	117	.285	8	1276	92	10	.993
1988	California (A.L.)	1B	158	597	81	176	31	2	13	85	.295	8	*1369	*143	8	.995
1989	California (A.L.)	1B	159	593	78	167	30	2	16	79	.282	3	*1487	99	4	*.997
1990	California (A.L.)	1B	83	310	35	83	15	0	8	41	.268	2	727	62	4	.995
1991	California (A.L.)	1B	143	551	79	166	34	3	21	96	.301	2	*1335	98	8	.994
Major league totals (6 years)			846	3208	455	925	170	11	114	518	.288	28	7416	633	49	.994

JUDEN, JEFF
P, ASTROS

PERSONAL: Born January 19, 1971, at Salem, Mass.... 6-7/245.... Throws right, bats right.... Full name: Jeffrey Daniel Juden.
HIGH SCHOOL: Salem (Mass.).
TRANSACTIONS/CAREER NOTES: Selected by Houston Astros organization in first round (12th pick overall) of free-agent draft (June 5, 1989).

Year	Team (League)	G	W	L	Pct.	ERA	Sv.	IP	H	R	ER	BB	SO
1989	Sarasota (Florida State)	9	1	4	.200	3.40	0	39⅔	33	21	15	17	49
1990	Osceola (Florida State)	15	10	1	*.909	2.27	0	91	72	37	23	42	85
	Columbus (Southern)	11	1	3	.250	5.37	0	52	55	36	31	42	40
1991	Jackson (Texas)	16	6	3	.667	3.10	0	95⅔	84	43	33	44	75
	Tucson (Pacific Coast)	10	3	2	.600	3.18	0	56⅔	56	28	20	25	51
	Houston (N.L.)	4	0	2	.000	6.00	0	18	19	14	12	7	11
Major league totals (1 year)		4	0	2	.000	6.00	0	18	19	14	12	7	11

JUSTICE, DAVID
OF, BRAVES

PERSONAL: Born April 14, 1966, at Cincinnati.... 6-3/200.... Throws left, bats left.... Full name: David Christopher Justice.
HIGH SCHOOL: Covington Latin (Covington, Ky.).
COLLEGE: Thomas More College (Ky.).
TRANSACTIONS/CAREER NOTES: Selected by Atlanta Braves organization in fourth round of free-agent draft (June 3, 1985).... On Atlanta disabled list (June 27-August 20, 1991); included rehabilitation disability assignment to Macon (August 16-20, 1991).
RECORDS/HONORS: Named N.L. Rookie Player of the Year by THE SPORTING NEWS (1990).... Named N.L. Rookie of the Year

by Baseball Writers' Association of America (1990).
STATISTICAL NOTES: Tied for Appalachian League lead with five sacrifice flies in 1985.

Year	Team (League)	Pos.	G	AB	R	H	2B	3B	HR	RBI	Avg.	SB	PO	A	E	Avg.
							BATTING							FIELDING		
1985—Pulaski (Appalachian)		OF	66	204	39	50	8	0	•10	46	.245	0	86	2	4	.957
1986—Sumter (South Atlantic)....		OF	61	220	48	66	16	0	10	61	.300	10	124	7	4	.970
—Durham (Carolina)		OF-1B	67	229	47	64	9	1	12	44	.279	2	163	5	1	.994
1987—Greenville (Southern)		OF	93	348	38	79	12	4	6	40	.227	3	199	4	8	.962
1988—Richmond (Int'l)		OF	70	227	27	46	9	1	8	28	.203	4	136	5	4	.972
—Greenville (Southern)		OF	58	198	34	55	13	1	9	37	.278	6	100	3	5	.954
1989—Richmond (Int'l)		OF-1B	115	391	47	102	24	3	12	58	.261	12	220	15	6	.975
—Atlanta (N.L.)		OF	16	51	7	12	3	0	1	3	.235	2	24	0	0	1.000
1990—Richmond (Int'l)		OF-1B	12	45	7	16	5	1	2	7	.356	0	23	4	2	.931
—Atlanta (N.L.)		1B-OF	127	439	76	124	23	2	28	78	.282	11	604	42	14	.979
1991—Atlanta (N.L.)		OF	109	396	67	109	25	1	21	87	.275	8	204	9	7	.968
—Macon (South Atlantic)		OF	3	10	2	2	0	0	2	5	.200	0	1	0	0	1.000
Major league totals (3 years)			252	886	150	245	51	3	50	168	.277	21	832	51	21	.977

CHAMPIONSHIP SERIES RECORD

Year	Team (League)	Pos.	G	AB	R	H	2B	3B	HR	RBI	Avg.	SB	PO	A	E	Avg.
							BATTING							FIELDING		
1991—Atlanta (N.L.)		OF	7	25	4	5	1	0	1	2	.200	0	17	0	1	.944

WORLD SERIES RECORD

Year	Team (League)	Pos.	G	AB	R	H	2B	3B	HR	RBI	Avg.	SB	PO	A	E	Avg.
							BATTING							FIELDING		
1991—Atlanta (N.L.)		OF	7	27	5	7	0	0	2	6	.259	2	21	1	1	.957

KAISER, JEFF
P

PERSONAL: Born July 24, 1960, at Wyandotte, Mich. ... 6-3/195. ... Throws left, bats right. ... Full name: Jeffrey Patrick Kaiser.
HIGH SCHOOL: Aquinas (Southgate, Mich.).
COLLEGE: Western Michigan (bachelor of arts degree in business administration).
TRANSACTIONS/CAREER NOTES: Selected by Toronto Blue Jays organization in seventh round of free-agent draft (June 8, 1981). ... Selected by Oakland Athletics organization in 10th round of free-agent draft (June 7, 1982). ... On Tacoma disabled list (July 20-August 3, 1984; June 21-July 7, 1985; and May 4-14, 1986). ... Traded by A's organization to Cleveland Indians for P Curt Wardle (February 23, 1987). ... On Cleveland disabled list (August 9-31, 1987). ... Granted free agency (April 5, 1990). ... Re-signed by Indians organization (April 11, 1990). ... On Cleveland disabled list (July 8-September 4, 1990); included rehabilitation disability assignment to Colorado Springs (August 8-September 4, 1990). ... Granted free agency (October 4, 1990). ... Signed by Milwaukee Brewers organization (January 1, 1991). ... Released by Denver, Brewers organization (May 9, 1991). ... Signed by Toledo, Detroit Tigers organization (June 11, 1991). ... Granted free agency (December 20, 1991).

Year	Team (League)	G	W	L	Pct.	ERA	Sv.	IP	H	R	ER	BB	SO
1982—Medford (Northwest)	15	8	1	.889	5.31	0	78	91	56	46	57	69
1983—Modesto (California)	25	12	9	.571	3.83	0	164⅔	160	84	70	80	102
1984—Albany (Eastern)	7	5	1	.833	1.89	0	47⅔	36	11	10	15	20
—Tacoma (Pacific Coast)	14	4	7	.364	4.58	1	74⅔	81	52	38	28	38
1985—Oakland (A.L.)	15	0	0	...	14.58	0	16⅔	25	32	27	20	10
—Tacoma (Pacific Coast)	27	4	2	.667	1.75	5	46⅓	33	10	9	18	36
1986—Tacoma (Pacific Coast)	34	4	4	.500	4.31	2	110⅔	123	70	53	52	63
1987—Buffalo (American Assoc.)■	22	5	3	.625	5.17	1	71⅓	87	52	41	32	53
—Cleveland (A.L.)	2	0	0	...	16.20	0	3⅓	4	6	6	3	2
1988—Colorado Springs (Pac. Coast) ..	36	3	2	.600	3.74	6	53	56	23	22	19	47
—Cleveland (A.L.)	3	0	0	...	0.00	0	2⅔	2	0	0	1	0
1989—Colorado Springs (Pac. Coast) ..	31	3	6	.333	4.37	3	45⅓	64	29	22	18	46
—Cleveland (A.L.)	6	0	1	.000	7.36	0	3⅔	5	5	3	5	4
1990—Colorado Springs (Pac. Coast) ..	25	2	2	.500	2.93	3	43	36	16	14	22	46
—Cleveland (A.L.)	5	0	0	...	3.55	0	12⅔	16	5	5	7	9
1991—Denver (American Assoc.)■	8	0	1	.000	3.86	0	18⅔	16	9	8	13	12
—Toledo (International)■	16	3	0	1.000	2.08	1	34⅔	35	9	8	11	28
—Detroit (A.L.)	10	0	1	.000	9.00	2	5	6	5	5	5	4
Major league totals (6 years)	41	0	2	.000	9.41	2	44	58	53	46	41	29

KAMIENIECKI, SCOTT
P, YANKEES

PERSONAL: Born April 19, 1964, at Mt. Clemens, Mich. ... 6-0/197. ... Throws right, bats right. ... Full name: Scott Andrew Kamieniecki. ... Name pronounced KAM-ah-NIK-ee.
HIGH SCHOOL: Redford St. Mary's (Detroit).
COLLEGE: Michigan (bachelor of arts degree in physical education).
TRANSACTIONS/CAREER NOTES: Selected by Detroit Tigers organization in second round of free-agent draft (June 7, 1982). ... Selected by Milwaukee Brewers organization in 23 round of free-agent draft (June 3, 1985). ... Selected by New York Yankees organization in 14th round of free-agent draft (June 2, 1986). ... On New York disabled list (August 3, 1991-remainder of season).

Year	Team (League)	G	W	L	Pct.	ERA	Sv.	IP	H	R	ER	BB	SO
1987	—Albany (Eastern)	10	1	3	.250	5.35	0	37	41	25	22	33	19
	—Prince William (Carolina)	19	9	5	.643	4.17	0	112⅓	91	61	52	78	84
1988	—Prince William (Carolina)	15	6	7	.462	4.40	0	100⅓	115	62	49	50	72
	—Fort Lauderdale (Florida St.)	12	3	6	.333	3.62	0	77	71	36	31	40	51
1989	—Albany (Eastern)	24	10	9	.526	3.70	1	151	142	67	62	57	★140
1990	—Albany (Eastern)	22	10	9	.526	3.20	0	132	113	55	47	61	99
1991	—Columbus (International)	11	6	3	.667	2.36	0	76⅓	61	25	20	20	58
	—New York (A.L.)	9	4	4	.500	3.90	0	55⅓	54	24	24	22	34
Major league totals (1 year)		9	4	4	.500	3.90	0	55⅓	54	24	24	22	34

KARCHNER, MATT
P, EXPOS

PERSONAL: Born June 28, 1967, at Berwick, Pa. . . . 6-4/215. . . . Throws right, bats right. . . . Full name: Mathew Dean Karchner.
HIGH SCHOOL: Berwick (Pa.).
COLLEGE: Bloomsburg (Pa.).
TRANSACTIONS/CAREER NOTES: Selected by Kansas City Royals organization in eighth round of free-agent draft (June 5, 1989). . . . On disabled list (August 1-8, 1991). . . . Drafted by Montreal Expos (December 9, 1991).

Year	Team (League)	G	W	L	Pct.	ERA	Sv.	IP	H	R	ER	BB	SO
1989	—Eugene (Northwest)	8	1	1	.500	3.90	0	30	30	19	13	8	25
1990	—Appleton (Midwest)	27	2	7	.222	4.82	0	71	70	42	38	31	58
1991	—Baseball City (Florida State)	38	6	3	.667	1.97	5	73	49	28	16	25	65

KARKOVICE, RON
C, WHITE SOX

PERSONAL: Born August 8, 1963, at Union, N.J. . . . 6-1/215. . . . Throws right, bats right. . . . Full name: Ronald Joseph Karkovice. . . . Name pronounced CAR-ko-VICE.
HIGH SCHOOL: Boone (Orlando, Fla.).
TRANSACTIONS/CAREER NOTES: Selected by Chicago White Sox organization in first round (14th pick overall) of free-agent draft (June 7, 1982). . . . On disabled list (May 20-July 3, 1991).
STATISTICAL NOTES: Led Gulf Coast League catchers with 394 total chances and tied for lead with five double plays in 1982. . . . Led Gulf Coast League batters with 73 strikeouts in 1982. . . . Led Midwest League catchers with .996 fielding percentage in 1983. . . . Led Eastern League catchers with 13 double plays in 1985.

Year	Team (League)	Pos.	G	AB	R	H	2B	3B	HR	RBI	Avg.	SB	PO	A	E	Avg.
1982	—Sara. White Sox (GCL)	C	60	214	34	56	6	0	7	32	.262	5	★331	★51	12	.970
1983	—Appleton (Midwest)	C-OF	97	326	54	78	17	3	13	48	.239	10	682	91	4	†.995
1984	—Glens Falls (Eastern)	C	88	260	37	56	9	1	13	39	.215	3	442	★68	11	.979
	—Denver (Am. Assoc.)	C	31	86	7	19	1	0	2	10	.221	1	149	28	3	.983
1985	—Glens Falls (Eastern)	C	99	324	37	70	9	3	11	37	.216	6	573	★103	★14	.980
1986	—Birmingham (Southern)	C	97	319	63	90	13	1	20	53	.282	2	463	72	10	.982
	—Chicago (A.L.)	C	37	97	13	24	7	0	4	13	.247	1	227	19	1	.996
1987	—Chicago (A.L.)	C	39	85	7	6	0	0	2	7	.071	3	147	20	3	.982
	—Hawaii (Pacific Coast)	C-OF	34	104	15	19	3	0	4	11	.183	3	108	13	3	.976
1988	—Vancouver (Pac. Coast)	C	39	116	12	29	10	0	2	13	.250	2	202	16	3	.986
	—Chicago (A.L.)	C	46	115	10	20	4	0	3	9	.174	1	190	24	1	.995
1989	—Chicago (A.L.)	C	71	182	21	48	9	2	3	24	.264	0	299	47	5	.986
1990	—Chicago (A.L.)	C	68	183	30	45	10	0	6	20	.246	2	296	31	2	.994
1991	—Chicago (A.L.)	C-OF	75	167	25	41	13	0	5	22	.246	0	309	28	4	.988
Major league totals (6 years)			336	829	106	184	43	2	23	95	.222	10	1468	169	16	.990

KARROS, ERIC
1B, DODGERS

PERSONAL: Born November 4, 1967, at Hackensack, N.J. . . . 6-4/205. . . . Throws right, bats right. . . . Full name: Eric Peter Karros.
HIGH SCHOOL: Patrick Henry (San Diego).
COLLEGE: UCLA.
TRANSACTIONS/CAREER NOTES: Selected by Los Angeles Dodgers organization in sixth round of free-agent draft (June 1, 1988).
STATISTICAL NOTES: Led Pioneer League first basemen with 14 errors in 1988. . . . Led California League first basemen with 1,232 putouts, 110 assists and 1,358 total chances in 1989. . . . Led Texas League with 282 total bases in 1990. . . . Led Texas League first basemen with 1,337 total chances and 129 double plays in 1990. . . . Led Pacific Coast League with 269 total bases in 1991. . . . Tied for Pacific Coast League lead with eight intentional bases on balls received in 1991. . . . Led Pacific Coast League first basemen with 1,095 putouts, 109 assists and 1,215 total chances in 1991.

Year	Team (League)	Pos.	G	AB	R	H	2B	3B	HR	RBI	Avg.	SB	PO	A	E	Avg.
1988	—Great Falls (Pioneer)	1B-3B	66	268	68	98	12	1	12	55	.366	8	516	31	†19	.966
1989	—Bakersfield (California)	1B-3B	★142	545	86	★165	★40	1	15	86	.303	18	†1238	†113	19	.986
1990	—San Antonio (Texas)	1B	•131	509	91	★179	★45	2	18	78	★.352	8	★1223	★106	8	★.994
1991	—Albuquerque (PCL)	1B-3B	132	488	88	154	33	8	22	101	.316	3	†1095	†109	11	.991
	—Los Angeles (N.L.)	1B	14	14	0	1	1	0	0	1	.071	0	33	2	0	1.000
Major league totals (1 year)			14	14	0	1	1	0	0	1	.071	0	33	2	0	1.000

KELLY, PAT
2B/3B, YANKEES

PERSONAL: Born October 14, 1967, at Philadelphia. . . . 6-0/180. . . . Throws right, bats right. . . . Full name: Patrick Franklin Kelly.
HIGH SCHOOL: Catashuqua (Pa.).
COLLEGE: West Chester State (Pa.).

TRANSACTIONS/CAREER NOTES: Selected by New York Yankees organization in ninth round of free-agent draft (June 1, 1988).
STATISTICAL NOTES: Led Carolina League second basemen with 76 double plays and tied for lead with 641 total chances in 1989.
. . . Led Eastern League second basemen with 667 total chances and 97 double plays in 1990.

Year Team (League)	Pos.	G	AB	R	H	2B	3B	HR	RBI	Avg.	SB	PO	A	E	Avg.
1988—Oneonta (N.Y.-Penn)	2B-SS	71	280	49	92	11	6	2	34	.329	25	124	207	16	.954
1989—Prince William (Caro.).......	2B	124	436	61	116	21	*7	3	45	.266	31	244	*372	25	.961
1990—Albany (Eastern).............	2B	126	418	67	113	19	6	8	44	.270	31	*266	*381	*20	.970
1991—Columbus (Int'l)	2B	31	116	27	39	9	2	3	19	.336	8	53	97	4	.974
—New York (A.L.)	3B-2B	96	298	35	72	12	4	3	23	.242	12	78	204	18	.940
Major league totals (1 year)		96	298	35	72	12	4	3	23	.242	12	78	204	18	.940

KELLY, ROBERTO
OF, YANKEES

PERSONAL: Born October 1, 1964, at Panama City, Panama. . . . 6-2/192. . . . Throws right, bats right. . . . Full name: Roberto Conrado Kelly.
HIGH SCHOOL: Panama City (Panama).
COLLEGE: Jose Dolores Moscote College (Panama).
TRANSACTIONS/CAREER NOTES: Signed as free agent by New York Yankees organization (February 21, 1982). . . . On disabled list (July 10-August 23, 1986). . . . On New York disabled list (June 29-September 1, 1988; May 26-June 12, 1989; and July 6-August 13, 1991).
RECORDS/HONORS: Shares major league single-season record for fewest double plays by outfielder (150 or more games)—0 (1990).
STATISTICAL NOTES: Led International League outfielders with 345 total chances in 1987. . . . Led A.L. outfielders with 430 total chances in 1990.
MISCELLANEOUS: Batted as switch-hitter (1985).

Year Team (League)	Pos.	G	AB	R	H	2B	3B	HR	RBI	Avg.	SB	PO	A	E	Avg.
1982—Braden. Yankeees (GCL) ...	SS-OF	31	86	13	17	1	1	1	18	.198	3	47	79	19	.869
1983—Oneonta (N.Y.-Penn)	OF-3B	48	167	17	36	1	2	2	17	.216	12	70	3	5	.936
—Greensboro (S. Atlantic) ...	OF-SS	20	49	6	13	0	0	0	3	.265	3	30	2	0	1.000
1984—Greensboro (S. Atlantic) ...	OF-1B	111	361	68	86	13	2	1	26	.238	42	228	5	4	.983
1985—Fort Lauderdale (FSL)	OF	114	417	86	103	4	*13	3	38	.247	49	187	1	1	.995
1986—Albany (Eastern)..............	OF	86	299	42	87	11	4	2	43	.291	10	206	8	7	.968
1987—Columbus (Int'l)	OF	118	471	77	131	19	8	13	62	.278	*51	*331	4	10	.971
—New York (A.L.)	OF	23	52	12	14	3	0	1	7	.269	9	42	0	2	.955
1988—New York (A.L.)	OF	38	77	9	19	4	1	1	7	.247	5	70	1	1	.986
—Columbus (Int'l)	OF	30	120	25	40	8	1	3	16	.333	11	51	1	0	1.000
1989—New York (A.L.)	OF	137	441	65	133	18	3	9	48	.302	35	353	9	6	.984
1990—New York (A.L.)	OF	*162	641	85	183	32	4	15	61	.285	42	420	5	5	.988
1991—New York (A.L.)	OF	126	486	68	130	22	2	20	69	.267	32	268	8	8	.986
Major league totals (5 years)		486	1697	239	479	79	10	46	192	.282	123	1153	23	18	.985

KENNEDY, TERRY
C

PERSONAL: Born June 4, 1956, at Euclid, O. . . . 6-4/220. . . . Throws right, bats left. . . . Full name: Terrence Edward Kennedy. . . . Son of Bob Kennedy, major league outfielder-third baseman for five teams (1939-42 and 1946-57); manager, Chicago Cubs (1963-65); coach, Atlanta Braves (1967); and manager, Oakland A's (1968).
COLLEGE: Florida State.
TRANSACTIONS/CAREER NOTES: Selected by St. Louis Cardinals organization in first round (sixth pick overall) of free-agent draft (June 7, 1977). . . . Traded by Cardinals with C Steve Swisher, P John Littlefield, P Al Olmsted, P Kim Seaman, P John Urrea and IF Mike Phillips to San Diego Padres for P Rollie Fingers, P Bob Shirley, C-1B Gene Tenace and a player to be named later (December 8, 1980); Cardinals organization acquired C Bob Geren to complete deal (December 10, 1980). . . . Traded by Padres with P Mark Williamson to Baltimore Orioles for P Storm Davis (October 30, 1986). . . . Traded by Orioles to San Francisco Giants for C Bob Melvin (January 24, 1989). . . . Granted free agency (November 13, 1989). . . . Re-signed by Giants (December 8, 1989). . . . Granted free agency (November 4, 1991).
RECORDS/HONORS: Shares N.L. single-season record for most doubles by catcher—40 (1982). . . . Named catcher on THE SPORTING NEWS college All-America team (1976-77). . . . Named College Player of the Year by THE SPORTING NEWS (1977). . . . Named catcher on THE SPORTING NEWS N.L. Silver Slugger team (1983).
STATISTICAL NOTES: Led N.L. catchers with 12 double plays in 1981 and tied for lead with 11 in 1982 and 12 in 1985.

Year Team (League)	Pos.	G	AB	R	H	2B	3B	HR	RBI	Avg.	SB	PO	A	E	Avg.
1977—Johnson City (Appal.)	C-1B	12	39	14	23	7	2	3	15	.590	0	66	3	1	.986
—St. Petersburg (Fla. St.)	C	45	166	22	41	8	0	4	22	.247	0	168	22	6	.969
1978—Arkansas (Texas)	C-OF	69	239	55	69	14	0	10	54	.289	1	365	30	7	.983
—Springfield (Midwest)	C-1B	64	230	35	76	13	0	10	46	.330	1	331	26	7	.981
—St. Louis (N.L.)	C	10	29	0	5	0	0	0	2	.172	0	46	4	1	.980
1979—Springfield (Midwest)	C	84	294	35	86	18	1	13	64	.293	0	434	38	13	.973
—St. Louis (N.L.)	C	33	109	11	31	7	0	2	17	.284	0	135	7	1	.993
1980—St. Louis (N.L.)	C-OF	84	248	28	63	12	3	4	34	.254	0	231	22	7	.973
1981—San Diego (N.L.)■	C	101	382	32	115	24	1	2	41	.301	0	465	63	*20	.964
1982—San Diego (N.L.)	C-1B	153	562	55	166	42	1	21	97	.295	1	777	66	9	.989
1983—San Diego (N.L.)	C-1B	149	549	47	156	27	2	17	98	.284	1	807	82	12	.987
1984—San Diego (N.L.)	C	148	530	54	127	16	1	14	57	.240	1	708	54	14	.982

Year	Team (League)	Pos.	G	AB	R	H	2B	3B	HR	RBI	Avg.	SB	PO	A	E	Avg.
1985—San Diego (N.L.)		C-1B	143	532	54	139	27	1	10	74	.261	0	662	68	10	.986
1986—San Diego (N.L.)		C	141	432	46	114	22	1	12	57	.264	0	692	70	8	.990
1987—Baltimore (A.L.)■...............		C	143	512	51	128	13	1	18	62	.250	1	750	*58	6	.993
1988—Baltimore (A.L.)		C	85	265	20	60	10	0	3	16	.226	0	332	23	2	.994
1989—San Francisco (N.L.)■........		C-1B	125	355	19	85	15	0	5	34	.239	1	519	47	8	.986
1990—San Francisco (N.L.)		C	107	303	25	84	22	0	2	26	.277	1	390	38	4	.991
1991—San Francisco (N.L.)		C-1B	69	171	12	40	7	1	3	13	.234	0	240	36	6	.979
American League totals (2 years)			228	777	71	188	23	1	21	78	.242	1	1082	81	8	.993
National League totals (12 years)			1263	4202	403	1125	221	11	92	550	.268	5	5672	557	100	.984
Major league totals (14 years)			1491	4979	474	1313	244	12	113	628	.264	6	6754	638	108	.986

CHAMPIONSHIP SERIES RECORD

Year	Team (League)	Pos.	G	AB	R	H	2B	3B	HR	RBI	Avg.	SB	PO	A	E	Avg.
1984—San Diego (N.L.)		C	5	18	2	4	0	0	0	1	.222	0	28	4	0	1.000
1989—San Francisco (N.L.)		C	5	16	0	3	1	0	0	0	.188	0	26	1	0	1.000
Championship Series totals (2 years)			10	34	2	7	1	0	0	1	.206	0	54	5	0	1.000

WORLD SERIES RECORD

Year	Team (League)	Pos.	G	AB	R	H	2B	3B	HR	RBI	Avg.	SB	PO	A	E	Avg.
1984—San Diego (N.L.)		C	5	19	2	4	1	0	1	3	.211	0	30	2	0	1.000
1989—San Francisco (N.L.)		C	4	12	1	2	0	0	0	2	.167	0	23	1	1	.960
World Series totals (2 years)			9	31	3	6	1	0	1	5	.194	0	53	3	1	.982

ALL-STAR GAME RECORD

Year	League	Pos.	AB	R	H	2B	3B	HR	RBI	Avg.	SB	PO	A	E	Avg.
1981—National		PH	1	0	0	0	0	0	0	.000	0	0	0	0	...
1983—National								Did not play							
1985—National		C	2	0	1	0	0	0	1	.500	0	0	0	1	.000
1987—American		C	2	0	0	0	0	0	0	.000	0	3	1	0	1.000
All-Star Game totals (3 years)			5	0	1	0	0	0	1	.200	0	3	1	1	.800

KENT, JEFF

2B, BLUE JAYS

PERSONAL: Born March 7, 1968, at Bellflower, Calif. . . . 6-1/185. . . . Throws right, bats right. . . . Full name: Jeffrey Franklin Kent.
HIGH SCHOOL: Edison (Huntington Beach, Calif.).
COLLEGE: California.
TRANSACTIONS/CAREER NOTES: Selected by Toronto Blue Jays organization in 20th round of free-agent draft (June 5, 1989).
STATISTICAL NOTES: Led Florida State League second basemen with 680 total chances and 83 double plays in 1990. . . . Led Southern League second basemen with 673 total chances and 96 double plays in 1991.

Year	Team (League)	Pos.	G	AB	R	H	2B	3B	HR	RBI	Avg.	SB	PO	A	E	Avg.
1989—St. Catharines (NYP).........		SS-3B	73	268	34	60	14	1	*13	37	.224	5	103	178	29	.906
1990—Dunedin (Florida State)		2B	132	447	72	124	32	2	16	60	.277	17	*261	*404	15	.978
1991—Knoxville (Southern)		2B	•139	445	68	114	*34	1	2	61	.256	25	249	*395	*29	.957

KEY, JIMMY

P, BLUE JAYS

PERSONAL: Born April 22, 1961, at Huntsville, Ala. . . . 6-1/185. . . . Throws left, bats right. . . . Full name: James Edward Key.
HIGH SCHOOL: Butler (Huntsville, Ala.).
COLLEGE: Clemson.
TRANSACTIONS/CAREER NOTES: Selected by Chicago White Sox organization in 10th round of free-agent draft (June 5, 1979). . . . Selected by Toronto Blue Jays organization in third round of free-agent draft (June 7, 1982). . . . On Toronto disabled list (April 15-June 29, 1988); included rehabilitation disability assignment to Dunedin (June 10-27, 1988). . . . On disabled list (August 4-19, 1989). . . . On Toronto disabled list (May 23-June 22, 1990); included rehabilitation disability assignment to Dunedin (June 7-18, 1990).
RECORDS/HONORS: Named A.L. Pitcher of the Year by THE SPORTING NEWS (1987). . . . Named lefthanded pitcher on THE SPORTING NEWS A.L. All-Star team (1987).
MISCELLANEOUS: Appeared in one game as a pinch-runner (1985).

Year	Team (League)	G	W	L	Pct.	ERA	Sv.	IP	H	R	ER	BB	SO
1982—Medicine Hat (Pioneer)		5	2	1	.667	2.30	0	31⅓	27	12	8	10	25
—Florence (South Atlantic)		9	5	2	.714	3.72	0	58	59	33	24	18	49
1983—Knoxville (Southern)		14	6	5	.545	2.85	0	101	86	35	32	40	57
—Syracuse (International)		16	4	8	.333	4.13	0	89⅓	87	58	41	33	71
1984—Toronto (A.L.)		63	4	5	.444	4.65	10	62	70	37	32	32	44
1985—Toronto (A.L.)		35	14	6	.700	3.00	0	212⅔	188	77	71	50	85
1986—Toronto (A.L.)		36	14	11	.560	3.57	0	232	222	98	92	74	141
1987—Toronto (A.L.)		36	17	8	.680	*2.76	0	261	210	93	80	66	161

Year Team (League)	G	W	L	Pct.	ERA	Sv.	IP	H	R	ER	BB	SO
1988 —Toronto (A.L.)..........................	21	12	5	.706	3.29	0	131⅓	127	55	48	30	65
—Dunedin (Florida State)	4	2	0	1.000	0.00	0	21⅓	15	2	0	1	11
1989 —Toronto (A.L.)..........................	33	13	14	.481	3.88	0	216	226	99	93	27	118
1990 —Toronto (A.L.)..........................	27	13	7	.650	4.25	0	154⅔	169	79	73	22	88
—Dunedin (Florida State)	3	2	0	1.000	2.50	0	18	21	7	5	3	14
1991 —Toronto (A.L.)..........................	33	16	12	.571	3.05	0	209⅓	207	84	71	44	125
Major league totals (8 years)	284	103	68	.602	3.41	10	1479	1419	622	560	345	827

CHAMPIONSHIP SERIES RECORD

Year Team (League)	G	W	L	Pct.	ERA	Sv.	IP	H	R	ER	BB	SO
1985 —Toronto (A.L.)..........................	2	0	1	.000	5.19	0	8⅔	15	5	5	2	5
1989 —Toronto (A.L.)..........................	1	1	0	1.000	4.50	0	6	7	3	3	2	2
1991 —Toronto (A.L.)..........................	1	0	0	. . .	3.00	0	6	5	2	2	1	1
Championship Series totals (3 years)	4	1	1	.500	4.35	0	20⅔	27	10	10	5	8

ALL-STAR GAME RECORD

Year League	W	L	Pct.	ERA	Sv.	IP	H	R	ER	BB	SO
1985 —American	0	0	. . .	0.00	0	⅓	0	0	0	0	0
1991 —American	1	0	1.000	0.00	0	1	1	0	0	0	1
All-Star totals (2 years)	1	0	1.000	0.00	0	1⅓	1	0	0	0	1

KIECKER, DANA
P, RED SOX

PERSONAL: Born February 25, 1961, at Sleepy Eye, Minn.... 6-3/195.... Throws right, bats right.... Full name: Dana Ervin Kiecker.... Name pronounced KICK-er.
HIGH SCHOOL: Fairfax (Minn.).
COLLEGE: St. Cloud State (Minn.).
TRANSACTIONS/CAREER NOTES: Selected by Boston Red Sox organization in eighth round of free-agent draft (June 6, 1983)....
On Boston disabled list (May 27-July 21, 1991); included rehabilitation disability assignment to Pawtucket (June 24-July 21, 1991).
STATISTICAL NOTES: Led Florida State League pitchers with 29 games started in 1985.... Tied for Eastern League lead with five balks in 1986.

Year Team (League)	G	W	L	Pct.	ERA	Sv.	IP	H	R	ER	BB	SO
1983 —Elmira (New York-Penn)	16	11	5	.688	2.74	0	★111⅔	92	50	34	44	78
1984 —Winston-Salem (Carolina)	29	6	11	.353	4.38	1	137⅔	142	86	67	55	82
1985 —Winter Haven (Florida State) ...	29	12	•12	.500	2.60	0	★193⅔	176	72	56	59	60
1986 —New Britain (Eastern)	24	7	12	.368	4.14	0	156⅓	★171	88	72	48	71
1987 —New Britain (Eastern)	39	7	10	.412	3.82	6	153	164	76	65	66	66
1988 —Pawtucket (International)	23	7	7	.500	3.67	0	132⅓	120	65	54	46	74
—New Britain (Eastern)	1	1	0	1.000	0.00	0	6	3	0	0	0	1
1989 —Pawtucket (International)	28	8	9	.471	3.67	0	147⅓	163	83	60	36	87
1990 —Boston (A.L.)	32	8	9	.471	3.97	0	152	145	74	67	54	93
1991 —Boston (A.L.)	18	2	3	.400	7.36	0	40⅓	56	34	33	23	21
—Pawtucket (International)	8	2	3	.400	3.79	0	38	42	24	16	19	23
Major league totals (2 years)	50	10	12	.455	4.68	0	192⅓	201	108	100	77	114

CHAMPIONSHIP SERIES RECORD

Year Team (League)	G	W	L	Pct.	ERA	Sv.	IP	H	R	ER	BB	SO
1990 —Boston (A.L.)	1	0	0	. . .	1.59	0	5⅔	6	1	1	1	2

KIEFER, MARK
P, BREWERS

PERSONAL: Born November 13, 1968, at Orange, Calif.... 6-4/175.... Throws right, bats right.... Full name: Mark Andrew Kiefer.
HIGH SCHOOL: Garden Grove (Calif.).
COLLEGE: Cal State Fullerton.
TRANSACTIONS/CAREER NOTES: Selected by Milwaukee Brewers organization in 21st round of free-agent draft (June 2, 1987).

Year Team (League)	G	W	L	Pct.	ERA	Sv.	IP	H	R	ER	BB	SO
1988 —Helena (Pioneer)	15	4	4	.500	2.65	0	68	76	30	20	17	51
1989 —Beloit (Midwest)	30	9	6	.600	2.32	1	131⅔	106	44	34	32	100
1990 —Peoria Brewers (Arizona)	1	0	0	. . .	3.38	0	2⅔	3	1	1	1	2
—Stockton (California)	11	5	2	.714	3.30	0	60	65	23	22	17	37
1991 —El Paso (Texas)	12	7	1	.875	3.33	0	75⅔	62	33	28	43	72
—Denver (American Assoc.)	17	9	5	.643	4.62	0	101⅓	104	55	52	41	68

KIELY, JOHN
P, TIGERS

PERSONAL: Born October 4, 1964, at Boston. ... 6-3/210. ... Throws right, bats right. ... Full name: John F. Kiely.
TRANSACTIONS/CAREER NOTES: Signed as free agent by the Detroit Tigers organization (September 7, 1987).... Loaned by Tigers organization to Milwaukee Brewers organization (June 20, 1988); returned (August 4, 1988).

Year Team (League)	G	W	L	Pct.	ERA	Sv.	IP	H	R	ER	BB	SO
1988 —Peoria (Midwest)	9	3	2	.600	4.56	1	47⅓	42	25	24	12	50
—Bristol (Eastern)■	8	2	2	.500	6.17	1	11⅔	9	9	8	7	14

Year	Team (League)	G	W	L	Pct.	ERA	Sv.	IP	H	R	ER	BB	SO
1989	—Lakeland (Florida State)■	36	4	3	.571	2.40	8	63⅔	52	26	17	27	56
1990	—London (Eastern)	46	3	0	1.000	1.76	12	76⅔	62	17	15	42	52
1991	—Toledo (International)	42	4	2	.667	2.13	6	72	55	25	17	35	60
	—Detroit (A.L.)	7	0	1	.000	14.85	0	6⅔	13	11	11	9	1
	Major league totals (1 year)	7	0	1	.000	14.85	0	6⅔	13	11	11	9	1

KILE, DARRYL

P, ASTROS

PERSONAL: Born December 2, 1968, at Garden Grove, Calif. . . . 6-5/185. . . . Throws right, bats right. . . . Full name: Darryl Andrew Kile.
COLLEGE: Chaffey Junior College (Calif.).
TRANSACTIONS/CAREER NOTES: Selected by Houston Astros organization in 30th round of free-agent draft (June 2, 1987).
STATISTICAL NOTES: Tied for Southern League lead with two shutouts in 1989.

Year	Team (League)	G	W	L	Pct.	ERA	Sv.	IP	H	R	ER	BB	SO
1988	—Sarasota Astros (Gulf Coast)	12	5	3	.625	3.17	0	59⅔	48	34	21	33	54
1989	—Columbus (Southern)	20	11	6	.647	2.58	0	125⅔	74	47	36	68	108
	—Tucson (Pacific Coast)	6	2	1	.667	5.96	0	25⅔	33	20	17	13	18
1990	—Tucson (Pacific Coast)	26	5	10	.333	6.64	0	123⅓	147	97	91	68	77
1991	—Houston (N.L.)	37	7	11	.389	3.69	0	153⅔	144	81	63	84	100
	Major league totals (1 year)	37	7	11	.389	3.69	0	153⅔	144	81	63	84	100

KILGUS, PAUL

P

PERSONAL: Born February 2, 1962, at Bowling Green, Ky. . . . 6-1/185. . . . Throws left, bats left. . . . Full name: Paul Nelson Kilgus.
HIGH SCHOOL: Bowling Green (Ky.).
COLLEGE: Kentucky (bachelor of science degree in biology, 1984).
TRANSACTIONS/CAREER NOTES: Selected by Texas Rangers organization in 43rd round of free-agent draft (June 4, 1984). . . . Traded by Rangers with P Mitch Williams, P Steve Wilson, IF Curtis Wilkerson, IF Luis Benitez and OF Pablo Delgado to Chicago Cubs for OF Rafael Palmeiro, P Jamie Moyer and P Drew Hall (December 5, 1988). . . . Traded by Cubs organization to Toronto Blue Jays for P Jose Nunez (December 7, 1989). . . . Traded by Blue Jays to Baltimore Orioles for P Mickey Weston (December 14, 1990). . . . Released by Orioles (October 16, 1991).

Year	Team (League)	G	W	L	Pct.	ERA	Sv.	IP	H	R	ER	BB	SO
1984	—Tri-Cities (Northwest)	14	7	5	.583	2.87	0	78⅓	87	38	25	31	60
1985	—Salem (Carolina)	38	3	1	.750	2.03	10	84⅓	69	28	19	26	67
1986	—Tulsa (Texas)	41	3	7	.300	3.73	8	103⅔	102	56	43	36	59
1987	—Oklahoma City (Am. Assoc.)	21	2	0	1.000	4.01	7	24⅔	23	12	11	10	14
	—Texas (A.L.)	25	2	7	.222	4.13	0	89⅓	95	45	41	31	42
1988	—Texas (A.L.)	32	12	15	.444	4.16	0	203⅓	190	105	94	71	88
1989	—Chicago (N.L.)■	35	6	10	.375	4.39	2	145⅔	164	90	71	49	61
	—Iowa (American Association)	1	1	0	1.000	3.00	0	9	9	3	3	2	5
1990	—Toronto (A.L.)■	11	0	0	...	6.06	0	16⅓	19	11	11	7	7
	—Syracuse (International)	20	6	8	.429	2.94	0	125⅔	116	47	41	39	75
1991	—Baltimore (A.L.)■	38	0	2	.000	5.08	1	62	60	38	35	24	32
	—Rochester (International)	9	2	2	.500	5.76	0	45⅓	58	32	29	10	29
	American League totals (4 years)	106	14	24	.368	4.39	1	371	364	199	181	133	169
	National League totals (1 year)	35	6	10	.375	4.39	2	145⅔	164	90	71	49	61
	Major league totals (5 years)	141	20	34	.370	4.39	3	516⅔	528	289	252	182	230

CHAMPIONSHIP SERIES RECORD

Year	Team (League)	G	W	L	Pct.	ERA	Sv.	IP	H	R	ER	BB	SO
1989	—Chicago (N.L.)	1	0	0	...	0.00	0	3	4	0	0	1	1

KING, ERIC

P, TIGERS

PERSONAL: Born April 10, 1964, at Oxnard, Calif. . . . 6-2/218. . . . Throws right, bats right. . . . Full name: Eric Steven King.
HIGH SCHOOL: Royal (Simi Valley, Calif.).
TRANSACTIONS/CAREER NOTES: Signed as free agent by San Francisco Giants organization (June 11, 1983). . . . On suspended list (July 3-13, 1985), then transferred to disabled list (July 13-27, 1985). . . . Traded by Giants organization with P Dave LaPoint and C Matt Nokes to Detroit Tigers for P Juan Berenguer, C Bob Melvin and a player to be named later (October 7, 1985); Giants acquired P Scott Medvin to complete deal (December 11, 1985). . . . Traded by Tigers to Chicago White Sox for OF Kenny Williams (March 23, 1989). . . . On Chicago disabled list (June 9-July 16, 1989); included rehabiliation disability assignment to Sarasota and Gulf Coast White Sox. . . . On Chicago disabled list (August 1-September 1, 1990); included rehabilitation disability assignment to Sarasota (August 23-31, 1990). . . . Traded by White Sox with P Shawn Hillegas to Cleveland Indians for OF Cory Snyder and IF Lindsay Foster (December 4, 1990). . . . On Cleveland disabled list (June 16-July 31, 1991); included rehabilitation disability assignment to Colorado Springs (July 14-31, 1991). . . . Granted free agency (December 20, 1991). . . . Signed by Tigers (January 29, 1992).
RECORDS/HONORS: Shares major league single-game (nine innings) record for most putouts by pitcher—6 (July 8, 1986).

Year	Team (League)	G	W	L	Pct.	ERA	Sv.	IP	H	R	ER	BB	SO
1983	—Great Falls (Pioneer)	20	3	4	.429	4.31	2	56⅓	58	31	27	14	61
1984	—Clinton (Midwest)	35	5	10	.333	3.36	3	147⅓	142	74	55	76	124
1985	—Shreveport (Texas)	15	5	3	.625	2.32	0	104⅔	74	34	27	30	80
1986	—Nashville (American Assoc.)■	6	3	2	.600	3.52	0	38⅓	29	16	15	16	38
	—Detroit (A.L.)	33	11	4	.733	3.51	3	138⅓	108	54	54	63	79

Year	Team (League)	G	W	L	Pct.	ERA	Sv.	IP	H	R	ER	BB	SO
1987 —Detroit (A.L.)		55	6	9	.400	4.89	9	116	111	67	63	60	89
1988 —Toledo (International)		10	3	4	.429	3.26	0	69	54	26	25	23	51
—Detroit (A.L.)		23	4	1	.800	3.41	3	68⅔	60	28	26	34	45
1989 —Chicago (A.L.)■		25	9	10	.474	3.39	0	159⅓	144	69	60	64	72
—Sarasota (Florida State)		1	1	0	1.000	1.00	0	9	9	1	1	0	7
—Sarasota White Sox (GCL)		2	1	1	.500	4.09	0	11	13	8	5	3	8
1990 —Chicago (A.L.)		25	12	4	.750	3.28	0	151	135	59	55	40	70
—Sarasota (Florida State)		2	1	0	1.000	2.25	0	8	8	4	2	2	5
1991 —Cleveland (A.L.)■		25	6	11	.353	4.60	0	150⅔	166	83	77	44	59
—Colorado Springs (Pac. Coast) ..		3	1	0	1.000	9.53	0	11⅓	18	12	12	5	3
Major league totals (6 years)		186	48	39	.552	3.85	15	784	724	360	335	305	414

CHAMPIONSHIP SERIES RECORD

Year	Team (League)	G	W	L	Pct.	ERA	Sv.	IP	H	R	ER	BB	SO
1987 —Detroit (A.L.)		2	0	0	. . .	1.69	0	5⅓	3	1	1	2	4

KING, JEFF

3B, PIRATES

PERSONAL: Born December 26, 1964, at Marion, Ind. . . . 6-1/185. . . . Throws right, bats right. . . . Full name: Jeffrey Wayne King. . . . Son of Jack King, minor league catcher (1954-55).
HIGH SCHOOL: Rampart (Colorado Springs, Colo.).
COLLEGE: Arkansas.
TRANSACTIONS/CAREER NOTES: Selected by Chicago Cubs organization in 23rd round of free-agent draft (June 6, 1983). . . . Selected by Pittsburgh Pirates organization in first round (first pick overall) of free-agent draft (June 2, 1986). . . . On Pittsburgh disabled list (May 5-31, 1991); included rehabilitation disability assignment to Buffalo (May 25-31, 1991). . . . On Pittsburgh disabled list (June 13-October 7, 1991); included rehabilitation disability assignment to Buffalo (August 28-September 6, 1991).
RECORDS/HONORS: Named College Player of the Year by THE SPORTING NEWS (1986). . . . Named third baseman on THE SPORTING NEWS college All-America team (1986).
STATISTICAL NOTES: Led Carolina League with .565 slugging percentage in 1987.

Year	Team (League)	Pos.	G	AB	R	H	2B	3B	HR	RBI	Avg.	SB	PO	A	E	Avg.
1986 —Prince William (Caro.).......		3B	37	132	18	31	4	1	6	20	.235	1	25	50	8	.904
1987 —Salem (Carolina)		1B-3B	90	310	68	86	9	1	26	71	.277	6	572	106	13	.981
—Harrisburg (Eastern)		1B	26	100	12	24	7	0	2	25	.240	0	107	10	1	.992
1988 —Harrisburg (Eastern)		3B	117	411	49	105	21	1	14	66	.255	5	97	208	24	.927
1989 —Buffalo (Am. Assoc.)		1B-3B	51	169	26	43	5	2	6	29	.254	11	213	61	8	.972
—Pittsburgh (N.L.)		1-3-2-S	75	215	31	42	13	3	5	19	.195	4	403	59	4	.991
1990 —Pittsburgh (N.L.)		3B-1B	127	371	46	91	17	1	14	53	.245	3	61	215	18	.939
1991 —Pittsburgh (N.L.)		3B	33	109	16	26	1	1	4	18	.239	3	15	62	2	.975
—Buffalo (Am. Assoc.)		3B	9	18	3	4	1	1	0	2	.222	1	2	8	1	.909
Major league totals (3 years)			235	695	93	159	31	5	23	90	.229	10	479	336	24	.971

CHAMPIONSHIP SERIES RECORD

Year	Team (League)	Pos.	G	AB	R	H	2B	3B	HR	RBI	Avg.	SB	PO	A	E	Avg.
1990 —Pittsburgh (N.L.)		PH-3B	5	10	0	1	0	0	0	0	.100	0	1	4	0	1.000

KINGERY, MIKE

OF/1B, ATHLETICS

PERSONAL: Born March 29, 1961, at St. James, Minn. . . . 6-0/185. . . . Throws left, bats left. . . . Full name: Michael Scott Kingery.
HIGH SCHOOL: Atwater (Minn.).
COLLEGE: Wilmar Community College (Minn.) and St. Cloud State (Minn.).
TRANSACTIONS/CAREER NOTES: Signed as free agent by Kansas City Royals organization (August 27, 1979). . . . On disabled list (July 29-August 15, 1981). . . . Traded by Royals with P Scott Bankhead and P Steve Shields to Seattle Mariners for OF Danny Tartabull and P Rick Luecken (December 10, 1986). . . . Granted free agency (April 6, 1990). . . . Signed by Phoenix, San Francisco Giants organization (April 14, 1990). . . . Released by Giants (October 6, 1991). . . . Signed by Oakland Athletics organization (December 27, 1991).
STATISTICAL NOTES: Tied for South Atlantic League lead in double plays by outfielders with five in 1982. . . . Led Florida State League with 11 intentional bases on balls received in 1983.

Year	Team (League)	Pos.	G	AB	R	H	2B	3B	HR	RBI	Avg.	SB	PO	A	E	Avg.
1980 —Sara. Royals-Gold (GCL) ..		OF	44	143	12	32	3	3	0	13	.224	4	78	5	2	.976
1981 —Charleston, S.C. (S. Atl.) ...		OF	69	213	33	57	3	4	3	25	.268	12	80	7	4	.956
1982 —Charleston, S.C. (S. Atl.) ...		OF	140	513	65	163	19	4	8	75	.318	25	250	21	7	.975
1983 —Fort Myers (Florida St.)		OF	123	436	68	116	9	7	2	51	.266	31	200	16	5	.977
1984 —Memphis (Southern)		OF	139	455	65	135	19	3	4	58	.297	18	291	18	6	.981
1985 —Omaha (Am. Assoc.)		OF	132	444	51	113	25	6	2	49	.255	16	247	17	5	.981
1986 —Omaha (Am. Assoc.)		OF	79	298	47	99	14	8	3	47	.332	22	171	10	1	.995
—Kansas City (A.L.)		OF	62	209	25	54	8	5	3	14	.258	7	102	6	3	.973
1987 —Seattle (A.L.)■		OF	120	354	38	99	25	4	9	52	.280	7	226	15	2	.992
1988 —Seattle (A.L.)		OF-1B	57	123	21	25	6	0	1	9	.203	3	102	6	2	.982
—Calgary (Pacific Coast)		OF-1B	47	170	29	54	12	2	1	14	.318	5	144	4	3	.980
1989 —Calgary (Pacific Coast)		OF-1B	107	396	72	115	22	9	4	47	.290	7	289	10	1	.997
—Seattle (A.L.)		OF	31	76	14	17	3	0	2	6	.224	1	70	0	0	1.000

Year	Team (League)	Pos.	G	AB	R	H	2B	3B	HR	RBI	Avg.	SB	PO	A	E	Avg.
1990	—Phoenix (Pacific Coast)■..	OF	35	100	12	24	9	2	1	16	.240	2	61	4	1	.985
	—San Francisco (N.L.)	OF	105	207	24	61	7	1	0	24	.295	6	126	7	3	.978
1991	—San Francisco (N.L.)	OF-1B	91	110	13	20	2	2	0	8	.182	1	60	2	1	.984
	—Phoenix (Pacific Coast)	OF	13	44	8	15	3	0	1	13	.341	0	32	0	0	1.000
	American League totals (4 years)		270	762	98	195	42	9	15	81	.256	18	500	27	7	.987
	National League totals (2 years)		196	317	37	81	9	3	0	32	.256	7	186	9	4	.980
	Major league totals (6 years)		466	1079	135	276	51	12	15	113	.256	25	686	36	11	.985

KIPPER, BOB
P, TWINS

PERSONAL: Born July 8, 1964, at Aurora, Ill. . . . 6-2/180. . . . Throws left, bats right. . . . Full name: Robert Wayne Kipper.
HIGH SCHOOL: Aurora Central Catholic (Ill.).
TRANSACTIONS/CAREER NOTES: Selected by California Angels organization in first round (eighth pick overall) of free-agent draft (June 7, 1982). . . . On Peoria disabled list (July 20-August 8, 1983). . . . On Midland disabled list (May 31-June 10, 1985). . . . Loaned by Angels organization to Hawaii, Pittsburgh Pirates organization (August 2, 1985); returned (August 16, 1985). . . . Traded by Angels organization to Pirates organization (August 16, 1985), completing deal in which Pirates traded P John Candelaria, P Al Holland and OF George Hendrick to Angels for P Pat Clements, OF Mike Brown and a player to be named later (August 2, 1985). . . . On Pittsburgh disabled list (June 29-September 1, 1986); included rehabilitation disability assignment to Nashua (August 14-September 1, 1986). . . . On disabled list (July 31-September 1, 1989). . . . On Pittsburgh disabled list (March 30-May 7, 1990); included rehabilitation disability assignment to Buffalo (April 26-May 7, 1990). . . . Granted free agency (October 28, 1991). . . . Signed by Minnesota Twins (December 17, 1991).
RECORDS/HONORS: Named California League Pitcher of the Year (1984).
STATISTICAL NOTES: Pitched seven-inning, 9-0 no-hit victory against San Jose (June 10, 1984, second game). . . . Tied for N.L. lead with five balks in 1990.

Year	Team (League)	G	W	L	Pct.	ERA	Sv.	IP	H	R	ER	BB	SO
1982	—Salem (Northwest)	13	6	5	.545	4.46	1	76⅔	62	46	38	52	65
1983	—Peoria (Midwest)	22	5	8	.385	4.65	0	127⅔	112	77	66	52	105
1984	—Redwood (California)	26	*18	8	.692	*2.04	0	185	147	61	42	65	98
1985	—California (A.L.)	2	0	1	.000	21.60	0	3⅓	7	8	8	3	0
	—Midland (Texas)	9	3	3	.500	3.08	0	49⅔	52	22	17	10	31
	—Edmonton-Hawaii (PCL)■	7	3	0	1.000	1.99	0	49⅔	36	15	11	12	42
	—Pittsburgh (N.L.)	5	1	2	.333	5.11	0	24⅔	21	16	14	7	13
1986	—Pittsburgh (N.L.)	20	6	8	.429	4.03	0	114	123	60	51	34	81
	—Nashua (Eastern)	4	0	1	.000	3.44	0	18⅓	14	7	7	3	19
1987	—Pittsburgh (N.L.)	24	5	9	.357	5.94	0	110⅔	117	74	73	52	83
	—Vancouver (Pacific Coast)	6	0	2	.000	1.78	1	25⅓	23	7	5	4	22
1988	—Pittsburgh (N.L.)	50	2	6	.250	3.74	0	65	54	33	27	26	39
1989	—Pittsburgh (N.L.)	52	3	4	.429	2.93	4	83	55	29	27	33	58
1990	—Buffalo (American Assoc.)	5	0	0	. . .	7.71	0	4⅔	6	4	4	1	6
	—Pittsburgh (N.L.)	41	5	2	.714	3.02	3	62⅔	44	24	21	26	35
1991	—Pittsburgh (N.L.)	52	2	2	.500	4.65	4	60	66	34	31	22	38
	American League totals (1 year)	2	0	1	.000	21.60	0	3⅓	7	8	8	3	0
	National League totals (7 years)	244	24	33	.421	4.22	11	520	480	270	244	200	347
	Major league totals (7 years)	246	24	34	.414	4.33	11	523⅓	487	278	252	203	347

CHAMPIONSHIP SERIES RECORD

Year	Team (League)	G	W	L	Pct.	ERA	Sv.	IP	H	R	ER	BB	SO
1991	—Pittsburgh (N.L.)	1	0	0	. . .	4.50	0	2	2	1	1	0	1

KIRBY, WAYNE
OF, INDIANS

PERSONAL: Born January 22, 1964, at Williamsburg, Va. . . . 5-10/185. . . . Throws right, bats left. . . . Full name: Wayne Edward Kirby.
HIGH SCHOOL: Tabb (Va.).
COLLEGE: Newport News Apprentice School (Va.).
TRANSACTIONS/CAREER NOTES: Selected by Los Angeles Dodgers organization in 13th round of free-agent draft (January 11, 1983). . . . Granted free agency (October 15, 1990). . . . Signed by Cleveland Indians organization (December 3, 1990). . . . Granted free agency (October 15, 1991). . . . Signed by Colorado Springs, Indians organization (December 12, 1991).

Year	Team (League)	Pos.	G	AB	R	H	2B	3B	HR	RBI	Avg.	SB	PO	A	E	Avg.
1983	—Bradenton (Gulf Coast)	P	60	216	43	63	7	1	0	13	.292	23	89	9	1	.990
1984	—Vero Beach (Florida St.) ...	OF	76	224	39	61	6	3	0	21	.272	11	101	3	5	.954
	—Great Falls (Pioneer)	OF	20	84	19	26	2	2	1	11	.310	19	35	3	2	.950
	—Bakersfield (California)	OF	23	84	14	23	3	0	0	10	.274	8	10	1	3	.786
1985	—Vero Beach (Florida St.) ...	OF	122	437	70	123	9	3	0	28	.281	31	231	10	4	.984
1986	—Vero Beach (Florida St.) ...	OF-2B	114	387	60	101	9	4	2	31	.261	28	264	18	4	.986
1987	—Bakersfield (California)	OF	105	416	77	112	14	3	0	34	.269	56	213	13	12	.950
	—San Antonio (Texas)	OF	24	80	7	19	1	2	1	9	.238	6	47	1	3	.941
1988	—Bakersfield (California)	OF	12	47	12	13	0	1	0	4	.277	9	20	2	2	.917
	—San Antonio (Texas)	OF	100	334	50	80	9	2	0	21	.240	26	181	4	2	.989
1989	—San Antonio (Texas)	OF	44	140	14	30	3	1	0	7	.214	11	77	3	4	.952

Year Team (League)	Pos.	G	AB	R	H	2B	3B	HR	RBI	Avg.	SB	PO	A	E	Avg.
1990—Albuquerque (PCL)	OF	119	342	56	95	14	5	0	30	.278	29	185	11	9	.956
1991—Colorado Springs (PCL)■..	OF-2B	118	385	66	113	14	4	1	39	.294	29	227	14	6	.976
—Cleveland (A.L.)	OF	21	43	4	9	2	0	0	5	.209	1	40	1	0	1.000
Major league totals (1 year)		21	43	4	9	2	0	0	5	.209	1	40	1	0	1.000

KISER, GARLAND
P, INDIANS

PERSONAL: Born July 8, 1968, at Charlotte, N.C.... 6-3/190.... Throws left, bats left.... Full name: Garland Rauthard Kiser Jr.
HIGH SCHOOL: Sullivan Central (Blountville, Tenn.).
TRANSACTIONS/CAREER NOTES: Selected by Philadelphia Phillies organization in 24th round of free-agent draft (June 2, 1986).... Released by Phillies organization (March 29, 1988).... Signed by Cleveland Indians (April 6, 1988).

Year Team (League)	G	W	L	Pct.	ERA	Sv.	IP	H	R	ER	BB	SO
1986—Bend (Northwest)	14	4	5	.444	5.48	0	70 2/3	79	58	43	48	46
1987—Spartanburg (South Atlantic)	21	0	5	.000	6.49	1	43	49	37	31	24	27
1988—Sarasota Indians (Gulf Coast)■	7	5	1	.833	*1.29	0	56	31	12	8	17	45
—Burlington (Appalachian)	7	2	2	.500	2.03	0	31	22	11	7	9	29
1989—Watertown (New York-Penn)	12	7	1	.875	3.41	0	74	66	36	28	18	74
—Kinston (Carolina)	6	0	1	.000	7.11	0	12 2/3	14	10	10	7	7
1990—Kinston (Carolina)	55	5	3	.625	1.71	9	94 2/3	81	25	18	27	82
1991—Canton/Akron (Eastern)	17	2	3	.400	2.03	0	44 1/3	35	13	10	11	34
—Cleveland (A.L.)	7	0	0	...	9.64	0	4 2/3	7	5	5	4	3
—Kinston (Carolina)	31	6	1	.857	1.49	5	48 1/3	35	11	8	14	52
Major league totals (1 year)	7	0	0	...	9.64	0	4 2/3	7	5	5	4	3

KITTLE, RON
DH/1B

PERSONAL: Born January 5, 1958, at Gary, Ind.... 6-4/230.... Throws right, bats right.... Full name: Ronald Dale Kittle.
HIGH SCHOOL: Wirt (Gary, Ind.).
TRANSACTIONS/CAREER NOTES: Signed as free agent by Los Angeles Dodgers organization (July 5, 1977).... On Clinton disabled list (April 30-May 14, 1977).... Released by Dodgers organization (July 7, 1978).... Signed by Knoxville, Chicago White Sox organization (September 4, 1978).... On Glens Falls disabled list (July 27-August 31, 1980 and April 21-May 10, 1981).... On Chicago disabled list (July 4-25, 1985); included rehabilitation disability assignment to Buffalo (July 19-25, 1985).... Traded by White Sox with IF Wayne Tolleson and C Joel Skinner to New York Yankees for C Ron Hassey, SS Carlos Martinez and a player to be named later (July 30, 1986); Yankees traded C Bill Lindsey to White Sox organization to complete deal (December 24, 1986).... On New York disabled list (July 7-August 16, 1987); included rehabilitation disability assignment to Columbus (August 14-16, 1987).... Released by Yankees organization (December 21, 1987).... Signed by Cleveland Indians (February 9, 1988).... Granted free agency (November 4, 1988).... Signed by Chicago White Sox (November 26, 1988).... On disabled list (June 11, 1989-remainder of season).... Traded by White Sox to Baltimore Orioles for OF Phil Bradley (July 30, 1990).... Granted free agency (December 15, 1990).... Signed by Indians organization (January 20, 1991).... Released by Indians (April 1, 1991).... Signed by White Sox organization (June 19, 1991).... On Vancouver disabled list (June 21-29, 1991).... Released by White Sox (August 15, 1991).
RECORDS/HONORS: Shares major league record for most home runs in month of October—4 (1985).... Named Eastern League Most Valuable Player (1981).... Named Minor League Player of the Year by THE SPORTING NEWS (1982).... Named Pacific Coast League Most Valuable Player (1982).... Named A.L. Rookie Player of the Year by THE SPORTING NEWS (1983).... Named A.L. Rookie of the Year by Baseball Writers' Association of America (1983).
STATISTICAL NOTES: Led Eastern League with 270 total bases and .694 slugging percentage in 1981.... Led Pacific Coast League with 355 total bases and .752 slugging percentage and tied for lead in being hit by pitch with 10 in 1982.... Led A.L. batters with 150 strikeouts in 1983.

Year Team (League)	Pos.	G	AB	R	H	2B	3B	HR	RBI	Avg.	SB	PO	A	E	Avg.
1977—Clinton (Midwest)	OF	22	53	9	10	4	0	0	3	.189	1	16	0	0	1.000
—Lethbridge (Pioneer)	OF	34	100	22	25	3	0	7	21	.250	3	29	2	6	.838
1978—Clinton (Midwest)	OF	13	35	2	5	2	1	0	4	.143	1	4	1	1	.833
1979—Knoxville (Southern)■	OF-C	53	157	28	43	9	1	6	26	.274	0	44	1	6	.882
—Appleton (Midwest)	OF-C	35	120	18	31	3	1	2	12	.258	0	33	1	2	.944
1980—Appleton (Midwest)	C-OF	61	209	31	66	15	3	12	56	.316	0	56	9	1	.985
—Glens Falls (Eastern)	OF	17	65	11	20	3	1	4	9	.308	00	24	4	3	.903
1981—Glens Falls (Eastern)	OF	109	389	97	127	17	3	*40	*103	.326	0	28	0	3	.903
1982—Edmonton (Pac. Coast)	OF-C	127	472	*121	163	22	10	*50	*144	.345	5	149	15	8	.953
—Chicago (A.L.)	OF	20	29	3	7	2	0	1	7	.241	0	3	0	0	1.000
1983—Chicago (A.L.)	OF	145	520	75	132	19	3	35	100	.254	8	234	7	9	.964
1984—Chicago (A.L.)	OF	139	466	67	100	15	0	32	74	.215	3	226	14	7	.972
1985—Chicago (A.L.)	OF	116	379	51	87	12	0	26	58	.230	1	88	2	1	.989
—Buffalo (Am. Assoc.)	OF	6	21	3	7	0	2	0	5	.333	0	2	0	0	1.000
1986—Chicago-N.Y. (A.L.)■	OF	116	376	42	82	13	0	21	60	.218	4	39	3	0	1.000
1987—New York (A.L.)	OF	59	159	21	44	5	0	12	28	.277	0	4	1	0	1.000
—Columbus (Int'l)	DH	4	18	3	4	0	0	0	1	.222	0	0	0	0	...
1988—Cleveland (A.L.)■	DH	75	225	31	58	8	0	18	43	.258	0	0	0	0	...
1989—Chicago (A.L.)■	1B-OF	51	169	26	51	10	0	11	37	.302	0	216	12	4	.983
1990—Chicago-Balt. (A.L.)■..	1B	105	338	33	78	16	0	18	46	.231	2	176	6	2	.989
1991—Vancouver (Pac. Coast)■..	1B	17	71	9	22	4	1	4	21	.310	1	87	7	2	.979
—Chicago (A.L.)	1B	17	47	7	9	0	0	2	7	.191	0	101	6	2	.982
Major league totals (10 years)		843	2708	356	648	100	3	176	460	.239	18	1087	51	25	.979

Year	Team (League)	Pos.	G	AB	R	H	2B	3B	HR	RBI	Avg.	SB	PO	A	E	Avg.
1983 —Chicago (A.L.)		OF	3	7	1	2	1	0	0	0	.286	0	3	0	0	1.000

ALL-STAR GAME RECORD

Year	League	Pos.	AB	R	H	2B	3B	HR	RBI	Avg.	SB	PO	A	E	Avg.
1983 —American		OF	1	1	1	0	0	0	0	1.000	0	1	0	0	1.000

KLINK, JOE
P, ATHLETICS

PERSONAL: Born February 3, 1962, at Johnstown, Pa. . . . 5-11/175. . . . Throws left, bats left. . . . Full name: Joseph Charles Klink.
HIGH SCHOOL: Chaminade (Hollywood, Fla.).
COLLEGE: Biscayne College (Fla.).
TRANSACTIONS/CAREER NOTES: Selected by New York Mets organization in 36th round of free-agent draft (June 6, 1983). . . . Traded by Mets organization with P Bill Latham and OF Billy Beane to Minnesota Twins for 2B Tim Teufel and OF Pat Crosby (January 16, 1986). . . . Traded by Twins organization to Oakland Athletics for a player to be named later (March 31, 1988); Twins organization acquired P Russ Kibler to complete deal (June 25, 1988). . . . On Oakland disabled list (June 6-July 11, 1991); included rehabilitation disability assignment to Modesto (July 4-11, 1991).

Year	Team (League)	G	W	L	Pct.	ERA	Sv.	IP	H	R	ER	BB	SO
1983 —Columbia (South Atlantic)		12	2	2	.500	4.62	0	25⅓	24	16	13	14	14
1984 —Columbia (South Atlantic)		31	5	4	.556	3.49	11	38⅔	30	19	15	28	49
1985 —Lynchburg (Carolina)		44	3	3	.500	2.26	5	51⅔	41	16	13	26	59
1986 —Orlando (Southern)■		45	4	5	.444	2.51	11	68	59	24	19	37	63
1987 —Portland (Pacific Coast)		12	0	0	. . .	4.30	0	23	25	14	11	13	14
—Minnesota (A.L.)		12	0	1	.000	6.65	0	23	37	18	17	11	17
1988 —Huntsville (Southern)■		21	1	2	.333	0.78	3	34⅔	25	6	3	14	30
—Tacoma (Pacific Coast)		27	2	1	.667	5.12	1	38⅔	47	29	22	17	32
1989 —Huntsville (Southern)		57	4	4	.500	2.82	★26	60⅔	46	19	19	23	59
—Tacoma (Pacific Coast)		6	0	0	. . .	0.00	0	6⅔	2	0	0	2	5
1990 —Oakland (A.L.)		40	0	0	. . .	2.04	1	39⅔	34	9	9	18	19
1991 —Oakland (A.L.)		62	10	3	.769	4.35	2	62	60	30	30	21	34
—Modesto (California)		3	0	0	. . .	3.60	0	5	4	2	2	1	1
Major league totals (3 years)		**114**	**10**	**4**	**.714**	**4.04**	**3**	**124⅔**	**131**	**57**	**56**	**50**	**70**

WORLD SERIES RECORD

Year	Team (League)	G	W	L	Pct.	ERA	Sv.	IP	H	R	ER	BB	SO
1990 —Oakland (A.L.)		1	0	0	. . .	0.00	0	0	0	0	0	1	0

KMAK, JOE
C, BREWERS

PERSONAL: Born May 3, 1963, at Napa, Calif. . . . 6-0/185. . . . Throws right, bats right. . . . Name pronounced KAY-mak.
HIGH SCHOOL: Serra (San Mateo, Calif.).
COLLEGE: UC Santa Barbara.
TRANSACTIONS/CAREER NOTES: Selected by San Francisco Giants organization in tenth round of free-agent draft (June 3, 1985). . . . Signed as a free agent by Milwaukee Brewers organization (January 20, 1990).
STATISTICAL NOTES: Led American Association catchers with 10 double plays in 1991.

Year	Team (League)	Pos.	G	AB	R	H	2B	3B	HR	RBI	Avg.	SB	PO	A	E	Avg.
1985 —Everett (Northwest)		C	40	129	21	40	10	1	1	14	.310	0	175	21	3	.985
1986 —Fresno (California)		C	60	163	23	44	5	1	1	9	.270	3	203	26	3	.987
1987 —Fresno (California)		C	48	154	18	34	8	0	0	12	.221	1	323	35	4	.989
—Shreveport (Texas)		C	15	41	5	8	0	1	0	3	.195	0	87	11	2	.980
1988 —Shreveport (Texas)		C	71	178	16	40	5	2	1	14	.225	0	325	35	6	.984
1989 —Reno (California)		C	78	248	39	68	10	5	4	34	.274	8	459	60	5	.990
1990 —El Paso (Texas)■		C	35	109	8	31	3	2	2	11	.284	0	194	28	2	.991
—Denver (Am. Assoc.)		C	28	95	12	22	3	0	1	10	.232	2	160	20	6	.968
1991 —Denver (Am. Assoc.)		C	100	295	34	70	17	2	1	33	.237	7	579	★77	5	★.992

KNACKERT, BRENT
P, MARINERS

PERSONAL: Born August 1, 1969, at Los Angeles. . . . 6-3/190. . . . Throws right, bats right. . . . Full name: Brent Bradley Knackert.
TRANSACTIONS/CAREER NOTES: Selected by Chicago White Sox organization in second round of free-agent draft (June 2, 1987). . . . Drafted by New York Mets (December 4, 1989). . . . Claimed on waivers by Seattle Mariners (April 5, 1990). . . . On Calgary disabled list (April 11-June 16, 1991). . . . On San Bernardino disabled list (June 17, 1991-remainder of season).

Year	Team (League)	G	W	L	Pct.	ERA	Sv.	IP	H	R	ER	BB	SO
1987 —Sarasota White Sox (GCL)		12	6	2	.750	2.85	0	72⅔	55	28	23	15	60
1988 —Tampa (Florida State)		23	10	8	.556	3.17	0	142	132	58	50	46	78
1989 —Sarasota (Florida State)		35	8	5	.615	2.94	12	98	85	41	32	35	80
1990 —Seattle (A.L.)■		24	1	1	.500	6.51	0	37⅓	50	28	27	21	28
1991 —San Bernardino (California)		2	0	0	. . .	2.08	0	4⅓	3	1	1	3	7
Major league totals (1 year)		**24**	**1**	**1**	**.500**	**6.51**	**0**	**37⅓**	**50**	**28**	**27**	**21**	**28**

KNOBLAUCH, CHUCK
2B, TWINS

PERSONAL: Born July 7, 1968, at Houston. . . . 5-9/175. . . . Throws right, bats right. . . . Full name: Edward Charles Knoblauch. . . . Son of Ray Knoblauch, minor league pitcher (1947-56); and nephew of Ed Knoblauch, minor league outfielder (1938-42 and 1947-55). . . . Name pronounced NOB-lock.

HIGH SCHOOL: Bellaire (Houston).
COLLEGE: Texas A&M.
TRANSACTIONS/CAREER NOTES: Selected by Philadelphia Phillies organization in 18th round of free-agent draft (June 2, 1986). . . . Selected by Minnesota Twins organization in first round (25th pick overall) of free-agent draft (June 5, 1989).
RECORDS/HONORS: Named A.L. Rookie Player of the Year by THE SPORTING NEWS (1991). . . . Named A.L. Rookie of the Year by Baseball Writers' Association of America (1991).

Year	Team (League)	Pos.	G	AB	R	H	2B	3B	HR	RBI	Avg.	SB	PO	A	E	Avg.
1989 —Kenosha (Midwest)		SS	51	196	29	56	13	1	2	19	.286	9	60	124	21	.898
—Visalia (California)		SS	18	77	20	28	10	0	0	21	.364	2	23	52	10	.882
1990 —Orlando (Southern)		2B	118	432	74	125	23	6	2	53	.289	23	275	300	20	.966
1991 —Minnesota (A.L.)		2B	151	565	78	159	24	6	1	50	.281	25	249	460	18	.975
Major league totals (1 year)			151	565	78	159	24	6	1	50	.281	25	249	460	18	.975

CHAMPIONSHIP SERIES RECORD

Year	Team (League)	Pos.	G	AB	R	H	2B	3B	HR	RBI	Avg.	SB	PO	A	E	Avg.
1991 —Minnesota (A.L.)		2B	5	20	5	7	2	0	0	3	.350	2	8	14	0	1.000

WORLD SERIES RECORD

Year	Team (League)	Pos.	G	AB	R	H	2B	3B	HR	RBI	Avg.	SB	PO	A	E	Avg.
1991 —Minnesota (A.L.)		2B	7	26	3	8	1	0	0	2	.308	4	15	14	1	.967

KNORR, RANDY
C, BLUE JAYS

PERSONAL: Born November 12, 1968, at San Gabriel, Calif. . . . 6-2/205. . . . Throws right, bats right. . . . Full name: Randy Duane Knorr.
HIGH SCHOOL: Baldwin Park (Calif.).
TRANSACTIONS/CAREER NOTES: Selected by Toronto Blue Jays organization in 10th round of free-agent draft (June 2, 1986). . . . On disabled list (June 24-July 4, 1986 and May 10, 1989-remainder of season).
STATISTICAL NOTES: Led South Atlantic League catchers with 960 total chances and 25 passed balls in 1988.

Year	Team (League)	Pos.	G	AB	R	H	2B	3B	HR	RBI	Avg.	SB	PO	A	E	Avg.
1986 —Medicine Hat (Pioneer)		1B	55	215	21	58	13	0	4	52	.270	0	451	29	10	.980
1987 —Myrtle Beach (S. Atl.)	C-1B-2B	46	129	17	34	4	0	6	21	.264	0	95	7	1	.990
—Medicine Hat (Pioneer)		C	26	106	21	31	7	0	10	24	.292	0	70	5	4	.949
1988 —Myrtle Beach (S. Atl.)		C	117	364	43	85	13	0	9	42	.234	0	★870	75	15	.984
1989 —Dunedin (Florida State)		C	33	122	13	32	6	0	6	23	.262	0	186	20	2	.990
1990 —Knoxville (Southern)		C	116	392	51	108	12	1	13	64	.276	0	599	72	15	.978
1991 —Knoxville (Southern)	C-1B	24	74	7	13	4	0	0	4	.176	2	136	16	2	.987
—Syracuse (International) ..		C	91	342	29	89	20	0	5	44	.260	1	477	49	7	.987
—Toronto (A.L.)		C	3	1	0	0	0	0	0	0	.000	0	6	1	0	1.000
Major league totals (1 year)			3	1	0	0	0	0	0	0	.000	0	6	1	0	1.000

KNUDSEN, KURT
P, TIGERS

PERSONAL: Born February 20, 1967, at Arlington Heights, Ill. . . . 6-2/185. . . . Throws right, bats right. . . . Full name: Kurt David Knudsen.
HIGH SCHOOL: Del Campo (Fair Oaks, Calif.).
COLLEGE: American River (Calif.) and Miami (Fla.).
TRANSACTIONS/CAREER NOTES: Selected by Pittsburgh Pirates organization in eighth round of free-agent draft (June 2, 1987). . . . Selected by Detroit Tigers organization in ninth round of free-agent draft (June 1, 1988).

Year	Team (League)	G	W	L	Pct.	ERA	Sv.	IP	H	R	ER	BB	SO
1988 —Bristol (Appalachian)	2	0	0	. . .	0.00	0	2⅓	4	3	0	1	0
—Fayetteville (South Atlantic)	12	3	1	.750	1.35	1	20	8	4	3	9	22
—Lakeland (Florida State)	7	0	0	. . .	0.96	0	9⅓	7	2	1	7	6
1989 —Lakeland (Florida State)	45	3	2	.600	2.15	10	54⅓	43	16	13	22	68
1990 —Lakeland (Florida State)	14	5	0	1.000	2.28	3	67	42	18	17	22	70
—London (Eastern)	15	2	1	.667	2.08	1	26	15	6	6	11	26
1991 —London (Eastern)	34	2	3	.400	3.48	6	51⅔	42	29	20	30	56
—Toledo (International)	12	1	2	.333	1.47	0	18⅓	13	11	3	10	28

KNUDSON, MARK
P

PERSONAL: Born October 28, 1960, at Denver. . . . 6-5/200. . . . Throws right, bats right. . . . Full name: Mark Richard Knudson. . . . Name pronounced NOOD-sun.
HIGH SCHOOL: Natrona County (Casper, Wyo.).
COLLEGE: Colorado State.
TRANSACTIONS/CAREER NOTES: Selected by Houston Astros organization in third round of free-agent draft (June 7, 1982). . . . On Houston disabled list (July 15-August 5, 1985). . . . Traded by Astros organization to Milwaukee Brewers organization

(August 21, 1986), completing deal in which Brewers traded P Danny Darwin to Astros for P Don August and a player to be named later (August 15, 1986).... On Milwaukee disabled list (May 2-June 7, 1991); included rehabilitation disability assignment to Denver (May 28-June 7, 1991).... Granted free agency (October 16, 1991).

Year	Team (League)	G	W	L	Pct.	ERA	Sv.	IP	H	R	ER	BB	SO
1982	—Daytona Beach (Florida State)..	12	2	6	.250	4.77	0	60⅓	75	35	32	23	15
1983	—Daytona Beach (Florida State)..	12	5	3	.625	2.40	0	78⅔	80	29	21	22	47
	—Columbus (Southern)	13	4	5	.444	4.26	0	69⅔	82	40	33	21	28
1984	—Columbus (Southern)	14	4	5	.444	2.23	0	101	100	32	25	27	54
	—Tucson (Pacific Coast)	13	4	6	.400	3.64	0	84	93	41	34	20	42
1985	—Tucson (Pacific Coast)	24	8	5	.615	4.01	0	146	171	69	65	37	68
	—Houston (N.L.)	2	0	2	.000	9.00	0	11	21	11	11	3	4
1986	—Tucson-Vancouver (PCL)■．．．．．	17	6	6	.500	4.13	0	106⅔	124	54	49	26	63
	—Houston (N.L.)	9	1	5	.167	4.22	0	42⅔	48	23	20	15	20
	—Milwaukee (A.L.)	4	0	1	.000	7.64	0	17⅔	22	15	15	5	9
1987	—Denver (American Assoc.)	14	7	2	.778	5.86	0	78⅓	89	53	51	30	37
	—Milwaukee (A.L.)	15	4	4	.500	5.37	0	62	88	46	37	14	26
1988	—Denver (American Assoc.)	24	11	8	.579	3.40	0	164⅓	180	67	62	33	66
	—Milwaukee (A.L.)	5	0	0	...	1.13	0	16	17	3	2	2	7
1989	—Milwaukee (A.L.)	40	8	5	.615	3.35	0	123⅔	110	50	46	29	47
1990	—Milwaukee (A.L.)	30	10	9	.526	4.12	0	168⅓	187	84	77	40	56
1991	—Milwaukee (A.L.)	12	1	3	.250	7.97	0	35	54	33	31	15	23
	—Denver (American Assoc.)	13	4	4	.500	5.40	1	51⅔	73	34	31	13	28
American League totals (6 years)		106	23	22	.511	4.43	0	422⅔	478	231	208	105	168
National League totals (2 years)		11	1	7	.125	5.20	0	53⅔	69	34	31	18	24
Major league totals (7 years)		117	24	29	.453	4.52	0	476⅓	547	265	239	123	192

KOMMINSK, BRAD
OF, WHITE SOX

PERSONAL: Born April 4, 1961, at Lima, O.... 6-2/205.... Throws right, bats right.... Full name: Brad Lynn Komminsk.... Name pronounced KOMM-insk.
HIGH SCHOOL: Shawnee (Lima, O.).
TRANSACTIONS/CAREER NOTES: Selected by Atlanta Braves organization in first round (fourth pick overall) of free-agent draft (June 5, 1979).... Traded by Braves to Milwaukee Brewers for OF Dion James (January 20, 1987).... Granted free agency (October 15, 1988).... Signed by Colorado Springs, Cleveland Indians organization (December 21, 1988).... On Cleveland disabled list (April 9-May 4, 1989).... Claimed on waivers by San Francisco Giants (April 5, 1990).... Claimed on waivers by Baltimore Orioles (May 2, 1990).... Granted free agency (October 5, 1990).... Signed by Oakland Athletics (January 25, 1991).... On Tacoma disabled list (June 16-28, 1991).... Granted free agency (October 5, 1991).... Signed by Chicago White Sox organization (December 6, 1991).
RECORDS/HONORS: Named Carolina League Most Valuable Player (1981).
STATISTICAL NOTES: Led Appalachian League batters with 74 strikeouts in 1979.... Led Carolina League in total bases with 278 and grounding into double plays with 24 in 1981.... Led International League with .596 slugging percentage in 1983.... Led International League third basemen with 28 errors in 1986.... Led International League batters with 124 strikeouts in 1986.... Led American Association batters with 127 strikeouts in 1987.

Year	Team (League)	Pos.	G	AB	R	H	2B	3B	HR	RBI	Avg.	SB	PO	A	E	Avg.
1979	—Kingsport (Appalachian)	OF	59	185	37	41	9	1	7	34	.222	20	112	1	2	.983
1980	—Anderson (S. Atlantic)	OF	121	425	86	111	17	5	20	67	.261	27	217	5	12	.949
1981	—Durham (Carolina)	OF	132	459	108	•148	27	2	33	★104	★.322	35	154	7	10	.942
1982	—Savannah (Southern)	OF	133	454	88	124	18	7	26	78	.273	14	158	6	10	.943
	—Richmond (Int'l)	OF	5	17	4	6	1	0	2	5	.353	0	10	0	0	1.000
1983	—Richmond (Int'l)	OF	117	413	94	138	24	6	24	103	.334	26	179	4	3	.984
	—Atlanta (N.L.)	OF	19	36	2	8	2	0	0	4	.222	0	16	1	1	.944
1984	—Richmond (Int'l)	OF	42	144	23	37	11	3	5	28	.257	8	66	4	3	.959
	—Atlanta (N.L.)	OF	90	301	37	61	10	0	8	36	.203	18	135	2	1	.993
1985	—Atlanta (N.L.)	OF	106	300	52	68	12	3	4	21	.227	10	161	2	7	.959
1986	—Richmond (Int'l)	3B-OF-1B	133	465	67	109	22	4	13	65	.234	29	127	200	†30	.916
	—Atlanta (N.L.)	3B-OF	5	5	1	2	0	0	0	1	.400	0	1	2	0	1.000
1987	—Denver (Am. Assoc.)■	OF	135	494	110	147	31	4	★32	95	.298	18	269	16	5	.983
	—Milwaukee (A.L.)	OF	7	15	0	1	0	0	0	1	.067	1	10	0	0	1.000
1988	—Denver (Am. Assoc.)	OF	105	348	55	83	18	3	16	57	.239	7	210	6	4	.982
1989	—Colorado Springs (PCL)■..	OF	54	190	30	55	17	0	9	34	.289	7	119	0	1	.992
	—Cleveland (A.L.)	OF	71	198	27	47	8	2	8	33	.237	8	181	3	1	.995
1990	—San Francisco (N.L.)■	OF	8	5	2	1	0	0	0	0	.200	0	3	0	0	1.000
	—Baltimore (A.L.)■	OF	46	101	18	24	4	0	3	8	.238	1	67	2	0	1.000
	—Rochester (Int'l)	OF	28	79	7	23	2	0	1	8	.291	0	38	2	2	.952
1991	—Tacoma (Pacific Coast)■..	OF	74	270	38	79	15	4	5	43	.293	11	124	6	1	.992
	—Oakland (A.L.)	OF	24	25	1	3	1	0	0	2	.120	1	18	1	0	1.000
American League totals (4 years)			148	339	46	75	13	2	11	43	.221	11	276	6	1	.996
National League totals (5 years)			228	647	94	140	24	3	12	62	.216	28	316	7	9	.973
Major league totals (8 years)			376	986	140	215	37	5	23	105	.218	39	592	13	10	.984

KOSLOFSKI, KEVIN
OF, ROYALS

PERSONAL: Born September 24, 1966, at Decatur, Ill.... 5-8/165.... Throws right, bats left.... Full name: Kevin Craig Koslofski.
HIGH SCHOOL: Maroa-Forsythe (Maroa, Ill.).
TRANSACTIONS/CAREER NOTES: Selected by Kansas City Royals organization in 20th round of free-agent draft (June 4, 1984).... On Memphis disabled list (May 15-27, 1991).

Year	Team (League)	Pos.	G	AB	R	H	2B	3B	HR	RBI	Avg.	SB	PO	A	E	Avg.
1984	Eugene (Northwest)	OF	53	155	23	29	2	2	1	10	.187	10	46	1	2	.959
1985	Sarasota Royals (GCL)	OF	33	108	17	27	4	2	0	11	.250	7	43	3	1	.979
1986	Fort Myers (Florida St.)	OF	103	331	44	84	13	5	0	29	.254	12	178	★16	7	.965
1987	Fort Myers (Florida St.)	OF	109	330	46	80	12	3	0	25	.242	25	185	10	6	.970
1988	Baseball City (Fla. St.)	OF	108	368	52	97	7	8	3	30	.264	32	174	14	2	.989
1989	Baseball City (Fla. St.)	OF	116	343	65	89	10	3	4	33	.259	41	224	7	8	.967
1990	Memphis (Southern)	OF	118	367	52	78	11	5	3	32	.213	12	221	★16	6	.975
1991	Memphis (Southern)	OF	81	287	41	93	15	3	7	39	.324	10	176	12	5	.974
	Omaha (Am. Assoc.)	OF	25	94	13	28	3	2	2	19	.298	4	61	3	1	.985

KRAMER, TOM
P, INDIANS

PERSONAL: Born January 9, 1968, at Cincinnati. . . . 6-0/185. . . . Throws right, bats both. . . . Full name: Thomas Joseph Kramer.
HIGH SCHOOL: Roger Bacon (Cincinnati).
COLLEGE: John A. Logan College (Ill.).
TRANSACTIONS/CAREER NOTES: Selected by Cleveland Indians organization in fifth round of free-agent draft (June 2, 1987).
STATISTICAL NOTES: Led Midwest League with 10 complete games in 1988.

Year	Team (League)	G	W	L	Pct.	ERA	Sv.	IP	H	R	ER	BB	SO
1987	Burlington (West. Carolinas)....	12	7	3	.700	3.01	1	71⅔	57	31	24	26	71
1988	Waterloo (Midwest)	27	14	7	.667	2.54	0	★198⅔	173	70	56	60	152
1989	Kinston (Carolina)	18	9	5	.643	2.60	0	131⅔	97	44	38	44	89
	Canton/Akron (Eastern)	10	1	6	.143	6.23	0	43⅓	58	34	30	20	26
1990	Kinston (Carolina)	16	7	4	.636	2.85	0	98	82	34	31	29	96
	Canton/Akron (Eastern)	12	6	3	.667	3.00	0	72	67	25	24	14	46
1991	Canton/Akron (Eastern)	35	7	3	.700	2.38	6	79⅓	61	23	21	34	61
	Colorado Springs (Pac. Coast) ..	10	1	0	1.000	0.79	4	11⅓	5	1	1	5	18
	Cleveland (A.L.)	4	0	0	. . .	17.36	0	4⅔	10	9	9	6	4
Major league totals (1 year)		4	0	0	. . .	17.36	0	4⅔	10	9	9	6	4

KREMERS, JIMMY
C/1B, EXPOS

PERSONAL: Born October 8, 1965, at Little Rock, Ark. . . . 6-3/210. . . . Throws right, bats left. . . . Full name: James Edward Kremers.
HIGH SCHOOL: Catholic (Little Rock, Ark.).
COLLEGE: Arkansas.
TRANSACTIONS/CAREER NOTES: Selected by Cincinnati Reds organization in eighth round of free-agent draft (June 2, 1987). . . . Selected by Atlanta Braves organization in second round of free-agent draft (June 1, 1988). . . . Traded by Braves with a player to be named later to Montreal Expos for OF Otis Nixon and 3B Boi Rodriguez (April 1, 1991); Sumter (Expos organization) acquired P Keith Morrison to complete deal (June 3, 1991).
STATISTICAL NOTES: Led Southern League catchers with 743 total chances and 19 passed balls in 1989. . . . Led American Association catchers with 13 errors and 15 passed balls in 1991.

Year	Team (League)	Pos.	G	AB	R	H	2B	3B	HR	RBI	Avg.	SB	PO	A	E	Avg.
1988	Sumter (South Atlantic)....	C	72	256	30	68	12	3	5	42	.266	1	51	13	0	1.000
1989	Greenville (Southern)........	C	121	388	41	91	19	1	16	58	.235	5	★649	★86	8	.989
1990	Richmond (Int'l)	C-1B	63	190	25	44	8	0	6	24	.232	1	309	40	4	.989
	Atlanta (N.L.)	C	29	73	7	8	1	1	1	2	.110	0	107	10	1	.992
1991	Indianapolis (A.A.)■.........	C-1B	98	290	34	70	14	0	11	42	.241	1	600	82	†15	.978
Major league totals (1 year)			29	73	7	8	1	1	1	2	.110	0	107	10	1	.992

KREUTER, CHAD
C, TIGERS

PERSONAL: Born August 26, 1964, at Marin County, Calif. . . . 6-2/190. . . . Throws right, bats right. . . . Full name: Chad Michael Kreuter. . . . Name pronounced CREW-ter.
HIGH SCHOOL: Redwood (Calif.).
COLLEGE: Pepperdine.
TRANSACTIONS/CAREER NOTES: Selected by Texas Rangers organization in fifth round of free-agent draft (June 3, 1985). . . . Granted free agency (October 15, 1991). . . . Signed by Toledo, Detroit Tigers organization (January 2, 1992).
RECORDS/HONORS: Shares major league record for most hits in one inning in first major league game—2 (September 14, 1988, fifth inning).
STATISTICAL NOTES: Led Carolina League catchers with 21 errors and 17 double plays and tied for lead with 113 assists in 1986. . . . Tied for Texas League lead in double plays by catchers with nine in 1988. . . . Led A.L. with 21 passed balls in 1989.
MISCELLANEOUS: Batted as switch-hitter (1986-89).

Year	Team (League)	Pos.	G	AB	R	H	2B	3B	HR	RBI	Avg.	SB	PO	A	E	Avg.
1985	Burlington (W. Caro.)........	C	69	199	25	53	9	0	4	26	.266	3	349	34	8	.980
1986	Salem (Carolina)	C-OF-3B	125	387	55	85	21	2	6	49	.220	5	613	‡115	†21	.972
1987	Charlotte (Florida State) ...	C-OF-3B	85	281	36	61	18	1	9	40	.217	1	380	54	8	.982
1988	Tulsa (Texas)	C	108	358	46	95	24	6	3	51	.265	2	603	71	•13	.981
	Texas (A.L.)....................	C	16	51	3	14	2	1	1	5	.275	0	93	8	1	.990
1989	Texas (A.L.)....................	C	87	158	16	24	3	0	5	9	.152	0	453	26	4	.992
	Oklahoma City (A.A.)	C	26	87	10	22	3	0	0	6	.253	1	146	14	2	.988

Year Team (League)	Pos.	G	AB	R	H	2B	3B	HR	RBI	Avg.	SB	PO	A	E	Avg.
1990—Texas (A.L.)	C	22	22	2	1	1	0	0	2	.045	0	39	4	1	.977
—Oklahoma City (A.A.)	C	92	291	41	65	17	1	7	35	.223	0	559	64	10	.984
1991—Texas (A.L.)	C	3	4	0	0	0	0	0	0	.000	0	5	0	1	1.000
—Oklahoma City (A.A.)	C	24	70	14	19	6	0	0	12	.271	2	146	23	7	.960
—Tulsa (Texas)	C	42	128	23	30	5	1	2	10	.234	1	269	27	4	.987
Major league totals (4 years)		128	235	21	39	6	1	6	16	.166	0	590	38	6	.991

KRUEGER, BILL
P, TWINS

PERSONAL: Born April 24, 1958, at Waukegan, Ill. . . . 6-5/205. . . . Throws left, bats left. . . . Full name: William Culp Krueger. . . . Name pronounced CREW-ger.
HIGH SCHOOL: McMinnville (Ore.).
COLLEGE: Portland (bachelor of arts degree in business administration, 1979).
TRANSACTIONS/CAREER NOTES: Signed as free agent by Oakland Athletics organization (July 12, 1980). . . . On disabled list (August 5, 1983-remainder of season). . . . On Oakland disabled list (May 6 to August 8, 1986); included rehabilitation disability assignment to Madison (July 4-8, 1986) and Tacoma (July 10-18 and July 21-27, 1986). . . . Traded by A's organization to Los Angeles Dodgers organization for P Tim Meeks (June 23, 1987). . . . Released by Dodgers (November 12, 1987). . . . Re-signed by Dodgers organization (January 1, 1988). . . . Traded by Dodgers to Pittsburgh Pirates for P Jim Neidlinger (October 3, 1988). . . . Released by Pirates (March 28, 1989). . . . Signed by Denver, Milwaukee Brewers organization (April 7, 1989). . . . On Milwaukee disabled list (August 10-31, 1990); included rehabilitation disability assignment to Beloit (August 29-31, 1990). . . . Granted free agency (November 5, 1990). . . . Signed by Seattle Mariners (December 19, 1990). . . . Granted free agency (October 30, 1991). . . . Signed by Minnesota Twins organization (January 29, 1992).
STATISTICAL NOTES: Tied for Eastern League lead in games started by pitcher with 27 and shutouts with three in 1982. . . . Pitched seven-inning 2-0 no-hit victory against Phoenix (August 14, 1987, second game). . . . Led Pacific Coast League with four shutouts in 1988.

Year Team (League)	G	W	L	Pct.	ERA	Sv.	IP	H	R	ER	BB	SO
1980—Medford (Northwest)	9	0	4	.000	5.11	1	44	54	38	25	29	48
1981—Modesto (California)	16	3	5	.375	3.67	0	98	87	49	40	52	76
—West Haven (Eastern)	11	3	6	.333	3.57	0	68	74	36	27	31	36
1982—West Haven (Eastern)	28	15	9	.625	2.83	0	181	160	69	57	81	163
1983—Oakland (A.L.)	17	7	6	.538	3.61	0	109⅔	104	54	44	53	58
1984—Tacoma (Pacific Coast)	5	2	2	.500	3.69	0	31⅔	29	17	13	21	20
—Oakland (A.L.)	26	10	10	.500	4.75	0	142	156	95	75	85	61
1985—Oakland (A.L.)	32	9	10	.474	4.52	0	151⅓	165	95	76	69	56
—Tacoma (Pacific Coast)	2	0	1	.000	9.31	0	9⅔	12	10	10	6	10
1986—Oakland (A.L.)	11	1	2	.333	6.03	1	34⅓	40	25	23	13	10
—Madison (Midwest)	1	0	0	. . .	0.00	0	2	1	0	0	1	1
—Tacoma (Pacific Coast)	8	3	3	.500	4.64	0	52⅓	53	32	27	27	41
1987—Oakland (A.L.)	9	0	3	.000	9.53	0	5⅔	9	7	6	8	2
—Tacoma-Albuquerque (PCL)■..	24	9	7	.563	4.06	0	146⅓	158	74	66	66	97
—Los Angeles (N.L.)	2	0	0	. . .	0.00	0	2⅓	3	2	0	1	2
1988—Albuquerque (Pacific Coast)	27	★15	5	.750	★3.01	0	173⅓	167	74	58	69	114
—Los Angeles (N.L.)	1	0	0	. . .	11.57	0	2⅓	4	3	3	2	1
1989—Denver (American Assoc.)■	2	1	1	.500	2.03	0	13⅓	10	4	3	6	9
—Milwaukee (A.L.)	34	3	2	.600	3.84	3	93⅔	96	43	40	33	72
1990—Milwaukee (A.L.)	30	6	8	.429	3.98	0	129	137	70	57	54	64
—Beloit (Midwest)	1	1	0	1.000	1.50	0	6	4	1	1	0	4
1991—Seattle (A.L.)■	35	11	8	.579	3.60	0	175	194	82	70	60	91
American League totals (8 years)	194	47	49	.490	4.19	4	840⅔	901	471	391	375	414
National League totals (2 years)	3	0	0	. . .	5.79	0	4⅔	7	5	3	3	3
Major league totals (9 years)	197	47	49	.490	4.19	4	845⅓	908	476	394	378	417

KRUK, JOHN
1B, PHILLIES

PERSONAL: Born February 9, 1961, at Charleston, W.Va. . . . 5-10/200. . . . Throws left, bats left. . . . Full name: John Martin Kruk.
HIGH SCHOOL: Keyser (W.Va.).
COLLEGE: Allegany Community College (Md.).
TRANSACTIONS/CAREER NOTES: Selected by Pittsburgh Pirates organization in third round of free-agent draft (January 13, 1981). . . . Selected by San Diego Padres organization in secondary phase of free-agent draft (June 8, 1981). . . . On disabled list (May 5-21, 1989). . . . Traded by Padres with IF Randy Ready to Philadelphia Phillies for OF Chris James (June 2, 1989). . . . On disabled list (July 3-July 28, 1989).
STATISTICAL NOTES: Led Texas League in sacrifice flies with 13 in 1983. . . . Led Pacific Coast League outfielders in double plays with four in 1984.

Year Team (League)	Pos.	G	AB	R	H	2B	3B	HR	RBI	Avg.	SB	PO	A	E	Avg.
1981—Walla Walla (Northwest)	OF-1B	63	157	31	38	10	0	1	13	.242	7	108	5	2	.983
1982—Reno (California)	OF-1B	125	441	82	137	30	8	11	92	.311	17	253	11	7	.974
1983—Beaumont (Texas)	OF-1B-P	133	498	94	170	41	9	10	88	.341	13	304	22	8	.976
1984—Las Vegas (Pac. Coast)	OF	115	340	56	111	25	6	11	57	.326	2	183	7	2	.990
1985—Las Vegas (Pac. Coast)	OF-1B	123	422	61	148	29	4	7	59★	.351	2	356	18	7	.982
1986—San Diego (N.L.)	OF-1B	122	278	33	86	16	2	4	38	.309	2	139	6	3	.980
—Las Vegas (Pac. Coast)	OF-1B	6	28	6	13	3	1	0	9	.464	0	22	1	0	1.000

Year	Team (League)	Pos.	G	AB	R	H	2B	3B	HR	RBI	Avg.	SB	PO	A	E	Avg.
							BATTING							FIELDING		
1987 —San Diego (N.L.)		1B-OF	138	447	72	140	14	2	20	91	.313	18	911	78	5	.995
1988 —San Diego (N.L.)		1B-OF	120	378	54	91	17	1	9	44	.241	5	634	37	3	.996
1989 —San Diego-Phil. (N.L.)■....		OF-1B	112	357	53	107	13	6	8	44	.300	3	212	9	4	.982
1990 —Philadelphia (N.L.)		OF-1B	142	443	52	129	25	8	7	67	.291	10	543	45	4	.993
1991 —Philadelphia (N.L.)		1B-OF	152	538	84	158	27	6	21	92	.294	7	848	53	3	.997
Major league totals (6 years)			786	2441	348	711	112	25	69	376	.291	45	3287	228	22	.994

ALL-STAR GAME

Year	League	Pos.	AB	R	H	2B	3B	HR	RBI	Avg.	SB	PO	A	E	Avg.
						BATTING							FIELDING		
1991 —National							Did not play								

RECORD AS PITCHER

Year	Team (League)	G	W	L	Pct.	ERA	Sv.	IP	H	R	ER	BB	SO
1983 —Beaumont (Texas)	3	0	0	...	0.00	0	5	5	0	0	2	3

LaCOSS, MIKE
P

PERSONAL: Born May 30, 1956, at Glendale, Calif. . . . 6-4/200. . . . Throws right, bats right. . . . Full name: Michael James LaCoss.

HIGH SCHOOL: Mount Whitney (Visalia, Calif.).

TRANSACTIONS/CAREER NOTES: Selected by Cincinnati Reds organization in third round of free-agent draft (June 5, 1974). . . . Sold by Reds on waivers to Houston Astros (April 4, 1982). . . . On disabled list (June 17-July 8, 1983). . . . Granted free agency (November 8, 1984). . . . Signed by Kansas City Royals organization (February 19, 1985). . . . Released by Royals organization (November 6, 1985). . . . Signed by San Francisco Giants organization (February 3, 1986). . . . Granted free agency (November 12, 1986). . . . Re-signed by Giants (December 12, 1986). . . . Granted free agency (November 9, 1987). . . . Re-signed by Giants (November 24, 1987). . . . On disabled list (July 17-September 8, 1988). . . . On San Francisco disabled list (May 3-August 9, 1990); included rehabilitation disability assignment to San Jose (August 5-9, 1990). . . . Granted free agency (December 7, 1990); remained under current contract with Giants. . . . Released by Giants (July 3, 1991).

STATISTICAL NOTES: Tied for American Association lead with three shutouts in 1978.

Year	Team (League)	G	W	L	Pct.	ERA	Sv.	IP	H	R	ER	BB	SO
1974 —Billing (Pioneer)	13	6	5	.545	2.79	0	87	81	40	27	38	58
1975 —Tampa (Florida State)	23	4	7	.364	2.86	0	151	131	61	48	41	72
1976 —Three Rivers (Eastern)	25	12	10	.545	2.94	0	162	148	66	53	53	80
1977 —Indianapolis (Am. Assoc.)	27	11	*13	.458	3.87	0	186	181	93	80	65	104
1978 —Indianapolis (Am. Assoc.)	19	11	5	.688	3.46	0	130	129	62	50	49	67
—Cincinnati (N.L.)	16	4	8	.333	4.50	0	96	104	56	48	46	31
1979 —Cincinnati (N.L.)	35	14	8	.636	3.50	0	206	202	92	80	79	73
1980 —Cincinnati (N.L.)	34	10	12	.455	4.63	0	169	207	101	87	68	59
1981 —Cincinnati (N.L.)	20	4	7	.364	6.12	1	78	102	55	53	30	22
1982 —Houston (N.L.)■	41	6	6	.500	2.90	1	115	107	41	37	54	51
1983 —Houston (N.L.)	38	5	7	.417	4.43	1	138	142	81	68	56	53
1984 —Houston (N.L.)	39	7	5	.583	4.02	3	132	132	64	59	55	86
1985 —Kansas City (A.L.)■	21	1	1	.500	5.09	1	40⅔	49	25	23	29	26
—Omaha (American Assoc.)	4	1	2	.333	3.22	0	22⅓	23	12	8	15	11
1986 —San Francisco (N.L.)■	37	10	13	.435	3.57	0	204⅓	179	99	81	70	86
1987 —San Francisco (N.L.)	39	13	10	.565	3.68	0	171	184	78	70	63	79
1988 —San Francisco (N.L.)	19	7	7	.500	3.62	0	114⅓	99	55	46	47	70
1989 —San Francisco (N.L.)	45	10	10	.500	3.17	6	150⅓	143	62	53	65	78
1990 —San Francisco (N.L.)	13	6	4	.600	3.94	0	77⅔	75	37	34	39	39
—San Jose (Pacific Coast)	1	1	0	1.000	1.50	0	6	5	1	1	0	6
1991 —San Francisco (N.L.)	18	1	5	.167	7.23	0	47⅓	61	39	38	24	30
American League totals (1 year)	21	1	1	.500	5.09	1	40⅔	49	25	23	29	26
National League totals (13 years)	394	97	102	.487	3.99	11	1699	1737	860	754	696	757
Major league totals (14 years)	415	98	103	.488	4.02	12	1739⅔	1786	885	777	725	783

CHAMPIONSHIP SERIES RECORD

Year	Team (League)	G	W	L	Pct.	ERA	Sv.	IP	H	R	ER	BB	SO
1979 —Cincinnati (N.L.)	1	0	1	.000	10.80	0	1⅔	1	2	2	4	0
1987 —San Francisco (N.L.)	2	0	0	...	0.00	0	3⅓	1	0	0	3	2
1989 —San Francisco (N.L.)	1	0	0	...	9.00	0	3	7	3	3	0	2
Championship Series totals (3 years)	4	0	1	.000	5.63	0	8	9	5	5	7	4

WORLD SERIES RECORD

Year	Team (League)	G	W	L	Pct.	ERA	Sv.	IP	H	R	ER	BB	SO
1989 —San Francisco (N.L.)	2	0	0	...	6.23	0	4⅓	4	3	3	3	2

ALL-STAR GAME RECORD

Year	League	W	L	Pct.	ERA	Sv.	IP	H	R	ER	BB	SO
1979 —National	0	0	...	0.00	0	1⅓	1	0	0	0	0

LAKE, STEVE
C, GIANTS

PERSONAL: Born March 14, 1957, at Inglewood, Calif. . . . 6-1/199. . . . Throws right, bats right. . . . Full name: Steven Michael Lake.

HIGH SCHOOL: Lennox (Calif.).

TRANSACTIONS/CAREER NOTES: Selected by Baltimore Orioles organization in third round of free-agent draft (June 4, 1975).... On disabled list (April 17-May 16, 1978).... Sold by Orioles organization to Milwaukee Brewers organization (December 21, 1978).... On disabled list (June 20-July 6, 1979).... Loaned by Brewers organization to Tucson, Houston Astros organization (April 5, 1982); returned (September 7, 1982).... Traded by Brewers organization to Chicago Cubs for a player to be named later (April 1, 1983); Brewers organization acquired P Rich Buonantony to complete deal (October 24, 1983).... On Chicago disabled list (May 14-August 3, 1984); included rehabilitation disability assignment to Midland (July 23-August 3, 1984).... Released by Cubs (July 15, 1986).... Signed by Louisville, St. Louis Cardinals organization (July 24, 1986).... Traded by Cardinals with OF Curt Ford to Philadelphia Phillies for OF Milt Thompson (December 16, 1988).... On disabled list (August 28, 1989-remainder of season).... Granted free agency (November 13, 1989).... Re-signed by Phillies (December 6, 1989).... On disabled list (July 21-September 1, 1990).... Granted free agency (October 28, 1991).... Signed by San Francisco Giants (January 14, 1992).

STATISTICAL NOTES: Led Appalachian League with 15 passed balls in 1975.

Year — Team (League)	Pos.	G	AB	R	H	2B	3B	HR	RBI	Avg.	SB	PO	A	E	Avg.
1975 — Bluefield (Appalachian)	C	49	162	17	45	12	0	3	24	.278	3	254	*39	9	.970
1976 — Miami (Florida State)	PH	1	1	0	1	0	0	0	1	1.000	0	0	0	0	...
1977 — Miami (Florida State)	C	79	232	25	55	10	1	2	24	.237	2	357	47	6	.985
1978 — Miami (Florida State)	C	69	223	19	57	10	0	2	26	.256	2	300	49	6	.983
1979 — Stockton (California)■	C	94	329	36	93	12	3	6	40	.283	2	504	73	8	.986
1980 — Holyoke (Eastern)	C-OF	102	325	26	84	9	2	2	44	.258	3	445	107	10	.982
1981 — Vancouver (Pac. Coast)	C	109	348	27	80	14	1	2	38	.230	2	502	102	7	.989
1982 — Tucson (Pacific Coast)■...	C	112	378	42	100	15	4	3	45	.265	5	504	91	12	.980
1983 — Chicago (N.L.)■.............	C	38	85	9	22	4	1	1	7	.259	0	115	22	0	1.000
1984 — Chicago (N.L.)	C	25	54	4	12	4	0	2	7	.222	0	72	13	4	.955
— Midland (Texas)	C	9	25	2	4	0	0	0	1	.160	0	46	7	0	1.000
1985 — Chicago (N.L.)	C	58	119	5	18	2	0	1	11	.151	1	182	25	1	.995
1986 — Chicago-St. Louis (N.L.)■	C	36	68	8	20	2	0	2	14	.294	0	105	9	2	.983
— Iowa-Louisville (A.A.)......	C	33	98	5	24	6	0	0	13	.245	0	140	21	2	.988
1987 — St. Louis (N.L.)	C	74	179	19	45	7	2	2	19	.251	0	253	21	1	.996
1988 — St. Louis (N.L.)	C	36	54	5	15	3	0	1	4	.278	0	51	8	1	.983
1989 — Philadelphia (N.L.)■.........	C	58	155	9	39	5	1	2	14	.252	0	262	33	3	.990
1990 — Philadelphia (N.L.)	C	29	80	4	20	2	0	0	6	.250	0	115	19	1	.993
1991 — Philadelphia (N.L.)	C	58	158	12	36	4	1	1	11	.228	0	277	25	2	.993
Major league totals (9 years)		412	952	75	227	33	5	12	93	.238	1	1432	175	15	.991

CHAMPIONSHIP SERIES RECORD

Year — Team (League)	Pos.	G	AB	R	H	2B	3B	HR	RBI	Avg.	SB	PO	A	E	Avg.
1984 — Chicago (N.L.)	C	1	1	0	1	1	0	0	0	1.000	0	0	0	0	...

WORLD SERIES RECORD

Year — Team (League)	Pos.	G	AB	R	H	2B	3B	HR	RBI	Avg.	SB	PO	A	E	Avg.
1987 — St. Louis (N.L.)	C	3	3	0	1	0	0	0	1	.333	0	8	1	0	1.000

LAKER, TIM
C, EXPOS

PERSONAL: Born November 27, 1969, at Encino, Calif.... 6-2/185.... Throws right, bats right.... Full name: Timothy John Laker.
HIGH SCHOOL: Simi Valley (Calif.).
COLLEGE: Oxnard College (Calif.).
TRANSACTIONS/CAREER NOTES: Selected by Kansas City Royals organization in 49th round of free-agent draft (June 2, 1987). ... Selected by Montreal Expos organization in sixth round of free-agent draft (June 1, 1988).
STATISTICAL NOTES: Led New York-Pennsylvania League with 16 passed balls in 1989.... Led Midwest League catchers with 125 assists, 18 errors and 944 total chances in 1990.

Year — Team (League)	Pos.	G	AB	R	H	2B	3B	HR	RBI	Avg.	SB	PO	A	E	Avg.
1988 — Jamestown (N.Y.-Penn) ...	C-OF	47	152	14	34	9	0	0	17	.224	2	236	22	2	.992
1989 — Rockford (Midwest)	C	14	48	4	11	1	1	0	4	.229	1	91	6	4	.960
— Jamestown (N.Y.-Penn) ...	C	58	216	25	48	9	1	2	24	.222	8	437	61	8	.984
1990 — Rockford (Midwest)	C-OF	120	425	46	94	18	3	7	57	.221	7	802	†125	†18	.981
— West Palm Beach (FSL)	C	2	3	0	0	0	0	0	0	.000	0	2	0	0	1.000
1991 — Harrisburg (Eastern)	C	11	35	4	10	1	0	1	5	.286	0	67	4	3	.959
— West Palm Beach (FSL)	C	100	333	35	77	15	2	5	33	.231	10	560	87	*14	.979

LAMP, DENNIS
P

PERSONAL: Born September 23, 1952, at Los Angeles.... 6-3/215.... Throws right, bats right.... Full name: Dennis Patrick Lamp.
HIGH SCHOOL: St. John Bosco (Bellflower, Calif.).
TRANSACTIONS/CAREER NOTES: Selected by Chicago Cubs organization in third round of free-agent draft (June 8, 1971).... Traded by Cubs to Chicago White Sox for P Ken Kravec (March 28, 1981).... Granted free agency (November 7, 1983).... Signed by Toronto Blue Jays as Type A player (January 10, 1984). P Tom Seaver selected from player compensation pool by White Sox (January 20, 1984).... Released by Blue Jays (October 20, 1986).... Signed by Cleveland Indians (February 5, 1987).... Released by Indians (March 23, 1987).... Signed by Oakland Athletics organization (April 27, 1987).... Granted free agency (October 19, 1987).... Signed by Pawtucket, Boston Red Sox organization (January 5, 1988).... On disabled list (August 9-27, 1988).... Granted free agency (November 4, 1988).... Re-signed by Red Sox

(November 20, 1988). . . . Granted free agency (November 13, 1989). . . . Re-signed by Red Sox (December 6, 1989). . . . Granted free agency (November 4, 1991).

Year	Team (League)	G	W	L	Pct.	ERA	Sv.	IP	H	R	ER	BB	SO
1971	Caldwell (Pioneer)	14	1	2	.333	6.46	0	46	51	39	33	32	43
1972	Bradenton Cubs (Gulf Coast)	14	7	2	.778	1.93	0	70	56	20	15	21	56
1973	Quincy (Midwest)	13	6	4	.600	2.63	0	89	67	32	26	29	71
	Midland (Texas)	9	2	4	.333	4.69	0	48	54	29	25	11	23
1974	Key West (Florida State)	8	1	5	.167	1.47	0	49	39	15	8	14	20
	Midland (Texas)	24	1	1	.500	4.65	0	60	70	38	31	22	42
1975	Midland (Texas)	37	7	5	.583	3.33	0	127	112	52	47	54	71
1976	Wichita (American Assoc.)	30	8	*14	.364	4.06	0	153	182	94	69	52	98
1977	Wichita (American Assoc.)	20	11	4	.733	2.93	0	129	116	54	42	23	52
	Chicago (N.L.)	11	0	2	.000	6.30	0	30	43	21	21	8	12
1978	Chicago (N.L.)	37	7	15	.318	3.29	0	224	221	96	82	56	73
1979	Chicago (N.L.)	38	11	10	.524	3.51	0	200	223	96	78	46	86
1980	Chicago (N.L.)	41	10	14	.417	5.19	0	203	259	*123	*117	82	83
1981	Chicago (A.L.)■	27	7	6	.538	2.41	0	127	103	41	34	43	71
1982	Chicago (A.L.)	44	11	8	.579	3.99	5	189⅔	206	96	84	59	78
1983	Chicago (A.L.)	49	7	7	.500	3.71	15	116⅓	123	52	48	29	44
1984	Toronto (A.L.)■	56	8	8	.500	4.55	9	85	97	53	43	38	45
1985	Toronto (A.L.)	53	11	0	1.000	3.32	2	105⅔	96	42	39	27	68
1986	Toronto (A.L.)	40	2	6	.250	5.05	2	73	93	50	41	23	30
1987	Tacoma (Pacific Coast)■	6	1	0	1.000	2.92	0	12⅓	9	4	4	8	10
	Oakland (A.L.)	36	1	3	.250	5.08	3	56⅔	76	38	32	22	36
1988	Boston (A.L.)■	46	7	6	.538	3.48	0	82⅔	92	39	32	19	49
1989	Boston (A.L.)	42	4	2	.667	2.32	2	112⅓	96	37	29	27	61
1990	Boston (A.L.)	47	3	5	.375	4.68	0	105⅔	114	61	55	30	49
1991	Boston (A.L.)	51	6	3	.667	4.70	0	92	100	54	48	31	57
American League totals (11 years)		491	67	54	.554	3.81	38	1146	1196	563	485	348	588
National League totals (4 years)		127	28	41	.406	4.08	0	657	746	336	298	192	254
Major league totals (15 years)		618	95	95	.500	3.91	38	1803	1942	899	783	540	842

CHAMPIONSHIP SERIES RECORD

Year	Team (League)	G	W	L	Pct.	ERA	Sv.	IP	H	R	ER	BB	SO
1983	Chicago (A.L.)	3	0	0	. . .	0.00	0	2	0	1	0	2	1
1985	Toronto (A.L.)	3	0	0	. . .	0.00	0	9⅓	2	0	0	1	10
1990	Boston (A.L.)	1	0	0	. . .	108.00	0	⅓	2	4	4	2	0
Championship Series totals (3 years)		7	0	0	. . .	3.09	0	11⅔	4	5	4	5	11

LAMPKIN, TOM
C, PADRES

PERSONAL: Born March 4, 1964, at Cincinnati. . . . 5-11/185. . . . Throws right, bats left. . . . Full name: Thomas Michael Lampkin.
HIGH SCHOOL: Blanchet (Seattle).
COLLEGE: Portland.
TRANSACTIONS/CAREER NOTES: Selected by Cleveland Indians organization in 11th round of free-agent draft (June 2, 1986). . . . On disabled list (July 6, 1989-remainder of season). . . . Traded by Indians organization to San Diego Padres for OF Alex Cole (July 11, 1990).

Year	Team (League)	Pos.	G	AB	R	H	2B	3B	HR	RBI	Avg.	SB	PO	A	E	Avg.
							BATTING							FIELDING		
1986	Batavia (N.Y.-Penn)	C	63	190	24	49	5	1	1	20	.258	4	323	36	8	.978
1987	Waterloo (Midwest)	C	118	398	49	106	19	2	7	55	.266	5	689	*100	15	.981
1988	Williamsport (NYP)	C	80	263	38	71	10	0	3	23	.270	1	431	60	9	.982
	Colorado Springs (PCL)	C	34	107	14	30	5	0	0	7	.280	0	171	28	5	.975
	Cleveland (A.L.)	C	4	4	0	0	0	0	0	0	.000	0	3	0	0	1.000
1989	Colorado Springs (PCL)	C	63	209	26	67	10	3	4	32	.321	4	305	21	8	.976
1990	Colo. Spgs.-L.V. (PCL)■	C-2B	70	201	32	45	7	5	1	18	.224	7	315	36	12	.967
	San Diego (N.L.)	C	26	63	4	14	0	1	1	4	.222	0	91	10	3	.971
1991	San Diego (N.L.)	C	38	58	4	11	3	1	0	3	.190	0	49	5	0	1.000
	Las Vegas (Pac. Coast)	C-1B-OF	45	164	25	52	11	1	2	29	.317	2	211	26	6	.975
American League totals (1 year)			4	4	0	0	0	0	0	0	.000	0	3	0	0	1.000
National League totals (2 years)			64	121	8	25	3	2	1	7	.207	0	140	15	3	.981
Major league totals (3 years)			68	125	8	25	3	2	1	7	.200	0	143	15	3	.981

LANCASTER, LES
P, CUBS

PERSONAL: Born April 21, 1962, at Dallas.. . . . 6-2/200. . . . Throws right, bats right. . . . Full name: Lester Wayne Lancaster.
HIGH SCHOOL: Nimitz (Irving, Tex.).
COLLEGE: Arkansas and Dallas Baptist College (Tex.).
TRANSACTIONS/CAREER NOTES: Selected by New York Yankees organization in 24th round of free-agent draft (June 8, 1981). . . . Selected by Texas Rangers organization in 39th round of free-agent draft (June 6, 1983). . . . Signed as free agent by Chicago Cubs organization (June 13, 1985). . . . On disabled list (July 24-August 14 and August 20-September 4, 1988).
STATISTICAL NOTES: Led Appalachian League with seven complete games in 1985. . . . Tied for N.L. lead with eight balks in 1987.
MISCELLANEOUS: Appeared in one game with Cubs as an outfielder with no chances (1990).

Year Team (League)	G	W	L	Pct.	ERA	Sv.	IP	H	R	ER	BB	SO
1985 —Wytheville (Appalachian)	20	7	4	.636	3.62	3	*102	*98	49	41	24	*81
1986 —Winston-Salem (Carolina)	13	8	3	.727	2.78	0	97	88	37	30	30	52
—Pittsfield (Eastern)	14	5	6	.455	4.19	0	88	105	46	41	34	49
1987 —Chicago (N.L.)	27	8	3	.727	4.90	0	132⅓	138	76	72	51	78
—Iowa (American Association)	15	5	3	.625	3.22	4	67	59	24	24	17	62
1988 —Chicago (N.L.)	44	4	6	.400	3.78	5	85⅔	89	42	36	34	36
1989 —Iowa (American Association)	17	5	7	.417	2.66	0	91⅓	76	38	27	43	56
—Chicago (N.L.)	42	4	2	.667	1.36	8	72⅔	60	12	11	15	56
1990 —Chicago (N.L.)	55	9	5	.643	4.62	6	109	121	57	56	40	65
—Iowa (American Association)	6	0	1	.000	4.08	1	17⅔	20	10	8	5	15
1991 —Chicago (N.L.)	64	9	7	.563	3.52	3	156	150	68	61	49	102
Major league totals (5 years)	232	34	23	.596	3.82	22	555⅔	558	255	236	189	337

CHAMPIONSHIP SERIES RECORD

Year Team (League)	G	W	L	Pct.	ERA	Sv.	IP	H	R	ER	BB	SO
1989 —Chicago (N.L.)	3	1	1	.500	6.00	000	6	6	4	4	1	3

LANDRUM, BILL
P, PIRATES

PERSONAL: Born August 17, 1958, at Columbia, S.C. . . . . 6-2/205. . . . Throws right, bats right. . . . Full name: Thomas William Landrum. . . . Son of Joe Landrum, pitcher, Brooklyn Dodgers (1950 and 1952).
HIGH SCHOOL: Spring Valley (Calif.).
COLLEGE: Spartanburg Methodist College (S.C.) and South Carolina (bachelor of science degree, 1980).
TRANSACTIONS/CAREER NOTES: Signed as free agent by Chicago Cubs organization (June 22, 1980). . . . Released by Cubs organization (October 20, 1980). . . . Signed by Billings, Cincinnati Reds organization (February 7, 1981). . . . On Indianapolis disabled list (July 19-August 4, 1983). . . . Drafted by Chicago White Sox (December 3, 1984); returned to Reds organization (March 30, 1985). . . . On Denver disabled list (April 29-June 21, 1986). . . . Traded by Reds organization to Chicago Cubs for IF Luis Quinones (April 1, 1988). . . . Granted free agency (October 15, 1988). . . . Signed by Pittsburgh Pirates (January 12, 1989).

Year Team (League)	G	W	L	Pct.	ERA	Sv.	IP	H	R	ER	BB	SO
1980 —Sarasota Cubs (Gulf Coast)	11	2	0	1.000	4.14	0	37	37	21	17	11	27
1981 —Tampa (Florida State)■	17	6	8	.429	3.80	0	83	87	44	35	22	52
1982 —Waterbury (Eastern)	*58	10	6	.625	4.09	6	112⅓	109	63	51	65	104
1983 —Waterbury (Eastern)	17	1	1	.500	1.52	3	29⅔	17	5	5	14	33
—Indianapolis (Am. Assoc.)	15	1	3	.250	3.06	2	17⅔	20	6	6	6	21
1984 —Wichita (Texas)	47	7	4	.636	3.45	2	130⅓	12	58	50	52	120
1985 —Denver (American Assoc.)	29	6	6	.500	3.98	2	138	148	72	61	49	88
1986 —Denver (American Assoc.)	24	1	3	.250	3.47	8	36⅓	36	20	14	25	36
—Cincinnati (N.L.)	10	0	0	. . .	6.75	0	13⅓	23	11	10	4	14
1987 —Cincinnati (N.L.)	44	3	2	.600	4.71	2	65	68	35	34	34	42
—Nashville (American Assoc.)	19	4	0	1.000	2.09	1	38⅔	30	9	9	19	47
1988 —Iowa (American Association)■	9	1	0	1.000	2.95	3	21⅓	13	7	7	6	22
—Chicago (N.L.)	7	1	0	1.000	5.84	0	12⅓	19	8	8	3	6
1989 —Pittsburgh (N.L.)■	56	2	3	.400	1.67	26	81	60	18	15	28	51
—Buffalo (American Assoc.)	5	3	0	1.000	0.71	0	25⅓	16	2	2	6	20
1990 —Pittsburgh (N.L.)	54	7	3	.700	2.13	13	71⅔	69	22	17	21	39
1991 —Pittsburgh (N.L.)	61	4	4	.500	3.18	17	76⅓	76	32	27	19	45
Major league totals (6 years)	232	17	12	.586	3.13	58	319⅔	315	126	111	109	197

CHAMPIONSHIP SERIES RECORD

Year Team (League)	G	W	L	Pct.	ERA	Sv.	IP	H	R	ER	BB	SO
1990 —Pittsburgh (N.L.)	2	0	0	. . .	0.00	0	2	0	0	0	0	1
1991 —Pittsburgh (N.L.)	1	0	0	. . .	9.00	0	1	2	1	1	2	2
Championship Series totals (2 years)	3	0	0	. . .	3.00	0	3	2	1	1	2	3

LANDRUM, CED
OF, CUBS

PERSONAL: Born September 3, 1963, at Butler, Ala. . . . 5-9/170. . . . Throws right, bats left. . . . Full name: Cedric Bernard Landrum.
HIGH SCHOOL: Sweet Water (Ala.).
COLLEGE: North Alabama.
TRANSACTIONS/CAREER NOTES: Signed as a free agent by Chicago Cubs organization (November 9, 1985).
STATISTICAL NOTES: Led Carolina League outfielders with 316 total chances and four double plays in 1987. . . . Led American Association in caught stealing with 17 in 1988. . . . Led Eastern League outfielders with 15 assists in 1988.

Year Team (League)	Pos.	G	AB	R	H	2B	3B	HR	RBI	Avg.	SB	PO	A	E	Avg.
1986 —Geneva (N.Y.-Penn)	OF	64	213	51	67	6	2	3	16	.315	*49	96	5	8	.927
1987 —Winston-Salem (Caro.)	OF	126	458	82	129	13	7	4	49	.282	79	*286	11	19	.940
1988 —Pittsfield (Eastern)	OF-2B	128	445	*82	109	15	8	1	39	.245	*69	227	†16	8	.968
1989 —Charlotte (Florida State)	OF	123	361	72	92	11	2	6	37	.255	45	226	5	8	.967
1990 —Iowa (American Assoc.)	OF	123	372	71	110	10	4	0	24	.296	*46	214	3	4	.982
1991 —Iowa (American Assoc.)	OF	38	131	14	44	8	2	1	11	.336	13	43	4	3	.940
—Chicago (N.L.)	OF	56	86	28	20	2	1	0	6	.233	27	61	0	2	.968
Major league totals (1 year)		56	86	28	20	2	1	0	6	.233	27	61	0	2	.968

LANE, BRIAN

3B, REDS

PERSONAL: Born June 15, 1969, at Waco, Tex. . . . 6-3/215. . . . Throws right, bats right. . . . Full name: Brian Conley Lane.
HIGH SCHOOL: Waco Midway (Tex.).
TRANSACTIONS/CAREER NOTES: Selected by Cincinnati Reds organization in third round of free-agent draft (June 2, 1987). . . . On disabled list (March 14, 1991-entire season).

						BATTING							FIELDING		
Year Team (League)	Pos.	G	AB	R	H	2B	3B	HR	RBI	Avg.	SB	PO	A	E	Avg.
1987—Billings (Pioneer).............	3B	56	175	19	35	6	1	3	16	.200	2	35	107	12	.922
1988—Greensboro (S. Atlantic) ...	3B	115	451	55	127	17	3	3	52	.282	9	93	196	21	.932
1989—Chattanooga (Southern)...	3B	130	464	59	117	19	4	11	89	.252	6	94	223	27	.922
1990—Chattanooga (Southern)...	3B	79	293	41	70	13	2	6	51	.239	2	71	157	10	.958
—Nashville (Am. Assoc.)	3B	48	161	17	31	8	0	6	20	.193	3	36	83	5	.960
1991—							Did not play								

LANGSTON, MARK

P, ANGELS

PERSONAL: Born August 20, 1960, at San Diego. . . . 6-2/184. . . . Throws left, bats right. . . . Full name: Mark Edward Langston.
HIGH SCHOOL: Buchser (Santa Clara, Calif.).
COLLEGE: San Jose State.
TRANSACTIONS/CAREER NOTES: Selected by Chicago Cubs organization in 15th round of free-agent draft (June 6, 1978). . . . Selected by Seattle Mariners organization in third round of free-agent draft (June 8, 1981). . . . On disabled list (June 7-July 22, 1985). . . . Traded by Mariners with a player to be named later to Montreal Expos for P Randy Johnson, P Brian Holman and P Gene Harris (May 25, 1989); Indianapolis (Expos organization) acquired P Mike Campbell to complete deal (July 31, 1989). . . . Granted free agency (November 13, 1989). . . . Signed by California Angels (December 1, 1989).
RECORDS/HONORS: Holds major league single-season record for fewest assists by pitcher who led league in assists—42 (1990). . . . Named A.L. Rookie Pitcher of the Year by THE SPORTING NEWS (1984). . . . Won A.L. Gold Glove at pitcher (1987-88 and 1991).
STATISTICAL NOTES: Pitched seven innings, combining with Mike Witt in 1-0 nine-inning no-hit victory against Seattle Mariners (April 11, 1990).

Year Team (League)	G	W	L	Pct.	ERA	Sv.	IP	H	R	ER	BB	SO
1981—Bellingham (Northwest)............	13	7	3	.700	3.39	0	85	81	37	32	46	97
1982—Bakersfield (California)	26	12	7	.632	2.54	0	177⅓	143	71	50	102	161
1983—Chattanooga (Southern)..........	28	14	9	.609	3.59	0	198	187	104	79	102	142
1984—Seattle (A.L.)	35	17	10	.630	3.40	0	225	188	99	85	*118	*204
1985—Seattle (A.L.)	24	7	14	.333	5.47	0	126⅔	122	85	77	91	72
1986—Seattle (A.L.)	37	12	14	.462	4.85	0	239⅓	234	*142	*129	123	*245
1987—Seattle (A.L.)	35	19	13	.594	3.84	0	272	242	132	116	114	*262
1988—Seattle (A.L.)	35	15	11	.577	3.34	0	261⅓	222	108	97	110	235
1989—Seattle (A.L.) ■	10	4	5	.444	3.56	0	73⅓	60	30	29	19	60
—Montreal (N.L.) ■	24	12	9	.571	2.39	0	176⅔	138	57	47	93	175
1990—California (A.L.) ■	33	10	17	.370	4.40	0	223	215	120	109	104	195
1991—California (A.L.)	34	19	8	.704	3.00	0	246⅓	190	89	82	96	183
American League totals (8 years)..........	243	103	92	.528	3.91	0	1667	1473	805	724	775	1456
National League totals (1 year).............	24	12	9	.571	2.39	0	176⅔	138	57	47	93	175
Major league totals (8 years).................	267	115	101	.532	3.76	0	1843⅔	1611	862	771	868	1631

ALL-STAR GAME RECORD												
Year League	W	L	Pct.	ERA	Sv.	IP	H	R	ER	BB	SO	
1987—American	0	0	. . .	0.00	0	2	0	0	0	0	3	
1991—American					Did not play							

LANKFORD, RAY

OF, CARDINALS

PERSONAL: Born June 5, 1967, at Modesto, Calif. . . . 5-11/198. . . . Throws left, bats left. . . . Full name: Raymond Lewis Lankford.
HIGH SCHOOL: Grace Davis (Modesto, Calif.).
COLLEGE: Modesto Junior College (Calif.).
TRANSACTIONS/CAREER NOTES: Selected by Chicago Cubs organization in third round of free-agent draft (January 14, 1986). . . . Selected by St. Louis Cardinals organization in third round of free-agent draft (June 2, 1987).
RECORDS/HONORS: Named Texas League Most Valuable Player (1989).
STATISTICAL NOTES: Led Appalachian League outfielders with 155 total chances in 1987. . . . Led Appalachian League in caught stealing with 11 in 1987. . . . Led Midwest League with 242 total bases in 1988. . . . Led Texas League outfielders with 387 total chances in 1989. . . . Led American Association outfielders with 352 total chances in 1990. . . . Tied for American Association lead with nine intentional bases on balls received in 1990. . . . Hit for the cycle (September 15, 1991).

						BATTING							FIELDING		
Year Team (League)	Pos.	G	AB	R	H	2B	3B	HR	RBI	Avg.	SB	PO	A	E	Avg.
1987—Johnson City (Appal.)	OF	66	253	45	78	17	4	3	32	.308	14	*143	7	5	.968
1988—Springfield (Midwest)	OF	135	532	90	151	26	*16	11	66	.284	33	284	5	7	.976
1989—Arkansas (Texas)	OF	*134	498	98	*158	28	*12	11	98	.317	38	*367	9	11	.972
1990—Louisville (Am. Assoc.)	OF	132	473	61	123	25	8	10	72	.260	30	*333	8	•11	.969
—St. Louis (N.L.)	OF	39	126	12	36	10	1	3	12	.286	8	92	1	1	.989
1991—St. Louis (N.L.)	OF	151	566	83	142	23	*15	9	69	.251	44	367	7	6	.984
Major league totals (2 years)		190	692	95	178	33	16	12	81	.257	52	459	8	7	.985

LANSFORD, CARNEY

3B, ATHLETICS

PERSONAL: Born February 7, 1957, at San Jose, Calif. . . . 6-2/195. . . . Throws right, bats right. . . . Full name: Carney Ray Lansford. . . . Brother of Joe Lansford, first baseman, San Diego Padres, 1982-83; and brother of Phil Lansford, minor league infielder (1978-81).

HIGH SCHOOL: Wilcox (Santa Clara, Calif.).

TRANSACTIONS/CAREER NOTES: Selected by California Angels organization in third round of free-agent draft (June 4, 1975). . . . On disabled list (July 21-September 30, 1975 and June 11-July 7, 1978). . . . Traded by Angels with P Mark Clear and OF Rick Miller to Boston Red Sox for SS Rick Burleson and 3B Butch Hobson (December 10, 1980). . . . On disabled list (June 24-July 21, 1982). . . . Traded by Red Sox with OF Garry Hancock and a player to be named later to Oakland Athletics for OF Tony Armas and C Jeff Newman (December 6, 1982); A's acquired P Jerry King to complete deal (December 20, 1982). . . . On disabled list (May 19-June 7, 1983; July 26-August 28, 1985; and July 12-27, 1990). . . . On Oakland disabled list (April 1-July 19, 1991); included rehabilitation disability assignment to Tacoma (July 11-19, 1991). . . . On Oakland disabled list (July 25, 1991-remainder of season). . . . Granted free agency (November 6, 1991). . . . Re-signed by A's (December 9, 1991).

RECORDS/HONORS: Named third baseman on THE SPORTING NEWS A.L. Silver Slugger team (1981). . . . Named third baseman on THE SPORTING NEWS A.L. All-Star team (1989).

STATISTICAL NOTES: Led Texas League third basemen with 16 double plays in 1977. . . . Hit three home runs in a game (September 1, 1979). . . . Led A.L. with 11 sacrifice flies in 1980. . . . Led A.L. third basemen with .980 fielding percentage in 1987, .979 in 1988 and .970 in 1990.

Year — Team (League)	Pos.	G	AB	R	H	2B	3B	HR	RBI	Avg.	SB	PO	A	E	Avg.
1975 —Idaho Falls (Pioneer)	3B-SS	8	27	5	6	2	0	1	1	.222	2	8	14	9	.710
1976 —Quad Cities (Midwest)	3B-OF-SS	121	418	87	120	19	5	14	86	.287	26	130	215	36	.906
1977 —El Paso (Texas)	3B	120	443	98	147	17	3	18	94	.332	20	★110	★210	15	★.955
1978 —California (A.L.)	3B-SS	121	453	63	133	23	2	8	52	.294	20	94	186	18	.940
1979 —California (A.L.)	3B	157	654	114	188	30	5	19	79	.287	20	★135	263	7	★.983
1980 —California (A.L.)	3B	151	602	87	157	27	3	15	80	.261	14	★151	250	19	.955
1981 —Boston (A.L.)■	3B	102	399	61	134	23	3	4	52	★.336	15	70	180	13	.951
1982 —Boston (A.L.)	3B	128	482	65	145	28	4	11	63	.301	9	83	216	10	.968
1983 —Oakland (A.L.)■	3B-SS	80	299	43	92	16	2	10	45	.308	3	60	163	10	.957
1984 —Oakland (A.L.)	3B	151	597	70	179	31	5	14	74	.300	9	137	268	18	.957
1985 —Oakland (A.L.)	3B	98	401	51	111	18	2	13	46	.277	2	85	119	5	.976
1986 —Oakland (A.L.)	3B-1B-2B	151	591	80	168	16	4	19	72	.284	16	480	170	6	.991
1987 —Oakland (A.L.)	3B-1B	151	554	89	160	27	4	19	76	.289	27	156	258	7	†.983
1988 —Oakland (A.L.)	3B-1B-2B	150	556	80	155	20	2	7	57	.279	29	125	221	7	†.980
1989 —Oakland (A.L.)	3B-1B	148	551	81	185	28	2	2	52	.336	37	195	188	13	.967
1990 —Oakland (A.L.)	3B-1B	134	507	58	136	15	1	3	50	.268	16	128	195	9	†.973
1991 —Tacoma (Pacific Coast)	3B	8	23	1	7	1	1	0	1	.304	0	1	4	0	1.000
—Oakland (A.L.)	3B	5	16	0	1	0	0	0	1	.063	0	0	3	0	1.000
Major league totals (14 years)		1727	6662	942	1944	302	39	144	799	.292	217	1899	2680	142	.970

CHAMPIONSHIP SERIES RECORD

Year — Team (League)	Pos.	G	AB	R	H	2B	3B	HR	RBI	Avg.	SB	PO	A	E	Avg.
1979 —California (A.L.)	3B	4	17	2	5	0	0	0	3	.294	1	4	8	0	1.000
1988 —Oakland (A.L.)	3B	4	17	4	5	1	0	1	2	.294	0	7	8	0	1.000
1989 —Oakland (A.L.)	3B	3	11	2	5	0	0	0	4	.455	2	1	2	0	1.000
1990 —Oakland (A.L.)	3B	4	16	2	7	1	0	0	2	.438	0	3	11	0	1.000
Championship Series totals (4 years)		15	61	10	22	2	0	1	11	.361	3	15	29	0	1.000

WORLD SERIES RECORD

WORLD SERIES NOTES: Shares single-game record for most runs—4 (October 27, 1989).

Year — Team (League)	Pos.	G	AB	R	H	2B	3B	HR	RBI	Avg.	SB	PO	A	E	Avg.
1988 —Oakland (A.L.)	3B	5	18	2	3	0	0	0	1	.167	0	8	7	0	1.000
1989 —Oakland (A.L.)	3B	4	16	5	7	1	0	1	4	.438	0	5	5	0	1.000
1990 —Oakland (A.L.)	3B	4	15	0	4	0	0	0	1	.267	1	1	14	0	1.000
World Series totals (3 years)		13	49	7	14	1	0	1	6	.286	1	14	26	0	1.000

ALL-STAR GAME RECORD

Year — League	Pos.	AB	R	H	2B	3B	HR	RBI	Avg.	SB	PO	A	E	Avg.
1988 —American	3B	1	0	0	0	0	0	0	.000	0	0	1	0	1.000

LaPOINT, DAVE

P

PERSONAL: Born July 29, 1959, at Glens Falls, N.Y. . . . 6-3/231. . . . Throws left, bats left. . . . Full name: David Jeffrey LaPoint.

HIGH SCHOOL: Glens Falls (N.Y.).

TRANSACTIONS/CAREER NOTES: Selected by Milwaukee Brewers organization in 10th round of free-agent draft (June 7, 1977). . . . On Vancouver disabled list (May 6-17 and June 6-July 15, 1980). . . . Traded by Brewers with P Lary Sorensen, OF Sixto Lezcano and OF David Green to St. Louis Cardinals for P Pete Vuckovich, P Rollie Fingers and C Ted Simmons (December 12, 1980). . . . On disabled list (June 15-30, 1984). . . . Traded by Cardinals with 1B David Green, 1B Gary Rajsich and SS Jose Gonzalez (Jose Uribe) to San Francisco Giants for OF-1B Jack Clark (February 1, 1985). . . . Traded by Giants with C Matt Nokes and P Eric King to Detroit Tigers for P Juan Berenguer, C Bob Melvin and a player to be named (October 7, 1985); Giants acquired P Scott Medvin to complete deal (December 11, 1985). . . . Traded by Tigers to San Diego

Padres for P Mark Thurmond (July 9, 1986).... Released by Padres (December 20, 1986).... Signed by St. Louis Cardinals (January 19, 1987).... Traded by Cardinals to Chicago White Sox for P Bryce Hulstrom (July 30, 1987).... Granted free agency (November 9, 1987).... Re-signed by White Sox (February 9, 1988).... Traded by White Sox to Pittsburgh Pirates for P Barry Jones (August 13, 1988).... Granted free agency (November 4, 1988).... Signed by New York Yankees (December 3, 1988).... On disabled list (June 30-July 17 and August 3, 1989-remainder of season).... Granted free agency (December 7, 1990); remained with Yankees.... Released by Yankees (February 17, 1991).... Signed by Philadelphia Phillies (April 7, 1991).... Released by Phillies (April 23, 1991).... Signed by Milwaukee Brewers organization (May 9, 1991).... Released by Brewers organization (June 23, 1991).... Signed by Iowa, Chicago Cubs organization (June 28, 1991).... Granted free agency (October 15, 1991).

STATISTICAL NOTES: Tied for Midwest League lead with 20 home runs allowed in 1978.... Pitched 4-0 no-hit victory against Reno (July 25, 1979).... Tied for California League lead with three shutouts and 11 complete games in 1979.... Tied for American Association lead with nine complete games in 1981.... Led N.L. with 15 wild pitches in 1984.

Year	Team (League)	G	W	L	Pct.	ERA	Sv.	IP	H	R	ER	BB	SO
1977	Newark (New York-Penn)	13	5	2	.714	4.70	0	69	73	40	36	22	60
1978	Burlington (Midwest)	25	12	12	.500	4.02	0	161	177	98	72	41	134
1979	Stockton (California)	27	12	10	.545	3.15	0	180	144	74	63	85	★208
1980	Vancouver (Pacific Coast)	17	7	4	.636	2.81	0	93	71	48	29	45	64
—	Milwaukee (A.L.)	5	1	0	1.000	6.00	1	15	17	14	10	13	5
1981	Springfield (American Assoc.)■	25	13	9	.591	3.19	0	172	160	83	61	66	★129
—	St. Louis (N.L.)	3	1	0	1.000	4.09	0	11	12	5	5	2	4
1982	St. Louis (N.L.)	42	9	3	.750	3.42	0	152⅔	170	63	58	52	81
1983	St. Louis (N.L.)	37	12	9	.571	3.95	0	191⅓	191	92	84	84	113
1984	St. Louis (N.L.)	33	12	10	.545	3.96	0	193	205	94	85	77	130
1985	San Francisco (N.L.)■	31	7	17	.292	3.57	0	206⅔	215	99	82	74	122
1986	Detroit (A.L.)■	16	3	6	.333	5.72	0	67⅔	85	49	43	32	36
—	San Diego (N.L.)■	24	1	4	.200	4.26	0	61⅓	67	37	29	24	41
1987	St. Louis (N.L.)■	6	1	1	.500	6.75	0	16	26	12	12	5	8
—	Louisville (American Assoc.) ...	14	5	5	.500	4.03	0	91⅔	93	45	41	27	70
—	Chicago (A.L.)■	14	6	3	.667	2.94	0	82⅔	69	29	27	31	43
1988	Chicago (A.L.)	25	10	11	.476	3.40	0	161⅓	151	69	61	47	79
—	Pittsburgh (N.L.)■	8	4	2	.667	2.77	0	52	54	18	16	10	19
1989	New York (A.L.)■	20	6	9	.400	5.62	0	113⅔	146	73	71	45	51
1990	New York (A.L.)	28	7	10	.412	4.11	0	157⅔	180	84	72	57	67
1991	Philadelphia (N.L.)■	2	0	1	.000	16.20	0	5	10	10	9	6	3
—	Denver-Iowa (Am. Assoc.)■.....	33	3	2	.600	6.47	1	65⅓	85	56	47	25	42
American League totals (6 years)		108	33	39	.458	4.27	1	598	648	318	284	225	281
National League totals (9 years)		186	47	47	.500	3.85	0	889	950	430	380	334	521
Major league totals (12 years)		294	80	86	.482	4.02	1	1487	1598	748	664	559	802

WORLD SERIES RECORD

Year	Team (League)	G	W	L	Pct.	ERA	Sv.	IP	H	R	ER	BB	SO
1982	St. Louis (N.L.)	2	0	0	...	3.24	0	8⅓	10	6	3	2	3

LARKIN, BARRY
SS, REDS

PERSONAL: Born April 28, 1964, at Cincinnati.... 6-0/190.... Throws right, bats right.... Full name: Barry Louis Larkin.
HIGH SCHOOL: Moeller (Cincinnati).
COLLEGE: Michigan.

TRANSACTIONS/CAREER NOTES: Selected by Cincinnati Reds organization in second round of free-agent draft (June 7, 1982).... Selected by Reds organization in first round (fourth pick overall) of free-agent draft (June 3, 1985).... On disabled list (April 13-May 2, 1987).... On disabled list (July 11-September 1, 1989); included rehabilitation disability assignment to Nashville (August 27-September 1, 1989).... On disabled list (May 18-June 4, 1991).

RECORDS/HONORS: Shares major league record for most home runs in two consecutive games—5 (June 27-28, 1991).... Named shortstop on THE SPORTING NEWS college All-America team (1985).... Named American Association Most Valuable Player (1986).... Named shortstop on THE SPORTING NEWS N.L. All-Star team (1988-91).... Named shortstop on THE SPORTING NEWS N.L. Silver Slugger team (1988-91).

STATISTICAL NOTES: Led American Association with .525 slugging percentage in 1986.... Tied for N.L. lead in double plays by shortstops with 86 in 1990.... Hit three home runs in a game (June 28, 1991).

MISCELLANEOUS: Member of 1984 U.S. Olympic baseball team.

							BATTING						FIELDING			
Year	Team (League)	Pos.	G	AB	R	H	2B	3B	HR	RBI	Avg.	SB	PO	A	E	Avg.
1985	Vermont (Eastern)	SS	72	255	42	68	13	2	1	31	.267	12	110	166	17	.942
1986	Denver (Am. Assoc.)	SS-2B	103	413	67	136	31	10	10	51	.329	19	172	287	18	.962
—	Cincinnati (N.L.)	SS-2B	41	159	27	45	4	3	3	19	.283	8	51	125	4	.978
1987	Cincinnati (N.L.)	SS	125	439	64	107	16	2	12	43	.244	21	168	358	19	.965
1988	Cincinnati (N.L.)	SS	151	588	91	174	32	5	12	56	.296	40	231	470	•29	.960
1989	Cincinnati (N.L.)	SS	97	325	47	111	14	4	4	36	.342	10	142	267	10	.976
—	Nashville (Am. Assoc.)	SS	2	5	2	5	1	0	0	0	1.000	0	1	3	0	1.000
1990	Cincinnati (N.L.)	SS	158	614	85	185	25	6	7	67	.301	30	254	★469	17	.977
1991	Cincinnati (N.L.)	SS	123	464	88	140	27	4	20	69	.302	24	226	372	15	.976
Major league totals (6 years)			695	2589	402	762	118	24	58	290	.294	133	1072	2061	94	.971

CHAMPIONSHIP SERIES RECORD

Year	Team (League)	Pos.	G	AB	R	H	2B	3B	HR	RBI	Avg.	SB	PO	A	E	Avg.
							BATTING						FIELDING			
1990 —Cincinnati (N.L.)		SS	6	23	5	6	2	0	0	1	.261	3	21	15	1	.973

WORLD SERIES RECORD

WORLD SERIES NOTES: Shares record for most at-bats in one inning—2 (October 19, 1990, third inning).

Year	Team (League)	Pos.	G	AB	R	H	2B	3B	HR	RBI	Avg.	SB	PO	A	E	Avg.
							BATTING						FIELDING			
1990 —Cincinnati (N.L.)		SS	4	17	3	6	1	1	0	1	.353	0	1	14	0	1.000

ALL-STAR GAME RECORD

Year	League	Pos.	AB	R	H	2B	3B	HR	RBI	Avg.	SB	PO	A	E	Avg.
						BATTING						FIELDING			
1988 —National	SS	2	0	0	0	0	0	0		.000	0	0	1	0	1.000
1989 —National					Did not play										
1990 —National	PR-SS	0	0	0	0	0	0	0		. . .	1	1	2	0	1.000
1991 —National	SS	1	0	0	0	0	0	0		.000	0	0	2	0	1.000
All-Star Game totals (3 years)		3	0	0	0	0	0	0		.000	1	1	5	0	1.000

LARKIN, GENE
1B/OF, TWINS

PERSONAL: Born October 24, 1962, at Flushing, N.Y. . . . 6-3/199. . . . Throws right, bats both. . . . Full name: Eugene Thomas Larkin.
HIGH SCHOOL: Chaminade (Mineola, N.Y.).
COLLEGE: Columbia (received degree).
TRANSACTIONS/CAREER NOTES: Selected by Minnesota Twins organization in 20th round of free-agent draft (June 4, 1984). . . . On disabled list (July 14-30, 1990 and July 2-17, 1991).
STATISTICAL NOTES: Led Appalachian League first basemen with 54 double plays in 1984. . . . Led California League with 14 sacrifice flies in 1985. . . . Led California League first basemen with 140 double plays in 1985. . . . Tied for Southern League lead with 13 sacrifice flies in 1986. . . . Led A.L. in being hit by pitch with 15 in 1988.

Year	Team (League)	Pos.	G	AB	R	H	2B	3B	HR	RBI	Avg.	SB	PO	A	E	Avg.
							BATTING						FIELDING			
1984 —Elizabethton (Appal.)	1B	57	193	29	63	13	1	6	37	.326	1	478	19	6	*.988
1985 —Visalia (California)	1B	•142	528	90	161	25	3	13	•106	.305	0	•1227	62	12	.991
1986 —Orlando (Southern)	1B-3B	142	529	85	•170	29	6	15	104	.321	1	923	53	13	.987
1987 —Portland (Pacific Coast)	1B-OF	35	129	17	39	9	0	1	14	.302	0	191	22	4	.982
—Minnesota (A.L.)	1B	85	233	23	62	11	2	4	28	.266	1	165	10	2	.989
1988 —Minnesota (A.L.)	1B	149	505	56	135	30	2	8	70	.267	3	466	28	3	.994
1989 —Minnesota (A.L.)	1B-OF	136	446	61	119	25	1	6	46	.267	5	524	28	4	.993
1990 —Minnesota (A.L.)	OF-1B	119	401	46	108	26	4	5	42	.269	5	299	18	2	.994
1991 —Minnesota (A.L.)	0-1-2-3	98	255	34	73	14	1	2	19	.286	2	340	20	3	.992
Major league totals (5 years)		587	1840	220	497	106	10	25	205	.270	16	1794	104	14	.993

CHAMPIONSHIP SERIES RECORD

Year	Team (League)	Pos.	G	AB	R	H	2B	3B	HR	RBI	Avg.	SB	PO	A	E	Avg.
							BATTING						FIELDING			
1987 —Minnesota (A.L.)	PH	1	1	0	1	1	0	0	1	1.000	0	0	0	0	. . .
1991 —Minnesota (A.L.)	PH	3	3	0	0	0	0	0	0	.000	0	0	0	0	. . .
Championship Series totals (2 years)		4	4	0	1	1	0	0	1	.250	0	0	0	0	. . .

WORLD SERIES RECORD

Year	Team (League)	Pos.	G	AB	R	H	2B	3B	HR	RBI	Avg.	SB	PO	A	E	Avg.
							BATTING						FIELDING			
1987 —Minnesota (A.L.)	1B-PH	5	3	1	0	0	0	0	0	.000	0	1	0	0	1.000
1991 —Minnesota (A.L.)	PH	4	4	0	2	0	0	0	1	.500	0	0	0	0	. . .
World Series totals (2 years)		9	7	1	2	0	0	0	1	.286	0	1	0	0	1.000

LaVALLIERE, MIKE
C, PIRATES

PERSONAL: Born August 18, 1960, at Charlotte, N.C. . . . 5-10/205. . . . Throws right, bats left. . . . Full name: Michael Eugene LaValliere. . . . Son of Guy LaValliere, minor league catcher (1952 and 1955-61). . . . Name pronounced luh-VAL-yur.
HIGH SCHOOL: Trinity (Manchester, N.H.).
COLLEGE: Lowell (Mass.).
TRANSACTIONS/CAREER NOTES: Signed as free agent by Philadelphia Phillies organization (July 12, 1981). . . . Traded by Phillies to St. Louis Cardinals for a player to be named later (December 3, 1984); returned to Phillies due to injured status (December 13, 1984). . . . Granted free agency (December 23, 1984). . . . Signed by Louisville, Cardinals organization (January 23, 1985). . . . On Louisville disabled list (July 18-29, 1985). . . . Traded by Cardinals with OF Andy Van Slyke and P Mike Dunne to Pittsburgh Pirates for C Tony Pena (April 1, 1987). . . . On Pittsburgh disabled list (April 17-July 4, 1989); included rehabilitation disability assignment to Buffalo (June 26-July 4, 1989). . . . Granted free agency (October 31, 1991). . . . Re-signed by Pirates (January 3, 1992).
RECORDS/HONORS: Won N.L. Gold Glove at catcher (1987). . . . Named catcher on THE SPORTING NEWS N.L. All-Star team (1988).

Year	Team (League)	Pos.	G	AB	R	H	2B	3B	HR	RBI	Avg.	SB	PO	A	E	Avg.
1981—Spartanburg (S. Atl.)	3B-OF	39	123	15	33	9	0	2	23	.268	3	16	32	5	.906
1982—Peninsula (Carolina)	C-3B	66	178	20	49	4	2	2	23	.275	3	306	35	6	.983
1983—Reading (Eastern)	C-3B-P	81	218	24	64	16	2	4	43	.294	1	243	59	4	.987
1984—Reading (Eastern)	C-3-2-P	55	147	19	37	6	0	6	22	.252	0	113	45	2	.988
—Portland (Pacific Coast) ...	C	37	122	20	38	6	3	5	21	.311	0	186	16	1	.995
—Philadelphia (N.L.)	C	6	7	0	0	0	0	0	0	.000	0	20	2	0	1.000
1985—St. Louis (N.L.)■............	C	12	34	2	5	1	0	0	6	.147	0	48	5	0	1.000
—Louisville (Am. Assoc.)	C	83	231	19	47	12	1	4	26	.203	0	420	53	5	.990
1986—St. Louis (N.L.)	C	110	303	18	71	10	2	3	30	.234	0	468	47	6	.988
1987—Pittsburgh (N.L.)■............	C	121	340	33	102	19	0	1	36	.300	0	584	70	5	.992
1988—Pittsburgh (N.L.)	C	120	352	24	92	18	0	2	47	.261	0	565	55	8	.987
1989—Pittsburgh (N.L.)	C	68	190	15	60	10	0	2	23	.316	0	306	24	3	.991
—Buffalo (Am. Assoc.)	C	7	18	0	2	0	0	0	1	.111	0	15	1	0	1.000
1990—Pittsburgh (N.L.)	C	96	279	27	72	15	0	3	31	.258	0	478	36	5	.990
1991—Pittsburgh (N.L.)	C	108	336	25	97	11	2	3	41	.289	2	565	46	1	★.998
Major league totals (8 years)		641	1841	144	499	84	4	14	214	.271	5	3034	285	28	.992

CHAMPIONSHIP SERIES RECORD

Year	Team (League)	Pos.	G	AB	R	H	2B	3B	HR	RBI	Avg.	SB	PO	A	E	Avg.
1990—Pittsburgh (N.L.)	C	3	6	1	0	0	0	0	0	.000	0	17	2	0	1.000
1991—Pittsburgh (N.L.)	C-PH	3	6	0	2	0	0	0	1	.333	0	14	3	0	1.000
Championship Series totals (2 years)		6	12	1	2	0	0	0	1	.167	0	31	5	0	1.000

RECORD AS PITCHER

Year	Team (League)	G	W	L	Pct.	ERA	Sv.	IP	H	R	ER	BB	SO
1983—Reading (Eastern)	4	0	0	...	5.40	0	3⅓	3	3	2	2	2
1984—Reading (Eastern)	1	0	0	...	18.00	0	1	3	2	2	1	1

LAW, VANCE
3B

PERSONAL: Born October 1, 1956, at Boise, Idaho. . . . 6-1/190. . . . Throws right, bats right. . . . Full name: Vance Aaron Law. . . . Son of Vern Law, pitcher, Pittsburgh Pirates (1950-51 and 1954-67).

HIGH SCHOOL: Provo (Utah).

COLLEGE: Brigham Young.

TRANSACTIONS/CAREER NOTES: Selected by Pittsburgh Pirates organization in 38th round of free-agent draft (June 6, 1978). . . . On Portland disabled list (July 5-15, 1981). . . . Traded by Pirates organization with P Ernie Camacho to Chicago White Sox for P Ross Baumgarten and P Butch Edge (March 21, 1982). . . . Traded by White Sox to Montreal Expos for P Bob James (December 7, 1984). . . . Granted free agency (November 9, 1987). . . . Signed by Chicago Cubs (December 14, 1987). . . . Released by Cubs (January 2, 1990). . . . Signed by Chunichi Dragons of Japan Central League (January 4, 1990). . . . Signed by Oakland Athletics (January 11, 1991). . . . On Oakland disabled list (April 27-May 12, 1991). . . . Released by A's (October 11, 1991).

RECORDS/HONORS: Holds A.L. record for longest errorless game by third baseman—25 innings (May 8, finished May 9, 1984). . . . Shares A.L. single-game record for most innings played by third baseman—25 (May 8, finished May 9, 1984).

STATISTICAL NOTES: Led Pacific Coast League with 14 sacrifice hits in 1979.

Year	Team (League)	Pos.	G	AB	R	H	2B	3B	HR	RBI	Avg.	SB	PO	A	E	Avg.
1978—Bradenton Pirates (GCL) ..	SS	1	3	0	1	0	0	0	0	.333	0	2	5	0	1.000
—Salem (Carolina)	SS	60	213	48	68	13	7	2	30	.319	4	96	180	22	.926
1979—Portland (Pacific Coast) ...	SS-3B-2B	131	448	62	139	16	8	2	52	.310	8	201	308	22	.959
1980—Portland (Pacific Coast) ...	SS	96	339	59	100	23	5	5	54	.295	9	169	295	14	.971
—Pittsburgh (N.L.)	2B-SS-3B	25	74	11	17	2	2	0	3	.230	2	31	54	3	.966
1981—Pittsburgh (N.L.)	2B-SS-3B	30	67	1	9	0	1	0	3	.134	8	50	58	0	1.000
—Portland (Pacific Coast) ...	2B-SS-3B	88	310	55	86	14	9	5	43	.277	1	168	218	9	.977
1982—Chicago (A.L.)■................	S-3-2-0	114	359	40	101	20	1	5	54	.281	4	156	313	26	.947
1983—Chicago (A.L.)	3-2-S-0	145	408	55	99	21	5	4	42	.243	4	94	311	14	.967
1984—Chicago (A.L.)	3-2-0-S	151	481	60	121	18	2	17	59	.252	4	119	246	16	.958
1985—Montreal (N.L.)■...............	2-1-3-0	147	519	75	138	30	6	10	52	.266	6	420	402	12	.986
1986—Montreal (N.L.)	2-1-3-P-0	112	360	37	81	17	2	5	44	.225	3	273	299	4	.993
1987—Montreal (N.L.)	2-1-3-P	133	436	52	119	27	1	12	56	.273	8	258	308	11	.981
1988—Chicago (N.L.)■...............	3B-OF	151	556	73	163	29	2	11	78	.293	1	112	272	19	.953
1989—Chicago (N.L.)	3B-OF	130	408	38	96	22	3	7	42	.235	2	76	168	13	.949
1990—Chunichi (Jap. Cen.)■.......		122	457	...	143	...	...	29	78	.313	...	...	...	...	...
1991—Oakland (A.L.)■...............	3-S-0-1-P	74	134	11	28	7	1	0	9	.209	0	39	66	5	.955
—Tacoma (Pacific Coast)	3B	18	65	7	13	1	0	0	6	.200	0	5	34	2	.951
American League totals (4 years)		484	1382	166	349	66	9	26	164	.253	11	408	936	61	.957
National League totals (7 years)		728	2420	287	623	127	17	45	278	.257	30	1220	1561	62	.978
Major league totals (11 years)		1212	3802	453	972	193	26	71	442	.256	41	1628	2497	123	.971

CHAMPIONSHIP SERIES RECORD

Year	Team (League)	Pos.	G	AB	R	H	2B	3B	HR	RBI	Avg.	SB	PO	A	E	Avg.
1983—Chicago (A.L.)	3B	4	11	0	2	0	0	0	1	.182	0	1	9	1	.909
1989—Chicago (N.L.)	PH-3B	2	3	0	0	0	0	0	0	.000	0	0	0	0	...
Championship Series totals (2 years)		6	14	0	2	0	0	0	1	.143	0	1	9	1	.909

ALL-STAR GAME RECORD

Year	League	Pos.	AB	R	H	2B	3B	HR	RBI	Avg.	SB	PO	A	E	Avg.
						BATTING							**FIELDING**		
1988	National	2B	0	0	0	0	0	0	0	...	0	0	0	0	...

RECORD AS PITCHER

Year	Team (League)	G	W	L	Pct.	ERA	Sv.	IP	H	R	ER	BB	SO
1986	Montreal (N.L.)	3	0	0	...	2.25	0	4	3	2	1	2	0
1987	Montreal (N.L.)	3	0	0	...	5.40	0	3⅓	5	2	2	0	2
1991	Oakland (A.L.)■	1	0	0	...	0.00	0	⅔	1	0	0	1	0
	American League totals (1 year)	1	0	0	...	0.00	0	⅔	1	0	0	1	0
	National League totals (2 years)	6	0	0	...	3.68	0	7⅓	8	4	3	2	2
	Major league totals (3 years)	7	0	0	...	3.38	0	8	9	4	3	3	2

LAYANA, TIM
P, REDS

PERSONAL: Born March 2, 1964, at Inglewood, Calif.... 6-2/190.... Throws right, bats right.... Full name: Timothy Joseph Layana.
HIGH SCHOOL: Loyola (Los Angeles).
COLLEGE: Loyola Marymount.
TRANSACTIONS/CAREER NOTES: Selected by Chicago White Sox organization in 28th round of free-agent draft (June 7, 1982).... Selected by New York Mets organization in fifth round of free-agent draft (June 3, 1985).... Selected by New York Yankees organization in third round of free-agent draft (June 2, 1986).... Drafted by Cincinnati Reds (December 4, 1989).
MISCELLANEOUS: Appeared in one game as pinch-runner (1991).

Year	Team (League)	G	W	L	Pct.	ERA	Sv.	IP	H	R	ER	BB	SO
1986	Oneonta (New York-Penn)	3	2	0	1.000	2.37	0	19	10	5	5	5	24
	Fort Lauderdale (Florida St.)	11	5	4	.556	2.24	1	68⅓	59	19	17	19	52
1987	Columbus (International)	13	4	5	.444	4.76	0	70	77	37	37	37	36
	Albany (Eastern)	8	2	4	.333	5.05	0	46⅓	51	28	26	18	19
	Prince William (Carolina)	7	2	1	.667	6.35	0	22⅔	29	22	16	11	17
1988	Columbus (International)	11	1	7	.125	6.04	0	47⅔	54	34	32	25	25
	Albany (Eastern)	14	5	7	.417	4.34	0	87	90	52	42	30	42
1989	Albany (Eastern)	40	7	4	.636	1.73	★17	67⅔	53	17	13	15	48
1990	Cincinnati (N.L.)■	55	5	3	.625	3.49	2	80	71	33	31	44	53
1991	Cincinnati (N.L.)	22	0	2	.000	6.97	0	20⅔	23	18	16	11	14
	Nashville (American Assoc.)	26	3	1	.750	3.23	1	47⅓	41	17	17	28	43
	Major league totals (2 years)	77	5	5	.500	4.20	2	100⅔	94	51	47	55	67

LEACH, TERRY
P, EXPOS

PERSONAL: Born March 13, 1954, at Selma, Ala.... 6-0/191.... Throws right, bats right.... Full name: Terry Hester Leach.
HIGH SCHOOL: Selma (Ala.).
COLLEGE: Auburn (business administration degree in personnel management-industrial relations).
TRANSACTIONS/CAREER NOTES: Selected by Boston Red Sox organization in seventh round of free-agent draft (January 7, 1976).... Signed as free agent by Baton Rouge, independent (June 29, 1976); released when Baton Rouge withdrew from league (August 13, 1976).... Signed as free agent by Greenwood, Atlanta Braves organization (May 28, 1977).... Loaned by Braves organization to Kinston, independent (June 3, 1978); returned (October 28, 1978).... On Savannah disabled list (June 12-July 23, 1980).... Released by Braves organization (July 23, 1980).... Signed by Jackson, New York Mets organization (July 27, 1980).... Traded by Mets organization to Chicago Cubs organization for P Jim Adamczak and P Mitch Cook (September 28, 1983).... Traded by Chicago Cubs organization to Braves organization for P Ron Meridith (April 4, 1984).... Released by Braves organization (May 25, 1984).... Signed by Mets organization (May 26, 1984).... On disabled list (July 12-27, 1987).... Traded by Mets to Kansas City Royals for a player to be named later (June 9, 1989); Mets acquired P Aguedo Vasquez to complete deal (October 1, 1989).... Released by Royals (April 2, 1990).... Signed by Minnesota Twins (April 7, 1990).... Granted free agency (November 7, 1991).... Signed by Montreal Expos organization (January 28, 1992).
STATISTICAL NOTES: Led Gulf States League with 12 home runs allowed in 1976.

Year	Team (League)	G	W	L	Pct.	ERA	Sv.	IP	H	R	ER	BB	SO
1976	Baton Rouge (Gulf States)	5	2	0	1.000	6.16	0	19	43	21	13	14	15
1977	Greenwood (W. Carolinas)■	20	3	2	.600	2.55	3	67	47	25	19	24	67
1978	Savannah (Southern)	9	1	0	1.000	5.04	0	25	24	17	14	13	21
	Kinston (Carolina)■	34	5	4	.556	3.27	8	66	57	29	24	25	46
1979	Savannah (Southern)■	40	2	9	.182	1.96	2	92	77	33	20	26	68
	Richmond (International)	7	3	1	.750	1.93	1	14	14	3	3	4	12
1980	Savannah (Southern)	22	5	1	.833	3.21	1	87	83	36	31	17	58
	Jackson (Texas)■	8	5	1	.833	1.50	0	54	50	16	9	15	30
1981	Tidewater (International)	15	5	2	.714	2.72	1	76	63	27	23	19	42
	Jackson (Texas)	8	5	1	.833	1.71	0	58	47	14	11	12	43
	New York (N.L.)	21	1	1	.500	2.57	0	35	26	11	10	12	16
1982	Tidewater (International)	30	4	1	.800	2.96	5	48⅔	48	20	16	19	34
	New York (N.L.)	21	2	1	.667	4.17	3	45⅓	46	22	21	18	30
1983	Tidewater (International)	37	5	7	.417	4.46	6	113	120	66	56	42	66
1984	Richmond-Tidewater (Int'l)■	43	11	4	.733	3.03	1	95	98	42	32	30	59
1985	Tidewater (International)	24	1	0	1.000	1.59	4	45⅓	33	12	8	8	25
	New York (N.L.)	22	3	4	.429	2.91	1	55⅔	48	19	18	14	30

— 276 —

Year	Team (League)	G	W	L	Pct.	ERA	Sv.	IP	H	R	ER	BB	SO
1986	—Tidewater (International)	34	4	4	.500	2.49	7	79⅔	69	30	22	21	55
	—New York (N.L.)	6	0	0	...	2.70	0	6⅔	6	3	2	3	4
1987	—New York (N.L.)	44	11	1	.917	3.22	0	131⅓	132	54	47	29	61
1988	—New York (N.L.)	52	7	2	.778	2.54	3	92	95	32	26	24	51
1989	—New York (N.L.)	10	0	0	...	4.22	0	21⅓	19	11	10	4	2
	—Kansas City (A.L.)	30	5	6	.455	4.15	0	73⅔	78	46	34	36	34
1990	—Minnesota (A.L.)■	55	2	5	.286	3.20	2	81⅔	84	31	29	21	46
1991	—Minnesota (A.L.)	50	1	2	.333	3.61	0	67⅓	82	28	27	14	32
	American League totals (3 years)	135	8	13	.381	3.64	2	222⅔	244	105	90	71	112
	National League totals (7 years)	176	24	9	.727	3.11	7	387⅓	372	152	134	104	194
	Major league totals (9 years)	311	32	22	.593	3.30	9	610	616	257	224	175	306

CHAMPIONSHIP SERIES RECORD

Year	Team (League)	G	W	L	Pct.	ERA	Sv.	IP	H	R	ER	BB	SO
1988	—New York (N.L.)	3	0	0	...	0.00	0	5	4	0	0	1	4
1991	—Minnesota (A.L.)						Did not play						

WORLD SERIES RECORD

Year	Team (League)	G	W	L	Pct.	ERA	Sv.	IP	H	R	ER	BB	SO
1991	—Minnesota (A.L.)	2	0	0	...	3.86	0	2⅓	2	1	1	0	2

LEARY, TIM
P, YANKEES

PERSONAL: Born December 23, 1958, at Santa Monica, Calif. ... 6-3/218. ... Throws right, bats right. ... Full name: Timothy James Leary.
HIGH SCHOOL: Santa Monica (Calif.).
COLLEGE: UCLA.

TRANSACTIONS/CAREER NOTES: Selected by New York Mets organization in first round (second pick overall) of free-agent draft (June 5, 1979). ... On disabled list (July 19-October 1, 1979). ... On New York disabled list (April 16-August 1, 1981). ... On disabled list (April 13, 1982-remainder of season). ... Traded by Mets organization to Milwaukee Brewers organization as part of a six-player, four-team deal in which Kansas City Royals acquired C Jim Sundberg from Brewers, Texas Rangers acquired C Don Slaught from Royals, Mets organization acquired P Frank Wills from Royals and Brewers acquired P Danny Darwin and a player to be named later from Rangers (January 18, 1985); Brewers organization acquired C Bill Hance from Rangers to complete deal (January 30, 1985). ... Traded by Brewers with P Tim Crews to Los Angeles Dodgers for 1B Greg Brock (December 10, 1986). ... Traded by Dodgers with SS Mariano Duncan to Cincinnati Reds for OF Kal Daniels and IF Lenny Harris (July 18, 1989). ... Traded by Reds with OF Van Snider to New York Yankees for 1B Hal Morris and P Rodney Imes (December 12, 1989). ... Granted free agency (November 5, 1990). ... Re-signed by Yankees (November 19, 1990).

RECORDS/HONORS: Named righthanded pitcher on THE SPORTING NEWS college All-America team (1979). ... Named Texas League Most Valuable Player (1980). ... Named N.L. Comeback Player of the Year by THE SPORTING NEWS (1988). ... Named pitcher on N.L. Silver Slugger team (1988).

STATISTICAL NOTES: Led Texas League with six shutouts in 1980. ... Led A.L. with 23 wild pitches in 1990.

Year	Team (League)	G	W	L	Pct.	ERA	Sv.	IP	H	R	ER	BB	SO
1979	—						Did not play						
1980	—Jackson (Texas)	26	•15	8	.652	2.76	0	173	150	67	53	62	138
1981	—New York (N.L.)	1	0	0	...	0.00	0	2	0	0	0	1	3
	—Tidewater (International)	6	1	3	.250	3.71	0	34	27	16	14	27	15
1982	—						Did not play						
1983	—Tidewater (International)	27	8	★16	.333	4.38	0	160⅓	170	100	78	73	106
	—New York (N.L.)	2	1	1	.500	3.38	0	10⅔	15	10	4	4	9
1984	—New York (N.L.)	20	3	3	.500	4.02	0	53⅔	61	28	24	18	29
	—Tidewater (International)	10	4	4	.500	4.05	0	53⅓	47	26	24	42	27
1985	—Vancouver (Pacific Coast)■	27	10	7	.588	4.00	0	177⅔	174	85	79	57	136
	—Milwaukee (A.L.)	5	1	4	.200	4.05	0	33⅓	40	18	15	8	29
1986	—Milwaukee (A.L.)	33	12	12	.500	4.21	0	188⅓	216	97	88	53	110
1987	—Los Angeles (N.L.)■	39	3	11	.214	4.76	1	107⅔	121	62	57	36	61
1988	—Los Angeles (N.L.)	35	17	11	.607	2.91	0	228⅔	201	87	74	56	180
1989	—Los Angeles-Cincinnati (N.L.)■	33	8	14	.364	3.52	0	207	205	84	81	68	123
1990	—New York (A.L.)■	31	9	★19	.321	4.11	0	208	202	105	95	78	138
1991	—New York (A.L.)	28	4	10	.286	6.49	0	120⅔	150	89	87	57	83
	American League totals (4 years)	97	26	45	.366	4.66	0	550⅓	608	309	285	196	360
	National League totals (6 years)	130	32	40	.444	3.54	1	609⅔	603	271	240	183	405
	Major league totals (10 years)	227	58	85	.406	4.07	1	1160	1211	580	525	379	765

CHAMPIONSHIP SERIES RECORD

Year	Team (League)	G	W	L	Pct.	ERA	Sv.	IP	H	R	ER	BB	SO
1988	—Los Angeles (N.L.)	2	0	1	.000	6.23	0	4⅓	8	4	3	3	3

WORLD SERIES RECORD

Year	Team (League)	G	W	L	Pct.	ERA	Sv.	IP	H	R	ER	BB	SO
1988	—Los Angeles (N.L.)	2	0	0	...	1.35	0	6⅔	6	1	1	2	4

LEE, DEREK
OF, WHITE SOX

PERSONAL: Born July 28, 1966, at Chicago. ... 6-0/195. ... Throws right, bats left. ... Full name: Derek Gerald Lee.
HIGH SCHOOL: South Lakes (Reston, Va.).
COLLEGE: Manatee (Fla.) and South Florida.

TRANSACTIONS/CAREER NOTES: Selected by Pittsburgh Pirates organization in ninth round of free-agent draft (January 9, 1985).... Selected by Chicago Cubs organization in fifth round of free-agent draft (January 14, 1986).... Selected by Philadelphia Phillies organization in secondary phase of free-agent draft (June 2, 1986).... Selected by Detroit Tigers organization in eighth round of free-agent draft (June 2, 1987).... Selected by Chicago White Sox organization in 42nd round of free-agent draft (June 1, 1988).

Year — Team (League)	Pos.	G	AB	R	H	2B	3B	HR	RBI	Avg.	SB	PO	A	E	Avg.
1988 — Utica (New York-Penn)	OF-3B	76	252	51	86	7	5	2	47	.341	54	130	10	7	.952
1989 — South Bend (Midwest)	OF	125	448	★89	128	24	7	11	48	.286	45	187	6	8	.960
1990 — Birmingham (Southern)	OF	126	411	68	105	21	3	7	75	.255	14	188	6	8	.960
1991 — Birmingham (Southern)	OF	45	154	36	50	10	2	5	16	.325	9	65	5	1	.986
— Vancouver (Pac. Coast)....	OF-1B	87	318	54	94	28	5	6	44	.296	4	162	8	7	.960

LEE, MANNY
SS, BLUE JAYS

PERSONAL: Born June 17, 1965, at San Pedro de Macoris, Dominican Republic.... 5-9/166.... Throws right, bats both.... Full name: Manuel Lora Lee.

TRANSACTIONS/CAREER NOTES: Signed as free agent by New York Mets organization (May 10, 1982).... On disabled list (April 9-22, 1984).... Traded by Mets organization with OF Gerald Young to Houston Astros (August 31, 1984) as partial completion of deal in which Mets acquired IF Ray Knight from Astros for three players to be named later (August 28, 1984); Astros acquired P Mitch Cook to complete deal (September 10, 1984).... Drafted by Toronto Blue Jays (December 3, 1984).... On disabled list (March 28-April 12 and May 12-June 1, 1988; and April 30-June 6, 1989).

STATISTICAL NOTES: Led A.L. second basemen with .993 fielding percentage in 1990.

Year — Team (League)	Pos.	G	AB	R	H	2B	3B	HR	RBI	Avg.	SB	PO	A	E	Avg.
1982 — Kingsport (Appalachian) ..	2B-SS	16	54	2	12	1	0	0	3	.222	0	34	34	6	.919
1983 — Sarasota Mets (GCL)	2B-SS	32	97	8	24	2	1	0	12	.247	2	44	79	8	.939
— Little Falls (N.Y.-Penn)	2B	17	45	10	13	0	0	0	5	.289	2	34	40	3	.961
1984 — Columbia (S. Atlantic)	SS-2B	102	346	84	114	12	5	2	33	★.329	24	126	277	34	.922
1985 — Toronto (A.L.)■................	2B-SS-3B	64	40	9	8	0	0	0	0	.200	1	34	56	3	.968
1986 — Syracuse (International) ..	SS-2B	76	236	34	58	6	1	1	19	.246	7	132	237	18	.953
— Knoxville (Southern)	SS-2B	41	158	21	43	1	2	0	11	.272	8	70	117	8	.959
— Toronto (A.L.)..................	2B-SS-3B	35	78	8	16	0	1	1	7	.205	0	36	76	2	.982
1987 — Toronto (A.L.)................	2B-SS	56	121	14	31	2	3	1	11	.256	2	77	110	5	.974
— Syracuse (International) ..	SS	74	251	25	71	9	5	3	26	.283	2	120	177	23	.928
1988 — Toronto (A.L.)................	2B-SS-3B	116	381	38	111	16	3	2	38	.291	3	250	308	12	.979
1989 — Toronto (A.L.)................	2-S-3-O	99	300	27	78	9	2	3	34	.260	4	152	201	11	.970
1990 — Toronto (A.L.)................	2B-SS	117	391	45	95	12	4	6	41	.243	3	265	301	4 †	.993
1991 — Toronto (A.L.)................	SS	138	445	41	104	18	3	0	29	.234	7	194	360	19	.967
Major league totals (7 years)		625	1756	182	443	57	16	13	160	.252	20	1008	1412	56	.977

CHAMPIONSHIP SERIES RECORD

Year — Team (League)	Pos.	G	AB	R	H	2B	3B	HR	RBI	Avg.	SB	PO	A	E	Avg.
1985 — Toronto (A.L.)..................	PR-2B	1	0	0	0	0	0	0	0	...	0	0	0	0	...
1989 — Toronto (A.L.)..................	2B	2	8	2	2	0	0	0	0	.250	0	4	1	0	1.000
1991 — Toronto (A.L.)..................	SS	5	16	3	2	0	0	0	0	.125	0	8	16	1	.960
Championship Series totals (3 years)		8	24	5	4	0	0	0	0	.167	0	12	17	1	.967

LEE, MARK
P, BREWERS

PERSONAL: Born July 20, 1964, at Williston, N.D.... 6-3/200.... Throws left, bats left.... Full name: Mark Owen Lee.

HIGH SCHOOL: Natrona County (Casper, Wyo.).

COLLEGE: Trinidad State Junior College (Colo.) and Florida International.

TRANSACTIONS/CAREER NOTES: Selected by Detroit Tigers organization in 15th round of free-agent draft (June 3, 1985).... Traded by Tigers organization with C Rey Palacios to Kansas City Royals for P Ted Power (August 31, 1988).... Released by Royals organization (March 31, 1990).... Signed by Stockton, Milwaukee Brewers organization (May 23, 1990).

Year — Team (League)	G	W	L	Pct.	ERA	Sv.	IP	H	R	ER	BB	SO
1985 — Bristol (Eastern)	15	3	0	1.000	1.09	5	33	18	5	4	12	40
1986 — Lakeland (Florida State)	41	2	5	.286	5.17	10	62⅔	73	44	36	21	39
1987 — Glens Falls (Eastern)	7	0	0	...	8.64	0	8⅓	13	9	8	1	3
— Lakeland (Florida State)	30	3	2	.600	2.55	4	53	48	17	15	18	42
1988 — Lakeland (Florida State)	10	1	0	1.000	1.42	1	19	16	7	3	4	15
— Glens Falls (Eastern)	14	3	0	1.000	2.42	1	26	27	10	7	4	25
— Toledo (International)	22	0	1	.000	2.79	0	19⅓	18	7	6	7	13
— Kansas City (A.L.)■..............	4	0	0	...	3.60	0	5	6	2	2	1	0
1989 — Memphis (Southern)	25	5	11	.313	5.21	0	122⅔	149	84	71	44	79
1990 — Stockton (California)■	5	1	0	1.000	2.35	1	7⅔	5	2	2	3	7
— Denver (American Assoc.)	20	3	1	.750	2.25	4	28	25	7	7	6	35
— Milwaukee (A.L.)	11	1	0	1.000	2.11	0	21⅓	20	5	5	4	14
1991 — Milwaukee (A.L.)	62	2	5	.286	3.86	1	67⅔	72	33	29	31	43
Major league totals (3 years)	77	3	5	.375	3.45	1	94	98	40	36	36	57

LEE, TERRY
1B

PERSONAL: Born March 13, 1962, at San Francisco. . . . 6-5/220. . . . Throws right, bats right. . . . Full name: Terry James Lee.
HIGH SCHOOL: Churchill (Eugene, Ore.).
COLLEGE: Chemeketa Community College (Ore.) and Boise State.
TRANSACTIONS/CAREER NOTES: Signed as free agent by Cincinnati Reds organization (July 30, 1982). . . . On disabled list (June 9, 1986-remainder of season and April 1, 1987-entire season). . . . Released by Reds (November 20, 1991).
STATISTICAL NOTES: Led Midwest League first basemen with .992 fielding percentage in 1983. . . . Led Eastern League first basemen with 93 double plays in 1984. . . . Led American Association first basemen with .991 fielding percentage in 1991.

Year	Team (League)	Pos.	G	AB	R	H	2B	3B	HR	RBI	Avg.	SB	PO	A	E	Avg.
1982—Eugene (Northwest)		OF-1B	32	117	23	30	5	3	4	21	.256	4	123	7	1	.992
1983—Cedar Rapids (Midwest)		1B-OF-3B	123	405	60	106	*31	1	19	67	.262	11	946	64	8	†.992
1984—Vermont (Eastern)		1B	134	422	56	102	10	2	11	47	.242	2	*1105	85	*16	.987
1985—Vermont (Eastern)		1B-OF-3B	121	409	56	118	20	2	12	62	.289	4	599	59	10	.985
1986—Denver (Am. Assoc.)		1B	34	104	10	25	2	1	2	10	.240	0	240	25	1	.996
1987—							Did not play									
1988—Greensboro (S. Atlantic)		1B	25	56	8	18	5	0	2	9	.321	0	39	2	0	1.000
1989—Chattanooga (Southern)		OF-1B	51	177	23	46	13	0	5	27	.260	0	66	3	1	.986
—Nashville (Am. Assoc.)		1B	13	47	5	11	4	0	0	3	.234	0	118	13	2	.985
1990—Chattanooga (Southern)		1B	43	156	25	51	8	1	8	20	.327	4	331	27	6	.984
—Nashville (Am. Assoc.)		1B	72	260	38	79	18	1	15	67	.304	3	592	47	5	.992
—Cincinnati (N.L.)		1B	12	19	1	4	1	0	0	3	.211	0	28	3	0	1.000
1991—Nashville (Am. Assoc.)		1B-OF	126	437	70	133	21	4	15	67	.304	12	954	75	9	†.991
—Cincinnati (N.L.)		1B	3	6	0	0	0	0	0	0	.000	0	8	4	0	1.000
Major league totals (2 years)			15	25	1	4	1	0	0	3	.160	0	36	7	0	1.000

LEFFERTS, CRAIG
P, PADRES

PERSONAL: Born September 29, 1957, at Munich, West Germany. . . . 6-1/210. . . . Throws left, bats left. . . . Full name: Craig Lindsay Lefferts.
HIGH SCHOOL: Northeast (St. Petersburg, Fla.).
COLLEGE: Arizona.
TRANSACTIONS/CAREER NOTES: Selected by Kansas City Royals organization in sixth round of free-agent draft (June 5, 1979). . . . Selected by Chicago Cubs organization in ninth round of free-agent draft (June 3, 1980). . . . On disabled list (April 24-June 4, 1982). . . . Traded by Cubs with 1B Carmelo Martinez and 3B Fritz Connally to San Diego Padres for P Scott Sanderson (December 7, 1983). . . . Traded by Padres with P Dave Dravecky and IF Kevin Mitchell to San Francisco Giants for 3B Chris Brown, P Keith Comstock, P Mark Davis and P Mark Grant (July 4, 1987). . . . Granted free agency (November 13, 1989). . . . Signed by San Diego Padres (December 6, 1989).

Year	Team (League)	G	W	L	Pct.	ERA	Sv.	IP	H	R	ER	BB	SO
1980—Geneva (New York-Penn)	12	9	1	*.900	2.78	0	94	74	35	29	24	*99
1981—Midland (Texas)	26	12	•12	.500	4.14	0	185	203	95	85	36	135
1982—Iowa (American Association)	18	8	5	.615	3.05	0	97⅓	97	50	33	25	71
1983—Chicago (N.L.)	56	3	4	.429	3.13	1	89	80	35	31	29	60
1984—San Diego (N.L.)■	62	3	4	.429	2.13	10	105⅔	88	29	25	24	56
1985—San Diego (N.L.)	60	7	6	.538	3.35	2	83⅓	75	34	31	30	48
1986—San Diego (N.L.)	*83	9	8	.529	3.09	4	107⅔	98	41	37	44	72
1987—San Diego-San Fran. (N.L.)■	77	5	5	.500	3.83	6	98⅔	92	47	42	33	57
1988—San Francisco (N.L.)	64	3	8	.273	2.92	11	92⅓	74	33	30	23	58
1989—San Francisco (N.L.)	70	2	4	.333	2.69	20	107	93	38	32	22	71
1990—San Diego (N.L.)■	56	7	5	.583	2.52	23	78⅔	68	26	22	22	60
1991—San Diego (N.L.)	54	1	6	.143	3.91	23	69	74	35	30	14	48
Major league totals (9 years)	582	40	50	.444	3.03	100	831⅓	742	318	280	241	530

CHAMPIONSHIP SERIES RECORD

Year	Team (League)	G	W	L	Pct.	ERA	Sv.	IP	H	R	ER	BB	SO
1984—San Diego (N.L.)	3	2	0	1.000	0.00	0	4	1	0	0	1	1
1987—San Francisco (N.L.)	3	0	0	...	0.00	0	2	3	0	0	1	0
1989—San Francisco (N.L.)	2	0	0	...	9.00	0	1	1	1	1	2	1
Championship Series totals (3 years)	8	2	0	1.000	1.29	0	7	5	1	1	4	2

WORLD SERIES RECORD

Year	Team (League)	G	W	L	Pct.	ERA	Sv.	IP	H	R	ER	BB	SO
1984—San Diego (N.L.)	3	0	0	...	0.00	1	6	2	0	0	1	7
1989—San Francisco (N.L.)	3	0	0	...	3.38	0	2⅔	2	1	1	2	1
World Series totals (2 years)	6	0	0	...	1.04	1	8⅔	4	1	1	3	8

LEIBRANDT, CHARLIE
P, BRAVES

PERSONAL: Born October 4, 1956, at Chicago. . . . 6-3/200. . . . Throws left, bats right. . . . Full name: Charlie Louis Leibrandt Jr.
HIGH SCHOOL: Loyola Academy (Wilmette, Ill.).
COLLEGE: Miami of Ohio (bachelor of science degree in business management).
TRANSACTIONS/CAREER NOTES: Selected by Cincinnati Reds organization in ninth round of free-agent draft (June 6, 1978). . . . Traded by Reds to Kansas City Royals for P Bob Tufts (June 7, 1983). . . . Granted free agency (November 9, 1987). . . . Re-signed by Royals (January 7, 1988). . . . Traded by Royals with P Rick Luecken to Atlanta Braves for 1B Gerald Perry and P Jim

Lemasters (December 15, 1989).... On Atlanta disabled list (March 26-June 3, 1990); included rehabilitation disability assignment to Greenville (May 21-June 3, 1990).... Granted free agency (December 7, 1990).... Re-signed by Braves (December 20, 1990).

STATISTICAL NOTES: Tied for American Association lead in games started by pitcher with 26 in 1979.... Tied for American Association lead with three shutouts in 1984.

Year	Team (League)	G	W	L	Pct.	ERA	Sv.	IP	H	R	ER	BB	SO
1978	—Eugene (Northwest)	3	2	0	1.000	4.05	0	20	24	13	9	5	18
	—Tampa (Florida State)	6	4	1	.800	0.77	0	47	26	4	4	17	40
	—Indianapolis (Am. Assoc.)	4	2	1	.667	2.79	0	29	20	9	9	12	12
1979	—Indianapolis (Am. Assoc.)	27	8	*14	.364	2.94	0	162	146	67	53	65	100
	—Cincinnati (N.L.)	3	0	0	...	0.00	0	4	2	2	0	2	1
1980	—Cincinnati (N.L.)	36	10	9	.526	4.24	0	174	200	84	82	54	62
1981	—Indianapolis (Am. Assoc.)	25	9	7	.563	2.93	0	169	149	76	55	75	101
	—Cincinnati (N.L.)	7	1	1	.500	3.60	0	30	28	12	12	15	9
1982	—Cincinnati (N.L.)	36	5	7	.417	5.10	2	107⅔	130	68	61	48	34
1983	—Indianapolis-Omaha (A.A.)■	27	9	10	.474	4.27	0	185⅓	181	113	88	77	128
1984	—Omaha (American Assoc.)	9	7	1	.875	1.24	0	72⅔	51	14	10	16	38
	—Kansas City (A.L.)	23	11	7	.611	3.63	0	143⅓	158	65	58	38	53
1985	—Kansas City (A.L.)	33	17	9	.654	2.69	0	237⅔	223	86	71	68	108
1986	—Kansas City (A.L.)	35	14	11	.560	4.09	0	231⅓	238	112	105	63	108
1987	—Kansas City (A.L.)	35	16	11	.593	3.41	0	240⅓	235	104	91	74	151
1988	—Kansas City (A.L.)	35	13	12	.520	3.19	0	243	244	98	86	62	125
1989	—Kansas City (A.L.)	33	5	11	.313	5.14	0	161	196	98	92	54	73
1990	—Greenville (Southern)■	2	1	0	1.000	0.00	0	13	5	4	0	5	12
	—Atlanta (N.L.)	24	9	11	.450	3.16	0	162⅓	164	72	57	35	76
1991	—Atlanta (N.L.)	36	15	13	.536	3.49	0	229⅔	212	105	89	56	128
American League totals (6 years)		194	76	61	.555	3.60	0	1257	1294	563	503	359	618
National League totals (6 years)		142	40	41	.494	3.83	2	707⅔	736	343	301	210	310
Major league totals (12 years)		336	116	102	.532	3.68	2	1964⅔	2030	906	804	569	928

CHAMPIONSHIP SERIES RECORD

CHAMPIONSHIP SERIES NOTES: Shares single-series record for most games lost—2 (1985).

Year	Team (League)	G	W	L	Pct.	ERA	Sv.	IP	H	R	ER	BB	SO
1979	—Cincinnati (N.L.)	1	0	0	...	0.00	0	⅓	0	0	0	0	0
1984	—Kansas City (A.L.)	1	0	1	.000	1.13	0	8	3	1	1	4	6
1985	—Kansas City (A.L.)	3	1	2	.333	5.28	0	15⅓	17	9	9	4	6
1991	—Atlanta (N.L.)	1	0	0	...	1.35	0	6⅔	8	2	1	3	6
Championship Series totals (4 years)		6	1	3	.250	3.26	0	30⅓	28	12	11	11	18

WORLD SERIES RECORD

Year	Team (League)	G	W	L	Pct.	ERA	Sv.	IP	H	R	ER	BB	SO
1985	—Kansas City (A.L.)	2	0	1	.000	2.76	0	16⅓	10	5	5	4	10
1991	—Atlanta (N.L.)	2	0	2	.000	11.25	0	4	8	5	5	1	3
World Series totals (2 years)		4	0	3	.000	4.43	0	20⅓	18	10	10	5	13

LEITER, AL
P, BLUE JAYS

PERSONAL: Born October 23, 1965, at Toms River, N.J.... 6-3/215.... Throws left, bats left.... Full name: Alois Terry Leiter.... Brother of Mark Leiter, pitcher, Detroit Tigers; and brother of Kurt Leiter, minor league pitcher (1982-84 and 1986).... Name pronounced LIE-ter.

HIGH SCHOOL: Central Regional (Bayville, N.J.).

TRANSACTIONS/CAREER NOTES: Selected by New York Yankees organization in second round of free-agent draft (June 4, 1984). ...On New York disabled list (June 22-July 26, 1988); included rehabilitation disability assignment to Columbus (July 17-25, 1988).... Traded by Yankees to Toronto Blue Jays for OF Jesse Barfield (April 30, 1989).... On Toronto disabled list (May 11, 1989-remainder of season); included rehabilitation disability assignment to Dunedin (August 12-29, 1989).... On Syracuse disabled list (May 20-June 13, 1990).... On Toronto disabled list (April 27, 1991-remainder of season); included rehabilitation disability assignment to Dunedin (May 20-28 and July 19-August 7, 1991).

Year	Team (League)	G	W	L	Pct.	ERA	Sv.	IP	H	R	ER	BB	SO
1984	—Oneonta (New York-Penn)	10	3	2	.600	3.63	0	57	52	32	23	26	48
1985	—Oneonta (New York-Penn)	6	3	2	.600	2.37	0	38	27	14	10	25	34
	—Fort Lauderdale (Florida St.)	17	1	6	.143	6.48	0	82	87	70	59	57	44
1986	—Fort Lauderdale (Florida St.)	22	4	8	.333	4.05	0	117⅔	96	64	53	90	101
1987	—Columbus (International)	5	1	4	.200	6.17	0	23⅓	21	18	16	15	23
	—Albany (Eastern)	15	3	3	.500	3.35	0	78	64	34	29	37	71
	—New York (A.L.)	4	2	2	.500	6.35	0	22⅔	24	16	16	15	28
1988	—New York (A.L.)	14	4	4	.500	3.92	0	57⅓	49	27	25	33	60
	—Columbus (International)	4	0	2	.000	3.46	0	13	5	7	5	14	12
1989	—New York-Toronto (A.L.)■	5	1	2	.333	5.67	0	33⅓	32	23	21	23	26
	—Dunedin (Florida State)	3	0	2	.000	5.63	0	8	11	5	5	5	4
1990	—Dunedin (Florida State)	6	0	0	...	2.63	0	24	18	8	7	12	14
	—Syracuse (International)	15	3	8	.273	4.62	0	78	59	43	40	68	69
	—Toronto (A.L.)	4	0	0	...	0.00	0	6⅓	1	0	0	2	5
1991	—Toronto (A.L.)	3	0	0	...	27.00	0	1⅔	3	5	5	5	1
	—Dunedin (Florida State)	4	0	0	...	1.86	0	9⅔	5	2	2	7	5
Major league totals (5 years)		30	7	8	.467	4.97	0	121⅓	109	71	67	78	120

— 280 —

LEITER, MARK
P, TIGERS

PERSONAL: Born April 13, 1963, at Joliet, Ill. . . . 6-3/210. . . . Throws right, bats right. . . . Full name: Mark Edward Leiter. . . . Brother of Al Leiter, pitcher, Toronto Blue Jays organization; and brother of Kurt Leiter, minor league pitcher (1982-84 and 1986). . . . Name pronounced LIE-ter.

TRANSACTIONS/CAREER NOTES: Selected by Baltimore Orioles organization in fourth round of free-agent draft (January 11, 1983). . . . On disabled list (April 10, 1986-entire season; April 10, 1987-entire season; and April 10, 1988-entire season). . . . Released by Orioles organization (June 13, 1988). . . . Signed by Fort Lauderdale, New York Yankees organization (September 29, 1988). . . . Traded by Yankees to Detroit Tigers for IF Torey Lovullo (March 19, 1991). . . . On Detroit disabled list (June 6-23, 1991).

Year	Team (League)	G	W	L	Pct.	ERA	Sv.	IP	H	R	ER	BB	SO
1983	Bluefield (Appalachian)	6	2	1	.667	2.70	0	36⅔	33	17	11	13	35
	Hagerstown (Carolina)	8	1	5	.167	7.25	0	36	42	31	29	28	18
1984	Hagerstown (Carolina)	27	8	•13	.381	5.62	0	139⅓	132	96	87	★108	105
1985	Hagerstown (Carolina)	34	2	8	.200	3.46	8	83⅓	77	44	32	29	82
	Charlotte (Southern)	5	0	1	.000	1.42	1	6⅓	3	1	1	2	8
1986	—						Did not play						
1987	—						Did not play						
1988	—						Did not play						
1989	Fort Lauderdale (Florida St.)■	6	2	2	.500	1.53	1	35⅓	27	9	6	5	22
	Columbus (International)	22	9	6	.600	5.00	0	90	102	50	50	34	70
1990	Columbus (International)	30	9	4	.692	3.60	1	122⅔	114	56	49	27	115
	New York (A.L.)	8	1	1	.500	6.84	0	26⅓	33	20	20	9	21
1991	Toledo (International)■	5	1	0	1.000	0.00	1	6⅔	6	0	0	3	7
	Detroit (A.L.)	38	9	7	.563	4.21	1	134⅔	125	66	63	50	103
Major league totals (2 years)		46	10	8	.556	4.64	1	161	158	86	83	59	124

LEIUS, SCOTT
3B/SS, TWINS

PERSONAL: Born September 24, 1965, at Yonkers, N.Y. . . . 6-3/180. . . . Throws right, bats right. . . . Full name: Scott Thomas Leius. . . . Name pronounced LAY-us.
HIGH SCHOOL: Mamaroneck (N.Y.).
COLLEGE: Concordia College (N.Y.).
TRANSACTIONS/CAREER NOTES: Selected by Minnesota Twins organization in 13th round of free-agent draft (June 2, 1986). . . . On disabled list (August 3, 1989-remainder of season).
STATISTICAL NOTES: Led Appalachian League shortstops with 174 assists and 33 double plays in 1986. . . . Led Midwest League shortstops with 74 double plays in 1987.

Year	Team (League)	Pos.	G	AB	R	H	2B	3B	HR	RBI	Avg.	SB	PO	A	E	Avg.
1986	Elizabethton (Appal.)	SS-3B	61	237	37	66	14	1	4	23	.278	5	67	†176	18	.931
1987	Kenosha (Midwest)	SS	126	414	65	99	16	4	8	51	.239	6	183	331	31	.943
1988	Visalia (California)	SS	93	308	44	73	14	4	3	46	.237	3	154	234	15	.963
1989	Orlando (Southern)	SS	99	346	49	105	22	2	4	45	★.303	3	148	257	22	.948
1990	Portland (Pacific Coast)	SS-2B	103	352	34	81	13	5	2	23	.230	5	155	323	18	.964
	Minnesota (A.L.)	SS-3B	14	25	4	6	1	0	1	4	.240	0	20	25	0	1.000
1991	Minnesota (A.L.)	3B-SS-0F	109	199	35	57	7	2	5	20	.286	5	56	129	7	.964
Major league totals (2 years)			123	224	39	63	8	2	6	24	.281	5	76	154	7	.970

CHAMPIONSHIP SERIES RECORD

Year	Team (League)	Pos.	G	AB	R	H	2B	3B	HR	RBI	Avg.	SB	PO	A	E	Avg.
1991	Minnesota (A.L.)	PH-3B	3	4	0	0	0	0	0	0	.000	0	1	4	0	1.000

WORLD SERIES RECORD

Year	Team (League)	Pos.	G	AB	R	H	2B	3B	HR	RBI	Avg.	SB	PO	A	E	Avg.
1991	Minnesota (A.L.)	3B-PH-SS	7	14	2	5	0	0	1	2	.357	0	5	8	1	.929

LEMKE, MARK
2B, BRAVES

PERSONAL: Born August 13, 1965, at Utica, N.Y. . . . 5-9/167. . . . Throws right, bats both. . . . Full name: Mark Alan Lemke. . . . Name pronounced LEM-kee.
HIGH SCHOOL: Notre Dame (Utica, N.Y.).
TRANSACTIONS/CAREER NOTES: Selected by Atlanta Braves organization in 27th round of free-agent draft (June 6, 1983). . . . On Atlanta disabled list (May 29-July 17, 1990); included rehabilitation disability assignment to Bradenton (July 9-17, 1990).
STATISTICAL NOTES: Led Gulf Coast League second basemen with .977 fielding percentage, 175 putouts, 207 assists, 391 total chances and 39 double plays in 1984. . . . Led Carolina League second basemen with .982 fielding percentage, 355 assists and 83 double plays in 1987. . . . Led Southern League with 239 total bases in 1988. . . . Led Southern League second basemen with 739 total chances and 105 double plays in 1988. . . . Led International League second basemen with 731 total chances and 105 double plays in 1989.

Year	Team (League)	Pos.	G	AB	R	H	2B	3B	HR	RBI	Avg.	SB	PO	A	E	Avg.
1983	Bradenton Braves (GCL)	2B	53	209	37	55	6	0	0	19	.263	10	81	101	11	.943
1984	Anderson (S. Atlantic)	2B-3B	42	121	18	18	2	0	0	5	.149	3	67	83	4	.974
	Bradenton Braves (GCL)	2B-SS	•63	★243	41	67	11	0	3	32	.276	2	†175	†209	9	†.977

Year	Team (League)	Pos.	G	AB	R	H	2B	3B	HR	RBI	Avg.	SB	PO	A	E	Avg.
1985 —Sumter (South Atlantic)....		2B	90	231	25	50	6	0	0	20	.216	2	119	174	11	.964
1986 —Sumter (South Atlantic).....		3B-2B	126	448	99	122	24	2	18	66	.272	11	134	274	16	.962
1987 —Durham (Carolina)		2B-3B	127	489	75	143	28	3	20	68	.292	10	248	†355	11	†.982
—Greenville (Southern)		3B	6	26	0	6	0	0	0	4	.231	0	4	12	1	.941
1988 —Greenville (Southern)		2B	•143	*567	81	*153	30	4	16	80	.270	18	*281	*440	18	.976
—Atlanta (N.L.)		2B	16	58	8	13	4	0	0	2	.224	0	47	51	3	.970
1989 —Richmond (Int'l)		2B	*146	*518	69	143	22	7	5	61	.276	4	*299	*417	*15	.979
—Atlanta (N.L.)		2B	14	55	4	10	2	1	2	10	.182	0	25	40	0	1.000
1990 —Atlanta (N.L.)		3B-2B-SS	102	239	22	54	13	0	0	21	.226	0	90	193	4	.986
—Bradenton Braves (GCL)...		2B-3B	4	11	2	4	0	0	1	5	.364	0	5	11	1	.941
1991 —Atlanta (N.L.)		2B-3B	136	269	36	63	11	2	2	23	.234	1	162	215	10	.974
Major league totals (4 years)			268	621	70	140	30	3	4	56	.225	1	324	499	17	.980

CHAMPIONSHIP SERIES RECORD

Year	Team (League)	Pos.	G	AB	R	H	2B	3B	HR	RBI	Avg.	SB	PO	A	E	Avg.
1991 —Atlanta (N.L.)		2B	7	20	1	4	1	0	0	1	.200	0	12	10	1	.957

WORLD SERIES RECORD

WORLD SERIES NOTES: Shares single-game record for most triples—2 (October 24, 1991).

Year	Team (League)	Pos.	G	AB	R	H	2B	3B	HR	RBI	Avg.	SB	PO	A	E	Avg.
1991 —Atlanta (N.L.)		2B	6	24	4	10	1	3	0	4	.417	0	14	19	1	.971

LENNON, PATRICK
OF, MARINERS

PERSONAL: Born April 27, 1968, at Whiteville, N.C.... 6-2/200.... Throws right, bats right.... Full name: Patrick Orlando Lennon.
HIGH SCHOOL: Whiteville (N.C.).
TRANSACTIONS/CAREER NOTES: Selected by Seattle Mariners organization in first round (eighth pick overall) of free-agent draft (June 2, 1986).
STATISTICAL NOTES: Led Midwest League third basemen with 39 errors in 1987.

Year	Team (League)	Pos.	G	AB	R	H	2B	3B	HR	RBI	Avg.	SB	PO	A	E	Avg.
1986 —Bellingham (Northwest)....		SS-3B	51	169	35	41	5	2	3	27	.243	8	57	90	27	.845
1987 —Wausau (Midwest)		3B-SS	98	319	54	80	21	3	7	34	.251	25	73	190	†40	.868
1988 —Vermont (Eastern)		3B	95	321	44	83	9	3	9	40	.259	15	81	143	*28	.889
1989 —Williamsport (Eastern)		OF-3B	66	248	32	65	14	2	3	31	.262	7	67	20	14	.861
1990 —San Bernardino (Calif.)		3B-OF	44	163	29	47	6	2	8	30	.288	10	29	40	7	.908
—Williamsport (Eastern)		OF-3B	49	167	24	49	6	4	5	22	.293	6	62	40	10	.911
1991 —Calgary (Pacific Coast)		OF-3B	112	416	75	137	29	5	15	74	.329	12	114	3	6	.951
—Seattle (A.L.)		OF	9	8	2	1	1	0	0	1	.125	0	2	0	0	1.000
Major league totals (1 year)			9	8	2	1	1	0	0	1	.125	0	2	0	0	1.000

LEONARD, MARK
OF, GIANTS

PERSONAL: Born August 14, 1964, at Mountain View, Calif.... 6-1/195.... Throws right, bats left.... Full name: Mark David Leonard.
HIGH SCHOOL: Fremont (Calif.).
COLLEGE: UC Santa Barbara.
TRANSACTIONS/CAREER NOTES: Selected by San Francisco Giants organization in 29th round of free-agent draft (June 2, 1986). ... Loaned by Giants organization to Tri-Cities, co-op (June 23, 1986); returned (September 1, 1986).... On Phoenix disabled list (August 6, 1989-remainder of season).... On San Francisco disabled list (August 8-September 5, 1990); included rehabilitation disability assignment to Phoenix (August 27-September 5, 1990).
STATISTICAL NOTES: Led California League with 283 total bases, 11 sacrifice flies and 13 intentional bases on balls received in 1988.

Year	Team (League)	Pos.	G	AB	R	H	2B	3B	HR	RBI	Avg.	SB	PO	A	E	Avg.
1986 —Ever.-Tri-Cit. (N'west)■...		OF-1B-C	38	128	21	33	6	0	4	17	.258	4	63	2	4	.942
1987 —Clinton (Midwest)■..........		1B	128	413	57	132	31	2	15	80	.320	5	610	47	9	.986
1988 —San Jose (California)		OF-1B	*142	510	102	176	*50	6	15	*118	.345	11	178	120	9	.971
1989 —Shreveport (Texas)		OF	63	219	29	68	15	3	10	52	.311	1	90	5	0	1.000
—Phoenix (Pacific Coast)		OF	27	78	7	21	4	0	6	6	.269	1	29	1	3	.909
1990 —Phoenix (Pacific Coast)		OF	109	390	76	130	22	2	19	82	.333	6	120	3	1	.992
—San Francisco (N.L.)........		OF	11	17	3	3	1	0	1	2	.176	0	10	0	0	1.000
1991 —San Francisco (N.L.)........		OF	64	129	14	31	7	1	2	14	.240	0	41	0	0	1.000
—Phoenix (Pacific Coast)		OF	41	146	27	37	7	0	8	25	.253	1	45	3	3	.941
Major league totals (2 years)			75	146	17	34	8	1	3	16	.233	0	51	0	0	1.000

LEWIS, DARREN
OF, GIANTS

PERSONAL: Born August 28, 1967, at Berkeley, Calif.... 6-0/175.... Throws right, bats right.... Full name: Darren Joel Lewis.
HIGH SCHOOL: Moreau (Hayward, Calif.).
COLLEGE: Chabot College (Calif.) and California.

TRANSACTIONS/CAREER NOTES: Selected by Los Angeles Dodgers organization in sixth round of free-agent draft (January 14, 1986).... Selected by Toronto Blue Jays organization in 45th round of free-agent draft (June 2, 1987).... Selected by Oakland Athletics organization in 18th round of free-agent draft (June 1, 1988).... Traded by A's with a player to be named later to San Francisco Giants for IF Ernest Riles (December 4, 1990); Giants acquired P Pedro Pena to complete deal (December 17, 1990).

STATISTICAL NOTES: Led California League outfielders with 324 total chances in 1989.

Year	Team (League)	Pos.	G	AB	R	H	2B	3B	HR	RBI	Avg.	SB	PO	A	E	Avg.
1988	—Scottsdale A's (Arizona)...	OF	5	15	8	5	3	0	0	4	.333	4	15	1	0	1.000
	—Madison (Midwest)	OF-2B	60	199	38	49	4	1	0	11	.246	31	195	3	4	.980
1989	—Modesto (California)	OF	129	503	74	150	23	5	4	39	.298	27	★311	8	5	.985
	—Huntsville (Southern)	OF	9	31	7	10	1	1	1	7	.323	0	16	0	0	1.000
1990	—Huntsville (Southern)	OF	71	284	52	84	11	3	3	23	.296	21	186	6	0	1.000
	—Tacoma (Pacific Coast)	OF	60	247	32	72	5	2	2	26	.291	16	132	9	2	.986
	—Oakland (A.L.)	OF	25	35	4	8	0	0	0	1	.229	2	33	0	0	1.000
1991	—Phoenix (Pacific Coast)■..	OF	81	315	63	107	12	10	2	52	.340	32	243	5	2	.992
	—San Francisco (N.L.)	OF	72	222	41	55	5	3	1	15	.248	13	159	2	0	1.000
	American League totals (1 year)		25	35	4	8	0	0	0	1	.229	2	33	0	0	1.000
	National League totals (1 year)		72	222	41	55	5	3	1	15	.248	13	159	2	0	1.000
	Major league totals (2 years)		97	257	45	63	5	3	1	16	.245	15	192	2	0	1.000

LEWIS, JIM
P, PADRES

PERSONAL: Born July 20, 1964, at Jackson, Mich.... 6-2/215.... Throws right, bats right.... Full name: James Steven Lewis.
HIGH SCHOOL: Jonesville (Mich.).
COLLEGE: Citrus College (Calif.).
TRANSACTIONS/CAREER NOTES: Selected by San Diego Padres organization in fifth round of free-agent draft (January 9, 1985).

Year	Team (League)	G	W	L	Pct.	ERA	Sv.	IP	H	R	ER	BB	SO
1985	—Spokane (Northwest)	20	4	4	.500	3.88	0	67⅓	60	34	29	21	54
1986	—Charleston, S.C. (S. Atlantic)	51	4	8	.333	3.43	4	84	87	48	32	32	61
1987	—Reno (California)	13	2	2	.500	6.14	0	29⅓	34	26	20	21	28
1988	—Riverside (California)	44	7	7	.500	3.57	7	98⅓	99	57	39	54	80
1989	—Wichita (Texas)	★63	8	4	.667	2.70	18	83⅓	83	28	25	33	53
1990	—Las Vegas (Pacific Coast)	59	5	6	.455	4.55	5	93	109	60	47	46	54
1991	—Wichita (Texas)	2	0	0	...	0.00	1	2⅔	4	2	0	4	3
	—Las Vegas (Pacific Coast)	48	6	3	.667	3.38	3	85⅓	93	41	32	34	76
	—San Diego (N.L.)	12	0	0	...	4.15	0	13	14	7	6	11	10
	Major league totals (1 year)	12	0	0	...	4.15	0	13	14	7	6	11	10

LEWIS, MARK
SS/2B, INDIANS

PERSONAL: Born November 30, 1969, at Hamilton, O.... 6-1/190.... Throws right, bats right. ... Full name: Mark David Lewis.
HIGH SCHOOL: Hamilton (O.).
TRANSACTIONS/CAREER NOTES: Selected by Cleveland Indians organization in first round (second pick overall) of free-agent draft (June 1, 1988).... On Kinston disabled list (May 29-June 20, 1989).

Year	Team (League)	Pos.	G	AB	R	H	2B	3B	HR	RBI	Avg.	SB	PO	A	E	Avg.
1988	—Burlington (Appal.)	SS	61	227	39	60	13	1	7	43	.264	14	70	★177	23	.915
1989	—Kinston (Carolina)...........	SS	93	349	50	94	16	3	1	32	.269	17	130	244	32	.921
	—Canton/Akron (Eastern) ..	SS	7	25	4	5	1	0	0	1	.200	0	15	28	2	.956
1990	—Canton/Akron (Eastern) ..	SS	102	390	55	106	19	3	10	60	.272	8	152	286	31	.934
	—Colorado Springs (PCL) ...	SS	34	124	16	38	8	1	1	21	.306	2	52	84	11	.925
1991	—Colorado Springs (PCL)	SS-2B-3B	46	179	29	50	10	3	2	31	.279	3	65	135	10	.952
	—Cleveland (A.L.)	2B-SS	84	314	29	83	15	1	0	30	.264	2	129	231	9	.976
	Major league totals (1 year)		84	314	29	83	15	1	0	30	.264	2	129	231	9	.976

LEWIS, RICHIE
P, ORIOLES

PERSONAL: Born January 25, 1966, at Muncie, Ind.... 5-10/170.... Throws right, bats right. ... Full name: Richie Todd Lewis.
HIGH SCHOOL: South Side (Muncie, Ind.).
COLLEGE: Florida State (received degree, 1987).
TRANSACTIONS/CAREER NOTES: Selected by Montreal Expos organization in second round of free-agent draft (June 2, 1987).... On disabled list (June 2-August 12 and August 22, 1988-remainder of season; and July 28, 1989-remainder of season).... On Jacksonville disabled list (June 1-8 and June 11, 1990-remainder of season).... Traded by Expos to Baltimore Orioles for P Chris Myers (August 24, 1991).

Year	Team (League)	G	W	L	Pct.	ERA	Sv.	IP	H	R	ER	BB	SO
1987	—Indianapolis (Am. Assoc.)	2	0	0	...	9.82	0	3⅔	6	4	4	2	3
1988	—Jacksonville (Southern)	12	5	3	.625	3.38	0	61⅓	37	32	23	56	60
1989	—Jacksonville (Southern)	17	5	4	.556	2.58	0	94⅓	80	37	27	55	105
1990	—West Palm Beach (Florida St.) ..	10	0	1	.000	4.80	2	15	12	12	8	11	14
	—Jacksonville (Southern)	11	0	0	...	1.26	5	14⅓	7	2	2	5	14
1991	—Harrisburg (Eastern)	34	6	5	.545	3.74	5	74⅔	67	33	31	40	82
	—Indianapolis (Am. Assoc.)	5	1	0	1.000	3.58	0	27⅔	35	12	11	20	22
	—Rochester (International)■.......	2	1	0	1.000	2.81	0	16	13	5	5	7	18

LEWIS, SCOTT
P, ANGELS

PERSONAL: Born December 5, 1965, at Grants Pass, Ore. . . . 6-3/178. . . . Throws right, bats right. . . . Full name: Scott Allen Lewis.
HIGH SCHOOL: Medford (Ore.).
COLLEGE: UNLV.
TRANSACTIONS/CAREER NOTES: Selected by California Angels organization in 11th round of free-agent draft (June 1, 1988).
STATISTICAL NOTES: Led California League with nine balks in 1989. . . . Tied for Pacific Coast League lead with six complete games in 1990.

Year	Team (League)	G	W	L	Pct.	ERA	Sv.	IP	H	R	ER	BB	SO
1988	—Bend (Northwest)	9	5	3	.625	3.50	0	61⅔	63	33	24	12	53
	—Quad City (Midwest)	3	1	2	.333	4.64	0	21⅓	19	12	11	5	20
	—Palm Springs (California)	2	0	1	.000	5.63	0	8	12	5	5	2	7
1989	—Midland (Texas)	25	11	12	.478	4.93	0	162⅓	195	★121	89	55	104
1990	—Edmonton (Pacific Coast)	27	13	11	.542	3.90	0	177⅔	198	90	77	35	124
	—California (A.L.)	2	1	1	.500	2.20	0	16⅓	10	4	4	2	9
1991	—California (A.L.)	16	3	5	.375	6.27	0	60⅓	81	43	42	21	37
	—Edmonton (Pacific Coast)	17	3	9	.250	4.50	0	110	132	71	55	26	87
	Major league totals (2 years)	18	4	6	.400	5.40	0	76⅔	91	47	46	23	46

LEYRITZ, JIM
C/3B, YANKEES

PERSONAL: Born December 27, 1963, at Lakewood, O. . . . 6-0/190. . . . Throws right, bats right. . . . Full name: James Joseph Leyritz.
COLLEGE: Middle Georgia College and Kentucky.
TRANSACTIONS/CAREER NOTES: Signed as free agent by New York Yankees organization (August 24, 1985).
STATISTICAL NOTES: Led Florida State League with 25 passed balls in 1987. . . . Tied for Eastern League lead in being hit by pitch with nine in 1989.

Year	Team (League)	Pos.	G	AB	R	H	2B	3B	HR	RBI	Avg.	SB	PO	A	E	Avg.
1986	—Oneonta (N.Y.-Penn)	C	23	91	12	33	3	1	4	15	.363	1	170	21	2	.990
	—Fort Lauderdale (FSL)	C	12	34	3	10	1	1	0	1	.294	0	32	8	1	.976
1987	—Fort Lauderdale (FSL)	C	102	374	48	115	22	0	6	51	.307	2	458	★76	13	.976
1988	—Albany (Eastern)	C-3B-1B	112	382	40	92	18	3	5	50	.241	3	418	73	6	.988
1989	—Albany (Eastern)	C-OF-3B	114	375	53	118	18	2	10	66★	.315	2	421	41	3	.994
1990	—Columbus (Int'l)	3-2-1-0-C	59	204	36	59	11	1	8	32	.289	4	75	96	13	.929
	—New York (A.L.)	3B-OF-C	92	303	28	78	13	1	5	25	.257	2	117	107	13	.945
1991	—New York (A.L.)	3B-C-1B	32	77	8	14	3	0	0	4	.182	0	38	21	3	.952
	—Columbus (Int'l)	C-3-S-2	79	270	50	72	24	1	11	48	.267	1	209	48	5	.981
	Major league totals (2 years)		124	380	36	92	16	1	5	29	.242	2	155	128	16	.946

LILLIQUIST, DEREK
P, INDIANS

PERSONAL: Born February 20, 1966, at Winter Park, Fla. . . . 6-0/214. . . . Throws left, bats left. . . . Full name: Derek Jansen Lilliquist.
COLLEGE: Georgia.
TRANSACTIONS/CAREER NOTES: Selected by Boston Red Sox organization in 15th round of free-agent draft (June 4, 1984). . . . Selected by Atlanta Braves in first round (sixth pick overall) of free-agent draft (June 2, 1987). . . . Traded by Braves to San Diego Padres for P Mark Grant (July 12, 1990). . . . Claimed on waivers by Cleveland Indians (November 20, 1991).
RECORDS/HONORS: Named lefthanded pitcher on THE SPORTING NEWS college All-America team (1987).

Year	Team (League)	G	W	L	Pct.	ERA	Sv.	IP	H	R	ER	BB	SO
1987	—Bradenton Braves (GCL)	2	0	0	. . .	0.00	0	13	3	0	0	2	16
	—Durham (Carolina)	3	2	1	.667	2.88	0	25	13	9	8	6	29
1988	—Richmond (International)	28	10	12	.455	3.38	0	170⅔	179	70	64	36	80
1989	—Atlanta (N.L.)	32	8	10	.444	3.97	0	165⅔	202	87	73	34	79
1990	—Atlanta-San Diego (N.L.)■	28	5	11	.313	5.31	0	122	136	74	72	42	63
	—Richmond (International)	5	4	0	1.000	2.57	0	35	31	11	10	11	24
1991	—Las Vegas (Pacific Coast)	33	4	6	.400	5.38	2	105⅓	142	79	63	33	89
	—San Diego (N.L.)	6	0	2	.000	8.79	0	14⅓	25	14	14	4	7
	Major league totals (3 years)	66	13	23	.361	4.74	0	302	363	175	159	80	149

LIND, JOSE
2B, PIRATES

PERSONAL: Born May 1, 1964, at Toabaja, Puerto Rico. . . . 5-11/175. . . . Throws right, bats right. . . . Full name: Jose Salgado Lind. . . . Brother of Orlando Lind, pitcher, Minnesota Twins organization. . . . Name pronounced LEEND.
HIGH SCHOOL: Jose Alegria (Dorado, Puerto Rico).
TRANSACTIONS/CAREER NOTES: Signed as free agent by Pittsburgh Pirates organization (December 3, 1982).
STATISTICAL NOTES: Led Eastern League second basemen with 705 total chances and 84 double plays in 1986. . . . Led Pacific Coast League second basemen with 764 total chances and 84 double plays in 1987. . . . Led N.L. second basemen with 786 total chances in 1990 and 796 in 1991.

Year	Team (League)	Pos.	G	AB	R	H	2B	3B	HR	RBI	Avg.	SB	PO	A	E	Avg.
1983	—Bradenton Pirates (GCL)	2B-SS	45	163	26	49	3	4	0	18	.301	12	102	125	9	.962
1984	—Macon (South Atlantic)	2B-SS	121	396	39	82	5	2	0	30	.207	17	271	306	32	.947

Year	Team (League)	Pos.	G	AB	R	H	2B	3B	HR	RBI	Avg.	SB	PO	A	E	Avg.
1985—Prince William (Caro.)	2-S-3-0	105	377	42	104	9	4	0	28	.276	11	164	221	14	.965
1986—Nashua (Eastern)	2B	134	•520	58	137	18	5	1	33	.263	29	★314	★378	13	★.982
1987—Vancouver (Pac. Coast)	2B	128	★533	75	143	16	3	3	30	.268	21	★311	★432	21	.973
—Pittsburgh (N.L.)	2B	35	143	21	46	8	4	0	11	.322	2	53	139	1	.995
1988—Pittsburgh (N.L.)	2B	154	611	82	160	24	4	2	49	.262	15	333	473	11	.987
1989—Pittsburgh (N.L.)	2B	153	578	52	134	21	3	2	48	.232	15	309	438	18	.976
1990—Pittsburgh (N.L.)	2B	152	514	46	134	28	5	1	48	.261	8	★330	449	7	.991
1991—Pittsburgh (N.L.)	2B	150	502	53	133	16	6	3	54	.265	7	★349	438	9	.989
Major league totals (5 years)		644	2348	254	607	97	22	8	210	.259	47	1374	1937	46	.986

CHAMPIONSHIP SERIES RECORD

Year	Team (League)	Pos.	G	AB	R	H	2B	3B	HR	RBI	Avg.	SB	PO	A	E	Avg.
1990—Pittsburgh (N.L.)	2B	6	21	1	5	1	1	1	2	.238	0	19	19	0	1.000
1991—Pittsburgh (N.L.)	2B	7	25	0	4	0	0	0	3	.160	0	12	24	1	.973
Championship Series totals (2 years)		13	46	1	9	1	1	1	5	.196	0	31	43	1	.987

LINDEMAN, JIM
OF, PHILLIES

PERSONAL: Born January 10, 1962, at Evanston, Ill. . . . 6-1/200. . . . Throws right, bats right. . . . Full name: James William Lindeman.
HIGH SCHOOL: Maine West (Des Plaines, Ill.).
COLLEGE: Bradley.
TRANSACTIONS/CAREER NOTES: Selected by St. Louis Cardinals organization in first round (24th pick overall) of free-agent draft (June 6, 1983). . . . On St. Louis disabled list (May 12-29 and June 4-July 4, 1987); included rehabilitation disability assignment to Louisville (May 26-29 and June 17-July 4, 1987). . . . On St. Louis disabled list (April 22-July 5 1988); included rehabilitation disability assignment to Louisville (June 16-July 5, 1988). . . . On St. Louis disabled list (July 10-August 10, 1989); included rehabilitation disability assignment to Louisville (July 26-August 10, 1989). . . . Traded by Cardinals with P Matt Kinzer to Detroit Tigers for 2B Pat Austin, C Bill Henderson and P Marcus Betances (December 6, 1989). . . . Granted free agency (October 4, 1990). . . . Signed by Philadelphia Phillies organization (January 11, 1991).

Year	Team (League)	Pos.	G	AB	R	H	2B	3B	HR	RBI	Avg.	SB	PO	A	E	Avg.
1983—St. Petersburg (Fla. St.)	3B	70	232	45	64	13	1	8	37	.276	9	36	98	26	.838
1984—Springfield (Midwest)	3B-SS	94	354	69	96	15	2	18	66	.271	6	78	175	30	.894
—Arkansas (Texas)	3B	40	137	14	26	4	3	0	13	.190	3	26	67	6	.939
1985—Arkansas (Texas)	3B	128	450	54	127	30	6	10	63	.282	11	74	238	24	.929
1986—Louisville (Am. Assoc.)	1B-3B-OF	139	509	82	128	38	5	20	★96	.251	9	718	110	19	.978
—St. Louis (N.L.)	1B-3B-OF	19	55	7	14	1	0	1	6	.255	1	118	10	1	.992
1987—St. Louis (N.L.)	OF-1B	75	207	20	43	13	0	8	28	.208	3	196	14	3	.986
—Louisville (Am. Assoc.)	OF	20	78	11	24	3	1	4	10	.308	0	14	1	1	.938
1988—St. Louis (N.L.)	OF-1B	17	43	3	9	1	0	2	7	.209	0	36	2	1	.974
—Louisville (Am. Assoc.)	OF-1B	73	261	32	66	18	4	2	30	.253	2	308	23	4	.988
1989—St. Louis (N.L.)	1B-OF	73	45	8	5	1	0	0	2	.111	0	93	6	1	.990
—Louisville (Am. Assoc.)	OF-1B	29	109	18	33	8	1	5	20	.303	3	52	5	2	.966
1990—Toledo (International)■	1B-OF-3B	109	374	48	85	17	2	12	50	.227	2	709	53	8	.990
—Detroit (A.L.)	1B-OF	12	32	5	7	1	0	2	8	.219	0	5	0	0	1.000
1991—Scranton/W.B. (Int'l)■	OF-1B	11	40	7	11	1	1	2	7	.275	0	30	2	2	.941
—Philadelphia (N.L.)	OF-1B	65	95	13	32	5	0	0	12	.337	0	35	1	0	1.000
American League totals (1 year)		12	32	5	7	1	0	2	8	.219	0	5	0	0	1.000
National League totals (5 years)		249	445	51	103	21	0	11	55	.231	4	478	33	6	.988
Major league totals (6 years)		261	477	56	110	22	0	13	63	.231	4	483	33	6	.989

CHAMPIONSHIP SERIES RECORD

Year	Team (League)	Pos.	G	AB	R	H	2B	3B	HR	RBI	Avg.	SB	PO	A	E	Avg.
1987—St. Louis (N.L.)	1B-PH	5	13	1	4	0	0	1	3	.308	0	33	2	0	1.000

WORLD SERIES RECORD

Year	Team (League)	Pos.	G	AB	R	H	2B	3B	HR	RBI	Avg.	SB	PO	A	E	Avg.
1987—St. Louis (N.L.)	1B-PH-OF	6	15	3	5	1	0	0	2	.333	0	28	2	3	.909

LINDSEY, DOUG
C, PHILLIES

PERSONAL: Born September 22, 1967, at Austin, Tex. . . . 6-2/200. . . . Throws right, bats right. . . . Full name: Michael Douglas Lindsey.
HIGH SCHOOL: Harmony (Austin, Tex.).
COLLEGE: Seminole Junior College (Okla.).
TRANSACTIONS/CAREER NOTES: Selected by Philadelphia Phillies organization in sixth round of free-agent draft (June 2, 1987). . . . On Reading disabled list (May 29-June 5 and July 18-31, 1991).
STATISTICAL NOTES: Led Eastern League catchers with 12 double plays and tied for league lead with 11 passed balls in 1991.

Year	Team (League)	Pos.	G	AB	R	H	2B	3B	HR	RBI	Avg.	SB	PO	A	E	Avg.
1987 —Utica (New York-Penn)		C	52	169	23	41	7	0	1	25	.243	1	337	41	8	.979
1988 —Spartanburg (S. Atl.)		C	90	324	29	76	19	0	4	46	.235	4	461	59	9	.983
1989 —Spartanburg (S. Atl.)		C	39	136	14	31	7	0	3	17	.228	2	240	32	6	.978
—Clearwater (Florida St.)		C	36	118	8	23	3	0	0	9	.195	0	190	35	4	.983
1990 —Reading (Eastern)		C-1B	107	323	16	56	11	0	1	32	.173	2	574	70	8	.988
1991 —Reading (Eastern)		C	94	313	26	81	13	0	1	34	.259	1	571	75	3	★.995
—Philadelphia (N.L.)		C	1	3	0	0	0	0	0	0	.000	0	8	0	0	1.000
Major league totals (1 year)			1	3	0	0	0	0	0	0	.000	0	8	0	0	1.000

LINSKEY, MIKE

P, PADRES

PERSONAL: Born June 18, 1966, at Baltimore. . . . 6-5/220. . . . Throws left, bats left. . . . Full name: Michael Shawn Linskey.
HIGH SCHOOL: Loyola (Baltimore).
COLLEGE: James Madison (degree in sports management).
TRANSACTIONS/CAREER NOTES: Selected by Pittsburgh Pirates organization in 20th round of free-agent draft (June 4, 1984). . . . Selected by Baltimore Orioles organization in ninth round of free-agent draft (June 1, 1988). . . . On Rochester disabled list (April 10-19, 1991). . . . Claimed on waivers by San Diego Padres (November 20, 1991).

Year	Team (League)	G	W	L	Pct.	ERA	Sv.	IP	H	R	ER	BB	SO
1988 —Erie (New York-Penn)	10	3	3	.500	3.11	1	55	46	24	19	18	50
1989 —Frederick (Carolina)	9	2	2	.500	0.88	0	61⅓	47	7	6	16	46
—Hagerstown (Eastern)	18	10	6	.625	2.81	0	128	108	45	40	35	90
1990 —Hagerstown (Eastern)	8	7	1	.875	1.47	0	55	40	16	9	14	40
—Rochester (International)	19	7	9	.438	3.58	0	110⅔	116	60	44	28	54
1991 —Rochester (International)	10	1	5	.167	7.24	0	41	67	34	33	17	25
—Hagerstown (Eastern)	16	6	5	.545	4.46	0	107	128	62	53	37	71

LIRIANO, NELSON

IF

PERSONAL: Born June 3, 1964, at Puerto Plata, Dominican Republic. . . . 5-10/172. . . . Throws right, bats both. . . . Full name: Nelson Arturo Liriano. . . . Name pronounced LEER-ee-ON-oh.
HIGH SCHOOL: Jose Debeaw (Puerto Plata, Dominican Republic).
TRANSACTIONS/CAREER NOTES: Signed as free agent by Toronto Blue Jays organization (November 1, 1982). . . . Traded by Blue Jays with OF Pedro Munoz to Minnesota Twins for P John Candelaria (July 27, 1990). . . . Released by Twins (April 2, 1991). . . . Signed by Omaha, Kansas City Royals organization (May 1, 1991). . . . Granted free agency (October 15, 1991).
STATISTICAL NOTES: Led Carolina League second basemen with 79 double plays in 1985. . . . Led International League second basemen with 611 total chances and 96 double plays in 1987.

Year	Team (League)	Pos.	G	AB	R	H	2B	3B	HR	RBI	Avg.	SB	PO	A	E	Avg.
1983 —Florence (S. Atlantic)		2B	129	478	87	124	24	5	6	57	.259	27	214	323	34	.940
1984 —Kinston (Carolina)		2B	132	★512	68	126	22	4	5	50	.246	10	260	★357	★21	.967
1985 —Kinston (Carolina)		2B	134	451	68	130	23	1	6	36	.288	25	★261	328	★25	.959
1986 —Knoxville (Southern)	2B-3B-SS	135	557	88	159	25	★15	7	59	.285	35	239	324	22	.962
1987 —Syracuse (International) ..		2B	130	531	72	133	19	•10	10	55	.250	36	★246	★346	★19	.969
—Toronto (A.L.)		2B	37	158	29	38	6	2	2	10	.241	13	83	107	1	.995
1988 —Toronto (A.L.)	2B-3B	99	276	36	73	6	2	3	23	.264	12	121	177	12	.961
—Syracuse (International) ..		2B	8	31	2	6	1	1	0	1	.194	2	14	23	0	1.000
1989 —Toronto (A.L.)		2B	132	418	51	110	26	3	5	53	.263	16	267	330	12	.980
1990 —Toronto-Minn. (A.L.)■	2B-SS	103	355	46	83	12	9	1	28	.234	8	176	260	11	.975
1991 —Omaha (Am. Assoc.)■	2B-SS	86	292	50	80	16	9	2	36	.274	6	149	218	9	.976
—Kansas City (A.L.)		2B	10	22	5	9	0	0	0	1	.409	0	11	23	0	1.000
Major league totals (5 years)			381	1229	167	313	50	16	11	115	.255	49	658	897	36	.977

CHAMPIONSHIP SERIES RECORD

Year	Team (League)	Pos.	G	AB	R	H	2B	3B	HR	RBI	Avg.	SB	PO	A	E	Avg.
1989 —Toronto (A.L.)		2B	3	7	1	3	0	0	0	1	.429	3	4	3	1	.875

LISTACH, PAT

2B/SS, BREWERS

PERSONAL: Born September 12, 1967, at Natchitoches, La. . . . 5-9/170. . . . Throws right, bats right. . . . Full name: Patrick Alan Listach.
HIGH SCHOOL: Natchitoches (La.) Central.
COLLEGE: McLennan Community College (Tex.) and Arizona State.
TRANSACTIONS/CAREER NOTES: Selected by Seattle Mariners organization in 23rd round of free-agent draft (June 2, 1987). . . . Selected by Milwaukee Brewers organization in fifth round of free-agent draft (June 1, 1988).

Year	Team (League)	Pos.	G	AB	R	H	2B	3B	HR	RBI	Avg.	SB	PO	A	E	Avg.
1988 —Beloit (Midwest)		SS	53	200	40	48	5	1	1	18	.240	20	66	117	24	.884
1989 —Stockton (California)	2B-SS	132	480	73	110	11	4	2	34	.229	37	250	351	29	.954
1990 —Stockton (California)	2B-SS-OF	★139	503	★116	137	21	6	2	39	.272	78	319	356	25	.964
1991 —El Paso (Texas)		SS-2B	49	186	40	47	5	2	0	13	.253	14	86	131	22	.908
—Denver (Am. Assoc.)	2B-SS-OF	89	286	51	72	10	4	1	31	.252	23	182	237	9	.979

LITTON, GREG
IF/OF, GIANTS

PERSONAL: Born July 13, 1964, at New Orleans. . . . 6-0/190. . . . Throws right, bats right. . . . Full name: Jon Gregory Litton.
HIGH SCHOOL: Woodham (Pensacola, Fla.).
COLLEGE: Pensacola Junior College (Fla.).
TRANSACTIONS/CAREER NOTES: Selected by San Francisco Giants organization in first round (10th pick overall) of free-agent draft (January 17, 1984). . . . On San Francisco disabled list (March 28-April 21, 1990); included rehabilitation disability assignment to Phoenix (April 15-21, 1990). . . . On San Francisco disabled list (August 15-September 1, 1991).
STATISTICAL NOTES: Led California League second basemen with 453 assists and 749 total chances in 1985. . . . Led Texas League second basemen with 262 putouts, 369 assists, 655 total chances and 24 errors in 1986.

Year	Team (League)	Pos.	G	AB	R	H	2B	3B	HR	RBI	Avg.	SB	PO	A	E	Avg.
1984—Everett (Northwest)		2B-3B	62	243	29	57	12	2	4	26	.235	2	135	160	17	.946
1985—Fresno (California)		2B-OF	141	*564	88	150	*33	7	12	103	.266	8	269	†453	28	.963
1986—Shreveport (Texas)		2B-SS-OF	131	455	46	112	30	3	10	55	.246	1	†265	†373	†24	.964
1987—Shreveport (Texas)		2B-SS	72	254	34	66	6	3	8	33	.260	2	117	199	3	.991
—Phoenix (Pacific Coast)		2B-SS	60	203	24	44	8	2	1	22	.217	0	146	173	8	.976
1988—Shreveport (Texas)		3B-2B-SS	116	432	58	120	35	5	11	64	.278	2	116	247	13	.965
1989—Phoenix (Pacific Coast)		2-S-3-1-C	30	89	6	16	4	2	2	6	.180	1	48	50	4	.961
—San Francisco (N.L.)		3-2-S-O-C	71	143	12	36	5	3	4	17	.252	0	44	66	3	.973
1990—Phoenix (Pacific Coast)		OF-2B-3B	6	22	3	6	1	0	0	4	.273	0	6	7	2	.867
—San Francisco (N.L.)		O-2-S-3	93	204	17	50	9	1	1	24	.245	1	90	43	1	.993
1991—San Francisco (N.L.)		IF-O-C-P	59	127	13	23	7	1	1	15	.181	0	121	65	2	.989
—Phoenix (Pacific Coast)		SS-3B-2B	8	27	9	11	1	0	4	9	.407	0	6	23	4	.879
Major league totals (3 years)			223	474	42	109	21	5	6	56	.230	1	255	174	6	.986

CHAMPIONSHIP SERIES RECORD

Year	Team (League)	Pos.	G	AB	R	H	2B	3B	HR	RBI	Avg.	SB	PO	A	E	Avg.
1989—San Francisco (N.L.)		PH-3B	1	1	0	1	0	0	0	0	1.000	0	0	0	0	...

WORLD SERIES RECORD

Year	Team (League)	Pos.	G	AB	R	H	2B	3B	HR	RBI	Avg.	SB	PO	A	E	Avg.
1989—San Francisco (N.L.)		PH-2B-3B	2	6	1	3	1	0	1	3	.500	0	2	3	0	1.000

RECORD AS PITCHER

Year	Team (League)	G	W	L	Pct.	ERA	Sv.	IP	H	R	ER	BB	SO
1991—San Francisco (N.L.)		1	0	0	...	9.00	0	1	1	1	1	3	0

LIVERNOIS, DEREK
P, RED SOX

PERSONAL: Born April 17, 1967, at Inglewood, Calif. . . . 6-1/185. . . . Throws right, bats left. . . . Full name: Derek Robert Livernois.
HIGH SCHOOL: Lyman (Longwood, Fla.).
TRANSACTIONS/CAREER NOTES: Selected by Boston Red Sox organization in 15th round of free-agent draft (June 3, 1985). . . . On disabled list (July 7-19, 1987; June 16-July 26, 1988; and May 8-July 12, 1990).

Year	Team (League)	G	W	L	Pct.	ERA	Sv.	IP	H	R	ER	BB	SO
1985—Elmira (New York-Penn)	17	2	3	.400	3.83	2	47	44	26	20	18	55
1986—Greensboro (South Atlantic)	25	12	7	.632	2.65	0	159⅔	142	72	47	73	164
1987—Winter Haven (Florida State)	20	7	7	.500	4.92	0	113⅓	133	80	62	48	64
1988—Winter Haven (Florida State)	7	3	3	.500	3.15	0	40	39	18	14	12	25
1989—Lynchburg (Carolina)	26	10	8	.556	3.50	0	159⅓	147	75	62	48	*151
1990—New Britain (Eastern)	15	9	2	.818	1.98	0	95⅔	80	24	21	31	67
1991—Pawtucket (International)	5	1	2	.333	10.53	0	19⅔	27	25	23	17	14
—New Britain (Eastern)	5	3	2	.600	3.25	0	27⅔	28	14	10	10	31

LIVINGSTONE, SCOTT
3B, TIGERS

PERSONAL: Born July 15, 1965, at Dallas. . . . 6-0/190. . . . Throws right, bats left. . . . Full name: Scott Louis Livingstone.
COLLEGE: Texas A&M.
TRANSACTIONS/CAREER NOTES: Selected by Toronto Blue Jays organization in sixth round of free-agent draft (June 4, 1984). . . . Selected by New York Yankees organization in 26th round of free-agent draft (June 2, 1986). . . . Selected by Oakland Athletics organization in third round of free-agent draft (June 2, 1987). . . . Selected by Detroit Tigers organization in second round of free-agent draft (June 1, 1988). . . . On disabled list (July 14-23 and July 28-August 7, 1990).
RECORDS/HONORS: Named designated hitter on THE SPORTING NEWS college All-America team (1987-88).
STATISTICAL NOTES: Tied for Eastern League lead in total chances by third baseman with 360 in 1989.

Year	Team (League)	Pos.	G	AB	R	H	2B	3B	HR	RBI	Avg.	SB	PO	A	E	Avg.
1988—Lakeland (Florida State)		3B	53	180	28	51	8	1	2	25	.283	1	30	115	8	.948
1989—London (Eastern)		3B-SS	124	452	46	98	18	1	14	71	.217	1	100	265	25	.936
1990—Toledo (International)		3B	103	345	44	94	19	0	6	36	.272	0	66	181	13	.950
1991—Toledo (International)		3B-1B	92	331	48	100	13	3	3	62	.302	2	65	137	16	.927
—Detroit (A.L.)		3B	44	127	19	37	5	0	2	11	.291	2	32	67	2	.980
Major league totals (1 year)			44	127	19	37	5	0	2	11	.291	2	32	67	2	.980

LOFTON, KENNY
OF, INDIANS

PERSONAL: Born May 31, 1967, at East Chicago, Ind. . . . 6-0/180. . . . Throws left, bats left. . . . Full name: Kenneth Lofton. **HIGH SCHOOL:** Washington (East Chicago, Ind.). **COLLEGE:** Arizona.

TRANSACTIONS/CAREER NOTES: Selected by Houston Astros organization in 17th round of free-agent draft (June 1, 1988). . . . Traded by Astros with IF Dave Rohde to Cleveland Indians for P Willie Blair and C Eddie Taubensee (December 10, 1991). **STATISTICAL NOTES:** Tied for Pacific Coast League lead in caught stealing with 23 in 1991.

Year	Team (League)	Pos.	G	AB	R	H	2B	3B	HR	RBI	Avg.	SB	PO	A	E	Avg.
1988	—Auburn (N.Y.-Penn)	OF	48	187	23	40	6	1	1	14	.214	26	94	5	4	.961
1989	—Auburn (N.Y.-Penn)	OF	34	110	21	29	3	1	0	8	.264	26	37	4	8	.837
	—Asheville (S. Atlantic)	OF	22	82	14	27	2	0	1	9	.329	14	38	1	2	.951
1990	—Osceola (Florida State)	OF	124	481	98	*159	15	5	2	35	.331	62	246	13	7	.974
1991	—Tucson (Pacific Coast)	OF	130	*545	93	*168	19	*17	2	50	.308	40	*308	*27	9	.974
	—Houston (N.L.)	OF	20	74	9	15	1	0	0	0	.203	2	41	1	1	.977
Major league totals (1 year)			20	74	9	15	1	0	0	0	.203	2	41	1	1	.977

LONG, BILL
P

PERSONAL: Born February 29, 1960, at Cincinnati. . . . 6-0/190. . . . Throws right, bats right. . . . Full name: William Douglas Long. **COLLEGE:** Miami of Ohio.

TRANSACTIONS/CAREER NOTES: Selected by San Diego Padres organization in second round of free-agent draft (June 8, 1981). . . . Traded by Padres organization with P Tim Lollar, 3B Luis Salazar and SS Ozzie Guillen to Chicago White Sox for P LaMarr Hoyt, P Kevin Kristan and P Todd Simmons (December 6, 1984). . . . On disabled list (May 12-June 16, 1986). . . . Traded by White Sox to Chicago Cubs for P Frank Campos (April 30, 1990). . . . On Chicago disabled list (June 7-28, 1990). . . . Released by Cubs (December 18, 1990). . . . Signed by Montreal Expos (January 31, 1991). . . . On voluntarily retired list (June 1, 1991).

Year	Team (League)	G	W	L	Pct.	ERA	Sv.	IP	H	R	ER	BB	SO
1981	—Salem (Carolina)	14	9	2	.818	2.79	0	87	81	31	27	28	80
1982	—Amarillo (Texas)	27	12	10	.545	4.40	0	*198 1/3	*222	116	97	53	117
1983	—Las Vegas (Pacific Coast)	18	5	5	.500	7.65	0	62 1/3	99	66	53	28	41
	—Beaumont (Texas)	10	2	5	.286	5.65	0	65 1/3	80	47	41	28	33
1984	—Beaumont (Texas)	25	•14	5	.737	2.93	0	159 2/3	149	56	52	67	114
1985	—Buffalo (American Assoc.)■	25	*13	6	.684	3.51	0	151 1/3	146	69	59	43	71
	—Chicago (A.L.)	4	0	1	.000	10.29	0	14	25	17	16	5	13
1986	—Buffalo (American Assoc.)	22	9	9	.500	3.88	0	146	159	73	63	44	86
1987	—Hawaii (Pacific Coast)	2	2	0	1.000	4.15	0	13	15	7	6	4	6
	—Chicago (A.L.)	29	8	8	.500	4.37	1	169	179	85	82	28	72
1988	—Chicago (A.L.)	47	8	11	.421	4.03	2	174	187	89	78	43	77
1989	—Chicago (A.L.)	30	5	5	.500	3.92	1	98 2/3	101	49	43	37	51
	—Vancouver (Pacific Coast)	3	1	2	.333	2.77	0	26	17	8	8	2	14
1990	—Chicago (A.L.)	4	0	1	.000	6.35	0	5 2/3	6	5	4	2	2
	—Chicago (N.L.)■	42	6	1	.857	4.37	0	55 2/3	66	29	27	21	32
1991	—Montreal (N.L.)■	3	0	0	...	10.80	0	1 2/3	4	2	2	4	0
	—Indianapolis (Am. Assoc.)	10	1	4	.200	5.13	1	33 1/3	32	20	19	14	17
American League totals (5 years)		114	21	26	.447	4.35	4	461 1/3	498	245	223	115	215
National League totals (2 years)		45	6	1	.857	4.55	5	57 1/3	70	31	29	25	32
Major league totals (6 years)		159	27	27	.500	4.37	9	518 2/3	568	276	252	140	247

LONGMIRE, TONY
OF, PHILLIES

PERSONAL: Born August 12, 1968, at Vallejo, Calif. . . . 6-1/195. . . . Throws right, bats both. . . . Full name: Anthony Eugene Longmire. **HIGH SCHOOL:** Hogan (Vallejo, Calif.).

TRANSACTIONS/CAREER NOTES: Selected by Pittsburgh Pirates organization in eighth round of free-agent draft (June 2, 1986). . . . On Salem disabled list (August 27, 1988-remainder of season). . . . On disabled list (April 10-May 24 and June 25, 1990-remainder of season). . . . Traded by Pirates organization to Philadelphia Phillies (September 28, 1990), completing deal in which Phillies traded OF-1B Carmelo Martinez to Pirates for OF Wes Chamberlain, OF Julio Peguero and a player to be named later (August 30, 1990). **MISCELLANEOUS:** Batted lefthanded only at Salem (1988-89) and Harrisburg (1989).

Year	Team (League)	Pos.	G	AB	R	H	2B	3B	HR	RBI	Avg.	SB	PO	A	E	Avg.
1986	—Bradenton Pirates (GCL)	OF	15	40	6	11	2	1	0	6	.275	1	19	0	2	.905
1987	—Macon (South Atlantic)	OF	127	445	63	117	15	4	5	62	.263	18	167	5	8	.956
1988	—Salem (Carolina)	OF	64	218	46	60	12	2	11	40	.275	4	91	3	3	.969
	—Harrisburg (Eastern)	OF	32	94	7	14	2	2	0	4	.149	0	46	2	2	.960
1989	—Salem (Carolina)	OF	14	62	8	20	3	1	1	6	.323	0	14	3	0	1.000
	—Harrisburg (Eastern)	OF	37	127	15	37	7	0	3	22	.291	1	62	1	2	.969
1990	—Harrisburg (Eastern)	OF	24	91	9	27	6	0	1	13	.297	5	46	4	2	.962
1991	—Reading (Eastern)■	OF	85	323	43	93	22	1	9	56	.288	10	134	3	4	.972
	—Scranton/W.B. (Int'l)	OF	36	111	11	29	3	2	0	9	.261	4	54	1	4	.932

LOPEZ, JAVIER
C, BRAVES

PERSONAL: Born November 5, 1970, at Ponce, Puerto Rico. . . . 6-3/185. . . . Throws right, bats right. . . . Full name: Javier Torres Lopez. **HIGH SCHOOL:** Academia Cristo Rey (Urb la Ramble Ponce, Puerto Rico).

TRANSACTIONS/CAREER NOTES: Signed as free agent by Atlanta Braves organization (November 6, 1987).

STATISTICAL NOTES: Led Midwest League catchers with 11 double plays and 31 passed balls in 1990. . . . Led Carolina League catchers with 701 total chances and 14 double plays in 1991.

Year	Team (League)	Pos.	G	AB	R	H	2B	3B	HR	RBI	Avg.	SB	PO	A	E	Avg.
1988	—Bradenton Braves (GCL)...	C	31	94	8	18	4	0	1	9	.191	1	131	30	7	.958
1989	—Pulaski (Appalachian)	C	51	153	27	40	8	1	3	27	.261	3	264	26	5	.983
1990	—Burlington (Midwest)	C	116	422	48	112	17	3	11	55	.265	0	724	79	11	.986
1991	—Durham (Carolina)	C	113	384	43	94	14	2	11	51	.245	10	*610	85	6	.991

LOPEZ, LUIS
2B/SS, PADRES

PERSONAL: Born September 4, 1970, at Cidra, Puerto Rico. . . . 5-11/175. . . . Throws right, bats both. . . . Full name: Luis Lopez.

TRANSACTIONS/CAREER NOTES: Signed as free agent by San Diego Padres organization (September 9, 1987).

STATISTICAL NOTES: Led South Atlantic League shortstops with 703 total chances and 78 double plays in 1989.

Year	Team (League)	Pos.	G	AB	R	H	2B	3B	HR	RBI	Avg.	SB	PO	A	E	Avg.
1988	—Spokane (Northwest)	SS	70	312	50	95	13	1	0	35	.304	14	*118	217	*47	.877
1989	—Charleston, S.C. (S. Atl.) ...	SS	127	460	50	102	15	1	1	29	.222	12	*256	*373	*74	.895
1990	—Riverside (California)	SS	14	46	5	17	3	1	1	4	.370	4	18	38	6	.903
1991	—Wichita (Texas)	2B-SS	125	452	43	121	17	1	1	41	.268	6	274	339	26	.959

LOPEZ, LUIS
C/IF, INDIANS

PERSONAL: Born September 1, 1964, at Brooklyn, N.Y. . . . 6-1/190. . . . Throws right, bats right. . . . Full name: Luis Antonio Lopez.

HIGH SCHOOL: Lafayette (Brooklyn, N.Y.).

TRANSACTIONS/CAREER NOTES: Selected by Los Angeles Dodgers organization in second round of free-agent draft (June 6, 1983). . . . Released by Dodgers (December 13, 1990). . . . Signed by Cleveland Indians (January 11, 1991). . . . Granted free agency (October 15, 1991). . . . Signed by Colorado Springs, Indians organization (December 19, 1991).

RECORDS/HONORS: Named California League Most Valuable Player (1987).

STATISTICAL NOTES: Led Pioneer League first basemen with 16 errors in 1984. . . . Led California League with 276 total bases in 1987. . . . Led California League catchers with .989 fielding percentage in 1987. . . . Led Texas League in being hit by pitch with 13 in 1988.

Year	Team (League)	Pos.	G	AB	R	H	2B	3B	HR	RBI	Avg.	SB	PO	A	E	Avg.
1984	—Great Falls (Pioneer)	1B-C	68	275	60	90	15	5	6	61	.327	4	527	42	†17	.971
1985	—Vero Beach (Florida St.) ...	1B-C	120	382	47	106	18	2	1	43	.277	2	655	46	14	.980
1986	—Vero Beach (Florida St.) ...	C-1B	122	434	52	124	21	3	1	60	.286	5	688	72	15	.981
1987	—Bakersfield (California)	C-1B	*142	*550	89	*181	*43	2	16	96	.329	6	928	85	14	†.986
1988	—San Antonio (Texas)	1B-C-3B	124	470	56	116	16	3	7	65	.247	3	1036	87	18	.984
1989	—San Antonio (Texas)	0-1-3-C	99	327	46	87	17	0	10	51	.266	1	214	40	5	.981
	—Albuquerque (PCL)	3B-OF	19	75	17	37	7	0	2	16	.493	1	22	12	1	.971
1990	—Albuquerque (PCL)	1-C-3-S	128	448	65	158	23	2	11	81*	.353	3	494	33	7	.987
	—Los Angeles (N.L.)	1B	6	6	0	0	0	0	0	0	.000	0	4	0	0	1.000
1991	—Colorado Springs (PCL)■..	1B-3B-OF	41	176	29	61	11	4	1	31	.347	0	205	53	4	.985
	—Cleveland (A.L.)	C-1-3-0	35	82	7	18	4	1	0	7	.220	0	109	9	2	.983
	American League totals (1 year)		35	82	7	18	4	1	0	7	.220	0	109	9	2	.983
	National League totals (1 year)		6	6	0	0	0	0	0	0	.000	0	4	0	0	1.000
	Major league totals (2 years)		41	88	7	18	4	1	0	7	.205	0	113	9	2	.984

LOVULLO, TOREY
3B, YANKEES

PERSONAL: Born July 25, 1965, at Santa Monica, Calif. . . . 6-0/180. . . . Throws right, bats both. . . . Full name: Salvatore Anthony Lovullo.

COLLEGE: UCLA.

TRANSACTIONS/CAREER NOTES: Selected by Kansas City Royals organization in 27th round of free-agent draft (June 2, 1986). . . . Selected by Detroit Tigers organization in fifth round of free-agent draft (June 2, 1987). . . . Traded by Tigers to New York Yankees for P Mark Leiter (March 19, 1991).

RECORDS/HONORS: Named second baseman on THE SPORTING NEWS college All-America team (1987).

STATISTICAL NOTES: Tied for International League lead with 10 intentional bases on balls received in 1989.

Year	Team (League)	Pos.	G	AB	R	H	2B	3B	HR	RBI	Avg.	SB	PO	A	E	Avg.
1987	—Fayetteville (S. Atl.)	3B-2B	55	191	34	49	13	0	8	32	.257	6	41	133	22	.888
	—Lakeland (Florida State)	3B	18	60	11	16	3	0	1	16	.267	0	11	30	2	.953
1988	—Glens Falls (Eastern)	3B-2B	78	270	37	74	17	1	9	50	.274	2	63	173	21	.918
	—Toledo (International)	2B-3B-SS	57	177	18	41	8	1	5	20	.232	2	120	149	5	.982
	—Detroit (A.L.)	2B-3B	12	21	2	8	1	1	1	2	.381	0	12	19	0	1.000
1989	—Toledo (International)	1-3-2-S	112	409	48	94	23	2	10	52	.230	2	217	257	20	.960
	—Detroit (A.L.)	1B-3B	29	87	8	10	2	0	1	4	.115	1	134	24	1	.994
1990	—Toledo (International)	2B-3B-1B	141	486	71	131	*38	1	14	58	.270	4	280	352	18	.972
1991	—New York (A.L.)■..............	3B	22	51	0	9	2	0	0	2	.176	0	14	33	3	.940
	—Columbus (Int'l)	3-1-2-0	106	395	74	107	24	5	10	75	.271	4	277	164	16	.965
	Major league totals (3 years)		63	159	10	27	5	1	2	8	.170	1	160	76	4	.983

LUSADER, SCOTT
OF

PERSONAL: Born September 30, 1964, at Chicago. . . . 5-10/165. . . . Throws left, bats left. . . . Full name: Scott Edward Lusader. . . . Name pronounced loo-SAY-der.
HIGH SCHOOL: Twin Oaks (West Palm Beach, Fla.).
COLLEGE: Florida (bachelor of science degree in marketing).

TRANSACTIONS/CAREER NOTES: Selected by Detroit Tigers organization in sixth round of free-agent draft (June 3, 1985). . . . On Detroit disabled list (March 27-May 5, 1989); included rehabilitation disability assignment to Toledo (April 21-May 5, 1989). . . . Loaned by Tigers to Tucson, Houston Astros organization (July 13, 1989); returned (September 2, 1989). . . . Claimed on waivers by New York Yankees (April 5, 1991). . . . On New York disabled list (May 12-June 28, 1991); included rehabilitation disability assignment to Columbus (June 11-28, 1991). . . . Granted free agency (October 15, 1991).
RECORDS/HONORS: Shares major league record for most errors by outfielder in one inning—3 (September 9, 1989, first inning).

Year	Team (League)	Pos.	G	AB	R	H	2B	3B	HR	RBI	Avg.	SB	PO	A	E	Avg.
1985 —Lakeland (Florida State) ...		OF	27	97	16	28	5	1	2	22	.289	0	47	3	3	.943
—Birmingham (Southern)		OF	21	77	13	26	3	4	2	14	.338	0	49	1	0	1.000
1986 —Glens Falls (Eastern)		OF	136	479	74	134	23	3	11	59	.280	11	275	13	•11	.963
1987 —Toledo (International)		OF	136	505	78	136	29	8	17	80	.269	6	274	11	6	.979
—Detroit (A.L.)		OF	23	47	8	15	3	1	1	8	.319	1	29	0	1	.967
1988 —Toledo (International)		OF-1B	89	329	38	86	11	5	4	46	.261	3	193	0	3	.985
—Detroit (A.L.)		OF	16	16	3	1	0	0	1	3	.063	0	7	0	0	1.000
1989 —Toledo (International)		OF	44	153	17	37	9	1	2	15	.242	4	111	5	4	.967
—Detroit (A.L.)		OF	40	103	15	26	4	0	1	8	.252	4	56	0	4	.933
—Tucson (Pacific Coast)■...		OF	33	121	15	30	3	1	2	13	.248	4	80	2	4	.953
1990 —Toledo (International)■.....		OF	76	268	35	67	12	1	4	25	.250	4	140	5	4	.973
—Detroit (A.L.)		OF	45	87	13	21	2	0	2	16	.241	1	53	1	1	.982
1991 —New York (A.L.)■		OF	11	7	2	1	0	0	0	1	.143	0	3	0	0	1.000
—Columbus (Int'l)		OF	76	284	48	80	13	6	7	32	.282	7	109	9	3	.975
Major league totals (5 years)			135	260	41	64	9	1	5	36	.246	6	148	1	6	.961

LYONS, BARRY
C/1B, ASTROS

PERSONAL: Born June 3, 1960, at Biloxi, Miss. . . . 6-1/200. . . . Throws right, bats right. . . . Full name: Barry Stephen Lyons.
HIGH SCHOOL: Biloxi (Miss.).
COLLEGE: Delta State (Miss.).

TRANSACTIONS/CAREER NOTES: Selected by Detroit Tigers organization in 25th round of free-agent draft (June 8, 1981). . . . Selected by New York Mets organization in 15th round of free-agent draft (June 7, 1982). . . . On Tidewater disabled list (August 4, 1986-remainder of season). . . . On New York disabled list (June 27-July 25, 1989); included rehabilitation disability assignment to Tidewater (July 19-25, 1989). . . . On New York disabled list (May 16-July 9, 1990); included rehabilitation disability assignment to Tidewater (June 19-July 9, 1990). . . . Released by Mets (September 4, 1990). . . . Signed by Los Angeles Dodgers (September 21, 1990). . . . Granted free agency (June 12, 1991). . . . Signed by Edmonton, California Angels organization (June 19, 1991). . . . Released by Angels (October 24, 1991). . . . Signed by Houston Astros organization (January 15, 1992).
RECORDS/HONORS: Named Carolina League Player of the Year (1984).
STATISTICAL NOTES: Led Carolina League catchers with .989 fielding percentage and 72 assists in 1984. . . . Led Texas League in grounding into double plays with 19 in 1985. . . . Led Texas League catchers with 19 errors in 1985.

Year	Team (League)	Pos.	G	AB	R	H	2B	3B	HR	RBI	Avg.	SB	PO	A	E	Avg.
1982 —Shelby (South Atlantic)		C-1B	45	164	23	46	12	0	4	46	.280	0	226	21	8	.969
1983 —Lynchburg (Carolina)		C	2	7	0	1	0	0	0	2	.143	0	21	4	0	1.000
—Columbia (S. Atlantic)........		C-1B-OF	92	316	55	94	9	2	5	45	.297	3	387	33	17	.961
1984 —Lynchburg (Carolina)		C-1B-OF	115	412	59	130	17	3	12	87	.316	1	894	†86	13	†.987
1985 —Jackson (Texas)		C-1B	126	486	69	149	34	6	11	108	.307	3	834	65	†23	.975
1986 —New York (N.L.)		C	6	9	1	0	0	0	0	2	.000	0	16	0	1	.941
—Tidewater (Int'l)		1B-C	61	234	28	69	16	0	4	46	.295	0	423	25	6	.987
1987 —New York (N.L.)		C	53	130	15	33	4	1	4	24	.254	0	223	17	4	.984
1988 —New York (N.L.)		C-1B	50	91	5	21	7	1	0	11	.231	0	130	9	3	.979
1989 —New York (N.L.)		C	79	235	15	58	13	0	3	27	.247	0	463	29	10	.980
—Tidewater (Int'l)		C-1B	5	20	1	2	0	1	0	2	.100	0	43	5	1	.980
1990 —New York-L.A. (N.Y.)■......		C	27	85	9	20	0	0	3	9	.235	0	183	12	4	.980
—Tidewater (Int'l)		C-1B	57	164	8	28	5	0	0	17	.171	0	291	23	5	.984
1991 —Los Angeles (N.L.)		C	9	9	0	0	0	0	0	0	.000	0	12	1	0	1.000
—Edmonton (Pac. Coast)■...		C-1B	47	165	15	51	13	0	2	23	.309	0	247	26	8	.972
—California (A.L.)		1B	2	5	0	1	0	0	0	0	.200	0	10	1	0	1.000
American League totals (1 year)			2	5	0	1	0	0	0	0	.200	0	10	1	0	1.000
National League totals (6 years)			224	559	45	132	24	2	10	73	.236	0	1027	68	22	.980
Major league totals (6 years)			226	564	45	133	24	2	10	73	.236	0	1037	69	22	.980

LYONS, STEVE
IF/OF, BRAVES

PERSONAL: Born June 3, 1960, at Tacoma, Wash. . . . 6-3/195. . . . Throws right, bats left. . . . Full name: Stephen John Lyons.
HIGH SCHOOL: Marist (Eugene, Ore.), then Beaverton (Ore.).
COLLEGE: Oregon State.

TRANSACTIONS/CAREER NOTES: Selected by Boston Red Sox organization in first round (19th pick overall) of free-agent draft (June 8, 1981). . . . Traded by Red Sox to Chicago White Sox for P Tom Seaver (June 29, 1986). . . . Released by White Sox (April 13, 1991). . . . Signed by Red Sox (April 18, 1991). . . . Granted free agency (November 5, 1991). . . . Signed by Atlanta Braves (January 8, 1991).

STATISTICAL NOTES: Led International League third basemen with 98 putouts, 332 total chances and 25 errors in 1984. . . . Led A.L. third basemen with 36 double plays in 1988.

Year	Team (League)	Pos.	G	AB	R	H	2B	3B	HR	RBI	Avg.	SB	PO	A	E	Avg.
							BATTING							FIELDING		
1981	Winston-Salem (Caro.)	OF-SS	64	252	43	61	9	3	6	40	.242	19	137	23	8	.952
1982	Bristol (Eastern)	OF-SS	135	460	86	112	23	3	13	58	.243	35	275	11	9	.969
1983	New Britain (Eastern)	3-0-S-P	132	456	83	112	24	7	7	62	.246	47	145	207	17	.954
1984	Pawtucket (Int'l)	3B-OF-SS	131	444	80	119	21	2	17	62	.268	35	†141	211	†26	.931
1985	Boston (A.L.)	OF-3B-SS	133	371	52	98	14	3	5	30	.264	12	253	6	7	.974
1986	Boston-Chicago (A.L.)■..	OF-3B-1B	101	247	30	56	9	3	1	20	.227	4	175	11	4	.979
	Buffalo (Am. Assoc.)	3-S-0-1	20	74	18	22	5	1	3	8	.297	5	36	41	4	.951
1987	Chicago (A.L.)	3B-OF-2B	76	193	26	54	11	1	1	19	.280	3	69	101	4	.977
	Hawaii (Pacific Coast)	0-2-3-S	47	167	26	48	11	0	2	16	.287	7	73	71	3	.980
1988	Chicago (A.L.)	3-0-2-C-1	146	472	59	127	28	3	5	45	.269	1	128	243	29	.928
1989	Chicago (A.L.)	1B-OF-C	140	443	51	117	21	3	2	50	.264	9	414	245	15	.978
1990	Chicago (A.L.)	1B-OF-P	94	146	22	28	6	1	1	11	.192	1	244	54	5	.983
1991	Boston (A.L.)■................	OF-IF-P	87	212	15	51	10	1	4	17	.241	10	118	43	3	.982
	Major league totals (7 years)		777	2084	255	531	99	15	19	192	.255	40	1401	703	67	.969

RECORD AS PITCHER

Year	Team (League)	G	W	L	Pct.	ERA	Sv.	IP	H	R	ER	BB	SO
1983	New Britain (Eastern)	3	1	0	1.000	2.45	0	3⅔	3	1	1	1	2
1990	Chicago (A.L.)	1	0	0	. . .	4.50	0	2	2	1	1	4	1
1991	Boston (A.L.)■.........................	1	0	0	. . .	0.00	0	1	2	0	0	0	1
	Major league totals (2 years)	2	0	0	. . .	3.00	0	3	4	1	1	4	2

MAAS, KEVIN
DH/1B, YANKEES

PERSONAL: Born January 20, 1965, at Castro Valley, Calif. . . . 6-3/209. . . . Throws left, bats left. . . . Full name: Kevin Christian Maas. . . . Brother of Jason Maas, outfielder, New York Yankees organization.
HIGH SCHOOL: Bishop O'Dowd (Oakland, Calif.).
COLLEGE: California.
TRANSACTIONS/CAREER NOTES: Selected by New York Yankees organization in 22nd round of free-agent draft (June 2, 1986). . . . On disabled list (April 19-30 and July 27, 1989-remainder of season).

Year	Team (League)	Pos.	G	AB	R	H	2B	3B	HR	RBI	Avg.	SB	PO	A	E	Avg.
							BATTING							FIELDING		
1986	Oneonta (N.Y.-Penn)	1B	28	101	14	36	10	0	0	18	.356	5	222	19	1	.996
1987	Fort Lauderdale (FSL)	1B	116	439	77	122	28	4	11	73	.278	14	667	51	10	.986
1988	Prince William (Caro.).......	1B	29	108	24	32	7	0	12	35	.296	3	288	25	5	.984
	Albany (Eastern).............	1B	109	372	66	98	14	3	16	55	.263	5	902	73	12	.988
1989	Columbus (Int'l)	OF	83	291	42	93	23	2	6	45	.320	2	78	3	3	.964
1990	Columbus (Int'l)	1B	57	194	37	55	15	2	13	41	.284	2	219	19	4	.983
	New York (A.L.)	1B	79	254	42	64	9	0	21	41	.252	1	486	35	9	.983
1991	New York (A.L.)	1B	148	500	69	110	14	1	23	63	.220	5	317	23	6	.983
	Major league totals (2 years)		227	754	111	174	23	1	44	104	.231	6	803	58	15	.983

MacDONALD, BOB
P, BLUE JAYS

PERSONAL: Born April 27, 1965, at East Orange, N.J. . . . 6-3/208. . . . Throws left, bats left. . . . Full name: Robert Joseph MacDonald.
HIGH SCHOOL: Point Pleasant Beach (N.J.).
COLLEGE: Rutgers.
TRANSACTIONS/CAREER NOTES: Selected by Toronto Blue Jays organization in 19th round of free-agent draft (June 2, 1987).

Year	Team (League)	G	W	L	Pct.	ERA	Sv.	IP	H	R	ER	BB	SO
1987	St. Catharines (N.Y.-Penn)	1	0	0	. . .	4.50	0	4	8	4	2	0	4
	Myrtle Beach (South Atlantic) ..	10	2	1	.667	5.66	0	20⅔	24	18	13	7	12
1988	Myrtle Beach (South Atlantic) ..	52	3	4	.429	1.69	15	53⅓	42	13	10	18	43
1989	Knoxville (Southern)	43	3	5	.375	3.29	9	63	52	27	23	23	58
	Syracuse (International)	12	1	0	1.000	5.63	0	16	16	10	10	6	12
1990	Syracuse (International)	9	0	2	.000	5.40	2	8⅓	4	5	5	9	6
	Knoxville (Southern)	36	1	2	.333	1.89	15	57	37	17	12	29	54
	Toronto (A.L.)	4	0	0	. . .	0.00	0	2⅓	0	0	0	2	0
1991	Syracuse (International)	7	1	0	1.000	4.50	1	6	5	3	3	5	8
	Toronto (A.L.)......................	45	3	3	.500	2.85	0	53⅔	51	19	17	25	24
	Major league totals (2 years)	49	3	3	.500	2.73	0	56	51	19	17	27	24

CHAMPIONSHIP SERIES RECORD

Year	Team (League)	G	W	L	Pct.	ERA	Sv.	IP	H	R	ER	BB	SO
1991	Toronto (A.L.)...........................	1	0	0	. . .	9.00	0	1	1	1	1	1	0

MACFARLANE, MIKE
C, ROYALS

PERSONAL: Born April 12, 1964, at Stockton, Calif. . . . 6-1/205. . . . Throws right, bats right. . . . Full name: Michael Andrew Macfarlane.
HIGH SCHOOL: Lincoln (Stockton, Calif.).
COLLEGE: Santa Clara.

TRANSACTIONS/CAREER NOTES: Selected by Kansas City Royals organization in fourth round of free-agent draft (June 3, 1985). . . . On disabled list (April 9-July 9, 1986 and July 16-September 14, 1991).

							—BATTING—							—FIELDING—			
Year	Team (League)	Pos.	G	AB	R	H	2B	3B	HR	RBI	Avg.	SB	PO	A	E	Avg.
1985 —Memphis (Southern)		C	65	223	29	60	15	4	8	39	.269	0	295	24	9	.973
1986 —Memphis (Southern)		DH-OF	40	141	26	34	7	2	12	29	.241	0	0	0	0	...
1987 —Omaha (Am. Assoc.)		C	87	302	53	79	25	1	13	50	.262	0	408	37	6	.987
—Kansas City (A.L.)		C	8	19	0	4	1	0	0	3	.211	0	29	2	0	1.000
1988 —Kansas City (A.L.)		C	70	211	25	56	15	0	4	26	.265	0	309	18	2	.994
—Omaha (Am. Assoc.)		C	21	76	8	18	7	2	2	8	.237	0	85	5	1	.989
1989 —Kansas City (A.L.)		C	69	157	13	35	6	0	2	19	.223	0	249	17	1	.996
1990 —Kansas City (A.L.)		C	124	400	37	102	24	4	6	58	.255	1	660	23	6	.991
1991 —Kansas City (A.L.)		C	84	267	34	74	18	2	13	41	.277	1	391	28	3	.993
Major league totals (5 years)			355	1054	109	271	64	6	25	147	.257	2	1638	88	12	.993

MACHADO, JULIO
P, BREWERS

PERSONAL: Born December 1, 1965, at Zulia, Venezuela. . . . 5-9/165. . . . Throws right, bats right.

TRANSACTIONS/CAREER NOTES: Signed as free agent by Philadelphia Phillies organization (April 10, 1985). . . . Released by Phillies organization (March 3, 1989). . . . Signed by Jackson, New York Mets organization (April 5, 1989). . . . Loaned by Mets organization to Peninsula, independent (April 5, 1989); returned (April 16, 1989). . . . Traded by Mets organization with P Kevin Brown to Milwaukee Brewers (September 7, 1990) as partial completion of deal in which Brewers traded C Charlie O'Brien and a player to be named later to Mets for two players to be named later (August 30, 1990); Mets acquired P Kevin Carmody to complete deal (September 11, 1990).

Year	Team (League)	G	W	L	Pct.	ERA	Sv.	IP	H	R	ER	BB	SO
1985 —Spartanburg (South Atlantic) ..		32	4	5	.444	4.32	0	81⅓	75	50	39	38	71
1986 —Spartanburg (South Atlantic) ..		43	2	5	.286	3.73	7	79⅔	68	39	33	52	81
1987 —Clearwater (Florida State)		7	2	0	1.000	2.60	1	34⅔	31	11	10	19	32
—Reading (Eastern)		21	4	5	.444	4.74	0	108⅓	112	70	57	40	89
1988 —Reading (Eastern)		26	6	1	.857	5.43	5	63	69	41	38	34	52
—Clearwater (Florida State)		13	1	4	.200	2.95	3	36⅔	34	13	12	14	45
1989 —Peninsula (Carolina)■.............		4	1	0	1.000	0.00	2	3⅔	2	0	0	2	1
—St. Lucie (Florida State)■.........		4	1	0	1.000	0.00	2	10⅔	5	0	0	3	14
—Jackson (Texas)		32	3	5	.375	2.84	3	57	42	23	18	27	67
—Tidewater (International)		14	1	2	.333	0.62	5	29	16	2	2	17	37
—New York (N.L.)		10	0	1	.000	3.27	0	11	9	4	4	3	14
1990 —New York (N.L.)		27	4	1	.800	3.15	0	34⅓	32	13	12	17	27
—Tidewater (International)		16	0	1	.000	1.69	8	21⅓	16	7	4	8	24
—Milwaukee (A.L.)■.....................		10	0	0	...	0.69	3	13	9	1	1	8	12
1991 —Milwaukee (A.L.)		54	3	3	.500	3.45	3	88⅔	65	36	34	55	98
American League totals (2 years)		64	3	3	.500	3.10	6	101⅔	74	37	35	63	110
National League totals (2 years)		37	4	2	.667	3.18	0	45⅓	41	17	16	20	41
Major league totals (3 years)		101	7	5	.583	3.12	6	147	115	54	51	83	151

MACK, SHANE
OF, TWINS

PERSONAL: Born December 7, 1963, at Los Angeles. . . . 6-0/190. . . . Throws right, bats right. . . . Full name: Shane Lee Mack. . . . Brother of Quinn Mack, outfielder, Montreal Expos organization.

HIGH SCHOOL: Gahr (Cerritos, Calif.).

COLLEGE: UCLA.

TRANSACTIONS/CAREER NOTES: Selected by Kansas City Royals organization in fourth round of free-agent draft (June 8, 1981). . . . Selected by San Diego Padres organization in first round (11th pick overall) of free-agent draft (June 4, 1984). . . . On San Diego disabled list (March 25-May 4, 1989). . . . Drafted by Minnesota Twins (December 4, 1989).

RECORDS/HONORS: Named outfielder on THE SPORTING NEWS college All-America team (1984).

STATISTICAL NOTES: Tied for Texas League lead in being hit by pitch with seven in 1986. . . . Led Texas League outfielders with four double plays in 1986.

MISCELLANEOUS: Member of 1984 U.S. Olympic baseball team.

							—BATTING—							—FIELDING—			
Year	Team (League)	Pos.	G	AB	R	H	2B	3B	HR	RBI	Avg.	SB	PO	A	E	Avg.
1985 —Beaumont (Texas)		OF-3B	125	430	59	112	23	3	6	55	.260	12	252	12	7	.974
1986 —Beaumont (Texas)		OF	115	452	61	127	26	3	15	68	.281	14	255	•14	8	.971
—Las Vegas (Pac. Coast)		OF	19	69	13	25	1	6	0	6	.362	3	43	0	2	.956
1987 —Las Vegas (Pac. Coast)		OF	39	152	38	51	11	1	5	26	.336	13	97	3	1	.990
—San Diego (N.L.)		OF	105	238	28	57	11	3	4	25	.239	4	159	1	3	.982
1988 —Las Vegas (Pac. Coast)		OF	55	196	43	68	7	1	10	40	.347	7	116	7	3	.976
—San Diego (N.L.)		OF	56	119	13	29	3	0	0	12	.244	5	110	4	2	.983
1989 —Las Vegas (Pac. Coast)		OF	24	80	10	18	3	1	1	8	.225	4	59	3	1	.984
1990 —Minnesota (A.L.)■		OF	125	313	50	102	10	4	8	44	.326	13	230	8	3	.988
1991 —Minnesota (A.L.)		OF	143	442	79	137	27	8	18	74	.310	13	290	6	7	.977
American League totals (2 years)			268	755	129	239	37	12	26	118	.317	26	520	14	10	.982
National League totals (2 years)			161	357	41	86	14	3	4	37	.241	9	269	5	5	.982
Major league totals (4 years)			429	1112	170	325	51	15	30	155	.292	35	789	19	15	.982

CHAMPIONSHIP SERIES RECORD

					BATTING								FIELDING		
Year Team (League)	Pos.	G	AB	R	H	2B	3B	HR	RBI	Avg.	SB	PO	A	E	Avg.
1991—Minnesota (A.L.)	OF	5	18	4	6	1	1	0	3	.333	2	3	0	1	.750

WORLD SERIES RECORD

					BATTING								FIELDING		
Year Team (League)	Pos.	G	AB	R	H	2B	3B	HR	RBI	Avg.	SB	PO	A	E	Avg.
1991—Minnesota (A.L.)	OF	6	23	0	3	1	0	0	1	.130	0	11	0	0	1.000

MACLIN, LONNIE
OF, CARDINALS

PERSONAL: Born February 17, 1967, at Clayton, Mo. . . . 5-11/185. . . . Throws left, bats left. . . . Full name: Lonnie Lee Maclin Jr.
HIGH SCHOOL: Ritenour (St. Louis).
COLLEGE: St. Louis Community College at Meramec (Mo.).
TRANSACTIONS/CAREER NOTES: Selected by Cincinnati Reds organization in 10th round of free-agent draft (January 14, 1986). . . . Selected by St. Louis Cardinals organization in secondary phase of free-agent draft (June 2, 1986).

					BATTING								FIELDING		
Year Team (League)	Pos.	G	AB	R	H	2B	3B	HR	RBI	Avg.	SB	PO	A	E	Avg.
1987—Johnson City (Appal.)	OF	62	229	45	69	6	1	3	22	.301	21	70	1	6	.922
1988—St. Petersburg (Fla. St.)	OF	51	175	22	33	3	1	3	12	.189	9	79	1	0	1.000
—Savannah (S. Atlantic)	OF	46	119	10	28	3	0	0	9	.235	8	104	7	1	.991
1989—Springfield (Midwest)	OF	103	315	33	78	10	3	3	34	.248	18	135	7	5	.966
1990—St. Petersburg (Fla. St.)	OF	31	119	18	46	6	3	2	17	.387	6	65	3	4	.944
—Arkansas (Texas)	OF	74	264	32	82	14	5	2	25	.311	11	111	5	5	.959
—Louisville (Am. Assoc.)	OF	17	58	9	18	3	2	0	6	.310	1	39	0	1	.975
1991—Louisville (Am. Assoc.)	OF	84	327	35	94	12	2	4	37	.287	19	157	1	3	.981

MADDUX, GREG
P, CUBS

PERSONAL: Born April 14, 1966, at San Angelo, Tex. . . . 6-0/175. . . . Throws right, bats right. . . . Full name: Gregory Alan Maddux. . . . Brother of Mike Maddux, pitcher, San Diego Padres.
HIGH SCHOOL: Valley (Las Vegas).
TRANSACTIONS/CAREER NOTES: Selected by Chicago Cubs organization in second round of free-agent draft (June 4, 1984).
RECORDS/HONORS: Shares major league single-game record for most putouts by pitcher—7 (April 29, 1990). . . . Won N.L. Gold Glove at pitcher (1990-91).
STATISTICAL NOTES: Led Appalachian League with eight hit batsmen and tied for lead with two shutouts in 1984. . . . Tied for American Association lead with two shutouts in both 1986 and 1987. . . . Led American Association with 12 hit batsmen in 1986. . . . Tied for N.L. lead in games started by pitcher with 35 in 1990. . . . Led N.L. pitchers with 37 games started in 1991.
MISCELLANEOUS: Appeared as pinch-runner for Chicago Cubs (1989). . . . Singled and scored, struck out in two appearances as pinch-hitter (1991).

Year Team (League)	G	W	L	Pct.	ERA	Sv.	IP	H	R	ER	BB	SO
1984—Pikeville (Appalachian)	14	6	2	.750	2.63	0	85⅔	63	35	25	41	62
1985—Peoria (Midwest)	27	13	9	.591	3.19	0	186	176	86	66	52	125
1986—Pittsfield (Eastern)	8	4	3	.571	2.73	0	62⅔	49	22	19	15	35
—Iowa (American Association) ...	18	10	1	*.909	3.02	0	128⅓	127	49	43	30	65
—Chicago (N.L.)	6	2	4	.333	5.52	0	31	44	20	19	11	20
1987—Chicago (N.L.)	30	6	14	.300	5.61	0	155⅔	181	111	97	74	101
—Iowa (American Association) ...	4	3	0	1.000	0.98	0	27⅔	17	3	3	12	22
1988—Chicago (N.L.)	34	18	8	.692	3.18	0	249	230	97	88	81	140
1989—Chicago (N.L.)	35	19	12	.613	2.95	0	238⅓	222	90	78	82	135
1990—Chicago (N.L.)	35	15	15	.500	3.46	0	237	*242	*116	91	71	144
1991—Chicago (N.L.)	37	15	11	.577	3.35	0	*263	232	113	98	66	198
Major league totals (6 years)	177	75	64	.540	3.61	0	1174	1151	547	471	385	738

CHAMPIONSHIP SERIES RECORD

CHAMPIONSHIP SERIES NOTES: Shares single-series record for most earned runs allowed—11 (1989). . . . Holds N.L. single-series record for most runs allowed—12 (1989).

Year Team (League)	G	W	L	Pct.	ERA	Sv.	IP	H	R	ER	BB	SO
1989—Chicago (N.L.)	2	0	1	.000	13.50	0	7⅓	13	12	11	4	5

ALL-STAR GAME RECORD

Year League	W	L	Pct.	ERA	Sv.	IP	H	R	ER	BB	SO
1988—National					Did not play						

MADDUX, MIKE
P, PADRES

PERSONAL: Born August 27, 1961, at Dayton, O. . . . 6-2/190. . . . Throws right, bats right. . . . Full name: Michael Ausley Maddux. . . . Brother of Greg Maddux, pitcher, Chicago Cubs.
HIGH SCHOOL: Rancho (Las Vegas).
COLLEGE: Texas-El Paso.
TRANSACTIONS/CAREER NOTES: Selected by Cincinnati Reds organization in 36th round of free-agent draft (June 5, 1979). . . . Selected by Philadelphia Phillies organization in fifth round of free-agent draft (June 7, 1982). . . . On Philadelphia disabled list (April 21-June 1, 1988); included rehabilitation disability assignment to Maine (May 13-22, 1988). . . . Released by Phillies

organization (November 20, 1989).... Signed by Los Angeles Dodgers (December 21, 1989).... Granted free agency (October 15, 1990).... Signed by San Diego Padres (March 30, 1991).

Year	Team (League)	G	W	L	Pct.	ERA	Sv.	IP	H	R	ER	BB	SO
1982	Bend (Northwest)	11	3	6	.333	3.99	0	65⅓	68	35	29	26	59
1983	Spartanburg (South Atlantic)	13	4	6	.400	5.44	0	84⅓	98	62	51	47	85
	Peninsula (Carolina)	14	8	4	.667	3.62	0	99⅓	92	46	40	35	78
	Reading (Eastern)	1	0	0	...	6.00	0	3	4	2	2	1	2
1984	Reading (Eastern)	20	3	•12	.200	5.04	0	116	143	82	65	49	77
	Portland (Pacific Coast)	8	2	4	.333	5.84	0	44⅔	58	32	29	17	22
1985	Portland (Pacific Coast)	27	9	12	.429	5.31	0	166	195	106	98	51	96
1986	Portland (Pacific Coast)	12	5	2	.714	2.36	0	84	70	26	22	22	65
	Philadelphia (N.L.)	16	3	7	.300	5.42	0	78	88	56	47	34	44
1987	Maine (International)	18	6	6	.500	4.35	0	103⅓	116	58	50	26	71
	Philadelphia (N.L.)	7	2	0	1.000	2.65	0	17	17	5	5	5	15
1988	Philadelphia (N.L.)	25	4	3	.571	3.76	0	88⅔	91	41	37	34	59
	Maine (International)	5	0	2	.000	4.18	0	23⅔	25	18	11	10	18
1989	Philadelphia (N.L.)	16	1	3	.250	5.15	1	43⅔	52	29	25	14	26
	Scranton/Wilkes-Barre (Int'l)	19	7	7	.500	3.66	0	123	119	55	50	26	100
1990	Albuquerque (Pacific Coast)■	20	8	5	.615	4.25	0	108	122	59	51	32	85
	Los Angeles (N.L.)	11	0	1	.000	6.53	0	20⅔	24	15	15	4	11
1991	San Diego (N.L.)■	64	7	2	.778	2.46	5	98⅔	78	30	27	27	57
	Major league totals (6 years)	139	17	16	.515	4.05	6	346⅔	350	176	156	118	212

MAGADAN, DAVE

3B/1B, METS

PERSONAL: Born September 30, 1962, at Tampa, Fla.... 6-3/200.... Throws right, bats left.... Full name: David Joseph Magadan.... Cousin of Lou Piniella, manager, Cincinnati Reds.
HIGH SCHOOL: Jesuit (Tampa, Fla.).
COLLEGE: Alabama.
TRANSACTIONS/CAREER NOTES: Selected by Boston Red Sox organization in 12th round of free-agent draft (June 3, 1980).... Selected by New York Mets organization in second round of free-agent draft (June 6, 1983).... On disabled list (August 7-September 10, 1984; March 29-April 17, 1987; and May 5-20, 1988).
RECORDS/HONORS: Named designated hitter on THE SPORTING NEWS college All-America team (1983).
STATISTICAL NOTES: Led Carolina League with 10 intentional bases on balls received in 1984.... Led Texas League with 106 bases on balls received in 1985.... Led Texas League third basemen with 87 putouts, 275 assists, 393 total chances and 31 errors in 1985.... Led International League third basemen with .934 fielding percentage, 283 assists and 31 double plays in 1986.... Led N.L. first basemen with .998 fielding percentage in 1990.

Year	Team (League)	Pos.	G	AB	R	H	2B	3B	HR	RBI	Avg.	SB	PO	A	E	Avg.
1983	Columbia (S. Atlantic)	1B	64	220	41	74	13	1	3	32	.336	2	520	37	7	.988
1984	Lynchburg (Carolina)	1B	112	371	78	130	22	4	0	62	★.350	2	896	64	16	.984
1985	Jackson (Texas)	3B-1B	134	466	84	144	22	0	0	76	.309	0	†106	†276	†31	.925
1986	Tidewater (Int'l)	3B-1B	133	473	68	147	33	6	1	64	.311	2	78	†284	25	†.935
	New York (N.L.)	1B	10	18	3	8	0	0	0	3	.444	0	48	5	0	1.000
1987	New York (N.L.)	3B-1B	85	192	21	61	13	1	3	24	.318	0	88	92	4	.978
1988	New York (N.L.)	1B-3B	112	314	39	87	15	0	1	35	.277	0	459	99	10	.982
1989	New York (N.L.)	1B-3B	127	374	47	107	22	3	4	41	.286	1	587	89	7	.990
1990	New York (N.L.)	1B-3B	144	451	74	148	28	6	6	72	.328	2	837	99	3	†.997
1991	New York (N.L.)	1B	124	418	58	108	23	0	4	51	.258	1	1035	90	5	.996
	Major league totals (6 years)		602	1767	242	519	101	10	18	226	.294	4	3054	474	29	.992

CHAMPIONSHIP SERIES RECORD

Year	Team (League)	Pos.	G	AB	R	H	2B	3B	HR	RBI	Avg.	SB	PO	A	E	Avg.
1988	New York (N.L.)	PH	3	3	0	0	0	0	0	0	.000	0	0	0	0	...

MAGALLANES, EVER

2B/SS, WHITE SOX

PERSONAL: Born November 6, 1965, at Chihuahua, Mexico.... 5-10/165.... Throws right, bats left.... Full name: Everardo Magallanes.... Name pronounced MAG-a-YEA-nes.
COLLEGE: Texas A&M.
TRANSACTIONS/CAREER NOTES: Selected by New York Mets organization in 31st round of free-agent draft (June 2, 1986).... Selected by Cleveland Indians organization in 10th round of free-agent draft (June 2, 1987).... Granted free agency (October 16, 1991).... Signed by Chicago White Sox organization (December 6, 1991).

Year	Team (League)	Pos.	G	AB	R	H	2B	3B	HR	RBI	Avg.	SB	PO	A	E	Avg.
1987	Kinston (Carolina)	SS	58	205	20	50	4	3	2	23	.244	2	79	169	17	.936
1988	Kinston (Carolina)	SS-2B	119	396	67	104	13	3	1	45	.263	12	216	351	34	.943
1989	Canton/Akron (Eastern)	2B-SS	74	241	26	67	5	0	0	18	.278	1	155	199	11	.970
	Colorado Springs (PCL)	SS-2B	12	44	2	11	1	0	1	3	.250	1	16	37	2	.964
1990	Colorado Springs (PCL)	SS-2B-3B	125	377	60	116	17	3	1	63	.308	3	207	359	33	.945
1991	Colorado Springs (PCL)	2-S-3	94	305	37	87	13	1	1	33	.285	1	180	274	11	.975
	Cleveland (A.L.)	SS	3	2	0	0	0	0	0	0	.000	0	0	1	0	1.000
	Major league totals (1 year)		3	2	0	0	0	0	0	0	.000	0	0	1	0	1.000

MAGNANTE, MIKE
P, ROYALS

PERSONAL: Born June 17, 1965, at Glendale, Calif. . . . 6-1/180. . . . Throws left, bats left. . . . Full name: Michael Anthony Magnante. . . . Name pronounced mag-NAN-tee.
HIGH SCHOOL: John Burroughs (Burbank, Calif.).
COLLEGE: UCLA (bachelor of science in applied mathematics).
TRANSACTIONS/CAREER NOTES: Selected by Kansas City Royals organization in 11th round of free-agent draft (June 1, 1988). . . . On disabled list (June 17, 1990-remainder of season).

Year	Team (League)	G	W	L	Pct.	ERA	Sv.	IP	H	R	ER	BB	SO
1988	—Eugene (Northwest)	3	1	1	.500	0.56	0	16	10	6	1	2	26
	—Appleton (Midwest)	9	3	2	.600	3.21	0	47⅔	48	20	17	15	40
	—Baseball City (Florida State)	4	1	1	.500	4.13	0	24	19	12	11	8	19
1989	—Memphis (Southern)	26	8	9	.471	3.66	0	157⅓	137	70	64	53	118
1990	—Omaha (American Assoc.)	13	2	5	.286	4.11	0	76⅔	72	39	35	25	56
1991	—Omaha (American Assoc.)	10	6	1	.857	3.02	0	65⅔	53	23	22	23	50
	—Kansas City (A.L.)	38	0	1	.000	2.45	0	55	55	19	15	23	42
Major league totals (1 year)		**38**	**0**	**1**	**.000**	**2.45**	**0**	**55**	**55**	**19**	**15**	**23**	**42**

MAGRANE, JOE
P, CARDINALS

PERSONAL: Born July 2, 1964, at Des Moines, Ia. . . . 6-6/230. . . . Throws left, bats right. . . . Full name: Joseph David Magrane. . . . Name pronounced muh-GRAIN.
HIGH SCHOOL: Rowan (Morehead, Ky.).
COLLEGE: Arizona.
TRANSACTIONS/CAREER NOTES: Selected by Pittsburgh Pirates organization in third round of free-agent draft (June 7, 1982). . . . Selected by St. Louis Cardinals organization in first round (18th pick overall) of free-agent draft (June 3, 1985). . . . On St. Louis disabled list (May 30-June 18, 1987). . . . On St. Louis disabled list (April 17-June 11, 1988); included rehabilitation disability assignment to Louisville (May 23-June 11, 1988). . . . On disabled list (April 15-30, 1989 and March 19, 1991-entire season).
STATISTICAL NOTES: Tied for American Association lead with two shutouts and eight complete games in 1986. . . . Tied for N.L. lead with 10 hit batsmen in 1987.

Year	Team (League)	G	W	L	Pct.	ERA	Sv.	IP	H	R	ER	BB	SO
1985	—Johnson City (Appalachian)	6	2	1	.667	0.60	0	30	15	4	2	11	31
	—St. Petersburg (Florida State)	5	3	1	.750	1.04	0	34⅔	21	8	4	14	17
1986	—Arkansas (Texas)	13	8	4	.667	2.42	0	89⅓	66	29	24	31	66
	—Louisville (American Assoc.)	15	9	6	.600	2.06	0	113⅓	93	34	26	33	72
1987	—Louisville (American Assoc.)	3	1	0	1.000	1.93	0	23⅓	16	7	5	3	17
	—St. Louis (N.L.)	27	9	7	.563	3.54	0	170⅓	157	75	67	60	101
1988	—St. Louis (N.L.)	24	5	9	.357	*2.18	0	165⅓	133	57	40	51	100
	—Louisville (American Assoc.)	4	2	1	.667	3.15	0	20	19	7	7	7	18
1989	—St. Louis (N.L.)	34	18	9	.667	2.91	0	234⅔	219	81	76	72	127
1990	—St. Louis (N.L.)	31	10	17	.370	3.59	0	203⅓	204	86	81	59	100
1991	—						Did not play						
Major league totals (4 years)		**116**	**42**	**42**	**.500**	**3.07**	**0**	**773⅔**	**713**	**299**	**264**	**242**	**428**

CHAMPIONSHIP SERIES RECORD

Year	Team (League)	G	W	L	Pct.	ERA	Sv.	IP	H	R	ER	BB	SO
1987	—St. Louis (N.L.)	1	0	0	. . .	9.00	0	4	4	4	4	2	3

WORLD SERIES RECORD

Year	Team (League)	G	W	L	Pct.	ERA	Sv.	IP	H	R	ER	BB	SO
1987	—St. Louis (N.L.)	2	0	1	.000	8.59	0	7⅓	9	7	7	5	5

MAHLER, RICK
P

PERSONAL: Born August 5, 1953, at Austin, Tex. . . . 6-1/202. . . . Throws right, bats right. . . . Full name: Richard Keith Mahler. . . . Brother of Mickey Mahler, major league pitcher for seven teams (1977-82, 1985-86). . . . Name pronounced MAY-ler.
HIGH SCHOOL: John Jay (San Antonio).
COLLEGE: Trinity University (Tex.).
TRANSACTIONS/CAREER NOTES: Signed as free agent by Atlanta Braves organization (June 16, 1975). . . . Granted free agency (November 4, 1988). . . . Signed by Cincinnati Reds (December 2, 1988). . . . On Cincinnati disabled list (May 17-June 1, 1990); included rehabilitation disability assignment to Nashville (May 29 and May 30, 1990). . . . Granted free agency (November 5, 1990). . . . Signed by Montreal Expos organization (February 27, 1991). . . . Released by Expos (June 10, 1991). . . . Signed by Atlanta Braves (June 14, 1991). . . . Released by Braves (August 8, 1991).
RECORDS/HONORS: Holds major league single-season record for most game-winning runs batted in by pitcher—3 (1985). . . . Shares major league record for most years leading league in runs allowed—3.
STATISTICAL NOTES: Led N.L. pitchers with 39 games started in 1985 and tied for lead with 39 in 1986. . . . Led N.L. with 10 hit batsmen in 1989.

Year	Team (League)	G	W	L	Pct.	ERA	Sv.	IP	H	R	ER	BB	SO
1975	—Kingsport (Appalachian)	26	2	2	.500	2.95	5	64	52	23	21	26	58
1976	—Greenwood (W. Carolinas)	31	6	6	.500	2.91	2	105	96	49	34	49	68
1977	—Savannah (Southern)	17	6	2	.750	2.30	1	86	71	31	22	38	53
	—Richmond (International)	14	0	2	.000	6.08	0	40	45	29	27	23	25
1978	—Richmond (International)	32	9	5	.643	3.93	1	126	130	65	55	53	66
1979	—Richmond (International)	24	4	6	.400	3.33	4	54	46	26	20	18	40
	—Atlanta (N.L.)	15	0	0	. . .	6.14	0	22	28	16	15	11	12

Year	Team (League)	G	W	L	Pct.	ERA	Sv.	IP	H	R	ER	BB	SO
1980 —Richmond (International)		29	12	6	.667	2.59	0	188	172	68	54	80	101
—Atlanta (N.L.)		2	0	0	...	2.25	0	4	2	1	1	0	1
1981 —Atlanta (N.L.)		34	8	6	.571	2.81	2	112	109	41	35	43	54
1982 —Atlanta (N.L.)		39	9	10	.474	4.21	0	205⅓	213	105	96	62	105
1983 —Atlanta (N.L.)		10	0	0	...	5.02	0	14⅓	16	8	8	9	7
—Richmond (International)		24	12	7	.632	4.92	0	162⅔	165	102	89	85	103
1984 —Atlanta (N.L.)		38	13	10	.565	3.12	0	222	209	86	77	62	106
1985 —Atlanta (N.L.)		39	17	15	.531	3.48	0	266⅔	★272	116	103	79	107
1986 —Atlanta (N.L.)		39	14	★18	.438	4.88	0	237⅔	★283	★139	★129	95	137
1987 —Atlanta (N.L.)		39	8	13	.381	4.98	0	197	212	118	109	85	95
1988 —Atlanta (N.L.)		39	9	16	.360	3.69	0	249	★279	★125	★102	42	131
1989 —Cincinnati (N.L.)■...		40	9	13	.409	3.83	0	220⅔	★242	★113	94	51	102
1990 —Cincinnati (N.L.)		35	7	6	.538	4.28	4	134⅔	134	67	64	39	68
—Nashville (American Assoc.)		1	0	1	.000	2.45	0	7⅓	6	2	2	3	5
1991 —Montreal-Atlanta (N.L.)■		23	2	4	.333	4.50	0	66	70	37	33	28	27
Major league totals (13 years)		392	96	111	.464	3.99	6	1951⅓	2069	972	866	606	952

CHAMPIONSHIP SERIES RECORD

Year	Team (League)	G	W	L	Pct.	ERA	Sv.	IP	H	R	ER	BB	SO
1982 —Atlanta (N.L.)		1	0	0	...	0.00	0	1⅔	3	0	0	2	0
1990 —Cincinnati (N.L.)		1	0	0	...	0.00	0	1⅔	2	0	0	0	0
Championship Series totals (2 years)		2	0	0	...	0.00	0	3⅓	5	0	0	2	0

MAHOMES, PAT
P, TWINS

PERSONAL: Born August 9, 1970, at Bryan, Tex. . . . 6-1/175. . . . Throws right, bats right. . . . Full name: Patrick Lavon Mahomes.
HIGH SCHOOL: Lindale (Tex.).
TRANSACTIONS/CAREER NOTES: Selected by Minnesota Twins organization in sixth round of free-agent draft (June 1, 1988).
STATISTICAL NOTES: Led California League pitchers with 28 games started in 1990.

Year	Team (League)	G	W	L	Pct.	ERA	Sv.	IP	H	R	ER	BB	SO
1988 —Elizabethton (Appalachian)		13	6	3	.667	3.69	0	78	66	45	32	51	93
1989 —Kenosha (Midwest)		25	13	7	.650	3.28	0	156⅓	120	66	57	●100	167
1990 —Visalia (California)		28	11	11	.500	3.30	0	●185⅓	136	77	68	●118	178
1991 —Orlando (Southern)		18	8	5	.615	★1.78	0	116	77	30	23	57	136
—Portland (Pacific Coast)		9	3	5	.375	3.44	0	55	50	26	21	36	41

MALDONADO, CANDY
OF, BLUE JAYS

PERSONAL: Born September 5, 1960, at Humacao, Puerto Rico. . . . 6-0/195. . . . Throws right, bats right. . . . Full name: Candido Guadarrama Maldonado.
HIGH SCHOOL: Trina Padilla de Sanz (Humacao, Puerto Rico).
TRANSACTIONS/CAREER NOTES: Signed as free agent by Los Angeles Dodgers organization (June 6, 1978). . . . On disabled list (August 16-September 16, 1980). . . . Traded by Dodgers to San Francisco Giants for C Alex Trevino (December 11, 1985). . . . On disabled list (June 28-August 7, 1987). . . . Granted free agency (November 13, 1989). . . . Signed by Cleveland Indians (November 28, 1989). . . . Granted free agency (November 5, 1990). . . . Signed by Milwaukee Brewers (April 2, 1991). . . . On disabled list (April 11-June 25, 1991). . . . Traded by Brewers to Toronto Blue Jays for P Rob Wishnevski and a player to be named later (August 9, 1991); Brewers acquired IF William Suero to complete deal (August 14, 1991).
RECORDS/HONORS: Shares major league single-game record for most sacrifice flies—3 (August 29, 1987). . . . Named California League co-Most Valuable Player (1980).
STATISTICAL NOTES: Tied for Pioneer League lead with six sacrifice flies in 1978. . . . Led California League with 247 total bases in 1980. . . . Hit for the cycle (May 4, 1987).

Year	Team (League)	Pos.	G	AB	R	H	2B	3B	HR	RBI	Avg.	SB	PO	A	E	Avg.
1978 —Lethbridge (Pioneer)		OF	57	210	45	61	15	5	12	48	.290	2	112	6	8	.937
1979 —Clinton (Midwest)		OF	50	158	25	37	13	1	2	26	.234	5	81	5	2	.977
—Lethbridge (Pioneer)		OF	59	234	42	70	★20	3	5	33	.299	4	81	5	4	.956
1980 —Lodi (California)		OF	121	456	75	139	27	3	25	★102	.305	12	211	13	11	.953
1981 —Albuquerque (PCL)		OF	126	460	96	154	40	4	21	104	.335	13	221	21	8	.968
—Los Angeles (N.L.)		OF	11	12	0	1	0	0	0	0	.083	0	8	0	0	1.000
1982 —Albuquerque (PCL)		OF	138	541	91	163	28	6	24	96	.301	4	303	15	10	.970
—Los Angeles (N.L.)		OF	6	4	0	0	0	0	0	0	.000	0	5	0	0	1.000
1983 —Los Angeles (N.L.)		OF	42	62	5	12	1	1	1	6	.194	0	26	0	0	1.000
—Albuquerque (PCL)		OF-3B	38	144	23	46	6	1	4	20	.319	3	66	11	4	.951
1984 —Los Angeles (N.L.)		OF-3B	116	254	25	68	14	0	5	28	.268	0	124	5	8	.942
1985 —Los Angeles (N.L.)		OF	121	213	20	48	7	1	5	19	.225	1	121	6	2	.984
1986 —San Francisco (N.L.)■......		OF-3B	133	405	49	102	31	3	18	85	.252	4	161	11	3	.983
1987 —San Francisco (N.L.)		OF	118	442	69	129	28	4	20	85	.292	8	176	7	5	.973
1988 —San Francisco (N.L.)		OF	142	499	53	127	23	1	12	68	.255	6	251	5	10	.962
1989 —San Francisco (N.L.)		OF	129	345	39	75	23	0	9	41	.217	4	181	6	5	.974
1990 —Cleveland (A.L.)■...........		OF	155	590	76	161	32	2	22	95	.273	3	293	9	2	.993
1991 —Mil.-Toronto (A.L.)		OF	86	288	37	72	15	0	12	48	.250	4	139	2	2	.986
American League totals (2 years)			241	878	113	233	47	2	34	143	.265	7	432	11	4	.991
National League totals (9 years)			818	2236	260	562	127	10	70	332	.251	23	1053	40	33	.971
Major league totals (11 years)			1059	3114	373	795	174	12	104	475	.255	30	1485	51	37	.976

CHAMPIONSHIP SERIES RECORD

Year	Team (League)	Pos.	G	AB	R	H	2B	3B	HR	RBI	Avg.	SB	PO	A	E	Avg.
1983 — Los Angeles (N.L.)	PH	2	2	0	0	0	0	0	0	.000	0	0	0	0	...
1985 — Los Angeles (N.L.)	OF-PH	4	7	0	1	0	0	0	1	.143	0	4	0	1	.800
1987 — San Francisco (N.L.)	OF	5	19	2	4	1	0	0	2	.211	0	7	0	0	1.000
1989 — San Francisco (N.L.)	PH-OF	3	3	1	0	0	0	0	1	.000	0	2	0	0	1.000
1991 — Toronto (A.L.)	OF	5	20	1	2	1	0	0	1	.100	0	4	0	0	1.000
Championship Series totals (5 years)		19	51	4	7	2	0	0	5	.137	0	17	0	1	.944

WORLD SERIES RECORD

Year	Team (League)	Pos.	G	AB	R	H	2B	3B	HR	RBI	Avg.	SB	PO	A	E	Avg.
1989 — San Francisco (N.L.)	OF-PH	4	11	1	1	0	1	0	0	.091	0	5	0	0	1.000

MALDONADO, CARLOS
P, ROYALS

PERSONAL: Born October 18, 1966, at Chepo, Panama. .... 6-1/215. .... Throws right, bats right. .... Full name: Carlos Cesar Maldonado.
HIGH SCHOOL: Venancio Fenosa Pascual (Chepo, Panama).
TRANSACTIONS/CAREER NOTES: Signed as free agent by Kansas City Royals organization (April 28, 1986). .... On Appleton disabled list (April 7-May 12, 1989).

Year	Team (League)	G	W	L	Pct.	ERA	Sv.	IP	H	R	ER	BB	SO
1986 — Sarasota Royals (Gulf Coast) ...	10	0	2	.000	1.83	1	34⅓	29	10	7	10	16
1987 — Sarasota Royals (Gulf Coast) ...	20	5	1	.833	2.48	4	58	32	18	16	19	56
— Appleton (Midwest)	2	0	0	...	11.57	0	2⅓	4	3	3	3	4
1988 — Baseball City (Florida State) ...	16	1	5	.167	5.30	0	52⅔	46	35	31	39	44
1989 — Baseball City (Florida State)	28	11	3	.786	1.17	9	76⅔	47	14	10	24	66
1990 — Memphis (Southern)	55	4	5	.444	2.91	20	77⅓	61	29	25	37	77
— Kansas City (A.L.)	4	0	0	...	9.00	0	6	9	6	6	4	9
1991 — Omaha (American Assoc.)	41	1	1	.500	4.28	9	61	67	31	29	42	46
— Kansas City (A.L.)	5	0	0	...	8.22	0	7⅔	11	9	7	9	1
Major league totals (2 years)	9	0	0	...	8.56	0	13⅔	20	15	13	13	10

MALLICOAT, ROB
P, ASTROS

PERSONAL: Born November 16, 1964, at St. Helens, Ore. .... 6-3/180. .... Throws left, bats left. .... Full name: Robin Dale Mallicoat.
COLLEGE: Taft (Calif.).
TRANSACTIONS/CAREER NOTES: Selected by Detroit Tigers organization in eighth round of free-agent draft (June 6, 1983). .... Selected by Houston Astros organization in secondary phase of free-agent draft (January 17, 1984). .... On Columbus disabled list (June 24, 1986-remainder of season). .... On disabled list (April 8, 1988-entire season and April 7, 1989-entire season). .... On Sarasota disabled list (April 6-July 10, 1990).

Year	Team (League)	G	W	L	Pct.	ERA	Sv.	IP	H	R	ER	BB	SO
1984 — Auburn (New York-Penn)	1	0	0	...	5.40	0	5	8	3	3	3	6
— Asheville (South Atlantic)	11	3	4	.429	3.92	0	64⅓	49	30	28	36	57
1985 — Osceola (Florida State)	26	★16	6	.727	1.36	0	178⅔	119	41	27	74	★158
1986 — Tucson (Pacific Coast)	3	0	2	.000	6.43	0	14	18	14	10	8	9
— Columbus (Southern)	10	0	6	.000	4.81	0	58	61	38	31	45	52
1987 — Columbus (Southern)	24	10	7	.588	2.89	0	152⅓	132	68	49	78	141
— Tucson (Pacific Coast)	2	0	0	...	3.72	0	9⅔	9	5	4	7	8
— Houston (N.L.)	4	0	0	...	6.75	0	6⅔	8	5	5	6	4
1988 —					Did not play							
1989 —					Did not play							
1990 — Sarasota Astros (Gulf Coast) ...	7	0	1	.000	4.96	0	16⅓	15	15	9	15	21
— Osceola (Florida State)	3	0	0	...	0.00	0	12	8	2	0	9	10
1991 — Jackson (Texas)	18	4	1	.800	3.77	1	31	20	15	13	11	34
— Tucson (Pacific Coast)	19	4	4	.500	5.48	1	47⅔	43	32	29	38	32
— Houston (N.L.)	24	0	2	.000	3.86	1	23⅓	22	10	10	13	18
Major league totals (2 years)	28	0	2	.000	4.50	1	30	30	15	15	19	22

MANRIQUE, FRED
IF

PERSONAL: Born November 5, 1961, at Bolivar, Venezuela. .... 6-1/175. .... Throws right, bats right. .... Full name: Reyes Fred Eloy Manrique.
HIGH SCHOOL: Dellacosta (Venezuela).
TRANSACTIONS/CAREER NOTES: Signed as free agent by Toronto Blue Jays organization (November 24, 1978). .... On Knoxville disabled list (April 9-19, 1981). .... On Syracuse disabled list (June 27-July 12, 1982). .... Sold by Blue Jays to Montreal Expos (April 7, 1985). .... Traded by Expos to St. Louis Cardinals for C Tom Nieto (March 31, 1986). .... Traded by Cardinals to Chicago White Sox for P Bill Dawley (December 22, 1986). .... Traded by White Sox with OF Harold Baines to Texas Rangers for SS Scott Fletcher, OF Sammy Sosa and P Wilson Alvarez (July 29, 1989). .... Traded by Rangers to Minnesota Twins for P Jeff Satzinger and cash (April 13, 1990). .... Released by Twins organization (August 8, 1990). .... Signed by California Angels (December 7, 1990). .... Released by Angels (April 1, 1991). .... Signed by Tacoma, Oakland Athletics organization (April 19, 1991). .... Released by Tacoma (June 2, 1991).
STATISTICAL NOTES: Led International League second basemen with 22 errors in 1983 and 24 in 1984. .... Led American As-

sociation in grounding into double plays with 19 in 1986. . . . Led American Association shortstops with 25 errors and 86 double plays in 1986.

Year	Team (League)	Pos.	G	AB	R	H	2B	3B	HR	RBI	Avg.	SB	PO	A	E	Avg.
1979	—Dunedin (Florida State)	SS	5	15	0	2	0	0	0	0	.133	0	4	7	3	.786
	—Medicine Hat (Pioneer)	SS	66	270	47	81	8	•10	2	30	.300	4	103	208	★37	.894
1980	—Kinston (Carolina)...........	SS-OF	111	390	49	108	9	5	7	50	.277	6	120	192	37	.894
1981	—Knoxville (Southern)	SS	115	469	62	131	15	6	5	42	.279	7	161	330	45	.916
	—Toronto (A.L.).................	SS-3B	14	28	1	4	0	0	0	1	.143	0	10	27	3	.925
1982	—Syracuse (International) ..	2B-3B-SS	103	362	41	91	9	2	4	37	.251	5	186	255	24	.948
1983	—Syracuse (International) ..	2-S-3-0	128	485	55	130	22	8	10	50	.268	3	211	351	†36	.940
1984	—Syracuse (International) ..	2B-SS-3B	129	517	63	146	15	5	6	45	.282	14	233	389	†28	.957
	—Toronto (A.L.).................	2B	10	9	0	3	0	0	0	1	.333	0	5	10	1	.938
1985	—Indianapolis (A.A.)■...	3B-SS-2B	123	409	46	98	21	5	8	37	.240	2	126	249	19	.952
	—Montreal (N.L.)...............	2B-SS-3B	9	13	5	4	1	1	1	1	.308	0	5	10	0	1.000
1986	—Louisville (Am. Assoc.)■...	SS-2B	133	520	79	148	19	6	9	51	.285	15	208	421	†26	.960
	—St. Louis (N.L.)	3B-2B	13	17	2	3	0	0	1	1	.176	1	1	3	0	1.000
1987	—Chicago (A.L.)■.............	2B-SS	115	298	30	77	13	3	4	29	.258	5	176	286	7	.985
1988	—Chicago (A.L.)	2B-SS	140	345	43	81	10	6	5	37	.235	6	241	343	13	.978
1989	—Chicago-Texas (A.L.)■.....	2B-SS-3B	119	378	46	111	25	1	4	52	.294	4	177	250	21	.953
1990	—Minnesota (A.L.)■...........	2B	69	228	22	54	10	0	5	29	.237	2	104	155	7	.974
	—Portland (Pacific Coast) ...	PH	1	1	0	1	0	0	0	0	1 1.000	0	0	0	0	...
1991	—Tacoma (Pacific Coast)■..	3B-2B-SS	12	41	6	11	0	0	1	4	.268	0	9	26	1	.972
	—Oakland (A.L.)	SS-2B	9	21	2	3	0	0	0	0	.143	0	10	20	1	.968
	American League totals (7 years)		476	1307	144	333	58	10	18	149	.255	17	723	1091	53	.972
	National League totals (2 years)		22	30	7	7	1	1	2	2	.233	1	6	13	0	1.000
	Major league totals (9 years)		498	1337	151	340	59	11	20	151	.254	18	729	1104	53	.972

MANTO, JEFF
3B/1B

PERSONAL: Born August 23, 1964, at Bristol, Pa. . . . 6-3/210. . . . Throws right, bats right. . . . Full name: Jeffrey Paul Manto.
HIGH SCHOOL: Bristol (Pa.).
COLLEGE: Temple.
TRANSACTIONS/CAREER NOTES: Selected by New York Yankees organization in 35th round of free-agent draft (June 7, 1982). . . . Selected by California Angels organization in 14th round of free-agent draft (June 3, 1985). . . . On disabled list (July 16, 1986-remainder of season). . . . Traded by Angels organization with P Colin Charland to Cleveland Indians for P Scott Bailes (January 9, 1990). . . . Released by Indians (November 27, 1991).
RECORDS/HONORS: Named Texas League Most Valuable Player (1988).
STATISTICAL NOTES: Led California League third basemen with 245 assists and 365 total chances in 1987. . . . Tied for Texas League lead in errors by third basemen with 32 in 1988. . . . Led Texas League in grounding into double plays with 17 in 1988. . . . Led Pacific Coast League third basemen with .943 fielding percentage, 265 assists and 22 double plays in 1989.

Year	Team (League)	Pos.	G	AB	R	H	2B	3B	HR	RBI	Avg.	SB	PO	A	E	Avg.
1985	—Quad Cities (Midwest).......	OF-3B	74	233	34	46	5	2	11	34	.197	3	87	8	3	.969
1986	—Quad Cities (Midwest).......	3B	73	239	31	59	13	0	8	49	.247	2	48	114	28	.853
1987	—Palm Springs (Calif.)........	3B-1B	112	375	61	96	21	4	7	63	.256	8	93	†246	37	.902
1988	—Midland (Texas)	3B-2B-1B	120	408	88	123	23	3	24	101	.301	7	82	208	†32	.901
1989	—Edmonton (Pac. Coast)......	3B-1B	127	408	89	113	25	3	23	67	.277	4	140	†266	21	†.951
1990	—Colorado Springs (PCL)■..	3B-1B	96	316	73	94	27	1	18	82	.297	10	340	131	10	.979
	—Cleveland (A.L.)	1B-3B	30	76	12	17	5	1	2	14	.224	0	185	24	2	.991
1991	—Cleveland (A.L.)...............	3-1-C-0	47	128	15	27	7	0	2	13	.211	2	109	63	8	.956
	—Colorado Springs (PCL)	3-1-C-S-0	43	153	36	49	16	0	6	36	.320	1	169	53	11	.953
	Major league totals (2 years)		77	204	27	44	12	1	4	27	.216	2	294	87	10	.974

MANUEL, BARRY
P, RANGERS

PERSONAL: Born August 12, 1965, at Mamou, La. . . . 5-11/185. . . . Throws right, bats right. . . . Full name: Barry Paul Manuel. . . . Brother of Ferral Manuel, minor league catcher (1989).
HIGH SCHOOL: Mamou (La.).
COLLEGE: Louisiana State.
TRANSACTIONS/CAREER NOTES: Selected by Texas Rangers organization in second round of free-agent draft (June 2, 1987).
STATISTICAL NOTES: Pitched one inning, combining with Cedric Shaw and Everett Cunningham in 2-0 nine inning no-hit victory against Arkansas (April 18, 1991).

Year	Team (League)	G	W	L	Pct.	ERA	Sv.	IP	H	R	ER	BB	SO
1987	—Sarasota Rangers (GCL)	1	0	0	...	18.00	0	1	3	2	2	1	1
	—Charlotte (Florida State)	13	1	2	.333	6.60	0	30	33	24	22	18	19
1988	—Port Charlotte (Florida State) ...	37	4	3	.571	2.54	4	60⅓	47	24	17	32	55
1989	—Tulsa (Texas)	11	3	4	.429	7.48	0	49⅓	49	44	41	39	40
	—Port Charlotte (Florida State) ...	15	4	7	.364	4.72	0	76⅓	77	43	40	30	51
1990	—Charlotte (Florida State)	57	1	5	.167	2.88	★36	56⅓	39	23	18	30	60
1991	—Tulsa (Texas)	56	2	7	.222	3.29	★25	68⅓	63	29	25	34	45
	—Texas (A.L.)..............................	8	1	0	1.000	1.13	0	16	7	2	2	6	5
	Major league totals (1 year)	8	1	0	1.000	1.13	0	16	7	2	2	6	5

MANWARING, KIRT

C, GIANTS

PERSONAL: Born July 15, 1965, at Elmira, N.Y. . . . 5-11/190. . . . Throws right, bats right. . . . Full name: Kirt Dean Manwaring. **HIGH SCHOOL:** Horseheads (N.Y.). **COLLEGE:** Coastal Carolina (S.C.).

TRANSACTIONS/CAREER NOTES: Selected by Boston Red Sox organization in 12th round of free-agent draft (June 6, 1983). . . . Selected by San Francisco Giants organization in second round of free-agent draft (June 2, 1986). . . . On disabled list (August 31-September 15, 1989). . . . On San Francisco disabled list (May 30-July 11, 1991); included rehabilitation disability assignment to Phoenix (July 1-8, 1991) and San Jose (July 8-11, 1991).

STATISTICAL NOTES: Led Texas League catchers with 688 total chances and eight double plays in 1987.

Year	Team (League)	Pos.	G	AB	R	H	2B	3B	HR	RBI	Avg.	SB	PO	A	E	Avg.
1986	—Clinton (Midwest)	C	49	147	18	36	7	1	2	16	.245	1	243	31	5	.982
1987	—Shreveport (Texas)	C	98	307	27	82	13	2	2	22	.267	1	603	*81	4	.994
	—San Francisco (N.L.)	C	6	7	0	1	0	0	0	0	.143	0	9	1	1	.909
1988	—Phoenix (Pacific Coast)	C	81	273	29	77	12	2	2	35	.282	3	411	51	6	.987
	—San Francisco (N.L.)	C	40	116	12	29	7	0	1	15	.250	0	162	24	4	.979
1989	—San Francisco (N.L.)	C	85	200	14	42	4	2	0	18	.210	2	289	32	6	.982
1990	—Phoenix (Pacific Coast)	C	74	247	20	58	10	2	3	14	.235	0	352	45	4	*.990
	—San Francisco (N.L.)	C	8	13	0	2	0	1	0	1	.154	0	22	3	0	1.000
1991	—San Francisco (N.L.)	C	67	178	16	40	9	0	0	19	.225	1	315	28	4	.988
	—Phoenix (Pacific Coast)	C	24	81	8	18	0	0	4	14	.222	0	100	15	3	.975
	—San Jose (California)	C	1	3	1	0	0	0	0	0	.000	0	16	0	0	1.000
	Major league totals (5 years)		206	514	42	114	20	3	1	53	.222	3	797	88	15	.983

CHAMPIONSHIP SERIES RECORD

Year	Team (League)	Pos.	G	AB	R	H	2B	3B	HR	RBI	Avg.	SB	PO	A	E	Avg.
1989	—San Francisco (N.L.)	PH-C	3	2	0	0	0	0	0	0	.000	0	5	0	0	1.000

WORLD SERIES RECORD

Year	Team (League)	Pos.	G	AB	R	H	2B	3B	HR	RBI	Avg.	SB	PO	A	E	Avg.
1989	—San Francisco (N.L.)	C	1	1	1	1	1	0	0	0	1.000	0	0	0	0	...

MANZANILLO, JOSIAS

P, RED SOX

PERSONAL: Born October 16, 1967, at San Pedro de Macoris, Dominican Republic. . . . 6-0/190. . . . Throws right, bats right. . . . Full name: Josias Manzanillo. . . . Brother of Ravelo Manzanillo, pitcher, Toronto Blue Jays organization. . . . Name pronounced MAN-zan-EE-oh.

TRANSACTIONS/CAREER NOTES: Signed as free agent by Boston Red Sox organization (January 10, 1983). . . . On disabled list (June 8, 1987-remainder of season and April 8, 1988-entire season).

Year	Team (League)	G	W	L	Pct.	ERA	Sv.	IP	H	R	ER	BB	SO
1983	—Elmira (New York-Penn)	12	1	5	.167	7.98	0	38 1/3	52	44	34	20	19
1984	—Elmira (New York-Penn)	14	2	3	.400	5.26	1	25 2/3	27	24	15	26	15
1985	—Greensboro (South Atlantic)	7	1	1	.500	9.75	0	12	12	13	13	18	10
	—Elmira (New York-Penn)	19	2	4	.333	3.86	1	39 2/3	36	19	17	36	43
1986	—Winter Haven (Florida State)	23	13	5	.722	2.27	0	142 2/3	110	51	36	81	102
1987	—New Britain (Eastern)	2	2	0	1.000	4.50	0	10	8	5	5	8	12
1988	—						Did not play						
1989	—New Britain (Eastern)	26	9	10	.474	3.66	0	147 2/3	129	78	60	85	93
1990	—New Britain (Eastern)	12	4	4	.500	3.41	0	74	66	34	28	37	51
	—Pawtucket (International)	15	4	7	.364	5.55	0	82 2/3	75	57	51	45	77
1991	—Pawtucket (International)	20	5	5	.500	5.61	0	102 2/3	109	69	64	53	65
	—New Britain (Eastern)	7	2	2	.500	2.90	0	49 2/3	37	25	16	28	35
	—Boston (A.L.)	1	0	0	...	18.00	0	1	2	2	2	3	1
	Major league totals (1 year)	1	0	0	...	18.00	0	1	2	2	2	3	1

MARSHALL, MIKE

1B/OF

PERSONAL: Born January 12, 1960, at Libertyville, Ill. . . . 6-5/215. . . . Throws right, bats right. . . . Full name: Michael Allen Marshall. **HIGH SCHOOL:** Buffalo Grove (Ill.). **TRANSACTIONS/CAREER NOTES:** Selected by Los Angeles Dodgers organization in sixth round of free-agent draft (June 6, 1978). . . . On disabled list (May 13-June 3, 1984; June 20-July 18, 1985; July 20-August 4, 1986; May 6-29 and August 21-September 5, 1987). . . . Granted free agency (November 4, 1988). . . . Re-signed by Dodgers (November 13, 1988). . . . On disabled list (May 31-July 1, 1989). . . . Traded by Dodgers with P Alejandro Pena to New York Mets for OF Juan Samuel (December 20, 1989). . . . On disabled list (July 13-28, 1990). . . . Traded by Mets to Boston Red Sox for P Greg Hansell, OF Ed Perozo and a player to be named later (July 27, 1990); Mets acquired C Paul Williams to complete deal (November 19, 1990). . . . On Boston disabled list (June 3-19, 1991). . . . Released by Red Sox (July 20, 1991). . . . Signed by California Angels organization (July 27, 1991). . . . Released by Angels (August 7, 1991). . . . Signed by Nippon Ham Fighters of Japan Pacific League (December 20, 1991).

RECORDS/HONORS: Named California League co-Most Valuable Player (1979). . . . Named Minor League Player of the Year by THE SPORTING NEWS (1981). . . . Named Pacific Coast League Most Valuable Player (1981).

STATISTICAL NOTES: Led California League with 301 total bases in 1979. . . . Led Texas League first basemen with 120 double plays in 1980. . . . Led Pacific Coast League first basemen with 136 double plays in 1981.

Year	Team (League)	Pos.	G	AB	R	H	2B	3B	HR	RBI	Avg.	SB	PO	A	E	Avg.
1978 — Lethbridge (Pioneer)		1B-OF	65	256	48	83	15	2	12	70	.324	2	308	16	7	.979
1979 — Lodi (California)		1B	137	525	101 ★186	★37	3	24	116 ★.354		22	1173	71	20	.984
1980 — San Antonio (Texas)		1B	134	470	95	151	21	6	16	82	.321	6 ★1157	64	•16	.987
1981 — Albuquerque (PCL)		1B	128	467 ★114	174	25	7	★34 ★137 ★.373			21	1127	54	9	.992
— Los Angeles (N.L.)		1B-3B-OF	14	25	2	5	3	0	0	1	.200	0	14	2	0	1.000
1982 — Albuquerque (PCL)		OF-1B-3B	66	255	74	99	20	1	14	58	.388	11	113	3	4	.967
— Los Angeles (N.L.)		OF-1B	49	95	10	23	3	0	5	9	.242	2	122	5	2	.984
1983 — Los Angeles (N.L.)		OF-1B	140	465	47	132	17	1	17	65	.284	7	395	21	6	.986
1984 — Los Angeles (N.L.)		OF-1B	134	495	68	127	27	0	21	65	.257	4	331	17	5	.986
1985 — Los Angeles (N.L.)		OF-1B	135	518	72	152	27	2	28	95	.293	3	265	12	4	.986
1986 — Los Angeles (N.L.)		OF	103	330	47	77	11	0	19	53	.233	4	149	8	6	.963
1987 — Los Angeles (N.L.)		OF	104	402	45	118	19	0	16	72	.294	4	147	4	2	.987
1988 — Los Angeles (N.L.)		OF-1B	144	542	63	150	27	2	20	82	.277	4	605	49	7	.989
1989 — Los Angeles (N.L.)		OF	105	377	41	98	21	1	11	42	.260	2	179	2	4	.978
1990 — New York (N.L.)■		1B-OF	53	163	24	39	8	1	6	27	.239	2	277	24	2	.993
— Boston (A.L.)■		1B-OF	30	112	10	32	6	1	4	12	.286	0	55	7	1	.984
— Pawtucket (Int'l)		OF	6	23	5	7	0	0	2	4	.304	0	1	0	0	1.000
1991 — Boston (A.L.)		1B-OF	22	62	4	18	4	0	1	7	.290	0	49	0	1	.980
— Palm Springs (Calif.)■		OF	3	8	1	2	1	0	0	2	.250	0	0	0	0	. . .
— California (A.L.)		1B	2	7	0	0	0	0	0	0	.000	0	14	1	0	1.000
American League totals (2 years)			54	181	14	50	10	1	5	19	.276	0	118	8	2	.984
National League totals (10 years)			981	3412	419	921	163	7	143	511	.270	28	2484	144	38	.986
Major league totals (11 years)			1035	3593	433	971	173	8	148	530	.270	28	2602	152	40	.986

DIVISION SERIES RECORD

Year	Team (League)	Pos.	G	AB	R	H	2B	3B	HR	RBI	Avg.	SB	PO	A	E	Avg.
1981 — Los Angeles (N.L.)		PH	1	1	0	0	0	0	0	0	.000	0	0	0	0	. . .

CHAMPIONSHIP SERIES RECORD

CHAMPIONSHIP SERIES NOTES: Shares N.L. single-series record for most at-bats—30 (1988).

Year	Team (League)	Pos.	G	AB	R	H	2B	3B	HR	RBI	Avg.	SB	PO	A	E	Avg.
1983 — Los Angeles (N.L.)		1B-OF	4	15	1	2	1	0	1	2	.133	0	22	2	0	1.000
1985 — Los Angeles (N.L.)		OF	6	23	1	5	2	0	1	3	.217	0	8	0	0	1.000
1988 — Los Angeles (N.L.)		OF	7	30	3	7	1	1	0	5	.233	0	14	0	0	1.000
1990 — Boston (A.L.)		PH	3	3	0	1	0	0	0	0	.333	0	0	0	0	. . .
Championship Series totals (4 years)			20	71	5	15	4	1	2	10	.211	0	44	2	0	1.000

WORLD SERIES RECORD

Year	Team (League)	Pos.	G	AB	R	H	2B	3B	HR	RBI	Avg.	SB	PO	A	E	Avg.
1988 — Los Angeles (N.L.)		OF	5	13	2	3	0	1	1	3	.231	0	6	0	0	1.000

ALL-STAR GAME RECORD

Year	League	Pos.	AB	R	H	2B	3B	HR	RBI	Avg.	SB	PO	A	E	Avg.
1984 — National						Did not play									

MARTEL, ED
P, YANKEES

PERSONAL: Born March 2, 1969, at Mount Clemens, Mich. . . . 6-1/190. . . . Throws right, bats right. . . . Full name: Edward Joseph Martel.
HIGH SCHOOL: DeLaSalle Collegiate (Warren, Mich.).
TRANSACTIONS/CAREER NOTES: Selected by New York Yankees organization in 11th round of free-agent draft (June 2, 1987).

Year	Team (League)	G	W	L	Pct.	ERA	Sv.	IP	H	R	ER	BB	SO
1987 — Oneonta (New York-Penn)	2	1	0	1.000	3.00	0	3	2	1	1	3	2
1988 — Oneonta (New York-Penn)	9	2	2	.500	3.02	0	41⅔	53	20	14	8	24
1989 — Fort Lauderdale (Florida St.)	26	10	8	.556	4.04	0	144⅔	151	76	65	39	86
1990 — Prince William (Carolina)	25	8	13	.381	4.08	0	143⅓	134	77	65	65	95
1991 — Albany (Eastern)	25	•13	6	.684	2.81	0	163⅓	129	67	51	55	★141

MARTIN, AL
OF, PIRATES

PERSONAL: Born November 24, 1967, at West Covina, Calif. . . . 6-2/220. . . . Throws left, bats left. . . . Full name: Albert Lee Martin. . . . Formerly known as Albert Scales-Martin.
HIGH SCHOOL: Rowland Heights (Calif.).
TRANSACTIONS/CAREER NOTES: Selected by Atlanta Braves organization in eighth round of free-agent draft (June 3, 1985). . . . Granted free agency (October 15, 1991). . . . Signed by Pittsburgh Pirates organization (November 11, 1991).

STATISTICAL NOTES: Led Gulf Coast League first basemen with 15 errors in 1985.

Year	Team (League)	Pos.	G	AB	R	H	2B	3B	HR	RBI	Avg.	SB	PO	A	E	Avg.
1985	—Bradenton Braves (GCL)....	1B-OF	40	138	16	32	3	0	0	9	.232	1	246	13	†15	.945
1986	—Sumter (South Atlantic)....	1B	44	156	23	38	5	0	1	24	.244	6	299	12	8	.975
	—Idaho Falls (Pioneer)........	OF-1B	63	242	39	80	17	•6	4	44	.331	11	272	15	8	.973
1987	—Sumter (South Atlantic)....	OF-1B	117	375	59	95	18	5	12	64	.253	27	137	7	9	.941
1988	—Burlington (Midwest)........	OF	123	480	69	134	21	3	7	42	.279	40	224	4	8	.966
1989	—Durham (Carolina)	OF	128	457	*84	124	26	3	9	48	.271	27	169	7	7	.962
1990	—Greenville (Southern)........	OF	133	455	64	110	17	4	11	50	.242	20	200	8	7	.967
1991	—Greenville (Southern)	OF-1B	86	301	38	73	13	3	7	38	.243	19	134	7	6	.959
	—Richmond (Int'l)	OF	44	151	20	42	11	1	5	18	.278	11	73	4	2	.975

MARTIN, NORBERTO
2B/SS, WHITE SOX

PERSONAL: Born December 10, 1966, at Santo Domingo, Dominican Republic.... 5-10/164.... Throws right, bats both.... Full name: Norberto Edonal Martin.... Name pronounced mar-TEEN.

TRANSACTIONS/CAREER NOTES: Signed as free agent by Chicago White Sox organization (March 27, 1984).... On Peninsula disabled list (April 10-May 5, 1986).... On Appleton disabled list (May 14, 1986-remainder of season).... On disabled list (April 7, 1989-entire season and May 5-June 9, 1991).

STATISTICAL NOTES: Led Gulf Coast League shortstops with 37 errors in 1984.

Year	Team (League)	Pos.	G	AB	R	H	2B	3B	HR	RBI	Avg.	SB	PO	A	E	Avg.
1984	—Sara. White Sox (GCL)	SS-OF	56	205	36	56	8	2	1	30	.273	18	66	149	†37	.853
1985	—Appleton (Midwest)..........	SS	30	196	15	19	2	0	0	5	.097	2	39	86	12	.912
	—Niagara Falls (NYP)	SS	60	217	22	55	9	0	1	13	.253	6	85	173	35	.881
1986	—..................................						Did not play									
	—Appleton (Midwest)..........	SS	9	33	4	10	2	0	0	2	.303	1	13	16	6	.829
	—Sara. White Sox (GCL)	PR	1	0	0	0	0	0	0	0	...	0	0	0	0	...
1987	—Charleston, S.C. (S. Atl.) ...	SS-OF-2B	68	250	44	78	14	1	5	35	.312	14	84	152	25	.904
	—Peninsula (Carolina)	2B	41	162	21	42	6	1	1	18	.259	11	94	108	15	.931
1988	—Tampa (Florida State).......	2B	101	360	44	93	10	4	2	33	.258	24	196	268	20	.959
1989	—..................................						Did not play									
1990	—Vancouver (Pac. Coast)....	2B	130	508	77	135	20	4	3	45	.266	10	283	324	17	.973
1991	—Vancouver (Pac. Coast)....	2B-SS	93	338	39	94	9	0	0	20	.278	11	196	265	16	.966

MARTINEZ, CARLOS
1B/DH, INDIANS

PERSONAL: Born August 11, 1965, at La Guaira, Venezuela.... 6-5/175.... Throws right, bats right.... Full name: Carlos Alberto Martinez.

TRANSACTIONS/CAREER NOTES: Signed as free agent by New York Yankees organization (November 17, 1983).... On Fort Lauderdale disabled list (April 11-May 1, 1986).... Traded by Yankees organization with C Ron Hassey and a player to be named later to Chicago White Sox for C Joel Skinner, IF Wayne Tolleson and OF-DH Ron Kittle (July 30, 1986); Yankees traded C Bill Lindsey to White Sox organization to complete deal (December 24, 1986).... On Chicago disabled list (June 22-July 13, 1989); included rehabilitation disability assignment to South Bend (July 8-12, 1989).... Granted free agency (February 23, 1991).... Signed by Cleveland Indians (March 2, 1991).... On suspended list (October 5 and 6, 1991).

Year	Team (League)	Pos.	G	AB	R	H	2B	3B	HR	RBI	Avg.	SB	PO	A	E	Avg.
1984	—Sarasota Yankees (GCL) ..	SS	31	91	9	14	1	1	0	4	.154	3	53	103	14	.918
1985	—Fort Lauderdale (FSL)	SS	93	311	39	77	15	7	6	44	.248	8	123	254	25	.938
1986	—Fort Lauderdale (FSL)	SS	5	16	1	1	0	0	0	0	.063	0	7	18	0	1.000
	—Albany (Eastern).............	SS-3B	69	253	34	70	18	2	8	39	.277	2	120	161	32	.898
	—Buffalo (Am. Assoc.)■......	SS-3B	17	54	6	16	1	0	2	6	.296	0	24	20	5	.898
1987	—Birmingham (Southern)	3B	9	30	2	7	1	0	0	0	.233	2	5	17	2	.917
	—Hawaii (Pacific Coast)	OF-3B-SS	83	304	32	75	15	1	3	36	.247	3	109	91	18	.917
1988	—Birmingham (Southern)	OF-3B-SS	133	498	67	138	22	3	14	73	.277	25	196	139	20	.944
	—Chicago (A.L.)	3B	17	55	5	9	1	0	0	0	.164	1	7	33	4	.909
1989	—Vancouver (Pac. Coast)....	1B	18	64	12	25	3	1	2	9	.391	2	178	10	1	.995
	—Chicago (A.L.)	3B-1B-1OF	109	350	44	105	22	0	5	32	.300	4	283	134	20	.954
	—South Bend (Midwest)	3B	3	11	2	6	3	0	0	3	.545	2	0	9	3	.750
1990	—Chicago (A.L.)	1B-OF	92	272	18	61	6	5	4	24	.224	0	632	38	8	.988
1991	—Canton/Akron (Eastern)■	OF-1B	80	295	48	97	22	2	11	73	.329	11	37	1	2	.950
	—Cleveland (A.L.)	1B	72	257	22	73	14	0	5	30	.284	3	229	12	8	.968
Major league totals (4 years)			290	934	89	248	43	5	14	86	.266	8	1151	217	40	.972

MARTINEZ, CARMELO
1B/OF

PERSONAL: Born July 28, 1960, at Dorado, Puerto Rico.... 6-2/211.... Throws right, bats right.... Full name: Carmelo Salgado Martinez.... Cousin of Edgar Martinez, third baseman, Seattle Mariners.

HIGH SCHOOL: Jose S. Alegria (Dorado, Puerto Rico).

COLLEGE: Central College of Bayamon (Puerto Rico).

TRANSACTIONS/CAREER NOTES: Signed as free agent by Chicago Cubs organization (December 9, 1978).... Traded by Cubs with P Craig Lefferts and 3B Fritz Connally to San Diego Padres for P Scott Sanderson (December 7, 1983).... On disabled list

(March 31-April 15, 1985).... Granted free agency (November 13, 1989).... Signed by Philadelphia Phillies (December 1, 1989).... On Philadelphia disabled list (May 29-June 13, 1990).... Traded by Phillies to Pittsburgh Pirates for OF Wes Chamberlain, OF Julio Peguero and a player to be named later (August 30, 1990); Phillies acquired OF Tony Longmire to complete deal (September 28, 1990).... Traded by Pirates to Kansas City Royals for P Victor Cole (May 3, 1991).... Traded by Royals to Cincinnati Reds for 1B Todd Benzinger (July 11, 1991).... Granted free agency (November 5, 1991).

STATISTICAL NOTES: Led Texas League first basemen with 1,087 putouts, 1,180 total chances and 102 double plays in 1982.... Hit home run in first major league at-bat (August 22, 1983).... Led American Association first basemen with 1,191 putouts, 83 assists and 1,283 total chances and tied for lead with 99 double plays in 1983.... Tied for N.L. lead with 10 sacrifice flies in 1984.

Year	Team (League)	Pos.	G	AB	R	H	2B	3B	HR	RBI	Avg.	SB	PO	A	E	Avg.
							BATTING							FIELDING		
1979	—Sarasota Cubs (GCL)	OF-1B	40	143	18	29	4	0	1	23	.203	0	139	9	6	.961
1980	—Quad Cities (Midwest)	0-1-3-2-S	128	460	65	118	23	0	12	64	.257	8	433	99	13	.976
1981	—Midland (Texas)	3-0-2-1	116	392	65	116	22	1	21	84	.296	5	61	80	24	.855
1982	—Midland (Texas)	1B-OF	131	467	100	156	35	4	27	93	.334	1	†1098	78	17	.986
1983	—Iowa (American Assoc.)	1B-2B	123	458	76	115	25	1	★31	94	.251	8	†1191	†83	9	.993
	—Chicago (N.L.)	1B-3B-OF	29	89	8	23	3	0	6	16	.258	0	233	17	2	.992
1984	—San Diego (N.L.)■	OF-1B	149	488	64	122	28	2	13	66	.250	1	317	15	8	.976
1985	—San Diego (N.L.)	OF-1B	150	514	64	130	28	1	21	72	.253	0	302	14	7	.978
1986	—San Diego (N.L.)	OF-1B-3B	113	244	28	58	10	0	9	25	.238	1	142	14	2	.987
1987	—San Diego (N.L.)	OF-1B	139	447	59	122	21	2	15	70	.273	5	591	42	9	.986
1988	—San Diego (N.L.)	OF-1B	121	365	48	86	12	0	18	65	.236	1	430	32	4	.991
1989	—San Diego (N.L.)	OF-1B	111	267	23	59	12	2	6	39	.221	0	225	18	2	.992
1990	—Phil.-Pittsburgh (N.L.)■	1B-OF	83	217	26	52	9	0	10	35	.240	2	374	29	2	.995
1991	—Pitts.-Cin. (N.L.)■	1B-OF	64	154	13	36	5	0	6	19	.234	0	274	13	6	.980
	—Kansas City (A.L.)■	1B	44	121	17	25	6	0	4	17	.207	0	307	35	3	.991
	American League totals (1 year)		44	121	17	25	6	0	4	17	.207	0	307	35	3	.991
	National League totals (9 years)		959	2785	333	688	128	7	104	407	.247	10	2888	194	42	.987
	Major league totals (9 years)		1003	2906	350	713	134	7	108	424	.245	10	3195	229	45	.987

CHAMPIONSHIP SERIES RECORD

Year	Team (League)	Pos.	G	AB	R	H	2B	3B	HR	RBI	Avg.	SB	PO	A	E	Avg.
							BATTING							FIELDING		
1984	—San Diego (N.L.)	OF	5	17	1	3	0	0	0	0	.176	0	6	0	0	1.000
1990	—Pittsburgh (N.L.)	1B	2	8	0	2	2	0	0	2	.250	0	15	1	0	1.000
	Championship Series totals (2 years)		7	25	1	5	2	0	0	2	.200	0	21	1	0	1.000

WORLD SERIES RECORD

Year	Team (League)	Pos.	G	AB	R	H	2B	3B	HR	RBI	Avg.	SB	PO	A	E	Avg.
							BATTING							FIELDING		
1984	—San Diego (N.L.)	OF	5	17	0	3	0	0	0	0	.176	0	7	0	1	.875

MARTINEZ, CHITO
OF, ORIOLES

PERSONAL: Born December 19, 1965, at Belize.... 5-10/182.... Throws left, bats left. ... Full name: Reynaldo Ignacio Martinez.
HIGH SCHOOL: Brother Martin (New Orleans).
TRANSACTIONS/CAREER NOTES: Selected by Kansas City Royals organization in sixth round of free-agent draft (June 4, 1984).... On disabled list (July 28-August 15, 1986).... Granted free agency (October 15, 1990).... Signed by Baltimore Orioles organization (November 16, 1990).... On Rochester disabled list (May 5-16 and May 18-28, 1991).
STATISTICAL NOTES: Led Southern League outfielders with six double plays in 1988.... Led Southern League batters with 137 strikeouts in 1989.... Led American Association batters with 129 strikeouts in 1990.

Year	Team (League)	Pos.	G	AB	R	H	2B	3B	HR	RBI	Avg.	SB	PO	A	E	Avg.
							BATTING							FIELDING		
1984	—Eugene (Northwest)	OF	59	176	18	53	12	3	0	26	.301	4	78	2	8	.909
1985	—Fort Myers (Florida St.)	OF	76	248	35	65	9	5	0	29	.262	11	161	7	4	.977
1986	—Memphis (Southern)	OF	93	283	48	86	16	5	11	44	.304	4	115	6	8	.938
1987	—Omaha (Am. Assoc.)	OF	35	121	14	26	10	1	2	14	.215	0	43	3	1	.979
	—Memphis (Southern)	OF	78	283	34	74	10	3	9	43	.261	5	173	11	3	.984
1988	—Memphis (Southern)	OF	141	485	67	110	16	4	13	65	.227	20	267	★23	7	.976
1989	—Memphis (Southern)	OF	127	399	55	97	20	2	23	62	.243	3	257	★18	7	.975
1990	—Omaha (Am. Assoc.)	OF	122	364	59	96	12	8	21	67	.264	6	228	18	6	.976
1991	—Rochester (Int'l)■	OF-1B	60	211	42	68	8	1	20	50	.322	2	190	12	4	.981
	—Baltimore (A.L.)	OF-1B	67	216	32	58	12	1	13	33	.269	1	112	4	2	.983
	Major league totals (1 year)		67	216	32	58	12	1	13	33	.269	1	112	4	2	.983

MARTINEZ, DAVE
OF, REDS

PERSONAL: Born September 26, 1964, at New York.... 5-10/180.... Throws left, bats left.... Full name: David Martinez.
HIGH SCHOOL: Lake Howell (Maitland, Fla.).
COLLEGE: Valencia Community College (Fla.).
TRANSACTIONS/CAREER NOTES: Selected by Texas Rangers organization in 40th round of free-agent draft (June 7, 1982)....

Selected by Chicago Cubs organization in secondary phase of free-agent draft (January 11, 1983).... On disabled list (April 27, 1984-remainder of season).... Traded by Cubs to Montreal Expos for OF Mitch Webster (July 14, 1988).... On disqualified list (October 4, 1991); reinstated (October 5, 1991).... Traded by Expos with P Scott Ruskin and SS Willie Greene to Cincinnati Reds for P John Wetteland and P Bill Risley (December 11, 1991).

							BATTING						FIELDING			
Year	Team (League)	Pos.	G	AB	R	H	2B	3B	HR	RBI	Avg.	SB	PO	A	E	Avg.
1983	—Quad Cities (Midwest).......	OF	44	119	17	29	6	2	0	10	.244	10	47	8	1	.982
	—Geneva (N.Y.-Penn).........	OF	64	241	35	63	15	2	5	33	.261	16	132	6	8	.945
1984	—Quad Cities (Midwest).......	OF	12	41	6	9	2	2	0	5	.220	3	13	2	1	.938
1985	—Winston-Salem (Caro.) ...	OF	115	386	52	132	14	4	5	54 ★.342		38	206	11	7	.969
1986	—Iowa (American Assoc.) ...	OF	83	318	52	92	11	5	5	32	.289	42	214	7	2	.991
	—Chicago (N.L.)	OF	53	108	13	15	1	1	1	7	.139	4	77	2	1	.988
1987	—Chicago (N.L.)	OF	142	459	70	134	18	8	8	36	.292	16	283	10	6	.980
1988	—Chicago-Montreal (N.L.)■	OF	138	447	51	114	13	6	6	46	.255	23	281	4	6	.979
1989	—Montreal (N.L.)	OF	126	361	41	99	16	7	3	27	.274	23	199	7	7	.967
1990	—Montreal (N.L.)	OF-P	118	391	60	109	13	5	11	39	.279	13	257	6	3	.989
1991	—Montreal (N.L.)	OF	124	396	47	117	18	5	7	42	.295	16	213	10	4	.982
Major league totals (6 years)			701	2162	282	588	79	32	36	197	.272	95	1310	39	27	.980

RECORD AS PITCHER

Year	Team (League)	G	W	L	Pct.	ERA	Sv.	IP	H	R	ER	BB	SO
1990	—Montreal (N.L.)	1	0	0	...	54.00	0	⅓	2	2	2	2	0

MARTINEZ, DENNIS
P, EXPOS

PERSONAL: Born May 14, 1955, at Granada, Nicaragua. ... 6-1/180. ... Throws right, bats right.... Full name: Jose Dennis Martinez.

TRANSACTIONS/CAREER NOTES: Signed as free agent by Baltimore Orioles organization (December 10, 1973).... On Baltimore disabled list (March 28-April 20 and June 3-July 10, 1980); included rehabilitation disability assignment to Miami (July 1-10, 1980).... On Baltimore disabled list (April 28-June 16, 1986); included rehabilitation disability assignment to Rochester (May 21-June 10, 1986).... Traded by Orioles to Montreal Expos for a player to be named later (June 16, 1986); Orioles acquired IF Rene Gonzales to complete deal (December 16, 1986).... Granted free agency (November 12, 1986).... Signed by Miami, independent (April 14, 1987).... Released by Miami (May 6, 1987).... Signed by Montreal Expos organization (May 6, 1987).... Granted free agency (November 9, 1987).... Re-signed by Expos (December 18, 1987).

RECORDS/HONORS: Named International League Pitcher of the Year (1976).... Shares major league single-season record for fewest complete games by pitcher who led league—9 (1991).

STATISTICAL NOTES: Led International League with 16 complete games in 1976.... Led A.L. pitchers with 39 games started and 18 complete games in 1979.... Tied for N.L. lead with 10 balks in 1988.... Pitched 2-0 perfect game against Los Angeles Dodgers (July 28, 1991).... Led N.L. with five shutouts and tied for lead with nine complete games in 1991.

MISCELLANEOUS: Appeared in one game as pinch-hitter, sacrifice (1991).

Year	Team (League)	G	W	L	Pct.	ERA	Sv.	IP	H	R	ER	BB	SO
1974	—Miami (Florida State)	25	15	6	.714	2.06	0	179	124	48	41	53	162
1975	—Miami (Florida State)	20	12	4	.750	2.61	0	145	125	54	42	35	114
	—Asheville (South Atlantic)	6	4	1	.800	2.60	0	45	45	16	13	12	18
	—Rochester (International)	2	0	0	...	5.40	0	5	7	4	3	2	4
1976	—Rochester (International)	25	★14	8	.636	★2.50	0	180	148	64	50	50	★140
	—Baltimore (A.L.)	4	1	2	.333	2.57	0	28	23	8	8	8	18
1977	—Baltimore (A.L.)	42	14	7	.667	4.10	4	167	157	86	76	64	107
1978	—Baltimore (A.L.)	40	16	11	.593	3.52	0	276	257	121	108	93	142
1979	—Baltimore (A.L.)	40	15	16	.484	3.67	0	★292	279	129	119	78	132
1980	—Baltimore (A.L.)	25	6	4	.600	3.96	1	100	103	44	44	44	42
	—Miami (Florida State)	2	0	0	...	0.00	0	12	3	1	0	5	7
1981	—Baltimore (A.L.)	25	●14	5	.737	3.32	0	179	173	84	66	62	88
1982	—Baltimore (A.L.)	40	16	12	.571	4.21	0	252	262	123	118	87	111
1983	—Baltimore (A.L.)	32	7	16	.304	5.53	0	153	209	108	94	45	71
1984	—Baltimore (A.L.)	34	6	9	.400	5.02	0	141⅔	145	81	79	37	77
1985	—Baltimore (A.L.)	33	13	11	.542	5.15	0	180	203	110	103	63	68
1986	—Baltimore (A.L.)	4	0	0	...	6.75	0	6⅔	11	5	5	2	2
	—Rochester (International)	4	2	1	.667	6.05	0	19⅓	18	14	13	9	14
	—Montreal (N.L.)■	19	3	6	.333	4.59	0	98	103	52	50	28	63
1987	—Miami (Florida State)■	3	1	1	.500	6.16	0	19	21	14	13	3	11
	—Indianapolis (Am. Assoc.)■	7	3	2	.600	4.46	0	38⅓	32	20	19	13	30
	—Montreal (N.L.)	22	11	4	★.733	3.30	0	144⅔	133	59	53	40	84
1988	—Montreal (N.L.)	34	15	13	.536	2.72	0	235⅓	215	94	71	55	120
1989	—Montreal (N.L.)	34	16	7	.696	3.18	0	232	227	88	82	49	142
1990	—Montreal (N.L.)	32	10	11	.476	2.95	0	226	191	80	74	49	156
1991	—Montreal (N.L.)	31	14	11	.560	★2.39	0	222	187	70	59	62	123
American League totals (11 years)		319	108	93	.537	4.16	5	1775⅓	1822	899	820	583	858
National League totals (6 years)		172	69	52	.570	3.02	0	1158	1056	443	389	283	688
Major league totals (16 years)		491	177	145	.550	3.71	5	2933⅓	2878	1342	1209	866	1546

CHAMPIONSHIP SERIES RECORD

Year	Team (League)	G	W	L	Pct.	ERA	Sv.	IP	H	R	ER	BB	SO
1979	—Baltimore (A.L.)	1	0	0	...	3.24	0	8⅓	8	3	3	0	4

Year	Team (League)	G	W	L	Pct.	ERA	Sv.	IP	H	R	ER	BB	SO
1979 —Baltimore (A.L.)		2	0	0	...	18.00	0	2	6	4	4	0	0
1983 —Baltimore (A.L.)						Did not play							

ALL-STAR GAME RECORD

Year	League	W	L	Pct.	ERA	Sv.	IP	H	R	ER	BB	SO
1990 —National		0	0	...	0.00	0	1	0	0	0	0	1
1991 —National		0	1	.000	13.50	0	2	4	3	3	0	0
All-Star totals (2 years)		0	1	.000	9.00	0	3	4	3	3	0	1

MARTINEZ, DOMINGO
1B, BLUE JAYS

PERSONAL: Born August 4, 1967, at Santo Domingo, Dominican Republic. . . . 6-2/215. . . . Throws right, bats right. . . . Full name: Domingo Emelio Martinez.
TRANSACTIONS/CAREER NOTES: Signed as free agent by Toronto Blue Jays organization (August 23, 1984).
STATISTICAL NOTES: Led Gulf Coast League third basemen with 102 assists, 166 total chances and 27 errors and tied for lead with 37 putouts in 1985. . . . Led Southern League first basemen with 1,141 putouts, 87 assists, 21 errors and 1,249 total chances in 1988. . . . Led International League first basemen with 1,222 total chances and 106 double plays in 1991.

Year Team (League)	Pos.	G	AB	R	H	2B	3B	HR	RBI	Avg.	SB	PO	A	E	Avg.
1985 —Brad. Blue Jays (GCL).......	3B-2B	58	219	36	65	10	2	4	19	.297	3	‡39	†102	†27	.839
1986 —Ventura County (Calif.).....	1B-3B	129	455	51	113	19	6	9	57	.248	9	1004	79	16	.985
1987 —Dunedin (Florida State)	1B	118	435	53	112	*32	2	8	65	.257	8	1014	78	16	.986
1988 —Knoxville (Southern)	1B-3B	•143	516	54	136	25	2	13	70	.264	2	†1141	†88	†22	.982
1989 —Knoxville (Southern)	1B	120	415	56	102	19	2	10	53	.246	2	929	93	13	.987
1990 —Knoxville (Southern)	1B	128	463	53	119	20	3	17	66	.257	2	681	61	4	.995
1991 —Syracuse (International) ..	1B	126	467	61	146	16	2	17	83	.313	6	*1110	*103	*9	.993

MARTINEZ, EDGAR
3B, MARINERS

PERSONAL: Born January 2, 1963, at New York. . . . 5-11/175. . . . Throws right, bats right. . . . Full name: Edgar Martinez. . . . Cousin of Carmelo Martinez, first baseman-outfielder, Cincinnati Reds.
HIGH SCHOOL: Dorado (Puerto Rico).
COLLEGE: American College (Puerto Rico.).
TRANSACTIONS/CAREER NOTES: Signed as free agent by Seattle Mariners organization (December 19, 1982).
RECORDS/HONORS: Shares A.L. single-game record for most errors—4 (May 6, 1990).
STATISTICAL NOTES: Led Southern League third basemen with 360 total chances and 34 double plays in 1985. . . . Led Southern League with 12 sacrifice flies in 1985. . . . Led Southern League third basemen with .960 fielding percentage in 1986. . . . Led Pacific Coast League third basemen with 389 total chances and 31 double plays in 1987.

Year Team (League)	Pos.	G	AB	R	H	2B	3B	HR	RBI	Avg.	SB	PO	A	E	Avg.
1983 —Bellingham (Northwest)....	3B	32	104	14	18	1	1	0	5	.173	1	22	58	6	.930
1984 —Wausau (Midwest)...........	3B	126	433	72	131	32	2	15	66	.303	11	85	246	25	.930
1985 —Chattanooga (Southern)...	3B	111	357	43	92	15	5	3	47	.258	1	*94	*247	19	*.947
—Calgary (Pacific Coast) ...	3B-2B	20	68	8	24	7	1	0	14	.353	1	15	44	4	.937
1986 —Chattanooga (Southern)...	3B-2B	132	451	71	119	29	5	6	74	.264	2	94	263	15	†.960
1987 —Calgary (Pacific Coast)	3B	129	438	75	144	31	1	10	66	.329	3	*91	*278	20	.949
—Seattle (A.L.)	3B	13	43	6	16	5	2	0	5	.372	0	13	19	0	1.000
1988 —Calgary (Pacific Coast)	3B-2B	95	331	63	120	19	4	8	64	*.363	9	48	185	20	.921
—Seattle (A.L.)	3B	14	32	0	9	4	0	0	5	.281	0	5	8	1	.929
1989 —Seattle (A.L.)	3B	65	171	20	41	5	0	2	20	.240	2	40	72	6	.949
—Calgary (Pacific Coast)	3B-2B	32	113	30	39	11	0	3	23	.345	2	22	56	12	.867
1990 —Seattle (A.L.)	3B	144	487	71	147	27	2	11	49	.302	1	89	259	*27	.928
1991 —Seattle (A.L.)	3B	150	544	98	167	35	1	14	52	.307	0	84	299	15	.962
Major league totals (5 years)		386	1277	195	380	76	5	27	131	.298	3	231	657	49	.948

MARTINEZ, PEDRO
P, DODGERS

PERSONAL: Born July 25, 1971, at Manoguayabo, Dominican Republic. . . . 5-11/150. . . . Throws right, bats right. . . . Full name: Pedro Jaime Martinez. . . . Brother of Ramon Martinez, pitcher, Los Angeles Dodgers; and brother of Jesus Martinez, pitcher, Dodgers organization.
COLLEGE: Ohio Dominican College (Dominican Republic).
TRANSACTIONS/CAREER NOTES: Signed as a free agent by Los Angeles Dodgers organization (June 18, 1988). . . . Played in Dominican Republic (1988 and 1989).
RECORDS/HONORS: Named Minor League Player of the Year by THE SPORTING NEWS (1991).
STATISTICAL NOTES: Tied for Pioneer League lead in games started by pitcher with 14 in 1990. . . . Tied for Texas League lead with three shutouts in 1991.

Year Team (League)	G	W	L	Pct.	ERA	Sv.	IP	H	R	ER	BB	SO
1988 —..					Dominican Republic Summer League							
1989 —..					Dominican Republic Summer League							
1990 —Great Falls (Pioneer)	14	8	3	.727	3.62	0	77	74	39	31	40	82
1991 —Bakersfield (California)	10	8	0	1.000	2.05	0	61⅓	41	17	14	19	83
—San Antonio (Texas)	12	7	5	.583	1.76	0	76⅔	57	21	15	31	74
—Albuquerque (Pacific Coast)	6	3	3	.500	3.66	0	39⅓	28	17	16	16	35

MARTINEZ, RAMON
P, DODGERS

PERSONAL: Born March 22, 1968, at Santo Domingo, Dominican Republic. . . . 6-4/173. . . . Throws right, bats left. . . . Full name: Ramon Jaime Martinez. . . . Brother of Pedro Martinez and Jesus Martinez, pitchers, Los Angeles Dodgers organization.
HIGH SCHOOL: Liceo Secunderia Las Americas (Dominican Republic).
TRANSACTIONS/CAREER NOTES: Signed as free agent by Los Angeles Dodgers organization (September 1, 1984).
STATISTICAL NOTES: Led N.L. with 12 complete games in 1990.
MISCELLANEOUS: Member of 1984 Dominican Republic Olympic baseball team.

Year	Team (League)	G	W	L	Pct.	ERA	Sv.	IP	H	R	ER	BB	SO
1985	—Bradenton Dodgers (GCL)	23	4	1	.800	2.59	1	59	57	30	17	23	42
1986	—Bakersfield (California)	20	4	8	.333	4.75	0	106	119	73	56	63	78
1987	—Vero Beach (Florida State)	25	16	5	.762	2.17	0	170⅓	128	45	41	78	148
1988	—San Antonio (Texas)	14	8	4	.667	2.46	0	95	79	29	26	34	89
	—Albuquerque (Pacific Coast)	10	5	2	.714	2.76	0	58⅔	43	24	18	32	49
	—Los Angeles (N.L.)	9	1	3	.250	3.79	0	35⅔	27	17	15	22	23
1989	—Albuquerque (Pacific Coast)	18	10	2	.833	2.79	0	113	92	40	35	50	127
	—Los Angeles (N.L.)	15	6	4	.600	3.19	0	98⅔	79	39	35	41	89
1990	—Los Angeles (N.L.)	33	20	6	.769	2.92	0	234⅓	191	89	76	67	223
1991	—Los Angeles (N.L.)	33	17	13	.567	3.27	0	220⅓	190	89	80	69	150
	Major league totals (4 years)	90	44	26	.629	3.15	0	589	487	234	206	199	485

MARTINEZ, TINO
1B, MARINERS

PERSONAL: Born December 7, 1967, at Tampa, Fla. . . . 6-2/205. . . . Throws right, bats left. . . . Full name: Constantino Martinez.
HIGH SCHOOL: Jefferson (Tampa, Fla.).
COLLEGE: Tampa (Fla.).
TRANSACTIONS/CAREER NOTES: Selected by Boston Red Sox organization in third round of free-agent draft (June 3, 1985). . . . Selected by Seattle Mariners organization in first round (14th pick overall) of free-agent draft (June 1, 1988).
RECORDS/HONORS: Named first baseman on THE SPORTING NEWS college All-America team (1988). . . . Named Pacific Coast League Most Valuable Player (1991).
STATISTICAL NOTES: Led Eastern League first basemen with 1,348 total chances and 106 double plays in 1989. . . . Led Eastern League with 13 intentional bases on balls received in 1989. . . . Tied for Pacific Coast League lead with 11 intentional bases on balls received in 1990. . . . Led Pacific Coast League first basemen with .991 fielding percentage, 1,051 putouts, 98 assists, 1,159 total chances and 117 double plays in 1990. . . . Led Pacific Coast League first basemen with .992 fielding percentage and 122 double plays in 1991.
MISCELLANEOUS: Member of 1988 U.S. Olympic baseball team.

Year	Team (League)	Pos.	G	AB	R	H	2B	3B	HR	RBI	Avg.	SB	PO	A	E	Avg.
1989	—Williamsport (NYP)	1B	*137	*509	51	131	29	2	13	64	.257	7	*1260	*81	7	*.995
1990	—Calgary (Pacific Coast)	1B-3B	128	453	83	145	28	1	17	93	.320	8	†1051	†98	10	†.991
	—Seattle (A.L.)	1B	24	68	4	15	4	0	0	5	.221	0	155	12	0	1.000
1991	—Calgary (Pacific Coast)	1B-3B	122	442	94	144	34	5	18	86	.326	3	1078	106	9	†.992
	—Seattle (A.L.)	1B	36	112	11	23	2	0	4	9	.205	0	249	22	2	.993
	Major league totals (2 years)		60	180	15	38	6	0	4	14	.211	0	404	34	2	.995

MARZANO, JOHN
C, RED SOX

PERSONAL: Born February 14, 1963, at Philadelphia. . . . 5-11/195. . . . Throws right, bats right. . . . Full name: John Robert Marzano.
HIGH SCHOOL: Central (Philadelphia).
COLLEGE: Temple.
TRANSACTIONS/CAREER NOTES: Selected by Minnesota Twins organization in third round of free-agent draft (June 8, 1981). . . . Selected by Boston Red Sox organization in first round (14th pick overall) of free-agent draft (June 4, 1984). . . . On disabled list (June 13-28, 1986).
RECORDS/HONORS: Named catcher on THE SPORTING NEWS college All-America team (1984).
STATISTICAL NOTES: Led Eastern League in being hit by pitch with 12 in 1986.
MISCELLANEOUS: Member of 1984 U.S. Olympic baseball team.

Year	Team (League)	Pos.	G	AB	R	H	2B	3B	HR	RBI	Avg.	SB	PO	A	E	Avg.
1985	—New Britain (Eastern)	C	103	350	36	86	14	6	4	51	.246	4	530	70	12	.980
1986	—New Britain (Eastern)	C-3B	118	445	55	126	28	2	10	62	.283	2	509	76	14	.977
1987	—Pawtucket (Int'l)	C	70	255	46	72	22	0	10	35	.282	2	326	36	8	.978
	—Boston (A.L.)	C	52	168	20	41	11	0	5	24	.244	0	337	24	5	.986
1988	—Boston (A.L.)	C	10	29	3	4	1	0	0	1	.138	0	77	4	0	1.000
	—Pawtucket (Int'l)	C	33	111	7	22	2	1	0	5	.198	1	151	24	8	.956
	—New Britain (Eastern)	C	35	112	11	23	6	1	0	5	.205	1	117	11	3	.977
1989	—Pawtucket (Int'l)	C	106	322	27	68	11	0	8	36	.211	1	574	62	10	.985
	—Boston (A.L.)	C	7	18	5	8	3	0	1	3	.444	0	29	4	0	1.000
1990	—Boston (A.L.)	C	32	83	8	20	4	0	0	6	.241	0	153	14	0	1.000
	—Pawtucket (Int'l)	C-3B	26	75	16	24	4	1	2	8	.320	6	100	12	0	1.000
1991	—Boston (A.L.)	C	49	114	10	30	8	0	0	9	.263	0	174	20	3	.985
	Major league totals (5 years)		150	412	46	103	27	0	6	43	.250	0	770	66	8	.991

MASON, ROGER
P, PIRATES

PERSONAL: Born September 18, 1958, at Bellaire, Mich. . . . 6-6/220. . . . Throws right, bats right. . . . Full name: Roger LeRoy Mason.
HIGH SCHOOL: Bellaire (Mich.).
COLLEGE: Saginaw Valley State College (Mich.).

TRANSACTIONS/CAREER NOTES: Signed as a free agent by the Detroit Tigers organization (September 21, 1980).... On Evansville disabled list (May 3-19, 1984).... Traded by Tigers to San Francisco Giants organization for OF Alejandro Sanchez (April 5, 1985).... On Phoenix disabled list (May 2-23, 1985).... On San Francisco disabled list (May 30-July 20 and July 26, 1986-remainder of season); included rehabilitation assignment to Phoenix (July 9-17, 1986).... Granted free agency (October 15, 1988).... Signed by Tucson, Houston Astros organization (February 16, 1989).... Released by Astros organization (April 3, 1990).... Signed by Pittsburgh Pirates organization (May 18, 1990).

RECORDS/HONORS: Shares N.L. record for most consecutive home runs allowed in one inning—3 (April 13, 1987, first inning).

STATISTICAL NOTES: Pitched no-hitter for nine innings against Las Vegas (August 20, 1989); Tucson lost game in 11 innings, 1-0.

Year	Team (League)	G	W	L	Pct.	ERA	Sv.	IP	H	R	ER	BB	SO
1981	Macon (South Atlantic)	26	10	10	.500	3.89	0	148	153	77	64	50	105
1982	Lakeland (Florida State)	22	7	7	.500	3.46	0	132⅔	124	60	51	52	72
1983	Birmingham (Southern)	17	7	4	.636	★2.06	0	126⅔	116	45	29	43	83
	Evansville (Am. Assoc.)	11	5	5	.500	4.23	0	78⅓	84	39	37	21	43
1984	Evansville (Am. Assoc.)	25	9	7	.563	3.80	0	151⅔	175	78	64	64	88
	Detroit (A.L.)	5	1	1	.500	4.50	1	22	23	11	11	10	15
1985	Phoenix (Pacific Coast)■	24	12	1	★.923	3.33	0	167⅓	145	67	62	72	120
	San Francisco (N.L.)	5	1	3	.250	2.12	0	29⅔	28	13	7	11	26
1986	San Francisco (N.L.)	11	3	4	.429	4.80	0	60	56	35	32	30	43
	Phoenix (Pacific Coast)	1	1	0	1.000	0.00	0	6	2	0	0	1	2
1987	San Francisco (N.L.)	5	1	1	.500	4.50	0	26	30	15	13	10	18
	Phoenix (Pacific Coast)	10	5	1	.833	4.13	0	61	62	34	28	20	49
1988	Phoenix (Pacific Coast)	19	2	9	.182	4.86	0	90⅔	90	62	49	38	62
1989	Tucson (Pacific Coast)■	25	7	12	.368	3.54	0	155	125	71	61	46	105
	Houston (N.L.)	2	0	0	...	20.25	0	1⅓	2	3	3	2	3
1990	Buffalo (American Assoc.)■	29	3	5	.375	2.10	3	77	78	21	18	25	45
1991	Buffalo (American Assoc.)	34	9	5	.643	3.08	0	122⅔	115	47	42	44	80
	Pittsburgh (N.L.)	24	3	2	.600	3.03	3	29⅔	21	11	10	6	21
	American League totals (1 year)	5	1	1	.500	4.50	1	22	23	11	11	10	15
	National League totals (5 years)	47	8	10	.444	3.99	3	146⅔	137	77	65	59	111
	Major league totals (6 years)	52	9	11	.450	4.06	4	168⅔	160	88	76	69	126

CHAMPIONSHIP SERIES RECORD

Year	Team (League)	G	W	L	Pct.	ERA	Sv.	IP	H	R	ER	BB	SO
1991	Pittsburgh (N.L.)	3	0	0	...	0.00	1	4⅓	3	0	0	1	2

MASTERS, DAVE
P, GIANTS

PERSONAL: Born August 13, 1964, at San Diego.... 6-9/225.... Throws right, bats right. ... Full name: David William Masters.
HIGH SCHOOL: Lolani (Honolulu).
COLLEGE: California.

TRANSACTIONS/CAREER NOTES: Selected by Chicago Cubs organization in first round (24th pick overall) of free-agent draft (June 3, 1985).... On disabled list (May 2 through end of 1989 season).... Traded by Cubs organization to Montreal Expos organization for player to be named later (June 12, 1990); Cubs acquired P Mike Grace to complete trade (December 5, 1990). ... Granted free agency (July 26, 1991).... Signed by San Francisco Giants organization (July 28, 1991).

STATISTICAL NOTES: Led Carolina League with 12 hit batsmen and 22 wild pitches in 1986.... Led Eastern League 14 hit batsmen in 1987.

Year	Team (League)	G	W	L	Pct.	ERA	Sv.	IP	H	R	ER	BB	SO
1985	Winston-Salem (Carolina)	14	1	11	.083	5.59	0	67⅔	59	53	42	42	49
1986	Winston-Salem (Carolina)	30	8	9	.471	4.10	0	158	128	86	72	95	125
1987	Pittsfield (Eastern)	25	12	3	★.800	3.73	0	157	158	77	65	67	105
1988	Iowa (American Association)	28	14	8	.636	5.22	0	167⅓	164	★106	★97	★96	101
1989	Iowa (American Association)	4	0	1	.000	6.52	0	19⅓	21	17	14	18	22
1990	Iowa (American Association)	9	1	4	.200	12.30	0	26⅓	42	36	36	35	22
	Jacksonville (Southern)■	20	0	2	.000	3.46	0	41⅔	28	22	16	44	49
1991	Indianapolis (Am. Assoc.)	27	4	6	.400	6.04	1	70	82	56	47	63	64
	Phoenix (Pacific Coast)■	8	1	2	.333	6.46	0	30⅔	34	24	22	17	28

MATHEWS, TERRY
P, RANGERS

PERSONAL: Born October 5, 1964, at Alexandria, La.... 6-2/225.... Throws right, bats left.... Full name: Terry Alan Mathews.
HIGH SCHOOL: Menard (Alexandria, La.).
COLLEGE: Northeast Louisiana.

TRANSACTIONS/CAREER NOTES: Selected by Texas Rangers organization in fifth round of free-agent draft (June 2, 1987).

Year	Team (League)	G	W	L	Pct.	ERA	Sv.	IP	H	R	ER	BB	SO
1987	Gastonia (South Atlantic)	34	3	3	.500	5.59	0	48⅓	53	35	30	32	46
1988	Port Charlotte (Florida State)	27	13	6	.684	2.80	0	163⅔	141	68	51	49	94
1989	Tulsa (Texas)	10	2	5	.286	6.15	0	45⅓	53	40	31	24	32
	Port Charlotte (Florida State)	10	4	2	.667	3.64	0	59⅓	55	28	24	17	30
1990	Tulsa (Texas)	14	5	7	.417	4.27	0	86⅓	88	50	41	36	48
	Oklahoma City (Am. Assoc.)	12	2	7	.222	3.69	0	70⅔	81	39	29	15	36
1991	Oklahoma City (Am. Assoc.)	18	5	6	.455	3.49	1	95½	98	39	37	34	63
	Texas (A.L.)	34	4	0	1.000	3.61	1	57⅓	54	24	23	18	51
	Major league totals (1 year)	34	4	0	1.000	3.61	1	57⅓	54	24	23	18	51

MATTINGLY, DON

1B, YANKEES

PERSONAL: Born April 20, 1961, at Evansville, Ind. . . . . 6-0/192. . . . Throws left, bats left. . . . Full name: Donald Arthur Mattingly.
HIGH SCHOOL: Evansville Memorial (Ind.).
TRANSACTIONS/CAREER NOTES: Selected by New York Yankees organization in 19th round of free-agent draft (June 5, 1979). . . . On disabled list (June 9-24, 1987; May 27-June 14, 1988; and July 26-September 11, 1990).
RECORDS/HONORS: Holds major league records for most home runs in seven consecutive games—9 (July 8-17, 1987); eight consecutive games—10 (July 8-18, 1987). . . . Holds major league single-season records for most grand slams—6 (1987); most at bats without a stolen base—677 (1986). . . . Shares major league single-game records for most sacrifice flies—3 (May 3, 1986); most putouts and chances accepted by first baseman in nine-inning game—22 (July 20, 1987). . . . Shares major league record for most doubles in one inning—2 (April 11, 1987, seventh inning). . . . Holds A.L. single-season record for most consecutive games, one or more long hits—10 (July 7-19, 1987); most at-bats by lefthander—677 (1986). . . . Shares A.L. career record for highest fielding percentage for first baseman—.995; most consecutive games with one or more home runs—8 (July 8-18, 1987). . . . Named South Atlantic League Most Valuable Player (1980). . . . Named A.L. Player of the Year by THE SPORTING NEWS (1984-86). . . . Named first baseman on THE SPORTING NEWS A.L. All-Star team (1984-87). . . . Named Major League Player of the Year by THE SPORTING NEWS (1985). . . . Named first baseman on THE SPORTING NEWS A.L. Silver Slugger team (1985-87). . . . Won A.L. Gold Glove at first base (1985-89 and 1991). . . . Named A.L. Most Valuable Player by Baseball Writers' Association of America (1985).
STATISTICAL NOTES: Led South Atlantic League with 12 sacrifice flies in 1980. . . . Led A.L. first basemen with .996 fielding percentage in both 1984 and 1986. . . . Led A.L. with 370 total bases in 1985 and 388 in 1986. . . . Led A.L. with 21 game-winning RBIs in 1985 and tied for lead with 15 in 1986. . . . Led A.L. with 15 sacrifice flies in 1985. . . . Tied for A.L. lead in double plays by first basemen with 154 in 1985. . . . Led A.L. with .573 slugging percentage in 1986. . . . Led A.L. first basemen with 1,377 putouts and 1,483 total chances in 1986. . . . Led A.L. first basemen with 135 double plays in 1991.

Year—Team (League)	Pos.	G	AB	R	H	2B	3B	HR	RBI	Avg.	SB	PO	A	E	Avg.
1979—Oneonta (N.Y.-Penn)	OF-1B	53	166	20	58	10	2	3	31	.349	2	29	2	2	.939
1980—Greensboro (S. Atlantic)	OF-1B	133	494	92	*177	32	5	9	105	*.358	8	205	16	8	.965
1981—Nashville (Southern)	OF-1B	141	547	74	173	*35	4	7	98	.316	4	846	69	12	.987
1982—Columbus (Int'l)	OF-1B	130	476	67	150	24	2	10	75	.315	1	271	17	5	.983
—New York (A.L.)	OF-1B	7	12	0	2	0	0	0	1	.167	0	15	1	0	1.000
1983—New York (A.L.)	OF-1B-2B	91	279	34	79	15	4	4	32	.283	0	350	15	3	.992
—Columbus (Int'l)	1B-OF	43	159	35	54	11	3	8	37	.340	2	325	29	1	.997
1984—New York (A.L.)	1B-OF	153	603	91	*207	*44	2	23	110	*.343	0	1143	126	6	†.995
1985—New York (A.L.)	1B	159	652	107	211	*48	3	35	*145	.324	2	1318	87	7	*.995
1986—New York (A.L.)	1B-3B	162	677	117	*238	*53	2	31	113	.352	0	†1378	111	7	†.995
1987—New York (A.L.)	1B	141	569	93	186	38	2	30	115	.327	1	1239	91	5	*.996
1988—New York (A.L.)	1B-OF	144	599	94	186	37	0	18	88	.311	1	1250	99	9	.993
1989—New York (A.L.)	1B-OF	158	631	79	191	37	2	23	113	.303	3	1276	87	7	.995
1990—New York (A.L.)	1B-OF	102	394	40	101	16	0	5	42	.256	1	800	78	3	.997
1991—New York (A.L.)	1B	152	587	64	169	35	0	9	68	.288	2	1119	77	5	.996
Major league totals (10 years)		1269	5003	719	1570	323	15	178	827	.314	10	9888	772	52	.995

ALL-STAR GAME RECORD

Year—League	Pos.	AB	R	H	2B	3B	HR	RBI	Avg.	SB	PO	A	E	Avg.
1984—American	PH	1	0	0	0	0	0	0	.000	0	0	0	0	. . .
1985—American	1B	1	0	0	0	0	0	0	.000	0	4	0	0	1.000
1986—American	PH-1B	3	0	0	0	0	0	0	.000	0	7	0	0	1.000
1987—American	1B	0	0	0	0	0	0	0	. . .	0	10	0	0	1.000
1988—American	1B	2	0	0	0	0	0	0	.000	0	2	1	1	.750
1989—American	1B	1	0	1	1	0	0	0	1.000	0	4	0	0	1.000
All-Star Game totals (6 years)		8	0	1	1	0	0	0	.125	0	27	1	1	.966

MAURER, ROB

1B, RANGERS

PERSONAL: Born January 7, 1967, at Evansville, Ind. . . . . 6-3/210. . . . Throws left, bats left. . . . Full name: Robert John Maurer.
HIGH SCHOOL: Mater Dei (Evansville, Ind.).
COLLEGE: Evansville.
TRANSACTIONS/CAREER NOTES: Selected by Texas Rangers organization in sixth round of free-agent draft (June 1, 1988).
STATISTICAL NOTES: Tied for Pioneer League lead with three intentional bases on balls received in 1988. . . . Led Pioneer League first basemen with 65 double plays in 1988. . . . Led Florida State League first basemen with 105 double plays in 1989. . . . Led American Association with 245 total bases, .534 slugging percentage, .420 on base percentage and 96 base on balls received in 1991.

Year—Team (League)	Pos.	G	AB	R	H	2B	3B	HR	RBI	Avg.	SB	PO	A	E	Avg.
1988—Butte (Pioneer)	1B	63	233	65	91	18	3	8	60	*.391	0	519	*41	6	.989
1989—Port Charlotte (Fla. St.)	1B	132	456	69	126	18	9	6	51	.276	3	1094	*105	14	.988
1990—Tulsa (Texas)	1B	104	367	55	110	31	4	21	78	.300	4	939	72	11	.989
1991—Oklahoma City (A.A.)	1B	132	459	76	138	*41	3	20	77	.301	2	941	*84	*16	.985
—Texas (A.L.)	1B	13	16	0	1	1	0	0	2	.063	0	7	3	0	1.000
Major league totals (1 year)		13	16	0	1	1	0	0	2	.063	0	7	3	0	1.000

MAUSER, TIM

P, PHILLIES

PERSONAL: Born October 4, 1966, at Fort Worth, Tex. . . . . 6-0/185. . . . Throws right, bats right. . . . Full name: Timothy Edward Mauser.
HIGH SCHOOL: Arlington Heights (Tex.).
COLLEGE: Texas Christian.

TRANSACTIONS/CAREER NOTES: Selected by Philadelphia Phillies organization in third round of free-agent draft (June 1, 1988).
STATISTICAL NOTES: Pitched 9-0 no-hit victory against New Britain (August 30, 1989, second game).

Year	Team (League)	G	W	L	Pct.	ERA	Sv.	IP	H	R	ER	BB	SO
1988	—Spartanburg (South Atlantic) ..	4	2	1	.667	1.96	0	23	15	6	5	5	18
	—Reading (Eastern)	5	2	3	.400	3.49	0	28 ⅓	27	14	11	6	17
1989	—Clearwater (Florida State)	16	6	7	.462	2.69	0	107	105	40	32	40	73
	—Reading (Eastern)	11	7	4	.636	3.63	0	72	62	36	29	33	54
1990	—Reading (Eastern)	8	3	4	.429	3.30	0	46 ⅓	35	20	17	15	40
	—Scranton/Wilkes-Barre (Int'l) ..	16	5	7	.417	3.66	0	98 ⅓	75	48	40	34	54
1991	—Scranton/Wilkes-Barre (Int'l) ..	26	6	11	.353	3.72	1	128 ⅓	119	66	53	55	75
	—Philadelphia (N.L.)	3	0	0	. . .	7.59	0	10 ⅔	18	10	9	3	6
Major league totals (1 year)		**3**	**0**	**0**	. . .	**7.59**	**0**	**10 ⅔**	**18**	**10**	**9**	**3**	**6**

MAY, DERRICK
OF, CUBS

PERSONAL: Born July 14, 1968, at Rochester, N.Y. . . . 6-4/205. . . . Throws right, bats left. . . . Full name: Derrick Brant May. . . . Son of Dave May, major league outfielder for five teams (1967-78).
HIGH SCHOOL: Newark (Del.).
TRANSACTIONS/CAREER NOTES: Selected by Chicago Cubs organization in first round (ninth pick overall) of free-agent draft (June 2, 1986). . . . On Iowa disabled list (April 14-May 27 and June 6-24, 1991).
STATISTICAL NOTES: Tied for Carolina League lead in double plays by outfielders with four in 1988.

Year	Team (League)	Pos.	G	AB	R	H	2B	3B	HR	RBI	Avg.	SB	PO	A	E	Avg.
							BATTING						FIELDING			
1986	—Wytheville (Appal.)	OF	54	178	25	57	6	1	0	23	.320	17	47	3	5	.909
1987	—Peoria (Midwest)	OF	128	439	60	131	19	8	9	52	.298	5	181	13	8	.960
1988	—Winston-Salem (Caro.)	OF	130	485	76	•148	29	*9	8	65	.305	13	209	13	10	.957
1989	—Charlotte (Florida State)...	OF	136	491	72	145	26	5	9	70	.295	19	239	8	•13	.950
1990	—Iowa (American Assoc.) ...	OF-1B	119	459	55	136	27	1	8	69	.296	5	159	10	8	.955
	—Chicago (N.L.)	OF	17	61	8	15	3	0	1	11	.246	1	34	1	1	.972
1991	—Iowa (American Assoc.) ...	OF	82	310	47	92	18	4	3	49	.297	7	130	2	5	.964
	—Chicago (N.L.)	OF	15	22	4	5	2	0	1	3	.227	0	11	1	0	1.000
Major league totals (2 years)			**32**	**83**	**12**	**20**	**5**	**0**	**2**	**14**	**.241**	**1**	**45**	**2**	**1**	**.979**

MAY, SCOTT
P, CUBS

PERSONAL: Born November 11, 1961, at West Bend, Wis. . . . 6-0/185. . . . Throws right, bats right. . . . Full name: Scott Francis May.
HIGH SCHOOL: Almond (Wisc.).
COLLEGE: Wisconsin-Stevens Point.
TRANSACTIONS/CAREER NOTES: Selected by Los Angeles Dodgers in sixth round of free-agent draft (June 6, 1983). . . . Traded by Dodgers organization to Texas Rangers organization for OF Javier Ortiz (December 23, 1987). . . . Traded by Rangers organization with OF Mike Wilson to Milwaukee Brewers organization for P Todd Simmons and OF Lavel Freeman (June 29, 1989). . . . Granted free agency (October 15, 1990). . . . Signed by Chicago Cubs organization (January 21, 1991). . . . Released by Cubs (September 5, 1991). . . . Signed by Iowa, Cubs organization (December 14, 1991).

Year	Team (League)	G	W	L	Pct.	ERA	Sv.	IP	H	R	ER	BB	SO
1983	—Lethbridge (Pioneer)	13	2	1	.667	5.01	1	46 ⅔	46	29	26	30	36
1984	—Bakersfield (California)	25	8	10	.444	3.83	0	152 ⅔	128	78	65	81	107
1985	—San Antonio (Texas)	26	10	6	.625	3.47	0	191 ⅔	181	85	74	*99	125
1986	—Albuquerque (Pacific Coast)	27	0	7	.000	6.92	1	65	97	59	50	39	57
	—San Antonio (Texas)	4	2	0	1.000	5.25	0	24	31	15	14	7	12
1987	—San Antonio (Texas)	30	8	8	.500	5.98	0	111 ⅓	136	83	74	52	108
1988	—Oklahoma City (Am. Assoc.)■ ..	36	8	7	.533	2.97	0	151 ⅔	132	56	50	57	103
	—Texas (A.L.)	3	0	0	. . .	8.59	0	7 ⅓	8	7	7	4	4
1989	—Oklahoma City-Denver (A.A.)■..	29	9	13	.409	4.44	0	180 ⅓	180	*107	*89	79	129
1990	—Denver (American Assoc.)	7	1	1	.500	8.04	0	28	45	26	25	13	20
	—El Paso (Texas)	22	6	4	.600	3.79	0	99 ⅔	113	48	42	38	85
1991	—Iowa (American Association)■..	57	4	4	.500	2.97	10	94	75	38	31	54	93
	—Chicago (N.L.)	2	0	0	. . .	18.00	0	2	6	4	4	1	1
American League totals (1 year)		**3**	**0**	**0**	. . .	**8.59**	**0**	**7 ⅓**	**8**	**7**	**7**	**4**	**4**
National League totals (1 year)		**2**	**0**	**0**	. . .	**18.00**	**0**	**2**	**6**	**4**	**4**	**1**	**1**
Major league totals (2 years)		**5**	**0**	**0**	. . .	**10.61**	**0**	**9 ⅓**	**14**	**11**	**11**	**5**	**5**

MAYNE, BRENT
C, ROYALS

PERSONAL: Born April 19, 1968, at Loma Linda, Calif. . . . 6-1/190. . . . Throws right, bats left. . . . Full name: Brent Danem Mayne.
HIGH SCHOOL: Costa Mesa (Calif.).
COLLEGE: Orange Coast College (Calif.) and Cal State Fullerton.
TRANSACTIONS/CAREER NOTES: Selected by Kansas City Royals organization in first round (13th pick overall) of free-agent draft (June 5, 1989). . . . On disabled list (July 24, 1989-remainder of season).

Year	Team (League)	Pos.	G	AB	R	H	2B	3B	HR	RBI	Avg.	SB	PO	A	E	Avg.
1989—Baseball City (Fla. St.)		C	7	24	5	13	3	1	0	8	.542	0	31	2	0	1.000
1990—Kansas City (A.L.)		C	5	13	2	3	0	0	0	1	.231	0	29	3	1	.970
—Memphis (Southern)		C	115	412	48	110	16	3	2	61	.267	5	591	61	11	.983
1991—Kansas City (A.L.)		C	85	231	22	58	8	0	3	31	.251	2	425	38	6	.987
Major league totals (2 years)			90	244	24	61	8	0	3	32	.250	2	454	41	7	.986

McANDREW, JAMIE
P, DODGERS

PERSONAL: Born September 2, 1967, at Williamsport, Pa. ... 6-2/190. ... Throws right, bats right. ... Full name: Jamie Brian McAndrew. ... Son of Jim McAndrew, pitcher, New York Mets, San Diego Padres (1968-74). **HIGH SCHOOL:** Ponderosa (Fla.).

COLLEGE: Florida.

TRANSACTIONS/CAREER NOTES: Selected by Seattle Mariners organization in 23rd round of free-agent draft (June 2, 1986). ... Selected by Los Angeles Dodgers organization in first round (28th pick overall) of free-agent draft (June 5, 1989).

Year	Team (League)	G	W	L	Pct.	ERA	Sv.	IP	H	R	ER	BB	SO
1989—Great Falls (Pioneer)		13	*11	0	*1.000	1.65	0	76⅓	49	16	14	27	72
1990—San Antonio (Texas)		12	7	3	.700	1.93	0	79⅓	68	28	17	32	50
—Bakersfield (California)		14	10	3	.769	2.27	0	95	88	31	24	29	82
1991—Albuquerque (Pacific Coast)		28	12	10	.545	5.04	1	155⅓	167	105	87	76	91

McCASKILL, KIRK
P, WHITE SOX

PERSONAL: Born April 9, 1961, at Kapuskasing, Ontario, Canada. ... 6-1/205. ... Throws right, bats right. ... Full name: Kirk Edward McCaskill. ... Son of Ted McCaskill, National Hockey League and World Hockey Association player (1967-68, 1972-73 and 1973-74).

HIGH SCHOOL: Trinity Pawling (Pawling, N.Y.).
COLLEGE: Vermont.

TRANSACTIONS/CAREER NOTES: Selected by California Angels organization in fourth round of free-agent draft (June 7, 1982). ... On suspended list (August 30, 1983); then transferred to disqualified list (September 26, 1983-April 25, 1984). ... On California disabled list (April 24-July 11, 1987); included rehabilitation disability assignment to Palm Springs (June 24-July 2, 1987) and Edmonton (July 3-8, 1987). ... On disabled list (August 9, 1988-remainder of season). ... Granted free agency (October 30, 1991). ... Signed by Chicago White Sox (December 28, 1991).

Year	Team (League)	G	W	L	Pct.	ERA	Sv.	IP	H	R	ER	BB	SO
1982—Salem (Carolina)		11	5	5	.500	4.29	0	71⅓	63	43	34	51	87
1983—Redwood (California)		16	6	5	.545	2.33	0	108⅓	78	39	28	60	100
—Nashua (Eastern)		13	4	8	.333	4.45	0	87	90	47	43	43	63
1984—Edmonton (Pacific Coast)		24	7	11	.389	5.73	0	143	162	104	91	74	75
1985—Edmonton (Pacific Coast)		3	1	1	.500	2.04	0	17⅔	17	7	4	6	18
—California (A.L.)		30	12	12	.500	4.70	0	189⅔	189	105	99	64	102
1986—California (A.L.)		34	17	10	.630	3.36	0	246⅓	207	98	92	92	202
1987—California (A.L.)		14	4	6	.400	5.67	0	74⅔	84	52	47	34	56
—Palm Springs (California)		2	2	0	1.000	0.00	0	10	4	1	0	3	7
—Edmonton (Pacific Coast)		1	1	0	1.000	3.00	0	6	3	2	2	4	4
1988—California (A.L.)		23	8	6	.571	4.31	0	146⅓	155	78	70	61	98
1989—California (A.L.)		32	15	10	.600	2.93	0	212	202	73	69	59	107
1990—California (A.L.)		29	12	11	.522	3.25	0	174⅓	161	77	63	72	78
1991—California (A.L.)		30	10	*19	.345	4.26	0	177⅔	193	93	84	66	71
Major league totals (7 years)		192	78	74	.513	3.86	0	1221	1191	576	524	448	714

CHAMPIONSHIP SERIES RECORD

CHAMPIONSHIP SERIES NOTES: Holds single-series record for most runs allowed—13 (1986). ... Shares single-series record for most games lost—2 (1986). ... Shares record for most hits allowed in one inning—6 (October 14, 1986, third inning).

Year	Team (League)	G	W	L	Pct.	ERA	Sv.	IP	H	R	ER	BB	SO
1986—California (A.L.)		2	0	2	.000	7.71	0	9⅓	16	13	8	5	7

RECORD AS HOCKEY PLAYER

CAREER NOTES: Selected by Winnipeg Jets in fourth round (64th pick overall) of National Hockey League entry draft (June 1981).

Year	Team (League)	Games	Goals	Assists	Points	Penalty Minutes
1983-84—Sherbrooke Jets (AHL)		78	10	12	22	21

McCLELLAN, PAUL
P, GIANTS

PERSONAL: Born February 8, 1966, at San Mateo, Calif. ... 6-2/180. ... Throws right, bats right. ... Full name: Paul William McClellan. **HIGH SCHOOL:** Sequoia (Calif.). **COLLEGE:** College of San Mateo (Calif.).

TRANSACTIONS/CAREER NOTES: Selected by Atlanta Braves organization in 25th round of free-agent draft (June 3, 1985). ... Selected by San Francisco Giants organization in secondary phase of free-agent draft (January 14, 1986). **STATISTICAL NOTES:** Led Texas League with 22 balks in 1988.

Year	Team (League)	G	W	L	Pct.	ERA	Sv.	IP	H	R	ER	BB	SO
1986 —Everett (Northwest)		13	5	4	.556	3.34	0	86⅓	71	39	32	46	74
1987 —Clinton (Midwest)		28	12	10	.545	3.25	0	177⅓	141	86	64	100	*209
1988 —Shreveport (Texas)		27	10	12	.455	4.04	0	167	146	89	75	62	128
1989 —Shreveport (Texas)		12	8	3	.727	2.24	0	84⅓	56	26	21	35	56
—Phoenix (Pacific Coast)		9	3	4	.429	4.92	0	56⅔	56	34	31	29	25
1990 —Phoenix (Pacific Coast)		28	7	*16	.304	5.17	0	172⅓	192	112	99	78	102
—San Francisco (N.L.)		4	0	1	.000	11.74	0	7⅔	14	10	10	6	2
1991 —Shreveport (Texas)		14	11	1	.917	2.82	0	95⅔	75	33	30	30	63
—Phoenix (Pacific Coast)		5	2	2	.500	2.82	0	38⅓	27	12	12	21	18
—San Francisco (N.L.)		13	3	6	.333	4.56	0	71	68	41	36	25	44
Major league totals (2 years)		17	3	7	.300	5.26	0	78⅔	82	51	46	31	46

McCLENDON, LLOYD

OF/1B, PIRATES

PERSONAL: Born January 11, 1959, at Gary, Ind. . . . 5-11/210. . . . Throws right, bats right. . . . Full name: Lloyd Glenn McClendon.
HIGH SCHOOL: Roosevelt (Gary, Ind.).
COLLEGE: Valparaiso.
TRANSACTIONS/CAREER NOTES: Selected by New York Mets organization in eighth round of free-agent draft (June 3, 1980). . . . On disabled list (April 4-27, 1982). . . . Traded by Mets organization with P Charlie Puleo and OF Jason Felice to Cincinnati Reds for P Tom Seaver (December 16, 1982). . . . Traded by Reds organization to Chicago Cubs for OF Rolando Roomes (December 9, 1988). . . . Traded by Cubs to Pittsburgh Pirates for a player to be named later (September 7, 1990); Cubs acquired P Mike Pomeranz to complete deal (September 28, 1990).

						BATTING							FIELDING			
Year	Team (League)	Pos.	G	AB	R	H	2B	3B	HR	RBI	Avg.	SB	PO	A	E	Avg.
1980 —Kingsport (Appalachian) ..		C	14	46	7	15	2	0	1	9	.326	0	19	5	3	.889
—Little Falls (N.Y.-Penn)		C	40	117	25	32	9	1	3	20	.274	2	203	20	7	.970
1981 —Lynchburg (Carolina)		C-3B	103	363	55	91	12	6	7	57	.251	3	437	74	17	.968
1982 —Lynchburg (Carolina)		C-3B	108	384	61	105	25	1	18	78	.273	4	492	87	15	.975
1983 —Waterbury (Eastern)■		C-3B-1B	123	434	58	114	19	2	15	57	.263	4	466	99	8	.986
1984 —Vermont (Eastern)		C-1-3-0	60	202	36	56	16	0	7	27	.277	2	174	24	3	.985
—Wichita (Am. Assoc.)		3B-1B-C	48	152	28	45	13	1	6	28	.296	2	143	45	4	.979
1985 —Denver (Am. Assoc.)		1-3-C-0	114	379	57	105	18	5	16	79	.277	4	470	104	17	.971
1986 —Denver (Am. Assoc.)		1-0-C-3	132	433	75	112	30	1	*24	88	.259	2	656	45	11	.985
1987 —Cincinnati (N.L.)		C-1-3-0	45	72	8	15	5	0	2	13	.208	1	80	5	2	.977
—Nashville (Am. Assoc.)		1B-C	26	84	11	24	6	0	3	14	.286	1	72	3	1	.987
1988 —Cincinnati (N.L.)		C-0-1-3	72	137	9	30	4	0	3	14	.219	4	197	13	4	.981
—Nashville (Am. Assoc.)		OF-C	2	7	0	1	0	0	0	0	.143	0	12	2	0	1.000
1989 —Iowa (American Assoc.)■.		1B-OF-C	34	109	18	35	10	0	4	13	.321	4	115	6	6	.953
—Chicago (N.L.)		0-1-3-C	92	259	47	74	12	1	12	40	.286	6	310	18	6	.982
1990 —Chicago-Pitts. (N.L.)■		OF-1B-C	53	110	6	18	3	0	2	12	.164	1	120	9	1	.992
—Iowa (American Assoc.) ...		1-3-0-C	25	91	14	26	2	0	2	10	.286	3	125	12	2	.986
1991 —Pittsburgh (N.L.)		OF-1B-C	85	163	24	47	7	0	7	24	.288	2	163	12	3	.983
Major league totals (5 years)			347	741	94	184	31	1	26	103	.248	14	870	57	16	.983

CHAMPIONSHIP SERIES RECORD

						BATTING							FIELDING			
Year	Team (League)	Pos.	G	AB	R	H	2B	3B	HR	RBI	Avg.	SB	PO	A	E	Avg.
1989 —Chicago (N.L.)		PH-C-OF	3	3	0	2	0	0	0	0	.667	0	3	0	0	1.000
1991 —Pittsburgh (N.L.)		PH-1B	3	2	0	0	0	0	0	0	.000	0	0	0	0	. . .
Championship Series totals (2 years)			6	5	0	2	0	0	0	0	.400	0	3	0	0	1.000

McCLURE, BOB

P, CARDINALS

PERSONAL: Born April 29, 1953, at Oakland, Calif. . . . 5-11/188. . . . Throws left, bats right. . . . Full name: Robert Craig McClure.
HIGH SCHOOL: Terra Nova (Pacifica, Calif.).
COLLEGE: College of San Mateo (Calif.).
TRANSACTIONS/CAREER NOTES: Selected by Los Angeles Dodgers organization in third round of free-agent draft (January 10, 1973). . . . Selected by Kansas City Royals organization in secondary phase of free-agent draft (June 5, 1973). . . . On Jacksonville disabled list (April 15-May 13 and June 5-July 25, 1975). . . . Traded by Royals to Milwaukee Brewers (March 15, 1977), completing deal in which Royals traded IF Jamie Quirk, OF Jim Wohlford and a player to be named later to Brewers for P Jim Colborn and C Darrell Porter (December 6, 1976). . . . On Milwaukee disabled list (March 28-September 1, 1981); included rehabilitation disability assignment to Burlington (August 7-24, 1981). . . . Granted free agency (November 10, 1982). . . . Re-signed by Brewers (December 6, 1982). . . . On disabled list (August 22-September 12, 1983). . . . Sold by Brewers to Montreal Expos (June 8, 1986). . . . Granted free agency (November 9, 1987). . . . Re-signed by Expos (December 7, 1987). . . . Released by Expos (July 2, 1988). . . . Signed by New York Mets (July 13, 1988). . . . Released by Mets (October 27, 1988). . . . Signed by California Angels (January 12, 1989). . . . On California disabled list (April 6-August 14, 1990); included rehabilitation disability assignment to Palm Springs (August 3-14, 1990). . . . On disabled list (March 26-April 19, 1991). . . . Released by Angels (June 16, 1991). . . . Signed by St. Louis Cardinals (June 24, 1991).
STATISTICAL NOTES: Tied for Pioneer League lead with three shutouts in 1973. . . . Led A.L. with six balks in 1983.

Year	Team (League)	G	W	L	Pct.	ERA	Sv.	IP	H	R	ER	BB	SO
1973 —Billings (Pioneer)		14	*10	2	.833	2.11	0	94	64	41	22	67	110
1974 —Omaha (American Assoc.)		21	5	8	.385	3.84	0	136	140	71	58	65	88

Year Team (League)	G	W	L	Pct.	ERA	Sv.	IP	H	R	ER	BB	SO
1975—Jacksonville (Southern)	9	3	2	.600	2.36	0	42	31	18	11	23	39
—Kansas City (A.L.)	12	1	0	1.000	0.00	1	15	4	0	0	14	15
1976—Omaha (American Assoc.)........	21	9	8	.529	2.98	0	133	133	61	44	41	91
—Kansas City (A.L.)	8	0	0	...	9.00	0	4	3	4	4	8	3
1977—Milwaukee (A.L.)■	68	2	1	.667	2.54	6	71	64	25	20	34	57
1978—Milwaukee (A.L.)	44	2	6	.250	3.74	9	65	53	30	27	30	47
1979—Milwaukee (A.L.)	36	5	2	.714	3.88	5	51	53	29	22	24	37
1980—Milwaukee (A.L.)	52	5	8	.385	3.07	10	91	83	34	31	37	47
1981—Burlington (Midwest)	4	0	2	.000	9.64	0	14	19	15	15	11	11
—Milwaukee (A.L.)	4	0	0	...	3.38	0	8	7	3	3	4	6
1982—Milwaukee (A.L.)	34	12	7	.632	4.22	0	172⅔	160	90	81	74	99
1983—Milwaukee (A.L.)	24	9	9	.500	4.50	0	142	152	75	71	68	68
1984—Milwaukee (A.L.)	39	4	8	.333	4.38	1	139⅔	154	76	68	52	68
1985—Milwaukee (A.L.)	38	4	1	.800	4.31	3	85⅔	91	43	41	30	57
1986—Milwaukee (A.L.)	13	2	1	.667	3.86	0	16⅓	18	7	7	10	11
—Montreal (N.L.)■	52	2	5	.286	3.02	6	62⅔	53	22	21	23	42
1987—Montreal (N.L.)	52	6	1	.857	3.44	5	52⅓	47	30	20	20	33
1988—Montreal-New York (N.L.)■......	33	2	3	.400	5.40	3	30	35	18	18	8	19
1989—California (A.L.)■	48	6	1	.857	1.55	3	52⅓	39	14	9	15	36
1990—Palm Springs (California)	2	0	0	...	0.00	0	3	0	0	0	1	6
—California (A.L.)	11	2	0	1.000	6.43	0	7	7	6	5	3	6
1991—California (A.L.)	13	0	0	...	9.31	0	9⅔	13	11	10	5	5
—St. Louis (N.L.)	32	1	1	.500	3.13	0	23	24	8	8	8	15
American League totals (15 years)	444	54	44	.551	3.86	38	930⅓	901	447	399	408	562
National League totals (4 years)	169	11	10	.524	3.59	14	168	159	78	67	59	109
Major league totals (17 years)	613	65	54	.546	3.82	52	1098⅓	1060	525	466	467	671

DIVISION SERIES RECORD

Year Team (League)	G	W	L	Pct.	ERA	Sv.	IP	H	R	ER	BB	SO
1981—Milwaukee (A.L.)	3	0	0	...	0.00	0	3⅓	4	0	0	0	2

CHAMPIONSHIP SERIES RECORD

Year Team (League)	G	W	L	Pct.	ERA	Sv.	IP	H	R	ER	BB	SO
1982—Milwaukee (A.L.)	1	1	0	1.000	0.00	0	1⅔	2	0	0	0	0

WORLD SERIES RECORD

Year Team (League)	G	W	L	Pct.	ERA	Sv.	IP	H	R	ER	BB	SO
1982—Milwaukee (A.L.)	5	0	2	.000	4.15	2	4⅓	5	2	2	3	5

McCRAY, RODNEY
OF, METS

PERSONAL: Born September 13, 1963, at Detroit. . . . 5-10/175. . . . Throws right, bats right. . . . Full name: Rodney Duncan McCray.
COLLEGE: Santa Monica College (Calif.) and West Los Angeles College (Calif.).
TRANSACTIONS/CAREER NOTES: Selected by Chicago White Sox organization in first round (13th pick overall) of free-agent draft (January 12, 1982). . . . Selected by Oakland A's organization in secondary phase of free-agent draft (June 7, 1982). . . . Selected by Los Angeles Dodgers organization in secondary phase of free-agent draft (January 11, 1983). . . . Selected by San Diego Padres organization in ninth round of free-agent draft (January 17, 1984). . . . Drafted by White Sox organization (December 8, 1987). . . . On Vancouver disabled list (June 29-July 15, 1991). . . . Granted free agency (October 7, 1991). . . . Signed by New York Mets (December 13, 1991).
STATISTICAL NOTES: Led South Atlantic League in caught stealing with 32 in 1986. . . . Led California League outfielders with 271 total chances in 1987. . . . Led Florida State League with 96 bases on balls received in 1989. . . . Tied for Pacific Coast League lead in double plays by outfielders with five in 1991.

						—BATTING—							—FIELDING—		
Year Team (League)	Pos.	G	AB	R	H	2B	3B	HR	RBI	Avg.	SB	PO	A	E	Avg.
1984—Spokane (Northwest)	OF	71	244	40	50	6	1	1	20	.205	25	124	★13	4	.972
1985—Charleston, S.C. (S. Atl.) ...	OF	117	373	81	77	8	1	1	27	.206	49	177	13	13	.936
1986—Charleston, S.C. (S. Atl.) ...	OF	123	417	88	107	13	3	4	33	.257	★81	271	★17	6	.980
1987—Reno (California)	OF	117	413	69	87	11	5	0	26	.211	★65	★251	13	7	.974
1988—South Bend (Midwest)■ ..	OF	107	306	48	65	10	2	1	24	.212	55	218	15	10	.959
1989—Sarasota (Florida State) ...	OF	124	422	81	112	19	4	1	34	.265	44	296	9	4	★.987
1990—Birmingham (Southern)	OF	60	188	36	37	2	2	1	16	.197	26	156	8	4	.976
—Chicago (A.L.)	OF	32	6	4	0	0	0	0	0	.000	6	8	0	0	1.000
—Vancouver (Pac. Coast)....	OF	19	53	7	12	4	2	0	6	.226	4	50	4	2	.964
1991—Vancouver (Pac. Coast)....	OF	83	222	37	51	9	5	0	13	.230	14	186	8	3	.985
—Chicago (A.L.)	OF	17	7	2	2	0	0	0	0	.286	1	10	0	0	1.000
Major league totals (2 years)		49	13	10	2	0	0	0	0	.154	7	18	0	0	1.000

McDANIEL, TERRY
OF, PIRATES

PERSONAL: Born December 6, 1966, at Kansas City, Mo. . . . 5-9/205. . . . Throws right, bats right. . . . Full name: Terrence Keith McDaniel.
HIGH SCHOOL: Southeast (Kansas City, Mo.).
TRANSACTIONS/CAREER NOTES: Selected by New York Mets organization in sixth round of free-agent draft (January 14, 1986). . . . On disabled list (June 7-17, 1989; and May 17-June 5, July 15-August 8 and Au-

gust 12, 1990-remainder of season).... On Tidewater disabled list (April 10-19, 1991).... Claimed on waivers by Pittsburgh Pirates (November 19, 1991).

STATISTICAL NOTES: Tied for New York-Pennsylvania League lead in double plays by outfielders with three in 1987.... Led South Atlantic League batters with 173 strikeouts in 1988.... Led Florida State League outfielders with five double plays in 1989.

MISCELLANEOUS: Batted as switch-hitter (1987).

Year Team (League)	Pos.	G	AB	R	H	2B	3B	HR	RBI	Avg.	SB	PO	A	E	Avg.
1986—Kingsport (Appalachian) ..	OF	41	114	24	28	5	1	6	21	.246	14	68	*11	3	.963
1987—Little Falls (N.Y.-Penn)	OF	70	237	51	57	4	2	5	31	.241	20	101	*15	*9	.928
1988—Columbia (S. Atlantic).......	OF	127	449	76	111	16	6	5	43	.247	41	211	7	11	.952
—St. Lucie (Florida State)....	OF	4	12	1	3	0	0	0	0	.250	0	5	0	1	.833
1989—St. Lucie (Florida State).....	OF	105	351	70	81	17	11	7	43	.231	43	214	*16	4	.983
1990—Jackson (Texas)	OF	67	234	34	67	14	2	5	37	.286	19	129	3	4	.971
1991—Tidewater (Int'l)	OF	118	399	63	99	23	6	9	42	.248	18	207	8	9	.960
—New York (N.L.)	OF	23	29	3	6	1	0	0	2	.207	2	18	0	0	1.000
Major league totals (1 year)...........................		23	29	3	6	1	0	0	2	.207	2	18	0	0	1.000

McDONALD, BEN
P, ORIOLES

PERSONAL: Born November 24, 1967, at Baton Rouge, La.... 6-7/214.... Throws right, bats right.... Full name: Larry Benard McDonald.
HIGH SCHOOL: Denham Springs (La.).
COLLEGE: Louisiana State.

TRANSACTIONS/CAREER NOTES: Selected by Atlanta Braves organization in 27th round of free-agent draft (June 2, 1986).... Selected by Baltimore Orioles organization in first round (first pick overall) of free-agent draft (June 5, 1989).... On Baltimore disabled list (April 6-May 22, 1990); included rehabilitation disability assignment to Hagerstown (April 24-29 and May 14, 1990) and Rochester (April 30-May 13 and May 15-21, 1990).... On Baltimore disabled list (March 29-April 19 and May 23-July 1, 1991); included rehabilitation disability assignment to Rochester (June 19-July 1, 1991).
RECORDS/HONORS: Named College Player of the Year by THE SPORTING NEWS (1989).... Named righthanded pitcher on THE SPORTING NEWS college All-America team (1989).
MISCELLANEOUS: Member of 1988 U.S. Olympic baseball team.

Year Team (League)	G	W	L	Pct.	ERA	Sv.	IP	H	R	ER	BB	SO
1989—Frederick (Carolina).................	2	0	0	...	2.00	0	9	10	2	2	0	9
—Baltimore (A.L.)........................	6	1	0	1.000	8.59	0	7⅓	8	7	7	4	3
1990—Hagerstown (Eastern)	3	0	1	.000	6.55	0	11	11	8	8	3	15
—Rochester (International)	7	3	3	.500	2.86	0	44	33	18	14	21	37
—Baltimore (A.L.)........................	21	8	5	.615	2.43	0	118⅔	88	36	32	35	65
1991—Baltimore (A.L.)........................	21	6	8	.429	4.84	0	126⅓	126	71	68	43	85
—Rochester (International)	2	0	1	.000	7.71	0	7	10	7	6	5	7
Major league totals (3 years)	48	15	13	.536	3.82	0	252⅓	222	114	107	82	153

McDOWELL, JACK
P, WHITE SOX

PERSONAL: Born January 16, 1966, at Van Nuys, Calif.... 6-5/180.... Throws right, bats right.... Full name: Jack Burns McDowell.
HIGH SCHOOL: Notre Dame (Van Nuys, Calif.).
COLLEGE: Stanford.

TRANSACTIONS/CAREER NOTES: Selected by Boston Red Sox organization in 20th round of free-agent draft (June 4, 1984).... Selected by Chicago White Sox organization in first round (fifth pick overall) of free-agent draft (June 2, 1987).... On suspended list (August 20-24, 1991).
STATISTICAL NOTES: Tied for A.L. lead in games started by pitcher with 35 in 1991.

Year Team (League)	G	W	L	Pct.	ERA	Sv.	IP	H	R	ER	BB	SO
1987—Sarasota White Sox (GCL)........	2	0	1	.000	2.57	0	7	4	3	2	1	12
—Birmingham (Southern)	4	1	2	.333	7.84	0	20⅔	19	20	18	8	17
—Chicago (A.L.)	4	3	0	1.000	1.93	0	28	16	6	6	6	15
1988—Chicago (A.L.)	26	5	10	.333	3.97	0	158⅔	147	85	70	68	84
1989—Vancouver (Pacific Coast)	16	5	6	.455	6.13	0	86⅔	97	60	59	50	65
—Sarasota White Sox (GCL)........	4	2	0	1.000	0.75	0	24	19	2	2	4	25
1990—Chicago (A.L.)	33	14	9	.609	3.82	0	205	189	93	87	77	165
1991—Chicago (A.L.)	35	17	10	.630	3.41	0	253⅔	212	97	96	82	191
Major league totals (4 years)	98	39	29	.574	3.61	0	645⅓	564	281	259	233	455

ALL-STAR GAME RECORD

Year League	W	L	Pct.	ERA	Sv.	IP	H	R	ER	BB	SO
1991—American	0	0	...	0.00	0	2	1	0	0	2	0

McDOWELL, ROGER
P, DODGERS

PERSONAL: Born December 21, 1960, at Cincinnati.... 6-1/182.... Throws right, bats right.... Full name: Roger Alan McDowell.
HIGH SCHOOL: Colerain (Cincinnati).
COLLEGE: Bowling Green State.

TRANSACTIONS/CAREER NOTES: Selected by New York Mets organization in third round of free-agent draft (June 7, 1982).... On disabled list (April 10-August 14, 1984 and March 29-May 14, 1987).... Traded by Mets with OF Lenny Dykstra and a player to be named later to Philadelphia Phillies for OF Juan Samuel (June 18, 1989); Phillies organization acquired P Tom Edens to complete deal (July 27, 1989).... On disabled list (July 1-18, 1991).... Traded by Phillies to Los Angeles Dodgers for P Mike Hartley and OF Braulio Castillo (July 31, 1991).

MISCELLANEOUS: Appeared as outfielder in one game with no chances (1986) and two games with no chances (1991).

Year	Team (League)	G	W	L	Pct.	ERA	Sv.	IP	H	R	ER	BB	SO
1982 —Shelby (South Atlantic)	12	6	4	.600	3.28	0	71⅓	61	34	26	30	40
—Lynchburg (Carolina)	4	2	0	1.000	2.15	0	29½	26	12	7	11	23
1983 —Jackson (Texas)	27	11	12	.478	4.86	0	172⅓	203	111	93	71	115
1984 —Jackson (Texas)	3	0	0	...	3.68	0	7⅓	9	3	3	1	8
1985 —New York (N.L.)	62	6	5	.545	2.83	17	127⅓	108	43	40	37	70
1986 —New York (N.L.)	75	14	9	.609	3.02	22	128	107	48	43	42	65
1987 —New York (N.L.)	56	7	5	.583	4.16	25	88⅔	95	41	41	28	32
1988 —New York (N.L.)	62	5	5	.500	2.63	16	89	80	31	26	31	46
1989 —New York-Philadelphia (N.L.)■.	69	4	8	.333	1.96	23	92	79	36	20	38	47
1990 —Philadelphia (N.L.)	72	6	8	.429	3.86	22	86⅓	92	41	37	35	39
1991 —Phil.-Los Angeles (N.L.)■	71	9	9	.500	2.93	10	101⅓	100	40	33	48	50
Major league totals (7 years)	**467**	**51**	**49**	**.510**	**3.03**	**135**	**712⅔**	**661**	**280**	**240**	**259**	**349**

CHAMPIONSHIP SERIES RECORD

Year	Team (League)	G	W	L	Pct.	ERA	Sv.	IP	H	R	ER	BB	SO
1986 —New York (N.L.)	2	0	0	...	0.00	0	7	1	0	0	0	3
1988 —New York (N.L.)	4	0	1	.000	4.50	0	6	6	3	3	2	5
Championship Series totals (2 years)	**6**	**0**	**1**	**.000**	**2.08**	**0**	**13**	**7**	**3**	**3**	**2**	**8**

WORLD SERIES RECORD

Year	Team (League)	G	W	L	Pct.	ERA	Sv.	IP	H	R	ER	BB	SO
1986 —New York (N.L.)	5	1	0	1.000	4.91	0	7⅓	10	5	4	6	2

McELROY, CHUCK
P, CUBS

PERSONAL: Born October 1, 1967, at Galveston, Tex.... 6-0/160.... Throws left, bats left.... Full name: Charles Dwayne McElroy.
HIGH SCHOOL: Lincoln (Port Arthur, Tex.).
TRANSACTIONS/CAREER NOTES: Selected by Philadelphia Phillies organization in eighth round of free-agent draft (June 2, 1986).... Traded by Phillies with P Bob Scanlon to Chicago Cubs for P Mitch Williams (April 7, 1991).

Year	Team (League)	G	W	L	Pct.	ERA	Sv.	IP	H	R	ER	BB	SO
1986 —Utica (New York-Penn)	14	4	6	.400	2.95	0	94⅔	85	40	31	28	91
1987 —Spartanburg (South Atlantic) ..	24	14	4	.778	3.11	0	130⅓	117	51	45	48	115
—Clearwater (Florida State)	2	1	0	1.000	0.00	0	7⅓	1	1	0	4	7
1988 —Reading (Eastern)	28	9	12	.429	4.50	0	160	•173	89	∗80	70	92
1989 —Reading (Eastern)	32	3	1	.750	2.68	12	47	39	14	14	14	39
—Scranton/Wilkes-Barre (Int'l) ..	14	1	2	.333	2.93	3	15⅓	13	6	5	11	12
—Philadelphia (N.L.)	11	0	0	...	1.74	0	10⅓	12	2	2	4	8
1990 —Scranton/Wilkes-Barre (Int'l) ..	57	6	8	.429	2.72	7	76	62	24	23	34	78
—Philadelphia (N.L.)	16	0	1	.000	7.71	0	14	24	13	12	10	16
1991 —Chicago (N.L.)■	71	6	2	.750	1.95	3	101⅓	73	33	22	57	92
Major league totals (3 years)	**98**	**6**	**3**	**.667**	**2.58**	**3**	**125⅔**	**109**	**48**	**36**	**71**	**116**

McGAFFIGAN, ANDY
P

PERSONAL: Born October 25, 1956, at West Palm Beach, Fla.... 6-3/190.... Throws right, bats right.... Full name: Andrew Joseph McGaffigan.
HIGH SCHOOL: Twin Lakes (West Palm Beach, Fla.).
COLLEGE: Palm Beach Junior College (Fla.) and Florida Southern (received degree, 1978).
TRANSACTIONS/CAREER NOTES: Selected by Cincinnati Reds organization in 36th round of free-agent draft (June 5, 1974).... Selected by Chicago White Sox organization in fifth round of free-agent draft (January 7, 1976).... Selected by New York Yankees organization in sixth round of free-agent draft (June 6, 1978).... On disabled list (September 1-22, 1980).... On Columbus disabled list (April 10-June 14, 1981).... Traded by Yankees with OF Ted Wilborn to San Francisco Giants organization for P Doyle Alexander (March 30, 1982).... On Phoenix disabled list (June 20-August 13, 1982).... Traded by Giants to Montreal Expos (March 31, 1984) as compensation for the injury P Fred Breining arrived with in earlier trade. Giants had traded Breining and OF Max Venable to Expos for 1B Al Oliver (February 27, 1984); Breining remained with Expos.... Traded by Expos with P Jim Jefferson to Cincinnati Reds for 1B Dan Driessen (July 26, 1984).... Traded by Reds with P Jay Tibbs, P John Stuper and C Dann Bilardello to Expos for P Bill Gullickson and C Sal Butera (December 19, 1985).... On disabled list (June 15-July 2, 1988 and August 18-September 2, 1989).... Traded by Expos to Giants for a player to be named later (April 7, 1990).... Expos organization acquired IF Steve Hecht to complete deal (June 26, 1990).... Released by Giants (April 25, 1990).... Signed by Omaha, Kansas City Royals organization (May 9, 1990).... Granted free agency (November 5, 1990).... Re-signed by Royals (December 8, 1990).... Released by Royals (July 16, 1991).... Signed by Milwaukee Brewers organization (August 4, 1991).... Granted free agency (October 15, 1991).
RECORDS/HONORS: Named Southern League Pitcher of the Year (1980).

Year	Team (League)	G	W	L	Pct.	ERA	Sv.	IP	H	R	ER	BB	SO
1978 —Oneonta (New York-Penn)	2	0	1	.000	4.50	0	12	14	8	6	9	13
—Fort Lauderdale (Florida St.)	11	4	5	.444	2.86	1	66	45	28	21	20	36
1979 —West Haven (Eastern)	23	10	6	.625	3.81	0	144	136	75	61	54	113

Year	Team (League)	G	W	L	Pct.	ERA	Sv.	IP	H	R	ER	BB	SO
1980	—Nashville (Southern)	31	15	5	.750	*2.38	0	170	139	62	45	62	125
1981	—Columbus (International)	17	8	6	.571	3.23	0	103	85	45	37	37	57
	—New York (A.L.)	2	0	0	...	2.57	0	7	5	3	2	3	2
1982	—Phoenix (Pacific Coast)■	18	1	6	.143	6.00	0	96	115	72	64	51	64
	—San Francisco (N.L.)	4	1	0	1.000	0.00	0	8	5	1	0	1	4
1983	—San Francisco (N.L.)	43	3	9	.250	4.29	2	134⅓	131	67	64	39	93
1984	—Montreal-Cincinnati (N.L.)■	30	3	6	.333	3.52	1	69	60	28	27	23	57
1985	—Denver (American Assoc.)	26	11	5	.688	2.95	2	106⅔	105	43	35	37	91
	—Cincinnati (N.L.)	15	3	3	.500	3.72	0	94⅓	88	40	39	30	83
1986	—Montreal (N.L.)■	48	10	5	.667	2.65	2	142⅔	114	49	42	55	104
1987	—Montreal (N.L.)	69	5	2	.714	2.39	12	120⅓	105	38	32	42	100
1988	—Montreal (N.L.)	63	6	0	1.000	2.76	4	91⅓	81	31	28	37	71
1989	—Montreal (N.L.)	57	3	5	.375	4.68	2	75	85	40	39	30	40
1990	—San Francisco (N.L.)■	4	0	0	...	17.36	0	4⅔	10	9	9	4	4
	—Omaha (American Assoc.)■	10	2	1	.667	3.71	3	17	22	7	7	5	17
	—Kansas City (A.L.)	24	4	3	.571	3.09	1	78⅓	75	40	27	28	49
1991	—Omaha-Denver (Am. Assoc.)■.	33	0	2	.000	3.58	7	65⅓	72	33	26	26	45
	—Kansas City (A.L.)	4	0	0	...	4.50	0	8	14	5	4	2	3
American League totals (3 years)		30	4	3	.571	3.17	1	93⅔	94	48	33	33	54
National League totals (9 years)		333	34	30	.531	3.41	23	739⅔	679	303	280	261	556
Major league totals (11 years)		363	38	33	.535	3.38	24	833⅓	773	351	313	294	610

McGEE, WILLIE
OF, GIANTS

PERSONAL: Born November 2, 1958, at San Francisco. . . . 6-1/195. . . . Throws right, bats both. . . . Full name: Willie Dean McGee.
HIGH SCHOOL: Ellis (Richmond, Calif.).
COLLEGE: Diablo Valley College (Calif.).

TRANSACTIONS/CAREER NOTES: Selected by Chicago White Sox organization in seventh round of free-agent draft (June 8, 1976). . . . Selected by New York Yankees organization in secondary phase of free-agent draft (January 11, 1977). . . . On disabled list (May 22-June 7 and July 14-August 7, 1980; and April 24-June 4, 1981). . . . Traded by Yankees organization to St. Louis Cardinals organization for P Bob Sykes (October 21, 1981). . . . On Louisville disabled list (April 13-23, 1982). . . . On St. Louis disabled list (March 30-April 29, 1983); included rehabilitation disability assignment to Arkansas (April 18-29, 1983). . . . On disabled list (July 12-27, 1984 and August 3-27, 1986). . . . On disabled list (June 7-July 18 and July 26-August 14, 1989); included rehabilitation disability assignment to Louisville (July 8-18, 1989). . . . Traded by Cardinals to Oakland Athletics for OF Felix Jose, 3B Stan Royer and P Daryl Green (August 29, 1990). . . . Granted free agency (November 5, 1990). . . . Signed by San Francisco Giants (December 3, 1990). . . . On San Francisco disabled list (July 12-August 1, 1991); included rehabilitation disability assignment to Phoenix (July 28-August 1, 1991).
RECORDS/HONORS: Holds modern N.L. single-season record for highest batting average by switch-hitter (100 or more games)—.353 (1985). . . . Shares major league single-season record for fewest double plays by outfielder who led league in double plays—3 (1991). . . . Won N.L. Gold Glove as outfielder (1983, 1985-86). . . . Named N.L. Player of the Year by THE SPORTING NEWS (1985). . . . Named outfielder on THE SPORTING NEWS N.L. All-Star team (1985). . . . Named outfielder on THE SPORTING NEWS N.L. Silver Slugger team (1985). . . . Named N.L. Most Valuable Player by Baseball Writers' Association of America (1985).
STATISTICAL NOTES: Hit for the cycle (June 23, 1984). . . . Led N.L. in grounding into double plays with 24 in 1987. . . . Tied for N.L. lead in double plays by outfielders with three in 1991.

							—BATTING—							—FIELDING—		
Year	Team (League)	Pos.	G	AB	R	H	2B	3B	HR	RBI	Avg.	SB	PO	A	E	Avg.
1977	—Oneonta (N.Y.-Penn)	OF	65	225	31	53	4	3	2	22	.236	13	103	5	10	.915
1978	—Fort Lauderdale (FSL)	OF	124	423	62	106	6	6	0	37	.251	25	243	12	9	.966
1979	—West Haven (Eastern)	OF	49	115	21	28	3	1	1	8	.243	7	88	3	3	.968
	—Fort Lauderdale (FSL)	OF	46	176	25	56	8	3	1	18	.318	16	103	3	2	.981
1980	—Nashville (Southern)	OF	78	223	35	63	4	5	1	22	.283	7	127	6	6	.957
1981	—Nashville (Southern)	OF	100	388	77	125	20	5	7	63	.322	24	203	10	6	.973
1982	—Louisville (Am. Assoc.)■..	OF	13	55	11	16	2	2	1	3	.291	5	40	0	1	.976
	—St. Louis (N.L.)	OF	123	422	43	125	12	8	4	56	.296	24	245	3	11	.958
1983	—St. Louis (N.L.)	OF	147	601	75	172	22	8	5	75	.286	39	385	7	5	.987
	—Arkansas (Texas)	OF	7	29	5	8	1	1	0	2	.276	1	7	0	0	1.000
1984	—St. Louis (N.L.)	OF	145	571	82	166	19	11	6	50	.291	43	374	10	6	.985
1985	—St. Louis (N.L.)	OF	152	612	114	*216	26	*18	10	82	*.353	56	382	11	9	.978
1986	—St. Louis (N.L.)	OF	124	497	65	127	22	7	7	48	.256	19	325	9	3	*.991
1987	—St. Louis (N.L.)	OF-SS	153	620	76	177	37	11	11	105	.285	16	354	10	7	.981
1988	—St. Louis (N.L.)	OF	137	562	73	164	24	6	3	50	.292	41	348	9	9	.975
1989	—St. Louis (N.L.)	OF	58	199	23	47	10	2	3	17	.236	8	118	2	3	.976
	—Louisville (Am. Assoc.)	OF	8	27	5	11	4	0	0	4	.407	3	20	1	1	.955
1990	—St. Louis (N.L.)	OF	125	501	76	168	32	5	3	62	*.335	28	341	13	*16	.957
	—Oakland (A.L.)■	OF	29	113	23	31	3	2	0	15	.274	3	72	1	1	.986
1991	—San Francisco (N.L.)■	OF	131	497	67	155	30	3	4	43	.312	17	259	6	6	.978
	—Phoenix (Pacific Coast)	OF	4	10	4	5	1	0	0	1	.500	2	10	0	1	.909
American League totals (1 year)			29	113	23	31	3	2	0	15	.274	3	72	1	1	.986
National League totals (10 years)			1295	5082	694	1517	234	79	56	588	.299	291	3131	80	75	.977
Major league totals (10 years)			1324	5195	717	1548	237	81	56	603	.298	294	3203	81	76	.977

CHAMPIONSHIP SERIES RECORD
CHAMPIONSHIP SERIES NOTES: Shares single-series records for most triples—2 (1982); most times caught stealing—3 (1985). . . . Holds N.L. career record for most triples—3. . . . Shares N.L. career record for most times caught stealing—4.

Year Team (League)	Pos.	G	AB	R	H	2B	3B	HR	RBI	Avg.	SB	PO	A	E	Avg.
1982—St. Louis (N.L.)	OF	3	13	4	4	0	2	1	5	.308	0	12	0	1	.923
1985—St. Louis (N.L.)	OF	6	26	6	7	1	0	0	3	.269	2	18	0	0	1.000
1987—St. Louis (N.L.)	OF	7	26	2	8	1	1	0	2	.308	0	16	0	0	1.000
1990—Oakland (A.L.)	OF-PR-DH	3	9	3	2	1	0	0	0	.222	2	2	0	0	1.000
Championship Series totals (4 years)		19	74	15	21	3	3	1	10	.284	4	48	0	1	.980

WORLD SERIES RECORD

Year Team (League)	Pos.	G	AB	R	H	2B	3B	HR	RBI	Avg.	SB	PO	A	E	Avg.
1982—St. Louis (N.L.)	OF	6	25	6	6	0	0	2	5	.240	2	24	0	0	1.000
1985—St. Louis (N.L.)	OF	7	27	2	7	2	0	1	2	.259	1	15	0	0	1.000
1987—St. Louis (N.L.)	OF	7	27	2	10	2	0	0	4	.370	0	21	1	1	.957
1990—Oakland (A.L.)	OF-PH	4	10	1	2	1	0	0	0	.200	1	5	0	0	1.000
World Series totals (4 years)		24	89	11	25	5	0	3	11	.281	4	65	1	1	.985

ALL-STAR GAME RECORD

Year League	Pos.	AB	R	H	2B	3B	HR	RBI	Avg.	SB	PO	A	E	Avg.
1983—National	OF	2	0	1	0	0	0	0	.500	0	2	0	0	1.000
1985—National	OF	2	0	1	1	0	0	2	.500	0	1	0	0	1.000
1987—National	OF	4	0	0	0	0	0	0	.000	0	2	0	0	1.000
1988—National	PR-OF	2	0	0	0	0	0	0	.000	0	1	0	0	1.000
All-Star Game totals (4 years)		10	0	2	1	0	0	2	.200	0	6	0	0	1.000

McGRIFF, FRED
1B, PADRES

PERSONAL: Born October 31, 1963, at Tampa, Fla.... 6-3/210.... Throws left, bats left.... Full name: Frederick Stanley McGriff.
HIGH SCHOOL: Jefferson (Tampa, Fla.).
TRANSACTIONS/CAREER NOTES: Selected by New York Yankees organization in ninth round of free-agent draft (June 8, 1981).... Traded by Yankees organization with OF Dave Collins, P Mike Morgan and cash to Toronto Blue Jays for OF-C Tom Dodd and P Dale Murray (December 9, 1982).... On disabled list (June 5-August 14, 1985).... Traded by Blue Jays with SS Tony Fernandez to San Diego Padres for OF Joe Carter and 2B Roberto Alomar (December 5, 1990).
RECORDS/HONORS: Shares major league record for most grand slams in two consecutive games—2 (August 13 and 14, 1991). ... Named first baseman on THE SPORTING NEWS A.L. All-Star team (1989).... Named first baseman on THE SPORTING NEWS A.L. Silver Slugger team (1989).
STATISTICAL NOTES: Led Gulf Coast League with 48 bases on balls received in 1982.... Led International League first basemen with .992 fielding percentage, 1,219 putouts, 85 assists, 1,314 total chances and 108 double plays in 1986.... Tied for International League lead with eight intentional bases on balls received and grounding into double plays with 16 in 1986.... Led A.L. first basemen with 1,592 total chances and 148 double plays in 1989.... Led N.L. with 26 intentional base on balls received in 1991.

Year Team (League)	Pos.	G	AB	R	H	2B	3B	HR	RBI	Avg.	SB	PO	A	E	Avg.
1981—Braden. Yankeees (GCL)...	1B	29	81	6	12	2	0	0	9	.148	0	176	8	7	.963
1982—Braden. Yankeees (GCL)...	1B	62	217	38	59	11	1	★9	●41	.272	6	514	★56	8	.986
1983—Florence (S. Atlantic)■......	1B	33	119	26	37	3	1	7	26	.311	3	250	14	6	.978
—Kinston (Carolina)......	1B	94	350	53	85	14	1	21	57	.243	3	784	57	10	.988
1984—Knoxville (Southern)	1B	56	189	29	47	13	2	9	25	.249	0	481	45	10	.981
—Syracuse (International) ..	1B	70	238	28	56	10	1	13	28	.235	0	644	45	3	.996
1985—Syracuse (International) ..	1B	51	176	19	40	8	2	5	20	.227	0	433	37	5	.989
1986—Syracuse (International) ..	1B-OF	133	468	69	121	23	4	19	74	.259	0	†1219	†85	10	†.992
—Toronto (A.L.)	1B	3	5	1	1	0	0	0	0	.200	0	3	0	0	1.000
1987—Toronto (A.L.)	1B	107	295	58	73	16	0	20	43	.247	3	108	7	2	.983
1988—Toronto (A.L.)	1B	154	536	100	151	35	4	34	82	.282	6	1344	93	5	★.997
1989—Toronto (A.L.)	1B	161	551	98	148	27	3	★36	92	.269	7	1460	115	★17	.989
1990—Toronto (A.L.)	1B	153	557	91	167	21	1	35	88	.300	5	1246	126	6	.996
1991—San Diego (N.L.)■............	1B	153	528	84	147	19	1	31	106	.278	4	1370	87	14	.990
American League totals (5 years)		578	1944	348	540	99	8	125	305	.278	21	4161	341	30	.993
National League totals (1 year)		153	528	84	147	19	1	31	106	.278	4	1370	87	14	.990
Major league totals (6 years)		731	2472	432	687	118	9	156	411	.278	25	5531	428	44	.993

CHAMPIONSHIP SERIES RECORD

Year Team (League)	Pos.	G	AB	R	H	2B	3B	HR	RBI	Avg.	SB	PO	A	E	Avg.
1989—Toronto (A.L.)	1B	5	21	1	3	0	0	0	3	.143	0	35	2	1	.974

McGWIRE, MARK
1B, ATHLETICS

PERSONAL: Born October 1, 1963, at Pomona, Calif.... 6-5/225.... Throws right, bats right.... Full name: Mark David McGwire.
HIGH SCHOOL: Damien (Claremont, Calif.).
COLLEGE: Southern California.
TRANSACTIONS/CAREER NOTES: Selected by Montreal Expos organization in eighth round of free-agent draft (June 8, 1981)....

Selected by Oakland A's organization in first round (10th pick overall) of free-agent draft (June 4, 1984).... On disabled list (April 11-26, 1989).

RECORDS/HONORS: Holds major league rookie-season records for most home runs—49; extra bases on long hits—183 (1987). ... Shares major league record for most home runs in two consecutive games—5 (June 27 and 28, 1987).... Shares modern major league record for most runs in two consecutive games—9 (June 27 and 28, 1987).... Holds A.L. rookie season record for highest slugging percentage—.618 (1987).... Named College Player of the Year by THE SPORTING NEWS (1984).... Named first baseman on THE SPORTING NEWS college All-America team (1984).... Named A.L. Rookie Player of the Year by THE SPORTING NEWS (1987).... Won A.L. Gold Glove at first base (1990).... Named A.L. Rookie of the Year by Baseball Writers' Association of America (1987).

STATISTICAL NOTES: Led California League third basemen with 239 assists and 354 total chances in 1985.... Hit three home runs in a game (June 27, 1987).... Led A.L. with .618 slugging percentage in 1987.... Led A.L. with 110 bases on balls received in 1990.... Led A.L. first basemen with 1,429 total chances in 1990.

MISCELLANEOUS: Member of 1984 U.S. Olympic baseball team.

Year	Team (League)	Pos.	G	AB	R	H	2B	3B	HR	RBI	Avg.	SB	PO	A	E	Avg.
1984 —Modesto (California)	1B	16	55	7	11	3	0	1	1	.200	0	107	6	1	.991
1985 —Modesto (California)	3B-1B	138	489	95	134	23	3	•24	•106	.274	1	105	†240	33	.913
1986 —Huntsville (Southern)	3B	55	195	40	59	15	0	10	53	.303	3	34	124	16	.908
—Tacoma (Pacific Coast)	3B	78	280	42	89	21	5	13	59	.318	1	53	126	25	.877
—Oakland (A.L.)	3B	18	53	10	10	1	0	3	9	.189	0	10	20	6	.833
1987 —Oakland (A.L.)	1B-3B-0F	151	557	97	161	28	4	•49	118	.289	1	1176	101	13	.990
1988 —Oakland (A.L.)	1B-0F	155	550	87	143	22	1	32	99	.260	0	1228	88	9	.993
1989 —Oakland (A.L.)	1B	143	490	74	113	17	0	33	95	.231	1	1170	114	6	.995
1990 —Oakland (A.L.)	1B	156	523	87	123	16	0	39	108	.235	2	•1329	95	5	.997
1991 —Oakland (A.L.)	1B	154	483	62	97	22	0	22	75	.201	2	1191	•101	4	.997
Major league totals (6 years)		777	2656	417	647	106	5	178	504	.244	6	6104	519	43	.994

CHAMPIONSHIP SERIES RECORD

Year	Team (League)	Pos.	G	AB	R	H	2B	3B	HR	RBI	Avg.	SB	PO	A	E	Avg.
1988 —Oakland (A.L.)	1B	4	15	4	5	0	0	1	3	.333	0	24	2	0	1.000
1989 —Oakland (A.L.)	1B	5	18	3	7	1	0	1	3	.389	0	46	1	1	.979
1990 —Oakland (A.L.)	1B	4	13	2	2	0	0	0	2	.154	0	40	0	0	1.000
Championship Series totals (3 years)		13	46	9	14	1	0	2	8	.304	0	110	3	1	.991

WORLD SERIES RECORD

Year	Team (League)	Pos.	G	AB	R	H	2B	3B	HR	RBI	Avg.	SB	PO	A	E	Avg.
1988 —Oakland (A.L.)	1B	5	17	1	1	0	0	1	1	.059	0	40	3	0	1.000
1989 —Oakland (A.L.)	1B	4	17	0	5	1	0	0	1	.294	0	28	2	0	1.000
1990 —Oakland (A.L.)	1B	4	14	1	3	0	0	0	0	.214	0	42	1	2	.956
World Series totals (3 years)		13	48	2	9	1	0	1	2	.188	0	110	6	2	.983

ALL-STAR GAME RECORD

ALL-STAR GAME NOTES: Named to A.L. All-Star team for 1991 game; replaced due to injury by Rafael Palmeiro.

Year	League	Pos.	AB	R	H	2B	3B	HR	RBI	Avg.	SB	PO	A	E	Avg.
1987 —American	1B	3	0	0	0	0	0	0	.000	0	7	0	1	.875
1988 —American	1B	2	0	1	0	0	0	0	.500	0	8	0	0	1.000
1989 —American	1B	3	0	1	0	0	0	0	.333	0	5	0	0	1.000
1990 —American	1B	2	0	0	0	0	0	0	.000	0	7	0	0	1.000
All-Star Game totals (4 years)		10	0	2	0	0	0	0	.200	0	27	0	1	.964

McINTOSH, TIM

1B/OF, BREWERS

PERSONAL: Born March 21, 1965, at Crystal, Minn. ... 5-11/195. ... Throws right, bats right.... Full name: Timothy Allen McIntosh.

HIGH SCHOOL: Hopkins (Minnetonka, Minn.).

COLLEGE: Minnesota.

TRANSACTIONS/CAREER NOTES: Selected by Milwaukee Brewers organization in third round of free-agent draft (June 2, 1986). ... On Denver disabled list (July 22-29, 1991).

STATISTICAL NOTES: Led California League catchers with 99 assists and 14 double plays in 1988.... Led American Association catchers with 19 errors and 13 passed balls in 1990.

Year	Team (League)	Pos.	G	AB	R	H	2B	3B	HR	RBI	Avg.	SB	PO	A	E	Avg.
1986 —Beloit (Midwest)	OF	49	173	26	45	3	2	4	21	.260	0	98	4	4	.962
1987 —Beloit (Midwest)	C	130	461	83	139	30	3	20	85	.302	7	624	71	6	•.991
1988 —Stockton (California)	C-OF	138	519	81	147	32	6	15	92	.283	10	779	†101	17	.981
1989 —El Paso (Texas)	C-OF	120	463	72	139	30	3	17	93	.300	5	474	59	17	.969
1990 —Denver (Am. Assoc.)	C-OF	116	416	72	120	21	3	18	74	.288	6	577	72	†20	.970
—Milwaukee (A.L.)	C	5	5	1	1	0	0	1	1	.200	0	6	1	1	.875
1991 —Denver (Am. Assoc.)	1B-OF-C	122	462	69	135	19	9	18	•91	.292	2	698	64	8	.990
—Milwaukee (A.L.)	OF-1B	7	11	2	4	1	0	1	1	.364	0	1	0	0	1.000
Major league totals (2 years)		12	16	3	5	1	0	2	2	.313	0	7	1	1	.889

McKNIGHT, JEFF
OF/IF, METS

PERSONAL: Born February 18, 1963, at Conway, Ark. . . . 6-0/188. . . . Throws right, bats both. . . . Full name: Jefferson Alan McKnight. . . . Son of Jim McKnight, infielder, Chicago Cubs (1960 and 1962).
HIGH SCHOOL: South Side (Bee Branch, Ark.).
COLLEGE: Westark Community College (Ark.).
TRANSACTIONS/CAREER NOTES: Selected by Baltimore Orioles organization in 28th round of free-agent draft (June 7, 1982). . . . Selected by New York Mets organization in secondary phase of free-agent draft (January 11, 1983). . . . Released by Mets (September 29, 1989). . . . Signed by Rochester, Baltimore Orioles organization (December 5, 1989). . . . On disabled list (June 4, 1991-remainder of season). . . . Released by Orioles (October 16, 1991). . . . Signed by Tidewater, New York Mets organization (December 20, 1991).
STATISTICAL NOTES: Led International League with 79 bases on balls received in 1989.

Year	Team (League)	Pos.	G	AB	R	H	2B	3B	HR	RBI	Avg.	SB	PO	A	E	Avg.
1983	—Little Falls (N.Y.-Penn)	SS	39	115	10	25	3	1	0	9	.217	1	43	72	16	.878
1984	—Columbia (S. Atlantic)	S-2-3-1-0	95	251	31	64	10	1	1	27	.255	9	115	144	21	.925
1985	—Columbia (S. Atlantic)	OF-1B-P	67	159	26	42	6	1	1	24	.264	6	92	16	4	.964
	—Lynchburg (Carolina)	S-3-2-0	49	150	19	33	6	1	0	21	.220	0	47	106	12	.927
1986	—Jackson (Texas)	OF-IF-P	132	469	71	118	24	3	4	55	.252	5	400	154	19	.967
1987	—Jackson (Texas)	0-3-1-2-S	16	59	5	12	3	0	2	8	.203	1	22	27	1	.980
	—Tidewater (Int'l)	IF-OF-P	87	184	21	47	7	3	2	25	.255	0	141	119	9	.967
1988	—Tidewater (Int'l)	0-2-S-1-3	113	345	36	88	14	0	2	25	.255	0	180	155	15	.957
1989	—Tidewater (Int'l)	IF-OF-C	116	425	84	106	19	2	9	48	.249	3	665	172	15	.982
	—New York (N.L.)	2-1-S-3	6	12	2	3	0	0	0	0	.250	0	4	5	1	.900
1990	—Rochester (Int'l)■	0-S-1-2	100	339	56	95	21	3	7	45	.280	7	211	144	14	.962
	—Baltimore (A.L.)	1-0-2-S	29	75	11	15	2	0	1	4	.200	0	106	20	0	1.000
1991	—Rochester (Int'l)	SS-2B-OF	22	81	19	31	7	2	1	18	.383	1	34	60	5	.949
	—Baltimore (A.L.)	OF-1B	16	41	2	7	1	0	0	2	.171	1	22	2	0	1.000
	American League totals (2 years)		45	116	13	22	3	0	1	6	.190	1	128	22	0	1.000
	National League totals (1 year)		6	12	2	3	0	0	0	0	.250	0	4	5	1	.900
	Major league totals (3 years)		51	128	15	25	3	0	1	6	.195	1	132	27	1	.994

RECORD AS PITCHER

Year	Team (League)	G	W	L	Pct.	ERA	Sv.	IP	H	R	ER	BB	SO
1985	—Columbia (South Atlantic)	3	0	0	. . .	9.00	0	4	4	5	4	3	8
1986	—Jackson (Texas)	5	0	0	. . .	1.50	0	6	4	1	1	1	1
1987	—Tidewater (International)	1	0	0	. . .	0.00	0	2	0	0	0	0	0

McLEMORE, MARK
IF, ORIOLES

PERSONAL: Born October 4, 1964, at San Diego. . . . 5-11/195. . . . Throws right, bats both. . . . Full name: Mark Tremell McLemore.
HIGH SCHOOL: Morse (San Diego).
TRANSACTIONS/CAREER NOTES: Selected by California Angels organization in ninth round of free-agent draft (June 7, 1982). . . . On disabled list (May 15-27, 1985). . . . On California disabled list (May 24-August 2, 1988); included rehabilitation disability assignment to Palm Springs (July 7-21, 1988) and Edmonton (July 22-27, 1988). . . . On California disabled list (May 17-August 17, 1990); included rehabilitation disability assignment to Edmonton (May 24-June 6, 1990) and Palm Springs (August 9-13, 1990). . . . Traded by Angels to Colorado Springs, Cleveland Indians organization (August 17, 1990), completing deal in which Indians traded C Ron Tingley to Angels for a player to be named later (September 6, 1989). . . . Released by Indians organization (December 13, 1990). . . . Signed by Tucson, Houston Astros organization (March 6, 1991). . . . On Houston disabled list (May 9-June 25, 1991); included rehabilitation disablitity assignment to Tucson (May 24-29, 1991) and Jackson (June 14-22, 1991). . . . Released by Astros (June 25, 1991). . . . Signed by Baltimore Orioles (July 5, 1991). . . . Granted free agency (October 15, 1991). . . . Re-signed by Orioles organization (February 5, 1992).
STATISTICAL NOTES: Led California League second basemen with 400 assists and 84 double plays in 1984. . . . Led Pacific Coast League second basemen with 597 total chances and 95 double plays in 1989.

Year	Team (League)	Pos.	G	AB	R	H	2B	3B	HR	RBI	Avg.	SB	PO	A	E	Avg.
1982	—Salem (Northwest)	2B-SS	55	165	42	49	6	2	0	25	.297	14	81	125	11	.949
1983	—Peoria (Midwest)	2B-SS	95	329	42	79	7	3	0	18	.240	15	170	250	24	.946
1984	—Redwood (California)	2B-SS	134	482	102	142	8	3	0	45	.295	59	274	†429	25	.966
1985	—Midland (Texas)	2B-SS	117	458	80	124	17	6	2	46	.271	31	301	339	19	.971
1986	—Midland (Texas)	2B	63	237	54	75	9	1	1	29	.316	38	155	194	13	.964
	—Edmonton (Pac. Coast)	2B	73	286	41	79	13	1	0	23	.276	29	173	215	7	.982
	—California (A.L.)	2B	5	4	0	0	0	0	0	0	.000	0	3	10	0	1.000
1987	—California (A.L.)	2B-SS	138	433	61	102	13	3	3	41	.236	25	293	363	17	.975
1988	—California (A.L.)	2B-3B	77	233	38	56	11	2	2	16	.240	13	108	178	6	.979
	—Palm Springs (Calif.)	2B	11	44	9	15	3	1	0	6	.341	7	18	24	1	.977
	—Edmonton (Pac. Coast)	2B	12	45	7	12	3	0	0	6	.267	7	35	33	1	.986
1989	—Edmonton (Pac. Coast)	2B	114	430	60	105	13	2	2	34	.244	26	★264	323	10	★.983
	—California (A.L.)	2B	32	103	12	25	3	1	0	14	.243	6	55	88	5	.966
1990	—Calif.-Cleveland (A.L.)■	2B-SS-3B	28	60	6	9	2	0	0	2	.150	1	37	39	4	.950
	—L.V.-Colo. Spgs. (PCL)	2B-SS-3B	23	93	15	25	4	0	1	10	.269	5	47	72	6	.952
	—Palm Springs (Calif.)	2B	6	22	3	6	0	0	0	2	.273	0	20	22	0	1.000

Year	Team (League)	Pos.	G	AB	R	H	2B	3B	HR	RBI	Avg.	SB	PO	A	E	Avg.
1991—Houston (N.L.)■		2B	21	61	6	9	1	0	0	2	.148	0	25	54	2	.975
—Tucson (Pacific Coast)		2B	4	14	2	5	1	0	0	0	.357	0	8	6	0	1.000
—Jackson (Texas)		2B	7	22	6	5	3	0	1	4	.227	1	27	24	0	1.000
—Rochester (Int'l)■		2B	57	228	32	64	11	4	1	28	.281	12	134	166	5	.984
American League totals (5 years)			280	833	117	192	29	6	5	73	.230	45	496	678	32	.973
National League totals (1 year)			21	61	6	9	1	0	0	2	.148	0	25	54	2	.975
Major league totals (6 years)			301	894	123	201	30	6	5	75	.225	45	521	732	34	.974

McNEELY, JEFF
OF, RED SOX

PERSONAL: Born October 18, 1969, at Monroe, N.C. . . . 6-2/190. . . . Throws right, bats right. . . . Full name: Jeffrey Laverne McNeely.
HIGH SCHOOL: Monroe (N.C.).
COLLEGE: Spartanburg Methodist College (S.C.).
TRANSACTIONS/CAREER NOTES: Selected by Boston Red Sox organization in second round of free-agent draft (June 5, 1989).

Year	Team (League)	Pos.	G	AB	R	H	2B	3B	HR	RBI	Avg.	SB	PO	A	E	Avg.
1989—Sarasota Red Sox (GCL)		OF	9	32	10	13	1	1	0	4	.406	5	13	1	0	1.000
—Elmira (New York-Penn)		OF	61	208	20	52	7	0	2	21	.250	16	96	5	7	.935
1990—Winter Haven (Fla. St.)		OF	16	62	4	10	0	0	0	3	.161	7	41	3	1	.978
—Elmira (New York-Penn)		OF	73	246	41	77	4	5	6	37	.313	★39	124	8	7	.950
1991—Lynchburg (Carolina)		OF	106	382	58	123	16	5	4	38	★.322	38	237	5	8	.968

McRAE, BRIAN
OF, ROYALS

PERSONAL: Born August 27, 1967, at Bradenton, Fla. . . . 6-0/185. . . . Throws right, bats both. . . . Full name: Brian Wesley McRae. . . . Son of Hal McRae, outfielder, Cincinnati Reds and Kansas City Royals (1968 and 1970-87); coach, Royals (1987); coach, Montreal Expos (1990-91); and current manager, Royals.
HIGH SCHOOL: Blue Springs (Mo.).
TRANSACTIONS/CAREER NOTES: Selected by Kansas City Royals organization in first round (17th pick overall) of free-agent draft (June 3, 1985).
RECORDS/HONORS: Shares major league single-season record for fewest double plays by outfielder (150 or more games)—0 (1991).
STATISTICAL NOTES: Led Northwest League second basemen with 373 total chances in 1986. . . . Tied for Southern League lead in double plays by outfielders with five in 1989.

Year	Team (League)	Pos.	G	AB	R	H	2B	3B	HR	RBI	Avg.	SB	PO	A	E	Avg.
1985—Sarasota Royals (GCL)		2B-SS	60	217	40	58	6	5	0	23	.267	27	116	142	18	.935
1986—Eugene (Northwest)		2B	72	306	★66	82	10	3	1	29	.268	28	146	★214	13	★.965
1987—Fort Myers (Florida St.)		2B	131	481	62	121	14	1	1	31	.252	33	★284	346	18	.972
1988—Baseball City (Fla. St.)		2B	30	107	18	33	2	0	1	11	.308	8	70	103	4	.977
—Memphis (Southern)		2B	91	288	33	58	13	1	4	15	.201	13	147	231	18	.955
1989—Memphis (Southern)		OF	138	★533	72	121	18	8	5	42	.227	23	249	11	5	.981
1990—Memphis (Southern)		OF	116	470	78	126	24	6	10	64	.268	21	265	8	7	.975
—Kansas City (A.L.)		OF	46	168	21	48	8	3	2	23	.286	4	120	1	0	1.000
1991—Kansas City (A.L.)		OF	152	629	86	164	28	9	8	64	.261	20	405	2	3	.993
Major league totals (2 years)			198	797	107	212	36	12	10	87	.266	24	525	3	3	.994

McREYNOLDS, KEVIN
OF, ROYALS

PERSONAL: Born October 16, 1959, at Little Rock, Ark. . . . 6-1/215. . . . Throws right, bats right. . . . Full name: Walter Kevin McReynolds.
HIGH SCHOOL: Sylvan Hills (North Little Rock, Ark.).
COLLEGE: Arkansas.
TRANSACTIONS/CAREER NOTES: Selected by Milwaukee Brewers organization in 18th round of free-agent draft (June 6, 1978). . . . Selected by San Diego Padres organization in first round (sixth pick overall) of free-agent draft (June 8, 1981). . . . Traded by Padres with P Gene Walter and IF Adam Ging to New York Mets for OF Shawn Abner, OF Stanley Jefferson, OF Kevin Mitchell, P Kevin Armstrong and P Kevin Brown (December 11, 1986). . . . Traded by Mets with IF Gregg Jefferies and 2B Keith Miller to Kansas City Royals for P Bret Saberhagen and IF Bill Pecota (December 11, 1991).
RECORDS/HONORS: Holds major league single-season record for most stolen bases with no caught stealing—21 (1988). . . . Shares major league single-season records for fewest assists by outfielder who led league in assists—14 (1990); fewest double plays by outfielder (150 or more games)—0 (1987). . . . Named outfielder on THE SPORTING NEWS college All-America team (1981). . . . Named California League Most Valuable Player (1982). . . . Named Minor League Player of the Year by THE SPORTING NEWS (1983). . . . Named Pacific Coast League Player of the Year (1983). . . . Named outfielder on THE SPORTING NEWS N.L. All-Star team (1988).
STATISTICAL NOTES: Led Pacific Coast League with 328 total bases in 1983. . . . Led N.L. outfielders with 436 total chances in 1984 and 445 in 1985. . . . Led N.L. outfielders with five double plays in 1988. . . . Hit for the cycle (August 1, 1989).

Year	Team (League)	Pos.	G	AB	R	H	2B	3B	HR	RBI	Avg.	SB	PO	A	E	Avg.
1982—Reno (California)		OF	90	338	83	127	17	5	★28	98	★.376	0	52	7	3	.952
—Amarillo (Texas)		OF	40	162	30	57	8	3	5	39	.352	4	76	3	2	.975
1983—Las Vegas (Pac. Coast)		OF	113	446	98	168	★46	9	★32	116	.377	14	257	9	9	.967
—San Diego (N.L.)		OF	39	140	15	31	3	1	4	14	.221	2	87	4	1	.989

Year Team (League)	Pos.	G	AB	R	H	2B	3B	HR	RBI	Avg.	SB	PO	A	E	Avg.
						BATTING						FIELDING			
1984 —San Diego (N.L.)	OF	147	525	68	146	26	6	20	75	.278	3	*422	10	4	.991
1985 —San Diego (N.L.)	OF	152	564	61	132	24	4	15	75	.234	4	*430	12	3	.993
1986 —San Diego (N.L.)	OF	158	560	89	161	31	6	26	96	.288	8	332	9	8	.977
1987 —New York (N.L.)■..............	OF	151	590	86	163	32	5	29	95	.276	14	286	8	4	.987
1988 —New York (N.L.)	OF	147	552	82	159	30	2	27	99	.288	21	252	*18	4	.985
1989 —New York (N.L.)	OF	148	545	74	148	25	3	22	85	.272	15	307	10	•10	.969
1990 —New York (N.L.)	OF	147	521	75	140	23	1	24	82	.269	9	237	•14	3	.988
1991 —New York (N.L.)	OF	143	522	65	135	32	1	16	74	.259	6	281	9	2	.993
Major league totals (9 years)		1232	4519	615	1215	226	29	183	695	.269	82	2634	94	39	.986

CHAMPIONSHIP SERIES RECORD

CHAMPIONSHIP SERIES NOTES: Shares N.L. single-game record for most hits—4 (October 11, 1988).

Year Team (League)	Pos.	G	AB	R	H	2B	3B	HR	RBI	Avg.	SB	PO	A	E	Avg.
						BATTING						FIELDING			
1984 —San Diego (N.L.)	OF	4	10	2	3	0	0	1	4	.300	0	10	0	0	1.000
1988 —New York (N.L.)	OF	7	28	4	7	2	0	2	4	.250	2	19	0	0	1.000
Championship Series totals (2 years)		11	38	6	10	2	0	3	8	.263	2	29	0	0	1.000

MEACHAM, RUSTY
P, ROYALS

PERSONAL: Born January 27, 1968, at Stuart, Fla.... 6-2/165.... Throws right, bats right.... Full name: Russell Loren Meacham.
COLLEGE: Indian River Community College (Fla.).
TRANSACTIONS/CAREER NOTES: Selected by Detroit Tigers organization in 33rd round of free-agent draft (June 2, 1987).... Claimed on waivers by Kansas City Royals (October 23, 1991).
STATISTICAL NOTES: Tied for Appalachian League lead with two shutouts in 1988.... Tied for Eastern League lead with three shutouts and nine complete games in 1990.

Year Team (League)	G	W	L	Pct.	ERA	Sv.	IP	H	R	ER	BB	SO
1988 —Fayetteville (South Atlantic)	6	0	3	.000	6.20	0	24⅔	37	19	17	6	16
—Bristol (Appalachian)	13	•9	1	•.900	*1.43	0	75⅓	55	14	12	22	85
1989 —Fayetteville (South Atlantic)	16	10	3	.769	2.29	0	102	103	33	26	23	74
—Lakeland (Florida State)	11	5	4	.556	1.95	0	64⅔	59	15	14	12	39
1990 —London (Eastern)	26	*15	9	.625	3.13	0	178	161	70	62	36	123
1991 —Toledo (International)	26	9	7	.563	3.09	2	125⅓	117	53	43	40	70
—Detroit (A.L.)	10	2	1	.667	5.20	0	27⅔	35	17	16	11	14
Major league totals (1 year)	10	2	1	.667	5.20	0	27⅔	35	17	16	11	14

MEDINA, LUIS
1B, ROYALS

PERSONAL: Born March 26, 1963, at Santa Monica, Calif.... 6-3/195.... Throws left, bats right.... Full name: Luis Main Medina.
HIGH SCHOOL: Wareen (Downey, Calif.).
COLLEGE: Cerritos Junior College (Calif.) and Arizona State.
TRANSACTIONS/CAREER NOTES: Selected by New York Mets organization in 33rd round of free-agent draft (June 8, 1981).... Selected by New York Mets organization in secondary phase of free-agent draft (January 12, 1982).... Selected by New York Yankees organization in secondary phase of free-agent draft (June 7, 1982).... Selected by Cincinnati Reds organization in secondary phase of free-agent draft (January 11, 1983).... Selected by Oakland Athletics organization in secondary phase of free-agent draft (June 6, 1983).... Selected by Houston Astros organization in secondary phase of free-agent draft (June 4, 1984).... Selected by Cleveland Indians organization in ninth round of free-agent draft (June 3, 1985).... Granted free agency (October 16, 1991).... Signed by Kansas City Royals organization (January 6, 1992).
RECORDS/HONORS: Named Midwest League Most Valuable Player (1986).
STATISTICAL NOTES: Led Midwest League with 300 total bases in 1986.... Led Pacific Coast League with .616 slugging percentage in 1988 and .593 in 1991.

Year Team (League)	Pos.	G	AB	R	H	2B	3B	HR	RBI	Avg.	SB	PO	A	E	Avg.
						BATTING						FIELDING			
1985 —Batavia (N.Y.-Penn)	OF-1B	76	290	43	77	16	0	12	43	.266	7	101	3	1	.990
1986 —Waterloo (Midwest)	OF	136	505	*107	*160	25	5	*35	*110	.317	6	208	8	5	.977
1987 —Williamsport (NYP)	OF-1B	96	341	61	109	15	6	16	68	.320	10	260	10	4	.985
1988 —Colorado Springs (PCL)	OF-1B	111	406	81	126	*28	6	*28	81	.310	1	374	26	10	.976
—Cleveland (A.L.)	1B	16	51	10	13	0	0	6	8	.255	0	137	9	0	1.000
1989 —Cleveland (A.L.)	OF-1B	30	83	8	17	1	0	4	8	.205	0	4	0	2	.667
—Colorado Springs (PCL)	OF-1B	51	166	17	29	8	0	3	19	.175	0	141	8	5	.968
1990 —Colorado Springs (PCL)	1B	94	320	58	87	15	0	18	53	.272	7	29	2	1	.969
1991 —Colorado Springs (PCL)	1B	117	450	81	146	28	6	•27	98	.324	0	439	29	1	.998
—Cleveland (A.L.)	DH	5	16	0	1	0	0	0	0	.063	0	0	0	0	...
Major league totals (3 years)		51	150	18	31	1	0	10	16	.207	0	141	9	2	.987

MELENDEZ, JOSE
P, PADRES

PERSONAL: Born September 2, 1965, at Naguabo, Puerto Rico.... 6-2/175.... Throws right, bats right.... Full name: Jose Luis Melendez.
TRANSACTIONS/CAREER NOTES: Signed as free agent by Pittsburgh Pirates organization (August 29, 1983).... On disabled list (May 3-25 and June 9-August 12, 1985).... Drafted by Seattle Mariners organization (December 5, 1988).... Claimed on waivers by San Diego Padres (March 26, 1991).

Year	Team (League)	G	W	L	Pct.	ERA	Sv.	IP	H	R	ER	BB	SO
1984 — Watertwon (New York-Penn)...		15	5	7	.417	2.77	0	91	61	37	28	40	68
1985 — Prince William (Carolina)		9	3	2	.600	2.44	1	44⅓	25	17	12	26	41
1986 — Prince William (Carolina)		28	13	10	.565	2.61	0	186⅓	141	75	54	81	146
1987 — Harrisburg (Eastern)		6	1	3	.250	10.80	0	18⅓	28	24	22	11	13
— Salem (Carolina)		20	9	6	.600	4.56	0	116⅓	96	62	59	56	86
1988 — Salem (Carolina)		8	4	2	.667	4.02	0	53⅔	55	26	24	19	50
— Harrisburg (Eastern)		22	5	3	.625	2.27	1	71⅓	46	20	18	19	38
1989 — Williamsport (N.Y.-Penn)■......		11	3	4	.429	2.45	0	73⅓	54	23	20	22	56
— Calgary (Pacific Coast)		17	1	2	.333	5.75	0	40⅔	42	27	26	19	24
1990 — Calgary (Pacific Coast)		45	11	4	.733	3.90	2	124⅔	119	61	54	44	95
— Seattle (A.L.)		3	0	0	...	11.81	0	5⅓	8	8	7	3	7
1991 — Las Vegas (Pacific Coast)■......		9	7	0	1.000	3.99	0	58⅔	54	27	26	11	45
— San Diego (N.L.)		31	8	5	.615	3.27	3	93⅔	77	35	34	24	60
American League totals (1 year)		3	0	0	...	11.81	0	5⅓	8	8	7	3	7
National League totals (1 year)		31	8	5	.615	3.27	3	93⅔	77	35	34	24	60
Major league totals (2 years)		34	8	5	.615	3.73	3	99	85	43	41	27	67

MELVIN, BOB

C, ROYALS

PERSONAL: Born October 28, 1961, at Palo Alto, Calif. ... 6-4/207. ... Throws right, bats right. ... Full name: Robert Paul Melvin.
HIGH SCHOOL: Menlo-Atherton (Menlo Park, Calif.).
COLLEGE: California and Canada College (Calif.).
TRANSACTIONS/CAREER NOTES: Selected by Baltimore Orioles organization in third round of free-agent draft (June 5, 1979). ... Selected by Detroit Tigers organization in secondary phase of free-agent draft (January 13, 1981). ... On disabled list (May 1-25, 1982). ... Traded by Tigers with P Juan Berenguer and a player to be named later to San Francisco Giants for P Dave LaPoint, P Eric King and C Matt Nokes (October 7, 1985); Giants acquired P Scott Medvin to complete deal (December 11, 1985). ... On disabled list (July 11-26, 1987). ... Traded by Giants to Baltimore Orioles for C Terry Kennedy (January 24, 1989). ... On disabled list (April 22-May 7, 1989). ... Traded by Orioles to Kansas City Royals for P Storm Davis (December 11, 1991).
STATISTICAL NOTES: Led Southern League catchers with .987 fielding percentage in 1982.

Year	Team (League)	Pos.	G	AB	R	H	2B	3B	HR	RBI	Avg.	SB	PO	A	E	Avg.
1981 — Macon (South Atlantic)		C	114	412	56	112	19	1	14	64	.272	5	456	67	2	★.996
1982 — Birmingham (Southern)		C-1B-3B	98	364	33	86	12	1	13	52	.236	1	638	54	9	†.987
1983 — Birmingham (Southern)		C-1B-2B	78	285	43	82	14	2	10	56	.288	0	404	30	2	.995
— Evansville (A.A.)		C-1B	45	142	10	27	6	0	2	11	.190	0	213	16	1	.996
1984 — Evansville (A.A.)		C-1B	44	141	12	35	13	0	0	11	.248	0	214	21	1	.996
— Birmingham (Southern)		C-1B-3B	69	271	34	73	14	1	2	33	.269	1	341	38	4	.990
1985 — Nashville (Am. Assoc.)		C-1B-OF	53	177	27	48	7	1	9	24	.271	3	276	28	2	.993
— Detroit (A.L.)		C	41	82	10	18	4	1	0	4	.220	0	175	13	2	.989
1986 — San Francisco (N.L.)■.....		C-3B	89	268	24	60	14	2	5	25	.224	3	443	60	6	.988
1987 — San Francisco (N.L.)		C-1B	84	246	31	49	8	0	11	31	.199	0	414	44	1	.998
1988 — San Francisco (N.L.)		C-1B	92	273	23	64	13	1	8	27	.234	0	406	31	7	.984
— Phoenix (Pacific Coast)		C	21	75	11	23	5	0	2	9	.307	0	123	6	1	.992
1989 — Baltimore (A.L.)■.............		C	85	278	22	67	10	1	1	32	.241	1	303	20	3	.991
1990 — Baltimore (A.L.)		C-1B	93	301	30	73	14	1	5	37	.243	0	365	26	1	.997
1991 — Baltimore (A.L.)		C	79	228	11	57	10	0	1	23	.250	0	383	31	1	.998
American League totals (4 years)			298	889	73	215	38	3	7	96	.242	1	1226	90	7	.995
National League totals (3 years)			265	787	78	173	35	3	24	83	.220	3	1263	135	14	.990
Major league totals (7 years)			563	1676	151	388	73	6	31	179	.232	4	2489	225	21	.992

CHAMPIONSHIP SERIES RECORD

Year	Team (League)	Pos.	G	AB	R	H	2B	3B	HR	RBI	Avg.	SB	PO	A	E	Avg.
1987 — San Francisco (N.L.)		PH-C	3	7	0	3	0	0	0	0	.429	0	14	1	0	1.000

MERCED, ORLANDO

1B, PIRATES

PERSONAL: Born November 2, 1966, at San Juan, Puerto Rico. ... 5-11/175. ... Throws right, bats both. ... Full name: Orlando Luis Merced.
HIGH SCHOOL: University Garden (San Juan, Puerto Rico).
TRANSACTIONS/CAREER NOTES: Signed as free agent by Pittsburgh Pirates organization (February 22, 1985). ... On Macon disabled list (April 18-28, 1987). ... On Watertown disabled list (June 23, 1987-remainder of season).

Year	Team (League)	Pos.	G	AB	R	H	2B	3B	HR	RBI	Avg.	SB	PO	A	E	Avg.
1985 — Bradenton Pirates (GCL) ..		SS-3B	40	136	16	31	6	0	1	13	.228	3	46	78	28	.816
1986 — Macon (South Atlantic)		OF-3B	65	173	20	34	4	1	2	24	.197	5	53	15	13	.840
— Watertown (N.Y.-Penn)....		3B-1B-OF	27	89	12	16	0	1	3	9	.180	6	49	28	10	.885
1987 — Macon (South Atlantic)		OF	4	4	1	0	0	0	0	0	.000	1	1	1	0	1.000
— Watertown (N.Y.-Penn)....		2B	4	12	4	5	0	1	0	3	.417	1	11	7	2	.900
1988 — Augusta (S. Atlantic)		2B-3B-SS	37	136	19	36	6	3	1	17	.265	2	35	39	7	.914
— Salem (Carolina)		3-2-0-S	80	298	47	87	12	7	7	42	.292	13	77	183	31	.893

Year	Team (League)	Pos.	G	AB	R	H	2B	3B	HR	RBI	Avg.	SB	PO	A	E	Avg.
1989—Harrisburg (Eastern)		1B-OF-3B	95	341	43	82	16	4	6	48	.240	13	435	32	10	.979
—Buffalo (Am. Assoc.)		1B-OF-3B	35	129	18	44	5	3	1	16	.341	0	173	15	3	.984
1990—Buffalo (Am. Assoc.)		1B-3B-OF	101	378	52	99	12	6	9	55	.262	14	689	83	20	.975
—Pittsburgh (N.L.)		OF-C	25	24	3	5	1	0	0	0	.208	0	0	0	0	...
1991—Buffalo (Am. Assoc.)		1B	3	12	1	2	0	0	0	0	.167	1	29	2	0	1.000
—Pittsburgh (N.L.)		1B-OF	120	411	83	113	17	2	10	50	.275	8	916	60	12	.988
Major league totals (2 years)			145	435	86	118	18	2	10	50	.271	8	916	60	12	.988

CHAMPIONSHIP SERIES RECORD

CHAMPIONSHIP SERIES NOTES: Hit home run in first series at-bat (October 12, 1991).

Year	Team (League)	Pos.	G	AB	R	H	2B	3B	HR	RBI	Avg.	SB	PO	A	E	Avg.
1991—Pittsburgh (N.L.)		1B-PH	3	9	1	2	0	0	1	1	.222	0	13	0	1	.929

MERCEDES, HENRY
C, ATHLETICS

PERSONAL: Born July 23, 1969, at Santo Domingo, Dominican Republic.... 5-11/185. ... Throws right, bats right.... Full name: Henry Felipe Perez Mercedes.
TRANSACTIONS/CAREER NOTES: Signed as free agent by Oakland Athletics organization (June 22, 1987).
STATISTICAL NOTES: Led California League catchers with 21 errors in 1991.

Year	Team (League)	Pos.	G	AB	R	H	2B	3B	HR	RBI	Avg.	SB	PO	A	E	Avg.
1988—Scottsdale (Arizona)		C	2	5	1	2	0	0	0	0	.400	0	13	2	0	1.000
1989—South. Oregon (N'west)		C-3B	22	61	6	10	0	1	0	1	.164	0	129	15	3	.980
—Modesto (California)		C	16	37	6	3	0	0	1	3	.081	0	81	9	4	.957
—Madison (Midwest)		C	51	152	11	32	3	0	2	13	.211	0	304	40	5	.986
1990—Madison (Midwest)		C-3-2-0	90	282	29	64	13	2	3	37	.227	6	555	110	9	.987
—Tacoma (Pacific Coast)		C	12	31	3	6	1	0	0	2	.194	0	46	4	0	1.000
1991—Modesto (California)		C-3B-P	116	388	55	100	17	3	4	61	.258	5	551	86	†24	.964

RECORD AS PITCHER

Year	Team (League)	G	W	L	Pct.	ERA	Sv.	IP	H	R	ER	BB	SO
1991—Modesto (California)	1	0	1	.000	81.00	0	1	4	9	9	6	2

MERCEDES, LUIS
OF, ORIOLES

PERSONAL: Born February 20, 1968, at San Pedro de Macoris, Dominican Republic.... 6-0/193.... Throws right, bats right.... Full name: Luis Roberto Mercedes.
TRANSACTIONS/CAREER NOTES: Signed as free agent by Baltimore Orioles organization (February 16, 1987).... On Rochester disabled list (July 19-29, 1991).
STATISTICAL NOTES: Led International League with .435 on base percentage in 1991.

Year	Team (League)	Pos.	G	AB	R	H	2B	3B	HR	RBI	Avg.	SB	PO	A	E	Avg.
1988—Bluefield (Appalachian)		2B	59	215	36	59	8	4	0	20	.274	16	127	152	*26	.915
1989—Frederick (Carolina)		2B	108	401	62	124	12	5	3	36	*.309	29	204	305	25	.953
1990—Hagerstown (Eastern)		OF	108	416	71	139	12	4	3	37	.334	38	157	5	•9	.947
1991—Rochester (Int'l)		OF-1B	102	374	68	125	14	5	2	36	.334	23	175	10	8	.959
—Baltimore (A.L.)		OF	19	54	10	11	2	0	0	2	.204	0	20	0	0	1.000
Major league totals (1 year)			19	54	10	11	2	0	0	2	.204	0	20	0	0	1.000

MERCKER, KENT
P, BRAVES

PERSONAL: Born February 1, 1968, at Dublin, O.... 6-2/195.... Throws left, bats left.... Full name: Kent Franklin Mercker.
HIGH SCHOOL: Dublin (O.).
TRANSACTIONS/CAREER NOTES: Selected by Atlanta Braves organization in first round (fifth pick overall) of free-agent draft (June 2, 1986).... On disabled list (March 30-May 6, 1990 and August 9-24, 1991).
RECORDS/HONORS: Named Carolina League co-Pitcher of the Year (1988).
STATISTICAL NOTES: Tied for International League lead in games started by pitcher with 27 in 1989.... Pitched six innings, combining with Mark Wohlers and Alejandro Pena in 1-0 nine-inning no-hit victory against San Diego Padres (September 11, 1991).

Year	Team (League)	G	W	L	Pct.	ERA	Sv.	IP	H	R	ER	BB	SO
1986—Bradenton Braves (GCL)	9	4	3	.571	2.47	0	47⅓	37	21	13	16	42
1987—Durham (Carolina)	3	0	1	.000	5.40	0	11⅔	11	8	7	6	14
1988—Durham (Carolina)	19	11	4	.733	*2.75	0	127⅔	102	44	39	47	159
—Greenville (Southern)	9	3	1	.750	3.35	0	48⅓	36	20	18	26	60
1989—Richmond (International)	27	9	12	.429	3.20	0	168⅔	107	66	60	*95	*144
—Atlanta (N.L.)	2	0	0	...	12.46	0	4⅓	8	6	6	6	4
1990—Richmond (International)	12	5	4	.556	3.55	1	58⅓	60	30	23	27	69
—Atlanta (N.L.)	36	4	7	.364	3.17	7	48⅓	43	22	17	24	39
1991—Atlanta (N.L.)	50	5	3	.625	2.58	6	73⅓	56	23	21	35	62
Major league totals (3 years)	88	9	10	.474	3.14	13	126	107	51	44	65	105

CHAMPIONSHIP SERIES RECORD

Year	Team (League)	G	W	L	Pct.	ERA	Sv.	IP	H	R	ER	BB	SO
1991—Atlanta (N.L.)		1	0	1	.000	13.50	0	⅔	0	1	1	2	0

WORLD SERIES RECORD

Year	Team (League)	G	W	L	Pct.	ERA	Sv.	IP	H	R	ER	BB	SO
1991—Atlanta (N.L.)		2	0	0	...	0.00	0	1	0	0	0	0	1

MERULLO, MATT
C/1B, WHITE SOX

PERSONAL: Born August 4, 1965, at Winchester, Mass. . . . 6-2/200. . . . Throws right, bats left. . . . Full name: Matthew Bates Merullo. . . . Grandson of Lennie Merullo Sr., infielder, Chicago Cubs (1941-47); and son of Lennie Merullo Jr., minor league infielder (1961-64).

HIGH SCHOOL: Fairfield Prep (Conn.).
COLLEGE: North Carolina.
TRANSACTIONS/CAREER NOTES: Selected by Chicago White Sox organization in seventh round of free-agent draft (June 2, 1986).
STATISTICAL NOTES: Led Southern League with 21 passed balls in 1988. . . . Led Southern League catchers with 18 errors in 1990.

Year	Team (League)	Pos.	G	AB	R	H	2B	3B	HR	RBI	Avg.	SB	PO	A	E	Avg.
1986—Peninsula (Carolina)	C	64	208	21	63	12	2	3	35	.303	1	225	26	6	.977
1987—Daytona Beach (Fla. St.)	C-1B-OF	70	250	26	65	11	6	4	47	.260	1	227	28	6	.977
—Birmingham (Southern)	C	48	167	13	46	7	0	2	17	.275	1	278	24	8	.974
1988—Birmingham (Southern)	C-1B	125	449	58	117	26	0	6	60	.261	3	640	60	14	.980
1989—Vancouver (Pac. Coast)	C	3	9	0	2	1	0	0	2	.222	0	19	1	1	.952
—Chicago (A.L.)	C	31	81	5	18	1	0	1	8	.222	0	100	10	3	.973
—Birmingham (Southern)	C	33	119	19	35	6	0	3	23	.294	0	149	10	1	.994
1990—Birmingham (Southern)	C-1B	102	378	57	110	26	1	8	50	.291	2	561	51	†24	.962
1991—Chicago (A.L.)	C-1B	80	140	8	32	1	0	5	21	.229	0	159	14	2	.989
—Birmingham (Southern)	C	8	28	5	6	0	0	2	3	.214	0	25	3	1	.966
Major league totals (2 years)		111	221	13	50	2	0	6	29	.226	0	259	24	5	.983

MESA, JOSE
P, ORIOLES

PERSONAL: Born May 22, 1966, at Azua, Dominican Republic. . . . 6-3/222. . . . Throws right, bats right. . . . Full name: Jose Ramon Mesa.
HIGH SCHOOL: Santa School (Azua, Dominican Republic).
TRANSACTIONS/CAREER NOTES: Signed as free agent by Toronto Blue Jays organization (October 31, 1981). . . . On Kinston disabled list (August 27, 1984-remainder of season). . . . Traded by Blue Jays organization to Baltimore Orioles (September 4, 1987), completing deal in which Orioles traded P Mike Flanagan to Blue Jays for P Oswald Peraza and a player to be named later (August 31, 1987). . . . On Rochester disabled list (April 18-May 16 and June 30, 1988-remainder of season; May 27, 1989-remainder of season; and August 21-September 5, 1991).
STATISTICAL NOTES: Led Gulf Coast League with three shutouts in 1982. . . . Tied for Carolina League lead with nine hit batsmen in 1985. . . . Led Southern League pitchers with 35 games started in 1987.
MISCELLANEOUS: Appeared in one game as pinch-runner (1991).

Year	Team (League)	G	W	L	Pct.	ERA	Sv.	IP	H	R	ER	BB	SO
1982—Bradenton Blue Jays (GCL)	13	6	4	.600	2.70	1	83⅓	58	34	25	20	40
1983—Florence (South Atlantic)	28	6	12	.333	5.48	0	141⅓	153	★116	86	93	91
1984—Florence (South Atlantic)	7	4	3	.571	3.76	0	38⅓	38	24	16	25	35
—Kinston (Carolina)	10	5	2	.714	3.91	0	50⅔	51	23	22	28	24
1985—Kinston (Carolina)	30	5	10	.333	6.16	1	106⅔	110	89	73	79	71
1986—Ventura County (California)	24	10	6	.625	3.86	0	142⅓	141	71	61	58	113
—Knoxville (Southern)	9	2	2	.500	4.35	0	41⅓	40	32	20	23	30
1987—Knoxville (Southern)	35	10	•13	.435	5.21	0	★193⅓	★206	★131	★112	104	115
—Baltimore (A.L.)■	6	1	3	.250	6.03	0	31⅓	38	23	21	15	17
1988—Rochester (International)	11	0	3	.000	8.62	0	15⅔	21	20	15	14	15
1989—Rochester (International)	7	0	2	.000	5.40	0	10	10	6	6	6	3
—Hagerstown (Eastern)	3	0	0	...	1.38	0	13	9	2	2	4	12
1990—Hagerstown (Eastern)	15	5	5	.500	3.42	0	79	77	35	30	30	72
—Rochester (International)	4	1	2	.333	2.42	0	26	21	11	7	12	23
—Baltimore (A.L.)	7	3	2	.600	3.86	0	46⅔	37	20	20	27	24
1991—Baltimore (A.L.)	23	6	11	.353	5.97	0	123⅔	151	86	82	62	64
—Rochester (International)	8	3	3	.500	3.86	0	51⅓	37	25	22	30	48
Major league totals (3 years)	36	10	16	.385	5.49	0	201⅔	226	129	123	104	105

MEULENS, HENSLEY
OF/1B, YANKEES

PERSONAL: Born June 23, 1967, at Curacao, Netherlands Antilles. . . . 6-3/212. . . . Throws right, bats right. . . . Full name: Hensley Filemon Meulens.
TRANSACTIONS/CAREER NOTES: Signed as free agent by New York Yankees organization (October 31, 1985).
RECORDS/HONORS: Named International League Player of the Year (1990).
STATISTICAL NOTES: Led Gulf Coast League third basemen with 178 total chances in 1986. . . . Led Gulf Coast League batters with 66 strikeouts in 1986. . . . Tied for Eastern League lead in double plays by third basemen with 18 in 1988. . . . Tied for Eastern League lead in being hit by pitch with nine in 1989. . . . Led International League with 245 total bases in 1990.

— 322 —

Year Team (League)	Pos.	G	AB	R	H	2B	3B	HR	RBI	Avg.	SB	PO	A	E	Avg.
1986—Sarasota Yankees (GCL) ..	3B	59	219	36	51	10	4	4	31	.233	4	★40	★118	20	.888
1987—Prince William (Caro.)......	3B	116	430	76	129	23	2	28	103	.300	14	96	224	★37	.896
—Fort Lauderdale (FSL)	3B	17	58	2	10	3	0	0	2	.172	0	18	37	7	.887
1988—Albany (Eastern)..............	3B	79	278	50	68	9	1	13	40	.245	3	57	162	23	.905
—Columbus (Int'l)	3B	55	209	27	48	9	1	6	22	.230	0	39	111	14	.915
1989—Albany (Eastern)..............	3B	104	335	55	86	8	2	11	45	.257	3	67	172	★29	.892
—Columbus (Int'l)	3B	14	45	8	13	4	0	1	3	.289	0	11	27	3	.927
—New York (A.L.)	3B	8	28	2	5	0	0	0	1	.179	0	5	23	4	.875
1990—Columbus (Int'l)	OF-1B-3B	136	480	81	137	20	5	26	96	.285	6	359	51	13	.969
—New York (A.L.)	OF	23	83	12	20	7	0	3	10	.241	1	49	3	2	.963
1991—New York (A.L.)	OF-1B	96	288	37	64	8	1	6	29	.222	3	179	5	6	.968
Major league totals (3 years)		127	399	51	89	15	1	9	40	.223	4	233	31	12	.957

MILACKI, BOB

P, ORIOLES

PERSONAL: Born July 28, 1964, at Trenton, N.J. . . . 6-4/232. . . . Throws right, bats right. . . . Full name: Robert Milacki.
HIGH SCHOOL: Lake Havasu (Ariz.).
COLLEGE: Yavapai College (Ariz.).
TRANSACTIONS/CAREER NOTES: Selected by San Diego Padres organization in first round (ninth pick overall) of free-agent draft (January 11, 1983). . . . Selected by Baltimore Orioles organization in secondary phase of free-agent draft (June 6, 1983). . . . On disabled list (July 2-August 28, 1984). . . . On Daytona Beach disabled list (April 12-May 11, 1985). . . . On Hagerstown disabled list (July 5-August 24, 1985). . . . On disabled list (July 31-September 1, 1990).
STATISTICAL NOTES: Lost no-hitter in 12th inning against Chattanooga (May 28, 1987). . . . Led International League with 11 complete games and tied for lead with three shutouts in 1988. . . . Tied for A.L. lead in games started by pitcher with 36 in 1989. . . . Pitched six innings, combining with Mike Flanagan, Mark Williamson and Gregg Olson in 2-0 nine-inning no-hit victory against Oakland Athletics (July 13, 1991).

Year Team (League)	G	W	L	Pct.	ERA	Sv.	IP	H	R	ER	BB	SO
1984—Hagerstown (Carolina)	15	4	5	.444	3.36	0	77⅔	69	35	29	48	62
1985—Daytona Beach (Florida State)..	8	1	4	.200	3.99	0	38⅓	32	23	17	26	24
—Hagerstown (Carolina)	7	3	2	.600	2.66	0	40⅔	32	16	12	22	37
1986—Hagerstown (Carolina)	13	4	5	.444	4.75	0	60⅔	69	59	32	37	46
—Miami (Florida State)	12	4	4	.500	3.74	0	67⅓	70	36	28	27	41
—Charlotte (Southern)	1	0	1	.000	6.75	0	5⅓	7	4	4	4	6
1987—Charlotte (Southern)	29	11	9	.550	4.56	1	148	168	86	75	66	101
1988—Charlotte (Southern)	5	3	1	.750	2.39	0	37⅔	26	11	10	12	29
—Rochester (International)	24	12	8	.600	2.70	0	176⅔	174	62	53	65	103
—Baltimore (A.L.)	3	2	0	1.000	0.72	0	25	9	2	2	9	18
1989—Baltimore (A.L.)	37	14	12	.538	3.74	0	243	233	105	101	88	113
1990—Baltimore (A.L.)	27	5	8	.385	4.46	0	135⅓	143	73	67	61	60
1991—Hagerstown (Eastern)	3	3	0	1.000	1.06	0	17	14	3	2	3	18
—Baltimore (A.L.)	31	10	9	.526	4.01	0	184	175	86	82	53	108
Major league totals (4 years)	98	31	29	.517	3.86	0	587⅓	560	266	252	211	299

MILCHIN, MIKE

P, CARDINALS

PERSONAL: Born February 28, 1968, at Knoxville, Tenn. . . . 6-3/190. . . . Throws left, bats left. . . . Full name: Michael Wayne Milchin.
HIGH SCHOOL: Tucker (Richmond, Tenn.).
COLLEGE: Clemson.
TRANSACTIONS/CAREER NOTES: Selected by St. Louis Cardinals organization in second round of free-agent draft (June 5, 1989).
MISCELLANEOUS: Member of 1988 U.S. Olympic baseball team.

Year Team (League)	G	W	L	Pct.	ERA	Sv.	IP	H	R	ER	BB	SO
1989—Hamilton (New York-Penn)	8	1	2	.333	2.18	0	41⅓	35	11	10	9	46
—Springfield (Midwest)	6	3	2	.600	2.14	0	42	30	14	10	10	44
1990—St. Petersburg (Florida State) ..	11	6	1	.857	2.77	0	68⅓	57	25	21	20	66
—Arkansas (Texas)	17	6	8	.429	4.31	0	102⅓	103	62	49	47	75
1991—Arkansas (Texas)	6	3	2	.600	3.06	0	35⅓	27	13	12	8	38
—Louisville (American Assoc.) ...	18	5	9	.357	5.07	0	94	132	64	53	40	47

MILLER, KEITH

2B, ROYALS

PERSONAL: Born June 12, 1963, at Midland, Mich. . . . 5-11/185. . . . Throws right, bats right. . . . Full name: Keith Alan Miller.
HIGH SCHOOL: All Saints (Bay City, Mich.).
COLLEGE: Oral Roberts.
TRANSACTIONS/CAREER NOTES: Selected by Cleveland Indians organization in 24th round of free-agent draft (June 5, 1981). . . . Selected by New York Yankees organization in second round of free-agent draft (June 4, 1984); contract was later voided after it was discovered he had a pre-existing knee injury. . . . Signed as free agent by New York Mets organization (September 6, 1984). . . . On disabled list (April 8-May 20, 1986). . . . On New York disabled list (June 29-September 1, 1987); included rehabilitation disability assignment to Tidewater (August 21-September 1, 1987). . . . On disabled list (April 25-May 17 and August 15-September 1, 1990; and May 27-June 16, 1991). . . . Traded by Mets with OF Kevin McReynolds and IF Gregg Jefferies to Kansas City Royals for P Bret Saberhagen and IF Bill Pecota (December 11, 1991).
STATISTICAL NOTES: Tied for Texas League lead in being hit by pitch with seven in 1986.

Year	Team (League)	Pos.	G	AB	R	H	2B	3B	HR	RBI	Avg.	SB	PO	A	E	Avg.
1985 —Lynchburg (Carolina)	3B-2B-OF	89	325	51	98	16	5	7	54	.302	14	103	203	25	.924
—Jackson (Texas)	2B-SS	46	165	17	37	8	1	3	22	.224	8	108	132	8	.968
1986 —Jackson (Texas)	2B	94	353	80	116	23	4	5	36	.329	23	198	272	19	.961
1987 —Tidewater (Int'l)	2B-OF	53	202	29	50	9	1	6	22	.248	14	112	129	5	.980
—New York (N.L.)	2B	25	51	14	19	2	2	0	1	.373	8	21	38	2	.967
1988 —Tidewater (Int'l)	2-S-3-0	42	171	23	48	11	1	1	15	.281	8	81	111	12	.941
—New York (N.L.)	2-S-3-0	40	70	9	15	1	1	1	5	.214	0	34	24	5	.921
1989 —Tidewater (Int'l)	2-0-S-3	48	184	33	49	8	2	1	15	.266	12	89	109	8	.961
—New York (N.L.)	2-0-S-3	57	143	15	33	7	0	1	7	.231	6	90	52	5	.966
1990 —New York (N.L.)	0F-2B-SS	88	233	42	60	8	0	1	12	.258	16	168	21	4	.979
1991 —New York (N.L.)	2-0-3-S	98	275	41	77	22	1	4	23	.280	14	165	154	10	.970
Major league totals (5 years)		308	772	121	204	40	4	7	48	.264	44	478	289	26	.967

MILLER, ORLANDO
SS, ASTROS

PERSONAL: Born January 13, 1969, at Changionola, Panama.... 6-1/180.... Throws right, bats right.... Full name: Orlando Salmon Miller.
TRANSACTIONS/CAREER NOTES: Signed as a free agent by New York Yankees organization (September 17, 1987).... Traded by Yankees organization to Houston Astros organization for IF Dave Silvestri and a player to be named later (March 13, 1990); Yankees acquired P Daven Bond to complete deal (June 11, 1990).... On Jackson disabled list (May 10-June 8, 1991).

Year	Team (League)	Pos.	G	AB	R	H	2B	3B	HR	RBI	Avg.	SB	PO	A	E	Avg.
1988 —Fort Lauderdale (FSL)	SS	3	11	0	3	0	0	0	1	.273	1	0	4	4	0 1.000
—Sarasota Yankees (GCL)	2B-SS	14	44	5	8	1	0	0	5	.182	1	19	30	5	.907
1989 —Oneonta (N.Y.-Penn)	2-S-3-0	58	213	29	62	5	2	1	25	.291	8	96	124	9	.961
1990 —Asheville (S. Atlantic)■	SS	121	438	60	137	29	6	4	62	.313	12	208	348	*47	.922
1991 —Jackson (Texas)	SS	23	70	5	13	6	0	1	5	.186	0	31	66	12	.890
—Osceola (Florida State)	SS	74	272	27	81	11	2	0	36	.298	1	106	205	24	.928

MILLER, PAUL
P, PIRATES

PERSONAL: Born April 27, 1965, at Burlington, Wis.... 6-5/215.... Throws right, bats right. ... Full name: Paul Robert Miller.
HIGH SCHOOL: Burton (Richmond, Ill.).
COLLEGE: Carthage (Wis.).
TRANSACTIONS/CAREER NOTES: Selected by Cincinnati Reds organization in 27th round of free-agent draft (June 2, 1986).... Selected by Pittsburgh Pirates organization in 53rd round of free-agent draft (June 2, 1987).... On Carolina disabled list (May 24-June 8, 1991).
STATISTICAL NOTES: Pitched 2-0 no-hit victory against Sarasota Reds (July 27, 1987, first game).

Year	Team (League)	G	W	L	Pct.	ERA	Sv.	IP	H	R	ER	BB	SO
1987 —Bradenton Pirates (GCL)	12	3	6	.333	3.20	0	70⅓	55	34	25	26	62
1988 —Augusta (South Atlantic)	15	6	5	.545	2.89	0	90⅓	80	34	29	28	51
1989 —Salem (Carolina)	26	6	12	.333	4.17	0	133⅔	138	86	62	64	82
1990 —Salem (Carolina)	22	8	6	.571	2.45	0	150⅔	145	58	41	33	83
—Harrisburg (Eastern)	5	2	1	.667	2.19	0	37	27	9	9	10	11
1991 —Carolina (Southern)	15	7	2	.778	2.42	0	89⅓	69	29	24	35	69
—Buffalo (American Assoc.)	10	5	2	.714	1.48	0	67	41	17	11	29	30
—Pittsburgh (N.L.)	1	0	0	...	5.40	0	5	4	3	3	3	2
Major league totals (1 year)	1	0	0	...	5.40	0	5	4	3	3	3	2

MILLIGAN, RANDY
1B/OF, ORIOLES

PERSONAL: Born November 27, 1961, at San Diego.... 6-1/234.... Throws right, bats right.... Full name: Randall Andre Milligan.
HIGH SCHOOL: San Diego (Calif.).
COLLEGE: San Diego Mesa College (Calif.).
TRANSACTIONS/CAREER NOTES: Selected by New York Mets organization in first round (third pick overall) of free-agent draft (January 13, 1981).... On disabled list (July 11, 1984-remainder of season).... Traded by Mets with P Scott Henion to Pittsburgh Pirates for C Mackey Sasser and P Tim Drummond (March 26, 1988).... Traded by Pirates to Baltimore Orioles for a player to be named later (November 9, 1988); Pirates acquired P Pete Blohm to complete deal (December 7, 1988).... On disabled list (August 10-September 28, 1990).
RECORDS/HONORS: Named Minor League Player of the Year by THE SPORTING NEWS (1987).... Named International League Player of the Year (1987).
STATISTICAL NOTES: Led International League batters with 272 total bases, 91 bases on balls received and tied for lead with 10 intentional bases on balls received in 1987.... Hit three home runs in a game (June 9, 1990).

Year	Team (League)	Pos.	G	AB	R	H	2B	3B	HR	RBI	Avg.	SB	PO	A	E	Avg.
1981 —Shelby (South Atlantic)	OF-SS	130	406	90	115	16	6	7	58	.283	49	174	5	14	.927
1982 —Lynchburg (Carolina)	OF-1B	118	420	63	113	10	6	5	55	.269	25	341	12	11	.970
1983 —Lynchburg (Carolina)	1B-OF	106	349	60	102	13	5	5	56	.292	41	558	41	13	.979
1984 —Jackson (Texas)	1B	62	193	32	53	5	0	9	34	.275	15	475	67	8	.985
1985 —Jackson (Texas)	1B	119	391	60	121	22	2	13	77	.309	11	726	49	11	.986

Year	Team (League)	Pos.	G	AB	R	H	2B	3B	HR	RBI	Avg.	SB	PO	A	E	Avg.
1986 —Tidewater (Int'l)		1B	21	60	3	5	0	0	0	3	.083	0	60	4	1	.985
—Jackson (Texas)		1B	78	269	53	85	11	3	7	53	.316	13	684	62	6	.992
1987 —Tidewater (Int'l)		1B-OF	136	457	*99	149	28	4	29	*103	*.326	8	858	88	10	.990
—New York (N.L.)		PH-PR	3	1	0	0	0	0	0	0	.000	0	0	0	0	...
1988 —Pittsburgh (N.L.)■		1B-OF	40	82	10	18	5	0	3	8	.220	1	213	15	3	.987
—Buffalo (Am. Assoc.)		1B-OF	63	221	37	61	15	3	2	30	.276	1	551	48	5	.992
1989 —Baltimore (A.L.)■		1B	124	365	56	98	23	5	12	45	.268	9	914	83	5	.995
1990 —Baltimore (A.L.)		1B	109	362	64	96	20	1	20	60	.265	6	846	87	9	.990
1991 —Baltimore (A.L.)		1B-OF	141	483	57	127	17	2	16	70	.263	0	948	81	11	.989
American League totals (3 years)			374	1210	177	321	60	8	48	175	.265	15	2708	251	25	.992
National League totals (2 years)			43	83	10	18	5	0	3	8	.217	1	213	15	3	.987
Major league totals (5 years)			417	1293	187	339	65	8	51	183	.262	16	2921	266	28	.991

MILLS, ALAN

P, YANKEES

PERSONAL: Born October 18, 1966, at Lakeland, Fla. . . . 6-1/190. . . . Throws right, bats both. . . . Full name: Alan Bernard Mills. **HIGH SCHOOL:** Kathleen (Fla.). **COLLEGE:** Polk Community College (Fla.).

TRANSACTIONS/CAREER NOTES: Selected by Boston Red Sox organization in first round (13th pick overall) of free-agent draft (January 14, 1986). . . . Selected by California Angels organization in secondary phase of free-agent draft (June 2, 1986). . . . Traded by Angels organization to New York Yankees organization (June 22, 1987), completing deal in which Angels traded P Ron Romanick and a player to be named later to Yankees for C Butch Wynegar (December 19, 1986).

Year	Team (League)	G	W	L	Pct.	ERA	Sv.	IP	H	R	ER	BB	SO
1986 —Salem (Northwest)		14	6	6	.500	4.63	0	83⅔	77	58	43	60	50
1987 —Prince William (Carolina)■		35	2	11	.154	6.09	1	85⅔	102	75	58	64	53
1988 —Prince William (Carolina)		42	3	8	.273	4.13	4	93⅔	93	56	43	43	59
1989 —Prince William (Carolina)		26	6	1	.857	0.91	7	39⅔	22	5	4	13	44
—Fort Lauderdale (Florida St.)		22	1	4	.200	3.77	6	31	40	15	13	9	25
1990 —New York (A.L.)		36	1	5	.167	4.10	0	41⅔	48	21	19	33	24
—Columbus (International)		17	3	3	.500	3.38	6	29⅓	22	11	11	14	30
1991 —Columbus (International)		38	7	5	.583	4.43	8	113⅔	109	65	56	75	77
—New York (A.L.)		6	1	1	.500	4.41	0	16⅓	16	9	8	8	11
Major league totals (2 years)		42	2	6	.250	4.19	0	58	64	30	27	41	35

MINUTELLI, GINO

P, REDS

PERSONAL: Born May 23, 1964, at Wilmington, Del. . . . 6-0/190. . . . Throws left, bats left. . . . Full name: Gino Michael Minutelli. **HIGH SCHOOL:** Sweetwater (National City, Calif.). **COLLEGE:** Southwestern College (Calif.).

TRANSACTIONS/CAREER NOTES: Signed as free agent by Cincinnati Reds organization (May 19, 1985). . . . On disabled list (April 12-23 and April 27, 1988-remainder of season). . . . On Plant City disabled list (April 1-August 1, 1989). . . . On Nashville disabled list (June 3-23, 1991). . . . On Cincinnati disabled list (June 30-July 15, 1991); included rehabilitation disability assignment to Charleston, W.Va. (July 7-15, 1991).

STATISTICAL NOTES: Led Southern League with 13 balks in 1990.

Year	Team (League)	G	W	L	Pct.	ERA	Sv.	IP	H	R	ER	BB	SO
1985 —Tri-Cities (Northwest)		20	4	•8	.333	8.05	0	57	61	57	51	57	79
1986 —Cedar Rapids (Midwest)		27	15	5	.750	3.66	0	152⅔	133	73	62	76	149
1987 —Tampa (Florida State)		17	7	6	.538	3.80	0	104⅓	98	51	44	48	70
—Vermont (Eastern)		6	4	1	.800	3.18	0	39⅔	34	15	14	16	39
1988 —Chattanooga (Southern)		2	0	1	.000	1.59	0	5⅔	6	2	1	4	3
1989 —Plant City (Gulf Coast)		1	0	0	...	0.00	0	1	0	0	0	1	0
—Chattanooga (Southern)		6	1	1	.500	5.28	0	29	28	19	17	23	20
1990 —Chattanooga (Southern)		17	9	5	.643	3.99	0	108⅓	106	52	48	46	75
—Nashville (American Assoc.)		11	5	2	.714	3.22	0	78⅓	65	34	28	31	61
—Cincinnati (N.L.)		2	0	0	...	9.00	0	1	0	1	1	2	0
1991 —Nashville (American Assoc.)		13	4	7	.364	1.90	0	80⅓	57	25	17	35	64
—Cincinnati (N.L.)		16	0	2	.000	6.04	0	25⅓	30	17	17	18	21
—Charleston, W.Va. (S. Atl.)		2	1	0	1.000	0.00	0	8	2	0	0	4	8
Major league totals (2 years)		18	0	2	.000	6.15	0	26⅓	30	18	18	20	21

MIRANDA, ANGEL

P, BREWERS

PERSONAL: Born November 9, 1969, at Arecibo, Puerto Rico. . . . 6-1/160. . . . Throws left, bats left. . . . Full name: Angel Miranda. **HIGH SCHOOL:** Maria Cadillo (Arecibo, Puerto Rico).

TRANSACTIONS/CAREER NOTES: Signed as free agent by Milwaukee Brewers organization (March 4, 1987). . . . Loaned by Brewers organization to Butte, co-op (March 4, 1987); returned (Summer, 1987).

Year	Team (League)	G	W	L	Pct.	ERA	Sv.	IP	H	R	ER	BB	SO
1987 —Butte-Helena (Pioneer)■		25	1	2	.333	3.12	3	43⅓	27	22	15	26	60
1988 —Stockton (California)		16	0	1	.000	7.18	2	26⅓	20	30	21	37	36
—Helena (Pioneer)		14	5	2	.714	3.86	0	60⅔	54	32	26	58	75

Year	Team (League)	G	W	L	Pct.	ERA	Sv.	IP	H	R	ER	BB	SO
1989 — Beloit (Midwest)		43	6	5	.545	0.86	16	63	39	13	6	32	88
1990 — Stockton (California)		52	9	4	.692	2.66	24	108⅓	75	37	32	49	138
1991 — El Paso (Texas)		38	4	2	.667	2.54	11	74⅓	55	27	21	41	86
— Denver (American Assoc.)		11	0	1	.000	6.17	2	11⅔	10	9	8	17	14

MITCHELL, KEITH
OF, BRAVES

PERSONAL: Born August 6, 1969, at San Diego. . . . 5-10/180. . . . Throws right, bats right. . . . Full name: Keith Alexander Mitchell. . . . Cousin of Kevin Mitchell, outfielder, Seattle Mariners.
HIGH SCHOOL: Lincoln (San Diego).
TRANSACTIONS/CAREER NOTES: Selected by Atlanta Braves organization in fourth round of free-agent draft (June 2, 1987).
STATISTICAL NOTES: Led Gulf Coast League outfielders with 109 putouts and tied for lead with 117 total chances in 1987. . . . Tied for Carolina League lead in double plays by outfielder with four in 1990.

Year	Team (League)	Pos.	G	AB	R	H	2B	3B	HR	RBI	Avg.	SB	PO	A	E	Avg.
1987 — Bradenton Braves (GCL)	OF-2B	57	208	24	50	12	1	2	21	.240	7	†111	6	4	.967
1988 — Sumter (South Atlantic)	OF	98	341	35	85	16	1	5	33	.249	9	193	7	6	.971
1989 — Burlington (Midwest)	OF-3B	127	448	64	117	23	4	10	49	.261	12	250	18	8	.971
1990 — Durham (Carolina)	OF	129	456	81	134	24	3	6	48	.294	18	256	9	5	.981
1991 — Greenville (Southern)	OF	60	214	46	70	15	3	10	47	.327	12	99	4	4	.963
— Richmond (Int'l)	OF	25	95	16	31	6	1	2	17	.326	0	56	0	1	.982
— Atlanta (N.L.)	OF	48	66	11	21	0	0	2	5	.318	3	31	1	1	.970
Major league totals (1 year)		48	66	11	21	0	0	2	5	.318	3	31	1	1	.970

CHAMPIONSHIP SERIES RECORD

Year	Team (League)	Pos.	G	AB	R	H	2B	3B	HR	RBI	Avg.	SB	PO	A	E	Avg.
1991 — Atlanta (N.L.)	PR-OF-PH	5	4	0	0	0	0	0	0	.000	0	2	0	0	1.000

WORLD SERIES RECORD

Year	Team (League)	Pos.	G	AB	R	H	2B	3B	HR	RBI	Avg.	SB	PO	A	E	Avg.
1991 — Atlanta (N.L.)	OF-PR	3	2	0	0	0	0	0	0	.000	0	0	0	0	. . .

MITCHELL, KEVIN
OF, MARINERS

PERSONAL: Born January 13, 1962, at San Diego. . . . 5-11/210. . . . Throws right, bats right. . . . Full name: Kevin Darrell Mitchell. . . . Cousin of Keith Mitchell, outfielder, Atlanta Braves.
HIGH SCHOOL: Clairmont (San Diego).
TRANSACTIONS/CAREER NOTES: Signed as free agent by New York Mets organization (November 16, 1980). . . . On disabled list (July 21, 1982-remainder of season and July 12-30, 1985). . . . Traded by Mets with OF Shawn Abner, OF Stanley Jefferson, P Kevin Armstrong and P Kevin Brown to San Diego Padres for OF Kevin McReynolds, P Gene Walter and IF Adam Ging (December 11, 1986). . . . Traded by Padres with P Dave Dravecky and P Craig Lefferts to San Francisco Giants for 3B Chris Brown, P Keith Comstock, P Mark Davis and P Mark Grant (July 4, 1987). . . . On suspended list for one game (May 3, 1991). . . . On disabled list (June 3-25, 1991). . . . Traded by Giants with P Mike Remlinger to Seattle Mariners for P Bill Swift, P Mike Jackson and P Dave Burba (December 11, 1991).
RECORDS/HONORS: Holds major league single-season record for most intentional bases on balls received by righthanded batter—32 (1989). . . . Named Major League Player of the Year by The Sporting News (1989). . . . Named N.L. Player of the Year by The Sporting News (1989). . . . Named outfielder on The Sporting News N.L. All-Star team (1989). . . . Named outfielder on The Sporting News N.L. Silver Slugger team (1989). . . . Named N.L. Most Valuable Player by Baseball Writers' Association of American (1989).
STATISTICAL NOTES: Led Texas League third basemen with 224 assists in 1983. . . . Led International League third basemen with 215 assists in 1984. . . . Led International League third basemen with 22 errors in 1985. . . . Led N.L. with 345 total bases, 32 intentional bases on balls received and .635 slugging percentage in 1989. . . . Hit three home runs in a game (May 25, 1990).

Year	Team (League)	Pos.	G	AB	R	H	2B	3B	HR	RBI	Avg.	SB	PO	A	E	Avg.
1981 — Kingsport (Appalachian)	3B-OF	62	221	39	74	9	2	7	45	.335	5	44	102	18	.890
1982 — Lynchburg (Carolina)	3B	29	85	19	27	5	1	1	16	.318	0	11	33	10	.815
1983 — Jackson (Texas)	3B-OF	120	441	75	132	25	2	15	85	.299	11	81	†224	21	.936
1984 — Tidewater (Int'l)	3B-1B-OF	120	432	51	105	21	3	10	54	.243	1	114	†220	22	.938
— New York (N.L.)	3B	7	14	0	3	0	0	0	1	.214	0	1	4	1	.833
1985 — Tidewater (Int'l)	3B-1B	95	348	44	101	24	2	9	43	.290	3	56	209	†22	.923
1986 — New York (N.L.)	O-S-3-1	108	328	51	91	22	2	12	43	.277	3	158	69	10	.958
1987 — San Diego-S.F. (N.L.)■	3B-OF-SS	131	464	68	130	20	2	22	70	.280	9	76	240	15	.955
1988 — San Francisco (N.L.)	3B-OF	148	505	60	127	25	7	19	80	.251	5	118	205	22	.936
1989 — San Francisco (N.L.)	OF-3B	154	543	100	158	34	6	★47	★125	.291	3	305	10	7	.978
1990 — San Francisco (N.L.)	OF	140	524	90	152	24	2	35	93	.290	4	295	9	9	.971
1991 — San Francisco (N.L.)	OF-1B	113	371	52	95	13	1	27	69	.256	2	188	6	6	.970
Major league totals (7 years)		801	2749	421	756	138	20	162	481	.275	26	1141	543	70	.960

CHAMPIONSHIP SERIES RECORD

CHAMPIONSHIP SERIES NOTES: Shares N.L. single-series record for most at-bats—30 (1987).

Year	Team (League)	Pos.	G	AB	R	H	2B	3B	HR	RBI	Avg.	SB	PO	A	E	Avg.
1986 —New York (N.L.)	OF	2	8	1	2	0	0	0	0	.250	0	3	0	0	1.000
1987 —San Francisco (N.L.)	3B	7	30	2	8	1	0	1	2	.267	1	4	11	1	.938
1989 —San Francisco (N.L.)	OF	5	17	5	6	0	0	2	7	.353	0	15	1	1	.941
Championship Series totals (3 years)		14	55	8	16	1	0	3	9	.291	1	22	12	2	.944

WORLD SERIES RECORD

Year	Team (League)	Pos.	G	AB	R	H	2B	3B	HR	RBI	Avg.	SB	PO	A	E	Avg.
1986 —New York (N.L.)	PH-O-DH	5	8	1	2	0	0	0	0	.250	0	0	2	0	1.000
1989 —San Francisco (N.L.)	OF	4	17	2	5	0	0	1	2	.294	0	10	0	1	.909
World Series totals (2 years)		9	25	3	7	0	0	1	2	.280	0	10	2	1	.923

ALL-STAR GAME RECORD

Year	League	Pos.	AB	R	H	2B	3B	HR	RBI	Avg.	SB	PO	A	E	Avg.
1989 —National	OF	4	1	2	0	0	0	1	.500	0	0	0	0	. . .
1990 —National	OF	2	0	0	0	0	0	0	.000	0	1	0	0	1.000
All-Star Game totals (2 years)		6	1	2	0	0	0	1	.333	0	1	0	0	1.000

MOELLER, DENNIS
P, ROYALS

PERSONAL: Born September 15, 1967, at Tarzana, Calif. . . . 6-2/195. . . . Throws right, bats right. . . . Full name: Dennis Michael Moeller.
HIGH SCHOOL: Cleveland (Reseda, Calif.).
COLLEGE: Los Angeles Valley College (Calif.).
TRANSACTIONS/CAREER NOTES: Selected by Kansas City Royals organization in 17th round of free-agent draft (June 2, 1986). . . . On Memphis disabled list (July 26, 1989-remainder of season).

Year	Team (League)	G	W	L	Pct.	ERA	Sv.	IP	H	R	ER	BB	SO
1986 —Eugene (Northwest)	14	4	0	1.000	3.06	0	61⅔	54	22	21	34	65
1987 —Appleton (Midwest)	18	2	5	.286	7.20	0	55	72	63	44	45	49
1988 —Appleton (Midwest)	20	3	5	.375	3.18	0	99	94	46	35	34	88
1989 —Baseball City (Florida State)	12	9	0	1.000	1.77	0	71	59	17	14	20	64
—Memphis (Southern)	5	1	1	.500	2.84	0	25⅓	16	9	8	10	21
1990 —Omaha (American Assoc.)........	11	5	2	.714	4.02	0	65	63	29	29	30	53
—Memphis (Southern)	14	7	6	.538	6.25	0	67⅔	79	55	47	30	42
1991 —Omaha (American Assoc.)........	14	7	3	.700	3.22	0	78⅓	70	36	28	40	51
—Memphis (Southern)	10	4	5	.444	2.55	0	53	52	24	15	21	54

MOLITOR, PAUL
1B/DH, BREWERS

PERSONAL: Born August 22, 1956, at St. Paul, Minn. . . . 6-0/185. . . . Throws right, bats right. . . . Full name: Paul Leo Molitor.
HIGH SCHOOL: Cretin (St. Paul).
COLLEGE: Minnesota.
TRANSACTIONS/CAREER NOTES: Selected by St. Louis Cardinals organization in 28th round of free-agent draft (June 5, 1974). . . . Selected by Milwaukee Brewers organization in first round (third pick overall) of free-agent draft (June 7, 1977). . . . On disabled list (June 24-July 18, 1980; May 3-August 12, 1981; May 2, 1984-remainder of season; August 13-28, 1985; May 10-30, June 2-17 and June 19-July 8, 1986; and April 30-May 26 and June 27-July 16, 1987). . . . Granted free agency (November 9, 1987). . . . Re-signed by Brewers (January 5, 1988). . . . On disabled list (March 30-April 14, 1989). . . . On Milwaukee disabled list (April 2-27 and June 17-July 30, 1990); included rehabilitation disability assignment to Beloit (July 28, 1990).
RECORDS/HONORS: Shares major league record for most stolen bases in one inning—3 (July 26, 1987, first inning). . . . Named shortstop on THE SPORTING NEWS college All-America team (1977). . . . Named Midwest League Most Valuable Player (1977). . . . Named A.L. Rookie Player of the Year by THE SPORTING NEWS (1978). . . . Named designated hitter on THE SPORTING NEWS A.L. All-Star team (1987). . . . Named designated hitter on THE SPORTING NEWS A.L. Silver Slugger team (1987-88).
STATISTICAL NOTES: Hit three home runs in a game (May 12, 1982). . . . Led A.L. third basemen with 29 errors and 48 double plays in 1982. . . . Hit for the cycle (May 15, 1991).

Year	Team (League)	Pos.	G	AB	R	H	2B	3B	HR	RBI	Avg.	SB	PO	A	E	Avg.
1977 —Burlington (Midwest)	SS	64	228	52	79	12	0	8	50	.346	14	83	207	28	.912
1978 —Milwaukee (A.L.)	2B-SS-3B	125	521	73	142	26	4	6	45	.273	30	253	401	22	.967
1979 —Milwaukee (A.L.)	2B-SS	140	584	88	188	27	16	9	62	.322	33	309	440	16	.979
1980 —Milwaukee (A.L.)	2B-SS-3B	111	450	81	137	29	2	9	37	.304	34	260	336	20	.968
1981 —Milwaukee (A.L.)	OF	64	251	45	67	11	0	2	19	.267	10	119	4	3	.976
1982 —Milwaukee (A.L.)	3B-SS	160	★666	★136	201	26	8	19	71	.302	41	134	350	†32	.938
1983 —Milwaukee (A.L.)	3B	152	608	95	164	28	6	15	47	.270	41	105	343	16	.966
1984 —Milwaukee (A.L.)	3B	13	46	3	10	1	0	0	6	.217	1	7	21	2	.933
1985 —Milwaukee (A.L.)	3B	140	576	93	171	28	3	10	48	.297	21	126	263	19	.953
1986 —Milwaukee (A.L.)	3B-OF	105	437	62	123	24	6	9	55	.281	20	86	171	15	.945
1987 —Milwaukee (A.L.)	3B-2B	118	465	★114	164	★41	5	16	75	.353	45	60	113	5	.972
1988 —Milwaukee (A.L.)	3B-2B	154	609	115	190	34	6	13	60	.312	41	87	188	17	.942
1989 —Milwaukee (A.L.)	3B-2B	155	615	84	194	35	4	11	56	.315	27	106	287	18	.956
1990 —Milwaukee (A.L.)	2B-1B-3B	103	418	64	119	27	6	12	45	.285	18	463	222	10	.986
—Beloit (Midwest)	DH	1	4	1	2	0	0	1	1	.500	0	0	0	0	. . .
1991 —Milwaukee (A.L.)	1B	158	★665	★133	★216	32	•13	17	75	.325	19	389	32	6	.986
Major league totals (14 years)		1698	6911	1186	2086	369	79	148	701	.302	381	2504	3171	201	.966

DIVISION SERIES RECORD

Year Team (League)	Pos.	G	AB	R	H	2B	3B	HR	RBI	Avg.	SB	PO	A	E	Avg.
									BATTING				FIELDING		
1981—Milwaukee (A.L.)	OF	5	20	2	5	0	0	1	1	.250	0	12	0	0	1.000

CHAMPIONSHIP SERIES RECORD

Year Team (League)	Pos.	G	AB	R	H	2B	3B	HR	RBI	Avg.	SB	PO	A	E	Avg.
1982—Milwaukee (A.L.)	3B	5	19	4	6	1	0	2	5	.316	1	4	11	2	.882

WORLD SERIES NOTES: Holds single-game records for most hits—5; most singles—5 (October 12, 1982).... Shares single-game record (nine innings) for most at-bats—6 (October 12, 1982).

WORLD SERIES RECORD

Year Team (League)	Pos.	G	AB	R	H	2B	3B	HR	RBI	Avg.	SB	PO	A	E	Avg.
1982—Milwaukee (A.L.)	3B	7	31	5	11	0	0	0	3	.355	1	4	9	0	1.000

ALL-STAR GAME RECORD

ALL-STAR GAME NOTES: Named to A.L. All-Star team in 1980; replaced due to injury.

Year League	Pos.	AB	R	H	2B	3B	HR	RBI	Avg.	SB	PO	A	E	Avg.
1985—American	3B-OF	1	0	0	0	0	0	0	.000	0	0	0	0	...
1988—American	2B	3	0	0	0	0	0	0	.000	0	1	2	0	1.000
1991—American	3B	0	0	0	0	0	0	0	...	0	0	0	0	...
All-Star Game totals (3 years)		4	0	0	0	0	0	0	.000	0	1	2	0	1.000

MONDESI, RAUL
OF, DODGERS

PERSONAL: Born March 12, 1971, at San Cristobal, Dominican Republic.... 5-11/150.... Throws right, bats right.... Full name: Raul Mondesi.
HIGH SCHOOL: Liceo Manuel Maria Valencia (Dominican Republic).
TRANSACTIONS/CAREER NOTES: Signed as free agent by Los Angeles Dodgers organization (June 6, 1988).... On Bakersfield disabled list (May 8-July 5, 1991).

Year Team (League)	Pos.	G	AB	R	H	2B	3B	HR	RBI	Avg.	SB	PO	A	E	Avg.
1990—Great Falls (Pioneer)	OF	44	175	35	53	10	4	8	31	.303	30	65	4	1	.986
1991—Bakersfield (California)	OF	28	106	23	30	7	2	3	13	.283	9	42	5	3	.940
—San Antonio (Texas)	OF	53	213	32	58	11	5	5	26	.272	8	101	6	4	.964
—Albuquerque (PCL)	OF	2	9	3	3	0	1	0	0	.333	1	0	0	1	.000

MONTELEONE, RICH
P, YANKEES

PERSONAL: Born March 22, 1963, at Tampa, Fla.... 6-2/236.... Throws right, bats right. ... Full name: Richard Monteleone. ... Name pronounced MON-ta-lee-YONE.
HIGH SCHOOL: Tampa Catholic (Fla.).
TRANSACTIONS/CAREER NOTES: Selected by Detroit Tigers organization in first round (20th pick overall) of free-agent draft (June 7, 1982).... Traded by Tigers organization to Seattle Mariners for 3B Darnell Coles (December 12, 1985).... Released by Mariners organization (May 9, 1988).... Signed by Edmonton, California Angels organization (May 13, 1988).... Traded by Angels organization with OF Claudell Washington to New York Yankees for OF Luis Polonia (April 28, 1990).
STATISTICAL NOTES: Led Appalachian League pitchers with eight home runs allowed in 1982.

Year Team (League)	G	W	L	Pct.	ERA	Sv.	IP	H	R	ER	BB	SO
1982—Bristol (Appalachian)	12	4	6	.400	3.89	0	71⅔	66	41	31	23	52
1983—Lakeland (Florida State)	24	9	8	.529	4.11	0	142⅓	146	80	65	80	124
—Birmingham (Southern)	3	1	1	.500	7.20	0	15	25	12	12	6	9
1984—Birmingham (Southern)	19	7	8	.467	4.66	0	123⅔	116	69	64	67	74
—Evansville (Am. Assoc.)	11	5	3	.625	4.50	0	64	64	33	32	36	42
1985—Nashville (American Assoc.)	27	6	12	.333	5.08	0	145⅓	149	89	82	87	97
1986—Calgary (Pacific Coast)■	39	8	12	.400	5.28	0	158⅔	177	108	93	★89	101
1987—Seattle (A.L.)	3	0	0	...	6.43	0	7	10	5	5	4	2
—Calgary (Pacific Coast)	51	6	★13	.316	5.51	15	65⅓	59	45	40	63	38
1988—Calgary-Edmonton (PCL)■......	30	4	7	.364	5.08	0	122½	141	84	69	27	97
—California (A.L.)	3	0	0	...	0.00	0	4⅓	4	0	0	1	3
1989—Edmonton (Pacific Coast)........	13	3	6	.333	3.47	0	57	50	23	22	16	47
—California (A.L.)	24	2	2	.500	3.18	0	39⅔	39	15	14	13	27
1990—Edmonton (Pacific Coast)........	5	1	0	1.000	1.93	1	14	7	3	3	4	9
—Columbus (International)■	38	4	4	.500	2.24	9	64⅓	51	17	16	23	60
—New York (A.L.)	5	0	1	.000	6.14	0	7⅓	8	5	5	2	8
1991—Columbus (International)	32	1	3	.250	2.12	17	46⅔	36	15	11	7	52
—New York (A.L.)	26	3	1	.750	3.64	0	47	42	27	19	19	34
Major league totals (5 years)	61	5	4	.556	3.67	0	105⅓	103	52	43	39	74

MONTGOMERY, JEFF
P, ROYALS

PERSONAL: Born January 7, 1962, at Wellston, O.... 5-11/180.... Throws right, bats right.... Full name: Jeffrey Thomas Montgomery.
HIGH SCHOOL: Wellston (O.).
COLLEGE: Marshall (bachelor of science degree in computer science, 1984).

TRANSACTIONS/CAREER NOTES: Selected by Cincinnati Reds organization in ninth round of free-agent draft (June 6, 1983).... Traded by Reds to Kansas City Royals for OF Van Snider (February 15, 1988).
RECORDS/HONORS: Shares major league record for striking out side on nine pitches (April 29, 1990, eighth inning).

Year Team (League)	G	W	L	Pct.	ERA	Sv.	IP	H	R	ER	BB	SO
1983 — Billings (Pioneer)	20	6	2	.750	2.42	1	44 2/3	31	13	12	13	90
1984 — Tampa (Florida State)	31	5	3	.625	2.44	•14	44 1/3	29	15	12	30	56
— Vermont (Eastern)	22	2	0	1.000	2.13	4	25 1/3	14	7	6	24	20
1985 — Vermont (Eastern)	*53	5	3	.625	2.05	9	101	63	25	23	48	89
1986 — Denver (American Assoc.)	30	11	7	.611	4.39	1	151 2/3	162	88	74	57	78
1987 — Nashville (American Assoc.)	24	8	5	.615	4.14	0	139	132	76	64	51	121
— Cincinnati (N.L.)	14	2	2	.500	6.52	0	19 1/3	25	15	14	9	13
1988 — Omaha (American Assoc.)■	20	1	2	.333	1.91	13	28 1/3	15	6	6	11	36
— Kansas City (A.L.)	45	7	2	.778	3.45	1	62 2/3	54	25	24	30	47
1989 — Kansas City (A.L.)	63	7	3	.700	1.37	18	92	66	16	14	25	94
1990 — Kansas City (A.L.)	73	6	5	.545	2.39	24	94 1/3	81	36	25	34	94
1991 — Kansas City (A.L.)	67	4	4	.500	2.90	33	90	83	32	29	28	77
American League totals (4 years)	248	24	14	.632	2.44	76	339	284	109	92	117	312
National League totals (1 year)	14	2	2	.500	6.52	0	19 1/3	25	15	14	9	13
Major league totals (5 years)	262	26	16	.619	2.66	76	358 1/3	309	124	106	126	325

MOORE, BOBBY
OF, BRAVES

PERSONAL: Born October 27, 1965, at Cincinnati.... 5-9/165.... Throws right, bats right....
Full name: Robert Vincent Moore.
HIGH SCHOOL: Purcell-Marian (Cincinnati).
COLLEGE: Eastern Kentucky.

TRANSACTIONS/CAREER NOTES: Selected by Detroit Tigers organization in 29th round of free-agent draft (June 4, 1984).... Selected by Kansas City Royals organization in 16th round of free-agent draft (June 2, 1987).... Traded by Royals to Atlanta Braves for SS Rico Rossy (December 10, 1991).
STATISTICAL NOTES: Led American Association with 13 sacrifice hits in 1991.... Led American Association outfielders with six double plays in 1991.

Year Team (League)	Pos.	G	AB	R	H	2B	3B	HR	RBI	Avg.	SB	PO	A	E	Avg.
1987 — Eugene (Northwest)	OF	57	235	40	88	13	4	1	25	*.374	23	75	6	3	.964
1988 — Baseball City (Fla. St.)	OF	60	224	25	52	4	2	0	10	.232	12	121	5	3	.977
1989 — Baseball City (Fla. St.)	OF	131	483	*85	131	21	5	0	42	.271	34	304	11	7	.978
1990 — Memphis (Southern)	OF	112	422	93	128	20	6	2	36	.303	7	224	6	1	*.996
1991 — Omaha (Am. Assoc.)	OF	130	494	65	120	13	3	0	34	.243	35	296	15	2	.994
— Kansas City (A.L.)	OF	18	14	3	5	1	0	0	0	.357	3	11	0	0	1.000
Major league totals (1 year)		18	14	3	5	1	0	0	0	.357	3	11	0	0	1.000

MOORE, KERWIN
OF, ROYALS

PERSONAL: Born October 29, 1970, at Detroit.... 6-1/190.... Throws right, bats right....
Full name: Kerwin Lamar Moore.
HIGH SCHOOL: Martin Luther King (Detroit).
TRANSACTIONS/CAREER NOTES: Selected by Kansas City Royals organization in 16th round of free-agent draft (June 1, 1988).
STATISTICAL NOTES: Led Midwest League with 111 bases on balls received in 1990.... Led Florida State League batters with 141 strikeouts in 1991.

Year Team (League)	Pos.	G	AB	R	H	2B	3B	HR	RBI	Avg.	SB	PO	A	E	Avg.
1988 — Sarasota Royals (GCL)	OF	53	165	19	29	5	0	0	14	.176	20	80	2	4	.953
1989 — Eugene (Northwest)	OF	65	226	44	50	9	2	2	25	.221	20	127	3	6	.956
— Baseball City (Fla. St.)	OF	4	11	3	4	0	0	1	2	.364	2	7	0	0	1.000
1990 — Appleton (Midwest)	OF	128	451	*93	100	17	7	2	36	.222	57	257	11	12	.957
1991 — Baseball City (Fla. St.)	OF	*130	485	67	102	14	2	1	23	.210	*61	306	2	4	.987

MOORE, MIKE
P, ATHLETICS

PERSONAL: Born November 26, 1959, at Eakly, Okla.... 6-4/205.... Throws right, bats right....
Full name: Michael Wayne Moore.
HIGH SCHOOL: Eakly (Okla.).
COLLEGE: Oral Roberts.

TRANSACTIONS/CAREER NOTES: Selected by St. Louis Cardinals organization in third round of free-agent draft (June 6, 1978). ... Selected by Seattle Mariners organization in first round (first pick overall) of free-agent draft (June 8, 1981).... Granted free agency (November 4, 1988).... Signed by Oakland Athletics (November 28, 1988).... On disabled list (July 20-August 6, 1991).
RECORDS/HONORS: Named righthanded pitcher on THE SPORTING NEWS college All-America team (1981).
STATISTICAL NOTES: Tied for A.L. lead in games started by pitcher with 37 in 1986.
MISCELLANEOUS: Made an out in only appearance as pinch-hitter (1987).... Appeared in one game as pinch-runner (1991).

Year Team (League)	G	W	L	Pct.	ERA	Sv.	IP	H	R	ER	BB	SO
1981 — Lynn (Eastern)	13	6	5	.545	3.64	0	94	83	42	38	34	81
1982 — Seattle (A.L.)	28	7	14	.333	5.36	0	144 1/3	159	91	86	79	73
— Salt Lake City (Pacific Coast)	1	0	0	. . .	4.50	0	8	9	4	4	5	6

Year Team (League)	G	W	L	Pct.	ERA	Sv.	IP	H	R	ER	BB	SO
1983 —Seattle (A.L.)	22	6	8	.429	4.71	0	128	130	75	67	60	108
—Salt Lake City (Pacific Coast) ..	11	4	4	.500	3.61	0	82⅓	78	48	33	54	80
1984 —Seattle (A.L.)	34	7	17	.292	4.97	0	212	236	127	117	85	158
1985 —Seattle (A.L.)	35	17	10	.630	3.46	0	247	230	100	95	70	155
1986 —Seattle (A.L.)	38	11	13	.458	4.30	1	266	★279	141	127	94	146
1987 —Seattle (A.L.)	33	9	★19	.321	4.71	0	231	★268	145	★121	84	115
1988 —Seattle (A.L.)	37	9	15	.375	3.78	1	228⅔	196	104	96	63	182
1989 —Oakland (A.L.)■	35	19	11	.633	2.61	0	241⅔	193	82	70	83	172
1990 —Oakland (A.L.)	33	13	15	.464	4.65	0	199⅓	204	113	103	84	73
1991 —Oakland (A.L.)	33	17	8	.680	2.96	0	210	176	75	69	105	153
Major league totals (10 years)	328	115	130	.469	4.06	2	2108	2071	1053	951	807	1335

CHAMPIONSHIP SERIES RECORD

Year Team (League)	G	W	L	Pct.	ERA	Sv.	IP	H	R	ER	BB	SO
1989 —Oakland (A.L.)	1	1	0	1.000	0.00	0	7	3	1	0	2	3
1990 —Oakland (A.L.)	1	1	0	1.000	1.50	0	6	4	1	1	1	5
Championship Series totals (2 years)	2	2	0	1.000	0.69	0	13	7	2	1	3	8

WORLD SERIES RECORD

WORLD SERIES NOTES: Shares single-game record for most wild pitches—2 (October 15, 1989).

Year Team (League)	G	W	L	Pct.	ERA	Sv.	IP	H	R	ER	BB	SO
1989 —Oakland (A.L.)	2	2	0	1.000	2.08	0	13	9	3	3	3	10
1990 —Oakland (A.L.)	1	0	1	.000	6.75	0	2⅔	8	6	2	0	1
World Series totals (2 years)	3	2	1	.667	2.87	0	15⅔	17	9	5	3	11

ALL-STAR GAME RECORD

Year League	W	L	Pct.	ERA	Sv.	IP	H	R	ER	BB	SO
1989 —American	0	0	...	0.00	0	1	0	0	0	0	1

MORANDINI, MICKEY
2B, PHILLIES

PERSONAL: Born April 22, 1966, at Kittanning, Pa. ... 5-11/167. ... Throws right, bats left. ... Full name: Michael Robert Morandini.
HIGH SCHOOL: Leechburg Area (Pa.).
COLLEGE: Indiana.
TRANSACTIONS/CAREER NOTES: Selected by Pittsburgh Pirates organization in seventh round of free-agent draft (June 2, 1987). ... Selected by Philadelphia Phillies organization in fifth round of free-agent draft (June 1, 1988).
STATISTICAL NOTES: Led International League second basemen with 271 putouts, 419 assists and 701 total chances in 1990.
MISCELLANEOUS: Member of 1988 U.S. Olympic baseball team.

							BATTING					FIELDING			
Year Team (League)	Pos.	G	AB	R	H	2B	3B	HR	RBI	Avg.	SB	PO	A	E	Avg.
1989 —Spartanburg (S. Atl.)	SS	63	231	43	78	19	1	1	30	.338	18	87	198	10	.966
—Clearwater (Florida St.)	SS	17	63	14	19	4	1	0	4	.302	3	20	59	2	.975
—Reading (Eastern)	SS	48	188	39	66	12	1	5	29	.351	5	73	137	10	.955
1990 —Scranton/W.B. (Int'l)	2B-SS	139	503	76	131	24	★10	1	31	.260	16	†271	†419	11	.984
—Philadelphia (N.L.)	2B	25	79	9	19	4	0	1	3	.241	3	37	61	1	.990
1991 —Scranton/W.B. (Int'l)	2B	12	46	7	12	4	0	1	9	.261	2	19	38	1	.983
—Philadelphia (N.L.)	2B	98	325	38	81	11	4	1	20	.249	13	183	254	6	.986
Major league totals (2 years)		123	404	47	100	15	4	2	23	.248	16	220	315	7	.987

MORGAN, MIKE
P, CUBS

PERSONAL: Born October 8, 1959, at Tulare, Calif. ... 6-2/222. ... Throws right, bats right. ... Full name: Michael Thomas Morgan.
HIGH SCHOOL: Valley (Las Vegas).
TRANSACTIONS/CAREER NOTES: Selected by Oakland Athletics organization in first round (fourth pick overall) of free-agent draft (June 6, 1978). ... On disabled list (May 14-June 27, 1980). ... Traded by A's organization to New York Yankees for SS Fred Stanley and a player to be named later (November 3, 1980); A's acquired 2B Brian Doyle to complete deal (November 17, 1980). ... On disabled list (April 9-22, 1981). ... Traded by Yankees with OF-1B Dave Collins, 1B Fred McGriff and cash to Toronto Blue Jays for P Dale Murray and OF-C Tom Dodd (December 9, 1982). ... On Toronto disabled list (July 2-August 23, 1983); included rehabilitation disability assignment to Syracuse (August 1-18, 1983). ... Drafted by Seattle Mariners (December 3, 1984). ... On Seattle disabled list (April 17, 1985-remainder of season); included rehabilitation disability assignment to Calgary (July 19-22, 1985). ... Traded by Mariners to Baltimore Orioles for P Ken Dixon (December 9, 1987). ... On Baltimore disabled list (June 9-July 19 and August 12, 1988-remainder of season); included rehabilitation disability assignment to Rochester (June 30-July 17, 1988). ... Traded by Orioles to Los Angeles Dodgers for OF Mike Devereaux (March 12, 1989). ... Granted free agency (October 28, 1991). ... Signed by Chicago Cubs (December 3, 1991).
STATISTICAL NOTES: Tied for International League lead with four shutouts in 1984. ... Tied for N.L. lead with four shutouts in 1990.

Year Team (League)	G	W	L	Pct.	ERA	Sv.	IP	H	R	ER	BB	SO
1978 —Oakland (A.L.)	3	0	3	.000	7.50	0	12	19	12	10	8	0
—Vancouver (Pacific Coast)	14	5	6	.455	5.58	0	92	109	67	57	54	31
1979 —Ogden (Pacific Coast)	13	5	5	.500	3.48	0	101	93	48	39	49	42
—Oakland (A.L.)	13	2	10	.167	5.96	0	77	102	57	51	50	17

Year	Team (League)	G	W	L	Pct.	ERA	Sv.	IP	H	R	ER	BB	SO
1980 —Ogden (Pacific Coast)		20	6	9	.400	5.40	0	115	135	79	69	77	46
1981 —Nashville (Southern)■		26	8	7	.533	4.42	0	169	164	97	83	83	100
1982 —New York (A.L.)		30	7	11	.389	4.37	0	150⅓	167	77	73	67	71
1983 —Toronto (A.L.)■		16	0	3	.000	5.16	0	45⅓	48	26	26	21	22
—Syracuse (International)		5	0	3	.000	5.59	1	19⅓	20	12	12	13	17
1984 —Syracuse (International)		34	13	11	.542	4.07	1	★185⅔	167	•101	84	•100	105
1985 —Seattle (A.L.)■		2	1	1	.500	12.00	0	6	11	8	8	5	2
—Calgary (Pacific Coast)		1	0	0	. . .	4.50	0	2	3	1	1	0	0
1986 —Seattle (A.L.)		37	11	•17	.393	4.53	1	216⅓	243	122	109	86	116
1987 —Seattle (A.L.)		34	12	17	.414	4.65	0	207	245	117	107	53	85
1988 —Baltimore (A.L.)■		22	1	6	.143	5.43	1	71⅓	70	45	43	23	29
—Rochester (International)		3	0	2	.000	4.76	0	17	19	10	9	6	7
1989 —Los Angeles (N.L.)■		40	8	11	.421	2.53	0	152⅔	130	51	43	33	72
1990 —Los Angeles (N.L.)		33	11	15	.423	3.75	0	211	216	100	88	60	106
1991 —Los Angeles (N.L.)		34	14	10	.583	2.78	1	236⅓	197	85	73	61	140
American League totals (8 years)		157	34	68	.333	4.89	2	785⅓	905	464	427	313	342
National League totals (3 years)		107	33	36	.478	3.06	1	600	543	236	204	154	318
Major league totals (11 years)		264	67	104	.392	4.10	3	1385⅓	1448	700	631	467	660

ALL-STAR GAME RECORD

Year	League	W	L	Pct.	ERA	Sv.	IP	H	R	ER	BB	SO
1991 —National	0	0	. . .	0.00	0	1	0	0	0	0	1

MORMAN, RUSS
1B/OF, REDS

PERSONAL: Born April 28, 1962, at Independence, Mo. . . . 6-4/215. . . . Throws right, bats right. . . . Full name: Russell Lee Morman.
HIGH SCHOOL: William Chrisman (Independence, Mo.).
COLLEGE: Iowa Western Community College and Wichita State.
TRANSACTIONS/CAREER NOTES: Selected by Kansas City Royals organization in seventh round of free-agent draft (January 13, 1981). . . . Selected by Chicago White Sox organization in first round (28th pick overall) of free-agent draft (June 6, 1983). . . . Released by White Sox (November 20, 1989). . . . Signed by Omaha, Kansas City Royals organization (December 21, 1989). . . . Granted free agency (October 16, 1991). . . . Signed by Cincinnati Reds organization (November 12, 1991).
RECORDS/HONORS: Shares major league record for most hits in one inning in first major league game—2 (August 3, 1986, fourth inning). . . . Named first baseman on THE SPORTING NEWS college All-America team (1983).
STATISTICAL NOTES: Led Eastern League with .512 slugging percentage in 1985. . . . Led Eastern League first basemen with .988 fielding percentage and 79 assists in 1985. . . . Led American Association third basemen with 23 double plays in 1986.

								BATTING						FIELDING		
Year	Team (League)	Pos.	G	AB	R	H	2B	3B	HR	RBI	Avg.	SB	PO	A	E	Avg.
1983 —Glens Falls (Eastern)	1B	71	233	29	57	9	1	3	32	.245	8	591	43	7	.989
1984 —Appleton (Midwest)	1B-OF	122	424	68	111	17	7	7	80	.262	29	823	43	10	.989
1985 —Glens Falls (Eastern)	1-3-0	119	422	64	131	24	5	17	81	.310	11	905	†81	12	†.988
—Buffalo (Am. Assoc.)	1B	21	64	16	19	3	1	7	14	.297	2	144	7	2	.987
1986 —Buffalo (Am. Assoc.)	3B-OF	106	365	52	97	17	2	13	57	.266	3	87	201	24	.923
—Chicago (A.L.)	1B	49	159	18	40	5	0	4	17	.252	1	342	26	4	.989
1987 —Hawaii (Pacific Coast)	1B-OF	89	294	52	79	19	2	9	53	.269	5	410	28	3	.993
1988 —Vancouver (Pac. Coast)	1B-OF	69	257	40	77	8	1	5	45	.300	4	370	21	3	.992
—Chicago (A.L.)	1B-OF	40	75	8	18	2	0	0	3	.240	0	114	5	2	.983
1989 —Vancouver (Pac. Coast)	1B-OF	61	216	18	60	14	1	1	23	.278	1	163	12	3	.983
—Chicago (A.L.)	1B	37	58	5	13	2	0	0	8	.224	1	157	13	2	.988
1990 —Omaha (Am. Assoc.)■	1-0-3-2	121	436	67	130	14	9	13	81	.298	21	665	59	5	.993
—Kansas City (A.L.)	OF-1B	12	37	5	10	4	2	1	3	.270	0	27	4	0	1.000
1991 —Kansas City (A.L.)	1B-OF	12	23	1	6	0	0	0	1	.261	0	47	3	0	1.000
—Omaha (Am. Assoc.)	1B-OF-P	88	316	46	83	15	3	7	50	.263	10	564	41	7	.989
Major league totals (5 years)		150	352	37	87	13	2	5	32	.247	2	687	51	8	.989

RECORD AS PITCHER

Year	Team (League)	G	W	L	Pct.	ERA	Sv.	IP	H	R	ER	BB	SO
1991 —Omaha (American Assoc.)	1	0	0	. . .	0.00	0	1	0	0	0	0	0

MORRIS, HAL
1B, REDS

PERSONAL: Born April 9, 1965, at Fort Rucker, Ala. . . . 6-4/215. . . . Throws left, bats left. . . . Full name: William Harold Morris.
HIGH SCHOOL: Munster (Ind.).
COLLEGE: Michigan.
TRANSACTIONS/CAREER NOTES: Selected by New York Yankees organization in eighth round of free-agent draft (June 2, 1986). . . . On Albany disabled list (August 14, 1986-remainder of season). . . . Traded by Yankees with P Rodney Imes to Cincinnati Reds for P Tim Leary and OF Van Snider (December 12, 1989).

								BATTING						FIELDING		
Year	Team (League)	Pos.	G	AB	R	H	2B	3B	HR	RBI	Avg.	SB	PO	A	E	Avg.
1986 —Oneonta (N.Y.-Penn)	1B	36	127	26	48	9	2	3	30	.378	1	317	26	3	.991
—Albany (Eastern)	1B	25	79	7	17	5	0	0	4	.215	0	203	19	2	.991
1987 —Albany (Eastern)	1B-OF	135	★530	65	★173	31	4	5	73	.326	7	1086	79	17	.986

Year	Team (League)	Pos.	G	AB	R	H	2B	3B	HR	RBI	Avg.	SB	PO	A	E	Avg.
1988 —Columbus (Int'l)		OF-1B	121	452	41	134	19	4	3	38	.296	8	543	26	8	.986
—New York (A.L.)		OF	15	20	1	2	0	0	0	0	.100	0	7	0	0	1.000
1989 —Columbus (Int'l)		1B-OF	111	417	70	136	24	1	17	66 *.326		5	636	67	9	.987
—New York (A.L.)		OF-1B	15	18	2	5	0	0	0	4	.278	0	12	0	0	1.000
1990 —Cincinnati (N.L.)■..............		1B-OF	107	309	50	105	22	3	7	36	.340	9	595	53	4	.994
—Nashville (Am. Assoc.)		OF	16	64	8	22	5	0	1	10	.344	4	23	1	1	.960
1991 —Cincinnati (N.L.)		1B-OF	136	478	72	152	33	1	14	59	.318	10	979	100	9	.992
American League totals (2 years)			30	38	3	7	0	0	0	4	.184	0	19	0	0	1.000
National League totals (2 years)			243	787	122	257	55	4	21	95	.327	19	1574	153	13	.993
Major league totals (4 years)			273	825	125	264	55	4	21	99	.320	19	1593	153	13	.993

CHAMPIONSHIP SERIES RECORD

Year	Team (League)	Pos.	G	AB	R	H	2B	3B	HR	RBI	Avg.	SB	PO	A	E	Avg.
1990 —Cincinnati (N.L.)		1B-PH	5	12	3	5	1	0	0	1	.417	0	20	2	0	1.000

WORLD SERIES RECORD

Year	Team (League)	Pos.	G	AB	R	H	2B	3B	HR	RBI	Avg.	SB	PO	A	E	Avg.
1990 —Cincinnati (N.L.)		1B-DH	4	14	0	1	0	0	0	2	.071	0	18	1	0	1.000

MORRIS, JACK
P, BLUE JAYS

PERSONAL: Born May 16, 1955, at St. Paul, Minn.... 6-3/200.... Throws right, bats right.... Full name: John Scott Morris.
HIGH SCHOOL: Highland Park (St. Paul, Minn.).
COLLEGE: Brigham Young.
TRANSACTIONS/CAREER NOTES: Selected by Detroit Tigers organization in fifth round of free-agent draft (June 8, 1976).... Granted free agency (November 12, 1986).... Re-signed by Tigers (December 19, 1986).... Granted free agency (November 9, 1987).... Re-signed by Tigers (December 29, 1987).... On Detroit disabled list (May 25-July 24, 1989); included rehabilitation disability assignment to Lakeland (July 10-24, 1989).... Granted free agency (December 7, 1990).... Signed by Minnesota Twins (February 5, 1991).... Granted free agency (November 11, 1991).... Signed by Toronto Blue Jays (December 18, 1991).
RECORDS/HONORS: Holds A.L. career records for most consecutive starting assignments—431; most putouts by pitcher—344 and most wild pitches—170.... Holds A.L. single-season record for most wild pitches—24 (1987).... Holds A.L. record for most seasons leading league in wild pitches—5.... Shares A.L. single-season record for fewest complete games by pitcher who led league in complete games—11 (1990).... Shares A.L. record for most years allowing 30 or more home runs—4.... Shares A.L. single-game record for most wild pitches—5 (August 3, 1987, 10 innings).... Named A.L. Pitcher of the Year by THE SPORTING NEWS (1981).... Named righthanded pitcher on THE SPORTING NEWS A.L. All-Star team (1981).
STATISTICAL NOTES: Led A.L. with 18 wild pitches in 1983, 14 in 1984, 15 in 1985, 24 in 1987 and 15 in 1991..... Pitched 4-0 no-hit victory against Chicago White Sox (April 7, 1984).... Led A.L. with six shutouts in 1986.... Tied for A.L. lead in complete games with 11 and games started by pitcher with 36 in 1990.... Tied for A.L. lead in games started by pitcher with 35 in 1991.
MISCELLANEOUS: Appeared as pinch-runner in seven games (1983).... Appeared as pinch-runner in one game (1985).... Made an out in only appearance as pinch-hitter (1987).

Year	Team (League)	G	W	L	Pct.	ERA	Sv.	IP	H	R	ER	BB	SO
1976 —Montgomery (Southern)		12	2	3	.400	6.25	0	36	37	31	25	36	18
1977 —Evansville (Am. Assoc.)..........		20	6	7	.462	3.60	0	135	141	68	54	42	95
—Detroit (A.L.)		7	1	1	.500	3.72	0	46	38	20	19	23	28
1978 —Detroit (A.L.)		28	3	5	.375	4.33	0	106	107	57	51	49	48
1979 —Evansville (Am. Assoc.)..........		5	2	2	.500	2.38	0	34	22	13	9	18	28
—Detroit (A.L.)		27	17	7	.708	3.27	0	198	179	76	72	59	113
1980 —Detroit (A.L.)		36	16	15	.516	4.18	0	250	252	125	116	87	112
1981 —Detroit (A.L.)		25	•14	7	.667	3.05	0	198	153	69	67	*78	97
1982 —Detroit (A.L.)		37	17	16	.515	4.06	0	266⅓	247	131	120	96	135
1983 —Detroit (A.L.)		37	20	13	.606	3.34	0	*293⅔	257	117	109	83	*232
1984 —Detroit (A.L.)		35	19	11	.633	3.60	0	240⅓	221	108	96	87	148
1985 —Detroit (A.L.)		35	16	11	.593	3.33	0	257	212	102	95	110	191
1986 —Detroit (A.L.)		35	21	8	.724	3.27	0	267	229	105	97	82	223
1987 —Detroit (A.L.)		34	18	11	.621	3.38	0	266	227	111	100	93	208
1988 —Detroit (A.L.)		34	15	13	.536	3.94	0	235	225	115	103	83	168
1989 —Detroit (A.L.)		24	6	14	.300	4.86	0	170⅓	189	102	92	59	115
—Lakeland (Florida State)		3	0	0	...	2.25	0	8	7	2	2	0	2
1990 —Detroit (A.L.)		36	15	18	.455	4.51	0	249⅔	231	*144	*125	97	162
1991 —Minnesota (A.L.)■...................		35	18	12	.600	3.43	0	246⅔	226	107	94	92	163
Major league totals (15 years)		465	216	162	.571	3.71	0	3290	2993	1489	1356	1178	2143

CHAMPIONSHIP SERIES RECORD

CHAMPIONSHIP SERIES NOTES: Shares A.L. single-series record for most games won—2 (1991).... Appeared as pinch-runner for Detroit Tigers in one game (1987).

Year	Team (League)	G	W	L	Pct.	ERA	Sv.	IP	H	R	ER	BB	SO
1984 —Detroit (A.L.)		1	1	0	1.000	1.29	0	7	5	1	1	1	4
1987 —Detroit (A.L.)		1	0	1	.000	6.75	0	8	6	6	6	3	7
1991 —Minnesota (A.L.)		2	2	0	1.000	4.05	0	13⅓	17	6	6	1	7
Championship Series totals (3 years)		4	3	1	.750	4.13	0	28⅓	28	13	13	5	18

WORLD SERIES RECORD

WORLD SERIES NOTES: Shares single-game record for most wild pitches—2 (October 13, 1984).

Year	Team (League)	G	W	L	Pct.	ERA	Sv.	IP	H	R	ER	BB	SO
1984	Detroit (A.L.)	2	2	0	1.000	2.00	0	18	13	4	4	3	13
1991	Minnesota (A.L.)	3	2	0	1.000	1.17	0	23	18	3	3	9	15
	World Series totals (2 years)	5	4	0	1.000	1.54	0	41	31	7	7	12	28

ALL-STAR GAME RECORD

Year	League	W	L	Pct.	ERA	Sv.	IP	H	R	ER	BB	SO
1981	American	0	0	...	0.00	0	2	2	0	0	1	2
1984	American	0	0	...	0.00	0	2	2	0	0	1	2
1985	American	0	1	.000	6.75	0	2⅔	5	2	2	1	1
1987	American	0	0	...	0.00	0	2	1	0	0	1	2
1991	American	0	0	...	4.50	0	2	4	1	1	0	1
	All-Star totals (5 years)	0	1	.000	2.53	0	10⅔	14	3	3	4	8

MORRIS, JOHN
OF, ANGELS

PERSONAL: Born February 23, 1961, at Freeport, N.Y. . . . 6-1/185. . . . Throws left, bats left. . . . Full name: John Daniel Morris.
HIGH SCHOOL: W.C. Mepham (Bellmore, N.Y.).
COLLEGE: Seton Hall.
TRANSACTIONS/CAREER NOTES: Selected by Kansas City Royals organization in first round (10th pick overall) of free-agent draft (June 7, 1982). . . . Traded by Royals organization to St. Louis Cardinals organization for OF Lonnie Smith (May 17, 1985). . . . On Louisville disabled list (May 7-June 11 and June 28-July 8, 1986). . . . On St. Louis disabled list (March 20-September 2, 1988); included rehabilitation disability assignment to Louisville (August 17-September 2, 1988). . . . On disabled list (June 5, 1990-remainder of season). . . . Granted free agency (October 9, 1990). . . . Signed by Scranton/Wilkes-Barre, Philadelphia Phillies organization (January 10, 1991). . . . Granted free agency (October 9, 1991). . . . Signed by California Angels (December 16, 1991).
RECORDS/HONORS: Named outfielder on THE SPORTING NEWS college All-America team (1982). . . . Named Southern League Most Valuable Player (1983).
STATISTICAL NOTES: Led Southern League outfielders with 343 total chances in 1985.

							BATTING						FIELDING			
Year	Team (League)	Pos.	G	AB	R	H	2B	3B	HR	RBI	Avg.	SB	PO	A	E	Avg.
1982	Fort Myers (Florida St.)	OF	45	137	21	39	7	2	2	17	.285	11	64	2	2	.971
1983	Jacksonville (Southern)	OF	140	490	96	141	27	8	23	92	.288	30	260	8	3 *.989	
1984	Omaha (Am. Assoc.)	OF	148	492	77	133	24	4	15	60	.270	18	*359	7	4 *.989	
1985	Omaha-Louisville (A.A.)■	OF	130	466	64	117	25	6	5	50	.251	21	*330	11	2 *.994	
1986	Louisville (Am. Assoc.)	OF	60	213	30	50	13	7	1	24	.235	11	132	6	2	.986
	St. Louis (N.L.)	OF	39	100	8	24	0	1	1	14	.240	6	68	0	1	.986
1987	Louisville (Am. Assoc.)	OF	14	47	13	16	5	2	3	12	.340	2	20	2	0	1.000
	St. Louis (N.L.)	OF	101	157	22	41	6	4	3	23	.261	5	86	0	1	.989
1988	Louisville (Am. Assoc.)	OF	13	40	3	4	0	0	0	0	.100	0	8	0	0	1.000
	St. Louis (N.L.)	OF	20	38	3	11	2	1	0	3	.289	0	12	0	2	.857
1989	St. Louis (N.L.)	OF	96	117	18	28	4	1	2	14	.239	1	45	0	0	1.000
1990	St. Louis (N.L.)	OF	18	18	0	2	0	0	0	0	.111	0	4	0	0	1.000
1991	Philadelphia (N.L.)■	OF	85	127	15	28	2	1	1	6	.220	2	73	1	2	.974
	Major league totals (6 years)		359	557	56	134	14	8	7	60	.241	14	288	1	6	.980

CHAMPIONSHIP SERIES RECORD

							BATTING						FIELDING			
Year	Team (League)	Pos.	G	AB	R	H	2B	3B	HR	RBI	Avg.	SB	PO	A	E	Avg.
1987	St. Louis (N.L.)	OF	2	3	0	0	0	0	0	0	.000	0	1	0	0	1.000

WORLD SERIES RECORD

							BATTING						FIELDING			
Year	Team (League)	Pos.	G	AB	R	H	2B	3B	HR	RBI	Avg.	SB	PO	A	E	Avg.
1987	St. Louis (N.L.)	OF	1	2	0	0	0	0	0	0	.000	0	2	0	0	1.000

MORTON, KEVIN
P, RED SOX

PERSONAL: Born August 3, 1968, at Norwalk, Conn. . . . 6-2/185. . . . Throws left, bats right. . . . Full name: Kevin Joseph Morton.
HIGH SCHOOL: Brien McMahon (Norwalk, Conn.).
COLLEGE: Seton Hall.
TRANSACTIONS/CAREER NOTES: Selected by Boston Red Sox organization in first round (supplemental choice, 29th pick overall) of free-agent draft (June 5, 1989).
STATISTICAL NOTES: Pitched 1-0 perfect game victory against Reading (August 25, 1990, first game). . . . Led Eastern League with 14 hit batsmen in 1990.

Year	Team (League)	G	W	L	Pct.	ERA	Sv.	IP	H	R	ER	BB	SO
1989	Sarasota Red Sox (Gulf Coast)	2	1	0	1.000	0.00	1	6	2	0	0	1	11
	Elmira (New York-Penn)	3	1	1	.500	1.88	0	24	11	6	5	6	32
	Lynchburg (Carolina)	9	4	5	.444	2.35	0	65	42	20	17	17	68
1990	New Britain (Eastern)	26	8	*14	.364	3.81	0	163	151	86	69	48	131
1991	Pawtucket (International)	16	7	3	.700	3.49	0	98	91	41	38	30	80
	Boston (A.L.)	16	6	5	.545	4.59	0	86⅓	93	49	44	40	45
	Major league totals (1 year)	16	6	5	.545	4.59	0	86⅓	93	49	44	40	45

MOSEBY, LLOYD
OF

PERSONAL: Born November 5, 1959, at Portland, Ark. . . . 6-3/200. . . . Throws right, bats left. . . . Full name: Lloyd Anthony Moseby.
HIGH SCHOOL: Oakland (Calif.).
TRANSACTIONS/CAREER NOTES: Selected by Toronto Blue Jays organization in first round (second pick overall) of free-agent draft (June 6, 1978). . . . On disabled list (July 31-August 16, 1988). . . . Granted free agency (November 13, 1989). . . . Signed by Detroit Tigers (December 7, 1989). . . . On disabled list (June 26-July 13, 1990; and April 25-May 8, May 31-June 18 and August 5-20, 1991). . . . Granted free agency (November 5, 1991).
RECORDS/HONORS: Named outfielder on THE SPORTING NEWS A.L. All-Star team (1983). . . . Named outfielder on THE SPORTING NEWS A.L. Silver Slugger team (1983).
STATISTICAL NOTES: Led Pioneer League in being hit by pitch with 11 and tied for lead in caught stealing with seven in 1978. . . . Led Florida State League with 237 total bases and tied for lead in being hit by pitch with 10 in 1979.

Year	Team (League)	Pos.	G	AB	R	H	2B	3B	HR	RBI	Avg.	SB	PO	A	E	Avg.
1978 — Medicine Hat (Pioneer)		OF	67	253	65	77	12	4	10	38	.304	20	76	3	6	.929
1979 — Dunedin (Florida State)		OF	129	446	*89	*148	23	6	18	84	.332	16	190	11	9	.957
1980 — Syracuse (International) ..		OF	37	146	28	47	8	6	3	19	.322	9	83	1	3	.966
— Toronto (A.L.)		OF	114	389	44	89	24	1	9	46	.229	4	208	12	4	.982
1981 — Toronto (A.L.)		OF	100	378	36	88	16	2	9	43	.233	11	259	4	3	.989
1982 — Toronto (A.L.)		OF	147	487	51	115	20	9	9	52	.236	11	361	4	3	.992
1983 — Toronto (A.L.)		OF	151	539	104	170	31	7	18	81	.315	27	399	10	7	.983
1984 — Toronto (A.L.)		OF	158	592	97	166	28	•15	18	92	.280	39	473	8	5	.990
1985 — Toronto (A.L.)		OF	152	584	92	151	30	7	18	70	.259	37	394	7	8	.980
1986 — Toronto (A.L.)		OF	152	589	89	149	24	5	21	86	.253	32	371	6	6	.984
1987 — Toronto (A.L.)		OF	155	592	106	167	27	4	26	96	.282	39	294	7	6	.980
1988 — Toronto (A.L.)		OF	128	472	77	113	17	7	10	42	.239	31	304	2	5	.984
1989 — Toronto (A.L.)		OF	135	502	72	111	25	3	11	43	.221	24	288	3	4	.986
1990 — Detroit (A.L.)■		OF	122	431	64	107	16	5	14	51	.248	17	288	9	5	.983
1991 — Detroit (A.L.)		OF	74	260	37	68	15	1	6	35	.262	8	126	1	6	.955
Major league totals (12 years)			1588	5815	869	1494	273	66	169	737	.257	280	3765	73	62	.984

CHAMPIONSHIP SERIES RECORD

Year	Team (League)	Pos.	G	AB	R	H	2B	3B	HR	RBI	Avg.	SB	PO	A	E	Avg.
1985 — Toronto (A.L.)		OF	7	31	5	7	1	0	0	4	.226	1	16	0	0	1.000
1989 — Toronto (A.L.)		OF	5	16	4	5	0	0	1	2	.313	1	15	0	0	1.000
Championship Series totals (2 years)			12	47	9	12	1	0	1	6	.255	2	31	0	0	1.000

ALL-STAR GAME RECORD

Year	League	Pos.	AB	R	H	2B	3B	HR	RBI	Avg.	SB	PO	A	E	Avg.
1986 — American		OF	0	0	0	0	0	0	0	. . .	0	0	0	0	. . .

MOSES, JOHN
OF/1B

PERSONAL: Born August 9, 1957, at Los Angeles. . . . 5-10/170. . . . Throws left, bats both. . . . Full name: John William Moses.
HIGH SCHOOL: Western (Anaheim, Calif.).
COLLEGE: Golden West College (Calif.) and Arizona.
TRANSACTIONS/CAREER NOTES: Selected by Seattle Mariners organization in 16th round of free-agent draft (June 3, 1980). . . . Released by Mariners (December 21, 1987). . . . Signed by Cleveland Indians (January 19, 1988). . . . Released by Indians (March 29, 1988). . . . Signed by Portland, Minnesota Twins organization (April 5, 1988). . . . Granted free agency (November 5, 1990). . . . Signed by Boston Red Sox (February 1, 1991). . . . Released by Red Sox (April 1, 1991). . . . Signed by Colorado Springs, Indians organization (May 1, 1991). . . . Released by Colorado Springs (July 19, 1991). . . . Signed by Detroit Tigers (August 5, 1991). . . . Released by Tigers (August 25, 1991). . . . Signed by Buffalo, Pittsburgh Pirates organization (August 1, 1991). . . . Released by Buffalo (August 5, 1991).
STATISTICAL NOTES: Tied for Midwest League lead with 13 sacrifice hits in 1981. . . . Led Midwest League in caught stealing with 21 and with 103 bases on balls received in 1981. . . . Led Eastern League outfielders with six double plays in 1982. . . . Tied for A.L. lead in caught stealing with 18 in 1986.

Year	Team (League)	Pos.	G	AB	R	H	2B	3B	HR	RBI	Avg.	SB	PO	A	E	Avg.
1980 — Bellingham (Northwest)....		OF	60	227	55	60	5	2	2	32	.264	16	92	6	3	.970
1981 — Wausau (Midwest)		OF	123	429	*102	120	24	3	3	48	.280	50	204	10	5	.977
1982 — Lynn (Eastern)		OF	128	466	87	133	25	6	6	52	.285	50	259	*20	0	*1.000
— Seattle (A.L.)		OF	22	44	7	14	5	1	1	3	.318	1	16	2	1	.947
1983 — Seattle (A.L.)		OF	93	130	19	27	4	1	0	6	.208	11	87	8	2	.979
— Salt Lake City (PCL)		OF	16	65	14	17	4	0	0	10	.262	4	26	0	0	1.000
1984 — Chattanooga (Southern) ...		OF	53	182	27	46	6	3	0	12	.253	19	107	4	2	.982
— Salt Lake City (PCL)		OF	70	276	45	76	11	5	0	27	.275	21	161	8	1	.994
— Seattle (A.L.)		OF	19	35	3	12	1	1	0	2	.343	1	26	1	0	1.000
1985 — Calgary (Pacific Coast)		OF-1B	113	473	75	152	*37	1	5	47	.321	35	316	12	4	.988
— Seattle (A.L.)		OF	33	62	4	12	0	0	3	3	.194	5	35	1	0	1.000
1986 — Calgary (Pacific Coast)		OF	39	148	31	48	3	1	3	18	.324	15	93	3	1	.990
— Seattle (A.L.)		OF-1B	103	399	56	102	16	3	3	34	.256	25	249	11	5	.981
1987 — Seattle (A.L.)		OF-1B	116	390	58	96	16	4	3	38	.246	23	271	7	4	.986
1988 — Portland (Pacific Coast)■ .		OF	17	66	13	23	3	1	0	6	.348	0	40	0	0	1.000
— Minnesota (A.L.)		OF	105	206	33	65	10	3	2	12	.316	11	123	1	0	1.000

Year	Team (League)	Pos.	G	AB	R	H	2B	3B	HR	RBI	Avg.	SB	PO	A	E	Avg.
1989—Minnesota (A.L.)	OF-1B-P	129	242	33	68	12	3	1	31	.281	14	168	3	2	.988
1990—Minnesota (A.L.)	OF-1B-P	115	172	26	38	3	1	1	14	.221	2	108	2	0	1.000
1991—Colorado Springs (PCL)■..	OF-1B	74	298	58	88	18	3	3	31	.295	11	253	18	4	.985
—Detroit (A.L.)■	OF	13	21	5	1	1	0	0	1	.048	4	13	0	0	1.000
—Buffalo (Am. Assoc.)■	OF	3	11	2	3	0	0	0	0	.273	2	5	0	0	1.000
Major league totals (10 years)		748	1701	244	435	68	17	11	144	.256	101	1096	36	14	.988

RECORD AS PITCHER

Year	Team (League)	G	W	L	Pct.	ERA	Sv.	IP	H	R	ER	BB	SO
1989—Minnesota (A.L.)	1	0	0	...	0.00	0	1	0	0	0	1	0
1990—Minnesota (A.L.)	2	0	0	...	13.50	0	2	5	3	3	2	0
Major league totals (2 years)	3	0	0	...	9.00	0	3	5	3	3	3	0

MOTA, ANDY
2B, ASTROS

PERSONAL: Born March 4, 1966, at Santo Domingo, Dominican Republic.... 5-10/180.... Throws right, bats right.... Full name: Andres Alberto Mota.... Son of Manny Mota, Los Angeles Dodgers coach; major league outfielder for four teams (1962-80 and 1982); brother of Jose Mota, infielder, Kansas City Royals organization; brother of Domingo Mota, infielder, Royals organization; and brother of Rafael Mota, outfielder, Houston Astros organization.
HIGH SCHOOL: Calasanz (Santo Domingo, Dominican Republic).
COLLEGE: Golden West Junior College (Calif.) and Cal State Fullerton.
TRANSACTIONS/CAREER NOTES: Selected by Kansas City Royals organization in sixth round of free-agent draft (January 3, 1985).... Selected by Houston Astros organization in 12th round of free-agent draft (June 2, 1987).... On disabled list (August 2-September 1, 1990).
STATISTICAL NOTES: Led Florida State League in being hit by pitch with 11 in 1989.... Led Florida State League third baseman with 32 errors in 1989.

Year	Team (League)	Pos.	G	AB	R	H	2B	3B	HR	RBI	Avg.	SB	PO	A	E	Avg.
1987—Auburn (N.Y.-Penn).........	3-0-1-2	70	255	26	67	9	1	4	14	.263	6	33	111	12	.923
1988—Auburn (N.Y.-Penn).........	1-3-2-0	72	271	56	★95	15	3	3	47 ★.351		31	313	86	19	.955
1989—Osceola (Florida State)	3-1-0-S	131	505	68	★161	21	4	4	69 ★.319		28	213	186	†37	.915
1990—Columbus (Southern)	2B-3B	111	413	59	118	21	1	11	62	.286	17	247	258	22	.958
1991—Tucson (Pacific Coast)	2B	123	462	65	138	19	4	2	46	.299	14	214 ★307		18	.967
—Houston (N.L.)	2B	27	90	4	17	2	0	1	6	.189	2	30	66	3	.970
Major league totals (1 year)		27	90	4	17	2	0	1	6	.189	2	30	66	3	.970

MOTA, JOSE
IF/OF, ROYALS

PERSONAL: Born March 16, 1965, at Santo Domingo, Dominican Republic.... 5-9/155.... Throws right, bats both.... Full name: Jose Manuel Mota.... Son of Manny Mota, Los Angeles Dodgers coach; major league outfielder for four teams (1962-80 and 1982); brother of Andres Mota, infielder, Houston Astros; brother of Rafael Mota, outfielder, Houston Astros organization; and brother of Domingo Mota, infielder, Kansas City Royals organization.
COLLEGE: Cal State Fullerton.
TRANSACTIONS/CAREER NOTES: Selected by Chicago White Sox organization in second round of free-agent draft (June 3, 1985). ... Traded by White Sox organization to Texas Rangers organization (December 12, 1985), completing trade in which Rangers traded IF Wayne Tolleson and P Dave Schmidt to White Sox for IF Scott Fletcher, P Ed Correa and a player to be named later (November 25, 1985).... On Tulsa disabled list (May 14-24, 1986).... Sold by Rangers organization to Los Angeles Dodgers organization (June 24, 1987).... Drafted by Oakland Athletics (December 6, 1988).... Traded by Oakland A's to San Diego Padres organization as part of a three-way deal in which A's organization acquired OF Peter Kuld from Cleveland Indians organization (June 3, 1989); Indians organization acquired OF-P Brian Brooks to complete deal (June 11, 1989).... Granted free agency (October 15, 1991).... Signed by Kansas City Royals organization (November 22, 1991).

Year	Team (League)	Pos.	G	AB	R	H	2B	3B	HR	RBI	Avg.	SB	PO	A	E	Avg.
1985—Niagara Falls (NYP)	2B	65	254	35	77	9	2	0	27	.303	8	154	156	16	.951
—Buffalo (Am. Assoc.)	2B	6	18	3	5	0	0	0	1	.278	0	10	12	0	1.000
1986—Tulsa (Texas)■.................	3B	41	158	26	51	7	3	1	11	.323	14	53	102	8	.951
—Oklahoma City (A.A.)	2B	71	255	38	71	9	1	0	20	.278	7	129	201	★14	.959
1987—San Antonio (Texas)■........	2B	75	261	34	65	6	3	0	15	.249	5	138	190	8	.976
1988—San Antonio (Texas)	OF-2B-3B	82	214	32	56	11	1	1	18	.262	10	56	32	3	.967
—Albuquerque (PCL)	2B-SS	15	4	5	0	0	0	1	.333	1	2	10	0	1.000
1989—Wichita (Texas)■...............	S-0-2-3	41	109	17	35	5	1	1	9	.321	3	57	64	1	.992
1990—Las Vegas (Pac. Coast)	S-0-3-2	92	247	44	74	4	4	4	21	.300	2	64	117	8	.958
1991—Las Vegas (Pac. Coast)	2-S-3-0	107	377	56	109	10	2	1	37	.289	15	173	310	15	.970
—San Diego (N.L.)	2B	17	36	4	8	0	0	0	2	.222	0	24	27	2	.962
Major league totals (1 year)		17	36	4	8	0	0	0	2	.222	0	24	27	2	.962

MOYER, JAMIE
P, CUBS

PERSONAL: Born November 18, 1962, at Sellersville, Pa.... 6-0/170.... Throws left, bats left. ... Full name: Jamie Moyer.... Son-in-law of Digger Phelps, Notre Dame basketball coach (1971-72 through 1990-91).
HIGH SCHOOL: Souderton Area (Pa.).

COLLEGE: St. Joseph's (Pa.).
TRANSACTIONS/CAREER NOTES: Selected by Chicago Cubs organization in sixth round of free-agent draft (June 4, 1984). . . .
Traded by Cubs with OF Rafael Palmeiro and P Drew Hall to Texas Rangers for P Mitch Williams, P Paul Kilgus, P Steve Wilson,
IF Curtis Wilkerson, IF Luis Benitez and OF Pablo Delgado (December 5, 1988). . . . On Texas disabled list (May 31-September
1, 1989); included rehabilitation disability assignment to Sarasota Rangers (August 5-14, 1989) and Tulsa (August 15-24,
1989). . . . Released by Rangers (November 13, 1990). . . . Signed by Louisville, St. Louis Cardinals organization (January 9,
1991). . . . Released by Cardinals (October 14, 1991). . . . Signed by Cubs organization (January 8, 1992).
STATISTICAL NOTES: Led American Association with 16 home runs allowed in 1991.

Year	Team (League)	G	W	L	Pct.	ERA	Sv.	IP	H	R	ER	BB	SO
1984	—Geneva (New York-Penn)	14	•9	3	.750	1.89	0	★104⅔	59	27	22	31	★120
1985	—Winston-Salem (Carolina)	12	8	2	.800	2.30	0	94	82	36	24	22	94
	—Pittsfield (Eastern)	15	7	6	.538	3.72	0	96⅔	99	49	40	32	51
1986	—Pittsfield (Eastern)	6	3	1	.750	0.88	0	41	27	10	4	16	42
	—Iowa (American Association)	6	3	2	.600	2.55	0	42⅓	25	14	12	11	25
	—Chicago (N.L.)	16	7	4	.636	5.05	0	87⅓	107	52	49	42	45
1987	—Chicago (N.L.)	35	12	15	.444	5.10	0	201	210	127	★114	97	147
1988	—Chicago (N.L.)	34	9	15	.375	3.48	0	202	212	84	78	55	121
1989	—Texas (A.L.)■	15	4	9	.308	4.86	0	76	84	51	41	33	44
	—Sarasota Rangers (GCL)	3	1	0	1.000	1.64	0	11	8	4	2	1	18
	—Tulsa (Texas)	2	1	1	.500	5.11	0	12⅓	16	8	7	3	9
1990	—Texas (A.L.)	33	2	6	.250	4.66	0	102⅓	115	59	53	39	58
1991	—St. Louis (N.L.)■	8	0	5	.000	5.74	0	31⅓	38	21	20	16	20
	—Louisville (American Assoc.)	20	5	10	.333	3.80	0	125⅔	125	64	53	43	69
American League totals (2 years)		48	6	15	.286	4.74	0	178⅓	199	110	94	72	102
National League totals (4 years)		93	28	39	.418	4.50	0	521⅔	567	284	261	210	333
Major league totals (6 years)		141	34	54	.386	4.56	0	700	766	394	355	282	435

MULHOLLAND, TERRY
P, PHILLIES

PERSONAL: Born March 9, 1963, at Uniontown, Pa. . . . 6-3/206. . . . Throws
left, bats right. . . . Full name: Terence John Mulholland.
HIGH SCHOOL: Laurel Highlands (Uniontown, Pa.).
COLLEGE: Marietta College (O.).
TRANSACTIONS/CAREER NOTES: Selected by San Francisco Giants organization in first round (24th pick overall) of free-agent
draft (June 4, 1984). . . . On San Francisco disabled list (August 1, 1988-remainder of season). . . . Traded by Giants with P
Dennis Cook and 3B Charlie Hayes to Philadelphia Phillies for P Steve Bedrosian and a player to be named later (June 18,
1989); Giants organization acquired IF Rick Parker to complete deal (August 7, 1989). . . . On Philadelphia disabled list (June
12-28, 1990); included rehabilitation disability assignment to Scranton/Wilkes-Barre (June 23-24, 1990).
STATISTICAL NOTES: Led Texas League with three shutouts in 1985. . . . Led Pacific Coast League pitchers with 29 games started in 1987. . . . Pitched 6-0 no-hit victory against San Francisco (August 15, 1990).
MISCELLANEOUS: Appeared in one game as pinch-runner (1991).

Year	Team (League)	G	W	L	Pct.	ERA	Sv.	IP	H	R	ER	BB	SO
1984	—Everett (Northwest)	3	1	0	1.000	0.00	0	19	10	2	0	4	15
	—Fresno (California)	9	5	2	.714	2.95	0	42⅔	32	17	14	36	39
1985	—Shreveport (Texas)	26	9	8	.529	2.90	0	176⅔	166	79	57	87	122
1986	—Phoenix (Pacific Coast)	17	8	5	.615	4.46	0	111	112	60	55	56	77
	—San Francisco (N.L.)	15	1	7	.125	4.94	0	54⅔	51	33	30	35	27
1987	—Phoenix (Pacific Coast)	37	7	12	.368	5.07	1	172⅓	200	★124	•97	90	94
1988	—Phoenix (Pacific Coast)	19	7	3	.700	3.58	0	100⅔	116	45	40	44	57
	—San Francisco (N.L.)	9	2	1	.667	3.72	0	46	50	20	19	7	18
1989	—Phoenix (Pacific Coast)	13	4	5	.444	2.99	0	78⅓	67	30	26	26	61
	—San Francisco-Phil. (N.L.)■□	25	4	7	.364	4.92	0	115⅓	137	66	63	36	66
1990	—Philadelphia (N.L.)	33	9	10	.474	3.34	0	180⅔	172	78	67	42	75
	—Scranton/Wilkes-Barre (Int'l)	1	0	1	.000	3.00	0	6	9	4	2	2	2
1991	—Philadelphia (N.L.)	34	16	13	.552	3.61	0	232	231	100	93	49	142
Major league totals (5 years)		116	32	38	.457	3.89	0	628⅔	641	297	272	169	328

MULLINIKS, RANCE
DH/3B, BLUE JAYS

PERSONAL: Born January 15, 1956, at Tulare, Calif. . . . 6-0/175. . . . Throws right,
bats left. . . . Full name: Steven Rance Mulliniks. . . . Son of Harvey Mulliniks, minor
league pitcher (1956-57). . . . Name pronounced MULL-in-iks.
HIGH SCHOOL: Monache (Porterville, Calif.).
TRANSACTIONS/CAREER NOTES: Selected by California Angels organization in third round of free-agent draft (June 5, 1974). . . .
On disabled list (May 4-June 9 and September 2-24, 1976). . . . Traded by Angels with 1B Willie Aikens to Kansas City Royals
for OF Al Cowens, SS Todd Cruz and a player to be named later (December 6, 1979); Angels acquired P Craig Eaton to complete
deal (April 1, 1980). . . . Traded by Royals to Toronto Blue Jays for P Phil Huffman (March 25, 1982). . . . On disabled list (August 6-September 1, 1986 and April 12-May 2, 1988). . . . Granted free agency (November 5, 1990). . . . Re-signed by Blue
Jays (December 4, 1990). . . . On disabled list (April 27-May 28, 1991).
STATISTICAL NOTES: Led Pacific Coast League shortstops with .968 fielding percentage in 1979. . . . Led A.L. third basemen with
.968 fielding percentage in 1984 and .975 in 1986.

Year	Team (League)	Pos.	G	AB	R	H	2B	3B	HR	RBI	Avg.	SB	PO	A	E	Avg.
1974	—Idaho Falls (Pioneer)	SS	66	202	28	44	8	3	0	24	.218	14	★110	★170	★33	.895
1975	—Quad Cities (Midwest)	SS	52	186	34	50	6	2	1	21	.269	7	82	136	17	.928
	—Salinas (California)	SS-2B	59	209	38	54	8	0	0	10	.258	13	88	146	14	.944

Year	Team (League)	Pos.	G	AB	R	H	2B	3B	HR	RBI	Avg.	SB	PO	A	E	Avg.
1976	El Paso (Texas)	SS-2B	90	333	81	105	22	4	7	51	.315	20	140	247	20	.951
1977	Salt Lake City (PCL)	SS	58	220	48	68	17	3	11	51	.309	11	116	207	15	.956
	California (A.L.)	SS	78	271	36	73	13	2	3	21	.269	1	112	229	13	.963
1978	Salt Lake City (PCL)	SS	34	127	34	39	6	2	3	21	.307	0	65	109	12	.935
	California (A.L.)	SS	50	119	6	22	3	1	1	6	.185	2	68	93	8	.953
1979	Salt Lake City (PCL)	SS-2B	116	402	94	138	21	7	3	59	.343	21	204	331	17	†.969
	California (A.L.)	SS	22	68	7	10	0	0	1	8	.147	0	46	43	4	.957
1980	Kansas City (A.L.)■	SS-2B	36	54	8	14	3	0	0	6	.259	0	30	53	1	.988
1981	Kansas City (A.L.)	2B-SS-3B	24	44	6	10	3	0	0	5	.227	0	25	39	5	.928
1982	Toronto (A.L.)■	3B-SS	112	311	32	76	25	0	4	35	.244	3	69	154	14	.941
1983	Toronto (A.L.)	3B-SS-2B	129	364	54	100	34	3	10	49	.275	0	77	185	7	.974
1984	Toronto (A.L.)	3B-SS-2B	125	343	41	111	21	5	3	42	.324	2	67	152	8	†.965
1985	Toronto (A.L.)	3B	129	366	55	108	26	1	10	57	.295	2	75	162	7	★.971
1986	Toronto (A.L.)	3B-2B	117	348	50	90	22	0	11	45	.259	1	60	176	6	†.975
1987	Toronto (A.L.)	3B-SS	124	332	37	103	28	1	11	44	.310	1	29	137	13	.927
1988	Toronto (A.L.)	3B	119	337	49	101	21	1	12	48	.300	1	3	5	0	1.000
1989	Toronto (A.L.)	3B	103	273	25	65	11	2	3	29	.238	0	15	50	1	.985
1990	Toronto (A.L.)	3B-1B	57	97	11	28	4	0	2	16	.289	2	23	25	2	.960
1991	Toronto (A.L.)	3B	97	240	27	60	12	1	2	24	.250	0	2	3	0	1.000
Major league totals (15 years)			1322	3567	444	971	226	17	73	435	.272	15	701	1506	89	.961

CHAMPIONSHIP SERIES RECORD

Year	Team (League)	Pos.	G	AB	R	H	2B	3B	HR	RBI	Avg.	SB	PO	A	E	Avg.
1985	Toronto (A.L.)	PH-3B	5	11	1	4	1	0	1	3	.364	0	1	4	0	1.000
1989	Toronto (A.L.)	PH	1	1	0	0	0	0	0	0	.000	0	0	0	0	...
1991	Toronto (A.L.)	DH-PH	5	8	1	1	0	0	0	1	.125	0	0	0	0	...
Championship Series totals (3 years)			11	20	2	5	1	0	1	3	.250	0	1	4	0	1.000

MUNOZ, MIKE
P, TIGERS

PERSONAL: Born July 12, 1965, at Baldwin Park, Calif.... 6-3/195.... Throws left, bats left.... Full name: Michael Anthony Munoz.
COLLEGE: Cal Poly Pomona.
TRANSACTIONS/CAREER NOTES: Selected by Los Angeles Dodgers organization in third round of free-agent draft (June 2, 1986).... Traded by Dodgers organization to Detroit Tigers for P Mike Wilkins (September 30, 1990).

Year	Team (League)	G	W	L	Pct.	ERA	Sv.	IP	H	R	ER	BB	SO
1986	Great Falls (Pioneer)	14	4	4	.500	3.21	0	$81\frac{1}{3}$	85	44	29	38	49
1987	Bakersfield (California)	52	8	7	.533	3.74	9	118	125	68	49	43	80
1988	San Antonio (Texas)	56	7	2	.778	1.00	14	$71\frac{2}{3}$	63	18	8	24	71
1989	Albuquerque (Pacific Coast)	60	6	4	.600	3.08	6	79	72	32	27	40	81
	Los Angeles (N.L.)	3	0	0	...	16.88	0	$2\frac{2}{3}$	5	5	5	2	3
1990	Los Angeles (N.L.)	8	0	1	.000	3.18	0	$5\frac{2}{3}$	6	2	2	3	2
	Albuquerque (Pacific Coast)	49	4	1	.800	4.25	6	$59\frac{1}{3}$	65	33	28	19	40
1991	Toledo (International)■	38	2	3	.400	3.83	8	54	44	30	23	35	38
	Detroit (A.L.)	6	0	0	...	9.64	0	$9\frac{1}{3}$	14	10	10	5	3
American League totals (1 year)		6	0	0	...	9.64	0	$9\frac{1}{3}$	14	10	10	5	3
National League totals (2 years)		11	0	1	.000	7.56	0	$8\frac{1}{3}$	11	7	7	5	5
Major league totals (3 years)		17	0	1	.000	8.66	0	$17\frac{2}{3}$	25	17	17	10	8

MUNOZ, PEDRO
OF, TWINS

PERSONAL: Born September 19, 1968, at Ponce, Puerto Rico.... 5-10/208.... Throws right, bats right.... Full name: Pedro Javier Munoz.
HIGH SCHOOL: Dr. Pila (Ponce, Puerto Rico).
TRANSACTIONS/CAREER NOTES: Signed as free agent by Toronto Blue Jays organization (May 31, 1985).... On disabled list (July 30-August 28, 1987).... Traded by Blue Jays organization with 2B Nelson Liriano to Minnesota Twins for P John Candelaria (July 27, 1990).... On Minnesota disabled list (July 15-30, 1991).
STATISTICAL NOTES: Tied for South Atlantic League lead with four intentional bases on balls received in 1986.

Year	Team (League)	Pos.	G	AB	R	H	2B	3B	HR	RBI	Avg.	SB	PO	A	E	Avg.
1985	Brad. Blue Jays (GCL)	OF	40	145	14	38	3	0	2	17	.262	4	46	2	1	.980
1986	Florence (S. Atlantic)	OF	122	445	69	131	16	5	14	82	.294	9	197	14	9	.959
1987	Dunedin (Florida State)	OF	92	341	55	80	11	5	8	44	.235	13	4	1	0	1.000
1988	Dunedin (Florida State)	OF	133	481	59	141	21	7	8	73	.293	15	164	8	★15	.920
1989	Knoxville (Southern)	OF	122	442	54	118	15	4	19	65	.267	10	55	3	1	.983
1990	Syracuse (International)	OF	86	317	41	101	22	3	7	56	.319	16	110	4	6	.950
	Portland (Pacific Coast)■	OF	30	110	19	35	4	0	5	21	.318	8	51	1	3	.945
	Minnesota (A.L.)	OF	22	85	13	23	4	1	0	5	.271	3	34	1	1	.972
1991	Portland (Pacific Coast)	OF	56	212	33	67	19	2	5	28	.316	9	109	2	2	.982
	Minnesota (A.L.)	OF	51	138	15	39	7	1	2	26	.283	3	89	3	1	.989
Major league totals (2 years)			73	223	28	62	11	2	7	31	.278	6	123	4	2	.984

MUNOZ, ROBERTO
P, YANKEES

PERSONAL: Born March 3, 1968, at Rio Piedras, Puerto Rico. . . . 6-7/210. . . . Throws right, bats right. . . . Full name: Roberto Munoz.
COLLEGE: Palm Beach Junior College (Fla.).
TRANSACTIONS/CAREER NOTES: Selected by New York Yankees organization in 15th round of free-agent draft (June 1, 1988).

Year	Team (League)	G	W	L	Pct.	ERA	Sv.	IP	H	R	ER	BB	SO
1989	—Sarasota Yankees (GCL)	2	1	1	.500	3.48	0	10⅓	5	4	4	4	13
	—Fort Lauderdale (Florida St.)....	3	1	2	.333	4.73	0	13⅓	16	8	7	7	2
1990	—Greensboro (South Atlantic)	9	7	0	1.000	2.39	0	64	43	18	17	18	55
1991	—Fort Lauderdale (Florida St.)....	19	5	8	.385	2.33	0	108	91	45	28	40	53
	—Columbus (International)	1	0	1	.000	24.00	0	3	8	8	8	3	2

MURPHY, DALE
OF, PHILLIES

PERSONAL: Born March 12, 1956, at Portland, Ore. . . . 6-4/221. . . . Throws right, bats right. . . . Full name: Dale Bryan Murphy.
HIGH SCHOOL: Woodrow Wilson (Portland, Ore.).
COLLEGE: Portland Community College (Ore.) and Brigham Young.
TRANSACTIONS/CAREER NOTES: Selected by Atlanta Braves organization in first round (fifth pick overall) of free-agent draft (June 5, 1974). . . . On disabled list (May 25-July 19, 1979). . . . Traded by Braves with a player to be named later to Philadelphia Phillies for P Jeff Parrett and two players to be named later (August 3, 1990); Scranton/Wilkes-Barre (Phillies organization) acquired P Tommy Greene (August 9, 1990), and Braves acquired OF Jim Vatcher (August 9, 1990) and SS Victor Rosario (September 4, 1990) to complete deal.
RECORDS/HONORS: Shares major league record for most years leading league in games by outfielder—6. . . . Shares major league single-season record for fewest double plays by outfielder, season (150 or more games)—0 (1983). . . . Shares major league records for most home runs in one inning—2; runs batted in one inning—6 (July 27, 1989, sixth inning). . . . Shares N.L. single-season record for most intentional bases on balls received by righthanded batter—29 (1987). . . . Named N.L. Player of the Year by THE SPORTING NEWS (1982-83). . . . Named outfielder on THE SPORTING NEWS N.L. All-Star team (1982-85). . . . Won N.L. Gold Glove as outfielder (1982-86). . . . Named outfielder on THE SPORTING NEWS N.L. Silver Slugger team (1982-85). . . . Named N.L. Most Valuable Player by Baseball Writers' Association of America (1982-83).
STATISTICAL NOTES: Tied for International League lead with 249 total bases in 1977. . . . Led International League catchers with 510 putouts, 14 passed balls and tied for lead with seven double plays in 1977. . . . Led N.L. batters with 145 strikeouts in 1978, 133 in 1980 and tied for lead with 141 in 1985. . . . Led N.L. first basemen with 20 errors in 1978. . . . Hit three home runs in a game (May 18, 1979). . . . Tied for N.L. lead in double plays by outfielders with four in both 1981 and 1985. . . . Led N.L. with .540 slugging percentage in 1983 and .547 in 1984. . . . Led N.L. with 332 total bases in 1984. . . . Led N.L. with 90 bases on balls received in 1985. . . . Led N.L. with 29 intentional bases on balls received in 1987. . . . Led N.L. in grounding into double plays with 24 in 1988 and 22 in 1990.

							BATTING							FIELDING			
Year	Team (League)	Pos.	G	AB	R	H	2B	3B	HR	RBI	Avg.	SB	PO	A	E	Avg.
1974	—Kingsport (Appalachian) ..	C	54	181	28	46	7	0	5	31	.254	0	389	28	7	.983
1975	—Greenwood (W. Caro.).......	C-1B	131	443	48	101	20	1	5	48	.228	5	723	81	18	.978
1976	—Savannah (Southern)	C	104	352	37	94	13	5	12	55	.267	6	444	40	10	.980
	—Richmond (Int'l)	C-OF	18	50	10	13	1	1	4	8	.260	0	60	9	4	.945
	—Atlanta (N.L.)	C	19	65	3	17	6	0	0	9	.262	0	100	13	3	.974
1977	—Richmond (Int'l)	C-1B	127	466	71	142	*33	4	22	*90	.305	4	†600	50	15	.977
	—Atlanta (N.L.)	C	18	76	5	24	8	1	2	14	.316	0	114	11	6	.954
1978	—Atlanta (N.L.)	1B-C	151	530	66	120	14	3	23	79	.226	11	1220	105	†23	.983
1979	—Atlanta (N.L.)	1B-C	104	384	53	106	7	2	21	57	.276	6	812	57	20	.978
1980	—Atlanta (N.L.)	OF-1B	156	569	98	160	27	2	33	89	.281	9	384	15	6	.985
1981	—Atlanta (N.L.)	OF-1B	104	369	43	91	12	1	13	50	.247	14	264	11	5	.982
1982	—Atlanta (N.L.)	OF	*162	598	113	168	23	2	36	*109	.281	23	407	6	9	.979
1983	—Atlanta (N.L.)	OF	*162	589	131	178	24	4	36	*121	.302	30	373	10	6	.985
1984	—Atlanta (N.L.)	OF	*162	607	94	176	32	8	*36	100	.290	19	369	10	5	.987
1985	—Atlanta (N.L.)	OF	*162	616	*118	185	32	2	*37	111	.300	10	334	8	7	.980
1986	—Atlanta (N.L.)	OF	160	614	89	163	29	7	29	83	.265	7	303	6	6	.981
1987	—Atlanta (N.L.)	OF	159	566	115	167	27	1	44	105	.295	16	325	14	8	.977
1988	—Atlanta (N.L.)	OF	156	592	77	134	35	4	24	77	.226	3	340	15	3	.992
1989	—Atlanta (N.L.)	OF	154	574	60	131	16	0	20	84	.228	3	331	5	5	.985
1990	—Atlanta-Phil. (N.L.)■........	OF	154	563	60	138	23	1	24	83	.245	9	321	7	5	.985
1991	—Philadelphia (N.L.)	OF	153	544	66	137	33	1	18	81	.252	1	287	6	5	.983
Major league totals (16 years)			2136	7856	1191	2095	348	39	396	1252	.267	161	6284	299	122	.982

CHAMPIONSHIP SERIES RECORD

							BATTING							FIELDING			
Year	Team (League)	Pos.	G	AB	R	H	2B	3B	HR	RBI	Avg.	SB	PO	A	E	Avg.
1982	—Atlanta (N.L.)	OF	3	11	1	3	0	0	0	0	.273	1	8	0	0	1.000

ALL-STAR GAME RECORD

						BATTING							FIELDING			
Year	League	Pos.	AB	R	H	2B	3B	HR	RBI	Avg.	SB	PO	A	E	Avg.
1980	—National	OF	1	0	0	0	0	0	0	.000	0	0	0	0	...
1982	—National	OF	2	1	0	0	0	0	0	.000	0	2	0	0	1.000
1983	—National	OF	3	0	1	0	0	0	1	.333	0	0	0	0	...
1984	—National	OF	3	1	2	0	0	1	1	.667	0	0	0	0	...

Year	League	Pos.	AB	R	H	2B	3B	HR	RBI	Avg.	SB	PO	A	E	Avg.
						BATTING							FIELDING		
1985 —National		OF	3	0	1	1	0	0	0	.333	0	1	0	0	1.000
1986 —National		OF	2	0	0	0	0	0	0	.000	0	2	0	0	1.000
1987 —National		OF	1	0	0	0	0	0	0	.000	0	1	0	0	1.000
All-Star Game totals (7 years)			15	2	4	1	0	1	2	.267	0	6	0	0	1.000

MURPHY, ROB
P, ASTROS

PERSONAL: Born May 26, 1960, at Miami. . . . 6-2/215. . . . Throws left, bats left. . . . Full name: Robert Albert Murphy Jr.
HIGH SCHOOL: Christopher Columbus (Miami).
COLLEGE: Florida.
TRANSACTIONS/CAREER NOTES: Selected by Milwaukee Brewers organization in 29th round of free-agent draft (June 6, 1978). . . . Selected by Cincinnati Reds organization in secondary phase of free-agent draft (January 13, 1981). . . . Traded by Reds with 1B Nick Esasky to Boston Red Sox for 1B Todd Benzinger, P Jeff Sellers and a player to be named later (December 13, 1988); Reds acquired P Luis Vasquez to complete deal (January 12, 1989). . . . Traded by Red Sox to Seattle Mariners for P Mike Gardiner (April 1, 1991). . . . Granted free agency (December 20, 1991). . . . Signed by Houston Astros organization (January 27, 1992).

Year	Team (League)	G	W	L	Pct.	ERA	Sv.	IP	H	R	ER	BB	SO
1981 —Tampa (Florida State)		25	6	8	.429	4.54	0	105	109	73	53	67	58
1982 —Cedar Rapids (Midwest)		31	3	7	.300	4.04	0	89	92	62	40	61	96
1983 —Cedar Rapids (Midwest)		36	6	10	.375	3.33	2	140⅔	120	66	52	69	137
1984 —Vermont (Eastern)		45	2	3	.400	2.71	•15	69⅔	57	23	21	35	69
1985 —Denver (American Assoc.)		41	5	5	.500	4.61	5	84	94	55	43	57	66
—Cincinnati (N.L.)		2	0	0	. . .	6.00	0	3	2	2	2	2	1
1986 —Denver (American Assoc.)		27	3	4	.429	1.90	7	42⅔	33	12	9	24	36
—Cincinnati (N.L.)		34	6	0	1.000	0.72	1	50⅓	26	4	4	21	36
1987 —Cincinnati (N.L.)		87	8	5	.615	3.04	3	100⅔	91	37	34	32	99
1988 —Cincinnati (N.L.)		★76	0	6	.000	3.08	3	84⅔	69	31	29	38	74
1989 —Boston (A.L.)■		74	5	7	.417	2.74	9	105	97	38	32	41	107
1990 —Boston (A.L.)■		68	0	6	.000	6.32	7	57	85	46	40	32	54
1991 —Seattle (A.L.)■		57	0	1	.000	3.00	4	48	47	17	16	19	34
American League totals (3 years)		199	5	14	.263	3.77	20	210	229	101	88	92	195
National League totals (4 years)		199	14	11	.560	2.60	7	238⅔	188	74	69	93	210
Major league totals (7 years)		398	19	25	.432	3.15	27	448⅔	417	175	157	185	405

CHAMPIONSHIP SERIES RECORD

Year	Team (League)	G	W	L	Pct.	ERA	Sv.	IP	H	R	ER	BB	SO
1990 —Boston (A.L.)		1	0	0	. . .	13.50	0	⅔	2	1	1	1	0

MURRAY, EDDIE
1B, METS

PERSONAL: Born February 24, 1956, at Los Angeles. . . . 6-2/222. . . . Throws right, bats both. . . . Full name: Eddie Clarence Murray. . . . Brother of Rich Murray, first baseman, San Francisco Giants (1980, 1983); brother of Leon Murray, minor league first baseman (1970); brother of Charles Murray, minor league outfielder (1962-66 and 1969); and brother of Venice Murray, minor league first baseman (1978).
HIGH SCHOOL: Locke (Los Angeles).
COLLEGE: Cal State Los Angeles.
TRANSACTIONS/CAREER NOTES: Selected by Baltimore Orioles organization in third round of free-agent draft (June 5, 1973). . . . On disabled list (July 10-August 7, 1986). . . . Traded by Orioles to Los Angeles Dodgers for P Brian Holton, P Ken Howell and SS Juan Bell (December 4, 1988). . . . Granted free agency (October 29, 1991). . . . Signed by New York Mets (November 27, 1991).
RECORDS/HONORS: Shares major league career record for most games with switch-hit home runs— 10. . . . Shares major league single-season record for games with switch-hit home runs—2 (1982, 1987 and 1990). . . . Holds A.L. career record for most game-winning runs batted in—117. . . . Holds A.L. single-season records for most consecutive games with one or more hits by switch-hitter—22 (1984); most intentional bases on balls by switch-hitter—25 (1984). . . . Holds N.L. single-season record for fewest double plays by first baseman (150 or more games)—88 (1990). . . . Named Appalachian League Player of the Year (1973). . . . Named A.L. Rookie of the Year by Baseball Writers' Association of America (1977). . . . Won A.L. Gold Glove at first base (1982-84). . . . Named first baseman on THE SPORTING NEWS A.L. All-Star team (1983). . . . Named first baseman on THE SPORTING NEWS A.L. Silver Slugger team (1983-84). . . . Named first baseman on THE SPORTING NEWS N.L. All-Star team (1990). . . . Named first baseman on THE SPORTING NEWS N.L. Silver Slugger team (1990).
STATISTICAL NOTES: Led Florida State League with 212 total bases in 1974. . . . Led Florida State League first basemen with 113 double plays in 1974. . . . Switch-hit home runs in one game 10 times (August 3, 1977; August 29, 1979, two righthanded and one lefthanded; August 16, 1981; April 24, 1982; August 26, 1985, two lefthanded and one righthanded; May 8, 1987; May 9, 1987; April 18, 1990; and June 9, 1990). . . . Led A.L. first basemen with 1,615 total chances in 1978, 1,694 in 1984 and 1,526 in 1987. . . . Led A.L. first basemen with 1,504 putouts in 1978. . . . Hit three home runs in a game (August 29, 1979, second game; September 14, 1980, 13 innings, and August 26, 1985). . . . Led A.L. with .410 on base percentage, 107 bases on balls received and 19 game-winning RBIs in 1984. . . . Led A.L. with 25 intentional bases on balls received in 1984 and tied for lead with 18 in 1982. . . . Led A.L. first basemen with 152 double plays in 1984, 146 in 1987 and tied for lead with 154 in 1985. . . . Led N.L. first basemen with .996 fielding percentage, 137 assists and 122 double plays in 1989. . . . Tied for N.L. lead with 21 intentional bases on balls received in 1990.

Year	Team (League)	Pos.	G	AB	R	H	2B	3B	HR	RBI	Avg.	SB	PO	A	E	Avg.
1973 — Bluefield (Appalachian)		1B	50	188	34	54	6	0	11	32	.287	6	421	14	13	.971
1974 — Miami (Florida State)		1B	131	460	64	133	*29	7	12	63	.289	4	*1114	*51	*25	.979
— Asheville (W. Carolinas) ...		1B	2	7	1	2	2	0	0	2	.286	0	17	0	0	1.000
1975 — Asheville (W. Carolinas) ...		1B-3B	124	436	66	115	13	5	17	68	.264	7	637	58	15	.979
1976 — Charlotte (Southern)		1B	88	299	46	89	15	2	12	46	.298	11	746	45	9	.989
— Rochester (Int'l)		1B-OF-3B	54	168	35	46	6	2	11	40	.274	3	291	13	5	.984
1977 — Baltimore (A.L.)		OF-1B	160	611	81	173	29	2	27	88	.283	0	482	20	4	.992
1978 — Baltimore (A.L.)		1B-3B	161	610	85	174	32	3	27	95	.285	6	†1507	112	6	.996
1979 — Baltimore (A.L.)		1B	159	606	90	179	30	2	25	99	.295	10	*1456	107	10	.994
1980 — Baltimore (A.L.)		1B	158	621	100	186	36	2	32	116	.300	7	1369	77	9	.994
1981 — Baltimore (A.L.)		1B	99	378	57	111	21	2	*22	*78	.294	2	899	*91	1	*.999
1982 — Baltimore (A.L.)		1B	151	550	87	174	30	1	32	110	.316	7	1269	97	4	*.997
1983 — Baltimore (A.L.)		1B	156	582	115	178	30	3	33	111	.306	5	1393	114	10	.993
1984 — Baltimore (A.L.)		1B	•162	588	97	180	26	3	29	110	.306	10	*1538	*143	13	.992
1985 — Baltimore (A.L.)		1B	156	583	111	173	37	1	31	124	.297	5	1338	152	*19	.987
1986 — Baltimore (A.L.)		1B	137	495	61	151	25	1	17	84	.305	3	1045	88	13	.989
1987 — Baltimore (A.L.)		1B	160	618	89	171	28	3	30	91	.277	1	1371	145	10	.993
1988 — Baltimore (A.L.)		1B	161	603	75	171	27	2	28	84	.284	5	867	106	11	.989
1989 — Los Angeles (N.L.)■....		1B-3B	160	594	66	147	29	1	20	88	.247	7	1316	†137	6	†.996
1990 — Los Angeles (N.L.)		1B	155	558	96	184	22	3	26	95	.330	8	1180	113	10	.992
1991 — Los Angeles (N.L.)		1B-3B	153	576	69	150	23	1	19	96	.260	10	1327	128	7	.995
American League totals (12 years)			1820	6845	1048	2021	351	25	333	1190	.295	61	14534	1252	110	.993
National League totals (3 years)			468	1728	231	481	74	5	65	279	.278	25	3823	378	23	.995
Major league totals (15 years)			2288	8573	1279	2502	425	30	398	1469	.292	86	18357	1630	133	.993

CHAMPIONSHIP SERIES RECORD

CHAMPIONSHIP SERIES NOTES: Shares single-game record for most runs—4 (October 7, 1983).

Year	Team (League)	Pos.	G	AB	R	H	2B	3B	HR	RBI	Avg.	SB	PO	A	E	Avg.
1979 — Baltimore (A.L.)		1B	4	12	3	5	0	0	1	5	.417	0	44	3	2	.959
1983 — Baltimore (A.L.)		1B	4	15	5	4	0	0	1	3	.267	1	34	3	1	.974
Championship Series totals (2 years)			8	27	8	9	0	0	2	8	.333	1	78	6	3	.966

WORLD SERIES RECORD

Year	Team (League)	Pos.	G	AB	R	H	2B	3B	HR	RBI	Avg.	SB	PO	A	E	Avg.
1979 — Baltimore (A.L.)		1B	7	26	3	4	1	0	1	2	.154	1	60	7	0	1.000
1983 — Baltimore (A.L.)		1B	5	20	2	5	0	0	2	3	.250	0	46	1	1	.979
World Series totals (2 years)			12	46	5	9	1	0	3	5	.196	1	106	8	1	.991

ALL-STAR GAME RECORD

Year	League	Pos.	AB	R	H	2B	3B	HR	RBI	Avg.	SB	PO	A	E	Avg.
1978 — American							Did not play								
1981 — American		PH-1B	2	0	0	0	0	0	0	.000	0	2	1	0	1.000
1982 — American		PH-1B	1	0	0	0	0	0	0	.000	0	4	0	0	1.000
1983 — American		1B	2	0	0	0	0	0	0	.000	0	4	0	0	1.000
1984 — American		1B	2	0	1	1	0	0	0	.500	0	3	0	0	1.000
1985 — American		1B	3	0	0	0	0	0	0	.000	0	5	2	0	1.000
1986 — American							Did not play								
1991 — National		1B	1	0	0	0	0	0	0	.000	0	3	0	0	1.000
All-Star Game totals (6 years)			11	0	1	1	0	0	0	.091	0	21	3	0	1.000

MURRAY, MATT

P, BRAVES

PERSONAL: Born September 26, 1970, at Boston.... 6-6/200.... Throws right, bats left.... Full name: Matthew Michael Murray.
HIGH SCHOOL: Loomis Chaffee (Windsor, Conn.).
TRANSACTIONS/CAREER NOTES: Selected by Atlanta Braves organization in second round of free-agent draft (June 1, 1988).... On disabled list (May 1-July 10 and July 20, 1991-remainder of season).

Year	Team (League)	G	W	L	Pct.	ERA	Sv.	IP	H	R	ER	BB	SO
1988 — Pulaski (Appalachian)	13	2	4	.333	4.17	1	54	48	32	25	26	76
1989 — Bradenton Braves (GCL)	2	1	0	1.000	0.00	0	7	3	0	0	0	10
— Sumter (South Atlantic)	12	3	5	.375	4.33	0	72⅔	62	37	35	22	69
1990 — Burlington (Midwest)	26	11	7	.611	3.26	0	163	139	72	59	61	134
1991 — Durham (Carolina)	2	1	0	1.000	1.29	0	7	5	1	1	0	7

MUSSINA, MIKE

P, ORIOLES

PERSONAL: Born December 8, 1968, at Williamsport, Pa.... 6-2/182.... Throws right, bats right.... Full name: Michael Cole Mussina.
HIGH SCHOOL: Montoursville (Pa.).
COLLEGE: Stanford (degree in economics, 1990).

TRANSACTIONS/CAREER NOTES: Selected by Baltimore Orioles organization in 11th round of free-agent draft (June 2, 1987).... Selected by Orioles organization in first round (20th pick overall) of free-agent draft (June 4, 1990).... On Rochester disabled list (May 5-12, 1991).
RECORDS/HONORS: Named International League Most Valuable Pitcher (1991).

Year	Team (League)	G	W	L	Pct.	ERA	Sv.	IP	H	R	ER	BB	SO
1990	—Hagerstown (Eastern)	7	3	0	1.000	1.49	0	42⅓	34	10	7	7	40
	—Rochester (International)	2	0	0	...	1.35	0	13⅓	8	2	2	4	15
1991	—Rochester (International)	19	10	4	.714	2.87	0	122⅓	108	42	39	31	107
	—Baltimore (A.L.)	12	4	5	.444	2.87	0	87⅔	77	31	28	21	52
	Major league totals (1 year)	12	4	5	.444	2.87	0	87⅔	77	31	28	21	52

MUTIS, JEFF
P, INDIANS

PERSONAL: Born December 20, 1966, at Allentown, Pa.... 6-2/185.... Throws left, bats left.... Full name: Jeffrey Thomas Mutis.
COLLEGE: Lafayette College (Pa.).
TRANSACTIONS/CAREER NOTES: Selected by Cleveland Indians organization in 34th round of free-agent draft (June 3, 1985).... Selected by Indians organization in first round (27th pick overall) of free-agent draft (June 1, 1988).... On Kinston disabled list (July 20, 1988-remainder of season; July 6-31 and August 1, 1989-remainder of season).
STATISTICAL NOTES: Tied for Eastern League lead with three shutouts in 1990.... Led Eastern League pitchers with four shutouts and seven complete games in 1991.

Year	Team (League)	G	W	L	Pct.	ERA	Sv.	IP	H	R	ER	BB	SO
1988	—Burlington (Appalachian)	3	3	0	1.000	0.41	0	22	8	1	1	6	20
	—Kinston (Carolina)	1	1	0	1.000	1.59	0	5⅔	6	1	1	3	2
1989	—Kinston (Carolina)	16	7	3	.700	2.62	0	99⅔	87	42	29	20	68
1990	—Canton/Akron (Eastern)	26	11	10	.524	3.16	0	165	★178	73	58	44	94
1991	—Canton/Akron (Eastern)	25	11	5	.688	★1.80	0	★169⅔	138	42	34	51	89
	—Cleveland (A.L.)	3	0	3	.000	11.68	0	12⅓	23	16	16	7	6
	Major league totals (1 year)	3	0	3	.000	11.68	0	12⅓	23	16	16	7	6

MYERS, GREG
C, BLUE JAYS

PERSONAL: Born April 14, 1966, at Riverside, Calif.... 6-2/205.... Throws right, bats left.... Full name: Gregory Richard Myers.
HIGH SCHOOL: Riverside Polytechnical (Calif.).
TRANSACTIONS/CAREER NOTES: Selected by Toronto Blue Jays organization in third round of free-agent draft (June 4, 1984).... On disabled list (June 17, 1988-remainder of season).... On Toronto disabled list (March 26-June 5, 1989); included rehabilitation disability assignment to Knoxville (May 17-June 5, 1989).... On Toronto disabled list (May 5-25, 1990); included rehabilitation disability assignment to Syracuse (May 21-24, 1990).
STATISTICAL NOTES: Led California League catchers with 967 total chances in 1986.... Led International League catchers with 698 total chances in 1987.

Year	Team (League)	Pos.	G	AB	R	H	2B	3B	HR	RBI	Avg.	SB	PO	A	E	Avg.
1984	—Medicine Hat (Pioneer)	C	38	133	20	42	9	0	2	20	.316	0	216	24	4	.984
1985	—Florence (S. Atlantic)	C	134	489	52	109	19	2	5	62	.223	0	551	61	7	★.989
1986	—Ventura (California)	C	124	451	65	133	23	4	20	79	.295	9	★849	99	19	.980
1987	—Syracuse (International)	C	107	342	35	84	19	1	10	47	.246	3	★637	50	11	.984
	—Toronto (A.L.)	C	7	9	1	1	0	0	0	0	.111	0	24	1	0	1.000
1988	—Syracuse (International)	C	34	120	18	34	7	1	7	21	.283	1	63	9	1	.986
1989	—Knoxville (Southern)	C	29	90	11	30	10	0	5	19	.333	0	130	12	1	.993
	—Toronto (A.L.)	C	17	44	0	5	2	0	0	4	.114	0	46	6	0	1.000
	—Syracuse (International)	C	24	89	8	24	6	0	1	11	.270	0	60	7	1	.985
1990	—Toronto (A.L.)	C	87	250	33	59	7	1	5	22	.236	0	411	30	3	.993
	—Syracuse (International)	C	3	11	0	2	1	0	0	2	.182	0	14	0	0	1.000
1991	—Toronto (A.L.)	C	107	309	25	81	22	0	8	36	.262	0	484	37	11	.979
	Major league totals (4 years)		218	612	59	146	31	1	13	59	.239	0	965	74	14	.987

CHAMPIONSHIP SERIES RECORD

Year	Team (League)	Pos.	G	AB	R	H	2B	3B	HR	RBI	Avg.	SB	PO	A	E	Avg.
1991	—Toronto (A.L.)					Did not play										

MYERS, JIM
P, GIANTS

PERSONAL: Born April 28, 1969, at Oklahoma City.... 6-1/185.... Throws right, bats right.... Full name: James Xavier Myers.
HIGH SCHOOL: Crowder (Okla.).
TRANSACTIONS/CAREER NOTES: Selected by San Francisco Giants organization in 35th round of free-agent draft (June 2, 1987).
MISCELLANEOUS: Had no chances in one game as outfielder with San Jose (1990).

Year	Team (League)	G	W	L	Pct.	ERA	Sv.	IP	H	R	ER	BB	SO
1987	—Pocatello (Pioneer)	10	0	2	.000	8.69	0	19⅔	29	21	19	16	12
1988	—Pocatello (Pioneer)	12	4	5	.444	5.40	0	58⅓	72	50	35	32	39
1989	—Clinton (Midwest)	32	4	12	.250	3.73	0	137⅔	139	71	57	58	63
1990	—San Jose (California)	60	5	8	.385	3.21	25	84	80	44	30	34	61
1991	—Shreveport (Texas)	★62	6	4	.600	2.48	24	76⅓	71	22	21	30	51

MYERS, RANDY
P, PADRES

PERSONAL: Born September 19, 1962, at Vancouver, Wash.... 6-1/225.... Throws left, bats left.... Full name: Randall Kirk Myers.
HIGH SCHOOL: Evergreen (Vancouver, Wash.).
COLLEGE: Clark Community College (Wash.).

TRANSACTIONS/CAREER NOTES: Selected by Cincinnati Reds organization in third round of free-agent draft (January 12, 1982). ... Selected by New York Mets organization in secondary phase of free-agent draft (June 7, 1982).... Traded by Mets with P Kip Gross to Cincinnati Reds for P John Franco and OF Don Brown (December 6, 1989).... Traded by Reds to San Diego Padres for OF-2B Bip Roberts and a player to be named later (December 8, 1991); Reds acquired OF Craig Pueschner to complete deal (December 9, 1991).
RECORDS/HONORS: Shares N.L. single-game record for most consecutive strikeouts by relief pitcher—6 (September 8, 1990). ... Named Carolina League Pitcher of the Year (1984).
STATISTICAL NOTES: Tied for Appalachian League lead in games started by pitcher with 13 and balks with three in 1982.... Tied for South Atlantic League lead in games started by pitcher with 28 in 1983.... Tied for Carolina League lead with seven complete games in 1984.

Year Team (League)	G	W	L	Pct.	ERA	Sv.	IP	H	R	ER	BB	SO
1982—Kingsport (Appalachian)	13	6	3	.667	4.12	0	74⅓	68	49	34	69	•86
1983—Columbia (South Atlantic)	28	14	10	.583	3.63	0	173⅓	146	94	70	108	164
1984—Lynchburg (Carolina)	23	13	5	.722	*2.06	0	157	123	46	36	61	171
—Jackson (Texas)	5	2	1	.667	2.06	0	35	29	14	8	16	35
1985—Jackson (Texas)	19	4	8	.333	3.96	0	120⅓	99	61	53	69	116
—Tidewater (International)	8	1	1	.500	1.84	0	44	40	13	9	20	25
—New York (N.L.)	1	0	0	...	0.00	0	2	0	0	0	1	2
1986—Tidewater (International)	45	6	7	.462	2.35	12	65	44	19	17	44	79
—New York (N.L.)	10	0	0	...	4.22	0	10⅔	11	5	5	9	13
1987—New York (N.L.)	54	3	6	.333	3.96	6	75	61	36	33	30	92
—Tidewater (International)	5	0	0	...	4.91	3	7⅓	6	4	4	4	13
1988—New York (N.L.)	55	7	3	.700	1.72	26	68	45	15	13	17	69
1989—New York (N.L.)	65	7	4	.636	2.35	24	84⅓	62	23	22	40	88
1990—Cincinnati (N.L.) ■	66	4	6	.400	2.08	31	86⅔	59	24	20	38	98
1991—Cincinnati (N.L.)	58	6	13	.316	3.55	6	132	116	61	52	80	108
Major league totals (7 years)	309	27	32	.458	2.85	93	458⅔	354	164	145	215	470

CHAMPIONSHIP SERIES RECORD

CHAMPIONSHIP SERIES NOTES: Shares N.L. single-series record for most saves—3 (1990).

Year Team (League)	G	W	L	Pct.	ERA	Sv.	IP	H	R	ER	BB	SO
1988—New York (N.L.)	3	2	0	1.000	0.00	0	4⅔	1	0	0	2	0
1990—Cincinnati (N.L.)	4	0	0	...	0.00	3	5⅔	2	0	0	3	7
Championship Series totals (2 years)	7	2	0	1.000	0.00	3	10⅓	3	0	0	5	7

WORLD SERIES RECORD

Year Team (League)	G	W	L	Pct.	ERA	Sv.	IP	H	R	ER	BB	SO
1990—Cincinnati (N.L.)	3	0	0	...	0.00	1	3	2	0	0	0	3

ALL-STAR GAME RECORD

Year League	W	L	Pct.	ERA	Sv.	IP	H	R	ER	BB	SO
1990—National	0	0	...	0.00	0	1	1	0	0	2	0

NABHOLZ, CHRIS
P, EXPOS

PERSONAL: Born January 5, 1967, at Harrisburg, Pa.... 6-5/212.... Throws left, bats left.... Full name: Christopher William Nabholz.
HIGH SCHOOL: Pottsville (Pa.).
COLLEGE: Towson State.
TRANSACTIONS/CAREER NOTES: Selected by Cleveland Indians organization in 30th round of free-agent draft (June 3, 1985).... Selected by Montreal Expos organization in second round of free-agent draft (June 1, 1988).... On Montreal disabled list (June 16-August 4, 1991); included rehabilitation disability assignment to Indianapolis (July 16-August 4, 1991).

Year Team (League)	G	W	L	Pct.	ERA	Sv.	IP	H	R	ER	BB	SO
1989—Rockford (Midwest)	24	13	5	.722	2.18	0	161⅓	132	54	39	41	149
1990—Jacksonville (Southern)	11	7	2	.778	3.03	0	74⅓	62	28	25	27	77
—Montreal (N.L.)	11	6	2	.750	2.83	0	70	43	23	22	32	53
—Indianapolis (Am. Assoc.)	10	0	6	.000	4.83	0	63⅓	66	38	34	28	44
1991—Montreal (N.L.)	24	8	7	.533	3.63	0	153⅔	134	66	62	57	99
—Indianapolis (Am. Assoc.)	4	2	2	.500	1.86	0	19⅓	13	5	4	5	16
Major league totals (2 years)	35	14	9	.609	3.38	0	223⅔	177	89	84	89	152

NAEHRING, TIM
SS, RED SOX

PERSONAL: Born February 1, 1967, at Cincinnati.... 6-2/190.... Throws right, bats right. ... Full name: Timothy James Naehring.
HIGH SCHOOL: LaSalle (Cincinnati).
COLLEGE: Miami of Ohio.
TRANSACTIONS/CAREER NOTES: Selected by Boston Red Sox organization in eighth round of free-agent draft (June 1, 1988).... On Boston disabled list (August 16, 1990-remainder of season and May 18, 1991-remainder of season).

Year	Team (League)	Pos.	G	AB	R	H	2B	3B	HR	RBI	Avg.	SB	PO	A	E	Avg.
1988	—Elmira (New York-Penn) ..	SS	19	59	6	18	3	0	1	13	.305	0	25	51	6	.927
	—Winter Haven (Fla. St.)	SS	42	141	17	32	7	0	0		.227	1	77	136	20	.914
1989	—Lynchburg (Carolina)	SS	56	209	24	63	7	1	4	37	.301	2	72	131	12	.944
	—Pawtucket (Int'l)	SS-3B	79	273	32	75	16	1	3	31	.275	2	118	192	21	.937
1990	—Pawtucket (Int'l)	SS-3B-2B	82	290	45	78	16	1	15	47	.269	16	126	240	16	.958
	—Boston (A.L.)	SS-3B-2B	24	85	10	23	6	0	2	12	.271	9	36	66	9	.919
1991	—Boston (A.L.)	SS-3B-2B	20	55	1	6	1	0	0	3	.109	0	17	53	3	.959
	Major league totals (2 years)		44	140	11	29	7	0	2	15	.207	9	53	119	12	.935

NAGY, CHARLES
P, INDIANS

PERSONAL: Born May 5, 1967, at Bridgeport, Conn. . . . 6-3/200. . . . Throws right, bats left. . . . Full name: Charles Harrison Nagy.
HIGH SCHOOL: Roger Ludlowe (Fairfield, Conn.).
COLLEGE: Connecticut.
TRANSACTIONS/CAREER NOTES: Selected by Cleveland Indians organization in first round (17th pick overall) of free-agent draft (June 1, 1988).
RECORDS/HONORS: Named Carolina League Pitcher of the Year (1989).
STATISTICAL NOTES: Led Carolina League with four shutouts in 1989. . . . Tied for Eastern League lead with nine complete games in 1990.
MISCELLANEOUS: Member of 1988 U.S. Olympic baseball team.

Year	Team (League)	G	W	L	Pct.	ERA	Sv.	IP	H	R	ER	BB	SO
1989	—Kinston (Carolina)	13	8	4	.667	1.51	0	95⅓	69	22	16	24	99
	—Canton/Akron (Eastern)	15	4	5	.444	3.35	0	94	102	44	35	32	65
1990	—Canton/Akron (Eastern)	23	13	8	.619	2.52	0	175	132	62	49	39	99
	—Cleveland (A.L.)	9	2	4	.333	5.91	0	45⅔	58	31	30	21	26
1991	—Cleveland (A.L.)	33	10	15	.400	4.13	0	211⅓	228	103	97	66	109
	Major league totals (2 years)	42	12	19	.387	4.45	0	257	286	134	127	87	135

NATAL, ROB
C, EXPOS

PERSONAL: Born November 13, 1965, at Long Beach, Calif. . . . 5-11/190. . . . Throws right, bats right. . . . Full name: Robert Marcilino Natal.
HIGH SCHOOL: Hilltop (Chula Vista, Calif.).
COLLEGE: California.
TRANSACTIONS/CAREER NOTES: Selected by Montreal Expos organization in 13th round of free-agent draft (June 2, 1987).
STATISTICAL NOTES: Led Florida State League catchers with 765 total chances in 1988.

Year	Team (League)	Pos.	G	AB	R	H	2B	3B	HR	RBI	Avg.	SB	PO	A	E	Avg.
1987	—Jamestown (N.Y.-Penn) ...	C	57	180	26	58	8	4	7	32	.322	6	321	52	6	.984
1988	—West Palm Beach (FSL)	C	113	387	47	93	17	0	6	51	.240	3	★671	77	17	.978
1989	—Jacksonville (Southern) ...	C	46	141	12	29	8	1	0	11	.206	2	324	37	7	.981
	—West Palm Beach (FSL)	C	15	48	5	6	0	0	1	2	.125	1	68	24	3	.968
1990	—Jacksonville (Southern) ...	C	62	171	23	42	7	1	7	25	.246	0	344	46	10	.975
1991	—Indianapolis (A.A.)	C	16	41	2	13	4	0	0	9	.317	1	62	5	2	.971
	—Harrisburg (Eastern)	C	100	336	47	86	16	3	13	53	.256	1	453	45	4	.992

NAVARRO, JAIME
P, BREWERS

PERSONAL: Born March 27, 1967, at Bayamon, Puerto Rico. . . . 6-4/210. . . . Throws right, bats right. . . . Full name: Jaime Navarro. . . . Son of Julio Navarro, pitcher, Los Angeles Angels, Detroit Tigers and Atlanta Braves (1962-66 and 1970).
HIGH SCHOOL: Luis Pales Matos (Bayamon, Puerto Rico).
COLLEGE: Miami-Dade Community College-New World Center (Fla.).
TRANSACTIONS/CAREER NOTES: Selected by Baltimore Orioles organization in second round of free-agent draft (January 14, 1986). . . . Selected by Orioles organization in secondary phase of free-agent draft (June 2, 1986). . . . Selected by Milwaukee Brewers organization in third round of free-agent draft (June 2, 1987).
STATISTICAL NOTES: Led A.L. with five balks in 1990.

Year	Team (League)	G	W	L	Pct.	ERA	Sv.	IP	H	R	ER	BB	SO
1987	—Helena (Pioneer)	13	4	3	.571	3.57	0	85⅔	87	37	34	18	95
1988	—Stockton (California)	26	15	5	.750	3.09	0	174⅔	148	70	60	74	151
1989	—El Paso (Texas)	11	5	2	.714	2.47	0	76⅔	61	29	21	35	78
	—Denver (American Assoc.)	3	1	1	.500	3.60	0	20	24	8	8	7	17
	—Milwaukee (A.L.)	19	7	8	.467	3.12	0	109⅔	119	47	38	32	56
1990	—Milwaukee (A.L.)	32	8	7	.533	4.46	1	149⅓	176	83	74	41	75
	—Denver (American Assoc.)	6	2	3	.400	4.20	0	40⅔	41	27	19	14	28
1991	—Milwaukee (A.L.)	34	15	12	.556	3.92	0	234	237	117	102	73	114
	Major league totals (3 years)	85	30	27	.526	3.91	1	493	532	247	214	146	245

NAVARRO, TITO
SS, METS

PERSONAL: Born September 12, 1970, at Rio Pedras, Puerto Rico. . . . 5-10/155. . . . Throws right, bats right. . . . Full name: Roberto Rodriguez Navarro.
HIGH SCHOOL: Colegio del Carmen (Trujillo Alto, Puerto Rico).
TRANSACTIONS/CAREER NOTES: Signed as free agent by New York Mets organization (September 2, 1987).

STATISTICAL NOTES: Led South Atlantic League shortstops with 212 putouts, 440 assists and 692 total chances in 1990. . . . Led Eastern League shortstops with 617 total chances in 1991.

Year Team (League)	Pos.	G	AB	R	H	2B	3B	HR	RBI	Avg.	SB	PO	A	E	Avg.
1988—Kingsport (Appalachian)..	SS	54	172	26	42	3	2	0	23	.244	3	64	133	12 ★	.943
1989—Pittsfield (N.Y.-Penn)	SS-2B	46	157	26	44	6	2	0	14	.280	13	63	128	17	.918
1990—Columbia (S. Atlantic)	SS-1B	136	497	86	156	25	4	0	54	.314	50	†224	†440	40	.943
—Jackson (Texas)	SS	3	11	0	2	1	0	0	1	.182	0	4	11	2	.882
1991—Williamsport (Eastern)	SS	128	482	69	139	9	4	2	42	.288	42	★233	353	31 ★	.950

NEAGLE, DENNY
P, TWINS

PERSONAL: Born September 13, 1968, at Prince Georges County, Md. . . . 6-4/209. . . . Throws left, bats left. . . . Full name: Dennis Edward Neagle.
HIGH SCHOOL: Arundel (Gambrills, Md.).
COLLEGE: Minnesota.
TRANSACTIONS/CAREER NOTES: Selected by Minnesota Twins organization in third round of free-agent draft (June 5, 1989). . . . On Minnesota disabled list (July 28-August 12, 1991).

Year Team (League)	G	W	L	Pct.	ERA	Sv.	IP	H	R	ER	BB	SO
1989—Elizabethton (Appalachian)	6	1	2	.333	4.50	1	22	20	11	11	8	32
—Kenosha (Midwest)	6	2	1	.667	1.65	0	43⅔	25	9	8	16	40
1990—Visalia (California)	10	8	0	1.000	1.43	0	63	39	13	10	16	92
—Orlando (Southern)	17	12	3	.800	2.45	0	121⅓	94	40	33	31	94
1991—Minnesota (A.L.)	7	0	1	.000	4.05	0	20	28	9	9	7	14
—Portland (Pacific Coast)	19	9	4	.692	3.27	0	104⅔	101	41	38	32	94
Major league totals (1 year)	7	0	1	.000	4.05	0	20	28	9	9	7	14

NELSON, GENE
P, ATHLETICS

PERSONAL: Born December 3, 1960, at Tampa, Fla. . . . 6-0/174. . . . Throws right, bats right. . . . Full name: Wayland Eugene Nelson II.
HIGH SCHOOL: Pasco (Dade City, Fla.).
TRANSACTIONS/CAREER NOTES: Selected by Texas Rangers organization in 29th round of free-agent draft (June 6, 1978). . . . Traded by Rangers organization with P Ray Fontenot to New York Yankees organization for P Bob Polinsky, P Neal Mersch and P Mark Softy (October 8, 1979), completing deal in which Yankees traded OF Mickey Rivers and three players to be named later to Rangers for 3B Amos Lewis and two players to be named later (August 1, 1979). . . . On New York disabled list (April 10-May 4, 1981); included rehabilitation disability assignment to Fort Lauderdale (April 17-May 4, 1981). . . . Traded by Yankees organization with P Bill Caudill, a player to be named later and cash to Seattle Mariners for P Shane Rawley (April 1, 1982); Mariners organization acquired OF Bobby Brown to complete deal (April 6, 1982). . . . On Salt Lake City disabled list (June 25-July 31, 1983). . . . Traded by Mariners organization with P Jerry Don Gleaton to Chicago White Sox for P Salome Barojas (June 27, 1984). . . . Traded by White Sox with a player to be named later to Oakland Athletics for IF Donnie Hill (December 11, 1986); A's acquired P Bruce Tanner to complete deal (December 18, 1986). . . . On disabled list (April 8-23, 1989 and April 10-May 20, 1991).
STATISTICAL NOTES: Led Florida State League with five shutouts and 16 complete games in 1980.
MISCELLANEOUS: Had one at-bat with no hits (1985). . . . Appeared as pinch-runner in three games (1988). . . . Appeared in one game as pinch-runner (1989).

Year Team (League)	G	W	L	Pct.	ERA	Sv.	IP	H	R	ER	BB	SO
1978—Sarasota Rangers (GCL)	14	5	0	1.000	2.25	3	52	41	18	13	20	28
1979—Asheville (Western Carolinas)	33	13	5	.722	3.60	0	155	149	77	62	44	96
1980—Fort Lauderdale (Florida St.)■.	27	★20	3	★.870	1.97	0	196	146	51	43	70	130
1981—New York (A.L.)	8	3	1	.750	4.85	0	39	40	24	21	23	16
—Fort Lauderdale (Florida St.)	2	0	0	...	5.40	0	10	9	6	6	5	8
—Columbus (International)	5	4	0	1.000	2.53	1	32	25	9	9	14	37
1982—Seattle (A.L.)■	22	6	9	.400	4.62	0	122⅔	133	70	63	60	71
—Salt Lake City (Pacific Coast)	5	1	3	.250	3.35	0	37⅔	36	18	14	28	22
1983—Salt Lake City (Pacific Coast)	16	9	4	.692	5.18	0	99	115	65	57	28	74
—Seattle (A.L.)	10	0	3	.000	7.88	0	32	38	29	28	21	11
1984—Salt Lake City (Pacific Coast)	17	6	8	.429	5.63	0	112	138	75	70	54	89
—Chicago (A.L.)■	20	3	5	.375	4.46	1	74⅔	72	38	37	17	36
1985—Chicago (A.L.)	46	10	10	.500	4.26	2	145⅔	144	74	69	67	101
1986—Chicago (A.L.)	54	6	6	.500	3.85	6	114⅔	118	52	49	41	70
1987—Oakland (A.L.)■	54	6	5	.545	3.93	3	123⅔	120	58	54	35	94
1988—Oakland (A.L.)	54	9	6	.600	3.06	3	111⅔	93	42	38	38	67
1989—Oakland (A.L.)	50	3	5	.375	3.26	0	80	60	33	30	30	70
1990—Oakland (A.L.)	51	3	3	.500	1.57	5	74⅔	55	14	13	17	38
1991—Oakland (A.L.)	44	1	5	.167	6.84	0	48⅔	60	38	37	23	23
Major league totals (11 years)	413	50	58	.463	4.08	23	967⅓	933	472	438	372	597

CHAMPIONSHIP SERIES RECORD

CHAMPIONSHIP SERIES NOTES: Shares A.L. single-series record for most games won—2 (1988).

Year Team (League)	G	W	L	Pct.	ERA	Sv.	IP	H	R	ER	BB	SO
1988—Oakland (A.L.)	2	2	0	1.000	0.00	0	4⅔	5	0	0	1	0
1989—Oakland (A.L.)	1	0	0	...	0.00	0	1⅓	1	0	0	0	2
1990—Oakland (A.L.)	1	0	0	...	0.00	0	1⅔	3	0	0	0	0
Championship Series totals (3 years)	4	2	0	1.000	0.00	0	7⅔	9	0	0	1	2

Year Team (League)	G	W	L	Pct.	ERA	Sv.	IP	H	R	ER	BB	SO
1988—Oakland (A.L.)	3	0	0	...	1.42	0	6⅓	4	1	1	3	3
1989—Oakland (A.L.)	2	0	0	...	54.00	0	1	4	6	6	2	1
1990—Oakland (A.L.)	2	0	0	...	0.00	0	5	3	0	0	2	0
World Series totals (3 years)	7	0	0	...	5.11	0	12⅓	11	7	7	7	4

NELSON, JEFF
P, MARINERS

PERSONAL: Born November 17, 1966, at Baltimore. . . . 6-8/225. . . . Throws right, bats right. . . . Full name: Jeffrey Allen Nelson. **HIGH SCHOOL:** Catonsville (Md.). **COLLEGE:** Catonsville Community College (Md.).
TRANSACTIONS/CAREER NOTES: Selected by Los Angeles Dodgers organization in 22nd round of free-agent draft (June 4, 1984). . . . Drafted by Calgary, Seattle Mariners organization (December 9, 1986). . . . On disabled list (July 16, 1989-remainder of season).

Year Team (League)	G	W	L	Pct.	ERA	Sv.	IP	H	R	ER	BB	SO
1984—Great Falls (Pioneer)	1	0	0	...	54.00	0	⅔	3	4	4	3	1
—Bradenton Dodgers (GCL)	9	0	0	...	1.35	0	13⅓	6	3	2	6	7
1985—Bradenton Dodgers (GCL)	14	0	5	.000	5.51	0	47⅓	72	50	29	32	31
1986—Great Falls (Pioneer)	3	0	0	...	13.50	0	2	5	3	3	3	1
—Bakersfield (California)	24	0	7	.000	6.69	0	71⅓	79	83	53	84	37
1987—Salinas (California)■............	17	3	7	.300	5.74	0	80	80	61	51	71	43
1988—San Bernardino (California)	27	8	9	.471	5.54	0	149⅓	163	115	92	91	94
1989—Williamsport (Eastern)	15	7	5	.583	3.31	0	92⅓	72	41	34	53	61
1990—Williamsport (Eastern)	10	1	4	.200	6.44	0	43⅓	65	35	31	18	14
—Peninsula (Carolina)	18	2	2	.500	3.15	6	60	47	21	21	25	49
1991—Jacksonville (Southern)	21	4	0	1.000	1.27	12	28⅓	23	5	4	9	34
—Calgary (Pacific Coast)	28	3	4	.429	3.90	21	32⅓	39	19	14	15	26

NEN, ROBB
P, RANGERS

PERSONAL: Born January 28, 1969, at San Pedro, Calif. . . . 6-4/200. . . . Throws right, bats right. . . . Full name: Robert Allen Nen. . . . Son of Dick Nen, first baseman, Los Angeles Dodgers, Washington Senators and Chicago Cubs (1963, 1965-68 and 1970). **HIGH SCHOOL:** Los Alamitos (Calif.).
TRANSACTIONS/CAREER NOTES: Selected by Texas Rangers organization in 32nd round of free-agent draft (June 2, 1987). . . . On Charlotte disabled list (Beginning of season-April 26 and May 6-May 24, 1990). . . . On disabled list (April 23-June 10, June 28-July 8 and July 11-September 3, 1991).

Year Team (League)	G	W	L	Pct.	ERA	Sv.	IP	H	R	ER	BB	SO
1987—Sarasota Rangers (GCL)	2	0	0	...	7.71	0	2⅓	4	2	2	3	4
1988—Gastonia (South Atlantic)	14	0	5	.000	7.45	0	48⅓	69	57	40	45	36
—Butte (Pioneer)	14	4	5	.444	8.75	0	48⅓	65	55	47	45	30
1989—Gastonia (South Atlantic)	24	7	4	.636	2.41	0	138⅓	96	47	37	76	146
1990—Charlotte (Florida State)	11	1	4	.200	3.69	0	53⅔	44	28	22	36	38
—Tulsa (Texas)	7	0	5	.000	5.06	0	26⅔	23	20	15	21	21
1991—Tulsa (Texas)	6	0	2	.000	5.79	0	28	24	21	18	20	23

NEWLIN, JIM
P, MARINERS

PERSONAL: Born September 11, 1966, at New Orleans. . . . 6-2/205. . . . Throws right, bats right. . . . Full name: James Russell Newlin. **HIGH SCHOOL:** Shawnee Mission South (Overland Park, Kan.). **COLLEGE:** Wichita (Kan.).
TRANSACTIONS/CAREER NOTES: Selected by Seattle Mariners organization in 12th round of free-agent draft (June 5, 1989).

Year Team (League)	G	W	L	Pct.	ERA	Sv.	IP	H	R	ER	BB	SO
1989—San Bernardino (California)	19	1	2	.333	1.57	4	28⅔	13	6	5	15	25
1990—San Bernardino (California)	36	1	5	.167	3.60	12	45	35	24	18	21	56
—Williamsport (Eastern)	20	1	1	.500	3.49	0	38⅔	45	22	15	15	23
1991—Jacksonville (Southern)	47	6	5	.545	2.25	12	64	58	24	16	29	48

NEWMAN, AL
IF, REDS

PERSONAL: Born June 30, 1960, at Kansas City, Mo. . . . 5-9/188. . . . Throws right, bats left. . . . Full name: Albert Dwayne Newman. **HIGH SCHOOL:** Ontario (Calif.). **COLLEGE:** Chaffey College (Calif.) and San Diego State.
TRANSACTIONS/CAREER NOTES: Selected by California Angels organization in third round of free-agent draft (January 9, 1979). . . . Selected by Texas Rangers organization in third round of free-agent draft (January 8, 1980). . . . Selected by New York Mets organization in secondary phase of free-agent draft (June 3, 1980). . . . Selected by Montreal Expos organization in secondary phase of free-agent draft (June 8, 1981). . . . On Memphis disabled list (July 23-August 16, 1983). . . . Traded by Expos organization with P Scott Sanderson to San Diego Padres for P Gary Lucas (December 7, 1983). . . . Traded by Padres to Expos organization for P Greg A. Harris (July 20, 1984). . . . Traded by Expos to Minnesota Twins for P Mike Shade (February 20, 1987). . . . Granted free agency (November 11, 1991) . . . . Signed by Cincinnati Reds organization (January 28, 1992).
STATISTICAL NOTES: Led Southern League second basemen with 776 total chances in 1982. . . . Led Southern League with 18 sacrifice hits in 1982. . . . Led Texas League shortstops with 58 double plays in 1984.

Year Team (League)	Pos.	G	AB	R	H	2B	3B	HR	RBI	Avg.	SB	PO	A	E	Avg.
1982 — Memphis (Southern)	2B	142	494	85	136	16	8	1	41	.275	63	★356	●388	★32	.959
1983 — Wichita (Am. Assoc.)........	2B	38	124	20	30	6	1	0	16	.242	2	73	96	5	.971
— Memphis (Southern)	2B	52	194	18	49	5	2	0	13	.253	16	111	123	14	.944
1984 — Beaumont (Texas)■	SS	88	318	69	80	8	0	0	23	.252	33	138	250	27	.935
— Indianapolis (A.A.)■	2-3-0-S	37	123	13	37	3	0	0	11	.301	11	49	79	2	.985
1985 — Indianapolis (A.A.)	2B-SS	87	301	42	85	16	2	0	23	.282	31	144	250	10	.975
— Montreal (N.L.)	2B-SS	25	29	7	5	1	0	0	1	.172	2	19	36	0	1.000
1986 — Montreal (N.L.)	2B-SS	95	185	23	37	3	0	1	8	.200	11	98	161	11	.959
1987 — Minnesota (A.L.)■	S-2-3-0	110	307	44	68	15	5	0	29	.221	15	120	225	5	.986
1988 — Minnesota (A.L.)	3B-SS-2B	105	260	35	58	7	0	0	19	.223	12	97	155	6	.977
1989 — Minnesota (A.L.)	2-3-S-0	141	446	62	113	18	2	0	38	.253	25	191	282	16	.967
1990 — Minnesota (A.L.)	2-S-3-0	144	388	43	94	14	0	0	30	.242	13	190	304	13	.974
1991 — Minnesota (A.L.)	IF-OF	118	246	25	47	5	0	0	19	.191	4	130	184	4	.987
American League totals (5 years)		618	1647	209	380	59	7	0	135	.231	69	728	1150	44	.977
National League totals (2 years)		120	214	30	42	4	0	1	9	.196	13	117	197	11	.966
Major league totals (7 years)		738	1861	239	422	63	7	1	144	.227	82	845	1347	55	.976

CHAMPIONSHIP SERIES RECORD

Year Team (League)	Pos.	G	AB	R	H	2B	3B	HR	RBI	Avg.	SB	PO	A	E	Avg.
1987 — Minnesota (A.L.)	2B	1	2	0	0	0	0	0	0	.000	0	0	1	0	1.000
1991 — Minnesota (A.L.)	3B-SS	2	0	0	0	0	0	0	0	...	0	0	0	0	...
Championship Series totals (2 years)		3	2	0	0	0	0	0	0	.000	0	0	1	0	1.000

WORLD SERIES RECORD

Year Team (League)	Pos.	G	AB	R	H	2B	3B	HR	RBI	Avg.	SB	PO	A	E	Avg.
1987 — Minnesota (A.L.)	PR-2B-PH	4	5	0	1	0	0	0	0	.200	0	1	2	0	1.000
1991 — Minnesota (A.L.)	PH-IF-PR	4	2	0	1	0	1	0	1	.500	0	0	2	0	1.000
World Series totals (2 years)		8	7	0	2	0	1	0	1	.286	0	1	4	0	1.000

NEWMAN, ALAN

P, TWINS

PERSONAL: Born October 2, 1969, at La Habra, Calif.... 6-6/212.... Throws left, bats left. ... Full name: Alan Spencer Newman.
HIGH SCHOOL: La Habra (Calif.).
COLLEGE: Cal State Fullerton.
TRANSACTIONS/CAREER NOTES: Selected by San Diego Padres organization in 26th round of free-agent draft (June 2, 1987).... Selected by Minnesota Twins organization in second round of free-agent draft (June 1, 1988).
STATISTICAL NOTES: Led Appalachian League with 17 wild pitches in 1988.

Year Team (League)	G	W	L	Pct.	ERA	Sv.	IP	H	R	ER	BB	SO
1988 — Elizabethton (Appalachian)	13	2	●8	.200	8.13	0	55⅓	57	62	50	56	51
1989 — Kenosha (Midwest)	18	3	9	.250	2.84	0	88⅔	65	41	28	74	82
1990 — Kenosha (Midwest)	22	10	4	.714	★1.64	0	154	95	41	28	78	158
— Visalia (California)	5	3	1	.750	2.23	0	36⅓	29	15	9	22	42
1991 — Visalia (California)	15	6	5	.545	3.51	0	92⅓	86	49	36	49	79
— Orlando (Southern)	11	5	4	.556	2.69	0	67	53	28	20	30	53

NEWSON, WARREN

OF, WHITE SOX

PERSONAL: Born June 3, 1964, at Newnan, Ga.... 5-7/190.... Throws left, bats left. ... Full name: Warren Dale Newson.
HIGH SCHOOL: Newnan (Ga.).
COLLEGE: Middle Georgia.
TRANSACTIONS/CAREER NOTES: Selected by San Diego Padres organization in fourth round of free-agent draft (January 14, 1986).... Traded by Padres with IF Joey Cora and IF Kevin Garner to Chicago White Sox organization for P Adam Peterson and P Steve Rosenberg (March 31, 1991).
STATISTICAL NOTES: Led Texas League with 103 bases on balls received and 10 intentional bases on balls received in 1989.

Year Team (League)	Pos.	G	AB	R	H	2B	3B	HR	RBI	Avg.	SB	PO	A	E	Avg.
1986 — Spokane (Northwest)	OF	54	159	29	37	8	1	2	31	.233	3	54	3	3	.950
1987 — Charleston, S.C. (S. Atl.) ...	OF	58	191	50	66	12	2	7	32	.346	13	81	4	2	.977
— Reno (California)	OF	51	165	44	51	7	●7	6	28	.309	2	60	5	8	.890
1988 — Riverside (California)	OF	130	438	99	130	23	●7	★22	91	.297	36	182	7	11	.945
1989 — Wichita (Texas)	OF	128	427	94	130	20	6	18	70	.304	20	191	15	5	.976
1990 — Las Vegas (Pac. Coast)	OF	123	404	80	123	20	3	13	58	.304	13	146	4	10	.938
1991 — Vancouver (Pac. Coast)■.	OF	33	111	19	41	12	1	2	19	.369	5	53	1	0	1.000
— Chicago (A.L.)	OF	71	132	20	39	5	0	4	25	.295	2	48	3	2	.962
Major league totals (1 year)		71	132	20	39	5	0	4	25	.295	2	48	3	2	.962

NICHOLS, CARL

C

PERSONAL: Born October 14, 1962, at Los Angeles.... 6-0/192.... Throws right, bats right. ... Full name: Carl Edward Nichols.
HIGH SCHOOL: Compton (Calif.).
TRANSACTIONS/CAREER NOTES: Selected by Baltimore Orioles organization in fourth round of

free-agent draft (June 3, 1980).... Loaned by Orioles organization to Macon, Detroit Tigers organization (April 8, 1982); returned (September 15, 1982).... Loaned by Orioles organization to San Jose, independent (April 10, 1984); returned (June 9, 1984).... Loaned by Orioles organization to Redwood, California Angels organization (June 9, 1984); returned (September 10, 1984).... Traded by Orioles organization to Houston Astros for P Dave Johnson and OF Victor Hithe (March 31, 1989).... On disabled list (August 24-September 15, 1990).... Granted free agency (October 16, 1991).
STATISTICAL NOTES: Led New York-Pennsylvania League catchers with 47 assists and tied for lead with six double plays in 1983.... Led California League catchers with 769 putouts, 112 assists and 897 total chances in 1984.... Led Southern League catchers with 693 putouts, 110 assists and 818 total chances in 1986.... Led International League catchers with .988 fielding percentage, nine double plays and nine passed balls in 1987.... Led Pacific Coast League catchers with 76 assists in 1989.... Tied for Pacific Coast League lead in double plays by catcher with eight in 1991.

| | | | | | | | | —BATTING— | | | | | | —FIELDING— | | |
Year	Team (League)	Pos.	G	AB	R	H	2B	3B	HR	RBI	Avg.	SB	PO	A	E	Avg.
1980—Bluefield (Appalachian)		C-1B-OF	37	85	24	18	2	2	0	10	.212	4	129	13	2	.986
1981—Miami (Florida State)		C-1F-OF	16	31	1	6	0	0	0	3	.194	0	34	9	6	.878
—Hagerstown (Carolina)		C-O-S-2	38	81	8	22	4	0	1	6	.272	3	131	21	3	.981
1982—Macon (South Atlantic)■..		C-OF-1B	84	257	33	55	10	2	0	30	.214	7	391	49	21	.954
1983—San Jose (California)■......		C-OF-3B	54	152	16	31	4	0	1	12	.204	2	204	39	17	.935
—Newark (N.Y.-Penn)		C-O-3-S	66	217	40	63	14	0	5	26	.290	4	348	†56	10	.976
1984—San Jose-Red. (Calif.)■...		C-OF	121	389	53	88	14	2	4	54	.226	1	†769	†112	17	.981
1985—Charlotte (Southern)		C-OF-1B	115	331	45	78	11	2	2	37	.236	7	496	71	15	.974
1986—Charlotte (Southern)		C-OF	118	439	63	118	26	1	14	72	.269	8	†700	†110	16	.981
—Baltimore (A.L.)		C	5	5	0	0	0	0	0	0	.000	0	11	0	0	1.000
1987—Rochester (Int'l)		C-OF	108	364	45	93	15	3	11	52	.255	3	617	65	9	†.987
—Baltimore (A.L.)		C	13	21	4	8	1	0	0	3	.381	0	39	3	0	1.000
1988—Baltimore (A.L.)		C-OF	18	47	2	9	1	0	0	1	.191	0	71	13	1	.988
—Rochester (Int'l)		C-OF-3B	75	193	20	44	7	1	3	16	.228	0	335	44	8	.979
1989—Tucson (Pacific Coast)■...		C-OF	104	340	45	87	27	1	4	27	.256	0	553	†77	1	.998
—Houston (N.L.)		C	8	13	0	1	0	0	0	2	.077	0	16	1	0	1.000
1990—Tucson (Pacific Coast)		C-OF-1B	58	170	24	43	11	0	4	33	.253	1	242	36	6	.979
—Houston (N.L.)		C-1B-OF	32	49	7	10	3	0	0	11	.204	0	86	10	3	.970
1991—Houston (N.L.)		C	20	51	3	10	3	0	0	1	.196	0	86	14	3	.971
—Tucson (Pacific Coast)		C	36	121	13	26	4	1	3	17	.215	0	237	30	4	.985
American League totals (3 years)			36	73	6	17	2	0	0	4	.233	0	121	16	1	.993
National League totals (3 years)			60	113	10	21	6	0	0	14	.186	0	188	25	6	.973
Major league totals (6 years)			96	186	16	38	8	0	0	18	.204	0	309	41	7	.980

NICHOLS, ROD
P, INDIANS

PERSONAL: Born December 29, 1964, at Burlington, Ia. .... 6-2/190. .... Throws right, bats right.... Full name: Rodney Lea Nichols.
HIGH SCHOOL: Highland (Alberquerque, N.M.).
COLLEGE: New Mexico.
TRANSACTIONS/CAREER NOTES: Selected by Cleveland Indians organization in fifth round of free-agent draft (June 3, 1985)....
On disabled list (July 12-August 18, 1986).... On Cleveland disabled list (March 26-May 12, 1988).... On Cleveland disabled list (March 19-June 12, 1989); including rehabilitation disability assignment to Colorado Springs (May 24-June 12, 1989).
STATISTICAL NOTES: Tied for Pacific Coast League lead with two shutouts in 1990.

Year	Team (League)	G	W	L	Pct.	ERA	Sv.	IP	H	R	ER	BB	SO
1985—Batavia (New York-Penn)		13	5	5	.500	3.00	0	84	74	40	28	33	93
1986—Waterloo (Midwest)		20	8	5	.615	4.06	0	115⅓	128	56	52	21	83
1987—Kinston (Carolina)		9	4	2	.667	4.02	0	56	53	27	25	14	61
—Williamsport (N.Y.-Penn)		16	4	3	.571	3.69	0	100	107	53	41	33	60
1988—Kinston (Carolina)		4	3	1	.750	4.50	0	24	26	13	12	15	19
—Colorado Springs (Pac. Coast) ..		10	2	6	.250	5.68	0	58⅔	69	41	37	17	43
—Cleveland (A.L.)		11	1	7	.125	5.06	0	69⅓	73	41	39	23	31
1989—Colorado Springs (Pac. Coast) ..		10	8	1	.889	3.58	0	65⅓	57	28	26	30	41
—Cleveland (A.L.)		15	4	6	.400	4.40	0	71⅔	81	42	35	24	42
1990—Cleveland (A.L.)		4	0	3	.000	7.88	0	16	24	14	14	6	3
—Colorado Springs (Pac. Coast) ..		22	12	9	.571	5.13	0	133⅓	160	84	76	48	74
1991—Cleveland (A.L.)		31	2	11	.154	3.54	1	137⅓	145	63	54	30	76
Major league totals (4 years)		61	7	27	.206	4.34	1	294⅓	323	160	142	83	152

NIED, DAVE
P, BRAVES

PERSONAL: Born December 22, 1968, at Dallas. .... 6-2/175. .... Throws right, bats right.... Full name: David Glen Nied.
HIGH SCHOOL: Duncanville (Tex.).
TRANSACTIONS/CAREER NOTES: Selected by Atlanta Braves organization in 14th round of free-agent draft (June 2, 1987).
STATISTICAL NOTES: Tied for South Atlantic League lead with 15 home runs allowed in 1988.... Tied for Carolina League lead with two shutouts in 1991.

Year	Team (League)	G	W	L	Pct.	ERA	Sv.	IP	H	R	ER	BB	SO
1988—Sumter (South Atlantic)		27	12	9	.571	3.76	0	165⅓	156	78	69	53	133
1989—Durham (Carolina)		12	5	2	.714	6.63	0	58⅓	74	47	43	23	38
—Burlington (Midwest)		13	5	6	.455	3.83	0	80	78	38	34	23	73
1990—Durham (Carolina)		10	1	1	.500	3.83	0	42⅓	38	19	18	14	27
—Burlington (Midwest)		10	5	3	.625	2.25	0	64	55	21	16	10	66
1991—Greenville (Southern)		15	7	3	.700	2.41	0	89⅔	79	26	24	20	101
—Durham (Carolina)		13	8	3	.727	1.56	0	80⅔	46	19	14	23	77

NIEVES, MEL
OF, BRAVES

PERSONAL: Born December 28, 1971, at San Juan, Puerto Rico.... 6-2/186.... Throws right, bats both.... Full name: Melvin Ramos Nieves.
HIGH SCHOOL: Ivis Pales Matos (Santa Rosa, Puerto Rico).
TRANSACTIONS/CAREER NOTES: Signed as free agent by Atlanta Braves organization (May 20, 1988).

Year Team (League)	Pos.	G	AB	R	H	2B	3B	HR	RBI	Avg.	SB	PO	A	E	Avg.
1988—Bradenton Braves (GCL)...	OF	56	170	16	30	6	0	1	12	.176	5	100	1	2	.981
1989—Pulaski (Appalachian)	OF	64	231	43	64	16	3	9	46	.277	6	45	1	6	.885
1990—Sumter (South Atlantic)....	OF	126	459	60	130	24	7	9	59	.283	10	227	7	11	.955
1991—Durham (Carolina)	OF	64	201	31	53	11	0	9	25	.264	3	75	8	5	.943

NILSSON, DAVE
C/3B, BREWERS

PERSONAL: Born December 14, 1969, at Queensland, Australia.... 6-3/185.... Throws right, bats left.... Full name: David Wayne Nilsson.
HIGH SCHOOL: Kedron (Brisbane, Australia).
TRANSACTIONS/CAREER NOTES: Signed as free agent by Milwaukee Brewers organization (February 9, 1987).... On disabled list (April 30-May 26, 1990).

Year Team (League)	Pos.	G	AB	R	H	2B	3B	HR	RBI	Avg.	SB	PO	A	E	Avg.
1987—Helena (Pioneer)	C	55	188	36	74	13	0	1	21	.394	0	329	28	7	.981
1988—Beloit (Midwest)	C-1B	95	332	28	74	15	2	4	41	.223	2	526	64	6	.990
1989—Stockton (California)	C-2B	125	472	59	115	16	6	5	56	.244	2	703	66	13	.983
1990—Stockton (California)	C-1B-3B	107	359	70	104	22	3	7	47	.290	6	600	86	12	.983
1991—El Paso (Texas)	C-3B	65	249	52	104	24	3	5	57	.418	4	348	46	8	.980
—Denver (Am. Assoc.)	C-1B-3B	28	95	10	22	8	0	1	14	.232	1	146	16	2	.988

NIXON, OTIS
OF, BRAVES

PERSONAL: Born January 9, 1959, at Evergreen, N.C.... 6-2/180.... Throws right, bats both.... Full name: Otis Junior Nixon.... Brother of Donell Nixon, outfielder, Seattle Mariners, San Francisco Giants, Baltimore Orioles (1987-90).
HIGH SCHOOL: Columbus (N.C.).
COLLEGE: Louisburg College (N.C.).
TRANSACTIONS/CAREER NOTES: Selected by Cincinnati Reds organization in 21st round of free-agent draft (June 6, 1978).... Selected by California Angels organization in secondary phase of free-agent draft (January 9, 1979).... Selected by New York Yankees organization in secondary phase of free-agent draft (June 5, 1979).... Traded by Yankees with P George Frazier and a player to be named later to Cleveland Indians for 3B Toby Harrah and a player to be named later (February 5, 1984); Yankees organization acquired P Rick Browne and Indians organization acquired P Guy Elston to complete deal (February 8, 1984).... Granted free agency (October 15, 1987).... Signed by Indianapolis, Montreal Expos organization (March 5, 1988).... Traded by Expos with 3B Boi Rodriguez to Atlanta Braves for C Jimmy Kremers and a player to be named later (April 1, 1991); Sumter (Expos organization) acquired P Keith Morrison to complete deal (June 3, 1991).... On suspended list (August 13-16, 1991).... On disqualified list (September 16, 1991-remainder of season).... Granted free agency (November 11, 1991).... Re-signed by Braves (December 12, 1991).
RECORDS/HONORS: Shares modern major league single-game record for most stolen bases—6 (June 16, 1991).
STATISTICAL NOTES: Led Appalachian League with 57 bases on balls received in 1979.... Led Appalachian League third basemen with .945 fielding percentage, 120 putouts and 12 double plays in 1979.... Led South Atlantic League with 113 bases on balls received in 1980.... Led Southern League with 110 bases on balls received in 1981.... Led International League in caught stealing with 29 in 1983.... Led International League outfielders with .992 fielding percentage, 363 putouts and 371 total chances in 1983.

Year Team (League)	Pos.	G	AB	R	H	2B	3B	HR	RBI	Avg.	SB	PO	A	E	Avg.
1979—Paintsville (Appal.)	3B-SS	63	203	58	58	10	3	1	25	.286	5	54 †122		11 †.941	
1980—Greensboro (S. Atlantic) ...	3B-SS	136	493 ★124	137	12	5	3	48	.278	★67	164	308	36	.929	
1981—Nashville (Southern)	SS	127	407	89	102	9	2	0	20	.251	71	198	348	★56	.907
1982—Nashville (Am. Assoc.)	SS-2B	72	283	47	80	3	2	0	20	.283	61	126	211	23	.936
—Columbus (Int'l)	2B-SS	59	207	43	58	4	0	0	14	.280	46	104	169	14	.951
1983—Columbus (Int'l)	OF-2B	138	★557 ★129 ★162	11	6	0	41	.291	★94	†385	24	4 †.990			
—New York (A.L.)	OF	13	14	2	2	0	0	0	0	.143	2	14	1	1	.938
1984—Cleveland (A.L.)■	OF	49	91	16	14	0	0	0	1	.154	12	81	3	0	1.000
—Maine (International)	OF	72	253	42	70	5	1	0	22	.277	39	206	7	1	.995
1985—Cleveland (A.L.)	OF	104	162	34	38	4	0	3	9	.235	20	129	5	4	.971
1986—Cleveland (A.L.)	OF	105	95	33	25	4	1	0	8	.263	23	90	3	3	.969
1987—Cleveland (A.L.)	OF	19	17	2	1	0	0	0	1	.059	2	21	0	0	1.000
—Buffalo (Am. Assoc.)	OF	59	249	51	71	13	4	2	23	.285	36	170	3	3	.983
1988—Indianapolis (A.A.)■	OF	67	235	52	67	6	3	0	19	.285	40	130	1	1	.992
—Montreal (N.L.)	OF	90	271	47	66	8	2	0	15	.244	46	176	2	1	.994
1989—Montreal (N.L.)	OF	126	258	41	56	7	2	0	21	.217	37	160	2	2	.988
1990—Montreal (N.L.)	OF-SS	119	231	46	58	6	2	1	20	.251	50	149	6	1	.994
1991—Atlanta (N.L.)■	OF	124	401	81	119	10	1	0	26	.297	72	218	6	3	.987
American League totals (5 years)		290	379	87	80	8	1	3	19	.211	59	335	12	8	.977
National League totals (4 years)		459	1161	215	299	31	7	1	82	.258	205	703	16	7	.990
Major league totals (9 years)		749	1540	302	379	39	8	4	101	.246	264	1038	28	15	.986

NOBOA, JUNIOR
IF/OF, METS

PERSONAL: Born November 10, 1964, at Azua, Dominican Republic. . . . 5-10/165. . . . Throws right, bats right. . . . Full name: Milciades Arturo Noboa Jr. . . . Name pronounced nuh-BO-uh.
HIGH SCHOOL: Santa Barbara (Santo Domingo, Dominican Republic).
TRANSACTIONS/CAREER NOTES: Signed as free agent by Cleveland Indians organization (May 26, 1981). . . . Traded by Indians to California Angels for OF Ted Milner (March 30, 1988). . . . Granted free agency (October 15, 1988). . . . Signed by Indianapolis, Montreal Expos organization (January 4, 1989). . . . Claimed on waivers by New York Mets (October 8, 1991).
STATISTICAL NOTES: Led Midwest League second basemen with 257 putouts and 81 double plays in 1983. . . . Led Midwest League with 18 sacrifice hits in 1983. . . . Led Eastern League with 17 sacrifice hits in 1984. . . . Tied for American Association lead with eight sacrifice flies in 1989. . . . Led American Association second basemen with .986 fielding percentage in 1989.

Year	Team (League)	Pos.	G	AB	R	H	2B	3B	HR	RBI	Avg.	SB	PO	A	E	Avg.
1981	—Batavia (N.Y.-Penn)	2B	50	162	15	49	8	0	0	6	.302	11	82	100	★18	.910
1982	—Waterloo (Midwest)	SS	121	385	69	96	12	5	0	23	.249	44	★207	306	46	.918
1983	—Waterloo (Midwest)	2B-SS	132	449	64	115	22	3	1	29	.256	47	†260	355	24	.962
1984	—Buffalo (Eastern)	2B	117	383	55	97	18	4	1	45	.253	12	228	305	★18	.967
	—Cleveland (A.L.)	2B	23	11	3	4	0	0	0	0	.364	1	7	13	0	1.000
1985	—Maine (International)	2B	122	403	62	116	11	2	5	32	.288	13	270	379	14	.979
1986	—Maine (International)	2B-SS-3B	108	399	44	114	21	1	4	32	.286	10	160	252	13	.969
1987	—Buffalo (Am. Assoc.)	2B-SS-3B	43	149	26	47	6	2	0	14	.315	2	70	108	11	.942
	—Cleveland (A.L.)	2B-SS-3B	39	80	7	18	2	1	0	7	.225	1	28	66	3	.969
1988	—Edmonton (Pac. Coast)■.	2-S-0-3	50	159	24	47	6	1	0	17	.296	5	86	145	7	.971
	—California (A.L.)	2B-SS-3B	21	16	4	1	0	0	0	0	.063	0	8	24	1	.970
1989	—Indianapolis (A.A.)■	2B-SS	117	467	61	★159	21	8	2	62	★.340	14	170	305	10	†.979
	—Montreal (N.L.)	2B-SS-3B	21	44	3	10	0	0	0	1	.227	0	17	45	0	1.000
1990	—Montreal (N.L.)	IF-P	1	158	15	42	7	2	0	14	.266	4	47	52	2	.980
1991	—Montreal (N.L.)	OF-IF	67	95	5	23	3	0	1	2	.242	2	20	19	1	.975
	American League totals (3 years)		83	107	14	23	2	1	0	7	.215	2	43	103	4	.973
	National League totals (3 years)		89	297	23	75	10	2	1	17	.253	6	84	116	3	.985
	Major league totals (6 years)		172	404	37	98	12	3	1	24	.243	8	127	219	7	.980

RECORD AS PITCHER

Year	Team (League)	G	W	L	Pct.	ERA	Sv.	IP	H	R	ER	BB	SO
1990	—Montreal (N.L.)	1	0	0	...	0.00	0	2/3	0	0	0	1	0

NOKES, MATT
C, YANKEES

PERSONAL: Born October 31, 1963, at San Diego. . . . 6-1/198. . . . Throws right, bats left. . . . Full name: Matthew Dodge Nokes.
HIGH SCHOOL: Patrick Henry (San Diego).
TRANSACTIONS/CAREER NOTES: Selected by San Francisco Giants organization in 20th round of free-agent draft (June 8, 1981). . . . Traded by Giants with P Dave LaPoint and P Eric King to Detroit Tigers for P Juan Berenguer, C Bob Melvin and a player to be named (October 7, 1985); Giants acquired P Scott Medvin to complete deal (December 11, 1985). . . . On disabled list (June 19-August 3, 1989). . . . Traded by Tigers to New York Yankees for P Lance McCullers and P Clay Parker (June 4, 1990).
RECORDS/HONORS: Named catcher on THE SPORTING NEWS A.L. All-Star team (1987). . . . Named catcher on THE SPORTING NEWS A.L. Silver Slugger team (1987).
STATISTICAL NOTES: Led Pioneer League with 19 passed balls in 1981. . . . Led California League catchers with nine double plays in 1983. . . . Led Texas League catchers with six double plays in 1985. . . . Tied for American Association lead in errors by catchers with 13 in 1986.

Year	Team (League)	Pos.	G	AB	R	H	2B	3B	HR	RBI	Avg.	SB	PO	A	E	Avg.
1981	—Great Falls (Pioneer)	C	44	146	14	33	6	2	0	13	.226	0	288	35	★13	.961
1982	—Clinton (Midwest)	C	82	247	19	53	12	0	3	23	.215	1	363	41	13	.969
1983	—Fresno (California)	C	125	429	62	138	26	6	14	82	.322	0	595	62	16	.976
1984	—Shreveport (Texas)	C	97	308	32	89	19	2	11	61	.289	0	400	31	8	.982
1985	—Shreveport (Texas)	C	105	344	52	101	24	1	14	56	.294	2	520	40	12	.979
	—San Francisco (N.L.)	C	19	53	3	11	2	0	2	5	.208	0	84	2	2	.977
1986	—Nashville (Am. Assoc.)■	C-1B-OF	125	428	55	122	25	4	10	71	.285	2	502	50	‡18	.968
	—Detroit (A.L.)	C	7	24	2	8	1	0	1	2	.333	0	43	2	0	1.000
1987	—Detroit (A.L.)	C-OF-3B	135	461	69	133	14	2	32	87	.289	2	600	32	5	.992
1988	—Detroit (A.L.)	C	122	382	53	96	18	0	16	53	.251	0	574	45	7	.989
1989	—Detroit (A.L.)	C	87	268	15	67	10	0	9	39	.250	1	235	26	6	.978
1990	—Detroit-New York (A.L.)■	C-OF	136	351	33	87	9	1	11	40	.248	2	237	34	2	.993
1991	—New York (A.L.)	C	135	456	52	122	20	0	24	77	.268	3	690	48	6	.992
	American League totals (6 years)		622	1942	224	513	72	3	93	298	.264	8	2379	187	26	.990
	National League totals (1 year)		19	53	3	11	2	0	2	5	.208	0	84	2	2	.977
	Major league totals (7 years)		641	1995	227	524	74	3	95	303	.263	8	2463	189	28	.990

CHAMPIONSHIP SERIES RECORD

Year	Team (League)	Pos.	G	AB	R	H	2B	3B	HR	RBI	Avg.	SB	PO	A	E	Avg.
1987	—Detroit (A.L.)	PH-DH-C	5	14	2	2	0	0	1	2	.143	0	11	2	0	1.000

Year	League		Pos.	AB	R	H	2B	3B	HR	RBI	Avg.	SB	PO	A	E	Avg.
							BATTING							FIELDING		
1987	American	....	C	2	0	0	0	0	0	0	.000	0	8	0	0	1.000

NOLTE, ERIC

P, BREWERS

PERSONAL: Born April 28, 1964, at Canoga Park, Calif. . . . 6-3/200. . . . Throws left, bats left. . . . Full name: Eric Carl Nolte. . . . Name pronounced NOLT-ee.
HIGH SCHOOL: Hemet (Calif.).
COLLEGE: UCLA.
TRANSACTIONS/CAREER NOTES: Selected by Chicago Cubs organization in seventh round of free-agent draft (June 7, 1982). . . . Selected by San Diego Padres organization in sixth round of free-agent draft (June 3, 1985). . . . On Las Vegas disabled list (March 25-May 8, 1989). . . . Released by Padres (May 20, 1991). . . . Signed by Texas Rangers organization (May 23, 1991). . . . Granted free agency (October 15, 1991). . . . Signed by Denver, Milwaukee Brewers organization (December 9, 1991).
STATISTICAL NOTES: Tied for Northwest League lead with two balks in 1985.

Year	Team (League)	G	W	L	Pct.	ERA	Sv.	IP	H	R	ER	BB	SO
1985	Spokane (Northwest)	14	3	•8	.273	3.99	0	76⅔	79	50	34	46	52
1986	Charleston, S.C. (S. Atlantic)	26	12	9	.571	3.90	0	164	154	80	71	68	121
1987	Reno (California)	11	3	4	.429	4.36	0	64	76	38	31	24	47
	Wichita (American Assoc.)	10	4	2	.667	2.88	0	75	62	28	24	19	67
	San Diego (N.L.)	12	2	6	.250	3.21	0	67⅓	57	28	24	36	44
1988	San Diego (N.L.)	2	0	0	. . .	6.00	0	3	3	2	2	2	1
	Las Vegas (Pacific Coast)	27	8	7	.533	6.03	0	128⅓	168	97	86	53	68
1989	Las Vegas (Pacific Coast)	23	6	9	.400	5.18	0	116⅓	121	74	67	54	89
	San Diego (N.L.)	3	0	0	. . .	11.00	0	9	15	12	11	7	8
1990	Las Vegas (Pacific Coast)	33	2	11	.154	8.58	0	122⅔	187	★130	★117	49	79
1991	San Diego (N.L.)	6	3	2	.600	11.05	0	22	37	27	27	10	15
	Texas (A.L.)■..........................	3	0	0	. . .	3.38	0	2⅔	3	1	1	3	1
	Oklahoma City (Am. Assoc.).....	25	1	3	.250	5.91	1	56⅓	74	39	37	31	40
American League totals (1 year)	....	3	0	0	. . .	3.38	0	2⅔	3	1	1	3	1
National League totals (4 years)	....	23	5	8	.385	5.68	0	101⅓	112	69	64	55	68
Major league totals (4 years)	....	26	5	8	.385	5.63	0	104	115	70	65	58	69

NUNEZ, EDWIN

P, BREWERS

PERSONAL: Born May 27, 1963, at Humacao, Puerto Rico. . . . 6-5/240. . . . Throws right, bats right. . . . Full name: Edwin Martinez Nunez. . . . Name pronounced NOON-yez.
HIGH SCHOOL: Roque (Humacao, Puerto Rico).
TRANSACTIONS/CAREER NOTES: Signed as free agent by Seattle Mariners organization (March 17, 1979). . . . On Seattle disabled list (April 23-May 15, 1982). . . . On Salt Lake City disabled list (June 4-29, 1982; June 30-July 14, 1983; and May 12-June 3, 1984). . . . On Seattle disabled list (April 5-29 and May 1-16, 1986; and May 20-June 4, 1987). . . . Traded by Mariners organization to New York Mets for P Gene Walter (July 11, 1988). . . . Released by Mets (March 28, 1989). . . . Signed by Toledo, Detroit Tigers organization (April 1, 1989). . . . On disabled list (July 8-August 14, 1990). . . . Granted free agency (November 5, 1990). . . . Signed by Milwaukee Brewers (December 4, 1990). . . . On Milwaukee disabled list (May 7-August 1, 1991); included rehabilitation disability assignment to Beloit (July 16-August 1, 1991).
STATISTICAL NOTES: Led Midwest League with 13 complete games in 1981.

Year	Team (League)	G	W	L	Pct.	ERA	Sv.	IP	H	R	ER	BB	SO
1979	Bellingham (Northwest)............	6	4	1	.800	2.08	0	39	39	14	9	5	30
1980	Wausau (Midwest)	22	9	7	.563	3.72	0	138	145	71	57	58	91
1981	Wausau (Midwest)...................	25	★16	3	.842	2.47	0	★186	143	61	51	58	★205
1982	Seattle (A.L.)	8	1	2	.333	4.58	0	35⅓	36	18	18	16	27
	Salt Lake City (Pacific Coast) ..	11	4	3	.571	3.42	0	55⅓	40	26	21	23	42
1983	Seattle (A.L.)	14	0	4	.000	4.38	0	37	40	21	18	22	35
	Salt Lake City (Pacific Coast) ..	14	4	4	.500	7.10	0	77⅓	99	70	61	36	52
1984	Salt Lake City (Pacific Coast) ..	18	3	2	.600	3.58	3	27⅔	24	12	11	12	26
	Seattle (A.L.)	37	2	2	.500	3.19	7	67⅔	55	26	24	21	57
1985	Seattle (A.L.)	70	7	3	.700	3.09	16	90⅓	79	36	31	34	58
1986	Seattle (A.L.)	14	1	2	.333	5.82	0	21⅔	25	15	14	5	17
	Calgary (Pacific Coast)	6	1	2	.333	7.07	0	14	19	13	11	4	17
1987	Seattle (A.L.)	48	3	4	.429	3.80	12	47⅓	45	20	20	18	34
1988	Calgary (Pacific Coast)	3	2	0	1.000	4.70	0	15⅓	15	9	8	4	12
	Seattle (A.L.)	14	1	4	.200	7.98	0	29⅓	45	33	26	14	19
	New York (N.L.)■.....................	10	1	0	1.000	4.50	0	14	21	7	7	3	8
1989	Toledo (International)■..............	13	1	5	.167	2.58	1	59⅓	47	20	17	18	53
	Detroit (A.L.)	27	3	4	.429	4.17	1	54	49	33	25	36	41
1990	Detroit (A.L.)	42	3	1	.750	2.24	6	80⅓	65	26	20	37	66
1991	Milwaukee (A.L.)■....................	23	2	1	.667	6.04	8	25⅓	28	20	17	13	24
	Beloit (Midwest)	5	0	1	.000	4.00	1	9	9	5	4	0	9
American League totals (10 years)	....	297	23	27	.460	3.93	50	488⅓	467	248	213	216	378
National League totals (1 year)	....	10	1	0	1.000	4.50	0	14	21	7	7	3	8
Major league totals (10 years)	....	307	24	27	.471	3.94	50	502⅓	488	255	220	219	386

OBERKFELL, KEN
IF, ANGELS

PERSONAL: Born May 4, 1956, at Maryville, Ill. . . . 6-1/210. . . . Throws right, bats left. . . . Full name: Kenneth Ray Oberkfell. . . . Name pronounced OH-burk-fell. . . .
HIGH SCHOOL: Collinsville (Ill.).
COLLEGE: Belleville Area Junior College (Ill.).

TRANSACTIONS/CAREER NOTES: Signed as free agent by St. Louis Cardinals organization (May 4, 1975). . . . On disabled list (May 11-June 20, 1980 and March 31-April 23, 1982). . . . Traded by Cardinals to Atlanta Braves for P Ken Dayley and 1B Mike Jorgensen (June 15, 1984). . . . On Atlanta disabled list (August 27, 1984-remainder of season and June 26-July 11, 1987). . . . Traded by Braves with cash to Pittsburgh Pirates for a player to be named later (August 28, 1988); Braves acquired OF Tommy Gregg to complete deal (September 1, 1988). . . . Traded by Pirates to San Francisco Giants for P Roger Samuels (May 10, 1989). . . . Granted free agency (November 13, 1989). . . . Signed by Houston Astros (December 6, 1989). . . . On disabled list (June 19-July 4, 1990). . . . Released by Astros (July 27, 1991). . . . Signed by California Angels organization (February 2, 1992).

STATISTICAL NOTES: Led N.L. second basemen with .985 fielding percentage in 1979. . . . Led N.L. third basemen with 23 double plays and tied for lead with 338 total chances in 1981. . . . Led N.L. third basemen with .972 fielding percentage in 1982. . . . Led N.L. third basemen with .960 fielding percentage in 1983.

Year — Team (League)	Pos.	G	AB	R	H	2B	3B	HR	RBI	Avg.	SB	PO	A	E	Avg.
1975 —Johnson City (Appal.)	SS	17	54	15	19	3	0	1	8	.352	3	21	58	4	.952
—St. Petersburg (Fla. St.)	SS	41	134	14	47	6	1	0	22	.351	1	71	107	6	.967
1976 —Arkansas (Texas)	2B-SS	128	456	64	131	19	2	3	47	.287	2	259	321	18	.970
1977 —New Orleans (A.A.)	2B-SS	120	418	67	105	18	5	4	32	.251	19	205	325	17	.969
—St. Louis (N.L.)	2B	9	9	0	1	0	0	0	1	.111	0	3	4	0	1.000
1978 —Springfield (Am. Assoc.)	3B-2B-SS	64	242	41	69	13	4	6	38	.285	6	77	113	6	.969
—St. Louis (N.L.)	2B-3B	24	50	7	6	1	0	0	0	.120	0	30	48	1	.987
1979 —St. Louis (N.L.)	2B-3B-SS	135	369	53	111	19	5	1	35	.301	4	223	343	9	†.984
1980 —St. Louis (N.L.)	2B-3B	116	422	58	128	27	6	3	46	.303	4	227	340	7	.988
1981 —St. Louis (N.L.)	3B-SS	102	376	43	110	12	6	2	45	.293	13	77	247	15	.956
1982 —St. Louis (N.L.)	3B-2B	137	470	55	136	22	5	2	34	.289	11	80	305	11	†.972
1983 —St. Louis (N.L.)	3B-2B-SS	151	488	62	143	26	5	3	38	.293	12	132	303	18	†.960
1984 —St. Louis-Atlanta (N.L.)■	3B-2B-SS	100	324	38	87	19	2	1	21	.269	2	64	173	8	.967
1985 —Atlanta (N.L.)	3B-2B	134	412	30	112	19	4	3	35	.272	1	88	257	12	.966
1986 —Atlanta (N.L.)	3B-2B	151	503	62	136	24	3	5	48	.270	7	116	335	11	.976
1987 —Atlanta (N.L.)	3B-2B	135	508	59	142	29	2	3	48	.280	3	89	265	7	.981
1988 —Atlanta-Pitts. (N.L.)■	3-2-S-1	140	476	49	129	22	4	3	42	.271	4	107	237	15	.958
1989 —Pitts.-San Fran. (N.L.)■	3B-1B-2B	97	156	19	42	6	1	2	17	.269	0	131	47	4	.978
1990 —Houston (N.L.)■	3B-1B-2B	77	150	10	31	6	1	1	12	.207	1	93	52	4	.973
1991 —Houston (N.L.)	1B-3B	53	70	7	16	4	0	0	14	.229	0	70	13	2	.976
Major league totals (15 years)		1561	4783	552	1330	236	44	29	436	.278	62	1530	2969	124	.973

CHAMPIONSHIP SERIES RECORD

CHAMPIONSHIP SERIES NOTES: Shares record for most at-bats, three-game Series—15 (1982).

Year — Team (League)	Pos.	G	AB	R	H	2B	3B	HR	RBI	Avg.	SB	PO	A	E	Avg.
1982 —St. Louis (N.L.)	3B	3	15	1	3	0	0	0	2	.200	0	2	4	1	.857
1989 —San Francisco (N.L.)	PH-3B	3	4	0	0	0	0	0	0	.000	0	0	1	0	1.000
Championship Series totals (2 years)		6	19	1	3	0	0	0	2	.158	0	2	5	1	.875

WORLD SERIES RECORD

Year — Team (League)	Pos.	G	AB	R	H	2B	3B	HR	RBI	Avg.	SB	PO	A	E	Avg.
1982 —St. Louis (N.L.)	3B	7	24	4	7	1	0	0	1	.292	2	3	21	1	.960
1989 —San Francisco (N.L.)	PH-3B	4	6	1	2	0	0	0	0	.333	0	0	5	1	.833
World Series totals (2 years)		11	30	5	9	1	0	0	1	.300	2	3	26	2	.935

O'BRIEN, CHARLIE
C, METS

PERSONAL: Born May 1, 1961, at Tulsa, Okla. . . . 6-2/190. . . . Throws right, bats right. . . . Full name: Charles Hugh O'Brien.
HIGH SCHOOL: Bishop Kelley (Tulsa, Okla.).
COLLEGE: McClennan Community College (Tex.) and Wichita State.

TRANSACTIONS/CAREER NOTES: Selected by Texas Rangers organization in 14th round of free-agent draft (June 6, 1978). . . . Selected by Seattle Mariners organization in 21st round of free-agent draft (June 8, 1981). . . . Selected by Oakland Athletics organization in fifth round of free-agent draft (June 7, 1982). . . . On disabled list (July 31, 1983-remainder of season). . . . On Albany disabled list (April 13-May 15, 1984). . . . Traded by A's organization with IF Steve Kiefer, P Mike Fulmer and P Pete Kendrick to Milwaukee Brewers for P Moose Haas (March 30, 1986). . . . Traded by Brewers with a player to be named later to New York Mets for two players to be named later (August 30, 1990); Brewers acquired P Julio Machado and P Kevin Brown (September 7, 1990) and Mets acquired P Kevin Carmody (September 11, 1990) to complete deal.

Year — Team (League)	Pos.	G	AB	R	H	2B	3B	HR	RBI	Avg.	SB	PO	A	E	Avg.
1982 —Medford (Northwest)	C	17	60	11	17	3	0	3	14	.283	0	116	18	4	.971
—Modesto (California)	C	41	140	23	42	6	0	3	32	.300	7	239	44	5	.983
1983 —Albany (Eastern)	C-1B	92	285	50	83	12	1	14	56	.291	3	478	82	11	.981
1984 —Modesto (California)	C	9	32	8	9	2	0	1	5	.281	1	41	8	0	1.000
—Tacoma (Pacific Coast)	C-OF	69	195	33	44	11	0	9	22	.226	0	260	39	0	1.000
1985 —Huntsville (Southern)	C	33	115	20	24	5	0	7	16	.209	0	182	29	5	.977
—Oakland (A.L.)	C	16	11	3	3	1	0	1	1	.273	0	23	0	1	.958
—Modesto (California)	C	9	27	5	8	4	1	1	2	.296	0	33	8	1	.976
—Tacoma (Pacific Coast)	C	18	57	5	9	4	0	0	7	.158	0	110	9	3	.975

Year	Team (League)	Pos.	G	AB	R	H	2B	3B	HR	RBI	Avg.	SB	PO	A	E	Avg.
1986	— Vancouver (Pac. Coast)■..	C	6	17	1	2	0	0	0	1	.118	0	22	3	2	.926
	— El Paso (Texas)	C-OF-1B	92	336	72	109	20	3	15	75	.324	0	437	43	4	.992
1987	— Denver (Am. Assoc.)	C	80	266	37	75	12	1	8	35	.282	5	415	53	6	.987
	— Milwaukee (A.L.)	C	10	35	2	7	3	1	0	0	.200	0	78	11	0	1.000
1988	— Denver (Am. Assoc.)	C	48	153	16	43	5	0	4	25	.281	1	243	44	3	.990
	— Milwaukee (A.L.)	C	40	118	12	26	6	0	2	9	.220	0	210	20	2	.991
1989	— Milwaukee (A.L.)	C	62	188	22	44	10	0	6	35	.234	0	314	36	5	.986
1990	— Milwaukee (A.L.)■.............	C	46	145	11	27	7	2	0	11	.186	0	217	24	2	.992
	— New York (N.L.)■.............	C	28	68	6	11	3	0	0	9	.162	0	191	21	3	.986
1991	— New York (N.L.)	C	69	168	16	31	6	0	2	14	.185	0	396	37	4	.991
	American League totals (5 years)		174	497	50	107	27	3	8	56	.215	0	842	91	10	.989
	National League totals (2 years)		97	236	22	42	9	0	2	23	.178	0	587	58	7	.989
	Major league totals (6 years)		271	733	72	149	36	3	10	79	.203	0	1429	149	17	.989

O'BRIEN, PETE

1B, MARINERS

PERSONAL: Born February 9, 1958, at Santa Monica, Calif. . . . 6-2/195. . . . Throws left, bats left. . . . Full name: Peter Michael O'Brien.
HIGH SCHOOL: Carmel (Calif.).
COLLEGE: Monterrey Peninsula College (Calif.) and Nebraska.
TRANSACTIONS/CAREER NOTES: Selected by Texas Rangers organization in 15th round of free-agent draft (June 5, 1979). . . . Traded by Rangers with OF Oddibe McDowell and 2B Jerry Browne to Cleveland Indians for 2B Julio Franco (December 6, 1988). . . . Granted free agency (November 13, 1989). . . . Signed by Seattle Mariners (December 7, 1989). . . . On disabled list (May 5-June 19, 1990).
RECORDS/HONORS: Shares major league single-game record (nine innings) for most double plays started by first baseman—3 (May 22, 1984).
STATISTICAL NOTES: Led A.L. first basemen with 120 assists in 1983 and 146 in 1987. . . . Led A.L. first basemen with .997 fielding percentage in 1991.

Year	Team (League)	Pos.	G	AB	R	H	2B	3B	HR	RBI	Avg.	SB	PO	A	E	Avg.
1979	— Sarasota Rangers (GCL)...	1B	50	189	39	46	10	2	0	31	.243	1	★465	★44	7	.986
1980	— Asheville (S. Atlantic)	1B	134	505	98	149	34	2	17	94	.295	6 ★	1227	★96	14	.990
1981	— Tulsa (Texas)	1B	110	382	57	109	19	3	17	78	.285	3	973	95	11	.990
1982	— Denver (Am. Assoc.)	OF-1B	128	477	92	148	21	1	25	102	.310	0	418	37	8	.983
	— Texas (A.L.)	OF-1B	20	67	13	16	4	1	4	13	.239	1	39	3	0	1.000
1983	— Texas (A.L.)	1B-OF	154	524	53	124	24	5	8	53	.237	5	1191	†121	11	.992
1984	— Texas (A.L.)	1B-OF	142	520	57	149	26	2	18	80	.287	3	1271	105	11	.992
1985	— Texas (A.L.)	1B	159	573	69	153	34	3	22	92	.267	5	1457	98	8	.995
1986	— Texas (A.L.)	1B	156	551	86	160	23	3	23	90	.290	4	1224	115	11	.992
1987	— Texas (A.L.)	1B-OF	159	569	84	163	26	1	23	88	.286	0	1233	†146	11	.992
1988	— Texas (A.L.)	1B	156	547	57	149	24	1	16	71	.272	1	1346	140	8	.995
1989	— Cleveland (A.L.)■	1B	155	554	75	144	24	1	12	55	.260	3	1359	114	9	.994
1990	— Seattle (A.L.)■..............	1B-OF	108	366	32	82	18	0	5	27	.224	0	852	76	5	.995
1991	— Seattle (A.L.)	1B-OF	152	560	58	139	29	3	17	88	.248	0	1065	87	5	†.996
	Major league totals (10 years)		1361	4831	584	1279	232	20	148	657	.265	22	11037	1005	79	.993

OFFERMAN, JOSE

SS, DODGERS

PERSONAL: Born November 8, 1968, at San Pedro de Macoris, Dominican Republic. . . . 6-0/160. . . . Throws right, bats both. . . . Full name: Jose Antonio Dono Offerman.
COLLEGE: Colegio Biblico Cristiano (Dominican Republic).
TRANSACTIONS/CAREER NOTES: Signed as free agent by Los Angeles Dodgers organization (July 24, 1986).
RECORDS/HONORS: Named Minor League Player of the Year by THE SPORTING NEWS (1990). . . . Named Pacific Coast League Player of the Year (1990).
STATISTICAL NOTES: Tied for Pioneer League lead in caught stealing with 10 in 1988. . . . Tied for Pacific Coast League lead in caught stealing with 18 in 1990. . . . Hit home run in first major league at-bat (August 19, 1990). . . . Led Pacific Coast League shortstops with 36 errors in 1990.

Year	Team (League)	Pos.	G	AB	R	H	2B	3B	HR	RBI	Avg.	SB	PO	A	E	Avg.
1988	— Great Falls (Pioneer)	SS	60	251	75	83	11	5	2	28	.331	★57	82	143	18	★.926
1989	— Bakersfield (California)	SS	62	245	53	75	9	4	2	22	.306	37	94	179	30	.901
	— San Antonio (Texas)	SS	68	278	47	80	6	3	2	22	.288	32	106	168	20	.932
1990	— Albuquerque (PCL)	SS-2B	117	454	104	148	16	11	0	56	.326	★60	174	361	†36	.937
	— Los Angeles (N.L.)	SS	29	58	7	9	0	0	1	7	.155	1	30	40	4	.946
1991	— Albuquerque (PCL)	SS	79	289	58	86	8	4	0	29	.298	32	126	241	17	.956
	— Los Angeles (N.L.)	SS	52	113	10	22	2	0	0	3	.195	3	50	121	10	.945
	Major league totals (2 years)		81	171	17	31	2	0	1	10	.181	4	80	161	14	.945

OJEDA, BOB

P, DODGERS

PERSONAL: Born December 17, 1957, at Los Angeles. . . . 6-1/195. . . . Throws left, bats left. . . . Full name: Robert Michael Ojeda. . . . Name pronounced oh-HEE-duh.
HIGH SCHOOL: Redwood (Visalia, Calif.).
COLLEGE: College of the Sequoias (Calif.).

TRANSACTIONS/CAREER NOTES: Signed as free agent by Boston Red Sox organization (May 20, 1978).... On disabled list (August 20-September 10, 1982 and August 16-September 1, 1984).... Traded by Red Sox with P Tom McCarthy, P John Mitchell and P Chris Bayer to New York Mets for P Calvin Schiraldi, P Wes Gardner, OF John Christensen and OF LaSchelle Tarver (November 13, 1985).... On disabled list (May 11-September 1, 1987).... Traded by Mets with P Greg Hansell to Los Angeles Dodgers for OF Hubie Brooks (December 15, 1990).

RECORDS/HONORS: Named International League Pitcher of the Year (1981).

STATISTICAL NOTES: Tied for Florida State League lead in games started by pitcher with 29 in 1979.... Tied for International League lead with three balks in 1980.... Tied for A.L. lead with five shutouts in 1984.

Year	Team (League)	G	W	L	Pct.	ERA	Sv.	IP	H	R	ER	BB	SO
1978	—Elmira (New York-Penn)	18	1	6	.143	4.81	2	43	45	32	23	43	35
1979	—Winter Haven (Florida State)	29	15	7	.682	2.43	0	200	163	66	54	84	150
1980	—Pawtucket (International)	19	6	7	.462	3.22	0	123	107	54	44	56	78
	—Boston (A.L.)	7	1	1	.500	6.92	0	26	39	20	20	14	12
1981	—Pawtucket (International)	25	12	9	.571	*2.13	0	173	136	52	41	73	113
	—Boston (A.L.)	10	6	2	.750	3.14	0	66	50	25	23	25	28
1982	—Boston (A.L.)	22	4	6	.400	5.63	0	78⅓	95	53	49	29	52
1983	—Boston (A.L.)	29	12	7	.632	4.04	0	173⅔	173	85	78	73	94
1984	—Boston (A.L.)	33	12	12	.500	3.99	0	216⅔	211	106	96	96	137
1985	—Boston (A.L.)	39	9	11	.450	4.00	1	157⅔	166	74	70	48	102
1986	—New York (N.L.)■	32	18	5	.783	2.57	0	217⅓	185	72	62	52	148
1987	—New York (N.L.)	10	3	5	.375	3.88	0	46⅓	45	23	20	10	21
1988	—New York (N.L.)	29	10	13	.435	2.88	0	190⅓	158	74	61	33	133
1989	—New York (N.L.)	31	13	11	.542	3.47	0	192	179	83	74	78	95
1990	—New York (N.L.)	38	7	6	.538	3.66	0	118	123	53	48	40	62
1991	—Los Angeles (N.L.)■	31	12	9	.571	3.18	0	189⅓	181	78	67	70	120
	American League totals (6 years)	140	44	39	.530	4.21	1	718⅓	734	363	336	285	425
	National League totals (6 years)	171	63	49	.563	3.13	0	953⅓	871	383	332	283	579
	Major league totals (12 years)	311	107	88	.549	3.60	1	1671⅔	1605	746	668	568	1004

CHAMPIONSHIP SERIES RECORD

CHAMPIONSHIP SERIES NOTES: Shares N.L. single-game record for most hits allowed—10 (October 9, 1986).

Year	Team (League)	G	W	L	Pct.	ERA	Sv.	IP	H	R	ER	BB	SO
1986	—New York (N.L.)	2	1	0	1.000	2.57	0	14	15	4	4	4	6

WORLD SERIES RECORD

Year	Team (League)	G	W	L	Pct.	ERA	Sv.	IP	H	R	ER	BB	SO
1986	—New York (N.L.)	2	1	0	1.000	2.08	0	13	13	3	3	5	9

OLANDER, JIM
OF, BREWERS

PERSONAL: Born February 21, 1963, at Tuscon, Ariz.... 6-1/185.... Throws right, bats right. ... Full name: James Bentley Olander.

HIGH SCHOOL: Sahuaro (Tucson, Ariz.).

TRANSACTIONS/CAREER NOTES: Selected by Philadelphia Phillies organization in seventh round of free-agent draft (June 8, 1981).... Granted free agency (October 15, 1989).... Signed by Houston Astros organization (February 12, 1990).... Traded by Astros to Milwaukee Brewers organization for player to be named later (May 31, 1990).

RECORDS/HONORS: Named American Association Most Valuable Player (1991).

STATISTICAL NOTES: Led Carolina League outfielders with 328 total chances in 1983.

Year	Team (League)	Pos.	G	AB	R	H	2B	3B	HR	RBI	Avg.	SB	PO	A	E	Avg.
1981	—Helena (Pioneer)	OF	61	222	37	72	10	3	6	37	.324	5	114	5	7	.944
1982	—Spartanburg (S. Atl.)	OF	121	423	77	129	25	6	12	63	.305	12	227	16	7	.972
1983	—Peninsula (Carolina)	OF	126	503	62	125	21	3	15	79	.249	12	*296	*19	13	.960
1984	—Reading (Eastern)	OF-1B	117	362	44	95	12	2	8	47	.262	10	255	10	9	.967
1985	—Portland (Pacific Coast)	OF	44	72	6	16	2	0	0	6	.222	3	23	1	1	.960
	—Reading (Eastern)	OF	64	208	30	67	15	2	4	39	.322	2	125	6	2	.985
1986	—Reading (Eastern)	OF	129	464	77	151	*33	4	8	68	*.325	11	320	3	•11	.967
1987	—Maine (International)	OF	43	145	17	31	7	0	1	8	.214	2	89	2	0	1.000
1988	—Maine (International)	OF	25	71	5	15	3	0	0	4	.211	0	49	0	1	.980
1989	—Scranton/W.B. (Int'l)	OF	111	274	35	69	17	4	3	29	.252	5	208	5	1	*.995
1990	—Tucson (Pacific Coast)■..	OF	33	98	12	23	8	2	1	12	.235	0	65	5	2	.972
	—Denver (Am. Assoc.)■	OF	74	233	33	67	12	4	3	36	.288	2	163	2	3	.982
1991	—Denver (Am. Assoc.)	OF	134	498	*89	*162	32	10	9	78	*.325	14	307	3	3	.990
	—Milwaukee (A.L.)	OF	12	9	2	0	0	0	0	0	.000	0	9	0	0	1.000
	Major league totals (1 year)		12	9	2	0	0	0	0	0	.000	0	9	0	0	1.000

OLERUD, JOHN
1B, BLUE JAYS

PERSONAL: Born August 5, 1968, at Bellevue, Wash.... 6-5/218.... Throws left, bats left.... Full name: John Garrett Olerud.... Son of John E. Olerud, minor league catcher (1965-70). ... Name pronounced OH-luh-rude.

HIGH SCHOOL: Interlake (Bellevue, Wash.).

COLLEGE: Washington State.

TRANSACTIONS/CAREER NOTES: Selected by New York Mets organization in 27th round of free-agent draft (June 2, 1986).... Selected by Toronto Blue Jays organization in third round of free-agent draft (June 5, 1989).

STATISTICAL NOTES: Tied for A.L. lead with 10 sacrifice flies in 1991.

Year Team (League)	Pos.	G	AB	R	H	2B	3B	HR	RBI	Avg.	SB	PO	A	E	Avg.
						BATTING							FIELDING		
1989 — Toronto (A.L.)	1B	6	8	2	3	0	0	0	0	.375	0	19	2	0	1.000
1990 — Toronto (A.L.)	1B	111	358	43	95	15	1	14	48	.265	0	133	10	2	.986
1991 — Toronto (A.L.)	1B	139	454	64	116	30	1	17	68	.256	0	1120	78	5	.996
Major league totals (3 years)		256	820	109	214	45	2	31	116	.261	0	1272	90	7	.995

CHAMPIONSHIP SERIES RECORD

Year Team (League)	Pos.	G	AB	R	H	2B	3B	HR	RBI	Avg.	SB	PO	A	E	Avg.
						BATTING							FIELDING		
1991 — Toronto (A.L.)	1B	5	19	1	3	0	0	0	3	.158	0	40	3	0	1.000

OLIN, STEVE
P, INDIANS

PERSONAL: Born October 10, 1965, at Portland, Ore. . . . 6-2/190. . . . Throws right, bats right. . . . Full name: Steven Robert Olin.
HIGH SCHOOL: Beaverton (Ore.).
COLLEGE: Portland State (Ore.).
TRANSACTIONS/CAREER NOTES: Selected by Cleveland Indians organization in 16th round of free-agent draft (June 2, 1987).

Year Team (League)	G	W	L	Pct.	ERA	Sv.	IP	H	R	ER	BB	SO
1987 — Burlington (Appalachian)	•26	4	4	.500	2.35	7	57⅓	42	21	15	17	75
1988 — Waterloo (Midwest)	29	3	0	1.000	1.37	15	39⅓	26	7	6	14	48
— Kinston (Carolina)	33	5	2	.714	3.02	8	56⅔	49	23	19	15	45
1989 — Colorado Springs (Pac. Coast)	42	4	1	.800	3.22	★24	50⅓	34	18	18	15	46
— Cleveland (A.L.)	25	1	4	.200	3.75	1	36	35	16	15	14	24
1990 — Cleveland (A.L.)	50	4	4	.500	3.41	1	92⅓	96	41	35	26	64
— Colorado Springs (Pac. Coast)	14	3	1	.750	0.66	2	27⅓	18	9	2	15	30
1991 — Cleveland (A.L.)	48	3	6	.333	3.36	17	56⅓	61	26	21	23	38
— Colorado Springs (Pac. Coast)	22	3	2	.600	4.47	6	44⅓	45	25	22	10	36
Major league totals (3 years)	123	8	14	.364	3.46	19	184⅔	192	83	71	63	126

OLIVA, JOSE
3B, RANGERS

PERSONAL: Born March 3, 1971, at San Pedro de Macoris, Dominican Republic. . . . 6-1/160. . . . Throws right, bats right. . . . Full name: Jose Galvez Oliva.
TRANSACTIONS/CAREER NOTES: Signed as free agent by Texas Rangers organization (November 12, 1987). . . . On Charlotte disabled list (July 16-25, 1991).

Year Team (League)	Pos.	G	AB	R	H	2B	3B	HR	RBI	Avg.	SB	PO	A	E	Avg.
						BATTING							FIELDING		
1988 — Sarasota Rangers (GCL)	SS	27	70	5	15	3	0	1	11	.214	0	16	43	6	.908
1989 — Butte (Pioneer)	SS-3B	41	114	18	24	2	3	4	13	.211	4	38	94	15	.898
1990 — Gastonia (S. Atlantic)	S-3-2	120	387	43	81	25	1	10	52	.209	9	163	284	44	.910
1991 — Charlotte (Florida State)	3B-SS	108	383	55	92	17	4	14	59	.240	9	79	154	16	.936
— Sarasota Rangers (GCL)	3B	3	11	0	1	1	0	0	1	.091	0	4	3	0	1.000

OLIVARES, OMAR
P, CARDINALS

PERSONAL: Born July 6, 1967, at Mayaguez, Puerto Rico. . . . 6-1/193. . . . Throws right, bats right. . . . Full name: Omar Palqu Olivares. . . . Son of Ed Olivares, outfielder, St. Louis Cardinals (1960-61).
HIGH SCHOOL: Hostos (Mayaguez, Puerto Rico).
TRANSACTIONS/CAREER NOTES: Signed as free agent by San Diego Padres organization (September 15, 1986). . . . Traded by Padres organization to St. Louis Cardinals for OF Alex Cole and P Steve Peters (February 27, 1990).
STATISTICAL NOTES: Tied for Texas League lead with 10 hit batsmen in 1989.

Year Team (League)	G	W	L	Pct.	ERA	Sv.	IP	H	R	ER	BB	SO
1987 — Charleston, S.C. (S. Atlantic)	31	4	14	.222	4.60	0	170⅓	182	107	87	57	86
1988 — Charleston, S.C. (S. Atlantic)	24	13	6	.684	2.23	0	185⅓	166	63	46	43	94
— Riverside (California)	4	3	0	1.000	1.16	0	23⅓	18	9	3	9	16
1989 — Wichita (Texas)	26	12	11	.522	3.39	0	★185⅔	175	87	70	61	79
1990 — Louisville (American Assoc.)	23	10	11	.476	2.82	0	159⅓	127	58	50	59	88
— St. Louis (N.L.)	9	1	1	.500	2.92	0	49⅓	45	17	16	17	20
1991 — St. Louis (N.L.)	28	11	7	.611	3.71	1	167⅓	148	72	69	61	91
— Louisville (American Assoc.)	6	1	2	.333	3.47	0	36⅓	39	15	14	16	27
Major league totals (2 years)	37	12	8	.600	3.53	1	216⅔	193	89	85	78	111

OLIVER, JOE
C, REDS

PERSONAL: Born July 24, 1965, at Memphis, Tenn. . . . 6-3/210. . . . Throws right, bats right. . . . Full name: Joseph Melton Oliver.
HIGH SCHOOL: Boone (Orlando, Fla.).
TRANSACTIONS/CAREER NOTES: Selected by Cincinnati Reds organization in second round of free-agent draft (June 6, 1983). . . . On disabled list (April 23-May 6, 1986).
STATISTICAL NOTES: Led Pioneer League catchers with .989 fielding percentage, 425 putouts, 38 assists and 468 total chances in 1983. . . . Led Midwest League catchers with 30 passed balls and 855 total chances in 1984. . . . Led Florida State League catchers with 84 assists and 33 passed balls in 1985. . . . Led American Association catchers with 13 errors in 1989. . . . Tied for N.L. lead with 16 passed balls in 1990.

Year Team (League)	Pos.	G	AB	R	H	2B	3B	HR	RBI	Avg.	SB	PO	A	E	Avg.
1983 —Billings (Pioneer)	C-1B	56	186	21	40	4	0	4	28	.215	1	†426	†39	5	†.989
1984 —Cedar Rapids (Midwest)	C	102	335	34	73	11	0	3	29	.218	2	★757	85	13	.985
1985 —Tampa (Florida State)	C-1B	112	386	38	104	23	2	7	62	.269	1	615	†94	16	.978
1986 —Vermont (Eastern)	C	84	282	32	78	18	1	6	41	.277	2	383	62	14	.969
1987 —Vermont (Eastern)	C-1B	66	236	31	72	13	2	10	60	.305	0	247	35	10	.966
1988 —Nashville (Am. Assoc.)	C	73	220	19	45	7	2	4	24	.205	0	413	37	7	.985
—Chattanooga (Southern)	C	28	105	9	26	6	0	3	12	.248	0	176	15	0	1.000
1989 —Nashville (Am. Assoc.)	C-1B	71	233	22	68	13	0	6	31	.292	0	388	37	†13	.970
—Cincinnati (N.L.)	C	49	151	13	41	8	0	3	23	.272	0	260	21	4	.986
1990 —Cincinnati (N.L.)	C	121	364	34	84	23	0	8	52	.231	1	686	59	6	★.992
1991 —Cincinnati (N.L.)	C	94	269	21	58	11	0	11	41	.216	0	496	40	11	.980
Major league totals (3 years)		264	784	68	183	42	0	22	116	.233	1	1442	120	21	.987

CHAMPIONSHIP SERIES RECORD

Year Team (League)	Pos.	G	AB	R	H	2B	3B	HR	RBI	Avg.	SB	PO	A	E	Avg.
1990 —Cincinnati (N.L.)	C	5	14	1	2	0	0	0	0	.143	0	27	1	0	1.000

WORLD SERIES RECORD

Year Team (League)	Pos.	G	AB	R	H	2B	3B	HR	RBI	Avg.	SB	PO	A	E	Avg.
1990 —Cincinnati (N.L.)	C	4	18	2	6	3	0	0	2	.333	0	27	1	3	.903

OLIVERAS, FRANCISCO
P, GIANTS

PERSONAL: Born January 31, 1963, at Santurce, Puerto Rico. . . . 5-10/180. . . . Throws right, bats right. . . . Full name: Francisco Javier Noa Oliveras.
HIGH SCHOOL: Ramon Vilamayo (Santurce, Puerto Rico).
TRANSACTIONS/CAREER NOTES: Signed as free agent by Baltimore Orioles organization (September 10, 1980). . . . On disabled list (July 9-23, 1982 and April 22-May 9, 1983). . . . On Rochester disabled list (July 30-August 18, 1984). . . . Loaned by Orioles organization to Daytona Beach, co-op (June 1, 1985); returned (July 4, 1985). . . . Loaned by Orioles organization to Beaumont, San Diego Padres organization (July 31, 1985); returned (September 1, 1985). . . . Granted free agency (October 15, 1987). . . . Signed by Portland, Minnesota Twins organization (December, 1987). . . . Traded by Twins organization to San Francisco Giants for a player to be named later (May 30, 1990); Visalia (Twins organization) acquired P Ed Gustafson to complete deal (September 26, 1990). . . . On San Francisco disabled list (July 11-August 4, 1990); included rehabilitation disability assignment to San Jose (July 30-August 3, 1990).
STATISTICAL NOTES: Tied for Southern League lead with 27 home runs allowed in 1986.

Year Team (League)	G	W	L	Pct.	ERA	Sv.	IP	H	R	ER	BB	SO
1981 —Miami (Florida State)	19	6	5	.545	3.83	0	108	103	55	46	48	80
—Charlotte (Southern)	4	0	2	.000	5.63	0	16	23	10	10	7	10
1982 —Charlotte (Southern)	24	10	9	.526	3.55	0	162⅓	132	71	64	64	97
1983 —Charlotte (Southern)	25	8	★14	.364	4.64	0	151⅓	173	94	78	73	89
1984 —Charlotte (Southern)	19	3	7	.300	4.20	0	75	68	45	35	39	52
—Rochester (International)	12	1	3	.250	7.97	0	40⅔	58	37	36	19	39
1985 —Charlotte (Southern)	12	2	1	.667	4.74	0	57	57	40	30	25	20
—Daytona Beach (Florida State)■	3	3	0	1.000	1.90	0	23⅔	13	6	5	9	25
—Beaumont (Texas)■	7	3	1	.750	5.00	0	27	23	17	15	9	24
1986 —Charlotte (Southern)■	33	12	9	.571	4.18	0	194	185	112	90	71	127
1987 —Charlotte (Southern)	23	6	3	.667	3.60	2	100	99	43	40	21	67
—Rochester (International)	6	3	0	1.000	4.33	0	27	31	14	13	7	18
1988 —Orlando (Southern)■	7	3	1	.750	4.81	0	43	44	24	23	18	42
—Portland (Pacific Coast)	21	11	10	.524	4.31	0	133⅔	134	69	64	43	95
1989 —Portland (Pacific Coast)	17	6	4	.600	4.98	0	97⅔	108	54	54	24	54
—Minnesota (A.L.)	12	3	4	.429	4.53	0	55⅔	64	28	28	15	24
1990 —Portland (Pacific Coast)	11	3	4	.429	2.90	0	62	44	23	20	22	56
—San Francisco (N.L.)■	33	2	2	.500	2.77	2	55⅓	47	22	17	21	41
—San Jose (Pacific Coast)	1	0	0	...	2.45	0	3⅔	4	2	1	1	3
1991 —Phoenix (Pacific Coast)	3	2	0	1.000	2.45	0	18⅓	18	5	5	7	12
—San Francisco (N.L.)	55	6	6	.500	3.86	3	79⅓	69	36	34	22	48
American League totals (1 year)	12	3	4	.429	4.53	0	55⅔	64	28	28	15	24
National League totals (2 years)	88	8	8	.500	3.41	5	134⅔	116	58	51	43	89
Major league totals (3 years)	100	11	12	.478	3.74	5	190⅓	180	86	79	58	113

OLSON, GREG
C, BRAVES

PERSONAL: Born September 6, 1960, at Marshall, Minn. . . . 6-0/200. . . . Throws right, bats right. . . . Full name: Gregory William Olson.
HIGH SCHOOL: Edina East (Minn.).
COLLEGE: Minnesota.
TRANSACTIONS/CAREER NOTES: Selected by New York Mets organization in seventh round of free-agent draft (June 7, 1982). . . . Granted free agency (October 15, 1988). . . . Signed by Portland, Minnesota Twins organization (November 30, 1988). . . . Granted free agency (October 15, 1989). . . . Signed by Richmond, Atlanta Braves organization (November 6, 1989).
STATISTICAL NOTES: Led Carolina League catchers with 973 total chances in 1983. . . . Tied for International League lead with 15 passed balls in 1988.

Year	Team (League)	Pos.	G	AB	R	H	2B	3B	HR	RBI	Avg.	SB	PO	A	E	Avg.
1982	—Lynchburg (Carolina)	C-3B	32	91	10	24	1	0	0	5	.264	1	149	26	6	.967
1983	—Lynchburg (Carolina)	C	107	318	56	73	7	0	0	22	.230	0	*881	*82	10	*.990
1984	—Jackson (Texas)	C	74	234	27	55	9	0	0	22	.235	1	511	51	9	.984
1985	—Jackson (Texas)	C	69	211	21	57	7	0	1	32	.270	1	353	56	6	.986
1986	—Jackson (Texas)	C	64	196	28	39	5	1	2	16	.199	0	347	49	4	.990
	—Tidewater (Int'l)	C	19	55	11	18	1	0	0	7	.327	1	104	13	3	.975
1987	—Tidewater (Int'l)	C	47	120	15	34	8	1	2	15	.283	0	219	12	3	.987
1988	—Tidewater (Int'l)	C-OF	115	344	39	92	19	1	6	48	.267	0	600	64	7	.990
1989	—Portland (Pacific Coast)■	C-3B	79	247	38	58	8	2	6	38	.235	3	440	32	5	.990
	—Minnesota (A.L.)	C	3	2	0	1	0	0	0	0	.500	0	4	0	0	1.000
1990	—Richmond (Int'l)■	C	3	7	0	0	0	0	0	0	.000	0	17	2	0	1.000
	—Atlanta (N.L.)	C-3B	100	298	36	78	12	1	7	36	.262	0	501	43	7	.987
1991	—Atlanta (N.L.)	C	133	411	46	99	25	0	6	44	.241	1	721	48	4	.995
American League totals (1 year)			3	2	0	1	0	0	0	0	.500	0	4	0	0	1.000
National League totals (2 years)			233	709	82	177	37	1	13	80	.250	2	1222	91	11	.992
Major league totals (3 years)			236	711	82	178	37	1	13	80	.250	2	1226	91	11	.992

CHAMPIONSHIP SERIES RECORD

Year	Team (League)	Pos.	G	AB	R	H	2B	3B	HR	RBI	Avg.	SB	PO	A	E	Avg.
1991	—Atlanta (N.L.)	C	7	24	3	8	1	0	1	4	.333	1	62	1	0	1.000

WORLD SERIES RECORD

Year	Team (League)	Pos.	G	AB	R	H	2B	3B	HR	RBI	Avg.	SB	PO	A	E	Avg.
1991	—Atlanta (N.L.)	C	7	27	3	6	2	0	0	1	.222	1	47	6	0	1.000

ALL-STAR GAME RECORD

Year	League	Pos.	AB	R	H	2B	3B	HR	RBI	Avg.	SB	PO	A	E	Avg.
1990	—National	PH-C	1	0	0	0	0	0	0	.000	0	0	0	0	...

OLSON, GREGG
P, ORIOLES

PERSONAL: Born October 11, 1966, at Omaha, Neb. . . . 6-4/206. . . . Throws right, bats right. . . . Full name: Gregg William Olson.
HIGH SCHOOL: Omaha Northwest (Neb.).
COLLEGE: Auburn.
TRANSACTIONS/CAREER NOTES: Selected by Baltimore Orioles organization in first round (fourth pick overall) of free-agent draft (June 1, 1988).
RECORDS/HONORS: Holds A.L. rookie record for most saves—27 (1989). . . . Named righthanded pitcher on THE SPORTING NEWS college All-America team (1988). . . . Named A.L. Rookie of the Year by Baseball Writers' Association of America (1989).
STATISTICAL NOTES: Pitched one inning, combining with Bob Milacki, Mike Flanagan and Mark Williamson in 2-0 nine-inning no-hit victory against Oakland Athletics (July 13, 1991).

Year	Team (League)	G	W	L	Pct.	ERA	Sv.	IP	H	R	ER	BB	SO
1988	—Hagerstown (Carolina)	8	1	0	1.000	2.00	4	9	5	2	2	2	9
	—Charlotte (Southern)	8	0	1	.000	5.87	1	15⅓	24	13	10	6	22
	—Baltimore (A.L.)	10	1	1	.500	3.27	0	11	10	4	4	10	9
1989	—Baltimore (A.L.)	64	5	2	.714	1.69	27	85	57	17	16	46	90
1990	—Baltimore (A.L.)	64	6	5	.545	2.42	37	74⅓	57	20	20	31	74
1991	—Baltimore (A.L.)	72	4	6	.400	3.18	31	73⅔	74	28	26	29	72
Major league totals (4 years)		210	16	14	.533	2.43	95	244	198	69	66	116	245

ALL-STAR GAME RECORD

Year	League	W	L	Pct.	ERA	Sv.	IP	H	R	ER	BB	SO
1990	—American					Did not play							

O'NEILL, PAUL
OF, REDS

PERSONAL: Born February 25, 1963, at Columbus, O. . . . 6-4/215. . . . Throws left, bats left. . . . Full name: Paul Andrew O'Neill. . . . Son of Charles O'Neill, minor league pitcher (1945-48).
HIGH SCHOOL: Brookhaven (Columbus, O.).
COLLEGE: Otterbein College (O.).
TRANSACTIONS/CAREER NOTES: Selected by Cincinnati Reds organization in fourth round of free-agent draft (June 8, 1981). . . . On disabled list (May 10-July 16, 1986). . . . On Cincinnati disabled list (July 21-September 1, 1989); included rehabilitation disability assignment to Nashville (August 27-September 1, 1989).
STATISTICAL NOTES: Led American Association outfielders with 19 assists and eight double plays in 1985.

Year	Team (League)	Pos.	G	AB	R	H	2B	3B	HR	RBI	Avg.	SB	PO	A	E	Avg.
1981	—Billings (Pioneer)	OF	66	241	37	76	7	2	3	29	.315	6	87	4	5	.948
1982	—Cedar Rapids (Midwest)	OF	116	386	50	105	19	2	8	71	.272	12	137	7	8	.947
1983	—Tampa (Florida State)	OF-1B	121	413	62	115	23	7	8	51	.278	20	218	14	10	.959

Year	Team (League)	Pos.	G	AB	R	H	2B	3B	HR	RBI	Avg.	SB	PO	A	E	Avg.
	—Waterbury (Eastern)........	OF	14	43	6	12	0	0	0	6	.279	2	26	0	0	1.000
1984	—Vermont (Eastern)..........	OF	134	475	70	126	31	5	16	76	.265	29	246	5	7	.973
1985	—Denver (Am. Assoc.).......	OF-1B	*137	*509	63	*155	*32	3	7	74	.305	5	248	†20	7	.975
	—Cincinnati (N.L.)...............	OF	5	12	1	4	1	0	0	1	.333	0	3	1	0	1.000
1986	—Cincinnati (N.L.)..............	PH	3	2	0	0	0	0	0	0	.000	0	0	0	0	...
	—Denver (Am. Assoc.).......	OF	55	193	20	49	9	2	5	27	.254	1	98	7	4	.963
1987	—Cincinnati (N.L.).......	OF-1B-P	84	160	24	41	14	1	7	28	.256	2	90	2	4	.958
	—Nashville (Am. Assoc.)	OF	11	37	12	11	0	0	3	6	.297	1	19	1	0	1.000
1988	—Cincinnati (N.L.)............	OF-1B	145	485	58	122	25	3	16	73	.252	8	410	13	6	.986
1989	—Cincinnati (N.L.)..........	OF	117	428	49	118	24	2	15	74	.276	20	223	7	4	.983
	—Nashville (Am. Assoc.)	OF	4	12	1	4	0	0	0	0	.333	1	7	1	0	1.000
1990	—Cincinnati (N.L.)..........	OF	145	503	59	136	28	0	16	78	.270	13	271	12	2	.993
1991	—Cincinnati (N.L.)..........	OF	152	532	71	136	36	0	28	91	.256	12	301	13	2	.994
	Major league totals (7 years)		651	2122	262	557	128	6	82	345	.262	55	1298	48	18	.987

CHAMPIONSHIP SERIES RECORD

Year	Team (League)	Pos.	G	AB	R	H	2B	3B	HR	RBI	Avg.	SB	PO	A	E	Avg.
1990	—Cincinnati (N.L.)...............	OF	5	17	1	8	3	0	1	4	.471	1	9	2	0	1.000

WORLD SERIES RECORD

Year	Team (League)	Pos.	G	AB	R	H	2B	3B	HR	RBI	Avg.	SB	PO	A	E	Avg.
1990	—Cincinnati (N.L.)...............	OF	4	12	2	1	0	0	0	1	.083	1	11	0	0	1.000

ALL-STAR GAME RECORD

Year	League	Pos.	AB	R	H	2B	3B	HR	RBI	Avg.	SB	PO	A	E	Avg.
1991	—National	OF	2	0	0	0	0	0	0	.000	0	0	0	0	...

RECORD AS PITCHER

Year	Team (League)	G	W	L	Pct.	ERA	Sv.	IP	H	R	ER	BB	SO
1987	—Cincinnati (N.L.)......................	1	0	0	...	13.50	0	2	2	3	3	4	2

OQUENDO, JOSE
2B/SS, CARDINALS

PERSONAL: Born July 4, 1963, at Rio Piedras, Puerto Rico.... 5-10/171.... Throws right, bats left.... Full name: Jose Manuel Oquendo.... Name pronounced oh-KEN-doh.
HIGH SCHOOL: Villamallo (Rio Piedras, Puerto Rico).
TRANSACTIONS/CAREER NOTES: Signed as free agent by New York Mets organization (April 15, 1979).... Traded by Mets organization with P Mark Jason Davis to St. Louis Cardinals organization for SS Argenis Salazar and P John Young (April 2, 1985).
RECORDS/HONORS: Holds major league single-season records by second baseman (150 or more games) for highest fielding percentage—.996 (1990); fewest errors—3 (1990).... Shares major league single-season record for fewest double plays by second baseman (150 or more games)—65 (1990).... Holds N.L. single-season record for fewest chances accepted by second baseman (150 games or more)—678 (1990).
STATISTICAL NOTES: Led Northwest League shortstops with 40 errors in 1979.... Led Carolina League with 13 sacrifice hits in 1980.... Led International League with 14 sacrifice hits in 1982.... Led American Association shortstops with 591 total chances in 1985.... Led American Association with 15 sacrifice hits in 1985.... Led N.L. second basemen with 346 putouts, 500 assists, 851 total chances and 106 double plays in 1989.... Led N.L. second basemen with .994 fielding percentage in 1989 and .996 in 1990.

Year	Team (League)	Pos.	G	AB	R	H	2B	3B	HR	RBI	Avg.	SB	PO	A	E	Avg.
1979	—Grays Harbor (N'west)......	SS-2B	64	220	24	50	8	0	1	14	.227	9	90	177	†40	.870
1980	—Lynchburg (Carolina).......	SS	109	301	38	51	10	3	0	26	.169	14	126	358	31 ★	.940
1981	—Lynchburg (Carolina).......	SS	124	393	59	98	8	6	0	38	.249	38	169	390	23 ★	.960
1982	—Tidewater (Int'l)	SS	114	337	40	72	8	3	0	22	.214	24	186	337	25	.954
1983	—Tidewater (Int'l)	SS	13	34	3	4	0	0	0	3	.118	2	20	23	4	.915
	—New York (N.L.)	SS	120	328	29	70	7	0	1	17	.213	8	182	326	21	.960
1984	—New York (N.L.)	SS	81	189	23	42	5	0	0	10	.222	10	95	152	7	.972
	—Tidewater (Int'l)	SS	38	113	8	18	1	0	1	8	.159	8	54	111	2	.988
1985	—Louisville (Am. Assoc.)■...	SS	133	384	38	81	8	1	1	30	.211	13	★227	341	23	.961
1986	—St. Louis (N.L.)	S-2-3-0	76	138	20	41	4	1	0	13	.297	2	52	94	8	.948
1987	—St. Louis (N.L.)	IF-OF-P	116	248	43	71	9	4	1	24	.286	4	149	133	4	.986
1988	—St. Louis (N.L.)	IF-O-C-P	148	451	36	125	10	1	7	46	.277	4	268	315	11	.981
1989	—St. Louis (N.L.)	2B-SS-1B	•163	556	59	162	28	7	1	48	.291	3	†356	†523	6	†.993
1990	—St. Louis (N.L.)	2B-SS	156	469	38	118	17	5	1	37	.252	1	294	403	4	†.994
1991	—St. Louis (N.L.)	2B-SS-P	127	366	37	88	11	4	1	26	.240	1	271	368	9	.986
	Major league totals (8 years)		987	2745	285	717	91	18	12	221	.261	33	1667	2314	70	.983

CHAMPIONSHIP SERIES RECORD

Year	Team (League)	Pos.	G	AB	R	H	2B	3B	HR	RBI	Avg.	SB	PO	A	E	Avg.
1987	—St. Louis (N.L.)	OF-3B-PH	5	12	3	2	0	0	1	4	.167	0	7	0	0	1.000

Year	Team (League)	Pos.	G	AB	R	H	2B	3B	HR	RBI	Avg.	SB	PO	A	E	Avg.
							BATTING								FIELDING	
1987 —St. Louis (N.L.)	OF-3B	7	24	2	6	0	0	0	2	.250	0	8	10	0	1.000

RECORD AS PITCHER

Year	Team (League)	G	W	L	Pct.	ERA	Sv.	IP	H	R	ER	BB	SO
1987 —St. Louis (N.L.)	1	0	0	...	27.00	0	1	4	3	3	1	0
1988 —St. Louis (N.L.)	1	0	1	.000	4.50	0	4	4	2	2	6	1
1991 —St. Louis (N.L.)	1	0	0	...	27.00	0	1	2	3	3	0	1
Major league totals (3 years)	3	0	1	.000	12.00	0	6	10	8	8	7	2

OQUIST, MIKE
P, ORIOLES

PERSONAL: Born May 30, 1968, at La Junta, Colo.... 6-2/178.... Throws right, bats right.... Full name: Michael Lee Oquist.
HIGH SCHOOL: La Junta (Colo.).
COLLEGE: Arkansas.
TRANSACTIONS/CAREER NOTES: Selected by Baltimore Orioles organization in 13th round of free-agent draft (June 5, 1989).

Year	Team (League)	G	W	L	Pct.	ERA	Sv.	IP	H	R	ER	BB	SO
1989 —Erie (New York-Penn)	15	7	4	.636	3.59	0	97⅔	86	43	39	25	109
1990 —Frederick (Carolina)	25	9	8	.529	2.81	0	166⅓	134	64	52	48	★170
1991 —Hagerstown (Eastern)	27	10	9	.526	4.06	0	166⅓	168	82	75	62	136

OROSCO, JESSE
P, BREWERS

PERSONAL: Born April 21, 1957, at Santa Barbara, Calif.... 6-2/185.... Throws left, bats right.... Full name: Jesse Orosco.... Name pronounced oh-ROSS-koh.
HIGH SCHOOL: Santa Barbara (Calif.).
COLLEGE: Santa Barbara City College (Calif.).
TRANSACTIONS/CAREER NOTES: Selected by St. Louis Cardinals organization in seventh round of free-agent draft (January 11, 1977).... Selected by Minnesota Twins organization in second round of free-agent draft (January 10, 1978).... Traded by Twins organization to New York Mets (February 7, 1979), completing deal in which Twins traded P Greg Field and a player to be named later to Mets for P Jerry Koosman (December 8, 1978).... Traded by Mets as part of an eight-player, three-team deal in which Mets sent Orosco to Oakland Athletics (December 11, 1987). A's then traded Orosco, SS Alfredo Griffin and P Jay Howell to Los Angeles Dodgers for P Bob Welch, P Matt Young and P Jack Savage. A's then traded Savage, P Wally Whitehurst and P Kevin Tapani to Mets.... Granted free agency (November 4, 1988).... Signed by Cleveland Indians (December 3, 1988). ... Traded by Indians to Milwaukee Brewers for a player to be named later (December 6, 1991).
MISCELLANEOUS: Appeared as outfielder in one game with one putout (1986).

Year	Team (League)	G	W	L	Pct.	ERA	Sv.	IP	H	R	ER	BB	SO
1978 —Elizabethton (Appalachian)	20	4	4	.500	1.13	6	40	29	7	5	20	48
1979 —Tidewater (International)■	16	4	4	.500	3.89	0	81	82	45	35	43	55
—New York (N.L.)	18	1	2	.333	4.89	0	35	33	20	19	22	22
1980 —Jackson (Texas)	37	4	4	.500	3.68	3	71	52	36	29	62	85
1981 —Tidewater (International)	46	9	5	.643	3.31	8	87	80	39	32	32	81
—New York (N.L.)	8	0	1	.000	1.59	1	17	13	4	3	6	18
1982 —New York (N.L.)	54	4	10	.286	2.72	4	109⅓	92	37	33	40	89
1983 —New York (N.L.)	62	13	7	.650	1.47	17	110	76	27	18	38	84
1984 —New York (N.L.)	60	10	6	.625	2.59	31	87	58	29	25	34	85
1985 —New York (N.L.)	54	8	6	.571	2.73	17	79	66	26	24	34	68
1986 —New York (N.L.)	58	8	6	.571	2.33	21	81	64	23	21	35	62
1987 —New York (N.L.)	58	3	9	.250	4.44	16	77	78	41	38	31	78
1988 —Los Angeles (N.L.)■	55	3	2	.600	2.72	9	53	41	18	16	30	43
1989 —Cleveland (A.L.)■	69	3	4	.429	2.08	3	78	54	20	18	26	79
1990 —Cleveland (A.L.)	55	5	4	.556	3.90	2	64⅔	58	35	28	38	55
1991 —Cleveland (A.L.)	47	2	0	1.000	3.74	0	45⅔	52	20	19	15	36
American League totals (3 years)	171	10	8	.556	3.11	5	188⅓	164	75	65	79	170
National League totals (9 years)	427	50	49	.505	2.73	116	648⅓	521	225	197	270	549
Major league totals (12 years)	598	60	57	.513	2.82	121	836⅔	685	300	262	349	719

CHAMPIONSHIP SERIES RECORD

CHAMPIONSHIP SERIES NOTES: Holds single-series record for most games won—3 (1986).

Year	Team (League)	G	W	L	Pct.	ERA	Sv.	IP	H	R	ER	BB	SO
1986 —New York (N.L.)	4	3	0	1.000	3.38	0	8	5	3	3	2	10
1988 —Los Angeles (N.L.)	4	0	0	...	7.71	0	2⅓	4	2	2	3	0
Championship Series totals (2 years)	8	3	0	1.000	4.35	0	10⅓	9	5	5	5	10

WORLD SERIES RECORD

Year	Team (League)	G	W	L	Pct.	ERA	Sv.	IP	H	R	ER	BB	SO
1986 —New York (N.L.)	4	0	0	...	0.00	2	5⅔	2	0	0	0	6

ALL-STAR GAME RECORD

Year	League	W	L	Pct.	ERA	Sv.	IP	H	R	ER	BB	SO
1983 —National	0	0	...	0.00	0	⅓	0	0	0	0	1
1984 —National					Did not play						

ORSULAK, JOE
OF, ORIOLES

PERSONAL: Born May 31, 1962, at Glen Ridge, N.J. . . . . 6-1/210. . . . Throws left, bats left. . . . Full name: Joseph Michael Orsulak.
HIGH SCHOOL: Parsippany (N.J.).
TRANSACTIONS/CAREER NOTES: Selected by Pittsburgh Pirates organization in sixth round of free-agent draft (June 3, 1980). . . . On temporarily inactive list (July 10-27, 1981). . . . On disabled list (May 25-June 9, 1985). . . . On Pittsburgh disabled list (March 31-May 22, 1987); included rehabilitation disability assignment to Vancouver (May 4-22, 1987). . . . Traded by Pirates to Baltimore Orioles for SS Terry Crowley Jr. and 3B Rico Rossy (November 6, 1987).
STATISTICAL NOTES: Tied for South Atlantic League lead in double plays by outfielders with four in 1981. . . . Led Pacific Coast League outfielders with 367 total chances and eight double plays in 1983.

| | | | | | | | —BATTING— | | | | | | —FIELDING— | | |
Year Team (League)	Pos.	G	AB	R	H	2B	3B	HR	RBI	Avg.	SB	PO	A	E	Avg.
1981—Greenwood (S. Atlantic)....	OF	118	460	80	145	18	8	6	70	.315	18	249	16	4	★.985
1982—Alexandria (Carolina)	OF-1B	129	463	92	134	18	4	14	65	.289	28	286	7	10	.967
1983—Hawaii (Pacific Coast)	OF	139	538	87	154	12	•13	10	58	.286	38	★341	•18	8	.978
—Pittsburgh (N.L.)	OF	7	11	0	2	0	0	0	1	.182	0	2	2	0	1.000
1984—Hawaii (Pacific Coast)	OF	98	388	51	110	19	12	3	53	.284	14	258	6	2	.992
—Pittsburgh (N.L.)	OF	32	67	12	17	1	2	0	3	.254	3	41	1	0	1.000
1985—Pittsburgh (N.L.)	OF	121	397	54	119	14	6	0	21	.300	24	229	10	6	.976
1986—Pittsburgh (N.L.)	OF	138	401	60	100	19	6	2	19	.249	24	193	11	4	.981
1987—Vancouver (Pac. Coast)....	OF	39	143	20	33	6	1	1	12	.231	2	58	2	2	.968
1988—Baltimore (A.L.)■..........	OF	125	379	48	109	21	3	8	27	.288	9	228	6	5	.979
1989—Baltimore (A.L.)	OF	123	390	59	111	22	5	7	55	.285	5	250	10	4	.985
1990—Baltimore (A.L.)	OF	124	413	49	111	14	3	11	57	.269	6	267	5	3	.989
1991—Baltimore (A.L.)	OF	143	486	57	135	22	1	5	43	.278	6	273	★22	1	.997
American League totals (4 years)		515	1668	213	466	79	12	31	182	.279	26	1018	43	13	.988
National League totals (4 years)		298	876	126	238	34	14	2	44	.272	51	465	24	10	.980
Major league totals (8 years)		813	2544	339	704	113	26	33	226	.277	77	1483	67	23	.985

ORTIZ, JAVIER
OF

PERSONAL: Born January 22, 1963, at Boston. . . . 6-4/220. . . . Throws right, bats right. . . . Full name: Javier Victor Ortiz. . . . Name pronounced or-TEEZ.
HIGH SCHOOL: Hialeah-Miami Lakes (Hialeah, Fla.).
COLLEGE: Florida and Miami-Dade (South) Community College.
TRANSACTIONS/CAREER NOTES: Selected by Texas Rangers organization in first round (fourth pick overall) of free-agent draft (January 11, 1983). . . . On disabled list (April 9-May 21, 1985). . . . Traded by Rangers organization to Los Angeles Dodgers organization for P Scott May (December 12, 1987). . . . On disabled list (June 6-August 24, 1988). . . . Traded by Dodgers organization to Tucson (Houston Astros organization) for P Ed Vosberg (July 22, 1989). . . . On Houston disabled list (July 27, 1990-remainder of season). . . . Released by Astros (November 18, 1991).
STATISTICAL NOTES: Led Midwest League with .561 slugging percentage in 1983. . . . Tied for Texas League lead in being hit by pitch with seven in 1986. . . . Led American Association with 10 sacrifice flies in 1987.

| | | | | | | | —BATTING— | | | | | | —FIELDING— | | |
Year Team (League)	Pos.	G	AB	R	H	2B	3B	HR	RBI	Avg.	SB	PO	A	E	Avg.
1983—Burlington (Midwest)	OF	101	378	72	133	23	4	16	79	★.352	10	126	7	10	.930
1984—Tulsa (Texas)	OF	94	325	42	97	21	3	8	53	.298	4	115	13	9	.941
1985—Tulsa (Texas)	OF-1B	86	304	47	75	12	3	5	31	.247	11	264	15	9	.969
1986—Tulsa (Texas)	OF	110	378	52	114	29	3	14	65	.302	15	178	7	★11	.944
1987—Oklahoma City (A.A.)	OF	119	381	58	105	23	7	15	69	.276	5	209	16	6	.974
1988—San Antonio (Texas)■........	OF-1B	51	182	35	53	13	2	8	33	.291	6	116	2	2	.983
1989—Albuq.-Tucson (PCL)■	OF	81	260	47	66	10	0	11	36	.254	2	130	7	8	.945
1990—Tucson (Pacific Coast)	OF	49	179	36	63	16	2	5	39	.352	2	98	4	2	.981
—Houston (N.L.)	OF	30	77	7	21	5	1	1	10	.273	1	44	1	1	.978
1991—Tucson (Pacific Coast)	OF	34	127	20	41	13	0	3	22	.323	0	43	5	3	.941
—Houston (N.L.)	OF	47	83	7	23	4	1	1	5	.277	0	27	2	0	1.000
Major league totals (2 years)		77	160	14	44	9	2	2	15	.275	1	71	3	1	.987

ORTIZ, JUNIOR
C, INDIANS

PERSONAL: Born October 24, 1959, at Humacao, Puerto Rico. . . . 5-11/181. . . . Throws right, bats right. . . . Full name: Adalberto Colon Ortiz Jr. . . . Brother of Alexander Ortiz, minor league outfielder (1978-79). . . . Name pronounced or-TEEZ.
HIGH SCHOOL: Ana Roque (Humacao, Puerto Rico).
TRANSACTIONS/CAREER NOTES: Signed as free agent by Pittsburgh Pirates organization (January 18, 1977). . . . On Charleston temporary inactive list (June 18-22, 1977). . . . On disabled list (June 16-September 5, 1978). . . . Traded by Pirates with P Art Ray to New York Mets for OF Marvell Wynne and P Steve Senteney (June 14, 1983). . . . Drafted by Pittsburgh Pirates (December 3, 1984). . . . On disabled list (July 28-September 5, 1988). . . . Traded by Pirates with P Orlando Lind to Minnesota Twins for P Mike Pomeranz (April 4, 1990). . . . On disabled list (June 1-16, 1991). . . . Granted free agency (November 11, 1991). . . . Signed by Cleveland Indians organization (December 16, 1991).
STATISTICAL NOTES: Tied for Western Carolinas League lead with 22 passed balls in 1978. . . . Led Carolina League catchers with 84 assists, 17 errors and 12 double plays in 1979. . . . Led Pacific Coast League catchers with 744 putouts, 110 assists, 19 errors, 873 total chances and 17 double plays in 1982.

| | | | | | | | —BATTING— | | | | | | —FIELDING— | | |
Year Team (League)	Pos.	G	AB	R	H	2B	3B	HR	RBI	Avg.	SB	PO	A	E	Avg.
1977—Charles., S.C. (W. Caro.) ...	C	21	53	2	14	3	0	0	10	.264	0	93	13	4	.964
—Bradenton Pirates (GCL) ..	C	34	118	11	24	5	1	1	12	.203	1	76	14	4	.957

						BATTING							FIELDING		
Year Team (League)	Pos.	G	AB	R	H	2B	3B	HR	RBI	Avg.	SB	PO	A	E	Avg.
1978—Charleston, S.C. (W. Caro.)..	C	41	122	12	26	4	0	1	16	.213	1	198	44	7	.972
1979—Salem (Carolina)	C-1B	108	396	35	112	21	2	5	66	.283	0	632	†84	†17	.977
1980—Buffalo (Am. Assoc.)	C	126	515	79	*178	25	1	12	78*	.346	7	497	91	16	.974
—Portland (Pacific Coast) ...	C	8	27	1	3	0	1	0	3	.111	0	42	10	0	1.000
1981—Portland (Pacific Coast) ...	C	105	346	49	93	14	7	2	46	.269	5	606	76	15	.978
1982—Portland (Pacific Coast) ...	C-OF-1B	124	449	46	131	22	0	6	57	.292	4	†751	†110	†19	.978
—Pittsburgh (N.L.)	C	7	15	1	3	1	0	0	0	.200	0	27	3	0	1.000
1983—Pitts.-New York (N.L.)■....	C	73	193	11	48	5	0	0	12	.249	1	293	31	11	.967
1984—New York (N.L.)	C	40	91	6	18	3	0	0	11	.198	1	136	13	3	.980
1985—Pittsburgh (N.L.)■	C	23	72	4	21	2	0	1	5	.292	1	115	14	2	.985
1986—Pittsburgh (N.L.)	C	49	110	11	37	6	0	0	14	.336	0	165	13	3	.983
1987—Pittsburgh (N.L.)	C	75	192	16	52	8	1	1	22	.271	0	313	39	9	.975
1988—Pittsburgh (N.L.)	C	49	118	8	33	6	0	2	18	.280	1	152	23	3	.983
1989—Pittsburgh (N.L.)	C	91	230	16	50	6	1	1	22	.217	2	334	32	2	.995
1990—Minnesota (A.L.)■	C	71	170	18	57	7	1	0	18	.335	0	247	25	0	1.000
1991—Minnesota (A.L.)	C	61	134	9	28	5	1	0	11	.209	0	203	17	1	.995
American League totals (2 years)		132	304	27	85	12	2	0	29	.280	0	450	42	1	.998
National League totals (8 years)		407	1021	73	262	37	2	5	104	.257	6	1535	168	33	.981
Major league totals (10 years)		539	1325	100	347	49	4	5	133	.262	6	1985	210	34	.985

CHAMPIONSHIP SERIES RECORD

						BATTING							FIELDING		
Year Team (League)	Pos.	G	AB	R	H	2B	3B	HR	RBI	Avg.	SB	PO	A	E	Avg.
1991—Minnesota (A.L.)	C	3	3	0	0	0	0	0	0	.000	0	10	0	0	1.000

WORLD SERIES RECORD

						BATTING							FIELDING		
Year Team (League)	Pos.	G	AB	R	H	2B	3B	HR	RBI	Avg.	SB	PO	A	E	Avg.
1991—Minnesota (A.L.)	C	3	5	0	1	0	0	0	1	.200	0	9	0	0	1.000

ORTON, JOHN
C, ANGELS

PERSONAL: Born December 8, 1965, at Santa Cruz, Calif. ... 6-1/192. ... Throws right, bats right. ... Full name: John Andrew Orton.
HIGH SCHOOL: Soquel (Calif.).
COLLEGE: Cal Poly San Luis Obispo.
TRANSACTIONS/CAREER NOTES: Selected by New York Mets organization in 17th round of free-agent draft (June 4, 1984). ... Selected by California Angels organization in first round (25th pick overall) of free-agent draft (June 2, 1987). ... On disabled list (June 14-August 5, 1988).
STATISTICAL NOTES: Led Texas League catchers with .994 fielding percentage and 12 double plays in 1989.

						BATTING							FIELDING		
Year Team (League)	Pos.	G	AB	R	H	2B	3B	HR	RBI	Avg.	SB	PO	A	E	Avg.
1987—Salem (Northwest)	OF-C	51	176	31	46	8	1	8	36	.261	6	271	15	6	.979
—Midland (Texas)	C	5	13	1	2	1	0	0	0	.154	0	26	5	1	.969
1988—Palm Springs (Calif.)	C	68	230	42	46	6	1	1	28	.200	5	235	27	8	.970
1989—Midland (Texas)	C-1B	99	344	51	80	20	6	10	53	.233	2	466	56	4	†.992
—California (A.L.)	C	16	39	4	7	1	0	0	4	.179	0	76	7	1	.988
1990—California (A.L.)	C	31	84	8	16	5	0	1	6	.190	0	139	15	2	.987
—Edmonton (Pac. Coast)	C	50	174	29	42	8	0	6	26	.241	4	277	36	7	.978
1991—California (A.L.)	C	29	69	7	14	4	0	0	3	.203	0	145	23	1	.994
—Edmonton (Pac. Coast)	C	76	245	39	55	14	1	5	32	.224	5	397	49	7	.985
Major league totals (3 years)		76	192	19	37	10	0	1	13	.193	0	360	45	4	.990

OSTEEN, GAVIN
P, ATHLETICS

PERSONAL: Born November 27, 1969, at Orange City, Del. ... 6-0/195. ... Throws left, bats right. ... Full name: Gavin Edward Osteen. ... Son of Claude Osteen, major league pitcher for six teams (1957, 1959-75); and brother of Dave Osteen, pitcher, St. Louis Cardinals organization.
HIGH SCHOOL: Annville-Cleona (Annville, Pa.).
COLLEGE: Allegheny Community (Md.).
TRANSACTIONS/CAREER NOTES: Selected by Oakland Athletics organization in ninth round of free-agent draft (June 5, 1989).

Year Team (League)	G	W	L	Pct.	ERA	Sv.	IP	H	R	ER	BB	SO
1989—Southern Oregon (Northwest)..	16	2	2	.500	3.50	0	$46\frac{1}{3}$	44	24	18	29	42
1990—Madison (Midwest)	27	10	10	.500	3.10	0	154	126	69	53	80	120
1991—Huntsville (Southern)	28	13	9	.591	3.54	0	173	*176	82	68	65	105

OSUNA, AL
P, ASTROS

PERSONAL: Born August 10, 1965, at Inglewood, Calif. ... 6-3/200. ... Throws left, bats right. ... Full name: Alfonso Osuna Jr.
HIGH SCHOOL: Gahr (Cerritos, Calif.).
COLLEGE: Cerritos College (Calif.) and Stanford.
TRANSACTIONS/CAREER NOTES: Selected by Baltimore Orioles organization in fifth round of free-agent draft (January 9, 1985).

. . . Selected by San Diego Padres organization in secondary phase of free-agent draft (June 3, 1985). . . . Selected by Houston Astros organization in 16th round of free-agent draft (June 2, 1987).
RECORDS/HONORS: Named N.L. Rookie Pitcher of the Year by THE SPORTING NEWS (1991).

Year	Team (League)	G	W	L	Pct.	ERA	Sv.	IP	H	R	ER	BB	SO
1987	—Auburn (New York-Penn)	8	1	0	1.000	5.74	0	15 2/3	16	16	10	14	20
	—Asheville (South Atlantic)	14	2	0	1.000	2.75	2	19 2/3	20	6	6	6	20
1988	—Asheville (South Atlantic)	31	6	1	.857	1.98	3	50	41	19	11	25	41
	—Osceola (Florida State)	8	0	1	.000	6.94	0	11 2/3	12	9	9	9	5
1989	—Osceola (Florida State)	46	3	4	.429	2.66	7	67 2/3	50	27	20	27	62
1990	—Columbus (International)	•60	7	5	.583	3.38	6	69 1/3	57	30	26	33	82
	—Houston (N.L.)	12	2	0	1.000	4.76	0	11 1/3	10	6	6	6	6
1991	—Houston (N.L.)	71	7	6	.538	3.42	12	81 2/3	59	39	31	46	68
	Major league totals (2 years)	83	9	6	.600	3.58	12	93	69	45	37	52	74

OTTO, DAVE
P, INDIANS

PERSONAL: Born November 12, 1964, at Chicago. . . . 6-7/210. . . . Throws left, bats left. . . . Full name: David Alan Otto.
HIGH SCHOOL: Elk Grove (Ill.).
COLLEGE: Missouri.
TRANSACTIONS/CAREER NOTES: Selected by Baltimore Orioles organization in second round of free-agent draft (June 7, 1982). . . . Selected by Oakland A's organization in second round of free-agent draft (June 3, 1985). . . . On Oakland disabled list (April 29, 1990-remainder of season); included rehabilitation disability assignment to Tacoma (May 14-15, 1990). . . . Granted free agency (December 20, 1990). . . . Signed by Colorado Springs, Cleveland Indians organization (January 16, 1991).
STATISTICAL NOTES: Led Pacific Coast League with 18 wild pitches and tied for lead in games started by pitcher with 28 in 1989.

Year	Team (League)	G	W	L	Pct.	ERA	Sv.	IP	H	R	ER	BB	SO
1985	—Medford (Northwest)	11	2	2	.500	4.04	0	42 1/3	42	27	19	22	27
1986	—Madison (Midwest)	26	13	7	.650	2.66	0	169	154	72	50	71	125
1987	—Madison (Midwest)	1	0	0	...	0.00	0	3	2	0	0	0	2
	—Huntsville (Southern)	9	4	1	.800	2.34	0	50	36	14	13	11	25
	—Oakland (A.L.)	3	0	0	...	9.00	0	6	7	6	6	1	3
1988	—Tacoma (Pacific Coast)	21	4	9	.308	3.52	0	127 2/3	124	71	50	63	80
	—Oakland (A.L.)	3	0	0	...	1.80	0	10	9	2	2	6	7
1989	—Tacoma (Pacific Coast)	29	10	13	.435	3.67	0	169	164	84	69	61	122
	—Oakland (A.L.)	1	0	0	...	2.70	0	6 2/3	6	2	2	2	4
1990	—Oakland (A.L.)	2	0	0	...	7.71	0	2 1/3	3	3	2	3	2
	—Tacoma (Pacific Coast)	2	0	0	...	4.50	0	2	3	1	1	1	2
1991	—Colorado Springs (Pac. Coast)■	17	5	6	.455	4.75	0	94 2/3	110	56	50	43	62
	—Cleveland (A.L.)	18	2	8	.200	4.23	0	100	108	52	47	27	47
	Major league totals (5 years)	27	2	8	.200	4.25	0	125	133	65	59	39	63

OWEN, SPIKE
SS, EXPOS

PERSONAL: Born April 19, 1961, at Cleburne, Tex. . . . 5-10/170. . . . Throws right, bats both. . . . Full name: Spike Dee Owen. . . . Brother of Dave Owen, shortstop, Chicago Cubs, Kansas City Royals (1983-85 and 1988).
HIGH SCHOOL: Cleburne (Tex.).
COLLEGE: Texas.
TRANSACTIONS/CAREER NOTES: Selected by Seattle Mariners organization in first round (sixth pick overall) of free-agent draft (June 7, 1982). . . . On disabled list (July 15-August 1, 1985). . . . Traded by Mariners with OF Dave Henderson to Boston Red Sox for IF Rey Quinones, a player to be named later and cash (August 19, 1986); as part of deal, Mariners claimed P Mike Brown and P Mike Trujillo on waivers from Red Sox (August 22, 1986). Mariners acquired OF John Christensen to complete deal (September 25, 1986). . . . Traded by Red Sox with P Dan Gakeler to Montreal Expos for P John Dopson and SS Luis Rivera (December 8, 1988). . . . On disabled list (July 17-August 1, 1989).
RECORDS/HONORS: Shares modern major league single-game record for most runs—6 (August 21, 1986). . . . Holds N.L. single-season record for most consecutive errorless games by shortstop—63 (April 9-June 22, 1990). . . . Named shortstop on THE SPORTING NEWS college All-America team (1982).
STATISTICAL NOTES: Led A.L. shortstops with 767 total chances and 133 double plays in 1986.

Year	Team (League)	Pos.	G	AB	R	H	2B	3B	HR	RBI	Avg.	SB	PO	A	E	Avg.
1982	—Lynn (Eastern)	SS	78	241	32	64	9	2	1	27	.266	18	106	207	9	.972
1983	—Salt Lake City (PCL)	SS	72	256	58	68	8	9	1	32	.266	22	111	212	14	.958
	—Seattle (A.L.)	SS	80	306	36	60	11	3	2	21	.196	10	122	233	11	.970
1984	—Seattle (A.L.)	SS	152	530	67	130	18	8	3	43	.245	16	245	463	17	.977
1985	—Seattle (A.L.)	SS	118	352	41	91	10	6	6	37	.259	11	196	361	14	.975
1986	—Seattle-Boston (A.L.)■	SS	154	528	67	122	24	7	1	45	.231	4	279	467	21	.973
1987	—Boston (A.L.)	SS	132	437	50	113	17	7	2	48	.259	11	176	336	13	.975
1988	—Boston (A.L.)	SS	89	257	40	64	14	1	5	18	.249	0	102	192	10	.967
1989	—Montreal (N.L.)■	SS	142	437	52	102	17	4	6	41	.233	3	232	388	13	★.979
1990	—Montreal (N.L.)	SS	149	453	55	106	24	5	5	35	.234	8	216	340	6	★.989
1991	—Montreal (N.L.)	SS	139	424	39	108	22	3	3	26	.255	2	189	376	8	.986
	American League totals (6 years)		725	2410	301	580	94	32	19	212	.241	52	1120	2052	86	.974
	National League totals (3 years)		430	1314	146	316	63	17	14	102	.240	13	637	1104	27	.985
	Major league totals (9 years)		1155	3724	447	896	157	49	33	314	.241	65	1757	3156	113	.978

Year Team (League)	Pos.	G	AB	R	H	2B	3B	HR	RBI	Avg.	SB	PO	A	E	Avg.
1986 —Boston (A.L.)	SS	7	21	5	9	0	1	0	3	.429	1	12	21	5	.868
1988 —Boston (A.L.)	PH	1	0	0	0	0	0	0	0	...	0	0	0	0	...
Championship Series totals (2 years)		8	21	5	9	0	1	0	3	.429	1	12	21	5	.868

WORLD SERIES RECORD

Year Team (League)	Pos.	G	AB	R	H	2B	3B	HR	RBI	Avg.	SB	PO	A	E	Avg.
1986 —Boston (A.L.)	SS	7	20	2	6	0	0	0	2	.300	0	10	13	0	1.000

PAGLIARULO, MIKE
3B, TWINS

PERSONAL: Born March 15, 1960, at Medford, Mass. . . . 6-2/195. . . . Throws right, bats left. . . . Full name: Michael Timothy Pagliarulo. . . . Son of Charles Pagliarulo, minor league infielder (1958). . . . Name pronounced PAL-ya-ROO-lo.
HIGH SCHOOL: Medford (Mass.).
COLLEGE: Miami (Fla.).
TRANSACTIONS/CAREER NOTES: Selected by New York Yankees organization in sixth round of free-agent draft (June 8, 1981). . . . On disabled list (July 25-August 11, 1988). . . . Traded by Yankees with P Don Schulze to San Diego Padres for P Walt Terrell and a player to be named later (July 22, 1989); Yankees acquired P Fred Toliver to complete deal (September 27, 1989). . . . Granted free agency (November 5, 1990). . . . Signed by Minnesota Twins (January 25, 1991). . . . Granted free agency (November 11, 1991). . . . Re-signed by Twins (January 7, 1992).
STATISTICAL NOTES: Led New York-Pennsylvania League third basemen with 214 total chances in 1981. . . . Led New York-Pennsylvania League with eight intentional bases on balls received in 1981. . . . Led Southern League third basemen with 433 total chances in 1983.

Year Team (League)	Pos.	G	AB	R	H	2B	3B	HR	RBI	Avg.	SB	PO	A	E	Avg.
1981 —Oneonta (N.Y.-Penn)	3B	72	245	32	53	9	4	2	28	.216	13	40	*159	15	.930
1982 —Greensboro (S. Atlantic) ...	3B	123	403	79	113	22	0	22	79	.280	7	73	*278	27	.929
1983 —Nashville (Southern)	3B	135	450	82	117	19	4	19	80	.260	8	*98	*315	20	*.954
1984 —Columbus (Int'l)	3B-SS	58	146	24	31	5	1	7	25	.212	0	27	95	13	.904
—New York (A.L.)	3B	67	201	24	48	15	3	7	34	.239	0	44	106	7	.955
1985 —New York (A.L.)	3B	138	380	55	91	16	2	19	62	.239	0	67	187	13	.951
1986 —New York (A.L.)	3B-SS	149	504	71	120	24	3	28	71	.238	4	104	283	19	.953
1987 —New York (A.L.)	3B-1B	150	522	76	122	26	3	32	87	.234	1	97	297	17	.959
1988 —New York (A.L.)	3B	125	444	46	96	20	1	15	67	.216	1	82	232	19	.943
1989 —New York (A.L.)	3B	74	223	19	44	10	0	4	16	.197	1	25	122	10	.936
—San Diego (N.L.) ■	3B	50	148	12	29	7	0	3	14	.196	2	19	83	7	.936
1990 —San Diego (N.L.)	3B	128	398	29	101	23	2	7	38	.254	1	79	200	13	.955
1991 —Minnesota (A.L.) ■	3B-2B	121	365	38	102	20	0	6	36	.279	1	56	248	11	.965
American League totals (7 years)		824	2639	329	623	131	12	111	373	.236	8	475	1475	96	.953
National League totals (2 years)		178	546	41	130	30	2	10	52	.238	3	98	283	20	.950
Major league totals (8 years)		1002	3185	370	753	161	14	121	425	.236	11	573	1758	116	.953

CHAMPIONSHIP SERIES RECORD

Year Team (League)	Pos.	G	AB	R	H	2B	3B	HR	RBI	Avg.	SB	PO	A	E	Avg.
1991 —Minnesota (A.L.)	3B-PH	5	15	4	5	1	0	1	3	.333	0	4	10	0	1.000

WORLD SERIES RECORD

Year Team (League)	Pos.	G	AB	R	H	2B	3B	HR	RBI	Avg.	SB	PO	A	E	Avg.
1991 —Minnesota (A.L.)	PH-3B	6	11	1	3	0	0	1	2	.273	0	3	3	0	1.000

PAGNOZZI, TOM
C, CARDINALS

PERSONAL: Born July 30, 1962, at Tucson, Ariz. . . . 6-1/190. . . . Throws right, bats right. . . . Full name: Thomas Alan Pagnozzi. . . . Brother of Tim Pagnozzi, minor league shortstop (1976); and brother of Mike Pagnozzi, minor league pitcher (1975-78). . . . Name pronounced pag-NOHZ-ee.
HIGH SCHOOL: Rincon (Tucson, Ariz.).
COLLEGE: Central Arizona College and Arkansas.
TRANSACTIONS/CAREER NOTES: Selected by Milwaukee Brewers organization in 24th round of free-agent draft (January 12, 1982). . . . Selected by St. Louis Cardinals organization in eighth round of free-agent draft (June 6, 1983).
RECORDS/HONORS: Won N.L. Gold Glove at catcher (1991).

Year Team (League)	Pos.	G	AB	R	H	2B	3B	HR	RBI	Avg.	SB	PO	A	E	Avg.
1983 —Erie (New York-Penn)	C	45	168	28	52	9	1	6	22	.310	3	183	20	3	.985
—Macon (South Atlantic)	C	18	57	7	14	2	1	0	6	.246	3	125	18	8	.947
1984 —Springfield (Midwest)	C	114	396	57	112	20	4	10	68	.283	3	667	*90	12	.984
1985 —Arkansas (Texas)	C-1B	41	139	15	43	7	1	5	29	.309	4	243	27	1	.996
—Louisville (Am. Assoc.)	C	76	268	29	72	13	2	5	40	.269	0	266	25	4	.986
1986 —Louisville (Am. Assoc.)	C	30	106	12	31	4	0	1	18	.292	0	160	19	3	.984

Year	Team (League)	Pos.	G	AB	R	H	2B	3B	HR	RBI	Avg.	SB	PO	A	E	Avg.
1987	—Louisville (Am. Assoc.)	C-3B	84	320	53	100	20	2	14	71	.313	0	427	43	6	.987
	—St. Louis (N.L.)	C-1B	27	48	8	9	1	0	2	9	.188	1	61	5	0	1.000
1988	—St. Louis (N.L.)	1B-C-3B	81	195	17	55	9	0	0	15	.282	0	340	30	4	.989
1989	—St. Louis (N.L.)	C-1B-3B	52	80	3	12	2	0	0	3	.150	0	100	9	2	.982
1990	—St. Louis (N.L.)	C-1B	69	220	20	61	15	0	2	23	.277	1	345	39	4	.990
1991	—St. Louis (N.L.)	C-1B	140	459	38	121	24	5	2	57	.264	9	682	81	7	.991
	Major league totals (5 years)		369	1002	86	258	51	5	6	107	.257	11	1528	164	17	.990

CHAMPIONSHIP SERIES RECORD

Year	Team (League)	Pos.	G	AB	R	H	2B	3B	HR	RBI	Avg.	SB	PO	A	E	Avg.
1987	—St. Louis (N.L.)	PH	1	1	0	0	0	0	0	0	.000	0	0	0	0	...

WORLD SERIES RECORD

Year	Team (League)	Pos.	G	AB	R	H	2B	3B	HR	RBI	Avg.	SB	PO	A	E	Avg.
1987	—St. Louis (N.L.)	DH-PH	2	4	0	1	0	0	0	0	.250	0	0	0	0	...

PALACIOS, VINCE
P, PIRATES

PERSONAL: Born July 19, 1963, at Mataloma, Mexico. . . . 6-3/195. . . . Throws right, bats right. . . . Full name: Vicente Hernandez Palacios. . . . Name pronounced puh-LAH-see-os.
HIGH SCHOOL: Secundaria Tecnica (Soleda Vera Cruz, Mexico).
TRANSACTIONS/CAREER NOTES: Signed as free agent by Aguila of Mexican League (April 23, 1982). . . . Sold by Aguila to Chicago White Sox organization (July 20, 1984). . . . Loaned by White Sox organization to Mexico City Reds of Mexican League (May 28, 1985); returned (September 3, 1985). . . . Loaned by White Sox to Aguila of Mexican League (April 5, 1986); returned (September 1, 1986). . . . Released by White Sox organization (November 10, 1986). . . . Signed by Pittsburgh Pirates organization (December 4, 1986). . . . Drafted by Milwaukee Brewers (December 8, 1986). . . . Returned to Pirates (April 3, 1987). . . . On disabled list (April 1-June 12 and July 4, 1989-remainder of season). . . . On Pittsburgh disabled list (August 8-September 6, 1991); included rehabilitation disability assignment to Buffalo (August 28-September 6, 1991).
STATISTICAL NOTES: Led Mexican League with three balks in 1983. . . . Tied for Eastern League lead with four balks in 1985. . . . Led Pacific Coast League with five shutouts in 1987.

Year	Team (League)	G	W	L	Pct.	ERA	Sv.	IP	H	R	ER	BB	SO
1982	—						Did not play						
1983	—Aguila (Mexican)	22	12	6	.667	2.61	0	165⅓	121	53	48	60	125
1984	—Aguila (Mexican)	24	7	8	.467	3.52	4	128	117	64	50	79	120
	—Glens Falls (Eastern)■	5	1	2	.333	2.49	0	25⅓	23	12	7	11	10
1985	—Glens Falls (Eastern)	8	1	1	.500	4.76	1	39⅔	44	25	21	29	20
	—Mexico City Reds (Mexican)■...	13	7	2	.778	3.87	0	74⅓	86	44	32	44	49
1986	—Aguila (Mexican)■	23	5	14	.263	4.41	1	138⅔	157	75	68	78	121
1987	—Vancouver (Pacific Coast)■	27	13	5	.722	*2.58	0	*185	140	63	53	85	*148
	—Pittsburgh (N.L.)	6	2	1	.667	4.30	0	29⅓	27	14	14	9	13
1988	—Pittsburgh (N.L.)	7	1	2	.333	6.66	0	24⅓	28	18	18	15	15
	—Buffalo (American Assoc.)	5	3	0	1.000	1.99	0	31⅔	26	7	7	5	23
1989	—Buffalo (American Assoc.)	2	0	0	.000	7.20	0	10	9	8	8	8	8
1990	—Buffalo (American Assoc.)	28	13	7	.650	3.43	0	183⅔	173	77	70	53	137
	—Pittsburgh (N.L.)	7	0	0	...	0.00	3	15	4	0	0	2	8
1991	—Pittsburgh (N.L.)	36	6	3	.667	3.75	3	81⅔	69	34	34	38	64
	—Buffalo (American Assoc.)	3	0	0	...	1.42	2	6⅓	7	1	1	2	8
	Major league totals (4 years)	56	9	6	.600	3.95	6	150⅓	128	66	66	64	100

PALL, DONN
P, WHITE SOX

PERSONAL: Born January 11, 1962, at Chicago. . . . 6-1/183. . . . Throws right, bats right. . . . Full name: Donn Steven Pall.
HIGH SCHOOL: Evergreen Park (Ill.).
COLLEGE: Illinois (received degree, 1985).
TRANSACTIONS/CAREER NOTES: Selected by Chicago White Sox organization in 23rd round of free-agent draft (June 3, 1985). . . . On Chicago disabled list (May 19-June 2, 1989); included rehabilitation disability assignment to South Bend (May 30-June 2, 1989).
STATISTICAL NOTES: Tied for Gulf Coast League lead with four complete games and two shutouts in 1985.

Year	Team (League)	G	W	L	Pct.	ERA	Sv.	IP	H	R	ER	BB	SO
1985	—Sarasota White Sox (GCL)	13	•7	5	.583	1.67	0	*86	68	34	16	10	63
1986	—Appleton (Midwest)	11	5	5	.500	2.31	0	78	71	29	20	14	51
	—Birmingham (Southern)	21	3	4	.429	4.44	1	73	77	38	36	27	41
1987	—Birmingham (Southern)	30	8	11	.421	4.27	0	158	173	100	75	63	139
1988	—Vancouver (Pacific Coast)	44	5	2	.714	2.23	10	72⅔	61	21	18	20	41
	—Chicago (A.L.)	17	0	2	.000	3.45	0	28⅔	39	11	11	8	16
1989	—Chicago (A.L.)	53	4	5	.444	3.31	6	87	90	35	32	19	58
	—South Bend (Midwest)	2	0	0	...	0.00	0	3⅓	1	0	0	0	4
1990	—Chicago (A.L.)	56	3	5	.375	3.32	2	76	63	33	28	24	39
1991	—Chicago (A.L.)	51	7	2	.778	2.41	0	71	59	22	19	20	40
	Major league totals (4 years)	177	14	14	.500	3.08	8	262⅔	251	101	90	71	153

PALMEIRO, RAFAEL

1B, RANGERS

PERSONAL: Born September 24, 1964, at Havana, Cuba.... 6-0/188.... Throws left, bats left.... Full name: Rafael Corrales Palmeiro.... Name pronounced pal-MAIR-o.

HIGH SCHOOL: Jackson (Miami).

COLLEGE: Mississippi State (degree in commercial art).

TRANSACTIONS/CAREER NOTES: Selected by New York Mets organization in eighth round of free-agent draft (June 7, 1982).... Selected by Chicago Cubs organization in first round (22nd pick overall) of free-agent draft (June 3, 1985).... Traded by Cubs with P Jamie Moyer and P Drew Hall to Texas Rangers for P Mitch Williams, P Paul Kilgus, P Steve Wilson, IF Curtis Wilkerson, IF Luis Benitez and OF Pablo Delgado (December 5, 1988).

RECORDS/HONORS: Named outfielder on THE SPORTING NEWS college All-America team (1985).... Named Eastern League Most Valuable Player (1986).

STATISTICAL NOTES: Led Eastern League with 225 total bases, 13 sacrifice flies and 13 intentional bases on balls received in 1986.

Year	Team (League)	Pos.	G	AB	R	H	2B	3B	HR	RBI	Avg.	SB	PO	A	E	Avg.
1985 —Peoria (Midwest).............		OF	73	279	34	83	22	4	5	51	.297	9	113	7	1	.992
1986 —Pittsfield (Eastern)..........		OF	•140	509	66	*156	29	2	12	*95	.306	15	248	9	3	*.988
—Chicago (N.L.)............		OF	22	73	9	18	4	0	3	12	.247	1	34	2	4	.900
1987 —Iowa (American Assoc.) ...		OF-1B	57	214	36	64	14	3	11	41	.299	4	150	13	2	.988
—Chicago (N.L.)..........		OF-1B	84	221	32	61	15	1	14	30	.276	2	176	9	1	.995
1988 —Chicago (N.L.)..........		OF-1B	152	580	75	178	41	5	8	53	.307	12	322	11	5	.985
1989 —Texas (A.L.).■.........		1B	156	559	76	154	23	4	8	64	.275	4	1167	*119	12	.991
1990 —Texas (A.L.).............		1B	154	598	72	*191	35	6	14	89	.319	3	1215	91	7	.995
1991 —Texas (A.L.).............		1B	159	631	115	203	*49	3	26	88	.322	4	1305	96	*12	.992
American League totals (3 years)			469	1788	263	548	107	13	48	241	.306	11	3687	306	31	.992
National League totals (3 years)			258	874	116	257	60	6	25	95	.294	15	532	22	10	.982
Major league totals (6 years)			727	2662	379	805	167	19	73	336	.302	26	4219	328	41	.991

ALL-STAR GAME RECORD

Year	League	Pos.	AB	R	H	2B	3B	HR	RBI	Avg.	SB	PO	A	E	Avg.
1988 —National	PH-OF	0	0	0	0	0	0	0	...	0	1	0	0	1.000
1991 —American	1B	0	0	0	0	0	0	0	...	0	2	0	0	1.000
All-Star Game totals (2 years)		0	0	0	0	0	0	0	...	0	3	0	0	1.000

PALMER, DEAN

3B/OF, RANGERS

PERSONAL: Born December 27, 1968, at Tallahassee, Fla.... 6-2/195.... Throws right, bats right.... Full name: Dean William Palmer.

HIGH SCHOOL: Florida (Tallahassee, Fla.).

TRANSACTIONS/CAREER NOTES: Selected by Texas Rangers organization in third round of free-agent draft (June 2, 1986).... On disabled list (July 19, 1988-remainder of season).

STATISTICAL NOTES: Led Texas League batters with 152 strikeouts in 1989.... Led Texas League third baseman with 30 errors in 1989.

Year	Team (League)	Pos.	G	AB	R	H	2B	3B	HR	RBI	Avg.	SB	PO	A	E	Avg.
1986 —Sarasota Rangers (GCL) ...	3B	50	163	19	34	7	1	0	12	.209	6	25	75	13	.885
1987 —Gastonia (S. Atlantic)	3B	128	484	51	104	16	0	9	54	.215	5	58	209	*59	.819
1988 —Port Charlotte (Fla. St.)	3B	74	305	38	81	12	1	4	35	.266	0	49	144	28	.873
1989 —Tulsa (Texas)	3B-SS	133	498	82	125	32	5	*25	90	.251	15	85	213	†31	.906
—Texas (A.L.)..................	3B-SS-OF	16	19	0	2	2	0	0	1	.105	0	3	4	2	.778
1990 —Tulsa (Texas)	3B	7	24	4	7	0	1	3	9	.292	0	6	3	.833	
—Oklahoma City (A.A.)	3B-1B	88	316	33	69	17	4	12	39	.218	1	206	110	21	.938
1991 —Oklahoma City (A.A.)	3B-OF	60	234	45	70	11	2	*22	59	.299	4	49	105	11	.933
—Texas (A.L.)..................	3B-OF	81	268	38	50	9	2	15	37	.187	0	69	75	9	.941
Major league totals (2 years)		97	287	38	52	11	2	15	38	.181	0	72	79	11	.932

PAPPAS, ERIK

C/IF, ROYALS

PERSONAL: Born April 25, 1966, at Chicago.... 6-0/190.... Throws right, bats right.... Full name: Erik Daniel Pappas.

HIGH SCHOOL: Mount Carmel (Chicago).

TRANSACTIONS/CAREER NOTES: Selected by California Angels organization in first round (sixth pick overall) of free-agent draft (June 4, 1984).... On disabled list (April 8-July 20, 1986).... Drafted by Chicago Cubs organization (December 6, 1988).... Released by Cubs (November 5, 1991).... Signed by Kansas City Royals organization (December 2, 1991).

STATISTICAL NOTES: Led Northwest League catchers with 26 passed balls and tied for lead with six double plays in 1984.... Led California League catchers with 867 total chances and 37 passed balls in 1987.

Year	Team (League)	Pos.	G	AB	R	H	2B	3B	HR	RBI	Avg.	SB	PO	A	E	Avg.
1984 —Salem (Northwest)	C	56	177	24	43	3	3	1	15	.243	10	404	38	*20	.957
1985 —Quad City (Midwest)	C	100	317	53	76	8	4	2	29	.240	16	632	74	19	.974
1986 —Palm Springs (Calif.)	C	74	248	40	61	16	2	5	38	.246	9	445	48	5	.990
1987 —Palm Springs (Calif.)	C	119	395	50	96	20	3	3	64	.243	16	*775	82	10	.988

Year	Team (League)	Pos.	G	AB	R	H	2B	3B	HR	RBI	Avg.	SB	PO	A	E	Avg.
								BATTING						FIELDING		
1988—Midland (Texas)	C-1B	83	275	40	76	17	2	4	38	.276	16	467	56	12	.978
1989—Charlotte (Southern)■	C-0-1-2-3	119	354	69	106	31	1	16	49	.299	7	398	61	9	.981
1990—Iowa (American Assoc.)	C-0-1-2	131	405	56	101	19	2	16	55	.249	6	589	69	4	.994
1991—Chicago (N.L.)	C	7	17	1	3	0	0	0	2	.176	0	35	1	0	1.000
—Iowa (American Assoc.)	C-OF-1B	88	284	41	78	19	1	7	48	.275	5	420	58	6	.988
Major league totals (1 year)		7	17	1	3	0	0	0	2	.176	0	35	1	0	1.000

PAQUETTE, CRAIG
3B, ATHLETICS

PERSONAL: Born March 28, 1969, at Long Beach, Calif. . . . 6-0/185. . . . Throws right, bats right. . . . Full name: Craig Howard Paquette.
HIGH SCHOOL: Ranchos Alamitos (Garden Grove, Calif.).
COLLEGE: Golden West (Calif.).
TRANSACTIONS/CAREER NOTES: Selected by Minnesota Twins organization in 36th round of free-agent draft (June 2, 1987). . . . Selected by Oakland Athletics organization in eighth round of free-agent draft (June 5, 1989). . . . On Modesto disabled list (April 10-May 5, 1991). . . . On Huntsville disabled list (June 1-11, 1991).
STATISTICAL NOTES: Tied for Northwest League lead with 163 total bases in 1989. . . . Led Northwest League third basemen with .936 fielding percentage and 12 double plays in 1989.

Year	Team (League)	Pos.	G	AB	R	H	2B	3B	HR	RBI	Avg.	SB	PO	A	E	Avg.
								BATTING						FIELDING		
1989—South. Oregon (N'west)	3B-SS-2B	71	277	53	93	*22	3	14	56	.336	9	61	155	15	†.935
1990—Modesto (California)	3B	130	495	65	118	23	4	15	59	.238	8	*88	218	26	*.922
1991—Huntsville (Southern)	3B-1B	102	378	50	99	18	1	8	60	.262	0	51	132	16	.920

PAREDES, JOHNNY
2B

PERSONAL: Born September 2, 1962, at Maracaibo, Venezuela. . . . 5-11/175. . . . Throws right, bats right. . . . Full name: Johnny Alfonso Isambert Paredes.
HIGH SCHOOL: Tecnica Industrial (Venezuela).
TRANSACTIONS/CAREER NOTES: Signed as free agent by Philadelphia Phillies organization (June 22, 1982). . . . Released by Phillies organization (September 19, 1983). . . . Signed by Gastonia, Montreal Expos organization (January 12, 1984). . . . On disabled list (March 31-September 28, 1989). . . . Drafted by Detroit Tigers (December 4, 1989). . . . Returned to Expos organization (May 1, 1990). . . . Released by Expos (October 3, 1990). . . . Signed by Tigers (December, 1990). . . . Granted free agency (December 20, 1991).

Year	Team (League)	Pos.	G	AB	R	H	2B	3B	HR	RBI	Avg.	SB	PO	A	E	Avg.
								BATTING						FIELDING		
1982—Helena (Pioneer)	3B-2B-SS	34	105	17	32	4	1	1	7	.305	6	28	63	7	.929
1983—Spartanburg (S. Atl.)	3B-1B-2B	46	130	14	31	0	3	0	11	.238	10	98	59	11	.935
1984—West Palm Beach (FSL)■	2B	112	438	64	111	11	1	0	32	.253	23	275	295	15	*.974
1985—West Palm Beach (FSL)	2B	101	322	65	84	7	4	2	34	.261	31	184	281	9	*.981
—Jacksonville (Southern)	2B	21	73	11	23	2	0	0	5	.315	3	47	51	2	.980
1986—Jacksonville (Southern)	0-S-2-3-1	122	472	86	135	15	5	6	34	.286	22	230	189	19	.957
1987—Indianapolis (A.A.)	2B	130	493	80	154	19	6	8	47	.312	30	234	387	14	.978
1988—Indianapolis (A.A.)	2B-3B	101	400	69	118	17	3	4	46	.295	43	220	275	10	.980
—Montreal (N.L.)	2B-OF	35	91	6	17	2	0	1	10	.187	5	46	77	3	.976
1989—								Did not play								
1990—Detroit (A.L.)■	2B	6	8	2	1	0	0	0	0	.125	0	4	7	1	.917
—Indianapolis (A.A.)■	2B	94	322	46	84	7	1	3	17	.261	20	179	248	12	.973
—Montreal (N.L.)	2B	3	6	0	2	1	0	0	1	.333	0	1	7	1	.889
1991—Toledo (International)■	2B-OF	135	514	82	146	25	6	1	53	.284	36	293	422	18	.975
—Detroit (A.L.)	2B-3B-SS	16	18	4	6	0	0	0	0	.333	1	11	12	1	.958
American League totals (2 years)		22	26	6	7	0	0	0	0	.269	1	15	19	2	.944
National League totals (2 years)		38	97	6	19	3	0	1	11	.196	5	47	84	4	.970
Major league totals (3 years)		60	123	12	26	3	0	1	11	.211	6	62	103	6	.965

PARENT, MARK
C, ORIOLES

PERSONAL: Born September 16, 1961, at Ashland, Ore. . . . 6-5/240. . . . Throws right, bats right. . . . Full name: Mark Alan Parent.
HIGH SCHOOL: Anderson (Calif.).
TRANSACTIONS/CAREER NOTES: Selected by San Diego Padres organization in fourth round of free-agent draft (June 5, 1979). . . . On suspended list (August 27, 1983-remainder of season). . . . On disabled list (September 4, 1984-remainder of season). . . . Traded by Padres to Texas Rangers for 3B Scott Coolbaugh (December 12, 1990). . . . On Texas disabled list (March 9-September 6, 1991); included rehabilitation disability assignment to Oklahoma City (August 31-September 5, 1991). . . . Granted free agency (October 8, 1991). . . . Signed by Baltimore Orioles organization (February 5, 1992).
STATISTICAL NOTES: Led Northwest League catchers with .979 fielding percentage in 1980. . . . Led Carolina League catchers with 16 double plays in 1981. . . . Led Pacific Coast League catchers with .988 fielding percentage in 1987.

Year	Team (League)	Pos.	G	AB	R	H	2B	3B	HR	RBI	Avg.	SB	PO	A	E	Avg.
								BATTING						FIELDING		
1979—Walla Walla (Northwest)	C-OF	40	126	8	24	4	0	1	11	.190	8	229	34	6	.978
1980—Reno (California)	C	30	99	8	20	3	0	0	12	.202	0	128	23	2	.987
—Grays Harbor (N'west)	C-1B	66	230	29	55	11	2	7	32	.239	1	381	38	9	†.979
1981—Salem (Carolina)	C	123	438	44	103	16	3	6	47	.235	10	*694	87	*28	.965

Year Team (League)	Pos.	G	AB	R	H	2B	3B	HR	RBI	Avg.	SB	PO	A	E	Avg.
						BATTING							FIELDING		
1982 —Amarillo (Texas)	C	26	89	12	17	3	1	1	13	.191	2	100	6	2	.981
—Salem (Carolina)	C-1B	99	360	39	81	15	2	6	41	.225	2	475	64	12	.978
1983 —Beaumont (Texas)	C	81	282	38	71	22	1	7	33	.252	1	464	71	10	*.982
1984 —Beaumont (Texas)	C-1B	111	380	52	109	24	3	7	60	.287	1	674	68	7	.991
1985 —Las Vegas (Pac. Coast)	C-1B	105	361	36	87	23	3	7	45	.241	1	586	54	6	.991
1986 —Las Vegas (Pac. Coast)	C-1B	86	267	29	77	10	4	5	40	.288	0	344	40	5	.987
—San Diego (N.L.)	C	8	14	1	2	0	0	0	0	.143	0	16	0	2	.889
1987 —Las Vegas (Pac. Coast)	C-1-3-0	105	387	50	113	23	2	4	43	.292	2	556	58	8	†.987
—San Diego (N.L.)	C	12	25	0	2	0	0	0	2	.080	0	36	3	0	1.000
1988 —San Diego (N.L.)	C	41	118	9	23	3	0	6	15	.195	0	203	15	3	.986
1989 —San Diego (N.L.)	C-1B	52	141	12	27	4	0	7	21	.191	1	246	17	0	1.000
1990 —San Diego (N.L.)	C	65	189	13	42	11	0	3	16	.222	1	324	31	3	.992
1991 —Oklahoma City (A.A.)■	C	5	8	0	2	0	0	0	1	.250	0	4	0	0	1.000
—Texas (A.L.)	C	3	1	0	0	0	0	0	0	.000	0	5	0	0	1.000
American League totals (1 year)		3	1	0	0	0	0	0	0	.000	0	5	0	0	1.000
National League totals (5 years)		178	487	35	96	18	0	16	54	.197	2	825	66	8	.991
Major league totals (6 years)		181	488	35	96	18	0	16	54	.197	2	830	66	8	.991

PARKER, DAVE
DH

PERSONAL: Born June 9, 1951, at Jackson, Miss. . . . 6-5/230. . . . Throws right, bats left. . . . Full name: David Gene Parker.

HIGH SCHOOL: Courter Tech (Cincinnati).

TRANSACTIONS/CAREER NOTES: Selected by Pittsburgh Pirates organization in 14th round of free-agent draft (June 4, 1970). . . . On disabled list (June 7-28 and July 5-31, 1974; July 1-16, 1978; May 14-29, 1981; and May 12-June 7 and July 29-September 7, 1982). . . . Granted free agency (November 7, 1983). . . . Signed by Cincinnati Reds (December 7, 1983). . . . Traded by Reds to Oakland Athletics for P Jose Rijo and P Tim Birtsas (December 8, 1987). . . . On disabled list (July 5-August 21, 1988). . . . Granted free agency (November 13, 1989). . . . Signed by Milwaukee Brewers (December 3, 1989). . . . Traded by Brewers to California Angels for OF Dante Bichette (March 14, 1991). . . . Released by Angels (September 7, 1991). . . . Signed by Toronto Blue Jays (September 14, 1991). . . . Granted free agency (November 4, 1991).

RECORDS/HONORS: Shares major league record for most home runs in month of October—4 (1985). . . . Shares major league single-season record for fewest errors by outfielder who led league—9 (1986). . . . Named Carolina League Most Valuable Player (1972). . . . Named outfielder on THE SPORTING NEWS N.L. All-Star team (1975, 1977-78 and 1985-86). . . . Won N.L. Gold Glove as outfielder (1977-79). . . . Named N.L. Player of the Year by THE SPORTING NEWS (1978). . . . Named N.L. Most Valuable Player by Baseball Writers' Association of America (1978). . . . Named outfielder on THE SPORTING NEWS N.L. Silver Slugger team (1985-86). . . . Named designated hitter on THE SPORTING NEWS A.L. All-Star team (1990). . . . Named designated hitter on THE SPORTING NEWS A.L. Silver Slugger team (1990).

STATISTICAL NOTES: Tied for Gulf Coast League lead with 107 total bases in 1970. . . . Tied for Gulf Coast League lead in errors by outfielder with eight in 1970. . . . Led Carolina League with 270 total bases in 1972. . . . Led N.L. with .541 slugging percentage in 1975 and .585 in 1978. . . . Led N.L. outfielders with 389 putouts, 26 assists, 15 errors, 430 total chances and nine double plays in 1977. . . . Led N.L. with 23 intentional bases on balls received in 1978 and tied for lead with 24 in 1985. . . . Tied for N.L. lead with nine sacrifice flies in 1979. . . . Led N.L. with 340 total bases in 1978, 350 in 1985 and 304 in 1986. . . . Led N.L. in grounding into double plays with 26 in 1985. . . . Tied for N.L. lead with 16 game-winning RBIs in 1987. . . . Led A.L. with 14 sacrifice flies in 1990.

Year Team (League)	Pos.	G	AB	R	H	2B	3B	HR	RBI	Avg.	SB	PO	A	E	Avg.
						BATTING							FIELDING		
1970 —Bradenton Pirates (GCL)	OF-P	61	239	34	75	8	3	•6	41	.314	6	92	11	‡8	.928
1971 —Waterbury (Eastern)	OF	30	114	10	26	4	1	0	7	.228	1	43	5	6	.889
—Monroe (W. Carolinas)	OF	71	268	49	96	16	4	11	48	.358	18	104	8	10	.918
1972 —Salem (Carolina)	OF	135	*523	*91	*162	*30	6	22	*101	*.310	*38	*250	*20	*20	.931
1973 —Charleston, S.C. (S. Atl.)	OF	84	309	44	98	20	7	9	57	.317	6	144	11	7	.957
—Pittsburgh (N.L.)	OF	54	139	17	40	9	1	4	14	.288	1	77	3	3	.964
1974 —Pittsburgh (N.L.)	OF-1B	73	220	27	62	10	3	4	29	.282	3	154	8	4	.976
1975 —Pittsburgh (N.L.)	OF	148	558	75	172	35	10	25	101	.308	8	311	7	9	.972
1976 —Pittsburgh (N.L.)	OF	138	537	82	168	28	10	13	90	.313	19	294	13	14	.956
1977 —Pittsburgh (N.L.)	OF-2B	159	637	107	*215	*44	8	21	88	*.338	17	†389	†26	†15	.965
1978 —Pittsburgh (N.L.)	OF	148	581	102	194	32	12	30	117	*.334	20	302	12	*13	.960
1979 —Pittsburgh (N.L.)	OF	158	622	109	193	45	7	25	94	.310	20	341	15	*15	.960
1980 —Pittsburgh (N.L.)	OF	139	518	71	153	31	1	17	79	.295	10	235	14	9	.965
1981 —Pittsburgh (N.L.)	OF	67	240	29	62	14	3	9	48	.258	6	110	1	7	.941
1982 —Pittsburgh (N.L.)	OF	73	244	41	66	19	3	6	29	.270	7	108	2	5	.957
1983 —Pittsburgh (N.L.)	OF	144	552	68	154	29	4	12	69	.279	12	282	3	8	.973
1984 —Cincinnati (N.L.)■	OF	156	607	73	173	28	0	16	94	.285	11	296	6	8	.974
1985 —Cincinnati (N.L.)	OF	160	635	88	198	*42	4	34	*125	.312	5	329	12	10	.972
1986 —Cincinnati (N.L.)	OF	*162	637	89	174	31	3	31	116	.273	1	278	9	*9	.970
1987 —Cincinnati (N.L.)	OF-1B	153	589	77	149	28	0	26	97	.253	7	354	17	11	.971
1988 —Oakland (A.L.)■	OF-1B	101	377	43	97	18	1	12	55	.257	0	63	5	3	.958
1989 —Oakland (A.L.)	OF	144	553	56	146	27	0	22	97	.264	0	2	0	0	1.000
1990 —Milwaukee (A.L.)■	1B	157	610	71	176	30	3	21	92	.289	4	24	0	1	.960
1991 —Calif.-Toronto (A.L.)■	DH	132	502	47	120	26	2	11	59	.239	2	0	0	0	...
American League totals (4 years)		534	2042	217	539	101	6	66	303	.264	7	89	5	4	.959
National League totals (15 years)		1932	7316	1055	2173	425	69	273	1190	.297	147	3860	148	140	.966
Major league totals (19 years)		2466	9358	1272	2712	526	75	339	1493	.290	154	3949	153	144	.966

CHAMPIONSHIP SERIES RECORD

Year	Team (League)	Pos.	G	AB	R	H	2B	3B	HR	RBI	Avg.	SB	PO	A	E	Avg.
1974 — Pittsburgh (N.L.)	OF-PH	3	8	0	1	0	0	0	0	.125	0	4	1	0	1.000
1975 — Pittsburgh (N.L.)	OF	3	10	2	0	0	0	0	0	.000	0	13	1	0	1.000
1979 — Pittsburgh (N.L.)	OF	3	12	2	4	0	0	0	2	.333	1	9	0	0	1.000
1988 — Oakland (A.L.)	DH-OF	3	12	1	3	1	0	0	0	.250	0	1	0	1	.500
1989 — Oakland (A.L.)	DH	4	16	2	3	0	0	2	3	.188	0	0	0	0	...
Championship Series totals (5 years)		16	58	7	11	1	0	2	5	.190	1	27	2	1	.967

WORLD SERIES RECORD

Year	Team (League)	Pos.	G	AB	R	H	2B	3B	HR	RBI	Avg.	SB	PO	A	E	Avg.
1979 — Pittsburgh (N.L.)	OF	7	29	2	10	3	0	0	4	.345	0	13	1	1	.933
1988 — Oakland (A.L.)	OF-DH	4	15	0	3	0	0	0	0	.200	0	4	0	0	1.000
1989 — Oakland (A.L.)	DH-PH	3	9	2	2	1	0	1	2	.222	0	0	0	0	...
World Series totals (3 years)		14	53	4	15	4	0	1	6	.283	0	17	1	1	.947

ALL-STAR GAME RECORD

Year	League	Pos.	AB	R	H	2B	3B	HR	RBI	Avg.	SB	PO	A	E	Avg.
1977 — National	OF	3	1	1	0	0	0	0	.333	0	2	0	0	1.000
1979 — National	OF	3	0	1	0	0	0	1	.333	0	2	0	0	1.000
1980 — National	OF	2	0	0	0	0	0	0	.000	0	0	0	0	...
1981 — National	OF	3	1	1	0	0	1	1	.333	0	1	0	0	1.000
1985 — National	OF	2	0	0	0	0	0	0	.000	0	1	0	0	1.000
1986 — National	OF	2	0	1	0	0	0	0	.500	0	0	0	0	...
1990 — American							Did not play								
All-Star Game totals (6 years)		15	2	4	0	0	1	2	.267	0	4	2	0	1.000

PARKER, RICK
OF/IF, ASTROS

PERSONAL: Born March 20, 1963, at Kansas City, Mo.. : . 6-0/185. . . . Throws right, bats right. . . . Full name: Richard Allen Parker.
HIGH SCHOOL: Oak Park (Kansas City, Mo.).
COLLEGE: Southwest Missouri State and Texas.
TRANSACTIONS/CAREER NOTES: Selected by Philadelphia Phillies organization in 16th round of free-agent draft (June 3, 1985). . . . Traded by Phillies organization to Phoenix, San Francisco Giants organization (August 7, 1989), completing deal in which Phillies traded P Steve Bedrosian and a player to be named later to Giants for P Dennis Cook, P Terry Mulholland and 3B Charlie Hayes (June 18, 1989). . . . On San Francisco disabled list (March 25-May 16, 1991); included rehabilitation disability assignment to Phoenix (April 27-May 16, 1991). . . . Released by Giants (December 9, 1991). . . . Signed by Tucson, Houston Astros organization (January 3, 1992).

Year	Team (League)	Pos.	G	AB	R	H	2B	3B	HR	RBI	Avg.	SB	PO	A	E	Avg.
1985 — Bend (Northwest)	SS	55	205	45	51	9	1	2	20	.249	14	79	143	25	.899
1986 — Spartanburg (S. Atl.)	SS	62	233	39	69	7	3	5	28	.296	14	87	169	18	.934
— Clearwater (Florida St.)	SS	63	218	24	51	10	2	0	15	.234	8	94	197	21	.933
1987 — Clearwater (Florida St.)	2B-SS-3B	101	330	56	83	13	3	3	34	.252	6	130	234	27	.931
1988 — Reading (Eastern)	3-0-1-2-S	116	362	50	93	13	3	3	47	.257	24	174	114	18	.941
1989 — Reading (Eastern)	3B-OF-SS	103	388	59	92	7	*9	3	32	.237	17	123	91	22	.907
— Phoenix (Pacific Coast)■	3B-OF-SS	18	68	5	18	2	1	0	11	.265	1	25	32	1	.983
1990 — Phoenix (Pacific Coast)	3B-OF-2B	44	173	38	58	7	4	1	18	.335	13	57	51	2	.982
— San Francisco (N.L.)	0-2-S-3	54	107	19	26	5	0	2	14	.243	6	45	3	2	.960
1991 — Phoenix (Pacific Coast)	OF-3B-SS	85	297	41	89	10	9	6	41	.300	16	132	58	11	.945
— San Francisco (N.L.)	OF	13	14	0	1	0	0	0	1	.071	0	5	0	0	1.000
Major league totals (2 years)		67	121	19	27	5	0	2	15	.223	6	50	3	2	.964

PARKS, DEREK
C, TWINS

PERSONAL: Born September 29, 1968, at Covina, Calif. . . . 6-0/205. . . . Throws right, bats right. . . . Full name: Derek Gavin Parks.
HIGH SCHOOL: Montclair (Calif.).
TRANSACTIONS/CAREER NOTES: Selected by Minnesota Twins in first round (10th pick overall) of free-agent draft (June 2, 1986). . . . On disabled list (June 12-August 31, 1989 and August 5-15, 1991).
STATISTICAL NOTES: Led Southern League in being hit by pitch with 15 in 1988. . . . Led Appalachian League with 17 passed balls in 1986.

Year	Team (League)	Pos.	G	AB	R	H	2B	3B	HR	RBI	Avg.	SB	PO	A	E	Avg.
1986 — Elizabethton (Appal.)	C	62	224	39	53	10	1	10	40	.237	1	297	36	7	.979
1987 — Kenosha (Midwest)	C	129	466	70	115	19	2	4	94	.247	1	800	85	14	.984
1988 — Orlando (Southern)	C	118	400	52	94	15	0	7	42	.235	1	616	66	7	.990
1989 — Orlando (Southern)	C	31	95	16	18	3	0	2	10	.189	1	135	12	3	.980
1990 — Portland (Pacific Coast)	C	76	231	27	41	8	1	11	27	.177	0	488	45	13	.976
1991 — Orlando (Southern)	C	92	256	30	55	14	0	6	31	.215	0	476	37	8	.985

PARRETT, JEFF
P

PERSONAL: Born August 26, 1961, at Indianapolis. . . . 6-3/193. . . . Throws right, bats right. . . . Full name: Jeffrey Dale Parrett.
HIGH SCHOOL: Lafayette (Lexington, Ky.).
COLLEGE: Kentucky.
TRANSACTIONS/CAREER NOTES: Selected by Milwaukee Brewers organization in ninth round of free-agent draft (June 6, 1983). . . . Drafted by Montreal Expos (December 10, 1985). . . . On disabled list (July 16-August 14, 1988). . . . Traded by Expos with P Floyd Youmans to Philadelphia Phillies for P Kevin Gross (December 6, 1988). . . . On disabled list (April 29-May 22, 1989). . . . Traded by Phillies with two players to be named later to Atlanta Braves for OF Dale Murphy and a player to be named later (August 3, 1990); Scranton/Wilkes-Barre (Phillies organization) acquired P Tommy Greene (August 9, 1990) and Braves acquired OF Jim Vatcher (August 9, 1990) and SS Victor Rosario (September 4, 1990) to complete deal. . . . Released by Braves (December 9, 1991).

Year	Team (League)	G	W	L	Pct.	ERA	Sv.	IP	H	R	ER	BB	SO
1983	Paintsville (Appalachian)	3	2	0	1.000	2.12	0	17	12	6	4	8	21
	Beloit (Midwest)	10	2	2	.500	4.02	0	47	40	26	21	29	34
1984	Beloit (Midwest)	29	4	3	.571	4.52	2	91⅔	76	50	46	71	95
1985	Stockton (California)	45	7	4	.636	*2.75	11	127⅔	97	50	39	75	120
1986	Montreal (N.L.)■	12	0	1	.000	4.87	0	20⅓	19	11	11	13	21
	Indianapolis (Am. Assoc.)	25	2	5	.286	4.96	2	69	54	44	38	35	76
1987	Indianapolis (Am. Assoc.)	20	2	1	.667	2.01	9	22⅓	15	5	5	13	17
	Montreal (N.L.)	45	7	6	.538	4.21	6	62	53	33	29	30	56
1988	Montreal (N.L.)	61	12	4	.750	2.65	6	91⅔	66	29	27	45	62
1989	Philadelphia (N.L.)■	72	12	6	.667	2.98	6	105⅔	90	43	35	44	98
1990	Philadelphia-Atlanta (N.L.)■	67	5	10	.333	4.64	2	108⅔	119	62	56	55	86
1991	Atlanta (N.L.)	18	1	2	.333	6.33	1	21⅓	31	18	15	12	14
	Richmond (International)	19	2	7	.222	4.52	0	79⅔	72	45	40	46	88
Major league totals (6 years)		**275**	**37**	**29**	**.561**	**3.80**	**21**	**409⅔**	**378**	**196**	**173**	**199**	**337**

PARRISH, LANCE
C, ANGELS

PERSONAL: Born June 15, 1956, at McKeesport, Pa. . . . 6-3/224. . . . Throws right, bats right. . . . Full name: Lance Michael Parrish.
HIGH SCHOOL: Walnut (Calif.).
TRANSACTIONS/CAREER NOTES: Selected by Detroit Tigers organization in first round (16th pick overall) of free-agent draft (June 5, 1974). . . . On disabled list (July 31-September 29, 1986). . . . Granted free agency (November 12, 1986) . . . Signed by Philadelphia Phillies (March 13, 1987). . . . On disabled list (July 13-28, 1988). . . . Traded by Phillies to California Angels for P David Holdridge (October 3, 1988). . . . On disabled list (June 10-25, 1991).
RECORDS/HONORS: Named catcher on THE SPORTING NEWS A.L. Silver Slugger team (1980, 1982-84, 1986 and 1990). . . . Named catcher on THE SPORTING NEWS A.L. All-Star team (1982 and 1984). . . . Won A.L. Gold Glove at catcher (1983-85).
STATISTICAL NOTES: Led Appalachian League batters with 92 strikeouts in 1974. . . . Led Florida State League catchers with eight double plays and 31 passed balls in 1975. . . . Led Southern League with 22 passed balls in 1976. . . . Led American Association catchers with 10 double plays and 21 passed balls in 1977. . . . Led A.L. with 21 passed balls in 1979, 19 in 1991 and tied for lead with 17 in 1980. . . . Led A.L. catchers with 772 total chances in 1983. . . . Led A.L. with 13 sacrifice flies in 1983. . . . Led A.L. catchers with 11 double plays in 1984 and 15 in 1990. . . . Led N.L. catchers with 12 passed balls and tied for lead with 11 double plays in 1988. . . . Led A.L. catchers with 88 assists in 1990.

Year	Team (League)	Pos.	G	AB	R	H	2B	3B	HR	RBI	Avg.	SB	PO	A	E	Avg.
1974	Bristol (Appalachian)	3B-OF	68	253	45	54	11	1	11	46	.213	2	36	83	22	.844
1975	Lakeland (Florida State)	C	100	341	30	75	15	2	5	37	.220	0	460	50	7	.986
1976	Montgomery (Southern)	C	107	340	46	75	9	2	14	55	.221	0	*600	*79	11	*.984
1977	Evansville (A.A.)	C	115	416	74	116	21	2	25	90	.279	2	*722	*82	11	*.987
	Detroit (A.L.)	C	12	46	10	9	2	0	3	7	.196	0	76	6	0	1.000
1978	Detroit (A.L.)	C	85	288	37	63	11	3	14	41	.219	0	353	39	5	.987
1979	Detroit (A.L.)	C	143	493	65	136	26	3	19	65	.276	6	707	*79	9	.989
1980	Detroit (A.L.)	C-1B-OF	144	553	79	158	34	6	24	82	.286	6	607	67	7	.990
1981	Detroit (A.L.)	C	96	348	39	85	18	2	10	46	.244	2	407	40	3	.993
1982	Detroit (A.L.)	C-OF	133	486	75	138	19	2	32	87	.284	3	627	76	8	.989
1983	Detroit (A.L.)	C	155	605	80	163	42	3	27	114	.269	1	695	73	4	.995
1984	Detroit (A.L.)	C	147	578	75	137	16	2	33	98	.237	2	720	67	7	.991
1985	Detroit (A.L.)	C	140	549	64	150	27	1	28	98	.273	2	695	53	5	.993
1986	Detroit (A.L.)	C	91	327	53	84	6	1	22	62	.257	0	483	48	6	.989
1987	Philadelphia (N.L.)■	C	130	466	42	114	21	0	17	67	.245	0	724	66	9	.989
1988	Philadelphia (N.L.)	C-1B	123	424	44	91	17	2	15	60	.215	0	640	73	9	.988
1989	California (A.L.)■	C	124	433	48	103	12	1	17	50	.238	1	638	63	5	.993
1990	California (A.L.)	C-1B	133	470	54	126	14	0	24	70	.268	2	794	†90	6	.993
1991	California (A.L.)	C-1B	119	402	38	87	12	0	19	51	.216	0	670	57	2	.997
American League totals (13 years)			**1522**	**5578**	**717**	**1439**	**239**	**24**	**272**	**871**	**.258**	**25**	**7472**	**758**	**67**	**.992**
National League totals (2 years)			**253**	**890**	**86**	**205**	**38**	**2**	**32**	**127**	**.230**	**0**	**1364**	**139**	**18**	**.988**
Major league totals (15 years)			**1775**	**6468**	**803**	**1644**	**277**	**26**	**304**	**998**	**.254**	**25**	**8836**	**897**	**85**	**.991**

CHAMPIONSHIP SERIES RECORD

Year	Team (League)	Pos.	G	AB	R	H	2B	3B	HR	RBI	Avg.	SB	PO	A	E	Avg.
1984	Detroit (A.L.)	C	3	12	1	3	1	0	1	3	.250	0	21	2	0	1.000

Year	Team (League)	Pos.	G	AB	R	H	2B	3B	HR	RBI	Avg.	SB	PO	A	E	Avg.
							BATTING							FIELDING		
1984	—Detroit (A.L.)	C	5	18	3	5	1	0	1	2	.278	1	30	3	1	.971

ALL-STAR GAME RECORD

ALL-STAR GAME NOTES: Named to A.L. All-Star team for 1985 game; replaced due to injury by Rich Gedman.

Year	League	Pos.	AB	R	H	2B	3B	HR	RBI	Avg.	SB	PO	A	E	Avg.
						BATTING							FIELDING		
1980	—American	C	1	0	0	0	0	0	0	.000	0	0	0	0	...
1982	—American	C	2	0	1	1	0	0	0	.500	0	2	3	0	1.000
1983	—American	C	2	0	0	0	0	0	0	.000	0	1	0	0	1.000
1984	—American	C	2	0	0	0	0	0	0	.000	0	3	1	1	.800
1986	—American	C	3	0	0	0	0	0	0	.000	0	4	0	0	1.000
1988	—National	C	1	0	0	0	0	0	0	.000	0	0	0	0	...
1990	—American	PH-C	1	1	1	0	0	0	0	1.000	0	3	0	0	1.000
	All-Star Game totals (7 years)		12	1	2	1	0	0	0	.167	0	13	4	1	.944

PASQUA, DAN

OF/1B, WHITE SOX

PERSONAL: Born October 17, 1961, at Yonkers, N.Y. . . . 6-0/205. . . . Throws left, bats left. . . . Full name: Daniel Anthony Pasqua. . . . Name pronounced PASS-kwuh.
HIGH SCHOOL: Old Tappan (N.J.).
COLLEGE: William Paterson College (N.J.).
TRANSACTIONS/CAREER NOTES: Selected by New York Yankees organization in third round of free-agent draft (June 7, 1982). . . . Traded by Yankees organization with C Mark Salas and P Steve Rosenberg to Chicago White Sox for P Richard Dotson and P Scott Nielsen (November 12, 1987). . . . On disabled list (April 6-May 14 and August 21, 1989-remainder of season). . . . Granted free agency (October 31, 1991). . . . Re-signed by White Sox (December 4, 1991).
RECORDS/HONORS: Named Appalachian League Player of the Year (1982). . . . Named International League Player of the Year (1985).
STATISTICAL NOTES: Led Southern League batters with 148 strikeouts in 1984. . . . Led International League with .599 slugging percentage in 1985. . . . Led A.L. outfielders with .996 fielding percentage in 1988.

Year	Team (League)	Pos.	G	AB	R	H	2B	3B	HR	RBI	Avg.	SB	PO	A	E	Avg.
							BATTING							FIELDING		
1982	—Paintsville (Appal.)	OF	60	239	43	72	10	2	•16	•63	.301	1	114	4	4	.967
	—Oneonta (N.Y.-Penn)	OF	4	17	3	5	1	0	2	4	.294	1	2	1	1	.750
1983	—Fort Lauderdale (FSL)	OF	131	451	83	123	25	10	19	84	.273	12	213	8	5	.978
	—Columbus (Int'l)	OF	1	3	0	0	0	0	0	0	.000	0	5	0	0	1.000
1984	—Nashville (Southern)	OF	136	460	78	112	14	3	•33	91	.243	5	244	11	•12	.955
1985	—Columbus (Int'l)	OF	78	287	52	92	16	5	18	69	.321	5	141	9	4	.974
	—New York (A.L.)	OF	60	148	17	31	3	1	9	25	.209	0	72	2	0	1.000
1986	—Columbus (Int'l)	OF	32	110	25	32	3	3	6	20	.291	1	62	0	3	.954
	—New York (A.L.)	OF-1B	102	280	44	82	17	0	16	45	.293	2	172	4	2	.989
1987	—New York (A.L.)	OF-1B	113	318	42	74	7	1	17	42	.233	0	214	10	2	.991
	—Columbus (Int'l)	OF	23	85	16	29	6	0	6	15	.341	2	55	0	1	.982
1988	—Chicago (A.L.)■..............	OF-1B	129	422	48	96	16	2	20	50	.227	1	316	14	2	†.994
1989	—Chicago (A.L.)	OF	73	246	26	61	9	1	11	47	.248	1	149	3	1	.993
1990	—Chicago (A.L.)	OF	112	325	43	89	27	3	13	58	.274	1	71	5	3	.962
1991	—Chicago (A.L.)	1B-OF	134	417	71	108	22	5	18	66	.259	0	587	46	6	.991
	Major league totals (7 years)		723	2156	291	541	101	13	104	333	.251	5	1581	84	16	.990

PATTERSON, BOB

P, PIRATES

PERSONAL: Born May 16, 1959, at Jacksonville, Fla. . . . 6-2/192. . . . Throws left, bats right. . . . Full name: Robert Chandler Patterson.
HIGH SCHOOL: Wade Hampton (Greenville, S.C.).
COLLEGE: East Carolina (degree in industrial technology).
TRANSACTIONS/CAREER NOTES: Selected by San Diego Padres organization in 21st round of free-agent draft (June 7, 1982). . . . Traded by Padres to Pittsburgh Pirates for OF Marvell Wynne (April 3, 1986). . . . On disabled list (April 28, 1988-remainder of season).

Year	Team (League)	G	W	L	Pct.	ERA	Sv.	IP	H	R	ER	BB	SO
1982	—Sarasota Padres (Gulf Coast)...	8	4	3	.571	2.94	0	52	60	18	17	7	65
	—Reno (California)	4	1	0	1.000	3.55	0	25⅓	28	11	10	5	10
1983	—Beaumont (Texas)	43	8	4	.667	4.01	11	116⅔	107	61	52	36	97
1984	—Las Vegas (Pacific Coast)	*60	8	9	.471	3.27	13	143⅓	129	63	52	37	97
1985	—Las Vegas (Pacific Coast)	42	10	11	.476	3.14	6	186⅓	187	80	65	52	146
	—San Diego (N.L.)	3	0	0	...	24.75	0	4	13	11	11	3	1
1986	—Hawaii (Pacific Coast)■...........	25	9	6	.600	3.40	1	156	146	68	59	44	*137
	—Pittsburgh (N.L.)	11	2	3	.400	4.95	0	36⅓	49	20	20	5	20
1987	—Pittsburgh (N.L.)	15	1	4	.200	6.70	0	43	49	34	32	22	27
	—Vancouver (Pacific Coast)	14	5	2	.714	2.12	9	89	62	21	21	30	92
1988	—Buffalo (American Assoc.)	4	2	0	1.000	2.32	0	31	26	12	8	4	20
1989	—Buffalo (American Assoc.)	31	12	6	.667	3.35	1	177⅓	177	69	66	35	103
	—Pittsburgh (N.L.)	12	4	3	.571	4.05	1	26⅔	23	13	12	8	20
1990	—Pittsburgh (N.L.)	55	8	5	.615	2.95	5	94⅔	88	33	31	21	70
1991	—Pittsburgh (N.L.)	54	4	3	.571	4.11	2	65⅔	67	32	30	15	57
	Major league totals (6 years)	150	19	18	.514	4.53	8	270⅓	289	143	136	74	195

Year Team (League)	G	W	L	Pct.	ERA	Sv.	IP	H	R	ER	BB	SO
1990 —Pittsburgh (N.L.)	2	0	0	...	0.00	1	1	1	0	0	2	0
1991 —Pittsburgh (N.L.)	1	0	0	...	0.00	0	2	1	0	0	0	3
Championship Series totals (2 years)	3	0	0	...	0.00	1	3	2	0	0	2	3

PATTERSON, JOHN
2B, GIANTS

PERSONAL: Born February 11, 1960, at Key West, Fla. . . . 5-9/160. . . . Throws right, bats both. . . . Full name: John Allen Patterson.
HIGH SCHOOL: Trevor G. Browne (Phoenix).
COLLEGE: Central Arizona and Grand Canyon (Ariz.).
TRANSACTIONS/CAREER NOTES: Selected by San Diego Padres organization in third round of free-agent draft (January 14, 1986). . . . Selected by San Francisco Giants organization in 23rd round of free-agent draft (June 1, 1988).

Year Team (League)	Pos.	G	AB	R	H	2B	3B	HR	RBI	Avg.	SB	PO	A	E	Avg.
1988 —Everett (Northwest)	2B-SS	58	232	37	58	10	4	0	26	.250	21	89	97	9	.954
1989 —...							Did not play								
1990 —San Jose (California)	2B	131	530	91	160	23	6	4	66	.302	29	247	322	26	.956
1991 —Shreveport (Texas)	2B	117	464	81	137	31	13	4	56	.295	41	242	299	15	.973

PATTERSON, KEN
P, WHITE SOX

PERSONAL: Born July 8, 1964, at Costa Mesa, Calif. . . . 6-4/210. . . . Throws left, bats left. . . . Full name: Kenneth Brian Patterson.
COLLEGE: McLennan Community College (Tex.) and Baylor.
TRANSACTIONS/CAREER NOTES: Selected by Philadelphia Phillies organization in 29th round of free-agent draft (June 7, 1982). . . . Selected by Baltimore Orioles organization in secondary phase of free-agent draft (January 11, 1983). . . . Selected by Phillies organization in secondary phase of free-agent draft (June 6, 1983). . . . Selected by New York Yankees organization in third round of free-agent draft (June 3, 1985). . . . Traded by Yankees organization with a player to be named later to Chicago White Sox for IF-OF Jerry Royster and IF Mike Soper (August 26, 1987); White Sox acquired P Jeff Pries to complete deal (September 19, 1987).
STATISTICAL NOTES: Led New York-Pennsylvania League with four shutouts in 1986.

Year Team (League)	G	W	L	Pct.	ERA	Sv.	IP	H	R	ER	BB	SO
1985 —Oneonta (New York-Penn)	6	2	2	.500	4.84	0	22 1/3	23	14	12	14	21
1986 —Fort Lauderdale (Florida St.)	5	0	2	.000	7.71	0	18 2/3	30	20	16	16	13
—Oneonta (New York-Penn)	15	9	3	.750	*1.35	0	100 1/3	67	25	15	45	102
1987 —Fort Lauderdale (Florida St.)	9	1	3	.250	6.33	0	42 2/3	46	34	30	31	36
—Albany (Eastern)	24	3	6	.333	3.96	5	63 2/3	59	31	28	31	47
—Hawaii (Pacific Coast)■	3	0	0	...	0.00	2	3 1/3	1	0	0	3	5
1988 —Vancouver (Pacific Coast)	55	6	5	.545	3.23	12	86 1/3	64	37	31	36	89
—Chicago (A.L.)	9	0	2	.000	4.79	1	20 2/3	25	11	11	7	8
1989 —Vancouver (Pacific Coast)	2	0	1	.000	1.00	0	9	6	2	1	1	17
—Chicago (A.L.)	50	6	1	.857	4.52	0	65 2/3	64	37	33	28	43
1990 —Chicago (A.L.)	43	2	1	.667	3.39	2	66 1/3	58	27	25	34	40
1991 —Chicago (A.L.)	43	3	0	1.000	2.83	1	63 2/3	48	22	20	35	32
Major league totals (4 years)	145	11	4	.733	3.70	4	216 1/3	195	97	89	104	123

PAULINO, ELVIN
1B, CUBS

PERSONAL: Born November 6, 1967, at Moca, Dominican Republic. . . . 6-1/190. . . . Throws right, bats left. . . . Full name: Luis Ernesto Paulino.
TRANSACTIONS/CAREER NOTES: Signed as free agent by Chicago Cubs organization (April 25, 1986).
STATISTICAL NOTES: Led Midwest League first basemen with 102 double plays in 1989. . . . Led Southern League first basemen with 1,201 total chances and 105 double plays in 1991.

Year Team (League)	Pos.	G	AB	R	H	2B	3B	HR	RBI	Avg.	SB	PO	A	E	Avg.
1987 —Peoria (Midwest)	1B	49	117	22	24	2	0	1	13	.205	1	280	21	5	.984
—Wytheville (Appal.)	OF-1B	55	185	42	58	11	2	8	40	.314	4	190	20	12	.946
1988 —Peoria (Midwest)	1B	122	404	44	94	19	5	2	40	.233	3	1016	77	16	.986
1989 —Peoria (Midwest)	1B	119	414	57	122	29	2	8	72	.295	5	1073	*97	18	.985
1990 —Winston-Salem (Caro.)	1B	109	409	69	107	23	2	14	63	.262	5	885	77	17	.983
1991 —Charlotte (Southern)	1B	132	460	67	118	27	1	*24	*81	.257	8	*1105	*83	13	.989

PAVLAS, DAVE
P

PERSONAL: Born August 12, 1962, at Frankfurt, West Germany. . . . 6-7/195. . . . Throws right, bats right. . . . Full name: David Lee Pavlas.
HIGH SCHOOL: Shiner (Tex.).
COLLEGE: Rice.
TRANSACTIONS/CAREER NOTES: Signed as free agent by Chicago Cubs organization (December 15, 1984). . . . Traded by Cubs organization to Texas Rangers organization (June 6, 1987), completing deal in which Rangers traded P Mike Mason to Cubs for a player to be named later (May 15, 1987). . . . Sold by Rangers organization to Cubs organization (January 3, 1990). . . . Released by Cubs (September 5, 1991).

RECORDS/HONORS: Named Carolina League Pitcher of the Year (1986).
STATISTICAL NOTES: Led American Association with 10 hit batsmen in 1990.

Year	Team (League)	G	W	L	Pct.	ERA	Sv.	IP	H	R	ER	BB	SO
1985	—Peoria (Midwest)	17	8	3	.727	2.62	1	110	90	40	32	32	86
1986	—Winston-Salem (Carolina)	28	14	6	.700	3.84	0	173⅓	172	91	74	57	143
1987	—Pittsfield (Eastern)	7	6	1	.857	3.80	0	45	49	25	19	17	27
	—Tulsa (Texas)■	13	1	6	.143	7.69	0	59⅔	79	51	51	27	46
1988	—Tulsa (Texas)	26	5	2	.714	1.98	2	77⅓	52	26	17	18	69
	—Oklahoma City (Am. Assoc.)	13	3	1	.750	4.47	0	52⅓	59	29	26	28	40
1989	—Oklahoma City (Am. Assoc.)	29	2	*14	.125	4.70	0	143⅔	175	89	75	67	94
1990	—Iowa (American Association)■	53	8	3	.727	3.26	8	99⅓	84	38	36	48	96
	—Chicago (N.L.)	13	2	0	1.000	2.11	0	21⅓	23	7	5	6	12
1991	—Iowa (American Association)	61	5	6	.455	3.98	7	97⅓	92	49	43	43	54
	—Chicago (N.L.)	1	0	0	...	18.00	0	1	3	2	2	0	0
	Major league totals (2 years)	14	2	0	1.000	2.82	0	22⅓	26	9	7	6	12

PAVLIK, ROGER
P, RANGERS

PERSONAL: Born October 4, 1967, at Houston. . . . 6-2/220. . . . Throws right, bats right. . . . Full name: Roger Allen Pavlik.
HIGH SCHOOL: Aldine (Houston).
TRANSACTIONS/CAREER NOTES: Selected by Texas Rangers organization in second round of free-agent draft (June 2, 1986). . . . On disabled list (June 21, 1986-remainder of season; June 4-August 6, 1987; and April 29-May 6 and May 23-July 29, 1991).
STATISTICAL NOTES: Pitched 5⅓ innings, combining with Steve Peters for nine no-hit innings in a 1-0 loss to Indianapolis Indians (April 17, 1991).

Year	Team (League)	G	W	L	Pct.	ERA	Sv.	IP	H	R	ER	BB	SO
1986	—							Did not play					
1987	—Gastonia (South Atlantic)	15	2	7	.222	4.95	0	67⅓	66	46	37	42	55
1988	—Gastonia (South Atlantic)	18	2	12	.143	4.59	0	84⅓	94	65	43	58	89
	—Butte (Pioneer)	8	4	0	1.000	4.59	0	49	45	29	25	34	56
1989	—Port Charlotte (Florida State)	26	3	8	.273	3.41	1	118⅔	92	60	45	72	98
1990	—Charlotte (Florida State)	11	5	3	.625	2.44	0	66⅓	50	21	18	40	76
	—Tulsa (Texas)	16	6	5	.545	2.33	0	100⅓	66	29	26	71	91
1991	—Oklahoma City (Am. Assoc.)	8	0	5	.000	5.19	0	26	19	21	15	26	43

PECOTA, BILL
IF, METS

PERSONAL: Born February 16, 1960, at Redwood City, Calif. . . . 6-2/190. . . . Throws right, bats right. . . . Full name: William Joseph Pecota.
HIGH SCHOOL: Peterson (Sunnyvale, Calif.).
COLLEGE: De Anza College (Calif.).
TRANSACTIONS/CAREER NOTES: Selected by Kansas City Royals organization in 10th round of free-agent draft (January 13, 1981). . . . Traded by Royals with P Bret Saberhagen to New York Mets for OF Kevin McReynolds, IF Gregg Jefferies and 2B Keith Miller (December 11, 1991).
STATISTICAL NOTES: Led Southern League third basemen with 434 total chances in 1984. . . . Led American Association third basemen with .962 fielding percentage, 111 putouts, 247 assists, 372 total chances and 22 double plays in 1985. . . . Led American Association third basemen with 217 assists and 337 total chances in 1986.

Year	Team (League)	Pos.	G	AB	R	H	2B	3B	HR	RBI	Avg.	SB	PO	A	E	Avg.
1981	—Sara. Royals-Blue (GCL)	C-3B-2B	61	208	*61	66	11	4	3	22	.317	14	112	45	6	.963
1982	—Fort Myers (Florida St.)	3B	135	482	71	115	16	6	4	49	.239	39	109	243	15	.959
1983	—Fort Myers (Florida St.)	3B	65	234	48	63	7	2	5	33	.269	28	46	114	7	.958
	—Jacksonville (Southern)	3B-SS	72	260	38	63	9	1	5	25	.242	9	54	135	19	.909
1984	—Memphis (Southern)	3B	145	543	84	131	19	2	9	50	.241	43	*142	267	25	*.942
1985	—Omaha (Am. Assoc.)	3B-SS-OF	130	409	47	98	17	3	1	34	.240	21	†111	†247	14	†.962
1986	—Omaha (Am. Assoc.)	3B-SS-OF	139	474	48	125	26	2	4	54	.264	20	125	†238	11	.971
	—Kansas City (A.L.)	3B-SS	12	29	3	6	2	0	0	2	.207	0	7	31	1	.974
1987	—Omaha (Am. Assoc.)	3B-SS-2B	35	126	31	39	8	1	2	16	.310	7	38	78	8	.935
	—Kansas City (A.L.)	SS-3B-2B	66	156	22	43	5	1	3	14	.276	5	67	135	6	.971
1988	—Kansas City (A.L.)	IF-OF-C	90	178	25	37	3	3	1	15	.208	7	98	145	6	.976
1989	—Kansas City (A.L.)	S-O-2-3-1	65	83	21	17	4	2	3	5	.205	5	50	79	2	.985
	—Omaha (Am. Assoc.)	S-3-2-0	64	248	34	63	12	1	3	40	.254	10	96	206	8	.974
1990	—Kansas City (A.L.)	2-S-3-0-1	87	240	43	58	15	2	5	20	.242	8	160	195	5	.986
	—Omaha (Am. Assoc.)	3B-2B-SS	29	116	30	35	6	0	4	13	.302	11	32	80	1	.991
1991	—Kansas City (A.L.)	IF-OF-P	125	398	53	114	23	2	6	45	.286	16	163	206	4	.989
	Major league totals (6 years)		445	1084	167	275	52	10	18	101	.254	41	545	791	24	.982

RECORD AS PITCHER

Year	Team (League)	G	W	L	Pct.	ERA	Sv.	IP	H	R	ER	BB	SO
1991	—Kansas City (A.L.)	1	0	0	...	4.50	0	2	4	1	1	0	0

PEDRE, GEORGE
C, CUBS

PERSONAL: Born October 12, 1966, at Culver City, Calif. . . . 5-11/210. . . . Throws right, bats right. . . . Full name: Jorge Enrique Pedre.
HIGH SCHOOL: Culver City (Calif.).
COLLEGE: West Los Angeles College and Los Angeles Harbor Junior College.

TRANSACTIONS/CAREER NOTES: Selected by Atlanta Braves organization in 11th round of free-agent draft (January 14, 1986)...
... Selected by Kansas City Royals organization in 33rd round of free-agent draft (June 2, 1987).... On Memphis disabled list (June 23-July 1 and July 5-30, 1989; and May 30-June 7 and June 29 to July 7, 1990).... Claimed on waivers by Chicago Cubs (December 2, 1991).
STATISTICAL NOTES: Led Midwest League with 27 passed balls in 1988.

Year Team (League)	Pos.	G	AB	R	H	2B	3B	HR	RBI	Avg.	SB	PO	A	E	Avg.
1987—Eugene (Northwest)	C-1B	64	233	28	63	15	0	13	66	.270	2	300	28	6	.982
1988—Appleton (Midwest)	C-1B	111	412	44	112	20	2	6	54	.272	4	561	85	15	.977
1989—Baseball City (Fla. St.)	C-1B	55	208	39	68	17	2	5	40	.327	1	183	25	7	.967
—Memphis (Southern)	C-1B	38	141	17	33	5	0	2	16	.234	0	145	10	3	.981
1990—Memphis (Southern)	C-1B	99	360	55	93	14	1	9	54	.258	6	301	43	14	.961
1991—Memphis (Southern)	C-1B-3B	100	363	43	92	28	1	9	59	.253	1	415	61	8	.983
—Omaha (Am. Assoc.)	C-1B	31	116	12	25	4	0	1	4	.216	2	195	20	4	.982
—Kansas City (A.L.)	C-1B	10	19	2	5	1	1	0	3	.263	0	35	4	1	.975
Major league totals (1 year)		10	19	2	5	1	1	0	3	.263	0	35	4	1	.975

PEGUERO, JULIO
OF, PHILLIES

PERSONAL: Born September 7, 1968, at San Isidro, Dominican Republic.... 6-0/160.... Throws right, bats both.... Full name: Julio Cesar Peguero.... Name pronounced peh-GAIR-oh.
HIGH SCHOOL: Nuestra Senora del Perfecto Socorro (San Isidro, Dominican Republic).
TRANSACTIONS/CAREER NOTES: Signed as free agent by Pittsburgh Pirates organization (July 30, 1986).... On disabled list (July 9, 1989-remainder of season).... Traded by Pirates organization with OF Wes Chamberlain and a player to be named later to Philadelphia Phillies organization for 1B-OF Carmelo Martinez (August 30, 1990); Phillies acquired OF Tony Longmire to complete deal (September 28, 1990).
STATISTICAL NOTES: Led International League outfielders with 333 total chances in 1991.

Year Team (League)	Pos.	G	AB	R	H	2B	3B	HR	RBI	Avg.	SB	PO	A	E	Avg.
1987—Macon (South Atlantic)	OF-2B	132	520	88	148	11	6	4	53	.285	23	251	19	17	.941
1988—Salem (Carolina)	OF-2B	128	517	89	135	17	5	5	50	.261	43	291	15	8	.975
1989—Harrisburg (Eastern)	OF	76	284	34	70	14	1	2	21	.246	14	163	6	2	.988
1990—Harris.-Reading (East.)■.	OF	107	423	40	117	14	★9	1	28	.277	8	239	4	4	.984
1991—Scranton/W.B. (Int'l)	OF	133	506	71	138	20	9	2	39	.273	21	★317	12	4	.988

PEGUES, STEVE
OF, TIGERS

PERSONAL: Born May 21, 1968, at Pontotoc, Miss.... 6-2/172.... Throws right, bats right. ... Full name: Steven Antone Pegues.... Name pronounced peh-GEEZE.
HIGH SCHOOL: Pontotoc (Miss.).
TRANSACTIONS/CAREER NOTES: Selected by Detroit Tigers organization in first round (21st pick overall) of free-agent draft (June 2, 1987).

Year Team (League)	Pos.	G	AB	R	H	2B	3B	HR	RBI	Avg.	SB	PO	A	E	Avg.
1987—Bristol (Appalachian)	OF	59	236	36	67	6	5	2	23	.284	22	114	4	10	.922
1988—Fayetteville (S. Atl.)	OF	118	437	50	112	7	5	6	46	.256	21	240	13	12	.955
1989—Fayetteville (S. Atl.)	OF	70	269	35	83	11	6	1	38	.309	16	127	8	2	.985
—Lakeland (Florida State)	OF	55	193	24	49	7	2	0	15	.254	12	115	3	2	.983
1990—London (Eastern)	OF	126	483	48	131	22	5	8	63	.271	17	244	7	★9	.965
1991—London (Eastern)	OF	56	216	24	65	3	2	6	26	.301	4	69	4	1	.986
—Toledo (International)	OF	68	222	21	50	13	3	4	23	.225	8	84	7	4	.958

PELTIER, DAN
OF, RANGERS

PERSONAL: Born June 30, 1968, at Clifton Park, N.Y.... 6-1/200.... Throws left, bats left.... Full name: Daniel Edward Peltier.
HIGH SCHOOL: Shenedowa (Clifton Park, N.Y.).
COLLEGE: Notre Dame (degree in business administration).
TRANSACTIONS/CAREER NOTES: Selected by Texas Rangers organization in third round of free-agent draft (June 5, 1989).... On disabled list (July 29, 1989-remainder of season and June 24-August 2, 1991).

Year Team (League)	Pos.	G	AB	R	H	2B	3B	HR	RBI	Avg.	SB	PO	A	E	Avg.
1989—Butte (Pioneer)	OF	33	122	35	49	7	1	7	28	.402	10	28	4	2	.941
1990—Tulsa (Texas)	OF	117	448	66	125	20	4	11	57	.279	10	173	9	8	.958
1991—Oklahoma City (A.A.)	OF	94	345	38	79	16	4	3	32	.229	6	161	7	6	.966

PEMBERTON, RUDY
OF, TIGERS

PERSONAL: Born December 17, 1969, at San Pedro de Macoris, Dominican Republic. ... 6-1/185.... Throws right, bats right.
TRANSACTIONS/CAREER NOTES: Signed as free agent by Detroit Tigers organization (June 7, 1987).... Played in Dominican Republic Summer League (1987-88).

Year	Team (League)	Pos.	G	AB	R	H	2B	3B	HR	RBI	Avg.	SB	PO	A	E	Avg.
1987 —						Dominican Republic Summer League										
1988 —Bristol (Appalachian)		OF	6	5	2	0	0	0	0	0	.000	0	0	0	0	...
1989 —Bristol (Appalachian)		OF	56	214	40	58	9	2	6	39	.271	19	84	4	5	.946
1990 —Fayetteville (S. Atl.)		OF	127	454	59	126	14	5	6	61	.278	12	192	12	10	.953
1991 —Lakeland (Florida State)...		OF	111	375	40	86	15	2	3	36	.229	25	184	9	9	.955

PENA, ALEJANDRO
P, BRAVES

PERSONAL: Born June 25, 1959, at Cambiaso, Dominican Republic. . . . 6-1/203. . . . Throws right, bats right. . . . Full name: Alejandro Vasquez Pena.

TRANSACTIONS/CAREER NOTES: Signed as free agent by Los Angeles Dodgers organization (September 10, 1978). . . . On disabled list (April 8-September 5, 1985). . . . On Los Angeles disabled list (March 23-May 26, 1986; included rehabilitation disability assignment to Vero Beach (May 2-19, 1986). . . . On disabled list (July 27-August 17, 1987). . . . Granted free agency (November 4, 1988). . . . Re-signed by Dodgers (November 7, 1988). . . . On disabled list (July 8-23, 1989). . . . Traded by Dodgers with OF Mike Marshall to New York Mets for OF Juan Samuel (December 20, 1989). . . . Traded by Mets to Atlanta Braves for P Tony Castillo and a player to be named later (August 28, 1991); Mets acquired P Joe Roa to complete deal (August 29, 1991). . . . Granted free agency (November 1, 1991).

STATISTICAL NOTES: Tied for N.L. lead with four shutouts in 1984. . . . Pitched one-inning, combining with Kent Mercker and Mark Wohlers in 1-0 nine-inning no-hit victory against San Diego Padres (September 11, 1991).

Year	Team (League)	G	W	L	Pct.	ERA	Sv.	IP	H	R	ER	BB	SO
1979 —Clinton (Midwest)		21	3	3	.500	4.18	0	71	53	39	33	44	57
1980 —Vero Beach (Florida State)........		35	10	3	.769	3.21	8	73	57	32	26	41	46
1981 —Albuquerque (Pacific Coast)		38	2	5	.286	1.61	*22	56	36	12	10	21	40
—Los Angeles (N.L.)		14	1	1	.500	2.88	2	25	18	8	8	11	14
1982 —Los Angeles (N.L.)		29	0	2	.000	4.79	0	35⅔	37	24	19	21	20
—Albuquerque (Pacific Coast)		16	1	1	.500	5.34	5	28⅔	37	18	17	10	27
1983 —Los Angeles (N.L.)		34	12	9	.571	2.75	1	177	152	67	54	51	120
1984 —Los Angeles (N.L.)		28	12	6	.667	*2.48	0	199⅓	186	67	55	46	135
1985 —Los Angeles (N.L.)		2	0	1	.000	8.31	0	4⅓	7	5	4	3	2
1986 —Vero Beach (Florida State)		4	0	2	.000	7.47	0	15⅔	22	15	13	4	11
—Los Angeles (N.L.)		24	1	2	.333	4.89	1	70	74	40	38	30	46
1987 —Los Angeles (N.L.)		37	2	7	.222	3.50	11	87⅓	82	41	34	37	76
1988 —Los Angeles (N.L.)		60	6	7	.462	1.91	12	94⅓	75	29	20	27	83
1989 —Los Angeles (N.L.)		53	4	3	.571	2.13	5	76	62	20	18	18	75
1990 —New York (N.L.)■		52	3	3	.500	3.20	5	76	71	31	27	22	76
1991 —New York-Atlanta (N.L.)■		59	8	1	.889	2.40	15	82⅓	74	23	22	22	62
Major league totals (11 years)		392	49	42	.538	2.90	52	927⅓	838	355	299	288	709

CHAMPIONSHIP SERIES RECORD

CHAMPIONSHIP SERIES NOTES: Shares major league single-series record for most wild pitches—4 (1991). . . . Shares N.L. single series-record for most saves—3 (1991).

Year	Team (League)	G	W	L	Pct.	ERA	Sv.	IP	H	R	ER	BB	SO
1981 —Los Angeles (N.L.)		2	0	0	...	0.00	0	2⅓	1	0	0	0	0
1983 —Los Angeles (N.L.)		1	0	0	...	6.75	0	2⅔	4	2	2	1	3
1988 —Los Angeles (N.L.)		3	1	1	.500	4.15	1	4⅓	1	2	2	5	1
1991 —Atlanta (N.L.)		4	0	0	...	0.00	3	4⅓	1	0	0	0	4
Championship Series totals (4 years)		10	1	1	.500	2.63	4	13⅔	7	4	4	6	8

WORLD SERIES RECORD

Year	Team (League)	G	W	L	Pct.	ERA	Sv.	IP	H	R	ER	BB	SO
1981 —Los Angeles (N.L.)						Did not play							
1988 —Los Angeles (N.L.)		2	1	0	1.000	0.00	0	5	2	0	0	1	7
1991 —Atlanta (N.L.)		3	0	1	.000	3.38	0	5⅓	6	2	2	3	7
World Series totals (2 years)		5	1	1	.500	1.74	0	10⅓	8	2	2	4	14

PENA, GERONIMO
2B, CARDINALS

PERSONAL: Born March 29, 1967, at Distrito Nacional, Dominican Republic. . . . 6-1/195. . . . Throws right, bats left. . . . Full name: Geronimo Pena.

HIGH SCHOOL: Distrito Nacional (Dominican Republic).

TRANSACTIONS/CAREER NOTES: Signed as free agent by St. Louis Cardinals organization (August 9, 1984). . . . On St. Louis disabled list (March 25-June 5, 1989); included rehabilitation disability assignment to St. Petersburg (May 29-June 5, 1989).

STATISTICAL NOTES: Led Appalachian League with four intentional bases on balls received in 1986. . . . Led South Atlantic League second basemen with 324 putouts, 342 assists, 29 errors, 695 total chances and 80 double plays in 1987. . . . Led Florida State League second basemen with 723 total chances and 103 double plays in 1988. . . . Led American Association in being hit by pitch with 18 in 1990. . . . Led American Association third basemen with 20 errors in 1990.

MISCELLANEOUS: Batted righthanded only (1986-87).

Year	Team (League)	Pos.	G	AB	R	H	2B	3B	HR	RBI	Avg.	SB	PO	A	E	Avg.
1986 —Johnson City (Appal.)		2B	56	202	*55	60	7	4	3	20	.297	27	108	144	7	.973
1987 —Savannah (Southern)		2B-SS	134	505	95	136	28	3	9	51	.269	*80	†325	†343	†29	.958
1988 —St. Petersburg (Fla. St.)		2B	130	484	82	125	25	10	4	35	.258	35	*301	*402	20	*.972

Year	Team (League)	Pos.	G	AB	R	H	2B	3B	HR	RBI	Avg.	SB	PO	A	E	Avg.
1989	—St. Petersburg (Fla. St.)	2B	6	21	2	4	1	0	0	2	.190	2	9	19	1	.966
	—Arkansas (Texas)	2B	77	267	61	79	16	8	9	44	.296	14	177	208	14	.965
1990	—Louisville (Am. Assoc.)	2B-3B	118	390	65	97	24	6	6	35	.249	24	153	261	†27	.939
	—St. Louis (N.L.)	2B	18	45	5	11	2	0	0	2	.244	1	24	30	1	.982
1991	—St. Louis (N.L.)	2B-OF	104	185	38	45	8	3	5	17	.243	15	101	146	6	.976
	Major league totals (2 years)		122	230	43	56	10	3	5	19	.243	16	125	176	7	.977

PENA, TONY
C, RED SOX

PERSONAL: Born June 4, 1957, at Monte Cristi, Dominican Republic.... 6-0/185.... Throws right, bats right.... Full name: Antonio Francisco Padilla Pena.... Brother of Ramon Pena, pitcher, Detroit Tigers (1989).
HIGH SCHOOL: Liceo Marti (Monte Cristi, Dominican Republic).
TRANSACTIONS/CAREER NOTES: Signed as free agent by Pittsburgh Pirates organization (July 22, 1975).... Traded by Pirates to St. Louis Cardinals for OF Andy Van Slyke, C Mike LaValliere and P Mike Dunne (April 1, 1987).... On St. Louis disabled list (April 11-May 22, 1987); included rehabilitation disability assignment to Louisville (May 19-22, 1987).... Granted free agency (November 13, 1989).... Signed by Boston Red Sox (November 27, 1989).
RECORDS/HONORS: Named catcher on THE SPORTING NEWS N.L. All-Star team (1983).... Won N.L. Gold Glove at catcher (1983-85).... Won A.L. Gold Glove at catcher (1991).
STATISTICAL NOTES: Led Carolina League catchers with nine double plays and tied for lead with 16 passed balls in 1977..... Led Eastern League catchers with 14 double plays in 1979.... Led N.L. catchers with 1,075 total chances in 1983, 999 in 1984 and 1,034 in 1985.... Led N.L. catchers with 15 double plays in 1984 and 13 in 1989.... Led N.L. catchers with 100 assists in 1985. ... Led N.L. catchers with 18 errors in 1986.... Tied for N.L. lead in grounding into double plays with 21 in 1986.... Led N.L. catchers with .994 fielding percentage in 1988 and .997 in 1989.... Led A.L. catchers with 864 putouts and 943 total chances in 1990.... Led A.L. catchers with 929 total chances and 15 double plays in 1991.

Year	Team (League)	Pos.	G	AB	R	H	2B	3B	HR	RBI	Avg.	SB	PO	A	E	Avg.
1976	—Bradenton Pirates (GCL) ..	O-1-C-3	33	110	10	23	2	2	1	11	.209	5	108	14	4	.968
	—Charles., S.C. (W. Caro.) ...	C	14	49	4	11	2	0	1	8	.224	0	64	7	2	.973
1977	—Charles., S.C. (W. Caro.) ...	C	29	101	10	24	4	0	3	16	.238	2	172	19	6	.970
	—Salem (Carolina)	C	84	319	36	88	15	3	7	46	.276	3	*470	*66	*17	.969
1978	—Shreveport (Texas)	C	104	348	34	80	14	0	8	42	.230	3	637	54	*25	.965
1979	—Buffalo (Eastern)	C	134	515	89	161	16	4	34	97	.313	5	*768	*120	*26	.972
1980	—Portland (Pacific Coast) ..	C	124	452	57	148	24	13	9	77	.327	6	*639	85	*23	.969
	—Pittsburgh (N.L.)	C	8	21	1	9	1	1	0	1	.429	1	38	2	2	.952
1981	—Pittsburgh (N.L.)	C	66	210	16	63	9	1	2	17	.300	1	286	41	5	.985
1982	—Pittsburgh (N.L.)	C	138	497	53	147	28	4	11	63	.296	2	763	89	16	.982
1983	—Pittsburgh (N.L.)	C	151	542	51	163	22	3	15	70	.301	6	*976	90	9	.992
1984	—Pittsburgh (N.L.)	C	147	546	77	156	27	2	15	78	.286	12	*895	*95	9	.991
1985	—Pittsburgh (N.L.)	C-1B	147	546	53	136	27	2	10	59	.249	12	925	†102	12	.988
1986	—Pittsburgh (N.L.)	C-1B	144	510	56	147	26	2	10	52	.288	9	824	99	†18	.981
1987	—St. Louis (N.L.)■	C-1B-OF	116	384	40	82	13	4	5	44	.214	6	624	51	8	.988
	—Louisville (Am. Assoc.)	C	2	8	0	3	0	0	0	0	.375	0	7	1	0	1.000
1988	—St. Louis (N.L.)	C-1B	149	505	55	133	23	1	10	51	.263	6	796	72	6	†.993
1989	—St. Louis (N.L.)	C-OF	141	424	36	110	17	2	4	37	.259	5	675	70	2	†.997
1990	—Boston (A.L.)■	C-1B	143	491	62	129	19	1	7	56	.263	8	*866	74	5	.995
1991	—Boston (A.L.)	C	141	464	45	107	23	2	5	48	.231	8	*864	60	5	.995
	American League totals (2 years)		284	955	107	236	42	3	12	104	.247	16	1730	134	10	.995
	National League totals (10 years)		1207	4185	438	1146	193	22	82	472	.274	59	6802	711	87	.989
	Major league totals (12 years)		1491	5140	545	1382	235	25	94	576	.269	75	8532	845	97	.990

CHAMPIONSHIP SERIES RECORD

Year	Team (League)	Pos.	G	AB	R	H	2B	3B	HR	RBI	Avg.	SB	PO	A	E	Avg.
1987	—St. Louis (N.L.)	C	7	21	5	8	0	1	0	0	.381	1	55	5	0	1.000
1990	—Boston (A.L.)	C	4	14	0	3	0	0	0	0	.214	0	22	4	1	.963
	Championship Series totals (2 years)		11	35	5	11	0	1	0	0	.314	1	77	9	1	.989

WORLD SERIES RECORD

Year	Team (League)	Pos.	G	AB	R	H	2B	3B	HR	RBI	Avg.	SB	PO	A	E	Avg.
1987	—St. Louis (N.L.)	C-DH	7	22	2	9	1	0	0	4	.409	1	32	1	1	.971

ALL-STAR GAME RECORD

Year	League	Pos.	AB	R	H	2B	3B	HR	RBI	Avg.	SB	PO	A	E	Avg.
1982	—National	PR-C	1	0	0	0	0	0	0	.000	1	3	0	0	1.000
1984	—National	C	0	0	0	0	0	0	0	...	0	2	0	0	1.000
1985	—National	C	0	0	0	0	0	0	0	...	0	4	1	0	1.000
1986	—National	PR	0	0	0	0	0	0	0	...	0	0	0	0	...
1989	—National	PH-C	2	0	0	0	0	0	0	.000	0	2	1	0	1.000
	All-Star Game totals (5 years)		3	0	0	0	0	0	0	.000	1	11	1	0	1.000

PENDLETON, TERRY
3B, BRAVES

PERSONAL: Born July 16, 1960, at Los Angeles. . . . 5-9/195. . . . Throws right, bats left. . . . Full name: Terry Lee Pendleton.
HIGH SCHOOL: Channel Island (Oxnard, Calif.).
COLLEGE: Oxnard College (Calif.) and Fresno State.
TRANSACTIONS/CAREER NOTES: Selected by St. Louis Cardinals organization in seventh round of free-agent draft (June 7, 1982). . . . On disabled list (April 8-May 23 and July 16-September 5, 1983; June 15-30, 1985; May 28-June 24, 1988; and April 24-May 9, 1990). . . . Granted free agency (November 5, 1990). . . . Signed by Atlanta Braves (December 3, 1990).
RECORDS/HONORS: Won N.L. Gold Glove at third base (1987 and 1989). . . . Named N.L. Comeback Player of the Year by THE SPORTING NEWS (1991). . . . Named third baseman on THE SPORTING NEWS N.L. All-Star team (1991). . . . Named N.L. Most Valuable Player by Baseball Writers' Association of America (1991).
STATISTICAL NOTES: Led American Association third basemen with .964 fielding percentage and 88 putouts in 1984. . . . Led N.L. third basemen with 133 putouts and 371 assists in 1986. . . . Led N.L. third basemen 524 total chances in 1986, 512 in 1987, 520 in 1989 and 481 in 1991. . . . Led N.L. third basemen with 36 double plays in 1986 and 31 in 1991. . . . Tied for N.L. lead with 303 total bases in 1991.

Year Team (League)	Pos.	G	AB	R	H	2B	3B	HR	RBI	Avg.	SB	PO	A	E	Avg.
1982 —Johnson City (Appal.)	2B	43	181	38	58	14	•4	4	27	.320	13	79	105	17	.915
—St. Petersburg (Fla. St.)	2B	20	69	4	18	2	1	1	7	.261	1	41	51	2	.979
1983 —Arkansas (Texas)	2B	48	185	29	51	10	3	4	20	.276	7	94	135	7	.970
1984 —Louisville (Am. Assoc.)	3B-2B	91	330	52	98	23	5	4	44	.297	6	†91	157	10	†.961
—St. Louis (N.L.)	3B	67	262	37	85	16	3	1	33	.324	20	59	155	13	.943
1985 —St. Louis (N.L.)	3B	149	559	56	134	16	3	5	69	.240	17	129	361	18	.965
1986 —St. Louis (N.L.)	3B-OF	159	578	56	138	26	5	1	59	.239	24	†133	†371	20	.962
1987 —St. Louis (N.L.)	3B	159	583	82	167	29	4	12	96	.286	19	117	★369	26	.949
1988 —St. Louis (N.L.)	3B	110	391	44	99	20	2	6	53	.253	3	75	239	12	.963
1989 —St. Louis (N.L.)	3B	162	613	83	162	28	5	13	74	.264	9	113	★392	15	★.971
1990 —St. Louis (N.L.)	3B	121	447	46	103	20	2	6	58	.230	7	91	248	19	.947
1991 —Atlanta (N.L.)■	3B	153	586	94	★187	34	8	22	86	★.319	10	108	★349	24	.950
Major league totals (8 years)		1080	4019	498	1075	189	32	66	528	.267	109	825	2484	147	.957

CHAMPIONSHIP SERIES RECORD

CHAMPIONSHIP SERIES NOTES: Shares record for most at-bats in one inning—2 (October 13, 1985, second inning). . . . Shares N.L. single-series record for most at-bats—30 (1991).

Year Team (League)	Pos.	G	AB	R	H	2B	3B	HR	RBI	Avg.	SB	PO	A	E	Avg.
1985 —St. Louis (N.L.)	3B	6	24	2	5	1	0	0	4	.208	0	6	18	1	.960
1987 —St. Louis (N.L.)	3B	6	19	3	4	0	1	0	1	.211	0	3	11	0	1.000
1991 —Atlanta (N.L.)	3B	7	30	1	5	1	1	0	1	.167	0	5	11	0	1.000
Championship Series totals (3 years)		19	73	6	14	2	2	0	6	.192	0	14	40	1	.982

WORLD SERIES RECORD

Year Team (League)	Pos.	G	AB	R	H	2B	3B	HR	RBI	Avg.	SB	PO	A	E	Avg.
1985 —St. Louis (N.L.)	3B	7	23	3	6	1	1	0	3	.261	0	6	14	1	.952
1987 —St. Louis (N.L.)	DH-PH	3	7	2	3	0	0	0	1	.429	2	0	0	0	. . .
1991 —Atlanta (N.L.)	3B	7	30	6	11	3	0	2	3	.367	0	3	20	2	.920
World Series totals (3 years)		17	60	11	20	4	1	2	7	.333	2	9	34	3	.935

PENNINGTON, BRAD
P, ORIOLES

PERSONAL: Born April 14, 1969, at Salem, Ind. . . . 6-5/205. . . . Throws left, bats left. . . . Full name: Brad Lee Pennington.
HIGH SCHOOL: Eastern (Pekin, Ind.).
COLLEGE: Bellarmine College (Ky.) and Vincennes University (Ind.).
TRANSACTIONS/CAREER NOTES: Selected by Baltimore Orioles organization in 12th round of free-agent draft (June 5, 1989).
STATISTICAL NOTES: Tied for Appalachian League lead with 14 wild pitches in 1989.

Year Team (League)	G	W	L	Pct.	ERA	Sv.	IP	H	R	ER	BB	SO
1989 —Bluefield (Appalachian)	15	2	•7	.222	6.58	0	64⅓	50	58	47	★74	81
1990 —Wausau (Midwest)	32	4	9	.308	5.18	0	106	81	89	61	121	142
1991 —Frederick (Carolina)	36	1	4	.200	3.92	13	43⅔	32	23	19	44	58
—Kane County (Midwest)	23	0	2	.000	5.87	4	23	16	17	15	25	43

PEREZ, MELIDO
P, YANKEES

PERSONAL: Born February 15, 1966, at San Cristobal, Dominican Republic. . . . 6-4/180. . . . Throws right, bats right. . . . Full name: Melido T. Perez. . . . Brother of Pascual Perez, pitcher, New York Yankees; brother of Vladimir Perez, pitcher, San Francisco Giants organization; brother of Dario Perez, pitcher, Kansas City Royals organization; brother of Carlos Perez, pitcher, Montreal Expos organization; and brother of Valerio Perez, minor league pitcher (1983-84).
HIGH SCHOOL: San Gregorio de Nigua (San Cristobal, Dominican Republic).
TRANSACTIONS/CAREER NOTES: Signed as free agent by Kansas City Royals organization (July 22, 1983). . . . Traded by Royals with P John Davis, P Chuck Mount and P Greg Hibbard to Chicago White Sox for P Floyd Bannister and IF Dave Cochrane (December 10, 1987). . . . Traded by White Sox with P Robert Wickman and P Domingo Jean to New York Yankees for 2B Steve Sax (January 10, 1992).
STATISTICAL NOTES: Tied for Northwest League lead in games started by pitcher with 15, balks with two and home runs allowed

with 13 in 1985.... Led Midwest League with 13 complete games in 1986.... Pitched six-inning, 8-0 no-hit victory against New York Yankees (July 12, 1990).

Year	Team (League)	G	W	L	Pct.	ERA	Sv.	IP	H	R	ER	BB	SO
1984 —Charleston, S.C. (S. Atlantic)		16	5	7	.417	4.35	0	89	99	52	43	19	55
1985 —Eugene (Northwest)		17	6	7	.462	5.44	0	101	116	65	★61	35	88
1986 —Burlington (Midwest)		28	10	12	.455	3.70	0	170⅓	148	83	70	49	153
1987 —Fort Myers (Florida State)		8	4	3	.571	2.38	0	64⅓	51	20	17	7	51
—Memphis (Southern)		20	8	5	.615	3.43	0	133⅔	125	60	51	20	126
—Kansas City (A.L.)		3	1	1	.500	7.84	0	10⅓	18	12	9	5	5
1988 —Chicago (A.L.)■		32	12	10	.545	3.79	0	197	186	105	83	72	138
1989 —Chicago (A.L.)		31	11	14	.440	5.01	0	183⅓	187	106	102	90	141
1990 —Chicago (A.L.)		35	13	14	.481	4.61	0	197	177	111	101	86	161
1991 —Chicago (A.L.)		49	8	7	.533	3.12	1	135⅔	111	49	47	52	128
Major league totals (5 years)		150	45	46	.495	4.26	1	723⅓	679	383	342	305	573

PEREZ, MIKE
P, CARDINALS

PERSONAL: Born October 19, 1964, at Yauco, Puerto Rico.... 6-0/185.... Throws right, bats right. ... Full name: Michael Irvin Perez.
HIGH SCHOOL: Yauco (Puerto Rico).
COLLEGE: San Jose City College (Calif.) and Troy State (Ala.).
TRANSACTIONS/CAREER NOTES: Selected by St. Louis Cardinals organization in 12th round of free-agent draft (June 2, 1986).

Year	Team (League)	G	W	L	Pct.	ERA	Sv.	IP	H	R	ER	BB	SO
1986 —Johnson City (Appalachian).....		18	3	5	.375	2.97	3	72⅔	69	35	24	22	72
1987 —Springfield (Midwest)		58	6	2	.750	0.85	★41	84⅓	47	12	8	21	119
1988 —Arkansas (Texas)		11	1	3	.250	11.30	0	14⅓	18	18	18	13	17
—St. Petersburg (Florida State) ..		35	2	2	.500	2.08	17	43⅓	24	12	10	16	45
1989 —Arkansas (Texas)		57	4	6	.400	3.64	★33	76⅔	68	34	31	32	74
1990 —Louisville (American Assoc.) ...		★57	7	7	.500	4.28	★31	67⅓	64	34	32	33	69
—St. Louis (N.L.)		13	1	0	1.000	3.95	1	13⅔	12	6	6	3	5
1991 —St. Louis (N.L.)		14	0	2	.000	5.82	0	17	19	11	11	7	7
—Louisville (American Assoc.) ...		37	3	5	.375	6.13	4	47	54	38	32	25	39
Major league totals (2 years)		27	1	2	.333	4.99	1	30⅔	31	17	17	10	12

PEREZ, PASCUAL
P, YANKEES

PERSONAL: Born May 17, 1957, at San Cristobal, Dominican Republic.... 6-3/184.... Throws right, bats right.... Full name: Pascual Gross Perez.... Brother of Melido Perez, pitcher, New York Yankees; brother of Vladimir Perez, pitcher, San Francisco Giants organization; brother of Dario Perez, pitcher, Kansas City Royals organization; brother of Carlos Perez, pitcher, Montreal Expos organization; and brother of Valerio Perez, minor league pitcher (1983-84).
TRANSACTIONS/CAREER NOTES: Signed as free agent by Pittsburgh Pirates organization (January 27, 1976).... On suspended list (August 26-28, 1976).... On disabled list (July 16-August 14, 1979).... Traded by Pirates organization with a player to be named later to Atlanta Braves organization for P Larry McWilliams (June 30, 1982); Braves organization acquired SS Carlos Rios to complete deal (September 8, 1982).... On suspended list (April 3-May 1, 1984).... On disabled list (May 5-25, June 1-22 and August 13-September 3, 1985).... On suspended list (July 22, 1985); then transferred to restricted list (July 25-August 4, 1985).... Released by Braves (April 1, 1986).... Signed by Indianapolis, Montreal Expos organization (February 16, 1987).... On Montreal disabled list (May 8-June 21, 1988); included rehabilitation disability assignment to Indianapolis (June 13-21, 1988).... Granted free agency (November 13, 1989).... Signed by New York Yankees (November 21, 1989).... On New York disabled list (April 26, 1990-remainder of season); included rehabilitation disability assignment to Tampa (May 21-31, 1990) and Fort Lauderdale (June 5-10, 1990). Did not pitch while at Tampa.... On disabled list (March 30-May 14, 1991).... On New York disabled list (June 1-August 16, 1991); included rehabilitation disability assignment to Albany/Colonie (August 4-16, 1991).
RECORDS/HONORS: Named American Association Pitcher of the Year (1987).
STATISTICAL NOTES: Led Western Carolina League in balks with 6 in 1977.... Tied for Carolina League lead with five shutouts in 1978.... Tied for American Association lead with two shutouts in 1987.... Pitched five-inning, 1-0 no-hit victory against Philadelphia Phillies (September 24, 1988).... Tied for N.L. lead with 10 balks in 1988.

Year	Team (League)	G	W	L	Pct.	ERA	Sv.	IP	H	R	ER	BB	SO
1976 —Bradenton Pirates (GCL)		10	2	5	.286	4.66	0	56	51	41	29	35	34
1977 —Charleston, S.C. (W. Caro.).......		25	10	5	.667	3.98	0	156	153	80	69	60	96
1978 —Salem (Carolina)		24	11	7	.611	2.61	0	152	133	70	44	51	126
—Columbus (International)		1	0	0	. . .	0.00	0	5	4	0	0	1	4
1979 —Portland (Pacific Coast)		20	9	7	.563	5.50	0	103	121	70	63	47	51
1980 —Portland (Pacific Coast)		24	12	10	.545	4.05	0	160	172	76	72	48	105
—Pittsburgh (N.L.)		2	0	1	.000	3.75	0	12	15	6	5	2	7
1981 —Portland (Pacific Coast)		5	1	2	.333	4.94	0	31	40	19	17	14	11
—Pittsburgh (N.L.)		17	2	7	.222	3.98	0	86	92	50	38	34	46
1982 —Portland (Pacific Coast)		19	4	9	.308	4.82	0	106⅓	111	59	57	37	59
—Richmond (International)■		5	5	0	1.000	1.26	0	43	32	7	6	8	27
—Atlanta (N.L.)		16	4	4	.500	3.06	0	79⅓	85	35	27	17	29
1983 —Atlanta (N.L.)		33	15	8	.652	3.43	0	215⅓	213	88	82	51	144
1984 —Atlanta (N.L.)		30	14	8	.636	3.74	0	211⅔	208	96	88	51	145
1985 —Atlanta (N.L.)		22	1	13	.071	6.14	0	95⅓	115	72	65	57	57
1986 —													

Out of Organized Baseball

— 376 —

Year	Team (League)	G	W	L	Pct.	ERA	Sv.	IP	H	R	ER	BB	SO
1987	—Indianapolis (Am. Assoc.)■	19	9	7	.563	★3.79	0	133	128	65	56	34	125
	—Montreal (N.L.)	10	7	0	1.000	2.30	0	70⅓	52	21	18	16	58
1988	—Montreal (N.L.)	27	12	8	.600	2.44	0	188	133	59	51	44	131
	—Indianapolis (Am. Assoc.)	2	0	0	. . .	1.17	0	7⅔	4	1	1	4	7
1989	—Montreal (N.L.)	33	9	13	.409	3.31	0	198⅓	178	85	73	45	152
1990	—New York (A.L.)■	3	1	2	.333	1.29	0	14	8	3	2	3	12
	—Fort Lauderdale (Florida St.)	1	0	0	. . .	6.00	0	3	3	2	2	1	1
1991	—New York (A.L.)	14	2	4	.333	3.18	0	73⅔	68	26	26	24	41
	—Albany/Colonie (Eastern)	2	0	0	. . .	1.69	0	5⅓	5	1	1	1	6
American League totals (2 years)		17	3	6	.333	2.87	0	87⅔	76	29	28	27	53
National League totals (9 years)		190	64	62	.508	3.48	0	1156⅓	1091	512	447	317	769
Major league totals (11 years)		207	67	68	.496	3.44	0	1244	1167	541	475	344	822

CHAMPIONSHIP SERIES RECORD

Year	Team (League)	G	W	L	Pct.	ERA	Sv.	IP	H	R	ER	BB	SO
1982	—Atlanta (N.L.)	2	0	1	.000	5.19	0	8⅔	10	5	5	2	4

ALL-STAR GAME RECORD

Year	League	W	L	Pct.	ERA	Sv.	IP	H	R	ER	BB	SO
1983	—National	0	0	. . .	27.00	0	⅔	3	2	2	1	1

PEREZ, ROBERT
OF, BLUE JAYS

PERSONAL: Born June 4, 1969, at Bolivar, Venezuela. . . . 6-3/195. . . . Throws right, bats right. . . . Full name: Robert Alexander Jiminez Perez.
HIGH SCHOOL: Raul Leoni Otero (Bolivar, Venezuela).
TRANSACTIONS/CAREER NOTES: Signed as free agent by Toronto Blue Jay organization (May 1, 1989).

Year	Team (League)	Pos.	G	AB	R	H	2B	3B	HR	RBI	Avg.	SB	PO	A	E	Avg.
1990	—St. Catharines (NYP).........	OF	52	207	21	54	10	2	5	25	.261	7	80	5	1	.988
	—Myrtle Beach (S. Atl.)........	OF	21	72	8	21	2	0	1	10	.292	2	40	1	1	.976
1991	—Dunedin (Florida State)	OF	127	480	50	145	28	6	4	50	.302	8	160	10	5	.971
	—Syracuse (International) ..	OF	4	20	2	4	1	0	0	1	.200	0	5	0	1	.833

PEREZ, YORKIS
P

PERSONAL: Born September 30, 1967, at Bajos de Haina, Dominican Republic. . . . 6-0/180. . . . Throws left, bats left. . . . Full name: Yorkis Miguel Perez.
TRANSACTIONS/CAREER NOTES: Signed as free agent by Minnesota Twins organization (February 23, 1983). . . . Traded by Twins organization with P Neal Heaton, P Al Cardwood and C Jeff Reed to Montreal Expos for P Jeff Reardon and C Tom Nieto (February 3, 1987). . . . Granted free agecny (October 15, 1990). . . . Signed by Atlanta Braves organization (January, 1991). . . . Traded by Braves with P Turk Wendell to Chicago Cubs for P Mike Bielecki and C Damon Berryhill (September 29, 1991). . . . Released by Cubs (December 11, 1991). . . . Signed to play in Japan for 1992.

Year	Team (League)	G	W	L	Pct.	ERA	Sv.	IP	H	R	ER	BB	SO
1983	—Elizabethton (Appalachian)	3	0	1	.000	20.25	0	4	5	9	9	9	6
1984	—Elizabethton (Appalachian)	1	0	0	. . .	0.00	0	1⅓	1	0	0	1	1
1985	—Santiago (Dominican Repub.) ..	21	6	8	.429	3.17	1	122	104	58	43	63	69
1986	—Kenosha (Midwest)	31	4	11	.267	5.15	0	131	120	81	75	88	144
1987	—West Palm Beach (Florida St.)■	15	6	2	.750	2.34	0	100	78	36	26	46	111
	—Jacksonville (Southern)	12	2	7	.222	4.05	1	60	61	34	27	30	60
1988	—Jacksonville (Southern)	27	8	12	.400	5.82	0	130	142	96	84	94	105
1989	—West Palm Beach (Florida St.) ..	18	7	6	.538	2.76	1	94⅔	62	34	29	54	85
	—Jacksonville (Southern)	20	4	3	.571	3.60	0	35	25	16	14	34	50
1990	—Jacksonville (Southern)	28	2	2	.500	6.00	1	42	36	34	28	34	39
	—Indianapolis (Am. Assoc.)	9	1	1	.500	2.31	0	11⅔	8	5	3	6	8
1991	—Richmond (International)■	36	•12	3	.800	3.79	1	107	99	47	45	53	102
	—Chicago (N.L.)■	3	1	0	1.000	2.08	0	4⅓	2	1	1	2	3
Major league totals (1 year)		3	1	0	1.000	2.08	0	4⅓	2	1	1	2	3

PEREZCHICA, TONY
IF, INDIANS

PERSONAL: Born April 20, 1966, at Mexicali, Mexico. . . . 5-11/165. . . . Throws right, bats right. . . . Full name: Antonio Llamas Perezchica.
HIGH SCHOOL: Palm Springs (Calif.).
TRANSACTIONS/CAREER NOTES: Selected by San Francisco Giants organization in third round of free-agent draft (June 4, 1984). . . . On Phoenix disabled list (April 21-May 5 and August 19-31, 1989). . . . Claimed on waivers by Cleveland Indians (August 6, 1991).
STATISTICAL NOTES: Led Midwest League shortstops with 599 total chances in 1985.

Year	Team (League)	Pos.	G	AB	R	H	2B	3B	HR	RBI	Avg.	SB	PO	A	E	Avg.
1984	—Everett (Northwest)	SS	33	119	10	23	6	1	0	10	.193	0	45	73	18	.868
1985	—Clinton (Midwest)	SS	127	452	54	109	21	•8	4	40	.241	23	★224	332	43	.928
1986	—Fresno (California)	SS-3B	126	452	65	126	30	8	9	54	.279	18	224	303	42	.926

Year	Team (League)	Pos.	G	AB	R	H	2B	3B	HR	RBI	Avg.	SB	PO	A	E	Avg.
1987—Shreveport (Texas)	SS-2B	89	332	44	106	24	1	11	47	.319	3	144	258	16	.962
1988—Phoenix (Pacific Coast)	2B-SS-OF	134	517	79	158	18	•10	9	64	.306	10	255	381	29	.956
—San Francisco (N.L.)	2B	7	8	1	1	0	0	0	1	.125	0	5	5	0	1.000
1989—Phoenix (Pacific Coast) ...	2B-SS	94	307	40	71	11	3	8	33	.231	5	155	224	8	.979
1990—San Francisco (N.L.)	2B-SS	4	3	1	1	0	0	0	0	.333	0	2	0	0	1.000
—Phoenix (Pacific Coast) ...	2B-SS-3B	105	392	55	105	22	6	9	49	.268	8	199	325	22	.960
1991—Phoenix (Pacific Coast)	3B-2B-SS	51	191	41	56	10	4	8	34	.293	1	71	125	15	.929
—San Francisco (N.L.)	SS-2B	23	48	2	11	4	1	0	3	.229	0	20	29	2	.961
—Cleveland (A.L.)■	SS-3B-2B	17	22	4	8	2	0	0	0	.364	0	3	11	0	1.000
American League totals (1 year)		17	22	4	8	2	0	0	0	.364	0	3	11	0	1.000
National League totals (3 years)		34	59	4	13	4	1	0	4	.220	0	27	34	2	.968
Major league totals (3 years)		51	81	8	21	6	1	0	4	.259	0	30	45	2	.974

PERRY, GERALD
1B, CARDINALS

PERSONAL: Born October 30, 1960, at Savannah, Ga. . . . 6-0/201. . . . Throws right, bats left. . . . Full name: Gerald June Perry. . . . Nephew of Dan Driessen, major league first baseman for five teams (1973-1987).
HIGH SCHOOL: H.E. McCracken (Buffton, N.C.).

TRANSACTIONS/CAREER NOTES: Selected by Atlanta Braves' organization in 11th round of free-agent draft (June 6, 1978). . . . On disabled list (June 19-July 4, 1988; June 6-21 and July 10, 1989-remainder of season). . . . Traded by Atlanta Braves with P Jim Lemasters to Kansas City Royals for P Charlie Leibrandt and P Rick Luecken (December 15, 1989). . . . Granted free agency (November 5, 1990). . . . Signed by St. Louis Cardinals (December 13, 1990).
STATISTICAL NOTES: Led Gulf Coast League first basemen with 46 double plays in 1978. . . . Led Carolina League first basemen with 109 double plays in 1980.

Year	Team (League)	Pos.	G	AB	R	H	2B	3B	HR	RBI	Avg.	SB	PO	A	E	Avg.
1978—Bradenton Braves (GCL) ...	1B	*55	191	32	51	*12	3	1	26	.267	7	*479	*37	6	*.989
1979—Greenwood (W. Caro.)	1B	109	400	69	133	17	4	9	71	*.333	35	881	59	19	.980
1980—Durham (Carolina)	1B	138	497	102	124	19	5	15	92	.249	37	*1296	93	16	.989
1981—Savannah (Southern)	1B	137	476	71	132	18	3	19	84	.277	22	1221	86	18	.986
1982—Richmond (Int'l)	1B	133	492	94	146	22	4	15	92	.297	39	1110	94	•17	.986
1983—Richmond (Int'l)	1B	113	423	81	133	21	8	13	71	.314	26	943	88	11	.989
—Atlanta (N.L.)	1B-OF	27	39	5	14	2	0	1	6	.359	0	55	0	1	.982
1984—Atlanta (N.L.)	1B-OF	122	347	52	92	12	2	7	47	.265	15	550	28	12	.980
1985—Atlanta (N.L.)	1B-OF	110	238	22	51	5	0	3	13	.214	9	541	37	9	.985
1986—Richmond (Int'l)	OF-1B	107	384	69	125	30	5	10	75	.326	11	394	25	7	.984
—Atlanta (N.L.)	OF-1B	29	70	6	19	2	0	2	11	.271	0	24	1	2	.926
1987—Atlanta (N.L.)	1B-OF	142	533	77	144	35	2	12	74	.270	42	1297	72	14	.990
1988—Atlanta (N.L.)	1B	141	547	61	164	29	1	8	74	.300	29	1282	106	•17	.988
1989—Atlanta (N.L.)	1B	72	266	24	67	11	0	4	21	.252	10	618	51	9	.987
1990—Kansas City (A.L.)■	1B	133	465	57	118	22	2	8	57	.254	17	394	40	6	.986
1991—St. Louis (N.L.)■	1B-OF	109	242	29	58	8	4	6	36	.240	15	413	29	5	.989
American League totals (1 year)		133	465	57	118	22	2	8	57	.254	17	394	40	6	.986
National League totals (8 years)		752	2282	276	609	104	9	43	282	.267	120	4780	324	69	.987
Major league totals (9 years)		885	2747	333	727	126	11	51	339	.265	137	5174	364	75	.987

PERSCHKE, GREG
P, WHITE SOX

PERSONAL: Born August 3, 1967, at LaPorte, Ind. . . . 6-3/180. . . . Throws right, bats right. . . . Full name: Gregory Lee Perschke.
COLLEGE: Southwestern Michigan Community College and New Orleans.
TRANSACTIONS/CAREER NOTES: Selected by Toronto Blue Jays organization in 32nd round of free-agent draft (June 2, 1987). . . . Selected by Atlanta Braves organization in 23rd round of free-agent draft (June 1, 1988). . . . Selected by Chicago White Sox organization in 24th round of free-agent draft (June 5, 1989).

Year	Team (League)	G	W	L	Pct.	ERA	Sv.	IP	H	R	ER	BB	SO
1989—Utica (New York-Penn)	14	0	0	...	1.59	9	17	5	3	3	4	20
—South Bend (Midwest)	13	0	2	.000	3.10	1	20⅓	19	10	7	2	16
1990—Sarasota (Florida State)	42	7	3	.700	1.21	9	111⅓	83	32	15	29	107
—Birmingham (Southern)	4	3	1	.750	2.60	1	27⅔	20	9	8	6	18
1991—Vancouver (Pacific Coast)	27	7	•12	.368	4.65	0	176	170	104	91	62	98

PETERSON, ADAM
P, PADRES

PERSONAL: Born December 11, 1965, at Long Beach, Calif. . . . 6-3/190. . . . Throws right, bats right. . . . Full name: Adam Charles Peterson.
HIGH SCHOOL: Timpview (Provo, Utah).
TRANSACTIONS/CAREER NOTES: Selected by Chicago White Sox organization in fifth round of free-agent draft (June 4, 1984). . . . Traded by White Sox with P Steve Rosenberg to San Diego Padres for IF Joey Cora, IF Kevin Garner and OF Warren Newson (March 31, 1991).
STATISTICAL NOTES: Tied for Pacific Coast League lead with six complete games in 1989. . . . Tied for Pacific Coast League lead with two shutouts in 1990.

Year	Team (League)	G	W	L	Pct.	ERA	Sv.	IP	H	R	ER	BB	SO
1984 —Sarasota White Sox (GCL)		12	1	4	.200	5.44	0	43	49	39	26	19	31
1985 —Niagara Falls (N.Y.-Penn)		14	7	6	.538	3.02	0	92⅓	74	39	31	34	79
1986 —Peninsula (Carolina)		24	9	8	.529	4.59	0	147	150	92	75	58	84
—Birmingham (Southern)		6	1	3	.250	4.18	0	32⅓	34	16	15	16	21
1987 —Birmingham (Southern)		26	12	9	.571	3.90	0	170⅔	165	79	74	73	124
—Chicago (A.L.)		1	0	0	...	13.50	0	4	8	6	6	3	1
1988 —Vancouver (Pacific Coast)		28	14	7	.667	3.32	0	171	161	69	63	81	103
—Chicago (A.L.)		2	0	1	.000	13.50	0	6	6	9	9	6	5
1989 —Vancouver (Pacific Coast)		25	14	5	.737	2.72	0	172	141	60	52	71	116
—Chicago (A.L.)		3	0	1	.000	15.19	0	5⅓	13	9	9	2	3
1990 —Vancouver (Pacific Coast)		6	4	1	.800	2.09	0	43	26	11	10	15	30
—Chicago (A.L.)		20	2	5	.286	4.55	0	85	90	46	43	26	29
1991 —Las Vegas (Pacific Coast)■......		8	2	2	.500	4.50	0	42	41	25	21	20	37
—San Diego (N.L.)		13	3	4	.429	4.45	0	54⅔	50	33	27	28	37
American League totals (4 years)		26	2	7	.222	6.01	0	100⅓	117	70	67	37	38
National League totals (1 year)		13	3	4	.429	4.45	0	54⅔	50	33	27	28	37
Major league totals (5 years)		39	5	11	.313	5.46	0	155	167	103	94	65	75

PETKOVSEK, MARK
P, PIRATES

PERSONAL: Born November 18, 1965, at Beaumont, Tex. .... 6-0/185. .... Throws right, bats right. .... Full name: Mark Joseph Petkovsek. .... Name pronounced PET-kie-zeck.
HIGH SCHOOL: Kelly (Beaumont, Tex.).
COLLEGE: Texas.
TRANSACTIONS/CAREER NOTES: Selected by Texas Rangers organization in first round (29th pick overall) of free-agent draft (June 2, 1987). .... Granted free agency (October 16, 1991). .... Signed by Pittsburgh Pirates organization (January 22, 1992).
STATISTICAL NOTES: Tied for Florida State League lead with five shutouts in 1988.

Year	Team (League)	G	W	L	Pct.	ERA	Sv.	IP	H	R	ER	BB	SO
1987 —Sarasota Rangers (GCL)		3	0	0	...	3.18	0	5⅔	4	2	2	2	7
—Charlotte (Florida State)		11	3	4	.429	4.02	0	56	67	36	25	17	23
1988 —Port Charlotte (Florida State) ...		28	10	11	.476	2.97	0	175⅔	156	71	58	42	95
1989 —Tulsa (Texas)		21	8	5	.615	3.47	0	140	144	63	54	35	66
—Oklahoma City (Am. Assoc.).....		6	0	4	.000	7.34	0	30⅔	39	27	25	18	8
1990 —Oklahoma City (Am. Assoc.).....		28	7	★14	.333	5.25	0	151	★187	★103	88	42	81
1991 —Oklahoma City (Am. Assoc.).....		25	9	8	.529	4.93	0	149⅔	162	89	82	38	67
—Texas (A.L.).............................		4	0	1	.000	14.46	0	9⅓	21	16	15	4	6
Major league totals (1 year)		4	0	1	.000	14.46	0	9⅓	21	16	15	4	6

PETRALLI, GENO
C, RANGERS

PERSONAL: Born September 25, 1959, at Sacramento, Calif. .... 6-1/190. .... Throws right, bats left. .... Full name: Eugene James Petralli Jr. .... Son of Gene Petralli, minor league first baseman (1948-1951 and 1953). .... Name pronounced puh-TRA-lee.
HIGH SCHOOL: John F. Kennedy (Sacramento, Calif.).
COLLEGE: Sacramento City College (Calif.).
TRANSACTIONS/CAREER NOTES: Selected by Toronto Blue Jays organization in third round of free-agent draft (January 10, 1978). .... On Dunedin suspended list (April 13-27, 1979). .... On disabled list (May 6-June 1 and June 28-August 18, 1981). .... Sold by Blue Jays to Maine, Cleveland Indians organization (May 8, 1984). .... On Maine disabled list (July 11, 1984-remainder of season). .... Released by Indians organization (April 23, 1985). .... Signed by Oklahoma City, Texas Rangers organization (May 17, 1985). .... On Texas disabled list (May 27-June 11 and June 27-August 19, 1989); included rehabilitation disability assignment to Tulsa (August 14-19, 1989). .... On Texas disabled list (June 19-July 29, 1991); included rehabilitation disability assignment to Oklahoma City (July 25-29, 1991). .... Granted free agency (October 30, 1991). .... Re-signed by Rangers (December 7, 1991).
RECORDS/HONORS: Holds modern major league single-season record for most passed balls—35 (1987). .... Shares modern major league single-game record for most passed balls—6 (August 30, 1987). .... Shares modern major league record for most passed balls in one inning—4 (August 22, 1987, seventh inning).
STATISTICAL NOTES: Tied for Pioneer League lead with 27 passed balls in 1978. .... Led International League catchers with 633 putouts, 86 assists, 19 errors, 738 total chances and 10 double plays and in 1982. .... Led A.L. with 35 passed balls in 1987 and 20 in both 1988 and 1990.

Year	Team (League)	Pos.	G	AB	R	H	2B	3B	HR	RBI	Avg.	SB	PO	A	E	Avg.
1978 —Medicine Hat (Pioneer)		C-3B	65	242	42	68	14	5	2	40	.281	4	238	68	19	.942
1979 —Dunedin (Florida State)		C-3B-0F	52	184	18	53	13	0	1	24	.288	1	206	42	5	.980
—Syracuse (International) ..		C	18	56	6	13	0	1	0	7	.232	0	67	12	1	.988
1980 —Knoxville (Southern)		C-1B-0F	116	382	42	109	20	2	3	38	.285	0	569	82	18	.973
1981 —Syracuse (International) ..		C	45	151	17	40	11	0	0	16	.265	1	188	30	6	.973
1982 —Syracuse (International) ..		C-1B-3B	126	395	57	114	19	3	9	58	.289	2	†674	†89	†20	.974
—Toronto (A.L.)		C-3B	16	44	3	16	2	0	0	1	.364	0	51	4	1	.982
1983 —Syracuse (International) ..		C-1B	104	327	39	80	9	2	3	40	.245	0	541	68	7	.989
—Toronto (A.L.)		C	6	4	0	0	0	0	0	0	.000	0	7	0	1	1.000
1984 —Toronto (A.L.)		C	3	3	0	0	0	0	0	0	.000	0	1	1	0	1.000
—Maine (International)■......		C-0F-1B	23	83	9	18	3	0	0	5	.217	0	122	11	6	.957

Year	Team (League)	Pos.	G	AB	R	H	2B	3B	HR	RBI	Avg.	SB	PO	A	E	Avg.
1985	—Maine (International)	C	2	7	0	1	0	0	0	1	.143	0	12	1	1	.929
	—Oklahoma City (A.A.)■......	C	27	80	11	21	8	0	1	5	.263	0	108	14	3	.976
	—Texas (A.L.)......................	C	42	100	7	27	2	0	0	11	.270	1	179	16	2	.990
1986	—Texas (A.L.)....................	C-3B-2B	69	137	17	35	9	3	2	18	.255	3	163	14	4	.978
1987	—Texas (A.L.)....................	C-3-1-2-0	101	202	28	61	11	2	7	31	.302	0	370	34	5	.988
1988	—Texas (A.L.)....................	C-3-1-2	129	351	35	99	14	2	7	36	.282	0	421	54	10	.979
1989	—Texas (A.L.)....................	C	70	184	18	56	7	0	4	23	.304	0	258	15	3	.989
	—Tulsa (Texas)	C	5	13	2	3	0	0	1	1	.231	0	6	1	0	1.000
1990	—Texas (A.L.)....................	C-3B-2B	133	325	28	83	13	1	0	21	.255	0	602	46	6	.991
1991	—Texas (A.L.)....................	C-3B	87	199	21	54	8	1	2	20	.271	2	294	25	11	.967
	—Oklahoma City (A.A.)	C	4	15	1	4	1	0	0	2	.267	0	13	1	0	1.000
Major league totals (10 years)			656	1549	157	431	66	9	22	161	.278	6	2346	209	42	.984

PETRY, DAN

P

PERSONAL: Born November 13, 1958, at Palo Alto, Calif. . . . 6-4/215. . . . Throws right, bats right. . . . Full name: Daniel Joseph Petry. . . . Name pronounced PEE-tree.

HIGH SCHOOL: El Dorado (Placentia, Calif.).

TRANSACTIONS/CAREER NOTES: Selected by Detroit Tigers organization in fourth round of free-agent draft (June 8, 1976). . . . On Detroit disabled list (June 6-August 19, 1986); included rehabilitation disability assignment to Lakeland (July 30-August 19, 1986). . . . Traded by Tigers to California Angels for OF Gary Pettis (December 5, 1987). . . . On California disabled list (June 26-August 30, 1988); included rehabilitation disability assignment to Palm Springs (August 13-30, 1988). . . . Granted free agency (November 13, 1989). . . . Signed by Toledo, Tigers organization (January 22, 1990). . . . Granted free agency (November 5, 1990). . . . Re-signed by Tigers (December 19, 1990). . . . Traded by Tigers to Atlanta Braves for IF Victor Rosario (June 25, 1991). . . . Traded by Braves to Boston Red Sox for a player to be named later (August 16, 1991); Braves acquired OF Mickey Pina to complete deal (November 13, 1991). . . . Granted free agency (November 1, 1991).

STATISTICAL NOTES: Led A.L. pitchers with 38 games started and 37 home runs allowed in 1983.

Year	Team (League)	G	W	L	Pct.	ERA	Sv.	IP	H	R	ER	BB	SO
1976	—Bristol (Appalachian)	14	2	3	.400	3.76	0	79	54	42	33	*56	51
1977	—Lakeland (Florida State)	25	10	11	.476	3.41	0	145	139	68	55	68	68
1978	—Montgomery (Southern)	14	6	7	.462	2.45	0	92	70	38	25	41	69
	—Evansville (Am. Assoc.)	13	4	3	.571	4.56	0	71	59	38	36	33	50
1979	—Evansville (Am. Assoc.)	15	4	3	.571	4.85	0	91	92	60	49	37	55
	—Detroit (A.L.)	15	6	5	.545	3.95	0	98	90	46	43	33	43
1980	—Evansville (Am. Assoc.)	4	2	0	1.000	2.70	0	30	21	11	9	12	16
	—Detroit (A.L.)	27	10	9	.526	3.93	0	165	156	82	72	83	88
1981	—Detroit (A.L.)	23	10	9	.526	3.00	0	141	115	53	47	57	79
1982	—Detroit (A.L.)	35	15	9	.625	3.22	0	246	220	98	88	100	132
1983	—Detroit (A.L.)	38	19	11	.633	3.92	0	266⅓	256	126	116	99	122
1984	—Detroit (A.L.)	35	18	8	.692	3.24	0	233⅓	231	94	84	66	144
1985	—Detroit (A.L.)	34	15	13	.536	3.36	0	238⅔	190	98	89	81	109
1986	—Detroit (A.L.)	20	5	10	.333	4.66	0	116	122	78	60	53	56
	—Lakeland (Florida State)	3	1	1	.500	6.97	0	10⅓	13	8	8	1	6
1987	—Detroit (A.L.)	30	9	7	.563	5.61	0	134⅔	148	101	84	76	93
1988	—California (A.L.)■	22	3	9	.250	4.38	0	139⅔	139	70	68	59	64
	—Palm Springs (California)	3	1	2	.333	6.60	0	15	19	14	11	11	11
1989	—California (A.L.)	19	3	2	.600	5.47	0	51	53	32	31	23	21
1990	—Detroit (A.L.)■	32	10	9	.526	4.45	0	149⅔	148	78	74	77	73
1991	—Detroit-Boston (A.L.)■.	30	2	3	.400	4.79	1	77	87	52	41	31	30
	—Atlanta (N.L.)■	10	0	0	. . .	5.55	0	24⅓	29	17	15	14	9
American League totals (13 years)		360	125	104	.546	3.93	1	2056⅓	1955	1008	897	838	1054
National League totals (1 year)		10	0	0	. . .	5.55	0	24⅓	29	17	15	14	9
Major league totals (13 years)		370	125	104	.546	3.94	1	2080⅔	1984	1025	912	852	1063

CHAMPIONSHIP SERIES RECORD

Year	Team (League)	G	W	L	Pct.	ERA	Sv.	IP	H	R	ER	BB	SO
1984	—Detroit (A.L.)	1	0	0	. . .	2.57	0	7	4	2	2	1	4
1987	—Detroit (A.L.)	1	0	0	. . .	0.00	0	3⅓	1	1	0	0	1
Championship Series totals (2 years)		2	0	0	. . .	1.74	0	10⅓	5	3	2	1	5

WORLD SERIES RECORD

Year	Team (League)	G	W	L	Pct.	ERA	Sv.	IP	H	R	ER	BB	SO
1984	—Detroit (A.L.)	2	0	1	.000	9.00	0	8	14	8	8	5	4

ALL-STAR GAME RECORD

Year	League	W	L	Pct.	ERA	Sv.	IP	H	R	ER	BB	SO
1985	—American	0	0	. . .	54.00	0	⅓	0	2	2	3	1

PETTIS, GARY

OF, RANGERS

PERSONAL: Born April 3, 1958, at Oakland, Calif. . . . 6-1/160. . . . Throws right, bats both. . . . Full name: Gary George Pettis. . . . Brother of Stacey Pettis, minor league outfielder (1981-1987).

HIGH SCHOOL: Castlemont (Oakland, Calif.).

COLLEGE: Laney College (Calif.).
TRANSACTIONS/CAREER NOTES: Selected by California Angels organization in sixth round of free-agent draft (January 9, 1979). . . . On California disabled list (July 5-31, 1985). . . . Traded by Angels to Detroit Tigers for P Dan Petry (December 5, 1987). . . . On disabled list (July 30-August 15, 1988). . . . On Detroit disabled list (March 26-May 15, 1989); included rehabilitation disability assignment to Toledo (May 6-15, 1989). . . . Granted free agency (November 13, 1989). . . . Signed by Texas Rangers (November 24, 1989).
RECORDS/HONORS: Shares major league single-game record for most putouts by outfielder— 12 (June 4, 1985, 15 innings). . . . Shares A.L. single-game record for most chances accepted by outfielder— 12 (June 4, 1985, 15 innings). . . . Won A.L. Gold Glove as outfielder (1985-86 and 1988-90).
STATISTICAL NOTES: Led A.L. outfielders with 478 total chances in 1986.

Year	Team (League)	Pos.	G	AB	R	H	2B	3B	HR	RBI	Avg.	SB	PO	A	E	Avg.
1979 —Idaho Falls (Pioneer)		3B-SS-2B	50	198	39	63	10	•10	3	26	.318	15	59	94	24	.864
1980 —Salinas (California)		OF-SS-3B	118	393	71	94	15	3	2	31	.239	43	206	36	13	.949
1981 —Holyoke (Eastern)		OF	120	421	77	112	8	9	3	36	.266	55	237	5	4	.984
1982 —Spokane (Northwest)		OF	133	528	108	152	22	*14	1	59	.288	*53	*345	9	6	*.983
—California (A.L.)		OF	10	5	5	1	0	1	0	1	.200	0	5	1	0	1.000
1983 —Edmonton (Pac. Coast)		OF	132	529	*138	151	27	8	11	52	.285	52	325	10	5	.985
—California (A.L.)		OF	22	85	19	25	2	3	3	6	.294	8	49	5	1	.982
1984 —California (A.L.)		OF	140	397	63	90	11	6	2	29	.227	48	337	11	6	.983
1985 —California (A.L.)		OF	125	443	67	114	10	8	1	32	.257	56	368	13	4	.990
1986 —California (A.L.)		OF	154	539	93	139	23	4	5	58	.258	50	*462	9	7	.985
1987 —California (A.L.)		OF	133	394	49	82	13	2	1	17	.208	24	344	2	7	.980
—Edmonton (Pac. Coast)		OF	8	16	6	2	1	0	0	1	.125	3	7	1	1	.889
1988 —Detroit (A.L.)■		OF	129	458	65	96	14	4	3	36	.210	44	361	5	5	.987
1989 —Toledo (International)		OF	6	21	6	7	1	0	1	3	.333	4	9	1	0	1.000
—Detroit (A.L.)		OF	119	444	77	114	8	6	1	18	.257	43	325	1	4	.988
1990 —Texas (A.L.)■		OF	136	423	66	101	16	8	3	31	.239	38	285	10	2	.993
1991 —Texas (A.L.)		OF	137	282	37	61	7	5	0	19	.216	29	248	4	6	.977
Major league totals (10 years)			1105	3470	541	823	104	46	20	247	.237	340	2784	61	42	.985

CHAMPIONSHIP SERIES RECORD

Year	Team (League)	Pos.	G	AB	R	H	2B	3B	HR	RBI	Avg.	SB	PO	A	E	Avg.
1986 —California (A.L.)		OF	7	26	4	9	1	0	1	4	.346	0	28	0	1	.966

PHILLIPS, J.R.

1B, ANGELS

PERSONAL: Born April 29, 1970, at Moreno Valley, Calif. . . . 6-1/185. . . . Throws left, bats left. . . . Full name: Charles Gene Phillips.
HIGH SCHOOL: Bishop Amat (La Puente, Calif.).
TRANSACTIONS/CAREER NOTES: Selected by California Angels organization in fourth round of free-agent draft (June 1, 1988).
STATISTICAL NOTES: Led California League batters with 144 strikeouts in 1991. . . . Led California League first basemen with 1,166 putouts, 1,272 total chances and 117 double plays in 1991.

Year	Team (League)	Pos.	G	AB	R	H	2B	3B	HR	RBI	Avg.	SB	PO	A	E	Avg.
1988 —Bend (Northwest)		OF-1B	56	210	24	40	8	0	4	23	.190	3	197	9	3	.986
1989 —Quad City (Midwest)		1B-OF	125	442	41	85	29	1	8	50	.192	3	954	46	20	.980
1990 —Palm Springs (Calif.)		1B	46	162	14	32	4	1	1	15	.198	3	436	26	16	.967
—Boise (Northwest)		1B-OF	70	237	30	46	6	0	10	34	.194	1	642	42	8	.988
1991 —Palm Springs (Calif.)		1B-P	130	471	64	117	22	2	20	70	.248	15	†1166	94	12	.991

RECORD AS PITCHER

Year	Team (League)	G	W	L	Pct.	ERA	Sv.	IP	H	R	ER	BB	SO
1991 —Palm Springs (Calif.)		2	0	0	. . .	4.50	0	2.0	3	1	1	2	3

PHILLIPS, TONY

IF/OF, TIGERS

PERSONAL: Born April 25, 1959, at Atlanta. . . . 5-10/175. . . . Throws right, bats both. . . . Full name: Keith Anthony Phillips.
HIGH SCHOOL: Roswell (Ga.).
COLLEGE: New Mexico Military Institute.
TRANSACTIONS/CAREER NOTES: Selected by Seattle Mariners organization in 16th round of free-agent draft (June 7, 1977). . . . Selected by Montreal Expos organization in secondary phase of free-agent draft (January 10, 1978). . . . On West Palm Beach temporary inactive list (April 11-May 4, 1978). . . . Traded by Expos organization with cash to San Diego Padres for 1B Willie Montanez (August 31, 1980). . . . Traded by Padres organization with P Eric Mustad and IF Kevin Bell to Oakland Athletics organization for P Bob Lacey and P Roy Moretti (March 27, 1981). . . . On Oakland disabled list (March 26-August 22, 1985); included rehabilitation disability assignment to Tacoma (July 30-August 5 and August 7-20, 1985). . . . On disabled list (August 14-October 3, 1986). . . . On Oakland disabled list (July 12-August 28, 1987); included rehabilitation disability assignment to Tacoma (August 20-28, 1987). . . . Released by A's (December 21, 1987). . . . Re-signed by A's (March 9, 1988). . . . On A's disabled list (May 18-July 8, 1988); included rehabilitation disability assignment to Tacoma (June 16-July 4, 1988). . . . Granted free agency (November 13, 1989). . . . Signed by Detroit Tigers (December 5, 1989).
RECORDS/HONORS: Shares major league single-game record (nine innings) for most assists by second baseman— 12 (July 6, 1986).
STATISTICAL NOTES: Led Southern League with 98 bases on balls received in 1980. . . . Led Southern League shortstops with 42 errors in 1980. . . . Led Eastern League in being hit by pitch with 10 in 1981. . . . Hit for the cycle (May 16, 1986).

Year	Team (League)	Pos.	G	AB	R	H	2B	3B	HR	RBI	Avg.	SB	PO	A	E	Avg.
1978	—West Palm Beach (FSL)	3B-SS-2B	32	54	8	9	0	0	0	3	.167	2	13	33	5	.902
	—Jamestown (N.Y.-Penn) ...	SS-2B-3B	52	152	24	29	5	2	1	17	.191	3	73	146	16	.932
1979	—West Palm Beach (FSL)	2B-SS	60	203	30	47	5	1	0	18	.232	7	120	156	21	.929
	—Memphis (Southern)	SS-2B	52	156	31	44	4	2	3	11	.282	3	68	134	18	.918
1980	—Memphis (Southern)	SS-2B	136	502	100	125	18	4	5	41	.249	50	226	408	†42	.938
1981	—West Haven (Eastern)■ ...	SS	131	461	79	114	25	3	9	64	.247	40	200	391	★33	.947
	—Tacoma (Pacific Coast)	2B-SS	4	11	1	4	1	0	0	2	.364	0	8	10	0	1.000
1982	—Tacoma (Pacific Coast)	SS	86	300	76	89	18	5	4	47	.297	29	138	236	30	.926
	—Oakland (A.L.)	SS	40	81	11	17	2	2	0	8	.210	2	46	95	7	.953
1983	—Oakland (A.L.)	SS-2B-3B	148	412	54	102	12	3	4	35	.248	16	218	383	30	.952
1984	—Oakland (A.L.)	SS-2B-OF	154	451	62	120	24	3	4	37	.266	10	255	391	28	.958
1985	—Tacoma (Pacific Coast)	3B-2B	20	69	9	9	1	0	0	5	.130	3	15	36	4	.927
	—Oakland (A.L.)	3B-2B	42	161	23	45	12	2	4	17	.280	3	54	103	3	.981
1986	—Oakland (A.L.)	2-3-0-S	118	441	76	113	14	5	5	52	.256	15	191	326	13	.975
1987	—Oakland (A.L.)	2-3-S-0	111	379	48	91	20	0	10	46	.240	7	179	299	14	.972
	—Tacoma (Pacific Coast)	2B-3B	7	26	5	9	2	1	1	6	.346	1	8	10	0	1.000
1988	—Tacoma (Pacific Coast)	S-0-2-3	16	59	10	16	0	0	2	8	.271	0	25	27	2	.963
	—Oakland (A.L.)	3-0-2-S-1	79	212	32	43	8	4	2	17	.203	0	84	80	10	.943
1989	—Oakland (A.L.)	2-3-S-0-1	143	451	48	118	15	6	4	47	.262	3	184	321	15	.971
1990	—Detroit (A.L.)■	3-2-S-0	152	573	97	144	23	5	8	55	.251	19	180	368	23	.960
1991	—Detroit (A.L.)	0-3-2-S	146	564	87	160	28	4	17	72	.284	10	269	237	8	.984
Major league totals (10 years)			1133	3725	538	953	158	34	58	386	.256	85	1660	2603	151	.966

CHAMPIONSHIP SERIES RECORD

Year	Team (League)	Pos.	G	AB	R	H	2B	3B	HR	RBI	Avg.	SB	PO	A	E	Avg.
1988	—Oakland (A.L.)	OF-2B	2	7	0	2	1	0	0	0	.286	0	10	0	0	1.000
1989	—Oakland (A.L.)	2B-3B	5	18	1	3	1	0	0	1	.167	2	4	14	0	1.000
Championship Series totals (2 years)			7	25	1	5	2	0	0	1	.200	2	14	14	0	1.000

WORLD SERIES RECORD

Year	Team (League)	Pos.	G	AB	R	H	2B	3B	HR	RBI	Avg.	SB	PO	A	E	Avg.
1988	—Oakland (A.L.)	OF-2B	2	4	1	1	0	0	0	0	.250	2	3	5	0	1.000
1989	—Oakland (A.L.)	2B-3B-OF	4	17	2	4	1	0	1	3	.235	0	8	15	0	1.000
World Series totals (2 years)			6	21	3	5	1	0	1	3	.238	2	11	20	0	1.000

PIATT, DOUG
P, EXPOS

PERSONAL: Born September 26, 1965, at Beaver, Pa. ... 6-1/190. ... Throws right, bats left. ... Full name: Douglas William Piatt.
COLLEGE: Western Kentucky.
TRANSACTIONS/CAREER NOTES: Selected by St. Louis Cardinals organization in third round of free-agent draft (January 17, 1984). ... Signed as free agent by Cleveland Indians organization (February 3, 1988). ... Traded by Indians organization to Montreal Expos organization for P Rick Carriger (July 27, 1989).

Year	Team (League)	G	W	L	Pct.	ERA	Sv.	IP	H	R	ER	BB	SO
1988	—Burlington (Appalachian)	2	0	0	...	13.50	1	1⅓	4	2	2	1	1
	—Waterloo (Midwest)	26	2	1	.667	2.21	11	36⅔	33	18	9	11	40
1989	—Kinston (Carolina)	20	2	0	1.000	2.51	1	28⅔	24	8	8	8	31
	—Watertown (New York-Penn) ...	15	4	2	.667	0.51	6	35	21	5	2	9	43
	—Rockford (Midwest)■	11	2	2	.500	3.20	2	19⅔	19	7	7	11	24
1990	—West Palm Beach (Florida St.) ..	21	4	1	.800	0.99	9	27⅓	12	6	3	16	41
	—Jacksonville (Southern)	35	5	1	.833	2.20	6	49	30	17	12	29	51
1991	—Indianapolis (Am. Assoc.)	44	6	4	.600	3.45	13	47	40	24	18	27	61
	—Montreal (N.L.)	21	0	0	...	2.60	0	34⅔	29	11	10	17	29
Major league totals (1 year)		21	0	0	...	2.60	0	34⅔	29	11	10	17	29

PIAZZA, MIKE
C/1B, DODGERS

PERSONAL: Born September 4, 1968, at Norristown, Pa. ... 6-3/200. ... Throws right, bats right. ... Full name: Michael Joseph Piazza.
HIGH SCHOOL: Phoenixville Area (Phoenixville, Pa.).
COLLEGE: Miami-Dade (North) Community College (Fla.).
TRANSACTIONS/CAREER NOTES: Selected by Los Angeles Dodgers organization in 62nd round of free-agent draft (June 1, 1988).
STATISTICAL NOTES: Led California League with .540 slugging percentage and in grounding into double plays with 19 in 1991.

Year	Team (League)	Pos.	G	AB	R	H	2B	3B	HR	RBI	Avg.	SB	PO	A	E	Avg.
1989	—Salem (Northwest)	C	57	198	22	53	11	0	8	25	.268	0	230	21	6	.977
1990	—Vero Beach (Florida St.) ...	C-1B	88	272	27	68	20	0	6	45	.250	0	428	38	16	.967
1991	—Bakersfield (California)	C-1B	117	448	71	124	27	2	29	80	.277	0	723	69	15	.981

PICHARDO, HIPOLITO
P, ROYALS

PERSONAL: Born August 22, 1969, at Jicome Esperanza, Dominican Republic. . . . 6-1/160. . . . Throws right, bats right. . . . Full name: Hipolito Pichardo.
HIGH SCHOOL: Liceo Enriguillo (Jicome Esperanza, Dominican Republic).
TRANSACTIONS/CAREER NOTES: Signed as a free agent by Kansas City Royals organization (December 16, 1987).

Year	Team (League)	G	W	L	Pct.	ERA	Sv.	IP	H	R	ER	BB	SO
1988—Boardwalk Royals (GCL)		1	0	0	...	13.50	0	1 1/3	3	2	2	1	3
1989—Appleton (Midwest)..................		12	5	4	.556	2.97	0	75 2/3	58	29	25	18	50
1990—Baseball City (Florida State)		11	1	6	.143	3.80	0	45	47	28	19	25	40
1991—Memphis (Southern)		34	3	11	.214	4.27	0	99	116	56	47	38	75

PIERCE, ED
P, ROYALS

PERSONAL: Born October 6, 1968, at Arcadia, Calif. . . . 6-1/185. . . . Throws left, bats left. . . . Full name: Edward John Pierce.
HIGH SCHOOL: Glendora (Calif.).
COLLEGE: Orange Coast (Calif.) and California.
TRANSACTIONS/CAREER NOTES: Selected by Texas Rangers organization in 35th round of free-agent draft (June 2, 1987). . . . Selected by Kansas City Royals organization in seventh round of free-agent draft (June 5, 1989).

Year	Team (League)	G	W	L	Pct.	ERA	Sv.	IP	H	R	ER	BB	SO
1989—Eugene (Northwest)		27	2	2	.500	2.77	4	39	24	19	12	26	71
1990—Baseball City (Florida State)		37	3	1	.750	3.24	5	50	49	21	18	32	53
—Memphis (Southern)		1	0	0	...	0.00	0	1	0	0	0	1	1
1991—Memphis (Southern)		31	5	11	.313	3.84	0	136	136	73	58	61	90

PIRKL, GREG
C/1B, MARINERS

PERSONAL: Born August 7, 1970, at Long Beach, Calif. . . . 6-5/225. . . . Throws right, bats right. . . . Full name: Gregory Daniel Pirkl.
HIGH SCHOOL: Los Alamitos (Calif.).
TRANSACTIONS/CAREER NOTES: Selected by Seattle Mariners organization in second round of free-agent draft (June 1, 1988). . . . On disabled list (May 31-June 22 and July 3, 1990-remainder of season).
STATISTICAL NOTES: Led Northwest League with 22 passed balls in 1988.

Year	Team (League)	Pos.	G	AB	R	H	2B	3B	HR	RBI	Avg.	SB	PO	A	E	Avg.
1988—Bellingham (Northwest)....		C	65	246	22	59	6	0	6	35	.240	1	227	19	9	.965
1989—Bellingham (Northwest)....		C	70	265	31	68	6	0	8	36	.257	4	296	23	9	.973
1990—San Bernardino (Calif.)		C	58	207	37	61	10	0	5	28	.295	3	325	40	9	.976
1991—San Bernardino (Calif.)		C-1B	63	239	32	75	13	1	14	53	.314	4	412	33	11	.976
—Peninsula (Carolina)		C-1B	64	239	20	63	16	0	6	41	.264	0	322	31	5	.986

PLANTIER, PHIL
OF, RED SOX

PERSONAL: Born January 27, 1969, at Manchester, N.H. . . . 5-11/195. . . . Throws right, bats left. . . . Full name: Phillip Alan Plantier.
HIGH SCHOOL: Poway (Calif.).
TRANSACTIONS/CAREER NOTES: Selected by Boston Red Sox organization in 11th round of free-agent draft (June 2, 1987).
RECORDS/HONORS: Named Carolina League Most Valuable Player (1989).
STATISTICAL NOTES: Led Carolina League with 242 total bases, .546 slugging percentage and tied for lead with seven intentional bases on balls received with in 1989. . . . Led International League batters with .549 slugging percentage and 148 strikeouts in 1990.

Year	Team (League)	Pos.	G	AB	R	H	2B	3B	HR	RBI	Avg.	SB	PO	A	E	Avg.
1987—Elmira (New York-Penn) ..		3B	28	80	7	14	2	0	2	9	.175	2	12	34	12	.793
1988—Winter Haven (Fla. St.)	OF-3B-2B		111	337	29	81	13	1	4	32	.240	0	106	72	18	.908
1989—Lynchburg (Carolina)		OF	131	443	73	133	26	1	*27	*105	.300	4	140	10	8	.949
1990—Pawtucket (Int'l)		OF	123	430	83	109	22	3	*33	79	.253	1	245	8	*14	.948
—Boston (A.L.)		OF	14	15	1	2	1	0	0	3	.133	0	0	0	0	...
1991—Pawtucket (Int'l)	OF-3B		84	298	69	91	19	4	16	61	.305	6	173	6	0	1.000
—Boston (A.L.)		OF	53	148	27	49	7	1	11	35	.331	1	80	1	2	.976
Major league totals (2 years)			67	163	28	51	8	1	11	38	.313	1	80	1	2	.976

PLESAC, DAN
P, BREWERS

PERSONAL: Born February 4, 1962, at Gary, Ind. . . . 6-5/215. . . . Throws left, bats left. . . . Full name: Daniel Thomas Plesac. . . . Name pronounced PLEE-sack.
HIGH SCHOOL: Crown Point (Ind.).
COLLEGE: North Carolina State.
TRANSACTIONS/CAREER NOTES: Selected by St. Louis Cardinals organization in second round of free-agent draft (June 3, 1980). . . . Selected by Milwaukee Brewers organization in first round (26th pick overall) of free-agent draft (June 6, 1983).
STATISTICAL NOTES: Led Appalachian League pitchers with three balks and tied for lead in games started with 14 in 1983.

Year	Team (League)	G	W	L	Pct.	ERA	Sv.	IP	H	R	ER	BB	SO
1983—Paintsville (Appalachian)		14	*9	1	.900	3.50	0	82 1/3	76	44	32	57	*85
1984—Stockton (California)		16	6	6	.500	3.32	0	108 1/3	106	51	40	50	101
—El Paso (Texas)		7	2	2	.500	3.46	0	39	43	19	15	16	24

Year	Team (League)	G	W	L	Pct.	ERA	Sv.	IP	H	R	ER	BB	SO
1985	El Paso (Texas)	25	12	5	.706	4.97	0	150⅓	171	91	83	68	128
1986	Milwaukee (A.L.)	51	10	7	.588	2.97	14	91	81	34	30	29	75
1987	Milwaukee (A.L.)	57	5	6	.455	2.61	23	63	63	30	23	23	89
1988	Milwaukee (A.L.)	50	1	2	.333	2.41	30	52⅓	46	14	14	12	52
1989	Milwaukee (A.L.)	52	3	4	.429	2.35	33	61⅓	47	16	16	17	52
1990	Milwaukee (A.L.)	66	3	7	.300	4.43	24	69	67	36	34	31	65
1991	Milwaukee (A.L.)	45	2	7	.222	4.29	8	92⅓	92	49	44	39	61
Major league totals (6 years)		321	24	33	.421	3.25	132	445⅓	396	179	161	151	394

ALL-STAR GAME RECORD

Year	League	W	L	Pct.	ERA	Sv.	IP	H	R	ER	BB	SO
1987	American	0	0	...	0.00	0	1	0	0	0	0	1
1988	American	0	0	...	0.00	0	⅓	0	0	0	0	1
1989	American	0	0	...	...	0	0	1	0	0	0	0
All-Star totals (3 years)		0	0	...	0.00	0	1⅓	1	0	0	0	2

PLUNK, ERIC
P, BLUE JAYS

PERSONAL: Born September 3, 1963, at Wilmington, Calif. . . . 6-5/217. . . . Throws right, bats right. . . . Full name: Eric Vaughn Plunk.
HIGH SCHOOL: Bellflower (Calif.).
COLLEGE: Cal State Dominguez Hills.
TRANSACTIONS/CAREER NOTES: Selected by New York Yankees organization in fourth round of free-agent draft (June 8, 1981). . . . On disabled list (August 11-26, 1983). . . . Traded by Yankees with OF Stan Javier, P Jay Howell, P Jose Rijo and P Tim Birtsas to Oakland Athletics for OF Rickey Henderson, P Bert Bradley and cash (December 5, 1984). . . . On disabled list (July 2-17, 1988). . . . Traded by A's with P Greg Cadaret and OF Luis Polonia to New York Yankees for OF Rickey Henderson (June 21, 1989). . . . Released by Yankees (November 20, 1991). . . . Signed by Syracuse, Toronto Blue Jays organization (December 12, 1991).
STATISTICAL NOTES: Tied for Florida State League lead with four shutouts in 1983. . . . Tied for Florida State League lead with seven balks in 1984. . . . Led A.L. with six balks in 1986.

Year	Team (League)	G	W	L	Pct.	ERA	Sv.	IP	H	R	ER	BB	SO
1981	Bradenton Yankees (GCL)	11	3	4	.429	3.83	0	54	56	29	23	20	47
1982	Paintsville (Appalachian)	12	6	3	.667	4.64	0	64	63	35	33	30	59
1983	Fort Lauderdale (Florida St.)	20	8	10	.444	2.74	0	125	115	55	38	63	109
1984	Fort Lauderdale (Florida St.)	28	12	12	.500	2.86	0	176⅓	153	85	56	★123	★152
1985	Huntsville (Southern)■	13	8	2	.800	3.40	0	79⅓	61	36	30	56	68
	Tacoma (Pacific Coast)	11	0	5	.000	5.77	0	53	51	41	34	50	43
1986	Tacoma (Pacific Coast)	6	2	3	.400	4.68	0	32⅔	25	18	17	33	31
	Oakland (A.L.)	26	4	7	.364	5.31	0	120⅓	91	75	71	102	98
1987	Oakland (A.L.)	32	4	6	.400	4.74	2	95	91	53	50	62	90
	Tacoma (Pacific Coast)	24	1	1	.500	1.56	9	34⅔	21	8	6	17	56
1988	Oakland (A.L.)	49	7	2	.778	3.00	5	78	62	27	26	39	79
1989	Oakland-New York (A.L.)■	50	8	6	.571	3.28	1	104⅓	82	43	38	64	85
1990	New York (A.L.)	47	6	3	.667	2.72	0	72⅔	58	27	22	43	67
1991	New York (A.L.)	43	2	5	.286	4.76	0	111⅔	128	69	59	62	103
Major league totals (6 years)		247	31	29	.517	4.11	8	582	512	294	266	372	522

CHAMPIONSHIP SERIES RECORD

Year	Team (League)	G	W	L	Pct.	ERA	Sv.	IP	H	R	ER	BB	SO
1988	Oakland (A.L.)	1	0	0	...	0.00	0	⅓	1	0	0	0	1

WORLD SERIES RECORD

Year	Team (League)	G	W	L	Pct.	ERA	Sv.	IP	H	R	ER	BB	SO
1988	Oakland (A.L.)	2	0	0	...	0.00	0	1⅔	0	0	0	0	3

PLYMPTON, JEFF
P, RED SOX

PERSONAL: Born November 24, 1965, at Framingham, Mass. . . . 6-2/205. . . . Throws right, bats right. . . . Full name: Jeffrey Hunter Plympton.
HIGH SCHOOL: King Phillip Regional (Wrentham, Mass.).
COLLEGE: Maine.
TRANSACTIONS/CAREER NOTES: Selected by Cleveland Indians organization in 45th round of free-agent draft (June 4, 1984). . . . Selected by Boston Red Sox organization in 10th round of free-agent draft (June 2, 1987).

Year	Team (League)	G	W	L	Pct.	ERA	Sv.	IP	H	R	ER	BB	SO
1987	New Britain (Eastern)	23	4	1	.800	3.82	1	63⅔	61	35	27	34	60
1988	Lynchburg (Carolina)	41	5	4	.556	2.60	12	83	69	30	24	45	105
1989	New Britain (Eastern)	38	4	4	.500	3.72	5	72⅔	72	36	30	39	63
1990	New Britain (Eastern)	37	3	4	.429	2.67	13	64	62	31	19	16	155
	Pawtucket (International)	11	1	0	1.000	0.00	3	17⅓	10	0	0	11	11
1991	Pawtucket (International)	41	2	6	.250	3.12	7	69⅓	65	31	24	29	63
	Boston (A.L.)	4	0	0	...	0.00	0	5⅓	5	0	0	4	2
Major league totals (1 year)		4	0	0	...	0.00	0	5⅓	5	0	0	4	2

POLONIA, LUIS

OF, ANGELS

PERSONAL: Born October 12, 1964, at Santiago City, Dominican Republic. . . . 5-8/150. . . . Throws left, bats left. . . . Full name: Luis Andrew Almonte Polonia.
HIGH SCHOOL: San Francisco (Santiago City, Dominican Republic).
TRANSACTIONS/CAREER NOTES: Signed as free agent by Oakland Athletics organization (January 3, 1984). . . . Traded by A's with P Greg Cadaret and P Eric Plunk to New York Yankees for OF Rickey Henderson (June 21, 1989). . . . Traded by Yankees to California Angels for OF Claudell Washington and P Rich Monteleone (April 28, 1990).
STATISTICAL NOTES: Led Midwest League in caught stealing with 24 in 1984. . . . Led Pacific Coast League in caught stealing with 21 in 1986. . . . Led A.L. in caught stealing with 23 in 1991.
MISCELLANEOUS: Batted as switch-hitter (1984-1986 and Tacoma, 1987-88).

						BATTING						FIELDING		
Year	Team (League)	Pos.	G	AB	R	H	2B	3B	HR	RBI	Avg.	SB	PO	A	E	Avg.
1984 — Madison (Midwest)		OF	135	*528	103	*162	21	10	8	64	.307	55	202	9	10	.955
1985 — Huntsville (Southern)		OF	130	515	82	149	15	*18	2	36	.289	39	236	13	12	.954
1986 — Tacoma (Pacific Coast)		OF	134	*549	98	*165	20	4	3	63	.301	36	*318	8	10	.970
1987 — Tacoma (Pacific Coast)		OF	14	56	18	18	1	2	0	8	.321	4	28	1	1	.967
— Oakland (A.L.)		OF	125	435	78	125	16	10	4	49	.287	29	235	2	5	.979
1988 — Tacoma (Pacific Coast)		OF	65	254	58	85	13	5	2	27	.335	31	129	7	7	.951
— Oakland (A.L.)		OF	84	288	51	84	11	4	2	27	.292	24	155	3	2	.988
1989 — Oak.-New York (A.L.)■....		OF	125	433	70	130	17	6	3	46	.300	22	231	9	4	.984
1990 — New York-Calif. (A.L.)■....		OF	120	403	52	135	7	9	2	35	.335	21	142	3	3	.980
1991 — California (A.L.)		OF	150	604	92	179	28	8	2	50	.296	48	246	9	5	.981
Major league totals (5 years)			604	2163	343	653	79	37	13	207	.302	144	1009	26	19	.982

CHAMPIONSHIP SERIES RECORD

						BATTING						FIELDING		
Year	Team (League)	Pos.	G	AB	R	H	2B	3B	HR	RBI	Avg.	SB	PO	A	E	Avg.
1988 — Oakland (A.L.)		PR-OF-PH	3	5	0	2	0	0	0	0	.400	0	2	0	0	1.000

WORLD SERIES RECORD

						BATTING						FIELDING		
Year	Team (League)	Pos.	G	AB	R	H	2B	3B	HR	RBI	Avg.	SB	PO	A	E	Avg.
1988 — Oakland (A.L.)		PH-OF	3	9	1	1	0	0	0	0	.111	0	2	0	0	1.000

POOLE, JIM

P, ORIOLES

PERSONAL: Born April 28, 1966, at Rochester, N.Y. . . . 6-2/203. . . . Throws left, bats left. . . . Full name: James Richard Poole.
HIGH SCHOOL: South College (Philadelphia).
COLLEGE: Georgia Tech.
TRANSACTIONS/CAREER NOTES: Selected by Los Angeles Dodgers organization in 34th round of free-agent draft (June 2, 1987). . . . Selected by Dodgers organization in ninth round of free-agent draft (June 1, 1988). . . . Traded by Dodgers with cash to Texas Rangers for P Steve Allen and P David Lynch (December 30, 1990). . . . Claimed on waivers by Baltimore Orioles (May 31, 1991).

Year	Team (League)	G	W	L	Pct.	ERA	Sv.	IP	H	R	ER	BB	SO
1988 — Vero Beach (Florida State)	10	1	1	.500	3.77	0	14⅓	13	7	6	9	12
1989 — Vero Beach (Florida State)	*60	11	4	.733	1.61	19	78⅓	57	16	14	24	93
— Bakersfield (California)	1	0	0	. . .	0.00	0	1⅔	2	1	0	0	1
1990 — San Antonio (Texas)	54	6	7	.462	2.40	16	63⅔	55	31	17	27	77
— Los Angeles (N.L.)	16	0	0	. . .	4.22	0	10⅔	7	5	5	8	6
1991 — Oklahoma City (Am. Assoc.)	10	0	0	. . .	0.00	3	12⅓	4	0	0	1	14
— Texas-Baltimore (A.L.)■	29	3	2	.600	2.36	1	42	29	14	11	12	38
— Rochester (International)	27	3	2	.600	2.79	9	29	29	11	9	9	25
American League totals (1 year)	29	3	2	.600	2.36	1	42	29	14	11	12	38
National League totals (1 year)	16	0	0	. . .	4.22	0	10⅔	7	5	5	8	6
Major league totals (2 years)	45	3	2	.600	2.73	1	52⅔	36	19	16	20	44

PORTUGAL, MARK

P, ASTROS

PERSONAL: Born October 30, 1962, at Los Angeles. . . . 6-0/190. . . . Throws right, bats right. . . . Full name: Mark Steven Portugal.
HIGH SCHOOL: Norwalk (Calif.).
TRANSACTIONS/CAREER NOTES: Signed as free agent by Minnesota Twins organization (October 23, 1980). . . . On Toledo disabled list (July 22-August 2, 1985). . . . On Minnesota disabled list (August 7-28, 1988). . . . Traded by Twins to Houston Astros for a player to be named later (December 4, 1988); Twins organization acquired P Todd McClure to complete deal (December 7, 1988). . . . On disabled list (July 18-August 13, 1991).
STATISTICAL NOTES: Led Appalachian League with 12 wild pitches, 11 home runs allowed and tied for lead with five hit batsmen in 1981.
MISCELLANEOUS: Appeared in one game as pinch-runner (1991).

Year	Team (League)	G	W	L	Pct.	ERA	Sv.	IP	H	R	ER	BB	SO
1981 — Elizabethton (Appalachian)	14	7	1	.875	3.71	1	85	65	41	35	39	65
1982 — Wisconsin Rapids (Midwest)....	36	9	8	.529	4.01	2	119	110	62	53	62	95
1983 — Visalia (California)	24	10	5	.667	4.18	0	131⅓	142	77	61	84	132
1984 — Orlando (Southern)	27	14	7	.667	2.98	0	196	171	80	65	113	110
1985 — Toledo (International)	19	8	5	.615	3.78	0	128⅔	129	60	54	60	89
— Minnesota (A.L.)	6	1	3	.250	5.55	0	24⅓	24	16	15	14	12

Year	Team (League)	G	W	L	Pct.	ERA	Sv.	IP	H	R	ER	BB	SO
1986	Toledo (International)	6	5	1	.833	2.60	0	45	34	15	13	23	30
	Minnesota (A.L.)	27	6	10	.375	4.31	1	112⅔	112	56	54	50	67
1987	Minnesota (A.L.)	13	1	3	.250	7.77	0	44	58	40	38	24	28
	Portland (Pacific Coast)	17	1	10	.091	6.00	0	102	108	75	68	50	69
1988	Portland (Pacific Coast)	3	2	0	1.000	1.37	0	19⅔	15	3	3	8	9
	Minnesota (A.L.)	26	3	3	.500	4.53	3	57⅔	60	30	29	17	31
1989	Tucson (Pacific Coast)■	17	7	5	.583	3.78	0	116⅔	107	55	49	32	90
	Houston (N.L.)	20	7	1	.875	2.75	0	108	91	34	33	37	86
1990	Houston (N.L.)	32	11	10	.524	3.62	0	196⅔	187	90	79	67	136
1991	Houston (N.L.)	32	10	12	.455	4.49	1	168⅓	163	91	84	59	120
American League totals (4 years)		72	11	19	.367	5.13	4	238⅔	254	142	136	105	138
National League totals (3 years)		84	28	23	.549	3.73	1	473	441	215	196	163	342
Major league totals (7 years)		156	39	42	.481	4.20	5	711⅔	695	357	332	268	480

POUGH, CLYDE
OF, INDIANS

PERSONAL: Born December 25, 1969, at Avon Park, Fla. . . . 6-0/173. . . . Throws right, bats right. . . . Full name: Clyde Gary Pough. **HIGH SCHOOL:** Avon Park (Fla.). **TRANSACTIONS/CAREER NOTES:** Selected by Cleveland Indians organization in third round of free-agent draft (June 1, 1988). **STATISTICAL NOTES:** Led New York-Pennsylvania League third basemen with 249 total chances and 15 double plays in 1990.

						BATTING						FIELDING			
Year	Team (League)	Pos.	G	AB	R	H	2B	3B	HR	RBI	Avg.	SB	PO	A	E	Avg.
1988	Sarasota Indians (GCL)	SS-3B-P	52	173	28	45	11	0	3	21	.260	1	54	92	10	.936
1989	Burlington (Appal.)	3B	67	225	39	58	15	1	8	37	.258	9	42	116	*25	.863
1990	Reno (California)	3B	16	53	1	8	0	1	0	2	.151	0	9	27	2	.947
	Watertown (N.Y.-Penn)	3B	76	285	47	72	15	1	9	48	.253	21	51	*170	28	.888
1991	Columbus (S. Atlantic)	OF-3B	115	414	77	126	35	3	11	73	.304	11	79	8	7	.926
	Kinston (Carolina)	OF	11	30	2	5	1	0	0	2	.167	1	4	0	0	1.000
	Colorado Springs (PCL)	OF	2	2	0	0	0	0	0	0	.000	0	0	0	0	...

RECORD AS PITCHER

Year	Team (League)	G	W	L	Pct.	ERA	Sv.	IP	H	R	ER	BB	SO
1988	Sarasota Indians (Gulf Coast)	1	1	0	1.000	9.00	0	2	2	2	2	4	1

POWELL, ALONZO
OF/1B, MARINERS

PERSONAL: Born December 12, 1964, at San Francisco. . . . 6-2/190. . . . Throws right, bats right. . . . Full name: Alonzo Sidney Powell. **HIGH SCHOOL:** Lincoln (San Francisco). **TRANSACTIONS/CAREER NOTES:** Signed as free agent by San Francisco Giants organization (February 3, 1983). . . . Loaned by Giants organization to San Jose, independent (April 9, 1985); returned (September 10, 1985). . . . Traded by Giants organization with P George Riley to Montreal Expos organization for P Bill Laskey (October 24, 1985). . . . On disabled list (August 8, 1988-remainder of season). . . . Traded by Expos organization to Minnesota Twins (September 16, 1989), completing deal in which Twins traded OF Jim Dwyer to Expos for a player to be named later (August 28, 1989). . . . Granted free agency (October 15, 1990). . . . Signed by Seattle Mariners organization (December 21, 1990). **STATISTICAL NOTES:** Led California League outfielders with 21 assists in 1985.

						BATTING						FIELDING			
Year	Team (League)	Pos.	G	AB	R	H	2B	3B	HR	RBI	Avg.	SB	PO	A	E	Avg.
1983	Clinton (Midwest)	OF	36	113	14	22	5	1	0	9	.195	2	66	2	5	.932
	Great Falls (Pioneer)	OF-1B-3B	51	149	13	33	2	2	1	16	.221	10	127	15	8	.947
1984	Everett (Northwest)	1B	6	17	2	3	1	0	1	4	.176	0	38	2	3	.930
	Clinton (Midwest)	OF-1B-2B	47	149	22	37	3	2	1	10	.248	0	166	9	5	.972
1985	San Jose (California)■	OF-1B	136	473	79	122	27	6	9	62	.258	34	292	†21	10	.969
1986	West Palm Beach (FSL)■	OF	23	76	20	25	7	1	4	18	.329	5	56	1	0	1.000
	Jacksonville (Southern)	OF	105	402	67	121	21	5	15	80	.301	15	256	4	3	.989
1987	Montreal (N.L.)	OF	14	41	3	8	3	0	0	4	.195	0	13	0	0	1.000
	Indianapolis (A.A.)	OF-1B	90	331	64	99	14	10	19	74	.299	8	163	6	5	.971
1988	Indianapolis (A.A.)	OF	88	282	31	74	18	3	4	39	.262	10	148	6	1	.994
1989	West Palm Beach (FSL)	DH	12	41	7	7	4	3	1	8	.171	1	0	0	0	...
	Indianapolis (A.A.)	OF-1B	121	423	50	98	26	5	13	59	.232	9	300	15	5	.984
1990	Portland (Pacific Coast)■	OF-1B	107	376	56	121	25	3	8	62	.322	23	254	10	6	.978
1991	Calgary (Pacific Coast)■	OF-1B	53	192	45	72	18	7	7	43	.375	2	110	8	2	.983
	Seattle (A.L.)	OF-1B	57	111	16	24	6	1	3	12	.216	0	66	2	2	.971
American League totals (1 year)			57	111	16	24	6	1	3	12	.216	0	66	2	2	.971
National League totals (1 year)			14	41	3	8	3	0	0	4	.195	0	13	0	0	1.000
Major league totals (2 years)			71	152	19	32	9	1	3	16	.211	0	79	2	2	.976

POWELL, ROSS
P, REDS

PERSONAL: Born January 24, 1968, at Grand Rapids, Mich. . . . 5-11/180. . . . Throws left, bats left. . . . Full name: Ross John Powell. **HIGH SCHOOL:** Cedar Springs (Mich.). **COLLEGE:** Michigan.

TRANSACTIONS/CAREER NOTES: Selected by Cincinnati Reds organization in third round of free-agent draft (June 5, 1989).
STATISTICAL NOTES: Tied for Southern League lead with six complete games in 1990.

Year	Team (League)	G	W	L	Pct.	ERA	Sv.	IP	H	R	ER	BB	SO
1989	Cedar Rapids (Midwest)	13	7	4	.636	3.54	0	76⅓	68	37	30	23	58
1990	Chattanooga (Southern)..........	29	8	•14	.364	1.31	0	185	172	29	27	57	132
	Nashville (American Assoc.)....	3	0	0	...	3.38	0	2⅔	1	1	1	0	4
1991	Nashville (American Assoc.)....	24	8	8	.500	4.37	0	129⅔	125	74	63	63	82

POWER, TED
P

PERSONAL: Born January 31, 1955, at Guthrie, Okla.... 6-4/220.... Throws right, bats right....
Full name: Ted Henry Power.
HIGH SCHOOL: Abilene (Kan.).
COLLEGE: Kansas State.
TRANSACTIONS/CAREER NOTES: Selected by Los Angeles Dodgers organization in fifth round of free-agent draft (June 8, 1976).
... On disabled list (July 18-29 and August 20-September 4, 1977; and July 5-21, 1978).... Traded by Dodgers organization to Cincinnati Reds for cash and IF Michael James Ramsey (October 15, 1982).... Traded by Reds with SS Kurt Stillwell to Kansas City Royals for P Danny Jackson and SS Angel Salazar (November 6, 1987).... On disabled list (June 18-July 4, 1988). ... Traded by Royals to Detroit Tigers for C Rey Palacios and P Mark Lee (August 31, 1988).... Granted free agency (November 4, 1988).... Re-signed by Tigers (December 7, 1988).... Released by Tigers (March 25, 1989).... Signed by Louisville, St. Louis Cardinals organization (March 28, 1989).... On St. Louis disabled list (May 17-June 19, 1989); included rehabilitation disability assignment to Louisville (June 9-19, 1989).... Granted free agency (November 13, 1989).... Signed by Pittsburgh Pirates (November 20, 1989).... On disabled list (June 5-July 14 and August 5-20, 1990).... Granted free agency (November 5, 1990).... Signed by Reds (December 14, 1990).... Granted free agency (November 4, 1991).

Year	Team (League)	G	W	L	Pct.	ERA	Sv.	IP	H	R	ER	BB	SO
1976	Lodi (California)	13	1	3	.250	4.59	1	51	46	34	26	44	58
1977	San Antonio (Texas)	12	5	3	.625	3.88	0	72	51	35	31	55	60
1978	San Antonio (Texas)	25	6	5	.545	4.01	3	101	92	57	45	75	97
1979	San Antonio (Texas)	10	5	1	.833	5.20	0	64	69	44	37	43	52
	Albuquerque (Pacific Coast)	18	5	5	.500	4.63	0	101	95	59	52	82	69
1980	Albuquerque (Pacific Coast)	26	13	7	.650	4.53	0	155	160	93	78	95	113
1981	Albuquerque (Pacific Coast)	27	★18	3	.857	3.56	0	187	165	84	74	★103	111
	Los Angeles (N.L.).....................	5	1	3	.250	3.21	0	14	16	6	5	7	7
1982	Los Angeles (N.L.)	12	1	1	.500	6.68	0	33⅔	38	27	25	23	15
	Albuquerque (Pacific Coast)	14	5	4	.556	5.18	0	73	77	51	42	49	54
1983	Cincinnati (N.L.)■...................	49	5	6	.455	4.54	2	111	120	62	56	49	57
1984	Cincinnati (N.L.)	★78	9	7	.563	2.82	11	108⅔	93	37	34	46	81
1985	Cincinnati (N.L.)	64	8	6	.571	2.70	27	80	65	27	24	45	42
1986	Cincinnati (N.L.)	56	10	6	.625	3.70	1	129	115	59	53	52	95
1987	Cincinnati (N.L.)	34	10	13	.435	4.50	0	204	213	115	102	71	133
1988	Kansas City-Detroit (A.L.)■....	26	6	7	.462	5.91	0	99	121	67	65	38	57
1989	Louisville (American Assoc.)■	8	4	3	.571	3.16	0	37	29	13	13	15	36
	St. Louis (N.L.)	23	7	7	.500	3.71	0	97	96	47	40	21	43
1990	Pittsburgh (N.L.)■...................	40	1	3	.250	3.66	7	51⅔	50	23	21	17	42
1991	Cincinnati (N.L.)■...................	68	5	3	.625	3.62	3	87	87	37	35	31	51
	American League totals (1 year)	26	6	7	.462	5.91	0	99	121	67	65	38	57
	National League totals (10 years)	429	57	55	.509	3.88	51	916	893	440	395	362	566
	Major league totals (11 years)	455	63	62	.504	4.08	51	1015	1014	507	460	400	623

CHAMPIONSHIP SERIES RECORD

Year	Team (League)	G	W	L	Pct.	ERA	Sv.	IP	H	R	ER	BB	SO
1990	Pittsburgh (N.L.)	3	0	0	...	3.60	1	5	6	2	2	2	3

PRATT, TODD
C/1B, PHILLIES

PERSONAL: Born February 9, 1967, at Bellevue, Neb.... 6-3/195.... Throws right, bats right....
Full name: Todd Alan Pratt.
HIGH SCHOOL: Hilltop (Chula Vista, Calif.).
TRANSACTIONS/CAREER NOTES: Selected by Boston Red Sox organization in sixth round of free-agent draft (June 3, 1985).... Drafted by Cleveland Indians organization (December 7, 1987).... Returned to Red Sox organization (March, 1988).... Granted free agency (October 15, 1991).... Signed by Baltimore Orioles organization (November 13, 1991).... Drafted by Philadelphia Phillies organization (December 9, 1991).
STATISTICAL NOTES: Led South Atlantic League catchers with 660 putouts and nine double plays and tied for lead in errors with 13 in 1986.... Led Eastern League catchers with 11 errors in 1989.

						BATTING							FIELDING			
Year	Team (League)	Pos.	G	AB	R	H	2B	3B	HR	RBI	Avg.	SB	PO	A	E	Avg.
1985	Elmira (New York-Penn) ..	C	39	119	7	16	1	1	0	5	.134	0	254	29	6	.979
1986	Greensboro (S. Atlantic) ...	C-1B	107	348	63	84	16	0	12	56	.241	0	†826	55	‡15	.983
1987	Winter Haven (Fla. St.)	C-1B-OF	118	407	57	105	22	0	12	65	.258	0	672	64	15	.980
1988	New Britain (Eastern)	C-1B	124	395	41	89	15	2	8	49	.225	1	540	46	15	.975
1989	New Britain (Eastern)	C-1B	109	338	30	77	17	1	2	35	.228	1	435	42	†11	.977
1990	New Britain (Eastern)	C-1B	70	195	15	45	14	1	2	22	.231	0	166	15	4	.978
1991	Pawtucket (Int'l)	C-1B	68	219	68	64	16	0	11	41	.292	0	236	21	4	.985

PRESLEY, JIM

3B

PERSONAL: Born October 23, 1961, at Pensacola, Fla.... 6-1/190.... Throws right, bats right. ... Full name: James Arthur Presley.
HIGH SCHOOL: Escambia (Pensacola, Fla.).
COLLEGE: Pensacola Junior College (Fla.).
TRANSACTIONS/CAREER NOTES: Selected by Seattle Mariners organization in fourth round of free-agent draft (June 5, 1979).... Traded by Mariners to Atlanta Braves for P Gary Eave and 3B Ken Pennington (January 24, 1990).... Granted free agency (November 5, 1990).... Signed by San Diego Padres (February 8, 1991).... Released by Padres (June 8, 1991).... Signed by Oklahoma City, Texas Rangers organization (July 18, 1991).... Granted free agency (October 15, 1991).
RECORDS/HONORS: Holds major league single-season record for fewest putouts by third baseman (150 or more games)—82 (1985).
STATISTICAL NOTES: Led Midwest League in being hit by pitch with 12 in 1980.... Led Eastern League third basemen with 247 assists, 35 errors and 365 total chances in 1982.... Led Southern League third basemen with 29 double plays in 1983.... Hit three home runs in a game (September 1, 1986).... Led A.L. third basemen with 311 assists and 445 total chances in 1987.... Led N.L. third basemen with 25 errors in 1990.

Year	Team (League)	Pos.	G	AB	R	H	2B	3B	HR	RBI	Avg.	SB	PO	A	E	Avg.
1979 —Bellingham (Northwest)....		SS	48	138	20	27	4	1	1	12	.196	7	42	127	27	.862
1980 —Wausau (Midwest)..........		3-S-2-1	126	429	45	105	21	1	12	52	.245	9	161	235	22	.947
1981 —Wausau (Midwest)..........		3B	57	208	48	58	10	0	12	53	.279	9	32	105	9	.938
—Lynn (Eastern)		3B-2B	64	210	32	54	7	1	8	36	.257	4	49	110	11	.935
1982 —Lynn (Eastern)		3B-OF	133	462	65	123	24	0	22	79	.266	12	84 +250		+35	.905
1983 —Chattanooga (Southern)....		3B-SS	131	461	70	122	31	5	14	90	.265	9	122	329	27	.944
1984 —Salt Lake City (PCL).......		3B	69	265	43	84	13	4	13	56	.317	1	53	140	12	.941
—Seattle (A.L.)		3B	70	251	27	57	12	1	10	36	.227	1	48	113	7	.958
1985 —Seattle (A.L.)		3B	155	570	71	157	33	1	28	84	.275	2	82	335	17	.961
1986 —Seattle (A.L.)		3B	155	616	83	163	33	4	27	107	.265	0	110	308	15	.965
1987 —Seattle (A.L.)		3B-SS	152	575	78	142	23	6	24	88	.247	2	113 +315		21	.953
1988 —Seattle (A.L.)		3B	150	544	50	125	26	0	14	62	.230	3	112	234	22	.940
1989 —Seattle (A.L.)		3B-1B	117	390	42	92	20	1	12	41	.236	0	222	169	18	.956
1990 —Atlanta (N.L.)■		3B-1B	140	541	59	131	34	1	19	72	.242	1	178	242	+26	.942
1991 —San Diego (N.L.)■		3B	20	59	3	8	0	0	1	5	.136	0	13	23	3	.923
—Oklahoma City (A.A.)■.....		3B	51	207	30	56	10	2	6	29	.271	1	31	82	5	.958
American League totals (6 years)			799	2946	351	736	147	13	115	418	.250	8	687	1474	100	.956
National League totals (2 years)			160	600	62	139	34	1	20	77	.232	1	191	265	29	.940
Major league totals (8 years)			959	3546	413	875	181	14	135	495	.247	9	878	1739	129	.953

ALL-STAR GAME RECORD

Year	League	Pos.	AB	R	H	2B	3B	HR	RBI	Avg.	SB	PO	A	E	Avg.
1986 —American							Did not play								

PRINCE, TOM

C, PIRATES

PERSONAL: Born August 13, 1964, at Kankakee, Ill.... 5-11/185.... Throws right, bats right.... Full name: Thomas Albert Prince.
HIGH SCHOOL: Bradley Bourbonnais (Kankakee, Ill.).
COLLEGE: Kankakee Community College (Ill.).
TRANSACTIONS/CAREER NOTES: Selected by Atlanta Braves organization in eighth round of free-agent draft (January 11, 1983). ... Selected by Braves organization in secondary phase of free-agent draft (June 6, 1983).... Selected by Pittsburgh Pirates organization in secondary phase of free-agent draft (January 17, 1984).... On Pittsburgh disabled list (August 13-September 1, 1991); included rehabilitation disability assignment to Buffalo (August 28-September 1, 1991).
STATISTICAL NOTES: Led South Atlantic League catchers with 930 total chances, 10 double plays and 27 passed balls in 1985. ... Led Carolina League catchers with 954 total chances and 15 passed balls in 1986.... Led Eastern League catchers with 721 total chances and nine double plays in 1987.

Year	Team (League)	Pos.	G	AB	R	H	2B	3B	HR	RBI	Avg.	SB	PO	A	E	Avg.
1984 —Watertown (N.Y.-Penn)....		C-3B	23	69	6	14	3	0	2	13	.203	0	155	26	2	.989
—Bradenton Pirates (GCL) ..		C-1B	18	48	4	11	0	0	1	6	.229	1	75	16	4	.958
1985 —Macon (South Atlantic)		C	124	360	60	75	20	1	10	42	.208	13	*810	*101	*19	.980
1986 —Prince William (Caro.)....		C	121	395	59	100	34	1	10	47	.253	4	*821	•113	20	.979
1987 —Harrisburg (Eastern)		C	113	365	41	112	23	2	6	54	.307	6	*622	*88	•11	.985
—Pittsburgh (N.L.)		C	4	9	1	2	1	0	1	2	.222	0	14	3	0	1.000
1988 —Buffalo (Am. Assoc.)		C	86	304	35	79	16	0	14	42	.260	3	456	51	*12	.977
—Pittsburgh (N.L.)		C	29	74	3	13	2	0	0	6	.176	0	108	8	2	.983
1989 —Buffalo (Am. Assoc.)		C	65	183	21	37	8	1	6	33	.202	2	312	22	5	.985
—Pittsburgh (N.L.)		C	21	52	1	7	4	0	0	5	.135	1	85	11	4	.960
1990 —Pittsburgh (N.L.)		C	4	10	1	1	0	0	0	0	.100	0	16	1	0	1.000
—Buffalo (Am. Assoc.)		C-1B	94	284	38	64	13	0	7	37	.225	4	461	62	8	.985
1991 —Pittsburgh (N.L.)		C-1B	26	34	4	9	3	0	1	2	.265	0	53	9	1	.984
—Buffalo (Am. Assoc.)		C	80	221	29	46	8	3	6	32	.208	3	379	61	5	.989
Major league totals (5 years)			84	179	10	32	10	0	2	15	.179	1	276	32	7	.978

PUCKETT, KIRBY

OF, TWINS

PERSONAL: Born March 14, 1961, at Chicago.... 5-8/226.... Throws right, bats right.... Full name: Kirby Puckett.
HIGH SCHOOL: Calumet (Chicago).
COLLEGE: Bradley and Triton College (Ill.).

TRANSACTIONS/CAREER NOTES: Selected by Minnesota Twins organization in first round (third pick overall) of free-agent draft (January 12, 1982).

RECORDS/HONORS: Shares major league single-game records for most doubles—4 (May 13, 1989); most doubles in two consecutive games—6 (May 13 [4], 14 [2], 1989).... Shares major league single-season record for most at-bats with no sacrifice flies—680 (1986).... Shares modern major league record for most hits in first game in majors (nine innings)—4 (May 8, 1984).... Holds A.L. record for most hits in two consecutive nine-inning games—10 (August 29 and 30, 1987).... Shares A.L. record for most seasons with 400 or more putouts by outfielder—5.... Named California League Player of the Year (1983).... Named outfielder on THE SPORTING NEWS A.L. All-Star team (1986-89).... Won A.L. Gold Glove as outfielder (1986-89 and 1991).... Named outfielder on THE SPORTING NEWS A.L. Silver Slugger team (1986-89).

STATISTICAL NOTES: Led Appalachian League with 135 total bases in 1982.... Led California League outfielders with five double plays in 1983.... Led A.L. outfielders with 492 total chances in 1985, 465 in 1988 and 455 in 1989.... Hit for the cycle (August 1, 1986).... Collected six hits in one game (August 30, 1987 and May 23, 1991).... Led A.L. with 358 total bases in 1988.... Led A.L. in grounding into double plays with 27 in 1991.

Year	Team (League)	Pos.	G	AB	R	H	2B	3B	HR	RBI	Avg.	SB	PO	A	E	Avg.
1982	—Elizabethton (Appal.)	OF	65	*275	*65	*105	15	3	3	35	*.382	*43	133	*11	5	.966
1983	—Visalia (California)	OF	138	*548	105	172	29	7	9	97	.314	48	253	*22	5	.982
1984	—Toledo (International)	OF	21	80	9	21	2	0	1	5	.263	8	35	1	3	.923
	—Minnesota (A.L.)	OF	128	557	63	165	12	5	0	31	.296	14	438	*16	3	.993
1985	—Minnesota (A.L.)	OF	161	*691	80	199	29	13	4	74	.288	21	*465	19	8	.984
1986	—Minnesota (A.L.)	OF	161	680	119	223	37	6	31	96	.328	20	429	8	6	.986
1987	—Minnesota (A.L.)	OF	157	624	96	*207	32	5	28	99	.332	12	341	8	5	.986
1988	—Minnesota (A.L.)	OF	158	*657	109	*234	42	5	24	121	.356	6	*450	12	3	.994
1989	—Minnesota (A.L.)	OF	159	635	75	*215	45	4	9	85	*.339	11	*438	13	4	.991
1990	—Minnesota (A.L.)	0-2-3-S	146	551	82	164	40	3	12	80	.298	5	354	9	4	.989
1991	—Minnesota (A.L.)	OF	152	611	92	195	29	6	15	89	.319	11	373	13	6	.985
Major league totals (8 years)			1222	5006	716	1602	266	47	123	675	.320	100	3288	98	39	.989

CHAMPIONSHIP SERIES RECORD

CHAMPIONSHIP SERIES NOTES: Shares A.L. single-game record for most at-bats—6 (October 12, 1987).

Year	Team (League)	Pos.	G	AB	R	H	2B	3B	HR	RBI	Avg.	SB	PO	A	E	Avg.
1987	—Minnesota (A.L.)	OF	5	24	3	5	1	0	1	3	.208	1	7	0	0	1.000
1991	—Minnesota (A.L.)	OF	5	21	4	9	1	0	2	6	.429	0	13	1	0	1.000
Championship Series totals (2 years)			10	45	7	14	2	0	3	9	.311	1	20	1	0	1.000

WORLD SERIES RECORD

WORLD SERIES NOTES: Shares record for most at-bats in one inning—2 (October 18, 1987, fourth inning).... Shares single-game record for most runs—4 (October 24, 1987).

Year	Team (League)	Pos.	G	AB	R	H	2B	3B	HR	RBI	Avg.	SB	PO	A	E	Avg.
1987	—Minnesota (A.L.)	OF	7	28	5	10	1	1	0	3	.357	1	15	1	1	.941
1991	—Minnesota (A.L.)	OF	7	24	4	6	0	1	2	4	.250	1	16	1	0	1.000
World Series totals (2 years)			14	52	9	16	1	2	2	7	.308	2	31	2	1	.971

ALL-STAR GAME RECORD

Year	League	Pos.	AB	R	H	2B	3B	HR	RBI	Avg.	SB	PO	A	E	Avg.
1986	—American	OF	3	0	1	0	0	0	0	.333	1	5	0	0	1.000
1987	—American	PH-OF	4	0	0	0	0	0	0	.000	0	1	0	0	1.000
1988	—American	OF	1	0	0	0	0	0	0	.000	0	1	0	0	1.000
1989	—American	OF	3	1	1	0	0	0	0	.333	0	0	0	0	...
1990	—American	PH-OF	1	0	1	0	0	0	0	1.000	0	1	0	0	1.000
1991	—American	OF	1	0	0	0	0	0	0	.000	0	0	0	0	...
All-Star Game totals (6 years)			13	1	3	0	0	0	0	.231	1	8	0	0	1.000

PUGH, TIM

P, REDS

PERSONAL: Born January 26, 1967, at Lake Tahoe, Calif.... 6-6/225.... Throws right, bats right.... Full name: Timothy Dean Pugh.

HIGH SCHOOL: Bartlesville (Okla.).

COLLEGE: Oklahoma State.

TRANSACTIONS/CAREER NOTES: Selected by Toronto Blue Jays organization in eighth round of free-agent draft (June 1, 1988).... Selected by Cincinnati Reds organization in sixth round of free-agent draft (June 5, 1989).

STATISTICAL NOTES: Led South Atlantic League with eight complete games in 1990.

Year	Team (League)	G	W	L	Pct.	ERA	Sv.	IP	H	R	ER	BB	SO
1989	—Billings (Pioneer)	13	2	6	.250	3.94	0	77⅔	81	44	34	25	72
1990	—Charleston, W.Va. (S. Atl.)	27	*15	6	.714	1.93	0	177⅓	142	58	38	56	153
1991	—Chattanooga (Southern)	5	3	1	.750	1.64	0	38⅓	20	7	7	11	24
	—Nashville (American Assoc.)	23	7	11	.389	3.81	0	148⅔	130	68	63	56	89

PUHL, TERRY
OF

PERSONAL: Born July 8, 1956, at Melville, Saskatchewan).... 6-2/197.... Throws right, bats left.... Full name: Terrance Stephen Puhl.... Name pronounced POOL.
HIGH SCHOOL: Melville (Saskatchewan).
TRANSACTIONS/CAREER NOTES: Signed as free agent by Houston Astros organization (September 19, 1973).... On disabled list (April 13-30, 1984; April 22-May 7, June 13-28, July 19-August 15 and August 26, 1985-remainder of season; March 30-April 15 and July 2-23, 1986; May 10-June 28 and August 7, 1990-remainder of season).... Granted free agency (November 5, 1990).... Signed by New York Mets (December 13, 1990).... Released by Mets (April 1, 1991).... Signed by Kansas City Royals (April 25, 1991).... Released by Royals (June 9, 1991).
RECORDS/HONORS: Holds major league career record for highest fielding percentage by outfielder (1,000 or more games)—.993. ... Shares major league single-season records for highest fielding percentage by outfielder (150 or more games)—1.000 (1979); fewest errors by outfielder (150 or more games)—0 (1979).

Year	Team (League)	Pos.	G	AB	R	H	2B	3B	HR	RBI	Avg.	SB	PO	A	E	Avg.
1974 —Covington (Appal.)		OF	59	211	42	60	11	0	0	21	.284	17	89	2	2	.978
1975 —Dubuque (Midwest)		OF-1B	104	346	57	115	10	2	0	28	.332	20	230	11	7	.972
1976 —Columbus (Southern)		OF	28	98	13	28	5	0	1	14	.286	11	76	1	2	.975
—Memphis (International)		OF	105	372	50	99	17	3	1	39	.266	18	191	5	3	.985
1977 —Charleston, W.Va. (Int'l)		OF	78	285	53	87	12	6	4	33	.305	12	189	4	3	.985
—Houston (N.L.)		OF	60	229	40	69	13	5	0	10	.301	10	119	3	1	.992
1978 —Houston (N.L.)		OF	149	585	87	169	25	6	3	35	.289	32	386	6	3	.992
1979 —Houston (N.L.)		OF	157	600	87	172	22	4	8	49	.287	30	352	7	0	*1.000
1980 —Houston (N.L.)		OF	141	535	75	151	24	5	13	55	.282	27	311	14	3	.991
1981 —Houston (N.L.)		OF	96	350	43	88	19	4	3	28	.251	22	185	5	0	•1.000
1982 —Houston (N.L.)		OF	145	507	64	133	17	9	8	50	.262	17	257	4	3	.989
1983 —Houston (N.L.)		OF	137	465	66	136	25	7	8	44	.292	24	220	4	2	.991
1984 —Houston (N.L.)		OF	132	449	66	135	19	7	9	55	.301	13	213	6	3	.986
1985 —Houston (N.L.)		OF	57	194	34	55	14	3	2	23	.284	6	92	3	0	1.000
1986 —Houston (N.L.)		OF	81	172	17	42	10	0	3	14	.244	3	65	0	0	1.000
1987 —Houston (N.L.)		OF	90	122	9	28	5	0	2	15	.230	1	48	0	1	.980
1988 —Houston (N.L.)		OF	113	234	42	71	7	2	3	19	.303	22	116	2	2	.983
1989 —Houston (N.L.)		OF-1B	121	354	41	96	25	4	0	27	.271	9	212	3	0	1.000
1990 —Houston (N.L.)		OF-1B	37	41	5	12	1	0	0	8	.293	1	9	0	0	1.000
1991 —Kansas City (A.L.)■		OF	15	18	0	4	0	0	0	3	.222	0	0	0	0	...
American League totals (1 year)			15	18	0	4	0	0	0	3	.222	0	0	0	0	...
National League totals (14 years)			1516	4837	676	1357	226	56	62	432	.281	217	2585	57	18	.993
Major league totals (15 years)			1531	4855	676	1361	226	56	62	435	.280	217	2585	57	18	.993

DIVISION SERIES RECORD

Year	Team (League)	Pos.	G	AB	R	H	2B	3B	HR	RBI	Avg.	SB	PO	A	E	Avg.
1981 —Houston (N.L.)		OF	5	21	2	4	1	0	0	0	.190	1	7	1	0	1.000

CHAMPIONSHIP SERIES RECORD

CHAMPIONSHIP SERIES NOTES: Shares single-game record for most singles—4 (October 12, 1980, 10 innings).... Shares N.L. single-series record for most singles—8 (1980).

Year	Team (League)	Pos.	G	AB	R	H	2B	3B	HR	RBI	Avg.	SB	PO	A	E	Avg.
1980 —Houston (N.L.)		PH-OF	5	19	4	10	2	0	0	3	.526	2	13	0	0	1.000
1986 —Houston (N.L.)		PH	3	3	0	2	0	0	0	0	.667	1	0	0	0	...
Championship Series totals (2 years)			8	22	4	12	2	0	0	3	.545	3	13	0	0	1.000

ALL-STAR GAME RECORD

Year	League	Pos.	AB	R	H	2B	3B	HR	RBI	Avg.	SB	PO	A	E	Avg.
1978 —National									Did not play						

PULLIAM, HARVEY
OF, ROYALS

PERSONAL: Born October 20, 1967, at San Francisco.... 6-0/210.... Throws right, bats right.... Full name: Harvey Jerome Pulliam Jr.
HIGH SCHOOL: McAteer (San Francisco).
TRANSACTIONS/CAREER NOTES: Selected by Kansas City Royals organization in third round of free-agent draft (June 2, 1986).

Year	Team (League)	Pos.	G	AB	R	H	2B	3B	HR	RBI	Avg.	SB	PO	A	E	Avg.
1986 —Sarasota Royals (GCL)		OF	48	168	14	35	3	0	4	23	.208	3	62	5	4	.944
1987 —Appleton (Midwest)		OF	110	395	54	109	20	1	9	55	.276	21	195	8	6	.971
1988 —Baseball City (Fla. St.)		OF	132	457	56	111	19	4	4	42	.243	21	289	9	6	.980
1989 —Memphis (Southern)		OF	116	417	67	121	28	8	10	67	.290	5	157	8	5	.971
—Omaha (Am. Assoc.)		OF	7	22	3	4	2	0	0	2	.182	0	12	1	0	1.000
1990 —Omaha (Am. Assoc.)		OF	123	436	72	117	18	5	16	72	.268	9	188	12	4	.980
1991 —Omaha (Am. Assoc.)		OF	104	346	35	89	18	2	6	39	.257	2	162	12	3	.983
—Kansas City (A.L.)		OF	18	33	4	9	1	0	3	4	.273	0	21	1	2	.917
Major league totals (1 year)			18	33	4	9	1	0	3	4	.273	0	21	1	2	.917

QUANTRILL, PAUL
P, RED SOX

PERSONAL: Born November 3, 1968, at London, Ont. . . . 6-1/175. . . . Throws right, bats left. . . . Full name: Paul John Quantrill.
HIGH SCHOOL: Okemos (Mich.).
COLLEGE: Wisconsin.
TRANSACTIONS/CAREER NOTES: Selected by Los Angeles Dodgers organization in 26th round of free-agent draft (June 2, 1986). . . . Selected by Boston Red Sox organization in sixth round of free-agent draft (June 5, 1989).
STATISTICAL NOTES: Led International League pitchers with six complete games in 1991.

Year	Team (League)	G	W	L	Pct.	ERA	Sv.	IP	H	R	ER	BB	SO
1989	—Sarasota Red Sox (Gulf Coast) ..	2	0	0	...	0.00	2	5	2	0	0	0	5
	—Elmira (New York-Penn)	20	5	4	.556	3.43	2	76	90	37	29	12	57
1990	—Winter Haven (Florida State) ...	7	2	5	.286	4.14	0	45⅔	46	24	21	6	14
	—New Britain (Eastern)	22	7	11	.389	3.53	0	132⅔	148	65	52	23	53
1991	—New Britain (Eastern)	5	2	1	.667	2.06	0	35	32	14	8	8	18
	—Pawtucket (International)	25	10	7	.588	4.45	0	155⅔	169	81	77	30	75

QUINLAN, TOM
3B, BLUE JAYS

PERSONAL: Born March 27, 1968, at St. Paul, Minn. . . . 6-3/210. . . . Throws right, bats right. . . . Full name: Thomas Raymond Quinlan.
HIGH SCHOOL: Hill-Murray (St. Paul, Minn.).
TRANSACTIONS/CAREER NOTES: Selected by Toronto Blue Jays organization in 27th round of free-agent draft (June 2, 1986). . . . On disabled list (June 10-July 14, 1989).
STATISTICAL NOTES: Led South Atlantic League third basemen with 96 putouts and 29 double plays and tied for lead in total chances with 368 in 1989. . . . Tied for Southern League lead in double plays by third basemen with 21 in 1989. . . . Led Southern League batters with 157 strikeouts in 1990. . . . Led Southern League third basemen with 103 putouts in 1990. . . . Led International League batters with 163 strikeouts in 1991. . . . Led International League third basemen with .942 fielding percentage and 26 double plays in 1991.

Year	Team (League)	Pos.	G	AB	R	H	2B	3B	HR	RBI	Avg.	SB	PO	A	E	Avg.
1987	—Myrtle Beach (S. Atl.)........	3B-1B	132	435	42	97	20	3	5	51	.223	0	†107	232	40	.894
1988	—Knoxville (Southern)	3B-1B	98	326	33	71	19	1	8	44	.218	4	87	188	25	.917
1989	—Knoxville (Southern)	3B	139	452	62	95	21	3	16	57	.210	6	81	259	34	.909
1990	—Knoxville (Southern)	3B-SS	141	481	70	124	24	6	15	51	.258	8	†106	259	31	.922
	—Toronto (A.L.)...................	3B	1	2	0	1	0	0	0	0	.500	0	0	1	0	1.000
1991	—Syracuse (International) ..	3B-1B	132	466	56	112	24	6	10	49	.240	9	138	222	23	†.940
	Major league totals (1 year)		1	2	0	1	0	0	0	0	.500	0	0	1	0	1.000

QUINONES, LUIS
IF, TWINS

PERSONAL: Born April 28, 1962, at Ponce, Puerto Rico. . . . 5-11/180. . . . Throws right, bats both. . . . Full name: Luis Raul Quinones. . . . Name pronounced kee-NO-nez.
HIGH SCHOOL: Dr. Pila (Ponce, Puerto Rico).
TRANSACTIONS/CAREER NOTES: Signed as free agent by San Diego Padres organization (April 28, 1980). . . . Drafted by Oakland Athletics (December 6, 1982). . . . Traded by A's organization to Cleveland Indians (December 8, 1983), completing deal in which Indians traded C Jim Essian to A's for a player to be named later (December 5, 1983). . . . Traded by Indians organization with P Mike Jeffcoat to San Francisco Giants organization for SS Johnnie LeMaster (May 7, 1985). . . . Released by Giants (November 10, 1986). . . . Signed by Tacoma, A's organization (January 22, 1987). . . . Traded by A's to Chicago Cubs for 3B Ron Cey (January 30, 1987). . . . Traded by Cubs to Cincinnati Reds for P Bill Landrum (April 1, 1988). . . . Released by Reds (November 20, 1991). . . . Signed by Minnesota Twins organization (January 3, 1992).
RECORDS/HONORS: Shares major league record for most plate appearances in one inning—3 (August 3, 1989, first inning).
STATISTICAL NOTES: Tied for Northwest League lead in double plays by shortstops with 33 in 1980. . . . Tied for Carolina League lead in errors by shortstop with 53 in 1981. . . . Led Carolina League shortstops with 77 double plays in 1981. . . . Led International League shortstops with 43 errors in 1984.

Year	Team (League)	Pos.	G	AB	R	H	2B	3B	HR	RBI	Avg.	SB	PO	A	E	Avg.
1980	—Grays Harbor (N'west)	SS	56	156	33	35	2	2	0	11	.224	13	70	157	24	.904
1981	—Salem (Carolina)	SS-2B	123	455	64	102	10	4	7	37	.224	18	208	341	‡53	.912
1982	—Salem (Carolina)	SS	41	173	32	48	1	4	5	28	.277	6	41	99	15	.903
	—Amarillo (Texas)	SS	95	411	69	120	19	7	11	60	.292	8	164	288	31	.936
1983	—Albany (Eastern)■............	2B-OF-SS	56	213	35	51	5	2	6	23	.239	4	101	138	13	.948
	—Oakland (A.L.)	2-0-3-S	19	42	5	8	2	1	0	4	.190	1	22	24	1	.979
	—Tacoma (Pacific Coast) ...	SS-OF-2B	45	133	14	35	3	1	2	14	.263	5	62	97	9	.946
1984	—Maine (International)■........	SS-OF-2B	131	473	71	127	27	3	8	60	.268	5	217	330	†43	.927
1985	—Maine (International)	SS-OF	14	45	4	8	2	1	1	2	.178	0	19	12	0	1.000
	—Phoenix (Pacific Coast)■..	SS-2B-3B	85	304	46	78	13	7	8	47	.257	4	106	236	13	.963
1986	—Phoenix (Pacific Coast) ...	SS	14	55	7	14	4	1	0	7	.255	2	23	37	3	.952
	—San Francisco (N.L.)	SS-3B-2B	71	106	13	19	1	3	0	11	.179	3	28	66	8	.922
1987	—Iowa (American Assoc.)■.	SS-2B	77	287	44	91	14	∗12	11	62	.317	2	93	122	14	.939
	—Chicago (N.L.)	SS-2B-3B	49	101	12	22	6	0	0	8	.218	0	35	58	3	.969
1988	—Nashville (Am. Assoc.)■...	SS-3B-1B	114	417	42	115	28	6	9	53	.276	3	164	285	25	.947
	—Cincinnati (N.L.)	SS-2B-3B	23	52	4	12	3	0	1	11	.231	1	15	37	2	.963
1989	—Nashville (Am. Assoc.) ...	3B-2B-SS	45	176	19	40	9	2	4	24	.227	1	38	75	13	.897
	—Cincinnati (N.L.)	2B-3B-SS	97	340	43	83	13	4	12	34	.244	2	112	213	10	.970
1990	—Cincinnati (N.L.)	3-2-S-1	83	145	10	35	7	0	2	17	.241	1	44	85	6	.956
1991	—Cincinnati (N.L.)	2B-3B-SS	97	212	15	47	4	3	4	20	.222	1	68	106	7	.961
	American League totals (1 year)		19	42	5	8	2	1	0	4	.190	1	22	24	1	.979
	National League totals (6 years)		420	956	97	218	34	10	19	101	.228	8	302	565	36	.960
	Major league totals (7 years)		439	998	102	226	36	11	19	105	.226	9	324	589	37	.961

Year	Team (League)	Pos.	G	AB	R	H	2B	3B	HR	RBI	Avg.	SB	PO	A	E	Avg.
1990 —Cincinnati (N.L.)		PH	3	2	1	1	0	0	0	2	.500	1	0	0	0	...

QUINTANA, CARLOS
1B, RED SOX

PERSONAL: Born August 26, 1965, at Estado Miranda, Venezuela.... 6-2/220.... Throws right, bats right.... Full name: Carlos Narcis Quintana. **HIGH SCHOOL:** Mamparal Miranda (Venezuela). **TRANSACTIONS/CAREER NOTES:** Signed as free agent by Boston Red Sox organization (November 26, 1984).... On Boston disabled list (June 22-July 7, 1989). **RECORDS/HONORS:** Shares major league record for most runs batted in in one inning—6 (July 30, 1991, third inning). **STATISTICAL NOTES:** Led International League outfielders with 15 assists in 1988.... Led A.L. first basemen with 137 assists and 17 errors in 1990.... Tied for A.L. lead in assists by first baseman with 101 in 1991.

Year	Team (League)	Pos.	G	AB	R	H	2B	3B	HR	RBI	Avg.	SB	PO	A	E	Avg.
1985 —Elmira (New York-Penn) ..		OF	65	220	27	61	8	0	4	35	.277	3	55	5	3	.952
1986 —Greensboro (S. Atlantic) ...		OF-1B	126	443	97	144	19	4	11	81	.325	26	224	12	9	.963
1987 —New Britain (Eastern)		OF	56	206	31	64	11	3	2	31	.311	3	100	4	2	.981
1988 —Pawtucket (Int'l)		OF-1B	131	471	67	134	25	3	16	66	.285	3	525	†44	11	.981
—Boston (A.L.)		OF	5	6	1	2	0	0	0	2	.333	0	4	0	0	1.000
1989 —Pawtucket (Int'l)		1B-OF	82	272	45	78	11	2	11	52	.287	6	398	27	2	.995
—Boston (A.L.)		OF-1B	34	77	6	16	5	0	0	6	.208	0	31	0	2	.939
1990 —Boston (A.L.)		1B-OF	149	512	56	147	28	0	7	67	.287	1	1190	†137	†17	.987
1991 —Boston (A.L.)		1B-OF	149	478	69	141	21	1	11	71	.295	1	1041	‡102	9	.992
Major league totals (4 years)			337	1073	132	306	54	1	18	146	.285	2	2266	239	28	.989

CHAMPIONSHIP SERIES RECORD

Year	Team (League)	Pos.	G	AB	R	H	2B	3B	HR	RBI	Avg.	SB	PO	A	E	Avg.
1990 —Boston (A.L.)		1B	4	13	0	0	0	0	0	1	.000	0	29	2	0	1.000

QUIRICO, RAFAEL
P, GIANTS

PERSONAL: Born September 7, 1969, at Santo Domingo, Dominican Republic.... 6-2/185.... Throws left, bats left.... Full name: Rafael Quirico. **TRANSACTIONS/CAREER NOTES:** Signed as free agent by New York Yankees organization (May 15, 1987).... Drafted by San Francisco Giants (December 9, 1991). **STATISTICAL NOTES:** Led New York-Pennsylvania League with nine balks in 1990.... Led South Atlantic League with 10 balks in 1990.... Tied for South Atlantic League lead in balks with nine in 1991.

Year	Team (League)	G	W	L	Pct.	ERA	Sv.	IP	H	R	ER	BB	SO
1989 —Sarasota Yankees (GCL)	17	2	2	.500	3.82	1	63⅔	61	32	27	20	55
1990 —Oneonta (New York-Penn)	14	6	3	.667	3.21	0	87	69	38	31	39	69
—Greensboro (South Atlantic)	13	2	6	.250	5.00	0	72	74	60	40	30	52
1991 —Greensboro (South Atlantic) ...	26	12	8	.600	2.26	0	155⅓	103	59	39	80	162

QUIRK, JAMIE
C, ATHLETICS

PERSONAL: Born October 22, 1954, at Whittier, Calif.... 6-4/200.... Throws right, bats left.... Full name: James Patrick Quirk. **HIGH SCHOOL:** St. Paul (Sante Fe Springs, Calif.). **COLLEGE:** Whittier College (Calif.). **TRANSACTIONS/CAREER NOTES:** Selected by Kansas City Royals organization in first round (18th pick overall) of free-agent draft (June 6, 1972).... Traded by Royals with OF Jim Wohlford and a player to be named later to Milwaukee Brewers for P Jim Colborn and C Darrell Porter (December 6, 1976); Brewers acquired P Bob McClure to complete deal (March 15, 1977).... Traded by Brewers organization to Kansas City Royals for P Gerry Ako and cash (August 3, 1978).... On Kansas City disabled list (August 14-September 5, 1978 and August 10-September 1, 1982).... Granted free agency (November 10, 1982).... Signed by St. Louis Cardinals (February 16, 1983).... Released by Cardinals (March 26, 1984).... Named Cardinals coach (April 13, 1984).... Signed by Chicago White Sox organization (May 23, 1984).... Sold by White Sox to Cleveland Indians (September 24, 1984).... Released by Indians (October 15, 1984).... Signed by Royals organization (February 25, 1985).... Granted free agency (November 12, 1985).... Re-signed by Royals (November 27, 1985).... Granted free agency (November 12, 1986).... Re-signed by Royals (December 17, 1986).... On disabled list (July 21-August 5, 1987).... Granted free agency (November 9, 1987).... Re-signed by Royals (January 25, 1988).... Granted free agency (November 4, 1988).... Signed by New York Yankees (December 20, 1988).... Released by Yankees (May 16, 1989).... Signed by Tacoma, Oakland Athletics organization (May 27, 1989).... Released by A's (July 24, 1989).... Signed by Baltimore Orioles (August 5, 1989). ... Released by Orioles (November 2, 1989).... Signed by A's (December 13, 1989).... Granted free agency (November 5, 1990).... Re-signed by Athletics (November 28, 1990). **STATISTICAL NOTES:** Led Pioneer League shortstops with 16 double plays in 1972.... Led American Association third basemen with 31 double plays in 1975.... Led American Association with 23 passed balls in 1985.

Year	Team (League)	Pos.	G	AB	R	H	2B	3B	HR	RBI	Avg.	SB	PO	A	E	Avg.
1972 —Billings (Pioneer)		SS	55	208	29	53	9	4	5	37	.255	4	*63	*162	*28	*.889
1973 —San Jose (Pacific Coast) ...		SS	132	429	58	99	12	7	8	45	.231	7	160	330	39	.926

Year	Team (League)	Pos.	G	AB	R	H	2B	3B	HR	RBI	Avg.	SB	PO	A	E	Avg.
1974	—Jacksonville (Southern) ...	SS	46	163	16	37	7	2	3	21	.227	2	75	133	20	.912
	—Omaha (Am. Assoc.)	SS-3B-2B	53	203	27	57	10	2	10	31	.281	2	64	141	14	.936
1975	—Omaha (Am. Assoc.)	3B	127	445	62	122	23	4	13	64	.274	4	109	*254	16	*.958
	—Kansas City (A.L.)	OF-3B	14	39	2	10	0	0	1	5	.256	0	19	3	2	.917
1976	—Kansas City (A.L.)	SS-3B-1B	64	114	11	28	6	0	1	15	.246	0	9	14	2	.920
1977	—Milwaukee (A.L.)■	OF-3B	93	221	16	48	14	1	3	13	.217	0	19	4	2	.920
1978	—Spokane (Northwest)	3B-1B	97	343	58	100	20	2	12	63	.292	2	235	142	20	.950
	—Kansas City (A.L.)■	3B-SS	17	29	3	6	2	0	0	2	.207	0	11	16	2	.931
1979	—Kansas City (A.L.)	C-SS-3B	51	79	8	24	6	1	1	11	.304	0	16	9	1	.962
1980	—Kansas City (A.L.)	C-3-0-1	62	163	13	45	5	0	5	21	.276	3	78	66	8	.947
1981	—Kansas City (A.L.)	C-3-2-0	46	100	8	25	7	0	0	10	.250	0	63	23	4	.956
1982	—Kansas City (A.L.)	C-1-3-0	36	78	8	18	3	0	1	5	.231	0	110	12	0	1.000
1983	—St. Louis (N.L.)■	C-3B-SS	48	86	3	18	2	1	2	11	.209	0	68	13	6	.931
1984	—Denver (Am. Assoc.)■ C-3-0-1-P	70	201	23	42	6	3	2	24	.209	0	212	67	11	.962
	—Chicago-Clev. (A.L.)■	3B-C	4	3	1	1	0	0	1	2	.333	0	1	0	0	1.000
1985	—Omaha (Am. Assoc.)■	C-1B-3B	104	324	33	79	5	1	8	48	.244	0	525	67	14	.977
	—Kansas City (A.L.)	C-1B	19	57	3	16	3	1	0	4	.281	0	66	8	1	.987
1986	—Kansas City (A.L.)	C-3-1-0	80	219	24	47	10	0	8	26	.215	0	303	64	4	.989
1987	—Kansas City (A.L.)	C-SS	109	296	24	70	17	0	5	33	.236	1	532	40	8	.986
1988	—Kansas City (A.L.)	C-1B-3B	84	196	22	47	7	1	8	25	.240	1	412	34	8	.982
1989	—N.Y.-Oak.-Balt. (A.L.)■ C-3-1-0-S	47	85	6	15	2	0	1	10	.176	0	129	15	1	.993
	—Tacoma (Pacific Coast)	C	14	47	5	8	2	0	1	5	.170	0	89	7	2	.980
1990	—Oakland (A.L.)■	C-1-3-0	56	121	12	34	5	1	3	26	.281	0	168	18	5	.974
1991	—Oakland (A.L.)	C-1B-3B	76	203	16	53	4	0	1	17	.261	0	337	38	6	.984
American League totals (16 years)			858	2003	177	487	91	5	39	225	.243	5	2273	364	54	.980
National League totals (1 year)			48	86	3	18	2	1	2	11	.209	0	68	13	6	.931
Major league totals (17 years)			906	2089	180	505	93	6	41	236	.242	5	2341	377	60	.978

CHAMPIONSHIP SERIES RECORD

Year	Team (League)	Pos.	G	AB	R	H	2B	3B	HR	RBI	Avg.	SB	PO	A	E	Avg.
1976	—Kansas City (A.L.)	PH-DH	4	7	1	1	0	1	0	2	.143	0	0	0	0	...
1985	—Kansas City (A.L.)	PH	1	1	0	0	0	0	0	0	.000	0	0	0	0	...
1990	—Oakland (A.L.)	PH	1	1	0	1	0	0	0	0	1.000	0	0	0	0	...
Championship Series totals (3 years)			6	9	1	2	0	1	0	2	.222	0	0	0	0	...

WORLD SERIES RECORD

Year	Team (League)	Pos.	G	AB	R	H	2B	3B	HR	RBI	Avg.	SB	PO	A	E	Avg.
1980	—Kansas City (A.L.)						Did not play									
1985	—Kansas City (A.L.)						Did not play									
1990	—Oakland (A.L.)	C	1	3	0	0	0	0	0	0	.000	0	2	2	0	1.000

RECORD AS PITCHER

Year	Team (League)	G	W	L	Pct.	ERA	Sv.	IP	H	R	ER	BB	SO
1984	—Denver (American Assoc.)	2	0	0	...	13.50	0	2	6	3	3	0	0

RADINSKY, SCOTT
P, WHITE SOX

PERSONAL: Born March 3, 1968, at Glendale, Calif. . . . . 6-3/190. . . . Throws left, bats left. . . . Full name: Scott David Radinsky.
HIGH SCHOOL: Simi Valley (Calif.).
TRANSACTIONS/CAREER NOTES: Selected by Chicago White Sox organization in third round of free-agent draft (June 2, 1986).

Year	Team (League)	G	W	L	Pct.	ERA	Sv.	IP	H	R	ER	BB	SO
1986	—Sarasota White Sox (GCL)	7	1	0	1.000	3.38	0	26⅔	24	20	10	17	18
1987	—Peninsula (Carolina)	12	1	7	.125	5.77	0	39	43	30	25	32	37
	—Sarasota White Sox (GCL)	11	3	3	.500	2.31	0	58⅓	43	23	15	39	41
1988	—Sarasota White Sox (GCL)	5	0	0	...	5.40	0	3⅓	2	2	2	4	7
1989	—South Bend (Midwest)	53	7	5	.583	1.75	31	61⅔	39	21	12	19	83
1990	—Chicago (A.L.)	62	6	1	.857	4.82	4	52⅓	47	29	28	36	46
1991	—Chicago (A.L.)	67	5	5	.500	2.02	8	71⅓	53	18	16	23	49
Major league totals (2 years)	129	11	6	.647	3.20	12	123⅔	100	47	44	59	95

RAINES, TIM
OF, WHITE SOX

PERSONAL: Born September 16, 1959, at Sanford, Fla. . . . 5-8/185. . . . Throws right, bats both. . . . Full name: Timothy Raines. . . . Brother of Ned Raines, minor league outfielder (1978-80).
HIGH SCHOOL: Seminole (Sanford, Fla.).
TRANSACTIONS/CAREER NOTES: Selected by Montreal Expos organization in fifth round of free-agent draft (June 7, 1977). . . . On disabled list (May 23-June 5, 1981). . . . Granted free agency (November 12, 1986). . . . Re-signed by Expos (May 2, 1987). . . . On disabled list (June 24-July 9, 1988 and June 25-July 10, 1990). . . . Traded by Expos with P Jeff Carter and a player to be named later to Chicago White Sox for OF Ivan Calderon and P Barry Jones (December 23, 1990);

White Sox acquired P Mario Brito to complete deal (February 15, 1991).

RECORDS/HONORS: Holds major league career record for highest stolen base percentage (300 or more attempts)—.850.... Holds major league single-season record for most intentional bases on balls received by switch-hitter—26 (1987).... Holds N.L. career record for highest stolen base percentage (300 or more attempts)—.857.... Named Minor League Player of the Year by THE SPORTING NEWS (1980).... Named N.L. Rookie Player of the Year by THE SPORTING NEWS (1981).... Named outfielder on THE SPORTING NEWS N.L. All-Star team (1983 and 1986).... Won THE SPORTING NEWS Gold Shoe Award (1984).... Named outfielder on THE SPORTING NEWS N.L. Silver Slugger team (1986).

STATISTICAL NOTES: Led N.L. outfielders with 21 assists in 1983.... Led N.L. with .413 on base percentage in 1986.... Hit for the cycle (August 16, 1987).... Switch-hit home runs in one game (July 16, 1988).

Year	Team (League)	Pos.	G	AB	R	H	2B	3B	HR	RBI	Avg.	SB	PO	A	E	Avg.
1977—Sarasota Expos (GCL)		2B-3B-OF	49	161	28	45	6	2	0	21	.280	29	79	72	13	.921
1978—West Palm Beach (FSL)		2B-SS	100	359	67	103	10	0	0	23	.287	57	219	273	24	.953
1979—Memphis (Southern)		2B	•145	552	*104	160	25	10	5	50	.290	59	*341	*413	*23	.970
1980—Denver (Am. Assoc.)		2B	108	429	105	152	23	•11	6	64	*.354	*77	226	338	16	.972
—Montreal (N.L.)		2B-OF	15	20	5	1	0	0	0	0	.050	5	15	16	0	1.000
1981—Montreal (N.L.)		OF-2B	88	313	61	95	13	7	5	37	.304	*71	162	8	4	.977
1982—Montreal (N.L.)		OF-2B	156	647	90	179	32	8	4	43	.277	*78	293	126	8	.981
1983—Montreal (N.L.)		OF-2B	156	615	*133	183	32	8	11	71	.298	*90	314	†23	4	.988
1984—Montreal (N.L.)		OF-2B	160	622	106	192	•38	9	6	60	.309	*75	420	8	6	.986
1985—Montreal (N.L.)		OF	150	575	115	184	30	13	11	41	.320	70	284	8	2	.993
1986—Montreal (N.L.)		OF	151	580	91	194	35	10	9	62	*.334	70	270	13	6	.979
1987—Montreal (N.L.)		OF	139	530	*123	175	34	8	18	68	.330	50	297	9	4	.987
1988—Montreal (N.L.)		OF	109	429	66	116	19	7	12	48	.270	33	235	5	3	.988
1989—Montreal (N.L.)		OF	145	517	76	148	29	6	9	60	.286	41	253	7	1	.996
1990—Montreal (N.L.)		OF	130	457	65	131	11	5	9	62	.287	49	239	3	6	.976
1991—Chicago (A.L.)■		OF	155	609	102	163	20	6	5	50	.268	51	273	12	3	.990
American League totals (1 year)			155	609	102	163	20	6	5	50	.268	51	273	12	3	.990
National League totals (11 years)			1399	5305	931	1598	273	81	96	552	.301	632	2782	226	44	.986
Major league totals (12 years)			1554	5914	1033	1761	293	87	101	602	.298	683	3055	238	47	.986

CHAMPIONSHIP SERIES RECORD

Year	Team (League)	Pos.	G	AB	R	H	2B	3B	HR	RBI	Avg.	SB	PO	A	E	Avg.
1981—Montreal (N.L.)		OF	5	21	1	5	2	0	0	1	.238	0	9	0	0	1.000

ALL-STAR GAME RECORD

Year	League	Pos.	AB	R	H	2B	3B	HR	RBI	Avg.	SB	PO	A	E	Avg.
1981—National		PR-OF	0	0	0	0	0	0	0	...	0	1	0	0	1.000
1982—National		OF	1	0	0	0	0	0	0	.000	1	0	0	0	...
1983—National		OF	3	0	0	0	0	0	0	.000	1	2	0	0	1.000
1984—National		OF	1	0	0	0	0	0	0	.000	0	4	0	0	1.000
1985—National		PH-OF	0	1	0	0	0	0	0	...	0	0	0	0	...
1986—National		PH-OF	2	0	0	0	0	0	0	.000	0	1	0	0	1.000
1987—National		OF	3	0	3	0	1	0	2	1.000	1	1	0	0	1.000
All-Star Game totals (7 years)			10	1	3	0	1	0	2	.300	3	9	0	0	1.000

RAMIREZ, RAFAEL
SS, ASTROS

PERSONAL: Born February 18, 1959, at San Pedro de Macoris, Dominican Republic.... 5-11/190.... Throws right, bats right.... Full name: Rafael Emilio Peguero Ramirez.

TRANSACTIONS/CAREER NOTES: Signed as free agent by Atlanta Braves organization (September 28, 1976).... On disabled list (April 16-27, 1979; June 23-July 17, 1980; and July 2-September 25, 1987).... Traded by Braves with cash to Houston Astros for 3B Ed Whited and P Mike Stoker (December 8, 1987).... On disabled list (July 12-27, 1990).... Granted free agency (October 31, 1991).... Re-signed by Astros organization (January 10, 1992).

RECORDS/HONORS: Shares major league record for most years leading league in errors by shortstop—6.... Shares major league single-game records for most doubles—4 (May 21, 1986, 13 innings); most double plays by shortstop—6 (June 27, 1982, 14 innings).... Holds N.L single-season record for fewest putouts by shortstop who led league in putouts—251 (1984).

STATISTICAL NOTES: Led N.L. shortstops with 130 double plays in 1982, 116 in 1983, 115 in 1985 and tied for lead with 94 in 1984.... Led N.L. shortstops with 866 total chances in 1982 and 724 in 1984.

Year	Team (League)	Pos.	G	AB	R	H	2B	3B	HR	RBI	Avg.	SB	PO	A	E	Avg.
1977—Bradenton Braves (GCL)		SS-OF	49	175	20	31	2	1	4	19	.177	2	52	94	32	.820
1978—Greenwood (W. Caro.)		SS	81	282	54	77	15	3	6	46	.273	4	119	229	*43	.890
—Savannah (Southern)		SS	38	131	14	27	4	0	2	13	.206	1	61	123	15	.925
1979—Savannah (Southern)		SS	113	386	47	80	17	3	10	39	.207	7	134	282	*38	.916
1980—Richmond (Int'l)		SS	80	281	33	79	15	3	5	38	.281	4	117	294	23	.947
—Atlanta (N.L.)		SS	50	165	17	44	6	1	2	11	.267	2	63	140	11	.949
1981—Atlanta (N.L.)		SS	95	307	30	67	16	2	2	20	.218	7	181	306	*30	.942
1982—Atlanta (N.L.)		SS	157	609	74	169	24	4	10	52	.278	27	*300	528	*38	.956
1983—Atlanta (N.L.)		SS	152	622	82	185	13	5	7	58	.297	16	232	490	*39	.949
1984—Atlanta (N.L.)		SS	145	591	51	157	22	4	2	48	.266	14	*251	443	*30	.959
1985—Atlanta (N.L.)		SS	138	568	54	141	25	4	5	58	.248	2	214	451	*32	.954

Year	Team (League)	Pos.	G	AB	R	H	2B	3B	HR	RBI	Avg.	SB	PO	A	E	Avg.
							BATTING							FIELDING		
1986 —Atlanta (N.L.)	SS-3B-OF	134	496	57	119	21	1	8	33	.240	19	156	371	29	.948
1987 —Atlanta (N.L.)	SS-3B	56	179	22	47	12	0	1	21	.263	6	66	110	10	.946
1988 —Houston (N.L.)■.............	SS	155	566	51	156	30	5	6	59	.276	3	232	408	23	.965
1989 —Houston (N.L.)	SS	151	537	46	132	20	2	6	54	.246	3	189	326	*30	.945
1990 —Houston (N.L.)	SS	132	445	44	116	19	3	2	37	.261	10	190	321	25	.953
1991 —Houston (N.L.)	SS-2B-3B	101	233	17	55	10	0	1	20	.236	3	86	124	8	.963
Major league totals (12 years)		1466	5318	545	1388	218	31	52	471	.261	112	2160	4018	305	.953

CHAMPIONSHIP SERIES RECORD

Year	Team (League)	Pos.	G	AB	R	H	2B	3B	HR	RBI	Avg.	SB	PO	A	E	Avg.
							BATTING							FIELDING		
1982 —Atlanta (N.L.)	SS	3	11	1	2	0	0	0	1	.182	0	5	11	1	.941

ALL-STAR GAME RECORD

Year	League	Pos.	AB	R	H	2B	3B	HR	RBI	Avg.	SB	PO	A	E	Avg.
						BATTING							FIELDING		
1984 —National						Did not play									

RAMOS, JOHN
C, YANKEES

PERSONAL: Born August 6, 1965, at Tampa, Fla. . . . 6-0/ 190. . . . Throws right, bats right. . . . Full name: John Joseph Ramos.
HIGH SCHOOL: Henry B. Plant (Tampa, Fla.).
COLLEGE: Stanford.
TRANSACTIONS/CAREER NOTES: Selected by Cleveland Indians organization in 23rd round of free-agent draft (June 6, 1986). . . . Selected by New York Yankees organization in fifth round of free-agent draft (June 2, 1986).
STATISTICAL NOTES: Led Carolina League catchers with 25 errors in 1988. . . . Led International League with nine sacrifice flies in 1991.

Year	Team (League)	Pos.	G	AB	R	H	2B	3B	HR	RBI	Avg.	SB	PO	A	E	Avg.
							BATTING							FIELDING		
1986 —Fort Lauderdale (FSL)	C	54	184	25	49	10	1	2	28	.266	8	197	19	9	.960
—Oneonta (N.Y.-Penn)	C	3	8	3	4	2	1	0	1	.500	0	22	0	0	1.000
1987 —Prince William (Caro.)	C	76	235	26	51	6	1	2	27	.217	8	283	24	19	.942
1988 —Prince William (Caro.)	C-OF	109	391	47	119	18	2	8	57	.304	8	585	37	†26	.960
—Albany (Eastern)	3B-OF-C	21	72	11	16	1	3	1	13	.222	2	24	27	2	.962
1989 —Albany (Eastern)	C-OF	105	359	55	98	21	0	9	60	.273	7	561	46	11	.982
1990 —Albany (Eastern)	C-3B	84	287	38	90	20	1	4	46	.314	1	230	21	4	.984
—Columbus (Int'l)	C	2	6	0	0	0	0	0	1	.000	0	2	1	0	1.000
1991 —Columbus (Int'l)	C	104	377	52	116	18	3	10	63	.308	1	487	41	6	.989
—New York (A.L.)	C	10	26	4	8	1	0	0	3	.308	0	23	1	0	1.000
Major league totals (1 year)		10	26	4	8	1	0	0	3	.308	0	23	1	0	1.000

RANDOLPH, WILLIE
2B, METS

PERSONAL: Born July 6, 1954, at Holly Hill, S.C. . . . 5-11/ 171. . . . Throws right, bats right. . . . Full name: William Larry Randolph Jr. . . . Brother of Terry Randolph, National Football League player (1977).
HIGH SCHOOL: Tilden (Brooklyn, N.Y.).
TRANSACTIONS/CAREER NOTES: Selected by Pittsburgh Pirates organization in seventh round of free-agent draft (June 6, 1972). . . . Traded to Pirates with P Ken Brett and P Dock Ellis to New York Yankees for P Doc Medich (December 11, 1975). . . . On disabled list (June 23-July 14, 1978; June 27-July 12 and July 13 to August 5, 1983). . . . Granted free agency (November 12, 1986). . . . Re-signed by Yankees (January 8, 1987). . . . On disabled list (July 15-August 14, 1987; June 10-25 and August 3-28, 1988). . . . Granted free agency (October 24, 1988). . . . Signed by Los Angeles Dodgers (December 10, 1988). . . . Traded by Dodgers to Oakland Athletics for OF Stan Javier (May 13, 1990). . . . On disabled list (July 15-August 1, 1990). . . . Granted free agency (November 5, 1990). . . . Signed by Milwaukee Brewers (April 2, 1991). . . . Granted free agency (October 31, 1991). . . . Signed by New York Mets (December 20, 1991).
RECORDS/HONORS: Shares major league single-game record (19 innings) for most assists by second baseman—13 (August 25, 1976). . . . Holds A.L. single-game record (19 innings) for most chances accepted by second baseman—20 (August 25, 1976). . . . Named second baseman on THE SPORTING NEWS A.L. All-Star team (1977, 1980 and 1987). . . . Named second baseman on THE SPORTING NEWS A.L. Silver Slugger team (1980).
STATISTICAL NOTES: Led Western Carolinas League with 90 bases on balls received and tied for lead with eight sacrifice flies in 1973. . . . Led Eastern League with 110 bases on balls received in 1974. . . . Led A.L. second basemen with 846 total chances in 1979. . . . Led A.L. second basemen with 128 double plays in 1979 and 112 in 1984. . . . Led A.L. in bases on balls received with 119 in 1980.

Year	Team (League)	Pos.	G	AB	R	H	2B	3B	HR	RBI	Avg.	SB	PO	A	E	Avg.
							BATTING							FIELDING		
1972 —Bradenton Pirates (GCL) ..	SS-OF	44	167	21	53	6	5	0	10	.317	10	85	116	24	.893
1973 —Charles., S.C. (W. Caro.) ..	2B	121	428	93	120	25	6	8	51	.280	43	*285	308	*24	.961
1974 —Thetford Mines (East.)	2B	135	461	*103	117	28	6	12	53	.254	38	269	319	21	.966
1975 —Charleston, W.Va. (Int'l) ...	2B	91	313	44	106	13	5	7	42	.339	14	189	250	16	.965
—Pittsburgh (N.L.)	2B-3B	30	61	9	10	1	0	0	3	.164	1	34	45	6	.929
1976 —New York (A.L.)■.............	2B	125	430	59	115	15	4	1	40	.267	37	307	415	19	.974
1977 —New York (A.L.)	2B	147	551	91	151	28	11	4	40	.274	13	350	454	16	.980

Year	Team (League)	Pos.	G	AB	R	H	2B	3B	HR	RBI	Avg.	SB	PO	A	E	Avg.
							BATTING							FIELDING		
1978 —New York (A.L.)	2B	134	499	87	139	18	6	3	42	.279	36	296	400	16	.978
1979 —New York (A.L.)	2B	153	574	98	155	15	13	5	61	.270	33	*355	*478	13	.985
1980 —New York (A.L.)	2B	138	513	99	151	23	7	7	46	.294	30	361	401	19	.976
1981 —New York (A.L.)	2B	93	357	59	83	14	3	2	24	.232	14	205	268	*11	.977
1982 —New York (A.L.)	2B	144	553	85	155	21	4	3	36	.280	16	352	380	14	.981
1983 —New York (A.L.)	2B	104	420	73	117	21	1	2	38	.279	12	265	298	12	.979
1984 —New York (A.L.)	2B	142	564	86	162	24	2	2	31	.287	10	334	419	13	.983
1985 —New York (A.L.)	2B	143	497	75	137	21	2	5	40	.276	16	303	425	11	.985
1986 —New York (A.L.)	2B	141	492	76	136	15	2	5	50	.276	15	313	381	*20	.972
1987 —New York (A.L.)	2B	120	449	96	137	24	2	7	67	.305	11	286	338	12	.981
1988 —New York (A.L.)■	2B	110	404	43	93	20	1	2	34	.230	8	254	339	7	.988
1989 —Los Angeles (N.L.)■	2B	145	549	62	155	18	0	2	36	.282	7	260	412	9	.987
1990 —Los Angeles (N.L.)	2B	26	96	15	26	4	0	1	9	.271	1	50	73	4	.969
—Oakland (A.L.)■	2B	93	292	37	75	9	3	1	21	.257	6	148	240	7	.982
1991 —Milwaukee (A.L.)■	2B	124	431	60	141	14	3	0	54	.327	4	237	378	*20	.969
American League totals (15 years)		1911	7026	1124	1947	282	64	49	624	.277	261	4366	5614	210	.979
National League totals (3 years)		201	706	86	191	23	0	3	48	.271	9	344	530	19	.979
Major league totals (17 years)		2112	7732	1210	2138	305	64	52	672	.277	270	4710	6144	229	.979

DIVISION SERIES RECORD

Year	Team (League)	Pos.	G	AB	R	H	2B	3B	HR	RBI	Avg.	SB	PO	A	E	Avg.
							BATTING							FIELDING		
1981 —New York (A.L.)	2B	5	20	0	4	0	0	0	1	.200	0	7	10	0	1.000

CHAMPIONSHIP SERIES RECORD

CHAMPIONSHIP SERIES NOTES: Shares A.L. career record for most times grounding into double play—4.

Year	Team (League)	Pos.	G	AB	R	H	2B	3B	HR	RBI	Avg.	SB	PO	A	E	Avg.
							BATTING							FIELDING		
1975 —Pittsburgh (N.L.)	PH-PR-2B	2	2	1	0	0	0	0	0	.000	0	0	1	0	1.000
1976 —New York (A.L.)	2B	5	17	0	2	0	0	0	1	.118	1	8	14	0	1.000
1977 —New York (A.L.)	2B	5	18	4	5	1	0	0	2	.278	0	13	9	0	1.000
1980 —New York (A.L.)	2B	3	13	0	5	2	0	0	1	.385	0	2	9	0	1.000
1981 —New York (A.L.)	2B	3	12	2	4	0	0	1	2	.333	0	12	12	0	1.000
1990 —Oakland (A.L.)	PR-2B	4	8	1	3	0	0	0	3	.375	0	5	9	0	1.000
Championship Series totals (6 years)		22	70	8	19	3	0	1	9	.271	1	40	54	0	1.000

WORLD SERIES RECORD

Year	Team (League)	Pos.	G	AB	R	H	2B	3B	HR	RBI	Avg.	SB	PO	A	E	Avg.
							BATTING							FIELDING		
1976 —New York (A.L.)	2B	4	14	1	1	0	0	0	0	.071	0	13	8	0	1.000
1977 —New York (A.L.)	2B	6	25	5	4	2	0	1	1	.160	0	13	14	0	1.000
1981 —New York (A.L.)	2B	6	18	5	4	1	1	2	3	.222	1	13	11	0	1.000
1990 —Oakland (A.L.)	2B	4	15	0	4	0	0	0	0	.267	0	14	12	0	1.000
World Series totals (4 years)		20	72	11	13	3	1	3	4	.181	1	53	45	0	1.000

ALL-STAR GAME RECORD

ALL-STAR GAME NOTES: Shares single-game record for most at-bats (nine-inning game)—5 (July 19, 1977).... Named to A.L. All-Star team for 1976 game; replaced due to injury.

Year	League	Pos.	AB	R	H	2B	3B	HR	RBI	Avg.	SB	PO	A	E	Avg.
						BATTING							FIELDING		
1977 —American	2B	5	0	1	0	0	0	1	.200	0	2	6	0	1.000
1980 —American	2B	4	0	2	0	0	0	0	.500	0	0	3	2	.600
1981 —American	2B	3	0	1	0	0	0	0	.333	0	0	5	0	1.000
1987 —American	2B	1	0	0	0	0	0	0	.000	0	0	1	0	1.000
1989 —National	2B	1	0	0	0	0	0	0	.000	0	0	0	0	...
All-Star Game totals (5 years)		14	0	4	0	0	0	1	.286	0	2	15	2	.895

RASMUSSEN, DENNIS
P, ORIOLES

PERSONAL: Born April 18, 1959, at Los Angeles.... 6-7/233.... Throws left, bats left.... Full name: Dennis Lee Rasmussen.... Grandson of Bill Brubaker, infielder, Pittsburgh Pirates and Boston Braves (1932-40 and 1943).
HIGH SCHOOL: Bear Creek (Lakewood, Colo.).
COLLEGE: Creighton.
TRANSACTIONS/CAREER NOTES: Selected by Pittsburgh Pirates organization in 18th round of free-agent draft (June 7, 1977).... Selected by California Angels organization in first round (17th pick overall) of free-agent draft (June 3, 1980).... Traded by Angels organization to New York Yankees (November 24, 1982), completing deal in which Yankees traded P Tommy John to Angels for a player to be named later (August 31, 1982).... Traded by Yankees organization with 2B Edwin Rodriguez to San Diego Padres (September 12, 1983), completing deal in which Padres traded P John Montefusco to Yankees for two players to be named later (August 26, 1983).... Traded by Padres with a player to be named later to Yankees organization for 3B Graig Nettles (March 30, 1984); Yankees organization acquired P Darin Cloninger to complete deal (April 26, 1984).... Traded by Yankees to Cincinnati Reds for P Bill Gullickson (August 26, 1987).... Traded by Reds to San Diego Padres for P Candy Sierra (June 8, 1988).... Granted free agency (November 5, 1990).... Re-signed by Padres (January 9, 1991).... On San Diego

disabled list (March 31-May 25, 1991); included rehabilitation disability assignment to Las Vegas (April 23-May 22, 1991). . . . Granted free agency (October 28, 1991). . . . Signed by Rochester, Baltimore Orioles organization (January 31, 1992).
STATISTICAL NOTES: Led Eastern League with 18 wild pitches in 1981. . . . Tied for International League lead in games started by pitcher with 28 in 1983. . . . Led N.L. with 28 home runs allowed in 1990.
MISCELLANEOUS: Struck out in only appearance as pinch-hitter (1991).

Year	Team (League)	G	W	L	Pct.	ERA	Sv.	IP	H	R	ER	BB	SO
1980 —Salinas (California)		11	4	6	.400	5.45	0	76	69	51	46	52	63
1981 —Holyoke (Eastern)		24	8	12	.400	3.98	0	156	134	95	69	99	125
1982 —Spokane (Pacific Coast)		27	11	8	.579	5.03	0	171⅔	166	110	96	★113	162
1983 —Columbus (International)■		28	•13	10	.565	4.57	0	181	161	106	92	108	★187
—San Diego (N.L.)■		4	0	0	. . .	1.98	0	13⅔	10	5	3	8	13
1984 —Columbus (International)■		6	4	1	.800	3.09	0	43⅔	24	15	15	27	30
—New York (A.L.)		24	9	6	.600	4.57	0	147⅓	127	79	75	60	110
1985 —New York (A.L.)		22	3	5	.375	3.98	0	101⅔	97	56	45	42	63
—Columbus (International)		7	0	3	.000	3.80	0	45	41	24	19	25	43
1986 —New York (A.L.)		31	18	6	.750	3.88	0	202	160	91	87	74	131
1987 —New York (A.L.)		26	9	7	.563	4.75	0	146	145	78	77	55	89
—Columbus (International)		1	1	0	1.000	1.29	0	7	5	1	1	0	4
—Cincinnati (N.L.)■		7	4	1	.800	3.97	0	45⅓	39	22	20	12	39
1988 —Cincinnati-San Diego (N.L.)■...		31	16	10	.615	3.43	0	204⅔	199	84	78	58	112
1989 —San Diego (N.L.)		33	10	10	.500	4.26	0	183⅔	190	100	87	72	87
1990 —San Diego (N.L.)		32	11	15	.423	4.51	0	187⅓	217	110	94	62	86
1991 —Las Vegas (Pacific Coast)		5	1	3	.250	5.47	0	26⅓	23	18	16	15	12
—San Diego (N.L.)		24	6	13	.316	3.74	0	146⅔	155	74	61	49	75
American League totals (4 years)		103	39	24	.619	4.28	0	597⅓	529	304	284	231	393
National League totals (6 years)		131	47	49	.490	3.95	0	781⅔	810	395	343	261	412
Major league totals (9 years)		234	86	73	.541	4.09	0	1379	1339	699	627	492	805

RATLIFF, DARYL
OF, PIRATES

PERSONAL: Born October 15, 1969, at Santa Cruz, Calif. . . . 6-1/180. . . . Throws right, bats right. . . . Full name: Daryl Reynard Ratliff.
HIGH SCHOOL: Santa Cruz (Calif.).
TRANSACTIONS/CAREER NOTES: Selected by Pittsburgh Pirates organization in fifth round of free-agent draft (June 1, 1988).
STATISTICAL NOTES: Led Appalachian League outfielders with three double plays in 1989.

Year	Team (League)	Pos.	G	AB	R	H	2B	3B	HR	RBI	Avg.	SB	PO	A	E	Avg.
1989 —Princeton (Appalachian) ..		OF	66	208	28	51	2	0	0	21	.245	10	110	9	4	.967
1990 —Augusta (S. Atlantic)		OF	122	417	70	123	11	6	1	55	.295	24	218	13	9	.963
1991 —Salem (Carolina)		OF	88	352	60	103	8	4	2	23	.293	35	181	15	10	.951
—Carolina (Southern)		OF	24	93	10	20	3	0	0	9	.215	8	43	0	1	.977

READY, RANDY
IF, ATHLETICS

PERSONAL: Born January 8, 1960, at San Mateo, Calif. . . . 5-11/184. . . . Throws right, bats right. . . . Full name: Randy Max Ready.
HIGH SCHOOL: John F. Kennedy (Fremont, Calif.).
COLLEGE: Cal State Hayward and Mesa College (Colo.).
TRANSACTIONS/CAREER NOTES: Selected by Milwaukee Brewers organization in fifth round of free-agent draft (June 3, 1980). . . . On Vancouver disabled list (August 21, 1984-remainder of season). . . . On Milwaukee disabled list (April 30-June 19, 1985); included rehabilitation disability assignment to Vancouver (June 1-19, 1985). . . . Traded by Brewers to San Diego Padres for a player to be named later (June 12, 1986); Brewers organization acquired IF Tim Pyznarski to complete deal (October 29, 1986). . . . On San Diego disabled list (June 19-July 7, 1986). . . . On Las Vegas disabled list (July 22, 1986-remainder of season). . . . Traded by Padres with OF John Kruk to Philadelphia Phillies for OF Chris James (June 2, 1989). . . . On disabled list (June 7-July 11, 1991). . . . Granted free agency (October 28, 1991). . . . Signed by Oakland A's (January 14, 1992).
RECORDS/HONORS: Shares A.L. single-game record for most innings played by third baseman—25 (May 8, finished May 9, 1984; fielded 24⅓ innings).
STATISTICAL NOTES: Led Midwest League third basemen with 22 double plays in 1981. . . . Led Texas League with 281 total bases in 1982. . . . Led Texas League third basemen with 456 total chances and 27 double plays in 1982. . . . Led Pacific Coast League with 99 bases on balls received in 1983.

Year	Team (League)	Pos.	G	AB	R	H	2B	3B	HR	RBI	Avg.	SB	PO	A	E	Avg.
1980 —Butte (Pioneer)		SS-2B-3B	61	226	★65	85	★23	4	8	50	★.376	2	86	174	22	.922
1981 —Burlington (W. Caro.)		3B	110	367	74	113	17	0	17	56	.308	7	72	216	21	★.932
1982 —El Paso (Texas)		3B	132	475	★122	★178	33	5	20	99	★.375	13	★115	★312	•29	.936
1983 —Vancouver (Pac. Coast)		3B	116	407	82	134	28	1	13	59	.329	24	136	231	24	.939
—Milwaukee (A.L.)		3B	12	37	8	15	3	2	1	6	.405	0	5	8	0	1.000
1984 —Milwaukee (A.L.)		3B	37	123	13	23	6	1	3	13	.187	0	29	76	6	.946
—Vancouver (Pac. Coast)		3B	43	151	48	49	7	4	3	18	.325	10	74	125	6	.971
1985 —Milwaukee (A.L.)		OF-3B-2B	48	181	29	48	9	5	1	21	.265	0	93	14	1	.991
—Vancouver (Pac. Coast)		OF-3B-2B	52	190	33	62	12	3	4	29	.326	14	60	35	7	.931
1986 —Milwaukee (A.L.)		OF-2B-3B	23	79	8	15	4	0	1	4	.190	2	35	21	3	.949
—San Diego (N.L.)■		3B	1	3	0	0	0	0	0	0	.000	0	0	2	1	.667
—Las Vegas (Pac. Coast)		3B-OF	10	38	5	14	4	0	1	8	.368	1	12	10	0	1.000

Year Team (League)	Pos.	G	AB	R	H	2B	3B	HR	RBI	Avg.	SB	PO	A	E	Avg.
1987—San Diego (N.L.)	3B-2B-OF	124	350	69	108	26	6	12	54	.309	7	124	220	15	.958
1988—San Diego (N.L.)	3B-2B-OF	114	331	43	88	16	2	7	39	.266	6	112	153	11	.960
1989—San Diego-Phil. (N.L.)■	OF-3B-2B	100	254	37	67	13	2	8	26	.264	4	80	72	9	.944
1990—Philadelphia (N.L.)	OF-2B	101	217	26	53	9	1	1	26	.244	3	78	86	2	.988
1991—Philadelphia (N.L.)	2B	76	205	32	51	10	1	1	20	.249	2	127	145	3	.989
American League totals (4 years)		120	420	58	101	22	8	6	44	.240	2	162	119	10	.966
National League totals (6 years)		516	1360	207	367	74	12	29	165	.270	22	521	678	41	.967
Major league totals (9 years)		636	1780	265	468	96	20	35	209	.263	24	683	797	51	.967

REARDON, JEFF
P, RED SOX

PERSONAL: Born October 1, 1955, at Pittsfield, Mass. . . . 6-0/205. . . . Throws right, bats right. . . . Full name: Jeffrey James Reardon.
HIGH SCHOOL: Wahconah (Dalton, Mass.).
COLLEGE: Massachusetts.
TRANSACTIONS/CAREER NOTES: Selected by Montreal Expos organization in 23rd round of free-agent draft (June 5, 1973). . . . Signed as free agent by New York Mets organization (June 14, 1977). . . . On Tidewater disabled list (June 13-24 and June 29-July 26, 1979). . . . Traded by Mets with OF Dan Norman to Montreal Expos for OF Ellis Valentine (May 29, 1981). . . . Traded by Expos with C Tom Nieto to Minnesota Twins for P Neal Heaton, P Al Cardwood, P Yorkis Perez and C Jeff Reed (February 3, 1987). . . . Granted free agency (November 13, 1989). . . . Signed by Boston Red Sox (December 6, 1989). . . . On disabled list (July 30-September 12, 1990).
RECORDS/HONORS: Named N.L. Fireman of the Year by THE SPORTING NEWS (1985). . . . Named A.L. Co-Fireman of the Year by THE SPORTING NEWS (1987).
STATISTICAL NOTES: Led Carolina League with three shutouts in 1977.

Year Team (League)	G	W	L	Pct.	ERA	Sv.	IP	H	R	ER	BB	SO
1977—Lynchburg (Carolina)	16	8	3	.727	3.30	0	101	89	42	37	30	60
1978—Jackson (Texas)	28	★17	4	★.810	2.54	0	163	128	56	46	65	115
1979—Tidewater (International)	30	5	2	.714	2.09	0	69	46	18	16	21	64
—New York (N.L.)	18	1	2	.333	1.71	2	21	12	7	4	9	10
1980—New York (N.L.)	61	8	7	.533	2.62	6	110	96	36	32	47	101
1981—New York-Montreal (N.L.)■	43	3	0	1.000	2.19	8	70	48	17	17	21	49
1982—Montreal (N.L.)	75	7	4	.636	2.06	26	109	87	28	25	36	86
1983—Montreal (N.L.)	66	7	9	.438	3.03	21	92	87	34	31	44	78
1984—Montreal (N.L.)	68	7	7	.500	2.90	23	87	70	31	28	37	79
1985—Montreal (N.L.)	63	2	8	.200	3.18	★41	87⅔	68	31	31	26	67
1986—Montreal (N.L.)	62	7	9	.438	3.94	35	89	83	42	39	26	67
1987—Minnesota (A.L.)■	63	8	8	.500	4.48	31	80⅓	70	41	40	28	83
1988—Minnesota (A.L.)	63	2	4	.333	2.47	42	73	68	21	20	15	56
1989—Minnesota (A.L.)	65	5	4	.556	4.07	31	73	68	33	33	12	46
1990—Boston (A.L.)■	47	5	3	.625	3.16	21	51⅓	39	19	18	19	33
1991—Boston (A.L.)	57	1	4	.200	3.03	40	59⅓	54	21	20	16	44
American League totals (5 years)	295	21	23	.477	3.50	165	337	299	135	131	90	262
National League totals (8 years)	456	42	46	.477	2.80	162	665⅔	551	226	207	246	537
Major league totals (13 years)	751	63	69	.477	3.03	327	1002⅔	850	361	338	336	799

DIVISION SERIES RECORD

Year Team (League)	G	W	L	Pct.	ERA	Sv.	IP	H	R	ER	BB	SO
1981—Montreal (N.L.)	3	0	1	.000	2.08	2	4⅓	1	1	1	1	2

CHAMPIONSHIP SERIES RECORD

CHAMPIONSHIP SERIES NOTES: Shares A.L. single-series record for most games pitched—4 (1987).

Year Team (League)	G	W	L	Pct.	ERA	Sv.	IP	H	R	ER	BB	SO
1981—Montreal (N.L.)	1	0	0	...	27.00	0	1	3	3	3	0	0
1987—Minnesota (A.L.)	4	1	1	.500	5.06	2	5⅓	7	3	3	3	5
1990—Boston (A.L.)	1	0	0	...	9.00	0	2	3	2	2	1	0
Championship Series totals (3 years)	6	1	1	.500	8.64	2	8⅓	13	8	8	4	5

WORLD SERIES RECORD

Year Team (League)	G	W	L	Pct.	ERA	Sv.	IP	H	R	ER	BB	SO
1987—Minnesota (A.L.)	4	0	0	...	0.00	1	4⅔	5	0	0	0	3

ALL-STAR GAME RECORD

Year League	W	L	Pct.	ERA	Sv.	IP	H	R	ER	BB	SO
1985—National	0	0	...	0.00	0	1	1	0	0	0	1
1986—National						Did not play					
1988—American						Did not play					
1991—American	0	0	...	0.00	0	⅔	1	0	0	0	0
All-Star totals (2 years)	0	0	...	0.00	0	1⅔	2	0	0	0	1

REDFIELD, JOE
IF/OF, PIRATES

PERSONAL: Born January 14, 1961, at Doylestown, Pa. . . . 6-2/185. . . . Throws right, bats right. . . . Full name: Joseph Randall Redfield.
HIGH SCHOOL: Miraleste (Rancho Palos Verdes, Calif.).
COLLEGE: California.

TRANSACTIONS/CAREER NOTES: Selected by New York Mets organization in ninth round of free-agent draft (June 7, 1982)....
On Jackson disabled list (April 9-May 9, 1985)....Traded by Mets organization to Baltimore Orioles organization for 3B Rick
Lockwood (April 25, 1986)....Drafted by Richmond, Atlanta Braves organization (December 8, 1986)....Traded by Braves
organization to California Angels for P Stan Cliburn (April 7, 1987)....Granted free agency (October 15, 1988)....Signed by
Philadelphia Phillies organization (November 17, 1989)....Granted free agency (October 22, 1989)....Signed by Milwaukee
Brewers organization (December 8, 1989)....Granted free agency (October 15, 1990)....Signed by Pittsburgh Pirates organization (December 22, 1990)....Granted free agency (October 16, 1991)....Signed by Pirates organization (January 22,
1992).
STATISTICAL NOTES: Led International League third basemen with 85 putouts in 1989....Led American Association third basemen with 83 putouts, 165 assists and 260 total chances in 1990....Tied for American Association lead in being hit by pitch
with 15 in 1991....Led American Association third basemen with .947 fielding percentage in 1991.

					BATTING								FIELDING			
Year	Team (League)	Pos.	G	AB	R	H	2B	3B	HR	RBI	Avg.	SB	PO	A	E	Avg.
1982—Little Falls (N.Y.-Penn)	SS-3B	54	206	44	59	14	5	8	57	.286	11	100	130	26	.898
1983—Jackson (Texas)	SS-OF-1B	36	127	16	25	4	1	2	12	.197	0	47	94	12	.922
—Lynchburg (Carolina)	IF-OF	62	192	32	39	4	7	4	27	.203	5	115	103	15	.936
1984—Lynchburg (Carolina)	3-S-2-1	122	428	80	115	18	7	11	58	.269	14	133	269	29	.933
1985—Jackson (Texas)	1B-3B-SS	39	73	12	10	4	0	1	5	.137	0	88	21	5	.956
—Tidewater (Int'l)	3B	4	10	0	3	1	0	0	0	.300	0	0	2	0	1.000
—Lynchburg (Carolina)	3B-2B	41	132	22	32	8	0	3	18	.242	10	37	76	7	.942
1986—Jackson (Texas)	3B	15	60	8	17	1	2	0	3	.283	2	10	19	4	.879
—Charlotte (Southern)■	IF-OF	95	344	65	102	16	4	14	49	.297	8	91	153	22	.917
1987—Midland (Texas)■	3B-1B-2B	128	498	108	160	31	7	•30	•108	.321	17	132	137	23	.921
1988—Edmonton (Pac. Coast)	3B-1B-OF	118	417	67	121	★38	1	3	52	.290	11	377	154	14	.974
—California (A.L.)	3B	1	2	0	0	0	0	0	0	.000	0	0	1	0	1.000
1989—Scranton/W.B. (Int'l)■	3B-1B-SS	123	428	45	103	13	6	9	49	.241	21	†264	206	22	.955
1990—Denver (Am. Assoc.)■	IF-OF	137	525	★87	144	23	10	17	71	.274	34	†136	†205	14	.961
1991—Buffalo (Am. Assoc.)■	3-1-2-S	105	356	60	98	21	6	7	50	.275	21	112	162	14	†.951
—Pittsburgh (N.L.)	3B	11	18	1	2	0	0	0	0	.111	0	4	7	1	.917
American League totals (1 year)		1	2	0	0	0	0	0	0	.000	0	0	1	0	1.000
National League totals (1 year)		11	18	1	2	0	0	0	0	.111	0	4	7	1	.917
Major league totals (2 years)		12	20	1	2	0	0	0	0	.100	0	4	8	1	.923

REDINGTON, TOM
3B, PADRES

PERSONAL: Born February 13, 1969, at Fullerton, Calif....6-1/200....Throws right,
bats right....Full name: Thomas Richard Redington.
TRANSACTIONS/CAREER NOTES: Selected by Atlanta Braves organization in third round of
free agent draft (June 2, 1987)....Claimed on waivers by San Diego Padres (November
16, 1990).
RECORDS/HONORS: Named Midwest League Most Valuable Player (1989).
STATISTICAL NOTES: Led South Atlantic League third basemen with 103 putouts, 243 assists, 376 total chances and 20 double
plays in 1988....Led Texas League third basemen with 360 total chances in 1991.

					BATTING								FIELDING			
Year	Team (League)	Pos.	G	AB	R	H	2B	3B	HR	RBI	Avg.	SB	PO	A	E	Avg.
1987—Sumter (South Atlantic)	3B	18	56	9	18	2	0	0	5	.321	1	12	29	3	.932
1988—Sumter (South Atlantic)	3B-SS	129	429	45	84	13	1	11	60	.196	4	†104	†246	30	.921
1989—Burlington (Midwest)	3B-SS	85	298	49	89	14	0	★17	52	.299	4	57	183	21	.920
—Greenville (Southern)	3B	33	110	9	27	4	0	3	13	.245	1	19	90	7	.940
1990—Greenville (Southern)	3B	124	409	55	103	13	1	12	52	.252	2	60	258	18	★.946
1991—Wichita (Texas)■	3B	116	394	54	112	23	0	5	57	.284	2	77	★257	★26	.928

REDUS, GARY
1B/OF, PIRATES

PERSONAL: Born November 1, 1956, at Athens, Ala....6-1/195....Throws right, bats right....
Full name: Gary Eugene Redus....Name pronounced REE-dus.
HIGH SCHOOL: Tanner (Ala.).
TRANSACTIONS/CAREER NOTES: Selected by Boston Red Sox organization in 17th round of free-
agent draft (June 7, 1977)....Selected by Cincinnati Reds organization in 15th round of free-agent draft (June 6, 1978)....
Traded by Reds with P Tom Hume to Philadelphia Phillies for P John Denny and P Jeff Gray (December 11, 1985)....On Phila-
delphia disabled list (April 28-July 1, 1986); included rehabilitation disability assignment to Reading (June 23-30, 1986)....
Traded by Phillies to Chicago White Sox for P Joe Cowley and cash (March 26, 1987)....Traded by White Sox to Pittsburgh
Pirates for OF Mike Diaz (August 19, 1988)....Granted free agency (November 4, 1988)....Re-signed by Pirates (November
15, 1988)....On disabled list (March 27-April 11 and July 25-August 9, 1989)....Granted free agency (November 5, 1990).
...Re-signed by Pirates (December 10, 1990).
RECORDS/HONORS: Named Pioneer League Player of the Year (1978).
STATISTICAL NOTES: Led Pioneer League with 199 total bases and tied for lead in sacrifice flies with six in 1978....Tied for
Western Carolinas League lead in errors by second basemen with 20 in 1979....Led Florida State League with 220 total bases
in 1980....Tied for American Association lead with nine sacrifice flies in 1981....Hit for the cycle (August 25, 1989).

					BATTING								FIELDING			
Year	Team (League)	Pos.	G	AB	R	H	2B	3B	HR	RBI	Avg.	SB	PO	A	E	Avg.
1978—Billings (Pioneer)	2B	68	253	★100	★117	19	6	17	62	★.462	★42	124	★185	★28	.917
1979—Nashville (Southern)	OF	36	109	7	19	2	1	0	7	.174	8	74	3	3	.963
—Greensboro (W. Caro.)	2B-OF	83	309	79	86	17	1	16	52	.278	41	172	193	†21	.946
1980—Tampa (Florida State)	OF-3B-1B	128	452	78	136	18	9	16	68	.301	50	213	84	27	.917

Year	Team (League)	Pos.	G	AB	R	H	2B	3B	HR	RBI	Avg.	SB	PO	A	E	Avg.
1981	— Waterbury (Eastern)	OF-1B	138	477	71	119	26	4	20	75	.249	48	667	34	14	.980
1982	— Indianapolis (A.A.)	OF	122	439	112	146	29	9	24	93	.333	*54	223	10	7	.971
	— Cincinnati (N.L.)	OF	20	83	12	18	3	2	1	7	.217	11	29	3	1	.970
1983	— Cincinnati (N.L.)	OF	125	453	90	112	20	9	17	51	.247	39	235	11	7	.972
1984	— Cincinnati (N.L.)	OF	123	394	69	100	21	3	7	22	.254	48	200	6	7	.967
1985	— Cincinnati (N.L.)	OF	101	246	51	62	14	4	6	28	.252	48	140	3	2	.986
1986	— Philadelphia (N.L.)■	OF	90	340	62	84	22	4	11	33	.247	25	185	8	4	.980
	— Reading (Eastern)	OF	6	24	4	6	1	0	0	6	.250	1	11	1	1	.923
1987	— Chicago (A.L.)■	OF	130	475	78	112	26	6	12	48	.236	52	262	13	6	.979
1988	— Chicago (A.L.)	OF	77	262	42	69	10	4	6	34	.263	26	140	7	2	.987
	— Pittsburgh (N.L.)■	OF	30	71	12	14	2	0	2	4	.197	5	42	2	2	.957
1989	— Pittsburgh (N.L.)	1B-OF	98	279	42	79	18	7	6	33	.283	25	583	55	9	.986
1990	— Pittsburgh (N.L.)	1B-OF	96	227	32	56	15	3	6	23	.247	11	461	36	8	.984
1991	— Pittsburgh (N.L.)	1B-OF	98	252	45	62	12	2	7	24	.246	17	403	26	6	.986
	American League totals (2 years)		207	737	120	181	36	10	18	82	.246	78	402	20	8	.981
	National League totals (9 years)		781	2345	415	587	127	34	63	225	.250	229	2278	150	46	.981
	Major league totals (10 years)		988	3082	535	768	163	44	81	307	.249	307	2680	170	54	.981

CHAMPIONSHIP SERIES RECORD

Year	Team (League)	Pos.	G	AB	R	H	2B	3B	HR	RBI	Avg.	SB	PO	A	E	Avg.
1990	— Pittsburgh (N.L.)	PH-1B	5	8	1	2	0	0	0	0	.250	1	16	0	0	1.000
1991	— Pittsburgh (N.L.)	1B	5	19	1	3	0	0	0	0	.158	2	51	0	2	.962
	Championship Series totals (2 years)		10	27	2	5	0	0	0	0	.185	3	67	0	2	.971

REED, DARREN

OF, EXPOS

PERSONAL: Born October 16, 1965, at Ventura, Calif.... 6-1/205.... Throws right, bats right. ... Full name: Darren Douglas Reed.
HIGH SCHOOL: Ventura (Calif.).
COLLEGE: Ventura College (Calif.).
TRANSACTIONS/CAREER NOTES: Selected by Oakland Athletics organization in 10th round of free-agent draft (January 17, 1984).... Selected by New York Yankees organization in secondary phase of free-agent draft (June 4, 1984).... On disabled list (June 17, 1986-remainder of season).... Traded by Yankees organization with C Phil Lombardi and P Steve Frey to New York Mets for SS Rafael Santana and P Victor Garcia (December 11, 1987).... Traded by Mets with OF Alex Diaz to Montreal Expos for OF Terrel Hansen and P David Sommer (April 2, 1991).... On disabled list (April 5, 1991-entire season).
STATISTICAL NOTES: Led International League in grounding into double plays with 15 in 1989.

Year	Team (League)	Pos.	G	AB	R	H	2B	3B	HR	RBI	Avg.	SB	PO	A	E	Avg.
1984	— Oneonta (N.Y.-Penn)	OF-C	40	113	17	26	7	0	2	9	.230	1	41	2	2	.956
1985	— Fort Lauderdale (FSL)	OF	100	369	63	117	21	4	10	61	.317	13	191	8	7	.966
1986	— Albany (Eastern)	OF	51	196	22	45	11	1	4	27	.230	1	78	2	5	.941
1987	— Albany (Eastern)	OF	107	404	68	129	23	4	20	79	.319	7	174	6	4	.978
	— Columbus (Int'l)	OF	21	79	15	26	3	3	8	16	.329	0	33	2	1	.972
1988	— Tidewater (Int'l)■	OF-C	101	345	31	83	26	0	9	47	.241	0	170	5	4	.978
1989	— Tidewater (Int'l)	OF	133	444	57	119	30	6	4	50	.268	11	232	*19	5	.980
1990	— Tidewater (Int'l)	OF	104	359	58	95	21	4	6	17	74	.265	16	222	11	4	.983
	— New York (N.L.)	OF	26	39	5	8	4	1	1	2	.205	1	20	1	1	.955
1991	—■						Did not play									
	Major league totals (1 year)		26	39	5	8	4	1	1	2	.205	1	20	1	1	.955

REED, JEFF

C, REDS

PERSONAL: Born November 12, 1962, at Joliet, Ill.... 6-2/190.... Throws right, bats left.... Full name: Jeffrey Scott Reed.... Brother of Curtis Reed, minor league outfielder (1977-84).
HIGH SCHOOL: West (Joliet, Ill.).
TRANSACTIONS/CAREER NOTES: Selected by Minnesota Twins organization in first round (12th pick overall) of free-agent draft (June 3, 1980).... Traded by Twins organizatioin with P Neal Heaton, P Al Cardwood and P Yorkis Perez to Montreal Expos for P Jeff Reardon and C Tom Nieto (February 3, 1987).... On Montreal disabled list (April 20-May 25, 1987); included rehabilitation disability assignment to Indianapolis (May 19-25, 1987).... Traded by Expos with OF Herm Winningham and P Randy St. Claire to Cincinnati Reds for OF Tracy Jones and P Pat Pacillo (July 13, 1988).... On disabled list (July 1-19, 1991).
RECORDS/HONORS: Holds modern N.L. record for most errors by catcher in one inning—3 (July 28, 1987, seventh inning).
STATISTICAL NOTES: Led California League catchers with 758 total chances and tied for lead in double plays with nine in 1982. ... Led Southern League catchers with 714 total chances and 12 double plays in 1983.... Led International League catchers with 720 total chances in 1985.

Year	Team (League)	Pos.	G	AB	R	H	2B	3B	HR	RBI	Avg.	SB	PO	A	E	Avg.
1980	— Elizabethton (Appal.)	C	65	225	39	64	15	1	1	20	.284	2	269	*41	9	.972
1981	— Wis. Rapids (Midwest)	C	106	312	63	73	12	1	4	34	.234	4	547	*93	7	.989
	— Orlando (Southern)	C	3	4	0	1	0	0	0	0	.250	0	4	1	0	1.000
1982	— Visalia (California)	C	125	395	69	130	19	2	5	54	.329	1	*642	•106	10	.987
1983	— Orlando (Southern)	C	118	379	52	100	16	5	6	45	.264	2	*618	*88	8	*.989
	— Toledo (International)	C	14	41	5	7	1	1	0	3	.171	0	77	6	1	.988

Year	Team (League)	Pos.	G	AB	R	H	2B	3B	HR	RBI	Avg.	SB	PO	A	E	Avg.
1984—Minnesota (A.L.)		C	18	21	3	3	3	0	0	1	.143	0	41	2	1	.977
—Toledo (International)		C	94	301	30	80	16	3	3	35	.266	1	546	43	5	*.992
1985—Toledo (International)		C	122	404	53	100	15	3	5	36	.248	1	*627	*81	12	.983
—Minnesota (A.L.)		C	7	10	2	2	0	0	0	0	.200	0	9	3	0	1.000
1986—Minnesota (A.L.)		C	68	165	13	39	6	1	2	9	.236	1	332	19	2	.994
—Toledo (International)		C	25	71	10	22	5	3	1	14	.310	0	108	22	2	.985
1987—Montreal (N.L.)■		C	75	207	15	44	11	0	1	21	.213	0	357	36	12	.970
—Indianapolis (A.A.)		C	5	17	0	3	0	0	0	0	.176	0	27	2	0	1.000
1988—Montreal-Cin. (N.L.)■		C	92	265	20	60	9	2	1	16	.226	1	468	38	3	.994
—Indianapolis (A.A.)		C	8	22	1	7	3	0	0	1	.318	0	30	11	0	1.000
1989—Cincinnati (N.L.)		C	102	287	16	64	11	0	3	23	.223	0	504	50	7	.988
1990—Cincinnati (N.L.)		C	72	175	12	44	8	1	3	16	.251	0	358	26	5	.987
1991—Cincinnati (N.L.)		C	91	270	20	72	15	2	3	31	.267	0	527	29	5	.991
American League totals (3 years)			93	196	18	44	9	1	2	10	.224	1	382	24	3	.993
National League totals (5 years)			432	1204	83	284	54	5	11	107	.236	1	2214	179	32	.987
Major league totals (8 years)			525	1400	101	328	63	6	13	117	.234	2	2596	203	35	.988

CHAMPIONSHIP SERIES RECORD

Year	Team (League)	Pos.	G	AB	R	H	2B	3B	HR	RBI	Avg.	SB	PO	A	E	Avg.
1990—Cincinnati (N.L.)		C	4	7	0	0	0	0	0	0	.000	0	24	1	0	1.000

REED, JODY

2B, RED SOX

PERSONAL: Born July 26, 1962, at Tampa, Fla. . . . 5-9/165. . . . Throws right, bats right. . . . Full name: Jody Eric Reed.

HIGH SCHOOL: Brandon (Fla.).

COLLEGE: Manatee Junior College (Fla.) and Florida State (degree in criminology, 1985).

TRANSACTIONS/CAREER NOTES: Selected by Texas Rangers organization in third round of free-agent draft (January 12, 1982). . . . Selected by San Francisco Giants organization in secondary phase of free-agent draft (June 7, 1982). . . . Selected by Texas Rangers organization in secondary phase of free-agent draft (June 6, 1983). . . . Selected by Boston Red Sox organization in eighth round of free-agent draft (June 4, 1984).

RECORDS/HONORS: Shares major league record for most doubles in one inning—2 (September 8, 1991, third inning). . . . Shares modern major league record for most long hits in one inning—2 (September 8, 1991, third inning).

STATISTICAL NOTES: Led Florida State League with 94 bases on balls received in 1985. . . . Led Florida State League shortstops with 101 double plays in 1985. . . . Led International League shortstops with 683 total chances and 86 double plays in 1987.

Year	Team (League)	Pos.	G	AB	R	H	2B	3B	HR	RBI	Avg.	SB	PO	A	E	Avg.
1984—Winter Haven (Fla. St.)		SS	77	273	46	74	14	1	0	20	.271	9	128	271	26	.939
1985—Winter Haven (Fla. St.)		SS	134	489	*95	157	25	1	0	45	*.321	16	*256	*478	37	*.952
1986—New Britain (Eastern)		SS	60	218	33	50	12	1	0	11	.229	10	114	190	14	.956
—Pawtucket (Int'l)		SS	69	227	27	64	11	0	1	30	.282	8	115	222	12	.966
1987—Pawtucket (Int'l)		SS	136	510	77	151	22	2	7	51	.296	9	*236	*427	20	.971
—Boston (A.L.)		SS-2B-3B	9	30	4	9	1	1	0	8	.300	1	11	26	0	1.000
1988—Boston (A.L.)		SS-2B-3B	109	338	60	99	23	1	1	28	.293	1	147	282	11	.975
1989—Boston (A.L.)		S-2-3-0	146	524	76	151	42	2	3	40	.288	4	255	423	19	.973
1990—Boston (A.L.)		2B-SS	155	598	70	173	∗45	0	5	51	.289	4	278	478	16	.979
1991—Boston (A.L.)		2B	153	618	87	175	42	2	5	60	.283	6	312	444	14	.982
Major league totals (5 years)			572	2108	297	607	153	6	14	187	.288	16	1003	1653	60	.978

CHAMPIONSHIP SERIES RECORD

Year	Team (League)	Pos.	G	AB	R	H	2B	3B	HR	RBI	Avg.	SB	PO	A	E	Avg.
1988—Boston (A.L.)		SS	4	11	0	3	1	0	0	0	.273	0	3	10	0	1.000
1990—Boston (A.L.)		2B-SS	4	15	0	2	0	0	0	1	.133	0	11	11	0	1.000
Championship Series totals (2 years)			8	26	0	5	1	0	0	1	.192	0	14	21	0	1.000

REED, RICK

P, PIRATES

PERSONAL: Born August 16, 1964, at Huntington, W.Va. . . . 6-0/205. . . . Throws right, bats right. . . . Full name: Richard Allen Reed.

HIGH SCHOOL: Huntington (W.Va.).

COLLEGE: Marshall (W.Va.).

TRANSACTIONS/CAREER NOTES: Selected by Pittsburgh Pirates organization in 26th round of free-agent draft (June 2, 1986). . . . On Buffalo disabled list (May 2-13, 1991).

RECORDS/HONORS: Named American Association Most Valuable Pitcher (1991).

Year	Team (League)	G	W	L	Pct.	ERA	Sv.	IP	H	R	ER	BB	SO
1986—Bradenton Pirates (GCL)	8	0	2	.000	3.75	0	24	20	12	10	6	15
—Macon (South Atlantic)	1	0	0	. . .	2.84	0	6 1/3	5	3	2	2	1
1987—Macon (South Atlantic)	46	8	4	.667	2.50	7	93 2/3	80	38	26	29	92
1988—Salem (Carolina)	15	6	2	.750	2.74	0	72 1/3	56	28	22	17	73
—Harrisburg (Eastern)	2	1	0	1.000	1.13	0	16	11	2	2	2	17
—Buffalo (American Assoc.)	10	5	2	.714	1.64	0	77	62	15	14	12	50
—Pittsburgh (N.L.)	2	1	0	1.000	3.00	0	12	10	4	4	2	6

Year	Team (League)	G	W	L	Pct.	ERA	Sv.	IP	H	R	ER	BB	SO
1989	—Buffalo (American Assoc.)	20	9	8	.529	3.72	0	125 2/3	130	58	52	28	75
	—Pittsburgh (N.L.)	15	1	4	.200	5.60	0	54 2/3	62	35	34	11	34
1990	—Buffalo (American Assoc.)	15	7	4	.636	3.46	0	91	82	37	35	21	63
	—Pittsburgh (N.L.)	13	2	3	.400	4.36	1	53 2/3	62	32	26	12	27
1991	—Buffalo (American Assoc.)	25	*14	4	*.778	*2.15	0	167 2/3	151	45	40	26	102
	—Pittsburgh (N.L.)	1	0	0	...	10.38	0	4 1/3	8	6	5	1	2
Major league totals (4 years)		31	4	7	.364	4.98	1	124 2/3	142	77	69	26	69

REIMER, KEVIN
OF/DH, RANGERS

PERSONAL: Born June 28, 1964, at Macon, Ga. . . . 6-2/230. . . . Throws right, bats left. . . . Full name: Kevin Michael Reimer. . . . Son of Gerry Reimer, minor league first baseman-outfielder (1958-68).
HIGH SCHOOL: A.L. Fortune (Enderby, B.C.).
COLLEGE: Orange Coast College (Calif.) and Cal State Fullerton.
TRANSACTIONS/CAREER NOTES: Selected by Texas Rangers organization in 11th round of free-agent draft (June 3, 1985). . . . On suspended list (August 28-31, 1991).
STATISTICAL NOTES: Tied for Texas League lead with nine intentional bases on balls received in 1988.

							—BATTING—							—FIELDING—			
Year	Team (League)	Pos.	G	AB	R	H	2B	3B	HR	RBI	Avg.	SB	PO	A	E	Avg.
1985	—Burlington (Midwest)	1B-OF	80	292	25	67	12	0	8	33	.229	0	685	29	15	.979
1986	—Salem (Carolina)	OF-1B	133	453	57	111	21	2	16	76	.245	4	412	27	32	.932
1987	—Charlotte (Florida State) ...	OF	74	271	36	66	13	7	6	34	.244	2	31	0	2	.939
1988	—Tulsa (Texas)	OF	133	486	74	147	30	*11	21	76	.302	4	63	1	7	.901
	—Texas (A.L.)	OF	12	25	2	3	0	0	1	2	.120	0	0	0	0	...
1989	—Oklahoma City (A.A.)	OF	133	514	59	137	37	7	10	73	.267	4	73	2	6	.926
	—Texas (A.L.)	DH-PH	3	5	0	0	0	0	0	0	.000	0	0	0	0	...
1990	—Oklahoma City (A.A.)	1B-OF	51	198	24	56	18	2	4	33	.283	2	170	11	2	.989
	—Texas (A.L.)	OF	64	100	5	26	9	1	2	15	.260	0	12	0	2	.857
1991	—Texas (A.L.)	OF	136	394	46	106	22	0	20	69	.269	0	110	0	6	.948
Major league totals (4 years)			215	524	53	135	31	1	23	86	.258	0	122	0	8	.938

REMLINGER, MIKE
P, MARINERS

PERSONAL: Born March 23, 1966, at Middletown, N.Y. . . . 6-0/195. . . . Throws left, bats left. . . . Full name: Michael John Remlinger.
HIGH SCHOOL: Carver (Plymouth, Mass.).
COLLEGE: Dartmouth.
TRANSACTIONS/CAREER NOTES: Selected by San Francisco Giants organization in first round (16th pick overall) of free-agent draft (June 2, 1987). . . . On disabled list (April 30-remainder of season, 1988). . . . Traded by Giants with OF Kevin Mitchell to Seattle Mariners for P Bill Swift, P Mike Jackson and P Dave Burba (December 11, 1991).
RECORDS/HONORS: Shares major league record for pitching shutout in first major league game (June 15, 1991).

Year	Team (League)	G	W	L	Pct.	ERA	Sv.	IP	H	R	ER	BB	SO
1987	—Everett (Northwest)	2	0	0	...	3.60	0	5	1	2	2	5	11
	—Clinton (Midwest)	6	2	1	.667	3.30	0	30	21	12	11	14	43
	—Shreveport (Texas)	6	4	2	.667	2.36	0	34 1/3	14	11	9	22	51
1988	—Shreveport (Texas)	3	1	0	1.000	0.69	0	13	7	4	1	4	18
1989	—Shreveport (Texas)	16	4	6	.400	2.98	0	90 2/3	68	43	30	73	92
	—Phoenix (Pacific Coast)	11	1	6	.143	9.21	0	43	51	47	44	52	28
1990	—Shreveport (Texas)	25	9	11	.450	3.90	0	147 2/3	149	82	64	72	75
1991	—Phoenix (Pacific Coast)	19	5	5	.500	6.38	0	108 2/3	134	86	77	59	68
	—San Francisco (N.L.)	8	2	1	.667	4.37	0	35	36	17	17	20	19
Major league totals (1 year)		8	2	1	.667	4.37	0	35	36	17	17	20	19

RENFROE, LADDIE
P, CUBS

PERSONAL: Born May 9, 1962, at Natchez, Miss. . . . 5-11/200. . . . Throws right, bats right. . . . Full name: Cohen Williams Renfroe.
HIGH SCHOOL: Nashua (N.H.).
COLLEGE: Mississippi.
TRANSACTIONS/CAREER NOTES: Selected by Chicago Cubs organization in 25th round of free-agent draft (June 4, 1984).
RECORDS/HONORS: Named Outstanding Pitcher in Southern League (1989).

Year	Team (League)	G	W	L	Pct.	ERA	Sv.	IP	H	R	ER	BB	SO
1984	—Geneva (New York-Penn)	24	3	3	.500	1.38	10	39	34	10	6	10	33
1985	—Peoria (Midwest)	57	10	6	.625	3.20	8	95 2/3	79	36	34	39	56
1986	—Winston-Salem (Carolina)	*65	6	6	.500	2.93	*21	83	84	37	27	27	51
1987	—Pittsfield (Eastern)	40	4	5	.444	4.08	16	46 1/3	56	22	21	18	27
	—Iowa (American Association) ...	8	0	1	.000	5.02	0	14 1/3	8	9	8	5	9
1988	—Iowa (American Association) ...	16	1	3	.250	4.88	0	24	28	13	13	11	12
	—Pittsfield (Eastern)	29	9	4	.692	1.96	1	110 1/3	102	32	24	24	57
1989	—Charlotte (Southern)	*78	*19	7	.731	3.14	15	132	127	52	46	34	85
1990	—Iowa (American Association) ...	44	7	3	.700	4.98	9	118	146	68	65	30	56
1991	—Iowa (American Association) ...	*63	8	5	.615	4.21	*18	98 1/3	101	52	46	32	52
	—Chicago (N.L.)	4	0	1	.000	13.50	0	4 2/3	11	7	7	2	4
Major league totals (1 year)		4	0	1	.000	13.50	0	4 2/3	11	7	7	2	4

REUSCHEL, RICK
P

PERSONAL: Born May 16, 1949, at Quincy, Ill. . . . 6-3/250. . . . Throws right, bats right. . . . Full name: Ricky Eugene Reuschel. . . . Brother of Paul Reuschel, pitcher, Chicago Cubs and Cleveland Indians (1975-79). . . . Name pronounced RUSH-ul.
HIGH SCHOOL: Central (Camp Point, Ill.).
COLLEGE: Western Illinois.
TRANSACTIONS/CAREER NOTES: Selected by Chicago Cubs organization in third round of free-agent draft (June 4, 1970). . . . On temporary inactive list (July 2, 1971); transferred to military list (July 8, 1971-April 10, 1972). . . . Traded by Cubs to New York Yankees for P Doug Bird, $400,000 and a player to be named later (June 12, 1981); Cubs acquired P Mike Griffin to complete deal (August 5, 1981). . . . On disabled list (March 23, 1982-remainder of season). . . . On New York disabled list (April 4-June 9, 1983); included rehabilitation disability assignment to Columbus (May 23-June 9, 1983). . . . Released by Yankees (June 9, 1983). . . . Signed by Quad Cities, Cubs organization (June 28, 1983). . . . On disabled list (March 27-April 21 and August 23-September 1, 1984). . . . Granted free agency (November 8, 1984). . . . Signed by Pittsburgh Pirates organization (February 28, 1985). . . . Traded by Pirates to San Francisco Giants for P Jeff Robinson and P Scott Medvin (August 21, 1987). . . . On disabled list (July 30-August 16, 1989; May 30-September 17, 1990; and April 23-June 19, 1991). . . . Released by Giants (June 19, 1991).
RECORDS/HONORS: Shares major league record for most putouts by pitcher in one inning—3 (April 25, 1975, third inning). . . . Named righthanded pitcher on THE SPORTING NEWS N.L. All-Star team (1977). . . . Named N.L. Comeback Player of the Year by THE SPORTING NEWS (1985). . . . Won N.L. Gold Glove at pitcher (1985 and 1987).
STATISTICAL NOTES: Led Northern League pitchers with seven complete games and tied for lead with 14 games started in 1970. . . . Tied for N.L. lead in games started by pitcher with 38 in 1980 and 36 in 1988. . . . Tied for N.L. lead with eight hit batsmen in 1986. . . . Tied for N.L. lead with 12 complete games and four shutouts in 1987. . . . Tied for N.L. lead in sacrifice hits by batters with 19 in 1988.

Year Team (League)	G	W	L	Pct.	ERA	Sv.	IP	H	R	ER	BB	SO
1970—Huron (Northern)	14	9	2	.818	3.53	0	102	96	52	40	22	88
1971—San Antonio (Texas)	16	8	4	.667	2.31	0	121	105	40	31	15	81
1972—Wichita (American Assoc.)	12	9	2	.818	1.32	0	102	78	30	15	30	72
—Chicago (N.L.)	21	10	8	.556	2.93	0	129	127	46	42	29	87
1973—Chicago (N.L.)	36	14	15	.483	3.00	0	237	244	95	79	62	168
1974—Chicago (N.L.)	41	13	12	.520	4.29	0	241	262	130	115	83	160
1975—Chicago (N.L.)	38	11	★17	.393	3.73	1	234	244	116	97	67	155
1976—Chicago (N.L.)	38	14	12	.538	3.46	1	260	260	★117	100	64	146
1977—Chicago (N.L.)	39	20	10	.667	2.79	1	252	233	84	78	74	166
1978—Chicago (N.L.)	35	14	15	.483	3.41	0	243	235	98	92	54	115
1979—Chicago (N.L.)	36	18	12	.600	3.62	0	239	251	104	96	75	125
1980—Chicago (N.L.)	38	11	13	.458	3.40	0	257	★281	111	97	76	140
1981—Chicago (N.L.)	13	4	7	.364	3.45	0	86	87	40	33	23	53
—New York (A.L.)■	12	4	4	.500	2.66	0	71	75	24	21	10	22
1982—						Did not play						
1983—Columbus (International)	4	0	1	.000	5.06	0	16	21	9	9	6	7
—Quad Cities (Midwest)■	13	3	4	.429	2.42	0	70⅔	73	29	19	9	56
—Chicago (N.L.)	4	1	1	.500	3.92	0	20⅔	18	9	9	10	9
1984—Chicago (N.L.)	19	5	5	.500	5.17	0	92⅓	123	57	53	23	43
1985—Hawaii (Pacific Coast)■	8	6	2	.750	2.50	0	54	52	18	15	12	46
—Pittsburgh (N.L.)	31	14	8	.636	2.27	1	194	153	58	49	52	138
1986—Pittsburgh (N.L.)	35	9	16	.360	3.96	0	215⅔	232	106	95	57	125
1987—Pitts.-San Francisco (N.L.)■	34	13	9	.591	3.09	0	227	207	91	78	42	107
1988—San Francisco (N.L.)	36	19	11	.633	3.12	0	245	242	88	85	42	92
1989—San Francisco (N.L.)	32	17	8	.680	2.94	0	208⅓	195	75	68	54	111
1990—San Francisco (N.L.)	15	3	6	.333	3.93	1	87	102	40	38	31	49
1991—San Francisco (N.L.)	4	0	2	.000	4.22	0	10⅔	17	5	5	7	4
American League totals (1 year)	12	4	4	.500	2.66	0	71	75	24	21	10	22
National League totals (19 years)	545	210	187	.529	3.39	5	3478⅔	3513	1470	1309	925	1993
Major league totals (19 years)	557	214	191	.528	3.37	5	3549⅔	3588	1494	1330	935	2015

DIVISION SERIES RECORD

Year Team (League)	G	W	L	Pct.	ERA	Sv.	IP	H	R	ER	BB	SO
1981—New York (A.L.)	1	0	1	.000	3.00	0	6	4	2	2	1	3

CHAMPIONSHIP SERIES RECORD
CHAMPIONSHIP SERIES NOTES: Tied N.L. single-series record (seven games) for most earned runs allowed—7 (1987).

Year Team (League)	G	W	L	Pct.	ERA	Sv.	IP	H	R	ER	BB	SO
1987—San Francisco (N.L.)	2	0	1	.000	6.30	0	10	15	8	7	2	2
1989—San Francisco (N.L.)	2	1	1	.500	5.19	0	8⅔	12	6	5	2	5
Championship Series totals (2 years)	4	1	2	.333	5.79	0	18⅔	27	14	12	4	7

WORLD SERIES RECORD

Year Team (League)	G	W	L	Pct.	ERA	Sv.	IP	H	R	ER	BB	SO
1981—New York (A.L.)	2	0	0	. . .	4.91	0	3⅔	7	3	2	3	2
1989—San Francisco (N.L.)	1	0	1	.000	11.25	0	4	5	5	5	4	2
World Series totals (2 years)	3	0	1	.000	8.22	0	7⅔	12	8	7	7	4

ALL-STAR GAME RECORD
ALL-STAR GAME NOTES: Shares single-inning record for most home runs allowed—2 (July 11, 1989, first inning).

Year — League	W	L	Pct.	ERA	Sv.	IP	H	R	ER	BB	SO
1977 — National	0	0	...	0.00	0	1	1	0	0	0	0
1987 — National	0	0	...	0.00	0	1⅓	1	0	0	0	1
1989 — National	0	0	...	18.00	0	1	3	2	2	0	0
All-Star totals (3 years)	0	0	...	5.40	0	3⅓	5	2	2	0	1

REYES, GIL
C, EXPOS

PERSONAL: Born December 10, 1963, at Santo Domingo, Dominican Republic.... 6-2/212.... Throws right, bats right.... Name pronounced RAY-us.
HIGH SCHOOL: San Martin de Porres (Dominican Republic).
TRANSACTIONS/CAREER NOTES: Signed as free agent by Los Angeles Dodgers organization (January 15, 1980).... On San Antonio disabled list (May 11-June 1, 1983).... Traded by Dodgers to Indianapolis (Montreal Expos organization) for P Jeff Fischer (March 27, 1989).
STATISTICAL NOTES: Tied for California League lead in assists by catchers with 106 and double plays with nine in 1982.... Led Texas League catchers with 718 total chances, 13 double plays and 31 passed balls in 1984.... Tied for Pacific Coast League lead in sacrifice flies with eight in 1985.... Led Pacific Coast League catchers with 65 assists and 21 errors in 1985.... Led Pacific Coast League with 24 passed balls in 1985 and 17 in 1986.... Led Pacific Coast League catchers with 62 assists in 1988.... Led American Association catchers with 742 total chances and tied for lead in double plays with 10 in 1989.

					BATTING							FIELDING			
Year — Team (League)	Pos.	G	AB	R	H	2B	3B	HR	RBI	Avg.	SB	PO	A	E	Avg.
1980 — Lethbridge (Pioneer)	1B	6	11	0	2	0	0	0	1	.182	0	16	0	2	.889
1981 — Vero Beach (Florida St.)	1B-C	21	58	3	12	3	0	1	6	.207	0	71	6	2	.975
— Lethbridge (Pioneer)	C-1B	44	155	28	40	9	0	6	24	.258	1	240	24	4	.985
1982 — Lodi (California)	C-3B	127	424	65	119	18	1	15	55	.281	5	493	‡106	20	.968
1983 — San Antonio (Texas)	C	33	124	10	35	7	0	1	16	.282	0	167	30	5	.975
— Los Angeles (N.L.)	C	19	31	1	5	2	0	0	0	.161	0	59	9	4	.944
— Albuquerque (PCL)	C	20	62	8	19	1	2	2	15	.306	0	103	17	8	.938
1984 — San Antonio (Texas)	C	120	433	55	131	16	2	10	78	.303	1	*598	*101	*19	.974
— Los Angeles (N.L.)	C	4	5	0	0	0	0	0	0	.000	0	5	0	0	1.000
1985 — Albuquerque (PCL)	C-1B	*111	366	35	97	20	0	6	54	.265	0	439	✝66	✝21	.960
— Los Angeles (N.L.)	C	6	1	0	0	0	0	0	0	.000	0	6	4	0	1.000
1986 — Albuquerque (PCL)	C-1B	104	306	36	70	13	1	7	36	.229	1	423	69	14	.972
1987 — Albuquerque (PCL)	C-1B-P	89	265	42	72	18	2	5	46	.272	0	414	66	12	.976
1988 — Albuquerque (PCL)	C-1B-3B	98	318	40	93	14	0	12	66	.292	2	459	✝70	16	.971
— Los Angeles (N.L.)	C	5	9	1	1	0	0	0	0	.111	0	16	0	0	1.000
1989 — Indianapolis (A.A.)■	C	106	314	35	71	8	0	9	35	.226	0	*647	*86	9	.988
— Montreal (N.L.)	C	4	5	0	1	0	0	0	1	.200	0	10	1	0	1.000
1990 — Indianapolis (A.A.)	C	89	309	22	72	14	1	9	45	.233	2	504	*78	*13	.978
1991 — Montreal (N.L.)	C	83	207	11	45	9	0	0	13	.217	2	375	61	11	.975
Major league totals (6 years)		121	258	13	52	11	0	0	14	.202	2	471	75	15	.973

RECORD AS PITCHER

Year — Team (League)	G	W	L	Pct.	ERA	Sv.	IP	H	R	ER	BB	SO
1987 — Albuquerque (Pacific Coast)	89	0	0	...	0.00	0	⅓	0	0	0	1	1

REYNOLDS, HAROLD
2B, MARINERS

PERSONAL: Born November 26, 1960, at Eugene, Ore.... 5-11/165.... Throws right, bats both.... Full name: Harold Craig Reynolds.... Brother of Don Reynolds, outfielder, San Diego Padres (1978-79); and brother of Larry Reynolds, minor league shortstop-outfielder (1979-84).
HIGH SCHOOL: Corvallis (Ore.).
COLLEGE: San Diego State, Canada College (Calif.) and Cal State Long Beach.
TRANSACTIONS/CAREER NOTES: Selected by San Diego Padres organization in fifth round of free-agent draft (June 5, 1979).... Selected by Seattle Mariners organization in secondary phase of free-agent draft (June 3, 1980).
RECORDS/HONORS: Shares major league single-game record (nine innings) for most assists by second baseman—12 (August 27, 1986).... Shares A.L. record for most years leading league in errors by second baseman—4.... Won A.L. Gold Glove at second base (1988-90).
STATISTICAL NOTES: Led Midwest League second basemen with 82 double plays in 1981.... Led Eastern League in caught stealing with 20 in 1982.... Led Pacific Coast League with 14 sacrifice hits 14 in 1983.... Led Pacific Coast League second basemen with 286 putouts, 410 assists, 27 errors and 723 total chances in 1983.... Led Pacific Coast League second basemen with 104 double plays and 747 total chances in 1984.... Tied for Pacific Coast League lead in caught stealing with 17 in 1984.... Led A.L. second basemen with 111 double plays in 1986, 1987, 1988 and 133 in 1991.... Led A.L. in caught stealing with 20 in 1987 and 29 in 1988.... Led A.L. second basemen with 874 total chances in 1987, 792 in 1988, 834 in 1989, 848 in 1990 and 829 in 1991.

					BATTING							FIELDING			
Year — Team (League)	Pos.	G	AB	R	H	2B	3B	HR	RBI	Avg.	SB	PO	A	E	Avg.
1981 — Wausau (Midwest)	2B-OF-3B	127	493	98	146	23	3	11	59	.296	*69	259	386	27	.960
1982 — Lynn (Eastern)	2B	102	375	58	102	14	4	2	48	.272	39	202	232	19	.958
1983 — Salt Lake City (PCL)	2B-SS	136	534	84	165	20	9	1	72	.309	54	✝287	*410	*27	.963
— Seattle (A.L.)	2B	20	59	8	12	4	1	0	1	.203	0	30	48	2	.975
1984 — Salt Lake City (PCL)	2B	135	*558	94	165	22	6	3	54	.296	37	*326	*396	*25	*.967
— Seattle (A.L.)	2B	10	10	3	3	0	0	0	0	.300	1	8	12	0	1.000
1985 — Seattle (A.L.)	2B	67	104	15	15	3	1	0	6	.144	3	69	123	8	.960
— Calgary (Pacific Coast)	2B	52	212	36	77	11	3	5	30	.363	9	119	171	13	.957

— 404 —

Year	Team (League)	Pos.	G	AB	R	H	2B	3B	HR	RBI	Avg.	SB	PO	A	E	Avg.
								BATTING							**FIELDING**		
1986	—Calgary (Pacific Coast)	2B	29	118	20	37	7	0	1	7	.314	10	64	83	4	.974
	—Seattle (A.L.)	2B	126	445	46	99	19	4	1	24	.222	30	278	415	16	.977
1987	—Seattle (A.L.)	2B	160	530	73	146	31	8	1	35	.275	★60	★347	★507	★20	.977
1988	—Seattle (A.L.)	2B	158	598	61	169	26	•11	4	41	.283	35	303	★471	★18	.977
1989	—Seattle (A.L.)	2B	153	613	87	184	24	9	0	43	.300	25	311	★506	★17	.980
1990	—Seattle (A.L.)	2B	160	★642	100	162	36	5	5	55	.252	31	★330	★499	•19	.978
1991	—Seattle (A.L.)	2B	161	631	95	160	34	6	3	57	.254	28	★348	★463	18	.978
	Major league totals (9 years)		1015	3632	488	950	177	45	14	262	.262	213	2024	3044	118	.977

ALL-STAR GAME RECORD

Year	League	Pos.	AB	R	H	2B	3B	HR	RBI	Avg.	SB	PO	A	E	Avg.
							BATTING						**FIELDING**		
1987	—American	2B	3	0	0	0	0	0	0	.000	0	4	4	0	1.000
1988	—American	2B	1	0	0	0	0	0	0	.000	0	1	1	0	1.000
	All-Star Game totals (2 years)		4	0	0	0	0	0	0	.000	0	5	5	0	1.000

REYNOLDS, SHANE
P, ASTROS

PERSONAL: Born March 26, 1968, at Bastrop, La. ... 6-3/210. ... Throws right, bats right. ... Full name: Richard Shane Reynolds.
COLLEGE: Faulkner State Junior College (Ala.) and Texas.
TRANSACTIONS/CAREER NOTES: Selected by Houston Astros organization in third round of free-agent draft (June 5, 1989).
STATISTICAL NOTES: Tied for Texas League lead in games started by pitcher with 27 in 1991.

Year	Team (League)	G	W	L	Pct.	ERA	Sv.	IP	H	R	ER	BB	SO
1989	—Auburn (New York-Penn)	6	3	2	.600	2.31	0	35	36	16	9	14	23
	—Asheville (South Atlantic)	8	5	3	.625	3.68	0	51⅓	53	25	21	21	33
1990	—Columbus (Southern)	29	9	10	.474	4.81	0	155⅓	•181	104	83	70	92
1991	—Jackson (Texas)	27	8	9	.471	4.47	0	151	165	93	75	62	116

REYNOSO, ARMANDO
P, BRAVES

PERSONAL: Born May 1, 1966, at San Luis Potosi, Mexico. ... 6-0/186. ... Throws right, bats right. ... Full name: Martia Armando Gutierrez Reynoso.
HIGH SCHOOL: Escuela Secandaria Mita del Estado (Jalisco, Mexico).
TRANSACTIONS/CAREER NOTES: Signed as free agent by Saltillo of Mexican League. ... Sold by Saltillo to Atlanta Braves organization (August 15, 1990).
STATISTICAL NOTES: Led International League with six balks in 1991. ... Tied for International League lead with three shutouts and 10 hit batsmen in 1991.

Year	Team (League)	G	W	L	Pct.	ERA	Sv.	IP	H	R	ER	BB	SO
1988	—Saltillo (Mexican)	32	11	11	.500	4.30	2	180	176	98	86	85	92
1989	—Saltillo (Mexican)	27	13	9	.591	3.48	0	160⅓	155	78	62	64	107
1990	—Richmond (International)■	30	6	9	.400	4.55	0	140⅓	159	83	71	73	56
1991	—Richmond (International)	22	10	6	.625	★2.61	0	131	117	44	38	39	97
	—Atlanta (N.L.)	6	2	1	.667	6.17	0	23⅓	26	18	16	10	10
	Major league totals (1 year)	6	2	1	.667	6.17	0	23⅓	26	18	16	10	10

CHAMPIONSHIP SERIES RECORD

Year	Team (League)	G	W	L	Pct.	ERA	Sv.	IP	H	R	ER	BB	SO
1991	—Atlanta (N.L.)						Did not play						

WORLD SERIES RECORD

Year	Team (League)	G	W	L	Pct.	ERA	Sv.	IP	H	R	ER	BB	SO
1991	—Atlanta (N.L.)						Did not play						

RHODES, ARTHUR
P, ORIOLES

PERSONAL: Born October 24, 1969, at Waco, Tex. ... 6-2/204. ... Throws left, bats left. ... Full name: Arthur Lee Rhodes Jr. ... Brother of Ricky Rhodes, pitcher, New York Yankees organization.
HIGH SCHOOL: LaVega (Waco, Tex.).
TRANSACTIONS/CAREER NOTES: Selected by Baltimore Orioles organization in second round of free-agent draft (June 1, 1988). ... On Hagerstown disabled list (May 13-June 5, 1991).
RECORDS/HONORS: Named Eastern League Pitcher of the Year (1991).

Year	Team (League)	G	W	L	Pct.	ERA	Sv.	IP	H	R	ER	BB	SO
1988	—Bluefield (Appalachian)	11	3	4	.429	3.31	0	35⅓	29	17	13	15	44
1989	—Erie (New York-Penn)	5	2	0	1.000	1.16	0	31	13	7	4	10	45
	—Frederick (Carolina)	7	2	2	.500	5.18	0	24⅓	19	16	14	19	28
1990	—Frederick (Carolina)	13	4	6	.400	2.12	0	80⅔	62	25	19	21	103
	—Hagerstown (Eastern)	12	3	4	.429	3.73	0	72⅓	62	32	30	39	60
1991	—Hagerstown (Eastern)	19	7	4	.636	2.70	0	106⅔	73	37	32	47	115
	—Baltimore (A.L.)	8	0	3	.000	8.00	0	36	47	35	32	23	23
	Major league totals (1 year)	8	0	3	.000	8.00	0	36	47	35	32	23	23

RHODES, KARL
OF, ASTROS

PERSONAL: Born August 21, 1968, at Cincinnati. . . . 5-11/170. . . . Throws left, bats left. . . . Full name: Karl Derrick Rhodes.
HIGH SCHOOL: Western Hills (Cincinnati).
TRANSACTIONS/CAREER NOTES: Selected by Houston Astros organization in third round of free-agent draft (June 2, 1986).
STATISTICAL NOTES: Tied for Southern League lead in double plays by outfielders with five in 1989.

Year Team (League)	Pos.	G	AB	R	H	2B	3B	HR	RBI	Avg.	SB	PO	A	E	Avg.
1986 —Sarasota Astros (GCL)......	OF	*62	222	36	65	10	3	0	22	.293	14	113	6	0	*1.000
1987 —Asheville (S. Atlantic).......	OF	129	413	62	104	16	4	3	50	.252	43	163	14	9	.952
1988 —Osceola (Florida State).....	OF-2B	132	452	69	128	4	2	1	34	.283	64	232	14	2	.992
1989 —Columbus (Southern)........	OF	•143	520	81	134	25	5	4	63	.258	18	262	15	11	.962
1990 —Tucson (Pacific Coast)	OF	107	385	68	106	24	11	3	59	.275	24	214	*20	8	.967
—Houston (N.L.)	OF	39	86	12	21	6	1	1	3	.244	4	61	2	3	.955
1991 —Houston (N.L.)	OF	44	136	7	29	3	1	1	12	.213	2	87	4	4	.958
—Tucson (Pacific Coast)	OF	84	308	45	80	17	1	1	46	.260	5	140	11	9	.944
Major league totals (2 years)		83	222	19	50	9	2	2	15	.225	6	148	6	7	.957

RICE, PAT
P, MARINERS

PERSONAL: Born November 2, 1963, at Rapid City, S.D. . . . 6-2/200. . . . Throws right, bats right. . . . Full name: Patrick Edward Rice.
HIGH SCHOOL: Air Academy (Colorado Springs, Colo.).
COLLEGE: Cochise County Community College (Ariz.) and Arkansas.
TRANSACTIONS/CAREER NOTES: Signed as free agent by Salt Lake City, independent (June 19, 1986). . . . Sold by Salt Lake City to Seattle Mariners organization (September 5, 1986).

Year Team (League)	G	W	L	Pct.	ERA	Sv.	IP	H	R	ER	BB	SO
1986 —Salt Lake City (Pacific Coast) ..	18	1	3	.250	3.34	0	59⅓	67	33	22	15	39
1987 —Wausau (Midwest)■.................	28	12	11	.522	3.84	0	166⅓	192	100	71	43	127
1988 —San Bernardino (California)	33	7	7	.500	3.42	3	121	121	56	46	32	114
—Vermont (Eastern)	6	3	0	1.000	1.04	0	26	22	7	3	7	16
1989 —Williamsport (Eastern)	5	0	0	...	12.15	0	6⅔	13	9	9	4	5
—Calgary (Pacific Coast)	17	6	3	.667	4.85	1	55⅓	63	32	30	21	35
1990 —Calgary (Pacific Coast)	15	1	1	.500	6.35	2	28⅓	34	21	20	13	27
—Williamsport (Eastern)	25	4	4	.500	3.98	0	72⅓	77	36	32	24	58
1991 —Calgary (Pacific Coast)	21	13	4	.765	5.03	0	121⅔	138	70	68	37	59
—Seattle (A.L.)	7	1	1	.500	3.00	0	21	18	10	7	10	12
Major league totals (1 year)	7	1	1	.500	3.00	0	21	18	10	7	10	12

RICHARDSON, JEFF
IF, PIRATES

PERSONAL: Born August 26, 1965, at Grand Island, Neb. . . . 6-2/180. . . . Throws right, bats right. . . . Full name: Jeffrey Scott Richardson.
HIGH SCHOOL: Grand Island (Neb.).
COLLEGE: Arkansas and Louisiana Tech.
TRANSACTIONS/CAREER NOTES: Selected by Cincinnati Reds organization in seventh round of free-agent draft (June 2, 1986). . . . Traded by Reds with P Mike Roesler to Pittsburgh Pirates organization for OF Billy Hatcher (April 3, 1990). . . . On Buffalo disabled list (June 14-August 1, 1991).

Year Team (League)	Pos.	G	AB	R	H	2B	3B	HR	RBI	Avg.	SB	PO	A	E	Avg.
1986 —Billings (Pioneer)..............	2B-SS	47	162	42	51	14	4	0	20	.315	12	48	64	6	.949
1987 —Tampa (Florida State).......	2B-3B-SS	100	374	44	112	9	2	0	37	.299	10	180	228	17	.960
—Vermont (Eastern)	2B-3B	35	134	24	28	4	0	0	8	.209	5	73	76	4	.974
1988 —Chattanooga (Southern)...	SS	88	399	50	100	17	1	1	37	.251	1	186	321	23	*.957
1989 —Nashville (Am. Assoc.)	SS	88	286	36	78	19	2	1	25	.273	3	132	218	16	.956
—Cincinnati (N.L.)..............	SS-3B	53	125	10	21	4	0	2	11	.168	0	50	81	4	.970
1990 —Buffalo (Am. Assoc.)■........	S-2-3-1	66	164	15	34	4	0	1	15	.207	1	103	142	12	.953
1991 —Buffalo (Am. Assoc.)	2B-SS	62	186	21	48	16	2	1	24	.258	5	121	179	5	.984
—Pittsburgh (N.L.)	3B-SS	6	4	0	1	0	0	0	0	.250	0	0	1	0	1.000
Major league totals (2 years)		59	129	10	22	4	0	2	11	.171	0	50	82	4	.971

RIESGO, NIKCO
1B/3B/OF, PHILLIES

PERSONAL: Born January 11, 1967, at Long Beach, Calif. . . . 6-2/185. . . . Throws right, bats right. . . . Full name: Damon Nikco Riesgo. . . . Name pronounced ree-ESS-go.
COLLEGE: San Diego State.
TRANSACTIONS/CAREER NOTES: Selected by Milwaukee Brewers organization in 25th round of free-agent draft (June 3, 1985). . . . Selected by San Diego Padres organization in eighth round of free-agent draft (June 1, 1988). . . . Traded by Padres organization to New York Mets organization for 3B-OF Craig Ropez (January 5, 1990). . . . Traded by Mets organization with P Rocky Elli to Philadelphia Phillies organization for 2B Tommy Herr (August 30, 1990). . . . Drafted by Montreal Expos organization (December 4, 1990). . . . On Montreal disabled list (March 31-April 18, 1991); included rehabilitation assignment to West Palm Beach (April 11-18, 1991). . . . Returned to Phillies organization (May 8, 1991).
RECORDS/HONORS: Named Florida State League Most Valuable Player (1990).
STATISTICAL NOTES: Led Florida State League with 219 total bases in 1990.

Year	Team (League)	Pos.	G	AB	R	H	2B	3B	HR	RBI	Avg.	SB	PO	A	E	Avg.
								BATTING						FIELDING			
1988	—Spokane (Northwest)	OF-3B	65	219	45	55	8	3	7	51	.251	24	80	5	3	.966
1989	—Charleston, S.C. (S. Atl.) ...	OF	119	402	74	96	25	1	13	53	.239	34	134	7	9	.940
1990	—St. Lucie (Florida State)■..	1B-3B-OF	131	456	93	136	★35	3	14	★94	.298	46	785	56	14	.984
1991	—West Palm Beach (FSL)■..	1B-OF	5	18	4	5	1	0	1	1	.278	0	37	3	1	.976
	—Montreal (N.L.)	OF	4	7	1	1	0	0	0	0	.143	0	0	1	1	.500
	—Reading (Eastern)■..........	OF-1B	98	356	61	92	18	2	14	66	.258	8	295	22	10	.969
Major league totals (1 year)			**4**	**7**	**1**	**1**	**0**	**0**	**0**	**0**	**.143**	**0**	**0**	**1**	**1**	**.500**

RIGHETTI, DAVE
P, GIANTS

PERSONAL: Born November 28, 1958, at San Jose, Calif. . . . 6-4/212. . . . Throws left, bats left. . . . Full name: David Allen Righetti. . . . Son of Leo Righetti, minor league infielder (1944-49 and 1951-57); and brother of Steven Righetti, minor league third baseman (1977-79). . . . Name pronounced rih-GET-tee.

HIGH SCHOOL: San Jose Pioneer (Calif.).

COLLEGE: San Jose City College (Calif.).

TRANSACTIONS/CAREER NOTES: Selected by Texas Rangers organization in first round (ninth pick overall) of free-agent draft (January 11, 1977). . . . On disabled list (July 31-September 2, 1978). . . . Traded by Rangers organization with P Mike Griffin, P Paul Mirabella, OF Juan Beniquez and OF Greg Jemison to New York Yankees for P Sparky Lyle, P Larry McCall, P Dave Rajsich, C Mike Heath, SS Domingo Ramos and cash (November 10, 1978). . . . On West Haven disabled list (May 21-June 28, 1979). . . . On Columbus disabled list (June 28-July 20 and August 2-23, 1979). . . . On disabled list (June 17-July 2, 1984). . . . Granted free agency (November 9, 1987). . . . Re-signed by Yankees (December 23, 1987). . . . Granted free agency (November 5, 1990). . . . Signed by San Francisco Giants (December 4, 1990).

RECORDS/HONORS: Named A.L. Rookie Pitcher of the Year by THE SPORTING NEWS (1981). . . . Named A.L. Rookie of the Year by Baseball Writers' Association of America (1981). . . . Named A.L. Fireman of the Year by THE SPORTING NEWS (1986). . . . Named A.L. co-Fireman of the Year by THE SPORTING NEWS (1987).

STATISTICAL NOTES: Pitched 4-0 no-hit victory against Boston Red Sox (July 4, 1983).

Year	Team (League)	G	W	L	Pct.	ERA	Sv.	IP	H	R	ER	BB	SO
1977	—Asheville (Western Carolinas) ..	17	11	3	★.786	3.14	0	109	98	47	38	53	101
1978	—Tulsa (Texas)	13	5	5	.500	3.16	0	91	66	40	32	49	127
1979	—West Haven (Eastern)■	11	4	3	.571	1.96	0	69	45	23	15	45	78
	—Columbus (International)	8	3	2	.600	2.93	0	40	22	13	13	19	44
	—New York (A.L.)	3	0	1	.000	3.71	0	17	10	7	7	10	13
1980	—Columbus (International)	24	6	10	.375	4.63	0	142	124	79	73	★101	139
1981	—Columbus (International)	7	5	0	1.000	1.00	0	45	30	8	5	26	50
	—New York (A.L.)	15	8	4	.667	2.06	0	105	75	25	24	38	89
1982	—New York (A.L.)	33	11	10	.524	3.79	1	183	155	88	77	★108	163
	—Columbus (International)	4	1	0	1.000	2.81	0	25⅔	22	11	8	12	33
1983	—New York (A.L.)	31	14	8	.636	3.44	0	217	194	96	83	67	169
1984	—New York (A.L.)	64	5	6	.455	2.34	31	96⅓	79	29	25	37	90
1985	—New York (A.L.)	74	12	7	.632	2.78	29	107	96	36	33	45	92
1986	—New York (A.L.)	74	8	8	.500	2.45	★46	106⅔	88	31	29	35	83
1987	—New York (A.L.)	60	8	6	.571	3.51	31	95	95	45	37	44	77
1988	—New York (A.L.)	60	5	4	.556	3.52	25	87	86	35	34	37	70
1989	—New York (A.L.)	55	2	6	.250	3.00	25	69	73	32	23	26	51
1990	—New York (A.L.)	53	1	1	.500	3.57	36	53	48	24	21	26	43
1991	—San Francisco (N.L.)■..............	61	2	7	.222	3.39	24	71⅔	64	29	27	28	51
American League totals (11 years)		**522**	**74**	**61**	**.548**	**3.11**	**224**	**1136**	**999**	**448**	**393**	**473**	**940**
National League totals (1 year)		**61**	**2**	**7**	**.222**	**3.39**	**24**	**71⅔**	**64**	**29**	**27**	**28**	**51**
Major league totals (12 years)		**583**	**76**	**68**	**.528**	**3.13**	**248**	**1207⅔**	**1063**	**477**	**420**	**501**	**991**

DIVISION SERIES RECORD

Year	Team (League)	G	W	L	Pct.	ERA	Sv.	IP	H	R	ER	BB	SO
1981	—New York (A.L.)	2	2	0	1.000	1.00	0	9	8	1	1	3	10

CHAMPIONSHIP SERIES RECORD

Year	Team (League)	G	W	L	Pct.	ERA	Sv.	IP	H	R	ER	BB	SO
1981	—New York (A.L.)	1	1	0	1.000	0.00	0	6	4	0	0	2	4

WORLD SERIES RECORD

Year	Team (League)	G	W	L	Pct.	ERA	Sv.	IP	H	R	ER	BB	SO
1981	—New York (A.L.)	1	0	0	. . .	13.50	0	2	5	3	3	2	1

ALL-STAR GAME RECORD

Year	League	W	L	Pct.	ERA	Sv.	IP	H	R	ER	BB	SO
1986	—American	0	0	. . .	0.00	0	⅔	2	0	0	0	0
1987	—American	0	0	. . .	0.00	0	⅓	1	0	0	0	0
All-Star totals (2 years)		**0**	**0**	**. . .**	**0.00**	**0**	**1**	**3**	**0**	**0**	**0**	**0**

RIJO, JOSE
P, REDS

PERSONAL: Born May 13, 1965, at San Cristobal, Dominican Republic. . . . 6-2/210. . . . Throws right, bats right. . . . Full name: Jose Antonio Abreau Rijo. . . . Son-in-law of Juan Marichal, Hall of Fame pitcher, San Francisco Giants, Boston Red Sox and Los Angeles Dodgers (1960-75). . . . Name pronounced REE-ho.

TRANSACTIONS/CAREER NOTES: Signed as free agent by New York Yankees organization (August 1, 1980).... Traded by Yankees organization with OF Stan Javier, P Jay Howell, P Eric Plunk and P Tim Birtsas to Oakland Athletics for OF Rickey Henderson, P Bert Bradley and cash (December 5, 1984).... Traded by A's organization with P Tim Birtsas to Cincinnati Reds for OF Dave Parker (December 8, 1987).... On disabled list (August 18-September 8, 1988 and July 17-September 1, 1989).... On disabled list (June 29-July 21, 1990); included rehabilitation disability assignment to Nashville (July 16-20, 1990).... On disabled list (June 21-July 25, 1991).

RECORDS/HONORS: Named Florida State League Most Valuable Player (1983).... Named righthanded pitcher on THE SPORTING NEWS N.L. All-Star team (1991).

STATISTICAL NOTES: Led Florida State League with 15 complete games and tied for lead with four shutouts in 1983.... Led Pacific Coast League with 11 balks in 1985.... Tied for N.L. lead with five balks in 1990.

MISCELLANEOUS: Struck out in only appearance as pinch-hitter (1991).

Year — Team (League)	G	W	L	Pct.	ERA	Sv.	IP	H	R	ER	BB	SO
1981 — Bradenton Yankees (GCL)	11	3	3	.500	4.50	1	22	37	16	11	7	22
1982 — Paintsville (Appalachian)	13	8	4	.667	2.50	0	79⅓	76	33	22	22	66
1983 — Fort Lauderdale (Florida St.)	21	★15	5	.750	★1.68	0	160⅓	129	38	30	43	152
— Nashville (Southern)	5	3	2	.600	2.68	0	40⅓	31	12	12	22	32
1984 — New York (A.L.)	24	2	8	.200	4.76	2	62⅓	74	40	33	33	47
— Columbus (International)	11	3	3	.500	4.41	0	65⅓	67	35	32	40	47
1985 — Tacoma (Pacific Coast)■	24	7	10	.412	2.90	0	149	116	64	48	★108	★179
— Oakland (A.L.)	12	6	4	.600	3.53	0	63⅔	57	26	25	28	65
1986 — Oakland (A.L.)	39	9	11	.450	4.65	1	193⅔	172	116	100	108	176
1987 — Oakland (A.L.)	21	2	7	.222	5.90	0	82½	106	67	54	41	67
— Tacoma (Pacific Coast)	9	2	4	.333	3.95	0	54⅔	44	27	24	28	67
1988 — Cincinnati (N.L.)■	49	13	8	.619	2.39	0	162	120	47	43	63	160
1989 — Cincinnati (N.L.)	19	7	6	.538	2.84	0	111	101	39	35	48	86
1990 — Cincinnati (N.L.)	29	14	8	.636	2.70	0	197	151	65	59	78	152
— Nashville (American Assoc.)	1	0	0	. . .	8.31	0	4⅓	5	4	4	2	2
1991 — Cincinnati (N.L.)	30	15	6	.714	2.51	0	204⅓	165	69	57	55	172
American League totals (4 years)	96	19	30	.388	4.75	3	402	409	249	212	210	355
National League totals (4 years)	127	49	28	.636	2.59	0	674⅓	537	220	194	244	570
Major league totals (8 years)	223	68	58	.540	3.39	3	1076⅓	946	469	406	454	925

CHAMPIONSHIP SERIES RECORD

Year Team (League)	G	W	L	Pct.	ERA	Sv.	IP	H	R	ER	BB	SO
1990 — Cincinnati (N.L.)	2	1	0	1.000	4.38	0	12⅓	10	6	6	7	15

WORLD SERIES RECORD

Year Team (League)	G	W	L	Pct.	ERA	Sv.	IP	H	R	ER	BB	SO
1990 — Cincinnati (N.L.)	2	2	0	1.000	0.59	0	15⅓	9	1	1	5	14

RILES, ERNEST

IF, ASTROS

PERSONAL: Born October 2, 1960, at Bainbridge, Ga.... 6-1/175.... Throws right, bats left. ... Full name: Ernest Riles.
HIGH SCHOOL: Bainbridge (Ga.).
COLLEGE: Middle Georgia College.

TRANSACTIONS/CAREER NOTES: Selected by Seattle Mariners organization in 21st round of free-agent draft (June 3, 1980).... Selected by Milwaukee Brewers organization in secondary phase of free-agent draft (January 13, 1981).... On Milwaukee disabled list (March 26-June 3, 1987); included rehabilitation disability assignment to El Paso (May 13-June 2, 1987).... Traded by Brewers to San Francisco Giants for OF Jeffrey Leonard (June 8, 1988).... Traded by Giants to Oakland Athletics for OF Darren Lewis and a player to be named later (December 4, 1990); Giants acquired P Pedro Pena to complete deal (December 17, 1990).... Granted free agency (October 28, 1991).... Signed by Houston Astros organization (January 27, 1992).

STATISTICAL NOTES: Led California League with 84 bases on balls received in 1982.... Led California League shortstops with 95 double plays and tied for lead in total chances with 692 in 1982.... Led Texas League shortstops with 670 total chances and 77 double plays in 1983.

						BATTING							FIELDING			
Year — Team (League)	Pos.	G	AB	R	H	2B	3B	HR	RBI	Avg.	SB	PO	A	E	Avg.
1981 — Butte (Pioneer)	SS-3B-2B	67	256	63	89	11	2	4	43	.348	9	97	217	27	.921
1982 — Stockton (California)	SS	138	447	60	128	23	6	2	56	.286	21	204	★451	37	.947
1983 — El Paso (Texas)	SS	130	476	109	166	31	3	13	91	★.349	9	★193	★445	32	★.952
1984 — Vancouver (Pac. Coast)	SS	123	424	59	113	19	7	3	54	.267	1	★190	316	17	.967
1985 — Vancouver (Pac. Coast)	SS	30	118	19	41	7	1	2	20	.347	2	47	120	6	.965
— Milwaukee (A.L.)	SS	116	448	54	128	12	7	5	45	.286	2	183	310	22	.957
1986 — Milwaukee (A.L.)	SS	145	524	69	132	24	2	9	47	.252	7	212	327	20	.964
1987 — El Paso (Texas)	SS	41	153	45	52	10	0	6	24	.340	1	70	127	10	.952
— Milwaukee (A.L.)	3B-SS	83	276	38	72	11	1	4	38	.261	3	76	152	13	.946
1988 — Milwaukee (A.L.)	3B-SS	41	127	7	32	6	1	1	9	.252	2	36	64	4	.962
— San Francisco (N.L.)■ ..	3B-2B-SS	79	187	26	55	7	2	3	28	.294	1	46	133	3	.984
1989 — San Francisco (N.L.)	3-2-S-O	122	302	43	84	13	2	7	40	.278	0	69	144	9	.959
1990 — San Francisco (N.L.)	SS-2B-3B	92	155	22	31	2	1	8	21	.200	0	53	105	3	.981
1991 — Oakland (A.L.)■	3-S-2-1	108	281	30	60	8	4	5	32	.214	3	113	143	11	.959
American League totals (5 years)		493	1656	198	424	61	15	24	171	.256	17	620	996	70	.958
National League totals (3 years)		293	644	91	170	22	5	18	89	.264	1	168	382	15	.973
Major league totals (7 years)		786	2300	289	594	83	20	42	260	.258	18	788	1378	85	.962

CHAMPIONSHIP SERIES RECORD

Year	Team (League)	Pos.	G	AB	R	H	2B	3B	HR	RBI	Avg.	SB	PO	A	E	Avg.
							BATTING						FIELDING			
1989 —San Francisco (N.L.)		PH	1	1	0	0	0	0	0	0	.000	0	0	0	0	...

WORLD SERIES RECORD

Year	Team (League)	Pos.	G	AB	R	H	2B	3B	HR	RBI	Avg.	SB	PO	A	E	Avg.
							BATTING						FIELDING			
1989 —San Francisco (N.L.)		DH-PH	4	8	0	0	0	0	0	0	.000	0	0	0	0	...

RIPKEN, BILLY
2B, ORIOLES

PERSONAL: Born December 16, 1964, at Havre de Grace, Md. . . . 6-1/186. . . . Throws right, bats right. . . . Full name: William Oliver Ripken. . . . Son of Cal Ripken Sr., manager, Baltimore Orioles (1987-88), coach, Orioles (1976-86 and 1989-91); brother of Cal Ripken Jr., Orioles shortstop.

HIGH SCHOOL: Aberdeen (Md.).

TRANSACTIONS/CAREER NOTES: Selected by Baltimore Orioles organization in 11th round of free-agent draft (June 7, 1982). . . . On disabled list (April 20-May 3, 1984; June 23-July 6, 1985; March 27-April 14 and August 23-September 7, 1989; and August 5-20, 1990). . . . On Baltimore disabled list (July 15-August 15, 1991); included rehabilitation disability assignment to Frederick (August 12-13, 1991) and Hagerstown (August 13-15, 1991).

STATISTICAL NOTES: Led Southern League second basemen with 723 total chances and 79 double plays in 1986. . . . Tied for Southern League lead in grounding into double plays with 21 in 1986. . . . Tied for A.L. lead with 17 sacrifice hits in 1990.

Year	Team (League)	Pos.	G	AB	R	H	2B	3B	HR	RBI	Avg.	SB	PO	A	E	Avg.
							BATTING						FIELDING			
1982 —Bluefield (Appalachian)		SS-3B-2B	27	45	8	11	1	0	0	4	.244	0	15	17	3	.914
1983 —Bluefield (Appalachian)		SS-3B	48	152	24	33	6	0	0	13	.217	7	82	145	23	.908
1984 —Hagerstown (Carolina)		SS-2B	115	409	48	94	15	3	2	40	.230	3	187	358	28	.951
1985 —Charlotte (Southern)		SS	18	51	2	7	1	0	0	3	.137	0	18	52	4	.946
—Daytona Beach (Fla. St.) ..		SS-3B-2B	67	222	23	51	11	0	0	18	.230	7	90	198	8	.973
1986 —Charlotte (Southern)		2B	141	530	58	142	20	3	5	62	.268	9	*305	*395	*23	.968
1987 —Rochester (Int'l)		2B-SS	74	238	32	68	15	0	0	11	.286	7	154	200	9	.975
—Baltimore (A.L.)		2B	58	234	27	72	9	0	2	20	.308	4	133	162	3	.990
1988 —Baltimore (A.L.)		2B-3B	150	512	52	106	18	1	2	34	.207	8	310	440	12	.984
1989 —Baltimore (A.L.)		2B	115	318	31	76	11	2	2	26	.239	1	255	335	9	.985
1990 —Baltimore (A.L.)		2B	129	406	48	118	28	1	3	38	.291	5	250	366	8	.987
1991 —Baltimore (A.L.)		2B	104	287	24	62	11	1	0	14	.216	0	201	284	7	.986
—Frederick (Carolina)		DH	1	4	2	1	0	0	0	1	.250	0	0	0	0	...
—Hagerstown (Eastern)		2B	1	5	1	3	0	0	0	0	.600	1	2	1	0	1.000
Major league totals (5 years)			556	1757	182	434	77	5	9	132	.247	18	1149	1587	39	.986

RIPKEN, CAL
SS, ORIOLES

PERSONAL: Born August 24, 1960, at Havre de Grace, Md. . . . 6-4/224. . . . Throws right, bats right. . . . Full name: Calvin Edwin Ripken Jr. . . . Son of Cal Ripken Sr., manager, Baltimore Orioles (1987-88), coach, Orioles (1976-86 and 1989-91); and brother of Billy Ripken, second baseman, Orioles.

HIGH SCHOOL: Aberdeen (Md.).

TRANSACTIONS/CAREER NOTES: Selected by Baltimore Orioles organization in second round of free-agent draft (June 6, 1978).

RECORDS/HONORS: Holds major league record for most years leading league in games by shortstop—7; most consecutive games by shortstop—1,546. . . . Holds major league single-season records for most at-bats without a triple—646 (1989); highest fielding percentage by shortstop—.996 (1990); fewest errors by shortstop (150 or more games)—3 (1990); most consecutive errorless games by shortstop—95 (April 14-July 27, 1990); most consecutive chances accepted by shortstop without an error—431 (April 14-July 28, 1990, first game). . . . Holds A.L. career records for most home runs by shortstop—251; most years leading league in putouts by shortstop—5. . . . Holds A.L. single-season record for most assists by shortstop—583 (1984). . . . Named A.L. Rookie Player of the Year by THE SPORTING NEWS (1982). . . . Named A.L. Rookie of the Year by Baseball Writers' Association of America (1982). . . . Named Major League Player of the Year by THE SPORTING NEWS (1983 and 1991). . . . Named A.L. Player of the Year by THE SPORTING NEWS (1983 and 1991). . . . Named shortstop on THE SPORTING NEWS A.L. All-Star team (1983-85, 1989 and 1991). . . . Named shortstop on THE SPORTING NEWS Silver Slugger team (1983-86, 1989 and 1991) . . . Named A.L. Most Valuable Player by Baseball Writers' Association of America (1983 and 1991). . . . Won A.L. Gold Glove at shortstop (1991).

STATISTICAL NOTES: Tied for Appalachian League lead in double plays by shortstops with 31 in 1978. . . . Led Southern League third basemen with .933 fielding percentage, 119 putouts, 268 assists, and 34 double plays in 1980. . . . Tied for Southern League lead in sacrifice flies with nine in 1980. . . . Led A.L. shortstops with 831 total chances in 1983, 906 in 1984, 815 in 1989 and 806 in 1991. . . . Led A.L. shortstops with 113 double plays in 1983, 122 in 1984, 123 in 1985, 119 in 1989 and 114 in 1991. . . . Hit for the cycle (May 6, 1984). . . . Tied for A.L. lead with 15 game-winning RBIs in 1986. . . . Tied for A.L. lead with 10 sacrifice flies in 1988. . . . Led A.L. with 368 total bases in 1991.

Year	Team (League)	Pos.	G	AB	R	H	2B	3B	HR	RBI	Avg.	SB	PO	A	E	Avg.
							BATTING						FIELDING			
1978 —Bluefield (Appalachian)		SS	63	239	27	63	7	1	0	24	.264	1	*92	204	*33	.900
1979 —Miami (Florida State)		3B-SS-2B	105	393	51	119	*28	1	5	54	.303	4	149	260	30	.932
—Charlotte (Southern)		3B	17	61	6	11	0	1	3	8	.180	1	13	26	3	.929
1980 —Charlotte (Southern)		3B-SS	•144	522	91	144	28	5	25	78	.276	4	†151	†341	35	†.934
1981 —Rochester (Int'l)		3B-SS	114	437	74	126	31	4	23	75	.288	0	128	320	21	.955
—Baltimore (A.L.)		SS-3B	23	39	1	5	0	0	0	0	.128	0	13	30	3	.935
1982 —Baltimore (A.L.)		SS-3B	160	598	90	158	32	5	28	93	.264	3	221	440	19	.972

Year	Team (League)	Pos.	G	AB	R	H	2B	3B	HR	RBI	Avg.	SB	PO	A	E	Avg.
							BATTING							FIELDING		
1983 —Baltimore (A.L.)		SS	•162	*663	*121	*211	*47	2	27	102	.318	0	272	*534	25	.970
1984 —Baltimore (A.L.)		SS	•162	641	103	195	37	7	27	86	.304	2	*297	*583	26	.971
1985 —Baltimore (A.L.)		SS	161	642	116	181	32	5	26	110	.282	2	*286	474	26	.967
1986 —Baltimore (A.L.)		SS	162	627	98	177	35	1	25	81	.282	4	240	*482	13	.982
1987 —Baltimore (A.L.)		SS	*162	624	97	157	28	3	27	98	.252	3	240	*480	20	.973
1988 —Baltimore (A.L.)		SS	161	575	87	152	25	1	23	81	.264	2	*284	480	21	.973
1989 —Baltimore (A.L.)		SS	•162	646	80	166	30	0	21	93	.257	3	*276	*531	8	.990
1990 —Baltimore (A.L.)		SS	161	600	78	150	28	4	21	84	.250	3	242	435	3	*.996
1991 —Baltimore (A.L.)		SS	•162	650	99	210	46	5	34	114	.323	6	*267	*528	11	*.986
Major league totals (11 years)			1638	6305	970	1762	340	33	259	942	.279	28	2638	4997	175	.978

CHAMPIONSHIP SERIES RECORD

Year	Team (League)	Pos.	G	AB	R	H	2B	3B	HR	RBI	Avg.	SB	PO	A	E	Avg.
							BATTING							FIELDING		
1983 —Baltimore (A.L.)		SS	4	15	5	6	2	0	0	1	.400	0	7	11	0	1.000

WORLD SERIES RECORD

Year	Team (League)	Pos.	G	AB	R	H	2B	3B	HR	RBI	Avg.	SB	PO	A	E	Avg.
							BATTING							FIELDING		
1983 —Baltimore (A.L.)		SS	5	18	2	3	0	0	0	1	.167	0	6	14	0	1.000

ALL-STAR GAME RECORD

Year	League	Pos.	AB	R	H	2B	3B	HR	RBI	Avg.	SB	PO	A	E	Avg.
						BATTING							FIELDING		
1983 —American		SS	0	0	0	0	0	0	0	. . .	0	1	0	0	1.000
1984 —American		SS	3	0	0	0	0	0	0	.000	0	0	0	0	. . .
1985 —American		SS	3	0	1	0	0	0	0	.333	0	2	1	0	1.000
1986 —American		SS	4	0	0	0	0	0	0	.000	0	0	1	0	1.000
1987 —American		SS	2	0	1	0	0	0	0	.500	0	5	0	0	1.000
1988 —American		SS	3	0	0	0	0	0	0	.000	0	1	4	0	1.000
1989 —American		SS	3	0	1	1	0	0	0	.333	0	0	0	0	. . .
1990 —American		SS	2	0	0	0	0	0	0	.000	0	1	1	0	1.000
1991 —American		SS	3	1	2	0	0	1	3	.667	0	2	1	0	1.000
All-Star Game totals (9 years)			23	1	5	1	0	1	3	.217	0	7	13	0	1.000

RISLEY, BILL

P, EXPOS

PERSONAL: Born May 29, 1967, at Chicago. . . . 6-2/215. . . . Throws right, bats right. . . . Full name: William Charles Risley. . . . Name pronounced RIZZ-lee.
HIGH SCHOOL: Marist (Chicago).
TRANSACTIONS/CAREER NOTES: Selected by Cincinnati Reds organization in 14th round of free-agent draft (June 2, 1987). . . . Traded by Reds with P John Wetteland to Montreal Expos for OF Dave Martinez, P Scott Ruskin and SS Willie Greene (December 11, 1991).
STATISTICAL NOTES: Tied for Southern League lead with five balks in 1991.

Year	Team (League)	G	W	L	Pct.	ERA	Sv.	IP	H	R	ER	BB	SO
1987 —Sarasota Reds (Gulf Coast)		11	1	4	.200	1.89	0	52⅓	38	24	11	26	50
1988 —Greensboro (South Atlantic)		23	8	4	.667	4.11	0	120⅓	82	60	55	84	135
1989 —Cedar Rapids (Midwest)		27	9	10	.474	3.90	0	140⅔	87	72	61	81	128
1990 —Cedar Rapids (Midwest)		22	8	9	.471	2.81	0	137⅔	99	51	43	68	123
1991 —Chattanooga (Southern)		19	5	7	.417	3.16	0	108⅓	81	48	38	60	77
—Nashville (American Assoc.)		8	3	5	.375	4.91	0	44	45	27	24	26	32

RITCHIE, WALLY

P, PHILLIES

PERSONAL: Born July 12, 1965, at Glendale, Calif. . . . 6-2/180. . . . Throws left, bats left. . . . Full name: Wallace Reid Ritchie.
HIGH SCHOOL: Hoover (Glendale, Calif.).
COLLEGE: Glendale Community College (Calif.) and Brigham Young.
TRANSACTIONS/CAREER NOTES: Selected by Philadelphia Phillies organization in fourth round of free-agent draft (June 3, 1985). . . . On Philadelphia disabled list (June 5-27, 1991). . . . On suspended list for one game (June 27, 1991).
STATISTICAL NOTES: Pitched a 1-0 no-hit victory vs. Syracuse (June 25, 1990); allowed one hit in the eighth (an extra) inning.

Year	Team (League)	G	W	L	Pct.	ERA	Sv.	IP	H	R	ER	BB	SO
1985 —Bend (Northwest)		2	1	0	1.000	4.50	0	10	10	11	5	5	3
—Clearwater (Florida State)		14	3	1	.750	3.47	1	46⅔	49	30	18	12	24
1986 —Clearwater (Florida State)		32	4	1	.800	2.25	10	52	40	15	13	16	39
—Reading (Eastern)		28	4	1	.800	2.70	4	30	29	13	9	9	13
1987 —Maine (International)		13	3	1	.750	2.05	2	22	17	6	5	8	16
—Philadelphia (N.L.)		49	3	2	.600	3.75	3	62⅓	60	27	26	29	45
1988 —Philadelphia (N.L.)		19	0	0	. . .	3.12	0	26	19	14	9	17	8
—Maine (International)		16	4	5	.444	4.69	0	78⅔	88	49	41	29	49
1989 —Scranton/Wilkes-Barre (Int'l)		34	7	4	.636	4.18	0	135⅔	143	70	63	38	73
1990 —Scranton/Wilkes-Barre (Int'l)		20	4	3	.571	4.15	0	82⅓	75	46	38	28	47
1991 —Scranton/Wilkes-Barre (Int'l)		7	1	0	1.000	2.42	2	26	17	8	7	7	25
—Philadelphia (N.L.)		39	1	2	.333	2.50	0	50⅓	44	17	14	17	26
Major league totals (3 years)		107	4	4	.500	3.18	3	138⅔	123	58	49	63	79

RITZ, KEVIN
P, TIGERS

PERSONAL: Born June 8, 1965, at Eatonstown, N.J.... 6-4/210.... Throws right, bats right.
HIGH SCHOOL: Davis County (Ia.).
COLLEGE: William Penn (Ia.) and Indian Hills Community College (Ia.).
TRANSACTIONS/CAREER NOTES: Selected by San Francisco Giants organization in fourth round of free-agent draft (January 9, 1985).... Selected by Detroit Tigers organization in secondary phase of free-agent draft (June 3, 1985).

Year	Team (League)	G	W	L	Pct.	ERA	Sv.	IP	H	R	ER	BB	SO
1986 —Gastonia (South Atlantic)		7	1	2	.333	4.21	0	36⅓	29	19	17	21	34
—Lakeland (Florida State)		18	3	9	.250	5.57	1	85⅔	114	60	53	45	39
1987 —Glens Falls (Eastern)		25	8	8	.500	4.89	0	152⅔	171	95	83	71	78
1988 —Glens Falls (Eastern)		26	8	10	.444	3.82	0	136⅔	115	68	58	70	75
1989 —Toledo (International)		16	7	8	.467	3.16	0	102⅔	95	48	36	60	74
—Detroit (A.L.)		12	4	6	.400	4.38	0	74	75	41	36	44	56
1990 —Toledo (International)		20	3	6	.333	5.22	0	89⅔	93	68	52	59	57
—Detroit (A.L.)		4	0	4	.000	11.05	0	7⅓	14	12	9	14	3
1991 —Toledo (International)		20	8	7	.533	3.28	0	126⅓	116	50	46	60	105
—Detroit (A.L.)		11	0	3	.000	11.74	0	15⅓	17	22	20	22	9
Major league totals (3 years)		**27**	**4**	**13**	**.235**	**6.05**	**0**	**96⅔**	**106**	**75**	**65**	**80**	**68**

RIVERA, BEN
P, BRAVES

PERSONAL: Born January 11, 1969, at San Pedro de Macoris, Dominican Republic.... 6-6/210.... Throws right, bats right.... Full name: Bienvenido Santana Rivera.
TRANSACTIONS/CAREER NOTES: Signed as free agent by Atlanta Braves organization (November 15, 1986).

Year	Team (League)	G	W	L	Pct.	ERA	Sv.	IP	H	R	ER	BB	SO
1987 —Bradenton Braves (GCL)		16	1	5	.167	3.26	0	49⅔	55	26	18	19	29
1988 —Sumter (South Atlantic)		27	9	11	.450	3.17	0	173⅓	167	77	61	52	99
1989 —Durham (Carolina)		23	5	7	.417	4.49	0	102⅓	113	55	51	51	58
1990 —Greenville (Southern)		13	1	4	.200	6.58	0	52	68	40	38	26	32
—Durham (Carolina)		16	5	3	.625	3.60	1	75	69	41	30	33	64
1991 —Greenville (Southern)		26	11	8	.579	3.57	0	158⅔	155	76	63	75	116

RIVERA, LUIS
SS, RED SOX

PERSONAL: Born January 3, 1964, at Cidra, Puerto Rico.... 5-9/175.... Throws right, bats right.... Full name: Luis Antonio Rivera.
HIGH SCHOOL: Luis Munoz Iglesias (Cidra, Puerto Rico).
TRANSACTIONS/CAREER NOTES: Signed as free agent by Montreal Expos organization (September 22, 1981).... Traded by Expos with P John Dopson to Boston Red Sox for SS Spike Owen and P Dan Gakeler (December 8, 1988).
RECORDS/HONORS: Shares A.L. single-season record for fewest errors by shortstop who led league in errors—24 (1991).
STATISTICAL NOTES: Led Florida State League shortstops with 704 total chances and 95 double plays in 1983.... Tied for Florida State League lead in total chances by shortstops with 626 in 1984.... Led Southern League shortstops with 643 total chances and 107 double plays in 1985.... Led American Association shortstops with 84 double plays in 1987.

Year	Team (League)	Pos.	G	AB	R	H	2B	3B	HR	RBI	Avg.	SB	PO	A	E	Avg.
1982 —San Jose (California)		SS	130	476	53	123	20	3	3	49	.258	12	226	389	55	.918
1983 —West Palm Beach (FSL)		SS	129	419	63	95	18	5	5	53	.227	6	217	★436	★51	.928
1984 —West Palm Beach (FSL)		SS	124	439	54	100	23	0	6	43	.228	14	★198	★389	39	.938
1985 —Jacksonville (Southern)		SS	138	★538	74	129	20	2	16	72	.240	18	★198	★412	33	.949
1986 —Indianapolis (A.A.)		SS	108	407	60	100	17	5	7	43	.246	18	178	330	24	.955
—Montreal (N.L.)		SS	55	166	20	34	11	1	0	13	.205	1	64	119	9	.953
1987 —Indianapolis (A.A.)		SS	108	433	73	135	26	3	8	53	.312	24	190	291	18	.964
—Montreal (N.L.)		SS	18	32	0	5	2	0	0	1	.156	0	9	27	3	.923
1988 —Montreal (N.L.)		SS	123	371	35	83	17	3	4	30	.224	3	160	301	18	.962
1989 —Pawtucket (Int'l)■		SS-3B	43	175	22	44	9	0	1	13	.251	5	53	106	9	.946
—Boston (A.L.)		SS-2B	93	323	35	83	17	1	5	29	.257	2	127	240	16	.958
1990 —Boston (A.L.)		SS-2B-3B	118	346	38	78	20	0	7	45	.225	4	187	310	18	.965
1991 —Boston (A.L.)		SS	129	414	64	107	22	3	8	40	.258	4	180	386	★24	.959
American League totals (3 years)			**340**	**1083**	**137**	**268**	**59**	**4**	**20**	**114**	**.247**	**10**	**494**	**936**	**58**	**.961**
National League totals (3 years)			**196**	**569**	**55**	**122**	**30**	**4**	**4**	**44**	**.214**	**4**	**233**	**447**	**30**	**.958**
Major league totals (6 years)			**536**	**1652**	**192**	**390**	**89**	**8**	**24**	**158**	**.236**	**14**	**727**	**1383**	**88**	**.960**

CHAMPIONSHIP SERIES RECORD

Year	Team (League)	Pos.	G	AB	R	H	2B	3B	HR	RBI	Avg.	SB	PO	A	E	Avg.
1990 —Boston (A.L.)		SS	4	9	1	2	1	0	0	0	.222	0	6	16	1	.957

ROBERSON, KEVIN
OF, CUBS

PERSONAL: Born January 29, 1968, at Decatur, Ill.... 6-4/210.... Throws right, bats both.... Full name: Kevin Lynn Roberson.
HIGH SCHOOL: Eisenhower (Decatur, Ill).
COLLEGE: Parkland College (Ill.).

TRANSACTIONS/CAREER NOTES: Selected by Chicago Cubs organization in 16th round of free-agent draft (June 1, 1988).
STATISTICAL NOTES: Led South Atlantic league outfielders with seven double plays in 1989. . . . Tied for South Atlantic League lead in strikeouts by batters with 149 in 1989. . . . Led Southern League batters with 129 strikeouts in 1991.

Year	Team (League)	Pos.	G	AB	R	H	2B	3B	HR	RBI	Avg.	SB	PO	A	E	Avg.
1988	Wytheville (Appal.)	OF	63	225	39	47	12	2	3	29	.209	3	93	4	6	.942
1989	Charleston, W.Va. (SAL) ..	OF	126	429	49	109	19	1	13	57	.254	3	210	18	7	.970
1990	Winston-Salem (Caro.)	OF	85	313	49	84	23	3	5	45	.268	7	136	4	6	.959
	Charlotte (Southern)	OF	31	119	14	29	6	2	5	16	.244	2	63	1	0	1.000
1991	Charlotte (Southern)	OF	136	507	77	130	24	2	19	67	.256	17	259	7	4	.985

ROBERTS, BIP
OF/2B, REDS

PERSONAL: Born October 27, 1963, at Berkeley, Calif. . . . 5-7/165. . . . Throws right, bats both. . . . Full name: Leon Joseph Roberts III.
HIGH SCHOOL: Skyline (Oakland, Calif.).
COLLEGE: Chabot College (Calif.) and UNLV.
TRANSACTIONS/CAREER NOTES: Selected by Pittsburgh Pirates organization in fifth round of free-agent draft (June 8, 1981). . . . Selected by Pirates organization in secondary phase of free-agent draft (June 7, 1982). . . . On suspended list (June 30-July 3, 1985). . . . Drafted by San Diego Padres (December 10, 1985). . . . On disabled list (May 21-June 5, 1986 and August 17-September 9, 1991). . . . Traded by Padres with a player to be named later to Cincinnati Reds for P Randy Myers (December 8, 1991); Reds acquired OF Craig Pueschner to complete deal (December 9, 1991).
STATISTICAL NOTES: Led South Atlantic League second basemen with .962 fielding percentage and tied for lead in double plays with 76 in 1983. . . . Led Carolina League second basemen with 654 total chances and 91 double plays in 1984.

Year	Team (League)	Pos.	G	AB	R	H	2B	3B	HR	RBI	Avg.	SB	PO	A	E	Avg.
1982	Bradenton Pirates (GCL) ..	2B	6	23	4	7	1	0	0	1	.304	4	14	15	0	1.000
	Greenwood (S. Atlantic)....	2B	33	107	15	23	3	1	0	6	.215	10	52	82	7	.950
1983	Greenwood (S. Atlantic)....	2B-SS	122	438	78	140	20	5	6	63	.320	27	273	311	24 †.961
1984	Prince William (Caro.)	2B	134	498	81	★150	25	5	8	77	.301	50	★282	352	20	★.969
1985	Nashua (Eastern)	2B	105	401	64	109	19	5	1	23	.272	40	217	249	•29	.941
1986	San Diego (N.L.) ■	2B	101	241	34	61	5	2	1	12	.253	14	166	172	10	.971
1987	Las Vegas (Pac. Coast)	2B-OF-3B	98	359	66	110	18	10	1	38	.306	27	147	150	8	.974
1988	Las Vegas (Pac. Coast)	3B-OF-2B	100	343	73	121	21	8	7	51	.353	29	103	130	17	.932
	San Diego (N.L.)	2B-3B	5	9	1	3	0	0	0	0	.333	0	2	3	1	.833
1989	San Diego (N.L.)	O-3-S-2	117	329	81	99	15	8	3	25	.301	21	134	113	9	.965
1990	San Diego (N.L.)	O-3-S-2	149	556	104	172	36	3	9	44	.309	46	227	160	13	.968
1991	San Diego (N.L.)	OF-2B	117	424	66	119	13	3	3	32	.281	26	239	185	10	.977
Major league totals (5 years)			489	1559	286	454	69	16	16	113	.291	107	768	633	43	.970

ROBINSON, DON
P, ANGELS

PERSONAL: Born June 8, 1957, at Ashland, Ky. . . . 6-4/240. . . . Throws right, bats right. . . . Full name: Don Allen Robinson.
HIGH SCHOOL: Ceredo-Kenova (Kenova, W.Va.).
TRANSACTIONS/CAREER NOTES: Selected by Pittsburgh Pirates organization in third round of free-agent draft (June 4, 1975). . . . On Columbus disabled list (July 28-September 6, 1977). . . . On disabled list (March 31-May 1, 1980; May 2-June 6 and August 2-26, 1981). . . . On Pittsburgh disabled list (March 29-June 10 and July 29-September 2, 1983); included rehabilitation disability assignment to Lynn (April 29-May 18, 1983). . . . On Pittsburgh disabled list (April 21-June 7, 1986); included rehabilitation disability assignment to Prince William (May 24-June 7, 1986). . . . Traded by Pirates to San Francisco Giants for C Mackey Sasser and $50,000 (July 31, 1987). . . . On San Francisco disabled list (March 28-May 23, 1990); included rehabilitation disability assignment to San Jose (May 9-22, 1990). . . . On disabled list (July 20-August 5, 1991). . . . Granted free agency (October 31, 1991). . . . Signed by California Angels (January 3, 1992).
RECORDS/HONORS: Named N.L. Rookie Pitcher of the Year by THE SPORTING NEWS (1978). . . . Named pitcher on THE SPORTING NEWS N.L. Silver Slugger team (1982, 1989-90).
STATISTICAL NOTES: Tied for Gulf Coast League lead with six hit batsmen in 1975. . . . Led Western Carolinas League with 11 complete games in 1976. . . . Tied for N.L. lead with 26 home runs allowed in 1982.
MISCELLANEOUS: Appeared in one game as outfielder with two putouts (1984). . . . Appeared in two games as pinch-hitter (1991).

Year	Team (League)	G	W	L	Pct.	ERA	Sv.	IP	H	R	ER	BB	SO
1975	Bradenton Pirates (GCL)	10	2	3	.400	2.45	0	66	51	23	18	31	★70
1976	Charleston, S.C. (W. Caro.).......	25	12	9	.571	3.24	0	★172	146	79	62	64	132
1977	Shreveport (Texas)	18	7	6	.538	4.10	0	112	113	58	51	41	103
	Columbus (International)	1	1	0	1.000	0.00	0	5	7	0	0	1	3
1978	Pittsburgh (N.L.)	35	14	6	.700	3.47	1	228	203	98	88	57	135
1979	Pittsburgh (N.L.)	29	8	8	.500	3.86	0	161	171	74	69	52	96
1980	Pittsburgh (N.L.)	29	7	10	.412	3.99	1	160	157	74	71	45	103
1981	Pittsburgh (N.L.)	16	0	3	.000	5.92	2	38	47	27	25	23	17
1982	Pittsburgh (N.L.)	38	15	13	.536	4.28	0	227	213	★123	108	103	165
1983	Pittsburgh (N.L.)	9	2	2	.500	4.46	0	36⅓	43	21	18	21	28
	Lynn (Eastern)	2	0	1	.000	8.10	0	6⅔	9	6	6	2	5
1984	Pittsburgh (N.L.)	51	5	6	.455	3.02	10	122	99	45	41	49	110
1985	Pittsburgh (N.L.)	44	5	11	.313	3.87	3	95⅓	95	49	41	42	65
1986	Pittsburgh (N.L.)	50	3	4	.429	3.38	14	69⅓	61	27	26	27	53
	Prince William (Carolina)	3	1	1	.500	0.71	0	12⅔	13	7	1	1	13

Year	Team (League)	G	W	L	Pct.	ERA	Sv.	IP	H	R	ER	BB	SO
1987	—Pitts.-San Francisco (N.L.)■....	67	11	7	.611	3.42	19	108	105	42	41	40	79
1988	—San Francisco (N.L.)	51	10	5	.667	2.45	6	176⅔	152	63	48	49	122
1989	—San Francisco (N.L.)	34	12	11	.522	3.43	0	197	184	80	75	37	96
1990	—San Jose (Pacific Coast)	2	1	0	1.000	3.86	0	7	6	3	3	1	8
	—San Francisco (N.L.)	26	10	7	.588	4.57	0	157⅔	173	84	80	41	78
1991	—San Francisco (N.L.)	34	5	9	.357	4.38	1	121⅓	123	64	59	50	78
	Major league totals (14 years)	513	107	102	.512	3.75	57	1897⅔	1826	871	790	636	1225

CHAMPIONSHIP SERIES RECORD

Year	Team (League)	G	W	L	Pct.	ERA	Sv.	IP	H	R	ER	BB	SO
1979	—Pittsburgh (N.L.)	2	1	0	1.000	0.00	1	2	0	0	0	1	3
1987	—San Francisco (N.L.)	3	0	1	.000	9.00	0	3	3	3	3	0	3
1989	—San Francisco (N.L.)	1	1	0	1.000	0.00	0	1⅔	3	1	0	0	0
	Championship Series totals (3 years)	6	2	1	.667	4.05	1	6⅔	6	4	3	1	6

WORLD SERIES RECORD

Year	Team (League)	G	W	L	Pct.	ERA	Sv.	IP	H	R	ER	BB	SO
1979	—Pittsburgh (N.L.)	4	1	0	1.000	5.40	0	5	4	3	3	6	3
1989	—San Francisco (N.L.)	1	0	1	.000	21.60	0	1⅔	4	4	4	1	0
	World Series totals (2 years)	5	1	1	.500	9.45	0	6⅔	8	7	7	7	3

ROBINSON, JEFF
P, CUBS

PERSONAL: Born December 13, 1960, at Santa Ana, Calif.... 6-4/200.... Throws right, bats right.... Full name: Jeffrey Daniel Robinson.
HIGH SCHOOL: Troy (Fullerton, Calif.).
COLLEGE: Cal State Fullerton.
TRANSACTIONS/CAREER NOTES: Selected by Toronto Blue Jays organization in 17th round of free-agent draft (June 5, 1979).... Selected by Detroit Tigers organization in 14th round of free-agent draft (June 7, 1982).... Selected by San Francisco Giants organization in second round of free-agent draft (June 6, 1983).... Traded by Giants with P Scott Medvin to Pittsburgh Pirates for P Rick Reuschel (August 21, 1987).... Traded by Pirates with P Willie Smith to New York Yankees for C Don Slaught (December 4, 1989).... Granted free agency (November 5, 1990).... Signed by California Angels (January 17, 1991).... Granted free agency (October 29, 1991).... Signed by Chicago Cubs organization (January 7, 1992).
RECORDS/HONORS: Shares major league record by striking out side on nine pitches (September 7, 1987, eighth inning).
STATISTICAL NOTES: Tied for N.L. lead with seven hit batsmen in 1984.... Tied for Pacific Coast League lead in games started by pitcher with 29 in 1985.
MISCELLANEOUS: Had no chances in one game as outfielder (1986).

Year	Team (League)	G	W	L	Pct.	ERA	Sv.	IP	H	R	ER	BB	SO
1983	—Fresno (California)	14	7	6	.538	2.28	0	94⅔	88	35	24	21	78
1984	—San Francisco (N.L.)	34	7	15	.318	4.56	0	171⅔	195	99	87	52	102
1985	—Phoenix (Pacific Coast)	29	9	9	.500	5.14	0	161	192	107	92	60	80
	—San Francisco (N.L.)	8	0	0	...	5.11	0	12⅓	16	11	7	10	8
1986	—San Francisco (N.L.)	64	6	3	.667	3.36	8	104⅓	92	46	39	32	90
1987	—San Francisco-Pitts. (N.L.)■..	81	8	9	.471	2.85	14	123⅓	89	43	39	54	101
1988	—Pittsburgh (N.L.)	75	11	5	.688	3.03	9	124⅔	113	44	42	39	87
1989	—Pittsburgh (N.L.)	50	7	13	.350	4.58	4	141⅓	161	92	72	59	95
1990	—New York (A.L.)	54	3	6	.333	3.45	0	88⅔	82	35	34	34	43
1991	—California (A.L.)■	39	0	3	.000	5.37	3	57	56	34	34	29	57
	American League totals (2 years)	93	3	9	.250	4.20	3	145⅔	138	69	68	63	100
	National League totals (6 years)	312	39	45	.464	3.80	35	677⅔	666	335	286	246	483
	Major league totals (8 years)	405	42	54	.438	3.87	38	823⅓	804	404	354	309	583

ROBINSON, JEFF
P, RANGERS

PERSONAL: Born December 14, 1961, at Ventura, Calif.... 6-6/240.... Throws right, bats right.... Full name: Jeffrey Mark Robinson.
HIGH SCHOOL: Christian (El Cajon, Calif.).
COLLEGE: Azusa Pacific University (Calif.).
TRANSACTIONS/CAREER NOTES: Selected by San Diego Padres organization in 40th round of free-agent draft (June 3, 1980).... Selected by Detroit Tigers organization in third round of free-agent draft (June 6, 1983).... On disabled list (June 28-July 10, 1985 and August 24, 1988-remainder of season).... On Detroit disabled list (May 15-31 and June 11-July 26, 1989); included rehabilitation disability assignment to Lakeland (July 10-26, 1989).... Traded by Tigers to Baltimore Orioles for C Mickey Tettleton (January 11, 1991).... Released by Orioles (November 13, 1991).... Signed by Texas Rangers organization (January 3, 1992).

Year	Team (League)	G	W	L	Pct.	ERA	Sv.	IP	H	R	ER	BB	SO
1983	—Lakeland (Florida State)	11	2	5	.286	5.94	0	50	61	38	33	19	23
1984	—Lakeland (Florida State)	10	2	3	.400	3.36	0	61⅔	62	30	23	26	33
	—Birmingham (Southern)	20	6	6	.500	4.70	0	113	111	64	59	56	47
1985	—Birmingham (Southern)	22	4	8	.333	5.09	0	115	142	79	65	59	67
1986	—Nashville (American Assoc.)	25	10	7	.588	4.38	0	150	162	85	73	72	72
1987	—Detroit (A.L.)	29	9	6	.600	5.37	0	127⅓	132	86	76	54	98
1988	—Detroit (A.L.)	24	13	6	.684	2.98	0	172	121	61	57	72	114
1989	—Detroit (A.L.)	16	4	5	.444	4.73	0	78	76	47	41	46	40
	—Lakeland (Florida State)	4	0	0	...	6.55	0	11	12	8	8	4	5

Year	Team (League)	G	W	L	Pct.	ERA	Sv.	IP	H	R	ER	BB	SO
1990 —Detroit (A.L.)		27	10	9	.526	5.96	0	145	141	101	96	88	76
1991 —Baltimore (A.L.)■.....................		21	4	9	.308	5.18	0	104⅓	119	62	60	51	65
—Rochester (International)		8	1	2	.333	6.43	1	21	23	18	15	15	13
Major league totals (5 years)		117	40	35	.533	4.74	0	626⅔	589	357	330	311	393

CHAMPIONSHIP SERIES RECORD

Year	Team (League)	G	W	L	Pct.	ERA	Sv.	IP	H	R	ER	BB	SO
1987 —Detroit (A.L.)		1	0	0	...	0.00	0	⅓	1	0	0	0	0

ROBINSON, RON
P, BREWERS

PERSONAL: Born March 24, 1962, at Exeter, Calif. . . . 6-4/235. . . . Throws right, bats right. . . . Full name: Ronald Dean Robinson.
HIGH SCHOOL: Woodlake (Calif.).
TRANSACTIONS/CAREER NOTES: Selected by Cincinnati Reds organization in first round (19th pick overall) of free-agent draft (June 3, 1980). . . . On Cincinnati disabled list (June 25-July 18 and July 20-September 2, 1988); included rehabilitation disability assignment to Nashville (August 15-September 2, 1988). . . . On Cincinnati disabled list (March 19-July 17, 1989); included rehabilitation disability assignment to Nashville (June 26-July 2, 1989); then transferred to Chattanooga (July 3, 1989). . . . Traded by Reds with P Bob Sebra to Milwaukee Brewers for OF Glenn Braggs and IF Billy Bates (June 9, 1990). . . . On disabled list (April 12, 1991-remainder of season).

Year	Team (League)	G	W	L	Pct.	ERA	Sv.	IP	H	R	ER	BB	SO
1980 —Tampa (Florida State)...............		13	4	6	.400	3.32	0	76	76	32	28	16	44
1981 —Cedar Rapids (Midwest)		24	10	8	.556	2.24	0	169	136	58	42	55	165
1982 —Waterbury (Eastern)...............		32	13	7	.650	3.28	1	178⅓	166	78	65	65	149
1983 —Waterbury (Eastern)...............		20	7	9	.438	3.60	0	142⅔	132	66	57	60	82
—Indianapolis (Am. Assoc.)		4	4	0	1.000	3.23	0	30⅔	22	13	11	7	20
1984 —Wichita (American Assoc.)		25	9	6	.600	4.61	0	150⅓	168	86	77	60	98
—Cincinnati (N.L.)		12	1	2	.333	2.72	0	39⅔	35	18	12	13	24
1985 —Denver (American Assoc.)		6	2	1	.667	2.72	0	39⅔	39	17	12	12	24
—Cincinnati (N.L.)		33	7	7	.500	3.99	1	108⅓	107	53	48	32	76
1986 —Cincinnati (N.L.)		70	10	3	.769	3.24	14	116⅔	110	44	42	43	117
1987 —Cincinnati (N.L.)		48	7	5	.583	3.68	4	154	148	71	63	43	99
1988 —Cincinnati (N.L.)		17	3	7	.300	4.12	0	78⅔	88	47	36	26	38
—Nashville (American Assoc.)		2	0	0	...	7.36	0	3⅔	4	3	3	3	4
1989 —Nashville (American Assoc.)		3	2	0	1.000	1.89	0	19	12	5	4	6	11
—Chattanooga (Southern)		1	0	0	...	1.80	0	5	3	1	1	1	5
—Cincinnati (N.L.)		15	5	3	.625	3.35	0	83⅓	80	36	31	28	36
1990 —Cincinnati (N.L.)		6	2	2	.500	4.88	0	31⅓	36	18	17	14	14
—Milwaukee (A.L.)■.................		22	12	5	.706	2.91	0	148⅓	158	60	48	37	57
1991 —Milwaukee (A.L.)		1	0	1	.000	6.23	0	4⅓	6	3	3	3	0
American League totals (2 years)		23	12	6	.667	3.01	0	152⅔	164	63	51	40	57
National League totals (7 years)		201	35	29	.547	3.66	19	612	604	287	249	199	404
Major league totals (8 years)		224	47	35	.573	3.53	19	764⅔	768	350	300	239	461

RODRIGUEZ, CARLOS
SS, YANKEES

PERSONAL: Born November 1, 1967, at Mexico City, Mexico. . . . 5-9/160. . . . Throws right, bats both. . . . Full name: Carlos Marquez Rodriguez.
TRANSACTIONS/CAREER NOTES: Sold by Mexico City Tigers of Mexican League to New York Yankees organization (March 20, 1987).
STATISTICAL NOTES: Led Gulf Coast League shortstops with .950 fielding percentage, 78 putouts, 167 assists and 258 total chances in 1987. . . . Led Florida State League with 21 sacrifice hits in 1989.

Year	Team (League)	Pos.	G	AB	R	H	2B	3B	HR	RBI	Avg.	SB	PO	A	E	Avg.
1987 —Sarasota Yankees (GCL) ..		SS-2B	50	115	15	18	0	0	0	11	.157	2	†79	†168	13	†.950
1988 —Fort Lauderdale (FSL)		SS-2B	124	461	39	110	15	1	0	36	.239	3	241	363	18	.971
1989 —Fort Lauderdale (FSL)		SS	102	353	48	85	15	1	0	26	.241	9	180	279	14	★.970
—Albany (Eastern)		SS	36	107	15	27	4	2	0	8	.252	1	46	107	5	.968
1990 —Albany (Eastern)		SS	18	75	10	21	4	0	0	7	.280	1	23	58	3	.964
—Columbus (Int'l)		SS	71	220	31	60	12	0	0	16	.273	3	90	232	6	.982
1991 —Columbus (Int'l)		SS	73	212	32	54	9	3	0	21	.255	1	138	236	11	.971
—New York (A.L.)		SS-2B	15	37	1	7	0	0	0	2	.189	0	11	34	2	.957
Major league totals (1 year)			15	37	1	7	0	0	0	2	.189	0	11	34	2	.957

RODRIGUEZ, HENRY
OF, DODGERS

PERSONAL: Born November 8, 1967, at Santo Domingo, Dominican Republic. . . . 6-1/180. . . . Throws left, bats left. . . . Full name: Henry Anderson Lorenzo Rodriguez.
HIGH SCHOOL: Liceo Republica de Paraguay.
TRANSACTIONS/CAREER NOTES: Signed as free agent by Los Angeles Dodgers organization (July 14, 1985).
RECORDS/HONORS: Named Texas League Most Valuable Player (1990).
STATISTICAL NOTES: Tied for Gulf Coast League lead with seven intentional bases on balls received in 1987. . . . Led Texas League with 14 sacrifice flies in 1990.

Year	Team (League)	Pos.	G	AB	R	H	2B	3B	HR	RBI	Avg.	SB	PO	A	E	Avg.
1987	—Sarasota Dodgers (GCL) ...	1B-SS	49	148	23	49	7	3	0	15	*.331	3	309	23	6	.982
1988	—Salem (Carolina)	1B	72	291	47	84	14	4	2	39	.289	14	585	*38	7	.989
1989	—Vero Beach (Florida St.) ...	1B-OF	126	433	53	123	*33	1	10	73	.284	7	1072	66	12	.990
	—Bakersfield (California)	1B	3	9	2	2	0	0	1	2	.222	0	8	0	0	1.000
1990	—San Antonio (Texas)	OF	129	495	82	144	22	9	*28	*109	.291	5	223	5	10	.958
1991	—Albuquerque (PCL)	OF-1B	121	446	61	121	22	5	10	67	.271	4	234	12	5	.980

RODRIGUEZ, IVAN
C, RANGERS

PERSONAL: Born November 30, 1971, at Vega Baja, Puerto Rico. . . . 5-9/205. . . . Throws right, bats right. . . . Full name: Ivan Rodriguez.
HIGH SCHOOL: Lina Padron Rivera (Vega Baja, Puerto Rico).
TRANSACTIONS/CAREER NOTES: Signed as free agent by Texas Rangers organization (July 27, 1988).
STATISTICAL NOTES: Led South Atlantic League catchers with 34 double plays in 1989. . . . Led Florida State League catchers with 842 total chances in 1990.

Year	Team (League)	Pos.	G	AB	R	H	2B	3B	HR	RBI	Avg.	SB	PO	A	E	Avg.
1989	—Gastonia (S. Atlantic)	C	112	386	38	92	22	1	7	42	.238	2	691	*96	11	.986
1990	—Charlotte (Florida State) ...	C	109	408	48	117	17	7	2	55	.287	1	*727	101	14	.983
1991	—Tulsa (Texas)	C	50	175	16	48	7	2	3	28	.274	1	210	33	3	.988
	—Texas (A.L.)	C	88	280	24	74	16	0	3	27	.264	0	517	62	10	.983
Major league totals (1 year)			88	280	24	74	16	0	3	27	.264	0	517	62	10	.983

RODRIGUEZ, RICH
P, PADRES

PERSONAL: Born March 1, 1963, at Los Angeles. . . . 6-0/200. . . . Throws left, bats left. . . . Full name: Richard Anthony Rodriguez.
HIGH SCHOOL: Mountain View (El Monte, Calif.).
COLLEGE: Tennessee.
TRANSACTIONS/CAREER NOTES: Selected by Kansas City Royals organization in 17th round of free-agent draft (June 8, 1981). . . . Selected by New York Mets organization in ninth round of free-agent draft (June 4, 1984). . . . Traded by Mets organization to Wichita (San Diego Padres organization) for 1B Brad Pounders and 1B Bill Stevenson (January 13, 1989).
MISCELLANEOUS: Appeared as pinch-runner in one game (1991).

Year	Team (League)	G	W	L	Pct.	ERA	Sv.	IP	H	R	ER	BB	SO
1984	—Little Falls (New York-Penn)	25	2	1	.667	2.80	0	35⅓	28	21	11	36	27
1985	—Columbia (South Atlantic)	49	6	3	.667	4.03	6	80⅓	89	41	36	36	71
1986	—Lynchburg (Carolina)	36	2	1	.667	3.57	3	45⅓	37	20	18	19	38
	—Jackson (Texas)	13	3	4	.429	9.00	0	33	51	35	33	15	15
1987	—Lynchburg (Carolina)	*69	3	1	.750	2.78	5	68	69	23	21	26	59
1988	—Jackson (Texas) ■	47	2	7	.222	2.87	6	78⅓	66	35	25	42	68
1989	—Wichita (Texas)■	54	8	3	.727	3.63	8	74⅓	74	30	30	37	40
1990	—Las Vegas (Pacific Coast)	27	3	4	.429	3.51	8	59	50	24	23	22	46
	—San Diego (N.L.)	32	1	1	.500	2.83	1	47⅔	52	17	15	16	22
1991	—San Diego (N.L.)	64	3	1	.750	3.26	0	80	66	31	29	44	40
Major league totals (2 years)		96	4	2	.667	3.10	1	127⅔	118	48	44	60	62

RODRIGUEZ, ROSARIO
P, PIRATES

PERSONAL: Born July 8, 1969, at Los Moches, Mexico. . . . 6-0/195. . . . Throws left, bats right. . . . Full name: Rosario Rodriguez.
HIGH SCHOOL: Pasteje Academy (Mexico City, Mexico).
TRANSACTIONS/CAREER NOTES: Signed as free agent by Cincinnati Reds organization (March 16, 1987). . . . Claimed on waivers by Pittsburgh Pirates (December 20, 1990).

Year	Team (League)	G	W	L	Pct.	ERA	Sv.	IP	H	R	ER	BB	SO
1987	—Sarasota Reds (Gulf Coast)	17	1	5	.167	3.08	1	64⅓	64	32	22	21	33
1988	—Greensboro (South Atlantic)	23	6	4	.600	1.52	2	65⅓	49	15	11	24	53
	—Cedar Rapids (Midwest)	13	3	4	.429	3.99	0	70	73	41	31	25	47
1989	—Chattanooga (Southern)	28	3	0	1.000	4.47	2	44⅓	48	24	22	18	36
	—Cincinnati (N.L.)	7	1	1	.500	4.15	0	4⅓	3	2	2	3	0
1990	—Nashville (American Assoc.)	5	0	1	.000	10.38	0	4⅓	4	5	5	3	1
	—Chattanooga (Southern)	36	2	2	.500	4.36	7	53⅔	52	29	26	48	39
	—Cincinnati (N.L.)	9	0	0	. . .	6.10	0	10⅓	15	7	7	2	8
1991	—Buffalo (American Assoc.)■	48	4	3	.571	3.00	8	51	38	22	17	31	43
	—Pittsburgh (N.L.)	18	1	1	.500	4.11	6	15⅓	14	7	7	8	10
Major league totals (3 years)		34	2	2	.500	4.80	6	30	32	16	16	13	18

CHAMPIONSHIP SERIES RECORD

Year	Team (League)	G	W	L	Pct.	ERA	Sv.	IP	H	R	ER	BB	SO
1991	—Pittsburgh (N.L.)	1	0	0	. . .	27.00	0	1	1	3	3	2	1

ROESLER, MIKE
P, PIRATES

PERSONAL: Born September 12, 1963, at Fort Wayne, Ind. . . . 6-5/200. . . . Throws right, bats right. . . . Full name: Michael Joseph Roesler. . . . Name pronounced RESS-ler.
HIGH SCHOOL: Bishop Luers (Fort Wayne, Ind.).
COLLEGE: Ball State.

TRANSACTIONS/CAREER NOTES: Selected by Cincinnati Reds organization in 17th round of free-agent draft (June 3, 1985). . . . Traded by Reds with IF Jeff Richardson to Pittsburgh Pirates for OF Billy Hatcher (April 3, 1990).

Year	Team (League)	G	W	L	Pct.	ERA	Sv.	IP	H	R	ER	BB	SO
1985	Billings (Pioneer)	13	8	2	.800	2.33	0	88⅔	72	32	23	28	73
1986	Cedar Rapids (Midwest)	32	9	13	.409	4.58	3	163	165	95	83	80	135
1987	Tampa (Florida State)	28	7	2	.778	2.23	11	36⅓	30	14	9	15	29
	Vermont (Eastern)	22	4	2	.667	3.29	11	27⅓	28	10	10	10	19
1988	Chattanooga (Southern)	16	1	1	.500	2.21	9	20⅓	16	5	5	8	13
	Nashville (American Assoc.)	32	3	2	.600	5.01	1	41⅓	44	25	23	27	31
1989	Nashville (American Assoc.)	40	6	4	.600	3.25	10	69⅓	63	30	25	39	53
	Cincinnati (N.L.)	17	0	1	.000	3.96	0	25	22	11	11	9	14
1990	Pittsburgh (N.L.)■	5	1	0	1.000	3.00	0	6	5	2	2	2	4
	Buffalo (American Assoc.)	24	0	3	.000	4.29	0	42	50	25	20	17	19
	Harrisburg (Eastern)	10	2	1	.667	4.56	0	23⅔	29	14	12	6	11
1991	Carolina (Southern)	20	2	4	.333	4.91	6	25⅔	20	15	14	15	31
	Buffalo (American Assoc.)	33	5	4	.556	3.56	8	48	46	19	19	21	34
Major league totals (2 years)		22	1	1	.500	3.77	0	31	27	13	13	11	18

ROGERS, KENNY
P, RANGERS

PERSONAL: Born November 10, 1964, at Savannah, Ga. . . . 6-1/205. . . . Throws left, bats left. . . . Full name: Kenneth Scott Rogers.
HIGH SCHOOL: Plant City (Fla.).
TRANSACTIONS/CAREER NOTES: Selected by Texas Rangers organization in 39th round of free-agent draft (June 7, 1982). . . . On Tulsa disabled list (April 12-30, 1986).

Year	Team (League)	G	W	L	Pct.	ERA	Sv.	IP	H	R	ER	BB	SO
1982	Sarasota Rangers (GCL)	2	0	0	. . .	0.00	0	3	0	0	0	0	4
1983	Sarasota Rangers (GCL)	15	4	1	.800	2.36	1	53⅓	40	21	14	20	36
1984	Burlington (Midwest)	39	4	7	.364	3.98	3	92⅔	87	52	41	33	93
1985	Daytona Beach (Florida State)	6	0	1	.000	7.20	0	10	12	9	8	11	9
	Burlington (Midwest)	33	2	5	.286	2.84	4	95	67	34	30	62	96
1986	Tulsa (Texas)	10	0	3	.000	9.91	0	26⅓	39	30	29	18	23
	Salem (Carolina)	12	2	7	.222	6.27	0	66	75	54	46	26	46
1987	Charlotte (Florida State)	5	0	3	.000	4.76	0	17	17	13	9	8	14
	Tulsa (Texas)	28	1	5	.167	5.35	2	69	80	51	41	35	59
1988	Tulsa (Texas)	13	4	6	.400	4.00	0	83⅓	73	43	37	34	76
	Port Charlotte (Florida State)	8	2	0	1.000	1.27	1	35⅓	22	8	5	11	26
1989	Texas (A.L.)	73	3	4	.429	2.93	2	73⅔	60	28	24	42	63
1990	Texas (A.L.)	69	10	6	.625	3.13	15	97⅔	93	40	34	42	74
1991	Texas (A.L.)	63	10	10	.500	5.42	5	109⅔	121	80	66	61	73
Major league totals (3 years)		205	23	20	.535	3.97	22	281	274	148	124	145	210

ROGERS, KEVIN
P, GIANTS

PERSONAL: Born August 20, 1968, at Cleveland, Miss. . . . 6-2/190. . . . Throws left, bats both. . . . Full name: Charles Kevin Rogers.
HIGH SCHOOL: Cleveland (Miss.).
COLLEGE: Mississippi Delta Junior College.
TRANSACTIONS/CAREER NOTES: Selected by San Francisco Giants organization in ninth round of free-agent draft (June 1, 1988).
STATISTICAL NOTES: Tied for Midwest League lead in games started by pitcher with 28 in 1989.

Year	Team (League)	G	W	L	Pct.	ERA	Sv.	IP	H	R	ER	BB	SO
1988	Pocatello (Pioneer)	13	2	8	.200	6.20	0	69⅔	73	51	48	35	71
1989	Clinton (Midwest)	29	13	8	.619	2.55	0	169⅓	128	74	48	78	168
1990	San Jose (California)	28	14	5	.737	3.61	0	172	143	86	69	68	★186
1991	Shreveport (Texas)	22	4	6	.400	3.36	0	118	124	63	44	54	108

ROHDE, DAVE
IF, INDIANS

PERSONAL: Born May 8, 1964, at Los Altos, Calif. . . . 6-2/182. . . . Throws right, bats both. . . . Full name: David Grant Rohde. . . . Name pronounced ROH-dee.
HIGH SCHOOL: Corona Del Mar (Newport Beach, Calif.).
COLLEGE: Saddleback Community College (Calif.) and Arizona.
TRANSACTIONS/CAREER NOTES: Selected by Houston Astros organization in fifth round of free-agent draft (June 2, 1986). . . . Traded by Astros with OF Kenny Lofton to Cleveland Indians for P Willie Blair and C Eddie Taubensee (December 10, 1991).
STATISTICAL NOTES: Led Southern League second basemen with .987 fielding percentage in 1988.
MISCELLANEOUS: Batted righthanded only (1986-88).

Year	Team (League)	Pos.	G	AB	R	H	2B	3B	HR	RBI	Avg.	SB	PO	A	E	Avg.
1986	Auburn (N.Y.-Penn)	SS	61	207	41	54	6	4	2	22	.261	28	90	158	16	.939
1987	Osceola (Florida State)	2B-SS-C	103	377	57	108	15	1	5	42	.286	12	165	305	20	.959
1988	Columbus (Southern)	2B-SS	142	486	76	130	20	2	4	53	.267	36	251	356	25	†.960
1989	Columbus (Southern)	3B-2B-SS	67	254	40	71	5	2	2	27	.280	15	70	127	17	.921
	Tucson (Pacific Coast)	SS-3B	75	234	35	68	7	3	1	30	.291	11	108	232	13	.963
1990	Houston (N.L.)	2B-3B-SS	58	98	8	18	4	0	0	5	.184	0	28	70	0	1.000
	Tucson (Pacific Coast)	2B-SS	47	170	42	60	10	2	0	20	.353	5	76	137	7	.968

Year	Team (League)	Pos.	G	AB	R	H	2B	3B	HR	RBI	Avg.	SB	PO	A	E	Avg.
1991—Houston (N.L.)	2-3-S-1	29	41	3	5	0	0	0	0	.122	0	13	23	0	1.000
—Tucson (Pacific Coast)	IF-OF	73	253	36	94	10	4	1	40	.372	15	144	208	11	.970
Major league totals (2 years)			87	139	11	23	4	0	0	5	.165	0	41	93	0	1.000

ROJAS, MEL
P, EXPOS

PERSONAL: Born December 10, 1966, at Haina, Dominican Republic. . . . 5-11/185. . . . Throws right, bats right. . . . Full name: Melquiades Rojas. . . . Nephew of Felipe Alou, major league outfielder-first baseman (1958-74); nephew of Matty Alou, major league outfielder (1960-74); and nephew of Jesus Alou, major league outfielder (1963-75 and 1978-79). . . . Name pronounced ROH-hass.
HIGH SCHOOL: Liceo Manresa (Santo Domingo, Dominican Republic).
TRANSACTIONS/CAREER NOTES: Signed as free agent by Montreal Expos organization (November 7, 1985). . . . On Rockford disabled list (May 7-June 14, 1988). . . . On West Palm Beach disabled list (August 8, 1988-remainder of season). . . . On Indianapolis disabled list (June 26-July 5, 1991).

Year	Team (League)	G	W	L	Pct.	ERA	Sv.	IP	H	R	ER	BB	SO
1986—Bradenton Expos (Gulf Coast)	13	4	5	.444	4.88	0	55⅓	63	39	30	37	34
1987—Burlington (Midwest)	25	8	9	.471	3.80	0	158⅔	146	84	67	67	100
1988—Rockford (Midwest)	12	6	4	.600	2.45	0	73⅓	52	30	20	29	72
—West Palm Beach (Florida St.)	2	1	0	1.000	3.60	0	5	4	2	2	1	4
1989—Jacksonville (Southern)	34	10	7	.588	2.49	5	112	62	39	31	57	104
1990—Indianapolis (Am. Assoc.)	17	2	4	.333	3.13	0	97⅔	84	42	34	47	64
—Montreal (N.L.)	23	3	1	.750	3.60	1	40	34	17	16	24	26
1991—Montreal (N.L.)	37	3	3	.500	3.75	6	48	42	21	20	13	37
—Indianapolis (Am. Assoc.)	14	4	2	.667	4.10	1	52⅔	50	29	24	14	55
Major league totals (2 years)	60	6	4	.600	3.68	7	88	76	38	36	37	63

ROMERO, MANDY
C, PIRATES

PERSONAL: Born October 19, 1967, at Miami. . . . 5-11/196. . . . Throws right, bats both. . . . Full name: Armando Romero. . . . Brother of Andy Romero, minor league first baseman-outfielder (1977-80).
HIGH SCHOOL: Miami Jackson (Fla.).
COLLEGE: Brevard Community College (Fla.).
TRANSACTIONS/CAREER NOTES: Selected by Pittsburgh Pirates in 19th round of free-agent draft (June 1, 1988). . . . On disabled list (April 11-29 and June 20-28, 1991).
STATISTICAL NOTES: Led South Atlantic League catchers with .989 fielding percentage in 1989. . . . Led Carolina League with 222 total bases in 1990. . . . Tied for Southern League lead with 14 passed balls in 1991.

Year	Team (League)	Pos.	G	AB	R	H	2B	3B	HR	RBI	Avg.	SB	PO	A	E	Avg.
1988—Princeton (Appalachian)	C	30	71	7	22	6	0	2	11	.310	1	143	14	2	.987
1989—Augusta (S. Atlantic)	C-3B	121	388	58	87	26	3	4	55	.224	8	629	74	9	†.987
1990—Salem (Carolina)	C	124	460	62	134	31	3	17	*90	.291	0	565	60	7	.989
1991—Carolina (Southern)	C	98	323	29	70	12	0	3	31	.217	1	552	63	4	*.994

ROMINE, KEVIN
OF

PERSONAL: Born May 23, 1961, at Exeter, N.H. . . . 5-11/204. . . . Throws right, bats right. . . . Full name: Kevin Andrew Romine. . . . Name pronounced ro-MINE.
HIGH SCHOOL: Fountain Valley (Calif.).
COLLEGE: Orange Coast College (Calif.) and Arizona State.
TRANSACTIONS/CAREER NOTES: Selected by California Angels organization in third round of free-agent draft (January 8, 1980). . . . Selected by Philadelphia Phillies organization in secondary phase of free-agent draft (June 3, 1980). . . . Selected by Boston Red Sox organization in second round of free-agent draft (June 7, 1982). . . . On Pawtucket disabled list (July 18-31, 1984 and July 6-17, 1985). . . . Released by Red Sox (August 9, 1991).
RECORDS/HONORS: Named outfielder on THE SPORTING NEWS college All-America team (1982).
STATISTICAL NOTES: Tied for Eastern League lead in double plays by outfielders with four in 1983.

Year	Team (League)	Pos.	G	AB	R	H	2B	3B	HR	RBI	Avg.	SB	PO	A	E	Avg.
1982—Winter Haven (Fla. St.)	OF	55	201	24	51	4	4	3	22	.254	8	97	6	3	.972
1983—New Britain (Eastern)	OF	132	467	74	122	26	5	11	80	.261	20	211	12	4	.982
1984—Pawtucket (Int'l)	OF	113	336	62	85	10	1	12	72	.253	13	202	12	5	.977
1985—Pawtucket (Int'l)	OF	106	403	43	98	20	1	5	33	.243	19	246	9	8	.970
—Boston (A.L.)	OF	24	28	3	6	2	0	0	1	.214	1	20	1	0	1.000
1986—Pawtucket (Int'l)	OF	71	257	30	75	8	3	4	32	.292	11	162	2	2	.988
—Boston (A.L.)	OF	35	35	6	9	2	0	0	2	.257	2	45	1	0	1.000
1987—Pawtucket (Int'l)	OF	129	491	72	131	24	1	11	52	.267	21	311	6	3	.991
—Boston (A.L.)	OF	9	24	5	7	2	0	0	2	.292	0	10	1	0	1.000
1988—Boston (A.L.)	OF	57	78	17	15	2	1	1	6	.192	2	44	0	2	.957
—Pawtucket (Int'l)	OF	41	148	18	53	6	1	4	26	.358	0	71	5	0	1.000
1989—Pawtucket (Int'l)	OF-1B	27	90	9	27	3	0	2	7	.300	0	49	4	1	.981
—Boston (A.L.)	OF	92	274	30	75	13	0	1	23	.274	1	157	9	3	.982
1990—Boston (A.L.)	OF	70	136	21	37	7	0	2	14	.272	4	81	0	2	.976
1991—Boston (A.L.)	OF	44	55	7	9	2	0	1	7	.164	1	27	0	1	.964
Major league totals (7 years)		331	630	89	158	30	1	5	55	.251	11	384	12	8	.980

Year	Team (League)	Pos.	G	AB	R	H	2B	3B	HR	RBI	Avg.	SB	PO	A	E	Avg.
							BATTING							FIELDING		
1988 —Boston (A.L.)		PR	2	0	1	0	0	0	0	0	...	3	0	0	0	...

ROSARIO, VICTOR
SS, TIGERS

PERSONAL: Born August 26, 1966, at Hato Mayor del Rey, Dominican Republic. . . . 5-11/ 155. . . . Throws right, bats right. . . . Full name: Victor Manuel Rosario.
TRANSACTIONS/CAREER NOTES: Signed as free agent by Boston Red Sox organization (December 5, 1983). . . . Loaned by Red Sox organization to Daytona Beach, Texas Rangers organization (July, 1986); returned (July, 1986). . . . Traded by Red Sox organization to Jacksonville (Montreal Expos organization) for P John Trautwein (August 31, 1988). . . . Traded by Expos organization to Philadelphia Phillies organization for P Tim Sossamon (March 28, 1989). . . . Traded by Phillies organization to Atlanta Braves (September 4, 1990) as partial completion of deal in which Braves traded OF Dale Murphy and a player to be named later to Phillies for P Jeff Parrett and two players to be named later (August 3, 1990); Scranton/Wilkes-Barre (Phillies organization) acquired P Tommy Greene and Braves acquired OF Jim Vatcher to complete deal (August 9, 1990). . . . Traded by Braves to Detroit Tigers for P Dan Petry (June 25, 1991). . . . On Toledo disabled list (August 1-11, 1991).
STATISTICAL NOTES: Led International League shortstops with 638 total chances and 76 double plays in 1990.
MISCELLANEOUS: Batted as switch-hitter (1986).

Year	Team (League)	Pos.	G	AB	R	H	2B	3B	HR	RBI	Avg.	SB	PO	A	E	Avg.
							BATTING							FIELDING		
1984 —Elmira (New York-Penn) ..		SS	23	27	2	3	0	0	0	0	.111	0	8	22	4	.882
1985 —Elmira (New York-Penn) ..		SS	59	177	11	36	8	1	1	14	.203	11	70	130	24	.893
1986 —Greensboro (S. Atlantic) ..		SS	26	93	12	28	5	1	4	19	.301	3	37	65	9	.919
—Day. B.-Win. Hav. (FSL)■.		SS-2B	20	55	6	12	2	0	0	5	.218	0	25	30	6	.902
1987 —Greensboro (S. Atlantic) ..		SS	109	370	43	81	9	0	10	48	.219	2	155	303	44	.912
1988 —New Britain (Eastern)		SS	101	347	28	90	14	1	1	26	.259	4	159	274	25	.945
1989 —Reading (Eastern)■.........		SS	64	213	16	50	8	0	3	16	.235	7	91	171	13	.953
—Scranton/W.B. (Int'l)........		SS	56	151	16	39	7	0	0	16	.258	3	58	127	11	.944
1990 —Scranton/W.B. (Int'l)........		SS	•143	477	45	120	23	6	5	42	.252	8	★206	★396	★36	.944
—Atlanta (N.L.)■		SS-2B	9	7	3	1	0	0	0	0	.143	0	3	4	0	1.000
1991 —Richmond (Int'l)		SS	60	206	28	63	9	6	0	26	.306	4	85	145	13	.947
—Toledo (International)■.....		SS	56	217	31	64	11	6	1	22	.295	8	103	160	16	.943
Major league totals (1 year)			9	7	3	1	0	0	0	0	.143	0	3	4	0	1.000

ROSE, BOBBY
IF/OF, ANGELS

PERSONAL: Born March 15, 1967, at Covina, Calif. . . . 5-11/185. . . . Throws right, bats right. . . . Full name: Robert Richard Rose.
HIGH SCHOOL: San Dimas (Calif.).
TRANSACTIONS/CAREER NOTES: Selected by California Angels organization in fifth round of free-agent draft (June 3, 1985). . . . On California disabled list (August 24, 1991-remainder of season).
STATISTICAL NOTES: Led Texas League with .541 slugging percentage in 1989. . . . Led Pacific Coast League second basemen with 21 errors in 1990.

Year	Team (League)	Pos.	G	AB	R	H	2B	3B	HR	RBI	Avg.	SB	PO	A	E	Avg.
							BATTING							FIELDING		
1985 —Salem (Northwest)		SS-1B	50	167	15	37	6	2	0	16	.222	8	58	112	22	.885
1986 —Quad Cities (Midwest).......		SS-2B	129	467	67	118	21	5	7	56	.253	3	176	297	40	.922
1987 —						Out of Organized Baseball											
1988 —Quad City (Midwest)		I-C-O-P	135	483	75	137	23	3	13	78	.284	14	186	188	31	.923
—Palm Springs (Calif.)		DH	1	3	0	1	0	0	0	1	.333	0	0	0	0	...
1989 —Midland (Texas)		3B-2B	99	351	64	126	21	5	11	73★	.359	4	102	203	17	.947
—California (A.L.)		3B-2B	14	38	4	8	1	2	1	3	.211	0	10	21	2	.939
1990 —Edmonton (Pac. Coast)		2B-3B-SS	134	502	84	142	27	10	9	68	.283	6	225	376	†25	.960
—California (A.L.)		2B-3B	7	13	5	5	0	0	1	2	.385	0	3	7	0	1.000
1991 —Edmonton (Pac. Coast)		3B-2B-1B	62	242	35	72	14	5	6	55	.298	3	81	130	9	.959
—California (A.L.)		2-0-3-1	22	65	5	18	5	1	1	8	.277	0	44	31	0	1.000
Major league totals (3 years)			43	116	14	31	6	3	3	13	.267	0	57	59	2	.983

RECORD AS PITCHER

Year	Team (League)	G	W	L	Pct.	ERA	Sv.	IP	H	R	ER	BB	SO
1988 —Quad City (Midwest)	1	0	0	...	0.00	0	⅓	0	0	0	0	0

ROSENBERG, STEVE
P, METS

PERSONAL: Born October 31, 1964, at Brooklyn, N.Y. . . . 6-0/185. . . . Throws left, bats left. . . . Full name: Steven Alan Rosenberg.
HIGH SCHOOL: Coral Springs (Fla.).
COLLEGE: Florida.
TRANSACTIONS/CAREER NOTES: Selected by New York Yankees organization in fourth round of free-agent draft (June 2, 1986). . . . Traded by Yankees organization with OF Dan Pasqua and C Mark Salas to Chicago White Sox for P Richard Dotson and P Scott Nielsen (November 12, 1987). . . . Traded by White Sox with P Adam Peterson to San Diego Padres for IF Joey Cora, IF Kevin Garner and OF Warren Newson (March 31, 1991). . . . Traded by Padres to New York Mets for SS-2B Jeff Gardner (December 11, 1991).

Year	Team (League)	G	W	L	Pct.	ERA	Sv.	IP	H	R	ER	BB	SO
1986	—Oneonta (New York-Penn)	4	0	0	...	1.00	3	9	4	1	1	2	10
	—Fort Lauderdale (Florida St.)	25	6	1	.857	2.12	3	29⅔	24	7	7	18	26
1987	—Albany (Eastern)	32	4	4	.500	2.25	15	40	33	11	10	12	24
	—Columbus (International)	21	4	1	.800	4.08	2	35⅓	43	17	16	18	27
1988	—Vancouver (Pacific Coast)■	20	2	0	1.000	3.33	3	24⅓	15	9	9	11	17
	—Chicago (A.L.)	33	0	1	.000	4.30	1	46	53	22	22	19	28
1989	—Chicago (A.L.)	38	4	13	.235	4.94	0	142	148	92	78	58	77
1990	—Vancouver (Pacific Coast)	40	6	5	.545	3.57	8	88⅓	66	43	35	44	74
	—Chicago (A.L.)	6	1	0	1.000	5.40	0	10	10	6	6	5	4
1991	—Las Vegas (Pacific Coast)■	36	2	4	.333	7.54	0	68	95	62	57	26	61
	—San Diego (N.L.)	10	1	1	.500	6.94	0	11⅔	11	9	9	5	6
	American League totals (3 years)	77	5	14	.263	4.82	1	198	211	120	106	82	109
	National League totals (1 year)	10	1	1	.500	6.94	0	11⅔	11	9	9	5	6
	Major league totals (4 years)	87	6	15	.286	4.94	1	209⅔	222	129	115	87	115

ROSENTHAL, WAYNE
P, RANGERS

PERSONAL: Born February 19, 1965, at Brooklyn, N.Y. ... 6-5/220. ... Throws right, bats right. ... Full name: Wayne Scott Rosenthal.
HIGH SCHOOL: South Shore (Brooklyn, N.Y.).
COLLEGE: St. John's (N.Y.).
TRANSACTIONS/CAREER NOTES: Selected by Texas Rangers organization in 24th round of free-agent draft (June 2, 1986).

Year	Team (League)	G	W	L	Pct.	ERA	Sv.	IP	H	R	ER	BB	SO
1986	—Sarasota Rangers (GCL)	23	4	2	.667	★0.73	9	61⅔	36	9	5	11	73
1987	—Gastonia (South Atlantic)	56	1	5	.167	1.70	★30	68⅔	44	19	13	25	101
1988	—Port Charlotte (Florida State) ...	23	1	2	.333	2.05	7	26½	20	6	6	4	21
1989	—Port Charlotte (Florida State) ...	20	2	1	.667	2.22	10	24⅓	13	8	6	8	26
	—Tulsa (Texas)	31	2	4	.333	3.06	10	50	40	20	17	21	47
1990	—Tulsa (Texas)	12	2	2	.500	2.40	4	15	9	6	4	9	18
	—Oklahoma City (Am. Assoc.)	42	3	4	.429	3.00	14	48	40	24	16	18	39
1991	—Oklahoma City (Am. Assoc.)	32	3	2	.600	4.03	5	51⅓	52	24	23	22	59
	—Texas (A.L.)	36	1	4	.200	5.25	1	70⅓	72	43	41	36	61
	Major league totals (1 year)	36	1	4	.200	5.25	1	70⅓	72	43	41	36	61

ROSSY, RICO
SS, ROYALS

PERSONAL: Born February 16, 1964, at Santurce, Puerto Rico. ... 5-10/170. ... Throws right, bats right. ... Full name: Elam Jose Rossy.
HIGH SCHOOL: Frontier (Ind.).
COLLEGE: Purdue.
TRANSACTIONS/CAREER NOTES: Selected by Baltimore Orioles organization in 33rd round of free-agent draft (June 3, 1985). ... Traded by Orioles organization with SS Terry Crowley Jr. to Pittsburgh Pirates organization for OF Joe Orsulak (November 6, 1987). ... Traded by Pirates organization to Atlanta Braves organization for OF Greg Tubbs (May 2, 1990). ... Traded by Braves to Kansas City Royals for OF Bobby Moore (December 10, 1991).
STATISTICAL NOTES: Led New York-Pennsylvania League third basemen with 67 putouts, 159 assists, 252 total chances and 15 double plays in 1985.

Year	Team (League)	Pos.	G	AB	R	H	2B	3B	HR	RBI	Avg.	SB	PO	A	E	Avg.
1985	—Newark (N.Y.-Penn)	3B-SS-2B	73	246	38	53	14	2	3	25	.215	17	†67	†159	26	.897
1986	—Miami (Florida State)	3B-SS	38	134	26	34	7	1	1	9	.254	10	30	95	8	.940
	—Charlotte (Southern)	S-3-2-0	77	232	40	68	16	2	3	25	.293	13	121	149	10	.964
1987	—Charlotte (Southern)	3B-2B-OF	127	471	69	135	22	3	4	50	.287	20	129	255	19	.953
1988	—Buffalo (Am. Assoc.)■	SS-3B-2B	68	187	12	46	4	0	1	20	.246	1	101	152	10	.962
1989	—Harrisburg (Eastern)	SS-3B	78	238	20	60	16	1	2	25	.252	2	107	175	12	.959
	—Buffalo (Am. Assoc.)	SS-C-2B	38	109	11	21	5	0	0	10	.193	4	85	98	6	.968
1990	—Buffalo (Am. Assoc.)	SS	8	17	3	3	0	1	0	2	.176	1	9	20	2	.935
	—Greenville (Southern)■......	SS	5	21	4	4	1	0	0	0	.190	0	9	23	2	.941
	—Richmond (Int'l)	SS	107	380	58	88	13	0	4	32	.232	11	144	290	18	★.960
1991	—Richmond (Int'l)	2B-SS-3B	★139	482	58	124	25	1	2	48	.257	4	286	408	17	.976
	—Atlanta (N.L.)	SS	5	1	0	0	0	0	0	0	.000	0	0	0	0	...
	Major league totals (1 year)		5	1	0	0	0	0	0	0	.000	0	0	0	0	...

ROWLAND, RICH
C, TIGERS

PERSONAL: Born February 25, 1967, at Cloverdale, Calif. ... 6-1/210. ... Throws right, bats right. ... Full name: Richard Garnet Rowland.
COLLEGE: Mendocino Community College (Calif.).
TRANSACTIONS/CAREER NOTES: Selected by Detroit Tigers organization in 17th round of free-agent draft (June 1, 1988). ... On Toledo disabled list (May 3-27, 1991).

Year	Team (League)	Pos.	G	AB	R	H	2B	3B	HR	RBI	Avg.	SB	PO	A	E	Avg.
1988	—Bristol (Appalachian)	C	56	186	29	51	10	1	4	41	.274	1	253	31	7	.976
1989	—Fayetteville (S. Atl.)	C	108	375	43	102	17	1	9	59	.272	4	527	66	11	.982

Year	Team (League)	Pos.	G	AB	R	H	2B	3B	HR	RBI	Avg.	SB	PO	A	E	Avg.
1990	—London (Eastern)	C	47	161	22	46	10	0	8	30	.286	1	231	24	3	.988
	—Toledo (International)	C	62	192	28	50	12	0	7	22	.260	2	305	39	★13	.964
	—Detroit (A.L.)	C	7	19	3	3	1	0	0	0	.158	0	29	0	1	.967
1991	—Toledo (International)	C	109	383	56	104	26	0	13	68	.272	4	614	78	4	★.994
	—Detroit (A.L.)	C	4	4	0	1	0	0	0	1	.250	0	2	1	0	1.000
	Major league totals (2 years)		11	23	3	4	1	0	0	1	.174	0	31	1	1	.970

ROYER, STAN

3B, CARDINALS

PERSONAL: Born August 31, 1967, at Olney, Ill. . . . 6-3/221. . . . Throws right, bats right. . . . Full name: Stanley Dean Royer.
HIGH SCHOOL: Charleston (Ill.).
COLLEGE: Eastern Illinois.
TRANSACTIONS/CAREER NOTES: Selected by Atlanta Braves organization in 10th round of free-agent draft (June 3, 1985). . . . Selected by Oakland Athletics organization in first round (16th pick overall) of free-agent draft (June 1, 1988). . . . Traded by A's organization with Felix Jose and P Daryl Green to St. Louis Cardinals for OF Willie McGee (August 29, 1990).
RECORDS/HONORS: Named Northwest League Most Valuable Player (1988).
STATISTICAL NOTES: Led Northwest League third basemen with 231 total chances in 1988. . . . Led California League third basemen with 342 total chances in 1989. . . . Led Southern League third basemen with 269 assists, 387 total chances, 38 errors and 28 double plays in 1990. . . . Led American Association third basemen with 100 putouts, 299 assists, 428 total chances, 29 errors and 32 double plays in 1991.

Year	Team (League)	Pos.	G	AB	R	H	2B	3B	HR	RBI	Avg.	SB	PO	A	E	Avg.
1988	—South. Oregon (N'west).....	3B	73	286	47	91	19	3	6	48	.318	1	★50	★158	23	★.900
1989	—Modesto (California)	3B	127	476	54	120	28	1	11	69	.252	3	★99	220	23	★.933
	—Tacoma (Pacific Coast)	3B	6	19	2	5	1	0	0	2	.263	0	4	9	4	.765
1990	—Huntsville (Southern)	3B-OF-SS	137	527	69	136	29	3	14	89	.258	4	88	†271	†38	.904
	—Louisville (Am. Assoc.)■..	3B	4	15	1	4	1	0	0	4	.267	0	0	7	0	1.000
1991	—Louisville (Am. Assoc.).....	3B-C	★138	★523	48	133	30	6	14	74	.254	1	†100	†299	†29	.932
	—St. Louis (N.L.)	3B	9	21	1	6	1	0	0	1	.286	0	5	4	0	1.000
	Major league totals (1 year)		9	21	1	6	1	0	0	1	.286	0	5	4	0	1.000

RUFFIN, BRUCE

P, BREWERS

PERSONAL: Born October 4, 1963, at Lubbock, Tex. . . . 6-2/209. . . . Throws left, bats both. . . . Full name: Bruce Wayne Ruffin.
HIGH SCHOOL: J.M. Hanks (El Paso, Tex.).
COLLEGE: Texas.
TRANSACTIONS/CAREER NOTES: Selected by Philadelphia Phillies organization in 31st round of free-agent draft (June 7, 1982). . . . Selected by Phillies organization in second round of free-agent draft (June 3, 1985). . . . Traded by Phillies to Milwaukee Brewers for SS-3B Dale Sveum (December 11, 1991).

Year	Team (League)	G	W	L	Pct.	ERA	Sv.	IP	H	R	ER	BB	SO
1985	—Clearwater (Florida State)	14	5	5	.500	2.88	0	97	87	33	31	34	74
1986	—Reading (Eastern)	16	8	4	.667	3.29	0	90⅓	89	41	33	26	68
	—Philadelphia (N.L.)	21	9	4	.692	2.46	0	146⅓	138	53	40	44	70
1987	—Philadelphia (N.L.)	35	11	14	.440	4.35	0	204⅔	236	118	99	73	93
1988	—Philadelphia (N.L.)	55	6	10	.375	4.43	3	144⅓	151	86	71	80	82
1989	—Philadelphia (N.L.)	24	6	10	.375	4.44	0	125⅔	152	69	62	62	70
	—Scranton/Wilkes-Barre (Int'l) ..	9	5	1	.833	4.68	0	50	44	28	26	39	44
1990	—Philadelphia (N.L.)	32	6	13	.316	5.38	0	149	178	99	89	62	79
1991	—Scranton/Wilkes-Barre (Int'l) ..	13	4	5	.444	4.66	0	75⅓	82	43	39	41	50
	—Philadelphia (N.L.)	31	4	7	.364	3.78	0	119	125	52	50	38	85
	Major league totals (6 years)	198	42	58	.420	4.16	3	889	980	477	411	359	479

RUFFIN, JOHNNY

P, WHITE SOX

PERSONAL: Born July 29, 1971, at Butler, Ala. . . . 6-3/172. . . . Throws right, bats right. . . . Full name: Johnny Renando Ruffin.
HIGH SCHOOL: Choctaw County (Butler, Ala.).
TRANSACTIONS/CAREER NOTES: Selected by Chicago White Sox organization in fourth round of free-agent draft (June 1, 1988).

Year	Team (League)	G	W	L	Pct.	ERA	Sv.	IP	H	R	ER	BB	SO
1988	—Sarasota White Sox (GCL)	13	4	2	.667	2.30	0	58⅔	43	27	15	22	31
1989	—Utica (New York-Penn)	15	4	8	.333	3.36	0	88⅓	67	43	33	46	92
1990	—South Bend (Midwest)	24	7	6	.538	4.17	0	123	117	86	57	82	92
1991	—Sarasota (Florida State)	26	11	4	.733	3.23	0	158⅔	126	68	57	62	117

RUSKIN, SCOTT

P, REDS

PERSONAL: Born June 6, 1963, at Jacksonville, Fla. . . . 6-1/192. . . . Throws left, bats right. . . . Full name: Scott Drew Ruskin.
HIGH SCHOOL: Sandalwood (Jacksonville, Fla.).
COLLEGE: Florida.
TRANSACTIONS/CAREER NOTES: Selected by Cincinnati Reds organization in 14th round of free-agent draft (June 8, 1981). . . .

Selected by Texas Rangers organization in fourth round of free-agent draft (June 4, 1984).... Selected by Cleveland Indians organization in third round of free-agent draft (June 3, 1985).... Selected by Montreal Expos organization in secondary phase of free-agent draft (January 14, 1986).... Selected by Pittsburgh Pirates organization in secondary phase of free-agent draft (June 2, 1986).... On Macon disabled list (April 7-28, 1987).... Traded by Pirates with SS Willie Greene and a player to be named later to Montreal Expos for P Zane Smith (August 8, 1990); Expos acquired OF Moises Alou to complete deal (August 16, 1990).... Traded by Expos with OF Dave Martinez and SS Willie Greene to Cincinnati Reds for P John Wetteland and P Bill Risley (December 11, 1991).

Year	Team (League)	G	W	L	Pct.	ERA	Sv.	IP	H	R	ER	BB	SO
1989	—Salem (Carolina)	14	4	5	.444	2.23	1	84²/₃	71	35	21	33	92
	—Harrisburg (Eastern)	12	2	3	.400	4.86	0	63	64	38	34	32	56
1990	—Pittsburgh-Montreal (N.L.)■....	67	3	2	.600	2.75	2	75¹/₃	75	28	23	38	57
1991	—Montreal (N.L.)	64	4	4	.500	4.24	6	63²/₃	57	31	30	30	46
Major league totals (2 years)		131	7	6	.538	3.43	8	139	132	59	53	68	103

RECORD AS POSITION PLAYER

Year	Team (League)	Pos.	G	AB	R	H	2B	3B	HR	RBI	Avg.	SB	PO	A	E	Avg.
							BATTING						FIELDING			
1986	—Bradenton Pirates (GCL) ..	DH	11	31	3	11	1	0	0	4	.355	1	0	0	0	...
1987	—Macon (South Atlantic)	OF-1B	81	239	37	71	9	2	9	42	.297	7	183	11	6	.970
	—Salem (Carolina)	1B-OF	23	83	16	25	3	1	3	11	.301	10	154	16	1	.994
1988	—Salem (Carolina)	OF-1B	26	96	16	28	8	2	4	16	.292	6	83	6	4	.957
	—Harrisburg (Eastern)	OF-1B	90	309	27	69	14	3	3	32	.223	11	233	12	8	.968

RUSSELL, JEFF
P, RANGERS

PERSONAL: Born September 2, 1961, at Cincinnati.... 6-3/205.... Throws right, bats right. ... Full name: Jeffrey Lee Russell.
HIGH SCHOOL: Wyoming (Cincinnati).
COLLEGE: Gulf Coast Community College (Fla.).

TRANSACTIONS/CAREER NOTES: Selected by Cincinnati Reds organization in fifth round of free-agent draft (June 5, 1979).... On disabled list (May 5-June 10 and July 28, 1982-remainder of season).... On Denver disabled list (May 22-June 10, 1985).... Traded by Reds to Texas Rangers organization (July 23, 1985), completing deal in which Rangers traded 3B Buddy Bell to Reds for OF Duane Walker and a player to be named later (July 19, 1985).... On Texas disabled list (March 25-May 15, 1987); included rehabilitation disability assignment to Port Charlotte (April 26-May 4, 1987) and Oklahoma City (May 5-15, 1987).... On Texas disabled list (May 29-September 10, 1990); included rehabilitation disability assignment to Charlotte (July 30-August 3, 1990).

RECORDS/HONORS: Named A.L. Fireman of the Year by THE SPORTING NEWS (1989).
MISCELLANEOUS: Made an out in only appearance as a pinch-hitter (1988).

Year	Team (League)	G	W	L	Pct.	ERA	Sv.	IP	H	R	ER	BB	SO
1980	—Eugene (Northwest)	13	6	5	.545	3.00	0	90	80	47	30	50	75
1981	—Tampa (Florida State)	22	10	4	.714	2.01	0	143	109	51	32	48	92
1982	—Waterbury (Eastern)	14	6	4	.600	2.37	0	79²/₃	67	27	21	23	88
1983	—Indianapolis (Am. Assoc.)	18	5	5	.500	3.55	1	119	106	51	47	44	98
	—Cincinnati (N.L.)	10	4	5	.444	3.03	0	68¹/₃	58	30	23	22	40
1984	—Cincinnati (N.L.)	33	6	*18	.250	4.26	0	181²/₃	186	97	86	65	101
1985	—Denver-Oklahoma City (A.A.)■	18	7	4	.636	4.06	0	115¹/₃	105	55	52	51	94
	—Texas (A.L.)	13	3	6	.333	7.55	0	62	85	55	52	27	44
1986	—Oklahoma City (Am. Assoc.)	11	4	1	.800	3.95	0	70²/₃	63	32	31	38	34
	—Texas (A.L.)	37	5	2	.714	3.40	2	82	74	40	31	31	54
1987	—Port Charlotte (Florida State)	2	0	0	...	2.45	0	11	8	3	3	5	3
	—Oklahoma City (Am. Assoc.)	4	0	0	...	1.42	0	6¹/₃	5	1	1	1	5
	—Texas (A.L.)	52	5	4	.556	4.44	3	97¹/₃	109	56	48	52	56
1988	—Texas (A.L.)	34	10	9	.526	3.82	0	188²/₃	183	86	80	66	88
1989	—Texas (A.L.)	71	6	4	.600	1.98	*38	72²/₃	45	21	16	24	77
1990	—Texas (A.L.)	27	1	5	.167	4.26	10	25¹/₃	23	15	12	16	16
1991	—Texas (A.L.)	68	6	4	.600	3.29	30	79¹/₃	71	36	29	26	52
American League totals (7 years)		302	36	34	.514	3.97	83	607¹/₃	590	309	268	242	387
National League totals (2 years)		43	10	23	.303	3.92	0	250	244	127	109	87	141
Major league totals (9 years)		345	46	57	.447	3.96	83	857¹/₃	834	436	377	329	528

ALL-STAR GAME RECORD

Year	League	W	L	Pct.	ERA	Sv.	IP	H	R	ER	BB	SO
1988	—American	0	0	...	0.00	0	1	1	0	0	1	0
1989	—American	0	0	...	9.00	0	1	1	1	1	1	0
All-Star totals (2 years)		0	0	...	4.50	0	2	2	1	1	2	0

RUSSELL, JOHN
OF

PERSONAL: Born January 5, 1961, at Oklahoma City.... 6-0/195.... Throws right, bats right.... Full name: John William Russell.
HIGH SCHOOL: Norman (Okla.).
COLLEGE: Oklahoma.

TRANSACTIONS/CAREER NOTES: Selected by Montreal Expos organization in fourth round of free-agent draft (June 5, 1979).... Selected by Philadelphia Phillies organization in first round (13th pick overall) of free-agent draft (June 7, 1982).... Sold by Phillies to Atlanta Braves (March 25, 1989).... Released by Braves (April 6, 1990).... Signed by Oklahoma City, Texas

Rangers organization (May 8, 1990).... Granted free agency (October 22, 1990).... Re-signed by Oklahoma City (February 1, 1991).... On disabled list (May 1-June 6 and July 29-September 1, 1991).... Granted free agency (October 28, 1991).

STATISTICAL NOTES: Tied for Pacific Coast League lead with 13 passed balls in 1983.... Led N.L. with 17 passed balls in 1986.

Year	Team (League)	Pos.	G	AB	R	H	2B	3B	HR	RBI	Avg.	SB	PO	A	E	Avg.
1982	—Reading (Eastern)	C-OF-1B	77	263	26	53	10	5	6	30	.202	3	354	44	12	.971
1983	—Portland (Pacific Coast)	C-OF-3B	128	445	71	113	23	3	27	76	.254	3	551	58	12	.981
1984	—Portland (Pacific Coast)	OF-1B-C	93	350	75	101	22	5	19	77	.289	1	182	18	5	.976
	—Philadelphia (N.L.)	OF-C	39	99	11	28	8	1	2	11	.283	0	51	1	0	1.000
1985	—Philadelphia (N.L.)	OF-1B	81	216	22	47	12	0	9	23	.218	2	170	9	4	.978
	—Portland (Pacific Coast)	OF-C-1B	16	49	8	15	2	2	4	11	.306	0	24	1	1	.962
1986	—Philadelphia (N.L.)	C	93	315	35	76	21	2	13	60	.241	0	498	39	13	.976
1987	—Philadelphia (N.L.)	OF-C	24	62	5	9	1	0	3	8	.145	0	48	1	1	.980
	—Maine (International)	OF-C-3B	44	143	15	29	6	1	7	24	.203	2	107	14	2	.984
1988	—Maine (International)	C-0-3-1	110	394	50	90	18	0	13	52	.228	4	363	54	10	.977
	—Philadelphia (N.L.)	C	22	49	5	12	1	0	2	4	.245	0	77	9	5	.945
1989	—Atlanta (N.L.)■	C-0-I-P	74	159	14	29	2	0	2	9	.182	0	196	28	4	.982
1990	—Oklahoma City (A.A.)■	C	6	22	7	9	4	0	2	6	.409	0	30	1	1	.969
	—Texas (A.L.)	C-0-1-3	68	128	16	35	4	0	2	8	.273	1	148	11	3	.981
1991	—Texas (A.L.)	OF-C	22	27	3	3	0	0	0	1	.111	0	24	0	0	1.000
American League totals (2 years)			90	155	19	38	4	0	2	9	.245	1	172	11	3	.984
National League totals (6 years)			333	900	92	201	45	3	31	115	.223	2	1040	87	27	.977
Major league totals (8 years)			423	1055	111	239	49	3	33	124	.227	3	1212	98	30	.978

RECORD AS PITCHER

Year	Team (League)	G	W	L	Pct.	ERA	Sv.	IP	H	R	ER	BB	SO
1989	—Atlanta (N.L.)	1	0	0	...	0.00	0	⅓	0	0	0	0	0

RYAN, NOLAN
P, RANGERS

PERSONAL: Born January 31, 1947, at Refugio, Tex.... 6-2/212.... Throws right, bats right.... Full name: Lynn Nolan Ryan Jr.
HIGH SCHOOL: Alvin (Tex.).
COLLEGE: Alvin Junior College (Tex.).

TRANSACTIONS/CAREER NOTES: Selected by New York Mets organization in eighth round of free-agent draft (June, 1965).... On military list (January 3-May 13, 1967).... On Jacksonville disabled list (July 16-August 30, 1967).... On disabled list (July 30-August 30, 1968 and May 12-June 8, 1969).... On military list (August 11-September 1, 1969).... Traded by Mets with P Don Rose, OF Leroy Stanton and C Francisco Estrada to California Angels for IF Jim Fregosi (December 10, 1971).... On disabled list (June 14-July 5, 1978).... Granted free agency (November 1, 1979).... Signed by Houston Astros (November 19, 1979).... On disabled list (March 25-April 17 and May 3-June 6, 1983; June 2-17 and June 18-July 3, 1984; June 1-24 and July 28-August 12, 1986).... Granted free agency (November 4, 1988).... Signed by Texas Rangers (December 7, 1988).... On disabled list (May 18-June 6, 1990; May 14-29 and July 29-August 19, 1991).

RECORDS/HONORS: Holds major league career records for most strikeouts—5,511; most years with 100 or more strikeouts—23; most consecutive seasons, 300 or more strikeouts—3; most games with 15 or more strikeouts—26; most games with 10 or more strikeouts—213; most years with 300 or more strikeouts—6; most years with 200 or more strikeouts—15; most bases on balls allowed—2,686; most no-hit games—7; most low-hit (one or zero) games—19; most wild-pitches—265.... Holds major league single-season record for most games with 10 or more strikeouts—23 (1973); most seasons leading league in bases on balls allowed—8; most strikeouts—383 (1973).... Holds major league records for most strikeouts, three consecutive games—47 (August 12, 16 and 20, 1974, 27⅓ innings); most strikeouts by losing pitcher, extra-inning game—19 (August 20, 1974, 11 innings).... Holds modern major league records for most consecutive starting assignments—554 (July 30, 1974 through 1991).... Shares major league records for striking out side on nine pitches (April 19, 1968, third inning and July 9, 1972, second inning; most no-hit games, season—2 (1973); most clubs shut out, season—8 (1972); most consecutive seasons leading major leagues in bases on balls allowed—3; most strikeouts, three consecutive nine-inning games—41 (August 7, 12 and 16, 1974).... Holds A.L. career record for most years with 200 or more strikeouts—10; most games 10 or more strikeouts—146; most games 15 or more strikeouts—23; most no-hit games—6; and most low-hit games (one or zero)—15. ... Shares A.L. records for most consecutive strikeouts, game—8 (July 9, 1972 and July 15, 1973); most strikeouts, two consecutive games—32 (August 7 [13], 12 and 16, 1974); most no-hit games (one or zero), season—3 (1973); most seasons leading league in errors by pitcher—4.... Named Western Carolinas Pitcher of the Year (1966).... Named A.L. Pitcher of the Year by THE SPORTING NEWS (1977).... Named righthanded pitcher on THE SPORTING NEWS A.L. All-Star team (1977). ... Named Man of the Year by THE SPORTING NEWS (1990).

STATISTICAL NOTES: Tied for Appalachian League lead with eight hit batsmen in 1965.... Led Western Carolinas League pitchers with 28 games started in 1966.... Led A.L. with nine shutouts in 1972, seven in 1976, and tied for lead with five in 1979.... Led A.L. with 18 wild pitches in 1972, 21 in 1977, 13 in 1978 and 19 in 1989.... Pitched 3-0 no-hit victory against Kansas City Royals (May 15, 1973).... Pitched 6-0 no-hit victory against Detroit Tigers (July 15, 1973).... Pitched 4-0 no-hit victory against Minnesota Twins (September 28, 1974).... Pitched 1-0 no-hit victory against Baltimore Orioles (June 1, 1975).... Tied for A.L. lead with 22 complete games in 1977.... Pitched 5-0 no-hit victory against Los Angeles Dodgers (September 26, 1981).... Led N.L. with 16 wild pitches in 1981 and 15 in 1986.... Led N.L. with eight hit batsmen in 1982.... Tied for N.L. lead with 14 sacrifice hits in 1985.... Pitched 5-0 no-hit victory against Oakland Athletics (June 11, 1990).... Pitched 3-0 no-hit victory against Toronto Blue Jays (May 1, 1991).

Year	Team (League)	G	W	L	Pct.	ERA	Sv.	IP	H	R	ER	BB	SO
1965	—Marion (Appalachian)	13	3	6	.333	4.38	0	78	61	47	38	56	115
1966	—Greenville (W. Caro.)	29	*17	2	.895	2.51	0	183	109	59	51	*127	*272
	—Williamsport (Eastern)	3	0	2	.000	0.95	0	19	9	6	2	12	35
	—New York (N.L.)	2	0	1	.000	15.00	0	3	5	5	5	3	6
1967	—Winter Haven (Florida State)	1	0	0	...	2.25	0	4	1	1	1	2	5
	—Jacksonville (International)	3	1	0	1.000	0.00	0	7	3	1	0	3	18

Year Team (League)	G	W	L	Pct.	ERA	Sv.	IP	H	R	ER	BB	SO
1968 — New York (N.L.)	21	6	9	.400	3.09	0	134	93	50	46	75	133
1969 — New York (N.L.)	25	6	3	.667	3.54	1	89	60	38	35	53	92
1970 — New York (N.L.)	27	7	11	.389	3.41	1	132	86	59	50	97	125
1971 — New York (N.L.)	30	10	14	.417	3.97	0	152	125	78	67	116	137
1972 — California (A.L.)■	39	19	16	.543	2.28	0	284	166	80	72	*157	*329
1973 — California (A.L.)	41	21	16	.568	2.87	1	326	238	113	104	*162	*383
1974 — California (A.L.)	42	22	16	.579	2.89	0	*333	221	127	107	*202	*367
1975 — California (A.L.)	28	14	12	.538	3.45	0	198	152	90	76	132	186
1976 — California (A.L.)	39	17	*18	.486	3.36	0	284	193	117	106	*183	*327
1977 — California (A.L.)	37	19	16	.543	2.77	0	299	198	110	92	*204	*341
1978 — California (A.L.)	31	10	13	.435	3.71	0	235	183	106	97	*148	*260
1979 — California (A.L.)	34	16	14	.533	3.59	0	223	169	104	89	114	*223
1980 — Houston (N.L.)■	35	11	10	.524	3.35	0	234	205	100	87	*98	200
1981 — Houston (N.L.)	21	11	5	.688	*1.69	0	149	99	34	28	68	140
1982 — Houston (N.L.)	35	16	12	.571	3.16	0	250⅓	196	100	88	*109	245
1983 — Houston (N.L.)	29	14	9	.609	2.98	0	196⅓	134	74	65	101	183
1984 — Houston (N.L.)	30	12	11	.522	3.04	0	183⅔	143	78	62	69	197
1985 — Houston (N.L.)	35	10	12	.455	3.80	0	232	205	108	98	95	209
1986 — Houston (N.L.)	30	12	8	.600	3.34	0	178	119	72	66	82	194
1987 — Houston (N.L.)	34	8	16	.333	*2.76	0	211⅔	154	75	65	87	*270
1988 — Houston (N.L.)	33	12	11	.522	3.52	0	220	186	98	86	87	*228
1989 — Texas (A.L.)■	32	16	10	.615	3.20	0	239⅓	162	96	85	98	*301
1990 — Texas (A.L.)	30	13	9	.591	3.44	0	204	137	86	78	74	*232
1991 — Texas (A.L.)	27	12	6	.667	2.91	0	173	102	58	56	72	203
American League totals (11 years)	380	179	146	.551	3.09	1	2798⅓	1921	1087	962	1546	3152
National League totals (14 years)	387	135	132	.506	3.23	2	2365	1810	969	848	1140	2359
Major league totals (25 years)	767	314	278	.530	3.15	3	5163⅓	3731	2056	1810	2686	5511

DIVISION SERIES RECORD

Year Team (League)	G	W	L	Pct.	ERA	Sv.	IP	H	R	ER	BB	SO
1981 — Houston (N.L.)	2	1	1	.500	1.80	0	15	6	4	3	3	14

CHAMPIONSHIP SERIES RECORD

CHAMPIONSHIP SERIES NOTES: Shares career record for most strikeouts—46. . . . Shares single-game record for most consecutive strikeouts—4 (October 3, 1979).

Year Team (League)	G	W	L	Pct.	ERA	Sv.	IP	H	R	ER	BB	SO
1969 — New York (N.L.)	1	1	0	1.000	2.57	0	7	3	2	2	2	7
1979 — California (A.L.)	1	0	0	. . .	1.29	0	7	4	3	1	3	8
1980 — Houston (N.L.)	2	0	0	. . .	5.40	0	13⅓	16	8	8	3	14
1986 — Houston (N.L.)	2	0	1	.000	3.86	0	14	9	6	6	1	17
Championship Series totals (4 years)	6	1	1	.500	3.70	0	41⅓	32	19	17	9	46

WORLD SERIES RECORD

Year Team (League)	G	W	L	Pct.	ERA	Sv.	IP	H	R	ER	BB	SO
1969 — New York (N.L.)	1	0	0	0.00	0.00	0	2⅓	1	0	0	2	3

ALL-STAR GAME RECORD

ALL-STAR GAME NOTES: Named to A.L. All-Star team to replace Frank Tanana for 1977 game; declined.

Year League	W	L	Pct.	ERA	Sv.	IP	H	R	ER	BB	SO
1972 — American				Did not play							
1975 — American				Did not play							
1973 — American	0	0	. . .	9.00	0	2	2	2	2	2	2
1979 — American	0	0	. . .	13.50	0	2	5	3	3	1	2
1981 — National	0	0	. . .	0.00	0	1	0	0	0	0	1
1985 — National	0	0	. . .	0.00	0	3	2	0	0	2	2
1989 — American	1	0	1.000	0.00	0	2	1	0	0	0	3
All-Star totals (5 years)	1	0	1.000	4.50	0	10	10	5	5	5	10

SABERHAGEN, BRET
P, METS

PERSONAL: Born April 11, 1964, at Chicago Heights, Ill. . . . 6-1/200. . . . Throws right, bats right. . . . Full name: Bret William Saberhagen.

HIGH SCHOOL: Cleveland (Reseda, Calif.).

TRANSACTIONS/CAREER NOTES: Selected by Kansas City Royals organization in 19th round of free-agent draft (June 7, 1982). . . . On disabled list (August 10-September 1, 1986; July 16-September 10, 1990; and June 15-July 13, 1991). . . . Traded by Royals with IF Bill Pecota to New York Mets for OF Kevin McReynolds, IF Gregg Jefferies and 2B Keith Miller (December 11, 1991).

RECORDS/HONORS: Named A.L. Pitcher of the Year by THE SPORTING NEWS (1985 and 1989). . . . Named righthanded pitcher on THE SPORTING NEWS A.L. All-Star team (1985 and 1989). . . . Named A.L. Cy Young Award winner by Baseball Writers' Association of America (1985 and 1989). . . . Named A.L. Comeback Player of the Year by THE SPORTING NEWS (1987). . . . Won A.L. Gold Glove at pitcher (1989).

STATISTICAL NOTES: Led A.L. with 12 complete games in 1989. . . . Pitched 7-0 no-hit victory against Chicago White Sox (August 26, 1991).

MISCELLANEOUS: Appeared in one game as pinch-runner (1984). . . . Appeared in three games as pinch-runner (1989).

Year	Team (League)	G	W	L	Pct.	ERA	Sv.	IP	H	R	ER	BB	SO
1983—	Fort Myers (Florida State)	16	10	5	.667	2.30	0	109 2/3	98	34	28	19	82
—	Jacksonville (Southern)	11	6	2	.750	2.91	0	77 1/3	66	31	25	29	48
1984—	Kansas City (A.L.)..................	38	10	11	.476	3.48	1	157 2/3	138	71	61	36	73
1985—	Kansas City (A.L.)..................	32	20	6	.769	2.87	0	235 1/3	211	79	75	38	158
1986—	Kansas City (A.L.)..................	30	7	12	.368	4.15	0	156	165	77	72	29	112
1987—	Kansas City (A.L.)..................	33	18	10	.643	3.36	0	257	246	99	96	53	163
1988—	Kansas City (A.L.)..................	35	14	16	.467	3.80	0	260 2/3	*271	122	110	59	171
1989—	Kansas City (A.L.)..................	36	*23	6	.793	*2.16	0	*262 1/3	209	74	63	43	193
1990—	Kansas City (A.L.)..................	20	5	9	.357	3.27	0	135	146	52	49	28	87
1991—	Kansas City (A.L.)..................	28	13	8	.619	3.07	0	196 1/3	165	76	67	45	136
Major league totals (8 years)		252	110	78	.585	3.21	1	1660 1/3	1551	650	593	331	1093

CHAMPIONSHIP SERIES RECORD

Year	Team (League)	G	W	L	Pct.	ERA	Sv.	IP	H	R	ER	BB	SO
1984—	Kansas City (A.L.)..................	1	0	0	. . .	2.25	0	8	6	3	2	1	5
1985—	Kansas City (A.L.)..................	2	0	0	. . .	6.14	0	7 1/3	12	5	5	2	6
Championship Series totals (2 years)		3	0	0	. . .	4.11	0	15 1/3	18	8	7	3	11

WORLD SERIES RECORD

Year	Team (League)	G	W	L	Pct.	ERA	Sv.	IP	H	R	ER	BB	SO
1985—	Kansas City (A.L.)..................	2	2	0	1.000	0.50	0	18	11	1	1	1	10

ALL-STAR GAME RECORD

Year	League	W	L	Pct.	ERA	Sv.	IP	H	R	ER	BB	SO
1987—	American	0	0	. . .	0.00	0	3	1	0	0	0	0
1990—	American	1	0	1.000	0.00	0	2	0	0	0	0	1
All-Star totals (2 years)	1	0	1.000	0.00	0	5	1	0	0	0	1

SABO, CHRIS
3B, REDS

PERSONAL: Born January 19, 1962, at Detroit. . . . 6-0/185. . . . Throws right, bats right. . . . Full name: Christopher Andrew Sabo. . . . Name pronounced SAY-bo.
HIGH SCHOOL: Detroit Catholic Central (Mich.).
COLLEGE: Michigan.
TRANSACTIONS/CAREER NOTES: Selected by Montreal Expos organization in 30th round of free-agent draft (June 3, 1980). . . . Selected by Cincinnati Reds organization in second round of free-agent draft (June 6, 1983). . . . On Cincinnati disabled list (June 27-September 1, 1989); included rehabilitation disability assignment to Nashville (August 7-11, 1989).
RECORDS/HONORS: Shares major league single-game record for most assists by third baseman (nine innings)—11 (April 7, 1988). . . . Shares N.L. single-season record for fewest putouts by third baseman (150 or more games)—86 (1991). . . . Named third baseman on THE SPORTING NEWS college All-America team (1983). . . . Named N.L. Rookie of the Year by Baseball Writers' Association of America (1988).
STATISTICAL NOTES: Led Eastern League third basemen with .943 fielding percentage in 1984. . . . Led Eastern League third basemen with 236 assists in 1985. . . . Led N.L. third basemen with .966 fielding percentage and 31 double plays in 1988.

						—BATTING—						—FIELDING—			
Year	Team (League)	Pos.	G	AB	R	H	2B	3B	HR	RBI	Avg.	SB	PO	A	E	Avg.
1983—	Cedar Rapids (Midwest) ...	3B	77	274	43	75	11	6	12	37	.274	15	43	130	9	.951
1984—	Vermont (Eastern)	3B-2B	125	441	44	94	19	1	5	38	.213	15	80	210	21	†.932
1985—	Vermont (Eastern)	3B-SS	124	428	66	119	19	0	11	46	.278	7	97	†236	18	.949
1986—	Denver (Am. Assoc.)	3B	129	432	83	118	26	2	10	60	.273	9	83	202	9	*.969
1987—	Nashville (Am. Assoc.)	3B	91	315	56	92	19	3	7	51	.292	23	43	137	12	.938
1988—	Cincinnati (N.L.)..............	3B-SS	137	538	74	146	40	2	11	44	.271	46	75	318	14	†.966
1989—	Cincinnati (N.L.)..............	3B	82	304	40	79	21	1	6	29	.260	14	36	145	11	.943
—	Nashville (Am. Assoc.)	3B	7	30	0	5	2	0	0	3	.167	0	5	5	1	.923
1990—	Cincinnati (N.L.)..............	3B	148	567	95	153	38	2	25	71	.270	25	70	273	12	*.966
1991—	Cincinnati (N.L.)..............	3B	153	582	91	175	35	3	26	88	.301	19	86	255	12	.966
Major league totals (4 years)			520	1991	300	553	134	8	68	232	.278	104	267	991	49	.963

CHAMPIONSHIP SERIES RECORD

						—BATTING—						—FIELDING—			
Year	Team (League)	Pos.	G	AB	R	H	2B	3B	HR	RBI	Avg.	SB	PO	A	E	Avg.
1990—	Cincinnati (N.L.)..............	3B	6	22	1	5	0	0	1	3	.227	0	7	7	0	1.000

WORLD SERIES RECORD

WORLD SERIES NOTES: Shares record for most home runs in two consecutive innings—2 (October 19, 1990, second and third innings).

						—BATTING—						—FIELDING—			
Year	Team (League)	Pos.	G	AB	R	H	2B	3B	HR	RBI	Avg.	SB	PO	A	E	Avg.
1990—	Cincinnati (N.L.)..............	3B	4	16	2	9	1	0	2	5	.563	0	3	14	0	1.000

ALL-STAR GAME RECORD

					—BATTING—						—FIELDING—		
Year	League	Pos.	AB	R	H	2B	3B	HR	RBI	Avg.	SB	PO	A	E	Avg.
1988—	National	PR	0	0	0	0	0	0	0	. . .	1	0	0	0	. . .
1990—	National	3B	2	0	0	0	0	0	0	.000	0	0	2	0	1.000
1991—	National	3B	2	0	0	0	0	0	0	.000	0	1	0	0	1.000
All-Star Game totals (3 years)		4	0	0	0	0	0	0	.000	1	1	2	0	1.000

SALAS, MARK
C/1B

PERSONAL: Born March 8, 1961, at Montebello, Calif. . . . 6-0/205. . . . Throws right, bats left. . . . Full name: Mark Bruce Salas. . . . Name pronounced SAL-us.
HIGH SCHOOL: Nogales (La Puente, Calif.).
TRANSACTIONS/CAREER NOTES: Selected by St. Louis Cardinals organization in 18th round of free-agent draft (June 5, 1979). . . . Loaned by Cardinals organization to Nashville, New York Yankees organization (June 30, 1982); returned (September 13, 1982). . . . Drafted by Minnesota Twins (December 3, 1984). . . . On disabled list (May 24-June 17, 1986). . . . Traded by Twins to New York Yankees for P Joe Niekro and cash (June 7, 1987). . . . Traded by Yankees organization with OF Dan Pasqua and P Steve Rosenberg to Chicago White Sox for P Richard Dotson and P Scott Nielsen (November 12, 1987). . . . Released by White Sox (March 28, 1989). . . . Signed by Cleveland Indians (April 1, 1989). . . . Released by Indians (December 1, 1989). . . . Signed by Detroit Tigers (April 8, 1990). . . . Granted free agency (October 29, 1991).
STATISTICAL NOTES: Tied for Appalachian League lead with 10 passed balls in 1979. . . . Tied for Florida State League lead with 10 sacrifice flies and errors by catcher with 13 in 1981.

Year	Team (League)	Pos.	G	AB	R	H	2B	3B	HR	RBI	Avg.	SB	PO	A	E	Avg.
1979—Johnson City (Appal.)		C	53	144	23	35	4	2	5	23	.243	2	194	19	6	.973
1980—Gastonia (S. Atlantic)		C	98	267	42	67	8	3	9	46	.251	3	452	41	5	★.990
1981—St. Petersburg (Fla. St.)		C-1B	100	321	26	78	9	2	2	52	.243	9	387	66	‡13	.972
1982—Arkansas (Texas)		C	27	76	4	17	4	0	0	5	.224	1	88	15	1	.990
—Louisville (Am. Assoc.)		C	7	22	1	4	0	0	1	1	.182	0	16	3	1	.950
—Nashville (Southern)■		C	43	137	19	35	7	0	6	20	.255	0	267	24	7	.977
1983—Arkansas (Texas)		C-OF	131	473	76	144	25	4	20	82	.304	7	334	41	4	.989
1984—Louisville (Am. Assoc.)		C-OF	95	316	28	77	20	2	12	48	.244	2	260	28	7	.976
—St. Louis (N.L.)		C-OF	14	20	1	2	1	0	0	1	.100	0	13	2	0	1.000
1985—Minnesota (A.L.)■		C	120	360	51	108	20	5	9	41	.300	0	529	39	5	.991
1986—Minnesota (A.L.)		C	91	258	28	60	7	4	8	33	.233	3	358	32	8	.980
1987—Minn.-New York (A.L.)■		C-OF	72	160	21	40	6	0	6	21	.250	0	258	16	1	.996
—Columbus (Int'l)		C	12	43	5	10	1	0	2	4	.233	0	46	5	0	1.000
1988—Chicago (A.L.)■		C	75	196	17	49	7	0	3	9	.250	0	251	35	6	.979
1989—Colorado Springs (PCL)■		C-1B-OF	46	146	27	46	10	2	6	20	.315	0	86	5	1	.989
—Cleveland (A.L.)		C	30	77	4	17	4	1	2	7	.221	0	3	1	0	1.000
1990—Detroit (A.L.)■		C-3B	74	164	18	38	3	0	9	24	.232	0	227	23	3	.988
1991—Detroit (A.L.)		C-1B	33	57	2	5	1	0	1	7	.088	0	28	2	0	1.000
American League totals (7 years)			495	1272	141	317	48	10	38	142	.249	3	1654	148	23	.987
National League totals (1 year)			14	20	1	2	1	0	0	1	.100	0	13	2	0	1.000
Major league totals (8 years)			509	1292	142	319	49	10	38	143	.247	3	1667	150	23	.988

SALAZAR, LUIS
3B, CUBS

PERSONAL: Born May 19, 1956, at Barcelona, Venezuela. . . . 5-10/190. . . . Throws right, bats right. . . . Full name: Luis Ernesto Garcia Salazar.
HIGH SCHOOL: Jose Antonio Anzoategui (Barcelona, Venezuela).
TRANSACTIONS/CAREER NOTES: Signed as free agent by Kansas City Royals organization (November 29, 1973). . . . Released by Royals organization (July 8, 1974). . . . Signed by Pittsburgh Pirates organization (November 23, 1975). . . . Traded by Pirates organization with OF Rick Lancellotti to San Diego Padres organization for IF Kurt Bevacqua and a player to be named later (August 4, 1980); Pirates organization acquired P Mark Lee to complete deal (August 12, 1980). . . . On disabled list (May 15-June 11, 1984). . . . Traded by Padres with P Tim Lollar, P Bill Long and SS Ozzie Guillen to Chicago White Sox for P LaMarr Hoyt, P Kevin Kristan and P Todd Simmons (December 6, 1984). . . . On Chicago disabled list (April 4-August 8, August 16-September 1 and September 8, 1986-remainder of season); included rehabilitation disability assignment to Appleton (July 17-August 6, 1986). . . . Released by White Sox (December 19, 1986). . . . Signed by San Diego Padres organization (April 2, 1987). . . . Granted free agency (October 20, 1987). . . . Signed by Toledo, Detroit Tigers organization (February 20, 1988). . . . Traded by Tigers to Padres for SS Mike Brumley (March 23, 1989). . . . Traded by Padres with OF Marvell Wynne to Chicago Cubs for P Calvin Schiraldi, OF Darrin Jackson and a player to be named later (August 30, 1989); Padres acquired 1B Phil Stephenson to complete deal (September 5, 1989).
STATISTICAL NOTES: Led Eastern League outfielders with 312 putouts and tied for lead with three double plays in 1979. . . . Led N.L. third basemen with 26 errors and tied for lead with 28 double plays in 1982.

Year	Team (League)	Pos.	G	AB	R	H	2B	3B	HR	RBI	Avg.	SB	PO	A	E	Avg.
1974—Sarasota Royals (GCL)		SS	2	4	0	1	0	0	0	1	.250	0	0	2	0	1.000
1976—Niagara Falls (NYP)■		SS-OF	42	151	18	36	3	4	1	17	.238	7	71	49	17	.876
1977—Salem (Carolina)		SS-3B-2B	116	433	72	117	17	5	11	48	.270	9	157	294	45	.909
1978—Salem (Carolina)		OF-3B-SS	126	472	55	138	20	4	3	49	.292	22	160	77	19	.926
1979—Buffalo (Eastern)		OF-3B	★139	★561	★108	★181	17	5	27	86	.323	21	†321	42	13	.965
1980—Portland-Hawaii (PCL)■		OF	127	497	91	157	23	15	9	64	.316	43	304	11	8	.975
—San Diego (N.L.)		3B-OF	44	169	28	57	4	7	1	25	.337	11	39	88	7	.948
1981—San Diego (N.L.)		3B-OF	109	400	37	121	19	6	3	38	.303	11	108	191	14	.955
1982—San Diego (N.L.)		3B-SS-OF	145	524	55	127	15	5	8	62	.242	32	133	326	†29	.941
1983—San Diego (N.L.)		3B-SS	134	481	52	124	16	2	14	45	.258	24	122	274	21	.950
1984—San Diego (N.L.)		3B-OF-SS	93	228	20	55	7	2	3	17	.241	11	87	97	6	.968
1985—Chicago (A.L.)■		OF-3B-1B	122	327	39	80	18	2	10	45	.245	14	180	57	10	.960
1986—Appleton (Midwest)		3B	21	79	9	16	1	0	2	4	.203	0	9	39	5	.906
—Chicago (A.L.)		DH-PH	4	7	1	1	0	0	0	0	.143	0	0	0	0	. . .
1987—Las Vegas (Pac. Coast)■		OF	4	17	2	5	2	0	1	3	.294	1	5	0	0	1.000
—San Diego (N.L.)		3-S-O-P-1	84	189	13	48	5	0	3	17	.254	3	56	95	9	.944
1988—Detroit (A.L.)■		O-S-3-2-1	130	452	61	122	14	1	12	62	.270	6	199	151	10	.972

Year Team (League)	Pos.	G	AB	R	H	2B	3B	HR	RBI	Avg.	SB	PO	A	E	Avg.
						BATTING							FIELDING		
1989—San Diego-Chi. (N.L.)■	3-O-S-1	121	326	34	92	12	2	9	34	.282	1	79	154	10	.959
1990—Chicago (N.L.)	3B-OF	115	410	44	104	13	3	12	47	.254	3	96	137	12	.951
1991—Chicago (N.L.)	3B-1B-OF	103	333	34	86	14	1	14	38	.258	0	76	152	10	.958
American League totals (3 years)		256	786	101	203	32	3	22	107	.258	20	379	208	20	.967
National League totals (9 years)		948	3060	317	814	105	28	67	323	.266	96	796	1514	118	.951
Major league totals (12 years)		1204	3846	418	1017	137	31	89	430	.264	116	1175	1722	138	.955

CHAMPIONSHIP SERIES RECORD

Year Team (League)	Pos.	G	AB	R	H	2B	3B	HR	RBI	Avg.	SB	PO	A	E	Avg.
						BATTING							FIELDING		
1984—San Diego (N.L.)	3B-PH-OF	3	5	0	1	0	1	0	0	.200	0	1	3	0	1.000
1989—Chicago (N.L.)	3B	5	19	2	7	0	1	1	2	.368	0	4	5	1	.900
Championship Series totals (2 years)		8	24	2	8	0	2	1	2	.333	0	5	8	1	.929

WORLD SERIES RECORD

WORLD SERIES NOTES: Appeared as pinch-runner and pinch-hitter (1984).

Year Team (League)	Pos.	G	AB	R	H	2B	3B	HR	RBI	Avg.	SB	PO	A	E	Avg.
						BATTING							FIELDING		
1984—San Diego (N.L.)	3B-OF	4	3	0	1	0	0	0	0	.333	0	1	0	0	1.000

RECORD AS PITCHER

Year Team (League)	G	W	L	Pct.	ERA	Sv.	IP	H	R	ER	BB	SO
1987—San Diego (N.L.)	2	0	0	...	4.50	0	2	2	1	1	1	0

SALMON, TIM
OF, ANGELS

PERSONAL: Born August 24, 1968, at Long Beach, Calif. ... 6-3/200. ... Throws right, bats right. ... Full name: Timothy James Salmon.
HIGH SCHOOL: Greenway (Phoenix).
COLLEGE: Grand Canyon University (Ariz.).
TRANSACTIONS/CAREER NOTES: Selected by Atlanta Braves organization in 18th round of free-agent draft (June 2, 1986). ... Selected by California Angels organization in third round of free-agent draft (June 5, 1989). ... On disabled list (May 12-May 23 and May 27-August 7, 1990).
STATISTICAL NOTES: Led Texas League with 89 bases on balls and 166 strikeouts in 1991.

Year Team (League)	Pos.	G	AB	R	H	2B	3B	HR	RBI	Avg.	SB	PO	A	E	Avg.
						BATTING							FIELDING		
1989—Bend (Northwest)	OF	55	196	37	48	6	5	6	31	.245	2	84	7	4	.958
1990—Palm Springs (Calif.)	OF	36	118	19	34	6	0	2	21	.288	11	63	3	1	.985
—Midland (Texas)	OF	27	97	17	26	3	1	3	16	.268	1	51	6	3	.950
1991—Midland (Texas)	OF	131	465	100	114	26	4	23	94	.245	12	265	16	10	.966

SAMPEN, BILL
P, EXPOS

PERSONAL: Born January 18, 1963, at Lincoln, Ill. ... 6-2/195. ... Throws right, bats right. ... Full name: William Albert Sampen.
HIGH SCHOOL: Hartem (Hartsburg, Ill.).
COLLEGE: MacMurray College (Ill.).
TRANSACTIONS/CAREER NOTES: Selected by Pittsburgh Pirates organization in 12th round of free-agent draft (June 3, 1985). ... On Harrisburg disabled list (April 6-May 5, 1988). ... Drafted by Montreal Expos (December 4, 1989).
STATISTICAL NOTES: Tied for Eastern League lead in games started by pitcher with 26 in 1989.

Year Team (League)	G	W	L	Pct.	ERA	Sv.	IP	H	R	ER	BB	SO
1985—Watertown (New York-Penn)...	5	0	0	...	1.80	1	10	9	3	2	7	11
1986—Watertown (New York-Penn)...	9	0	3	.000	4.25	2	29⅔	27	18	14	13	29
1987—Salem (Carolina)	26	9	8	.529	3.84	0	152⅓	126	77	65	72	137
1988—Harrisburg (Eastern)	13	6	3	.667	3.70	0	82⅔	72	38	34	27	65
—Salem (Carolina)	8	3	3	.500	3.33	0	51⅓	47	22	19	14	59
1989—Harrisburg (Eastern)	26	11	9	.550	3.21	0	165⅔	148	75	59	40	134
1990—Montreal (N.L.)■	59	12	7	.632	2.99	2	90⅓	94	34	30	33	69
1991—Montreal (N.L.)	43	9	5	.643	4.00	0	92⅓	96	49	41	46	52
—Indianapolis (Am. Assoc.)	7	4	0	1.000	2.04	0	39⅔	33	13	9	19	41
Major league totals (2 years)	102	21	12	.636	3.50	2	182⅔	190	83	71	79	121

SAMUEL, JUAN
2B, DODGERS

PERSONAL: Born December 9, 1960, at San Pedro de Macoris, Dominican Republic. ... 5-11/170. ... Throws right, bats right. ... Full name: Juan Milton Samuel. ... Name pronounced sam-WELL.
HIGH SCHOOL: Licey Puerto Rico.
TRANSACTIONS/CAREER NOTES: Signed as free agent by Philadelphia Phillies organization (April 29, 1980). ... On disabled list (April 13-May 2, 1986 and April 1-19, 1989). ... Traded by Phillies to New York Mets for OF Lenny Dykstra, P Roger McDowell and a player to be named later (June 18, 1989); Phillies organization acquired P Tom Edens to complete deal (July 27, 1989). ... Traded by Mets to Los Angeles Dodgers for P Alejandro Pena and OF Mike Marshall (December 20, 1989). ... Granted free agency (November 5, 1990). ... Re-signed by Dodgers (December 16, 1990). ... Granted free agency (October 28, 1991).

RECORDS/HONORS: Holds major league single-season records for most at-bats by righthander—701 (1984); fewest sacrifice hits with most at-bats—0 (1984). . . . Shares major league record for most consecutive seasons leading league in strikeouts—4 (1984-1987). . . . Shares major league single-game record (nine innings) for most assists by second baseman—12 (April 20, 1985). . . . Holds N.L. single-season record for most at-bats—701 (1984). . . . Named Carolina League Most Valuable Player (1982). . . . Named N.L. Rookie Player of the Year by THE SPORTING NEWS (1984). . . . Named second baseman on THE SPORTING NEWS N.L. All-Star team (1987). . . . Named second baseman on THE SPORTING NEWS N.L. Silver Slugger team (1987).

STATISTICAL NOTES: Led Northwest League batters with 87 strikeouts and caught stealing with 10 in 1980. . . . Led South Atlantic League second basemen with 737 total chances and 82 double plays in 1981. . . . Led Carolina League second basemen with 721 total chances and 82 double plays in 1982. . . . Led Carolina League with 283 total bases and tied for lead in being hit by pitch with 15 in 1982. . . . Led N.L. batters with 168 strikeouts in 1984, 142 in 1986, 162 in 1987 and tied for lead with 141 in 1985. . . . Led N.L. second basemen with 826 total chances in 1987. . . . Led N.L. second basemen with 343 putouts and 92 double plays in 1988.

Year	Team (League)	Pos.	G	AB	R	H	2B	3B	HR	RBI	Avg.	SB	PO	A	E	Avg.
1980	Central Oregon (N'West) ..	2B	69	*298	66	84	11	2	17	44	.282	25	162	188	*30	.921
1981	Spartanburg (S. Atl.)	2B	135	512	88	127	22	8	11	74	.248	53	*280	*409	*50	.932
1982	Peninsula (Carolina)	2B	135	494	*111	158	29	6	28	94	.320	64	*244	*442	*35	.951
1983	Reading (Eastern)	2B	47	184	36	43	10	0	11	39	.234	19	121	127	14	.947
	Portland (Pacific Coast) ...	2B	65	261	59	86	14	8	15	52	.330	33	110	168	15	.949
	Philadelphia (N.L.)	2B	18	65	14	18	1	2	2	5	.277	3	44	54	9	.916
1984	Philadelphia (N.L.)	2B	160	*701	105	191	36	•19	15	69	.272	72	388	438	*33	.962
1985	Philadelphia (N.L.)	2B	161	*663	101	175	31	13	19	74	.264	53	*389	463	15	.983
1986	Philadelphia (N.L.)	2B	145	591	90	157	36	12	16	78	.266	42	290	440	*25	.967
1987	Philadelphia (N.L.)	2B	160	*655	113	178	37	*15	28	100	.272	35	*374	434	*18	.978
1988	Philadelphia (N.L.)	2B-OF-3B	157	629	68	153	32	9	12	67	.243	33	†351	387	16	.979
1989	Phil.-New York (N.L.)■	OF	137	532	69	125	16	2	11	48	.235	42	339	6	4	.989
1990	Los Angeles (N.L.)■...	2B-OF	143	492	62	119	24	3	13	52	.242	38	273	262	16	.971
1991	Los Angeles (N.L.)	2B	153	594	74	161	22	6	12	58	.271	23	300	442	17	.978
	Major league totals (9 years)		1234	4922	696	1277	235	81	128	551	.259	341	2748	2926	153	.974

CHAMPIONSHIP SERIES RECORD

Year	Team (League)	Pos.	G	AB	R	H	2B	3B	HR	RBI	Avg.	SB	PO	A	E	Avg.
1983	Philadelphia (N.L.)	PR	1	0	0	0	0	0	0	0	...	0	0	0	0	...

WORLD SERIES RECORD

Year	Team (League)	Pos.	G	AB	R	H	2B	3B	HR	RBI	Avg.	SB	PO	A	E	Avg.
1983	Philadelphia (N.L.)	PR-PH	3	1	0	0	0	0	0	0	.000	0	0	0	0	...

ALL-STAR GAME RECORD

ALL-STAR GAME NOTES: Holds single-game record for most putouts by second baseman—7 (July 14, 1987). . . . Shares single-game record for most chances accepted by second baseman—9 (July 14, 1987).

Year	League	Pos.	AB	R	H	2B	3B	HR	RBI	Avg.	SB	PO	A	E	Avg.
1984	National							Did not play							
1987	National	2B	4	0	0	0	0	0	0	.000	0	7	2	0	1.000
1991	National	2B	1	0	1	0	0	0	0	1.000	0	2	1	0	1.000
	All-Star Game totals (2 years)		5	0	1	0	0	0	0	.200	0	9	3	0	1.000

SANCHEZ, ALEX
P, ROYALS

PERSONAL: Born April 8, 1966, at Antioch, Calif. . . . 6-2/185. . . . Throws right, bats right. . . . Full name: Alex Anthony Sanchez.
HIGH SCHOOL: Antioch (Calif.).
COLLEGE: UCLA.

TRANSACTIONS/CAREER NOTES: Selected by Chicago Cubs organization in 20th round of free-agent draft (June 4, 1984). . . . Selected by Toronto Blue Jays organization in first round (17th pick overall) of free-agent draft (June 2, 1987). . . . On disabled list (May 16-24 and July 19-August 15, 1990). . . . Traded by Blue Jays organization to Cleveland Indians (September 24, 1990), completing deal in which Blue Jays traded P Mauro Gozzo and two players to be named later to Indians for P Bud Black (September 16, 1990); P Steve Cummings sent by Blue Jays to Indians as partial completion of trade (September 21, 1990). . . . Traded by Indians to Blue Jays for P Willie Blair (November 6, 1990). . . . Claimed on waivers by Kansas City Royals (October 17, 1991).
RECORDS/HONORS: Named International League Pitcher of the Year (1989).
STATISTICAL NOTES: Led New York-Pennsylvania League pitchers with 17 games started in 1987. . . . Tied for International League lead in games started by pitcher with 27 in 1989.

Year	Team (League)	G	W	L	Pct.	ERA	Sv.	IP	H	R	ER	BB	SO
1987	St. Catharines (N.Y.-Penn)	17	8	3	.727	2.64	0	95⅓	72	33	28	38	*116
	Myrtle Beach (South Atlantic) ..	1	0	0	...	3.00	1	3	2	1	1	0	4
1988	Knoxville (Southern)	24	12	5	.706	2.53	0	149⅓	100	56	42	74	166
	Syracuse (International)	10	4	3	.571	3.59	0	57⅔	47	26	23	43	57
1989	Syracuse (International)	28	•13	7	.650	3.13	0	169⅔	125	68	59	74	141
	Toronto (A.L.)............................	4	0	1	.000	10.03	0	11⅔	16	13	13	14	4

Year Team (League)	G	W	L	Pct.	ERA	Sv.	IP	H	R	ER	BB	SO
1990 —Syracuse (International)■	22	5	9	.357	5.71	0	112	111	77	71	79	65
1991 —Syracuse (International)	14	1	4	.200	10.29	1	28	33	33	32	35	12
—Knoxville (Southern)	14	4	2	.667	3.07	0	58⅔	43	26	20	36	38
Major league totals (1 year)	**4**	**0**	**1**	**.000**	**10.03**	**0**	**11⅔**	**16**	**13**	**13**	**14**	**4**

SANCHEZ, REY
SS, CUBS

PERSONAL: Born October 5, 1967, at Rio Piedras, Puerto Rico. . . . 5-0/165. . . . Throws right, bats right. . . . Full name: Rey Francisco Guadalupe Sanchez.
HIGH SCHOOL: Live Oak (Morgan Hill, Calif.).
TRANSACTIONS/CAREER NOTES: Selected by Texas Rangers organization in 13th round of free-agent draft (June 2, 1986). . . . Traded by Rangers organization to Chicago Cubs organization for IF Bryan House (January 3, 1990). . . . On disabled list (entire 1990 season).
STATISTICAL NOTES: Led Gulf Coast League shortstops with .938 fielding percentage in 1986. . . . Led American Association shortstops with 104 double plays in 1989.

Year Team (League)	Pos.	G	AB	R	H	2B	3B	HR	RBI	Avg.	SB	PO	A	E	Avg.
							BATTING						FIELDING		
1986 —Sarasota Rangers (GCL) ...	SS-2B	52	169	27	49	3	1	0	23	.290	10	69	158	15	†.938
1987 —Gastonia (S. Atlantic)	SS	50	160	19	35	1	2	1	10	.219	6	88	162	18	.933
—Butte (Pioneer)	SS	49	189	36	69	10	6	0	25	.365	22	84	162	12	.953
1988 —Port Charlotte (Fla. St.)	SS	128	418	60	128	6	5	0	38	.306	29	226	*415	35	.948
1989 —Oklahoma City (A.A.)	SS	134	464	38	104	10	4	1	39	.224	4	*237	*418	29	*.958
1990 —■							Did not play								
1991 —Iowa (American Assoc.) ...	SS	126	417	60	121	16	5	2	46	.290	13	204	375	17	.971
—Chicago (N.L.)	SS-2B	13	23	1	6	0	0	0	2	.261	0	11	25	0	1.000
Major league totals (1 year)		**13**	**23**	**1**	**6**	**0**	**0**	**0**	**2**	**.261**	**0**	**11**	**25**	**0**	**1.000**

SANDBERG, RYNE
2B, CUBS

PERSONAL: Born September 18, 1959, at Spokane, Wash. . . . 6-2/185. . . . Throws right, bats right. . . . Full name: Ryne Dee Sandberg.
HIGH SCHOOL: North Central (Spokane, Wash.).
TRANSACTIONS/CAREER NOTES: Selected by Philadelphia Phillies organization in 20th round of free-agent draft (June 6, 1978). . . . Traded by Phillies with SS Larry Bowa to Chicago Cubs for SS Ivan DeJesus (January 27, 1982). . . . On disabled list (June 14-July 15, 1987).
RECORDS/HONORS: Holds major league career records for highest fielding percentage by second baseman—.990; most consecutive errorless games by a second baseman— 123 (June 21, 1989-May 17, 1990). . . . Holds major league single-season record for most consecutive errorless games by second baseman—90 (June 21-October 1, 1989). . . . Shares major league single-game record for most assists by second baseman— 12 (June 12, 1983). . . . Shares N.L. record for most years with 500 or more assists by second baseman—5. . . . Won N.L. Gold Glove at second base (1983-91). . . . Named Major League Player of the Year by THE SPORTING NEWS (1984). . . . Named N.L. Player of the Year by THE SPORTING NEWS (1984). . . . Named second baseman on THE SPORTING NEWS N.L. All-Star team (1984 and 1988-91). . . . Named second baseman on THE SPORTING NEWS N.L. Silver Slugger team (1984-85 and 1988-91). . . . Named N.L. Most Valuable Player by Baseball Writers' Association of America (1984).
STATISTICAL NOTES: Led Pioneer League shortstops with 39 double plays in 1978. . . . Led Western Carolinas League shortstops with 80 double plays in 1979. . . . Led Eastern League shortstops with .964 fielding percentage, 386 assists and 81 double plays in 1980. . . . Led N.L. second basemen with .986 fielding percentage, 571 assists and 126 double plays in 1983. . . . Led N.L. second basemen with 914 total chances in 1983, 870 in 1984 and 824 in 1988. . . . Led N.L. with 344 total bases in 1990.

Year Team (League)	Pos.	G	AB	R	H	2B	3B	HR	RBI	Avg.	SB	PO	A	E	Avg.
							BATTING						FIELDING		
1978 —Helena (Pioneer)	SS	56	190	34	59	6	6	1	23	.311	15	92	*200	24	.924
1979 —Spartanburg (W. Caro.)	SS	*138	*539	83	133	21	7	4	47	.247	21	134	*467	35	*.945
1980 —Reading (Eastern)	SS-3B	129	490	95	152	21	12	11	79	.310	32	156	†388	20	†.965
1981 —Oklahoma City (A.A.)	SS-2B	133	519	78	152	17	5	9	62	.293	32	229	396	21	.967
—Philadelphia (N.L.)	SS-2B	13	6	2	1	0	0	0	0	.167	0	7	7	0	1.000
1982 —Chicago (N.L.)■	3B-2B	156	635	103	172	33	5	7	54	.271	32	136	373	12	.977
1983 —Chicago (N.L.)	2B-SS	158	633	94	165	25	4	8	48	.261	37	330	572	13	†.986
1984 —Chicago (N.L.)	2B	156	636	*114	200	36	•19	19	84	.314	32	314	*550	6	*.993
1985 —Chicago (N.L.)	2B-SS	153	609	113	186	31	6	26	83	.305	54	353	501	12	.986
1986 —Chicago (N.L.)	2B	154	627	68	178	28	5	14	76	.284	34	309	*492	5	*.994
1987 —Chicago (N.L.)	2B	132	523	81	154	25	2	16	59	.294	21	294	375	10	.985
1988 —Chicago (N.L.)	2B	155	618	77	163	23	8	19	69	.264	25	291	*522	11	.987
1989 —Chicago (N.L.)	2B	157	606	*104	176	25	5	30	76	.290	15	294	466	6	.992
1990 —Chicago (N.L.)	2B	155	615	*116	188	30	3	*40	100	.306	25	278	*469	8	.989
1991 —Chicago (N.L.)	2B	158	585	104	170	32	2	26	100	.291	22	267	*515	4	*.995
Major league totals (11 years)		**1547**	**6093**	**976**	**1753**	**288**	**59**	**205**	**749**	**.288**	**297**	**2873**	**4842**	**87**	**.989**

CHAMPIONSHIP SERIES RECORD

Year Team (League)	Pos.	G	AB	R	H	2B	3B	HR	RBI	Avg.	SB	PO	A	E	Avg.
							BATTING						FIELDING		
1984 —Chicago (N.L.)	2B	5	19	3	7	2	0	0	2	.368	3	13	18	1	.969
1989 —Chicago (N.L.)	2B	5	20	6	8	3	1	1	4	.400	0	7	11	0	1.000
Championship Series totals (2 years)		**10**	**39**	**9**	**15**	**5**	**1**	**1**	**6**	**.385**	**3**	**20**	**29**	**1**	**.980**

ALL-STAR GAME RECORD

Year	League	Pos.	AB	R	H	2B	3B	HR	RBI	Avg.	SB	PO	A	E	Avg.
1984 —National		2B	4	0	1	0	0	0	0	.250	1	0	0	0	...
1985 —National		2B	1	1	0	0	0	0	0	.000	0	0	3	0	1.000
1986 —National		2B	3	0	0	0	0	0	0	.000	0	0	2	1	.667
1987 —National		2B	2	0	0	0	0	0	0	.000	0	0	2	0	1.000
1988 —National		2B	4	0	1	0	0	0	0	.250	0	2	2	0	1.000
1989 —National		2B	3	0	0	0	0	0	0	.000	0	2	4	0	1.000
1990 —National		2B	3	0	0	0	0	0	0	.000	0	1	2	0	1.000
1991 —National		2B	3	0	1	1	0	0	0	.333	0	2	1	0	1.000
All-Star Game totals (8 years)			23	1	3	1	0	0	0	.130	1	7	16	1	.958

SANDERS, DEION
OF, BRAVES

PERSONAL: Born August 9, 1967, at Fort Myers, Fla. . . . 6-1/195. . . . Throws left, bats left. . . . Full name: Deion Luwynn Sanders.
HIGH SCHOOL: North Ft. Myers (Fla.).
COLLEGE: Florida State.
TRANSACTIONS/CAREER NOTES: Selected by Kansas City Royals organization in sixth round of free-agent draft (June 3, 1985). . . . Selected by New York Yankees organization in 30th round of free-agent draft (June 1, 1988). . . . On disqualified list (August 1-September 24, 1990). . . . Released by Yankees organization (September 24, 1990). . . . Signed by Atlanta Braves (January 29, 1991). . . . Placed on Richmond temporary inactive list (August 1, 1991).

Year	Team (League)	Pos.	G	AB	R	H	2B	3B	HR	RBI	Avg.	SB	PO	A	E	Avg.
1988 —Sarasota Yankees (GCL) ..		OF	17	75	7	21	4	2	0	6	.280	11	33	1	2	.944
—Fort Lauderdale (FSL)		OF	6	21	5	9	2	0	0	2	.429	2	22	2	0	1.000
—Columbus (Int'l)		OF	5	20	3	3	1	0	0	0	.150	1	13	0	0	1.000
1989 —Albany (Eastern)		OF	33	119	28	34	2	2	1	6	.286	17	79	3	0	1.000
—New York (A.L.)		OF	14	47	7	11	2	0	2	7	.234	1	30	1	1	.969
—Columbus (Int'l)		OF	70	259	38	72	12	7	5	30	.278	16	165	0	4	.976
1990 —New York (A.L.)		OF	57	133	24	21	2	2	3	9	.158	8	69	2	2	.973
—Columbus (Int'l)		OF	22	84	21	27	7	1	2	10	.321	9	49	1	0	1.000
1991 —Atlanta (N.L.)■		OF	54	110	16	21	1	2	4	13	.191	11	57	3	3	.952
—Richmond (Int'l)		OF	29	130	20	34	6	3	5	16	.262	12	73	1	1	.987
American League totals (2 years)			71	180	31	32	4	2	5	16	.178	9	99	3	3	.971
National League totals (1 year)			54	110	16	21	1	2	4	13	.191	11	57	3	3	.952
Major league totals (3 years)			125	290	47	53	5	4	9	29	.183	20	156	6	6	.964

RECORD AS FOOTBALL PLAYER
TRANSACTIONS/CAREER NOTES: Selected by Atlanta Falcons in first round (fifth pick overall) of 1989 NFL draft. . . . Signed by Falcons (September 7, 1989). . . . On reserve/did not report list (July 27-August 13, 1990).
RECORDS/HONORS: Named as defensive back on THE SPORTING NEWS college All-America team (1986-1988). . . . Named to THE SPORTING NEWS NFL All-Pro team (1991).
PRO STATISTICS: 1989—Recovered one fumble and caught one pass for minus eight yards. 1990—Recovered two fumbles. 1991—Ran with a lateral from an interception for 55 yards and a touchdown and caught one pass for 17 yards.

			—INTERCEPTIONS—				—PUNT RETURNS—				–KICKOFF RETURNS–				—TOTAL—		
Year	Team	G	No.	Yds.	Avg.	TD	No.	Yds.	Avg.	TD	No.	Yds.	Avg.	TD	TD	Pts.	F.
1989 —Atlanta NFL		15	5	52	10.4	0	28	307	11.0	*1	35	725	20.7	0	1	6	2
1990 —Atlanta NFL		16	3	153	51.0	2	29	250	8.6	*1	39	851	21.8	0	3	18	4
1991 —Atlanta NFL		16	6	115	19.2	1	21	170	8.1	0	26	576	22.2	*1	2	12	1
Pro totals (3 years)		47	14	320	22.3	3	78	727	9.3	2	100	2152	21.5	1	6	36	7

SANDERS, REGGIE
OF, REDS

PERSONAL: Born December 1, 1967, at Florence, S.C. . . . 6-1/180. . . . Throws right, bats right. . . . Full name: Reginald Laverne Sanders.
HIGH SCHOOL: Wilson (Florence, S.C.).
COLLEGE: Spartanburg Methodist (S.C.).
TRANSACTIONS/CAREER NOTES: Selected by Cincinnati Reds organization in seventh round of free-agent draft (June 2, 1987). . . . On disabled list (July 11-September 15, 1988 and July 15-September 5, 1989). . . . On Chattanooga disabled list (June 30-July 26, 1991). . . . On Cincinnati disabled list (August 24-September 20, 1991).
RECORDS/HONORS: Named Midwest League Most Valuable Player (1990).

Year	Team (League)	Pos.	G	AB	R	H	2B	3B	HR	RBI	Avg.	SB	PO	A	E	Avg.
1988 —Billings (Pioneer)		SS	17	64	11	15	1	1	0	3	.234	10	18	33	3	.944
1989 —Greensboro (S. Atlantic) ...		SS	81	315	53	91	18	5	9	53	.289	21	125	169	42	.875
1990 —Cedar Rapids (Midwest) ...		OF	127	466	89	133	21	4	17	63	.285	40	241	10	10	.962
1991 —Chattanooga (Southern) ...		OF	86	302	50	95	15	8	8	49	.315	15	158	2	3	.982
—Cincinnati (N.L.)		OF	9	40	6	8	0	0	1	3	.200	1	22	0	0	1.000
Major league totals (1 year)			9	40	6	8	0	0	1	3	.200	1	22	0	0	1.000

SANDERSON, SCOTT
P, YANKEES

PERSONAL: Born July 22, 1956, at Dearborn, Mich. . . . 6-5/192. . . . Throws right, bats right. . . . Full name: Scott Douglas Sanderson.
HIGH SCHOOL: Glenbrook North (Northbrook, Ill.).
COLLEGE: Vanderbilt.

TRANSACTIONS/CAREER NOTES: Selected by Kansas City Royals organization in 11th round of free-agent draft (June 5, 1974). . . . Selected by Montreal Expos organization in third round of free-agent draft (June 7, 1977). . . . On disabled list (July 5-September 1, 1983). . . . Traded by Expos with IF Al Newman to San Diego Padres for P Gary Lucas (December 7, 1983); traded by Padres to Chicago Cubs for 1B Carmelo Martinez, P Craig Lefferts and 3B Fritz Connally (December 7, 1983). . . . On Chicago disabled list (June 1-July 5, 1984); included rehabilitation disability assignment to Lodi (June 29-July 5, 1984). . . . On disabled list (August 14, 1985-remainder of season; March 29-April 24 and June 22-July 7, 1987). . . . On Chicago disabled list (April 5-August 23, 1988); included rehabilitation disability assignment to Peoria (June 25-29, 1988) and Iowa (June 30-July 11, 1988). . . . Granted free agency (November 4, 1988). . . . Re-signed by Cubs (December 7, 1988). . . . Granted free agency (November 13, 1989). . . . Signed by Oakland Athletics (December 13, 1989). . . . Granted free agency (November 5, 1990). . . . Re-signed by A's (December 19, 1990). . . . Sold by A's to New York Yankees (December 31, 1990).

RECORDS/HONORS: Shares N.L. record for most consecutive home runs allowed in one inning—3 (July 11, 1982, second inning).

Year	Team (League)	G	W	L	Pct.	ERA	Sv.	IP	H	R	ER	BB	SO
1977	—West Palm Beach (Florida St.) ..	10	5	2	.714	2.68	0	57	58	22	17	23	37
1978	—Memphis (Southern)	9	5	3	.625	4.03	0	58	55	32	26	19	44
	—Denver (American Assoc.)	9	4	2	.667	6.06	0	49	47	35	33	30	36
	—Montreal (N.L.)	10	4	2	.667	2.51	0	61	52	20	17	21	50
1979	—Montreal (N.L.)	34	9	8	.529	3.43	1	168	148	69	64	54	138
1980	—Montreal (N.L.)	33	16	11	.593	3.11	0	211	206	76	73	56	125
1981	—Montreal (N.L.)	22	9	7	.563	2.96	0	137	122	50	45	31	77
1982	—Montreal (N.L.)	32	12	12	.500	3.46	0	224	212	98	86	58	158
1983	—Montreal (N.L.)	18	6	7	.462	4.65	1	81⅓	98	50	42	20	55
1984	—Chicago (N.L.)■	24	8	5	.615	3.14	0	140⅔	140	54	49	24	76
	—Lodi (California)	1	0	1	.000	3.60	0	5	7	2	2	0	2
1985	—Chicago (N.L.)	19	5	6	.455	3.12	0	121	100	49	42	27	80
1986	—Chicago (N.L.)	37	9	11	.450	4.19	1	169⅔	165	85	79	37	124
1987	—Chicago (N.L.)	32	8	9	.471	4.29	2	144⅔	156	72	69	50	106
1988	—Peoria (Midwest)	1	0	0	...	0.00	0	5	4	1	0	0	3
	—Iowa (American Association) ...	3	1	0	1.000	4.73	0	13⅓	13	7	7	4	4
	—Chicago (N.L.)	11	1	2	.333	5.28	0	15⅓	13	9	9	3	6
1989	—Chicago (N.L.)	37	11	9	.550	3.94	0	146⅓	155	69	64	31	86
1990	—Oakland (A.L.)■	34	17	11	.607	3.88	0	206⅓	205	99	89	66	128
1991	—New York (A.L.)■	34	16	10	.615	3.81	0	208	200	95	88	29	130
	American League totals (2 years)	68	33	21	.611	3.84	0	414⅓	405	194	177	95	258
	National League totals (12 years)	309	98	89	.524	3.55	5	1620	1567	701	639	412	1081
	Major league totals (14 years)	377	131	110	.544	3.61	5	2034⅓	1972	895	816	507	1339

DIVISION SERIES RECORD

Year	Team (League)	G	W	L	Pct.	ERA	Sv.	IP	H	R	ER	BB	SO
1981	—Montreal (N.L.)	1	0	0	...	6.75	0	2⅔	4	4	2	2	2

CHAMPIONSHIP SERIES RECORD

Year	Team (League)	G	W	L	Pct.	ERA	Sv.	IP	H	R	ER	BB	SO
1984	—Chicago (N.L.)	1	0	0	...	5.79	0	4⅔	6	3	3	1	2
1989	—Chicago (N.L.)	1	0	0	...	0.00	0	2	2	0	0	0	1
	Championship Series totals (2 years)	2	0	0	...	4.05	0	6⅔	8	3	3	1	3

WORLD SERIES RECORD

Year	Team (League)	G	W	L	Pct.	ERA	Sv.	IP	H	R	ER	BB	SO
1990	—Oakland (A.L.)	2	0	0	...	10.80	0	1⅔	4	2	2	1	0

ALL-STAR GAME RECORD

Year	League	W	L	Pct.	ERA	Sv.	IP	H	R	ER	BB	SO
1991	—American					Did not play							

SANFORD, MO
P, REDS

PERSONAL: Born December 24, 1966, at Americus, Ga. . . . 6-6/225. . . . Throws right, bats right. . . . Full name: Meredith Leroy Sanford Jr.
HIGH SCHOOL: Starkville (Miss.).
COLLEGE: Alabama.
TRANSACTIONS/CAREER NOTES: Selected by New York Yankees organization in third round of free-agent draft (June 4, 1984). . . . Selected by Cincinnati Reds organization in 32nd round of free-agent draft (June 1, 1988).
STATISTICAL NOTES: Pitched 7-0 no-hit victory against Myrtle Beach (June 2, 1989).

Year	Team (League)	G	W	L	Pct.	ERA	Sv.	IP	H	R	ER	BB	SO
1988	—Sarasota Reds (Gulf Coast)	14	3	4	.429	3.23	1	53	34	24	19	25	64
1989	—Greensboro (South Atlantic)	25	12	6	.667	2.81	0	153⅔	112	52	48	64	160
1990	—Cedar Rapids (Midwest)	25	13	4	.765	2.74	0	157⅔	112	50	48	55	180
1991	—Chattanooga (Southern)	16	7	4	.636	2.74	0	95⅓	69	37	29	55	124
	—Nashville (American Assoc.)	5	3	0	1.000	1.60	0	33⅔	19	7	6	22	38
	—Cincinnati (N.L.)	5	1	2	.333	3.86	0	28	19	14	12	15	31
	Major league totals (1 year)	5	1	2	.333	3.86	0	28	19	14	12	15	31

SANTANA, ANDRES
2B/SS, GIANTS

PERSONAL: Born March 19, 1968, at San Pedro de Macoris, Dominican Republic. . . . 5-11/150. . . . Throws right, bats both. . . . Full name: Andres Confesor Santana.
TRANSACTIONS/CAREER NOTES: Signed as free agent by San Francisco Giants organization (November 22, 1985). . . . On disabled list (May 18-31, 1991).

STATISTICAL NOTES: Led Pioneer League shortstops with 337 total chances in 1987.... Led Pioneer League in caught stealing with 10 in 1987.... Led Midwest League in caught stealing with 23 in 1988.... Led Pacific Coast League second basemen with 21 errors in 1991.

Year Team (League)	Pos.	G	AB	R	H	2B	3B	HR	RBI	Avg.	SB	PO	A	E	Avg.
1987—Pocatello (Pioneer)...........	SS	67	256	51	67	2	3	0	9	.262	*45	94	*202	*41	.878
1988—Clinton (Midwest).............	SS	118	450	77	126	4	1	0	24	.280	88	154	301	50	.901
—Shreveport (Texas)	SS	11	36	3	6	0	0	0	3	.167	3	20	29	1	.980
1989—San Jose (California)	SS	18	69	14	18	3	0	0	3	.261	10	22	46	8	.895
1990—Shreveport (Texas)	SS	92	336	50	98	5	4	0	24	.292	31	131	207	33	.911
—San Francisco (N.L.)	SS	6	2	0	0	0	0	0	1	.000	0	2	1	0	1.000
1991—Phoenix (Pacific Coast)	2B-SS	113	456	84	144	7	5	1	35	.316	45	213	302	†32	.941
Major league totals (1 year)		6	2	0	0	0	0	0	1	.000	0	2	1	0	1.000

SANTIAGO, BENITO
C, PADRES

PERSONAL: Born March 9, 1965, at Ponce, Puerto Rico.... 6-1/185.... Throws right, bats right. ... Full name: Benito Rivera Santiago. ... Name pronounced SAHN-tee-AH-go.
HIGH SCHOOL: John F. Kennedy (Ponce, Puerto Rico).
TRANSACTIONS/CAREER NOTES: Signed as free agent by San Diego Padres organization (September 1, 1982).... On disabled list (June 21-July 2, 1985).... On San Diego disabled list (June 15-August 10, 1990); included rehabilitation disability assignment to Las Vegas (August 2-9, 1990).
RECORDS/HONORS: Holds major league rookie-season record for most consecutive games batted safely—34 (August 25-October 2, 1987).... Named N.L. Rookie Player of the Year by THE SPORTING NEWS (1987).... Named catcher on THE SPORTING NEWS N.L. All-Star team (1987, 1989 and 1991).... Named catcher on THE SPORTING NEWS N.L. Silver Slugger team (1987-88 and 1990-91).... Named N.L. Rookie of the Year by Baseball Writers' Association of America (1987).... Won N.L. Gold Glove at catcher (1988-90).
STATISTICAL NOTES: Led Florida State League catchers with 26 passed balls and 12 double plays in 1983.... Led Texas League catchers with 78 assists and 16 passed balls in 1985.... Led Pacific Coast League catchers with 655 total chances in 1986. ... Led N.L. with 22 passed balls in 1987 and 14 in 1989.... Tied for N.L. lead in double plays by catchers with 11 in 1988 and 14 in 1991.... Led N.L. catchers with 100 assists and 14 errors in 1991.... Led N.L. in grounding into double plays with 21 in 1991.

Year Team (League)	Pos.	G	AB	R	H	2B	3B	HR	RBI	Avg.	SB	PO	A	E	Avg.
1983—Miami (Florida State)	C	122	429	34	106	25	3	5	56	.247	3	471	*69	*21	.963
1984—Reno (California)	C	114	416	64	116	20	6	16	83	.279	5	692	96	25	.969
1985—Beaumont (Texas)	C-1B-3B	101	372	55	111	16	6	5	52	.298	12	525	†78	15	.976
1986—Las Vegas (Pac. Coast)	C	117	437	55	125	26	3	17	71	.286	19	*563	71	*21	.968
—San Diego (N.L.)	C	17	62	10	18	2	0	3	6	.290	0	80	7	5	.946
1987—San Diego (N.L.)	C	146	546	64	164	33	2	18	79	.300	21	817	80	*22	.976
1988—San Diego (N.L.)	C	139	492	49	122	22	2	10	46	.248	15	725	*75	*12	.985
1989—San Diego (N.L.)	C	129	462	50	109	16	3	16	62	.236	11	685	81	*20	.975
1990—San Diego (N.L.)	C	100	344	42	93	8	5	11	53	.270	5	538	51	12	.980
—Las Vegas (Pac. Coast)	C	6	20	5	6	2	0	1	8	.300	0	25	5	0	1.000
1991—San Diego (N.L.)	C-OF	152	580	60	155	22	3	17	87	.267	8	830	†100	†14	.985
Major league totals (6 years)		683	2486	275	661	103	15	75	333	.266	60	3675	394	85	.980

ALL-STAR GAME RECORD
ALL-STAR GAME NOTES: Named to N.L. All-Star team for 1990 game; replaced due to injury.

Year League	Pos.	AB	R	H	2B	3B	HR	RBI	Avg.	SB	PO	A	E	Avg.
1989—National	C	1	0	0	0	0	0	0	.000	0	0	0	1	.000
1991—National	C	3	0	0	0	0	0	0	.000	0	4	0	0	1.000
All-Star Game totals (2 years)		4	0	0	0	0	0	0	.000	0	4	0	1	.800

SANTOVENIA, NELSON
C/1B, WHITE SOX

PERSONAL: Born July 27, 1961, at Pino del Rio, Cuba.... 6-3/210.... Throws right, bats right.... Full name: Nelson Gil Santovenia.... Name pronounced SAN-toe-VAYN-yuh.
HIGH SCHOOL: Miami Southbridge (Fla.).
COLLEGE: Miami-Dade (South) Community College and Miami (Fla.).
TRANSACTIONS/CAREER NOTES: Selected by Philadelphia Phillies organization in 29th round of free-agent draft (June 5, 1979). ... Selected by Montreal Expos organization in third round of free-agent draft (June 8, 1981).... Selected by Expos organization in secondary phase of free-agent draft (June 7, 1982).... On suspended list (May 24-31, 1984).... On Montreal disabled list (June 4-20, 1988; May 13-June 13, 1989; and July 13-September 1, 1990).... On Indianapolis disqualified list (June 11, 1991); reinstated (June 11, 1991).... Released by Expos (December 9, 1991).... Signed by Chicago White Sox organization (February 3, 1992).
STATISTICAL NOTES: Led Southern League with 21 passed balls in 1983.... Tied for Southern League lead in double plays by catchers with nine in 1984.... Led Southern League catchers with 785 putouts and 867 total chances in 1987.

Year Team (League)	Pos.	G	AB	R	H	2B	3B	HR	RBI	Avg.	SB	PO	A	E	Avg.
1982—West Palm Beach (FSL)	C	40	118	8	29	4	0	1	12	.246	0	127	21	5	.967
1983—Memphis (Southern)	C	94	318	27	77	13	0	3	44	.242	1	490	69	*15	.974
1984—Jacksonville (Southern) ...	C	90	255	27	55	9	0	5	29	.216	0	464	•64	4	.992

Year	Team (League)	Pos.	G	AB	R	H	2B	3B	HR	RBI	Avg.	SB	PO	A	E	Avg.
1985	—Jacksonville (Southern) ...	C	57	184	15	40	6	0	2	15	.217	2	281	20	9	.971
	—Indianapolis (A.A.)	C	28	75	5	16	2	0	0	4	.213	1	135	20	1	.994
1986	—Jacksonville (Southern) ...	C-OF	31	72	15	22	7	0	4	11	.306	0	97	14	1	.991
	—Indianapolis (A.A.)	C	18	57	6	12	1	0	1	2	.211	0	80	14	1	.989
1987	—Jacksonville (Southern) ...	C-1B	117	394	56	110	17	0	19	63	.279	3	†790	71	11	.987
	—Montreal (N.L.)	C	2	1	0	0	0	0	0	0	.000	0	1	0	0	1.000
1988	—Indianapolis (A.A.)	C	27	91	9	28	5	0	2	13	.308	0	198	23	3	.987
	—Montreal (N.L.)	C-1B	92	309	26	73	20	2	8	41	.236	2	465	63	9	.983
1989	—Montreal (N.L.)	C-1B	97	304	30	76	14	1	5	31	.250	2	564	66	12	.981
1990	—Montreal (N.L.)	C	59	163	13	31	3	1	6	28	.190	0	264	24	6	.980
	—Indianapolis (A.A.)	C	11	44	3	14	2	0	1	10	.318	0	40	7	1	.979
1991	—Montreal (N.L.)	C-1B	41	96	7	24	5	0	2	14	.250	0	140	16	3	.981
	—Indianapolis (A.A.)	C-1B	61	195	23	51	7	1	6	26	.262	0	333	33	5	.987
Major league totals (5 years)			291	873	76	204	42	4	21	114	.234	4	1434	169	30	.982

SASSER, MACKEY
C/OF/1B, METS

PERSONAL: Born August 3, 1962, at Fort Gaines, Ga. ... 6-1/210. ... Throws right, bats left. ... Full name: Mack Daniel Sasser Jr.
HIGH SCHOOL: Godby (Tallahassee, Fla.).
COLLEGE: George C. Wallace Community College (Ala.) and Troy State (Ala.).
TRANSACTIONS/CAREER NOTES: Selected by San Francisco Giants organization in fifth round of free-agent draft (January 17, 1984). ... Traded by Giants organization with $50,000 to Pittsburgh Pirates organization for P Don Robinson (July 31, 1987). ... Traded by Pirates with P Tim Drummond to New York Mets for 1B Randy Milligan and P Scott Henion (March 26, 1988).
STATISTICAL NOTES: Led California League with 245 total bases in 1985. ... Led California League with 19 passed balls in 1985. ... Led Texas League with 13 intentional bases on balls received in 1986. ... Led Pacific Coast League catchers with 584 put-outs, 663 total chances and 16 errors in 1987. ... Led N.L. catchers with 14 errors in 1990.

Year	Team (League)	Pos.	G	AB	R	H	2B	3B	HR	RBI	Avg.	SB	PO	A	E	Avg.
1984	—Clinton (Midwest)	1-3-0-C	118	428	57	125	20	5	6	65	.292	15	526	95	17	.973
	—Fresno (California)	OF-3B-1B	16	62	8	17	1	1	0	6	.274	1	24	15	4	.907
1985	—Fresno (California)	O-C-1-3	133	497	79	168	27	4	14	102	.338	3	402	44	14	.969
1986	—Shreveport (Texas)	C-1B-OF	120	441	52	129	29	5	5	72	.293	4	577	66	10	.985
1987	—Phoenix-Vanc. (PCL)■....	C-3B-1B	115	400	53	127	24	1	3	56	.318	3	†588	72	†18	.973
	—San Fran.-Pitts. (N.L.)	C	14	27	2	5	0	0	0	2	.185	0	29	0	0	1.000
1988	—New York (N.L.)■.............	C-3B-OF	60	123	9	35	10	1	1	17	.285	0	235	17	6	.977
1989	—New York (N.L.)	C-3B	72	182	17	53	14	2	1	22	.291	0	335	19	3	.992
1990	—New York (N.L.)	C-1B	100	270	31	83	14	0	6	41	.307	0	501	43	†14	.975
1991	—New York (N.L.)	C-OF-1B	96	228	18	62	14	2	5	35	.272	0	271	21	3	.990
Major league totals (5 years)			342	830	77	238	52	5	13	117	.287	0	1371	100	26	.983

CHAMPIONSHIP SERIES RECORD

Year	Team (League)	Pos.	G	AB	R	H	2B	3B	HR	RBI	Avg.	SB	PO	A	E	Avg.
1988	—New York (N.L.)	PH-C	4	5	0	1	0	0	0	0	.200	0	2	0	0	1.000

SATRE, JASON
P, REDS

PERSONAL: Born August 24, 1970, at Tampa, Fla. ... 6-1/180. ... Throws right, bats right. ... Full name: Jason Robert Satre.
HIGH SCHOOL: Cooper (Abilene, Tex.).
TRANSACTIONS/CAREER NOTES: Selected by Cincinnati Reds organization in 27th round of free-agent draft (June 1, 1988).

Year	Team (League)	G	W	L	Pct.	ERA	Sv.	IP	H	R	ER	BB	SO
1988	—Sarasota Reds (Gulf Coast)	11	0	3	.000	2.49	0	47	31	16	13	29	44
1989	—Greensboro (South Atlantic)	27	7	•13	.350	5.72	0	133⅔	128	95	85	87	106
1990	—Charleston, W.Va. (S. Atl.)	24	6	12	.333	4.73	0	116	99	70	61	75	105
1991	—Cedar Rapids (Midwest)	21	8	6	.571	2.58	1	132⅔	101	48	38	67	130
	—Chattanooga (Southern)..........	8	1	7	.125	5.11	0	44	37	26	25	26	44

SAUVEUR, RICH
P, METS

PERSONAL: Born November 23, 1963, at Arlington, Va. ... 6-4/170. ... Throws left, bats left. ... Full name: Richard Daniel Sauveur. ... Name pronounced SO-vurr.
HIGH SCHOOL: Falls Church (Va.).
COLLEGE: Manatee Junior College (Fla.).
TRANSACTIONS/CAREER NOTES: Selected by Pittsburgh Pirates organization in 11th round of free-agent draft (January 11, 1983). ... Selected by Pirates organization in secondary phase of free-agent draft (June 6, 1983). ... On Prince William disabled list (May 25-July 5, 1984). ... On Hawaii disabled list (August 10-September 5, 1986). ... Drafted by Montreal Expos organization (December 7, 1987). ... On disabled list (May 4, 1989-remainder of season). ... Granted free agency (October 15, 1989). ... Signed by Pittsburgh Pirates organization (December 15, 1989). ... Released by Pirates organization (March 31, 1990). ... Signed by Miami, Independent (May 17, 1990). ... Released by Miami (July 11, 1990). ... Signed by Expos organization (July 16, 1990). ... Granted free agency (October 15, 1990). ... Signed by New York Mets organization (January 22, 1991). ... On Tidewater disabled list (August 8-20, 1991).

STATISTICAL NOTES: Tied for New York-Pennsylvania League lead with four balks in 1983. . . . Led Eastern League with four balks in 1984 and tied for lead with four in 1985. . . . Tied for Eastern League lead in games started by pitcher with 27 in 1987.

Year	Team (League)	G	W	L	Pct.	ERA	Sv.	IP	H	R	ER	BB	SO
1983	Watertown (New York-Penn)...	16	7	5	.583	2.31	0	93⅔	80	41	24	31	73
1984	Prince William (Carolina)	10	3	3	.500	3.13	0	54⅔	43	22	19	31	54
	Nashua (Eastern)......................	10	5	3	.625	2.93	0	70⅔	54	27	23	34	48
1985	Nashua (Eastern)....................	25	9	10	.474	3.55	0	157⅓	146	73	62	78	85
1986	Nashua (Eastern)....................	5	3	1	.750	1.18	0	38	21	5	5	11	28
	Hawaii (Pacific Coast)	14	7	6	.538	3.03	0	92	73	40	31	45	68
	Pittsburgh (N.L.)	3	0	0	...	6.00	0	12	17	8	8	6	6
1987	Harrisburg (Eastern)	30	13	6	.684	2.86	0	★195	174	71	62	96	★160
1988	Jacksonville (Southern)■	8	0	2	.000	4.05	1	6⅔	7	5	3	5	8
	Indianapolis (Am. Assoc.)	43	7	4	.636	2.43	10	81⅓	60	26	22	28	58
	Montreal (N.L.).......................	4	0	0	...	6.00	0	3	3	2	2	2	3
1989	Indianapolis (Am. Assoc.)	8	0	1	.000	7.45	1	9⅔	10	8	8	6	8
1990	Miami (Florida State)■.............	11	0	4	.000	3.32	0	40⅔	41	16	15	17	34
	Indianapolis (Am. Assoc.)■.......	14	2	2	.500	1.93	0	56	45	14	12	25	24
1991	Tidewater (International)■.......	42	2	2	.500	2.38	6	45⅓	31	14	12	23	49
	New York (N.L.)	6	0	0	...	10.80	0	3⅓	7	4	4	2	4
Major league totals (3 years)		13	0	0	...	6.87	0	18⅓	27	14	14	10	13

SAX, STEVE

2B, WHITE SOX

PERSONAL: Born January 29, 1960, at Sacramento, Calif. . . . 6-0/188. . . . Throws right, bats right. . . . Full name: Stephen Louis Sax. . . . Brother of Dave Sax, first baseman-catcher, New York Yankees organization.
HIGH SCHOOL: James Marshall (West Sacramento, Calif.).
TRANSACTIONS/CAREER NOTES: Selected by Los Angeles Dodgers organization in ninth round of free-agent draft (June 6, 1978). . . . On disabled list (April 19-May 4, 1985). . . . Granted free agency (November 4, 1988). . . . Signed by New York Yankees (November 23, 1988). . . . Traded by Yankees to Chicago White Sox for P Melido Perez, P Robert Wickman and P Domingo Jean (January 10, 1992).
RECORDS/HONORS: Named Texas League Most Valuable Player (1981). . . . Named N.L. Rookie of the Year by Baseball Writers' Association of America (1982). . . . Named second baseman on THE SPORTING NEWS N.L. All-Star team (1986). . . . Named second baseman on THE SPORTING NEWS N.L. Silver Slugger team (1986).
STATISTICAL NOTES: Led Florida State League second basemen with .976 fielding percentage, 360 putouts, 438 assists and 91 double plays in 1980. . . . Led N.L. in caught stealing with 30 in 1983. . . . Led N.L. second basemen with 22 errors in 1985. . . . Led A.L. second basemen with 117 double plays in 1989.

Year	Team (League)	Pos.	G	AB	R	H	2B	3B	HR	RBI	Avg.	SB	PO	A	E	Avg.
1978	Lethbridge (Pioneer)	SS	39	131	24	43	6	3	0	21	.328	0	21	40	9	.871
1979	Clinton (Midwest).............	OF-2B-3B	115	386	64	112	15	2	2	52	.290	25	111	75	18	.912
1980	Vero Beach (Florida St.) ...	2B-OF	•139	•530	78	150	18	8	3	61	.283	33	†360	†438	20	†.976
1981	San Antonio (Texas)........	2B	115	485	94	168	23	3	8	52	★.346	34	255	298	17	.970
	Los Angeles (N.L.)............	2B	31	119	15	33	2	0	2	9	.277	5	64	93	4	.975
1982	Los Angeles (N.L.)............	2B	150	638	88	180	23	7	4	47	.282	49	347	452	19	.977
1983	Los Angeles (N.L.)............	2B	155	623	94	175	18	5	5	41	.281	58	331	339	★30	.957
1984	Los Angeles (N.L.)............	2B	145	569	70	138	24	4	1	35	.243	34	318	450	21	.973
1985	Los Angeles (N.L.)............	2B-3B	136	488	62	136	8	4	1	42	.279	27	330	358	†22	.969
1986	Los Angeles (N.L.)............	2B	·157	633	91	210	43	4	6	56	.332	40	•367	432	16	.980
1987	Los Angeles (N.L.)............	2B-OF-3B	157	610	84	171	22	7	6	46	.280	37	343	420	14	.982
1988	Los Angeles (N.L.)............	2B	160	★632	70	175	19	4	5	57	.277	42	276	429	14	.981
1989	New York (A.L.)■..............	2B	158	•651	88	205	26	3	5	63	.315	43	312	460	10	★.987
1990	New York (A.L.)..............	2B	155	615	70	160	24	2	4	42	.260	43	292	457	10	.987
1991	New York (A.L.)..............	2B-3B	158	652	85	198	38	2	10	56	.304	31	277	454	10	.987
American League totals (3 years)			471	1918	243	563	88	7	19	161	.294	117	881	1371	30	.987
National League totals (8 years)			1091	4312	574	1218	159	35	30	333	.282	292	2376	2973	140	.974
Major league totals (11 years)			1562	6230	817	1781	247	42	49	494	.286	409	3257	4344	170	.978

DIVISION SERIES RECORD

Year	Team (League)	Pos.	G	AB	R	H	2B	3B	HR	RBI	Avg.	SB	PO	A	E	Avg.
1981	Los Angeles (N.L.)............	2B	1	0	0	0	0	0	0	0	...	0	0	0	0	...

CHAMPIONSHIP SERIES RECORD

CHAMPIONSHIP SERIES NOTES: Shares record for most stolen bases in one inning—2 (October 9, 1988, third inning). . . . Holds N.L. single-series records for most runs—7 (1988). . . . Shares N.L. single-series records for most at-bats—30; singles—8; stolen bases—5 (1988). . . . Shares N.L. single-game record for most stolen bases—3 (October 9, 1988, 12 innings).

Year	Team (League)	Pos.	G	AB	R	H	2B	3B	HR	RBI	Avg.	SB	PO	A	E	Avg.
1981	Los Angeles (N.L.)............	2B	1	0	0	0	0	0	0	0	...	0	0	1	0	1.000
1983	Los Angeles (N.L.)............	2B	4	16	0	4	0	0	0	0	.250	1	11	12	0	1.000
1985	Los Angeles (N.L.)............	2B	6	20	1	6	3	0	0	1	.300	0	11	21	0	1.000
1988	Los Angeles (N.L.)............	2B	7	30	7	8	0	0	0	3	.267	5	12	22	0	1.000
Championship Series totals (4 years)			18	66	8	18	3	0	0	4	.273	6	34	56	0	1.000

WORLD SERIES RECORD

Year	Team (League)	Pos.	G	AB	R	H	2B	3B	HR	RBI	Avg.	SB	PO	A	E	Avg.
1981	Los Angeles (N.L.)	PH-PR-2B	2	1	0	0	0	0	0	0	.000	0	0	0	0	...
1988	Los Angeles (N.L.)	2B	5	20	3	6	0	0	0	0	.300	1	11	11	0	1.000
World Series totals (2 years)			7	21	3	6	0	0	0	0	.286	1	11	11	0	1.000

ALL-STAR GAME RECORD

Year	League	Pos.	AB	R	H	2B	3B	HR	RBI	Avg.	SB	PO	A	E	Avg.
1982	National	PR-2B	1	0	1	0	0	0	0	1.000	0	2	0	1	.667
1983	National	2B	3	1	1	0	0	0	1	.333	1	2	0	1	.667
1986	National	2B	1	0	1	0	0	0	1	1.000	1	0	1	0	1.000
1989	American	2B	1	0	0	0	0	0	0	.000	0	1	3	0	1.000
1990	American	2B	1	0	0	0	0	0	0	.000	1	0	1	0	1.000
All-Star Game totals (5 years)			7	1	3	0	0	0	2	.429	3	5	5	2	.833

SCANLAN, BOB
P, CUBS

PERSONAL: Born August 9, 1966, at Los Angeles.... 6-7/215.... Throws right, bats right... Full name: Robert Guy Scanlan Jr.
HIGH SCHOOL: Harvard (North Hollywood, Calif.).
TRANSACTIONS/CAREER NOTES: Selected by Philadelphia Phillies organization in 25th round of free-agent draft (June 4, 1984).... Traded by Phillies with P Chuck McElroy to Chicago Cubs organization for P Mitch Williams (April 7, 1991).
STATISTICAL NOTES: Led International League with 17 wild pitches in 1988.

Year	Team (League)	G	W	L	Pct.	ERA	Sv.	IP	H	R	ER	BB	SO
1984	Sarasota Phillies (Gulf Coast)	13	0	2	.000	6.48	0	33⅓	43	31	24	30	17
1985	Spartanburg (South Atlantic)	26	8	12	.400	4.14	0	152⅓	160	95	70	53	108
1986	Clearwater (Florida State)	24	8	12	.400	4.15	0	125⅔	146	73	58	45	51
1987	Reading (Eastern)	27	*15	5	.750	5.10	0	164	187	98	93	55	91
1988	Maine (International)	28	5	*18	.217	5.59	0	161	181	*110	*100	50	79
1989	Reading (Eastern)	31	6	10	.375	5.78	0	118⅓	124	88	•76	58	63
1990	Scranton/Wilkes-Barre (Int'l)	23	8	1	.889	4.85	0	130	128	79	70	59	74
1991	Iowa (American Association)■	4	2	0	1.000	2.95	0	18⅓	14	8	6	10	15
	Chicago (N.L.)	40	7	8	.467	3.89	1	111	114	60	48	40	44
Major league totals (1 year)		40	7	8	.467	3.89	1	111	114	60	48	40	44

SCHAEFER, JEFF
IF, MARINERS

PERSONAL: Born May 31, 1960, at Patchogue, N.Y. .... 5-10/170. ... Throws right, bats right.... Full name: Jeffrey Scott Schaefer.
HIGH SCHOOL: Patchogue-Medford (Medford, N.Y.).
COLLEGE: Maryland.
TRANSACTIONS/CAREER NOTES: Selected by Baltimore Orioles organization in 12th round of free-agent draft (June 8, 1981)....
Sold by Orioles organization to Edmonton, California Angels organization (January 21, 1986).... On disabled list (May 21-31, 1986).... Drafted by San Antonio, Los Angeles Dodgers organization (December 9, 1986).... Granted free agency (October 15, 1987).... Signed by Vancouver, Chicago White Sox organization (November 16, 1987).... Granted free agency (October 15, 1989).... Signed by Calgary, Seattle Mariners organization (November 13, 1989).
STATISTICAL NOTES: Led Appalachian League second basemen with 365 total chances and 56 double plays in 1981.... Led Southern League second basemen with .982 fielding percentage in 1984.... Led Texas League shortstops with 521 total chances and 73 double plays in 1987.... Led Pacific Coast League shortstops with 679 total chances in 1988.

Year	Team (League)	Pos.	G	AB	R	H	2B	3B	HR	RBI	Avg.	SB	PO	A	E	Avg.
1981	Bluefield (Appalachian)	2B	62	250	45	67	7	2	1	31	.268	17	*170	*189	6	.984
1982	Hagerstown (Carolina)	2B	18	60	4	6	0	0	0	7	.100	1	39	41	3	.964
	Charlotte (Southern)	2-3-0-S	106	331	35	83	15	0	3	32	.251	16	231	232	22	.955
1983	Hagerstown (Carolina)	2B-SS	68	229	32	61	15	4	1	16	.266	8	145	197	7	.980
	Charlotte (Southern)	2B-SS	51	182	20	43	7	2	4	28	.236	4	102	166	11	.961
1984	Rochester (Int'l)	SS-3B-2B	31	91	10	24	5	1	0	3	.264	0	44	84	2	.985
	Charlotte (Southern)	2B-SS-P	99	383	47	90	8	0	4	31	.235	8	249	264	9	†.983
1985	Charlotte (Southern)	S-2-3-0	49	181	19	47	7	1	2	19	.260	6	84	112	7	.966
	Rochester (Int'l)	2B-SS	68	187	17	37	4	0	2	12	.198	1	134	195	5	.985
1986	Midland (Texas)■	SS-2B	114	406	50	109	17	1	6	41	.268	1	192	342	31	.945
1987	San Antonio (Texas)■	SS	101	368	39	112	18	2	0	37	.304	2	165	*330	26	.950
1988	Vancouver (Pac. Coast)■	SS	131	450	53	111	30	2	1	59	.247	7	*227	*417	*35	.948
1989	Vancouver (Pac. Coast)	2B-SS-OF	88	294	32	67	13	2	3	22	.228	10	177	232	10	.976
	Chicago (A.L.)	SS-2B-3B	15	10	2	1	0	0	0	0	.100	1	5	7	2	.857
1990	Calgary (Pacific Coast)■	SS-3B-OF	49	170	24	41	9	2	0	19	.241	8	86	139	8	.966
	Seattle (A.L.)	3B-SS-2B	55	107	11	22	3	0	0	6	.206	4	52	87	5	.965
1991	Seattle (A.L.)	SS-3B-2B	84	164	19	41	7	1	1	11	.250	3	79	120	6	.971
Major league totals (3 years)			154	281	32	64	10	1	1	17	.228	8	136	214	13	.964

RECORD AS PITCHER

Year	Team (League)	G	W	L	Pct.	ERA	Sv.	IP	H	R	ER	BB	SO
1984	Charlotte (Southern)	1	0	0	...	18.00	0	1	2	2	2	2	0

SCHATZEDER, DAN
P

PERSONAL: Born December 1, 1954, at Elmhurst, Ill. . . . 6-0/195. . . . Throws left, bats left. . . . Full name: Daniel Ernest Schatzeder. . . . Name pronounced SHOT-zay-dur.
HIGH SCHOOL: Willowbrook (Villa Park, Ill.).
COLLEGE: Denver (degree in business administration, 1976).

TRANSACTIONS/CAREER NOTES: Selected by Montreal Expos organization in third round of free-agent draft (June 8, 1976). . . . On Denver disabled list (July 5-August 30, 1977). . . . Traded by Expos to Detroit Tigers for OF Ron LeFlore (December 7, 1979). . . . On disabled list (May 27-June 17, 1980). . . . Traded by Tigers with P Mike Chris to San Francisco Giants for OF Larry Herndon (December 9, 1981). . . . Sold by Giants to Expos (June 15, 1982). . . . Granted free agency (November 7, 1983). . . . Re-signed by Expos (December 19, 1983). . . . On Montreal disabled list (June 21-July 23 and August 7-September 1, 1985); included rehabilitation disability assignment to Indianapolis (July 19-23, 1985). . . . Traded by Expos with IF Skeeter Barnes to Philadelphia Phillies for IF Tom Foley and P Lary Sorensen (July 24, 1986). . . . Traded by Phillies with cash to Minnesota Twins for P Danny Clay and 3B Tom Schwarz (June 24, 1987). . . . Released by Twins (December 21, 1987). . . . Signed by Cleveland Indians (February 9, 1988). . . . Released by Indians (June 22, 1988). . . . Signed by Portland, Twins organization (June 27, 1988). . . . Granted free agency (November 4, 1988). . . . Signed by Houston Astros (January 30, 1989). . . . On Houston disabled list (July 19-September 6, 1989); included rehabilitation disability assignment to Tucson (August 18-31, 1989). . . . Granted free agency (November 13, 1989). . . . Re-signed by Astros (December 19, 1989). . . . Traded by Astros to New York Mets for P Steve LaRose and IF Nick Davis (September 10, 1990). . . . Granted free agency (November 5, 1990). . . . Signed by Kansas City Royals (December 4, 1990). . . . Released by Royals (May 29, 1991). . . . Signed by Tidewater, New York Mets organization (June 6, 1991). . . . Released by Tidewater (June 16, 1991).

Year	Team (League)	G	W	L	Pct.	ERA	Sv.	IP	H	R	ER	BB	SO
1976	West Palm Beach (Florida St.) ..	10	5	3	.625	2.67	0	64	49	22	19	20	49
	Quebec City (Eastern)	5	2	3	.400	4.50	0	28	38	16	14	10	19
1977	Quebec City (Eastern)	8	5	3	.625	2.76	0	62	39	20	19	15	59
	Denver (American Assoc.)	9	2	2	.500	6.00	0	36	45	25	24	14	28
	Montreal (N.L.)	6	2	1	.667	2.45	0	22	16	6	6	13	14
1978	Denver (American Assoc.)	4	3	0	1.000	2.89	0	28	24	11	9	11	19
	Montreal (N.L.)	29	7	7	.500	3.06	0	144	108	54	49	68	69
1979	Montreal (N.L.)	32	10	5	.667	2.83	1	162	136	57	51	59	106
1980	Detroit (A.L.)■	32	11	13	.458	4.01	0	193	178	88	86	58	94
1981	Detroit (A.L.)	17	6	8	.429	6.08	0	71	74	49	48	29	20
1982	San Fran.-Montreal (N.L.)■	39	1	6	.143	5.32	0	69⅓	84	46	41	24	33
	Phoenix (Pacific Coast)	1	0	0	. . .	12.27	0	3⅔	10	6	5	3	1
1983	Montreal (N.L.)	58	5	2	.714	3.21	0	87	88	34	31	25	48
1984	Montreal (N.L.)	36	7	7	.500	2.71	1	136	112	44	41	36	89
1985	Montreal (N.L.)	24	3	5	.375	3.80	0	104⅓	101	52	44	31	64
	Indianapolis (Am. Assoc.)	1	0	0	. . .	0.00	0	3	2	0	0	1	3
1986	Montreal-Philadelphia (N.L.)■..	55	6	5	.545	3.26	2	88⅓	81	43	32	35	47
1987	Philadelphia (N.L.)	26	3	1	.750	4.06	0	37⅔	40	21	17	14	28
	Minnesota (A.L.)■	30	3	1	.750	6.39	0	43⅔	64	37	31	18	30
1988	Cleveland-Minnesota (A.L.)■..	25	0	3	.000	6.49	3	26⅓	34	21	19	7	17
	Portland (Pacific Coast)■	13	6	4	.600	2.60	0	86⅔	82	26	25	24	55
1989	Tucson (Pacific Coast)	11	0	2	.000	3.94	1	16	15	8	7	10	15
	Houston (N.L.)■	36	4	1	.800	4.45	1	56⅔	64	33	28	28	46
1990	Houston-New York (N.L.)■....	51	1	3	.250	2.20	0	69⅔	66	23	17	23	39
1991	Kansas City (A.L.)■	8	0	0	. . .	9.45	0	6⅔	11	9	7	7	4
	Tidewater (International)■	9	0	0	. . .	7.36	0	14⅔	22	13	12	13	10
American League totals (5 years)		112	20	25	.444	5.05	3	340⅔	361	204	191	119	165
National League totals (11 years)		392	49	43	.533	3.29	5	977	896	413	357	356	583
Major league totals (15 years)		504	69	68	.504	3.74	8	1317⅔	1257	617	548	475	748

CHAMPIONSHIP SERIES RECORD

Year	Team (League)	G	W	L	Pct.	ERA	Sv.	IP	H	R	ER	BB	SO
1987	Minnesota (A.L.)	2	0	0	. . .	0.00	0	4⅓	2	0	0	0	5

WORLD SERIES RECORD

Year	Team (League)	G	W	L	Pct.	ERA	Sv.	IP	H	R	ER	BB	SO
1987	Minnesota (A.L.)	3	1	0	1.000	6.23	0	4⅓	4	3	3	3	3

SCHEID, RICH
P, WHITE SOX

PERSONAL: Born February 3, 1965, at Staten Island, N.Y. . . . 6-3/185. . . . Throws left, bats left. . . . Full name: Richard Paul Scheid.
COLLEGE: Seton Hall.
TRANSACTIONS/CAREER NOTES: Selected by New York Yankees organization in second round of free-agent draft (June 2, 1986). . . . Traded by Yankees organization with P Bob Tewksbury and P Dean Wilkins to Chicago Cubs organization for P Steve Trout (July 13, 1987). . . . Traded by Cubs to Chicago White Sox organization for P Chuck Mount (December 22, 1989).

Year	Team (League)	G	W	L	Pct.	ERA	Sv.	IP	H	R	ER	BB	SO
1986	Oneonta (New York-Penn)	15	9	3	.750	2.23	0	93	62	30	23	32	100
1987	Fort Lauderdale (Florida St.)	9	7	0	1.000	2.95	0	55	43	25	18	29	49
	Albany-Pittsfield (Eastern)■....	20	4	3	.571	6.16	0	76	88	60	52	52	46
1988	Pittsfield (Eastern)	24	6	6	.500	3.73	1	118⅓	119	58	49	62	75
1989	Iowa (American Association) ...	7	0	0	. . .	4.91	0	7⅓	8	6	4	10	7
	Charlotte (Southern)	17	4	1	.800	4.08	0	46⅓	43	30	21	27	37
1990	Birmingham (Southern)■	25	2	1	.667	2.22	4	44⅔	37	17	11	21	37
	Vancouver (Pacific Coast)	20	2	2	.500	3.20	0	39⅓	37	19	14	24	38
1991	Vancouver (Pacific Coast)	47	6	7	.462	6.08	3	66⅔	65	46	45	33	57

SCHILLING, CURT
P, ASTROS

PERSONAL: Born November 14, 1966, at Phoenix. . . . 6-4/215. . . . Throws right, bats right. . . . Full name: Curtis Montague Schilling.
HIGH SCHOOL: Shadow Mountain (Phoenix).
COLLEGE: Yavapai College (Ariz.).
TRANSACTIONS/CAREER NOTES: Selected by Boston Red Sox organization in second round of free-agent draft (January 14, 1986). . . . Traded by Red Sox organization with OF Brady Anderson to Baltimore Orioles for P Mike Boddicker (July 29, 1988). . . . Traded by Orioles with P Pete Harnisch and OF Steve Finley to Houston Astros for 1B Glenn Davis (January 10, 1991).
STATISTICAL NOTES: Tied for International League lead in games started by pitcher with 27, shutouts with three, complete games with nine and balks with six in 1989.

Year	Team (League)	G	W	L	Pct.	ERA	Sv.	IP	H	R	ER	BB	SO
1986	Elmira (New York-Penn)	16	7	3	.700	2.59	0	93⅔	92	34	27	30	75
1987	Greensboro (South Atlantic)	29	8	*15	.348	3.82	0	184	179	96	78	65	*189
1988	New Britain (Eastern)	21	8	5	.615	2.97	0	106	91	44	35	40	62
	Charlotte (Southern)■............	7	5	2	.714	3.18	0	45⅓	36	19	16	23	32
	Baltimore (A.L.)	4	0	3	.000	9.82	0	14⅔	22	19	16	10	4
1989	Rochester (International)	27	•13	11	.542	3.21	0	*185⅓	176	76	66	59	109
	Baltimore (A.L.)	5	0	1	.000	6.23	0	8⅔	10	6	6	3	6
1990	Rochester (International)	15	4	4	.500	3.92	0	87⅓	95	46	38	25	83
	Baltimore (A.L.)	35	1	2	.333	2.54	3	46	38	13	13	19	32
1991	Houston (N.L.)■	56	3	5	.375	3.81	8	75⅔	79	35	32	39	71
	Tucson (Pacific Coast)	13	0	1	.000	3.42	3	23⅔	16	9	9	12	21
	American League totals (3 years)	44	1	6	.143	4.54	3	69⅓	70	38	35	32	42
	National League totals (1 year) ...	56	3	5	.375	3.81	8	75⅔	79	35	32	39	71
	Major league totals (4 years)	100	4	11	.267	4.16	11	145	149	73	67	71	113

SCHIRALDI, CALVIN
P

PERSONAL: Born June 16, 1962, at Houston. . . . 6-5/215. . . . Throws right, bats right. . . . Full name: Calvin Drew Schiraldi. . . . Name pronounced shur-ALL-dee.
HIGH SCHOOL: Westlake (Austin, Tex.).
COLLEGE: Texas.
TRANSACTIONS/CAREER NOTES: Selected by Chicago White Sox organization in 17th round of free-agent draft (June 3, 1980). . . . Selected by New York Mets organization in first round (27th pick overall) of free-agent draft (June 6, 1983). . . . On New York disabled list (May 15-30, 1985). . . . Traded by Mets with P Wes Gardner, OF John Christensen and OF LaSchelle Tarver to Boston Red Sox for P Bob Ojeda, P Tom McCarthy, P John Mitchell and P Chris Bayer (November 13, 1985). . . . Traded by Red Sox with P Al Nipper to Chicago Cubs for P Lee Smith (December 8, 1987). . . . On disabled list (May 13-28 and August 5-20, 1988). . . . Traded by Cubs with OF Darrin Jackson and a player to be named later to San Diego Padres for OF Marvell Wynne and IF Luis Salazar (August 30, 1989); Padres acquired 1B Phil Stephenson to complete deal (September 5, 1989). . . . Released by Padres (March 30, 1991). . . . Signed by Tucson, Houston Astros organization (April 17, 1991). . . . Traded by Astros to Texas Rangers for a player to be named later (June 20, 1991). . . . Granted free agency (October 16, 1991).
RECORDS/HONORS: Named Texas League Pitcher of the Year (1984).

Year	Team (League)	G	W	L	Pct.	ERA	Sv.	IP	H	R	ER	BB	SO
1983	Jackson (Texas)	7	3	3	.500	5.82	0	38⅔	41	28	25	29	26
	Lynchburg (Carolina)	6	4	1	.800	4.45	0	30⅓	28	16	15	17	41
1984	Jackson (Texas)	23	•14	3	.824	2.88	0	156⅓	118	58	50	69	131
	Tidewater (International)	4	3	1	.750	1.15	0	31⅓	18	6	4	10	24
	New York (N.L.)	5	0	2	.000	5.71	0	17⅓	20	13	11	10	16
1985	Tidewater (International)	17	4	5	.444	3.50	0	100⅓	91	50	39	56	76
	New York (N.L.)	10	2	1	.667	8.89	0	26⅓	43	27	26	11	21
1986	Pawtucket (International)■	31	4	3	.571	2.86	12	44	32	19	14	20	59
	Boston (A.L.)	25	4	2	.667	1.41	9	51	36	8	8	15	55
1987	Boston (A.L.)	62	8	5	.615	4.41	6	83⅔	75	45	41	40	93
1988	Chicago (N.L.)■	29	9	13	.409	4.38	1	166⅓	166	87	81	63	140
1989	Chicago-San Diego (N.L.)■	59	6	7	.462	3.51	4	100	72	40	39	63	71
1990	San Diego (N.L.)	42	3	8	.273	4.41	1	104	105	59	51	60	74
1991	Tucson (Pacific Coast)■	15	3	2	.600	4.47	0	54⅓	62	28	27	21	49
	Texas (A.L.)■	3	0	1	.000	11.57	0	4⅔	5	6	6	5	1
	Oklahoma City (Am. Assoc.)	18	1	2	.333	5.64	0	30⅓	32	19	19	23	24
	American League totals (3 years)	90	12	8	.600	3.55	15	139⅓	116	59	55	60	149
	National League totals (5 years)	145	20	31	.392	4.52	6	414	406	226	208	207	322
	Major league totals (8 years)	235	32	39	.451	4.28	21	553⅓	522	285	263	267	471

CHAMPIONSHIP SERIES RECORD

CHAMPIONSHIP SERIES NOTES: Shares A.L. single-series record for most games pitched—4 (1986).

Year	Team (League)	G	W	L	Pct.	ERA	Sv.	IP	H	R	ER	BB	SO
1986	Boston (A.L.)	4	0	1	.000	1.50	1	6	5	2	1	3	9

WORLD SERIES RECORD

Year	Team (League)	G	W	L	Pct.	ERA	Sv.	IP	H	R	ER	BB	SO
1986	Boston (A.L.)	3	0	2	.000	13.50	1	4	7	7	6	3	2

SCHMIDT, DAVE
P

PERSONAL: Born April 22, 1957, at Niles, Mich. . . . 6-1/194. . . . Throws right, bats right. . . . Full name: David Joseph Schmidt.
HIGH SCHOOL: Granada Hills (Calif.).
COLLEGE: Los Angeles Valley College (Calif.) and UCLA.

TRANSACTIONS/CAREER NOTES: Selected by Texas Rangers organization in 26th round of free-agent draft (June 5, 1979). . . . On disabled list (March 25-May 1, 1983). . . . Traded by Rangers with IF Wayne Tolleson to Chicago White Sox for P Ed Correa, IF Scott Fletcher and a player to be named later (November 25, 1985); Rangers acquired IF Jose Mota to complete deal (December 12, 1985). . . . Released by White Sox (December 19, 1986). . . . Signed by Baltimore Orioles (January 22, 1987). . . . Granted free agency (November 13, 1989). . . . Signed by Montreal Expos (December 13, 1989). . . . On Montreal disabled list (March 29-May 2 and July 26, 1990-remainder of season); included rehabilitation disability assignment to Jacksonville (April 24-29, 1990). . . . Granted free agency (November 5, 1990). . . . Signed by West Palm Beach, Expos organization (April 7, 1991). . . . Released by Expos (August 2, 1991). . . . Signed by Oklahoma City, Rangers organization (August 8, 1991). . . . Released by Rangers organization (October 9, 1991).

Year	Team (League)	G	W	L	Pct.	ERA	Sv.	IP	H	R	ER	BB	SO
1979	—Sarasota Rangers (GCL)	7	2	2	.500	4.20	0	30	30	19	14	8	27
1980	—Asheville (South Atlantic)	12	8	1	.889	1.98	3	91	76	32	20	13	67
	—Tulsa (Texas)	12	4	6	.400	4.44	0	73	90	42	36	28	46
1981	—Tulsa (Texas)	3	1	1	.500	1.88	0	24	17	5	5	6	17
	—Texas (A.L.)	14	0	1	.000	3.09	1	32	31	11	11	11	13
	—Wichita (Texas)	12	2	5	.286	4.86	0	87	90	47	47	26	49
1982	—Texas (A.L.)	33	4	6	.400	3.20	6	109 2/3	118	45	39	25	69
1983	—Texas (A.L.)	31	3	3	.500	3.88	2	46 1/3	42	20	20	14	29
1984	—Texas (A.L.)	43	6	6	.500	2.56	12	70 1/3	69	30	20	20	46
1985	—Texas (A.L.)	51	7	6	.538	3.15	5	85 2/3	81	36	30	22	46
1986	—Chicago (A.L.)■	49	3	6	.333	3.31	8	92 1/3	94	37	34	27	67
1987	—Baltimore (A.L.)■	35	10	5	.667	3.77	1	124	128	57	52	26	70
1988	—Baltimore (A.L.)	41	8	5	.615	3.40	2	129 2/3	129	58	49	38	67
1989	—Baltimore (A.L.)	38	10	13	.435	5.69	0	156 2/3	196	102	99	36	46
1990	—Jacksonville (Southern)■	3	0	1	.000	4.50	0	6	4	3	3	0	4
	—Montreal (N.L.)	34	3	3	.500	4.31	13	48	58	26	23	13	22
1991	—West Palm Beach (Florida St.) ..	9	1	1	.500	3.21	1	14	12	9	5	0	11
	—Ind.-Oklahoma City (A.A.)■.....	24	0	3	.000	2.92	1	37	39	17	12	17	19
	—Montreal (N.L.)	4	0	1	.000	10.38	0	4 1/3	9	5	5	2	3
American League totals (9 years)		335	51	51	.500	3.76	37	846 2/3	888	396	354	219	453
National League totals (2 years)		38	3	4	.429	4.82	13	52 1/3	67	31	28	15	25
Major league totals (11 years)		373	54	55	.495	3.82	50	899	955	427	382	234	478

SCHOFIELD, DICK
SS, ANGELS

PERSONAL: Born November 21, 1962, at Springfield, Ill. . . . 5-10/179. . . . Throws right, bats right. . . . Full name: Richard Craig Schofield. . . . Son of John Richard (Dick) Schofield, major league infielder for seven teams (1953-71).
HIGH SCHOOL: Sacred Heart-Griffin (Springfield, Ill.).
TRANSACTIONS/CAREER NOTES: Selected by California Angels organization in first round (third pick overall) of free-agent draft (June 8, 1981). . . . On disabled list (July 1-24, 1984; July 13-August 11, 1987; April 12-May 6 and August 11-September 21, 1989). . . . On California disabled list (March 31-June 6, 1990); included rehabilitation disability assignment to Edmonton (May 31-June 5, 1990). . . . Granted free agency (November 1, 1991).
STATISTICAL NOTES: Led Pioneer League shortstops with 102 putouts in 1981. . . . Led Pioneer League with 68 bases on balls received in 1981. . . . Led A.L. shortstops with .984 fielding percentage in 1987. . . . Led A.L. shortstops with 125 double plays in 1988.

					—————BATTING—————								———FIELDING———			
Year	Team (League)	Pos.	G	AB	R	H	2B	3B	HR	RBI	Avg.	SB	PO	A	E	Avg.
1981	—Idaho Falls (Pioneer)	SS-2B	66	226	59	63	10	1	6	31	.279	13	†102	201	22	.932
1982	—Danville (Midwest)	SS	92	308	80	111	21	★10	12	53	★.360	17	129	249	23	.943
	—Redwood (California)	SS	33	102	15	25	3	3	1	8	.245	6	35	103	3	.979
	—Spokane (Northwest)	SS-3B	7	30	4	9	4	1	1	12	.300	0	7	20	0	1.000
1983	—Edmonton (Pac. Coast)	SS-3B	139	521	91	148	30	7	16	94	.284	9	220	402	30	.954
	—California (A.L.)	SS	21	54	4	11	2	0	3	4	.204	0	24	67	7	.929
1984	—California (A.L.)	SS	140	400	39	77	10	3	4	21	.193	5	218	420	12	★.982
1985	—California (A.L.)	SS	147	438	50	96	19	3	8	41	.219	11	261	397	25	.963
1986	—California (A.L.)	SS	139	458	67	114	17	6	13	57	.249	23	246	389	18	.972
1987	—California (A.L.)	SS-2B	134	479	52	120	17	3	9	46	.251	19	205	351	9	†.984
1988	—California (A.L.)	SS	155	527	61	126	11	6	6	34	.239	20	278	492	13	★.983
1989	—California (A.L.)	SS	91	302	42	69	11	2	4	26	.228	9	118	276	7	.983
1990	—Edmonton (Pac. Coast)	SS	5	18	4	7	1	0	1	4	.389	0	6	14	1	.952
	—California (A.L.)	SS	99	310	41	79	8	1	1	18	.255	3	170	318	17	.966
1991	—California (A.L.)	SS	134	427	44	96	9	3	0	31	.225	8	186	398	15	.975
Major league totals (9 years)			1060	3395	400	788	104	27	48	278	.232	98	1706	3108	123	.975

CHAMPIONSHIP SERIES RECORD

					—————BATTING—————								———FIELDING———			
Year	Team (League)	Pos.	G	AB	R	H	2B	3B	HR	RBI	Avg.	SB	PO	A	E	Avg.
1986	—California (A.L.)	SS	7	30	4	9	1	0	1	2	.300	1	13	23	2	.947

SCHOOLER, MIKE
P, MARINERS

PERSONAL: Born August 10, 1962, at Anaheim, Calif. . . . 6-3/220. . . . Throws right, bats right. . . . Full name: Michael Ralph Schooler.
HIGH SCHOOL: Garden Grove (Calif.).
COLLEGE: Golden West College (Calif.) and Cal State Fullerton.

Selected by Seattle Mariners organization in second round of free-agent draft (June 3, 1985). . . . On disabled list (August 25, 1990-remainder of season). . . . On Seattle disabled list (March 30-July 8, 1991); included rehabilitation disability assignment to Jacksonville (June 9-July 3, 1991).

Year Team (League)	G	W	L	Pct.	ERA	Sv.	IP	H	R	ER	BB	SO
1985—Bellingham (Northwest)	10	4	3	.571	2.93	0	55⅓	42	24	18	15	48
1986—Wausau (Midwest)	26	12	10	.545	3.35	0	166⅓	166	83	62	44	171
1987—Chattanooga (Southern)	28	13	8	.619	3.96	0	175	183	87	77	48	144
1988—Calgary (Pacific Coast)	26	4	4	.500	3.21	0	33⅔	33	19	12	6	47
—Seattle (A.L.)	40	5	8	.385	3.54	15	48⅓	45	21	19	24	54
1989—Seattle (A.L.)	67	1	7	.125	2.81	33	77	81	27	24	19	69
1990—Seattle (A.L.)	49	1	4	.200	2.25	30	56	47	18	14	16	45
1991—Jacksonville (Southern)	11	1	1	.500	5.56	0	11⅓	13	9	7	3	12
—Seattle (A.L.)	34	3	3	.500	3.67	7	34⅓	25	14	14	10	31
Major league totals (4 years)	190	10	22	.313	2.96	85	215⅔	198	80	71	69	199

SCHOUREK, PETE
P, METS

PERSONAL: Born May 10, 1969, at Austin, Tex. . . . 6-5/195. . . . Throws left, bats left. . . . Full name: Peter Alan Schourek. . . . Name pronounced SHUR-ek.
HIGH SCHOOL: George C. Marshall (Falls Church, Va.).
TRANSACTIONS/CAREER NOTES: Selected by New York Mets organization in second round of free-agent draft (June 2, 1987). . . . On disabled list (June 17, 1988-remainder of season).

Year Team (League)	G	W	L	Pct.	ERA	Sv.	IP	H	R	ER	BB	SO
1987—Kingsport (Appalachian)	12	4	5	.444	3.68	0	78⅓	70	37	32	34	57
1988—						Did not play						
1989—Columbia (South Atlantic)	27	5	9	.357	2.85	1	136	120	66	43	66	131
—St. Lucie (Florida State)	2	0	0	. . .	2.25	0	4	3	1	1	2	4
1990—St. Lucie (Florida State)	5	4	1	.800	0.97	0	37	29	4	4	8	28
—Tidewater (International)	2	1	0	1.000	2.57	0	14	9	4	4	5	14
—Jackson (Texas)	19	11	4	.733	3.04	0	124⅓	109	53	42	39	94
1991—Tidewater (International)	4	1	1	.500	2.52	0	25	18	7	7	10	17
—New York (N.L.)	35	5	4	.556	4.27	2	86⅓	82	49	41	43	67
Major league totals (1 year)	35	5	4	.556	4.27	2	86⅓	82	49	41	43	67

SCHU, RICK
IF, PHILLIES

PERSONAL: Born January 26, 1962, at Philadelphia. . . . 6-0/185. . . . Throws right, bats right. . . . Full name: Richard Spencer Schu. . . . Son of Ken Schu, minor league pitcher (1955-56). . . . Name pronounced SHOO.
HIGH SCHOOL: Del Campo (Carmichael, Calif.).
COLLEGE: Sacramento City College (Calif.).
TRANSACTIONS/CAREER NOTES: Signed as free agent by Philadelphia Phillies organization (November 25, 1980). . . . On disabled list (August 19-September 3, 1987). . . . Traded by Phillies with OF Jeff Stone and OF Keith Hughes to Baltimore Orioles for OF Mike Young and a player to be named later (March 21, 1988); Phillies acquired OF Frank Bellino to complete deal (June 14, 1988). . . . On disabled list (April 22-May 7, June 6-21 and August 12-29, 1988). . . . Sold by Orioles to Detroit Tigers (May 19, 1989). . . . Released by Tigers (December 8, 1989). . . . Signed by Edmonton, California Angels organization (February 5, 1990). . . . Released by Angels (April 1, 1991). . . . Signed by Scranton/Wilkes-Barre, Phillies organization (April 10, 1991). . . . Granted free agency (October 31, 1991). . . . Re-signed by Phillies organization (January 8, 1992).
RECORDS/HONORS: Shares major league record for most doubles in one inning—2 (October 3, 1985, third inning).
STATISTICAL NOTES: Led Pacific Coast League third basemen with 390 total chances in 1984. . . . Led International League with .552 slugging percentage and 49 extra base hits in 1991.

Year Team (League)	Pos.	G	AB	R	H	2B	3B	HR	RBI	Avg.	SB	PO	A	E	Avg.
1981—Bend (Northwest)	3B-2B-SS	68	258	41	69	10	0	2	42	.267	15	55	137	24	.889
1982—Spartanburg (S. Atl.)	3B-2B-SS	125	429	78	117	28	1	12	60	.273	37	157	257	45	.902
1983—Peninsula (Carolina)	3B-SS-2B	122	444	69	119	22	3	14	63	.268	29	82	252	30	.918
—Portland (Pacific Coast)	3B-SS	9	29	7	11	2	1	1	3	.379	0	6	12	2	.900
1984—Portland (Pacific Coast)	3B	140	552	70	166	35	•14	12	82	.301	7	*109	*254	*27	.931
—Philadelphia (N.L.)	3B	17	29	12	8	2	1	2	5	.276	0	7	13	1	.952
1985—Portland (Pacific Coast)	SS-3B	42	150	19	42	8	3	4	22	.280	1	36	91	11	.920
—Philadelphia (N.L.)	3B	112	416	54	105	21	4	7	24	.252	8	86	191	20	.933
1986—Philadelphia (N.L.)	3B	92	208	32	57	10	1	8	25	.274	2	42	94	13	.913
1987—Philadelphia (N.L.)	3B-1B	92	196	24	46	6	3	7	23	.235	0	193	71	10	.964
1988—Baltimore (A.L.)■	3B-1B	89	270	22	69	9	4	4	20	.256	0	94	110	11	.949
1989—Baltimore-Detroit (A.L.)■	3-2-1-S	99	266	25	57	11	0	7	21	.214	1	59	126	12	.939
—Rochester (Int'l)	3B-1B	28	94	11	21	6	1	1	10	.223	3	50	39	5	.947
1990—California (A.L.)■	3-1-0-2	61	157	19	42	8	0	6	14	.268	0	104	81	11	.944
—Edmonton (Pac. Coast)	1B-3B-0F	18	60	8	18	7	0	1	8	.300	0	83	20	2	.981
1991—Scranton/W.B. (Int'l)■	1-3-2-0	106	355	69	114	*30	5	14	57	.321	7	534	69	8	.987
—Philadelphia (N.L.)	3B-1B	17	22	1	2	0	0	2	0	.091	0	15	1	1	.941
American League totals (3 years)		249	693	66	168	28	4	17	55	.242	7	257	317	34	.944
National League totals (5 years)		330	871	123	218	39	9	24	79	.250	10	343	370	45	.941
Major league totals (8 years)		579	1564	189	386	67	13	41	134	.247	17	600	687	79	.942

SCHULZ, JEFF
OF/1B, REDS

PERSONAL: Born June 2, 1961, at Evansville, Ind. . . . 6-1/190. . . . Throws right, bats left. . . . Full name: Jeffrey Alan Schulz.
HIGH SCHOOL: Memorial (Evansville, Ind.).
COLLEGE: Western Kentucky and Indiana State.
TRANSACTIONS/CAREER NOTES: Selected by Kansas City Royals organization in 23rd round of free-agent draft (June 6, 1983). . . . On Kansas City disabled list (August 7-September 5, 1990). . . . Released by Royals (December 3, 1990). . . . Signed by Pittsburgh Pirates organization (January 25, 1991). . . . Granted free agency (October 16, 1991). . . . Signed by Cincinnati Reds organization (November 12, 1991).
STATISTICAL NOTES: Tied for American Association lead with eight sacrifice flies in 1991.

Year	Team (League)	Pos.	G	AB	R	H	2B	3B	HR	RBI	Avg.	SB	PO	A	E	Avg.
1983	—Butte (Pioneer)	OF	61	211	44	69	12	2	7	55	.327	8	59	6	4	.942
1984	—Charleston, S.C. (S. Atl.) ...	OF	69	265	52	89	14	3	5	54	.336	4	115	12	4	.969
	—Fort Myers (Florida St.)	OF	59	204	23	64	10	0	0	26	.314	8	110	10	0	1.000
1985	—Memphis (Southern)	OF	136	488	73	149	15	5	4	53	.305	8	263	12	11	.962
1986	—Omaha (Am. Assoc.)	OF	123	400	40	121	19	4	2	61	.303	0	119	5	5	.961
1987	—Omaha (Am. Assoc.)	OF-1B	99	316	25	81	12	7	4	36	.256	1	163	8	2	.988
1988	—Omaha (Am. Assoc.)	OF	101	359	37	103	20	3	5	41	.287	1	105	7	7	.941
1989	—Omaha (Am. Assoc.)	OF	95	331	31	92	19	5	2	37	.278	2	132	6	3	.979
	—Kansas City (A.L.)	OF	7	9	0	2	0	0	0	1	.222	0	6	0	0	1.000
1990	—Omaha (Am. Assoc.)	OF-1B	69	231	35	69	16	1	4	27	.299	2	86	2	0	1.000
	—Kansas City (A.L.)	OF	30	66	5	17	5	1	0	6	.258	0	33	0	2	.943
1991	—Buffalo (Am. Assoc.)■......	OF-1B	122	437	55	131	20	4	2	54	.300	7	205	11	2	.991
	—Pittsburgh (N.L.)	PH	3	3	0	0	0	0	0	0	.000	0	0	0	0	...
	American League totals (2 years)		37	75	5	19	5	1	0	7	.253	0	39	0	2	.951
	National League totals (1 year)		3	3	0	0	0	0	0	0	.000	0	0	0	0	...
	Major league totals (3 years)		40	78	5	19	5	1	0	7	.244	0	39	0	2	.951

SCIOSCIA, MIKE
C, DODGERS

PERSONAL: Born November 27, 1958, at Upper Darby, Pa. . . . 6-2/220. . . . Throws right, bats left. . . . Full name: Michael Lorri Scioscia. . . . Name pronounced SO-sha.
HIGH SCHOOL: Springfield (Pa.).
COLLEGE: Penn State.
TRANSACTIONS/CAREER NOTES: Selected by Los Angeles Dodgers organization in first round (19th pick overall) of free-agent draft (June 8, 1976). . . . On disabled list (May 19-August 4, 1978; April 10-20, 1980; May 15, 1983-remainder of season; May 6-21, 1984; June 10-July 15, 1986; June 1-16, 1987; and July 5-20, 1991).
RECORDS/HONORS: Named catcher on THE SPORTING NEWS N.L. All-Star team (1990).
STATISTICAL NOTES: Led Midwest League catchers with 20 errors and 12 double plays in 1977. . . . Led Pacific Coast League catchers with 19 double plays and 22 passed balls in 1979. . . . Tied for Pacific Coast League lead in being hit by pitch with seven in 1979. . . . Led N.L. with 11 passed balls in 1981. . . . Led N.L. catchers with 1,016 total chances in 1987, 915 in 1989 and 910 in 1990.

Year	Team (League)	Pos.	G	AB	R	H	2B	3B	HR	RBI	Avg.	SB	PO	A	E	Avg.
1976	—Bellingham (Northwest)....	C	46	151	25	42	6	0	7	26	.278	2	202	35	14	.944
1977	—Clinton (Midwest)	C-1B	121	364	58	92	20	1	7	44	.253	9	764	95	†22	.975
1978	—San Antonio (Texas)	C	58	204	29	61	16	0	2	34	.299	3	214	17	4	.983
1979	—Albuquerque (PCL)	C	143	461	80	155	34	0	3	68	.336	5	★690	★86	★15	.981
1980	—Albuquerque (PCL)	C	52	160	33	53	11	1	3	33	.331	3	207	19	5	.978
	—Los Angeles (N.L.)	C	54	134	8	34	5	1	1	8	.254	1	226	26	2	.992
1981	—Los Angeles (N.L.)	C	93	290	27	80	10	0	2	29	.276	0	493	48	7	.987
1982	—Los Angeles (N.L.)	C	129	365	31	80	11	1	5	38	.219	2	631	57	10	.986
1983	—Los Angeles (N.L.)	C	12	35	3	11	3	0	1	7	.314	0	55	4	0	1.000
1984	—Los Angeles (N.L.)	C	114	341	29	93	18	0	5	38	.273	2	701	64	12	.985
1985	—Los Angeles (N.L.)	C	141	429	47	127	26	3	7	53	.296	3	818	66	•13	.986
1986	—Los Angeles (N.L.)	C	122	374	36	94	18	1	5	26	.251	3	756	64	15	.982
1987	—Los Angeles (N.L.)	C	142	461	44	122	26	1	6	38	.265	7	★925	80	11	.989
1988	—Los Angeles (N.L.)	C	130	408	29	105	18	0	3	35	.257	0	748	63	7	.991
1989	—Los Angeles (N.L.)	C	133	408	40	102	16	0	10	44	.250	0	★822	★82	11	.988
1990	—Los Angeles (N.L.)	C	135	435	46	115	25	0	12	66	.264	4	★842	58	10	.989
1991	—Los Angeles (N.L.)	C	119	345	39	91	16	2	8	40	.264	4	677	51	7	.990
	Major league totals (12 years)		1324	4025	379	1054	192	9	65	422	.262	26	7694	663	105	.988

DIVISION SERIES RECORD

Year	Team (League)	Pos.	G	AB	R	H	2B	3B	HR	RBI	Avg.	SB	PO	A	E	Avg.
1981	—Los Angeles (N.L.)	C	4	13	0	2	0	0	0	1	.154	0	21	3	0	1.000

CHAMPIONSHIP SERIES RECORD

Year	Team (League)	Pos.	G	AB	R	H	2B	3B	HR	RBI	Avg.	SB	PO	A	E	Avg.
1981	—Los Angeles (N.L.)	C	5	15	1	2	0	0	1	1	.133	0	27	1	0	1.000
1985	—Los Angeles (N.L.)	C	6	16	2	4	0	0	0	1	.250	0	31	4	1	.972
1988	—Los Angeles (N.L.)	C	7	22	3	8	1	0	1	2	.364	0	37	4	0	1.000
	Championship Series totals (3 years)		18	53	6	14	1	0	2	4	.264	0	95	9	1	.990

Year	Team (League)	Pos.	G	AB	R	H	2B	3B	HR	RBI	Avg.	SB	PO	A	E	Avg.
1981—Los Angeles (N.L.)...........		C-PH	3	4	1	1	0	0	0	0	.250	0	7	1	0	1.000
1988—Los Angeles (N.L.)...........		C	4	14	0	3	0	0	0	1	.214	0	28	0	1	.966
World Series totals (2 years)			7	18	1	4	0	0	0	1	.222	0	35	1	1	.973

ALL-STAR GAME RECORD

Year	League	Pos.	AB	R	H	2B	3B	HR	RBI	Avg.	SB	PO	A	E	Avg.
1989—National		C	1	0	0	0	0	0	0	.000	0	3	0	0	1.000
1990—National		C	2	0	0	0	0	0	0	.000	0	6	0	0	1.000
All-Star Game totals (2 years)			3	0	0	0	0	0	0	.000	0	9	0	0	1.000

SCOTT, DONNIE
C/1B

PERSONAL: Born August 16, 1961, at Dunedin, Fla. . . . 5-11/200. . . . Throws right, bats both. . . . Full name: Donald Malcolm Scott.
HIGH SCHOOL: Tampa Catholic (Fla.).
TRANSACTIONS/CAREER NOTES: Selected by Texas Rangers organization in second round of free-agent draft (June 5, 1979). . . . Traded by Rangers to Seattle Mariners organization for C Orlando Mercado (April 4, 1985). . . . Released by Mariners (March 20, 1986). . . . Signed by Rochester, Baltimore Orioles organization (March 29, 1986). . . . Released by Orioles organization (April 7, 1987). . . . Signed by El Paso, Milwaukee Brewers organization (May 6, 1987). . . . Granted free agency (October 22, 1988). . . . Signed by Brewers organization (January 23, 1989). . . . Granted free agency (October 15, 1989). . . . Signed by Nashville, Cincinnati Reds organization (November 6, 1989). . . . On Nashville disabled list (April 22-May 6, and August 5-12, 1991). . . . On Cincinnati voluntarily retired list (October 7, 1991). . . . Named manager of Billings (Reds organization) of Pioneer League for 1992.
STATISTICAL NOTES: Led South Atlantic League with 41 passed balls and tied for lead in double plays by catchers with seven in 1980. . . . Led Texas League with 21 passed balls in 1982. . . . Led American Association with 22 passed balls in 1983. . . . Led A.L. with 18 passed balls in 1984. . . . Switch-hit home runs in one game (April 29, 1985).

Year	Team (League)	Pos.	G	AB	R	H	2B	3B	HR	RBI	Avg.	SB	PO	A	E	Avg.
1979—Sarasota Rangers (GCL) ...		C-OF	45	146	18	45	7	1	1	29	.308	4	190	19	4	*.981
1980—Asheville (S. Atlantic)		C	115	421	57	124	22	1	13	78	.295	0	593	*81	17	.975
1981—Tulsa (Texas)		C-3B-OF	114	385	44	91	16	2	5	41	.236	4	509	103	19	.970
1982—Tulsa (Texas)		C-3B	108	367	55	104	19	3	12	61	.283	1	537	75	*21	.967
1983—Oklahoma City (A.A.)		C	112	371	44	94	14	3	4	54	.253	0	596	*74	12	.982
—Texas (A.L.)		C	2	4	0	0	0	0	0	0	.000	0	8	2	0	1.000
1984—Oklahoma City (A.A.)		C	46	168	25	55	14	2	3	25	.327	0	222	46	4	.985
—Texas (A.L.)		C	81	235	16	52	9	0	3	20	.221	0	400	41	12	.974
1985—Calgary (Pacific Coast)■..		C	7	26	6	12	3	1	0	9	.462	0	39	5	3	.936
—Seattle (A.L.)		C	80	185	18	41	13	0	4	23	.222	1	277	31	6	.981
1986—Rochester (Int'l)■.............		C-3B	59	173	17	47	7	1	1	16	.272	0	306	22	3	.991
1987—El Paso (Texas)■.............		C	5	20	4	9	0	0	1	1	.450	0	27	5	1	.970
—Denver (Am. Assoc.)		C-1B	65	196	21	44	8	4	3	33	.224	0	217	24	5	.980
1988—Denver (Am. Assoc.)		C	29	68	3	14	2	0	0	3	.206	0	84	11	3	.969
—El Paso (Texas)		C-3B	13	50	15	17	0	1	1	7	.340	1	69	14	0	1.000
1989—Denver (Am. Assoc.)		C-3B	111	330	36	84	15	0	3	31	.255	4	546	22	12	.979
1990—Nashville (Am. Assoc.)■..		C-1B	78	243	36	55	12	3	0	21	.226	0	356	55	6	.986
1991—Nashville (Am. Assoc.) ...		C-3B-OF	84	225	19	40	8	0	3	18	.178	0	411	49	12	.975
—Cincinnati (N.L.)		C	10	19	0	3	0	0	0	0	.158	0	19	0	0	1.000
American League totals (3 years)			163	424	34	93	22	0	7	43	.219	1	685	74	18	.977
National League totals (1 year)			10	19	0	3	0	0	0	0	.158	0	19	0	0	1.000
Major league totals (4 years)			173	443	34	96	22	0	7	43	.217	1	704	74	18	.977

SCOTT, GARY
3B, CUBS

PERSONAL: Born August 22, 1968, at New Rochelle, N.Y. . . . 6-0/175. . . . Throws right, bats right. . . . Full name: Gary Thomas Scott.
HIGH SCHOOL: John Bowne (Flushing, N.Y.).
COLLEGE: Villanova.
TRANSACTIONS/CAREER NOTES: Selected by Chicago Cubs organization in second round of free-agent draft (June 5, 1989). . . . On Iowa disabled list (July 31, 1991-remainder of season).

Year	Team (League)	Pos.	G	AB	R	H	2B	3B	HR	RBI	Avg.	SB	PO	A	E	Avg.
1989—Geneva (N.Y.-Penn)		3B	48	175	33	49	10	1	10	42	.280	4	23	69	14	.868
1990—Winston-Salem (Caro.)		3B	102	380	63	112	22	0	12	70	.295	17	63	184	29	.895
—Charlotte (Southern)		3B	35	143	21	44	9	0	4	17	.308	4	25	102	8	.941
1991—Chicago (N.L.)		3B	31	79	8	13	3	0	1	5	.165	0	13	50	2	.969
—Iowa (American Assoc.) ...		3B-SS	63	231	21	48	10	2	3	34	.208	0	47	116	8	.953
Major league totals (1 year)			31	79	8	13	3	0	1	5	.165	0	13	50	2	.969

SCOTT, MIKE
P

PERSONAL: Born April 26, 1955, at Santa Monica, Calif. . . . 6-3/215. . . . Throws right, bats right. . . . Full name: Michael Warren Scott.
HIGH SCHOOL: Hawthorne (Calif.).
COLLEGE: Pepperdine.

TRANSACTIONS/CAREER NOTES: Selected by New York Mets organization in second round of free-agent draft (June 8, 1976)....
Traded by Mets to Houston Astros for OF-1B Danny Heep (December 10, 1982).... On disabled list (April 5-May 4, 1983; June
22-July 13, 1988; and April 14, 1991-remainder of season).... On voluntarily retired list (November 18, 1991).
RECORDS/HONORS: Shares major league record for most strikeouts in one inning—4 (September 3, 1986, fifth inning)....
Named N.L. Pitcher of the Year by THE SPORTING NEWS (1986).... Named righthanded pitcher on THE SPORTING NEWS
N.L. All-Star team (1986 and 1989).... Named N.L. Cy Young Award winner by Baseball Writers' Association of America
(1986).
STATISTICAL NOTES: Led Texas League with 14 complete games and tied for lead with three balks in 1977.... Tied for Interna-
tional League lead in games started by pitcher with 29 in 1978.... Tied for International League lead with three balks in 1980.
... Pitched 2-0 no-hit victory against San Francisco Giants (September 25, 1986).... Tied for N.L. lead with five shutouts in
1986.... Tied for N.L. lead in games started by pitcher with 36 in 1987.

Year	Team (League)	G	W	L	Pct.	ERA	Sv.	IP	H	R	ER	BB	SO
1976	—Jackson (Texas)	7	3	3	.500	2.86	0	44	34	20	14	14	19
1977	—Jackson (Texas)	25	*14	10	.583	2.94	0	*187	132	77	61	55	97
	—Tidewater (International)	2	0	1	.000	18.00	0	2	4	5	4	3	0
1978	—Tidewater (International)	29	10	10	.500	3.94	0	192	196	105	84	83	93
1979	—Tidewater (International)	18	8	4	.667	3.18	0	99	103	37	35	27	40
	—New York (N.L.)	18	1	3	.250	5.37	0	52	59	35	31	20	21
1980	—Tidewater (International)	27	13	7	.650	2.96	0	170	165	69	56	64	88
	—New York (N.L.)	6	1	1	.500	4.34	0	29	40	14	14	8	13
1981	—New York (N.L.)	23	5	10	.333	3.90	0	136	130	65	59	34	54
1982	—New York (N.L.)	37	7	13	.350	5.14	3	147	185	100	84	60	63
1983	—Houston (N.L.)■	24	10	6	.625	3.72	0	145	143	67	60	46	73
1984	—Houston (N.L.)	31	5	11	.313	4.68	0	154	179	96	80	43	83
1985	—Houston (N.L.)	36	18	8	.692	3.29	0	221⅔	194	91	81	80	137
1986	—Houston (N.L.)	37	18	10	.643	*2.22	0	*275⅓	182	73	68	72	*306
1987	—Houston (N.L.)	36	16	13	.552	3.23	0	247⅔	199	94	89	79	233
1988	—Houston (N.L.)	32	14	8	.636	2.92	0	218⅔	162	74	71	53	190
1989	—Houston (N.L.)	33	*20	10	.667	3.10	0	229	180	87	79	62	172
1990	—Houston (N.L.)	32	9	13	.409	3.81	0	205⅔	194	102	87	66	121
1991	—Houston (N.L.)	2	0	2	.000	12.86	0	7	11	10	10	4	3
Major league totals (13 years)		347	124	108	.534	3.54	3	2068	1858	908	813	627	1469

CHAMPIONSHIP SERIES RECORD

CHAMPIONSHIP SERIES NOTES: Shares single-series records for most complete games—2 (1986).... Shares single-game
record for most strikeouts—14; consecutive strikeouts—4 (October 8, 1986).... Shares N.L. career record for most complete
games—2.

Year	Team (League)	G	W	L	Pct.	ERA	Sv.	IP	H	R	ER	BB	SO
1986	—Houston (N.L.)	2	2	0	1.000	0.50	0	18	8	1	1	1	19

ALL-STAR GAME RECORD

ALL-STAR GAME NOTES: Named to N.L. All-Star team for 1989 game; replaced due to injury by Rick Sutcliffe.

Year	League	W	L	Pct.	ERA	Sv.	IP	H	R	ER	BB	SO
1986	—National	0	0	...	9.00	0	1	1	1	1	0	2
1987	—National	0	0	...	0.00	0	2	1	0	0	0	1
All-Star totals (2 years)		0	0	...	3.00	0	3	2	1	1	0	3

SCOTT, TIM
P, PADRES

PERSONAL: Born November 16, 1966, at Hanford, Calif.... 6-2/185.... Throws right, bats right....
Full name: Timothy Dale Scott.
HIGH SCHOOL: Hanford (Calif.).
TRANSACTIONS/CAREER NOTES: Selected by Los Angeles Dodgers organization in second round of
free-agent draft (June 4, 1984).... On disabled list (July 23, 1985-remainder of season and April 11-May 15, 1986)....
Granted free agency (October 15, 1990).... Signed by San Diego Padres organization (November 1, 1990).

Year	Team (League)	G	W	L	Pct.	ERA	Sv.	IP	H	R	ER	BB	SO
1984	—Great Falls (Pioneer)	13	5	4	.556	4.38	0	78	90	58	38	44	38
1985	—Bakersfield (California)	12	3	4	.429	5.80	0	63⅔	84	46	41	28	31
1986	—Vero Beach (Florida State)	20	5	4	.556	3.40	0	95⅓	113	44	36	24	37
1987	—Bakersfield (California)	7	2	3	.400	4.45	0	32⅓	33	19	16	10	29
	—San Antonio (Texas)	2	0	1	.000	16.88	0	5⅓	14	10	10	2	6
1988	—Bakersfield (California)	36	4	7	.364	3.64	7	64⅓	52	34	26	26	59
1989	—San Antonio (Texas)	48	4	2	.667	3.71	4	68	71	30	28	36	64
1990	—San Antonio (Texas)	30	3	3	.500	2.85	7	47⅓	35	17	15	14	52
	—Albuquerque (Pacific Coast)	17	2	1	.667	4.20	3	15	14	9	7	14	15
1991	—Las Vegas (Pacific Coast)■	41	8	8	.500	5.19	0	111	133	78	64	39	74
	—San Diego (N.L.)	2	0	0	...	9.00	0	1	2	2	1	0	1
Major league totals (1 year)		2	0	0	...	9.00	0	1	2	2	1	0	1

SCRUGGS, TONY
OF, RANGERS

PERSONAL: Born March 19, 1966, at Riverside, Calif.... 6-1/210.... Throws right, bats
right.... Full name: Anthony Raymond Scruggs.
HIGH SCHOOL: Palo Alto (Calif.).
COLLEGE: UCLA.

TRANSACTIONS/CAREER NOTES: Selected by California Angels organization in seventh round of free-agent draft (June 2, 1986). . . . Selected by Texas Rangers organization in seventh round of free-agent draft (June 2, 1987). . . . On Oklahoma City disabled list (July 19-September 6, 1991).

Year	Team (League)	Pos.	G	AB	R	H	2B	3B	HR	RBI	Avg.	SB	PO	A	E	Avg.
1987	—Sarasota Rangers (GCL)...	OF	30	119	24	41	5	0	6	24	.345	12	39	6	2	.957
	—Charlotte (Florida State)...	OF	23	86	14	28	4	0	3	11	.326	4	41	1	5	.894
1988	—Sarasota Rangers (GCL)...	OF	5	12	1	1	0	0	0	0	.083	1	4	0	0	1.000
	—Charlotte (Florida State)...	OF	67	240	35	70	11	4	6	42	.292	6	119	4	6	.953
1989	—Tulsa (Texas)	OF	60	195	19	38	3	3	1	21	.195	3	108	4	1	.991
	—Charlotte (Florida State)...	OF	60	197	29	58	9	4	3	34	.294	15	100	7	3	.973
1990	—Gastonia (S. Atlantic)	OF	75	274	50	84	16	0	8	48	.307	20	118	0	5	.959
	—Tulsa (Texas)	OF	53	195	28	67	5	6	4	37	.344	4	112	2	1	.991
1991	—Texas (A.L.)	OF	5	6	1	0	0	0	0	0	.000	0	5	0	0	1.000
	—Oklahoma City (A.A.)	OF	53	182	19	37	4	0	3	21	.203	4	128	1	0	1.000
Major league totals (1 year)			5	6	1	0	0	0	0	0	.000	0	5	0	0	1.000

SCUDDER, SCOTT
P, INDIANS

PERSONAL: Born February 14, 1968, at Paris, Tex. . . . 6-2/185. . . . Throws right, bats right. . . . Full name: William Scott Scudder.
HIGH SCHOOL: Prairieland (Pattonville, Tex.).
TRANSACTIONS/CAREER NOTES: Selected by Cincinnati Reds organization in first round (17th pick overall) of free-agent draft (June 2, 1986). . . . On disabled list (May 31-June 17 and June 27-August 17, 1991). . . . Traded by Reds with P Jack Armstrong and P Joe Turek to Cleveland Indians for P Greg Swindell (November 15, 1991).
STATISTICAL NOTES: Pitched 4-0 no-hit victory against Wausau (May 20, 1988).

Year	Team (League)	G	W	L	Pct.	ERA	Sv.	IP	H	R	ER	BB	SO
1986	—Billings (Pioneer)	12	1	3	.250	4.78	0	52⅔	43	34	28	36	38
1987	—Cedar Rapids (Midwest)	26	7	12	.368	4.10	0	153⅔	129	86	70	76	128
1988	—Cedar Rapids (Midwest)	16	7	3	.700	2.02	0	102⅓	61	30	23	41	126
	—Chattanooga (Southern)	11	7	0	1.000	2.96	0	70	53	24	23	30	52
1989	—Nashville (American Assoc.)	12	6	2	.750	2.68	0	80⅔	54	27	24	48	64
	—Cincinnati (N.L.)	23	4	9	.308	4.49	0	100⅓	91	54	50	61	66
1990	—Nashville (American Assoc.)	11	7	1	.875	2.34	0	80⅔	53	27	21	32	60
	—Cincinnati (N.L.)	21	5	5	.500	4.90	0	71⅔	74	41	39	30	42
1991	—Cincinnati (N.L.)	27	6	9	.400	4.35	1	101⅓	91	52	49	56	51
Major league totals (3 years)		71	15	23	.395	4.54	1	273⅓	256	147	138	147	159

CHAMPIONSHIP SERIES RECORD

Year	Team (League)	G	W	L	Pct.	ERA	Sv.	IP	H	R	ER	BB	SO
1990	—Cincinnati (N.L.)	1	0	0	. . .	0.00	0	1	1	0	0	0	1

WORLD SERIES RECORD

Year	Team (League)	G	W	L	Pct.	ERA	Sv.	IP	H	R	ER	BB	SO
1990	—Cincinnati (N.L.)	1	0	0	. . .	0.00	0	1⅓	0	0	0	2	2

SEANEZ, RUDY
P, DODGERS

PERSONAL: Born October 20, 1968, at Brawley, Calif. . . . 5-10/185. . . . Throws right, bats right. . . . Full name: Rudy Caballero Seanez.
HIGH SCHOOL: Brawley Union (Calif.).
TRANSACTIONS/CAREER NOTES: Selected by Cleveland Indians organization in fourth round of free-agent draft (June 10, 1986). . . . On disabled list (May 4-July 11 and August 9-29, 1987). . . . On Cleveland disabled list (April 1-16 and July 30-September 2, 1991); included rehabilitation disability assignment to Colorado Springs (August 14-September 2, 1991). . . . Traded by Indians to Los Angeles Dodgers for P Dennis Cook and P Mike Christopher (December 10, 1991).
STATISTICAL NOTES: Pitched 4-0 no-hit victory against Pulaski (August 2, 1986).

Year	Team (League)	G	W	L	Pct.	ERA	Sv.	IP	H	R	ER	BB	SO
1986	—Burlington (Appalachian)	13	5	2	.714	3.20	0	76	59	37	27	32	56
1987	—Waterloo (Midwest)	10	0	4	.000	6.75	0	34⅔	35	29	26	23	23
1988	—Waterloo (Midwest)	22	6	6	.500	4.69	0	113⅓	98	69	59	68	93
1989	—Kinston (Carolina)	25	8	10	.444	4.14	0	113	94	66	52	★111	149
	—Colorado Springs (Pac. Coast) ..	1	0	0	. . .	0.00	0	1	1	0	0	0	0
	—Cleveland (A.L.)	5	0	0	. . .	3.60	0	5	1	2	2	4	7
1990	—Canton/Akron (Eastern)	15	1	0	1.000	2.16	5	16⅔	9	4	4	12	27
	—Cleveland (A.L.)	24	2	1	.667	5.60	0	27⅓	22	17	17	25	24
	—Colorado Springs (Pac. Coast) ..	12	1	4	.200	6.75	1	12	15	10	9	10	7
1991	—Colorado Springs (Pac. Coast) ..	16	0	0	. . .	7.27	0	17⅓	17	14	14	22	19
	—Canton/Akron (Eastern)	25	4	2	.667	2.58	7	38⅓	17	12	11	30	73
	—Cleveland (A.L.)	5	0	0	. . .	16.20	0	5	10	12	9	7	7
Major league totals (3 years)		34	2	1	.667	6.75	0	37⅓	33	31	28	36	38

SEARCY, STEVE
P, PHILLIES

PERSONAL: Born June 4, 1964, at Knoxville, Tenn. . . . 6-1/195. . . . Throws left, bats left. . . . Full name: William Stephen Searcy.
COLLEGE: Tennessee.
TRANSACTIONS/CAREER NOTES: Selected by Detroit Tigers organization in third round of free-

agent draft (June 3, 1985).... On Detroit disabled list (March 27-May 5, 1989).... Granted free agency (July 12, 1991)....
Signed by Philadelphia Phillies (July 15, 1991).
RECORDS/HONORS: Named International League Pitcher of the Year (1988).
STATISTICAL NOTES: Tied for Eastern League lead in games started by pitcher with 27 in 1986.... Led International League with
12 hit batsmen in 1988.

Year	Team (League)	G	W	L	Pct.	ERA	Sv.	IP	H	R	ER	BB	SO
1985	—Bristol (Appalachian)	4	1	1	.500	2.05	0	22	15	6	5	2	24
	—Birmingham (Southern)	7	2	2	.500	3.19	0	36⅔	39	17	13	23	19
1986	—Glens Falls (Eastern)	27	11	6	.647	3.30	0	172	166	79	63	74	*139
1987	—Toledo (International)	10	3	4	.429	4.22	0	53⅓	49	26	25	32	54
1988	—Toledo (International)	27	•13	7	.650	2.59	0	170	131	61	49	79	*176
	—Detroit (A.L.)	2	0	2	.000	5.63	0	8	8	6	5	4	5
1989	—Toledo (International)	9	2	3	.400	7.54	0	37	41	36	31	37	26
	—Lakeland (Florida State)	9	2	3	.400	2.56	0	52⅔	40	21	15	33	44
	—Detroit (A.L.)	8	1	1	.500	6.04	0	22⅓	27	16	15	12	11
1990	—Toledo (International)	17	10	5	.667	2.92	0	104⅔	71	40	34	52	105
	—Detroit (A.L.)	16	2	7	.222	4.66	0	75⅓	76	44	39	51	66
1991	—Detroit (A.L.)	16	1	2	.333	8.41	0	40⅔	52	40	38	30	32
	—Philadelphia (N.L.)■	18	2	1	.667	4.15	0	30⅓	29	16	14	14	21
American League totals (4 years)		42	4	12	.250	5.97	0	146⅓	163	106	97	97	114
National League totals (1 year)		18	2	1	.667	4.15	0	30⅓	29	16	14	14	21
Major league totals (4 years)		60	6	13	.316	5.65	0	176⅔	192	122	111	111	135

SEGUI, DAVID
1B/OF, ORIOLES

PERSONAL: Born July 19, 1966, at Kansas City, Kan.... 6-1/200.... Throws left, bats both....
Full name: David Vincent Segui.... Son of Diego Segui, major league pitcher for five teams
(1962-75 and 1977); and brother of Dan Segui, infielder in New York Mets organization.
HIGH SCHOOL: Bishop Ward (Kansas City, Kan.).
COLLEGE: Kansas City Community College (Kan.) and Louisiana Tech.
TRANSACTIONS/CAREER NOTES: Selected by Baltimore Orioles organization in 18th round of free-agent draft (June 2, 1987)....
On Rochester disabled list (April 19-26, 1991).

Year	Team (League)	Pos.	G	AB	R	H	2B	3B	HR	RBI	Avg.	SB	PO	A	E	Avg.
1988	—Hagerstown (Carolina)	1B-OF	60	190	35	51	12	4	3	31	.268	0	342	25	9	.976
1989	—Frederick (Carolina)	1B	83	284	43	90	19	0	10	50	.317	2	707	47	4	.995
	—Hagerstown (Eastern)	1B	44	173	22	56	14	1	1	27	.324	0	381	30	1	.998
1990	—Rochester (Int'l)	1B-OF	86	307	55	103	28	0	2	51	.336	5	704	62	3	.996
	—Baltimore (A.L.)	1B	40	123	14	30	7	0	2	15	.244	5	283	26	3	.990
1991	—Rochester (Int'l)	1B-OF	28	96	9	26	2	0	1	10	.271	1	165	15	0	1.000
	—Baltimore (A.L.)	OF-1B	86	212	15	59	7	0	2	22	.278	1	264	23	3	.990
Major league totals (2 years)			126	335	29	89	14	0	4	37	.266	6	547	49	6	.990

SEGURA, JOSE
P, REDS

PERSONAL: Born January 26, 1963, at Fundacion, Dominican Republic.... 5-11/180....
Throws right, bats right.... Full name: Jose Altagracia Mota Segura.... Name pronounced
suh-GOOR-uh.
HIGH SCHOOL: Cuba Jai (Fundacion, Dominican Republic).
TRANSACTIONS/CAREER NOTES: Signed as a free agent by Philadelphia Phillies organization (June 22, 1981).... Drafted by Syracuse, Toronto Blue Jays organization (December 6, 1983).... On disabled list (July 14, 1986-August 9, 1986).... Granted
free agency (October 15, 1987).... Signed by Chicago White Sox (January 29, 1988).... Released by White Sox organization
(November 20, 1988).... Re-signed by White Sox organization (December 22, 1988).... On disabled list (August 13, 1990-
remainder of season).... Granted free agency (September 4, 1990).... Signed by San Francisco Giants organization (November 26, 1990).... Granted free agency (October 15, 1991).... Signed by Nashville, Cincinnati Reds organization (January
7, 1992).

Year	Team (League)	G	W	L	Pct.	ERA	Sv.	IP	H	R	ER	BB	SO
1981	—Helena (Pioneer)	25	2	3	.400	4.37	4	35	42	26	17	15	27
1982	—Spartanburg (South Atlantic)	20	2	2	.500	7.76	4	29	32	28	25	18	17
	—Bend (Northwest)	24	4	4	.500	1.72	3	36⅔	27	16	7	28	43
1983	—Spartanburg (South Atlantic)	40	1	6	.143	6.44	5	65⅔	77	59	47	42	54
1984	—Kinston (Carolina)■	16	7	4	.636	3.98	0	97⅓	88	48	43	35	55
	—Knoxville (Southern)	12	4	6	.400	4.43	0	69	75	47	34	47	26
1985	—Kinston (Carolina)	34	4	•13	.235	4.16	1	110⅓	109	62	51	69	73
1986	—Knoxville (Southern)	24	4	7	.364	4.22	2	106⅔	101	72	50	72	55
1987	—Syracuse (International)	43	5	8	.385	6.56	4	107	136	90	78	59	54
1988	—Chicago (A.L.)■	4	0	0	...	13.50	0	8⅔	19	17	13	8	2
	—Vancouver (Pacific Coast)	20	6	6	.500	4.54	0	111	127	69	56	60	39
1989	—Vancouver (Pacific Coast)	44	1	2	.333	2.30	17	66⅔	50	21	17	19	52
	—Chicago (A.L.)	7	0	1	.000	15.00	0	6	13	11	10	3	4
1990	—Vancouver (Pacific Coast)	40	1	3	.250	5.10	8	54⅔	49	34	31	35	47
1991	—Phoenix (Pacific Coast)■	32	5	5	.500	3.43	4	39⅓	46	15	15	17	21
	—San Francisco (N.L.)	11	0	1	.000	4.41	0	16⅓	20	11	8	5	10
American League totals (2 years)		11	0	1	.000	14.11	0	14⅔	32	28	23	11	6
National League totals (1 year)		11	0	1	.000	4.41	0	16⅓	20	11	8	5	10
Major league totals (3 years)		22	0	2	.000	9.00	0	31	52	39	31	16	16

SEITZER, KEVIN
3B, ROYALS

PERSONAL: Born March 26, 1962, at Springfield, Ill. . . . 5-11/190. . . . Throws right, bats right. . . . Full name: Kevin Lee Seitzer.
HIGH SCHOOL: Lincoln (Ill.).
COLLEGE: Eastern Illinois (bachelor of science degree in industrial electronics).
TRANSACTIONS/CAREER NOTES: Selected by Kansas City Royals organization in 11th round of free-agent draft (June 6, 1983). . . . On disabled list (April 27-May 31, 1991).
RECORDS/HONORS: Named South Atlantic League Most Valuable Player (1984).
STATISTICAL NOTES: Led Pioneer League third basemen with 122 assists and 172 total chances in 1983. . . . Led South Atlantic League third basemen with 409 total chances in 1984. . . . Led South Atlantic League with 118 bases on balls received in 1984. . . . Tied for American Association lead in being hit by pitch with nine in 1986. . . . Collected six hits in one game (August 2, 1987). . . . Led A.L. third basemen with 22 errors in 1987 and 26 in 1988.

														BATTING									FIELDING	
Year	Team (League)	Pos.	G	AB	R	H	2B	3B	HR	RBI	Avg.	SB	PO	A	E	Avg.
1983—Butte (Pioneer)		3B-SS	68	238	60	82	14	1	2	45	.345	11	52 †124	21	.893
1984—Charleston, S.C. (S. Atl.) ...		3B	•141	489	*96	•145	26	5	8	79	.297	23	80 *279	*50	.878
1985—Fort Myers (Florida St.)		1B-3B	90	290	61	91	10	5	3	46	.314	28	569	88	9	.986
—Memphis (Southern)		3B-1B-OF	52	187	26	65	6	2	1	20	.348	9	79	51	10	.929
1986—Memphis (Southern)		1B	4	11	4	3	0	0	0	1	.273	2	28	3	1	.969
—Omaha (Am. Assoc.)		OF-1B-3B	129	432	86	138	20	11	13	74	.319	20	338	39	9	.977
—Kansas City (A.L.)		1B-OF-3B	28	96	16	31	4	1	2	11	.323	0	224	19	3	.988
1987—Kansas City (A.L.)		3B-1B-OF	161	641	105	•207	33	8	15	83	.323	12	290	315	†24	.962
1988—Kansas City (A.L.)		3B-OF	149	559	90	170	32	5	5	60	.304	10	93	297	†26	.938
1989—Kansas City (A.L.)		3-S-0-1	160	597	78	168	17	2	4	48	.281	17	118	277	20	.952
1990—Kansas City (A.L.)		3B-2B	158	622	91	171	31	5	6	38	.275	7	118	281	19	.955
1991—Kansas City (A.L.)		3B	85	234	28	62	11	3	1	25	.265	4	45	127	11	.940
Major league totals (6 years)			741	2749	408	809	128	24	33	265	.294	50	888	1316	103	.955

ALL-STAR GAME RECORD

					BATTING								FIELDING	
Year	League	Pos.	AB	R	H	2B	3B	HR	RBI	Avg.	SB	PO	A	E	Avg.
1987—American		3B	2	0	0	0	0	0	0	.000	0	0	0	0	...

SEMINARA, FRANK
P, PADRES

PERSONAL: Born May 16, 1967, at Brooklyn, N.Y. . . . 6-2/205. . . . Throws right, bats right. . . . Full name: Frank Peter Seminara. . . . Name pronounced SEM-ah-NAIR-ah.
COLLEGE: Columbia.
TRANSACTIONS/CAREER NOTES: Selected by New York Yankees organization in 12th round of free-agent draft (June 1, 1988). . . . Drafted by San Diego Padres (December 3, 1990).
RECORDS/HONORS: Named Carolina League Pitcher of the Year (1990).
STATISTICAL NOTES: Led Texas League with six complete games and tied for lead with nine hit batsmen and games started by pitcher with 27 in 1991.

Year	Team (League)	G	W	L	Pct.	ERA	Sv.	IP	H	R	ER	BB	SO
1988—Oneonta (New York-Penn)		16	4	7	.364	4.37	1	78⅓	86	49	38	32	60
1989—Oneonta (New York-Penn)		11	7	2	.778	2.06	0	70	51	25	16	18	70
—Prince William (Carolina)		21	2	4	.333	3.68	2	36⅔	26	23	15	22	23
1990—Prince William (Carolina)		25	*16	8	.667	*1.90	0	170⅓	136	51	36	52	132
1991—Wichita (Texas)■		27	*15	10	.600	3.38	0	*176	173	86	66	68	107

SERVAIS, SCOTT
C, ASTROS

PERSONAL: Born June 4, 1967, at LaCrosse, Wis. . . . 6-2/195. . . . Throws right, bats right. . . . Full name: Scott Daniel Servais.
COLLEGE: Creighton.
TRANSACTIONS/CAREER NOTES: Selected by New York Mets organization in second round of free-agent draft (June 3, 1985). . . . Selected by Houston Astros organization in third round of free-agent draft (June 1, 1988). . . . On Houston disabled list (August 4-September 7, 1991).
STATISTICAL NOTES: Tied for Pacific Coast League in double plays by catcher with nine in 1990.
MISCELLANEOUS: Member of 1988 U.S. Olympic baseball team.

										BATTING					FIELDING	
Year	Team (League)	Pos.	G	AB	R	H	2B	3B	HR	RBI	Avg.	SB	PO	A	E	Avg.
1989—Osceola (Florida State)		C-1B	46	153	16	41	9	0	2	23	.268	0	168	24	4	.980
—Columbus (Southern)		C	63	199	20	47	5	0	1	22	.236	0	330	45	3	.992
1990—Tucson (Pacific Coast)		C	89	303	37	66	11	3	5	37	.218	0	453	63	9	.983
1991—Tucson (Pacific Coast)		C	60	219	34	71	12	0	2	27	.324	0	350	33	6	.985
—Houston (N.L.)		C	16	37	0	6	3	0	0	6	.162	0	77	4	1	.988
Major league totals (1 year)			16	37	0	6	3	0	0	6	.162	0	77	4	1	.988

SHARPERSON, MIKE
3B/SS, DODGERS

PERSONAL: Born October 4, 1961, at Orangeburg, S.C. . . . 6-3/190. . . . Throws right, bats right. . . . Full name: Michael Tyrone Sharperson.
COLLEGE: DeKalb Community College South (Ga.).
TRANSACTIONS/CAREER NOTES: Selected by Pittsburgh Pirates organization in 41st

round of free-agent draft (June 5, 1979).... Selected by Montreal Expos organization in secondary phase of free-agent draft (January 8, 1980).... Selected by Detroit Tigers organization in fourth round of free-agent draft (January 13, 1981).... Selected by Toronto Blue Jays organization in secondary phase of free-agent draft (June 8, 1981).... On disabled list (August 14, 1983-remainder of season).... Traded by Blue Jays organization to Los Angeles Dodgers for P Juan Guzman (September 22, 1987).... On disabled list (May 8-30, 1991).

STATISTICAL NOTES: Led Southern League second basemen with 775 total chances and 103 double plays in 1984.... Led International League second basemen with 286 putouts and 666 total chances in 1985.... Tied for International League lead in double plays by third basemen with 16 in 1987.

Year	Team (League)	Pos.	G	AB	R	H	2B	3B	HR	RBI	Avg.	SB	PO	A	E	Avg.
1982	—Florence (S. Atlantic)	SS-3B	111	326	51	83	16	1	3	33	.255	28	136	261	33	.923
1983	—Kinston (Carolina)	S-3-2-C	90	361	55	96	8	1	5	41	.266	20	148	286	19	.958
1984	—Knoxville (Southern)	2B	140	542	86	165	25	7	4	48	.304	20	★331	★423	21	.973
1985	—Syracuse (International)	2B-SS	134	★536	★86	★155	19	★7	1	59	.289	14	†291	372	17	.975
1986	—Syracuse (International)	2B-SS	133	519	★86	★150	18	★9	4	45	.289	17	258	376	18	.972
1987	—Toronto (A.L.)	2B	32	96	4	20	4	1	0	9	.208	2	64	69	4	.971
	—Syracuse (International)	3B-2B	88	338	67	101	21	5	5	26	.299	13	81	152	8	.967
	—Los Angeles (N.L.)■	3B-2B	10	33	7	9	2	0	0	1	.273	0	4	28	1	.970
1988	—Albuquerque (PCL)	2B-3B-SS	56	210	55	67	10	2	0	30	.319	19	88	173	12	.956
	—Los Angeles (N.L.)	2B-3B-SS	46	59	8	16	1	0	0	4	.271	0	19	31	2	.962
1989	—Albuquerque (PCL)	2B-3B-SS	98	359	81	111	15	7	3	48	.309	17	114	250	14	.963
	—Los Angeles (N.L.)	2-1-3-S	27	28	2	7	3	0	0	5	.250	0	11	8	0	1.000
1990	—Los Angeles (N.L.)	3-S-2-1	129	357	42	106	14	2	3	36	.297	15	152	193	15	.958
1991	—Los Angeles (N.L.)	3-S-1-2	105	216	24	60	11	2	2	20	.278	1	89	107	4	.980
	American League totals (1 year)		32	96	4	20	4	1	0	9	.208	2	64	69	4	.971
	National League totals (5 years)		317	693	83	198	31	4	5	66	.286	16	275	367	22	.967
	Major league totals (5 years)		349	789	87	218	35	5	5	75	.276	18	339	436	26	.968

CHAMPIONSHIP SERIES RECORD

Year	Team (League)	Pos.	G	AB	R	H	2B	3B	HR	RBI	Avg.	SB	PO	A	E	Avg.
1988	—Los Angeles (N.L.)	PH-SS-3B	2	1	0	0	0	0	0	1	.000	0	1	0	0	1.000

SHAW, JEFF
P, INDIANS

PERSONAL: Born July 7, 1966, at Washington Courthouse, O.... 6-2/185.... Throws right, bats right.... Full name: Jeffrey Lee Shaw.
HIGH SCHOOL: Washington Senior (O.).
COLLEGE: Cuyahoga Community College-Western Campus (O.).
TRANSACTIONS/CAREER NOTES: Selected by Cleveland Indians organization in first round (first pick overall) of free-agent draft (January 14, 1986).
STATISTICAL NOTES: Led Midwest League pitchers with 28 games started and four shutouts in 1987.... Tied for Eastern League lead in games started by pitcher with 27 in 1988.... Led Eastern League with 14 hit batsmen in 1989.... Pitched seven innings, combining with Everett Cunningham and Barry Manuel in 2-0 nine inning no-hit victory against Arkansas (April 18, 1991).

Year	Team (League)	G	W	L	Pct.	ERA	Sv.	IP	H	R	ER	BB	SO
1986	—Batavia (New York-Penn)	14	8	4	.667	2.44	0	88⅔	79	32	24	35	71
1987	—Waterloo (Midwest)	28	11	11	.500	3.52	0	184⅓	192	89	72	56	117
1988	—Williamsport (Eastern)	27	5	★19	.208	3.63	0	163⅔	★173	★94	66	75	61
1989	—Canton/Akron (Eastern)	30	7	10	.412	3.62	0	154⅓	134	84	62	67	95
1990	—Colorado Springs (Pac. Coast)	17	10	3	.769	4.29	0	98⅔	98	54	47	52	55
	—Cleveland (A.L.)	12	3	4	.429	6.66	0	48⅔	73	38	36	20	25
1991	—Colorado Springs (Pac. Coast)	12	6	3	.667	4.64	0	75⅔	77	47	39	25	55
	—Cleveland (A.L.)	29	0	5	.000	3.36	1	72⅓	72	34	27	27	31
	Major league totals (2 years)	41	3	9	.250	4.69	1	121	145	72	63	47	56

SHEFFIELD, GARY
3B, BREWERS

PERSONAL: Born November 18, 1968, at Tampa, Fla.... 5-11/190.... Throws right, bats right.... Full name: Gary Antonian Sheffield.... Nephew of Dwight Gooden, pitcher, New York Mets.
HIGH SCHOOL: Hillsborough (Tampa, Fla.).
TRANSACTIONS/CAREER NOTES: Selected by Milwaukee Brewers organization in first round (sixth pick overall) of free-agent draft (June 2, 1986).... On Milwaukee disabled list (July 14-September 9, 1989).... On suspended list (August 31-September 3, 1990).... On disabled list (June 15-July 3 and July 25, 1991-remainder of season).
RECORDS/HONORS: Named Minor League co-Player of the Year by THE SPORTING NEWS (1988).
STATISTICAL NOTES: Led Pioneer League shortstops with 34 double plays in 1986.... Led California League shortstops with 77 double plays in 1987.

Year	Team (League)	Pos.	G	AB	R	H	2B	3B	HR	RBI	Avg.	SB	PO	A	E	Avg.
1986	—Helena (Pioneer)	SS	57	222	53	81	12	2	15	★71	.365	14	97	149	24	.911
1987	—Stockton (California)	SS	129	469	84	130	23	3	17	★103	.277	25	235	345	39	.937
1988	—El Paso (Texas)	SS-3B-OF	77	296	70	93	19	3	19	65	.314	5	130	206	23	.936
	—Denver (Am. Assoc.)	3B-SS	57	212	42	73	9	5	9	54	.344	8	54	97	8	.950
	—Milwaukee (A.L.)	SS	24	80	12	19	1	0	4	12	.238	3	39	48	3	.967

Year Team (League)	Pos.	G	AB	R	H	2B	3B	HR	RBI	Avg.	SB	PO	A	E	Avg.
1989—Milwaukee (A.L.)	SS-3B	95	368	34	91	18	0	5	32	.247	10	100	238	16	.955
—Denver (Am. Assoc.)	SS	7	29	3	4	1	1	0	0	.138	0	2	6	0	1.000
1990—Milwaukee (A.L.)	3B	125	487	67	143	30	1	10	67	.294	25	98	254	25	.934
1991—Milwaukee (A.L.)	3B	50	175	25	34	12	2	2	22	.194	5	29	65	8	.922
Major league totals (4 years)		294	1110	138	287	61	3	21	133	.259	43	266	605	52	.944

SHELBY, JOHN
OF

PERSONAL: Born February 23, 1958, at Lexington, Ky. . . . 6-1/175. . . . Throws right, bats both.
HIGH SCHOOL: Henry Clay (Lexington, Ky.).
COLLEGE: Columbia State Community College (Tenn.).
TRANSACTIONS/CAREER NOTES: Selected by Baltimore Orioles organization in first round (19th pick overall) of free-agent draft (January 11, 1977). . . . Traded by Orioles organization with P Brad Havens to Los Angeles Dodgers for P Tom Niedenfuer (May 22, 1987). . . . On disabled list (April 22-May 12, 1988). . . . Granted free agency (November 13, 1989). . . . Re-signed by Dodgers (December 19, 1989). . . . Released by Dodgers (June 2, 1990). . . . Signed by Toledo, Detroit Tigers organization (June 13, 1990). . . . Granted free agency (November 5, 1990). . . . Re-signed by Tigers (November 26, 1990). . . . Released by Tigers (August 13, 1991).
RECORDS/HONORS: Holds N.L. single-season record for most strikeouts by switch-hitter— 128 (1988).
STATISTICAL NOTES: Led Appalachian League outfielders with three double plays in 1978. . . . Led Florida State League outfielders with seven double plays in 1979.

Year Team (League)	Pos.	G	AB	R	H	2B	3B	HR	RBI	Avg.	SB	PO	A	E	Avg.
1977—Bluefield (Appalachian)	OF	60	211	28	54	9	1	0	1	.256	6	90	•12	7	.936
1978—Miami (Florida State)	OF	13	26	4	6	1	0	0	3	.231	0	14	2	2	.889
—Bluefield (Appalachian)	OF	64	248	49	70	9	1	6	25	.282	7	128	★11	6	.959
1979—Miami (Florida State)	OF	132	478	50	96	11	6	3	38	.201	13	★252	•22	8	.972
1980—Charlotte (Southern)	OF	134	★560	66	135	27	11	6	51	.241	34	★361	21	★16	.960
1981—Charlotte (Southern)	OF	62	251	40	59	11	4	2	21	.235	24	120	3	10	.925
—Rochester (Int'l)	OF	76	326	42	86	21	8	3	32	.264	18	189	8	6	.970
—Baltimore (A.L.)	OF	7	2	2	0	0	0	0	0	.000	2	1	0	0	1.000
1982—Rochester (Int'l)	OF	133	★548	92	153	26	6	16	52	.279	34	331	13	8	.977
—Baltimore (A.L.)	OF	26	35	8	11	3	0	1	2	.314	0	20	1	0	1.000
1983—Baltimore (A.L.)	OF	126	325	52	84	15	2	5	27	.258	15	200	9	4	.981
1984—Baltimore (A.L.)	OF	128	383	44	80	12	5	6	30	.209	12	261	9	2	.993
1985—Rochester (Int'l)	OF	52	206	31	59	16	4	8	21	.286	14	124	4	1	.992
—Baltimore (A.L.)	OF-2B	69	205	28	58	6	2	7	27	.283	5	148	4	3	.981
1986—Baltimore (A.L.)	OF	135	404	54	92	14	4	11	49	.228	18	222	5	5	.978
1987—Baltimore (A.L.)	OF	21	32	4	6	0	0	1	3	.188	0	25	0	0	1.000
—Rochester (Int'l)	OF	6	24	5	6	2	0	1	2	.250	1	14	0	0	1.000
—Los Angeles (N.L.)■	OF	120	476	61	132	26	0	21	69	.277	16	269	9	8	.972
1988—Los Angeles (N.L.)	OF	140	494	65	130	23	6	10	64	.263	16	329	7	6	.982
1989—Los Angeles (N.L.)	OF	108	345	28	63	11	1	1	12	.183	10	220	3	2	.991
—Albuquerque (PCL)	OF	32	126	20	36	7	3	4	21	.286	12	75	2	1	.987
1990—Los Angeles (N.L.)	OF	25	24	2	6	1	0	0	2	.250	4	8	0	0	1.000
—Toledo (International)■	OF	5	19	2	6	1	0	0	1	.316	4	17	0	0	1.000
—Detroit (A.L.)	OF	78	222	22	55	9	3	4	20	.248	4	138	5	4	.973
1991—Detroit (A.L.)	OF	53	143	19	22	8	1	3	8	.154	0	108	4	2	.982
American League totals (9 years)		643	1751	233	408	67	17	38	166	.233	56	1123	37	20	.983
National League totals (4 years)		393	1339	156	331	61	7	32	147	.247	46	826	19	16	.981
Major league totals (11 years)		1036	3090	389	739	128	24	70	313	.239	102	1949	56	36	.982

CHAMPIONSHIP SERIES RECORD

CHAMPIONSHIP SERIES NOTES: Shares single-series record for most strikeouts— 12 (1988).

Year Team (League)	Pos.	G	AB	R	H	2B	3B	HR	RBI	Avg.	SB	PO	A	E	Avg.
1983—Baltimore (A.L.)	OF-PH	3	9	1	2	0	0	0	0	.222	1	3	0	0	1.000
1988—Los Angeles (N.L.)	OF	7	24	3	4	0	0	0	3	.167	2	19	0	0	1.000
Championship Series totals (2 years)		10	33	4	6	0	0	0	3	.182	3	22	0	0	1.000

WORLD SERIES RECORD

Year Team (League)	Pos.	G	AB	R	H	2B	3B	HR	RBI	Avg.	SB	PO	A	E	Avg.
1983—Baltimore (A.L.)	PH-OF	5	9	1	4	0	0	0	1	.444	0	10	0	0	1.000
1988—Los Angeles (N.L.)	OF	5	18	0	4	1	0	0	1	.222	1	14	0	0	1.000
World Series totals (2 years)		10	27	1	8	1	0	0	2	.296	1	24	0	0	1.000

SHELTON, BEN
1B/OF, PIRATES

PERSONAL: Born September 21, 1969, at Chicago. . . . 6-3/210. . . . Throws left, bats right. . . . Full name: Benjamin Davis Shelton.
HIGH SCHOOL: River Forest (Oak Park, Ill.).
TRANSACTIONS/CAREER NOTES: Selected by Pittsburgh Pirates organization in second round of free-agent draft (June 2, 1987).

Year	Team (League)	Pos.	G	AB	R	H	2B	3B	HR	RBI	Avg.	SB	PO	A	E	Avg.
1987	Bradenton Pirates (GCL) ..	1B	38	119	22	34	8	3	4	16	.286	7	290	15	3	.990
1988	Princeton (Appalachian) ..	1B	63	204	34	45	7	3	4	20	.221	8	475	29	*14	.973
	Augusta (S. Atlantic)	1B	38	128	25	25	2	2	5	20	.195	3	192	12	6	.971
1989	Augusta (S. Atlantic)	1B	122	386	67	95	16	4	8	50	.246	18	976	69	*27	.975
1990	Salem (Carolina)	1B	109	320	44	66	10	2	10	36	.206	1	923	55	*18	.982
1991	Salem (Carolina)	1B-OF	65	203	37	53	10	2	14	56	.261	4	444	43	7	.986
	Carolina (Southern)	1B-OF	55	169	19	39	8	3	1	19	.231	2	463	27	9	.982

SHERIDAN, PAT
OF

PERSONAL: Born December 4, 1957, at Ann Arbor, Mich. . . . 6-3/175. . . . Throws right, bats left. . . . Full name: Patrick Arthur Sheridan. . . . Son of Arthur Sheridan, minor league pitcher (1952-56).
HIGH SCHOOL: Wayne Memorial (Wayne, Mich.).
COLLEGE: Eastern Michigan.
TRANSACTIONS/CAREER NOTES: Selected by Cincinnati Reds organization in 36th round of free-agent draft (June 8, 1976). . . . Selected by Kansas City Royals organization in third round of free-agent draft (June 5, 1979). . . . On Jacksonville disabled list (May 16-June 2, 1980). . . . On Omaha disabled list (May 25-June 25, 1981; April 27-June 25 and June 27-July 19, 1982). . . . On Kansas City disabled list (June 19-July 4 and August 5-September 3, 1985); included rehabilitation disability assignment to Omaha (August 26-September 3, 1985). . . . Released by Royals (March 28, 1986). . . . Signed by Detroit Tigers (April 25, 1986). . . . Traded by Tigers to San Francisco Giants for OF Tracy Jones (June 18, 1989). . . . Granted free agency (November 13, 1989). . . . Signed by Royals organization (February 15, 1990). . . . Released by Royals organization (April 3, 1990). . . . Signed by Iowa, Chicago Cubs organization (April 25, 1990). . . . Placed on suspended list (May 26, 1990). . . . Left team (June 18, 1990). . . . Granted free agency (October 15, 1990). . . . Signed by New York Yankees organization (January 24, 1991). . . . Released by Yankees (October 15, 1991).

Year	Team (League)	Pos.	G	AB	R	H	2B	3B	HR	RBI	Avg.	SB	PO	A	E	Avg.
1979	Fort Myers (Florida St.)	OF	67	235	25	66	4	3	0	16	.281	14	142	8	1	.993
1980	Fort Myers (Florida St.)	OF-C	20	79	17	32	1	0	1	13	.405	8	37	4	1	.976
	Jacksonville (Southern) ...	OF	97	367	63	112	17	7	5	42	.305	14	201	7	9	.959
1981	Omaha (Am. Assoc.)	OF	86	315	49	94	15	8	5	31	.298	12	193	2	3	.985
	Kansas City (A.L.)	OF	3	1	0	0	0	0	0	0	.000	0	2	0	0	1.000
1982	Omaha (Am. Assoc.)	OF	41	135	8	34	8	1	0	13	.252	2	92	3	0	1.000
1983	Omaha (Am. Assoc.)	OF	20	75	16	23	4	5	4	14	.307	2	53	2	0	1.000
	Kansas City (A.L.)	OF	109	333	43	90	12	2	7	36	.270	3	237	6	3	.988
1984	Kansas City (A.L.)	OF	138	481	64	136	24	4	8	53	.283	19	273	8	4	.986
1985	Kansas City (A.L.)	OF	78	206	18	47	9	2	3	17	.228	11	116	3	2	.983
	Omaha (Am. Assoc.)	OF	8	28	1	10	1	0	0	1	.357	0	8	1	0	1.000
1986	Nashville (Am. Assoc.)■ ...	OF	9	35	4	10	2	0	1	5	.286	2	16	0	0	1.000
	Detroit (A.L.)	OF	98	236	41	56	9	1	6	19	.237	9	172	1	4	.977
1987	Detroit (A.L.)	OF	141	421	57	109	19	3	6	49	.259	18	236	6	6	.976
1988	Detroit (A.L.)	OF	127	347	47	88	9	5	1	47	.254	8	203	2	4	.981
1989	Detroit (A.L.)	OF	50	120	16	29	3	0	3	15	.242	4	52	2	1	.982
	San Francisco (N.L.)	OF	70	161	20	33	3	4	3	14	.205	4	111	2	2	.983
1990	Iowa (American Assoc.)■ .	OF	23	70	16	23	3	0	4	10	.329	2	32	0	0	1.000
1991	Columbus (Int'l)■	OF	21	70	15	19	3	2	2	12	.271	2	34	0	0	1.000
	New York (A.L.)	OF	62	113	13	23	3	0	4	7	.204	1	46	3	0	1.000
American League totals (9 years)			806	2258	299	578	88	17	38	243	.256	73	1337	31	24	.983
National League totals (1 year)			70	161	20	33	3	4	3	14	.205	4	111	2	2	.983
Major league totals (9 years)			876	2419	319	611	91	21	41	257	.253	77	1448	33	26	.983

CHAMPIONSHIP SERIES RECORD

Year	Team (League)	Pos.	G	AB	R	H	2B	3B	HR	RBI	Avg.	SB	PO	A	E	Avg.
1984	Kansas City (A.L.)	OF	3	6	1	0	0	0	0	0	.000	0	9	0	1	.900
1985	Kansas City (A.L.)	OF-PH	7	20	4	3	0	0	2	3	.150	0	13	0	0	1.000
1987	Detroit (A.L.)	OF-PR	5	10	2	3	1	0	1	2	.300	1	7	1	0	1.000
1989	San Francisco (N.L.)	OF	5	13	1	2	0	1	0	0	.154	0	9	1	0	1.000
Championship Series totals (4 years)			20	49	8	8	1	1	3	5	.163	1	38	2	1	.976

WORLD SERIES RECORD

Year	Team (League)	Pos.	G	AB	R	H	2B	3B	HR	RBI	Avg.	SB	PO	A	E	Avg.
1985	Kansas City (A.L.)	PH-OF	5	18	0	4	2	0	0	1	.222	0	6	0	0	1.000
1989	San Francisco (N.L.)	OF	1	2	0	0	0	0	0	0	.000	0	0	0	0	...
World Series totals (2 years)			6	20	0	4	2	0	0	1	.200	0	6	0	0	1.000

SHERMAN, DARRELL
OF, ORIOLES

PERSONAL: Born December 4, 1967, at Los Angeles. . . . 5-9/160. . . . Throws left, bats left. . . . Full name: Darrell Edward Sherman.
COLLEGE: California.
TRANSACTIONS/CAREER NOTES: Selected by San Diego Padres organization in sixth round of free-agent draft (June 5, 1989). . . . Drafted by Baltimore Orioles (December 9, 1991).

Year	Team (League)	Pos.	G	AB	R	H	2B	3B	HR	RBI	Avg.	SB	PO	A	E	Avg.
1989 —Spokane (Northwest)		OF	70	258	★70	82	13	1	0	29	.318	★58	137	•9	3	.980
1990 —Riverside (California)		OF	131	483	97	140	10	4	0	35	.290	74	★303	14	11	.966
—Las Vegas (Pac. Coast)		OF	4	12	1	0	0	0	0	1	.000	1	5	1	0	1.000
1991 —Wichita (Texas)		OF	131	502	93	148	17	3	3	48	.295	43	★323	1	8	.976

SHERRILL, TIM
P, CARDINALS

PERSONAL: Born September 10, 1965, at Harrison, Ark. . . . 5-11/170. . . . Throws left, bats left. . . . Full name: Timothy Shawn Sherrill.
HIGH SCHOOL: Valley Springs (Ark.).
COLLEGE: North Arkansas Community College and Arkansas.
TRANSACTIONS/CAREER NOTES: Selected by St. Louis Cardinals organization in 18th round of free-agent draft (June 2, 1987).

Year	Team (League)	G	W	L	Pct.	ERA	Sv.	IP	H	R	ER	BB	SO
1987 —Johnson City (Appalachian).....	25	3	4	.429	3.00	•8	42	25	18	14	18	62
1988 —Savannah (South Atlantic).......	31	3	2	.600	1.79	16	45⅓	26	12	9	13	62
—St. Petersburg (Florida State) ..	16	2	0	1.000	1.54	6	23⅓	14	4	4	8	25
1989 —St. Petersburg (Florida State) .	52	4	0	1.000	2.12	6	68	52	19	16	23	48
—Savannah (South Atlantic) ...	3	0	0	. . .	0.00	2	3⅔	3	0	0	2	6
1990 —Louisville (American Assoc.) ...	52	4	3	.571	2.49	2	61⅓	49	17	17	21	57
—St. Louis (N.L.)	8	0	0	. . .	6.23	0	4⅓	10	5	3	3	3
1991 —Louisville (American Assoc.) ...	42	5	5	.500	3.13	10	60⅓	56	21	21	26	37
—St. Louis (N.L.)	10	0	0	. . .	8.16	0	14⅓	20	13	13	3	4
Major league totals (2 years)	18	0	0	. . .	7.71	0	18⅔	30	18	16	6	7

SHINALL, ZAK
P, DODGERS

PERSONAL: Born October 14, 1968, at St. Louis. . . . 6-4/220. . . . Throws right, bats right. . . . Full name: Zakary Sebastian Shinall.
HIGH SCHOOL: El Segundo (Calif.).
COLLEGE: El Camino Junior College (Calif.).
TRANSACTIONS/CAREER NOTES: Selected by Los Angeles Dodgers organization in 29th round of free-agent draft (June 2, 1987).

Year	Team (League)	G	W	L	Pct.	ERA	Sv.	IP	H	R	ER	BB	SO
1987 —Sarasota Dodgers (GCL)	8	1	2	.333	5.04	0	30⅓	27	17	17	15	29
1988 —Bakersfield (California)	28	7	8	.467	4.22	0	113	90	65	53	104	63
1989 —Vero Beach (Florida State)	47	5	7	.417	2.51	7	86	71	32	24	29	69
1990 —San Antonio (Texas)	20	6	3	.667	3.55	0	91⅓	93	44	36	41	43
1991 —San Antonio (Texas)	25	2	4	.333	2.96	9	54⅔	53	31	18	21	29
—Albuquerque (Pacific Coast)	29	2	0	1.000	3.07	1	41	48	15	14	10	22

SHIPLEY, CRAIG
2B/SS, PADRES

PERSONAL: Born January 7, 1963, at Parramatta, Australia. . . . 6-1/185. . . . Throws right, bats right. . . . Full name: Craig Barry Shipley.
HIGH SCHOOL: Epping (Sydney, Australia).
COLLEGE: Alabama.
TRANSACTIONS/CAREER NOTES: Signed as free agent by Los Angeles Dodgers organization (May 28, 1984). . . . On Albuquerque disabled list (May 5-June 6, 1986). . . . Traded by Dodgers to New York Mets organization for C John Gibbons (April 1, 1988). . . . On disabled list (beginning of season-August 20, 1990). . . . Drafted by San Diego Padres organization (December 2, 1990). . . . On Las Vegas disabled list (April 11-May 2, 1991).

Year	Team (League)	Pos.	G	AB	R	H	2B	3B	HR	RBI	Avg.	SB	PO	A	E	Avg.
1984 —Vero Beach (Florida St.) ...	SS	85	293	56	82	11	2	0	28	.280	18	137	216	17	.954
1985 —Albuquerque (PCL)	SS	124	414	50	100	9	2	0	30	.242	24	202	367	21	.964
1986 —Albuquerque (PCL)	SS	61	203	33	59	8	2	0	16	.291	6	99	173	18	.938
—Los Angeles (N.L.)	SS-2B-3B	12	27	3	3	1	0	0	4	.111	0	16	18	3	.919
1987 —Albuquerque (PCL)	SS	49	139	17	31	6	1	1	15	.223	6	70	101	9	.950
—San Antonio (Texas)	3B	33	127	14	30	5	3	2	9	.236	0	19	56	3	.962
—Los Angeles (N.L.)	SS-3B	26	35	3	9	1	0	0	2	.257	0	15	28	3	.935
1988 —Jackson (Texas)■.............	SS	89	335	41	8	14	3	6	41	.024	6	141	266	16	.962
—Tidewater (Int'l)	2B-SS-3B	40	151	12	41	5	0	1	13	.272	0	54	110	2	.988
1989 —Tidewater (Int'l)	SS-3B-2B	44	131	6	27	1	0	2	9	.206	0	48	110	6	.963
—New York (N.L.)	SS-3B	4	7	3	1	0	0	0	0	.143	0	0	4	0	1.000
1990 —Tidewater (Int'l)	PH-PR	4	3	1	0	0	0	0	0	.000	0	0	0	0	. . .
1991 —Las Vegas (Pac. Coast)■..	SS-2B	65	230	27	69	9	5	5	34	.300	2	83	177	6	.977
—San Diego (N.L.)	SS-2B	37	91	6	25	3	0	1	6	.275	0	39	70	7	.940
Major league totals (4 years)		79	160	15	38	5	0	1	12	.238	0	70	120	13	.936

SHOW, ERIC
P, ATHLETICS

PERSONAL: Born May 19, 1956, at Riverside, Calif. . . . 6-1/185. . . . Throws right, bats right. . . . Full name: Eric Vaughn Show. . . . Name pronounced like 'CHOW'.
COLLEGE: California Riverside.
TRANSACTIONS/CAREER NOTES: Selected by Minnesota Twins organization in 36th round of free-

agent draft (June 5, 1974). . . . Selected by San Diego Padres organization in 18th round of free-agent draft (June 6, 1978). . . . On disabled list (July 8-31 and August 28, 1986-remainder of season; and July 6, 1989-remainder of season). . . . Granted free agency (November 5, 1990). . . . Signed by Oakland Athletics (December 10, 1990). . . . On Oakland disabled list (April 7-May 3, 1991); included rehabilitation disability assignment to Tacoma (April 21-27, 1991) and Modesto (April 27-May 3, 1991).
STATISTICAL NOTES: Led Texas League with 10 hit batsmen in 1980.

Year	Team (League)	G	W	L	Pct.	ERA	Sv.	IP	H	R	ER	BB	SO
1978	—Walla Walla (Northwest)	11	5	2	.714	2.85	0	60	47	28	19	20	43
1979	—Reno (California)	28	13	9	.591	3.57	0	169	144	79	67	92	186
1980	—Amarillo (Texas)	26	12	6	.667	3.74	0	166	141	81	69	81	144
1981	—Hawaii (Pacific Coast)	34	7	3	.700	2.54	0	85	67	30	24	35	70
	—San Diego (N.L.)	15	1	3	.250	3.13	3	23	17	9	8	9	22
1982	—San Diego (N.L.)	47	10	6	.625	2.64	3	150	117	49	44	48	88
1983	—San Diego (N.L.)	35	15	12	.556	4.17	0	200⅔	201	97	93	74	120
1984	—San Diego (N.L.)	32	15	9	.625	3.40	0	206⅔	175	88	78	88	104
1985	—San Diego (N.L.)	35	12	11	.522	3.09	0	233	212	95	80	87	141
1986	—San Diego (N.L.)	24	9	5	.643	2.97	0	136⅓	109	47	45	69	94
1987	—San Diego (N.L.)	34	8	16	.333	3.84	0	206⅓	188	99	88	85	117
1988	—San Diego (N.L.)	32	16	11	.593	3.26	0	234⅔	201	86	85	53	144
1989	—San Diego (N.L.)	16	8	6	.571	4.23	0	106⅓	113	59	50	39	66
1990	—San Diego (N.L.)	39	6	8	.429	5.76	1	106⅓	131	74	68	41	55
1991	—Tacoma (Pacific Coast)■	8	3	2	.600	2.68	0	40⅓	36	15	12	9	27
	—Modesto (California)	1	0	1	.000	16.88	0	2⅔	6	6	5	1	1
	—Oakland (A.L.)	23	1	2	.333	5.92	0	51⅔	62	36	34	17	20
American League totals (1 year)		23	1	2	.333	5.92	0	51⅔	62	36	34	17	20
National League totals (10 years)		309	100	87	.535	3.59	7	1603⅓	1464	703	639	593	951
Major league totals (11 years)		332	101	89	.532	3.66	7	1655	1526	739	673	610	971

CHAMPIONSHIP SERIES RECORD

Year	Team (League)	G	W	L	Pct.	ERA	Sv.	IP	H	R	ER	BB	SO
1984	—San Diego (N.L.)	2	0	1	.000	13.50	0	5⅓	8	8	8	4	2

WORLD SERIES RECORD

Year	Team (League)	G	W	L	Pct.	ERA	Sv.	IP	H	R	ER	BB	SO
1984	—San Diego (N.L.)	1	0	1	.000	10.13	0	2⅔	4	4	3	1	2

SHUMPERT, TERRY
2B, ROYALS

PERSONAL: Born August 16, 1966, at Paducah, Ky. . . . 5-11/190. . . . Throws right, bats right. . . . Full name: Terrance Darnell Shumpert.
HIGH SCHOOL: Paducah Tilghman (Paducah, Ky.).
COLLEGE: Kentucky.
TRANSACTIONS/CAREER NOTES: Selected by Kansas City Royals organization in second round of free-agent draft (June 2, 1987). . . . On Kansas City disabled list (June 3-September 10, 1990); included rehabilitation disability assignment to Omaha (August 7-25, 1990).

						BATTING						FIELDING			
Year	Team (League)	Pos.	G	AB	R	H	2B	3B	HR	RBI	Avg.	SB	PO	A	E	Avg.
1987	—Eugene (Northwest)	2B	48	186	38	54	16	1	4	22	.290	16	81	107	11	.945
1988	—Appleton (Midwest)	2B-OF	114	422	64	102	★37	2	7	38	.242	36	235	266	20	.962
1989	—Omaha (Am. Assoc.)	2B	113	355	54	88	29	2	4	22	.248	23	218	295	★22	.959
1990	—Omaha (Am. Assoc.)	2B	39	153	24	39	6	4	2	12	.255	18	72	95	7	.960
	—Kansas City (A.L.)	2B	32	91	7	25	6	1	0	8	.275	3	56	74	3	.977
1991	—Kansas City (A.L.)	2B	144	369	45	80	16	4	5	34	.217	17	249	368	16	.975
Major league totals (2 years)			176	460	52	105	22	5	5	42	.228	20	305	442	19	.975

SIERRA, RUBEN
OF, RANGERS

PERSONAL: Born October 6, 1965, at Rio Piedras, Puerto Rico. . . . 6-1/200. . . . Throws right, bats both. . . . Full name: Ruben Angel Garcia Sierra.
HIGH SCHOOL: Dr. Secario Rosario (Rio Piedras, Puerto Rico).
TRANSACTIONS/CAREER NOTES: Signed as free agent by Texas Rangers organization (November 21, 1982).
RECORDS/HONORS: Named A.L. Player of the Year by THE SPORTING NEWS (1989). . . . Named outfielder on THE SPORTING NEWS A.L. All-Star team (1989). . . . Named outfielder on THE SPORTING NEWS A.L. Silver Slugger team (1989).
STATISTICAL NOTES: Switch-hit home runs in one game (September 13, 1986; August 27, 1988 and June 8, 1989). . . . Led A.L. with 12 sacrifice flies in 1987. . . . Led A.L. outfielders with six double plays in 1987. . . . Led A.L. with 344 total bases and .543 slugging percentage in 1989.
MISCELLANEOUS: Batted righthanded only (1983).

						BATTING						FIELDING			
Year	Team (League)	Pos.	G	AB	R	H	2B	3B	HR	RBI	Avg.	SB	PO	A	E	Avg.
1983	—Sarasota Rangers (GCL) ...	OF	48	182	26	44	7	3	1	26	.242	3	67	6	4	.948
1984	—Burlington (Midwest)	OF	★138	482	55	127	33	5	6	75	.263	13	239	18	★20	.928
1985	—Tulsa (Texas)	OF	★137	★545	63	138	34	★8	13	74	.253	22	234	12	★15	.943
1986	—Oklahoma City (A.A.)	OF	46	189	31	56	11	2	9	41	.296	8	114	4	2	.983
	—Texas (A.L.)	OF	113	382	50	101	13	10	16	55	.264	7	200	7	6	.972
1987	—Texas (A.L.)	OF	158	★643	97	169	35	4	30	109	.263	16	272	•17	11	.963

Year	Team (League)	Pos.	G	AB	R	H	2B	3B	HR	RBI	Avg.	SB	PO	A	E	Avg.
								BATTING						FIELDING		
1988 —Texas (A.L.)		OF	156	615	77	156	32	2	23	91	.254	18	310	11	7	.979
1989 —Texas (A.L.)		OF	•162	634	101	194	35	*14	29	*119	.306	8	313	13	9	.973
1990 —Texas (A.L.)		OF	159	608	70	170	37	2	16	96	.280	9	283	7	10	.967
1991 —Texas (A.L.)		OF	161	661	110	203	44	5	25	116	.307	16	305	15	7	.979
Major league totals (6 years)			909	3543	505	993	196	37	139	586	.280	74	1683	70	50	.972

ALL-STAR GAME RECORD

Year	League	Pos.	AB	R	H	2B	3B	HR	RBI	Avg.	SB	PO	A	E	Avg.
					BATTING							FIELDING			
1989 —American		OF	3	1	2	0	0	0	1	.667	0	1	0	0	1.000
1991 —American		OF	2	0	0	0	0	0	0	.000	0	0	0	0	. . .
All-Star Game totals (2 years)			5	1	2	0	0	0	1	.400	0	1	0	0	1.000

SILVESTRI, DAVE
SS, YANKEES

PERSONAL: Born September 29, 1967, at St. Louis. . . . 6-0/180. . . . Throws right, bats right. . . . Full name: David Joseph Silvestri.
HIGH SCHOOL: Parkway Central (Chesterfield, Mo.).
COLLEGE: Missouri.
TRANSACTIONS/CAREER NOTES: Selected by Houston Astros in second round of free-agent draft (June 1, 1988). . . . Traded by Astros organization with a player to be named later to New York Yankees organization for IF Orlando Miller (March 13, 1990); Yankees acquired P Daven Bond to complete deal (June 11, 1990).
STATISTICAL NOTES: Led Florida State League shortstops with 221 putouts, 473 assists, 726 total chances and 93 double plays in 1989. . . . Led Carolina League shortstops with 622 total chances and 96 double plays in 1990. . . . Led Eastern League shortstops with 84 double plays in 1991. . . . Led Eastern League with 58 extra base hits in 1991.
MISCELLANEOUS: Member of 1988 U.S. Olympic baseball team.

Year	Team (League)	Pos.	G	AB	R	H	2B	3B	HR	RBI	Avg.	SB	PO	A	E	Avg.
								BATTING						FIELDING		
1989 —Osceola (Florida State)		SS-1B	129	437	67	111	20	1	2	50	.254	28	†238	*475	32	.957
1990 —Prince William (Caro.)■		SS	131	465	74	120	30	7	5	56	.258	37	218	*382	22	*.965
—Albany (Eastern)		SS	2	7	0	2	0	0	0	2	.286	0	3	5	1	.889
1991 —Albany (Eastern)		SS	*140	512	*97	134	31	8	19	83	.262	20	218	*362	•32	.948

SIMMS, MIKE
OF, ASTROS

PERSONAL: Born January 12, 1967, at Orange, Calif. . . . 6-4/185. . . . Throws right, bats right. . . . Full name: Michael Howard Simms.
HIGH SCHOOL: Esperanza (Calif.).
TRANSACTIONS/CAREER NOTES: Selected by Houston Astros organization in sixth round of free-agent draft (June 3, 1985).
STATISTICAL NOTES: Led South Atlantic League batters with 264 total bases and 167 strikeouts in 1987. . . . Led South Atlantic League first basemen with 1,089 putouts, 1,158 total chances and 19 errors in 1987. . . . Led Pacific Coast League batters with 135 strikeouts in 1990. . . . Led Pacific Coast League first basemen with 19 errors in 1990.

Year	Team (League)	Pos.	G	AB	R	H	2B	3B	HR	RBI	Avg.	SB	PO	A	E	Avg.
								BATTING						FIELDING		
1985 —Sarasota Astros (GCL)		1B	21	70	10	19	2	1	3	18	.271	0	186	7	5	.975
1986 —Sarasota Astros (GCL)		1B	54	181	33	47	14	1	4	37	.260	2	433	28	7	.985
1987 —Asheville (S. Atlantic)		1B-3B	133	469	93	128	19	0	*39	100	.273	7	†1089	52	†19	.984
1988 —Osceola (Florida State)		1B	123	428	63	104	19	1	16	73	.243	9	1143	41	22	.982
1989 —Columbus (Southern)		1B	109	378	64	97	21	3	20	81	.257	12	938	44	10	.990
1990 —Tucson (Pacific Coast)		1B-3B-OF	124	421	75	115	34	5	13	72	.273	3	1013	75	†19	.983
—Houston (N.L.)		1B	12	13	3	4	1	0	1	2	.308	0	20	1	0	1.000
1991 —Tucson (Pacific Coast)		OF-1B	85	297	53	73	20	2	15	59	.246	2	325	25	8	.978
—Houston (N.L.)		OF	49	123	18	25	5	0	3	16	.203	1	44	4	6	.889
Major league totals (2 years)			61	136	21	29	6	0	4	18	.213	1	64	5	6	.920

SIMON, RICHIE
P, ASTROS

PERSONAL: Born November 29, 1965, at Brookyln, N.Y. . . . 6-2/200. . . . Throws right, bats right. . . . Full name: Richard Simon.
HIGH SCHOOL: Grady (Brooklyn, N.Y.).
COLLEGE: St. Francis (N.Y.).
TRANSACTIONS/CAREER NOTES: Selected by Houston Astros in sixth round of free-agent draft (June 2, 1986).

Year	Team (League)	G	W	L	Pct.	ERA	Sv.	IP	H	R	ER	BB	SO
1986 —Auburn (New York-Penn)		15	4	6	.400	2.92	0	89⅓	76	35	29	34	54
1987 —Auburn (New York-Penn)		16	8	2	.800	2.59	0	107⅔	104	41	31	43	80
—Osceola (Florida State)		5	1	3	.250	4.76	0	22⅔	26	14	12	12	9
1988 —Asheville (South Atlantic)		23	9	9	.500	3.32	0	149	144	71	55	53	100
—Osceola (Florida State)		6	2	2	.500	2.81	0	41⅔	38	18	13	16	19
1989 —Osceola (Florida State)		19	6	8	.429	3.79	0	121	126	60	51	33	66
1990 —Columbus (Southern)		49	5	2	.714	3.32	2	86⅔	88	41	32	34	59
1991 —Jackson (Texas)		56	4	2	.667	2.18	20	70⅓	55	23	17	30	54

SIMONS, DOUG

P, METS

PERSONAL: Born September 15, 1966, at Bakersfield, Calif.... 6-0/160.... Throws left, bats left.... Full name: Douglas Eugene Simons.
HIGH SCHOOL: Calabasas (Calif.).
COLLEGE: Oxnard College (Calif.) and Pepperdine.

TRANSACTIONS/CAREER NOTES: Selected by Los Angeles Dodgers organization in 45th round of free-agent draft (June 2, 1987).... Selected by Minnesota Twins organization in ninth round of free-agent draft (June 1, 1988).... Drafted by New York Mets (December 3, 1990).

Year — Team (League)	G	W	L	Pct.	ERA	Sv.	IP	H	R	ER	BB	SO
1988 — Visalia (California)	17	6	5	.545	3.94	0	107⅓	100	59	47	46	123
1989 — Visalia (California)	14	6	2	.750	1.49	0	90⅔	77	33	15	33	79
— Orlando (Southern)	14	7	3	.700	3.81	0	87⅓	83	39	37	37	58
1990 — Orlando (Southern)	29	*15	12	.556	2.54	0	188	160	76	53	43	109
1991 — New York (N.L.)■	42	2	3	.400	5.19	1	60⅔	55	40	35	19	38
Major league totals (1 year)	42	2	3	.400	5.19	1	60⅔	55	40	35	19	38

SINATRO, MATT

C, MARINERS

PERSONAL: Born March 22, 1960, at West Hartford, Conn.... 5-9/174.... Throws right, bats right.... Full name: Matthew Stephen Sinatro.
HIGH SCHOOL: Conard (West Hartford, Conn.).
TRANSACTIONS/CAREER NOTES: Selected by Atlanta Braves organization in second round of free-agent draft (June 6, 1978).... Granted free agency (October 15, 1984).... Re-signed by Braves organization (December 11, 1984).... On Richmond disabled list (July 2-August 1, 1985).... On Richmond suspended list (July 6-August 15, 1986).... Released by Braves organization (August 15, 1986).... Signed by Buffalo, Chicago White Sox organization (August 20, 1986).... Granted free agency (October 15, 1986).... Signed by Tacoma, Oakland Athletics organization (April 1, 1987).... Released by A's (October 15, 1987).... Re-signed by A's organization (January 5, 1988).... On Oakland disabled list (August 19-September 3, 1988).... Traded by A's organization to Tucson (Houston Astros organization) for C-OF Troy Afenir (April 6, 1989).... Sold by Astros organization to Detroit Tigers (June 19, 1989).... Sold by Tigers organization to Calgary, Seattle Mariners organization (August 5, 1989).... Granted free agency (October 5, 1990).... Re-signed by Mariners organization (November 5, 1990).... Granted free agency (October 16, 1991).... Re-signed by Mariners (January 21, 1992).
STATISTICAL NOTES: Tied for Western Carolinas League lead in caught stealing with 15 in 1979.... Led Southern League catchers with 10 double plays in 1980.... Led International League catchers with 710 total chances in 1983.... Led Southern League catchers with 537 total chances in 1984.

Year — Team (League)	Pos.	G	AB	R	H	2B	3B	HR	RBI	Avg.	SB	PO	A	E	Avg.
1978 — Kingsport (Appalachian)	C	35	112	15	23	7	0	0	6	.205	4	198	26	2	.991
1979 — Greenwood (W. Caro.)	C	120	385	54	97	16	4	7	57	.252	25	639	69	11	.985
1980 — Savannah (Southern)	C	122	449	76	125	16	1	11	50	.278	17	514	70	15	.975
1981 — Richmond (Int'l)	C	121	430	43	101	13	2	6	53	.235	18	738	78	12	.986
— Atlanta (N.L.)	C	12	32	4	9	1	1	0	4	.281	1	56	10	0	1.000
1982 — Atlanta (N.L.)	C	37	81	10	11	2	0	1	4	.136	0	112	25	0	1.000
— Richmond (Int'l)	C	72	246	39	62	7	1	8	29	.252	13	423	53	5	.990
1983 — Richmond (Int'l)	C	110	365	36	77	11	1	4	41	.211	6	*642	60	8	.989
— Atlanta (N.L.)	C	7	12	0	2	0	0	0	2	.167	0	24	5	1	.967
1984 — Atlanta (N.L.)	C	2	4	0	0	0	0	0	0	.000	0	4	0	0	1.000
— Greenville (Southern)	C	101	352	36	80	16	1	5	49	.227	6	*466	•64	7	.987
1985 — Greenville (Southern)	C	49	172	25	48	4	1	6	28	.279	4	265	49	7	.978
— Richmond (Int'l)	C	24	67	7	19	3	0	1	8	.284	1	89	8	3	.970
1986 — Richmond (Int'l)	C-3B	28	66	8	13	2	0	2	7	.197	0	124	18	2	.986
— Buffalo (Am. Assoc.)■	C	11	32	4	8	3	0	0	3	.250	0	60	7	4	.944
1987 — Tacoma (Pacific Coast)■	C-3B-OF	79	215	30	54	13	0	5	32	.251	6	370	50	12	.972
— Oakland (A.L.)	C	6	3	0	0	0	0	0	0	.000	0	4	0	0	1.000
1988 — Tacoma (Pacific Coast)	C-OF	77	234	28	54	8	1	2	23	.231	2	361	48	7	.983
— Oakland (A.L.)	C	10	9	1	3	2	0	0	5	.333	0	21	2	0	1.000
1989 — Tucson-Calgary (PCL)■	C	46	128	13	33	6	0	0	12	.258	1	224	28	6	.977
— Detroit (A.L.)■	C	13	25	2	3	0	0	0	1	.120	0	42	2	0	1.000
1990 — Seattle (A.L.)■	C	30	50	2	15	1	0	0	4	.300	1	112	16	1	.992
— Calgary (Pacific Coast)	C	9	20	1	6	0	0	1	2	.300	0	33	1	0	1.000
1991 — Seattle (A.L.)■	C	5	8	1	2	0	0	0	1	.250	0	18	3	0	1.000
— Calgary (Pacific Coast)	C	40	131	13	34	8	0	3	19	.260	1	199	17	9	.960
American League totals (5 years)		64	95	6	23	3	0	0	11	.242	1	197	23	1	.995
National League totals (4 years)		58	129	14	22	3	1	1	10	.171	1	196	40	1	.996
Major league totals (9 years)		122	224	20	45	6	1	1	21	.201	2	393	63	2	.996

SISK, DOUG

P

PERSONAL: Born September 26, 1957, at Renton, Wash.... 6-2/210.... Throws right, bats right.... Full name: Douglas Randall Sisk.
HIGH SCHOOL: Stadium (Renton, Wash.).
COLLEGE: Green River Community College (Wash.) and Washington State (bachelor of science degree in criminal justice).
TRANSACTIONS/CAREER NOTES: Signed as free agent by New York Mets organization (June 10, 1980).... On disabled list (August 9-29, 1984).... Traded by Mets to Baltimore Orioles for P Blaine Beatty and a player to be named later (December 8, 1987); Mets acquired P Greg Talamantez to complete deal (December 11, 1987).... On Baltimore disabled list (June 27-July 22, 1988); included rehabilitation disability assignment to Rochester (July 3-21, 1988).... Released by Orioles (October 3, 1988).... Signed by Colorado Springs, Cleveland Indians organization (December 15, 1989).... Released by Indians organi-

zation (June 9, 1990).... Signed by Tidewater, Mets organization (June 12, 1990).... Traded by Mets organization to Atlanta Braves for P Tony Valle (July 22, 1990).... On Atlanta disabled list (July 28-August 28, 1990).... Released by Braves (August 28, 1990).... Re-signed by Braves (January 25, 1991).... On Atlanta disabled list (May 24, 1991-remainder of season); included rehabilitaion disability assignment to Richmond (June 12-27, 1991).... Granted free agency (October 28, 1991).

STATISTICAL NOTES: Led Appalachian League pitchers with 15 games started in 1980.

Year	Team (League)	G	W	L	Pct.	ERA	Sv.	IP	H	R	ER	BB	SO
1980 —Kingsport (Appalachian)	15	•8	5	.615	2.66	0	*98	*91	46	29	45	41
1981 —Lynchburg (Carolina)	36	3	2	.600	3.25	7	83	78	35	30	32	61
—Jackson (Texas)	14	3	0	1.000	3.60	4	25	23	11	10	12	15
1982 —Jackson (Texas)	44	11	8	.579	*2.67	5	138	136	59	41	58	53
—New York (N.L.)	8	0	1	.000	1.04	1	8⅔	5	1	1	4	4
1983 —New York (N.L.)	67	5	4	.556	2.24	11	104⅓	88	38	26	59	33
1984 —New York (N.L.)	50	1	3	.250	2.09	15	77⅔	57	24	18	54	32
1985 —New York (N.L.)	42	4	5	.444	5.30	0	73	86	48	43	40	26
—Tidewater (International)	4	0	2	.000	7.20	0	15	15	12	12	13	4
1986 —Tidewater (International)	9	2	3	.400	4.20	2	30	34	16	14	9	19
—New York (N.L.)	41	4	2	.667	3.06	1	70⅔	77	31	24	31	31
1987 —New York (N.L.)	55	3	1	.750	3.46	3	78	83	38	30	22	37
1988 —Baltimore (A.L.)■......................	52	3	3	.500	3.72	6	94⅓	109	43	39	45	26
—Rochester (International)	6	0	2	.000	5.91	3	10⅔	15	7	7	3	5
1989 —					Out of Organized Baseball							
1990 —Colorado Springs (Pac. Coast)■	8	1	0	1.000	7.04	0	7⅔	8	8	6	5	7
—Tidewater (International)■......	8	5	1	.833	2.81	0	41⅔	39	16	13	10	20
—Atlanta (N.L.)■......................	3	0	0	...	3.86	0	2⅓	1	1	1	4	1
1991 —Atlanta (N.L.)	14	2	1	.667	5.02	0	14⅓	21	14	8	8	5
—Richmond (International)	9	0	0	...	1.59	2	11⅓	14	3	2	4	2
American League totals (1 year)	52	3	3	.500	3.72	6	94⅓	109	43	39	45	26
National League totals (8 years)	280	19	17	.528	3.17	31	429	418	195	151	222	169
Major league totals (9 years)	332	22	20	.524	3.27	31	523⅓	527	238	190	267	195

CHAMPIONSHIP SERIES RECORD

Year	Team (League)	G	W	L	Pct.	ERA	Sv.	IP	H	R	ER	BB	SO
1986 —New York (N.L.)	1	0	0	...	0.00	0	1	1	0	0	1	0

WORLD SERIES RECORD

Year	Team (League)	G	W	L	Pct.	ERA	Sv.	IP	H	R	ER	BB	SO
1986 —New York (N.L.)	1	0	0	...	0.00	0	⅔	0	0	0	1	1

SKINNER, JOEL
C, INDIANS

PERSONAL: Born February 21, 1961, at La Jolla, Calif.... 6-4/204.... Throws right, bats right.... Full name: Joel Patrick Skinner.... Son of Bob Skinner, outfielder-first baseman, Pittsburgh Pirates, Cincinnati Reds and St. Louis Cardinals (1954 and 1956-66); manager, Philadelphia Phillies (1968-69); coach, San Diego Padres (1977); coach, California Angels (1978); coach, Pirates (1979-85); and coach, Atlanta Braves (1986-88).

HIGH SCHOOL: Mission Bay (Calif.).

COLLEGE: San Diego Mesa College (Calif.).

TRANSACTIONS/CAREER NOTES: Selected by Pittsburgh Pirates organization in 36th round of free-agent draft (June 5, 1979).... On disabled list (June 1-13, 1981).... Selected by Chicago White Sox organization in player compensation pool draft (February 2, 1982). White Sox received compensation for Philadelphia Phillies signing free agent P Ed Farmer, a Type A player (January 28, 1982).... On Denver disabled list (July 23, 1984-remainder of season).... Traded by White Sox with OF-DH Ron Kittle and IF Wayne Tolleson to New York Yankees for C Ron Hassey, SS Carlos Martinez and a player to be named later (July 30, 1986); Yankees traded C Bill Lindsey to White Sox organization to complete deal (December 24, 1986).... Traded by Yankees with OF Turner Ward to Cleveland Indians for OF Mel Hall (March 19, 1989).

STATISTICAL NOTES: Tied for South Atlantic League lead in double plays by catchers with seven in 1980.... Led American Association catchers with 698 total chances and 13 double plays in 1985.... Led American Association batters with 115 strikeouts and tied for lead in grounding into double plays with 16 in 1985.

Year	Team (League)	Pos.	G	AB	R	H	2B	3B	HR	RBI	Avg.	SB	PO	A	E	Avg.
1980 —Shelby (South Atlantic)	C	100	324	36	73	15	2	7	27	.225	0	536	63	18	.971
1981 —Greenwood (S. Atlantic)....	C	117	428	48	114	25	2	11	63	.266	2	766	42	*22	.973
1982 —Glens Falls (Eastern)■......	C	120	422	49	107	11	6	7	65	.254	1	726	80	12	.985
1983 —Denver (Am. Assoc.)	C	108	361	55	94	15	5	12	50	.260	0	550	54	5	.992
—Chicago (A.L.)	C	6	11	2	3	0	0	0	1	.273	0	20	4	1	.960
1984 —Denver (Am. Assoc.)	C	42	141	27	40	6	0	10	27	.284	1	255	24	5	.982
—Chicago (A.L.)	C	43	80	4	17	2	0	0	3	.213	1	171	11	2	.989
1985 —Buffalo (Am. Assoc.)	C	115	390	47	94	13	0	12	59	.241	0	*623	*65	10	.986
—Chicago (A.L.)	C	22	44	9	15	4	1	1	5	.341	0	94	8	3	.971
1986 —Chicago-N.Y. (A.L.)■......	C	114	315	23	73	9	1	5	37	.232	1	507	37	9	.984
1987 —New York (A.L.)	C	64	139	9	19	4	0	3	14	.137	0	232	18	4	.984
—Columbus (Int'l)	C	49	178	19	43	10	2	6	27	.242	0	226	25	4	.984
1988 —New York (A.L.)	C-OF-1B	88	251	23	57	15	0	4	23	.227	0	396	16	4	.990
1989 —Cleveland (A.L.)■	C	79	178	10	41	10	0	1	13	.230	1	280	22	3	.990
1990 —Cleveland (A.L.)	C	49	139	16	35	4	1	2	16	.252	0	222	16	1	.996
1991 —Cleveland (A.L.)	C	99	284	23	69	14	0	1	24	.243	0	504	38	5	.991
Major league totals (9 years)		564	1441	119	329	62	3	17	136	.228	3	2426	170	32	.988

SLAUGHT, DON
C, PIRATES

PERSONAL: Born September 11, 1958, at Long Beach, Calif. . . . 6-1/190. . . . Throws right, bats right. . . . Full name: Donald Martin Slaught.
HIGH SCHOOL: Rolling Hills (Palos Verdes, Calif.).
COLLEGE: El Camino College (Calif.) and UCLA (bachelor of science degree in economics, 1983).
TRANSACTIONS/CAREER NOTES: Selected by Milwaukee Brewers organization in 19th round of free-agent draft (June 5, 1979). . . . Selected by Kansas City Royals organization in seventh round of free-agent draft (June 3, 1980). . . . On Omaha disabled list (August 16-September 29, 1981 and April 21-May 15, 1982). . . . On disabled list (May 16-June 1, 1983). . . . Traded by Royals to Texas Rangers as part of a six-player, four-team deal in which Royals acquired C Jim Sundberg from Brewers, Mets organization acquired P Frank Wills from Royals, Brewers acquired P Danny Darwin and a player to be named later from Rangers and P Tim Leary from Mets (January 18, 1985); Brewers organization acquired C Bill Hance from Rangers to complete deal (January 30, 1985). . . . On disabled list (August 9-26, 1985). . . . On Texas disabled list (May 18-July 4, 1986); included rehabilitation disability assignment to Oklahoma City (July 1-4, 1986). . . . Traded by Rangers to New York Yankees for a player to be named later (November 2, 1987); Rangers acquired P Brad Arnsberg to complete deal (November 10, 1987). . . . On disabled list (May 15-June 20, 1988). . . . Traded by Yankees to Pittsburgh Pirates for P Jeff Robinson and P Willie Smith (December 4, 1989). . . . On disabled list (June 30-July 16, 1990). . . . Granted free agency (November 5, 1990). . . . Re-signed by Pirates (December 19, 1990). . . . On disabled list (July 22-August 13, 1991).

Year — Team (League)	Pos.	G	AB	R	H	2B	3B	HR	RBI	Avg.	SB	PO	A	E	Avg.
1980 — Fort Myers (Florida St.)	C	50	176	13	46	9	0	2	16	.261	3	175	34	4	.981
1981 — Jacksonville (Southern) ...	C-1B	96	379	45	127	21	2	6	44	.335	13	482	61	9	.984
— Omaha (Am. Assoc.)	C	22	71	10	21	4	0	2	8	.296	3	91	7	3	.970
1982 — Omaha (Am. Assoc.)	C	53	206	29	55	10	1	4	16	.267	6	216	25	5	.980
— Kansas City (A.L.)	C	43	115	14	32	6	0	3	8	.278	0	156	7	1	.994
1983 — Kansas City (A.L.)	C	83	276	21	86	13	4	0	28	.312	3	299	18	12	.964
1984 — Kansas City (A.L.)	C	124	409	48	108	27	4	4	42	.264	0	547	44	11	.982
1985 — Texas (A.L.)■	C	102	343	34	96	17	4	8	35	.280	5	550	33	6	.990
1986 — Texas (A.L.)	C	95	314	39	83	17	1	13	46	.264	3	533	40	4	.993
— Oklahoma City (A.A.)	C	3	12	2	4	1	0	0	1	.333	0	6	1	0	1.000
1987 — Texas (A.L.)	C	95	237	25	53	15	2	8	16	.224	0	429	39	7	.985
1988 — New York (A.L.)■	C	97	322	33	91	25	1	9	43	.283	1	496	24	•11	.979
1989 — New York (A.L.)	C	117	350	34	88	21	3	5	38	.251	1	493	44	5	.991
1990 — Pittsburgh (N.L.)■	C	84	230	27	69	18	3	4	29	.300	0	345	36	8	.979
1991 — Pittsburgh (N.L.)	C-3B	77	220	19	65	17	1	1	29	.295	1	338	31	5	.987
American League totals (8 years)		756	2366	248	637	141	19	50	256	.269	13	3503	249	57	.985
National League totals (2 years)		161	450	46	134	35	4	5	58	.298	1	683	67	13	.983
Major league totals (10 years)		917	2816	294	771	176	23	55	314	.274	14	4186	316	70	.985

CHAMPIONSHIP SERIES RECORD

Year — Team (League)	Pos.	G	AB	R	H	2B	3B	HR	RBI	Avg.	SB	PO	A	E	Avg.
1984 — Kansas City (A.L.)	C	3	11	0	4	0	0	0	0	.364	0	17	0	3	.850
1990 — Pittsburgh (N.L.)	C	4	11	0	1	1	0	0	1	.091	0	22	1	1	.958
1991 — Pittsburgh (N.L.)	C-PH	6	17	0	4	0	0	0	1	.235	0	30	5	0	1.000
Championship Series totals (3 years)		13	39	0	9	1	0	0	2	.231	0	69	6	4	.949

SLOCUMB, HEATHCLIFF
P, CUBS

PERSONAL: Born June 7, 1966, at Jamaica, N.Y. . . . 6-3/210. . . . Throws right, bats right. . . . Full name: Heathcliff Slocumb.
HIGH SCHOOL: John Bowne (Flushing, N.Y.).
TRANSACTIONS/CAREER NOTES: Signed as free agent by New York Mets organization (July 10, 1984). . . . Drafted by Chicago Cubs organization (December 9, 1986).
STATISTICAL NOTES: Led Carolina League with 19 wild pitches in 1988.

Year — Team (League)	G	W	L	Pct.	ERA	Sv.	IP	H	R	ER	BB	SO
1984 — Kingsport (Appalachian)	1	0	0	. . .	0.00	0	1/3	0	1	0	1	0
— Little Falls (New York-Penn)....	4	0	0	. . .	11.00	0	9	8	11	11	16	10
1985 — Kingsport (Appalachian)	11	3	2	.600	3.78	0	52 1/3	47	32	22	31	29
1986 — Little Falls (New York-Penn)....	25	3	1	.750	1.65	1	43 2/3	24	17	8	36	41
1987 — Winston-Salem (Carolina)■	9	1	2	.333	6.26	0	27 1/3	26	25	19	26	27
— Peoria (Midwest)	16	10	4	.714	2.60	0	103 2/3	97	44	30	42	81
1988 — Winston-Salem (Carolina)	25	6	6	.500	4.96	1	119 2/3	122	75	66	90	78
1989 — Peoria (Midwest)	49	5	3	.625	1.78	22	55 2/3	31	16	11	33	52
1990 — Charlotte (Southern)	43	3	1	.750	2.15	12	50 1/3	50	20	12	32	37
— Iowa (American Association) ...	20	3	2	.600	2.00	1	27	16	10	6	18	21
1991 — Chicago (N.L.)	52	2	1	.667	3.45	1	62 2/3	53	29	24	30	34
— Iowa (American Association) ...	12	1	0	1.000	4.05	1	13 1/3	10	8	6	6	9
Major league totals (1 year)	52	2	1	.667	3.45	1	62 2/3	53	29	24	30	34

SLUSARSKI, JOE
P, ATHLETICS

PERSONAL: Born December 19, 1966, at Indianapolis. . . . 6-4/195. . . . Throws right, bats right. . . . Full name: Joseph Andrew Slusarski.
HIGH SCHOOL: Griffin (Springfield, Ill.).
COLLEGE: Lincoln Land Community College (Ill.) and New Orleans.

TRANSACTIONS/CAREER NOTES: Selected by Seattle Mariners organization in sixth round of free-agent draft (June 2, 1987)....
Selected by Oakland Athletics organization in second round of free-agent draft (June 1, 1988).... On Huntsville disabled list
(May 18-25, 1990).
STATISTICAL NOTES: Led California League with 15 home runs allowed in 1989.
MISCELLANEOUS: Member of 1988 U.S. Olympic baseball team.

Year	Team (League)	G	W	L	Pct.	ERA	Sv.	IP	H	R	ER	BB	SO
1989	—Modesto (California)	27	•13	10	.565	3.18	0	184	155	78	65	50	160
1990	—Huntsville (Southern)	17	6	8	.429	4.47	0	108⅔	114	65	54	35	75
	—Tacoma (Pacific Coast)	9	4	2	.667	3.40	0	55⅔	54	24	21	22	37
1991	—Oakland (A.L.)	20	5	7	.417	5.27	0	109⅓	121	69	64	52	60
	—Tacoma (Pacific Coast)	7	4	2	.667	2.72	0	46⅓	42	20	14	10	25
Major league totals (1 year)		20	5	7	.417	5.27	0	109⅓	121	69	64	52	60

SMILEY, JOHN
P, PIRATES

PERSONAL: Born March 17, 1965, at Phoenixville, Pa.... 6-4/200.... Throws left, bats left.
... Full name: John Patrick Smiley.
HIGH SCHOOL: Perkiomen Valley (Graterford, Pa.).
TRANSACTIONS/CAREER NOTES: Selected by Pittsburgh Pirates organization in 12th round of
free-agent draft (June 6, 1983).... On disabled list (April 27-May 27, 1984 and May 19-July 1, 1990).
STATISTICAL NOTES: Tied for Gulf Coast League lead with five home runs allowed in 1983.

Year	Team (League)	G	W	L	Pct.	ERA	Sv.	IP	H	R	ER	BB	SO
1983	—Bradenton Pirates (GCL)	12	3	4	.429	5.92	0	65⅓	69	45	43	27	42
1984	—Macon (South Atlantic)	21	5	11	.313	3.95	1	130	119	73	57	41	73
1985	—Prince William (Carolina)	10	2	2	.500	5.14	0	56	64	36	32	27	45
	—Macon (South Atlantic)	16	3	8	.273	4.67	0	88⅔	84	55	46	37	70
1986	—Prince William (Carolina)	48	2	4	.333	3.10	14	90	64	35	31	40	93
	—Pittsburgh (N.L.)	12	1	0	1.000	3.86	0	11⅔	4	6	5	4	9
1987	—Pittsburgh (N.L.)	63	5	5	.500	5.76	4	75	69	49	48	50	58
1988	—Pittsburgh (N.L.)	34	13	11	.542	3.25	0	205	185	81	74	46	129
1989	—Pittsburgh (N.L.)	28	12	8	.600	2.81	0	205⅓	174	78	64	49	123
1990	—Pittsburgh (N.L.)	26	9	10	.474	4.64	0	149⅓	161	83	77	36	86
1991	—Pittsburgh (N.L.)	33	•20	8	★.714	3.08	0	207⅔	194	78	71	44	129
Major league totals (6 years)		196	60	42	.588	3.57	4	854	787	375	339	229	534

CHAMPIONSHIP SERIES RECORD
CHAMPIONSHIP SERIES NOTES: Shares single-series record for most games lost—2 (1991).

Year	Team (League)	G	W	L	Pct.	ERA	Sv.	IP	H	R	ER	BB	SO
1990	—Pittsburgh (N.L.)	1	0	0	...	0.00	0	2	2	0	0	0	0
1991	—Pittsburgh (N.L.)	2	0	2	.000	23.63	0	2⅔	8	8	7	1	3
Championship Series totals (2 years)		3	0	2	.000	13.50	0	4⅔	10	8	7	1	3

ALL-STAR GAME RECORD

Year	League	W	L	Pct.	ERA	Sv.	IP	H	R	ER	BB	SO
1991	—National	0	0	...	0.00	0	0	1	1	1	0	0

SMITH, BRYN
P, CARDINALS

PERSONAL: Born August 11, 1955, at Marietta, Ga.... 6-2/205.... Throws right, bats right....
Full name: Bryn Nelson Smith.... Name pronounced BRIN.
HIGH SCHOOL: Santa Maria (Calif.).
COLLEGE: Allan Hancock College (Calif.).
TRANSACTIONS/CAREER NOTES: Selected by St. Louis Cardinals organization in the 49th round of free-agent draft (June 5,
1973).... Signed as free agent by Baltimore Orioles organization (December 18, 1974).... Traded by Orioles organization with
P Rudy May and P Randy Miller to Montreal Expos organization for P Don Stanhouse, P Joe Kerrigan and OF Gary Roenicke
(December 7, 1977).... On Memphis disabled list (August 5-17, 1978).... Released by Expos (December 20, 1986).... Re-
signed by Expos (February 27, 1987).... On Montreal disabled list (March 23-May 1, 1987); included rehabilitation disability
assignment to West Palm Beach (April 10, 1987).... Granted free agency (November 9, 1987).... Re-signed by Expos (De-
cember 16, 1987).... Granted free agency (November 13, 1989).... Signed by St. Louis Cardinals (November 28, 1989)....
On disabled list (July 28-September 6, 1990).
RECORDS/HONORS: Named American Association Pitcher of the Year (1981).
STATISTICAL NOTES: Tied for Southern League Lead with 16 complete games in 1977 and 12 in 1980.... Tied for American Association lead with nine complete games in 1981.

Year	Team (League)	G	W	L	Pct.	ERA	Sv.	IP	H	R	ER	BB	SO
1975	—Miami (Florida State)	26	11	7	.611	2.14	1	139	117	48	33	59	93
1976	—Miami (Florida State)	23	10	10	.500	2.80	0	164	140	72	51	62	119
1977	—Charlotte (Southern)	27	★15	11	.577	2.75	0	★206	★195	78	63	57	103
1978	—Denver (American Assoc.)■.....	11	0	6	.000	6.83	0	54	79	48	41	14	25
	—Memphis (Southern)	11	4	6	.400	2.48	0	69	53	28	19	31	48
1979	—Memphis (Southern)	27	11	10	.524	3.38	0	184	175	80	69	74	115
1980	—Memphis (Southern)	27	10	9	.526	2.78	0	181	179	75	56	54	110
1981	—Denver (American Assoc.)	29	★15	5	.750	3.05	1	★183	166	80	62	42	127
	—Montreal (N.L.)	7	1	0	1.000	2.77	0	13	14	4	4	3	9
1982	—Wichita (American Assoc.)	3	2	0	1.000	1.90	0	23⅔	21	5	5	2	15
	—Montreal (N.L.)	47	2	4	.333	4.20	3	79⅓	81	43	37	23	50

Year Team (League)	G	W	L	Pct.	ERA	Sv.	IP	H	R	ER	BB	SO
1983 —Montreal (N.L.)	49	6	11	.353	2.49	3	155⅓	142	51	43	43	101
1984 —Montreal (N.L.)	28	12	13	.480	3.32	0	179	178	72	66	51	101
1985 —Montreal (N.L.)	32	18	5	.783	2.91	0	222⅓	193	85	72	41	127
1986 —Montreal (N.L.)	30	10	8	.556	3.94	0	187⅓	182	101	82	63	105
1987 —West Palm Beach (Florida St.) ..	4	0	2	.000	4.08	0	17⅔	19	10	8	1	16
—Montreal (N.L.)	26	10	9	.526	4.37	0	150⅓	164	81	73	31	94
1988 —Montreal (N.L.)	32	12	10	.545	3.00	0	198	179	79	66	32	122
1989 —Montreal (N.L.)	33	10	11	.476	2.84	0	215⅔	177	76	68	54	129
1990 —St. Louis (N.L.) ■.....................	26	9	8	.529	4.27	0	141⅓	160	81	67	30	78
1991 —St. Louis (N.L.)	31	12	9	.571	3.85	0	198⅔	188	95	85	45	94
Major league totals (11 years)	341	102	88	.537	3.43	6	1740⅓	1658	768	663	416	1010

SMITH, DAVE
P, CUBS

PERSONAL: Born January 21, 1955, at San Francisco. . . . 6-1/195. . . . Throws right, bats right. . . . Full name: David Stanley Smith Jr.
HIGH SCHOOL: Poway (Calif.).
COLLEGE: San Diego State.
TRANSACTIONS/CAREER NOTES: Selected by Houston Astros organization in eighth round of free-agent draft (June 8, 1976). . . . On disabled list (June 27-July 18, 1982). . . . Granted free agency (November 9, 1987). . . . Re-signed by Astros (January 8, 1988). . . . Granted free agency (December 7, 1990). . . . Signed by Chicago Cubs (December 17, 1990). . . . On disabled list (July 23-September 1, 1991).
STATISTICAL NOTES: Tied for N.L. lead with five balks in 1990.

Year Team (League)	G	W	L	Pct.	ERA	Sv.	IP	H	R	ER	BB	SO
1976 —Covington (Appalachian)	15	5	5	.500	2.69	2	97	80	40	29	28	71
1977 —Cocoa (Florida State)	14	7	5	.583	3.10	0	93	97	40	32	31	81
—Columbus (Southern)	9	3	5	.375	3.50	0	54	52	2	21	24	29
1978 —Columbus (Southern)	26	10	13	.435	3.48	0	181	170	89	70	88	114
1979 —Charleston, W.Va. (Int'l)	34	7	8	.467	3.66	1	160	159	80	65	44	90
1980 —Houston (N.L.)	57	7	5	.583	1.92	10	103	90	24	22	32	85
1981 —Houston (N.L.)	42	5	3	.625	2.76	8	75	54	26	23	23	52
1982 —Houston (N.L.)	49	5	4	.556	3.84	11	63⅓	69	30	27	31	28
1983 —Houston (N.L.)	42	3	1	.750	3.10	6	72⅔	72	32	25	36	41
1984 —Houston (N.L.)	53	5	4	.556	2.21	5	77⅓	60	22	19	20	45
1985 —Houston (N.L.)	64	9	5	.643	2.27	27	79⅓	69	26	20	17	40
1986 —Houston (N.L.)	54	4	7	.364	2.73	33	56	39	17	17	22	46
1987 —Houston (N.L.)	50	2	3	.400	1.65	24	60	39	13	11	21	73
1988 —Houston (N.L.)	51	4	5	.444	2.67	27	57⅓	60	26	17	19	38
1989 —Houston (N.L.)	52	3	4	.429	2.64	25	58	49	20	17	19	31
1990 —Houston (N.L.)	49	6	6	.500	2.39	23	60⅓	45	18	16	20	50
1991 —Chicago (N.L.) ■.....................	35	0	6	.000	6.00	17	33	39	22	22	19	16
Major league totals (12 years)	598	53	53	.500	2.67	216	795⅓	685	276	236	279	545

DIVISION SERIES RECORD

Year Team (League)	G	W	L	Pct.	ERA	Sv.	IP	H	R	ER	BB	SO
1981 —Houston (N.L.)	2	0	0	. . .	3.86	0	2⅓	2	1	1	0	4

CHAMPIONSHIP SERIES RECORD

Year Team (League)	G	W	L	Pct.	ERA	Sv.	IP	H	R	ER	BB	SO
1980 —Houston (N.L.)	3	1	0	1.000	3.86	0	2⅓	4	1	1	2	4
1986 —Houston (N.L.)	2	0	1	.000	9.00	0	2	2	2	2	3	2
Championship Series totals (2 years)	5	1	1	.500	6.23	0	4⅓	6	3	3	5	6

ALL-STAR GAME RECORD

Year League	W	L	Pct.	ERA	Sv.	IP	H	R	ER	BB	SO
1986 —National					Did not play						
1990 —National	0	0	. . .	0.00	0	⅔	1	0	0	2	1

SMITH, DWIGHT
OF, CUBS

PERSONAL: Born November 8, 1963, at Tallahassee, Fla. . . . 5-11/175. . . . Throws right, bats left. . . . Full name: John Dwight Smith.
HIGH SCHOOL: Wade Hampton (Varnville, S.C.).
COLLEGE: Spartanburg Methodist (S.C.).
TRANSACTIONS/CAREER NOTES: Selected by Toronto Blue Jays organization in third round of free-agent draft (January 17, 1984). . . . Selected by Chicago Cubs organization in secondary phase of free-agent draft (June 4, 1984).
STATISTICAL NOTES: Tied for Appalachian League lead in double plays by outfielders with three in 1984. . . . Led Midwest League outfielders with 296 total chances in 1986. . . . Led Eastern League with 270 total bases and tied for lead in caught stealing with 18 in 1987.

Year Team (League)	Pos.	G	AB	R	H	2B	3B	HR	RBI	Avg.	SB	PO	A	E	Avg.
						BATTING								**FIELDING**	
1984 —Pikeville (Appalachian)	OF	61	195	42	46	6	2	1	17	.236	★39	77	8	•9	.904
1985 —Geneva (N.Y.-Penn)	OF	73	232	44	67	11	2	4	32	.289	30	81	4	7	.924
1986 —Peoria (Midwest)	OF	124	471	92	146	22	★11	11	57	.310	53	★272	11	13	.956

Year	Team (League)	Pos.	G	AB	R	H	2B	3B	HR	RBI	Avg.	SB	PO	A	E	Avg.
1987	—Pittsfield (Eastern)..........	OF	130	498	*111	168	28	10	18	72	.337	*60	214	8	•14	.941
1988	—Iowa (American Assoc.) ...	OF	129	505	76	148	26	3	9	48	.293	25	216	11	*15	.938
1989	—Iowa (American Assoc.) ...	OF	21	83	11	27	7	3	2	7	.325	6	39	2	4	.911
	—Chicago (N.L.).................	OF	109	343	52	111	19	6	9	52	.324	9	188	7	5	.975
1990	—Chicago (N.L.).................	OF	117	290	34	76	15	0	6	27	.262	11	139	4	2	.986
1991	—Chicago (N.L.).................	OF	90	167	16	38	7	2	3	21	.228	2	73	3	3	.962
Major league totals (3 years)			316	800	102	225	41	8	18	100	.281	22	400	14	10	.976

CHAMPIONSHIP SERIES RECORD

CHAMPIONSHIP SERIES NOTES: Shares record for most at-bats in one inning—2 (October 5, 1989, first inning).

Year	Team (League)	Pos.	G	AB	R	H	2B	3B	HR	RBI	Avg.	SB	PO	A	E	Avg.
1989	—Chicago (N.L.)	OF	4	15	2	3	1	0	0	0	.200	1	10	0	0	1.000

SMITH, GREG
2B, DODGERS

PERSONAL: Born April 5, 1967, at Baltimore. . . . 5-11/170. . . . Throws right, bats both. . . . Full name: Gregory Allen Smith.
HIGH SCHOOL: Gleneig (Md.).
TRANSACTIONS/CAREER NOTES: Selected by Chicago Cubs organization in second round of free-agent draft (June 3, 1985). . . . Traded by Cubs organization to Los Angeles Dodgers for IF Jose Vizcaino (December 14, 1990). . . . On Albuquerque disabled list (June 1-June 19 and July 8, 1991-remainder of season).
STATISTICAL NOTES: Led Midwest League shortstops with 48 errors and tied for lead with 189 putouts in 1987. . . . Led Southern League second basemen with 621 total chances and 59 double plays in 1989.

Year	Team (League)	Pos.	G	AB	R	H	2B	3B	HR	RBI	Avg.	SB	PO	A	E	Avg.
1985	—Wytheville (Appal.)	SS	51	179	28	42	6	2	0	15	.235	8	56	160	24	.900
1986	—Peoria (Midwest)	SS-2B	53	170	24	43	6	3	2	26	.253	9	65	101	15	.917
1987	—Peoria (Midwest)	SS-2B	124	444	69	120	23	5	6	56	.270	26	†193	347	†49	.917
1988	—Winston-Salem (Caro.)	2B-1B	95	361	62	101	12	2	4	29	.280	52	162	236	16	.961
1989	—Charlotte (Southern)	2B	126	467	59	138	23	6	5	64	.296	38	*253	*348	20	.968
	—Chicago (N.L.)	2B	4	5	1	2	0	0	0	2	.400	0	4	3	2	.778
1990	—Chicago (N.L.)	SS-2B	18	44	4	9	2	1	0	5	.205	1	20	38	3	.951
	—Iowa (American Assoc.) ...	SS-3B	105	398	54	116	19	1	5	44	.291	26	155	303	18	.962
1991	—Albuquerque (PCL)■	2B-SS	48	161	25	35	3	2	0	17	.217	11	80	145	9	.962
	—Los Angeles (N.L.)...........	2B	5	3	1	0	0	0	0	0	.000	0	0	0	0	...
Major league totals (3 years)			27	52	6	11	2	1	0	7	.212	1	24	41	5	.929

SMITH, LEE
P, CARDINALS

PERSONAL: Born December 4, 1957, at Jamestown, La. . . . 6-6/269. . . . Throws right, bats right. . . . Full name: Lee Arthur Smith.
HIGH SCHOOL: Castor (La.).
COLLEGE: Northwestern State (La.).
TRANSACTIONS/CAREER NOTES: Selected by Chicago Cubs organization in second round of free-agent draft (June 4, 1975). . . . On disabled list (April 21-May 6, 1986). . . . Traded by Cubs to Boston Red Sox for P Al Nipper and P Calvin Schiraldi (December 8, 1987). . . . Traded by Red Sox to St. Louis Cardinals for OF Tom Brunansky (May 4, 1990).
RECORDS/HONORS: Holds major league career record for most consecutive errorless games by pitcher—484 (July 5, 1982 through 1991). . . . Holds N.L. single-season record for most saves—47 (1991). . . . Named N.L. co-Fireman of the Year by THE SPORTING NEWS (1983). . . . Named N.L Fireman of the Year by THE SPORTING NEWS (1991).
STATISTICAL NOTES: Tied for American Association lead with 16 wild pitches in 1980.

Year	Team (League)	G	W	L	Pct.	ERA	Sv.	IP	H	R	ER	BB	SO
1975	—Bradenton Cubs (Gulf Coast)	10	3	6	.375	2.32	0	62	35	23	16	*49	35
1976	—Pompano Beach (Florida St.)....	26	4	8	.333	5.35	0	101	120	76	60	74	52
1977	—Pompano Beach (Florida St.)....	26	10	4	.714	4.29	0	130	131	67	62	85	82
1978	—Midland (Texas)	30	8	10	.444	5.98	0	155	161	122	103	*128	71
1979	—Midland (Texas)	35	9	5	.643	4.93	1	104	122	65	57	85	46
1980	—Wichita (American Assoc.)	50	4	7	.364	3.70	15	90	70	49	37	56	63
	—Chicago (N.L.)	18	2	0	1.000	2.86	0	22	21	9	7	14	17
1981	—Chicago (N.L.)	40	3	6	.333	3.49	1	67	57	31	26	31	50
1982	—Chicago (N.L.)	72	2	5	.286	2.69	17	117	105	38	35	37	99
1983	—Chicago (N.L.)	66	4	10	.286	1.65	*29	103⅓	70	23	19	41	91
1984	—Chicago (N.L.)	69	9	7	.563	3.65	33	101	98	42	41	35	86
1985	—Chicago (N.L.)	65	7	4	.636	3.04	33	97⅔	87	35	33	32	112
1986	—Chicago (N.L.)	66	9	9	.500	3.09	31	90⅓	69	32	31	42	93
1987	—Chicago (N.L.)	62	4	10	.286	3.12	36	83⅔	84	30	29	32	96
1988	—Boston (A.L.)■	64	4	5	.444	2.80	29	83⅔	72	34	26	37	96
1989	—Boston (A.L.)	64	6	1	.857	3.57	25	70⅔	53	30	28	33	96
1990	—Boston (A.L.)	11	2	1	.667	1.88	4	14⅓	13	4	3	9	17
	—St. Louis (N.L.)■	53	3	4	.429	2.10	27	68⅔	58	20	16	20	70
1991	—St. Louis (N.L.)	67	6	3	.667	2.34	*47	73	70	19	19	13	67
American League totals (3 years)		139	12	7	.632	3.04	58	168⅔	138	68	57	79	209
National League totals (10 years)		578	49	58	.458	2.80	254	823⅔	719	279	256	297	781
Major league totals (12 years)		717	61	65	.484	2.84	312	992⅓	857	347	313	376	990

CHAMPIONSHIP SERIES RECORD

Year	Team (League)	G	W	L	Pct.	ERA	Sv.	IP	H	R	ER	BB	SO
1984 —Chicago (N.L.)		2	0	1	.000	9.00	1	2	3	2	2	0	3
1988 —Boston (A.L.)		2	0	1	.000	8.10	0	3⅓	6	3	3	1	4
Championship Series totals (2 years)		4	0	2	.000	8.44	1	5⅓	9	5	5	1	7

ALL-STAR GAME RECORD

Year	League	W	L	Pct.	ERA	Sv.	IP	H	R	ER	BB	SO
1983 —National	0	0	. . .	9.00	0	1	2	2	1	0	1
1987 —National	1	0	1.000	0.00	0	3	2	0	0	0	4
1991 —National					Did not play						
All-Star totals (2 years)	1	0	1.000	2.25	0	4	4	2	1	0	5

SMITH, LONNIE

OF, BRAVES

PERSONAL: Born December 22, 1955, at Chicago. . . . 5-9/170. . . . Throws right, bats right. . . . Full name: Lonnie Smith.
HIGH SCHOOL: Centennial (Compton, Calif.).
TRANSACTIONS/CAREER NOTES: Selected by Philadelphia Phillies organization in first round (third pick overall) of free-agent draft (June 5, 1974). . . . On Oklahoma City disabled list (April 14-25, 1978). . . . Traded by Phillies with a player to be named later to Cleveland Indians for C Bo Diaz (November 20, 1981); traded by Indians to St. Louis Cardinals for P Lary Sorensen and P Silvio Martinez (November 20, 1981). Indians organization acquired P Scott Munninghoff to complete first deal (December 9, 1981). . . . On disabled list (June 11-July 8, 1983). . . . Traded by Cardinals to Kansas City Royals for OF John Morris (May 17, 1985). . . . On disabled list (April 13-May 4, 1986). . . . Granted free agency (November 12, 1986). . . . Re-signed by Royals organization (May 8, 1987). . . . Released by Royals (December 15, 1987). . . . Signed by Richmond, Atlanta Braves organization (March 12, 1988). . . . On disabled list (May 20-June 13, 1989 and March 30-April 28, 1991).
RECORDS/HONORS: Shares major league single-season record for fewest double plays by outfielder who led league in double plays—4 (1983). . . . Named outfielder on THE SPORTING NEWS N.L. All-Star team (1982). . . . Named N.L. Rookie Player of the Year by THE SPORTING NEWS (1980). . . . Named N.L. Comeback Player of the Year by THE SPORTING NEWS (1989).
STATISTICAL NOTES: Tied for Western Carolinas League lead in caught stealing with 14 in 1975. . . . Led American Association outfielders with five double plays in 1978. . . . Led American Association in caught stealing with 19 in 1978. . . . Led N.L. in being hit by pitch with nine in 1982 and 1984 and tied for lead with nine in 1983. . . . Tied for N.L. lead in caught stealing with 26 in 1982. . . . Tied for N.L. lead in double plays by outfielders with four in 1983. . . . Led International League with 66 bases on balls received in 1988. . . . Led N.L. with .415 on base percentage in 1989.

						BATTING							FIELDING			
Year	Team (League)	Pos.	G	AB	R	H	2B	3B	HR	RBI	Avg.	SB	PO	A	E	Avg.
1974 —Auburn (N.Y.-Penn)	OF	61	210	48	60	10	4	5	27	.286	12	143	6	•9	.943
1975 —Spartanburg (W. Caro.)	OF	131	465	*114	*150	23	4	7	40	.323	56	*317	9	11	.967
1976 —Oklahoma City (A.A.)	OF	134	483	*93	149	24	9	8	54	.308	26	200	4	*14	.936
1977 —Oklahoma City (A.A.)	OF	125	477	91	132	14	10	4	41	.277	45	231	8	*13	.948
1978 —Oklahoma City (A.A.)	OF	125	480	103	151	20	5	7	43	.315	66	274	*21	*12	.961
—Philadelphia (N.L.)	OF	17	4	6	0	0	0	0	0	.000	4	5	1	0	1.000
1979 —Oklahoma City (A.A.)	OF	110	451	*106	149	26	9	7	44	.330	34	268	13	*12	.959
—Philadelphia (N.L.)	OF	17	30	4	5	2	0	0	3	.167	2	19	1	0	1.000
1980 —Philadelphia (N.L.)	OF	100	298	69	101	14	4	3	20	.339	33	121	2	4	.969
1981 —Philadelphia (N.L.)	OF	62	176	40	57	14	3	2	11	.324	21	91	10	3	.971
1982 —St. Louis (N.L.)■	OF	156	592	*120	182	35	8	8	69	.307	68	303	•16	10	.970
1983 —St. Louis (N.L.)	OF	130	492	83	158	31	5	8	45	.321	43	225	14	*15	.941
1984 —St. Louis (N.L.)	OF	145	504	77	126	20	4	6	49	.250	50	184	*18	•11	.948
1985 —St. Louis (N.L.)	OF	28	96	15	25	2	2	0	7	.260	12	43	1	0	1.000
—Kansas City (A.L.)■	OF	120	448	77	115	23	4	6	41	.257	40	195	10	9	.958
1986 —Kansas City (A.L.)	OF	134	508	80	146	25	7	8	44	.287	26	245	5	9	.965
1987 —Omaha (Am. Assoc.)	OF	40	149	36	49	9	1	7	33	.329	8	51	1	3	.945
—Kansas City (A.L.)	OF	48	167	26	42	7	1	3	8	.251	9	52	2	5	.915
1988 —Richmond (Int'l)■	OF	93	290	58	87	13	5	9	51	.300	26	120	6	2	.984
—Atlanta (N.L.)	OF	43	114	14	27	3	0	3	9	.237	4	59	2	2	.968
1989 —Atlanta (N.L.)	OF	134	482	89	152	34	4	21	79	.315	25	289	3	2	.993
1990 —Atlanta (N.L.)	OF	135	466	72	142	27	9	9	42	.305	10	254	6	12	.956
1991 —Atlanta (N.L.)	OF	122	353	58	97	19	1	7	44	.275	9	134	5	5	.965
American League totals (3 years)		302	1123	183	303	55	12	17	93	.270	75	492	17	23	.957
National League totals (12 years)		1089	3607	647	1072	201	40	67	378	.297	281	1727	79	64	.966
Major league totals (14 years)		1391	4730	830	1375	256	52	84	471	.291	356	2219	96	87	.964

DIVISION SERIES RECORD

						BATTING							FIELDING			
Year	Team (League)	Pos.	G	AB	R	H	2B	3B	HR	RBI	Avg.	SB	PO	A	E	Avg.
1981 —Philadelphia (N.L.)	OF	5	19	1	5	1	0	0	0	.263	0	6	1	0	1.000

CHAMPIONSHIP SERIES RECORD

						BATTING							FIELDING			
Year	Team (League)	Pos.	G	AB	R	H	2B	3B	HR	RBI	Avg.	SB	PO	A	E	Avg.
1980 —Philadelphia (N.L.)	PR-OF	3	5	2	3	0	0	0	0	.600	1	2	1	0	1.000
1982 —St. Louis (N.L.)	OF	3	11	1	3	0	0	0	1	.273	0	2	0	0	1.000

Year	Team (League)	Pos.	G	AB	R	H	2B	3B	HR	RBI	Avg.	SB	PO	A	E	Avg.
1985 — Kansas City (A.L.)		OF	7	28	2	7	2	0	0	1	.250	2	8	3	1	.917
1991 — Atlanta (N.L.)		OF	7	24	3	6	3	0	0	0	.250	1	10	2	0	1.000
Championship Series totals (4 years)			20	68	8	19	5	0	0	2	.279	4	22	6	1	.966

WORLD SERIES RECORD

WORLD SERIES NOTES: Holds career record for most clubs played with—4. . . . Shares record for most at-bats in one inning—2 (October 24, 1991, seventh inning).

Year	Team (League)	Pos.	G	AB	R	H	2B	3B	HR	RBI	Avg.	SB	PO	A	E	Avg.
1980 — Philadelphia (N.L.)		PR-O-DH	6	19	2	5	1	0	0	1	.263	0	4	1	0	1.000
1982 — St. Louis (N.L.)		OF-DH	7	28	6	9	4	1	0	1	.321	2	11	0	0	1.000
1985 — Kansas City (A.L.)		OF	7	27	4	9	3	0	0	4	.333	2	7	2	0	1.000
1991 — Atlanta (N.L.)		DH-OF	7	26	5	6	0	0	3	3	.231	1	2	0	0	1.000
World Series totals (4 years)			27	100	17	29	8	1	3	9	.290	5	24	3	0	1.000

ALL-STAR GAME RECORD

Year	League	Pos.	AB	R	H	2B	3B	HR	RBI	Avg.	SB	PO	A	E	Avg.
1982 — National		OF	0	0	0	0	0	0	0	. . .	0	1	0	0	1.000

SMITH, OZZIE

SS, CARDINALS

PERSONAL: Born December 26, 1954, at Mobile, Ala. . . . 5-10/168. . . . Throws right, bats both. . . . Full name: Osborne Earl Smith.

HIGH SCHOOL: Locke (Los Angeles).

COLLEGE: Cal Poly San Luis Obispo (received degree).

TRANSACTIONS/CAREER NOTES: Selected by Detroit Tigers organization in seventh round of free-agent draft (June 8, 1976). . . . Selected by San Diego Padres organization in fourth round of free-agent draft (June 7, 1977). . . . Traded by Padres to St. Louis Cardinals for SS Garry Templeton (February 11, 1982). . . . On disabled list (July 14-August 19, 1984 and March 31-April 15, 1989).

RECORDS/HONORS: Holds major league records for most years with 500 or more assists by shortstop—8; most years leading league in assists and chances accepted by shortstop—8. . . . Holds major league single-season records for most assists by shortstop—621 (1980); fewest chances accepted by shortstop who led league in chances accepted—692 (1989); fewest double plays by shortstop who led league in double plays—79 (1991). . . . Shares Major League record for most double plays by shortstop in extra-inning game—6 (August 25, 1979, 19 innings). . . . Holds N.L. single-season record for fewest errors by shortstop (150 or more games)—8 (1991). . . . Holds N.L. records for most years leading league in fielding percentage by shortstop (100 or more games)—7. . . . Shares N.L. records for most consecutive years leading league in assists by shortstop—4 (1979-82); highest fielding average by shortstop (150 or more games)—.987 (1987 and 1991); and most years leading league in double plays by shortstop—5. . . . Shares modern N.L. record for most consecutive years leading league in fielding average by shortstop (100 or more games)—4 (1984-87). . . . Won N.L. Gold Glove at shortstop (1980-91). . . . Named shortstop on THE SPORTING NEWS N.L. All-Star team (1982, 1984-87). . . . Named shortstop on THE SPORTING NEWS N.L. Silver Slugger team (1987).

STATISTICAL NOTES: Led Northwest League shortstops with 40 double plays in 1977. . . . Led N.L. with 28 sacrifice hits in 1978 and 23 in 1980. . . . Led N.L. shortstops with 933 total chances in 1980, 658 in 1981, 844 in 1983, 827 in 1985, 771 in 1987, 775 in 1988 and 709 in 1989. . . . Led N.L. shortstops with 113 double plays in 1980, 111 in 1987, 79 in 1991 and tied for lead with 94 in 1984 and 96 in 1986.

Year	Team (League)	Pos.	G	AB	R	H	2B	3B	HR	RBI	Avg.	SB	PO	A	E	Avg.
1977 — Walla Walla (Northwest) ..		SS	•68	*287	*69	87	10	2	1	35	.303	30	130	*254	23	*.943
1978 — San Diego (N.L.)		SS	159	590	69	152	17	6	1	46	.258	40	264	548	25	.970
1979 — San Diego (N.L.)		SS	156	587	77	124	18	6	0	27	.211	28	256	*555	20	.976
1980 — San Diego (N.L.)		SS	158	609	67	140	18	5	0	35	.230	57	*288	*621	24	.974
1981 — San Diego (N.L.)		SS	•110	*450	53	100	11	2	0	21	.222	22	220	*422	16	*.976
1982 — St. Louis (N.L.)■		SS	140	488	58	121	24	1	2	43	.248	25	279	*535	13	*.984
1983 — St. Louis (N.L.)		SS	159	552	69	134	30	6	3	50	.243	34	*304	519	21	.975
1984 — St. Louis (N.L.)		SS	124	412	53	106	20	5	1	44	.257	35	233	437	12	*.982
1985 — St. Louis (N.L.)		SS	158	537	70	148	22	3	6	54	.276	31	264	*549	14	*.983
1986 — St. Louis (N.L.)		SS	153	514	67	144	19	4	0	54	.280	31	229	453	15	*.978
1987 — St. Louis (N.L.)		SS	158	600	104	182	40	4	0	75	.303	43	245	*516	10	*.987
1988 — St. Louis (N.L.)		SS	153	575	80	155	27	1	3	51	.270	57	234	*519	22	.972
1989 — St. Louis (N.L.)		SS	155	593	82	162	30	8	2	50	.273	29	209	*483	17	.976
1990 — St. Louis (N.L.)		SS	143	512	61	130	21	1	1	50	.254	32	212	378	12	.980
1991 — St. Louis (N.L.)		SS	150	550	96	157	30	3	3	50	.285	35	244	387	8	*.987
Major league totals (14 years)			2076	7569	1006	1955	327	55	22	650	.258	499	3481	6922	229	.978

CHAMPIONSHIP SERIES RECORD

Year	Team (League)	Pos.	G	AB	R	H	2B	3B	HR	RBI	Avg.	SB	PO	A	E	Avg.
1982 — St. Louis (N.L.)		SS	3	9	0	5	0	0	0	3	.556	1	4	11	0	1.000
1985 — St. Louis (N.L.)		SS	6	23	4	10	1	1	1	3	.435	1	6	16	0	1.000
1987 — St. Louis (N.L.)		SS	7	25	2	5	0	1	0	1	.200	0	10	19	1	.967
Championship Series totals (3 years)			16	57	6	20	1	2	1	7	.351	2	20	46	1	.985

WORLD SERIES RECORD

Year	Team (League)	Pos.	G	AB	R	H	2B	3B	HR	RBI	Avg.	SB	PO	A	E	Avg.
1982 —St. Louis (N.L.)		SS	7	24	3	5	0	0	0	1	.208	1	22	17	0	1.000
1985 —St. Louis (N.L.)		SS	7	23	1	2	0	0	0	0	.087	1	10	16	1	.963
1987 —St. Louis (N.L.)		SS	7	28	3	6	0	0	0	2	.214	2	7	19	0	1.000
World Series totals (3 years)			21	75	7	13	0	0	0	3	.173	4	39	52	1	.989

ALL-STAR GAME RECORD

Year	League	Pos.	AB	R	H	2B	3B	HR	RBI	Avg.	SB	PO	A	E	Avg.
1981 —National		SS	0	0	0	0	0	0	0	. . .	0	1	0	0	1.000
1982 —National		PR-SS	0	0	0	0	0	0	0	. . .	0	0	1	0	1.000
1983 —National		SS	2	1	1	0	0	0	0	.500	0	0	0	0	. . .
1984 —National		SS	3	0	0	0	0	0	0	.000	1	3	0	0	1.000
1985 —National		SS	4	0	0	0	0	0	0	.000	0	1	3	0	1.000
1986 —National		SS	1	0	0	0	0	0	0	.000	0	3	2	0	1.000
1987 —National		SS	2	0	0	0	0	0	0	.000	0	3	2	1	.833
1988 —National		SS	2	0	0	0	0	0	0	.000	0	1	4	0	1.000
1989 —National		SS	4	0	1	0	0	0	0	.250	0	1	3	0	1.000
1990 —National		SS	1	0	0	0	0	0	0	.000	0	1	1	0	1.000
1991 —National		SS	1	0	0	0	0	0	0	.000	0	0	1	0	1.000
All-Star Game totals (11 years)			20	1	2	0	0	0	0	.100	1	14	17	1	.969

SMITH, PETE
P, BRAVES

PERSONAL: Born February 27, 1966, at Abington, Mass. . . . 6-2/200. . . . Throws right, bats right. . . . Full name: Peter John Smith.
HIGH SCHOOL: Burlington (Mass.).
TRANSACTIONS/CAREER NOTES: Selected by Philadelphia Phillies organization in first round (21st pick overall) of free-agent draft (June 4, 1984). . . . Traded by Phillies organization with C Ozzie Virgil to Atlanta Braves for P Steve Bedrosian and OF Milt Thompson (December 10, 1985). . . . On Atlanta disabled list (June 25-September 3, 1990); included rehabilitation disability assignment to Greenville (August 26-September 2, 1990). . . . On Atlanta disabled list (April 4-May 23, 1991); included rehabilitation disability assignment to Macon (April 12-24) and Richmond (April 24-May 9 and May 13-14, 1991).
STATISTICAL NOTES: Led N.L. with seven balks in 1989.

Year	Team (League)	G	W	L	Pct.	ERA	Sv.	IP	H	R	ER	BB	SO
1984 —Sarasota Phillies (Gulf Coast) ..		8	1	2	.333	1.46	0	37	28	11	6	16	35
1985 —Clearwater (Florida State)		26	12	10	.545	3.29	0	153	135	68	56	80	86
1986 —Greenville (Southern)■..............		24	1	8	.111	5.85	0	104⅔	117	88	68	78	64
1987 —Greenville (Southern)		29	9	9	.500	3.35	1	177⅓	162	76	66	67	119
—Atlanta (N.L.)		6	1	2	.333	4.83	0	31⅔	39	21	17	14	11
1988 —Atlanta (N.L.)		32	7	15	.318	3.69	0	195⅓	183	89	80	88	124
1989 —Atlanta (N.L.)		28	5	14	.263	4.75	0	142	144	83	75	57	115
1990 —Atlanta (N.L.)		13	5	6	.455	4.79	0	77	77	45	41	24	56
—Greenville (Southern)		2	0	0	. . .	0.00	0	3⅓	1	0	0	0	2
1991 —Macon (South Atlantic)		3	0	0	. . .	8.38	0	9⅔	15	11	9	2	14
—Richmond (International)		10	3	3	.500	7.24	0	51	66	44	41	24	41
—Atlanta (N.L.)		14	1	3	.250	5.06	0	48	48	33	27	22	29
Major league totals (5 years)		93	19	40	.322	4.37	0	494	491	271	240	205	335

SMITH, ROY
P

PERSONAL: Born September 6, 1961, at Mount Vernon, N.Y. . . . 6-3/212. . . . Throws right, bats right. . . . Full name: LeRoy Purdy Smith III.
HIGH SCHOOL: Mount Vernon (N.Y.).
COLLEGE: Mercy (N.Y.) and Fordham.
TRANSACTIONS/CAREER NOTES: Selected by Philadelphia Phillies organization in third round of free-agent draft (June 5, 1979). . . . Traded by Phillies organization with P Jerry Reed and OF Wil Culmer to Cleveland Indians for P John Denny (September 12, 1982). . . . On Cleveland disabled list (July 3-August 1, 1985); included rehabilitation disability assignment to Maine (July 27-30, 1985). . . . Traded by Indians with P Ramon Romero to Minnesota Twins for P Ken Schrom and P Bryan Oeklers (January 7, 1986). . . . On Toledo disabled list (June 7-July 3, 1986). . . . Released by Twins organization (December 20, 1986). . . . Re-signed by Twins organization (February 24, 1987). . . . Released by Twins (December 2, 1990). . . . Signed by Baltimore Orioles organization (January 1, 1991). . . . Granted free agency (October 16, 1991).
RECORDS/HONORS: Named Carolina League Pitcher of the Year (1980).
STATISTICAL NOTES: Tied for Carolina League lead with three shutouts in 1980.

Year	Team (League)	G	W	L	Pct.	ERA	Sv.	IP	H	R	ER	BB	SO
1979 —Helena (Pioneer)		5	5	0	1.000	2.50	0	36	21	16	10	16	42
1980 —Peninsula (Carolina)		27	★17	6	.739	2.60	0	163	101	54	47	63	134
1981 —Reading (Eastern)		27	11	8	.579	4.42	0	161	123	92	79	97	117
1982 —Reading (Eastern)		26	10	8	.556	3.85	0	166	141	81	71	82	122
1983 —Charleston, W.Va. (Int'l)■........		27	6	8	.429	5.16	0	155⅓	166	101	89	75	95
1984 —Maine (International)		12	5	4	.556	4.35	0	80⅔	77	47	39	29	48
—Cleveland (A.L.)		22	5	4	.556	4.59	0	86⅓	91	49	44	40	55
1985 —Maine (International)		15	10	4	.714	2.39	0	109⅓	84	33	29	29	65
—Cleveland (A.L.)		12	1	4	.200	5.34	0	62⅓	84	40	37	17	28

Year	Team (League)	G	W	L	Pct.	ERA	Sv.	IP	H	R	ER	BB	SO
1986	—Minnesota (A.L.)■	5	0	2	.000	6.97	0	10⅓	13	8	8	5	8
	—Toledo (International)	9	2	1	.667	1.51	0	53⅔	42	12	9	16	39
1987	—Portland (Pacific Coast)	24	9	12	.429	3.79	0	166⅓	176	84	70	41	106
	—Minnesota (A.L.)	7	1	0	1.000	4.96	0	16⅓	20	10	9	6	8
1988	—Portland (Pacific Coast)	22	12	9	.571	4.32	0	150	152	82	72	31	110
	—Minnesota (A.L.)	9	3	0	1.000	2.68	0	37	29	12	11	12	17
1989	—Minnesota (A.L.)	32	10	6	.625	3.92	1	172⅓	180	82	75	51	92
1990	—Minnesota (A.L.)	32	5	10	.333	4.81	0	153⅓	191	91	82	47	87
1991	—Rochester (International)■	11	6	2	.750	3.50	0	74⅔	65	31	29	17	40
	—Baltimore (A.L.)	17	5	4	.556	5.60	0	80⅓	99	52	50	24	25
	Major league totals (8 years)	136	30	31	.492	4.60	1	618⅓	707	344	316	202	320

SMITH, WILLIE

P, YANKEES

PERSONAL: Born January 27, 1967, at Savannah, Ga. . . . 6-7/240. . . . Throws right, bats right. . . . Full name: Willie Everett Smith.
HIGH SCHOOL: Savannah (Ga.).
TRANSACTIONS/CAREER NOTES: Signed as free agent by Pittsburgh Pirates organization (July 13, 1986). . . . On disabled list (June 12-July 15, 1988). . . . Traded by Pirates organization with P Jeff D. Robinson to New York Yankees organization for C Don Slaught (December 4, 1989).

Year	Team (League)	G	W	L	Pct.	ERA	Sv.	IP	H	R	ER	BB	SO
1986	—Bradenton Pirates (GCL)	7	1	0	1.000	2.49	1	21⅔	16	8	6	6	13
1987	—Bradenton Pirates (GCL)	10	2	1	.667	0.93	4	19⅓	12	4	2	11	27
	—Watertown (New York-Penn)	5	2	0	1.000	4.43	1	20⅓	15	13	10	10	24
1988	—Augusta (South Atlantic)	30	1	4	.200	2.98	6	48⅓	35	20	16	29	48
1989	—Salem (Carolina)	23	4	5	.444	2.94	4	64⅓	46	26	21	40	58
	—Harrisburg (Eastern)	12	3	0	1.000	2.45	0	18⅓	11	5	5	10	21
1990	—Albany (Eastern)■	9	1	1	.500	0.00	4	8⅔	6	1	0	5	12
	—Columbus (International)	33	3	1	.750	6.23	7	34⅔	38	24	24	29	47
1991	—Albany (Eastern)	21	7	7	.500	4.15	0	108⅓	99	65	50	72	104

SMITH, ZANE

P, PIRATES

PERSONAL: Born December 28, 1960, at Madison, Wis. . . . 6-2/200. . . . Throws left, bats left. . . . Full name: Zane William Smith.
HIGH SCHOOL: North Platte (Neb.).
COLLEGE: Indiana State.
TRANSACTIONS/CAREER NOTES: Selected by Atlanta Braves organization in third round of free-agent draft (June 7, 1982). . . . On disabled list (August 5-September 1, 1985 and August 25, 1988-remainder of season). . . . Traded by Braves to Montreal Expos for P Sergio Valdez, P Nate Minshey and OF Kevin Dean (July 2, 1989). . . . Traded by Expos to Pittsburgh Pirates for P Scott Ruskin, SS Willie Greene and a player to be named later (August 8, 1990); Expos acquired OF Moises Alou to complete deal (August 16, 1990). . . . Granted free agency (November 5, 1990). . . . Re-signed by Pirates (December 6, 1990).
RECORDS/HONORS: Named lefthanded pitcher on THE SPORTING NEWS N.L. All-Star team (1987).
STATISTICAL NOTES: Tied for N.L. lead in games started by pitcher with 36 in 1987. . . . Led N.L. batters with 14 sacrifice hits in 1987.
MISCELLANEOUS: Struck out in only at-bat as pinch-hitter (1991).

Year	Team (League)	G	W	L	Pct.	ERA	Sv.	IP	H	R	ER	BB	SO
1982	—Anderson (South Atlantic)	12	5	3	.625	6.86	1	63	65	53	48	34	32
1983	—Durham (Carolina)	27	9	•15	.375	4.90	0	170⅔	183	109	93	83	126
1984	—Greenville (Southern)	9	7	0	1.000	1.65	0	60	47	13	11	23	35
	—Richmond (International)	19	7	4	.636	4.15	0	123⅔	113	62	57	65	68
	—Atlanta (N.L.)	3	1	0	1.000	2.25	0	20	16	7	5	13	16
1985	—Atlanta (N.L.)	42	9	10	.474	3.80	0	147	135	70	62	80	85
1986	—Atlanta (N.L.)	38	8	16	.333	4.05	1	204⅔	209	109	92	105	139
1987	—Atlanta (N.L.)	36	15	10	.600	4.09	0	242	245	*130	110	91	130
1988	—Atlanta (N.L.)	23	5	10	.333	4.30	0	140⅓	159	72	67	44	59
1989	—Atlanta-Montreal (N.L.)■	48	1	13	.071	3.49	2	147	141	76	57	52	93
1990	—Montreal-Pittsburgh (N.L.)■	33	12	9	.571	2.55	0	215⅓	196	77	61	50	130
1991	—Pittsburgh (N.L.)	35	16	10	.615	3.20	0	228	234	95	81	29	120
	Major league totals (8 years)	258	67	78	.462	3.58	3	1344⅓	1335	636	535	464	772

CHAMPIONSHIP SERIES RECORD

Year	Team (League)	G	W	L	Pct.	ERA	Sv.	IP	H	R	ER	BB	SO
1990	—Pittsburgh (N.L.)	2	0	2	.000	6.00	0	9	14	6	6	1	8
1991	—Pittsburgh (N.L.)	2	1	1	.500	0.61	0	14⅔	15	1	1	3	10
	Championship Series totals (2 years)	4	1	3	.250	2.66	0	23⅔	29	7	7	4	18

SMOLTZ, JOHN

P, BRAVES

PERSONAL: Born May 15, 1967, at Detroit. . . . 6-3/185. . . . Throws right, bats right. . . . Full name: John Andrew Smoltz.
HIGH SCHOOL: Waverly (Lansing, Mich.).
TRANSACTIONS/CAREER NOTES: Selected by Detroit Tigers organization in 22nd round of free-agent draft (June 3, 1985). . . . Traded by Tigers organization to Atlanta Braves for P Doyle Alexander (August 12, 1987).

STATISTICAL NOTES: Tied for Florida State League lead with six balks in 1986.... Led N.L. with 14 wild pitches in 1990 and 20 in 1991.

MISCELLANEOUS: Appeared in two games as pinch-runner (1991).

Year	Team (League)	G	W	L	Pct.	ERA	Sv.	IP	H	R	ER	BB	SO
1986	—Lakeland (Florida State)	17	7	8	.467	3.56	0	96	86	44	38	31	47
1987	—Glens Falls (Eastern)	21	4	10	.286	5.68	0	130	131	89	82	81	86
	—Richmond (International)■	3	0	1	.000	6.19	0	16	17	11	11	11	5
1988	—Richmond (International)	20	10	5	.667	2.79	0	135⅓	118	49	42	37	115
	—Atlanta (N.L.)	12	2	7	.222	5.48	0	64	74	40	39	33	37
1989	—Atlanta (N.L.)	29	12	11	.522	2.94	0	208	160	79	68	72	168
1990	—Atlanta (N.L.)	34	14	11	.560	3.85	0	231⅓	206	109	99	*90	170
1991	—Atlanta (N.L.)	36	14	13	.519	3.80	0	229⅔	206	101	97	77	148
	Major league totals (4 years)	111	42	42	.500	3.72	0	733	646	329	303	272	523

CHAMPIONSHIP SERIES RECORD

Year	Team (League)	G	W	L	Pct.	ERA	Sv.	IP	H	R	ER	BB	SO
1991	—Atlanta (N.L.)	2	2	0	1.000	1.76	0	15⅓	14	3	3	3	15

WORLD SERIES RECORD

Year	Team (League)	G	W	L	Pct.	ERA	Sv.	IP	H	R	ER	BB	SO
1991	—Atlanta (N.L.)	2	0	0	...	1.26	0	14⅓	13	2	2	1	11

ALL-STAR GAME RECORD

Year	League	W	L	Pct.	ERA	Sv.	IP	H	R	ER	BB	SO
1989	—National	0	1	.000	9.00	0	1	2	1	1	0	0

SNOW, J.T.
1B, YANKEES

PERSONAL: Born February 26, 1968, at Long Beach, Calif.... 6-2/202.... Throws left, bats both.... Full name: Jack Thomas Snow Jr.... Son of Jack Snow, National Football League player (1965-75).

HIGH SCHOOL: Los Alamitos (Calif.).

COLLEGE: Arizona.

TRANSACTIONS/CAREER NOTES: Selected by New York Yankees organization in fifth round of free-agent draft (June 5, 1989).

STATISTICAL NOTES: Led New York-Pennsylvania League first basemen with 649 total chances in 1989.... Led Carolina League first basemen with 1,298 total chances and 120 double plays in 1990.... Tied for Eastern League lead with 10 sacrifice flies in 1991.... Led Eastern League first basemen with 1,200 total chances in 1991.

							————BATTING————						————FIELDING————			
Year	Team (League)	Pos.	G	AB	R	H	2B	3B	HR	RBI	Avg.	SB	PO	A	E	Avg.
1989	—Oneonta (N.Y.-Penn)	1B	73	274	41	80	18	2	8	51	.292	4	*590	53	6	*.991
1990	—Prince William (Caro.)	1B	*138	520	57	133	25	1	8	72	.256	2	*1208	*78	12	.991
1991	—Albany/Colonie (East.)	1B	132	477	78	133	33	3	13	76	.279	5	*1102	90	8	*.993

SNYDER, CORY
OF/1B, GIANTS

PERSONAL: Born November 11, 1962, at Englewood, Calif.... 6-3/185.... Throws right, bats right.... Full name: James Cory Snyder.... Son of Jim Snyder, minor league infielder (1961-62).

HIGH SCHOOL: Canyon (Canyon Country, Calif.).

COLLEGE: Brigham Young.

TRANSACTIONS/CAREER NOTES: Selected by Cleveland Indians organization in first round (fourth pick overall) of free-agent draft (June 4, 1984).... On Cleveland disabled list (July 14-30, 1989); included rehabilitation disability assignment to Canton-Akron (July 24-30, 1989).... Traded by Indians with IF Lindsay Foster to Chicago White Sox for P Eric King and P Shawn Hillegas (December 4, 1990).... Traded by White Sox to Toronto Blue Jays for OF Shawn Jeter and a player to be named later (July 14, 1991); White Sox acquired P Steve Wapnick to complete deal (September 4, 1991).... Released by Blue Jays (October 28, 1991).... Signed by San Francisco Giants organization (January 13, 1992).

RECORDS/HONORS: Named shortstop on THE SPORTING NEWS college All-America team (1984).... Named Eastern League Most Valuable Player (1985).

STATISTICAL NOTES: Led Eastern League with 255 total bases and 12 sacrifice flies in 1985.... Led Eastern League third basemen with 132 putouts, 391 total chances and 26 double plays in 1985.... Hit three home runs in a game (May 21, 1987).... Led A.L. outfielders with .997 fielding percentage in 1989.

MISCELLANEOUS: Member of 1984 U.S. Olympic baseball team.

							————BATTING————						————FIELDING————			
Year	Team (League)	Pos.	G	AB	R	H	2B	3B	HR	RBI	Avg.	SB	PO	A	E	Avg.
1985	—Waterbury (Eastern)	3B-SS	*139	512	77	144	25	1	*28	*94	.281	5	†134	231	33	.917
1986	—Maine (International)	3B-SS	49	192	25	58	19	0	9	32	.302	2	46	87	8	.943
	—Cleveland (A.L.)	OF-SS-3B	103	416	58	113	21	1	24	69	.272	2	213	84	10	.967
1987	—Cleveland (A.L.)	OF-SS	157	577	74	136	24	2	33	82	.236	5	313	53	15	.961
1988	—Cleveland (A.L.)	OF	142	511	71	139	24	3	26	75	.272	5	314	*16	5	.985
1989	—Cleveland (A.L.)	OF-SS	132	489	49	105	17	0	18	59	.215	6	297	32	1	†.997
	—Canton/Akron (Eastern)	OF	4	11	3	5	0	0	0	2	.455	1	5	2	0	1.000
1990	—Cleveland (A.L.)	OF-SS	123	438	46	102	27	3	14	55	.233	1	229	18	7	.972
1991	—Chicago-Toronto (A.L.)■.	OF-1B-3B	71	166	14	29	4	1	3	17	.175	0	198	17	3	.986
	—Syracuse (International)	OF	17	67	11	18	3	0	6	17	.269	0	25	0	0	1.000
	Major league totals (6 years)		728	2597	312	624	117	10	118	357	.240	19	1564	220	41	.978

SOJO, LUIS
2B, ANGELS

PERSONAL: Born January 3, 1966, at Barquisimeto, Venezuela. . . . 5-11/174. . . . Throws right, bats right. . . . Full name: Luis Sojo. . . . Name pronounced SOW-ho.
TRANSACTIONS/CAREER NOTES: Signed as free agent by Toronto Blue Jays organization (January 3, 1986). . . . Played in Dominican Republic (1986). . . . Traded by Blue Jays with OF Junior Felix and a player to be named later to California Angels for OF Devon White, P Willie Fraser and a player to be named later (December 2, 1990); Blue Jays acquired P Marcus Moore and Angels acquired C Ken Rivers to complete deal (December 4, 1990).
STATISTICAL NOTES: Led International League shortstops with .957 fielding percentage in 1989. . . . Led International League with nine sacrifice flies in 1990. . . . Led A.L. with 19 sacrifice hits in 1991.

Year	Team (League)	Pos.	G	AB	R	H	2B	3B	HR	RBI	Avg.	SB	PO	A	E	Avg.
1986 —	....					Dominican Republic Summer League										
1987 —	Myrtle Beach (S. Atl.)........	S-2-3-0	72	223	23	47	5	4	2	15	.211	5	104	123	14	.942
1988 —	Myrtle Beach (S. Atl.)........	SS	135	*536	83	*155	22	5	5	56	.289	14	191	407	28	.955
1989 —	Syracuse (International) ..	SS-2B	121	482	54	133	20	5	3	54	.276	9	170	348	23	†.957
1990 —	Syracuse (International) ..	2B-SS	75	297	39	88	12	3	6	25	.296	10	138	212	10	.972
	—Toronto (A.L.)..................	2-S-0-3	33	80	14	18	3	0	1	9	.225	1	34	31	5	.929
1991 —	California (A.L.)■.............	2-S-3-0	113	364	38	94	14	1	3	20	.258	4	233	335	11	.981
	Major league totals (2 years)		146	444	52	112	17	1	4	29	.252	5	267	366	16	.975

SORRENTO, PAUL
1B, TWINS

PERSONAL: Born November 17, 1965, at Somerville, Mass. . . . 6-2/223. . . . Throws right, bats left. . . . Full name: Paul Anthony Sorrento.
HIGH SCHOOL: St. John's Preparatory (Danvers, Mass.).
COLLEGE: Florida State.
TRANSACTIONS/CAREER NOTES: Selected by California Angels organization in fourth round of free-agent draft (June 2, 1986). . . . Traded by Angels organization with P Mike Cook and P Rob Wassenaar to Minnesota Twins for P Bert Blyleven and P Kevin Trudeau (November 3, 1988).
STATISTICAL NOTES: Led Southern League first basemen with 103 double plays in 1989. . . . Led Pacific Coast League first basemen with 14 errors in 1991.

Year	Team (League)	Pos.	G	AB	R	H	2B	3B	HR	RBI	Avg.	SB	PO	A	E	Avg.
1986 —	Quad Cities (Midwest).......	OF	53	177	33	63	11	2	6	34	.356	0	83	7	1	.989
	—Palm Springs (Calif.)........	OF	16	62	5	15	3	0	1	7	.242	0	16	1	1	.944
1987 —	Palm Springs (Calif.)........	OF	114	370	66	83	14	2	8	45	.224	1	123	10	4	.971
1988 —	Palm Springs (Calif.)........	1B-OF	133	465	91	133	30	6	14	99	.286	3	719	55	18	.977
1989 —	Orlando (Southern)■........	1B	140	509	81	130	*35	2	27	*112	.255	1	1070	41	*24	.979
	—Minnesota (A.L.)	1B	14	21	2	5	0	0	0	1	.238	0	13	0	0	1.000
1990 —	Portland (Pacific Coast) ...	1B-OF	102	354	59	107	27	1	19	72	.302	3	695	52	13	.983
	—Minnesota (A.L.)	1B	41	121	11	25	4	1	5	13	.207	1	118	7	1	.992
1991 —	Portland (Pacific Coast) ...	1B-OF	113	409	59	126	30	2	13	79	.308	1	933	58	†14	.986
	—Minnesota (A.L.)	1B	26	47	6	12	2	0	4	13	.255	0	70	7	0	1.000
	Major league totals (3 years)		81	189	19	42	6	1	9	27	.222	1	201	14	1	.995

CHAMPIONSHIP SERIES RECORD

Year	Team (League)	Pos.	G	AB	R	H	2B	3B	HR	RBI	Avg.	SB	PO	A	E	Avg.
1991 —	Minnesota (A.L.)	PH	1	1	0	0	0	0	0	0	.000	0	0	0	0	...

WORLD SERIES RECORD

Year	Team (League)	Pos.	G	AB	R	H	2B	3B	HR	RBI	Avg.	SB	PO	A	E	Avg.
1991 —	Minnesota (A.L.)	PH-1B	3	2	0	0	0	0	0	0	.000	0	1	1	0	1.000

SOSA, SAMMY
OF, WHITE SOX

PERSONAL: Born November 10, 1968, at San Pedro de Macoris, Dominican Republic. . . . 6-0/175. . . . Throws right, bats right. . . . Full name: Samuel Sosa.
TRANSACTIONS/CAREER NOTES: Signed as free agent by Texas Rangers organization (July 30, 1985). . . . Traded by Rangers with SS Scott Fletcher and P Wilson Alvarez to Chicago White Sox for OF Harold Baines and IF Fred Manrique (July 29, 1989).
STATISTICAL NOTES: Led Gulf Coast League with 96 total bases in 1986. . . . Tied for South Atlantic League lead in double plays by outfielders with four in 1987.

Year	Team (League)	Pos.	G	AB	R	H	2B	3B	HR	RBI	Avg.	SB	PO	A	E	Avg.
1986 —	Sarasota Rangers (GCL)...	OF	61	229	38	63	*19	1	4	28	.275	11	92	9	•6	.944
1987 —	Gastonia (S. Atlantic)	OF	129	519	73	145	27	4	11	59	.279	22	183	12	17	.920
1988 —	Port Charlotte (Fla. St.)	OF	131	507	70	116	13	*12	9	51	.229	42	227	11	7	.971
1989 —	Tulsa (Texas)	OF	66	273	45	81	15	4	7	31	.297	16	110	7	4	.967
	—Texas-Chicago (A.L.)■...	OF	58	183	27	47	8	0	4	13	.257	10	94	2	4	.960
	—Oklahoma City (A.A.)	OF	10	39	2	4	2	0	0	3	.103	4	22	0	2	.917
	—Vancouver (Pac. Coast) ...	OF	13	49	7	18	3	0	1	5	.367	0	43	1	0	1.000
1990 —	Chicago (A.L.)	OF	153	532	72	124	26	10	15	70	.233	32	315	14	*13	.962
1991 —	Chicago (A.L.)	OF	116	316	39	64	10	1	10	33	.203	13	214	6	6	.973
	—Vancouver (Pac. Coast)....	OF	32	116	19	31	7	2	3	19	.267	1	95	2	3	.970
	Major league totals (3 years)		327	1031	138	235	44	11	29	116	.228	55	623	22	23	.966

SPEHR, TIM
C, ROYALS

PERSONAL: Born July 2, 1966, at Excelsior Springs, Mo. . . . 6-2/205. . . . Throws right, bats right. . . . Full name: Timothy Joseph Spehr.
HIGH SCHOOL: Richfield (Waco, Tex.).
COLLEGE: Arizona State.
TRANSACTIONS/CAREER NOTES: Selected by Kansas City Royals organization in fifth round of free-agent draft (June 1, 1988). . . . On disabled list (June 25-July 27, 1988). . . . On Baseball City disabled list (April 7-May 21, 1989).
STATISTICAL NOTES: Led American Association catchers with 730 total chances and 14 double plays in 1990.

						BATTING							FIELDING		
Year	Team (League)	Pos.	G	AB	R	H	2B	3B	HR	RBI	Avg.	SB	PO	A	E	Avg.
1988—Appleton (Midwest)		C	31	110	15	29	3	0	5	22	.264	3	146	14	7	.958
1989—Baseball City (Fla. St.)		C	18	64	8	16	5	0	1	7	.250	1	63	7	1	.986
—Memphis (Southern)		C	61	216	22	42	9	0	8	23	.194	1	274	36	5	.984
1990—Omaha (Am. Assoc.)		C	102	307	42	69	10	2	6	34	.225	5	*658	67	5	*.993
1991—Omaha (Am. Assoc.)		C	72	215	27	59	14	2	6	26	.274	3	402	53	8	.983
—Kansas City (A.L.)		C	37	74	7	14	5	0	3	14	.189	1	190	19	3	.986
Major league totals (1 year)			37	74	7	14	5	0	3	14	.189	1	190	19	3	.986

SPIERS, BILL
SS, BREWERS

PERSONAL: Born June 5, 1966, at Orangeburg, S.C. . . . 6-2/190. . . . Throws right, bats left. . . . Full name: William James Spiers III. . . . Name pronounced SPY-ers.
HIGH SCHOOL: Wade Hampton Academy (Orangeburg, S.C.).
COLLEGE: Clemson.
TRANSACTIONS/CAREER NOTES: Selected by Milwaukee Brewers organization in first round (13th pick overall) of free-agent draft (June 2, 1987). . . . On Milwaukee disabled list (April 6-May 15, 1990); included rehabilitation disability assignment to Denver (April 27-May 14, 1990).
RECORDS/HONORS: Named shortstop on THE SPORTING NEWS college All-America team (1987).

						BATTING							FIELDING		
Year	Team (League)	Pos.	G	AB	R	H	2B	3B	HR	RBI	Avg.	SB	PO	A	E	Avg.
1987—Helena (Pioneer)		SS	6	22	4	9	1	0	0	3	.409	2	8	6	6	.700
—Beloit (Midwest)		SS	64	258	43	77	10	1	3	26	.298	11	111	160	20	.931
1988—Stockton (California)		SS	84	353	68	95	17	3	5	52	.269	27	140	240	19	.952
—El Paso (Texas)		SS	47	168	22	47	5	2	3	21	.280	4	73	141	13	.943
1989—Milwaukee (A.L.)		S-3-2-1	114	345	44	88	9	3	4	33	.255	10	164	295	21	.956
—Denver (Am. Assoc.)		SS	14	47	9	17	2	1	2	8	.362	1	32	33	2	.970
1990—Denver (Am. Assoc.)		SS	11	38	6	12	0	0	1	7	.316	1	22	23	2	.957
—Milwaukee (A.L.)		SS	112	363	44	88	15	3	2	36	.242	11	159	326	12	.976
1991—Milwaukee (A.L.)		SS-OF	133	414	71	117	13	6	8	54	.283	14	201	345	17	.970
Major league totals (3 years)			359	1122	159	293	37	12	14	123	.261	35	524	966	50	.968

SPRAGUE, ED
C/3B/1B, BLUE JAYS

PERSONAL: Born July 25, 1967, at Castro Valley, Calif. . . . 6-2/215. . . . Throws right, bats right. . . . Full name: Edward Nelson Sprague. . . . Son of Ed Sprague, major league pitcher for four teams (1968-69 and 1971-76).
HIGH SCHOOL: St. Mary's (Stockton, Calif.).
COLLEGE: Stanford.
TRANSACTIONS/CAREER NOTES: Selected by Boston Red Sox organization in 26th round of free-agent draft (June 3, 1985). . . . Selected by Toronto Blue Jays organization in first round (25th pick overall) of free-agent draft (June 1, 1988).
MISCELLANEOUS: Member of 1988 U.S. Olympic baseball team.

						BATTING							FIELDING		
Year	Team (League)	Pos.	G	AB	R	H	2B	3B	HR	RBI	Avg.	SB	PO	A	E	Avg.
1989—Dunedin (Florida State)		3B	52	192	21	42	9	2	7	23	.219	1	33	86	14	.895
—Syracuse (International) ..		3B	86	288	23	60	14	1	5	33	.208	0	51	149	*25	.889
1990—Syracuse (International) ..		3B-1B-C	142	*519	60	124	23	5	20	75	.239	4	171	246	35	.923
1991—Syracuse (International) ..		C-3B	23	88	24	32	8	0	5	25	.364	2	111	17	6	.955
—Toronto (A.L.)		3B-1B-C	61	160	17	44	7	0	4	20	.275	0	167	72	14	.945
Major league totals (1 year)			61	160	17	44	7	0	4	20	.275	0	167	72	14	.945

SPRINGER, RUSS
P, YANKEES

PERSONAL: Born November 7, 1968, at Alexandria, La. . . . 6-4/195. . . . Throws right, bats right. . . . Full name: Russell Paul Springer.
HIGH SCHOOL: Grant (Dry Prong, La.).
COLLEGE: Louisiana State.
TRANSACTIONS/CAREER NOTES: Selected by New York Yankees organization in seventh round of free-agent draft (June 5, 1989).

Year	Team (League)	G	W	L	Pct.	ERA	Sv.	IP	H	R	ER	BB	SO
1989—Sarasota Yankees (GCL)		6	3	0	1.000	1.50	0	24	14	8	4	10	34
1990—Tampa Yankees (Gulf Coast)....		4	0	2	.000	1.20	0	15	10	6	2	4	17
—Greensboro (South Atlantic) ..		10	2	3	.400	3.67	0	56⅓	51	33	23	31	51
1991—Fort Lauderdale (Florida St.)		25	5	9	.357	3.49	0	152⅓	118	68	59	62	139
—Albany (Eastern)		2	1	0	1.000	1.80	0	15	9	4	3	6	16

ST. CLAIRE, RANDY
P

PERSONAL: Born August 23, 1960, at Glens Falls, N.Y. . . . 6-2/190. . . . Throws right, bats right. . . . Full name: Randy Anthony St. Claire. . . . Son of Ebba St. Claire, catcher, Boston/Milwaukee Braves, New York Giants (1951-54); and brother of Steve St. Claire, minor league outfielder (1984-88).

HIGH SCHOOL: Central (Whitehall, N.Y.).
TRANSACTIONS/CAREER NOTES: Signed as free agent by Montreal Expos organization (September 9, 1978). . . . On Indianapolis disabled list (May 7-17, 1985). . . . Traded by Expos with C Jeff Reed and OF Herm Winningham to Cincinnati Reds for OF Tracy Jones and P Pat Pacillo (July 13, 1988). . . . Released by Reds organization (March 28, 1989). . . . Signed by Portland, Minnesota Twins organization (April 1, 1989). . . . Granted free agency (October 22, 1989). . . . Signed by Oklahoma City, Texas Rangers organization (June 14, 1990). . . . Released by Oklahoma City (September 4, 1990). . . . Signed by Atlanta Braves organization (March 9, 1991). . . . Released by Braves (November 20, 1991).

Year — Team (League)	G	W	L	Pct.	ERA	Sv.	IP	H	R	ER	BB	SO
1979 — Calgary (Pacific Coast)	6	1	2	.333	4.36	0	33	30	22	16	15	17
1980 — Calgary (Pacific Coast)	21	5	7	.417	4.26	0	57	65	36	27	23	51
1981 — Jamestown (New York-Penn) ..	13	4	1	.800	1.94	0	51	53	22	11	17	36
1982 — San Jose (California)	9	2	5	.286	4.13	0	61	58	32	28	20	44
— West Palm Beach (Florida St.) ..	19	3	8	.273	5.26	2	65	74	41	38	17	38
1983 — West Palm Beach (Florida St.) ..	42	5	7	.417	2.11	11	98	72	33	23	31	77
1984 — Jacksonville (Southern)	48	10	7	.588	2.88	15	75	64	35	24	29	56
— Indianapolis (Am. Assoc.)	13	1	1	.500	1.02	8	17 2/3	15	2	2	6	17
— Montreal (N.L.)	4	0	0	...	4.50	0	8	11	4	4	2	4
1985 — Indianapolis (Am. Assoc.)	11	0	1	.000	1.83	6	19 2/3	21	5	4	3	11
— Montreal (N.L.)	42	5	3	.625	3.93	0	68 2/3	69	32	30	26	25
1986 — Indianapolis (Am. Assoc.)	*57	5	7	.417	3.99	15	99 1/3	105	49	44	29	72
— Montreal (N.L.)	11	2	0	1.000	2.37	1	19	13	5	5	6	21
1987 — Montreal (N.L.)	44	3	3	.500	4.03	7	67	64	31	30	20	43
— Indianapolis (Am. Assoc.)	18	0	1	.000	2.18	7	20 2/3	12	5	5	12	15
1988 — Montreal-Cincinnati (N.L.)■...	16	1	0	1.000	3.86	0	21	24	13	9	10	14
— Nashville (American Assoc.)	36	0	3	.000	2.68	13	40 1/3	35	15	12	9	27
1989 — Portland (Pacific Coast) ■.......	27	4	0	1.000	3.18	3	45 1/3	39	21	16	17	48
— Minnesota (A.L.)	14	1	0	1.000	5.24	1	22 1/3	19	13	13	10	14
1990 — Oklahoma City (Am. Assoc.)■..	29	1	2	.333	2.01	1	53 2/3	45	15	12	12	68
1991 — Richmond (International)■.......	29	6	2	.750	1.19	2	68	39	10	9	11	60
— Atlanta (N.L.)	19	0	0	...	4.08	0	28 2/3	31	17	13	9	30
American League totals (1 year)	14	1	0	1.000	5.24	1	22 1/3	19	13	13	10	14
National League totals (6 years)	136	11	6	.647	3.86	8	212 1/3	212	102	91	73	137
Major league totals (7 years)	150	12	6	.667	3.99	9	234 2/3	231	115	104	83	151

CHAMPIONSHIP SERIES RECORD

Year — Team (League)	G	W	L	Pct.	ERA	Sv.	IP	H	R	ER	BB	SO
1991 — Atlanta (N.L.)					Did not play							

WORLD SERIES RECORD

Year — Team (League)	G	W	L	Pct.	ERA	Sv.	IP	H	R	ER	BB	SO
1991 — Atlanta (N.L.)	1	0	0	...	9.00	0	1	1	1	1	0	0

STAIRS, MATT
2B/3B, EXPOS

PERSONAL: Born February 27, 1969, at St. John, New Brunswick, Canada. . . . 5-9/175. . . . Throws right, bats right. . . . Full name: Matthew Wade Stairs.
TRANSACTIONS/CAREER NOTES: Signed as free agent by Montreal Expos organization (January 17, 1989). . . . On disabled list (May 16-23, 1991).
RECORDS/HONORS: Named Eastern League Most Valuable Player (1991).
STATISTICAL NOTES: Led Eastern League with .509 slugging percentage, 257 total bases and tied for lead with eight intentional bases on balls received in 1991.
MISCELLANEOUS: Member of 1988 Canadian Olympic baseball team.

Year — Team (League)	Pos.	G	AB	R	H	2B	3B	HR	RBI	Avg.	SB	PO	A	E	Avg.
1989 — West Palm Beach (FSL) 3B-SS-2B		36	111	12	21	3	1	1	9	.189	0	21	66	4	.956
— Jamestown (N.Y.-Penn)	2B-3B	14	43	8	11	1	0	1	5	.256	1	15	35	6	.893
— Rockford (Midwest)	3B	44	141	20	40	9	2	2	14	.284	5	30	62	7	.929
1990 — West Palm Beach (FSL)	3B-2B	55	183	30	62	9	3	3	30	.339	15	40	112	17	.899
— Jacksonville (Southern)	3-0-2-S	79	280	26	71	17	0	3	34	.254	5	76	107	22	.893
1991 — Harrisburg (Eastern)	2B-3B-OF	129	505	87	*168	30	*10	13	78	.333	23	193	314	22	.958

STANFORD, LARRY
P, YANKEES

PERSONAL: Born September 26, 1967, at Manchester, Conn. . . . 6-3/205. . . . Throws right, bats right. . . . Full name: Lawrence Charles Stanford.
COLLEGE: Indian River Community College (Fla.), Louisiana State and Florida International.
TRANSACTIONS/CAREER NOTES: Selected by New York Yankees organization in sixth round of free-agent draft (June 5, 1989).
STATISTICAL NOTES: Tied for Eastern League lead with three balks in 1991.

Year — Team (League)	G	W	L	Pct.	ERA	Sv.	IP	H	R	ER	BB	SO
1989 — Oneonta (New York-Penn)	15	4	3	.571	3.83	0	80	75	41	34	30	60
1990 — Fort Lauderdale (Florida St.)	57	3	1	.750	1.31	29	61 2/3	40	15	9	18	60
1991 — Albany (Eastern)	52	2	3	.400	1.89	•24	62	41	18	13	36	61

STANLEY, MIKE
C/IF, YANKEES

PERSONAL: Born June 25, 1963, at Fort Lauderdale, Fla. . . . 6-1/185. . . . Throws right, bats right. . . . Full name: Robert Michael Stanley.
HIGH SCHOOL: St. Thomas Aquinas (Ft. Lauderdale, Fla.).
COLLEGE: Florida.

TRANSACTIONS/CAREER NOTES: Selected by Texas Rangers organization in 16th round of free-agent draft (June 3, 1985). . . . On disabled list (July 24-August 14, 1988 and August 18-September 2, 1989). . . . Granted free agency (November 15, 1990). . . . Re-signed by Rangers organization (February 4, 1991). . . . Granted free agency (October 14, 1991). . . . Signed by Columbus, New York Yankees organization (January 21, 1992).

Year	Team (League)	Pos.	G	AB	R	H	2B	3B	HR	RBI	Avg.	SB	PO	A	E	Avg.
1985	—Salem (Carolina)	1B-C	4	9	2	5	0	0	0	3	.556	0	19	1	1	.952
	—Burlington (Midwest)	C-1B-OF	13	42	8	13	2	0	1	6	.310	0	45	2	0	1.000
	—Tulsa (Texas)	C-1-0-2	46	165	24	51	10	0	3	17	.309	6	289	18	6	.981
1986	—Tulsa (Texas)	C-1B-3B	67	235	41	69	16	2	6	35	.294	5	379	45	2	.995
	—Texas (A.L.)	3B-C-OF	15	30	4	10	3	0	1	1	.333	1	14	8	1	.957
	—Oklahoma City (A.A.)	C-3B-1B	56	202	37	74	13	3	5	49	.366	1	206	55	9	.967
1987	—Oklahoma City (A.A.)	C-1B	46	182	43	61	8	3	13	54	.335	2	277	32	2	.994
	—Texas (A.L.)	C-1B-OF	78	216	34	59	8	1	6	37	.273	3	389	26	7	.983
1988	—Texas (A.L.)	C-1B-3B	94	249	21	57	8	0	3	27	.229	0	342	17	4	.989
1989	—Texas (A.L.)	C-1B-3B	67	122	9	30	3	1	1	11	.246	1	117	8	3	.977
1990	—Texas (A.L.)	C-3B-1B	103	189	21	47	8	1	2	19	.249	1	261	25	4	.986
1991	—Texas (A.L.)	C-1-3-0	95	181	25	45	13	1	3	25	.249	0	288	20	6	.981
Major league totals (6 years)			452	987	114	248	43	4	16	120	.251	6	1411	104	25	.984

STANTON, MIKE
P, BRAVES

PERSONAL: Born June 2, 1967, at Houston. . . . 6-1/190. . . . Throws left, bats left. . . . Full name: William Michael Stanton.
HIGH SCHOOL: Midland (Tex.).
COLLEGE: Alvin Community College (Tex.).

TRANSACTIONS/CAREER NOTES: Selected by Atlanta Braves organization in 13th round of free-agent draft (June 2, 1987). . . . On Atlanta disabled list (April 27, 1990-remainder of season); included rehabilitation disability assignment to Greenville (May 31-June 5 and August 21-29, 1990).

Year	Team (League)	G	W	L	Pct.	ERA	Sv.	IP	H	R	ER	BB	SO
1987	—Pulaski (Appalachian)	15	4	8	.333	3.24	0	83⅓	64	37	30	42	82
1988	—Burlington (Midwest)	30	11	5	.688	3.62	0	154	154	86	62	69	160
	—Durham (Carolina)	2	1	0	1.000	1.46	0	12⅓	14	3	2	5	14
1989	—Greenville (Southern)	47	4	1	.800	1.58	19	51⅓	32	10	9	31	58
	—Richmond (International)	13	2	0	1.000	0.00	8	20	6	0	0	13	20
	—Atlanta (N.L.)	20	0	1	.000	1.50	7	24	17	4	4	8	27
1990	—Atlanta (N.L.)	7	0	3	.000	18.00	2	7	16	16	14	4	7
	—Greenville (Southern)	4	0	1	.000	1.59	0	5⅔	7	1	1	3	4
1991	—Atlanta (N.L.)	74	5	5	.500	2.88	7	78	62	27	25	21	54
Major league totals (3 years)		101	5	9	.357	3.55	16	109	95	47	43	33	88

CHAMPIONSHIP SERIES RECORD

Year	Team (League)	G	W	L	Pct.	ERA	Sv.	IP	H	R	ER	BB	SO
1991	—Atlanta (N.L.)	3	0	0	...	2.45	0	3⅔	4	1	1	3	3

WORLD SERIES RECORD

Year	Team (League)	G	W	L	Pct.	ERA	Sv.	IP	H	R	ER	BB	SO
1991	—Atlanta (N.L.)	5	1	0	1.000	0.00	0	7⅓	5	0	0	2	7

STATON, DAVID
1B/3B, PADRES

PERSONAL: Born April 12, 1968, at Seattle. . . . 6-5/215. . . . Throws right, bats right. . . . Full name: David Allen Staton.
HIGH SCHOOL: Tustin (Calif.).
COLLEGE: Orange Coast College (Calif.), then California.

TRANSACTIONS/CAREER NOTES: Selected by Pittsburgh Pirates organization in 22nd round of free-agent draft (June 1, 1988). . . . Selected by San Diego Padres organization in fifth round of free-agent draft (June 5, 1989). . . . On disabled list (July 20-27, 1991).
STATISTICAL NOTES: Tied for Northwest League lead with 163 total bases in 1989.

Year	Team (League)	Pos.	G	AB	R	H	2B	3B	HR	RBI	Avg.	SB	PO	A	E	Avg.
1989	—Spokane (Northwest)	3B	70	260	52	94	18	0	*17	*72	*.362	1	30	116	25	.854
1990	—Riverside (California)	3B-1B	92	335	56	97	16	1	20	64	.290	4	149	162	13	.960
	—Wichita (Texas)	1B-3B	45	164	26	50	11	0	6	31	.305	1	326	35	4	.989
1991	—Las Vegas (Pac. Coast)	1B-3B	107	375	61	100	19	1	22	74	.267	1	553	116	24	.965

STEINBACH, TERRY
C, ATHLETICS

PERSONAL: Born March 2, 1962, at New Ulm, Minn. . . . 6-1/195. . . . Throws right, bats right. . . . Full name: Terry Lee Steinbach. . . . Brother of Tom Steinbach, minor league outfielder (1983).
HIGH SCHOOL: New Ulm (Minn.).
COLLEGE: Minnesota.

TRANSACTIONS/CAREER NOTES: Selected by Cleveland Indians organization in 16th round of free-agent draft (June 3, 1980). . . . Selected by Oakland A's organization in ninth round of free-agent draft (June 6, 1983). . . . On disabled list (May 6-June 1, 1988 and July 3-28, 1990).

RECORDS/HONORS: Named Southern League Most Valuable Player (1986).
STATISTICAL NOTES: Led Northwest League third basemen with 122 assists and tied for lead with 17 errors in 1983. . . . Led Midwest League third basemen with 31 double plays in 1984. . . . Hit home run in first major league at-bat (September 12, 1986). . . . Led Southern League with 22 passed balls in 1986. . . . Led A.L. catchers with 15 errors in 1991.

Year	Team (League)	Pos.	G	AB	R	H	2B	3B	HR	RBI	Avg.	SB	PO	A	E	Avg.
1983 —Medford (Northwest)	3B-0F-1B	62	219	42	69	16	0	6	38	.315	8	105	†124	†21	.916
1984 —Madison (Midwest)	3B-1B-P	135	474	57	140	24	6	11	79	.295	5	107	257	27	.931
1985 —Huntsville (Southern) ...	C-3-1-0-P	128	456	64	124	31	3	9	72	.272	4	187	43	6	.975
1986 —Huntsville (Southern)	C-1B-3B	138	505	113	164	33	2	24	★132	.325	10	620	73	14	.980
—Oakland (A.L.)	C	6	15	3	5	0	0	2	4	.333	0	21	4	1	.962
1987 —Oakland (A.L.)	C-3B-1B	122	391	66	111	16	3	16	56	.284	1	642	44	10	.986
1988 —Oakland (A.L.)	C-3-1-0	104	351	42	93	19	1	9	51	.265	3	536	58	9	.985
1989 —Oakland (A.L.)	C-0-1-3	130	454	37	124	13	1	7	42	.273	1	612	47	11	.984
1990 —Oakland (A.L.)	C-1B	114	379	32	95	15	2	9	57	.251	0	401	31	5	.989
1991 —Oakland (A.L.)	C-1B	129	456	50	125	31	1	6	67	.274	2	639	53	†15	.979
Major league totals (6 years)		605	2046	230	553	94	8	49	277	.270	7	2851	237	51	.984

CHAMPIONSHIP SERIES RECORD

Year	Team (League)	Pos.	G	AB	R	H	2B	3B	HR	RBI	Avg.	SB	PO	A	E	Avg.
1988 —Oakland (A.L.)	C	2	4	0	1	0	0	0	0	.250	0	12	0	0	1.000
1989 —Oakland (A.L.)	C-DH	4	15	0	3	0	0	0	1	.200	0	17	0	0	1.000
1990 —Oakland (A.L.)	C	3	11	2	5	0	0	0	1	.455	0	11	0	0	1.000
Championship Series totals (3 years)		9	30	2	9	0	0	0	2	.300	0	40	0	0	1.000

WORLD SERIES RECORD

Year	Team (League)	Pos.	G	AB	R	H	2B	3B	HR	RBI	Avg.	SB	PO	A	E	Avg.
1988 —Oakland (A.L.)	C-DH	3	11	0	4	1	0	0	0	.364	0	11	3	0	1.000
1989 —Oakland (A.L.)	C	4	16	3	4	0	1	1	7	.250	0	27	2	0	1.000
1990 —Oakland (A.L.)	C	3	8	0	1	0	0	0	0	.125	0	8	1	0	1.000
World Series totals (3 years)		10	35	3	9	1	1	1	7	.257	0	46	6	0	1.000

ALL-STAR GAME RECORD

ALL-STAR GAME NOTES: Hit home run in first at-bat (July 12, 1988).

Year	League	Pos.	AB	R	H	2B	3B	HR	RBI	Avg.	SB	PO	A	E	Avg.
1988 —American	C	1	1	1	0	0	1	2	1.000	0	3	1	1	.800
1989 —American	C	3	0	1	0	0	0	0	.333	0	6	1	0	1.000
All-Star Game totals (2 years)		4	1	2	0	0	1	2	.500	0	9	2	1	.917

RECORD AS PITCHER

Year	Team (League)	G	W	L	Pct.	ERA	Sv.	IP	H	R	ER	BB	SO
1984 —Madison (Midwest)	2	0	0	. . .	9.00	0	3	2	4	3	4	0
1985 —Huntsville (Southern)	1	0	0	. . .	0.00	0	1	0	0	0	0	0

STEPHENS, RAY
C, PHILLIES

PERSONAL: Born September 22, 1962, at Houston. . . . 6-0/190. . . . Throws right, bats right. . . . Full name: Carl Ray Stephens Jr.
HIGH SCHOOL: Bradley Central (Cleveland, Tenn.).
COLLEGE: Middle Georgia College and Troy State (Ala.).
TRANSACTIONS/CAREER NOTES: Selected by St. Louis Cardinals organization in sixth round of free-agent draft (June 3, 1985). . . . Released by Cardinals (November 12, 1991). . . . Signed by Philadelphia Phillies organization (December 16, 1991).
STATISTICAL NOTES: Led American Association catchers with 661 total chances and 13 passed balls in 1988.

Year	Team (League)	Pos.	G	AB	R	H	2B	3B	HR	RBI	Avg.	SB	PO	A	E	Avg.
1985 —Erie (New York-Penn).......	C	9	31	3	9	1	1	1	5	.290	0	68	17	1	.988
—Savannah (S. Atlantic)	C	39	127	11	26	6	0	0	6	.205	1	229	30	4	.985
1986 —Savannah (S. Atlantic)	C	95	325	52	71	10	0	13	56	.218	2	570	★70	12	.982
—Louisville (Am. Assoc.)	C	12	31	2	6	1	0	1	2	.194	0	38	6	1	.978
1987 —Arkansas (Texas)	C	100	307	35	77	20	0	8	42	.251	6	553	75	5	.992
—Louisville (Am. Assoc.)	C	9	30	1	4	0	0	0	2	.133	0	53	4	1	.983
1988 —Louisville (Am. Assoc.)	C	115	355	26	67	13	2	3	25	.189	2	★590	★64	7	★.989
1989 —Arkansas (Texas)	C	112	363	49	95	14	0	7	44	.262	2	545	63	9	.985
1990 —Louisville (Am. Assoc.)	C	98	294	20	65	8	1	3	27	.221	0	552	55	8	.987
—St. Louis (N.L.)	C	5	15	2	2	1	0	1	1	.133	0	31	2	0	1.000
1991 —Louisville (Am. Assoc.)	C	60	165	16	46	7	0	7	28	.279	2	261	28	6	.980
—St. Louis (N.L.)	C	6	7	0	2	0	0	0	0	.286	0	16	2	0	1.000
Major league totals (2 years)		11	22	2	4	1	0	1	1	.182	0	47	4	0	1.000

STEPHENSON, PHIL
1B/OF, PADRES

PERSONAL: Born September 19, 1960, at Guthrie, Okla. . . . 6-1/200. . . . Throws left, bats left. . . . Full name: Phillip Raymond Stephenson. . . . Brother of Gene Stephenson, baseball coach, Wichita State University.
HIGH SCHOOL: Guthrie (Okla.).

COLLEGE: Wichita State (bachelor of arts degree in business management).

TRANSACTIONS/CAREER NOTES: Selected by Montreal Expos organization in fifth round of free-agent draft (June 8, 1981)....
Selected by Oakland Athletics organization in third round of free-agent draft (June 7, 1982).... Loaned by A's organization to
Midland, California Angels organization (July 7, 1985); returned (September 10, 1985).... Traded by A's with 3B Bob Bathe to
Chicago Cubs for 2B Gary Jones and P John Cox (January 17, 1986).... On Chicago disabled list (May 27-June 11, 1989)....
Traded by Cubs to San Diego Padres (September 5, 1989), completing deal in which Cubs traded P Calvin Schiraldi, OF Darrin
Jackson and a player to be named later to Padres for OF Marvell Wynne and IF Luis Salazar (August 30, 1989).... On San
Diego disabled list (April 7-July 11 and August 9, 1991-remainder of season); included rehabilitation disability assignment to
Las Vegas (June 17-25, 1991) and Wichita (June 25-July 6, 1991).... Granted free agency (December 20, 1991).... Re-
signed by Padres organization (January 30, 1992).

RECORDS/HONORS: Named first baseman on THE SPORTING NEWS college All-America team (1981).

STATISTICAL NOTES: Led Eastern League with 114 bases on balls received in 1983 and 129 in 1986.... Tied for Eastern League
lead with 10 sacrifice flies in 1983.... Tied for Eastern League lead in errors by first basemen with 14 in 1983.... Led Eastern
League first basemen with .996 fielding percentage, 1,164 putouts, 163 assists and 1,332 total chances in 1986.... Led American Association with .566 slugging percentage in 1988.... Led American Association first basemen with 103 double plays in
1988.... Led American Association with nine intentional bases on balls received in 1989 and tied for lead with nine in 1988.

							BATTING						FIELDING			
Year	Team (League)	Pos.	G	AB	R	H	2B	3B	HR	RBI	Avg.	SB	PO	A	E	Avg.
1982 —Modesto (California)		1B	64	212	39	60	14	2	5	26	.283	18	436	39	4	.992
1983 —Albany (Eastern)		1B-OF	133	436	90	122	•30	3	19	77	.280	17	771	85	‡14	.984
1984 —Tacoma (Pacific Coast)		OF-1B	124	398	70	120	25	1	10	69	.302	15	418	40	9	.981
1985 —Tacoma (Pacific Coast)		OF-1B	56	171	30	36	11	0	5	24	.211	5	117	6	5	.961
—Midland (Texas)■		1B-OF	50	176	39	52	14	0	7	41	.295	5	340	27	3	.992
1986 —Pittsfield (Eastern)■........		1B-OF-P	•140	423	72	115	29	2	12	68	.272	30	†1165	†163	5	†.996
1987 —Iowa (American Assoc.) ...		1B-OF	105	298	53	91	24	2	10	56	.305	4	735	71	10	.988
1988 —Iowa (American Assoc.) ...		1B	118	426	69	125	28	11	22	81	.293	9	925	•88	10	.990
1989 —Chicago-S.D. (N.L.)■		1B-OF	27	38	4	9	0	0	2	2	.237	2	42	4	1	.979
—Iowa (American Assoc.) ...		1B-OF	84	290	52	87	17	3	13	62	.300	28	648	51	7	.990
1990 —San Diego (N.L.)		1B	103	182	26	38	9	1	4	19	.209	2	345	36	1	.997
1991 —Las Vegas (Pac. Coast)		PH	7	18	1	4	0	1	0	5	.222	0	0	0	0	...
—Wichita (Texas)		PH	12	34	4	16	5	0	0	8	.471	0	0	0	0	...
—San Diego (N.L.)		PH	11	7	0	2	0	0	0	0	.286	0	0	0	0	...
Major league totals (3 years)			141	227	30	49	9	1	6	21	.216	4	387	40	2	.995

RECORD AS PITCHER

Year	Team (League)	G	W	L	Pct.	ERA	Sv.	IP	H	R	ER	BB	SO
1986 —Pittsfield (Eastern)..................	3	0	0	...	0.00	0	4	1	0	0	2	1

STEVENS, LEE

1B/OF, ANGELS

PERSONAL: Born July 10, 1967, at Kansas City, Mo.... 6-4/219.... Throws left, bats left....
Full name: DeWain Lee Stevens.

HIGH SCHOOL: Lawrence (Kan.).

TRANSACTIONS/CAREER NOTES: Selected by California Angels organization in first round (22nd
pick overall) of free-agent draft (June 2, 1986).

STATISTICAL NOTES: Led California League first basemen with 1,028 putouts, 66 assists and .986 fielding percentage in 1987.
... Led Texas League outfielders with 12 errors in 1988.... Tied for Pacific Coast League lead with 11 intentional bases on
balls received in 1990.

							BATTING						FIELDING			
Year	Team (League)	Pos.	G	AB	R	H	2B	3B	HR	RBI	Avg.	SB	PO	A	E	Avg.
1986 —Salem (Northwest)		OF-1B	72	267	45	75	18	2	6	47	.281	13	231	18	5	.980
1987 —Palm Springs (Calif.)		1B-OF	140	532	82	130	29	2	19	97	.244	1	†1031	†68	18	†.984
1988 —Midland (Texas)		OF-1B	116	414	79	123	26	2	23	76	.297	0	217	16	†14	.943
1989 —Edmonton (Pac. Coast)		1B-OF	127	446	72	110	29	9	14	74	.247	5	635	40	7	.990
1990 —Edmonton (Pac. Coast)		OF-1B	90	338	57	99	31	2	16	66	.293	1	284	10	6	.980
—California (A.L.)		1B	67	248	28	53	10	0	7	32	.214	1	597	36	4	.994
1991 —Edmonton (Pac. Coast)		OF-1B	123	481	75	151	29	3	19	96	.314	3	519	33	7	.987
—California (A.L.)		OF-1B	18	58	8	17	7	0	0	9	.293	1	100	6	1	.991
Major league totals (2 years)			85	306	36	70	17	0	7	41	.229	2	697	42	5	.993

STEWART, DAVE

P, ATHLETICS

PERSONAL: Born February 19, 1957, at Oakland, Calif.... 6-2/200.... Throws right, bats
right.... Full name: David Keith Stewart.

HIGH SCHOOL: St. Elizabeth (Oakland, Calif.).

COLLEGE: Merritt College (Calif.) and Cal State Hayward.

TRANSACTIONS/CAREER NOTES: Selected by Los Angeles Dodgers organization in 16th round of free-agent draft (June 4, 1975).
... Traded by Dodgers with a player to be named later to Texas Rangers for P Rick Honeycutt (August 19, 1983); Rangers acquired P Ricky Wright to complete deal (September 16, 1983).... Traded by Rangers to Philadelphia Phillies for P Rick Surhoff
(September 13, 1985).... Released by Phillies (May 9, 1986).... Signed by Tacoma, Oakland A's organization (May 23,
1986).... On disabled list (May 9-26, 1991).

RECORDS/HONORS: Shares A.L. single-season record for fewest complete games by pitcher who led league in complete
games—11 (1990).... Named righthanded pitcher on THE SPORTING NEWS A.L. All-Star team (1988).

STATISTICAL NOTES: Tied for Midwest League lead with 15 complete games, three shutouts and three balks in 1977.... Tied for
Texas League lead in games started by pitcher with 28 in 1978.... Led Pacific Coast League pitchers with 29 games started in
1980.... Led A.L. pitchers with 37 games started in 1988 and tied for lead with 36 in 1989 and 1990 and with 35 in 1991....
Tied for A.L. lead in complete games with 14 in 1988 and 11 in 1990.... Led A.L. with 16 balks in 1988.... Pitched 5-0 no-hit
victory against Toronto Blue Jays (June 29, 1990).... Tied for A.L. lead with four in shutouts in 1990.

Year	Team (League)	G	W	L	Pct.	ERA	Sv.	IP	H	R	ER	BB	SO
1975	Bellingham (Northwest)	22	0	5	.000	5.51	2	49	59	46	30	49	37
1976	Danville (Midwest)	4	0	2	.000	16.20	0	10	17	20	18	16	10
	Bellingham (Northwest)	24	1	1	.500	5.04	1	50	47	35	28	58	53
1977	Clinton (Midwest)	24	★17	4	★.810	2.15	0	176	152	52	42	72	144
	Albuquerque (Pacific Coast)	1	1	0	1.000	4.50	0	6	4	3	3	6	3
1978	San Antonio (Texas)	28	14	12	.538	3.68	0	★193	181	99	79	97	130
	Los Angeles (N.L.)	1	0	0	...	0.00	0	2	1	0	0	0	1
1979	Albuquerque (Pacific Coast)	28	11	12	.478	5.24	1	170	198	112	99	81	105
1980	Albuquerque (Pacific Coast)	31	★15	10	.600	3.70	1	★202	189	94	83	89	125
1981	Los Angeles (N.L.)	32	4	3	.571	2.51	6	43	40	13	12	14	29
1982	Los Angeles (N.L.)	45	9	8	.529	3.81	1	146⅓	137	72	62	49	80
1983	Los Angeles (N.L.)	46	5	2	.714	2.96	8	76	67	28	25	33	54
	Texas (A.L.)■	8	5	2	.714	2.14	0	59	50	15	14	17	24
1984	Texas (A.L.)	32	7	14	.333	4.73	0	192⅓	193	106	101	87	119
1985	Texas (A.L.)	42	0	6	.000	5.42	4	81⅓	86	53	49	37	64
	Philadelphia (N.L.)■	4	0	0	...	6.23	0	4⅓	5	4	3	4	2
1986	Philadelphia (N.L.)	8	0	0	...	6.57	0	12⅓	15	9	9	4	9
	Tacoma (Pacific Coast)■	1	0	0	...	0.00	0	3	4	1	0	1	3
	Oakland (A.L.)	29	9	5	.643	3.74	0	149⅓	137	67	62	65	102
1987	Oakland (A.L.)	37	★20	13	.606	3.68	0	261⅓	224	121	107	105	205
1988	Oakland (A.L.)	37	21	12	.636	3.23	0	★275⅔	240	111	99	110	192
1989	Oakland (A.L.)	36	21	9	.700	3.32	0	257⅔	★260	105	95	69	155
1990	Oakland (A.L.)	36	22	11	.667	2.56	0	★267	226	84	76	83	166
1991	Oakland (A.L.)	35	11	11	.500	5.18	0	226	245	★135	★130	105	144
	American League totals (9 years)	292	116	83	.583	3.73	4	1769⅔	1661	797	733	678	1171
	National League totals (6 years)	136	18	13	.581	3.52	15	284	265	126	111	104	175
	Major league totals (12 years)	428	134	96	.583	3.70	19	2053⅔	1926	923	844	782	1346

DIVISION SERIES RECORD

Year	Team (League)	G	W	L	Pct.	ERA	Sv.	IP	H	R	ER	BB	SO
1981	Los Angeles (N.L.)	2	0	2	.000	40.50	0	⅔	4	3	3	0	1

CHAMPIONSHIP SERIES RECORD

CHAMPIONSHIP SERIES NOTES: Holds career record for most games won—5.... Shares A.L. single-series record for most games won—2 (1989-90).

Year	Team (League)	G	W	L	Pct.	ERA	Sv.	IP	H	R	ER	BB	SO
1988	Oakland (A.L.)	2	1	0	1.000	1.35	0	13⅓	9	2	2	6	11
1989	Oakland (A.L.)	2	2	0	1.000	2.81	0	16	13	5	5	3	9
1990	Oakland (A.L.)	2	2	0	1.000	1.13	0	16	8	2	2	2	4
	Championship Series totals (3 years)	6	5	0	1.000	1.79	0	45⅓	30	9	9	11	24

WORLD SERIES RECORD

Year	Team (League)	G	W	L	Pct.	ERA	Sv.	IP	H	R	ER	BB	SO
1981	Los Angeles (N.L.)	2	0	0	...	0.00	0	1⅔	1	0	0	2	1
1988	Oakland (A.L.)	2	0	1	.000	3.14	0	14⅓	12	7	5	5	5
1989	Oakland (A.L.)	2	2	0	1.000	1.69	0	16	10	3	3	2	14
1990	Oakland (A.L.)	2	0	2	.000	2.77	0	13	10	6	4	6	5
	World Series totals (4 years)	8	2	3	.400	2.40	0	45	33	16	12	15	25

ALL-STAR GAME RECORD

Year	League	W	L	Pct.	ERA	Sv.	IP	H	R	ER	BB	SO
1989	American	0	0	...	18.00	0	1	3	2	2	2	0

STIEB, DAVE
P, BLUE JAYS

PERSONAL: Born July 22, 1957, at Santa Ana, Calif.... 6-1/195.... Throws right, bats right.... Full name: David Andrew Stieb.... Brother of Steve Stieb, minor league catcher (1979-81).... Name pronounced STEEB.

HIGH SCHOOL: Oak Grove (San Jose, Calif.).

COLLEGE: Santa Ana College (Calif.) and Southern Illinois.

TRANSACTIONS/CAREER NOTES: Selected by Toronto Blue Jays organization in fifth round of free-agent draft (June 6, 1978).... On disabled list (May 23, 1991-remainder of season).

RECORDS/HONORS: Shares major league record for most consecutive one-hit games—2 (September 24 and 30, 1988).... Shares A.L. single-season record for most low-hit (no-hit and one-hit) games—3 (1988).... Named outfielder on THE SPORTING NEWS college All-America team (1978).... Named A.L. Pitcher of the Year by THE SPORTING NEWS (1982).... Named righthanded pitcher on THE SPORTING NEWS A.L. All-Star team (1982).

STATISTICAL NOTES: Led A.L. with 19 complete games and five shutouts in 1982.... Led A.L. with 14 hit batsmen in 1983, 11 in 1984, 15 in 1986, 13 in 1989 and tied for lead with 11 in 1981.... Pitched 3-0 no-hit victory against Cleveland Indians (September 2, 1990).

MISCELLANEOUS: Appeared in one game as outfielder with no chances and had one at-bat (1980).... Appeared in one game as pinch-runner (1986 and 1988).

Year	Team (League)	G	W	L	Pct.	ERA	Sv.	IP	H	R	ER	BB	SO
1979	Dunedin (Florida State)	8	5	0	1.000	4.24	0	51	54	30	24	28	38
	Syracuse (International)	7	5	2	.714	2.12	0	51	39	15	12	14	20

Year	Team (League)	G	W	L	Pct.	ERA	Sv.	IP	H	R	ER	BB	SO
	—Toronto (A.L.).........................	18	8	8	.500	4.33	0	129	139	70	62	48	52
1980	—Toronto (A.L.).........................	34	12	15	.444	3.70	0	243	232	108	100	83	108
1981	—Toronto (A.L.).........................	25	11	10	.524	3.18	0	184	148	70	65	61	89
1982	—Toronto (A.L.).........................	38	17	14	.548	3.25	0	★288⅓	★271	116	104	75	141
1983	—Toronto (A.L.).........................	36	17	12	.586	3.04	0	278	223	105	94	93	187
1984	—Toronto (A.L.).........................	35	16	8	.667	2.83	0	★267	215	87	84	88	198
1985	—Toronto (A.L.).........................	36	14	13	.519	★2.48	0	265	206	89	73	96	167
1986	—Toronto (A.L.).........................	37	7	12	.368	4.74	1	205	239	128	108	87	127
1987	—Toronto (A.L.).........................	33	13	9	.591	4.09	0	185	164	92	84	87	115
1988	—Toronto (A.L.).........................	32	16	8	.667	3.04	0	207⅓	157	76	70	79	147
1989	—Toronto (A.L.).........................	33	17	8	.680	3.35	0	206⅔	164	83	77	76	101
1990	—Toronto (A.L.).........................	33	18	6	.750	2.93	0	208⅔	179	73	68	64	125
1991	—Toronto (A.L.).........................	9	4	3	.571	3.17	0	59⅔	52	22	21	23	29
	Major league totals (13 years)	399	170	126	.574	3.33	1	2726⅔	2389	1119	1010	960	1586

CHAMPIONSHIP SERIES RECORD

CHAMPIONSHIP SERIES NOTES: Holds A.L. single-series record for most strikeouts—18 (1985).... Shares single-series record for most games lost—2 (1989).

Year	Team (League)	G	W	L	Pct.	ERA	Sv.	IP	H	R	ER	BB	SO
1985	—Toronto (A.L.).........................	3	1	1	.500	3.10	0	20⅓	11	7	7	10	18
1989	—Toronto (A.L.).........................	2	0	2	.000	6.35	0	11⅓	12	8	8	6	10
	Championship Series totals (2 years)	5	1	3	.250	4.26	0	31⅔	23	15	15	16	28

ALL-STAR GAME RECORD

ALL-STAR GAME NOTES: Shares single-game record for most wild pitches—2 (July 8, 1980).... Shares record for most wild pitches in one inning—2 (July 8, 1980, seventh inning).

Year	League	W	L	Pct.	ERA	Sv.	IP	H	R	ER	BB	SO
1980	—American	0	0	...	0.00	0	1	1	1	0	2	0
1981	—American	0	0	...	0.00	0	1⅔	1	0	0	1	1
1983	—American	1	0	1.000	0.00	0	3	0	1	0	1	4
1984	—American	0	1	.000	4.50	0	2	3	2	1	0	2
1985	—American	0	0	...	0.00	0	1	0	0	0	1	2
1988	—American	0	0	...	0.00	0	1	1	0	0	0	0
1990	—American	0	0	...	0.00	0	2	0	0	0	1	1
	All-Star totals (7 years)	1	1	.500	0.77	0	11⅔	6	4	1	6	10

RECORD AS POSITION PLAYER

						BATTING							FIELDING			
Year	Team (League)	Pos.	G	AB	R	H	2B	3B	HR	RBI	Avg.	SB	PO	A	E	Avg.
1978	—Dunedin (Florida State)	OF-P	35	99	10	19	3	0	1	9	.192	2	85	7	3	.968

STILLWELL, KURT
SS

PERSONAL: Born June 4, 1965, at Glendale, Calif.... 5-11/175.... Throws right, bats both.... Full name: Kurt Andrew Stillwell.... Son of Ron Stillwell, infielder, Washington Senators (1961-62); and brother of Rod Stillwell, minor league shortstop (1989-90).

HIGH SCHOOL: Thousand Oaks (Calif.).

TRANSACTIONS/CAREER NOTES: Selected by Cincinnati Reds organization in first round (second pick overall) of free-agent draft (June 6, 1983).... On disabled list (August 9, 1985-remainder of season).... Traded by Reds with P Ted Power to Kansas City Royals for P Danny Jackson and SS Angel Salazar (November 6, 1987).... On disabled list (July 6-August 3, 1989 and August 5-21, 1991).... Granted free agency (October 29, 1991).

RECORDS/HONORS: Shares A.L. single-season record for fewest errors by shortstop who led league—24 (1990).

						BATTING							FIELDING			
Year	Team (League)	Pos.	G	AB	R	H	2B	3B	HR	RBI	Avg.	SB	PO	A	E	Avg.
1983	—Billings (Pioneer).............	SS	65	250	47	81	10	1	2	44	.324	5	73	137	★30	.875
1984	—Cedar Rapids (Midwest) ...	SS	112	382	63	96	15	1	4	33	.251	24	156	245	25	.941
1985	—Denver (Am. Assoc.)	SS-3B	59	182	28	48	7	4	1	22	.264	5	103	135	25	.905
1986	—Cincinnati (N.L.)	SS	104	279	31	64	6	1	0	26	.229	6	107	205	16	.951
	—Denver (Am. Assoc.)	SS	10	30	2	7	0	0	0	2	.233	2	14	21	5	.875
1987	—Cincinnati (N.L.)	SS-2B-3B	131	395	54	102	20	7	4	33	.258	4	144	247	23	.944
1988	—Kansas City (A.L.)■.........	SS	128	459	63	115	28	5	10	53	.251	6	170	349	13	.976
1989	—Kansas City (A.L.)...........	SS	130	463	52	121	20	7	7	54	.261	9	179	334	16	.970
1990	—Kansas City (A.L.)..........	SS	144	506	60	126	35	4	3	51	.249	0	181	350	★24	.957
1991	—Kansas City (A.L.)..........	SS	122	385	44	102	17	1	6	51	.265	3	163	263	18	.959
	American League totals (4 years)		524	1813	219	464	100	17	26	209	.256	18	693	1296	71	.966
	National League totals (2 years)		235	674	85	166	26	8	4	59	.246	10	251	452	39	.947
	Major league totals (6 years)		759	2487	304	630	126	25	30	268	.253	28	944	1748	110	.961

ALL-STAR GAME RECORD

						BATTING					FIELDING			
Year	League	Pos.	AB	R	H	2B	3B	HR	RBI	Avg.	SB	PO	A	E	Avg.
1988	—American	SS	0	0	0	0	0	0	0	...	0	1	0	0	1.000

STOTTLEMYRE, TODD
P, BLUE JAYS

PERSONAL: Born May 20, 1965, at Yakima, Wash. ... 6-3/195. ... Throws right, bats left. ... Full name: Todd Vernon Stottlemyre. ... Son of Mel Stottlemyre Sr., pitcher, New York Yankees (1964-74); coach, New York Mets (1984-91); and brother of Mel Stottlemyre Jr., pitcher, Kansas City Royals.

HIGH SCHOOL: A.C. Davis (Yakima, Wash.).
COLLEGE: Yakima Valley College (Wash.).
TRANSACTIONS/CAREER NOTES: Selected by New York Yankees organization in fifth round of free-agent draft (June 6, 1983). ... Selected by St. Louis Cardinals organization in secondary phase of free-agent draft (January 9, 1985). ... Selected by Toronto Blue Jays organization in secondary phase of free-agent draft (June 3, 1985).
STATISTICAL NOTES: Led International League pitchers with 34 games started in 1987.

Year	Team (League)	G	W	L	Pct.	ERA	Sv.	IP	H	R	ER	BB	SO
1986	—Ventura County (California)	17	9	4	.692	2.43	0	103⅔	76	39	28	36	104
	—Knoxville (Southern)	18	8	7	.533	4.18	0	99	93	56	46	49	81
1987	—Syracuse (International)	34	11	•13	.458	4.44	0	186⅔	189	•103	*92	*87	143
1988	—Toronto (A.L.)	28	4	8	.333	5.69	0	98	109	70	62	46	67
	—Syracuse (International)	7	5	0	1.000	2.05	0	48⅓	36	12	11	8	51
1989	—Toronto (A.L.)	27	7	7	.500	3.88	0	127⅔	137	56	55	44	63
	—Syracuse (International)	10	3	2	.600	3.23	0	55⅔	46	23	20	15	45
1990	—Toronto (A.L.)	33	13	17	.433	4.34	0	203	214	101	98	69	115
1991	—Toronto (A.L.)	34	15	8	.652	3.78	0	219	194	97	92	75	116
	Major league totals (4 years)	122	39	40	.494	4.27	0	647⅔	654	324	307	234	361

CHAMPIONSHIP SERIES RECORD

Year	Team (League)	G	W	L	Pct.	ERA	Sv.	IP	H	R	ER	BB	SO
1989	—Toronto (A.L.)	1	0	1	.000	7.20	0	5	7	4	4	2	3
1991	—Toronto (A.L.)	1	0	1	.000	9.82	0	3⅔	7	4	4	1	3
	Championship Series totals (2 years)	2	0	2	.000	8.31	0	8⅔	14	8	8	3	6

STRANGE, DOUG
IF, CUBS

PERSONAL: Born April 13, 1964, at Greenville, S.C. ... 6-2/170. ... Throws right, bats both. ... Full name: Joseph Douglas Strange.
HIGH SCHOOL: Wade Hampton (Greenville, S.C.).
COLLEGE: North Carolina State.
TRANSACTIONS/CAREER NOTES: Selected by Detroit Tigers organization in seventh round of free-agent draft (June 3, 1985). ... Traded by Tigers to Houston Astros organization for IF-OF Lou Frazier (March 30, 1990). ... Released by Astros organization (May 25, 1990). ... Signed by Chicago Cubs organization (June 11, 1990).
STATISTICAL NOTES: Led Florida State League third baseman with 116 putouts and tied for lead with 20 double plays in 1986. ... Led American Association third baseman with 16 double plays in 1990. ... Led American Association with 10 intentional base on balls received in 1991.
MISCELLANEOUS: Batted righthanded only at Glens Falls in 1987.

Year	Team (League)	Pos.	G	AB	R	H	2B	3B	HR	RBI	Avg.	SB	PO	A	E	Avg.
1985	—Bristol (Eastern)	OF-2B-3B	65	226	43	69	16	1	6	45	.305	6	84	59	11	.929
1986	—Lakeland (Florida State) ...	3B-1B	126	466	59	119	29	4	2	63	.255	18	†202	215	37	.919
1987	—Glens Falls (Eastern)	3-2-0-S	115	431	63	130	31	1	13	70	.302	5	110	214	20	.942
	—Toledo (International)	3B	16	45	7	11	2	0	1	5	.244	3	14	28	3	.933
1988	—Toledo (International) ...	3B-SS-1B	82	278	23	56	8	2	6	19	.201	9	52	126	13	.932
	—Glens Falls (Eastern)	3B	57	218	32	61	11	1	1	36	.280	11	45	112	12	.929
1989	—Toledo (International) ...	3B-SS	83	304	38	75	15	2	8	42	.247	8	108	197	17	.947
	—Detroit (A.L.)	3B-2B-SS	64	196	16	42	4	1	1	14	.214	3	53	118	19	.900
1990	—Tucson (Pacific Coast)■...	3B-SS	37	98	7	22	3	0	0	7	.224	0	9	47	9	.862
	—Iowa (American Assoc.)■ .	3B-2B-SS	82	269	31	82	17	1	5	35	.305	6	58	149	16	.928
1991	—Iowa (American Assoc.) ...	3-2-1-S-0	131	509	76	149	35	5	8	56	.293	10	263	273	21	.962
	—Chicago (N.L.)	3B	3	9	0	4	1	0	0	1	.444	1	1	3	1	.800
	American League totals (1 year)		64	196	16	42	4	1	1	14	.214	3	53	118	19	.900
	National League totals (1 year)		3	9	0	4	1	0	0	1	.444	1	1	3	1	.800
	Major league totals (2 years)		67	205	16	46	5	1	1	15	.224	4	54	121	20	.897

STRAWBERRY, DARRYL
OF, DODGERS

PERSONAL: Born March 12, 1962, at Los Angeles. ... 6-6/200. ... Throws left, bats left. ... Full name: Darryl Eugene Strawberry. ... Brother of Michael Strawberry, minor league outfielder (1980-81).
HIGH SCHOOL: Crenshaw (Los Angeles).
TRANSACTIONS/CAREER NOTES: Selected by New York Mets organization in first round (first pick overall) of free-agent draft (June 3, 1980). ... On disabled list (May 12-June 28, 1985). ... Granted free agency (November 5, 1990). ... Signed by Los Angeles Dodgers (November 8, 1990). ... On disabled list (June 18-July 3, 1991).
RECORDS/HONORS: Named Texas League Most Valuable Player (1982). ... Named N.L. Rookie Player of the Year by THE SPORTING NEWS (1983). ... Named N.L. Rookie of the Year by Baseball Writers' Association of America (1983). ... Named outfielder on THE SPORTING NEWS N.L. All-Star team (1988 and 1990). ... Named outfielder on THE SPORTING NEWS N.L. Silver Slugger team (1988 and 1990).
STATISTICAL NOTES: Led Texas League in slugging percentage with .602, bases on balls received with 100 and caught stealing with 22 in 1982. ... Hit three home runs in a game (August 5, 1985). ... Led N.L. with .545 slugging percentage in 1988.

Year	Team (League)	Pos.	G	AB	R	H	2B	3B	HR	RBI	Avg.	SB	PO	A	E	Avg.
1980—Kingsport (Appalachian) ..	OF	44	157	27	42	5	2	5	20	.268	5	55	4	3	.952
1981—Lynchburg (Carolina)	OF	123	420	84	107	22	6	13	78	.255	31	173	8	13	.933
1982—Jackson (Texas)	OF	129	435	93	123	19	9	★34	97	.283	45	211	8	9	.961
1983—Tidewater (Int'l)	OF	16	57	12	19	4	1	3	13	.333	7	22	0	4	.846
—New York (N.L.)	OF	122	420	63	108	15	7	26	74	.257	19	232	8	4	.984
1984—New York (N.L.)	OF	147	522	75	131	27	4	26	97	.251	27	276	11	6	.980
1985—New York (N.L.)	OF	111	393	78	109	15	4	29	79	.277	26	211	5	2	.991
1986—New York (N.L.)	OF	136	475	76	123	27	5	27	93	.259	28	226	10	6	.975
1987—New York (N.L.)	OF	154	532	108	151	32	5	39	104	.284	36	272	6	8	.972
1988—New York (N.L.)	OF	153	543	101	146	27	3	★39	101	.269	29	297	4	9	.971
1989—New York (N.L.)	OF	134	476	69	107	26	1	29	77	.225	11	272	4	8	.972
1990—New York (N.L.)	OF	152	542	92	150	18	1	37	108	.277	15	268	10	3	.989
1991—Los Angeles (N.L.)■.........	OF	139	505	86	134	22	4	28	99	.265	10	209	11	5	.978
Major league totals (9 years)		1248	4408	748	1159	209	34	280	832	.263	201	2263	69	51	.979

CHAMPIONSHIP SERIES RECORD

CHAMPIONSHIP SERIES NOTES: Shares single-series record for most strikeouts—12 (1986).... Shares N.L. single-series record for most at-bats—30 (1988).

Year	Team (League)	Pos.	G	AB	R	H	2B	3B	HR	RBI	Avg.	SB	PO	A	E	Avg.
1986—New York (N.L.)	OF	6	22	4	5	1	0	2	5	.227	1	9	0	0	1.000
1988—New York (N.L.)	OF	7	30	5	9	2	0	1	6	.300	0	11	0	0	1.000
Championship Series totals (2 years)		13	52	9	14	3	0	3	11	.269	1	20	0	0	1.000

WORLD SERIES RECORD

Year	Team (League)	Pos.	G	AB	R	H	2B	3B	HR	RBI	Avg.	SB	PO	A	E	Avg.
1986—New York (N.L.)	OF	7	24	4	5	1	0	1	1	.208	3	19	0	0	1.000

ALL-STAR GAME RECORD

ALL-STAR GAME NOTES: Named to N.L. All-Star team for 1989 and 1991 games; replaced due to injury.

Year	League	Pos.	AB	R	H	2B	3B	HR	RBI	Avg.	SB	PO	A	E	Avg.
1984—National	OF	2	0	1	0	0	0	0	.500	0	0	0	0	...
1985—National	OF	1	2	1	0	0	0	0	1.000	1	3	0	0	1.000
1986—National	OF	2	0	1	0	0	0	0	.500	0	1	0	0	1.000
1987—National	OF	2	0	0	0	0	0	0	.000	0	0	0	0	...
1988—National	OF	4	0	1	0	0	0	0	.250	0	4	0	0	1.000
1990—National	OF	1	0	0	0	0	0	0	.000	0	3	1	1	.800
All-Star Game totals (6 years)		12	2	4	0	0	0	0	.333	1	11	1	1	.923

STUBBS, FRANKLIN

1B, BREWERS

PERSONAL: Born October 21, 1960, at Laurinburg, N.C.... 6-2/209.... Throws left, bats left.... Full name: Franklin Lee Stubbs. **HIGH SCHOOL:** Richmond (Hamlet, N.C.). **COLLEGE:** Virginia Tech.

TRANSACTIONS/CAREER NOTES: Selected by Los Angeles Dodgers organization in first round (19th pick overall) of free-agent draft (June 7, 1982).... On disabled list (July 5, 1982-remainder of season; August 3-24, 1987; and August 20, 1989-remainder of season).... Traded by Dodgers to Houston Astros for P Terry Wells (April 1, 1990).... Granted free agency (November 5, 1990).... Signed by Milwaukee Brewers (December 5, 1990).

RECORDS/HONORS: Shares major league single-game record for fewest putouts by first baseman—0 (July 25, 1990).... Named first baseman on THE SPORTING NEWS college All-America team (1982).

STATISTICAL NOTES: Led N.L. first basemen with .994 fielding percentage in 1987.

Year	Team (League)	Pos.	G	AB	R	H	2B	3B	HR	RBI	Avg.	SB	PO	A	E	Avg.
1982—Vero Beach (Florida St.) ..	1B	16	54	6	11	1	1	3	5	.204	2	134	3	3	.979
1983—San Antonio (Texas)	1B-OF	47	173	35	54	8	3	12	52	.312	5	425	23	5	.989
—Albuquerque (PCL)	OF-1B	76	267	49	74	16	3	16	58	.277	3	106	3	6	.948
1984—Los Angeles (N.L.)	1B-OF	87	217	22	42	2	3	8	17	.194	2	417	37	4	.991
—Albuquerque (PCL)	OF-1B	29	108	26	35	5	5	6	24	.324	3	36	4	2	.952
1985—Albuquerque (PCL)	1B-OF	132	421	86	118	23	5	32	93	.280	23	945	87	14	.987
—Los Angeles (N.L.)	1B	10	9	0	2	0	0	0	2	.222	0	11	0	0	1.000
1986—Los Angeles (N.L.)	OF-1B	132	420	55	95	11	1	23	58	.226	7	244	14	7	.974
1987—Los Angeles (N.L.)	1B-OF	129	386	48	90	16	3	16	52	.233	8	830	79	5	+.995
1988—Los Angeles (N.L.)	1B-OF	115	242	30	54	13	0	8	34	.223	11	530	57	13	.978
1989—Los Angeles (N.L.)	OF-1B	69	103	11	30	6	0	4	15	.291	3	70	5	3	.962
1990—Houston (N.L.)■...........	1B-OF	146	448	59	117	23	2	23	71	.261	19	609	43	6	.991
1991—Milwaukee (A.L.)■...........	1B-OF	103	362	48	77	16	2	11	38	.213	13	828	82	9	.990
American League totals (1 year)		103	362	48	77	16	2	11	38	.213	13	828	82	9	.990
National League totals (7 years)		688	1825	225	430	71	9	82	249	.236	50	2711	235	38	.987
Major league totals (8 years)		791	2187	273	507	87	11	93	287	.232	63	3539	317	47	.988

CHAMPIONSHIP SERIES RECORD

Year	Team (League)	Pos.	G	AB	R	H	2B	3B	HR	RBI	Avg.	SB	PO	A	E	Avg.
1988 —Los Angeles (N.L.)............		1B-PH	4	8	0	2	0	0	0	0	.250	0	16	2	0	1.000

WORLD SERIES RECORD

Year	Team (League)	Pos.	G	AB	R	H	2B	3B	HR	RBI	Avg.	SB	PO	A	E	Avg.
1988 —Los Angeles (N.L.)............		1B	5	17	3	5	2	0	0	2	.294	0	34	0	0	1.000

SUERO, WILLIAM
2B, BREWERS

PERSONAL: Born November 7, 1966, at Santo Domingo, Dominican Republic.... 5-9/175. ... Throws right, bats right.... Full name: William Urban Suero.... Name pronounced SWEAR-o.
HIGH SCHOOL: Francisco Rosario Sanchez (Santo Domingo, Dominican Republic).
TRANSACTIONS/CAREER NOTES: Signed as free agent by Toronto Blue Jays organization (May 1, 1985).... On disabled list (June 21, 1985-remainder of season).... Traded by Blue Jays to Milwaukee Brewers (August 14, 1991) to complete deal in which Brewers traded OF Candy Maldonado to Blue Jays in exchange for P Rob Wishnevski and a player to be named later (August 9, 1991).
STATISTICAL NOTES: Led Pioneer League second basemen with 360 total chances and 34 double plays in 1986.... Led New York-Pennsylvania League second basemen with 362 total chances in 1987.... Led Southern League in caught stealing with 22 in 1990.

Year	Team (League)	Pos.	G	AB	R	H	2B	3B	HR	RBI	Avg.	SB	PO	A	E	Avg.
1985 —..							Did not play									
1986 —Medicine Hat (Pioneer)		2B	64	273	39	76	7	5	2	28	.278	13	★159	★182	★19	★.947
1987 —St. Catharines (NYP).........		2B	•77	297	43	94	12	4	4	24	.316	23	★149	197	★16	.956
1988 —Myrtle Beach (S. Atl.)........		2B	125	493	88	140	21	6	6	52	.284	21	254	303	26	.955
1989 —Dunedin (Florida State)		2B	51	206	35	60	10	5	2	17	.291	9	92	155	10	.961
—Knoxville (Southern)		2B	87	324	42	84	17	5	4	29	.259	7	146	228	15	.961
1990 —Knoxville (Southern)		2B	133	483	80	127	29	7	16	60	.263	40	259	333	23	.963
1991 —Syracuse (International) ..		2B	98	393	49	78	18	1	1	28	.198	17	178	318	★19	.963
—Denver (Am. Assoc.)■.......		2B	20	70	20	27	3	2	0	15	.386	3	63	57	3	.976

SURHOFF, B.J.
C/IF, BREWERS

PERSONAL: Born August 4, 1964, at Bronx, N.Y.... 6-1/200.... Throws right, bats left.... Full name: William James Surhoff.... Son of Dick Surhoff, National Basketball Association player (1952-53 and 1953-54); and brother of Rich Surhoff, pitcher, Philadelphia Phillies and Texas Rangers (1985).
HIGH SCHOOL: Rye (N.Y.).
COLLEGE: North Carolina.
TRANSACTIONS/CAREER NOTES: Selected by New York Yankees organization in fifth round of free-agent draft (June 7, 1982).... Selected by Milwaukee Brewers organization in first round (first pick overall) of free-agent draft (June 3, 1985).... On suspended list (August 23-25, 1990).
RECORDS/HONORS: Named College Player of the Year by THE SPORTING NEWS (1985).... Named catcher on THE SPORTING NEWS college All-America team (1985).
STATISTICAL NOTES: Tied for Pacific Coast League lead in double plays by catchers with 10 in 1986.... Led A.L. catchers with 68 assists in 1991.
MISCELLANEOUS: Member of 1984 U.S. Olympic baseball team.

Year	Team (League)	Pos.	G	AB	R	H	2B	3B	HR	RBI	Avg.	SB	PO	A	E	Avg.
1985 —Beloit (Midwest)		C	76	289	39	96	13	4	7	58	.332	10	475	44	3	.994
1986 —Vancouver (Pac. Coast)....		C	116	458	71	141	19	3	5	59	.308	21	539	70	7	★.989
1987 —Milwaukee (A.L.)		C-3B-1B	115	395	50	118	22	3	7	68	.299	11	648	56	11	.985
1988 —Milwaukee (A.L.)		C-3-1-S-0	139	493	47	121	21	0	5	38	.245	21	550	94	8	.988
1989 —Milwaukee (A.L.)		C-3B	126	436	42	108	17	4	5	55	.248	14	530	58	10	.983
1990 —Milwaukee (A.L.)		C-3B	135	474	55	131	21	4	6	59	.276	14	619	62	12	.983
1991 —Milwaukee (A.L.)		C-3-0-2	143	505	57	146	19	4	5	68	.289	5	665	†71	4	.995
Major league totals (5 years)			658	2303	251	624	100	15	28	288	.271	65	3012	341	45	.987

SUTCLIFFE, RICK
P, ORIOLES

PERSONAL: Born June 21, 1956, at Independence, Mo.... 6-7/215.... Throws right, bats left.... Full name: Richard Lee Sutcliffe.... Brother of Terry Sutcliffe, minor league pitcher (1979-81).
HIGH SCHOOL: Van Horn (Independence, Mo.).
TRANSACTIONS/CAREER NOTES: Selected by Los Angeles Dodgers organization in first round (21st pick overall) of free-agent draft (June 5, 1974).... On disabled list (May 3-24, 1977 and August 14-September 5, 1981).... Traded by Dodgers with 2B Jack Perconte to Cleveland Indians for OF Jorge Orta, C Jack Fimple and P Larry White (December 9, 1981).... Traded by Indians with C Ron Hassey and P George Frazier to Chicago Cubs for OF Mel Hall, OF Joe Carter, P Don Schulze and P Darryl Banks (June 13, 1984).... Granted free agency (November 8, 1984).... Re-signed by Cubs (December 14, 1984).... On disabled list (May 20-June 7, July 8-23 and July 29-September 27, 1985; June 30-August 3, 1986; and May 21-June 11, 1988). ... On Chicago disabled list (March 31-August 29, 1990); included rehabilitation disability assignment to Iowa (April 26-May 1, 1990).... On Chicago disabled list (April 2-18 and June 9-August 6, 1991); included rehabilitation disability assignment to

Peoria (July 10-11, 1991) and Iowa (July 15-20, 1991 and July 29-30, 1991).... Granted free agency (October 28, 1991)....
Signed by Baltimore Orioles (December 19, 1991).
RECORDS/HONORS: Shares major league single-season record for fewest games won by pitcher who led league—18 (1987)....
Named N.L. Rookie Pitcher of the Year by THE SPORTING NEWS (1979).... Named N.L. Rookie of the Year by Baseball Writers' Association of America (1979).... Named N.L. Pitcher of the Year by THE SPORTING NEWS (1984).... Named right-handed pitcher on THE SPORTING NEWS N.L. All-Star team (1984).... Named N.L. Cy Young Award winner by Baseball Writers' Association of America (1984).... Named N.L. Comeback Player of the Year by THE SPORTING NEWS (1987).
STATISTICAL NOTES: Tied for Northwest League lead with two shutouts in 1974. ... Led California League pitchers with 28 games started in 1975.
MISCELLANEOUS: Received base on balls in only appearance as pinch-hitter (1991).

Year	Team (League)	G	W	L	Pct.	ERA	Sv.	IP	H	R	ER	BB	SO
1974	—Bellingham (Northwest)	17	10	3	.769	3.32	1	95	79	42	35	48	69
1975	—Bakersfield (California)	28	8	*16	.333	4.15	0	193	*214	*115	*89	68	91
1976	—Waterbury (Eastern)	30	10	11	.476	3.18	0	187	*187	90	66	45	121
	—Los Angeles (N.L.)	1	0	0	...	0.00	0	5	2	0	0	1	3
1977	—Albuquerque (Pacific Coast)	17	3	10	.231	6.43	5	77	96	67	55	63	48
1978	—Albuquerque (Pacific Coast)	30	13	6	.684	4.45	0	184	179	101	91	92	99
	—Los Angeles (N.L.)	2	0	0	...	0.00	0	2	2	0	0	1	0
1979	—Los Angeles (N.L.)	39	17	10	.630	3.46	0	242	217	104	93	97	117
1980	—Los Angeles (N.L.)	42	3	9	.250	5.56	5	110	122	73	68	55	59
1981	—Los Angeles (N.L.)	14	2	2	.500	4.02	0	47	41	24	21	20	16
1982	—Cleveland (A.L.)■	34	14	8	.636	*2.96	1	216	174	81	71	98	142
1983	—Cleveland (A.L.)	36	17	11	.607	4.29	0	243⅓	251	131	116	102	160
1984	—Cleveland (A.L.)	15	4	5	.444	5.15	0	94⅓	111	60	54	46	58
	—Chicago (N.L.)■	20	16	1	.941	2.69	0	150⅓	123	53	45	39	155
1985	—Chicago (N.L.)	20	8	8	.500	3.18	0	130	119	51	46	44	102
1986	—Chicago (N.L.)	28	5	14	.263	4.64	0	176⅔	166	92	91	96	122
1987	—Chicago (N.L.)	34	*18	10	.643	3.68	0	237⅓	223	106	97	106	174
1988	—Chicago (N.L.)	32	13	14	.481	3.86	0	226	232	97	97	70	144
1989	—Chicago (N.L.)	35	16	11	.593	3.66	0	229	202	98	93	69	153
1990	—Iowa (American Association)	2	0	2	.000	7.82	0	12⅔	18	13	11	7	12
	—Chicago (N.L.)	5	0	2	.000	5.82	0	21⅔	25	14	14	12	7
1991	—Chicago (N.L.)	19	6	5	.545	4.10	0	96⅔	96	52	44	45	52
	—Peoria (Midwest)	1	0	0	...	6.00	0	9	12	6	6	2	6
	—Iowa (American Association)	3	1	2	.333	9.69	0	13	23	14	14	6	8
American League totals (3 years)		85	35	24	.593	3.92	1	553⅔	536	272	241	246	360
National League totals (13 years)		291	104	86	.547	3.81	5	1673⅔	1570	764	709	655	1104
Major league totals (15 years)		376	139	110	.558	3.84	6	2227⅓	2106	1036	950	901	1464

CHAMPIONSHIP SERIES RECORD
CHAMPIONSHIP SERIES NOTES: Hit home run in first series at-bat (October 2, 1984).

Year	Team (League)	G	W	L	Pct.	ERA	Sv.	IP	H	R	ER	BB	SO
1984	—Chicago (N.L.)	2	1	1	.500	3.38	0	13⅓	9	6	5	8	10
1989	—Chicago (N.L.)	1	0	0	...	4.50	0	6	5	3	3	4	2
Championship Series totals (2 years)		3	1	1	.500	3.72	0	19⅓	14	9	8	12	12

ALL-STAR GAME RECORD

Year	League	W	L	Pct.	ERA	Sv.	IP	H	R	ER	BB	SO
1983	—American				Did not play								
1987	—National	0	0	...	0.00	0	2	1	0	0	1	0
1989	—National	0	0	...	18.00	0	1	4	2	2	0	0
All-Star totals (2 years)		0	0	...	6.00	0	3	5	2	2	1	0

SUTKO, GLENN
C, REDS

PERSONAL: Born May 9, 1968, at Atlanta.... 6-3/225.... Throws right, bats right.... Full name: Glenn Edward Sutko.
HIGH SCHOOL: Forsyth (Cumming, Ga.).
COLLEGE: Spartanburg Methodist (S.C.) and Dekalb College (Ga.).
TRANSACTIONS/CAREER NOTES: Selected by Cincinnati Reds organization in 45th round of free-agent draft (June 2, 1987)....
On Cedar Rapids disabled list (May 29-July 12, 1990).... On Nashville disabled list (July 27-August 5, 1991).

						BATTING							FIELDING			
Year	Team (League)	Pos.	G	AB	R	H	2B	3B	HR	RBI	Avg.	SB	PO	A	E	Avg.
1988	—Billings (Pioneer)	C	30	84	3	13	2	1	1	8	.155	3	141	15	5	.969
1989	—Greensboro (S. Atlantic)	C	109	333	44	78	21	0	7	41	.234	1	676	77	11	.986
1990	—Cedar Rapids (Midwest)	C	4	10	0	3	0	0	0	0	.300	0	21	2	0	1.000
	—Chattanooga (Southern)	C-1B	53	174	12	29	7	1	2	11	.167	1	351	33	4	.990
	—Cincinnati (N.L.)	C	1	1	0	0	0	0	0	0	.000	0	3	0	0	1.000
1991	—Nashville (Am. Assoc.)	C	45	134	9	28	2	1	3	15	.209	1	228	39	4	.985
	—Cincinnati (N.L.)	C	10	10	0	1	0	0	0	1	.100	0	16	5	3	.875
Major league totals (2 years)			11	11	0	1	0	0	0	1	.091	0	19	5	3	.889

SVEUM, DALE
SS/3B, PHILLIES

PERSONAL: Born November 23, 1963, at Richmond, Calif.... 6-3/185.... Throws right, bats both.... Full name: Dale Curtis Sveum.... Name pronounced SWAIM.
HIGH SCHOOL: Pinole Valley (Calif.).
TRANSACTIONS/CAREER NOTES: Selected by Milwaukee Brewers organization in first round (25th

pick overall) of free-agent draft (June 7, 1982).... On Milwaukee disabled list (July 23-August 9, 1986).... On Milwaukee disabled list (March 19, 1989-entire season); included rehabilitation disability assignment to Beloit (June 30-July 5, 1989); then transferred to Stockton (July 6-18, 1989).... Traded by Brewers to Philadelphia Phillies for P Bruce Ruffin (December 11, 1991).

STATISTICAL NOTES: Led California League third basemen with 261 assists in 1983.... Led Texas League with 256 total bases in 1984.... Led Texas League third basemen with 111 putouts and 30 errors in 1984....... Led American League third basemen in errors with 26 in 1986.... Hit three home runs in a game (July 17, 1987).... Switch-hit home runs in one game (July 17, 1987 and June 12, 1988).... Led American League shortstops with 27 errors in 1988.

Year	Team (League)	Pos.	G	AB	R	H	2B	3B	HR	RBI	Avg.	SB	PO	A	E	Avg.
1982 —Pikeville (Appalachian)		SS-3B	58	223	29	52	13	1	2	21	.233	6	84	158	36	.871
1983 —Stockton (California)		3B-SS	135	533	70	139	26	5	5	70	.261	15	105	†281	40	.906
1984 —El Paso (Texas)		3B-SS	131	523	92	★172	★41	8	9	84	.329	6	†113	259	†30	.925
1985 —Vancouver (Pac. Coast)....		3B-SS	122	415	42	98	17	3	6	48	.236	4	81	200	26	.915
1986 —Vancouver (Pac. Coast)....		3B	28	105	16	31	3	2	1	23	.295	0	22	54	4	.950
—Milwaukee (A.L.)	3B-SS-2B		91	317	35	78	13	2	7	35	.246	4	92	179	†30	.900
1987 —Milwaukee (A.L.)		SS-2B	153	535	86	135	27	3	25	95	.252	2	242	396	23	.965
1988 —Milwaukee (A.L.)		SS-2B	129	467	41	113	14	4	9	51	.242	1	209	375	†27	.956
1989 —Beloit (Midwest)		DH	6	15	0	2	1	0	0	2	.133	0	0	0	0	...
—Stockton (California)		DH	11	43	5	8	0	0	1	5	.186	0	0	0	0	...
1990 —Milwaukee (A.L.)		3-2-1-S	48	117	15	23	7	0	1	12	.197	0	59	63	6	.953
—Denver (Am. Assoc.)		3-S-1-2	57	218	25	63	17	2	2	26	.289	1	134	102	12	.952
1991 —Milwaukee (A.L.)		SS-3B-2B	90	266	33	64	19	1	4	43	.241	2	85	189	10	.965
Major league totals (5 years)			511	1702	210	413	80	10	46	236	.243	9	687	1202	96	.952

SWAN, RUSS
P, MARINERS

PERSONAL: Born January 3, 1964, at Fremont, Calif.... 6-4/215.... Throws left, bats left.... Full name: Russell Howard Swan.
HIGH SCHOOL: Kennewick (Wash.).
COLLEGE: Spokane Falls Community College (Wash.) and Texas A&M.
TRANSACTIONS/CAREER NOTES: Selected by Houston Astros organization in second round of free-agent draft (January 17, 1984).... Selected by Seattle Mariners'organization in secondary phase of free-agent draft (June 4, 1984).... Selected by San Francisco Giants organization in ninth round of free-agent draft (June 2, 1986).... Traded by Giants organization to Seattle Mariners for P Gary Eave (May 24, 1990).... On Seattle disabled list (July 8-September 1, 1990); included rehabilitation disability assignment to Calgary (August 16-31, 1990).... On disabled list (August 3-18, 1991).

Year	Team (League)	G	W	L	Pct.	ERA	Sv.	IP	H	R	ER	BB	SO
1986 —Everett (Northwest)	7	5	0	1.000	2.15	0	46	30	17	11	22	45
—Clinton (Midwest)	7	3	3	.500	3.09	0	43⅔	36	18	15	8	37
1987 —Fresno (California)	12	6	3	.667	3.80	0	64	54	40	27	29	59
1988 —San Jose (Pacific Coast)	11	7	0	1.000	2.23	0	76⅔	53	28	19	26	62
1989 —Shreveport (Texas)	11	2	3	.400	2.63	0	75⅓	62	25	22	22	56
—San Francisco (N.L.)	2	0	2	.000	10.80	0	6⅔	11	10	8	4	2
—Phoenix (Pacific Coast)	14	4	3	.571	3.36	0	83	75	37	31	29	49
1990 —San Francisco (N.L.)	2	0	1	.000	3.86	0	2⅓	6	4	1	4	1
—Phoenix-Calgary (Pac. Coast)■	11	3	6	.333	4.45	0	56⅔	69	35	28	27	35
—Seattle (A.L.)	11	2	3	.400	3.64	0	47	42	22	19	18	15
1991 —Seattle (A.L.)	63	6	2	.750	3.43	2	78⅔	81	35	30	28	33
American League totals (2 years)	74	8	5	.615	3.51	2	125⅔	123	57	49	46	48
National League totals (2 years)	4	0	3	.000	9.00	0	9	17	14	9	8	3
Major league totals (3 years)	78	8	8	.500	3.88	2	134⅔	140	71	58	54	51

SWIFT, BILL
P, GIANTS

PERSONAL: Born October 27, 1961, at Portland, Me. ... 6-0/180. ... Throws right, bats right.... Full name: William Charles Swift.
HIGH SCHOOL: South Portland (Portland, Me.).
COLLEGE: Maine.
TRANSACTIONS/CAREER NOTES: Selected by Minnesota Twins organization in second round of free-agent draft (June 6, 1983). ... Selected by Seattle Mariners organization in first round (second pick overall) of free-agent draft (June 4, 1984).... On disabled list (May 6-21, 1985 and April 22, 1987-remainder of season).... On Seattle disabled list (March 28-April 27, 1989); included rehabilitation disability assignment to San Bernardino (April 18-27, 1989).... On disabled list (April 11-26, 1991). ... Traded by Mariners with P Mike Jackson and P Dave Burba to San Francisco Giants for OF Kevin Mitchell and P Mike Remlinger (December 11, 1991).
MISCELLANEOUS: Member of 1984 U.S. Olympic baseball team.

Year	Team (League)	G	W	L	Pct.	ERA	Sv.	IP	H	R	ER	BB	SO
1985 —Chattanooga (Southern)	7	2	1	.667	3.69	0	39	34	16	16	21	21
—Seattle (A.L.)	23	6	10	.375	4.77	0	120⅔	131	71	64	48	55
1986 —Seattle (A.L.)	29	2	9	.182	5.46	0	115⅓	148	85	70	55	55
—Calgary (Pacific Coast)	10	4	4	.500	3.95	1	57	57	33	25	22	29
1987 —Calgary (Pacific Coast)	5	0	0	...	8.84	0	18⅓	32	22	18	13	5
1988 —Seattle (A.L.)	38	8	12	.400	4.59	0	174⅔	199	99	89	65	47
1989 —San Bernardino (California)	2	1	0	1.000	0.00	0	10	8	0	0	2	4
—Seattle (A.L.)	37	7	3	.700	4.43	1	130	140	72	64	38	45
1990 —Seattle (A.L.)	55	6	4	.600	2.39	6	128	135	46	34	21	42
1991 —Seattle (A.L.)	71	1	2	.333	1.99	17	90⅓	74	22	20	26	48
Major league totals (6 years)	253	30	40	.429	4.04	24	759	827	395	341	253	292

SWINDELL, GREG
P, REDS

PERSONAL: Born January 2, 1965, at Fort Worth, Tex. . . . 6-3/225. . . . Throws left, bats both. . . . Full name: Forest Gregory Swindell. . . . Name pronounced swin-DELL.
HIGH SCHOOL: Sharpstown (Tex.).
COLLEGE: Texas.
TRANSACTIONS/CAREER NOTES: Selected by Cleveland Indians organization in first round (second pick overall) of free-agent draft (June 2, 1986). . . . On disabled list (June 30, 1987-remainder of season and July 26-August 30, 1989). . . . Traded by Indians to Cincinnati Reds for P Jack Armstrong, P Scott Scudder and P Joe Turek (November 15, 1991).
RECORDS/HONORS: Named lefthanded pitcher on THE SPORTING NEWS college All-America team (1985-86).

Year	Team (League)	G	W	L	Pct.	ERA	Sv.	IP	H	R	ER	BB	SO
1986	—Waterloo (Midwest)	3	2	1	.667	1.00	0	18	12	2	2	3	25
	—Cleveland (A.L.)	9	5	2	.714	4.23	0	61⅔	57	35	29	15	46
1987	—Cleveland (A.L.)	16	3	8	.273	5.10	0	102⅓	112	62	58	37	97
1988	—Cleveland (A.L.)	33	18	14	.563	3.20	0	242	234	97	86	45	180
1989	—Cleveland (A.L.)	28	13	6	.684	3.37	0	184⅓	170	71	69	51	129
1990	—Cleveland (A.L.)	34	12	9	.571	4.40	0	214⅔	245	110	105	47	135
1991	—Cleveland (A.L.)	33	9	16	.360	3.48	0	238	241	112	92	31	169
	Major league totals (6 years)	153	60	55	.522	3.79	0	1043	1059	487	439	226	756

ALL-STAR GAME RECORD

Year	League	W	L	Pct.	ERA	Sv.	IP	H	R	ER	BB	SO
1989	—American	0	0	. . .	0.00	0	1⅔	2	0	0	0	3

SWINGLE, PAUL
P, ANGELS

PERSONAL: Born December 21, 1966, at Inglewood, Calif. . . . 6-0/185. . . . Throws right, bats right. . . . Full name: Paul Christopher Swingle.
HIGH SCHOOL: Dobson (Mesa, Ariz.).
COLLEGE: Grand Canyon College (Ariz.).
TRANSACTIONS/CAREER NOTES: Selected by California Angels organization in 29th round of free-agent draft (June 3, 1989).

Year	Team (League)	G	W	L	Pct.	ERA	Sv.	IP	H	R	ER	BB	SO
1989	—Bend (Northwest)	9	1	0	1.000	2.95	0	18⅓	7	9	6	19	26
1990	—Boise (Northwest)	14	0	1	.000	0.66	6	13⅔	5	1	1	4	25
1991	—Palm Springs (California)	43	5	4	.556	4.42	10	57	51	37	28	41	63

SZEKELY, JOE
C

PERSONAL: Born June 28, 1961, at Paris, Tex. . . . 6-1/195. . . . Throws right, bats left. . . . Full name: Joseph Szekely Jr. . . . Son of Joseph Szekely Sr., outfielder, Cincinnati Reds (1953).
HIGH SCHOOL: Paris (Tex.).
COLLEGE: Texas A&M.
TRANSACTIONS/CAREER NOTES: Selected by Kansas City Royals organization in second round of free-agent draft (June 7, 1982). . . . Traded by Royals organization with P Jose Torres and P John Serritella to Los Angeles Dodgers organization for P Joe Beckwith (December 8, 1983). . . . On disabled list (April 29-May 14, 1985 and April 8, 1988-entire season). . . . Granted free agency (October 22, 1989). . . . Signed by Pittsburgh Pirates organization (November 20, 1989). . . . Traded by Pirates organization to Toronto Blue Jays organization for OF Brian Morrison (April 10, 1990). . . . Granted free agency (October 15, 1990). . . . Signed by Atlanta Braves organization (January 14, 1991). . . . Granted free agency (October 15, 1991).
RECORDS/HONORS: Named catcher on THE SPORTING NEWS college All-America team (1982).
STATISTICAL NOTES: Led South Atlantic League catchers with nine double plays in 1983. . . . Led California League catchers with 15 double plays in 1984. . . . Led Texas League catchers with 586 total chances and 14 passed balls in 1986.

							BATTING							FIELDING			
Year	Team (League)	Pos.	G	AB	R	H	2B	3B	HR	RBI	Avg.	SB	PO	A	E	Avg.
1982	—Butte (Pioneer)	C	53	164	35	46	12	1	4	30	.280	4	298	39	7	.980
1983	—Charleston, S.C. (S. Atl.)	C	142	*521	83	144	17	5	15	87	.276	12	624	69	19	.973
1984	—Bakersfield (California)■	C	110	353	54	97	26	3	4	61	.275	4	563	88	14	.979
1985	—Vero Beach (Florida St.)	C	68	211	24	52	8	4	0	25	.246	3	337	46	7	.982
	—San Antonio (Texas)	C	30	106	9	28	9	0	1	18	.264	0	136	12	1	.993
1986	—San Antonio (Texas)	C	98	299	28	73	7	1	1	23	.244	2	*508	*75	3	*.995
1987	—San Antonio (Texas)	C-1B	113	417	54	124	22	2	4	49	.297	4	591	54	5	.992
1988								Did not play									
1989	—Albuquerque (PCL)	C	66	170	22	40	11	0	1	17	.235	2	286	16	5	.984
1990	—Buffalo (Am. Assoc.)■	C	2	4	1	0	0	0	0	0	.000	0	7	3	0	1.000
	—Syracuse (International)■	C	50	155	17	27	3	2	5	16	.174	1	258	19	6	.979
1991	—Richmond (Int'l)■	C-1B	83	227	24	59	10	1	3	30	.260	1	327	39	2	.995

TABLER, PAT
DH/1B, BLUE JAYS

PERSONAL: Born February 2, 1958, at Hamilton, O. . . . 6-2/200. . . . Throws right, bats right. . . . Full name: Patrick Sean Tabler.
HIGH SCHOOL: McNicholas (Cincinnati).
TRANSACTIONS/CAREER NOTES: Selected by New York Yankees organization in first round (16th pick overall) of free-agent draft (June 8, 1976). . . . Loaned by Yankees organization to Iowa, Chicago Cubs organization (June 12, 1981); returned (August 19, 1981). . . . Acquired on waivers by Chicago Cubs for two players to be named later (August 19, 1981); Yankees acquired P Bill Caudill (April 1, 1982) and Yankees organization acquired P Jay Howell (August 2, 1982) to complete deal. . . . Traded by Cubs with P Dick Tidrow, P Randy Martz and IF Scott Fletcher to Chicago White Sox for P Steve Trout and P Warren Brusstar (January 25, 1983). . . . Traded by White Sox to Cleveland Indians for SS Jerry Dybzinski (April 1, 1983). . . . On Cleveland disabled list (June 11-30, 1986); included rehabilitation disability assignment to Maine (June 26-30,

1986).... Traded by Indians to Kansas City Royals for P Bud Black (June 3, 1988).... Traded by Royals to New York Mets for P Archie Corbin (August 30, 1990).... Granted free agency (November 5, 1990).... Signed by Toronto Blue Jays (December 5, 1990).

STATISTICAL NOTES: Tied for American Association lead with nine sacrifice flies in 1982.... Led American Association third basemen with 112 putouts, 215 assists, 34 errors and 361 total chances in 1982.

						BATTING							FIELDING		
Year	Team (League)	Pos.	G	AB	R	H	2B	3B	HR	RBI	Avg.	SB	PO	A	E	Avg.
1976 —Oneonta (N.Y.-Penn)	3B-OF	65	238	27	55	3	0	1	20	.231	6	79	71	12	.926
1977 —Fort Lauderdale (FSL)	3B	110	391	35	93	7	1	1	36	.238	4	87	209	★35	.894
1978 —Fort Lauderdale (FSL)	1B-3B-OF	138	455	56	124	9	5	5	70	.273	5	855	88	15	.984
1979 —Fort Lauderdale (FSL)	0-3-2-1	75	247	39	78	12	4	2	33	.316	4	102	41	11	.929
—West Haven (Eastern)......	2B-OF	56	190	33	57	15	3	6	36	.300	9	124	169	13	.958
1980 —Nashville (Am. Assoc.)	2B	136	479	82	142	38	8	16	83	.296	9	262	361	★27	.958
1981 —Columbus (Int'l)	2B-3B	52	179	41	53	14	3	11	33	.296	0	66	116	14	.929
—Iowa (American Assoc.)■.	2B	63	222	41	68	13	3	6	37	.306	2	110	141	4	.984
—Chicago (N.L.)	2B	35	101	11	19	3	1	1	5	.188	0	70	93	3	.982
1982 —Iowa (American Assoc.) ...	3B-1B	129	441	89	151	32	★11	17	105	.342	0	†112	†215	†34	.906
—Chicago (N.L.)	3B	25	85	9	20	4	2	1	7	.235	15	23	33	3	.949
1983 —Charleston, S.C. (S. Atl.)■.	3B	4	14	2	3	0	1	0	2	.214	0	2	4	3	.667
—Cleveland (A.L.)	OF-3B-2B	124	430	56	125	23	5	6	65	.291	2	197	55	11	.958
1984 —Cleveland (A.L.)	1-0-3-2	144	473	66	137	21	3	10	68	.290	3	532	89	7	.989
1985 —Cleveland (A.L.)	1B-3B-2B	117	404	47	111	18	3	5	59	.275	0	744	77	14	.983
1986 —Cleveland (A.L.)	1B	130	473	61	154	29	2	6	48	.326	3	846	84	9	.990
—Maine (International)........	DH	3	12	5	3	1	0	0	1	.250	0	0	0	0	...
1987 —Cleveland (A.L.)	1B	151	553	66	170	34	3	11	86	.307	5	650	75	•12	.984
—Cleveland-K.C. (A.L.)■..	OF-1B-3B	130	444	53	125	22	3	2	66	.282	3	182	10	5	.975
1989 —Kansas City (A.L.)............	0-1-2-3	123	390	36	101	11	1	2	42	.259	2	217	25	4	.984
1990 —Kansas City (A.L.)	OF-3B-1B	75	195	12	53	14	0	1	19	.272	0	101	10	2	.982
—New York (N.L.)■.............	OF	17	43	6	12	1	1	1	10	.279	0	20	1	0	1.000
1991 —Toronto (A.L.)	1B-OF	82	185	20	40	5	1	1	21	.216	0	183	14	3	.985
American League totals (9 years)		1076	3547	417	1016	177	21	44	474	.286	16	3652	439	67	.984
National League totals (3 years)		77	229	26	51	8	4	3	22	.223	15	113	127	6	.976
Major league totals (11 years)		1153	3776	443	1067	185	25	47	496	.283	31	3765	566	73	.983

CHAMPIONSHIP SERIES RECORD

						BATTING							FIELDING		
Year	Team (League)	Pos.	G	AB	R	H	2B	3B	HR	RBI	Avg.	SB	PO	A	E	Avg.
1991 —Toronto (A.L.)............	PH-DH	2	1	0	0	0	0	0	0	.000	0	0	0	0	...

ALL-STAR GAME RECORD

				BATTING								FIELDING		
Year	League	Pos.	AB	R	H	2B	3B	HR	RBI	Avg.	SB	PO	A	E	Avg.
1987 —American	PH	0	0	0	0	0	0	0	...	0	0	0	0	...

TACKETT, JEFF
C, ORIOLES

PERSONAL: Born December 1, 1965, at Fresno, Calif.... 6-2/206.... Throws right, bats right. ... Full name: Jeffery Wilson Tackett.... Son of Terry Tackett, minor league pitcher (1961-65).

HIGH SCHOOL: Camarillo (Calif.).

TRANSACTIONS/CAREER NOTES: Selected by Baltimore Orioles organization in second round of free-agent draft (June 4, 1984). ... On disabled list (May 22-31, 1987).

STATISTICAL NOTES: Led New York-Pennsylvania League catchers with 489 total chances in 1985.... Led International League catchers with 570 putouts, 62 assists, 644 total chances and 11 double plays in 1990.... Led International League catchers with 761 putouts, 85 assists, 852 total chances and 14 passed balls and tied for lead with 12 double plays in 1991.

						BATTING							FIELDING		
Year	Team (League)	Pos.	G	AB	R	H	2B	3B	HR	RBI	Avg.	SB	PO	A	E	Avg.
1984 —Bluefield (Appalachian)	C	34	98	9	16	2	0	0	12	.163	1	215	22	5	.979
1985 —Daytona Beach (Fla. St.) ..	C-1B	40	103	8	20	5	2	0	10	.194	1	173	21	5	.975
—Newark (N.Y.-Penn)	C	62	187	21	39	6	0	0	22	.209	2	★412	★63	★14	.971
1986 —Hagerstown (Carolina)	C-1B	83	246	53	70	15	1	0	21	.285	16	465	38	9	.982
1987 —Charlotte (Southern)........	C	61	205	18	46	6	1	0	13	.224	5	379	27	10	.976
1988 —Charlotte (Southern)........	C	81	272	24	56	9	0	0	18	.206	6	543	57	11	.982
1989 —Rochester (Int'l)	C-3B	67	199	13	36	3	1	2	17	.181	3	339	42	9	.977
1990 —Rochester (Int'l)	C-3B-1B	108	306	37	73	8	3	4	33	.239	4	†573	†63	12	.981
1991 —Rochester (Int'l)	C-3B-1B	126	433	64	102	18	2	6	50	.236	3	†779	†90	8	.991
—Baltimore (A.L.)	C	6	8	1	1	0	0	0	0	.125	0	22	0	0	1.000
Major league totals (1 year)		6	8	1	1	0	0	0	0	.125	0	22	0	0	1.000

TANANA, FRANK
P, TIGERS

PERSONAL: Born July 3, 1953, at Detroit.... 6-3/195.... Throws left, bats left.... Full name: Frank Daryl Tanana.... Son of Frank Richard Tanana, minor league outfielder (1952-56).... Name pronounced tuh-NAN-uh.

HIGH SCHOOL: Detroit Catholic Central (Mich.).

COLLEGE: Cal State Fullerton.

TRANSACTIONS/CAREER NOTES: Selected by California Angels organization in first round (13th pick overall) of free-agent draft (June 8, 1971).... On disabled list (July 9-September 4, 1979).... Traded by Angels with P Jim Dorsey and OF Joe Rudi to Boston Red Sox for OF Fred Lynn and P Steve Renko (January 23, 1981).... Granted free agency (November 13, 1981).... Signed by Texas Rangers (January 6, 1982).... Traded by Rangers to Detroit Tigers for P Duane James (June 20, 1985).... Granted free agency (November 9, 1987).... Re-signed by Detroit (February 17, 1988).... Granted free agency (November 13, 1989).... Re-signed by Tigers (November 20, 1989).

RECORDS/HONORS: Shares A.L. record for most consecutive hits allowed, start of game—5 (May 18, 1980).... Named Texas League Pitcher of the Year (1973).... Named A.L. Rookie Pitcher of the Year by THE SPORTING NEWS (1974).... Named lefthanded pitcher on THE SPORTING NEWS A.L. All-Star team (1976-77).

STATISTICAL NOTES: Led Texas League with 15 complete games in 1973.... Led A.L. with seven shutouts in 1977.... Led A.L. with eight balks in 1978 and tied for lead with four in 1984.

MISCELLANEOUS: Appeared in one game as pinch-runner (1971); did not pitch due to a sore arm.... Struck out in only at-bat (1991).

Year	Team (League)	G	W	L	Pct.	ERA	Sv.	IP	H	R	ER	BB	SO
1971 —..						Did not pitch							
1972 —Quad Cities (Midwest)..............	19	7	2	.778	2.79	0	129	111	48	40	57	134
1973 —El Paso (Texas)........................	26	16	6	.727	2.71	0	*206	170	72	62	63	*197
—Salt Lake City (Pacific Coast) ..	2	1	0	1.000	2.57	0	14	11	5	4	2	15
—California (A.L.)	4	2	2	.500	3.12	0	26	20	11	9	8	22
1974 —California (A.L.)	39	14	19	.424	3.11	0	269	262	104	93	77	180
1975 —California (A.L.)	34	16	9	.640	2.63	0	257	211	80	75	73	*269
1976 —California (A.L.)	34	19	10	.655	2.44	0	288	212	88	78	73	261
1977 —California (A.L.)	31	15	9	.625	*2.54	0	241	201	72	68	61	205
1978 —California (A.L.)	33	18	12	.600	3.65	0	239	239	108	97	60	137
1979 —California (A.L.)	18	7	5	.583	3.90	0	90	93	44	39	25	46
1980 —California (A.L.)	32	11	12	.478	4.15	0	204	223	107	94	45	113
1981 —Boston (A.L.)■........................	24	4	10	.286	4.02	0	141	142	70	63	43	78
1982 —Texas (A.L.)■........................	30	7	•18	.280	4.21	0	194 ⅓	199	102	91	55	87
1983 —Texas (A.L.)	29	7	9	.438	3.16	0	159 ⅓	144	70	56	49	108
1984 —Texas (A.L.)	35	15	15	.500	3.25	0	246 ⅓	234	117	89	81	141
1985 —Texas-Detroit (A.L.)■........................	33	12	14	.462	4.27	0	215	220	112	102	57	159
1986 —Detroit (A.L.)	32	12	9	.571	4.16	0	188 ⅓	196	95	87	65	119
1987 —Detroit (A.L.)	34	15	10	.600	3.91	0	218 ⅔	216	106	95	56	146
1988 —Detroit (A.L.)	32	14	11	.560	4.21	0	203	213	105	95	64	127
1989 —Detroit (A.L.)	33	10	14	.417	3.58	0	223 ⅔	227	105	89	74	147
1990 —Detroit (A.L.)	34	9	8	.529	5.31	1	176 ⅓	190	104	104	66	114
1991 —Detroit (A.L.)	33	13	12	.520	3.77	0	217 ⅓	217	98	91	78	107
Major league totals (19 years)	**574**	**220**	**208**	**.514**	**3.59**	**1**	**3797 ⅓**	**3659**	**1698**	**1515**	**1110**	**2566**

CHAMPIONSHIP SERIES RECORD

CHAMPIONSHIP SERIES NOTES: Holds career record for most hit batsmen—4.... Holds single-season record for most hit batsmen—3 (1987).... Holds single-game record for most hit batsmen—3 (October 11, 1987).

Year	Team (League)	G	W	L	Pct.	ERA	Sv.	IP	H	R	ER	BB	SO
1979 —California (A.L.)	1	0	0	...	3.60	0	5	6	2	2	2	3
1987 —Detroit (A.L.)	1	0	1	.000	5.06	0	5 ⅓	6	4	3	4	1
Championship Series totals (2 years)	**2**	**0**	**1**	**.000**	**4.35**	**0**	**10 ⅓**	**12**	**6**	**5**	**6**	**4**

ALL-STAR GAME RECORD

ALL-STAR GAME NOTES: Named to A.L. All-Star team for the 1977 game; replaced due to injury.

Year	League	W	L	Pct.	ERA	Sv.	IP	H	R	ER	BB	SO
1976 —American	0	0	...	13.50	0	2	3	3	3	1	0
1978 —American				Did not play							

TAPANI, KEVIN

P, TWINS

PERSONAL: Born February 18, 1964, at Des Moines, Ia. ... 6-0/ 187. ... Throws right, bats right.... Full name: Kevin Ray Tapani.... Name pronounced TAP-uh-nee.

HIGH SCHOOL: Escanaba (Mich.).

COLLEGE: Central Michigan (degree in finance, 1987).

TRANSACTIONS/CAREER NOTES: Selected by Chicago Cubs organization in ninth round of free-agent draft (June 3, 1985).... Selected by Oakland Athletics organization in second round of free-agent draft (June 2, 1986).... Traded by A's as part of an eight-player, three-team deal in which New York Mets traded P Jesse Orosco to A's (December 11, 1987). A's traded Orosco, SS Alfredo Griffin and P Jay Howell to Los Angeles Dodgers for P Bob Welch, P Matt Young and P Jack Savage. A's then traded Savage, P Wally Whitehurst and Tapani to Mets.... Traded by Mets with P Tim Drummond to Portland, Minnesota Twins organization (August 1, 1989) as partial completion of deal in which Twins traded P Frank Viola to Mets for P Rick Aguilera, P David West and three players to be named later (July 31, 1989); Twins acquired P Jack Savage to complete deal (October 16, 1989). ... On disabled list (August 17-September 10, 1990).

Year	Team (League)	G	W	L	Pct.	ERA	Sv.	IP	H	R	ER	BB	SO
1986 —Medford (Northwest)	2	1	0	1.000	0.00	0	8 ⅓	6	3	0	3	9
—Modesto (California)	11	6	1	.857	2.48	0	69	74	26	19	22	44
—Huntsville (Southern)	1	1	0	1.000	6.00	0	6	8	4	4	1	2
—Tacoma (Pacific Coast)	1	0	1	.000	15.43	0	2 ⅓	5	6	4	1	1
1987 —Modesto (California)	24	10	7	.588	3.76	0	148 ⅓	122	74	62	60	121
1988 —St. Lucie (Florida State)■..........	3	1	0	1.000	1.42	0	19	17	5	3	4	11
—Jackson (Texas)	24	5	1	.833	2.74	3	62 ⅓	46	23	19	19	35

Year	Team (League)	G	W	L	Pct.	ERA	Sv.	IP	H	R	ER	BB	SO
1989	—Tidewater (International)	17	7	5	.583	3.47	0	109	113	49	42	25	63
	—New York (N.L.)	3	0	0	...	3.68	0	7⅓	5	3	3	4	2
	—Portland (Pacific Coast)■	6	4	2	.667	2.20	0	41	38	15	10	12	30
	—Minnesota (A.L.)	5	2	2	.500	3.86	0	32⅔	34	15	14	8	21
1990	—Minnesota (A.L.)	28	12	8	.600	4.07	0	159⅓	164	75	72	29	101
1991	—Minnesota (A.L.)	34	16	9	.640	2.99	0	244	225	84	81	40	135
American League totals (3 years)		67	30	19	.612	3.45	0	436	423	174	167	77	257
National League totals (1 year)		3	0	0	...	3.68	0	7⅓	5	3	3	4	2
Major league totals (3 years)		70	30	19	.612	3.45	0	443⅓	428	177	170	81	259

CHAMPIONSHIP SERIES RECORD

Year	Team (League)	G	W	L	Pct.	ERA	Sv.	IP	H	R	ER	BB	SO
1991	—Minnesota (A.L.)	2	0	1	.000	7.84	0	10⅓	16	9	9	3	9

WORLD SERIES RECORD

Year	Team (League)	G	W	L	Pct.	ERA	Sv.	IP	H	R	ER	BB	SO
1991	—Minnesota (A.L.)	2	1	1	.500	4.50	0	12	13	6	6	2	7

TARTABULL, DANNY
OF, YANKEES

PERSONAL: Born October 30, 1962, at Miami. . . . 6-1/205. . . . Throws right, bats right. . . . Full name: Danilo Mora Tartabull. . . . Son of Jose Tartabull, outfielder, Kansas City A's, Boston Red Sox, Oakland A's (1962-70); and brother of Jose Tartabull Jr., minor league outfielder (1986-88).

HIGH SCHOOL: Carol City (Miami).
TRANSACTIONS/CAREER NOTES: Selected by Cincinnati Reds organization in third round of free-agent draft (June 3, 1980). . . . Selected by Seattle Mariners organization in player compensation pool draft (January 20, 1983); Mariners received compensation for Chicago White Sox signing free-agent P Floyd Bannister (December 13, 1982). . . . On disabled list (May 15-30, 1986). . . . Traded by Mariners with P Rick Luecken to Kansas City Royals for P Scott Bankhead, P Steve Shields and OF Mike Kingery (December 10, 1986). . . . On disabled list (June 15-30, 1989; April 11-May 18 and July 14-31, 1990). . . . Granted free agency (October 28, 1991). . . . Signed by New York Yankees (January 6, 1992).
RECORDS/HONORS: Named Florida State League Most Valuable Player (1981). . . . Named Pacific Coast League Player of the Year (1985).
STATISTICAL NOTES: Led Florida State League third basemen with 29 errors in 1981. . . . Led Pacific Coast League shortstops with 68 double plays in 1984. . . . Led Pacific Coast League with .615 slugging percentage and 291 total bases in 1985. . . . Led Pacific Coast League shortstops with 35 errors in 1985. . . . Led A.L. with 21 game-winning RBIs in 1987. . . . Hit three home runs in a game (July 6, 1991). . . . Led A.L. with .593 slugging percentage in 1991.

							BATTING							FIELDING		
Year	Team (League)	Pos.	G	AB	R	H	2B	3B	HR	RBI	Avg.	SB	PO	A	E	Avg.
1980	—Billings (Pioneer)	3B-OF-2B	59	157	33	47	10	0	2	27	.299	7	34	54	14	.863
1981	—Tampa (Florida State).......	3B-2B	127	422	86	131	*28	10	14	81*	.310	11	150	248	*39	.911
1982	—Waterbury (Eastern)........	2B	126	409	64	93	17	3	17	63	.227	12	237	306	*32	.944
1983	—Chattanooga (Southern)■.	2B	128	481	95	145	32	7	13	66	.301	25	252	405	23	.966
1984	—Salt Lake City (PCL).........	SS	116	418	69	127	22	9	13	73	.304	11	181	333	24	.955
	—Seattle (A.L.)	SS-2B	10	20	3	6	1	0	2	7	.300	0	8	21	2	.935
1985	—Calgary (Pacific Coast)	SS-3B	125	473	102	142	14	3	*43	*109	.300	17	181	399	†36	.942
	—Seattle (A.L.)	SS-3B	19	61	8	20	7	1	1	7	.328	1	28	43	4	.947
1986	—Seattle (A.L.)	0F-2B-3B	137	511	76	138	25	6	25	96	.270	4	233	111	18	.950
1987	—Kansas City (A.L.)■..........	OF	158	582	95	180	27	3	34	101	.309	9	228	11	6	.976
1988	—Kansas City (A.L.)	OF	146	507	80	139	38	3	26	102	.274	8	227	8	9	.963
1989	—Kansas City (A.L.)	OF	133	441	54	118	22	0	18	62	.268	4	108	3	2	.982
1990	—Kansas City (A.L.)	OF	88	313	41	84	19	0	15	60	.268	1	81	1	3	.965
1991	—Kansas City (A.L.)	OF	132	484	78	153	35	3	31	100	.316	6	190	4	7	.965
Major league totals (8 years)			823	2919	435	838	174	16	152	535	.287	33	1103	202	51	.962

ALL-STAR GAME RECORD

						BATTING						FIELDING		
Year	League	Pos.	AB	R	H	2B	3B	HR	RBI	Avg.	SB	PO	A	E	Avg.
1991	—American	DH	2	0	0	0	0	0	0	.000	0	0	0	0	...

TATUM, JIM
SS/3B/1B, BREWERS

PERSONAL: Born October 9, 1967, at Grossmont, Calif. . . . 6-2/200. . . . Throws right, bats right. . . . Full name: James Ray Tatum Jr.
HIGH SCHOOL: Santana (Santee, Calif.).
TRANSACTIONS/CAREER NOTES: Selected by San Diego Padres organization in third round of free-agent draft (June 3, 1985). . . . Signed as free agent by Milwaukee Brewers organization (June 21, 1990).
STATISTICAL NOTES: Led Northwest League third basemen with 149 assists, 27 errors, 214 total chances and 11 double plays in 1985. . . . Led South Atlantic League third basemen with 35 errors and 29 double plays in 1986. . . . Led South Atlantic League third basemen with 257 assists and tied for lead with 368 total chances in 1987. . . . Led Texas League in sacrifice flies with 20, being hit by pitch with 15 and grounding into double plays with 21 in 1991.

							BATTING							FIELDING		
Year	Team (League)	Pos.	G	AB	R	H	2B	3B	HR	RBI	Avg.	SB	PO	A	E	Avg.
1985	—Spokane (Northwest)	3B-SS	74	281	21	64	9	1	1	32	.228	0	51	†168	†30	.880
1986	—Charleston, S.C. (S. Atl.) ...	3B-2B-SS	120	431	55	112	19	2	10	62	.260	2	81	232	†41	.884

Year	Team (League)	Pos.	G	AB	R	H	2B	3B	HR	RBI	Avg.	SB	PO	A	E	Avg.
1987 —Charleston, S.C. (S. Atl.) ...	3B-SS-2B	128	468	52	131	22	2	9	72	.280	8	87	†259	24	.935
1988 —Wichita (Texas)	3B	118	402	38	105	26	1	8	54	.261	2	*97	195	27	.915
1990 —Canton/Akron (Eastern)■	3B-1B	30	106	6	19	6	0	2	11	.179	1	57	51	12	.900
—Stockton (California)■.....	3B-1B	70	260	41	68	16	0	12	59	.262	4	160	108	7	.975
1991 —El Paso (Texas)	IF-C-P	130	493	99	158	27	8	18	128	.320	5	190	263	31	.936

RECORD AS PITCHER

Year	Team (League)	G	W	L	Pct.	ERA	Sv.	IP	H	R	ER	BB	SO
1991 —El Paso (Texas)	1	0	0	...	0.00	0	1	1	0	00	0	0

TAUBENSEE, EDDIE
C, ASTROS

PERSONAL: Born October 31, 1968, at Beeville, Tex. . . . 6-4/205. . . . Throws right, bats left. . . . Full name: Edward Kenneth Taubensee. . . . Name pronounced TAW-ben-see.
HIGH SCHOOL: Lake Howell (Maitland, Fla.).
TRANSACTIONS/CAREER NOTES: Selected by Cincinnati Reds organization in sixth round of free-agent draft (June 2, 1986). . . . Drafted by Oakland Athletics (December 3, 1990). . . . Claimed on waivers by Cleveland Indians (April 4, 1991). . . . Traded by Indians with P Willie Blair to Houston Astros for OF Kenny Lofton and IF Dave Rohde (December 10, 1991).
STATISTICAL NOTES: Led Pioneer League with 19 passed balls in 1987. . . . Tied for South Atlantic League lead in double plays by catchers with seven in 1988.

Year	Team (League)	Pos.	G	AB	R	H	2B	3B	HR	RBI	Avg.	SB	PO	A	E	Avg.
1986 —Sarasota Reds (GCL)	C-1B	35	107	8	21	3	0	1	11	.196	0	208	27	8	.967
1987 —Billings (Pioneer)	C	55	162	24	43	7	0	5	28	.265	2	344	29	6	.984
1988 —Greensboro (S. Atlantic) ...	C	103	330	36	85	16	1	10	41	.258	8	640	70	15	.979
—Chattanooga (Southern) ...	C	5	12	2	2	0	0	1	1	.167	0	17	5	1	.957
1989 —Cedar Rapids (Midwest) ...	C	59	196	25	39	5	0	8	22	.199	4	400	9	1	.998
—Chattanooga (Southern) ...	C	45	127	11	24	2	0	3	13	.189	0	213	31	6	.976
1990 —Cedar Rapids (Midwest) ...	C	122	417	57	108	21	1	16	62	.259	11	795	94	16	.982
1991 —Cleveland (A.L.)■	C	26	66	5	16	2	1	0	8	.242	0	89	6	2	.979
—Colorado Springs (PCL)	C	91	287	53	89	23	3	13	39	.310	0	412	47	12	.975
Major league totals (1 year)		26	66	5	16	2	1	0	8	.242	0	89	6	2	.979

TAYLOR, SCOTT
P, RED SOX

PERSONAL: Born August 2, 1967, at Defiance, O. . . . 6-1/185. . . . Throws left, bats left. . . . Full name: Rodney Scott Taylor.
HIGH SCHOOL: Defiance (O.).
COLLEGE: Bowling Green State.
TRANSACTIONS/CAREER NOTES: Selected by Boston Red Sox organization in 28th round of free-agent draft (June 1, 1988). . . . On disabled list (June 15-July 4, 1989). . . . On New Britain disabled list (July 13, 1990-remainder of season).

Year	Team (League)	G	W	L	Pct.	ERA	Sv.	IP	H	R	ER	BB	SO
1988 —Elmira (New York-Penn)	2	1	0	1.000	0.00	0	3⅔	2	0	0	3	8
1989 —Lynchburg (Carolina)	19	5	3	.625	2.89	1	81	61	33	26	25	99
1990 —Lynchburg (Carolina)	13	5	6	.455	2.73	0	89	76	36	27	30	120
—New Britain (Eastern)	5	0	2	.000	1.65	0	27⅓	23	8	5	13	27
1991 —Pawtucket (International)	7	3	3	.500	3.46	0	39	32	19	15	17	35
—New Britain (Eastern)	4	2	0	1.000	0.62	0	29	20	2	2	9	38

TAYLOR, WADE
P, YANKEES

PERSONAL: Born October 19, 1965, at Mobile, Ala. . . . 6-1/193. . . . Throws right, bats right. . . . Full name: Wade Eric Taylor.
COLLEGE: Jefferson Davis Junior College (Ala.) and Miami (Fla.).
TRANSACTIONS/CAREER NOTES: Selected by Toronto Blue Jays organization in ninth round of free-agent draft (January 14, 1986). . . . Selected by Los Angeles Dodgers organization in secondary phase of free-agent draft (June 2, 1986). . . . Signed as free agent by Seattle Mariners organization (June 30, 1987). . . . Traded by Mariners with P Lee Guetterman and P Clay Parker to New York Yankees for P Steve Trout and OF Henry Cotto (December 22, 1987).
STATISTICAL NOTES: Tied for International League lead with three shutouts in 1990.

Year	Team (League)	G	W	L	Pct.	ERA	Sv.	IP	H	R	ER	BB	SO
1987 —Bellingham (Northwest)............	12	3	5	.375	4.47	1	58⅓	58	31	29	22	53
1988 —Fort Lauderdale (Florida St.)■...	24	4	11	.267	3.45	0	122⅔	109	53	47	57	90
1989 —Prince William (Carolina)	25	9	8	.529	3.34	0	142⅔	131	63	53	56	104
1990 —Albany (Eastern)	12	6	4	.600	2.88	0	84⅓	71	30	27	18	44
—Columbus (International)	14	6	4	.600	2.19	0	98⅔	91	25	24	30	57
1991 —Columbus (International)	9	4	1	.800	3.54	0	61	59	27	24	22	36
—New York (A.L.)	23	7	12	.368	6.27	0	116⅓	144	85	81	53	72
Major league totals (1 year)	23	7	12	.368	6.27	0	116⅓	144	85	81	53	72

TAYLOR, WILL
OF, PADRES

PERSONAL: Born August 19, 1968, at Alexandria, La. . . . 6-2/170. . . . Throws right, bats right. . . . Full name: William Christopher Taylor.
TRANSACTIONS/CAREER NOTES: Selected by San Diego Padres organization in second round of free-agent draft (June 2, 1986).

STATISTICAL NOTES: Led California League in caught stealing with 28 in 1989. . . . Led Texas League in caught stealing with 29 in 1990.
MISCELLANEOUS: Batted as switch-hitter (1989-90).

							—BATTING—						—FIELDING—		
Year	Team (League)	Pos.	G	AB	R	H	2B	3B	HR	RBI	Avg.	SB	PO	A	E	Avg.
1986 —Spokane (Northwest)		OF	59	202	38	57	6	1	0	20	.282	18	113	2	9	.927
1987 —Charleston, S.C. (S. Atl.) ...		OF	120	416	70	120	5	1	1	40	.288	56	204	10	11	.951
1988 —Riverside (California)		OF	112	295	40	54	5	1	0	16	.183	31	172	6	10	.947
1989 —Riverside (California)		OF	131	530	81	135	16	7	2	31	.255	60	182	7	7	.964
1990 —Wichita (Texas)		OF	102	414	57	110	18	7	4	31	.266	51	169	13	7	.963
1991 —Las Vegas (Pac. Coast)		OF	125	468	82	121	11	5	4	33	.259	∗62	246	6	8	.969

TELFORD, ANTHONY
P, ORIOLES

PERSONAL: Born March 6, 1966, at San Jose, Calif. . . . 6-0/ 189. . . . Throws right, bats right. . . . Full name: Anthony Charles Telford.
HIGH SCHOOL: Silver Creek (Calif.).
COLLEGE: San Jose State.
TRANSACTIONS/CAREER NOTES: Selected by Baltimore Orioles organization in third round of free-agent draft (June 2, 1987). . . . On disabled list (April 20, 1988-remainder of season). . . . On Frederick disabled list (April 7-18, 1989). . . . On Erie disabled list (June 16-30, 1989).

Year	Team (League)	G	W	L	Pct.	ERA	Sv.	IP	H	R	ER	BB	SO
1987 —Newark (New York-Penn)		6	1	0	1.000	1.02	0	17 2/3	16	2	2	3	27
—Hagerstown (Eastern)		2	1	0	1.000	1.59	0	11 1/3	9	2	2	5	10
—Rochester (International)		1	0	0	. . .	0.00	0	2	0	0	0	3	3
1988 —Hagerstown (Eastern)		1	1	0	1.000	0.00	0	7	3	0	0	0	10
1989 —Frederick (Carolina)		9	2	1	.667	4.21	1	25 2/3	25	15	12	12	19
1990 —Frederick (Carolina)		8	4	2	.667	1.68	0	53 2/3	35	15	10	11	49
—Hagerstown (Eastern)		14	10	2	.833	1.97	0	96	80	26	21	25	73
—Baltimore (A.L.)		8	3	3	.500	4.95	0	36 1/3	43	22	20	19	20
1991 —Rochester (International)		27	∗12	9	.571	3.95	0	157 1/3	166	82	69	48	115
—Baltimore (A.L.)		9	0	0	. . .	4.05	0	26 2/3	27	12	12	6	24
Major league totals (2 years)		17	3	3	.500	4.57	0	63	70	34	32	25	44

TEMPLETON, GARRY
IF

PERSONAL: Born March 24, 1956, at Lockney, Tex. . . . 6-0/209. . . . Throws right, bats both. . . . Full name: Garry Lewis Templeton. . . . Brother of Ken Templeton, minor league outfielder (1972-74).
HIGH SCHOOL: Santa Ana Valley (Calif.).
TRANSACTIONS/CAREER NOTES: Selected by St. Louis Cardinals organization in first round (13th pick overall) of free-agent draft (June 5, 1974). . . . On disabled list (July 24-August 14 and August 24-September 8, 1980). . . . On suspended list (August 26, 1981); then transferred to disabled list (August 28-September 14, 1981). . . . Traded by Cardinals to San Diego Padres for SS Ozzie Smith (February 11, 1982). . . . On disabled list (April 28-May 17, 1983). . . . Granted free agency (November 4, 1988). . . . Re-signed by Padres (December 6, 1988). . . . Traded by Padres to New York Mets for IF Tim Teufel (May 31, 1991). . . . Granted free agency (November 4, 1991).
RECORDS/HONORS: Shares major league single-season records by collecting 100 or more hits righthanded and lefthanded (1979); most consecutive seasons leading league, three-base hits—3 (1977-79). . . . Named shortstop on THE SPORTING NEWS N.L. All-Star team (1977, 1979-80). . . . Named shortstop on THE SPORTING NEWS N.L. Silver Slugger team (1980, 84).
STATISTICAL NOTES: Led American Association shortstops with 177 putouts in 1976. . . . Tied for N.L. lead in caught stealing with 24 in 1977. . . . Led N.L. shortstops with 848 total chances in 1978 and 851 in 1979. . . . Led N.L. shortstops with 108 double plays in 1978. . . . Tied for N.L. lead in double plays by shortstops with 102 in 1979. . . . Led N.L. with 23 intentional bases on balls received in 1984 and tied for lead with 24 in 1985.

							—BATTING—						—FIELDING—		
Year	Team (League)	Pos.	G	AB	R	H	2B	3B	HR	RBI	Avg.	SB	PO	A	E	Avg.
1974 —Sara. Cardinals (GCL)		SS	18	71	11	19	1	0	3	10	.268	8	15	41	3	.949
—St. Petersburg (Fla. St.)		SS	23	95	3	20	1	0	0	2	.211	4	42	64	7	.938
1975 —St. Petersburg (Fla. St.)		SS	82	349	50	92	7	8	1	32	.264	18	130	253	29	.930
—Arkansas (Texas)		SS	42	177	36	71	9	4	2	20	.401	16	60	131	18	.914
1976 —Tulsa (American Assoc.) ..		S-3-0	106	443	65	142	24	∗15	6	38	.321	25	†178	319	34	.936
—St. Louis (N.L.)		SS	53	213	32	62	8	2	1	17	.291	11	111	172	24	.922
1977 —St. Louis (N.L.)		SS	153	621	94	200	19	∗18	8	79	.322	28	285	453	32	.958
1978 —St. Louis (N.L.)		SS	155	647	82	181	31	∗13	2	47	.280	34	∗285	523	∗40	.953
1979 —St. Louis (N.L.)		SS	154	672	105	∗211	32	∗19	9	62	.314	26	∗292	525	∗34	.960
1980 —St. Louis (N.L.)		SS	118	504	83	161	19	9	4	43	.319	31	223	451	∗29	.959
1981 —St. Louis (N.L.)		SS	80	333	47	96	16	8	1	33	.288	8	160	272	18	.960
1982 —San Diego (N.L.)■		SS	141	563	76	139	25	8	6	64	.247	27	220	422	26	.961
1983 —San Diego (N.L.)		SS	126	460	39	121	20	2	3	40	.263	16	219	355	24	.960
1984 —San Diego (N.L.)		SS	148	493	40	127	19	3	2	35	.258	8	225	407	26	.960
1985 —San Diego (N.L.)		SS	148	546	63	154	30	2	6	55	.282	16	245	460	23	.968
1986 —San Diego (N.L.)		SS	147	510	42	126	21	2	2	44	.247	10	207	358	20	.966
1987 —San Diego (N.L.)		SS	148	510	42	113	13	5	5	48	.222	14	∗253	447	20	.972
1988 —San Diego (N.L.)		SS-3B	110	362	35	90	15	7	3	36	.249	8	170	316	16	.968
1989 —San Diego (N.L.)		SS	142	506	43	129	26	3	6	40	.255	1	232	409	20	.970
1990 —San Diego (N.L.)		SS	144	505	45	125	25	3	9	59	.248	1	214	367	∗26	.957
1991 —S.D.-New York (N.L.)■■...		S-3-1-0	112	276	25	61	10	2	3	26	.221	3	210	141	8	.978
Major league totals (16 years)			2079	7721	893	2096	329	106	70	728	.271	242	3551	6078	386	.961

CHAMPIONSHIP SERIES RECORD

Year	Team (League)	Pos.	G	AB	R	H	2B	3B	HR	RBI	Avg.	SB	PO	A	E	Avg.
1984 — San Diego (N.L.)		SS	5	15	2	5	1	0	0	2	.333	1	19	11	1	.968

WORLD SERIES RECORD

Year	Team (League)	Pos.	G	AB	R	H	2B	3B	HR	RBI	Avg.	SB	PO	A	E	Avg.
1984 — San Diego (N.L.)		SS	5	19	1	6	1	0	0	0	.316	0	8	11	0	1.000

ALL-STAR GAME RECORD

ALL-STAR GAME NOTES: Named to N.L. All-Star team for 1979 game; declined.

Year	League	Pos.	AB	R	H	2B	3B	HR	RBI	Avg.	SB	PO	A	E	Avg.
1977 — National		SS	1	1	1	1	0	0	0	1.000	0	1	2	1	.750
1985 — National		PH	1	0	1	0	0	0	0	1.000	0	0	0	0	...
All-Star Game totals (2 years)			2	1	2	1	0	0	0	1.000	0	1	2	1	.750

TERRELL, WALT
P, TIGERS

PERSONAL: Born May 11, 1958, at Jeffersonville, Ind. . . . . 6-1/205. . . . Throws right, bats left. . . . Full name: Charles Walter Terrell. . . . Name pronounced TAIR-el.
HIGH SCHOOL: Jeffersonville (Ind.).
COLLEGE: Morehead State (degree in 1980).
TRANSACTIONS/CAREER NOTES: Selected by New York Mets organization in 15th round of free-agent draft (June 5, 1979). . . . Selected by Texas Rangers organization in 33rd round of free-agent draft (June 3, 1980). . . . Traded by Rangers organization with P Ron Darling to New York Mets organization for OF Lee Mazzilli (April 1, 1982). . . . On Tidewater disabled list (July 19-August 2, 1982). . . . Traded by Mets to Detroit Tigers for 3B Howard Johnson (December 7, 1984). . . . On Detroit disabled list (April 1-30, 1988); included rehabilitation disability assignment to Lakeland (April 16-26, 1988). . . . Traded by Tigers to San Diego Padres for IF Chris Brown and IF Keith Moreland (October 28, 1988). . . . Traded by Padres with a player to be named later to New York Yankees for 3B Mike Pagliarulo and P Don Schulze (July 22, 1989); Yankees acquired P Fred Toliver to complete deal (September 27, 1989). . . . Granted free agency (November 13, 1989). . . . Signed by Pittsburgh Pirates (November 29, 1989). . . . Released by Pirates (July 24, 1990). . . . Signed by Tigers (July 28, 1990).
RECORDS/HONORS: Named International League Pitcher of the Year (1983).

Year	Team (League)	G	W	L	Pct.	ERA	Sv.	IP	H	R	ER	BB	SO
1980 — Sarasota Rangers (GCL)	7	3	2	.600	1.42	0	38	20	11	6	12	23
— Asheville (South Atlantic)	3	1	1	.500	6.75	0	8	11	9	6	8	5
1981 — Tulsa (Texas)	27	•15	7	.682	3.10	0	174	158	74	60	63	123
1982 — Tidewater (International)■	21	7	8	.467	3.96	0	138⅔	130	69	61	72	74
— New York (N.L.)	3	0	3	.000	3.43	0	21	22	12	8	14	8
1983 — Tidewater (International)	12	10	1	.909	3.12	0	86⅔	76	34	30	44	58
— New York (N.L.)	21	8	8	.500	3.57	0	133⅔	123	57	53	55	59
1984 — New York (N.L.)	33	11	12	.478	3.52	0	215	232	99	84	80	114
1985 — Detroit (A.L.)■	34	15	10	.600	3.85	0	229	221	107	98	95	130
1986 — Detroit (A.L.)	34	15	12	.556	4.56	0	217⅓	199	116	110	98	93
1987 — Detroit (A.L.)	35	17	10	.630	4.05	0	244⅔	254	123	110	94	143
1988 — Lakeland (Florida State)	2	1	1	.500	6.52	0	9⅔	13	7	7	1	6
— Detroit (A.L.)	29	7	16	.304	3.97	0	206⅓	199	101	91	78	84
1989 — San Diego (N.L.)■	19	5	13	.278	4.01	0	123⅓	134	65	55	26	63
— New York (A.L.)■	13	6	5	.545	5.20	0	83	102	52	48	24	30
1990 — Pittsburgh (N.L.)■	16	2	7	.222	5.88	0	82⅔	98	59	54	33	34
— Detroit (A.L.)■	13	6	4	.600	4.54	0	75⅓	86	39	38	24	30
1991 — Detroit (A.L.)	35	12	14	.462	4.24	0	218⅔	★257	115	103	79	80
American League totals (7 years)	193	78	71	.523	4.22	0	1274⅓	1318	653	598	492	590
National League totals (5 years)	92	26	43	.377	3.97	0	575⅔	609	292	254	208	278
Major league totals (10 years)	285	104	114	.477	4.14	0	1850	1927	945	852	700	868

CHAMPIONSHIP SERIES RECORD

Year	Team (League)	G	W	L	Pct.	ERA	Sv.	IP	H	R	ER	BB	SO
1987 — Detroit (A.L.)	1	0	0	...	9.00	0	6	7	6	6	4	4

TERRY, SCOTT
P, CARDINALS

PERSONAL: Born November 21, 1959, at Hobbs, N.M. . . . 5-11/195. . . . Throws right, bats right. . . . Full name: Scott Ray Terry.
HIGH SCHOOL: Gregory-Portland (Gregory, Tex.).
COLLEGE: Southwestern University, Tex. (received degree, 1982).
TRANSACTIONS/CAREER NOTES: Selected by Cincinnati Reds organization in 12th round of free-agent draft (June 3, 1980). . . . On Wichita disabled list (August 8-September 18, 1984). . . . Traded by Reds organization to St. Louis Cardinals (September 3, 1987), completing deal in which Cardinals traded P Pat Perry to Reds for a player to be named later (August 31, 1987). . . . On St. Louis disabled list (June 27-July 24, 1988); included rehabilitation disability assignment to Louisville (July 18-24, 1988). . . . On disabled list (August 14-September 5, 1989). . . . Granted free agency (December 20, 1991). . . . Re-signed by Cardinals (January 4, 1992).
STATISTICAL NOTES: Led Eastern League with six shutouts in 1984. . . . Tied for American Association lead in games started by pitcher with 28 and wild pitches with 14 in 1985. . . . Led American Association with 10 complete games in 1987.

Year Team (League)	G	W	L	Pct.	ERA	Sv.	IP	H	R	ER	BB	SO
1983 —Tampa (Florida State)	30	3	3	.500	4.25	6	59⅓	60	34	28	30	52
1984 —Vermont (Eastern)	20	14	3	.824	★1.50	0	144	110	31	24	43	100
—Wichita (American Assoc.)	2	0	0	...	5.79	0	9⅓	13	6	6	7	6
1985 —Denver (American Assoc.)	28	11	12	.478	4.43	0	178⅔	★203	★105	★88	76	101
1986 —Denver (American Assoc.)	10	1	2	.333	2.33	2	19⅓	22	13	5	8	13
—Cincinnati (N.L.)	28	1	2	.333	6.14	0	55⅔	66	40	38	32	32
1987 —Nashville (American Assoc.)	27	11	10	.524	3.96	0	★181⅔	199	94	80	48	91
—St. Louis (N.L.)■	11	0	0	...	3.38	0	13⅓	13	5	5	8	9
1988 —St. Louis (N.L.)	51	9	6	.600	2.92	3	129⅓	119	48	42	34	65
—Louisville (American Assoc.)	3	0	0	...	0.00	0	5	2	0	0	1	1
1989 —St. Louis (N.L.)	31	8	10	.444	3.57	2	148⅔	142	65	59	43	69
1990 —St. Louis (N.L.)	50	2	6	.250	4.75	2	72	75	45	38	27	35
1991 —St. Louis (N.L.)	65	4	4	.500	2.80	1	80⅓	76	31	25	32	52
Major league totals (6 years)	236	24	28	.462	3.73	8	499⅓	491	234	207	176	262

RECORD AS POSITION PLAYER

Year Team (League)	Pos.	G	AB	R	H	2B	3B	HR	RBI	Avg.	SB	PO	A	E	Avg.
1980 —Billings (Pioneer)	OF	67	251	39	65	9	3	4	45	.259	7	104	•10	5	.958
1981 —Cedar Rapids (Midwest)	OF	113	351	32	68	9	0	5	31	.194	10	147	5	5	.968
1982 —Cedar Rapids (Midwest)	OF	108	335	50	85	16	3	12	54	.254	13	156	10	8	.954
1983 —Tampa (Florida State)	OF-P	66	105	14	25	6	2	0	12	.238	0	60	16	3	.962

TETTLETON, MICKEY
C, TIGERS

PERSONAL: Born September 16, 1960, at Oklahoma City.... 6-2/212.... Throws right, bats both.... Full name: Mickey Lee Tettleton.
HIGH SCHOOL: Southeast (Oklahoma City).
COLLEGE: Oklahoma State.
TRANSACTIONS/CAREER NOTES: Selected by Oakland A's organization in fifth round of free-agent draft (June 8, 1981).... On disabled list (July 16-August 13, 1982).... On Oakland disabled list (August 4-25, 1985); included rehabilitation disability assignment to Modesto (August 21-25, 1985).... On Oakland disabled list (May 9-June 16, 1986); included rehabilitation disability assignment to Modesto (May 23-June 13, 1986).... On Oakland disabled list (July 22-August 6, 1987); included rehabilitation disability assignment to Modesto (August 2-6, 1987).... Released by A's (March 28, 1988).... Signed by Rochester, Baltimore Orioles organization (April 5, 1988).... On disabled list (August 5-September 2, 1989).... Granted free agency (November 5, 1990).... Re-signed by Orioles (December 19, 1990).... Traded by Orioles to Detroit Tigers for P Jeff M. Robinson (January 11, 1991).
RECORDS/HONORS: Holds major league single-season record for most strikeouts by switch-hitter—160 (1990).... Named catcher on THE SPORTING NEWS A.L. All-Star team (1989 and 1991).... Named catcher on THE SPORTING NEWS A.L. Silver Slugger team (1989 and 1991).
STATISTICAL NOTES: Tied for Eastern League lead with eight intentional bases on balls received in 1984.... Led Eastern League catchers with .993 fielding percentage in 1984.... Switch-hit home runs in one game (June 13, 1988).

Year Team (League)	Pos.	G	AB	R	H	2B	3B	HR	RBI	Avg.	SB	PO	A	E	Avg.
1981 —Modesto (California)	C-OF-1B	48	138	28	34	3	0	5	19	.246	2	235	31	14	.950
1982 —Modesto (California)	C-OF	88	253	44	63	18	0	8	37	.249	4	424	36	8	.983
1983 —Modesto (California)	C-OF	124	378	55	92	18	2	7	62	.243	1	582	46	11	.983
1984 —Albany (Eastern)	C-OF-IF	86	281	32	65	18	0	5	47	.231	2	368	42	3	†.993
—Oakland (A.L.)	C	33	76	10	20	2	1	1	5	.263	0	112	10	1	.992
1985 —Oakland (A.L.)	C	78	211	23	53	12	0	3	15	.251	2	344	24	4	.989
—Modesto (California)	C	4	14	1	3	3	0	0	2	.214	0	20	1	0	1.000
1986 —Oakland (A.L.)	C	90	211	26	43	9	0	10	35	.204	7	463	32	8	.984
—Modesto (California)	C	15	42	14	10	1	0	2	8	.238	2	40	3	2	.956
1987 —Oakland (A.L.)	C-1B	82	211	19	41	3	0	8	26	.194	1	435	29	6	.987
—Modesto (California)	C	3	11	4	4	1	0	2	2	.364	0	5	0	0	1.000
1988 —Rochester (Int'l)■	C-OF	19	41	9	10	3	1	1	4	.244	0	71	7	3	.963
—Baltimore (A.L.)	C	86	283	31	74	11	1	11	37	.261	0	361	31	3	.992
1989 —Baltimore (A.L.)	C	117	411	72	106	21	2	26	65	.258	3	297	42	2	.994
1990 —Baltimore (A.L.)	C-1B-OF	135	444	68	99	21	2	15	51	.223	2	458	39	5	.990
1991 —Detroit (A.L.)■	C-OF-1B	154	501	85	132	17	2	31	89	.263	3	562	55	6	.990
Major league totals (8 years)		775	2348	334	568	96	8	105	323	.242	18	3032	262	35	.989

ALL-STAR GAME RECORD

Year League	Pos.	AB	R	H	2B	3B	HR	RBI	Avg.	SB	PO	A	E	Avg.
1989 —American	C	1	0	0	0	0	0	0	.000	0	2	0	0	1.000

TEUFEL, TIM
3B/2B, PADRES

PERSONAL: Born July 7, 1958, at Greenwich, Conn.... 6-0/175.... Throws right, bats right.... Full name: Timothy Shawn Teufel.... Name pronounced TUFF-el.
HIGH SCHOOL: St. Mary's (Greenwich, Conn.).
COLLEGE: St. Petersburg Junior College (Fla.) and Clemson.
TRANSACTIONS/CAREER NOTES: Selected by Milwaukee Brewers organization in 16th round of free-agent draft (June 6, 1978). ... Selected by Chicago White Sox organization in secondary phase of free-agent draft (June 5, 1979).... Selected by Minnesota Twins organization in second round of free-agent draft (June 3, 1980).... Traded by Twins with OF Pat Crosby to New York Mets for OF Billy Beane, P Bill Latham and P Joe Klink (January 16, 1986).... On disabled list (June 16-July 1, 1987;

May 17-June 11, 1988; and June 5-23, 1989).... Traded by Mets to San Diego Padres for SS Garry Templeton (May 31, 1991).... Granted free agency (October 30, 1991).... Re-signed by Padres (January 8, 1991).

RECORDS/HONORS: Holds A.L. single-season record for fewest double plays by second baseman (150 or more games)—81 (1984).... Named second baseman on THE SPORTING NEWS college All-America team (1980).... Named International League Player of the Year (1983).

STATISTICAL NOTES: Led International League second basemen with 304 putouts, 394 assists, 711 total chances and 109 double plays in 1983.

Year	Team (League)	Pos.	G	AB	R	H	2B	3B	HR	RBI	Avg.	SB	PO	A	E	Avg.
1980 —Orlando (Southern)		2B	86	287	38	76	15	3	11	47	.265	3	196	246	17	.963
1981 —Orlando (Southern)		2B	128	416	69	103	21	5	17	60	.248	4	312	376	20	.972
1982 —Orlando (Southern)		2B	100	340	52	96	12	4	9	56	.282	16	231	185	15	.965
—Toledo (International)		2B	45	149	25	42	10	4	6	20	.282	1	99	139	3	.988
1983 —Toledo (International)		2B-SS	136	471	103	152	27	6	27	100	.323	13	+306	+401	14	.981
—Minnesota (A.L.)		2B-SS	21	78	11	24	7	1	3	6	.308	0	47	58	1	.991
1984 —Minnesota (A.L.)		2B	157	568	76	149	30	3	14	61	.262	1	315 ★485		13	.984
1985 —Minnesota (A.L.)		2B	138	434	58	113	24	3	10	50	.260	4	237	352	12	.980
1986 —New York (N.L.)■...........	2B-1B-3B		93	279	35	69	20	1	4	31	.247	1	143	174	9	.972
1987 —New York (N.L.)	2B-1B		97	299	55	92	29	0	14	61	.308	3	139	214	11	.970
1988 —New York (N.L.)	2B-1B		90	273	35	64	20	0	4	31	.234	0	175	213	7	.982
1989 —New York (N.L.)	2B-1B		83	219	27	56	7	2	2	15	.256	1	261	112	10	.974
1990 —New York (N.L.)	1B-2B-3B		80	175	28	43	11	0	10	24	.246	2	141	58	4	.980
1991 —New York-S.D. (N.L.)■....2B-3B-1B			117	341	41	74	16	0	12	44	.217	9	178	205	9	.977
American League totals (3 years)			316	1080	145	286	61	7	27	117	.265	5	599	895	26	.983
National League totals (6 years)			560	1586	221	398	103	3	46	206	.251	14	1037	976	50	.976
Major league totals (9 years)			876	2666	366	684	164	10	73	323	.257	19	1636	1871	76	.979

CHAMPIONSHIP SERIES RECORD

Year	Team (League)	Pos.	G	AB	R	H	2B	3B	HR	RBI	Avg.	SB	PO	A	E	Avg.
1986 —New York (N.L.)		2B	2	6	0	1	0	0	0	0	.167	0	2	8	0	1.000
1988 —New York (N.L.)		2B	1	3	0	0	0	0	0	0	.000	0	1	3	0	1.000
Championship Series totals (2 years)			3	9	0	1	0	0	0	0	.111	0	3	11	0	1.000

WORLD SERIES RECORD

Year	Team (League)	Pos.	G	AB	R	H	2B	3B	HR	RBI	Avg.	SB	PO	A	E	Avg.
1986 —New York (N.L.)		2B	3	9	1	4	1	0	1	1	.444	0	3	3	1	.857

TEWKSBURY, BOB
P, CARDINALS

PERSONAL: Born November 30, 1960, at Concord, N.H.... 6-4/208.... Throws right, bats right.... Full name: Robert Alan Tewksbury.

HIGH SCHOOL: Merrimack (Penacook, N.H.).

COLLEGE: Rutgers and St. Leo College (Fla.).

TRANSACTIONS/CAREER NOTES: Selected by New York Yankees organization in 19th round of free-agent draft (June 8, 1981).... On Fort Lauderdale disabled list (April 8-June 7, 1983).... On disabled list (April 9-27, 1984).... On Albany disabled list (June 10-25, 1985).... Traded by Yankees with P Rich Scheid and P Dean Wilkins to Chicago Cubs for P Steve Trout (July 13, 1987).... On Chicago disabled list (August 13, 1987-remainder of season and May 22-June 12, 1988).... Granted free agency (October 15, 1988).... Signed by St. Louis Cardinals (December 16, 1988).

STATISTICAL NOTES: Led Florida State League with five shutouts and tied for lead with 13 complete games in 1982.

Year	Team (League)	G	W	L	Pct.	ERA	Sv.	IP	H	R	ER	BB	SO
1981 —Oneonta (New York-Penn)	14	7	3	.700	3.60	0	85	85	43	34	37	62
1982 —Fort Lauderdale (Florida St.)	24	★15	4	.789	★1.88	1	182⅓	146	46	38	47	92
1983 —Fort Lauderdale (Florida St.)	2	2	0	1.000	0.00	0	16	6	1	0	1	5
—Nashville (Southern)	7	5	1	.833	2.82	0	51	49	20	16	10	15
1984 —Nashville (Southern)	26	11	9	.550	2.83	0	172	185	69	54	42	78
1985 —Albany (Eastern)	17	6	5	.545	3.54	0	106⅔	101	48	42	19	63
—Columbus (International)	6	3	0	1.000	1.02	0	44	27	5	5	5	21
1986 —New York (A.L.)	23	9	5	.643	3.31	0	130⅓	144	58	48	31	49
—Columbus (International)	2	1	0	1.000	2.70	0	10	6	3	3	2	4
1987 —New York (A.L.)	8	1	4	.200	6.75	0	33⅓	47	26	25	7	12
—Columbus (International)	11	6	1	.857	2.53	0	74⅔	68	23	21	11	32
—Chicago (N.L.)■........................	7	0	4	.000	6.50	0	18	32	15	13	13	10
1988 —Iowa (American Association) ...	10	4	2	.667	3.76	0	67	73	28	28	10	43
—Chicago (N.L.)	1	0	0	....	8.10	0	3⅓	6	5	3	2	1
1989 —Louisville (American Assoc.)■ ..	28	★13	5	.722	2.43	0	★189	170	63	51	34	72
—St. Louis (N.L.)	7	1	0	1.000	3.30	0	30	25	12	11	10	17
1990 —St. Louis (N.L.)	28	10	9	.526	3.47	1	145⅓	151	67	56	15	50
—Louisville (American Assoc.) ...	6	3	2	.600	2.43	0	40⅔	41	15	11	3	22
1991 —St. Louis (N.L.)	30	11	12	.478	3.25	0	191	206	86	69	38	75
American League totals (2 years)	31	10	9	.526	4.01	0	163⅔	191	84	73	38	61
National League totals (5 years)	73	22	25	.468	3.53	1	387⅔	420	185	152	78	153
Major league totals (6 years)	104	32	34	.485	3.67	1	551⅓	611	269	225	116	214

THIGPEN, BOBBY
P, WHITE SOX

PERSONAL: Born July 17, 1963, at Tallahassee, Fla. . . . 6-3/195. . . . Throws right, bats right. . . . Full name: Robert Thomas Thigpen.
HIGH SCHOOL: Aucilla Christian Academy (Monticello, Fla.).
COLLEGE: Seminole Community College (Fla.) and Mississippi State.
TRANSACTIONS/CAREER NOTES: Selected by Milwaukee Brewers organization in seventh round of free-agent draft (January 11, 1983). . . . Selected by Chicago White Sox organization in fourth round of free-agent draft (June 3, 1985).
RECORDS/HONORS: Holds major league single-season record for most saves—57 (1990). . . . Named A.L. Fireman of the Year by THE SPORTING NEWS (1990).
STATISTICAL NOTES: Led Southern League with 11 hit batsmen in 1986.

Year	Team (League)	G	W	L	Pct.	ERA	Sv.	IP	H	R	ER	BB	SO
1985	—Niagara Falls (N.Y.-Penn)	28	2	3	.400	1.72	9	52⅓	30	12	10	19	74
	—Appleton (Midwest)	1	1	0	1.000	0.00	0	2⅔	1	0	0	1	4
1986	—Birmingham (Southern)	25	8	11	.421	4.68	0	159⅔	182	97	83	54	90
	—Chicago (A.L.)	20	2	0	1.000	1.77	7	35⅔	26	7	7	12	20
1987	—Chicago (A.L.)	51	7	5	.583	2.73	16	89	86	30	27	24	52
	—Hawaii (Pacific Coast)	9	2	3	.400	6.15	0	52⅔	72	38	36	14	17
1988	—Chicago (A.L.)	68	5	8	.385	3.30	34	90	96	38	33	33	62
1989	—Chicago (A.L.)	61	2	6	.250	3.76	34	79	62	34	33	40	47
1990	—Chicago (A.L.)	*77	4	6	.400	1.83	*57	88⅔	60	20	18	32	70
1991	—Chicago (A.L.)	67	7	5	.583	3.49	30	69⅔	63	32	27	38	47
Major league totals (6 years)		344	27	30	.474	2.89	178	452	393	161	145	179	298

ALL-STAR GAME RECORD

Year	League	W	L	Pct.	ERA	Sv.	IP	H	R	ER	BB	SO
1990	—American	0	0	. . .	0.00	0	1	0	0	0	0	1

THOMAS, FRANK
1B, WHITE SOX

PERSONAL: Born May 27, 1968, at Columbus, Ga. . . . 6-5/240. . . . Throws right, bats right. . . . Full name: Frank Edward Thomas.
HIGH SCHOOL: Columbus (Ga.).
COLLEGE: Auburn.
TRANSACTIONS/CAREER NOTES: Selected by Chicago White Sox organization in first round (seventh pick overall) of free-agent draft (June 5, 1989).
RECORDS/HONORS: Named first baseman on THE SPORTING NEWS college All-America team (1989). . . . Named designated hitter on THE SPORTING NEWS A.L. All-Star team (1991). . . . Named designated hitter on THE SPORTING NEWS Silver Slugger team (1991).
STATISTICAL NOTES: Led Southern League with 112 bases on balls received and .581 slugging percentage in 1990. . . . Led A.L. with 138 bases on balls received and .453 on base percentage in 1991.

Year	Team (League)	Pos.	G	AB	R	H	2B	3B	HR	RBI	Avg.	SB	PO	A	E	Avg.
1989	—Sara. White Sox (GCL)	1B	17	52	8	19	5	0	1	11	.365	4	130	8	2	.986
	—Sarasota (Florida State)	1B	55	188	27	52	9	1	4	30	.277	0	420	31	7	.985
1990	—Birmingham (Southern)	1B	109	353	85	114	27	5	18	71	.323	7	954	77	14	.987
	—Chicago (A.L.)	1B	60	191	39	63	11	3	7	31	.330	0	428	26	5	.989
1991	—Chicago (A.L.)	1B	158	559	104	178	31	2	32	109	.318	1	459	27	2	.996
Major league totals (2 years)			218	750	143	241	42	5	39	140	.321	1	887	53	7	.993

THOMAS, MIKE
P, INDIANS

PERSONAL: Born September 2, 1969, at Sacramento, Calif. . . . 6-2/175. . . . Throws left, bats left. . . . Full name: Michael Steven Thomas.
COLLEGE: Labette (Kan.).
TRANSACTIONS/CAREER NOTES: Selected by New York Mets organization in 23rd round of free-agent draft (June 5, 1989). . . . Traded with P Ron Darling to Montreal Expos organization for P Tim Burke (July 15, 1991). . . . Drafted by Cleveland Indians (December 9, 1991).

Year	Team (League)	G	W	L	Pct.	ERA	Sv.	IP	H	R	ER	BB	SO
1989	—Sarasota Mets (Gulf Coast)	8	2	0	1.000	1.44	0	31⅓	23	5	5	14	34
	—Kingsport (Appalachian)	6	1	2	.333	6.52	0	19⅓	13	16	14	17	17
1990	—Pittsfield (New York-Penn)	28	3	3	.500	2.67	3	64	51	23	19	29	80
1991	—Columbia-Sumter (S. Atl.)■	49	8	3	.727	3.03	20	68⅓	53	28	23	48	89

THOME, JIM
3B, INDIANS

PERSONAL: Born August 27, 1990, at Peoria, Ill. . . . 6-3/200. . . . Throws right, bats left. . . . Full name: James Howard Thome. . . . Name pronounced TOE-me.
HIGH SCHOOL: Limestone (Ill.).
COLLEGE: Illinois Central.
TRANSACTIONS/CAREER NOTES: Selected by Cleveland Indians organization in 13th round of free-agent draft (June 5, 1989).

Year	Team (League)	Pos.	G	AB	R	H	2B	3B	HR	RBI	Avg.	SB	PO	A	E	Avg.
1989	—Sarasota Indians (GCL)	SS-3B	55	186	22	44	5	3	0	22	.237	6	65	144	21	.909
1990	—Burlington (Appal.)	3B	34	118	31	44	7	1	12	34	.373	6	28	79	11	.907
	—Kinston (Carolina)	3B	33	117	19	36	4	1	4	16	.308	4	10	66	8	.905

Year Team (League)	Pos.	G	AB	R	H	2B	3B	HR	RBI	Avg.	SB	PO	A	E	Avg.
1991—Canton/Akron (Eastern) ..	3B	84	294	47	99	20	2	5	45	.337	8	41	167	17	.924
—Colorado Springs (PCL)	3B	41	151	20	43	7	3	2	28	.285	0	28	84	6	.949
—Cleveland (A.L.)	3B	27	98	7	25	4	2	1	9	.255	1	12	60	8	.900
Major league totals (1 year)		27	98	7	25	4	2	1	9	.255	1	12	60	8	.900

THOMPSON, MILT
OF, CARDINALS

PERSONAL: Born January 5, 1959, at Washington, D.C. . . . 5-11/200. . . . Throws right, bats left. . . . Full name: Milton Bernard Thompson.
HIGH SCHOOL: Zadok Magruder (Washington, D.C.).
COLLEGE: Howard (Washington, D.C.).
TRANSACTIONS/CAREER NOTES: Selected by Atlanta Braves organization in second round of free-agent draft (January 9, 1979). . . . Traded by Braves with P Steve Bedrosian to Philadelphia Phillies for C Ozzie Virgil and P Pete Smith (December 10, 1985). . . . Traded by Phillies to St. Louis Cardinals for C Steve Lake and OF Curt Ford (December 16, 1988).
STATISTICAL NOTES: Led Southern League outfielders with 336 total chances in 1982. . . . Led Southern League in caught stealing with 19 in 1982. . . . Led International League outfielders with 341 total chances in 1984.

Year Team (League)	Pos.	G	AB	R	H	2B	3B	HR	RBI	Avg.	SB	PO	A	E	Avg.
1979—Greenwood (W. Caro.)	OF	53	145	31	27	4	1	2	16	.186	16	85	8	3	.969
—Kingsport (Appalachian) ..	OF	26	94	22	31	8	4	1	11	.330	13	58	4	1	.984
1980—Durham (Carolina)	OF	68	255	49	74	12	3	2	36	.290	38	159	8	5	.971
—Savannah (Southern)	OF	71	278	35	83	7	3	1	15	.299	22	133	11	6	.960
1981—Savannah (Southern)	OF	140	493	92	135	18	2	4	31	.274	46	226	17	8	.968
1982—Savannah (Southern)	OF	•144	526	83	132	20	7	6	45	.251	*68	*312	10	14	.958
—Richmond (Int'l)	OF	3	6	2	1	0	0	0	0	.167	1	4	0	0	1.000
1983—Richmond (Int'l)	OF	12	32	12	8	1	0	0	3	.250	6	30	0	1	.968
—Savannah (Southern)	OF-1B	115	386	84	117	21	4	5	36	.303	46	295	15	7	.978
1984—Richmond (Int'l)	OF	134	503	•91	145	11	3	4	40	.288	47	*317	13	11	.968
—Atlanta (N.L.)	OF	25	99	16	30	1	0	2	4	.303	14	37	6	2	.956
1985—Richmond (Int'l)	OF	82	312	52	98	10	1	2	22	.314	34	209	3	4	.981
—Atlanta (N.L.)	OF	73	182	17	55	7	2	0	6	.302	9	78	2	3	.964
1986—Philadelphia (N.L.)■	OF	96	299	38	75	7	1	6	23	.251	19	212	1	2	.991
—Portland (Pacific Coast) ...	OF	41	161	26	56	10	2	1	16	.348	21	101	1	1	.990
1987—Philadelphia (N.L.)	OF	150	527	86	159	26	9	7	43	.302	46	354	4	4	.989
1988—Philadelphia (N.L.)	OF	122	378	53	109	16	2	2	33	.288	17	278	5	5	.983
1989—St. Louis (N.L.)■	OF	155	545	60	158	28	8	4	68	.290	27	348	5	8	.978
1990—St. Louis (N.L.)	OF	135	418	42	91	14	7	6	30	.218	25	232	4	7	.971
1991—St. Louis (N.L.)	OF	115	326	55	100	16	5	6	34	.307	16	207	8	2	.991
Major league totals (8 years)		871	2774	367	777	115	34	33	241	.280	173	1746	35	33	.982

THOMPSON, ROBBY
2B, GIANTS

PERSONAL: Born May 10, 1962, at West Palm Beach, Fla. . . . 5-11/170. . . . Throws right, bats right. . . . Full name: Robert Randall Thompson.
HIGH SCHOOL: Forest Hill (West Palm Beach, Fla.).
COLLEGE: Palm Beach Junior College (Fla.) and Florida.
TRANSACTIONS/CAREER NOTES: Selected by Oakland A's organization in second round of free-agent draft (January 12, 1982). . . . Selected by Seattle Mariners organization in secondary phase of free-agent draft (June 7, 1982). . . . Selected by San Francisco Giants organization in secondary phase of free-agent draft (June 6, 1983). . . . On disabled list (April 28-May 13, 1987).
RECORDS/HONORS: Holds major league single-game record for most times caught stealing—4 (June 27, 1986, 12 innings). . . . Named N.L. Rookie Player of the Year by THE SPORTING NEWS (1986).
STATISTICAL NOTES: Led Texas League second basemen with .982 fielding percentage, 291 putouts, 664 total chances and 91 double plays in 1985. . . . Led N.L. with 18 sacrifice hits in 1986. . . . Tied for N.L. lead in being hit by pitch with 13 in 1989. . . . Tied for N.L. lead in double plays by second basemen with 94 in 1990. . . . Hit for the cycle (April 22, 1991). . . . Led N.L. second basemen with 98 double plays in 1991.

Year Team (League)	Pos.	G	AB	R	H	2B	3B	HR	RBI	Avg.	SB	PO	A	E	Avg.
1983—Fresno (California)	2B	64	220	33	57	8	1	4	23	.259	4	118	185	11	.965
1984—Fresno (California)	2B-SS-3B	102	325	53	81	11	0	8	43	.249	21	182	280	24	.951
1985—Shreveport (Texas)	2B-SS	121	449	85	117	20	7	9	40	.261	28	+292	366	12	+.982
1986—San Francisco (N.L.)	2B-SS	149	549	73	149	27	3	7	47	.271	12	255	451	17	.976
1987—San Francisco (N.L.)	2B	132	420	62	110	26	5	10	44	.262	16	246	341	17	.972
1988—San Francisco (N.L.)	2B	138	477	66	126	24	6	7	48	.264	14	255	365	14	.978
1989—San Francisco (N.L.)	2B	148	547	91	132	26	*11	13	50	.241	12	307	425	8	.989
1990—San Francisco (N.L.)	2B	144	498	67	122	22	3	15	56	.245	14	287	441	8	.989
1991—San Francisco (N.L.)	2B	144	492	74	129	24	5	19	48	.262	14	320	402	11	.985
Major league totals (6 years)		855	2983	433	768	149	33	71	293	.257	82	1670	2425	75	.982

CHAMPIONSHIP SERIES RECORD

Year Team (League)	Pos.	G	AB	R	H	2B	3B	HR	RBI	Avg.	SB	PO	A	E	Avg.
1987—San Francisco (N.L.)	2B-PH	7	20	4	2	0	1	1	2	.100	2	11	19	1	.968
1989—San Francisco (N.L.)	2B	5	18	5	5	0	0	2	3	.278	0	10	13	0	1.000
Championship Series totals (2 years)		12	38	9	7	0	1	3	5	.184	2	21	32	1	.981

WORLD SERIES RECORD

Year	Team (League)	Pos.	G	AB	R	H	2B	3B	HR	RBI	Avg.	SB	PO	A	E	Avg.
							BATTING							FIELDING		
1989 —San Francisco (N.L.)	2B-PH	4	11	0	1	0	0	0	2	.091	0	4	10	0	1.000

ALL-STAR GAME RECORD

ALL-STAR GAME NOTES: Named to N.L. All-Star team for 1988 game; replaced due to injury by Bob Walk.

THOMPSON, RYAN
OF, BLUE JAYS

PERSONAL: Born November 4, 1967, at Chestertown, Md. ... 6-3/200. ... Throws right, bats right. ... Full name: Ryan Orlando Thompson.
HIGH SCHOOL: Kent County (Rock Hall, Md.).
TRANSACTIONS/CAREER NOTES: Selected by Toronto Blue Jays organization in 13th round of free-agent draft (June 2, 1987). ... On disabled list (May 29-June 7, 1991).

Year	Team (League)	Pos.	G	AB	R	H	2B	3B	HR	RBI	Avg.	SB	PO	A	E	Avg.
							BATTING							FIELDING		
1987 —Medicine Hat (Pioneer)	OF	40	110	13	27	3	1	1	9	.245	1	56	2	4	.935
1988 —St. Catharines (NYP).........	OF	23	57	13	10	4	0	0	2	.175	2	29	1	4	.882
—Dunedin (Florida State)	OF	17	29	2	4	0	0	1	2	.138	0	11	0	0	1.000
1989 —St. Catharines (NYP)	OF	74	278	39	76	14	1	6	36	.273	9	111	•11	5	.961
1990 —Dunedin (Florida State)	OF	117	438	56	101	15	5	6	37	.231	18	237	7	7	.972
1991 —Knoxville (Southern)	OF	114	403	48	97	14	3	8	40	.241	17	222	5	4	.983

THON, DICKIE
SS, RANGERS

PERSONAL: Born June 20, 1958, at South Bend, Ind. ... 5-11/175. ... Throws right, bats right. ... Full name: Richard William Thon.
HIGH SCHOOL: San Antonio (Rio Piedras, Puerto Rico).
TRANSACTIONS/CAREER NOTES: Signed as free agent by California Angels organization (November 23, 1975). ... Traded by Angels to Houston Astros for P Ken Forsch (April 1, 1981). ... On disabled list (April 9, 1984-remainder of season and May 19-June 8, 1985). ... Granted free agency (November 12, 1985). ... Re-signed by Astros (January 7, 1986). ... On disabled list (June 6-23, 1986). ... On Houston restricted list (April 3-18, 1987), then transferred to disabled list (April 19-May 10, 1987); included rehabilitation disability assignment to Tucson (April 19-May 8, 1987). ... On disqualified list (July 4, 1987-remainder of season). ... Granted free agency (November 9, 1987). ... Signed by San Diego Padres (February 18, 1988). ... Sold by Padres to Philadelphia Phillies (January 27, 1989). ... On suspended list (June 29-July 1, 1990). ... Granted free agency (November 4, 1991). ... Signed by Texas Rangers (December 16, 1991).
RECORDS/HONORS: Shares N.L. single-season record for fewest triples for league leader—10 (1982). ... Named shortstop on THE SPORTING NEWS N.L. All-Star team (1983). ... Named shortstop on THE SPORTING NEWS N.L. Silver Slugger team (1983).
STATISTICAL NOTES: Led N.L. with 18 game-winning RBIs in 1983. ... Tied for N.L. lead in double plays by shortstops with 86 in 1990.

Year	Team (League)	Pos.	G	AB	R	H	2B	3B	HR	RBI	Avg.	SB	PO	A	E	Avg.
							BATTING							FIELDING		
1976 —Quad Cities (Midwest).......	SS	69	246	46	68	11	4	1	32	.276	19	96	193	32	.900
1977 —Salinas (California)	SS	56	225	48	71	13	2	4	44	.316	10	95	162	13	.952
—Salt Lake City (PCL).........	SS	77	274	47	79	9	3	8	43	.288	14	129	242	26	.935
1978 —Salt Lake City (PCL).........	2B-SS	130	439	67	113	17	3	1	47	.257	15	273	380	26	.962
1979 —Salt Lake City (PCL).........	SS-2B	38	162	25	47	3	1	2	21	.290	14	70	120	11	.945
—California (A.L.)	2B-SS-3B	35	56	6	19	3	0	0	8	.339	0	38	46	8	.913
1980 —Salt Lake City (PCL).........	2B-SS	40	155	28	61	14	2	2	28	.394	9	81	107	12	.940
—California (A.L.)	S-2-3-1	80	267	32	68	12	2	0	15	.255	7	70	124	10	.951
1981 —Houston (N.L.)■.............	2B-SS-3B	49	95	13	26	6	0	0	3	.274	6	53	63	6	.951
1982 —Houston (N.L.)	SS-3B-2B	136	496	73	137	31	★10	3	36	.276	37	183	412	17	.972
1983 —Houston (N.L.)	SS	154	619	81	177	28	9	20	79	.286	34	258	★533	28	.966
1984 —Houston (N.L.)	SS	5	17	3	6	0	1	0	1	.353	0	8	13	0	1.000
1985 —Houston (N.L.)	SS	84	251	26	63	6	1	6	29	.251	8	106	218	11	.967
1986 —Houston (N.L.)	SS	106	278	24	69	13	1	3	21	.248	6	142	210	10	.972
1987 —Tucson (Pacific Coast)	SS	14	48	10	13	4	0	0	6	.271	1	22	40	7	.899
—Houston (N.L.)	SS	32	66	6	14	1	0	1	3	.212	3	21	53	6	.925
1988 —San Diego (N.L.)■...........	SS-2B-3B	95	258	36	68	12	2	1	18	.264	19	84	171	12	.955
1989 —Philadelphia (N.L.)■........	SS	136	435	45	118	18	4	15	60	.271	6	174	380	16	.972
1990 —Philadelphia (N.L.)	SS	149	552	54	141	20	4	8	48	.255	12	222	439	25	.964
1991 —Philadelphia (N.L.)	SS	146	539	44	136	18	4	9	44	.252	11	234	412	21	.969
American League totals (2 years)		115	323	38	87	15	2	0	23	.269	7	108	170	18	.939
National League totals (11 years)		1092	3606	405	955	153	36	66	342	.265	142	1485	2904	152	.967
Major league totals (13 years)		1207	3929	443	1042	168	38	66	365	.265	149	1593	3074	170	.965

DIVISION SERIES RECORD

Year	Team (League)	Pos.	G	AB	R	H	2B	3B	HR	RBI	Avg.	SB	PO	A	E	Avg.
							BATTING							FIELDING		
1981 —Houston (N.L.)	SS-PH	4	11	0	2	0	0	0	0	.182	0	5	10	1	.938

CHAMPIONSHIP SERIES RECORD

| | | | | | | —BATTING— | | | | | | | —FIELDING— | | | |
Year	Team (League)	Pos.	G	AB	R	H	2B	3B	HR	RBI	Avg.	SB	PO	A	E	Avg.
1979 —California (A.L.)		PR-SS	1	0	1	0	0	0	0	0	...	0	0	0	0	...
1986 —Houston (N.L.)		SS-PH	6	12	1	3	0	0	1	1	.250	0	6	9	0	1.000
Championship Series totals (2 years)			7	12	2	3	0	0	1	1	.250	0	6	9	0	1.000

ALL-STAR GAME RECORD

| | | | | | —BATTING— | | | | | | —FIELDING— | | |
Year	League	Pos.	AB	R	H	2B	3B	HR	RBI	Avg.	SB	PO	A	E	Avg.
1983 —National		PH-SS	3	0	1	0	0	0	0	.333	0	0	2	0	1.000

THURMAN, GARY
OF, ROYALS

PERSONAL: Born November 12, 1964, at Indianapolis. ... 5-10/175. ... Throws right, bats right. ... Full name: Gary Montez Thurman Jr.
HIGH SCHOOL: Indianapolis North Central (Ind.).
TRANSACTIONS/CAREER NOTES: Selected by Kansas City Royals organization in first round (21st pick overall) of free-agent draft (June 6, 1983). ... On Kansas City disabled list (March 26-April 13 and May 10-July 26, 1989); included rehabilitation disability assignment to Omaha (June 15-July 26, 1989). ... On disabled list (August 6-September 9, 1991).
RECORDS/HONORS: Shares A.L. single-season record for most stolen bases with no caught stealing— 16 (1989).
STATISTICAL NOTES: Led Gulf Coast League batters with 58 strikeouts in 1983. ... Led Gulf Coast League outfielders with 143 total chances in 1983. ... Tied for South Atlantic League lead in caught stealing with 17 in 1984. ... Led South Atlantic League outfielders with 329 total chances in 1984. ... Led Florida State League outfielders with 396 total chances in 1985. ... Tied for American Association lead in double plays by outfielder with six in 1987.

| | | | | | | —BATTING— | | | | | | | —FIELDING— | | |
Year	Team (League)	Pos.	G	AB	R	H	2B	3B	HR	RBI	Avg.	SB	PO	A	E	Avg.
1983 —Sarasota Royals (GCL)		OF	59	203	32	52	8	2	0	19	.256	31	★127	★13	3	.979
1984 —Charleston, S.C. (S. Atl.) ...		OF	129	478	71	109	6	8	6	51	.228	44	★311	5	13	.960
1985 —Fort Myers (Florida St.)		OF	134	453	68	137	9	9	0	45	.302	★70	★368	18	10	.975
1986 —Memphis (Southern)		OF	131	525	88	164	24	12	7	62	.312	53	277	5	11	.962
—Omaha (Am. Assoc.)		OF	3	2	1	1	0	0	0	0	.500	2	2	0	0	1.000
1987 —Omaha (Am. Assoc.)		OF	115	450	88	132	14	9	8	39	.293	★58	283	11	●8	.974
—Kansas City (A.L.)		OF	27	81	12	24	2	0	0	5	.296	7	61	5	2	.971
1988 —Omaha (Am. Assoc.)		OF	106	422	77	106	12	6	3	40	.251	35	195	16	6	.972
—Kansas City (A.L.)		OF	35	66	6	11	1	0	0	2	.167	5	36	1	2	.949
1989 —Kansas City (A.L.)		OF	72	87	24	17	2	1	0	5	.195	16	54	2	3	.949
—Omaha (Am. Assoc.)		OF	17	64	5	14	3	2	0	3	.219	5	34	1	2	.946
1990 —Kansas City (A.L.)		OF	23	60	5	14	3	0	0	3	.233	1	32	0	0	1.000
—Omaha (Am. Assoc.)		OF	98	381	65	126	14	8	0	26	.331	39	163	6	6	.966
1991 —Kansas City (A.L.)		OF	80	184	24	51	9	0	2	13	.277	15	129	2	4	.970
Major league totals (5 years)			237	478	71	117	17	1	2	28	.245	44	312	10	11	.967

TIMLIN, MIKE
P, BLUE JAYS

PERSONAL: Born March 10, 1966, at Midland, Tex. ... 6-4/205. ... Throws right, bats right. ... Full name: Michael August Timlin.
HIGH SCHOOL: Midland (Tex.).
COLLEGE: Southwestern University (Tex.).
TRANSACTIONS/CAREER NOTES: Selected by Toronto Blue Jays organization in fifth round of free-agent draft (June 2, 1987). ... On disabled list (August 2-17, 1991).
STATISTICAL NOTES: Led South Atlantic League with 19 hit batsmen in 1988.

Year	Team (League)	G	W	L	Pct.	ERA	Sv.	IP	H	R	ER	BB	SO
1987 —Medicine Hat (Pioneer)		13	4	8	.333	5.14	0	75⅓	79	50	43	26	66
1988 —Myrtle Beach (South Atlantic) ..		35	10	6	.625	2.86	0	151	119	68	48	77	106
1989 —Dunedin (Florida State)		33	5	8	.385	3.25	7	88⅔	90	44	32	36	64
1990 —Dunedin (Florida State)		42	7	2	.778	1.43	22	50⅓	36	11	8	16	46
—Knoxville (Southern)		17	1	2	.333	1.73	8	26	20	6	5	7	21
1991 —Toronto (A.L.)		63	11	6	.647	3.16	3	108⅓	94	43	38	50	85
Major league totals (1 year)		63	11	6	.647	3.16	3	108⅓	94	43	38	50	85

CHAMPIONSHIP SERIES RECORD

Year	Team (League)	G	W	L	Pct.	ERA	Sv.	IP	H	R	ER	BB	SO
1991 —Toronto (A.L.)		4	0	1	.000	3.18	0	5⅔	5	4	2	2	5

TINGLEY, RON
C, ANGELS

PERSONAL: Born May 27, 1959, at Presque Isle, Me. ... 6-2/194. ... Throws right, bats right. ... Full name: Ronald Irvin Tingley.
HIGH SCHOOL: Ramona (Riverside, Calif.).
TRANSACTIONS/CAREER NOTES: Selected by San Diego Padres organization in 10th round of free-agent draft (June 7, 1977). ... On disabled list (April 10-29, 1980). ... Traded by Padres organization to Seattle Mariners organization for SS Bill Wrona (April 1, 1984). ... On disabled list (April 7-August 10, 1984). ... Granted free agency (October 15, 1984). ... Signed by Calgary, Mariners organization (January 15, 1985). ... Granted free agency (October 15, 1985). ...

Signed by Richmond, Atlanta Braves organization (November 19, 1985).... Released by Braves organization (June 19, 1986). ... Signed by Maine, Cleveland Indians organization (June 23, 1986).... Traded by Indians organization to California Angels for a player to be named later (September 6, 1989); Colorado Springs (Indians organization) acquired IF Mark McLemore to complete deal (August 17, 1990).... On California disabled list (August 4-September 1, 1990).... Granted free agency (October 15, 1990).... Signed by Edmonton, Angels organization (December 6, 1990).

Year	Team (League)	Pos.	G	AB	R	H	2B	3B	HR	RBI	Avg.	SB	PO	A	E	Avg.
1977 —Walla Walla (Northwest) ..		OF	21	33	8	5	0	0	1	3	.152	0	5	2	0	1.000
1978 —Walla Walla (Northwest) ..		OF-C	43	140	22	29	2	0	2	21	.207	2	149	16	8	.954
1979 —Santa Clara (California)....		C-OF-P	52	143	11	29	4	1	0	17	.203	0	258	42	8	.974
—Amarillo (Texas)		C-OF	30	90	16	23	4	1	1	6	.256	2	133	17	4	.974
1980 —Reno (California)		C-OF	65	204	37	61	3	3	3	35	.299	46	333	46	10	.974
1981 —Amarillo (Texas)		C-1B-OF	116	379	72	109	9	★10	13	60	.288	8	607	47	11	.983
1982 —Hawaii (Pacific Coast)		C	115	362	45	95	13	8	6	42	.262	11	540	77	12	.981
—San Diego (N.L.)		C	8	20	0	2	0	0	0	0	.100	0	40	4	2	.957
1983 —Las Vegas (Pac. Coast)		C	92	294	44	83	15	6	10	48	.282	9	449	55	12	.977
1984 —Salt Lake City (PCL)■..		C	3	2	1	1	0	0	1	1	.500	0	3	0	0	1.000
1985 —Calgary (Pacific Coast)		C-OF	83	277	36	70	11	3	11	47	.253	3	399	51	10	.978
1986 —Richmond-Maine (Int'l)■..		C	58	174	13	35	2	1	3	13	.201	1	280	23	6	.981
1987 —Buffalo (Am. Assoc.)		C-1B-3B	57	167	27	45	8	5	5	30	.269	1	306	37	6	.983
1988 —Colorado Springs (PCL)		C	44	130	11	37	5	1	3	20	.285	1	234	22	0	1.000
—Cleveland (A.L.)		C	9	24	1	4	0	0	1	2	.167	0	48	6	0	1.000
1989 —Colorado Springs (PCL)		C-1B	66	207	28	54	8	2	6	39	.261	2	349	45	12	.970
—California (A.L.)■		C	4	3	0	1	0	0	0	0	.333	0	7	1	1	.889
1990 —Edmonton (Pac. Coast)		C	54	172	27	46	9	2	5	23	.267	1	284	35	8	.976
—California (A.L.)		C	5	3	0	0	0	0	0	0	.000	0	12	0	0	1.000
1991 —Edmonton (Pac. Coast)		C	17	55	11	16	5	0	3	15	.291	1	65	9	3	.961
—California (A.L.)		C	45	115	11	23	7	0	1	13	.200	1	222	32	3	.988
American League totals (4 years)			63	145	12	28	7	0	2	15	.193	1	289	39	4	.988
National League totals (1 year)			8	20	0	2	0	0	0	0	.100	0	40	4	2	.957
Major league totals (5 years)			71	165	12	30	7	0	2	15	.182	1	329	43	6	.984

RECORD AS PITCHER

Year	Team (League)	G	W	L	Pct.	ERA	Sv.	IP	H	R	ER	BB	SO
1979 —Santa Clara (California)...........	1	0	0	...	9.00	0	1	4	5	1	2	2

TINSLEY, LEE
OF, INDIANS

PERSONAL: Born March 4, 1969, at Shelbyville, Ky.... 5-10/180.... Throws right, bats both.... Full name: Lee Owen Tinsley.
HIGH SCHOOL: Shelby County (Ky.).
TRANSACTIONS/CAREER NOTES: Selected by Oakland Athletics organization in first round (11th pick overall) of free-agent draft (June 2, 1987).... Traded by A's with P Apolinar Garcia to Cleveland Indians for 3B Brook Jacoby (July 26, 1991).
STATISTICAL NOTES: Led Northwest League batters with 106 strikeouts and 66 bases on balls received and tied for lead in caught stealing 10 in 1988.... Led Midwest League batters with 177 strikeouts in 1989 and 175 in 1990.... Led Midwest League outfielders with 320 total chances in 1990.

Year	Team (League)	Pos.	G	AB	R	H	2B	3B	HR	RBI	Avg.	SB	PO	A	E	Avg.
1987 —Medford (Northwest)	OF	45	132	22	23	3	2	0	13	.174	9	77	2	4	.952
1988 —South. Oregon (N'west).....	OF	72	256	56	64	8	2	3	28	.250	★42	127	6	6	.957
1989 —Madison (Midwest)	OF	123	397	51	72	10	2	6	31	.181	19	274	7	8	.972
1990 —Madison (Midwest)	OF	132	482	88	121	14	12	12	59	.251	44	★302	7	11	.966
1991 —Huntsville (Southern)	OF	92	303	47	68	7	6	2	24	.224	36	175	3	7	.962
—Canton/Akron (Eastern)■	OF	38	139	26	41	7	2	3	8	.295	18	56	1	2	.966

TOLENTINO, JOSE
OF/1B, PIRATES

PERSONAL: Born June 3, 1961, at Mexico City, Mexico. ... 6-1/195. ... Throws left, bats left.... Full name: Jose Franco Tolentino.
COLLEGE: Seminole Junior College (Okla.) and Texas.
TRANSACTIONS/CAREER NOTES: Selected by San Francisco Giants organization in 36th round of free-agent draft (June 7, 1982).... Selected by Oakland Athletics organization in sventh round of free-agent draft (June 13, 1983).... Traded by A's organization to Texas Rangers organization for P Kris Killingworth and P Tom Duggan (December 12, 1987).... Released by Rangers organization (June 13, 1988).... Signed as free agent by Houston Astros organization (June 17, 1988).... Granted free agency (October 15, 1990).... Re-signed by Astros organization (March 6, 1991).... Released by Astros (November 18, 1991).... Signed by Pittsburgh Pirates (January 7, 1992).
STATISTICAL NOTES: Led Southern League first baseman with 1,356 total chances in 1986.... Tied for Pacific Coast League lead with eight intentional base on balls received in 1991.

Year	Team (League)	Pos.	G	AB	R	H	2B	3B	HR	RBI	Avg.	SB	PO	A	E	Avg.
1983 —Medford (Northwest)	1B	49	181	33	60	11	1	7	39	.331	1	425	27	8	★.983
1984 —Modesto (California)	1B	66	251	40	71	17	1	14	54	.283	4	566	54	5	.992
—Albany (Eastern)..............	1B	71	257	32	73	13	1	5	43	.284	2	602	52	5	.992
1985 —Tacoma (Pacific Coast)	1B	106	339	38	87	24	1	6	41	.257	1	801	77	11	.988

Year	Team (League)	Pos.	G	AB	R	H	2B	3B	HR	RBI	Avg.	SB	PO	A	E	Avg.
1986—Huntsville (Southern)		1B	137	540	80	•170	28	0	16	105	.315	7	*1253	*95	8	.994
1987—Tacoma (Pacific Coast)		1B	59	202	16	46	8	0	3	26	.228	0	279	15	7	.977
—Huntsville (Southern)		1B-3B	49	173	20	41	6	0	6	25	.237	1	387	30	7	.983
1988—Oklahoma City (A.A.)■...		1B	48	131	6	28	4	0	0	8	.214	0	366	26	3	.992
—Columbus (Southern)■......		1B-OF	72	259	33	79	10	3	9	53	.305	1	535	39	6	.990
1989—Tucson (Pacific Coast)		1B-OF	128	408	61	111	27	1	9	64	.272	2	995	71	6	.994
1990—Tucson (Pacific Coast)		OF-1B	116	377	69	116	32	3	21	78	.308	0	309	20	6	.982
1991—Tucson (Pacific Coast)		1B	90	303	44	88	24	5	6	51	.290	2	690	55	12	.984
—Houston (N.L.)		1B-OF	44	54	6	14	4	0	1	6	.259	0	53	5	1	.983
Major league totals (1 year)			44	54	6	14	4	0	1	6	.259	0	53	5	1	.983

TOMLIN, RANDY
P, PIRATES

PERSONAL: Born June 14, 1966, at Bainbridge, Md. . . . 5-11/179. . . . Throws left, bats left. . . . Full name: Randy Leon Tomlin.
COLLEGE: Liberty (Va.).
TRANSACTIONS/CAREER NOTES: Selected by Pittsburgh Pirates organization in 18th round of free-agent draft (June 1, 1988).
STATISTICAL NOTES: Pitched 1-0 no-hit victory against Kinston (May 28, 1989). . . . Tied for Eastern League lead with three shutouts in 1990.
MISCELLANEOUS: Appeared in one game as pinch-runner (1991).

Year	Team (League)	G	W	L	Pct.	ERA	Sv.	IP	H	R	ER	BB	SO
1988—Watertown (New York-Penn)...		15	7	5	.583	2.18	0	103⅓	75	31	25	25	87
1989—Salem (Carolina)		21	12	6	.667	3.25	0	138⅔	131	60	50	43	99
—Harrisburg (Eastern)		5	2	2	.500	0.84	0	32	18	6	3	6	31
1990—Harrisburg (Eastern)		19	9	6	.600	2.28	0	126⅓	101	43	32	34	92
—Buffalo (American Assoc.)		3	0	0	...	3.38	0	8	12	3	3	1	3
—Pittsburgh (N.L.)		12	4	4	.500	2.55	0	77⅔	62	24	22	12	42
1991—Pittsburgh (N.L.)		31	8	7	.533	2.98	0	175	170	75	58	54	104
Major league totals (2 years)		43	12	11	.522	2.85	0	252⅔	232	99	80	66	146

CHAMPIONSHIP SERIES RECORD

Year	Team (League)	G	W	L	Pct.	ERA	Sv.	IP	H	R	ER	BB	SO
1991—Pittsburgh (N.L.)		1	0	0	...	3.00	0	6	6	2	2	2	1

TORVE, KELVIN
1B/OF

PERSONAL: Born January 10, 1960, at Rapid City, S.D. . . . 6-3/185. . . . Throws right, bats left. . . . Full name: Kelvin Curtis Torve.
HIGH SCHOOL: Stevens (Rapid City, S.D.).
COLLEGE: Oral Roberts (bachelor of science degree in marketing).
TRANSACTIONS/CAREER NOTES: Selected by San Francisco Giants organization in second round of free-agent draft (June 8, 1981). . . . Traded by Giants organization to Baltimore Orioles organization for P Tommy Alexander (April 9, 1985). . . . Granted free agency (October 15, 1987). . . . Signed by Portland, Minnesota Twins organization (January 18, 1988). . . . Granted free agency (October 15, 1989). . . . Signed by Tidewater, New York Mets organization (December 13, 1989). . . . Granted free agency (October 15, 1990). . . . Re-signed by Mets organization (January 10, 1991). . . . Released by Mets organization (December 13, 1991).
STATISTICAL NOTES: Led Texas League with 11 intentional bases on balls received and tied for lead with nine sacrifice flies in 1982. . . . Led Pacific Coast League first basemen with 1,310 total chances and 111 double plays in 1989.

Year	Team (League)	Pos.	G	AB	R	H	2B	3B	HR	RBI	Avg.	SB	PO	A	E	Avg.
1981—Clinton (Midwest)		1B	57	211	27	55	10	0	1	27	.261	7	538	41	4	.993
1982—Shreveport (Texas)		1B	127	449	66	137	29	7	15	84	.305	9	1040	*96	17	.985
1983—Phoenix (Pacific Coast)		1B	115	392	58	102	21	5	4	54	.260	6	730	53	10	.987
1984—Shreveport (Texas)		1B-SS	114	316	59	94	21	5	16	62	.297	2	668	58	4	.995
1985—Charlotte (Southern)■......		1B-OF	134	482	85	140	•34	1	15	77	.290	5	1077	68	9	.992
1986—Rochester (Int'l)		1B	109	356	39	86	16	1	4	41	.242	5	555	51	5	.992
1987—Rochester (Int'l)		1B	86	252	27	66	10	0	9	32	.262	10	632	48	3	.996
1988—Portland (Pacific Coast)■.		1B	103	385	58	116	28	2	9	47	.301	5	864	62	2	*.998
—Minnesota (A.L.)		1B	12	16	1	3	0	0	1	2	.188	0	14	1	0	1.000
1989—Portland (Pacific Coast) ...		1B	137	499	62	145	*41	2	8	62	.291	10	*1206	*102	2	*.998
1990—Tidewater (Int'l)■.............		1B-OF	115	402	62	122	25	1	11	76	.303	9	839	77	15	.984
—New York (N.L.)		1B	20	38	0	11	4	0	0	2	.289	0	65	0	0	1.000
1991—Tidewater (Int'l)		1B-OF-3B	103	336	57	92	20	2	9	49	.274	4	416	24	4	.991
—New York (N.L.)		1B	10	8	0	0	0	0	0	0	.000	0	0	2	0	1.000
American League totals (1 year)			12	16	1	3	0	0	1	2	.188	0	14	1	0	1.000
National League totals (2 years)			30	46	0	11	4	0	0	2	.239	0	65	2	0	1.000
Major league totals (3 years)			42	62	1	14	4	0	1	4	.226	0	79	3	0	1.000

TRAMMELL, ALAN
SS, TIGERS

PERSONAL: Born February 21, 1958, at Garden Grove, Calif. . . . 6-0/175. . . . Throws right, bats right. . . . Full name: Alan Stuart Trammell. . . . Name pronounced TRAM-ull.
HIGH SCHOOL: Kearney (San Diego).

TRANSACTIONS/CAREER NOTES: Selected by Detroit Tigers organization in second round of free-agent draft (June 8, 1976).... On disabled list (July 9-31, 1984; June 29-July 17, 1988; June 4-23, 1989; and July 18-August 13, 1991).

RECORDS/HONORS: Named Southern League Most Valuable Player (1977).... Won A.L. Gold Glove at shortstop (1980-81 and 1983-84).... Named A.L. Comeback Player of the Year by THE SPORTING NEWS (1983).... Named shortstop on THE SPORTING NEWS A.L. All-Star team (1987-88 and 1990).... Named shortstop on THE SPORTING NEWS A.L. Silver Slugger team (1987-88 and 1990).

STATISTICAL NOTES: Led A.L. with 16 sacrifice hits in 1981 and 15 in 1983.... Led A.L. shortstops with 102 double plays in 1990.

Year	Team (League)	Pos.	G	AB	R	H	2B	3B	HR	RBI	Avg.	SB	PO	A	E	Avg.
1976	—Bristol (Appalachian)	SS	41	140	27	38	2	2	0	7	.271	8	59	131	12	.941
	—Montgomery (Southern)	SS	21	56	4	10	0	0	0	2	.179	3	40	64	2	.981
1977	—Montgomery (Southern)	SS	134	454	78	132	9	★19	3	50	.291	4	188	397	27	.956
	—Detroit (A.L.)	SS	19	43	6	8	0	0	0	0	.186	0	15	34	2	.961
1978	—Detroit (A.L.)	SS	139	448	49	120	14	6	2	34	.268	3	239	421	14	.979
1979	—Detroit (A.L.)	SS	142	460	68	127	11	4	6	50	.276	17	245	388	26	.961
1980	—Detroit (A.L.)	SS	146	560	107	168	21	5	9	65	.300	12	225	412	13	.980
1981	—Detroit (A.L.)	SS	105	392	52	101	15	3	2	31	.258	10	181	347	9	.983
1982	—Detroit (A.L.)	SS	157	489	66	126	34	3	9	57	.258	19	259	459	16	.978
1983	—Detroit (A.L.)	SS	142	505	83	161	31	2	14	66	.319	30	236	367	13	.979
1984	—Detroit (A.L.)	SS	139	555	85	174	34	5	14	69	.314	19	180	314	10	.980
1985	—Detroit (A.L.)	SS	149	605	79	156	21	7	13	57	.258	14	225	400	15	.977
1986	—Detroit (A.L.)	SS	151	574	107	159	33	7	21	75	.277	25	238	445	22	.969
1987	—Detroit (A.L.)	SS	151	597	109	205	34	3	28	105	.343	21	222	421	19	.971
1988	—Detroit (A.L.)	SS	128	466	73	145	24	1	15	69	.311	7	195	355	11	.980
1989	—Detroit (A.L.)	SS	121	449	54	109	20	3	5	43	.243	10	188	396	9	.985
1990	—Detroit (A.L.)	SS	146	559	71	170	37	1	14	89	.304	12	232	409	14	.979
1991	—Detroit (A.L.)	SS-3B	101	375	57	93	20	0	9	55	.248	11	131	296	9	.979
Major league totals (15 years)			1936	7077	1066	2022	349	50	161	865	.286	210	3011	5464	202	.977

CHAMPIONSHIP SERIES RECORD

Year	Team (League)	Pos.	G	AB	R	H	2B	3B	HR	RBI	Avg.	SB	PO	A	E	Avg.
1984	—Detroit (A.L.)	SS	3	11	2	4	0	1	1	3	.364	0	1	8	0	1.000
1987	—Detroit (A.L.)	SS	5	20	3	4	1	0	0	2	.200	0	6	9	1	.938
Championship Series totals (2 years)			8	31	5	8	1	1	1	5	.258	0	7	17	1	.960

WORLD SERIES RECORD

WORLD SERIES NOTES: Shares single-series record for most hits, five-game series—9 (1984).... Shares single-game record for batting in all club's runs—4 (October 13, 1984).

Year	Team (League)	Pos.	G	AB	R	H	2B	3B	HR	RBI	Avg.	SB	PO	A	E	Avg.
1984	—Detroit (A.L.)	SS	5	20	5	9	1	0	2	6	.450	1	8	9	1	.944

ALL-STAR GAME RECORD

ALL-STAR GAME NOTES: Named to A.L. All-Star team for 1984 game; replaced due to injury by Alfredo Griffin.... Named to A.L. All-Star team for 1988 game; replaced due to injury by Cal Ripken Jr.

Year	League	Pos.	AB	R	H	2B	3B	HR	RBI	Avg.	SB	PO	A	E	Avg.
1980	—American	SS	0	0	0	0	0	0	0	...	0	0	0	0	...
1985	—American	SS	1	0	0	0	0	0	0	.000	0	0	0	0	...
1987	—American	PH	1	0	0	0	0	0	0	.000	0	0	0	0	...
1990	—American	PH	1	0	0	0	0	0	0	.000	0	0	0	0	...
All-Star Game totals (4 years)			3	0	0	0	0	0	0	.000	0	0	0	0	...

TREADWAY, JEFF
2B, BRAVES

PERSONAL: Born January 22, 1963, at Columbus, Ga.... 5-11/170.... Throws right, bats left.... Full name: Hugh Jeffery Treadway.

HIGH SCHOOL: Griffin (Ga.).

COLLEGE: Middle Georgia College and Georgia.

TRANSACTIONS/CAREER NOTES: Selected by Montreal Expos organization in 18th round of free-agent draft (January 13, 1981).... Signed as free agent by Cincinnati Reds organization (January 29, 1984).... On disabled list (August 28-September 24, 1988).... Sold by Reds to Atlanta Braves (March 25, 1989).

STATISTICAL NOTES: Hit three home runs in a game (May 26, 1990).

Year	Team (League)	Pos.	G	AB	R	H	2B	3B	HR	RBI	Avg.	SB	PO	A	E	Avg.
1984	—Tampa (Florida State)	3B-2B	119	372	44	115	16	0	0	44	.309	13	128	184	25	.926
1985	—Vermont (Eastern)	2B	129	431	63	130	17	1	2	49	.302	6	271	332	15	.976
1986	—Vermont (Eastern)	2B	33	122	18	41	8	1	1	16	.336	3	68	102	5	.971
	—Denver (Am. Assoc.)	2B-3B	72	204	20	67	11	4	3	23	.328	3	75	153	6	.974
1987	—Nashville (Am. Assoc.)	2B	123	409	66	129	28	5	7	59	.315	2	236	362	12	★.980
	—Cincinnati (N.L.)	2B	23	84	9	28	4	0	2	4	.333	1	44	48	4	.958
1988	—Cincinnati (N.L.)	2B-3B	103	301	30	76	19	4	2	23	.252	2	189	253	8	.982
1989	—Atlanta (N.L.)■	2B-3B	134	473	58	131	18	3	8	40	.277	3	273	341	12	.981

Year Team (League)	Pos.	G	AB	R	H	2B	3B	HR	RBI	Avg.	SB	PO	A	E	Avg.
1990—Atlanta (N.L.)	2B	128	474	56	134	20	2	11	59	.283	3	241	360	15	.976
1991—Atlanta (N.L.)	2B	106	306	41	98	17	2	3	32	.320	2	155	206	15	.960
Major league totals (5 years)		494	1638	194	467	78	11	26	158	.285	11	902	1208	54	.975

CHAMPIONSHIP SERIES RECORD

Year Team (League)	Pos.	G	AB	R	H	2B	3B	HR	RBI	Avg.	SB	PO	A	E	Avg.
1991—Atlanta (N.L.)	2B	1	3	0	1	0	0	0	0	.333	0	2	2	0	1.000

WORLD SERIES RECORD

Year Team (League)	Pos.	G	AB	R	H	2B	3B	HR	RBI	Avg.	SB	PO	A	E	Avg.
1991—Atlanta (N.L.)	2B-PH	3	4	1	1	0	0	0	0	.250	0	1	3	1	.800

TRLICEK, RICK
P, BLUE JAYS

PERSONAL: Born April 26, 1969, at Houston. . . . 6-3/200. . . . Throws right, bats right. . . . Full name: Richard Alan Trlicek. . . . Name pronounced TRILL-a-CHECK.
HIGH SCHOOL: LaGrange (Tex.).
TRANSACTIONS/CAREER NOTES: Selected by Philadelphia Phillies organization in fourth round of free-agent draft (June 2, 1987). . . . Released by Phillies organization (March 23, 1989). . . . Signed by Atlanta Braves organization (April 2, 1989). . . . Traded by Braves organization to Toronto Blue Jays for C Ernie Whitt and OF Kevin Batiste (December 17, 1989). . . . On disabled list (August 4, 1991-remainder of season).

Year Team (League)	G	W	L	Pct.	ERA	Sv.	IP	H	R	ER	BB	SO
1987—Utica (New York-Penn)	10	2	5	.286	4.10	0	37⅓	43	28	17	31	22
1988—Batavia (New York-Penn)	8	2	3	.400	7.39	0	31⅔	27	32	26	31	26
1989—Sumter (South Atlantic)■	15	6	5	.545	2.59	0	93⅔	73	40	27	40	72
—Durham (Carolina)	1	0	0	. . .	1.13	0	8	3	2	1	1	4
1990—Dunedin (Florida State)■	26	5	8	.385	3.73	0	154⅓	128	74	64	72	125
1991—Knoxville (Southern)	41	2	5	.286	2.45	16	51⅓	36	26	14	22	55

TROMBLEY, MIKE
P, TWINS

PERSONAL: Born April 14, 1967, at Springfield, Mass. . . . 6-2/200. . . . Throws right, bats right. . . . Full name: Michael Scott Trombley.
HIGH SCHOOL: Minnechaug Regional (Wilbraham, Mass.).
COLLEGE: Duke.
TRANSACTIONS/CAREER NOTES: Selected by Minnesota Twins organization in 14th round of free-agent draft (June 5, 1989).

Year Team (League)	G	W	L	Pct.	ERA	Sv.	IP	H	R	ER	BB	SO
1989—Kenosha (Midwest)	12	5	1	.833	3.12	2	49	45	23	17	13	41
—Visalia (California)	6	2	2	.500	2.14	0	42	31	12	10	11	36
1990—Visalia (California)	27	14	6	.700	3.43	0	176	163	79	67	50	164
1991—Orlando (Southern)	27	12	7	.632	2.54	0	★191	153	65	54	57	★175

TSAMIS, GEORGE
P, TWINS

PERSONAL: Born June 14, 1967, at Campbell, Calif. . . . 6-2/175. . . . Throws left, bats right. . . . Full name: George Alex Tsamis.
HIGH SCHOOL: Countryside Senior (Clearwater, Fla.).
COLLEGE: Stetson.
TRANSACTIONS/CAREER NOTES: Selected by Toronto Blue Jays organization in 33rd round of free-agent draft (June 1, 1988). . . . Selected by Minnesota Twins organization in 15th round of free-agent draft (June 5, 1989).
STATISTICAL NOTES: Led California League with three shutouts in 1990.

Year Team (League)	G	W	L	Pct.	ERA	Sv.	IP	H	R	ER	BB	SO
1989—Visalia (California)	15	6	3	.667	3.05	0	94⅓	85	36	32	34	87
1990—Visalia (California)	26	★17	4	.810	2.21	0	183⅔	168	62	45	61	145
1991—Orlando (Southern)	1	0	0	. . .	0.00	0	7	3	2	0	4	5
—Portland (Pacific Coast)	29	10	8	.556	3.27	0	167⅔	183	75	61	66	71

TUCKER, SCOOTER
C, ASTROS

PERSONAL: Born November 18, 1966, at Greenville, Miss. . . . 6-2/205. . . . Throws right, bats right. . . . Full name: Eddie Jack Tucker.
HIGH SCHOOL: Washington (Everett, Washington).
COLLEGE: Delta State (Miss.).
TRANSACTIONS/CAREER NOTES: Selected by San Francisco Giants organization in fifth round of free-agent draft (June 1, 1988). . . . Claimed on waivers by Houston Astros (September 25, 1991).
STATISTICAL NOTES: Led Texas League catchers with .995 fielding percentage, 673 putouts, 70 assists and 747 total chances in 1991.

Year Team (League)	Pos.	G	AB	R	H	2B	3B	HR	RBI	Avg.	SB	PO	A	E	Avg.
1988—Everett (Northwest)	C	45	153	24	40	5	0	3	23	.261	0	237	23	1	.996
1989—Clinton (Midwest)	C-OF	126	426	44	105	20	2	3	43	.246	6	649	60	10	.986
1990—San Jose (California)	C-OF	123	439	59	123	28	2	5	71	.280	9	599	88	11	.984
1991—Shreveport (Texas)	C-3B	110	352	49	100	29	1	4	49	.284	3	†673	†71	4	†.995

TURNER, MATT
P, ASTROS

PERSONAL: Born February 18, 1967, at Lexington, Ky. . . . 6-5/215. . . . Throws right, bats right. . . . Full name: William Matthew Turner.
HIGH SCHOOL: Lexington Catholic, then Lafayette (Lexington, Ky.).
COLLEGE: Middle Georgia.
TRANSACTIONS/CAREER NOTES: Signed as free agent by Atlanta Braves organization (May 21, 1986). . . . Traded by Braves with a player to be named later to Houston Astros for P Jim Clancy (July 31, 1991); Astros acquired P Earl Sanders to complete deal (November 15, 1991).
STATISTICAL NOTES: Tied for South Atlantic League lead with six balks in 1987.

Year	Team (League)	G	W	L	Pct.	ERA	Sv.	IP	H	R	ER	BB	SO
1986	—Pulaski (Appalachian)	18	1	3	.250	4.62	2	48²/₃	55	36	25	28	48
1987	—Sumter (South Atlantic)	39	2	3	.400	4.71	0	93²/₃	91	61	49	48	102
1988	—Burlington (Midwest)	7	1	3	.250	6.55	0	34¹/₃	43	27	25	16	26
	—Sumter (South Atlantic)	7	1	0	1.000	4.60	0	15²/₃	17	8	8	3	7
1989	—Durham (Carolina)	53	9	9	.500	2.44	1	118	95	38	32	47	114
1990	—Greenville (Southern)	40	6	4	.600	2.66	4	67²/₃	59	24	20	29	60
	—Richmond (International)	22	2	3	.400	3.86	2	42	44	20	18	16	36
1991	—Richmond (International)	23	1	3	.250	4.75	5	36	33	21	19	20	33
	—Tucson (Pacific Coast)■	13	1	1	.500	4.15	1	26	27	12	12	14	25

TURNER, SHANE
OF/IF

PERSONAL: Born January 8, 1963, at Los Angeles. . . . 5-10/180. . . . Throws left, bats left. . . . Full name: Shane Lee Turner.
HIGH SCHOOL: Carey (Pomona, Calif.).
COLLEGE: Cal State Fullerton.
TRANSACTIONS/CAREER NOTES: Selected by New York Yankees organization in sixth round of free-agent draft (June 3, 1985). . . . On disabled list (June 3-June 14 and July 5, 1986-remainder of season). . . . Traded by Yankees organization with OF Keith Hughes to Philadelphia Phillies organization for OF Mike Easler (June 10, 1987). . . . Traded by Phillies organization to Baltimore Orioles organization for C John Posey (June 1, 1989). . . . Granted free agency (October 15, 1991).

Year	Team (League)	Pos.	G	AB	R	H	2B	3B	HR	RBI	Avg.	SB	PO	A	E	Avg.
1985	—Oneonta (N.Y.-Penn)	SS-2B	64	228	35	56	7	3	0	26	.246	12	109	164	15	+.948
1986	—Fort Lauderdale (FSL)	SS	66	222	48	71	12	2	2	36	.320	12	121	200	16	.953
1987	—Columbus (Int'l)	SS	25	76	10	17	0	2	0	7	.224	2	35	53	8	.917
	—Albany-Reading (East.)■	3B-2B-SS	94	356	69	119	19	7	4	55	.334	5	106	172	9	.969
1988	—Maine (International)	3-S-2-0	38	117	10	21	3	1	0	9	.179	14	38	100	9	.939
	—Reading (Eastern)	3B-2B-SS	78	295	52	88	11	6	3	21	.298	2	102	150	10	.962
	—Philadelphia (N.L.)	3B-SS	18	35	1	6	0	0	0	1	.171	0	8	14	1	.957
1989	—Reading (Eastern)	1B-3B-2B	46	141	18	28	5	1	1	11	.199	13	216	37	7	.973
	—Rochester (Int'l)■	3B-OF-2B	59	194	31	43	6	1	2	19	.222	6	76	72	8	.949
1990	—Rochester (Int'l)	0-2-S-3	86	209	29	59	7	0	1	19	.282	3	117	70	6	.969
1991	—Rochester (Int'l)	1-0-C-P	110	404	49	114	13	2	1	57	.282	6	151	168	16	.952
	—Baltimore (A.L.)	2B	4	1	0	0	0	0	0	0	.000	0	0	1	0	1.000
American League totals (1 year)			4	1	0	0	0	0	0	0	.000	0	0	1	0	1.000
National League totals (1 year)			18	35	1	6	0	0	0	1	.171	0	8	14	1	.957
Major league totals (2 years)			22	36	1	6	0	0	0	1	.167	0	8	15	1	.958

RECORD AS PITCHER

Year	Team (League)	G	W	L	Pct.	ERA	Sv.	IP	H	R	ER	BB	SO
1991	—Rochester (International)	1	0	0	. . .	0.00	0	1	0	0	0	1	0

URIBE, JOSE
SS, GIANTS

PERSONAL: Born January 21, 1960, at San Cristobal, Dominican Republic. . . . 5-10/170. . . . Throws right, bats both. . . . Full name: Jose Alta Uribe. . . . Formerly known as Jose Alta Gonzalez. . . . Name pronounced yoo-REE-bay.
TRANSACTIONS/CAREER NOTES: Signed as free agent by New York Yankees organization (February 18, 1977). . . . Released by Yankees organization (July 5, 1977). . . . Signed by St. Louis Cardinals organization (August 18, 1980). . . . Traded by Cardinals with 1B David Green, 1B Gary Rajsich and P Dave LaPoint to San Francisco Giants for OF-1B Jack Clark (February 1, 1985). . . . On disabled list (April 11-30, May 5-20 and May 28-July 4, 1987; and May 31-June 16, 1988). . . . On San Francisco disabled list (April 4-19 and June 18-July 23, 1991); included rehabilitation disability assignment to San Jose (July 4-10, 1991) and Phoenix (July 10-23, 1991).
STATISTICAL NOTES: Led Texas League shortstops with 88 double plays in 1982. . . . Led American Association shortstops with 664 total chances and 90 double plays in 1983. . . . Led American Association with 14 sacrifice hits in 1983. . . . Led American Association shortstops with 720 total chances and 96 double plays in 1984. . . . Led N.L. shortstops 85 double plays in 1989.

Year	Team (League)	Pos.	G	AB	R	H	2B	3B	HR	RBI	Avg.	SB	PO	A	E	Avg.
1981	—St. Petersburg (Fla. St.)	SS	128	463	54	124	15	2	0	40	.268	12	171	*387	32	.946
1982	—Arkansas (Texas)	SS	123	465	73	115	17	7	0	41	.247	16	185	385	36	.941
	—Louisville (Am. Assoc.)	SS	8	28	5	10	2	0	0	4	.357	0	15	18	1	.971
1983	—Louisville (Am. Assoc.)	SS	122	423	64	120	19	6	3	44	.284	26	206	425	*33	.950
1984	—Louisville (Am. Assoc.)	SS	145	484	68	135	20	2	3	46	.279	11	*233	*455	*32	*.956
	—St. Louis (N.L.)	SS-2B	8	19	4	4	0	0	0	3	.211	1	7	15	1	.957
1985	—San Francisco (N.L.)■	SS-2B	147	476	46	113	20	4	3	26	.237	8	209	438	26	.961
1986	—San Francisco (N.L.)	SS	157	453	46	101	15	1	3	43	.223	22	249	444	16	.977

Year	Team (League)	Pos.	G	AB	R	H	2B	3B	HR	RBI	Avg.	SB	PO	A	E	Avg.
							BATTING							FIELDING		
1987—San Francisco (N.L.)		SS	95	309	44	90	16	5	5	30	.291	12	145	286	13	.971
1988—San Francisco (N.L.)		SS	141	493	47	124	10	7	3	35	.252	10	212	404	19	.970
1989—San Francisco (N.L.)		SS	151	453	34	100	12	6	1	30	.221	6	225	436	18	.973
1990—San Francisco (N.L.)		SS	138	415	35	103	8	6	1	24	.248	5	182	373	20	.965
1991—San Francisco (N.L.)		SS	90	231	23	51	8	4	1	12	.221	3	98	218	11	.966
—San Jose (California)		SS	3	9	0	1	0	1	0	1	.111	0	5	6	0	1.000
—Phoenix (Pacific Coast)		SS	11	41	7	14	1	1	0	4	.341	0	16	34	1	.980
Major league totals (8 years)			927	2849	279	686	89	33	17	203	.241	67	1327	2614	124	.969

CHAMPIONSHIP SERIES RECORD

Year	Team (League)	Pos.	G	AB	R	H	2B	3B	HR	RBI	Avg.	SB	PO	A	E	Avg.
							BATTING							FIELDING		
1987—San Francisco (N.L.)		SS	7	26	1	7	1	0	0	2	.269	1	11	20	1	.969
1989—San Francisco (N.L.)		SS	5	17	2	4	1	0	0	1	.235	1	6	9	2	.882
Championship Series totals (2 years)			12	43	3	11	2	0	0	3	.256	2	17	29	3	.939

WORLD SERIES RECORD

Year	Team (League)	Pos.	G	AB	R	H	2B	3B	HR	RBI	Avg.	SB	PO	A	E	Avg.
							BATTING							FIELDING		
1989—San Francisco (N.L.)		SS	3	5	1	1	0	0	0	0	.200	0	1	3	0	1.000

VALDEZ, EFRAIN
P, BREWERS

PERSONAL: Born June 11, 1966, at Nizao de Bani, Dominican Republic.... 5-11/170.... Throws left, bats left.... Full name: Efrain Antonio Valdez.
HIGH SCHOOL: Aliro Paulino (Nizao de Bani, Dominican Republic).
TRANSACTIONS/CAREER NOTES: Signed as free agent by San Diego Padres organization (May 4, 1983).... Sold by Padres organization to Texas Rangers organization (December 10, 1984).... Played in Dominican Republic League (1985).... Loaned by Rangers organization to San Luis Potosi of Mexican League (1986).... Drafted by Cleveland Indians organization (December 6, 1988).... Claimed on waivers by Toronto Blue Jays (July 3, 1991).... Granted free agency (October 15, 1991).... Signed by Denver, Milwaukee Brewers organization (November 29, 1991).

Year	Team (League)	G	W	L	Pct.	ERA	Sv.	IP	H	R	ER	BB	SO
1983—Spokane (Northwest)		13	0	0	...	6.98	0	29⅔	40	32	23	17	27
1984—Spokane (Northwest)		13	1	2	.333	7.56	0	16⅔	26	18	14	8	15
1985—						Dominican Republic Summer League							
1986—San Luis (Mexican)■		26	11	8	.579	4.60	0	164⅓	176	105	84	76	82
—Tulsa (Texas)■		4	0	1	.000	5.84	0	12⅓	12	8	8	6	4
1987—Tulsa (Texas)		11	1	4	.200	7.11	0	49⅓	62	44	39	24	38
—Charlotte (Florida State)		17	3	6	.333	3.71	0	70⅓	67	32	29	27	45
1988—Tulsa (Texas)		43	6	5	.545	4.55	6	63⅓	63	37	32	24	52
1989—Canton/Akron (Eastern)■		44	2	4	.333	2.15	1	75⅓	60	26	18	13	55
1990—Colorado Springs (Pac. Coast) ..		46	4	2	.667	3.81	6	75⅔	72	38	32	30	52
—Cleveland (A.L.)		13	1	1	.500	3.04	0	23⅔	20	10	8	14	13
1991—Colorado Springs (Pac. Coast) ..		14	3	1	.750	3.82	1	30⅔	26	15	13	13	25
—Cleveland (A.L.)		7	0	0	...	1.50	0	6	5	1	1	3	1
—Syracuse (International)■		21	3	2	.600	5.36	0	43⅔	50	27	26	25	30
Major league totals (2 years)		20	1	1	.500	2.73	0	29⅔	25	11	9	17	14

VALDEZ, RAFAEL
P, PADRES

PERSONAL: Born December 17, 1968, at Nizao Boni, Dominican Republic.... 5-11/185.... Throws right, bats right.... Full name: Rafael Emilio Diaz Valdez.
HIGH SCHOOL: Aliro Paulino (Nizao Boni, Dominican Republic).
TRANSACTIONS/CAREER NOTES: Signed as free agent by San Diego Padres organization (March 6, 1985).... On disabled list (April 11-May 11 and June 13, 1991-remainder of season).
STATISTICAL NOTES: Led South Atlantic League shortstops with 46 errors in 1986.... Pitched 2-0 perfect game against Reno (July 20, 1989).

Year	Team (League)	G	W	L	Pct.	ERA	Sv.	IP	H	R	ER	BB	SO
1988—Charleston, S.C. (S. Atlantic)		28	11	4	.733	2.25	0	152⅓	117	42	38	46	100
1989—Riverside (California)		21	10	5	.667	2.26	0	143⅓	89	40	36	58	137
—Wichita (Texas)		6	5	0	1.000	1.94	0	41⅔	28	10	9	24	26
1990—San Diego (N.L.)		3	0	1	.000	11.12	0	5⅔	11	7	7	2	3
—Las Vegas (Pacific Coast)		17	4	7	.364	4.92	0	86	82	58	47	65	79
1991—Las Vegas (Pacific Coast)		5	0	2	.000	5.94	0	16⅔	22	13	11	16	9
Major league totals (1 year)		3	0	1	.000	11.12	0	5⅔	11	7	7	2	3

RECORD AS POSITION PLAYER

Year	Team (League)	Pos.	G	AB	R	H	2B	3B	HR	RBI	Avg.	SB	PO	A	E	Avg.
							BATTING							FIELDING		
1986—Charleston, S.C. (S. Atl.) ...		SS-2B	90	260	25	55	15	3	3	27	.212	2	112	204	†47	.871
1987—Charleston, S.C. (S. Atl.) ...		SS	127	435	42	115	16	2	5	44	.264	4	145	343	53	.902

VALDEZ, SERGIO
P, EXPOS

PERSONAL: Born September 7, 1965, at Elias Pina, Dominican Republic.... 6-1/190.... Throws right, bats right.... Full name: Sergio Sanchez Valdez.
TRANSACTIONS/CAREER NOTES: Signed as free agent by Montreal Expos organization (June 18, 1983).... On West Palm Beach disabled list (May 17-June 3, 1984).... Traded by

Expos organization with P Nate Minchey and OF Kevin Dean to Atlanta Braves for P Zane Smith (July 2, 1989).... Claimed on waivers by Cleveland Indians (April 30, 1990).... Released by Indians (March 25, 1991).... Re-signed by Indians organization (April 3, 1991).... Granted free agency (October 16, 1991).... Signed by Montreal Expos organization (December 10, 1991).

STATISTICAL NOTES: Tied for New York-Pennsylvania League lead in games started by pitcher with 15 in 1985.... Tied for Florida State League lead with four shutouts in 1986.... Tied for American Association lead with two shutouts in 1987.

Year	Team (League)	G	W	L	Pct.	ERA	Sv.	IP	H	R	ER	BB	SO
1983	—Calgary (Pioneer)	13	6	3	.667	5.57	0	72⅔	88	55	45	31	41
1984	—West Palm Beach (Florida St.) ..	5	0	0	...	8.74	0	11⅓	15	11	11	8	6
	—Jamestown (New York-Penn)..	13	2	7	.222	4.03	0	76	78	47	34	33	46
1985	—Utica (New York-Penn)	15	6	5	.545	3.07	0	105⅔	98	53	36	36	86
1986	—West Palm Beach (Florida St.) ..	24	★16	6	.727	2.47	0	145⅓	119	48	40	46	108
	—Montreal (N.L.)	5	0	4	.000	6.84	0	25	39	20	19	11	20
1987	—Indianapolis (Am. Assoc.)	27	10	7	.588	5.12	0	158⅓	191	108	90	64	★128
1988	—Indianapolis (Am. Assoc.)	14	5	4	.556	3.43	0	84	80	38	32	28	61
1989	—Indianapolis (Am. Assoc.)	19	6	3	.667	3.28	1	90⅔	78	38	33	26	81
	—Atlanta (N.L.)■	19	1	2	.333	6.06	0	32⅔	31	24	22	17	26
1990	—Atlanta (N.L.)	6	0	0	...	6.75	0	5⅓	6	4	4	3	3
	—Cleveland (A.L.)■	24	6	6	.500	4.75	0	102⅓	109	62	54	35	63
	—Colorado Springs (Pac. Coast) ..	7	4	3	.571	5.19	0	43⅓	55	29	25	13	33
1991	—Colorado Springs (Pac. Coast) ..	26	4	•12	.250	4.11	0	131⅓	139	67	60	27	71
	—Cleveland (A.L.)	6	1	0	1.000	5.51	0	16⅓	15	11	10	5	11
American League totals (2 years)		30	7	6	.538	4.85	0	118⅔	124	73	64	40	74
National League totals (3 years)		30	1	6	.143	6.43	0	63	76	48	45	31	49
Major league totals (4 years)		60	8	12	.400	5.40	0	181⅔	200	121	109	71	123

VALENTIN, JOHN
SS, RED SOX

PERSONAL: Born February 18, 1967, at Mineola, N.Y.... 6-0/170.... Throws right, bats right.... Full name: John William Valentin.
HIGH SCHOOL: St. Anthony's (Jersey City, N.J.).
COLLEGE: Seton Hall.
TRANSACTIONS/CAREER NOTES: Selected by Boston Red Sox organization in fifth round of free-agent draft (June 1, 1988).
STATISTICAL NOTES: Led New York-Pennsylvania League shortstops with .949 fielding with in 1988.

Year	Team (League)	Pos.	G	AB	R	H	2B	3B	HR	RBI	Avg.	SB	PO	A	E	Avg.
1988	—Elmira (New York-Penn) ..	SS-3B	60	207	18	45	5	1	2	16	.217	5	96	175	14	+.951
1989	—Winter Haven (Fla. St.)	SS-3B	55	215	27	58	13	1	3	18	.270	4	99	177	12	.958
	—Lynchburg (Carolina)	SS	75	264	47	65	7	2	8	34	.246	5	105	220	16	.953
1990	—New Britain (Eastern)	SS	94	312	20	68	18	1	2	31	.218	1	139	266	21	.951
1991	—New Britain (Eastern)	SS	23	81	8	16	3	0	0	5	.198	1	50	65	3	.975
	—Pawtucket (Int'l)	SS	100	329	52	87	22	4	9	49	.264	0	184	300	25	.951

VALENTIN, JOSE
SS, PADRES

PERSONAL: Born October 12, 1969, at Manati, Puerto Rico.... 5-10/175.... Throws right, bats both.... Full name: Jose Valentin.
TRANSACTIONS/CAREER NOTES: Signed as free agent by San Diego Padres organization (October 12, 1986).... On disabled list (April 16-May 1 and May 18-July 11, 1990).
STATISTICAL NOTES: Led Texas League shortstops with 658 total chances in 1991.

Year	Team (League)	Pos.	G	AB	R	H	2B	3B	HR	RBI	Avg.	SB	PO	A	E	Avg.
1987	—Spokane (Northwest)	SS	70	244	52	61	8	2	2	24	.250	8	101	175	26	.914
1988	—Charleston, S.C. (S. Atl.) ...	SS	133	444	56	103	20	1	6	44	.232	11	204	412	60	.911
1989	—Riverside (California)	SS	114	381	40	74	10	5	10	41	.194	8	★227	333	★46	.924
	—Wichita (Texas)	SS-3B	18	49	8	12	1	0	2	5	.245	1	26	45	8	.899
1990	—Wichita (Texas)	SS	11	36	4	10	2	0	0	2	.278	2	14	33	2	.959
1991	—Wichita (Texas)	SS	129	447	73	112	22	5	17	68	.251	8	176	★442	40	.939

VALENZUELA, FERNANDO
P

PERSONAL: Born November 1, 1960, at Navajoa, Sonora, Mexico.... 5-11/202.... Throws left, bats left.... Full name: Fernando Anguamea Valenzuela.... Name pronounced VAL-en-ZWAY-luh.
TRANSACTIONS/CAREER NOTES: Sold by Puebla of Mexican League to Los Angeles Dodgers organization (July 6, 1979).... On disabled list (July 31-September 26, 1988).... Granted free agency (November 13, 1989).... Re-signed by Dodgers (December 15, 1989).... Granted free agency (November 5, 1990).... Re-signed by Dodgers (December 19, 1990).... Released by Dodgers (March 28, 1991).... Signed by California Angels organization (May 20, 1991).... On California disabled list (June 13-July 5, 1991).... Released by Angels (July 5, 1991).... Re-signed by Angels organization (July 10, 1991).... Released by Angels organization (September 10, 1991).
RECORDS/HONORS: Shares modern major league rookie-season record for most shutout games won or tied—8 (1981).... Shares N.L. single-season record for fewest assists by pitcher who led league in assists—47 (1986).... Named Major League Player of the Year by THE SPORTING NEWS (1981).... Named N.L. Pitcher of the Year by THE SPORTING NEWS (1981).... Named N.L. Rookie Pitcher of the Year by THE SPORTING NEWS (1981).... Named lefthanded pitcher on THE SPORTING NEWS N.L. All-Star team (1981 and 1986).... Named pitcher on THE SPORTING NEWS N.L. Silver Slugger team (1981 and 1983).... Named N.L. Cy Young Award winner by Baseball Writers' Association of America (1981).... Named N.L. Rookie of

the Year by Baseball Writers' Association of America (1981).... Won N.L. Gold Glove at pitcher (1986).
STATISTICAL NOTES: Led Mexican Center League with 13 wild pitches in 1978.... Led N.L. with 11 complete games in 1981, 20 in 1986 and tied for lead with 12 in 1987.... Led N.L. with eight shutouts in 1981.... Tied for N.L. lead in games started by pitcher with 25 in 1981.... Led N.L. with 14 wild pitches in 1987.... Pitched 6-0 no-hit victory against St. Louis Cardinals (June 29, 1990).
MISCELLANEOUS: Appeared in one game as an outfielder with no chances (1982).... Appeared in one game as a first baseman with two putouts (1989).

Year	Team (League)	G	W	L	Pct.	ERA	Sv.	IP	H	R	ER	BB	SO
1978	Guanajuato (Mexican Center) ..	16	5	6	.455	2.23	1	93	88	46	23	46	*91
1979	Yucatan (Mexican)	26	10	12	.455	2.49	0	181	157	68	50	70	141
	Lodi (California)■...............	3	1	2	.333	1.13	0	24	21	10	3	3	18
1980	San Antonio (Texas)	27	13	9	.591	3.10	0	174	156	70	60	70	*162
	Los Angeles (N.L.)	10	2	0	1.000	0.00	1	18	8	2	0	5	16
1981	Los Angeles (N.L.)	25	13	7	.650	2.48	0	*192	140	55	53	61	*180
1982	Los Angeles (N.L.)	37	19	13	.594	2.87	0	285	247	105	91	83	199
1983	Los Angeles (N.L.)	35	15	10	.600	3.75	0	257	245	*122	107	99	189
1984	Los Angeles (N.L.)	34	12	17	.414	3.03	0	261	218	109	88	*106	240
1985	Los Angeles (N.L.)	35	17	10	.630	2.45	0	272⅓	211	92	74	101	208
1986	Los Angeles (N.L.)	34	*21	11	.656	3.14	0	269⅓	226	104	94	85	242
1987	Los Angeles (N.L.)	34	14	14	.500	3.98	0	251	*254	120	111	*124	190
1988	Los Angeles (N.L.)	23	5	8	.385	4.24	1	142⅓	142	71	67	76	64
1989	Los Angeles (N.L.)	31	10	13	.435	3.43	0	196⅔	185	89	75	98	116
1990	Los Angeles (N.L.)	33	13	13	.500	4.59	0	204	223	112	*104	77	115
1991	Palm Springs (California)■.......	1	0	0	. . .	0.00	0	4	4	1	0	3	2
	Midland (Texas)	4	3	1	.750	1.96	0	23	18	5	5	6	17
	California (A.L.)	2	0	2	.000	12.15	0	6⅔	14	10	9	3	5
	Edmonton (Pacific Coast).........	7	3	3	.500	7.12	0	36⅔	48	34	29	17	36
American League totals (1 year)		2	0	2	.000	12.15	0	6⅔	14	10	9	3	5
National League totals (11 years)		331	141	116	.549	3.31	2	2348⅔	2099	981	864	915	1759
Major league totals (12 years)		333	141	118	.544	3.34	2	2355⅓	2113	991	873	918	1764

DIVISION SERIES RECORD

Year	Team (League)	G	W	L	Pct.	ERA	Sv.	IP	H	R	ER	BB	SO
1981	Los Angeles (N.L.)	2	1	0	1.000	1.06	0	17	10	2	2	3	10

CHAMPIONSHIP SERIES RECORD

CHAMPIONSHIP SERIES NOTES: Holds N.L. single-series record for most bases on balls allowed—10 (1985).... Holds N.L. single-game record for most bases on balls allowed—8 (October 14, 1985).

Year	Team (League)	G	W	L	Pct.	ERA	Sv.	IP	H	R	ER	BB	SO
1981	Los Angeles (N.L.)	2	1	1	.500	2.45	0	14⅔	10	4	4	5	10
1983	Los Angeles (N.L.)	1	1	0	1.000	1.13	0	8	7	1	1	4	5
1985	Los Angeles (N.L.)	2	1	0	1.000	1.88	0	14⅓	11	3	3	10	13
Championship Series totals (3 years)		5	3	1	.750	1.95	0	37	28	8	8	19	28

WORLD SERIES RECORD

Year	Team (League)	G	W	L	Pct.	ERA	Sv.	IP	H	R	ER	BB	SO
1981	Los Angeles (N.L.)	1	1	0	1.000	4.00	0	9	9	4	4	7	6

ALL-STAR GAME RECORD

ALL-STAR GAME NOTES: Shares single-game record for most consecutive strikeouts—5 (July 15, 1986).

Year	League	W	L	Pct.	ERA	Sv.	IP	H	R	ER	BB	SO
1981	National	0	0	. . .	0.00	0	1	2	0	0	0	0
1982	National	0	0	. . .	0.00	0	⅔	0	0	0	2	0
1983	National					Did not play						
1984	National	0	0	. . .	0.00	0	2	2	0	0	0	3
1985	National	0	0	. . .	0.00	0	1	0	0	0	1	1
1986	National	0	0	. . .	0.00	0	3	1	0	0	0	5
All-Star totals (5 years)		0	0	. . .	0.00	0	7⅔	5	0	0	3	9

VALERA, JULIO
P, METS

PERSONAL: Born October 13, 1968, at San Sebastian, Puerto Rico.... 6-2/215.... Throws right, bats right.
HIGH SCHOOL: Manual Mendez Liciago (San Sebastian, Puerto Rico).
TRANSACTIONS/CAREER NOTES: Signed as free agent by New York Mets organization (February 6, 1986).

Year	Team (League)	G	W	L	Pct.	ERA	Sv.	IP	H	R	ER	BB	SO
1986	Kingsport (Appalachian)	13	3	*10	.231	5.19	0	76⅓	91	58	44	29	64
1987	Columbia (South Atlantic)	22	8	7	.533	2.80	0	125⅓	114	53	39	31	97
1988	Columbia (South Atlantic)	30	15	11	.577	3.20	1	191	171	77	68	51	144
1989	St. Lucie (Florida State)...........	6	4	2	.667	1.00	0	45	34	5	5	6	45
	Jackson (Texas)	19	10	6	.625	*2.49	0	137⅓	123	47	38	36	107
	Tidewater (International)	2	1	1	.500	2.08	0	13	8	3	3	5	10
1990	Tidewater (International)	24	10	10	.500	3.02	1	158	146	66	53	39	133
	New York (N.L.)	3	1	1	.500	6.92	0	13	20	11	10	7	4

Year	Team (League)	G	W	L	Pct.	ERA	Sv.	IP	H	R	ER	BB	SO
1991 — Tidewater (International)		26	10	10	.500	3.83	0	★176⅓	152	79	75	70	117
— New York (N.L.)		2	0	0	...	0.00	0	2	1	0	0	4	3
Major league totals (2 years)		5	1	1	.500	6.00	0	15	21	11	10	11	7

VALLE, DAVE
C, MARINERS

PERSONAL: Born October 30, 1960, at Bayside, N.Y.... 6-2/200.... Throws right, bats right.... Full name: David Valle.... Brother of John Valle, minor league outfielder (1972-84).... Name pronounced VALLEY.
HIGH SCHOOL: Holy Cross (Flushing, N.Y.).
TRANSACTIONS/CAREER NOTES: Selected by Seattle Mariners organization in second round of free-agent draft (June 6, 1978). ... On disabled list (July 26-August 25, 1979; June 24-July 3, 1981; April 13-June 20 and June 27-July 7, 1983).... On Salt Lake City disabled list (May 4-17 and June 9-25, 1984).... On Seattle disabled list (April 26-July 19, 1985); included rehabilitation disability assignment to Calgary (June 26-July 12, 1985).... On disabled list (April 17-May 7, 1987 and July 23-September 2, 1988).... On Seattle disabled list (May 30-July 6, 1989); included rehabilitation disability assignment to Calgary (July 4-6, 1989).... On disabled list (May 18-June 17, 1990).... On suspended list (July 21-24, 1991).
STATISTICAL NOTES: Led Northwest League catchers with six double plays and tied for lead with 23 passed balls in 1978.... Led California League catchers with 102 assists in 1980.... Led A.L. catchers with .997 fielding percentage in 1990.

							BATTING							FIELDING			
Year	Team (League)	Pos.	G	AB	R	H	2B	3B	HR	RBI	Avg.	SB	PO	A	E	Avg.
1978 — Bellingham (Northwest)....		C	57	167	12	34	2	0	2	21	.204	3	★338	65	10	.976
1979 — Alexandria (Carolina)		C	58	169	17	36	5	0	6	25	.213	1	290	44	11	.968
1980 — San Jose (California)		C-P	119	430	81	126	14	0	12	70	.293	6	570	†102	17	.975
1981 — Lynn (Eastern)		C	93	318	38	82	16	0	11	54	.258	3	445	56	6	.988
1982 — Salt Lake City (PCL).........		C-1B	75	234	28	49	11	1	4	28	.209	4	347	49	11	.973
1983 — Chattanooga (Southern) ...		C-1B	53	176	20	42	11	0	3	22	.239	0	239	24	4	.985
1984 — Salt Lake City (PCL).........		C	86	284	54	79	13	1	12	54	.278	0	433	34	6	.987
— Seattle (A.L.)		C	13	27	4	8	1	0	1	4	.296	0	56	5	0	1.000
1985 — Seattle (A.L.)		C	31	70	2	11	1	0	0	4	.157	00	117	7	3	.976
— Calgary (Pacific Coast)		C	42	131	17	45	8	0	6	26	.344	0	202	11	1	.995
1986 — Calgary (Pacific Coast)		C	105	353	71	110	21	2	21	72	.312	5	404	61	6	.987
— Seattle (A.L.)		C-1B	22	53	10	18	3	0	5	15	.340	0	90	3	2	.979
1987 — Seattle (A.L.)		C-1B-OF	95	324	40	83	16	3	12	53	.256	2	422	34	5	.989
1988 — Seattle (A.L.)		C-1B	93	290	29	67	15	2	10	50	.231	0	490	47	6	.989
1989 — Seattle (A.L.)		C	94	316	32	75	10	3	7	34	.237	0	496	52	4	.993
— Calgary (Pacific Coast)		C	2	6	0	0	0	0	0	0	.000	0	6	0	0	1.000
1990 — Seattle (A.L.)		C-1B	107	308	37	66	15	0	7	33	.214	1	633	44	2	†.997
1991 — Seattle (A.L.)		C	132	324	38	63	8	1	8	32	.194	0	676	52	6	.992
Major league totals (8 years)			587	1712	192	391	69	9	50	225	.228	3	2980	244	28	.991

RECORD AS PITCHER

Year	Team (League)	G	W	L	Pct.	ERA	Sv.	IP	H	R	ER	BB	SO
1980 — San Jose (California)		1	0	0	...	0.00	0	1	1	0	0	2	2

VanderWAL, JOHN
OF, EXPOS

PERSONAL: Born April 29, 1966, at Grand Rapids, Mich.... 6-2/190.... Throws left, bats left.... Full name: John Henry VanderWal.
HIGH SCHOOL: Hudsonville (Mich.).
COLLEGE: Western Michigan.
TRANSACTIONS/CAREER NOTES: Selected by Houston Astros organization in eighth round of free-agent draft (June 4, 1984).... Selected by Montreal Expos organization in third round of free-agent draft (June 2, 1987).

							BATTING							FIELDING			
Year	Team (League)	Pos.	G	AB	R	H	2B	3B	HR	RBI	Avg.	SB	PO	A	E	Avg.
1987 — Jamestown (N.Y.-Penn) ...		OF	18	69	24	33	12	3	3	15	.478	3	20	0	0	1.000
— West Palm Beach (FSL)		OF	50	189	29	54	11	2	2	22	.286	8	103	1	3	.972
1988 — West Palm Beach (FSL)		OF	62	231	50	64	15	2	10	33	.277	11	109	3	1	.991
— Jacksonville (Southern) ...		OF	58	208	22	54	14	0	3	14	.260	3	99	0	0	1.000
1989 — Jacksonville (Southern) ...		OF	71	217	30	55	9	2	6	24	.253	2	72	3	1	.987
1990 — Indianapolis (A.A.)		OF	51	135	16	40	6	0	2	14	.296	0	48	4	2	.963
— Jacksonville (Southern) ...		OF	77	277	45	84	25	3	8	40	.303	6	106	4	1	.991
1991 — Indianapolis (A.A.)		OF	133	478	84	140	36	8	15	71	.293	8	197	7	1	★.995
— Montreal (N.L.)		OF	21	61	4	13	4	1	1	8	.213	0	29	0	0	1.000
Major league totals (1 year)			21	61	4	13	4	1	1	8	.213	0	29	0	0	1.000

VAN POPPEL, TODD
P, ATHLETICS

PERSONAL: Born December 9, 1971, at Hinsdale, Ill.... 6-5/210.... Throws right, bats right.... Full name: Todd Matthew Van Poppel.
HIGH SCHOOL: St. Martin (Arlington, Tex.).
TRANSACTIONS/CAREER NOTES: Selected by Oakland Athletics organization in first round (14th pick overall) of free-agent draft (June 4, 1990).

Year	Team (League)	G	W	L	Pct.	ERA	Sv.	IP	H	R	ER	BB	SO
1990 — Southern Oregon (Northwest) ..		5	1	1	.500	1.13	0	24	10	5	3	9	32
— Madison (Midwest)		3	2	1	.667	3.95	0	13⅔	8	11	6	10	17

Year	Team (League)	G	W	L	Pct.	ERA	Sv.	IP	H	R	ER	BB	SO
1991—Huntsville (Southern)		24	6	*13	.316	3.47	0	132⅓	118	69	51	90	115
—Oakland (A.L.)		1	0	0	...	9.64	0	4⅔	7	5	5	2	6
Major league totals (1 year)		1	0	0	...	9.64	0	4⅔	7	5	5	2	6

VAN SLYKE, ANDY
OF, PIRATES

PERSONAL: Born December 21, 1960, at Utica, N.Y. . . . 6-2/195. . . . Throws right, bats left. . . . Full name: Andrew James Van Slyke.
HIGH SCHOOL: New Hartford (N.Y.).
TRANSACTIONS/CAREER NOTES: Selected by St. Louis Cardinals organization in first round (sixth pick overall) of free-agent draft (June 5, 1979). . . . On disabled list (June 8, 1979-entire season and April 10-May 14, 1981). . . . Traded by Cardinals with C Mike LaValliere and P Mike Dunne to Pittsburgh Pirates for C Tony Pena (April 1, 1987). . . . On disabled list (April 17-May 12, 1989).
RECORDS/HONORS: Named N.L. Player of the Year by THE SPORTING NEWS (1988). . . . Named outfielder on THE SPORTING NEWS N.L. All-Star team (1988). . . . Won N.L. Gold Glove as outfielder (1988-91). . . . Named outfielder on THE SPORTING NEWS N.L. Silver Slugger team (1988).
STATISTICAL NOTES: Tied for N.L. lead in double plays by outfielders with four in 1985, six in 1987 and five in 1989. . . . Led N.L. with 13 sacrifice flies in 1988. . . . Led N.L. outfielders with 422 total chances in 1988.

Year	Team (League)	Pos.	G	AB	R	H	2B	3B	HR	RBI	Avg.	SB	PO	A	E	Avg.
1979 —							Did not play									
1980—Gastonia (S. Atlantic)	OF	126	426	62	115	15	4	8	59	.270	19	177	16	•16	.923
1981—St. Petersburg (Fla. St.)	OF	94	282	42	62	11	3	1	25	.220	10	168	10	5	.973
1982—Arkansas (Texas)	OF	123	416	83	116	13	*11	16	70	.279	37	266	17	7	.976
1983—Louisville (Am. Assoc.)	3B-1B-OF	54	220	52	81	21	4	6	41	.368	13	201	78	16	.946
—St. Louis (N.L.)	OF-3B-1B	101	309	51	81	15	5	8	38	.262	21	203	59	6	.978
1984—St. Louis (N.L.)	OF-3B-1B	137	361	45	88	16	4	7	50	.244	28	357	82	8	.982
1985—St. Louis (N.L.)	OF-1B	146	424	61	110	25	6	13	55	.259	34	237	13	1	.996
1986—St. Louis (N.L.)	OF-1B	137	418	48	113	23	7	13	61	.270	21	415	34	8	.982
1987—Pittsburgh (N.L.)■	OF-1B	157	564	93	165	36	11	21	82	.293	34	338	10	4	.989
1988—Pittsburgh (N.L.)	OF	154	587	101	169	23	*15	25	100	.288	30	*406	12	4	.991
1989—Pittsburgh (N.L.)	OF-1B	130	476	64	113	18	9	9	53	.237	16	344	9	4	.989
1990—Pittsburgh (N.L.)	OF	136	493	67	140	26	6	17	77	.284	14	326	6	8	.976
1991—Pittsburgh (N.L.)	OF	138	491	87	130	24	7	17	83	.265	10	273	8	1	.996
Major league totals (9 years)		1236	4123	617	1109	206	70	130	599	.269	208	2899	233	44	.986

CHAMPIONSHIP SERIES RECORD

Year	Team (League)	Pos.	G	AB	R	H	2B	3B	HR	RBI	Avg.	SB	PO	A	E	Avg.
1985—St. Louis (N.L.)	OF-PR	5	11	1	1	0	0	0	1	.091	0	6	0	0	1.000
1990—Pittsburgh (N.L.)	OF	6	24	3	5	1	1	0	3	.208	1	13	1	0	1.000
1991—Pittsburgh (N.L.)	OF	7	25	3	4	2	0	1	2	.160	1	18	1	0	1.000
Championship Series totals (3 years)		18	60	7	10	3	1	1	6	.167	2	37	2	0	1.000

WORLD SERIES RECORD

Year	Team (League)	Pos.	G	AB	R	H	2B	3B	HR	RBI	Avg.	SB	PO	A	E	Avg.
1985—St. Louis (N.L.)	OF-PH-PR	6	11	0	1	0	0	0	0	.091	0	8	0	0	1.000

ALL-STAR GAME RECORD

Year	League	Pos.	AB	R	H	2B	3B	HR	RBI	Avg.	SB	PO	A	E	Avg.
1988—National	OF	2	0	0	0	0	0	.000	0	2	0	0	1.000

VARSHO, GARY
OF, PIRATES

PERSONAL: Born June 20, 1961, at Marshfield, Wis. . . . 5-11/190. . . . Throws right, bats left. . . . Full name: Gary Andrew Varsho.
HIGH SCHOOL: Marshfield (Wis.).
COLLEGE: Wisconsin Oshkosh.
TRANSACTIONS/CAREER NOTES: Selected by Chicago Cubs organization in fifth round of free-agent draft (June 7, 1982). . . . On disabled list (August 13, 1986-remainder of season). . . . Traded by Cubs to Pittsburgh Pirates for OF Steve Carter (March 29, 1991).
STATISTICAL NOTES: Led California League second basemen with 71 double plays in 1983. . . . Led Texas League second basemen with 650 total chances in 1984. . . . Led American Association in caught stealing with 17 in 1987.

Year	Team (League)	Pos.	G	AB	R	H	2B	3B	HR	RBI	Avg.	SB	PO	A	E	Avg.
1982—Quad Cities (Midwest)	2B	76	271	52	68	9	4	3	40	.251	30	190	180	14	.964
1983—Salinas (California)	2B	131	490	69	129	16	*13	6	57	.263	46	284	339	★33	.950
1984—Midland (Texas)	2B	128	429	65	112	15	6	8	50	.261	27	*286	335	*29	.955
1985—Pittsfield (Eastern)	1B-OF	115	418	62	101	14	6	3	37	.242	•40	670	51	6	.992
1986—Pittsfield (Eastern)	OF-1B-2B	107	399	75	106	18	5	13	44	.266	★45	213	14	6	.974
1987—Iowa (American Assoc.)	OF	132	504	87	152	23	9	9	48	.302	37	227	18	6	.976
1988—Iowa (American Assoc.)	OF	66	234	46	65	16	5	4	26	.278	8	120	6	2	.984
—Chicago (N.L.)	OF	46	73	6	20	3	0	0	5	.274	5	29	0	3	.906

Year	Team (League)	Pos.	G	AB	R	H	2B	3B	HR	RBI	Avg.	SB	PO	A	E	Avg.
1989	—Chicago (N.L.)	OF	61	87	10	16	4	2	0	6	.184	3	25	1	2	.929
	—Iowa (American Assoc.)	OF	31	112	13	26	3	1	2	13	.232	6	67	4	3	.959
1990	—Iowa (American Assoc.)	OF-1B-3B	63	229	35	69	9	0	7	33	.301	18	202	15	7	.969
	—Chicago (N.L.)	OF	46	48	10	12	4	0	0	1	.250	2	2	0	0	1.000
1991	—Pittsburgh (N.L.)■	OF-1B	99	187	23	51	11	2	4	23	.273	9	95	2	1	.990
	Major league totals (4 years)		252	395	49	99	22	4	4	35	.251	19	151	3	6	.963

CHAMPIONSHIP SERIES RECORD

Year	Team (League)	Pos.	G	AB	R	H	2B	3B	HR	RBI	Avg.	SB	PO	A	E	Avg.
1991	—Pittsburgh (N.L.)	PH	2	2	0	1	0	0	0	0	.500		0	0	0	...

VASQUEZ, JULIAN
P, METS

PERSONAL: Born May 24, 1968, at Puerto Plata, Dominican Republic.... 6-3/165.... Throws right, bats right.... Full name: Julian Vasquez. **HIGH SCHOOL:** Escuela Antera Mota (Puerto Plata, Dominican Republic). **TRANSACTIONS/CAREER NOTES:** Signed as a free agent by New York Mets organization (July 22, 1986).

Year	Team (League)	G	W	L	Pct.	ERA	Sv.	IP	H	R	ER	BB	SO
1987	—Kingsport (Appalachian)	25	2	3	.400	3.29	3	41	36	20	15	22	36
1988	—Kingsport (Appalachian)	19	0	1	.000	3.19	10	31	19	13	11	13	30
1989	—Columbia (South Atlantic)	37	1	5	.167	3.88	7	58	47	30	25	32	61
1990	—Columbia (South Atlantic)	25	1	4	.200	2.17	9	29	28	15	7	17	37
1991	—St. Lucie (Florida State)	56	3	2	.600	0.28	•25	64	35	6	2	39	56

VATCHER, JIM
OF, PADRES

PERSONAL: Born May 27, 1966, at Santa Monica, Calif.... 5-9/175.... Throws right, bats right.... Full name: James Ernest Vatcher. **HIGH SCHOOL:** Palisades (Calif.). **COLLEGE:** West Los Angeles College (Calif.) and Cal State Northridge. **TRANSACTIONS/CAREER NOTES:** Selected by Philadelphia Phillies organization in 20th round of free-agent draft (June 2, 1987). ... Traded by Phillies to Atlanta Braves (August 9, 1990) as partial completion of deal in which Braves traded OF Dale Murphy and a player to be named later to Phillies for P Jeff Parrett and two players to be named later (August 3, 1990); Scranton/Wilkes-Barre (Phillies organization) acquired P Tommy Greene (August 9, 1990) and Braves acquired SS Victor Rosario (September 4, 1990) to complete deal.... Claimed on waivers by San Diego Padres (February 8, 1991). **STATISTICAL NOTES:** Tied for New York-Pennsylvania League lead in double plays by outfielders with three in 1987.... Led South Atlantic League with 89 bases on balls received in 1988.

Year	Team (League)	Pos.	G	AB	R	H	2B	3B	HR	RBI	Avg.	SB	PO	A	E	Avg.
1987	—Utica (New York-Penn)	OF-SS	67	249	44	67	15	2	3	21	.269	10	116	12	3	.977
1988	—Spartanburg (S. Atl.)	OF	•137	496	*90	150	32	2	12	72	.302	26	224	13	4	.983
1989	—Clearwater (Florida St.)	OF-2B-3B	92	349	51	105	30	5	4	46	.301	7	163	35	8	.961
	—Reading (Eastern)	OF	48	171	27	56	11	3	4	32	.327	2	76	5	1	.988
1990	—Scranton/W.B. (Int'l)	OF-3B	55	181	30	46	12	4	5	22	.254	1	88	24	2	.982
	—Phil.-Atlanta (N.L.)■	OF	57	73	7	19	2	1	1	7	.260	0	27	0	0	1.000
1991	—Las Vegas (Pac. Coast)■	OF-2B-P	117	395	67	105	28	6	17	67	.266	4	206	18	8	.966
	—San Diego (N.L.)	OF	17	20	3	4	0	0	0	2	.200	1	8	1	1	.900
	Major league totals (2 years)		74	93	10	23	2	1	1	9	.247	1	35	1	1	.973

RECORD AS PITCHER

Year	Team (League)	G	W	L	Pct.	ERA	Sv.	IP	H	R	ER	BB	SO
1991	—Las Vegas (Pacific Coast)	1	1	0	1.000	0.00	0	3	1	0	0	2	1

VAUGHN, GREG
OF, BREWERS

PERSONAL: Born July 3, 1965, at Sacramento, Calif.... 6-0/193.... Throws right, bats right. ... Full name: Gregory Lamont Vaughn. **HIGH SCHOOL:** John F. Kennedy (Sacramento, Calif.). **COLLEGE:** Sacramento City College (Calif.) and Miami (Fla.). **TRANSACTIONS/CAREER NOTES:** Selected by St. Louis Cardinals organization in fifth round of free-agent draft (January 17, 1984).... Selected by Milwaukee Brewers organization in secondary phase of free-agent draft (June 4, 1984).... Selected by Pittsburgh Pirates organization in secondary phase of free-agent draft (January 9, 1985).... Selected by California Angels organization in secondary phase of free-agent draft (June 3, 1985).... Selected by Brewers organization in secondary phase of free-agent draft (June 2, 1986).... On disabled list (May 26-June 10, 1990). **RECORDS/HONORS:** Named Midwest League co-Most Valuable Player (1987).... Named American Association Most Valuable Player (1989). **STATISTICAL NOTES:** Led Midwest League with 292 total bases in 1987.... Led Texas League with 279 total bases in 1988.... Led American Association with .548 slugging percentage in 1989.

Year	Team (League)	Pos.	G	AB	R	H	2B	3B	HR	RBI	Avg.	SB	PO	A	E	Avg.
1986	—Helena (Pioneer)	OF	66	258	64	75	13	2	16	54	.291	23	99	5	3	.972
1987	—Beloit (Midwest)	OF	139	492	*120	150	31	6	*33	105	.305	36	247	11	10	.963

Year Team (League)	Pos.	G	AB	R	H	2B	3B	HR	RBI	Avg.	SB	PO	A	E	Avg.
1988 — El Paso (Texas)	OF	131	505	*104	152	*39	2	*28	*105	.301	22	216	12	7	.970
1989 — Denver (Am. Assoc.)	OF	110	387	74	107	17	5	*26	*92	.276	20	140	4	3	.980
— Milwaukee (A.L.)	OF	38	113	18	30	3	0	5	23	.265	4	32	1	2	.943
1990 — Milwaukee (A.L.)	OF	120	382	51	84	26	2	17	61	.220	7	195	8	7	.967
1991 — Milwaukee (A.L.)	OF	145	542	81	132	24	5	27	98	.244	2	315	5	2	.994
Major league totals (3 years)		303	1037	150	246	53	7	49	182	.237	13	542	14	11	.981

VAUGHN, MO

1B/DH, RED SOX

PERSONAL: Born December 15, 1967, at Norwalk, Conn. . . . 6-1/230. . . . Throws right, bats left. . . . Full name: Maurice Samuel Vaughn.
HIGH SCHOOL: Trinity Pawling Prep (Pawling, N.Y.).
COLLEGE: Seton Hall.
TRANSACTIONS/CAREER NOTES: Selected by Boston Red Sox organization in first round (23rd pick overall) of free-agent draft (June 9, 1989).

Year Team (League)	Pos.	G	AB	R	H	2B	3B	HR	RBI	Avg.	SB	PO	A	E	Avg.
1989 — New Britain (Eastern)	1B	73	245	28	68	15	0	8	38	.278	1	541	45	•10	.983
1990 — Pawtucket (Int'l)	1B	108	386	62	114	26	1	22	72	.295	8	828	60	11	.988
1991 — Pawtucket (Int'l)	1B	69	234	35	64	10	0	14	50	.274	2	432	24	3	.993
— Boston (A.L.)	1B	74	219	21	57	12	0	4	32	.260	2	378	26	6	.985
Major league totals (1 year)		74	219	21	57	12	0	4	32	.260	2	378	26	6	.985

VELARDE, RANDY

3B/SS, YANKEES

PERSONAL: Born November 24, 1962, at Midland, Tex. . . . 6-0/190. . . . Throws right, bats right. . . . Full name: Randy Lee Velarde. . . . Name pronounced vel-ARE-dee.
HIGH SCHOOL: Robert E. Lee (Midland, Tex.).
COLLEGE: Lubbock Christian College (Tex.).
TRANSACTIONS/CAREER NOTES: Selected by Chicago White Sox organization in 19th round of free-agent draft (June 3, 1985). . . . Traded by White Sox organization with P Pete Filson to New York Yankees for P Scott Nielsen and IF Mike Soper (January 5, 1987). . . . On New York disabled list (August 9-29, 1989).
STATISTICAL NOTES: Led Midwest League shortstops with 52 errors in 1986.

Year Team (League)	Pos.	G	AB	R	H	2B	3B	HR	RBI	Avg.	SB	PO	A	E	Avg.
1985 — Niagara Falls (NYP)	0-S-2-3	67	218	28	48	7	3	1	16	.220	8	124	117	15	.941
1986 — Appleton (Midwest)	SS-3B-OF	124	417	55	105	31	4	11	50	.252	13	205	300	†54	.903
— Buffalo (Am. Assoc.)	SS	9	20	2	4	1	0	0	2	.200	1	9	28	3	.925
1987 — Albany (Eastern)■............	SS-OF	71	263	40	83	20	2	7	32	.316	8	128	254	17	.957
— Columbus (Int'l)	SS	49	185	21	59	10	6	5	33	.319	8	100	164	16	.943
— New York (A.L.)	SS	8	22	1	4	0	0	0	1	.182	0	8	20	2	.933
1988 — Columbus (Int'l)	SS-2B-3B	78	293	39	79	23	4	5	37	.270	7	123	271	25	.940
— New York (A.L.)	2B-SS-3B	48	115	18	20	6	0	5	12	.174	1	72	98	8	.955
1989 — Columbus (Int'l)	SS-3B	103	387	59	103	26	3	11	53	.266	3	150	295	22	.953
— New York (A.L.)	3B-SS	33	100	12	34	4	2	2	11	.340	0	26	61	4	.956
1990 — New York (A.L.)	3-S-0-2	95	229	21	48	6	2	5	19	.210	0	70	159	12	.950
1991 — New York (A.L.)	3B-SS-OF	80	184	19	45	11	1	1	15	.245	3	64	148	15	.934
Major league totals (5 years)		264	650	71	151	27	5	13	58	.232	4	240	486	41	.947

VELASQUEZ, GUILLERMO

1B, PADRES

PERSONAL: Born April 23, 1968, at Mexicali, Mexico. . . . 6-3/220. . . . Throws right, bats left. . . . Full name: Guillermo Velasquez.
TRANSACTIONS/CAREER NOTES: Signed as free agent by Monterrey of the Mexican League prior to 1986 season. . . . Signed as free agent by San Diego Padres organization (December, 1986).
STATISTICAL NOTES: Led Texas League first basemen with 1,173 total chances in 1991.

Year Team (League)	Pos.	G	AB	R	H	2B	3B	HR	RBI	Avg.	SB	PO	A	E	Avg.
1986 — Monterrey (Mexican)	1B	62	146	19	39	8	2	3	21	.267	1	353	11	4	.989
1987 — Charleston, S.C. (S. Atl.)■.	1B	102	295	32	65	12	0	3	30	.220	2	695	58	12	.984
1988 — Charleston, S.C. (S. Atl.) ...	1B	135	520	55	149	28	3	11	90	.287	1	*1186	85	13	.990
1989 — Riverside (California)	1B	139	544	73	152	30	2	9	69	.279	4	1073	95	*19	.984
1990 — Wichita (Texas)	1B	105	377	48	102	21	2	12	72	.271	0	631	50	14	.980
1991 — Wichita (Texas)	1B	130	501	72	148	26	3	21	100	.295	4	*1092	69	12	.990

VENABLE, MAX

OF

PERSONAL: Born June 6, 1957, at Phoenix. . . . 5-10/185. . . . Throws right, bats left. . . . Full name: William McKinley Venable Jr.
HIGH SCHOOL: Cordova (Rancho Cordova, Calif.).
TRANSACTIONS/CAREER NOTES: Selected by Los Angeles Dodgers organization in third round of free-agent draft (June 8, 1976). . . . On disabled list (June 26-July 10, 1976). . . . Drafted by San Francisco Giants (December 4, 1978). . . . On Phoenix disabled list (April 23-May 16, 1981). . . . On San Francisco disabled list (April 21-June 1, 1982); in-

cluded rehabilitation disability assignment to Phoenix (May 22-June 1, 1982).... Traded by Giants to Montreal Expos organization (March 31, 1984), completing deal in which Expos traded 1B Al Oliver to Giants for P Fred Breining and a player to be named later (February 27, 1984). Giants traded P Andy McGaffigan to Expos (March 31, 1984) as compensation for Breining arriving with an injury; Breining remained with Expos.... Traded by Expos organization to Cincinnati Reds organization for IF Skeeter Barnes (April 26, 1985).... Released by Reds (March 29, 1987).... Re-signed by Reds organization (April 9, 1987).... Granted free agency (October 15, 1987).... Signed by Baltimore Orioles (February, 1988).... Released by Orioles (March, 1988).... Signed by Nashville, Reds organization (July 11, 1988).... Loaned by Reds organization to Yucatan of Mexican League (July, 1988); returned (September, 1988).... Granted free agency (October 15, 1988).... Signed by Edmonton, California Angels organization (January 11, 1989).... Granted free agency (November 5, 1990).... Re-signed by Angels (December 13, 1990).... Granted free agency (November 11, 1991).... Signed by Chiba Lotte Mariners of Japan Pacific League (December 16, 1991).

STATISTICAL NOTES: Led American Association with 11 sacrifice hits in 1987.

Year	Team (League)	Pos.	G	AB	R	H	2B	3B	HR	RBI	Avg.	SB	PO	A	E	Avg.
1976	—Bellingham (Northwest)....	OF	51	162	25	35	2	0	1	16	.216	9	58	4	8	.886
1977	—Clinton (Midwest)............	OF-2B	125	425	72	115	19	4	9	63	.271	17	149	13	13	.926
1978	—Lodi (California)	OF	•140	566	134	180	30	9	17	101	.318	46	220	8	8	.966
1979	—San Francisco (N.L.)■.......	OF	55	85	12	14	1	1	0	3	.165	3	30	2	3	.914
	—Shreveport (Texas)	OF	18	69	11	16	1	2	0	3	.232	5	28	2	1	.968
	—Phoenix (Pacific Coast)	OF	38	150	27	46	5	4	0	11	.307	17	96	4	3	.971
1980	—Phoenix (Pacific Coast)	OF	78	312	52	89	10	10	5	40	.285	15	179	7	4	.979
	—San Francisco (N.L.)........	OF	64	138	13	37	5	0	0	10	.268	8	61	0	0	1.000
1981	—Phoenix (Pacific Coast)	OF	104	428	81	122	24	10	8	48	.285	33	263	6	3	.989
	—San Francisco (N.L.)........	OF	18	32	2	6	0	2	0	1	.188	3	12	0	0	1.000
1982	—San Francisco (N.L.)........	OF	71	125	17	28	2	1	1	7	.224	9	66	6	1	.986
	—Phoenix (Pacific Coast)	OF	8	32	5	8	1	2	0	3	.250	1	16	0	0	1.000
1983	—San Francisco (N.L.)........	OF	94	228	28	50	7	4	6	27	.219	15	141	5	1	.993
1984	—Indianapolis (A.A.)■........	OF	99	330	57	82	13	3	9	47	.248	22	183	4	4	.979
	—Montreal (N.L.)	OF	38	71	7	17	2	0	2	7	.239	1	33	0	0	1.000
1985	—Ind.-Denver (A.A.)■........	OF	46	172	27	42	7	5	4	19	.244	10	93	2	1	.990
	—Cincinnati (N.L.)	OF	77	135	21	39	12	3	0	10	.289	11	60	3	0	1.000
1986	—Cincinnati (N.L.)	OF	108	147	17	31	7	1	2	15	.211	7	63	0	2	.969
	—Cincinnati (N.L.)	OF	7	7	2	1	0	0	0	2	.143	0	3	0	0	1.000
1987	—Nashville (Am. Assoc.)	OF	116	400	57	108	16	4	2	28	.270	20	212	5	5	.977
1988	—Yucatan (Mexican)■........	OF	13	47	14	15	0	1	1	8	.319	1	31	1	0	1.000
1989	—Edmonton (Pac. Coast)■...	OF	95	329	52	89	14	4	1	45	.271	13	189	9	2	.990
	—California (A.L.)	OF	20	53	7	19	4	0	0	4	.358	0	21	0	0	1.000
1990	—California (A.L.)	OF	93	189	26	49	9	3	4	21	.259	5	112	3	3	.975
1991	—California (A.L.)	OF	82	187	24	46	8	2	3	21	.246	2	86	3	3	.967
American League totals (3 years)			195	429	57	114	21	5	7	46	.266	7	219	6	6	.974
National League totals (9 years)			532	968	119	223	36	12	11	82	.230	57	469	16	7	.986
Major league totals (12 years)			727	1397	176	337	57	17	18	128	.241	64	688	22	13	.982

VENTURA, ROBIN

3B, WHITE SOX

PERSONAL: Born July 14, 1967, at Santa Maria, Calif.... 6-1/192.... Throws right, bats left.... Full name: Robin Mark Ventura.
HIGH SCHOOL: Righetti (Santa Maria, Calif.).
COLLEGE: Oklahoma State.
TRANSACTIONS/CAREER NOTES: Selected by Chicago White Sox organization in first round (10th pick overall) of free-agent draft (June 1, 1988).
RECORDS/HONORS: Named College Player of the Year by THE SPORTING NEWS (1987-88).... Named third baseman on THE SPORTING NEWS college All-America team (1987-1988).... Won A.L. Gold Glove at third base (1991).
STATISTICAL NOTES: Led Southern League with 12 intentional bases on balls received in 1989.... Led Southern League third basemen with .930 fielding percentage and tied for lead with 21 double plays in 1989.... Led A.L. third basemen with 134 putouts and 18 errors in 1991.
MISCELLANEOUS: Member of 1988 U.S. Olympic baseball team.

Year	Team (League)	Pos.	G	AB	R	H	2B	3B	HR	RBI	Avg.	SB	PO	A	E	Avg.
1989	—Birmingham (Southern)	3-1-2	129	454	75	126	25	2	3	67	.278	9	108	249	27	+.930
	—Chicago (A.L.)	3B	16	45	5	8	3	0	0	7	.178	0	17	33	2	.962
1990	—Chicago (A.L.)	3B-1B	150	493	48	123	17	1	5	54	.249	1	116	268	25	.939
1991	—Chicago (A.L.)	3B-1B	157	606	92	172	25	1	23	100	.284	2	†225	291	†18	.966
Major league totals (3 years)			323	1144	145	303	45	2	28	161	.265	3	358	592	45	.955

VILLANUEVA, HECTOR

C/1B, CUBS

PERSONAL: Born October 2, 1964, at San Juan, Puerto Rico.... 6-1/220.... Throws right, bats right.... Full name: Hector Balasquide Villanueva.
HIGH SCHOOL: Cupeyville (Rio Piedras, Puerto Rico).
COLLEGE: Alabama.
TRANSACTIONS/CAREER NOTES: Signed as free agent by Chicago Cubs organization (March 26, 1985).... On disabled list (June 7-22, 1987).... On Chicago disabled list (April 1-21, 1991).
STATISTICAL NOTES: Led Carolina League with 12 sacrifice flies in 1986.... Led Eastern League with 71 bases on balls received in 1988.

Year	Team (League)	Pos.	G	AB	R	H	2B	3B	HR	RBI	Avg.	SB	PO	A	E	Avg.
1985 —Peoria (Midwest)		C-P	65	193	22	45	7	0	1	19	.233	0	322	43	12	.968
1986 —Winston-Salem (Caro.)		C-1B	125	412	58	131	20	2	13	100	.318	6	653	72	6	.992
1987 —Pittsfield (Eastern)		C-1B	109	391	59	107	31	0	14	70	.274	3	489	58	4	.993
1988 —Pittsfield (Eastern)		1-C-3-P	127	436	50	137	24	3	10	75	.314	5	840	98	11	.988
1989 —Iowa (American Assoc.)		C-1B-P	120	444	46	112	25	1	12	57	.252	1	618	67	6	.991
1990 —Iowa (American Assoc.)		C-1B	52	177	20	47	7	1	8	34	.266	0	263	27	0	1.000
—Chicago (N.L.)		C-1B	52	114	14	31	4	1	7	18	.272	1	170	10	2	.989
1991 —Chicago (N.L.)		C-1B	71	192	23	53	10	1	13	32	.276	0	276	27	6	.981
—Iowa (American Assoc.)		C	6	25	2	9	3	0	2	9	.360	0	15	0	0	1.000
Major league totals (2 years)			123	306	37	84	14	2	20	50	.275	1	446	37	8	.984

RECORD AS PITCHER

Year	Team (League)	G	W	L	Pct.	ERA	Sv.	IP	H	R	ER	BB	SO
1985 —Peoria (Midwest)		1	0	0	...	0.00	0	1	0	0	0	1	1
1988 —Pittsfield (Eastern)		1	0	0	...	9.00	0	1	2	1	1	0	1
1989 —Iowa (American Association)		1	0	0	...	18.00	0	1	3	2	2	1	0

VIOLA, FRANK

P, RED SOX

PERSONAL: Born April 19, 1960, at Hempstead, N.Y. . . . 6-4/209. . . . Throws left, bats left. . . . Full name: Frank John Viola Jr. . . . Name pronounced vy-OH-luh.
HIGH SCHOOL: East Meadow (New York).
COLLEGE: St. John's (N.Y.).
TRANSACTIONS/CAREER NOTES: Selected by Kansas City Royals organization in 16th round of free-agent draft (June 6, 1978). . . . Selected by Minnesota Twins organization in second round of free-agent draft (June 8, 1981). . . . Traded by Twins to New York Mets for P Rick Aguilera, P David West and three players to named later (July 31, 1989); Portland, Twins organization, acquired P Kevin Tapani and P Tim Drummond (August 1, 1989), and Twins acquired P Jack Savage to complete deal (October 16, 1989). . . . Granted free agency (October 28, 1991). . . . Signed by Boston Red Sox (January 2, 1992).
RECORDS/HONORS: Holds major league single-season record for fewest innings pitched for league leader—249 ⅔ (1990). . . . Named A.L. Pitcher of the Year by THE SPORTING NEWS (1988). . . . Named lefthanded pitcher on THE SPORTING NEWS A.L. All-Star team (1988). . . . Named A.L. Cy Young Award winner by Baseball Writers' Association of America (1988). . . . Named lefthanded pitcher on THE SPORTING NEWS N.L. All-Star team (1990).
STATISTICAL NOTES: Tied for A.L. lead in games started by pitcher with 37 in 1986. . . . Tied for N.L. lead in games started by pitcher with 35 in 1990.

Year	Team (League)	G	W	L	Pct.	ERA	Sv.	IP	H	R	ER	BB	SO
1981 —Orlando (Southern)		17	5	4	.556	3.43	0	97	112	47	37	33	50
1982 —Toledo (International)		8	2	3	.400	3.88	0	58	61	27	25	18	34
—Minnesota (A.L.)		22	4	10	.286	5.21	0	126	152	77	73	38	84
1983 —Minnesota (A.L.)		35	7	15	.318	5.49	0	210	242	*141	*128	92	127
1984 —Minnesota (A.L.)		35	18	12	.600	3.21	0	257⅔	225	101	92	73	149
1985 —Minnesota (A.L.)		36	18	14	.563	4.09	0	250⅔	262	*136	114	68	135
1986 —Minnesota (A.L.)		37	16	13	.552	4.51	0	245⅔	257	136	123	83	191
1987 —Minnesota (A.L.)		36	17	10	.630	2.90	0	251⅔	230	91	81	66	197
1988 —Minnesota (A.L.)		35	*24	7	*.774	2.64	0	255⅓	236	80	75	54	193
1989 —Minnesota (A.L.)		24	8	12	.400	3.79	0	175⅔	171	80	74	47	138
—New York (N.L.)■		12	5	5	.500	3.38	0	85⅓	75	35	32	27	73
1990 —New York (N.L.)		35	20	12	.625	2.67	0	*249⅔	227	83	74	60	182
1991 —New York (N.L.)		35	13	15	.464	3.97	0	231⅓	*259	112	102	54	132
American League totals (8 years)		260	112	93	.546	3.86	0	1772⅔	1775	842	760	521	1214
National League totals (3 years)		82	38	32	.543	3.31	0	566⅓	561	230	208	141	387
Major league totals (10 years)		342	150	125	.545	3.72	0	2339	2336	1072	968	662	1601

CHAMPIONSHIP SERIES RECORD

Year	Team (League)	G	W	L	Pct.	ERA	Sv.	IP	H	R	ER	BB	SO
1987 —Minnesota (A.L.)		2	1	0	1.000	5.25	0	12	14	8	7	5	9

WORLD SERIES RECORD

Year	Team (League)	G	W	L	Pct.	ERA	Sv.	IP	H	R	ER	BB	SO
1987 —Minnesota (A.L.)		3	2	1	.667	3.72	0	19⅓	17	8	8	3	16

ALL-STAR GAME RECORD

Year	League	W	L	Pct.	ERA	Sv.	IP	H	R	ER	BB	SO
1988 —American		1	0	1.000	0.00	0	2	0	0	0	0	1
1990 —National		0	0	...	0.00	0	1	1	0	0	0	0
1991 —National		0	0	...	0.00	0	1	0	0	0	1	0
All-Star totals (3 years)		1	0	1.000	0.00	0	4	1	0	0	1	1

VITKO, JOSEPH

P, METS

PERSONAL: Born February 7, 1970, at Somerville, N.J. . . . 6-8/210. . . . Throws right, bats right. . . . Full name: Joseph John Vitko III.
HIGH SCHOOL: Central Cambria (Ebensburg, Pa.).
COLLEGE: St. Francis (Pa.).
TRANSACTIONS/CAREER NOTES: Selected by New York Mets organization in 38th round of free-agent draft (June 1, 1988). . . . Selected by New York Mets organization in 24th round of free-agent draft (June 5, 1989).

Year Team (League)	G	W	L	Pct.	ERA	Sv.	IP	H	R	ER	BB	SO
1989 — Sarasota Mets (Gulf Coast)	8	4	1	.800	3.29	0	41	28	20	15	16	33
— Pittsfield (New York-Penn)	5	2	1	.667	0.91	0	29²⁄₃	24	6	3	8	29
1990 — Columbia (South Atlantic)	16	8	1	.889	2.49	1	90¹⁄₃	70	29	25	30	72
1991 — St. Lucie (Florida State)	22	11	8	.579	2.24	0	140¹⁄₃	102	40	35	39	105

VIZCAINO, JOSE
3B/SS, CUBS

PERSONAL: Born March 26, 1968, at Palenque, Dominican Republic. .... 6-1/180. .... Throws right, bats both. .... Full name: Jose Luis Pimental Vizcaino. .... Name pronounced VIS-ky-EE-no.
HIGH SCHOOL: Americo Tolentino (Palenque de San Cristobal, Dominican Republic).
TRANSACTIONS/CAREER NOTES: Signed as free agent by Los Angeles Dodgers organization (February 18, 1986). .... Traded by Dodgers to Chicago Cubs for IF Greg Smith (December 14, 1990).
STATISTICAL NOTES: Led Gulf Coast League shortstops with 23 double plays in 1987. .... Led Pacific Coast League shortstops with 611 total chances and 82 double plays in 1989.

Year Team (League)	Pos.	G	AB	R	H	2B	3B	HR	RBI	Avg.	SB	PO	A	E	Avg.
1987 — Sarasota Dodgers (GCL) ...	SS-1B	49	150	26	38	5	1	0	12	.253	8	73	107	13	.933
1988 — Bakersfield (California)	SS	122	433	77	126	11	4	0	38	.291	13	185	340	30	.946
1989 — Albuquerque (PCL)	SS	129	434	60	123	10	4	1	44	.283	16	*191	*390	*30	.951
— Los Angeles (N.L.)	SS	7	10	2	2	0	0	0	0	.200	0	6	9	2	.882
1990 — Albuquerque (PCL)	2B-SS	81	276	46	77	10	2	2	38	.279	13	141	229	14	.964
— Los Angeles (N.L.)	SS-2B	37	51	3	14	1	1	0	2	.275	1	23	27	2	.962
1991 — Chicago (N.L.)■	3B-SS-2B	93	145	7	38	5	0	0	10	.262	2	49	118	7	.960
Major league totals (3 years)		137	206	12	54	6	1	0	12	.262	3	78	154	11	.955

VIZQUEL, OMAR
SS, MARINERS

PERSONAL: Born April 24, 1967, at Caracas, Venezuela. .... 5-9/165. .... Throws right, bats both. .... Full name: Omar Enrique Vizquel. .... Name pronounced vis-KEL.
HIGH SCHOOL: Francisco Espejo (Caracas, Venezuela).
TRANSACTIONS/CAREER NOTES: Signed as free agent by Seattle Mariners organization (April 1, 1984). .... On Seattle disabled list (April 7-May 13, 1990); included rehabilitation disability assignment to Calgary (May 3-7, 1990) and San Bernardino (May 8-12, 1990).
STATISTICAL NOTES: Led Midwest League shortstops with .969 fielding percentage in 1986.
MISCELLANEOUS: Batted righthanded only (1984-88).

Year Team (League)	Pos.	G	AB	R	H	2B	3B	HR	RBI	Avg.	SB	PO	A	E	Avg.
1984 — Butte (Pioneer)	SS-2B	15	45	7	14	2	0	0	4	.311	2	13	29	5	.894
1985 — Bellingham (Northwest)....	SS-2B	50	187	24	42	9	0	5	17	.225	4	85	175	19	.932
1986 — Wausau (Midwest)	SS-2B	105	352	60	75	13	2	4	28	.213	19	153	328	16	†.968
1987 — Salinas (California)	SS-2B	114	407	61	107	12	8	0	38	.263	25	81	295	25	.938
1988 — Vermont (Eastern)	SS	103	374	54	95	18	2	2	35	.254	30	173	268	19	*.959
— Calgary (Pacific Coast)	SS	33	107	10	24	2	3	1	12	.224	2	43	92	6	.957
1989 — Calgary (Pacific Coast)	SS	7	28	3	6	2	0	0	3	.214	0	15	14	0	1.000
— Seattle (A.L.)	SS	143	387	45	85	7	3	1	20	.220	1	208	388	18	.971
1990 — Calgary (Pacific Coast)	SS	48	150	18	35	6	2	0	8	.233	4	70	142	6	.972
— San Bernardino (Calif.)	SS	6	28	5	7	0	0	0	3	.250	1	11	21	3	.914
— Seattle (A.L.)	SS	81	255	19	63	3	2	2	18	.247	4	103	239	7	.980
1991 — Seattle (A.L.)	SS-2B	142	426	42	98	16	4	1	41	.230	7	224	422	13	.980
Major league totals (3 years)		366	1068	106	246	26	9	4	79	.230	12	535	1049	38	.977

WAGNER, HECTOR
P, ROYALS

PERSONAL: Born November 26, 1968, at Los Mamelles, Santo Domingo, Dominican Republic. .... 6-3/200. .... Throws right, bats right. .... Full name: Hector Raul Wagner.
TRANSACTIONS/CAREER NOTES: Signed as free agent by Kansas City Royals organization (May 13, 1986). .... On Omaha disabled list (August 3, 1991-remainder of season).

Year Team (League)	G	W	L	Pct.	ERA	Sv.	IP	H	R	ER	BB	SO
1987 — Sarasota Royals (Gulf Coast) ...	13	1	3	.250	3.06	0	53	63	26	18	12	28
1988 — Eugene (Northwest)	15	4	•9	.308	3.68	0	85²⁄₃	76	46	35	28	67
1989 — Appleton (Midwest)	24	6	11	.353	4.56	0	130¹⁄₃	149	79	66	29	71
1990 — Memphis (Southern)	40	12	4	.750	2.03	1	133¹⁄₃	114	37	30	41	63
— Kansas City (A.L.)	5	0	2	.000	8.10	0	23¹⁄₃	32	24	21	11	14
1991 — Omaha (American Assoc.)........	17	5	6	.455	3.44	0	86¹⁄₃	88	45	33	38	36
— Kansas City (A.L.)	2	1	1	.500	7.20	0	10	16	10	8	3	5
Major league totals (2 years)	7	1	3	.250	7.83	0	33¹⁄₃	48	34	29	14	19

WAINHOUSE, DAVE
P, EXPOS

PERSONAL: Born November 7, 1967, at Toronto. .... 6-2/185. .... Throws right, bats left. .... Full name: David Paul Wainhouse.
HIGH SCHOOL: Mercer Island (Wash.).
COLLEGE: Washington State.

TRANSACTIONS/CAREER NOTES: Selected by Montreal Expos organization in first round (19th pick overall) of free-agent draft (June 1, 1988).... On Harrisburg disabled list (April 25-May 3, 1991).
MISCELLANEOUS: Member of 1988 Canadian Olympic baseball team.

Year Team (League)	G	W	L	Pct.	ERA	Sv.	IP	H	R	ER	BB	SO
1989—West Palm Beach (Florida St.)..	13	1	5	.167	4.07	0	66⅓	75	35	30	19	26
1990—West Palm Beach (Florida St.)..	12	6	3	.667	2.11	0	76⅔	68	28	18	34	58
—Jacksonville (Southern)	17	7	7	.500	4.33	0	95⅔	97	59	46	47	59
1991—Harrisburg (Eastern)	33	2	2	.500	2.60	11	52	49	17	15	17	46
—Indianapolis (Am. Assoc.)	14	2	0	1.000	4.08	1	28⅔	28	14	13	15	13
—Montreal (N.L.)	2	0	1	.000	6.75	0	2⅔	2	2	2	4	1
Major league totals (1 year)	2	0	1	.000	6.75	0	2⅔	2	2	2	4	1

WAKAMATSU, DON
C, DODGERS

PERSONAL: Born February 22, 1963, at Hood River, Ore.... 6-2/200.... Throws right, bats right.... Full name: Wilbur Donald Wakamatsu.
HIGH SCHOOL: Hayward (Calif.).
COLLEGE: Arizona State.
TRANSACTIONS/CAREER NOTES: Selected by Cincinnati Reds organization in 11th round of free-agent draft (June 7, 1985).... Released by Reds organization (March 29, 1989).... Signed by Birmingham, Chicago White Sox organization (April 4, 1989). ... Granted free agency (October 7, 1991).... Signed by Los Angeles Dodgers (December 10, 1991).
STATISTICAL NOTES: Led Pioneer League catchers with 416 total chances in 1985.... Led Southern League catchers with .990 fielding percentage in 1989.

Year Team (League)	Pos.	G	AB	R	H	2B	3B	HR	RBI	Avg.	SB	PO	A	E	Avg.
1985—Billings (Pioneer)	C	58	196	20	49	7	0	0	24	.250	1	367	44	5	★.988
1986—Tampa (Florida State)	1B-C	112	361	41	100	18	2	1	66	.277	6	623	58	14	.980
1987—Cedar Rapids (Midwest)	C-1B	103	365	33	79	13	1	7	41	.216	3	690	69	11	.986
1988—Chattanooga (Southern)	C-1B-3B	79	235	22	56	9	1	1	26	.238	0	418	59	8	.984
1989—Birmingham (Southern)■	C-1B-3B	92	287	45	73	15	0	2	45	.254	7	503	57	8	†.986
1990—Vancouver (Pac. Coast)	C	62	187	20	49	10	0	0	13	.262	2	285	33	2	.994
1991—Vancouver (Pac. Coast)	C-1B	55	172	20	34	8	0	4	19	.198	0	267	31	3	.990
—Chicago (A.L.)	C	18	31	2	7	0	0	0	0	.226	0	47	2	0	1.000
Major league totals (1 year)		18	31	2	7	0	0	0	0	.226	0	47	2	0	1.000

WALK, BOB
P, PIRATES

PERSONAL: Born November 26, 1956, at Van Nuys, Calif.... 6-4/217.... Throws right, bats right.... Full name: Robert Vernon Walk.
HIGH SCHOOL: Hart (Calif.).
COLLEGE: College of the Canyons (Calif.).
TRANSACTIONS/CAREER NOTES: Selected by California Angels organization in fifth round of free-agent draft (January 9, 1975). ... Selected by Philadelphia Phillies organization in fifth round of free-agent draft (January 7, 1976).... Selected by Phillies organization in secondary phase of free-agent draft (June 8, 1976).... Traded by Phillies to Atlanta Braves for OF Gary Matthews (March 25, 1981).... On Atlanta disabled list (May 26-August 9, 1981).... Released by Braves (March 26, 1984).... Signed by Pittsburgh Pirates organization (April 3, 1984).... On Pittsburgh disabled list (July 23, 1984-remainder of season). ... Granted free agency (November 4, 1988).... Re-signed by Pirates (November 27, 1988).... On disabled list (June 9-24, 1989; June 20-July 14 and August 6-25, 1990).... On Pittsburgh disabled list (April 15-May 14 and July 27-September 1, 1991); included rehabilitation disability assignment to Carolina (August 28-30, 1991).... Granted free agency (November 4, 1991).... Re-signed by Pirates (December 31, 1991).
STATISTICAL NOTES: Led Carolina League with 13 hit batsmen in 1978.... Led International League pitchers with 11 complete games and tied for lead with 28 games started and 22 home runs allowed in 1983.... Led Pacific Coast League with 12 complete games in 1985.... Led N.L. with 13 wild pitches in 1988.

Year Team (League)	G	W	L	Pct.	ERA	Sv.	IP	H	R	ER	BB	SO
1977—Spartanburg (W. Carolinas)	15	6	9	.400	3.64	0	99	90	55	40	46	66
—Peninsula (Carolina)	8	0	2	.000	4.25	0	36	44	31	17	20	23
1978—Peninsula (Carolina)	26	13	8	.619	2.12	0	187	147	58	44	64	150
1979—Reading (Eastern)	24	12	7	.632	★2.24	0	185	156	62	46	77	★135
1980—Oklahoma City (Am. Assoc.)	8	5	1	.833	2.94	0	49	39	21	16	17	36
—Philadelphia (N.L.)	27	11	7	.611	4.56	0	152	163	82	77	71	94
1981—Atlanta (N.L.)■	12	1	4	.200	4.60	0	43	41	25	22	23	16
—Richmond (International)	4	2	1	.667	2.45	0	22	18	7	6	11	13
1982—Atlanta (N.L.)	32	11	9	.550	4.87	0	164⅓	179	101	89	59	84
1983—Richmond (International)	28	11	12	.478	5.21	0	★185	179	★119	★107	102	123
—Atlanta (N.L.)	1	0	0	...	7.36	0	3⅔	7	3	3	2	4
1984—Hawaii (Pacific Coast)■	18	9	5	.643	★2.26	0	127⅓	100	39	32	42	85
—Pittsburgh (N.L.)	2	1	1	.500	2.61	0	10⅓	8	5	3	4	10
1985—Hawaii (Pacific Coast)	24	★16	5	.762	★2.65	0	173	143	57	51	61	124
—Pittsburgh (N.L.)	9	2	3	.400	3.68	0	58⅔	60	27	24	18	40
1986—Pittsburgh (N.L.)	44	7	8	.467	3.75	2	141⅔	129	66	59	64	78
1987—Pittsburgh (N.L.)	39	8	2	.800	3.31	0	117	107	52	43	51	78
1988—Pittsburgh (N.L.)	32	12	10	.545	2.71	0	212⅔	183	75	64	65	81
1989—Pittsburgh (N.L.)	33	13	10	.565	4.41	0	196	208	106	96	65	83
1990—Pittsburgh (N.L.)	26	7	5	.583	3.75	1	129⅔	136	59	54	36	73
1991—Pittsburgh (N.L.)	25	9	2	.818	3.60	0	115	104	53	46	35	67
—Carolina (Southern)	1	0	1	.000	1.80	0	5	5	1	1	2	3
Major league totals (12 years)	282	82	61	.573	3.88	3	1344	1325	654	580	493	708

CHAMPIONSHIP SERIES RECORD

Year	Team (League)	G	W	L	Pct.	ERA	Sv.	IP	H	R	ER	BB	SO
1982 — Atlanta (N.L.)		1	0	0	...	9.00	0	1	2	1	1	1	1
1990 — Pittsburgh (N.L.)		2	1	1	.500	4.85	0	13	11	7	7	2	8
1991 — Pittsburgh (N.L.)		3	0	0	...	1.93	1	9⅓	5	2	2	3	5
Championship Series totals (3 years)		6	1	1	.500	3.86	1	23⅓	18	10	10	6	14

WORLD SERIES RECORD

Year	Team (League)	G	W	L	Pct.	ERA	Sv.	IP	H	R	ER	BB	SO
1980 — Philadelphia (N.L.)		1	1	0	1.000	7.71	0	7	8	6	6	3	3

ALL-STAR GAME RECORD

Year	League	W	L	Pct.	ERA	Sv.	IP	H	R	ER	BB	SO
1988 — National		0	0	...	0.00	0	⅓	0	0	0	0	0

WALKER, CHICO
OF/3B, CUBS

PERSONAL: Born November 25, 1957, at Jackson, Miss. ... 5-9/185. ... Throws right, bats both. ... Full name: Cleotha Walker.
HIGH SCHOOL: Tilden (Chicago).
TRANSACTIONS/CAREER NOTES: Selected by Boston Red Sox organization in 22nd round of free-agent draft (June 8, 1976). ... On disabled list (August 22-September 19, 1979). ... Granted free agency (October 15, 1984). ... Signed by Iowa, Chicago Cubs organization (November 9, 1984). ... Traded by Cubs organization to California Angels for P Todd Fischer (October 16, 1987). ... Granted free agency (October 15, 1988). ... Signed by Toronto Blue Jays organization (January 28, 1989). ... Granted free agency (October 22, 1989). ... Signed by Chicago Cubs organization (April 25, 1990). ... Granted free agency (December 20, 1991). ... Re-signed by Cubs (December 23, 1991).
STATISTICAL NOTES: Led Eastern League in caught stealing with 16 in 1979. ... Led International League second basemen with 667 total chances and tied for lead with 74 double plays in 1980. ... Led International League with nine intentional bases on balls received in 1984. ... Led American Association in total bases with 258 and caught stealing with 22 in 1986. ... Led American Association outfielders with 16 assists in 1986.

Year	Team (League)	Pos.	G	AB	R	H	2B	3B	HR	RBI	Avg.	SB	PO	A	E	Avg.
1976 — Elmira (New York-Penn)		2B	22	28	9	5	1	2	0	1	.179	0	9	18	3	.900
1977 — Elmira (New York-Penn)		2B-SS	64	227	26	50	4	3	1	14	.220	10	122	196	15	.955
1978 — Winter Haven (Fla. St.)		SS-3B-2B	133	480	66	134	10	6	3	52	.279	17	172	380	42	.929
1979 — Bristol (Eastern)		2B	123	498	75	132	19	★12	8	57	.265	29	252	357	23	.964
1980 — Pawtucket (Int'l)		2B	139	536	59	146	18	7	8	52	.272	21	252	★394	★21	.969
— Boston (A.L.)		2B	19	57	3	12	0	0	1	5	.211	3	15	31	2	.958
1981 — Pawtucket (Int'l)		OF-2B-3B	138	535	50	148	21	5	17	68	.277	24	209	178	13	.968
— Boston (A.L.)		2B	6	17	3	6	0	0	0	2	.353	0	4	10	0	1.000
1982 — Pawtucket (Int'l)		O-2-3-S	133	494	71	124	22	2	15	66	.251	25	209	48	11	.959
1983 — Pawtucket (Int'l)		3-O-S-2	125	442	78	119	18	1	18	56	.269	27	122	126	16	.939
— Boston (A.L.)		OF	4	5	2	2	0	0	2	1	.400	0	4	1	0	1.000
1984 — Pawtucket (Int'l)		2B-OF-3B	130	499	•91	131	26	5	18	51	.263	42	223	241	20	.959
— Boston (A.L.)		2B	3	2	1	0	0	0	0	0	.000	0	0	1	0	1.000
1985 — Iowa (American Assoc.)■		OF-3B	89	331	47	94	17	8	5	46	.284	42	177	6	5	.973
— Chicago (N.L.)		2B	21	12	3	1	0	0	0	0	.083	1	4	0	0	1.000
1986 — Iowa (American Assoc.)		OF-2B	138	530	97	•158	30	11	16	65	.298	•67	286	†38	8	.976
— Chicago (N.L.)		OF	28	101	21	28	3	2	1	7	.277	15	42	1	2	.956
1987 — Chicago (N.L.)		OF-3B	47	105	15	21	4	0	0	7	.200	11	37	0	1	.974
— Iowa (American Assoc.)		O-2-3-S	90	315	64	77	13	3	8	31	.244	28	146	90	8	.967
1988 — Edmonton (Pac. Coast)■		OF	79	304	58	88	17	4	7	39	.289	25	174	5	7	.962
— California (A.L.)		OF-2B-3B	33	78	8	12	1	0	0	2	.154	2	33	20	2	.964
1989 — Syracuse (International)■		OF-2B	123	431	61	103	11	5	12	63	.239	37	177	30	3	.986
1990 — Charlotte (Southern)■		OF-2B	88	310	49	82	15	1	12	45	.265	10	107	50	4	.975
— Iowa (American Assoc.)		OF	32	114	30	41	7	1	6	19	.360	9	37	6	2	.956
1991 — Chicago (N.L.)		3B-OF-2B	124	374	51	96	10	1	6	34	.257	13	106	89	8	.961
American League totals (5 years)			65	159	17	32	1	2	1	10	.201	5	56	63	4	.967
National League totals (4 years)			220	592	90	146	17	3	7	48	.247	40	189	90	11	.962
Major league totals (9 years)			285	751	107	178	18	5	8	58	.237	45	245	153	15	.964

WALKER, LARRY
OF/1B, EXPOS

PERSONAL: Born December 1, 1966, at Maple Ridge, British Columbia. ... 6-3/215. ... Throws right, bats left. ... Full name: Larry Kenneth Robert Walker.
HIGH SCHOOL: Maple Ridge Senior Secondary School (British Columbia).
TRANSACTIONS/CAREER NOTES: Signed as free agent by Montreal Expos organization (November 14, 1984). ... On disabled list (April 4, 1988-entire season and June 28-July 13, 1991).

Year	Team (League)	Pos.	G	AB	R	H	2B	3B	HR	RBI	Avg.	SB	PO	A	E	Avg.
1985 — Utica (New York-Penn)		1B-3B	62	215	24	48	8	2	2	26	.223	12	354	62	8	.981
1986 — Burlington (Midwest)		OF-3B	95	332	67	96	12	6	29	74	.289	16	106	51	10	.940
— West Palm Beach (FSL)		OF	38	113	20	32	7	5	4	16	.283	2	44	5	0	1.000
1987 — Jacksonville (Southern)		OF	128	474	91	136	25	7	26	83	.287	24	263	9	9	.968
1988 —							Did not play									
1989 — Indianapolis (A.A.)		OF	114	385	68	104	18	2	12	59	.270	36	241	★18	★11	.959
— Montreal (N.L.)		OF	20	47	4	8	0	0	0	4	.170	1	19	2	0	1.000

Year	Team (League)	Pos.	G	AB	R	H	2B	3B	HR	RBI	Avg.	SB	PO	A	E	Avg.
							BATTING							FIELDING		
1990 —Montreal (N.L.)............		OF	133	419	59	101	18	3	19	51	.241	21	249	12	4	.985
1991 —Montreal (N.L.)............		OF-1B	137	487	59	141	30	2	16	64	.290	14	536	36	6	.990
Major league totals (3 years)................			290	953	122	250	48	5	35	119	.262	36	804	50	10	.988

WALKER, MIKE
P, TIGERS

PERSONAL: Born October 4, 1966, at Brooksville, Fla.... 6-1/195.... Throws right, bats right. ... Full name: Michael Charles Walker.
HIGH SCHOOL: Hernando (Brooksville, Fla.).
COLLEGE: Seminole Community College (Fla.).
TRANSACTIONS/CAREER NOTES: Selected by Montreal Expos organization in 14th round of free-agent draft (June 4, 1984).... Selected by Expos organization in secondary phase of free-agent draft (January 9, 1985).... Selected by Cleveland Indians organization in second round of free-agent draft (January 14, 1986).... Released by Indians (November 27, 1991).... Signed by Detroit Tigers organization (December 19, 1991).
STATISTICAL NOTES: Led Midwest League with eight complete games in 1987.... Led Eastern League pitchers with 17 wild pitches and tied for lead with 27 games started in 1988.... Led Pacific Coast League pitchers with 21 home runs allowed and 14 hit batsmen and tied for lead with 28 games started in 1989.

Year	Team (League)	G	W	L	Pct.	ERA	Sv.	IP	H	R	ER	BB	SO
1986 —Burlington (Appalachian).........		14	4	6	.400	5.89	0	70⅓	75	*65	*46	45	42
1987 —Waterloo (Midwest)		23	11	7	.611	3.59	0	145⅓	133	74	58	68	144
—Kinston (Carolina).....................		3	3	0	1.000	2.61	0	20⅔	17	7	6	14	19
1988 —Williamsport (N.Y.-Penn).........		28	*15	7	.682	3.72	0	*164⅓	162	82	68	74	*144
—Cleveland (A.L.)......................		3	0	1	.000	7.27	0	8⅔	8	7	7	10	7
1989 —Colorado Springs (Pac. Coast) ..		28	6	*15	.286	5.79	0	168	193	*124	*108	*93	97
1990 —Colorado Springs (Pac. Coast) ..		18	2	7	.222	5.58	1	79	96	62	49	36	50
—Canton/Akron (Eastern)...........		1	1	0	1.000	0.00	0	7	4	0	0	4	3
—Cleveland (A.L.)		18	2	6	.250	4.88	0	75⅔	82	49	41	42	34
1991 —Canton/Akron (Eastern)		45	9	4	.692	2.79	11	77⅓	68	36	24	45	42
—Cleveland (A.L.)		5	0	1	.000	2.08	0	4⅓	6	1	1	2	2
Major league totals (3 years)		26	2	8	.200	4.97	0	88⅔	96	57	49	54	43

WALLACH, TIM
3B, EXPOS

PERSONAL: Born September 14, 1957, at Huntington Park, Calif.... 6-3/202.... Throws right, bats right.... Full name: Timothy Charles Wallach.
HIGH SCHOOL: University (Irvine, Calif.).
COLLEGE: Saddleback Junior College (Calif.) and Cal State Fullerton.
TRANSACTIONS/CAREER NOTES: Selected by California Angels organization in eighth round of free-agent draft (June 6, 1978). ... Selected by Montreal Expos organization in first round (10th pick overall) of free-agent draft (June 5, 1979).
RECORDS/HONORS: Named College Player of the Year by THE SPORTING NEWS (1979).... Named first baseman on THE SPORTING NEWS college All-America team (1979).... Named third baseman on THE SPORTING NEWS N.L. All-Star team (1985 and 1987).... Won N.L. Gold Glove at third base (1985, 1988 and 1990).... Named third baseman on THE SPORTING NEWS N.L. Silver Slugger team (1985 and 1987).
STATISTICAL NOTES: Hit home run in first major league at-bat (September 6, 1980).... Led American Association with 295 total bases and tied for lead with nine sacrifice flies in 1980.... Led N.L. third basemen with 132 putouts in 1982.... Led N.L. third basemen with 162 putouts and 332 assists in 1984.... Led N.L. third basemen with 515 total chances in 1984 and 549 in 1985. ... Led N.L. third basemen with 29 double plays in 1984, 34 in 1985 and tied for lead with 31 in 1988.... Led N.L. in being hit by pitch with 10 in 1986.... Tied for N.L. lead with 16 game-winning RBIs in 1987.... Hit three home runs in a game (May 4, 1987).... Led N.L. third basemen with 128 putouts in 1987 and 123 in 1988.... Led N.L. in grounding into double plays with 21 in 1989.

Year	Team (League)	Pos.	G	AB	R	H	2B	3B	HR	RBI	Avg.	SB	PO	A	E	Avg.
							BATTING							FIELDING		
1979 —Memphis (Southern)	1B-3B	75	257	50	84	16	4	18	51	.327	0	290	35	4	.988
1980 —Denver (Am. Assoc.)	3B-OF-1B	134	512	103	144	29	7	36	124	.281	1	222	147	21	.946
—Montreal (N.L.)	OF-1B	5	11	1	2	0	0	1	2	.182	0	12	0	0	1.000
1981 —Montreal (N.L.)	OF-1B-3B	71	212	19	50	9	1	4	13	.236	0	207	31	1	.996
1982 —Montreal (N.L.)	3B-OF-1B	158	596	89	160	31	3	28	97	.268	6	†132	287	23	.948
1983 —Montreal (N.L.)	3B	156	581	54	156	33	3	19	70	.269	0	*151	262	19	.956
1984 —Montreal (N.L.)	3B-SS	160	582	55	143	25	4	18	72	.246	3	†162	†332	21	.959
1985 —Montreal (N.L.)	3B	155	569	70	148	36	3	22	81	.260	9	*148	*383	18	.967
1986 —Montreal (N.L.)	3B	134	480	50	112	22	1	18	71	.233	8	94	270	16	.958
1987 —Montreal (N.L.)	3B-P	153	593	89	177	*42	4	26	123	.298	9	†128	292	21	.952
1988 —Montreal (N.L.)	3B-2B	159	592	52	152	32	5	12	69	.257	2	†124	329	18	.962
1989 —Montreal (N.L.)	3B-P	154	573	76	159	*42	0	13	77	.277	3	113	302	18	.958
1990 —Montreal (N.L.)	3B	161	626	69	185	37	5	21	98	.296	6	128	309	21	.954
1991 —Montreal (N.L.)	3B	151	577	60	130	22	1	13	73	.225	2	107	310	14	*.968
Major league totals (12 years)		1617	5992	684	1574	331	30	195	846	.263	48	1506	3107	190	.960

DIVISION SERIES RECORD

Year	Team (League)	Pos.	G	AB	R	H	2B	3B	HR	RBI	Avg.	SB	PO	A	E	Avg.
							BATTING							FIELDING		
1981 —Montreal (N.L.)	OF	4	4	1	1	1	0	0	0	.250	0	4	0	0	1.000

CHAMPIONSHIP SERIES RECORD

Year	Team (League)	Pos.	G	AB	R	H	2B	3B	HR	RBI	Avg.	SB	PO	A	E	Avg.
							BATTING							FIELDING		
1981 —Montreal (N.L.)	PH	1	1	0	0	0	0	0	0	.000	0	0	0	0	...

ALL-STAR GAME RECORD

Year	League	Pos.	AB	R	H	2B	3B	HR	RBI	Avg.	SB	PO	A	E	Avg.
1984 —National		3B	1	0	0	0	0	0	0	.000	0	0	0	0	...
1985 —National		3B	2	1	1	1	0	0	0	.500	0	1	1	0	1.000
1987 —National		3B	3	0	0	0	0	0	0	.000	0	0	2	0	1.000
1989 —National		3B	1	0	0	0	0	0	0	.000	0	0	0	0	...
1990 —National		3B	2	0	0	0	0	0	0	.000	0	0	0	0	...
All-Star Game totals (5 years)			9	1	1	1	0	0	0	.111	0	1	3	0	1.000

RECORD AS PITCHER

Year	Team (League)	G	W	L	Pct.	ERA	Sv.	IP	H	R	ER	BB	SO
1987 —Montreal (N.L.)	1	0	0	...	0.00	0	1	1	0	0	0	0
1989 —Montreal (N.L.)	1	0	0	...	9.00	0	1	2	1	1	0	0
Major league totals (2 years)	2	0	0	...	4.50	0	2	3	1	1	0	0

WALLING, DENNY
IF/OF, ASTROS

PERSONAL: Born April 17, 1954, at Neptune, N.J. . . . 6-1/185. . . . Throws right, bats left. . . . Full name: Dennis Martin Walling. . . . Brother of Gregory Walling, minor league outfielder (1967).
HIGH SCHOOL: Howell (Farmingdale, N.J.).
COLLEGE: Brookdale Community College (N.J.) and Clemson.
TRANSACTIONS/CAREER NOTES: Selected by San Francisco Giants organization in eighth round of free-agent draft (June 5, 1974). . . . Selected by Oakland Athletics organization in secondary phase of free-agent draft (June 4, 1975). . . . On San Jose disabled list (April 18-June 15, 1977). . . . Traded by A's organization with cash to Houston Astros organization for OF Willie Crawford (June 15, 1977). . . . Granted free agency (November 7, 1983). . . . Re-signed by Astros (December 20, 1983). . . . On disabled list (May 2-24, 1984 and March 28-April 17, 1987). . . . On Houston disabled list (June 20-August 6, 1988); included rehabilitation disability assignment to Tucson (July 29-August 3, 1988). . . . Traded by Astros to St. Louis Cardinals for P Bob Forsch (August 31, 1988). . . . On disabled list (May 24-June 8, 1989). . . . Granted free agency (November 5, 1990). . . . Signed by Texas Rangers (April 7, 1991). . . . On Texas disabled list (April 13-May 4, 1991); included rehabilitation disability assignment to Oklahoma City (April 29-May 4, 1991). . . . Released by Rangers (June 22, 1991). . . . Signed by Astros organization (January 27, 1992).
RECORDS/HONORS: Named outfielder on THE SPORTING NEWS college All-America team (1975).

Year	Team (League)	Pos.	G	AB	R	H	2B	3B	HR	RBI	Avg.	SB	PO	A	E	Avg.
1975 —Oakland (A.L.)		OF	6	8	0	1	1	0	0	2	.125	0	3	0	0	1.000
1976 —Chattanooga (Southern)		OF	115	369	48	95	15	5	9	42	.257	20	241	8	2 *.992
—Oakland (A.L.)		OF	3	11	1	3	0	0	0	0	.273	0	8	0	1	.889
1977 —San Jose (Pacific Coast)		OF	3	10	1	3	0	0	0	4	.300	0	8	0	0	1.000
—Charleston, W.Va. (Int'l)■		OF	29	89	17	31	4	1	4	14	.348	2	66	0	0	1.000
—Houston (N.L.)		OF	6	21	1	6	0	1	0	6	.286	0	14	0	0	1.000
1978 —Houston (N.L.)		OF	120	247	30	62	11	3	3	36	.251	9	140	4	3	.980
1979 —Houston (N.L.)		OF	82	147	21	48	8	4	3	31	.327	3	65	2	1	.985
1980 —Houston (N.L.)		1B-OF	100	284	30	85	6	5	3	29	.299	4	525	31	6	.989
1981 —Houston (N.L.)		1B-OF	65	158	23	37	6	0	5	23	.234	2	226	9	2	.992
1982 —Houston (N.L.)		OF-1B	85	146	22	30	4	1	1	14	.205	4	167	11	1	.994
1983 —Houston (N.L.)		1B-3B-OF	100	135	24	40	5	3	3	19	.296	2	134	29	6	.964
1984 —Houston (N.L.)		3B-1B-OF	87	249	37	70	11	5	3	31	.281	7	116	102	7	.969
1985 —Houston (N.L.)		3B-1B-OF	119	345	44	93	20	1	7	45	.270	5	326	124	12	.974
1986 —Houston (N.L.)		3B-OF-1B	130	382	54	119	23	1	13	58	.312	1	108	161	9	.968
1987 —Houston (N.L.)		3B-1B-OF	110	325	45	92	21	4	5	33	.283	5	175	119	10	.967
1988 —Houston-St. Louis (N.L.)■		3B-OF-1B	84	234	22	56	13	2	1	21	.239	2	73	112	9	.954
—Tucson (Pacific Coast)		3B	5	16	2	3	1	0	0	4	.188	0	4	10	1	.933
1989 —St. Louis (N.L.)		1B-3B-OF	69	79	9	24	7	0	1	11	.304	0	67	9	4	.950
1990 —St. Louis (N.L.)		3B-1B-OF	78	127	7	28	5	0	1	19	.220	0	103	26	0	1.000
1991 —Texas (A.L.)■		3B-OF	24	44	1	4	1	0	0	2	.091	0	10	13	1	.958
—Oklahoma City (A.A.)		DH	3	10	0	5	1	0	0	3	.500	0	0	0	0	...
American League totals (3 years)			33	63	2	8	2	0	0	4	.127	0	21	13	2	.944
National League totals (14 years)			1235	2879	369	790	140	30	49	376	.274	44	2239	739	70	.977
Major league totals (17 years)			1268	2942	371	798	142	30	49	380	.271	44	2260	752	72	.977

DIVISION SERIES RECORD

Year	Team (League)	Pos.	G	AB	R	H	2B	3B	HR	RBI	Avg.	SB	PO	A	E	Avg.
1981 —Houston (N.L.)		PH-1B	3	6	0	2	0	0	0	1	.333	0	6	1	1	.875

CHAMPIONSHIP SERIES RECORD

Year	Team (League)	Pos.	G	AB	R	H	2B	3B	HR	RBI	Avg.	SB	PO	A	E	Avg.
1980 —Houston (N.L.)		1B-OF-PH	3	9	2	1	0	0	0	2	.111	0	6	0	0	1.000
1986 —Houston (N.L.)		3B-PH	5	19	1	3	1	0	0	2	.158	0	3	6	0	1.000
Championship Series totals (2 years)			8	28	3	4	1	0	0	4	.143	0	9	6	0	1.000

WALTON, BRUCE
P, ATHLETICS

PERSONAL: Born December 25, 1962, at Bakersfield, Calif.... 6-2/195.... Throws right, bats right.... Full name: Bruce Kenneth Walton. **HIGH SCHOOL:** North Bakersfield (Calif.). **COLLEGE:** Hawaii.
TRANSACTIONS/CAREER NOTES: Selected by St. Louis Cardinals organization in 10th round of free-agent draft (June 8, 1981). ... Selected by Oakland Athletics organization in 16th round of free-agent draft (June 3, 1985).
STATISTICAL NOTES: Tied for California League lead in games started by pitcher with 27 in 1986.

Year	Team (League)	G	W	L	Pct.	ERA	Sv.	IP	H	R	ER	BB	SO
1985	Pocatello (Pioneer)	18	3	7	.300	4.11	3	76⅔	89	46	35	27	69
1986	Madison (Midwest)	1	0	0	...	5.40	0	5	5	3	3	1	1
	Modesto (California)	27	13	7	.650	4.09	0	176	*204	96	80	41	107
1987	Modesto (California)	16	8	6	.571	2.88	0	106⅓	97	44	34	27	84
	Huntsville (Southern)	18	2	2	.500	3.10	2	58	61	24	20	13	40
1988	Huntsville (Southern)	42	4	5	.444	4.56	3	116⅓	126	64	59	23	82
1989	Tacoma (Pacific Coast)	32	8	6	.571	3.76	1	107⅔	118	59	45	27	76
1990	Tacoma (Pacific Coast)	46	5	5	.500	3.11	7	98⅓	103	42	34	23	67
1991	Tacoma (Pacific Coast)	38	1	1	.500	1.35	20	46⅔	39	11	7	5	49
	Oakland (A.L.)	12	1	0	1.000	6.23	0	13	11	9	9	6	10
Major league totals (1 year)		12	1	0	1.000	6.23	0	13	11	9	9	6	10

WALTON, JEROME
OF, CUBS

PERSONAL: Born July 8, 1965, at Newnan, Ga.... 6-1/175.... Throws right, bats right.... Full name: Jerome O'Terrell Walton. **HIGH SCHOOL:** Enterprise (Ala.). **COLLEGE:** Enterprise State Junior College (Ala.).
TRANSACTIONS/CAREER NOTES: Selected by Chicago Cubs organization in second round of free-agent draft (January 14, 1986). ... On Chicago disabled list (May 11-June 11, 1989); included rehabilitation disability assignment to Iowa (June 6-11, 1989). ... On Chicago disabled list (June 18-August 2, 1990); included rehabilitation disability assignment to Iowa (July 29-August 1, 1990).
RECORDS/HONORS: Named N.L. Rookie Player of the Year by THE SPORTING NEWS (1989).... Named N.L. Rookie of the Year by Baseball Writers' Association of America (1989).
STATISTICAL NOTES: Led Appalachian League outfielders with 128 putouts and 131 total chances and tied for lead with two double plays in 1986.... Led Midwest League in caught stealing with 25 in 1987.

Year	Team (League)	Pos.	G	AB	R	H	2B	3B	HR	RBI	Avg.	SB	PO	A	E	Avg.
1986	Wytheville (Appal.)	OF-3B	62	229	48	66	7	4	5	34	.288	21	+130	7	3	.979
1987	Peoria (Midwest)	OF	128	472	102	158	24	11	6	38	.335	49	255	9	7	.974
1988	Pittsfield (Eastern)	OF	120	414	64	137	26	2	3	49	.331	42	270	11	2	*.993
1989	Chicago (N.L.)	OF	116	475	64	139	23	3	5	46	.293	24	289	2	3	.990
	Iowa (American Assoc.)	OF	4	18	4	6	1	0	1	3	.333	2	8	0	0	1.000
1990	Chicago (N.L.)	OF	101	392	63	103	16	2	2	21	.263	14	247	3	6	.977
	Iowa (American Assoc.)	OF	4	16	3	3	0	0	1	1	.188	0	6	1	0	1.000
1991	Chicago (N.L.)	OF	123	270	42	59	13	1	5	17	.219	7	170	2	3	.983
Major league totals (3 years)			340	1137	169	301	52	6	12	84	.265	45	706	7	12	.983

CHAMPIONSHIP SERIES RECORD
CHAMPIONSHIP SERIES NOTES: Shares records for most at-bats in one inning—2; hits in one inning—2; and singles in one inning—2 (October 5, 1989, first inning).

Year	Team (League)	Pos.	G	AB	R	H	2B	3B	HR	RBI	Avg.	SB	PO	A	E	Avg.
1989	Chicago (N.L.)	OF	5	22	4	8	0	0	0	2	.364	0	11	0	0	1.000

WAPNICK, STEVE
P, WHITE SOX

PERSONAL: Born September 25, 1965, at Panorama City, Calif.... 6-2/200.... Throws right, bats right.... Full name: Steven Lee Wapnick. **COLLEGE:** Moorpark College (Calif.) and Fresno State.
TRANSACTIONS/CAREER NOTES: Selected by San Diego Padres organization in second round of free-agent draft (January 9, 1985).... Selected by Oakland Athletics organization in secondary phase of free-agent draft (June 3, 1985).... Selected by Toronto Blue Jays organization in 30th round of free-agent draft (June 2, 1987).... Drafted by Detroit Tigers (December 4, 1989).... Returned to Syracuse, Blue Jays organization (May 1, 1990).... Traded by Blue Jays to Chicago White Sox (September 4, 1991), completing deal in which Blue Jays traded OF Shawn Jeter and a player to be named later to White Sox for OF Cory Snyder (July 14, 1991).

Year	Team (League)	G	W	L	Pct.	ERA	Sv.	IP	H	R	ER	BB	SO
1987	St. Catharines (N.Y.-Penn)	20	3	4	.429	3.02	1	65⅔	53	28	22	21	63
1988	Myrtle Beach (South Atlantic)	*54	4	3	.571	2.24	12	60⅓	44	18	15	31	69
1989	Dunedin (Florida State)	24	4	0	1.000	2.05	7	66	48	19	15	22	59
	Knoxville (Southern)	12	1	0	1.000	0.49	2	18⅓	12	1	1	7	20
	Syracuse (International)	6	1	0	1.000	0.69	0	13	9	1	1	5	10
1990	Detroit (A.L.) ■	4	0	0	...	6.43	0	7	8	5	5	10	6
	Syracuse (International) ■	11	0	1	.000	5.06	2	16	16	9	9	6	19
1991	Syracuse (International)	53	6	3	.667	2.76	*20	71⅔	68	23	22	25	58
	Chicago (A.L.) ■	6	0	1	.000	1.80	0	5	2	1	1	4	1
Major league totals (2 years)		10	0	1	.000	4.50	0	12	10	6	6	14	7

WARD, DUANE
P, BLUE JAYS

PERSONAL: Born May 28, 1964, at Parkview, N.M. . . . 6-4/215. . . . Throws right, bats right. . . . Full name: Roy Duane Ward.
HIGH SCHOOL: Farmington (N.M.).
TRANSACTIONS/CAREER NOTES: Selected by Atlanta Braves organization in first round (ninth pick overall) of free-agent draft (June 7, 1982). . . . On disabled list (May 7-29 and July 14-August 7, 1984). . . . Traded by Braves organization to Toronto Blue Jays for P Doyle Alexander (July 6, 1986).

Year	Team (League)	G	W	L	Pct.	ERA	Sv.	IP	H	R	ER	BB	SO
1982	—Bradenton Braves (GCL)	8	2	3	.400	4.53	0	45⅔	45	25	23	24	31
	—Anderson (South Atlantic)	5	1	2	.333	5.32	0	23⅔	24	16	14	15	18
1983	—Durham (Carolina)	28	11	13	.458	4.29	0	178⅓	165	103	85	75	115
1984	—Greenville (Southern)	21	4	9	.308	4.99	0	104⅔	108	71	58	57	54
1985	—Greenville (Southern)	28	11	10	.524	4.20	0	150	141	83	70	*105	100
	—Richmond (International)	5	0	1	.000	11.81	0	5⅓	8	9	7	8	3
1986	—Atlanta (N.L.)	10	0	1	.000	7.31	0	16	22	13	13	8	8
	—Richmond-Syracuse (Int'l)■	20	7	5	.583	3.98	0	117⅔	125	56	52	52	67
	—Toronto (A.L.)	2	0	1	.000	13.50	0	2	3	4	3	4	1
1987	—Toronto (A.L.)	12	1	0	1.000	6.94	0	11⅔	14	9	9	12	10
	—Syracuse (International)	46	2	2	.500	3.89	14	76⅓	59	35	33	42	67
1988	—Toronto (A.L.)	64	9	3	.750	3.30	15	111⅓	101	46	41	60	91
1989	—Toronto (A.L.)	66	4	10	.286	3.77	15	114⅔	94	55	48	58	122
1990	—Toronto (A.L.)	73	2	8	.200	3.45	11	127⅔	101	51	49	42	112
1991	—Toronto (A.L.)	*81	7	6	.538	2.77	23	107⅓	80	36	33	33	132
	American League totals (6 years)	298	23	28	.451	3.47	64	475	393	201	183	209	468
	National League totals (1 year)	10	0	1	.000	7.31	0	16	22	13	13	8	8
	Major league totals (6 years)	308	23	29	.442	3.59	64	491	415	214	196	217	476

CHAMPIONSHIP SERIES RECORD

Year	Team (League)	G	W	L	Pct.	ERA	Sv.	IP	H	R	ER	BB	SO
1989	—Toronto (A.L.)	2	0	0	. . .	7.36	0	3⅔	6	3	3	3	5
1991	—Toronto (A.L.)	2	0	1	.000	6.23	1	4⅓	4	3	3	1	6
	Championship Series totals (2 years)	4	0	1	.000	6.75	1	8	10	6	6	4	11

WARD, KEVIN
OF/1B, PADRES

PERSONAL: Born September 28, 1961, at Lansdale, Pa. . . . 6-1/195. . . . Throws right, bats right. . . . Full name: Kevin Michael Ward.
HIGH SCHOOL: Central Bucks (Doylestown, Pa.).
COLLEGE: Arizona.
TRANSACTIONS/CAREER NOTES: Selected by St. Louis Cardinals organization in 29th round of free-agent draft (June 7, 1982). . . . Selected by Philadelphia Phillies organization in sixth round of free-agent draft (June 6, 1983). . . . On disabled list (June 2, 1985-remainder of season and April 11-25, 1986). . . . Granted free agency (October 15, 1987). . . . Signed by Oakland Athletics organization (November 11, 1988). . . . Granted free agency (October 15, 1990). . . . Signed by San Diego Padres organization (January 28, 1991).
STATISTICAL NOTES: Led Pacific Coast League outfielders with 11 errors in 1990.

								BATTING						FIELDING			
Year	Team (League)	Pos.	G	AB	R	H	2B	3B	HR	RBI	Avg.	SB	PO	A	E	Avg.
1983	—Bend (Northwest)	OF	55	199	33	61	12	2	2	29	.307	18	70	3	•9	.890
1984	—Peninsula (Carolina)	OF	130	456	84	119	18	5	13	69	.261	21	217	4	10	.957
1985	—Reading (Eastern)	OF	42	132	23	40	9	6	1	21	.303	7	84	1	0	1.000
1986	—Reading (Eastern)	OF	119	398	79	109	27	6	7	59	.274	28	155	3	5	.969
1987	—Reading (Eastern)	OF	16	56	9	14	5	1	0	6	.250	5	30	0	2	.938
	—Maine (International)	OF	106	326	48	68	13	3	13	37	.209	14	151	7	7	.958
1988	—Maine (International)	OF	134	456	60	105	22	8	11	63	.230	17	234	6	5	.980
1989	—Huntsville (Southern)■	OF	27	84	20	26	4	4	3	18	.310	15	42	5	0	1.000
1990	—Tacoma (Pacific Coast)	OF-1B	123	421	83	125	30	14	10	60	.297	24	169	7	†12	.936
1991	—Las Vegas (Pac. Coast)■	OF	83	276	51	89	17	6	6	43	.322	10	129	3	5	.964
	—San Diego (N.L.)	OF	44	107	13	26	7	2	2	8	.243	1	54	0	1	.982
	Major league totals (1 year)		44	107	13	26	7	2	2	8	.243	1	54	0	1	.982

WARD, TURNER
OF, BLUE JAYS

PERSONAL: Born April 11, 1965, at Orlando, Fla. . . . 6-2/200. . . . Throws right, bats both. . . . Full name: Turner Max Ward.
HIGH SCHOOL: Satsuma (Ala.).
COLLEGE: South Alabama.
TRANSACTIONS/CAREER NOTES: Selected by New York Yankees organization in 18th round of free-agent draft (June 2, 1986). . . . Traded by Yankees organization with C Joel Skinner to Cleveland Indians organization for OF Mel Hall (March 19, 1989). . . . On Sarasota Indians disabled list (April 7-July 24, 1989). . . . Traded by Indians with P Tom Candiotti to Toronto Blue Jays for P Denis Boucher, OF Glenallen Hill, OF Mark Whiten and a player to be named later (June 27, 1991); Indians acquired cash instead of player to complete deal (October 15, 1991).
STATISTICAL NOTES: Led Pacific Coast League outfielders with 292 putouts and 308 total chances in 1990.

								BATTING						FIELDING			
Year	Team (League)	Pos.	G	AB	R	H	2B	3B	HR	RBI	Avg.	SB	PO	A	E	Avg.
1986	—Oneonta (N.Y.-Penn)	OF-1B-3B	63	221	42	62	4	1	1	19	.281	6	97	6	5	.954
1987	—Fort Lauderdale (FSL)	OF-3B	130	493	83	145	15	2	7	55	.294	25	332	11	8	.977

Year	Team (League)	Pos.	G	AB	R	H	2B	3B	HR	RBI	Avg.	SB	PO	A	E	Avg.
1988 —Columbus (Int'l)		OF	134	490	55	123	24	1	7	50	.251	28	223	5	1	*.996
1989 —Sarasota Indians (GCL)■..		DH	4	15	2	3	0	0	0	1	.200	1	0	0	0	...
—Canton/Akron (Eastern) ..		OF	30	93	19	28	5	1	0	3	.301	1	2	0	0	1.000
1990 —Colorado Springs (PCL)		OF-2B	133	495	89	148	24	9	6	65	.299	22	†292	7	9	.971
—Cleveland (A.L.)		OF	14	46	10	16	2	1	1	10	.348	3	20	2	1	.957
1991 —Clev.-Toronto (A.L.)■.......		OF	48	113	12	27	7	0	0	7	.239	0	70	1	0	1.000
—Colorado Springs (PCL) ...		OF	14	51	5	10	1	1	1	3	.196	2	30	0	1	.968
—Syracuse (International) ..		OF	59	218	40	72	11	3	7	32	.330	9	136	5	0	1.000
Major league totals (2 years)			62	159	22	43	9	1	1	17	.270	3	90	3	1	.989

WASSENAAR, ROB

P, TWINS

PERSONAL: Born April 28, 1965, at Denver. . . . 6-2/200. . . . Throws right, bats right. . . . Full name: Robert Michael Wassenaar.
HIGH SCHOOL: Edina (Minn.).
COLLEGE: Stanford.
TRANSACTIONS/CAREER NOTES: Selected by California Angels organization in 21st round of free-agent draft (June 2, 1987). . . . Traded by Angels organization with P Mike Cook and 1B Paul Sorrento to Minnesota Twins organization for P Kevin Trudeau and P Bert Blyleven (November 3, 1988).

Year	Team (League)	G	W	L	Pct.	ERA	Sv.	IP	H	R	ER	BB	SO
1987 —Salem (Northwest)	31	3	4	.429	2.14	8	54⅔	48	18	13	18	65
1988 —Quad City (Midwest)	48	2	5	.286	3.14	11	48⅔	47	24	17	14	50
1989 —Visalia (California)■.................	28	6	7	.462	3.49	3	80	88	38	31	29	60
—Orlando (Southern)	13	5	5	.500	4.85	0	81⅔	93	51	44	26	47
1990 —Orlando (Southern)	52	8	5	.615	2.98	6	96⅔	85	39	32	20	65
1991 —Orlando (Southern)	15	2	2	.500	1.44	1	25	18	6	4	7	2
—Portland (Pacific Coast)	40	4	4	.500	3.26	5	77⅓	75	31	28	25	62

WAYNE, GARY

P, TWINS

PERSONAL: Born November 30, 1962, at Dearborn, Mich. . . . 6-3/200. . . . Throws left, bats left. . . . Full name: Gary Anthony Wayne.
HIGH SCHOOL: Crestwood (Dearborn Heights, Mich.).
COLLEGE: Michigan.
TRANSACTIONS/CAREER NOTES: Selected by Oakland A's organization in 23rd round of free-agent draft (June 6, 1983). . . . Selected by Montreal Expos organization in fourth round of free-agent draft (June 4, 1984). . . . On disabled list (April 7-August 24, 1988). . . . Drafted by Minnesota Twins (December 5, 1988).

Year	Team (League)	G	W	L	Pct.	ERA	Sv.	IP	H	R	ER	BB	SO
1984 —West Palm Beach (Florida St.) ..	13	3	5	.375	3.87	0	74⅓	70	38	32	49	46
1985 —Jacksonville (Southern)	21	3	12	.200	5.29	0	102	108	67	60	70	62
—West Palm Beach (Florida St.) ..	8	2	2	.500	5.58	0	30⅔	37	23	19	22	18
1986 —West Palm Beach (Florida St.) ..	47	2	5	.286	1.61	*25	61⅓	48	16	11	25	55
1987 —Jacksonville (Southern)	56	5	1	.833	2.35	10	80⅓	56	23	21	35	78
1988 —Indianapolis (Am. Assoc.)	8	0	0	...	6.14	1	7⅓	9	5	5	3	6
1989 —Minnesota (A.L.)■	60	3	4	.429	3.30	1	71	55	28	26	36	41
1990 —Minnesota (A.L.)	38	1	1	.500	4.19	1	38⅔	38	19	18	13	28
—Portland (Pacific Coast)	22	2	4	.333	3.41	5	31⅔	29	14	12	13	30
1991 —Portland (Pacific Coast)	51	4	5	.444	2.79	8	67⅔	63	27	21	31	66
—Minnesota (A.L.)	8	1	0	1.000	5.11	1	12⅓	11	7	7	4	7
Major league totals (3 years)	106	5	5	.500	3.76	3	122	104	54	51	53	76

WEATHERS, DAVE

P, BLUE JAYS

PERSONAL: Born September 25, 1969, at Lawrenceburg, Tenn. . . . 6-3/205. . . . Throws right, bats right. . . . Full name: John David Weathers.
HIGH SCHOOL: Loretto (Tenn.).
COLLEGE: Motlow State Community College (Tenn.).
TRANSACTIONS/CAREER NOTES: Selected by Toronto Blue Jays organization in third round of free-agent draft (June 1, 1988).
STATISTICAL NOTES: Led South Atlantic League pitchers with 31 games started in 1989. . . . Tied for Florida State League lead in games started by pitcher with 27 in 1990.

Year	Team (League)	G	W	L	Pct.	ERA	Sv.	IP	H	R	ER	BB	SO
1988 —St. Catharines (N.Y.-Penn)	15	4	4	.500	3.02	0	62⅔	58	30	21	26	36
1989 —Myrtle Beach (South Atlantic) ..	31	11	•13	.458	3.86	0	172⅔	163	99	74	86	111
1990 —Dunedin (Florida State)	27	10	7	.588	3.70	0	158	158	82	65	59	96
1991 —Knoxville (Southern)	24	10	7	.588	2.45	0	139⅓	121	51	38	49	114
—Toronto (A.L.)	15	1	0	1.000	4.91	0	14⅔	15	9	8	17	13
Major league totals (1 year)	15	1	0	1.000	4.91	0	14⅔	15	9	8	17	13

WEBSTER, LENNY

C, TWINS

PERSONAL: Born February 10, 1965, at New Orleans. . . . 5-9/192. . . . Throws right, bats right. . . . Full name: Leonard Irell Webster.
HIGH SCHOOL: Lutcher (La.).
COLLEGE: Grambling State.

TRANSACTIONS/CAREER NOTES: Selected by Minnesota Twins organization in 16th round of free-agent draft (June 7, 1982).... Selected by Twins organization in 21st round of free-agent draft (June 3, 1985).
RECORDS/HONORS: Named Midwest League Most Valuable Player (1988).

Year	Team (League)	Pos.	G	AB	R	H	2B	3B	HR	RBI	Avg.	SB	PO	A	E	Avg.
1986	—Kenosha (Midwest)	C	22	65	2	10	2	0	0	8	.154	0	87	9	0	1.000
	—Elizabethton (Appal.)	C	48	152	29	35	4	0	3	14	.230	1	88	11	3	.971
1987	—Kenosha (Midwest)	C	52	140	17	35	7	0	3	17	.250	2	228	29	5	.981
1988	—Kenosha (Midwest)	C	129	465	82	134	23	2	11	87	.288	3	606	96	14	.980
1989	—Visalia (California)	C	63	231	36	62	7	0	5	39	.268	2	352	57	4	.990
	—Orlando (Southern)	C	59	191	29	45	7	0	2	17	.236	2	293	46	4	.988
	—Minnesota (A.L.)	C	14	20	3	6	2	0	0	1	.300	0	32	0	0	1.000
1990	—Orlando (Southern)	C	126	455	69	119	31	0	8	71	.262	0	629	70	9	.987
	—Minnesota (A.L.)	C	2	6	1	2	1	0	0	0	.333	0	9	0	0	1.000
1991	—Portland (Pacific Coast) ...	C	87	325	43	82	18	0	7	34	.252	1	477	65	6	*.989
	—Minnesota (A.L.)	C	18	34	7	10	1	0	3	8	.294	0	61	10	1	.986
Major league totals (3 years)			34	60	11	18	4	0	3	9	.300	0	102	10	1	.991

WEBSTER, MITCH
OF, DODGERS

PERSONAL: Born May 16, 1959, at Larned, Kan.... 6-1/185.... Throws left, bats both. ... Full name: Mitchell Dean Webster.
HIGH SCHOOL: Larned (Kan.).
TRANSACTIONS/CAREER NOTES: Selected by Los Angeles Dodgers organization in 23rd round of free-agent draft (June 7, 1977).... Drafted by Syracuse, Toronto Blue Jays organization (December 4, 1979).... Traded by Blue Jays organization to Montreal Expos for a player to be named later (June 22, 1985); Blue Jays organization acquired P Cliff Young to complete deal (September 10, 1985).... Traded by Expos to Chicago Cubs for OF Dave Martinez (July 14, 1988).... On disabled list (May 14-29, 1989).... Traded by Cubs to Cleveland Indians for OF Dave Clark (November 20, 1989).... Traded by Indians to Pittsburgh Pirates for P Mike York (May 16, 1991).... Traded by Pirates to Dodgers for OF Jose Gonzales (July 3, 1991).... Granted free agency (October 30, 1991).... Re-signed by Dodgers (December 6, 1991).
RECORDS/HONORS: Shares major league single-season record for fewest double plays by outfielder (150 or more games)—0 (1987).
STATISTICAL NOTES: Led International League outfielders with 385 total chances and five double plays in 1982.

Year	Team (League)	Pos.	G	AB	R	H	2B	3B	HR	RBI	Avg.	SB	PO	A	E	Avg.
1977	—Lethbridge (Pioneer)	OF	55	168	45	59	4	0	0	31	.351	13	81	3	8	.913
1978	—Clinton (Midwest)	OF	45	157	18	38	3	1	0	9	.242	8	92	6	7	.933
	—Lethbridge (Pioneer)	OF	55	182	58	58	5	1	0	18	.319	18	77	3	0	*1.000
1979	—Clinton (Midwest)	OF	123	473	95	*154	17	7	2	40	*.326	10	*272	10	10	.966
1980	—Syracuse (International)■	OF	49	161	23	35	4	2	1	12	.217	4	112	3	5	.958
	—Kinston (Carolina)	OF	65	258	43	76	7	3	0	28	.295	16	129	8	5	.965
1981	—Knoxville (Southern)	OF	140	554	89	163	26	6	1	42	.294	52	317	7	10	.970
1982	—Syracuse (International) ..	OF	137	513	95	144	21	7	13	68	.281	12	*367	16	2	*.995
1983	—Syracuse (International) ..	OF-1B	135	462	77	120	26	8	9	45	.260	21	266	16	10	.966
	—Toronto (A.L.)	OF-1B	11	11	2	2	0	0	0	0	.182	0	5	0	0	1.000
1984	—Toronto (A.L.)	OF-1B	26	22	9	5	2	1	0	4	.227	0	16	0	2	.889
	—Syracuse (International) ..	OF	95	360	60	108	24	5	3	25	.300	16	239	7	7	.972
1985	—Toronto (A.L.)	OF	4	1	0	0	0	0	0	0	.000	0	0	0	0	...
	—Syracuse (International) ..	OF	47	189	32	52	5	3	3	23	.275	5	83	10	1	.989
	—Montreal (N.L.)■	OF	74	212	32	58	8	2	11	30	.274	15	133	3	1	.993
1986	—Montreal (N.L.)	OF	151	576	89	167	31	*13	8	49	.290	36	325	12	8	.977
1987	—Montreal (N.L.)	OF	156	588	101	165	30	8	15	63	.281	33	266	8	5	.982
1988	—Mont.-Chi. (N.L.)■	OF	151	523	69	136	16	8	6	39	.260	22	322	3	6	.982
1989	—Chicago (N.L.)	OF	98	272	40	70	12	4	3	19	.257	14	161	3	6	.965
1990	—Cleveland (A.L.)■	OF-1B	128	437	58	110	20	6	12	55	.252	22	345	3	5	.986
1991	—Cleveland (A.L.)	OF	13	32	2	4	0	0	0	0	.125	0	24	0	0	1.000
	—Pitts.-Los Angeles (N.L.)■	OF-1B	94	171	21	38	8	5	2	19	.222	0	87	2	2	.978
American League totals (5 years)			182	503	71	121	22	7	12	59	.241	24	390	3	7	.983
National League totals (6 years)			724	2342	352	634	105	40	45	219	.271	120	1294	31	28	.979
Major league totals (9 years)			906	2845	423	755	127	47	57	278	.265	144	1684	34	35	.980

CHAMPIONSHIP SERIES RECORD

Year	Team (League)	Pos.	G	AB	R	H	2B	3B	HR	RBI	Avg.	SB	PO	A	E	Avg.
1989	—Chicago (N.L.)	PH-OF	3	3	0	1	0	0	0	0	.333	0	0	0	0	...

WEDGE, ERIC
C, RED SOX

PERSONAL: Born January 27, 1968, at Fort Wyane, Ind.... 6-3/215.... Throws right, bats right. . . Full name: Eric Michael Wedge.
HIGH SCHOOL: Northrop (Fort Wayne, Ind.).
COLLEGE: Wichita State.
TRANSACTIONS/CAREER NOTES: Selected by Boston Red Sox organization in third round of free-agent draft (June 5, 1989).
STATISTICAL NOTES: Led Eastern League catchers with eight double plays in 1990.

Year	Team (League)	Pos.	G	AB	R	H	2B	3B	HR	RBI	Avg.	SB	PO	A	E	Avg.
1989	—Elmira (New York-Penn) ..	C	41	145	20	34	6	2	7	22	.234	1	283	30	2	.994
	—New Britain (Eastern)	C	14	40	3	8	2	0	0	2	.200	0	83	9	0	1.000
1990	—New Britain (Eastern)	C	103	339	36	77	13	1	5	47	.227	1	583	62	9	.986
1991	—Pawtucket (Int'l)	C	53	163	24	38	14	1	5	18	.233	0	282	36	6	.981
	—New Britain (Eastern)	C	2	8	0	2	0	0	0	0	.250	0	6	1	0	1.000
	—Winter Haven (Fla. St.)	C	8	21	2	5	0	0	1	1	.238	1	17	2	0	1.000
	—Boston (A.L.)	PH	1	1	0	1	0	0	0	0	1.000	0	0	0	0	...
Major league totals (1 year)			1	1	0	1	0	0	0	0	1.000	0	0	0	0	...

WEGMAN, BILL
P, BREWERS

PERSONAL: Born December 19, 1962, at Cincinnati. . . . 6-5/220. . . . Throws right, bats right. . . . Full name: William Edward Wegman.
HIGH SCHOOL: Oak Hill (Cincinnati).
TRANSACTIONS/CAREER NOTES: Selected by Milwaukee Brewers organization in fifth round of free-agent draft (June 8, 1981). . . . On Vancouver disabled list (June 18-August 11, 1984). . . . On disabled list (August 7-22, 1987; May 21-June 7, 1988; and June 1, 1989-remainder of season). . . . On Milwaukee disabled list (June 3, 1990-remainder of season); included rehabilitation disability assignment to Beloit (June 27, 1990). . . . On Milwaukee disabled list (April 5-May 3, 1991); included rehabilitation disability assignment to Beloit (April 13-30, 1991) and Denver (April 30-May 3, 1991).
STATISTICAL NOTES: Led California League with five balks and tied for lead with 15 complete games and four shutouts in 1983. . . . Led Pacific Coast League with 21 home runs allowed in 1985.
MISCELLANEOUS: Appeared in two games as a pinch-runner (1986). . . . Appeared in one game as a pinch-runner (1988).

Year	Team (League)	G	W	L	Pct.	ERA	Sv.	IP	H	R	ER	BB	SO
1981	—Butte (Pioneer)	14	6	5	.545	4.17	0	82	94	51	38	44	47
1982	—Beloit (Midwest)	25	12	6	.667	2.81	0	179⅔	176	77	56	38	129
1983	—Stockton (California)	24	*16	5	.762	*1.30	0	186⅔	149	33	27	45	135
1984	—El Paso (Texas)	10	4	5	.444	2.67	0	64	62	25	19	15	42
	—Vancouver (Pacific Coast)	6	0	3	.000	1.95	1	27⅔	30	11	6	8	16
1985	—Vancouver (Pacific Coast)	28	10	11	.476	4.02	0	188	187	93	84	52	113
	—Milwaukee (A.L.)	3	2	0	1.000	3.57	0	17⅔	17	8	7	3	6
1986	—Milwaukee (A.L.)	35	5	12	.294	5.13	0	198⅓	217	120	113	43	82
1987	—Milwaukee (A.L.)	34	12	11	.522	4.24	0	225	229	113	106	53	102
1988	—Milwaukee (A.L.)	32	13	13	.500	4.12	0	199	207	104	91	50	84
1989	—Milwaukee (A.L.)	11	2	6	.250	6.71	0	51	69	44	38	21	27
1990	—Denver (American Assoc.)	3	1	0	1.000	3.29	0	13⅔	10	5	5	7	14
	—Milwaukee (A.L.)	8	2	2	.500	4.85	0	29⅔	37	21	16	6	20
	—Beloit (Midwest)	1	0	0	...	0.00	0	2	1	0	0	1	2
1991	—Beloit (Midwest)	3	0	2	.000	1.64	0	11	11	5	2	1	12
	—Denver (American Assoc.)	1	0	0	...	2.57	0	7	6	2	2	1	1
	—Milwaukee (A.L.)	28	15	7	.682	2.84	0	193⅓	176	76	61	40	89
Major league totals (7 years)		151	51	51	.500	4.25	0	914	952	486	432	216	410

WEHNER, JOHN
3B, PIRATES

PERSONAL: Born June 29, 1967, at Pittsburgh. . . . 6-3/204. . . . Throws right, bats right. . . . Full name: John Paul Wehner. . . . Name pronounced WAY-ner.
HIGH SCHOOL: Carrick (Pittsburgh).
COLLEGE: Indiana.
TRANSACTIONS/CAREER NOTES: Selected by Pittsburgh Pirates organization in seventh round of free-agent draft (June 1, 1988). . . . On Pittsburgh disabled list (August 29-October 7, 1991).
STATISTICAL NOTES: Led New York-Pennsylvania League third basemen with 219 total chances and 14 double plays in 1988. . . . Led Carolina League third basemen with 403 total chances and tied for lead with 24 double plays in 1989. . . . Led Eastern League third basemen with 476 total chances and 40 double plays in 1990.

Year	Team (League)	Pos.	G	AB	R	H	2B	3B	HR	RBI	Avg.	SB	PO	A	E	Avg.
1988	—Watertown (N.Y.-Penn)....	3B	70	265	41	73	6	0	3	31	.275	18	*65	137	17	.922
1989	—Salem (Carolina)	3B	*137	*515	69	*155	32	6	14	73	.301	21	*89	*278	36	.911
1990	—Harrisburg (Eastern)	3B	•138	*511	71	147	27	1	4	62	.288	24	*109	*317	*50	.895
1991	—Carolina (Southern)	3B-1B	61	234	30	62	5	1	3	21	.265	17	182	134	10	.969
	—Buffalo (Am. Assoc.)	3B	31	112	18	34	9	2	1	15	.304	6	30	69	8	.925
	—Pittsburgh (N.L.)	3B	37	106	15	36	7	0	0	7	.340	3	23	65	6	.936
Major league totals (1 year)			37	106	15	36	7	0	0	7	.340	3	23	65	6	.936

WEISS, WALT
SS, ATHLETICS

PERSONAL: Born November 28, 1963, at Tuxedo, N.Y. . . . 6-0/175. . . . Throws right, bats both. . . . Full name: Walter William Weiss Jr.
HIGH SCHOOL: Suffern (N.Y.).
COLLEGE: North Carolina.
TRANSACTIONS/CAREER NOTES: Selected by Baltimore Orioles organization in 10th round of free-agent draft (June 7, 1982). . . . Selected by Oakland Athletics organization in first round (11th pick overall) of free-agent draft (June 3, 1985). . . . On Oakland disabled list (May 18-July 31, 1989); included rehabilitation disability assignment to Tacoma (July 18-25, 1989) and Modesto (July 26-31, 1989). . . . On disabled list (August 23-September 7, 1990; April 15-30 and June 7, 1991-remainder of season).

RECORDS/HONORS: Named A.L. Rookie Player of the Year by THE SPORTING NEWS (1988).... Named A.L. Rookie of the Year by Baseball Writers' Association of American (1988).

Year	Team (League)	Pos.	G	AB	R	H	2B	3B	HR	RBI	Avg.	SB	PO	A	E	Avg.
1985	—Pocatello (Pioneer)	SS	40	158	19	49	9	3	0	21	.310	6	51	126	11	.941
	—Modesto (California)	SS	30	122	17	24	4	1	0	7	.197	3	36	97	7	.950
1986	—Madison (Midwest)	SS	84	322	50	97	15	5	2	54	.301	12	143	251	20	.952
	—Huntsville (Southern)	SS	46	160	19	40	2	1	0	13	.250	5	72	142	11	.951
1987	—Huntsville (Southern)	SS	91	337	43	96	16	2	1	32	.285	23	152	259	17	.960
	—Oakland (A.L.)	SS	16	26	3	12	4	0	0	1	.462	1	8	30	1	.974
	—Tacoma (Pacific Coast)	SS	46	179	35	47	4	3	0	17	.263	8	76	140	11	.952
1988	—Oakland (A.L.)	SS	147	452	44	113	17	3	3	39	.250	4	254	431	15	.979
1989	—Oakland (A.L.)	SS	84	236	30	55	11	0	3	21	.233	6	106	195	15	.953
	—Tacoma (Pacific Coast)	SS	2	9	1	1	1	0	0	1	.111	0	0	3	1	.750
	—Modesto (California)	SS	5	8	1	3	0	0	1	1	.375	0	6	9	0	1.000
1990	—Oakland (A.L.)	SS	138	445	50	118	17	1	2	35	.265	9	194	373	12	.979
1991	—Oakland (A.L.)	SS	40	133	15	30	6	1	0	13	.226	6	64	99	5	.970
Major league totals (5 years)			425	1292	142	328	55	5	8	109	.254	26	626	1128	48	.973

CHAMPIONSHIP SERIES RECORD

Year	Team (League)	Pos.	G	AB	R	H	2B	3B	HR	RBI	Avg.	SB	PO	A	E	Avg.
1988	—Oakland (A.L.)	SS	4	15	2	5	2	0	0	2	.333	0	7	10	0	1.000
1989	—Oakland (A.L.)	SS-PR	4	9	2	1	1	0	0	0	.111	1	5	9	0	1.000
1990	—Oakland (A.L.)	SS	2	7	2	0	0	0	0	0	.000	0	2	7	1	.900
Championship Series totals (3 years)			10	31	6	6	3	0	0	2	.194	1	14	26	1	.976

WORLD SERIES RECORD

Year	Team (League)	Pos.	G	AB	R	H	2B	3B	HR	RBI	Avg.	SB	PO	A	E	Avg.
1988	—Oakland (A.L.)	SS	5	16	1	1	0	0	0	0	.063	0	5	11	1	.941
1989	—Oakland (A.L.)	SS	4	15	3	2	0	0	1	1	.133	0	7	8	0	1.000
World Series totals (2 years)			9	31	4	3	0	0	1	1	.097	0	12	19	1	.969

WELCH, BOB
P, ATHLETICS

PERSONAL: Born November 3, 1956, at Detroit.... 6-3/198.... Throws right, bats right.... Full name: Robert Lynn Welch.
HIGH SCHOOL: Hazel Park (Ferndale, Mich.).
COLLEGE: Eastern Michigan.

TRANSACTIONS/CAREER NOTES: Selected by Chicago Cubs organization in 14th round of free-agent draft (June 5, 1974).... Selected by Los Angeles Dodgers organization in first round (20th pick overall) of free-agent draft (June 7, 1977).... On Los Angeles disabled list (April 29-June 5, 1985); included rehabilitation disability assignment to Vero Beach (May 21-June 5, 1985).... Traded by Dodgers as part of an eight-player, three-team deal in which New York Mets sent P Jesse Orosco to Oakland Athletics. A's traded Orosco, SS Alfredo Griffin and P Jay Howell to Dodgers for Welch, P Matt Young and P Jack Savage. A's then traded Savage, P Wally Whitehurst and P Kevin Tapani to Mets (December 11, 1987).... On disabled list (June 13-30, 1989).... Granted free agency (November 5, 1990).... Re-signed by A's (December 15, 1990).
RECORDS/HONORS: Named A.L. Pitcher of the Year by THE SPORTING NEWS (1990).... Named righthanded pitcher on THE SPORTING NEWS A.L. All-Star team (1990).... Named A.L. Cy Young Award winner by Baseball Writers' Association of America (1990).
STATISTICAL NOTES: Tied for N.L. lead with four shutouts in 1987.... Tied for A.L. lead in games started by pitcher with 35 in 1991.
MISCELLANEOUS: Appeared in one game as outfielder with no chances (1982).... Appeared in one game as pinch-runner (1991).

Year	Team (League)	G	W	L	Pct.	ERA	Sv.	IP	H	R	ER	BB	SO
1977	—San Antonio (Texas)	14	4	5	.444	4.44	0	71	94	44	35	17	56
1978	—Albuquerque (Pacific Coast)	11	5	1	.833	3.78	0	69	72	33	29	19	53
	—Los Angeles (N.L.)	23	7	4	.636	2.03	3	111	92	28	25	26	66
1979	—Los Angeles (N.L.)	25	5	6	.455	4.00	5	81	82	42	36	32	64
1980	—Los Angeles (N.L.)	32	14	9	.609	3.28	0	214	190	85	78	79	141
1981	—Los Angeles (N.L.)	23	9	5	.643	3.45	0	141	141	56	54	41	88
1982	—Los Angeles (N.L.)	36	16	11	.593	3.36	0	235²/₃	199	94	88	81	176
1983	—Los Angeles (N.L.)	31	15	12	.556	2.65	0	204	164	73	60	72	156
1984	—Los Angeles (N.L.)	31	13	13	.500	3.78	0	178²/₃	191	86	75	58	126
1985	—Los Angeles (N.L.)	23	14	4	.778	2.31	0	167¹/₃	141	49	43	35	96
	—Vero Beach (Florida State)	3	0	0	...	2.12	0	17	15	4	4	1	9
1986	—Los Angeles (N.L.)	33	7	13	.350	3.28	0	235²/₃	227	95	86	55	183
1987	—Los Angeles (N.L.)	35	15	9	.625	3.22	0	251²/₃	204	94	90	86	196
1988	—Oakland (A.L.)■	36	17	9	.654	3.64	0	244²/₃	237	107	99	81	158
1989	—Oakland (A.L.)	33	17	8	.680	3.00	0	209²/₃	191	82	70	78	137
1990	—Oakland (A.L.)	35	*27	6	*.818	2.95	0	238	214	90	78	77	127
1991	—Oakland (A.L.)	35	12	13	.480	4.58	0	220	220	124	112	91	101
American League totals (4 years)		139	73	36	.670	3.54	0	912¹/₃	862	403	359	327	523
National League totals (10 years)		292	115	86	.572	3.14	8	1820	1631	702	635	565	1292
Major league totals (14 years)		431	188	122	.606	3.27	8	2732¹/₃	2493	1105	994	892	1815

DIVISION SERIES RECORD

Year Team (League)	G	W	L	Pct.	ERA	Sv.	IP	H	R	ER	BB	SO
1981—Los Angeles (N.L.)	1	0	0	...	0.00	0	1	0	0	0	1	1

CHAMPIONSHIP SERIES RECORD

Year Team (League)	G	W	L	Pct.	ERA	Sv.	IP	H	R	ER	BB	SO
1978—Los Angeles (N.L.)	1	1	0	1.000	2.08	0	4⅓	2	1	1	0	5
1981—Los Angeles (N.L.)	3	0	0	...	5.40	1	1⅔	2	1	1	0	2
1983—Los Angeles (N.L.)	1	0	1	.000	6.75	0	1⅓	0	2	1	2	0
1985—Los Angeles (N.L.)	1	0	1	.000	6.75	0	2⅔	5	4	2	6	2
1988—Oakland (A.L.)	1	0	0	...	27.00	0	1⅔	6	5	5	2	0
1989—Oakland (A.L.)	1	1	0	1.000	3.18	0	5⅔	8	2	2	1	4
1990—Oakland (A.L.)	1	1	0	1.000	1.23	0	7⅓	6	1	1	3	4
Championship Series totals (7 years)	9	3	2	.600	4.74	1	24⅔	29	16	13	14	17

WORLD SERIES RECORD

Year Team (League)	G	W	L	Pct.	ERA	Sv.	IP	H	R	ER	BB	SO
1978—Los Angeles (N.L.)	3	0	1	.000	6.23	1	4⅓	4	3	3	2	6
1981—Los Angeles (N.L.)	1	0	0	...	0.00	0	0	3	2	2	1	0
1988—Oakland (A.L.)	1	0	0	...	1.80	0	5	6	1	1	3	8
1989—Oakland (A.L.)					Did not play							
1990—Oakland (A.L.)	1	0	0	...	4.91	0	7⅓	9	4	4	2	2
World Series totals (4 years)	6	0	1	.000	5.40	1	16⅔	22	10	10	8	16

ALL-STAR GAME RECORD

Year League	W	L	Pct.	ERA	Sv.	IP	H	R	ER	BB	SO
1980—National	0	0	...	6.00	0	3	5	2	2	1	4
1990—American	0	0	...	0.00	0	2	1	0	0	0	1
All-Star totals (2 years)	0	0	...	3.60	0	5	6	2	2	1	5

WELLS, DAVID
P, BLUE JAYS

PERSONAL: Born May 20, 1963, at Torrance, Calif. . . . 6-4/225. . . . Throws left, bats left. . . . Full name: David Lee Wells.
HIGH SCHOOL: Point Loma (San Diego).
TRANSACTIONS/CAREER NOTES: Selected by Toronto Blue Jays organization in second round of free-agent draft (June 7, 1982). . . . On Knoxville disabled list (June 28, 1984-remainder of season). . . . On disabled list (April 10, 1985-entire season). . . . On Knoxville disabled list (July 7-August 20, 1986).

Year Team (League)	G	W	L	Pct.	ERA	Sv.	IP	H	R	ER	BB	SO
1982—Medicine Hat (Pioneer)	12	4	3	.571	5.18	0	64⅓	71	42	37	32	53
1983—Kinston (Carolina)	25	6	5	.545	3.73	0	157	141	81	65	71	115
1984—Kinston (Carolina)	7	1	6	.143	4.71	0	42	51	29	22	19	44
—Knoxville (Southern)	8	3	2	.600	2.59	0	59	58	22	17	17	34
1985—					Did not play							
1986—Florence (South Atlantic)	4	0	0	...	3.55	0	12⅔	7	6	5	9	14
—Ventura (California)	5	2	1	.667	1.89	0	19	13	5	4	4	26
—Knoxville (Southern)	10	1	3	.250	4.05	0	40	42	24	18	18	32
—Syracuse (International)	3	0	1	.000	9.82	0	3⅔	6	4	4	1	2
1987—Syracuse (International)	43	4	6	.400	3.87	6	109⅓	102	49	47	32	106
—Toronto (A.L.)	18	4	3	.571	3.99	1	29⅓	37	14	13	12	32
1988—Toronto (A.L.)	41	3	5	.375	4.62	4	64⅓	65	36	33	31	56
—Syracuse (International)	6	0	0	...	0.00	3	5⅔	7	1	0	2	8
1989—Toronto (A.L.)	54	7	4	.636	2.40	2	86⅓	66	25	23	28	78
1990—Toronto (A.L.)	43	11	6	.647	3.14	3	189	165	72	66	45	115
1991—Toronto (A.L.)	40	15	10	.600	3.72	1	198⅓	188	88	82	49	106
Major league totals (5 years)	196	40	28	.588	3.44	11	567⅓	521	235	217	165	387

CHAMPIONSHIP SERIES RECORD

Year Team (League)	G	W	L	Pct.	ERA	Sv.	IP	H	R	ER	BB	SO
1989—Toronto (A.L.)	1	0	0	...	0.00	0	1	0	1	0	2	1
1991—Toronto (A.L.)	4	0	0	...	2.35	0	7⅔	6	2	2	2	9
Championship Series totals (2 years)	5	0	0	...	2.08	0	8⅔	6	3	2	4	10

WENDELL, TURK
P, CUBS

PERSONAL: Born May 19, 1967, at Pittsfield, Mass. . . . 6-2/175. . . . Throws right, bats left. . . . Full name: Steven John Wendell.
HIGH SCHOOL: Wahconah Regional (Mass.).
COLLEGE: Quinnipiac College (Conn.).
TRANSACTIONS/CAREER NOTES: Selected by Atlanta Braves organization in fifth round of free-agent draft (June 1, 1988). . . . Traded by Braves with P Yorkis Perez to Chicago Cubs for P Mike Bielecki and C Damon Berryhill (September 29, 1991).
STATISTICAL NOTES: Led Appalachian League with six complete games in 1988. . . . Led Midwest League with five shutouts and tied for lead with nine complete games in 1989.

Year	Team (League)	G	W	L	Pct.	ERA	Sv.	IP	H	R	ER	BB	SO
1988	—Pulaski (Appalachian)	14	3	•8	.273	3.83	0	*101	85	50	43	30	87
1989	—Burlington (Midwest)	22	9	11	.450	2.21	0	159	127	63	39	41	153
	—Greenville (Southern)	1	0	0	...	9.82	0	3⅔	7	5	4	1	3
	—Durham (Carolina)	3	2	0	1.000	1.13	0	24	13	4	3	6	27
1990	—Durham (Carolina)	6	1	3	.250	1.86	0	38⅔	24	10	8	15	26
	—Greenville (Southern)	36	4	9	.308	5.74	2	91	105	70	58	48	85
1991	—Greenville (Southern)	25	11	3	*.786	2.56	0	147⅔	130	47	42	51	122
	—Richmond (International)	3	0	2	.000	3.43	0	21	20	9	8	16	18

WEST, DAVID
P, TWINS

PERSONAL: Born September 1, 1964, at Memphis, Tenn.... 6-6/231.... Throws left, bats left.... Full name: David Lee West.
HIGH SCHOOL: Craigmont (Memphis, Tenn.).
TRANSACTIONS/CAREER NOTES: Selected by New York Mets organization in fourth round of free-agent draft (June 6, 1983).... Traded by Mets with P Rick Aguilera and three players to be named later to Minnesota Twins for P Frank Viola (July 31, 1989); Portland (Twins organization) acquired P Kevin Tapani and P Tim Drummond (August 1, 1989), and Twins acquired P Jack Savage to complete deal (October 16, 1989).... On disabled list (September 7, 1990-remainder of season).... On Minnesota disabled list (April 7-July 2, 1991); included rehabilitation disability assignment to Orlando (May 12-15, 1991) and Portland (June 14-July 2, 1991).
STATISTICAL NOTES: Led New York-Pennsylvania League with 16 wild pitches in 1984.... Won 3-0 no-hit victory against Spartanburg (August 14, 1985).... Tied for Texas League lead with two shutouts in 1987.

Year	Team (League)	G	W	L	Pct.	ERA	Sv.	IP	H	R	ER	BB	SO
1983	—Sarasota Mets (Gulf Coast)	12	2	4	.333	2.85	0	53⅔	41	28	17	52	56
1984	—Columbia (South Atlantic)	12	3	5	.375	6.23	0	60⅔	41	47	42	68	60
	—Little Falls (New York-Penn)	13	6	4	.600	3.34	0	62	43	35	23	62	79
1985	—Columbia (South Atlantic)	26	10	9	.526	4.56	0	150	105	97	76	*111	194
1986	—Lynchburg (Carolina)	13	1	6	.143	5.16	0	75	76	50	43	53	70
	—Columbia (South Atlantic)	13	10	3	.769	2.91	0	92⅔	74	41	30	56	101
1987	—Jackson (Texas)	25	10	7	.588	2.81	0	166⅔	152	67	52	*81	*186
1988	—Tidewater (International)	23	12	4	*.750	*1.80	0	160⅓	106	42	32	*97	143
	—New York (N.L.)	2	1	0	1.000	3.00	0	6	6	2	2	3	3
1989	—Tidewater (International)	12	7	4	.636	2.37	0	87⅓	60	31	23	29	69
	—New York (N.L.)	11	0	2	.000	7.40	0	24⅓	25	20	20	14	19
	—Minnesota (A.L.)■	10	3	2	.600	6.41	0	39⅓	48	29	28	19	31
1990	—Minnesota (A.L.)	29	7	9	.438	5.10	0	146⅓	142	88	83	78	92
1991	—Minnesota (A.L.)	15	4	4	.500	4.54	0	71⅓	66	37	36	28	52
	—Orlando (Southern)	1	0	0	...	0.00	0	0⅓	0	0	0	0	0
	—Portland (Pacific Coast)	4	1	1	.500	6.32	0	15⅔	12	11	11	12	15
American League totals (3 years)		54	14	15	.483	5.15	0	257	256	154	147	125	175
National League totals (2 years)		13	1	2	.333	6.53	0	30⅓	31	22	22	17	22
Major league totals (4 years)		67	15	17	.469	5.29	0	287⅓	287	176	169	142	197

CHAMPIONSHIP SERIES RECORD

Year	Team (League)	G	W	L	Pct.	ERA	Sv.	IP	H	R	ER	BB	SO
1991	—Minnesota (A.L.)	2	1	0	1.000	0.00	0	5⅔	1	0	0	4	4

WORLD SERIES RECORD

Year	Team (League)	G	W	L	Pct.	ERA	Sv.	IP	H	R	ER	BB	SO
1991	—Minnesota (A.L.)	2	0	0	...	...	0	0	2	4	4	4	0

WESTON, MICKEY
P, PHILLIES

PERSONAL: Born March 26, 1961, at Flint, Mich.... 6-1/187.... Throws right, bats right.... Full name: Michael Lee Weston.
HIGH SCHOOL: Lake Fenton (Fenton, Mich.).
COLLEGE: Eastern Michigan.
TRANSACTIONS/CAREER NOTES: Selected by New York Mets organization in 12th round of free-agent draft (June 7, 1982).... On disabled list (April 8-18 and May 23-June 25, 1986).... Granted free agency (October 15, 1988).... Signed by Rochester, Baltimore Orioles organization (November 28, 1988).... On Baltimore disabled list (June 23-August 22, 1989); included rehabilitation disability assignment to Rochester (August 2-21, 1989).... Traded by Orioles to Toronto Blue Jays for P Paul Kilgus (December 14, 1990).... Granted free agency (October 16, 1991).... Signed by Scranton/Wilkes-Barre, Philadelphia Phillies organization (December 18, 1991).

Year	Team (League)	G	W	L	Pct.	ERA	Sv.	IP	H	R	ER	BB	SO
1982	—Little Falls (New York-Penn)	17	7	6	.538	5.07	0	92⅓	105	63	52	22	67
1983	—Columbia (South Atlantic)	37	2	2	.500	4.34	6	74⅔	87	48	36	22	46
1984	—Columbia (South Atlantic)	32	6	5	.545	1.84	2	63⅔	58	27	13	27	40
1985	—Lynchburg (Carolina)	49	6	5	.545	2.15	10	100⅓	81	29	24	22	62
1986	—Jackson (Texas)	34	4	4	.500	4.33	2	70⅔	73	40	34	27	36
1987	—Jackson (Texas)	58	8	4	.667	3.40	3	82	96	39	31	18	50
1988	—Jackson (Texas)	30	8	5	.615	*2.23	0	125⅓	127	50	31	20	61
	—Tidewater (International)	4	2	1	.667	1.52	0	29⅔	21	6	5	5	16
1989	—Rochester (International)■	23	8	3	.727	2.09	4	112	103	30	26	19	51
	—Baltimore (A.L.)	7	1	0	1.000	5.54	1	13	18	8	8	2	7
1990	—Rochester (International)	29	11	1	.917	1.98	6	109⅓	93	36	24	22	58
	—Baltimore (A.L.)	9	0	1	.000	7.71	0	21	28	20	18	6	9

Year	Team (League)	G	W	L	Pct.	ERA	Sv.	IP	H	R	ER	BB	SO
1991	—Syracuse (International)■	27	•12	6	.667	3.74	0	166	193	85	69	36	60
	—Toronto (A.L.)...........................	2	0	0	...	0.00	0	2	1	0	0	1	1
Major league totals (3 years)		18	1	1	.500	6.50	1	36	47	28	26	9	17

WETTELAND, JOHN
P, EXPOS

PERSONAL: Born August 21, 1966, at San Mateo, Calif. ... 6-2/195. ... Throws right, bats right. ... Full name: John Karl Wetteland.
HIGH SCHOOL: Cardinal Newman (Santa Rosa, Calif.).
COLLEGE: College of San Mateo (Calif.).
TRANSACTIONS/CAREER NOTES: Selected by New York Mets organization in 12th round of free-agent draft (June 4, 1984). ... Selected by Los Angeles Dodgers organization in secondary phase of free-agent draft (January 9, 1985). ... Drafted by Detroit Tigers (December 7, 1987). ... Returned to Dodgers organization (March 29, 1988). ... On Albuquerque disabled list (May 1-8 and June 3-29, 1991). ... Traded by Dodgers with P Tim Belcher to Cincinnati Reds for OF Eric Davis and P Kip Gross (November 25, 1991). ... Traded by Reds with P Bill Risley to Montreal Expos for OF Dave Martinez, P Scott Ruskin and SS Willie Greene (December 11, 1991).
STATISTICAL NOTES: Tied for Florida State League lead with 11 home runs allowed and 17 wild pitches in 1987. ... Led Texas League with 22 wild pitches in 1988.

Year	Team (League)	G	W	L	Pct.	ERA	Sv.	IP	H	R	ER	BB	SO
1985	—Great Falls (Pioneer)	11	1	1	.500	3.92	0	20 2/3	17	10	9	15	23
1986	—Bakersfield (California)	15	0	7	.000	5.78	0	67	71	50	43	46	38
	—Great Falls (Pioneer)	12	4	3	.571	5.45	0	69 1/3	70	51	42	40	59
1987	—Vero Beach (Florida State)	27	12	7	.632	3.13	0	175 2/3	150	81	61	92	144
1988	—San Antonio (Texas)	25	10	8	.556	3.88	0	162 1/3	141	74	70	•77	140
1989	—Albuquerque (Pacific Coast)	10	5	3	.625	3.65	0	69	61	28	28	20	73
	—Los Angeles (N.L.)....................	31	5	8	.385	3.77	1	102 2/3	81	46	43	34	96
1990	—Los Angeles (N.L.)....................	22	2	4	.333	4.81	0	43	44	28	23	17	36
	—Albuquerque (Pacific Coast)	8	2	2	.500	5.59	0	29	27	19	18	13	26
1991	—Albuquerque (Pacific Coast)	41	4	3	.571	2.79	20	61 1/3	48	22	19	26	55
	—Los Angeles (N.L.)....................	6	1	0	1.000	0.00	0	9	5	2	0	3	9
Major league totals (3 years)		59	8	12	.400	3.84	1	154 2/3	130	76	66	54	141

WHITAKER, LOU
2B, TIGERS

PERSONAL: Born May 12, 1957, at Brooklyn, N.Y. ... 5-11/180. ... Throws right, bats left. ... Full name: Louis Rodman Whitaker.
HIGH SCHOOL: Martinsville (Va.).
TRANSACTIONS/CAREER NOTES: Selected by Detroit Tigers organization in fifth round of free-agent draft (June 4, 1975). ... On disabled list (May 3-14, 1977 and June 13-28, 1979).
RECORDS/HONORS: Named Florida State League Most Valuable Player (1976). ... Named A.L. Rookie of the Year by Baseball Writers' Association of America (1978). ... Named second baseman on THE SPORTING NEWS A.L. All-Star team (1983-84). ... Won A.L. Gold Glove at second base (1983-85). ... Named second baseman on THE SPORTING NEWS A.L. Silver Slugger team (1983-85 and 1987).
STATISTICAL NOTES: Led Florida State League second basemen with 30 double plays in 1976. ... Led A.L. second basemen with 811 total chances and 120 double plays in 1982.

Year	Team (League)	Pos.	G	AB	R	H	2B	3B	HR	RBI	Avg.	SB	PO	A	E	Avg.
1975	—Bristol (Appalachian)	3B-SS	42	114	17	27	6	1	1	17	.237	1	38	82	16	.882
1976	—Lakeland (Florida State) ...	3B	124	343	•70	129	12	5	1	62	.376	48	•99	•267	•30	•.924
1977	—Montgomery (Southern) ...	2B	107	396	•81	111	13	4	3	48	.280	38	208	285	15	.970
	—Detroit (A.L.)	2B	11	32	5	8	1	0	0	2	.250	2	17	18	0	1.000
1978	—Detroit (A.L.)	2B	139	484	71	138	12	7	3	58	.285	7	301	458	17	.978
1979	—Detroit (A.L.)	2B	127	423	75	121	14	8	3	42	.286	20	280	369	9	.986
1980	—Detroit (A.L.)	2B	145	477	68	111	19	1	1	45	.233	8	340	428	12	.985
1981	—Detroit (A.L.)	2B	•109	335	48	88	14	4	5	36	.263	5	227	•354	9	.985
1982	—Detroit (A.L.)	2B	152	560	76	160	22	8	15	65	.286	11	331	•470	10	•.988
1983	—Detroit (A.L.)	2B	161	643	94	206	40	6	12	72	.320	17	299	447	13	.983
1984	—Detroit (A.L.)	2B	143	558	90	161	25	1	13	56	.289	6	290	405	15	.979
1985	—Detroit (A.L.)	2B	152	609	102	170	29	8	21	73	.279	6	314	414	11	.985
1986	—Detroit (A.L.)	2B	144	584	95	157	26	6	20	73	.269	13	276	421	11	.984
1987	—Detroit (A.L.)	2B	149	604	110	160	38	6	16	59	.265	13	275	416	17	.976
1988	—Detroit (A.L.)	2B	115	403	54	111	18	2	12	55	.275	2	218	284	8	.984
1989	—Detroit (A.L.)	2B	148	509	77	128	21	1	28	85	.251	6	•327	393	11	.985
1990	—Detroit (A.L.)	2B	132	472	75	112	22	2	18	60	.237	8	286	372	6	.991
1991	—Detroit (A.L.)	2B	138	470	94	131	26	2	23	78	.279	4	255	361	4	•.994
Major league totals (15 years)			1965	7163	1134	1962	327	62	190	859	.274	128	4036	5610	153	.984

CHAMPIONSHIP SERIES RECORD

Year	Team (League)	Pos.	G	AB	R	H	2B	3B	HR	RBI	Avg.	SB	PO	A	E	Avg.
1984	—Detroit (A.L.)	2B	3	14	3	2	0	0	0	0	.143	0	5	6	0	1.000
1987	—Detroit (A.L.)	2B	5	17	4	3	0	0	1	1	.176	1	11	14	0	1.000
Championship Series totals (2 years)			8	31	7	5	0	0	1	1	.161	1	16	20	0	1.000

Year	Team (League)	Pos.	G	AB	R	H	2B	3B	HR	RBI	Avg.	SB	PO	A	E	Avg.
1984 —Detroit (A.L.)		2B	5	18	6	5	2	0	0	0	.278	0	15	18	0	1.000

ALL-STAR GAME RECORD

ALL-STAR GAME NOTES: Named to A.L. All-Star team for 1987 game; replaced due to injury by Harold Reynolds.

Year	League	Pos.	AB	R	H	2B	3B	HR	RBI	Avg.	SB	PO	A	E	Avg.
1983 —American	PH-2B	1	1	1	0	1	0	2	1.000	0	1	0	0	1.000
1984 —American	2B	3	0	2	1	0	0	0	.667	0	0	5	0	1.000
1985 —American	2B	2	0	0	0	0	0	0	.000	0	1	1	0	1.000
1986 —American	2B	2	1	1	0	0	1	2	.500	0	0	3	0	1.000
All-Star Game totals (4 years)		8	2	4	1	1	1	4	.500	0	2	9	0	1.000

WHITE, DEVON
OF, BLUE JAYS

PERSONAL: Born December 29, 1962, at Kingston, Jamaica. . . . 6-2/182. . . . Throws right, bats both. . . . Full name: Devon Markes White. . . . Name pronounced de-VON.
HIGH SCHOOL: Park West (New York).
TRANSACTIONS/CAREER NOTES: Selected by California Angels organization in sixth round of free-agent draft (June 8, 1981). . . . On suspended list (June 11-12 and July 19, 1982-remainder of season). . . . On Edmonton disabled list (May 12-22, 1986). . . . On disabled list (May 7-June 10, 1988). . . . Traded by Angels organization with P Willie Fraser and a player to be named later to Toronto Blue Jays for OF Junior Felix, IF Luis Sojo and a player to be named later (December 2, 1990); Blue Jays acquired P Marcus Moore and Angels acquired C Ken Rivers to complete deal (December 4, 1990).
RECORDS/HONORS: Shares major league record for most stolen bases in one inning—3 (September 9, 1989, sixth inning). . . . Won A.L. Gold Glove as outfielder (1988-89 and 1991).
STATISTICAL NOTES: Led Midwest League outfielders with 286 total chances in 1983. . . . Led California League outfielders with 351 total chances in 1984. . . . Led Pacific Coast League outfielders with 339 total chances in 1986. . . . Switch-hit home runs in one game (June 23, 1987 and June 29, 1990). . . . Led A.L. outfielders with 449 total chances in 1987 and 448 in 1991.

Year	Team (League)	Pos.	G	AB	R	H	2B	3B	HR	RBI	Avg.	SB	PO	A	E	Avg.
1981 —Idaho Falls (Pioneer)	OF-3B-1B	30	106	10	19	2	0	0	10	.179	4	33	10	3	.935
1982 —Danville (Midwest)	OF	57	186	21	40	6	1	1	11	.215	11	89	3	8	.920
1983 —Peoria (Midwest)	OF	117	430	69	109	17	6	13	66	.253	32	267	8	11	.962
—Nashua (Eastern)	OF	17	70	11	18	7	2	0	2	.257	5	37	0	3	.925
1984 —Redwood (California)	OF	138	520	101	147	25	5	7	55	.283	36	*322	16	13	.963
1985 —Midland (Texas)	OF	70	260	52	77	10	4	4	35	.296	38	176	10	4	.979
—Edmonton (Pac. Coast)	OF	66	277	53	70	16	5	4	39	.253	21	205	6	2	.991
—California (A.L.)	OF	21	7	7	1	0	0	0	0	.143	3	10	1	0	1.000
1986 —Edmonton (Pac. Coast)	OF	112	461	84	134	25	10	14	60	.291	*42	317	•16	6	.982
—California (A.L.)	OF	29	51	8	12	1	1	1	3	.235	13	49	0	2	.961
1987 —California (A.L.)	OF	159	639	103	168	33	5	24	87	.263	32	*424	16	9	.980
1988 —California (A.L.)	OF	122	455	76	118	22	2	11	51	.259	17	364	7	9	.976
1989 —California (A.L.)	OF	156	636	86	156	18	13	12	56	.245	44	430	10	5	.989
1990 —California (A.L.)	OF	125	443	57	96	17	3	11	44	.217	21	302	11	9	.972
—Edmonton (Pac. Coast)	OF	14	55	9	20	4	4	0	6	.364	4	31	1	3	.914
1991 —Toronto (A.L.) ■..........	OF	156	642	110	181	40	10	17	60	.282	33	*439	8	1	*.998
Major league totals (7 years)		768	2873	447	732	131	34	76	301	.255	163	2018	53	35	.983

CHAMPIONSHIP SERIES RECORD

Year	Team (League)	Pos.	G	AB	R	H	2B	3B	HR	RBI	Avg.	SB	PO	A	E	Avg.
1986 —California (A.L.)	OF-PR	4	2	2	1	0	0	0	0	.500	0	3	0	0	1.000
1991 —Toronto (A.L.)	OF	5	22	5	8	1	0	0	0	.364	3	16	0	0	1.000
Championship Series totals (2 years)		9	24	7	9	1	0	0	0	.375	3	19	0	0	1.000

ALL-STAR GAME RECORD

Year	League	Pos.	AB	R	H	2B	3B	HR	RBI	Avg.	SB	PO	A	E	Avg.
1989 —American	OF	1	0	0	0	0	0	0	.000	0	0	0	0	. . .

WHITEHURST, WALLY
P, METS

PERSONAL: Born April 11, 1964, at Shreveport, La. . . . 6-3/195. . . . Throws right, bats right. . . . Full name: Walter Richard Whitehurst.
HIGH SCHOOL: Terrebonne (Houma, La.).
COLLEGE: New Orleans.
TRANSACTIONS/CAREER NOTES: Selected by Oakland Athletics organization in third round of free-agent draft (June 3, 1985). . . . Traded by A's as part of an eight-player, three-team deal in which New York Mets sent P Jesse Orosco to A's. A's traded Orosco, SS Alfedo Griffin and P Jay Howell to Los Angeles Dodgers for P Bob Welch, P Matt Young and P Jack Savage. A's then traded Savage, Whitehurst and P Kevin Tapani to Mets (December 11, 1987). . . . On disabled list (July 26-August 10, 1991).
STATISTICAL NOTES: Tied for Northwest League lead with seven hit batsmen and two balks in 1985. . . . Tied for Midwest League lead with four shutouts in 1986. . . . Tied for Southern League lead with three shutouts in 1987.

Year	Team (League)	G	W	L	Pct.	ERA	Sv.	IP	H	R	ER	BB	SO
1985	—Medford (Northwest)	14	7	5	.583	3.58	0	88	92	51	35	29	•91
	—Modesto (California)	2	1	0	1.000	1.80	0	10	10	3	2	5	5
1986	—Madison (Midwest)	8	6	1	.857	0.59	0	61	42	8	4	16	57
	—Huntsville (Southern)	19	9	5	.643	4.64	0	104⅔	114	66	54	46	54
1987	—Huntsville (Southern)	28	11	10	.524	3.98	0	183⅓	192	104	81	42	106
1988	—Tidewater (International)■	26	10	11	.476	3.05	0	165	145	65	56	32	113
1989	—Tidewater (International)	21	8	7	.533	3.25	0	133	123	54	48	32	95
	—New York (N.L.)	9	0	1	.000	4.50	0	14	17	7	7	5	9
1990	—New York (N.L.)	38	1	0	1.000	3.29	2	65⅔	63	27	24	9	46
	—Tidewater (International)	2	1	0	1.000	2.00	0	9	7	2	2	1	10
1991	—New York (N.L.)	36	7	12	.368	4.19	1	133⅓	142	67	62	25	87
	Major league totals (3 years)	83	8	13	.381	3.93	3	213	222	101	93	39	142

WHITEN, MARK

OF, INDIANS

PERSONAL: Born November 25, 1966, at Pensacola, Fla.... 6-3/215.... Throws right, bats both.... Full name: Mark Anthony Whiten.... Name pronounced WHITT-en.
HIGH SCHOOL: Pensacola (Fla.).
COLLEGE: Pensacola Junior College (Fla.).
TRANSACTIONS/CAREER NOTES: Selected by Toronto Blue Jays organization in fifth round of free-agent draft (January 14, 1986).... On suspended list (May 23-25, 1991).... Traded by Blue Jays with P Denis Boucher, OF Glenallen Hill and a player to be named later (June 27, 1991); Indians acquired cash instead of player to complete deal (October 15, 1991).
STATISTICAL NOTES: Tied for Pioneer League lead in being hit by pitch with six in 1986.... Led South Atlantic League outfielders with 322 total chances and tied for lead with four double plays in 1987.... Led South Atlantic League in being hit by pitch with 16 and tied for lead with 10 intentional bases on balls received in 1987.... Led Southern League in being hit by pitch with 11 in 1989.
MISCELLANEOUS: Batted righthanded only (1988-89).

						BATTING							FIELDING			
Year	Team (League)	Pos.	G	AB	R	H	2B	3B	HR	RBI	Avg.	SB	PO	A	E	Avg.
1986	—Medicine Hat (Pioneer)	OF	•70	270	53	81	16	3	10	44	.300	22	111	9	•10	.923
1987	—Myrtle Beach (S. Atl.)	OF	★139	494	90	125	22	5	15	64	.253	49	★292	★18	12	.963
1988	—Dunedin (Florida State)	OF	99	385	61	97	8	5	7	37	.252	17	200	★21	9	.961
	—Knoxville (Southern)	OF	28	108	20	28	3	1	2	9	.259	6	62	3	4	.942
1989	—Knoxville (Southern)	OF	129	423	75	109	13	6	12	47	.258	11	223	17	8	.968
1990	—Syracuse (International)	OF	104	390	65	113	19	4	14	48	.290	2	158	14	6	.966
	—Toronto (A.L.)	OF	33	88	12	24	1	1	2	7	.273	14	60	3	0	1.000
1991	—Toronto (A.L.)	OF	46	149	12	33	4	3	2	19	.221	0	90	2	0	1.000
	—Cleveland (A.L.)■	OF	70	258	34	66	14	4	7	26	.256	4	166	11	7	.962
	Major league totals (2 years)		149	495	58	123	19	8	11	52	.248	18	316	16	7	.979

WHITSON, ED

P, PADRES

PERSONAL: Born May 19, 1955, at Johnson City, Tenn.... 6-3/200.... Throws right, bats right. ... Full name: Eddie Lee Whitson.
HIGH SCHOOL: Unicoi County (Erwin, Tenn.).
TRANSACTIONS/CAREER NOTES: Selected by Pittsburgh Pirates organization in sixth round of free-agent draft (June 5, 1974).... Traded by Pirates with P Fred Breining and P Al Holland to San Francisco Giants for IF Bill Madlock, IF Lenny Randle and P Dave Roberts (June 28, 1979).... Traded by Giants to Cleveland Indians for 2B Duane Kuiper (November 16, 1981).... Traded by Indians to San Diego Padres for P Juan Eichelberger and 1B-OF Broderick Perkins (November 18, 1982).... On San Diego disabled list (April 18-May 28, 1983); included rehabilitation disability assignment to Las Vegas (May 10-28, 1983).... Granted free agency (November 8, 1984).... Signed by New York Yankees (December 27, 1984).... On New York disabled list (April 30-May 21, 1986).... Traded by Yankees to Padres for P Tim Stoddard (July 9, 1986).... On disabled list (May 27-June 29 and July 6-September 26, 1991).
STATISTICAL NOTES: Led Western Carolinas League with 15 hit batsmen in 1975.... Led Carolina League with 16 complete games in 1976.... Led N.L. with 36 home runs allowed in 1987.

Year	Team (League)	G	W	L	Pct.	ERA	Sv.	IP	H	R	ER	BB	SO
1974	—Bradenton Pirates (GCL)	8	1	4	.200	4.30	0	44	45	28	21	15	25
1975	—Charleston, S.C. (W. Caro.)	24	8	★15	.348	5.07	0	142	140	★96	★80	99	120
1976	—Salem (Carolina)	26	•15	9	.625	2.53	0	★203	168	75	57	65	★186
1977	—Columbus (International)	26	8	13	.381	3.34	0	175	175	74	65	68	120
	—Pittsburgh (N.L.)	5	1	0	1.000	3.38	0	16	11	6	6	9	10
1978	—Columbus (International)	7	2	2	.500	3.71	0	51	56	25	21	10	55
	—Pittsburgh (N.L.)	43	5	6	.455	3.28	4	74	66	31	27	37	64
1979	—Pitts.-San Francisco (N.L.)■...	37	7	11	.389	4.10	1	158	151	83	72	75	93
1980	—San Francisco (N.L.)	34	11	13	.458	3.10	0	212	222	88	73	56	90
1981	—San Francisco (N.L.)	22	6	9	.400	4.02	0	123	130	61	55	47	65
1982	—Cleveland (A.L.)■	40	4	2	.667	3.26	2	107⅔	91	43	39	58	61
1983	—San Diego (N.L.)■	31	5	7	.417	4.30	1	144⅓	143	73	69	50	81
	—Las Vegas (Pacific Coast)	3	1	0	1.000	6.75	0	12	15	9	9	5	11
1984	—San Diego (N.L.)	31	14	8	.636	3.24	0	189	181	72	68	42	103
1985	—New York (A.L.)■	30	10	8	.556	4.88	0	158⅔	201	100	86	43	89
1986	—New York (A.L.)	14	5	2	.714	7.54	0	37	54	37	31	23	27
	—San Diego (N.L.)■	17	1	7	.125	5.62	0	75⅓	85	48	47	37	46
1987	—San Diego (N.L.)	36	10	13	.435	4.73	0	205⅔	197	113	108	64	135
1988	—San Diego (N.L.)	34	13	11	.542	3.77	0	205⅓	202	93	86	45	118
1989	—San Diego (N.L.)	33	16	11	.593	2.66	0	227	198	77	67	48	117

Year Team (League)	G	W	L	Pct.	ERA	Sv.	IP	H	R	ER	BB	SO
1990 —San Diego (N.L.)	32	14	9	.609	2.60	0	228⅔	215	73	66	47	127
1991 —San Diego (N.L.)	13	4	6	.400	5.03	0	78⅔	93	47	44	17	40
American League totals (3 years)	84	19	12	.613	4.63	2	303⅓	346	180	156	124	177
National League totals (13 years)	368	107	111	.491	3.66	6	1937	1894	865	788	574	1089
Major league totals (15 years)	452	126	123	.506	3.79	8	2240⅓	2240	1045	944	698	1266

CHAMPIONSHIP SERIES RECORD

Year Team (League)	G	W	L	Pct.	ERA	Sv.	IP	H	R	ER	BB	SO
1984 —San Diego (N.L.)	1	1	0	1.000	1.13	0	8	5	1	1	2	6

WORLD SERIES RECORD

Year Team (League)	G	W	L	Pct.	ERA	Sv.	IP	H	R	ER	BB	SO
1984 —San Diego (N.L.)	1	0	0	...	40.50	0	⅔	5	3	3	0	0

ALL-STAR GAME RECORD

Year League	W	L	Pct.	ERA	Sv.	IP	H	R	ER	BB	SO
1980 —National					Did not play						

WHITT, ERNIE
C

PERSONAL: Born June 13, 1952, at Detroit.... 6-2/205.... Throws right, bats left.... Full name: Leo Ernest Whitt.
HIGH SCHOOL: Carl Brablec (Roseville, Mich.).
COLLEGE: Macomb County Community College (Mich.).
TRANSACTIONS/CAREER NOTES: Selected by Boston Red Sox organization in 15th round of free-agent draft (June 6, 1972).... On disabled list (April 11-June 13, 1975).... Selected by Toronto Blue Jays in A.L. expansion draft (November 5, 1976).... On Toronto disabled list (August 17-September 27, 1977 and June 16-July 1, 1984).... On Toronto disabled list (April 15-30, 1986); included rehabilitation disability assignment to Syracuse (April 28-30, 1986).... Granted free agency (November 12, 1986).... Re-signed by Blue Jays (January 8, 1987).... Traded by Blue Jays with OF Kevin Batiste to Atlanta Braves for P Rick Trlicek (December 17, 1989).... On Atlanta disabled list (June 3-July 30, 1990); included rehabilitation disability assignment to Greenville (July 24-29, 1990).... Released by Braves (October 15, 1990).... Signed by Baltimore Orioles (April 7, 1991).... Released by Orioles (July 5, 1991).
RECORDS/HONORS: Named catcher on THE SPORTING NEWS A.L. All-Star team (1988).
STATISTICAL NOTES: Tied for Carolina League lead in double plays by catcher with seven in 1973.... Led Eastern League catchers with .992 fielding percentage in 1974.... Led International League with 16 passed balls in 1978.... Led International League catchers with .995 fielding percentage in 1979.... Hit three home runs in a game (September 14, 1987).... Led A.L. catchers with 863 total chances in 1987.

Year Team (League)	Pos.	G	AB	R	H	2B	3B	HR	RBI	Avg.	SB	PO	A	E	Avg.
1972 —Williamsport (NYP)	1B	1	4	1	2	1	0	0	0	.500	0	8	1	0	1.000
—Winter Haven (Fla. St.)	C-1B-OF	31	82	3	15	1	1	0	7	.183	0	151	14	5	.971
1973 —Winston-Salem (Caro.)	C-OF-1B	130	424	63	123	23	3	1	50	.290	7	686	70	15	.981
1974 —Bristol (Eastern)	C-OF-1B	111	385	55	96	10	1	9	56	.249	12	557	50	6	†.990
1975 —Bristol (Eastern)	C-OF	82	252	29	64	9	1	2	19	.254	2	357	36	7	.983
1976 —Bristol (Eastern)	C	26	87	12	19	2	3	1	10	.218	0	127	25	1	.993
—Rhode Island (Int'l)	C-1-0-3	90	304	33	81	16	2	7	42	.266	1	487	59	9	.984
—Boston (A.L.)	C	8	18	4	4	2	0	1	3	.222	0	24	0	0	1.000
1977 —Charleston, W.Va. (Int'l)■	C-3B	29	94	12	24	6	0	0	7	.255	0	129	28	7	.957
—Toronto (A.L.)	C	23	41	4	7	3	0	0	6	.171	0	62	4	0	1.000
1978 —Syracuse (International)	C-1B-OF	121	399	50	98	16	3	12	53	.246	0	673	79	7	.991
—Toronto (A.L.)	C	2	4	0	0	0	0	0	0	.000	0	7	1	0	1.000
1979 —Syracuse (International)	C-OF-3B	114	382	32	95	18	4	7	43	.249	2	494	69	3	†.995
1980 —Toronto (A.L.)	C	106	295	23	70	12	2	6	34	.237	1	436	56	7	.986
1981 —Toronto (A.L.)	C	74	195	16	46	9	0	1	16	.236	5	297	46	3	.991
1982 —Toronto (A.L.)	C	105	284	28	74	14	2	11	42	.261	3	406	30	8	.982
1983 —Toronto (A.L.)	C	123	344	53	88	15	2	17	56	.256	1	554	50	5	.992
1984 —Toronto (A.L.)	C	124	315	35	75	12	1	15	46	.238	0	583	40	4	.994
1985 —Toronto (A.L.)	C	139	412	55	101	21	2	19	64	.245	3	649	38	8	.988
1986 —Toronto (A.L.)	C	131	395	48	106	19	2	16	56	.268	0	717	41	7	.991
1987 —Toronto (A.L.)	C	135	446	57	120	24	1	19	75	.269	0	*803	55	5	.994
1988 —Toronto (A.L.)	C	127	398	63	100	11	2	16	70	.251	4	643	43	4	.994
1989 —Toronto (A.L.)	C	129	385	42	101	24	1	11	53	.262	5	550	43	5	.992
1990 —Atlanta (N.L.)■	C	67	180	14	31	8	0	2	10	.172	0	296	42	3	.991
—Greenville (Southern)	C	4	12	1	4	1	0	0	0	.333	0	14	1	0	1.000
1991 —Baltimore (A.L.)■	C	35	62	5	15	2	0	0	3	.242	0	72	8	0	1.000
American League totals (14 years)		1261	3594	433	907	168	15	132	524	.252	22	5795	455	56	.991
National League totals (1 year)		67	180	14	31	8	0	2	10	.172	0	296	42	3	.991
Major league totals (15 years)		1328	3774	447	938	176	15	134	534	.249	22	6091	497	59	.991

CHAMPIONSHIP SERIES RECORD

Year Team (League)	Pos.	G	AB	R	H	2B	3B	HR	RBI	Avg.	SB	PO	A	E	Avg.
1985 —Toronto (A.L.)	C	7	21	1	4	1	0	0	2	.190	0	50	3	0	1.000
1989 —Toronto (A.L.)	C	5	16	1	2	0	0	1	3	.125	0	32	2	0	1.000
Championship Series totals (2 years)		12	37	2	6	1	0	1	5	.162	0	82	5	0	1.000

Year	League	Pos.	AB	R	H	2B	3B	HR	RBI	Avg.	SB	PO	A	E	Avg.
1985—American		C	0	0	0	0	0	0	0	...	0	2	0	0	1.000

WICKANDER, KEVIN
P, INDIANS

PERSONAL: Born January 4, 1965, at Fort Dodge, Ia. . . . 6-2/202. . . . Throws left, bats left. . . . Full name: Kevin Dean Wickander. **HIGH SCHOOL:** Cortez (Phoenix). **COLLEGE:** Grand Canyon College (Ariz.).

TRANSACTIONS/CAREER NOTES: Selected by Cleveland Indians organization in second round of free-agent draft (June 2, 1986). . . . On disabled list (May 31, 1990-remainder of season).

Year	Team (League)	G	W	L	Pct.	ERA	Sv.	IP	H	R	ER	BB	SO
1986—Batavia (New York-Penn)		11	3	4	.429	2.72	0	46⅓	30	19	14	27	63
1987—Kinston (Carolina)		25	9	6	.600	3.42	0	147⅓	128	69	56	75	118
1988—Williamsport (Eastern)		24	1	0	1.000	0.63	16	28⅔	14	3	2	9	33
—Colorado Springs (Pac. Coast) ..		19	0	2	.000	7.16	0	32⅔	44	30	26	27	22
1989—Colorado Springs (Pac. Coast) ..		45	1	3	.250	2.95	11	42⅔	40	14	14	27	41
—Cleveland (A.L.)		2	0	0	...	3.38	0	2⅔	6	1	1	2	0
1990—Cleveland (A.L.)		10	0	1	.000	3.65	0	12⅓	14	6	5	4	10
1991—Canton/Akron (Eastern)		20	1	2	.333	3.96	0	25	24	14	11	13	21
—Colorado Springs (Pac. Coast) ..		11	1	0	1.000	2.45	2	11	8	3	3	5	9
Major league totals (2 years)		12	0	1	.000	3.60	0	15	20	7	6	6	10

WILKERSON, CURT
IF, ROYALS

PERSONAL: Born April 26, 1961, at Petersburg, Va. . . . 5-9/173. . . . Throws right, bats both. . . . Full name: Curtis Vernon Wilkerson. **HIGH SCHOOL:** Dinwiddie (Va.). **TRANSACTIONS/CAREER NOTES:** Selected by Texas Rangers organization in fourth round of free-agent draft (June 3, 1980). . . . On disabled list (May 19-June 21, 1983). . . . Traded by Rangers with P Mitch Williams, P Paul Kilgus, P Steve Wilson, IF Luis Benitez and OF Pablo Delgado to Chicago Cubs for OF Rafael Palmeiro, P Jamie Moyer and P Drew Hall (December 5, 1988). . . . Granted free agency (November 5, 1990). . . . Signed by Pittsburgh Pirates (January 9, 1991). . . . Granted free agency (November 5, 1991). . . . Signed by Kansas City Royals organization (January 28, 1992).

STATISTICAL NOTES: Tied for Texas League lead with 11 sacrifice hits in 1982.

Year	Team (League)	Pos.	G	AB	R	H	2B	3B	HR	RBI	Avg.	SB	PO	A	E	Avg.
1980—Sarasota Rangers (GCL) ...		SS-2B	37	105	15	20	2	0	0	8	.190	1	38	86	17	.879
1981—Asheville (S. Atlantic)		SS-2B	106	333	45	68	7	3	0	19	.204	12	188	372	28	.952
1982—Burlington (Midwest)		SS-2B	56	198	18	50	6	0	0	13	.253	21	78	159	16	.937
—Tulsa (Texas)		SS	72	266	32	71	6	3	2	14	.267	12	102	225	18	.948
1983—Oklahoma City (A.A.)		SS	89	343	51	107	19	4	3	31	.312	14	135	272	19	.955
—Texas (A.L.)		SS-2B-3B	16	35	7	6	0	1	0	1	.171	3	18	31	1	.980
1984—Texas (A.L.)		SS-2B	153	484	47	120	12	0	1	26	.248	12	227	391	30	.954
1985—Texas (A.L.)		SS-2B	129	360	35	88	11	6	0	22	.244	14	165	328	21	.959
1986—Texas (A.L.)		2B-SS	110	236	27	56	10	3	0	15	.237	9	125	199	13	.961
1987—Texas (A.L.)		SS-2B-3B	85	138	28	37	5	3	2	14	.268	6	79	98	6	.967
1988—Texas (A.L.)		2B-SS-3B	117	338	41	99	12	5	0	28	.293	9	186	299	15	.970
1989—Chicago (N.L.)■		3-2-S-O	77	160	18	39	4	2	1	10	.244	4	42	91	'8	.943
1990—Chicago (N.L.)		3-2-S-O	77	186	21	41	5	1	0	16	.220	2	49	93	14	.910
1991—Pittsburgh (N.L.)■		2B-SS-3B	85	191	20	36	9	1	2	18	.188	2	73	124	2	.990
American League totals (6 years)			610	1591	185	406	50	18	3	106	.255	53	800	1346	86	.961
National League totals (3 years)			239	537	59	116	18	4	3	44	.216	8	164	308	24	.952
Major league totals (9 years)			849	2128	244	522	68	22	6	150	.245	61	964	1654	110	.960

CHAMPIONSHIP SERIES RECORD

Year	Team (League)	Pos.	G	AB	R	H	2B	3B	HR	RBI	Avg.	SB	PO	A	E	Avg.
1989—Chicago (N.L.)		PR-3B-PH	3	2	1	1	0	0	0	0	.500	0	0	0	0	...
1991—Pittsburgh (N.L.)		PH	4	4	0	0	0	0	0	0	.000	0	0	0	0	...
Championship Series totals (2 years)			7	6	1	1	0	0	0	0	.167	0	0	0	0	...

WILKINS, DEAN
P, EXPOS

PERSONAL: Born August 24, 1966, at Chicago. . . . 6-1/170. . . . Throws right, bats right. . . . Full name: Dean Allan Wilkins. **HIGH SCHOOL:** Mira Mesa (Calif.). **COLLEGE:** San Diego Mesa College (Calif.).

TRANSACTIONS/CAREER NOTES: Selected by New York Yankees organization in second round of free-agent draft (January 14, 1986). . . . Traded by Yankees organization with P Rick Scheid and P Bob Tewksbury to Chicago Cubs for P Steve Trout (July 13, 1987). . . . Drafted by Houston Astros (December 3, 1990). . . . Rights retained in exchange for Astros organization sending outright OF-1B Jeff Baldwin to Iowa, Cubs organization (April 24, 1991). . . . Granted free agency (October 16, 1991). . . . Signed by Montreal Expos organization (December 10, 1991).

Year	Team (League)	G	W	L	Pct.	ERA	Sv.	IP	H	R	ER	BB	SO
1986	—Oneonta (New York-Penn)	15	9	0	*1.000	3.13	1	83⅓	64	32	29	24	80
1987	—Fort Lauderdale (Florida St.) ...	15	8	5	.615	2.73	0	105⅔	95	41	32	39	76
	—Albany (Eastern)	2	0	0	...	6.75	0	12	18	11	9	1	8
	—Winston-Salem (Carolina)■	13	4	4	.500	4.11	1	50⅓	49	31	23	24	29
1988	—Pittsfield (Eastern)	*59	5	7	.417	1.63	*26	71⅔	53	25	13	30	59
1989	—Iowa (American Association) ...	38	8	11	.421	4.24	3	138	149	74	65	58	82
	—Chicago (N.L.)	11	1	0	1.000	5.17	0	15⅔	13	9	9	9	14
1990	—Iowa (American Association) ...	52	6	2	.750	3.70	11	73	75	37	30	38	61
	—Chicago (N.L.)	7	0	0	...	9.82	1	7⅓	11	8	8	7	3
1991	—Tucson (Pacific Coast)■	*65	8	7	.533	4.20	*21	83⅔	84	47	39	43	65
	—Houston (N.L.)	7	2	1	.667	11.25	1	8	16	14	10	10	4
	Major league totals (3 years)	25	3	1	.750	7.84	2	31	40	31	27	26	21

WILKINS, RICK
C, CUBS

PERSONAL: Born July 4, 1967, at Jacksonville, Fla. ... 6-2/210. ... Throws right, bats left. ... Full name: Richard David Wilkins.
HIGH SCHOOL: Bolles (Jacksonville, Fla.).
COLLEGE: Florida Community College and Furman.
TRANSACTIONS/CAREER NOTES: Selected by Chicago Cubs organization in 23rd round of free-agent draft (June 2, 1986).
STATISTICAL NOTES: Led Appalachian League with eight intentional bases on balls received in 1987. ... Led Appalachian League catchers with .989 fielding percentage, 483 putouts and 540 total chances and tied for lead with six double plays in 1987. ... Led Midwest League catchers with 984 total chances in 1988. ... Led Carolina League catchers with 860 total chances and tied for lead with eight double plays in 1989. ... Led Southern League catchers with 857 total chances, 11 double plays and 15 passed balls in 1990.

Year	Team (League)	Pos.	G	AB	R	H	2B	3B	HR	RBI	Avg.	SB	PO	A	E	Avg.
1987	—Geneva (N.Y.-Penn)	C-1B	75	243	35	61	8	2	8	43	.251	7	†503	51	7	†.988
1988	—Peoria (Midwest)	C	137	490	54	119	30	1	8	63	.243	4	*864	101	*19	.981
1989	—Winston-Salem (Caro.)	C	132	445	61	111	24	1	12	54	.249	4	*764	*78	*18	.979
1990	—Charlotte (Southern)	C	127	449	48	102	18	1	17	71	.227	4	*740	*103	14	.984
1991	—Iowa (American Assoc.) ...	C-OF	38	107	12	29	3	1	5	14	.271	1	204	24	3	.987
	—Chicago (N.L.)	C	86	203	21	45	9	0	6	22	.222	3	373	42	3	.993
	Major league totals (1 year)		86	203	21	45	9	0	6	22	.222	3	373	42	3	.993

WILLARD, JERRY
C, BRAVES

PERSONAL: Born March 14, 1960, at Oxnard, Calif. ... 6-2/195. ... Throws right, bats left. ... Full name: Gerald Duane Willard Jr.
HIGH SCHOOL: Hueneme (Calif.).
COLLEGE: Oxnard College (Calif.).
TRANSACTIONS/CAREER NOTES: Signed as free agent by Philadelphia Phillies organization (December 20, 1979). ... Traded by Phillies organization with 2B Manny Trillo, IF Julio Franco, OF George Vukovich and P Jay Baller to Cleveland Indians for OF Von Hayes (December 9, 1982). ... Released by Indians organization (April 1, 1986). ... Signed by Tacoma, Oakland A's organization (April 4, 1986). ... On Oakland disabled list (May 11-June 29, 1987). ... Released by A's (October 12, 1987). ... Signed by Vancouver, Chicago White Sox organization (February 10, 1989). ... On Vancouver disabled list (May 10-24, 1989). ... Released by White Sox (November 30, 1990). ... Signed by Atlanta Braves (January 19, 1991).
STATISTICAL NOTES: Led International League catchers with 78 assists in 1983. ... Led Pacific Coast League catchers with 12 double plays in 1989. ... Led Pacific Coast League with 18 passed balls in 1990.

Year	Team (League)	Pos.	G	AB	R	H	2B	3B	HR	RBI	Avg.	SB	PO	A	E	Avg.
1980	—Central Oregon (N'West) ..	C	65	231	53	85	21	1	5	59	.368	2	283	37	*18	.947
1981	—Peninsula (Carolina)	C	107	334	43	87	17	1	12	60	.260	6	319	28	3	.991
1982	—Reading (Eastern)	C	81	281	43	82	10	1	12	51	.292	1	534	64	13	.979
	—Oklahoma City (A.A.)	C	36	95	13	22	5	0	2	14	.232	1	169	35	8	.962
1983	—Charleston, W.Va. (Int'l)■.	C-3B-OF	127	396	61	119	22	2	19	77	.301	0	613	†79	12	.983
1984	—Cleveland (A.L.)	C	87	246	21	55	8	1	10	37	.224	1	335	35	7	.981
1985	—Cleveland (A.L.)	C	104	300	39	81	13	0	7	36	.270	1	427	52	5	.990
	—Maine (International)	C	11	40	5	9	3	0	1	4	.225	1	56	11	2	.971
1986	—Tacoma (Pacific Coast)■..	C	22	62	7	16	5	0	1	12	.258	0	100	7	1	.991
	—Oakland (A.L.)	C	75	161	17	43	7	0	4	26	.267	0	300	12	2	.994
1987	—Tacoma (Pacific Coast) ...	O-C-1-3	67	215	42	64	15	0	6	38	.298	0	117	14	4	.970
	—Oakland (A.L.)	1B-3B	7	6	1	1	0	0	0	0	.167	0	1	0	1	1.000
1988							Out of Organized Baseball										
1989	—Birmingham (Southern)■..	C	5	10	5	3	1	0	0	1	.300	0	38	4	2	.955
	—Vancouver (Pac. Coast)....	C-1B	90	283	32	78	18	1	7	38	.276	0	435	56	1	.998
1990	—Vancouver (Pac. Coast)....	C-1B	121	380	66	106	21	0	20	76	.279	2	550	74	12	.981
	—Chicago (A.L.)	C	3	3	0	0	0	0	0	0	.000	0	0	0	0	...
1991	—Richmond (Int'l)■	C	91	277	42	83	24	0	8	39	.300	1	411	37	6	.987
	—Atlanta (N.L.)	C	17	14	1	3	0	0	1	4	.214	0	3	0	0	1.000
	American League totals (5 years)		276	716	78	180	28	1	21	99	.251	1	1063	99	14	.988
	National League totals (1 year)		17	14	1	3	0	0	1	4	.214	0	3	0	0	1.000
	Major league totals (6 years)		293	730	79	183	28	1	22	103	.251	1	1066	99	14	.988

CHAMPIONSHIP SERIES RECORD

Year	Team (League)	Pos.	G	AB	R	H	2B	3B	HR	RBI	Avg.	SB	PO	A	E	Avg.
1991 — Atlanta (N.L.)		PH	2	2	0	0	0	0	0	0	.000	0	0	0	0	...

WORLD SERIES RECORD

Year	Team (League)	Pos.	G	AB	R	H	2B	3B	HR	RBI	Avg.	SB	PO	A	E	Avg.
1991 — Atlanta (N.L.)		PH	1	0	0	0	0	0	0	1	...	0	0	0	0	...

WILLIAMS, BERNIE
OF, YANKEES

PERSONAL: Born September 13, 1968, at San Juan, Puerto Rico. . . . 6-2/196. . . . Throws right, bats both. . . . Full name: Bernabe Figueroa Williams.
TRANSACTIONS/CAREER NOTES: Signed as free agent by New York Yankees organization (September 13, 1985). . . . On disabled list (July 15, 1988-remainder of season).
RECORDS/HONORS: Shares major league single-game record (nine innings) for most strikeouts—5 (August 21, 1991).
STATISTICAL NOTES: Led Gulf Coast League outfielders with 123 total chances in 1986. . . . Tied for Gulf Coast League lead in caught stealing with 12 in 1986. . . . Led Eastern League in bases on balls received with 98 and caught stealing with 18 in 1990. . . . Led Eastern League outfielders with 307 total chances and tied for lead with four double plays in 1990.
MISCELLANEOUS: Batted righthanded only (1986-88).

Year	Team (League)	Pos.	G	AB	R	H	2B	3B	HR	RBI	Avg.	SB	PO	A	E	Avg.
1986 — Sarasota Yankees (GCL) ..		OF	61	230	*45	62	5	3	2	25	.270	33	*117	3	3	.976
1987 — Fort Lauderdale (FSL)		OF	25	71	11	11	3	0	0	4	.155	9	49	1	0	1.000
— Oneonta (N.Y.-Penn)		OF	25	93	13	32	4	0	0	15	.344	9	40	0	2	.952
1988 — Prince William (Caro.).......		OF	92	337	72	113	16	7	7	45	*.335	29	186	8	5	.975
1989 — Columbus (Int'l)		OF	50	162	21	35	8	1	2	16	.216	11	112	2	1	.991
— Albany (Eastern)		OF	91	314	63	79	11	8	11	42	.252	26	180	5	5	.974
1990 — Albany (Eastern)		OF	134	466	*91	131	28	5	8	54	.281	*39	*288	15	4	.987
1991 — Columbus (Int'l)		OF	78	306	52	90	14	6	8	37	.294	9	164	2	1	.994
— New York (A.L.)		OF	85	320	43	76	19	4	3	34	.238	10	230	3	5	.979
Major league totals (1 year)			85	320	43	76	19	4	3	34	.238	10	230	3	5	.979

WILLIAMS, BRIAN
P, ASTROS

PERSONAL: Born February 15, 1969, at Lancaster, S.C. . . . 6-2/195. . . . Throws right, bats right. . . . Full name: Brian O'Neal Williams.
COLLEGE: South Carolina.
TRANSACTIONS/CAREER NOTES: Selected by Pittsburgh Pirates organization in third round of free-agent draft (June 2, 1987). . . . Selected by Houston Astros organization in first round (31st pick overall) of free-agent draft (June 4, 1990).

Year	Team (League)	G	W	L	Pct.	ERA	Sv.	IP	H	R	ER	BB	SO
1990 — Auburn (New York-Penn)		3	0	0	...	4.05	0	6⅔	6	5	3	6	7
1991 — Jackson (Texas)		3	2	1	.667	4.20	0	15	17	8	7	7	15
— Tucson (Pacific Coast)		7	0	1	.000	4.93	0	38⅓	39	25	21	22	29
— Houston (N.L.)		2	0	1	.000	3.75	0	12	11	5	5	4	4
Major league totals (1 year)		2	0	1	.000	3.75	0	12	11	5	5	4	4

WILLIAMS, CARY
OF, PHILLIES

PERSONAL: Born June 14, 1967, at Florence, Ala. . . . 6-3/190. . . . Throws right, bats right. . . . Full name: Cary Wayne Williams.
HIGH SCHOOL: Bradshaw (Florence, Ala.).
COLLEGE: John C. Calhoun Community College (Ala.) and Alabama.
TRANSACTIONS/CAREER NOTES: Selected by Philadelphia Phillies organization in 10th round of free-agent draft (June 5, 1989).

Year	Team (League)	Pos.	G	AB	R	H	2B	3B	HR	RBI	Avg.	SB	PO	A	E	Avg.
1989 — Clearwater (Florida St.)		OF	52	187	35	50	14	0	2	14	.267	9	124	7	2	.985
1990 — Clearwater (Florida St.)		OF	63	245	20	64	12	3	1	21	.261	2	144	9	3	.981
— Reading (Eastern)		OF	49	179	16	44	10	0	2	18	.246	0	107	4	3	.974
1991 — Reading (Eastern)		OF	116	421	55	117	21	3	6	62	.278	12	228	5	5	.979

WILLIAMS, GERALD
OF, YANKEES

PERSONAL: Born August 10, 1966, at New Orleans. . . . 6-2/190. . . . Throws right, bats right. . . . Full name: Gerald Floyd Williams.
COLLEGE: Grambling State.
TRANSACTIONS/CAREER NOTES: Selected by New York Yankees organization in 14th round of free-agent draft (June 2, 1987).
STATISTICAL NOTES: Led Carolina League outfielders with 307 total chances in 1989.

Year	Team (League)	Pos.	G	AB	R	H	2B	3B	HR	RBI	Avg.	SB	PO	A	E	Avg.
1987 — Oneonta (N.Y.-Penn)		OF	29	115	26	42	6	2	2	29	.365	6	68	3	3	.959
1988 — Prince William (Caro.).......		OF	54	159	20	29	3	0	2	18	.182	6	71	2	3	.961
— Fort Lauderdale (FSL)		OF	63	212	21	40	7	2	2	17	.189	4	163	2	6	.965

Year	Team (League)	Pos.	G	AB	R	H	2B	3B	HR	RBI	Avg.	SB	PO	A	E	Avg.
1989 —Prince William (Caro.).......		OF	134	454	63	104	19	6	13	69	.229	15	*292	7	8	.974
1990 —Fort Lauderdale (FSL)		OF	50	204	25	59	4	5	7	43	.289	19	115	1	3	.975
—Albany (Eastern)..............		OF	96	324	54	81	17	2	13	58	.250	18	210	6	7	.969
1991 —Albany/Colonie (East.).....		OF	45	175	28	50	15	0	5	32	.286	18	109	4	3	.974
—Columbus (Int'l)		OF	61	198	20	51	8	3	2	27	.258	9	124	1	3	.977

WILLIAMS, KENNY
OF

PERSONAL: Born April 6, 1964, at Berkeley, Calif.... 6-1/195.... Throws right, bats right.... Full name: Kenneth Royal Williams.
HIGH SCHOOL: Mount Pleasant (San Jose, Calif.).
COLLEGE: Stanford.
TRANSACTIONS/CAREER NOTES: Selected by Chicago White Sox organization in third round of free-agent draft (June 7, 1982). ... On Chicago disabled list (May 25-June 30, 1988).... Traded by White Sox to Detroit Tigers for P Eric King (March 23, 1989).... On Detroit disabled list (June 23-July 29, 1989); included rehabilitation disability assignment to Toledo (July 14-29, 1989).... Claimed on waivers by Toronto Blue Jays (June 18, 1990).... Claimed on waivers by Montreal Expos (June 4, 1991).... On Montreal disabled list (June 13-28, 1991).... Released by Expos (November 18, 1991).

Year	Team (League)	Pos.	G	AB	R	H	2B	3B	HR	RBI	Avg.	SB	PO	A	E	Avg.
1982 —Sara. White Sox (GCL)		OF	31	104	19	31	2	1	1	11	.298	9	61	2	0	1.000
1983 — Appleton (Midwest).........		OF	124	415	60	96	18	2	12	53	.231	27	218	10	10	.958
1984 — Appleton (Midwest).........		OF	38	147	23	42	11	2	5	26	.286	13	58	5	2	.969
—Glens Falls (Eastern)		OF	97	309	35	76	7	5	8	47	.246	16	173	10	5	.973
1985 —Glens Falls (Eastern)		OF	133	*520	*87	130	16	6	16	66	.250	27	296	*20	*14	.958
1986 —Buffalo (Am. Assoc.)		OF	50	189	21	40	4	2	4	15	.212	5	100	8	1	.991
—Birmingham (Southern)		OF	68	272	41	90	16	5	6	40	.331	26	192	3	8	.961
—Chicago (A.L.)		OF	15	31	2	4	0	0	1	1	.129	1	18	1	0	1.000
1987 —Hawaii (Pacific Coast)		OF	35	134	19	36	4	4	3	14	.269	5	75	1	2	.974
—Chicago (A.L.)		OF	116	391	48	110	18	2	11	50	.281	21	303	5	6	.981
1988 —Chicago (A.L.)	OF-3B	73	220	18	35	4	2	8	28	.159	5	87	69	17	.902
—Vancouver (Pac. Coast)		OF	16	60	8	15	2	1	1	7	.250	2	23	0	0	1.000
1989 —Detroit (A.L.)■...............	OF-1B	94	258	29	53	5	1	6	23	.205	9	180	11	4	.979
—Toledo (International)		OF	14	51	8	13	2	0	3	8	.255	2	27	1	0	1.000
1990 —Detroit-Toronto (A.L.)■....		OF	106	155	23	25	8	1	0	13	.161	9	103	5	0	1.000
1991 —Syracuse (International) ..		OF	15	54	14	18	1	0	7	19	.333	4	31	1	0	1.000
—Toronto (A.L.).................		OF	13	29	5	6	2	0	1	3	.207	1	16	1	0	1.000
—Montreal (N.L.)■.............		OF	34	70	11	19	5	2	0	1	.271	2	42	3	2	.957
—Indianapolis (A.A.)...........		OF	18	47	7	11	3	1	2	7	.234	1	30	3	0	1.000
American League totals (6 years)			417	1084	125	233	37	6	27	118	.215	46	707	92	27	.967
National League totals (1 year)			34	70	11	19	5	2	0	1	.271	2	42	3	2	.957
Major league totals (6 years)			451	1154	136	252	42	8	27	119	.218	48	749	95	29	.967

WILLIAMS, MATT
3B, GIANTS

PERSONAL: Born November 28, 1965, at Bishop, Calif.... 6-2/210.... Throws right, bats right.... Full name: Matthew Derrick Williams.
HIGH SCHOOL: Carson (Nev.).
COLLEGE: UNLV.
TRANSACTIONS/CAREER NOTES: Selected by New York Mets organization in 27th round of free-agent draft (June 6, 1983).... Selected by San Francisco Giants organization in first round (third pick overall) of free-agent draft (June 2, 1986).
RECORDS/HONORS: Named shortstop on THE SPORTING NEWS college All-America team (1986).... Named third baseman on THE SPORTING NEWS N.L. All-Star team (1990).... Named third baseman on THE SPORTING NEWS N.L. Silver Slugger team (1990).... Won N.L. Gold Glove at third base (1991).
STATISTICAL NOTES: Led N.L. third basemen with 33 double plays and tied for lead with 465 total chances in 1990.... Led N.L. third basemen with 131 putouts in 1991.

Year	Team (League)	Pos.	G	AB	R	H	2B	3B	HR	RBI	Avg.	SB	PO	A	E	Avg.
1986 —Everett (Northwest)		SS	4	17	3	4	0	1	1	10	.235	0	5	10	2	.882
—Clinton (Midwest).............		SS	68	250	32	60	14	3	7	29	.240	3	89	150	10	.960
1987 —Phoenix (Pacific Coast) ..	3B-2B-SS	56	211	36	61	15	2	6	37	.289	6	53	136	14	.931
—San Francisco (N.L.)	SS-3B	84	245	28	46	9	2	8	21	.188	4	110	234	9	.975
1988 —Phoenix (Pacific Coast) ..	3-S-2-0	82	306	45	83	19	1	12	51	.271	6	56	173	13	.946
—San Francisco (N.L.)	3B-SS	52	156	17	32	6	1	8	19	.205	0	48	108	7	.957
1989 —San Francisco (N.L.)	3B-SS	84	292	31	59	18	1	18	50	.202	1	90	168	10	.963
—Phoenix (Pacific Coast) ..	3B-SS-OF	76	284	61	91	20	2	26	61	.320	9	57	197	11	.958
1990 —San Francisco (N.L.)	3B	159	617	87	171	27	2	33	*122	.277	7	*140	306	19	.959
1991 —San Francisco (N.L.)	3B-SS	157	589	72	158	24	5	34	98	.268	5	†134	295	16	.964
Major league totals (5 years)			536	1899	235	466	84	11	101	310	.245	17	522	1111	61	.964

CHAMPIONSHIP SERIES RECORD
CHAMPIONSHIP SERIES NOTES: Holds N.L. single-series record for most runs batted in—9 (1989).

Year	Team (League)	Pos.	G	AB	R	H	2B	3B	HR	RBI	Avg.	SB	PO	A	E	Avg.
1989 —San Francisco (N.L.)	3B-SS	5	20	2	6	1	0	2	9	.300	0	5	12	0	1.000

WORLD SERIES RECORD

Year	Team (League)	Pos.	G	AB	R	H	2B	3B	HR	RBI	Avg.	SB	PO	A	E	Avg.
						BATTING								**FIELDING**		
1989	San Francisco (N.L.)	3B-SS	4	16	1	2	0	0	1	1	.125	0	4	12	0	1.000

ALL-STAR GAME RECORD

Year	League	Pos.	AB	R	H	2B	3B	HR	RBI	Avg.	SB	PO	A	E	Avg.
					BATTING								**FIELDING**		
1990	National	PH	0	0	0	0	0	0	0	...	0	0	0	0	...

WILLIAMS, MITCH
P, PHILLIES

PERSONAL: Born November 17, 1964, at Santa Ana, Calif.... 6-4/205.... Throws left, bats left.... Full name: Mitchell Steven Williams.... Brother of Bruce Williams, minor league pitcher (1981-85).
HIGH SCHOOL: West Linn (Ore.).

TRANSACTIONS/CAREER NOTES: Selected by San Diego Padres organization in eighth round of free-agent draft (June 7, 1982). ... Drafted by Texas Rangers (December 3, 1984).... Returned to Padres organization (April 6, 1985).... Traded by Padres organization to Rangers for 3B Randy Asadoor (April 6, 1985).... On suspended list (May 2-4, 1988).... Traded by Rangers with P Paul Kilgus, P Steve Wilson, IF Curtis Wilkerson, IF Luis Benitez and OF Pablo Delgado to Chicago Cubs for OF Rafael Palmeiro, P Jamie Moyer and P Drew Hall (December 5, 1988).... On disabled list (June 12-July 12, 1990).... Traded by Cubs to Philadelphia Phillies for P Chuck McElroy and P Bob Scanlon (April 7, 1991).... Granted free agency (October 31, 1991).... Re-signed by Phillies (December 18, 1991).
RECORDS/HONORS: Holds major league rookie-season record for most games pitched—80 (1986).
STATISTICAL NOTES: Led Northwest League pitchers with 14 wild pitches and tied for lead with 14 games started and two balks in 1983.

Year	Team (League)	G	W	L	Pct.	ERA	Sv.	IP	H	R	ER	BB	SO
1982	Walla Walla (Northwest)	12	3	4	.429	4.78	0	58⅓	37	37	31	*72	66
1983	Reno (California)	11	1	7	.125	7.14	0	58	58	56	46	60	44
	Spokane (Northwest)	14	7	6	.538	4.48	0	92⅓	84	51	•46	55	87
1984	Reno (California)	26	9	8	.529	4.99	0	164	163	113	91	127	165
1985	Salem (Carolina)■	22	6	9	.400	5.45	0	99	57	64	60	*117	138
	Tulsa (Texas)	6	2	2	.500	4.64	0	33	17	24	17	48	37
1986	Texas (A.L.)	*80	8	6	.571	3.58	8	98	69	39	39	79	90
1987	Texas (A.L.)	85	8	6	.571	3.23	6	108⅔	63	47	39	94	129
1988	Texas (A.L.)	67	2	7	.222	4.63	18	68	48	38	35	47	61
1989	Chicago (N.L.)■	*76	4	4	.500	2.64	36	81⅓	71	27	24	52	67
1990	Chicago (N.L.)	59	1	8	.111	3.93	16	66⅓	60	38	29	50	55
1991	Philadelphia (N.L.)■	69	12	5	.706	2.34	30	88⅓	56	24	23	62	84
American League totals (3 years)		232	18	19	.486	3.70	32	274⅔	180	124	113	220	280
National League totals (3 years)		204	17	17	.500	2.89	82	236⅓	187	89	76	164	206
Major league totals (6 years)		436	35	36	.493	3.33	114	511	367	213	189	384	486

CHAMPIONSHIP SERIES RECORD

Year	Team (League)	G	W	L	Pct.	ERA	Sv.	IP	H	R	ER	BB	SO
1989	Chicago (N.L.)	2	0	0	...	0.00	0	1	1	0	0	0	2

ALL-STAR GAME RECORD

Year	League	W	L	Pct.	ERA	Sv.	IP	H	R	ER	BB	SO
1989	National	0	0	...	0.00	0	1	0	0	0	1	1

WILLIAMSON, MARK
P, ORIOLES

PERSONAL: Born July 21, 1959, at Corpus Christi, Tex.... 6-0/177.... Throws right, bats right.... Full name: Mark Alan Williamson.
HIGH SCHOOL: Mt. Miguel (Calif.).
COLLEGE: Grossmont College (Calif.) and San Diego State (degree in mechanical engineering).
TRANSACTIONS/CAREER NOTES: Selected by Kansas City Royals organization in 12th round of free-agent draft (June 8, 1981). ... Selected by San Diego Padres organization in fourth round of free-agent draft (June 7, 1982).... Traded by Padres organization with C Terry Kennedy to Baltimore Orioles for P Storm Davis (October 30, 1986).... On disabled list (March 31-April 22 and August 19, 1990-remainder of season; and August 14-September 1, 1991).
STATISTICAL NOTES: Pitched one inning, combining with Bob Milacki, Mike Flanagan and Gregg Olson in 2-0 nine-inning no-hit victory against Oakland Athletics (July 13, 1991).

Year	Team (League)	G	W	L	Pct.	ERA	Sv.	IP	H	R	ER	BB	SO
1982	Reno (California)	26	7	5	.583	4.39	9	41	34	24	20	18	30
1983	Beaumont (Texas)	47	6	3	.667	4.03	3	82⅔	90	45	37	30	39
1984	Reno (California)	56	10	12	.455	2.90	15	93	105	41	30	23	69
1985	Beaumont (Texas)	42	10	9	.526	2.86	8	78⅔	72	27	25	23	64
1986	Las Vegas (Pacific Coast)	*65	10	3	*.769	3.36	•16	104⅓	103	47	39	36	81
1987	Baltimore (A.L.)■	61	8	9	.471	4.03	3	125	122	59	56	41	73
	Rochester (International)	1	0	1	.000	6.75	0	4	6	3	3	1	1
1988	Baltimore (A.L.)	37	5	8	.385	4.90	2	117⅔	125	70	64	40	69
	Rochester (International)	12	2	3	.400	3.34	2	29⅔	38	11	11	5	25
1989	Baltimore (A.L.)	65	10	5	.667	2.93	9	107⅓	105	35	35	30	55
1990	Baltimore (A.L.)	49	8	2	.800	2.21	1	85⅓	65	25	21	28	60
1991	Baltimore (A.L.)	65	5	5	.500	4.48	4	80⅓	87	42	40	35	53
Major league totals (5 years)		277	36	29	.554	3.77	19	515⅔	504	231	216	174	310

WILLIS, CARL

P, TWINS

PERSONAL: Born December 28, 1960, at Danville, Va. . . . 6-4/212. . . . Throws right, bats left. . . . Full name: Carl Blake Willis.
HIGH SCHOOL: Piedmont Academy (Providence, N.C.).
COLLEGE: UNC Wilmington.
TRANSACTIONS/CAREER NOTES: Selected by San Francisco Giants organization in 31st round of free-agent draft (June 7, 1982). . . . Selected by Detroit Tigers organization in 23rd round of free-agent draft (June 6, 1983). . . . Traded by Tigers to Cincinnati Reds (September 1, 1984), completing deal in which Reds traded P Bill Scherrer to Tigers for cash and a player to be named later (August 27, 1984). . . . Drafted by California Angels (December 10, 1985). . . . Returned to Reds organization (April 6, 1986). . . . Traded by Reds organization to Chicago White Sox for OF Darrell Pruitt (January 19, 1988). . . . Drafted by Edmonton, Angels organization (December 6, 1988). . . . Granted free agency (October 22, 1989). . . . Signed by Colorado Springs, Cleveland Indians organization (December 20, 1989). . . . Granted free agency (October 15, 1990). . . . Signed by Portland, Minnesota Twins organization (December 12, 1990).

Year	Team (League)	G	W	L	Pct.	ERA	Sv.	IP	H	R	ER	BB	SO
1983	Bristol (Appalachian)	2	0	1	.000	3.38	0	2 2/3	0	1	1	4	3
	Lakeland (Florida State)	4	3	0	1.000	0.00	0	9 2/3	6	0	0	5	7
	Birmingham (Southern)	14	3	1	.750	3.98	2	20 1/3	16	9	9	7	13
1984	Evansville (Am. Assoc.)	40	5	3	.625	3.73	16	60 1/3	59	26	25	20	27
	Detroit (A.L.)	10	0	2	.000	7.31	0	16	25	13	13	5	4
	Cincinnati (N.L.)■	7	0	1	.000	3.72	1	9 2/3	8	4	4	2	3
1985	Cincinnati (N.L.)	11	1	0	1.000	9.22	1	13 2/3	21	18	14	5	6
	Denver (American Assoc.)	37	4	4	.500	4.15	8	78	82	39	36	30	27
1986	Denver (American Assoc.)	20	1	3	.250	4.68	8	32 2/3	39	22	17	16	16
	Cincinnati (N.L.)	29	1	3	.250	4.47	0	52 1/3	54	29	26	32	24
1987	Nashville (American Assoc.)	53	6	4	.600	3.33	5	83 2/3	97	39	31	30	54
1988	Vancouver (Pacific Coast)■	40	4	4	.500	4.22	4	64	77	36	30	16	44
	Chicago (A.L.)	6	0	0	. . .	8.25	0	12	17	12	11	7	6
1989	Edmonton (Pacific Coast)■	36	5	7	.417	3.69	5	112 1/3	137	54	46	36	47
1990	Colorado Springs (Pac. Coast)■	41	5	3	.625	6.39	2	98 2/3	136	80	70	32	42
1991	Portland (Pacific Coast)■	3	1	1	.500	1.64	0	11	5	4	2	0	0
	Minnesota (A.L.)	40	8	3	.727	2.63	2	89	76	31	26	19	53
	American League totals (3 years)	56	8	5	.615	3.85	2	117	118	56	50	31	63
	National League totals (3 years)	47	2	4	.333	5.23	2	75 2/3	83	51	44	39	33
	Major league totals (5 years)	103	10	9	.526	4.39	4	192 2/3	201	107	94	70	96

CHAMPIONSHIP SERIES RECORD

Year	Team (League)	G	W	L	Pct.	ERA	Sv.	IP	H	R	ER	BB	SO
1991	Minnesota (A.L.)	3	0	0	. . .	0.00	0	5 1/3	2	0	0	0	3

WORLD SERIES RECORD

Year	Team (League)	G	W	L	Pct.	ERA	Sv.	IP	H	R	ER	BB	SO
1991	Minnesota (A.L.)	4	0	0	. . .	5.14	0	7	6	4	4	2	2

WILLS, FRANK

P

PERSONAL: Born October 26, 1958, at New Orleans. . . . 6-2/210. . . . Throws right, bats right. . . . Full name: Frank Lee Wills Jr.
HIGH SCHOOL: De La Salle (La.).
COLLEGE: Tulane.
TRANSACTIONS/CAREER NOTES: Selected by Kansas City Royals organization in first round (16th pick overall) of free-agent draft (June 3, 1980). . . . On Kansas City disabled list (August 1-16, 1984). . . . Traded by Royals to New York Mets organization as part of a six-player, four-team deal in which Royals acquired C Jim Sundberg from Brewers, Rangers acquired C Don Slaught from Royals, Brewers acquired P Danny Darwin and a player to be named later from Rangers and P Tim Leary from Mets (January 18, 1985); Brewers organization acquired C Bill Hance from Rangers to complete deal (January 30, 1985). . . . Traded by Mets to Seattle Mariners organization for P Wray Bergendahl (March 29, 1985). . . . Released by Mariners (March 20, 1986). . . . Signed by Maine, Cleveland Indians organization (March 27, 1986). . . . On Maine disabled list (May 4-31, 1986). . . . Released by Indians (March 29, 1988). . . . Signed by Knoxville, Toronto Blue Jays organization (April 7, 1988). . . . Released by Blue Jays (October 28, 1988). . . . Re-signed by Blue Jays organization (January 12, 1989). . . . Granted free agency (October 16, 1991).
RECORDS/HONORS: Named righthanded pitcher on THE SPORTING NEWS college All-America team (1980).
STATISTICAL NOTES: Tied for Southern League lead with 15 wild pitches in 1981. . . . Pitched seven-inning, 1-0 no-hit victory against Tacoma (May 31, 1985, first game).

Year	Team (League)	G	W	L	Pct.	ERA	Sv.	IP	H	R	ER	BB	SO
1980	Sarasota Royals-Blue (GCL)	4	2	0	1.000	1.96	0	23	18	7	5	8	20
	Charleston, S.C. (S. Atlantic)	9	2	5	.286	3.63	0	57	59	33	23	32	48
1981	Jacksonville (Southern)	27	9	14	.391	3.98	0	192	199	104	85	91	174
1982	Omaha (American Assoc.)	41	7	10	.412	5.20	3	107 1/3	110	71	62	*81	77
1983	Jacksonville (Southern)	8	5	2	.714	2.48	0	54 1/3	44	19	15	23	40
	Omaha (American Assoc.)	16	4	11	.267	4.74	0	95	96	56	50	45	65
	Kansas City (A.L.)	6	2	1	.667	4.15	0	34 2/3	35	17	16	15	23
1984	Omaha (American Assoc.)	15	7	4	.636	2.81	0	89 2/3	75	32	28	49	69
	Kansas City (A.L.)	10	2	3	.400	5.11	0	37	39	21	21	13	21
1985	Calgary (Pacific Coast)■	9	4	3	.571	4.86	0	46 1/3	44	27	25	25	31
	Seattle (A.L.)	24	5	11	.313	6.00	1	123	122	85	82	68	67
1986	Maine (International)■	22	4	3	.571	2.87	6	31 1/3	37	10	10	10	21
	Cleveland (A.L.)	26	4	4	.500	4.91	4	40 1/3	43	23	22	16	32

Year	Team (League)	G	W	L	Pct.	ERA	Sv.	IP	H	R	ER	BB	SO
1987 —Buffalo (American Assoc.)		36	3	2	.600	3.34	6	56⅔	53	28	21	22	45
—Cleveland (A.L.)		6	0	1	.000	5.06	1	5⅓	3	3	3	7	4
1988 —Syracuse (International)■		25	6	4	.600	3.24	3	80⅔	70	40	29	25	53
—Toronto (A.L.)........................		10	0	0	....	5.23	0	20⅔	22	12	12	6	19
1989 —Syracuse (International)		14	1	0	1.000	1.59	5	17	8	7	3	8	13
—Toronto (A.L.)........................		24	3	1	.750	3.66	0	71⅓	65	31	29	30	41
1990 —Toronto (A.L.)........................		44	6	4	.600	4.73	0	99	101	54	52	38	72
1991 —Toronto (A.L.)........................		4	0	1	.000	16.62	0	4⅓	8	8	8	5	2
—Syracuse (International)		22	3	5	.375	4.84	1	61⅓	71	35	33	21	38
Major league totals (9 years)		**154**	**22**	**26**	**.458**	**5.06**	**6**	**435⅔**	**438**	**254**	**245**	**198**	**281**

WILSON, CRAIG
IF/OF, CARDINALS

PERSONAL: Born November 28, 1964, at Anne Arundel County, Md. . . . 5-11/208. . . . Throws right, bats right. . . . Full name: Craig Wilson.
HIGH SCHOOL: Annapolis (Md.).
COLLEGE: Anne Arundel Community College (Md.).
TRANSACTIONS/CAREER NOTES: Selected by St. Louis Cardinals organization in 20th round of free-agent draft (June 4, 1984).
STATISTICAL NOTES: Led Midwest League third basemen with .932 fielding percentage in 1985. . . . Led Midwest League second basemen with 653 total chances and 86 double plays in 1986. . . . Led American Association third basemen with 264 assists, 26 errors, 386 total chances and 28 double plays in 1988.

						BATTING						FIELDING			
Year	Team (League)	Pos.	G	AB	R	H	2B	3B	HR	RBI	Avg.	SB	PO	A	E	Avg.
1984 —Erie (New York-Penn)	2B-3B-SS	72	282	53	83	18	4	7	46	.294	10	169	206	14	.964
1985 —Springfield (Midwest)	3B-2B	133	504	64	132	16	4	8	52	.262	33	156	293	27 †.943
1986 —Springfield (Midwest)	2B	127	496	106	136	17	6	1	49	.274	44	*292 *343	18 *.972
1987 —St. Petersburg (Fla. St.)	3B-2B	38	162	35	58	6	4	0	28	.358	12	35	91	6	.955
—Louisville (Am. Assoc.)	2B-3B	21	70	10	15	2	0	1	8	.214	0	22	51	2	.973
—Arkansas (Texas)	2-3-S-0	66	238	37	69	13	1	1	26	.290	9	117	164	8	.972
1988 —Louisville (Am. Assoc.)	3B-2B	133	497	59	127	27	2	1	46	.256	6	98 †271	†26	.934
1989 —Arkansas (Texas)	2B-3B	55	224	41	71	12	1	1	40	.317	8	127	150	12	.958
—Louisville (Am. Assoc.)	2B-3B	75	278	37	81	18	3	1	30	.291	1	130	151	18	.940
—St. Louis (N.L.)	3B	6	4	1	1	0	0	0	1	.250	0	1	0	1	.500
1990 —Louisville (Am. Assoc.)	2B-3B	57	204	30	57	9	2	2	23	.279	5	78	139	12	.948
—St. Louis (N.L.)	3-0-2-1	55	121	13	30	2	0	0	7	.248	0	45	30	1	.987
1991 —St. Louis (N.L.)	3-0-1-2	60	82	5	14	2	0	0	13	.171	0	30	14	2	.957
Major league totals (3 years)		**121**	**207**	**19**	**45**	**4**	**0**	**0**	**21**	**.217**	**0**	**76**	**44**	**4**	**.968**

WILSON, MOOKIE
OF

PERSONAL: Born February 9, 1956, at Bamberg, S.C. . . . 5-10/175. . . . Throws right, bats both. . . . Full name: William Hayward Wilson. . . . Brother of John Wilson, minor league outfielder (1982-87); and brother of Phil Wilson, minor league outfielder (1984-89).
HIGH SCHOOL: Bamberg-Erhardt (Bamberg, S.C.).
COLLEGE: Spartanburg Methodist (S.C.) and South Carolina.
TRANSACTIONS/CAREER NOTES: Selected by Los Angeles Dodgers organization in fourth round of free-agent draft (January 7, 1976). . . . Selected by New York Mets organization in second round of free-agent draft (June 7, 1977). . . . On disabled list (July 2-September 1, 1985). . . . On New York disabled list (March 30-May 9, 1986); included rehabilitation disability assignment to Tidewater (April 26-May 9, 1986). . . . Traded by Mets to Toronto Blue Jays (August 1, 1989), completing deal in which Blue Jays traded P Jeff Musselman and P Mike Brady to Mets for a player to be named later (July 31, 1989). . . . Granted free agency (November 13, 1989). . . . Re-signed by Blue Jays (November 27, 1989). . . . Granted free agency (October 29, 1991).
STATISTICAL NOTES: Led N.L. outfielders with six double plays in 1984.

						BATTING						FIELDING			
Year	Team (League)	Pos.	G	AB	R	H	2B	3B	HR	RBI	Avg.	SB	PO	A	E	Avg.
1977 —Wausau (Midwest)	OF	68	245	50	71	10	2	6	32	.290	23	150	8	9	.946
1978 —Jackson (Texas)	OF	132	497	72	145	13	*15	7	72	.292	38	282	10	7	.977
1979 —Tidewater (Int'l)	OF	*141	529	84	141	22	10	5	36	.267	49	317	11	7	.979
1980 —Tidewater (Int'l)	OF	132	515	*92 *152	11	*14	4	44	.295	50	*350	11	7	.981
—New York (N.L.)	OF	27	105	16	26	5	3	0	4	.248	7	72	1	2	.973
1981 —New York (N.L.)	OF	92	328	49	89	8	8	3	14	.271	24	226	3	4	.983
1982 —New York (N.L.)	OF	159	639	90	178	25	9	5	55	.279	58	415	12	5	.988
1983 —New York (N.L.)	OF	152	*638	91	176	25	6	7	51	.276	54	422	5	7	.984
1984 —New York (N.L.)	OF	154	587	88	162	28	10	10	54	.276	46	396	8	4	.990
1985 —New York (N.L.)	OF	93	337	56	93	16	8	6	26	.276	24	216	0	8	.964
1986 —Tidewater (Int'l)	OF	9	31	4	8	1	0	0	4	.258	4	19	1	0	1.000
—New York (N.L.)	OF	123	381	61	110	17	5	9	45	.289	25	228	7	5	.979
1987 —New York (N.L.)	OF	124	385	58	115	19	7	9	34	.299	21	205	3	8	.963
1988 —New York (N.L.)	OF	112	378	61	112	17	5	8	41	.296	15	200	4	5	.976
1989 —New York (N.L.)	OF	80	249	22	51	10	1	3	18	.205	7	152	2	4	.975
—Toronto (A.L.)■	OF	54	238	32	71	9	1	2	17	.298	12	111	2	1	.991
1990 —Toronto (A.L.)	OF	147	588	81	156	36	4	3	51	.265	23	370	5	3	.992
1991 —Toronto (A.L.)	OF	86	241	26	58	12	4	2	28	.241	11	71	2	2	.973
American League totals (3 years)		**287**	**1067**	**139**	**285**	**57**	**9**	**7**	**96**	**.267**	**46**	**552**	**9**	**6**	**.989**
National League totals (10 years)		**1116**	**4027**	**592**	**1112**	**170**	**62**	**60**	**342**	**.276**	**281**	**2532**	**45**	**52**	**.980**
Major league totals (12 years)		**1403**	**5094**	**731**	**1397**	**227**	**71**	**67**	**438**	**.274**	**327**	**3084**	**54**	**58**	**.982**

CHAMPIONSHIP SERIES NOTES: Shares single-game record for most at-bats—7 (October 15, 1986, 16 innings).

Year	Team (League)	Pos.	G	AB	R	H	2B	3B	HR	RBI	Avg.	SB	PO	A	E	Avg.
1986 —New York (N.L.)		OF	6	26	2	3	0	0	0	1	.115	1	16	1	0	1.000
1988 —New York (N.L.)		OF-PH	4	13	2	2	0	0	0	1	.154	1	6	0	0	1.000
1989 —Toronto (A.L.)		OF	5	19	2	5	0	0	0	2	.263	1	10	0	0	1.000
1991 —Toronto (A.L.)		PR-DH-O	3	8	1	2	0	0	0	0	.250	1	4	0	0	1.000
Championship Series totals (4 years)			18	66	7	12	0	0	0	4	.182	4	36	1	0	1.000

WORLD SERIES RECORD

Year	Team (League)	Pos.	G	AB	R	H	2B	3B	HR	RBI	Avg.	SB	PO	A	E	Avg.
1986 —New York (N.L.)		OF	7	26	3	7	1	0	0	0	.269	3	15	2	0	1.000

WILSON, NIGEL
OF, BLUE JAYS

PERSONAL: Born January 12, 1970, at Oshawa, Ont. . . . 6-1/185. . . . Throws left, bats left. . . . Full name: Nigel Edward Wilson.
HIGH SCHOOL: Ajax (Ont.).
TRANSACTIONS/CAREER NOTES: Signed as free agent by Toronto Blue Jays organization (July 30, 1987).
STATISTICAL NOTES: Led Florida State League with 217 total bases and .477 slugging percentage in 1991.

Year	Team (League)	Pos.	G	AB	R	H	2B	3B	HR	RBI	Avg.	SB	PO	A	E	Avg.
1988 —St. Catharines (NYP)		OF	40	103	12	21	1	2	2	11	.204	8	50	3	5	.914
1989 —St. Catharines (NYP)		OF	42	161	17	35	5	2	4	18	.217	8	37	2	3	.929
1990 —Myrtle Beach (S. Atl.)		OF	110	440	77	120	23	9	16	62	.273	22	127	7	10	.931
1991 —Dunedin (Florida State)		OF	119	455	64	137	18	*13	12	55	.301	27	196	7	8	.962

WILSON, STEVE
P, DODGERS

PERSONAL: Born December 13, 1964, at Victoria, B.C. . . . 6-4/195. . . . Throws left, bats left. . . . Full name: Stephen Douglas Wilson.
HIGH SCHOOL: Eric Hamber (Vancouver, B.C.).
COLLEGE: Portland.
TRANSACTIONS/CAREER NOTES: Selected by Texas Rangers organization in fourth round of free-agent draft (June 3, 1985). . . . Traded by Rangers with P Mitch Williams, P Paul Kilgus, IF Curtis Wilkerson, IF Luis Benitez and OF Pablo Delgado to Chicago Cubs for OF Rafael Palmeiro, P Jamie Moyer and P Drew Hall (December 5, 1988). . . . Traded by Cubs to Los Angeles Dodgers for P Jeff Hartsock (September 6, 1991).
MISCELLANEOUS: Appeared in one game as pinch-runner with Chicago Cubs (1991).

Year	Team (League)	G	W	L	Pct.	ERA	Sv.	IP	H	R	ER	BB	SO
1985 —Burlington (Midwest)		21	3	5	.375	4.58	0	72⅔	71	44	37	27	76
1986 —Tulsa (Texas)		24	7	13	.350	4.87	0	136⅔	117	83	74	*103	95
1987 —Charlotte (Florida State)		20	9	5	.643	2.44	0	107	81	41	29	44	80
1988 —Tulsa (Texas)		25	15	7	.682	3.16	0	165⅓	147	72	58	53	132
—Texas (A.L.)		3	0	0	. . .	5.87	0	7⅔	7	5	5	4	1
1989 —Chicago (N.L.)■		53	6	4	.600	4.20	2	85⅔	83	43	40	31	65
1990 —Chicago (N.L.)		45	4	9	.308	4.79	1	139	140	77	74	43	95
1991 —Iowa (American Association)		25	3	8	.273	3.87	0	114	102	55	49	45	84
—Chicago-Los Angeles (N.L.)■		19	0	0	. . .	2.61	2	20⅔	14	7	6	9	14
American League totals (1 year)		3	0	0	. . .	5.87	0	7⅔	7	5	5	4	1
National League totals (3 years)		117	10	13	.435	4.40	5	245⅓	237	127	120	83	174
Major league totals (4 years)		120	10	13	.435	4.45	5	253	244	132	125	87	175

CHAMPIONSHIP SERIES RECORD

Year	Team (League)	G	W	L	Pct.	ERA	Sv.	IP	H	R	ER	BB	SO
1989 —Chicago (N.L.)		2	0	1	.000	4.91	0	3⅔	3	5	2	1	4

WILSON, TREVOR
P, GIANTS

PERSONAL: Born June 7, 1966, at Torrance, Calif. . . . 6-0/195. . . . Throws left, bats left. . . . Full name: Trevor Kirk Wilson.
HIGH SCHOOL: Oregon City (Ore.).
COLLEGE: Oregon State.
TRANSACTIONS/CAREER NOTES: Selected by San Francisco Giants organization in eighth round of free-agent draft (June 3, 1985). . . . On San Francisco disabled list (August 22-September 6, 1990).
STATISTICAL NOTES: Tied for Northwest League lead with two balks in 1985.

Year	Team (League)	G	W	L	Pct.	ERA	Sv.	IP	H	R	ER	BB	SO
1985 —Everett (Northwest)		17	2	4	.333	4.23	3	55⅓	67	36	26	26	50
1986 —Clinton (Midwest)		34	6	11	.353	4.27	2	130⅔	126	70	62	64	84
1987 —Clinton (Midwest)		26	10	6	.625	2.01	0	161⅓	130	60	36	77	146
1988 —Shreveport (Texas)		12	5	4	.556	1.86	0	72⅔	55	19	15	23	53
—Phoenix (Pacific Coast)		11	2	3	.400	5.05	0	51⅔	49	35	29	33	49
—San Francisco (N.L.)		4	0	2	.000	4.09	0	22	25	14	10	8	15

Year	Team (League)	G	W	L	Pct.	ERA	Sv.	IP	H	R	ER	BB	SO
1989	—Phoenix (Pacific Coast)	23	7	7	.500	3.12	0	115⅓	109	49	40	76	77
	—San Francisco (N.L.)	14	2	3	.400	4.35	0	39⅓	28	20	19	24	22
1990	—Phoenix (Pacific Coast)	11	5	5	.500	3.82	0	66	63	31	28	44	45
	—San Francisco (N.L.)	27	8	7	.533	4.00	0	110⅓	87	52	49	49	66
1991	—San Francisco (N.L.)	44	13	11	.542	3.56	0	202	173	87	80	77	139
Major league totals (4 years)		89	23	23	.500	3.81	0	373⅔	313	173	158	158	242

WILSON, WILLIE
OF, ATHLETICS

PERSONAL: Born July 9, 1955, at Montgomery, Ala. . . . 6-3/200. . . . Throws right, bats both. . . . Full name: Willie James Wilson.
HIGH SCHOOL: Summit (N.J.).
TRANSACTIONS/CAREER NOTES: Selected by Kansas City Royals organization in first round (18th pick overall) of free-agent draft (June 5, 1974). . . . On disabled list (August 21-September 6, 1983). . . . On suspended list (December 15, 1983-May 15, 1984). . . . On disabled list (May 27-June 17, 1989). . . . Granted free agency (November 13, 1989). . . . Re-signed by Royals (December 7, 1989). . . . Granted free agency (November 5, 1990). . . . Signed by Oakland Athletics (December 3, 1990). . . . On disabled list (August 15-September 1, 1991).
RECORDS/HONORS: Holds major league single-season records for most at-bats—705 (1980); most at-bats by switch-hitter—705 (1980). . . . Shares major league single-season records by collecting 100 or more hits righthanded and lefthanded (1980); most hits by switch-hitter—230 (1980). . . . Holds A.L. career record for stolen base percentage (300 or more attempts)—.836. . . . Holds A.L. single-season record for most triples by a switch-hitter—21 (1985). . . . Shares A.L. records for most years leading league in triples—5; most consecutive stolen bases without caught stealing—32 (July 23-September 23, 1980). . . . Shares A.L. single-season record for fewest times caught stealing (50 or more stolen bases)—8 (1983). . . . Named Midwest League Most Valuable Player (1975). . . . Named outfielder on THE SPORTING NEWS A.L. Silver Slugger team (1980 and 1982). . . . Won A.L. Gold Glove as outfielder (1980).
STATISTICAL NOTES: Led Midwest League in being hit by pitch with 13 in 1975. . . . Switch-hit home runs in one game (June 15, 1979).

						BATTING						FIELDING			
Year	Team (League)	Pos.	G	AB	R	H	2B	3B	HR	RBI	Avg.	SB	PO	A	E	Avg.
1974	—Sarasota Royals (GCL)	OF	47	155	30	39	3	5	1	14	.252	★24	92	8	4	.962
1975	—Waterloo (Midwest)	OF	127	486	92	★132	18	4	8	73	.272	★76	249	★17	17	.940
1976	—Jacksonville (Southern)	OF	107	388	54	98	13	6	1	35	.253	37	273	5	8	.972
	—Kansas City (A.L.)	OF	12	6	0	1	0	0	0	0	.167	2	6	1	1	.875
1977	—Omaha (Am. Assoc.)	OF	132	495	67	139	10	6	4	47	.281	★74	★278	7	11	.963
	—Kansas City (A.L.)	OF	13	34	10	11	2	0	0	1	.324	6	24	0	1	.960
1978	—Kansas City (A.L.)	OF	127	198	43	43	8	2	0	16	.217	46	171	6	4	.978
1979	—Kansas City (A.L.)	OF	154	588	113	185	18	13	6	49	.315	★83	384	12	6	.985
1980	—Kansas City (A.L.)	OF	161	★705	★133	★230	28	•15	3	49	.326	79	482	9	6	.988
1981	—Kansas City (A.L.)	OF	102	439	54	133	10	7	1	32	.303	34	299	★14	4	.987
1982	—Kansas City (A.L.)	OF	136	585	87	194	19	★15	3	46	★.332	37	215	8	3	.987
1983	—Kansas City (A.L.)	OF	137	576	90	159	22	8	2	33	.276	59	354	3	9	.975
1984	—Kansas City (A.L.)	OF	128	541	81	163	24	9	2	44	.301	47	383	6	4	.990
1985	—Kansas City (A.L.)	OF	141	605	87	168	25	★21	4	43	.278	43	378	4	2	.995
1986	—Kansas City (A.L.)	OF	156	631	77	170	20	7	9	44	.269	34	408	4	3	.993
1987	—Kansas City (A.L.)	OF	146	610	97	170	18	★15	4	30	.279	59	342	3	1	★.997
1988	—Kansas City (A.L.)	OF	147	591	81	155	17	•11	1	37	.262	35	365	1	4	.989
1989	—Kansas City (A.L.)	OF	112	383	58	97	17	7	3	43	.253	24	252	2	6	.977
1990	—Kansas City (A.L.)	OF	115	307	49	89	13	3	2	42	.290	24	187	2	0	1.000
1991	—Oakland (A.L.)■	OF	113	294	38	70	14	4	0	28	.238	20	176	2	3	.983
Major league totals (16 years)			1900	7093	1098	2038	255	137	40	537	.287	632	4426	77	57	.988

DIVISION SERIES RECORD

						BATTING						FIELDING			
Year	Team (League)	Pos.	G	AB	R	H	2B	3B	HR	RBI	Avg.	SB	PO	A	E	Avg.
1981	—Kansas City (A.L.)	OF	3	13	0	4	0	0	0	1	.308	0	6	0	0	1.000

CHAMPIONSHIP SERIES RECORD

						BATTING						FIELDING			
Year	Team (League)	Pos.	G	AB	R	H	2B	3B	HR	RBI	Avg.	SB	PO	A	E	Avg.
1978	—Kansas City (A.L.)	PR-OF	3	4	0	1	0	0	0	0	.250	0	2	0	0	1.000
1980	—Kansas City (A.L.)	OF	3	13	2	4	2	1	0	4	.308	0	6	1	0	1.000
1984	—Kansas City (A.L.)	OF	3	13	0	2	0	0	0	0	.154	0	10	0	0	1.000
1985	—Kansas City (A.L.)	OF	7	29	5	9	0	0	1	2	.310	1	12	0	0	1.000
Championship Series totals (4 years)			16	59	7	16	2	1	1	6	.271	1	30	1	0	1.000

WORLD SERIES RECORD

WORLD SERIES NOTES: Holds single-series record for most strikeouts—12 (1980). . . . Shares record for most at-bats in one inning—2 (October 18, 1980, first inning).

						BATTING						FIELDING			
Year	Team (League)	Pos.	G	AB	R	H	2B	3B	HR	RBI	Avg.	SB	PO	A	E	Avg.
1980	—Kansas City (A.L.)	OF	6	26	3	4	1	0	0	0	.154	2	15	1	0	1.000
1985	—Kansas City (A.L.)	OF	7	30	2	11	0	1	0	3	.367	3	19	1	0	1.000
World Series totals (2 years)			13	56	5	15	1	1	0	3	.268	5	34	2	0	1.000

ALL-STAR GAME RECORD

Year	League	Pos.	AB	R	H	2B	3B	HR	RBI	Avg.	SB	PO	A	E	Avg.
1982 — American		OF	2	0	0	0	0	0	0	.000	0	1	0	0	1.000
1983 — American		OF	1	0	1	1	0	0	1	1.000	0	2	0	0	1.000
All-Star Game totals (2 years)			3	0	1	1	0	0	1	.333	0	3	0	0	1.000

WINFIELD, DAVE
OF, BLUE JAYS

PERSONAL: Born October 3, 1951, at St. Paul, Minn. . . . 6-6/220. . . . Throws right, bats right. . . . Full name: David Mark Winfield.
HIGH SCHOOL: St. Paul Central (Minn).
COLLEGE: Minnesota (received degree).
TRANSACTIONS/CAREER NOTES: Selected by Baltimore Orioles organization in 40th round of free-agent draft (June 5, 1969). . . . Selected by San Diego Padres organization in first round (fourth pick overall) of free-agent draft (June 5, 1973). . . . Granted free agency (October 22, 1980). . . . Signed by New York Yankees (December 15, 1980). . . . On disabled list (May 20-June 4, 1982; April 16-May 1, 1984; and March 19, 1989-entire season). . . . Traded by Yankees to California Angels for P Mike Witt (May 11, 1990). . . . Granted free agency (October 30, 1991). . . . Signed by Toronto Blue Jays (December 19, 1991).
RECORDS/HONORS: Named outfielder on THE SPORTING NEWS college All-America team (1973). . . . Named outfielder on THE SPORTING NEWS N.L. All-Star team (1979). . . . Won N.L. Gold Glove as outfielder (1979-80). . . . Named outfielder on THE SPORTING NEWS A.L. Silver Slugger team (1981-85). . . . Named outfielder on THE SPORTING NEWS A.L. All-Star team (1982-84). . . . Won A.L. Gold Glove as outfielder (1982-85 and 1987). . . . Named A.L. Comeback Player of the Year by THE SPORTING NEWS (1990).
STATISTICAL NOTES: Led N.L. with 333 total bases and 24 intentional bases on balls received in 1979. . . . Hit three home runs in a game (April 13, 1991).
MISCELLANEOUS: Selected by Atlanta Hawks in fifth round (79th pick overall) of 1973 NBA draft. . . . Selected by Utah Stars in sixth round (58th pick overall) of 1973 ABA draft. . . . Selected by Minnesota Vikings in 17th round (429th pick overall) of 1973 NFL draft.

Year	Team (League)	Pos.	G	AB	R	H	2B	3B	HR	RBI	Avg.	SB	PO	A	E	Avg.
1973 — San Diego (N.L.)		OF-1B	56	141	9	39	4	1	3	12	.277	0	65	1	3	.957
1974 — San Diego (N.L.)		OF	145	498	57	132	18	4	20	75	.265	9	276	11	•12	.960
1975 — San Diego (N.L.)		OF	143	509	74	136	20	2	15	76	.267	23	302	9	9	.972
1976 — San Diego (N.L.)		OF	137	492	81	139	26	4	13	69	.283	26	304	*15	6	.982
1977 — San Diego (N.L.)		OF	157	615	104	169	29	7	25	92	.275	16	368	15	11	.972
1978 — San Diego (N.L.)		OF-1B	158	587	88	181	30	5	24	97	.308	21	328	8	7	.980
1979 — San Diego (N.L.)		OF	159	597	97	184	27	10	34	*118	.308	15	344	14	5	.986
1980 — San Diego (N.L.)		OF	162	558	89	154	25	6	20	87	.276	23	273	20	4	.987
1981 — New York (A.L.)■		OF	105	388	52	114	25	1	13	68	.294	11	196	1	3	.985
1982 — New York (A.L.)		OF	140	539	84	151	24	8	37	106	.280	5	279	*17	8	.974
1983 — New York (A.L.)		OF	152	598	99	169	26	8	32	116	.283	15	313	5	7	.978
1984 — New York (A.L.)		OF	141	567	106	193	34	4	19	100	.340	6	306	3	2	.994
1985 — New York (A.L.)		OF	155	633	105	174	34	6	26	114	.275	19	316	13	3	.991
1986 — New York (A.L.)		OF-3B	154	565	90	148	31	5	24	104	.262	6	292	9	5	.984
1987 — New York (A.L.)		OF	156	575	83	158	22	1	27	97	.275	5	253	6	3	.989
1988 — New York (A.L.)		OF	149	559	96	180	37	2	25	107	.322	9	276	3	3	.989
1989 —							Did not play									
1990 — New York-Calif. (A.L.)■		OF	132	475	70	127	21	2	21	78	.267	0	177	7	2	.989
1991 — California (A.L.)		OF	150	568	75	149	27	4	28	86	.262	7	198	7	2	.990
American League totals (10 years)			1434	5467	860	1563	281	41	252	976	.286	83	2606	71	38	.986
National League totals (8 years)			1117	3997	599	1134	179	39	154	626	.284	133	2260	93	57	.976
Major league totals (18 years)			2551	9464	1459	2697	460	80	406	1602	.285	216	4866	164	95	.981

DIVISION SERIES RECORD

Year	Team (League)	Pos.	G	AB	R	H	2B	3B	HR	RBI	Avg.	SB	PO	A	E	Avg.
1981 — New York (A.L.)		OF	5	20	2	7	3	0	0	0	.350	0	10	1	0	1.000

CHAMPIONSHIP SERIES RECORD

Year	Team (League)	Pos.	G	AB	R	H	2B	3B	HR	RBI	Avg.	SB	PO	A	E	Avg.
1981 — New York (A.L.)		OF	3	13	2	2	1	0	0	2	.154	1	6	0	0	1.000

WORLD SERIES RECORD

Year	Team (League)	Pos.	G	AB	R	H	2B	3B	HR	RBI	Avg.	SB	PO	A	E	Avg.
1981 — New York (A.L.)		OF	6	22	0	1	0	0	0	1	.045	1	13	1	0	1.000

ALL-STAR GAME NOTES: Holds career record for most doubles—7. . . . Shares record for most consecutive games with one or more hits—7. . . . Shares single-game record for most at-bats in nine-inning game—5 (July 17, 1979).

ALL-STAR GAME RECORD

Year	League	Pos.	AB	R	H	2B	3B	HR	RBI	Avg.	SB	PO	A	E	Avg.
1977 — National		OF	2	0	2	1	0	0	2	1.000	0	1	0	0	1.000
1978 — National		OF	2	1	1	0	0	0	0	.500	0	1	0	0	1.000

Year	League	Pos.	AB	R	H	2B	3B	HR	RBI	Avg.	SB	PO	A	E	Avg.
1979 — National		OF	5	1	1	1	0	0	1	.200	0	3	0	0	1.000
1980 — National		OF	2	0	0	0	0	0	1	.000	0	2	0	0	1.000
1981 — American		OF	4	0	0	0	0	0	0	.000	0	0	1	0	1.000
1982 — American		OF	2	0	1	0	0	0	0	.500	0	0	0	0	...
1983 — American		OF	3	2	3	1	0	0	1	1.000	0	3	0	0	1.000
1984 — American		OF	4	0	1	1	0	0	0	.250	0	2	1	0	1.000
1985 — American		OF	3	0	1	0	0	0	0	.333	1	0	0	0	...
1986 — American		OF	1	1	1	0	0	0	0	1.000	0	0	0	0	...
1987 — American		OF	5	0	1	1	0	0	0	.200	0	2	0	0	1.000
1988 — American		OF	3	1	1	1	0	0	0	.333	0	1	0	0	1.000
All-Star Game totals (12 years)			36	6	13	7	0	0	5	.361	1	15	2	0	1.000

WINNINGHAM, HERM
OF, RED SOX

PERSONAL: Born December 1, 1961, at Orangeburg, S.C. . . . 5-11/185. . . . Throws right, bats left.
HIGH SCHOOL: Orangeburg (S.C.).
COLLEGE: DeKalb Community College South (Ga.).

TRANSACTIONS/CAREER NOTES: Selected by Pittsburgh Pirates organization in 38th round of free-agent draft (June 5, 1979). . . . Selected by Milwaukee Brewers organization in secondary phase of free-agent draft (January 8, 1980). . . . Selected by Montreal Expos organization in secondary phase of free-agent draft (June 3, 1980). . . . Selected by New York Mets organization in secondary phase of free-agent draft (January 13, 1981). . . . On Tidewater disabled list (August 9-September 20, 1983). . . . Traded by Mets with IF Hubie Brooks, C Mike Fitzgerald and P Floyd Youmans to Expos for C Gary Carter (December 10, 1984). . . . On Montreal disabled list (June 24-July 13, 1985); included rehabilitation disability assignment to Indianapolis (July 4-13, 1985). . . . Traded by Expos with C Jeff Reed and P Randy St. Claire to Cincinnati Reds for OF Tracy Jones and P Pat Pacillo (July 13, 1988). . . . On disabled list (June 6-21, 1989). . . . Granted free agency (November 5, 1991). . . . Signed by Boston Red Sox (January 29, 1992).

RECORDS/HONORS: Shares modern major league single-game record for most triples—3 (August 15, 1990, 12 innings).

Year	Team (League)	Pos.	G	AB	R	H	2B	3B	HR	RBI	Avg.	SB	PO	A	E	Avg.
1981 — Kingsport (Appalachian)		OF	58	204	44	52	7	4	2	14	.255	20	128	3	2	*.985
1982 — Lynchburg (Carolina)		OF	120	430	65	127	20	5	6	61	.295	50	235	6	5	.980
1983 — Jackson (Texas)		OF	78	288	54	102	13	6	4	41	.354	17	157	5	6	.964
— Tidewater (Int'l)		OF	29	113	18	30	5	2	1	11	.265	6	70	1	3	.959
1984 — Tidewater (Int'l)		OF	115	406	50	114	20	3	3	47	.281	23	228	8	4	.983
— New York (N.L.)		OF	14	27	5	11	1	1	0	5	.407	2	7	0	0	1.000
1985 — Montreal (N.L.)■		OF	125	312	30	74	6	5	3	21	.237	20	229	6	4	.983
— Indianapolis (A.A.)		OF	11	35	3	6	0	0	0	2	.171	2	22	0	1	.957
1986 — Montreal (N.L.)		OF-SS	90	185	23	40	6	3	4	11	.216	12	97	2	2	.980
— Indianapolis (A.A.)		OF	51	201	35	54	5	7	4	24	.269	23	106	3	1	.991
1987 — Montreal (N.L.)		OF	137	347	34	83	20	3	4	41	.239	29	225	5	6	.975
1988 — Montreal-Cin. (N.L.)■		OF	100	203	16	47	3	4	0	21	.232	12	128	1	1	.992
— Indianapolis (A.A.)		OF	3	10	2	2	0	1	0	1	.200	1	6	0	0	1.000
1989 — Cincinnati (N.L.)		OF	115	251	40	63	11	3	3	13	.251	14	146	3	3	.980
1990 — Cincinnati (N.L.)		OF	84	160	20	41	8	5	3	17	.256	4	89	3	0	1.000
1991 — Cincinnati (N.L.)		OF	98	169	17	38	6	1	1	4	.225	4	99	2	5	.953
Major league totals (8 years)			763	1654	185	397	61	25	18	133	.240	99	1020	22	21	.980

CHAMPIONSHIP SERIES RECORD

Year	Team (League)	Pos.	G	AB	R	H	2B	3B	HR	RBI	Avg.	SB	PO	A	E	Avg.
1990 — Cincinnati (N.L.)		PH-OF	3	7	1	2	1	0	0	1	.286	1	7	0	0	1.000

WORLD SERIES RECORD

Year	Team (League)	Pos.	G	AB	R	H	2B	3B	HR	RBI	Avg.	SB	PO	A	E	Avg.
1990 — Cincinnati (N.L.)		PH-OF	2	4	1	2	0	0	0	0	.500	0	3	0	0	1.000

WITMEYER, RON
1B, ATHLETICS

PERSONAL: Born June 28, 1967, at West Islip, N.Y. . . . 6-3/215. . . . Throws left, bats left. . . . Full name: Ronald Herman Witmeyer.
HIGH SCHOOL: East Islip (N.Y.).
COLLEGE: Stanford.

TRANSACTIONS/CAREER NOTES: Selected by Oakland Athletics organization in seventh round of free-agent draft (June 1, 1988).

Year	Team (League)	Pos.	G	AB	R	H	2B	3B	HR	RBI	Avg.	SB	PO	A	E	Avg.
1989 — Modesto (California)		1B	134	457	54	93	22	1	8	43	.204	5	1111	100	13	.989
1990 — Modesto (California)		1B	92	333	38	78	14	5	10	45	.234	0	709	43	8	.989
— Huntsville (Southern)		1B	27	91	18	29	4	0	5	18	.319	0	220	15	3	.987
— Tacoma (Pacific Coast)		1B	10	31	5	9	2	0	1	7	.290	0	81	2	2	.976
1991 — Tacoma (Pacific Coast)		1B	122	431	64	113	18	4	15	80	.262	2	955	58	8	.992
— Oakland (A.L.)		1B	11	19	0	1	0	0	0	0	.053	0	32	3	0	1.000
Major league totals (1 year)			11	19	0	1	0	0	0	0	.053	0	32	3	0	1.000

WITT, BOBBY
P, RANGERS

PERSONAL: Born May 11, 1964, at Canton, Mass. . . . 6-2/205. . . . Throws right, bats right. . . . Full name: Robert Andrew Witt.
HIGH SCHOOL: Canton (Mass.).
COLLEGE: Oklahoma.
TRANSACTIONS/CAREER NOTES: Selected by Cincinnati Reds organization in seventh round of free-agent draft (June 7, 1982). . . . Selected by Texas Rangers organization in first round (third pick overall) of free-agent draft (June 3, 1985). . . . On Texas disabled list (May 21-June 20, 1987); included rehabilitation disability assignment to Oklahoma City (June 7-12, 1987) and Tulsa (June 13, 1987). . . . On Texas disabled list (May 27-July 31, 1991); included rehabilitation disability assignment to Oklahoma City (July 22-29, 1991).
RECORDS/HONORS: Shares major league record for most strikeouts in one inning—4 (August 2, 1987, second inning). . . . Named righthanded pitcher on THE SPORTING NEWS college All-America team (1985).
STATISTICAL NOTES: Led A.L. with 22 wild pitches in 1986 and tied for lead with 16 in 1988.
MISCELLANEOUS: Member of 1984 U.S. Olympic baseball team. . . . Struck out in only appearance as pinch-hitter (1987). . . . Appeared in two games as pinch-runner (1990).

Year	Team (League)	G	W	L	Pct.	ERA	Sv.	IP	H	R	ER	BB	SO
1985	—Tulsa (Texas)	11	0	6	.000	6.43	0	35	26	26	25	44	39
1986	—Texas (A.L.)	31	11	9	.550	5.48	0	157⅔	130	104	96	*143	174
1987	—Texas (A.L.)	26	8	10	.444	4.91	0	143	114	82	78	*140	160
	—Oklahoma City (Am. Assoc.)	1	1	0	1.000	9.00	0	5	5	5	5	3	2
	—Tulsa (Texas)	1	0	1	.000	5.40	0	5	5	9	3	6	2
1988	—Texas (A.L.)	22	8	10	.444	3.92	0	174⅓	134	83	76	101	148
	—Oklahoma City (Am. Assoc.)	11	4	6	.400	4.34	0	76⅔	69	42	37	47	70
1989	—Texas (A.L.)	31	12	13	.480	5.14	0	194⅓	182	123	•111	*114	166
1990	—Texas (A.L.)	33	17	10	.630	3.36	0	222	197	98	83	110	221
1991	—Texas (A.L.)	17	3	7	.300	6.09	0	88⅔	84	66	60	74	82
	—Oklahoma City (Am. Assoc.)	2	1	1	.500	1.13	0	8	3	1	1	8	12
Major league totals (6 years)		**160**	**59**	**59**	**.500**	**4.63**	**0**	**980**	**841**	**556**	**504**	**682**	**951**

WITT, MIKE
P, YANKEES

PERSONAL: Born July 20, 1960, at Fullerton, Calif. . . . 6-7/203. . . . Throws right, bats right. . . . Full name: Michael Atwater Witt.
HIGH SCHOOL: Servite (Calif.).
COLLEGE: Cypress Junior College (Calif.).
TRANSACTIONS/CAREER NOTES: Selected by California Angels organization in fourth round of free-agent draft (June 6, 1978). . . . Granted free agency (November 9, 1987). . . . Re-signed by Angels (December 22, 1987). . . . Traded by Angels to New York Yankees for OF Dave Winfield (May 11, 1990). . . . On New York disabled list (June 9-August 7, 1990). . . . Granted free agency (December 7, 1990). . . . Re-signed by Yankees (January 2, 1991). . . . On New York disabled list (March 29-June 7, 1991); included rehabilitation disability assignment to Columbus (June 1-2, 1991). . . . On New York disabled list (June 14, 1991-remainder of season); included rehabilitation disability assignment to Albany/Colonie (July 17-19, 1991).
STATISTICAL NOTES: Tied for A.L. lead with 11 hit batsmen in 1981. . . . Pitched 1-0 perfect game against Texas Rangers (September 30, 1984). . . . Pitched two innings, combining with Mark Langston in 1-0 nine-inning no-hit victory against Seattle Mariners (April 11, 1990).

Year	Team (League)	G	W	L	Pct.	ERA	Sv.	IP	H	R	ER	BB	SO
1978	—Idaho Falls (Pioneer)	13	7	1	.875	3.56	0	86	88	45	34	26	79
1979	—Salinas (California)	30	8	10	.444	5.11	0	141	156	96	80	70	94
1980	—Salinas (California)	13	7	3	.700	2.10	0	90	85	30	21	35	76
	—El Paso (Texas)	12	5	5	.500	5.79	0	70	72	53	45	39	64
1981	—California (A.L.)	22	8	9	.471	3.28	0	129	123	60	47	47	75
1982	—California (A.L.)	33	8	6	.571	3.51	0	179⅔	177	77	70	47	85
1983	—California (A.L.)	43	7	14	.333	4.91	5	154	173	90	84	75	77
1984	—California (A.L.)	34	15	11	.577	3.47	0	246⅔	227	103	95	84	196
1985	—California (A.L.)	35	15	9	.625	3.56	0	250	228	115	99	98	180
1986	—California (A.L.)	34	18	10	.643	2.84	0	269	218	95	85	73	208
1987	—California (A.L.)	36	16	14	.533	4.01	0	247	252	128	110	84	192
1988	—California (A.L.)	34	13	16	.448	4.15	0	249⅔	263	*130	115	87	133
1989	—California (A.L.)	33	9	15	.375	4.54	0	220	252	119	•111	48	123
1990	—California-New York (A.L.)■	26	5	9	.357	4.00	1	117	106	62	52	47	74
1991	—Columbus (International)	1	0	0	. . .	9.00	0	4	7	4	4	3	5
	—New York (A.L.)	2	0	1	.000	10.13	0	5⅓	8	7	6	1	0
	—Albany/Colonie (Eastern)	1	0	0	. . .	9.00	0	2	2	2	2	2	2
Major league totals (11 years)		**332**	**114**	**114**	**.500**	**3.80**	**6**	**2067⅓**	**2027**	**986**	**874**	**691**	**1343**

CHAMPIONSHIP SERIES RECORD

Year	Team (League)	G	W	L	Pct.	ERA	Sv.	IP	H	R	ER	BB	SO
1982	—California (A.L.)	1	0	0	. . .	6.00	0	3	2	2	2	2	3
1986	—California (A.L.)	2	1	0	1.000	2.55	0	17⅔	13	5	5	2	8
Championship Series totals (2 years)		**3**	**1**	**0**	**1.000**	**3.05**	**0**	**20⅔**	**15**	**7**	**7**	**4**	**11**

ALL-STAR GAME RECORD

Year	League	W	L	Pct.	ERA	Sv.	IP	H	R	ER	BB	SO
1986	—American				Did not play							
1987	—American				Did not play							

— 530 —

WOHLERS, MARK
P, BRAVES

PERSONAL: Born January 23, 1970, at Holyoke, Mass.... 6-4/205.... Throws right, bats right.... Full name: Mark Edward Wohlers.
HIGH SCHOOL: Holyoke (Mass.).
TRANSACTIONS/CAREER NOTES: Selected by Atlanta Braves organization in eighth round of free-agent draft (June 1, 1988).
RECORDS/HONORS: Named Southern League Outstanding Pitcher (1991).
STATISTICAL NOTES: Pitched two innings, combining with Kent Mercker and Alejandro Pena in 1-0 nine-inning no-hit victory against San Diego Padres (September 11, 1991).

Year	Team (League)	G	W	L	Pct.	ERA	Sv.	IP	H	R	ER	BB	SO
1988—Pulaski (Appalachian)		13	5	3	.625	3.32	0	59⅔	47	37	22	50	49
1989—Sumter (South Atlantic)		14	2	7	.222	6.49	0	68	74	55	49	59	51
—Pulaski (Appalachian)		14	1	1	.500	5.48	0	46	48	36	28	28	50
1990—Greenville (Southern)		14	0	1	.000	4.02	6	15⅔	14	7	7	14	20
—Sumter (South Atlantic)		37	5	4	.556	1.88	5	52⅔	27	13	11	20	85
1991—Greenville (Southern)		28	0	0	...	0.57	21	31⅓	9	4	2	13	44
—Richmond (International)		23	1	0	1.000	1.03	11	26⅓	23	4	3	12	22
—Atlanta (N.L.)		17	3	1	.750	3.20	2	19⅔	17	7	7	13	13
Major league totals (1 year)		17	3	1	.750	3.20	2	19⅔	17	7	7	13	13

CHAMPIONSHIP SERIES RECORD

Year	Team (League)	G	W	L	Pct.	ERA	Sv.	IP	H	R	ER	BB	SO
1991—Atlanta (N.L.)		3	0	0	...	0.00	0	1⅔	3	0	0	1	1

WORLD SERIES RECORD

Year	Team (League)	G	W	L	Pct.	ERA	Sv.	IP	H	R	ER	BB	SO
1991—Atlanta (N.L.)		3	0	0	...	0.00	0	1⅔	2	0	0	2	1

WOOD, TED
OF, GIANTS

PERSONAL: Born January 4, 1967, at Mansfield, O.... 6-2/178.... Throws left, bats left.... Full name: Edward Robert Wood Jr.
COLLEGE: New Orleans.
TRANSACTIONS/CAREER NOTES: Selected by San Francisco Giants in first round (29th pick overall) of free-agent draft (June 1, 1988).
RECORDS/HONORS: Named outfielder on THE SPORTING NEWS college All-America team (1988).
STATISTICAL NOTES: Led Pacific Coast League with 86 bases on balls received in 1991.
MISCELLANEOUS: Member of 1988 U.S. Olympic Baseball team.

Year	Team (League)	Pos.	G	AB	R	H	2B	3B	HR	RBI	Avg.	SB	PO	A	E	Avg.
													BATTING			FIELDING
1989—Shreveport (Texas)		OF	114	349	44	90	13	1	0	43	.258	9	200	4	3	.986
1990—Shreveport (Texas)		OF	131	456	81	121	22	*11	17	72	.265	17	247	8	6	.977
1991—Phoenix (Pacific Coast)		OF	*137	512	90	159	38	6	11	*109	.311	12	275	8	10	.966
—San Francisco (N.L.)		OF	10	25	0	3	0	0	0	1	.120	0	10	0	1	.909
Major league totals (1 year)			10	25	0	3	0	0	0	1	.120	0	10	0	1	.909

WOODSON, KERRY
P, MARINERS

PERSONAL: Born May 18, 1969, at Jacksonville, Fla.... 6-2/190.... Throws right, bats right.... Full name: Walter Browne Woodson IV.
HIGH SCHOOL: Carmel (Calif.).
COLLEGE: San Jose City (Calif.).
TRANSACTIONS/CAREER NOTES: Selected by Seattle Mariners organization in 29th round of free-agent draft (June 1, 1988).
STATISTICAL NOTES: Led California League with 12 hit batsmen in 1990.

Year	Team (League)	G	W	L	Pct.	ERA	Sv.	IP	H	R	ER	BB	SO
1989—Bellingham (Northwest)		12	3	4	.429	4.75	0	60⅔	63	42	32	27	53
1990—San Bernardino (California)		27	8	6	.571	3.10	0	136⅔	111	62	47	83	131
1991—San Bernardino (California)		5	2	0	1.000	1.95	0	27⅔	33	13	6	16	14
—Jacksonville (Southern)		13	4	6	.400	3.06	0	79⅓	73	35	27	39	50

WORRELL, TODD
P, CARDINALS

PERSONAL: Born September 28, 1959, at Arcadia, Calif.... 6-5/222.... Throws right, bats right.... Full name: Todd Roland Worrell.... Brother of Tim Worrell, pitcher, San Diego Padres organization.... Name pronounced wor-RELL.
HIGH SCHOOL: Maranatta (Arcadia, Calif.).
COLLEGE: Biola College, Calif. (bachelor of science degree in Christian education).
TRANSACTIONS/CAREER NOTES: Selected by St. Louis Cardinals organization in first round (21st pick overall) of free-agent draft (June 7, 1982).... On St. Louis disabled list (May 14-June 7, 1989); included rehabilitation disability assignment to Louisville (June 6-7, 1989).... On disabled list (March 31, 1990-entire season).... On St. Louis disabled list (April 4, 1991-entire season); included rehabilitation disability assignment to Louisville (May 4-10, 1991).
RECORDS/HONORS: Holds major league rookie-season record for most saves—36 (1986).... Named righthanded pitcher on THE SPORTING NEWS college All-America team (1982).... Named N.L. Rookie Pitcher of the Year by THE SPORTING NEWS (1986).... Named N.L. Fireman of the Year by THE SPORTING NEWS (1986).... Named N.L. Rookie of the Year by Baseball Writers' Association of America (1986).
MISCELLANEOUS: Appeared as outfielder in two games with no chances (1986).... Had no chances in one game as outfielder (1987 and 1989).

Year	Team (League)	G	W	L	Pct.	ERA	Sv.	IP	H	R	ER	BB	SO
1982 —Erie (New York-Penn)		9	4	1	.800	3.31	0	51⅔	52	23	19	15	57
1983 —Louisville (American Assoc.)		15	4	2	.667	4.74	0	79⅔	76	49	42	42	46
—Arkansas (Texas)		10	5	2	.714	3.07	0	70⅓	57	33	24	37	74
1984 —Arkansas (Texas)		18	3	10	.231	4.49	0	100⅓	109	72	50	67	88
—St. Petersburg (Florida State)		8	3	2	.600	2.09	0	47⅓	41	22	11	24	33
1985 —Louisville (American Assoc.)		34	8	6	.571	3.60	11	127⅔	114	59	51	47	★126
—St. Louis (N.L.)		17	3	0	1.000	2.91	5	21⅔	17	7	7	7	17
1986 —St. Louis (N.L.)		74	9	10	.474	2.08	★36	103⅔	86	29	24	41	73
1987 —St. Louis (N.L.)		75	8	6	.571	2.66	33	94⅔	86	29	28	34	92
1988 —St. Louis (N.L.)		68	5	9	.357	3.00	32	90	69	32	30	34	78
1989 —St. Louis (N.L.)		47	3	5	.375	2.96	20	51⅔	42	21	17	26	41
—Louisville (American Assoc.)		1	0	0	. . .	0.00	0	1	0	0	0	0	1
1990 —								Did not play					
1991 —Louisville (American Assoc.)		3	0	0	. . .	18.00	0	3	4	6	6	3	4
Major league totals (5 years)		281	28	30	.483	2.64	126	361⅔	300	118	106	142	301

CHAMPIONSHIP SERIES RECORD

CHAMPIONSHIP SERIES NOTES: Appeared as outfielder in one game (1987).

Year	Team (League)	G	W	L	Pct.	ERA	Sv.	IP	H	R	ER	BB	SO
1985 —St. Louis (N.L.)		4	1	0	1.000	1.42	0	6⅓	4	1	1	2	3
1987 —St. Louis (N.L.)		3	0	0	. . .	2.08	1	4⅓	4	1	1	1	6
Championship Series totals (2 years)		7	1	0	1.000	1.69	1	10⅔	8	2	2	3	9

WORLD SERIES RECORD

WORLD SERIES NOTES: Shares single-game record for most consecutive strikeouts—6 (October 24, 1985).

Year	Team (League)	G	W	L	Pct.	ERA	Sv.	IP	H	R	ER	BB	SO
1985 —St. Louis (N.L.)		3	0	1	.000	3.86	1	4⅔	4	2	2	2	6
1987 —St. Louis (N.L.)		4	0	0	. . .	1.29	2	7	6	1	1	4	3
World Series totals (2 years)		7	0	1	.000	2.31	3	11⅔	10	3	3	6	9

ALL-STAR GAME RECORD

Year	League	W	L	Pct.	ERA	Sv.	IP	H	R	ER	BB	SO
1988 —National		0	0	. . .	0.00	0	1	0	0	0	0	0

WORTHINGTON, CRAIG
3B, ORIOLES

PERSONAL: Born April 17, 1965, at Los Angeles. . . . 6-0/200. . . . Throws right, bats right. . . . Full name: Craig Richard Worthington.
HIGH SCHOOL: Cantwell (Pico Rivera, Calif.).
COLLEGE: Cerritos College (Calif.).
TRANSACTIONS/CAREER NOTES: Selected by New York Mets organization in sixth round of free-agent draft (January 17, 1984). . . . Selected by Houston Astros organization in secondary phase of free-agent draft (June 4, 1984). . . . Selected by Chicago Cubs organization in secondary phase of free-agent draft (January 9, 1985). . . . Selected by Baltimore Orioles organization in secondary phase of free-agent draft (June 3, 1985). . . . On Baltimore disabled list (May 21-June 29, 1991); included rehabilitation disability assignment to Rochester (June 11-29, 1991).
RECORDS/HONORS: Named International League Player of the Year (1988). . . . Named A.L. Rookie Player of the Year by THE SPORTING NEWS (1989).
STATISTICAL NOTES: Led International League third basemen with 310 total chances and tied for lead with 16 double plays in 1987. . . . Led International League third basemen with 91 putouts and 319 total chances in 1988.

Year	Team (League)	Pos.	G	AB	R	H	2B	3B	HR	RBI	Avg.	SB	PO	A	E	Avg.
1985 —Bluefield (Appalachian)	3B	39	129	33	44	9	1	7	20	.341	3	32	68	12	.893
1986 —Hagerstown (Carolina)	3B	132	480	85	144	35	1	15	★105	.300	7	92	249	32	.914
1987 —Rochester (Int'l)	3B	109	383	46	99	14	1	7	50	.258	0	★79	★211	★20	★.935
1988 —Rochester (Int'l)	3B-SS	121	430	53	105	25	1	16	73	.244	3	†91	209	19	.940
—Baltimore (A.L.)	3B	26	81	5	15	2	0	2	4	.185	1	20	53	3	.961
1989 —Baltimore (A.L.)	3B	145	497	57	123	23	0	15	70	.247	1	113	277	20	.951
1990 —Baltimore (A.L.)	3B	133	425	46	96	17	0	8	44	.226	1	90	218	18	.945
1991 —Baltimore (A.L.)	3B	31	102	11	23	3	0	4	12	.225	0	26	51	2	.975
—Rochester (Int'l)	3B	19	57	10	17	4	0	2	9	.298	0	10	13	1	.958
Major league totals (4 years)		335	1105	119	257	45	0	29	130	.233	3	249	599	43	.952

YELDING, ERIC
SS, ASTROS

PERSONAL: Born February 22, 1965, at Montrose, Ala. . . . 5-11/165. . . . Throws right, bats right. . . . Full name: Eric Girard Yelding.
HIGH SCHOOL: Fairhope (Montrose, Ala.).
COLLEGE: Chipola Junior College (Fla.).
TRANSACTIONS/CAREER NOTES: Selected by Toronto Blue Jays organization in first round (19th pick overall) of free-agent draft (January 17, 1984). . . . Drafted by Chicago Cubs (December 5, 1988). . . . Claimed on waivers by Houston Astros (April 3, 1989). . . . On suspended list for one game (April 19, 1991).
STATISTICAL NOTES: Led Pioneer League in caught stealing with 11 in 1984. . . . Led Carolina League in caught stealing with 26 in 1985. . . . Led California League shortstops with 573 total chances in 1986. . . . Led International League in caught stealing with 23 in 1988. . . . Led International League second basemen with 21 errors in 1988. . . . Led N.L. in caught stealing with 25 in 1990.

Year	Team (League)	Pos.	G	AB	R	H	2B	3B	HR	RBI	Avg.	SB	PO	A	E	Avg.
1984 — Medicine Hat (Pioneer)		OF	67	★304	61	94	14	6	4	29	.309	31	99	9	13	.893
1985 — Kinston (Carolina)............		OF	135	526	59	137	14	4	2	31	.260	★62	310	10	9	.973
1986 — Ventura County (Calif.).....		SS	131	★560	83	157	14	7	4	40	.280	41	★231	284	★58	.899
1987 — Myrtle Beach (S. Atl.)........		SS	88	357	53	109	12	2	1	31	.305	73	126	226	45	.887
— Knoxville (Southern)		SS	39	150	23	30	6	1	0	7	.200	10	64	92	14	.918
1988 — Syracuse (International) ..		2B-SS	★138	★556	•69	139	15	2	1	38	.250	★59	222	310	†35	.938
1989 — Houston (N.L.)■..............		SS-2B-OF	70	90	19	21	2	0	0	9	.233	11	37	57	3	.969
1990 — Houston (N.L.)		O-S-2-3	142	511	69	130	9	5	1	28	.254	64	315	124	17	.963
1991 — Houston (N.L.)		SS-OF	78	276	19	67	11	1	1	20	.243	11	114	166	20	.933
— Tucson (Pacific Coast)		SS	11	43	6	17	3	0	0	3	.395	4	22	24	2	.958
Major league totals (3 years)			290	877	107	218	22	6	2	57	.249	86	466	347	40	.953

YORK, MIKE
P, PADRES

PERSONAL: Born September 6, 1964, at Oak Park, Ill. . . . 6-1/192. . . . Throws right, bats right. . . . Full name: Michael David York.
HIGH SCHOOL: Argo Community (Chicago).
TRANSACTIONS/CAREER NOTES: Selected by New York Yankees organization in 40th round of free-agent draft (June 7, 1982). . . . Released by Yankees organization (July 22, 1983). . . . Signed by Sarasota White Sox, Chicago White Sox organization (July 18, 1984). . . . Released by White Sox organization (April 8, 1985). . . . Signed by Lakeland, Detroit Tigers organization (June 9, 1985). . . . Released by Tigers organization (August 29, 1986). . . . Signed by Pittsburgh Pirates organization (October 11, 1986). . . . Traded by Pirates to Cleveland Indians organization for OF Mitch Webster (May 16, 1991). . . . On disabled list (August 17-October 7, 1991). . . . Released by Indians (October 7, 1991). . . . Signed by San Diego Padres organization (December 19, 1991).

Year	Team (League)	G	W	L	Pct.	ERA	Sv.	IP	H	R	ER	BB	SO
1983 — Oneonta (New York-Penn)		9	0	0	. . .	8.18	0	11	19	13	10	8	3
1984 — Sarasota White Sox (GCL)■......		5	1	0	1.000	3.68	0	14⅔	18	9	6	9	19
1985 — Bristol (Appalachian)■		21	•9	2	.818	2.37	2	38	24	12	10	34	31
1986 — Lakeland (Florida State)		16	1	3	.250	6.42	1	40⅔	49	42	29	43	29
— Gastonia (South Atlantic)		22	2	2	.500	3.44	9	34	26	15	13	27	27
1987 — Macon (South Atlantic)■		28	★17	6	.739	3.04	0	165⅔	129	71	56	★88	169
1988 — Salem (Carolina)		13	9	2	.818	2.68	0	84	65	31	25	52	77
— Harrisburg (Eastern)		13	0	5	.000	3.72	0	82⅓	92	43	34	45	61
1989 — Harrisburg (Eastern)		18	11	5	.688	2.31	0	121	105	37	31	40	106
— Buffalo (American Assoc.)		8	1	3	.250	5.93	0	41	48	29	27	25	28
1990 — Buffalo (American Assoc.)		27	8	7	.533	4.20	0	158⅔	165	87	74	•78	130
— Pittsburgh (N.L.)		4	1	1	.500	2.84	0	12⅔	13	5	4	5	4
1991 — Buffalo (American Assoc.)		7	5	1	.833	2.91	0	43⅓	36	17	14	23	22
— Colorado Springs (Pac. Coast)■		5	0	1	.000	5.88	0	26	40	19	17	16	13
— Cleveland (A.L.)		14	1	4	.200	6.75	0	34⅔	45	29	26	19	19
American League totals (1 year)		14	1	4	.200	6.75	0	34⅔	45	29	26	19	19
National League totals (1 year)		4	1	1	.500	2.84	0	12⅔	13	5	4	5	4
Major league totals (2 years)		18	2	5	.286	5.70	0	47⅓	58	34	30	24	23

YOUNG, ANTHONY
P, METS

PERSONAL: Born January 19, 1966, at Houston. . . . 6-2/200. . . . Throws right, bats right. . . . Full name: Anthony Wayne Young.
HIGH SCHOOL: Furr (Houston).
COLLEGE: Houston.
TRANSACTIONS/CAREER NOTES: Selected by Montreal Expos organization in 10th round of free-agent draft (June 4, 1984). . . . Selected by New York Mets organization in 38th round of free-agent draft (June 2, 1987). . . . On disabled list (July 19, 1989-remainder of season and June 11-18, 1990).
RECORDS/HONORS: Named Texas League Pitcher of the Year (1990).

Year	Team (League)	G	W	L	Pct.	ERA	Sv.	IP	H	R	ER	BB	SO
1987 — Little Falls (New York-Penn)....		14	3	4	.429	4.53	0	53⅔	58	37	27	25	48
1988 — Little Falls (New York-Penn)....		15	3	5	.375	2.20	0	73⅔	51	33	18	34	75
1989 — Columbia (South Atlantic)		21	9	6	.600	3.49	0	129	115	60	50	55	127
1990 — Jackson (Texas)		23	★15	3	.833	★1.65	0	158	116	38	29	52	95
1991 — Tidewater (International)		25	7	9	.438	3.73	0	164	172	74	68	67	93
— New York (N.L.)		10	2	5	.286	3.10	0	49⅓	48	20	17	12	20
Major league totals (1 year)		10	2	5	.286	3.10	0	49⅓	48	20	17	12	20

YOUNG, CLIFF
P, ANGELS

PERSONAL: Born August 2, 1964, at Willis, Tex. . . . 6-4/210. . . . Throws left, bats left. . . . Full name: Clifford Raphael Young.
HIGH SCHOOL: Willis (Tex.).
TRANSACTIONS/CAREER NOTES: Selected by Montreal Expos organization in fifth round of free-agent draft (June 6, 1983). . . . On suspended list (May 23-30, 1984). . . . Traded by Expos organization to Toronto Blue Jays organization (September 10, 1985), completing deal in which Blue Jays traded OF Mitch Webster to Expos for a player to be named later (June 22, 1985). . . . On disabled list (August 20-30, 1986). . . . Drafted by Oakland Athletics (December 8, 1986). . . . Returned to Blue Jays organization (April 6, 1987). . . . Traded by Blue Jays organization to California Angels for P DeWayne Buice (March 9, 1989).

STATISTICAL NOTES: Led Southern League pitchers with 31 games started in 1986. . . . Led Florida State League with 13 home runs allowed in 1986.

Year	Team (League)	G	W	L	Pct.	ERA	Sv.	IP	H	R	ER	BB	SO
1983	—Calgary (Pioneer)	13	7	1	.875	5.11	0	79⅓	98	55	45	32	72
1984	—Gastonia (South Atlantic)	24	8	10	.444	4.18	0	144⅓	117	77	67	68	121
1985	—West Palm Beach (Florida St.)	25	15	5	.750	3.98	0	153⅔	149	77	68	57	112
1986	—Knoxville (Southern)■	31	12	★14	.462	3.89	0	★203⅔	★232	111	88	71	121
1987	—Knoxville (Southern)	42	8	9	.471	4.45	1	119⅓	148	76	59	43	81
1988	—Syracuse (International)	33	9	6	.600	3.42	1	147⅓	133	68	56	32	75
1989	—Edmonton (Pacific Coast)■	31	8	9	.471	4.79	0	139	158	80	74	32	89
1990	—Edmonton (Pacific Coast)	30	7	4	.636	2.42	4	52	45	15	14	10	30
	—California (A.L.)	17	1	1	.500	3.52	0	30⅔	40	14	12	7	19
1991	—California (A.L.)	11	1	0	1.000	4.26	0	12⅔	12	6	6	3	6
	—Edmonton (Pacific Coast)	34	4	8	.333	4.90	5	71⅔	88	53	39	25	39
Major league totals (2 years)		28	2	1	.667	3.74	0	43⅓	52	20	18	10	25

YOUNG, CURT

P, ROYALS

PERSONAL: Born April 16, 1960, at Saginaw, Mich. . . . 6-1/175. . . . Throws left, bats right. . . . Full name: Curtis Allen Young.
HIGH SCHOOL: Arthur Hill (Saginaw, Mich.).
COLLEGE: Central Michigan.
TRANSACTIONS/CAREER NOTES: Selected by Oakland A's organization in fourth round of free-agent draft (June 8, 1981). . . . On Oakland disabled list (May 3-July 5, 1985); included rehabilitation disability assignment to Modesto (June 29-July 5, 1985). . . . On disabled list (June 30-July 20, 1987 and June 2-17, 1991). . . . Granted free agency (October 28, 1991). . . . Signed by Kansas City Royals organization (February 2, 1992).
STATISTICAL NOTES: Led California League pitchers with 28 games started in 1982.
MISCELLANEOUS: Appeared in one game as a pinch-runner (1990). . . . Had one at-bat with no hits (1991).

Year	Team (League)	G	W	L	Pct.	ERA	Sv.	IP	H	R	ER	BB	SO
1981	—Medford (Northwest)	8	2	2	.500	4.25	0	53	45	27	25	32	49
	—Modesto (California)	5	2	1	.667	3.48	0	31	28	15	12	16	22
1982	—Modesto (California)	28	15	8	.652	3.47	0	205	189	90	79	81	162
1983	—Tacoma (Pacific Coast)	27	12	9	.571	5.05	0	158⅔	175	94	89	52	109
	—Oakland (A.L.)	8	0	1	.000	16.00	0	9	17	17	16	5	5
1984	—Tacoma (Pacific Coast)	14	6	4	.600	3.78	0	95⅓	88	45	40	28	61
	—Oakland (A.L.)	20	9	4	.692	4.06	0	108⅔	118	53	49	31	41
1985	—Oakland (A.L.)	19	0	4	.000	7.24	0	46	57	38	37	22	19
	—Modesto (California)	2	0	0	. . .	4.76	0	5⅔	7	4	3	6	3
	—Tacoma (Pacific Coast)	3	2	0	1.000	3.60	0	15	10	7	6	7	8
1986	—Tacoma (Pacific Coast)	4	4	0	1.000	2.00	0	27	16	7	6	6	28
	—Oakland (A.L.)	29	13	9	.591	3.45	0	198	176	88	76	57	116
1987	—Oakland (A.L.)	31	13	7	.650	4.08	0	203	194	102	92	44	124
1988	—Oakland (A.L.)	26	11	8	.579	4.14	0	156⅓	162	77	72	50	69
1989	—Oakland (A.L.)	25	5	9	.357	3.73	0	111	117	56	46	47	55
1990	—Oakland (A.L.)	26	9	6	.600	4.85	0	124⅓	124	70	67	53	56
1991	—Oakland (A.L.)	41	4	2	.667	5.00	0	68⅓	74	38	38	34	27
Major league totals (9 years)		225	64	50	.561	4.33	0	1024⅔	1039	539	493	343	512

CHAMPIONSHIP SERIES RECORD

Year	Team (League)	G	W	L	Pct.	ERA	Sv.	IP	H	R	ER	BB	SO
1988	—Oakland (A.L.)	1	0	0	. . .	0.00	0	1⅓	1	1	0	0	2

WORLD SERIES RECORD

Year	Team (League)	G	W	L	Pct.	ERA	Sv.	IP	H	R	ER	BB	SO
1988	—Oakland (A.L.)	1	0	0	. . .	0.00	0	1	1	0	0	0	0
1989	—Oakland (A.L.)						Did not play						
1990	—Oakland (A.L.)	1	0	0	. . .	0.00	0	1	1	0	0	0	0
World Series totals (2 years)		2	0	0	. . .	0.00	0	2	2	0	0	0	0

YOUNG, ERIC

2B, DODGERS

PERSONAL: Born May 18, 1967, at New Brunswick, N.J. . . . 5-9/180. . . . Throws right, bats right. . . . Full name: Eric Orlando Young.
HIGH SCHOOL: New Brunswick (N.J.).
COLLEGE: Rutgers.
TRANSACTIONS/CAREER NOTES: Selected by Los Angeles Dodgers organization in 43rd round of free-agent draft (June 5, 1989).
STATISTICAL NOTES: Led Florida State League second basemen with 24 errors in 1990. . . . Led Texas League in caught stealing with 26 in 1991. . . . Led Texas League second basemen with .974 fielding percentage in 1991.

Year	Team (League)	Pos.	G	AB	R	H	2B	3B	HR	RBI	Avg.	SB	PO	A	E	Avg.
1989	—Kissimm. Dodgers (GCL)	2B	56	197	53	65	11	5	2	22	.330	★41	104	128	★15	.939
1990	—Vero Beach (Florida St.)	2B-OF	127	460	101	132	23	7	2	50	.287	★76	156	218	†25	.937
1991	—San Antonio (Texas)	2B-OF	127	461	82	129	17	4	3	35	.280	★70	206	282	13	†.974
	—Albuquerque (PCL)	2B	1	5	0	2	0	0	0	0	.400	0	1	2	0	1.000

YOUNG, GERALD

OF, ASTROS

PERSONAL: Born October 22, 1964, at Tele, Honduras. . . . 6-2/185. . . . Throws right, bats both. . . . Full name: Gerald Anthony Young.
HIGH SCHOOL: Valley (Santa Ana, Calif.).
TRANSACTIONS/CAREER NOTES: Selected by New York Mets organization in fifth round of free-agent draft (June 7, 1982). . . . Traded by Mets organization with IF Manny Lee to Houston Astros (August 31, 1984) as partial completion of deal in which Mets acquired IF Ray Knight for three players to be named later (August 28, 1984); Astros acquired P Mitch Cook to complete deal (September 10, 1984).
STATISTICAL NOTES: Tied for Appalachian League lead in being hit by pitch with six in 1982. . . . Led Appalachian League shortstops with 38 errors in 1982. . . . Tied for Florida State League lead in double plays by outfielders with five in 1985. . . . Led Southern League in caught stealing with 27 in 1986. . . . Led N.L. in caught stealing with 25 in 1989 and tied for lead with 27 in 1988. . . . Led N.L. outfielders with 428 total chances and tied for lead with five double plays in 1989.

							BATTING						FIELDING		
Year — Team (League)	Pos.	G	AB	R	H	2B	3B	HR	RBI	Avg.	SB	PO	A	E	Avg.
1982 —Kingsport (Appalachian) ..	SS-2B-3B	59	197	27	35	6	1	0	15	.178	7	79	170	+39	.865
1983 —Sarasota Mets (GCL)	OF-SS	56	177	34	42	7	2	1	14	.237	11	88	9	7	.933
1984 —Columbia (S. Atlantic).......	OF	124	396	69	84	14	3	1	52	.212	43	254	7	4	.985
1985 —Osceola (Florida State)■...	OF	133	474	88	121	20	9	3	48	.255	31	251	11	5	.981
1986 —Columbus (Southern)	OF	136	539	101	151	30	4	9	62	.280	*54	317	22	13	.963
1987 —Tucson (Pacific Coast)	OF	86	340	59	99	15	5	2	31	.291	43	232	7	7	.972
—Houston (N.L.)	OF	71	274	44	88	9	2	1	15	.321	26	143	5	3	.980
1988 —Houston (N.L.)	OF	149	576	79	148	21	9	0	37	.257	65	357	10	3	.992
1989 —Houston (N.L.)	OF	146	533	71	124	17	3	0	38	.233	34	*412	*15	1	*.998
1990 —Houston (N.L.)	OF	57	154	15	27	4	1	1	4	.175	6	99	4	1	.990
—Tucson (Pacific Coast)	OF	49	183	37	61	7	4	0	24	.333	14	112	8	6	.952
1991 —Tucson (Pacific Coast)	OF	24	79	14	24	2	3	0	17	.304	3	45	4	0	1.000
—Houston (N.L.)	OF	108	142	26	31	3	1	1	11	.218	16	96	4	0	1.000
Major league totals (5 years)		531	1679	235	418	54	16	3	105	.249	147	1107	38	8	.993

YOUNG, MATT

P, RED SOX

PERSONAL: Born August 9, 1958, at Pasadena, Calif. . . . 6-3/210. . . . Throws left, bats left. . . . Full name: Matthew John Young.
HIGH SCHOOL: St. Francis (La Canada, Calif.).
COLLEGE: Pasadena City College (Calif.) and UCLA.
TRANSACTIONS/CAREER NOTES: Selected by Boston Red Sox organization in second round of free-agent draft (January 10, 1978). . . . Selected by Seattle Mariners organization in second round of free-agent draft (June 3, 1980). . . . On Seattle disabled list (July 4-29, 1984). . . . Traded by Mariners to Los Angeles Dodgers for P Dennis Powell and IF Mike Watters (December 10, 1986). . . . Traded by Dodgers as part of an eight-player, three-team deal in which New York Mets traded P Jesse Orosco to Oakland Athletics (December 11, 1987). A's traded Orosco with SS Alfredo Griffin and P Jay Howell to Dodgers for Young, P Bob Welch and P Jack Savage. A's then traded Savage with P Wally Whitehurst and P Kevin Tapani to Mets. . . . On disabled list (April 3, 1988-entire season). . . . Released by A's (December 21, 1988). . . . Re-signed by A's (January 19, 1989). . . . On Oakland disabled list (March 19-June 13, 1989); included rehabilitation disability assignment to Modesto (May 16 and May 25-June 2, 1989) and Tacoma (June 3-9, 1989). . . . Granted free agency (November 13, 1989). . . . Signed by Seattle Mariners (December 15, 1989). . . . Granted free agency (November 5, 1990). . . . Signed by Boston Red Sox (December 4, 1990). . . . On Boston disabled list (June 5-August 1, 1991); included rehabilitation disability assignment to Pawtucket (July 22-August 1, 1991).
RECORDS/HONORS: Shares major league record for most strikeouts in one inning—4 (September 9, 1990, first inning).

Year — Team (League)	G	W	L	Pct.	ERA	Sv.	IP	H	R	ER	BB	SO
1980 —Bellingham (Northwest)...........	12	4	5	.444	4.93	0	73	73	46	40	62	53
1981 —Lynn (Eastern)	14	3	9	.250	4.00	0	81	80	47	36	38	57
1982 —Salt Lake City (Pacific Coast) ..	29	12	10	.545	4.65	1	176	192	113	91	75	118
1983 —Seattle (A.L.)	33	11	15	.423	3.27	0	203⅔	178	86	74	79	130
1984 —Seattle (A.L.)	22	6	8	.429	5.72	0	113⅓	141	81	72	57	73
—Salt Lake City (Pacific Coast) ..	6	6	0	1.000	1.51	0	41⅔	32	9	7	20	37
1985 —Seattle (A.L.)	37	12	*19	.387	4.91	1	218⅓	242	135	119	76	136
1986 —Seattle (A.L.)	65	8	6	.571	3.82	13	103⅔	108	50	44	46	82
1987 —Los Angeles (N.L.)■...............	47	5	8	.385	4.47	11	54⅓	62	30	27	17	42
1988 —■					Did not play							
1989 —Modesto (California)	3	0	0	. . .	0.75	0	12	9	1	1	6	13
—Tacoma (Pacific Coast)	2	1	1	.500	2.45	0	11	8	4	3	5	6
—Oakland (A.L.)	26	1	4	.200	6.75	0	37⅓	42	31	28	31	27
1990 —Seattle (A.L.)■.....................	34	8	18	.308	3.51	0	225⅓	198	106	88	107	176
1991 —Boston (A.L.)■.....................	19	3	7	.300	5.18	0	88⅔	92	55	51	53	69
—Pawtucket (International)	2	1	0	1.000	4.50	0	8	8	4	4	6	7
American League totals (7 years)	236	49	77	.389	4.33	14	990⅓	1001	544	476	449	693
National League totals (1 year)	47	5	8	.385	4.47	11	54⅓	62	30	27	17	42
Major league totals (8 years)	283	54	85	.388	4.33	25	1044⅔	1063	574	503	466	735

CHAMPIONSHIP SERIES RECORD

Year — Team (League)	G	W	L	Pct.	ERA	Sv.	IP	H	R	ER	BB	SO
1989 —Oakland (A.L.)	1	0	0	. . .	0.00	0	⅓	0	0	0	2	0

WORLD SERIES RECORD

Year — Team (League)	G	W	L	Pct.	ERA	Sv.	IP	H	R	ER	BB	SO
1989 —Oakland (A.L.)					Did not play							

Year	League	W	L	Pct.	ERA	Sv.	IP	H	R	ER	BB	SO
1983 —American		0	0	...	0.00	0	1	0	0	0	0	1

YOUNG, PETE
P, EXPOS

PERSONAL: Born March 19, 1968, at Meadville, Miss. . . . 6-0/225. . . . Throws right, bats right. . . . Full name: Bryan Owen Young.
HIGH SCHOOL: McComb (Miss.).
COLLEGE: Mississippi State.
TRANSACTIONS/CAREER NOTES: Selected by Cincinnati Reds organization in 22nd round of free-agent draft (June 2, 1986). . . . Selected by Montreal Expos organization in sixth round of free-agent draft (June 5, 1989).

Year	Team (League)	G	W	L	Pct.	ERA	Sv.	IP	H	R	ER	BB	SO
1989 —Jamestown (New York-Penn) ..		18	5	2	.714	1.94	4	65	63	18	14	14	62
1990 —West Palm Beach (Florida St.) ..		39	8	3	.727	2.47	19	109⅓	106	36	30	27	62
1991 —Sumter (South Atlantic)...........		1	0	0	...	9.00	0	1	1	1	1	1	2
—Harrisburg (Eastern)		54	7	5	.583	2.60	13	90	82	28	26	24	74

YOUNT, ROBIN
OF, BREWERS

PERSONAL: Born September 16, 1955, at Danville, Ill. . . . 6-0/180. . . . Throws right, bats right. . . . Brother of Larry Yount, pitcher, Houston Astros (1971).
HIGH SCHOOL: Taft (Woodland Hills, Calif.).
TRANSACTIONS/CAREER NOTES: Selected by Milwaukee Brewers organization in first round (third pick overall) of free-agent draft (June 5, 1973). . . . On disabled list (March 28-May 3, 1978). . . . Granted free agency (November 13, 1989). . . . Re-signed by Brewers (December 19, 1989). . . . On disabled list (July 6-30, 1991).
RECORDS/HONORS: Named shortstop on THE SPORTING NEWS A.L. All-Star team (1978, 1980 and 1982). . . . Named shortstop on THE SPORTING NEWS A.L. Silver Slugger team (1980 and 1982). . . . Named Major League Player of the Year by THE SPORTING NEWS (1982). . . . Named A.L. Player of the Year by THE SPORTING NEWS (1982). . . . Won A.L. Gold Glove at shortstop (1982). . . . Named A.L. Most Valuable Player by Baseball Writers' Association of America (1982 and 1989). . . . Named outfielder on THE SPORTING NEWS A.L. All-Star team (1989). . . . Named outfielder on THE SPORTING NEWS A.L. Silver Slugger team (1989).
STATISTICAL NOTES: Led A.L. shortstops with 831 total chances and 104 double plays and tied for lead with 290 putouts in 1976. . . . Led A.L. with 367 total bases and .578 slugging percentage in 1982. . . . Led A.L. outfielders with .997 fielding percentage in 1986. . . . Hit for the cycle (June 12, 1988).

Year	Team (League)	Pos.	G	AB	R	H	2B	3B	HR	RBI	Avg.	SB	PO	A	E	Avg.
1973 —Newark (N.Y.-Penn)		SS	64	242	29	69	15	3	3	25	.285	8	43	85	18	.877
1974 —Milwaukee (A.L.)		SS	107	344	48	86	14	5	3	26	.250	7	148	327	19	.962
1975 —Milwaukee (A.L.)		SS	147	558	67	149	28	2	8	52	.267	12	273	402	★44	.939
1976 —Milwaukee (A.L.)		SS-OF	●161	638	59	161	19	3	2	54	.252	16	‡290	510	31	.963
1977 —Milwaukee (A.L.)		SS	154	605	66	174	34	4	4	49	.288	16	256	449	29	.960
1978 —Milwaukee (A.L.)		SS	127	502	66	147	23	9	9	71	.293	16	246	453	30	.959
1979 —Milwaukee (A.L.)		SS	149	577	72	154	26	5	8	51	.267	11	267	517	25	.969
1980 —Milwaukee (A.L.)		SS	143	611	121	179	★49	10	23	87	.293	20	239	455	28	.961
1981 —Milwaukee (A.L.)		SS	96	377	50	103	15	5	10	49	.273	4	161	370	8	★.985
1982 —Milwaukee (A.L.)		SS	156	635	129	★210	●46	12	29	114	.331	14	253	★489	24	.969
1983 —Milwaukee (A.L.)		SS	149	578	102	178	42	★10	17	80	.308	12	256	420	19	.973
1984 —Milwaukee (A.L.)		SS	160	624	105	186	27	7	16	80	.298	14	199	402	18	.971
1985 —Milwaukee (A.L.)		OF-1B	122	466	76	129	26	3	15	68	.277	10	267	5	8	.971
1986 —Milwaukee (A.L.)		OF-1B	140	522	82	163	31	7	9	46	.312	14	365	9	2	+.995
1987 —Milwaukee (A.L.)		OF	158	635	99	198	25	9	21	103	.312	19	380	5	5	.987
1988 —Milwaukee (A.L.)		OF	★162	621	92	190	38	●11	13	91	.306	22	444	12	2	.996
1989 —Milwaukee (A.L.)		OF	160	614	101	195	38	9	21	103	.318	19	361	8	7	.981
1990 —Milwaukee (A.L.)		OF	158	587	98	145	17	5	17	77	.247	15	★422	3	4	.991
1991 —Milwaukee (A.L.)		OF	130	503	66	131	20	4	10	77	.260	6	315	1	2	.994
Major league totals (18 years)			2579	9997	1499	2878	518	120	235	1278	.288	247	5142	4837	305	.970

DIVISION SERIES RECORD

Year	Team (League)	Pos.	G	AB	R	H	2B	3B	HR	RBI	Avg.	SB	PO	A	E	Avg.
1981 —Milwaukee (A.L.)		SS	5	19	4	6	0	1	0	1	.316	1	6	16	1	.957

CHAMPIONSHIP SERIES RECORD

Year	Team (League)	Pos.	G	AB	R	H	2B	3B	HR	RBI	Avg.	SB	PO	A	E	Avg.
1982 —Milwaukee (A.L.)		SS	5	16	1	4	0	0	0	0	.250	0	11	12	1	.958

WORLD SERIES RECORD

WORLD SERIES NOTES: Shares single-game record for most at-bats in nine-inning game—6 (October 12, 1982).

Year	Team (League)	Pos.	G	AB	R	H	2B	3B	HR	RBI	Avg.	SB	PO	A	E	Avg.
1982 —Milwaukee (A.L.)		SS	7	29	6	12	3	0	1	6	.414	0	20	19	3	.929

Year	League	Pos.	AB	R	H	2B	3B	HR	RBI	Avg.	SB	PO	A	E	Avg.
						BATTING							FIELDING		
1980 — American		SS	2	0	0	0	0	0	0	.000	0	3	2	0	1.000
1982 — American		SS	3	0	0	0	0	0	0	.000	0	0	2	0	1.000
1983 — American		SS	2	1	0	0	0	0	1	.000	0	0	1	0	1.000
All-Star Game totals (3 years)			7	1	0	0	0	0	1	.000	0	3	5	0	1.000

ZAPPELLI, MARK
P, ANGELS

PERSONAL: Born July 21, 1966, at Santa Rosa, Calif. . . . 6-0/160. . . . Throws right, bats right. . . . Full name: Mark John Zappelli.
HIGH SCHOOL: Cardinal Newman (Santa Rosa, Calif.).
COLLEGE: Cal Poly San Luis Obispo.
TRANSACTIONS/CAREER NOTES: Signed as free agent by California Angels organization (February 21, 1989). . . . On Midland disabled list (May 8-19, 1991).

Year	Team (League)	G	W	L	Pct.	ERA	Sv.	IP	H	R	ER	BB	SO
1989 — Quad City (Midwest)		48	5	3	.625	1.85	22	68	44	15	14	21	71
1990 — Midland (Texas)		57	3	4	.429	4.40	6	45	57	28	22	14	35
— Palm Springs (California)		21	0	1	.000	2.45	6	22	17	7	6	9	25
1991 — Midland (Texas)		32	2	2	.500	2.48	11	32⅔	26	15	9	13	31
— Edmonton (Pacific Coast)		17	2	1	.667	4.44	0	24⅓	24	16	12	19	16

ZAVARAS, CLINT
P, MARINERS

PERSONAL: Born January 4, 1967, at Denver. . . . 6-1/175. . . . Throws right, bats right. . . . Full name: Clinton Wayne Zavaras.
HIGH SCHOOL: Mullen (Denver).
TRANSACTIONS/CAREER NOTES: Selected by Seattle Mariners organization in third round of free-agent draft (June 3, 1985). . . . On disabled list (April 2, 1990-entire season). . . . On Calgary disabled list (April 11-27, 1991). . . . On San Bernardino disabled list (May 11-June 10, 1991).

Year	Team (League)	G	W	L	Pct.	ERA	Sv.	IP	H	R	ER	BB	SO
1985 — Bellingham (Northwest)		12	4	7	.364	5.59	0	56⅓	49	37	35	47	62
1986 — Wausau (Midwest)		17	6	6	.500	3.35	0	91⅓	68	45	34	67	98
1987 — Salinas (California)		26	7	12	.368	4.45	0	139⅔	102	87	69	101	180
1988 — Vermont (Eastern)		24	10	7	.588	3.92	0	128⅔	115	67	56	54	120
1989 — Calgary (Pacific Coast)		21	6	9	.400	6.04	0	110⅓	105	77	74	56	89
— Seattle (A.L.)		10	1	6	.143	5.19	0	52	49	33	30	30	31
1990 — Seattle (A.L.)							Did not play						
1991 — San Bernardino (California)		11	1	3	.250	3.79	0	40⅓	35	25	17	37	38
— Jacksonville (Southern)		6	2	2	.500	4.60	0	31⅓	36	18	16	10	21
Major league totals (1 year)		10	1	6	.143	5.19	0	52	49	33	30	30	31

ZEILE, TODD
3B, CARDINALS

PERSONAL: Born September 9, 1965, at Van Nuys, Calif. . . . 6-1/190. . . . Throws right, bats right. . . . Full name: Todd Edward Zeile. . . . Husband of Julianne McNamara, Olympic gold-medal gymnast (1984). . . . Name pronounced ZEEL.
HIGH SCHOOL: Hart (Newhall, Calif.).
COLLEGE: UCLA.
TRANSACTIONS/CAREER NOTES: Selected by Kansas City Royals organization in 30th round of free-agent draft (June 6, 1983). . . . Selected by St. Louis Cardinals organization in second round of free-agent draft (June 2, 1986).
RECORDS/HONORS: Named Midwest League Co-Most Valuable Player (1987).
STATISTICAL NOTES: Led New York-Pennsylvania League with six sacrifice flies in 1986. . . . Tied for New York-Pennsylvania League lead in double plays by catchers with seven in 1986. . . . Led Texas League catchers with 687 putouts and 761 total chances in 1988. . . . Led American Association catchers with .992 fielding percentage and 17 passed balls in 1989.

Year	Team (League)	Pos.	G	AB	R	H	2B	3B	HR	RBI	Avg.	SB	PO	A	E	Avg.
						BATTING							FIELDING			
1986 — Erie (New York-Penn)		C	70	248	40	64	14	1	14	*63	.258	5	407	*66	8	.983
1987 — Springfield (Midwest)	C-3B	130	487	94	142	24	4	25	*106	.292	1	867	79	14	.985
1988 — Arkansas (Texas)	C-OF-1B	129	430	95	117	33	2	19	75	.272	6	+697	66	10	.987
1989 — Louisville (Am. Assoc.)	C-3B-1B	118	453	71	131	26	3	19	85	.289	0	583	71	6	+.991
— St. Louis (N.L.)		C	28	82	7	21	3	1	1	8	.256	0	125	10	4	.971
1990 — St. Louis (N.L.)	C-3-1-O	144	495	62	121	25	3	15	57	.244	2	648	106	15	.980
1991 — St. Louis (N.L.)	3B	155	565	76	158	36	3	11	81	.280	17	124	290	*25	.943
Major league totals (3 years)			327	1142	145	300	64	7	27	146	.263	19	897	406	44	.967

ZOSKY, EDDIE
SS, BLUE JAYS

PERSONAL: Born February 10, 1968, at Whittier, Calif. . . . 6-0/175. . . . Throws right, bats right. . . . Full name: Edward James Zosky.
HIGH SCHOOL: St. Paul's (Sante Fe Springs, Calif.).
COLLEGE: Fresno State.
TRANSACTIONS/CAREER NOTES: Selected by New York Mets organization in fifth round of free-agent draft (June 2, 1986). . . . Selected by Toronto Blue Jays organization in first round (19th pick overall) of free-agent draft (June 5, 1989).

Named shortstop on THE SPORTING NEWS college All-America team (1989).
STATISTICAL NOTES: Led Southern League shortstops with 80 double plays in 1990.... Led International League shortstops with 616 total chances and 88 double plays in 1991.

Year	Team (League)	Pos.	G	AB	R	H	2B	3B	HR	RBI	Avg.	SB	PO	A	E	Avg.
1989—Knoxville (Southern)		SS	56	208	21	46	5	3	2	14	.221	1	94	135	8	.966
1990—Knoxville (Southern)		SS	115	450	53	122	20	7	3	45	.271	3	*196	295	31	*.941
1991—Syracuse (International)		SS	119	511	69	135	18	4	6	39	.264	9	*221	*371	24	*.961
—Toronto (A.L.)		SS	18	27	2	4	1	1	0	2	.148	0	12	26	0	1.000
Major league totals (1 year)			18	27	2	4	1	1	0	2	.148	0	12	26	0	1.000

ZUPCIC, BOB
OF, RED SOX

PERSONAL: Born August 18, 1966, at Pittsburgh.... 6-4/225.... Throws right, bats right.... Full name: Robert Zupcic.
HIGH SCHOOL: Bishop Egan (Fairless Hills, Pa.).
COLLEGE: Oral Roberts.
TRANSACTIONS/CAREER NOTES: Selected by Boston Red Sox in first round (32nd pick overall) of free-agent draft (June 2, 1987).
RECORDS/HONORS: Named outfielder on THE SPORTING NEWS college All-America team (1987).

Year	Team (League)	Pos.	G	AB	R	H	2B	3B	HR	RBI	Avg.	SB	PO	A	E	Avg.
1987—Elmira (New York-Penn)		OF	66	238	39	72	12	2	7	37	.303	5	131	1	4	.971
1988—Lynchburg (Carolina)		OF	135	482	69	143	33	5	13	97	.297	10	250	9	3	.989
1989—New Britain (Eastern)		OF	94	346	37	75	12	2	2	28	.217	15	186	12	6	.971
—Pawtucket (Int'l)		OF	27	94	8	24	7	1	1	11	.255	1	61	4	0	1.000
1990—New Britain (Eastern)		OF	132	461	45	98	26	1	2	41	.213	10	286	10	4	.987
1991—Pawtucket (Int'l)		OF	129	429	70	103	27	1	18	70	.240	11	255	13	2	.993
—Boston (A.L.)		OF	18	25	3	4	0	0	1	3	.160	0	14	0	2	.875
Major league totals (1 year)			18	25	3	4	0	0	1	3	.160	0	14	0	2	.875

ZUVELLA, PAUL
SS

PERSONAL: Born October 31, 1958, at San Mateo, Calif.... 6-0/178.... Throws right, bats right.... Full name: Paul Zuvella.... Name pronounced zoo-VELL-uh.
HIGH SCHOOL: Samuel Ayer (Milpitas, Calif.).
COLLEGE: Stanford (bachelor of arts degree in communications, 1980).
TRANSACTIONS/CAREER NOTES: Selected by Milwaukee Brewers organization in 11th round of free-agent draft (June 5, 1979). ... Selected by Atlanta Braves organization in 15th round of free-agent draft (June 3, 1980).... On Durham disabled list (August 27, 1980-remainder of season).... Traded by Braves organization with OF Claudell Washington to New York Yankees for OF Ken Griffey (June 30, 1986).... Granted free agency (October 15, 1987).... Signed by Colorado Springs, Cleveland Indians organization (January 8, 1988).... Released by Indians (April 2, 1990).... Signed by Omaha, Kansas City Royals organization (April 13, 1991).... Granted free agency (October 15, 1990).... Re-signed by Royals (January 21, 1991).... On Omaha disabled list (July 2-August 3, 1991).... Granted free agency (October 16, 1991).
STATISTICAL NOTES: Led Southern League shortstops with 661 total chances in 1981.... Led International League shortstops with 664 total chances and 85 double plays in 1984.... Led International League in being hit by pitch with eight in 1984.... Led American Association shortstops with 78 double plays in 1990.

Year	Team (League)	Pos.	G	AB	R	H	2B	3B	HR	RBI	Avg.	SB	PO	A	E	Avg.
1980—Bradenton Braves (GCL)		SS	2	8	0	1	0	0	0	1	.125	0	4	9	1	.929
—Durham (Carolina)		SS	48	149	21	47	7	0	2	19	.315	3	58	140	12	.943
1981—Savannah (Southern)		SS	138	485	61	145	17	2	11	68	.299	10	220	*406	35	.947
1982—Richmond (Int'l)		SS	133	455	63	128	15	2	9	54	.281	8	245	335	22	.963
—Atlanta (N.L.)		SS	2	1	0	0	0	0	00	0	.000	0	0	4	1	.800
1983—Richmond (Int'l)		SS	117	415	53	119	13	2	6	64	.287	4	169	324	18	*.965
—Atlanta (N.L.)		SS	3	5	0	0	0	0	0	0	.000	0	1	2	1	.750
1984—Richmond (Int'l)		SS	127	462	77	140	18	•6	6	55	.303	14	*219	*405	16	*.975
—Atlanta (N.L.)	2B-SS		11	25	2	5	1	0	0	1	.200	0	13	21	0	1.000
1985—Richmond (Int'l)		SS	8	32	3	7	0	0	1	3	.219	0	10	30	3	.930
—Atlanta (N.L.)	2B-SS-3B		81	190	16	48	8	1	0	4	.253	2	112	173	8	.973
1986—Rich.-Col. (Int'l)■	SS-2B		89	334	56	101	13	1	2	31	.302	11	149	231	10	.974
—New York (A.L.)		SS	21	48	2	4	1	0	0	2	.083	0	30	54	3	.966
1987—New York (A.L.)	2B-SS-3B		14	34	2	6	0	0	0	0	.176	0	20	25	0	1.000
—Columbus (Int'l)	SS-2B		69	269	47	81	15	4	2	25	.301	13	131	178	11	.966
1988—Colorado Springs (PCL)■	SS-2B		68	232	33	67	11	3	1	28	.289	6	105	190	16	.949
—Cleveland (A.L.)		SS	51	130	9	30	5	1	0	7	.231	0	77	112	8	.959
1989—Colorado Springs (PCL)		SS	96	387	61	128	23	3	10	66	.331	8	139	321	12	*.975
—Cleveland (A.L.)	SS-3B		24	58	10	16	2	0	2	6	.276	0	14	24	2	.950
1990—Omaha (Am. Assoc.)■		SS	111	407	47	115	16	1	5	41	.283	11	184	314	15	.971
1991—Omaha (Am. Assoc.)	SS-2B-3B		64	219	28	59	14	1	1	20	.269	3	99	173	10	.965
American League totals (4 years)			110	270	23	56	8	1	2	15	.207	0	141	215	13	.965
National League totals (4 years)			97	221	18	53	9	1	0	5	.240	2	126	200	10	.970
Major league totals (8 years)			207	491	41	109	17	2	2	20	.222	2	267	415	23	.967

MAJOR LEAGUE MANAGERS

ANDERSON, SPARKY
TIGERS

PERSONAL: Born February 22, 1934, at Bridgewater, S.D. . . . 5-9/168. . . . Threw and batted righthanded. . . . Full name: George Lee Anderson.
TRANSACTIONS/CAREER NOTES: Signed by Santa Barbara, Brooklyn Dodgers organization (January 30, 1953). . . . Dodgers franchise transferred to Los Angeles for 1958. . . . Recalled by Los Angeles Dodgers and traded to Philadelphia Phillies for P Jim Golden, P Gene Snyder and OF Eldon (Rip) Repulski (December 23, 1958). . . . On Toronto disabled list (August 13-September 13, 1961 and August 12-23, 1962).
STATISTICAL NOTES: Led California League shortstops with 83 double plays in 1953. . . . Led Western League with 20 sacrifice hits in 1954. . . . Tied for Texas League lead with 22 sacrifice hits in 1955. . . . Led Texas League second basemen with 117 double plays in 1955. . . . Led Pacific Coast League second basemen with .985 fielding percentage, 523 putouts, 486 assists and 135 double plays and tied for lead with 15 errors in 1957. . . . Led International League second basemen with 104 double plays in 1958 and 89 in 1960. . . . Led International League with 15 sacrifice hits in 1960.

							BATTING							FIELDING			
Year	Team (League)	Pos.	G	AB	R	H	2B	3B	HR	RBI	Avg.	SB	PO	A	E	Avg.
1953 — Santa Barbara (Calif.)		SS	•141	*598	98	157	21	4	5	55	.263	13	*277	395	32	.955
1954 — Pueblo (Western)		2B	147	497	72	147	13	5	0	62	.296	14	*397	432	20	•.976
1955 — Fort Worth (Texas)		2B	158	594	86	158	24	1	0	42	.266	6	*456	*469	18	*.981
1956 — Montreal (International)		2B	140	453	65	135	17	5	0	47	.298	4	372	391	15	.981
1957 — Los Angeles (PCL)		2B-SS	•168	619	74	161	15	0	2	35	.260	8	†524	†488	‡15	†.985
1958 — Montreal (International)		2B	•155	580	78	156	35	5	2	56	.269	21	*387	*464	10	*.988
1959 — Philadelphia (N.L.)■		2B	152	477	42	104	9	3	0	34	.218	6	343	403	12	.984
1960 — Toronto (International)■		2B	148	543	67	123	11	5	5	21	.227	12	319	*416	12	.984
1961 — Toronto (International)		2B	97	275	30	66	17	0	0	22	.240	5	189	203	6	.985
1962 — Toronto (International)		2B	124	432	56	111	18	2	2	38	.257	2	282	327	8	*.987
1963 — Toronto (International)		2B	116	358	56	89	12	5	3	25	.249	3	226	256	6	*.988
Major league totals (1 year)			152	477	42	104	9	3	0	34	.218	6	343	403	12	.984

RECORD AS MANAGER

BACKGROUND: Coach, San Diego Padres (1969).
HONORS: Coach, N.L. All-Star team (1974). . . . Coach, A.L. All-Star team (1982 and 1984). . . . Named A.L. Manager of the Year by THE SPORTING NEWS (1987).

		REGULAR SEASON				Playoff		Champ. Series		World Series		All-Star Game	
Year	Team (League)	W	L	Pct.	Pos.	W	L	W	L	W	L	W	L
1964 — Toronto (International)		80	72	.526	5th	—	—	—	—	—	—	—	—
1965 — Rock Hill (Western Carolinas)		24	40	.375	8th	—	—	—	—	—	—	—	—
— (Second half)		35	23	.603	1st	2	0	—	—	—	—	—	—
1966 — St. Petersburg (Florida State)		42	24	.636	2nd	—	—	—	—	—	—	—	—
— (Second half)		49	21	.700	1st	2	3	—	—	—	—	—	—
1967 — Modesto (California)		38	32	.543	T2nd	—	—	—	—	—	—	—	—
— (Second half)		41	29	.586	1st	0	2	—	—	—	—	—	—
1968 — Asheville (Southern)		86	54	.614	1st	—	—	—	—	—	—	—	—
1970 — Cincinnati (N.L.)		102	60	.630	1st (W)	—	—	3	0	1	4	—	—
1971 — Cincinnati (N.L.)		79	83	.488	T4th (W)	—	—	—	—	—	—	0	1
1972 — Cincinnati (N.L.)		95	59	.619	1st (W)	—	—	3	2	3	4	—	—
1973 — Cincinnati (N.L.)		99	63	.611	1st (W)	—	—	2	3	—	—	1	0
1974 — Cincinnati (N.L.)		98	64	.605	2nd (W)	—	—	—	—	—	—	—	—
1975 — Cincinnati (N.L.)		108	54	.667	1st (W)	—	—	3	0	4	3	—	—
1976 — Cincinnati (N.L.)		102	60	.630	1st (W)	—	—	3	0	4	0	1	0
1977 — Cincinnati (N.L.)		88	74	.543	2nd (W)	—	—	—	—	—	—	1	0
1978 — Cincinnati (N.L.)		92	69	.571	2nd (W)	—	—	—	—	—	—	—	—
1979 — Detroit (A.L.)		56	50	.528	5th (E)	—	—	—	—	—	—	—	—
1980 — Detroit (A.L.)		84	78	.519	5th (E)	—	—	—	—	—	—	—	—
1981 — Detroit (A.L.)		31	26	.544	4th (E)	—	—	—	—	—	—	—	—
— (Second half)		29	23	.558	3rd (E)	—	—	—	—	—	—	—	—
1982 — Detroit (A.L.)		83	79	.512	4th (E)	—	—	—	—	—	—	—	—
1983 — Detroit (A.L.)		92	70	.568	2nd (E)	—	—	—	—	—	—	—	—
1984 — Detroit (A.L.)		104	58	.642	1st (E)	—	—	3	0	4	1	—	—
1985 — Detroit (A.L.)		84	77	.522	3rd (E)	—	—	—	—	—	—	0	1
1986 — Detroit (A.L.)		87	75	.537	3rd (E)	—	—	—	—	—	—	—	—
1987 — Detroit (A.L.)		98	64	.605	1st (E)	—	—	1	4	—	—	—	—
1988 — Detroit (A.L.)		88	74	.543	2nd (E)	—	—	—	—	—	—	—	—
1989 — Detroit (A.L.)		59	103	.364	7th (E)	—	—	—	—	—	—	—	—
1990 — Detroit (A.L.)		79	83	.488	3rd (E)	—	—	—	—	—	—	—	—
1991 — Detroit (A.L.)		84	78	.519	T2nd (E)	—	—	—	—	—	—	—	—
American League totals (13 years)		1058	938	.530		—	—	4	4	4	1	0	1
National League totals (9 years)		863	586	.596		—	—	14	5	12	11	3	1
Major league totals (22 years)		1921	1524	.558		—	—	18	9	16	12	3	2

NOTES:
1965 — Won playoff against Salisbury (first-half winner).
1966 — Lost playoff against Leesburg (first-half winner).

1967— Lost playoff against San Jose (first-half winner).
1970— Defeated Pittsburgh in N.L. Championship Series; lost to Baltimore in World Series.
1972— Defeated Pittsburgh in N.L. Championship Series; lost to Oakland in World Series.
1973— Lost to New York Mets in N.L. Championship Series.
1975— Defeated Pittsburgh in N.L. Championship Series; defeated Boston in World Series.
1976— Defeated Philadelphia in N.L. Championship Series; defeated New York Yankees in World Series.
1979— Replaced Detroit manager Les Moss (and interim manager Dick Tracewski) with club in fifth place and record of 29-26 (June 14, 1979).
1984— Defeated Kansas City in A.L. Championship Series; defeated San Diego in World Series.
1987— Lost to Minnesota in A.L. Championship Series.
1989— Record includes period in which Anderson took time off and was replaced temporarily by Dick Tracewski (May 19-June 4); Tigers were 9-8 under Tracewski.

COX, BOBBY
BRAVES

PERSONAL: Born May 21, 1941, at Tulsa, Okla.... 6-0/185.... Threw and batted righthanded.... Full name: Robert Joe Cox.
HIGH SCHOOL: Selma (Calif.).
COLLEGE: Reedley Junior College (Calif.).

TRANSACTIONS/CAREER NOTES: Signed by Los Angeles Dodgers organization (1959).... Drafted by Chicago Cubs organization (November 30, 1964).... Acquired by Atlanta Braves organization (1966).... On Austin disabled list (May 8-18 and May 30-June 9, 1966).... On disabled list (May 1-June 12, 1967).... Traded by Braves to New York Yankees for C Bob Tillman and P Dale Roberts (December 7, 1967); Roberts later was transferred to Richmond.... On disabled list (May 28-June 18, 1970).
STATISTICAL NOTES: Led Alabama-Florida League shortstops with 71 double plays in 1961.... Led Pacific Coast League third basemen with .954 fielding percentage in 1965.

Year	Team (League)	Pos.	G	AB	R	H	2B	3B	HR	RBI	Avg.	SB	PO	A	E	Avg.
1960 —Reno (California)		2B	125	440	99	112	20	5	13	75	.255	28	282	*385	*39	.945
1961 —Salem (Northwest)		2B	14	44	3	9	2	0	0	2	.205	0	25	25	2	.962
—Panama City (Ala.-Fla.) ...		2B	92	335	66	102	27	4	17	73	.304	17	220	247	8	*.983
1962 —Salem (Northwest)		3B-2B	*141	514	83	143	26	7	16	82	.278	7	174	296	28	.944
1963 —Albuquerque (Texas)		3B	17	53	5	15	2	0	2	5	.283	1	8	27	1	.972
—Great Falls (Pioneer)		3B	109	407	103	137	*31	4	19	85	.337	7	82	211	21	*.933
1964 —Albuquerque (Texas)		2B	138	523	98	152	29	13	16	91	.291	8	*322	*415	*28	.963
1965 —Salt Lake City (PCL)■.		3B-2B	136	473	58	125	32	1	12	55	.264	1	133	337	22	+.955
1966 —Tacoma (Pacific Coast)		3B-2B	10	34	2	4	1	0	0	4	.118	0	23	15	0	1.000
—Austin (Texas)■.............		2B-3B	92	339	35	77	11	1	7	30	.227	7	140	216	12	.967
1967 —Richmond (Int'l)		3B-1B	99	350	52	104	17	4	14	51	.297	3	84	136	8	.965
1968 —New York (A.L.)■.............		3B	135	437	33	100	15	1	7	41	.229	3	98	279	17	.957
1969 —New York (A.L.)		3B-2B	85	191	17	41	7	1	2	17	.215	0	50	147	11	.947
1970 —Syracuse (International) ..	3B-SS-2B	90	251	34	55	15	0	9	30	.219	0	86	163	13	.950
1971 —Fort Lauderdale (FSL)		2B-P	4	9	1	1	0	0	0	0	.111	0	4	5	0	1.000
Major league totals (2 years)			220	628	50	141	22	2	9	58	.225	3	148	426	28	.953

RECORD AS PITCHER

Year	Team (League)	G	W	L	Pct.	ERA	Sv.	IP	H	R	ER	BB	SO
1971 —Fort Lauderdale (Florida St.)	3	1	0	1.000	5.40	0	10	15	9	6	5	4

RECORD AS MANAGER

BACKGROUND: Minor league instructor, New York Yankees (October 28, 1970-March 24, 1971).... Coach, New York Yankees (1977).
HONORS: Coach, A.L. All-Star team (1985).... Named Major League Manager of the Year by THE SPORTING NEWS (1985).... Named N.L. Manager of the Year by THE SPORTING NEWS (1991).

		REGULAR SEASON				POSTSEASON							
						Playoff		Champ. Series		World Series		All-Star Game	
Year	Team (League)	W	L	Pct.	Pos.	W	L	W	L	W	L	W	L
1971 —Fort Lauderdale (Florida State).............		71	70	.504	4th (E)	—	—	—	—	—	—	—	—
1972 —West Haven (Eastern)...........................		84	56	.600	1st (A)	3	0	—	—	—	—	—	—
1973 —Syracuse (International)		76	70	.521	3rd (A)	—	—	—	—	—	—	—	—
1974 —Syracuse (International)		74	70	.514	2nd (N)	—	—	—	—	—	—	—	—
1975 —Syracuse (International)		72	64	.529	3rd	—	—	—	—	—	—	—	—
1976 —Syracuse (International)		82	57	.590	2nd	6	1	—	—	—	—	—	—
1978 —Atlanta (N.L.)		69	93	.426	6th (W)	—	—	—	—	—	—	—	—
1979 —Atlanta (N.L.)		66	94	.413	6th (W)	—	—	—	—	—	—	—	—
1980 —Atlanta (N.L.)		81	80	.503	4th (W)	—	—	—	—	—	—	—	—
1981 —Atlanta (N.L.)		25	29	.463	4th (W)	—	—	—	—	—	—	—	—
—(Second half)		25	27	.481	5th (W)	—	—	—	—	—	—	—	—
1982 —Toronto (A.L.)		78	84	.481	T6th (E)	—	—	—	—	—	—	—	—
1983 —Toronto (A.L.)		89	73	.549	4th (E)	—	—	—	—	—	—	—	—
1984 —Toronto (A.L.)		89	73	.549	2nd (E)	—	—	—	—	—	—	—	—
1985 —Toronto (A.L.)		99	62	.615	1st (E)	—	—	3	4	—	—	—	—
1990 —Atlanta (N.L.)		40	57	.412	6th (W)	—	—	—	—	—	—	—	—
1991 —Atlanta (N.L.)		94	68	.580	1st (W)	—	—	4	3	3	4	—	—
American League totals (4 years)		355	292	.549		—	—	3	4	—	—	—	—
National League totals (6 years)		400	448	.472		—	—	4	3	3	4	—	—
Major league totals (10 years)		755	740	.505		—	—	7	7	3	4	—	—

NOTES:
1971— Served as player/manager.
1972— Defeated Three Rivers in playoff.
1976— Won playoffs by defeating Memphis three games to none and Richmond (finals) three games to one.
1985— Lost to Kansas City in A.L. Championship Series.
1990— Replaced Atlanta manager Russ Nixon with club in sixth place and record of 25-40 (June 22, 1990).
1991— Defeated Pittsburgh in N.L. Championship Series; lost to Minnesota in World Series.

CRAIG, ROGER
GIANTS

PERSONAL: Born February 17, 1931, at Durham, N.C. . . . 6-4/196. . . . Threw and batted right-handed. . . . Full name: Roger Lee Craig.
COLLEGE: North Carolina State.
TRANSACTIONS/CAREER NOTES: On disabled list (May 3-June 16, 1960). . . . Selected by New York Mets in N.L. expansion draft (October 10, 1961). . . . Traded by Mets to St. Louis Cardinals for P Bill Wakefield and OF George Altman (November 4, 1963). . . . Traded by Cardinals to Cincinnati Reds with OF Charlie James for P Bob Purkey and a player to be named later (December 14, 1964). . . . Released by Reds and signed by Philadelphia Phillies (April 11, 1966). . . . On Philadelphia disabled list (May 26-June 10, 1966).
RECORDS/HONORS: Shares major league single-season record for most 1-0 games lost—5 (1963). . . . Shares N.L. single-season record for most consecutive losses—18 (May 4-August 4, 1963).
STATISTICAL NOTES: Tied for N.L. lead with four shutouts in 1959.

Year Team (League)	G	W	L	Pct.	ERA	Sv.	IP	H	R	ER	BB	SO
1950 —Newport News (Piedmont)	6	0	1	.000	7.11	...	19	22	17	15	23	7
—Valdosta (Georgia-Florida)	23	14	7	.667	3.13	...	167	136	86	58	150	152
1951 —Newport News (Piedmont)	38	14	11	.560	3.67	...	221	175	109	90	*175	119
1952 —					In military service							
1953 —					In military service							
1954 —Elmira (New York-Penn)	3	0	0	...	9.00	...	2	4	6	2	2	1
—Pueblo (Western)	6	1	1	.500	9.64	...	14	14	17	15	19	8
—Newport News (Piedmont) ...	20	8	3	.727	2.52	...	125	107	44	35	56	108
1955 —Montreal (International)	22	10	2	.833	3.54	...	117	105	48	46	64	68
—Brooklyn (N.L.)	21	5	3	.625	2.77	...	91	81	37	28	43	48
1956 —Brooklyn (N.L.)	35	12	11	.522	3.71	...	199	169	90	82	87	109
1957 —Brooklyn (N.L.)	32	6	9	.400	4.62	...	111	102	58	57	47	69
1958 —Los Angeles (N.L.)	9	2	1	.667	4.50	...	32	30	20	16	12	16
—St. Paul (American Assoc.)	28	5	•17	.227	3.91	...	182	180	100	79	77	119
1959 —Spokane (Pacific Coast)	14	6	7	.462	3.19	...	96	86	39	34	26	46
—Los Angeles (N.L.)	29	11	5	.688	2.06	...	153	122	49	35	45	76
1960 —Los Angeles (N.L.)	21	8	3	.727	3.26	...	116	99	48	42	43	69
1961 —Los Angeles (N.L.)	40	5	6	.455	6.13	...	113	130	87	77	52	63
1962 —New York (N.L.)■	42	10	*24	.294	4.52	...	233	261	133	117	70	118
1963 —New York (N.L.)	46	5	*22	.185	3.78	...	236	249	117	99	58	108
1964 —St. Louis (N.L.)■	39	7	9	.438	3.25	...	166	180	76	60	35	84
1965 —Cincinnati (N.L.)■	40	1	4	.200	3.66	...	64	74	33	26	25	30
1966 —Philadelphia (N.L.)■	14	2	1	.667	5.48	...	23	31	15	14	5	13
—Seattle (Pacific Coast)	6	0	1	.000	2.45	...	22	15	11	6	9	11
1967 —					Did not play							
1968 —Albuquerque (Texas)	1	0	0	...	0.00	...	4	3	0	0	2	2
Major league totals (12 years)	368	74	98	.430	3.82	0	1537	1528	763	653	522	803

WORLD SERIES RECORD

Year Team (League)	G	W	L	Pct.	ERA	Sv.	IP	H	R	ER	BB	SO
1955 —Brooklyn (N.L.)	1	1	0	1.000	3.00	...	6	4	2	2	5	4
1956 —Brooklyn (N.L.)	2	0	1	.000	12.00	...	6	10	8	8	3	4
1959 —Los Angeles (N.L.)	2	0	1	.000	8.68	...	9 ⅓	15	9	9	5	8
1964 —St. Louis (N.L.)	2	1	0	1.000	0.00	...	5	2	0	0	3	9
World Series totals (4 years)	7	2	2	.500	6.49	0	26 ⅓	31	19	19	16	25

RECORD AS MANAGER

BACKGROUND: Scout, Los Angeles Dodgers (1967). . . . Coach, San Diego Padres (1969-72). . . . Minor league pitching instructor, Los Angeles Dodgers organization (1973). . . . Coach, Houston Astros (1974-75). . . . Coach, San Diego Padres (1976-77). . . . Named manager of Padres, replacing Alvin Dark (March 21, 1978). . . . Coach, Detroit Tigers (1980-84). . . . Scout, Detroit Tigers (March 2, 1985-September 18, 1985).
HONORS: Coach, N.L. All-Star team (1987-88).

					Playoff		Champ. Series		World Series		All-Star Game	
Year Team (League)	W	L	Pct.	Pos.	W	L	W	L	W	L	W	L
1968 —Albuquerque (Texas)	70	69	.504	2nd (W)	—	—	—	—	—	—	—	—
1978 —San Diego (N.L.)	84	78	.519	4th (W)	—	—	—	—	—	—	—	—
1979 —San Diego (N.L.)	68	93	.422	5th (W)	—	—	—	—	—	—	—	—
1985 —San Francisco (N.L.)	6	12	.333	6th (W)	—	—	—	—	—	—	—	—
1986 —San Francisco (N.L.)	83	79	.512	3rd (W)	—	—	—	—	—	—	—	—
1987 —San Francisco (N.L.)	90	72	.556	1st (W)	—	—	3	4	—	—	—	—
1988 —San Francisco (N.L.)	83	79	.512	4th (W)	—	—	—	—	—	—	—	—
1989 —San Francisco (N.L.)	92	70	.568	1st (W)	—	—	4	1	0	4	—	—

						REGULAR SEASON				POSTSEASON					
									Playoff		Champ. Series		World Series		All-Star Game
Year	Team (League)		W	L	Pct.	Pos.	W	L	W	L	W	L	W	L	
1990 —San Francisco (N.L.)			85	77	.525	3rd (W)	—	—	—	—	—	—	0	1	
1991 —San Francisco (N.L.)			75	87	.463	4th (W)	—	—	—	—	—	—	—	—	
Major league totals (9 years)			666	647	.507		—	—	7	5	0	4	0	1	

NOTES:
1985— Replaced San Francisco manager Jim Davenport with club in sixth place and record of 56-88 (September 18).
1987— Lost to St. Louis in N.L. Championship Series.
1989— Defeated Chicago Cubs in N.L. Championship Series; lost to Oakland in World Series.

FREGOSI, JIM
PHILLIES

PERSONAL: Born April 4, 1942, at San Francisco. . . . 6-2/197. . . . Threw and batted righthanded. . . . Full name: James Louis Fregosi. . . . Father of Jim Fregosi Jr., minor league shortstop (1985-87).
HIGH SCHOOL: Serra (San Mateo, Calif.).
COLLEGE: Menlo College (Calif.).
TRANSACTIONS/CAREER NOTES: Signed by Boston Red Sox organization (September 6, 1959). . . . Selected by Los Angeles Angels off Red Sox roster in A.L. expansion draft (December 14, 1960). . . . On disabled list (July 12-August 5, 1961). . . . Traded by Angels to New York Mets for P Nolan Ryan, P Don Rose, OF Leroy Stanton and C Francisco Estrada (December 10, 1971). . . . Traded by Mets to Texas Rangers for a player to be named later (July 11, 1973); deal settled with cash. . . . On disabled list (April 22-May 12, 1977). . . . Traded by Rangers to Pittsburgh Pirates for 1B-C Ed Kirkpatrick (June 15, 1977). . . . Released by Pirates in order to accept managerial position with California Angels (June 1, 1978).
RECORDS/HONORS: Shares major league single-game record for most double plays started by shortstop (nine-inning game)—5 (May 1, 1966, first game). . . . Named shortstop on THE SPORTING NEWS A.L. All-Star Team (1964 and 1967). . . . Won A.L. Gold Glove at shortstop (1967).
STATISTICAL NOTES: Tied for American Association lead in double plays by shortstops with 100 in 1961. . . . Led American League with 15 sacrifice hits in 1965. . . . Led American League shortstops with 125 double plays in 1966 and tied for lead with 92 in 1968. . . . Led American League shortstops with 531 assists and tied for lead in errors with 35 in 1966.

							BATTING							FIELDING			
Year	Team (League)	Pos.	G	AB	R	H	2B	3B	HR	RBI	Avg.	SB	PO	A	E	Avg.
1960 —Alpine (Sophomore)	IF-OF	112	404	96	108	17	7	6	58	.267	4	198	261	39	.922
1961 —Dallas/Fort Worth (A.A.)	SS	150	516	54	131	18	4	6	50	.254	6	247 *495	*53	.933
—Los Angeles (A.L.)	SS	11	27	7	6	0	0	0	3	.222	0	12	22	2	.944
1962 —Dallas/Fort Worth (A.A.)	SS-OF	64	219	25	62	9	3	1	14	.283	1	94	164	22	.921
—Los Angeles (A.L.)	SS	58	175	15	51	3	4	3	23	.291	2	96	150	15	.943
1963 —Los Angeles (A.L.)	SS	154	592	83	170	29	12	9	50	.287	2	271	446	27	.964
1964 —Los Angeles (A.L.)	SS	147	505	86	140	22	9	18	72	.277	8	225	421	23	.966
1965 —California (A.L.)	SS	161	602	66	167	19	7	15	64	.277	13	*312	481	26	.968
1966 —California (A.L.)	SS-1B	162	611	78	154	32	7	13	67	.252	17	299 †531	†35	.960
1967 —California (A.L.)	SS	151	590	75	171	23	6	9	56	.290	9	258	435	25	.965
1968 —California (A.L.)	SS	159	614	77	150	21	*13	9	49	.244	9	273	454	29	.962
1969 —California (A.L.)	SS	161	580	78	151	22	6	12	47	.260	9	255	465	21	.972
1970 —California (A.L.)	SS-1B	158	601	95	167	33	5	22	82	.278	9	313	475	20	.975
1971 —California (A.L.)	SS-1B-OF	107	347	31	81	15	1	5	33	.233	2	241	251	22	.957
1972 —New York (N.L.)■	3B-SS-1B	101	340	31	79	15	4	5	32	.232	0	91	162	15	.944
1973 —New York (N.L.)	S-3-1-0	45	124	7	29	4	1	0	11	.234	1	47	70	9	.929
—Texas (A.L.)■	3B-1B-SS	45	157	25	42	6	2	6	16	.268	0	98	53	5	.968
1974 —Texas (A.L.)	1B-3B	78	230	31	60	5	0	12	34	.261	0	331	73	5	.988
1975 —Texas (A.L.)	1B-3B	77	191	25	50	5	0	7	33	.262	0	356	35	6	.985
1976 —Texas (A.L.)	1B-2B	58	133	17	31	7	0	2	12	.233	2	183	18	2	.990
1977 —Texas (A.L.)	1B	13	28	4	7	1	0	1	5	.250	0	31	4	0	1.000
—Pittsburgh (N.L.)■	1B-3B	36	56	10	16	1	1	3	16	.286	2	99	5	2	.981
1978 —Pittsburgh (N.L.)	3B-1B-2B	20	20	3	4	1	0	0	1	.200	0	14	4	2	.900
American League totals (16 years)		1700	5983	793	1598	243	72	143	646	.267	73	3554	4314	263	.968
National League totals (4 years)		202	540	51	128	21	6	8	60	.237	3	251	241	28	.946
Major league totals (18 years)		1902	6523	844	1726	264	78	151	706	.265	76	3805	4555	291	.966

ALL-STAR GAME RECORD

					BATTING						FIELDING			
Year	League	Pos.	AB	R	H	2B	3B	HR	RBI	Avg.	SB	PO	A	E	Avg.
1964 —American	SS	4	1	1	0	0	0	1	.250	0	4	1	0	1.000
1966 —American	SS	2	0	0	0	0	0	0	.000	0	0	1	0	1.000
1967 —American	SS	4	0	1	0	0	0	0	.250	0	2	3	0	1.000
1968 —American	SS	3	0	1	1	0	0	0	.333	0	1	6	0	1.000
1969 —American	SS	1	0	0	0	0	0	0	.000	0	0	0	0	. . .
1970 —American	PH	1	0	0	0	0	0	0	.000	0	0	0	0	. . .
All-Star Game totals (6 years)		15	1	3	1	0	0	1	.200	0	7	11	0	1.000

RECORD AS MANAGER
BACKGROUND: Special assignment scout and coach, Philadelphia Phillies (1989-1990). . . . Minor league pitching instructor and special assignment scout, Phillies (beginning of 1991 season-April 23, 1991).
HONORS: Named American Association Manager of the Year (1983). . . . Named American Association Co-Manager of the Year (1985). . . . Named Minor League Manager of the Year by THE SPORTING NEWS (1985). . . . Coach, A.L. All-Star team (1987).

| | | | REGULAR SEASON | | | | POSTSEASON | | | | | |
Year	Team (League)		W	L	Pct.	Pos.	Playoff W	Playoff L	Champ. Series W	Champ. Series L	World Series W	World Series L	All-Star Game W	All-Star Game L
1978	California (A.L.)		62	54	.534	T2nd (W)	—	—	—	—	—	—	—	—
1979	California (A.L.)		88	74	.543	1st (W)	—	—	1	3	—	—	—	—
1980	California (A.L.)		65	95	.406	6th (W)	—	—	—	—	—	—	—	—
1981	California (A.L.)		22	25	.468	4th (W)	—	—	—	—	—	—	—	—
1983	Louisville (American Association)		78	57	.578	1st (E)	3	6	—	—	—	—	—	—
1984	Louisville (American Association)		79	76	.510	4th	8	3	—	—	—	—	—	—
1985	Louisville (American Association)		74	68	.521	1st (E)	4	1	—	—	—	—	—	—
1986	Louisville (American Association)		32	34	.485	3rd (E)	—	—	—	—	—	—	—	—
	Chicago (A.L.)		45	51	.469	5th (W)	—	—	—	—	—	—	—	—
1987	Chicago (A.L.)		77	85	.475	5th (W)	—	—	—	—	—	—	—	—
1988	Chicago (A.L.)		71	90	.441	5th (W)	—	—	—	—	—	—	—	—
1991	Philadelphia (N.L.)		74	75	.497	3rd (E)	—	—	—	—	—	—	—	—
	American League totals (7 years)		430	474	.476		—	—	1	3	—	—	—	—
	National League totals (1 year)		74	75	.497		—	—	—	—	—	—	—	—
	Major league totals (8 years)		504	549	.479		—	—	1	3	—	—	—	—

NOTES:
1978— Replaced California manager Dave Garcia with club in third place and record of 25-21 (June 1).
1979— Lost to Baltimore in A.L. Championship Series.
1981— Replaced as California manager by Gene Mauch (May 28).
1983— Won playoff against Oklahoma City three games to two; lost championship playoff to Denver four games to none.
1984— Won playoff against Indianapolis four games to two; won championship playoff against Denver four games to one.
1985— Won championship playoff against Oklahoma City four games to one.
1986— Replaced Chicago manager Tony La Russa (record of 26-38) and interim manager Doug Rader (record of 1-1) with club in fifth place and record of 27-39 (June 22).
1991— Replaced Philadelphia manager Nick Leyva with club in sixth place and record of 4-9 (April 23).

GARNER, PHIL

BREWERS

PERSONAL: Born April 30, 1949, at Jefferson City, Tenn.... 5-10/177.... Threw and batted righthanded.... Full name: Philip Mason Garner.
HIGH SCHOOL: Beardon (Knoxville, Tenn.).
COLLEGE: Tennessee (received bachelor of science degree in general business, 1973).
TRANSACTIONS/CAREER NOTES: Selected by Montreal Expos organization in eighth round of free-agent draft (June 4, 1970)....
Selected by Oakland Athletics organization in secondary phase of free-agent draft (January 13, 1971).... Traded by A's with IF Tommy Helms and P Chris Batton to Pittsburgh Pirates for P Doc Medich, P Dave Guisti, P Rick Langford, P Doug Bair, OF Mitchell Page and OF Tony Armas (March 15, 1977).... On Pittsburgh disabled list (April 2-23, 1981).... Traded by Pirates to Houston Astros for 2B Johnny Ray and two players to be named later (August 31, 1981); Pirates organization acquired OF Kevin Houston and P Randy Niemann to complete deal (September 9, 1981).... Granted free agency (November 12, 1986).... Re-signed by Astros (January 6, 1987).... Traded by Astros to Los Angeles Dodgers for a player to be named later (June 19, 1987); Astros organization acquired P Jeff Edwards to complete deal (June 26, 1987).... Granted free agency (November 9, 1987).... Signed by San Francisco Giants (January 28, 1988).... On San Francisco disabled list (April 13-September 2, 1988); included rehabilitation disability assignment to Phoenix (August 5-24, 1988).... Granted free agency (November 3, 1988).
RECORDS/HONORS: Shares major league record for most grand slams in two consecutive games—2 (September 14 and 15, 1978).... Shares N.L. single-month record for most grand slams—2 (September, 1978).
STATISTICAL NOTES: Led Pacific Coast League third basemen with 104 putouts, 261 assists, 35 errors, 400 total chances and 23 double plays in 1973.... Led A.L. second basemen with 26 errors in 1975.... Led A.L. second basemen with 865 total chances in 1976.... Led N.L. second basemen with 499 assists, 21 errors, 869 total chances and 116 double plays in 1980.

| | | | | | | | BATTING | | | | | | FIELDING | | | |
Year	Team (League)	Pos.	G	AB	R	H	2B	3B	HR	RBI	Avg.	SB	PO	A	E	Avg.
1971	Burlington (Midwest)	3B	116	439	73	122	22	4	11	70	.278	8	*122	203	29	.918
1972	Birmingham (Southern)	3B	71	264	45	74	10	6	12	40	.280	3	74	116	13	.936
	Iowa (American Assoc.)	3B	70	247	33	60	18	4	9	22	.243	7	50	140	10	.950
1973	Tucson (Pacific Coast)	3B-2B	138	516	87	149	23	12	14	73	.289	3	+107	+270	+35	.915
	Oakland (A.L.)	3B	9	5	0	0	0	0	0	0	.000	0	2	3	0	1.000
1974	Tucson (Pacific Coast)	3B-SS	96	388	78	128	29	10	11	51	.330	3	92	182	15	.948
	Oakland (A.L.)	3B-SS-2B	30	28	4	5	1	0	0	1	.179	1	11	24	1	.972
1975	Oakland (A.L.)	2B-SS	•160	488	46	120	21	5	6	54	.246	4	355	427	+26	.968
1976	Oakland (A.L.)	2B	159	555	54	145	29	12	8	74	.261	35	378	*465	22	.975
1977	Pittsburgh (N.L.)■	3B-2B-SS	153	585	99	152	35	10	17	77	.260	32	223	351	17	.971
1978	Pittsburgh (N.L.)	3B-2B-SS	154	528	66	138	25	9	10	66	.261	27	258	389	28	.959
1979	Pittsburgh (N.L.)	3B-2B-SS	150	549	76	161	32	8	11	59	.293	17	234	396	22	.966
1980	Pittsburgh (N.L.)	2B-SS	151	548	62	142	27	6	5	58	.259	32	349	+500	+21	.976
1981	Pitts.-Houston (N.L.)■	2B	87	294	35	73	9	3	1	26	.248	10	183	250	12	.973
1982	Houston (N.L.)	2B-3B	155	588	65	161	33	8	13	83	.274	24	285	464	17	.978
1983	Houston (N.L.)	3B	154	567	76	135	24	2	14	79	.238	18	100	311	24	.945
1984	Houston (N.L.)	3B-2B	128	374	60	104	17	6	4	45	.278	3	136	251	12	.970
1985	Houston (N.L.)	3B-2B	135	463	65	124	23	10	6	51	.268	4	101	229	21	.940
1986	Houston (N.L.)	3B-2B	107	313	43	83	14	3	9	41	.265	12	66	152	23	.905

Year	Team (League)	Pos.	G	AB	R	H	2B	3B	HR	RBI	Avg.	SB	PO	A	E	Avg.
							BATTING							FIELDING		
1987—Houston-L.A. (N.L.)■		3B-2B-SS	113	238	29	49	9	0	5	23	.206	6	65	144	13	.941
1988—San Francisco (N.L.)■		3B	15	13	0	2	0	0	0	1	.154	0	0	0	0	...
—Phoenix (Pacific Coast)		2B-3B	17	45	5	12	2	1	1	5	.267	0	12	22	0	1.000
American League totals (4 years)			358	1076	104	270	51	17	14	129	.251	40	746	919	49	.971
National League totals (12 years)			1502	5060	676	1324	248	65	95	609	.262	185	2000	3437	210	.963
Major league totals (16 years)			1860	6136	780	1594	299	82	109	738	.260	225	2746	4356	259	.965

DIVISION SERIES RECORD

Year	Team (League)	Pos.	G	AB	R	H	2B	3B	HR	RBI	Avg.	SB	PO	A	E	Avg.
							BATTING							FIELDING		
1981—Houston (N.L.)		2B	5	18	1	2	0	0	0	0	.111	0	6	8	1	.933

CHAMPIONSHIP SERIES RECORD

Year	Team (League)	Pos.	G	AB	R	H	2B	3B	HR	RBI	Avg.	SB	PO	A	E	Avg.
							BATTING							FIELDING		
1975—Oakland (A.L.)		2B	3	5	0	0	0	0	0	0	.000	0	7	4	1	.917
1979—Pittsburgh (N.L.)		2B-SS	3	12	4	5	0	1	1	1	.417	0	8	9	0	1.000
1986—Houston (N.L.)		3B	3	9	1	2	1	0	0	2	.222	0	1	9	0	1.000
Championship Series totals (3 years)			9	26	5	7	1	1	1	3	.269	0	16	22	1	.974

WORLD SERIES RECORD

WORLD SERIES NOTES: Holds single-series record (seven games) for most double plays by second basemen—9 (1979).... Shares single-series records for highest batting average (seven games)—.500 (1979); one or more hits in each game, seven-game series (1979).... Shares record for most assists by second baseman in one inning—3 (October 13, 1979, ninth inning).

Year	Team (League)	Pos.	G	AB	R	H	2B	3B	HR	RBI	Avg.	SB	PO	A	E	Avg.
							BATTING							FIELDING		
1979—Pittsburgh (N.L.)		2B	7	24	4	12	4	0	0	5	.500	0	21	23	2	.957

ALL-STAR GAME RECORD

Year	League	Pos.	AB	R	H	2B	3B	HR	RBI	Avg.	SB	PO	A	E	Avg.
						BATTING							FIELDING		
1976—American		2B	1	0	0	0	0	0	0	.000	0	1	1	0	1.000
1980—National		2B	2	1	1	0	0	0	0	.500	1	1	3	0	1.000
1981—National		2B	0	0	0	0	0	0	0	...	0	0	0	0	...
All-Star Game totals (3 years)			3	1	1	0	0	0	0	.333	1	2	4	0	1.000

RECORD AS MANAGER

BACKGROUND: Coach, Houston Astros (1989-91).

GASTON, CITO
BLUE JAYS

PERSONAL: Born March 17, 1944, at San Antonio.... 6-4/210.... Threw and batted right-handed.... Full name: Clarence Edwin Gaston.

HIGH SCHOOL: Holy Cross (Corpus Christi, Tex.).

TRANSACTIONS/CAREER NOTES: Signed by Milwaukee Braves organization (March 22, 1964).... On Binghamton disabled list (May 26-July 6, 1964).... On disabled list (August 2-29, 1965).... Selected by San Diego Padres from Atlanta in expansion draft (October 14, 1968).... On disabled list (May 17-June 2, 1972).... Traded by Padres to Atlanta Braves for P Danny Frisella (November 7, 1974).... Sold by Braves to Pittsburgh Pirates (September 22, 1978).... Granted free agency (November 2, 1978).... Signed by Santo Domingo of Inter-American League (April 10, 1979).... On suspended list (June 21-30, 1979).... Granted free agency when Inter-American League folded (June 30, 1979).... Signed by Leon of Mexican League (July 22, 1979).

STATISTICAL NOTES: Led New York-Pennsylvania League with 255 total bases in 1966.

Year	Team (League)	Pos.	G	AB	R	H	2B	3B	HR	RBI	Avg.	SB	PO	A	E	Avg.
							BATTING							FIELDING		
1964—Binghamton (N.Y.-Penn)		OF	11	21	1	5	2	0	1	4	.238	0	8	0	1	.889
—Greenville (W. Carolinas)		OF	49	165	15	38	6	3	0	16	.230	1	62	5	5	.931
1965—West Palm Beach (FSL)		OF	70	202	14	38	5	3	0	9	.188	0	111	4	5	.958
1966—Batavia (N.Y.-Penn)		OF	114	433	84	143	18	5	*28	*104	.330	8	214	12	13	.946
—Austin (Texas)		OF	4	10	2	3	1	1	0	4	.300	0	10	0	0	1.000
1967—Austin (Texas)		OF	136	505	72	154	24	6	10	70	.305	6	274	8	12	.959
—Atlanta (N.L.)		OF	9	25	1	3	0	1	0	1	.120	1	7	1	2	.800
1968—Richmond (Int'l)		OF	21	71	9	17	4	0	2	8	.239	0	43	0	0	1.000
—Shreveport (Texas)		OF	96	340	49	95	15	4	6	57	.279	12	203	3	9	.958
1969—San Diego (N.L.)■		OF	129	391	20	90	11	7	2	28	.230	4	243	12	11	.959
1970—San Diego (N.L.)		OF	146	584	92	186	26	9	29	93	.318	4	310	7	8	.975
1971—San Diego (N.L.)		OF	141	518	57	118	13	9	17	61	.228	1	271	8	5	.982
1972—San Diego (N.L.)		OF	111	379	30	102	14	0	7	44	.269	2	158	10	4	.977
1973—San Diego (N.L.)		OF	133	476	51	119	18	4	16	57	.250	0	198	16	*12	.947
1974—San Diego (N.L.)		OF	106	267	19	57	11	0	6	33	.213	0	119	7	1	.992
1975—Atlanta (N.L.)■		OF-1B	64	141	17	34	4	0	6	15	.241	1	80	2	3	.965
1976—Atlanta (N.L.)		OF-1B	69	134	15	39	4	0	4	25	.291	1	58	2	1	.984
1977—Atlanta (N.L.)		OF-1B	56	85	6	23	4	0	3	21	.271	1	44	4	1	.980
1978—Atlanta-Pitts. (N.L.)■		OF-1B	62	120	6	28	1	0	1	9	.233	0	66	2	3	.958

			BATTING										FIELDING			
Year Team (League)	Pos.	G	AB	R	H	2B	3B	HR	RBI	Avg.	SB	PO	A	E	Avg.
1979—Santo Domingo (I-A)■......		40	148	22	48	5	0	1	14	.324	1	...	...	...	...
—Leon (Mexican)■.............	OF	24	83	5	28	2	0	1	8	.337	0	24	0	0	1.000
1980—Leon (Mexican)...............	1B	48	185	16	44	5	0	4	27	.238	0	126	3	3	.977
Major league totals (11 years)......		1026	3120	314	799	106	30	91	387	.256	13	1554	71	51	.970

ALL-STAR GAME RECORD

		BATTING									FIELDING			
Year League	Pos.	AB	R	H	2B	3B	HR	RBI	Avg.	SB	PO	A	E	Avg.
1970—National................	OF	2	0	0	0	0	0	0	.000	0	2	0	0	1.000

BACKGROUND: Minor league instructor, Atlanta Braves organization (1981).... Coach, Toronto Blue Jays (1982-May 15, 1989).
HONORS: Coach, A.L. All-Star team (1991).

		REGULAR SEASON				POSTSEASON					
						Playoff		Champ. Series		World Series		All-Star Game
Year Team (League)	W	L	Pct.	Pos.	W	L	W	L	W	L	W	L
1989—Toronto (A.L.).................	77	49	.611	1st (E)	—	—	1	4	—	—	—	—
1990—Toronto (A.L.).................	86	76	.531	2nd (E)	—	—	—	—	—	—	—	—
1991—Toronto (A.L.).................	91	71	.562	1st (E)	—	—	1	4	—	—	—	—
Major league totals (3 years).........	254	196	.564		—	—	2	8	—	—	—	—

NOTES:
1989— Replaced Toronto manager Jimy Williams with club in seventh place and record of 12-24 (May 15); lost to Oakland in A.L. Championship Series.
1991— Record includes time taken off because of back injury (August 21-September 27); Blue Jays were 19-14 under temporary manager Gene Tenace during that time. Lost to Minnesota in A.L. Championship Series.

HARGROVE, MIKE
INDIANS

PERSONAL: Born October 26, 1949, at Perryton, Tex.... 6-0/195.... Throws left, bats left.... Full name: Dudley Michael Hargrove.
HIGH SCHOOL: Perryton (Tex.).
COLLEGE: Northwestern State, Okla. (received bachelor of science degree in physical education and social sciences).
TRANSACTIONS/CAREER NOTES: Selected by Texas Rangers organization in 25th round of free-agent draft (June 6, 1972).... Traded by Rangers with 3B Kurt Bevacqua and C Bill Fahey to San Diego Padres for OF Oscar Gamble, C Dave Roberts and cash (October 25, 1978).... Traded by Padres to Cleveland Indians for OF Paul Dade (June 14, 1979).... Granted free agency (November 12, 1985).
RECORDS/HONORS: Named Western Carolinas League Player of the Year (1973).... Named A.L. Rookie Player of the Year by THE SPORTING NEWS (1974).... Named A.L. Rookie of the Year by the Baseball Writers' Association of America (1974).
STATISTICAL NOTES: Led New York-Pennsylvania League first basemen with 58 double plays in 1972.... Led Western Carolinas League with 247 total bases in 1973.... Led Western Carolinas League first basemen with 118 double plays in 1973.... Led A.L. with 97 bases on balls received in 1976 and 107 in 1978.... Led A.L. first basemen with 1,489 total chances in 1980.... Led A.L. with .432 on base percentage in 1981.

			BATTING									FIELDING			
Year Team (League)	Pos.	G	AB	R	H	2B	3B	HR	RBI	Avg.	SB	PO	A	E	Avg.
1972—Geneva (N.Y.-Penn)..........	1B	•70	243	38	65	8	0	4	37	.267	3	★537	▪40	10	★.983
1973—Gastonia (W. Carolinas) ...	1B	•130	456	88	★160	★35	8	12	82★	.351	10	★1121	•77	14	★.988
1974—Texas (A.L.).....................	1B-OF	131	415	57	134	18	6	4	66	.323	0	638	72	9	.987
1975—Texas (A.L.).....................	OF-1B	145	519	82	157	22	2	11	62	.303	4	513	45	13	.977
1976—Texas (A.L.).....................	1B	151	541	80	155	30	1	7	58	.287	2	1222	110	★21	.984
1977—Texas (A.L.).....................	1B	153	525	98	160	28	4	18	69	.305	2	1393	100	11	.993
1978—Texas (A.L.).....................	1B	146	494	63	124	24	1	7	40	.251	2	1221	★116	▪17	.987
1979—San Diego (N.L.)■.............	1B	52	125	15	24	5	0	0	8	.192	0	323	17	5	.986
—Cleveland (A.L.)■	OF-1B	100	338	60	110	21	4	10	56	.325	2	356	16	2	.995
1980—Cleveland (A.L.).............	1B	160	589	86	179	22	2	11	85	.304	4	★1391	88	10	.993
1981—Cleveland (A.L.).............	1B	94	322	43	102	21	0	2	49	.317	5	766	76	▪9	.989
1982—Cleveland (A.L.).............	1B	160	591	67	160	26	1	4	65	.271	2	1293	★123	5	.996
1983—Cleveland (A.L.).............	1B	134	469	57	134	21	4	3	57	.286	0	1098	115	7	.994
1984—Cleveland (A.L.).............	1B	133	352	44	94	14	2	2	44	.267	0	790	83	8	.991
1985—Cleveland (A.L.).............	1B-OF	107	284	31	81	14	1	1	27	.285	1	599	66	6	.991
American League totals (12 years).................	1614	5439	768	1590	261	28	80	678	.292	24	11280	1010	118	.990
National League totals (1 year)......................	52	125	15	24	5	0	0	8	.192	0	323	17	5	.986
Major league totals (12 years).........................	1666	5564	783	1614	266	28	80	686	.290	24	11603	1027	123	.990

ALL-STAR GAME RECORD

		BATTING									FIELDING			
Year League	Pos.	AB	R	H	2B	3B	HR	RBI	Avg.	SB	PO	A	E	Avg.
1975—American...............	PH	1	0	0	0	0	0	0	.000	0	0	0	0	...

BACKGROUND: Minor league coach, Cleveland Indians organization (1986).... Coach, Cleveland Indians (1990-July 6, 1991).
HONORS: Named Carolina League Manager of the Year (1987).... Named Pacific Coast League Manager of the Year (1989).

		REGULAR SEASON				POSTSEASON							
						Playoff		Champ. Series		World Series		All-Star Game	
Year Team (League)	W	L	Pct.	Pos.	W	L	W	L	W	L	W	L	
1987 —Kinston (Carolina)	33	37	.471	T3rd (S)	—	—	—	—	—	—	—	—	
—(Second half)	42	28	.600	1st (S)	3	3	—	—	—	—	—	—	
1988 —Williamsport (Eastern)	66	73	.475	6th	—	—	—	—	—	—	—	—	
1989 —Colorado Springs (Pacific Coast)	44	26	.629	1st (S)	—	—	—	—	—	—	—	—	
—(Second half)	34	38	.472	3rd (S)	2	3	—	—	—	—	—	—	
1991 —Cleveland (A.L.)	32	53	.376	7th (E)	—	—	—	—	—	—	—	—	
Major league totals (1 year)	32	53	.376		—	—	—	—	—	—	—	—	

NOTES:
1987— Defeated Winston-Salem two games to none in playoffs; lost to Salem three games to one for league championship.
1989— Lost to Albuquerque in playoffs.
1991— Replaced Cleveland manager John McNamara with club in seventh place and record of 25-52 (July 6).

HOBSON, BUTCH
RED SOX

PERSONAL: Born August 17, 1951, at Tuscaloosa, Ala. . . . 6-1/190. . . . Threw and batted righthanded. . . . Full name: Clell Lavern Hobson Jr. . . . Son of Clell Hobson, minor league infielder (1953-57).
HIGH SCHOOL: Bessemer (Ala.).
COLLEGE: Alabama.
TRANSACTIONS/CAREER NOTES: Selected by Boston Red Sox organization in eighth round of free-agent draft (June 5, 1973). . . . On disabled list (July 27-August 11 and August 23-September 7, 1980). . . . Traded by Red Sox with SS Rick Burleson to California Angels for 3B Carney Lansford, P Mark Clear and OF Rick Miller (December 10, 1980). . . . Traded by Angels to New York Yankees for P Bill Castro (March 24, 1982). . . . On disabled list (April 1-24, 1982 and August 1-14, 1985). . . . Released by Yankees organization (September 17, 1985).
STATISTICAL NOTES: Led Eastern League with 201 total bases in 1975. . . . Led International League third basemen with 89 putouts and 204 assists in 1976. . . . Led A.L. batters with 162 strikeouts in 1977.

					BATTING								FIELDING			
Year Team (League)	Pos.	G	AB	R	H	2B	3B	HR	RBI	Avg.	SB	PO	A	E	Avg.
1973 —Winston-Salem (Caro.)	3B-OF	17	39	8	7	2	1	0	5	.179	0	10	10	1	.952
1974 —Winston-Salem (Caro.)	OF-3B-1B	119	423	66	120	18	8	14	74	.284	2	211	79	12	.960
1975 —Bristol (Eastern)	3B	•138	471	68	125	25	3	15	73	.265	6	102	309	28	.936
—Boston (A.L.)	3B	2	4	0	1	0	0	0	0	.250	0	1	3	0	1.000
1976 —Rhode Island (Int'l)	3B-SS	90	360	56	103	21	1	25	72	.286	1	†91	•204	15	.952
—Boston (A.L.)	3B	76	269	34	63	7	5	8	34	.234	0	60	146	14	.936
1977 —Boston (A.L.)	3B	159	593	77	157	33	5	30	112	.265	5	128	272	23	.946
1978 —Boston (A.L.)	3B	147	512	65	128	26	2	17	80	.250	1	122	261	*43	.899
1979 —Boston (A.L.)	3B-2B	146	528	74	138	26	7	28	93	.261	3	110	251	25	.935
1980 —Boston (A.L.)	3B	93	324	35	74	6	0	11	39	.228	1	52	109	16	.910
1981 —California (A.L.)■	3B	85	268	27	63	7	4	4	36	.235	1	85	139	•17	.929
1982 —New York (A.L.)■	1B	30	58	2	10	2	0	0	3	.172	0	37	2	2	.951
—Columbus (Int'l)	1B-3B	27	83	17	27	5	1	4	20	.325	0	44	14	4	.935
1983 —Columbus (Int'l)	3B-1B	112	379	68	93	17	4	19	63	.245	2	91	149	11	.956
1984 —Columbus (Int'l)	3B-1B	116	382	49	96	18	1	13	56	.251	0	207	121	12	.965
1985 —Columbus (Int'l)	3B-1B	107	347	44	82	9	1	12	56	.236	0	123	138	16	.942
Major league totals (8 years)		738	2556	314	634	107	23	98	397	.248	11	595	1183	140	.927

RECORD AS MANAGER
HONORS: Named International League Manager of the Year (1991).

		REGULAR SEASON				POSTSEASON							
						Playoff		Champ. Series		World Series		All-Star Game	
Year Team (League)	W	L	Pct.	Pos.	W	L	W	L	W	L	W	L	
1987 —Columbia (South Atlantic)	35	35	.500	5th (S)	—	—	—	—	—	—	—	—	
—(Second half)	29	40	.420	6th (S)	—	—	—	—	—	—	—	—	
1988 —Columbia (South Atlantic)	38	32	.543	4th (S)	—	—	—	—	—	—	—	—	
—(Second half)	36	31	.537	2nd (S)	—	—	—	—	—	—	—	—	
1989 —New Britain (Eastern)	60	76	.441	8th	—	—	—	—	—	—	—	—	
1990 —New Britain (Eastern)	72	67	.518	4th	3	5	—	—	—	—	—	—	
1991 —Pawtucket (International)	79	64	.552	1st (E)	0	3	—	—	—	—	—	—	

NOTES:
1990— Defeated Albany three games to two in playoffs; lost to London three games to none in league championship.
1991— Lost to Columbus in playoffs.

HOWE, ART
ASTROS

PERSONAL: Born December 15, 1946, at Pittsburgh. . . . 6-1/185. . . . Threw and batted righthanded. . . . Full name: Arthur Henry Howe Jr.
HIGH SCHOOL: Shaler (Glenshaw, Pa.).
COLLEGE: Wyoming (bachelor of science degree in business administration, 1969).
TRANSACTIONS/CAREER NOTES: Signed as free agent by Pittsburgh Pirates organization (June, 1971). . . . On disabled list (August 17-September 2, 1972 and April 13-May 6, 1973). . . . Traded by Pirates to Houston Astros (January 6, 1976), completing deal in which Astros traded 2B Tommy Helms to Pirates for a player to be named later (December 12, 1975). . . . On disabled list (May 12-June 19, 1982 and March 27, 1983-entire season). . . . Granted free agency (November 7, 1983). . . . Signed by St. Louis Cardinals (March 21, 1984). . . . Released by Cardinals (April 22, 1985).
STATISTICAL NOTES: Tied for Carolina League lead in putouts by third basemen with 95 in 1971. . . . Led International League third basemen with 22 errors and 24 double plays in 1972.

Year	Team (League)	Pos.	G	AB	R	H	2B	3B	HR	RBI	Avg.	SB	PO	A	E	Avg.
1971 —Salem (Carolina)	3B-SS	114	382	77	133	27	7	12	79	★.348	11	‡110	221	21	.940
1972 —Charleston, W.Va. (Int'l) ...	3B-2B-SS	109	365	68	99	21	3	14	53	.271	8	105	248	†24	.936
1973 —Charleston, W.Va. (Int'l) ...	3B-2B-SS	119	372	50	85	20	1	8	44	.228	6	141	229	21	.946
1974 —Charleston, W.Va. (Int'l) ...	3B	60	207	26	70	17	4	8	36	.338	4	35	90	9	.933
—Pittsburgh (N.L.)	3B-SS	29	74	10	18	4	1	1	5	.243	0	11	49	4	.938
1975 —Charleston, W.Va. (Int'l) ...	3B-2B	11	42	4	15	1	3	0	3	.357	0	15	23	1	.974
—Pittsburgh (N.L.)	3B	63	146	13	25	9	0	1	10	.171	1	19	89	7	.939
1976 —Memphis (International)■.	3B-1B	74	259	50	92	21	3	12	59	.355	1	93	120	14	.938
—Houston (N.L.)	3B-2B	21	29	0	4	1	0	0	0	.138	0	17	16	1	.971
1977 —Houston (N.L.)	2B-3B-SS	125	413	44	109	23	7	8	58	.264	0	213	333	8	.986
1978 —Houston (N.L.)	2B-3B-1B	119	420	46	123	33	3	7	55	.293	2	240	302	13	.977
1979 —Houston (N.L.)	2B-3B-1B	118	355	32	88	15	2	6	33	.248	3	188	261	7	.985
1980 —Houston (N.L.)	1-3-2-S	110	321	34	91	12	5	10	46	.283	1	598	86	10	.986
1981 —Houston (N.L.)	3B-1B	103	361	43	107	22	4	3	36	.296	1	67	206	9	.968
1982 —Houston (N.L.)	3B-1B	110	365	29	87	15	1	5	38	.238	2	344	174	7	.987
1983 —						Did not play									
1984 —St. Louis (N.L.)■	3-1-2-S	89	139	17	30	5	0	2	12	.216	0	71	80	3	.981
1985 —St. Louis (N.L.)	1B-3B	4	3	0	0	0	0	0	0	.000	0	5	1	0	1.000
Major league totals (11 years)		891	2626	268	682	139	23	43	293	.260	10	1773	1597	69	.980

DIVISION SERIES RECORD

Year	Team (League)	Pos.	G	AB	R	H	2B	3B	HR	RBI	Avg.	SB	PO	A	E	Avg.
1981 —Houston (N.L.)	3B	5	17	1	4	0	0	1	1	.235	0	6	9	0	1.000

CHAMPIONSHIP SERIES RECORD

Year	Team (League)	Pos.	G	AB	R	H	2B	3B	HR	RBI	Avg.	SB	PO	A	E	Avg.
1974 —Pittsburgh (N.L.)	PH	1	1	0	0	0	0	0	0	.000	0	0	0	0	...
1980 —Houston (N.L.)	1B-PH	5	15	0	3	1	1	0	2	.200	0	29	3	0	1.000
Championship Series totals (2 years)		6	16	0	3	1	1	0	2	.188	0	29	3	0	1.000

RECORD AS MANAGER

BACKGROUND: Coach, Texas Rangers (May 21, 1985-1988).
HONORS: Coach, N.L. All-Star team (1991).

	REGULAR SEASON				POSTSEASON							
						Playoff		Champ. Series		World Series		All-Star Game
Year	Team (League)	W	L	Pct.	Pos.	W	L	W	L	W	L	W	L
1989 —Houston (N.L.)		86	76	.531	3rd (W)	—	—	—	—	—	—	—	—
1990 —Houston (N.L.)		75	87	.463	T4th (W)	—	—	—	—	—	—	—	—
1991 —Houston (N.L.)		65	97	.401	6th (W)	—	—	—	—	—	—	—	—
Major league totals (3 years)		226	260	.465		—	—	—	—	—	—	—	—

KELLY, TOM
TWINS

PERSONAL: Born August 15, 1950, at Graceville, Minn.... 5-11/185.... Threw and batted lefthanded.... Full name: Jay Thomas Kelly.
HIGH SCHOOL: St. Mary's (South Amboy, N.J.).
COLLEGE: Mesa (Ariz.) Community College and Monmouth College (N.J.).
TRANSACTIONS/CAREER NOTES: Selected by Seattle Pilots organization in eighth round of free-agent draft (June 7, 1968).... Seattle franchise transferred to Milwaukee for 1970.... On temporary inactive list (April 16-20, April 25-30 and August 21, 1970-remainder of season).... On military list (August 27, 1970-February 3, 1971).... Released by Jacksonville (April 6, 1971).... Signed by Charlotte, Minnesota Twins organization (April 28, 1971).... Loaned by Twins organization to Rochester, Baltimore Orioles organization (April 5, 1976); returned (September 22, 1976).... On temporary inactive list (April 15-19, 1977).... On disabled list (July 25-August 4, 1977).... Released by Toledo (December 18, 1978).... Signed by Visalia, Twins organization (January 2, 1979).... Released by Visalia (December 2, 1980).
STATISTICAL NOTES: Led Pacific Coast League outfielders with six double plays in 1972.... Led International League with 91 bases on balls received in 1978.

Year	Team (League)	Pos.	G	AB	R	H	2B	3B	HR	RBI	Avg.	SB	PO	A	E	Avg.
1968 —Newark (N.Y.-Penn)	OF	65	218	50	69	11	4	2	10	.317	16	★144	★9	3	.981
1969 —Clinton (Midwest)	OF	100	269	47	60	10	2	6	35	.223	10	158	15	4	.977
1970 —Jacksonville (Southern) ...	OF-1B	93	266	33	64	10	1	8	38	.241	2	204	19	4	.982
1971 —Charlotte (Florida State)■.	1B-OF	100	303	50	89	17	0	6	41	.294	2	508	38	9	.984
1972 —Tacoma (Pacific Coast)	OF-1B	132	407	76	114	19	2	10	52	.280	4	282	19	10	.968
1973 —Tacoma (Pacific Coast)	OF-1B	114	337	67	87	19	2	17	49	.258	4	200	20	6	.973
1974 —Tacoma (Pacific Coast)	OF-1B	115	357	68	110	16	0	18	69	.308	4	514	41	3	.995
1975 —Tacoma (Pacific Coast)	OF-1B	62	202	38	51	5	0	9	29	.252	6	185	12	6	.970
—Minnesota (A.L.)	1B-OF	49	127	11	23	5	0	1	11	.181	0	360	28	6	.985
1976 —Rochester (Int'l)■	OF-1B	127	405	71	117	19	3	18	70	.289	2	323	28	4	.989
1977 —Tacoma (Pacific Coast)■..	1B-OF-P	113	363	80	99	12	1	12	64	.273	11	251	15	6	.978
1978 —Toledo (International)	1B-OF	119	325	47	74	13	0	10	49	.228	2	556	46	5	.992
1979 —Visalia (California)	1B-P	2	0	0	0	0	0	0	0	.000	0	3	4	0	1.000
Major league totals (1 year)		49	127	11	23	5	0	1	11	.181	0	360	28	6	.985

Year Team (League)	G	W	L	Pct.	ERA	Sv.	IP	H	R	ER	BB	SO
1977—Tacoma (Pacific Coast)	1	0	0	...	6.00	0	3	2	2	2	3	0
1979—Visalia (California)	1	1	0	1.000	2.25	0	8	5	3	2	7	2
1980—Visalia (California)	2	0	0	...	0.69	0	13	12	1	1	6	2

RECORD AS MANAGER

BACKGROUND: Player/manager, Tacoma, Minnesota Twins organization (1977).... Player/coach, Toledo, Twins organization (1978).... Player/manager, Visalia, Twins organization (1979-80).... Coach, Twins (1983-September 11, 1986).
HONORS: Named California League Manager of the Year (1979).... Named California League Co-Manager of the Year (1980). ... Named Southern League Manager of the Year (1981).... Coach, A.L. All-Star team (1991).... Named A.L. Manager of the Year by THE SPORTING NEWS (1991).

		REGULAR SEASON				POSTSEASON					
						Playoff		Champ. Series		World Series		All-Star Game	
Year Team (League)	W	L	Pct.	Pos.	W	L	W	L	W	L	W	L
1977—Tacoma (Pacific Coast)	28	26	.519	3rd (W)	—	—	—	—	—	—	—	—
1979—Visalia (California)	44	26	.629	1st (S)	1	2	—	—	—	—	—	—
—(Second half)	42	28	.600	2nd (S)	—	—	—	—	—	—	—	—
1980—Visalia (California)	27	43	.386	4th (S)	—	—	—	—	—	—	—	—
—(Second half)	44	26	.629	1st (S)	2	3	—	—	—	—	—	—
1981—Orlando (Southern)	42	27	.609	1st (E)	6	2	—	—	—	—	—	—
—(Second half)	37	36	.507	3rd (E)	—	—	—	—	—	—	—	—
1982—Orlando (Southern)	31	38	.449	5th (E)	—	—	—	—	—	—	—	—
—(Second half)	43	32	.573	2nd (E)	—	—	—	—	—	—	—	—
1986—Minnesota (A.L.)	12	11	.522	6th (W)	—	—	—	—	—	—	—	—
1987—Minnesota (A.L.)	85	77	.525	1st (W)	—	—	4	1	4	3	—	—
1988—Minnesota (A.L.)	91	71	.562	2nd (W)	—	—	—	—	—	—	1	0
1989—Minnesota (A.L.)	80	82	.494	5th (W)	—	—	—	—	—	—	—	—
1990—Minnesota (A.L.)	74	88	.457	7th (W)	—	—	—	—	—	—	—	—
1991—Minnesota (A.L.)	95	67	.586	1st (W)	—	—	4	1	4	3	—	—
Major league totals (6 years)	437	396	.525		—	—	8	2	8	6	1	0

NOTES:
1977— Replaced Tacoma manager Del Wilber with record of 40-49 and became player/manager (June, 1977).
1979— Lost to San Jose in semifinals.
1980— Defeated Fresno two games to one in semifinals; lost to Stockton three games to none in championship.
1981— Defeated Savannah three games to one in semifinals; defeated Nashville three games to one for championship.
1986— Replaced Minnesota manager Ray Miller with club in seventh place and record of 59-80 (September 12, 1986).
1987— Defeated Detroit in A.L. Championship Series; defeated St. Louis in World Series.
1991— Defeated Toronto in A.L. Championship Series; defeated Atlanta in World Series.

LAMONT, GENE

WHITE SOX

PERSONAL: Born December 25, 1946, at Rockford, Ill. ... 6-1/190. ... Threw right and batted both. ... Full name: Gene William Lamont.
HIGH SCHOOL: Hiawatha (Kirkland, Ill.).
COLLEGE: Northern Illinois and Western Illinois.
TRANSACTIONS/CAREER NOTES: Selected by Detroit Tigers organization in first round (13th pick overall) of free-agent draft (June 29, 1965).... On disabled list (May 18-28, 1966).... On temporarily inactive list (May 20-25, 1967).... On military list (May 25, 1967-remainder of season).... On temporarily inactive list (July 15-31, 1972).... Traded by Tigers to Atlanta Braves organization for C Bob Didier (May 14, 1973).... Drafted by Tigers (December 3, 1973).
STATISTICAL NOTES: Led Southern League catchers with nine errors in 1969.... Led Southern League catchers with 730 put-outs, 72 assists, 814 total chances, 9 double plays and 15 passed balls in 1972.... Led American Association catchers with eight double plays in 1976.

Year Team (League)	Pos.	G	AB	R	H	2B	3B	HR	RBI	Avg.	SB	PO	A	E	Avg.
1965—Syracuse (International) ..	C	5	9	1	1	0	0	1	1	.111	0	...	...	...	...
—Daytona Beach (Fla. St.) ..	C	38	104	9	24	5	1	1	16	.231	1	222	19	3	.988
1966—Statesville (W. Caro.)	C	45	137	14	27	4	2	3	19	.197	1	283	28	8	.975
—Rocky Mount (Carolina)....	C	36	102	9	26	4	1	2	9	.255	0	213	19	5	.979
1967—Rocky Mount (Carolina)....	C	19	56	4	8	2	0	1	5	.143	0	107	16	1	.992
1968—Rocky Mount (Carolina)....	C-OF-3B	101	304	36	76	10	0	4	39	.250	1	498	72	7	.988
1969—Montgomery (Southern) ...	C-3B	86	268	24	63	15	1	3	29	.235	0	410	92	†16	.969
1970—Toledo (International)	C-3B-OF	74	230	27	61	9	1	4	32	.265	1	313	59	5	.987
—Detroit (A.L.)	C	15	44	3	13	3	1	1	4	.295	0	87	8	0	1.000
1971—Toledo (International)	C	63	180	17	41	8	1	5	19	.228	0	321	43	9	.976
—Detroit (A.L.)	C	7	15	2	1	0	0	0	1	.067	0	38	2	2	.952
1972—Montgomery (Southern) ...	C-OF	119	385	47	105	19	1	6	51	.273	1	†731	†72	12	.985
1973—Richmond (Int'l)■	C-1B	101	275	29	69	11	1	2	25	.251	0	411	34	3	.993
1974—Detroit (A.L.)■	C	60	92	9	20	4	0	3	8	.217	0	204	21	6	.974
1975—Detroit (A.L.)	C	4	8	1	3	1	0	0	1	.375	1	14	3	1	.944
—Evansville (A.A.)	C	49	130	15	40	9	0	3	20	.308	1	211	23	4	.983
1976—Evansville (A.A.)	C	96	269	23	63	13	0	5	25	.234	2	467	47	7	.987
1977—Evansville (A.A.)	C	3	5	0	2	1	0	0	0	.400	0	4	1	0	1.000
Major league totals (4 years)		86	159	15	37	8	1	4	14	.233	1	343	34	9	.977

RECORD AS MANAGER

BACKGROUND: Coach, Pittsburgh Pirates (1986-91).

HONORS: Named Southern League Manager of the Year (1982).

		REGULAR SEASON					POSTSEASON					
						Playoff		Champ. Series		World Series		All-Star Game
Year	Team (League)	W	L	Pct.	Pos.	W	L	W	L	W	L	W	L
1978	—Fort Myers (Florida State)	38	30	.559	1st (S)	0	1	—	—	—	—	—	—
	—(Second half)	33	36	.478	5th (S)	—	—	—	—	—	—	—	—
1979	—Fort Myers (Florida State)	38	32	.543	3rd (S)	—	—	—	—	—	—	—	—
	—(Second half)	31	37	.456	4th (S)	—	—	—	—	—	—	—	—
1980	—Jacksonville (Southern)	31	40	.437	4th (E)	—	—	—	—	—	—	—	—
	—(Second half)	32	41	.438	5th (E)	—	—	—	—	—	—	—	—
1981	—Jacksonville (Southern)	34	36	.486	4th (E)	—	—	—	—	—	—	—	—
	—(Second half)	31	41	.431	4th (E)	—	—	—	—	—	—	—	—
1982	—Jacksonville (Southern)	41	31	.569	1st (E)	—	—	—	—	—	—	—	—
	—(Second half)	42	30	.583	1st (E)	4	4	—	—	—	—	—	—
1983	—Jacksonville (Southern)	36	36	.500	2nd (E)	—	—	—	—	—	—	—	—
	—(Second half)	41	32	.562	1st (E)	4	4	—	—	—	—	—	—
1984	—Omaha (American Association)	68	86	.442	8th	—	—	—	—	—	—	—	—
1985	—Omaha (American Association)	73	69	.514	3rd (W)	—	—	—	—	—	—	—	—

NOTES:
1978— Lost to Miami for Southern Division championship.
1981— Jacksonville tied one game.
1982— Defeated Columbus three games to one for Eastern Division championship; lost to Nashville three games to one for league championship.
1983— Defeated Savannah three games to one for Eastern Division championship; lost to Birmingham three games to one for league championship.

LA RUSSA, TONY

ATHLETICS

PERSONAL: Born October 4, 1944, at Tampa, Fla. . . . 6-0/185. . . . Threw and batted right-handed. . . . Full name: Anthony La Russa Jr.
HIGH SCHOOL: Jefferson (Tampa, Fla.).
TRANSACTIONS/CAREER NOTES: Signed by Kansas City Athletics organization (June 6, 1962). . . . On disabled list (May 9-September 8, 1964; June 3-July 15, 1965; and April 12-May 6 and July 3-September 5, 1967). . . . Kansas City franchise transferred to Oakland (October, 1967). . . . Sold by Oakland A's to Atlanta Braves (August 14, 1971). . . . Traded by Braves to Chicago Cubs for P Tom Phoebus (October 20, 1972). . . . Sold by Cubs to Pittsburgh Pirates organization (March 23, 1974). . . . Released by Pirates organization (April 4, 1975). . . . Signed by Chicago White Sox organization (April 7, 1975). . . . On disabled list (August 8-18, 1976). . . . Sold by White Sox to St. Louis Cardinals organization (December 13, 1976). . . . Named Cardinals coach (June 20, 1977). . . . Released by Cardinals organization (September 29, 1977).
STATISTICAL NOTES: Led International League in being hit by pitch with 11 in 1972.

						BATTING							FIELDING			
Year	Team (League)	Pos.	G	AB	R	H	2B	3B	HR	RBI	Avg.	SB	PO	A	E	Avg.
1962	—Daytona Beach (Fla. St.) ..	SS	64	225	37	58	7	0	1	32	.258	11	135	173	38	.890
	—Binghamton (Eastern)	SS-2B	12	43	3	8	0	0	0	4	.186	2	20	27	8	.855
1963	—Kansas City (A.L.)	SS-2B	34	44	4	11	1	1	0	1	.250	0	29	25	2	.964
1964	—Lewiston (Northwest)	2B-SS	90	329	50	77	22	1	1	25	.234	14	188	218	18	.958
1965	—Birmingham (Southern)	2B	75	259	24	50	11	2	1	18	.193	5	202	161	21	.945
1966	—Modesto (California)	2B	81	316	67	92	20	1	7	54	.291	18	201	212	20	.954
	—Mobile (Southern)	2B	51	170	20	50	9	4	4	26	.294	4	117	133	10	.962
1967	—Birmingham (Southern)	2B	41	139	12	32	6	1	5	22	.230	3	88	120	5	.977
1968	—Oakland (A.L.)	PH	5	3	0	1	0	0	0	0	.333	0	0	0	0	. . .
	—Vancouver (Pac. Coast)	2B	122	455	55	109	16	8	5	29	.240	4	249	321	14	*.976
1969	—Iowa (American Assoc.)	2B	67	235	37	72	11	1	4	27	.306	5	177	222	15	.964
	—Oakland (A.L.)	PH	8	8	0	0	0	0	0	0	.000	0	0	0	0	. . .
1970	—Iowa (American Assoc.)	2B	22	88	13	22	5	0	2	5	.250	0	52	59	3	.974
	—Oakland (A.L.)	2B	52	106	6	21	4	1	0	6	.198	0	67	89	5	.969
1971	—Iowa (American Assoc.)	2-3-S-O	28	107	21	31	5	1	2	11	.290	0	70	85	2	.987
	—Oakland (A.L.)	2B-SS-3B	23	8	3	0	0	0	0	0	.000	0	8	7	2	.882
	—Atlanta (N.L.)	2B	9	7	1	2	0	0	0	0	.286	0	8	6	1	.933
1972	—Richmond (Int'l)	2B	122	389	68	120	13	2	10	42	.308	0	305	289	20	.967
1973	—Wichita (Texas)■	2B-1B-3B	106	392	82	123	16	0	5	75	.314	10	423	213	26	.961
1974	—Charleston, S.C. (S. Atl.)■.	2B	139	457	50	119	17	1	8	35	.260	4	262	*378	17	.974
1975	—Denver (Am. Assoc.)■	3-O-S-2	118	354	87	99	23	2	7	46	.280	13	95	91	10	.949
1976	—Iowa (American Assoc.)	IF-OF-P	107	332	53	86	11	0	4	34	.259	10	132	160	22	.930
1977	—New Orleans (A.A.)■	2B-3B	50	128	17	24	2	2	3	6	.188	0	66	87	7	.956
	American League totals (5 years)		122	169	13	33	5	2	0	7	.195	0	104	121	9	.962
	National League totals (1 year)		9	7	1	2	0	0	0	0	.286	0	8	6	1	.933
	Major league totals (5 years)		131	176	14	35	5	2	0	7	.199	0	112	127	10	.960

RECORD AS PITCHER

Year	Team (League)	G	W	L	Pct.	ERA	Sv.	IP	H	R	ER	BB	SO
1976	—Iowa (American Association) ...	3	0	0	. . .	3.00	0	3	3	1	1	0	0

RECORD AS MANAGER

BACKGROUND: Coach, St. Louis Cardinals organization (June 20-September 29, 1977). . . . Coach, Chicago White Sox (July 3, 1978-remainder of season).
HONORS/RECORDS: Named Major League Manager of the Year by THE SPORTING NEWS (1983). . . . Coach, A.L. All-Star team

(1984 and 1987).... Shares major league record for most clubs managed, season—2 (1986).... Named A.L. Manager of the Year by The Sporting News (1988).

| | | | | | REGULAR SEASON | | | | POSTSEASON | | | | | |
| | | | | | | | | Playoff | | Champ. Series | | World Series | | All-Star Game | |
Year	Team (League)	W	L	Pct.	Pos.			W	L	W	L	W	L	W	L
1978	—Knoxville (Southern)	49	21	.700	1st (W)			—	—	—	—	—	—	—	—
	—(Second half)	4	4	.500	3rd (W)			—	—	—	—	—	—	—	—
1979	—Iowa (American Association)	54	52	.509	2nd (E)			—	—	—	—	—	—	—	—
	—Chicago (A.L.)	27	27	.500	5th (W)			—	—	—	—	—	—	—	—
1980	—Chicago (A.L.)	70	90	.438	5th (W)			—	—	—	—	—	—	—	—
1981	—Chicago (A.L.)	31	22	.585	3rd (W)			—	—	—	—	—	—	—	—
	—(Second half)	23	30	.434	6th (W)			—	—	—	—	—	—	—	—
1982	—Chicago (A.L.)	87	75	.537	3rd (W)			—	—	—	—	—	—	—	—
1983	—Chicago (A.L.)	99	63	.611	1st (W)			—	—	1	3	—	—	—	—
1984	—Chicago (A.L.)	74	88	.457	T5th (W)			—	—	—	—	—	—	—	—
1985	—Chicago (A.L.)	85	77	.525	3rd (W)			—	—	—	—	—	—	—	—
1986	—Chicago (A.L.)	26	38	.406	6th (W)			—	—	—	—	—	—	—	—
	—Oakland (A.L.)	45	34	.570	T3rd (W)			—	—	—	—	—	—	—	—
1987	—Oakland (A.L.)	81	81	.500	3rd (W)			—	—	—	—	—	—	—	—
1988	—Oakland (A.L.)	104	58	.642	1st (W)			—	—	4	0	1	4	—	—
1989	—Oakland (A.L.)	99	63	.611	1st (W)			—	—	4	1	4	0	1	0
1990	—Oakland (A.L.)	103	59	.636	1st (W)			—	—	4	0	0	4	1	0
1991	—Oakland (A.L.)	84	78	.519	4th (W)			—	—	—	—	—	—	1	0
	Major league totals (13 years)	1038	883	.540				—	—	13	4	5	8	3	0

NOTES:
1978— Became Chicago coach and replaced as Knoxville manager by Joe Jones (July 3).
1979— Replaced as Iowa manager by Joe Sparks (August 3); replaced Chicago manager Don Kessinger with club in fifth place and record of 46-60 (August 3).
1983— Lost to Baltimore in A.L. Championship Series.
1986— Replaced as White Sox manager by interim manager Doug Rader (June 20); replaced Oakland manager Jackie Moore (record of 29-44) and interim manager Jeff Newman (record of 2-8) with club in seventh place and record of 31-52 (July 7).
1988— Defeated Boston in A.L. Championship Series; lost to Los Angeles in World Series.
1989— Defeated Toronto in A.L. Championship Series; defeated San Francisco in World Series.
1990— Defeated Boston in A.L. Championship Series; lost to Cincinnati in World Series.

LASORDA, TOM
DODGERS

PERSONAL: Born September 22, 1927, at Norristown, Pa.... 5-9/195.... Threw and batted lefthanded.... Full name: Thomas Charles Lasorda.... Name pronounced luh-SORR-duh.
TRANSACTIONS/CAREER NOTES: On National Defense list (May 14, 1946-February 2, 1948). ... On disabled list (July 9-19, 1948).... Drafted by Nashua (Brooklyn Dodgers organization) from Philadelphia Phillies organization (November 24, 1948).... Sold by Brooklyn Dodgers organization to Kansas City Athletics (March 2, 1956).... Traded by Athletics to New York Yankees for P Wally Burnette and cash (July 11, 1956).... Sold by Yankees organization to Brooklyn Dodgers organization (May 26, 1957).... Released (July 9, 1960).
RECORDS/HONORS: Shares N.L. record for most wild pitches in one inning—3 (May 5, 1955, first inning).... Named International League Pitcher of the Year (1958).
STATISTICAL NOTES: Led Canadian-American League with 20 wild pitches in 1948.... Led International League with 14 wild pitches in 1953.... Led International League with 16 complete games and tied for lead with five shutouts in 1958.

Year	Team (League)	G	W	L	Pct.	ERA	Sv.	IP	H	R	ER	BB	SO
1945	—Concord (N. Carolina St.)	27	3	12	.200	4.09	...	121	115	84	55	100	91
1946	—						In military service						
1947	—						In military service						
1948	—Schenectady (Can.-Am.)	32	9	12	.429	4.64	...	192	180	122	99	153	195
1949	—Greenville (Sally)	45	7	7	.500	2.93	...	178	141	81	58	138	151
1950	—Montreal (International)	31	9	4	.692	3.70	...	146	136	73	60	82	85
1951	—Montreal (International)	31	12	8	.600	3.49	...	165	145	75	64	87	80
1952	—Montreal (International)	33	14	5	.737	3.66	...	182	156	90	74	93	77
1953	—Montreal (International)	36	17	8	.680	2.81	...	208	171	77	65	94	122
1954	—Montreal (International)	23	14	5	.737	3.51	...	154	142	66	60	79	75
	—Brooklyn (N.L.)	4	0	0	...	5.00	...	9	8	5	5	5	5
1955	—Brooklyn (N.L.)	4	0	0	...	13.50	...	4	5	6	6	6	4
	—Montreal (International)	22	9	8	.529	3.27	...	143	125	58	52	62	92
1956	—Kansas City (A.L.)■	18	0	4	.000	6.20	...	45	40	38	31	45	28
	—Denver (American Assoc.)■	16	3	4	.429	4.99	...	83	94	54	46	34	54
1957	—Denver (American Assoc.)	6	0	2	.000	12.18	...	17	29	25	23	6	8
	—Los Angeles (Pacific Coast)■	29	7	10	.412	3.89	...	132	134	73	57	59	72
1958	—Montreal (International)	34	★18	6	.750	2.50	...	★230	191	77	64	76	126
1959	—Montreal (International)	29	12	8	.600	3.83	...	188	192	93	80	77	64
1960	—Montreal (International)	12	2	5	.286	8.20	...	45	79	48	41	24	17
	American League totals (1 year)	18	0	4	.000	6.20	...	45	40	38	31	45	28
	National League totals (2 years)	8	0	0	...	7.62	...	13	13	11	11	11	9
	Major league totals (3 years)	26	0	4	.000	6.52	...	58	53	49	42	56	37

RECORD AS MANAGER

BACKGROUND: Scout, Los Angeles Dodgers (1961-65).... Manager, Los Angeles farm team in Arizona Instructional League (1969).... Coach, Los Angeles Dodgers (1973-76).
HONORS: Named Pioneer League Manager of the Year (1967).... Named Pacific Coast League Co-Manager of the Year (1970). ... Named Minor League Manager of the Year by THE SPORTING NEWS (1970).... Coach, N.L. All-Star team (1977, 1983-84 and 1986).... Named N.L. Co-Manager of the Year by THE SPORTING NEWS (1988).

							POSTSEASON					
		REGULAR SEASON					Champ.		World		All-Star	
						Playoff	Series		Series		Game	
Year Team (League)	W	L	Pct.	Pos.	W	L	W	L	W	L	W	L
1965—Pocatello (Pioneer)	33	33	.500	T2nd	—	—	—	—	—	—	—	—
1966—Ogden (Pioneer)	39	27	.591	1st	—	—	—	—	—	—	—	—
1967—Ogden (Pioneer)	41	25	.621	1st	—	—	—	—	—	—	—	—
1968—Ogden (Pioneer)	39	25	.609	1st	—	—	—	—	—	—	—	—
1969—Spokane (Pacific Coast)	71	73	.493	2nd (N)	—	—	—	—	—	—	—	—
1970—Spokane (Pacific Coast)	94	52	.630	1st (N)	4	0	—	—	—	—	—	—
1971—Spokane (Pacific Coast)	69	76	.476	3rd (N)	—	—	—	—	—	—	—	—
1972—Albuquerque (Pacific Coast)	92	56	.622	1st (E)	3	1	—	—	—	—	—	—
1976—Los Angeles (N.L.)	2	2	.500	2nd (W)	—	—	—	—	—	—	—	—
1977—Los Angeles (N.L.)	98	64	.605	1st (W)	—	—	3	1	2	4	—	—
1978—Los Angeles (N.L.)	95	67	.586	1st (W)	—	—	3	1	2	4	1	0
1979—Los Angeles (N.L.)	79	83	.488	3rd (W)	—	—	—	—	—	—	1	0
1980—Los Angeles (N.L.)	92	71	.564	2nd (W)	—	—	—	—	—	—	—	—
1981—Los Angeles (N.L.)	36	21	.632	1st (W)	—	—	—	—	—	—	—	—
—(Second half)	27	26	.509	4th (W)	3	2	3	2	4	2	—	—
1982—Los Angeles (N.L.)	88	74	.543	2nd (W)	—	—	—	—	—	—	1	0
1983—Los Angeles (N.L.)	91	71	.562	1st (W)	—	—	1	3	—	—	—	—
1984—Los Angeles (N.L.)	79	83	.488	4th (W)	—	—	—	—	—	—	—	—
1985—Los Angeles (N.L.)	95	67	.586	1st (W)	—	—	2	4	—	—	—	—
1986—Los Angeles (N.L.)	73	89	.451	5th (W)	—	—	—	—	—	—	—	—
1987—Los Angeles (N.L.)	73	89	.451	4th (W)	—	—	—	—	—	—	—	—
1988—Los Angeles (N.L.)	94	67	.584	1st (W)	—	—	4	3	4	1	—	—
1989—Los Angeles (N.L.)	77	83	.481	4th (W)	—	—	—	—	—	—	0	1
1990—Los Angeles (N.L.)	86	76	.531	2nd (W)	—	—	—	—	—	—	—	—
1991—Los Angeles (N.L.)	93	69	.574	2nd (W)	—	—	—	—	—	—	—	—
Major league totals (16 years)	1278	1102	.537		3	2	16	14	12	11	3	1

NOTES:
1970— Won championship playoff against Hawaii.
1972— Won championship playoff against Eugene.
1976— Replaced retiring Los Angeles manager Walter Alston with club in second place and record of 90-68 (September 29).
1977— Defeated Philadelphia in N.L. Championship Series; lost to New York Yankees in World Series.
1978— Defeated Philadelphia in N.L. Championship Series; lost to New York Yankees in World Series.
1981— Defeated Houston in divisional playoffs; defeated Montreal in N.L. Championship Series; defeated New York Yankees in World Series.
1983— Lost to Philadelphia in N.L. Championship Series.
1985— Lost to St. Louis in N.L. Championship Series.
1988— Defeated New York Mets in N.L. Championship Series; defeated Oakland in World Series.

LEFEBVRE, JIM

CUBS

PERSONAL: Born January 7, 1942, at Inglewood, Calif.... 6-0/185.... Threw right and batted both.... Full name: James Kenneth Lefebvre.... Name pronounced luh-FEE-ver.
HIGH SCHOOL: Morningside (Inglewood, Calif.).
TRANSACTIONS/CAREER NOTES: Signed as free agent by Los Angeles Dodgers organization (1962).... On military list (March 15-July 19, 1964 and July 25-August 8, 1969).... Released by Dodgers (November 27, 1972).... Signed by Lotte Orions of Japan (1973).
RECORDS/HONORS: Named N.L. Rookie of the Year by Baseball Writers' Association of America (1965).
STATISTICAL NOTES: Led California League second basemen with 79 double plays in 1962.... Led Northwest League second basemen with 109 double plays in 1963.

| | | | | | | BATTING | | | | | | | FIELDING | | | |
Year Team (League)	Pos.	G	AB	R	H	2B	3B	HR	RBI	Avg.	SB	PO	A	E	Avg.
1962—Reno (California)	2B	138	541	139	177	33	4	39	130	.327	23	345	313	27	.961
1963—Salem (Northwest)	2B	139	474	82	134	29	9	17	92	.283	6	*316	327	*35	.948
1964—Spokane (Pacific Coast) ...	2B	55	200	26	53	10	1	6	31	.265	2	123	126	8	.969
1965—Los Angeles (N.L.)	2B	157	544	57	136	21	4	12	69	.250	3	349	429	24	.970
1966—Los Angeles (N.L.)	2B-3B	152	544	69	149	23	3	24	74	.274	1	268	389	16	.976
1967—Los Angeles (N.L.)	3B-2B-1B	136	494	51	129	18	5	8	50	.261	1	173	321	18	.965
1968—Los Angeles (N.L.)	2-3-0-1	84	286	23	69	12	1	5	31	.241	0	179	161	8	.977
1969—Los Angeles (N.L.)	3B-2B-1B	95	275	29	65	15	2	4	44	.236	2	154	185	6	.983
1970—Los Angeles (N.L.)	2B-3B-1B	109	314	33	79	15	1	4	44	.252	1	168	212	6	.984
1971—Los Angeles (N.L.)	2B-3B	119	388	40	95	14	2	12	68	.245	0	247	274	9	.983
1972—Los Angeles (N.L.)	2B-3B	70	169	11	34	8	0	5	24	.201	0	70	99	4	.977
1973—Lotte Orions (Jap. Pac.)■.	1-2-3-0	111	400	50	106	12	2	29	63	.265	...	763	77	7	.992
1974—Lotte Orions (Jap. Pac.)	1B-3B	82	279	37	79	12	2	14	52	.283	...	580	32	4	.994
1975—Lotte Orions (Jap. Pac.)	1B	47	151	13	39	5	0	9	24	.258	...	252	13	0	1.000
1976—Lotte Orions (Jap. Pac.)	1B	90	268	22	65	8	0	8	37	.243	...	506	32	3	.994
Major league totals (8 years)		922	3014	313	756	126	18	74	404	.251	8	1608	2070	91	.976

WORLD SERIES RECORD

Year	Team (League)	Pos.	G	AB	R	H	2B	3B	HR	RBI	Avg.	SB	PO	A	E	Avg.
1965 —Los Angeles (N.L.)		2B	3	10	2	4	0	0	0	0	.400	0	3	7	1	.909
1966 —Los Angeles (N.L.)		2B	4	12	1	2	0	0	1	1	.167	0	10	10	0	1.000
World Series totals (2 years)			7	22	3	6	0	0	1	1	.273	0	13	17	1	.968

ALL-STAR GAME RECORD

Year	League	Pos.	AB	R	H	2B	3B	HR	RBI	Avg.	SB	PO	A	E	Avg.
1966 —National		2B	2	0	0	0	0	0	0	.000	0	2	0	0	1.000

RECORD AS MANAGER

BACKGROUND: Coach, Lotte Orions of Japan (1977).... Coach, Los Angeles Dodgers (September 24, 1978-1979).... Coach, San Francisco Giants (1980 and 1982).... Director of player development, San Francisco Giants (1983-84).... Coach, Oakland Athletics (1987-88).

HONORS: Named Pacific Coast League Manager of the Year (1985-86).... Coach, A.L. All-Star team (1990).

Year	Team (League)	W	L	Pct.	Pos.	Playoff W	Playoff L	Champ. Series W	Champ. Series L	World Series W	World Series L	All-Star Game W	All-Star Game L
1978 —Lethbridge (Pioneer)	33	35	.485	5th	—	—	—	—	—	—	—	—
1985 —Phoenix (Pacific Coast)	37	33	.529	2nd (S)	—	—	—	—	—	—	—	—
—(Second half)	43	29	.597	1st (S)	3	3	—	—	—	—	—	—
1986 —Phoenix (Pacific Coast)	43	28	.606	1st (S)	2	3	—	—	—	—	—	—
—(Second half)	38	33	.535	2nd (S)	—	—	—	—	—	—	—	—
1989 —Seattle (A.L.)	73	89	.451	6th (W)	—	—	—	—	—	—	—	—
1990 —Seattle (A.L.)	77	85	.475	5th (W)	—	—	—	—	—	—	—	—
1991 —Seattle (A.L.)	83	79	.512	5th (W)	—	—	—	—	—	—	—	—
Major league totals (3 years)	233	253	.479		—	—	—	—	—	—	—	—

NOTES:
1985— Defeated Hawaii three games to none in semifinals; lost to Vancouver three games to none for championship.
1986— Lost to Las Vegas in semifinals.

LEYLAND, JIM
PIRATES

PERSONAL: Born December 15, 1944, at Toledo, O.... 5-11/ 170.... Threw and batted right-handed.... Full name: James Richard Leyland.... Name pronounced LEE-lund.

HIGH SCHOOL: Perrysburg (O.).

TRANSACTIONS/CAREER NOTES: Signed as free agent by Detroit Tigers organization (September 21, 1963).... On disabled list (June 15-27, 1964).

Year	Team (League)	Pos.	G	AB	R	H	2B	3B	HR	RBI	Avg.	SB	PO	A	E	Avg.
1964 —Lakeland (Florida State) ...	C	52	129	8	25	0	1	0	8	.194	1	268	17	6	.979
—Cocoa Tigers (Coc. Rk.)	C	24	52	2	12	1	1	0	4	.231	1	122	15	3	.979
1965 —Jamestown (N.Y.-Penn) ...	C-3B-P	82	211	18	50	7	2	1	21	.237	2	318	36	6	.983
1966 —Rocky Mount (Carolina)	C	67	173	24	42	6	0	0	16	.243	0	369	23	1	.997
1967 —Montgomery (Southern) ...	C	62	171	11	40	3	0	1	16	.234	0	350	25	6	.984
1968 —Montgomery (Southern) ...	C-3B-SS	81	264	19	51	3	0	1	20	.193	2	511	43	7	.988
1969 —Montgomery (Southern) ...	C	16	39	1	8	0	0	0	1	.205	0	64	6	3	.959
—Lakeland (Florida State) ...	C-P	60	179	20	43	8	0	1	16	.240	0	321	28	4	.989
1970 —Montgomery (Southern) ...	C	2	3	0	0	0	0	0	0	.000	0	6	0	1	.857

RECORD AS PITCHER

Year	Team (League)	G	W	L	Pct.	ERA	Sv.	IP	H	R	ER	BB	SO
1965 —Jamestown (New York-Penn) ..	1	0	0	...	0.00	...	2	2	0	0	0	1
1969 —Lakeland (Florida State)	1	0	0	...	9.00	0	2	4	2	2	0	1

RECORD AS MANAGER

BACKGROUND: Coach, Detroit Tigers organization (1970-June 5, 1971); served as player/coach (1970).... Coach, Chicago White Sox (1982-85).

HONORS: Named Florida State League Manager of the Year (1977-78).... Named American Association Manager of the Year (1979).... Named N.L. Co-Manager of the Year by THE SPORTING NEWS (1988).... Coach, N.L. All-Star team (1990-91). ... Named N.L. Manager of the Year by THE SPORTING NEWS (1990).

Year	Team (League)	W	L	Pct.	Pos.	Playoff W	Playoff L	Champ. Series W	Champ. Series L	World Series W	World Series L	All-Star Game W	All-Star Game L
1971 —Bristol (Appalachian)	31	35	.470	3rd (S)	—	—	—	—	—	—	—	—
1972 —Clinton (Midwest)	22	41	.349	5th (N)	—	—	—	—	—	—	—	—
—(Second half)	27	36	.429	4th (N)	—	—	—	—	—	—	—	—
1973 —Clinton (Midwest)	36	26	.581	2nd (N)	—	—	—	—	—	—	—	—
—(Second half)	37	25	.597	1st (N)	0	2	—	—	—	—	—	—
1974 —Montgomery (Southern)	61	76	.445	3rd (W)	—	—	—	—	—	—	—	—
1975 —Clinton (Midwest)	29	31	.483	4th (S)	—	—	—	—	—	—	—	—
—(Second half)	38	30	.559	2nd (S)	—	—	—	—	—	—	—	—
1976 —Lakeland (Florida State)	74	64	.536	2nd (N)	4	0	—	—	—	—	—	—

| | REGULAR SEASON | | | | POSTSEASON | | | | | | | |
| | | | | | Playoff | | Champ. Series | | World Series | | All-Star Game | |
Year Team (League)	W	L	Pct.	Pos.	W	L	W	L	W	L	W	L
1977 — Lakeland (Florida State)	85	53	.616	1st (N)	5	1	—	—	—	—	—	—
1978 — Lakeland (Florida State)	31	38	.449	4th (N)	—	—	—	—	—	—	—	—
— (Second half)	47	22	.681	1st (N)	2	2	—	—	—	—	—	—
1979 — Evansville (American Association)	78	58	.574	1st (E)	4	2	—	—	—	—	—	—
1980 — Evansville (American Association)	61	74	.452	2nd (E)	—	—	—	—	—	—	—	—
1981 — Evansville (American Association)	73	63	.537	1st (E)	1	3	—	—	—	—	—	—
1986 — Pittsburgh (N.L.)	64	98	.395	6th (E)	—	—	—	—	—	—	—	—
1987 — Pittsburgh (N.L.)	80	82	.494	T4th (E)	—	—	—	—	—	—	—	—
1988 — Pittsburgh (N.L.)	85	75	.525	2nd (E)	—	—	—	—	—	—	—	—
1989 — Pittsburgh (N.L.)	74	88	.457	5th (E)	—	—	—	—	—	—	—	—
1990 — Pittsburgh (N.L.)	95	67	.586	1st (E)	—	—	2	4	—	—	—	—
1991 — Pittsburgh (N.L.)	98	64	.605	1st (E)	—	—	3	4	—	—	—	—
Major league totals (6 years)	496	474	.511		—	—	5	8	—	—	—	—

NOTES:
1973 — Lost playoff to Wisconsin Rapids.
1976 — Defeated Miami two games to none in semifinals; defeated Tampa two games to none for championship.
1977 — Defeated Miami two games to none in semifinals; defeated St. Petersburg three games to one for championship.
1978 — Defeated St. Petersburg one game to none for Northern Division championship; lost to Miami two games to one for championship.
1979 — Defeated Oklahoma City for championship.
1981 — Lost to Denver in semifinals.
1985 — Served as acting manager of Chicago White Sox (record of 1-1), with club in fourth place, while manager Tony La Russa served a suspension (August 10 and 11).
1990 — Lost to Cincinnati in N.L. Championship Series.
1991 — Lost to Atlanta in N.L. Championship Series.

McRAE, HAL
ROYALS

PERSONAL: Born June 10, 1945, at Avon Park, Fla. . . . 5-11/185. . . . Threw and batted righthanded. . . . Full name: Harold Abraham McRae. . . . Father of Brian McRae, outfielder, Kansas City Royals.
HIGH SCHOOL: Douglas (Sebring, Fla.).
COLLEGE: Florida A&M.
TRANSACTIONS/CAREER NOTES: Selected by Cincinnati Reds organization in sixth round of free-agent draft (June, 1965). . . . On disabled list (June 23-July 6, 1966; April 26-May 7, 1967; April 18-May 28 and July 4-August 5, 1969). . . . Traded with P Wayne Simpson to Kansas City Royals for P Roger Nelson and OF Richie Scheinblum (November 30, 1972). . . . On disabled list (June 11-August 2, 1979; May 13-June 2, 1980). . . . Granted free agency (November 10, 1982). . . . Re-signed by Royals (November 15, 1982). . . . Granted free agency (November 12, 1985). . . . Re-signed by Royals (December 8, 1985). . . . Released by Royals (December 19, 1986). . . . Re-signed by Royals as a player-coach (January 12, 1987). . . . Released as a player (July 21, 1987).
RECORDS/HONORS: Shares major league doubleheader record for most long hits—6 (5 doubles, 1 home run) (August 27, 1974). . . . Named designated hitter on THE SPORTING NEWS A.L. All-Star Team (1976-77 and 1982). . . . Named designated hitter on THE SPORTING NEWS A.L. Silver Slugger Team (1982).
STATISTICAL NOTES: Led A.L. with .406 on base percentage in 1976. . . . Led A.L. in being hit by pitch with 13 in 1977.

| | | | | | | BATTING | | | | | | | FIELDING | | | |
Year Team (League)	Pos.	G	AB	R	H	2B	3B	HR	RBI	Avg.	SB	PO	A	E	Avg.
1965 — Tampa (Florida State)	OF	22	65	3	10	3	0	0	4	.154	1	19	0	0	1.000
1966 — Peninsula (Carolina)	2B	109	394	65	113	19	4	11	56	.287	10	252	226	*28	.945
1967 — Buffalo (International)	2B	73	259	30	65	14	3	10	34	.251	7	133	208	23	.937
— Knoxville (Southern)	2B	51	186	26	54	10	3	6	25	.290	2	140	136	12	.958
1968 — Indianapolis (PCL)	2B-OF	119	444	64	131	31	11	16	65	.295	15	222	307	14	.974
— Cincinnati (N.L.)	2B	17	51	1	10	1	0	0	2	.196	1	33	30	5	.926
1969 — Indianapolis (A.A.)	OF	17	41	2	9	1	0	0	4	.220	0	0	0	0	. . .
1970 — Cincinnati (N.L.)	OF-3B-2B	70	165	18	41	6	1	8	23	.248	0	53	7	1	.984
1971 — Cincinnati (N.L.)	OF	99	337	39	89	24	2	9	34	.264	3	167	6	6	.966
1972 — Cincinnati (N.L.)	OF-3B	61	97	9	27	4	0	5	26	.278	0	16	14	6	.833
1973 — Kansas City (A.L.)■	OF-3B	106	338	36	79	18	3	9	50	.234	2	101	6	5	.955
1974 — Kansas City (A.L.)	OF-3B	148	539	71	167	36	4	15	88	.310	11	132	3	7	.951
1975 — Kansas City (A.L.)	OF-3B	126	480	57	147	38	6	5	71	.306	11	207	7	3	.986
1976 — Kansas City (A.L.)	OF	149	527	75	175	34	5	8	73	.332	22	63	2	2	.970
1977 — Kansas City (A.L.)	OF	*162	641	104	191	*54	11	21	92	.298	18	81	8	4	.957
1978 — Kansas City (A.L.)	OF	156	623	90	170	39	5	16	72	.273	17	3	1	0	1.000
1979 — Kansas City (A.L.)	DH	101	393	55	113	32	4	10	74	.288	5	0	0	0	. . .
1980 — Kansas City (A.L.)	OF	124	489	73	145	39	5	14	83	.297	10	17	0	0	1.000
1981 — Kansas City (A.L.)	OF	101	389	38	106	23	2	7	36	.272	3	10	0	1	.909
1982 — Kansas City (A.L.)	OF	159	613	91	189	*46	8	27	*133	.308	4	1	0	1	.500
1983 — Kansas City (A.L.)	DH	157	589	84	183	41	6	12	82	.311	2	0	0	0	. . .
1984 — Kansas City (A.L.)	DH	106	317	30	96	13	4	3	42	.303	0	0	0	0	. . .
1985 — Kansas City (A.L.)	DH	112	320	41	83	19	0	14	70	.259	0	0	0	0	. . .
1986 — Kansas City (A.L.)	DH	112	278	22	70	14	0	7	37	.252	0	0	0	0	. . .
1987 — Kansas City (A.L.)	DH	18	32	5	10	3	0	1	9	.313	0	0	0	0	. . .
American League totals (15 years)		1837	6568	872	1924	449	63	169	1012	.293	105	615	27	23	.965
National League totals (4 years)		247	650	67	167	35	3	22	85	.257	4	269	57	18	.948
Major league totals (19 years)		2084	7218	939	2091	484	66	191	1097	.290	109	884	84	41	.959

DIVISION SERIES RECORD

Year	Team (League)	Pos.	G	AB	R	H	2B	3B	HR	RBI	Avg.	SB	PO	A	E	Avg.
				BATTING									FIELDING			
1981	—Kansas City (A.L.)	DH	3	11	0	1	1	0	0	0	.091	0	0	0	0	...

CHAMPIONSHIP SERIES RECORD

CHAMPIONSHIP SERIES NOTES: Holds record for most runs, five-game series—6 (1977).... Shares career record for most doubles—7.

Year	Team (League)	Pos.	G	AB	R	H	2B	3B	HR	RBI	Avg.	SB	PO	A	E	Avg.
				BATTING									FIELDING			
1970	—Cincinnati (N.L.)	OF	2	4	0	0	0	0	0	0	.000	0	2	0	0	1.000
1972	—Cincinnati (N.L.)	PH	1	0	0	0	0	0	0	0	...	0	0	0	0	...
1976	—Kansas City (A.L.)	OF	5	17	2	2	1	1	0	1	.118	0	5	1	0	1.000
1977	—Kansas City (A.L.)	OF	5	18	6	8	3	0	1	2	.444	0	2	1	0	1.000
1978	—Kansas City (A.L.)	DH	4	14	0	3	0	0	0	2	.214	1	0	0	0	...
1980	—Kansas City (A.L.)	DH	3	10	0	2	0	0	0	0	.200	0	0	0	0	...
1984	—Kansas City (A.L.)	PH	2	2	0	2	1	0	0	1	1.000	0	0	0	0	...
1985	—Kansas City (A.L.)	DH	6	23	1	6	2	0	0	3	.261	0	0	0	0	...
Championship Series totals (8 years)			28	88	9	23	7	1	1	9	.261	1	9	2	0	1.000

WORLD SERIES RECORD

Year	Team (League)	Pos.	G	AB	R	H	2B	3B	HR	RBI	Avg.	SB	PO	A	E	Avg.
				BATTING									FIELDING			
1970	—Cincinnati (N.L.)	OF	3	11	1	5	2	0	0	3	.455	0	2	1	0	1.000
1972	—Cincinnati (N.L.)	OF	5	9	1	4	1	0	0	2	.444	0	4	0	0	1.000
1980	—Kansas City (A.L.)	DH	6	24	3	9	3	0	0	1	.375	0	0	0	0	...
1985	—Kansas City (A.L.)	PH	3	1	0	0	0	0	0	0	.000	0	0	0	0	...
World Series totals (4 years)			17	45	5	18	6	0	0	6	.400	0	6	1	0	1.000

ALL-STAR GAME RECORD

Year	League	Pos.	AB	R	H	2B	3B	HR	RBI	Avg.	SB	PO	A	E	Avg.
			BATTING									FIELDING			
1975	—American	PH	1	0	0	0	0	0	0	.000	0	0	0	0	...
1976	—American	PH	1	0	0	0	0	0	0	.000	0	0	0	0	...
1982	—American	PH	0	0	0	0	0	0	0	...	0	0	0	0	...
All-Star Game totals (3 years)			2	0	0	0	0	0	0	.000	0	0	0	0	...

RECORD AS MANAGER

BACKGROUND: Player/hitting coach, Kansas City Royals (beginning of 1987 season-July 21, 1987).... Hitting coach, Kansas City Royals (July 21, 1987-remainder of season).... Minor league hitting instructor, Pittsburgh Pirates (1988-89).... Hitting instructor, Montreal Expos (1990-May 24, 1991).

Year	Team (League)	W	L	Pct.	Pos.	Playoff W	Playoff L	Champ. Series W	Champ. Series L	World Series W	World Series L	All-Star Game W	All-Star Game L
		REGULAR SEASON				POSTSEASON							
1991	—Kansas City (A.L.)	66	58	.532	6th (W)	—	—	—	—	—	—	—	—
Major league totals (1 year)		66	58	.532		—	—	—	—	—	—	—	—

NOTES:

1991— Replaced Kansas City manager John Wathan (15-22) and interim manager Bob Schaefer (1-0) with club in seventh place and record of 16-22 (May 24).... Placed on suspended list (August 13); reinstated (August 14).

OATES, JOHNNY

ORIOLES

PERSONAL: Born January 21, 1946, at Sylva, N.C.... 5-11/185.... Threw right and batted lefthanded.... Full name: Johnny Lane Oates.

HIGH SCHOOL: Prince George (Va.).

COLLEGE: Virginia Tech (received bachelor of science degree in health and physical education).

TRANSACTIONS/CAREER NOTES: Selected by Chicago White Sox organization in second round of free-agent draft (June, 1966).... Selected by Baltimore Orioles organization in secondary phase of free-agent draft (January 28, 1967).... On military list (April 21-August 22, 1970).... Traded by Orioles with P Pat Dobson, P Roric Harrison and 2B Dave Johnson to Atlanta Braves for C Earl Williams and IF Taylor Duncan (November 30, 1972).... On disabled list (July 17-September 2, 1973).... Traded by Braves with 1B Dick Allen to Philadelphia Phillies for C Jim Essian, OF Barry Bonnell and cash (May 7, 1975).... On disabled list (April 14-June 1, 1976).... Traded by Phillies with P R. Quency Hill to Los Angeles Dodgers for IF Ted Sizemore (December 20, 1976).... Released by Dodgers (March 27, 1980).... Signed by New York Yankees (April 4, 1980).... Granted free agency (November 13, 1980).... Re-signed by Yankees organization (January 23, 1981).... On disabled list (August 3-August 25, 1981).... Released by Yankees organization (October 27, 1981).

STATISTICAL NOTES: Led International League catchers with 727 total chances in 1971.... Led National League with 15 passed balls in 1974.... Tied for National League lead in double plays by catchers with 10 in 1975.

Year	Team (League)	Pos.	G	AB	R	H	2B	3B	HR	RBI	Avg.	SB	PO	A	E	Avg.
				BATTING									FIELDING			
1967	—Bluefield (Appalachian)	C	5	12	5	5	1	0	1	4	.417	0	23	5	0	1.000
	—Miami (Florida State)	C-OF	48	156	22	45	5	2	3	19	.288	2	271	37	8	.975
1968	—Miami (Florida State)	C-OF	70	194	24	51	9	3	0	23	.263	2	384	42	3	.993
1969	—Dallas/Fort Worth (Tex.)	C	66	191	24	55	12	2	1	18	.288	0	253	42	4	.987

Year Team (League)	Pos.	G	AB	R	H	2B	3B	HR	RBI	Avg.	SB	PO	A	E	Avg.
1970 —Rochester (Int'l)	C	9	16	1	6	1	0	0	4	.375	0	24	2	0	1.000
—Baltimore (A.L.)	C	5	18	2	5	0	1	0	2	.278	0	30	1	2	.939
1971 —Rochester (Int'l)	C	114	346	49	96	16	3	7	44	.277	10	*648	*73	6	.992
1972 —Baltimore (A.L.)	C	85	253	20	66	12	1	4	21	.261	5	391	31	2	*.995
1973 —Atlanta (N.L.)■	C	93	322	27	80	6	0	4	27	.248	1	409	57	9	.981
1974 —Atlanta (N.L.)	C	100	291	22	65	10	0	1	21	.223	2	434	55	4	.992
1975 —Atlanta-Phil. (N.L.)■.......	C	98	287	28	81	15	0	1	25	.282	1	450	45	5	.990
1976 —Philadelphia (N.L.)	C	37	99	10	25	2	0	0	8	.253	0	155	15	1	.994
1977 —Los Angeles (N.L.)■.........	C	60	156	18	42	4	0	3	11	.269	1	258	37	4	.987
1978 —Los Angeles (N.L.)	C	40	75	5	23	1	0	0	6	.307	0	77	10	4	.956
1979 —Los Angeles (N.L.)	C	26	46	4	6	2	0	0	2	.130	0	64	13	2	.975
1980 —New York (A.L.)■	C	39	64	6	12	3	0	1	3	.188	1	99	10	1	.991
1981 —Columbus (Int'l)							Did not play								
American League totals (3 years)		129	335	28	83	15	2	5	26	.248	6	520	42	5	.991
National League totals (7 years) ...		454	1276	114	322	40	0	9	100	.252	5	1847	232	29	.986
Major league totals (10 years)		583	1611	142	405	55	2	14	126	.251	11	2367	274	34	.987

CHAMPIONSHIP SERIES RECORD

Year Team (League)	Pos.	G	AB	R	H	2B	3B	HR	RBI	Avg.	SB	PO	A	E	Avg.
1976 —Philadelphia (N.L.)	C	1	1	0	0	0	0	0	0	.000	0	1	0	0	1.000

WORLD SERIES RECORD

Year Team (League)	Pos.	G	AB	R	H	2B	3B	HR	RBI	Avg.	SB	PO	A	E	Avg.
1977 —Los Angeles (N.L.)...........	C	1	1	0	0	0	0	0	0	.000	0	1	0	0	1.000
1978 —Los Angeles (N.L.)...........	C	1	1	0	1	0	0	0	0	1.000	0	3	1	0	1.000
World Series totals (2 years)		2	2	0	1	0	0	0	0	.500	0	4	1	0	1.000

RECORD AS MANAGER

BACKGROUND: Player/coach, Columbus, International League (July 30, 1981-remainder of season).... Coach, Chicago Cubs (1984-87).... Coach, Baltimore Orioles (1989-May 23, 1991).

HONORS: Named International League Manager of the Year (1988).

						POSTSEASON					
	REGULAR SEASON				Playoff		Champ. Series		World Series		All-Star Game
Year Team (League)	W	L	Pct.	Pos.	W	L	W	L	W	L	W	L
1982 —Nashville (Southern)	32	38	.457	4th (W)	—	—	—	—	—	—	—	—
—(Second half)	45	29	.608	1st (W)	6	2	—	—	—	—	—	—
1983 —Columbus (International)	83	57	.593	1st	2	3	—	—	—	—	—	—
1988 —Rochester (International)	77	64	.546	1st (W)	5	5	—	—	—	—	—	—
1991 —Baltimore (A.L.)	54	71	.432	6th (E)	—	—	—	—	—	—	—	—
Major league totals (1 year)	54	71	.432		—	—	—	—	—	—	—	—

NOTES:

1982—Defeated Knoxville three games to one in playoffs; defeated Jacksonville three games to one for league championship.

1983—Lost to Tidewater in playoffs.

1988—Defeated Tidewater three games to one for league championship; lost to Indianapolis (American Association) four games to two in AAA-Alliance championship.

1991—Replaced Baltimore manager Frank Robinson with club in seventh place and record of 13-24 (May 23).

PINIELLA, LOU
REDS

PERSONAL: Born August 28, 1943, at Tampa, Fla.... 6-2/199.... Threw and batted right-handed.... Full name: Louis Victor Piniella.... Cousin of Dave Magadan, infielder, New York Mets.... Name pronounced pin-ELL-uh.

HIGH SCHOOL: Jesuit (Tampa, Fla.).

COLLEGE: Tampa.

TRANSACTIONS/CAREER NOTES: Signed as free agent by Cleveland Indians organization (June 9, 1962).... Drafted by Washington Senators (November 26, 1962).... On military list (March 9-July 20, 1964).... Traded by Senators organization to Baltimore Orioles organization (August 4, 1964), completing deal in which Orioles traded P Lester (Buster) Narum to Senators for cash and a player to be named later (March 31, 1964).... On suspended list (June 27-29, 1965).... Traded by Orioles organization to Indians organization for C Cam Carreon (March 10, 1966).... On temporary inactive list (May 19-22, 1967).... On disabled list (May 22-June 6, 1968).... On temporary inactive list (June 6-25, 1968).... Selected by Seattle Pilots in expansion draft (October 15, 1968).... Traded by Pilots to Kansas City Royals for OF Steve Whitaker and P John Gelnar (April 1, 1969).... On military list (August 7-22, 1969).... On disabled list (May 5-June 8, 1971).... Traded by Royals with P Ken Wright to New York Yankees for P Lindy McDaniel (December 7, 1973).... On disabled list (June 17-July 6, 1975; August 23-September 7, 1981; and March 30-April 22, 1983).... On voluntarily retired list (June 17, 1984).

RECORDS/HONORS: Shares major league record for most assists by outfielder in one inning—2 (May 27, 1974, third inning).... Named A.L. Rookie of the Year by Baseball Writers' Association of America (1969).

STATISTICAL NOTES: Led A.L. in grounding into double plays with 25 in 1972.

Year Team (League)	Pos.	G	AB	R	H	2B	3B	HR	RBI	Avg.	SB	PO	A	E	Avg.
1962 —Selma (Ala.-Fla.)	OF	70	278	40	75	10	5	8	44	.270	4	94	6	9	.917
1963 —Peninsula (Carolina)■.......	OF	143	548	71	170	29	4	16	77	.310	8	271	*23	8	.974

Year	Team (League)	Pos.	G	AB	R	H	2B	3B	HR	RBI	Avg.	SB	PO	A	E	Avg.
1964	—Aberdeen (Northern)	OF	20	74	8	20	8	3	0	12	.270	1	37	1	1	.974
	—Baltimore (A.L.)■	PH	4	1	0	0	0	0	0	0	.000	0	0	0	0	...
1965	—Elmira (Eastern)	OF	126	490	64	122	29	6	11	64	.249	5	176	5	7	.963
1966	—Portland (Pacific Coast)■	OF	133	457	47	132	22	3	7	52	.289	6	177	11	11	.945
1967	—Portland (Pacific Coast)	OF	113	396	46	122	20	1	8	56	.308	2	199	7	6	.972
1968	—Portland (Pacific Coast)	OF	88	331	49	105	15	3	13	62	.317	0	167	6	7	.961
	—Cleveland (A.L.)	OF	6	5	1	0	0	0	0	1	.000	1	1	0	0	1.000
1969	—Kansas City (A.L.)■	OF	135	493	43	139	21	6	11	68	.282	2	278	13	7	.977
1970	—Kansas City (A.L.)	OF-1B	144	542	54	163	24	5	11	88	.301	3	250	6	4	.985
1971	—Kansas City (A.L.)	OF	126	448	43	125	21	5	3	51	.279	5	201	6	3	.986
1972	—Kansas City (A.L.)	OF	151	574	65	179	*33	4	11	72	.312	7	275	8	7	.976
1973	—Kansas City (A.L.)	OF	144	513	53	128	28	1	9	69	.250	5	196	9	3	.986
1974	—New York (A.L.)■	OF-1B	140	518	71	158	26	0	9	70	.305	1	270	16	3	.990
1975	—New York (A.L.)	OF	74	199	7	39	4	1	0	22	.196	0	65	5	1	.986
1976	—New York (A.L.)	OF	100	327	36	92	16	6	3	38	.281	0	199	10	4	.981
1977	—New York (A.L.)	OF-1B	103	339	47	112	19	3	12	45	.330	2	86	3	2	.978
1978	—New York (A.L.)	OF	130	472	67	148	34	5	6	69	.314	3	213	4	7	.969
1979	—New York (A.L.)	OF	130	461	49	137	22	2	11	69	.297	3	204	13	4	.982
1980	—New York (A.L.)	OF	116	321	39	92	18	0	2	27	.287	0	157	8	5	.971
1981	—New York (A.L.)	OF	60	159	16	44	9	0	5	18	.277	0	69	2	1	.986
1982	—New York (A.L.)	OF	102	261	33	80	17	1	6	37	.307	0	68	2	0	1.000
1983	—New York (A.L.)	OF	53	148	19	43	9	1	2	16	.291	3	67	4	3	.959
1984	—New York (A.L.)	OF	29	86	8	26	4	1	1	6	.302	0	40	3	0	1.000
Major league totals (18 years)			1747	5867	651	1705	305	41	102	766	.291	35	2639	112	54	.981

DIVISION SERIES RECORD

Year	Team (League)	Pos.	G	AB	R	H	2B	3B	HR	RBI	Avg.	SB	PO	A	E	Avg.
1981	—New York (A.L.)	DH-PH	4	10	1	2	1	0	1	3	.200	0	0	0	0	...

CHAMPIONSHIP SERIES RECORD

Year	Team (League)	Pos.	G	AB	R	H	2B	3B	HR	RBI	Avg.	SB	PO	A	E	Avg.
1976	—New York (A.L.)	DH-PH	4	11	1	3	1	0	0	0	.273	0	0	0	0	...
1977	—New York (A.L.)	OF-DH	5	21	1	7	3	0	0	2	.333	0	9	1	0	1.000
1978	—New York (A.L.)	OF	4	17	2	4	0	0	0	0	.235	0	13	0	0	1.000
1980	—New York (A.L.)	OF	2	5	1	1	0	0	1	1	.200	0	5	0	0	1.000
1981	—New York (A.L.)	PH-DH-OF	3	5	2	3	0	0	1	3	.600	0	0	0	0	...
Championship Series totals (5 years)			18	59	7	18	4	0	2	6	.305	0	27	1	0	1.000

WORLD SERIES RECORD

WORLD SERIES NOTES: Shares single-series record for one or more hits in each game (1978).

Year	Team (League)	Pos.	G	AB	R	H	2B	3B	HR	RBI	Avg.	SB	PO	A	E	Avg.
1976	—New York (A.L.)	DH-OF-PH	4	9	1	3	1	0	0	0	.333	0	1	0	0	1.000
1977	—New York (A.L.)	OF	6	22	1	6	0	0	0	3	.273	0	16	1	1	.944
1978	—New York (A.L.)	OF	6	25	3	7	0	0	0	4	.280	1	14	1	0	1.000
1981	—New York (A.L.)	OF-PH	6	16	2	7	1	0	0	3	.438	1	7	0	0	1.000
World Series totals (4 years)			22	72	7	23	2	0	0	10	.319	2	38	2	1	.976

ALL-STAR GAME RECORD

Year	League	Pos.	AB	R	H	2B	3B	HR	RBI	Avg.	SB	PO	A	E	Avg.
1972	—American	PH	1	0	0	0	0	0	0	.000	0	0	0	0	...

RECORD AS MANAGER

BACKGROUND: Coach, New York Yankees (June 25, 1984-1985).... Vice president and general manager, New York Yankees (beginning of 1988 season-June 22, 1988).... Special adviser, New York Yankees (1989).

			REGULAR SEASON				POSTSEASON						
							Playoff		Champ. Series		World Series		All-Star Game	
Year	Team (League)	W	L	Pct.	Pos.	W	L	W	L	W	L	W	L
1986	—New York (A.L.)	90	72	.556	2nd (E)	—	—	—	—	—	—	—	—
1987	—New York (A.L.)	89	73	.549	4th (E)	—	—	—	—	—	—	—	—
1988	—New York (A.L.)	45	48	.484	5th (E)	—	—	—	—	—	—	—	—
1990	—Cincinnati (N.L.)	91	71	.562	1st (W)	—	—	4	2	4	0	—	—
1991	—Cincinnati (N.L.)	74	88	.457	5th (W)	—	—	—	—	—	—	0	1
American League totals (3 years)		224	193	.537		—	—	—	—	—	—	—	—
National League totals (2 years)		165	159	.509		—	—	4	2	4	0	0	1
Major league totals (5 years)		389	352	.525		—	—	4	2	4	0	0	1

NOTES:
1988— Replaced New York manager Billy Martin with club in second place and record of 40-28 (June 23).
1990— Defeated Pittsburgh in N.L. Championship Series; defeated Oakland in World Series.

PLUMMER, BILL

MARINERS

PERSONAL: Born March 21, 1947, at Oakland, Calif. . . . 6-2/200. . . . Threw and batted righthanded. . . . Full name: William Francis Plummer. . . . Son of William L. Plummer, minor league pitcher (1921-27).
HIGH SCHOOL: Anderson Union (Anderson, Calif.).
COLLEGE: Shasta College (Calif.) and Sacramento State (Calif.).
TRANSACTIONS/CAREER NOTES: Signed as free agent by St. Louis Cardinals organization (April 25, 1965). . . . Drafted by Chicago Cubs from Tulsa, Cardinals organization (November 28, 1967). . . . Traded by Cubs with OF Clarence Jones and P Ken Myette to Cincinnati Reds organization for P Ted Abernathy (January 9, 1969). . . . On disabled list (March 30-May 5, 1972). . . . Released by Reds (March 30, 1978). . . . Signed by Seattle Mariners organization (April 6, 1978). . . . Granted free agency (November 2, 1978). . . . Re-signed by Mariners (February 1, 1979).
STATISTICAL NOTES: Led Florida Rookie League catchers with 220 total chances in 1965. . . . Led American Association catchers with 653 putouts, 64 assists and 725 total chances in 1969. . . . Led American Association catchers with .994 fielding percentage, 641 putouts and 697 total chances in 1970. . . . Led American Association catchers with 55 assists in 1971.

							BATTING							FIELDING			
Year — Team (League)	Pos.	G	AB	R	H	2B	3B	HR	RBI	Avg.	SB	PO	A	E	Avg.
1965 — Cedar Rapids (Midwest) ...	C	7	15	2	2	1	0	0	0	.133	0	46	3	1	.980
— Sara. Cards (Fla. Rk.)	C	42	102	10	27	5	0	0	7	.265	2	*189	26	5	.977
1966 — Eugene (Northwest)	C	46	125	6	18	3	0	1	11	.144	0	276	29	10	.968
1967 — Modesto (California)	C-1B-3B	120	397	48	93	8	6	11	56	.234	6	851	69	18	.981
1968 — Chicago (N.L.)■...............	C	2	2	0	0	0	0	0	0	.000	0	2	0	0	1.000
1969 — Indianapolis (A.A.)■.........	C-OF-P	104	355	41	88	8	3	7	41	.248	4	†653	†64	8	.989
1970 — Indianapolis (A.A.)	C-OF-1B	115	365	37	95	12	1	7	42	.260	1	†653	52	4	†.994
— Cincinnati (N.L.)	C	4	8	0	1	0	0	0	0	.125	0	6	0	1	.857
1971 — Indianapolis (A.A.)	C-3B-1B	104	372	50	99	15	5	17	65	.266	2	569	†66	9	.986
— Cincinnati (N.L.)	C-3B	10	19	0	0	0	0	0	0	.000	0	8	6	0	1.000
1972 — Cincinnati (N.L.)	C-1B-3B	38	102	8	19	4	0	2	9	.186	0	156	9	1	.994
1973 — Cincinnati (N.L.)	C-3B	50	119	8	18	3	0	2	11	.151	1	172	10	2	.989
1974 — Cincinnati (N.L.)	C-3B	50	120	7	27	7	0	2	10	.225	1	208	14	6	.974
1975 — Cincinnati (N.L.)	C	65	159	17	29	7	0	1	19	.182	1	186	14	2	.990
1976 — Cincinnati (N.L.)	C	56	153	16	38	6	1	4	19	.248	1	0	235	21	6	.977
1977 — Cincinnati (N.L.)	C	51	117	10	16	5	0	1	7	.137	1	194	15	3	.986
1978 — San Jose (Pacific Coast)■.	C	24	78	9	14	2	0	2	8	.179	0	101	9	2	.982
— Seattle (A.L.)	C	41	93	6	20	5	0	2	7	.215	0	127	9	3	.978
1979 — Spokane (Pacific Coast) ...	C-1B-P	116	369	37	94	12	2	4	46	.255	1	489	49	14	.975
American League totals (1 year)		41	93	6	20	5	0	2	7	.215	0	127	9	3	.978
National League totals (9 years)		326	799	66	148	32	1	12	75	.185	4	1167	89	21	.984
Major league totals (10 years)		367	892	72	168	37	1	14	82	.188	4	1294	98	24	.983

RECORD AS PITCHER

Year — Team (League)	G	W	L	Pct.	ERA	Sv.	IP	H	R	ER	BB	SO
1969 — Indianapolis (Am. Assoc.)	1	0	0	...	0.00	0	2	2	0	0	1	0
1979 — Spokane (Pacific Coast)	2	0	0	...	18.00	0	1	3	2	2	0	0

RECORD AS MANAGER

BACKGROUND: Player/coach, Spokane, Pacific Coast League (1979). . . . Coach, Seattle Mariners (1982-83). . . . Coach, Seattle Mariners (July 14, 1988-1991).

		REGULAR SEASON				POSTSEASON					
						Playoff		Champ. Series		World Series		All-Star Game	
Year — Team (League)	W	L	Pct.	Pos.	W	L	W	L	W	L	W	L
1980 — San Jose (California)	32	37	.464	2nd (S)	—	—	—	—	—	—	—	—
— (Second half)	41	29	.586	2nd (S)	—	—	—	—	—	—	—	—
1981 — Wausau (Midwest)	41	23	.641	1st (N)	—	—	—	—	—	—	—	—
— (Second half)	43	25	.632	1st (N)	4	1	—	—	—	—	—	—
1984 — Chattanooga (Southern)	32	34	.485	4th (W)	—	—	—	—	—	—	—	—
— (Second half)	31	47	.397	4th (W)	—	—	—	—	—	—	—	—
1985 — Chattanooga (Southern)	36	35	.507	3rd (W)	—	—	—	—	—	—	—	—
— (Second half)	30	42	.417	5th (W)	—	—	—	—	—	—	—	—
1986 — Calgary (Pacific Coast)	36	35	.507	2nd (N)	—	—	—	—	—	—	—	—
— (Second half)	30	42	.417	5th (N)	—	—	—	—	—	—	—	—
1987 — Calgary (Pacific Coast)	38	32	.543	2nd (N)	—	—	—	—	—	—	—	—
— (Second half)	46	25	.648	1st (N)	4	5	—	—	—	—	—	—
1988 — Calgary (Pacific Coast)	33	38	.489	3rd (N)	—	—	—	—	—	—	—	—
— (Second half)	11	8	.579		—	—	—	—	—	—	—	—

NOTES:
1981— Wausau tied one game during regular season; defeated Waterloo two games to one in playoffs; defeated Quad Cities two games to none for league championship.
1987— Defeated Tacoma three games to two in playoffs; lost to Albuquerque three games to one for league championship.
1988— Left Calgary to coach for Seattle (July 14); replaced by Orlando Martinez.

RIDDOCH, GREG

PADRES

PERSONAL: Born July 17, 1946, at Greeley, Colo. . . . 5-11/175. . . . Threw and batted righthanded. . . . Full name: Gregory Lee Riddoch. . . . Name pronounced ri-DOCK.
HIGH SCHOOL: Garden Grove (Calif.).
COLLEGE: Northern Colorado (bachelor of arts degree in business administration and master's degree in education).

TRANSACTIONS/CAREER NOTES: Selected by Baltimore Orioles organization in 49th round of free-agent draft (June 8, 1965).... Selected by Orioles organization in secondary phase of free-agent draft (June 7, 1966).... Selected by Orioles organization in secondary phase of free-agent draft (January 28, 1967).... Selected by Cincinnati Reds organization in secondary phase of free-agent draft (June 7, 1967).... On Tampa restricted list (April 16-June 21, 1969).... Released by Reds organization (January 6, 1972).

STATISTICAL NOTES: Led Northern League third basemen with .937 fielding percentage in 1969.

						BATTING								**FIELDING**		
Year	Team (League)	Pos.	G	AB	R	H	2B	3B	HR	RBI	Avg.	SB	PO	A	E	Avg.
1967—Tampa (Florida State)		SS	63	213	19	38	6	3	1	19	.178	5	101	149	14	.947
1968—Tampa (Florida State)		SS-3B	89	199	16	35	5	0	2	20	.176	1	95	115	14	.938
1969—Sioux Falls (Northern)		3B-1B	64	253	42	81	8	4	8	30	.320	6	92	100	12	†.941
1970—Asheville (Southern)		3B	132	448	25	92	16	1	1	22	.205	9	262	21	21	.931
1971—Three Rivers (Eastern)		SS-3B-1B	78	201	14	34	8	1	1	8	.169	2	54	106	12	.930

RECORD AS MANAGER

BACKGROUND: Scouting supervisor, Cincinnati Reds (1982-83).... Assistant director of player development, Reds (1984).... Director of minor league clubs, Reds (1985).... Associate director of minor leagues and scouting, San Diego Padres (January 1, 1986-February 25, 1986).... Director of minor leagues and scouting, Padres (February 26, 1986-October 27, 1986).... Coach, San Diego Padres (October 28, 1986-July 10, 1990).

HONORS: Named Northwest League Manager of the Year (1975).

									Champ.		World		All-Star	
		REGULAR SEASON				**POSTSEASON**								
						Playoff		Series		Series		Game		
Year	Team (League)	W	L	Pct.	Pos.	W	L	W	L	W	L	W	L	
1974—Seattle (Northwest)	45	39	.536	3rd (W)	—	—	—	—	—	—	—	—	
1975—Eugene (Northwest)	54	25	.684	1st (S)	2	0	—	—	—	—	—	—	
1976—Eugene (Northwest)	37	34	.521	2nd (S)	—	—	—	—	—	—	—	—	
1977—Billings (Pioneer)	23	46	.333	6th	—	—	—	—	—	—	—	—	
1978—Eugene (Northwest)	36	34	.514	1st (S)	0	1	—	—	—	—	—	—	
1979—Eugene (Northwest)	30	41	.423	4th (S)	—	—	—	—	—	—	—	—	
1980—Eugene (Northwest)	37	33	.529	1st (S)	1	1	—	—	—	—	—	—	
1981—Eugene (Northwest)	33	37	.471	3rd (S)	—	—	—	—	—	—	—	—	
1990—San Diego (N.L.)	38	44	.463	T5th (W)	—	—	—	—	—	—	—	—	
1991—San Diego (N.L.)	84	78	.519	3rd (W)	—	—	—	—	—	—	—	—	
Major league totals (2 years)	122	122	.500		—	—	—	—	—	—	—	—	

NOTES:
1975— Won championship playoff against Portland.
1978— Lost playoffs to Grays Harbor after one game (balance of playoff cancelled due to rain and wet grounds).
1980— Playoff series against Bellingham was tied at one game each when series was canceled due to rain and wet grounds; Eugene and Bellingham were declared co-champions.
1990— Replaced San Diego manager Jack McKeon with club in fourth place and record of 37-43 (July 11).

RODGERS, BUCK

ANGELS

PERSONAL: Born August 16, 1938, at Delaware, O.... 6-1/190.... Threw right and batted both.... Full name: Robert Leroy Rodgers.

COLLEGE: Ohio Wesleyan University and Ohio Northern University.

TRANSACTIONS/CAREER NOTES: Signed by Detroit Tigers organization (July 14, 1956).... On Knoxville disabled list (May 24-June 3, 1959).... Selected by Los Angeles Angels from Tigers in A.L. expansion draft (December 14, 1960).... On Hawaii disabled list (May 4-June 11, 1969).

RECORDS/HONORS: Holds A.L. rookie-season record for most games by catcher—150 (1962).... Shares A.L. single-season record for fewest assists by catcher (150 or more games)—73 (1962).

STATISTICAL NOTES: Led New York-Pennsylvania League catchers with 77 assists and 24 errors in 1957.... Led Pioneer League catchers with 16 errors in 1958.... Led South Atlantic League catchers with 11 errors in 1959.... Led A.L. catchers with 14 double plays in 1962 and 14 in 1964.... Led A.L. catchers with 73 assists in 1967.

						BATTING								**FIELDING**		
Year	Team (League)	Pos.	G	AB	R	H	2B	3B	HR	RBI	Avg.	SB	PO	A	E	Avg.
1956—Jamestown (Pony)		OF	48	153	28	36	8	1	6	26	.235	3	43	6	3	.942
1957—Erie (New York-Penn)		C-OF	114	430	79	127	26	4	12	80	.295	6	568	†77	*25	.963
1958—Lancaster (Eastern)		C	19	63	8	16	3	0	3	8	.254	1	111	11	2	.984
—Idaho Falls (Pioneer)		C-OF	99	378	73	115	15	6	12	74	.304	3	524	45	†20	.966
1959—Birmingham (Southern)		C	3	13	1	1	0	1	0	2	.077	0	28	0	1	.966
—Knoxville (South Atlantic)		OF-C	105	355	53	102	18	6	7	55	.287	3	565	60	†13	.980
1960—Denver (Am. Assoc.)		C	23	84	12	20	7	1	3	12	.238	0	127	15	4	.973
—Birmingham (Southern)		C	93	313	36	77	14	1	5	38	.246	0	456	*68	7	.987
1961—Dallas/Fort Worth (A.A.)■		C	124	427	55	122	22	3	3	62	.286	2	*595	*70	11	.984
—Los Angeles (A.L.)		C	16	56	8	18	2	0	2	13	.321	0	71	11	3	.965
1962—Los Angeles (A.L.)		C	155	565	65	146	34	6	6	61	.258	1	826	73	•10	.989
1963—Los Angeles (A.L.)		C	100	300	24	70	6	0	4	23	.233	2	416	48	*10	.979
1964—Los Angeles (A.L.)		C	148	514	35	125	18	3	4	54	.243	4	884	*87	*13	.987
1965—California (A.L.)		C	132	411	33	86	14	3	1	32	.209	4	682	52	7	.991
1966—California (A.L.)		C	133	454	45	107	20	3	7	48	.236	3	662	*69	6	.992
1967—California (A.L.)		C-OF	139	429	29	94	13	3	6	41	.219	1	728	†73	7	.991
1968—California (A.L.)		C	91	258	13	49	6	0	1	14	.190	2	407	50	7	.985
1969—Hawaii (Pacific Coast)		C-3B	44	145	15	37	5	0	0	12	.255	0	215	26	4	.984
—California (A.L.)		C	18	46	4	9	1	0	0	2	.196	2	74	9	0	1.000

Year	Team (League)	Pos.	G	AB	R	H	2B	3B	HR	RBI	Avg.	SB	PO	A	E	Avg.
							BATTING							FIELDING		
1975	—Salinas (California)	PH	4	3	1	1	0	0	0	0	.333	0	0	0	0	...
1977	—El Paso (Texas)	PH	1	0	0	0	0	0	0	0	...	0	0	0	0	...
	Major league totals (9 years)		932	3033	259	704	114	18	31	288	.232	19	4750	472	63	.988

RECORD AS MANAGER

BACKGROUND: Player/manager, Salinas, California Angels organization (August 24-September 15, 1975).... Player/manager, El Paso, Angels organization (July 15-August 14, 1977).... Coach, Minnesota Twins (1970-74).... Coach, San Francisco Giants (1976).... Coach, Milwaukee Brewers (1978-80).

RECORDS/HONORS: Shares major league record for most clubs managed, season—2 (1990).... Named Texas League Manager of the Year (1977).... Named American Association Manager of the Year (1984).... Named Minor League Manager of the Year by THE SPORTING NEWS (1984).... Named N.L. Manager of the Year by THE SPORTING NEWS (1987).... Coach, N.L. All-Star team (1988-89).

Year	Team (League)	W	L	Pct.	Pos.	Playoff W	Playoff L	Champ. Series W	Champ. Series L	World Series W	World Series L	All-Star Game W	All-Star Game L
		REGULAR SEASON				POSTSEASON							
1975	—Salinas (California)	35	35	.500	5th	—	—	—	—	—	—	—	—
	—(Second half)	32	38	.457	6th	—	—	—	—	—	—	—	—
1977	—El Paso (Texas)	38	24	.613	1st (W)	—	—	—	—	—	—	—	—
	—(Second half)	40	28	.588	1st (W)	0	2	—	—	—	—	—	—
1980	—Milwaukee (A.L.)	13	10	.565	3rd (E)	—	—	—	—	—	—	—	—
1981	—Milwaukee (A.L.)	31	25	.554	3rd (E)	—	—	—	—	—	—	—	—
	—(Second half)	31	22	.585	1st (E)	2	3	—	—	—	—	—	—
1982	—Milwaukee (A.L.)	23	24	.489	T5th (E)	—	—	—	—	—	—	—	—
1984	—Indianapolis (American Association)	91	63	.591	1st	2	4	—	—	—	—	—	—
1985	—Montreal (N.L.)	84	77	.522	3rd (E)	—	—	—	—	—	—	—	—
1986	—Montreal (N.L.)	78	83	.484	4th (E)	—	—	—	—	—	—	—	—
1987	—Montreal (N.L.)	91	71	.562	3rd (E)	—	—	—	—	—	—	—	—
1988	—Montreal (N.L.)	81	81	.500	3rd (E)	—	—	—	—	—	—	—	—
1989	—Montreal (N.L.)	81	81	.500	4th (E)	—	—	—	—	—	—	—	—
1990	—Montreal (N.L.)	85	77	.525	3rd (E)	—	—	—	—	—	—	—	—
1991	—Montreal (N.L.)	20	29	.408	6th (E)	—	—	—	—	—	—	—	—
	—California (A.L.)	20	18	.526	7th (W)	—	—	—	—	—	—	—	—
	American League totals (4 years)	118	99	.544		2	3	—	—	—	—	—	—
	National League totals (7 years)	520	499	.510		—	—	—	—	—	—	—	—
	Major league totals (10 years)	638	598	.516		2	3	—	—	—	—	—	—

NOTES:
1977— Lost league championship to Arkansas.
1980— Began season as temporary Milwaukee manager for George Bamberger, who was ill. Bamberger returned with club in second place and record of 26-21 (June 6). Rodgers named manager after Bamberger retired with club in fourth place and record of 73-66 (September 7).
1981— Lost to New York Yankees in divisional playoff.
1982— Replaced as Milwaukee manager by Harvey Kuenn (June 2).
1984— Lost semifinal playoff series to Louisville.
1990— Replaced as Montreal manager by Tom Runnells (June 3); replaced Doug Rader as California manager with club in seventh place and record of 61-63 (August 26).

RUNNELLS, TOM

EXPOS

PERSONAL: Born April 17, 1955, at Greeley, Colo.... 6-0/175.... Threw right and batted both.... Full name: Thomas William Runnells.
HIGH SCHOOL: Greeley West (Colo.).
COLLEGE: Northern Colorado (received bachelor of arts degree in physical education).
TRANSACTIONS/CAREER NOTES: Signed as free agent by San Francisco Giants organization (June 16, 1977).... On disabled list (July 24-remainder of season, 1983).... Granted free agency (October 20, 1983).... Signed by Indianapolis, Cincinnati Reds organization (October 30, 1983).
STATISTICAL NOTES: Led American Association second basemen with .993 fielding percentage in 1984.... Led American Association second basemen with 654 total chances and 83 double plays in 1985.
MISCELLANEOUS: Batted righthanded only (1977).

Year	Team (League)	Pos.	G	AB	R	H	2B	3B	HR	RBI	Avg.	SB	PO	A	E	Avg.
							BATTING							FIELDING		
1977	—Great Falls (Pioneer)	2-3-0-S	63	241	61	70	8	1	1	53	.290	17	117	144	16	.942
1978	—Fresno (California)	2B-SS-3B	139	564	83	163	15	7	0	55	.289	32	289	437	37	.952
1979	—Shreveport (Texas)	SS	128	435	45	102	10	2	4	32	.234	4	190	413	19	*.969
1980	—Shreveport (Texas)	SS	73	258	27	50	4	1	0	10	.194	9	117	240	18	.952
	—Phoenix (Pacific Coast)	SS-2B	37	149	21	45	4	0	0	10	.302	2	51	121	4	.977
1981	—Phoenix (Pacific Coast)	SS-OF-2B	131	467	40	128	11	2	0	51	.274	13	240	392	28	.958
1982	—Phoenix (Pacific Coast)	S-3-2-0	108	347	52	93	8	11	0	48	.268	15	164	259	23	.948
1983	—Phoenix (Pacific Coast)	SS-2B-1B	74	244	43	74	11	4	1	28	.303	7	119	188	13	.959
1984	—Wichita (Am. Assoc.)■......	2-3-0-S	125	438	67	108	21	3	6	61	.247	8	229	350	5	†.991
1985	—Denver (Am. Assoc.)	2B	114	466	55	135	22	8	5	51	.290	5	256	*391	7	*.986
	—Cincinnati (N.L.)	SS-2B	28	35	3	7	1	0	0	0	.200	0	10	22	0	1.000
1986	—Denver (Am. Assoc.)	2-S-0-3	95	298	34	68	12	4	3	28	.228	1	159	248	10	.976
	—Cincinnati (N.L.)	2B-3B	12	11	1	1	1	0	0	0	.091	0	4	5	0	1.000
	Major league totals (2 years)		40	46	4	8	2	0	0	0	.174	0	14	27	0	1.000

BACKGROUND: Coach, Montreal Expos (1990-June 3, 1991).
HONORS: Named American Association Manager of the Year (1989).

| | | | REGULAR SEASON | | | | POSTSEASON | | | | | |
| | | | | | | Playoff | | Champ. Series | | World Series | | All-Star Game |
Year	Team (League)	W	L	Pct.	Pos.	W	L	W	L	W	L	W	L
1987	—Vermont (Eastern)	73	67	.521	4th	4	4	—	—	—	—	—	—
1988	—Chattanooga (Southern)	43	30	.589	1st (W)	—	—	—	—	—	—	—	—
	—(Second half)	38	32	.543	2nd (W)	6	1	—	—	—	—	—	—
1989	—Indianapolis (American Association)	87	59	.596	1st (E)	7	2	—	—	—	—	—	—
1991	—Montreal (N.L.)	51	61	.455	6th (E)	—	—	—	—	—	—	—	—
	Major league totals (1 year)	51	61	.455		—	—	—	—	—	—	—	—

NOTES:
1987— Defeated Pittsfield three games to one in playoffs; lost to Harrisburg three games to one in league championship.
1988— Defeated Memphis three games to one in playoffs; defeated Greenville three games to none for league championship.
1989— Defeated Omaha three games to two for league championship; defeated Richmond (International League) four games to none for AAA-Alliance championship.
1991— Replaced Montreal manager Buck Rodgers with club in sixth place and record of 20-29 (June 3).

SHOWALTER, BUCK
YANKEES

PERSONAL: Born May 23, 1956, at DeFuniak Springs, Fla. . . . 5-9/195. . . . Threw and batted lefthanded. . . . Full name: William Nathaniel Showalter III.
COLLEGE: Chipola Junior College (Fla.) and Mississippi State.
TRANSACTIONS/CAREER NOTES: Selected by New York Yankees organization in fifth round of free-agent draft (June 7, 1977). . . . On disabled list (July 1-11 and July 19-August 4, 1981).
STATISTICAL NOTES: Led Southern League first basemen with 1,281 putouts in 1982.

| | | | | | | BATTING | | | | | | | FIELDING | | |
Year	Team (League)	Pos.	G	AB	R	H	2B	3B	HR	RBI	Avg.	SB	PO	A	E	Avg.
1977	—Fort Lauderdale (FSL)	OF	56	196	32	71	8	1	1	25	.362	4	96	2	2	.980
1978	—West Haven (Eastern)	OF	123	429	52	124	13	2	3	46	.289	19	192	•15	7	.967
1979	—West Haven (Eastern)	1B-OF	129	469	71	131	7	3	6	51	.279	8	575	52	7	.989
1980	—Nashville (Southern)	OF-1B	142	550	84	•178	19	3	1	82	.324	6	71	2	1	.986
1981	—Columbus (Int'l)	OF	14	37	6	7	1	0	1	3	.189	0	11	0	1	.917
	—Nashville (Southern)	OF-1B	90	307	46	81	17	6	0	38	.264	3	201	14	7	.968
1982	—Nashville (Southern)	1B-OF	132	517	66	•152	29	3	3	46	.294	2†1282	51	13	.990
1983	—Nashville (Southern)	1B-OF-P	89	297	35	82	13	4	1	37	.276	1	127	6	2	.985
	—Columbus (Int'l)	1B-P	18	63	9	15	3	0	1	8	.238	1	139	14	1	.994

RECORD AS PITCHER

Year	Team (League)	G	W	L	Pct.	ERA	Sv.	IP	H	R	ER	BB	SO
1983	—Nashville (Southern)	1	0	0	. . .	9.00	0	1	2	1	1	0	1
	—Columbus (International)	1	0	0	. . .	0.00	0	2	0	0	0	0	2

RECORD AS MANAGER

BACKGROUND: Minor league coach, New York Yankees organization (1984). . . . Coach, Yankees (1990-91).
HONORS: Named New York-Pennsylvania League Manager of the Year (1985). . . . Named Eastern League Manager of the Year (1989).

| | | | REGULAR SEASON | | | | POSTSEASON | | | | | |
| | | | | | | Playoff | | Champ. Series | | World Series | | All-Star Game |
Year	Team (League)	W	L	Pct.	Pos.	W	L	W	L	W	L	W	L
1985	—Oneonta (New York-Pennsylvania)	55	23	.705	1st (N)	3	0	—	—	—	—	—	—
1986	—Oneonta (New York-Pennsylvania)	59	18	.766	1st (Y)	0	1	—	—	—	—	—	—
1987	—Fort Lauderdale (Florida State)	85	53	.616	1st (S)	5	1	—	—	—	—	—	—
1988	—Fort Lauderdale (Florida State)	39	29	.574	3rd (E)	—	—	—	—	—	—	—	—
	—(Second half)	30	36	.455	T3rd (E)	—	—	—	—	—	—	—	—
1989	—Albany/Colonie (Eastern)	92	48	.657	1st	6	2	—	—	—	—	—	—

NOTES:
1985— Defeated Geneva in one-game semifinal playoff; defeated Auburn two games to none for league championship.
1986— Lost to Newark in playoffs.
1987— Defeated Lakeland two games to none in playoffs; defeated Osceola three games to one for league championship.
1989— Defeated Reading three games to one in playoffs; defeated Harrisburg three games to one for league championship.

TORBORG, JEFF
METS

PERSONAL: Born November 26, 1941, at Westfield, N.J. . . . 6-0/195. . . . Threw and batted righthanded. . . . Full name: Jeffrey Allen Torborg. . . . Father of Doug Torborg, minor league pitcher (1987-88).
HIGH SCHOOL: Westfield (N.J.).
COLLEGE: Rutgers (bachelor of science degree in education) and Montclair State College, N.J. (master's degree in athletic administration).
TRANSACTIONS/CAREER NOTES: Signed as free agent by Los Angeles Dodgers organization (May 22, 1963). . . . Sold by Dodgers to California Angels (March 13, 1971). . . . On disabled list (June 25-July 27, 1971; May 21-June 13, 1972; and July 13-August 10, 1973). . . . Traded by Angels to St. Louis Cardinals for P John Andrews (December 6, 1973). . . . Released by Cardinals (March 25, 1974).

Year	Team (League)	Pos.	G	AB	R	H	2B	3B	HR	RBI	Avg.	SB	PO	A	E	Avg.
1963	—Albuquerque (Texas)	C	64	184	19	41	10	3	1	18	.223	0	349	27	6	.984
1964	—Los Angeles (N.L.)	C	28	43	4	10	1	1	0	4	.233	0	80	4	2	.977
1965	—Los Angeles (N.L.)	C	56	150	8	36	5	1	3	13	.240	0	300	19	3	.991
1966	—Los Angeles (N.L.)	C	46	120	4	27	3	0	1	13	.225	0	269	17	4	.986
1967	—Los Angeles (N.L.)	C	76	196	11	42	4	1	2	12	.214	1	413	30	5	.989
1968	—Los Angeles (N.L.)	C	37	93	2	15	2	0	0	4	.161	0	206	20	2	.991
1969	—Los Angeles (N.L.)	C	51	124	7	23	4	0	0	7	.185	1	251	26	1	.996
1970	—Los Angeles (N.L.)	C	64	134	11	31	8	0	1	17	.231	1	275	16	5	.983
1971	—California (A.L.)■	C	55	123	6	25	5	0	0	5	.203	0	208	17	3	.987
1972	—California (A.L.)	C	59	153	5	32	3	0	0	8	.209	0	383	28	1	.998
1973	—California (A.L.)	C	102	255	20	56	7	0	1	18	.220	0	611	37	6	.991
	American League totals (3 years)		216	531	31	113	15	0	1	31	.213	0	1202	82	10	.992
	National League totals (7 years)		358	860	47	184	27	3	7	70	.214	3	1794	132	22	.989
	Major league totals (10 years)		574	1391	78	297	42	3	8	101	.214	3	2996	214	32	.990

RECORD AS MANAGER

BACKGROUND: Coach, Cleveland Indians (1975-June 18, 1977).... Coach, New York Yankees (July 26, 1979-1988).
HONORS: Named A.L. Manager of the Year by THE SPORTING NEWS (1990).

		—REGULAR SEASON—				Playoff		Champ. Series		World Series		All-Star Game	
Year	Team (League)	W	L	Pct.	Pos.	W	L	W	L	W	L	W	L
1977	—Cleveland (A.L.)	45	59	.433	5th (E)	—	—	—	—	—	—	—	—
1978	—Cleveland (A.L.)	69	90	.434	6th (E)	—	—	—	—	—	—	—	—
1979	—Cleveland (A.L.)	43	52	.453	6th (E)	—	—	—	—	—	—	—	—
1989	—Chicago (A.L.)	69	92	.429	7th (W)	—	—	—	—	—	—	—	—
1990	—Chicago (A.L.)	94	68	.580	2nd (W)	—	—	—	—	—	—	—	—
1991	—Chicago (A.L.)	87	75	.537	2nd (W)	—	—	—	—	—	—	—	—
	Major league totals (6 years)	407	436	.483		—	—	—	—	—	—	—	—

NOTES:
1977— Replaced Frank Robinson as Cleveland manager with club in sixth place and record of 26-31 (June 19).
1979— Replaced as Cleveland manager by Dave Garcia (July 23).

TORRE, JOE
CARDINALS

PERSONAL: Born July 18, 1940, at Brooklyn, N.Y.... 6-1/2 10.... Threw and batted righthanded.... Full name: Joseph Paul Torre.... Brother of Frank Torre, first baseman, Milwaukee Braves, Philadelphia Phillies (1956-60, 1962-63).... Name pronounced TORE-ee.

TRANSACTIONS/CAREER NOTES: Signed by Jacksonville, Milwaukee Braves organization (August 24, 1959).... On military list (September 30, 1962-March 26, 1963).... Braves franchise transferred to Atlanta (1966).... On disabled list (April 18-May 9, 1968).... Traded by Atlanta Braves to St. Louis Cardinals for 1B Orlando Cepeda (March 17, 1969).... Traded by Cardinals to New York Mets for P Tommy Moore and P Ray Sadecki (October 13, 1974).... Released as player by Mets (June 18, 1977).

RECORDS/HONORS: Shares major league single-game record for most times grounded into double play—4 (July 21, 1975).... Named catcher on THE SPORTING NEWS N.L. All-Star team (1964-1966).... Won N.L. Gold Glove at catcher (1965).... Named Major League Player of the Year by THE SPORTING NEWS (1971).... Named N.L. Player of the Year by THE SPORTING NEWS (1971).... Named third baseman on THE SPORTING NEWS N.L. All-Star team (1971).... Named N.L. Most Valuable Player by Baseball Writers' Association of America (1971).

STATISTICAL NOTES: Led N.L. catchers with .995 fielding percentage in 1964 and .996 in 1968.... Led N.L. in grounding into double plays with 26 in 1964, 22 in 1965, 22 in 1967 and 21 in 1968.... Led N.L. catchers with 12 double plays in 1967.... Led N.L. with 352 total bases in 1971.... Hit for the cycle (June 27, 1973).... Led N.L. first basemen with 102 assists and 144 double plays in 1974.

Year	Team (League)	Pos.	G	AB	R	H	2B	3B	HR	RBI	Avg.	SB	PO	A	E	Avg.
1960	—Eau Claire (Northern)	C	117	369	63	127	23	3	16	74	★.344	7	636	64	9	.987
	—Milwaukee (N.L.)	PH	2	2	0	1	0	0	0	0	.500	0	0	0	0	...
1961	—Louisville (Am. Assoc.)	C	27	111	18	38	8	2	3	24	.342	0	185	14	2	.990
	—Milwaukee (N.L.)	C	113	406	40	113	21	4	10	42	.278	3	494	50	10	.982
1962	—Milwaukee (N.L.)	C	80	220	23	62	8	1	5	26	.282	1	325	39	5	.986
1963	—Milwaukee (N.L.)	C-1B-OF	142	501	57	147	19	4	14	71	.293	1	919	76	6	.994
1964	—Milwaukee (N.L.)	C-1B	154	601	87	193	36	5	20	109	.321	4	1081	94	7	†.994
1965	—Milwaukee (N.L.)	C-1B	148	523	68	152	21	1	27	80	.291	0	1022	73	8	.993
1966	—Atlanta (N.L.)	C-1B	148	546	83	172	20	3	36	101	.315	0	874	87	12	.988
1967	—Atlanta (N.L.)	C-1B	135	477	67	132	18	1	20	68	.277	2	785	81	8	.991
1968	—Atlanta (N.L.)	C-1B	115	424	45	115	11	2	10	55	.271	1	733	48	2	†.997
1969	—St. Louis (N.L.)■	1B-C	159	602	72	174	29	6	18	101	.289	0	1360	91	7	.995
1970	—St. Louis (N.L.)	C-3B-1B	•161	624	89	203	27	9	21	100	.325	2	651	162	13	.984
1971	—St. Louis (N.L.)	3B	161	634	97	★230	34	8	24	★137	★.363	4	★136	271	•21	.951
1972	—St. Louis (N.L.)	3B-1B	149	544	71	157	26	6	11	81	.289	3	336	198	15	.973
1973	—St. Louis (N.L.)	1B-3B	141	519	67	149	17	2	13	69	.287	2	881	128	12	.988
1974	—St. Louis (N.L.)	1B-3B	147	529	59	149	28	1	11	70	.282	1	1173	†124	14	.989
1975	—New York (N.L.)■	3B-1B	114	361	33	89	16	3	6	35	.247	0	172	157	15	.956
1976	—New York (N.L.)	1B-3B	114	310	36	95	10	3	5	31	.306	1	593	52	7	.989
1977	—New York (N.L.)	1B-3B	26	51	2	9	3	0	1	9	.176	0	83	3	1	.989
	Major league totals (18 years)		2209	7874	996	2342	344	59	252	1185	.297	25	11618	1731	163	.988

ALL-STAR GAME RECORD

Year	League	Pos.	AB	R	H	2B	3B	HR	RBI	Avg.	SB	PO	A	E	Avg.
							BATTING						FIELDING		
1964 —National		C	2	0	0	0	0	0	0	.000	0	5	0	0	1.000
1965 —National		C	4	1	1	0	0	1	2	.250	0	5	1	0	1.000
1966 —National		C	3	0	0	0	0	0	0	.000	0	5	0	0	1.000
1967 —National		C	2	0	0	0	0	0	0	.000	0	4	1	0	1.000
1970 —National		PH	1	0	0	0	0	0	0	.000	0	0	0	0	...
1971 —National		3B	3	0	0	0	0	0	0	.000	0	1	0	0	1.000
1972 —National		3B	3	0	0	0	0	0	0	.000	0	1	2	0	1.000
1973 —National		1B-3B	3	0	0	0	0	0	0	.000	0	5	0	0	1.000
All-Star Game totals (9 years)			21	1	1	0	0	1	2	.048	0	26	4	0	1.000

HONORS: Coach, N.L. All-Star team (1983).

MANAGERIAL RECORD

Year	Team (League)	W	L	Pct.	Pos.	Playoff W	L	Champ. Series W	L	World Series W	L	All-Star Game W	L
			REGULAR SEASON						POSTSEASON					
1977 —New York (N.L.)		49	68	.419	6th (E)	—	—	—	—	—	—	—	—
1978 —New York (N.L.)		66	96	.407	6th (E)	—	—	—	—	—	—	—	—
1979 —New York (N.L.)		63	99	.389	6th (E)	—	—	—	—	—	—	—	—
1980 —New York (N.L.)		67	95	.414	5th (E)	—	—	—	—	—	—	—	—
1981 —New York (N.L.)		17	34	.333	5th (E)	—	—	—	—	—	—	—	—
— (Second half)		24	28	.462	4th (E)	—	—	—	—	—	—	—	—
1982 —Atlanta (N.L.)		89	73	.549	1st (W)	—	—	0	3	—	—	—	—
1983 —Atlanta (N.L.)		88	74	.543	2nd (W)	—	—	—	—	—	—	—	—
1984 —Atlanta (N.L.)		80	82	.494	T2nd (W)	—	—	—	—	—	—	—	—
1990 —St. Louis (N.L.)		24	34	.414	6th (E)	—	—	—	—	—	—	—	—
1991 —St. Louis (N.L.)		84	78	.519	2nd (E)	—	—	—	—	—	—	—	—
Major league totals (10 years)		651	761	.461		—	—	0	3	—	—	—	—

NOTES:

1977 — Replaced New York Manager Joe Frazier with club in sixth place and record of 15-30 (May 31); served as player/manager (May 31-until released as player, June 18).

1982 — Lost to St. Louis in N.L. Championship Series.

1990 — Replaced St. Louis manager Whitey Herzog (33-47) and interim manager Red Schoendienst (13-11) with club in sixth place and record of 46-58 (August 1).

VALENTINE, BOBBY
RANGERS

PERSONAL: Born May 13, 1950, at Stamford, Conn. . . . 5-10/185. . . . Threw and batted righthanded. . . . Full name: Robert John Valentine. . . . Son-in-law of Ralph Branca, pitcher, Brooklyn Dodgers, Detroit Tigers, New York Yankees (1944-54, 1956).

HIGH SCHOOL: Rippowan (Stamford, Conn.).

COLLEGE: Arizona State and Southern California.

TRANSACTIONS/CAREER NOTES: Selected by Los Angeles Dodgers organization in first round (fifth pick overall) of free-agent draft (June 7, 1968). . . . Traded by Dodgers with IF Billy Grabarkewitz, OF Frank Robinson, P Bill Singer and P Mike Strahler to California Angels for P Andy Messersmith and 3B Ken McMullen (November 28, 1972). . . . On disabled list (May 17, 1973-remainder of season and May 29-June 13, 1974). . . . Loaned by Angels to Charleston, Pittsburgh Pirates organization (April 4, 1975); returned (June 20, 1975). . . . Traded by Angels with a player to be named later to San Diego Padres for P Gary Ross (September 17, 1975); Padres acquired IF Rudy Meoli to complete deal (November 4, 1975). . . . Traded by Padres with P Paul Siebert to New York Mets for IF-OF Dave Kingman (June 15, 1977). . . . Released by Mets (March 26, 1979). . . . Signed by Seattle Mariners (April 10, 1979). . . . Granted free agency (November 1, 1979).

RECORDS/HONORS: Named Pacific Coast League Player of the Year (1970).

STATISTICAL NOTES: Led Pioneer League outfielders with 107 putouts and tied for lead with eight assists in 1968. . . . Led Pacific Coast League shortstops with 38 errors in 1969. . . . Led Pacific Coast League in total bases with 324, in sacrifice flies with 10 and double plays by shortstop with 106 in 1970. . . . Led Pacific Coast League shortstops with 217 putouts and 54 errors in 1970.

Year	Team (League)	Pos.	G	AB	R	H	2B	3B	HR	RBI	Avg.	SB	PO	A	E	Avg.
							BATTING						FIELDING			
1968 —Ogden (Pioneer)		OF-SS	62	224	*62	63	14	4	6	26	.281	*20	†111	‡10	6	.953
1969 —Spokane (Pacific Coast)		SS-OF	111	402	61	104	19	5	3	35	.259	34	166	254	†38	.917
1970 —Spokane (Pacific Coast)		SS-2B	•146	*621	*122	*211	*39	*16	14	80	*.340	29	†217	474	†54	.928
1971 —Spokane (Pacific Coast)		SS	7	30	7	10	2	0	1	2	.333	3	13	18	3	.912
—Los Angeles (N.L.)		S-3-2-0	101	281	32	70	10	2	1	25	.249	5	123	176	16	.949
1972 —Los Angeles (N.L.)		2-3-0-S	119	391	42	107	11	2	3	32	.274	5	178	245	23	.948
1973 —California (A.L.)		SS-OF	32	126	12	38	5	2	1	13	.302	6	63	75	6	.958
1974 —California (A.L.)		OF-SS-3B	117	371	39	97	10	3	3	39	.261	8	160	116	17	.942
1975 —Charleston, W.Va. (Int'l)■		3B	56	175	27	41	4	0	1	17	.234	8	44	74	6	.952
—Salt Lake City (PCL)■		1-0-3-2	46	147	29	45	6	1	0	17	.306	13	92	14	3	.972
—California (A.L.)		1B-3B-OF	26	57	5	16	2	0	0	5	.281	0	27	1	2	.933
—San Diego (N.L.)■		OF	7	15	1	2	0	0	1	1	.133	1	4	0	0	1.000
1976 —Hawaii (Pacific Coast)		1-0-3-S	120	395	67	120	23	2	13	89	.304	9	578	47	4	.994
—San Diego (N.L.)■		OF-1B	15	49	3	18	4	0	0	4	.367	0	55	6	0	1.000
1977 —S.D.-New York (N.L.)■		SS-1B-3B	86	150	13	23	4	0	2	13	.153	0	119	64	3	.984

Year	Team (League)	Pos.	G	AB	R	H	2B	3B	HR	RBI	Avg.	SB	PO	A	E	Avg.
							BATTING							FIELDING		
1978 —New York (N.L.)		2B-3B	69	160	17	43	7	0	1	18	.269	1	78	109	6	.969
1979 —Seattle (A.L.)■		S-O-2-3-C	62	98	9	27	6	0	0	7	.276	1	32	38	2	.972
American League totals (4 years)			237	652	65	178	23	5	4	64	.273	15	282	230	27	.950
National League totals (6 years)			397	1046	108	263	36	4	8	93	.251	12	557	600	48	.960
Major league totals (9 years)			634	1698	173	441	59	9	12	157	.260	27	839	830	75	.957

RECORD AS MANAGER

BACKGROUND: Scout and minor league instructor, San Diego Padres (1981). . . . Minor league instructor, New York Mets (1982). . . . Coach, Mets (1983-May 15, 1985).

HONORS: Coach, A.L. All-Star team (1988).

Year	Team (League)	W	L	Pct.	Pos.	Playoff W	Playoff L	Champ. Series W	Champ. Series L	World Series W	World Series L	All-Star Game W	All-Star Game L
						REGULAR SEASON		POSTSEASON					
1985 —Texas (A.L.)		53	76	.411	7th (W)	—	—	—	—	—	—	—	—
1986 —Texas (A.L.)		87	75	.537	2nd (W)	—	—	—	—	—	—	—	—
1987 —Texas (A.L.)		75	87	.463	T6th (W)	—	—	—	—	—	—	—	—
1988 —Texas (A.L.)		70	91	.435	6th (W)	—	—	—	—	—	—	—	—
1989 —Texas (A.L.)		83	79	.512	4th (W)	—	—	—	—	—	—	—	—
1990 —Texas (A.L.)		83	79	.512	3rd (W)	—	—	—	—	—	—	—	—
1991 —Texas (A.L.)		85	77	.525	3rd (W)	—	—	—	—	—	—	—	—
Major league totals (7 years)		536	564	.487		—	—	—	—	—	—	—	—

NOTES:

1985— Replaced Texas manager Doug Rader with club in seventh place and record of 9-23 (May 16).

1992
HALL OF FAME ENSHRINEES

FINGERS, ROLLIE
P

PERSONAL: Born August 25, 1946, at Steubenville, O. . . . 6-4/200. . . . Threw and batted righthanded. . . . Full name: Roland Glen Fingers. . . . Brother of Gordon Fingers, minor league pitcher (1970).
COLLEGE: Chaffey Junior College (Calif.).
TRANSACTIONS/CAREER NOTES: Signed as free agent by Kansas City Athletics organization (December 24, 1964). . . . On disabled list (April 18-June 1, 1967). . . . A's franchise transferred to Oakland (October, 1967). . . . On military list (December 29, 1967-May 12, 1968). . . . On Birmingham disabled list (June 3-12, 1968). . . . Granted free agency (November 1, 1976). . . . Signed by San Diego Padres (December 14, 1976). . . . Traded by Padres with P Bob Shirley, C-1B Gene Tenace and a player to be named later to St. Louis Cardinals for C Terry Kennedy, C Steve Swisher, P John Littlefield, P Al Olmsted, P Kim Seaman, P John Urrea and IF Mike Phillips (December 8, 1980); Cardinals organization acquired C Bob Geren to complete deal (December 10, 1980). . . . Traded by Cardinals with C Ted Simmons and P Pete Vuckovich to Milwaukee Brewers for OF Sixto Lezcano, OF David Green, P Lary Sorensen and P Dave LaPoint (December 12, 1980). . . . On disabled list (March 26, 1983-remainder of season and July 24, 1984-remainder of season). . . . Granted free agency (November 8, 1984). . . . Re-signed by Brewers (January 16, 1985). . . . Released by Brewers (November 14, 1985).
RECORDS/HONORS: Holds major league career record for most saves—341. . . . Named N.L. Fireman of the Year by THE SPORTING NEWS (1977-78). . . . Named N.L. co-Fireman of the Year by THE SPORTING NEWS (1980). . . . Named A.L. Fireman of the Year by THE SPORTING NEWS (1981). . . . Named A.L. Most Valuable Player by Baseball Writers' Association of America (1981). . . . Won A.L. Cy Young Award (1981).
STATISTICAL NOTES: Tied for Southern League lead with three shutouts in 1968.

Year	Team (League)	G	W	L	Pct.	ERA	Sv.	IP	H	R	ER	BB	SO
1965	Leesburg (Florida State)	25	8	15	.348	2.98	. . .	175	148	83	58	69	108
1966	Modesto (California)	22	11	6	.647	2.77	. . .	159	120	61	49	43	152
1967	Birmingham (Southern)	18	6	5	.545	2.21	. . .	102	75	34	25	36	61
1968	Birmingham (Southern)	18	10	4	.714	3.00	. . .	108	94	38	36	28	93
	Oakland (A.L.)	1	0	0	. . .	36.00	. . .	1	4	4	4	1	0
1969	Oakland (A.L.)	60	6	7	.462	3.71	12	119	116	60	49	41	61
1970	Oakland (A.L.)	45	7	9	.438	3.65	2	148	137	65	60	48	79
1971	Oakland (A.L.)	48	4	6	.400	3.00	17	129	94	46	43	30	98
1972	Oakland (A.L.)	65	11	9	.550	2.51	21	111	85	35	31	32	113
1973	Oakland (A.L.)	62	7	8	.467	1.91	22	127	107	41	27	39	110
1974	Oakland (A.L.)	*76	9	5	.643	2.65	18	119	104	41	35	29	95
1975	Oakland (A.L.)	*75	10	6	.625	2.98	24	127	95	43	42	33	115
1976	Oakland (A.L.)	70	13	11	.542	2.47	20	135	118	40	37	40	113
1977	San Diego (N.L.)■	*78	8	9	.471	3.00	*35	132	123	47	44	36	113
1978	San Diego (N.L.)	67	6	13	.316	2.52	*37	107	84	33	30	29	72
1979	San Diego (N.L.)	54	9	9	.500	4.50	13	84	91	47	42	37	65
1980	San Diego (N.L.)	66	11	9	.550	2.80	23	103	101	35	32	32	69
1981	Milwaukee (A.L.)■	47	6	3	.667	1.04	*28	78	55	9	9	13	61
1982	Milwaukee (A.L.)	50	5	6	.455	2.60	29	79²/₃	63	23	23	20	71
1983	Milwaukee (A.L.)						Did not play						
1984	Milwaukee (A.L.)	33	1	2	.333	1.96	23	46	38	13	10	13	40
1985	Milwaukee (A.L.)	47	1	6	.143	5.04	17	55¹/₃	59	33	31	19	24
American League totals (13 years)		679	80	78	.506	2.83	233	1275	1075	453	401	358	980
National League totals (4 years)		265	34	40	.459	3.13	108	426	399	162	148	134	319
Major league totals (17 years)		944	114	118	.491	2.90	341	1701	1474	615	549	492	1299

DIVISION SERIES RECORD

Year	Team (League)	G	W	L	Pct.	ERA	Sv.	IP	H	R	ER	BB	SO
1981	Milwaukee (A.L.)	3	1	0	1.000	3.86	1	4²/₃	7	3	2	1	5

CHAMPIONSHIP SERIES RECORD
CHAMPIONSHIP SERIES NOTES: Shares A.L. career record for most games pitched—11.

Year	Team (League)	G	W	L	Pct.	ERA	Sv.	IP	H	R	ER	BB	SO
1971	Oakland (A.L.)	2	0	0	. . .	7.71	0	2¹/₃	2	2	2	1	2
1972	Oakland (A.L.)	3	1	0	1.000	1.69	0	5¹/₃	4	1	1	1	3
1973	Oakland (A.L.)	3	0	1	.000	1.93	1	4²/₃	4	1	1	2	4
1974	Oakland (A.L.)	2	0	0	. . .	3.00	1	3	3	1	1	1	3
1975	Oakland (A.L.)	4	0	1	.000	6.75	0	4	5	3	3	1	3
Championship Series totals (5 years)		14	1	2	.333	3.72	2	19¹/₃	18	8	8	6	15

WORLD SERIES RECORD
WORLD SERIES NOTES: Holds major league career records for most saves—6; most games as relief pitcher—16. . . . Shares major league record for most saves, five-game Series—2 (1974).

Year	Team (League)	G	W	L	Pct.	ERA	Sv.	IP	H	R	ER	BB	SO
1972	Oakland (A.L.)	6	1	1	.500	1.74	2	10¹/₃	4	2	2	4	11
1973	Oakland (A.L.)	6	0	1	.000	0.66	2	13²/₃	13	5	1	4	8

Year	Team (League)	G	W	L	Pct.	ERA	Sv.	IP	H	R	ER	BB	SO
1974 —Oakland (A.L.)		4	1	0	1.000	1.93	2	9⅓	8	2	2	2	6
1982 —Milwaukee (A.L.)						Did not play							
World Series totals (4 years)		16	2	2	.500	1.35	6	33⅓	25	9	5	10	25

ALL-STAR GAME RECORD

Year	League	W	L	Pct.	ERA	Sv.	IP	H	R	ER	BB	SO
1973 —American		0	0	...	0.00	0	1	0	0	0	0	0
1974 —American		0	0	...	18.00	0	1	1	2	2	1	0
1975 —American					Did not play							
1976 —American					Did not play							
1978 —National		0	0	...	0.00	0	2	1	0	0	0	1
1981 —American		0	1	.000	54.00	0	⅓	2	2	2	2	0
1982 —American		0	0	...	0.00	0	1	2	0	0	0	0
All-Star totals (7 years)		0	1	.000	6.75	0	5⅓	6	4	4	3	1

SEAVER, TOM
P

PERSONAL: Born November 17, 1944, at Fresno, Calif.... 6-1/210.... Threw and batted right-handed.... Full name: George Thomas Seaver.... Son of Charles Seaver, former U.S. Walker Cup golfer.

COLLEGE: Fresno City College (Calif.) and Southern California (bachelor of science degree in public relations, 1974).

TRANSACTIONS/CAREER NOTES: Selected by Los Angeles Dodgers organization in 22nd round of free-agent draft (June, 1965). ... Selected by Atlanta Braves in free-agent draft (January, 1966).... Signed by Braves organization to Richmond contract (February, 1966); Commissioner William Eckert nullified contract because the signing violated the college rule. Since Southern California declared Seaver ineligible, Eckert decreed that any club other than the Braves willing to match terms of Richmond contract would be eligible to draw for negotiation rights. Cleveland, Philadelphia and New York Mets expressed willingness, and Eckert drew Mets in a special drawing (April 3, 1966); Mets then signed Seaver to Jacksonville contract.... Traded by Mets to Cincinnati Reds for IF Doug Flynn, P Pat Zachry, OF Dan Norman and OF Steve Henderson (June 15, 1977).... On disabled list (July 1-August 4, 1980).... Traded by Reds to Mets for P Charlie Puleo, C Lloyd McClendon and OF Jason Felice (December 16, 1982).... Selected by Chicago White Sox in player compensation pool draft (January 20, 1984). White Sox received compensation for Toronto Blue Jays' signing of P Dennis Lamp, a Type A player (January 10, 1984).... On disabled list (May 18-June 4, 1986).... Traded by White Sox to Boston Red Sox for OF Steve Lyons (June 29, 1986).... Granted free agency (November 12, 1986).... Signed by New York Mets (June 6, 1987).... Placed on voluntarily retired list (June 22, 1987).

RECORDS/HONORS: Established major league records for most consecutive seasons, 200 or more strikeouts—9 (1968-1976); most consecutive strikeouts, game— 10 (April 22, 1970); most times pitched opening game of season— 16.... Established N.L. records for lowest earned run average, 200 or more games won, lifetime—2.73; most strikeouts, righthanded pitcher, life-time—3,272; most seasons, 200 or more strikeouts— 10.... Tied N.L. record for most strikeouts, game— 19 (April 22, 1970). ... Named N.L. Rookie of the Year by Baseball Writers' Association of America (1967).... Named N.L. Pitcher of the Year by THE SPORTING NEWS (1969 and 1975).... Named righthanded pitcher on THE SPORTING NEWS N.L. All-Star Team (1969, 1973, 1975 and 1981).... Won N.L. Cy Young Award (1969, 1973 and 1975).

STATISTICAL NOTES: Led International League pitchers with 32 games started in 1966.... Tied for N.L. lead with 18 complete games in 1973.... Led N.L. with seven shutouts in 1977.... Pitched 4-0 no-hit victory against St. Louis (June 16, 1978).... Tied for N.L. lead with five shutouts in 1979.

Year	Team (League)	G	W	L	Pct.	ERA	Sv.	IP	H	R	ER	BB	SO
1966 —Jacksonville (International)		34	12	12	.500	3.13	0	210	184	87	73	66	188
1967 —New York (N.L.)		35	16	13	.552	2.76	0	251	224	85	77	78	170
1968 —New York (N.L.)		36	16	12	.571	2.20	0	278	224	73	68	48	205
1969 —New York (N.L.)		36	*25	7	*.781	2.21	0	273	202	75	67	82	208
1970 —New York (N.L.)		37	18	12	.600	*2.81	0	291	230	103	91	83	*283
1971 —New York (N.L.)		36	20	10	.667	*1.76	0	286	210	61	56	61	*289
1972 —New York (N.L.)		35	21	12	.636	2.92	0	262	215	92	85	77	249
1973 —New York (N.L.)		36	19	10	.655	*2.08	0	290	219	74	67	64	*251
1974 —New York (N.L.)		32	11	11	.500	3.20	0	236	199	89	84	75	201
1975 —New York (N.L.)		36	*22	9	.710	2.38	0	280	217	81	74	88	*243
1976 —New York (N.L.)		35	14	11	.560	2.59	0	271	211	83	78	77	*235
1977 —New York-Cincinnati (N.L.)■		33	21	6	.778	2.59	0	261	199	78	75	66	196
1978 —Cincinnati (N.L.)		36	16	14	.533	2.87	0	260	218	97	83	89	226
1979 —Cincinnati (N.L.)		32	16	6	.727	3.14	0	215	187	85	75	61	131
1980 —Cincinnati (N.L.)		26	10	8	.556	3.64	0	168	140	74	68	59	101
1981 —Cincinnati (N.L.)		23	14	2	*.875	2.55	0	166	120	51	47	66	87
1982 —Cincinnati (N.L.)		21	5	13	.278	5.50	0	111⅓	136	75	68	44	62
1983 —New York (N.L.)■		34	9	14	.391	3.55	0	231	201	104	91	86	135
1984 —Chicago (A.L.)■		34	15	11	.577	3.95	0	236⅔	216	108	104	61	131
1985 —Chicago (A.L.)		35	16	11	.593	3.17	0	238⅓	223	103	84	69	134
1986 —Chicago-Boston (A.L.)■		28	7	13	.350	4.03	0	176⅓	180	83	79	56	103
American League totals (3 years)		97	38	35	.521	3.69	0	651⅔	619	294	267	186	368
National League totals (17 years)		559	273	170	.616	2.73	0	4130⅓	3352	1380	1254	1204	3272
Major league totals (20 years)		656	311	205	.603	2.86	0	4782	3971	1674	1521	1390	3640

CHAMPIONSHIP SERIES RECORD

CHAMPIONSHIP SERIES NOTES: Established Championship Series record for most strikeouts, five-game series— 17 (1973).

Year	Team (League)	G	W	L	Pct.	ERA	Sv.	IP	H	R	ER	BB	SO
1969 —New York (N.L.)		1	1	0	1.000	6.43	0	7	8	5	5	3	2

Year	Team (League)	G	W	L	Pct.	ERA	Sv.	IP	H	R	ER	BB	SO
1973	—New York (N.L.)	2	1	1	.500	1.62	0	16⅔	13	4	3	5	17
1979	—Cincinnati (N.L.)	1	0	0	...	2.25	0	8	5	2	2	2	5
Championship Series totals (3 years)		4	2	1	.667	2.84	0	31⅔	26	11	10	10	24

WORLD SERIES RECORD

Year	Team (League)	G	W	L	Pct.	ERA	Sv.	IP	H	R	ER	BB	SO
1969	—New York (N.L.)	2	1	1	.500	3.00	0	15	12	5	5	3	9
1973	—New York (N.L.)	2	0	1	.000	2.40	0	15	13	4	4	3	18
World Series totals (2 years)		4	1	2	.333	2.70	0	30	25	9	9	6	27

ALL-STAR GAME RECORD

Year	League	W	L	Pct.	ERA	Sv.	IP	H	R	ER	BB	SO
1967	—National	0	0	...	0.00	0	1	0	0	0	1	1
1968	—National	0	0	...	0.00	0	2	2	0	0	0	5
1969	—National					Did not play						
1970	—National	0	0	...	0.00	0	3	1	0	0	0	4
1971	—National					Did not play						
1972	—National					Did not play						
1973	—National	0	0	...	0.00	0	1	0	0	0	1	0
1975	—National	0	0	...	27.00	0	1	2	3	3	1	2
1976	—National	0	0	...	4.50	0	2	2	1	1	0	1
1977	—National	0	0	...	9.00	0	2	4	3	2	1	2
1978	—National					Did not play						
1981	—National	0	0	...	9.00	0	1	3	1	1	0	1
All-Star totals (12 years)		0	0	...	4.85	0	13	14	8	7	4	16

OTHER BOOKS AVAILABLE
FROM THE SPORTING NEWS LIBRARY
Take your pick!